PUBLISHER'S NOTE

The One Year Bible has been prepared especially for regular Bible readers who wish to read through the entire Bible in one year.

Each day you will read a passage from the Old Testament and one from the New, along with a Psalm and one or two Proverbs. This gives variety and freshness to your daily reading.

Instead of following a Bible reading chart and experiencing the delay of turning from place to place, you will find the text here in sequence, ready for your quiet reading and meditation.

May this year and every year be enriched as you enjoy daily portions from God's Word.

WAYS TO USE THE ONE YEAR BIBLE

The One Year Bible is divided into daily readings. For each day there is a portion of the Old Testament, the New Testament, Psalms, and Proverbs. These four separate daily readings are grouped on consecutive pages, giving freshness and diversity to each day's reading. This also makes it easy to use *The One Year Bible* in a variety of ways.

The One Year Bible has led thousands of readers through the Bible in one year. Its arrangement, however, is equally useful for guiding a reader through the Bible in two, or even three, years. If you feel too rushed or want to spend more time on each day's selections, here are a few other suggested reading plans:

The Revised One-Year Plan
Schedule some time both in the morning and evening. Then read the New Testament selection with the Psalms in the morning and the Old Testament selection with the Proverbs in the evening.

The Two-Year Plan
During the first year just read the Old Testament selection with the Proverbs. Then during the second year, read the New Testament with the Psalms.

The Three-Year Plan
Read the Old Testament selection the first year, the New Testament the second year, and the Psalms and Proverbs selections during the third.

Words of Praise and Wisdom in One Year
Read the Psalms and Proverbs selected for each day. This will take you through the Psalms twice and Proverbs once during the year, giving you words of praise and wisdom to live by each day.

And you need not limit yourself to these suggested plans, either. The arrangement of *The One Year Bible* makes it easy to devise any number of Bible reading plans to meet your particular needs.

INDEX
TO THE BOOKS OF THE BIBLE

ALPHABETICAL INDEX
TO THE BOOKS OF THE BIBLE

Where Can I Find It?

Great Passages from The Bible

Great Stories from The Bible

JANUARY 1

GENESIS 1:1—2:25

IN the beginning God created the heaven and the earth.

2And the earth was without form, and void; and darkness *was* upon the face of the deep. And the Spirit of God moved upon the face of the waters.

3And God said, Let there be light: and there was light.

4And God saw the light, that *it was* good: and God divided the light from the darkness.

5And God called the light Day, and the darkness he called Night. And the evening and the morning were the first day.

6And God said, Let there be a firmament in the midst of the waters, and let it divide the waters from the waters.

7And God made the firmament, and divided the waters which *were* under the firmament from the waters which *were* above the firmament: and it was so.

8And God called the firmament Heaven. And the evening and the morning were the second day.

9And God said, Let the waters under the heaven be gathered together unto one place, and let the dry *land* appear: and it was so.

10And God called the dry *land* Earth; and the gathering together of the waters called he Seas: and God saw that *it was* good.

11And God said, Let the earth bring forth grass, the herb yielding seed, *and* the fruit tree yielding fruit after his kind, whose seed *is* in itself, upon the earth: and it was so.

12And the earth brought forth grass, *and* herb yielding seed after his kind, and the tree yielding fruit, whose seed *was* in itself, after his kind: and God saw that *it was* good.

13And the evening and the morning were the third day.

14And God said, Let there be lights in the firmament of the heaven to divide the day from the night; and let them be for signs, and for seasons, and for days, and years:

15And let them be for lights in the firmament of the heaven to give light upon the earth: and it was so.

16And God made two great lights; the greater light to rule the day, and the lesser light to rule the night: *he made* the stars also.

17And God set them in the firmament of the heaven to give light upon the earth,

18And to rule over the day and over the night, and to divide the light from the darkness: and God saw that *it was* good.

19And the evening and the morning were the fourth day.

20And God said, Let the waters bring forth abundantly the moving creature that hath life, and fowl *that* may fly above the earth in the open firmament of heaven.

21And God created great whales, and every living creature that moveth, which the waters brought forth abundantly, after their kind, and every winged fowl after his kind: and God saw that *it was* good.

22And God blessed them, saying, Be fruitful, and multiply, and fill the waters in the seas, and let fowl multiply in the earth.

23And the evening and the morning were the fifth day.

24And God said, Let the earth bring forth the living creature after his kind, cattle, and creeping thing, and beast of the earth after his kind: and it was so.

25And God made the beast of the earth after his kind, and cattle after their kind, and every thing that creepeth upon the earth after his kind: and God saw that *it was* good.

26And God said, Let us make man in our image, after our likeness: and let them have dominion over the fish of the sea, and over the fowl of the air, and over the cattle, and over all the earth, and over every creeping thing that creepeth upon the earth.

27So God created man in his *own* image, in the image of God created he him; male and female created he them.

28And God blessed them, and God said unto them, Be fruitful, and multiply, and replenish the earth, and subdue it: and have dominion over the fish of the sea, and over the fowl of the air, and over every living thing that moveth upon the earth.

29And God said, Behold, I have given you every herb bearing seed, which *is* upon the face of all the earth, and every tree, in the which *is* the fruit of a tree yielding seed; to you it shall be for meat.

30And to every beast of the earth, and to every fowl of the air, and to every thing that creepeth upon the earth, wherein *there is* life, *I have given* every green herb for meat: and it was so.

31And God saw every thing that he had made, and, behold, *it was* very good. And the evening and the morning were the sixth day.

THUS the heavens and the earth were finished, and all the host of them.

2And on the seventh day God ended his work which he had made; and he rested on the seventh day from all his work which he had made.

3And God blessed the seventh day, and sanctified it: because that in it he had rested from all his work which God created and made.

4These *are* the generations of the heavens and of the earth when they were created, in the day that the LORD God made the earth and the heavens,

5And every plant of the field before it was in the earth, and every herb of the field before it grew: for the LORD God had not caused it to rain upon the earth, and *there was* not a man to till the ground.

6But there went up a mist from the earth, and watered the whole face of the ground.

7And the LORD God formed man *of* the dust of the ground, and breathed into his nostrils the breath of life; and man became a living soul.

8And the LORD God planted a garden eastward in Eden; and there he put the man whom he had formed.

9And out of the ground made the LORD God to grow every tree that is pleasant to the sight, and good for food; the tree of life also in the midst of the garden, and the tree of knowledge of good and evil.

10And a river went out of Eden to water the garden; and from thence it was parted, and became into four heads.

11The name of the first *is* Pison: that *is* it which compasseth the whole land of Havilah, where *there is* gold;

12And the gold of that land *is* good: there *is* bdellium and the onyx stone.

13And the name of the second river *is* Gihon: the same *is* it that compasseth the whole land of Ethiopia.

14And the name of the third river *is* Hiddekel: that *is* it which goeth toward the east of Assyria. And the fourth river *is* Euphrates.

15And the LORD God took the man, and put him into the garden of Eden to dress it and to keep it.

16And the LORD God commanded the man, saying, Of every tree of the garden thou mayest freely eat:

17But of the tree of the knowledge of good and evil, thou shalt not eat of it: for in the day that thou eatest thereof thou shalt surely die.

18And the LORD God said, *It is* not good that the man should be alone; I will make him an help meet for him.

19And out of the ground the LORD God formed every beast of the field, and every fowl of the air; and brought *them* unto Adam to see what he would call them: and whatsoever Adam called every living creature, that *was* the name thereof.

20And Adam gave names to all cattle, and to the fowl of the air, and to every beast of the field; but for Adam there was not found an help meet for him.

21And the LORD God caused a deep sleep to fall upon Adam, and he slept: and he took one of his ribs, and closed up the flesh instead thereof;

22And the rib, which the LORD God had taken from man, made he a woman, and brought her unto the man.

23And Adam said, This *is* now bone of my bones, and flesh of my flesh: she shall be called Woman, because she was taken out of Man.

24Therefore shall a man leave his father and his mother, and shall cleave unto his wife: and they shall be one flesh.

25And they were both naked, the man and his wife, and were not ashamed.

MATTHEW 1:1—2:12

THE book of the generation of Jesus Christ, the son of David, the son of Abraham.

2Abraham begat Isaac; and Isaac begat Jacob; and Jacob begat Judas and his brethren;

3And Judas begat Phares and Zara of Thamar; and Phares begat Esrom; and Esrom begat Aram;

4And Aram begat Aminadab; and Aminadab begat Naasson; and Naasson begat Salmon;

5And Salmon begat Booz of Rachab; and Booz begat Obed of Ruth; and Obed begat Jesse;

6And Jesse begat David the king; and David the king begat Solomon of her *that had been the wife* of Urias;

7And Solomon begat Roboam; and Roboam begat Abia; and Abia begat Asa;

8And Asa begat Josaphat; and Josaphat begat Joram; and Joram begat Ozias;

9And Ozias begat Joatham; and Joatham begat Achaz; and Achaz begat Ezekias;

10And Ezekias begat Manasses; and Manasses begat Amon; and Amon begat Josias;

11And Josias begat Jechoniah and his brethren, about the time they were carried away to Babylon:

12And after they were brought to Babylon, Jechoniah begat Salathiel; and Salathiel begat Zorobabel;

13And Zorobabel begat Abiud; and Abiud begat Eliakim; and Eliakim begat Azor;

14And Azor begat Sadoc; and Sadoc begat Achim; and Achim begat Eliud;

15And Eliud begat Eleazar; and Eleazar begat Matthan; and Matthan begat Jacob;

16And Jacob begat Joseph the husband of Mary, of whom was born Jesus, who is called Christ.

17So all the generations from Abraham to David *are* fourteen generations; and from David until the carrying away into Babylon *are* fourteen generations; and from the carrying away into Babylon unto Christ *are* fourteen generations.

18Now the birth of Jesus Christ was on this wise: When as his mother Mary was espoused to Joseph, before they came together, she was found with child of the Holy Ghost.

19Then Joseph her husband, being a just *man,* and not willing to make her a publick example, was minded to put her away privily.

20But while he thought on these things, behold, the angel of the Lord appeared unto him in a dream, saying, Joseph, thou son of David, fear not to take unto thee Mary thy wife; for that which is conceived in her is of the Holy Ghost.

21And she shall bring forth a son, and thou shalt call his name JESUS: for he shall save his people from their sins.

22Now all this was done, that it might be fulfilled which was spoken of the Lord by the prophet, saying,

23Behold, a virgin shall be with child, and shall bring forth a son, and they shall call his name Emmanuel, which being interpreted is, God with us.

24Then Joseph being raised from sleep did as the angel of the Lord had bidden him, and took unto him his wife:

25And knew her not till she had brought forth her firstborn son: and he called his name JESUS.

Now when Jesus was born in Beth-lehem of Judaea in the days of Herod the king, behold, there came wise men from the east to Jerusalem,

2Saying, Where is he that is born King of the Jews? for we have seen his star in the east, and are come to worship him.

3When Herod the king had heard *these things,* he was troubled, and all Jerusalem with him.

4And when he had gathered all the chief priests and scribes of the people together, he demanded of them where Christ should be born.

5And they said unto him, In Beth-lehem of Judaea: for thus it is written by the prophet,

6And thou Beth-lehem, *in* the land of Juda, art not least among the princes of Juda: for out of thee shall come a Governor, that shall rule my people Israel.

7Then Herod, when he had privily called the wise men, enquired of them diligently what time the star appeared.

8And he sent them to Beth–lehem, and said, Go and search diligently for the young child; and when ye have found *him*, bring me word again, that I may come and worship him also.

9When they had heard the king, they departed; and, lo, the star, which they saw in the east, went before them, till it came and stood over where the young child was.

10When they saw the star, they rejoiced with exceeding great joy.

11And when they were come into the house, they saw the young child with Mary his mother, and fell down, and worshipped him: and when they had opened their treasures, they presented unto him gifts; gold, and frankincense, and myrrh.

12And being warned of God in a dream that they should not return to Herod, they departed into their own country another way.

PSALM 1:1–6

BLESSED *is* the man that walketh not in the counsel of the ungodly, nor standeth in the way of sinners, nor sitteth in the seat of the scornful.

2But his delight *is* in the law of the LORD; and in his law doth he meditate day and night.

3And he shall be like a tree planted by the rivers of water, that bringeth forth his fruit in his season; his leaf also shall not wither; and whatsoever he doeth shall prosper.

4The ungodly *are* not so: but *are* like the chaff which the wind driveth away.

5Therefore the ungodly shall not stand in the judgment, nor sinners in the congregation of the righteous.

6For the LORD knoweth the way of the righteous: but the way of the ungodly shall perish.

PROVERBS FOR TODAY/ 1:1–6

The proverbs of Solomon the son of David, king of Israel; To know wisdom and instruction; to perceive the words of understanding; To receive the instruction of wisdom, justice, and judgment, and equity; To give subtilty to the simple, to the young man knowledge and discretion. A wise man *will hear, and will increase learning; and a man of understanding shall attain unto wise counsels: To understand a proverb, and the interpretation; the words of the wise, and their dark sayings.*

JANUARY 2

GENESIS 3:1—4:26

NOW the serpent was more subtil than any beast of the field which the LORD God had made. And he said unto the woman, Yea, hath God said, Ye shall not eat of every tree of the garden?

2And the woman said unto the serpent, We may eat of the fruit of the trees of the garden:

3But of the fruit of the tree which *is* in the midst of the garden, God hath said, Ye shall not eat of it, neither shall ye touch it, lest ye die.

4And the serpent said unto the woman, Ye shall not surely die:

5For God doth know that in the day ye eat thereof, then your eyes shall be opened, and ye shall be as gods, knowing good and evil.

6And when the woman saw that the tree *was* good for food, and that it *was* pleasant to the eyes, and a tree to be desired to make *one* wise, she took of the fruit thereof, and did eat, and gave also unto her husband with her; and he did eat.

7And the eyes of them both were opened, and they knew that they *were* naked; and they sewed fig leaves together, and made themselves aprons.

8And they heard the voice of the LORD God walking in the garden in the cool of the day: and Adam and his wife hid themselves from the presence of the LORD God amongst the trees of the garden.

9And the LORD God called unto Adam, and said unto him, Where *art* thou?

10And he said, I heard thy voice in the garden, and I was afraid, because I *was* naked; and I hid myself.

11And he said, Who told thee that thou *wast* naked? Hast thou eaten of the tree, whereof I commanded thee that thou shouldest not eat?

12And the man said, The woman whom thou gavest *to be* with me, she gave me of the tree, and I did eat.

13And the LORD God said unto the woman, What *is* this *that* thou hast done? And the woman said, The serpent beguiled me, and I did eat.

14And the LORD God said unto the serpent, Because thou hast done this, thou *art* cursed above all cattle, and above every beast of the field; upon thy belly shalt thou go, and dust shalt thou eat all the days of thy life:

15And I will put enmity between thee and the woman, and between thy seed and her seed; it shall bruise thy head, and thou shalt bruise his heel.

16Unto the woman he said, I will greatly multiply thy sorrow and thy conception; in sorrow thou shalt bring forth children; and thy desire *shall be* to thy husband, and he shall rule over thee.

17And unto Adam he said, Because thou hast hearkened unto the voice of thy wife, and hast eaten of the tree, of which I commanded thee, saying, Thou shalt not eat of it: cursed *is* the ground for thy sake; in sorrow shalt thou eat *of* it all the days of thy life;

18Thorns also and thistles shall it bring forth to thee; and thou shalt eat the herb of the field;

19In the sweat of thy face shalt thou eat bread, till thou return unto the ground; for out of it wast thou taken: for dust thou *art*, and unto dust shalt thou return.

20And Adam called his wife's name Eve; because she was the mother of all living.

21Unto Adam also and to his wife did the LORD God make coats of skins, and clothed them.

22And the LORD God said, Behold, the man is become as one of us, to know good and evil: and now, lest he put forth his hand, and take also of the tree of life, and eat, and live for ever:

23Therefore the LORD God sent him forth from the garden of Eden, to till the ground from whence he was taken.

24So he drove out the man; and he placed at the east of the garden of Eden Cherubims, and a flaming sword which turned every way, to keep the way of the tree of life.

AND Adam knew Eve his wife; and she conceived, and bare Cain, and said, I have gotten a man from the LORD.

2And she again bare his brother Abel. And Abel was a keeper of sheep, but Cain was a tiller of the ground.

3And in process of time it came to pass, that Cain brought of the fruit of the ground an offering unto the LORD.

4And Abel, he also brought of the firstlings of his flock and of the fat thereof. And the LORD had respect unto Abel and to his offering:

5But unto Cain and to his offering he had not respect. And Cain was very wroth, and his countenance fell.

6And the LORD said unto Cain, Why art thou wroth? and why is thy countenance fallen?

7If thou doest well, shalt thou not be accepted? and if thou doest not well, sin lieth at the door. And unto thee *shall be* his desire, and thou shalt rule over him.

8And Cain talked with Abel his brother: and it came to pass, when they were in the field, that Cain rose up against Abel his brother, and slew him.

9And the LORD said unto Cain, Where *is* Abel thy brother? And he said, I know not: *Am* I my brother's keeper?

10And he said, What hast thou done? the voice of thy brother's blood crieth unto me from the ground.

11And now *art* thou cursed from the earth, which hath opened her mouth to receive thy brother's blood from thy hand;

12When thou tillest the ground, it shall not henceforth yield unto thee her strength; a fugitive and a vagabond shalt thou be in the earth.

13And Cain said unto the LORD, My punishment *is* greater than I can bear.

14Behold, thou hast driven me out this day from the face of the earth; and from thy face shall I be hid; and I shall be a fugitive and a vagabond in the earth; and it shall come to pass, *that* every one that findeth me shall slay me.

15And the LORD said unto him, Therefore whosoever slayeth Cain, vengeance shall be taken on him sevenfold. And the LORD set a mark upon Cain, lest any finding him should kill him.

16And Cain went out from the presence of the LORD, and dwelt in the land of Nod, on the east of Eden.

17And Cain knew his wife; and she conceived, and bare Enoch: and he builded a city, and called the name of the city, after the name of his son, Enoch.

18And unto Enoch was born Irad: and Irad begat Mehujael: and Mehujael begat Methusael: and Methusael begat Lamech.

19And Lamech took unto him two wives: the name of the one *was* Adah, and the name of the other Zillah.

20And Adah bare Jabal: he was the father of such as dwell in tents, and *of such as have* cattle.

21And his brother's name *was* Jubal: he was the father of all such as handle the harp and organ.

22And Zillah, she also bare Tubal-cain, an instructer of every artificer in brass and iron: and the sister of Tubal-cain *was* Naamah.

23And Lamech said unto his wives, Adah and Zillah, Hear my voice; ye wives of Lamech, hearken unto my speech: for I have slain a man to my wounding, and a young man to my hurt.

24If Cain shall be avenged sevenfold, truly Lamech seventy and sevenfold.

25And Adam knew his wife again; and she bare a son, and called his name Seth: For God, *said she,* hath appointed me another seed instead of Abel, whom Cain slew.

26And to Seth, to him also there was born a son; and he called his name Enos: then began men to call upon the name of the LORD.

MATTHEW 2:13—3:6

AND when they [the wise men] were departed, behold, the angel of the Lord appeareth to Joseph in a dream, saying, Arise, and take the young child and his mother, and flee into Egypt, and be thou there until I bring thee word: for Herod will seek the young child to destroy him.

14When he arose, he took the young child and his mother by night, and departed into Egypt:

15And was there until the death of Herod: that it might be fulfilled which was spoken of the Lord by the prophet, saying, Out of Egypt have I called my son.

16Then Herod, when he saw that he was mocked of the wise men, was exceeding wroth, and sent forth, and slew all the children that were in Beth-lehem, and in all the coasts thereof, from two years old and under, according to the time which he had diligently enquired of the wise men.

17Then was fulfilled that which was spoken by Jeremy the prophet, saying,

18In Rama was there a voice heard, lamentation, and weeping, and great mourning, Rachel weeping *for* her children, and would not be comforted, because they are not.

19But when Herod was dead, behold, an angel of the Lord appeareth in a dream to Joseph in Egypt,

20Saying, Arise, and take the young child and his mother, and go into the land of Israel: for they are dead which sought the young child's life.

21And he arose, and took the young child and his mother, and came into the land of Israel.

22But when he heard that Archelaus did reign in Judaea in the room of his father Herod, he was afraid to go thither: notwithstanding, being warned of God in a dream, he turned aside into the parts of Galilee:

23And he came and dwelt in a city called Nazareth: that it might be fulfilled which was spoken by the prophets, He shall be called a Nazarene.

IN those days came John the Baptist, preaching in the wilderness of Judaea,

2And saying, Repent ye: for the kingdom of heaven is at hand.

3For this is he that was spoken of by the prophet Esaias, saying, The voice of one crying in the wilderness, Prepare ye the way of the Lord, make his paths straight.

4And the same John had his raiment of camel's hair, and a leathern girdle about his loins; and his meat was locusts and wild honey.

5Then went out to him Jerusalem, and all Judaea, and all the region round about Jordan,

6And were baptized of him in Jordan, confessing their sins.

PSALM 2:1-12

WHY do the heathen rage, and the people imagine a vain thing?

2The kings of the earth set themselves, and the rulers take counsel together, against the LORD, and against his anointed, *saying,*

3Let us break their bands asunder, and cast away their cords from us.

4He that sitteth in the heavens shall laugh: the Lord shall have them in derision.

5Then shall he speak unto them in his wrath, and vex them in his sore displeasure.

6Yet have I set my king upon my holy hill of Zion.

7I will declare the decree: the LORD hath said unto me, Thou *art* my Son; this day have I begotten thee.

8Ask of me, and I shall give *thee* the

heathen *for* thine inheritance, and the uttermost parts of the earth *for* thy possession.

9Thou shalt break them with a rod of iron; thou shalt dash them in pieces like a potter's vessel.

10Be wise now therefore, O ye kings:

be instructed, ye judges of the earth.

11Serve the LORD with fear, and rejoice with trembling.

12Kiss the Son, lest he be angry, and ye perish *from* the way, when his wrath is kindled but a little. Blessed *are* all they that put their trust in him.

PROVERBS FOR TODAY/ 1:7–9

The fear of the LORD is *the beginning of knowledge:* but *fools despise wisdom and instruction.* □ *My son, hear the instruction of thy father, and forsake not the law of thy mother: For they* shall be *an ornament of grace unto thy head, and chains about thy neck.*

JANUARY 3

GENESIS 5:1—7:24

THIS *is* the book of the generations of Adam. In the day that God created man, in the likeness of God made he him;

2Male and female created he them; and blessed them, and called their name Adam, in the day when they were created.

3And Adam lived an hundred and thirty years, and begat *a son* in his own likeness, after his image; and called his name Seth:

4And the days of Adam after he had begotten Seth were eight hundred years: and he begat sons and daughters:

5And all the days that Adam lived were nine hundred and thirty years: and he died.

6And Seth lived an hundred and five years, and begat Enos:

7And Seth lived after he begat Enos eight hundred and seven years, and begat sons and daughters:

8And all the days of Seth were nine hundred and twelve years: and he died.

9And Enos lived ninety years, and begat Cainan:

10And Enos lived after he begat Cainan eight hundred and fifteen years, and begat sons and daughters:

11And all the days of Enos were nine hundred and five years: and he died.

12And Cainan lived seventy years, and begat Mahalaleel:

13And Cainan lived after he begat Mahalaleel eight hundred and forty years, and begat sons and daughters:

14And all the days of Cainan were nine hundred and ten years: and he died.

15And Mahalaleel lived sixty and five years, and begat Jared:

16And Mahalaleel lived after he begat Jared eight hundred and thirty years, and begat sons and daughters:

17And all the days of Mahalaleel were eight hundred ninety and five years: and he died.

18And Jared lived an hundred sixty and two years, and he begat Enoch:

19And Jared lived after he begat Enoch eight hundred years, and begat sons and daughters:

20And all the days of Jared were nine hundred sixty and two years: and he died.

21And Enoch lived sixty and five years, and begat Methuselah:

22And Enoch walked with God after he begat Methuselah three hundred years, and begat sons and daughters:

23And all the days of Enoch were three hundred sixty and five years:

24And Enoch walked with God: and he *was* not; for God took him.

25And Methuselah lived an hundred eighty and seven years, and begat Lamech:

26And Methuselah lived after he begat Lamech seven hundred eighty and two years, and begat sons and daughters:

27And all the days of Methuselah were nine hundred sixty and nine years: and he died.

28And Lamech lived an hundred eighty and two years, and begat a son:

29And he called his name Noah, saying, This *same* shall comfort us concerning our work and toil of our hands, because of the ground which the Lord hath cursed.

30And Lamech lived after he begat Noah five hundred ninety and five years, and begat sons and daughters:

31And all the days of Lamech were seven hundred seventy and seven years: and he died.

32And Noah was five hundred years old: and Noah begat Shem, Ham, and Japheth.

And it came to pass, when men began to multiply on the face of the earth, and daughters were born unto them,

2That the sons of God saw the daughters of men that they *were* fair; and they took them wives of all which they chose.

3And the Lord said, My spirit shall not always strive with man, for that he also *is* flesh: yet his days shall be an hundred and twenty years.

4There were giants in the earth in those days; and also after that, when the sons of God came in unto the daughters of men, and they bare *children* to them, the same *became* mighty men which *were* of old, men of renown.

5And God saw that the wickedness of man *was* great in the earth, and *that* every imagination of the thoughts of his heart *was* only evil continually.

6And it repented the Lord that he had made man on the earth, and it grieved him at his heart.

7And the Lord said, I will destroy man whom I have created from the face of the earth; both man, and beast, and the creeping thing, and the fowls of the air; for it repenteth me that I have made them.

8But Noah found grace in the eyes of the Lord.

9These *are* the generations of Noah: Noah was a just man *and* perfect in his generations, *and* Noah walked with God.

10And Noah begat three sons, Shem, Ham, and Japheth.

11The earth also was corrupt before God, and the earth was filled with violence.

12And God looked upon the earth, and, behold, it was corrupt; for all flesh had corrupted his way upon the earth.

13And God said unto Noah, The end

of all flesh is come before me; for the earth is filled with violence through them; and, behold, I will destroy them with the earth.

14Make thee an ark of gopher wood; rooms shalt thou make in the ark, and shalt pitch it within and without with pitch.

15And this *is the fashion* which thou shalt make it *of:* The length of the ark *shall be* three hundred cubits, the breadth of it fifty cubits, and the height of it thirty cubits.

16A window shalt thou make to the ark, and in a cubit shalt thou finish it above; and the door of the ark shalt thou set in the side thereof; *with* lower, second, and third *stories* shalt thou make it.

17And, behold, I, even I, do bring a flood of waters upon the earth, to destroy all flesh, wherein *is* the breath of life, from under heaven; *and* every thing that *is* in the earth shall die.

18But with thee will I establish my covenant; and thou shalt come into the ark, thou, and thy sons, and thy wife, and thy sons' wives with thee.

19And of every living thing of all flesh, two of every *sort* shalt thou bring into the ark, to keep *them* alive with thee; they shall be male and female.

20Of fowls after their kind, and of cattle after their kind, of every creeping thing of the earth after his kind, two of every *sort* shall come unto thee, to keep *them* alive.

21And take thou unto thee of all food that is eaten, and thou shalt gather *it* to thee; and it shall be for food for thee, and for them.

22Thus did Noah; according to all that God commanded him, so did he.

AND the LORD said unto Noah, Come thou and all thy house into the ark; for thee have I seen righteous before me in this generation.

2Of every clean beast thou shalt take to thee by sevens, the male and his female: and of beasts that *are* not clean by two, the male and his female.

3Of fowls also of the air by sevens, the male and the female; to keep seed alive upon the face of all the earth.

4For yet seven days, and I will cause it to rain upon the earth forty days and forty nights; and every living substance that I have made will I destroy from off the face of the earth.

5And Noah did according unto all that the LORD commanded him.

6And Noah *was* six hundred years old when the flood of waters was upon the earth.

7And Noah went in, and his sons, and his wife, and his sons' wives with him, into the ark, because of the waters of the flood.

8Of clean beasts, and of beasts that *are* not clean, and of fowls, and of every thing that creepeth upon the earth,

9There went in two and two unto Noah into the ark, the male and the female, as God had commanded Noah.

10And it came to pass after seven days, that the waters of the flood were upon the earth.

11In the six hundredth year of Noah's life, in the second month, the seventeenth day of the month, the same day were all the fountains of the great deep broken up, and the windows of heaven were opened.

12And the rain was upon the earth forty days and forty nights.

13In the selfsame day entered Noah, and Shem, and Ham, and Japheth, the sons of Noah, and Noah's wife, and the three wives of his sons with them, into the ark;

14They, and every beast after his kind, and all the cattle after their kind, and every creeping thing that creepeth upon the earth after his kind, and every fowl after his kind, every bird of every sort.

15And they went in unto Noah into

the ark, two and two of all flesh, wherein *is* the breath of life.

16And they that went in, went in male and female of all flesh, as God had commanded him: and the LORD shut him in.

17And the flood was forty days upon the earth; and the waters increased, and bare up the ark, and it was lift up above the earth.

18And the waters prevailed, and were increased greatly upon the earth; and the ark went upon the face of the waters.

19And the waters prevailed exceedingly upon the earth; and all the high hills, that *were* under the whole heaven, were covered.

20Fifteen cubits upward did the waters prevail; and the mountains were covered.

21And all flesh died that moved upon the earth, both of fowl, and of cattle, and of beast, and of every creeping thing that creepeth upon the earth, and every man:

22All in whose nostrils *was* the breath of life, of all that *was* in the dry *land,* died.

23And every living substance was destroyed which was upon the face of the ground, both man, and cattle, and the creeping things, and the fowl of the heaven; and they were destroyed from the earth: and Noah only remained *alive,* and they that *were* with him in the ark.

24And the waters prevailed upon the earth an hundred and fifty days.

MATTHEW 3:7—4:11

BUT when he [John the Baptist] saw many of the Pharisees and Sadducees come to his baptism, he said unto them, O generation of vipers, who hath warned you to flee from the wrath to come?

8Bring forth therefore fruits meet for repentance:

9And think not to say within yourselves, We have Abraham to *our* father: for I say unto you, that God is able of these stones to raise up children unto Abraham.

10And now also the axe is laid unto the root of the trees: therefore every tree which bringeth not forth good fruit is hewn down, and cast into the fire.

11I indeed baptize you with water unto repentance: but he that cometh after me is mightier than I, whose shoes I am not worthy to bear: he shall baptize you with the Holy Ghost, and *with* fire:

12Whose fan *is* in his hand, and he will throughly purge his floor, and gather his wheat into the garner; but he will burn up the chaff with unquenchable fire.

13Then cometh Jesus from Galilee to Jordan unto John, to be baptized of him.

14But John forbad him, saying, I have need to be baptized of thee, and comest thou to me?

15And Jesus answering said unto him, Suffer *it to be so* now: for thus it becometh us to fulfil all righteousness. Then he suffered him.

16And Jesus, when he was baptized, went up straightway out of the water: and, lo, the heavens were opened unto him, and he saw the Spirit of God descending like a dove, and lighting upon him:

17And lo a voice from heaven, saying, This is my beloved Son, in whom I am well pleased.

THEN was Jesus led up of the spirit into the wilderness to be tempted of the devil.

2And when he had fasted forty days and forty nights, he was afterward an hungred.

3And when the tempter came to him, he said, If thou be the Son of God, command that these stones be made bread.

4But he answered and said, It is writ-

Sarai; and the name of Nahor's wife, Milcah, the daughter of Haran, the father of Milcah, and the father of Iscah.

30But Sarai was barren; she *had* no child.

31And Terah took Abram his son, and Lot the son of Haran his son's son, and Sarai his daughter in law, his son Abram's wife; and they went forth with them from Ur of the Chaldees, to go into the land of Canaan; and they came unto Haran, and dwelt there.

32And the days of Terah were two hundred and five years: and Terah died in Haran.

Now the LORD had said unto Abram, Get thee out of thy country, and from thy kindred, and from thy father's house, unto a land that I will shew thee:

2And I will make of thee a great nation, and I will bless thee, and make thy name great; and thou shalt be a blessing:

3And I will bless them that bless thee, and curse him that curseth thee: and in thee shall all families of the earth be blessed.

4So Abram departed, as the LORD had spoken unto him; and Lot went with him: and Abram *was* seventy and five years old when he departed out of Haran.

5And Abram took Sarai his wife, and Lot his brother's son, and all their substance that they had gathered, and the souls that they had gotten in Haran; and they went forth to go into the land of Canaan; and into the land of Canaan they came.

6And Abram passed through the land unto the place of Sichem, unto the plain of Moreh. And the Canaanite *was* then in the land.

7And the LORD appeared unto Abram, and said, Unto thy seed will I give this land: and there builded he an altar unto the LORD, who appeared unto him.

8And he removed from thence unto a mountain on the east of Beth–el, and pitched his tent, *having* Beth–el on the west, and Hai on the east: and there he builded an altar unto the LORD, and called upon the name of the LORD.

9And Abram journeyed, going on still toward the south.

10And there was a famine in the land: and Abram went down into Egypt to sojourn there; for the famine *was* grievous in the land.

11And it came to pass, when he was come near to enter into Egypt, that he said unto Sarai his wife, Behold now, I know that thou *art* a fair woman to look upon:

12Therefore it shall come to pass, when the Egyptians shall see thee, that they shall say, This *is* his wife: and they will kill me, but they will save thee alive.

13Say, I pray thee, thou *art* my sister: that it may be well with me for thy sake; and my soul shall live because of thee.

14And it came to pass, that, when Abram was come into Egypt, the Egyptians beheld the woman that she *was* very fair.

15The princes also of Pharaoh saw her, and commended her before Pharaoh: and the woman was taken into Pharaoh's house.

16And he entreated Abram well for her sake; and he had sheep, and oxen, and he asses, and menservants, and maidservants, and she asses, and camels.

17And the LORD plagued Pharaoh and his house with great plagues because of Sarai Abram's wife.

18And Pharaoh called Abram, and said, What *is* this *that* thou hast done unto me? why didst thou not tell me that she *was* thy wife?

19Why saidst thou, She *is* my sister?

so I might have taken her to me to wife: now therefore behold thy wife, take *her,* and go thy way.

20And Pharaoh commanded *his* men concerning him: and they sent him away, and his wife, and all that he had.

AND Abram went up out of Egypt, he, and his wife, and all that he had, and Lot with him, into the south.

2And Abram *was* very rich in cattle, in silver, and in gold.

3And he went on his journeys from the south even to Beth–el, unto the place where his tent had been at the beginning, between Beth–el and Hai;

4Unto the place of the altar, which he had made there at the first: and there Abram called on the name of the LORD.

MATTHEW 5:1–26

AND seeing the multitudes, he [Jesus] went up into a mountain: and when he was set, his disciples came unto him:

2And he opened his mouth, and taught them, saying,

3Blessed *are* the poor in spirit: for theirs is the kingdom of heaven.

4Blessed *are* they that mourn: for they shall be comforted.

5Blessed *are* the meek: for they shall inherit the earth.

6Blessed *are* they which do hunger and thirst after righteousness: for they shall be filled.

7Blessed *are* the merciful: for they shall obtain mercy.

8Blessed *are* the pure in heart: for they shall see God.

9Blessed *are* the peacemakers: for they shall be called the children of God.

10Blessed *are* they which are persecuted for righteousness' sake: for theirs is the kingdom of heaven.

11Blessed are ye, when *men* shall revile you, and persecute *you,* and shall say all manner of evil against you falsely, for my sake.

12Rejoice, and be exceeding glad: for great *is* your reward in heaven: for so persecuted they the prophets which were before you.

13Ye are the salt of the earth: but if the salt have lost his savour, wherewith shall it be salted? it is thenceforth good for nothing, but to be cast out, and to be trodden under foot of men.

14Ye are the light of the world. A city that is set on an hill cannot be hid.

15Neither do men light a candle, and put it under a bushel, but on a candlestick; and it giveth light unto all that are in the house.

16Let your light so shine before men, that they may see your good works, and glorify your Father which is in heaven.

17Think not that I am come to destroy the law, or the prophets: I am not come to destroy, but to fulfil.

18For verily I say unto you, Till heaven and earth pass, one jot or one tittle shall in no wise pass from the law, till all be fulfilled.

19Whosoever therefore shall break one of these least commandments, and shall teach men so, he shall be called the least in the kingdom of heaven: but whosoever shall do and teach *them,* the same shall be called great in the kingdom of heaven.

20For I say unto you, That except your righteousness shall exceed *the righteousness* of the scribes and Pharisees, ye shall in no case enter into the kingdom of heaven.

21Ye have heard that it was said by them of old time, Thou shalt not kill; and whosoever shall kill shall be in danger of the judgment:

22But I say unto you, That whosoever is angry with his brother without a cause shall be in danger of the judgment: and whosoever shall say to his brother, Raca, shall be in danger of the council: but whosoever shall say, Thou fool, shall be in danger of hell fire.

23Therefore if thou bring thy gift to the altar, and there rememberest that thy brother hath ought against thee;

24Leave there thy gift before the altar, and go thy way; first be reconciled to thy brother, and then come and offer thy gift.

25Agree with thine adversary quickly, whiles thou art in the way with him; lest at any time the adversary deliver thee to the judge, and the judge deliver thee to the officer, and thou be cast into prison.

26Verily I say unto thee, Thou shalt by no means come out thence, till thou hast paid the uttermost farthing.

PSALM 5:1–12

GIVE ear to my words, O LORD, consider my meditation.

2Hearken unto the voice of my cry, my King, and my God: for unto thee will I pray.

3My voice shalt thou hear in the morning, O LORD; in the morning will I direct *my prayer* unto thee, and will look up.

4For thou *art* not a God that hath pleasure in wickedness: neither shall evil dwell with thee.

5The foolish shall not stand in thy sight: thou hatest all workers of iniquity.

6Thou shalt destroy them that speak leasing: the LORD will abhor the bloody and deceitful man.

7But as for me, I will come *into* thy house in the multitude of thy mercy: *and* in thy fear will I worship toward thy holy temple.

8Lead me, O LORD, in thy righteousness because of mine enemies; make thy way straight before my face.

9For *there is* no faithfulness in their mouth; their inward part *is* very wickedness; their throat *is* an open sepulchre; they flatter with their tongue.

10Destroy thou them, O God; let them fall by their own counsels; cast them out in the multitude of their transgressions; for they have rebelled against thee.

11But let all those that put their trust in thee rejoice: let them ever shout for joy, because thou defendest them: let them also that love thy name be joyful in thee.

12For thou, LORD, wilt bless the righteous; with favour wilt thou compass him as *with* a shield.

PROVERBS FOR TODAY/ 1:24–28

Because I have called, and ye refused; I have stretched out my hand, and no man regarded; But ye have set at nought all my counsel, and would none of my reproof: I also will laugh at your calamity; I will mock when your fear cometh; When your fear cometh as desolation, and your destruction cometh as a whirlwind; when distress and anguish cometh upon you. Then shall they call upon me, but I will not answer; they shall seek me early, but they shall not find me:

JANUARY 6

GENESIS 13:5—15:21

AND Lot also, which went with Abram, had flocks, and herds, and tents.

6And the land was not able to bear them, that they might dwell together: for their substance was great, so that they could not dwell together.

7And there was a strife between the herdmen of Abram's cattle and the herdmen of Lot's cattle: and the Canaanite and the Perizzite dwelled then in the land.

8And Abram said unto Lot, Let there be no strife, I pray thee, between me and thee, and between my herdmen and thy herdmen; for we *be* brethren.

9*Is* not the whole land before thee? separate thyself, I pray thee, from me: if *thou wilt take* the left hand, then I will go to the right; or if *thou depart* to the right hand, then I will go to the left.

10And Lot lifted up his eyes, and beheld all the plain of Jordan, that it *was* well watered every where, before the LORD destroyed Sodom and Gomorrah, *even* as the garden of the LORD, like the land of Egypt, as thou comest unto Zoar.

11Then Lot chose him all the plain of Jordan; and Lot journeyed east: and they separated themselves the one from the other.

12Abram dwelled in the land of Canaan, and Lot dwelled in the cities of the plain, and pitched *his* tent toward Sodom.

13But the men of Sodom *were* wicked and sinners before the LORD exceedingly.

14And the LORD said unto Abram, after that Lot was separated from him, Lift up now thine eyes, and look from the place where thou art northward, and southward, and eastward, and westward:

15For all the land which thou seest, to thee will I give it, and to thy seed for ever.

16And I will make thy seed as the dust of the earth: so that if a man can number the dust of the earth, *then* shall thy seed also be numbered.

17Arise, walk through the land in the length of it and in the breadth of it; for I will give it unto thee.

18Then Abram removed *his* tent, and came and dwelt in the plain of Mamre, which *is* in Hebron, and built there an altar unto the LORD.

AND it came to pass in the days of Amraphel king of Shinar, Arioch king of Ellasar, Chedorlaomer king of Elam, and Tidal king of nations;

2*That these* made war with Bera king of Sodom, and with Birsha king of Gomorrah, Shinab king of Admah, and Shemeber king of Zeboiim, and the king of Bela, which is Zoar.

3All these were joined together in the vale of Siddim, which is the salt sea.

4Twelve years they served Chedorlaomer, and in the thirteenth year they rebelled.

5And in the fourteenth year came Chedorlaomer, and the kings that *were* with him, and smote the Rephaims in Ashteroth Karnaim, and the Zuzims in Ham, and the Emims in Shaveh Kiriathaim,

6And the Horites in their mount Seir, unto Elparan, which *is* by the wilderness.

7And they returned, and came to Enmishpat, which *is* Kadesh, and smote all the country of the Amalekites, and also the Amorites, that dwelt in Haze-zon–tamar.

8And there went out the king of Sodom, and the king of Gomorrah, and the king of Admah, and the king of Zeboiim, and the king of Bela (the same *is* Zoar;) and they joined battle with them in the vale of Siddim;

9With Chedorlaomer the king of Elam, and with Tidal king of nations, and Amraphel king of Shinar, and Arioch king of Ellasar; four kings with five.

10And the vale of Siddim *was full of* slimepits; and the kings of Sodom and Gomorrah fled, and fell there; and they that remained fled to the mountain.

11And they took all the goods of Sodom and Gomorrah, and all their victuals, and went their way.

12And they took Lot, Abram's brother's son, who dwelt in Sodom, and his goods, and departed.

13And there came one that had escaped, and told Abram the Hebrew; for he dwelt in the plain of Mamre the Amorite, brother of Eshcol, and brother of Aner: and these *were* confederate with Abram.

14And when Abram heard that his brother was taken captive, he armed his trained *servants,* born in his own house, three hundred and eighteen, and pursued *them* unto Dan.

15And he divided himself against them, he and his servants, by night, and smote them, and pursued them unto Hobah, which *is* on the left hand of Damascus.

16And he brought back all the goods, and also brought again his brother Lot, and his goods, and the women also, and the people.

17And the king of Sodom went out to meet him after his return from the slaughter of Chedorlaomer, and of the kings that *were* with him, at the valley of Shaveh, which *is* the king's dale.

18And Melchizedek king of Salem brought forth bread and wine: and he *was* the priest of the most high God.

19And he blessed him, and said, Blessed *be* Abram of the most high God, possessor of heaven and earth:

20And blessed be the most high God, which hath delivered thine enemies into thy hand. And he gave him tithes of all.

21And the king of Sodom said unto Abram, Give me the persons, and take the goods to thyself.

22And Abram said to the king of Sodom, I have lift up mine hand unto the LORD, the most high God, the possessor of heaven and earth,

23That I will not *take* from a thread even to a shoelatchet, and that I will not take any thing that *is* thine, lest thou shouldest say, I have made Abram rich:

24Save only that which the young men have eaten, and the portion of the men which went with me, Aner, Eshcol, and Mamre; let them take their portion.

AFTER these things the word of the LORD came unto Abram in a vision, saying, Fear not, Abram: I *am* thy shield, *and* thy exceeding great reward.

2And Abram said, LORD GOD, what wilt thou give me, seeing I go childless, and the steward of my house *is* this Eliezer of Damascus?

3And Abram said, Behold, to me thou hast given no seed: and, lo, one born in my house is mine heir.

4And, behold, the word of the LORD *came* unto him, saying, This shall not be thine heir; but he that shall come forth out of thine own bowels shall be thine heir.

5And he brought him forth abroad, and said, Look now toward heaven, and tell the stars, if thou be able to number them: and he said unto him, So shall thy seed be.

6And he believed in the LORD; and he counted it to him for righteousness.

7And he said unto him, I *am* the LORD that brought thee out of Ur of the Chaldees, to give thee this land to inherit it.

8And he said, Lord GOD, whereby shall I know that I shall inherit it?

9And he said unto him, Take me an heifer of three years old, and a she goat of three years old, and a ram of three years old, and a turtledove, and a young pigeon.

10And he took unto him all these, and divided them in the midst, and laid each piece one against another: but the birds divided he not.

11And when the fowls came down upon the carcases, Abram drove them away.

12And when the sun was going down, a deep sleep fell upon Abram; and, lo, an horror of great darkness fell upon him.

13And he said unto Abram, Know of a surety that thy seed shall be a stranger in a land *that is* not theirs, and shall serve them; and they shall afflict them four hundred years;

14And also that nation, whom they shall serve, will I judge: and afterward shall they come out with great substance.

15And thou shalt go to thy fathers in peace; thou shalt be buried in a good old age.

16But in the fourth generation they shall come hither again: for the iniquity of the Amorites *is* not yet full.

17And it came to pass, that, when the sun went down, and it was dark, behold a smoking furnace, and a burning lamp that passed between those pieces.

18In the same day the LORD made a covenant with Abram, saying, Unto thy seed have I given this land, from the river of Egypt unto the great river, the river Euphrates:

19The Kenites, and the Kenizzites, and the Kadmonites,

20And the Hittites, and the Perizzites, and the Rephaims,

21And the Amorites, and the Canaanites, and the Girgashites, and the Jebusites.

MATTHEW 5:27–48

YE have heard that it was said by them of old time, Thou shalt not commit adultery:

28But I say unto you, That whosoever looketh on a woman to lust after her hath committed adultery with her already in his heart.

29And if thy right eye offend thee, pluck it out, and cast *it* from thee: for it is profitable for thee that one of thy members should perish, and not *that* thy whole body should be cast into hell.

30And if thy right hand offend thee, cut it off, and cast *it* from thee: for it is profitable for thee that one of thy members should perish, and not *that* thy whole body should be cast into hell.

31It hath been said, Whosoever shall put away his wife, let him give her a writing of divorcement:

32But I say unto you, That whosoever shall put away his wife, saving for the cause of fornication, causeth her to commit adultery: and whosoever shall marry her that is divorced committeth adultery.

33Again, ye have heard that it hath been said by them of old time, Thou shalt not forswear thyself, but shalt perform unto the Lord thine oaths:

34But I say unto you, Swear not at all; neither by heaven; for it is God's throne:

35Nor by the earth; for it is his footstool: neither by Jerusalem; for it is the city of the great King.

36Neither shalt thou swear by thy

head, because thou canst not make one hair white or black.

37But let your communication be, Yea, yea; Nay, nay: for whatsoever is more than these cometh of evil.

38Ye have heard that it hath been said, An eye for an eye, and a tooth for a tooth:

39But I say unto you, That ye resist not evil: but whosoever shall smite thee on thy right cheek, turn to him the other also.

40And if any man will sue thee at the law, and take away thy coat, let him have *thy* cloak also.

41And whosoever shall compel thee to go a mile, go with him twain.

42Give to him that asketh thee, and from him that would borrow of thee turn not thou away.

43Ye have heard that it hath been said, Thou shalt love thy neighbour, and hate thine enemy.

44But I say unto you, Love your enemies, bless them that curse you, do good to them that hate you, and pray for them which despitefully use you, and persecute you;

45That ye may be the children of your Father which is in heaven: for he maketh his sun to rise on the evil and on the good, and sendeth rain on the just and on the unjust.

46For if ye love them which love you, what reward have ye? do not even the publicans the same?

47And if ye salute your brethren only, what do ye more *than others?* do not even the publicans so?

48Be ye therefore perfect, even as your Father which is in heaven is perfect.

PSALM 6:1–10

O LORD, rebuke me not in thine anger, neither chasten me in thy hot displeasure.

2Have mercy upon me, O LORD; for I *am* weak: O LORD, heal me; for my bones are vexed.

3My soul is also sore vexed: but thou, O LORD, how long?

4Return, O LORD, deliver my soul: oh save me for thy mercies' sake.

5For in death *there is* no remembrance of thee: in the grave who shall give thee thanks?

6I am weary with my groaning; all the night make I my bed to swim; I water my couch with my tears.

7Mine eye is consumed because of grief; it waxeth old because of all mine enemies.

8Depart from me, all ye workers of iniquity; for the LORD hath heard the voice of my weeping.

9The LORD hath heard my supplication; the LORD will receive my prayer.

10Let all mine enemies be ashamed and sore vexed: let them return *and* be ashamed suddenly.

PROVERBS FOR TODAY/ 1:29–33

For that they hated knowledge, and did not choose the fear of the LORD: They would none of my counsel: they despised all my reproof. Therefore shall they eat of the fruit of their own way, and be filled with their own devices. For the turning away of the simple shall slay them, and the prosperity of fools shall destroy them. But whoso hearkeneth unto me shall dwell safely, and shall be quiet from fear of evil.

JANUARY 7

GENESIS 16:1—18:19

Now Sarai Abram's wife bare him no children: and she had an handmaid, an Egyptian, whose name *was* Hagar.

2And Sarai said unto Abram, Behold now, the LORD hath restrained me from bearing: I pray thee, go in unto my maid; it may be that I may obtain children by her. And Abram hearkened to the voice of Sarai.

3And Sarai Abram's wife took Hagar her maid the Egyptian, after Abram had dwelt ten years in the land of Canaan, and gave her to her husband Abram to be his wife.

4And he went in unto Hagar, and she conceived: and when she saw that she had conceived, her mistress was despised in her eyes.

5And Sarai said unto Abram, My wrong *be* upon thee: I have given my maid into thy bosom; and when she saw that she had conceived, I was despised in her eyes: the LORD judge between me and thee.

6But Abram said unto Sarai, Behold, thy maid *is* in thy hand; do to her as it pleaseth thee. And when Sarai dealt hardly with her, she fled from her face.

7And the angel of the LORD found her by a fountain of water in the wilderness, by the fountain in the way to Shur.

8And he said, Hagar, Sarai's maid, whence camest thou? and whither wilt thou go? And she said, I flee from the face of my mistress Sarai.

9And the angel of the LORD said unto her, Return to thy mistress, and submit thyself under her hands.

10And the angel of the LORD said unto her, I will multiply thy seed exceedingly, that it shall not be numbered for multitude.

11And the angel of the LORD said unto her, Behold, thou *art* with child, and shalt bear a son, and shalt call his name Ishmael; because the LORD hath heard thy affliction.

12And he will be a wild man; his hand *will be* against every man, and every man's hand against him; and he shall dwell in the presence of all his brethren.

13And she called the name of the LORD that spake unto her, Thou God seest me: for she said, Have I also here looked after him that seeth me?

14Wherefore the well was called Beer–lahai–roi; behold, *it is* between Kadesh and Bered.

15And Hagar bare Abram a son: and Abram called his son's name, which Hagar bare, Ishmael.

16And Abram *was* fourscore and six years old, when Hagar bare Ishmael to Abram.

AND when Abram was ninety years old and nine, the LORD appeared to Abram, and said unto him, I *am* the Almighty God; walk before me, and be thou perfect.

2And I will make my covenant between me and thee, and will multiply thee exceedingly.

3And Abram fell on his face: and God talked with him, saying,

4As for me, behold, my covenant *is* with thee, and thou shalt be a father of many nations.

5Neither shall thy name any more be called Abram, but thy name shall be Abraham; for a father of many nations have I made thee.

6And I will make thee exceeding fruitful, and I will make nations of thee, and kings shall come out of thee.

7And I will establish my covenant between me and thee and thy seed after thee in their generations for an everlasting covenant, to be a God unto thee, and to thy seed after thee.

8And I will give unto thee, and to thy seed after thee, the land wherein thou art a stranger, all the land of Canaan, for an everlasting possession; and I will be their God.

9And God said unto Abraham, Thou shalt keep my covenant therefore, thou, and thy seed after thee in their generations.

10This *is* my covenant, which ye shall keep, between me and you and thy seed after thee; Every man child among you shall be circumcised.

11And ye shall circumcise the flesh of your foreskin; and it shall be a token of the covenant betwixt me and you.

12And he that is eight days old shall be circumcised among you, every man child in your generations, he that is born in the house, or bought with money of any stranger, which *is* not of thy seed.

13He that is born in thy house, and he that is bought with thy money, must needs be circumcised: and my covenant shall be in your flesh for an everlasting covenant.

14And the uncircumcised man child whose flesh of his foreskin is not circumcised, that soul shall be cut off from his people; he hath broken my covenant.

15And God said unto Abraham, As for Sarai thy wife, thou shalt not call her name Sarai, but Sarah *shall* her name *be.*

16And I will bless her, and give thee a son also of her: yea, I will bless her, and she shall be *a mother* of nations; kings of people shall be of her.

17Then Abraham fell upon his face, and laughed, and said in his heart, Shall *a child* be born unto him that is an hundred years old? and shall Sarah, that is ninety years old, bear?

18And Abraham said unto God, O that Ishmael might live before thee!

19And God said, Sarah thy wife shall bear thee a son indeed; and thou shalt call his name Isaac: and I will establish my covenant with him for an everlasting covenant, *and* with his seed after him.

20And as for Ishmael, I have heard thee: Behold, I have blessed him, and will make him fruitful, and will multiply him exceedingly; twelve princes shall he beget, and I will make him a great nation.

21But my covenant will I establish with Isaac, which Sarah shall bear unto thee at this set time in the next year.

22And he left off talking with him, and God went up from Abraham.

23And Abraham took Ishmael his son, and all that were born in his house, and all that were bought with his money, every male among the men of Abraham's house; and circumcised the flesh of their foreskin in the selfsame day, as God had said unto him.

24And Abraham *was* ninety years old and nine, when he was circumcised in the flesh of his foreskin.

25And Ishmael his son *was* thirteen years old, when he was circumcised in the flesh of his foreskin.

26In the selfsame day was Abraham circumcised, and Ishmael his son.

27And all the men of his house, born in the house, and bought with money of the stranger, were circumcised with him.

AND the LORD appeared unto him in the plains of Mamre: and he sat in the tent door in the heat of the day;

2And he lift up his eyes and looked, and, lo, three men stood by him: and when he saw *them,* he ran to meet them from the tent door, and bowed himself toward the ground,

3And said, My Lord, if now I have found favour in thy sight, pass not away, I pray thee, from thy servant:

4Let a little water, I pray you, be fetched, and wash your feet, and rest yourselves under the tree:

5And I will fetch a morsel of bread,

and comfort ye your hearts; after that ye shall pass on: for therefore are ye come to your servant. And they said, So do, as thou hast said.

6And Abraham hastened into the tent unto Sarah, and said, Make ready quickly three measures of fine meal, knead *it,* and make cakes upon the hearth.

7And Abraham ran unto the herd, and fetcht a calf tender and good, and gave *it* unto a young man; and he hasted to dress it.

8And he took butter, and milk, and the calf which he had dressed, and set *it* before them; and he stood by them under the tree, and they did eat.

9And they said unto him, Where *is* Sarah thy wife? And he said, Behold, in the tent.

10And he said, I will certainly return unto thee according to the time of life; and, lo, Sarah thy wife shall have a son. And Sarah heard *it* in the tent door, which *was* behind him.

11Now Abraham and Sarah *were* old *and* well stricken in age; *and* it ceased to be with Sarah after the manner of women.

12Therefore Sarah laughed within herself, saying, After I am waxed old shall I have pleasure, my lord being old also?

13And the LORD said unto Abraham, Wherefore did Sarah laugh, saying, Shall I of a surety bear a child, which am old?

14Is any thing too hard for the LORD? At the time appointed I will return unto thee, according to the time of life, and Sarah shall have a son.

15Then Sarah denied, saying, I laughed not; for she was afraid. And he said, Nay; but thou didst laugh.

16And the men rose up from thence, and looked toward Sodom: and Abraham went with them to bring them on the way.

17And the LORD said, Shall I hide from Abraham that thing which I do;

18Seeing that Abraham shall surely become a great and mighty nation, and all the nations of the earth shall be blessed in him?

19For I know him, that he will command his children and his household after him, and they shall keep the way of the LORD, to do justice and judgment; that the LORD may bring upon Abraham that which he hath spoken of him.

MATTHEW 6:1–24

TAKE heed that ye do not your alms before men, to be seen of them: otherwise ye have no reward of your Father which is in heaven.

2Therefore when thou doest *thine* alms, do not sound a trumpet before thee, as the hypocrites do in the synagogues and in the streets, that they may have glory of men. Verily I say unto you, They have their reward.

3But when thou doest alms, let not thy left hand know what thy right hand doeth:

4That thine alms may be in secret: and thy Father which seeth in secret himself shall reward thee openly.

5And when thou prayest, thou shalt not be as the hypocrites *are:* for they love to pray standing in the synagogues and in the corners of the streets, that they may be seen of men. Verily I say unto you, They have their reward.

6But thou, when thou prayest, enter into thy closet, and when thou hast shut thy door, pray to thy Father which is in secret; and thy Father which seeth in secret shall reward thee openly.

7But when ye pray, use not vain repetitions, as the heathen *do:* for they think that they shall be heard for their much speaking.

8Be not ye therefore like unto them: for your Father knoweth what things ye have need of, before ye ask him.

9After this manner therefore pray

ye: Our Father which art in heaven, Hallowed be thy name.

¹⁰Thy kingdom come. Thy will be done in earth, as *it is* in heaven.

¹¹Give us this day our daily bread.

¹²And forgive us our debts, as we forgive our debtors.

¹³And lead us not into temptation, but deliver us from evil: For thine is the kingdom, and the power, and the glory, for ever. Amen.

¹⁴For if ye forgive men their trespasses, your heavenly Father will also forgive you:

¹⁵But if ye forgive not men their trespasses, neither will your Father forgive your trespasses.

¹⁶Moreover when ye fast, be not, as the hypocrites, of a sad countenance: for they disfigure their faces, that they may appear unto men to fast. Verily I say unto you, They have their reward.

¹⁷But thou, when thou fastest, anoint thine head, and wash thy face;

¹⁸That thou appear not unto men to fast, but unto thy Father which is in secret: and thy Father, which seeth in secret, shall reward thee openly.

¹⁹Lay not up for yourselves treasures upon earth, where moth and rust doth corrupt, and where thieves break through and steal:

²⁰But lay up for yourselves treasures in heaven, where neither moth nor rust doth corrupt, and where thieves do not break through nor steal:

²¹For where your treasure is, there will your heart be also.

²²The light of the body is the eye: if therefore thine eye be single, thy whole body shall be full of light.

²³But if thine eye be evil, thy whole body shall be full of darkness. If therefore the light that is in thee be darkness, how great *is* that darkness!

²⁴No man can serve two masters: for either he will hate the one, and love the other; or else he will hold to the one, and despise the other. Ye cannot serve God and mammon.

PSALM 7:1–17

O LORD my God, in thee do I put my trust: save me from all them that persecute me, and deliver me:

²Lest he tear my soul like a lion, rending *it* in pieces, while *there is* none to deliver.

³O LORD my God, if I have done this; if there be iniquity in my hands;

⁴If I have rewarded evil unto him that was at peace with me; (yea, I have delivered him that without cause is mine enemy:)

⁵Let the enemy persecute my soul, and take *it;* yea, let him tread down my life upon the earth, and lay mine honour in the dust. Selah.

⁶Arise, O LORD, in thine anger, lift up thyself because of the rage of mine enemies: and awake for me *to* the judgment *that* thou hast commanded.

⁷So shall the congregation of the people compass thee about: for their sakes therefore return thou on high.

⁸The LORD shall judge the people: judge me, O LORD, according to my righteousness, and according to mine integrity *that is* in me.

⁹Oh let the wickedness of the wicked come to an end; but establish the just: for the righteous God trieth the hearts and reins.

¹⁰My defence *is* of God, which saveth the upright in heart.

¹¹God judgeth the righteous, and God is angry *with the wicked* every day.

¹²If he turn not, he will whet his sword; he hath bent his bow, and made it ready.

¹³He hath also prepared for him the instruments of death; he ordaineth his arrows against the persecutors.

¹⁴Behold, he travaileth with iniquity, and hath conceived mischief, and brought forth falsehood.

¹⁵He made a pit, and digged it, and is fallen into the ditch *which* he made.

16His mischief shall return upon his own head, and his violent dealing shall come down upon his own pate.

17I will praise the LORD according to his righteousness: and will sing praise to the name of the LORD most high.

PROVERBS FOR TODAY/ 2:1–5

My son, if thou wilt receive my words, and hide my commandments with thee; So that thou incline thine ear unto wisdom, and apply thine heart to understanding; Yea, if thou criest after knowledge, and liftest up thy voice for understanding; If thou seekest her as silver, and searchest for her as for hid treasures; Then shalt thou understand the fear of the LORD, and find the knowledge of God.

JANUARY 8

GENESIS 18:20—19:38

AND the LORD said, Because the cry of Sodom and Gomorrah is great, and because their sin is very grievous;

21I will go down now, and see whether they have done altogether according to the cry of it, which is come unto me; and if not, I will know.

22And the men turned their faces from thence, and went toward Sodom: but Abraham stood yet before the LORD.

23And Abraham drew near, and said, Wilt thou also destroy the righteous with the wicked?

24Peradventure there be fifty righteous within the city; wilt thou also destroy and not spare the place for the fifty righteous that *are* therein?

25That be far from thee to do after this manner, to slay the righteous with the wicked: and that the righteous should be as the wicked, that be far from thee: Shall not the Judge of all the earth do right?

26And the LORD said, If I find in Sodom fifty righteous within the city, then I will spare all the place for their sakes.

27And Abraham answered and said, Behold now, I have taken upon me to speak unto the Lord, which *am but* dust and ashes:

28Peradventure there shall lack five of the fifty righteous: wilt thou destroy all the city for *lack of* five? And he said, If I find there forty and five, I will not destroy *it*.

29And he spake unto him yet again, and said, Peradventure there shall be forty found there: And he said, I will not do *it* for forty's sake.

30And he said *unto him,* Oh let not the Lord be angry, and I will speak: Peradventure there shall thirty be found there. And he said, I will not do *it,* if I find thirty there.

31And he said, Behold now, I have taken upon me to speak unto the Lord: Peradventure there shall be twenty found there. And he said, I will not destroy *it* for twenty's sake.

32And he said, Oh let not the Lord be angry, and I will speak yet but this once: Peradventure ten shall be found there. And he said, I will not destroy *it* for ten's sake.

33And the LORD went his way, as soon as he had left communing with Abraham: and Abraham returned unto his place.

AND there came two angels to Sodom at even; and Lot sat in the gate of Sodom: and Lot seeing *them* rose up to meet them; and he bowed himself with his face toward the ground;

2And he said, Behold now, my lords, turn in, I pray you, into your servant's house, and tarry all night, and wash your feet, and ye shall rise up early, and go on your ways. And they said, Nay; but we will abide in the street all night.

3And he pressed upon them greatly; and they turned in unto him, and entered into his house; and he made them a feast, and did bake unleavened bread, and they did eat.

4But before they lay down, the men of the city, *even* the men of Sodom, compassed the house round, both old and young, all the people from every quarter:

5And they called unto Lot, and said unto him, Where *are* the men which came in to thee this night? bring them out unto us, that we may know them.

6And Lot went out at the door unto them, and shut the door after him,

7And said, I pray you, brethren, do not so wickedly.

8Behold now, I have two daughters which have not known man; let me, I pray you, bring them out unto you, and do ye to them as *is* good in your eyes: only unto these men do nothing; for therefore came they under the shadow of my roof.

9And they said, Stand back. And they said *again*, This one *fellow* came in to sojourn, and he will needs be a judge: now will we deal worse with thee, than with them. And they pressed sore upon the man, *even* Lot, and came near to break the door.

10But the men put forth their hand, and pulled Lot into the house to them, and shut to the door.

11And they smote the men that *were* at the door of the house with blindness, both small and great: so that they wea-ried themselves to find the door.

12And the men said unto Lot, Hast thou here any besides? son in law, and thy sons, and thy daughters, and whatsoever thou hast in the city, bring *them* out of this place:

13For we will destroy this place, because the cry of them is waxen great before the face of the LORD; and the LORD hath sent us to destroy it.

14And Lot went out, and spake unto his sons in law, which married his daughters, and said, Up, get you out of this place; for the LORD will destroy this city. But he seemed as one that mocked unto his sons in law.

15And when the morning arose, then the angels hastened Lot, saying, Arise, take thy wife, and thy two daughters, which are here; lest thou be consumed in the iniquity of the city.

16And while he lingered, the men laid hold upon his hand, and upon the hand of his wife, and upon the hand of his two daughters; the LORD being merciful unto him: and they brought him forth, and set him without the city.

17And it came to pass, when they had brought them forth abroad, that he said, Escape for thy life; look not behind thee, neither stay thou in all the plain; escape to the mountain, lest thou be consumed.

18And Lot said unto them, Oh, not so, my Lord:

19Behold now, thy servant hath found grace in thy sight, and thou hast magnified thy mercy, which thou hast shewed unto me in saving my life; and I cannot escape to the mountain, lest some evil take me, and I die:

20Behold now, this city *is* near to flee unto, and it *is* a little one: Oh, let me escape thither, (*is* it not a little one?) and my soul shall live.

21And he said unto him, See, I have accepted thee concerning this thing also, that I will not overthrow this city, for the which thou hast spoken.

22Haste thee, escape thither; for I cannot do any thing till thou be come thither. Therefore the name of the city was called Zoar.

23The sun was risen upon the earth when Lot entered into Zoar.

24Then the LORD rained upon Sodom and upon Gomorrah brimstone and fire from the LORD out of heaven;

25And he overthrew those cities, and all the plain, and all the inhabitants of the cities, and that which grew upon the ground.

26But his wife looked back from behind him, and she became a pillar of salt.

27And Abraham gat up early in the morning to the place where he stood before the LORD:

28And he looked toward Sodom and Gomorrah, and toward all the land of the plain, and beheld, and, lo, the smoke of the country went up as the smoke of a furnace.

29And it came to pass, when God destroyed the cities of the plain, that God remembered Abraham, and sent Lot out of the midst of the overthrow, when he overthrew the cities in the which Lot dwelt.

30And Lot went up out of Zoar, and dwelt in the mountain, and his two daughters with him; for he feared to dwell in Zoar: and he dwelt in a cave, he and his two daughters.

31And the firstborn said unto the younger, Our father *is* old, and *there is* not a man in the earth to come in unto us after the manner of all the earth:

32Come, let us make our father drink wine, and we will lie with him, that we may preserve seed of our father.

33And they made their father drink wine that night: and the firstborn went in, and lay with her father; and he perceived not when she lay down, nor when she arose.

34And it came to pass on the morrow, that the firstborn said unto the younger, Behold, I lay yesternight with my father: let us make him drink wine this night also; and go thou in, *and* lie with him, that we may preserve seed of our father.

35And they made their father drink wine that night also: and the younger arose, and lay with him; and he perceived not when she lay down, nor when she arose.

36Thus were both the daughters of Lot with child by their father.

37And the firstborn bare a son, and called his name Moab: the same *is* the father of the Moabites unto this day.

38And the younger, she also bare a son, and called his name Benammi: the same *is* the father of the children of Ammon unto this day.

MATTHEW 6:25—7:14

THEREFORE I say unto you, Take no thought for your life, what ye shall eat, or what ye shall drink; nor yet for your body, what ye shall put on. Is not the life more than meat, and the body than raiment?

26Behold the fowls of the air: for they sow not, neither do they reap, nor gather into barns; yet your heavenly Father feedeth them. Are ye not much better than they?

27Which of you by taking thought can add one cubit unto his stature?

28And why take ye thought for raiment? Consider the lilies of the field, how they grow; they toil not, neither do they spin:

29And yet I say unto you, That even Solomon in all his glory was not arrayed like one of these.

30Wherefore, if God so clothe the grass of the field, which to day is, and to morrow is cast into the oven, *shall he* not much more *clothe* you, O ye of little faith?

31Therefore take no thought, saying, What shall we eat? or, What shall we drink? or, Wherewithal shall we be clothed?

32(For after all these things do the Gentiles seek:) for your heavenly Father knoweth that ye have need of all these things.

33But seek ye first the kingdom of God, and his righteousness; and all these things shall be added unto you.

34Take therefore no thought for the morrow: for the morrow shall take thought for the things of itself. Sufficient unto the day is the evil thereof.

JUDGE not, that ye be not judged.

2For with what judgment ye judge, ye shall be judged: and with what measure ye mete, it shall be measured to you again.

3And why beholdest thou the mote that is in thy brother's eye, but considerest not the beam that is in thine own eye?

4Or how wilt thou say to thy brother, Let me pull out the mote out of thine eye; and, behold, a beam is in thine own eye?

5Thou hypocrite, first cast out the beam out of thine own eye; and then shalt thou see clearly to cast out the mote out of thy brother's eye.

6Give not that which is holy unto the dogs, neither cast ye your pearls before swine, lest they trample them under their feet, and turn again and rend you.

7Ask, and it shall be given you; seek, and ye shall find; knock, and it shall be opened unto you:

8For every one that asketh receiveth; and he that seeketh findeth; and to him that knocketh it shall be opened.

9Or what man is there of you, whom if his son ask bread, will he give him a stone?

10Or if he ask a fish, will he give him a serpent?

11If ye then, being evil, know how to give good gifts unto your children, how much more shall your Father which is in heaven give good things to them that ask him?

12Therefore all things whatsoever ye would that men should do to you, do ye even so to them: for this is the law and the prophets.

13Enter ye in at the strait gate: for wide is the gate, and broad is the way, that leadeth to destruction, and many there be which go in thereat:

14Because strait is the gate, and narrow is the way, which leadeth unto life, and few there be that find it.

PSALM 8:1-9

O LORD our Lord, how excellent is thy name in all the earth! who hast set thy glory above the heavens.

2Out of the mouth of babes and sucklings hast thou ordained strength because of thine enemies, that thou mightest still the enemy and the avenger.

3When I consider thy heavens, the work of thy fingers, the moon and the stars, which thou hast ordained;

4What is man, that thou art mindful of him? and the son of man, that thou visitest him?

5For thou hast made him a little lower than the angels, and hast crowned him with glory and honour.

6Thou madest him to have dominion over the works of thy hands: thou hast put all things under his feet:

7All sheep and oxen, yea, and the beasts of the field;

8The fowl of the air, and the fish of the sea, and whatsoever passeth through the paths of the seas.

9O LORD our Lord, how excellent is thy name in all the earth!

PROVERBS FOR TODAY/ 2:6–17

For the LORD giveth wisdom: out of his mouth cometh *knowledge and understanding. He layeth up sound wisdom for the righteous:* he is *a buckler to them that walk uprightly. He keepeth the paths of judgment, and preserveth the way of his saints. Then shalt thou understand righteousness, and judgment, and equity;* yea, *every good path. When wisdom entereth into thine heart, and knowledge is pleasant unto thy soul; Discretion shall preserve thee, understanding shall keep thee: To deliver thee from the way of the evil* man, *from the man that speaketh froward things; Who leave the paths of uprightness, to walk in the ways of darkness; Who rejoice to do evil,* and *delight in the frowardness of the wicked; Whose ways* are *crooked, and* they *froward in their paths: To deliver thee from the strange woman,* even *from the stranger* which *flattereth with her words; Which forsaketh the guide of her youth, and forgetteth the covenant of her God.*

JANUARY 9

GENESIS 20:1—22:24

AND Abraham journeyed from thence toward the south country, and dwelled between Kadesh and Shur, and sojourned in Gerar.

2And Abraham said of Sarah his wife, She *is* my sister: and Abimelech king of Gerar sent, and took Sarah.

3But God came to Abimelech in a dream by night, and said to him, Behold, thou *art but* a dead man, for the woman which thou hast taken; for she *is* a man's wife.

4But Abimelech had not come near her: and he said, Lord, wilt thou slay also a righteous nation?

5Said he not unto me, She *is* my sister? and she, even she herself said, He *is* my brother: in the integrity of my heart and innocency of my hands have I done this.

6And God said unto him in a dream, Yea, I know that thou didst this in the integrity of thy heart; for I also withheld thee from sinning against me: therefore suffered I thee not to touch her.

7Now therefore restore the man *his* wife; for he *is* a prophet, and he shall pray for thee, and thou shalt live: and if thou restore *her* not, know thou that thou shalt surely die, thou, and all that *are* thine.

8Therefore Abimelech rose early in the morning, and called all his servants, and told all these things in their ears: and the men were sore afraid.

9Then Abimelech called Abraham, and said unto him, What hast thou done unto us? and what have I offended thee, that thou hast brought on me and on my kingdom a great sin? thou hast done deeds unto me that ought not to be done.

10And Abimelech said unto Abraham, What sawest thou, that thou hast done this thing?

11And Abraham said, Because I thought, Surely the fear of God *is* not in this place; and they will slay me for my wife's sake.

12And yet indeed *she is* my sister; she *is* the daughter of my father, but not the daughter of my mother; and she became my wife.

13And it came to pass, when God caused me to wander from my father's house, that I said unto her, This *is* thy kindness which thou shalt shew unto me; at every place whither we shall come, say of me, He *is* my brother.

14And Abimelech took sheep, and oxen, and menservants, and womenservants, and gave *them* unto Abraham, and restored him Sarah his wife.

15And Abimelech said, Behold, my land *is* before thee: dwell where it pleaseth thee.

16And unto Sarah he said, Behold, I have given thy brother a thousand *pieces* of silver: behold, he *is* to thee a covering of the eyes, unto all that *are* with thee, and with all *other:* thus she was reproved.

17So Abraham prayed unto God: and God healed Abimelech, and his wife, and his maidservants; and they bare *children.*

18For the LORD had fast closed up all the wombs of the house of Abimelech, because of Sarah Abraham's wife.

AND the LORD visited Sarah as he had said, and the LORD did unto Sarah as he had spoken.

2For Sarah conceived, and bare Abraham a son in his old age, at the set time of which God had spoken to him.

3And Abraham called the name of his son that was born unto him, whom Sarah bare to him, Isaac.

4And Abraham circumcised his son Isaac being eight days old, as God had commanded him.

5And Abraham was an hundred years old, when his son Isaac was born unto him.

6And Sarah said, God hath made me to laugh, *so that* all that hear will laugh with me.

7And she said, Who would have said unto Abraham, that Sarah should have given children suck? for I have born *him* a son in his old age.

8And the child grew, and was weaned: and Abraham made a great feast the *same* day that Isaac was weaned.

9And Sarah saw the son of Hagar the Egyptian, which she had born unto Abraham, mocking.

10Wherefore she said unto Abraham, Cast out this bondwoman and her son: for the son of this bondwoman shall not be heir with my son, *even* with Isaac.

11And the thing was very grievous in Abraham's sight because of his son.

12And God said unto Abraham, Let it not be grievous in thy sight because of the lad, and because of thy bondwoman; in all that Sarah hath said unto thee, hearken unto her voice; for in Isaac shall thy seed be called.

13And also of the son of the bondwoman will I make a nation, because he *is* thy seed.

14And Abraham rose up early in the morning, and took bread, and a bottle of water, and gave *it* unto Hagar, putting *it* on her shoulder, and the child, and sent her away: and she departed, and wandered in the wilderness of Beersheba.

15And the water was spent in the bottle, and she cast the child under one of the shrubs.

16And she went, and sat her down over against *him* a good way off, as it were a bowshot: for she said, Let me not see the death of the child. And she sat over against *him,* and lift up her voice, and wept.

17And God heard the voice of the lad; and the angel of God called to Hagar out of heaven, and said unto her, What aileth thee, Hagar? fear not; for God hath heard the voice of the lad where he *is.*

18Arise, lift up the lad, and hold him in thine hand; for I will make him a great nation.

19And God opened her eyes, and she saw a well of water; and she went, and filled the bottle with water, and gave the lad drink.

20And God was with the lad; and he grew, and dwelt in the wilderness, and became an archer.

21And he dwelt in the wilderness of Paran: and his mother took him a wife out of the land of Egypt.

22And it came to pass at that time, that Abimelech and Phichol the chief captain of his host spake unto Abraham, saying, God *is* with thee in all that thou doest:

23Now therefore swear unto me here by God that thou wilt not deal falsely with me, nor with my son, nor with my son's son: *but* according to the kindness that I have done unto thee, thou shalt do unto me, and to the land wherein thou hast sojourned.

24And Abraham said, I will swear.

25And Abraham reproved Abimelech because of a well of water, which Abimelech's servants had violently taken away.

26And Abimelech said, I wot not who hath done this thing: neither didst thou tell me, neither yet heard I *of it*, but to day.

27And Abraham took sheep and oxen, and gave them unto Abimelech; and both of them made a covenant.

28And Abraham set seven ewe lambs of the flock by themselves.

29And Abimelech said unto Abraham, What *mean* these seven ewe lambs which thou hast set by themselves?

30And he said, For *these* seven ewe lambs shalt thou take of my hand, that they may be a witness unto me, that I have digged this well.

31Wherefore he called that place Beer–sheba; because there they sware both of them.

32Thus they made a covenant at Beer–sheba: then Abimelech rose up, and Phichol the chief captain of his host, and they returned into the land of the Philistines.

33And *Abraham* planted a grove in Beer–sheba, and called there on the name of the LORD, the everlasting God.

34And Abraham sojourned in the Philistines' land many days.

AND it came to pass after these things, that God did tempt Abraham, and said unto him, Abraham: and he said, Behold, *here* I *am*.

2And he said, Take now thy son, thine only *son* Isaac, whom thou lovest, and get thee into the land of Moriah; and offer him there for a burnt offering upon one of the mountains which I will tell thee of.

3And Abraham rose up early in the morning, and saddled his ass, and took two of his young men with him, and Isaac his son, and clave the wood for the burnt offering, and rose up, and went unto the place of which God had told him.

4Then on the third day Abraham lifted up his eyes, and saw the place afar off.

5And Abraham said unto his young men, Abide ye here with the ass; and I and the lad will go yonder and worship, and come again to you.

6And Abraham took the wood of the burnt offering, and laid *it* upon Isaac his son; and he took the fire in his hand, and a knife; and they went both of them together.

7And Isaac spake unto Abraham his father, and said, My father: and he said, Here *am* I, my son. And he said, Behold the fire and the wood: but where *is* the lamb for a burnt offering?

8And Abraham said, My son, God will provide himself a lamb for a burnt offering: so they went both of them together.

9And they came to the place which God had told him of; and Abraham built an altar there, and laid the wood in order, and bound Isaac his son, and laid him on the altar upon the wood.

10And Abraham stretched forth his hand, and took the knife to slay his son.

11And the angel of the LORD called

unto him out of heaven, and said, Abraham, Abraham: and he said, Here *am* I.

¹²And he said, Lay not thine hand upon the lad, neither do thou any thing unto him: for now I know that thou fearest God, seeing thou hast not withheld thy son, thine only *son* from me.

¹³And Abraham lifted up his eyes, and looked, and behold behind *him* a ram caught in a thicket by his horns: and Abraham went and took the ram, and offered him up for a burnt offering in the stead of his son.

¹⁴And Abraham called the name of that place Jehovah–jireh: as it is said *to* this day, In the mount of the Lord it shall be seen.

¹⁵And the angel of the Lord called unto Abraham out of heaven the second time,

¹⁶And said, By myself have I sworn, saith the Lord, for because thou hast done this thing, and hast not withheld thy son, thine only *son:*

¹⁷That in blessing I will bless thee, and in multiplying I will multiply thy seed as the stars of the heaven, and as the sand which *is* upon the sea shore; and thy seed shall possess the gate of his enemies;

¹⁸And in thy seed shall all the nations of the earth be blessed; because thou hast obeyed my voice.

¹⁹So Abraham returned unto his young men, and they rose up and went together to Beer–sheba; and Abraham dwelt at Beer–sheba.

²⁰And it came to pass after these things, that it was told Abraham, saying, Behold, Milcah, she hath also born children unto thy brother Nahor;

²¹Huz his firstborn, and Buz his brother, and Kemuel the father of Aram,

²²And Chesed, and Hazo, and Pildash, and Jidlaph, and Bethuel.

²³And Bethuel begat Rebekah: these eight Milcah did bear to Nahor, Abraham's brother.

²⁴And his concubine, whose name *was* Reumah, she bare also Tebah, and Gaham, and Thahash, and Maachan.

MATTHEW 7:15–29

BEWARE of false prophets, which come to you in sheep's clothing, but inwardly they are ravening wolves.

¹⁶Ye shall know them by their fruits. Do men gather grapes of thorns, or figs of thistles?

¹⁷Even so every good tree bringeth forth good fruit; but a corrupt tree bringeth forth evil fruit.

¹⁸A good tree cannot bring forth evil fruit, neither *can* a corrupt tree bring forth good fruit.

¹⁹Every tree that bringeth not forth good fruit is hewn down, and cast into the fire.

²⁰Wherefore by their fruits ye shall know them.

²¹Not every one that saith unto me, Lord, Lord, shall enter into the kingdom of heaven; but he that doeth the will of my Father which is in heaven.

²²Many will say to me in that day, Lord, Lord, have we not prophesied in thy name? and in thy name have cast out devils? and in thy name done many wonderful works?

²³And then will I profess unto them, I never knew you: depart from me, ye that work iniquity.

²⁴Therefore whosoever heareth these sayings of mine, and doeth them, I will liken him unto a wise man, which built his house upon a rock:

²⁵And the rain descended, and the floods came, and the winds blew, and beat upon that house; and it fell not; for it was founded upon a rock.

²⁶And every one that heareth these sayings of mine, and doeth them not, shall be likened unto a foolish man, which built his house upon the sand:

²⁷And the rain descended, and the floods came, and the winds blew, and

beat upon that house; and it fell: and great was the fall of it.

28And it came to pass, when Jesus had ended these sayings, the people were astonished at his doctrine:

29For he taught them as *one* having authority, and not as the scribes.

PSALM 9:1–12

I will praise *thee*, O LORD, with my whole heart; I will shew forth all thy marvellous works.

2I will be glad and rejoice in thee: I will sing praise to thy name, O thou most High.

3When mine enemies are turned back, they shall fall and perish at thy presence.

4For thou hast maintained my right and my cause; thou satest in the throne judging right.

5Thou hast rebuked the heathen, thou hast destroyed the wicked, thou hast put out their name for ever and ever.

6O thou enemy, destructions are come to a perpetual end: and thou hast destroyed cities; their memorial is perished with them.

7But the LORD shall endure for ever: he hath prepared his throne for judgment.

8And he shall judge the world in righteousness, he shall minister judgment to the people in uprightness.

9The LORD also will be a refuge for the oppressed, a refuge in times of trouble.

10And they that know thy name will put their trust in thee: for thou, LORD, hast not forsaken them that seek thee.

11Sing praises to the LORD, which dwelleth in Zion: declare among the people his doings.

12When he maketh inquisition for blood, he remembereth them: he forgetteth not the cry of the humble.

PROVERBS FOR TODAY/ 2:18–22

For her house inclineth unto death, and her paths unto the dead. None that go unto her return again, neither take they hold of the paths of life. That thou mayest walk in the way of good men, and keep the paths of the righteous. For the upright shall dwell in the land, and the perfect shall remain in it. But the wicked shall be cut off from the earth, and the transgressors shall be rooted out of it.

JANUARY 10

GENESIS 23:1—24:51

AND Sarah was an hundred and seven and twenty years old: *these were* the years of the life of Sarah.

2And Sarah died in Kirjath–arba; the same *is* Hebron in the land of Canaan: and Abraham came to mourn for Sarah, and to weep for her.

3And Abraham stood up from before his dead, and spake unto the sons of Heth, saying,

4I *am* a stranger and a sojourner with you: give me a possession of a burying-place with you, that I may bury my dead out of my sight.

5And the children of Heth answered Abraham, saying unto him,

6Hear us, my lord: thou *art* a mighty prince among us: in the choice of our sepulchres bury thy dead; none of us shall withhold from thee his sepulchre, but that thou mayest bury thy dead.

7And Abraham stood up, and bowed himself to the people of the land, *even* to the children of Heth.

8And he communed with them, saying, If it be your mind that I should bury my dead out of my sight; hear me, and intreat for me to Ephron the son of Zohar,

9That he may give me the cave of Machpelah, which he hath, which *is* in the end of his field; for as much money as it is worth he shall give it me for a possession of a buryingplace amongst you.

10And Ephron dwelt among the children of Heth: and Ephron the Hittite answered Abraham in the audience of the children of Heth, *even* of all that went in at the gate of his city, saying,

11Nay, my lord, hear me: the field give I thee, and the cave that *is* therein, I give it thee; in the presence of the sons of my people give I it thee: bury thy dead.

12And Abraham bowed down himself before the people of the land.

13And he spake unto Ephron in the audience of the people of the land, saying, But if thou *wilt give it,* I pray thee, hear me: I will give thee money for the field; take *it* of me, and I will bury my dead there.

14And Ephron answered Abraham, saying unto him,

15My lord, hearken unto me: the land *is worth* four hundred shekels of silver; what *is* that betwixt me and thee? bury therefore thy dead.

16And Abraham hearkened unto Ephron; and Abraham weighed to Ephron the silver, which he had named in the audience of the sons of Heth, four hundred shekels of silver, current *money* with the merchant.

17And the field of Ephron, which *was* in Machpelah, which *was* before Mamre, the field, and the cave which *was* therein, and all the trees that *were* in the field, that *were* in all the borders round about, were made sure

18Unto Abraham for a possession in the presence of the children of Heth, before all that went in at the gate of his city.

19And after this, Abraham buried Sarah his wife in the cave of the field of Machpelah before Mamre: the same *is* Hebron in the land of Canaan.

20And the field, and the cave that *is* therein, were made sure unto Abraham for a possession of a buryingplace by the sons of Heth.

AND Abraham was old, *and* well stricken in age: and the LORD had blessed Abraham in all things.

2And Abraham said unto his eldest servant of his house, that ruled over all that he had, Put, I pray thee, thy hand under my thigh:

3And I will make thee swear by the LORD, the God of heaven, and the God of the earth, that thou shalt not take a wife unto my son of the daughters of the Canaanites, among whom I dwell:

4But thou shalt go unto my country, and to my kindred, and take a wife unto my son Isaac.

5And the servant said unto him, Peradventure the woman will not be willing to follow me unto this land: must I needs bring thy son again unto the land from whence thou camest?

6And Abraham said unto him, Beware thou that thou bring not my son thither again.

7The LORD God of heaven, which took me from my father's house, and from the land of my kindred, and which spake unto me, and that sware unto me, saying, Unto thy seed will I give this land; he shall send his angel before thee, and thou shalt take a wife unto my son from thence.

8And if the woman will not be willing to follow thee, then thou shalt be clear from this my oath: only bring not my son thither again.

9And the servant put his hand under the thigh of Abraham his master, and sware to him concerning that matter.

10And the servant took ten camels of the camels of his master, and departed; for all the goods of his master *were* in his hand: and he arose, and went to Mesopotamia, unto the city of Nahor.

11And he made his camels to kneel down without the city by a well of water at the time of the evening, *even* the time that women go out to draw *water.*

12And he said, O LORD God of my master Abraham, I pray thee, send me good speed this day, and shew kindness unto my master Abraham.

13Behold, I stand *here* by the well of water; and the daughters of the men of the city come out to draw water:

14And let it come to pass, that the damsel to whom I shall say, Let down thy pitcher, I pray thee, that I may drink; and she shall say, Drink, and I will give thy camels drink also: *let the same be* she *that* thou hast appointed for thy servant Isaac; and thereby shall I know that thou hast shewed kindness unto my master.

15And it came to pass, before he had done speaking, that, behold, Rebekah came out, who was born to Bethuel, son of Milcah, the wife of Nahor, Abraham's brother, with her pitcher upon her shoulder.

16And the damsel *was* very fair to look upon, a virgin, neither had any man known her: and she went down to the well, and filled her pitcher, and came up.

17And the servant ran to meet her, and said, Let me, I pray thee, drink a little water of thy pitcher.

18And she said, Drink, my lord: and she hasted, and let down her pitcher upon her hand, and gave him drink.

19And when she had done giving him drink, she said, I will draw *water* for

thy camels also, until they have done drinking.

20And she hasted, and emptied her pitcher into the trough, and ran again unto the well to draw *water,* and drew for all his camels.

21And the man wondering at her held his peace, to wit whether the LORD had made his journey prosperous or not.

22And it came to pass, as the camels had done drinking, that the man took a golden earring of half a shekel weight, and two bracelets for her hands of ten *shekels* weight of gold;

23And said, Whose daughter *art* thou? tell me, I pray thee: is there room *in* thy father's house for us to lodge in?

24And she said unto him, I *am* the daughter of Bethuel the son of Milcah, which she bare unto Nahor.

25She said moreover unto him, We have both straw and provender enough, and room to lodge in.

26And the man bowed down his head, and worshipped the LORD.

27And he said, Blessed *be* the LORD God of my master Abraham, who hath not left destitute my master of his mercy and his truth: I *being* in the way, the LORD led me to the house of my master's brethren.

28And the damsel ran, and told *them of* her mother's house these things.

29And Rebekah had a brother, and his name *was* Laban: and Laban ran out unto the man, unto the well.

30And it came to pass, when he saw the earring and bracelets upon his sister's hands, and when he heard the words of Rebekah his sister, saying, Thus spake the man unto me; that he came unto the man; and, behold, he stood by the camels at the well.

31And he said, Come in, thou blessed of the LORD; wherefore standest thou without? for I have prepared the house, and room for the camels.

32And the man came into the house: and he ungirded his camels, and gave straw and provender for the camels, and water to wash his feet, and the men's feet that *were* with him.

³³And there was set *meat* before him to eat: but he said, I will not eat, until I have told mine errand. And he said, Speak on.

³⁴And he said, I *am* Abraham's servant.

³⁵And the LORD hath blessed my master greatly; and he is become great: and he hath given him flocks, and herds, and silver, and gold, and menservants, and maidservants, and camels, and asses.

³⁶And Sarah my master's wife bare a son to my master when she was old: and unto him hath he given all that he hath.

³⁷And my master made me swear, saying, Thou shalt not take a wife to my son of the daughters of the Canaanites, in whose land I dwell:

³⁸But thou shalt go unto my father's house, and to my kindred, and take a wife unto my son.

³⁹And I said unto my master, Peradventure the woman will not follow me.

⁴⁰And he said unto me, The LORD, before whom I walk, will send his angel with thee, and prosper thy way; and thou shalt take a wife for my son of my kindred, and of my father's house:

⁴¹Then shalt thou be clear from *this* my oath, when thou comest to my kindred; and if they give not thee *one,* thou shalt be clear from my oath.

⁴²And I came this day unto the well, and said, O LORD God of my master Abraham, if now thou do prosper my way which I go:

⁴³Behold, I stand by the well of water; and it shall come to pass, that when the virgin cometh forth to draw *water,* and I say to her, Give me, I pray thee, a little water of thy pitcher to drink;

⁴⁴And she say to me, Both drink thou, and I will also draw for thy camels:

let the same *be* the woman whom the LORD hath appointed out for my master's son.

⁴⁵And before I had done speaking in mine heart, behold, Rebekah came forth with her pitcher on her shoulder; and she went down unto the well, and drew *water:* and I said unto her, Let me drink, I pray thee.

⁴⁶And she made haste, and let down her pitcher from her *shoulder,* and said, Drink, and I will give thy camels drink also: so I drank, and she made the camels drink also.

⁴⁷And I asked her, and said, Whose daughter *art* thou? And she said, The daughter of Bethuel, Nahor's son, whom Milcah bare unto him: and I put the earring upon her face, and the bracelets upon her hands.

⁴⁸And I bowed down my head, and worshipped the LORD, and blessed the LORD God of my master Abraham, which had led me in the right way to take my master's brother's daughter unto his son.

⁴⁹And now if ye will deal kindly and truly with my master, tell me: and if not, tell me; that I may turn to the right hand, or to the left.

⁵⁰Then Laban and Bethuel answered and said, the thing proceedeth from the LORD: we cannot speak unto thee bad or good.

⁵¹Behold, Rebekah *is* before thee, take *her,* and go, and let her be thy master's son's wife, as the LORD hath spoken.

MATTHEW 8:1–17

WHEN he [Jesus] was come down from the mountain, great multitudes followed him.

²And, behold, there came a leper and worshipped him, saying, Lord, if thou wilt, thou canst make me clean.

³And Jesus put forth *his* hand, and

touched him, saying, I will; be thou clean. And immediately his leprosy was cleansed.

4And Jesus saith unto him, See thou tell no man; but go thy way, shew thyself to the priest, and offer the gift that Moses commanded, for a testimony unto them.

5And when Jesus was entered into Capernaum, there came unto him a centurion, beseeching him,

6And saying, Lord, my servant lieth at home sick of the palsy, grievously tormented.

7And Jesus saith unto him, I will come and heal him.

8The centurion answered and said, Lord, I am not worthy that thou shouldest come under my roof: but speak the word only, and my servant shall be healed.

9For I am a man under authority, having soldiers under me: and I say to this *man,* Go, and he goeth; and to another, Come, and he cometh; and to my servant, Do this, and he doeth *it.*

10When Jesus heard *it,* he marvelled, and said to them that followed, Verily I say unto you, I have not found so great faith, no, not in Israel.

11And I say unto you, That many shall come from the east and west, and shall sit down with Abraham, and Isaac, and Jacob, in the kingdom of heaven.

12But the children of the kingdom shall be cast out into outer darkness: there shall be weeping and gnashing of teeth.

13And Jesus said unto the centurion, Go thy way; and as thou hast believed, *so* be it done unto thee. And his servant was healed in the selfsame hour.

14And when Jesus was come into Peter's house, he saw his wife's mother laid, and sick of a fever.

15And he touched her hand, and the fever left her: and she arose, and ministered unto them.

16When the even was come, they brought unto him many that were possessed with devils: and he cast out the spirits with *his* word, and healed all that were sick:

17That it might be fulfilled which was spoken by Esaias the prophet, saying, Himself took our infirmities, and bare *our* sicknesses.

PSALM 9:13–20

HAVE mercy upon me, O LORD; consider my trouble *which I suffer* of them that hate me, thou that liftest me up from the gates of death:

14That I may shew forth all thy praise in the gates of the daughter of Zion: I will rejoice in thy salvation.

15The heathen are sunk down in the pit *that* they made: in the net which they hid is their own foot taken.

16The LORD is known *by* the judgment *which* he executeth: the wicked is snared in the work of his own hands. Higgaion. Selah.

17The wicked shall be turned into hell, *and* all the nations that forget God.

18For the needy shall not alway be forgotten: the expectation of the poor shall *not* perish for ever.

19Arise, O LORD; let not man prevail: let the heathen be judged in thy sight.

20Put them in fear, O LORD: *that* the nations may know themselves *to be but* men. Selah.

PROVERBS FOR TODAY/ 3:1–6

My son, forget not my law; but let thine heart keep my commandments: For length of days, and long life, and peace, shall they add to thee. □ *Let not mercy and truth forsake thee: bind them about thy neck; write them upon the table of*

thine heart: So shalt thou find favour and good understanding in the sight of God and man. ☐ *Trust in the* LORD *with all thine heart; and lean not unto thine own understanding. In all thy ways acknowledge him, and he shall direct thy paths.*

JANUARY 11

GENESIS 24:52—26:16

And it came to pass, that, when Abraham's servant heard their [Laban's and Bethuel's] words, he worshipped the LORD, *bowing himself* to the earth.

53And the servant brought forth jewels of silver, and jewels of gold, and raiment, and gave *them* to Rebekah: he gave also to her brother and to her mother precious things.

54And they did eat and drink, he and the men that *were* with him, and tarried all night; and they rose up in the morning, and he said, Send me away unto my master.

55And her brother and her mother said, Let the damsel abide with us *a few* days, at the least ten; after that she shall go.

56And he said unto them, Hinder me not, seeing the LORD hath prospered my way; send me away that I may go to my master.

57And they said, We will call the damsel, and enquire at her mouth.

58And they called Rebekah, and said unto her, Wilt thou go with this man? And she said, I will go.

59And they sent away Rebekah their sister, and her nurse, and Abraham's servant, and his men.

60And they blessed Rebekah, and said unto her, Thou *art* our sister, be thou *the mother* of thousands of millions, and let thy seed possess the gate of those which hate them.

61And Rebekah arose, and her dam-sels, and they rode upon the camels, and followed the man: and the servant took Rebekah, and went his way.

62And Isaac came from the way of the well Lahairoi; for he dwelt in the south country.

63And Isaac went out to meditate in the field at the eventide: and he lifted up his eyes, and saw, and, behold, the camels *were* coming.

64And Rebekah lifted up her eyes, and when she saw Isaac, she lighted off the camel.

65For she *had* said unto the servant, What man *is* this that walketh in the field to meet us? And the servant *had* said, It *is* my master: therefore she took a vail, and covered herself.

66And the servant told Isaac all things that he had done.

67And Isaac brought her into his mother Sarah's tent, and took Rebekah, and she became his wife; and he loved her: and Isaac was comforted after his mother's *death.*

THEN again Abraham took a wife, and her name *was* Keturah.

2And she bare him Zimran, and Jokshan, and Medan, and Midian, and Ishbak, and Shuah.

3And Jokshan begat Sheba, and Dedan. And the sons of Dedan were Asshurim, and Letushim, and Leummim.

4And the sons of Midian; Ephah, and Epher, and Hanoch, and Abidah, and Eldaah. All these *were* the children of Keturah.

5And Abraham gave all that he had unto Isaac.

6But unto the sons of the concubines, which Abraham had, Abraham gave gifts, and sent them away from Isaac his son, while he yet lived, eastward, unto the east country.

7And these *are* the days of the years of Abraham's life which he lived, an hundred threescore and fifteen years.

8Then Abraham gave up the ghost, and died in a good old age, an old man, and full *of years;* and was gathered to his people.

9And his sons Isaac and Ishmael buried him in the cave of Machpelah, in the field of Ephron the son of Zohar the Hittite, which *is* before Mamre;

10The field which Abraham purchased of the sons of Heth: there was Abraham buried, and Sarah his wife.

11And it came to pass after the death of Abraham, that God blessed his son Isaac; and Isaac dwelt by the well Lahai-roi.

12Now these *are* the generations of Ishmael, Abraham's son, whom Hagar the Egyptian, Sarah's handmaid, bare unto Abraham:

13And these *are* the names of the sons of Ishmael, by their names, according to their generations: the firstborn of Ishmael, Nebajoth; and Kedar, and Adbeel, and Mibsam,

14And Mishma, and Dumah, and Massa,

15Hadar, and Tema, Jetur, Naphish, and Kedemah:

16These *are* the sons of Ishmael, and these *are* their names, by their towns, and by their castles; twelve princes according to their nations.

17And these *are* the years of the life of Ishmael, an hundred and thirty and seven years: and he gave up the ghost and died; and was gathered unto his people.

18And they dwelt from Havilah unto Shur, that *is* before Egypt, as thou goest toward Assyria: *and* he died in the presence of all his brethren.

19And these *are* the generations of Isaac, Abraham's son: Abraham begat Isaac:

20And Isaac was forty years old when he took Rebekah to wife, the daughter of Bethuel the Syrian of Padan-aram, the sister to Laban the Syrian.

21And Isaac intreated the LORD for his wife, because she *was* barren: and the LORD was intreated of him, and Rebekah his wife conceived.

22And the children struggled together within her; and she said, If *it be* so, why *am* I thus? And she went to enquire of the LORD.

23And the LORD said unto her, Two nations *are* in thy womb, and two manner of people shall be separated from thy bowels; and *the one* people shall be stronger than *the other* people; and the elder shall serve the younger.

24And when her days to be delivered were fulfilled, behold, *there were* twins in her womb.

25And the first came out red, all over like an hairy garment; and they called his name Esau.

26And after that came his brother out, and his hand took hold on Esau's heel; and his name was called Jacob: and Isaac *was* threescore years old when she bare them.

27And the boys grew: and Esau was a cunning hunter, a man of the field; and Jacob *was* a plain man, dwelling in tents.

28And Isaac loved Esau, because he did eat of *his* venison: but Rebekah loved Jacob.

29And Jacob sod pottage: and Esau came from the field, and he *was* faint:

30And Esau said to Jacob, Feed me, I pray thee, with that same red *pottage;* for I *am* faint: therefore was his name called Edom.

31And Jacob said, Sell me this day thy birthright.

32And Esau said, Behold, I *am* at

the point to die: and what profit shall this birthright do to me?

33And Jacob said, Swear to me this day; and he sware unto him: and he sold his birthright unto Jacob.

34Then Jacob gave Esau bread and pottage of lentiles; and he did eat and drink, and rose up, and went his way: thus Esau despised *his* birthright.

AND there was a famine in the land, beside the first famine that was in the days of Abraham. And Isaac went unto Abimelech king of the Philistines unto Gerar.

2And the LORD appeared unto him, and said, Go not down into Egypt; dwell in the land which I shall tell thee of:

3Sojourn in this land, and I will be with thee, and will bless thee; for unto thee, and unto thy seed, I will give all these countries, and I will perform the oath which I sware unto Abraham thy father;

4And I will make thy seed to multiply as the stars of heaven, and will give unto thy seed all these countries; and in thy seed shall all the nations of the earth be blessed;

5Because that Abraham obeyed my voice, and kept my charge, my commandments, my statutes, and my laws.

6And Isaac dwelt in Gerar:

7And the men of the place asked *him* of his wife; and he said, She *is* my sister: for he feared to say, *She is* my wife; lest, *said he,* the men of the place should kill me for Rebekah; because she *was* fair to look upon.

8And it came to pass, when he had been there a long time, that Abimelech king of the Philistines looked out at a window, and saw, and, behold, Isaac *was* sporting with Rebekah his wife.

9And Abimelech called Isaac, and said, Behold, of a surety she *is* thy wife: and how saidst thou, She *is* my sister? And Isaac said unto him, Because I said, Lest I die for her.

10And Abimelech said, What *is* this thou hast done unto us? one of the people might lightly have lien with thy wife, and thou shouldest have brought guiltiness upon us.

11And Abimelech charged all *his* people, saying, He that toucheth this man or his wife shall surely be put to death.

12Then Isaac sowed in that land, and received in the same year an hundredfold: and the LORD blessed him.

13And the man waxed great, and went forward, and grew until he became very great:

14For he had possession of flocks, and possession of herds, and great store of servants: and the Philistines envied him.

15For all the wells which his father's servants had digged in the days of Abraham his father, the Philistines had stopped them, and filled them with earth.

16And Abimelech said unto Isaac, Go from us; for thou art much mightier than we.

MATTHEW 8:18–34

Now when Jesus saw great multitudes about him, he gave commandment to depart unto the other side.

19And a certain scribe came, and said unto him, Master, I will follow thee whithersoever thou goest.

20And Jesus saith unto him, The foxes have holes, and the birds of the air *have* nests; but the Son of man hath not where to lay *his* head.

21And another of his disciples said unto him, Lord, suffer me first to go and bury my father.

22But Jesus said unto him, Follow me; and let the dead bury their dead.

23And when he was entered into a ship, his disciples followed him,

24And, behold, there arose a great tempest in the sea, insomuch that the ship was covered with the waves: but he was asleep.

25And his disciples came to *him* and awoke him, saying, Lord, save us: we perish.

26And he saith unto them, Why are ye fearful, O ye of little faith? Then he arose, and rebuked the winds and the sea; and there was a great calm.

27But the men marvelled, saying, What manner of man is this, that even the winds and the sea obey him!

28And when he was come to the other side into the country of the Gergesenes, there met him two possessed with devils, coming out of the tombs, exceeding fierce, so that no man might pass by that way.

29And, behold, they cried out, saying, What have we to do with thee, Jesus, thou Son of God? art thou come hither to torment us before the time?

30And there was a good way off from them an herd of many swine feeding.

31So the devils besought him, saying, If thou cast us out, suffer us to go away into the herd of swine.

32And he said unto them, Go. And when they were come out, they went into the herd of swine: and, behold, the whole herd of swine ran violently down a steep place into the sea, and perished in the waters.

33And they that kept them fled, and went their ways into the city, and told every thing, and what was befallen to the possessed of the devils.

34And, behold, the whole city came out to meet Jesus: and when they saw him, they besought *him* that he would depart out of their coasts.

PSALM 10:1–15

WHY standest thou afar off, O LORD? *why* hidest thou *thyself* in times of trouble?

2The wicked in *his* pride doth perse-cute the poor: let them be taken in the devices that they have imagined.

3For the wicked boasteth of his heart's desire, and blesseth the covetous, *whom* the LORD abhorreth.

4The wicked, through the pride of his countenance, will not seek *after God:* God *is* not in all his thoughts.

5His ways are always grievous; thy judgments *are* far above out of his sight: *as for* all his enemies, he puffeth at them.

6He hath said in his heart, I shall not be moved: for *I shall* never *be* in adversity.

7His mouth is full of cursing and deceit and fraud: under his tongue *is* mischief and vanity.

8He sitteth in the lurking places of the villages: in the secret places doth he murder the innocent: his eyes are privily set against the poor.

9He lieth in wait secretly as a lion in his den: he lieth in wait to catch the poor: he doth catch the poor, when he draweth him into his net.

10He croucheth, *and* humbleth himself, that the poor may fall by his strong ones.

11He hath said in his heart, God hath forgotten: he hideth his face; he will never see *it.*

12Arise, O LORD; O God, lift up thine hand: forget not the humble.

13Wherefore doth the wicked contemn God? he hath said in his heart, Thou wilt not require *it.*

14Thou hast seen *it;* for thou beholdest mischief and spite, to requite *it* with thy hand: the poor committeth himself unto thee; thou art the helper of the fatherless.

15Break thou the arm of the wicked and the evil *man:* seek out his wickedness *till* thou find none.

PROVERBS FOR TODAY/ 3:7–8

Be not wise in thine own eyes: fear the LORD, and depart from evil. It shall be health to thy navel, and marrow to thy bones.

JANUARY 12

GENESIS 26:17—27:46

AND Isaac departed thence, and pitched his tent in the valley of Gerar, and dwelt there.

18And Isaac digged again the wells of water, which they had digged in the days of Abraham his father; for the Philistines had stopped them after the death of Abraham: and he called their names after the names by which his father had called them.

19And Isaac's servants digged in the valley, and found there a well of springing water.

20And the herdmen of Gerar did strive with Isaac's herdmen, saying, The water *is* ours: and he called the name of the well Esek; because they strove with him.

21And they digged another well, and strove for that also: and called the name of it Sitnah.

22And he removed from thence, and digged another well; and for that they strove not: and he called the name of it Rehoboth; and he said, For now the LORD hath made room for us, and we shall be fruitful in the land.

23And he went up from thence to Beer-sheba.

24And the LORD appeared unto him the same night, and said, I *am* the God of Abraham thy father: fear not, for I *am* with thee, and will bless thee, and multiply thy seed for my servant Abraham's sake.

25And he builded an altar there, and called upon the name of the LORD, and pitched his tent there: and there Isaac's servants digged a well.

26Then Abimelech went to him from Gerar, and Ahuzzath one of his friends, and Phichol the chief captain of his army.

27And Isaac said unto them, Where-fore come ye to me, seeing ye hate me, and have sent me away from you?

28And they said, We saw certainly that the LORD was with thee: and we said, Let there be now an oath betwixt us, *even* betwixt us and thee, and let us make a covenant with thee;

29That thou wilt do us no hurt, as we have not touched thee, and as we have done unto thee nothing but good, and have sent thee away in peace: thou *art* now the blessed of the LORD.

30And he made them a feast, and they did eat and drink.

31And they rose up betimes in the morning, and sware one to another: and Isaac sent them away, and they departed from him in peace.

32And it came to pass the same day, that Isaac's servants came, and told him concerning the well which they had digged, and said unto him, We have found water.

33And he called it Shebah: therefore the name of the city *is* Beer-sheba unto this day.

34And Esau was forty years old when he took to wife Judith the daughter of Beeri the Hittite, and Bashemath the daughter of Elon the Hittite:

35Which were a grief of mind unto Isaac and to Rebekah.

AND it came to pass, that when Isaac was old, and his eyes were dim, so that he could not see, he called Esau his eldest son, and said unto him, My son: and he said unto him, Behold, *here am* I.

2And he said, Behold now, I am old, I know not the day of my death:

3Now therefore take, I pray thee, thy weapons, thy quiver and thy bow, and go out to the field, and take me *some* venison;

4And make me savoury meat, such as I love, and bring *it* to me, that I may eat; that my soul may bless thee before I die.

5And Rebekah heard when Isaac spake to Esau his son. And Esau went to the field to hunt *for* venison, *and* to bring *it*.

6And Rebekah spake unto Jacob her son, saying, Behold, I heard thy father speak unto Esau thy brother, saying,

7Bring me venison, and make me savoury meat, that I may eat, and bless thee before the LORD before my death.

8Now therefore, my son, obey my voice according to that which I command thee.

9Go now to the flock, and fetch me from thence two good kids of the goats; and I will make them savoury meat for thy father, such as he loveth:

10And thou shalt bring *it* to thy father, that he may eat, and that he may bless thee before his death.

11And Jacob said to Rebekah his mother, Behold, Esau my brother *is* a hairy man, and I *am* a smooth man:

12My father peradventure will feel me, and I shall seem to him as a deceiver; and I shall bring a curse upon me, and not a blessing.

13And his mother said unto him, Upon me *be* thy curse, my son: only obey my voice, and go fetch me *them*.

14And he went, and fetched, and brought *them* to his mother: and his mother made savoury meat, such as his father loved.

15And Rebekah took goodly raiment of her eldest son Esau, which *were* with her in the house, and put them upon Jacob her younger son:

16And she put the skins of the kids of the goats upon his hands, and upon the smooth of his neck:

17And she gave the savoury meat and the bread, which she had prepared, into the hand of her son Jacob.

18And he came unto his father, and said, My father: and he said, Here *am* I; who *art* thou, my son?

19And Jacob said unto his father, I *am* Esau thy firstborn; I have done according as thou badest me: arise, I pray thee, sit and eat of my venison, that thy soul may bless me.

20And Isaac said unto his son, How *is it* that thou hast found *it* so quickly, my son? And he said, Because the LORD thy God brought *it* to me.

21And Isaac said unto Jacob, Come near, I pray thee, that I may feel thee, my son, whether thou *be* my very son Esau or not.

22And Jacob went near unto Isaac his father; and he felt him, and said, The voice *is* Jacob's voice, but the hands *are* the hands of Esau.

23And he discerned him not, because his hands were hairy, as his brother Esau's hands: so he blessed him.

24And he said, *Art* thou my very son Esau? And he said, I *am*.

25And he said, Bring *it* near to me, and I will eat of my son's venison, that my soul may bless thee. And he brought *it* near to him, and he did eat: and he brought him wine, and he drank.

26And his father Isaac said unto him, Come near now, and kiss me, my son.

27And he came near, and kissed him: and he smelled the smell of his raiment, and blessed him, and said, See, the smell of my son *is* as the smell of a field which the LORD hath blessed:

28Therefore God give thee of the dew of heaven, and the fatness of the earth, and plenty of corn and wine:

29Let people serve thee, and nations bow down to thee: be lord over thy brethren, and let thy mother's sons bow down to thee: cursed *be* every one that curseth thee, and blessed *be* he that blesseth thee.

30And it came to pass, as soon as Isaac had made an end of blessing Jacob, and Jacob was yet scarce gone out from the presence of Isaac his father, that Esau his brother came in from his hunting.

31And he also had made savoury meat, and brought it unto his father, and said unto his father, Let my father arise, and eat of his son's venison, that thy soul may bless me.

32And Isaac his father said unto him, Who *art* thou? And he said, I *am* thy son, thy firstborn Esau.

33And Isaac trembled very exceedingly, and said, Who? where *is* he that hath taken venison, and brought *it* me, and I have eaten of all before thou camest, and have blessed him? yea, and he shall be blessed.

34And when Esau heard the words of his father, he cried with a great and exceeding bitter cry, and said unto his father, Bless me, *even* me also, O my father.

35And he said, Thy brother came with subtilty, and hath taken away thy blessing.

36And he said, Is not he rightly named Jacob? for he hath supplanted me these two times: he took away my birthright; and, behold, now he hath taken away my blessing. And he said, Hath thou not reserved a blessing for me?

37And Isaac answered and said unto Esau, Behold, I have made him thy lord, and all his brethren have I given to him for servants; and with corn and wine have I sustained him: and what shall I do now unto thee, my son?

38And Esau said unto his father, Hast thou but one blessing, my father? bless me, *even* me also, O my father. And Esau lifted up his voice, and wept.

39And Isaac his father answered and said unto him, Behold, thy dwelling shall be the fatness of the earth, and of the dew of heaven from above;

40And by thy sword shalt thou live, and shalt serve thy brother; and it shall come to pass when thou shalt have the dominion, that thou shalt break his yoke from off thy neck.

41And Esau hated Jacob because of the blessing wherewith his father blessed him: and Esau said in his heart, The days of mourning for my father are at hand; then will I slay my brother Jacob.

42And these words of Esau her elder son were told to Rebekah: and she sent and called Jacob her younger son, and said unto him, Behold, thy brother Esau, as touching thee, doth comfort himself, *purposing* to kill thee.

43Now therefore, my son, obey my voice; and arise, flee thou to Laban my brother to Haran;

44And tarry with him a few days, until thy brother's fury turn away;

45Until thy brother's anger turn away from thee, and he forget *that* which thou hast done to him: then I will send, and fetch thee from thence: why should I be deprived also of you both in one day?

46And Rebekah said to Isaac, I am weary of my life because of the daughters of Heth: if Jacob take a wife of the daughters of Heth, such as these *which are* of the daughters of the land, what good shall my life do me?

MATTHEW 9:1-17

AND he [Jesus] entered into a ship, and passed over, and came into his own city.

2And, behold, they brought to him a man sick of the palsy, lying on a bed: and Jesus seeing their faith said unto the sick of the palsy; Son, be of good cheer; thy sins be forgiven thee.

3And, behold, certain of the scribes said within themselves, This *man* blasphemeth.

4And Jesus knowing their thoughts said, Wherefore think ye evil in your hearts?

5For whether is easier, to say, *Thy* sins be forgiven thee; or to say, Arise, and walk?

6But that ye may know that the Son of man hath power on earth to forgive sins, (then saith he to the sick of the palsy,) Arise, take up thy bed, and go unto thine house.

7And he arose, and departed to his house.

8But when the multitudes saw *it,* they marvelled, and glorified God, which had given such power unto men.

9And as Jesus passed forth from thence, he saw a man, named Matthew, sitting at the receipt of custom: and he saith unto him, Follow me. And he arose, and followed him.

10And it came to pass, as Jesus sat at meat in the house, behold, many publicans and sinners came and sat down with him and his disciples.

11And when the Pharisees saw *it,* they said unto his disciples, Why eateth your Master with publicans and sinners?

12But when Jesus heard *that,* he said unto them, They that be whole need not a physician, but they that are sick.

13But go ye and learn what *that* meaneth, I will have mercy, and not sacrifice:

for I am not come to call the righteous, but sinners to repentance.

14Then came to him the disciples of John, saying, Why do we and the Pharisees fast oft, but thy disciples fast not?

15And Jesus said unto them, Can the children of the bridechamber mourn, as long as the bridegroom is with them? but the days will come, when the bridegroom shall be taken from them, and then shall they fast.

16No man putteth a piece of new cloth unto an old garment, for that which is put in to fill it up taketh from the garment, and the rent is made worse.

17Neither do men put new wine into old bottles: else the bottles break, and the wine runneth out, and the bottles perish: but they put new wine into new bottles, and both are preserved.

PSALM 10:16–18

THE LORD *is* King for ever and ever: the heathen are perished out of his land.

17LORD, thou hast heard the desire of the humble: thou wilt prepare their heart, thou wilt cause thine ear to hear:

18To judge the fatherless and the oppressed, that the man of the earth may no more oppress.

PROVERBS FOR TODAY/ 3:9–10

Honour the LORD with thy substance, and with the firstfruits of all thine increase: So shall thy barns be filled with plenty, and thy presses shall burst out with new wine.

JANUARY 13

GENESIS 28:1—29:35

AND Isaac called Jacob, and blessed him, and charged him, and said unto him, Thou shalt not take a wife of the daughters of Canaan.

2Arise, go to Padan-aram, to the house of Bethuel thy mother's father; and take thee a wife from thence of the daughters of Laban thy mother's brother.

3And God Almighty bless thee, and make thee fruitful, and multiply thee, that thou mayest be a multitude of people;

4And give thee the blessing of Abraham, to thee, and to thy seed with thee; that thou mayest inherit the land wherein thou art a stranger, which God gave unto Abraham.

5And Isaac sent away Jacob: and he went to Padan-aram unto Laban, son of Bethuel the Syrian, the brother of Rebekah, Jacob's and Esau's mother.

6When Esau saw that Isaac had blessed Jacob, and sent him away to Padan-aram, to take him a wife from thence; and that as he blessed him he gave him a charge, saying, Thou shalt not take a wife of the daughters of Canaan;

7And that Jacob obeyed his father and his mother, and was gone to Padan-aram;

8And Esau seeing that the daughters of Canaan pleased not Isaac his father;

9Then went Esau unto Ishmael, and took unto the wives which he had Mahalath the daughter of Ishmael Abraham's son, the sister of Nebajoth, to be his wife.

10And Jacob went out from Beer-sheba, and went toward Haran.

11And he lighted upon a certain place, and tarried there all night, because the sun was set; and he took of the stones of that place, and put *them for* his pillows, and lay down in that place to sleep.

12And he dreamed, and behold a ladder set up on the earth, and the top of it reached to heaven: and behold the angels of God ascending and descending on it.

13And, behold, the LORD stood above it, and said, I *am* the LORD God of Abraham thy father, and the God of Isaac: the land whereon thou liest, to thee will I give it, and to thy seed;

14And thy seed shall be as the dust of the earth, and thou shalt spread abroad to the west, and to the east, and to the north, and to the south: and in thee and in thy seed shall all the families of the earth be blessed.

15And, behold, I *am* with thee, and will keep thee in all *places* whither thou goest, and will bring thee again into this land; for I will not leave thee, until I have done *that* which I have spoken to thee of.

16And Jacob awaked out of his sleep, and he said, Surely the LORD is in this place; and I knew *it* not.

17And he was afraid, and said, How dreadful *is* this place! this *is* none other but the house of God, and this *is* the gate of heaven.

18And Jacob rose up early in the morning, and took the stone that he had put *for* his pillows, and set it up *for* a pillar, and poured oil upon the top of it.

19And he called the name of that place Beth-el: but the name of that city *was called* Luz at the first.

20And Jacob vowed a vow, saying, If God will be with me, and will keep me in this way that I go, and will give me bread to eat, and raiment to put on,

21So that I come again to my father's house in peace; then shall the LORD be my God:

22And this stone, which I have set *for* a pillar, shall be God's house: and of all that thou shalt give me I will surely give the tenth unto thee.

THEN Jacob went on his journey, and came into the land of the people of the east.

2And he looked, and behold a well in the field, and, lo, there *were* three flocks of sheep lying by it; for out of that well they watered the flocks: and a great stone *was* upon the well's mouth.

3And thither were all the flocks gathered: and they rolled the stone from the well's mouth, and watered the sheep, and put the stone again upon the well's mouth in his place.

4And Jacob said unto them, My brethren, whence *be* ye? and they said, Of Haran *are* we.

5And he said unto them, Know ye Laban the son of Nahor? And they said, We know *him.*

6And he said unto them, *Is* he well? And they said, *He is* well: and, behold, Rachel his daughter cometh with the sheep.

7And he said, Lo, *it is* yet high day, neither *is it* time that the cattle should be gathered together: water ye the sheep, and go *and* feed *them.*

8And they said, We cannot, until all the flocks be gathered together, and *till* they roll the stone from the well's mouth; then we water the sheep.

9And while he yet spake with them, Rachel came with her father's sheep: for she kept them.

10And it came to pass, when Jacob saw Rachel the daughter of Laban his mother's brother, and the sheep of Laban his mother's brother, that Jacob went near, and rolled the stone from the well's mouth, and watered the flock of Laban his mother's brother.

11And Jacob kissed Rachel, and lifted up his voice, and wept.

12And Jacob told Rachel that he *was* her father's brother, and that he *was* Rebekah's son: and she ran and told her father.

13And it came to pass, when Laban heard the tidings of Jacob his sister's son, that he ran to meet him, and embraced him, and kissed him, and brought him to his house. And he told Laban all these things.

14And Laban said to him, Surely thou *art* my bone and my flesh. And he abode with him the space of a month.

15And Laban said unto Jacob, Because thou *art* my brother, shouldest thou therefore serve me for nought? tell me, what *shall* thy wages *be?*

16And Laban had two daughters: the name of the elder *was* Leah, and the name of the younger *was* Rachel.

17Leah *was* tender eyed; but Rachel was beautiful and well favoured.

18And Jacob loved Rachel; and said, I will serve thee seven years for Rachel thy younger daughter.

19And Laban said, *It is* better that I give her to thee, than that I should give her to another man: abide with me.

20And Jacob served seven years for Rachel; and they seemed unto him *but* a few days, for the love he had to her.

21And Jacob said unto Laban, Give *me* my wife, for my days are fulfilled, that I may go in unto her.

22And Laban gathered together all the men of the place, and made a feast.

23And it came to pass in the evening, that he took Leah his daughter, and brought her to him; and he went in unto her.

24And Laban gave unto his daughter Leah Zilpah his maid *for* an handmaid.

25And it came to pass, that in the morning, behold, it *was* Leah: and he said to Laban, What *is* this thou hast done unto me? did not I serve with thee for Rachel? wherefore then hast thou beguiled me?

26And Laban said, It must not be so done in our country, to give the younger before the firstborn.

27Fulfil her week, and we will give thee this also for the service which thou shalt serve with me yet seven other years.

28And Jacob did so, and fulfilled her week: and he gave him Rachel his daughter to wife also.

29And Laban gave to Rachel his daughter Bilhah his handmaid to be her maid.

30And he went in also unto Rachel, and he loved also Rachel more than Leah, and served with him yet seven other years.

31And when the Lord saw that Leah *was* hated, he opened her womb: but Rachel *was* barren.

32And Leah conceived, and bare a son, and she called his name Reuben: for she said, Surely the LORD hath looked upon my affliction; now therefore my husband will love me.

33And she conceived again, and bare a son; and said, Because the LORD hath heard that I *was* hated, he hath therefore given me this *son* also: and she called his name Simeon.

34And she conceived again, and bare a son; and said, Now this time will my husband be joined unto me, because I have born him three sons: therefore was his name called Levi.

35And she conceived again, and bare a son: and she said, Now will I praise the LORD: therefore she called his name Judah; and left bearing.

MATTHEW 9:18–38

WHILE he [Jesus] spake these things unto them, behold, there came a certain ruler, and worshipped him, saying, My daugh-ter is even now dead: but come and lay thy hand upon her, and she shall live.

19And Jesus arose, and followed him, and *so did* his disciples.

20And, behold, a woman, which was diseased with an issue of blood twelve years, came behind *him,* and touched the hem of his garment:

21For she said within herself, If I may but touch his garment, I shall be whole.

22But Jesus turned him about, and when he saw her, he said, Daughter, be of good comfort; thy faith hath made thee whole. And the woman was made whole from that hour.

23And when Jesus came into the rul-er's house, and saw the minstrels and the people making a noise,

24He said unto them, Give place: for the maid is not dead, but sleepeth. And they laughed him to scorn.

25But when the people were put forth, he went in, and took her by the hand, and the maid arose.

26And the fame hereof went abroad into all that land.

27And when Jesus departed thence, two blind men followed him, crying, and saying, *Thou* son of David, have mercy on us.

28And when he was come into the house, the blind men came to him: and Jesus saith unto them, Believe ye that I am able to do this? They said unto him, Yea, Lord.

29Then touched he their eyes, say-ing, According to your faith be it unto you.

30And their eyes were opened; and Jesus straitly charged them, saying, See *that* no man know *it.*

31But they, when they were de-parted, spread abroad his fame in all that country.

32As they went out, behold, they brought to him a dumb man possessed with a devil.

33And when the devil was cast out,

the dumb spake: and the multitudes marvelled, saying, It was never so seen in Israel.

34But the Pharisees said, He casteth out devils through the prince of the devils.

35And Jesus went about all the cities and villages, teaching in their synagogues, and preaching the gospel of the kingdom, and healing every sickness and every disease among the people.

36But when he saw the multitudes, he was moved with compassion on them, because they fainted, and were scattered abroad, as sheep having no shepherd.

37Then saith he unto his disciples, The harvest truly *is* plenteous, but the labourers *are* few;

38Pray ye therefore the Lord of the harvest, that he will send forth labourers into his harvest.

PSALM 11:1–7

IN the LORD put I my trust: how say ye to my soul, Flee *as* a bird to your mountain?

2For, lo, the wicked bend *their* bow, they make ready their arrow upon the string, that they may privily shoot at the upright in heart.

3If the foundations be destroyed, what can the righteous do?

4The LORD *is* in his holy temple, the LORD's throne *is* in heaven: his eyes behold, his eyelids try, the children of men.

5The LORD trieth the righteous: but the wicked and him that loveth violence his soul hateth.

6Upon the wicked he shall rain snares, fire and brimstone, and an horrible tempest: *this shall be* the portion of their cup.

7For the righteous LORD loveth righteousness; his countenance doth behold the upright.

PROVERBS FOR TODAY/ 3:11–12

My son, despise not the chastening of the LORD; neither be weary of his correction: For whom the LORD loveth he correcteth; even as a father the son in whom *he delighteth.*

JANUARY 14

GENESIS 30:1—31:16

AND when Rachel saw that she bare Jacob no children, Rachel envied her sister; and said unto Jacob, Give me children, or else I die.

2And Jacob's anger was kindled against Rachel: and he said, *Am* I in God's stead, who hath withheld from thee the fruit of the womb?

3And she said, Behold my maid Bilhah, go in unto her; and she shall bear upon my knees, that I may also have children by her.

4And she gave him Bilhah her handmaid to wife: and Jacob went in unto her.

5And Bilhah conceived, and bare Jacob a son.

6And Rachel said, God hath judged me, and hath also heard my voice, and hath given me a son: therefore called she his name Dan.

7And Bilhah Rachel's maid conceived again, and bare Jacob a second son.

8And Rachel said, With great wrestlings have I wrestled with my sister, and I have prevailed: and she called his name Naphtali.

9When Leah saw that she had left bearing, she took Zilpah her maid, and gave her Jacob to wife.

10And Zilpah Leah's maid bare Jacob a son.

11And Leah said, A troop cometh: and she called his name Gad.

12And Zilpah Leah's maid bare Jacob a second son.

13And Leah said, Happy am I, for the daughters will call me blessed: and she called his name Asher.

14And Reuben went in the days of wheat harvest, and found mandrakes in the field, and brought them unto his mother Leah. Then Rachel said to Leah, Give me, I pray thee, of thy son's mandrakes.

15And she said unto her, *Is it* a small matter that thou hast taken my husband? and wouldest thou take away my son's mandrakes also? And Rachel said, Therefore he shall lie with thee to night for thy son's mandrakes.

16And Jacob came out of the field in the evening, and Leah went out to meet him, and said, Thou must come in unto me; for surely I have hired thee with my son's mandrakes. And he lay with her that night.

17And God hearkened unto Leah, and she conceived, and bare Jacob the fifth son.

18And Leah said, God hath given me my hire, because I have given my maiden to my husband: and she called his name Issachar.

19And Leah conceived again, and bare Jacob the sixth son.

20And Leah said, God hath endued me *with* a good dowry; now will my husband dwell with me, because I have born him six sons: and she called his name Zebulun.

21And afterwards she bare a daughter, and called her name Dinah.

22And God remembered Rachel, and God hearkened to her, and opened her womb.

23And she conceived, and bare a son; and said, God hath taken away my reproach:

24And she called his name Joseph; and said, The LORD shall add to me another son.

25And it came to pass, when Rachel had born Joseph, that Jacob said unto Laban, Send me away, that I may go unto mine own place, and to my country.

26Give *me* my wives and my children, for whom I have served thee, and let me go: for thou knowest my service which I have done thee.

27And Laban said unto him, I pray thee, if I have found favour in thine eyes, *tarry; for* I have learned by experience that the LORD hath blessed me for thy sake.

28And he said, Appoint me thy wages, and I will give *it.*

29And he said unto him, Thou knowest how I have served thee, and how thy cattle was with me.

30For *it was* little which thou hadst before I *came,* and it is *now* increased unto a multitude; and the LORD hath blessed thee since my coming: and now when shall I provide for mine own house also?

31And he said, What shall I give thee? And Jacob said, Thou shalt not give me any thing: if thou wilt do this thing for me, I will again feed *and* keep thy flock.

32I will pass through all thy flock to day, removing from thence all the speckled and spotted cattle, and all the brown cattle among the sheep, and the spotted and speckled among the goats: and *of such* shall be my hire.

33So shall my righteousness answer for me in time to come, when it shall come for my hire before thy face: every one that *is* not speckled and spotted among the goats, and brown among the sheep, that shall be counted stolen with me.

34And Laban said, Behold, I would it might be according to thy word.

35And he removed that day the he goats that were ringstraked and spotted, and all the she goats that were speckled and spotted, *and* every one that had *some* white in it, and all the brown among the sheep, and gave *them* into the hand of his sons.

36And he set three days' journey betwixt himself and Jacob: and Jacob fed the rest of Laban's flocks.

37And Jacob took him rods of green poplar, and of the hazel and chestnut tree; and pilled white stakes in them, and made the white appear which *was* in the rods.

38And he set the rods which he had pilled before the flocks in the gutters in the watering troughs when the flocks came to drink, that they should conceive when they came to drink.

39And the flocks conceived before the rods, and brought forth cattle ringstraked, speckled, and spotted.

40And Jacob did separate the lambs, and set the faces of the flocks toward the ringstraked, and all the brown in the flock of Laban; and he put his own flocks by themselves, and put them not unto Laban's cattle.

41And it came to pass, whensoever the stronger cattle did conceive, that Jacob laid the rods before the eyes of the cattle in the gutters, that they might conceive among the rods.

42But when the cattle were feeble, he put *them* not in: so the feebler were Laban's, and the stronger Jacob's.

43And the man increased exceedingly, and had much cattle, and maidservants, and menservants, and camels, and asses.

AND he [Jacob] heard the words of Laban's sons, saying, Jacob hath taken away all that *was* our father's; and of *that* which *was* our father's hath he gotten all this glory.

2And Jacob beheld the countenance of Laban, and, behold, it *was* not toward him as before.

3And the LORD said unto Jacob, Return unto the land of thy fathers, and to thy kindred; and I will be with thee.

4And Jacob sent and called Rachel and Leah to the field unto his flock.

5And said unto them, I see your father's countenance, that it *is* not toward me as before; but the God of my father hath been with me.

6And ye know that with all my power I have served your father.

7And your father hath deceived me, and changed my wages ten times; but God suffered him not to hurt me.

8If he said thus, The speckled shall be thy wages; then all the cattle bare speckled: and if he said thus, The ringstraked shall be thy hire; then bare all the cattle ringstraked.

9Thus God hath taken away the cattle of your father, and given *them* to me.

10And it came to pass at the time that the cattle conceived, that I lifted up mine eyes, and saw in a dream, and, behold, the rams which leaped upon the cattle *were* ringstraked, speckled, and grisled.

11And the angel of God spake unto me in a dream, *saying*, Jacob: and I said, Here *am* I.

12And he said, Lift up now thine eyes, and see, all the rams which leap upon the cattle *are* ringstraked, speckled, and grisled: for I have seen all that Laban doeth unto thee.

13I *am* the God of Beth–el, where thou anointedst the pillar, *and* where thou vowedst a vow unto me: now arise, get thee out from this land, and return unto the land of thy kindred.

14And Rachel and Leah answered and said unto him, *Is there* yet any portion or inheritance for us in our father's house?

15Are we not counted of him strangers? for he hath sold us, and hath quite devoured also our money.

16For all the riches which God hath taken from our father, that *is* ours, and our children's: now then, whatsoever God hath said unto thee, do.

MATTHEW 10:1–26

AND when he [Jesus] had called unto *him* his twelve disciples, he gave them power *against* unclean spirits, to cast them out, and to heal all manner of sickness and all manner of disease.

2Now the names of the twelve apostles are these; The first, Simon, who is called Peter, and Andrew his brother; James *the son* of Zebedee, and John his brother;

3Philip, and Bartholomew; Thomas, and Matthew the publican; James *the son* of Alphaeus, and Lebbaeus whose surname was Thaddaeus;

4Simon the Canaanite, and Judas Iscariot, who also betrayed him.

5These twelve Jesus sent forth, and commanded them, saying, Go not into the way of the Gentiles, and into *any* city of the Samaritans enter ye not:

6But go rather to the lost sheep of the house of Israel.

7And as ye go, preach, saying, The kingdom of heaven is at hand.

8Heal the sick, cleanse the lepers, raise the dead, cast out devils: freely ye have received, freely give.

9Provide neither gold, nor silver, nor brass in your purses,

10Nor scrip for *your* journey, neither two coats, neither shoes, nor yet staves: for the workman is worthy of his meat.

11And into whatsoever city or town ye shall enter, enquire who in it is worthy; and there abide till ye go thence.

12And when ye come into an house, salute it.

13And if the house be worthy, let your peace come upon it: but if it be not worthy, let your peace return to you.

14And whosoever shall not receive you, nor hear your words, when ye depart out of that house or city, shake off the dust of your feet.

15Verily I say unto you, It shall be more tolerable for the land of Sodom and Gomorrha in the day of judgment, than for that city.

16Behold, I send you forth as sheep in the midst of wolves: be ye therefore wise as serpents, and harmless as doves.

17But beware of men: for they will deliver you up to the councils, and they will scourge you in their synagogues;

18And ye shall be brought before governors and kings for my sake, for a testimony against them and the Gentiles.

19But when they deliver you up, take no thought how or what ye shall speak: for it shall be given you in that same hour what ye shall speak.

20For it is not ye that speak, but the Spirit of your Father which speaketh in you.

21And the brother shall deliver up the brother to death, and the father the child: and the children shall rise up against *their* parents, and cause them to be put to death.

22And ye shall be hated of all *men* for my name's sake: but he that endureth to the end shall be saved.

23But when they persecute you in this city, flee ye into another: for verily I say unto you, Ye shall not have gone over the cities of Israel, till the Son of man be come.

24The disciple is not above *his* master, nor the servant above his lord.

25It is enough for the disciple that he be as his master, and the servant as his lord. If they have called the master of the house Beelzebub, how much more *shall they call* them of his household?

26Fear them not therefore: for there

is nothing covered, that shall not be revealed; and hid, that shall not be known.

PSALM 12:1–8

HELP, LORD; for the godly man ceaseth; for the faithful fail from among the children of men.

²They speak vanity every one with his neighbour: *with* flattering lips *and* with a double heart do they speak.

³The LORD shall cut off all flattering lips, *and* the tongue that speaketh proud things:

⁴Who have said, With our tongue will we prevail; our lips *are* our own: who *is* lord over us?

⁵For the oppression of the poor, for the sighing of the needy, now will I arise, saith the LORD; I will set *him* in safety *from him that* puffeth at him.

⁶The words of the LORD *are* pure words: *as* silver tried in a furnace of earth, purified seven times.

⁷Thou shalt keep them, O LORD, thou shalt preserve them from this generation for ever.

⁸The wicked walk on every side, when the vilest men are exalted.

PROVERBS FOR TODAY/ 3:13–15

Happy is *the man* that *findeth wisdom, and the man* that *getteth understanding. For the merchandise of it* is *better than the merchandise of silver, and the gain thereof than fine gold. She* is *more precious than rubies: and all the things thou canst desire are not to be compared unto her.*

JANUARY 15

GENESIS 31:17—32:12

THEN Jacob rose up, and set his sons and his wives upon camels; ¹⁸And he carried away all his cattle, and all his goods which he had gotten, the cattle of his getting, which he had gotten in Padan–aram, for to go to Isaac his father in the land of Canaan.

¹⁹And Laban went to shear his sheep: and Rachel had stolen the images that *were* her father's.

²⁰And Jacob stole away unawares to Laban the Syrian, in that he told him not that he fled.

²¹So he fled with all that he had; and he rose up, and passed over the river, and set his face *toward* the mount Gilead.

²²And it was told Laban on the third day that Jacob was fled.

²³And he took his brethren with him, and pursued after him seven days' journey; and they overtook him in the mount Gilead.

²⁴And God came to Laban the Syrian in a dream by night, and said unto him, Take heed that thou speak not to Jacob either good or bad.

²⁵Then Laban overtook Jacob. Now Jacob had pitched his tent in the mount: and Laban with his brethren pitched in the mount of Gilead.

²⁶And Laban said to Jacob, What hast thou done, that thou hast stolen away unawares to me, and carried away my daughters, as captives *taken* with the sword?

²⁷Wherefore didst thou flee away secretly, and steal away from me; and

didst not tell me, that I might have sent thee away with mirth, and with songs, with tabret, and with harp?

28And hast not suffered me to kiss my sons and my daughters? thou hast now done foolishly in *so* doing.

29It is in the power of my hand to do you hurt: but the God of your father spake unto me yesternight, saying, Take thou heed that thou speak not to Jacob either good or bad.

30And now, *though* thou wouldest needs be gone, because thou sore long-edst after thy father's house, *yet* wherefore hast thou stolen my gods?

31And Jacob answered and said to Laban, Because I was afraid: for I said, Peradventure thou wouldest take by force thy daughters from me.

32With whomsoever thou findest thy gods, let him not live: before our breth-ren discern thou what *is* thine with me, and take *it* to thee. For Jacob knew not that Rachel had stolen them.

33And Laban went into Jacob's tent, and into Leah's tent, and into the two maidservants' tents; but he found *them* not. Then went he out of Leah's tent, and entered into Rachel's tent.

34Now Rachel had taken the images, and put them in the camel's furniture, and sat upon them. And Laban searched all the tent, but found *them* not.

35And she said to her father, Let it not displease my lord that I cannot rise up before thee; for the custom of women *is* upon me. And he searched, but found not the images.

36And Jacob was wroth, and chode with Laban: and Jacob answered and said to Laban, What *is* my trespass? what *is* my sin, that thou hast so hotly pursued after me?

37Whereas thou hast searched all my stuff, what hast thou found of all thy household stuff? set *it* here before my brethren and thy brethren, that they may judge betwixt us both.

38This twenty years *have I been* with thee; thy ewes and thy she goats have not cast their young, and the rams of thy flock have I not eaten.

39That which was torn *of beasts* I brought not unto thee; I bare the loss of it; of my hand didst thou require it, *whether* stolen by day, or stolen by night.

40*Thus* I was; in the day the drought consumed me, and the frost by night; and my sleep departed from mine eyes.

41Thus have I been twenty years in thy house; I served thee fourteen years for thy two daughters, and six years for thy cattle: and thou hast changed my wages ten times.

42Except the God of my father, the God of Abraham, and the fear of Isaac, had been with me, surely thou hadst sent me away now empty. God hath seen mine affliction and the labour of my hands, and rebuked *thee* yester-night.

43And Laban answered and said unto Jacob, *These* daughters *are* my daugh-ters, and *these* children *are* my children, and *these* cattle *are* my cattle, and all that thou seest *is* mine: and what can I do this day unto these my daughters, or unto their children which they have born?

44Now therefore come thou, let us make a covenant, I and thou; and let it be for a witness between me and thee.

45And Jacob took a stone, and set it up *for* a pillar.

46And Jacob said unto his brethren, Gather stones; and they took stones, and made an heap: and they did eat there upon the heap.

47And Laban called it Jegar–sahadu-tha: but Jacob called it Galeed.

48And Laban said, This heap *is* a wit-ness between me and thee this day. Therefore was the name of it called Galeed;

49And Mizpah; for he said, The LORD watch between me and thee, when we are absent one from another.

50If thou shalt afflict my daughters,

or if thou shalt take *other* wives beside my daughters, no man *is* with us; see, God *is* witness betwixt me and thee.

51And Laban said to Jacob, Behold this heap, and behold *this* pillar, which I have cast betwixt me and thee:

52This heap *be* witness, and *this* pillar *be* witness, that I will not pass over this heap to thee, and that thou shalt not pass over this heap and this pillar unto me, for harm.

53The God of Abraham, and the God of Nahor, the God of their father, judge betwixt us. And Jacob sware by the fear of his father Isaac.

54Then Jacob offered sacrifice upon the mount, and called his brethren to eat bread: and they did eat bread, and tarried all night in the mount.

55And early in the morning Laban rose up, and kissed his sons and his daughters, and blessed them: and Laban departed, and returned unto his place.

And Jacob went on his way, and the angels of God met him.

2And when Jacob saw them, he said, This *is* God's host: and he called the name of that place Mahanaim.

3And Jacob sent messengers before him to Esau his brother unto the land of Seir, the country of Edom.

4And he commanded them, saying, Thus shall ye speak unto my lord Esau; Thy servant Jacob saith thus, I have sojourned with Laban, and stayed there until now:

5And I have oxen, and asses, flocks, and menservants, and womenservants: and I have sent to tell my lord, that I may find grace in thy sight.

6And the messengers returned to Jacob, saying, We came to thy brother Esau, and also he cometh to meet thee, and four hundred men with him.

7Then Jacob was greatly afraid and distressed: and he divided the people that *was* with him, and the flocks, and herds, and the camels, into two bands;

8And said, If Esau come to the one company, and smite it, then the other company which is left shall escape.

9And Jacob said, O God of my father Abraham, and God of my father Isaac, the LORD which saidst unto me, Return unto thy country, and to thy kindred, and I will deal well with thee:

10I am not worthy of the least of all the mercies, and of all the truth, which thou hast shewed unto thy servant; for with my staff I passed over this Jordan; and now I am become two bands.

11Deliver me, I pray thee, from the hand of my brother, from the hand of Esau: for I fear him, lest he will come and smite me, *and* the mother with the children.

12And thou saidst, I will surely do thee good, and make thy seed as the sand of the sea, which cannot be numbered for multitude.

MATTHEW 10:27—11:6

What I tell you in darkness, *that* speak ye in light: and what ye hear in the ear, *that* preach ye upon the housetops.

28And fear not them which kill the body, but are not able to kill the soul: but rather fear him which is able to destroy both soul and body in hell.

29Are not two sparrows sold for a farthing? and one of them shall not fall on the ground without your Father.

30But the very hairs of your head are all numbered.

31Fear ye not therefore, ye are of more value than many sparrows.

32Whosoever therefore shall confess me before men, him will I confess also before my Father which is in heaven.

33But whosoever shall deny me before men, him will I also deny before my Father which is in heaven.

34Think not that I am come to send peace on earth: I came not to send peace, but a sword.

35For I am come to set a man at variance against his father, and the daughter against her mother, and the daughter in law against her mother in law.

36And a man's foes *shall be* they of his own household.

37He that loveth father or mother more than me is not worthy of me: and he that loveth son or daughter more than me is not worthy of me.

38And he that taketh not his cross, and followeth after me, is not worthy of me.

39He that findeth his life shall lose it: and he that loseth his life for my sake shall find it.

40He that receiveth you receiveth me, and he that receiveth me receiveth him that sent me.

41He that receiveth a prophet in the name of a prophet shall receive a prophet's reward; and he that receiveth a righteous man in the name of a righteous man shall receive a righteous man's reward.

42And whosoever shall give to drink unto one of these little ones a cup of cold *water* only in the name of a disciple, verily I say unto you, he shall in no wise lose his reward.

AND it came to pass, when Jesus had made an end of commanding his twelve disciples, he departed thence to teach and to preach in their cities.

2Now when John had heard in the prison the works of Christ, he sent two of his disciples,

3And said unto him, Art thou he that should come, or do we look for another?

4Jesus answered and said unto them, Go and shew John again those things which ye do hear and see:

5The blind receive their sight, and the lame walk, the lepers are cleansed, and the deaf hear, the dead are raised up, and the poor have the gospel preached to them.

6And blessed is *he,* whosoever shall not be offended in me.

PSALM 13:1–6

How long wilt thou forget me, O LORD? for ever? how long wilt thou hide thy face from me?

2How long shall I take counsel in my soul, *having* sorrow in my heart daily? how long shall mine enemy be exalted over me?

3Consider *and* hear me, O LORD my God: lighten mine eyes, lest I sleep the *sleep of* death;

4Lest mine enemy say, I have prevailed against him; *and* those that troubled me rejoice when I am moved.

5But I have trusted in thy mercy; my heart shall rejoice in thy salvation.

6I will sing unto the LORD, because he hath dealt bountifully with me.

PROVERBS FOR TODAY/ 3:16–18

Length of days is *in her right hand;* and *in her left hand riches and honour. Her ways* are *ways of pleasantness, and all her paths* are *peace. She* is *a tree of life to them that lay hold upon her: and happy* is *every one that retaineth her.*

JANUARY 16

GENESIS 32:13—34:31

AND he [Jacob] lodged there that same night; and took of that which came to his hand a present for Esau his brother;

14Two hundred she goats, and twenty he goats, two hundred ewes, and twenty rams,

15Thirty milch camels with their colts, forty kine, and ten bulls, twenty she asses, and ten foals.

16And he delivered *them* into the hand of his servants, every drove by themselves; and said unto his servants, Pass over before me, and put a space betwixt drove and drove.

17And he commanded the foremost, saying, When Esau my brother meeteth thee, and asketh thee, saying, Whose *art* thou? and whither goest thou? and whose *are* these before thee?

18Then thou shalt say, *They be* thy servant Jacob's; it *is* a present sent unto my lord Esau: and, behold, also he *is* behind us.

19And so commanded he the second, and the third, and all that followed the droves, saying, On this manner shall ye speak unto Esau, when ye find him.

20And say ye moreover, Behold, thy servant Jacob *is* behind us. For he said, I will appease him with the present that goeth before me, and afterward I will see his face; peradventure he will accept of me.

21So went the present over before him: and himself lodged that night in the company.

22And he rose up that night, and took his two wives, and his two womenservants, and his eleven sons, and passed over the ford Jabbok.

23And he took them, and sent them over the brook, and sent over that he had.

24And Jacob was left alone; and there wrestled a man with him until the breaking of the day.

25And when he saw that he prevailed not against him, he touched the hollow of his thigh; and the hollow of Jacob's thigh was out of joint, as he wrestled with him.

26And he said, Let me go, for the day breaketh. And he said, I will not let thee go, except thou bless me.

27And he said unto him, What *is* thy name? And he said, Jacob.

28And he said, Thy name shall be called no more Jacob, but Israel: for as a prince hast thou power with God and with men, and hast prevailed.

29And Jacob asked *him,* and said, Tell *me,* I pray thee, thy name. And he said, Wherefore *is* it *that* thou dost ask after my name? And he blessed him there.

30And Jacob called the name of the place Peniel: for I have seen God face to face, and my life is preserved.

31And as he passed over Penuel the sun rose upon him, and he halted upon his thigh.

32Therefore the children of Israel eat not *of* the sinew which shrank, which *is* upon the hollow of the thigh, unto this day: because he touched the hollow of Jacob's thigh in the sinew that shrank.

AND Jacob lifted up his eyes and looked, and, behold, Esau came, and with him four hundred men. And he divided the children unto Leah, and unto Rachel, and unto the two handmaids.

2And he put the handmaids and their children foremost, and Leah and her children after, and Rachel and Joseph hindermost.

3And he passed over before them, and bowed himself to the ground seven times, until he came near to his brother.

4And Esau ran to meet him, and embraced him, and fell on his neck, and kissed him: and they wept.

5And he lifted up his eyes, and saw the women and the children; and said, Who *are* those with thee? And he said, The children which God hath graciously given thy servant.

6Then the handmaidens came near, they and their children, and they bowed themselves.

7And Leah also with her children came near, and bowed themselves: and after came Joseph near and Rachel, and they bowed themselves.

8And he said, What *meanest* thou by all this drove which I met? And he said, *These are* to find grace in the sight of my lord.

9And Esau said, I have enough, my brother; keep that thou hast unto thyself.

10And Jacob said, Nay, I pray thee, if now I have found grace in thy sight, then receive my present at my hand: for therefore I have seen thy face, as though I had seen the face of God, and thou wast pleased with me.

11Take, I pray thee, my blessing that is brought to thee; because God hath dealt graciously with me, and because I have enough. And he urged him, and he took *it.*

12And he said, Let us take our journey, and let us go, and I will go before thee.

13And he said unto him, My lord knoweth that the children *are* tender, and the flocks and herds with young *are* with me: and if men should overdrive them one day, all the flock will die.

14Let my lord, I pray thee, pass over before his servant: and I will lead on softly, according as the cattle that goeth before me and the children be able to endure, until I come unto my lord unto Seir.

15And Esau said, Let me now leave with thee *some* of the folk that *are* with me. And he said, What needeth it? let me find grace in the sight of my lord.

16So Esau returned that day on his way unto Seir.

17And Jacob journeyed to Succoth, and built him an house, and made booths for his cattle: therefore the name of the place is called Succoth.

18And Jacob came to Shalem, a city of Shechem, which *is* in the land of Canaan, when he came from Padan–aram; and pitched his tent before the city.

19And he bought a parcel of a field, where he had spread his tent, at the hand of the children of Hamor, Shechem's father, for an hundred pieces of money.

20And he erected there an altar, and called it El–elohe–Israel.

AND Dinah the daughter of Leah, which she bare unto Jacob, went out to see the daughters of the land.

2And when Shechem the son of Hamor the Hivite, prince of the country, saw her, he took her, and lay with her, and defiled her.

3And his soul clave unto Dinah the daughter of Jacob, and he loved the damsel, and spake kindly unto the damsel.

4And Shechem spake unto his father Hamor, saying, Get me this damsel to wife.

5And Jacob heard that he had defiled Dinah his daughter: now his sons were with his cattle in the field: and Jacob held his peace until they were come.

6And Hamor the father of Shechem went out unto Jacob to commune with him.

7And the sons of Jacob came out of the field when they heard *it:* and the men were grieved, and they were very wroth, because he had wrought folly in Israel in lying with Jacob's daughter;

which thing ought not to be done.

8And Hamor communed with them, saying, The soul of my son Shechem longeth for your daughter: I pray you give her him to wife.

9And make ye marriages with us, *and* give your daughters unto us, and take our daughters unto you.

10And ye shall dwell with us: and the land shall be before you; dwell and trade ye therein, and get you possessions therein.

11And Shechem said unto her father and unto her brethren, Let me find grace in your eyes, and what ye shall say unto me I will give.

12Ask me never so much dowry and gift, and I will give according as ye shall say unto me: but give me the damsel to wife.

13And the sons of Jacob answered Shechem and Hamor his father deceitfully, and said, because he had defiled Dinah their sister:

14And they said unto them, We cannot do this thing, to give our sister to one that is uncircumcised; for that *were* a reproach unto us:

15But in this will we consent unto you: If ye will be as we *be,* that every male of you be circumcised:

16Then will we give our daughters unto you, and we will take your daughters to us, and we will dwell with you, and we will become one people.

17But if ye will not hearken unto us, to be circumcised; then will we take our daughter, and we will be gone.

18And their words pleased Hamor, and Shechem Hamor's son.

19And the young man deferred not to do the thing, because he had delight in Jacob's daughter: and he *was* more honourable than all the house of his father.

20And Hamor and Shechem his son came unto the gate of their city, and communed with the men of their city, saying,

21These men *are* peaceable with us;

therefore let them dwell in the land, and trade therein; for the land, behold, *it is* large enough for them; let us take their daughters to us for wives, and let us give them our daughters.

22Only herein will the men consent unto us for to dwell with us, to be one people, if every male among us be circumcised, as they *are* circumcised.

23*Shall* not their cattle and their substance and every beast of theirs *be* ours? only let us consent unto them, and they will dwell with us.

24And unto Hamor and unto Shechem his son hearkened all that went out of the gate of his city; and every male was circumcised, all that went out of the gate of his city.

25And it came to pass on the third day, when they were sore, that two of the sons of Jacob, Simeon and Levi, Dinah's brethren, took each man his sword, and came upon the city boldly, and slew all the males.

26And they slew Hamor and Shechem his son with the edge of the sword, and took Dinah out of Shechem's house, and went out.

27The sons of Jacob came upon the slain, and spoiled the city, because they had defiled their sister.

28They took their sheep, and their oxen, and their asses, and that which *was* in the city, and that which *was* in the field,

29And all their wealth, and all their little ones, and their wives took they captive, and spoiled even all that *was* in the house.

30And Jacob said to Simeon and Levi, Ye have troubled me to make me to stink among the inhabitants of the land, among the Canaanites and the Perizzites: and I *being* few in number, they shall gather themselves together against me, and slay me; and I shall be destroyed, I and my house.

31And they said, Should he deal with our sister as with an harlot?

MATTHEW 11:7–30

A ND as they departed, Jesus began to say unto the multitudes concerning John, What went ye out into the wilderness to see? A reed shaken with the wind?

8But what went ye out for to see? A man clothed in soft raiment? behold, they that wear soft *clothing* are in kings' houses.

9But what went ye out for to see? A prophet? yea, I say unto you, and more than a prophet.

10For this is *he,* of whom it is written, Behold, I send my messenger before thy face, which shall prepare thy way before thee.

11Verily I say unto you, Among them that are born of women there hath not risen a greater than John the Baptist: notwithstanding he that is least in the kingdom of heaven is greater than he.

12And from the days of John the Baptist until now the kingdom of heaven suffereth violence, and the violent take it by force.

13For all the prophets and the law prophesied until John.

14And if ye will receive *it,* this is Elias, which was for to come.

15He that hath ears to hear, let him hear.

16But whereunto shall I liken this generation? It is like unto children sitting in the markets, and calling unto their fellows,

17And saying, We have piped unto you, and ye have not danced; we have mourned unto you, and ye have not lamented.

18For John came neither eating nor drinking, and they say, He hath a devil.

19The Son of man came eating and drinking, and they say, Behold a man gluttonous, and a winebibber, a friend of publicans and sinners. But wisdom is justified of her children.

20Then began he to upbraid the cities wherein most of his mighty works were done, because they repented not:

21Woe unto thee, Chorazin! woe unto thee, Bethsaida! for if the mighty works, which were done in you, had been done in Tyre and Sidon, they would have repented long ago in sackcloth and ashes.

22But I say unto you, It shall be more tolerable for Tyre and Sidon at the day of judgment, than for you.

23And thou, Capernaum, which art exalted unto heaven, shalt be brought down to hell: for if the mighty works, which have been done in thee, had been done in Sodom, it would have remained until this day.

24But I say unto you, That it shall be more tolerable for the land of Sodom, in the day of judgment, than for thee.

25At that time Jesus answered and said, I thank thee, O Father, Lord of heaven and earth, because thou hast hid these things from the wise and prudent, and hast revealed them unto babes.

26Even so, Father: for so it seemed good in thy sight.

27All things are delivered unto me of my Father: and no man knoweth the Son, but the Father; neither knoweth any man the Father, save the Son, and *he* to whomsoever the Son will reveal *him.*

28Come unto me, all *ye* that labour and are heavy laden, and I will give you rest.

29Take my yoke upon you, and learn of me; for I am meek and lowly in heart: and ye shall find rest unto your souls.

30For my yoke *is* easy, and my burden is light.

PSALM 14:1–7

T HE fool hath said in his heart, *There is* no God. They are corrupt, they have done abominable works, *there is* none that doeth good.

2The LORD looked down from heaven upon the children of men, to see if there were any that did understand, *and* seek God.

3They are all gone aside, they are *all* together become filthy: *there is* none that doeth good, no, not one.

4Have all the workers of iniquity no knowledge? who eat up my people *as* they eat bread, and call not upon the LORD.

5There were they in great fear: for God *is* in the generation of the righteous.

6Ye have shamed the counsel of the poor, because the LORD *is* his refuge.

7Oh that the salvation of Israel *were* come out of Zion! when the LORD bringeth back the captivity of his people, Jacob shall rejoice, *and* Israel shall be glad.

PROVERBS FOR TODAY/ 3:19–20

The LORD by wisdom hath founded the earth; by understanding hath he established the heavens. By his knowledge the depths are broken up, and the clouds drop down the dew.

JANUARY 17

GENESIS 35:1—36:43

AND God said unto Jacob, Arise, go up to Beth–el, and dwell there: and make there an altar unto God, that appeared unto thee when thou fleddest from the face of Esau thy brother.

2Then Jacob said unto his household, and to all that *were* with him, Put away the strange gods that *are* among you, and be clean, and change your garments:

3And let us arise, and go up to Beth–el; and I will make there an altar unto God, who answered me in the day of my distress, and was with me in the way which I went.

4And they gave unto Jacob all the strange gods which *were* in their hand, and *all their* earrings which *were* in their ears; and Jacob hid them under the oak which *was* by Shechem.

5And they journeyed: and the terror of God was upon the cities that *were* round about them, and they did not pursue after the sons of Jacob.

6So Jacob came to Luz, which *is* in the land of Canaan, that *is,* Beth–el, he and all the people that *were* with him.

7And he built there an altar, and called the place El–beth–el: because there God appeared unto him, when he fled from the face of his brother.

8But Deborah Rebekah's nurse died, and she was buried beneath Beth–el under an oak: and the name of it was called Allon–bachuth.

9And God appeared unto Jacob again, when he came out of Padan–aram, and blessed him.

10And God said unto him, Thy name *is* Jacob: thy name shall not be called any more Jacob, but Israel shall be thy name: and he called his name Israel.

11And God said unto him, I *am* God Almighty: be fruitful and multiply; a nation and a company of nations shall be of thee, and kings shall come out of thy loins;

12And the land which I gave Abraham and Isaac, to thee I will give it, and to thy seed after thee will I give the land.

¹³And God went up from him in the place where he talked with him.

¹⁴And Jacob set up a pillar in the place where he talked with him, *even* a pillar of stone: and he poured a drink offering thereon, and he poured oil thereon.

¹⁵And Jacob called the name of the place where God spake with him, Beth–el.

¹⁶And they journeyed from Beth–el; and there was but a little way to come to Ephrath: and Rachel travailed, and she had hard labour.

¹⁷And it came to pass, when she was in hard labour, that the midwife said unto her, Fear not; thou shalt have this son also.

¹⁸And it came to pass, as her soul was in departing, (for she died) that she called his name Ben–oni: but his father called him Benjamin.

¹⁹And Rachel died, and was buried in the way to Ephrath, which *is* Bethlehem.

²⁰And Jacob set a pillar upon her grave: that *is* the pillar of Rachel's grave unto this day.

²¹And Israel journeyed, and spread his tent beyond the tower of Edar.

²²And it came to pass, when Israel dwelt in that land, that Reuben went and lay with Bilhah his father's concubine: and Israel heard *it*. Now the sons of Jacob were twelve:

²³The sons of Leah; Reuben, Jacob's firstborn, and Simeon, and Levi, and Judah, and Issachar, and Zebulun:

²⁴The sons of Rachel; Joseph, and Benjamin:

²⁵And the sons of Bilhah, Rachel's handmaid; Dan, and Naphtali:

²⁶And the sons of Zilpah, Leah's handmaid; Gad, and Asher: these *are* the sons of Jacob, which were born to him in Padan–aram.

²⁷And Jacob came unto Isaac his father unto Mamre, unto the city of Ar-

bah, which *is* Hebron, where Abraham and Isaac sojourned.

²⁸And the days of Isaac were an hundred and fourscore years.

²⁹And Isaac gave up the ghost, and died, and was gathered unto his people, *being* old and full of days: and his sons Esau and Jacob buried him.

Now these *are* the generations of Esau, who is Edom.

²Esau took his wives of the daughters of Canaan; Adah the daughter of Elon the Hittite, and Aholibamah the daughter of Anah the daughter of Zibeon the Hivite;

³And Bashemath Ishmael's daughter, sister of Nebajoth.

⁴And Adah bare to Esau Eliphaz; and Bashemath bare Reuel;

⁵And Aholibamah bare Jeush, and Jaalam, and Korah: these *are* the sons of Esau, which were born unto him in the land of Canaan.

⁶And Esau took his wives, and his sons, and his daughters, and all the persons of his house, and his cattle, and all his beasts, and all his substance, which he had got in the land of Canaan; and went into the country from the face of his brother Jacob.

⁷For their riches were more than that they might dwell together; and the land wherein they were strangers could not bear them because of their cattle.

⁸Thus dwelt Esau in mount Seir: Esau *is* Edom.

⁹And these *are* the generations of Esau the father of the Edomites in mount Seir:

¹⁰These *are* the names of Esau's sons; Eliphaz the son of Adah the wife of Esau, Reuel the son of Bashemath the wife of Esau.

¹¹And the sons of Eliphaz were Teman, Omar, Zepho, and Gatam, and Kenaz.

¹²And Timna was concubine to Eliphaz Esau's son; and she bare to Eliphaz

Amalek: these *were* the sons of Adah Esau's wife.

13And these *are* the sons of Reuel; Nahath, and Zerah, Shammah, and Mizzah: these were the sons of Bashemath Esau's wife.

14And these were the sons of Aholibamath, the daughter of Anah the daughter of Zibeon, Esau's wife: and she bare to Esau Jeush, and Jaalam, and Korah.

15These *were* dukes of the sons of Esau: the sons of Eliphaz the firstborn *son* of Esau; duke Teman, duke Omar, duke Zepho, duke Kenaz,

16Duke Korah, duke Gatam, *and* duke Amalek: these *are* the dukes *that came* of Eliphaz in the land of Edom; these *were* the sons of Adah.

17And these *are* the sons of Reuel Esau's son; duke Nahath, duke Zerah, duke Shammah, duke Mizzah: these *are* the dukes *that came* of Reuel in the land of Edom; these *are* the sons of Bashemath Esau's wife.

18And these *are* the sons of Aholibamah Esau's wife; duke Jeush, duke Jaalam, duke Korah: these *were* the dukes *that came* of Aholibamah the daughter of Anah, Esau's wife.

19These are the sons of Esau, who *is* Edom, and these *are* their dukes.

20These *are* the sons of Seir the Horite, who inhabited the land; Lotan, and Shobal, and Zibeon, and Anah.

21And Dishon, and Ezer, and Dishan: these *are* the dukes of the Horites, the children of Seir in the land of Edom.

22And the children of Lotan were Hori and Hemam; and Lotan's sister *was* Timna.

23And the children of Shobal *were* these; Alvan, and Manahath, and Ebal, Shepho, and Onam.

24And these *are* the children of Zibeon; both Ajah, and Anah: this *was* that Anah that found the mules in the wilderness, as he fed the asses of Zibeon his father.

25And the children of Anah *were* these; Dishon, and Aholibamah the daughter of Anah.

26And these *are* the children of Dishon; Hemdan, and Eshban, and Ithran, and Cheran.

27The children of Ezer *are* these; Bilhan, and Zaavan, and Akan.

28The children of Dishan *are* these; Uz, and Aran.

29These *are* the dukes *that came* of the Horites; duke Lotan, duke Shobal, duke Zibeon, duke Anah.

30Duke Dishon, duke Ezer, duke Dishan: these *are* the dukes *that came* of Hori, among their dukes in the land of Seir.

31And these *are* the kings that reigned in the land of Edom, before there reigned any king over the children of Israel.

32And Bela the son of Beor reigned in Edom: and the name of his city *was* Dinhabah.

33And Bela died, and Jobab the son of Zerah of Bozrah reigned in his stead.

34And Jobab died, and Husham of the land of Temani reigned in his stead.

35And Husham died, and Hadad the son of Bedad, who smote Midian in the field of Moab, reigned in his stead: and the name of his city *was* Avith.

36And Hadad died, and Samlah of Masrekah reigned in his stead.

37And Samlah died, and Saul of Rehoboth *by* the river reigned in his stead.

38And Saul died, and Baal–hanan the son of Achbor reigned in his stead.

39And Baal–hanan the son of Achbor died, and Hadar reigned in his stead; and the name of his city *was* Pau; and his wife's name *was* Mehetabel, the daughter of Matred, the daughter of Mezahab.

40And these *are* the names of the dukes *that came* of Esau, according to their families, after their places, by their names; duke Timnah, duke Alvah, duke Jetheth,

41Duke Aholibamah, duke Elah, duke Pinon,

⁴²Duke Kenaz, duke Teman, duke Mibzar,

⁴³Duke Magdiel, duke Iram: these *be* the dukes of Edom, according to their habitations in the land of their possession: he *is* Esau the father of the Edomites.

MATTHEW 12:1–21

A T that time Jesus went on the sabbath day through the corn; and his disciples were an hungred, and began to pluck the ears of corn, and to eat.

²But when the Pharisees saw *it,* they said unto him, Behold, thy disciples do that which is not lawful to do upon the sabbath day.

³But he said unto them, Have ye not read what David did, when he was an hungred, and they that were with him;

⁴How he entered into the house of God, and did eat the shewbread, which was not lawful for him to eat, neither for them which were with him, but only for the priests?

⁵Or have ye not read in the law, how that on the sabbath days the priests in the temple profane the sabbath, and are blameless?

⁶But I say unto you, That in this place is *one* greater than the temple.

⁷But if ye had known what *this* meaneth, I will have mercy, and not sacrifice, ye would not have condemned the guiltless.

⁸For the Son of man is Lord even of the sabbath day.

⁹And when he was departed thence, he went into their synagogue:

¹⁰And, behold, there was a man which had *his* hand withered. And they asked him, saying, Is it lawful to heal on the sabbath days? that they might accuse him.

¹¹And he said unto them, What man shall there be among you, that shall have one sheep, and if it fall into a pit on the sabbath day, will he not lay hold on it, and lift *it* out?

¹²How much then is a man better than a sheep? Wherefore it is lawful to do well on the sabbath days.

¹³Then saith he to the man, Stretch forth thine hand. And he stretched *it* forth; and it was restored whole, like as the other.

¹⁴Then the Pharisees went out, and held a council against him, how they might destroy him.

¹⁵But when Jesus knew *it,* he withdrew himself from thence: and great multitudes followed him, and he healed them all;

¹⁶And charged them that they should not make him known:

¹⁷That it might be fulfilled which was spoken by Esaias the prophet, saying,

¹⁸Behold my servant, whom I have chosen; my beloved, in whom my soul is well pleased: I will put my spirit upon him, and he shall shew judgment to the Gentiles.

¹⁹He shall not strive, nor cry; neither shall any man hear his voice in the streets.

²⁰A bruised reed shall he not break, and smoking flax shall he not quench, till he send forth judgment unto victory.

²¹And in his name shall the Gentiles trust.

PSALM 15:1–5

L ORD, who shall abide in thy tabernacle? who shall dwell in thy holy hill?

²He that walketh uprightly, and worketh righteousness, and speaketh the truth in his heart.

³*He that* backbiteth not with his tongue, nor doeth evil to his neighbour, nor taketh up a reproach against his neighbour.

⁴In whose eyes a vile person is contemned; but he honoureth them that

fear the LORD. *He that* sweareth to his own hurt, and changeth not.

5*He that* putteth not out his money to usury, nor taketh reward against the innocent. He that doeth these *things* shall never be moved.

PROVERBS FOR TODAY/ 3:21–26

My son, let not them depart from thine eyes: keep sound wisdom and discretion: So shall they be life unto thy soul, and grace to thy neck. Then shalt thou walk in thy way safely, and thy foot shall not stumble. When thou liest down, thou shalt not be afraid: yea, thou shalt lie down, and thy sleep shall be sweet. Be not afraid of sudden fear, neither of the desolation of the wicked, when it cometh. For the LORD shall be thy confidence, and shall keep thy foot from being taken.

JANUARY 18

GENESIS 37:1—38:30

AND Jacob dwelt in the land wherein his father was a stranger, in the land of Canaan. 2These *are* the generations of Jacob. Joseph, *being* seventeen years old, was feeding the flock with his brethren; and the lad *was* with the sons of Bilhah, and with the sons of Zilpah, his father's wives: and Joseph brought unto his father their evil report.

3Now Israel loved Joseph more than all his children, because he *was* the son of his old age: and he made him a coat of *many* colours.

4And when his brethren saw that their father loved him more than all his brethren, they hated him, and could not speak peaceably unto him.

5And Joseph dreamed a dream, and he told *it* his brethren: and they hated him yet the more.

6And he said unto them, Hear, I pray you, this dream which I have dreamed:

7For, behold, we *were* binding sheaves in the field, and, lo, my sheaf arose, and also stood upright; and, behold, your sheaves stood round about, and made obeisance to my sheaf.

8And his brethren said to him, Shalt thou indeed reign over us? or shalt thou indeed have dominion over us? And they hated him yet the more for his dreams, and for his words.

9And he dreamed yet another dream, and told it his brethren, and said, Behold, I have dreamed a dream more; and, behold, the sun and the moon and the eleven stars made obeisance to me.

10And he told *it* to his father, and to his brethren: and his father rebuked him, and said unto him, What *is* this dream that thou hast dreamed? Shall I and thy mother and thy brethren indeed come to bow down ourselves to thee to the earth?

11And his brethren envied him; but his father observed the saying.

12And his brethren went to feed their father's flock in Shechem.

13And Israel said unto Joseph, Do not thy brethren feed *the flock* in Shechem? come, and I will send thee unto them. And he said to him, Here *am I.*

14And he said to him, Go, I pray thee, see whether it be well with thy brethren, and well with the flocks; and bring me word again. So he sent him out of the vale of Hebron, and he came to Shechem.

15And a certain man found him, and, behold, *he was* wandering in the field: and the man asked him, saying, What seekest thou?

16And he said, I seek my brethren: tell me, I pray thee, where they feed *their flocks.*

17And the man said, They are departed hence; for I heard them say, Let us go to Dothan. And Joseph went after his brethren, and found them in Dothan.

18And when they saw him afar off, even before he came near unto them, they conspired against him to slay him.

19And they said one to another, Behold, this dreamer cometh.

20Come now therefore, and let us slay him, and cast him into some pit, and we will say, Some evil beast hath devoured him: and we shall see what will become of his dreams.

21And Reuben heard *it,* and he delivered him out of their hands; and said, Let us not kill him.

22And Reuben said unto them, Shed no blood, *but* cast him into this pit that *is* in the wilderness, and lay no hand upon him; that he might rid him out of their hands, to deliver him to his father again.

23And it came to pass, when Joseph was come unto his brethren, that they stript Joseph out of his coat, *his* coat of *many* colours that *was* on him;

24And they took him, and cast him into a pit: and the pit *was* empty, *there was* no water in it.

25And they sat down to eat bread: and they lifted up their eyes and looked, and, behold, a company of Ishmeelites came from Gilead with their camels bearing spicery and balm and myrrh, going to carry *it* down to Egypt.

26And Judah said unto his brethren, What profit *is it* if we slay our brother, and conceal his blood?

27Come, and let us sell him to the Ishmeelites, and let not our hand be upon him; for he *is* our brother *and* our flesh. And his brethren were content.

28Then there passed by Midianites merchantmen; and they drew and lifted up Joseph out of the pit, and sold Joseph to the Ishmeelites for twenty *pieces* of silver: and they brought Joseph into Egypt.

29And Reuben returned unto the pit; and, behold, Joseph *was* not in the pit; and he rent his clothes.

30And he returned unto his brethren, and said, The child *is* not; and I, whither shall I go?

31And they took Joseph's coat, and killed a kid of the goats, and dipped the coat in the blood;

32And they sent the coat of *many* colours, and they brought *it* to their father; and said, This have we found: know now whether it *be* thy son's coat or no.

33And he knew it, and said, *It is* my son's coat; an evil beast hath devoured him; Joseph is without doubt rent in pieces.

34And Jacob rent his clothes, and put sackcloth upon his loins, and mourned for his son many days.

35And all his sons and all his daughters rose up to comfort him; but he refused to be comforted; and he said, For I will go down into the grave unto my son mourning. Thus his father wept for him.

36And the Midianites sold him into Egypt unto Potiphar, an officer of Pharaoh's, *and* captain of the guard.

AND it came to pass at that time, that Judah went down from his brethren, and turned in to a certain Adullamite, whose name *was* Hirah.

2And Judah saw there a daughter of a certain Canaanite, whose name *was* Shuah; and he took her, and went in unto her.

3And she conceived, and bare a son; and he called his name Er.

4And she conceived again, and bare a son; and she called his name Onan.

5And she yet again conceived, and bare a son; and called his name Shelah: and he was at Chezib, when she bare him.

6And Judah took a wife for Er his firstborn, whose name *was* Tamar.

7And Er, Judah's firstborn, was wicked in the sight of the LORD; and the LORD slew him.

8And Judah said unto Onan, Go in unto thy brother's wife, and marry her, and raise up seed to thy brother.

9And Onan knew that the seed should not be his; and it came to pass, when he went in unto his brother's wife, that he spilled *it* on the ground, lest that he should give seed to his brother.

10And the thing which he did displeased the LORD: wherefore he slew him also.

11Then said Judah to Tamar his daughter in law, Remain a widow at thy father's house, till Shelah my son be grown: for he said, Lest peradventure he die also, as his brethren *did*. And Tamar went and dwelt in her father's house.

12And in process of time the daughter of Shuah Judah's wife died; and Judah was comforted, and went up unto his sheepshearers to Timnath, he and his friend Hirah the Adullamite.

13And it was told Tamar, saying, Behold thy father in law goeth up to Timnath to shear his sheep.

14And she put her widow's garments off from her, and covered her with a vail, and wrapped herself, and sat in an open place, which *is* by the way to Timnath; for she saw that Shelah was grown, and she was not given unto him to wife.

15When Judah saw her, he thought her *to be* an harlot; because she had covered her face.

16And he turned unto her by the way, and said, Go to, I pray thee, let me come in unto thee; (for he knew not that she *was* his daughter in law.) And she said, What wilt thou give me, that thou mayest come in unto me?

17And he said, I will send *thee* a kid from the flock. And she said, Wilt thou give *me* a pledge, till thou send *it?*

18And he said, What pledge shall I give thee? And she said, Thy signet, and thy bracelets, and thy staff that *is* in thine hand. And he gave *it* her, and came in unto her, and she conceived by him.

19And she arose, and went away, and laid by her vail from her, and put on the garments of her widowhood.

20And Judah sent the kid by the hand of his friend the Adullamite, to receive *his* pledge from the woman's hand: but he found her not.

21Then he asked the men of that place, saying, Where *is* the harlot, that *was* openly by the way side? And they said, There was no harlot in this *place.*

22And he returned to Judah, and said, I cannot find her; and also the men of the place said, *that* there was no harlot in this *place.*

23And Judah said, Let her take *it* to her, lest we be shamed: behold, I sent this kid, and thou hast not found her.

24And it came to pass about three months after, that it was told Judah, saying, Tamar thy daughter in law hath played the harlot; and also, behold, she *is* with child by whoredom. And Judah said, Bring her forth, and let her be burnt.

25When she *was* brought forth, she sent to her father in law, saying, By the man, whose these *are, am* I with child: and she said, Discern, I pray thee, whose *are* these, the signet, and bracelets, and staff.

26And Judah acknowledged *them,* and said, She hath been more righteous than I; because that I gave her not to Shelah my son. And he knew her again no more.

27And it came to pass in the time of her travail, that, behold, twins *were* in her womb.

28And it came to pass, when she travailed, that *the one* put out *his* hand: and the midwife took and bound upon his hand a scarlet thread, saying, This came out first.

29And it came to pass, as he drew back his hand, that, behold, his brother came out: and she said, How hast thou broken forth? *this* breach *be* upon thee: therefore his name was called Pharez.

30And afterward came out his brother, that had the scarlet thread upon his hand: and his name was called Zarah.

MATTHEW 12:22–45

THEN was brought unto him one possessed with a devil, blind, and dumb: and he healed him, insomuch that the blind and dumb both spake and saw.

23And all the people were amazed, and said, Is not this the son of David?

24But when the Pharisees heard *it,* they said, This *fellow* doth not cast out devils, but by Beelzebub the prince of the devils.

25And Jesus knew their thoughts, and said unto them, Every kingdom divided against itself is brought to desolation; and every city or house divided against itself shall not stand:

26And if Satan cast out Satan, he is divided against himself; how shall then his kingdom stand?

27And if I by Beelzebub cast out devils, by whom do your children cast *them* out? therefore they shall be your judges.

28But if I cast out devils by the Spirit of God, then the kingdom of God is come unto you.

29Or else how can one enter into a strong man's house, and spoil his goods, except he first bind the strong man? and then he will spoil his house.

30He that is not with me is against me; and he that gathereth not with me scattereth abroad.

31Wherefore I say unto you, All manner of sin and blasphemy shall be forgiven unto men: but the blasphemy *against* the *Holy* Ghost shall not be forgiven unto men.

32And whosoever speaketh a word against the Son of man, it shall be forgiven him: but whosoever speaketh against the Holy Ghost, it shall not be forgiven him, neither in this world, neither in the *world* to come.

33Either make the tree good, and his fruit good; or else make the tree corrupt, and his fruit corrupt: for the tree is known by *his* fruit.

34O generation of vipers, how can ye, being evil, speak good things? for out of the abundance of the heart the mouth speaketh.

35A good man out of the good treasure of the heart bringeth forth good things: and an evil man out of the evil treasure bringeth forth evil things.

36But I say unto you, That every idle word that men shall speak, they shall give account thereof in the day of judgment.

37For by thy words thou shalt be justified, and by thy words thou shalt be condemned.

38Then certain of the scribes and of the Pharisees answered, saying, Master, we would see a sign from thee.

39But he answered and said unto them, An evil and adulterous generation seeketh after a sign; and there shall no sign be given to it, but the sign of the prophet Jonas:

40For as Jonas was three days and three nights in the whale's belly; so shall the Son of man be three days and three nights in the heart of the earth.

41The men of Nineveh shall rise in judgment with this generation, and shall condemn it: because they repented at the preaching of Jonas; and, behold, a greater than Jonas *is* here.

42The queen of the south shall rise up in the judgment with this generation, and shall condemn it: for she came from the uttermost parts of the earth to hear the wisdom of Solomon; and, behold, a greater than Solomon *is* here.

43When the unclean spirit is gone out of a man, he walketh through dry places, seeking rest, and findeth none.

44Then he saith, I will return into my house from whence I came out; and when he is come, he findeth *it* empty, swept, and garnished.

45Then goeth he, and taketh with himself seven other spirits more wicked than himself, and they enter in and dwell there: and the last *state* of that man is worse than the first. Even so shall it be also unto this wicked generation.

PSALM 16:1–11

PRESERVE me, O God: for in thee do I put my trust.

2*O my soul,* thou hast said unto the LORD, Thou *art* my Lord: my goodness *extendeth* not to thee;

3*But* to the saints that *are* in the earth, and *to* the excellent, in whom *is* all my delight.

4Their sorrows shall be multiplied *that* hasten *after* another *god:* their drink offerings of blood will I not offer, nor take up their names into my lips.

5The LORD *is* the portion of mine inheritance and of my cup: thou maintainest my lot.

6The lines are fallen unto me in pleasant *places;* yea, I have a goodly heritage.

7I will bless the LORD, who hath given me counsel: my reins also instruct me in the night seasons.

8I have set the LORD always before me: because *he is* at my right hand, I shall not be moved.

9Therefore my heart is glad, and my glory rejoiceth: my flesh also shall rest in hope.

10For thou wilt not leave my soul in hell; neither wilt thou suffer thine Holy One to see corruption.

11Thou wilt shew me the path of life: in thy presence *is* fulness of joy; at thy right hand *there are* pleasures for evermore.

PROVERBS FOR TODAY/ 3:27–32

Withhold not good from them to whom it is due, when it is in the power of thine hand to do it. Say not unto thy neighbour, Go, and come again, and to morrow I will give; when thou hast it by thee. □ *Devise not evil against thy neighbour, seeing he dwelleth securely by thee. Strive not with a man without cause, if he have done thee no harm.* □ *Envy thou not the oppressor, and choose none of his ways. For the froward* is *abomination to the LORD: but his secret* is *with the righteous.*

GENESIS 39:1—41:16

ND Joseph was brought down to Egypt; and Potiphar, an officer of Pharoah, captain of the guard, an Egyptian, bought him of the hands of the Ishmeelites, which had brought him down thither.

2And the Lord was with Joseph, and he was a prosperous man; and he was in the house of his master the Egyptian.

3And his master saw that the Lord *was* with him, and that the Lord made all that he did to prosper in his hand.

4And Joseph found grace in his sight, and he served him: and he made him overseer over his house, and all *that* he had he put into his hand.

5And it came to pass from the time *that* he had made him overseer in his house, and over all that he had, that the Lord blessed the Egyptian's house for Joseph's sake; and the blessing of the Lord was upon all that he had in the house, and in the field.

6And he left all that he had in Joseph's hand; and he knew not ought he had, save the bread which he did eat. And Joseph was a goodly *person,* and well favoured.

7And it came to pass after these things, that his master's wife cast her eyes upon Joseph; and she said, Lie with me.

8But he refused, and said unto his master's wife, Behold, my master wotteth not what *is* with me in the house, and he hath committed all that he hath to my hand;

9*There is* none greater in this house than I; neither hath he kept back any thing from me but thee, because thou *art* his wife: how then can I do this great wickedness, and sin against God?

10And it came to pass, as she spake to Joseph day by day, that he hearkened not unto her, to lie by her, *or* to be with her.

11And it came to pass about this time, that *Joseph* went into the house to do his business; and *there was* none of the men of the house there within.

12And she caught him by his garment, saying, Lie with me: and he left his garment in her hand, and fled, and got him out.

13And it came to pass, when she saw that he had left his garment in her hand, and was fled forth,

14That she called unto the men of her house, and spake unto them, saying, See, he hath brought in an Hebrew unto us to mock us; he came in unto me to lie with me, and I cried with a loud voice:

15And it came to pass, when he heard that I lifted up my voice and cried, that he left his garment with me, and fled, and got him out.

16And she laid up his garment by her, until his lord came home.

17And she spake unto him according to these words, saying, The Hebrew servant, which thou hast brought unto us, came in unto me to mock me:

18And it came to pass, as I lifted up my voice and cried, that he left his garment with me, and fled out.

19And it came to pass, when his master heard the words of his wife, which she spake unto him, saying, After this manner did thy servant to me; that his wrath was kindled.

20And Joseph's master took him, and put him into the prison, a place where the king's prisoners *were* bound: and he was there in the prison.

21But the Lord was with Joseph, and shewed him mercy, and gave him favour in the sight of the keeper of the prison.

22And the keeper of the prison committed to Joseph's hand all the prisoners that *were* in the prison; and whatsoever they did there, he was the doer *of it.*

23The keeper of the prison looked not to any thing *that was* under his hand; because the LORD was with him, and *that* which he did, the LORD made *it* to prosper.

AND it came to pass after these things, *that* the butler of the king of Egypt and *his* baker had offended their lord the king of Egypt.

2And Pharaoh was wroth against two *of* his officers, against the chief of the butlers, and against the chief of the bakers.

3And he put them in ward in the house of the captain of the guard, into the prison, the place where Joseph *was* bound.

4And the captain of the guard charged Joseph with them, and he served them: and they continued a season in ward.

5And they dreamed a dream both of them, each man his dream in one night, each man according to the interpretation of his dream, the butler and the baker of the king of Egypt, which *were* bound in the prison.

6And Joseph came in unto them in the morning, and looked upon them, and, behold, they *were* sad.

7And he asked Pharaoh's officers that *were* with him in the ward of his lord's house, saying, Wherefore look ye *so* sadly to day?

8And they said unto him, We have dreamed a dream, and *there is* no interpreter of it. And Joseph said unto them, *Do* not interpretations *belong* to God? tell me *them,* I pray you.

9And the chief butler told his dream to Joseph, and said to him, In my dream, behold, a vine *was* before me;

10And in the vine *were* three branches: and it *was* as though it budded, *and* her blossoms shot forth; and the clusters thereof brought forth ripe grapes:

11And Pharaoh's cup *was* in my hand: and I took the grapes, and pressed them into Pharaoh's cup, and I gave the cup into Pharaoh's hand.

12And Joseph said unto him, This *is* the interpretation of it: The three branches *are* three days:

13Yet within three days shall Pharaoh lift up thine head, and restore thee unto thy place: and thou shalt deliver Pharaoh's cup into his hand, after the former manner when thou wast his butler.

14But think on me when it shall be well with thee, and shew kindness, I pray thee, unto me, and make mention of me unto Pharaoh, and bring me out of this house:

15For indeed I was stolen away out of the land of the Hebrews: and here also have I done nothing that they should put me into the dungeon.

16When the chief baker saw that the interpretation was good, he said unto Joseph, I also *was* in my dream, and, behold, I *had* three white baskets on my head:

17And in the uppermost basket *there was* of all manner of bakemeats for Pharaoh; and the birds did eat them out of the basket upon my head

18And Joseph answered and said, This *is* the interpretation thereof: The three baskets *are* three days:

19Yet within three days shall Pharaoh lift up thy head from off thee, and shall hang thee on a tree; and the birds shall eat thy flesh from off thee.

20And it came to pass the third day, *which was* Pharaoh's birthday, that he made a feast unto all his servants: and he lifted up the head of the chief butler and of the chief baker among his servants.

21And he restored the chief butler unto his butlership again; and he gave the cup into Pharaoh's hand:

22But he hanged the chief baker: as Joseph had interpreted to them.

23Yet did not the chief butler remember Joseph, but forgat him.

AND it came to pass at the end of two full years, that Pharaoh dreamed: and, behold, he stood by the river.

2And, behold, there came up out of the river seven well favoured kine and fatfleshed; and they fed in a meadow.

3And, behold, seven other kine came up after them out of the river, ill favoured and leanfleshed; and stood by the *other* kine upon the brink of the river.

4And the ill favoured and leanfleshed kine did eat up the seven well favoured and fat kine. So Pharaoh awoke.

5And he slept and dreamed the second time: and, behold, seven ears of corn came up upon one stalk, rank and good.

6And, behold, seven thin ears and blasted with the east wind sprung up after them.

7And the seven thin ears devoured the seven rank and full ears. And Pharaoh awoke, and, behold, *it was* a dream.

8And it came to pass in the morning that his spirit was troubled; and he sent and called for all the magicians of Egypt, and all the wise men thereof: and Pharaoh told them his dream; but *there was* none that could interpret them unto Pharaoh.

9Then spake the chief butler unto Pharaoh, saying, I do remember my faults this day:

10Pharaoh was wroth with his servants, and put me in ward in the captain of the guard's house, *both* me and the chief baker:

11And we dreamed a dream in one night, I and he; we dreamed each man according to the interpretation of his dream.

12And *there was* there with us a young man, an Hebrew, servant to the captain of the guard; and we told him, and he interpreted to us our dreams; to each man according to his dream he did interpret.

13And it came to pass, as he inter-

preted to us, so it was; me he restored unto mine office, and him he hanged.

14Then Pharaoh sent and called Joseph, and they brought him hastily out of the dungeon: and he shaved *himself,* and changed his raiment, and came in unto Pharaoh.

15And Pharaoh said unto Joseph, I have dreamed a dream, and *there is* none that can interpret it: and I have heard say of thee, *that* thou canst understand a dream to interpret it.

16And Joseph answered Pharaoh, saying, *It is* not in me: God shall give Pharaoh an answer of peace.

MATTHEW 12:46—13:23

WHILE he [Jesus] yet talked to the people, behold, *his* mother and his brethren stood without, desiring to speak with him.

47Then one said unto him, Behold, thy mother and thy brethren stand without, desiring to speak with thee.

48But he answered and said unto him that told him, Who is my mother? and who are my brethren?

49And he stretched forth his hand toward his disciples, and said, Behold my mother and my brethren!

50For whosoever shall do the will of my Father which is in heaven, the same is my brother, and sister, and mother.

THE same day went Jesus out of the house, and sat by the sea side.

2And great multitudes were gathered together unto him, so that he went into a ship, and sat; and the whole multitude stood on the shore.

3And he spake many things unto them in parables, saying, Behold, a sower went forth to sow;

4And when he sowed, some *seeds* fell by the way side, and the fowls came and devoured them up:

5Some fell upon stony places, where they had not much earth: and forthwith they sprung up, because they had no deepness of earth:

6And when the sun was up, they were scorched; and because they had no root, they withered away.

7And some fell among thorns; and the thorns sprung up, and choked them:

8But other fell into good ground, and brought forth fruit, some an hundredfold, some sixtyfold, some thirtyfold.

9Who hath ears to hear, let him hear.

10And the disciples came, and said unto him, Why speakest thou unto them in parables?

11He answered and said unto them, Because it is given unto you to know the mysteries of the kingdom of heaven, but to them it is not given.

12For whosoever hath, to him shall be given, and he shall have more abundance: but whosoever hath not, from him shall be taken away even that he hath.

13Therefore speak I to them in parables: because they seeing see not; and hearing they hear not, neither do they understand.

14And in them is fulfilled the prophecy of Esaias, which saith, By hearing ye shall hear, and shall not understand; and seeing ye shall see, and shall not perceive:

15For this people's heart is waxed gross, and *their* ears are dull of hearing, and their eyes they have closed; lest at any time they should see with *their* eyes, and hear with *their* ears, and should understand with *their* heart, and should be converted, and I should heal them.

16But blessed *are* your eyes, for they see: and your ears, for they hear.

17For verily I say unto you, That many prophets and righteous *men* have desired to see *those things* which ye see, and have not seen *them;* and to hear *those things* which ye hear, and have not heard *them.*

18Hear ye therefore the parable of the sower.

19When any one heareth the word of the kingdom, and understandeth *it* not, then cometh the wicked *one,* and catcheth away that which was sown in his heart. This is he which received seed by the way side.

20But he that received the seed into stony places, the same is he that heareth the word, and anon with joy receiveth it;

21Yet hath he not root in himself, but dureth for a while: for when tribulation or persecution ariseth because of the word, by and by he is offended.

22He also that received seed among the thorns is he that heareth the word; and the care of this world, and the deceitfulness of riches, choke the word, and he becometh unfruitful.

23But he that received seed into the good ground is he that heareth the word, and understandeth *it;* which also beareth fruit, and bringeth forth, some an hundredfold, some sixty, some thirty.

PSALM 17:1–15

HEAR the right, O Lord, attend unto my cry, give ear unto my prayer, *that goeth* not out of feigned lips.

2Let my sentence come forth from thy presence; let thine eyes behold the things that are equal.

3Thou hast proved mine heart; thou hast visited *me* in the night; thou hast tried me, *and* shalt find nothing; I am purposed *that* my mouth shall not transgress.

4Concerning the works of men, by the word of thy lips I have kept *me from* the paths of the destroyer.

5Hold up my goings in thy paths, *that* my footsteps slip not.

6I have called upon thee, for thou wilt hear me, O God: incline thine ear unto me, *and hear* my speech.

7Shew thy marvellous lovingkindness, O thou that savest by thy right hand them which put their trust *in thee* from those that rise up *against them.*

8Keep me as the apple of the eye, hide me under the shadow of thy wings,

9From the wicked that oppress me, *from* my deadly enemies, *who* compass me about.

10They are inclosed in their own fat: with their mouth they speak proudly.

11They have now compassed us in our steps: they have set their eyes bowing down to the earth;

12Like as a lion *that* is greedy of his prey, and as it were a young lion lurking in secret places.

13Arise, O LORD, disappoint him, cast him down: deliver my soul from the wicked, *which is* thy sword:

14From men *which are* thy hand, O LORD, from men of the world, *which have* their portion in *this* life, and whose belly thou fillest with thy hid *treasure:* they are full of children, and leave the rest of their *substance* to their babes.

15As for me, I will behold thy face in righteousness: I shall be satisfied, when I awake, with thy likeness.

PROVERBS FOR TODAY/ 3:33–35

The curse of the LORD is in the house of the wicked: but he blesseth the habitation of the just. Surely he scorneth the scorners: but he giveth grace unto the lowly. The wise shall inherit glory: but shame shall be the promotion of fools.

JANUARY 20

GENESIS 41:17—42:17

AND Pharaoh said unto Joseph, In my dream, behold, I stood upon the bank of the river:

18And, behold, there came up out of the river seven kine, fatfleshed and well favoured; and they fed in a meadow:

19And, behold, seven other kine came up after them, poor and very ill favoured and leanfleshed, such as I never saw in all the land of Egypt for badness:

20And the lean and the ill favoured kine did eat up the first seven fat kine:

21And when they had eaten them up, it could not be known that they had eaten them; but they *were* still ill favoured, as at the beginning. So I awoke.

22And I saw in my dream, and, behold, seven ears came up in one stalk, full and good:

23And, behold, seven ears, withered, thin, *and* blasted with the east wind, sprung up after them:

24And the thin ears devoured the seven good ears: and I told *this* unto the magicians; but *there was* none that could declare *it* to me.

25And Joseph said unto Pharaoh, The dream of Pharaoh *is* one: God hath shewed Pharaoh what he *is* about to do.

26The seven good kine *are* seven years; and the seven good ears *are* seven years: the dream *is* one.

27And the seven thin and ill favoured kine that came up after them *are* seven years; and the seven empty ears blasted with the east wind shall be seven years of famine.

28This *is* the thing which I have spoken unto Pharaoh: What God *is* about to do he sheweth unto Pharaoh.

29Behold, there come seven years

of great plenty throughout all the land of Egypt:

30And there shall arise after them seven years of famine; and all the plenty shall be forgotten in the land of Egypt; and the famine shall consume the land;

31And the plenty shall not be known in the land by reason of that famine following; for it *shall be* very grievous.

32And for that the dream was doubled unto Pharaoh twice; *it is* because the thing *is* established by God, and God will shortly bring it to pass.

33Now therefore let Pharaoh look out a man discreet and wise, and set him over the land of Egypt.

34Let Pharaoh do *this,* and let him appoint officers over the land, and take up the fifth part of the land of Egypt in the seven plenteous years.

35And let them gather all the food of those good years that come, and lay up corn under the hand of Pharaoh, and let them keep food in the cities.

36And that food shall be for store to the land against the seven years of famine, which shall be in the land of Egypt; that the land perish not through the famine.

37And the thing was good in the eyes of Pharaoh, and in the eyes of all his servants.

38And Pharaoh said unto his servants, Can we find *such a one* as this *is,* a man in whom the Spirit of God *is?*

39And Pharaoh said unto Joseph, Forasmuch as God hath shewed thee all this, *there is* none so discreet and wise as thou *art:*

40Thou shalt be over my house, and according unto thy word shall all my people be ruled: only in the throne will I be greater than thou.

41And Pharaoh said unto Joseph, See, I have set thee over all the land of Egypt.

42And Pharaoh took off his ring from his hand, and put it upon Joseph's hand, and arrayed him in vestures of fine linen, and put a gold chain about his neck;

43And he made him to ride in the second chariot which he had; and they cried before him, Bow the knee: and he made him *ruler* over all the land of Egypt.

44And Pharaoh said unto Joseph, I *am* Pharaoh, and without thee shall no man lift up his hand or foot in all the land of Egypt.

45And Pharaoh called Joseph's name Zaphnath–paaneah; and he gave him to wife Asenath the daughter of Poti–pherah priest of On. And Joseph went out over *all* the land of Egypt.

46And Joseph *was* thirty years old when he stood before Pharaoh king of Egypt. And Joseph went out from the presence of Pharaoh, and went throughout all the land of Egypt.

47And in the seven plenteous years the earth brought forth by handfuls.

48And he gathered up all the food of the seven years, which were in the land of Egypt, and laid up the food in the cities: the food of the field, which *was* round about every city, laid he up in the same.

49And Joseph gathered corn as the sand of the sea, very much, until he left numbering; for *it was* without number.

50And unto Joseph were born two sons before the years of famine came, which Asenath the daughter of Poti–pherah priest of On bare unto him.

51And Joseph called the name of the firstborn Manasseh: For God, *said he,* hath made me forget all my toil, and all my father's house.

52And the name of the second called he Ephraim: For God hath caused me to be fruitful in the land of my affliction.

53And the seven years of plenteousness, that was in the land of Egypt, were ended.

54And the seven years of dearth began to come, according as Joseph had said: and the dearth was in all lands; but in all the land of Egypt there was bread.

55And when all the land of Egypt was famished, the people cried to Pharaoh for bread: and Pharaoh said unto all the Egyptians, Go unto Joseph; what he saith to you, do.

56And the famine was over all the face of the earth: And Joseph opened all the storehouses, and sold unto the Egyptians; and the famine waxed sore in the land of Egypt.

57And all countries came into Egypt to Joseph for to buy *corn;* because that the famine was *so* sore in all lands.

Now when Jacob saw that there was corn in Egypt, Jacob said unto his sons, Why do ye look one upon another?

2And he said, Behold, I have heard that there is corn in Egypt: get you down thither, and buy for us from thence; that we may live, and not die.

3And Joseph's ten brethren went down to buy corn in Egypt.

4But Benjamin, Joseph's brother, Jacob sent not with his brethren; for he said, Lest peradventure mischief befall him.

5And the sons of Israel came to buy *corn* among those that came: for the famine was in the land of Canaan.

6And Joseph *was* the governor over the land, *and* he *it was* that sold to all the people of the land: and Joseph's brethren came, and bowed down themselves before him *with* their faces to the earth.

7And Joseph saw his brethren, and he knew them, but made himself strange unto them, and spake roughly unto them; and he said unto them, Whence come ye? And they said, From the land of Canaan to buy food.

8And Joseph knew his brethren, but they knew not him.

9And Joseph remembered the dreams which he dreamed of them, and said unto them, Ye *are* spies; to see the nakedness of the land ye are come.

10And they said unto him, Nay, my lord, but to buy food are thy servants come.

11We *are* all one man's sons; we *are* true *men,* thy servants are no spies.

12And he said unto them, Nay, but to see the nakedness of the land ye are come.

13And they said, Thy servants *are* twelve brethren, the sons of one man in the land of Canaan; and, behold, the youngest *is* this day with our father, and one *is* not.

14And Joseph said unto them, That *is it* that I spake unto you, saying, Ye *are* spies:

15Hereby ye shall be proved: By the life of Pharaoh ye shall not go forth hence, except your youngest brother come hither.

16Send one of you, and let him fetch your brother, and ye shall be kept in prison, that your words may be proved, whether *there be any* truth in you: or else by the life of Pharaoh surely ye *are* spies.

17And he put them all together into ward three days.

MATTHEW 13:24–46

ANOTHER parable put he [Jesus] forth unto them, saying, The kingdom of heaven is likened unto a man which sowed good seed in his field:

25But while men slept, his enemy came and sowed tares among the wheat, and went his way.

26But when the blade was sprung up, and brought forth fruit, then appeared the tares also.

27So the servants of the householder came and said unto him, Sir, didst not thou sow good seed in thy field? from whence then hath it tares?

28He said unto them, An enemy hath done this. The servants said unto him, Wilt thou then that we go and gather them up?

29But he said, Nay; lest while ye

gather up the tares, ye root up also the wheat with them.

30Let both grow together until the harvest: and in the time of harvest I will say to the reapers, Gather ye together first the tares, and bind them in bundles to burn them: but gather the wheat into my barn.

31Another parable put he forth unto them, saying, The kingdom of heaven is like to a grain of mustard seed, which a man took, and sowed in his field:

32Which indeed is the least of all seeds: but when it is grown, it is the greatest among herbs, and becometh a tree, so that the birds of the air come and lodge in the branches thereof.

33Another parable spake he unto them; The kingdom of heaven is like unto leaven, which a woman took, and hid in three measures of meal, till the whole was leavened.

34All these things spake Jesus unto the multitude in parables; and without a parable spake he not unto them:

35That it might be fulfilled which was spoken by the prophet, saying, I will open my mouth in parables; I will utter things which have been kept secret from the foundation of the world.

36Then Jesus sent the multitude away, and went into the house: and his disciples came unto him, saying, Declare unto us the parable of the tares of the field.

37He answered and said unto them, He that soweth the good seed is the Son of man;

38The field is the world; the good seed are the children of the kingdom; but the tares are the children of the wicked one;

39The enemy that sowed them is the devil; the harvest is the end of the world; and the reapers are the angels.

40As therefore the tares are gathered and burned in the fire; so shall it be in the end of this world.

41The Son of man shall send forth his angels, and they shall gather out of his kingdom all things that offend, and them which do iniquity;

42And shall cast them into a furnace of fire: there shall be wailing and gnashing of teeth.

43Then shall the righteous shine forth as the sun in the kingdom of their Father. Who hath ears to hear, let him hear.

44Again, the kingdom of heaven is like unto treasure hid in a field; the which when a man hath found, he hideth, and for joy thereof goeth and selleth all that he hath, and buyeth that field.

45Again, the kingdom of heaven is like unto a merchant man, seeking goodly pearls:

46Who, when he had found one pearl of great price, went and sold all that he had, and bought it.

PSALM 18:1–15

I will love thee, O LORD, my strength.

2The LORD is my rock, and my fortress, and my deliverer; my God, my strength, in whom I will trust; my buckler, and the horn of my salvation, and my high tower.

3I will call upon the LORD, who is worthy to be praised: so shall I be saved from mine enemies.

4The sorrows of death compassed me, and the floods of ungodly men made me afraid.

5The sorrows of hell compassed me about: the snares of death prevented me.

6In my distress I called upon the LORD, and cried unto my God: he heard my voice out of his temple, and my cry came before him, even into his ears.

7Then the earth shook and trembled; the foundations also of the hills moved and were shaken, because he was wroth.

8There went up a smoke out of his

nostrils, and fire out of his mouth devoured: coals were kindled by it.

⁹He bowed the heavens also, and came down: and darkness *was* under his feet.

¹⁰And he rode upon a cherub, and did fly: yea, he did fly upon the wings of the wind.

¹¹He made darkness his secret place; his pavilion round about him *were* dark waters *and* thick clouds of the skies.

¹²At the brightness *that was* before him his thick clouds passed, hail *stones* and coals of fire.

¹³The LORD also thundered in the heavens, and the Highest gave his voice; hail *stones* and coals of fire.

¹⁴Yea, he sent out his arrows, and scattered them; and he shot out lightnings, and discomfited them.

¹⁵Then the channels of waters were seen, and the foundations of the world were discovered at thy rebuke, O LORD, at the blast of the breath of thy nostrils.

PROVERBS FOR TODAY/ 4:1–6

Hear, ye children, the instruction of a father, and attend to know understanding. For I give you good doctrine, forsake ye not my law. For I was my father's son, tender and only beloved in the sight of my mother. He taught me also, and said unto me, Let thine heart retain my words: keep my commandments, and live. Get wisdom, get understanding: forget it not; neither decline from the words of my mouth. Forsake her not, and she shall preserve thee: love her, and she shall keep thee.

JANUARY 21

GENESIS 42:18—43:34

AND Joseph said unto them [his brothers] the third day, This do, and live; *for* I fear God:

¹⁹If ye *be* true *men*, let one of your brethren be bound in the house of your prison: go ye, carry corn for the famine of your houses:

²⁰But bring your youngest brother unto me; so shall your words be verified, and ye shall not die. And they did so.

²¹And they said one to another, We *are* verily guilty concerning our brother, in that we saw the anguish of his soul, when he besought us, and we would not hear; therefore is this distress come upon us.

²²And Reuben answered them, saying, Spake I not unto you, saying, Do

not sin against the child; and ye would not hear? therefore, behold, also his blood is required.

²³And they knew not that Joseph understood *them;* for he spake unto them by an interpreter.

²⁴And he turned himself about from them, and wept; and returned to them again, and communed with them, and took from them Simeon, and bound him before their eyes.

²⁵Then Joseph commanded to fill their sacks with corn, and to restore every man's money into his sack, and to give them provision for the way: and thus did he unto them.

²⁶And they laded their asses with the corn, and departed thence.

²⁷And as one of them opened his sack to give his ass provender in the inn,

he espied his money; for, behold, it *was* in his sack's mouth.

28And he said unto his brethren, My money is restored; and, lo, *it is* even in my sack: and their heart failed *them,* and they were afraid, saying one to another, What *is* this *that* God hath done unto us?

29And they came unto Jacob their father unto the land of Canaan, and told him all that befell unto them; saying,

30This man, *who is* the lord of the land, spake roughly to us, and took us for spies of the country.

31And we said unto him, We *are* true *men;* we are no spies:

32We *be* twelve brethren, sons of our father; one *is* not, and the youngest *is* this day with our father in the land of Canaan.

33And the man, the lord of the country, said unto us, Hereby shall I know that ye *are* true *men;* leave one of your brethren *here* with me, and take *food for* the famine of your households, and be gone:

34And bring your youngest brother unto me: then shall I know that ye *are* no spies, but *that* ye *are* true *men: so* will I deliver you your brother, and ye shall traffick in the land.

35And it came to pass as they emptied their sacks, that, behold, every man's bundle of money *was* in his sack: and when *both* they and their father saw the bundles of money, they were afraid.

36And Jacob their father said unto them, Me have ye bereaved *of my children:* Joseph *is* not, and Simeon *is* not, and ye will take Benjamin *away:* all these things are against me.

37And Reuben spake unto his father, saying, Slay my two sons, if I bring him not to thee: deliver him into my hand, and I will bring him to thee again.

38And he said, My son shall not go down with you; for his brother is dead, and he is left alone: if mischief befall him by the way in the which ye go,

then shall ye bring down my gray hairs with sorrow to the grave.

AND the famine *was* sore in the land.

2And it came to pass, when they had eaten up the corn which they had brought out of Egypt, their father said unto them, Go again, buy us a little food.

3And Judah spake unto him, saying, The man did solemnly protest unto us, saying, Ye shall not see my face, except your brother *be* with you.

4If thou wilt send our brother with us, we will go down and buy thee food:

5But if thou wilt not send *him,* we will not go down: for the man said unto us, Ye shall not see my face, except your brother *be* with you.

6And Israel said, Wherefore dealt ye *so* ill with me, *as* to tell the man whether ye had yet a brother?

7And they said, The man asked us straitly of our state, and of our kindred, saying, *Is* your father yet alive? have ye *another* brother? and we told him according to the tenor of these words: could we certainly know that he would say, Bring your brother down?

8And Judah said unto Israel his father, Send the lad with me, and we will arise and go; that we may live, and not die, both we, and thou, *and* also our little ones.

9I will be surety for him; of my hand shalt thou require him: if I bring him not unto thee, and set him before thee, then let me bear the blame for ever:

10For except we had lingered, surely now we had returned this second time.

11And their father Israel said unto them, If *it must be* so now, do this; take of the best fruits in the land in your vessels, and carry down the man a present, a little balm, and a little honey, spices, and myrrh, nuts, and almonds:

12And take double money in your

hand; and the money that was brought again in the mouth of your sacks, carry *it* again in your hand; peradventure it *was* an oversight:

13Take also your brother, and arise, go again unto the man:

14And God Almighty give you mercy before the man, that he may send away your other brother, and Benjamin. If I be bereaved *of my children,* I am bereaved.

15And the men took that present, and they took double money in their hand, and Benjamin; and rose up, and went down to Egypt, and stood before Joseph.

16And when Joseph saw Benjamin with them, he said to the ruler of his house, Bring *these* men home, and slay, and make ready; for *these* men shall dine with me at noon.

17And the man did as Joseph bade; and the man brought the men into Joseph's house.

18And the men were afraid, because they were brought unto Joseph's house; and they said, Because of the money that was returned in our sacks at the first time are we brought in; that he may seek occasion against us, and fall upon us, and take us for bondmen, and our asses.

19And they came near to the steward of Joseph's house, and they communed with him at the door of the house,

20And said, O sir, we came indeed down at the first time to buy food:

21And it came to pass, when we came to the inn, that we opened our sacks, and, behold, *every* man's money *was* in the mouth of his sack, our money in full weight: and we have brought it again in our hand.

22And other money have we brought down in our hands to buy food: we cannot tell who put our money in our sacks.

23And he said, Peace *be* to you, fear not: your God, and the God of your father, hath given you treasure in your sacks: I had your money. And he brought Simeon out unto them.

24And the man brought the men into Joseph's house, and gave *them* water, and they washed their feet; and he gave their asses provender.

25And they made ready the present against Joseph came at noon: for they heard that they should eat bread there.

26And when Joseph came home, they brought him the present which *was* in their hand into the house, and bowed themselves to him to the earth.

27And he asked them of *their* welfare, and said, *Is* your father well, the old man of whom ye spake? *Is* he yet alive?

28And they answered, Thy servant our father *is* in good health, he *is* yet alive. And they bowed down their heads, and made obeisance.

29And he lifted up his eyes, and saw his brother Benjamin, his mother's son, and said, *Is* this your younger brother, of whom ye spake unto me? And he said, God be gracious unto thee, my son.

30And Joseph made haste; for his bowels did yearn upon his brother: and he sought *where* to weep; and he entered into *his* chamber, and wept there.

31And he washed his face, and went out, and refrained himself, and said, Set on bread.

32And they set on for him by himself, and for them by themselves, and for the Egyptians, which did eat with him, by themselves: because the Egyptians might not eat bread with the Hebrews; for that *is* an abomination unto the Egyptians.

33And they sat before him, the firstborn according to his birthright, and the youngest according to his youth: and the men marvelled one at another.

34And he took *and sent* messes unto them from before him: but Benjamin's mess was five times so much as any of theirs. And they drank, and were merry with him.

MATTHEW 13:47—14:13

AGAIN, the kingdom of heaven is like unto a net, that was cast into the sea, and gathered of every kind:

48Which, when it was full, they drew to shore, and sat down, and gathered the good into vessels, but cast the bad away.

49So shall it be at the end of the world: the angels shall come forth, and sever the wicked from among the just,

50And shall cast them into the furnace of fire: there shall be wailing and gnashing of teeth.

51Jesus saith unto them, Have ye understood all these things? They say unto him, Yea, Lord.

52Then said he unto them, Therefore every scribe *which is* instructed unto the kingdom of heaven is like unto a man *that is* an householder, which bringeth forth out of his treasure *things* new and old.

53And it came to pass, *that* when Jesus had finished these parables, he departed thence.

54And when he was come into his own country, he taught them in their synagogue, insomuch that they were astonished, and said, Whence hath this *man* this wisdom, and *these* mighty works?

55Is not this the carpenter's son? is not his mother called Mary? and his brethren, James, and Joses, and Simon, and Judas?

56And his sisters, are they not all with us? Whence then hath this *man* all these things?

57And they were offended in him. But Jesus said unto them, A prophet is not without honour, save in his own country, and in his own house.

58And he did not many mighty works there because of their unbelief.

AT that time Herod the tetrarch heard of the fame of Jesus,

2And said unto his servants, This is John the Baptist; he is risen from the dead; and therefore mighty works do shew forth themselves in him.

3For Herod had laid hold on John, and bound him, and put *him* in prison for Herodias' sake, his brother Philip's wife.

4For John said unto him, It is not lawful for thee to have her.

5And when he would have put him to death, he feared the multitude, because they counted him as a prophet.

6But when Herod's birthday was kept, the daughter of Herodias danced before them, and pleased Herod.

7Whereupon he promised with an oath to give her whatsoever she would ask.

8And she, being before instructed of her mother, said, Give me here John Baptist's head in a charger.

9And the king was sorry: nevertheless for the oath's sake, and them which sat with him at meat, he commanded *it* to be given *her*.

10And he sent, and beheaded John in the prison.

11And his head was brought in a charger, and given to the damsel: and she brought *it* to her mother.

12And his disciples came, and took up the body, and buried it, and went and told Jesus.

13When Jesus heard *of it,* he departed thence by ship into a desert place apart: and when the people had heard *thereof,* they followed him on foot out of the cities.

PSALM 18:16–34

HE sent from above, he took me, he drew me out of many waters. 17He delivered me from my strong enemy, and from them which hated me: for they were too strong for me.

18They prevented me in the day of my calamity: but the LORD was my stay.

19He brought me forth also into a large place; he delivered me, because he delighted in me.

20The LORD rewarded me according to my righteousness; according to the cleanness of my hands hath he recompensed me.

21For I have kept the ways of the LORD, and have not wickedly departed from my God.

22For all his judgments *were* before me, and I did not put away his statutes from me.

23I was also upright before him, and I kept myself from mine iniquity.

24Therefore hath the LORD recompensed me according to my righteousness, according to the cleanness of my hands in his eyesight.

25With the merciful thou wilt shew thyself merciful; with an upright man thou wilt shew thyself upright;

26With the pure thou wilt shew thyself pure; and with the froward thou wilt shew thyself froward.

27For thou wilt save the afflicted people; but wilt bring down high looks.

28For thou wilt light my candle: the LORD my God will enlighten my darkness.

29For by thee I have run through a troop; and by my God have I leaped over a wall.

30*As for* God, his way *is* perfect: the word of the LORD is tried: he *is* a buckler to all those that trust in him.

31For who *is* God save the LORD? or who *is* a rock save our God?

32*It is* God that girdeth me with strength, and maketh my way perfect.

33He maketh my feet like hinds' *feet,* and setteth me upon my high places.

34He teacheth my hands to war, so that a bow of steel is broken by mine arms.

PROVERBS FOR TODAY/ 4:7–10

Wisdom is *the principal thing; therefore get wisdom: and with all thy getting get understanding. Exalt her, and she shall promote thee: she shall bring thee to honour, when thou dost embrace her. She shall give to thine head an ornament of grace: a crown of glory shall she deliver to thee.* □ *Hear, O my son, and receive my sayings; and the years of thy life shall be many.*

JANUARY 22

GENESIS 44:1—45:28

AND he [Joseph] commanded the steward of his house, saying, Fill the men's sacks *with* food, as much as they can carry, and put every man's money in his sack's mouth.

2And put my cup, the silver cup, in the sack's mouth of the youngest, and his corn money. And he did according to the word that Joseph had spoken.

3As soon as the morning was light, the men were sent away, they and their asses.

4*And* when they were gone out of the city, *and* not *yet* far off, Joseph said unto his steward, Up, follow after the men; and when thou dost overtake them, say unto them, Wherefore have ye rewarded evil for good?

5*Is* not this *it* in which my lord drinketh, and whereby indeed he divineth? ye have done evil in so doing.

6And he overtook them, and he spake unto them these same words.

7And they said unto him, Wherefore saith my lord these words? God forbid that thy servants should do according to this thing:

8Behold, the money, which we found in our sacks' mouths, we brought again unto thee out of the land of Canaan: how then should we steal out of thy lord's house silver or gold?

9With whomsoever of thy servants it be found, both let him die, and we also will be my lord's bondmen.

10And he said, Now also *let* it *be* according unto your words: he with whom it is found shall be my servant; and ye shall be blameless.

11Then they speedily took down every man his sack to the ground, and opened every man his sack.

12And he searched, *and* began at the eldest, and left at the youngest: and the cup was found in Benjamin's sack.

13Then they rent their clothes, and laded every man his ass, and returned to the city.

14And Judah and his brethren came to Joseph's house; for he *was* yet there: and they fell before him on the ground.

15And Joseph said unto them, What deed *is* this that ye have done? wot ye not that such a man as I can certainly divine?

16And Judah said, What shall we say unto my lord? what shall we speak? or how shall we clear ourselves? God hath found out the iniquity of thy servants: behold, we *are* my lord's servants, both we, and *he* also with whom the cup is found.

17And he said, God forbid that I should do so: *but* the man in whose hand the cup is found, he shall be my servant; and as for you, get you up in peace unto your father.

18Then Judah came near unto him, and said, Oh my lord, let thy servant, I pray thee, speak a word in my lord's ears, and let not thine anger burn against thy servant: for thou *art* even as Pharaoh.

19My lord asked his servants, saying, Have ye a father, or a brother?

20And we said unto my lord, We have a father, an old man, and a child of his old age, a little one; and his brother is dead, and he alone is left of his mother, and his father loveth him.

21And thou saidst unto thy servants, Bring him down unto me, that I may set mine eyes upon him.

22And we said unto my lord, The lad cannot leave his father: for *if* he should leave his father, *his father* would die.

23And thou saidst unto thy servants, Except your youngest brother come down with you, ye shall see my face no more.

24And it came to pass when we came up unto thy servant my father, we told him the words of my lord.

25And our father said, Go again, *and* buy us a little food.

26And we said, We cannot go down: if our youngest brother be with us, then will we go down: for we may not see the man's face, except our youngest brother *be* with us.

27And thy servant my father said unto us, Ye know that my wife bare me two *sons:*

28And the one went out from me, and I said, Surely he is torn in pieces; and I saw him not since:

29And if ye take this also from me, and mischief befall him, ye shall bring down my gray hairs with sorrow to the grave.

30Now therefore when I come to thy servant my father, and the lad *be* not with us; seeing that his life is bound up in the lad's life;

31It shall come to pass, when he seeth that the lad is not *with us,* that he will die: and thy servants shall bring down the gray hairs of thy servant our father with sorrow to the grave.

32For thy servant became surety for

the lad unto my father, saying, If I bring him not unto thee, then I shall bear the blame to my father for ever.

33Now therefore, I pray thee, let thy servant abide instead of the lad a bondman to my lord; and let the lad go up with his brethren.

34For how shall I go up to my father, and the lad *be* not with me? lest peradventure I see the evil that shall come on my father.

THEN Joseph could not refrain himself before all them that stood by him; and he cried, Cause every man to go out from me. And there stood no man with him, while Joseph made himself known unto his brethren.

2And he wept aloud: and the Egyptians and the house of Pharaoh heard.

3And Joseph said unto his brethren, I *am* Joseph; doth my father yet live? And his brethren could not answer him; for they were troubled at his presence.

4And Joseph said unto his brethren, Come near to me, I pray you. And they came near. And he said, I *am* Joseph your brother, whom ye sold into Egypt.

5Now therefore be not grieved, nor angry with yourselves, that ye sold me hither: for God did send me before you to preserve life.

6For these two years *hath* the famine *been* in the land: and yet *there are* five years, in the which *there shall* neither *be* earing nor harvest.

7And God sent me before you to preserve you a posterity in the earth, and to save your lives by a great deliverance.

8So now *it was* not you *that* sent me hither, but God: and he hath made me a father to Pharaoh, and lord of all his house, and a ruler throughout all the land of Egypt.

9Haste ye, and go up to my father, and say unto him, Thus saith thy son Joseph, God hath made me lord of all Egypt: come down unto me, tarry not:

10And thou shalt dwell in the land of Goshen, and thou shalt be near unto me, thou, and thy children, and thy children's children, and thy flocks, and thy herds, and all that thou hast:

11And there will I nourish thee; for yet *there are* five years of famine; lest thou, and thy household, and all that thou hast, come to poverty.

12And, behold, your eyes see, and the eyes of my brother Benjamin, that *it is* my mouth that speaketh unto you.

13And ye shall tell my father of all my glory in Egypt, and of all that ye have seen; and ye shall haste and bring down my father hither.

14And he fell upon his brother Benjamin's neck, and wept; and Benjamin wept upon his neck.

15Moreover he kissed all his brethren, and wept upon them: and after that his brethren talked with him.

16And the fame thereof was heard in Pharaoh's house, saying, Joseph's brethren are come: and it pleased Pharaoh well, and his servants.

17And Pharaoh said unto Joseph, Say unto thy brethren, This do ye; lade your beasts, and go, get you unto the land of Canaan;

18And take your father and your households, and come unto me: and I will give you the good of the land of Egypt, and ye shall eat the fat of the land.

19Now thou art commanded, this do ye; take you wagons out of the land of Egypt for your little ones, and for your wives, and bring your father, and come.

20Also regard not your stuff; for the good of all the land of Egypt *is* yours.

21And the children of Israel did so: and Joseph gave them wagons, according to the commandment of Pharaoh, and gave them provision for the way.

22To all of them he gave each man changes of raiment; but to Benjamin he gave three hundred *pieces* of silver, and five changes of raiment.

23And to his father he sent after this *manner;* ten asses laden with the good things of Egypt, and ten she asses laden with corn and bread and meat for his father by the way.

24So he sent his brethren away, and they departed: and he said unto them, See that ye fall not out by the way.

25And they went up out of Egypt, and came into the land of Canaan unto Jacob their father,

26And told him, saying, Joseph *is* yet alive, and he *is* governor over all the land of Egypt. And Jacob's heart fainted, for he believed them not.

27And they told him all the words of Joseph, which he had said unto them: and when he saw the wagons which Joseph had sent to carry him, the spirit of Jacob their father revived:

28And Israel said, *It is* enough; Joseph my son *is* yet alive: I will go and see him before I die.

MATTHEW 14:14–36

AND Jesus went forth, and saw a great multitude, and was moved with compassion toward them, and he healed their sick.

15And when it was evening, his disciples came to him, saying, This is a desert place, and the time is now past; send the multitude away, that they may go into the villages, and buy themselves victuals.

16But Jesus said unto them, They need not depart; give ye them to eat.

17And they say unto him, We have here but five loaves, and two fishes.

18He said, Bring them hither to me.

19And he commanded the multitude to sit down on the grass, and took the five loaves, and the two fishes, and looking up to heaven, he blessed, and brake, and gave the loaves to *his* disciples, and the disciples to the multitude.

20And they did all eat, and were filled: and they took up of the fragments that remained twelve baskets full.

21And they that had eaten were about five thousand men, beside women and children.

22And straightway Jesus constrained his disciples to get into a ship, and to go before him unto the other side, while he sent the multitudes away.

23And when he had sent the multitudes away, he went up into a mountain apart to pray: and when the evening was come, he was there alone.

24But the ship was now in the midst of the sea, tossed with waves: for the wind was contrary.

25And in the fourth watch of the night Jesus went unto them, walking on the sea.

26And when the disciples saw him walking on the sea, they were troubled, saying, It is a spirit; and they cried out for fear.

27But straightway Jesus spake unto them, saying, Be of good cheer; it is I; be not afraid.

28And Peter answered him and said, Lord, if it be thou, bid me come unto thee on the water.

29And he said, Come. And when Peter was come down out of the ship, he walked on the water, to go to Jesus.

30But when he saw the wind boisterous, he was afraid; and beginning to sink, he cried, saying, Lord, save me.

31And immediately Jesus stretched forth *his* hand, and caught him, and said unto him, O thou of little faith, wherefore didst thou doubt?

32And when they were come into the ship, the wind ceased.

33Then they that were in the ship came and worshipped him, saying, Of a truth thou art the Son of God.

34And when they were gone over, they came into the land of Gennesaret.

35And when the men of that place had knowledge of him, they sent out into all that country round about, and brought unto him all that were diseased;

36And besought him that they might only touch the hem of his garment:

and as many as touched were made perfectly whole.

PSALM 18:35–50

THOU hast also given me the shield of thy salvation: and thy right hand hath holden me up, and thy gentleness hath made me great.

36Thou hast enlarged my steps under me, that my feet did not slip.

37I have pursued mine enemies, and overtaken them: neither did I turn again till they were consumed.

38I have wounded them that they were not able to rise: they are fallen under my feet.

39For thou hast girded me with strength unto the battle: thou hast subdued under me those that rose up against me.

40Thou hast also given me the necks of mine enemies; that I might destroy them that hate me.

41They cried, *but there was* none to save *them: even* unto the LORD, but he answered them not.

42Then did I beat them small as the dust before the wind: I did cast them out as the dirt in the streets.

43Thou hast delivered me from the strivings of the people; *and* thou hast made me the head of the heathen: a people *whom* I have not known shall serve me.

44As soon as they hear of me, they shall obey me: the strangers shall submit themselves unto me.

45The strangers shall fade away, and be afraid out of their close places.

46The LORD liveth; and blessed *be* my rock; and let the God of my salvation be exalted.

47*It is* God that avengeth me, and subdueth the people under me.

48He delivereth me from mine enemies: yea, thou liftest me up above those that rise up against me: thou hast delivered me from the violent man.

49Therefore will I give thanks unto thee, O LORD, among the heathen, and sing praises unto thy name.

50Great deliverance giveth he to his king; and sheweth mercy to his anointed, to David, and to his seed for evermore.

PROVERBS FOR TODAY/ 4:11–13

I have taught thee in the way of wisdom; I have led thee in right paths. When thou goest, thy steps shall not be straitened; and when thou runnest, thou shalt not stumble. Take fast hold of instruction; let her *not go: keep her; for she* is *thy life.*

JANUARY 23

GENESIS 46:1—47:31

AND Israel took his journey with all that he had, and came to Beer–sheba, and offered sacrifices unto the God of his father Isaac.

2And God spake unto Israel in the visions of the night, and said, Jacob, Jacob. And he said, Here *am* I.

3And he said, I *am* God, the God of thy father: fear not to go down into Egypt; for I will there make of thee a great nation:

4I will go down with thee into Egypt; and I will also surely bring thee up *again:*

and Joseph shall put his hand upon thine eyes.

5And Jacob rose up from Beer-sheba: and the sons of Israel carried Jacob their father, and their little ones, and their wives, in the wagons which Pharaoh had sent to carry him.

6And they took their cattle, and their goods, which they had gotten in the land of Canaan, and came into Egypt, Jacob, and all his seed with him:

7His sons, and his sons' sons with him, his daughters, and his son's daughters, and all his seed brought he with him into Egypt.

8And these *are* the names of the children of Israel, which came into Egypt, Jacob and his sons: Reuben, Jacob's firstborn.

9And the sons of Reuben; Hanoch, and Phallu, and Hezron, and Carmi.

10And the sons of Simeon; Jemuel, and Jamin, and Ohad, and Jachin, and Zohar, and Shaul the son of a Canaanitish woman.

11And the sons of Levi; Gershon, Kohath, and Merari.

12And the sons of Judah; Er, and Onan, and Shelah, and Pharez, and Zarah: but Er and Onan died in the land of Canaan. And the sons of Pharez were Hezron and Hamul.

13And the sons of Issachar; Tola, and Phuvah, and Job, and Shimron.

14And the sons of Zebulun; Sered, and Elon, and Jahleel.

15These *be* the sons of Leah, which she bare unto Jacob in Padan-aram, with his daughter Dinah: all the souls of his sons and his daughters *were* thirty and three.

16And the sons of Gad; Ziphion, and Haggi, Shuni, and Ezbon, Eri, and Arodi, and Areli.

17And the sons of Asher; Jimnah, and Ishuah, and Isui, and Beriah, and Serah their sister: and the sons of Beriah; Heber, and Malchiel.

18These *are* the sons of Zilpah, whom Laban gave to Leah his daughter, and these she bare unto Jacob, *even* sixteen souls.

19The sons of Rachel Jacob's wife; Joseph, and Benjamin.

20And unto Joseph in the land of Egypt were born Manasseh and Ephraim, which Asenath the daughter of Potipherah priest of On bare unto him.

21And the sons of Benjamin *were* Belah, and Becher, and Ashbel, Gera, and Naaman, Ehi, and Rosh, Muppim, and Huppim, and Ard.

22These *are* the sons of Rachel, which were born to Jacob: all the souls *were* fourteen.

23And the sons of Dan; Hushim.

24And the sons of Naphtali; Jahzeel, and Guni, and Jezer, and Shillem.

25These *are* the sons of Bilhah, which Laban gave unto Rachel his daughter, and she bare these unto Jacob: all the souls *were* seven.

26And the souls that came with Jacob into Egypt, which came out of his loins, besides Jacob's sons' wives, all the souls *were* threescore and six;

27And the sons of Joseph, which were born him in Egypt, *were* two souls: all the souls of the house of Jacob, which came into Egypt, *were* threescore and ten.

28And he sent Judah before him unto Joseph, to direct his face unto Goshen; and they came into the land of Goshen.

29And Joseph made ready his chariot, and went up to meet Israel his father, to Goshen, and presented himself unto him; and he fell on his neck, and wept on his neck a good while.

30And Israel said unto Joseph, Now let me die, since I have seen thy face, because thou *art* yet alive.

31And Joseph said unto his brethren, and unto his father's house, I will go up, and shew Pharaoh, and say unto him, My brethren, and my father's house, which *were* in the land of Canaan, are come unto me;

32And the men *are* shepherds, for their trade hath been to feed cattle;

and they have brought their flocks, and their herds, and all that they have.

33And it shall come to pass, when Pharaoh shall call you, and shall say, What *is* your occupation?

34That ye shall say, Thy servants' trade hath been about cattle from our youth even until now, both we, *and* also our fathers: that ye may dwell in the land of Goshen; for every shepherd *is* an abomination unto the Egyptians.

THEN Joseph came and told Pharaoh, and said, My father and my brethren, and their flocks, and their herds, and all that they have, are come out of the land of Canaan; and, behold, they *are* in the land of Goshen.

2And he took some of his brethren, *even* five men, and presented them unto Pharaoh.

3And Pharaoh said unto his brethren, What *is* your occupation? And they said unto Pharaoh, Thy servants *are* shepherds, both we, *and* also our fathers.

4They said moreover unto Pharaoh, For to sojourn in the land are we come; for thy servants have no pasture for their flocks; for the famine *is* sore in the land of Canaan: now therefore, we pray thee, let thy servants dwell in the land of Goshen.

5And Pharaoh spake unto Joseph, saying, Thy father and thy brethren are come unto thee:

6The land of Egypt *is* before thee; in the best of the land make thy father and brethren to dwell; in the land of Goshen let them dwell: and if thou knowest *any* men of activity among them, then make them rulers over my cattle.

7And Joseph brought in Jacob his father, and set him before Pharaoh: and Jacob blessed Pharaoh.

8And Pharaoh said unto Jacob, How old *art* thou?

9And Jacob said unto Pharaoh, The days of the years of my pilgrimage *are* an hundred and thirty years: few and evil have the days of the years of my life been, and have not attained unto the days of the years of the life of my fathers in the days of their pilgrimage.

10And Jacob blessed Pharaoh, and went out from before Pharaoh.

11And Joseph placed his father and his brethren, and gave them a possession in the land of Egypt, in the best of the land, in the land of Rameses, as Pharaoh had commanded.

12And Joseph nourished his father, and his brethren, and all his father's household, with bread, according to *their* families.

13And *there was* no bread in all the land; for the famine *was* very sore, so that the land of Egypt and *all* the land of Canaan fainted by reason of famine.

14And Joseph gathered up all the money that was found in the land of Egypt, and in the land of Canaan, for the corn which they bought: and Joseph brought the money into Pharaoh's house.

15And when money failed in the land of Egypt, and in the land of Canaan, all the Egyptians came unto Joseph, and said, Give us bread: for why should we die in thy presence? for the money faileth.

16And Joseph said, Give your cattle; and I will give you for your cattle, if money fail.

17And they brought their cattle unto Joseph: and Joseph gave them bread *in exchange* for horses, and for the flocks, and for the cattle of the herds, and for the asses: and he fed them with bread for all their cattle for that year.

18When that year was ended, they came unto him the second year, and said unto him, We will not hide *it* from my lord, how that our money is spent; my lord also hath our herds of cattle; there is not ought left in the sight of my lord, but our bodies, and our lands:

19Wherefore shall we die before thine

eyes, both we and our land? buy us and our land for bread, and we and our land will be servants unto Pharaoh: and give *us* seed, that we may live, and not die, that the land be not desolate.

20And Joseph bought all the land of Egypt for Pharaoh; for the Egyptians sold every man his field, because the famine prevailed over them: so the land became Pharaoh's.

21And as for the people, he removed them to cities from *one* end of the borders of Egypt even to the *other* end thereof.

22Only the land of the priests bought he not; for the priests had a portion *assigned them* of Pharaoh, and did eat their portion which Pharaoh gave them: wherefore they sold not their lands.

23Then Joseph said unto the people, Behold, I have bought you this day and your land for Pharaoh: lo, *here is* seed for you, and ye shall sow the land.

24And it shall come to pass in the increase, that ye shall give the fifth *part* unto Pharaoh, and four parts shall be your own, for seed of the field, and for your food, and for them of your households, and for food for your little ones.

25And they said, Thou hast saved our lives: let us find grace in the sight of my lord, and we will be Pharaoh's servants.

26And Joseph made it a law over the land of Egypt unto this day, *that* Pharaoh should have the fifth *part;* except the land of the priests only, *which* became not Pharaoh's.

27And Israel dwelt in the land of Egypt, in the country of Goshen; and they had possessions therein, and grew, and multiplied exceedingly.

28And Jacob lived in the land of Egypt seventeen years: so the whole age of Jacob was an hundred forty and seven years.

29And the time drew nigh that Israel must die: and he called his son Joseph, and said unto him, If now I have found grace in thy sight, put, I pray thee, thy hand under my thigh, and deal kindly and truly with me; bury me not, I pray thee, in Egypt:

30But I will lie with my fathers, and thou shalt carry me out of Egypt, and bury me in their buryingplace. And he said, I will do as thou hast said:

31And he said, Swear unto me. And he sware unto him. And Israel bowed himself upon the bed's head.

MATTHEW 15:1–28

THEN came to Jesus scribes and Pharisees, which were of Jerusalem, saying,

2Why do thy disciples transgress the tradition of the elders? for they wash not their hands when they eat bread.

3But he answered and said unto them, Why do ye also transgress the commandment of God by your tradition?

4For God commanded, saying, Honour thy father and mother: and, He that curseth father or mother, let him die the death.

5But ye say, Whosoever shall say to *his* father or *his* mother, *It is* a gift, by whatsoever thou mightest be profited by me;

6And honour not his father or his mother, *he shall be free.* Thus have ye made the commandment of God of none effect by your tradition.

7*Ye* hypocrites, well did Esaias prophesy of you, saying,

8This people draweth nigh unto me with their mouth, and honoureth me with *their* lips; but their heart is far from me.

9But in vain they do worship me, teaching *for* doctrines the commandments of men.

10And he called the multitude, and said unto them, Hear, and understand:

11Not that which goeth into the mouth defileth a man; but that which cometh out of the mouth, this defileth a man.

12Then came his disciples, and said unto him, Knowest thou that the Pharisees were offended, after they heard this saying?

13But he answered and said, Every plant, which my heavenly Father hath not planted, shall be rooted up.

14Let them alone: they be blind leaders of the blind. And if the blind lead the blind, both shall fall into the ditch.

15Then answered Peter and said unto him, Declare unto us this parable.

16And Jesus said, Are ye also yet without understanding?

17Do not ye yet understand, that whatsoever entereth in at the mouth goeth into the belly, and is cast out into the draught?

18But those things which proceed out of the mouth come forth from the heart; and they defile the man.

19For out of the heart proceed evil thoughts, murders, adulteries, fornications, thefts, false witness, blasphemies:

20These are *the things* which defile a man: but to eat with unwashen hands defileth not a man.

21Then Jesus went thence, and departed into the coasts of Tyre and Sidon.

22And, behold, a woman of Canaan came out of the same coasts, and cried unto him, saying, Have mercy on me, O Lord, *thou* son of David; my daughter is grievously vexed with a devil.

23But he answered her not a word. And his disciples came and besought him, saying, Send her away; for she crieth after us.

24But he answered and said, I am not sent but unto the lost sheep of the house of Israel.

25Then came she and worshipped him, saying, Lord, help me.

26But he answered and said, It is not meet to take the children's bread, and to cast *it* to dogs.

27And she said, Truth, Lord: yet the dogs eat of the crumbs which fall from their masters' table.

28Then Jesus answered and said unto her, O woman, great *is* thy faith: be it unto thee even as thou wilt. And her daughter was made whole from that very hour.

PSALM 19:1–14

THE heavens declare the glory of God; and the firmament sheweth his handywork.

2Day unto day uttereth speech, and night unto night sheweth knowledge.

3*There is* no speech nor language, *where* their voice is not heard.

4Their line is gone out through all the earth, and their words to the end of the world. In them hath he set a tabernacle for the sun,

5Which *is* as a bridegroom coming out of his chamber, *and* rejoiceth as a strong man to run a race.

6His going forth *is* from the end of the heaven, and his circuit unto the ends of it: and there is nothing hid from the heat thereof.

7The law of the LORD *is* perfect, converting the soul: the testimony of the LORD *is* sure, making wise the simple.

8The statutes of the LORD *are* right, rejoicing the heart: the commandment of the LORD *is* pure, enlightening the eyes.

9The fear of the LORD *is* clean, enduring for ever: the judgments of the LORD *are* true *and* righteous altogether.

10More to be desired *are they* than gold, yea, than much fine gold: sweeter also than honey and the honeycomb.

11Moreover by them is thy servant warned: *and* in keeping of them *there is* great reward.

12Who can understand *his* errors? cleanse thou me from secret *faults.*

13Keep back thy servant also from presumptuous *sins;* let them not have dominion over me: then shall I be upright, and I shall be innocent from the great transgression.

14Let the words of my mouth, and the meditation of my heart, be acceptable in thy sight, O LORD, my strength, and my redeemer.

PROVERBS FOR TODAY/ 4:14–19

Enter not into the path of the wicked, and go not in the way of evil men. Avoid it, pass not by it, turn from it, and pass away. For they sleep not, except they have done mischief; and their sleep is taken away, unless they cause some to fall. For they eat the bread of wickedness, and drink the wine of violence. But the path of the just is as the shining light, that shineth more and more unto the perfect day. The way of the wicked is as darkness: they know not at what they stumble.

JANUARY 24

GENESIS 48:1—49:33

AND it came to pass after these things, that *one* told Joseph, Behold, thy father *is* sick: and he took with him his two sons, Manasseh and Ephraim.

2And *one* told Jacob, and said, Behold, thy son Joseph cometh unto thee: and Israel strengthened himself, and sat upon the bed.

3And Jacob said unto Joseph, God Almighty appeared unto me at Luz in the land of Canaan, and blessed me,

4And said unto me, Behold, I will make thee fruitful, and multiply thee, and I will make of thee a multitude of people; and will give this land to thy seed after thee *for* an everlasting possession.

5And now thy two sons, Ephraim and Manasseh, which were born unto thee in the land of Egypt before I came unto thee into Egypt, *are* mine; as Reuben and Simeon, they shall be mine.

6And thy issue, which thou begettest after them, shall be thine, *and* shall be called after the name of their brethren in their inheritance.

7And as for me, when I came from Padan, Rachel died by me in the land of Canaan in the way, when yet *there was* but a little way to come unto Ephrath: and I buried her there in the way of Ephrath; the same *is* Beth–lehem.

8And Israel beheld Joseph's sons, and said, Who *are* these?

9And Joseph said unto his father, They *are* my sons, whom God hath given me in this *place*. And he said, Bring them, I pray thee, unto me, and I will bless them.

10Now the eyes of Israel were dim for age, *so that* he could not see. And he brought them near unto him; and he kissed them, and embraced them.

11And Israel said unto Joseph, I had not thought to see thy face: and, lo, God hath shewed me also thy seed.

12And Joseph brought them out from between his knees, and he bowed himself with his face to the earth.

13And Joseph took them both, Ephraim in his right hand toward Israel's left hand, and Manasseh in his left hand toward Israel's right hand, and brought *them* near unto him.

14And Israel stretched out his right

hand, and laid *it* upon Ephraim's head, who *was* the younger, and his left hand upon Manasseh's head, guiding his hands wittingly; for Manasseh *was* the firstborn.

15And he blessed Joseph, and said, God, before whom my fathers Abraham and Isaac did walk, the God which fed me all my life long unto this day,

16The Angel which redeemed me from all evil, bless the lads; and let my name be named on them, and the name of my fathers Abraham and Isaac; and let them grow into a multitude in the midst of the earth.

17And when Joseph saw that his father laid his right hand upon the head of Ephraim, it displeased him: and he held up his father's hand, to remove it from Ephraim's head unto Manasseh's head.

18And Joseph said unto his father, Not so, my father: for this *is* the firstborn; put thy right hand upon his head.

19And his father refused, and said, I know *it,* my son, I know *it;* he also shall become a people, and he also shall be great: but truly his younger brother shall be greater than he, and his seed shall become a multitude of nations.

20And he blessed them that day, saying, In thee shall Israel bless, saying, God make thee as Ephraim and as Manasseh: and he set Ephraim before Manasseh.

21And Israel said unto Joseph, Behold, I die: but God shall be with you, and bring you again unto the land of your fathers.

22Moreover I have given to thee one portion above thy brethren, which I took out of the hand of the Amorite with my sword and with my bow.

AND Jacob called unto his sons, and said, Gather yourselves together, that I may tell you *that* which shall befall you in the last days.

2Gather yourselves together, and hear, ye sons of Jacob; and hearken unto Israel your father.

3Reuben, thou *art* my firstborn, my might, and the beginning of my strength, the excellency of dignity, and the excellency of power:

4Unstable as water, thou shalt not excel; because thou wentest up to thy father's bed; then defiledst thou *it:* he went up to my couch.

5Simeon and Levi *are* brethren; instruments of cruelty *are in* their habitations.

6O my soul, come not thou into their secret; unto their assembly, mine honour, be not thou united: for in their anger they slew a man, and in their selfwill they digged down a wall.

7Cursed *be* their anger, for *it was* fierce; and their wrath, for it was cruel: I will divide them in Jacob, and scatter them in Israel.

8Judah, thou *art he* whom thy brethren shall praise: thy hand *shall be* in the neck of thine enemies; thy father's children shall bow down before thee.

9Judah *is* a lion's whelp: from the prey, my son, thou art gone up: he stooped down, he couched as a lion, and as an old lion; who shall rouse him up?

10The sceptre shall not depart from Judah, nor a lawgiver from between his feet, until Shiloh come; and unto him *shall* the gathering of the people *be.*

11Binding his foal unto the vine, and his ass's colt unto the choice vine; he washed his garments in wine, and his clothes in the blood of grapes:

12His eyes *shall be* red with wine, and his teeth white with milk.

13Zebulun shall dwell at the haven of the sea; and he *shall be* for an haven of ships; and his border *shall be* unto Zidon.

14Issachar *is* a strong ass couching down between two burdens:

15And he saw that rest *was* good, and the land that *it was* pleasant; and bowed his shoulder to bear, and became a servant unto tribute.

16Dan shall judge his people, as one of the tribes of Israel.

17Dan shall be a serpent by the way, an adder in the path, that biteth the horse heels, so that his rider shall fall backward.

18I have waited for thy salvation, O LORD.

19Gad, a troop shall overcome him: but he shall overcome at the last.

20Out of Asher his bread *shall be* fat, and he shall yield royal dainties.

21Naphtali *is* a hind let loose: he giveth goodly words.

22Joseph *is* a fruitful bough, *even* a fruitful bough by a well; *whose* branches run over the wall:

23The archers have sorely grieved him, and shot *at him,* and hated him:

24But his bow abode in strength, and the arms of his hands were made strong by the hands of the mighty *God* of Jacob; (from thence *is* the shepherd, the stone of Israel:)

25*Even* by the God of thy father, who shall help thee; and by the Almighty, who shall bless thee with blessings of heaven above, blessings of the deep that lieth under, blessings of the breasts, and of the womb:

26The blessings of thy father have prevailed above the blessings of my progenitors unto the utmost bound of the everlasting hills: they shall be on the head of Joseph, and on the crown of the head of him that was separate from his brethren.

27Benjamin shall ravin *as* a wolf: in the morning he shall devour the prey, and at night he shall divide the spoil.

28All these *are* the twelve tribes of Israel: and this *is it* that their father spake unto them, and blessed them; every one according to his blessing he blessed them.

29And he charged them, and said unto them, I am to be gathered unto my people: bury me with my fathers in the cave that *is* in the field of Ephron the Hittite,

30In the cave that *is* in the field of Machpelah, which *is* before Mamre, in the land of Canaan, which Abraham bought with the field of Ephron the Hittite for a possession of a burying place.

31There they buried Abraham and Sarah his wife; there they buried Isaac and Rebekah his wife; and there I buried Leah.

32The purchase of the field and of the cave that *is* therein *was* from the children of Heth.

33And when Jacob had made an end of commanding his sons, he gathered up his feet into the bed, and yielded up the ghost, and was gathered unto his people.

MATTHEW 15:29—16:12

AND Jesus departed from thence, and came nigh unto the sea of Galilee; and went up into a mountain, and sat down there.

30And great multitudes came unto him, having with them *those that were* lame, blind, dumb, maimed, and many others, and cast them down at Jesus' feet; and he healed them:

31Insomuch that the multitude wondered, when they saw the dumb to speak, the maimed to be whole, the lame to walk, and the blind to see: and they glorified the God of Israel.

32Then Jesus called his disciples *unto him,* and said, I have compassion on the multitude, because they continue with me now three days, and have nothing to eat: and I will not send them away fasting, lest they faint in the way.

33And his disciples say unto him, Whence should we have so much bread in the wilderness, as to fill so great a multitude?

34And Jesus saith unto them, How many loaves have ye? And they said, Seven, and a few little fishes.

35And he commanded the multitude to sit down on the ground.

36And he took the seven loaves and the fishes, and gave thanks, and brake *them,* and gave to his disciples, and the disciples to the multitude.

37And they did all eat, and were filled: and they took up of the broken *meat* that was left seven baskets full.

38And they that did eat were four thousand men, beside women and children.

39And he sent away the multitude, and took ship, and came into the coasts of Magdala.

THE Pharisees also with the Sadducees came, and tempting desired him that he would shew them a sign from heaven.

2He answered and said unto them, When it is evening, ye say, *It will be* fair weather: for the sky is red.

3And in the morning, *It will be* foul weather to day: for the sky is red and lowring. O *ye* hypocrites, ye can discern the face of the sky; but can ye not *discern* the signs of the times?

4A wicked and adulterous generation seeketh after a sign; and there shall no sign be given unto it, but the sign of the prophet Jonas. And he left them, and departed.

5And when his disciples were come to the other side, they had forgotten to take bread.

6Then Jesus said unto them, Take heed and beware of the leaven of the Pharisees and of the Sadducees.

7And they reasoned among themselves, saying, *It is* because we have taken no bread.

8*Which* when Jesus perceived, he said unto them, O ye of little faith, why reason ye among yourselves, because ye have brought no bread?

9Do ye not yet understand, neither remember the five loaves of the five thousand, and how many baskets ye took up?

10Neither the seven loaves of the four thousand, and how many baskets ye took up?

11How is it that ye do not understand that I spake *it* not to you concerning bread, that ye should beware of the leaven of the Pharisees and of the Sadducees?

12Then understood they how that he bade *them* not beware of the leaven of bread, but of the doctrine of the Pharisees and of the Sadducees.

PSALM 20:1–9

THE LORD hear thee in the day of trouble; the name of the God of Jacob defend thee;

2Send thee help from the sanctuary, and strengthen thee out of Zion;

3Remember all thy offerings, and accept thy burnt sacrifice; Selah.

4Grant thee according to thine own heart, and fulfil all thy counsel.

5We will rejoice in thy salvation, and in the name of our God we will set up *our* banners: the LORD fulfil all thy petitions.

6Now know I that the LORD saveth his anointed; he will hear him from his holy heaven with the saving strength of his right hand.

7Some *trust* in chariots, and some in horses: but we will remember the name of the LORD our God.

8They are brought down and fallen: but we are risen, and stand upright.

9Save, LORD: let the king hear us when we call.

PROVERBS FOR TODAY/ 4:20–27

My son, attend to my words; incline thine ear unto my sayings. Let them not depart from thine eyes; keep them in the midst of thine heart. For they are life unto those that find them, and health to all their flesh. Keep thy heart with all diligence; for out of it are the issues of life. Put away from thee a froward mouth, and perverse lips put far from thee. Let thine eyes look right on, and let thine eyelids look straight before thee. Ponder the path of thy feet, and let all thy ways be established. Turn not to the right hand nor to the left: remove thy foot from evil.

JANUARY 25

GENESIS 50:1—EXODUS 2:10

A ND Joseph fell upon his father's face, and wept upon him, and kissed him.

2And Joseph commanded his servants the physicians to embalm his father: and the physicians embalmed Israel.

3And forty days were fulfilled for him; for so are fulfilled the days of those which are embalmed: and the Egyptians mourned for him threescore and ten days.

4And when the days of his mourning were past, Joseph spake unto the house of Pharaoh, saying, If now I have found grace in your eyes, speak, I pray you, in the ears of Pharaoh, saying,

5My father made me swear, saying, Lo, I die: in my grave which I have digged for me in the land of Canaan, there shalt thou bury me. Now therefore let me go up, I pray thee, and bury my father, and I will come again.

6And Pharaoh said, Go up, and bury thy father, according as he made thee swear.

7And Joseph went up to bury his father: and with him went up all the servants of Pharaoh, the elders of his house, and all the elders of the land of Egypt,

8And all the house of Joseph, and his brethren, and his father's house: only their little ones, and their flocks, and their herds, they left in the land of Goshen.

9And there went up with him both chariots and horsemen: and it was a very great company.

10And they came to the threshingfloor of Atad, which *is* beyond Jordan, and there they mourned with a great and very sore lamentation: and he made a mourning for his father seven days.

11And when the inhabitants of the land, the Canaanites, saw the mourning in the floor of Atad, they said, This *is* a grievous mourning to the Egyptians: wherefore the name of it was called Abel-mizraim, which *is* beyond Jordan.

12And his sons did unto him according as he commanded them:

13For his sons carried him into the land of Canaan, and buried him in the cave of the field of Machpelah, which Abraham bought with the field for a possession of a buryingplace of Ephron the Hittite, before Mamre.

14And Joseph returned into Egypt, he, and his brethren, and all that went up with him to bury his father, after he had buried his father.

15And when Joseph's brethren saw that their father was dead, they said, Joseph will peradventure hate us, and will certainly requite us all the evil which we did unto him.

16And they sent a messenger unto Joseph, saying, Thy father did command before he died, saying,

17So shall ye say unto Joseph, Forgive, I pray thee now, the trespass of thy brethren, and their sin; for they did unto thee evil: and now, we pray thee, forgive the trespass of the servants of the God of thy father. And Joseph wept when they spake unto him.

18And his brethren also went and fell down before his face; and they said, Behold, we *be* thy servants.

19And Joseph said unto them, Fear not: for *am* I in the place of God?

20But as for you, ye thought evil against me; *but* God meant it unto good, to bring to pass, as *it is* this day, to save much people alive.

21Now therefore fear ye not: I will nourish you, and your little ones. And he comforted them, and spake kindly unto them.

22And Joseph dwelt in Egypt, he, and his father's house: and Joseph lived an hundred and ten years.

23And Joseph saw Ephraim's children of the third *generation:* the children also of Machir the son of Manasseh were brought up upon Joseph's knees.

24And Joseph said unto his brethren, I die: and God will surely visit you, and bring you out of this land unto the land which he sware to Abraham, to Isaac, and to Jacob.

25And Joseph took an oath of the children of Israel, saying, God will surely visit you, and ye shall carry up my bones from hence.

26So Joseph died, *being* an hundred and ten years old: and they embalmed him, and he was put in a coffin in Egypt.

Now these *are* the names of the children of Israel, which came into Egypt; every man and his household came with Jacob.

2Reuben, Simeon, Levi, and Judah,

3Issachar, Zebulun, and Benjamin,

4Dan, and Naphtali, Gad, and Asher.

5And all the souls that came out of the loins of Jacob were seventy souls: for Joseph was in Egypt *already.*

6And Joseph died, and all his brethren, and all that generation.

7And the children of Israel were fruitful, and increased abundantly, and multiplied, and waxed exceeding mighty; and the land was filled with them.

8Now there arose up a new king over Egypt, which knew not Joseph.

9And he said unto his people, Behold, the people of the children of Israel *are* more and mightier than we:

10Come on, let us deal wisely with them; lest they multiply, and it come to pass, that, when there falleth out any war, they join also unto our enemies, and fight against us, and *so* get them up out of the land.

11Therefore they did set over them taskmasters to afflict them with their burdens. And they built for Pharaoh treasure cities, Pithom and Raamses.

12But the more they afflicted them, the more they multiplied and grew. And they were grieved because of the children of Israel.

13And the Egyptians made the children of Israel to serve with rigour:

14And they made their lives bitter with hard bondage, in morter, and in brick, and in all manner of service in the field: all their service, wherein they made them serve, *was* with rigour.

15And the king of Egypt spake to the Hebrew midwives, of which the name of the one *was* Shiphrah, and the name of the other Puah:

16And he said, When ye do the office of a midwife to the Hebrew women, and see *them* upon the stools; if it *be* a son, then ye shall kill him: but if it *be* a daughter, then she shall live.

17But the midwives feared God, and did not as the king of Egypt commanded them, but saved the men children alive.

18And the king of Egypt called for the midwives, and said unto them, Why have ye done this thing, and have saved the men children alive?

19And the midwives said unto Pharaoh, Because the Hebrew women *are* not as the Egyptain women; for they *are* lively, and are delivered ere the midwives come in unto them.

20Therefore God dealt well with the midwives: and the people multiplied, and waxed very mighty.

21And it came to pass, because the midwives feared God, that he made them houses.

22And Pharaoh charged all his people, saying, Every son that is born ye shall cast into the river, and every daughter ye shall save alive.

AND there went a man of the house of Levi, and took *to wife* a daughter of Levi.

2And the woman conceived, and bare a son: and when she saw him that he *was a* goodly *child,* she hid him three months.

3And when she could not longer hide him, she took for him an ark of bulrushes, and daubed it with slime and with pitch, and put the child therein; and she laid *it* in the flags by the river's brink.

4And his sister stood afar off, to wit what would be done to him.

5And the daughter of Pharaoh came down to wash *herself* at the river; and her maidens walked along by the river's side; and when she saw the ark among the flags, she sent her maid to fetch it.

6And when she had opened *it,* she saw the child: and, behold, the babe wept. And she had compassion on him, and said, This *is one* of the Hebrews' children.

7Then said his sister to Pharaoh's daughter, Shall I go and call to thee a nurse of the Hebrew women, that she may nurse the child for thee?

8And Pharaoh's daughter said to her, Go. And the maid went and called the child's mother.

9And Pharaoh's daughter said unto her, Take this child away, and nurse it for me, and I will give *thee* thy wages.

And the woman took the child, and nursed it.

10And the child grew, and she brought him unto Pharaoh's daughter, and he became her son. And she called his name Moses: and she said, Because I drew him out of the water.

MATTHEW 16:13—17:9

WHEN Jesus came into the coasts of Caesarea Philippi, he asked his disciples, saying, Whom do men say that I the Son of man am?

14And they said, Some *say that thou art* John the Baptist: some, Elias; and others, Jeremias, or one of the prophets.

15He saith unto them, But whom say ye that I am?

16And Simon Peter answered and said, Thou art the Christ, the Son of the living God.

17And Jesus answered and said unto him, Blessed art thou, Simon Bar–jona: for flesh and blood hath not revealed *it* unto thee, but my Father which is in heaven.

18And I say also unto thee, That thou art Peter, and upon this rock I will build my church; and the gates of hell shall not prevail against it.

19And I will give unto thee the keys of the kingdom of heaven: and whatsoever thou shalt bind on earth shall be bound in heaven: and whatsoever thou shalt loose on earth shall be loosed in heaven.

20Then charged he his disciples that they should tell no man that he was Jesus the Christ.

21From that time forth began Jesus to shew unto his disciples, how that he must go unto Jerusalem, and suffer many things of the elders and chief priests and scribes, and be killed, and be raised again the third day.

22Then Peter took him, and began

to rebuke him, saying, Be it far from thee, Lord: this shall not be unto thee.

23But he turned, and said unto Peter, Get thee behind me, Satan: thou art an offence unto me: for thou savourest not the things that be of God, but those that be of men.

24Then said Jesus unto his disciples, If any *man* will come after me, let him deny himself, and take up his cross, and follow me.

25For whosoever will save his life shall lose it: and whosoever will lose his life for my sake shall find it.

26For what is a man profited, if he shall gain the whole world, and lose his own soul? or what shall a man give in exchange for his soul?

27For the Son of man shall come in the glory of his Father with his angels; and then he shall reward every man according to his works.

28Verily I say unto you, There be some standing here, which shall not taste of death, till they see the Son of man coming in his kingdom.

AND after six days Jesus taketh Peter, James, and John his brother, and bringeth them up into an high mountain apart,

2And was transfigured before them: and his face did shine as the sun, and his raiment was white as the light.

3And, behold, there appeared unto them Moses and Elias talking with him.

4Then answered Peter, and said unto Jesus, Lord, it is good for us to be here: if thou wilt, let us make here three tabernacles; one for thee, and one for Moses, and one for Elias.

5While he yet spake, behold, a bright cloud overshadowed them: and behold a voice out of the cloud, which said, This is my beloved Son, in whom I am well pleased; hear ye him.

6And when the disciples heard *it,* they fell on their face, and were sore afraid.

7And Jesus came and touched them, and said, Arise, and be not afraid.

8And when they had lifted up their eyes, they saw no man, save Jesus only.

9And as they came down from the mountain, Jesus charged them, saying, Tell the vision to no man, until the Son of man be risen again from the dead.

PSALM 21:1–13

THE king shall joy in thy strength, O LORD; and in thy salvation how greatly shall he rejoice!

2Thou hast given him his heart's desire, and hast not withholden the request of his lips. Selah.

3For thou preventest him with the blessings of goodness: thou settest a crown of pure gold on his head.

4He asked life of thee, *and* thou gavest *it* him, *even* length of days for ever and ever.

5His glory *is* great in thy salvation: honour and majesty hast thou laid upon him.

6For thou hast made him most blessed for ever: thou hast made him exceeding glad with thy countenance.

7For the king trusteth in the LORD, and through the mercy of the most High he shall not be moved.

8Thine hand shall find out all thine enemies: thy right hand shall find out those that hate thee.

9Thou shalt make them as a fiery oven in the time of thine anger: the LORD shall swallow them up in his wrath, and the fire shall devour them.

10Their fruit shalt thou destroy from the earth, and their seed from among the children of men.

11For they intended evil against thee: they imagined a mischievous device, *which* they are not able *to perform.*

12Therefore shalt thou make them

turn their back, *when* thou shalt make ready *thine arrows* upon thy strings against the face of them.

13Be thou exalted, LORD, in thine own strength: *so* will we sing and praise thy power.

PROVERBS FOR TODAY/ 5:1–6

My son, attend unto my wisdom, and bow thine ear to my understanding: That thou mayest regard discretion, and that thy lips may keep knowledge. For the lips of a strange woman drop as an honeycomb, and her mouth is smoother than oil: But her end is bitter as wormwood, sharp as a two-edged sword. Her feet go down to death; her steps take hold on hell. Lest thou shouldest ponder the path of life, her ways are moveable, that thou canst not know them.

JANUARY 26

EXODUS 2:11—3:22

AND it came to pass in those days, when Moses was grown, that he went out unto his brethren, and looked on their burdens: and he spied an Egyptian smiting an Hebrew, one of his brethren.

12And he looked this way and that way, and when he saw that *there was* no man, he slew the Egyptian, and hid him in the sand.

13And when he went out the second day, behold, two men of the Hebrews strove together: and he said to him that did the wrong, Wherefore smitest thou thy fellow?

14And he said, Who made thee a prince and a judge over us? intendest thou to kill me, as thou killedst the Egyptian? And Moses feared, and said, Surely this thing is known.

15Now when Pharaoh heard this thing, he sought to slay Moses. But Moses fled from the face of Pharaoh, and dwelt in the land of Midian: and he sat down by a well.

16Now the priest of Midian had seven daughters: and they came and drew

water, and filled the troughs to water their father's flock.

17And the shepherds came and drove them away: but Moses stood up and helped them, and watered their flock.

18And when they came to Reuel their father, he said, How *is it that* ye are come so soon to day?

19And they said, An Egyptian delivered us out of the hand of the shepherds, and also drew *water* enough for us, and watered the flock.

20And he said unto his daughters, And where *is* he? why *is* it *that* ye have left the man? call him, that he may eat bread.

21And Moses was content to dwell with the man: and he gave Moses Zipporah his daughter.

22And she bare *him* a son, and he called his name Gershom: for he said, I have been a stranger in a strange land.

23And it came to pass in process of time, that the king of Egypt died: and the children of Israel sighed by reason of the bondage, and they cried, and their cry came up unto God by reason of the bondage.

24And God heard their groaning, and God remembered his covenant with Abraham, with Isaac, and with Jacob.

25And God looked upon the children of Israel, and God had respect unto *them*.

Now Moses kept the flock of Jethro his father in law, the priest of Midian: and he led the flock to the backside of the desert, and came to the mountain of God, *even* to Horeb.

2And the angel of the LORD appeared unto him in a flame of fire out of the midst of a bush: and he looked, and, behold, the bush burned with fire, and the bush *was* not consumed.

3And Moses said, I will now turn aside, and see this great sight, why the bush is not burnt.

4And when the LORD saw that he turned aside to see, God called unto him out of the midst of the bush, and said, Moses, Moses. And he said, Here *am* I.

5And he said, Draw not nigh hither: put off thy shoes from off thy feet, for the place whereon thou standest is holy ground.

6Moreover he said, I *am* the God of thy father, the God of Abraham, the God of Isaac, and the God of Jacob. And Moses hid his face; for he was afraid to look upon God.

7And the LORD said, I have surely seen the affliction of my people which *are* in Egypt, and have heard their cry by reason of their taskmasters; for I know their sorrows;

8And I am come down to deliver them out of the hand of the Egyptians, and to bring them up out of that land unto a good land and a large, unto a land flowing with milk and honey; unto the place of the Canaanites, and the Hittites, and the Amorites, and the Perizzites, and the Hivites, and the Jebusites.

9Now therefore, behold, the cry of the children of Israel is come unto me: and I have also seen the oppression wherewith the Egyptians oppress them.

10Come now therefore, and I will send thee unto Pharaoh, that thou mayest bring forth my people the children of Israel out of Egypt.

11And Moses said unto God, Who *am* I, that I should go unto Pharaoh, and that I should bring forth the children of Israel out of Egypt?

12And he said, Certainly I will be with thee; and this *shall be* a token unto thee, that I have sent thee: When thou hast brought forth the people out of Egypt, ye shall serve God upon this mountain.

13And Moses said unto God, Behold, *when* I come unto the children of Israel, and shall say unto them, The God of your fathers hath sent me unto you; and they shall say to me, What *is* his name? what shall I say unto them?

14And God said unto Moses, I AM THAT I AM: and he said, Thus shalt thou say unto the children of Israel, I AM hath sent me unto you.

15And God said moreover unto Moses, Thus shalt thou say unto the children of Israel, the LORD God of your fathers, the God of Abraham, the God of Isaac, and the God of Jacob, hath sent me unto you: this *is* my name for ever, and this *is* my memorial unto all generations.

16Go, and gather the elders of Israel together, and say unto them, The LORD God of your fathers, the God of Abraham, of Isaac, and of Jacob, appeared unto me, saying, I have surely visited you, and *seen* that which is done to you in Egypt:

17And I have said, I will bring you up out of the affliction of Egypt unto the land of the Canaanites, and the Hittites, and the Amorites, and the Perizzites, and the Hivites, and the Jebusites, unto a land flowing with milk and honey.

18And they shall hearken to thy voice: and thou shalt come, thou and the elders of Israel, unto the king of Egypt, and ye shall say unto him, The LORD God of the Hebrews hath met with us: and now let us go, we beseech thee, three days' journey into the wilderness, that we may sacrifice to the LORD our God.

19And I am sure that the king of Egypt will not let you go, no, not by a mighty hand.

20And I will stretch out my hand, and smite Egypt with all my wonders which I will do in the midst thereof: and after that he will let you go.

21And I will give this people favour in the sight of the Egyptians: and it shall come to pass, that, when ye go, ye shall not go empty:

22But every woman shall borrow of her neighbour, and of her that sojourneth in her house, jewels of silver, and jewels of gold, and raiment: and ye shall put *them* upon your sons, and upon your daughters; and ye shall spoil the Egyptians.

MATTHEW 17:10–27

AND his [Jesus'] disciples asked him, saying, Why then say the scribes that Elias must first come?

11And Jesus answered and said unto them, Elias truly shall first come, and restore all things.

12But I say unto you, That Elias is come already, and they knew him not, but have done unto him whatsoever they listed. Likewise shall also the Son of man suffer of them.

13Then the disciples understood that he spake unto them of John the Baptist.

14And when they were come to the multitude, there came to him a *certain* man, kneeling down to him, and saying,

15Lord, have mercy on my son: for he is lunatick, and sore vexed: for ofttimes he falleth into the fire, and oft into the water.

16And I brought him to thy disciples, and they could not cure him.

17Then Jesus answered and said, O faithless and perverse generation, how long shall I be with you? how long shall I suffer you? bring him hither to me.

18And Jesus rebuked the devil; and he departed out of him: and the child was cured from that very hour.

19Then came the disciples to Jesus apart, and said, Why could not we cast him out?

20And Jesus said unto them, Because of your unbelief: for verily I say unto you, If ye have faith as a grain of mustard seed, ye shall say unto this mountain, Remove hence to yonder place; and it shall remove; and nothing shall be impossible unto you.

21Howbeit this kind goeth not out but by prayer and fasting.

22And while they abode in Galilee, Jesus said unto them, The Son of man shall be betrayed into the hands of men:

23And they shall kill him, and the third day he shall be raised again. And they were exceeding sorry.

24And when they were come to Capernaum, they that received tribute *money* came to Peter, and said, Doth not your master pay tribute?

25He saith, Yes. And when he was come into the house, Jesus prevented him, saying, What thinkest thou, Simon? of whom do the kings of the earth take custom or tribute? of their own children, or of strangers?

26Peter saith unto him, Of strangers. Jesus saith unto him, Then are the children free.

27Notwithstanding, lest we should offend them, go thou to the sea, and cast an hook, and take up the fish that first cometh up; and when thou hast opened his mouth, thou shalt find a piece of money: that take, and give unto them for me and thee.

PSALM 22:1–18

MY God, my God, why hast thou forsaken me? *why art thou so far* from helping me, *and from* the words of my roaring?

2O my God, I cry in the daytime, but thou hearest not; and in the night season, and am not silent.

3But thou *art* holy, *O thou* that inhabitest the praises of Israel.

4Our fathers trusted in thee: they trusted, and thou didst deliver them.

5They cried unto thee, and were delivered: they trusted in thee, and were not confounded.

6But I *am* a worm, and no man; a reproach of men, and despised of the people.

7All they that see me laugh me to scorn: they shoot out the lip, they shake the head, *saying,*

8He trusted on the Lord *that* he would deliver him: let him deliver him, seeing he delighted in him.

9But thou *art* he that took me out of the womb: thou didst make me hope *when I was* upon my mother's breasts.

10I was cast upon thee from the womb: thou *art* my God from my mother's belly.

11Be not far from me; for trouble *is* near; for *there is* none to help.

12Many bulls have compassed me: strong *bulls* of Bashan have beset me round.

13They gaped upon me *with* their mouths, *as* a ravening and a roaring lion.

14I am poured out like water, and all my bones are out of joint: my heart is like wax; it is melted in the midst of my bowels.

15My strength is dried up like a potsherd; and my tongue cleaveth to my jaws; and thou hast brought me into the dust of death.

16For dogs have compassed me: the assembly of the wicked have inclosed me: they pierced my hands and my feet.

17I may tell all my bones: they look *and* stare upon me.

18They part my garments among them, and cast lots upon my vesture.

PROVERBS FOR TODAY/ 5:7–14

Hear me now therefore, O ye children, and depart not from the words of my mouth. Remove thy way far from her, and come not nigh the door of her house: Lest thou give thine honour unto others, and thy years unto the cruel: Lest strangers be filled with thy wealth; and thy labours be *in the house of a stranger; And thou mourn at the last, when thy flesh and thy body are consumed, And say, How have I hated instruction, and my heart despised reproof; And have not obeyed the voice of my teachers, nor inclined mine ear to them that instructed me! I was almost in all evil in the midst of the congregation and assembly.*

JANUARY 27

EXODUS 4:1—5:21

AND Moses answered and said, But, behold, they will not believe me, nor hearken unto my voice: for they will say, The LORD hath not appeared unto thee.

2And the LORD said unto him, What *is* that in thine hand? And he said, A rod.

3And he said, Cast it on the ground. And he cast it on the ground, and it became a serpent; and Moses fled from before it.

4And the LORD said unto Moses, Put forth thine hand, and take it by the tail. And he put forth his hand, and caught it, and it became a rod in his hand:

5That they may believe that the LORD God of their fathers, the God of Abraham, the God of Isaac, and the God of Jacob, hath appeared unto thee.

6And the LORD said furthermore unto him, Put now thine hand into thy bosom. And he put his hand into his bosom: and when he took it out, behold, his hand *was* leprous as snow.

7And he said, Put thine hand into thy bosom again. And he put his hand into his bosom again; and plucked it out of his bosom, and, behold, it was turned again as his *other* flesh.

8And it shall come to pass, if they will not believe thee, neither hearken to the voice of the first sign, that they will believe the voice of the latter sign.

9And it shall come to pass, if they will not believe also these two signs, neither hearken unto thy voice, that thou shalt take of the water of the river, and pour *it* upon the dry *land:* and the water which thou takest out of the river shall become blood upon the dry *land.*

10And Moses said unto the LORD, O my Lord, I *am* not eloquent, neither heretofore, nor since thou hast spoken unto thy servant: but I *am* slow of speech, and of a slow tongue.

11And the LORD said unto him, Who hath made man's mouth? or who maketh the dumb, or deaf, or the seeing, or the blind? have not I the LORD?

12Now therefore go, and I will be with thy mouth, and teach thee what thou shalt say.

13And he said, O my Lord, send, I pray thee, by the hand *of him whom* thou wilt send.

14And the anger of the LORD was kindled against Moses, and he said, *Is* not Aaron the Levite thy brother? I know that he can speak well. And also, behold, he cometh forth to meet thee: and when he seeth thee, he will be glad in his heart.

15And thou shalt speak unto him, and put words in his mouth: and I will be with thy mouth, and with his mouth, and will teach you what ye shall do.

16And he shall be thy spokesman unto the people: and he shall be, *even* he shall be to thee instead of a mouth, and thou shalt be to him instead of God.

17And thou shalt take this rod in thine hand, wherewith thou shalt do signs.

18And Moses went and returned to Jethro his father in law, and said unto him, Let me go, I pray thee, and return unto my brethren which *are* in Egypt, and see whether they be yet alive. And Jethro said to Moses, Go in peace.

19And the LORD said unto Moses in Midian, Go, return into Egypt: for all the men are dead which sought thy life.

20And Moses took his wife and his sons, and set them upon an ass, and he returned to the land of Egypt: and Moses took the rod of God in his hand.

21And the LORD said unto Moses,

When thou goest to return into Egypt, see that thou do all those wonders before Pharaoh, which I have put in thine hand: but I will harden his heart, that he shall not let the people go.

22And thou shalt say unto Pharaoh, Thus saith the LORD, Israel *is* my son, *even* my firstborn:

23And I say unto thee, Let my son go, that he may serve me: and if thou refuse to let him go, behold, I will slay thy son, *even* thy firstborn.

24And it came to pass by the way in the inn, that the LORD met him, and sought to kill him.

25Then Zipporah took a sharp stone, and cut off the foreskin of her son, and cast *it* at his feet, and said, Surely a bloody husband *art* thou to me.

26So he let him go: then she said, A bloody husband *thou art,* because of the circumcision.

27And the LORD said to Aaron, Go into the wilderness to meet Moses. And he went and met him in the mount of God, and kissed him.

28And Moses told Aaron all the words of the LORD who had sent him, and all the signs which he had commanded him.

29And Moses and Aaron went and gathered together all the elders of the children of Israel:

30And Aaron spake all the words which the LORD had spoken unto Moses, and did the signs in the sight of the people.

31And the people believed: and when they heard that the LORD had visited the children of Israel, and that he had looked upon their affliction, then they bowed their heads and worshipped.

AND afterward Moses and Aaron went in, and told Pharaoh, Thus saith the LORD God of Israel, Let my people go, that they may hold a feast unto me in the wilderness.

2And Pharaoh said, Who *is* the LORD, that I should obey his voice to let Israel go? I know not the LORD, neither will I let Israel go.

3And they said, The God of the Hebrews hath met with us: let us go, we pray thee, three days' journey into the desert, and sacrifice unto the LORD our God; lest he fall upon us with pestilence, or with the sword.

4And the king of Egypt said unto them, Wherefore do ye, Moses and Aaron, let the people from their works? get you unto your burdens.

5And Pharaoh said, Behold, the people of the land now *are* many, and ye make them rest from their burdens.

6And Pharaoh commanded the same day the taskmasters of the people, and their officers, saying,

7Ye shall no more give the people straw to make brick, as heretofore: let them go and gather straw for themselves.

8And the tale of the bricks, which they did make heretofore, ye shall lay upon them; ye shall not diminish *ought* thereof: for they *be* idle; therefore they cry, saying, Let us go *and* sacrifice to our God.

9Let there more work be laid upon the men, that they may labour therein; and let them not regard vain words.

10And the taskmasters of the people went out, and their officers, and they spake to the people, saying, Thus saith Pharaoh, I will not give you straw.

11Go ye, get you straw where ye can find it: yet not ought of your work shall be diminished.

12So the people were scattered abroad throughout all the land of Egypt to gather stubble instead of straw.

13And the taskmasters hasted *them,* saying, Fulfil your works, *your* daily tasks, as when there was straw.

14And the officers of the children of Israel, which Pharaoh's taskmasters had set over them, were beaten, *and* demanded, Wherefore have ye not fulfilled your task in making brick both yesterday and to day, as heretofore?

15Then the officers of the children of Israel came and cried unto Pharaoh, saying, Wherefore dealest thou thus with thy servants?

16There is no straw given unto thy servants, and they say to us, Make brick: and, behold, thy servants *are* beaten; but the fault *is* in thine own people.

17But he said, Ye *are* idle, *ye are* idle: therefore ye say, Let us go *and* do sacrifice to the LORD.

18Go therefore now, *and* work; for there shall no straw be given you, yet shall ye deliver the tale of bricks.

19And the officers of the children of Israel did see *that* they *were* in evil *case,* after it was said, Ye shall not minish *ought* from your bricks of your daily task.

20And they met Moses and Aaron, who stood in the way, as they came forth from Pharaoh:

21And they said unto them, The LORD look upon you, and judge; because ye have made our savour to be abhorred in the eyes of Pharaoh, and in the eyes of his servants, to put a sword in their hand to slay us.

MATTHEW 18:1–22

At the same time came the disciples unto Jesus, saying, Who is the greatest in the kingdom of heaven?

2And Jesus called a little child unto him, and set him in the midst of them,

3And said, Verily I say unto you, Except ye be converted, and become as little children, ye shall not enter into the kingdom of heaven.

4Whosoever therefore shall humble himself as this little child, the same is greatest in the kingdom of heaven.

5And whoso shall receive one such little child in my name receiveth me.

6But whoso shall offend one of these little ones which believe in me, it were better for him that a millstone were hanged about his neck, and *that* he were drowned in the depth of the sea.

7Woe unto the world because of offences! for it must needs be that offences come; but woe to that man by whom the offence cometh!

8Wherefore if thy hand or thy foot offend thee, cut them off, and cast *them* from thee: it is better for thee to enter into life halt or maimed, rather than having two hands or two feet to be cast into everlasting fire.

9And if thine eye offend thee, pluck it out, and cast *it* from thee: it is better for thee to enter into life with one eye, rather than having two eyes to be cast into hell fire.

10Take heed that ye despise not one of these little ones; for I say unto you, That in heaven their angels do always behold the face of my Father which is in heaven.

11For the Son of man is come to save that which was lost.

12How think ye? if a man have an hundred sheep, and one of them be gone astray, doth he not leave the ninety and nine, and goeth into the mountains, and seeketh that which is gone astray?

13And if so be that he find it, verily I say unto you, he rejoiceth more of that *sheep,* than of the ninety and nine which went not astray.

14Even so it is not the will of your Father which is in heaven, that one of these little ones should perish.

15Moreover if thy brother shall trespass against thee, go and tell him his fault between thee and him alone: if he shall hear thee, thou hast gained thy brother.

16But if he will not hear *thee, then* take with thee one or two more, that in the mouth of two or three witnesses every word may be established.

17And if he shall neglect to hear them, tell *it* unto the church: but if he neglect to hear the church, let him be unto thee as an heathen man and a publican.

18Verily I say unto you, Whatsoever ye shall bind on earth shall be bound in heaven: and whatsoever ye shall loose on earth shall be loosed in heaven.

19Again I say unto you, That if two of you shall agree on earth as touching any thing that they shall ask, it shall be done for them of my Father which is in heaven.

20For where two or three are gathered together in my name, there am I in the midst of them.

21Then came Peter to him, and said, Lord, how oft shall my brother sin against me, and I forgive him? till seven times?

22Jesus saith unto him, I say not unto thee, Until seven times: but, Until seventy times seven.

PSALM 22:19–31

BUT be not thou far from me, O LORD: O my strength, haste thee to help me.

20Deliver my soul from the sword; my darling from the power of the dog.

21Save me from the lion's mouth: for thou hast heard me from the horns of the unicorns.

22I will declare thy name unto my brethren: in the midst of the congregation will I praise thee.

23Ye that fear the LORD, praise him; all ye the seed of Jacob, glorify him; and fear him, all ye the seed of Israel.

24For he hath not despised nor abhorred the affliction of the afflicted; neither hath he hid his face from him; but when he cried unto him, he heard.

25My praise *shall be* of thee in the great congregation: I will pay my vows before them that fear him.

26The meek shall eat and be satisfied: they shall praise the LORD that seek him: your heart shall live for ever.

27All the ends of the world shall remember and turn unto the LORD: and all the kindreds of the nations shall worship before thee.

28For the kingdom *is* the LORD'S: and he *is* the governor among the nations.

29All *they that be* fat upon earth shall eat and worship: all they that go down to the dust shall bow before him: and none can keep alive his own soul.

30A seed shall serve him; it shall be accounted to the Lord for a generation.

31They shall come, and shall declare his righteousness unto a people that shall be born, that he hath done *this*.

PROVERBS FOR TODAY/ 5:15–21

Drink waters out of thine own cistern, and running waters out of thine own well. Let thy fountains be dispersed abroad, and rivers of waters in the streets. Let them be only thine own, and not strangers' with thee. Let thy fountain be blessed: and rejoice with the wife of thy youth. Let her be as the loving hind and pleasant roe; let her breasts satisfy thee at all times; and be thou ravished always with her love. And why wilt thou, my son, be ravished with a strange woman, and embrace the bosom of a stranger? For the ways of man are before the eyes of the LORD, and he pondereth all his goings.

JANUARY 28

EXODUS 5:22—7:25

AND Moses returned unto the LORD, and said, Lord, wherefore hast thou *so* evil entreated this people? why *is* it *that* thou hast sent me?

23For since I came to Pharaoh to speak in thy name, he hath done evil to this people; neither hast thou delivered thy people at all.

THEN the LORD said unto Moses, Now shalt thou see what I will do to Pharaoh: for with a strong hand shall he let them go, and with a strong hand shall he drive them out of his land.

2And God spake unto Moses, and said unto him, I *am* the LORD:

3And I appeared unto Abraham, unto Isaac, and unto Jacob, by *the name of* God Almighty, but by my name JEHOVAH was I not known to them.

4And I have also established my covenant with them, to give them the land of Canaan, the land of their pilgrimage, wherein they were strangers.

5And I have also heard the groaning of the children of Israel, whom the Egyptians keep in bondage; and I have remembered my covenant.

6Wherefore say unto the children of Israel, I *am* the LORD, and I will bring you out from under the burdens of the Egyptians, and I will rid you out of their bondage, and I will redeem you with a stretched out arm, and with great judgments:

7And I will take you to me for a people, and I will be to you a God: and ye shall know that I *am* the LORD your God, which bringeth you out from under the burdens of the Egyptians.

8And I will bring you in unto the land, concerning the which I did swear to give it to Abraham, to Isaac, and to Jacob; and I will give it you for an heritage: I *am* the LORD.

9And Moses spake so unto the children of Israel: but they hearkened not unto Moses for anguish of spirit, and for cruel bondage.

10And the LORD spake unto Moses, saying,

11Go in, speak unto Pharaoh king of Egypt, that he let the children of Israel go out of his land.

12And Moses spake before the LORD, saying, Behold, the children of Israel have not hearkened unto me; how then shall Pharaoh hear me, who *am* of uncircumcised lips?

13And the LORD spake unto Moses and unto Aaron, and gave them a charge unto the children of Israel, and unto Pharaoh king of Egypt, to bring the children of Israel out of the land of Egypt.

14These *be* the heads of their fathers' houses: The sons of Reuben the firstborn of Israel; Hanoch, and Pallu, Hezron, and Carmi: these *be* the families of Reuben.

15And the sons of Simeon; Jemuel, and Jamin, and Ohad, and Jachin, and Zohar, and Shaul the son of a Canaanitish woman: these *are* the families of Simeon.

16And these *are* the names of the sons of Levi according to their generations; Gershon, and Kohath, and Merari: and the years of the life of Levi *were* an hundred thirty and seven years.

17The sons of Gershon; Libni, and Shimi, according to their families.

18And the sons of Kohath; Amram, and Izhar, and Hebron, and Uzziel: and the years of the life of Kohath *were* an hundred thirty and three years.

19And the sons of Merari; Mahali and Mushi: these *are* the families of Levi according to their generations.

20And Amram took him Jochebed his father's sister to wife; and she bare him Aaron and Moses: and the years of the life of Amram *were* an hundred and thirty and seven years.

21And the sons of Izhar; Korah, and Nepheg, and Zichri.

22And the sons of Uzziel; Mishael, and Elzaphan, and Zithri.

23And Aaron took him Elisheba, daughter of Amminadab, sister of Naashon, to wife; and she bare him Nadab, and Abihu, Eleazar, and Ithamar.

24And the sons of Korah; Assir, and Elkanah, and Abiasaph: these *are* the families of the Korhites.

25And Eleazar Aaron's son took him *one* of the daughters of Putiel to wife; and she bare him Phinehas: these *are* the heads of the fathers of the Levites according to their families.

26These *are* that Aaron and Moses, to whom the LORD said, Bring out the children of Israel from the land of Egypt according to their armies.

27These *are* they which spake to Pharaoh king of Egypt, to bring out the children of Israel from Egypt: these *are* that Moses and Aaron.

28And it came to pass on the day *when* the LORD spake unto Moses in the land of Egypt,

29That the LORD spake unto Moses, saying, I *am* the LORD: speak thou unto Pharaoh king of Egypt all that I say unto thee.

30And Moses said before the LORD, Behold, I *am* of uncircumcised lips, and how shall Pharaoh hearken unto me?

AND the LORD said unto Moses, See, I have made thee a god to Pharaoh: and Aaron thy brother shall be thy prophet.

2Thou shalt speak all that I command thee: and Aaron thy brother shall speak unto Pharaoh, that he send the children of Israel out of his land.

3And I will harden Pharaoh's heart, and multiply my signs and my wonders in the land of Egypt.

4But Pharaoh shall not hearken unto you, that I may lay my hand upon Egypt, and bring forth mine armies, *and* my people the children of Israel, out of the land of Egypt by great judgments.

5And the Egyptians shall know that I *am* the LORD, when I stretch forth mine hand upon Egypt, and bring out the children of Israel from among them.

6And Moses and Aaron did as the LORD commanded them, so did they.

7And Moses *was* fourscore years old, and Aaron fourscore and three years old, when they spake unto Pharaoh.

8And the LORD spake unto Moses and unto Aaron, saying,

9When Pharaoh shall speak unto you, saying, Shew a miracle for you: then thou shalt say unto Aaron, Take thy rod, and cast *it* before Pharaoh, *and* it shall become a serpent.

10And Moses and Aaron went in unto Pharaoh, and they did so as the LORD had commanded: and Aaron cast down his rod before Pharaoh, and before his servants, and it became a serpent.

11Then Pharaoh also called the wise men and the sorcerers: now the magicians of Egypt, they also did in like manner with their enchantments.

12For they cast down every man his rod, and they became serpents: but Aaron's rod swallowed up their rods.

13And he hardened Pharaoh's heart, that he hearkened not unto them; as the LORD had said.

14And the LORD said unto Moses, Pharaoh's heart *is* hardened, he refuseth to let the people go.

15Get thee unto Pharaoh in the morning; lo, he goeth out unto the water; and thou shalt stand by the river's brink against he come; and the rod which was turned to a serpent shalt thou take in thine hand.

16And thou shalt say unto him, The LORD God of the Hebrews hath sent me unto thee, saying, Let my people go, that they may serve me in the wilderness: and, behold, hitherto thou wouldest not hear.

17Thus saith the LORD, In this thou shalt know that I *am* the LORD: behold, I will smite with the rod that *is* in mine hand upon the waters which *are* in the river, and they shall be turned to blood.

18And the fish that *is* in the river shall die, and the river shall stink; and the Egyptians shall lothe to drink of the water of the river.

19And the LORD spake unto Moses, Say unto Aaron, Take thy rod, and stretch out thine hand upon the waters of Egypt, upon their streams, upon their rivers, and upon their ponds, and upon all their pools of water, that they may become blood; and *that* there may be blood throughout all the land of Egypt, both in *vessels of* wood, and in *vessels* of stone.

20And Moses and Aaron did so, as the LORD commanded; and he lifted up the rod, and smote the waters that *were* in the river, in the sight of Pharaoh, and in the sight of his servants; and all the waters that *were* in the river were turned to blood.

21And the fish that *was* in the river died; and the river stank, and the Egyptians could not drink of the water of the river; and there was blood throughout all the land of Egypt.

22And the magicians of Egypt did so with their enchantments: and Pharaoh's heart was hardened, neither did he hearken unto them; as the LORD had said.

23And Pharaoh turned and went into his house, neither did he set his heart to this also.

24And all the Egyptians digged round about the river for water to drink; for they could not drink of the water of the river.

25And seven days were fulfilled, after that the LORD had smitten the river.

MATTHEW 18:23—19:12

THEREFORE is the kingdom of heaven likened unto a certain king, which would take account of his servants.

24And when he had begun to reckon, one was brought unto him, which owed him ten thousand talents.

25But forasmuch as he had not to pay, his lord commanded him to be sold, and his wife, and children, and all that he had, and payment to be made.

26The servant therefore fell down, and worshipped him, saying, Lord, have patience with me, and I will pay thee all.

27Then the lord of that servant was moved with compassion, and loosed him, and forgave him the debt.

28But the same servant went out, and found one of his fellowservants, which owed him an hundred pence: and he laid hands on him, and took *him* by the throat, saying, Pay me that thou owest.

29And his fellowservant fell down at his feet, and besought him, saying, Have patience with me, and I will pay thee all.

30And he would not: but went and cast him into prison, till he should pay the debt.

31So when his fellowservants saw what was done, they were very sorry, and came and told unto their lord all that was done.

32Then his lord, after that he had called him, said unto him, O thou wicked servant, I forgave thee all that debt, because thou desiredst me:

33Shouldest not thou also have had compassion on thy fellowservant, even as I had pity on thee?

34And his lord was wroth, and delivered him to the tormentors, till he should pay all that was due unto him.

35So likewise shall my heavenly Father do also unto you, if ye from your hearts forgive not every one his brother their trespasses.

AND it came to pass, *that* when Jesus had finished these sayings, he departed from Galilee, and came into the coasts of Judaea beyond Jordan;

2And great multitudes followed him; and he healed them there.

3The Pharisees also came unto him, tempting him, and saying unto him, Is it lawful for a man to put away his wife for every cause?

4And he answered and said unto them, Have ye not read, that he which made *them* at the beginning made them male and female,

5And said, For this cause shall a man leave father and mother, and shall cleave to his wife: and they twain shall be one flesh?

6Wherefore they are no more twain, but one flesh. What therefore God hath joined together, let not man put asunder.

7They say unto him, Why did Moses then command to give a writing of divorcement, and to put her away?

8He saith unto them, Moses because of the hardness of your hearts suffered you to put away your wives: but from the beginning it was not so.

9And I say unto you, Whosoever shall put away his wife, except *it be* for fornication, and shall marry another, committeth adultery: and whoso marrieth her which is put away doth commit adultery.

10His disciples say unto him, If the case of the man be so with *his* wife, it is not good to marry.

11But he said unto them, All *men* cannot receive this saying, save *they* to whom it is given.

12For there are some eunuchs, which were so born from *their* mother's womb: and there are some eunuchs, which were made eunuchs of men: and there be eunuchs, which have made themselves eunuchs for the kingdom of heaven's sake. He that is able to receive *it,* let him receive *it.*

PSALM 23:1–6

THE LORD *is* my shepherd; I shall not want.

2He maketh me to lie down in green pastures: he leadeth me beside the still waters.

3He restoreth my soul: he leadeth me in the paths of righteousness for his name's sake.

4Yea, though I walk through the valley of the shadow of death, I will fear no evil: for thou *art* with me; thy rod and thy staff they comfort me.

5Thou preparest a table before me in the presence of mine enemies: thou anointest my head with oil; my cup runneth over.

6Surely goodness and mercy shall follow me all the days of my life: and I will dwell in the house of the LORD for ever.

PROVERBS FOR TODAY/ 5:22–23

His own iniquities shall take the wicked himself, and he shall be holden with the cords of his sins. He shall die without instruction; and in the greatness of his folly he shall go astray.

JANUARY 29

EXODUS 8:1—9:35

AND the LORD spake unto Moses, Go unto Pharaoh, and say unto him, Thus saith the LORD, Let my people go, that they may serve me.

2And if thou refuse to let *them* go, behold, I will smite all thy borders with frogs:

3And the river shall bring forth frogs abundantly, which shall go up and come into thine house, and into thy bedchamber, and upon thy bed, and into the house of thy servants, and upon thy people, and into thine ovens, and into thy kneading troughs:

4And the frogs shall come up both on thee, and upon thy people, and upon all thy servants.

5And the LORD spake unto Moses, Say unto Aaron, Stretch forth thine hand with thy rod over the streams, over the rivers, and over the ponds, and cause frogs to come up upon the land of Egypt.

6And Aaron stretched out his hand over the waters of Egypt; and the frogs came up, and covered the land of Egypt.

7And the magicians did so with their enchantments, and brought up frogs upon the land of Egypt.

8Then Pharaoh called for Moses and Aaron, and said, Intreat the LORD, that he may take away the frogs from me, and from my people; and I will let the people go, that they may do sacrifice unto the LORD.

9And Moses said unto Pharaoh, Glory over me: when shall I intreat for thee, and for thy servants, and for thy people, to destroy the frogs from thee and thy houses, *that* they may remain in the river only?

10And he said, To morrow. And he said, *Be it* according to thy word: that thou mayest know that *there is* none like unto the LORD our God.

11And the frogs shall depart from thee, and from thy houses, and from thy servants, and from thy people; they shall remain in the river only.

12And Moses and Aaron went out from Pharaoh: and Moses cried unto the LORD because of the frogs which he had brought against Pharaoh.

13And the LORD did according to the word of Moses; and the frogs died out of the houses, out of the villages, and out of the fields.

14And they gathered them together upon heaps: and the land stank.

15But when Pharaoh saw that there was respite, he hardened his heart, and hearkened not unto them; as the LORD had said.

16And the LORD said unto Moses, Say unto Aaron, Stretch out thy rod, and smite the dust of the land, that it may become lice throughout all the land of Egypt.

17And they did so; for Aaron stretched out his hand with his rod, and smote the dust of the earth, and it became lice in man, and in beast; all the dust of the land became lice throughout all the land of Egypt.

18And the magicians did so with their enchantments to bring forth lice, but they could not: so there were lice upon man, and upon beast.

19Then the magicians said unto Pharaoh, This *is* the finger of God: and Pharaoh's heart was hardened, and he hearkened not unto them; as the LORD had said.

20And the LORD said unto Moses, Rise up early in the morning, and stand before Pharaoh; lo, he cometh forth to the water; and say unto him, Thus saith the LORD, Let my people go, that they may serve me.

21Else, if thou wilt not let my people go, behold, I will send swarms *of flies* upon thee, and upon thy servants, and upon thy people, and into thy houses: and the houses of the Egyptians shall be full of swarms *of flies,* and also the ground whereon they *are.*

22And I will sever in that day the land of Goshen, in which my people dwell, that no swarms *of flies* shall be there; to the end thou mayest know that I *am* the LORD in the midst of the earth.

23And I will put a division between my people and thy people: to morrow shall this sign be.

24And the LORD did so; and there came a grievous swarm *of flies* into the house of Pharaoh, and *into* his servants' houses, and into all the land of Egypt: the land was corrupted by reason of the swarm *of flies.*

25And Pharaoh called for Moses and for Aaron, and said, Go ye, sacrifice to your God in the land.

26And Moses said, It is not meet so to do, for we shall sacrifice the abomination of the Egyptians to the LORD our God: lo, shall we sacrifice the abomination of the Egyptians before their eyes, and will they not stone us?

27We will go three days' journey into the wilderness, and sacrifice to the LORD our God, as he shall command us.

28And Pharaoh said, I will let you go, that ye may sacrifice to the LORD your God in the wilderness; only ye shall not go very far away: intreat for me.

29And Moses said, Behold, I go out from thee, and I will intreat the LORD that the swarms *of flies* may depart from Pharaoh, from his servants, and from his people, to morrow: but let not Pharaoh deal deceitfully any more in not letting the people go to sacrifice to the LORD.

30And Moses went out from Pharaoh, and intreated the LORD.

31And the LORD did according to the word of Moses; and he removed the swarms *of flies* from Pharaoh, from his servants, and from his people; there remained not one.

32And Pharaoh hardened his heart at this time also, neither would he let the people go.

THEN the LORD said unto Moses, Go in unto Pharaoh, and tell him, Thus saith the LORD God of the Hebrews, Let my people go, that they may serve me.

2For if thou refuse to let *them* go, and wilt hold them still,

3Behold, the hand of the LORD is upon thy cattle which *is* in the field, upon the horses, upon the asses, upon the camels, upon the oxen, and upon the sheep: *there shall be* a very grievous murrain.

4And the LORD shall sever between the cattle of Israel and the cattle of Egypt: and there shall nothing die of all *that is* the children's of Israel.

5And the LORD appointed a set time, saying, To morrow the LORD shall do this thing in the land.

6And the LORD did that thing on the morrow, and all the cattle of Egypt died: but of the cattle of the children of Israel died not one.

7And Pharaoh sent, and, behold, there was not one of the cattle of the Israelites dead. And the heart of Pharaoh was hardened, and he did not let the people go.

8And the LORD said unto Moses and unto Aaron, Take to you handfuls of ashes of the furnace, and let Moses sprinkle it toward the heaven in the sight of Pharaoh.

9And it shall become small dust in all the land of Egypt, and shall be a boil breaking forth *with* blains upon man, and upon beast, throughout all the land of Egypt.

¹⁰And they took ashes of the furnace, and stood before Pharaoh; and Moses sprinkled it up toward heaven; and it became a boil breaking forth *with* blains upon man, and upon beast.

¹¹And the magicians could not stand before Moses because of the boils; for the boil was upon the magicians, and upon all the Egyptians.

¹²And the LORD hardened the heart of Pharaoh, and he hearkened not unto them; as the LORD had spoken unto Moses.

¹³And the LORD said unto Moses, Rise up early in the morning, and stand before Pharaoh, and say unto him, Thus saith the LORD God of the Hebrews, Let my people go, that they may serve me.

¹⁴For I will at this time send all my plagues upon thine heart, and upon thy servants, and upon thy people; that thou mayest know that *there is* none like me in all the earth.

¹⁵For now I will stretch out my hand, that I may smite thee and thy people with pestilence; and thou shalt be cut off from the earth.

¹⁶And in very deed for this *cause* have I raised thee up, for to shew *in* thee my power; and that my name may be declared throughout all the earth.

¹⁷As yet exaltest thou thyself against my people, that thou wilt not let them go?

¹⁸Behold, to morrow about this time I will cause it to rain a very grievous hail, such as hath not been in Egypt since the foundation thereof even until now.

¹⁹Send therefore now, *and* gather thy cattle, and all that thou hast in the field; *for upon* every man and beast which shall be found in the field, and shall not be brought home, the hail shall come down upon them, and they shall die.

²⁰He that feared the word of the LORD among the servants of Pharaoh made his servants and his cattle flee into the houses:

²¹And he that regarded not the word of the LORD left his servants and his cattle in the field.

²²And the LORD said unto Moses, Stretch forth thine hand toward heaven, that there may be hail in all the land of Egypt, upon man, and upon beast, and upon every herb of the field, throughout the land of Egypt.

²³And Moses stretched forth his rod toward heaven: and the LORD sent thunder and hail, and the fire ran along upon the ground; and the LORD rained hail upon the land of Egypt.

²⁴So there was hail, and fire mingled with the hail, very grievous, such as there was none like it in all the land of Egypt since it became a nation.

²⁵And the hail smote throughout all the land of Egypt all that *was* in the field, both man and beast; and the hail smote every herb of the field, and brake every tree of the field.

²⁶Only in the land of Goshen, where the children of Israel *were,* was there no hail.

²⁷And Pharaoh sent, and called for Moses and Aaron, and said unto them, I have sinned this time: the LORD *is* righteous, and I and my people *are* wicked.

²⁸Intreat the LORD (for *it is* enough) that there be no *more* mighty thunderings and hail; and I will let you go, and ye shall stay no longer.

²⁹And Moses said unto him, As soon as I am gone out of the city, I will spread abroad my hands unto the LORD; *and* the thunder shall cease, neither shall there be any more hail; that thou mayest know how that the earth *is* the LORD'S.

³⁰But as for thee and thy servants, I know that ye will not yet fear the LORD God.

³¹And the flax and the barley was smitten: for the barley *was* in the ear, and the flax *was* bolled.

32But the wheat and the rie were not smitten: for they *were* not grown up.

33And Moses went out of the city from Pharaoh, and spread abroad his hands unto the LORD: and the thunders and hail ceased, and the rain was not poured upon the earth.

34And when Pharaoh saw that the rain and the hail and the thunders were ceased, he sinned yet more, and hardened his heart, he and his servants.

35And the heart of Pharaoh was hardened, neither would he let the children of Israel go; as the LORD had spoken by Moses.

MATTHEW 19:13–30

THEN were there brought unto him [Jesus] little children, that he should put *his* hands on them, and pray: and the disciples rebuked them.

14But Jesus said, Suffer little children, and forbid them not, to come unto me: for of such is the kingdom of heaven.

15And he laid *his* hands on them, and departed thence.

16And, behold, one came and said unto him, Good Master, what good thing shall I do, that I may have eternal life?

17And he said unto him, Why callest thou me good? *there is* none good but one, *that is,* God: but if thou wilt enter into life, keep the commandments.

18He saith unto him, Which? Jesus said, Thou shalt do no murder, Thou shalt not commit adultery, Thou shalt not steal, Thou shalt not bear false witness,

19Honour thy father and *thy* mother: and, Thou shalt love thy neighbour as thyself.

20The young man saith unto him, All these things have I kept from my youth up: what lack I yet?

21Jesus said unto him, If thou wilt be perfect, go *and* sell that thou hast, and give to the poor, and thou shalt have treasure in heaven: and come *and* follow me.

22But when the young man heard that saying, he went away sorrowful: for he had great possessions.

23Then said Jesus unto his disciples, Verily I say unto you, That a rich man shall hardly enter into the kingdom of heaven.

24And again I say unto you, It is easier for a camel to go through the eye of a needle, than for a rich man to enter into the kingdom of God.

25When his disciples heard *it,* they were exceedingly amazed, saying, Who then can be saved?

26But Jesus beheld *them,* and said unto them, With men this is impossible; but with God all things are possible.

27Then answered Peter and said unto him, Behold, we have forsaken all, and followed thee; what shall we have therefore?

28And Jesus said unto them, Verily I say unto you, That ye which have followed me, in the regeneration when the Son of man shall sit in the throne of his glory, ye also shall sit upon twelve thrones, judging the twelve tribes of Israel.

29And every one that hath forsaken houses, or brethren, or sisters, or father, or mother, or wife, or children, or lands, for my name's sake, shall receive an hundredfold, and shall inherit everlasting life.

30But many *that are* first shall be last; and the last *shall be* first.

PSALM 24:1–10

THE earth *is* the LORD's, and the fulness thereof; the world, and they that dwell therein.

2For he hath founded it upon the seas, and established it upon the floods.

3Who shall ascend into the hill of the LORD? or who shall stand in his holy place?

4He that hath clean hands, and a pure heart; who hath not lifted up his soul unto vanity, nor sworn deceitfully.

5He shall receive the blessing from the LORD, and righteousness from the God of his salvation.

6This is the generation of them that seek him, that seek thy face, O Jacob. Selah.

7Lift up your heads, O ye gates; and be ye lift up, ye everlasting doors; and the King of glory shall come in.

8Who is this King of glory? The LORD strong and mighty, the LORD mighty in battle.

9Lift up your heads, O ye gates; even lift them up, ye everlasting doors; and the King of glory shall come in.

10Who is this King of glory? The LORD of hosts, he is the King of glory. Selah.

PROVERBS FOR TODAY/ 6:1–5

My son, if thou be surety for thy friend, if thou hast stricken thy hand with a stranger, Thou art snared with the words of thy mouth, thou art taken with the words of thy mouth. Do this now, my son, and deliver thyself, when thou art come into the hand of thy friend; go, humble thyself, and make sure thy friend. Give not sleep to thine eyes, nor slumber to thine eyelids. Deliver thyself as a roe from the hand of the hunter, and as a bird from the hand of the fowler.

JANUARY 30

EXODUS 10:1—12:13

AND the LORD said unto Moses, Go in unto Pharaoh: for I have hardened his heart, and the heart of his servants, that I might shew these my signs before him:

2And that thou mayest tell in the ears of thy son, and of thy son's son, what things I have wrought in Egypt, and my signs which I have done among them; that ye may know how that I am the LORD.

3And Moses and Aaron came in unto Pharaoh, and said unto him, Thus saith the LORD God of the Hebrews, How long wilt thou refuse to humble thyself before me? let my people go, that they may serve me.

4Else, if thou refuse to let my people go, behold, to morrow will I bring the locusts into thy coast:

5And they shall cover the face of the earth, that one cannot be able to see the earth: and they shall eat the residue of that which is escaped, which remaineth unto you from the hail, and shall eat every tree which groweth for you out of the field:

6And they shall fill thy houses, and the houses of all thy servants, and the houses of all the Egyptians; which neither thy fathers, nor thy fathers' fathers have seen, since the day that they were upon the earth unto this day. And he turned himself, and went out from Pharaoh.

7And Pharaoh's servants said unto him, How long shall this man be a snare unto us? let the men go, that they may serve the LORD their God: knowest thou not yet that Egypt is destroyed?

8And Moses and Aaron were brought again unto Pharaoh: and he said unto them, Go, serve the LORD your God: but who are they that shall go?

9And Moses said, We will go with

our young and with our old, with our sons and with our daughters, with our flocks and with our herds will we go; for we *must hold* a feast unto the LORD.

10And he said unto them, Let the LORD be so with you, as I will let you go, and your little ones: look *to it;* for evil *is* before you.

11Not so: go now ye *that are* men, and serve the LORD; for that ye did desire. And they were driven out from Pharaoh's presence.

12And the LORD said unto Moses, Stretch out thine hand over the land of Egypt for the locusts, that they may come up upon the land of Egypt, and eat every herb of the land, *even* all that the hail hath left.

13And Moses stretched forth his rod over the land of Egypt, and the LORD brought an east wind upon the land all that day, and all *that* night; *and* when it was morning, the east wind brought the locusts.

14And the locusts went up over all the land of Egypt, and rested in all the coasts of Egypt: very grievous *were they;* before them there were no such locusts as they, neither after them shall be such.

15For they covered the face of the whole earth, so that the land was darkened; and they did eat every herb of the land, and all the fruit of the trees which the hail had left: and there remained not any green thing in the trees, or in the herbs of the field, through all the land of Egypt.

16Then Pharaoh called for Moses and Aaron in haste; and he said, I have sinned against the LORD your God, and against you.

17Now therefore forgive, I pray thee, my sin only this once, and intreat the LORD your God, that he may take away from me this death only.

18And he went out from Pharaoh, and intreated the LORD.

19And the LORD turned a mighty strong west wind, which took away the locusts, and cast them into the Red sea; there remained not one locust in all the coasts of Egypt.

20But the LORD hardened Pharaoh's heart, so that he would not let the children of Israel go.

21And the LORD said unto Moses, Stretch out thine hand toward heaven, that there may be darkness over the land of Egypt, even darkness *which* may be felt.

22And Moses stretched forth his hand toward heaven; and there was a thick darkness in all the land of Egypt three days:

23They saw not one another, neither rose any from his place for three days: but all the children of Israel had light in their dwellings.

24And Pharaoh called unto Moses, and said, Go ye, serve the LORD; only let your flocks and your herds be stayed: let your little ones also go with you.

25And Moses said, Thou must give us also sacrifices and burnt offerings, that we may sacrifice unto the LORD our God.

26Our cattle also shall go with us; there shall not an hoof be left behind; for thereof must we take to serve the LORD our God; and we know not with what we must serve the LORD, until we come thither.

27But the LORD hardened Pharaoh's heart, and he would not let them go.

28And Pharaoh said unto him, Get thee from me, take heed to thyself, see my face no more; for in *that* day thou seest my face thou shalt die.

29And Moses said, Thou hast spoken well, I will see thy face again no more.

AND the LORD said unto Moses, Yet will I bring one plague *more* upon Pharaoh, and upon Egypt; afterwards he will let you go hence: when he shall let *you* go, he shall surely thrust you out hence altogether.

2Speak now in the ears of the people, and let every man borrow of his neighbour, and every woman of her neighbour, jewels of silver, and jewels of gold.

3And the Lord gave the people favour in the sight of the Egyptians. Moreover the man Moses *was* very great in the land of Egypt, in the sight of Pharaoh's servants, and in the sight of the people.

4And Moses said, Thus saith the Lord, About midnight will I go out into the midst of Egypt:

5And all the firstborn in the land of Egypt shall die, from the firstborn of Pharaoh that sitteth upon his throne, even unto the firstborn of the maidservant that *is* behind the mill; and all the firstborn of beasts.

6And there shall be a great cry throughout all the land of Egypt, such as there was none like it, nor shall be like it any more.

7But against any of the children of Israel shall not a dog move his tongue, against man or beast: that ye may know how that the Lord doth put a difference between the Egyptians and Israel.

8And all these thy servants shall come down unto me, and bow down themselves unto me, saying, Get thee out, and all the people that follow thee: and after that I will go out. And he went out from Pharaoh in a great anger.

9And the Lord said unto Moses, Pharaoh shall not hearken unto you; that my wonders may be multiplied in the land of Egypt.

10And Moses and Aaron did all these wonders before Pharaoh: and the Lord hardened Pharaoh's heart, so that he would not let the children of Israel go out of his land.

And the Lord spake unto Moses and Aaron in the land of Egypt, saying,

2This month *shall be* unto you the beginning of months: it *shall be* the first month of the year to you.

3Speak ye unto all the congregation of Israel, saying, In the tenth *day* of this month they shall take to them every man a lamb, according to the house of *their* fathers, a lamb for an house:

4And if the household be too little for the lamb, let him and his neighbour next unto his house take *it* according to the number of the souls; every man according to his eating shall make your count for the lamb.

5Your lamb shall be without blemish, a male of the first year: ye shall take *it* out from the sheep, or from the goats:

6And ye shall keep it up until the fourteenth day of the same month: and the whole assembly of the congregation of Israel shall kill it in the evening.

7And they shall take of the blood, and strike *it* on the two side posts and on the upper door post of the houses, wherein they shall eat it.

8And they shall eat the flesh in that night, roast with fire, and unleavened bread; *and* with bitter *herbs* they shall eat it.

9Eat not of it raw, nor sodden at all with water, but roast *with* fire; his head with his legs, and with the purtenance thereof.

10And ye shall let nothing of it remain until the morning; and that which remaineth of it until the morning ye shall burn with fire.

11And thus shall ye eat it; *with* your loins girded, your shoes on your feet, and your staff in your hand; and ye shall eat it in haste: it *is* the Lord's passover.

12For I will pass through the land of Egypt this night, and will smite all the firstborn in the land of Egypt, both man and beast; and against all the gods of Egypt I will execute judgment: I *am* the Lord.

13And the blood shall be to you for a token upon the houses where ye *are:* and when I see the blood, I will pass over you, and the plague shall not be upon you to destroy *you*, when I smite the land of Egypt.

MATTHEW 20:1–28

For the kingdom of heaven is like unto a man *that is* an householder, which went out early in the morning to hire labourers into his vineyard.

2And when he had agreed with the labourers for a penny a day, he sent them into his vineyard.

3And he went out about the third hour, and saw others standing idle in the marketplace,

4And said unto them; Go ye also into the vineyard, and whatsoever is right I will give you. And they went their way.

5Again he went out about the sixth and ninth hour, and did likewise.

6And about the eleventh hour he went out, and found others standing idle, and saith unto them, Why stand ye here all the day idle?

7They say unto him, Because no man hath hired us. He saith unto them, Go ye also into the vineyard; and whatsoever is right, *that* shall ye receive.

8So when even was come, the lord of the vineyard saith unto his steward, Call the labourers, and give them *their* hire, beginning from the last unto the first.

9And when they came that *were hired* about the eleventh hour, they received every man a penny.

10But when the first came, they supposed that they should have received more; and they likewise received every man a penny.

11And when they had received *it,* they murmured against the goodman of the house,

12Saying, These last have wrought *but* one hour, and thou hast made them equal unto us, which have borne the burden and heat of the day.

13But he answered one of them, and said, Friend, I do thee no wrong: didst not thou agree with me for a penny?

14Take *that* thine *is,* and go thy way:

I will give unto this last, even as unto thee.

15Is it not lawful for me to do what I will with mine own? Is thine eye evil, because I am good?

16So the last shall be first, and the first last: for many be called, but few chosen.

17And Jesus going up to Jerusalem took the twelve disciples apart in the way, and said unto them,

18Behold, we go up to Jerusalem: and the Son of man shall be betrayed unto the chief priests and unto the scribes, and they shall condemn him to death,

19And shall deliver him to the Gentiles to mock, and to scourge, and to crucify *him:* and the third day he shall rise again.

20Then came to him the mother of Zebedee's children with her sons, worshipping *him,* and desiring a certain thing of him.

21And he said unto her, What wilt thou? She saith unto him, Grant that these my two sons may sit, the one on thy right hand, and the other on the left, in thy kingdom.

22But Jesus answered and said, Ye know not what ye ask. Are ye able to drink of the cup that I shall drink of, and to be baptized with the baptism that I am baptized with? They say unto him, We are able.

23And he saith unto them, Ye shall drink indeed of my cup, and be baptized with the baptism that I am baptized with: but to sit on my right hand, and on my left, is not mine to give, but *it shall be given to them* for whom it is prepared of my Father.

24And when the ten heard *it,* they were moved with indignation against the two brethren.

25But Jesus called them *unto him,* and said, Ye know that the princes of the Gentiles exercise dominion over them, and they that are great exercise authority upon them.

26But it shall not be so among you: but whosoever will be great among you, let him be your minister;

27And whosoever will be chief among you, let him be your servant:

28Even as the Son of man came not to be ministered unto, but to minister, and to give his life a ransom for many.

PSALM 25:1–11

Unto thee, O Lord, do I lift up my soul.

2O my God, I trust in thee: let me not be ashamed, let not mine enemies triumph over me.

3Yea, let none that wait on thee be ashamed: let them be ashamed which transgress without cause.

4Shew me thy ways, O Lord; teach me thy paths.

5Lead me in thy truth, and teach me: for thou *art* the God of my salvation; on thee do I wait all the day.

6Remember, O Lord, thy tender mercies and thy lovingkindnesses; for they *have been* ever of old.

7Remember not the sins of my youth, nor my transgressions: according to thy mercy remember thou me for thy goodness' sake, O Lord.

8Good and upright *is* the Lord: therefore will he teach sinners in the way.

9The meek will he guide in judgment: and the meek will he teach his way.

10All the paths of the Lord *are* mercy and truth unto such as keep his covenant and his testimonies.

11For thy name's sake, O Lord, pardon mine iniquity; for it *is* great.

PROVERBS FOR TODAY/ 6:6–11

Go to the ant, thou sluggard; consider her ways, and be wise: Which having no guide, overseer, or ruler, Provideth her meat in the summer, and *gathereth her food in the harvest.* □ *How long wilt thou sleep, O sluggard? when wilt thou arise out of thy sleep? Yet a little sleep, a little slumber, a little folding of the hands to sleep: So shall thy poverty come as one that travelleth, and thy want as an armed man.*

JANUARY 31

EXODUS 12:14—13:16

And this day shall be unto you for a memorial; and ye shall keep it a feast to the Lord throughout your generations; ye shall keep it a feast by an ordinance for ever.

15Seven days shall ye eat unleavened bread; even the first day ye shall put away leaven out of your houses: for whosoever eateth leavened bread from the first day until the seventh day, that soul shall be cut off from Israel.

16And in the first day *there shall be* an holy convocation, and in the seventh day there shall be an holy convocation to you; no manner of work shall be done in them, save *that* which every man must eat, that only may be done of you.

17And ye shall observe *the feast of* unleavened bread; for in this selfsame day have I brought your armies out of the land of Egypt: therefore shall ye observe this day in your generations by an ordinance for ever.

18In the first *month,* on the fourteenth day of the month at even, ye shall eat unleavened bread, until the one and twentieth day of the month at even.

19Seven days shall there be no leaven found in your houses: for whosoever eateth that which is leavened, even that soul shall be cut off from the congregation of Israel, whether he be a stranger, or born in the land.

20Ye shall eat nothing leavened; in all your habitations shall ye eat unleavened bread.

21Then Moses called for all the elders of Israel, and said unto them, Draw out and take you a lamb according to your families, and kill the passover.

22And ye shall take a bunch of hyssop, and dip *it* in the blood that *is* in the bason, and strike the lintel and the two side posts with the blood that *is* in the bason: and none of you shall go out at the door of his house until the morning.

23For the LORD will pass through to smite the Egyptians; and when he seeth the blood upon the lintel, and on the two side posts, the LORD will pass over the door, and will not suffer the destroyer to come in unto your houses to smite *you.*

24And ye shall observe this thing for an ordinance to thee and to thy sons for ever.

25And it shall come to pass, when ye be come to the land which the LORD will give you, according as he hath promised, that ye shall keep this service.

26And it shall come to pass, when your children shall say unto you, What mean ye by this service?

27That ye shall say, It *is* the sacrifice of the LORD'S passover, who passed over the houses of the children of Israel in Egypt, when he smote the Egyptians, and delivered our houses. And the people bowed the head and worshipped.

28And the children of Israel went away, and did as the LORD had commanded Moses and Aaron, so did they.

29And it came to pass, that at midnight the LORD smote all the firstborn in the land of Egypt, from the firstborn of Pharaoh that sat on his throne unto the firstborn of the captive that *was* in the dungeon; and all the firstborn of cattle.

30And Pharaoh rose up in the night, he, and all his servants, and all the Egyptians; and there was a great cry in Egypt; for *there was* not a house where *there was* not one dead.

31And he called for Moses and Aaron by night, and said, Rise up, *and* get you forth from among my people, both ye and the children of Israel; and go, serve the LORD, as ye have said.

32Also take your flocks and your herds, as ye have said, and be gone; and bless me also.

33And the Egyptians were urgent upon the people, that they might send them out of the land in haste; for they said, We *be* all dead *men.*

34And the people took their dough before it was leavened, their kneading troughs being bound up in their clothes upon their shoulders.

35And the children of Israel did according to the word of Moses; and they borrowed of the Egyptians jewels of silver, and jewels of gold, and raiment:

36And the LORD gave the people favour in the sight of the Egyptians, so that they lent unto them *such things as they required.* And they spoiled the Egyptians.

37And the children of Israel journeyed from Rameses to Succoth, about six hundred thousand on foot *that were* men, beside children.

38And a mixed multitude went up also with them; and flocks, and herds, *even* very much cattle.

39And they baked unleavened cakes of the dough which they brought forth out of Egypt, for it was not leavened;

because they were thrust out of Egypt, and could not tarry, neither had they prepared for themselves any victual.

40Now the sojourning of the children of Israel, who dwelt in Egypt, *was* four hundred and thirty years.

41And it came to pass at the end of the four hundred and thirty years, even the selfsame day it came to pass, that all the hosts of the LORD went out from the land of Egypt.

42It *is* a night to be much observed unto the LORD for bringing them out from the land of Egypt: this *is* that night of the LORD to be observed of all the children of Israel in their generations.

43And the LORD said unto Moses and Aaron, This *is* the ordinance of the passover: There shall no stranger eat thereof:

44But every man's servant that is bought for money, when thou hast circumcised him, then shall he eat thereof.

45A foreigner and an hired servant shall not eat thereof.

46In one house shall it be eaten; thou shalt not carry forth ought of the flesh abroad out of the house; neither shall ye break a bone thereof.

47All the congregation of Israel shall keep it.

48And when a stranger shall sojourn with thee, and will keep the passover to the LORD, let all his males be circumcised, and then let him come near and keep it; and he shall be as one that is born in the land: for no uncircumcised person shall eat thereof.

49One law shall be to him that is homeborn, and unto the stranger that sojourneth among you.

50Thus did all the children of Israel; as the LORD commanded Moses and Aaron, so did they.

51And it came to pass the selfsame day, *that* the LORD did bring the children of Israel out of the land of Egypt by their armies.

AND the LORD spake unto Moses, saying,

2Sanctify unto me all the firstborn, whatsoever openeth the womb among the children of Israel, *both* of man and of beast: it *is* mine.

3And Moses said unto the people, Remember this day, in which ye came out from Egypt, out of the house of bondage; for by strength of hand the LORD brought you out from this *place:* there shall no leavened bread be eaten.

4This day came ye out in the month Abib.

5And it shall be when the LORD shall bring thee into the land of the Canaanites, and the Hittites, and the Amorites, and the Hivites, and the Jebusites, which he sware unto thy fathers to give thee, a land flowing with milk and honey, that thou shalt keep this service in this month.

6Seven days thou shalt eat unleavened bread, and in the seventh day *shall be* a feast to the LORD.

7Unleavened bread shall be eaten seven days; and there shall no leavened bread be seen with thee, neither shall there be leaven seen with thee in all thy quarters.

8And thou shalt shew thy son in that day, saying, *This is done* because of that *which* the LORD did unto me when I came forth out of Egypt.

9And it shall be for a sign unto thee upon thine hand, and for a memorial between thine eyes, that the LORD'S law may be in thy mouth: for with a strong hand hath the LORD brought thee out of Egypt.

10Thou shalt therefore keep this ordinance in his season from year to year.

11And it shall be when the LORD shall bring thee into the land of the Canaanites, as he sware unto thee and to thy fathers, and shall give it thee,

12That thou shalt set apart unto the LORD all that openeth the matrix, and every firstling that cometh of a beast which thou hast; the male *shall be* the LORD'S.

13And every firstling of an ass thou shalt redeem with a lamb; and if thou wilt not redeem it, then thou shalt break his neck: and all the firstborn of man among thy children shalt thou redeem.

14And it shall be when thy son asketh thee in time to come, saying, What *is* this? that thou shalt say unto him, By strength of hand, the LORD brought us out from Egypt, from the house of bondage:

15And it came to pass, when Pharaoh would hardly let us go, that the LORD slew all the firstborn in the land of Egypt, both the firstborn of man, and the firstborn of beast: therefore I sacrifice to the LORD all that openeth the matrix, being males; but all the firstborn of my children I redeem.

16And it shall be for a token upon thine hand, and for frontlets between thine eyes: for by strength of hand the LORD brought us forth out of Egypt.

MATTHEW 20:29—21:22

AND as they [Jesus and his disciples] departed from Jericho, a great multitude followed him.
30And, behold, two blind men sitting by the way side, when they heard that Jesus passed by, cried out, saying, Have mercy on us, O Lord, *thou* son of David.

31And the multitude rebuked them, because they should hold their peace: but they cried the more, saying, Have mercy on us, O Lord, *thou* son of David.

32And Jesus stood still, and called them, and said, What will ye that I shall do unto you?

33They say unto him, Lord, that our eyes may be opened.

34So Jesus had compassion *on them,* and touched their eyes: and immediately their eyes received sight, and they followed him.

AND when they drew nigh unto Jerusalem, and were come to Bethphage, unto the mount of Olives, then sent Jesus two disciples,

2Saying unto them, Go into the village over against you, and straightway ye shall find an ass tied, and a colt with her: loose *them,* and bring *them* unto me.

3And if any *man* say ought unto you, ye shall say, The Lord hath need of them; and straightway he will send them.

4All this was done, that it might be fulfilled which was spoken by the prophet, saying,

5Tell ye the daughter of Sion, Behold, thy king cometh unto thee, meek, and sitting upon an ass, and a colt the foal of an ass.

6And the disciples went, and did as Jesus commanded them,

7And brought the ass, and the colt, and put on them their clothes, and they set *him* thereon.

8And a very great multitude spread their garments in the way; others cut down branches from the trees, and strawed *them* in the way.

9And the multitudes that went before, and that followed, cried, saying, Hosanna to the son of David: Blessed *is* he that cometh in the name of the Lord; Hosanna in the highest.

10And when he was come into Jerusalem, all the city was moved, saying, Who is this?

11And the multitude said, This is Jesus the prophet of Nazareth of Galilee.

12And Jesus went into the temple of God, and cast out all them that sold and bought in the temple, and overthrew the tables of the moneychangers, and the seats of them that sold doves,

13And said unto them, It is written, My house shall be called the house of prayer; but ye have made it a den of thieves.

14And the blind and the lame came

to him in the temple; and he healed them.

15And when the chief priests and scribes saw the wonderful things that he did, and the children crying in the temple, and saying, Hosanna to the son of David; they were sore displeased,

16And said unto him, Hearest thou what these say? And Jesus saith unto them, Yea; have ye never read, Out of the mouth of babes and sucklings thou hast perfected praise?

17And he left them, and went out of the city into Bethany; and he lodged there.

18Now in the morning as he returned into the city, he hungered.

19And when he saw a fig tree in the way, he came to it, and found nothing thereon, but leaves only, and said unto it, Let no fruit grow on thee henceforward for ever. And presently the fig tree withered away.

20And when the disciples saw *it,* they marvelled, saying, How soon is the fig tree withered away!

21Jesus answered and said unto them, Verily I say unto you, If ye have faith, and doubt not, ye shall not only do this *which is done* to the fig tree, but also if ye shall say unto this mountain, Be thou removed, and be thou cast into the sea; it shall be done.

22And all things, whatsoever ye shall ask in prayer, believing, ye shall receive.

PSALM 25:12–22

WHAT man *is* he that feareth the LORD? him shall he teach in the way *that* he shall choose.

13His soul shall dwell at ease; and his seed shall inherit the earth.

14The secret of the LORD *is* with them that fear him; and he will shew them his covenant.

15Mine eyes *are* ever toward the LORD; for he shall pluck my feet out of the net.

16Turn thee unto me, and have mercy upon me; for I *am* desolate and afflicted.

17The troubles of my heart are enlarged: *O* bring thou me out of my distresses.

18Look upon mine affliction and my pain; and forgive all my sins.

19Consider mine enemies; for they are many; and they hate me with cruel hatred.

20O keep my soul, and deliver me: let me not be ashamed; for I put my trust in thee.

21Let integrity and uprightness preserve me; for I wait on thee.

22Redeem Israel, O God, out of all his troubles.

PROVERBS FOR TODAY/ 6:12–15

A naughty person, a wicked man, walketh with a froward mouth. He winketh with his eyes, he speaketh with his feet, he teacheth with his fingers; Frowardness is in his heart, he deviseth mischief continually; he soweth discord. Therefore shall his calamity come suddenly; suddenly shall he be broken without remedy.

EXODUS 13:17—15:19

ND it came to pass, when Pharaoh had let the people go, that God led them not *through* the way of the land of the Philistines, although that *was* near; for God said, Lest peradventure the people repent when they see war, and they return to Egypt:

18But God led the people about, *through* the way of the wilderness of the Red sea: and the children of Israel went up harnessed out of the land of Egypt.

19And Moses took the bones of Joseph with him: for he had straitly sworn the children of Israel, saying, God will surely visit you; and ye shall carry up my bones away hence with you.

20And they took their journey from Succoth, and encamped in Etham, in the edge of the wilderness.

21And the LORD went before them by day in a pillar of a cloud, to lead them the way; and by night in a pillar of fire, to give them light; to go by day and night:

22He took not away the pillar of the cloud by day, nor the pillar of fire by night, *from* before the people.

AND the LORD spake unto Moses, saying,

2Speak unto the children of Israel, that they turn and encamp before Pi–hahiroth, between Migdol and the sea, over against Baal–zephon: before it shall ye encamp by the sea.

3For Pharaoh will say of the children of Israel, They *are* entangled in the land, the wilderness hath shut them in.

4And I will harden Pharaoh's heart, that he shall follow after them; and I will be honoured upon Pharaoh, and

upon all his host; that the Egyptians may know that I *am* the LORD. And they did so.

5And it was told the king of Egypt that the people fled: and the heart of Pharaoh and of his servants was turned against the people, and they said, Why have we done this, that we have let Israel go from serving us?

6And he made ready his chariot, and took his people with him:

7And he took six hundred chosen chariots, and all the chariots of Egypt, and captains over every one of them.

8And the LORD hardened the heart of Pharaoh king of Egypt, and he pursued after the children of Israel: and the children of Israel went out with an high hand.

9But the Egyptians pursued after them, all the horses *and* chariots of Pharaoh, and his horsemen, and his army, and overtook them encamping by the sea, beside Pi–hahiroth, before Baal–zephon.

10And when Pharaoh drew nigh, the children of Israel lifted up their eyes, and, behold, the Egyptians marched after them; and they were sore afraid: and the children of Israel cried out unto the LORD.

11And they said unto Moses, Because *there were* no graves in Egypt, hast thou taken us away to die in the wilderness? wherefore hast thou dealt thus with us, to carry us forth out of Egypt?

12*Is* not this the word that we did tell thee in Egypt, saying, Let us alone, that we may serve the Egyptians? For *it had been* better for us to serve the Egyptians, than that we should die in the wilderness.

13And Moses said unto the people, Fear ye not, stand still, and see the salvation of the LORD, which he will shew to you to day: for the Egyptians whom ye have seen to day, ye shall see them again no more for ever.

14The LORD shall fight for you, and ye shall hold your peace.

15And the LORD said unto Moses, Wherefore criest thou unto me? speak unto the children of Israel, that they go forward:

16But lift thou up thy rod, and stretch out thine hand over the sea, and divide it: and the children of Israel shall go on dry *ground* through the midst of the sea.

17And I, behold, I will harden the hearts of the Egyptians, and they shall follow them: and I will get me honour upon Pharaoh, and upon all his host, upon his chariots, and upon his horsemen.

18And the Egyptians shall know that I *am* the LORD, when I have gotten me honour upon Pharaoh, upon his chariots, and upon his horsemen.

19And the angel of God, which went before the camp of Israel, removed and went behind them; and the pillar of the cloud went from before their face, and stood behind them:

20And it came between the camp of the Egyptians and the camp of Israel; and it was a cloud and darkness *to them,* but it gave light by night *to these:* so that the one came not near the other all the night.

21And Moses stretched out his hand over the sea; and the LORD caused the sea to go *back* by a strong east wind all that night, and made the sea dry *land,* and the waters were divided.

22And the children of Israel went into the midst of the sea upon the dry *ground:* and the waters *were* a wall unto them on their right hand, and on their left.

23And the Egyptians pursued, and went in after them to the midst of the sea, *even* all Pharaoh's horses, his chariots, and his horsemen.

24And it came to pass, that in the morning watch the LORD looked unto the host of the Egyptians through the pillar of fire and of the cloud, and troubled the host of the Egyptians,

25And took off their chariot wheels, that they drave them heavily: so that the Egyptians said, Let us flee from the face of Israel; for the LORD fighteth for them against the Egyptians.

26And the LORD said unto Moses, Stretch out thine hand over the sea, that the waters may come again upon the Egyptians, upon their chariots, and upon their horsemen.

27And Moses stretched forth his hand over the sea, and the sea returned to his strength when the morning appeared; and the Egyptians fled against it; and the LORD overthrew the Egyptians in the midst of the sea.

28And the waters returned, and covered the chariots, and the horsemen, *and* all the host of Pharaoh that came into the sea after them; there remained not so much as one of them.

29But the children of Israel walked upon dry *land* in the midst of the sea; and the waters *were* a wall unto them on their right hand, and on their left.

30Thus the LORD saved Israel that day out of the hand of the Egyptians; and Israel saw the Egyptians dead upon the sea shore.

31And Israel saw that great work which the LORD did upon the Egyptians: and the people feared the LORD, and believed the LORD, and his servant Moses.

THEN sang Moses and the children of Israel this song unto the LORD, and spake, saying, I will sing unto the LORD, for he hath triumphed gloriously: the horse and his rider hath he thrown into the sea.

2The LORD *is* my strength and song, and he is become my salvation: he *is* my God, and I will prepare him an habitation; my father's God, and I will exalt him.

3The LORD *is* a man of war: the LORD *is* his name.

4Pharaoh's chariots and his host hath he cast into the sea: his chosen captains also are drowned in the Red sea.

5The depths have covered them: they sank into the bottom as a stone.

6Thy right hand, O LORD, is become glorious in power: thy right hand, O LORD, hath dashed in pieces the enemy.

7And in the greatness of thine excellency thou hast overthrown them that rose up against thee: thou sentest forth thy wrath, *which* consumed them as stubble.

8And with the blast of thy nostrils the waters were gathered together, the floods stood upright as an heap, *and* the depths were congealed in the heart of the sea.

9The enemy said, I will pursue, I will overtake, I will divide the spoil; my lust shall be satisfied upon them; I will draw my sword, my hand shall destroy them.

10Thou didst blow with thy wind, the sea covered them: they sank as lead in the mighty waters.

11Who *is* like unto thee, O LORD, among the gods? who *is* like thee, glorious in holiness, fearful *in* praises, doing wonders?

12Thou stretchedst out thy right hand, the earth swallowed them.

13Thou in thy mercy hast led forth the people *which* thou hast redeemed: thou hast guided *them* in thy strength unto thy holy habitation.

14The people shall hear, *and* be afraid: sorrow shall take hold on the inhabitants of Palestina.

15Then the dukes of Edom shall be amazed; the mighty men of Moab, trembling shall take hold upon them; all the inhabitants of Canaan shall melt away.

16Fear and dread shall fall upon them; by the greatness of thine arm they shall be *as* still as a stone; till thy people pass over, O LORD, till the people pass over, *which* thou hast purchased.

17Thou shalt bring them in, and plant them in the mountain of thine inheritance, *in* the place, O LORD, *which* thou hast made for thee to dwell in, *in* the Sanctuary, O LORD, *which* thy hands have established.

18The LORD shall reign for ever and ever.

19For the horse of Pharaoh went in with his chariots and with his horsemen into the sea, and the LORD brought again the waters of the sea upon them; but the children of Israel went on dry *land* in the midst of the sea.

MATTHEW 21:23–46

AND when he [Jesus] was come into the temple, the chief priests and the elders of the people came unto him as he was teaching, and said, By what authority doest thou these things? and who gave thee this authority?

24And Jesus answered and said unto them, I also will ask you one thing, which if ye tell me, I in like wise will tell you by what authority I do these things.

25The baptism of John, whence was it? from heaven, or of men? And they reasoned with themselves, saying, If we shall say, From heaven; he will say unto us, Why did ye not then believe him?

26But if we shall say, Of men; we fear the people; for all hold John as a prophet.

27And they answered Jesus, and said, We cannot tell. And he said unto them, Neither tell I you by what authority I do these things.

28But what think ye? A *certain* man had two sons; and he came to the first, and said, Son, go work to day in my vineyard.

29He answered and said, I will not:

but afterward he repented, and went.

30And he came to the second, and said likewise. And he answered and said, I *go,* sir: and went not.

31Whether of them twain did the will of *his* father? They say unto him, The first. Jesus saith unto them, Verily I say unto you, That the publicans and the harlots go into the kingdom of God before you.

32For John came unto you in the way of righteousness, and ye believed him not; but the publicans and the harlots believed him: and ye, when ye had seen *it,* repented not afterward, that ye might believe him.

33Hear another parable: There was a certain householder, which planted a vineyard, and hedged it round about, and digged a winepress in it, and built a tower, and let it out to husbandmen, and went into a far country:

34And when the time of the fruit drew near, he sent his servants to the husbandmen, that they might receive the fruits of it.

35And the husbandmen took his servants, and beat one, and killed another, and stoned another.

36Again, he sent other servants more than the first: and they did unto them likewise.

37But last of all he sent unto them his son, saying, They will reverence my son.

38But when the husbandmen saw the son, they said among themselves, This is the heir; come, let us kill him, and let us seize on his inheritance.

39And they caught him, and cast *him* out of the vineyard, and slew *him.*

40When the lord therefore of the vineyard cometh, what will he do unto those husbandmen?

41They say unto him, He will miserably destroy those wicked men, and will let out *his* vineyard unto other husbandmen, which shall render him the fruits in their seasons.

42Jesus saith unto them, Did ye never read in the scriptures, The stone which the builders rejected, the same is become the head of the corner: this is the Lord's doing, and it is marvellous in our eyes?

43Therefore say I unto you, The kingdom of God shall be taken from you, and given to a nation bringing forth the fruits thereof.

44And whosoever shall fall on this stone shall be broken: but on whomsoever it shall fall, it will grind him to powder.

45And when the chief priests and Pharisees had heard his parables, they perceived that he spake of them.

46But when they sought to lay hands on him, they feared the multitude, because they took him for a prophet.

PSALM 26:1–12

JUDGE me, O LORD; for I have walked in mine integrity: I have trusted also in the LORD; *therefore* I shall not slide.

2Examine me, O LORD, and prove me; try my reins and my heart.

3For thy lovingkindness *is* before mine eyes: and I have walked in thy truth.

4I have not sat with vain persons, neither will I go in with dissemblers.

5I have hated the congregation of evil doers; and will not sit with the wicked.

6I will wash mine hands in innocency: so will I compass thine altar, O LORD:

7That I may publish with the voice of thanksgiving, and tell of all thy wondrous works.

8LORD, I have loved the habitation of thy house, and the place where thine honour dwelleth.

9Gather not my soul with sinners, nor my life with bloody men:

10In whose hands *is* mischief, and their right hand is full of bribes.

11But as for me, I will walk in mine integrity: redeem me, and be merciful unto me.

12My foot standeth in an even place: in the congregations will I bless the LORD.

PROVERBS FOR TODAY/ 6:16–19

These six things *doth the* LORD *hate: yea, seven* are *an abomination unto him: A proud look, a lying tongue, and hands that shed innocent blood, An heart that deviseth wicked imaginations, feet that be swift in running to mischief, A false witness* that *speaketh lies, and he that soweth discord among brethren.*

FEBRUARY 2

EXODUS 15:20—17:7

AND Miriam the prophetess, the sister of Aaron, took a timbrel in her hand; and all the women went out after her with timbrels and with dances.

21And Miriam answered them, Sing ye to the LORD, for he hath triumphed gloriously; the horse and his rider hath he thrown into the sea.

22So Moses brought Israel from the Red sea, and they went out into the wilderness of Shur; and they went three days in the wilderness, and found no water.

23And when they came to Marah, they could not drink of the waters of Marah, for they *were* bitter: therefore the name of it was called Marah.

24And the people murmured against Moses, saying, What shall we drink?

25And he cried unto the LORD; and the LORD shewed him a tree, *which* when he had cast into the waters, the waters were made sweet: there he made for them a statute and an ordinance, and there he proved them,

26And said, If thou wilt diligently hearken to the voice of the LORD thy God, and wilt do that which is right in his sight, and wilt give ear to his commandments, and keep all his stat-utes, I will put none of these diseases upon thee, which I have brought upon the Egyptians: for I *am* the LORD that healeth thee.

27And they came to Elim, where *were* twelve wells of water, and threescore and ten palm trees: and they encamped there by the waters.

AND they took their journey from Elim, and all the congregation of the children of Israel came unto the wilderness of Sin, which *is* between Elim and Sinai, on the fifteenth day of the second month after their departing out of the land of Egypt.

2And the whole congregation of the children of Israel murmured against Moses and Aaron in the wilderness:

3And the children of Israel said unto them, Would to God we had died by the hand of the LORD in the land of Egypt, when we sat by the flesh pots, *and* when we did eat bread to the full; for ye have brought us forth into this wilderness, to kill this whole assembly with hunger.

4Then said the LORD unto Moses, Behold, I will rain bread from heaven for you; and the people shall go out and gather a certain rate every day, that I may prove them, whether they will walk in my law, or no.

5And it shall come to pass, that on the sixth day they shall prepare *that* which they bring in; and it shall be twice as much as they gather daily.

6And Moses and Aaron said unto all the children of Israel, At even, then ye shall know that the LORD hath brought you out from the land of Egypt:

7And in the morning, then ye shall see the glory of the LORD; for that he heareth your murmurings against the LORD: and what *are* we, that ye murmur against us?

8And Moses said, *This shall be,* when the LORD shall give you in the evening flesh to eat, and in the morning bread to the full; for that the LORD heareth your murmurings which ye murmur against him: and what *are* we? your murmurings *are* not against us, but against the LORD.

9And Moses spake unto Aaron, Say unto all the congregation of the children of Israel, Come near before the LORD: for he hath heard your murmurings.

10And it came to pass, as Aaron spake unto the whole congregation of the children of Israel, that they looked toward the wilderness, and, behold, the glory of the LORD appeared in the cloud.

11And the LORD spake unto Moses, saying,

12I have heard the murmurings of the children of Israel: speak unto them, saying, At even ye shall eat flesh, and in the morning ye shall be filled with bread; and ye shall know that I *am* the LORD your God.

13And it came to pass, that at even the quails came up, and covered the camp: and in the morning the dew lay round about the host.

14And when the dew that lay was gone up, behold, upon the face of the wilderness *there lay* a small round thing, *as* small as the hoar frost on the ground.

15And when the children of Israel saw

it, they said one to another, It *is* manna: for they wist not what it *was.* And Moses said unto them, This *is* the bread which the LORD hath given you to eat.

16This *is* the thing which the LORD hath commanded, Gather of it every man according to his eating, an omer for every man, *according to* the number of your persons; take ye every man for *them* which *are* in his tents.

17And the children of Israel did so, and gathered, some more, some less.

18And when they did mete *it* with an omer, he that gathered much had nothing over, and he that gathered little had no lack; they gathered every man according to his eating.

19And Moses said, Let no man leave of it till the morning.

20Notwithstanding they hearkened not unto Moses; but some of them left of it until the morning, and it bred worms, and stank: and Moses was wroth with them.

21And they gathered it every morning, every man according to his eating: and when the sun waxed hot, it melted.

22And it came to pass, *that* on the sixth day they gathered twice as much bread, two omers for one *man:* and all the rulers of the congregation came and told Moses.

23And he said unto them, This *is that* which the LORD hath said, To morrow *is* the rest of the holy sabbath unto the LORD: bake *that* which ye will bake *to day,* and seethe that ye will seethe; and that which remaineth over lay up for you to be kept until the morning.

24And they laid it up till the morning, as Moses bade: and it did not stink, neither was there any worm therein.

25And Moses said, Eat that to day; for to day *is* a sabbath unto the LORD: to day ye shall not find it in the field.

26Six days ye shall gather it; but on the seventh day, *which is* the sabbath, in it there shall be none.

27And it came to pass, *that* there went out *some* of the people on the seventh day for to gather, and they found none.

28And the LORD said unto Moses, How long refuse ye to keep my commandments and my laws?

29See, for that the LORD hath given you the sabbath, therefore he giveth you on the sixth day the bread of two days; abide ye every man in his place, let no man go out of his place on the seventh day.

30So the people rested on the seventh day.

31And the house of Israel called the name thereof Manna: and it *was* like coriander seed, white; and the taste of it *was* like wafers *made* with honey.

32And Moses said, This *is* the thing which the LORD commandeth, Fill an omer of it to be kept for your generations; that they may see the bread wherewith I have fed you in the wilderness, when I brought you forth from the land of Egypt.

33And Moses said unto Aaron, Take a pot, and put an omer full of manna therein, and lay it up before the LORD, to be kept for your generations.

34As the LORD commanded Moses, so Aaron laid it up before the Testimony, to be kept.

35And the children of Israel did eat manna forty years, until they came to a land inhabited; they did eat manna, until they came unto the borders of the land of Canaan.

36Now an omer *is* the tenth *part* of an ephah.

AND all the congregation of the children of Israel journeyed from the wilderness of Sin, after their journeys, according to the commandment of the LORD, and pitched in Rephidim: and *there was* no water for the people to drink.

2Wherefore the people did chide with Moses, and said, Give us water that we may drink. And Moses said unto them, Why chide ye with me? wherefore do ye tempt the LORD?

3And the people thirsted there for water; and the people murmured against Moses, and said, Wherefore *is* this *that* thou hast brought us up out of Egypt, to kill us and our children and our cattle with thirst?

4And Moses cried unto the LORD, saying, What shall I do unto this people? they be almost ready to stone me.

5And the LORD said unto Moses, Go on before the people, and take with thee of the elders of Israel; and thy rod, wherewith thou smotest the river, take in thine hand, and go.

6Behold, I will stand before thee there upon the rock in Horeb; and thou shalt smite the rock, and there shall come water out of it, that the people may drink. And Moses did so in the sight of the elders of Israel.

7And he called the name of the place Massah, and Meribah, because of the chiding of the children of Israel, and because they tempted the LORD, saying, Is the LORD among us, or not?

MATTHEW 22:1–32

AND Jesus answered and spake unto them again by parables, and said,

2The kingdom of heaven is like unto a certain king, which made a marriage for his son.

3And sent forth his servants to call them that were bidden to the wedding: and they would not come.

4Again, he sent forth other servants, saying, Tell them which are bidden, Behold, I have prepared my dinner: my oxen and *my* fatlings *are* killed, and all things *are* ready: come unto the marriage.

5But they made light of *it,* and went their ways, one to his farm, another to his merchandise:

6And the remnant took his servants, and entreated *them* spitefully, and slew *them.*

7But when the king heard *thereof,*

ne was wroth: and he sent forth his armies, and destroyed those murderers, and burned up their city.

8Then saith he to his servants, The wedding is ready, but they which were bidden were not worthy.

9Go ye therefore into the highways, and as many as ye shall find, bid to the marriage.

10So those servants went out into the highways, and gathered together all as many as they found, both bad and good: and the wedding was furnished with guests.

11And when the king came in to see the guests, he saw there a man which had not on a wedding garment:

12And he saith unto him, Friend, how camest thou in hither not having a wedding garment? And he was speechless.

13Then said the king to the servants, Bind him hand and foot, and take him away, and cast *him* into outer darkness; there shall be weeping and gnashing of teeth.

14For many are called, but few *are* chosen.

15Then went the Pharisees, and took counsel how they might entangle him in *his* talk.

16And they sent out unto him their disciples with the Herodians, saying, Master, we know that thou art true, and teachest the way of God in truth, neither carest thou for any *man:* for thou regardest not the person of men.

17Tell us therefore, What thinkest thou? Is it lawful to give tribute unto Caesar, or not?

18But Jesus perceived their wickedness, and said, Why tempt ye me, *ye* hypocrites?

19Shew me the tribute money. And they brought unto him a penny.

20And he saith unto them, Whose *is* this image and superscription?

21They say unto him, Caesar's. Then saith he unto them, Render therefore unto Caesar the things which are Cae-

sar's; and unto God the things that are God's.

22When they had heard *these words,* they marvelled, and left him, and went their way.

23The same day came to him the Sadducees, which say that there is no resurrection, and asked him,

24Saying, Master, Moses said, If a man die, having no children, his brother shall marry his wife, and raise up seed unto his brother.

25Now there were with us seven brethren: and the first, when he had married a wife, deceased, and, having no issue, left his wife unto his brother:

26Likewise the second also, and the third, unto the seventh.

27And last of all the woman died also.

28Therefore in the resurrection whose wife shall she be of the seven? for they all had her.

29Jesus answered and said unto them, Ye do err, not knowing the scriptures, nor the power of God.

30For in the resurrection they neither marry, nor are given in marriage, but are as the angels of God in heaven.

31But as touching the resurrection of the dead, have ye not read that which was spoken unto you by God, saying,

32I am the God of Abraham, and the God of Isaac, and the God of Jacob? God is not the God of the dead, but of the living.

PSALM 27:1–7

THE LORD *is* my light and my salvation; whom shall I fear? the LORD *is* the strength of my life; of whom shall I be afraid?

2When the wicked, *even* mine enemies and my foes, came upon me to eat up my flesh, they stumbled and fell.

3Though an host should encamp against me, my heart shall not fear: though war should rise against me, in this *will* I *be* confident.

4One *thing* have I desired of the LORD, that will I seek after; that I may dwell in the house of the LORD all the days of my life, to behold the beauty of the LORD, and to enquire in his temple.

5For in the time of trouble he shall hide me in his pavilion: in the secret of his tabernacle shall he hide me; he shall set me up upon a rock.

6And now shall mine head be lifted up above mine enemies round about me: therefore will I offer in his tabernacle sacrifices of joy; I will sing, yea, I will sing praises unto the LORD.

7Hear, O LORD, *when* I cry with my voice: have mercy also upon me, and answer me.

PROVERBS FOR TODAY/ 6:20–26

My son, keep thy father's commandment, and forsake not the law of thy mother: Bind them continually upon thine heart, and tie them about thy neck. When thou goest, it shall lead thee; when thou sleepest, it shall keep thee; and when thou awakest, it shall talk with thee. For the commandment is a lamp; and the law is light; and reproofs of instruction are the way of life: To keep thee from the evil woman, from the flattery of the tongue of a strange woman. Lust not after her beauty in thine heart; neither let her take thee with her eyelids. For by means of a whorish woman a man is brought to a piece of bread: and the adulteress will hunt for the precious life.

FEBRUARY 3

EXODUS 17:8—19:15

THEN came Amalek, and fought with Israel in Rephidim.

9And Moses said unto Joshua, Choose us out men, and go out, fight with Amalek: to morrow I will stand on the top of the hill with the rod of God in mine hand.

10So Joshua did as Moses had said to him, and fought with Amalek: and Moses, Aaron, and Hur went up to the top of the hill.

11And it came to pass, when Moses held up his hand, that Israel prevailed: and when he let down his hand, Amalek prevailed.

12But Moses' hands *were* heavy; and they took a stone, and put *it* under him, and he sat thereon; and Aaron and Hur stayed up his hands, the one on the one side, and the other on the other side; and his hands were steady until the going down of the sun.

13And Joshua discomfited Amalek and his people with the edge of the sword.

14And the LORD said unto Moses, Write this *for* a memorial in a book, and rehearse *it* in the ears of Joshua: for I will utterly put out the remembrance of Amalek from under heaven.

15And Moses built an altar, and called the name of it Jehovah–nissi:

16For he said, Because the LORD hath sworn *that* the LORD *will have* war with Amalek from generation to generation.

WHEN Jethro, the priest of Midian, Moses' father in law, heard of all that God had done for Moses, and for Israel his people, *and* that the LORD had brought Israel out of Egypt;

2Then Jethro, Moses' father in law,

took Zipporah, Moses' wife, after he had sent her back,

3And her two sons; of which the name of the one *was* Gershom; for he said, I have been an alien in a strange land:

4And the name of the other *was* Eliezer; for the God of my father, *said he, was* mine help, and delivered me from the sword of Pharaoh:

5And Jethro, Moses' father in law, came with his sons and his wife unto Moses into the wilderness, where he encamped at the mount of God:

6And he said unto Moses, I thy father in law Jethro am come unto thee, and thy wife, and her two sons with her.

7And Moses went out to meet his father in law, and did obeisance, and kissed him; and they asked each other of *their* welfare; and they came into the tent.

8And Moses told his father in law all that the LORD had done unto Pharaoh and to the Egyptians for Israel's sake, *and* all the travail that had come upon them by the way, and *how* the LORD delivered them.

9And Jethro rejoiced for all the goodness which the LORD had done to Israel, whom he had delivered out of the hand of the Egyptians.

10And Jethro said, Blessed *be* the LORD, who hath delivered you out of the hand of the Egyptians, and out of the hand of Pharaoh, who hath delivered the people from under the hand of the Egyptians.

11Now I know that the LORD *is* greater than all gods: for in the thing wherein they dealt proudly *he was* above them.

12And Jethro, Moses' father in law, took a burnt offering and sacrifices for God: and Aaron came, and all the elders of Israel, to eat bread with Moses' father in law before God.

13And it came to pass on the morrow, that Moses sat to judge the people: and the people stood by Moses from the morning unto the evening.

14And when Moses' father in law saw all that he did to the people, he said, What *is* this thing that thou doest to the people? why sittest thou thyself alone, and all the people stand by thee from morning unto even?

15And Moses said unto his father in law, Because the people come unto me to enquire of God:

16When they have a matter, they come unto me; and I judge between one and another, and I do make *them* know the statutes of God, and his laws.

17And Moses' father in law said unto him, The thing that thou doest *is* not good.

18Thou wilt surely wear away, both thou, and this people that *is* with thee: for this thing *is* too heavy for thee; thou art not able to perform it thyself alone.

19Hearken now unto my voice, I will give thee counsel, and God shall be with thee: Be thou for the people to Godward, that thou mayest bring the causes unto God:

20And thou shalt teach them ordinances and laws, and shalt shew them the way wherein they must walk, and the work that they must do.

21Moreover thou shalt provide out of all the people able men, such as fear God, men of truth, hating covetousness; and place *such* over them, *to be* rulers of thousands, *and* rulers of hundreds, rulers of fifties, and rulers of tens:

22And let them judge the people at all seasons: and it shall be, *that* every great matter they shall bring unto thee, but every small matter they shall judge: so shall it be easier for thyself, and they shall bear *the burden* with thee.

23If thou shalt do this thing, and God command thee *so,* then thou shalt be able to endure, and all this people shall also go to their place in peace.

24So Moses hearkened to the voice of his father in law, and did all that he had said.

25And Moses chose able men out of

all Israel, and made them heads over the people, rulers of thousands, rulers of hundreds, rulers of fifties, and rulers of tens.

26And they judged the people at all seasons: the hard causes they brought unto Moses, but every small matter they judged themselves.

27And Moses let his father in law depart; and he went his way into his own land.

IN the third month, when the children of Israel were gone forth out of the land of Egypt, the same day came they *into* the wilderness of Sinai.

2For they were departed from Rephidim, and were come *to* the desert of Sinai, and had pitched in the wilderness; and there Israel camped before the mount.

3And Moses went up unto God, and the LORD called unto him out of the mountain, saying, Thus shalt thou say to the house of Jacob, and tell the children of Israel;

4Ye have seen what I did unto the Egyptians, and *how* I bare you on eagles' wings, and brought you unto myself.

5Now therefore, if ye will obey my voice indeed, and keep my covenant, then ye shall be a peculiar treasure unto me above all people: for all the earth *is* mine:

6And ye shall be unto me a kingdom of priests, and an holy nation. These *are* the words which thou shalt speak unto the children of Israel.

7And Moses came and called for the elders of the people, and laid before their faces all these words which the LORD commanded him.

8And all the people answered together, and said, All that the LORD hath spoken we will do. And Moses returned the words of the people unto the LORD.

9And the LORD said unto Moses, Lo, I come unto thee in a thick cloud, that the people may hear when I speak with thee, and believe thee for ever. And

Moses told the words of the people unto the LORD.

10And the LORD said unto Moses, Go unto the people, and sanctify them today and tomorrow, and let them wash their clothes,

11And be ready against the third day: for the third day the LORD will come down in the sight of all the people upon mount Sinai.

12And thou shalt set bounds unto the people round about, saying, Take heed to yourselves, *that ye* go *not* up into the mount, or touch the border of it: whosoever toucheth the mount shall be surely put to death:

13There shall not an hand touch it, but he shall surely be stoned, or shot through; whether *it be* beast or man, it shall not live: when the trumpet soundeth long, they shall come up to the mount.

14And Moses went down from the mount unto the people, and sanctified the people; and they washed their clothes.

15And he said unto the people, Be ready against the third day: come not at *your* wives.

MATTHEW 22:33—23:12

AND when the multitude heard *this,* they were astonished at his [Jesus'] doctrine.

34But when the Pharisees had heard that he had put the Sadducees to silence, they were gathered together.

35Then one of them, *which was* a lawyer, asked *him a question,* tempting him, and saying,

36Master, which *is* the great commandment in the law?

37Jesus said unto him, Thou shalt love the Lord thy God with all thy heart, and with all thy soul, and with all thy mind.

38This is the first and great commandment.

39And the second *is* like unto it, Thou

...alt love thy neighbour as thyself.

40On these two commandments hang all the law and the prophets.

41While the Pharisees were gathered together, Jesus asked them,

42Saying, What think ye of Christ? whose son is he? They say unto him, *The son* of David.

43He saith unto them, How then doth David in spirit call him Lord, saying,

44The LORD said unto my Lord, Sit thou on my right hand, till I make thine enemies thy footstool?

45If David then call him, Lord, how is he his son?

46And no man was able to answer him a word, neither durst any *man* from that day forth ask him any more *questions.*

THEN spake Jesus to the multitude, and to his disciples,

2Saying, The scribes and the Pharisees sit in Moses' seat:

3All therefore whatsoever they bid you observe, *that* observe and do; but do not ye after their works: for they say, and do not.

4For they bind heavy burdens and grievous to be borne, and lay *them* on men's shoulders; but they *themselves* will not move them with one of their fingers.

5But all their works they do for to be seen of men: they make broad their phylacteries, and enlarge the borders of their garments,

6And love the uppermost rooms at feasts, and the chief seats in the synagogues,

7And greetings in the markets, and

to be called of men, Rabbi, Rabbi.

8But be not ye called Rabbi: for one is your Master, *even* Christ; and all ye are brethren.

9And call no *man* your father upon the earth: for one is your Father, which is in heaven.

10Neither be ye called masters: for one is your Master, *even* Christ.

11But he that is greatest among you shall be your servant.

12And whosoever shall exalt himself shall be abased; and he that shall humble himself shall be exalted.

PSALM 27:8–14

WHEN *thou saidst,* Seek ye my face; my heart said unto thee, Thy face, LORD, will I seek.

9Hide not thy face *far* from me; put not thy servant away in anger: thou hast been my help; leave me not, neither forsake me, O God of my salvation.

10When my father and my mother forsake me, then the LORD will take me up.

11Teach me thy way, O LORD, and lead me in a plain path, because of mine enemies.

12Deliver me not over unto the will of mine enemies: for false witnesses are risen up against me, and such as breathe out cruelty.

13*I had fainted,* unless I had believed to see the goodness of the LORD in the land of the living.

14Wait on the LORD: be of good courage, and he shall strengthen thine heart: wait, I say, on the LORD.

PROVERBS FOR TODAY/ 6:27–35

Can a man take fire in his bosom, and his clothes not be burned? Can one go upon hot coals, and his feet not be burned? So he that goeth in to his neighbour's wife; whosoever toucheth her shall not be innocent. □ Men *do not despise a thief, if he steal to satisfy his soul when he is hungry; But* if *he be found, he shall restore sevenfold; he shall give all the substance of his house. But whoso committeth adultery with a woman lacketh understanding: he that doeth it destroyeth his own soul. A wound and dishonour shall he get; and his reproach shall not be wiped away. For jealousy is the rage of a man: therefore he will not spare in the day of vengeance. He will not regard any ransom; neither will he rest content, though thou givest many gifts.*

FEBRUARY 4

EXODUS 19:16—21:21

AND it came to pass on the third day in the morning, that there were thunders and lightnings, and a thick cloud upon the mount, and the voice of the trumpet exceeding loud; so that all the people that *was* in the camp trembled.

17And Moses brought forth the people out of the camp to meet with God; and they stood at the nether part of the mount.

18And mount Sinai was altogether on a smoke, because the LORD descended upon it in fire: and the smoke thereof ascended as the smoke of a furnace, and the whole mount quaked greatly.

19And when the voice of the trumpet sounded long, and waxed louder and louder, Moses spake, and God answered him by a voice.

20And the LORD came down upon mount Sinai, on the top of the mount: and the LORD called Moses *up* to the top of the mount; and Moses went up.

21And the LORD said unto Moses, Go down, charge the people, lest they break through unto the LORD to gaze, and many of them perish.

22And let the priests also, which come near to the LORD, sanctify themselves, lest the LORD break forth upon them.

23And Moses said unto the LORD, The people cannot come up to mount Sinai: for thou chargedst us, saying, Set bounds about the mount, and sanctify it.

24And the LORD said unto him, Away, get thee down, and thou shalt come up, thou, and Aaron with thee: but let not the priests and the people break through to come up unto the LORD, lest he break forth upon them.

25So Moses went down unto the people, and spake unto them.

AND God spake all these words, saying,

2I *am* the LORD thy God, which have brought thee out of the land of Egypt, out of the house of bondage.

3Thou shalt have no other gods before me.

4Thou shalt not make unto thee any graven image, or any likeness *of any thing* that *is* in heaven above, or that *is* in the earth beneath, or that *is* in the water under the earth:

5Thou shalt not bow down thyself to them, nor serve them: for I the LORD thy God *am* a jealous God, visiting the iniquity of the fathers upon the children unto the third and fourth *generation* of them that hate me;

6And shewing mercy unto thousands of them that love me, and keep my commandments.

7Thou shalt not take the name of the LORD thy God in vain; for the LORD will not hold him guiltless that taketh his name in vain.

8Remember the sabbath day, to keep it holy.

9Six days shalt thou labour, and do all thy work:

10But the seventh day *is* the sabbath of the LORD thy God: *in it* thou shalt not do any work, thou, nor thy son, nor thy daughter, thy manservant, nor thy maidservant, nor thy cattle, nor thy stranger that *is* within thy gates:

11For *in* six days the LORD made heaven and earth, the sea, and all that in them *is,* and rested the seventh day: wherefore the LORD blessed the sabbath day, and hallowed it.

12Honour thy father and thy mother: that thy days may be long upon the land which the LORD thy God giveth thee.

13Thou shalt not kill.

14Thou shalt not commit adultery.

15Thou shalt not steal.

16Thou shalt not bear false witness against thy neighbour.

17Thou shalt not covet thy neighbour's house, thou shalt not covet thy neighbour's wife, nor his manservant, nor his maidservant, nor his ox, nor his ass, nor any thing that *is* thy neighbour's.

18And all the people saw the thunderings, and the lightnings, and the noise of the trumpet, and the mountain smoking: and when the people saw *it,* they removed, and stood afar off.

19And they said unto Moses, Speak thou with us, and we will hear: but let not God speak with us, lest we die.

20And Moses said unto the people, Fear not: for God is come to prove you, and that his fear may be before your faces, that ye sin not.

21And the people stood afar off, and Moses drew near unto the thick darkness where God *was*.

22And the LORD said unto Moses, Thus thou shalt say unto the children of Israel, Ye have seen that I have talked with you from heaven.

23Ye shall not make with me gods of silver, neither shall ye make unto you gods of gold.

24An altar of earth thou shalt make unto me, and shalt sacrifice thereon thy burnt offerings, and thy peace offerings, thy sheep, and thine oxen: in all places where I record my name I will come unto thee, and I will bless thee.

25And if thou wilt make me an altar of stone, thou shalt not build it of hewn stone: for if thou lift up thy tool upon it, thou hast polluted it.

26Neither shalt thou go up by steps unto mine altar, that thy nakedness be not discovered thereon.

Now these *are* the judgments which thou shalt set before them.

2If thou buy an Hebrew servant, six years he shall serve: and in the seventh he shall go out free for nothing.

3If he came in by himself, he shall go out by himself: if he were married, then his wife shall go out with him.

4If his master have given him a wife, and she have born him sons or daughters; the wife and her children shall be her master's, and he shall go out by himself.

5And if the servant shall plainly say, I love my master, my wife, and my children; I will not go out free:

6Then his master shall bring him unto the judges; he shall also bring him to the door, or unto the door post; and his master shall bore his ear through with an aul; and he shall serve him for ever.

7And if a man sell his daughter to be a maidservant, she shall not go out as the menservants do.

8If she please not her master, who hath betrothed her to himself, then shall he let her be redeemed: to sell her unto a strange nation he shall have no power, seeing he hath dealt deceitfully with her.

9And if he have betrothed her unto his son, he shall deal with her after the manner of daughters.

10If he take him another *wife;* her food, her raiment, and her duty of marriage, shall he not diminish.

11And if he do not these three unto

her, then shall she go out free without money.

12He that smiteth a man, so that he die, shall be surely put to death.

13And if a man lie not in wait, but God deliver *him* into his hand; then I will appoint thee a place whither he shall flee.

14But if a man come presumptuously upon his neighbour, to slay him with guile; thou shalt take him from mine altar, that he may die.

15And he that smiteth his father, or his mother, shall be surely put to death.

16And he that stealeth a man, and selleth him, or if he be found in his hand, he shall surely be put to death.

17And he that curseth his father, or his mother, shall surely be put to death.

18And if men strive together, and one smite another with a stone, or with *his* fist, and he die not, but keepeth *his* bed:

19If he rise again, and walk abroad upon his staff, then shall he that smote *him* be quit: only he shall pay *for* the loss of his time, and shall cause *him* to be thoroughly healed.

20And if a man smite his servant, or his maid, with a rod, and he die under his hand; he shall be surely punished.

21Notwithstanding, if he continue a day or two, he shall not be punished: for he *is* his money.

MATTHEW 23:13–39

BUT woe unto you, scribes and Pharisees, hypocrites! for ye shut up the kingdom of heaven against men: for ye neither go in *yourselves,* neither suffer ye them that are entering to go in.

14Woe unto you, scribes and Pharisees, hypocrites! for ye devour widows' houses, and for a pretence make long prayer: therefore ye shall receive the greater damnation.

15Woe unto you, scribes and Pharisees, hypocrites! for ye compass sea and land to make one proselyte, and when he is made, ye make him twofold more the child of hell than yourselves.

16Woe unto you, *ye* blind guides, which say, Whosoever shall swear by the temple, it is nothing; but whosoever shall swear by the gold of the temple, he is a debtor!

17*Ye* fools and blind: for whether is greater, the gold, or the temple that sanctifieth the gold?

18And, Whosoever shall swear by the altar, it is nothing; but whosoever sweareth by the gift that is upon it, he is guilty.

19*Ye* fools and blind: for whether *is* greater, the gift, or the altar that sanctifieth the gift?

20Whoso therefore shall swear by the altar, sweareth by it, and by all things thereon.

21And whoso shall swear by the temple, sweareth by it, and by him that dwelleth therein.

22And he that shall swear by heaven, sweareth by the throne of God, and by him that sitteth thereon.

23Woe unto you, scribes and Pharisees, hypocrites! for ye pay tithe of mint and anise and cummin, and have omitted the weightier *matters* of the law, judgment, mercy, and faith: these ought ye to have done, and not to leave the other undone.

24*Ye* blind guides, which strain at a gnat, and swallow a camel.

25Woe unto you, scribes and Pharisees, hypocrites! for ye make clean the outside of the cup and of the platter, but within they are full of extortion and excess.

26*Thou* blind Pharisee, cleanse first that *which is* within the cup and platter, that the outside of them may be clean also.

27Woe unto you, scribes and Pharisees, hypocrites! for ye are like unto whited sepulchres, which indeed appear beautiful outward, but are within full of dead *men's* bones, and of all uncleanness.

28Even so ye also outwardly appear righteous unto men, but within ye are full of hypocrisy and iniquity.

29Woe unto you, scribes and Pharisees, hypocrites! because ye build the tombs of the prophets, and garnish the sepulchres of the righteous,

30And say, If we had been in the days of our fathers, we would not have been partakers with them in the blood of the prophets.

31Wherefore ye be witnesses unto yourselves, that ye are the children of them which killed the prophets.

32Fill ye up then the measure of your fathers.

33*Ye* serpents, *ye* generation of vipers, how can ye escape the damnation of hell?

34Wherefore, behold, I send unto you prophets, and wise men, and scribes: and *some* of them ye shall kill and crucify; and *some* of them shall ye scourge in your synagogues, and persecute *them* from city to city:

35That upon you may come all the righteous blood shed upon the earth, from the blood of righteous Abel unto the blood of Zacharias son of Barachias, whom ye slew between the temple and the altar.

36Verily I say unto you, All these things shall come upon this generation.

37O Jerusalem, Jerusalem, *thou* that killest the prophets, and stonest them which are sent unto thee, how often would I have gathered thy children together, even as a hen gathereth her chickens under *her* wings, and ye would not!

38Behold, your house is left unto you desolate.

39For I say unto you, Ye shall not see me henceforth, till ye shall say, Blessed *is* he that cometh in the name of the Lord.

PSALM 28:1–9

UNTO thee will I cry, O LORD my rock; be not silent to me: lest, *if* thou be silent to me, I become like them that go down into the pit.

2Hear the voice of my supplications, when I cry unto thee, when I lift up my hands toward thy holy oracle.

3Draw me not away with the wicked, and with the workers of iniquity, which speak peace to their neighbours, but mischief *is* in their hearts.

4Give them according to their deeds, and according to the wickedness of their endeavours: give them after the work of their hands; render to them their desert.

5Because they regard not the works of the LORD, nor the operation of his hands, he shall destroy them, and not build them up.

6Blessed *be* the LORD, because he hath heard the voice of my supplications.

7The LORD *is* my strength and my shield; my heart trusted in him, and I am helped: therefore my heart greatly rejoiceth; and with my song will I praise him.

8The LORD *is* their strength, and he *is* the saving strength of his anointed.

9Save thy people, and bless thine inheritance: feed them also, and lift them up for ever.

PROVERBS FOR TODAY/ 7:1–5

My son, keep my words, and lay up my commandments with thee. Keep my commandments, and live; and my law as the apple of thine eye. Bind them upon thy fingers, write them upon the table of thine heart. Say unto wisdom, Thou art *my*

sister; and call understanding thy kinswoman: That they may keep thee from the strange woman, from the stranger which flattereth with her words.

FEBRUARY 5

EXODUS 21:22—23:13

IF men strive, and hurt a woman with child, so that her fruit depart *from her,* and yet no mischief follow: he shall be surely punished, according as the woman's husband will lay upon him; and he shall pay as the judges *determine.*

23And if *any* mischief follow, then thou shalt give life for life,

24Eye for eye, tooth for tooth, hand for hand, foot for foot,

25Burning for burning, wound for wound, stripe for stripe.

26And if a man smite the eye of his servant, or the eye of his maid, that it perish; he shall let him go free for his eye's sake.

27And if he smite out his manservant's tooth, or his maidservant's tooth; he shall let him go free for his tooth's sake.

28If an ox gore a man or a woman, that they die: then the ox shall be surely stoned, and his flesh shall not be eaten; but the owner of the ox *shall be* quit.

29But if the ox were wont to push with his horn in time past, and it hath been testified to his owner, and he hath not kept him in, but that he hath killed a man or a woman; the ox shall be stoned, and his owner also shall be put to death.

30If there be laid on him a sum of money, then he shall give for the ransom of his life whatsoever is laid upon him.

31Whether he have gored a son, or have gored a daughter, according to this judgment shall it be done unto him.

32If the ox shall push a manservant or a maidservant; he shall give unto their master thirty shekels of silver, and the ox shall be stoned.

33And if a man shall open a pit, or a man shall dig a pit, and not cover it, and an ox or an ass fall therein;

34The owner of the pit shall make *it* good, *and* give money unto the owner of them; and the dead *beast* shall be his.

35And if one man's ox hurt another's, that he die; then they shall sell the live ox, and divide the money of it; and the dead *ox* also they shall divide.

36Or if it be known that the ox hath used to push in time past, and his owner hath not kept him in; he shall surely pay ox for ox; and the dead shall be his own.

IF a man shall steal an ox, or a sheep, and kill it, or sell it; he shall restore five oxen for an ox, and four sheep for a sheep.

2If a thief be found breaking up, and be smitten that he die, *there shall* no blood *be shed* for him.

3If the sun be risen upon him, *there shall be* blood *shed* for him; *for* he should make full restitution; if he have nothing, then he shall be sold for his theft.

4If the theft be certainly found in his hand alive, whether it be ox, or ass, or sheep; he shall restore double.

5If a man shall cause a field or vineyard to be eaten, and shall put in his beast, and shall feed in another man's field; of the best of his own field, and of the best of his own vineyard, shall he make restitution.

⁶If fire break out, and catch in thorns, so that the stacks of corn, or the standing corn, or the field, be consumed *therewith;* he that kindled the fire shall surely make restitution.

⁷If a man shall deliver unto his neighbour money or stuff to keep, and it be stolen out of the man's house; if the thief be found, let him pay double.

⁸If the thief be not found, then the master of the house shall be brought unto the judges, *to see* whether he have put his hand unto his neighbour's goods.

⁹For all manner of trespass, *whether it be* for ox, for ass, for sheep, for raiment, *or* for any manner of lost thing, which *another* challengeth to be his, the cause of both parties shall come before the judges; *and* whom the judges shall condemn, he shall pay double unto his neighbour.

¹⁰If a man deliver unto his neighbour an ass, or an ox, or a sheep, or any beast, to keep; and it die, or be hurt, or driven away, no man seeing *it:*

¹¹*Then* shall an oath of the LORD be between them both, that he hath not put his hand unto his neighbour's goods; and the owner of it shall accept *thereof,* and he shall not make *it* good.

¹²And if it be stolen from him, he shall make restitution unto the owner thereof.

¹³If it be torn in pieces, *then* let him bring it *for* witness, *and* he shall not make good that which was torn.

¹⁴And if a man borrow *ought* of his neighbour, and it be hurt, or die, the owner thereof *being* not with it, he shall surely make *it* good.

¹⁵*But* if the owner thereof *be* with it, he shall not make *it* good: if it *be* an hired *thing,* it came for his hire.

¹⁶And if a man entice a maid that is not betrothed, and lie with her, he shall surely endow her to be his wife.

¹⁷If her father utterly refuse to give her unto him, he shall pay money according to the dowry of virgins.

¹⁸Thou shalt not suffer a witch to live.

¹⁹Whosoever lieth with a beast shall surely be put to death.

²⁰He that sacrificeth unto *any* god, save unto the LORD only, he shall be utterly destroyed.

²¹Thou shalt neither vex a stranger, nor oppress him: for ye were strangers in the land of Egypt.

²²Ye shall not afflict any widow, or fatherless child.

²³If thou afflict them in any wise, and they cry at all unto me, I will surely hear their cry;

²⁴And my wrath shall wax hot, and I will kill you with the sword; and your wives shall be widows, and your children fatherless.

²⁵If thou lend money to *any of* my people *that is* poor by thee, thou shalt not be to him as an usurer, neither shalt thou lay upon him usury.

²⁶If thou at all take thy neighbour's raiment to pledge, thou shalt deliver it unto him by that the sun goeth down:

²⁷For that *is* his covering only, it *is* his raiment for his skin: wherein shall he sleep? and it shall come to pass, when he crieth unto me, that I will hear; for I *am* gracious.

²⁸Thou shalt not revile the gods, nor curse the ruler of thy people.

²⁹Thou shalt not delay *to offer* the first of thy ripe fruits, and of thy liquors: the firstborn of thy sons shalt thou give unto me.

³⁰Likewise shalt thou do with thine oxen, *and* with thy sheep: seven days it shall be with his dam; on the eighth day thou shalt give it me.

³¹And ye shall be holy men unto me: neither shall ye eat *any* flesh *that is* torn of beasts in the field; ye shall cast it to the dogs.

THOU shalt not raise a false report: put not thine hand with the wicked to be an unrighteous witness.

2Thou shalt not follow a multitude to *do* evil; neither shalt thou speak in a cause to decline after many to wrest *judgment:*

3Neither shalt thou countenance a poor man in his cause.

4If thou meet thine enemy's ox or his ass going astray, thou shalt surely bring it back to him again.

5If thou see the ass of him that hateth thee lying under his burden, and wouldest forbear to help him, thou shalt surely help with him.

6Thou shalt not wrest the judgment of thy poor in his cause.

7Keep thee far from a false matter; and the innocent and righteous slay thou not: for I will not justify the wicked.

8And thou shalt take no gift: for the gift blindeth the wise, and perverteth the words of the righteous.

9Also thou shalt not oppress a stranger: for ye know the heart of a stranger, seeing ye were strangers in the land of Egypt.

10And six years thou shalt sow thy land, and shalt gather in the fruits thereof:

11But the seventh *year* thou shalt let it rest and lie still; that the poor of thy people may eat: and what they leave the beasts of the field shall eat. In like manner thou shalt deal with thy vineyard, *and* with thy olive yard.

12Six days thou shalt do thy work, and on the seventh day thou shalt rest: that thine ox and thine ass may rest, and the son of thy handmaid, and the stranger, may be refreshed.

13And in all *things* that I have said unto you be circumspect: and make no mention of the name of other gods, neither let it be heard out of thy mouth.

MATTHEW 24:1–28

AND Jesus went out, and departed from the temple: and his disciples came to *him* for to shew him the buildings of the temple.

2And Jesus said unto them, See ye not all these things? verily I say unto you, There shall not be left here one stone upon another, that shall not be thrown down.

3And as he sat upon the mount of Olives, the disciples came unto him privately, saying, Tell us, when shall these things be? and what *shall be* the sign of thy coming, and of the end of the world?

4And Jesus answered and said unto them, Take heed that no man deceive you.

5For many shall come in my name, saying, I am Christ; and shall deceive many.

6And ye shall hear of wars and rumours of wars: see that ye be not troubled: for all *these things* must come to pass, but the end is not yet.

7For nation shall rise against nation, and kingdom against kingdom: and there shall be famines, and pestilences, and earthquakes, in divers places.

8All these *are* the beginning of sorrows.

9Then shall they deliver you up to be afflicted, and shall kill you: and ye shall be hated of all nations for my name's sake.

10And then shall many be offended, and shall betray one another, and shall hate one another.

11And many false prophets shall rise, and shall deceive many.

12And because iniquity shall abound, the love of many shall wax cold.

13But he that shall endure unto the end, the same shall be saved.

14And this gospel of the kingdom shall be preached in all the world for a witness unto all nations; and then shall the end come.

15When ye therefore shall see the abomination of desolation, spoken of by Daniel the prophet, stand in the holy place, (whoso readeth, let him understand:)

16Then let them which be in Judaea

flee into the mountains:

17Let him which is on the housetop not come down to take any thing out of his house:

18Neither let him which is in the field return back to take his clothes.

19And woe unto them that are with child, and to them that give suck in those days!

20But pray ye that your flight be not in the winter, neither on the sabbath day:

21For then shall be great tribulation, such as was not since the beginning of the world to this time, no, nor ever shall be.

22And except those days should be shortened, there should no flesh be saved: but for the elect's sake those days shall be shortened.

23Then if any man shall say unto you, Lo, here *is* Christ, or there; believe *it* not.

24For there shall arise false Christs, and false prophets, and shall shew great signs and wonders; insomuch that, if *it were* possible, they shall deceive the very elect.

25Behold, I have told you before.

26Wherefore if they shall say unto you, Behold, he is in the desert; go not forth: behold, *he is* in the secret chambers; believe *it* not.

27For as the lightning cometh out of the east, shineth even unto the west; so shall also the coming of the Son of man be.

28For wheresoever the carcase is, there will the eagles be gathered together.

PSALM 29:1–11

Give unto the Lord, O ye mighty, give unto the Lord glory and strength.

2Give unto the Lord the glory due unto his name; worship the Lord in the beauty of holiness.

3The voice of the Lord *is* upon the waters: the God of glory thundereth: the Lord *is* upon many waters.

4The voice of the Lord *is* powerful; the voice of the Lord *is* full of majesty.

5The voice of the Lord breaketh the cedars; yea, the Lord breaketh the cedars of Lebanon.

6He maketh them also to skip like a calf; Lebanon and Sirion like a young unicorn.

7The voice of the Lord divideth the flames of fire.

8The voice of the Lord shaketh the wilderness; the Lord shaketh the wilderness of Kadesh.

9The voice of the Lord maketh the hinds to calve, and discovereth the forests: and in his temple doth every one speak of *his* glory.

10The Lord sitteth upon the flood; yea, the Lord sitteth King for ever.

11The Lord will give strength unto his people; the Lord will bless his people with peace.

PROVERBS FOR TODAY/ 7:6–23

For at the window of my house I looked through my casement, And beheld among the simple ones, I discerned among the youths, a young man void of understanding, Passing through the street near her corner; and he went the way to her house, In the twilight, in the evening, in the black and dark night: And, behold, there met him a woman with *the attire of an harlot, and subtil of heart. (She* is *loud and stubborn; her feet abide not in her house: Now* is *she* without, *now in the streets, and lieth in wait at every corner.) So she caught him, and kissed him,* and *with an impudent face said unto him,* I have *peace offerings with me; this day have I payed my vows. Therefore came I forth to meet thee, diligently to seek thy face, and I have found thee. I have decked my bed with coverings of tapestry, with carved* works, *with fine linen of Egypt. I have perfumed my bed with myrrh, aloes, and cinnamon. Come, let us take our fill of love until the morning: let us solace ourselves with loves. For the goodman* is *not at home, he is gone a long journey: He hath taken a bag of money with him,* and *will come home at the day appointed. With her much fair speech she caused him to yield, with the flattering of her lips she forced him. He goeth after her straightway, as an ox goeth to the slaughter, or as a fool to the correction of the stocks; Till a dart strike through his liver; as a bird hasteth to the snare, and knoweth not that it* is *for his life.*

FEBRUARY 6

EXODUS 23:14—25:40

THREE times thou shalt keep a feast unto me in the year.

15Thou shalt keep the feast of unleavened bread: (thou shalt eat unleavened bread seven days, as I commanded thee, in the time appointed of the month Abib; for in it thou camest out from Egypt: and none shall appear before me empty:)

16And the feast of harvest, the firstfruits of thy labours, which thou hast sown in the field: and the feast of ingathering, *which is* in the end of the year, when thou hast gathered in thy labours out of the field.

17Three times in the year all thy males shall appear before the Lord GOD.

18Thou shalt not offer the blood of my sacrifice with leavened bread; neither shall the fat of my sacrifice remain until the morning.

19The first of the firstfruits of thy land thou shalt bring into the house of the LORD thy God. Thou shalt not seethe a kid in his mother's milk.

20Behold, I send an Angel before thee, to keep thee in the way, and to bring thee into the place which I have prepared.

21Beware of him, and obey his voice, provoke him not; for he will not pardon your transgressions: for my name *is* in him.

22But if thou shalt indeed obey his voice, and do all that I speak; then I will be an enemy unto thine enemies, and an adversary unto thine adversaries.

23For mine Angel shall go before thee, and bring thee in unto the Amorites, and the Hittites, and the Perizzites, and the Canaanites, the Hivites, and the Jebusites: and I will cut them off.

24Thou shalt not bow down to their gods, nor serve them, nor do after their works: but thou shalt utterly overthrow them, and quite break down their images.

25And ye shall serve the LORD your God, and he shall bless thy bread, and thy water; and I will take sickness away from the midst of thee.

26There shall nothing cast their young, nor be barren, in thy land: the number of thy days I will fulfil.

27I will send my fear before thee, and will destroy all the people to whom thou shalt come, and I will make all thine enemies turn their backs unto thee.

28And I will send hornets before thee, which shall drive out the Hivite, the Canaanite, and the Hittite, from before thee.

29I will not drive them out from before thee in one year; lest the land become desolate, and the beast of the field multiply against thee.

30By little and little I will drive them out from before thee, until thou be increased, and inherit the land.

31And I will set thy bounds from the Red sea even unto the sea of the Philistines, and from the desert unto the river: for I will deliver the inhabitants of the land into your hand; and thou shalt drive them out before thee.

32Thou shalt make no covenant with them, nor with their gods.

33They shall not dwell in thy land, lest they make thee sin against me: for if thou serve their gods, it will surely be a snare unto thee.

AND he said unto Moses, Come up unto the LORD, thou, and Aaron, Nadab, and Abihu, and seventy of the elders of Israel; and worship ye afar off.

2And Moses alone shall come near the LORD: but they shall not come nigh; neither shall the people go up with him.

3And Moses came and told the people all the words of the LORD, and all the judgments: and all the people answered with one voice, and said, All the words which the LORD hath said will we do.

4And Moses wrote all the words of the LORD, and rose up early in the morning, and builded an altar under the hill, and twelve pillars, according to the twelve tribes of Israel.

5And he sent young men of the children of Israel, which offered burnt offerings, and sacrificed peace offerings of oxen unto the LORD.

6And Moses took half of the blood, and put *it* in basons; and half of the blood he sprinkled on the altar.

7And he took the book of the covenant, and read in the audience of the people: and they said, All that the LORD hath said will we do, and be obedient.

8And Moses took the blood, and sprinkled *it* on the people, and said, Behold the blood of the covenant, which the LORD hath made with you concerning all these words.

9Then went up Moses, and Aaron, Nadab, and Abihu, and seventy of the elders of Israel:

10And they saw the God of Israel: and *there was* under his feet as it were a paved work of a sapphire stone, and as it were the body of heaven in *his* clearness.

11And upon the nobles of the children of Israel he laid not his hand: also they saw God, and did eat and drink.

12And the LORD said unto Moses, Come up to me into the mount, and be there: and I will give thee tables of stone, and a law, and commandments which I have written; that thou mayest teach them.

13And Moses rose up, and his minister Joshua: and Moses went up into the mount of God.

14And he said unto the elders, Tarry ye here for us, until we come again unto you: and, behold, Aaron and Hur *are* with you: if any man have any matters to do, let him come unto them.

15And Moses went up into the mount, and a cloud covered the mount.

16And the glory of the LORD abode upon mount Sinai, and the cloud covered it six days: and the seventh day he called unto Moses out of the midst of the cloud.

17And the sight of the glory of the LORD *was* like devouring fire on the top of the mount in the eyes of the children of Israel.

18And Moses went into the midst of the cloud, and gat him up into the mount: and Moses was in the mount forty days and forty nights.

AND the LORD spake unto Moses, saying,

2Speak unto the children of Israel, that they bring me an offering: of every man that giveth it willingly with his heart ye shall take my offering.

3And this *is* the offering which ye

shall take of them; gold, and silver, and brass,

4And blue, and purple, and scarlet, and fine linen, and goats' *hair,*

5And rams' skins dyed red, and badgers' skins, and shittim wood,

6Oil for the light, spices for anointing oil, and for sweet incense,

7Onyx stones, and stones to be set in the ephod, and in the breastplate.

8And let them make me a sanctuary; that I may dwell among them.

9According to all that I shew thee, *after* the pattern of the tabernacle, and the pattern of all the instruments thereof, even so shall ye make *it.*

10And they shall make an ark *of* shittim wood: two cubits and a half *shall be* the length thereof, and a cubit and a half the breadth thereof, and a cubit and a half the height thereof.

11And thou shalt overlay it with pure gold, within and without shalt thou overlay it, and shalt make upon it a crown of gold round about.

12And thou shalt cast four rings of gold for it, and put *them* in the four corners thereof; and two rings *shall be* in the one side of it, and two rings in the other side of it.

13And thou shalt make staves *of* shittim wood, and overlay them with gold.

14And thou shalt put the staves into the rings by the sides of the ark, that the ark may be borne with them.

15The staves shall be in the rings of the ark: they shall not be taken from it.

16And thou shalt put into the ark the testimony which I shall give thee.

17And thou shalt make a mercy seat *of* pure gold: two cubits and a half *shall be* the length thereof, and a cubit and a half the breadth thereof.

18And thou shalt make two cherubims *of* gold, *of* beaten work shalt thou make them, in the two ends of the mercy seat.

19And make one cherub on the one

end, and the other cherub on the other end: *even* of the mercy seat shall ye make the cherubims on the two ends thereof.

20And the cherubims shall stretch forth *their* wings on high, covering the mercy seat with their wings, and their faces *shall look* one to another; toward the mercy seat shall the faces of the cherubims be.

21And thou shalt put the mercy seat above upon the ark; and in the ark thou shalt put the testimony that I shall give thee.

22And there I will meet with thee, and I will commune with thee from above the mercy seat, from between the two cherubims which *are* upon the ark of the testimony, of all *things* which I will give thee in commandment unto the children of Israel.

23Thou shalt also make a table *of* shittim wood: two cubits *shall be* the length thereof, and a cubit the breadth thereof, and a cubit and a half the height thereof.

24And thou shalt overlay it with pure gold, and make thereto a crown of gold round about.

25And thou shalt make unto it a border of an hand breadth round about, and thou shalt make a golden crown to the border thereof round about.

26And thou shalt make for it four rings of gold, and put the rings in the four corners that *are* on the four feet thereof.

27Over against the border shall the rings be for places of the staves to bear the table.

28And thou shalt make the staves *of* shittim wood, and overlay them with gold, that the table may be borne with them.

29And thou shalt make the dishes thereof, and spoons thereof, and covers thereof, and bowls thereof, to cover withal: *of* pure gold shalt thou make them.

30And thou shalt set upon the table shewbread before me alway.

31And thou shalt make a candlestick *of* pure gold: *of* beaten work shall the candlestick be made: his shaft, and his branches, his bowls, his knops, and his flowers, shall be of the same.

32And six branches shall come out of the sides of it; three branches of the candlestick out of the one side, and three branches of the candlestick out of the other side:

33Three bowls made like unto almonds, *with* a knop and a flower in one branch; and three bowls made like almonds in the other branch, *with* a knop and a flower: so in the six branches that come out of the candlestick.

34And in the candlestick *shall be* four bowls made like unto almonds, *with* their knops and their flowers.

35And *there shall be* a knop under two branches of the same, and a knop under two branches of the same, and a knop under two branches of the same, according to the six branches that proceed out of the candlestick.

36Their knops and their branches shall be of the same: all it *shall be* one beaten work *of* pure gold.

37And thou shalt make the seven lamps thereof: and they shall light the lamps thereof, that they may give light over against it.

38And the tongs thereof, and the snuffdishes thereof, *shall be of* pure gold.

39*Of* a talent of pure gold shall he make it, with all these vessels.

40And look that thou make *them* after their pattern, which was shewed thee in the mount.

MATTHEW 24:29–51

IMMEDIATELY after the tribulation of those days shall the sun be darkened, and the moon shall not give her light, and the stars shall fall from heaven, and the powers of the heavens shall be shaken:

30And then shall appear the sign of the Son of man in heaven: and then shall all the tribes of the earth mourn, and they shall see the Son of man coming in the clouds of heaven with power and great glory.

31And he shall send his angels with a great sound of a trumpet, and they shall gather together his elect from the four winds, from one end of heaven to the other.

32Now learn a parable of the fig tree; When his branch is yet tender, and putteth forth leaves, ye know that summer *is* nigh:

33So likewise ye, when ye shall see all these things, know that it is near, *even* at the doors.

34Verily I say unto you, This generation shall not pass, till all these things be fulfilled.

35Heaven and earth shall pass away, but my words shall not pass away.

36But of that day and hour knoweth no *man*, no, not the angels of heaven, but my Father only.

37But as the days of Noe *were,* so shall also the coming of the Son of man be.

38For as in the days that were before the flood they were eating and drinking, marrying and giving in marriage, until the day that Noe entered into the ark,

39And knew not until the flood came, and took them all away; so shall also the coming of the Son of man be.

40Then shall two be in the field; the one shall be taken, and the other left.

41Two *women shall be* grinding at the mill; the one shall be taken, and the other left.

42Watch therefore: for ye know not what hour your Lord doth come.

43But know this, that if the goodman of the house had known in what watch the thief would come, he would have watched, and would not have suffered his house to be broken up.

44Therefore be ye also ready: for in such an hour as ye think not the Son of man cometh.

45Who then is a faithful and wise servant, whom his lord hath made ruler over his household, to give them meat in due season?

46Blessed *is* that servant, whom his lord when he cometh shall find so doing.

47Verily I say unto you, That he shall make him ruler over all his goods.

48But and if that evil servant shall say in his heart, My lord delayeth his coming;

49And shall begin to smite *his* fellow-servants, and to eat and drink with the drunken;

50The lord of that servant shall come in a day when he looketh not for *him,* and in an hour that he is not aware of,

51And shall cut him asunder, and appoint *him* his portion with the hypocrites: there shall be weeping and gnashing of teeth.

PSALM 30:1–12

I will extol thee, O LORD; for thou hast lifted me up, and hast not made my foes to rejoice over me.

2O LORD my God, I cried unto thee, and thou hast healed me.

3O LORD, thou hast brought up my soul from the grave: thou hast kept me alive, that I should not go down to the pit.

4Sing unto the LORD, O ye saints of his, and give thanks at the remembrance of his holiness.

5For his anger *endureth but* a moment; in his favour *is* life: weeping may endure for a night, but joy *cometh* in the morning.

6And in my prosperity I said, I shall never be moved.

7LORD, by thy favour thou hast made my mountain to stand strong: thou didst hide thy face, *and* I was troubled.

8I cried to thee, O LORD; and unto the LORD I made supplication.

9What profit *is there* in my blood, when I go down to the pit? Shall the dust praise thee? shall it declare thy truth?

10Hear, O LORD, and have mercy upon me: LORD, be thou my helper.

11Thou hast turned for me my mourning into dancing: thou hast put off my sackcloth, and girded me with gladness;

12To the end that *my* glory may sing praise to thee, and not be silent. O LORD my God, I will give thanks unto thee for ever.

PROVERBS FOR TODAY/ 7:24–27

Hearken unto me now therefore, O ye children, and attend to the words of my mouth. Let not thine heart decline to her ways, go not astray in her paths. For she hath cast down many wounded: yea, many strong men have been slain by her. Her house is *the way to hell, going down to the chambers of death.*

FEBRUARY 7

EXODUS 26:1—27:21

Moreover thou shalt make the tabernacle *with* ten curtains *of* fine twined linen, and blue, and purple, and scarlet: *with* cherubims of cunning work shalt thou make them.

2The length of one curtain *shall be* eight and twenty cubits, and the breadth of one curtain four cubits: and every one of the curtains shall have one measure.

3The five curtains shall be coupled together one to another; and *other* five curtains *shall be* coupled one to another.

4And thou shalt make loops of blue upon the edge of the one curtain from the selvedge in the coupling; and likewise shalt thou make in the uttermost edge of *another* curtain, in the coupling of the second.

5Fifty loops shalt thou make in the one curtain, and fifty loops shalt thou make in the edge of the curtain that *is* in the coupling of the second; that the loops may take hold one of another.

6And thou shalt make fifty taches of gold, and couple the curtains together with the taches: and it shall be one tabernacle.

7And thou shalt make curtains *of* goats' *hair* to be a covering upon the tabernacle: eleven curtains shalt thou make.

8The length of one curtain *shall be* thirty cubits, and the breadth of one curtain four cubits: and the eleven curtains *shall be all* of one measure.

9And thou shalt couple five curtains by themselves, and six curtains by themselves, and shalt double the sixth curtain in the forefront of the tabernacle.

10And thou shalt make fifty loops on the edge of the one curtain *that is* outmost in the coupling, and fifty loops in the edge of the curtain which coupleth the second.

11And thou shalt make fifty taches of brass, and put the taches into the loops, and couple the tent together, that it may be one.

12And the remnant that remaineth of the curtains of the tent, the half curtain that remaineth, shall hang over the backside of the tabernacle.

13And a cubit on the one side, and a cubit on the other side of that which remaineth in the length of the curtains of the tent, it shall hang over the sides

of the tabernacle on this side and on that side, to cover it.

14And thou shalt make a covering for the tent *of* rams' skins dyed red, and a covering above *of* badgers' skins.

15And thou shalt make boards for the tabernacle *of* shittim wood standing up.

16Ten cubits *shall be* the length of a board, and a cubit and a half *shall be* the breadth of one board.

17Two tenons *shall there be* in one board, set in order one against another: thus shalt thou make for all the boards of the tabernacle.

18And thou shalt make the boards for the tabernacle, twenty boards on the south side southward.

19And thou shalt make forty sockets of silver under the twenty boards; two sockets under one board for his two tenons, and two sockets under another board for his two tenons.

20And for the second side of the tabernacle on the north side *there shall be* twenty boards:

21And their forty sockets *of* silver; two sockets under one board, and two sockets under another board.

22And for the sides of the tabernacle westward thou shalt make six boards.

23And two boards shalt thou make for the corners of the tabernacle in the two sides.

24And they shall be coupled together beneath, and they shall be coupled together above the head of it unto one ring: thus shall it be for them both; they shall be for the two corners.

25And they shall be eight boards, and their sockets *of* silver, sixteen sockets; two sockets under one board, and two sockets under another board.

26And thou shalt make bars *of* shittim wood; five for the boards of the one side of the tabernacle,

27And five bars for the boards of the other side of the tabernacle, and five bars for the boards of the side of the tabernacle, for the two sides westward.

28And the middle bar in the midst

of the boards shall reach from end to end.

29And thou shalt overlay the boards with gold, and make their rings *of* gold *for* places for the bars: and thou shalt overlay the bars with gold.

30And thou shalt rear up the tabernacle according to the fashion thereof which was shewed thee in the mount.

31And thou shalt make a vail *of* blue, and purple, and scarlet, and fine twined linen of cunning work: with cherubims shall it be made:

32And thou shalt hang it upon four pillars of shittim *wood* overlaid with gold: their hooks *shall be of* gold, upon the four sockets of silver.

33And thou shalt hang up the vail under the taches, that thou mayest bring in thither within the vail the ark of the testimony: and the vail shall divide unto you between the holy *place* and the most holy.

34And thou shalt put the mercy seat upon the ark of the testimony in the most holy *place.*

35And thou shalt set the table without the vail, and the candlestick over against the table on the side of the tabernacle toward the south: and thou shalt put the table on the north side.

36And thou shalt make an hanging for the door of the tent, *of* blue, and purple, and scarlet, and fine twined linen, wrought with needlework.

37And thou shalt make for the hanging five pillars *of* shittim *wood,* and overlay them with gold, *and* their hooks *shall be of* gold: and thou shalt cast five sockets of brass for them.

AND thou shalt make an altar *of* shittim wood, five cubits long, and five cubits broad; the altar shall be foursquare: and the height thereof *shall be* three cubits.

2And thou shalt make the horns of it upon the four corners thereof: his horns shall be of the same: and thou shalt overlay it with brass.

3And thou shalt make his pans to receive his ashes, and his shovels, and his basons, and his fleshhooks, and his firepans: all the vessels thereof thou shalt make *of* brass.

4And thou shalt make for it a grate of network *of* brass; and upon the net shalt thou make four brasen rings in the four corners thereof.

5And thou shalt put it under the compass of the altar beneath, that the net may be even to the midst of the altar.

6And thou shalt make staves for the altar, staves *of* shittim wood, and overlay them with brass.

7And the staves shall be put into the rings, and the staves shall be upon the two sides of the altar, to bear it.

8Hollow with boards shalt thou make it: as it was shewed thee in the mount, so shall they make *it.*

9And thou shalt make the court of the tabernacle: for the south side southward *there shall be* hangings for the court *of* fine twined linen of an hundred cubits long for one side:

10And the twenty pillars thereof and their twenty sockets *shall be of* brass; the hooks of the pillars and their fillets *shall be of* silver.

11And likewise for the north side in length *there shall be* hangings of an hundred *cubits* long, and his twenty pillars and their twenty sockets *of* brass; the hooks of the pillars and their fillets *of* silver.

12And *for* the breadth of the court on the west side *shall be* hangings of fifty cubits: their pillars ten, and their sockets ten.

13And the breadth of the court on the east side eastward *shall be* fifty cubits.

14The hangings of one side *of the gate shall be* fifteen cubits: their pillars three, and their sockets three.

15And on the other side *shall be* hangings fifteen *cubits:* their pillars three, and their sockets three.

16And for the gate of the court *shall*

be an hanging of twenty cubits, *of* blue, and purple, and scarlet, and fine twined linen, wrought with needlework: *and* their pillars *shall be* four, and their sockets four.

17All the pillars round about the court *shall be* filleted with silver; their hooks *shall be of* silver, and their sockets *of* brass.

18The length of the court *shall be* an hundred cubits, and the breadth fifty every where, and the height five cubits *of* fine twined linen, and their sockets *of* brass.

19All the vessels of the tabernacle in all the service thereof, and all the pins thereof, and all the pins of the court, *shall be of* brass.

20And thou shalt command the children of Israel, that they bring thee pure oil olive beaten for the light, to cause the lamp to burn always.

21In the tabernacle of the congregation without the vail, which *is* before the testimony, Aaron and his sons shall order it from evening to morning before the LORD: *it shall be* a statute for ever unto their generations on the behalf of the children of Israel.

MATTHEW 25:1–30

THEN shall the kingdom of heaven be likened unto ten virgins, which took their lamps, and went forth to meet the bridegroom.

2And five of them were wise, and five *were* foolish.

3They that *were* foolish took their lamps, and took no oil with them:

4But the wise took oil in their vessels with their lamps.

5While the bridegroom tarried, they all slumbered and slept.

6And at midnight there was a cry made, Behold, the bridegroom cometh; go ye out to meet him.

7Then all those virgins arose, and trimmed their lamps.

8And the foolish said unto the wise, Give us of your oil; for our lamps are gone out.

9But the wise answered, saying, *Not so;* lest there be not enough for us and you: but go ye rather to them that sell, and buy for yourselves.

10And while they went to buy, the bridegroom came; and they that were ready went in with him to the marriage: and the door was shut.

11Afterward came also the other virgins, saying, Lord, Lord, open to us.

12But he answered and said, Verily I say unto you, I know you not.

13Watch therefore, for ye know neither the day nor the hour wherein the Son of man cometh.

14For *the kingdom of heaven is* as a man travelling into a far country, *who* called his own servants, and delivered unto them his goods.

15And unto one he gave five talents, to another two, and to another one; to every man according to his several ability; and straightway took his journey.

16Then he that had received the five talents went and traded with the same, and made *them* other five talents.

17And likewise he that *had received* two, he also gained other two.

18But he that had received one went and digged in the earth, and hid his lord's money.

19After a long time the lord of those servants cometh, and reckoneth with them.

20And so he that had received five talents came and brought other five talents, saying, Lord, thou deliveredst unto me five talents: behold, I have gained beside them five talents more.

21His lord said unto him, Well done, *thou* good and faithful servant: thou hast been faithful over a few things, I will make thee ruler over many things: enter thou into the joy of thy lord.

22He also that had received two talents came and said, Lord, thou deliveredst unto me two talents: behold, I have gained two other talents beside them.

23His lord said unto him, Well done, good and faithful servant; thou has been faithful over a few things, I will make thee ruler over many things: enter thou into the joy of thy lord.

24Then he which had received the one talent came and said, Lord, I knew thee that thou art an hard man, reaping where thou hast not sown, and gathering where thou hast not strawed:

25And I was afraid, and went and hid thy talent in the earth: lo, *there* thou hast *that is* thine.

26His lord answered and said unto him, *Thou* wicked and slothful servant, thou knewest that I reap where I sowed not, and gather where I have not strawed:

27Thou oughtest therefore to have put my money to the exchangers, and *then* at my coming I should have received mine own with usury.

28Take therefore the talent from him, and give *it* unto him which hath ten talents.

29For unto every one that hath shall be given, and he shall have abundance: but from him that hath not shall be taken away even that which he hath.

30And cast ye the unprofitable servant into outer darkness: there shall be weeping and gnashing of teeth.

PSALM 31:1–8

IN thee, O LORD, do I put my trust; let me never be ashamed: deliver me in thy righteousness.

2Bow down thine ear to me; deliver me speedily: be thou my strong rock, for an house of defence to save me.

3For thou *art* my rock and my fortress; therefore for thy name's sake lead me, and guide me.

4Pull me out of the net that they have laid privily for me: for thou *art* my strength.

5Into thine hand I commit my spirit: thou hast redeemed me, O LORD God of truth.

6I have hated them that regard lying vanities: but I trust in the LORD.

7I will be glad and rejoice in thy mercy: for thou hast considered my trouble; thou hast known my soul in adversities;

8And hast not shut me up into the hand of the enemy: thou hast set my feet in a large room.

PROVERBS FOR TODAY/ 8:1–10

Doth not wisdom cry? and understanding put forth her voice? She standeth in the top of high places, by the way in the places of the paths. She crieth at the gates, at the entry of the city, at the coming in at the doors. Unto you, O men, I call; and my voice is to the sons of man. O ye simple, understand wisdom: and, ye fools, be ye of an understanding heart. Hear; for I will speak of excellent things; and the opening of my lips shall be right things. For my mouth shall speak truth; and wickedness is an abomination to my lips. All the words of my mouth are in righteousness; there is nothing froward or perverse in them. They are all plain to him that understandeth, and right to them that find knowledge. Receive my instruction, and not silver; and knowledge rather than choice gold.

FEBRUARY 8

EXODUS 28:1–43

AND take thou unto thee Aaron thy brother, and his sons with him, from among the children of Israel, that he may minister unto me in the priest's office, *even* Aaron, Nadab and Abihu, Eleazar and Ithamar, Aaron's sons.

2And thou shalt make holy garments for Aaron thy brother for glory and for beauty.

3And thou shalt speak unto all *that are* wise hearted, whom I have filled with the spirit of wisdom, that they may make Aaron's garments to consecrate him, that he may minister unto me in the priest's office.

4And these *are* the garments which they shall make; a breastplate, and an ephod, and a robe, and a broidered coat, a mitre, and a girdle: and they shall make holy garments for Aaron thy brother, and his sons, that he may minister unto me in the priest's office.

5And they shall take gold, and blue, and purple, and scarlet, and fine linen.

6And they shall make the ephod *of* gold, *of* blue, and *of* purple, *of* scarlet, and fine twined linen, with cunning work.

7It shall have the two shoulderpieces thereof joined at the two edges thereof; and *so* it shall be joined together.

8And the curious girdle of the ephod, which *is* upon it, shall be of the same, according to the work thereof; *even of* gold, *of* blue, and purple, and scarlet, and fine twined linen.

9And thou shalt take two onyx stones, and grave on them the names of the children of Israel:

10Six of their names on one stone, and *the other* six names of the rest on the other stone, according to their birth.

11With the work of an engraver in stone, *like* the engravings of a signet, shalt thou engrave the two stones with the names of the children of Israel: thou shalt make them to be set in ouches of gold.

12And thou shalt put the two stones upon the shoulders of the ephod *for* stones of memorial unto the children of Israel: and Aaron shall bear their names before the LORD upon his two shoulders for a memorial.

13And thou shalt make ouches *of* gold;

14And two chains *of* pure gold at the ends; *of* wreathen work shalt thou make them, and fasten the wreathen chains to the ouches.

15And thou shalt make the breastplate of judgment with cunning work; after the work of the ephod thou shalt make it; *of* gold, *of* blue, and *of* purple, and *of* scarlet, and *of* fine twined linen, shalt thou make it.

16Foursquare *it* shall be *being* doubled; a span *shall be* the length thereof, and a span *shall be* the breadth thereof.

17And thou shalt set in it settings of stones, *even* four rows of stones: *the first* row *shall be* a sardius, a topaz, and a carbuncle: *this shall be* the first row.

18And the second row *shall be* an emerald, a sapphire, and a diamond.

19And the third row a ligure, an agate, and an amethyst.

20And the fourth row a beryl, and an onyx, and a jasper: they shall be set in gold in their inclosings.

21And the stones shall be with the names of the children of Israel, twelve, according to their names, *like* the engravings of a signet; every one with his name shall they be according to the twelve tribes.

22And thou shalt make upon the

breastplate chains at the ends *of* wreathen work *of* pure gold.

23And thou shalt make upon the breastplate two rings of gold, and shalt put the two rings on the two ends of the breastplate.

24And thou shalt put the two wreathen *chains* of gold in the two rings *which are* on the ends of the breastplate.

25And *the other* two ends of the two wreathen *chains* thou shalt fasten in the two ouches, and put *them* on the shoulderpieces of the ephod before it.

26And thou shalt make two rings of gold, and thou shalt put them upon the two ends of the breastplate in the border thereof, which *is* in the side of the ephod inward.

27And two *other* rings of gold thou shalt make, and shalt put them on the two sides of the ephod underneath, toward the forepart thereof, over against the *other* coupling thereof, above the curious girdle of the ephod.

28And they shall bind the breastplate by the rings thereof unto the rings of the ephod with a lace of blue, that *it* may be above the curious girdle of the ephod, and that the breastplate be not loosed from the ephod.

29And Aaron shall bear the names of the children of Israel in the breastplate of judgment upon his heart, when he goeth in unto the holy *place,* for a memorial before the Lord continually.

30And thou shalt put in the breastplate of judgment the Urim and the Thummim; and they shall be upon Aaron's heart, when he goeth in before the Lord: and Aaron shall bear the judgment of the children of Israel upon his heart before the Lord continually.

31And thou shalt make the robe of the ephod all *of* blue.

32And there shall be an hole in the top of it, in the midst thereof: it shall have a binding of woven work round about the hole of it, as it were the hole of an habergeon, that it be not rent.

33And *beneath* upon the hem of it thou shalt make pomegranates *of* blue, and *of* purple, and *of* scarlet, round about the hem thereof; and bells of gold between them round about:

34A golden bell and a pomegranate, a golden bell and a pomegranate, upon the hem of the robe round about.

35And it shall be upon Aaron to minister: and his sound shall be heard when he goeth in unto the holy *place* before the Lord, and when he cometh out, that he die not.

36And thou shalt make a plate *of* pure gold, and grave upon it, *like* the engravings of a signet, HOLINESS TO THE LORD.

37And thou shalt put it on a blue lace, that it may be upon the mitre; upon the forefront of the mitre it shall be.

38And it shall be upon Aaron's forehead, that Aaron may bear the iniquity of the holy things, which the children of Israel shall hallow in all their holy gifts; and it shall be always upon his forehead, that they may be accepted before the Lord.

39And thou shalt embroider the coat of fine linen, and thou shalt make the mitre *of* fine linen, and thou shalt make the girdle *of* needlework.

40And for Aaron's sons thou shalt make coats, and thou shalt make for them girdles, and bonnets shalt thou make for them, for glory and for beauty.

41And thou shalt put them upon Aaron thy brother, and his sons with him; and shalt anoint them, and consecrate them, and sanctify them, that they may minister unto me in the priest's office.

42And thou shalt make them linen breeches to cover their nakedness; from the loins even unto the thighs they shall reach.

43And they shall be upon Aaron, and upon his sons, when they come in unto the tabernacle of the congregation, or when they come near unto the altar to minister in the holy *place;* that they bear not iniquity, and die: *it shall be* a statute for ever unto him and his seed after him.

MATTHEW 25:31—26:13

WHEN the Son of man shall come in his glory, and all the holy angels with him, then shall he sit upon the throne of his glory:

32And before him shall be gathered all nations: and he shall separate them one from another, as a shepherd divideth *his* sheep from the goats:

33And he shall set the sheep on his right hand, but the goats on the left.

34Then shall the King say unto them on his right hand, Come, ye blessed of my Father, inherit the kingdom prepared for you from the foundation of the world:

35For I was an hungred, and ye gave me meat: I was thirsty, and ye gave me drink: I was a stranger, and ye took me in:

36Naked, and ye clothed me: I was sick, and ye visited me: I was in prison, and ye came unto me.

37Then shall the righteous answer him, saying, Lord, when saw we thee an hungred, and fed *thee?* or thirsty, and gave *thee* drink?

38When saw we thee a stranger, and took *thee* in? or naked, and clothed *thee?*

39Or when saw we thee sick, or in prison, and came unto thee?

40And the King shall answer and say unto them, Verily I say unto you, Inasmuch as ye have done *it* unto one of the least of these my brethren, ye have done *it* unto me.

41Then shall he say also unto them on the left hand, Depart from me, ye cursed, into everlasting fire, prepared for the devil and his angels:

42For I was an hungred, and ye gave me no meat: I was thirsty, and ye gave me no drink:

43I was a stranger, and ye took me not in: naked, and ye clothed me not:

sick, and in prison, and ye visited me not.

44Then shall they also answer him, saying, Lord, when saw we thee an hungred, or athirst, or a stranger, or naked, or sick, or in prison, and did not minister unto thee?

45Then shall he answer them, saying, Verily I say unto you, Inasmuch as ye did *it* not to one of the least of these, ye did *it* not to me.

46And these shall go away into everlasting punishment: but the righteous into life eternal.

AND it came to pass, when Jesus had finished all these sayings, he said unto his disciples,

2Ye know that after two days is *the feast of* the passover, and the Son of man is betrayed to be crucified.

3Then assembled together the chief priests, and the scribes, and the elders of the people, unto the palace of the high priest, who was called Caiaphas,

4And consulted that they might take Jesus by subtilty, and kill *him.*

5But they said, Not on the feast *day,* lest there be an uproar among the people.

6Now when Jesus was in Bethany, in the house of Simon the leper,

7There came unto him a woman having an alabaster box of very precious ointment, and poured it on his head, as he sat *at meat.*

8But when his disciples saw *it,* they had indignation, saying, To what purpose *is* this waste?

9For this ointment might have been sold for much, and given to the poor.

10When Jesus understood *it,* he said unto them, Why trouble ye the woman? for she hath wrought a good work upon me.

11For ye have the poor always with you; but me ye have not always.

12For in that she hath poured this ointment on my body, she did *it* for my burial.

13Verily I say unto you, Wheresoever this gospel shall be preached in the whole world, *there* shall also this, that this woman hath done, be told for a memorial of her.

PSALM 31:9–18

Have mercy upon me, O Lord, for I am in trouble: mine eye is consumed with grief, *yea* my soul and my belly.

10For my life is spent with grief, and my years with sighing: my strength faileth because of mine iniquity, and my bones are consumed.

11I was a reproach among all mine enemies, but especially among my neighbours, and a fear to mine acquaintance: they that did see me without fled from me.

12I am forgotten as a dead man out of mind: I am like a broken vessel.

13For I have heard the slander of many: fear *was* on every side: while they took counsel together against me, they devised to take away my life.

14But I trusted in thee, O Lord: I said, Thou *art* my God.

15My times *are* in thy hand: deliver me from the hand of mine enemies, and from them that persecute me.

16Make thy face to shine upon thy servant: save me for thy mercies' sake.

17Let me not be ashamed, O Lord; for I have called upon thee: let the wicked be ashamed, *and* let them be silent in the grave.

18Let the lying lips be put to silence; which speak grievous things proudly and contemptuously against the righteous.

PROVERBS FOR TODAY/ 8:11–13

For wisdom is *better than rubies; and all the things that may be desired are not to be compared to it. I wisdom dwell with prudence, and find out knowledge of witty inventions. The fear of the Lord* is *to hate evil: pride, and arrogancy, and the evil way, and the froward mouth, do I hate.*

FEBRUARY 9

EXODUS 29:1—30:10

And this *is* the thing that thou shalt do unto them to hallow them, to minister unto me in the priest's office: Take one young bullock, and two rams without blemish,

2And unleavened bread, and cakes unleavened tempered with oil, and wafers unleavened anointed with oil: *of* wheaten flour shalt thou make them.

3And thou shalt put them into one basket, and bring them in the basket, with the bullock and the two rams.

4And Aaron and his sons thou shalt bring unto the door of the tabernacle of the congregation, and shalt wash them with water.

5And thou shalt take the garments, and put upon Aaron the coat, and the robe of the ephod, and the ephod, and the breastplate, and gird him with the curious girdle of the ephod:

6And thou shalt put the mitre upon his head, and put the holy crown upon the mitre.

7Then shalt thou take the anointing

oil, and pour *it* upon his head, and anoint him.

8And thou shalt bring his sons, and put coats upon them.

9And thou shalt gird them with girdles, Aaron and his sons, and put the bonnets on them: and the priest's office shall be theirs for a perpetual statute: and thou shalt consecrate Aaron and his sons.

10And thou shalt cause a bullock to be brought before the tabernacle of the congregation: and Aaron and his sons shall put their hands upon the head of the bullock.

11And thou shalt kill the bullock before the LORD, *by* the door of the tabernacle of the congregation.

12And thou shalt take of the blood of the bullock, and put *it* upon the horns of the altar with thy finger, and pour all the blood beside the bottom of the altar.

13And thou shalt take all the fat that covereth the inwards, and the caul *that is* above the liver, and the two kidneys, and the fat that *is* upon them, and burn *them* upon the altar.

14But the flesh of the bullock, and his skin, and his dung, shalt thou burn with fire without the camp: it *is* a sin offering.

15Thou shalt also take one ram; and Aaron and his sons shall put their hands upon the head of the ram.

16And thou shalt slay the ram, and thou shalt take his blood, and sprinkle *it* round about upon the altar.

17And thou shalt cut the ram in pieces, and wash the inwards of him, and his legs, and put *them* unto his pieces, and unto his head.

18And thou shalt burn the whole ram upon the altar: it *is* a burnt offering unto the LORD: it *is* a sweet savour, an offering made by fire unto the LORD.

19And thou shalt take the other ram; and Aaron and his sons shall put their hands upon the head of the ram.

20Then shalt thou kill the ram, and take of his blood, and put *it* upon the tip of the right ear of Aaron, and upon the tip of the right ear of his sons, and upon the thumb of their right hand, and upon the great toe of their right foot, and sprinkle the blood upon the altar round about.

21And thou shalt take of the blood that *is* upon the altar, and of the anointing oil, and sprinkle *it* upon Aaron, and upon his garments, and upon his sons, and upon the garments of his sons with him: and he shall be hallowed, and his garments, and his sons, and his sons' garments with him.

22Also thou shalt take of the ram the fat and the rump, and the fat that covereth the inwards, and the caul *above* the liver, and the two kidneys, and the fat that *is* upon them, and the right shoulder; for it *is* a ram of consecration:

23And one loaf of bread, and one cake of oiled bread, and one wafer out of the basket of the unleavened bread that *is* before the LORD:

24And thou shalt put all in the hands of Aaron, and in the hands of his sons; and shalt wave them *for* a wave offering before the LORD.

25And thou shalt receive them of their hands, and burn *them* upon the altar for a burnt offering, for a sweet savour before the LORD: it *is* an offering made by fire unto the LORD.

26And thou shalt take the breast of the ram of Aaron's consecration, and wave it *for* a wave offering before the LORD: and it shall be thy part.

27And thou shalt sanctify the breast of the wave offering, and the shoulder of the heave offering, which is waved, and which is heaved up, of the ram of the consecration, *even* of *that* which *is* for Aaron, and of *that* which is for his sons:

28And it shall be Aaron's and his sons' by a statute for ever from the children of Israel: for it *is* an heave offering: and it shall be an heave offering from the children of Israel of the sacrifice of their peace offerings, *even* their heave offering unto the LORD.

29And the holy garments of Aaron shall be his sons' after him, to be anointed therein, and to be consecrated in them.

30*And* that son that is priest in his stead shall put them on seven days, when he cometh into the tabernacle of the congregation to minister in the holy *place.*

31And thou shalt take the ram of the consecration, and seethe his flesh in the holy place.

32And Aaron and his sons shall eat the flesh of the ram, and the bread that *is* in the basket, *by* the door of the tabernacle of the congregation.

33And they shall eat those things wherewith the atonement was made, to consecrate *and* to sanctify them: but a stranger shall not eat *thereof,* because they *are* holy.

34And if ought of the flesh of the consecrations, or of the bread, remain unto the morning, then thou shalt burn the remainder with fire: it shall not be eaten, because it *is* holy.

35And thus shalt thou do unto Aaron, and to his sons, according to all *things* which I have commanded thee: seven days shalt thou consecrate them.

36And thou shalt offer every day a bullock *for* a sin offering for atonement: and thou shalt cleanse the altar, when thou hast made an atonement for it, and thou shalt anoint it, to sanctify it.

37Seven days thou shalt make an atonement for the altar, and sanctify it; and it shall be an altar most holy: whatsoever toucheth the altar shall be holy.

38Now this *is that* which thou shalt offer upon the altar; two lambs of the first year day by day continually.

39The one lamb thou shalt offer in the morning; and the other lamb thou shalt offer at even:

40And with the one lamb a tenth deal of flour mingled with the fourth part of an hin of beaten oil; and the fourth part of an hin of wine *for* a drink offering.

41And the other lamb thou shalt offer at even, and shalt do thereto according to the meat offering of the morning, and according to the drink offering thereof, for a sweet savour, an offering made by fire unto the LORD.

42*This shall be* a continual burnt offering throughout your generations *at* the door of the tabernacle of the congregation before the LORD: where I will meet you, to speak there unto thee.

43And there I will meet with the children of Israel, and *the tabernacle* shall be sanctified by my glory.

44And I will sanctify the tabernacle of the congregation, and the altar: I will sanctify also both Aaron and his sons, to minister to me in the priest's office.

45And I will dwell among the children of Israel, and will be their God.

46And they shall know that I *am* the LORD their God, that brought them forth out of the land of Egypt, that I may dwell among them: I *am* the LORD their God.

AND thou shalt make an altar to burn incense upon: *of* shittim wood shalt thou make it.

2A cubit *shall be* the length thereof, and a cubit the breadth thereof; foursquare shall it be: and two cubits *shall be* the height thereof: the horns thereof *shall be* of the same.

3And thou shalt overlay it with pure gold, the top thereof, and the sides thereof round about, and the horns thereof; and thou shalt make unto it a crown of gold round about.

4And two golden rings shalt thou make to it under the crown of it, by the two corners thereof, upon the two sides of it shalt thou make *it;* and they shall be for places for the staves to bear it withal.

5And thou shalt make the staves *of*

shittim wood, and overlay them with gold.

6And thou shalt put it before the vail that *is* by the ark of the testimony, before the mercy seat that *is* over the testimony, where I will meet with thee.

7And Aaron shall burn thereon sweet incense every morning: when he dresseth the lamps, he shall burn incense upon it.

8And when Aaron lighteth the lamps at even, he shall burn incense upon it, a perpetual incense before the LORD throughout your generations.

9Ye shall offer no strange incense thereon, nor burnt sacrifice, nor meat offering; neither shall ye pour drink offering thereon.

10And Aaron shall make an atonement upon the horns of it once in a year with the blood of the sin offering of atonements: once in the year shall he make atonement upon it throughout your generations: it *is* most holy unto the LORD.

MATTHEW 26:14–46

THEN one of the twelve, called Judas Iscariot, went unto the chief priests,

15And said *unto them,* What will ye give me, and I will deliver him unto you? And they covenanted with him for thirty pieces of silver.

16And from that time he sought opportunity to betray him.

17Now the first *day* of the *feast of* unleavened bread the disciples came to Jesus, saying unto him, Where wilt thou that we prepare for thee to eat the passover?

18And he said, Go into the city to such a man, and say unto him, The Master saith, My time is at hand; I will keep the passover at thy house with my disciples.

19And the disciples did as Jesus had appointed them; and they made ready the passover.

20Now when the even was come, he sat down with the twelve.

21And as they did eat, he said, Verily I say unto you, that one of you shall betray me.

22And they were exceeding sorrowful, and began every one of them to say unto him, Lord, is it I?

23And he answered and said, He that dippeth *his* hand with me in the dish, the same shall betray me.

24The Son of man goeth as it is written of him: but woe unto that man by whom the Son of man is betrayed! it had been good for that man if he had not been born.

25Then Judas, which betrayed him, answered and said, Master, is it I? He said unto him, Thou hast said.

26And as they were eating, Jesus took bread, and blessed *it,* and brake *it,* and gave *it* to the disciples, and said, Take, eat; this is my body.

27And he took the cup, and gave thanks, and gave *it* to them, saying, Drink ye all of it;

28For this is my blood of the new testament, which is shed for many for the remission of sins.

29But I say unto you, I will not drink henceforth of this fruit of the vine, until that day when I drink it new with you in my Father's kingdom.

30And when they had sung an hymn, they went out into the mount of Olives.

31Then saith Jesus unto them, All ye shall be offended because of me this night: for it is written, I will smite the shepherd, and the sheep of the flock shall be scattered abroad.

32But after I am risen again, I will go before you into Galilee.

33Peter answered and said unto him, Though all *men* shall be offended because of thee, *yet* will I never be offended.

34Jesus said unto him, Verily I say unto thee, That this night, before the cock crow, thou shalt deny me thrice.

35Peter said unto him, Though I

should die with thee, yet will I not deny thee. Likewise also said all the disciples.

36Then cometh Jesus with them unto a place called Gethsemane, and saith unto the disciples, Sit ye here, while I go and pray yonder.

37And he took with him Peter and the two sons of Zebedee, and began to be sorrowful and very heavy.

38Then saith he unto them, My soul is exceeding sorrowful, even unto death: tarry ye here, and watch with me.

39And he went a little farther, and fell on his face, and prayed, saying, O my Father, if it be possible, let this cup pass from me: nevertheless not as I will, but as thou *wilt*.

40And he cometh unto the disciples, and findeth them asleep, and saith unto Peter, What, could ye not watch with me one hour?

41Watch and pray, that ye enter not into temptation: the spirit indeed *is* willing, but the flesh *is* weak.

42He went away again the second time, and prayed, saying, O my Father, if this cup may not pass away from me, except I drink it, thy will be done.

43And he came and found them asleep again: for their eyes were heavy.

44And he left them, and went away again, and prayed the third time, saying the same words.

45Then cometh he to his disciples, and saith unto them, Sleep on now, and take *your* rest: behold, the hour is at hand, and the Son of man is betrayed into the hands of sinners.

46Rise, let us be going: behold, he is at hand that doth betray me.

PSALM 31:19–24

Oh how great *is* thy goodness, which thou hast laid up for them that fear thee; *which* thou hast wrought for them that trust in thee before the sons of men!

20Thou shalt hide them in the secret of thy presence from the pride of man: thou shalt keep them secretly in a pavilion from the strife of tongues.

21Blessed *be* the Lord: for he hath shewed me his marvellous kindness in a strong city.

22For I said in my haste, I am cut off from before thine eyes: nevertheless thou heardest the voice of my supplications when I cried unto thee.

23O love the Lord, all ye his saints: *for* the Lord preserveth the faithful, and plentifully rewardeth the proud doer.

24Be of good courage, and he shall strengthen your heart, all ye that hope in the Lord.

PROVERBS FOR TODAY/ 8:14–26

Counsel is *mine, and sound wisdom:.I* am *understanding: I have strength. By me kings reign, and princes decree justice. By me princes rule, and nobles,* even *all the judges of the earth. I love them that love me; and those that seek me early shall find me. Riches and honour* are *with me:* yea, *durable riches and righteousness. My fruit* is *better than gold, yea, than fine gold; and my revenue than choice silver. I lead in the way of righteousness, in the midst of the paths of judgment: That I may cause those that love me to inherit substance; and I will fill their treasures.* □ *The Lord possessed me in the beginning of his way, before his works of old. I was set up from everlasting, from the beginning, or ever the earth was. When* there were *no depths, I was brought forth; when* there were *no fountains abounding with water. Before the mountains were settled, before the hills was I brought forth: While as yet he had not made the earth, nor the fields, nor the highest part of the dust of the world.*

EXODUS 30:11—31:18

AND the LORD spake unto Moses, saying,

12When thou takest the sum of the children of Israel after their number, then shall they give every man a ransom for his soul unto the LORD, when thou numberest them; that there be no plague among them, when *thou* numberest them.

13This they shall give, every one that passeth among them that are numbered, half a shekel after the shekel of the sanctuary: (a shekel *is* twenty gerahs:) an half shekel *shall be* the offering of the LORD.

14Every one that passeth among them that are numbered, from twenty years old and above, shall give an offering unto the LORD.

15The rich shall not give more, and the poor shall not give less than half a shekel, when *they* give an offering unto the LORD, to make an atonement for your souls.

16And thou shalt take the atonement money of the children of Israel, and shalt appoint it for the service of the tabernacle of the congregation; that it may be a memorial unto the children of Israel before the LORD, to make an atonement for your souls.

17And the LORD spake unto Moses, saying,

18Thou shalt also make a laver *of* brass, and his foot *also of* brass, to wash *withal:* and thou shalt put it between the tabernacle of the congregation and the altar, and thou shalt put water therein.

19For Aaron and his sons shall wash their hands and their feet thereat:

20When they go into the tabernacle of the congregation, they shall wash with water, that they die not; or when they come near to the altar to minister, to burn offering made by fire unto the LORD:

21So they shall wash their hands and their feet, that they die not: and it shall be a statute for ever to them, *even* to him and to his seed throughout their generations.

22Moreover the LORD spake unto Moses, saying,

23Take thou also unto thee principal spices, of pure myrrh five hundred *shekels,* and of sweet cinnamon half so much, *even* two hundred and fifty *shekels,* and of sweet calamus two hundred and fifty *shekels,*

24And of cassia five hundred *shekels,* after the shekel of the sanctuary, and of oil olive an hin:

25And thou shalt make it an oil of holy ointment, an ointment compound after the art of the apothecary: it shall be an holy anointing oil.

26And thou shalt anoint the tabernacle of the congregation therewith, and the ark of testimony,

27And the table and all his vessels, and the candlestick and his vessels, and the altar of incense,

28And the altar of burnt offering with all his vessels, and the laver and his foot.

29And thou shalt sanctify them, that they may be most holy: whatsoever toucheth them shall be holy.

30And thou shalt anoint Aaron and his sons, and consecrate them, that *they* may minister unto me in the priest's office.

31And thou shalt speak unto the children of Israel, saying, This shall be an holy anointing oil unto me throughout your generations.

32Upon man's flesh shall it not be poured, neither shall ye make *any other* like it, after the composition of it: it *is* holy, *and* it shall be holy unto you.

33Whosoever compoundeth *any* like it, or whosoever putteth *any* of it upon a stranger, shall even be cut off from his people.

34And the LORD said unto Moses, Take unto thee sweet spices, stacte, and onycha, and galbanum; *these* sweet spices with pure frankincense: of each shall there be a like *weight:*

35And thou shalt make it a perfume, a confection after the art of the apothecary, tempered together, pure *and* holy:

36And thou shalt beat *some* of it very small, and put of it before the testimony in the tabernacle of the congregation, where I will meet with thee: it shall be unto you most holy.

37And *as for* the perfume which thou shalt make, ye shall not make to yourselves according to the composition thereof: it shall be unto thee holy for the LORD.

38Whosoever shall make like unto that, to smell thereto, shall even be cut off from his people.

AND the LORD spake unto Moses, saying,

2See, I have called by name Bezaleel the son of Uri, the son of Hur, of the tribe of Judah:

3And I have filled him with the spirit of God, in wisdom, and in understanding, and in knowledge, and in all manner of workmanship,

4To devise cunning works, to work in gold, and in silver, and in brass,

5And in cutting of stones, to set *them,* and in carving of timber, to work in all manner of workmanship.

6And I, behold, I have given with him Aholiab, the son of Ahisamach, of the tribe of Dan: and in the hearts of all that are wise hearted I have put wisdom, that they may make all that I have commanded thee;

7The tabernacle of the congregation, and the ark of the testimony, and the mercy seat that *is* thereupon, and all the furniture of the tabernacle,

8And the table and his furniture, and the pure candlestick with all his furniture, and the altar of incense,

9And the altar of burnt offering with all his furniture, and the laver and his foot,

10And the cloths of service, and the holy garments for Aaron the priest, and the garments of his sons, to minister in the priest's office,

11And the anointing oil, and sweet incense for the holy *place:* according to all that I have commanded thee shall they do.

12And the LORD spake unto Moses, saying,

13Speak thou also unto the children of Israel, saying, Verily my sabbaths ye shall keep: for it *is* a sign between me and you throughout your generations; that *ye* may know that I *am* the LORD that doth sanctify you.

14Ye shall keep the sabbath therefore; for it *is* holy unto you: every one that defileth it shall surely be put to death: for whosoever doeth *any* work therein, that soul shall be cut off from among his people.

15Six days may work be done; but in the seventh *is* the sabbath of rest, holy to the LORD: whosoever doeth *any* work in the sabbath day, he shall surely be put to death.

16Wherefore the children of Israel shall keep the sabbath, to observe the sabbath throughout their generations, *for* a perpetual covenant.

17It *is* a sign between me and the children of Israel for ever: for *in* six days the LORD made heaven and earth, and on the seventh day he rested, and was refreshed.

18And he gave unto Moses, when he had made an end of communing with him upon mount Sinai, two tables of testimony, tables of stone, written with the finger of God.

MATTHEW 26:47–68

A ND while he [Jesus] yet spake, lo, Judas, one of the twelve, came, and with him a great multitude with swords and staves, from the chief priests and elders of the people.

48Now he that betrayed him gave them a sign, saying, Whomsoever I shall kiss, that same is he: hold him fast.

49And forthwith he came to Jesus, and said, Hail, master; and kissed him.

50And Jesus said unto him, Friend, wherefore art thou come? Then came they, and laid hands on Jesus, and took him.

51And, behold, one of them which were with Jesus stretched out *his* hand, and drew his sword, and struck a servant of the high priest's, and smote off his ear.

52Then said Jesus unto him, Put up again thy sword into his place: for all they that take the sword shall perish with the sword.

53Thinkest thou that I cannot now pray to my Father, and he shall presently give me more than twelve legions of angels?

54But how then shall the scriptures be fulfilled, that thus it must be?

55In that same hour said Jesus to the multitudes, Are ye come out as against a thief with swords and staves for to take me? I sat daily with you teaching in the temple, and ye laid no hold on me.

56But all this was done, that the scriptures of the prophets might be fulfilled. Then all the disciples forsook him, and fled.

57And they that had laid hold on Jesus led *him* away to Caiaphas the high priest, where the scribes and the elders were assembled.

58But Peter followed him afar off unto the high priest's palace, and went in, and sat with the servants, to see the end.

59Now the chief priests, and elders, and all the council, sought false witness against Jesus, to put him to death;

60But found none: yea, though many false witnesses came, *yet* found they none. At the last came two false witnesses,

61And said, this *fellow* said, I am able to destroy the temple of God, and to build it in three days.

62And the high priest arose, and said unto him, Answerest thou nothing? what *is it which* these witness against thee?

63But Jesus held his peace. And the high priest answered and said unto him, I adjure thee by the living God, that thou tell us whether thou be the Christ, the Son of God.

64Jesus saith unto him, Thou hast said: nevertheless I say unto you, Hereafter shall ye see the Son of man sitting on the right hand of power, and coming in the clouds of heaven.

65Then the high priest rent his clothes, saying, He hath spoken blasphemy; what further need have we of witnesses? behold, now ye have heard his blasphemy.

66What think ye? They answered and said, He is guilty of death.

67Then did they spit in his face, and buffeted him; and others smote *him* with the palms of their hands,

68Saying, Prophesy unto us, thou Christ, Who is he that smote thee?

PSALM 32:1–11

B LESSED *is he whose* transgression is forgiven, *whose* sin *is* covered.

2Blessed *is* the man unto whom the LORD imputeth not iniquity, and in whose spirit *there is* no guile.

3When I kept silence, my bones waxed old through my roaring all the day long.

4For day and night thy hand was heavy upon me: my moisture is turned into the drought of summer. Selah.

5I acknowledged my sin unto thee, and mine iniquity have I not hid. I said, I will confess my transgressions unto the LORD; and thou forgavest the iniquity of my sin. Selah.

6For this shall every one that is godly pray unto thee in a time when thou mayest be found: surely in the floods of great waters they shall not come nigh unto him.

7Thou *art* my hiding place; thou shalt preserve me from trouble; thou shalt compass me about with songs of deliverance. Selah.

8I will instruct thee and teach thee in the way which thou shalt go: I will guide thee with mine eye.

9Be ye not as the horse, *or* as the mule, *which* have no understanding: whose mouth must be held in with bit and bridle, lest they come near unto thee.

10Many sorrows *shall be* to the wicked: but he that trusteth in the LORD, mercy shall compass him about.

11Be glad in the LORD, and rejoice, ye righteous: and shout for joy, all *ye that are* upright in heart.

PROVERBS FOR TODAY/ 8:27–32

When he prepared the heavens, I was *there: when he set a compass upon the face of the depth: When he established the clouds above: when he strengthened the fountains of the deep: When he gave to the sea his decree, that the waters should not pass his commandment: when he appointed the foundations of the earth: Then I was by him,* as *one brought up* with him: *and I was daily* his *delight, rejoicing always before him; Rejoicing in the habitable part of his earth; and my delights* were *with the sons of men. Now therefore hearken unto me, O ye children: for blessed* are they that *keep my ways.*

FEBRUARY 11

EXODUS 32:1—33:23

AND when the people saw that Moses delayed to come down out of the mount, the people gathered themselves together unto Aaron, and said unto him, Up, make us gods, which shall go before us; for *as for* this Moses, the man that brought us up out of the land of Egypt, we wot not what is become of him.

2And Aaron said unto them, Break off the golden earrings, which *are* in the ears of your wives, of your sons, and of your daughters, and bring *them* unto me.

3And all the people brake off the golden earrings which *were* in their ears, and brought *them* unto Aaron.

4And he received *them* at their hand, and fashioned it with a graving tool, after he had made it a molten calf: and they said, These *be* thy gods, O Israel, which brought thee up out of the land of Egypt.

5And when Aaron saw *it,* he built an altar before it; and Aaron made proclamation, and said, To morrow *is* a feast to the LORD.

6And they rose up early on the morrow, and offered burnt offerings, and brought peace offerings; and the people sat down to eat and to drink, and rose up to play.

7And the Lord said unto Moses, Go, get thee down; for thy people, which thou broughtest out of the land of Egypt, have corrupted *themselves:*

8They have turned aside quickly out of the way which I commanded them: they have made them a molten calf, and have worshipped it, and have sacrificed thereunto, and said, These *be* thy gods, O Israel, which have brought thee up out of the land of Egypt.

9And the Lord said unto Moses, I have seen this people, and, behold, it *is* a stiffnecked people:

10Now therefore let me alone, that my wrath may wax hot against them, and that I may consume them: and I will make of thee a great nation.

11And Moses besought the Lord his God, and said, Lord, why doth thy wrath wax hot against thy people, which thou hast brought forth out of the land of Egypt with great power, and with a mighty hand?

12Wherefore should the Egyptians speak, and say, For mischief did he bring them out, to slay them in the mountains, and to consume them from the face of the earth? Turn from thy fierce wrath, and repent of this evil against thy people.

13Remember Abraham, Isaac, and Israel, thy servants, to whom thou swarest by thine own self, and saidst unto them, I will multiply your seed as the stars of heaven, and all this land that I have spoken of will I give unto your seed, and they shall inherit *it* for ever.

14And the Lord repented of the evil which he thought to do unto his people.

15And Moses turned, and went down from the mount, and the two tables of the testimony *were* in his hand: the tables *were* written on both their sides; on the one side and on the other *were* they written.

16And the tables *were* the work of God, and the writing *was* the writing of God, graven upon the tables.

17And when Joshua heard the noise of the people as they shouted, he said unto Moses, *There is* a noise of war in the camp.

18And he said, *It is* not the voice of *them that* shout for mastery, neither *is it* the voice of *them that* cry for being overcome: *but* the noise of *them that* sing do I hear.

19And it came to pass, as soon as he came nigh unto the camp, that he saw the calf, and the dancing: and Moses' anger waxed hot, and he cast the tables out of his hands, and brake them beneath the mount.

20And he took the calf which they had made, and burnt *it* in the fire, and ground *it* to powder, and strawed *it* upon the water, and made the children of Israel drink *of it.*

21And Moses said unto Aaron, What did this people unto thee, that thou hast brought so great a sin upon them?

22And Aaron said, Let not the anger of my lord wax hot: thou knowest the people, that they *are set* on mischief.

23For they said unto me, Make us gods, which shall go before us: for *as for* this Moses, the man that brought us up out of the land of Egypt, we wot not what is become of him.

24And I said unto them, Whosoever hath any gold, let them break *it* off. So they gave *it* me: then I cast it into the fire, and there came out this calf.

25And when Moses saw that the people *were* naked; (for Aaron had made them naked unto *their* shame among their enemies:)

26Then Moses stood in the gate of the camp, and said, Who *is* on the Lord's side? *let him come* unto me. And all the sons of Levi gathered themselves together unto him.

27And he said unto them, Thus saith the Lord God of Israel, Put every man his sword by his side, *and* go in and out from gate to gate throughout the camp, and slay every man his brother, and every man his companion, and every man his neighbour.

28And the children of Levi did according to the word of Moses: and there fell of the people that day about three thousand men.

29For Moses had said, Consecrate yourselves to day to the LORD, even every man upon his son, and upon his brother; that he may bestow upon you a blessing this day.

30And it came to pass on the morrow, that Moses said unto the people, Ye have sinned a great sin: and now I will go up unto the LORD; peradventure I shall make an atonement for your sin.

31And Moses returned unto the LORD, and said, oh, this people have sinned a great sin, and have made them gods of gold.

32Yet now, if thou wilt forgive their sin—; and if not, blot me, I pray thee, out of thy book which thou hast written.

33And the LORD said unto Moses, Whosoever hath sinned against me, him will I blot out of my book.

34Therefore now go, lead the people unto *the place* of which I have spoken unto thee: behold, mine Angel shall go before thee: nevertheless in the day when I visit I will visit their sin upon them.

35And the LORD plagued the people, because they made the calf, which Aaron made.

AND the LORD said unto Moses, Depart, *and* go up hence, thou and the people which thou has brought up out of the land of Egypt, unto the land which I sware unto Abraham, to Isaac, and to Jacob, saying, Unto thy seed will I give it:

2And I will send an angel before thee; and I will drive out the Canaanite, the Amorite, and the Hittite, and the Perizzite, the Hivite, and the Jebusite:

3Unto a land flowing with milk and honey: for I will not go up in the midst of thee; for thou *art* a stiffnecked people: lest I consume thee in the way.

4And when the people heard these evil tidings, they mourned: and no man did put on him his ornaments.

5For the LORD had said unto Moses, Say unto the children of Israel, Ye *are* a stiffnecked people: I will come up into the midst of thee in a moment, and consume thee: therefore now put off thy ornaments from thee, that I may know what to do unto thee.

6And the children of Israel stripped themselves of their ornaments by the mount Horeb.

7And Moses took the tabernacle, and pitched it without the camp, afar off from the camp, and called it the Tabernacle of the congregation. And it came to pass, *that* every one which sought the LORD went out unto the tabernacle of the congregation, which *was* without the camp.

8And it came to pass, when Moses went out unto the tabernacle, *that* all the people rose up, and stood every man *at* his tent door, and looked after Moses, until he was gone into the tabernacle.

9And it came to pass, as Moses entered into the tabernacle, the cloudy pillar descended, and stood *at* the door of the tabernacle, and *the LORD talked with Moses.*

10And all the people saw the cloudy pillar stand *at* the tabernacle door: and all the people rose up and worshipped, every man *in* his tent door.

11And the LORD spake unto Moses face to face, as a man speaketh unto his friend. And he turned again into the camp: but his servant Joshua, the son of Nun, a young man, departed not out of the tabernacle.

12And Moses said unto the LORD, See, thou sayest unto me, Bring up this people: and thou hast not let me know whom thou wilt send with me. Yet thou hast said, I know thee by name, and thou hast also found grace in my sight.

13Now therefore, I pray thee, if I have found grace in thy sight, shew me now thy way, that I may know thee, that I may find grace in thy sight: and consider that this nation *is* thy people.

14And he said, My presence shall go *with thee,* and I will give thee rest.

15And he said unto him, If thy presence go not *with me,* carry us not up hence.

16For wherein shall it be known here that I and thy people have found grace in thy sight? *is it* not in that thou goest with us? so shall we be separated, I and thy people, from all the people that *are* upon the face of the earth.

17And the LORD said unto Moses, I will do this thing also that thou hast spoken: for thou hast found grace in my sight, and I know thee by name.

18And he said, I beseech thee, shew me thy glory.

19And he said, I will make all my goodness pass before thee, and I will proclaim the name of the LORD before thee; and will be gracious to whom I will be gracious, and will shew mercy on whom I will shew mercy.

20And he said, Thou canst not see my face: for there shall no man see me, and live.

21And the LORD said, Behold, *there* is a place by me, and thou shalt stand upon a rock:

22And it shall come to pass, while my glory passeth by, that I will put thee in a clift of the rock, and will cover thee with my hand while I pass by:

23And I will take away mine hand, and thou shalt see my back parts: but my face shall not be seen.

MATTHEW 26:69—27:14

Now Peter sat without in the palace: and a damsel came unto him, saying, Thou also wast with Jesus of Galilee.

70But he denied before *them* all, saying, I know not what thou sayest.

71And when he was gone out into the porch, another *maid* saw him, and said unto them that were there, This *fellow* was also with Jesus of Nazareth.

72And again he denied with an oath, I do not know the man.

73And after a while came unto *him* they that stood by, and said to Peter, Surely thou also art *one* of them; for thy speech bewrayeth thee.

74Then began he to curse and to swear, *saying,* I know not the man. And immediately the cock crew.

75And Peter remembered the word of Jesus, which said unto him, Before the cock crow, thou shalt deny me thrice. And he went out, and wept bitterly.

WHEN the morning was come, all the chief priests and elders of the people took counsel against Jesus to put him to death:

2And when they had bound him, they led *him* away, and delivered him to Pontius Pilate the governor.

3Then Judas, which had betrayed him, when he saw that he was condemned, repented himself, and brought again the thirty pieces of silver to the chief priests and elders,

4Saying, I have sinned in that I have betrayed the innocent blood. And they said, What *is that* to us? see thou *to that.*

5And he cast down the pieces of silver in the temple, and departed, and went and hanged himself.

6And the chief priests took the silver pieces, and said, It is not lawful for to put them into the treasury, because it is the price of blood.

7And they took counsel, and bought with them the potter's field, to bury strangers in.

8Wherefore that field was called, The field of blood, unto this day.

9Then was fulfilled that which was

spoken by Jeremy the prophet, saying, And they took the thirty pieces of silver, the price of him that was valued, whom they of the children of Israel did value;

¹⁰And gave them for the potter's field, as the Lord appointed me.

¹¹And Jesus stood before the governor: and the governor asked him, saying, Art thou the King of the Jews? And Jesus said unto him, Thou sayest.

¹²And when he was accused of the chief priests and elders, he answered nothing.

¹³Then said Pilate unto him, Hearest thou not how many things they witness against thee?

¹⁴And he answered him to never a word; insomuch that the governor marvelled greatly.

PSALM 33:1—11

REJOICE in the LORD, O ye righteous: *for* praise is comely for the upright.

²Praise the LORD with harp: sing unto him with the psaltery *and* an instrument of ten strings.

³Sing unto him a new song; play skilfully with a loud noise.

⁴For the word of the LORD *is* right; and all his works *are done* in truth.

⁵He loveth righteousness and judgment: the earth is full of the goodness of the LORD.

⁶By the word of the LORD were the heavens made; and all the host of them by the breath of his mouth.

⁷He gathereth the waters of the sea together as an heap: he layeth up the depth in storehouses.

⁸Let all the earth fear the LORD: let all the inhabitants of the world stand in awe of him.

⁹For he spake, and it was *done;* he commanded, and it stood fast.

¹⁰The LORD bringeth the counsel of the heathen to nought: he maketh the devices of the people of none effect.

¹¹The counsel of the LORD standeth for ever, the thoughts of his heart to all generations.

PROVERBS FOR TODAY/ 8:33—36

Hear instruction, and be wise, and refuse it not. Blessed is *the man that heareth me, watching daily at my gates, waiting at the posts of my doors. For whoso findeth me findeth life, and shall obtain favour of the LORD. But he that sinneth against me wrongeth his own soul: all they that hate me love death.*

FEBRUARY 12

EXODUS 34:1—35:9

AND the LORD said unto Moses, Hew thee two tables of stone like unto the first: and I will write upon *these* tables the words that were in the first tables, which thou brakest.

²And be ready in the morning, and come up in the morning unto mount Sinai, and present thyself there to me in the top of the mount.

³And no man shall come up with thee, neither let any man be seen throughout all the mount; neither let the flocks nor herds feed before that mount.

⁴And he hewed two tables of stone like unto the first; and Moses rose up early in the morning, and went up unto

mount Sinai, as the LORD had commanded him, and took in his hand the two tables of stone.

5And the LORD descended in the cloud, and stood with him there, and proclaimed the name of the LORD.

6And the LORD passed by before him, and proclaimed, The LORD, The LORD God, merciful and gracious, longsuffering, and abundant in goodness and truth,

7Keeping mercy for thousands, forgiving iniquity and transgression and sin, and that will by no means clear *the guilty;* visiting the iniquity of the fathers upon the children, and upon the children's children, unto the third and to the fourth *generation.*

8And Moses made haste, and bowed his head toward the earth, and worshipped.

9And he said, If now I have found grace in thy sight, O Lord, let my Lord, I pray thee, go among us; for it *is* a stiffnecked people; and pardon our iniquity and our sin, and take us for thine inheritance.

10And he said, Behold, I make a covenant: before all thy people I will do marvels, such as have not been done in all the earth, nor in any nation: and all the people among which thou *art* shall see the work of the LORD: for it *is* a terrible thing that I will do with thee.

11Observe thou that which I command thee this day: behold, I drive out before thee the Amorite, and the Canaanite, and the Hittite, and the Perizzite, and the Hivite, and the Jebusite.

12Take heed to thyself, lest thou make a covenant with the inhabitants of the land whither thou goest, lest it be for a snare in the midst of thee:

13But he shall destroy their altars, break their images, and cut down their groves:

14For thou shalt worship no other god: for the LORD, whose name *is* Jealous, *is* a jealous God:

15Lest thou make a covenant with the inhabitants of the land, and they go a whoring after their gods, and do sacrifice unto their gods, and *one* call thee, and thou eat of his sacrifice;

16And thou take of their daughters unto thy sons, and their daughters go a whoring after their gods, and make thy sons go a whoring after their gods.

17Thou shalt make thee no molten gods.

18The feast of unleavened bread shalt thou keep. Seven days thou shalt eat unleavened bread, as I commanded thee, in the time of the month Abib: for in the month Abib thou camest out from Egypt.

19All that openeth the matrix *is* mine; and every firstling among thy cattle, *whether* ox or sheep, *that is male.*

20But the firstling of an ass thou shalt redeem with a lamb: and if thou redeem *him* not, then shalt thou break his neck. All the firstborn of thy sons thou shalt redeem. And none shall appear before me empty.

21Six days thou shalt work, but on the seventh day thou shalt rest: in earing time and in harvest thou shalt rest.

22And thou shalt observe the feast of weeks, of the firstfruits of wheat harvest, and the feast of ingathering at the year's end.

23Thrice in the year shall all your menchildren appear before the Lord GOD, the God of Israel.

24For I will cast out the nations before thee, and enlarge thy borders: neither shall any man desire thy land, when thou shalt go up to appear before the LORD thy God thrice in the year.

25Thou shalt not offer the blood of my sacrifice with leaven; neither shall the sacrifice of the feast of the passover be left unto the morning.

26The first of the firstfruits of thy land thou shalt bring unto the house of the LORD thy God. Thou shalt not seethe a kid in his mother's milk.

27And the LORD said unto Moses, Write thou these words: for after the tenor of these words I have made a covenant with thee and with Israel.

28And he was there with the LORD forty days and forty nights; he did neither eat bread, nor drink water. And he wrote upon the tables the words of the covenant, the ten commandments.

29And it came to pass, when Moses came down from mount Sinai with the two tables of testimony in Moses' hand, when he came down from the mount, that Moses wist not that the skin of his face shone while he talked with him.

30And when Aaron and all the children of Israel saw Moses, behold, the skin of his face shone; and they were afraid to come nigh him.

31And Moses called unto them; and Aaron and all the rulers of the congregation returned unto him: and Moses talked with them.

32And afterward all the children of Israel came nigh: and he gave them in commandment all that the LORD had spoken with him in mount Sinai.

33And *till* Moses had done speaking with them, he put a vail on his face.

34But when Moses went in before the LORD to speak with him, he took the vail off, until he came out. And he came out, and spake unto the children of Israel *that* which he was commanded.

35And the children of Israel saw the face of Moses, that the skin of Moses' face shone: and Moses put the vail upon his face again, until he went in to speak with him.

AND Moses gathered all the congregation of the children of Israel together, and said unto them, These *are* the words which the LORD hath commanded, that *ye* should do them.

2Six days shall work be done, but on the seventh day there shall be to you an holy day, a sabbath of rest to the LORD: whosoever doeth work therein shall be put to death.

3Ye shall kindle no fire throughout your habitations upon the sabbath day.

4And Moses spake unto all the congregation of the children of Israel, saying, This *is* the thing which the LORD commanded, saying,

5Take ye from among you an offering unto the LORD: whosoever *is* of a willing heart, let him bring it, an offering of the LORD: gold, and silver, and brass,

6And blue, and purple, and scarlet, and fine linen, and goats' *hair,*

7And rams' skins dyed red, and badgers' skins, and shittim wood,

8And oil for the light, and spices for anointing oil, and for the sweet incense,

9And onyx stones, and stones to be set for the ephod, and for the breastplate.

MATTHEW 27:15–34

Now at *that* feast the governor was wont to release unto the people a prisoner, whom they would.

16And they had then a notable prisoner, called Barabbas.

17Therefore when they were gathered together, Pilate said unto them, Whom will ye that I release unto you? Barabbas, or Jesus which is called Christ?

18For he knew that for envy they had delivered him.

19When he was set down on the judgment seat, his wife sent unto him, saying, Have thou nothing to do with that just man: for I have suffered many things this day in a dream because of him.

20But the chief priests and elders persuaded the multitude that they should ask Barabbas, and destroy Jesus.

21The governor answered and said unto them, Whether of the twain will ye that I release unto you? They said, Barabbas.

22Pilate saith unto them, What shall I do then with Jesus which is called

Christ? *They* all say unto him, Let him be crucified.

23And the governor said, Why, what evil hath he done? But they cried out the more, saying, Let him be crucified.

24When Pilate saw that he could prevail nothing, but *that* rather a tumult was made, he took water, and washed *his* hands before the multitude, saying, I am innocent of the blood of this just person: see ye *to it*.

25Then answered all the people, and said, His blood *be* on us, and on our children.

26Then released he Barabbas unto them: and when he had scourged Jesus, he delivered *him* to be crucified.

27Then the soldiers of the governor took Jesus into the common hall, and gathered unto him the whole band *of soldiers*.

28And they stripped him, and put on him a scarlet robe.

29And when they had platted a crown of thorns, they put *it* upon his head, and a reed in his right hand: and they bowed the knee before him, and mocked him, saying, Hail, King of the Jews!

30And they spit upon him, and took the reed, and smote him on the head.

31And after that they had mocked him, they took the robe off from him, and put his own raiment on him, and led him away to crucify *him*.

32And as they came out, they found a man of Cyrene, Simon by name: him they compelled to bear his cross.

33And when they were come unto a place called Golgotha, that is to say, a place of a skull,

34They gave him vinegar to drink mingled with gall: and when he had tasted *thereof*, he would not drink.

PSALM 33:12–22

Blessed *is* the nation whose God *is* the Lord: *and* the people *whom* he hath chosen for his own inheritance.

13The Lord looketh from heaven; he beholdeth all the sons of men.

14From the place of his habitation he looketh upon all the inhabitants of the earth.

15He fashioneth their hearts alike; he considereth all their works.

16There is no king saved by the multitude of an host: a mighty man is not delivered by much strength.

17An horse *is* a vain thing for safety: neither shall he deliver *any* by his great strength.

18Behold, the eye of the Lord *is* upon them that fear him, upon them that hope in his mercy;

19To deliver their soul from death, and to keep them alive in famine.

20Our soul waiteth for the Lord: he *is* our help and our shield.

21For our heart shall rejoice in him, because we have trusted in his holy name.

22Let thy mercy, O Lord, be upon us, according as we hope in thee.

PROVERBS FOR TODAY/ 9:1–6

Wisdom hath builded her house, she hath hewn out her seven pillars: She hath killed her beasts: she hath mingled her wine; she hath also furnished her table. She hath sent forth her maidens: she crieth upon the highest places of the city, Whoso is simple, let him turn in hither: as for him that wanteth understanding, she saith to him, Come, eat of my bread, and drink of the wine which I have mingled. Forsake the foolish, and live; and go in the way of understanding.

FEBRUARY 13

EXODUS 35:10—36:38

AND every wise hearted among you shall come, and make all that the LORD hath commanded;

11The tabernacle, his tent, and his covering, his taches, and his boards, his bars, his pillars, and his sockets,

12The ark, and the staves thereof, *with* the mercy seat, and the vail of the covering,

13The table, and his staves, and all his vessels, and the shewbread,

14The candlestick also for the light, and his furniture, and his lamps, with the oil for the light,

15And the incense altar, and his staves, and the anointing oil, and the sweet incense, and the hanging for the door at the entering in of the tabernacle,

16The altar of burnt offering, with his brasen grate, his staves, and all his vessels, the laver and his foot,

17The hangings of the court, his pillars, and their sockets, and the hanging for the door of the court,

18The pins of the tabernacle, and the pins of the court, and their cords,

19The cloths of service, to do service in the holy *place,* the holy garments for Aaron the priest, and the garments of his sons, to minister in the priest's office.

20And all the congregation of the children of Israel departed from the presence of Moses.

21And they came, every one whose heart stirred him up, and every one whom his spirit made willing, *and* they brought the LORD's offering to the work of the tabernacle of the congregation, and for all his service, and for the holy garments.

22And they came, both men and women, as many as were willing hearted, *and* brought bracelets, and earrings, and rings, and tablets, all jewels of gold: and every man that offered *offered* an offering of gold unto the LORD.

23And every man, with whom was found blue, and purple, and scarlet, and fine linen, and goats' *hair,* and red skins of rams, and badgers' skins, brought *them.*

24Every one that did offer an offering of silver and brass brought the LORD's offering: and every man, with whom was found shittim wood for any work of the service, brought *it.*

25And all the women that were wise hearted did spin with their hands, and brought that which they had spun, *both* of blue, and of purple, *and* of scarlet, and of fine linen.

26And all the women whose heart stirred them up in wisdom spun goats' *hair.*

27And the rulers brought onyx stones, and stones to be set, for the ephod, and for the breastplate;

28And spice, and oil for the light, and for the anointing oil, and for the sweet incense.

29The children of Israel brought a willing offering unto the LORD, every man and woman, whose heart made them willing to bring for all manner of work, which the LORD had commanded to be made by the hand of Moses.

30And Moses said unto the children of Israel, See, the LORD hath called by name Bezaleel the son of Uri, the son of Hur, of the tribe of Judah;

31And he hath filled him with the spirit of God, in wisdom, in understanding, and in knowledge, and in all manner of workmanship;

32And to devise curious works, to work in gold, and in silver, and in brass,

33And in the cutting of stones, to set *them,* and in carving of wood, to make any manner of cunning work.

34And he hath put in his heart that he may teach, *both* he, and Aholiab, the son of Ahisamach, of the tribe of Dan.

35Them hath he filled with wisdom of heart, to work all manner of work, of the engraver, and of the cunning workman, and of the embroiderer, in blue, and in purple, in scarlet, and in fine linen, and of the weaver, *even* of them that do any work, and of those that devise cunning work.

THEN wrought Bezaleel and Aholiab, and every wise hearted man, in whom the LORD put wisdom and understanding to know how to work all manner of work for the service of the sanctuary, according to all that the LORD had commanded.

2And Moses called Bezaleel and Aholiab, and every wise hearted man, in whose heart the LORD had put wisdom, *even* every one whose heart stirred him up to come unto the work to do it:

3And they received of Moses all the offering, which the children of Israel had brought for the work of the service of the sanctuary, to make it *withal*. And they brought yet unto him free offerings every morning.

4And all the wise men, that wrought all the work of the sanctuary, came every man from his work which they made;

5And they spake unto Moses, saying, The people bring much more than enough for the service of the work, which the LORD commanded to make.

6And Moses gave commandment, and they caused it to be proclaimed throughout the camp, saying, Let neither man nor woman make any more work for the offering of the sanctuary. So the people were restrained from bringing.

7For the stuff they had was sufficient for all the work to make it, and too much.

8And every wise hearted man among them that wrought the work of the tabernacle made ten curtains *of* fine twined linen, and blue, and purple, and scarlet: *with* cherubims of cunning work made he them.

9The length of one curtain *was* twenty and eight cubits, and the breadth of one curtain four cubits: the curtains *were* all of one size.

10And he coupled the five curtains one unto another: and *the other* five curtains he coupled one unto another.

11And he made loops of blue on the edge of one curtain from the selvedge in the coupling: likewise he made in the uttermost side of *another* curtain, in the coupling of the second.

12Fifty loops made he in one curtain, and fifty loops made he in the edge of the curtain which *was* in the coupling of the second: the loops held one *curtain* to another.

13And he made fifty taches of gold, and coupled the curtains one unto another with the taches: so it became one tabernacle.

14And he made curtains *of* goats' *hair* for the tent over the tabernacle: eleven curtains he made them.

15The length of one curtain *was* thirty cubits, and four cubits *was* the breadth of one curtain: the eleven curtains *were* of one size.

16And he coupled five curtains by themselves, and six curtains by themselves.

17And he made fifty loops upon the uttermost edge of the curtain in the coupling, and fifty loops made he upon the edge of the curtain which coupleth the second.

18And he made fifty taches *of* brass to couple the tent together, that it might be one.

19And he made a covering for the tent *of* rams' skins dyed red, and a covering *of* badgers' skins above *that*.

20And he made boards for the tabernacle *of* shittim wood, standing up.

21The length of a board *was* ten cubits, and the breadth of a board one cubit and a half.

22One board had two tenons, equally distant one from another: thus did he make for all the boards of the tabernacle.

23And he made boards for the tabernacle; twenty boards for the south side southward:

24And forty sockets of silver he made under the twenty boards; two sockets under one board for his two tenons, and two sockets under another board for his two tenons.

25And for the other side of the tabernacle, *which is* toward the north corner, he made twenty boards,

26And their forty sockets of silver; two sockets under one board, and two sockets under another board.

27And for the sides of the tabernacle westward he made six boards.

28And two boards made he for the corners of the tabernacle in the two sides.

29And they were coupled beneath, and coupled together at the head thereof, to one ring: thus he did to both of them in both the corners.

30And there were eight boards; and their sockets *were* sixteen sockets of silver, under every board two sockets.

31And he made bars of shittim wood; five for the boards of the one side of the tabernacle,

32And five bars for the board of the other side of the tabernacle, and five bars for the boards of the tabernacle for the sides westward.

33And he made the middle bar to shoot through the boards from the one end to the other.

34And he overlaid the boards with gold, and made their rings *of* gold *to be* places for the bars, and overlaid the bars with gold.

35And he made a vail *of* blue, and purple, and scarlet, and fine twined linen: *with* cherubims made he it of cunning work.

36And he made thereunto four pillars *of* shittim *wood,* and overlaid them with gold: their hooks *were of* gold; and he cast for them four sockets of silver.

37And he made an hanging for the tabernacle door *of* blue, and purple, and scarlet, and fine twined linen, of needlework;

38And the five pillars of it with their hooks: and he overlaid their chapiters and their fillets with gold: but their five sockets *were of* brass.

MATTHEW 27:35–66

AND they crucified him [Jesus], and parted his garments, casting lots: that it might be fulfilled which was spoken by the prophet, They parted my garments among them, and upon my vesture did they cast lots.

36And sitting down they watched him there;

37And set up over his head his accusation written, THIS IS JESUS THE KING OF THE JEWS.

38Then were there two thieves crucified with him, one on the right hand, and another on the left.

39And they that passed by reviled him, wagging their heads,

40And saying, Thou that destroyest the temple, and buildest *it* in three days, save thyself. If thou be the Son of God, come down from the cross.

41Likewise also the chief priests mocking *him,* with the scribes and elders, said,

42He saved others; himself he cannot save. If he be the King of Israel, let him now come down from the cross, and we will believe him.

43He trusted in God; let him deliver him now, if he will have him: for he said, I am the Son of God.

44The thieves also, which were crucified with him, cast the same in his teeth.

45Now from the sixth hour there was

darkness over all the land unto the ninth hour.

⁴⁶And about the ninth hour Jesus cried with a loud voice, saying, Eli, Eli, lama sabachthani? that is to say, My God, my God, why hast thou forsaken me?

⁴⁷Some of them that stood there, when they heard *that,* said, This *man* calleth for Elias.

⁴⁸And straightway one of them ran, and took a spunge, and filled *it* with vinegar, and put *it* on a reed, and gave him to drink.

⁴⁹The rest said, Let be, let us see whether Elias will come to save him.

⁵⁰Jesus, when he had cried again with a loud voice, yielded up the ghost.

⁵¹And, behold, the vail of the temple was rent in twain from the top to the bottom; and the earth did quake, and the rocks rent;

⁵²And the graves were opened; and many bodies of the saints which slept arose,

⁵³And came out of the graves after his resurrection, and went into the holy city, and appeared unto many.

⁵⁴Now when the centurion, and they that were with him, watching Jesus, saw the earthquake, and those things that were done, they feared greatly, saying, Truly this was the Son of God.

⁵⁵And many women were there beholding afar off, which followed Jesus from Galilee, ministering unto him:

⁵⁶Among which was Mary Magdalene, and Mary the mother of James and Joses, and the mother of Zebedee's children.

⁵⁷When the even was come, there came a rich man of Arimathaea, named Joseph, who also himself was Jesus' disciple:

⁵⁸He went to Pilate, and begged the body of Jesus. Then Pilate commanded the body to be delivered.

⁵⁹And when Joseph had taken the body, he wrapped it in a clean linen cloth,

⁶⁰And laid it in his own new tomb, which he had hewn out in the rock: and he rolled a great stone to the door of the sepulchre, and departed.

⁶¹And there was Mary Magdalene, and the other Mary, sitting over against the sepulchre.

⁶²Now the next day, that followed the day of the preparation, the chief priests and Pharisees came together unto Pilate,

⁶³Saying, Sir, we remember that that deceiver said, while he was yet alive, After three days I will rise again.

⁶⁴Command therefore that the sepulchre be made sure until the third day, lest his disciples come by night, and steal him away, and say unto the people, He is risen from the dead: so the last error shall be worse than the first.

⁶⁵Pilate said unto them, Ye have a watch: go your way, make *it* as sure as ye can.

⁶⁶So they went, and made the sepulchre sure, sealing the stone, and setting a watch.

PSALM 34:1–10

I will bless the LORD at all times: his praise *shall* continually *be* in my mouth.

²My soul shall make her boast in the LORD: the humble shall hear *thereof,* and be glad.

³O magnify the LORD with me, and let us exalt his name together.

⁴I sought the LORD, and he heard me, and delivered me from all my fears.

⁵They looked unto him, and were lightened: and their faces were not ashamed.

⁶This poor man cried, and the LORD heard *him,* and saved him out of all his troubles.

⁷The angel of the LORD encampeth round about them that fear him, and delivereth them.

⁸O taste and see that the LORD *is* good: blessed *is* the man *that* trusteth in him.

9O fear the LORD, ye his saints: for *there is* no want to them that fear him.

10The young lions do lack, and suffer hunger: but they that seek the LORD shall not want any good *thing.*

PROVERBS FOR TODAY/ 9:7–8

He that reproveth a scorner getteth to himself shame: and he that rebuketh a wicked man getteth himself a blot. Reprove not a scorner, lest he hate thee: rebuke a wise man, and he will love thee.

FEBRUARY 14

EXODUS 37:1—38:31

AND Bezaleel made the ark *of* shittim wood: two cubits and a half *was* the length of it, and a cubit and a half the breadth of it, and a cubit and a half the height of it:

2And he overlaid it with pure gold within and without, and made a crown of gold to it round about.

3And he cast for it four rings of gold, *to be set* by the four corners of it; even two rings upon the one side of it, and two rings upon the other side of it.

4And he made staves *of* shittim wood, and overlaid them with gold.

5And he put the staves into the rings by the sides of the ark, to bear the ark.

6And he made the mercy seat *of* pure gold: two cubits and a half *was* the length thereof, and one cubit and a half the breadth thereof.

7And he made two cherubims *of* gold, beaten out of one piece made he them, on the two ends of the mercy seat;

8One cherub on the end on this side, and another cherub on the *other* end on that side: out of the mercy seat made he the cherubims on the two ends thereof.

9And the cherubims spread out *their* wings on high, *and* covered with their wings over the mercy seat, with their faces one to another; *even* to the mercy

seatward were the faces of the cherubims.

10And he made the table *of* shittim wood: two cubits *was* the length thereof, and a cubit the breadth thereof, and a cubit and a half the height thereof:

11And he overlaid it with pure gold, and made thereunto a crown of gold round about.

12Also he made thereunto a border of an handbreadth round about; and made a crown of gold for the border thereof round about.

13And he cast for it four rings of gold, and put the rings upon the four corners that *were* in the four feet thereof.

14Over against the border were the rings, the places for the staves to bear the table.

15And he made the staves *of* shittim wood, and overlaid them with gold, to bear the table.

16And he made the vessels which *were* upon the table, his dishes, and his spoons, and his bowls, and his covers to cover withal, *of* pure gold.

17And he made the candlestick *of* pure gold: *of* beaten work made he the candlestick; his shaft, and his branch, his bowls, his knops, and his flowers, were of the same:

18And six branches going out of the sides thereof; three branches of the candlestick out of the one side thereof, and three branches of the candlestick out of the other side thereof:

19Three bowls made after the fashion of almonds in one branch, a knop and a flower; and three bowls made like almonds in another branch, a knop and a flower: so throughout the six branches going out of the candlestick.

20And in the candlestick *were* four bowls made like almonds, his knops, and his flowers:

21And a knop under two branches of the same, and a knop under two branches of the same, and a knop under two branches of the same, according to the six branches going out of it.

22Their knops and their branches were of the same: all of it *was* one beaten work *of* pure gold.

23And he made his seven lamps, and his snuffers, and his snuffdishes, *of* pure gold.

24*Of* a talent of pure gold made he it, and all the vessels thereof.

25And he made the incense altar *of* shittim wood: the length of it *was* a cubit, and the breadth of it a cubit; *it was* foursquare; and two cubits *was* the height of it; the horns thereof were of the same.

26And he overlaid it with pure gold, *both* the top of it, and the sides thereof round about, and the horns of it: also he made unto it a crown of gold round about.

27And he made two rings of gold for it under the crown thereof, by the two corners of it, upon the two sides thereof, to be places for the staves to bear it withal.

28And he made the staves *of* shittim wood, and overlaid them with gold.

29And he made the holy anointing oil, and the pure incense of sweet spices, according to the work of the apothecary.

AND he made the altar of burnt offering *of* shittim wood: five cubits *was* the length thereof, and five cubits the breadth thereof; *it was* foursquare; and three cubits the height thereof.

2And he made the horns thereof on the four corners of it; the horns thereof were of the same: and he overlaid it with brass.

3And he made all the vessels of the altar, the pots, and the shovels, and the basons, *and* the fleshhooks, and the firepans: all the vessels thereof made he *of* brass.

4And he made for the altar a brasen grate of network under the compass thereof beneath unto the midst of it.

5And he cast four rings for the four ends of the grate of brass, *to be* places for the staves.

6And he made the staves *of* shittim wood, and overlaid them with brass.

7And he put the staves into the rings on the sides of the altar, to bear it withal; he made the altar hollow with boards.

8And he made the laver *of* brass, and the foot of it *of* brass, of the lookingglasses of *the women* assembling, which assembled *at* the door of the tabernacle of the congregation.

9And he made the court: on the south side southward the hangings of the court *were of* fine twined linen, an hundred cubits:

10Their pillars *were* twenty, and their brasen sockets twenty; the hooks of the pillars and their fillets *were of* silver.

11And for the north side *the hangings were* an hundred cubits, their pillars *were* twenty, and their sockets of brass twenty; the hooks of the pillars and their fillets *of* silver.

12And for the west side *were* hangings of fifty cubits, their pillars ten, and their sockets ten; the hooks of the pillars and their fillets *of* silver.

13And for the east side eastward fifty cubits.

14The hangings of the one side *of the gate were* fifteen cubits; their pillars three, and their sockets three.

15And for the other side of the court

gate, on this hand and that hand, *were* hangings of fifteen cubits; their pillars three, and their sockets three.

16All the hangings of the court round about *were* of fine twined linen.

17And the sockets for the pillars *were of* brass; the hooks of the pillars and their fillets *of* silver; and the overlaying of their chapiters *of* silver; and all the pillars of the court *were* filleted with silver.

18And the hanging for the gate of the court *was* needlework, *of* blue, and purple, and scarlet, and fine twined linen: and twenty cubits *was* the length, and the height in the breadth *was* five cubits, answerable to the hangings of the court.

19And their pillars *were* four, and their sockets *of* brass four; their hooks *of* silver, and the overlaying of their chapiters and their fillets *of* silver.

20And all the pins of the tabernacle, and of the court round about, *were of* brass.

21This is the sum of the tabernacle, *even* of the tabernacle of testimony, as it was counted, according to the commandment of Moses, *for* the service of the Levites, by the hand of Ithamar, son to Aaron the priest.

22And Bezaleel the son of Uri, the son of Hur, of the tribe of Judah, made all that the LORD commanded Moses.

23And with him *was* Aholiab, son of Ahisamach, of the tribe of Dan, an engraver, and a cunning workman, and an embroiderer in blue, and in purple, and in scarlet, and fine linen.

24All the gold that was occupied for the work in all the work of the holy *place*, even the gold of the offering, was twenty and nine talents, and seven hundred and thirty shekels, after the shekel of the sanctuary.

25And the silver of them that were numbered of the congregation *was* an hundred talents, and a thousand seven hundred and threescore and fifteen shekels, after the shekel of the sanctuary:

26A bekah for every man, *that is,* half a shekel, after the shekel of the sanctuary, for every one that went to be numbered, from twenty years old and upward, for six hundred thousand and three thousand and five hundred and fifty *men.*

27And of the hundred talents of silver were cast the sockets of the sanctuary, and the sockets of the vail; an hundred sockets of the hundred talents, a talent for a socket.

28And of the thousand seven hundred seventy and five *shekels* he made hooks for the pillars, and overlaid their chapiters, and filleted them.

29And the brass of the offering *was* seventy talents, and two thousand and four hundred shekels.

30And therewith he made the sockets to the door of the tabernacle of the congregation, and the brasen altar, and the brasen grate for it, and all the vessels of the altar,

31And the sockets of the court round about, and the sockets of the court gate, and all the pins of the tabernacle, and all the pins of the court round about.

MATTHEW 28:1–20

IN the end of the sabbath, as it began to dawn toward the first *day* of the week, came Mary Magdalene and the other Mary to see the sepulchre.

2And, behold, there was a great earthquake: for the angel of the Lord descended from heaven, and came and rolled back the stone from the door, and sat upon it.

3His countenance was like lightning, and his raiment white as snow:

4And for fear of him the keepers did shake, and became as dead *men.*

5And the angel answered and said unto the women, Fear not ye: for I know that ye seek Jesus, which was crucified.

6He is not here: for he is risen, as

he said. Come, see the place where the Lord lay.

7And go quickly, and tell his disciples that he is risen from the dead; and, behold, he goeth before you into Galilee; there shall ye see him: lo, I have told you.

8And they departed quickly from the sepulchre with fear and great joy; and did run to bring his disciples word.

9And as they went to tell his disciples, behold, Jesus met them, saying, All hail. And they came and held him by the feet, and worshipped him.

10Then said Jesus unto them, Be not afraid: go tell my brethren that they go into Galilee, and there shall they see me.

11Now when they were going, behold, some of the watch came into the city, and shewed unto the chief priests all the things that were done.

12And when they were assembled with the elders, and had taken counsel, they gave large money unto the soldiers,

13Saying, Say ye, His disciples came by night, and stole him *away* while we slept.

14And if this come to the governor's ears, we will persuade him, and secure you.

15So they took the money, and did as they were taught: and this saying is commonly reported among the Jews until this day.

16Then the eleven disciples went away into Galilee, into a mountain where Jesus had appointed them.

17And when they saw him, they worshipped him: but some doubted.

18And Jesus came and spake unto them, saying, All power is given unto me in heaven and in earth.

19Go ye therefore, and teach all nations, baptizing them in the name of the Father, and of the Son, and of the Holy Ghost:

20Teaching them to observe all things whatsoever I have commanded you: and, lo, I am with you alway, *even* unto the end of the world. Amen.

PSALM 34:11–22

COME, ye children, hearken unto me: I will teach you the fear of the LORD.

12What man *is he that* desireth life, *and* loveth *many* days, that he may see good?

13Keep thy tongue from evil, and thy lips from speaking guile.

14Depart from evil, and do good; seek peace, and pursue it.

15The eyes of the LORD *are* upon the righteous, and his ears *are open* unto their cry.

16The face of the LORD *is* against them that do evil, to cut off the remembrance of them from the earth.

17*The righteous* cry, and the LORD heareth, and delivereth them out of all their troubles.

18The LORD *is* nigh unto them that are of a broken heart; and saveth such as be of a contrite spirit.

19Many *are* the afflictions of the righteous: but the LORD delivereth him out of them all.

20He keepeth all his bones: not one of them is broken.

21Evil shall slay the wicked: and they that hate the righteous shall be desolate.

22The LORD redeemeth the soul of his servants: and none of them that trust in him shall be desolate.

PROVERBS FOR TODAY/ 9:9–10

Give instruction *to a wise* man, *and he will be yet wiser: teach a just* man, *and he will increase in learning. The fear of the LORD* is *the beginning of wisdom: and the knowledge of the holy* is *understanding.*

EXODUS 39:1—40:38

A ND of the blue, and purple, and scarlet, they made cloths of service, to do service in the holy *place*, and made the holy garments for Aaron; as the LORD commanded Moses.

2And he made the ephod *of* gold, blue, and purple, and scarlet, and fine twined linen.

3And they did beat the gold into thin plates, and cut *it into* wires, to work *it* in the blue, and in the purple, and in the scarlet, and in the fine linen, *with* cunning work.

4They made shoulderpieces for it, to couple *it* together: by the two edges was it coupled together.

5And the curious girdle of his ephod, that *was* upon it, *was* of the same, according to the work thereof; *of* gold, blue, and purple, and scarlet, and fine twined linen; as the LORD commanded Moses.

6And they wrought onyx stones inclosed in ouches of gold, graven, as signets are graven, with the names of the children of Israel.

7And he put them on the shoulders of the ephod, *that they should be* stones for a memorial to the children of Israel; as the LORD commanded Moses.

8And he made the breastplate *of* cunning work, like the work of the ephod; *of* gold, blue, and purple, and scarlet, and fine twined linen.

9It was foursquare; they made the breastplate double: a span *was* the length thereof, and a span the breadth thereof, *being* doubled.

10And they set in it four rows of stones: *the first* row *was* a sardius, a topaz, and a carbuncle: this *was* the first row.

11And the second row, an emerald, a sapphire, and a diamond.

12And the third row, a ligure, an agate, and an amethyst.

13And the fourth row, a beryl, an onyx, and a jasper: *they were* inclosed in ouches of gold in their inclosings.

14And the stones *were* according to the names of the children of Israel, twelve, according to their names, *like* the engravings of a signet, every one with his name, according to the twelve tribes.

15And they made upon the breastplate chains at the ends, *of* wreathen work *of* pure gold.

16And they made two ouches *of* gold, and two gold rings; and put the two rings in the two ends of the breastplate.

17And they put the two wreathen chains of gold in the two rings on the ends of the breastplate.

18And the two ends of the two wreathen chains they fastened in the two ouches, and put them on the shoulderpieces of the ephod, before it.

19And they made two rings of gold, and put *them* on the two ends of the breastplate, upon the border of it, which *was* on the side of the ephod inward.

20And they made two *other* golden rings, and put them on the two sides of the ephod underneath, toward the forepart of it, over against the *other* coupling thereof, above the curious girdle of the ephod.

21And they did bind the breastplate by his rings unto the rings of the ephod with a lace of blue, that it might be above the curious girdle of the ephod, and that the breastplate might not be loosed from the ephod; as the LORD commanded Moses.

22And he made the robe of the ephod *of* woven work, all *of* blue.

23And *there was* an hole in the midst of the robe, as the hole of an habergeon, *with* a band round about the hole, that it should not rend.

24And they made upon the hems of the robe pomegranates *of* blue, and purple, and scarlet, *and* twined *linen.*

25And they made bells *of* pure gold, and put the bells between the pomegranates upon the hem of the robe, round about between the pomegranates;

26A bell and a pomegranate, a bell and a pomegranate, round about the hem of the robe to minister *in;* as the LORD commanded Moses.

27And they made coats *of* fine linen *of* woven work for Aaron, and for his sons,

28And a mitre *of* fine linen, and goodly bonnets *of* fine linen, and linen breeches *of* fine twined linen,

29And a girdle *of* fine twined linen, and blue, and purple, and scarlet, *of* needlework; as the LORD commanded Moses.

30And they made the plate of the holy crown *of* pure gold, and wrote upon it a writing, *like to* the engravings of a signet, HOLINESS TO THE LORD.

31And they tied unto it a lace of blue, to fasten *it* on high upon the mitre; as the LORD commanded Moses.

32Thus was all the work of the tabernacle of the tent of the congregation finished: and the children of Israel did according to all that the LORD commanded Moses, so did they.

33And they brought the tabernacle unto Moses, the tent, and all his furniture, his taches, his boards, his bars, and his pillars, and his sockets,

34And the covering of rams' skins dyed red, and the covering of badgers' skins, and the vail of the covering,

35The ark of the testimony, and the staves thereof, and the mercy seat,

36The table, *and* all the vessels thereof, and the shewbread,

37The pure candlestick, *with* the lamps thereof, *even with* the lamps to be set in order, and all the vessels thereof, and the oil for light,

38And the golden altar, and the anointing oil, and the sweet incense, and the hanging for the tabernacle door,

39The brasen altar, and his grate of brass, his staves, and all his vessels, the laver and his foot,

40The hangings of the court, his pillars, and his sockets, and the hanging for the court gate, his cords, and his pins, and all the vessels of the service of the tabernacle, for the tent of the congregation,

41The cloths of service to do service in the holy *place,* and the holy garments for Aaron the priest, and his sons' garments, to minister in the priest's office.

42According to all that the LORD commanded Moses, so the children of Israel made all the work.

43And Moses did look upon all the work, and, behold, they had done it as the LORD had commanded, even so had they done it: and Moses blessed them.

AND the LORD spake unto Moses, saying,

2On the first day of the first month shalt thou set up the tabernacle of the tent of the congregation.

3And thou shalt put therein the ark of the testimony, and cover the ark with the vail.

4And thou shalt bring in the table, and set in order the things that are to be set in order upon it; and thou shalt bring in the candlestick, and light the lamps thereof.

5And thou shalt set the altar of gold for the incense before the ark of the testimony, and put the hanging of the door to the tabernacle.

6And thou shalt set the altar of the burnt offering before the door of the tabernacle of the tent of the congregation.

7And thou shalt set the laver between the tent of the congregation and the altar, and shalt put water therein.

8And thou shalt set up the court round about, and hang up the hanging at the court gate.

9And thou shalt take the anointing oil, and anoint the tabernacle, and all that *is* therein, and shalt hallow it, and all the vessels thereof: and it shall be holy.

10And thou shalt anoint the altar of the burnt offering, and all his vessels, and sanctify the altar: and it shall be an altar most holy.

11And thou shalt anoint the laver and his foot, and sanctify it.

12And thou shalt bring Aaron and his sons unto the door of the tabernacle of the congregation, and wash them with water.

13And thou shalt put upon Aaron the holy garments, and anoint him, and sanctify him; that he may minister unto me in the priest's office.

14And thou shalt bring his sons, and clothe them with coats:

15And thou shalt anoint them, as thou didst anoint their father, that they may minister unto me in the priest's office: for their anointing shall surely be an everlasting priesthood throughout their generations.

16Thus did Moses: according to all that the LORD commanded him, so did he.

17And it came to pass in the first month in the second year, on the first *day* of the month, *that* the tabernacle was reared up.

18And Moses reared up the tabernacle, and fastened his sockets, and set up the boards thereof, and put in the bars thereof, and reared up his pillars.

19And he spread abroad the tent over the tabernacle, and put the covering of the tent above upon it; as the LORD commanded Moses.

20And he took and put the testimony into the ark, and set the staves on the ark, and put the mercy seat above upon the ark:

21And he brought the ark into the tabernacle, and set up the vail of the covering, and covered the ark of the testimony; as the LORD commanded Moses.

22And he put the table in the tent of the congregation, upon the side of the tabernacle northward, without the vail.

23And he set the bread in order upon *it* before the LORD; as the LORD had commanded Moses.

24And he put the candlestick in the tent of the congregation, over against the table, on the side of the tabernacle southward.

25And he lighted the lamps before the LORD; as the LORD commanded Moses.

26And he put the golden altar in the tent of the congregation before the vail:

27And he burnt sweet incense thereon; as the LORD commanded Moses.

28And he set up the hanging *at* the door of the tabernacle.

29And he put the altar of burnt offering *by* the door of the tabernacle of the tent of the congregation, and offered upon it the burnt offering and the meat offering; as the LORD commanded Moses.

30And he set the laver between the tent of the congregation and the altar, and put water there, to wash *withal.*

31And Moses and Aaron and his sons washed their hands and their feet thereat:

32When they went into the tent of the congregation, and when they came near unto the altar, they washed; as the LORD commanded Moses.

33And he reared up the court round about the tabernacle and the altar, and set up the hanging of the court gate. So Moses finished the work.

34Then a cloud covered the tent of the congregation, and the glory of the LORD filled the tabernacle.

35And Moses was not able to enter

into the tent of the congregation, because the cloud abode thereon, and the glory of the LORD filled the tabernacle.

36And when the cloud was taken up from over the tabernacle, the children of Israel went onward in all their journeys:

37But if the cloud were not taken up, then they journeyed not till the day that it was taken up.

38For the cloud of the LORD *was* upon the tabernacle by day, and fire was on it by night, in the sight of all the house of Israel, throughout all their journeys.

MARK 1:1–28

THE beginning of the gospel of Jesus Christ, the Son of God;
2As it is written in the prophets, Behold, I send my messenger before thy face, which shall prepare thy way before thee.

3The voice of one crying in the wilderness, Prepare ye the way of the Lord, make his paths straight.

4John did baptize in the wilderness, and preach the baptism of repentance for the remission of sins.

5And there went out unto him all the land of Judaea, and they of Jerusalem, and were all baptized of him in the river of Jordan, confessing their sins.

6And John was clothed with camel's hair, and with a girdle of a skin about his loins; and he did eat locusts and wild honey;

7And preached, saying, There cometh one mightier than I after me, the latchet of whose shoes I am not worthy to stoop down and unloose.

8I indeed have baptized you with water: but he shall baptize you with the Holy Ghost.

9And it came to pass in those days, that Jesus came from Nazareth of Galilee, and was baptized of John in Jordan.

10And straightway coming up out of the water, he saw the heavens opened, and the Spirit like a dove descending upon him:

11And there came a voice from heaven, *saying,* Thou art my beloved Son, in whom I am well pleased.

12And immediately the spirit driveth him into the wilderness.

13And he was there in the wilderness forty days, tempted of Satan; and was with the wild beasts; and the angels ministered unto him.

14Now after that John was put in prison, Jesus came into Galilee, preaching the gospel of the kingdom of God,

15And saying, The time is fulfilled, and the kingdom of God is at hand: repent ye, and believe the gospel.

16Now as he walked by the sea of Galilee, he saw Simon and Andrew his brother casting a net into the sea: for they were fishers.

17And Jesus said unto them, Come ye after me, and I will make you to become fishers of men.

18And straightway they forsook their nets, and followed him.

19And when he had gone a little farther thence, he saw James the *son* of Zebedee, and John his brother, who also were in the ship mending their nets.

20And straightway he called them: and they left their father Zebedee in the ship with the hired servants, and went after him.

21And they went into Capernaum; and straightway on the sabbath day he entered into the synagogue, and taught.

22And they were astonished at his doctrine: for he taught them as one that had authority, and not as the scribes.

23And there was in their synagogue a man with an unclean spirit; and he cried out,

24Saying, Let *us* alone; what have we to do with thee, thou Jesus of Nazareth? art thou come to destroy us? I know thee who thou art, the Holy One of God.

25And Jesus rebuked him, saying, Hold thy peace, and come out of him.

26And when the unclean spirit had torn him, and cried with a loud voice, he came out of him.

27And they were all amazed, insomuch that they questioned among themselves saying, What thing is this? what new doctrine *is* this? for with authority commandeth he even the unclean spirits, and they do obey him.

28And immediately his fame spread abroad throughout all the region round about Galilee.

PSALM 35:1–16

PLEAD *my cause,* O LORD, with them that strive with me: fight against them that fight against me.

2Take hold of shield and buckler, and stand up for mine help.

3Draw out also the spear, and stop *the way* against them that persecute me: say unto my soul, I *am* thy salvation.

4Let them be confounded and put to shame that seek after my soul: let them be turned back and brought to confusion that devise my hurt.

5Let them be as chaff before the wind: and let the angel of the LORD chase *them.*

6Let their way be dark and slippery: and let the angel of the LORD persecute them.

7For without cause have they hid for me their net *in* a pit, *which* without cause they have digged for my soul.

8Let destruction come upon him at unawares; and let his net that he hath hid catch himself: into that very destruction let him fall.

9And my soul shall be joyful in the LORD: it shall rejoice in his salvation.

10All my bones shall say, LORD, who *is* like unto thee, which deliverest the poor from him that is too strong for him, yea, the poor and the needy from him that spoileth him?

11False witnesses did rise up; they laid to my charge *things* that I knew not.

12They rewarded me evil for good *to* the spoiling of my soul.

13But as for me, when they were sick, my clothing *was* sackcloth: I humbled my soul with fasting; and my prayer returned into mine own bosom.

14I behaved myself as though *he had been* my friend *or* brother: I bowed down heavily, as one that mourneth *for his* mother.

15But in mine adversity they rejoiced, and gathered themselves together; *yea,* the abjects gathered themselves together against me, and I knew *it* not; they did tear *me,* and ceased not:

16With hypocritical mockers in feasts, they gnashed upon me with their teeth.

PROVERBS FOR TODAY/ 9:11–12

For by me thy days shall be multiplied, and the years of thy life shall be increased. If thou be wise, thou shalt be wise for thyself: but if thou scornest, thou alone shalt bear it.

FEBRUARY 16

AND the LORD called unto Moses, and spake unto him out of the tabernacle of the congregation, saying,

2Speak unto the children of Israel, and say unto them, If any man of you bring an offering unto the Lord, ye shall bring your offering of the cattle, *even* of the herd, and of the flock.

3If his offering *be* a burnt sacrifice of the herd, let him offer a male without blemish: he shall offer it of his own voluntary will at the door of the tabernacle of the congregation before the LORD.

4And he shall put his hand upon the head of the burnt offering; and it shall be accepted for him to make atonement for him.

5And he shall kill the bullock before the LORD: and the priests, Aaron's sons, shall bring the blood, and sprinkle the blood round about upon the altar that *is by* the door of the tabernacle of the congregation.

6And he shall flay the burnt offering, and cut it into his pieces.

7And the sons of Aaron the priest shall put fire upon the altar, and lay the wood in order upon the fire:

8And the priests, Aaron's sons, shall lay the parts, the head, and the fat, in order upon the wood that *is* on the fire which *is* upon the altar:

9But his inwards and his legs shall he wash in water: and the priest shall burn all on the altar, *to be* a burnt sacrifice, an offering made by fire, of a sweet savour unto the LORD.

10And if his offering *be* of the flocks, *namely,* of the sheep, or of the goats, for a burnt sacrifice; he shall bring it a male without blemish.

11And he shall kill it on the side of the altar northward before the LORD:

and the priests, Aaron's sons, shall sprinkle his blood round about upon the altar.

12And he shall cut it into his pieces, with his head and his fat: and the priest shall lay them in order on the wood that *is* on the fire which *is* upon the altar:

13But he shall wash the inwards and the legs with water: and the priest shall bring *it* all, and burn *it* upon the altar: it *is* a burnt sacrifice, an offering made by fire, of a sweet savour unto the LORD.

14And if the burnt sacrifice for his offering to the LORD *be* of fowls, then he shall bring his offering of turtledoves, or of young pigeons.

15And the priest shall bring it unto the altar, and wring off his head, and burn *it* on the altar; and the blood thereof shall be wrung out at the side of the altar:

16And he shall pluck away his crop with his feathers, and cast it beside the altar on the east part, by the place of the ashes:

17And he shall cleave it with the wings thereof, *but* shall not divide *it* asunder: and the priest shall burn it upon the altar, upon the wood that *is* upon the fire: it *is* a burnt sacrifice, an offering made by fire, of a sweet savour unto the LORD.

AND when any will offer a meat offering unto the LORD, his offering shall be *of* fine flour; and he shall pour oil upon it, and put frankincense thereon:

2And he shall bring it to Aaron's sons the priests: and he shall take thereout his handful of the flour thereof, and of the oil thereof, with all the frankincense thereof; and the priest shall burn the memorial of it upon the altar, *to be* an offering made by fire, of a sweet savour unto the LORD:

³And the remnant of the meat offering *shall be* Aaron's and his sons': *it is* a thing most holy of the offerings of the LORD made by fire.

⁴And if thou bring an oblation of a meat offering baken in the oven, *it shall be* unleavened cakes of fine flour mingled with oil, or unleavened wafers anointed with oil.

⁵And if thy oblation *be* a meat offering *baken* in a pan, it shall be *of* fine flour unleavened, mingled with oil.

⁶Thou shalt part it in pieces, and pour oil thereon: it *is* a meat offering.

⁷And if thy oblation *be* a meat offering *baken* in the fryingpan, it shall be made *of* fine flour with oil.

⁸And thou shalt bring the meat offering that is made of these things unto the LORD: and when it is presented unto the priest, he shall bring it unto the altar.

⁹And the priest shall take from the meat offering a memorial thereof, and shall burn *it* upon the altar: *it is* an offering made by fire, of a sweet savour unto the LORD.

¹⁰And that which is left of the meat offering *shall be* Aaron's and his sons': *it is* a thing most holy of the offerings of the LORD made by fire.

¹¹No meat offering, which ye shall bring unto the LORD, shall be made with leaven: for ye shall burn no leaven, nor any honey, in any offering of the LORD made by fire.

¹²As for the oblation of the firstfruits, ye shall offer them unto the LORD: but they shall not be burnt on the altar for a sweet savour.

¹³And every oblation of thy meat offering shalt thou season with salt; neither shalt thou suffer the salt of the covenant of thy God to be lacking from thy meat offering: with all thine offerings thou shalt offer salt.

¹⁴And if thou offer a meat offering of thy firstfruits unto the LORD, thou shalt offer for the meat offering of thy firstfruits green ears of corn dried by the fire, *even* corn beaten out of full ears.

¹⁵And thou shalt put oil upon it, and lay frankincense thereon: it *is* a meat offering.

¹⁶And the priest shall burn the memorial of it, *part* of the beaten corn thereof, and *part* of the oil thereof, with all the frankincense thereof: *it is* an offering made by fire unto the LORD.

AND if his oblation *be* a sacrifice of peace offering, if he offer *it* of the herd; whether *it be* a male or female, he shall offer it without blemish before the LORD.

²And he shall lay his hand upon the head of his offering, and kill it *at* the door of the tabernacle of the congregation: and Aaron's sons the priests shall sprinkle the blood upon the altar round about.

³And he shall offer of the sacrifice of the peace offering an offering made by fire unto the LORD; the fat that covereth the inwards, and all the fat that *is* upon the inwards,

⁴And the two kidneys, and the fat that *is* on them, which *is* by the flanks, and the caul above the liver, with the kidneys, it shall he take away.

⁵And Aaron's sons shall burn it on the altar upon the burnt sacrifice, which *is* upon the wood that *is* on the fire: *it is* an offering made by fire, of a sweet savour unto the LORD.

⁶And if his offering for a sacrifice of peace offering unto the LORD *be* of the flock; male or female, he shall offer it without blemish.

⁷If he offer a lamb for his offering, then shall he offer it before the LORD.

⁸And he shall lay his hand upon the head of his offering, and kill it before the tabernacle of the congregation: and Aaron's sons shall sprinkle the blood thereof round about upon the altar.

⁹And he shall offer of the sacrifice

of the peace offering an offering made by fire unto the LORD; the fat thereof, *and* the whole rump, it shall he take off hard by the backbone; and the fat that covereth the inwards, and all the fat that *is* upon the inwards,

10And the two kidneys, and the fat that *is* upon them, which *is* by the flanks, and the caul above the liver, with the kidneys, it shall he take away.

11And the priest shall burn it upon the altar: *it is* the food of the offering made by fire unto the LORD.

12And if his offering *be* a goat, then he shall offer it before the LORD.

13And he shall lay his hand upon the head of it, and kill it before the tabernacle of the congregation: and the sons of Aaron shall sprinkle the blood thereof upon the altar round about.

14And he shall offer thereof his offering, *even* an offering made by fire unto the LORD; the fat that covereth the inwards, and all the fat that *is* upon the inwards,

15And the two kidneys, and the fat that *is* upon them, which *is* by the flanks, and the caul above the liver, with the kidneys, it shall he take away.

16And the priest shall burn them upon the altar: *it is* the food of the offering made by fire for a sweet savour: all the fat *is* the LORD's.

17*It shall be* a perpetual statute for your generations throughout all your dwellings, that ye eat neither fat nor blood.

MARK 1:29—2:12

AND forthwith, when they [Jesus and his disciples] were come out of the synagogue, they entered into the house of Simon and Andrew, with James and John.

30But Simon's wife's mother lay sick of a fever, and anon they tell him of her.

31And he came and took her by the hand, and lifted her up; and immediately the fever left her, and she ministered unto them.

32And at even, when the sun did set, they brought unto him all that were diseased, and them that were possessed with devils.

33And all the city was gathered together at the door.

34And he healed many that were sick of divers diseases, and cast out many devils; and suffered not the devils to speak, because they knew him.

35And in the morning, rising up a great while before day, he went out, and departed into a solitary place, and there prayed.

36And Simon and they that were with him followed after him.

37And when they had found him, they said unto him, All *men* seek for thee.

38And he said unto them, Let us go into the next towns, that I may preach there also: for therefore came I forth.

39And he preached in their synagogues throughout all Galilee, and cast out devils.

40And there came a leper to him, beseeching him, and kneeling down to him, and saying unto him, If thou wilt, thou canst make me clean.

41And Jesus, moved with compassion, put forth *his* hand, and touched him, and saith unto him, I will; be thou clean.

42And, as soon as he had spoken, immediately the leprosy departed from him, and he was cleansed.

43And he straitly charged him, and forthwith sent him away;

44And saith unto him, See thou say nothing to any man: but go thy way, shew thyself to the priest, and offer for thy cleansing those things which Moses commanded, for a testimony unto them.

45But he went out, and began to publish *it* much, and to blaze abroad the matter, insomuch that Jesus could no more openly enter into the city, but was without in desert places: and they came to him from every quarter.

AND again he entered into Capernaum after *some* days; and it was noised that he was in the house.

2And straightway many were gathered together, insomuch that there was no room to receive *them,* no, not so much as about the door: and he preached the word unto them.

3And they come unto him, bringing one sick of the palsy, which was borne of four.

4And when they could not come nigh unto him for the press, they uncovered the roof where he was: and when they had broken *it* up, they let down the bed wherein the sick of the palsy lay.

5When Jesus saw their faith, he said unto the sick of the palsy, Son, thy sins be forgiven thee.

6But there were certain of the scribes sitting there, and reasoning in their hearts,

7Why doth this *man* thus speak blasphemies? who can forgive sins but God only?

8And immediately when Jesus perceived in his spirit that they so reasoned within themselves, he said unto them, Why reason ye these things in your hearts?

9Whether is it easier to say to the sick of the palsy, *Thy* sins be forgiven thee; or to say, Arise, and take up thy bed, and walk?

10But that ye may know that the Son of man hath power on earth to forgive sins, (he saith to the sick of the palsy,)

11I say unto thee, Arise, and take up thy bed, and go thy way into thine house.

12And immediately he arose, took up the bed, and went forth before them all; insomuch that they were all amazed, and glorified God, saying, We never saw it on this fashion.

PSALM 35:17–28

LORD, how long wilt thou look on? rescue my soul from their destructions, my darling from the lions.

18I will give thee thanks in the great congregation: I will praise thee among much people.

19Let not them that are mine enemies wrongfully rejoice over me: *neither* let them wink with the eye that hate me without a cause.

20For they speak not peace: but they devise deceitful matters against *them that are* quiet in the land.

21Yea, they opened their mouth wide against me, *and* said, Aha, aha, our eye hath seen *it.*

22*This* thou hast seen, O LORD: keep not silence: O Lord, be not far from me.

23Stir up thyself, and awake to my judgment, *even* unto my cause, my God and my Lord.

24Judge me, O LORD my God, according to thy righteousness; and let them not rejoice over me.

25Let them not say in their hearts, Ah, so would we have it: let them not say, We have swallowed him up.

26Let them be ashamed and brought to confusion together that rejoice at mine hurt: let them be clothed with shame and dishonour that magnify *themselves* against me.

27Let them shout for joy, and be glad, that favour my righteous cause: yea, let them say continually, Let the LORD be magnified, which hath pleasure in the prosperity of his servant.

28And my tongue shall speak of thy righteousness *and* of thy praise all the day long.

PROVERBS FOR TODAY/ 9:13–18

A foolish woman is clamorous: she is simple, and knoweth nothing. For she sitteth at the door of her house, on a seat in the high places of the city, To call passengers who go right on their ways: Whoso is simple, let him turn in hither: and as for him that wanteth understanding, she saith to him, Stolen waters are sweet, and bread eaten in secret is pleasant. But he knoweth not that the dead are there; and that her guests are in the depths of hell.

FEBRUARY 17

LEVITICUS 4:1—5:19

AND the LORD spake unto Moses, saying,

²Speak unto the children of Israel, saying, If a soul shall sin through ignorance against any of the commandments of the LORD *concerning things* which ought not to be done, and shall do against any of them:

³If the priest that is anointed do sin according to the sin of the people; then let him bring for his sin, which he hath sinned, a young bullock without blemish unto the LORD for a sin offering.

⁴And he shall bring the bullock unto the door of the tabernacle of the congregation before the LORD; and shall lay his hand upon the bullock's head, and kill the bullock before the LORD.

⁵And the priest that is anointed shall take of the bullock's blood, and bring it to the tabernacle of the congregation:

⁶And the priest shall dip his finger in the blood, and sprinkle of the blood seven times before the LORD, before the vail of the sanctuary.

⁷And the priest shall put *some* of the blood upon the horns of the altar of sweet incense before the LORD, which *is* in the tabernacle of the congregation; and shall pour all the blood of the bullock at the bottom of the altar of the burnt offering, which *is at* the door of the tabernacle of the congregation.

⁸And he shall take off from it all the fat of the bullock for the sin offering; the fat that covereth the inwards, and all the fat that *is* upon the inwards,

⁹And the two kidneys, and the fat that *is* upon them, which *is* by the flanks, and the caul above the liver, with the kidneys, it shall he take away,

¹⁰As it was taken off from the bullock of the sacrifice of peace offerings: and the priest shall burn them upon the altar of the burnt offering.

¹¹And the skin of the bullock, and all his flesh, with his head, and with his legs, and his inwards, and his dung,

¹²Even the whole bullock shall he carry forth without the camp unto a clean place, where the ashes are poured out, and burn him on the wood with fire: where the ashes are poured out shall he be burnt.

¹³And if the whole congregation of Israel sin through ignorance, and the thing be hid from the eyes of the assembly, and they have done *somewhat against* any of the commandments of the LORD *concerning things* which should not be done, and are guilty;

¹⁴When the sin, which they have sinned against it, is known, then the congregation shall offer a young bullock for the sin, and bring him before the tabernacle of the congregation.

¹⁵And the elders of the congregation

shall lay their hands upon the head of the bullock before the LORD: and the bullock shall be killed before the LORD.

16And the priest that is anointed shall bring of the bullock's blood to the tabernacle of the congregation:

17And the priest shall dip his finger *in some* of the blood, and sprinkle *it* seven times before the LORD, *even* before the vail.

18And he shall put *some* of the blood upon the horns of the altar which *is* before the LORD, that *is* in the tabernacle of the congregation, and shall pour out all the blood at the bottom of the altar of the burnt offering, which *is at* the door of the tabernacle of the congregation.

19And he shall take all his fat from him, and burn *it* upon the altar.

20And he shall do with the bullock as he did with the bullock for a sin offering, so shall he do with this: and the priest shall make an atonement for them, and it shall be forgiven them.

21And he shall carry forth the bullock without the camp, and burn him as he burned the first bullock: it *is* a sin offering for the congregation.

22When a ruler hath sinned, and done *somewhat* through ignorance *against* any of the commandments of the LORD his God *concerning things* which should not be done, and is guilty;

23Or if his sin, wherein he hath sinned, come to his knowledge; he shall bring his offering, a kid of the goats, a male without blemish:

24And he shall lay his hand upon the head of the goat, and kill it in the place where they kill the burnt offering before the LORD: it *is* a sin offering.

25And the priest shall take of the blood of the sin offering with his finger, and put *it* upon the horns of the altar of burnt offering, and shall pour out his blood at the bottom of the altar of burnt offering.

26And he shall burn all his fat upon the altar, as the fat of the sacrifice of peace offerings: and the priest shall make an atonement for him as concerning his sin, and it shall be forgiven him.

27And if any one of the common people sin through ignorance, while he doeth *somewhat against* any of the commandments of the LORD *concerning things* which ought not to be done, and be guilty;

28Or if his sin, which he hath sinned, come to his knowledge: then he shall bring his offering, a kid of the goats, a female without blemish, for his sin which he hath sinned.

29And he shall lay his hand upon the head of the sin offering, and slay the sin offering in the place of the burnt offering.

30And the priest shall take of the blood thereof with his finger, and put *it* upon the horns of the altar of burnt offering, and shall pour out all the blood thereof at the bottom of the altar.

31And he shall take away all the fat thereof, as the fat is taken away from off the sacrifice of peace offerings; and the priest shall burn *it* upon the altar for a sweet savour unto the LORD; and the priest shall make an atonement for him, and it shall be forgiven him.

32And if he bring a lamb for a sin offering, he shall bring it a female without blemish.

33And he shall lay his hand upon the head of the sin offering, and slay it for a sin offering in the place where they kill the burnt offering.

34And the priest shall take of the blood of the sin offering with his finger, and put *it* upon the horns of the altar of burnt offering, and shall pour out all the blood thereof at the bottom of the altar:

35And he shall take away all the fat thereof, as the fat of the lamb is taken away from the sacrifice of the peace offerings; and the priest shall burn them upon the altar, according to the offerings made by fire unto the LORD: and the priest shall make an atonement for his sin that he hath committed, and it shall be forgiven him.

AND if a soul sin, and hear the voice of swearing, and *is* a witness, whether he hath seen or known *of it;* if he do not utter *it,* then he shall bear his iniquity.

2Or if a soul touch any unclean thing, whether *it be* a carcase of an unclean beast, or a carcase of unclean cattle, or the carcase of unclean creeping things, and *if* it be hidden from him; he also shall be unclean, and guilty.

3Or if he touch the uncleanness of man, whatsoever uncleanness *it be* that a man shall be defiled withal, and it be hid from him; when he knoweth *of it,* then he shall be guilty.

4Or if a soul swear, pronouncing with *his* lips to do evil, or to do good, whatsoever *it be* that a man shall pronounce with an oath, and it be hid from him; when he knoweth *of it,* then he shall be guilty in one of these.

5And it shall be, when he shall be guilty in one of these *things,* that he shall confess that he hath sinned in that *thing:*

6And he shall bring his trespass offering unto the LORD for his sin which he hath sinned, a female from the flock, a lamb or a kid of the goats, for a sin offering; and the priest shall make an atonement for him concerning his sin.

7And if he be not able to bring a lamb, then he shall bring for his trespass, which he hath committed, two turtledoves, or two young pigeons, unto the LORD; one for a sin offering, and the other for a burnt offering.

8And he shall bring them unto the priest, who shall offer *that* which *is* for the sin offering first, and wring off his head from his neck, but shall not divide *it* asunder:

9And he shall sprinkle of the blood of the sin offering upon the side of the altar; and the rest of the blood shall be wrung out at the bottom of the altar: it *is* a sin offering.

10And he shall offer the second *for* a burnt offering, according to the manner: and the priest shall make an atonement for him for his sin which he hath sinned, and it shall be forgiven him.

11But if he be not able to bring two turtledoves, or two young pigeons, then he that sinned shall bring for his offering the tenth part of an ephah of fine flour for a sin offering; he shall put no oil upon it, neither shall he put *any* frankincense thereon: for it *is* a sin offering.

12Then shall he bring it to the priest, and the priest shall take his handful of it, *even* a memorial thereof, and burn *it* on the altar, according to the offerings made by fire unto the LORD: it *is* a sin offering.

13And the priest shall make an atonement for him as touching his sin that he hath sinned in one of these, and it shall be forgiven him: and *the remnant* shall be the priest's, as a meat offering.

14And the LORD spake unto Moses, saying,

15If a soul commit a trespass, and sin through ignorance, in the holy things of the LORD; then he shall bring for his trespass unto the LORD a ram without blemish out of the flocks, with thy estimation by shekels of silver, after the shekel of the sanctuary, for a trespass offering:

16And he shall make amends for the harm that he hath done in the holy thing, and shall add the fifth part thereto, and give it unto the priest: and the priest shall make an atonement for him with the ram of the trespass offering, and it shall be forgiven him.

17And if a soul sin, and commit any of these things which are forbidden to be done by the commandments of the LORD; though he wist *it* not, yet is he guilty, and shall bear his iniquity.

18And he shall bring a ram without blemish out of the flock, with thy estimation, for a trespass offering, unto the priest: and the priest shall make an atonement for him concerning his ignorance wherein he erred and wist *it* not, and it shall be forgiven him.

19It *is* a trespass offering: he hath certainly trespassed against the LORD.

MARK 2:13—3:6

AND he [Jesus] went forth again by the sea side; and all the multitude resorted unto him, and he taught them.

14And as he passed by, he saw Levi the *son* of Alphaeus sitting at the receipt of custom, and said unto him, Follow me. And he arose and followed him.

15And it came to pass, that, as Jesus sat at meat in his house, many publicans and sinners sat also together with Jesus and his disciples: for there were many, and they followed him.

16And when the scribes and Pharisees saw him eat with publicans and sinners, they said unto his disciples, How is it that he eateth and drinketh with publicans and sinners?

17When Jesus heard *it,* he saith unto them, They that are whole have no need of the physician, but they that are sick: I came not to call the righteous, but sinners to repentance.

18And the disciples of John and of the Pharisees used to fast: and they come and say unto him, Why do the disciples of John and of the Pharisees fast, but thy disciples fast not?

19And Jesus said unto them, Can the children of the bridechamber fast, while the bridegroom is with them? as long as they have the bridegroom with them, they cannot fast.

20But the days will come, when the bridegroom shall be taken away from them, and then shall they fast in those days.

21No man also seweth a piece of new cloth on an old garment: else the new piece that filled it up taketh away from the old, and the rent is made worse.

22And no man putteth new wine into old bottles: else the new wine doth burst the bottles, and the wine is spilled, and the bottles will be marred: but new wine must be put into new bottles.

23And it came to pass, that he went through the corn fields on the sabbath day; and his disciples began, as they went, to pluck the ears of corn.

24And the Pharisees said unto him, Behold, why do they on the sabbath day that which is not lawful?

25And he said unto them, Have ye never read what David did, when he had need, and was an hungred, he, and they that were with him?

26How he went into the house of God in the days of Abiathar the high priest, and did eat the shewbread, which is not lawful to eat but for the priests, and gave also to them which were with him?

27And he said unto them, The sabbath was made for man, and not man for the sabbath:

28Therefore the Son of man is Lord also of the sabbath.

AND he entered again into the synagogue; and there was a man there which had a withered hand.

2And they watched him, whether he would heal him on the sabbath day; that they might accuse him.

3And he saith unto the man which had the withered hand, Stand forth.

4And he saith unto them, Is it lawful to do good on the sabbath days, or to do evil? to save life, or to kill? But they held their peace.

5And when he had looked round about on them with anger, being grieved for the hardness of their hearts, he saith unto the man, Stretch forth thine hand. And he stretched *it* out: and his hand was restored whole as the other.

6And the Pharisees went forth, and straightway took counsel with the Herodians against him, how they might destroy him.

PSALM 36:1–12

THE transgression of the wicked saith within my heart, *that there is* no fear of God before his eyes.

2For he flattereth himself in his own eyes, until his iniquity be found to be hateful.

3The words of his mouth *are* iniquity and deceit: he hath left off to be wise, *and* to do good.

4He deviseth mischief upon his bed; he setteth himself in a way *that is* not good; he abhorreth not evil.

5Thy mercy, O Lord, *is* in the heavens; *and* thy faithfulness *reacheth* unto the clouds.

6Thy righteousness *is* like the great mountains; thy judgments *are* a great deep: O Lord, thou preservest man and beast.

7How excellent *is* thy lovingkindness, O God! therefore the children of men put their trust under the shadow of thy wings.

8They shall be abundantly satisfied with the fatness of thy house; and thou shalt make them drink of the river of thy pleasures.

9For with thee *is* the fountain of life: in thy light shall we see light.

10O continue thy lovingkindness unto them that know thee; and thy righteousness to the upright in heart.

11Let not the foot of pride come against me, and let not the hand of the wicked remove me.

12There are the workers of iniquity fallen: they are cast down, and shall not be able to rise.

PROVERBS FOR TODAY/ 10:1–2

The proverbs of Solomon. A wise son maketh a glad father: but a foolish son is *the heaviness of his mother.* □ *Treasures of wickedness profit nothing: but righteousness delivereth from death.*

FEBRUARY 18

LEVITICUS 6:1—7:27

AND the Lord spake unto Moses, saying,

2If a soul sin, and commit a trespass against the Lord, and lie unto his neighbour in that which was delivered him to keep, or in fellowship, or in a thing taken away by violence, or hath deceived his neighbour;

3Or have found that which was lost, and lieth concerning it, and sweareth falsely; in any of all these that a man doeth, sinning therein:

4Then it shall be, because he hath sinned, and is guilty, that he shall restore that which he took violently away, or the thing which he hath deceitfully gotten, or that which was delivered him to keep, or the lost thing which he found,

5Or all that about which he hath sworn falsely; he shall even restore it in the principal, and shall add the fifth part more thereto, *and* give it unto him to whom it appertaineth, in the day of his trespass offering.

6And he shall bring his trespass offering unto the Lord, a ram without blemish out of the flock, with thy estimation, for a trespass offering, unto the priest:

7And the priest shall make an atonement for him before the Lord: and it shall be forgiven him for any thing of all that he hath done in trespassing therein.

8And the Lord spake unto Moses, saying,

9Command Aaron and his sons, saying, This is the law of the burnt offering: It is the burnt offering, because of the burning upon the altar all night unto the morning, and the fire of the altar shall be burning in it.

10And the priest shall put on his linen garment, and his linen breeches shall he put upon his flesh, and take up the ashes which the fire hath consumed with the burnt offering on the altar, and he shall put them beside the altar.

11And he shall put off his garments, and put on other garments, and carry forth the ashes without the camp unto a clean place.

12And the fire upon the altar shall be burning in it; it shall not be put out: and the priest shall burn wood on it every morning, and lay the burnt offering in order upon it; and he shall burn thereon the fat of the peace offerings.

13The fire shall ever be burning upon the altar; it shall never go out.

14And this is the law of the meat offering: the sons of Aaron shall offer it before the Lord, before the altar.

15And he shall take of it his handful, of the flour of the meat offering, and of the oil thereof, and all the frankincense which is upon the meat offering, and shall burn it upon the altar for a sweet savour, even the memorial of it, unto the Lord.

16And the remainder thereof shall Aaron and his sons eat: with unleavened bread shall it be eaten in the holy place; in the court of the tabernacle of the congregation they shall eat it.

17It shall not be baken with leaven. I have given it unto them for their portion of my offerings made by fire; it is most holy, as is the sin offering, and as the trespass offering.

18All the males among the children of Aaron shall eat of it. It shall be a statute for ever in your generations concerning the offerings of the Lord made by fire: every one that toucheth them shall be holy.

19And the Lord spake unto Moses, saying,

20This is the offering of Aaron and of his sons, which they shall offer unto the Lord in the day when he is anointed; the tenth part of an ephah of fine flour for a meat offering perpetual, half of it in the morning, and half thereof at night.

21In a pan it shall be made with oil; and when it is baken, thou shalt bring it in: and the baken pieces of the meat offering shalt thou offer for a sweet savour unto the Lord.

22And the priest of his sons that is anointed in his stead shall offer it: it is a statute for ever unto the Lord; it shall be wholly burnt.

23For every meat offering for the priest shall be wholly burnt: it shall not be eaten.

24And the Lord spake unto Moses, saying,

25Speak unto Aaron and to his sons, saying, This is the law of the sin offering: In the place where the burnt offering is killed shall the sin offering be killed before the Lord: it is most holy.

26The priest that offereth it for sin shall eat it: in the holy place shall it be eaten, in the court of the tabernacle of the congregation.

27Whatsoever shall touch the flesh thereof shall be holy: and when there is sprinkled of the blood thereof upon any garment, thou shalt wash that whereon it was sprinkled in the holy place.

28But the earthen vessel wherein it is sodden shall be broken: and if it be sodden in a brasen pot, it shall be both scoured, and rinsed in water.

29All the males among the priests shall eat thereof: it *is* most holy.

30And no sin offering, whereof *any* of the blood is brought into the tabernacle of the congregation to reconcile *withal* in the holy *place,* shall be eaten: it shall be burnt in the fire.

LIKEWISE this *is* the law of the trespass offering: it *is* most holy.

2In the place where they kill the burnt offering shall they kill the trespass offering: and the blood thereof shall he sprinkle round about upon the altar.

3And he shall offer of it all the fat thereof; the rump, and the fat that covereth the inwards,

4And the two kidneys, and the fat that *is* on them, which *is* by the flanks, and the caul *that is* above the liver, with the kidneys, it shall he take away:

5And the priest shall burn them upon the altar *for* an offering made by fire unto the LORD: it *is* a trespass offering.

6Every male among the priests shall eat thereof: it shall be eaten in the holy place: it *is* most holy.

7As the sin offering *is,* so *is* the trespass offering: *there is* one law for them: the priest that maketh atonement therewith shall have *it.*

8And the priest that offereth any man's burnt offering, *even* the priest shall have to himself the skin of the burnt offering which he hath offered.

9And all the meat offering that is baken in the oven, and all that is dressed in the fryingpan, and in the pan, shall be the priest's that offereth it.

10And every meat offering, mingled with oil, and dry, shall all the sons of Aaron have, one *as much* as another.

11And this *is* the law of the sacrifice of peace offerings, which he shall offer unto the LORD.

12If he offer it for a thanksgiving, then he shall offer with the sacrifice of thanksgiving unleavened cakes mingled with oil, and unleavened wafers anointed with oil, and cakes mingled with oil, of fine flour, fried.

13Besides the cakes, he shall offer *for* his offering leavened bread with the sacrifice of thanksgiving of his peace offerings.

14And of it he shall offer one out of the whole oblation *for* an heave offering unto the LORD, *and* it shall be the priest's that sprinkleth the blood of the peace offerings.

15And the flesh of the sacrifice of his peace offerings for thanksgiving shall be eaten the same day that it is offered; he shall not leave any of it until the morning.

16But if the sacrifice of his offering *be* a vow, or a voluntary offering, it shall be eaten the same day that he offereth his sacrifice: and on the morrow also the remainder of it shall be eaten:

17But the remainder of the flesh of the sacrifice on the third day shall be burnt with fire.

18And if *any* of the flesh of the sacrifice of his peace offerings be eaten at all on the third day, it shall not be accepted, neither shall it be imputed unto him that offereth it: it shall be an abomination, and the soul that eateth of it shall bear his iniquity.

19And the flesh that toucheth any unclean *thing* shall not be eaten; it shall be burnt with fire: and as for the flesh, all that be clean shall eat thereof.

20But the soul that eateth *of* the flesh of the sacrifice of peace offerings, that *pertain* unto the LORD, having his uncleanness upon him, even that soul shall be cut off from his people.

21Moreover the soul that shall touch any unclean *thing, as* the uncleanness of man, or *any* unclean beast, or any abominable unclean *thing,* and eat of the flesh of the sacrifice of peace offerings, which *pertain* unto the LORD, even that soul shall be cut off from his people.

22And the LORD spake unto Moses, saying,

23Speak unto the children of Israel, saying, Ye shall eat no manner of fat, of ox, or of sheep, or of goat.

24And the fat of the beast that dieth of itself, and the fat of that which is torn with beasts, may be used in any other use: but ye shall in no wise eat of it.

25For whosoever eateth the fat of the beast, of which men offer an offering made by fire unto the LORD, even the soul that eateth *it* shall be cut off from his people.

26Moreover ye shall eat no manner of blood, *whether it be* of fowl or of beast, in any of your dwellings.

27Whatsoever soul *it be* that eateth any manner of blood, even that soul shall be cut off from his people.

MARK 3:7–30

BUT Jesus withdrew himself with his disciples to the sea: and a great multitude from Galilee followed him, and from Judaea,

8And from Jerusalem, and from Idumaea, and *from* beyond Jordan; and they about Tyre and Sidon, a great multitude, when they had heard what great things he did, came unto him.

9And he spake to his disciples, that a small ship should wait on him because of the multitude, lest they should throng him.

10For he had healed many; insomuch that they pressed upon him for to touch him, as many as had plagues.

11And unclean spirits, when they saw him, fell down before him, and cried, saying, Thou art the Son of God.

12And he straitly charged them that they should not make him known.

13And he goeth up into a mountain, and calleth *unto him* whom he would: and they came unto him.

14And he ordained twelve, that they should be with him, and that he might send them forth to preach,

15And to have power to heal sicknesses, and to cast out devils:

16And Simon he surnamed Peter;

17And James the *son* of Zebedee, and John the brother of James; and he surnamed them Boanerges, which is, The sons of thunder:

18And Andrew, and Philip, and Bartholomew, and Matthew, and Thomas, and James the *son* of Alphaeus, and Thaddaeus, and Simon the Canaanite,

19And Judas Iscariot, which also betrayed him: and they went into an house.

20And the multitude cometh together again, so that they could not so much as eat bread.

21And when his friends heard *of it,* they went out to lay hold on him: for they said, He is beside himself.

22And the scribes which came down from Jerusalem said, He hath Beelzebub, and by the prince of the devils casteth he out devils.

23And he called them *unto him,* and said unto them in parables, How can Satan cast out Satan?

24And if a kingdom be divided against itself, that kingdom cannot stand.

25And if a house be divided against itself, that house cannot stand.

26And if Satan rise up against himself, and be divided, he cannot stand, but hath an end.

27No man can enter into a strong man's house, and spoil his goods, except he will first bind the strong man; and then he will spoil his house.

28Verily I say unto you, All sins shall be forgiven unto the sons of men, and blasphemies wherewith soever they shall blaspheme:

29But he that shall blaspheme against the Holy Ghost hath never forgiveness, but is in danger of eternal damnation:

30Because they said, He hath an unclean spirit.

PSALM 37:1–11

FRET not thyself because of evil-doers, neither be thou envious against the workers of iniquity.

2For they shall soon be cut down like the grass, and wither as the green herb.

3Trust in the LORD, and do good; *so* shalt thou dwell in the land, and verily thou shalt be fed.

4Delight thyself also in the LORD; and he shall give thee the desires of thine heart.

5Commit thy way unto the LORD; trust also in him; and he shall bring *it* to pass.

6And he shall bring forth thy righteousness as the light, and thy judg-ment as the noonday.

7Rest in the LORD, and wait patiently for him: fret not thyself because of him who prospereth in his way, because of the man who bringeth wicked devices to pass.

8Cease from anger, and forsake wrath: fret not thyself in any wise to do evil.

9For evildoers shall be cut off: but those that wait upon the LORD, they shall inherit the earth.

10For yet a little while, and the wicked *shall* not *be:* yea, thou shalt diligently consider his place, and it *shall* not *be.*

11But the meek shall inherit the earth; and shall delight themselves in the abundance of peace.

PROVERBS FOR TODAY/ 10:3–4

The LORD will not suffer the soul of the righteous to famish: but he casteth away the substance of the wicked. □ *He becometh poor that dealeth* with *a slack hand: but the hand of the diligent maketh rich.*

FEBRUARY 19

LEVITICUS 7:28—9:6

AND the LORD spake unto Moses, saying,

29Speak unto the children of Israel, saying, He that offereth the sacrifice of his peace offerings unto the LORD shall bring his oblation unto the LORD of the sacrifice of his peace offerings.

30His own hands shall bring the offerings of the LORD made by fire, the fat with the breast, it shall he bring, that the breast may be waved *for* a wave offering before the LORD.

31And the priest shall burn the fat upon the altar: but the breast shall be Aaron's and his sons'.

32And the right shoulder shall ye give unto the priest *for* an heave offering of the sacrifices of your peace offerings.

33He among the sons of Aaron, that offereth the blood of the peace offerings, and the fat, shall have the right shoulder for *his* part.

34For the wave breast and the heave shoulder have I taken of the children of Israel from off the sacrifices of their peace offerings, and have given them unto Aaron the priest and unto his sons by a statute for ever from among the children of Israel.

35This *is the portion* of the anointing of Aaron, and of the anointing of his sons, out of the offerings of the LORD made by fire, in the day *when* he presented them to minister unto the LORD in the priest's office;

36Which the LORD commanded to be given them of the children of Israel, in the day that he anointed them, *by* a statute for ever throughout their generations.

37This *is* the law of the burnt offering, of the meat offering, and of the sin offering, and of the trespass offering, and of the consecrations, and of the sacrifice of the peace offerings;

38Which the LORD commanded Moses in mount Sinai, in the day that he commanded the children of Israel to offer their oblations unto the LORD, in the wilderness of Sinai.

AND the LORD spake unto Moses, saying,

2Take Aaron and his sons with him, and the garments, and the anointing oil, and a bullock for the sin offering, and two rams, and a basket of unleavened bread;

3And gather thou all the congregation together unto the door of the tabernacle of the congregation.

4And Moses did as the LORD commanded him; and the assembly was gathered together unto the door of the tabernacle of the congregation.

5And Moses said unto the congregation, This *is* the thing which the LORD commanded to be done.

6And Moses brought Aaron and his sons, and washed them with water.

7And he put upon him the coat, and girded him with the girdle, and clothed him with the robe, and put the ephod upon him, and he girded him with the curious girdle of the ephod, and bound *it* unto him therewith.

8And he put the breastplate upon him: also he put in the breastplate the Urim and the Thummim.

9And he put the mitre upon his head; also upon the mitre, *even* upon his forefront, did he put the golden plate, the holy crown; as the LORD commanded Moses.

10And Moses took the anointing oil, and anointed the tabernacle and all that *was* therein, and sanctified them.

11And he sprinkled thereof upon the altar seven times, and anointed the altar and all his vessels, both the laver and his foot, to sanctify them.

12And he poured of the anointing oil upon Aaron's head, and anointed him, to sanctify him.

13And Moses brought Aaron's sons, and put coats upon them, and girded them with girdles, and put bonnets upon them; as the LORD commanded Moses.

14And he brought the bullock for the sin offering: and Aaron and his sons laid their hands upon the head of the bullock for the sin offering.

15And he slew *it;* and Moses took the blood, and put *it* upon the horns of the altar round about with his finger, and purified the altar, and poured the blood at the bottom of the altar, and sanctified it, to make reconciliation upon it.

16And he took all the fat that *was* upon the inwards, and the caul *above* the liver, and the two kidneys, and their fat, and Moses burned *it* upon the altar.

17But the bullock, and his hide, his flesh, and his dung, he burnt with fire without the camp as the LORD commanded Moses.

18And he brought the ram for the burnt offering: and Aaron and his sons laid their hands upon the head of the ram.

19And he killed *it;* and Moses sprinkled the blood upon the altar round about.

20And he cut the ram into pieces; and Moses burnt the head, and the pieces, and the fat.

21And he washed the inwards and the legs in water; and Moses burnt the whole ram upon the altar: it *was* a burnt sacrifice for a sweet savour, *and* an offering made by fire unto the

LORD; as the LORD commanded Moses.

22And he brought the other ram, the ram of consecration: and Aaron and his sons laid their hands upon the head of the ram.

23And he slew *it;* and Moses took of the blood of it, and put *it* upon the tip of Aaron's right ear, and upon the thumb of his right hand, and upon the great toe of his right foot.

24And he brought Aaron's sons, and Moses put the blood upon the tip of their right ear, and upon the thumbs of their right hands, and upon the great toes of their right feet: and Moses sprinkled the blood upon the altar round about.

25And he took the fat, and the rump, and all the fat that *was* upon the inwards, and the caul *above* the liver, and the two kidneys, and their fat, and the right shoulder:

26And out of the basket of unleavened bread, that *was* before the LORD, he took one unleavened cake, and a cake of oiled bread, and one wafer, and put *them* on the fat, and upon the right shoulder:

27And he put all upon Aaron's hands, and upon his son's hands, and waved them *for* a wave offering before the LORD.

28And Moses took them from off their hands, and burnt *them* on the altar upon the burnt offering: they *were* consecrations for a sweet savour: it *is* an offering made by fire unto the LORD.

29And Moses took the breast, and waved it *for* a wave offering before the LORD: *for* of the ram of consecration it was Moses' part; as the LORD commanded Moses.

30And Moses took of the anointing oil, and of the blood which *was* upon the altar, and sprinkled *it* upon Aaron, *and* upon his garments, and upon his sons, and upon his sons' garments with him; and sanctified Aaron, *and* his garments, and his sons, and his sons' garments with him.

31And Moses said unto Aaron and to his sons, Boil the flesh *at* the door of the tabernacle of the congregation: and there eat it with the bread that *is* in the basket of consecrations, as I commanded, saying, Aaron and his sons shall eat it.

32And that which remaineth of the flesh and of the bread shall ye burn with fire.

33And ye shall not go out of the door of the tabernacle of the congregation *in* seven days, until the days of your consecration be at an end: for seven days shall he consecrate you.

34As he hath done this day, *so* the LORD hath commanded to do, to make an atonement for you.

35Therefore shall ye abide *at* the door of the tabernacle of the congregation day and night seven days, and keep the charge of the LORD, that ye die not: for so I am commanded.

36So Aaron and his sons did all things which the LORD commanded by the hand of Moses.

AND it came to pass on the eighth day, *that* Moses called Aaron and his sons, and the elders of Israel;

2And he said unto Aaron, Take thee a young calf for a sin offering, and a ram for a burnt offering, without blemish, and offer *them* before the LORD.

3And unto the children of Israel thou shalt speak, saying, Take ye a kid of the goats for a sin offering; and a calf and a lamb, *both* of the first year, without blemish, for a burnt offering;

4Also a bullock and a ram for peace offerings, to sacrifice before the LORD; and a meat offering mingled with oil: for to day the LORD will appear unto you.

5And they brought *that* which Moses commanded before the tabernacle of the congregation: and all the congregation drew near and stood before the LORD.

6And Moses said, This *is* the thing

which the LORD commanded that ye should do: and the glory of the LORD shall appear unto you.

MARK 3:31—4:25

THERE came then his [Jesus'] brethren and his mother, and, standing without, sent unto him, calling him.

32And the multitude sat about him, and they said unto him, Behold, thy mother and thy brethren without seek for thee.

33And he answered them, saying, Who is my mother, or my brethren?

34And he looked round about on them which sat about him, and said, Behold my mother and my brethren!

35For whosoever shall do the will of God, the same is my brother, and my sister, and mother.

AND he began again to teach by the sea side: and there was gathered unto him a great multitude, so that he entered into a ship, and sat in the sea; and the whole multitude was by the sea on the land.

2And he taught them many things by parables, and said unto them in his doctrine,

3Hearken; Behold, there went out a sower to sow:

4And it came to pass, as he sowed, some fell by the way side, and the fowls of the air came and devoured it up.

5And some fell on stony ground, where it had not much earth; and immediately it sprang up, because it had no depth of earth:

6But when the sun was up, it was scorched; and because it had no root, it withered away.

7And some fell among thorns, and the thorns grew up, and choked it, and it yielded no fruit.

8And other fell on good ground, and did yield fruit that sprang up and increased; and brought forth, some thirty, and some sixty, and some an hundred.

9And he said unto them, He that hath ears to hear, let him hear.

10And when he was alone, they that were about him with the twelve asked of him the parable.

11And he said unto them, Unto you it is given to know the mystery of the kingdom of God: but unto them that are without, all *these* things are done in parables:

12That seeing they may see, and not perceive; and hearing they may hear, and not understand; lest at any time they should be converted, and *their* sins should be forgiven them.

13And he said unto them, Know ye not this parable? and how then will ye know all parables?

14The sower soweth the word.

15And these are they by the way side, where the word is sown; but when they have heard, Satan cometh immediately, and taketh away the word that was sown in their hearts.

16And these are they likewise which are sown on stony ground; who, when they have heard the word, immediately receive it with gladness;

17And have no root in themselves, and so endure but for a time: afterward, when affliction or persecution ariseth for the word's sake, immediately they are offended.

18And these are they which are sown among thorns; such as hear the word,

19And the cares of this world, and the deceitfulness of riches, and the lusts of other things entering in, choke the word, and it becometh unfruitful.

20And these are they which are sown on good ground; such as hear the word, and receive *it,* and bring forth fruit, some thirtyfold, some sixty, and some an hundred.

21And he said unto them, Is a candle brought to be put under a bushel, or under a bed? and not to be set on a candlestick?

22For there is nothing hid, which shall not be manifested; neither was any thing kept secret, but that it should come abroad.

23If any man have ears to hear, let him hear.

24And he said unto them, Take heed what ye hear: with what measure ye mete, it shall be measured to you: and unto you that hear shall more be given.

25For he that hath, to him shall be given: and he that hath not, from him shall be taken even that which he hath.

PSALM 37:12–28

THE wicked plotteth against the just, and gnasheth upon him with his teeth.

13The Lord shall laugh at him: for he seeth that his day is coming.

14The wicked have drawn out the sword, and have bent their bow, to cast down the poor and needy, *and* to slay such as be of upright conversation.

15Their sword shall enter into their own heart, and their bows shall be broken.

16A little that a righteous man hath *is* better than the riches of many wicked.

17For the arms of the wicked shall be broken: but the LORD upholdeth the righteous.

18The LORD knoweth the days of the upright: and their inheritance shall be for ever.

19They shall not be ashamed in the evil time: and in the days of famine they shall be satisfied.

20But the wicked shall perish, and the enemies of the LORD *shall be* as the fat of lambs: they shall consume; into smoke shall they consume away.

21The wicked borroweth, and payeth not again: but the righteous sheweth mercy, and giveth.

22For *such as be* blessed of him shall inherit the earth; and *they that be* cursed of him shall be cut off.

23The steps of a *good* man are ordered by the LORD: and he delighteth in his way.

24Though he fall, he shall not be utterly cast down: for the LORD upholdeth *him with* his hand.

25I have been young, and *now* am old; yet have I not seen the righteous forsaken, nor his seed begging bread.

26*He is* ever merciful, and lendeth; and his seed *is* blessed.

27Depart from evil, and do good; and dwell for evermore.

28For the LORD loveth judgment, and forsaketh not his saints; they are preserved for ever: but the seed of the wicked shall be cut off.

PROVERBS FOR TODAY/ 10:5

He that gathereth in summer is *a wise son:* but *he that sleepeth in harvest* is *a son that causeth shame.*

FEBRUARY 20

LEVITICUS 9:7—10:20

AND Moses said unto Aaron, Go unto the altar, and offer thy sin offering, and thy burnt offering, and make an atonement for thyself, and for the people: and offer the offering of the people, and make an atonement for them; as the LORD commanded.

8Aaron therefore went unto the altar, and slew the calf of the sin offering, which *was* for himself.

9And the sons of Aaron brought the blood unto him: and he dipped his finger in the blood, and put *it* upon the horns of the altar, and poured out the blood at the bottom of the altar:

10But the fat, and the kidneys, and the caul above the liver of the sin offering, he burnt upon the altar; as the LORD commanded Moses.

11And the flesh and the hide he burnt with fire without the camp.

12And he slew the burnt offering; and Aaron's sons presented unto him the blood, which he sprinkled round about upon the altar.

13And they presented the burnt offering unto him, with the pieces thereof, and the head: and he burnt *them* upon the altar.

14And he did wash the inwards and the legs, and burnt *them* upon the burnt offering on the altar.

15And he brought the people's offering, and took the goat, which *was* the sin offering for the people, and slew it, and offered it for sin, as the first.

16And he brought the burnt offering, and offered it according to the manner.

17And he brought the meat offering, and took an handful thereof, and burnt *it* upon the altar, beside the burnt sacrifice of the morning.

18He slew also the bullock and the ram *for* a sacrifice of peace offerings, which *was* for the people: and Aaron's sons presented unto him the blood, which he sprinkled upon the altar round about,

19And the fat of the bullock and of the ram, the rump, and that which covereth *the inwards,* and the kidneys, and the caul *above* the liver:

20And they put the fat upon the breasts, and he burnt the fat upon the altar:

21And the breasts and the right shoulder Aaron waved *for* a wave offering before the LORD; as Moses commanded.

22And Aaron lifted up his hand toward the people, and blessed them, and came down from offering of the sin offering, and the burnt offering, and peace offerings.

23And Moses and Aaron went into the tabernacle of the congregation, and came out, and blessed the people: and the glory of the LORD appeared unto all the people.

24And there came a fire out from before the LORD, and consumed upon the altar the burnt offering and the fat: *which* when all the people saw, they shouted, and fell on their faces.

AND Nadab and Abihu, the sons of Aaron, took either of them his censer, and put fire therein, and put incense thereon, and offered strange fire before the LORD, which he commanded them not.

2And there went out fire from the LORD, and devoured them, and they died before the LORD.

3Then Moses said unto Aaron, This *is it* that the LORD spake, saying, I will be sanctified in them that come nigh me, and before all the people I will be glorified. And Aaron held his peace.

4And Moses called Mishael and Elzaphan, the sons of Uzziel the uncle of Aaron, and said unto them, Come near, carry your brethren from before the sanctuary out of the camp.

5So they went near, and carried them in their coats out of the camp; as Moses had said.

6And Moses said unto Aaron, and unto Eleazar and unto Ithamar, his sons, Uncover not your heads, neither rend your clothes; lest ye die, and lest wrath come upon all the people: but let your brethren, the whole house of Israel, bewail the burning which the LORD hath kindled.

7And ye shall not go out from the door of the tabernacle of the congregation, lest ye die: for the anointing oil of the LORD is upon you. And they did according to the word of Moses.

8And the LORD spake unto Aaron, saying,

9Do not drink wine nor strong drink, thou, nor thy sons with thee, when ye go into the tabernacle of the congregation, lest ye die: it shall be a statute for ever throughout your generations:

10And that ye may put difference between holy and unholy, and between unclean and clean;

11And that ye may teach the children of Israel all the statutes which the LORD hath spoken unto them by the hand of Moses.

12And Moses spake unto Aaron, and unto Eleazar and unto Ithamar, his sons that were left, Take the meat offering that remaineth of the offerings of the LORD made by fire, and eat it without leaven beside the altar: for it is most holy:

13And ye shall eat it in the holy place, because it is thy due, and thy sons' due, of the sacrifices of the LORD made by fire: for so I am commanded.

14And the wave breast and heave shoulder shall ye eat in a clean place; thou, and thy sons, and thy daughters with thee: for they be thy due, and thy sons' due, which are given out of the sacrifices of peace offerings of the children of Israel.

15The heave shoulder and the wave breast shall they bring with the offerings made by fire of the fat, to wave it for a wave offering before the LORD; and it shall be thine, and thy sons' with thee, by a statute for ever; as the LORD hath commanded.

16And Moses diligently sought the goat of the sin offering, and, behold, it was burnt: and he was angry with Eleazar and Ithamar, the sons of Aaron which were left alive, saying,

17Wherefore have ye not eaten the sin offering in the holy place, seeing it is most holy, and God hath given it you to bear the iniquity of the congregation, to make atonement for them before the LORD?

18Behold, the blood of it was not brought in within the holy place: ye should indeed have eaten it in the holy place, as I commanded.

19And Aaron said unto Moses, Behold, this day have they offered their sin offering and their burnt offering before the LORD; and such things have befallen me: and if I had eaten the sin offering to day, should it have been accepted in the sight of the LORD?

20And when Moses heard that, he was content.

MARK 4:26—5:20

AND he [Jesus] said, So is the kingdom of God, as if a man should cast seed into the ground;

27And should sleep, and rise night and day, and the seed should spring and grow up, he knoweth not how.

28For the earth bringeth forth fruit of herself; first the blade, then the ear, after that the full corn in the ear.

29But when the fruit is brought forth,

immediately he putteth in the sickle, because the harvest is come.

30And he said, Whereunto shall we liken the kingdom of God? or with what comparison shall we compare it?

31*It is* like a grain of mustard seed, which, when it is sown in the earth, is less than all the seeds that be in the earth:

32But when it is sown, it groweth up, and becometh greater than all herbs, and shooteth out great branches; so that the fowls of the air may lodge under the shadow of it.

33And with many such parables spake he the word unto them, as they were able to hear *it.*

34But without a parable spake he not unto them: and when they were alone, he expounded all things to his disciples.

35And the same day, when the even was come, he saith unto them, Let us pass over unto the other side.

36And when they had sent away the multitude, they took him even as he was in the ship. And there were also with him other little ships.

37And there arose a great storm of wind, and the waves beat into the ship, so that it was now full.

38And he was in the hinder part of the ship, asleep on a pillow: and they awake him, and say unto him, Master, carest thou not that we perish?

39And he arose, and rebuked the wind, and said unto the sea, Peace, be still. And the wind ceased, and there was a great calm.

40And he said unto them, Why are ye so fearful? how is it that ye have no faith?

41And they feared exceedingly, and said one to another, What manner of man is this, that even the wind and the sea obey him?

AND they came over unto the other side of the sea, into the country of the Gadarenes.

2And when he was come out of the ship, immediately there met him out of the tombs a man with an unclean spirit,

3Who had *his* dwelling among the tombs; and no man could bind him, no, not with chains:

4Because that he had been often bound with fetters and chains, and the chains had been plucked asunder by him, and the fetters broken in pieces: neither could any *man* tame him.

5And always, night and day, he was in the mountains, and in the tombs, crying, and cutting himself with stones.

6But when he saw Jesus afar off, he ran and worshipped him,

7And cried with a loud voice, and said, What have I to do with thee, Jesus, *thou* Son of the most high God? I adjure thee by God, that thou torment me not.

8For he said unto him, Come out of the man, *thou* unclean spirit.

9And he asked him, What *is* thy name? And he answered, saying, My name *is* Legion: for we are many.

10And he besought him much that he would not send them away out of the country.

11Now there was there nigh unto the mountains a great herd of swine feeding.

12And all the devils besought him, saying, Send us into the swine, that we may enter into them.

13And forthwith Jesus gave them leave. And the unclean spirits went out, and entered into the swine: and the herd ran violently down a steep place into the sea, (they were about two thousand;) and were choked in the sea.

14And they that fed the swine fled, and told *it* in the city, and in the country. And they went out to see what it was that was done.

15And they come to Jesus, and see him that was possessed with the devil, and had the legion, sitting, and clothed, and in his right mind: and they were afraid.

16And they that saw *it* told them how

it befell to him that was possessed with the devil, and *also* concerning the swine.

17And they began to pray him to depart out of their coasts.

18And when he was come into the ship, he that had been possessed with the devil prayed him that he might be with him.

19Howbeit Jesus suffered him not, but saith unto him, Go home to thy friends, and tell them how great things the Lord hath done for thee, and hath had compassion on thee.

20And he departed, and began to publish in Decapolis how great things Jesus had done for him: and all *men* did marvel.

PSALM 37:29–40

THE righteous shall inherit the land, and dwell therein for ever. 30The mouth of the righteous speaketh wisdom, and his tongue talketh of judgment.

31The law of his God *is* in his heart; none of his steps shall slide.

32The wicked watcheth the righ-teous, and seeketh to slay him.

33The LORD will not leave him in his hand, nor condemn him when he is judged.

34Wait on the LORD, and keep his way, and he shall exalt thee to inherit the land: when the wicked are cut off, thou shall see *it*.

35I have seen the wicked in great power, and spreading himself like a green bay tree.

36Yet he passed away, and, lo, he *was* not: yea, I sought him, but he could not be found.

37Mark the perfect *man,* and behold the upright: for the end of *that* man *is* peace.

38But the transgressors shall be destroyed together: the end of the wicked shall be cut off.

39But the salvation of the righteous *is* of the LORD: *he is* their strength in the time of trouble.

40And the LORD shall help them, and deliver them: he shall deliver them from the wicked, and save them, because they trust in him.

PROVERBS FOR TODAY/ 10:6–7

Blessings are *upon the head of the just: but violence covereth the mouth of the wicked.* □ *The memory of the just* is *blessed: but the name of the wicked shall rot.*

FEBRUARY 21

LEVITICUS 11:1—12:8

AND the LORD spake unto Moses and to Aaron, saying unto them, 2Speak unto the children of Israel, saying, These *are* the beasts which ye shall eat among all the beasts that *are* on the earth.

3Whatsoever parteth the hoof, and is clovenfooted, *and* cheweth the cud, among the beasts, that shall ye eat.

4Nevertheless these shall ye not eat of them that chew the cud, or of them that divide the hoof: *as* the camel, because he cheweth the cud, but divideth not the hoof; he *is* unclean unto you.

5And the coney, because he cheweth the cud, but divideth not the hoof; he *is* unclean unto you.

6And the hare, because he cheweth the cud, but divideth not the hoof; he *is* unclean unto you.

7And the swine, though he divide the hoof, and be clovenfooted, yet he cheweth not the cud; he *is* unclean to you.

8Of their flesh shall ye not eat, and their carcase shall ye not touch; they *are* unclean to you.

9These shall ye eat of all that *are* in the waters: whatsoever hath fins and scales in the waters, in the seas, and in the rivers, them shall ye eat.

10And all that have not fins and scales in the seas, and in the rivers, of all that move in the waters, and of any living thing which *is* in the waters, they *shall be* an abomination unto you:

11They shall be even an abomination unto you; ye shall not eat of their flesh, but ye shall have their carcases in abomination.

12Whatsoever hath no fins nor scales in the waters, that *shall be* an abomination unto you.

13And these *are they which* ye shall have in abomination among the fowls; they shall not be eaten, they *are* an abomination: the eagle, and the ossifrage, and the ospray,

14And the vulture, and the kite after his kind;

15Every raven after his kind;

16And the owl, and the night hawk, and the cuckow, and the hawk after his kind,

17And the little owl, and the cormorant, and the great owl,

18And the swan, and the pelican, and the gier eagle,

19And the stork, the heron after her kind, and the lapwing, and the bat.

20All fowls that creep, going upon *all* four, *shall be* an abomination unto you.

21Yet these may ye eat of every flying creeping thing that goeth upon *all* four, which have legs above their feet, to leap withal upon the earth;

22*Even* these of them ye may eat; the locust after his kind, and the bald locust after his kind, and the beetle after his kind, and the grasshopper after his kind.

23But all *other* flying creeping things, which have four feet, *shall be* an abomination unto you.

24And for these ye shall be unclean: whosoever toucheth the carcase of them shall be unclean until the even.

25And whosoever beareth *ought* of the carcase of them shall wash his clothes, and be unclean until the even.

26*The carcases* of every beast which divideth the hoof, and *is* not clovenfooted, nor cheweth the cud, *are* unclean unto you: every one that toucheth them shall be unclean.

27And whatsoever goeth upon his paws, among all manner of beasts that go on *all* four, those *are* unclean unto you: whoso toucheth their carcase shall be unclean until the even.

28And he that beareth the carcase of them shall wash his clothes, and be unclean until the even: they *are* unclean unto you.

29These also *shall be* unclean unto you among the creeping things that creep upon the earth; the weasel, and the mouse, and the tortoise after his kind,

30And the ferret, and the chameleon, and the lizard, and the snail, and the mole.

31These *are* unclean to you among all that creep: whosoever doth touch them, when they be dead, shall be unclean until the even.

32And upon whatsoever *any* of them, when they are dead, doth fall, it shall be unclean; whether *it be* any vessel of wood, or raiment, or skin, or sack, whatsoever vessel *it be,* wherein *any* work is done, it must be put into water, and it shall be unclean until the even; so it shall be cleansed.

33And every earthen vessel, whereinto *any* of them falleth, whatsoever *is* in it shall be unclean; and ye shall break it.

34Of all meat which may be eaten, *that* on which *such* water cometh shall be unclean: and all drink that may be drunk in every *such* vessel shall be unclean.

35And every *thing* whereupon *any part* of their carcase falleth shall be unclean; *whether it be* oven, or ranges for pots, they shall be broken down: *for* they *are* unclean, and shall be unclean unto you.

36Nevertheless a fountain or pit, *wherein there is* plenty of water, shall be clean: but that which toucheth their carcase shall be unclean.

37And if *any part* of their carcase fall upon any sowing seed which is to be sown, it *shall be* clean.

38But if *any* water be put upon the seed, and *any part* of their carcase fall thereon, it *shall be* unclean unto you.

39And if any beast, of which ye may eat, die; he that toucheth the carcase thereof shall be unclean until the even.

40And he that eateth of the carcase of it shall wash his clothes, and be unclean until the even: he also that beareth the carcase of it shall wash his clothes, and be unclean until the even.

41And every creeping thing that creepeth upon the earth *shall be* an abomination; it shall not be eaten.

42Whatsoever goeth upon the belly, and whatsoever goeth upon *all* four, or whatsoever hath more feet among all creeping things that creep upon the earth, them ye shall not eat; for they *are* an abomination.

43Ye shall not make yourselves abominable with any creeping thing that creepeth, neither shall ye make yourselves unclean with them, that ye should be defiled thereby.

44For I *am* the LORD your God: ye shall therefore sanctify yourselves, and ye shall be holy; for I *am* holy: neither shall ye defile yourselves with any man-

ner of creeping thing that creepeth upon the earth.

45For I *am* the LORD that bringeth you up out of the land of Egypt, to be your God: ye shall therefore be holy, for I *am* holy.

46This *is* the law of the beasts, and of the fowl, and of every living creature that moveth in the waters, and of every creature that creepeth upon the earth:

47To make a difference between the unclean and the clean, and between the beast that may be eaten and the beast that may not be eaten.

AND the LORD spake unto Moses, saying,

2Speak unto the children of Israel, saying, If a woman have conceived seed, and born a man child: then she shall be unclean seven days; according to the days of the separation for her infirmity shall she be unclean.

3And in the eighth day the flesh of his foreskin shall be circumcised.

4And she shall then continue in the blood of her purifying three and thirty days; she shall touch no hallowed thing, nor come into the sanctuary, until the days of her purifying be fulfilled.

5But if she bear a maid child, then she shall be unclean two weeks, as in her separation: and she shall continue in the blood of her purifying threescore and six days.

6And when the days of her purifying are fulfilled, for a son, or for a daughter, she shall bring a lamb of the first year for a burnt offering, and a young pigeon, or a turtledove, for a sin offering, unto the door of the tabernacle of the congregation, unto the priest:

7Who shall offer it before the LORD, and make an atonement for her; and she shall be cleansed from the issue of her blood. This *is* the law for her that hath born a male or a female.

8And if she be not able to bring a lamb, then she shall bring two turtles, or two young pigeons; the one for the burnt offering, and the other for a sin offering: and the priest shall make an atonement for her, and she shall be clean.

MARK 5:21–43

AND when Jesus was passed over again by ship unto the other side, much people gathered unto him: and he was nigh unto the sea.

22And, behold, there cometh one of the rulers of the synagogue, Jairus by name; and when he saw him, he fell at his feet,

23And besought him greatly, saying, My little daughter lieth at the point of death: I *pray thee,* come and lay thy hands on her, that she may be healed; and she shall live.

24And *Jesus* went with him; and much people followed him, and thronged him.

25And a certain woman, which had an issue of blood twelve years,

26And had suffered many things of many physicians, and had spent all that she had, and was nothing bettered, but rather grew worse,

27When she had heard of Jesus, came in the press behind, and touched his garment.

28For she said, If I may touch but his clothes, I shall be whole.

29And straightway the fountain of her blood was dried up; and she felt in *her* body that she was healed of that plague.

30And Jesus, immediately knowing in himself that virtue had gone out of him, turned him about in the press, and said, Who touched my clothes?

31And his disciples said unto him, Thou seest the multitude thronging thee, and sayest thou, Who touched me?

32And he looked round about to see her that had done this thing.

33But the woman fearing and trembling, knowing what was done in her, came and fell down before him, and told him all the truth.

34And he said unto her, Daughter, thy faith hath made thee whole; go in peace, and be whole of thy plague.

35While he yet spake, there came from the ruler of the synagogue's *house certain* which said, Thy daughter is dead: why troublest thou the Master any further?

36As soon as Jesus heard the word that was spoken, he saith unto the ruler of the synagogue, Be not afraid, only believe.

37And he suffered no man to follow him, save Peter, and James, and John the brother of James.

38And he cometh to the house of the ruler of the synagogue, and seeth the tumult, and them that wept and wailed greatly.

39And when he was come in, he saith unto them, Why make ye this ado, and weep? the damsel is not dead, but sleepeth.

40And they laughed him to scorn. But when he had put them all out, he taketh the father and the mother of the damsel, and them that were with him, and entereth in where the damsel was lying.

41And he took the damsel by the hand, and said unto her, Talitha cumi; which is, being interpreted, Damsel, I say unto thee, arise.

42And straightway the damsel arose, and walked; for she was *of the age of* twelve years. And they were astonished with a great astonishment.

43And he charged them straitly that no man should know it; and commanded that something should be given her to eat.

PSALM 38:1–22

O LORD, rebuke me not in thy wrath: neither chasten me in thy hot displeasure.

2For thine arrows stick fast in me, and thy hand presseth me sore.

3*There is* no soundness in my flesh because of thine anger; neither *is there any* rest in my bones because of my sin.

4For mine iniquities are gone over mine head: as an heavy burden they are too heavy for me.

5My wounds stink *and* are corrupt because of my foolishness.

6I am troubled; I am bowed down greatly; I go mourning all the day long.

7For my loins are filled with a loathsome *disease:* and *there is* no soundness in my flesh.

8I am feeble and sore broken: I have roared by reason of the disquietness of my heart.

9Lord, all my desire *is* before thee; and my groaning is not hid from thee.

10My heart panteth, my strength faileth me: as for the light of mine eyes, it also is gone from me.

11My lovers and my friends stand aloof from my sore; and my kinsmen stand afar off.

12They also that seek after my life lay snares *for me:* and they that seek my hurt speak mischievous things, and imagine deceits all the day long.

13But I, as a deaf *man,* heard not; and *I was* as a dumb man *that* openeth not his mouth.

14Thus I was as a man that heareth not, and in whose mouth *are* no reproofs.

15For in thee, O Lord, do I hope: thou wilt hear, O Lord my God.

16For I said, *Hear me,* lest *otherwise* they should rejoice over me: when my foot slippeth, they magnify *themselves* against me.

17For I *am* ready to halt, and my sorrow *is* continually before me.

18For I will declare mine iniquity; I will be sorry for my sin.

19But mine enemies *are* lively, *and* they are strong: and they that hate me wrongfully are multiplied.

20They also that render evil for good are mine adversaries; because I follow *the thing that* good *is.*

21Forsake me not, O Lord: O my God, be not far from me.

22Make haste to help me, O Lord my salvation.

PROVERBS FOR TODAY/ 10:8–9

The wise in heart will receive commandments: but a prating fool shall fall. □ *He that walketh uprightly walketh surely: but he that perverteth his ways shall be known.*

FEBRUARY 22

LEVITICUS 13:1–59

AND the Lord spake unto Moses and Aaron, saying,

2When a man shall have in the skin of his flesh a rising, a scab, or bright spot, and it be in the skin of his flesh *like* the plague of leprosy; then he shall be brought unto Aaron the priest, or unto one of his sons the priests:

3And the priest shall look on the plague in the skin of the flesh: and *when* the hair in the plague is turned white, and the plague in sight *be* deeper than the skin of his flesh, it *is* a plague of leprosy: and the priest shall look on him, and pronounce him unclean.

4If the bright spot *be* white in the skin of his flesh, and in sight *be* not deeper than the skin, and the hair thereof be not turned white; then the priest shall shut up *him that hath* the plague seven days:

5And the priest shall look on him the seventh day: and, behold, *if* the plague in his sight be at a stay, *and* the plague spread not in the skin; then the priest shall shut him up seven days more:

6And the priest shall look on him again the seventh day: and, behold, *if* the plague *be* somewhat dark, *and* the plague spread not in the skin, the priest shall pronounce him clean: it *is but* a scab: and he shall wash his clothes, and be clean.

7But if the scab spread much abroad in the skin, after that he hath been seen of the priest for his cleansing, he shall be seen of the priest again:

8And *if* the priest see that, behold, the scab spreadeth in the skin, then the priest shall pronounce him unclean: it *is* a leprosy.

9When the plague of leprosy is in a man, then he shall be brought unto the priest;

10And the priest shall see *him:* and, behold, *if* the rising *be* white in the skin, and it have turned the hair white, and *there be* quick raw flesh in the rising;

11It *is* an old leprosy in the skin of his flesh, and the priest shall pronounce him unclean, and shall not shut him up: for he *is* unclean.

12And if a leprosy break out abroad in the skin, and the leprosy cover all the skin of *him that hath* the plague from his head even to his foot, wheresoever the priest looketh;

13Then the priest shall consider: and, behold, *if* the leprosy have covered all his flesh, he shall pronounce *him* clean *that hath* the plague: it is all turned white: he *is* clean.

14But when raw flesh appeareth in him, he shall be unclean.

15And the priest shall see the raw flesh, and pronounce him to be unclean: *for* the raw flesh *is* unclean: it *is* a leprosy.

16Or if the raw flesh turn again, and be changed unto white, he shall come unto the priest;

17And the priest shall see him: and, behold, *if* the plague be turned into white; then the priest shall pronounce *him* clean *that hath* the plague: he *is* clean.

18The flesh also, in which, *even in* the skin thereof, was a boil, and is healed,

19And in the place of the boil there be a white rising, or a bright spot, white, and somewhat reddish, and it be shewed to the priest;

20And if, when the priest seeth it, behold, it *be* in sight lower than the skin, and the hair thereof be turned white; the priest shall pronounce him unclean: it *is* a plague of leprosy broken out of the boil.

21But if the priest look on it, and, behold, *there be* no white hairs therein, and *if* it *be* not lower than the skin, but *be* somewhat dark; then the priest shall shut him up seven days:

22And if it spread much abroad in the skin, then the priest shall pronounce him unclean: it *is* a plague.

23But if the bright spot stay in his place, *and* spread not, it *is* a burning boil; and the priest shall pronounce him clean.

24Or if there be *any* flesh, in the skin whereof *there is* a hot burning, and the quick *flesh* that burneth have a white bright spot, somewhat reddish, or white;

25Then the priest shall look upon it: and, behold, *if* the hair in the bright spot be turned white, and it *be in* sight deeper than the skin; it *is* a leprosy broken out of the burning: wherefore the priest shall pronounce him unclean: it *is* the plague of leprosy.

26But if the priest look on it, and,

behold, *there be* no white hair in the bright spot, and it *be* no lower than the *other* skin, but *be* somewhat dark; then the priest shall shut him up seven days:

27And the priest shall look upon him the seventh day: *and* if it be spread much abroad in the skin, then the priest shall pronounce him unclean: it *is* the plague of leprosy.

28And if the bright spot stay in his place, *and* spread not in the skin, but it *be* somewhat dark; it *is* a rising of the burning, and the priest shall pronounce him clean: for it *is* an inflammation of the burning.

29If a man or woman have a plague upon the head or the beard;

30Then the priest shall see the plague: and, behold, if it *be* in sight deeper than the skin; *and there be* in it a yellow thin hair; then the priest shall pronounce him unclean: it *is* a dry scall, *even* a leprosy upon the head or beard.

31And if the priest look on the plague of the scall, and, behold, it *be* not in sight deeper than the skin, and *that there is* no black hair in it; then the priest shall shut up *him that hath* the plague of the scall seven days:

32And in the seventh day the priest shall look on the plague: and, behold, *if* the scall spread not, and there be in it no yellow hair, and the scall *be* not in sight deeper than the skin;

33He shall be shaven, but the scall shall he not shave; and the priest shall shut up *him that hath* the scall seven days more:

34And in the seventh day the priest shall look on the scall: and, behold, *if* the scall be not spread in the skin, nor *be* in sight deeper than the skin; then the priest shall pronounce him clean: and he shall wash his clothes, and be clean.

35But if the scall spread much in the skin after his cleansing;

36Then the priest shall look on him: and, behold, if the scall be spread in the skin, the priest shall not seek for yellow hair; he *is* unclean.

37But if the scall be in his sight at a stay, and *that* there is black hair grown up therein; the scall is healed, he *is* clean: and the priest shall pronounce him clean.

38If a man also or a woman have in the skin of their flesh bright spots, *even* white bright spots;

39Then the priest shall look: and, behold, *if* the bright spots in the skin of their flesh *be* darkish white; it *is* a freckled spot *that* groweth in the skin; he *is* clean.

40And the man whose hair is fallen off his head, he is bald; *yet is* he clean.

41And he that hath his hair fallen off from the part of his head toward his face, he *is* forehead bald: *yet is* he clean.

42And if there be in the bald head, or bald forehead, a white reddish sore; it *is* a leprosy sprung up in his bald head, or his bald forehead.

43Then the priest shall look upon it: and, behold, *if* the rising of the sore *be* white reddish in his bald head, or in his bald forehead, as the leprosy appeareth in the skin of the flesh;

44He is a leprous man, he *is* unclean: the priest shall pronounce him utterly unclean; his plague *is* in his head.

45And the leper in whom the plague *is,* his clothes shall be rent, and his head bare, and he shall put a covering upon his upper lip, and shall cry, Unclean, unclean.

46All the days wherein the plague *shall be* in him he shall be defiled; he *is* unclean: he shall dwell alone; without the camp *shall* his habitation *be.*

47The garment also that the plague of leprosy is in, *whether it be* a woollen garment, or a linen garment;

48Whether *it be* in the warp, or woof; of linen, or of woollen; whether in a skin, or in any thing made of skin;

49And if the plague be greenish or reddish in the garment, or in the skin, either in the warp, or in the woof, or in any thing of skin; it *is* a plague of leprosy, and shall be shewed unto the priest:

50And the priest shall look upon the plague, and shut up *it that hath* the plague seven days:

51And he shall look on the plague on the seventh day: if the plague be spread in the garment, either in the warp, or in the woof, or in a skin, *or* in any work that is made of skin; the plague *is* a fretting leprosy; it *is* unclean.

52He shall therefore burn that garment, whether warp or woof, in woollen or in linen, or any thing of skin, wherein the plague is: for it *is* a fretting leprosy; it shall be burnt in the fire.

53And if the priest shall look, and, behold, the plague be not spread in the garment, either in the warp, or in the woof, or in any thing of skin;

54Then the priest shall command that they wash *the thing* wherein the plague *is,* and he shall shut it up seven days more:

55And the priest shall look on the plague, after that it is washed: and, behold, *if* the plague have not changed his colour, and the plague be not spread; it *is* unclean; thou shalt burn it in the fire; it *is* fret inward, *whether* it *be* bare within or without.

56And if the priest look, and, behold, the plague *be* somewhat dark after the washing of it; then he shall rend it out of the garment, or out of the skin, or out of the warp, or out of the woof:

57And if it appear still in the garment, either in the warp, or in the woof, or in any thing of skin; it *is* a spreading *plague:* thou shalt burn that wherein the plague *is* with fire.

58And the garment, either warp, or woof, or whatsoever thing of skin *it be,* which thou shalt wash, if the plague be departed from them, then it shall be washed the second time, and shall be clean.

59This *is* the law of the plague of leprosy in a garment of woollen or linen,

either in the warp, or woof, or any thing of skins, to pronounce it clean, or to pronounce it unclean.

MARK 6:1–29

AND he [Jesus] went out from thence, and came into his own country; and his disciples follow him.

2And when the sabbath day was come, he began to teach in the synagogue: and many hearing *him* were astonished, saying, From whence hath this *man* these things? and what wisdom *is* this which is given unto him, that even such mighty works are wrought by his hands?

3Is not this the carpenter, the son of Mary, the brother of James, and Joses, and of Juda, and Simon? and are not his sisters here with us? And they were offended at him.

4But Jesus said unto them, A prophet is not without honour, but in his own country, and among his own kin, and in his own house.

5And he could there do no mighty work, save that he laid his hands upon a few sick folk, and healed *them.*

6And he marvelled because of their unbelief. And he went round about the villages, teaching.

7And he called *unto him* the twelve, and began to send them forth by two and two; and gave them power over unclean spirits;

8And commanded them that they should take nothing for *their* journey, save a staff only; no scrip, no bread, no money in *their* purse;

9But *be* shod with sandals; and not put on two coats.

10And he said unto them, In what place soever ye enter into an house, there abide till ye depart from that place.

11And whosoever shall not receive you, nor hear you, when ye depart thence, shake off the dust under your feet for a testimony against them. Verily

I say unto you, It shall be more tolerable for Sodom and Gomorrha in the day of judgment, than for that city.

12And they went out, and preached that men should repent.

13And they cast out many devils, and anointed with oil many that were sick, and healed *them*.

14And king Herod heard *of him;* (for his name was spread abroad:) and he said, That John the Baptist was risen from the dead, and therefore mighty works do shew forth themselves in him.

15Others said, That it is Elias. And others said, That it is a prophet, or as one of the prophets.

16But when Herod heard *thereof,* he said, It is John, whom I beheaded: he is risen from the dead.

17For Herod himself had sent forth and laid hold upon John, and bound him in prison for Herodias' sake, his brother Philip's wife: for he had married her.

18For John had said unto Herod, It is not lawful for thee to have thy brother's wife.

19Therefore Herodias had a quarrel against him, and would have killed him; but she could not:

20For Herod feared John, knowing that he was a just man and an holy, and observed him; and when he heard him, he did many things, and heard him gladly.

21And when a convenient day was come, that Herod on his birthday made a supper to his lords, high captains, and chief *estates* of Galilee;

22And the daughter of the said Herodias came in, and danced, and pleased Herod and them that sat with him, the king said unto the damsel, Ask of me whatsoever thou wilt, and I will give *it* thee.

23And he sware unto her, Whatsoever thou shalt ask of me, I will give *it* thee, unto the half of my kingdom.

24And she went forth, and said unto her mother, What shall I ask? And she said, The head of John the Baptist.

25And she came in straightway with haste unto the king, and asked, saying, I will that thou give me by and by in a charger the head of John the Baptist.

26And the king was exceeding sorry; *yet* for his oath's sake, and for their sakes which sat with him, he would not reject her.

27And immediately the king sent an executioner, and commanded his head to be brought: and he went and beheaded him in the prison,

28And brought his head in a charger, and gave it to the damsel: and the damsel gave it to her mother.

29And when his disciples heard *of it,* they came and took up his corpse, and laid it in a tomb.

PSALM 39:1–13

I said, I will take heed to my ways, that I sin not with my tongue: I will keep my mouth with a bridle, while the wicked is before me.

2I was dumb with silence, I held my peace, *even* from good; and my sorrow was stirred.

3My heart was hot within me, while I was musing the fire burned: *then* spake I with my tongue,

4LORD, make me to know mine end, and the measure of my days, what it *is: that* I may know how frail I *am.*

5Behold, thou hast made my days *as* an handbreadth; and mine age *is* as nothing before thee: verily every man at his best state *is* altogether vanity. Selah.

6Surely every man walketh in a vain shew: surely they are disquieted in vain: he heapeth up *riches,* and knoweth not who shall gather them.

7And now, Lord, what wait I for? my hope *is* in thee.

8Deliver me from all my transgressions: make me not the reproach of the foolish.

9I was dumb, I opened not my mouth;

because thou didst *it.*

10Remove thy stroke away from me: I am consumed by the blow of thine hand.

11When thou with rebukes dost correct man for iniquity, thou makest his beauty to consume away like a moth: surely every man *is* vanity. Selah.

12Hear my prayer, O LORD, and give ear unto my cry; hold not thy peace at my tears: for I *am* a stranger with thee, *and* a sojourner, as all my fathers *were.*

13O spare me, that I may recover strength, before I go hence, and be no more.

PROVERBS FOR TODAY/ 10:10

He that winketh with the eye causeth sorrow: but a prating fool shall fall.

FEBRUARY 23

LEVITICUS 14:1–57

AND the LORD spake unto Moses, saying,

2This shall be the law of the leper in the day of his cleansing: He shall be brought unto the priest:

3And the priest shall go forth out of the camp; and the priest shall look, and, behold, *if* the plague of leprosy be healed in the leper;

4Then shall the priest command to take for him that is to be cleansed two birds alive *and* clean, and cedar wood, and scarlet, and hyssop:

5And the priest shall command that one of the birds be killed in an earthen vessel over running water:

6As for the living bird, he shall take it, and the cedar wood, and the scarlet, and the hyssop, and shall dip them and the living bird in the blood of the bird *that was* killed over the running water:

7And he shall sprinkle upon him that is to be cleansed from the leprosy seven times, and shall pronounce him clean, and shall let the living bird loose into the open field.

8And he that is to be cleansed shall wash his clothes, and shave off all his hair, and wash himself in water, that he may be clean: and after that he shall come into the camp, and shall tarry abroad out of his tent seven days.

9But it shall be on the seventh day, that he shall shave all his hair off his head and his beard and his eyebrows, even all his hair he shall shave off: and he shall wash his clothes, also he shall wash his flesh in water, and he shall be clean.

10And on the eighth day he shall take two he lambs without blemish, and one ewe lamb of the first year without blemish, and three tenth deals of fine flour *for* a meat offering, mingled with oil, and one log of oil.

11And the priest that maketh *him* clean shall present the man that is to be made clean, and those things, before the LORD, *at* the door of the tabernacle of the congregation:

12And the priest shall take one he lamb, and offer him for a trespass offering, and the log of oil, and wave them *for* a wave offering before the LORD:

13And he shall slay the lamb in the place where he shall kill the sin offering and the burnt offering, in the holy place: for as the sin offering *is* the priest's, *so is* the trespass offering: it *is* most holy:

14And the priest shall take *some* of the blood of the trespass offering, and the priest shall put *it* upon the tip of the right ear of him that is to be cleansed, and upon the thumb of his right hand, and upon the great toe of his right foot:

15And the priest shall take *some* of the log of oil, and pour *it* into the palm of his own left hand:

16And the priest shall dip his right finger in the oil that *is* in his left hand, and shall sprinkle of the oil with his finger seven times before the LORD:

17And of the rest of the oil that *is* in his hand shall the priest put upon the tip of the right ear of him that is to be cleansed, and upon the thumb of his right hand, and upon the great toe of his right foot, upon the blood of the trespass offering:

18And the remnant of the oil that *is* in the priest's hand he shall pour upon the head of him that is to be cleansed: and the priest shall make an atonement for him before the LORD.

19And the priest shall offer the sin offering, and make an atonement for him that is to be cleansed from his uncleanness; and afterward he shall kill the burnt offering:

20And the priest shall offer the burnt offering and the meat offering upon the altar: and the priest shall make an atonement for him, and he shall be clean.

21And if he *be* poor, and cannot get so much; then he shall take one lamb *for* a trespass offering to be waved, to make an atonement for him, and one tenth deal of fine flour mingled with oil for a meat offering, and a log of oil;

22And two turtledoves, or two young pigeons, such as he is able to get; and the one shall be a sin offering, and the other a burnt offering.

23And he shall bring them on the eighth day for his cleansing unto the priest, unto the door of the tabernacle of the congregation, before the LORD.

24And the priest shall take the lamb of the trespass offering, and the log of oil, and the priest shall wave them *for* a wave offering before the LORD:

25And he shall kill the lamb of the trespass offering, and the priest shall take *some* of the blood of the trespass offering, and put *it* upon the tip of the right ear of him that is to be cleansed, and upon the thumb of his right hand, and upon the great toe of his right foot:

26And the priest shall pour of the oil into the palm of his own left hand:

27And the priest shall sprinkle with his right finger *some* of the oil that *is* in his left hand seven times before the LORD:

28And the priest shall put of the oil that *is* in his hand upon the tip of the right ear of him that is to be cleansed, and upon the thumb of his right hand, and upon the great toe of his right foot, upon the place of the blood of the trespass offering:

29And the rest of the oil that *is* in the priest's hand he shall put upon the head of him that is to be cleansed, to make an atonement for him before the LORD.

30And he shall offer the one of the turtledoves, or of the young pigeons, such as he can get;

31*Even* such as he is able to get, the one *for* a sin offering, and the other *for* a burnt offering, with the meat offering: and the priest shall make an atonement for him that is to be cleansed before the LORD.

32This *is* the law *of him* in whom *is* the plague of leprosy, whose hand is not able to get *that which pertaineth* to his cleansing.

33And the LORD spake unto Moses and unto Aaron, saying,

34When ye be come into the land of Canaan, which I give to you for a possession, and I put the plague of leprosy in a house of the land of your possession;

35And he that owneth the house shall come and tell the priest, saying, It seemeth to me *there is* as it were a plague in the house:

36Then the priest shall command that they empty the house, before the priest go *into it* to see the plague, that all that *is* in the house be not made unclean: and afterward the priest shall go in to see the house:

37And he shall look on the plague, and, behold, *if* the plague *be* in the walls of the house with hollow strakes, greenish or reddish, which in sight *are* lower than the wall;

38Then the priest shall go out of the house to the door of the house, and shut up the house seven days:

39And the priest shall come again the seventh day, and shall look: and, behold, *if* the plague be spread in the walls of the house;

40Then the priest shall command that they take away the stones in which the plague *is,* and they shall cast them into an unclean place without the city:

41And he shall cause the house to be scraped within round about, and they shall pour out the dust that they scrape off without the city into an unclean place:

42And they shall take other stones, and put *them* in the place of those stones; and he shall take other morter, and shall plaister the house.

43And if the plague come again, and break out in the house, after that he hath taken away the stones, and after he hath scraped the house, and after it is plaistered;

44Then the priest shall come and look, and, behold, *if* the plague be spread in the house, it *is* a fretting leprosy in the house: it *is* unclean.

45And he shall break down the house, the stones of it, and the timber thereof, and all the morter of the house; and he shall carry *them* forth out of the city into an unclean place.

46Moreover he that goeth into the house all the while that it is shut up

shall be unclean until the even.

47And he that lieth in the house shall wash his clothes; and he that eateth in the house shall wash his clothes.

48And if the priest shall come in, and look *upon it,* and, behold, the plague hath not spread in the house, after the house was plaistered: then the priest shall pronounce the house clean, because the plague is healed.

49And he shall take to cleanse the house two birds, and cedar wood, and scarlet, and hyssop:

50And he shall kill the one of the birds in an earthen vessel over running water:

51And he shall take the cedar wood, and the hyssop, and the scarlet, and the living bird, and dip them in the blood of the slain bird, and in the running water, and sprinkle the house seven times:

52And he shall cleanse the house with the blood of the bird, and with the running water, and with the living bird, and with the cedar wood, and with the hyssop, and with the scarlet:

53But he shall let go the living bird out of the city into the open fields, and make an atonement for the house: and it shall be clean.

54This *is* the law for all manner of plague of leprosy, and scall,

55And for the leprosy of a garment, and of a house,

56And for a rising, and for a scab, and for a bright spot:

57To teach when *it is* unclean, and when *it is* clean: this *is* the law of leprosy.

MARK 6:30–56

AND the apostles gathered themselves together unto Jesus, and told him all things, both what they had done, and what they had taught.

31And he said unto them, Come ye yourselves apart into a desert place, and rest a while: for there were many coming and going, and they had no leisure so much as to eat.

32And they departed into a desert place by ship privately.

33And the people saw them departing, and many knew him, and ran afoot thither out of all cities, and outwent them, and came together unto him.

34And Jesus, when he came out, saw much people, and was moved with compassion toward them, because they were as sheep not having a shepherd: and he began to teach them many things.

35And when the day was now far spent, his disciples came unto him, and said, This is a desert place, and now the time is far passed:

36Send them away, that they may go into the country round about, and into the villages, and buy themselves bread: for they have nothing to eat.

37He answered and said unto them, Give ye them to eat. And they say unto him, Shall we go and buy two hundred pennyworth of bread, and give them to eat?

38He saith unto them, How many loaves have ye? go and see. And when they knew, they say, Five, and two fishes.

39And he commanded them to make all sit down by companies upon the green grass.

40And they sat down in ranks, by hundreds, and by fifties.

41And when he had taken the five loaves and the two fishes, he looked up to heaven, and blessed, and brake the loaves, and gave *them* to his disciples to set before them; and the two fishes divided he among them all.

42And they did all eat, and were filled.

43And they took up twelve baskets full of the fragments, and of the fishes.

44And they that did eat of the loaves were about five thousand men.

45And straightway he constrained his disciples to get into the ship, and to go to the other side before unto Beth-saida, while he sent away the people.

46And when he had sent them away, he departed into a mountain to pray.

47And when even was come, the ship was in the midst of the sea, and he alone on the land.

48And he saw them toiling in rowing; for the wind was contrary unto them: and about the fourth watch of the night he cometh unto them, walking upon the sea, and would have passed by them.

49But when they saw him walking upon the sea, they supposed it had been a spirit, and cried out:

50For they all saw him, and were troubled. And immediately he talked with them, and saith unto them, Be of good cheer: it is I; be not afraid.

51And he went up unto them into the ship; and the wind ceased: and they were sore amazed in themselves beyond measure, and wondered.

52For they considered not *the miracle* of the loaves: for their heart was hardened.

53And when they had passed over, they came into the land of Gennesaret, and drew to the shore.

54And when they were come out of the ship, straightway they knew him,

55And ran through that whole region round about, and began to carry about in beds those that were sick, where they heard he was.

56And whithersoever he entered, into villages, or cities, or country, they laid the sick in the streets, and besought him that they might touch if it were but the border of his garment: and as many as touched him were made whole.

PSALM 40:1–10

I waited patiently for the LORD; and he inclined unto me, and heard my cry.

2He brought me up also out of an horrible pit, out of the miry clay, and set my feet upon a rock, *and* established my goings.

3And he hath put a new song in my mouth, *even* praise unto our God: many shall see *it,* and fear, and shall trust in the LORD.

4Blessed *is* that man that maketh the LORD his trust, and respecteth not the proud, nor such as turn aside to lies.

5Many, O LORD my God, *are* thy wonderful works *which* thou hast done, and thy thoughts *which are* to us-ward: they cannot be reckoned up in order unto thee: *if* I would declare and speak *of them,* they are more than can be numbered.

6Sacrifice and offering thou didst not desire; mine ears hast thou opened: burnt offering and sin offering hast thou not required.

7Then said I, Lo, I come: in the volume of the book *it is* written of me,

8I delight to do thy will, O my God: yea, thy law *is* within my heart.

9I have preached righteousness in the great congregation: lo, I have not refrained my lips, O LORD, thou knowest.

10I have not hid thy righteousness within my heart; I have declared thy faithfulness and thy salvation: I have not concealed thy lovingkindness and thy truth from the great congregation.

PROVERBS FOR TODAY/ 10:11–12

The mouth of a righteous man is *a well of life: but violence covereth the mouth of the wicked.* □ *Hatred stirreth up strifes: but love covereth all sins.*

FEBRUARY 24

LEVITICUS 15:1—16:28

AND the LORD spake unto Moses and to Aaron, saying,

2Speak unto the children of Israel, and say unto them, When any man hath a running issue out of his flesh, *because of* his issue he *is* unclean.

3And this shall be his uncleanness in his issue: whether his flesh run with his issue, or his flesh be stopped from his issue, it *is* his uncleanness.

4Every bed, whereon he lieth that hath the issue, is unclean: and every thing, whereon he sitteth, shall be unclean.

5And whosoever toucheth his bed shall wash his clothes, and bathe *himself* in water, and be unclean until the even.

6And he that sitteth on *any* thing whereon he sat that hath the issue shall wash his clothes, and bathe *himself* in water, and be unclean until the even.

7And he that toucheth the flesh of him that hath the issue shall wash his clothes, and bathe *himself* in water, and be unclean until the even.

8And if he that hath the issue spit upon him that is clean; then he shall wash his clothes, and bathe *himself* in water, and be unclean until the even.

9And what saddle soever he rideth upon that hath the issue shall be unclean.

10And whosoever toucheth any thing that was under him shall be unclean until the even: and he that beareth *any* of those things shall wash his clothes, and bathe *himself* in water, and be unclean until the even.

11And whomsoever he toucheth that hath the issue, and hath not rinsed his hands in water, he shall wash his clothes, and bathe *himself* in water, and be unclean until the even.

12And the vessel of earth, that he toucheth which hath the issue, shall be broken: and every vessel of wood shall be rinsed in water.

13And when he that hath an issue is cleansed of his issue; then he shall number to himself seven days for his cleansing, and wash his clothes, and bathe his flesh in running water, and shall be clean.

14And on the eighth day he shall take to him two turtledoves, or two young pigeons, and come before the LORD unto the door of the tabernacle of the congregation, and give them unto the priest:

15And the priest shall offer them, the one *for* a sin offering, and the other *for* a burnt offering; and the priest shall make an atonement for him before the LORD for his issue.

16And if any man's seed of copulation go out from him, then he shall wash all his flesh in water, and be unclean until the even.

17And every garment, and every skin, whereon is the seed of copulation, shall be washed with water, and be unclean until the even.

18The woman also with whom man shall lie *with* seed of copulation, they shall *both* bathe *themselves* in water, and be unclean until the even.

19And if a woman have an issue, *and* her issue in her flesh be blood, she shall be put apart seven days: and whosoever toucheth her shall be unclean until the even.

20And every thing that she lieth upon in her separation shall be unclean: every thing also that she sitteth upon shall be unclean.

21And whosoever toucheth her bed shall wash his clothes, and bathe *himself* in water, and be unclean until the even.

22And whosoever toucheth any thing that she sat upon shall wash his clothes, and bathe *himself* in water, and be unclean until the even.

23And if it *be* on *her* bed, or on any thing whereon she sitteth, when he toucheth it, he shall be unclean until the even.

24And if any man lie with her at all, and her flowers be upon him, he shall be unclean seven days; and all the bed whereon he lieth shall be unclean.

25And if a woman have an issue of her blood many days out of the time of her separation, or if it run beyond the time of her separation; all the days of the issue of her uncleanness shall be as the days of her separation: she *shall be* unclean.

26Every bed whereon she lieth all the days of her issue shall be unto her as the bed of her separation: and whatsoever she sitteth upon shall be unclean, as the uncleanness of her separation.

27And whosoever toucheth those things shall be unclean, and shall wash his clothes, and bathe *himself* in water, and be unclean until the even.

28But if she be cleansed of her issue, then she shall number to herself seven days, and after that she shall be clean.

29And on the eighth day she shall take unto her two turtles, or two young pigeons, and bring them unto the priest, to the door of the tabernacle of the congregation.

30And the priest shall offer the one *for* a sin offering, and the other *for* a burnt offering; and the priest shall make an atonement for her before the LORD for the issue of her uncleanness.

31Thus shall ye separate the children of Israel from their uncleanness; that they die not in their uncleanness, when they defile my tabernacle that *is* among them.

32This *is* the law of him that hath an issue, and *of him* whose seed goeth from him, and is defiled therewith;

33And of her that is sick of her flowers, and of him that hath an issue, of the man, and of the woman, and of him that lieth with her that is unclean.

And the LORD spake unto Moses after the death of the two sons of Aaron, when they offered before the LORD, and died;

2And the LORD said unto Moses, Speak unto Aaron thy brother, that he come not at all times into the holy *place* within the vail before the mercy seat, which *is* upon the ark; that he die not: for I will appear in the cloud upon the mercy seat.

3Thus shall Aaron come into the holy *place:* with a young bullock for a sin offering, and a ram for a burnt offering.

4He shall put on the holy linen coat, and he shall have the linen breeches upon his flesh, and shall be girded with a linen girdle, and with the linen mitre shall he be attired: these *are* holy garments; therefore shall he wash his flesh in water, and *so* put them on.

5And he shall take of the congregation of the children of Israel two kids of the goats for a sin offering, and one ram for a burnt offering.

6And Aaron shall offer his bullock of the sin offering, which *is* for himself, and make an atonement for himself, and for his house.

7And he shall take the two goats, and present them before the LORD *at* the door of the tabernacle of the congregation.

8And Aaron shall cast lots upon the two goats; one lot for the LORD, and the other lot for the scapegoat.

9And Aaron shall bring the goat upon which the LORD's lot fell, and offer him *for* a sin offering.

10But the goat, on which the lot fell to be the scapegoat, shall be presented alive before the LORD, to make an atonement with him, *and* to let him go for a scapegoat into the wilderness.

11And Aaron shall bring the bullock of the sin offering, which *is* for himself, and shall make an atonement for himself, and for his house, and shall kill the bullock of the sin offering which *is* for himself:

12And he shall take a censer full of burning coals of fire from off the altar before the LORD, and his hands full of sweet incense beaten small, and bring *it* within the vail:

13And he shall put the incense upon the fire before the LORD, that the cloud of the incense may cover the mercy seat that *is* upon the testimony, that he die not:

14And he shall take of the blood of the bullock, and sprinkle *it* with his finger upon the mercy seat eastward; and before the mercy seat shall he sprinkle of the blood with his finger seven times.

15Then shall he kill the goat of the sin offering, that *is* for the people, and bring his blood within the vail, and do with that blood as he did with the blood of the bullock, and sprinkle it upon the mercy seat, and before the mercy seat:

16And he shall make an atonement for the holy *place,* because of the uncleanness of the children of Israel, and because of their transgressions in all their sins: and so shall he do for the tabernacle of the congregation, that remaineth among them in the midst of their uncleanness.

17And there shall be no man in the tabernacle of the congregation when he goeth in to make an atonement in the holy *place,* until he come out, and have made an atonement for himself, and for his household, and for all the congregation of Israel.

18And he shall go out unto the altar that *is* before the LORD, and make an atonement for it; and shall take of the blood of the bullock, and of the blood of the goat, and put *it* upon the horns of the altar round about.

19And he shall sprinkle of the blood upon it with his finger seven times, and cleanse it, and hallow it from the uncleanness of the children of Israel.

20And when he hath made an end

of reconciling the holy *place,* and the tabernacle of the congregation, and the altar, he shall bring the live goat:

21And Aaron shall lay both his hands upon the head of the live goat, and confess over him all the iniquities of the children of Israel, and all their transgressions in all their sins, putting them upon the head of the goat, and shall send *him* away by the hand of a fit man into the wilderness:

22And the goat shall bear upon him all their iniquities unto a land not inhabited: and he shall let go the goat in the wilderness.

23And Aaron shall come into the tabernacle of the congregation, and shall put off the linen garments, which he put on when he went into the holy *place,* and shall leave them there:

24And he shall wash his flesh with water in the holy place, and put on his garments, and come forth, and offer his burnt offering, and the burnt offering of the people, and make an atonement for himself, and for the people.

25And the fat of the sin offering shall he burn upon the altar.

26And he that let go the goat for the scapegoat shall wash his clothes, and bathe his flesh in water, and afterward come into the camp.

27And the bullock *for* the sin offering, and the goat *for* the sin offering, whose blood was brought in to make atonement in the holy *place,* shall *one* carry forth without the camp; and they shall burn in the fire their skins, and their flesh, and their dung.

28And he that burneth them shall wash his clothes, and bathe his flesh in water, and afterward he shall come into the camp.

MARK 7:1–23

THEN came together unto him [Jesus] the Pharisees, and certain of the scribes, which came from Jerusalem.

2And when they saw some of his disciples eat bread with defiled, that is to say, with unwashen, hands, they found fault.

3For the Pharisees, and all the Jews, except they wash *their* hands oft, eat not, holding the tradition of the elders.

4And *when they come* from the market, except they wash, they eat not. And many other things there be, which they have received to hold, *as* the washing of cups, and pots, brasen vessels, and of tables.

5Then the Pharisees and scribes asked him, Why walk not thy disciples according to the tradition of the elders, but eat bread with unwashen hands?

6He answered and said unto them, Well hath Esaias prophesied of you hypocrites, as it is written, This people honoureth me with *their* lips, but their heart is far from me.

7Howbeit in vain do they worship me, teaching *for* doctrines the commandments of men.

8For laying aside the commandment of God, ye hold the tradition of men, *as* the washing of pots and cups: and many other such like things ye do.

9And he said unto them, Full well ye reject the commandment of God, that ye may keep your own tradition.

10For Moses said, Honour thy father and thy mother; and, Whoso curseth father or mother, let him die the death:

11But ye say, If a man shall say to his father or mother, *It is* Corban, that is to say, a gift, by whatsoever thou mightest be profited by me; *he shall be free.*

12And ye suffer him no more to do ought for his father or his mother;

13Making the word of God of none effect through your tradition, which ye have delivered: and many such like things do ye.

14And when he had called all the people *unto him,* he said unto them,

Hearken unto me every one *of you,* and understand:

15There is nothing from without a man, that entering into him can defile him: but the things which come out of him, those are they that defile the man.

16If any man have ears to hear, let him hear.

17And when he was entered into the house from the people, his disciples asked him concerning the parable.

18And he saith unto them, Are ye so without understanding also? Do ye not perceive, that whatsoever thing from without entereth into the man, *it* cannot defile him;

19Because it entereth not into his heart, but into the belly, and goeth out into the draught, purging all meats?

20And he said, That which cometh out of the man, that defileth the man.

21For from within, out of the heart of men, proceed evil thoughts, adulteries, fornications, murders,

22Thefts, covetousness, wickedness, deceit, lasciviousness, an evil eye, blasphemy, pride, foolishness:

23All these evil things come from within, and defile the man.

PSALM 40:11–17

WITHHOLD not thou thy tender mercies from me, O LORD: let thy lovingkindness and thy truth continually preserve me.

12For innumerable evils have compassed me about: mine iniquities have taken hold upon me, so that I am not able to look up; they are more than the hairs of mine head: therefore my heart faileth me.

13Be pleased, O LORD, to deliver me: O LORD, make haste to help me.

14Let them be ashamed and confounded together that seek after my soul to destroy it; let them be driven backward and put to shame that wish me evil.

15Let them be desolate for a reward of their shame that say unto me, Aha, aha.

16Let all those that seek thee rejoice and be glad in thee: let such as love thy salvation say continually, The LORD be magnified.

17But I *am* poor and needy; *yet* the Lord thinketh upon me: thou *art* my help and my deliverer; make no tarrying, O my God.

PROVERBS FOR TODAY/ 10:13–14

In the lips of him that hath understanding wisdom is found: but a rod is *for the back of him that is void of understanding.* □ *Wise* men *lay up knowledge: but the mouth of the foolish* is *near destruction.*

FEBRUARY 25

LEVITICUS 16:29—18:30

AND *this* shall be a statute for ever unto you: *that* in the seventh month, on the tenth *day* of the month, ye shall afflict your souls, and do no work at all, *whether it be* one of your own country, or a stranger that sojourneth among you:

30For on that day shall *the priest* make an atonement for you, to cleanse you, *that* ye may be clean from all your sins before the LORD.

31It *shall be* a sabbath of rest unto you, and ye shall afflict your souls, by a statute for ever.

32And the priest, whom he shall anoint, and whom he shall consecrate to minister in the priest's office in his father's stead, shall make the atonement, and shall put on the linen clothes, *even* the holy garments:

33And he shall make an atonement for the holy sanctuary, and he shall make an atonement for the tabernacle of the congregation, and for the altar, and he shall make an atonement for the priests, and for all the people of the congregation.

34And this shall be an everlasting statute unto you, to make an atonement for the children of Israel for all their sins once a year. And he did as the LORD commanded Moses.

AND the LORD spake unto Moses, saying,

2Speak unto Aaron, and unto his sons, and unto all the children of Israel, and say unto them; This *is* the thing which the LORD hath commanded, saying,

3What man soever *there be* of the house of Israel, that killeth an ox, or lamb, or goat, in the camp, or that killeth *it* out of the camp,

4And bringeth it not unto the door of the tabernacle of the congregation, to offer an offering unto the LORD before the tabernacle of the LORD; blood shall be imputed unto that man; he hath shed blood; and that man shall be cut off from among his people:

5To the end that the children of Israel may bring their sacrifices, which they offer in the open field, even that they may bring them unto the LORD, unto the door of the tabernacle of the congregation, unto the priest, and offer them *for* peace offerings unto the LORD.

6And the priest shall sprinkle the blood upon the altar of the LORD *at* the door of the tabernacle of the congre-gation, and burn the fat for a sweet savour unto the LORD.

7And they shall no more offer their sacrifices unto devils, after whom they have gone a whoring. This shall be a statute for ever unto them throughout their generations.

8And thou shalt say unto them, Whatsoever man *there be* of the house of Israel, or of the strangers which sojourn among you, that offereth a burnt offering or sacrifice,

9And bringeth it not unto the door of the tabernacle of the congregation, to offer it unto the LORD; even that man shall be cut off from among his people.

10And whatsoever man *there be* of the house of Israel, or of the strangers that sojourn among you, that eateth any manner of blood; I will even set my face against that soul that eateth blood, and will cut him off from among his people.

11For the life of the flesh *is* in the blood: and I have given it to you upon the altar to make an atonement for your souls: for it *is* the blood *that* maketh an atonement for the soul.

12Therefore I said unto the children of Israel, No soul of you shall eat blood, neither shall any stranger that sojourneth among you eat blood.

13And whatsoever man *there be* of the children of Israel, or of the strangers that sojourn among you, which hunteth and catcheth any beast or fowl that may be eaten; he shall even pour out the blood thereof, and cover it with dust.

14For *it is* the life of all flesh; the blood of it *is* for the life thereof: therefore I said unto the children of Israel, Ye shall eat the blood of no manner of flesh: for the life of all flesh *is* the blood thereof: whosoever eateth it shall be cut off.

15And every soul that eateth that which died *of itself,* or that which was torn *with beasts, whether it be* one of your own country, or a stranger, he shall both wash his clothes, and bathe *himself* in water, and be unclean until the even: then shall he be clean.

16But if he wash *them* not, nor bathe his flesh; then he shall bear his iniquity.

AND the LORD spake unto Moses, saying,

2Speak unto the children of Israel, and say unto them, I am the LORD your God.

3After the doings of the land of Egypt, wherein ye dwelt, shall ye not do: and after the doings of the land of Canaan, whither I bring you, shall ye not do: neither shall ye walk in their ordinances.

4Ye shall do my judgments, and keep mine ordinances, to walk therein: I *am* the LORD your God.

5Ye shall therefore keep my statutes, and my judgments: which if a man do, he shall live in them: I *am* the LORD.

6None of you shall approach to any that is near of kin to him, to uncover *their* nakedness: I *am* the LORD.

7The nakedness of thy father, or the nakedness of thy mother, shalt thou not uncover: she *is* thy mother; thou shalt not uncover her nakedness.

8The nakedness of thy father's wife shalt thou not uncover: it *is* thy father's nakedness.

9The nakedness of thy sister, the daughter of thy father, or daughter of thy mother, *whether she be* born at home, or born abroad, *even* their nakedness thou shalt not uncover.

10The nakedness of thy son's daughter, or of thy daughter's daughter, *even* their nakedness thou shalt not uncover: for theirs *is* thine own nakedness.

11The nakedness of thy father's wife's daughter, begotten of thy father, she *is* thy sister, thou shalt not uncover her nakedness.

12Thou shalt not uncover the nakedness of thy father's sister: she *is* thy father's near kinswoman.

13Thou shalt not uncover the nakedness of thy mother's sister: for she *is* thy mother's near kinswoman.

14Thou shalt not uncover the nakedness of thy father's brother, thou shalt not approach to his wife: she *is* thine aunt.

15Thou shalt not uncover the nakedness of thy daughter in law: she *is* thy son's wife; thou shalt not uncover her nakedness.

16Thou shalt not uncover the nakedness of thy brother's wife: it *is* thy brother's nakedness.

17Thou shalt not uncover the nakedness of a woman and her daughter, neither shalt thou take her son's daughter, or her daughter's daughter, to uncover her nakedness; *for* they *are* her near kinswomen: it *is* wickedness.

18Neither shalt thou take a wife to her sister, to vex *her,* to uncover her nakedness, beside the other in her life *time.*

19Also thou shalt not approach unto a woman to uncover her nakedness, as long as she is put apart for her uncleanness.

20Moreover thou shalt not lie carnally with thy neighbour's wife, to defile thyself with her.

21And thou shalt not let any of thy seed pass through *the fire* to Molech, neither shalt thou profane the name of thy God: I *am* the LORD.

22Thou shalt not lie with mankind, as with womankind: it *is* abomination.

23Neither shalt thou lie with any beast to defile thyself therewith: neither shall any woman stand before a beast to lie down thereto: it *is* confusion.

24Defile not ye yourselves in any of these things: for in all these the nations are defiled which I cast out before you:

25And the land is defiled: therefore I do visit the iniquity thereof upon it, and the land itself vomiteth out her inhabitants.

26Ye shall therefore keep my statutes and my judgments, and shall not commit *any* of these abominations; *neither* any of your own nation, nor any stranger that sojourneth among you:

27(For all these abominations have the men of the land done, which *were* before you, and the land is defiled;)

28That the land spue not you out also, when ye defile it, as it spued out the nations that *were* before you.

29For whosoever shall commit any of these abominations, even the souls that commit *them* shall be cut off from among their people.

30Therefore shall ye keep mine ordinance, that *ye* commit not *any one* of these abominable customs, which were committed before you, and that ye defile not yourselves therein: I *am* the LORD your God.

MARK 7:24—8:9

A ND from thence he [Jesus] arose, and went into the borders of Tyre and Sidon, and entered into an house, and would have no man know *it*, but he could not be hid.

25For a *certain* woman, whose young daughter had an unclean spirit, heard of him, and came and fell at his feet:

26The woman was a Greek, a Syrophenician by nation; and she besought him that he would cast forth the devil out of her daughter.

27But Jesus said unto her, Let the children first be filled: for it is not meet to take the children's bread, and to cast *it* unto the dogs.

28And she answered and said unto him, Yes, Lord: yet the dogs under the table eat of the children's crumbs.

29And he said unto her, For this saying go thy way; the devil is gone out of thy daughter.

30And when she was come to her house, she found the devil gone out, and her daughter laid upon the bed.

31And again, departing from the coasts of Tyre and Sidon, he came unto the sea of Galilee, through the midst of the coasts of Decapolis.

32And they bring unto him one that was deaf, and had an impediment in his speech; and they beseech him to put his hand upon him.

33And he took him aside from the multitude, and put his fingers into his ears, and he spit, and touched his tongue;

34And looking up to heaven, he sighed, and saith unto him, Ephphatha, that is, Be opened.

35And straightway his ears were opened, and the string of his tongue was loosed, and he spake plain.

36And he charged them that they should tell no man: but the more he charged them, so much the more a great deal they published *it;*

37And were beyond measure astonished, saying, He hath done all things well: he maketh both the deaf to hear, and the dumb to speak.

IN those days the multitude being very great, and having nothing to eat, Jesus called his disciples *unto him,* and saith unto them,

2I have compassion on the multitude, because they have now been with me three days, and have nothing to eat:

3And if I send them away fasting to their own houses, they will faint by the way: for divers of them came from far.

4And his disciples answered him, From whence can a man satisfy these *men* with bread here in the wilderness?

5And he asked them, How many loaves have ye? And they said, Seven.

6And he commanded the people to sit down on the ground: and he took the seven loaves, and gave thanks, and brake, and gave to his disciples to set before *them;* and they did set *them* before the people.

7And they had a few small fishes: and he blessed, and commanded to set them also before *them.*

8So they did eat, and were filled: and they took up of the broken *meat* that was left seven baskets.

9And they that had eaten were about four thousand: and he sent them away.

PSALM 41:1–13

BLESSED is he that considereth the poor: the LORD will deliver him in time of trouble.

2The LORD will preserve him, and keep him alive; and he shall be blessed upon the earth: and thou wilt not deliver him unto the will of his enemies.

3The LORD will strengthen him upon the bed of languishing: thou wilt make all his bed in his sickness.

4I said, LORD, be merciful unto me: heal my soul; for I have sinned against thee.

5Mine enemies speak evil of me, When shall he die, and his name perish?

6And if he come to see me, he speaketh vanity: his heart gathereth iniquity to itself; when he goeth abroad, he telleth it.

7All that hate me whisper together against me: against me do they devise my hurt.

8An evil disease, say they, cleaveth fast unto him: and now that he lieth he shall rise up no more.

9Yea, mine own familiar friend, in whom I trusted, which did eat of my bread, hath lifted up his heel against me.

10But thou, O LORD, be merciful unto me, and raise me up, that I may requite them.

11By this I know that thou favourest me, because mine enemy doth not triumph over me.

12And as for me, thou upholdest me in mine integrity, and settest me before thy face for ever.

13Blessed be the LORD God of Israel from everlasting, and to everlasting. Amen, and Amen.

PROVERBS FOR TODAY/ 10:15–16

The rich man's wealth is *his strong city: the destruction of the poor* is *their poverty.* □ *The labour of the righteous* tendeth *to life: the fruit of the wicked to sin.*

FEBRUARY 26

LEVITICUS 19:1—20:21

AND the LORD spake unto Moses, saying,

2Speak unto all the congregation of the children of Israel, and say unto them, Ye shall be holy: for I the LORD your God am holy.

3Ye shall fear every man his mother, and his father, and keep my sabbaths: I am the LORD your God.

4Turn ye not unto idols, nor make to yourselves molten gods: I am the LORD your God.

5And if ye offer a sacrifice of peace offerings unto the LORD, ye shall offer it at your own will.

6It shall be eaten the same day ye offer it, and on the morrow: and if ought remain until the third day, it shall be burnt in the fire.

7And if it be eaten at all on the third day, it is abominable; it shall not be accepted.

8Therefore every one that eateth it shall bear his iniquity, because he hath profaned the hallowed thing of the

LORD: and that soul shall be cut off from among his people.

9And when ye reap the harvest of your land, thou shalt not wholly reap the corners of thy field, neither shalt thou gather the gleanings of thy harvest.

10And thou shalt not glean thy vineyard, neither shalt thou gather *every* grape of thy vineyard; thou shalt leave them for the poor and stranger: I *am* the LORD your God.

11Ye shall not steal, neither deal falsely, neither lie one to another.

12And ye shall not swear by my name falsely, neither shalt thou profane the name of thy God: I *am* the LORD.

13Thou shalt not defraud thy neighbour, neither rob *him:* the wages of him that is hired shall not abide with thee all night until the morning.

14Thou shalt not curse the deaf, nor put a stumblingblock before the blind, but shalt fear thy God: I *am* the LORD.

15Ye shall do no unrighteousness in judgment: thou shalt not respect the person of the poor, nor honour the person of the mighty: *but* in righteousness shalt thou judge thy neighbour.

16Thou shalt not go up and down *as* a talebearer among thy people: neither shalt thou stand against the blood of thy neighbour: I *am* the LORD.

17Thou shalt not hate thy brother in thine heart: thou shalt in any wise rebuke thy neighbour, and not suffer sin upon him.

18Thou shalt not avenge, nor bear any grudge against the children of thy people, but thou shalt love thy neighbour as thyself: I *am* the LORD.

19Ye shall keep my statutes. Thou shalt not let thy cattle gender with a diverse kind: thou shalt not sow thy field with mingled seed: neither shall a garment mingled of linen and woollen come upon thee.

20And whosoever lieth carnally with a woman, that *is* a bondmaid, betrothed to an husband, and not at all redeemed, nor freedom given her; she shall be scourged; they shall not be put to death, because she was not free.

21And he shall bring his trespass offering unto the LORD, unto the door of the tabernacle of the congregation, *even* a ram for a trespass offering.

22And the priest shall make an atonement for him with the ram of the trespass offering before the LORD for his sin which he hath done: and the sin which he hath done shall be forgiven him.

23And when ye shall come into the land, and shall have planted all manner of trees for food, then ye shall count the fruit thereof as uncircumcised: three years shall it be as uncircumcised unto you: it shall not be eaten of.

24But in the fourth year all the fruit thereof shall be holy to praise the LORD *withal.*

25And in the fifth year shall ye eat of the fruit thereof, that it may yield unto you the increase thereof: I *am* the LORD your God.

26Ye shall not eat *any thing* with the blood: neither shall ye use enchantment, nor observe times.

27Ye shall not round the corners of your heads, neither shalt thou mar the corners of thy beard.

28Ye shall not make any cuttings in your flesh for the dead, nor print any marks upon you: I *am* the LORD.

29Do not prostitute thy daughter, to cause her to be a whore; lest the land fall to whoredom, and the land become full of wickedness.

30Ye shall keep my sabbaths, and reverence my sanctuary: I *am* the LORD.

31Regard not them that have familiar spirits, neither seek after wizards, to be defiled by them: I *am* the LORD your God.

32Thou shalt rise up before the hoary head, and honour the face of the old man, and fear thy God: I *am* the LORD.

33And if a stranger sojourn with thee in your land, ye shall not vex him.

34*But* the stranger that dwelleth with

you shall be unto you as one born among you, and thou shalt love him as thyself; for ye were strangers in the land of Egypt: I *am* the Lord your God.

35Ye shall do no unrighteousness in judgment, in meteyard, in weight, or in measure.

36Just balances, just weights, a just ephah, and a just hin, shall ye have: I *am* the Lord your God, which brought you out of the land of Egypt.

37Therefore shall ye observe all my statutes, and all my judgments, and do them: I *am* the Lord.

And the Lord spake unto Moses, saying,

2Again, thou shalt say to the children of Israel, Whosoever *he be* of the children of Israel, or of the strangers that sojourn in Israel, that giveth *any* of his seed unto Molech: he shall surely be put to death: the people of the land shall stone him with stones.

3And I will set my face against that man, and will cut him off from among his people; because he hath given of his seed unto Molech, to defile my sanctuary, and to profane my holy name.

4And if the people of the land do any ways hide their eyes from the man, when he giveth of his seed unto Molech, and kill him not:

5Then I will set my face against that man, and against his family, and will cut him off, and all that go a whoring after him, to commit whoredom with Molech, from among their people.

6And the soul that turneth after such as have familiar spirits, and after wizards, to go a whoring after them, I will even set my face against that soul, and will cut him off from among his people.

7Sanctify yourselves therefore, and be ye holy: for I *am* the Lord your God.

8And ye shall keep my statutes, and do them: I *am* the Lord which sanctify you.

9For every one that curseth his father or his mother shall be surely put to death: he hath cursed his father or his mother; his blood *shall be* upon him.

10And the man that committeth adultery with *another* man's wife, *even he* that committeth adultery with his neighbour's wife, the adulterer and the adulteress shall surely be put to death.

11And the man that lieth with his father's wife hath uncovered his father's nakedness: both of them shall surely be put to death; their blood *shall be* upon them.

12And if a man lie with his daughter in law, both of them shall surely be put to death: they have wrought confusion; their blood *shall be* upon them.

13If a man also lie with mankind, as he lieth with a woman, both of them have committed an abomination: they shall surely be put to death; their blood *shall be* upon them.

14And if a man take a wife and her mother, it *is* wickedness: they shall be burnt with fire, both he and they; that there be no wickedness among you.

15And if a man lie with a beast, he shall surely be put to death: and ye shall slay the beast.

16And if a woman approach unto any beast, and lie down thereto, thou shalt kill the woman, and the beast: they shall surely be put to death; their blood *shall be* upon them.

17And if a man shall take his sister, his father's daughter, or his mother's daughter, and see her nakedness, and she see his nakedness; it *is* a wicked thing; and they shall be cut off in the sight of their people: he hath uncovered his sister's nakedness; he shall bear his iniquity.

18And if a man shall lie with a woman having her sickness, and shall uncover her nakedness; he hath discovered her fountain, and she had uncovered the fountain of her blood: and both of them shall be cut off from among their people.

19And thou shalt not uncover the nakedness of thy mother's sister, nor of thy father's sister: for he uncovereth his near kin: they shall bear their iniquity.

20And if a man shall lie with his uncle's wife, he hath uncovered his uncle's nakedness: they shall bear their sin; they shall die childless.

21And if a man shall take his brother's wife, it *is* an unclean thing: he hath uncovered his brother's nakedness; they shall be childless.

MARK 8:10–38

AND straightway he [Jesus] entered into a ship with his disciples, and came into the parts of Dalmanutha.

11And the Pharisees came forth, and began to question with him, seeking of him a sign from heaven, tempting him.

12And he sighed deeply in his spirit, and saith, Why doth this generation seek after a sign? verily I say unto you, There shall no sign be given unto this generation.

13And he left them, and entering into the ship again departed to the other side.

14Now *the disciples* had forgotten to take bread, neither had they in the ship with them more than one loaf.

15And he charged them, saying, Take heed, beware of the leaven of the Pharisees, and *of* the leaven of Herod.

16And they reasoned among themselves, saying, *It is* because we have no bread.

17And when Jesus knew *it,* he saith unto them, Why reason ye, because ye have no bread? perceive ye not yet, neither understand? have ye your heart yet hardened?

18Having eyes, see ye not? and having ears, hear ye not? and do ye not remember?

19When I brake the five loaves among five thousand, how many baskets full of fragments took ye up? They say unto him, Twelve.

20And when the seven among four thousand, how many baskets full of fragments took ye up? And they said, Seven.

21And he said unto them, How is it that ye do not understand?

22And he cometh to Bethsaida: and they bring a blind man unto him, and besought him to touch him.

23And he took the blind man by the hand, and led him out of the town; and when he had spit on his eyes, and put his hands upon him, he asked him if he saw ought.

24And he looked up, and said, I see men as trees, walking.

25After that he put *his* hands again upon his eyes, and made him look up: and he was restored, and saw every man clearly.

26And he sent him away to his house, saying, Neither go into the town, nor tell *it* to any in the town.

27And Jesus went out, and his disciples, into the towns of Caesarea Philippi: and by the way he asked his disciples, saying unto them, Whom do men say that I am?

28And they answered, John the Baptist: but some *say,* Elias; and others, One of the prophets.

29And he saith unto them, But whom say ye that I am? And Peter answereth and saith unto him, Thou art the Christ.

30And he charged them that they should tell no man of him.

31And he began to teach them, that the Son of man must suffer many things, and be rejected of the elders, and *of* the chief priests, and scribes, and be killed, and after three days rise again.

32And he spake that saying openly. And Peter took him, and began to rebuke him.

33But when he had turned about and looked on his disciples, he rebuked Peter, saying, Get thee behind me, Satan:

for thou savourest not the things that be of God, but the things that be of men.

34And when he had called the people *unto him* with his disciples also, he said unto them, Whosoever will come after me, let him deny himself, and take up his cross, and follow me.

35For whosoever will save his life shall lose it; but whosoever shall lose his life for my sake and the gospel's, the same shall save it.

36For what shall it profit a man, if he shall gain the whole world, and lose his own soul?

37Or what shall a man give in exchange for his soul?

38Whosoever therefore shall be ashamed of me and of my words in this adulterous and sinful generation; of him also shall the Son of man be ashamed, when he cometh in the glory of his Father with the holy angels.

PSALM 42:1–11

As the hart panteth after the water brooks, so panteth my soul after thee, O God.

2My soul thirsteth for God, for the living God: when shall I come and appear before God?

3My tears have been my meat day and night, while they continually say unto me, Where *is* thy God?

4When I remember these *things,* I pour out my soul in me: for I had gone with the multitude, I went with them to the house of God, with the voice of joy and praise, with a multitude that kept holyday.

5Why art thou cast down, O my soul? and *why* art thou disquieted in me? hope thou in God: for I shall yet praise him *for* the help of his countenance.

6O my God, my soul is cast down within me: therefore will I remember thee from the land of Jordan, and of the Hermonites, from the hill Mizar.

7Deep calleth unto deep at the noise of thy waterspouts: all thy waves and thy billows are gone over me.

8*Yet* the LORD will command his lovingkindness in the daytime, and in the night his song *shall be* with me, *and* my prayer unto the God of my life.

9I will say unto God my rock, Why hast thou forgotten me? why go I mourning because of the oppression of the enemy?

10*As* with a sword in my bones, mine enemies reproach me; while they say daily unto me, Where *is* thy God?

11Why art thou cast down, O my soul? and why art thou disquieted within me? hope thou in God: for I shall yet praise him, *who is* the health of my countenance, and my God.

PROVERBS FOR TODAY/ 10:17
He is in *the way of life that keepeth instruction: but he that refuseth reproof erreth.*

FEBRUARY 27

LEVITICUS 20:22—22:20

YE shall therefore keep all my statutes, and all my judgments, and do them: that the land, whither I bring you to dwell therein, spue you not out.

23And ye shall not walk in the manners of the nation, which I cast out before you: for they committed all these things, and therefore I abhorred them.

24But I have said unto you, Ye shall inherit their land, and I will give it unto you to possess it, a land that floweth with milk and honey: I *am* the LORD your God, which have separated you from *other* people.

25Ye shall therefore put difference between clean beasts and unclean, and between unclean fowls and clean: and ye shall not make your souls abominable by beast, or by fowl, or by any manner of living thing that creepeth on the ground, which I have separated from you as unclean.

26And ye shall be holy unto me: for I the LORD *am* holy, and have severed you from *other* people, that ye should be mine.

27A man also or woman that hath a familiar spirit, or that is a wizard, shall surely be put to death: they shall stone them with stones: their blood *shall be* upon them.

AND the LORD said unto Moses, Speak unto the priests the sons of Aaron, and say unto them, There shall none be defiled for the dead among his people:

2But for his kin, that is near unto him, *that is,* for his mother, and for his father, and for his son, and for his daughter, and for his brother,

3And for his sister a virgin, that is nigh unto him, which hath had no husband; for her may he be defiled.

4*But* he shall not defile himself, *being* a chief man among his people, to profane himself.

5They shall not make baldness upon their head, neither shall they shave off the corner of their beard, nor make any cuttings in their flesh.

6They shall be holy unto their God, and not profane the name of their God: for the offerings of the LORD made by fire, *and* the bread of their God, they do offer: therefore they shall be holy.

7They shall not take a wife *that is* a whore, or profane; neither shall they take a woman put away from her husband: for he *is* holy unto his God.

8Thou shalt sanctify him therefore; for he offereth the bread of thy God: he shall be holy unto thee: for I the LORD, which sanctify you, *am* holy.

9And the daughter of any priest, if she profane herself by playing the whore, she profaneth her father: she shall be burnt with fire.

10And *he that is* the high priest among his brethren, upon whose head the anointing oil was poured, and that is consecrated to put on the garments, shall not uncover his head, nor rend his clothes;

11Neither shall he go in to any dead body, nor defile himself for his father, or for his mother:

12Neither shall he go out of the sanctuary, nor profane the sanctuary of his God; for the crown of the anointing oil of his God *is* upon him: I *am* the LORD.

13And he shall take a wife in her virginity.

14A widow, or a divorced woman, or profane, *or* an harlot, these shall he not take: but he shall take a virgin of his own people to wife.

15Neither shall he profane his seed among his people: for I the Lord do sanctify him.

16And the Lord spake unto Moses, saying,

17Speak unto Aaron, saying, Whosoever *he be* of thy seed in their generations that hath *any* blemish, let him not approach to offer the bread of his God.

18For whatsoever man *he be* that hath a blemish, he shall not approach: a blind man, or a lame, or he that hath a flat nose, or any thing superfluous,

19Or a man that is brokenfooted, or brokenhanded,

20Or crookbackt, or a dwarf, or that hath a blemish in his eye, or be scurvy, or scabbed, or hath his stones broken;

21No man that hath a blemish of the seed of Aaron the priest shall come nigh to offer the offerings of the Lord made by fire: he hath a blemish; he shall not come nigh to offer the bread of his God.

22He shall eat the bread of his God, *both* of the most holy, and of the holy.

23Only he shall not go in unto the vail, nor come nigh unto the altar, because he hath a blemish; that he profane not my sanctuaries: for I the Lord do sanctify them.

24And Moses told *it* unto Aaron, and to his sons, and unto all the children of Israel.

And the Lord spake unto Moses, saying,

2Speak unto Aaron and to his sons, that they separate themselves from the holy things of the children of Israel, and that they profane not my holy name *in those things* which they hallow unto me: I *am* the Lord.

3Say unto them, Whosoever *he be* of all your seed among your generations, that goeth unto the holy things, which the children of Israel hallow unto the Lord, having his uncleanness upon him, that soul shall be cut off from my presence: I *am* the Lord.

4What man soever of the seed of Aaron *is* a leper, or hath a running issue; he shall not eat of the holy things, until he be clean. And whoso toucheth any thing *that is* unclean *by* the dead, or a man whose seed goeth from him;

5Or whosoever toucheth any creeping thing, whereby he may be made unclean, or a man of whom he may take uncleanness, whatsoever uncleanness he hath;

6The soul which hath touched any such shall be unclean until even, and shall not eat of the holy things, unless he wash his flesh with water.

7And when the sun is down, he shall be clean, and shall afterward eat of the holy things; because it *is* his food.

8That which dieth of itself, or is torn *with beasts,* he shall not eat to defile himself therewith: I *am* the Lord.

9They shall therefore keep mine ordinance, lest they bear sin for it, and die therefore, if they profane it: I the Lord do sanctify them.

10There shall no stranger eat *of* the holy thing: a sojourner of the priest, or an hired servant, shall not eat *of* the holy thing.

11But if the priest buy *any* soul with his money, he shall eat of it, and he that is born in his house: they shall eat of his meat.

12If the priest's daughter also be *married* unto a stranger, she may not eat of an offering of the holy things.

13But if the priest's daughter be a widow, or divorced, and have no child, and is returned unto her father's house, as in her youth, she shall eat of her father's meat: but there shall no stranger eat thereof.

14And if a man eat *of* the holy thing unwittingly, then he shall put the fifth *part* thereof unto it, and shall give *it* unto the priest with the holy thing.

15And they shall not profane the holy things of the children of Israel, which they offer unto the Lord;

16Or suffer them to bear the iniquity of trespass, when they eat their holy things: for I the LORD do sanctify them.

17And the LORD spake unto Moses, saying,

18Speak unto Aaron, and to his sons, and unto all the children of Israel, and say unto them, Whatsoever *he be* of the house of Israel, or of the strangers in Israel, that will offer his oblation for all his vows, and for all his freewill offerings, which they will offer unto the LORD for a burnt offering:

19*Ye shall offer* at your own will a male without blemish, of the beeves, of the sheep, or of the goats.

20*But* whatsoever hath a blemish, *that* shall ye not offer: for it shall not be acceptable for you.

MARK 9:1–29

AND he [Jesus] said unto them, Verily I say unto you, That there be some of them that stand here, which shall not taste of death, till they have seen the kingdom of God come with power.

2And after six days Jesus taketh *with him* Peter, and James, and John, and leadeth them up into an high mountain apart by themselves: and he was transfigured before them.

3And his raiment became shining, exceeding white as snow; so as no fuller on earth can white them.

4And there appeared unto them Elias with Moses: and they were talking with Jesus.

5And Peter answered and said to Jesus, Master, it is good for us to be here: and let us make three tabernacles; one for thee, and one for Moses, and one for Elias.

6For he wist not what to say; for they were sore afraid.

7And there was a cloud that overshadowed them: and a voice came out of the cloud, saying, This is my beloved Son: hear him.

8And suddenly, when they had looked round about, they saw no man any more, save Jesus only with themselves.

9And as they came down from the mountain, he charged them that they should tell no man what things they had seen, till the Son of man were risen from the dead.

10And they kept that saying with themselves, questioning one with another what the rising from the dead should mean.

11And they asked him, saying, Why say the scribes that Elias must first come?

12And he answered and told them, Elias verily cometh first, and restoreth all things; and how it is written of the Son of man, that he must suffer many things, and be set at nought.

13But I say unto you, That Elias is indeed come, and they have done unto him whatsoever they listed, as it is written of him.

14And when he came to *his* disciples, he saw a great multitude about them, and the scribes questioning with them.

15And straightway all the people, when they beheld him, were greatly amazed, and running to *him* saluted him.

16And he asked the scribes, What question ye with them?

17And one of the multitude answered and said, Master, I have brought unto thee my son, which hath a dumb spirit;

18And wheresoever he taketh him, he teareth him: and he foameth, and gnasheth with his teeth, and pineth away: and I spake to thy disciples that they should cast him out; and they could not.

19He answereth him, and saith, O faithless generation, how long shall I be with you? how long shall I suffer you? bring him unto me.

20And they brought him unto him: and when he saw him, straightway the spirit tare him; and he fell on the ground, and wallowed foaming.

21And he asked his father, How long is it ago since this came unto him? And he said, Of a child.

22And ofttimes it hath cast him into the fire, and into the waters, to destroy him: but if thou canst do any thing, have compassion on us, and help us.

23Jesus said unto him, If thou canst believe, all things *are* possible to him that believeth.

24And straightway the father of the child cried out, and said with tears, Lord, I believe; help thou mine unbelief.

25When Jesus saw that the people came running together, he rebuked the foul spirit, saying unto him, *Thou* dumb and deaf spirit, I charge thee, come out of him, and enter no more into him.

26And *the spirit* cried, and rent him sore, and came out of him: and he was as one dead; insomuch that many said, He is dead.

27But Jesus took him by the hand, and lifted him up; and he arose.

28And when he was come into the house, his disciples asked him privately, Why could not we cast him out?

29And he said unto them, This kind can come forth by nothing, but by prayer and fasting.

PSALM 43:1–5

JUDGE me, O God, and plead my cause against an ungodly nation: O deliver me from the deceitful and unjust man.

2For thou *art* the God of my strength: why dost thou cast me off? why go I mourning because of the oppression of the enemy?

3O send out thy light and thy truth: let them lead me; let them bring me unto thy holy hill, and to thy tabernacles.

4Then will I go unto the altar of God, unto God my exceeding joy: yea, upon the harp will I praise thee, O God, my God.

5Why art thou cast down, O my soul? and why art thou disquieted within me? hope in God: for I shall yet praise him, *who is* the health of my countenance, and my God.

PROVERBS FOR TODAY/ 10:18

He that hideth hatred with *lying lips, and he that uttereth a slander,* is *a fool.*

FEBRUARY 28

LEVITICUS 22:21—23:44

AND whosoever offereth a sacrifice of peace offerings unto the LORD to accomplish *his* vow, or a freewill offering in beeves or sheep, it shall be perfect to be accepted; there shall be no blemish therein.

22Blind, or broken, or maimed, or having a wen, or scurvy, or scabbed, ye shall not offer these unto the LORD, nor make an offering by fire of them upon the altar unto the LORD.

23Either a bullock or a lamb that hath any thing superfluous or lacking in his parts, that mayest thou offer *for* a freewill offering; but for a vow it shall not be accepted.

24Ye shall not offer unto the LORD that which is bruised, or crushed, or broken, or cut; neither shall ye make *any offering thereof* in your land.

25Neither from a stranger's hand shall

ye offer the bread of your God of any of these; because their corruption *is* in them, *and* blemishes *be* in them: they shall not be accepted for you.

26And the LORD spake unto Moses, saying,

27When a bullock, or a sheep, or a goat, is brought forth, then it shall be seven days under the dam; and from the eighth day and thenceforth it shall be accepted for an offering made by fire unto the LORD.

28And *whether it be* cow or ewe, ye shall not kill it and her young both in one day.

29And when ye will offer a sacrifice of thanksgiving unto the LORD, offer *it* at your own will.

30On the same day it shall be eaten up; ye shall leave none of it until the morrow: I *am* the LORD.

31Therefore shall ye keep my commandments, and do them: I *am* the LORD.

32Neither shall ye profane my holy name; but I will be hallowed among the children of Israel: I *am* the LORD which hallow you,

33That brought you out of the land of Egypt, to be your God: I *am* the LORD.

AND the LORD spake unto Moses, saying,

2Speak unto the children of Israel, and say unto them, *Concerning* the feasts of the LORD, which ye shall proclaim *to be* holy convocations, *even* these *are* my feasts.

3Six days shall work be done: but the seventh day *is* the sabbath of rest, and holy convocation; ye shall do no work *therein:* it *is* the sabbath of the LORD in all your dwellings.

4These *are* the feasts of the LORD, *even* holy convocations, which ye shall proclaim in their seasons.

5In the fourteenth *day* of the first month at even *is* the LORD'S passover.

6And on the fifteenth day of the same month *is* the feast of unleavened bread unto the LORD: seven days ye must eat unleavened bread.

7In the first day ye shall have an holy convocation: ye shall do no servile work therein.

8But ye shall offer an offering made by fire unto the LORD seven days: in the seventh day *is* an holy convocation: ye shall do no servile work *therein.*

9And the LORD spake unto Moses, saying,

10Speak unto the children of Israel, and say unto them, When ye be come into the land which I give unto you, and shall reap the harvest thereof, then ye shall bring a sheaf of the firstfruits of your harvest unto the priest:

11And he shall wave the sheaf before the LORD, to be accepted for you: on the morrow after the sabbath the priest shall wave it.

12And ye shall offer that day when ye wave the sheaf an he lamb without blemish of the first year for a burnt offering unto the LORD.

13And the meat offering thereof *shall be* two tenth deals of fine flour mingled with oil, an offering made by fire unto the LORD *for* a sweet savour: and the drink offering thereof *shall be* of wine, the fourth *part* of an hin.

14And ye shall eat neither bread, nor parched corn, nor green ears, until the selfsame day that ye have brought an offering unto your God: *it shall be* a statute for ever throughout your generations in all your dwellings.

15And ye shall count unto you from the morrow after the sabbath, from the day that ye brought the sheaf of the wave offering; seven sabbaths shall be complete:

16Even unto the morrow after the seventh sabbath shall ye number fifty days; and ye shall offer a new meat offering unto the LORD.

17Ye shall bring out of your habitations two wave loaves of two tenth deals: they shall be of fine flour; they shall be baken with leaven; *they are* the first-fruits unto the LORD.

18And ye shall offer with the bread seven lambs without blemish of the first year, and one young bullock, and two rams: they shall be *for* a burnt offering unto the LORD, with their meat offering, and their drink offerings, *even* an offering made by fire, of sweet savour unto the LORD.

19Then ye shall sacrifice one kid of the goats for a sin offering, and two lambs of the first year for a sacrifice of peace offerings.

20And the priest shall wave them with the bread of the firstfruits *for* a wave offering before the LORD, with the two lambs: they shall be holy to the LORD for the priest.

21And ye shall proclaim on the selfsame day, *that* it may be an holy convocation unto you: ye shall do no servile work *therein: it shall be* a statute for ever in all your dwellings throughout your generations.

22And when ye reap the harvest of your land, thou shalt not make clean riddance of the corners of thy field when thou reapest, neither shalt thou gather any gleaning of thy harvest: thou shalt leave them unto the poor, and to the stranger: I *am* the LORD your God.

23And the LORD spake unto Moses, saying,

24Speak unto the children of Israel, saying, In the seventh month, in the first *day* of the month, shall ye have a sabbath, a memorial of blowing of trumpets, an holy convocation.

25Ye shall do no servile work *therein:* but ye shall offer an offering made by fire unto the LORD.

26And the LORD spake unto Moses, saying,

27Also on the tenth *day* of this seventh month *there shall be* a day of atonement: it shall be an holy convocation unto you; and ye shall afflict your souls, and offer an offering made by fire unto the LORD.

28And ye shall do no work in that same day: for it *is* a day of atonement, to make an atonement for you before the LORD your God.

29For whatsoever soul *it be* that shall not be afflicted in that same day, he shall be cut off from among his people.

30And whatsoever soul *it be* that doeth any work in that same day, the same soul will I destroy from among his people.

31Ye shall do no manner of work: *it shall be* a statute for ever throughout your generations in all your dwellings.

32It *shall be* unto you a sabbath of rest, and ye shall afflict your souls: in the ninth *day* of the month at even, from even unto even, shall ye celebrate your sabbath.

33And the LORD spake unto Moses, saying,

34Speak unto the children of Israel, saying, The fifteenth day of this seventh month *shall be* the feast of tabernacles *for* seven days unto the LORD.

35On the first day *shall be* an holy convocation: ye shall do no servile work *therein.*

36Seven days ye shall offer an offering made by fire unto the LORD: on the eighth day shall be an holy convocation unto you; and ye shall offer an offering made by fire unto the LORD: it *is* a solemn assembly; *and* ye shall do no servile work *therein.*

37These *are* the feasts of the LORD, which ye shall proclaim *to be* holy convocations, to offer an offering made by fire unto the LORD, a burnt offering, and a meat offering, a sacrifice, and drink offerings, every thing upon his day:

38Beside the sabbaths of the LORD, and beside your gifts, and beside all your vows, and beside all your freewill offerings, which ye give unto the LORD.

39Also in the fifteenth day of the seventh month, when ye have gathered in the fruit of the land, ye shall keep a feast unto the LORD seven days: on the first day *shall be* a sabbath, and on the eighth day *shall be* a sabbath.

40And ye shall take you on the first day the boughs of goodly trees, branches of palm trees, and the boughs of thick trees, and willows of the brook; and ye shall rejoice before the LORD your God seven days.

41And ye shall keep it a feast unto the LORD seven days in the year. *It shall be* a statute for ever in your generations: ye shall celebrate it in the seventh month.

42Ye shall dwell in booths seven days; all that are Israelites born shall dwell in booths:

43That your generations may know that I made the children of Israel to dwell in booths, when I brought them out of the land of Egypt: I *am* the LORD your God.

44And Moses declared unto the children of Israel the feasts of the LORD.

MARK 9:30—10:12

ND they [Jesus and his disciples] departed thence, and passed through Galilee; and he would not that any man should know *it.*

31For he taught his disciples, and said unto them, The Son of man is delivered into the hands of men, and they shall kill him; and after that he is killed, he shall rise the third day.

32But they understood not that saying, and were afraid to ask him.

33And he came to Capernaum: and being in the house he asked them, What was it that ye disputed among yourselves by the way?

34But they held their peace: for by the way they had disputed among themselves, who *should be* the greatest.

35And he sat down, and called the twelve, and saith unto them, If any man desire to be first, *the same* shall be last of all, and servant of all.

36And he took a child, and set him in the midst of them: and when he had taken him in his arms, he said unto them,

37Whosoever shall receive one of such children in my name, receiveth me: and whosoever shall receive me, receiveth not me, but him that sent me.

38And John answered him, saying, Master, we saw one casting out devils in thy name, and he followeth not us: and we forbad him, because he followeth not us.

39But Jesus said, Forbid him not: for there is no man which shall do a miracle in my name, that can lightly speak evil of me.

40For he that is not against us is on our part.

41For whosoever shall give you a cup of water to drink in my name, because ye belong to Christ, verily I say unto you, he shall not lose his reward.

42And whosoever shall offend one of *these* little ones that believe in me, it is better for him that a millstone were hanged about his neck, and he were cast into the sea.

43And if thy hand offend thee, cut it off: it is better for thee to enter into life maimed, than having two hands to go into hell, into the fire that never shall be quenched:

44Where their worm dieth not, and the fire is not quenched.

45And if thy foot offend thee, cut it off: it is better for thee to enter halt into life, than having two feet to be cast into hell, into the fire that never shall be quenched:

46Where their worm dieth not, and the fire is not quenched.

47And if thine eye offend thee, pluck it out: it is better for thee to enter into the kingdom of God with one eye, than having two eyes to be cast into hell fire:

48Where their worm dieth not, and the fire is not quenched.

49For every one shall be salted with

fire, and every sacrifice shall be salted with salt.

50Salt *is* good: but if the salt have lost his saltness, wherewith will ye season it? Have salt in yourselves, and have peace one with another.

AND he arose from thence, and cometh into the coasts of Judaea by the farther side of Jordan: and the people resort unto him again; and, as he was wont, he taught them again.

2And the Pharisees came to him, and asked him, Is it lawful for a man to put away *his* wife? tempting him.

3And he answered and said unto them, What did Moses command you?

4And they said, Moses suffered to write a bill of divorcement, and to put *her* away.

5And Jesus answered and said unto them, For the hardness of your heart he wrote you this precept.

6But from the beginning of the creation God made them male and female.

7For this cause shall a man leave his father and mother, and cleave to his wife;

8And they twain shall be one flesh: so then they are no more twain, but one flesh.

9What therefore God hath joined together, let not man put asunder.

10And in the house his disciples asked him again of the same *matter*.

11And he saith unto them, Whosoever shall put away his wife, and marry another, committeth adultery against her.

12And if a woman shall put away her husband, and be married to another, she committeth adultery.

PSALM 44:1–7

WE have heard with our ears, O God, our fathers have told us, *what* work thou didst in their days, in the times of old.

2*How* thou didst drive out the heathen with thy hand, and plantedst them; *how* thou didst afflict the people, and cast them out.

3For they got not the land in possession by their own sword, neither did their own arm save them: but thy right hand, and thine arm, and the light of thy countenance, because thou hadst a favour unto them.

4Thou art my King, O God: command deliverances for Jacob.

5Through thee will we push down our enemies: through thy name will we tread them under that rise up against us.

6For I will not trust in my bow, neither shall my sword save me.

7But thou hast saved us from our enemies, and hast put them to shame that hated us.

PROVERBS FOR TODAY/ 10:19

In the multitude of words there wanteth not sin: but he that refraineth his lips is *wise.*

MARCH 1

LEVITICUS 24:1—25:46

AND the LORD spake unto Moses, saying,

2Command the children of Israel, that they bring unto thee pure oil olive beaten for the light, to cause the lamps to burn continually.

3Without the vail of the testimony, in the tabernacle of the congregation, shall Aaron order it from the evening unto the morning before the LORD continually: *it shall be* a statute for ever in your generations.

4He shall order the lamps upon the pure candlestick before the LORD continually.

5And thou shalt take fine flour, and bake twelve cakes thereof: two tenth deals shall be in one cake.

6And thou shalt set them in two rows, six on a row, upon the pure table before the LORD.

7And thou shalt put pure frankincense upon *each* row, that it may be on the bread for a memorial, *even* an offering made by fire unto the LORD.

8Every sabbath he shall set it in order before the LORD continually, *being taken* from the children of Israel by an everlasting covenant.

9And it shall be Aaron's and his sons'; and they shall eat it in the holy place: for it *is* most holy unto him of the offerings of the LORD made by fire by a perpetual statute.

10And the son of an Israelitish woman, whose father *was* an Egyptian, went out among the children of Israel: and this son of the Israelitish *woman* and a man of Israel strove together in the camp;

11And the Israelitish woman's son blasphemed the name *of the LORD, and cursed. And they brought him unto Moses: (and his mother's name was* Shelo-mith, the daughter of Dibri, of the tribe of Dan:)

12And they put him in ward, that the mind of the LORD might be shewed them.

13And the LORD spake unto Moses, saying,

14Bring forth him that hath cursed without the camp; and let all that heard *him* lay their hands upon his head, and let all the congregation stone him.

15And thou shalt speak unto the children of Israel, saying, Whosoever curseth his God shall bear his sin.

16And he that blasphemeth the name of the LORD, he shall surely be put to death, *and* all the congregation shall certainly stone him: as well the stranger, as he that is born in the land, when he blasphemeth the name *of the LORD, shall be put to death.*

17And he that killeth any man shall surely be put to death.

18And he that killeth a beast shall make it good; beast for beast.

19And if a man cause a blemish in his neighbour; as he hath done, so shall it be done to him;

20Breach for breach, eye for eye, tooth for tooth: as he hath caused a blemish in a man, so shall it be done to him *again.*

21And he that killeth a beast, he shall restore it: and he that killeth a man, he shall be put to death.

22Ye shall have one manner of law, as well for the stranger, as for one of your own country: for I *am* the LORD your God.

23And Moses spake to the children of Israel, that they should bring forth him that had cursed out of the camp, and stone him with stones. And the children of Israel did as the LORD commanded Moses.

AND the LORD spake unto Moses in Mount Sinai, saying,

2Speak unto the children of Israel, and say unto them, When ye come into the land which I give you, then shall the land keep a sabbath unto the LORD.

3Six years thou shalt sow thy field, and six years thou shalt prune thy vineyard, and gather in the fruit thereof;

4But in the seventh year shall be a sabbath of rest unto the land, a sabbath for the LORD: thou shalt neither sow thy field, nor prune thy vineyard.

5That which groweth of its own accord of thy harvest thou shalt not reap, neither gather the grapes of thy vine undressed: *for* it is a year of rest unto the land.

6And the sabbath of the land shall be meat for you; for thee, and for thy servant, and for thy maid, and for thy hired servant, and for thy stranger that sojourneth with thee,

7And for thy cattle, and for the beast that *are* in thy land, shall all the increase thereof be meat.

8And thou shalt number seven sabbaths of years unto thee, seven times seven years; and the space of the seven sabbaths of years shall be unto thee forty and nine years.

9Then shalt thou cause the trumpet of the jubilee to sound on the tenth *day* of the seventh month, in the day of atonement shall ye make the trumpet sound throughout all your land.

10And ye shall hallow the fiftieth year, and proclaim liberty throughout *all* the land unto all the inhabitants thereof: it shall be a jubilee unto you; and ye shall return every man unto his possession, and ye shall return every man unto his family.

11A jubilee shall that fiftieth year be unto you: ye shall not sow, neither reap that which groweth of itself in it, nor gather *the grapes* in it of thy vine undressed.

12For it *is* the jubilee; it shall be holy unto you: ye shall eat the increase thereof out of the field.

13In the year of this jubilee, ye shall return every man unto his possession.

14And if thou sell ought unto thy neighbour, or buyest *ought* of thy neighbour's hand, ye shall not oppress one another:

15According to the number of years after the jubilee, thou shalt buy of thy neighbour, *and* according unto the number of years of the fruits he shall sell unto thee:

16According to the multitude of years thou shalt increase the price thereof, and according to the fewness of years thou shalt diminish the price of it: for *according* to the number *of the years* of the fruits doth he sell unto thee.

17Ye shall not therefore oppress one another; but thou shalt fear thy God: for I *am* the LORD your God.

18Wherefore ye shall do my statutes, and keep my judgments, and do them; and ye shall dwell in the land in safety.

19And the land shall yield her fruit, and ye shall eat your fill, and dwell therein in safety.

20And if ye shall say, What shall we eat the seventh year? behold, we shall not sow, nor gather in our increase:

21Then I will command my blessing upon you in the sixth year, and it shall bring forth fruit for three years.

22And ye shall sow the eighth year, and eat *yet* of old fruit until the ninth year; until her fruits come in ye shall eat *of* the old *store*.

23The land shall not be sold for ever: for the land *is* mine; for ye *are* strangers and sojourners with me.

24And in all the land of your possession ye shall grant a redemption for the land.

25If thy brother be waxen poor, and hath sold away *some* of his possession, and if any of his kin come to redeem it, then shall he redeem that which his brother sold.

26And if the man have none to redeem it, and himself be able to redeem it;

27Then let him count the years of the sale thereof, and restore the overplus unto the man to whom he sold it; that he may return unto his possession.

28But if he be not able to restore *it* to him, then that which is sold shall remain in the hand of him that hath bought it until the year of jubilee: and in the jubilee it shall go out, and he shall return unto his possession.

29And if a man sell a dwelling house in a walled city, then he may redeem it within a whole year after it is sold; *within* a full year may he redeem it.

30And if it be not redeemed within the space of a full year, then the house that *is* in the walled city shall be established for ever to him that bought it throughout his generations: it shall not go out in the jubilee.

31But the houses of the villages which have no wall round about them shall be counted as the fields of the country: they may be redeemed, and they shall go out in the jubilee.

32Notwithstanding the cities of the Levites, *and* the houses of the cities of their possession, may the Levites redeem at any time.

33And if a man purchase of the Levites, then the house that was sold, and the city of his possession, shall go out in *the year of* jubilee: for the houses of the cities of the Levites *are* their possession among the children of Israel.

34But the field of the suburbs of their cities may not be sold; for it *is* their perpetual possession.

35And if thy brother be waxen poor, and fallen in decay with thee; then thou shalt relieve him: *yea, though he be* a stranger, or a sojourner; that he may live with thee.

36Take thou no usury of him, or increase: but fear thy God; that thy brother may live with thee.

37Thou shalt not give him thy money upon usury, nor lend him thy victuals for increase.

38I *am* the Lord your God, which brought you forth out of the land of Egypt, to give you the land of Canaan, *and* to be your God.

39And if thy brother *that dwelleth* by thee be waxen poor, and be sold unto thee; thou shalt not compel him to serve as a bondservant:

40*But* as an hired servant, *and* as a sojourner, he shall be with thee, *and* shall serve thee unto the year of jubilee:

41And *then* shall he depart from thee, *both* he and his children with him, and shall return unto his own family, and unto the possession of his fathers shall he return.

42For they *are* my servants, which I brought forth out of the land of Egypt: they shall not be sold as bondmen.

43Thou shalt not rule over him with rigour; but shalt fear thy God.

44Both thy bondmen, and thy bondmaids, which thou shalt have, *shall be* of the heathen that are round about you; of them shall ye buy bondmen and bondmaids.

45Moreover of the children of the strangers that do sojourn among you, of them shall ye buy, and of their families that *are* with you, which they begat in your land: and they shall be your possession.

46And ye shall take them as an inheritance for your children after you, to inherit *them for* a possession; they shall be your bondmen for ever: but over your brethren the children of Israel, ye shall not rule one over another with rigour.

MARK 10:13–31

AND they brought young children to him, that he should touch them: and *his* disciples rebuked those that brought *them.*

14But when Jesus saw *it,* he was much displeased, and said unto them, Suffer the little children to come unto me, and forbid them not: for of such is the kingdom of God.

15Verily I say unto you, Whosoever shall not receive the kingdom of God as a little child, he shall not enter therein.

16And he took them up in his arms, put *his* hands upon them, and blessed them.

17And when he was gone forth into the way, there came one running, and kneeled to him, and asked him, Good Master, what shall I do that I may inherit eternal life?

18And Jesus said unto him, Why callest thou me good? *there is* none good but one, *that is,* God.

19Thou knowest the commandments, Do not commit adultery, Do not kill, Do not steal, Do not bear false witness, Defraud not, Honour thy father and mother.

20And he answered and said unto him, Master, all these have I observed from my youth.

21Then Jesus beholding him loved him, and said unto him, One thing thou lackest: go thy way, sell whatsoever thou hast, and give to the poor, and thou shalt have treasure in heaven: and come, take up the cross, and follow me.

22And he was sad at that saying, and went away grieved: for he had great possessions.

23And Jesus looked round about, and saith unto his disciples, How hardly shall they that have riches enter into the kingdom of God!

24And the disciples were astonished at his words. But Jesus answereth again, and saith unto them, Children, how hard is it for them that trust in riches to enter into the kingdom of God!

25It is easier for a camel to go through the eye of a needle, than for a rich man to enter into the kingdom of God.

26And they were astonished out of measure, saying among themselves, Who then can be saved?

27And Jesus looking upon them saith, With men *it is* impossible, but not with God: for with God all things are possible.

28Then Peter began to say unto him, Lo, we have left all, and have followed thee.

29And Jesus answered and said, Verily I say unto you, There is no man that hath left house, or brethren, or sisters, or father, or mother, or wife, or children, or lands, for my sake, and the gospel's,

30But he shall receive an hundredfold now in this time, houses, and brethren, and sisters, and mothers, and children, and lands, with persecutions; and in the world to come eternal life.

31But many *that are* first shall be last; and the last first.

PSALM 44:8–26

IN God we boast all the day long, and praise thy name for ever. Selah.

9But thou hast cast off, and put us to shame; and goest not forth with our armies.

10Thou makest us to turn back from the enemy: and they which hate us spoil for themselves.

11Thou hast given us like sheep *appointed* for meat; and hast scattered us among the heathen.

12Thou sellest thy people for nought, and dost not increase *thy wealth* by their price.

13Thou makest us a reproach to our neighbours, a scorn and a derision to them that are round about us.

14Thou makest us a byword among the heathen, a shaking of the head among the people.

15My confusion *is* continually before me, and the shame of my face hath covered me,

16For the voice of him that reproacheth and blasphemeth; by reason of the enemy and avenger.

17All this is come upon us; yet have

we not forgotten thee, neither have we dealt falsely in thy covenant.

18Our heart is not turned back, neither have our steps declined from thy way;

19Though thou hast sore broken us in the place of dragons, and covered us with the shadow of death.

20If we have forgotten the name of our God, or stretched out our hands to a strange god;

21Shall not God search this out? for he knoweth the secrets of the heart.

22Yea, for thy sake are we killed all the day long; we are counted as sheep for the slaughter.

23Awake, why sleepest thou, O Lord? arise, cast *us* not off for ever.

24Wherefore hidest thou thy face, *and* forgettest our affliction and our oppression?

25For our soul is bowed down to the dust: our belly cleaveth unto the earth.

26Arise for our help, and redeem us for thy mercies' sake.

PROVERBS FOR TODAY/ 10:20–21

The tongue of the just is as choice silver: the heart of the wicked is little worth. □ *The lips of the righteous feed many: but fools die for want of wisdom.*

MARCH 2

LEVITICUS 25:47—27:13

AND if a sojourner or stranger wax rich by thee, and thy brother *that dwelleth* by him wax poor, and sell himself unto the stranger *or* sojourner by thee, or to the stock of the stranger's family:

48After that he is sold he may be redeemed again; one of his brethren may redeem him:

49Either his uncle, or his uncle's son, may redeem him, or *any* that is nigh of kin unto him of his family may redeem him; or if he be able, he may redeem himself.

50And he shall reckon with him that bought him from the year that he was sold to him unto the year of jubile: and the price of his sale shall be according unto the number of years, according to the time of an hired servant shall it be with him.

51If *there be* yet many years *behind,* according unto them he shall give again

the price of his redemption out of the money that he was bought for.

52And if there remain but few years unto the year of jubile, then he shall count with him, *and* according unto his years shall he give him again the price of his redemption.

53*And* as a yearly hired servant shall he be with him: *and the other* shall not rule with rigour over him in thy sight.

54And if he be not redeemed in these *years,* then he shall go out in the year of jubile, *both* he, and his children with him.

55For unto me the children of Israel *are* servants; they *are* my servants whom I brought forth out of the land of Egypt: I *am* the LORD your God.

YE shall make you no idols nor graven image, neither rear you up a standing image, neither shall ye set up *any* image of stone in your land, to bow down unto it: for I *am* the LORD your God.

2Ye shall keep my sabbaths, and reverence my sanctuary: I *am* the LORD.

3If ye walk in my statutes, and keep my commandments, and do them;

4Then I will give you rain in due season, and the land shall yield her increase, and the trees of the field shall yield their fruit.

5And your threshing shall reach unto the vintage, and the vintage shall reach unto the sowing time: and ye shall eat your bread to the full, and dwell in your land safely.

6And I will give peace in the land, and ye shall lie down, and none shall make *you* afraid: and I will rid evil beasts out of the land, neither shall the sword go through your land.

7And ye shall chase your enemies, and they shall fall before you by the sword.

8And five of you shall chase an hundred, and an hundred of you shall put ten thousand to flight: and your enemies shall fall before you by the sword.

9For I will have respect unto you, and make you fruitful, and multiply you, and establish my covenant with you.

10And ye shall eat old store, and bring forth the old because of the new.

11And I will set my tabernacle among you: and my soul shall not abhor you.

12And I will walk among you, and will be your God, and ye shall be my people.

13I *am* the LORD your God, which brought you forth out of the land of Egypt, that ye should not be their bondmen; and I have broken the bands of your yoke, and made you go upright.

14But if ye will not hearken unto me, and will not do all these commandments;

15And if ye shall despise my statutes, or if your soul abhor my judgments, so that ye will not do all my commandments, *but* that ye break my covenant:

16I also will do this unto you; I will even appoint over you terror, consumption, and the burning ague, that shall consume the eyes, and cause sorrow

of heart: and ye shall sow your seed in vain, for your enemies shall eat it.

17And I will set my face against you, and ye shall be slain before your enemies: they that hate you shall reign over you; and ye shall flee when none pursueth you.

18And if ye will not yet for all this hearken unto me, then I will punish you seven times more for your sins.

19And I will break the pride of your power; and I will make your heaven as iron, and your earth as brass:

20And your strength shall be spent in vain: for your land shall not yield her increase, neither shall the trees of the land yield their fruits.

21And if ye walk contrary unto me, and will not hearken unto me; I will bring seven times more plagues upon you according to your sins.

22I will also send wild beasts among you, which shall rob you of your children, and destroy your cattle, and make you few in number; and your *high* ways shall be desolate.

23And if ye will not be reformed by me by these things, but will walk contrary unto me;

24Then will I also walk contrary unto you, and will punish you yet seven times for your sins.

25And I will bring a sword upon you, that shall avenge the quarrel of *my* covenant: and when ye are gathered together within your cities, I will send the pestilence among you; and ye shall be delivered into the hand of the enemy.

26*And* when I have broken the staff of your bread, ten women shall bake your bread in one oven, and they shall deliver *you* your bread again by weight: and ye shall eat, and not be satisfied.

27And if ye will not for all this hearken unto me, but walk contrary unto me;

28Then I will walk contrary unto you also in fury; and I, even I, will chastise you seven times for your sins.

29And ye shall eat the flesh of your

sons, and the flesh of your daughters shall ye eat.

30And I will destroy your high places, and cut down your images, and cast your carcases upon the carcases of your idols, and my soul shall abhor you.

31And I will make your cities waste, and bring your sanctuaries unto desolation, and I will not smell the savour of your sweet odours.

32And I will bring the land into desolation: and your enemies which dwell therein shall be astonished at it.

33And I will scatter you among the heathen, and will draw out a sword after you: and your land shall be desolate, and your cities waste.

34Then shall the land enjoy her sabbaths, as long as it lieth desolate, and ye *be* in your enemies' land; *even* then shall the land rest, and enjoy her sabbaths.

35As long as it lieth desolate it shall rest; because it did not rest in your sabbaths, when ye dwelt upon it.

36And upon them that are left *alive* of you I will send a faintness into their hearts in the lands of their enemies; and the sound of a shaken leaf shall chase them; and they shall flee, as fleeing from a sword; and they shall fall when none pursueth.

37And they shall fall one upon another, as it were before a sword, when none pursueth: and ye shall have no power to stand before your enemies.

38And ye shall perish among the heathen, and the land of your enemies shall eat you up.

39And they that are left of you shall pine away in their iniquity in your enemies' lands; and also in the iniquities of their fathers shall they pine away with them.

40If they shall confess their iniquity, and the iniquity of their fathers, with their trespass which they trespassed against me, and that also they have walked contrary unto me;

41And *that* I also have walked contrary unto them, and have brought them into the land of their enemies; if then their uncircumcised hearts be humbled, and they then accept of the punishment of their iniquity:

42Then will I remember my covenant with Jacob, and also my covenant with Isaac, and also my covenant with Abraham will I remember; and I will remember the land.

43The land also shall be left of them, and shall enjoy her sabbaths, while she lieth desolate without them: and they shall accept of the punishment of their iniquity: because, even because they despised my judgments, and because their soul abhorred my statutes.

44And yet for all that, when they be in the land of their enemies, I will not cast them away, neither will I abhor them, to destory them utterly, and to break my covenant with them: for I *am* the LORD their God.

45But I will for their sakes remember the covenant of their ancestors whom I brought forth out of the land of Egypt in the sight of the heathen, that I might be their God: I *am* the LORD.

46These *are* the statutes and judgments and laws, which the LORD made between him and the children of Israel in mount Sinai by the hand of Moses.

AND the LORD spake unto Moses, saying,

2Speak unto the children of Israel, and say unto them, When a man shall make a singular vow, the persons *shall be* for the LORD by thy estimation.

3And thy estimation shall be of the male from twenty years old even unto sixty years old, even thy estimation shall be fifty shekels of silver, after the shekel of the sanctuary.

4And if it *be* a female, then thy estimation shall be thirty shekels.

5And if *it be* from five years old even unto twenty years old, then thy estimation shall be of the male twenty shekels, and for the female ten shekels.

⁶And if *it be* from a month old even unto five years old, then thy estimation shall be of the male five shekels of silver, and for the female thy estimation *shall be* three shekels of silver.

⁷And if *it be* from sixty years old and above; if *it be* a male, then thy estimation shall be fifteen shekels, and for the female ten shekels.

⁸But if he be poorer than thy estimation, then he shall present himself before the priest, and the priest shall value him; according to his ability that vowed shall the priest value him.

⁹And if *it be* a beast, whereof men bring an offering unto the LORD, all that *any man* giveth of such unto the LORD shall be holy.

¹⁰He shall not alter it, nor change it, a good for a bad, or a bad for a good: and if he shall at all change beast for beast, then it and the exchange thereof shall be holy.

¹¹And if *it be* any unclean beast, of which they do not offer a sacrifice unto the LORD, then he shall present the beast before the priest:

¹²And the priest shall value it, whether it be good or bad: as thou valuest it, *who art* the priest, so shall it be.

¹³But if he will at all redeem it, then he shall add a fifth *part* thereof unto thy estimation.

MARK 10:32–52

A ND they were in the way going up to Jerusalem; and Jesus went before them [the disciples]: and they were amazed; and as they followed, they were afraid. And he took again the twelve, and began to tell them what things should happen unto him,

³³*Saying*, Behold, we go up to Jerusalem; and the Son of man shall be delivered unto the chief priests, and unto the scribes; and they shall condemn him to death, and shall deliver him to the Gentiles:

³⁴And they shall mock him, and shall scourge him, and shall spit upon him, and shall kill him: and the third day he shall rise again.

³⁵And James and John, the sons of Zebedee, come unto him, saying, Master, we would that thou shouldest do for us whatsoever we shall desire.

³⁶And he said unto them, What would ye that I should do for you?

³⁷They said unto him, Grant unto us that we may sit, one on thy right hand, and the other on thy left hand, in thy glory.

³⁸But Jesus said unto them, Ye know not what ye ask: can ye drink of the cup that I drink of? and be baptized with the baptism that I am baptized with?

³⁹And they said unto him, We can. And Jesus said unto them, Ye shall indeed drink of the cup that I drink of; and with the baptism that I am baptized withal shall ye be baptized:

⁴⁰But to sit on my right hand and on my left hand is not mine to give; but *it shall be given to them* for whom it is prepared.

⁴¹And when the ten heard *it,* they began to be much displeased with James and John.

⁴²But Jesus called them *to him,* and saith unto them, Ye know that they which are accounted to rule over the Gentiles exercise lordship over them; and their great ones exercise authority upon them.

⁴³But so shall it not be among you: but whosoever will be great among you, shall be your minister:

⁴⁴And whosoever of you will be the chiefest, shall be servant of all.

⁴⁵For even the Son of man came not to be ministered unto, but to minister, and to give his life a ransom for many.

⁴⁶And they came to Jericho: and as he went out of Jericho with his disciples and a great number of people, blind Bartimaeus, the son of Timaeus, sat by the highway side begging.

47And when he heard that it was Jesus of Nazareth, he began to cry out, and say, Jesus, *thou* son of David, have mercy on me.

48And many charged him that he should hold his peace: but he cried the more a great deal, *Thou* son of David, have mercy on me.

49And Jesus stood still, and commanded him to be called. And they call the blind man, saying unto him, Be of good comfort, rise; he calleth thee.

50And he, casting away his garment, rose, and came to Jesus.

51And Jesus answered and said unto him, What wilt thou that I should do unto thee? The blind man said unto him, Lord, that I might receive my sight.

52And Jesus said unto him, Go thy way; thy faith hath made thee whole. And immediately he received his sight, and followed Jesus in the way.

PSALM 45:1–17

MY heart is inditing a good matter: I speak of the things which I have made touching the king: my tongue *is* the pen of a ready writer.

2Thou art fairer than the children of men: grace is poured into thy lips: therefore God hath blessed thee for ever.

3Gird thy sword upon *thy* thigh, O *most* mighty, with thy glory and thy majesty.

4And in thy majesty ride prosperously because of truth and meekness *and* righteousness; and thy right hand shall teach thee terrible things.

5Thine arrows *are* sharp in the heart of the king's enemies; *whereby* the people fall under thee.

6Thy throne, O God, *is* for ever and ever: the sceptre of thy kingdom *is* a right sceptre.

7Thou lovest righteousness, and hatest wickedness: therefore God, thy God, hath anointed thee with the oil of gladness above thy fellows.

8All thy garments *smell* of myrrh, and aloes, *and* cassia, out of the ivory palaces, whereby they have made thee glad.

9Kings' daughters *were* among thy honourable women: upon thy right hand did stand the queen in gold of Ophir.

10Hearken, O daughter, and consider, and incline thine ear; forget also thine own people, and thy father's house;

11So shall the king greatly desire thy beauty: for he *is* thy Lord; and worship thou him.

12And the daughter of Tyre *shall be there* with a gift; *even* the rich among the people shall intreat thy favour.

13The king's daughter *is* all glorious within: her clothing *is* of wrought gold.

14She shall be brought unto the king in raiment of needlework: the virgins her companions that follow her shall be brought unto thee.

15With gladness and rejoicing shall they be brought: they shall enter into the king's palace.

16Instead of thy fathers shall be thy children, whom thou mayest make princes in all the earth.

17I will make thy name to be remembered in all generations: therefore shall the people praise thee for ever and ever.

PROVERBS FOR TODAY/ 10:22

The blessing of the LORD, it maketh rich, and he addeth no sorrow with it

MARCH 3

LEVITICUS 27:14—NUMBERS 1:54

AND when a man shall sanctify his house *to be* holy unto the LORD, then the priest shall estimate it, whether it be good or bad: as the priest shall estimate it, so shall it stand.

15And if he that sanctified it will redeem his house, then he shall add the fifth *part* of the money of thy estimation unto it, and it shall be his.

16And if a man shall sanctify unto the LORD *some part* of a field of his possession, then thy estimation shall be according to the seed thereof: an homer of barley seed *shall be valued* at fifty shekels of silver.

17If he sanctify his field from the year of jubile, according to thy estimation it shall stand.

18But if he sanctify his field after the jubile, then the priest shall reckon unto him the money according to the years that remain, even unto the year of the jubile, and it shall be abated from thy estimation.

19And if he that sanctified the field will in any wise redeem it, then he shall add the fifth *part* of the money of thy estimation unto it, and it shall be assured to him.

20And if he will not redeem the field, or if he have sold the field to another man, it shall not be redeemed any more.

21But the field, when it goeth out in the jubile, shall be holy unto the LORD, as a field devoted; the possession thereof shall be the priest's.

22And if *a man* sanctify unto the LORD a field which he hath bought, which *is* not of the fields of his possession;

23Then the priest shall reckon unto him the worth of thy estimation, *even* unto the year of the jubile: and he shall give thine estimation in that day, *as* a holy thing unto the LORD.

24In the year of the jubile the field shall return unto him of whom it was bought, *even* to him to whom the possession of the land *did belong.*

25And all thy estimations shall be according to the shekel of the sanctuary: twenty gerahs shall be the shekel.

26Only the firstling of the beasts, which should be the LORD's firstling, no man shall sanctify it; whether *it be* ox, or sheep: it *is* the LORD's.

27And if *it be* of an unclean beast, then he shall redeem *it* according to thine estimation, and shall add a fifth *part* of it thereto: or if it be not redeemed, then it shall be sold according to thy estimation.

28Notwithstanding no devoted thing, that a man shall devote unto the LORD of all that he hath, *both* of man and beast, and of the field of his possession, shall be sold or redeemed: every devoted thing *is* most holy unto the LORD.

29None devoted, which shall be devoted of men, shall be redeemed; *but* shall surely be put to death.

30And all the tithe of the land, *whether* of the seed of the land, *or* of the fruit of the tree, *is* the LORD's: *it is* holy unto the LORD.

31And if a man will at all redeem *ought* of his tithes, he shall add thereto the fifth *part* thereof.

32And concerning the tithe of the herd, or of the flock, *even* of whatsoever passeth under the rod, the tenth shall be holy unto the LORD.

33He shall not search whether it be good or bad, neither shall he change it: and if he change it at all, then both it and the change thereof shall be holy; it shall not be redeemed.

34These *are* the commandments,

which the LORD commanded Moses for the children of Israel in mount Sinai.

AND the LORD spake unto Moses in the wilderness of Sinai, in the tabernacle of the congregation, on the first *day* of the second month, in the second year after they were come out of the land of Egypt, saying,

2Take ye the sum of all the congregation of the children of Israel, after their families, by the house of their fathers, with the number of *their* names, every male by their polls;

3From twenty years old and upward, all that are able to go forth to war in Israel: thou and Aaron shall number them by their armies.

4And with you there shall be a man of every tribe; every one head of the house of his fathers.

5And these *are* the names of the men that shall stand with you: of *the tribe of* Reuben; Elizur the son of Shedeur.

6Of Simeon; Shelumiel the son of Zurishaddai.

7Of Judah; Nahshon the son of Amminadab.

8Of Issachar; Nethaneel the son of Zuar.

9Of Zebulun; Eliab the son of Helon.

10Of the children of Joseph: of Ephraim; Elishama the son of Ammihud: of Manasseh; Gamaliel the son of Pedahzur.

11Of Benjamin; Abidan the son of Gideoni.

12Of Dan; Ahiezer the son of Ammishaddai.

13Of Asher; Pagiel the son of Ocran.

14Of Gad; Eliasaph the son of Deuel.

15Of Naphtali; Ahira the son of Enan.

16These *were* the renowned of the congregation, princes of the tribes of their fathers, heads of thousands in Israel.

17And Moses and Aaron took these men which are expressed by *their* names:

18And they assembled all the congregation together on the first *day* of the second month, and they declared their pedigrees after their families, by the house of their fathers, according to the number of the names, from twenty years old and upward, by their polls.

19As the LORD commanded Moses, so he numbered them in the wilderness of Sinai.

20And the children of Reuben, Israel's eldest son, by their generations, after their families, by the house of their fathers, according to the number of the names, by their polls, every male from twenty years old and upward, all that were able to go forth to war;

21Those that were numbered of them, *even* of the tribe of Reuben, *were* forty and six thousand and five hundred.

22Of the children of Simeon, by their generations, after their families, by the house of their fathers, those that were numbered of them, according to the number of the names, by their polls, every male from twenty years old and upward, all that were able to go forth to war;

23Those that were numbered of them, *even* of the tribe of Simeon, *were* fifty and nine thousand and three hundred.

24Of the children of Gad, by their generations, after their families, by the house of their fathers, according to the number of the names, from twenty years old and upward, all that were able to go forth to war;

25Those that were numbered of them, *even* of the tribe of Gad, *were* forty and five thousand six hundred and fifty.

26Of the children of Judah, by their generations, after their families, by the house of their fathers, according to the number of the names, from twenty years old and upward, all that were able to go forth to war;

27Those that were numbered of them, *even* of the tribe of Judah, *were* threescore and fourteen thousand and six hundred.

28Of the children of Issachar, by their generations, after their families, by the house of their fathers, according to the number of the names, from twenty years old and upward, all that were able to go forth to war;

29Those that were numbered of them, *even* of the tribe of Issachar, *were* fifty and four thousand and four hundred.

30Of the children of Zebulun, by their generations, after their families, by the house of their fathers, according to the number of the names, from twenty years old and upward, all that were able to go forth to war;

31Those that were numbered of them, *even* of the tribe of Zebulun, *were* fifty and seven thousand and four hundred.

32Of the children of Joseph, *namely,* of the children of Ephraim, by their generations, after their families, by the house of their fathers, according to the number of the names, from twenty years old and upward, all that were able to go forth to war;

33Those that were numbered of them, *even* of the tribe of Ephraim, *were* forty thousand and five hundred.

34Of the children of Manasseh, by their generations, after their families, by the house of their fathers, according to the number of the names, from twenty years old and upward, all that were able to go forth to war;

35Those that were numbered of them, *even* of the tribe of Manasseh, *were* thirty and two thousand and two hundred.

36Of the children of Benjamin, by their generations, after their families, by the house of their fathers, according to the number of the names, from twenty years old and upward, all that were able to go forth to war;

37Those that were numbered of them, *even* of the tribe of Benjamin, *were* thirty and five thousand and four hundred.

38Of the children of Dan, by their generations, after their families, by the house of their fathers, according to the number of the names, from twenty years old and upward, all that were able to go forth to war;

39Those that were numbered of them, *even* of the tribe of Dan, *were* threescore and two thousand and seven hundred.

40Of the children of Asher, by their generations, after their families, by the house of their fathers, according to the number of the names, from twenty years old and upward, all that were able to go forth to war;

41Those that were numbered of them, *even* of the tribe of Asher, *were* forty and one thousand and five hundred.

42Of the children of Naphtali, throughout their generations, after their families, by the house of their fathers, according to the number of the names, from twenty years old and upward, all that were able to go forth to war;

43Those that were numbered of them, *even* of the tribe of Naphtali, *were* fifty and three thousand and four hundred.

44These *are* those that were numbered, which Moses and Aaron numbered, and the princes of Israel, *being* twelve men: each one was for the house of his fathers.

45So were all those that were numbered of the children of Israel, by the house of their fathers, from twenty years old and upward, all that were able to go forth to war in Israel;

46Even all they that were numbered were six hundred thousand and three thousand and five hundred and fifty.

47But the Levites after the tribe of their fathers were not numbered among them.

48For the Lord had spoken unto Moses, saying,

49Only thou shalt not number the tribe of Levi, neither take the sum of them among the children of Israel:

50But thou shalt appoint the Levites over the tabernacle of testimony, and over all the vessels thereof, and over all things that *belong* to it: they shall bear the tabernacle, and all the vessels thereof; and they shall minister unto it, and shall encamp round about the tabernacle.

51And when the tabernacle setteth forward, the Levites shall take it down: and when the tabernacle is to be pitched, the Levites shall set it up: and the stranger that cometh nigh shall be put to death.

52And the children of Israel shall pitch their tents, every man by his own camp, and every man by his own standard, throughout their hosts.

53But the Levites shall pitch round about the tabernacle of testimony, that there be no wrath upon the congregation of the children of Israel: and the Levites shall keep the charge of the tabernacle of testimony.

54And the children of Israel did according to all that the Lord commanded Moses, so did they.

MARK 11:1–26

A ND when they came nigh to Jerusalem, unto Bethphage and Bethany, at the mount of Olives, he sendeth forth two of his disciples,

2And saith unto them, Go your way into the village over against you: and as soon as ye be entered into it, ye shall find a colt tied, whereon never man sat; loose him, and bring *him*.

3And if any man say unto you, Why do ye this? say ye that the Lord hath need of him; and straightway he will send him hither.

4And they went their way, and found the colt tied by the door without in a place where two ways met; and they loose him.

5And certain of them that stood there said unto them, What do ye, loosing the colt?

6And they said unto them even as Jesus had commanded: and they let them go.

7And they brought the colt to Jesus, and cast their garments on him; and he sat upon him.

8And many spread their garments in the way: and others cut down branches off the trees, and strawed *them* in the way.

9And they that went before, and they that followed, cried, saying, Hosanna; Blessed *is* he that cometh in the name of the Lord:

10Blessed *be* the kingdom of our father David, that cometh in the name of the Lord: Hosanna in the highest.

11And Jesus entered into Jerusalem, and into the temple: and when he had looked round about upon all things, and now the eventide was come, he went out unto Bethany with the twelve.

12And on the morrow, when they were come from Bethany, he was hungry:

13And seeing a fig tree afar off having leaves, he came, if haply he might find anything thereon: and when he came to it, he found nothing but leaves; for the time of figs was not *yet*.

14And Jesus answered and said unto it, No man eat fruit of thee hereafter for ever. And his disciples heard *it*.

15And they come to Jerusalem: and Jesus went into the temple, and began to cast out them that sold and bought in the temple, and overthrew the tables of the moneychangers, and the seats of them that sold doves;

16And would not suffer that any man should carry *any* vessel through the temple.

17And he taught, saying unto them, Is it not written, My house shall be called of all nations the house of prayer? but ye have made it a den of thieves.

18And the scribes and chief priests heard *it,* and sought how they might destroy him: for they feared him, because all the people was astonished at his doctrine.

19And when even was come, he went out of the city.

20And in the morning, as they passed by, they saw the fig tree dried up from the roots.

21And Peter calling to remembrance saith unto him, Master, behold, the fig tree which thou cursedst is withered away.

22And Jesus answering saith unto them, Have faith in God.

23For verily I say unto you, That whosoever shall say unto this mountain, Be thou removed, and be thou cast into the sea; and shall not doubt in his heart, but shall believe that those things which he saith shall come to pass; he shall have whatsoever he saith.

24Therefore I say unto you, What things soever ye desire, when ye pray, believe that ye receive *them,* and ye shall have *them.*

25And when ye stand praying, forgive, if ye have ought against any: that your Father also which is in heaven may forgive you your trespasses.

26But if ye do not forgive, neither will your Father which is in heaven forgive your trespasses.

PSALM 46:1–11

G OD *is* our refuge and strength, a very present help in trouble.

2Therefore will not we fear, though the earth be removed, and though the mountains be carried into the midst of the sea;

3*Though* the waters thereof roar *and* be troubled, *though* the mountains shake with the swelling thereof. Selah.

4*There is* a river, the streams whereof shall make glad the city of God, the holy *place* of the tabernacles of the most High.

5God *is* in the midst of her; she shall not be moved: God shall help her, *and that* right early.

6The heathen raged, the kingdoms were moved: he uttered his voice, the earth melted.

7The LORD of hosts *is* with us; the God of Jacob *is* our refuge. Selah.

8Come, behold the works of the LORD, what desolations he hath made in the earth.

9He maketh wars to cease unto the end of the earth; he breaketh the bow, and cutteth the spear in sunder; he burneth the chariot in the fire.

10Be still, and know that I *am* God: I will be exalted among the heathen, I will be exalted in the earth.

11The LORD of hosts *is* with us; the God of Jacob *is* our refuge. Selah.

PROVERBS FOR TODAY/ 10:23

It is *as sport to a fool to do mischief: but a man of understanding hath wisdom.*

MARCH 4

NUMBERS 2:1—3:51

ND the Lord spake unto Moses
and unto Aaron, saying,
2Every man of the children
of Israel shall pitch by his own standard,
with the ensign of their father's house:
far off about the tabernacle of the congregation shall they pitch.

3And on the east side toward the rising of the sun shall they of the standard of the camp of Judah pitch throughout their armies: and Nahshon the son of Amminadab *shall be* captain of the children of Judah.

4And his host, and those that were numbered of them, *were* threescore and fourteen thousand and six hundred.

5And those that do pitch next unto him *shall be* the tribe of Issachar: and Nethaneel the son of Zuar *shall be* captain of the children of Issachar.

6And his host, and those that were numbered thereof, *were* fifty and four thousand and four hundred.

7*Then* the tribe of Zebulun: and Eliab the son of Helon *shall be* captain of the children of Zebulun.

8And his host, and those that were numbered thereof, *were* fifty and seven thousand and four hundred.

9All that were numbered in the camp of Judah *were* an hundred thousand and fourscore thousand and six thousand and four hundred, throughout their armies. These shall first set forth.

10On the south side *shall be* the standard of the camp of Reuben according to their armies: and the captain of the children of Reuben *shall be* Elizur the son of Shedeur.

11And his host, and those that were numbered thereof, *were* forty and six thousand and five hundred.

12And those which pitch by him *shall be* the tribe of Simeon: and the captain of the children of Simeon *shall be* Shelumiel the son of Zurishadai.

13And his host, and those that were numbered of them, *were* fifty and nine thousand and three hundred.

14Then the tribe of Gad: and the captain of the sons of Gad *shall be* Eliasaph the son of Reuel.

15And his host, and those that were numbered of them, *were* forty and five thousand and six hundred and fifty.

16All that were numbered in the camp of Reuben *were* an hundred thousand and fifty and one thousand and four hundred and fifty, throughout their armies. And they shall set forth in the second rank.

17Then the tabernacle of the congregation shall set forward with the camp of the Levites in the midst of the camp: as they encamp, so shall they set forward, every man in his place by their standards.

18On the west side *shall be* the standard of the camp of Ephraim according to their armies: and the captain of the sons of Ephraim *shall be* Elishama the son of Ammihud.

19And his host, and those that were numbered of them, *were* forty thousand and five hundred.

20And by him *shall be* the tribe of Manasseh: and the captain of the children of Manasseh *shall be* Gamaliel the son of Pedahzur.

21And his host, and those that were numbered of them, *were* thirty and two thousand and two hundred.

22Then the tribe of Benjamin: and the captain of the sons of Benjamin *shall be* Abidan the son of Gideoni.

23And his host, and those that were numbered of them, *were* thirty and five thousand and four hundred.

24All that were numbered of the camp

of Ephraim *were* an hundred thousand and eight thousand and an hundred, throughout their armies. And they shall go forward in the third rank.

25The standard of the camp of Dan *shall be* on the north side by their armies: and the captain of the children of Dan *shall be* Ahiezer the son of Ammishaddai.

26And his host, and those that were numbered of them, *were* threescore and two thousand and seven hundred.

27And those that encamp by him *shall be* the tribe of Asher: and the captain of the children of Asher *shall be* Pagiel the son of Ocran.

28And his host, and those that were numbered of them, *were* forty and one thousand and five hundred.

29Then the tribe of Naphtali: and the captain of the children of Naphtali *shall be* Ahira the son of Enan.

30And his host, and those that were numbered of them, *were* fifty and three thousand and four hundred.

31All they that were numbered in the camp of Dan *were* an hundred thousand and fifty and seven thousand and six hundred. They shall go hindmost with their standards.

32These *are* those which were numbered of the children of Israel by the house of their fathers: all those that were numbered of the camps throughout their hosts *were* six hundred thousand and three thousand and five hundred and fifty.

33But the Levites were not numbered among the children of Israel; as the LORD commanded Moses.

34And the children of Israel did according to all that the LORD commanded Moses: so they pitched by their standards, and so they set forward, every one after their families, according to the house of their fathers.

THESE also *are* the generations of Aaron and Moses in the day *that* the LORD spake with Moses in mount Sinai.

2And these *are* the names of the sons of Aaron; Nadab the firstborn, and Abihu, Eleazar, and Ithamar.

3These *are* the names of the sons of Aaron, the priests which were anointed, whom he consecrated to minister in the priest's office.

4And Nadab and Abihu died before the LORD, when they offered strange fire before the LORD, in the wilderness of Sinai, and they had no children: and Eleazar and Ithamar ministered in the priest's office in the sight of Aaron their father.

5And the LORD spake unto Moses, saying,

6Bring the tribe of Levi near, and present them before Aaron the priest, that they may minister unto him.

7And they shall keep his charge, and the charge of the whole congregation before the tabernacle of the congregation, to do the service of the tabernacle.

8And they shall keep all the instruments of the tabernacle of the congregation, and the charge of the children of Israel, to do the service of the tabernacle.

9And thou shalt give the Levites unto Aaron and to his sons: they *are* wholly given unto him out of the children of Israel.

10And thou shalt appoint Aaron and his sons, and they shall wait on the priest's office: and the stranger that cometh nigh shall be put to death.

11And the LORD spake unto Moses, saying,

12And I, behold, I have taken the Levites from among the children of Israel instead of all the firstborn that openeth the matrix among the children of Israel: therefore the Levites shall be mine;

13Because all the firstborn *are* mine; *for* on the day that I smote all the firstborn in the land of Egypt I hallowed unto me all the firstborn in Israel, both man and beast: mine shall they be: I *am* the LORD.

14And the Lord spake unto Moses in the wilderness of Sinai, saying,

15Number the children of Levi after the house of their fathers, by their families: every male from a month old and upward shalt thou number them.

16And Moses numbered them according to the word of the Lord, as he was commanded.

17And these were the sons of Levi by their names; Gershon, and Kohath, and Merari.

18And these *are* the names of the sons of Gershon by their families; Libni, and Shimei.

19And the sons of Kohath by their families; Amram, and Izehar, Hebron, and Uzziel.

20And the sons of Merari by their families; Mahli, and Mushi. These *are* the families of the Levites according to the house of their fathers.

21Of Gershon *was* the family of the Libnites, and the family of the Shimites: these *are* the families of the Gershonites.

22Those that were numbered of them, according to the number of all the males, from a month old and upward, *even* those that were numbered of them *were* seven thousand and five hundred.

23The families of the Gershonites shall pitch behind the tabernacle westward.

24And the chief of the house of the father of the Gershonites *shall be* Eliasaph the son of Lael.

25And the charge of the sons of Gershon in the tabernacle of the congregation *shall be* the tabernacle, and the tent, the covering thereof, and the hanging for the door of the tabernacle of the congregation,

26And the hangings of the court, and the curtain for the door of the court, which *is* by the tabernacle, and by the altar round about, and the cords of it for all the service thereof.

27And of Kohath *was* the family of the Amramites, and the family of the Izeharites, and the family of the Hebronites, and the family of the Uzzielites: these *are* the families of the Kohathites.

28In the number of all the males, from a month old and upward, *were* eight thousand and six hundred, keeping the charge of the sanctuary.

29The families of the sons of Kohath shall pitch on the side of the tabernacle southward.

30And the chief of the house of the father of the families of the Kohathites *shall be* Elizaphan the son of Uzziel.

31And their charge *shall be* the ark, and the table, and the candlestick, and the altars, and the vessels of the sanctuary wherewith they minister, and the hanging, and all the service thereof.

32And Eleazar the son of Aaron the priest *shall be* chief over the chief of the Levites, *and have* the oversight of them that keep the charge of the sanctuary.

33Of Merari *was* the family of the Mahlites, and the family of the Mushites: these *are* the families of Merari.

34And those that were numbered of them, according to the number of all the males, from a month old and upward, *were* six thousand and two hundred.

35And the chief of the house of the father of the families of Merari *was* Zuriel the son of Abihail: *these* shall pitch on the side of the tabernacle northward.

36And *under* the custody and charge of the sons of Merari *shall be* the boards of the tabernacle, and the bars thereof, and the pillars thereof, and the sockets thereof, and all the vessels thereof, and all that serveth thereto,

37And the pillars of the court round about, and their sockets, and their pins, and their cords.

38But those that encamp before the tabernacle toward the east, *even* before the tabernacle of the congregation eastward, *shall be* Moses, and Aaron and his sons, keeping the charge of the sanctuary for the charge of the children of Israel; and the stranger that cometh nigh shall be put to death.

39All that were numbered of the Levites, which Moses and Aaron numbered at the commandment of the LORD, throughout their families, all the males from a month old and upward, *were* twenty and two thousand.

40And the LORD said unto Moses, Number all the firstborn of the males of the children of Israel from a month old and upward, and take the number of their names.

41And thou shalt take the Levites for me (I *am* the LORD) instead of all the firstborn among the children of Israel; and the cattle of the Levites instead of all the firstlings among the cattle of the children of Israel.

42And Moses numbered, as the LORD commanded him, all the firstborn among the children of Israel.

43And all the firstborn males by the number of names, from a month old and upward, of those that were numbered of them, were twenty and two thousand two hundred and threescore and thirteen.

44And the LORD spake unto Moses, saying,

45Take the Levites instead of all the firstborn among the children of Israel, and the cattle of the Levites instead of their cattle; and the Levites shall be mine: I *am* the LORD.

46And for those that are to be redeemed of the two hundred and threescore and thirteen of the firstborn of the children of Israel, which are more than the Levites;

47Thou shalt even take five shekels apiece by the poll, after the shekel of the sanctuary shalt thou take *them:* (the shekel *is* twenty gerahs:)

48And thou shalt give the money, wherewith the odd number of them is

to be redeemed, unto Aaron and to his sons.

49And Moses took the redemption money of them that were over and above them that were redeemed by the Levites:

50Of the firstborn of the children of Israel took he the money; a thousand three hundred and threescore and five *shekels,* after the shekel of the sanctuary:

51And Moses gave the money of them that were redeemed unto Aaron and to his sons, according to the word of the LORD, as the LORD commanded Moses.

MARK 11:27—12:17

ND they come again to Jerusalem: and as he was walking in the temple, there come to him the chief priests, and the scribes, and the elders,

28And say unto him, By what authority doest thou these things? and who gave thee this authority to do these things?

29And Jesus answered and said unto them, I will also ask of you one question, and answer me, and I will tell you by what authority I do these things.

30The baptism of John, was *it* from heaven, or of men? answer me.

31And they reasoned with themselves, saying, If we shall say, From heaven; he will say, Why then did ye not believe him?

32But if we shall say, Of men; they feared the people: for all *men* counted John, that he was a prophet indeed.

33And they answered and said unto Jesus, We cannot tell. And Jesus answering saith unto them, Neither do I tell you by what authority I do these things.

AND he began to speak unto them by parables. A *certain* man planted a vineyard, and set an hedge about *it,* and digged *a place for* the winefat, and built a tower, and let it out to husbandmen, and went into a far country.

2And at the season he sent to the husbandmen a servant, that he might receive from the husbandmen of the fruit of the vineyard.

3And they caught *him,* and beat him, and sent *him* away empty.

4And again he sent unto them another servant; and at him they cast stones, and wounded *him* in the head, and sent *him* away shamefully handled.

5And again he sent another; and him they killed, and many others; beating some, and killing some.

6Having yet therefore one son, his wellbeloved, he sent him also last unto them, saying, They will reverence my son.

7But those husbandmen said among themselves, This is the heir; come, let us kill him, and the inheritance shall be ours.

8And they took him, and killed *him,* and cast *him* out of the vineyard.

9What shall therefore the lord of the vineyard do? he will come and destroy the husbandmen, and will give the vineyard unto others.

10And have ye not read this scripture; The stone which the builders rejected is become the head of the corner:

11This was the Lord's doing, and it is marvellous in our eyes?

12And they sought to lay hold on him, but feared the people: for they knew that he had spoken the parable against them: and they left him, and went their way.

13And they send unto him certain of the Pharisees and of the Herodians, to catch him in *his* words.

14And when they were come, they say unto him, Master, we know that thou art true, and carest for no man: for thou regardest not the person of men, but teachest the way of God in truth: Is it lawful to give tribute to Caesar, or not?

15Shall we give, or shall we not give? But he, knowing their hypocrisy, said unto them, Why tempt ye me? bring me a penny, that I may see *it.*

16And they brought *it.* And he saith unto them, Whose *is* this image and superscription? And they said unto him, Caesar's.

17And Jesus answering said unto them, Render to Caesar the things that are Caesar's, and to God the things that are God's. And they marvelled at him.

PSALM 47:1–9

Oclap your hands, all ye people; shout unto God with the voice of triumph.

2For the LORD most high *is* terrible; *he is* a great King over all the earth.

3He shall subdue the people under us, and the nations under our feet.

4He shall choose our inheritance for us, the excellency of Jacob whom he loved. Selah.

5God is gone up with a shout, the LORD with the sound of a trumpet.

6Sing praises to God, sing praises: sing praises unto our King, sing praises.

7For God *is* the King of all the earth: sing ye praises with understanding.

8God reigneth over the heathen: God sitteth upon the throne of his holiness.

9The princes of the people are gathered together, *even* the people of the God of Abraham: for the shields of the earth *belong* unto God: he is greatly exalted.

PROVERBS FOR TODAY/ 10:24–25

The fear of the wicked, it shall come upon him: but the desire of the righteous shall be granted. □ *As the whirlwind passeth, so* is *the wicked no* more: *but the righteous* is *an everlasting foundation.*

MARCH 5

NUMBERS 4:1—5:31

AND the Lord spake unto Moses and unto Aaron, saying,

2Take the sum of the sons of Kohath from among the sons of Levi, after their families, by the house of their fathers,

3From thirty years old and upward even until fifty years old, all that enter into the host, to do the work in the tabernacle of the congregation.

4This *shall be* the service of the sons of Kohath in the tabernacle of the congregation, *about* the most holy things:

5And when the camp setteth forward, Aaron shall come, and his sons, and they shall take down the covering vail, and cover the ark of testimony with it:

6And shall put thereon the covering of badgers' skins, and shall spread over *it* a cloth wholly of blue, and shall put in the staves thereof.

7And upon the table of shewbread they shall spread a cloth of blue, and put thereon the dishes, and the spoons, and the bowls, and covers to cover withal: and the continual bread shall be thereon:

8And they shall spread upon them a cloth of scarlet, and cover the same with a covering of badgers' skins, and shall put in the staves thereof.

9And they shall take a cloth of blue, and cover the candlestick of the light, and his lamps, and his tongs, and his snuffdishes, and all the oil vessels thereof, wherewith they minister unto it:

10And they shall put it and all the vessels thereof within a covering of badgers' skins, and shall put *it* upon a bar.

11And upon the golden altar they shall spread a cloth of blue, and cover it with a covering of badgers' skins, and shall put to the staves thereof:

12And they shall take all the instruments of ministry, wherewith they minister in the sanctuary, and put *them* in a cloth of blue, and cover them with a covering of badgers' skins, and shall put *them* on a bar:

13And they shall take away the ashes from the altar, and spread a purple cloth thereon:

14And they shall put upon it all the vessels thereof, wherewith they minister about it, *even* the censers, the fleshhooks, and the shovels, and the basons, all the vessels of the altar; and they shall spread upon it a covering of badgers' skins, and put to the staves of it.

15And when Aaron and his sons have made an end of covering the sanctuary, and all the vessels of the sanctuary, as the camp is to set forward; after that, the sons of Kohath shall come to bear *it:* but they shall not touch *any* holy thing, lest they die. These *things are* the burden of the sons of Kohath in the tabernacle of the congregation.

16And to the office of Eleazar the son of Aaron the priest *pertaineth* the oil for the light, and the sweet incense, and the daily meat offering, and the anointing oil, *and* the oversight of all the tabernacle, and of all that therein *is,* in the sanctuary, and in the vessels thereof.

17And the Lord spake unto Moses and unto Aaron, saying,

18Cut ye not off the tribe of the families of the Kohathites from among the Levites:

19But thus do unto them, that they may live, and not die, when they approach unto the most holy things: Aaron and his sons shall go in, and appoint them every one to his service and to his burden:

20But they shall not go in to see when the holy things are covered, lest they die.

21And the LORD spake unto Moses, saying,

22Take also the sum of the sons of Gershon, throughout the houses of their fathers, by their families;

23From thirty years old and upward until fifty years old shalt thou number them; all that enter in to perform the service, to do the work in the tabernacle of the congregation.

24This *is* the service of the families of the Gershonites, to serve, and for burdens:

25And they shall bear the curtains of the tabernacle, and the tabernacle of the congregation, his covering, and the covering of the badgers' skins that *is* above upon it, and the hanging for the door of the tabernacle of the congregation,

26And the hangings of the court, and the hanging for the door of the gate of the court, which *is* by the tabernacle and by the altar round about, and their cords, and all the instruments of their service, and all that is made for them: so shall they serve.

27At the appointment of Aaron and his sons shall be all the service of the sons of the Gershonites, in all their burdens, and in all their service: and ye shall appoint unto them in charge all their burdens.

28This *is* the service of the families of the sons of Gershon in the tabernacle of the congregation: and their charge *shall be* under the hand of Ithamar the son of Aaron the priest.

29As for the sons of Merari, thou shalt number them after their families, by the house of their fathers;

30From thirty years old and upward even unto fifty years old shalt thou number them, every one that entereth into the service, to do the work of the tabernacle of the congregation.

31And this *is* the charge of their bur-den, according to all their service in the tabernacle of the congregation; the boards of the tabernacle, and the bars thereof, and the pillars thereof, and sockets thereof,

32And the pillars of the court round about, and their sockets, and their pins, and their cords, with all their instruments, and with all their service: and by name ye shall reckon the instruments of the charge of their burden.

33This *is* the service of the families of the sons of Merari, according to all their service, in the tabernacle of the congregation, under the hand of Ithamar the son of Aaron the priest.

34And Moses and Aaron and the chief of the congregation numbered the sons of the Kohathites after their families, and after the house of their fathers,

35From thirty years old and upward even unto fifty years old, every one that entereth into the service, for the work in the tabernacle of the congregation:

36And those that were numbered of them by their families were two thousand seven hundred and fifty.

37These *were* they that were numbered of the families of the Kohathites, all that might do service in the tabernacle of the congregation, which Moses and Aaron did number according to the commandment of the LORD by the hand of Moses.

38And those that were numbered of the sons of Gershon, throughout their families, and by the house of their fathers,

39From thirty years old and upward even unto fifty years old, every one that entereth into the service, for the work in the tabernacle of the congregation,

40Even those that were numbered of them, throughout their families, by the house of their fathers, were two thousand and six hundred and thirty.

41These *are* they that were numbered of the families of the sons of Gershon, of all that might do service in the tabernacle of the congregation, whom Moses and Aaron did number according to the commandment of the LORD.

42And those that were numbered of the families of the sons of Merari, throughout their families, by the house of their fathers,

43From thirty years old and upward even unto fifty years old, every one that entereth into the service, for the work in the tabernacle of the congregation,

44Even those that were numbered of them after their families, were three thousand and two hundred.

45These *be* those that were numbered of the families of the sons of Merari, whom Moses and Aaron numbered according to the word of the LORD by the hand of Moses.

46All those that were numbered of the Levites, whom Moses and Aaron and the chief of Israel numbered, after their families, and after the house of their fathers,

47From thirty years old and upward even unto fifty years old, every one that came to do the service of the ministry, and the service of the burden in the tabernacle of the congregation,

48Even those that were numbered of them, were eight thousand and five hundred and fourscore.

49According to the commandment of the LORD they were numbered by the hand of Moses, every one according to his service, and according to his burden: thus were they numbered of him, as the LORD commanded Moses.

AND the LORD spake unto Moses, saying,

2Command the children of Israel, that they put out of the camp every leper, and every one that hath an issue, and whosoever is defiled by the dead:

3Both male and female shall ye put out, without the camp shall ye put them; that they defile not their camps, in the midst whereof I dwell.

4And the children of Israel did so, and put them out without the camp: as the LORD spake unto Moses, so did the children of Israel.

5And the LORD spake unto Moses, saying,

6Speak unto the children of Israel, When a man or woman shall commit any sin that men commit, to do a trespass against the LORD, and that person be guilty;

7Then they shall confess their sin which they have done: and he shall recompense his trespass with the principal thereof, and add unto it the fifth *part* thereof, and give *it* unto *him* against whom he hath trespassed.

8But if a man have no kinsman to recompense the trespass unto, let the trespass be recompensed unto the LORD, *even* to the priest; beside the ram of the atonement, whereby an atonement shall be made for him.

9And every offering of all the holy things of the children of Israel, which they bring unto the priest, shall be his.

10And every man's hallowed things shall be his: whatsoever any man giveth the priest, it shall be his.

11And the LORD spake unto Moses, saying,

12Speak unto the children of Israel, and say unto them, If any man's wife go aside; and commit a trespass against him,

13And a man lie with her carnally, and it be hid from the eyes of her husband, and be kept close, and she be defiled, and *there be* no witness against her, neither she be taken *with the manner;*

14And the spirit of jealousy come upon him, and he be jealous of his wife, and she be defiled: or if the spirit of jealousy come upon him, and he be jealous of his wife, and she be not defiled:

15Then shall the man bring his wife unto the priest, and he shall bring her offering for her, the tenth *part* of an ephah of barley meal; he shall pour no oil upon it, nor put frankincense thereon; for it *is* an offering of jealousy, an offering of memorial, bringing iniquity to remembrance.

16And the priest shall bring her near, and set her before the LORD:

17And the priest shall take holy water in an earthen vessel; and of the dust that is in the floor of the tabernacle the priest shall take, and put *it* into the water:

18And the priest shall set the woman before the LORD, and uncover the woman's head, and put the offering of memorial in her hands, which *is* the jealousy offering: and the priest shall have in his hand the bitter water that causeth the curse:

19And the priest shall charge her by an oath, and say unto the woman, If no man have lain with thee, and if thou hast not gone aside to uncleanness *with another* instead of thy husband, be thou free from this bitter water that causeth the curse:

20But if thou hast gone aside *to another* instead of thy husband, and if thou be defiled, and some man have lain with thee beside thine husband:

21Then the priest shall charge the woman with an oath of cursing, and the priest shall say unto the woman, The LORD make thee a curse and an oath among thy people, when the LORD doth make thy thigh to rot, and thy belly to swell;

22And this water that causeth the curse shall go into thy bowels, to make *thy* belly to swell, and *thy* thigh to rot: And the woman shall say, Amen, amen.

23And the priest shall write these curses in a book, and he shall blot *them* out with the bitter water:

24And he shall cause the woman to drink the bitter water that causeth the curse: and the water that causeth the curse shall enter into her, *and become* bitter.

25Then the priest shall take the jealousy offering out of the woman's hand, and shall wave the offering before the LORD, and offer it upon the altar:

26And the priest shall take an handful of the offering, *even* the memorial thereof, and burn *it* upon the altar, and afterward shall cause the woman to drink the water.

27And when he hath made her to drink the water, then it shall come to pass, *that,* if she be defiled, and have done trespass against her husband, that the water that causeth the curse shall enter into her, *and become* bitter, and her belly shall swell, and her thigh shall rot: and the woman shall be a curse among her people.

28And if the woman be not defiled, but be clean; then she shall be free, and shall conceive seed.

29This *is* the law of jealousies, when a wife goeth aside *to another* instead of her husband, and is defiled:

30Or when the spirit of jealousy cometh upon him, and he be jealous over his wife, and shall set the woman before the LORD, and the priest shall execute upon her all this law.

31Then shall the man be guiltless from iniquity, and this woman shall bear her iniquity.

MARK 12:18–37

THEN come unto him [Jesus] the Sadducees, which say there is no resurrection; and they asked him, saying,

19Master, Moses wrote unto us, If a man's brother die, and leave *his* wife *behind him,* and leave no children, that his brother should take his wife, and raise up seed unto his brother.

20Now there were seven brethren: and the first took a wife, and dying left no seed.

21And the second took her, and died, neither left he any seed: and the third likewise.

22And the seven had her, and left

no seed: last of all the woman died also.

23In the resurrection therefore, when they shall rise, whose wife shall she be of them? for the seven had her to wife.

24And Jesus answering said unto them, Do ye not therefore err, because ye know not the scriptures, neither the power of God?

25For when they shall rise from the dead, they neither marry, nor are given in marriage; but are as the angels which are in heaven.

26And as touching the dead, that they rise: have ye not read in the book of Moses, how in the bush God spake unto him, saying, I *am* the God of Abraham, and the God of Isaac, and the God of Jacob?

27He is not the God of the dead, but the God of the living: ye therefore do greatly err.

28And one of the scribes came, and having heard them reasoning together, and perceiving that he had answered them well, asked him, Which is the first commandment of all?

29And Jesus answered him, The first of all the commandments *is,* Hear, O Israel; The Lord our God is one Lord:

30And thou shalt love the Lord thy God with all thy heart, and with all thy soul, and with all thy mind, and with all thy strength: this *is* the first commandment.

31And the second *is* like, *namely* this, Thou shalt love thy neighbour as thyself. There is none other commandment greater than these.

32And the scribe said unto him, Well, Master, thou hast said the truth: for there is one God; and there is none other but he:

33And to love him with all the heart and with all the understanding, and with all the soul, and with all the strength, and to love *his* neighbour as himself, is more than all whole burnt offerings and sacrifices.

34And when Jesus saw that he answered discreetly, he said unto him, Thou art not far from the kingdom of God. And no man after that durst ask him *any question.*

35And Jesus answered and said, while he taught in the temple, How say the scribes that Christ is the son of David?

36For David himself said by the Holy Ghost, the LORD said to my Lord, Sit thou on my right hand, till I make thine enemies thy footstool.

37David therefore himself calleth him Lord; and whence is he *then* his son? And the common people heard him gladly.

PSALM 48:1–14

G REAT *is* the LORD, and greatly to be praised in the city of our God, *in* the mountain of his holiness.

2Beautiful for situation, the joy of the whole earth, *is* mount Zion, *on* the sides of the north, the city of the great King.

3God is known in her palaces for a refuge.

4For, lo, the kings were assembled, they passed by together.

5They saw *it, and* so they marvelled; they were troubled, *and* hasted away.

6Fear took hold upon them there, *and* pain, as of a woman in travail.

7Thou breakest the ships of Tarshish with an east wind.

8As we have heard, so have we seen in the city of the LORD of hosts, in the city of our God: God will establish it for ever. Selah.

9We have thought of thy lovingkindness, O God, in the midst of thy temple.

10According to thy name, O God, so *is* thy praise unto the ends of the earth: thy right hand is full of righteousness.

11Let mount Zion rejoice, let the daughters of Judah be glad, because of thy judgments.

12Walk about Zion, and go round about her: tell the towers thereof.

13Mark ye well her bulwarks, consider her palaces; that ye may tell *it* to the generation following.

14For this God *is* our God for ever and ever: he will be our guide *even* unto death.

PROVERBS FOR TODAY/ 10:26

As vinegar to the teeth, and as smoke to the eyes, so is *the sluggard to them that send him.*

MARCH 6

NUMBERS 6:1—7:89

AND the LORD spake unto Moses, saying,

2Speak unto the children of Israel, and say unto them, When either man or woman shall separate *themselves* to vow a vow of a Nazarite, to separate *themselves* unto the LORD:

3He shall separate *himself* from wine and strong drink, and shall drink no vinegar of wine, or vinegar of strong drink, neither shall he drink any liquor of grapes, nor eat moist grapes, or dried.

4All the days of his separation shall he eat nothing that is made of the vine tree, from the kernels even to the husk.

5All the days of the vow of his separation there shall no razor come upon his head: until the days be fulfilled, in the which he separateth *himself* unto the LORD, he shall be holy, *and* shall let the locks of the hair of his head grow.

6All the days that he separateth *himself* unto the LORD he shall come at no dead body.

7He shall not make himself unclean for his father, or for his mother, for his brother, or for his sister, when they die: because the consecration of his God *is* upon his head.

8All the days of his separation he *is* holy unto the LORD.

9And if any man die very suddenly by him, and he hath defiled the head of his consecration; then he shall shave his head in the day of his cleansing, on the seventh day shall he shave it.

10And on the eighth day he shall bring two turtles, or two young pigeons, to the priest, to the door of the tabernacle of the congregation:

11And the priest shall offer the one for a sin offering, and the other for a burnt offering, and make an atonement for him, for that he sinned by the dead, and shall hallow his head that same day.

12And he shall consecrate unto the LORD the days of his separation, and shall bring a lamb of the first year for a trespass offering: but the days that were before shall be lost, because his separation was defiled.

13And this *is* the law of the Nazarite, when the days of his separation are fulfilled: he shall be brought unto the door of the tabernacle of the congregation:

14And he shall offer his offering unto the LORD, one he lamb of the first year without blemish for a burnt offering, and one ewe lamb of the first year without blemish for a sin offering, and one ram without blemish for peace offerings,

15And a basket of unleavened bread,

cakes of fine flour mingled with oil, and wafers of unleavened bread anointed with oil, and their meat offering, and their drink offerings.

16And the priest shall bring *them* before the LORD, and shall offer his sin offering, and his burnt offering:

17And he shall offer the ram *for* a sacrifice of peace offerings unto the LORD, with the basket of unleavened bread: the priest shall offer also his meat offering, and his drink offering.

18And the Nazarite shall shave the head of his separation *at* the door of the tabernacle of the congregation, and shall take the hair of the head of his separation, and put *it* in the fire which *is* under the sacrifice of the peace offerings.

19And the priest shall take the sodden shoulder of the ram, and one unleavened cake out of the basket, and one unleavened wafer, and shall put *them* upon the hands of the Nazarite, after *the hair of* his separation is shaven:

20And the priest shall wave them *for* a wave offering before the LORD: this *is* holy for the priest, with the wave breast and heave shoulder: and after that the Nazarite may drink wine.

21This *is* the law of the Nazarite who hath vowed, *and of* his offering unto the LORD for his separation, beside *that* that his hand shall get: according to the vow which he vowed, so he must do after the law of his separation.

22And the LORD spake unto Moses, saying,

23Speak unto Aaron and unto his sons, saying, On this wise ye shall bless the children of Israel, saying unto them,

24The LORD bless thee, and keep thee:

25The LORD make his face shine upon thee, and be gracious unto thee:

26The LORD lift up his countenance upon thee, and give thee peace.

27And they shall put my name upon the children of Israel; and I will bless them.

AND it came to pass on the day that Moses had fully set up the tabernacle, and had anointed it, and sanctified it, and all the instruments thereof, both the altar and all the vessels thereof, and had anointed them, and sanctified them;

2That the princes of Israel, heads of the house of their fathers, who *were* the princes of the tribes, and were over them that were numbered, offered:

3And they brought their offering before the LORD, six covered wagons, and twelve oxen; a wagon for two of the princes, and for each one an ox: and they brought them before the tabernacle.

4And the LORD spake unto Moses, saying,

5Take *it* of them, that they may be to do the service of the tabernacle of the congregation; and thou shalt give them unto the Levites, to every man according to his service.

6And Moses took the wagons and the oxen, and gave them unto the Levites.

7Two wagons and four oxen he gave unto the sons of Gershon, according to their service:

8And four wagons and eight oxen he gave unto the sons of Merari, according unto their service, under the hand of Ithamar the son of Aaron the priest.

9But unto the sons of Kohath he gave none: because the service of the sanctuary belonging unto them *was that* they should bear upon their shoulders.

10And the princes offered for dedicating of the altar in the day that it was anointed, even the princes offered their offering before the altar.

11And the LORD said unto Moses, They shall offer their offering, each prince on his day, for the dedicating of the altar.

12And he that offered his offering the first day was Nahshon the son of Amminadab, of the tribe of Judah:

13And his offering *was* one silver

charger, the weight thereof *was* an hundred and thirty *shekels,* one silver bowl of seventy shekels, after the shekel of the sanctuary; both of them *were* full of fine flour mingled with oil for a meat offering:

14One spoon of ten *shekels* of gold, full of incense:

15One young bullock, one ram, one lamb of the first year, for a burnt offering:

16One kid of the goats for a sin offering:

17And for a sacrifice of peace offerings, two oxen, five rams, five he goats, five lambs of the first year: this *was* the offering of Nahshon the son of Amminadab.

18On the second day Nethaneel the son of Zuar, prince of Issachar, did offer:

19He offered *for* his offering one silver charger, the weight whereof *was* an hundred and thirty *shekels,* one silver bowl of seventy shekels, after the shekel of the sanctuary; both of them full of fine flour mingled with oil for a meat offering:

20One spoon of gold of ten *shekels,* full of incense:

21One young bullock, one ram, one lamb of the first year, for a burnt offering:

22One kid of the goats for a sin offering:

23And for a sacrifice of peace offerings, two oxen, five rams, five he goats, five lambs of the first year: this *was* the offering of Nethaneel the son of Zuar.

24On the third day Eliab the son of Helon, prince of the children of Zebulun, *did offer:*

25His offering *was* one silver charger, the weight whereof *was* an hundred and thirty *shekels,* one silver bowl of seventy shekels, after the shekel of the sanctuary; both of them full of fine flour mingled with oil for a meat offering:

26One golden spoon of ten *shekels,* full of incense:

27One young bullock, one ram, one lamb of the first year, for a burnt offering:

28One kid of the goats for a sin offering:

29And for a sacrifice of peace offerings, two oxen, five rams, five he goats, five lambs of the first year: this *was* the offering of Eliab the son of Helon.

30On the fourth day Elizur the son of Shedeur, prince of the children of Reuben, *did offer:*

31His offering *was* one silver charger of the weight of an hundred and thirty *shekels,* one silver bowl of seventy shekels, after the shekel of the sanctuary; both of them full of fine flour mingled with oil for a meat offering:

32One golden spoon of ten *shekels,* full of incense:

33One young bullock, one ram, one lamb of the first year, for a burnt offering:

34One kid of the goats for a sin offering:

35And for a sacrifice of peace offerings, two oxen, five rams, five he goats, five lambs of the first year: this *was* the offering of Elizur the son of Shedeur.

36On the fifth day Shelumiel the son of Zurishaddai, prince of the children of Simeon, *did offer:*

37His offering *was* one silver charger, the weight whereof *was* an hundred and thirty *shekels,* one silver bowl of seventy shekels, after the shekel of the sanctuary; both of them full of fine flour mingled with oil for a meat offering:

38One golden spoon of ten *shekels,* full of incense:

39One young bullock, one ram, one lamb of the first year, for a burnt offering:

40One kid of the goats for a sin offering:

41And for a sacrifice of peace offerings, two oxen, five rams, five he goats, five lambs of the first year: this *was* the offering of Shelumiel the son of Zurishaddai.

⁴²On the sixth day Eliasaph the son of Deuel, prince of the children of Gad, *offered:*

⁴³His offering *was* one silver charger of the weight of an hundred and thirty *shekels,* a silver bowl of seventy shekels, after the shekel of the sanctuary; both of them full of fine flour mingled with oil for a meat offering:

⁴⁴One golden spoon of ten *shekels,* full of incense:

⁴⁵One young bullock, one ram, one lamb of the first year, for a burnt offering:

⁴⁶One kid of the goats for a sin offering:

⁴⁷And for a sacrifice of peace offerings, two oxen, five rams, five he goats, five lambs of the first year: this *was* the offering of Eliasaph the son of Deuel.

⁴⁸On the seventh day Elishama the son of Ammihud, prince of the children of Ephraim, *offered:*

⁴⁹His offering *was* one silver charger, the weight whereof *was* an hundred and thirty *shekels,* one silver bowl of seventy shekels, after the shekel of the sanctuary; both of them full of fine flour mingled with oil for a meat offering:

⁵⁰One golden spoon of ten *shekels,* full of incense:

⁵¹One young bullock, one ram, one lamb of the first year, for a burnt offering:

⁵²One kid of the goats for a sin offering:

⁵³And for a sacrifice of peace offerings, two oxen, five rams, five he goats, five lambs of the first year: this *was* the offering of Elishama the son of Ammihud.

⁵⁴On the eighth day *offered* Gamaliel the son of Pedahzur, prince of the children of Manasseh:

⁵⁵His offering *was* one silver charger of the weight of an hundred and thirty *shekels,* one silver bowl of seventy shekels, after the shekel of the sanctuary; both of them full of fine flour mingled with oil for a meat offering:

⁵⁶One golden spoon of ten *shekels,* full of incense:

⁵⁷One young bullock, one ram, one lamb of the first year, for a burnt offering:

⁵⁸One kid of the goats for a sin offering:

⁵⁹And for a sacrifice of peace offerings, two oxen, five rams, five he goats, five lambs of the first year: this *was* the offering of Gamaliel the son of Pedahzur.

⁶⁰On the ninth day Abidan the son of Gideoni, prince of the children of Benjamin, *offered:*

⁶¹His offering *was* one silver charger, the weight whereof *was* an hundred and thirty *shekels,* one silver bowl of seventy shekels, after the shekel of the sanctuary; both of them full of fine flour mingled with oil for a meat offering:

⁶²One golden spoon of ten *shekels,* full of incense:

⁶³One young bullock, one ram, one lamb of the first year, for a burnt offering:

⁶⁴One kid of the goats for a sin offering:

⁶⁵And for a sacrifice of peace offerings, two oxen, five rams, five he goats, five lambs of the first year: this *was* the offering of Abidan the son of Gideoni.

⁶⁶On the tenth day Ahiezer the son of Ammishaddai, prince of the children of Dan, *offered:*

⁶⁷His offering *was* one silver charger, the weight whereof *was* an hundred and thirty *shekels,* one silver bowl of seventy shekels, after the shekel of the sanctuary; both of them full of fine flour mingled with oil for a meat offering:

⁶⁸One golden spoon of ten *shekels,* full of incense:

⁶⁹One young bullock, one ram, one lamb of the first year, for a burnt offering:

⁷⁰One kid of the goats for a sin offering:

⁷¹And for a sacrifice of peace offer-

ings, two oxen, five rams, five he goats, five lambs of the first year: this *was* the offering of Ahiezer the son of Ammishaddai.

72On the eleventh day Pagiel the son of Ocran, prince of the children of Asher, *offered:*

73His offering *was* one silver charger, the weight whereof *was* an hundred and thirty *shekels,* one silver bowl of seventy shekels, after the shekel of the sanctuary; both of them full of fine flour mingled with oil for a meat offering:

74One golden spoon of ten *shekels,* full of incense:

75One young bullock, one ram, one lamb of the first year, for a burnt offering:

76One kid of the goats for a sin offering:

77And for a sacrifice of peace offerings, two oxen, five rams, five he goats, five lambs of the first year: this *was* the offering of Pagiel the son of Ocran.

78On the twelfth day Ahira the son of Enan, prince of the children of Naphtali, *offered:*

79His offering *was* one silver charger, the weight whereof *was* an hundred and thirty *shekels,* one silver bowl of seventy shekels, after the shekel of the sanctuary; both of them full of fine flour mingled with oil for a meat offering:

80One golden spoon of ten *shekels,* full of incense:

81One young bullock, one ram, one lamb of the first year, for a burnt offering:

82One kid of the goats for a sin offering:

83And for a sacrifice of peace offerings, two oxen, five rams, five he goats, five lambs of the first year: this *was* the offering of Ahira the son of Enan.

84This *was* the dedication of the altar, in the day when it was anointed, by the princes of Israel: twelve chargers of silver, twelve silver bowls, twelve spoons of gold:

85Each charger of silver *weighing* an hundred and thirty *shekels,* each bowl seventy: all the silver vessels *weighed* two thousand and four hundred *shekels,* after the shekel of the sanctuary:

86The golden spoons *were* twelve, full of incense, *weighing* ten *shekels* apiece, after the shekel of the sanctuary: all the gold of the spoons *was* an hundred and twenty *shekels.*

87All the oxen for the burnt offering *were* twelve bullocks, the rams twelve, the lambs of the first year twelve, with their meat offering: and the kids of the goats for sin offering twelve.

88And all the oxen for the sacrifice of the peace offerings *were* twenty and four bullocks, the rams sixty, the he goats sixty, the lambs of the first year sixty. This *was* the dedication of the altar, after that it was anointed.

89And when Moses was gone into the tabernacle of the congregation to speak with him, then he heard the voice of one speaking unto him from off the mercy seat that *was* upon the ark of testimony, from between the two cherubims: and he spake unto him.

MARK 12:38—13:13

AND he [Jesus] said unto them in his doctrine, Beware of the scribes, which love to go in long clothing, and *love* salutations in the marketplaces,

39And the chief seats in the synagogues, and the uppermost rooms at feasts:

40Which devour widows' houses, and for a pretence make long prayers: these shall receive greater damnation.

41And Jesus sat over against the treasury, and beheld how the people cast money into the treasury: and many that were rich cast in much.

42And there came a certain poor widow, and she threw in two mites, which make a farthing.

43And he called *unto him* his disciples, and saith unto them, Verily I say unto you, That this poor widow hath cast more in, than all they which have cast into the treasury:

44For all *they* did cast in of their abundance; but she of her want did cast in all that she had, *even* all her living.

AND as he went out of the temple, one of his disciples saith unto him, Master, see what manner of stones and what buildings *are here!*

2And Jesus answering said unto him, Seest thou these great buildings? there shall not be left one stone upon another, that shall not be thrown down.

3And as he sat upon the mount of Olives over against the temple, Peter and James and John and Andrew asked him privately,

4Tell us, when shall these things be? and what *shall be* the sign when all these things shall be fulfilled?

5And Jesus answering them began to say, Take heed lest any *man* deceive you:

6For many shall come in my name, saying, I am *Christ;* and shall deceive many.

7And when ye shall hear of wars and rumours of wars, be ye not troubled: for *such things* must needs be; but the end *shall* not *be* yet.

8For nation shall rise against nation, and kingdom against kingdom: and there shall be earthquakes in divers places, and there shall be famines and troubles: these *are* the beginnings of sorrows.

9But take heed to yourselves: for they shall deliver you up to councils; and in the synagogues ye shall be beaten: and ye shall be brought before rulers and kings for my sake, for a testimony against them.

10And the gospel must first be published among all nations.

11But when they shall lead *you,* and deliver you up, take no thought beforehand what ye shall speak, neither do ye premeditate: but whatsoever shall be given you in that hour, that speak ye: for it is not ye that speak, but the Holy Ghost.

12Now the brother shall betray the brother to death, and the father the son; and children shall rise up against *their* parents, and shall cause them to be put to death.

13And ye shall be hated of all *men* for my name's sake: but he that shall endure unto the end, the same shall be saved.

PSALM 49:1–20

HEAR this, all *ye* people; give ear, all *ye* inhabitants of the world:
2Both low and high, rich and poor, together.

3My mouth shall speak of wisdom; and the meditation of my heart *shall be* of understanding.

4I will incline mine ear to a parable: I will open my dark saying upon the harp.

5Wherefore should I fear in the days of evil, *when* the iniquity of my heels shall compass me about?

6They that trust in their wealth, and boast themselves in the multitude of their riches;

7None *of them* can by any means redeem his brother, nor give to God a ransom for him:

8(For the redemption of their soul *is* precious, and it ceaseth for ever:)

9That he should still live for ever, *and* not see corruption.

10For he seeth *that* wise men die, likewise the fool and the brutish person perish, and leave their wealth to others.

11Their inward thought *is, that* their houses *shall continue* for ever, *and* their dwelling places to all generations; they call *their* lands after their own names.

12Nevertheless man *being* in honour abideth not: he is like the beasts *that* perish.

13This their way *is* their folly: yet their posterity approve their sayings. Selah.

14Like sheep they are laid in the grave; death shall feed on them; and the upright shall have dominion over them in the morning; and their beauty shall consume in the grave from their dwelling.

15But God will redeem my soul from the power of the grave: for he shall receive me. Selah.

16Be not thou afraid when one is made rich, when the glory of his house is increased;

17For when he dieth he shall carry nothing away: his glory shall not descend after him.

18Though while he lived he blessed his soul: and *men* will praise thee, when thou doest well to thyself.

19He shall go to the generation of his fathers; they shall never see light.

20Man *that is* in honour, and understandeth not, is like the beasts *that* perish.

PROVERBS FOR TODAY/ 10:27–28

The fear of the Lord *prolongeth days: but the years of the wicked shall be shortened.* □ *The hope of the righteous* shall be *gladness: but the expectation of the wicked shall perish.*

MARCH 7

NUMBERS 8:1—9:23

And the Lord spake unto Moses, saying,

2Speak unto Aaron, and say unto him, When thou lightest the lamps, the seven lamps shall give light over against the candlestick.

3And Aaron did so; he lighted the lamps thereof over against the candlestick, as the Lord commanded Moses.

4And this work of the candlestick *was of* beaten gold, unto the shaft thereof, unto the flowers thereof, *was* beaten work: according unto the pattern which the Lord had shewed Moses, so he made the candlestick.

5And the Lord spake unto Moses, saying,

6Take the Levites from among the children of Israel, and cleanse them.

7And thus shalt thou do unto them, to cleanse them: Sprinkle water of purifying upon them, and let them shave all their flesh, and let them wash their clothes, and *so* make themselves clean.

8Then let them take a young bullock with his meat offering, *even* fine flour mingled with oil, and another young bullock shalt thou take for a sin offering.

9And thou shalt bring the Levites before the tabernacle of the congregation: and thou shalt gather the whole assembly of the children of Israel together:

10And thou shalt bring the Levites before the Lord: and the children of Israel shall put their hands upon the Levites:

11And Aaron shall offer the Levites before the Lord *for* an offering of the children of Israel, that they may execute the service of the Lord.

12And the Levites shall lay their hands upon the heads of the bullocks: and thou shalt offer the one *for* a sin offering, and the other *for* a burnt offering, unto the Lord, to make an atonement for the Levites.

13And thou shalt set the Levites before Aaron, and before his sons, and offer them *for* an offering unto the LORD.

14Thus shalt thou separate the Levites from among the children of Israel: and the Levites shall be mine.

15And after that shall the Levites go in to do the service of the tabernacle of the congregation: and thou shalt cleanse them, and offer them *for* an offering.

16For they *are* wholly given unto me from among the children of Israel; instead of such as open every womb, *even instead of* the firstborn of all the children of Israel, have I taken them unto me.

17For all the firstborn of the children of Israel *are* mine, *both* man and beast: on the day that I smote every firstborn in the land of Egypt I sanctified them for myself.

18And I have taken the Levites for all the firstborn of the children of Israel.

19And I have given the Levites *as* a gift to Aaron and to his sons from among the children of Israel, to do the service of the children of Israel in the tabernacle of the congregation, and to make an atonement for the children of Israel: that there be no plague among the children of Israel, when the children of Israel come nigh unto the sanctuary.

20And Moses, and Aaron, and all the congregation of the children of Israel, did to the Levites according unto all that the LORD commanded Moses concerning the Levites, so did the children of Israel unto them.

21And the Levites were purified, and they washed their clothes; and Aaron offered them *as* an offering before the LORD; and Aaron made an atonement for them to cleanse them.

22And after that went the Levites in to do their service in the tabernacle of the congregation before Aaron, and before his sons: as the LORD had commanded Moses concerning the Levites, so did they unto them.

23And the LORD spake unto Moses, saying,

24This *is it* that *belongeth* unto the Levites: from twenty and five years old and upward they shall go in to wait upon the service of the tabernacle of the congregation:

25And from the age of fifty years they shall cease waiting upon the service *thereof,* and shall serve no more:

26But shall minister with their brethren in the tabernacle of the congregation, to keep the charge, and shall do no service. Thus shalt thou do unto the Levites touching their charge.

AND the LORD spake unto Moses in the wilderness of Sinai, in the first month of the second year after they were come out of the land of Egypt, saying,

2Let the children of Israel also keep the passover at his appointed season.

3In the fourteenth day of this month, at even, ye shall keep it in his appointed season: according to all the rites of it, and according to all the ceremonies thereof, shall ye keep it.

4And Moses spake unto the children of Israel, that they should keep the passover.

5And they kept the passover on the fourteenth day of the first month at even in the wilderness of Sinai: according to all that the LORD commanded Moses, so did the children of Israel.

6And there were certain men, who were defiled by the dead body of a man, that they could not keep the passover on that day: and they came before Moses and before Aaron on that day:

7And those men said unto him, We *are* defiled by the dead body of a man: wherefore are we kept back, that we may not offer an offering of the LORD in his appointed season among the children of Israel?

8And Moses said unto them, Stand still, and I will hear what the LORD will command concerning you.

9And the LORD spake unto Moses, saying,

10Speak unto the children of Israel, saying, If any man of you or of your posterity shall be unclean by reason of a dead body, or *be* in a journey afar off, yet he shall keep the passover unto the LORD.

11The fourteenth day of the second month at even they shall keep it, *and* eat it with unleavened bread and bitter *herbs.*

12They shall leave none of it unto the morning, nor break any bone of it: according to all the ordinances of the passover they shall keep it.

13But the man that *is* clean, and is not in a journey, and forbeareth to keep the passover, even the same soul shall be cut off from among his people: because he brought not the offering of the LORD in his appointed season, that man shall bear his sin.

14And if a stranger shall sojourn among you, and will keep the passover unto the LORD; according to the ordinance of the passover, and according to the manner thereof, so shall he do: ye shall have one ordinance, both for the stranger, and for him that was born in the land.

15And on the day that the tabernacle was reared up the cloud covered the tabernacle, *namely,* the tent of the testimony: and at even there was upon the tabernacle as it were the appearance of fire, until the morning.

16So it was alway: the cloud covered it *by day,* and the appearance of fire by night.

17And when the cloud was taken up from the tabernacle, then after that the children of Israel journeyed: and in the place where the cloud abode, there the children of Israel pitched their tents.

18At the commandment of the LORD the children of Israel journeyed, and at the commandment of the LORD they pitched: as long as the cloud abode upon the tabernacle they rested in their tents.

19And when the cloud tarried long upon the tabernacle many days, then the children of Israel kept the charge of the LORD, and journeyed not.

20And *so* it was, when the cloud was a few days upon the tabernacle; according to the commandment of the LORD they abode in their tents, and according to the commandment of the LORD they journeyed.

21And *so* it was, when the cloud abode from even unto the morning, and *that* the cloud was taken up in the morning, then they journeyed: whether *it was* by day or by night that the cloud was taken up, they journeyed.

22Or *whether it were* two days, or a month, or a year, that the cloud tarried upon the tabernacle, remaining thereon, the children of Israel abode in their tents, and journeyed not: but when it was taken up, they journeyed.

23At the commandment of the LORD they rested in the tents, and at the commandment of the LORD they journeyed: they kept the charge of the LORD, at the commandment of the LORD by the hand of Moses.

MARK 13:14–37

BUT when ye shall see the abomination of desolation, spoken of by Daniel the prophet, standing where it ought not, (let him that readeth understand,) then let them that be in Judaea flee to the mountains:

15And let him that is on the housetop not go down into the house, neither enter *therein,* to take any thing out of his house:

16And let him that is in the field not turn back again for to take up his garment.

17But woe to them that are with child, and to them that give suck in those days!

18And pray ye that your flight be not in the winter.

19For *in* those days shall be affliction,

such as was not from the beginning of the creation which God created unto this time, neither shall be.

20And except that the Lord had shortened those days, no flesh should be saved: but for the elect's sake, whom he hath chosen, he hath shortened the days.

21And then if any man shall say to you, Lo, here *is* Christ; or, lo, *he is* there; believe *him* not:

22For false Christs and false prophets shall rise, and shall shew signs and wonders, to seduce, if *it were* possible, even the elect.

23But take ye heed: behold, I have foretold you all things.

24But in those days, after that tribulation, the sun shall be darkened, and the moon shall not give her light,

25And the stars of heaven shall fall, and the powers that are in heaven shall be shaken.

26And then shall they see the Son of man coming in the clouds with great power and glory.

27And then shall he send his angels, and shall gather together his elect from the four winds, from the uttermost part of the earth to the uttermost part of heaven.

28Now learn a parable of the fig tree; When her branch is yet tender, and putteth forth leaves, ye know that summer is near:

29So ye in like manner, when ye shall see these things come to pass, know that it is nigh, *even* at the doors.

30Verily I say unto you, that this generation shall not pass, till all these things be done.

31Heaven and earth shall pass away: but my words shall not pass away.

32But of that day and *that* hour knoweth no man, no, not the angels which are in heaven, neither the Son, but the Father.

33Take ye heed, watch and pray: for ye know not when the time is.

34*For the Son of man is* as a man taking a far journey, who left his house, and gave authority to his servants, and to every man his work, and commanded the porter to watch.

35Watch ye therefore: for ye know not when the master of the house cometh, at even, or at midnight, or at the cockcrowing, or in the morning:

36Lest coming suddenly he find you sleeping.

37And what I say unto you I say unto all, Watch.

PSALM 50:1–23

THE mighty God, *even* the LORD, hath spoken, and called the earth from the rising of the sun unto the going down thereof.

2Out of Zion, the perfection of beauty, God hath shined.

3Our God shall come, and shall not keep silence: a fire shall devour before him, and it shall be very tempestuous round about him.

4He shall call to the heavens from above, and to the earth, that he may judge his people.

5Gather my saints together unto me; those that have made a covenant with me by sacrifice.

6And the heavens shall declare his righteousness: for God *is* judge himself. Selah.

7Hear, O my people, and I will speak; O Israel, and I will testify against thee: I *am* God, *even* thy God.

8I will not reprove thee for thy sacrifices or thy burnt offerings, *to have been* continually before me.

9I will take no bullock out of thy house, *nor* he goats out of thy folds.

10For every beast of the forest *is* mine, *and* the cattle upon a thousand hills.

11I know all the fowls of the mountains: and the wild beasts of the field *are* mine.

12If I were hungry, I would not tell thee: for the world *is* mine, and the fulness thereof.

13Will I eat the flesh of bulls, or drink the blood of goats?

14Offer unto God thanksgiving; and pay thy vows unto the most High:

15And call upon me in the day of trouble: I will deliver thee, and thou shalt glorify me.

16But unto the wicked God saith, What hast thou to do to declare my statutes, or *that* thou shouldest take my covenant in thy mouth?

17Seeing thou hatest instruction, and casteth my words behind thee.

18When thou sawest a thief, then thou consentedst with him, and hast been partaker with adulterers.

19Thou givest thy mouth to evil, and thy tongue frameth deceit.

20Thou sittest *and* speakest against thy brother; thou slanderest thine own mother's son.

21These *things* hast thou done, and I kept silence; thou thoughtest that I was altogether *such an one* as thyself: *but* I will reprove thee, and set *them* in order before thine eyes.

22Now consider this, ye that forget God, lest I tear *you* in pieces, and *there be* none to deliver.

23Whoso offereth praise glorifieth me: and to him that ordereth *his* conversation *aright* will I shew the salvation of God.

PROVERBS FOR TODAY/ 10:29–30

The way of the LORD is *strength to the upright: but destruction* shall be *to the workers of iniquity.* □ *The righteous shall never be removed: but the wicked shall not inhabit the earth.*

MARCH 8

NUMBERS 10:1—11:23

AND the LORD spake unto Moses, saying,

2Make thee two trumpets of silver; of a whole piece shalt thou make them: that thou mayest use them for the calling of the assembly, and for the journeying of the camps.

3And when they shall blow with them, all the assembly shall assemble themselves to thee at the door of the tabernacle of the congregation.

4And if they blow *but* with one *trumpet,* then the princes, *which are* heads of the thousands of Israel, shall gather themselves unto thee.

5When ye blow an alarm, then the camps that lie on the east parts shall go forward.

6When ye blow an alarm the second time, then the camps that lie on the south side shall take their journey: they shall blow an alarm for their journeys.

7But when the congregation is to be gathered together, ye shall blow, but ye shall not sound an alarm.

8And the sons of Aaron, the priests, shall blow with the trumpets; and they shall be to you for an ordinance for ever throughout your generations.

9And if ye go to war in your land against the enemy that oppresseth you, then ye shall blow an alarm with the trumpets; and ye shall be remembered before the LORD your God, and ye shall be saved from your enemies.

10Also in the day of your gladness, and in your solemn days, and in the beginnings of your months, ye shall blow with the trumpets over your burnt offerings, and over the sacrifices of your peace offerings; that they may be to you for a memorial before your God: I *am* the LORD your God.

11And it came to pass on the twentieth *day* of the second month, in the second year, that the cloud was taken up from off the tabernacle of the testimony.

12And the children of Israel took their journeys out of the wilderness of Sinai: and the cloud rested in the wilderness of Paran.

13And they first took their journey according to the commandment of the LORD by the hand of Moses.

14In the first *place* went the standard of the camp of the children of Judah according to their armies: and over his host *was* Nahshon the son of Amminadab.

15And over the host of the tribe of the children of Issachar *was* Nethaneel the son of Zuar.

16And over the host of the tribe of the children of Zebulun *was* Eliab the son of Helon.

17And the tabernacle was taken down; and the sons of Gershon and the sons of Merari set forward, bearing the tabernacle.

18And the standard of the camp of Reuben set forward according to their armies: and over his host *was* Elizur the son of Shedeur.

19And over the host of the tribe of the children of Simeon *was* Shelumiel the son of Zurishaddai.

20And over the host of the tribe of the children of Gad *was* Eliasaph the son of Deuel.

21And the Kohathites set forward, bearing the sanctuary: and *the other* did set up the tabernacle against they came.

22And the standard of the camp of the children of Ephraim set forward according to their armies: and over his host *was* Elishama the son of Ammihud.

23And over the host of the tribe of the children of Manasseh *was* Gamaliel the son of Pedahzur.

24And over the host of the tribe of the children of Benjamin *was* Abidan the son of Gideoni.

25And the standard of the camp of the children of Dan set forward, *which was* the rereward of all the camps throughout their hosts: and over his host *was* Ahiezer the son of Ammishaddi.

26And over the host of the tribe of the children of Asher *was* Pagiel the son of Ocran.

27And over the host of the tribe of the children of Naphtali *was* Ahira the son of Enan.

28Thus *were* the journeyings of the children of Israel according to their armies, when they set forward.

29And Moses said unto Hobab, the son of Raguel the Midianite, Moses' father in law, We are journeying unto the place of which the LORD said, I will give it you: come thou with us, and we will do thee good: for the LORD hath spoken good concerning Israel.

30And he said unto him, I will not go; but I will depart to mine own land, and to my kindred.

31And he said, Leave us not, I pray thee; forasmuch as thou knowest how we are to encamp in the wilderness, and thou mayest be to us instead of eyes.

32And it shall be, if thou go with us, yea, it shall be, that what goodness the LORD shall do unto us, the same will we do unto thee.

33And they departed from the mount of the LORD three days' journey: and the ark of the covenant of the LORD went before them in the three days' journey, to search out a resting place for them.

34And the cloud of the LORD *was* upon them by day, when they went out of the camp.

35And it came to pass, when the ark set forward, that Moses said, Rise up, LORD, and let thine enemies be scattered; and let them that hate thee flee before thee.

36And when it rested, he said, Return, O LORD, unto the many thousands of Israel.

AND *when* the people complained, it displeased the LORD: and the LORD heard *it;* and his anger was kindled; and the fire of the LORD burnt among them, and consumed *them that were* in the uttermost parts of the camp.

2And the people cried unto Moses; and when Moses prayed unto the LORD, the fire was quenched.

3And he called the name of the place Taberah: because the fire of the LORD burnt among them.

4And the mixt multitude that *was* among them fell a lusting: and the children of Israel also wept again, and said, Who shall give us flesh to eat?

5We remember the fish, which we did eat in Egypt freely; the cucumbers, and the melons, and the leeks, and the onions, and the garlick:

6But now our soul *is* dried away: *there is* nothing at all, beside this manna, *before* our eyes.

7And the manna *was* as coriander seed, and the colour thereof as the colour of bdellium.

8*And* the people went about, and gathered *it,* and ground *it* in mills, or beat *it* in a mortar, and baked *it* in pans, and made cakes of it: and the taste of it was as the taste of fresh oil.

9And when the dew fell upon the camp in the night, the manna fell upon it.

10Then Moses heard the people weep throughout their families, every man in the door of his tent: and the anger of the LORD was kindled greatly; Moses also was displeased.

11And Moses said unto the LORD, Wherefore hast thou afflicted thy servant? and wherefore have I not found favour in thy sight, that thou layest the burden of all this people upon me?

12Have I conceived all this people? have I begotten them, that thou shouldest say unto me, Carry them in thy bosom, as a nursing father beareth the sucking child, unto the land which thou swarest unto their fathers?

13Whence should I have flesh to give unto all this people? for they weep unto me, saying, Give us flesh, that we may eat.

14I am not able to bear all this people alone, because *it is* too heavy for me.

15And if thou deal thus with me, kill me, I pray thee, out of hand, if I have found favour in thy sight; and let me not see my wretchedness.

16And the LORD said unto Moses, Gather unto me seventy men of the elders of the people, whom thou knowest to be the elders of the people, and officers over them; and bring them unto the tabernacle of the congregation, that they may stand there with thee.

17And I will come down and talk with thee there: and I will take of the spirit which *is* upon thee, and will put *it* upon them; and they shall bear the burden of the people with thee, that thou bear *it* not thyself alone.

18And say thou unto the people, Sanctify yourselves against to morrow, and ye shall eat flesh: for ye have wept in the ears of the LORD, saying, Who shall give us flesh to eat? for *it was* well with us in Egypt: therefore the LORD will give you flesh, and ye shall eat.

19Ye shall not eat one day, nor two days, nor five days, neither ten days, nor twenty days;

20*But* even a whole month, until it come out at your nostrils, and it be loathsome unto you: because that ye have despised the LORD which *is* among you, and have wept before him, saying,

Why came we forth out of Egypt?

21And Moses said, The people, among whom I *am, are* six hundred thousand footmen; and thou hast said, I will give them flesh, that they may eat a whole month.

22Shall the flocks and the herds be slain for them, to suffice them? or shall all the fish of the sea be gathered together for them, to suffice them?

23And the LORD said unto Moses, Is the LORD's hand waxed short? thou shalt see now whether my word shall come to pass unto thee or not.

MARK 14:1-21

AFTER two days was *the feast of* the passover, and of unleavened bread: and the chief priests and the scribes sought how they might take him [Jesus] by craft, and put *him* to death.

2But they said, Not on the feast *day,* lest there be an uproar of the people.

3And being in Bethany in the house of Simon the leper, as he sat at meat, there came a woman having an alabaster box of ointment of spikenard very precious; and she brake the box, and poured *it* on his head.

4And there were some that had indignation within themselves, and said, Why was this waste of the ointment made?

5For it might have been sold for more than three hundred pence, and have been given to the poor. And they murmured against her.

6And Jesus said, Let her alone; why trouble ye her? she hath wrought a good work on me.

7For ye have the poor with you always, and whensoever ye will ye may do them good: but me ye have not always.

8She hath done what she could: she is come aforehand to anoint my body to the burying.

9Verily I say unto you, Wheresoever this gospel shall be preached throughout the whole world, this also that she hath done shall be spoken of for a memorial of her.

10And Judas Iscariot, one of the twelve, went unto the chief priests, to betray him unto them.

11And when they heard *it,* they were glad, and promised to give him money. And he sought how he might conveniently betray him.

12And the first day of unleavened bread, when they killed the passover, his disciples said unto him, Where wilt thou that we go and prepare that thou mayest eat the passover?

13And he sendeth forth two of his disciples, and saith unto them, Go ye into the city, and there shall meet you a man bearing a pitcher of water: follow him.

14And wheresoever he shall go in, say ye to the goodman of the house, The Master saith, Where is the guestchamber, where I shall eat the passover with my disciples?

15And he will shew you a large upper room furnished *and* prepared: there make ready for us.

16And his disciples went forth, and came into the city, and found as he had said unto them: and they made ready the passover.

17And in the evening he cometh with the twelve.

18And as they sat and did eat, Jesus said, Verily I say unto you, One of you which eateth with me shall betray me.

19And they began to be sorrowful, and to say unto him one by one, *Is* it I? and another *said, Is* it I?

20And he answered and said unto them, *It is* one of the twelve, that dippeth with me in the dish.

21The Son of man indeed goeth, as it is written of him: but woe to that man by whom the Son of man is betrayed! good were it for that man if he had never been born.

PSALM 51:1–19

HAVE mercy upon me, O God, according to thy lovingkindness: according unto the multitude of thy tender mercies blot out my transgressions.

2Wash me throughly from mine iniquity, and cleanse me from my sin.

3For I acknowledge my transgressions: and my sin *is* ever before me.

4Against thee, thee only, have I sinned, and done *this* evil in thy sight: that thou mightest be justified when thou speakest, *and* be clear when thou judgest.

5Behold, I was shapen in iniquity; and in sin did my mother conceive me.

6Behold, thou desirest truth in the inward parts: and in the hidden *part* thou shalt make me to know wisdom.

7Purge me with hyssop, and I shall be clean: wash me, and I shall be whiter than snow.

8Make me to hear joy and gladness; *that* the bones *which* thou hast broken may rejoice.

9Hide thy face from my sins, and blot out all mine iniquities.

10Create in me a clean heart, O God;

and renew a right spirit within me.

11Cast me not away from thy presence; and take not thy holy spirit from me.

12Restore unto me the joy of thy salvation; and uphold me *with thy* free spirit.

13*Then* will I teach transgressors thy ways; and sinners shall be converted unto thee.

14Deliver me from bloodguiltiness, O God, thou God of my salvation: *and* my tongue shall sing aloud of thy righteousness.

15O Lord, open thou my lips; and my mouth shall shew forth thy praise.

16For thou desirest not sacrifice; else would I give *it:* thou delightest not in burnt offering.

17The sacrifices of God *are* a broken spirit: a broken and a contrite heart, O God, thou wilt not despise.

18Do good in thy good pleasure unto Zion: build thou the walls of Jerusalem.

19Then shalt thou be pleased with the sacrifices of righteousness, with burnt offering and whole burnt offering: then shall they offer bullocks upon thine altar.

PROVERBS FOR TODAY/ 10:31–32

The mouth of the just bringeth forth wisdom: but the froward tongue shall be cut out. The lips of the righteous know what is acceptable: but the mouth of the wicked speaketh frowardness.

MARCH 9

NUMBERS 11:24—13:33

AND Moses went out, and told the people the words of the LORD, and gathered the seventy men of the elders of the people, and set them round about the tabernacle.

25And the LORD came down in a cloud, and spake unto him, and took of the spirit that *was* upon him, and gave *it* unto the seventy elders: and it came to pass, *that,* when the spirit rested upon them, they prophesied, and did not cease.

26But there remained two *of the* men in the camp, the name of the one *was* Eldad, and the name of the other Medad: and the spirit rested upon them; and they *were* of them that were written, but went not out unto the tabernacle: and they prophesied in the camp.

27And there ran a young man, and told Moses, and said, Eldad and Medad do prophesy in the camp.

28And Joshua the son of Nun, the servant of Moses, *one* of his young men, answered and said, My lord Moses, forbid them.

29And Moses said unto him, Enviest thou for my sake? would God that all the LORD's people were prophets, *and* that the LORD would put his spirit upon them!

30And Moses gat him into the camp, he and the elders of Israel.

31And there went forth a wind from the LORD, and brought quails from the sea, and let *them* fall by the camp, as it were a day's journey on this side, and as it were a day's journey on the other side, round about the camp, and as it were two cubits *high* upon the face of the earth.

32And the people stood up all that day, and all *that* night, and all the next day, and they gathered the quails: he that gathered least gathered ten homers: and they spread *them* all abroad for themselves round about the camp.

33And while the flesh *was* yet between their teeth, ere it was chewed, the wrath of the LORD was kindled against the people, and the LORD smote the people with a very great plague.

34And he called the name of that place Kibroth–hattaavah: because there they buried the people that lusted.

35And the people journeyed from Kibroth–hattaavah unto Hazeroth; and abode at Hazeroth.

AND Miriam and Aaron spake against Moses because of the Ethiopian woman whom he had married: for he had married an Ethiopian woman.

2And they said, Hath the LORD indeed spoken only by Moses? hath he not spoken also by us? And the LORD heard *it.*

3(Now the man Moses *was* very meek, above all the men which *were* upon the face of the earth.)

4And the LORD spake suddenly unto Moses, and unto Aaron, and unto Miriam, Come out ye three unto the tabernacle of the congregation. And they three came out.

5And the LORD came down in the pillar of the cloud, and stood *in* the door of the tabernacle, and called Aaron and Miriam: and they both came forth.

6And he said, Hear now my words: If there be a prophet among you, *I* the LORD will make myself known unto him in a vision, *and* will speak unto him in a dream.

7My servant Moses *is* not so, who *is* faithful in all mine house.

8With him will I speak mouth to mouth, even apparently, and not in dark speeches; and the similitude of the LORD shall he behold: wherefore then were ye not afraid to speak against my servant Moses?

9And the anger of the LORD was kindled against them; and he departed.

10And the cloud departed from off the tabernacle; and, behold, Miriam *became* leprous, *white* as snow: and Aaron looked upon Miriam, and, behold, *she was* leprous.

11And Aaron said unto Moses, Alas, my lord, I beseech thee, lay not the sin upon us, wherein we have done foolishly, and wherein we have sinned.

12Let her not be as one dead, of whom the flesh is half consumed when he cometh out of his mother's womb.

13And Moses cried unto the LORD, saying Heal her now, O God, I beseech thee.

14And the LORD said unto Moses, If her father had but spit in her face, should she not be ashamed seven days? let her be shut out from the camp seven days, and after that let her be received in *again*.

15And Miriam was shut out from the camp seven days: and the people journeyed not till Miriam was brought in *again*.

16And afterward the people removed from Hazeroth, and pitched in the wilderness of Paran.

AND the LORD spake unto Moses, saying,

2Send thou men, that they may search the land of Canaan, which I give unto the children of Israel: of every tribe of their fathers shall ye send a man, every one a ruler among them.

3And Moses by the commandment of the LORD sent them from the wilderness of Paran: all those men *were* heads of the children of Israel.

4And these *were* their names: of the tribe of Reuben, Shammua the son of Zaccur.

5Of the tribe of Simeon, Shaphat the son of Hori.

6Of the tribe of Judah, Caleb the son of Jephunneh.

7Of the tribe of Issachar, Igal the son of Joseph.

8Of the tribe of Ephraim, Oshea the son of Nun.

9Of the tribe of Benjamin, Palti the son of Raphu.

10Of the tribe of Zebulun, Gaddiel the son of Sodi.

11Of the tribe of Joseph, *namely,* of the tribe of Manasseh, Gaddi the son of Susi.

12Of the tribe of Dan, Ammiel the son of Gemalli.

13Of the tribe of Asher, Sethur the son of Michael.

14Of the tribe of Naphtali, Nahbi the son of Vophsi.

15Of the tribe of Gad, Geuel the son of Machi.

16These *are* the names of the men which Moses sent to spy out the land. And Moses called Oshea the son of Nun Jehoshua.

17And Moses sent them to spy out the land of Canaan, and said unto them, Get you up this *way* southward, and go up into the mountain:

18And see the land, what it *is;* and the people that dwelleth therein, whether they *be* strong or weak, few or many;

19And what the land *is* that they dwell in, whether it *be* good or bad; and what cities *they be* that they dwell in, whether in tents, or in strong holds;

20And what the land *is,* whether it *be* fat or lean, whether there be wood therein, or not. And be ye of good courage, and bring of the fruit of the land. Now the time *was* the time of the firstripe grapes.

21So they went up, and searched the land from the wilderness of Zin unto Rehob, as men come to Hamath.

22And they ascended by the south, and came unto Hebron; where Ahiman, Sheshai, and Talmai, the children of Anak, *were.* (Now Hebron was built seven years before Zoan in Egypt.)

23And they came unto the brook of Eshcol, and cut down from thence a branch with one cluster of grapes, and they bare it between two upon a staff; and *they brought* of the pomegranates, and of the figs.

24The place was called the brook Eshcol, because of the cluster of grapes which the children of Israel cut down from thence.

25And they returned from searching of the land after forty days.

26And they went and came to Moses, and to Aaron, and to all the congregation of the children of Israel, unto the wilderness of Paran, to Kadesh; and brought back word unto them, and unto all the congregation, and shewed them the fruit of the land.

27And they told him, and said, We came unto the land whither thou sentest us, and surely it floweth with milk and honey; and this *is* the fruit of it.

28Nevertheless the people *be* strong that dwell in the land, and the cities *are* walled, *and* very great: and moreover we saw the children of Anak there.

29The Amalekites dwell in the land of the south: and the Hittites, and the Jebusites, and the Amorites, dwell in the mountains: and the Canaanites dwell by the sea, and by the coast of Jordan.

30And Caleb stilled the people before Moses, and said, Let us go up at once, and possess it; for we are well able to overcome it.

31But the men that went up with him said, We be not able to go up against the people; for they *are* stronger than we.

32And they brought up an evil report of the land which they had searched unto the children of Israel, saying, The land, through which we have gone to search it, is a land that eateth up the inhabitants thereof; and all the people that we saw in it *are* men of a great stature.

33And there we saw the giants, the sons of Anak, *which come* of the giants: and we were in our own sight as grasshoppers, and so we were in their sight.

MARK 14:22–52

AND as they did eat, Jesus took bread, and blessed, and brake *it,* and gave to them [the disciples], and said, Take, eat: this is my body.

23And he took the cup, and when he had given thanks, he gave *it* to them: and they all drank of it.

24And he said unto them, This is my blood of the new testament, which is shed for many.

25Verily I say unto you, I will drink no more of the fruit of the vine, until that day that I drink it new in the kingdom of God.

26And when they had sung an hymn, they went out into the mount of Olives.

27And Jesus saith unto them, All ye shall be offended because of me this night: for it is written, I will smite the shepherd, and the sheep shall be scattered.

28But after that I am risen, I will go before you into Galilee.

29But Peter said unto him, Although all shall be offended, yet *will* not I.

30And Jesus saith unto him, Verily I say unto thee, That this day, *even* in this night, before the cock crow twice, thou shalt deny me thrice.

31But he spake the more vehemently, If I should die with thee, I will not deny thee in any wise. Likewise also said they all.

32And they came to a place which was named Gethsemane: and he saith to his disciples, Sit ye here, while I shall pray.

33And he taketh with him Peter and James and John, and began to be sore amazed, and to be very heavy;

34And saith unto them, My soul is exceeding sorrowful unto death: tarry ye here, and watch.

35And he went forward a little, and fell on the ground, and prayed that, if it were possible, the hour might pass from him.

36And he said, Abba, Father, all things *are* possible unto thee; take away this cup from me: nevertheless not what I will, but what thou wilt.

37And he cometh, and findeth them sleeping, and saith unto Peter, Simon, sleepest thou? couldest not thou watch one hour?

38Watch ye and pray, lest ye enter into temptation. The spirit truly *is* ready, but the flesh *is* weak.

39And again he went away, and prayed, and spake the same words.

40And when he returned, he found them asleep again, (for their eyes were heavy,) neither wist they what to answer him.

41And he cometh the third time, and

saith unto them, Sleep on now, and take *your* rest: it is enough, the hour is come; behold, the Son of man is betrayed into the hands of sinners.

42Rise up, let us go; lo, he that betrayeth me is at hand.

43And immediately, while he yet spake, cometh Judas, one of the twelve, and with him a great multitude with swords and staves, from the chief priests and the scribes and the elders.

44And he that betrayed him had given them a token, saying, Whomsoever I shall kiss, that same is he; take him, and lead *him* away safely.

45And as soon as he was come, he goeth straightway to him, and saith, Master, master; and kissed him.

46And they laid their hands on him, and took him.

47And one of them that stood by drew a sword, and smote a servant of the high priest, and cut off his ear.

48And Jesus answered and said unto them, Are ye come out, as against a thief, with swords and *with* staves to take me?

49I was daily with you in the temple teaching, and ye took me not: but the scriptures must be fulfilled.

50And they all forsook him, and fled.

51And there followed him a certain young man, having a linen cloth cast about *his* naked *body;* and the young

men laid hold on him:

52And he left the linen cloth, and fled from them naked.

PSALM 52:1–9

WHY boastest thou thyself in mischief, O mighty man? the goodness of God *endureth* continually.

2Thy tongue deviseth mischiefs; like a sharp razor, working deceitfully.

3Thou lovest evil more than good; *and* lying rather than to speak righteousness. Selah.

4Thou lovest all devouring words, O *thou* deceitful tongue.

5God shall likewise destroy thee for ever, he shall take thee away, and pluck thee out of *thy* dwelling place, and root thee out of the land of the living. Selah.

6The righteous also shall see, and fear, and shall laugh at him:

7Lo, *this is* the man *that* made not God his strength; but trusted in the abundance of his riches, *and* strengthened himself in his wickedness.

8But I *am* like a green olive tree in the house of God: I trust in the mercy of God for ever and ever.

9I will praise thee for ever, because thou hast done *it:* and I will wait on thy name; for *it is* good before thy saints.

PROVERBS FOR TODAY/ 11:1–3

A false balance is *abomination to the LORD: but a just weight* is *his delight.* □ When *pride cometh, then cometh shame: but with the lowly* is *wisdom.* □ *The integrity of the upright shall guide them: but the perverseness of transgressors shall destroy them.*

MARCH 10

NUMBERS 14:1—15:16

AND all the congregation lifted up their voice, and cried; and the people wept that night.

2And all the children of Israel murmured against Moses and against Aaron: and the whole congregation said unto them, Would God that we had died in the land of Egypt! or would God we had died in this wilderness!

3And wherefore hath the LORD brought us unto this land, to fall by the sword, that our wives and our children should be a prey? were it not better for us to return into Egypt?

4And they said one to another, Let us make a captain, and let us return into Egypt.

5Then Moses and Aaron fell on their faces before all the assembly of the congregation of the children of Israel.

6And Joshua the son of Nun, and Caleb the son of Jephunneh, *which were* of them that searched the land, rent their clothes:

7And they spake unto all the company of the children of Israel, saying, The land, which we passed through to search it, *is* an exceeding good land.

8If the LORD delight in us, then he will bring us into this land, and give it us; a land which floweth with milk and honey.

9Only rebel not ye against the LORD, neither fear ye the people of the land; for they *are* bread for us: their defence is departed from them, and the LORD *is* with us: fear them not.

10But all the congregation bade stone them with stones. And the glory of the LORD appeared in the tabernacle of the congregation before all the children of Israel.

11And the LORD said unto Moses, How long will this people provoke me?

and how long will it be ere they believe me, for all the signs which I have shewed among them?

12I will smite them with the pestilence, and disinherit them, and will make of thee a greater nation and mightier than they.

13And Moses said unto the LORD, Then the Egyptians shall hear *it,* (for thou broughtest up this people in thy might from among them;)

14And they will tell *it* to the inhabitants of this land: *for* they have heard that thou LORD *art* among this people, that thou LORD art seen face to face, and *that* thy cloud standeth over them, and *that* thou goest before them, by day time in a pillar of a cloud, and in a pillar of fire by night.

15Now *if* thou shalt kill *all* this people as one man, then the nations which have heard the fame of thee will speak, saying,

16Because the LORD was not able to bring this people into the land which he sware unto them, therefore he hath slain them in the wilderness.

17And now, I beseech thee, let the power of my Lord be great, according as thou hast spoken, saying,

18The LORD *is* longsuffering, and of great mercy, forgiving iniquity and transgression, and by no means clearing *the guilty,* visiting the iniquity of the fathers upon the children unto the third and fourth *generation.*

19Pardon, I beseech thee, the iniquity of this people according unto the greatness of thy mercy, and as thou hast forgiven this people, from Egypt even until now.

20And the LORD said, I have pardoned according to thy word:

21But *as* truly *as* I live, all the earth shall be filled with the glory of the LORD.

22Because all those men which have seen my glory, and my miracles, which I did in Egypt and in the wilderness, and have tempted me now these ten times, and have not hearkened to my voice;

23Surely they shall not see the land which I sware unto the fathers, neither shall any of them that provoked me see it:

24But my servant Caleb, because he had another spirit with him, and hath followed me fully, him will I bring into the land whereinto he went; and his seed shall possess it.

25(Now the Amalekites and the Canaanites dwelt in the valley.) Tomorrow turn you, and get you into the wilderness by the way of the Red sea.

26And the LORD spake unto Moses and unto Aaron, saying,

27How long *shall I bear with* this evil congregation, which murmur against me? I have heard the murmurings of the children of Israel, which they murmur against me.

28Say unto them, *As truly as* I live, saith the LORD, as ye have spoken in mine ears, so will I do to you:

29Your carcases shall fall in this wilderness; and all that were numbered of you, according to your whole number, from twenty years old and upward, which have murmured against me,

30Doubtless ye shall not come into the land, *concerning* which I sware to make you dwell therein, save Caleb the son of Jephunneh, and Joshua the son of Nun.

31But your little ones, which ye said should be a prey, them will I bring in, and they shall know the land which ye have despised.

32But *as for* you, your carcases, they shall fall in this wilderness.

33And your children shall wander in the wilderness forty years, and bear your whoredoms, until your carcases be wasted in the wilderness.

34After the number of the days in which ye searched the land, *even* forty days, each day for a year, shall ye bear your iniquities, *even* forty years, and ye shall know my breach of promise.

35I the LORD have said, I will surely do it unto all this evil congregation, that are gathered together against me: in this wilderness they shall be consumed, and there they shall die.

36And the men, which Moses sent to search the land, who returned, and made all the congregation to murmur against him, by bringing up a slander upon the land,

37Even those men that did bring up the evil report upon the land, died by the plague before the LORD.

38But Joshua the son of Nun, and Caleb the son of Jephunneh, *which were* of the men that went to search the land, lived *still*.

39And Moses told these sayings unto all the children of Israel: and the people mourned greatly.

40And they rose up early in the morning, and gat them up into the top of the mountain, saying, Lo, we *be here,* and will go up unto the place which the LORD hath promised: for we have sinned.

41And Moses said, Wherefore now do ye transgress the commandment of the LORD? but it shall not prosper.

42Go not up, for the LORD *is* not among you; that ye be not smitten before your enemies.

43For the Amalekites and the Canaanites *are* there before you, and ye shall fall by the sword: because ye are turned away from the LORD, therefore the LORD will not be with you.

44But they presumed to go up unto the hill top: nevertheless the ark of the covenant of the LORD, and Moses, departed not out of the camp.

45Then the Amalekites came down, and the Canaanites which dwelt in that hill, and smote them, and discomfited them, *even* unto Hormah.

AND the LORD spake unto Moses, saying,

2Speak unto the children of Israel, and say unto them, When ye be come into the land of your habitations, which I give unto you,

3And will make an offering by fire unto the LORD, a burnt offering, or a sacrifice in performing a vow, or in a freewill offering, or in your solemn feasts, to make a sweet savour unto the LORD, of the herd, or of the flock:

4Then shall he that offereth his offering unto the LORD bring a meat offering of a tenth deal of flour mingled with the fourth *part* of an hin of oil.

5And the fourth *part* of an hin of wine for a drink offering shalt thou prepare with the burnt offering or sacrifice, for one lamb.

6Or for a ram, thou shalt prepare *for* a meat offering two tenths deals of flour mingled with the third *part* of an hin of oil.

7And for a drink offering thou shalt offer the third *part* of an hin of wine, *for* a sweet savour unto the LORD.

8And when thou preparest a bullock *for* a burnt offering, or *for* a sacrifice in performing a vow, or peace offerings unto the LORD:

9Then shall he bring with a bullock a meat offering of three tenth deals of flour mingled with half an hin of oil.

10And thou shalt bring for a drink offering half an hin of wine, *for* an offering made by fire, of a sweet savour unto the LORD.

11Thus shall it be done for one bullock, or for one ram, or for a lamb, or a kid.

12According to the number that ye shall prepare, so shall ye do every one according to their number.

13All that are born of the country shall do these things after this manner, in offering an offering made by fire, of a sweet savour unto the LORD.

14And if a stranger sojourn with you, or whosoever *be* among you in your generations, and will offer an offering made by fire, of a sweet savour unto the LORD; as ye do, so he shall do.

15One ordinance *shall be both* for you of the congregation, and also for the stranger that sojourneth *with you,* an ordinance for ever in your generations: as ye *are,* so shall the stranger be before the LORD.

16One law and one manner shall be for you, and for the stranger that sojourneth with you.

MARK 14:53–72

AND they led Jesus away to the high priest: and with him were assembled all the chief priests and the elders and the scribes.

54And Peter followed him afar off, even into the palace of the high priest: and he sat with the servants, and warmed himself at the fire.

55And the chief priests and all the council sought for witness against Jesus to put him to death; and found none.

56For many bare false witness against him, but their witness agreed not together.

57And there arose certain, and bare false witness against him, saying,

58We heard him say, I will destroy this temple that is made with hands, and within three days I will build another made without hands.

59But neither so did their witness agree together.

60And the high priest stood up in the midst, and asked Jesus, saying, Answerest thou nothing? what *is it which* these witness against thee?

61But he held his peace, and answered nothing. Again the high priest asked him, and said unto him, Art thou the Christ, the Son of the Blessed?

62And Jesus said, I am: and ye shall see the Son of man sitting on the right hand of power, and coming in the clouds of heaven.

63Then the high priest rent his

clothes, and saith, What need we any further witnesses?

64Ye have heard the blasphemy: what think ye? And they all condemned him to be guilty of death.

65And some began to spit on him, and to cover his face, and to buffet him, and to say unto him, Prophesy: and the servants did strike him with the palms of their hands.

66And as Peter was beneath in the palace, there cometh one of the maids of the high priest:

67And when she saw Peter warming himself, she looked upon him, and said, And thou also wast with Jesus of Nazareth.

68But he denied, saying, I know not, neither understand I what thou sayest. And he went out into the porch; and the cock crew.

69And a maid saw him again, and began to say to them that stood by, This is one of them.

70And he denied it again. And a little after, they that stood by said again to Peter, Surely thou art one of them: for thou art a Galilaean, and thy speech agreeth thereto.

71But he began to curse and to swear, saying, I know not this man of whom ye speak.

72And the second time the cock crew. And Peter called to mind the word that Jesus said unto him, Before the cock crow twice, thou shalt deny me thrice. And when he thought thereon, he wept.

PSALM 53:1–6

THE fool hath said in his heart, *There is* no God. Corrupt are they, and have done abominable iniquity: *there is* none that doeth good.

2God looked down from heaven upon the children of men, to see if there were *any* that did understand, that did seek God.

3Every one of them is gone back: they are altogether become filthy; *there is* none that doeth good, no, not one.

4Have the workers of iniquity no knowledge? who eat up my people *as* they eat bread: they have not called upon God.

5There were they in great fear, *where* no fear was: for God hath scattered the bones of him that encampeth *against* thee: thou hast put *them* to shame, because God hath despised them.

6Oh that the salvation of Israel *were* come out of Zion! When God bringeth back the captivity of his people, Jacob shall rejoice, *and* Israel shall be glad.

PROVERBS FOR TODAY/ 11:4
Riches profit not in the day of wrath: but righteousness delivereth from death.

MARCH 11

NUMBERS 15:17—16:40

AND the LORD spake unto Moses, saying,

18Speak unto the children of Israel, and say unto them, When ye come into the land whither I bring you,

19Then it shall be, that, when ye eat of the bread of the land, ye shall offer up an heave offering unto the LORD.

20Ye shall offer up a cake of the first of your dough *for* an heave offering: as *ye do* the heave offering of the threshingfloor, so shall ye heave it.

21Of the first of your dough ye shall give unto the LORD an heave offering in your generations.

22And if ye have erred, and not observed all these commandments, which the LORD hath spoken unto Moses,

23*Even* all that the LORD hath commanded you by the hand of Moses, from the day that the LORD commanded *Moses,* and henceforward among your generations;

24Then it shall be, if *ought* be committed by ignorance without the knowledge of the congregation, that all the congregation shall offer one young bullock for a burnt offering, for a sweet savour unto the LORD, with his meat offering, and his drink offering, according to the manner, and one kid of the goats for a sin offering.

25And the priest shall make an atonement for all the congregation of the children of Israel, and it shall be forgiven them; for it *is* ignorance: and they shall bring their offering, a sacrifice made by fire unto the LORD, and their sin offering before the LORD, for their ignorance:

26And it shall be forgiven all the congregation of the children of Israel, and the stranger that sojourneth among them; seeing all the people *were* in ignorance.

27And if any soul sin through ignorance, then he shall bring a she goat of the first year for a sin offering.

28And the priest shall make an atonement for the soul that sinneth ignorantly, when he sinneth by ignorance before the LORD, to make an atonement for him; and it shall be forgiven him.

29Ye shall have one law for him that sinneth through ignorance, *both for* him that is born among the children of Israel, and for the stranger that sojourneth among them.

30But the soul that doeth *ought* presumptuously, *whether he be* born in the land, or a stranger, the same reproacheth the LORD; and that soul shall be cut off from among his people.

31Because he hath despised the word of the LORD, and hath broken his commandment, that soul shall utterly be cut off; his iniquity *shall be* upon him.

32And while the children of Israel were in the wilderness, they found a man that gathered sticks upon the sabbath day.

33And they that found him gathering sticks brought him unto Moses and Aaron, and unto all the congregation.

34And they put him in ward, because it was not declared what should be done to him.

35And the LORD said unto Moses, The man shall be surely put to death: all the congregation shall stone him with stones without the camp.

36And all the congregation brought him without the camp, and stoned him with stones, and he died; as the LORD commanded Moses.

37And the LORD spake unto Moses, saying,

38Speak unto the children of Israel, and bid them that they make them fringes in the borders of their garments throughout their generations, and that they put upon the fringe of the borders a ribband of blue:

39And it shall be unto you for a fringe, that ye may look upon it, and remember all the commandments of the LORD, and do them; and that ye seek not after your own heart and your own eyes, after which ye use to go a whoring:

40That ye may remember, and do all my commandments, and be holy unto your God.

41I *am* the LORD your God, which brought you out of the land of Egypt, to be your God: I *am* the LORD your God.

Now Korah, the son of Izhar, the son of Kohath, the son of Levi, and Dathan and Abiram, the sons of Eliab, and On, the son of Peleth, sons of Reuben, took *men:*

2And they rose up before Moses, with certain of the children of Israel, two hundred and fifty princes of the assembly, famous in the congregation, men of renown:

3And they gathered themselves together against Moses and against Aaron, and said unto them, *Ye take* too much upon you, seeing all the congregation *are* holy, every one of them, and the LORD *is* among them: wherefore then lift ye up yourselves above the congregation of the LORD?

4And when Moses heard *it* he fell upon his face:

5And he spake unto Korah and unto all his company, saying, Even to morrow the LORD will shew who *are* his, and *who is* holy; and will cause *him* to come near unto him: even *him* whom he hath chosen will he cause to come near unto him.

6This do; Take you censers, Korah, and all his company;

7And put fire therein, and put incense in them before the LORD to morrow: and it shall be *that* the man whom the LORD doth choose, he *shall be* holy: *ye take* too much upon you, ye sons of Levi.

8And Moses said unto Korah, Hear, I pray you, ye sons of Levi:

9*Seemeth it but* a small thing unto you, that the God of Israel hath separated you from the congregation of Israel, to bring you near to himself to do the service of the tabernacle of the LORD, and to stand before the congregation to minister unto them?

10And he hath brought thee near *to him,* and all thy brethren the sons of Levi with thee: and seek ye the priesthood also?

11For which cause *both* thou and all thy company *are* gathered together against the LORD: and what *is* Aaron, that ye murmur against him?

12And Moses sent to call Dathan and Abiram, the sons of Eliab: which said, We will not come up:

13*Is it* a small thing that thou hast brought us up out of a land that floweth with milk and honey, to kill us in the wilderness, except thou make thyself altogether a prince over us?

14Moreover thou hast not brought us into a land that floweth with milk and honey, or given us inheritance of fields and vineyards: wilt thou put out the eyes of these men? we will not come up.

15And Moses was very wroth, and said unto the LORD, Respect not thou their offering: I have not taken one ass from them, neither have I hurt one of them.

16And Moses said unto Korah, Be thou and all thy company before the LORD, thou, and they, and Aaron, to morrow:

17And take every man his censer, and put incense in them, and bring ye before the LORD every man his censer, two hundred and fifty censers; thou also, and Aaron, each *of you* his censer.

18And they took every man his censer, and put fire in them, and laid incense thereon, and stood in the door of the tabernacle of the congregation with Moses and Aaron.

19And Korah gathered all the congregation against them unto the door of the tabernacle of the congregation: and the glory of the LORD appeared unto all the congregation.

20And the LORD spake unto Moses and unto Aaron, saying,

21Separate yourselves from among this congregation, that I may consume them in a moment.

22And they fell upon their faces, and said, O God, the God of the spirits of all flesh, shall one man sin, and wilt thou be wroth with all the congregation?

23And the LORD spake unto Moses, saying,

24Speak unto the congregation, saying, Get you up from about the tabernacle of Korah, Dathan, and Abiram.

25And Moses rose up and went unto Dathan and Abiram; and the elders of Israel followed him.

26And he spake unto the congregation, saying, Depart, I pray you, from the tents of these wicked men, and touch nothing of theirs, lest ye be consumed in all their sins.

27So they gat up from the tabernacle of Korah, Dathan, and Abiram, on every side: and Dathan and Abiram came out, and stood in the door of their tents, and their wives, and their sons, and their little children.

28And Moses said, Hereby ye shall know that the LORD hath sent me to do all these works; for *I have* not *done them* of mine own mind.

29If these men die the common death of all men, or if they be visited after the visitation of all men; *then* the LORD hath not sent me.

30But if the LORD make a new thing, and the earth open her mouth, and swallow them up, with all that *appertain* unto them, and they go down quick into the pit; then ye shall understand that these men have provoked the LORD.

31And it came to pass, as he had made an end of speaking all these words, that the ground clave asunder that *was* under them.

32And the earth opened her mouth, and swallowed them up, and their houses, and all the men that *appertained* unto Korah, and all *their* goods.

33They, and all that *appertained* to them, went down alive into the pit, and the earth closed upon them: and they perished from among the congregation.

34And all Israel that *were* round about them fled at the cry of them: for they said, Lest the earth swallow us up *also*.

35And there came out a fire from the LORD, and consumed the two hundred and fifty men that offered incense.

36And the LORD spake unto Moses, saying,

37Speak unto Eleazar the son of Aaron the priest, that he take up the censers out of the burning, and scatter thou the fire yonder; for they are hallowed.

38The censers of these sinners against their own souls, let them make them broad plates *for* a covering of the altar: for they offered them before the LORD, therefore they are hallowed: and they shall be a sign unto the children of Israel.

39And Eleazar the priest took the brasen censers, wherewith they that were burnt had offered; and they were made broad *plates* for a covering of the altar:

40*To be* a memorial unto the children of Israel, that no stranger, which *is* not of the seed of Aaron, come near to offer incense before the LORD; that he be not as Korah, and as his company: as the LORD said to him by the hand of Moses.

MARK 15:1–47

AND straightway in the morning the chief priests held a consultation with the elders and scribes and the whole council, and bound Jesus, and carried *him* away, and delivered *him* to Pilate.

2And Pilate asked him, Art thou the King of the Jews? And he answering said unto him, Thou sayest *it.*

3And the chief priests accused him of many things: but he answered nothing.

4And Pilate asked him again, saying, Answerest thou nothing? behold how many things they witness against thee.

5But Jesus yet answered nothing; so that Pilate marvelled.

6Now at *that* feast he released unto them one prisoner, whomsoever they desired.

7And there was *one* named Barabbas, *which lay* bound with them that had made insurrection with him, who had committed murder in the insurrection.

8And the multitude crying aloud began to desire *him to do* as he had ever done unto them.

9But Pilate answered them, saying, Will ye that I release unto you the King of the Jews?

10For he knew that the chief priests had delivered him for envy.

11But the chief priests moved the people, that he should rather release Barabbas unto them.

12And Pilate answered and said again unto them, What will ye then that I shall do *unto him* whom ye call the King of the Jews?

13And they cried out again, Crucify him.

14Then Pilate said unto them, Why, what evil hath he done? And they cried out the more exceedingly, Crucify him.

15And *so* Pilate, willing to content the people, released Barabbas unto them, and delivered Jesus, when he had scourged *him,* to be crucified.

16And the soldiers led him away into the hall, called Praetorium; and they call together the whole band.

17And they clothed him with purple, and platted a crown of thorns, and put it about his *head,*

18And began to salute him, Hail, King of the Jews!

19And they smote him on the head with a reed, and did spit upon him, and bowing *their* knees worshipped him.

20And when they had mocked him, they took off the purple from him, and put his own clothes on him, and led him out to crucify him.

21And they compel one Simon a Cyrenian, who passed by, coming out of the country, the father of Alexander and Rufus, to bear his cross.

22And they bring him unto the place Golgotha, which is, being interpreted, The place of a skull.

23And they gave him to drink wine mingled with myrrh: but he received *it* not.

24And when they had crucified him, they parted his garments, casting lots upon them, what every man should take.

25And it was the third hour, and they crucified him.

26And the superscription of his accusation was written over, THE KING OF THE JEWS.

27And with him they crucify two thieves; the one on his right hand, and the other on his left.

28And the scripture was fulfilled, which saith, And he was numbered with the transgressors.

29And they that passed by railed on him, wagging their heads, and saying, Ah, thou that destroyest the temple, and buildest *it* in three days,

30Save thyself, and come down from the cross.

31Likewise also the chief priests mocking said among themselves with the scribes, He saved others; himself he cannot save.

32Let Christ the King of Israel descend now from the cross, that we may see and believe. And they that were crucified with him reviled him.

33And when the sixth hour was come, there was darkness over the whole land until the ninth hour.

34And at the ninth hour Jesus cried with a loud voice, saying, Eloi, Eloi, lama sabachthani? which is, being interpreted, My God, my God, why hast thou forsaken me?

35And some of them that stood by, when they heard *it,* said, Behold, he calleth Elias.

36And one ran and filled a sponge full of vinegar, and put *it* on a reed, and gave him to drink, saying, Let alone; let us see whether Elias will come to take him down.

37And Jesus cried with a loud voice, and gave up the ghost.

38And the vail of the temple was rent

in twain from the top to the bottom.

39And when the centurion, which stood over against him, saw that he so cried out, and gave up the ghost, he said, Truly this man was the Son of God.

40There were also women looking on afar off: among whom was Mary Magdalene, and Mary the mother of James the less and of Joses, and Salome;

41(Who also, when he was in Galilee, followed him, and ministered unto him;) and many other women which came up with him unto Jerusalem.

42And now when the even was come, because it was the preparation, that is, the day before the sabbath,

43Joseph of Arimathaea, an honourable counsellor, which also waited for the kingdom of God, came, and went in boldly unto Pilate, and craved the body of Jesus.

44And Pilate marvelled if he were already dead: and calling *unto him* the centurion, he asked him whether he had been any while dead.

45And when he knew *it* of the centurion, he gave the body to Joseph.

46And he bought fine linen, and took him down, and wrapped him in the linen, and laid him in a sepulchre which was hewn out of a rock, and rolled a stone unto the door of the sepulchre.

47And Mary Magdalene and Mary *the mother* of Joses beheld where he was laid.

PSALM 54:1–7

Save me, O God, by thy name, and judge me by thy strength.
2Hear my prayer, O God; give ear to the words of my mouth.

3For strangers are risen up against me, and oppressors seek after my soul: they have not set God before them. Selah.

4Behold, God *is* mine helper: the Lord *is* with them that uphold my soul.

5He shall reward evil unto mine enemies: cut them off in thy truth.

6I will freely sacrifice unto thee: I will praise thy name, O LORD; for *it is* good.

7For he hath delivered me out of all trouble: and mine eye hath seen *his desire* upon mine enemies.

PROVERBS FOR TODAY/ 11:5–6

The righteousness of the perfect shall direct his way: but the wicked shall fall by his own wickedness. The righteousness of the upright shall deliver them: but transgressors shall be taken in their own *naughtiness.*

MARCH 12

NUMBERS 16:41—18:32

But on the morrow all the congregation of the children of Israel murmured against Moses and against Aaron, saying, Ye have killed the people of the LORD.

42And it came to pass, when the congregation was gathered against Moses and against Aaron, that they looked toward the tabernacle of the congregation: and, behold, the cloud covered it, and the glory of the LORD appeared.

43And Moses and Aaron came before the tabernacle of the congregation.

44And the LORD spake unto Moses, saying,

45Get you up from among this congregation, that I may consume them as in a moment. And they fell upon their faces.

46And Moses said unto Aaron, Take a censer, and put fire therein from off the altar, and put on incense, and go quickly unto the congregation, and make an atonement for them: for there is wrath gone out from the LORD; the plague is begun.

47And Aaron took as Moses commanded, and ran into the midst of the congregation; and, behold, the plague was begun among the people: and he put on incense, and made an atonement for the people.

48And he stood between the dead and the living; and the plague was stayed.

49Now they that died in the plague were fourteen thousand and seven hundred, beside them that died about the matter of Korah.

50And Aaron returned unto Moses unto the door of the tabernacle of the congregation: and the plague was stayed.

AND the LORD spake unto Moses, saying,

2Speak unto the children of Israel, and take of every one of them a rod according to the house of *their* fathers, of all their princes according to the house of their fathers twelve rods: write thou every man's name upon his rod.

3And thou shalt write Aaron's name upon the rod of Levi: for one rod *shall be* for the head of the house of their fathers.

4And thou shalt lay them up in the tabernacle of the congregation before the testimony, where I will meet with you.

5And it shall come to pass, *that* the man's rod, whom I shall choose, shall blossom: and I will make to cease from me the murmurings of the children of Israel, whereby they murmur against you.

6And Moses spake unto the children of Israel, and every one of their princes gave him a rod apiece, for each prince one, according to their fathers' houses, *even* twelve rods: and the rod of Aaron *was* among their rods.

7And Moses laid up the rods before the LORD in the tabernacle of witness.

8And it came to pass, that on the morrow Moses went into the tabernacle of witness; and, behold, the rod of Aaron for the house of Levi was budded, and brought forth buds, and bloomed blossoms, and yielded almonds.

9And Moses brought out all the rods from before the LORD unto all the children of Israel: and they looked, and took every man his rod.

10And the LORD said unto Moses, Bring Aaron's rod again before the testimony, to be kept for a token against the rebels; and thou shalt quite take away their murmurings from me, that they die not.

11And Moses did *so:* as the LORD commanded him, so did he.

12And the children of Israel spake unto Moses, saying, Behold, we die, we perish, we all perish.

13Whosoever cometh any thing near unto the tabernacle of the LORD shall die: shall we be consumed with dying?

AND the LORD said unto Aaron, Thou and thy sons and thy father's house with thee shall bear the iniquity of the sanctuary: and thou and thy sons with thee shall bear the iniquity of your priesthood.

2And thy brethren also of the tribe of Levi, the tribe of thy father, bring thou with thee, and they may be joined unto thee, and minister unto thee: but thou and thy sons with thee *shall minister* before the tabernacle of witness.

3And they shall keep thy charge, and the charge of all the tabernacle: only they shall not come nigh the vessels of the sanctuary and the altar, that neither they, nor ye also, die.

4And they shall be joined unto thee, and keep the charge of the tabernacle of the congregation, for all the service of the tabernacle: and a stranger shall not come nigh unto you.

5And ye shall keep the charge of the sanctuary, and the charge of the altar: that there be no wrath any more upon the children of Israel.

6And I, behold, I have taken your brethren the Levites from among the children of Israel: to you *they are* given *as* a gift for the LORD, to do the service of the tabernacle of the congregation.

7Therefore thou and thy sons with thee shall keep your priest's office for every thing of the altar, and within the vail; and ye shall serve: I have given your priest's office *unto you as* a service of gift: and the stranger that cometh nigh shall be put to death.

8And the LORD spake unto Aaron, Behold, I also have given thee the charge of mine heave offerings of all the hallowed things of the children of Israel; unto thee have I given them by reason of the anointing, and to thy sons, by an ordinance for ever.

9This shall be thine of the most holy things, *reserved* from the fire: every oblation of theirs, every meat offering of theirs, and every sin offering of theirs, and every trespass offering of theirs which they shall render unto me, *shall be* most holy for thee and for thy sons.

10In the most holy *place* shalt thou eat it; every male shall eat it: it shall be holy unto thee.

11And this *is* thine; the heave offering of their gift, with all the wave offerings of the children of Israel: I have given them unto thee, and to thy sons and to thy daughters with thee, by a statute for ever: every one that is clean in thy house shall eat of it.

12And the best of the oil, and all the best of the wine, and of the wheat, the firstfruits of them which they shall offer unto the LORD, them have I given thee.

13*And* whatsoever is first ripe in the land, which they shall bring unto the LORD, shall be thine; every one that is clean in thine house shall eat *of* it.

14Every thing devoted in Israel shall be thine.

15Every thing that openeth the matrix in all flesh, which they bring unto the LORD, *whether it be* of men or beasts, shall be thine: nevertheless the firstborn of man shalt thou surely redeem, and the firstling of unclean beasts shalt thou redeem.

16And those that are to be redeemed from a month old shalt thou redeem, according to thine estimation, for the money of five shekels, after the shekel of the sanctuary, which *is* twenty gerahs.

17But the firstling of a cow, or the firstling of a sheep, or the firstling of a goat, thou shalt not redeem; they *are* holy: thou shalt sprinkle their blood upon the altar, and shalt burn their fat *for* an offering made by fire, for a sweet savour unto the LORD.

18And the flesh of them shall be thine, as the wave breast and as the right shoulder are thine.

19All the heave offerings of the holy things, which the children of Israel offer unto the LORD, have I given thee, and thy sons and thy daughters with thee, by a statute for ever: it *is* a covenant of salt for ever before the LORD unto thee and to thy seed with thee.

20And the LORD spake unto Aaron, Thou shalt have no inheritance in their land, neither shalt thou have any part among them: I *am* thy part and thine inheritance among the children of Israel.

21And, behold, I have given the children of Levi all the tenth in Israel for an inheritance, for their service which they serve, *even* the service of the tabernacle of the congregation.

22Neither must the children of Israel henceforth come nigh the tabernacle of the congregation, lest they bear sin, and die.

23But the Levites shall do the service of the tabernacle of the congregation, and they shall bear their iniquity: *it shall be* a statute for ever throughout your generations, that among the children of Israel they have no inheritance.

24But the tithes of the children of Israel, which they offer *as* an heave offering unto the LORD, I have given to the Levites to inherit: therefore I have said unto them, Among the children of Israel they shall have no inheritance.

25And the LORD spake unto Moses, saying,

26Thus speak unto the Levites, and say unto them, When ye take of the children of Israel the tithes which I have given you from them for your inheritance, then ye shall offer up an heave offering of it for the LORD, *even* a tenth *part* of the tithe.

27And *this* your heave offering shall be reckoned unto you, as though *it were* the corn of the threshingfloor, and as the fulness of the winepress.

28Thus ye also shall offer an heave offering unto the LORD of all your tithes, which ye receive of the children of Israel; and ye shall give thereof the LORD'S heave offering to Aaron the priest.

29Out of all your gifts ye shall offer every heave offering of the LORD, of all the best thereof, *even* the hallowed part thereof out of it.

30Therefore thou shalt say unto them, When ye have heaved the best thereof from it, then it shall be counted unto the Levites as the increase of the threshingfloor, and as the increase of the winepress.

31And ye shall eat it in every place, ye and your households: for it *is* your reward for your service in the tabernacle of the congregation.

32And ye shall bear no sin by reason of it, when ye have heaved from it the best of it: neither shall ye pollute the holy things of the children of Israel, lest ye die.

MARK 16:1–20

AND when the sabbath was past, Mary Magdalene, and Mary the *mother* of James, and Salome, had bought sweet spices, that they might come and anoint him [Jesus].

2And very early in the morning the first *day* of the week, they came unto the sepulchre at the rising of the sun.

3And they said among themselves, Who shall roll us away the stone from the door of the sepulchre?

4And when they looked, they saw that the stone was rolled away: for it was very great.

5And entering into the sepulchre, they saw a young man sitting on the right side, clothed in a long white garment; and they were affrighted.

6And he saith unto them, Be not affrighted: Ye seek Jesus of Nazareth, which was crucified: he is risen; he is not here: behold the place where they laid him.

7But go your way, tell his disciples and Peter that he goeth before you into Galilee: there shall ye see him, as he said unto you.

8And they went out quickly, and fled from the sepulchre; for they trembled and were amazed: neither said they any thing to any *man;* for they were afraid.

9Now when *Jesus* was risen early the first *day* of the week, he appeared first to Mary Magdalene, out of whom he had cast seven devils.

10*And* she went and told them that had been with him, as they mourned and wept.

11And they, when they had heard that he was alive, and had been seen of her, believed not.

12After that he appeared in another

form unto two of them, as they walked, and went into the country.

13And they went and told *it* unto the residue: neither believed they them.

14Afterward he appeared unto the eleven as they sat at meat, and upbraided them with their unbelief and hardness of heart, because they believed not them which had seen him after he was risen.

15And he said unto them, Go ye into all the world, and preach the gospel to every creature.

16He that believeth and is baptized shall be saved; but he that believeth not shall be damned.

17And these signs shall follow them that believe; In my name shall they cast out devils; they shall speak with new tongues;

18They shall take up serpents; and if they drink any deadly thing, it shall not hurt them; they shall lay hands on the sick, and they shall recover.

19So then after the Lord had spoken unto them, he was received up into heaven, and sat on the right hand of God.

20And they went forth, and preached every where, the Lord working with *them,* and confirming the word with signs following. Amen.

PSALM 55:1–23

GIVE ear to my prayer, O God; and hide not thyself from my supplication.

2Attend unto me, and hear me: I mourn in my complaint, and make a noise;

3Because of the voice of the enemy, because of the oppression of the wicked: for they cast iniquity upon me, and in wrath they hate me.

4My heart is sore pained within me: and the terrors of death are fallen upon me.

5Fearfulness and trembling are come upon me, and horror hath overwhelmed me.

6And I said, Oh that I had wings like a dove! *for then* would I fly away, and be at rest.

7Lo, *then* would I wander far off, *and* remain in the wilderness. Selah.

8I would hasten my escape from the windy storm *and* tempest.

9Destroy, O Lord, *and* divide their tongues: for I have seen violence and strife in the city.

10Day and night they go about it upon the walls thereof: mischief also and sorrow *are* in the midst of it.

11Wickedness *is* in the midst thereof: deceit and guile depart not from her streets.

12For *it was* not an enemy *that* reproached me; then I could have borne *it:* neither *was it* he that hated me *that* did magnify *himself* against me; then I would have hid myself from him:

13But *it was* thou, a man mine equal, my guide, and mine acquaintance.

14We took sweet counsel together, *and* walked unto the house of God in company.

15Let death seize upon them, *and* let them go down quick into hell: for wickedness *is* in their dwellings, *and* among them.

16As for me, I will call upon God; and the LORD shall save me.

17Evening, and morning, and at noon, will I pray, and cry aloud: and he shall hear my voice.

18He hath delivered my soul in peace from the battle *that was* against me: for there were many with me.

19God shall hear, and afflict them, even he that abideth of old. Selah. Because they have no changes, therefore they fear not God.

20He hath put forth his hands against such as be at peace with him: he hath broken his covenant.

21*The words* of his mouth were smoother than butter, but war *was* in his heart: his words were softer than oil, yet *were* they drawn swords.

22Cast thy burden upon the LORD, and he shall sustain thee: he shall never suffer the righteous to be moved.

23But thou, O God, shalt bring them down into the pit of destruction: bloody and deceitful men shall not live out half their days; but I will trust in thee.

PROVERBS FOR TODAY/ 11:7

When a wicked man dieth, his *expectation shall perish: and the hope of unjust* men *perisheth.*

MARCH 13

NUMBERS 19:1—20:29

AND the LORD spake unto Moses and unto Aaron, saying,

2This *is* the ordinance of the law which the LORD hath commanded, saying, Speak unto the children of Israel, that they bring thee a red heifer without spot, wherein *is* no blemish, *and* upon which never came yoke:

3And ye shall give her unto Eleazar the priest, that he may bring her forth without the camp, and *one* shall slay her before his face:

4And Eleazar the priest shall take of her blood with his finger, and sprinkle of her blood directly before the tabernacle of the congregation seven times:

5And *one* shall burn the heifer in his sight; her skin, and her flesh, and her blood, with her dung, shall he burn:

6And the priest shall take cedar wood, and hyssop, and scarlet, and cast *it* into the midst of the burning of the heifer.

7Then the priest shall wash his clothes, and he shall bathe his flesh in water, and afterward he shall come into the camp, and the priest shall be unclean until the even.

8And he that burneth her shall wash his clothes in water, and bathe his flesh in water, and shall be unclean until the even.

9And a man *that is* clean shall gather up the ashes of the heifer, and lay *them* up without the camp in a clean place, and it shall be kept for the congregation of the children of Israel for a water of separation: it *is* a purification for sin.

10And he that gathereth the ashes of the heifer shall wash his clothes, and be unclean until the even: and it shall be unto the children of Israel, and unto the stranger that sojourneth among them, for a statute for ever.

11He that toucheth the dead body of any man shall be unclean seven days.

12He shall purify himself with it on the third day, and on the seventh day he shall be clean: but if he purify not himself the third day, then the seventh day he shall not be clean.

13Whosoever toucheth the dead body of any man that is dead, and purifieth not himself, defileth the tabernacle of the LORD; and that soul shall be cut off from Israel: because the water of separation was not sprinkled upon him, he shall be unclean; his uncleanness *is* yet upon him.

14This *is* the law, when a man dieth in a tent: all that come into the tent, and all that *is* in the tent, shall be unclean seven days.

15And every open vessel, which hath no covering bound upon it, *is* unclean.

16And whosoever toucheth one that is slain with a sword in the open fields, or a dead body, or a bone of a man, or a grave, shall be unclean seven days.

17And for an unclean *person* they shall take of the ashes of the burnt heifer of purification for sin, and running water shall be put thereto in a vessel:

18And a clean person shall take hyssop, and dip *it* in the water, and sprinkle *it* upon the tent, and upon all the vessels, and upon the persons that were there, and upon him that touched a bone, or one slain, or one dead, or a grave:

19And the clean *person* shall sprinkle upon the unclean on the third day, and on the seventh day: and on the seventh day he shall purify himself, and wash his clothes, and bathe himself in water, and shall be clean at even.

20But the man that shall be unclean, and shall not purify himself, that soul shall be cut off from among the congregation, because he hath defiled the sanctuary of the LORD: the water of separation hath not been sprinkled upon him; he *is* unclean.

21And it shall be a perpetual statute unto them, that he that sprinkleth the water of separation shall wash his clothes; and he that toucheth the water of separation shall be unclean until even.

22And whatsoever the unclean *person* toucheth shall be unclean; and the soul that toucheth *it* shall be unclean until even.

THEN came the children of Israel, *even* the whole congregation, into the desert of Zin in the first month: and the people abode in Kadesh; and Miriam died there, and was buried there.

2And there was no water for the congregation: and they gathered themselves together against Moses and against Aaron.

3And the people chode with Moses, and spake saying, Would God that we had died when our brethren died before the LORD!

4And why have ye brought up the congregation of the LORD into this wilderness, that we and our cattle should die there?

5And wherefore have ye made us to come up out of Egypt, to bring us in unto this evil place? it *is* no place of seed, or of figs, or of vines, or of pomegranates; neither *is* there any water to drink.

6And Moses and Aaron went from the presence of the assembly unto the door of the tabernacle of the congregation, and they fell upon their faces: and the glory of the LORD appeared unto them.

7And the LORD spake unto Moses, saying,

8Take the rod, and gather thou the assembly together, thou, and Aaron thy brother, and speak ye unto the rock before their eyes; and it shall give forth his water, and thou shalt bring forth to them water out of the rock: so thou shalt give the congregation and their beasts drink.

9And Moses took the rod from before the LORD, as he commanded him.

10And Moses and Aaron gathered the congregation together before the rock, and he said unto them, Hear now, ye rebels; must we fetch you water out of this rock?

11And Moses lifted up his hand, and with his rod he smote the rock twice: and the water came out abundantly, and the congregation drank, and their beasts *also.*

12And the LORD spake unto Moses and Aaron, Because ye believed me not, to sanctify me in the eyes of the children of Israel, therefore ye shall not bring this congregation into the land which I have given them.

13This *is* the water of Meribah; because the children of Israel strove with the LORD, and he was sanctified in them.

14And Moses sent messengers from Kadesh unto the king of Edom, Thus saith thy brother Israel, Thou knowest all the travail that hath befallen us:

15How our fathers went down into Egypt, and we have dwelt in Egypt a long time; and the Egyptians vexed us, and our fathers:

16And when we cried unto the LORD, he heard our voice, and sent an angel, and hath brought us forth out of Egypt: and, behold, we *are* in Kadesh, a city in the uttermost of thy border:

17Let us pass, I pray thee, through thy country: we will not pass through the fields, or through the vineyards, neither will we drink *of* the water of the wells: we will go by the king's *high* way, we will not turn to the right hand nor to the left, until we have passed thy borders.

18And Edom said unto him, Thou shalt not pass by me, lest I come out against thee with the sword.

19And the children of Israel said unto him, We will go by the high way: and if I and my cattle drink of thy water, then I will pay for it: I will only, without *doing* anything *else,* go through on my feet.

20And he said, Thou shalt not go through. And Edom came out against him with much people, and with a strong hand.

21Thus Edom refused to give Israel passage through his border: wherefore Israel turned away from him.

22And the children of Israel, *even* the whole congregation, journeyed from Kadesh, and came unto mount Hor.

23And the LORD spake unto Moses and Aaron in mount Hor, by the coast of the land of Edom, saying,

24Aaron shall be gathered unto his people: for he shall not enter into the land which I have given unto the children of Israel, because ye rebelled against my word at the water of Meribah.

25Take Aaron and Eleazar his son, and bring them up unto mount Hor:

26And strip Aaron of his garments, and put them upon Eleazar his son: and Aaron shall be gathered *unto his*

people, and shall die there.

27And Moses did as the LORD commanded: and they went up into mount Hor in the sight of all the congregation.

28And Moses stripped Aaron of his garments, and put them upon Eleazar his son; and Aaron died there in the top of the mount: and Moses and Eleazar came down from the mount.

29And when all the congregation saw that Aaron was dead, they mourned for Aaron thirty days, *even* all the house of Israel.

LUKE 1:1–25

FORASMUCH as many have taken in hand to set forth in order a declaration of those things which are most surely believed among us,

2Even as they delivered them unto us, which from the beginning were eyewitnesses, and ministers of the word;

3It seemed good to me also, having had perfect understanding of all things from the very first, to write unto thee in order, most excellent Theophilus,

4That thou mightest know the certainty of those things, wherein thou hast been instructed.

5There was in the days of Herod, the king of Judaea, a certain priest named Zacharias, of the course of Abia: and his wife *was* of the daughters of Aaron, and her name *was* Elisabeth.

6And they were both righteous before God, walking in all the commandments and ordinances of the Lord blameless.

7And they had no child, because that Elisabeth was barren, and they both were *now* well stricken in years.

8And it came to pass, that while he executed the priest's office before God in the order of his course,

9According to the custom of the priest's office, his lot was to burn incense when he went into the temple of the Lord.

10And the whole multitude of the people were praying without at the time of incense.

11And there appeared unto him an angel of the Lord standing on the right side of the altar of incense.

12And when Zacharias saw *him,* he was troubled, and fear fell upon him.

13But the angel said unto him, Fear not, Zacharias: for thy prayer is heard; and thy wife Elisabeth shall bear thee a son, and thou shalt call his name John.

14And thou shalt have joy and gladness; and many shall rejoice at his birth.

15For he shall be great in the sight of the Lord, and shall drink neither wine nor strong drink; and he shall be filled with the Holy Ghost, even from his mother's womb.

16And many of the children of Israel shall he turn to the Lord their God.

17And he shall go before him in the spirit and power of Elias, to turn the hearts of the fathers to the children, and the disobedient to the wisdom of the just; to make ready a people prepared for the Lord.

18And Zacharias said unto the angel, Whereby shall I know this? for I am an old man and my wife well stricken in years.

19And the angel answering said unto him, I am Gabriel, that stand in the presence of God; and am sent to speak unto thee, and to shew thee these glad tidings.

20And, behold, thou shalt be dumb, and not able to speak, until the day that these things shall be performed, because thou believest not my words, which shall be fulfilled in their season.

21And the people waited for Zacharias, and marvelled that he tarried so long in the temple.

22And when he came out, he could not speak unto them: and they perceived that he had seen a vision in the temple: for he beckoned unto them, and remained speechless.

23And it came to pass, that, as soon as the days of his ministration were accomplished, he departed to his own house.

24And after those days his wife Elisabeth conceived, and hid herself five months, saying,

25Thus hath the Lord dealt with me in the days wherein he looked on *me,* to take away my reproach among men.

PSALM 56:1–13

BE merciful unto me, O God: for man would swallow me up; he fighting daily oppresseth me.

2Mine enemies would daily swallow *me* up: for *they be* many that fight against me, O thou most High.

3What time I am afraid, I will trust in thee.

4In God I will praise his word, in God I have put my trust; I will not fear what flesh can do unto me.

5Every day they wrest my words: all their thoughts *are* against me for evil.

6They gather themselves together, they hide themselves, they mark my steps, when they wait for my soul.

7Shall they escape by iniquity? in *thine* anger cast down the people, O God.

8Thou tellest my wanderings: put thou my tears into thy bottle: *are they* not in thy book?

9When I cry *unto thee,* then shall mine enemies turn back: this I know; for God *is* for me.

10In God will I praise *his* word: in the Lord will I praise *his* word.

11In God have I put my trust: I will not be afraid what man can do unto me.

12Thy vows *are* upon me, O God: I will render praises unto thee.

13For thou hast delivered my soul from death: *wilt* not *thou deliver* my feet from falling, that I may walk before God in the light of the living?

PROVERBS FOR TODAY/ 11:8
The righteous is delivered out of trouble, and the wicked cometh in his stead.

MARCH 14

NUMBERS 21:1—22:20

AND *when* king Arad the Canaanite, which dwelt in the south, heard tell that Israel came by the way of the spies; then he fought against Israel, and took *some* of them prisoners.

2And Israel vowed a vow unto the LORD, and said, If thou wilt indeed deliver this people into my hand, then I will utterly destroy their cities.

3And the LORD hearkened to the voice of Israel, and delivered up the Canaanites; and they utterly destroyed them and their cities: and he called the name of the place Hormah.

4And they journeyed from mount Hor by the way of the Red sea, to compass the land of Edom: and the soul of the people was much discouraged because of the way.

5And the people spake against God, and against Moses, Wherefore have ye brought us up out of Egypt to die in the wilderness? for *there is* no bread, neither *is there any* water; and our soul loatheth this light bread.

6And the LORD sent fiery serpents among the people, and they bit the people; and much people of Israel died.

7Therefore the people came to Moses, and said, We have sinned, for we have spoken against the LORD, and against thee; pray unto the LORD, that he take away the serpents from us. And Moses prayed for the people.

8And the LORD said unto Moses, Make thee a fiery serpent, and set it upon a pole: and it shall come to pass,

that every one that is bitten, when he looketh upon it, shall live.

9And Moses made a serpent of brass, and put it upon a pole, and it came to pass, that if a serpent had bitten any man, when he beheld the serpent of brass, he lived.

10And the children of Israel set forward, and pitched in Oboth.

11And they journeyed from Oboth, and pitched at Ije–abarim, in the wilderness which *is* before Moab, toward the sunrising.

12From thence they removed, and pitched in the valley of Zared.

13From thence they removed, and pitched on the other side of Arnon, which *is* in the wilderness that cometh out of the coasts of the Amorites: for Arnon *is* the border of Moab, between Moab and the Amorites.

14Wherefore it is said in the book of the wars of the LORD, What he did in the Red sea, and in the brooks of Arnon,

15And at the stream of the brooks that goeth down to the dwelling of Ar, and lieth upon the border of Moab.

16And from thence *they went* to Beer: that *is* the well whereof the LORD spake unto Moses, Gather the people together, and I will give them water.

17Then Israel sang this song, Spring up, O well; sing ye unto it:

18The princes digged the well, the nobles of the people digged it, by *the direction of* the lawgiver, with their staves. And from the wilderness *they went* to Mattanah:

19And from Mattanah to Nahaliel: and from Nahaliel to Bamoth:

20And from Bamoth *in* the valley, that *is* in the country of Moab, to the top of Pisgah, which looketh toward Jeshimon.

21And Israel sent messengers unto Sihon king of the Amorites, saying,

22Let me pass through thy land: we will not turn into the fields, or into the vineyards; we will not drink *of* the waters of the well: *but* we will go along by the king's *high* way, until we be past thy borders.

23And Sihon would not suffer Israel to pass through his border: but Sihon gathered all his people together, and went out against Israel into the wilderness: and he came to Jahaz, and fought against Israel.

24And Israel smote him with the edge of the sword, and possessed his land from Arnon unto Jabbok, even unto the children of Ammon: for the border of the children of Ammon *was* strong.

25And Israel took all these cities: and Israel dwelt in all the cities of the Amorites, in Heshbon, and in all the villages thereof.

26For Heshbon *was* the city of Sihon the king of the Amorites, who had fought against the former king of Moab, and taken all his land out of his hand, even unto Arnon.

27Wherefore they that speak in proverbs say, Come into Heshbon, let the city of Sihon be built and prepared:

28For there is a fire gone out of Heshbon, a flame from the city of Sihon: it hath consumed Ar of Moab, *and* the lords of the high places of Arnon.

29Woe to thee, Moab! thou art undone, O people of Chemosh: he hath given his sons that escaped, and his daughters, into captivity unto Sihon king of the Amorites.

30We have shot at them; Heshbon is perished even unto Dibon, and we have laid them waste even unto Nophah, which *reacheth* unto Medeba.

31Thus Israel dwelt in the land of the Amorites.

32And Moses sent to spy out Jaazer, and they took the villages thereof, and drove out the Amorites that *were* there.

33And they turned and went up by the way of Bashan: and Og the king of Bashan went out against them, he, and all his people, to the battle at Edrei.

34And the LORD said unto Moses, Fear him not: for I have delivered him into thy hand, and all his people, and his land; and thou shalt do to him as thou didst unto Sihon king of the Amorites, ·which dwelt at Heshbon.

35So they smote him, and his sons, and all his people, until there was none left him alive: and they possessed his land.

AND the children of Israel set forward, and pitched in the plains of Moab on this side Jordan *by* Jericho.

2And Balak the son of Zippor saw all that Israel had done to the Amorites.

3And Moab was sore afraid of the people, because they *were* many: and Moab was distressed because of the children of Israel.

4And Moab said unto the elders of Midian, Now shall this company lick up all *that are* round about us, as the ox licketh up the grass of the field. And Balak the son of Zippor *was* king of the Moabites at that time.

5He sent messengers therefore unto Balaam the son of Beor to Pethor, which *is* by the river of the land of the children of his people, to call him, saying, Behold, there is a people come out from Egypt: behold, they cover the face of the earth, and they abide over against me:

6Come now therefore, I pray thee, curse me this people; for they *are* too mighty for me: peradventure I shall prevail, *that* we may smite them, and *that* I may drive them out of the land: for I wot that he whom thou blessest *is* blessed, and he whom thou cursest is cursed.

7And the elders of Moab and the elders of Midian departed with the rewards of divination in their hand; and they came unto Balaam, and spake unto him the words of Balak.

8And he said unto them, Lodge here this night, and I will bring you word again, as the LORD shall speak unto me: and the princes of Moab abode with Balaam.

9And God came unto Balaam, and said, What men *are* these with thee?

10And Balaam said unto God, Balak the son of Zippor, king of Moab, hath sent unto me, *saying,*

11Behold, *there is* a people come out of Egypt, which covereth the face of the earth: come now, curse me them; peradventure I shall be able to overcome them, and drive them out.

12And God said unto Balaam, Thou shalt not go with them; thou shalt not curse the people: for they *are* blessed.

13And Balaam rose up in the morning, and said unto the princes of Balak, Get you into your land: for the LORD refuseth to give me leave to go with you.

14And the princes of Moab rose up, and they went unto Balak, and said, Balaam refuseth to come with us.

15And Balak sent yet again princes, more, and more honourable than they.

16And they came to Balaam, and said to him, Thus saith Balak the son of Zippor, Let nothing, I pray thee, hinder thee from coming unto me:

17For I will promote thee unto very great honour, and I will do whatsoever thou sayest unto me: come therefore, I pray thee, curse me this people.

18And Balaam answered and said unto the servants of Balak, If Balak would give me his house full of silver and gold, I cannot go beyond the word of the LORD my God, to do less or more.

19Now therefore, I pray you, tarry ye also here this night, that I may know what the LORD will say unto me more.

20And God came unto Balaam at night, and said unto him, If the men come to call thee, rise up, *and* go with them; but yet the word which I shall say unto thee, that shalt thou do.

LUKE 1:26–56

AND in the sixth month the angel Gabriel was sent from God unto a city of Galilee, named Nazareth,

27To a virgin espoused to a man whose name was Joseph, of the house of David; and the virgin's name *was* Mary.

28And the angel came in unto her, and said, Hail, *thou that art* highly favoured, the Lord *is* with thee: blessed *art* thou among women.

29And when she saw *him,* she was troubled at his saying, and cast in her mind what manner of salutation this should be.

30And the angel said unto her, Fear not, Mary: for thou hast found favour with God.

31And, behold, thou shalt conceive in thy womb, and bring forth a son, and shalt call his name JESUS.

32He shall be great, and shall be called the Son of the Highest: and the Lord God shall give unto him the throne of his father David:

33And he shall reign over the house of Jacob for ever; and of his kingdom there shall be no end.

34Then said Mary unto the angel, How shall this be, seeing I know not a man?

35And the angel answered and said unto her, The Holy Ghost shall come upon thee, and the power of the Highest shall overshadow thee: therefore also that holy thing which shall be born of thee shall be called the Son of God.

36And, behold, thy cousin Elisabeth, she hath also conceived a son in her old age: and this is the sixth month with her, who was called barren.

37For with God nothing shall be impossible.

38And Mary said, Behold the handmaid of the Lord; be it unto me according to thy word. And the angel departed from her.

39And Mary arose in those days, and went into the hill country with haste, into a city of Judah;

40And entered into the house of Zacharias, and saluted Elisabeth.

41And it came to pass, that, when Elisabeth heard the salutation of Mary, the babe leaped in her womb; and Elisabeth was filled with the Holy Ghost:

42And she spake out with a loud voice, and said, Blessed *art* thou among women, and blessed *is* the fruit of thy womb.

43And whence *is* this to me, that the mother of my Lord should come to me?

44For, lo, as soon as the voice of thy salutation sounded in mine ears, the babe leaped in my womb for joy.

45And blessed *is* she that believed: for there shall be a performance of those things which were told her from the Lord.

46And Mary said, My soul doth magnify the Lord,

47And my spirit hath rejoiced in God my Saviour.

48For he hath regarded the low estate of his handmaiden: for, behold, from henceforth all generations shall call me blessed.

49For he that is mighty hath done to me great things; and holy *is* his name.

50And his mercy *is* on them that fear him from generation to generation.

51He hath shewed strength with his arm; he hath scattered the proud in the imagination of their hearts.

52He hath put down the mighty from *their* seats, and exalted them of low degree.

53He hath filled the hungry with good things; and the rich he hath sent empty away.

54He hath holpen his servant Israel, in remembrance of *his* mercy;

55As he spake to our fathers, to Abraham, and to his seed for ever.

56And Mary abode with her about three months, and returned to her own house.

PSALM 57:1–11

BE merciful unto me, O God, be merciful unto me: for my soul trusteth in thee: yea, in the shadow of thy wings will I make my refuge, until *these* calamities be overpast.

2I will cry unto God most high; unto God that performeth *all things* for me.

3He shall send from heaven, and save me *from* the reproach of him that would swallow me up. Selah. God shall send forth his mercy and his truth.

4My soul *is* among lions: *and* I lie *even among* them that are set on fire, *even* the sons of men, whose teeth *are* spears and arrows, and their tongue a sharp sword.

5Be thou exalted, O God, above the heavens; *let* thy glory *be* above all the earth.

6They have prepared a net for my steps; my soul is bowed down: they have digged a pit before me, into the midst whereof they are fallen *themselves*. Selah.

7My heart is fixed, O God, my heart is fixed: I will sing and give praise.

8Awake up, my glory; awake, psaltery and harp: I *myself* will awake early.

9I will praise thee, O Lord, among the people: I will sing unto thee among the nations.

10For thy mercy *is* great unto the heavens, and thy truth unto the clouds.

11Be thou exalted, O God, above the heavens: *let* thy glory *be* above all the earth.

PROVERBS FOR TODAY/ 11:9–11

An hypocrite with his mouth destroyeth his neighbour: but through knowledge shall the just be delivered. □ *When it goeth well with the righteous, the city rejoiceth: and when the wicked perish,* there is *shouting.* □ *By the blessing of the upright the city is exalted: but it is overthrown by the mouth of the wicked.*

MARCH 15

NUMBERS 22:21—23:30

A ND Balaam rose up in the morning, and saddled his ass, and went with the princes of Moab.

22And God's anger was kindled because he went: and the angel of the LORD stood in the way for an adversary against him. Now he was riding upon his ass, and his two servants *were* with him.

23And the ass saw the angel of the LORD standing in the way, and his sword drawn in his hand: and the ass turned aside out of the way, and went into the field: and Balaam smote the ass, to turn her into the way.

24But the angel of the LORD stood in a path of the vineyards, a wall *being* on this side, and a wall on that side.

25And when the ass saw the angel of the LORD, she thrust herself unto the wall, and crushed Balaam's foot against the wall: and he smote her again.

26And the angel of the LORD went further, and stood in a narrow place, where *was* no way to turn either to the right hand or to the left.

27And when the ass saw the angel of the LORD, she fell down under Balaam: and Balaam's anger was kindled, and he smote the ass with a staff.

28And the LORD opened the mouth of the ass, and she said unto Balaam, What have I done unto thee, that thou hast smitten me these three times?

29And Balaam said unto the ass, Because thou hast mocked me: I would there were a sword in mine hand, for now would I kill thee.

30And the ass said unto Balaam, *Am* not I thine ass, upon which thou hast ridden ever since *I was* thine unto this day? was I ever wont to do so unto thee? And he said, Nay.

31Then the LORD opened the eyes of Balaam, and he saw the angel of the LORD standing in the way, and his sword drawn in his hand: and he bowed down his head, and fell flat on his face.

32And the angel of the LORD said unto him, Wherefore hast thou smitten thine ass these three times? behold, I went out to withstand thee, because *thy* way is perverse before me:

33And the ass saw me, and turned from me these three times: unless she had turned from me, surely now also I had slain thee, and saved her alive.

34And Balaam said unto the angel of the LORD, I have sinned; for I knew not that thou stoodest in the way against me: now therefore, if it displease thee, I will get me back again.

35And the angel of the LORD said unto Balaam, Go with the men: but only the word that I shall speak unto thee, thou shalt speak. So Balaam went with the princes of Balak.

36And when Balak heard that Balaam was come, he went out to meet him unto a city of Moab, which *is* in the border of Arnon, which *is* in the utmost coast.

37And Balak said unto Balaam, Did I not earnestly send unto thee to call thee? wherefore camest thou not unto me? am I not able indeed to promote thee to honour?

38And Balaam said unto Balak, Lo, I am come unto thee: have I now any power at all to say any thing? the word that God putteth in my mouth, that shall I speak.

39And Balaam went with Balak, and they came unto Kirjath–huzoth.

40And Balak offered oxen and sheep, and sent to Balaam, and to the princes that *were* with him.

41And it came to pass on the morrow, that Balak took Balaam, and brought him up into the high places of Baal, that thence he might see the uttermost *part* of the people.

And Balaam said unto Balak, Build me here seven altars, and prepare me here seven oxen and seven rams.

2And Balak did as Balaam had spoken; and Balak and Balaam offered on *every* altar a bullock and a ram.

3And Balaam said unto Balak, Stand by thy burnt offering, and I will go: peradventure the Lord will come to meet me: and whatsoever he sheweth me I will tell thee. And he went to an high place.

4And God met Balaam: and he said unto him, I have prepared seven altars, and I have offered upon *every* altar a bullock and a ram.

5And the Lord put a word in Balaam's mouth, and said, Return unto Balak, and thus thou shalt speak.

6And he returned unto him, and, lo, he stood by his burnt sacrifice, he, and all the princes of Moab.

7And he took up his parable, and said, Balak the king of Moab hath brought me from Aram, out of the mountains of the east, *saying,* Come, curse me Jacob, and come, defy Israel.

8How shall I curse, whom God hath not cursed? or how shall I defy, *whom* the Lord hath not defied?

9For from the top of the rocks I see him, and from the hills I behold him: lo, the people shall dwell alone, and shall not be reckoned among the nations.

10Who can count the dust of Jacob, and the number of the fourth *part* of Israel? Let me die the death of the righteous, and let my last end be like his!

11And Balak said unto Balaam, What hast thou done unto me? I took thee to curse mine enemies, and, behold, thou hast blessed *them* altogether.

12And he answered and said, Must I not take heed to speak that which the Lord hath put in my mouth?

13And Balak said unto him, Come, I pray thee, with me unto another place, from whence thou mayest see them: thou shalt see but the utmost part of them, and shalt not see them all: and curse me them from thence.

14And he brought him into the field of Zophim, to the top of Pisgah, and built seven altars, and offered a bullock and a ram on *every* altar.

15And he said unto Balak, Stand here by thy burnt offering, while I meet *the* Lord yonder.

16And the Lord met Balaam, and put a word in his mouth, and said, Go again unto Balak, and say thus.

17And when he came to him, behold, he stood by his burnt offering, and the princes of Moab with him. And Balak said unto him, What hath the Lord spoken?

18And he took up his parable, and said, Rise up, Balak, and hear; hearken unto me, thou son of Zippor:

19God *is* not a man, that he should lie; neither the son of man, that he should repent: hath he said, and shall he not do *it?* or hath he spoken, and shall he not make it good?

20Behold, I have received *command-*

ment to bless: and he hath blessed; and I cannot reverse it.

21He hath not beheld iniquity in Jacob, neither hath he seen perverseness in Israel: the LORD his God *is* with him, and the shout of a king *is* among them.

22God brought them out of Egypt; he hath as it were the strength of an unicorn.

23Surely *there is* no enchantment against Jacob, neither *is there* any divination against Israel: according to this time it shall be said of Jacob and of Israel, What hath God wrought!

24Behold, the people shall rise up as a great lion, and lift up himself as a young lion: he shall not lie down until he eat *of* the prey, and drink the blood of the slain.

25And Balak said unto Balaam, Neither curse them at all, nor bless them at all.

26But Balaam answered and said unto Balak, Told not I thee, saying, All that the LORD speaketh, that I must do?

27And Balak said unto Balaam, Come, I pray thee, I will bring thee unto another place; peradventure it will please God that thou mayest curse me them from thence.

28And Balak brought Balaam unto the top of Peor, that looketh toward Jeshimon.

29And Balaam said unto Balak, Build me here seven altars, and prepare me here seven bullocks and seven rams.

30And Balak did as Balaam had said, and offered a bullock and a ram on *every* altar.

LUKE 1:57–80

Now Elisabeth's full time came that she should be delivered; and she brought forth a son.
58And her neighbours and her cousins heard how the Lord had shewed great mercy upon her; and they rejoiced with her.

59And it came to pass, that on the eighth day they came to circumcise the child; and they called him Zacharias, after the name of his father.

60And his mother answered and said, Not *so;* but he shall be called John.

61And they said unto her, There is none of thy kindred that is called by this name.

62And they made signs to his father, how he would have him called.

63And he asked for a writing table, and wrote, saying, His name is John. And they marvelled all.

64And his mouth was opened immediately, and his tongue *loosed,* and he spake, and praised God.

65And fear came on all that dwelt round about them: and all these sayings were noised abroad throughout all the hill country of Judaea.

66And all they that heard *them* laid *them* up in their hearts, saying, What manner of child shall this be! And the hand of the Lord was with him.

67And his father Zacharias was filled with the Holy Ghost, and prophesied, saying,

68Blessed *be* the Lord God of Israel; for he hath visited and redeemed his people,

69And hath raised up an horn of salvation for us in the house of his servant David;

70As he spake by the mouth of his holy prophets, which have been since the world began:

71That we should be saved from our enemies, and from the hand of all that hate us;

72To perform the mercy *promised* to our fathers, and to remember his holy covenant;

73The oath which he sware to our father Abraham,

74That he would grant unto us, that we being delivered out of the hand of our enemies might serve him without fear,

75In holiness and righteousness before him, all the days of our life.

76And thou, child, shalt be called the prophet of the Highest: for thou shalt go before the face of the Lord to prepare his ways;

77To give knowledge of salvation unto his people by the remission of their sins,

78Through the tender mercy of our God; whereby the dayspring from on high hath visited us,

79To give light to them that sit in darkness and *in* the shadow of death, to guide our feet into the way of peace.

80And the child grew, and waxed strong in spirit, and was in the deserts till the day of his shewing unto Israel.

PSALM 58:1–11

D o ye indeed speak righteousness, O congregation? do ye judge uprightly, O ye sons of men?

2Yea, in heart ye work wickedness; ye weigh the violence of your hands in the earth.

3The wicked are estranged from the womb: they go astray as soon as they be born, speaking lies.

4Their poison *is* like the poison of a serpent: *they are* like the deaf adder *that* stoppeth her ear;

5Which will not hearken to the voice of charmers, charming never so wisely.

6Break their teeth, O God, in their mouth: break out the great teeth of the young lions, O LORD.

7Let them melt away as waters *which* run continually: *when* he bendeth *his bow to shoot* his arrows, let them be as cut in pieces.

8As a snail *which* melteth, let *every one of them* pass away: *like* the untimely birth of a woman, *that* they may not see the sun.

9Before your pots can feel the thorns, he shall take them away as with a whirlwind, both living, and in *his* wrath.

10The righteous shall rejoice when he seeth the vengeance: he shall wash his feet in the blood of the wicked.

11So that a man shall say, Verily *there is* a reward for the righteous; verily he is a God that judgeth in the earth.

PROVERBS FOR TODAY/ 11:12–13

He that is void of wisdom despiseth his neighbour: but a man of understanding holdeth his peace. □ A talebearer revealeth secrets: but he that is of a faithful spirit concealeth the matter.

MARCH 16

NUMBERS 24:1—25:18

A ND when Balaam saw that it pleased the LORD to bless Israel, he went not, as at other times, to seek for enchantments, but he set his face toward the wilderness.

2And Balaam lifted up his eyes, and he saw Israel abiding *in his tents* according to their tribes; and the spirit of God came upon him.

3And he took up his parable, and said, Balaam the son of Beor hath said, and the man whose eyes are open hath said:

4He hath said, which heard the words of God, which saw the vision of the Almighty, falling *into a trance,* but having his eyes open:

5How goodly are thy tents, O Jacob,

and thy tabernacles, O Israel!

6As the valleys are they spread forth, as gardens by the river's side, as the trees of lign aloes which the LORD hath planted, *and* as cedar trees beside the waters.

7He shall pour the water out of his buckets, and his seed *shall be* in many waters, and his king shall be higher than Agag, and his kingdom shall be exalted.

8God brought him forth out of Egypt; he hath as it were the strength of an unicorn: he shall eat up the nations his enemies, and shall break their bones, and pierce *them* through with his arrows.

9He couched, he lay down as a lion, and as a great lion: who shall stir him up? Blessed *is* he that blesseth thee, and cursed *is* he that curseth thee.

10And Balak's anger was kindled against Balaam, and he smote his hands together: and Balak said unto Balaam, I called thee to curse mine enemies, and, behold, thou hast altogether blessed *them* these three times.

11Therefore now flee thou to thy place: I thought to promote thee unto great honor; but, lo, the LORD hath kept thee back from honour.

12And Balaam said unto Balak, Spake I not also to thy messengers which thou sentest unto me, saying,

13If Balak would give me his house full of silver and gold, I cannot go beyond the commandment of the LORD, to do *either* good or bad of mine own mind; *but* what the LORD saith, that will I speak?

14And now, behold, I go unto my people: come *therefore, and* I will advertise thee what this people shall do to thy people in the latter days.

15And he took up his parable, and said, Balaam the son of Beor hath said, and the man whose eyes are open hath said:

16He hath said, which heard the words of God, and knew the knowledge

of the most High, *which* saw the vision of the Almighty, falling *into a trance,* but having his eyes open:

17I shall see him, but not now: I shall behold him, but not nigh: there shall come a Star out of Jacob, and a Sceptre shall rise out of Israel, and shall smite the corners of Moab, and destroy all the children of Sheth.

18And Edom shall be a possession, Seir also shall be a possession for his enemies; and Israel shall do valiantly.

19Out of Jacob shall come he that shall have dominion, and shall destroy him that remaineth of the city.

20And when he looked on Amalek, he took up his parable, and said, Amalek *was* the first of the nations; but his latter end *shall be* that he perish for ever.

21And he looked on the Kenites, and took up his parable, and said, Strong is thy dwellingplace, and thou puttest thy nest in a rock.

22Nevertheless the Kenite shall be wasted, until Asshur shall carry thee away captive.

23And he took up his parable, and said, Alas, who shall live when God doeth this!

24And ships *shall come* from the coast of Chittim, and shall afflict Asshur, and shall afflict Eber, and he also shall perish for ever.

25And Balaam rose up, and went and returned to his place: and Balak also went his way.

AND Israel abode in Shittim, and the people began to commit whoredom with the daughters of Moab.

2And they called the people unto the sacrifices of their gods: and the people did eat, and bowed down to their gods.

3And Israel joined himself unto Baal–peor: and the anger of the LORD was kindled against Israel.

4And the LORD said unto Moses, Take all the heads of the people, and hang them up before the LORD against the sun, that the fierce anger of the LORD may be turned away from Israel.

5And Moses said unto the judges of Israel, Slay ye every one his men that were joined unto Baal–peor.

6And, behold, one of the children of Israel came and brought unto his brethren a Midianitish woman in the sight of Moses, and in the sight of all the congregation of the children of Israel, who *were* weeping *before* the door of the tabernacle of the congregation.

7And when Phinehas, the son of Eleazar, the son of Aaron the priest, saw *it,* he rose up from among the congregation, and took a javelin in his hand;

8And he went after the man of Israel into the tent, and thrust both of them through, the man of Israel, and the woman through her belly. So the plague was stayed from the children of Israel.

9And those that died in the plague were twenty and four thousand.

10And the LORD spake unto Moses, saying,

11Phinehas, the son of Eleazar, the son of Aaron the priest, hath turned my wrath away from the children of Israel, while he was zealous for my sake among them, that I consumed not the children of Israel in my jealousy.

12Wherefore say, Behold, I give unto him my covenant of peace:

13And he shall have it, and his seed after him, *even* the covenant of an everlasting priesthood; because he was zealous for his God, and made an atonement for the children of Israel.

14Now the name of the Israelite that was slain, *even* that was slain with the Midianitish woman, *was* Zimri, the son of Salu, a prince of a chief house among the Simeonites.

15And the name of the Midianitish woman that was slain *was* Cozbi, the daughter of Zur; he *was* head over a people, *and* of a chief house in Midian.

16And the LORD spake unto Moses, saying,

17Vex the Midianites, and smite them:

18For they vex you with their wiles, wherewith they have beguiled you in the matter of Peor, and in the matter of Cozbi, the daughter of a prince of Midian, their sister, which was slain in the day of the plague for Peor's sake.

LUKE 2:1–35

AND it came to pass in those days, that there went out a decree from Caesar Augustus, that all the world should be taxed.

2(*And* this taxing was first made when Cyrenius was governor of Syria.)

3And all went to be taxed, every one into his own city.

4And Joseph also went up from Galilee, out of the city of Nazareth, into Judaea, unto the city of David, which is called Bethlehem; (because he was of the house and lineage of David:)

5To be taxed with Mary his espoused wife, being great with child.

6And so it was, that, while they were there, the days were accomplished that she should be delivered.

7And she brought forth her firstborn son, and wrapped him in swaddling clothes, and laid him in a manger; because there was no room for them in the inn.

8And there were in the same country shepherds abiding in the field, keeping watch over their flock by night.

9And, lo, the angel of the Lord came upon them, and the glory of the Lord shone round about them: and they were sore afraid.

10And the angel said unto them, Fear not: for, behold, I bring you good tidings of great joy, which shall be to all people.

11For unto you is born this day in the city of David a Saviour, which is Christ the Lord.

12And this *shall be* a sign unto you; Ye shall find the babe wrapped in swaddling clothes, lying in a manger.

13And suddenly there was with the angel a multitude of the heavenly host praising God, and saying,

14Glory to God in the highest, and on earth peace, good will toward men.

15And it came to pass, as the angels were gone away from them into heaven, the shepherds said one to another, Let us now go even unto Bethlehem, and see this thing which is come to pass, which the Lord hath made known unto us.

16And they came with haste, and found Mary, and Joseph, and the babe lying in a manger.

17And when they had seen *it*, they made known abroad the saying which was told them concerning this child.

18And all they that heard *it* wondered at those things which were told them by the shepherds.

19But Mary kept all these things, and pondered *them* in her heart.

20And the shepherds returned, glorifying and praising God for all the things that they had heard and seen, as it was told unto them.

21And when eight days were accomplished for the circumcising of the child, his name was called JESUS, which was so named of the angel before he was conceived in the womb.

22And when the days of her purification according to the law of Moses were accomplished, they brought him to Jerusalem, to present *him* to the Lord;

23(As it is written in the law of the Lord, Every male that openeth the womb shall be called holy to the Lord;)

24And to offer a sacrifice according to that which is said in the law of the Lord, A pair of turtledoves, or two young pigeons.

25And, behold, there was a man in Jerusalem, whose name *was* Simeon; and the same man *was* just and devout, waiting for the consolation of Israel: and the Holy Ghost was upon him.

26And it was revealed unto him by the Holy Ghost, that he should not see death, before he had seen the Lord's Christ.

27And he came by the Spirit into the temple: and when the parents brought in the child Jesus, to do for him after the custom of the law,

28Then took he him up in his arms, and blessed God, and said,

29Lord, now lettest thou thy servant depart in peace, according to thy word:

30For mine eyes have seen thy salvation,

31Which thou hast prepared before the face of all people;

32A light to lighten the Gentiles, and the glory of thy people Israel.

33And Joseph and his mother marvelled at those things which were spoken of him.

34And Simeon blessed them, and said unto Mary his mother, Behold, this *child* is set for the fall and rising again of many in Israel; and for a sign which shall be spoken against;

35(Yea, a sword shall pierce through thy own soul also,) that the thoughts of many hearts may be revealed.

PSALM 59:1–17

DELIVER me from mine enemies, O my God: defend me from them that rise up against me.

2Deliver me from the workers of iniquity, and save me from bloody men.

3For, lo, they lie in wait for my soul: the mighty are gathered against me; not *for* my transgression, nor *for* my sin, O LORD.

4They run and prepare themselves without *my* fault: awake to help me, and behold.

5Thou therefore, O LORD God of hosts, the God of Israel, awake to visit all the heathen: be not merciful to any wicked transgressors. Selah.

6They return at evening: they make a noise like a dog, and go round about the city.

7Behold, they belch out with their

mouth: swords *are* in their lips: for who, *say they,* doth hear?

8But thou, O LORD, shalt laugh at them; thou shalt have all the heathen in derision.

9*Because of* his strength will I wait upon thee: for God *is* my defence.

10The God of my mercy shall prevent me: God shall let me see *my desire* upon mine enemies.

11Slay them not, lest my people forget: scatter them by thy power; and bring them down, O Lord our shield.

12*For* the sin of their mouth *and* the words of their lips let them even be taken in their pride: and for cursing and lying *which* they speak.

13Consume *them* in wrath, consume *them,* that they *may* not *be:* and let them know that God ruleth in Jacob unto the ends of the earth. Selah.

14And at evening let them return; *and* let them make a noise like a dog, and go round about the city.

15Let them wander up and down for meat, and grudge if they be not satisfied.

16But I will sing of thy power; yea, I will sing aloud of thy mercy in the morning: for thou hast been my defence and refuge in the day of my trouble.

17Unto thee, O my strength, will I sing: for God *is* my defence, *and* the God of my mercy.

PROVERBS FOR TODAY/ 11:14

Where no counsel is, *the people fall: but in the multitude of counsellors* there is *safety.*

MARCH 17

NUMBERS 26:1–51

AND it came to pass after the plague, that the LORD spake unto Moses and unto Eleazar the son of Aaron the priest, saying,

2Take the sum of all the congregation of the children of Israel, from twenty years old and upward, throughout their fathers' house, all that are able to go to war in Israel.

3And Moses and Eleazar the priest spake with them in the plains of Moab by Jordan *near* Jericho, saying,

4*Take the sum of the people,* from twenty years old and upward; as the LORD commanded Moses and the children of Israel, which went forth out of the land of Egypt.

5Reuben, the eldest son of Israel: the children of Reuben; Hanoch, *of*

whom cometh the family of the Hanochites: of Pallu, the family of the Palluites:

6Of Hezron, the family of the Hezronites: of Carmi, the family of the Carmites.

7These *are* the families of the Reubenites: and they that were numbered of them were forty and three thousand and seven hundred and thirty.

8And the sons of Pallu; Eliab.

9And the sons of Eliab; Nemuel, and Dathan, and Abiram. This *is that* Dathan and Abiram, *which were* famous in the congregation, who strove against Moses and against Aaron in the company of Korah, when they strove against the LORD:

10And the earth opened her mouth, and swallowed them up together with

Korah, when that company died, what time the fire devoured two hundred and fifty men: and they became a sign.

11Notwithstanding the children of Korah died not.

12The sons of Simeon after their families: of Nemuel, the family of the Nemuelites: of Jamin, the family of the Jaminites: of Jachin, the family of the Jachinites:

13Of Zerah, the family of the Zarhites: of Shaul, the family of the Shaulites.

14These *are* the families of the Simeonites, twenty and two thousand and two hundred.

15The children of Gad after their families: of Zephon, the family of the Zephonites: of Haggi, the family of the Haggites: of Shuni, the family of the Shunites:

16Of Ozni, the family of the Oznites: of Eri, the family of the Erites:

17Of Arod, the family of the Arodites: of Areli, the family of the Arelites.

18These *are* the families of the children of Gad according to those that were numbered of them, forty thousand and five hundred.

19The sons of Judah *were* Er and Onan: and Er and Onan died in the land of Canaan.

20And the sons of Judah after their families were; of Shelah, the family of the Shelanites: of Pharez, the family of the Pharzites: of Zerah, the family of the Zarhites.

21And the sons of Pharez were; of Hezron, the family of the Hezronites: of Hamul, the family of the Hamulites.

22These *are* the families of Judah according to those that were numbered of them, threescore and sixteen thousand and five hundred.

23Of the sons of Issachar after their families: *of* Tola, the family of the Tolaites: of Pua, the family of the Punites:

24Of Jashub, the family of the Jashubites: of Shimron, the family of the Shimronites.

25These *are* the families of Issachar according to those that were numbered of them, threescore and four thousand and three hundred.

26Of the sons of Zebulun after their families: of Sered, the family of the Sardites: of Elon, the family of the Elonites: of Jahleel, the family of the Jahleelites.

27These *are* the families of the Zebulunites according to those that were numbered of them, threescore thousand and five hundred.

28The sons of Joseph after their families *were* Manasseh and Ephraim.

29Of the sons of Manasseh: of Machir, the family of the Machirites: and Machir begat Gilead: of Gilead *come* the family of the Gileadites.

30These *are* the sons of Gilead: *of* Jeezer, the family of the Jeezerites: of Helek, the family of the Helekites:

31And *of* Asriel, the family of the Asrielites: and *of* Shechem, the family of the Shechemites:

32And *of* Shemida, the family of the Shemidaites: and *of* Hepher, the family of the Hepherites.

33And Zelophehad the son of Hepher had no sons, but daughters: and the names of the daughters of Zelophehad *were* Mahlah, and Noah, Hoglah, Milcah, and Tirzah.

34These *are* the families of Manasseh, and those that were numbered of them, fifty and two thousand and seven hundred.

35These *are* the sons of Ephraim after their families: of Shuthelah, the family of the Shuthalhites: of Becher, the family of the Bachrites: of Tahan, the family of the Tahanites.

36And these *are* the sons of Shuthelah: of Eran, the family of the Eranites.

37These *are* the families of the sons of Ephraim according to those that were numbered of them, thirty and two thousand and five hundred. These *are* the sons of Joseph after their families.

38The sons of Benjamin after their families: of Bela, the family of the Belaites: of Ashbel, the family of the Ashbelites: of Ahiram, the family of the Ahiramites:

39Of Shupham, the family of the Shuphamites: of Hupham, the family of the Huphamites.

40And the sons of Bela were Ard and Naaman: *of Ard,* the family of the Ardites: *and* of Naaman, the family of the Naamites.

41These *are* the sons of Benjamin after their families: and they that were numbered of them *were* forty and five thousand and six hundred.

42These *are* the sons of Dan after their families: of Shuham, the family of the Shuhamites. These *are* the families of Dan after their families.

43All the families of the Shuhamites, according to those that were numbered of them, *were* threescore and four thousand and four hundred.

44*Of* the children of Asher after their families: of Jimna, the family of the Jimnites: of Jesui, the family of the Jesuites: of Beriah, the family of the Beriites.

45Of the sons of Beriah: of Heber, the family of the Heberites: of Malchiel, the family of the Malchielites.

46And the name of the daughter of Asher *was* Sarah.

47These are the families of the sons of Asher according to those that were numbered of them; *who were* fifty and three thousand and four hundred.

48*Of* the sons of Naphtali after their families: of Jahzeel, the family of the Jahzeelites: of Guni, the family of the Gunites:

49Of Jezer, the family of the Jezerites: of Shillem, the family of the Shillemites.

50These *are* the families of Naphtali according to their families: and they that were numbered of them *were* forty and five thousand and four hundred.

51These *were* the numbered of the children of Israel, six hundred thousand and a thousand seven hundred and thirty.

LUKE 2:36–52

AND there was one Anna, a prophetess, the daughter of Phanuel, of the tribe of Aser: she was of a great age, and had lived with an husband seven years from her virginity;

37And she *was* a widow of about fourscore and four years, which departed not from the temple, but served *God* with fastings and prayers night and day.

38And she coming in that instant gave thanks likewise unto the Lord, and spake of him to all them that looked for redemption in Jerusalem.

39And when they had performed all things according to the law of the Lord, they returned into Galilee, to their own city Nazareth.

40And the child grew, and waxed strong in spirit, filled with wisdom: and the grace of God was upon him.

41Now his parents went to Jerusalem every year at the feast of the passover.

42And when he was twelve years old, they went up to Jerusalem after the custom of the feast.

43And when they had fulfilled the days, as they returned, the child Jesus tarried behind in Jerusalem; and Joseph and his mother knew not *of it.*

44But they, supposing him to have been in the company, went a day's journey; and they sought him among *their* kinsfolk and acquaintance.

45And when they found him not, they turned back again to Jerusalem, seeking him.

46And it came to pass, that after three days they found him in the temple, sitting in the midst of the doctors, both hearing them, and asking them questions.

47And all that heard him were astonished at his understanding and answers.

48And when they saw him, they were amazed: and his mother said unto him, Son, why hast thou thus dealt with us?

behold, thy father and I have sought thee sorrowing.

⁴⁹And he said unto them, How is it that ye sought me? wist ye not that I must be about my Father's business?

⁵⁰And they understood not the saying which he spake unto them.

⁵¹And he went down with them, and came to Nazareth, and was subject unto them: but his mother kept all these sayings in her heart.

⁵²And Jesus increased in wisdom and stature, and in favour with God and man.

PSALM 60:1–12

O GOD, thou hast cast us off, thou hast scattered us, thou hast been displeased; O turn thyself to us again.

²Thou hast made the earth to tremble; thou hast broken it: heal the breaches thereof; for it shaketh.

³Thou hast shewed thy people hard things: thou hast made us to drink the wine of astonishment.

⁴Thou hast given a banner to them that fear thee, that it may be displayed because of the truth. Selah.

⁵That thy beloved may be delivered; save *with* thy right hand, and hear me.

⁶God hath spoken in his holiness; I will rejoice, I will divide Shechem, and mete out the valley of Succoth.

⁷Gilead *is* mine, and Manasseh *is* mine; Ephraim also *is* the strength of mine head; Judah *is* my lawgiver;

⁸Moab *is* my washpot; over Edom will I cast out my shoe: Philistia, triumph thou because of me.

⁹Who will bring me *into* the strong city? who will lead me into Edom?

¹⁰*Wilt* not thou, O God, *which* hadst cast us off? and *thou,* O God, *which* didst not go out with our armies?

¹¹Give us help from trouble: for vain *is* the help of man.

¹²Through God we shall do valiantly: for he *it is that* shall tread down our enemies.

PROVERBS FOR TODAY/ 11:15

He that is surety for a stranger shall smart for it: *and he that hateth suretiship is sure.*

MARCH 18

NUMBERS 26:52—28:14

A ND the LORD spake unto Moses, saying,

⁵³Unto these the land shall be divided for an inheritance according to the number of names.

⁵⁴To many thou shalt give the more inheritance, and to few thou shalt give the less inheritance: to every one shall his inheritance be given according to those that were numbered of him.

⁵⁵Notwithstanding the land shall be divided by lot: according to the names of the tribes of their fathers they shall inherit.

⁵⁶According to the lot shall the possession thereof be divided between many and few.

⁵⁷And these *are* they that were numbered of the Levites after their families: of Gershon, the family of the Gershonites: of Kohath, the family of the Ko-

hathites: of Merari, the family of the Merarites.

58These *are* the families of the Levites: the family of the Libnites, the family of the Hebronites, the family of the Mahlites, the family of the Mushites, the family of the Korathites. And Kohath begat Amram.

59And the name of Amram's wife *was* Jochebed, the daughter of Levi, whom *her mother* bare to Levi in Egypt: and she bare unto Amram Aaron and Moses, and Miriam their sister.

60And unto Aaron was born Nadab, and Abihu, Eleazar, and Ithamar.

61And Nadab and Abihu died, when they offered strange fire before the LORD.

62And those that were numbered of them were twenty and three thousand, all males from a month old and upward: for they were not numbered among the children of Israel, because there was no inheritance given them among the children of Israel.

63These *are* they that were numbered by Moses and Eleazar the priest, who numbered the children of Israel in the plains of Moab by Jordan *near* Jericho.

64But among these there was not a man of them whom Moses and Aaron the priest numbered, when they numbered the children of Israel in the wilderness of Sinai.

65For the LORD had said of them, They shall surely die in the wilderness. And there was not left a man of them, save Caleb the son of Jephunneh, and Joshua the son of Nun.

THEN came the daughters of Zelophehad, the son of Hepher, the son of Gilead, the son of Machir, the son of Manasseh, of the families of Manasseh the son of Joseph: and these *are* the names of his daughters; Mahlah, Noah, and Hoglah, and Milcah, and Tirzah.

2And they stood before Moses, and before Eleazar the priest, and before the princes and all the congregation, *by* the door of the tabernacle of the congregation, saying,

3Our father died in the wilderness, and he was not in the company of them that gathered themselves together against the LORD in the company of Korah; but died in his own sin, and had no sons.

4Why should the name of our father be done away from among his family, because he hath no son? Give unto us *therefore* a possession among the brethren of our father.

5And Moses brought their cause before the LORD.

6And the LORD spake unto Moses, saying,

7The daughters of Zelophehad speak right: thou shalt surely give them a possession of an inheritance among their father's brethren; and thou shalt cause the inheritance of their father to pass unto them.

8And thou shalt speak unto the children of Israel, saying, If a man die, and have no son, then ye shall cause his inheritance to pass unto his daughter.

9And if he have no daughter, then ye shall give his inheritance unto his brethren.

10And if he have no brethren, then ye shall give his inheritance unto his father's brethren.

11And if his father have no brethren, then ye shall give his inheritance unto his kinsman that is next to him of his family, and he shall possess it: and it shall be unto the children of Israel a statute of judgment, as the LORD commanded Moses.

12And the LORD said unto Moses, Get thee up into this mount Abarim, and see the land which I have given unto the children of Israel.

13And when thou hast seen it, thou also shalt be gathered unto thy people, as Aaron thy brother was gathered.

14For ye rebelled against my commandment in the desert of Zin, in the strife of the congregation, to sanctify me at the water before their eyes: that *is* the water of Meribah in Kadesh in the wilderness of Zin.

15And Moses spake unto the LORD, saying,

16Let the LORD, the God of the spirits of all flesh, set a man over the congregation,

17Which may go out before them, and which may go in before them, and which may lead them out, and which may bring them in; that the congregation of the LORD be not as sheep which have no shepherd.

18And the LORD said unto Moses, Take thee Joshua the son of Nun, a man in whom *is* the spirit, and lay thine hand upon him;

19And set him before Eleazar the priest, and before all the congregation; and give him a charge in their sight.

20And thou shalt put *some* of thine honour upon him, that all the congregation of the children of Israel may be obedient.

21And he shall stand before Eleazar the priest, who shall ask *counsel* for him after the judgment of Urim before the LORD: at his word shall they go out, and at his word they shall come in, *both* he, and all the children of Israel with him, even all the congregation.

22And Moses did as the LORD commanded him: and he took Joshua, and set him before Eleazar the priest, and before all the congregation:

23And he laid his hands upon him, and gave him a charge, as the LORD commanded by the hand of Moses.

AND the LORD spake unto Moses, saying,

2Command the children of Israel, and say unto them, My offering, *and* my bread for my sacrifices made by fire, *for* a sweet savour unto me, shall ye observe to offer unto me in their due season.

3And thou shalt say unto them, This

is the offering made by fire which ye shall offer unto the LORD; two lambs of the first year without spot day by day, *for* a continual burnt offering.

4The one lamb shalt thou offer in the morning, and the other lamb shalt thou offer at even;

5And a tenth *part* of an ephah of flour for a meat offering, mingled with the fourth *part* of an hin of beaten oil.

6*It is* a continual burnt offering, which was ordained in mount Sinai for a sweet savour, a sacrifice made by fire unto the LORD.

7And the drink offering thereof *shall be* the fourth *part* of an hin for the one lamb: in the holy *place* shalt thou cause the strong wine to be poured unto the LORD *for* a drink offering.

8And the other lamb shalt thou offer at even: as the meat offering of the morning, and as the drink offering thereof, thou shalt offer *it,* a sacrifice made by fire, of a sweet savour unto the LORD.

9And on the sabbath day two lambs of the first year without spot, and two tenth deals of flour *for* a meat offering, mingled with oil, and the drink offering thereof:

10*This is* the burnt offering of every sabbath, beside the continual burnt offering, and his drink offering.

11And in the beginnings of your months ye shall offer a burnt offering unto the LORD; two young bullocks, and one ram, seven lambs of the first year without spot;

12And three tenth deals of flour *for* a meat offering, mingled with oil, for one bullock; and two tenth deals of flour *for* a meat offering, mingled with oil, for one ram;

13And a several tenth deal of flour mingled with oil *for* a meat offering unto one lamb; *for* a burnt offering of a sweet savour, a sacrifice made by fire unto the LORD.

14And their drink offerings shall be half an hin of wine unto a bullock, and the third *part* of an hin unto a ram, and a fourth *part* of an hin unto a lamb: this *is* the burnt offering of every month throughout the months of the year.

LUKE 3:1–22

Now in the fifteenth year of the reign of Tiberius Caesar, Pontius Pilate being governor of Judaea, and Herod being tetrarch of Galilee, and his brother Philip tetrarch of Ituraea and of the region of Trachonitis, and Lysanias the tetrarch of Abilene,

2Annas and Caiaphas being the high priests, the word of God came unto John the son of Zacharias in the wilderness.

3And he came into all the country about Jordan, preaching the baptism of repentance for the remission of sins;

4As it is written in the book of the words of Esaias the prophet, saying, The voice of one crying in the wilderness, Prepare ye the way of the Lord, make his paths straight.

5Every valley shall be filled, and every mountain and hill shall be brought low; and the crooked shall be made straight, and the rough ways *shall be* made smooth;

6And all flesh shall see the salvation of God.

7Then said he to the multitude that came forth to be baptized of him, O generation of vipers, who hath warned you to flee from the wrath to come?

8Bring forth therefore fruits worthy of repentance, and begin not to say within yourselves, We have Abraham to *our* father: for I say unto you, That God is able of these stones to raise up children unto Abraham.

9And now also the axe is laid unto the root of the trees: every tree therefore which bringeth not forth good fruit is hewn down, and cast into the fire.

10And the people asked him, saying, What shall we do then?

11He answereth and saith unto them, He that hath two coats, let him impart to him that hath none; and he that hath meat, let him do likewise.

12Then came also publicans to be baptized, and said unto him, Master, what shall we do?

13And he said unto them, Exact no more than that which is appointed you.

14And the soldiers likewise demanded of him, saying, And what shall we do? And he said unto them, Do violence to no man, neither accuse *any* falsely; and be content with your wages.

15And as the people were in expectation, and all men mused in their hearts of John, whether he were the Christ, or not;

16John answered, saying unto *them* all, I indeed baptize you with water; but one mightier than I cometh, the latchet of whose shoes I am not worthy to unloose: he shall baptize you with the Holy Ghost and with fire:

17Whose fan *is* in his hand, and he will throughly purge his floor, and will gather the wheat into his garner; but the chaff he will burn with fire unquenchable.

18And many other things in his exhortation preached he unto the people.

19But Herod the tetrarch, being reproved by him for Herodias his brother Philip's wife, and for all the evils which Herod had done,

20Added yet this above all, that he shut up John in prison.

21Now when all the people were baptized, it came to pass, that Jesus also being baptized, and praying, the heaven was opened,

22And the Holy Ghost descended in a bodily shape like a dove upon him, and a voice came from heaven, which said, Thou art my beloved Son; in thee I am well pleased.

PSALM 61:1–8

HEAR my cry, O God; attend unto my prayer.

2From the end of the earth will I cry unto thee, when my heart is overwhelmed: lead me to the rock *that* is higher than I.

3For thou hast been a shelter for me, *and* a strong tower from the enemy.

4I will abide in thy tabernacle for ever: I will trust in the covert of thy wings. Selah.

5For thou, O God, hast heard my vows: thou hast given *me* the heritage of those that fear thy name.

6Thou wilt prolong the king's life: *and* his years as many generations.

7He shall abide before God for ever: O prepare mercy and truth, *which* may preserve him.

8So will I sing praise unto thy name for ever, that I may daily perform my vows.

PROVERBS FOR TODAY/ 11:16–17

A gracious woman retaineth honour: and strong men *retain riches.*   □ *The merciful man doeth good to his own soul: but* he that is *cruel troubleth his own flesh.*

MARCH 19

NUMBERS 28:15—29:40

AND one kid of the goats for a sin offering unto the LORD shall be offered, beside the continual burnt offering, and his drink offering.

16And in the fourteenth day of the first month *is* the passover of the LORD.

17And in the fifteenth day of this month *is* the feast: seven days shall unleavened bread be eaten.

18In the first day *shall be* an holy convocation; ye shall do no manner of servile work *therein:*

19But ye shall offer a sacrifice made by fire *for* a burnt offering unto the LORD; two young bullocks, and one ram, and seven lambs of the first year: they shall be unto you without blemish:

20And their meat offering *shall be of* flour mingled with oil: three tenth deals shall ye offer for a bullock, and two tenth deals for a ram;

21A several tenth deal shalt thou offer for every lamb, throughout the seven lambs:

22And one goat *for* a sin offering, to make an atonement for you.

23Ye shall offer these beside the burnt offering in the morning, which *is* for a continual burnt offering.

24After this manner ye shall offer daily, throughout the seven days, the meat of the sacrifice made by fire, of a sweet savour unto the LORD: it shall be offered beside the continual burnt offering, and his drink offering.

25And on the seventh day ye shall have an holy convocation; ye shall do no servile work.

26Also in the day of the firstfruits, when ye bring a new meat offering unto the LORD, after your weeks *be out,* ye shall have an holy convocation; ye shall do no servile work:

27But he shall offer the burnt offering for a sweet savour unto the LORD; two young bullocks, one ram, seven lambs of the first year;

28And their meat offering of flour mingled with oil, three tenth deals unto one bullock, two tenth deals unto one ram,

29A several tenth deal unto one lamb, throughout the seven lambs;

30*And* one kid of the goats, to make an atonement for you.

31Ye shall offer *them* beside the continual burnt offering, and his meat offering, (they shall be unto you without blemish) and their drink offerings.

AND in the seventh month, on the first *day* of the month, ye shall have an holy convocation; ye shall do no servile work: it is a day of blowing the trumpets unto you.

2And ye shall offer a burnt offering for a sweet savour unto the LORD; one young bullock, one ram, *and* seven lambs of the first year without blemish:

3And their meat offering *shall be of* flour mingled with oil, three tenth deals for a bullock, *and* two tenth deals for a ram,

4And one tenth deal for one lamb, throughout the seven lambs:

5And one kid of the goats *for* a sin offering, to make an atonement for you:

6Beside the burnt offering of the month, and his meat offering, and the daily burnt offering, and his meat offering, and their drink offerings, according unto their manner, for a sweet savour, a sacrifice made by fire unto the LORD.

7And ye shall have on the tenth *day* of this seventh month an holy convocation; and ye shall afflict your souls: ye shall not do any work *therein:*

8But ye shall offer a burnt offering unto the LORD *for* a sweet savour; one young bullock, one ram, *and* seven lambs of the first year; they shall be unto you without blemish:

9And their meat offering *shall be of* flour mingled with oil, three tenth deals

to a bullock, *and* two tenth deals to one ram,

10A several tenth deal for one lamb, throughout the seven lambs:

11One kid of the goats *for* a sin offering; beside the sin offering of atonement, and the continual burnt offering, and the meat offering of it, and their drink offerings.

12And on the fifteenth day of the seventh month ye shall have an holy convocation; ye shall do no servile work, and ye shall keep a feast unto the LORD seven days:

13And ye shall offer a burnt offering, a sacrifice made by fire, of a sweet savour unto the LORD; thirteen young bullocks, two rams, *and* fourteen lambs of the first year; they shall be without blemish:

14And their meat offering *shall be of* flour mingled with oil, three tenth deals unto every bullock of the thirteen bullocks, two tenth deals to each ram of the two rams,

15And a several tenth deal to each lamb of the fourteen lambs:

16And one kid of the goats *for* a sin offering; beside the continual burnt offering, his meat offering, and his drink offering.

17And on the second day *ye shall offer* twelve young bullocks, two rams, fourteen lambs of the first year without spot:

18And their meat offering and their drink offerings for the bullocks, for the rams, and for the lambs, *shall be* according to their number, after the manner:

19And one kid of the goats *for* a sin offering; beside the continual burnt offering, and the meat offering thereof, and their drink offerings.

20And on the third day eleven bullocks, two rams, fourteen lambs of the first year without blemish;

21And their meat offering and their drink offerings for the bullocks, for the rams, and for the lambs, *shall be* according to their number, after the manner:

22And one goat *for* a sin offering; beside the continual burnt offering, and his meat offering, and his drink offering.

23And on the fourth day ten bullocks, two rams, *and* fourteen lambs of the first year without blemish:

24Their meat offering and their drink offerings for the bullocks, for the rams, and for the lambs, *shall be* according to their number, after the manner:

25And one kid of the goats *for* a sin offering; beside the continual burnt offering, his meat offering, and his drink offering.

26And on the fifth day nine bullocks, two rams, *and* fourteen lambs of the first year without spot:

27And their meat offering and their drink offerings for the bullocks, for the rams, and for the lambs, *shall be* according to their number, after the manner:

28And one goat *for* a sin offering; beside the continual burnt offering, and his meat offering, and his drink offering.

29And on the sixth day eight bullocks, two rams, *and* fourteen lambs of the first year without blemish:

30And their meat offering and their drink offerings for the bullocks, for the rams, and for the lambs, *shall be* according to their number, after the manner:

31And one goat *for* a sin offering; beside the continual burnt offering, his meat offering, and his drink offering.

32And on the seventh day seven bullocks, two rams, *and* fourteen lambs of the first year without blemish:

33And their meat offering and their drink offerings for the bullocks, for the rams, and for the lambs, *shall be* according to their number, after the manner:

34And one goat *for* a sin offering; beside the continual burnt offering, his meat offering, and his drink offering.

35On the eighth day ye shall have a solemn assembly: ye shall do no servile work *therein:*

36But ye shall offer a burnt offering, a sacrifice made by fire, of a sweet savour unto the LORD: one bullock, one ram, seven lambs of the first year without blemish:

37Their meat offering and their drink offerings for the bullock, for the ram, and for the lambs, *shall be* according to their number, after the manner:

38And one goat *for* a sin offering; beside the continual burnt offering, and his meat offering, and his drink offering.

39These *things* ye shall do unto the LORD in your set feasts, beside your vows, and your freewill offerings, for your burnt offerings, and for your meat offerings, and for your drink offerings, and for your peace offerings.

40And Moses told the children of Israel according to all that the LORD commanded Moses.

LUKE 3:23–38

AND Jesus himself began to be about thirty years of age, being (as was supposed) the son of Joseph, which was *the son* of Heli,

24Which was *the son* of Matthat, which was *the son* of Levi, which was *the son* of Melchi, which was *the son* of Janna, which was *the son* of Joseph,

25Which was *the son* of Mattathias, which was *the son* of Amos, which was *the son* of Naum, which was *the son* of Esli, which was *the son* of Nagge,

26Which was *the son* of Maath, which was *the son* of Mattathias, which was *the son* of Semei, which was *the son* of Joseph, which was *the son* of Juda,

27Which was *the son* of Joanna, which was *the son* of Rhesa, which was *the son* of Zorobabel, which was *the son* of Salathiel, which was *the son* of Neri,

28Which was *the son* of Melchi, which was *the son* of Addi, which was *the son* of Cosam, which was *the son* of Elmodam, which was *the son* of Er,

29Which was *the son* of Jose, which was *the son* of Eliezer, which was *the son* of Jorim, which was *the son* of Matthat, which was *the son* of Levi,

30Which was *the son* of Simeon, which was *the son* of Juda, which was *the son* of Joseph, which was *the son* of Jonan, which was *the son* of Eliakim,

31Which was *the son* of Melea, which was *the son* of Menan, which was *the son* of Mattatha, which was *the son* of Nathan, which was *the son* of David,

32Which was *the son* of Jesse, which was *the son* of Obed, which was *the son* of Booz, which was *the son* of Salmon, which was *the son* of Naasson,

33Which was *the son* of Aminadab, which was *the son* of Aram, which was *the son* of Esrom, which was *the son* of Phares, which was *the son* of Juda,

34Which was *the son* of Jacob, which was *the son* of Isaac, which was *the son* of Abraham, which was *the son* of Thara, which was *the son* of Nachor,

35Which was *the son* of Saruch, which was *the son* of Ragau, which was *the son* of Phalec, which was *the son* of Heber, which was *the son* of Sala,

36Which was *the son* of Cainan, which was *the son* of Arphaxad, which was *the son* of Sem, which was *the son* of Noe, which was *the son* of Lamech,

37Which was *the son* of Mathusala, which was *the son* of Enoch, which was *the son* of Jared, which was *the son* of Maleleel, which was *the son* of Cainan,

38Which was *the son* of Enos, which was *the son* of Seth, which was *the son* of Adam, which was *the son* of God.

PSALM 62:1–12

TRULY my soul waiteth upon God: from him *cometh* my salvation. 2He only *is* my rock and my salvation; *he is* my defence; I shall not be greatly moved.

3How long will ye imagine mischief against a man? ye shall be slain all of you: as a bowing wall *shall ye be, and as* a tottering fence.

4They only consult to cast *him* down from his excellency: they delight in lies: they bless with their mouth, but they curse inwardly. Selah.

5My soul, wait thou only upon God; for my expectation *is* from him.

6He only *is* my rock and my salvation: *he is* my defence; I shall not be moved.

7In God *is* my salvation and my glory: the rock of my strength, *and* my refuge, *is* in God.

8Trust in him at all times; ye people, pour out your heart before him: God *is* a refuge for us. Selah.

9Surely men of low degree *are* vanity, *and* men of the high degree *are* a lie: to be laid in the balance, they *are* altogether *lighter* than vanity.

10Trust not in oppression, and become not vain in robbery: if riches increase, set not your heart *upon them.*

11God hath spoken once; twice have I heard this; that power *belongeth* unto God.

12Also unto thee, O Lord, *belongeth* mercy: for thou renderest to every man according to his work.

PROVERBS FOR TODAY/ 11:18–19

The wicked worketh a deceitful work: but to him that soweth righteousness shall be *a sure reward.* □ *As righteousness* tendeth *to life: so he that pursueth evil* pursueth it *to his own death.*

MARCH 20

NUMBERS 30:1—31:54

AND Moses spake unto the heads of the tribes concerning the children of Israel, saying, This *is* the thing which the LORD hath commanded.

2If a man vow a vow unto the LORD, or swear an oath to bind his soul with a bond; he shall not break his word, he shall do according to all that proceedeth out of his mouth.

3If a woman also vow a vow unto the LORD, and bind *herself* by a bond, *being* in her father's house in her youth;

4And her father hear her vow, and her bond wherewith she hath bound her soul, and her father shall hold his peace at her: then all her vows shall stand, and every bond wherewith she hath bound her soul shall stand.

5But if her father disallow her in the day that he heareth; not any of her vows, or of her bonds wherewith she hath bound her soul, shall stand: and the LORD shall forgive her, because her father disallowed her.

6And if she had at all an husband, when she vowed, or uttered ought out of her lips, wherewith she bound her soul;

7And her husband heard *it,* and held his peace at her in the day that he heard *it:* then her vows shall stand, and her bonds wherewith she bound her soul shall stand.

8But if her husband disallowed her on the day that he heard *it;* then he shall make her vow which she vowed, and that which she uttered with her lips, wherewith she bound her soul, of none effect: and the LORD shall forgive her.

9But every vow of a widow, and of her that is divorced, wherewith they have bound their souls, shall stand against her.

10And if she vowed in her husband's house, or bound her soul by a bond with an oath;

11And her husband heard *it,* and held his peace at her, *and* disallowed her not: then all her vows shall stand, and every bond wherewith she bound her soul shall stand.

12But if her husband hath utterly made them void on the day he heard *them; then* whatsoever proceeded out of her lips concerning her vows, or concerning the bond of her soul, shall not stand: her husband hath made them void; and the LORD shall forgive her.

13Every vow, and every binding oath to afflict the soul, her husband may establish it, or her husband may make it void.

14But if her husband altogether hold his peace at her from day to day; then he establisheth all her vows, or all her bonds, which *are* upon her: he confirmeth them, because he held his peace at her in the day that he heard *them.*

15But if he shall any ways make them void after that he hath heard *them;* then he shall bear her iniquity.

16These *are* the statutes, which the LORD commanded Moses, between a man and his wife, between the father and his daughter, *being yet* in her youth in her father's house.

AND the LORD spake unto Moses, saying,

2Avenge the children of Israel of the Midianites: afterward shalt thou be gathered unto thy people.

3And Moses spake unto the people, saying, Arm some of yourselves unto the war, and let them go against the Midianites, and avenge the LORD of Midian.

4Of every tribe a thousand, throughout all the tribes of Israel, shall ye send to the war.

5So there were delivered out of the thousands of Israel, a thousand of *every* tribe, twelve thousand armed for war.

6And Moses sent them to the war, a thousand of *every* tribe, them and Phinehas the son of Eleazar the priest, to the war, with the holy instruments, and the trumpets to blow in his hand.

7And they warred against the Midianites, as the Lord commanded Moses; and they slew all the males.

8And they slew the kings of Midian, beside the rest of them that were slain; *namely,* Evi, and Rekem, and Zur, and Hur, and Reba, five kings of Midian: Balaam also the son of Beor they slew with the sword.

9And the children of Israel took *all* the women of Midian captives, and their little ones, and took the spoil of all their cattle, and all their flocks, and all their goods.

10And they burnt all their cities wherein they dwelt, and all their goodly castles, with fire.

11And they took all the spoil, and all the prey, *both* of men and of beasts.

12And they brought the captives, and the prey, and the spoil, unto Moses, and Eleazar the priest, and unto the congregation of the children of Israel, unto the camp at the plains of Moab, which *are* by Jordan *near* Jericho.

13And Moses, and Eleazar the priest, and all the princes of the congregation, went forth to meet them without the camp.

14And Moses was wroth with the officers of the host, *with* the captains over thousands, and captains over hundreds, which came from the battle.

15And Moses said unto them, Have ye saved all the women alive?

16Behold, these caused the children of Israel, through the counsel of Balaam, to commit trespass against the Lord in the matter of Peor, and there was a plague among the congregation of the Lord.

17Now therefore kill every male among the little ones, and kill every woman that hath known man by lying with him.

18But all the women children, that have not known a man by lying with him, keep alive for yourselves.

19And do ye abide without the camp seven days: whosoever hath killed any person, and whosoever hath touched any slain, purify *both* yourselves and your captives on the third day, and on the seventh day.

20And purify all *your* raiment, and all that is made of skins, and all work of goats' *hair,* and all things made of wood.

21And Eleazar the priest said unto the men of war which went to the battle, This *is* the ordinance of the law which the Lord commanded Moses;

22Only the gold, and the silver, the brass, the iron, the tin, and the lead,

23Every thing that may abide the fire, ye shall make *it* go through the fire, and it shall be clean: nevertheless it shall be purified with the water of separation: and all that abideth not the fire ye shall make go through the water.

24And ye shall wash your clothes on the seventh day, and ye shall be clean, and afterward ye shall come into the camp.

25And the Lord spake unto Moses, saying,

26Take the sum of the prey that was taken, *both* of man and of beast, thou, and Eleazar the priest, and the chief fathers of the congregation:

27And divide the prey into two parts; between them that took the war upon them, who went out to battle, and between all the congregation:

28And levy a tribute unto the Lord of the men of war which went out to battle; one soul of five hundred, *both* of the persons, and of the beeves, and of the asses, and of the sheep:

29Take *it* of their half, and give *it* unto Eleazar the priest, *for* an heave offering of the LORD.

30And of the children of Israel's half, thou shalt take one portion of fifty, of the persons, of the beeves, of the asses, and of the flocks, of all manner of beasts, and give them unto the Levites, which keep the charge of the tabernacle of the LORD.

31And Moses and Eleazar the priest did as the LORD commanded Moses.

32And the booty, *being* the rest of the prey which the men of war had caught, was six hundred thousand and seventy thousand and five thousand sheep,

33And threescore and twelve thousand beeves,

34And threescore and one thousand asses,

35And thirty and two thousand persons in all, of women that had not known man by lying with him.

36And the half, *which was* the portion of them that went out to war, was in number three hundred thousand and seven and thirty thousand and five hundred sheep:

37And the LORD's tribute of the sheep was six hundred and threescore and fifteen.

38And the beeves *were* thirty and six thousand; of which the LORD's tribute *was* threescore and twelve.

39And the asses *were* thirty thousand and five hundred; of which the LORD's tribute *was* threescore and one.

40And the persons *were* sixteen thousand; of which the LORD's tribute *was* thirty and two persons.

41And Moses gave the tribute, *which was* the LORD's heave offering, unto Eleazar the priest, as the LORD commanded Moses.

42And of the children of Israel's half, which Moses divided from the men that warred,

43(Now the half *that pertained unto* the congregation was three hundred thousand and thirty thousand *and* seven thousand and five hundred sheep,

44And thirty and six thousand beeves,

45And thirty thousand asses and five hundred,

46And sixteen thousand persons;)

47Even of the children of Israel's half, Moses took one portion of fifty, *both* of man and of beast, and gave them unto the Levites, which kept the charge of the tabernacle of the LORD; as the LORD commanded Moses.

48And the officers which *were* over thousands of the host, the captains of thousands, and captains of hundreds, came near unto Moses:

49And they said unto Moses, Thy servants have taken the sum of the men of war which *are* under our charge, and there lacketh not one man of us.

50We have therefore brought an oblation for the LORD, what every man hath gotten, of jewels of gold, chains, and bracelets, rings, earrings, and tablets, to make an atonement for our souls before the LORD.

51And Moses and Eleazar the priest took the gold of them, *even* all wrought jewels.

52And all the gold of the offering that they offered up to the LORD, of the captains of thousands, and of the captains of hundreds, was sixteen thousand seven hundred and fifty shekels.

53(*For* the men of war had taken spoil, every man for himself.)

54And Moses and Eleazar the priest took the gold of the captains of thousands and of hundreds, and brought it into the tabernacle of the congregation, *for* a memorial for the children of Israel before the LORD.

LUKE 4:1–32

AND Jesus being full of the Holy Ghost returned from Jordan, and was led by the Spirit into the wilderness,

2Being forty days tempted of the

devil. And in those days he did eat nothing: and when they were ended, he afterward hungered.

3And the devil said unto him, If thou be the Son of God, command this stone that it be made bread.

4And Jesus answered him, saying, It is written, That man shall not live by bread alone, but by every word of God.

5And the devil, taking him up into an high mountain, shewed unto him all the kingdoms of the world in a moment of time.

6And the devil said unto him, All this power will I give thee, and the glory of them: for that is delivered unto me; and to whomsoever I will I give it.

7If thou therefore wilt worship me, all shall be thine.

8And Jesus answered and said unto him, Get thee behind me, Satan: for it is written, Thou shalt worship the Lord thy God, and him only shalt thou serve.

9And he brought him to Jerusalem, and set him on a pinnacle of the temple, and said unto him, If thou be the Son of God, cast thyself down from hence:

10For it is written, He shall give his angels charge over thee, to keep thee:

11And in *their* hands they shall bear thee up, lest at any time thou dash thy foot against a stone.

12And Jesus answering said unto him, It is said, Thou shalt not tempt the Lord thy God.

13And when the devil had ended all the temptation, he departed from him for a season.

14And Jesus returned in the power of the Spirit into Galilee: and there went out a fame of him through all the region round about.

15And he taught in their synagogues, being glorified of all.

16And he came to Nazareth, where he had been brought up: and, as his custom was, he went into the synagogue on the sabbath day, and stood up for to read.

17And there was delivered unto him the book of the prophet Esaias. And when he had opened the book, he found the place where it was written,

18The Spirit of the Lord *is* upon me, because he hath anointed me to preach the gospel to the poor; he hath sent me to heal the brokenhearted, to preach deliverance to the captives, and recovering of sight to the blind, to set at liberty them that are bruised,

19To preach the acceptable year of the Lord.

20And he closed the book, and he gave *it* again to the minister, and sat down. And the eyes of all them that were in the synagogue were fastened on him.

21And he began to say unto them, This day is this scripture fulfilled in your ears.

22And all bare him witness, and wondered at the gracious words which proceeded out of his mouth. And they said, Is not this Joseph's son?

23And he said unto them, Ye will surely say unto me this proverb, Physician, heal thyself: whatsoever we have heard done in Capernaum, do also here in thy country.

24And he said, Verily I say unto you, No prophet is accepted in his own country,

25But I tell you of a truth, many widows were in Israel in the days of Elias, when the heaven was shut up three years and six months, when great famine was throughout all the land;

26But unto none of them was Elias sent, save unto Sarepta, *a city* of Sidon, unto a woman *that was* a widow.

27And many lepers were in Israel in the time of Eliseus the prophet; and none of them was cleansed, saving Naaman the Syrian.

28And all they in the synagogue, when they heard these things, were filled with wrath,

²⁹And rose up, and thrust him out of the city, and led him unto the brow of the hill whereon their city was built, that they might cast him down headlong.

³⁰But he passing through the midst of them went his way,

³¹And came down to Capernaum, a city of Galilee, and taught them on the sabbath days.

³²And they were astonished at his doctrine: for his word was with power.

PSALM 63:1–11

O God, thou *art* my God; early will I seek thee: my soul thirsteth for thee, my flesh longeth for thee in a dry and thirsty land, where no water is;

²To see thy power and thy glory, so *as* I have seen thee in the sanctuary.

³Because thy lovingkindness *is* better than life, my lips shall praise thee.

⁴Thus will I bless thee while I live: I will lift up my hands in thy name.

⁵My soul shall be satisfied as *with* marrow and fatness; and my mouth shall praise *thee* with joyful lips:

⁶When I remember thee upon my bed, *and* meditate on thee in the *night* watches.

⁷Because thou hast been my help, therefore in the shadow of thy wings will I rejoice.

⁸My soul followeth hard after thee: thy right hand upholdeth me.

⁹But those *that* seek my soul, to destroy *it,* shall go into the lower parts of the earth.

¹⁰They shall fall by the sword: they shall be a portion for foxes.

¹¹But the king shall rejoice in God; every one that sweareth by him shall glory: but the mouth of them that speak lies shall be stopped.

PROVERBS FOR TODAY/ 11:20–21

They that are of a froward heart are *abomination to the* LORD: *but* such as are *upright in* their *way* are *his delight.* □ Though *hand* join *in hand, the wicked shall not be unpunished: but the seed of the righteous shall be delivered.*

MARCH 21

NUMBERS 32:1—33:39

Now the children of Reuben and the children of Gad had a very great multitude of cattle: and when they saw the land of Jazer, and the land of Gilead, that, behold, the place *was* a place for cattle;

²The children of Gad and the children of Reuben came and spake unto Moses, and to Eleazar the priest, and unto the princes of the congregation, saying,

³Ataroth, and Dibon, and Jazer, and Nimrah, and Heshbon, and Elealeh, and Shebam, and Nebo, and Beon,

⁴*Even* the country which the LORD smote before the congregation of Israel, *is* a land for cattle, and thy servants have cattle:

⁵Wherefore, said they, if we have found grace in thy sight, let this land be given unto thy servants for a possession, *and* bring us not over Jordan.

⁶And Moses said unto the children of Gad and to the children of Reuben, Shall your brethren go to war, and shall ye sit here?

7And wherefore discourage ye the heart of the children of Israel from going over into the land which the Lord hath given them?

8Thus did your fathers, when I sent them from Kadesh–barnea to see the land.

9For when they went up unto the valley of Eshcol, and saw the land, they discouraged the heart of the children of Israel, that they should not go into the land which the Lord had given them.

10And the Lord's anger was kindled the same time, and he sware, saying,

11Surely none of the men that came up out of Egypt, from twenty years old and upward, shall see the land which I sware unto Abraham, unto Isaac, and unto Jacob; because they have not wholly followed me:

12Save Caleb the son of Jephunneh the Kenezite, and Joshua the son of Nun: for they have wholly followed the Lord.

13And the Lord's anger was kindled against Israel, and he made them wander in the wilderness forty years, until all the generation, that had done evil in the sight of the Lord, was consumed.

14And, behold, ye are risen up in your fathers' stead, an increase of sinful men, to augment yet the fierce anger of the Lord toward Israel.

15For if ye turn away from after him, he will yet again leave them in the wilderness; and ye shall destroy all this people.

16And they came near unto him, and said, We will build sheepfolds here for our cattle, and cities for our little ones:

17But we ourselves will go ready armed before the children of Israel, until we have brought them unto their place: and our little ones shall dwell in the fenced cities because of the inhabitants of the land.

18We will not return unto our houses, until the children of Israel have inherited every man his inheritance.

19For we will not inherit with them on yonder side Jordan, or forward; because our inheritance is fallen to us on this side Jordan eastward.

20And Moses said unto them, If ye will do this thing, if ye will go armed before the Lord to war,

21And will go all of you armed over Jordan before the Lord, until he hath driven out his enemies from before him,

22And the land be subdued before the Lord: then afterward ye shall return, and be guiltless before the Lord, and before Israel; and this land shall be your possession before the Lord.

23But if ye will not do so, behold, ye have sinned against the Lord: and be sure your sin will find you out.

24Build you cities for your little ones, and folds for your sheep; and do that which hath proceeded out of your mouth.

25And the children of Gad and the children of Reuben spake unto Moses, saying, Thy servants will do as my lord commandeth.

26Our little ones, our wives, our flocks, and all our cattle, shall be there in the cities of Gilead:

27But thy servants will pass over, every man armed for war, before the Lord to battle, as my lord saith.

28So concerning them Moses commanded Eleazar the priest, and Joshua the son of Nun, and the chief fathers of the tribes of the children of Israel:

29And Moses said unto them, If the children of Gad and the children of Reuben will pass with you over Jordan, every man armed to battle, before the Lord, and the land shall be subdued before you; then ye shall give them the land of Gilead for a possession:

30But if they will not pass over with you armed, they shall have possessions among you in the land of Canaan.

31And the children of Gad and the children of Reuben answered, saying, As the Lord hath said unto thy servants, so will we do.

32We will pass over armed before

the LORD into the land of Canaan, that the possession of our inheritance on this side Jordan *may be* ours.

33And Moses gave unto them, *even* to the children of Gad, and to the children of Reuben, and unto half the tribe of Manasseh the son of Joseph, the kingdom of Sihon king of the Amorites, and the kingdom of Og king of Bashan, the land, with the cities thereof in the coasts, *even* the cities of the country round about.

34And the children of Gad built Dibon, and Ataroth, and Aroer,

35And Atroth, Shophan, and Jaazer, and Jogbehah,

36And Beth–nimrah, and Beth–haran, fenced cities: and folds for sheep.

37And the children of Reuben built Heshbon, and Elealeh, and Kirjathaim,

38And Nebo, and Baal–meon, (their names being changed,) and Shibmah: and gave other names unto the cities which they builded.

39And the children of Machir the son of Manasseh went to Gilead, and took it, and dispossessed the Amorite which *was* in it.

40And Moses gave Gilead unto Machir the son of Manasseh; and he dwelt therein.

41And Jair the son of Manasseh went and took the small towns thereof, and called them Havoth–jair.

42And Nobah went and took Kenath, and the villages thereof, and called it Nobah, after his own name.

THESE *are* the journeys of the children of Israel, which went forth out of the land of Egypt with their armies under the hand of Moses and Aaron.

2And Moses wrote their goings out according to their journeys by the commandment of the LORD: and these *are* the journeys according to their goings out.

3And they departed from Rameses in the first month, on the fifteenth day of the first month; on the morrow after the passover the children of Israel went out with an high hand in the sight of all the Egyptians.

4For the Egyptians buried all *their* firstborn, which the LORD had smitten among them: upon their gods also the LORD executed judgments.

5And the children of Israel removed from Rameses, and pitched in Succoth.

6And they departed from Succoth, and pitched in Etham, which *is* in the edge of the wilderness.

7And they removed from Etham, and turned again unto Pi–hahiroth, which *is* before Baal–zephon: and they pitched before Migdol.

8And they departed from before Pi–hahiroth, and passed through the midst of the sea into the wilderness, and went three days' journey in the wilderness of Etham, and pitched in Marah.

9And they removed from Marah, and came unto Elim: and in Elim *were* twelve fountains of water, and threescore and ten palm trees; and they pitched there.

10And they removed from Elim, and encamped by the Red sea.

11And they removed from the Red sea, and encamped in the wilderness of Sin.

12And they took their journey out of the wilderness of Sin, and encamped in Dophkah.

13And they departed from Dophkah, and encamped in Alush.

14And they removed from Alush, and encamped at Rephidim, where was no water for the people to drink.

15And they departed from Rephidim, and pitched in the wilderness of Sinai.

16And they removed from the desert of Sinai, and pitched at Kibroth–hattaavah.

17And they departed from Kibroth–hattaavah, and encamped at Hazeroth.

18And they departed from Hazeroth,

and pitched in Rithmah.

19And they departed from Rithmah, and pitched at Rimmon–parez.

20And they departed from Rimmon–parez, and pitched in Libnah.

21And they removed from Libnah, and pitched at Rissah.

22And they journeyed from Rissah and pitched in Kehelathah.

23And they went from Kehelathah, and pitched in mount Shapher.

24And they removed from mount Shapher, and encamped in Haradah.

25And they removed from Haradah, and pitched in Makheloth.

26And they removed from Makheloth, and encamped at Tahath.

27And they departed from Tahath, and pitched at Tarah.

28And they removed from Tarah, and pitched in Mithcah.

29And they went from Mithcah, and pitched in Hashmonah.

30And they departed from Hashmonah, and encamped at Moseroth.

31And they departed from Moseroth, and pitched in Bene–jaakan.

32And they removed from Bene–jaakan, and encamped at Hor–hagidgad.

33And they went from Hor–hagidgad, and pitched in Jotbathah.

34And they removed from Jotbathah, and encamped at Ebronah.

35And they departed from Ebronah, and encamped at Ezion–gaber.

36And they removed from Ezion–gaber, and pitched in the wilderness of Zin, which is Kadesh.

37And they removed from Kadesh, and pitched in mount Hor, in the edge of the land of Edom.

38And Aaron the priest went up into mount Hor at the commandment of the LORD, and died there, in the fortieth year after the children of Israel were come out of the land of Egypt, in the first *day* of the fifth month.

39And Aaron *was* an hundred and twenty and three years old when he died in mount Hor.

LUKE 4:33—5:11

AND in the synagogue there was a man, which had a spirit of an unclean devil, and cried out with a loud voice,

34Saying, Let *us* alone; what have we to do with thee, *thou* Jesus of Nazareth? art thou come to destroy us? I know thee who thou art; the Holy One of God.

35And Jesus rebuked him, saying, Hold thy peace, and come out of him. And when the devil had thrown him in the midst, he came out of him, and hurt him not.

36And they were all amazed, and spake among themselves, saying, What a word *is* this! for with authority and power he commandeth the unclean spirits, and they come out.

37And the fame of him went out into every place of the country round about.

38And he arose out of the synagogue, and entered into Simon's house. And Simon's wife's mother was taken with a great fever; and they besought him for her.

39And he stood over her, and rebuked the fever; and it left her: and immediately she arose and ministered unto them.

40Now when the sun was setting, all they that had any sick with divers diseases brought them unto him; and he laid his hands on every one of them, and healed them.

41And devils also came out of many, crying out, and saying, Thou art Christ the Son of God. And he rebuking *them* suffered them not to speak: for they knew that he was Christ.

42And when it was day, he departed and went into a desert place: and the people sought him, and came unto him, and stayed him, that he should not depart from them.

43And he said unto them, I must preach the kingdom of God to other cities also: for therefore am I sent.

44And he preached in the synagogues of Galilee.

AND it came to pass, that, as the people pressed upon him to hear the word of God, he stood by the lake of Gennesaret,

2And saw two ships standing by the lake: but the fishermen were gone out of them, and were washing *their* nets.

3And he entered into one of the ships, which was Simon's, and prayed him that he would thrust out a little from the land. And he sat down, and taught the people out of the ship.

4Now when he had left speaking, he said unto Simon, Launch out into the deep, and let down your nets for a draught.

5And Simon answering said unto him, Master, we have toiled all the night, and have taken nothing: nevertheless at thy word I will let down the net.

6And when they had this done, they inclosed a great multitude of fishes: and their net brake.

7And they beckoned unto *their* partners, which were in the other ship, that they should come and help them. And they came, and filled both the ships, so that they began to sink.

8When Simon Peter saw *it,* he fell down at Jesus' knees, saying, Depart from me; for I am a sinful man, O Lord.

9For he was astonished, and all that were with him, at the draught of the fishes which they had taken:

10And so *was* also James, and John, the sons of Zebedee, which were partners with Simon. And Jesus said unto Simon, Fear not; from henceforth thou shalt catch men.

11And when they had brought their ships to land, they forsook all, and followed him.

PSALM 64:1–10

HEAR my voice, O God, in my prayer: preserve my life from fear of the enemy.

2Hide me from the secret counsel of the wicked; from the insurrection of the workers of iniquity:

3Who whet their tongue like a sword, *and* bend *their bows to shoot* their arrows, *even* bitter words:

4That they may shoot in secret at the perfect: suddenly do they shoot at him, and fear not.

5They encourage themselves *in* an evil matter: they commune of laying snares privily; they say, Who shall see them?

6They search out iniquities; they accomplish a diligent search: both the inward *thought* of every one *of them,* and the heart, *is* deep.

7But God shall shoot at them *with* an arrow; suddenly shall they be wounded.

8So they shall make their own tongue to fall upon themselves: all that see them shall flee away.

9And all men shall fear, and shall declare the work of God; for they shall wisely consider of his doing.

10The righteous shall be glad in the LORD, and shall trust in him; and all the upright in heart shall glory.

PROVERBS FOR TODAY/ 11:22

As *a jewel of gold in a swine's snout,* so is *a fair woman which is without discretion.*

NUMBERS 33:40—35:34

A ND king Arad the Canaanite, which dwelt in the south in the land of Canaan, heard of the coming of the children of Israel.

41And they departed from mount Hor, and pitched in Zalmonah.

42And they departed from Zalmonah, and pitched in Punon.

43And they departed from Punon, and pitched in Oboth.

44And they departed from Oboth, and pitched in Ije–abarim, in the border of Moab.

45And they departed from Iim, and pitched in Dibon–gad.

46And they removed from Dibon–gad, and encamped in Almon–diblathaim.

47And they removed from Almon–diblathaim, and pitched in the mountains of Abarim, before Nebo.

48And they departed from the mountains of Abarim, and pitched in the plains of Moab by Jordan *near* Jericho.

49And they pitched by Jordan, from Beth–jesimoth *even* unto Abel–shittim in the plains of Moab.

50And the LORD spake unto Moses in the plains of Moab by Jordan *near* Jericho, saying,

51Speak unto the children of Israel, and say unto them, When ye are passed over Jordan into the land of Canaan;

52Then ye shall drive out all the inhabitants of the land from before you, and destroy all their pictures, and destroy all their molten images, and quite pluck down all their high places:

53And ye shall dispossess *the inhabitants of* the land, and dwell therein: for I have given you the land to possess it.

54And ye shall divide the land by lot for an inheritance among your families:

and to the more ye shall give the more inheritance, and to the fewer ye shall give the less inheritance: every man's *inheritance* shall be in the place where his lot falleth; according to the tribes of your fathers ye shall inherit.

55But if ye will not drive out the inhabitants of the land from before you; then it shall come to pass, that those which ye let remain of them *shall be* pricks in your eyes, and thorns in your sides, and shall vex you in the land wherein ye dwell.

56Moreover it shall come to pass, *that* I shall do unto you, as I thought to do unto them.

A ND the LORD spake unto Moses, saying,

2Command the children of Israel, and say unto them, When ye come into the land of Canaan; (this *is* the land that shall fall unto you for an inheritance, *even* the land of Canaan with the coasts thereof:)

3Then your south quarter shall be from the wilderness of Zin along by the coast of Edom, and your south border shall be the outmost coast of the salt sea eastward:

4And your border shall turn from the south to the ascent of Akrabbim, and pass on to Zin: and the going forth thereof shall be from the south to Kadesh–barnea, and shall go on to Hazar–addar, and pass on to Azmon:

5And the border shall fetch a compass from Azmon unto the river of Egypt, and the goings out of it shall be at the sea.

6And *as for* the western border, ye shall even have the great sea for a border: this shall be your west border.

7And this shall be your north border:

from the great sea ye shall point out for you mount Hor:

8From mount Hor ye shall point out *your border* unto the entrance of Hamath; and the goings forth of the border shall be to Zedad:

9And the border shall go on to Ziphron, and the goings out of it shall be at Hazar–enan: this shall be your north border.

10And ye shall point out your east border from Hazar–enan to Shepham:

11And the coast shall go down from Shepham to Riblah, on the east side of Ain; and the border shall descend, and shall reach unto the side of the sea of Chinnereth eastward:

12And the border shall go down to Jordan, and the goings out of it shall be at the salt sea: this shall be your land with the coasts thereof round about.

13And Moses commanded the children of Israel, saying, This *is* the land which ye shall inherit by lot, which the LORD commanded to give unto the nine tribes, and to the half tribe:

14For the tribe of the children of Reuben according to the house of their fathers, and the tribe of the children of Gad according to the house of their fathers, have received *their inheritance;* and half the tribe of Manasseh have received their inheritance:

15The two tribes and the half tribe have received their inheritance on this side Jordan *near* Jericho eastward, toward the sunrising.

16And the LORD spake unto Moses, saying,

17These *are* the names of the men which shall divide the land unto you: Eleazar the priest, and Joshua the son of Nun.

18And ye shall take one prince of every tribe, to divide the land by inheritance.

19And the names of the men *are* these: Of the tribe of Judah, Caleb the son of Jephunneh.

20And of the tribe of the children of Simeon, Shemuel the son of Ammihud.

21Of the tribe of Benjamin, Elidad the son of Chislon.

22And the prince of the tribe of the children of Dan, Bukki the son of Jogli.

23The prince of the children of Joseph, for the tribe of the children of Manasseh, Hanniel the son of Ephod.

24And the prince of the tribe of the children of Ephraim, Kemuel the son of Shiphtan.

25And the prince of the tribe of the children of Zebulum, Elizaphan the son of Parnach.

26And the prince of the tribe of the children of Issachar, Paltiel the son of Azzan.

27And the prince of the tribe of the children of Asher, Ahihud the son of Shelomi.

28And the prince of the tribe of the children of Naphtali, Pedahel the son of Ammihud.

29These *are they* whom the LORD commanded to divide the inheritance unto the children of Israel in the land of Canaan.

AND the LORD spake unto Moses in the plains of Moab by Jordan *near* Jericho, saying,

2Command the children of Israel, that they give unto the Levites of the inheritance of their possession cities to dwell in; and ye shall give *also* unto the Levites suburbs for the cities round about them.

3And the cities shall they have to dwell in; and the suburbs of them shall be for their cattle, and for their goods, and for all their beasts.

4And the suburbs of the cities, which ye shall give unto the Levites, *shall reach* from the wall of the city and outward a thousand cubits round about.

5And ye shall measure from without the city on the east side two thousand cubits, and on the south side two thousand cubits, and on the west side two thousand cubits, and on the north side two thousand cubits; and the city *shall be* in the midst: this shall be to them the suburbs of the cities.

6And among the cities which ye shall give unto the Levites *there shall be* six cities for refuge, which ye shall appoint for the manslayer, that he may flee thither: and to them ye shall add forty and two cities.

7So all the cities which ye shall give to the Levites *shall be* forty and eight cities: them *shall ye give* with their suburbs.

8And the cities which ye shall give *shall be* of the possession of the children of Israel: from *them that have* many ye shall give many; but from *them that have* few ye shall give few: every one shall give of his cities unto the Levites according to his inheritance which he inheriteth.

9And the Lord spake unto Moses, saying,

10Speak unto the children of Israel, and say unto them, When ye be come over Jordan into the land of Canaan;

11Then ye shall appoint you cities to be cities of refuge for you; that the slayer may flee thither, which killeth any person at unawares.

12And they shall be unto you cities for refuge from the avenger; that the manslayer die not, until he stand before the congregation in judgment.

13And of these cities which ye shall give six cities shall ye have for refuge.

14Ye shall give three cities on this side Jordan, and three cities shall ye give in the land of Canaan, *which* shall be cities of refuge.

15These six cities shall be a refuge, *both* for the children of Israel, and for the stranger, and for the sojourner among them; that every one that killeth any person unawares may flee thither.

16And if he smite him with an instrument of iron, so that he die, he *is* a murderer: the murderer shall surely be put to death.

17And if he smite him with throwing a stone, wherewith he may die, and he die, he *is* a murderer: the murderer shall surely be put to death.

18Or *if* he smite him with an hand weapon of wood, wherewith he may die, and he die, he *is* a murderer: the murderer shall surely be put to death.

19The revenger of blood himself shall slay the murderer: when he meeteth him, he shall slay him.

20But if he thrust him of hatred, or hurl at him by laying of wait, that he die;

21Or in enmity smite him with his hand, that he die: he that smote *him* shall surely be put to death; *for* he *is* a murderer: the revenger of blood shall slay the murderer, when he meeteth him.

22But if he thrust him suddenly without enmity, or have cast upon him any thing without laying of wait,

23Or with any stone, wherewith a man may die, seeing *him* not, and cast *it* upon him, that he die, and *was* not his enemy, neither sought his harm:

24Then the congregation shall judge between the slayer and the revenger of blood according to these judgments:

25And the congregation shall deliver the slayer out of the hand of the revenger of blood, and the congregation shall restore him to the city of his refuge, whither he was fled: and he shall abide in it unto the death of the high priest, which was anointed with the holy oil.

26But if the slayer shall at any time come without the border of the city of his refuge, whither he was fled;

27And the revenger of blood find him without the borders of the city of his refuge, and the revenger of blood kill the slayer; he shall not be guilty of blood:

28Because he should have remained in the city of his refuge until the death of the high priest: but after the death of the high priest the slayer shall return into the land of his possession.

29So these *things* shall be for a statute of judgment unto you throughout your generations in all your dwellings.

30Whoso killeth any person, the murderer shall be put to death by the mouth of witnesses: but one witness shall not testify against any person *to cause him* to die.

31Moreover ye shall take no satisfaction for the life of a murderer, which *is* guilty of death: but he shall be surely put to death.

32And ye shall take no satisfaction for him that is fled to the city of his refuge, that he should come again to dwell in the land, until the death of the priest.

33So ye shall not pollute the land wherein ye *are:* for blood it defileth the land: and the land cannot be cleansed of the blood that is shed therein, but by the blood of him that shed it.

34Defile not therefore the land which ye shall inhabit, wherein I dwell: for I the LORD dwell among the children of Israel.

LUKE 5:12–28

And it came to pass, when he was in a certain city, behold a man full of leprosy: who seeing Jesus fell on *his* face, and besought him, saying, Lord, if thou wilt, thou canst make me clean.

13And he put forth *his* hand, and touched him, saying, I will: be thou clean. And immediately the leprosy departed from him.

14And he charged him to tell no man: but go, and shew thyself to the priest, and offer for thy cleansing, according as Moses commanded, for a testimony unto them.

15But so much the more went there a fame abroad of him: and great multitudes came together to hear, and to be healed by him of their infirmities.

16And he withdrew himself into the wilderness, and prayed.

17And it came to pass on a certain day, as he was teaching, that there were Pharisees and doctors of the law sitting by, which were come out of every town of Galilee, and Judaea, and Jerusalem: and the power of the Lord was *present* to heal them.

18And, behold, men brought in a bed a man which was taken with a palsy: and they sought *means* to bring him in, and to lay *him* before him.

19And when they could not find by what *way* they might bring him in because of the multitude, they went upon the housetop, and let him down through the tiling with *his* couch into the midst before Jesus.

20And when he saw their faith, he said unto him, Man, thy sins are forgiven thee.

21And the scribes and the Pharisees began to reason, saying, Who is this which speaketh blasphemies? Who can forgive sins, but God alone?

22But when Jesus perceived their thoughts, he answering said unto them, What reason ye in your hearts?

23Whether is easier, to say, Thy sins be forgiven thee; or to say, Rise up and walk?

24But that ye may know that the Son of man hath power upon earth to forgive sins, (he said unto the sick of the palsy,) I say unto thee, Arise, and take up thy couch, and go into thine house.

25And immediately he rose up before them, and took up that whereon he lay, and departed to his own house, glorifying God.

26And they were all amazed, and they glorified God, and were filled with fear, saying, We have seen strange things to day.

27And after these things he went forth, and saw a publican, named Levi, sitting at the receipt of custom: and he said unto him, Follow me.

28And he left all, rose up, and followed him.

PSALM 65:1–13

PRAISE waiteth for thee, O God, in Sion: and unto thee shall the vow be performed.

2O thou that hearest prayer, unto thee shall all flesh come.

3Iniquities prevail against me: *as for* our transgressions, thou shalt purge them away.

4Blessed *is the man whom* thou choosest, and causest to approach *unto thee, that* he may dwell in thy courts: we shall be satisfied with the goodness of thy house, *even* of thy holy temple.

5*By* terrible things in righteousness wilt thou answer us, O God of our salvation; *who art* the confidence of all the ends of the earth, and of them that are afar off *upon* the sea:

6Which by his strength setteth fast the mountains; *being* girded with power:

7Which stilleth the noise of the seas, the noise of their waves, and the tumult of the people.

8They also that dwell in the uttermost parts are afraid at thy tokens: thou makest the outgoings of the morning and evening to rejoice.

9Thou visitest the earth, and waterest it: thou greatly enrichest it with the river of God, *which* is full of water: thou preparest them corn, when thou hast so provided for it.

10Thou waterest the ridges thereof abundantly: thou settlest the furrows thereof: thou makest it soft with showers: thou blessest the springing thereof.

11Thou crownest the year with thy goodness; and thy paths drop fatness.

12They drop *upon* the pastures of the wilderness: and the little hills rejoice on every side.

13The pastures are clothed with flocks; the valleys also are covered over with corn; they shout for joy, they also sing.

PROVERBS FOR TODAY/ 11:23

The desire of the righteous is *only good:* but *the expectation of the wicked* is *wrath.*

MARCH 23

NUMBERS 36:1—DEUTERONOMY 1:46

AND the chief fathers of the families of the children of Gilead, the son of Machir, the son of Manasseh, of the families of the sons of Joseph, came near, and spake before Moses, and before the princes, the chief fathers of the children of Israel:

2And they said, The LORD commanded my lord to give the land for an inheritance by lot to the children of Israel: and my lord was commanded by the LORD to give the inheritance of Zelophehad our brother unto his daughters.

3And if they be married to any of the sons of the *other* tribes of the children of Israel, then shall their inheritance be taken from the inheritance of our fathers, and shall be put to the inheritance of the tribe whereunto they are received: so shall it be taken from the lot of our inheritance.

4And when the jubile of the children of Israel shall be, then shall their inheritance be put unto the inheritance of the tribe whereunto they are received: so shall their inheritance be taken away from the inheritance of the tribe of our fathers.

5And Moses commanded the children of Israel according to the word of the LORD, saying, The tribe of the sons of Joseph hath said well.

6This *is* the thing which the LORD doth command concerning the daughters of Zelophehad, saying, Let them marry to whom they think best; only to the family of the tribe of their father shall they marry.

7So shall not the inheritance of the children of Israel remove from tribe to tribe: for every one of the children of Israel shall keep himself to the inheritance of the tribe of his fathers.

8And every daughter, that possesseth an inheritance in any tribe of the children of Israel, shall be wife unto one of the family of the tribe of her father, that the children of Israel may enjoy every man the inheritance of his fathers.

9Neither shall the inheritance remove from *one* tribe to another tribe; but every one of the tribes of the children of Israel shall keep himself to his own inheritance.

10Even as the LORD commanded Moses, so did the daughters of Zelophehad:

11For Mahlah, Tirzah, and Hoglah, and Milcah, and Noah, the daughters of Zelophehad, were married unto their father's brothers' sons:

12*And* they were married into the families of the sons of Manasseh the son of Joseph, and their inheritance remained in the tribe of the family of their father.

13These *are* the commandments and the judgments, which the LORD commanded by the hand of Moses unto the children of Israel in the plains of Moab by Jordan *near* Jericho.

THESE *be* the words which Moses spake unto all Israel on this side Jordan in the wilderness, in the plain over against the Red *sea,* between Paran, and Tophel, and Laban, and Hazeroth, and Dizahab.

2(*There are* eleven days' *journey* from Horeb by the way of mount Seir unto Kadesh–barnea.)

3And it came to pass in the fortieth year, in the eleventh month, on the first *day* of the month, *that* Moses spake unto the children of Israel, according unto all that the LORD had given him in commandment unto them;

4After he had slain Sihon the king of the Amorites, which dwelt in Heshbon, and Og the king of Bashan, which dwelt at Astaroth in Edrei:

5On this side Jordan, in the land of Moab, began Moses to declare this law, saying,

6The LORD our God spake unto us in Horeb, saying, Ye have dwelt long enough in this mount:

7Turn you, and take your journey, and go to the mount of the Amorites, and unto all *the places* nigh thereunto, in the plain, in the hills, and in the vale, and in the south, and by the sea side, to the land of the Canaanites, and unto Lebanon, unto the great river, the river Euphrates.

8Behold, I have set the land before you: go in and possess the land which the LORD sware unto your fathers, Abraham, Isaac, and Jacob, to give unto them and to their seed after them.

9And I spake unto you at that time, saying, I am not able to bear you myself alone:

10The LORD your God hath multiplied you, and, behold, ye *are* this day as the stars of heaven for multitude.

11(The LORD God of your fathers make you a thousand times so many more as ye *are,* and bless you, as he hath promised you!)

12How can I myself alone bear your

cumbrance, and your burden, and your strife?

13Take you wise men, and understanding, and known among your tribes, and I will make them rulers over you.

14And ye answered me, and said, The thing which thou hast spoken *is* good *for us* to do.

15So I took the chief of your tribes, wise men, and known, and made them heads over you, captains over thousands, and captains over hundreds, and captains over fifties, and captains over tens, and officers among your tribes.

16And I charged your judges at that time, saying, Hear *the causes* between your brethren, and judge righteously between *every* man and his brother, and the stranger *that is* with him.

17Ye shall not respect persons in judgment; *but* ye shall hear the small as well as the great; ye shall not be afraid of the face of man; for the judgment *is* God's: and the cause that is too hard for you, bring *it* unto me, and I will hear it.

18And I commanded you at that time all the things which ye should do.

19And when we departed from Horeb, we went through all that great and terrible wilderness, which ye saw by the way of the mountain of the Amorites, as the LORD our God commanded us; and we came to Kadesh–barnea.

20And I said unto you, Ye are come unto the mountain of the Amorites, which the LORD our God doth give unto us.

21Behold, the LORD thy God hath set the land before thee: go up *and* possess *it,* as the LORD God of thy fathers hath said unto thee; fear not, neither be discouraged.

22And ye came near unto me every one of you, and said, We will send men before us, and they shall search us out the land, and bring us word again by what way we must go up, and into what cities we shall come.

23And the saying pleased me well: and I took twelve men of you, one of a tribe:

24And they turned and went up into the mountain, and came unto the valley of Eshcol, and searched it out.

25And they took of the fruit of the land in their hands, and brought *it* down unto us, and brought us word again, and said, *It is* a good land which the LORD our God doth give us.

26Notwithstanding ye would not go up, but rebelled against the commandment of the LORD your God:

27And ye murmured in your tents, and said, Because the LORD hated us, he hath brought us forth out of the land of Egypt, to deliver us into the hand of the Amorites, to destroy us.

28Whither shall we go up? our brethren have discouraged our heart, saying, The people *is* greater and taller than we; the cities *are* great and walled up to heaven; and moreover we have seen the sons of the Anakims there.

29Then I said unto you, Dread not, neither be afraid of them.

30The LORD your God which goeth before you, he shall fight for you, according to all that he did for you in Egypt before your eyes;

31And in the wilderness, where thou hast seen how that the LORD thy God bare thee, as a man doth bear his son, in all the way that ye went, until ye came into this place.

32Yet in this thing ye did not believe the LORD your God,

33Who went in the way before you, to search you out a place to pitch your tents *in,* in fire by night, to shew you by what way ye should go, and in a cloud by day.

34And the LORD heard the voice of your words, and was wroth, and sware, saying,

35Surely there shall not one of these

men of this evil generation see that good land, which I sware to give unto your fathers,

36Save Caleb the son of Jephunneh; he shall see it, and to him will I give the land that he hath trodden upon, and to his children, because he hath wholly followed the LORD.

37Also the LORD was angry with me for your sakes, saying, Thou also shalt not go in thither.

38*But* Joshua the son of Nun, which standeth before thee, he shall go in thither: encourage him: for he shall cause Israel to inherit it.

39Moreover your little ones, which ye said should be a prey, and your children, which in that day had no knowledge between good and evil, they shall go in thither, and unto them will I give it, and they shall possess it.

40But *as for* you, turn you, and take your journey into the wilderness by the way of the Red sea.

41Then ye answered and said unto me, We have sinned against the LORD, we will go up and fight, according to all that the LORD our God commanded us. And when ye had girded on every man his weapons of war, ye were ready to go up into the hill.

42And the LORD said unto me, Say unto them, Go not up, neither fight; for I *am* not among you; lest ye be smitten before your enemies.

43So I spake unto you; and ye would not hear, but rebelled against the commandment of the LORD, and went presumptuously up into the hill.

44And the Amorites, which dwelt in that mountain, came out against you, and chased you, as bees do, and destroyed you in Seir, *even* unto Hormah.

45And ye returned and wept before the LORD; but the LORD would not hearken to your voice, nor give ear unto you.

46So ye abode in Kadesh many days, according unto the days that ye abode *there*.

LUKE 5:29—6:11

AND Levi made him [Jesus] a great feast in his own house: and there was a great company of publicans and of others that sat down with them.

30But their scribes and Pharisees murmured against his disciples, saying, Why do ye eat and drink with publicans and sinners?

31And Jesus answering said unto them, They that are whole need not a physician: but they that are sick.

32I came not to call the righteous, but sinners to repentance.

33And they said unto him, Why do the disciples of John fast often, and make prayers, and likewise *the disciples* of the Pharisees; but thine eat and drink?

34And he said unto them, Can ye make the children of the bridechamber fast, while the bridegroom is with them?

35But the days will come, when the bridegroom shall be taken away from them, and then shall they fast in those days.

36And he spake also a parable unto them; No man putteth a piece of a new garment upon an old; if otherwise, then both the new maketh a rent, and the piece that was *taken* out of the new agreeth not with the old.

37And no man putteth new wine into old bottles; else the new wine will burst the bottles, and be spilled, and the bottles shall perish.

38But new wine must be put into new bottles; and both are preserved.

39No man also having drunk old *wine* straightway desireth new: for he saith, The old is better.

AND it came to pass on the second sabbath after the first, that he went through the corn fields; and his disciples plucked the ears of corn, and did eat, rubbing *them* in *their* hands.

2And certain of the Pharisees said unto them, Why do ye that which is not lawful to do on the sabbath days?

3And Jesus answering them said, Have ye not read so much as this, what David did, when himself was an hungred, and they which were with him;

4How he went into the house of God, and did take and eat the shewbread, and gave also to them that were with him; which it is not lawful to eat but for the priests alone?

5And he said unto them, That the Son of man is Lord also of the sabbath.

6And it came to pass also on another sabbath, that he entered into the synagogue and taught: and there was a man whose right hand was withered.

7And the scribes and Pharisees watched him, whether he would heal on the sabbath day; that they might find an accusation against him.

8But he knew their thoughts, and said to the man which had the withered hand, Rise up, and stand forth in the midst. And he arose and stood forth.

9Then said Jesus unto them, I will ask you one thing; Is it lawful on the sabbath days to do good, or to do evil? to save life, or to destroy it?

10And looking round about upon them all, he said unto the man, Stretch forth thy hand. And he did so: and his hand was restored whole as the other.

11And they were filled with madness; and communed one with another what they might do to Jesus.

PSALM 66:1–20

MAKE a joyful noise unto God, all ye lands:

2Sing forth the honour of his name: make his praise glorious.

3Say unto God, How terrible art thou in thy works! through the greatness of thy power shall thine enemies submit themselves unto thee.

4All the earth shall worship thee, and shall sing unto thee; they shall sing to thy name. Selah.

5Come and see the works of God: he is terrible in his doing toward the children of men.

6He turned the sea into dry land: they went through the flood on foot: there did we rejoice in him.

7He ruleth by his power for ever; his eyes behold the nations: let not the rebellious exalt themselves. Selah.

8O bless our God, ye people, and make the voice of his praise to be heard:

9Which holdeth our soul in life, and suffereth not our feet to be moved.

10For thou, O God, hast proved us: thou hast tried us, as silver is tried.

11Thou broughtest us into the net; thou laidst affliction upon our loins.

12Thou hast caused men to ride over our heads; we went through fire and through water: but thou broughtest us out into a wealthy place.

13I will go into thy house with burnt offerings: I will pay thee my vows,

14Which my lips have uttered, and my mouth hath spoken, when I was in trouble.

15I will offer unto thee burnt sacrifices of fatlings, with the incense of rams; I will offer bullocks with goats. Selah.

16Come and hear, all ye that fear God, and I will declare what he hath done for my soul.

17I cried unto him with my mouth, and he was extolled with my tongue.

18If I regard iniquity in my heart, the Lord will not hear me:

19But verily God hath heard me; he hath attended to the voice of my prayer.

20Blessed be God, which hath not turned away my prayer, nor his mercy from me.

PROVERBS FOR TODAY/ 11:24–26

There is that scattereth, and yet increaseth; and there is *that withholdeth more than is meet, but* it tendeth *to poverty.* □ *The liberal soul shall be made fat:*

and he that watereth shall be watered also himself. □ *He that withholdeth corn, the people shall curse him: but blessing* shall be *upon the head of him that selleth* it.

MARCH 24

DEUTERONOMY 2:1—3:29

THEN we turned, and took our journey into the wilderness by the way of the Red sea, as the LORD spake unto me: and we compassed mount Seir many days.

2And the LORD spake unto me, saying,

3Ye have compassed this mountain long enough: turn you northward.

4And command thou the people, saying, Ye *are* to pass through the coast of your brethren the children of Esau, which dwell in Seir; and they shall be afraid of you: take ye good heed unto yourselves therefore:

5Meddle not with them; for I will not give you of their land, no, not so much as a foot breadth; because I have given mount Seir unto Esau *for* a possession.

6Ye shall buy meat of them for money, that ye may eat; and ye shall also buy water of them for money, that ye may drink.

7For the LORD thy God hath blessed thee in all the works of thy hand: he knoweth thy walking through this great wilderness: these forty years the LORD thy God *hath been* with thee; thou hast lacked nothing.

8And when we passed by from our brethren the children of Esau, which dwelt in Seir, through the way of the plain from Elath, and from Ezion-gaber, we turned and passed by the way of the wilderness of Moab.

9And the LORD said unto me, Distress not the Moabites, neither contend with them in battle: for I will not give thee of their land *for* a possession; because I have given Ar unto the children of Lot *for* a possession.

10The Emims dwelt therein in times past, a people great, and many, and tall, as the Anakims;

11Which also were accounted giants, as the Anakims; but the Moabites call them Emims.

12The Horims also dwelt in Seir beforetime; but the children of Esau succeeded them, when they had destroyed them from before them, and dwelt in their stead; as Israel did unto the land of his possession, which the LORD gave unto them.

13Now rise up, *said I,* and get you over the brook Zered. And we went over the brook Zered.

14And the space in which we came from Kadesh-barnea, until we were come over the brook Zered, *was* thirty and eight years; until all the generation of the men of war were wasted out from among the host, as the LORD sware unto them.

15For indeed the hand of the LORD was against them, to destroy them from among the host, until they were consumed.

16So it came to pass, when all the men of war were consumed and dead from among the people,

17That the LORD spake unto me, saying,

18Thou art to pass over through Ar,

the coast of Moab, this day:

19And *when* thou comest nigh over against the children of Ammon, distress them not, nor meddle with them: for I will not give thee of the land of the children of Ammon *any* possession; because I have given it unto the children of Lot *for* a possession.

20(That also was accounted a land of giants: giants dwelt therein in old time; and the Ammonites call them Zamzummims:

21A people great, and many, and tall, as the Anakims; but the LORD destroyed them before them; and they succeeded them, and dwelt in their stead:

22As he did to the children of Esau, which dwelt in Seir, when he destroyed the Horims from before them; and they succeeded them, and dwelt in their stead even unto this day:

23And the Avims which dwelt in Hazerim, *even* unto Azzah, the Caphtorims, which came forth out of Caphtor, destroyed them, and dwelt in their stead.)

24Rise ye up, take your journey, and pass over the river Arnon: behold, I have given into thine hand Sihon the Amorite, king of Heshbon, and his land: begin to possess *it,* and contend with him in battle.

25This day will I begin to put the dread of thee and the fear of thee upon the nations *that are* under the whole heaven, who shall hear report of thee, and shall tremble, and be in anguish because of thee.

26And I sent messengers out of the wilderness of Kedemoth unto Sihon king of Heshbon with words of peace, saying,

27Let me pass through thy land: I will go along by the high way, I will neither turn unto the right hand nor to the left.

28Thou shalt sell me meat for money, that I may eat; and give me water for money, that I may drink: only I will pass through on my feet;

29(As the children of Esau which dwell in Seir, and the Moabites which dwell in Ar, did unto me;) until I shall pass over Jordan into the land which the LORD our God giveth us.

30But Sihon king of Heshbon would not let us pass by him: for the LORD thy God hardened his spirit, and made his heart obstinate, that he might deliver him into thy hand, as *appeareth* this day.

31And the LORD said unto me, Behold, I have begun to give Sihon and his land before thee: begin to possess, that thou mayest inherit his land.

32Then Sihon came out against us, he and all his people, to fight at Jahaz.

33And the LORD our God delivered him before us; and we smote him, and his sons, and all his people.

34And we took all his cities at that time, and utterly destroyed the men, and the women, and the little ones, of every city, we left none to remain:

35Only the cattle we took for a prey unto ourselves, and the spoil of the cities which we took.

36From Aroer, which *is* by the brink of the river of Arnon, and *from* the city that *is* by the river, even unto Gilead, there was not one city too strong for us: the LORD our God delivered all unto us:

37Only unto the land of the children of Ammon thou camest not, *nor* unto any place of the river Jabbok, nor unto the cities in the mountains, nor unto whatsoever the LORD our God forbad us.

THEN we turned, and went up the way to Bashan: and Og the king of Bashan came out against us, he and all his people, to battle at Edrei.

2And the LORD said unto me, Fear him not: for I will deliver him, and all his people, and his land, into thy hand; and thou shalt do unto him as thou didst unto Sihon king of the Amorites, which dwelt at Heshbon.

3So the LORD our God delivered into

our hands Og also, the king of Bashan, and all his people: and we smote him until none was left to him remaining.

4And we took all his cities at that time, there was not a city which we took not from them, threescore cities, all the region of Argob, the kingdom of Og in Bashan.

5All these cities *were* fenced with high walls, gates, and bars; beside unwalled towns a great many.

6And we utterly destroyed them, as we did unto Sihon king of Heshbon, utterly destroying the men, women, and children, of every city.

7But all the cattle, and the spoil of the cities, we took for a prey to ourselves.

8And we took at that time out of the hand of the two kings of the Amorites the land that *was* on this side Jordan, from the river of Arnon unto mount Hermon;

9(*Which* Hermon the Sidonians call Sirion; and the Amorites call it Shenir;)

10All the cities of the plain, and all Gilead, and all Bashan, unto Salchah and Edrei, cities of the kingdom of Og in Bashan.

11For only Og king of Bashan remained of the remnant of giants; behold, his bedstead *was* a bedstead of iron; *is* it not in Rabbath of the children of Ammon? nine cubits *was* the length thereof, and four cubits the breadth of it, after the cubit of a man.

12And this land, *which* we possessed at that time, from Aroer, which *is* by the river Arnon, and half mount Gilead, and the cities thereof, gave I unto the Reubenites and to the Gadites.

13And the rest of Gilead, and all Bashan, *being* the kingdom of Og, gave I unto the half tribe of Manasseh; all the region of Argob, with all Bashan, which was called the land of giants.

14Jair the son of Manasseh took all the country of Argob unto the coasts of Geshuri and Maachathi; and called them after his own name, Bashan-havoth-jair, unto this day.

15And I gave Gilead unto Machir.

16And unto the Reubenites and unto the Gadites I gave from Gilead even unto the river Arnon half the valley, and the border even unto the river Jabbok, *which is* the border of the children of Ammon;

17The plain also, and Jordan, and the coast *thereof,* from Chinnereth even unto the sea of the plain, *even* the salt sea, under Ashdoth-pisgah eastward.

18And I commanded you at that time, saying, The LORD your God hath given you this land to possess it: ye shall pass over armed before your brethren the children of Israel, all *that are* meet for the war.

19But your wives, and your little ones, and your cattle, (*for* I know that ye have much cattle,) shall abide in your cities which I have given you;

20Until the LORD have given rest unto your brethren, as well as unto you, and *until* they also possess the land which the LORD your God hath given them beyond Jordan: and *then* shall ye return every man unto his possession, which I have given you.

21And I commanded Joshua at that time, saying, Thine eyes have seen all that the LORD your God hath done unto these two kings: so shall the LORD do unto all the kingdoms whither thou passest.

22Ye shall not fear them: for the LORD your God he shall fight for you.

23And I besought the LORD at that time, saying,

24O Lord GOD, thou hast begun to shew thy servant thy greatness, and thy mighty hand: for what God *is there* in heaven or in earth, that can do according to thy works, and according to thy might?

25I pray thee, let me go over, and see the good land that *is* beyond Jordan, that goodly mountain, and Lebanon.

26But the LORD was wroth with me for your sakes, and would not hear me: and the LORD said unto me, Let it suffice thee; speak no more unto me of this matter.

27Get thee up into the top of Pisgah, and lift up thine eyes westward, and northward, and southward, and eastward, and behold *it* with thine eyes: for thou shalt not go over this Jordan.

28But charge Joshua, and encourage him, and strengthen him: for he shall go over before this people, and he shall cause them to inherit the land which thou shalt see.

29So we abode in the valley over against Beth–peor.

LUKE 6:12–38

AND it came to pass in those days, that he [Jesus] went out into a mountain to pray, and continued all night in prayer to God.

13And when it was day, he called *unto him* his disciples: and of them he chose twelve, whom also he named apostles;

14Simon, (whom he also named Peter,) and Andrew his brother, James and John, Philip and Bartholomew,

15Matthew and Thomas, James the *son* of Alphaeus, and Simon called Zelotes,

16And Judas *the brother* of James, and Judas Iscariot, which also was the traitor.

17And he came down with them, and stood in the plain, and the company of his disciples, and a great multitude of people out of all Judaea and Jerusalem, and from the sea coast of Tyre and Sidon, which came to hear him, and to be healed of their diseases;

18And they that were vexed with unclean spirits: and they were healed.

19And the whole multitude sought to touch him: for there went virtue out of him, and healed *them* all.

20And he lifted up his eyes on his disciples, and said, Blessed *be ye* poor: for yours is the kingdom of God.

21Blessed *are ye* that hunger now: for ye shall be filled. Blessed *are ye* that weep now: for ye shall laugh.

22Blessed are ye, when men shall hate you, and when they shall separate you *from their company,* and shall reproach *you,* and cast out your name as evil, for the Son of man's sake.

23Rejoice ye in that day, and leap for joy: for, behold, your reward *is* great in heaven: for in the like manner did their fathers unto the prophets.

24But woe unto you that are rich! for ye have received your consolation.

25Woe unto you that are full! for ye shall hunger. Woe unto you that laugh now! for ye shall mourn and weep.

26Woe unto you, when all men shall speak well of you! for so did their fathers to the false prophets.

27But I say unto you which hear, Love your enemies, do good to them which hate you,

28Bless them that curse you, and pray for them which despitefully use you.

29And unto him that smiteth thee on the *one* cheek offer also the other; and him that taketh away thy cloak forbid not *to take thy* coat also.

30Give to every man that asketh of thee; and of him that taketh away thy goods ask *them* not again.

31And as ye would that men should do to you, do ye also to them likewise.

32For if ye love them which love you, what thank have ye? for sinners also love those that love them.

33And if ye do good to them which do good to you, what thank have ye? for sinners also do even the same.

34And if ye lend *to them* of whom ye hope to receive, what thank have ye? for sinners also lend to sinners, to receive as much again.

35But love ye your enemies, and do good, and lend, hoping for nothing again; and your reward shall be great, and ye shall be the children of the Highest: for he is kind unto the unthankful and *to* the evil.

36Be ye therefore merciful, as your Father also is merciful.

37Judge not, and ye shall not be judged: condemn not, and ye shall not be condemned: forgive, and ye shall be forgiven:

38Give, and it shall be given unto you; good measure, pressed down, and shaken together, and running over, shall men give into your bosom. For with the same measure that ye mete withal it shall be measured to you again.

PSALM 67:1–7

Goﬔ be merciful unto us, and bless us; *and* cause his face to shine upon us; Selah.

2That thy way may be known upon earth, thy saving health among all nations.

3Let the people praise thee, O God; let all the people praise thee.

4O let the nations be glad and sing for joy: for thou shalt judge the people righteously, and govern the nations upon earth. Selah.

5Let the people praise thee, O God; let all the people praise thee.

6*Then* shall the earth yield her increase; *and* God, *even* our own God, shall bless us.

7God shall bless us; and all the ends of the earth shall fear him.

PROVERBS FOR TODAY/ 11:27

He that diligently seeketh good procureth favour: but he that seeketh mischief, it shall come unto him.

MARCH 25

DEUTERONOMY 4:1–49

Now therefore hearken, O Israel, unto the statutes and unto the judgments, which I teach you, for to do *them,* that ye may live, and go in and possess the land which the Lord God of your fathers giveth you.

2Ye shall not add unto the word which I command you, neither shall ye diminish *ought* from it, that ye may keep the commandments of the Lord your God which I command you.

3Your eyes have seen what the Lord did because of Baal–peor: for all the men that followed Baal–peor, the Lord

thy God hath destroyed them from among you.

4But ye that did cleave unto the Lord your God *are* alive every one of you this day.

5Behold, I have taught you statutes and judgments, even as the Lord my God commanded me, that ye should do so in the land whither ye go to possess it.

6Keep therefore and do *them;* for this *is* your wisdom and your understanding in the sight of the nations, which shall hear all these statutes, and say, Surely this great nation *is* a wise and understanding people.

7For what nation *is there* so great, who *hath* God *so* nigh unto them, as the LORD our God *is* in all *things that* we call upon him *for?*

8And what nation *is there so* great, that hath statutes and judgments *so* righteous as all this law, which I set before you this day?

9Only take heed to thyself, and keep thy soul diligently, lest thou forget the things which thine eyes have seen, and lest they depart from thy heart all the days of thy life: but teach them thy sons, and thy sons' sons;

10*Specially* the day that thou stoodest before the LORD thy God in Horeb, when the LORD said unto me, Gather me the people together, and I will make them hear my words, that they may learn to fear me all the days that they shall live upon the earth, and *that* they may teach their children.

11And ye came near and stood under the mountain; and the mountain burned with fire unto the midst of heaven, with darkness, clouds, and thick darkness.

12And the LORD spake unto you out of the midst of the fire: ye heard the voice of the words, but saw no similitude; only *ye heard* a voice.

13And he declared unto you his covenant, which he commanded you to perform, *even* ten commandments; and he wrote them upon two tables of stone.

14And the LORD commanded me at that time to teach you statutes and judgments, that ye might do them in the land whither ye go over to possess it.

15Take ye therefore good heed unto yourselves; for ye saw no manner of similitude on the day *that* the LORD spake unto you in Horeb out of the midst of the fire:

16Lest ye corrupt *yourselves,* and make you a graven image, the similitude of any figure, the likeness of male or female,

17The likeness of any beast that *is* on the earth, the likeness of any winged fowl that flieth in the air,

18The likeness of any thing that creepeth on the ground, the likeness of any fish that *is* in the waters beneath the earth:

19And lest thou lift up thine eyes unto heaven, and when thou seest the sun, and the moon, and the stars, *even* all the host of heaven, shouldest be driven to worship them, and serve them, which the LORD thy God hath divided unto all nations under the whole heaven.

20But the LORD hath taken you, and brought you forth out of the iron furnace, *even* out of Egypt, to be unto him a people of inheritance, as *ye are* this day.

21Furthermore the LORD was angry with me for your sakes, and sware that I should not go over Jordan, and that I should not go in unto that good land, which the LORD thy God giveth thee *for* an inheritance:

22But I must die in this land, I must not go over Jordan: but ye shall go over, and possess that good land.

23Take heed unto yourselves, lest ye forget the covenant of the LORD your God, which he made with you, and make you a graven image, *or* the likeness of any *thing,* which the LORD thy God hath forbidden thee.

24For the LORD thy God *is* a consuming fire, *even* a jealous God.

25When thou shalt beget children, and children's children, and ye shall have remained long in the land, and shall corrupt *yourselves,* and make a graven image, *or* the likeness of any *thing,* and shall do evil in the sight of the LORD thy God, to provoke him to anger:

26I call heaven and earth to witness against you this day, that ye shall soon utterly perish from off the land whereunto ye go over Jordan to possess it; ye shall not prolong *your* days upon it, but shall utterly be destroyed.

27And the LORD shall scatter you among the nations, and ye shall be left few in number among the heathen, whither the LORD shall lead you.

28And there ye shall serve gods, the work of men's hands, wood and stone, which neither see, nor hear, nor eat, nor smell.

29But if from thence thou shalt seek the LORD thy God, thou shalt find *him,* if thou seek him with all thy heart and with all thy soul.

30When thou art in tribulation, and all these things are come upon thee, *even* in the latter days, if thou turn to the LORD thy God, and shalt be obedient unto his voice;

31(For the LORD thy God *is* a merciful God;) he will not forsake thee, neither destroy thee, nor forget the covenant of thy fathers which he sware unto them.

32For ask now of the days that are past, which were before thee, since the day that God created man upon the earth, and *ask* from the one side of heaven unto the other, whether there hath been *any such thing* as this great thing *is,* or hath been heard like it?

33Did *ever* people hear the voice of God speaking out of the midst of the fire, as thou hast heard, and live?

34Or hath God assayed to go *and* take him a nation from the midst of *another* nation, by temptations, by signs, and by wonders, and by war, and by a mighty hand, and by a stretched out arm, and by great terrors, according to all that the LORD your God did for you in Egypt before your eyes?

35Unto thee it was shewed, that thou mightest know that the LORD he *is* God; *there is* none else beside him.

36Out of heaven he made thee to hear his voice, that he might instruct thee: and upon earth he shewed thee his great fire; and thou heardest his words out of the midst of the fire.

37And because he loved thy fathers, therefore he chose their seed after them, and brought thee out in his sight with his mighty power out of Egypt;

38To drive out nations from before thee greater and mightier than thou *art,* to bring thee in, to give thee their land *for* an inheritance, as *it is* this day.

39Know therefore this day, and consider *it* in thine heart, that the LORD he *is* God in heaven above, and upon the earth beneath: *there is* none else.

40Thou shalt keep therefore his statutes, and his commandments, which I command thee this day, that it may go well with thee, and with thy children after thee, and that thou mayest prolong *thy* days upon the earth, which the LORD thy God giveth thee, for ever.

41Then Moses severed three cities on this side Jordan toward the sunrising;

42That the slayer might flee thither, which should kill his neighbour unawares, and hated him not in times past; and that fleeing unto one of these cities he might live:

43*Namely,* Bezer in the wilderness, in the plain country, of the Reubenites; and Ramoth in Gilead, of the Gadites; and Golan in Bashan, of the Manassites.

44And this *is* the law which Moses set before the children of Israel:

45These *are* the testimonies, and the statutes, and the judgments, which Moses spake unto the children of Israel, after they came forth out of Egypt,

46On this side Jordan, in the valley over against Beth–peor, in the land of Sihon king of the Amorites, who dwelt at Heshbon, whom Moses and the children of Israel smote, after they were come forth out of Egypt:

47And they possessed his land, and the land of Og king of Bashan, two kings of the Amorites, which *were* on this side Jordan toward the sunrising;

48From Aroer, which *is* by the bank of the river Arnon, even unto mount Sion, which *is* Hermon,

49And all the plain on this side Jordan eastward, even unto the sea of the plain, under the springs of Pisgah.

LUKE 6:39—7:10

AND he [Jesus] spake a parable unto them, Can the blind lead the blind? shall they not both fall into the ditch?

40The disciple is not above his master: but every one that is perfect shall be as his master.

41And why beholdest thou the mote that is in thy brother's eye, but perceivest not the beam that is in thine own eye?

42Either how canst thou say to thy brother, Brother, let me pull out the mote that is in thine eye, when thou thyself beholdest not the beam that is in thine own eye? Thou hypocrite, cast out first the beam out of thine own eye, and then shalt thou see clearly to pull out the mote that is in thy brother's eye.

43For a good tree bringeth not forth corrupt fruit; neither doth a corrupt tree bring forth good fruit.

44For every tree is known by his own fruit. For of thorns men do not gather figs, nor of a bramble bush gather they grapes.

45A good man out of the good treasure of his heart bringeth forth that which is good; and an evil man out of the evil treasure of his heart bringeth forth that which is evil: for of the abundance of the heart his mouth speaketh.

46And why call ye me, Lord, Lord, and do not the things which I say?

47Whosoever cometh to me, and heareth my sayings, and doeth them, I will shew you to whom he is like:

48He is like a man which built an house, and digged deep, and laid the foundation on a rock: and when the flood arose, the stream beat vehemently upon that house, and could not shake it: for it was founded upon a rock.

49But he that heareth, and doeth not, is like a man that without a foundation built an house upon the earth; against which the stream did beat vehemently, and immediately it fell; and the ruin of that house was great.

Now when he had ended all his sayings in the audience of the people, he entered into Capernaum.

2And a certain centurion's servant, who was dear unto him, was sick, and ready to die.

3And when he heard of Jesus, he sent unto him the elders of the Jews, beseeching him that he would come and heal his servant.

4And when they came to Jesus, they besought him instantly, saying, That he was worthy for whom he should do this:

5For he loveth our nation, and he hath built us a synagogue.

6Then Jesus went with them. And when he was now not far from the house, the centurion sent friends to him, saying unto him, Lord, trouble not thyself: for I am not worthy that thou shouldest enter under my roof:

7Wherefore neither thought I myself worthy to come unto thee: but say in a word, and my servant shall be healed.

8For I also am a man set under authority, having under me soldiers, and I say unto one, Go, and he goeth; and to another, Come, and he cometh; and to my servant, Do this, and he doeth it.

9When Jesus heard these things, he marvelled at him, and turned him about, and said unto the people that followed him, I say unto you, I have not found so great faith, no, not in Israel.

10And they that were sent, returning to the house, found the servant whole that had been sick.

PSALM 68:1–18

LET God arise, let his enemies be scattered: let them also that hate him flee before him.

2As smoke is driven away, *so* drive

them away: as wax melteth before the fire, *so* let the wicked perish at the presence of God.

3But let the righteous be glad; let them rejoice before God: yea, let them exceedingly rejoice.

4Sing unto God, sing praises to his name: extol him that rideth upon the heavens by his name JAH, and rejoice before him.

5A father of the fatherless, and a judge of the widows, *is* God in his holy habitation.

6God setteth the solitary in families: he bringeth out those which are bound with chains: but the rebellious dwell in a dry *land.*

7O God, when thou wentest forth before thy people, when thou didst march through the wilderness; Selah:

8The earth shook, the heavens also dropped at the presence of God: *even* Sinai itself *was moved* at the presence of God, the God of Israel.

9Thou, O God, didst send a plentiful rain, whereby thou didst confirm thine inheritance, when it was weary.

10Thy congregation hath dwelt therein: thou, O God, hast prepared of thy goodness for the poor.

11The Lord gave the word: great *was* the company of those that published *it.*

12Kings of armies did flee apace: and she that tarried at home divided the spoil.

13Though ye have lien among the pots, *yet shall ye be as* the wings of a dove covered with silver, and her feathers with yellow gold.

14When the Almighty scattered kings in it, it was *white* as snow in Salmon.

15The hill of God *is as* the hill of Bashan; an high hill *as* the hill of Bashan.

16Why leap ye, ye high hills? *this is* the hill *which* God desireth to dwell in; yea, the LORD will dwell *in it* for ever.

17The chariots of God *are* twenty thousand, *even* thousands of angels: the Lord *is* among them, *as in* Sinai, in the holy *place.*

18Thou hast ascended on high, thou hast led captivity captive: thou hast received gifts for men; yea, *for* the rebellious also, that the LORD God might dwell *among them.*

PROVERBS FOR TODAY/ 11:28

He that trusteth in his riches shall fall; but the righteous shall flourish as a branch.

MARCH 26

DEUTERONOMY 5:1—6:25

AND Moses called all Israel, and said unto them, Hear, O Israel, the statutes and judgments which I speak in your ears this day, that ye may learn them, and keep, and do them.

2The LORD our God made a covenant with us in Horeb.

3The LORD made not this covenant with our fathers, but with us, *even* us, who *are* all of us here alive this day.

4The LORD talked with you face to face in the mount out of the midst of the fire,

5(I stood between the LORD and you at that time, to shew you the word of the LORD: for ye were afraid by reason of the fire, and went not up into the mount;) saying,

6I *am* the LORD thy God, which brought thee out of the land of Egypt, from the house of bondage.

7Thou shalt have none other gods before me.

8Thou shalt not make thee *any* graven image, *or* any likeness *of any thing* that *is* in heaven above, or that *is* in the earth beneath, or that *is* in the waters beneath the earth:

9Thou shalt not bow down thyself unto them, nor serve them: for I the LORD thy God *am* a jealous God, visiting the iniquity of the fathers upon the children unto the third and fourth *generation* of them that hate me,

10And shewing mercy unto thousands of them that love me and keep my commandments.

11Thou shalt not take the name of the LORD thy God in vain: for the LORD will not hold *him* guiltless that taketh his name in vain.

12Keep the sabbath day to sanctify it, as the LORD thy God hath commanded thee.

13Six days thou shalt labour, and do all thy work:

14But the seventh day *is* the sabbath of the LORD thy God: *in it* thou shalt not do any work, thou, nor thy son, nor thy daughter, nor thy manservant, nor thy maidservant, nor thine ox, nor thine ass, nor any of thy cattle, nor thy stranger that *is* within thy gates; that thy manservant and thy maidservant may rest as well as thou.

15And remember that thou wast a servant in the land of Egypt, and *that* the LORD thy God brought thee out thence through a mighty hand and by a stretched out arm: therefore the LORD thy God commanded thee to keep the sabbath day.

16Honour thy father and thy mother, as the LORD thy God hath commanded thee; that thy days may be prolonged, and that it may go well with thee, in the land which the LORD thy God giveth thee.

17Thou shalt not kill.

18Neither shalt thou commit adultery.

19Neither shalt thou steal.

20Neither shalt thou bear false witness against thy neighbour.

21Neither shalt thou desire thy neighbour's wife, neither shalt thou covet thy neighbour's house, his field, or his manservant, or his maidservant, his ox, or his ass, or any *thing* that *is* thy neighbour's.

22These words the LORD spake unto all your assembly in the mount out of the midst of the fire, of the cloud, and of the thick darkness, with a great voice: and he added no more. And he wrote them in two tables of stone, and delivered them unto me.

23And it came to pass, when ye heard the voice out of the midst of the darkness, (for the mountain did burn with fire,) that ye came near unto me, *even* all the heads of your tribes, and your elders:

24And ye said, Behold, the LORD our God hath shewed us his glory and his greatness, and we have heard his voice out of the midst of the fire: we have seen this day that God doth talk with man, and he liveth.

25Now therefore why should we die? for this great fire will consume us: if we hear the voice of the LORD our God any more, then we shall die.

26For who *is there of* all flesh, that hath heard the voice of the living God speaking out of the midst of the fire, as we *have,* and lived?

27Go thou near, and hear all that the LORD our God shall say: and speak thou unto us all that the LORD our God shall speak unto thee; and we will hear *it,* and do *it.*

28And the LORD heard the voice of your words, when ye spake unto me; and the LORD said unto me, I have heard the voice of the words of this people, which they have spoken unto thee: they have well said all that they have spoken.

29O that there were such an heart in them, that they would fear me, and keep all my commandments always, that it might be well with them, and with their children for ever!

30Go say to them, Get you into your tents again.

31But as for thee, stand thou here by me, and I will speak unto thee all the commandments, and the statutes, and the judgments, which thou shalt teach them, that they may do *them* in the land which I give them to possess it.

32Ye shall observe to do therefore as the Lord your God hath commanded you: ye shall not turn aside to the right hand or to the left.

33Ye shall walk in all the ways which the Lord your God hath commanded you, that ye may live, and *that it may be* well with you, and *that* ye may prolong *your* days in the land which ye shall possess.

Now these *are* the commandments, the statutes, and the judgments, which the Lord your God commanded to teach you, that ye might do *them* in the land whither ye go to possess it:

2That thou mightest fear the Lord thy God, to keep all his statutes and his commandments, which I command thee, thou, and thy son, and thy son's son, all the days of thy life; and that thy days may be prolonged.

3Hear therefore, O Israel, and observe to do *it;* that it may be well with thee, and that ye may increase mightily, as the Lord God of thy fathers hath promised thee, in the land that floweth with milk and honey.

4Hear, O Israel: The Lord our God *is* one Lord:

5And thou shalt love the Lord thy God with all thine heart, and with all thy soul, and with all thy might.

6And these words, which I command thee this day, shall be in thine heart:

7And thou shalt teach them diligently unto thy children, and shalt talk of them when thou sittest in thine house, and when thou walkest by the way, and when thou liest down, and when thou risest up.

8And thou shalt bind them for a sign upon thine hand, and they shall be as frontlets between thine eyes.

9And thou shalt write them upon the posts of thy house, and on thy gates.

10And it shall be, when the Lord thy God shall have brought thee into the land which he sware unto thy fathers, to Abraham, to Isaac, and to Jacob, to give thee great and goodly cities, which thou buildedst not,

11And houses full of all good *things,* which thou filledst not, and wells digged, which thou diggedst not, vineyards and olive trees, which thou plantedst not; when thou shalt have eaten and be full;

12*Then* beware lest thou forget the Lord, which brought thee forth out of the land of Egypt, from the house of bondage.

13Thou shalt fear the Lord thy God, and serve him, and shalt swear by his name.

14Ye shall not go after other gods, of the gods of the people which *are* round about you;

15(For the Lord thy God *is* a jealous God among you) lest the anger of the Lord thy God be kindled against thee, and destroy thee from off the face of the earth.

16Ye shall not tempt the Lord your God, as ye tempted *him* in Massah.

17Ye shall diligently keep the commandments of the Lord your God, and his testimonies, and his statutes, which he hath commanded thee.

18And thou shalt do *that which is* right and good in the sight of the Lord: that it may be well with thee, and that thou mayest go in and possess the good land which the Lord sware unto thy fathers,

19To cast out all thine enemies from before thee, as the Lord hath spoken.

20*And* when thy son asketh thee in time to come, saying, What *mean* the testimonies, and the statutes, and the judgments, which the LORD our God hath commanded you?

21Then thou shalt say unto thy son, We were Pharaoh's bondmen in Egypt; and the LORD brought us out of Egypt with a mighty hand:

22And the LORD shewed signs and wonders, great and sore, upon Egypt, upon Pharaoh, and upon all his household, before our eyes:

23And he brought us out from thence, that he might bring us in, to give us the land which he sware unto our fathers.

24And the LORD commanded us to do all these statutes, to fear the LORD our God, for our good always, that he might preserve us alive, as *it is* at this day.

25And it shall be our righteousness, if we observe to do all these commandments before the LORD our God, as he hath commanded us.

LUKE 7:11–35

AND it came to pass the day after, that he [Jesus] went into a city called Nain; and many of his disciples went with him, and much people.

12Now when he came nigh to the gate of the city, behold, there was a dead man carried out, the only son of his mother, and she was a widow: and much people of the city was with her.

13And when the Lord saw her, he had compassion on her, and said unto her, Weep not.

14And he came and touched the bier: and they that bare *him* stood still. And he said, Young man, I say unto thee, Arise.

15And he that was dead sat up, and began to speak. And he delivered him to his mother.

16And there came a fear on all: and they glorified God, saying, That a great prophet is risen up among us; and, That God hath visited his people.

17And this rumour of him went forth throughout all Judaea, and throughout all the region round about.

18And the disciples of John shewed him of all these things.

19And John calling *unto him* two of his disciples sent *them* to Jesus, saying, Art thou he that should come? or look we for another?

20When the men were come unto him, they said, John Baptist hath sent us unto thee, saying, Art thou he that should come? or look we for another?

21And in that same hour he cured many of *their* infirmities and plagues, and of evil spirits; and unto many *that were* blind he gave sight.

22Then Jesus answering said unto them, Go your way, and tell John what things ye have seen and heard; how that the blind see, the lame walk, the lepers are cleansed, the deaf hear, the dead are raised, to the poor the gospel is preached.

23And blessed is *he,* whosoever shall not be offended in me.

24And when the messengers of John were departed, he began to speak unto the people concerning John, What went ye out into the wilderness for to see? A reed shaken with the wind?

25But what went ye out for to see? A man clothed in soft raiment? Behold, they which are gorgeously apparelled, and live delicately, are in kings' courts.

26But what went ye out for to see? A prophet? Yea, I say unto you, and much more than a prophet.

27This is *he,* of whom it is written, Behold, I send my messenger before thy face, which shall prepare thy way before thee.

28For I say unto you, Among those that are born of women there is not a greater prophet than John the Baptist: but he that is least in the kingdom of God is greater than he.

29And all the people that heard *him,*

and the publicans, justified God, being baptized with the baptism of John.

30But the Pharisees and lawyers rejected the counsel of God against themselves, being not baptized of him.

31And the Lord said, Whereunto then shall I liken the men of this generation? and to what are they like?

32They are like unto children sitting in the marketplace, and calling one to another, and saying, We have piped unto you, and ye have not danced; we have mourned to you, and ye have not wept.

33For John the Baptist came neither eating bread nor drinking wine; and ye say, He hath a devil.

34The Son of man is come eating and drinking; and ye say, Behold a gluttonous man, and a winebibber, a friend of publicans and sinners!

35But wisdom is justified of all her children.

PSALM 68:19–35

BLESSED *be* the Lord, *who* daily loadeth us *with benefits, even* the God of our salvation. Selah.

20*He that is* our God *is* the God of salvation; and unto GOD the Lord *belong* the issues from death.

21But God shall wound the head of his enemies, *and* the hairy scalp of such an one as goeth on still in his trespasses.

22The Lord said, I will bring again from Bashan, I will bring *my people* again from the depths of the sea:

23That thy foot may be dipped in the blood of *thine* enemies, *and* the tongue of thy dogs in the same.

24They have seen thy goings, O God; *even* the goings of my God, my King, in the sanctuary.

25The singers went before, the players on instruments *followed* after; among *them were* the damsels playing with timbrels.

26Bless ye God in the congregations, *even* the Lord, from the fountain of Israel.

27There *is* little Benjamin *with* their ruler, the princes of Judah *and* their council, the princes of Zebulun, *and* the princes of Naphtali.

28Thy God hath commanded thy strength: strengthen, O God, that which thou hast wrought for us.

29Because of thy temple at Jerusalem shall kings bring presents unto thee.

30Rebuke the company of spearmen, the multitude of the bulls, with the calves of the people, *till every one* submit himself with pieces of silver: scatter thou the people *that* delight in war.

31Princes shall come out of Egypt; Ethiopia shall soon stretch out her hands unto God.

32Sing unto God, ye kingdoms of the earth; O sing praises unto the Lord; Selah:

33To him that rideth upon the heavens of heavens, *which were* of old; lo, he doth send out his voice, *and that* a mighty voice.

34Ascribe ye strength unto God: his excellency *is* over Israel, and his strength *is* in the clouds.

35O God, *thou art* terrible out of thy holy places: the God of Israel *is* he that giveth strength and power unto *his* people. Blessed *be* God.

PROVERBS FOR TODAY/ 11:29–31

He that troubleth his own house shall inherit the wind: and the fool shall be *servant to the wise of heart.* □ *The fruit of the righteous* is *a tree of life; and he that winneth souls* is *wise.* □ *Behold, the righteous shall be recompensed in the earth: much more the wicked and the sinner.*

MARCH 27

DEUTERONOMY 7:1—8:20

WHEN the LORD thy God shall bring thee into the land whither thou goest to possess it, and hath cast out many nations before thee, the Hittites, and the Girgashites, and the Amorites, and the Canaanites, and the Perizzites, and the Hivites, and the Jebusites, seven nations greater and mightier than thou;

2And when the LORD thy God shall deliver them before thee; thou shalt smite them, *and* utterly destroy them; thou shalt make no covenant with them, nor shew mercy unto them:

3Neither shalt thou make marriages with them; thy daughter thou shalt not give unto his son, nor his daughter shalt thou take unto thy son.

4For they will turn away thy son from following me, that they may serve other gods: so will the anger of the LORD be kindled against you, and destroy thee suddenly.

5But thus shall ye deal with them; ye shall destroy their altars, and break down their images, and cut down their groves, and burn their graven images with fire.

6For thou *art* an holy people unto the LORD thy God: the LORD thy God hath chosen thee to be a special people unto himself, above all people that *are* upon the face of the earth.

7The LORD did not set his love upon you, nor choose you, because ye were more in number than any people; for ye *were* the fewest of all people:

8But because the LORD loved you, and because he would keep the oath which he had sworn unto your fathers, hath the LORD brought you out with a mighty hand, and redeemed you out of the house of bondmen, from the hand of Pharaoh king of Egypt.

9Know therefore that the LORD thy God, he *is* God, the faithful God, which keepeth covenant and mercy with them that love him and keep his commandments to a thousand generations;

10And repayeth them that hate him to their face, to destroy them: he will not be slack to him that hateth him, he will repay him to his face.

11Thou shalt therefore keep the commandments, and the statutes, and the judgments, which I command thee this day, to do them.

12Wherefore it shall come to pass, if ye hearken to these judgments, and keep, and do them, that the LORD thy God shall keep unto thee the covenant and the mercy which he sware unto thy fathers:

13And he will love thee, and bless thee, and multiply thee: he will also bless the fruit of thy womb, and the fruit of thy land, thy corn, and thy wine, and thine oil, the increase of thy kine, and the flocks of thy sheep, in the land which he sware unto thy fathers to give thee.

14Thou shalt be blessed above all people: there shall not be male or female barren among you, or among your cattle.

15And the LORD will take away from thee all sickness, and will put none of the evil diseases of Egypt, which thou knowest, upon thee; but will lay them upon all *them* that hate thee.

16And thou shalt consume all the people which the LORD thy God shall deliver thee; thine eye shall have no pity upon them: neither shalt thou serve their gods; for that *will be* a snare unto thee.

17If thou shalt say in thine heart, These nations *are* more than I; how can I dispossess them?

18Thou shalt not be afraid of them:

but shalt well remember what the LORD thy God did unto Pharaoh, and unto all Egypt;

19The great temptations which thine eyes saw, and the signs, and the wonders, and the mighty hand, and the stretched out arm, whereby the LORD thy God brought thee out: so shall the LORD thy God do unto all the people of whom thou art afraid.

20Moreover the LORD thy God will send the hornet among them, until they that are left, and hide themselves from thee, be destroyed.

21Thou shalt not be affrighted at them: for the LORD thy God *is* among you, a mighty God and terrible.

22And the LORD thy God will put out those nations before thee by little and little: thou mayest not consume them at once, lest the beasts of the field increase upon thee.

23But the LORD thy God shall deliver them unto thee, and shall destroy them with a mighty destruction, until they be destroyed.

24And he shall deliver their kings into thine hand, and thou shalt destroy their name from under heaven: there shall no man be able to stand before thee, until thou have destroyed them.

25The graven images of their gods shall ye burn with fire: thou shalt not desire the silver or gold *that is* on them, nor take *it* unto thee, lest thou be snared therein: for it *is* an abomination to the LORD thy God.

26Neither shalt thou bring an abomination into thine house, lest thou be a cursed thing like it: *but* thou shalt utterly detest it, and thou shalt utterly abhor it; for it *is* a cursed thing.

ALL the commandments which I command thee this day shall ye observe to do, that ye may live, and multiply, and go in and possess the land which the LORD sware unto your fathers.

2And thou shalt remember all the way which the LORD thy God led thee these forty years in the wilderness, to humble thee, *and* to prove thee, to know what *was* in thine heart, whether thou wouldest keep his commandments, or no.

3And he humbled thee, and suffered thee to hunger, and fed thee with manna, which thou knewest not, neither did thy fathers know; that he might make thee know that man doth not live by bread only, but by every *word* that proceedeth out of the mouth of the LORD doth man live.

4Thy raiment waxed not old upon thee, neither did thy foot swell, these forty years.

5Thou shalt also consider in thine heart, that, as a man chasteneth his son, *so* the LORD thy God chasteneth thee.

6Therefore thou shalt keep the commandments of the LORD thy God, to walk in his ways, and to fear him.

7For the LORD thy God bringeth thee into a good land, a land of brooks of water, of fountains and depths that spring out of valleys and hills;

8A land of wheat, and barley, and vines, and fig trees, and pomegranates; a land of oil olive, and honey;

9A land wherein thou shalt eat bread without scarceness, thou shalt not lack any *thing* in it; a land whose stones *are* iron, and out of whose hills thou mayest dig brass.

10When thou hast eaten and art full, then thou shalt bless the LORD thy God for the good land which he hath given thee.

11Beware that thou forget not the LORD thy God, in not keeping his commandments, and his judgments, and his statutes, which I command thee this day:

12Lest *when* thou hast eaten and art full, and hast built goodly houses, and dwelt *therein;*

13And *when* thy herds and thy flocks multiply, and thy silver and thy gold is multiplied, and all that thou hast is multiplied;

14Then thine heart be lifted up, and thou forget the LORD thy God, which brought thee forth out of the land of Egypt, from the house of bondage;

15Who led thee through that great and terrible wilderness, *wherein were* fiery serpents, and scorpions, and drought, where *there was* no water; who brought thee forth water out of the rock of flint;

16Who fed thee in the wilderness with manna, which thy fathers knew not, that he might humble thee, and that he might prove thee, to do thee good at thy latter end;

17And thou say in thine heart, My power and the might of *mine* hand hath gotten me this wealth.

18But thou shalt remember the LORD thy God: for *it is* he that giveth thee power to get wealth, that he may establish his covenant which he sware unto thy fathers, as *it is* this day.

19And it shall be, if thou do at all forget the LORD thy God, and walk after other gods, and serve them, and worship them, I testify against you this day that ye shall surely perish.

20As the nations which the LORD destroyeth before your face, so shall ye perish; because ye would not be obedient unto the voice of the LORD your God.

LUKE 7:36—8:3

AND one of the Pharisees desired him [Jesus] that he would eat with him. And he went into the Pharisee's house, and sat down to meat.

37And, behold, a woman in the city, which was a sinner, when she knew that *Jesus* sat at meat in the Pharisee's house, brought an alabaster box of ointment,

38And stood at his feet behind *him* weeping, and began to wash his feet with tears, and did wipe *them* with the hairs of her head, and kissed his feet, and anointed *them* with the ointment.

39Now when the Pharisee which had bidden him saw *it*, he spake within himself, saying, This man, if he were a prophet, would have known who and what manner of woman *this is* that toucheth him: for she is a sinner.

40And Jesus answering said unto him, Simon, I have somewhat to say unto thee. And he saith, Master, say on.

41There was a certain creditor which had two debtors: the one owed five hundred pence, and the other fifty.

42And when they had nothing to pay, he frankly forgave them both. Tell me therefore, which of them will love him most?

43Simon answered and said, I suppose that *he*, to whom he forgave most. And he said unto him, Thou hast rightly judged.

44And he turned to the woman, and said unto Simon, Seest thou this woman? I entered into thine house, thou gavest me no water for my feet: but she hath washed my feet with tears, and wiped *them* with the hairs of her head.

45Thou gavest me no kiss: but this woman since the time I came in hath not ceased to kiss my feet.

46My head with oil thou didst not anoint: but this woman hath anointed my feet with ointment.

47Wherefore I say unto thee, Her sins, which are many, are forgiven; for she loved much: but to whom little is forgiven, *the same* loveth little.

48And he said unto her, Thy sins are forgiven.

49And they that sat at meat with him began to say within themselves, Who is this that forgiveth sins also?

50And he said to the woman, Thy faith hath saved thee; go in peace.

AND it came to pass afterward, that he went throughout every city and village, preaching and shewing the glad tidings of the kingdom of God: and the twelve *were* with him,

2And certain women, which had been healed of evil spirits and infirmities, Mary called Magdalene, out of whom went seven devils,

3And Joanna the wife of Chuza Herod's steward, and Susanna, and many others, which ministered unto him of their substance.

PSALM 69:1–14

Save me, O God; for the waters are come in unto *my* soul.

2I sink in deep mire, where *there is* no standing: I am come into deep waters, where the floods overflow me.

3I am weary of my crying: my throat is dried: mine eyes fail while I wait for my God.

4They that hate me without a cause are more than the hairs of mine head: they that would destroy me, *being* mine enemies wrongfully, are mighty: then I restored *that* which I took not away.

5O God, thou knowest my foolishness; and my sins are not hid from thee.

6Let not them that wait on thee, O Lord God of hosts, be ashamed for my sake: let not those that seek thee be confounded for my sake, O God of Israel.

7Because for thy sake I have borne reproach; shame hath covered my face.

8I am become a stranger unto my brethren, and an alien unto my mother's children.

9For the zeal of thine house hath eaten me up; and the reproaches of them that reproached thee are fallen upon me.

10When I wept, *and chastened* my soul with fasting, that was to my reproach.

11I made sackcloth also my garment; and I became a proverb to them.

12They that sit in the gate speak against me; and I *was* the song of the drunkards.

13But as for me, my prayer *is* unto thee, O Lord, *in* an acceptable time: O God, in the multitude of thy mercy hear me, in the truth of thy salvation.

14Deliver me out of the mire, and let me not sink: let me be delivered from them that hate me, and out of the deep waters.

PROVERBS FOR TODAY/ 12:1

Whoso loveth instruction loveth knowledge: but he that hateth reproof is *brutish.*

MARCH 28

DEUTERONOMY 9:1—10:22

Hear O Israel: Thou *art* to pass over Jordan this day, to go in to possess nations greater and mightier than thyself, cities great and fenced up to heaven,

2A people great and tall, the children of the Anakims, whom thou knowest, and *of whom* thou hast heard *say,* Who can stand before the children of Anak!

3Understand therefore this day, that the Lord thy God *is* he which goeth over before thee; *as* a consuming fire he shall destroy them, and he shall bring them down before thy face: so shalt thou drive them out, and destroy them quickly, as the LORD hath said unto thee.

4Speak not thou in thine heart, after that the LORD thy God hath cast them out from before thee, saying, For my righteousness the LORD hath brought me in to possess this land: but for the wickedness of these nations the LORD doth drive them out from before thee.

5Not for thy righteousness, or for the uprightness of thine heart, dost thou go to possess their land: but for the wickedness of these nations the LORD thy God doth drive them out from before thee, and that he may perform the word which the LORD sware unto thy fathers, Abraham, Isaac, and Jacob.

6Understand therefore, that the LORD thy God giveth thee not this good land to possess it for thy righteousness; for thou *art* a stiffnecked people.

7Remember, *and* forget not, how thou provokedst the LORD thy God to wrath in the wilderness: from the day that thou didst depart out of the land of Egypt, until ye came unto this place, ye have been rebellious against the LORD.

8Also in Horeb ye provoked the LORD to wrath, so that the LORD was angry with you to have destroyed you.

9When I was gone up into the mount to receive the tables of stone, *even* the tables of the covenant which the LORD made with you, then I abode in the mount forty days and forty nights, I neither did eat bread nor drink water.

10And the LORD delivered unto me two tables of stone written with the finger of God; and on them *was written* according to all the words, which the LORD spake with you in the mount out of the midst of the fire in the day of the assembly.

11And it came to pass at the end of forty days and forty nights, *that* the LORD gave me the two tables of stone, *even* the tables of the covenant.

12And the LORD said unto me, Arise, get thee down quickly from hence; for thy people which thou hast brought forth out of Egypt have corrupted *themselves;* they are quickly turned aside out of the way which I commanded them; they have made them a molten image.

13Furthermore the LORD spake unto me, saying, I have seen this people, and, behold, it *is* a stiffnecked people:

14Let me alone, that I may destroy them, and blot out their name from under heaven: and I will make of thee a nation mightier and greater than they.

15So I turned and came down from the mount, and the mount burned with fire: and the two tables of the covenant *were* in my two hands.

16And I looked, and, behold, ye had sinned against the LORD your God, *and* had made you a molten calf: ye had turned aside quickly out of the way which the LORD had commanded you.

17And I took the two tables, and cast them out of my two hands, and brake them before your eyes.

18And I fell down before the LORD, as at the first, forty days and forty nights: I did neither eat bread, nor drink water, because of all your sins which ye sinned, in doing wickedly in the sight of the LORD, to provoke him to anger.

19For I was afraid of the anger and hot displeasure, wherewith the LORD was wroth against you to destroy you. But the LORD hearkened unto me at that time also.

20And the LORD was very angry with Aaron to have destroyed him: and I prayed for Aaron also the same time.

21And I took your sin, the calf which ye had made, and burnt it with fire, and stamped it, *and* ground *it* very small, *even* until it was as small as dust: and I cast the dust thereof into the brook that descended out of the mount.

22And at Taberah, and at Massah, and at Kibrothhattaavah, ye provoked the LORD to wrath.

23Likewise when the LORD sent you from Kadeshbarnea, saying, Go up and possess the land which I have given you; then ye rebelled against the commandment of the LORD your God, and ye believed him not, nor hearkened to his voice.

24Ye have been rebellious against the LORD from the day that I knew you.

25Thus I fell down before the LORD forty days and forty nights, as I fell down *at the first;* because the LORD had said he would destroy you.

26I prayed therefore unto the LORD, and said, O Lord GOD, destroy not thy people and thine inheritance, which thou hast redeemed through thy greatness, which thou hast brought forth out of Egypt with a mighty hand.

27Remember thy servants, Abraham, Isaac, and Jacob; look not unto the stubbornness of this people, nor to their wickedness, nor to their sin:

28Lest the land whence thou broughtest us out say, Because the LORD was not able to bring them into the land which he promised them, and because he hated them, he hath brought them out to slay them in the wilderness.

29Yet they *are* thy people and thine inheritance, which thou broughtest out by thy mighty power and by thy stretched out arm.

AT that time the LORD said unto me, Hew thee two tables of stone like unto the first, and come up unto me into the mount, and make thee an ark of wood.

2And I will write on the tables the words that were in the first tables which thou brakest, and thou shalt put them in the ark.

3And I made an ark *of* shittim wood, and hewed two tables of stone like unto the first, and went up into the mount, having the two tables in mine hand.

4And he wrote on the tables, according to the first writing, the ten commandments, which the LORD spake unto you in the mount out of the midst of the fire in the day of the assembly:

and the LORD gave them unto me.

5And I turned myself and came down from the mount, and put the tables in the ark which I had made; and there they be, as the LORD commanded me.

6And the children of Israel took their journey from Beeroth of the children of Jaakan to Mosera: there Aaron died, and there he was buried; and Eleazar his son ministered in the priest's office in his stead.

7From thence they journeyed unto Gudgodah; and from Gudgodah to Jotbath, a land of rivers of waters.

8At that time the LORD separated the tribe of Levi, to bear the ark of the covenant of the LORD, to stand before the LORD to minister unto him, and to bless in his name, unto this day.

9Wherefore Levi hath no part nor inheritance with his brethren; the LORD *is* his inheritance, according as the LORD thy God promised him.

10And I stayed in the mount, according to the first time, forty days and forty nights; and the LORD hearkened unto me at that time also, *and* the LORD would not destroy thee.

11And the LORD said unto me, Arise, take *thy* journey before the people, that they may go in and possess the land, which I sware unto their fathers to give unto them.

12And now, Israel, what doth the LORD thy God require of thee, but to fear the LORD thy God, to walk in all his ways, and to love him, and to serve the LORD thy God with all thy heart and with all thy soul,

13To keep the commandments of the LORD, and his statutes, which I command thee this day for thy good?

14Behold, the heaven and the heaven of heavens *is* the LORD's thy God, the earth *also*, with all that therein *is*.

15Only the LORD had a delight in thy fathers to love them, and he chose their seed after them, *even* you above all people, as *it is* this day.

16Circumcise therefore the foreskin of your heart, and be no more stiff-necked.

17For the LORD your God *is* God of gods, and Lord of lords, a great God, a mighty, and a terrible, which regardeth not persons, nor taketh reward:

18He doth execute the judgment of the fatherless and widow, and loveth the stranger, in giving him food and raiment.

19Love ye therefore the stranger: for ye were strangers in the land of Egypt.

20Thou shalt fear the LORD thy God; him shalt thou serve, and to him shalt thou cleave, and swear by his name.

21He *is* thy praise, and he *is* thy God, that hath done for thee these great and terrible things, which thine eyes have seen.

22Thy fathers went down into Egypt with threescore and ten persons; and now the LORD thy God hath made thee as the stars of heaven for multitude.

LUKE 8:4–21

AND when much people were gathered together, and were come to him out of every city, he [Jesus] spake by a parable:

5A sower went out to sow his seed: and as he sowed, some fell by the way side; and it was trodden down, and the fowls of the air devoured it.

6And some fell upon a rock; and as soon as it was sprung up, it withered away, because it lacked moisture.

7And some fell among thorns; and the thorns sprang up with it, and choked it.

8And other fell on good ground, and sprang up, and bare fruit an hundredfold. And when he had said these things, he cried, He that hath ears to hear, let him hear.

9And his disciples asked him, saying, What might this parable be?

10And he said, Unto you it is given to know the mysteries of the kingdom of God: but to others in parables; that seeing they might not see, and hearing they might not understand.

11Now the parable is this: The seed is the word of God.

12Those by the way side are they that hear; then cometh the devil, and taketh away the word out of their hearts, lest they should believe and be saved.

13They on the rock *are they,* which, when they hear, receive the word with joy; and these have no root, which for a while believe, and in time of temptation fall away.

14And that which fell among thorns are they, which, when they have heard, go forth, and are choked with cares and riches and pleasures of *this* life, and bring no fruit to perfection.

15But that on the good ground are they, which in an honest and good heart, having heard the word, keep *it,* and bring forth fruit with patience.

16No man, when he hath lighted a candle, covereth it with a vessel, or putteth *it* under a bed; but setteth *it* on a candlestick, that they which enter in may see the light.

17For nothing is secret, that shall not be made manifest; neither *any thing* hid, that shall not be known and come abroad.

18Take heed therefore how ye hear: for whosoever hath, to him shall be given; and whosoever hath not, from him shall be taken even that which he seemeth to have.

19Then came to him *his* mother and his brethren, and could not come at him for the press.

20And it was told him *by certain* which said, Thy mother and thy brethren stand without, desiring to see thee.

21And he answered and said unto them, My mother and my brethren are these which hear the word of God, and do it.

PSALM 69:15–36

L ET not the waterflood overflow me, neither let the deep swallow me up, and let not the pit shut her mouth upon me.

16Hear me, O LORD; for thy lovingkindness *is* good: turn unto me according to the multitude of thy tender mercies.

17And hide not thy face from thy servant; for I am in trouble; hear me speedily.

18Draw nigh unto my soul, *and* redeem it: deliver me because of mine enemies.

19Thou hast known my reproach, and my shame, and my dishonour: mine adversaries *are* all before thee.

20Reproach hath broken my heart; and I am full of heaviness: and I looked *for some* to take pity, but *there was* none; and for comforters, but I found none.

21They gave me also gall for my meat; and in my thirst they gave me vinegar to drink.

22Let their table become a snare before them: and *that which should have been* for *their* welfare, *let it become* a trap.

23Let their eyes be darkened, that they see not; and make their loins continually to shake.

24Pour out thine indignation upon them, and let thy wrathful anger take hold of them.

25Let their habitation be desolate; *and* let none dwell in their tents.

26For they persecute *him* whom thou hast smitten; and they talk to the grief of those whom thou hast wounded.

27Add iniquity unto their iniquity: and let them not come into thy righteousness.

28Let them be blotted out of the book of the living, and not be written with the righteous.

29But I *am* poor and sorrowful: let thy salvation, O God, set me up on high.

30I will praise the name of God with a song, and will magnify him with thanksgiving.

31*This* also shall please the LORD better than an ox *or* bullock that hath horns and hoofs.

32The humble shall see *this, and* be glad: and your heart shall live that seek God.

33For the LORD heareth the poor, and despiseth not his prisoners.

34Let the heaven and earth praise him, the seas, and every thing that moveth therein.

35For God will save Zion, and will build the cities of Judah: that they may dwell there, and have it in possession.

36The seed also of his servants shall inherit it: and they that love his name shall dwell therein.

PROVERBS FOR TODAY/ 12:2–3

A good man *obtaineth favour of the* LORD: *but a man of wicked devices will he* condemn. □*A man shall not be established by wickedness: but the root of the righteous shall not be moved.*

MARCH 29

DEUTERONOMY 11:1—12:32

THEREFORE thou shalt love the LORD thy God, and keep his charge, and his statutes, and his judgments, and his commandments, alway.

2And know ye this day: for *I speak* not with your children which have not known, and which have not seen the chastisement of the LORD your God, his greatness, his mighty hand, and his stretched out arm,

3And his miracles, and his acts, which he did in the midst of Egypt unto Pharaoh the king of Egypt, and unto all his land;

4And what he did unto the army of Egypt, unto their horses, and to their chariots; how he made the water of the Red sea to overflow them as they pursued after you, and *how* the LORD hath destroyed them unto this day;

5And what he did unto you in the wilderness, until ye came into this place;

6And what he did unto Dathan and Abiram, the sons of Eliab, the son of Reuben: how the earth opened her mouth, and swallowed them up, and their households, and their tents, and all the substance that *was* in their possession, in the midst of all Israel:

7But your eyes have seen all the great acts of the LORD which he did.

8Therefore shall ye keep all the commandments which I command you this day, that ye may be strong, and go in and possess the land, whither ye go to possess it;

9And that ye may prolong *your* days in the land, which the LORD sware unto your fathers to give unto them and to their seed, a land that floweth with milk and honey.

10For the land, whither thou goest in to possess it, *is* not as the land of Egypt, from whence ye came out, where thou sowedst thy seed, and wateredst *it* with thy foot, as a garden of herbs:

11But the land, whither ye go to possess it, *is* a land of hills and valleys, *and* drinketh water of the rain of heaven:

12A land which the LORD thy God careth for: the eyes of the LORD thy God *are* always upon it, from the beginning of the year even unto the end of the year.

13And it shall come to pass, if ye shall hearken diligently unto my commandments which I command you this day, to love the LORD your God, and to serve him with all your heart and with all your soul,

14That I will give *you* the rain of your land in his due season, the first' rain and the latter rain, that thou mayest gather in thy corn, and thy wine, and thine oil.

15And I will send grass in thy fields for thy cattle, that thou mayest eat and be full.

16Take heed to yourselves, that your heart be not deceived, and ye turn aside, and serve other gods, and worship them;

17And *then* the LORD'S wrath be kindled against you, and he shut up the heaven, that there be no rain, and that the land yield not her fruit; and *lest* ye perish quickly from off the good land which the LORD giveth you.

18Therefore shall ye lay up these my words in your heart and in your soul, and bind them for a sign upon your hand, that they may be as frontlets between your eyes.

19And ye shall teach them your children, speaking of them when thou sittest in thine house, and when thou walkest by the way, when thou liest down, and when thou risest up.

20And thou shalt write them upon the door posts of thine house, and upon thy gates:

21That your days may be multiplied, and the days of your children, in the land which the LORD sware unto your fathers to give them, as the days of heaven upon the earth.

22For if ye shall diligently keep all these commandments which I command you, to do them, to love the LORD your God, to walk in all his ways, and to cleave unto him;

23Then will the LORD drive out all these nations from before you, and ye shall possess greater nations and mightier than yourselves.

24Every place whereon the soles of your feet shall tread shall be yours: from the wilderness and Lebanon, from the river, the river Euphrates, even unto the uttermost sea shall your coast be.

25There shall no man be able to stand before you: for the LORD your God shall lay the fear of you and the dread of you upon all the land that ye shall tread upon, as he hath said unto you.

26Behold, I set before you this day a blessing and a curse;

27A blessing, if ye obey the commandments of the LORD your God, which I command you this day:

28And a curse, if ye will not obey the commandments of the LORD your God, but turn aside out of the way which I command you this day, to go after other gods, which ye have not known.

29And it shall come to pass, when the LORD thy God hath brought thee in unto the land whither thou goest to possess it, that thou shalt put the blessing upon mount Gerizim, and the curse upon mount Ebal.

30Are they not on the other side Jordan, by the way where the sun goeth down, in the land of the Canaanites, which dwell in the champaign over against Gilgal, beside the plains of Moreh?

31For ye shall pass over Jordan to go in to possess the land which the LORD your God giveth you, and ye shall possess it, and dwell therein.

32And ye shall observe to do all the statutes and judgments which I set before you this day.

THESE *are* the statutes and judgments, which ye shall observe to do in the land, which the LORD God of thy fathers giveth thee to possess it, all the days that ye live upon the earth.

2Ye shall utterly destroy all the places, wherein the nations which ye shall possess served their gods, upon the high mountains, and upon the hills, and under every green tree:

3And ye shall overthrow their altars, and break their pillars, and burn their groves with fire; and ye shall hew down the graven images of their gods, and destroy the names of them out of that place.

4Ye shall not do so unto the LORD your God.

5But unto the place which the LORD your God shall choose out of all your tribes to put his name there, *even* unto his habitation shall ye seek, and thither thou shalt come:

6And thither ye shall bring your burnt offerings, and your sacrifices, and your tithes, and heave offerings of your hand, and your vows, and your freewill offerings, and the firstlings of your herds and of your flocks:

7And there ye shall eat before the LORD your God, and ye shall rejoice in all that ye put your hand unto, ye and your households, wherein the LORD thy God hath blessed thee.

8Ye shall not do after all *the things* that we do here this day, every man whatsoever *is* right in his own eyes.

9For ye are not as yet come to the

rest and to the inheritance, which the LORD your God giveth you.

10But *when* ye go over Jordan, and dwell in the land which the LORD your God giveth you to inherit, and *when* he giveth you rest from all your enemies round about, so that ye dwell in safety;

11Then there shall be a place which the LORD your God shall choose to cause his name to dwell there; thither shall ye bring all that I command you; your burnt offerings, and your sacrifices, your tithes, and the heave offering of your hand, and all your choice vows which ye vow unto the LORD:

12And ye shall rejoice before the LORD your God, ye, and your sons, and your daughters, and your menservants, and your maidservants, and the Levite that *is* within your gates; forasmuch as he hath no part nor inheritance with you.

13Take heed to thyself that thou offer not thy burnt offerings in every place that thou seest:

14But in the place which the LORD shall choose in one of thy tribes, there thou shalt offer thy burnt offerings, and there thou shalt do all that I command thee.

15Notwithstanding thou mayest kill and eat flesh in all thy gates, whatsoever thy soul lusteth after, according to the blessing of the LORD thy God which he hath given thee: the unclean and the clean may eat thereof, as of the roebuck, and as of the hart.

16Only ye shall not eat the blood; ye shall pour it upon the earth as water.

17Thou mayest not eat within thy gates the tithe of thy corn, or of thy wine, or of thy oil, or the firstlings of thy herds or of thy flock, nor any of thy vows which thou vowest, nor thy freewill offerings, or heave offering of thine hand:

18But thou must eat them before the LORD thy God in the place which the LORD thy God shall choose, thou, and thy son, and thy daughter, and thy manservant, and thy maidservant, and the Levite that *is* within thy gates: and thou shalt rejoice before the LORD thy God in all that thou puttest thine hands unto.

19Take heed to thyself that thou forsake not the Levite as long as thou livest upon the earth.

20When the LORD thy God shall enlarge thy border, as he hath promised thee, and thou shalt say, I will eat flesh, because thy soul longeth to eat flesh; thou mayest eat flesh, whatsoever thy soul lusteth after.

21If the place which the LORD thy God hath chosen to put his name there be too far from thee, then thou shalt kill of thy herd and of thy flock, which the LORD hath given thee, as I have commanded thee, and thou shalt eat in thy gates whatsoever thy soul lusteth after.

22Even as the roebuck and the hart is eaten, so thou shalt eat them: the unclean and the clean shall eat *of* them alike.

23Only be sure that thou eat not the blood: for the blood *is* the life; and thou mayest not eat the life with the flesh.

24Thou shalt not eat it; thou shalt pour it upon the earth as water.

25Thou shalt not eat it; that it may go well with thee, and with thy children after thee, when thou shalt do *that which is* right in the sight of the LORD.

26Only thy holy things which thou hast, and thy vows, thou shalt take, and go unto the place which the LORD shall choose:

27And thou shalt offer thy burnt offerings, the flesh and the blood, upon the altar of the LORD thy God: and the blood of thy sacrifices shall be poured out upon the altar of the LORD thy God, and thou shalt eat the flesh.

28Observe and hear all these words which I command thee, that it may go well with thee, and with thy children after thee for ever, when thou doest *that which is* good and right in the sight of the LORD thy God.

29When the LORD thy God shall cut off the nations from before thee, whither thou goest to possess them, and thou succeedest them, and dwellest in their land;

30Take heed to thyself that thou be not snared by following them, after that they be destroyed from before thee; and that thou enquire not after their gods, saying, How did these nations serve their gods? even so will I do likewise.

31Thou shalt not do so unto the LORD thy God: for every abomination to the LORD, which he hateth, have they done unto their gods; for even their sons and their daughters they have burnt in the fire to their gods.

32What thing soever I command you, observe to do it: thou shalt not add thereto, nor diminish from it.

LUKE 8:22–40

Now it came to pass on a certain day, that he [Jesus] went into a ship with his disciples: and he said unto them, Let us go over unto the other side of the lake. And they launched forth.

23But as they sailed he fell asleep: and there came down a storm of wind on the lake; and they were filled *with water,* and were in jeopardy.

24And they came to him, and awoke him, saying, Master, master, we perish. Then he arose, and rebuked the wind and the raging of the water: and they ceased, and there was a calm.

25And he said unto them, Where is your faith? And they being afraid wondered, saying one to another, What manner of man is this! for he commandeth even the winds and water, and they obey him.

26And they arrived at the country

of the Gadarenes, which is over against Galilee.

27And when he went forth to land, there met him out of the city a certain man, which had devils long time, and ware no clothes, neither abode in *any* house, but in the tombs.

28When he saw Jesus, he cried out, and fell down before him, and with a loud voice said, What have I to do with thee, Jesus, *thou* Son of God most high? I beseech thee, torment me not.

29(For he had commanded the unclean spirit to come out of the man. For oftentimes it had caught him: and he was kept bound with chains and in fetters; and he brake the bands, and was driven of the devil into the wilderness.)

30And Jesus asked him, saying, What is thy name? And he said, Legion: because many devils were entered into him.

31And they besought him that he would not command them to go out into the deep.

32And there was there an herd of many swine feeding on the mountain: and they besought him that he would suffer them to enter into them. And he suffered them.

33Then went the devils out of the man, and entered into the swine: and the herd ran violently down a steep place into the lake, and were choked.

34When they that fed *them* saw what was done, they fled, and went and told *it* in the city and in the country.

35Then they went out to see what was done; and came to Jesus, and found the man, out of whom the devils were departed, sitting at the feet of Jesus, clothed, and in his right mind: and they were afraid.

36They also which saw *it* told them by what means he that was possessed of the devils was healed.

37Then the whole multitude of the

country of the Gadarenes round about besought him to depart from them; for they were taken with great fear: and he went up into the ship, and returned back again.

38Now the man out of whom the devils were departed besought him that he might be with him: but Jesus sent him away, saying,

39Return to thine own house, and shew how great things God hath done unto thee. And he went his way and published throughout the whole city how great things Jesus had done unto him.

40And it came to pass, that, when Jesus was returned, the people *gladly* received him: for they were all waiting for him.

PSALM 70:1–5

MAKE *haste,* O God, to deliver me; make haste to help me, O LORD.

2Let them be ashamed and confounded that seek after my soul: let them be turned backward, and put to confusion, that desire my hurt.

3Let them be turned back for a reward of shame that say, Aha, aha.

4Let all those that seek thee rejoice and be glad in thee: and let such as love thy salvation say continually, Let God be magnified.

5But I *am* poor and needy: make haste unto me, O God: thou *art* my help and my deliverer; O LORD, make no tarrying.

PROVERBS FOR TODAY/ 12:4

A virtuous woman is *a crown to her husband: but she that maketh ashamed* is *as rottenness in his bones.*

MARCH 30

DEUTERONOMY 13:1—15:23

IF there arise among you a prophet, or a dreamer of dreams, and giveth thee a sign or a wonder,

2And the sign or the wonder come to pass, whereof he spake unto thee, saying, Let us go after other gods, which thou hast not known, and let us serve them;

3Thou shalt not hearken unto the words of that prophet, or that dreamer of dreams: for the LORD your God proveth you, to know whether ye love the LORD your God with all your heart and with all your soul.

4Ye shall walk after the LORD your God, and fear him, and keep his commandments, and obey his voice, and ye shall serve him, and cleave unto him.

5And that prophet, or that dreamer of dreams, shall be put to death; because he hath spoken to turn *you* away from the LORD your God, which brought you out of the land of Egypt, and redeemed you out of the house of bondage, to thrust thee out of the way which the LORD thy God commanded thee to walk in. So shalt thou put the evil away from the midst of thee.

6If thy brother, the son of thy mother, or thy son, or thy daughter, or the wife of thy bosom, or thy friend, which *is* as thine own soul, entice thee secretly, saying, Let us go and serve other gods, which thou hast not known, thou, nor thy fathers;

7*Namely,* of the gods of the people which *are* round about you, nigh unto thee, or far off from thee, from the *one* end of the earth even unto the *other* end of the earth;

8Thou shalt not consent unto him, nor hearken unto him; neither shall thine eye pity him, neither shalt thou spare, neither shalt thou conceal him:

9But thou shalt surely kill him; thine hand shall be first upon him to put him to death, and afterwards the hand of all the people.

10And thou shalt stone him with stones, that he die; because he hath sought to thrust thee away from the LORD thy God, which brought thee out of the land of Egypt, from the house of bondage.

11And all Israel shall hear, and fear, and shall do no more any such wickedness as this is among you.

12If thou shalt hear *say* in one of thy cities, which the LORD thy God hath given thee to dwell there, saying,

13*Certain* men, the children of Belial, are gone out from among you, and have withdrawn the inhabitants of their city, saying, Let us go and serve other gods, which ye have not known;

14Then shalt thou enquire, and make search, and ask diligently, and, behold, *if it be* truth, *and* the thing certain, *that* such abomination is wrought among you;

15Thou shalt surely smite the inhabitants of that city with the edge of the sword, destroying it utterly, and all that *is* therein, and the cattle thereof, with the edge of the sword.

16And thou shalt gather all the spoil of it into the midst of the street thereof, and shalt burn with fire the city, and all the spoil thereof every whit, for the LORD thy God: and it shall be an heap for ever; it shall not be built again.

17And there shall cleave nought of the cursed thing to thine hand: that the LORD may turn from the fierceness of his anger, and shew thee mercy, and have compassion upon thee, and multiply thee, as he hath sworn unto thy fathers;

18When thou shalt hearken to the voice of the LORD thy God, to keep all his commandments which I command thee this day, to do *that which is* right in the eyes of the LORD thy God.

YE *are* the children of the LORD your God: ye shall not cut yourselves, nor make any baldness between your eyes for the dead.

2For thou *art* an holy people unto the LORD thy God, and the LORD hath chosen thee to be a peculiar people unto himself, above all the nations that *are* upon the earth.

3Thou shalt not eat any abominable thing.

4These *are* the beasts which ye shall eat: the ox, the sheep, and the goat,

5The hart, and the roebuck, and the fallow deer, and the wild goat, and the pygarg, and the wild ox, and the chamois.

6And every beast that parteth the hoof, and cleaveth the cleft into two claws, *and* cheweth the cud among the beasts, that ye shall eat.

7Nevertheless these ye shall not eat of them that chew the cud, or of them that divide the cloven hoof; *as* the camel, and the hare, and the coney: for they chew the cud, but divide not the hoof; *therefore* they *are* unclean unto you.

8And the swine, because it divideth the hoof, yet cheweth not the cud, it *is* unclean unto you: ye shall not eat of their flesh, nor touch their dead carcase.

9These ye shall eat of all that *are* in the waters: all that have fins and scales shall ye eat:

10And whatsoever hath not fins and scales ye may not eat; it *is* unclean unto you.

11*Of* all clean birds ye shall eat.

¹²But these *are they* of which ye shall not eat: the eagle, and the ossifrage, and the ospray,

¹³And the glede, and the kite, and the vulture after his kind,

¹⁴And every raven after his kind,

¹⁵And the owl, and the night hawk, and the cuckow, and the hawk after his kind,

¹⁶The little owl, and the great owl, and the swan,

¹⁷And the pelican, and the gier eagle, and the cormorant,

¹⁸And the stork, and the heron after her kind, and the lapwing, and the bat.

¹⁹And every creeping thing that flieth *is* unclean unto you: they shall not be eaten.

²⁰*But of* all clean fowls ye may eat.

²¹Ye shall not eat *of* any thing that dieth of itself: thou shalt give it unto the stranger that *is* in thy gates, that he may eat it; or thou mayest sell it unto an alien: for thou *art* an holy people unto the Lᴏʀᴅ thy God. Thou shalt not seethe a kid in his mother's milk.

²²Thou shalt truly tithe all the increase of thy seed, that the field bringeth forth year by year.

²³And thou shalt eat before the Lᴏʀᴅ thy God, in the place which he shall choose to place his name there, the tithe of thy corn, of thy wine, and of thine oil, and the firstlings of thy herds and of thy flocks; that thou mayest learn to fear the Lᴏʀᴅ thy God always.

²⁴And if the way be too long for thee, so that thou art not able to carry it; *or* if the place be too far from thee, which the Lᴏʀᴅ thy God shall choose to set his name there, when the Lᴏʀᴅ thy God hath blessed thee:

²⁵Then shalt thou turn *it* into money, and bind up the money in thine hand, and shalt go unto the place which the Lᴏʀᴅ thy God shall choose:

²⁶And thou shalt bestow that money for whatsoever thy soul lusteth after, for oxen, or for sheep, or for wine, or for strong drink, or for whatsoever

thy soul desireth: and thou shalt eat there before the Lᴏʀᴅ thy God, and thou shalt rejoice, thou, and thine household,

²⁷And the Levite that *is* within thy gates; thou shalt not forsake him; for he hath no part nor inheritance with thee.

²⁸At the end of three years thou shalt bring forth all the tithe of thine increase the same year, and shalt lay *it* up within thy gates:

²⁹And the Levite, (because he hath no part nor inheritance with thee,) and the stranger, and the fatherless, and the widow, which *are* within thy gates, shall come, and shall eàt and be satisfied; that the Lᴏʀᴅ thy God may bless thee in all the work of thine hand which thou doest.

Aᴛ the end of *every* seven years thou shalt make a release.

²And this *is* the manner of the release: Every creditor that lendeth *ought* unto his neighbour shall release *it;* he shall not exact *it* of his neighbour, or of his brother; because it is called the Lᴏʀᴅ's release.

³Of a foreigner thou mayest exact *it again:* but *that* which is thine with thy brother thine hand shall release;

⁴Save when there shall be no poor among you; for the Lᴏʀᴅ shall greatly bless thee in the land which the Lᴏʀᴅ thy God giveth thee *for* an inheritance to possess it:

⁵Only if thou carefully hearken unto the voice of the Lᴏʀᴅ thy God, to observe to do all these commandments which I command thee this day.

⁶For the Lᴏʀᴅ thy God blesseth thee, as he promised thee: and thou shalt lend unto many nations, but thou shalt not borrow; and thou shalt reign over many nations, but they shall not reign over thee.

⁷If there be among you a poor man of one of thy brethren within any of thy gates in thy land which the Lᴏʀᴅ

thy God giveth thee, thou shalt not harden thine heart, nor shut thine hand from thy poor brother:

8But thou shalt open thine hand wide unto him, and shalt surely lend him sufficient for his need, *in that* which he wanteth.

9Beware that there be not a thought in thy wicked heart, saying, The seventh year, the year of release, is at hand; and thine eye be evil against thy poor brother, and thou givest him nought; and he cry unto the LORD against thee, and it be sin unto thee.

10Thou shalt surely give him, and thine heart shall not be grieved when thou givest unto him: because that for this thing the LORD thy God shall bless thee in all thy works, and in all that thou puttest thine hand unto.

11For the poor shall never cease out of the land: therefore I command thee, saying, Thou shalt open thine hand wide unto thy brother, to thy poor, and to thy needy, in thy land.

12*And* if thy brother, an Hebrew man, or an Hebrew woman, be sold unto thee, and serve thee six years; then in the seventh year thou shalt let him go free from thee.

13And when thou sendest him out free from thee, thou shalt not let him go away empty:

14Thou shalt furnish him liberally out of thy flock, and out of thy floor, and out of thy winepress: *of that* wherewith the LORD thy God hath blessed thee thou shalt give unto him.

15And thou shalt remember that thou wast a bondman in the land of Egypt, and the LORD thy God redeemed thee: therefore I command thee this thing to day.

16And it shall be, if he say unto thee, I will not go away from thee; because he loveth thee and thine house, because he is well with thee;

17Then thou shalt take an aul, and thrust *it* through his ear unto the door, and he shall be thy servant for ever.

And also unto thy maidservant thou shalt do likewise.

18It shall not seem hard unto thee, when thou sendest him away free from thee; for he hath been worth a double hired servant *to thee,* in serving thee six years: and the LORD thy God shall bless thee in all that thou doest.

19All the firstling males that come of thy herd and of thy flock thou shalt sanctify unto the LORD thy God: thou shalt do no work with the firstling of thy bullock, nor shear the firstling of thy sheep.

20Thou shalt eat *it* before the LORD thy God year by year in the place which the LORD shall choose, thou and thy household.

21And if there be *any* blemish therein, *as if it be* lame, or blind, *or have* any ill blemish, thou shalt not sacrifice it unto the LORD thy God.

22Thou shalt eat it within thy gates: the unclean and the clean *person shall eat it* alike, as the roebuck, and as the hart.

23Only thou shalt not eat the blood thereof; thou shalt pour it upon the ground as water.

LUKE 8:41—9:6

AND, behold, there came a man named Jairus, and he was a ruler of the synagogue: and he fell down at Jesus' feet, and besought him that he would come into his house:

42For he had one only daughter, about twelve years of age, and she lay a dying. But as he went the people thronged him.

43And a woman having an issue of blood twelve years, which had spent all her living upon physicians, neither could be healed of any,

44Came behind *him,* and touched the border of his garment: and immediately her issue of blood stanched.

45And Jesus said, Who touched me? When all denied, Peter and they that were with him said, Master, the multitude throng thee and press *thee,* and sayest thou, Who touched me?

46And Jesus said, Somebody hath touched me: for I perceive that virtue is gone out of me.

47And when the woman saw that she was not hid, she came trembling, and falling down before him, she declared unto him before all the people for what cause she had touched him, and how she was healed immediately.

48And he said unto her, Daughter, be of good comfort: thy faith hath made thee whole; go in peace.

49While he yet spake, there cometh one from the ruler of the synagogue's *house,* saying to him, Thy daughter is dead; trouble not the Master.

50But when Jesus heard *it,* he answered him, saying, Fear not: believe only, and she shall be made whole.

51And when he came into the house, he suffered no man to go in, save Peter, and James, and John, and the father and the mother of the maiden.

52And all wept, and bewailed her: but he said, Weep not; she is not dead, but sleepeth.

53And they laughed him to scorn, knowing that she was dead.

54And he put them all out, and took her by the hand, and called, saying, Maid, arise.

55And her spirit came again, and she arose straightway: and he commanded to give her meat.

56And her parents were astonished: but he charged them that they should tell no man what was done.

THEN he called his twelve disciples together, and gave them power and authority over all devils, and to cure diseases.

2And he sent them to preach the kingdom of God, and to heal the sick.

3And he said unto them, Take nothing for *your* journey, neither staves, nor scrip, neither bread, neither money;

neither have two coats apiece.

4And whatsoever house ye enter into, there abide, and thence depart.

5And whosoever will not receive you, when ye go out of that city, shake off the very dust from your feet for a testimony against them.

6And they departed, and went through the towns, preaching the gospel, and healing every where.

PSALM 71:1-24

IN thee, O LORD, do I put my trust: let me never be put to confusion.

2Deliver me in thy righteousness, and cause me to escape: incline thine ear unto me, and save me.

3Be thou my strong habitation, whereunto I may continually resort: thou hast given commandment to save me; for thou *art* my rock and my fortress.

4Deliver me, O my God, out of the hand of the wicked, out of the hand of the unrighteous and cruel man.

5For thou *art* my hope, O Lord GOD: *thou art* my trust from my youth.

6By thee have I been holden up from the womb: thou art he that took me out of my mother's bowels: my praise *shall be* continually of thee.

7I am as a wonder unto many; but thou *art* my strong refuge.

8Let my mouth be filled *with* thy praise *and with* thy honour all the day.

9Cast me not off in the time of old age; forsake me not when my strength faileth.

10For mine enemies speak against me; and they that lay wait for my soul take counsel together,

11Saying, God hath forsaken him: persecute and take him; for *there is* none to deliver *him.*

12O God, be not far from me: O my God, make haste for my help.

13Let them be confounded *and* consumed that are adversaries to my soul; let them be covered *with* reproach and dishonour that seek my hurt.

14But I will hope continually, and will yet praise thee more and more.

15My mouth shall shew forth thy righteousness *and* thy salvation all the day; for I know not the numbers *thereof.*

16I will go in the strength of the Lord GOD: I will make mention of thy righteousness, *even* of thine only.

17O God, thou hast taught me from my youth: and hitherto have I declared thy wondrous works.

18Now also when I am old and greyheaded, O God, forsake me not; until I have shewed thy strength unto *this* generation, *and* thy power to every one *that* is to come.

19Thy righteousness also, O God, *is* very high, who hast done great things: O God, who *is* like unto thee!

20*Thou,* which hast shewed me great and sore troubles, shalt quicken me again, and shalt bring me up again from the depths of the earth.

21Thou shalt increase my greatness, and comfort me on every side.

22I will also praise thee with the psaltery, *even* thy truth, O my God: unto thee will I sing with the harp, O thou Holy One of Israel.

23My lips shall greatly rejoice when I sing unto thee; and my soul, which thou hast redeemed.

24My tongue also shall talk of thy righteousness all the day long: for they are confounded, for they are brought unto shame, that seek my hurt.

PROVERBS FOR TODAY/ 12:5–7

The thoughts of the righteous are *right:* but *the counsels of the wicked* are *deceit.* □ *The words of the wicked* are *to lie in wait for blood: but the mouth of the upright shall deliver them.* □ *The wicked are overthrown, and* are *not: but the house of the righteous shall stand.*

MARCH 31

DEUTERONOMY 16:1—17:20

OBSERVE the month of Abib, and keep the passover unto the LORD thy God: for in the month of Abib the LORD thy God brought thee forth out of Egypt by night.

2Thou shalt therefore sacrifice the passover unto the LORD thy God, of the flock and the herd, in the place which the LORD shall choose to place his name there.

3Thou shalt eat no leavened bread with it; seven days shalt thou eat unleavened bread therewith, *even* the bread of affliction; for thou camest forth out of the land of Egypt in haste: that thou mayest remember the day when thou camest forth out of the land of Egypt all the days of thy life.

4And there shall be no leavened bread seen with thee in all thy coast seven days; neither shall there *any thing* of the flesh, which thou sacrificedst the first day at even, remain all night until the morning.

5Thou mayest not sacrifice the passover within any of thy gates, which the LORD thy God giveth thee:

6But at the place which the LORD thy God shall choose to place his name in, there thou shalt sacrifice the passover at even, at the going down of the sun, at the season that thou camest forth out of Egypt.

7And thou shalt roast and eat *it* in the place which the LORD thy God shall choose: and thou shalt turn in the morning, and go unto thy tents.

8Six days thou shalt eat unleavened bread: and on the seventh day *shall be* a solemn assembly to the LORD thy God: thou shalt do no work *therein.*

9Seven weeks shalt thou number unto thee: begin to number the seven weeks from *such time as* thou beginnest *to put* the sickle to the corn.

10And thou shalt keep the feast of weeks unto the LORD thy God with a tribute of a freewill offering of thine hand, which thou shalt give *unto the LORD thy God,* according as the LORD thy God hath blessed thee:

11And thou shalt rejoice before the LORD thy God, thou, and thy son, and thy daughter, and thy manservant, and thy maidservant, and the Levite that *is* within thy gates, and the stranger, and the fatherless, and the widow, that *are* among you, in the place which the LORD thy God hath chosen to place his name there.

12And thou shalt remember that thou wast a bondman in Egypt: and thou shalt observe and do these statutes.

13Thou shalt observe the feast of tabernacles seven days, after that thou hast gathered in thy corn and thy wine:

14And thou shalt rejoice in thy feast, thou, and thy son, and thy daughter, and thy manservant, and thy maidservant, and the Levite, the stranger, and the fatherless, and the widow, that *are* within thy gates.

15Seven days shalt thou keep a solemn feast unto the LORD thy God in the place which the LORD shall choose: because the LORD thy God shall bless thee in all thine increase, and in all the works of thine hands, therefore thou shalt surely rejoice.

16Three times in a year shall all thy males appear before the LORD thy God in the place which he shall choose; in the feast of unleavened bread, and in the feast of weeks, and in the feast of tabernacles: and they shall not appear before the LORD empty:

17Every man *shall give* as he is able, according to the blessing of the LORD thy God which he hath given thee.

18Judges and officers shalt thou make thee in all thy gates, which the LORD thy God giveth thee, throughout thy tribes: and they shall judge the people with just judgment.

19Thou shalt not wrest judgment; thou shalt not respect persons, neither take a gift: for a gift doth blind the eyes of the wise, and pervert the words of the righteous.

20That which is altogether just shalt thou follow, that thou mayest live, and inherit the land which the LORD thy God giveth thee.

21Thou shalt not plant thee a grove of any trees near unto the altar of the LORD thy God, which thou shalt make thee.

22Neither shalt thou set thee up *any* image; which the LORD thy God hateth.

THOU shalt not sacrifice unto the LORD thy God *any* bullock, or sheep, wherein *is* blemish *or* any evilfavouredness: for that *is* an abomination unto the LORD thy God.

2If there be found among you, within any of thy gates which the LORD thy God giveth thee, man or woman, that hath wrought wickedness in the sight of the LORD thy God, in transgressing his covenant,

3And hath gone and served other gods, and worshipped them, either the sun, or moon, or any of the host of heaven, which I have not commanded;

4And it be told thee, and thou hast heard *of it,* and enquired diligently, and, behold, *it be* true, *and* the thing certain, *that* such abomination is wrought in Israel:

5Then shalt thou bring forth that man

or that woman, which have committed that wicked thing, unto thy gates, *even* that man or that woman, and shalt stone them with stones, till they die.

6At the mouth of two witnesses, or three witnesses, shall he that is worthy of death be put to death; *but* at the mouth of one witness he shall not be put to death.

7The hands of the witnesses shall be first upon him to put him to death, and afterward the hands of all the people. So thou shalt put the evil away from among you.

8If there arise a matter too hard for thee in judgment, between blood and blood, between plea and plea, and between stroke and stroke, *being* matters of controversy within thy gates: then shalt thou arise, and get thee up into the place which the LORD thy God shall choose;

9And thou shalt come unto the priests the Levites, and unto the judge that shall be in those days, and enquire; and they shall shew thee the sentence of judgment:

10And thou shalt do according to the sentence, which they of that place which the LORD shall choose shall shew thee; and thou shalt observe to do according to all that they inform thee;

11According to the sentence of the law which they shall teach thee, and according to the judgment which they shall tell thee, thou shalt do: thou shalt not decline from the sentence which they shall shew thee, *to* the right hand, nor *to* the left.

12And the man that will do presumptuously, and will not hearken unto the priest that standeth to minister there before the LORD thy God, or unto the judge, even that man shall die: and thou shalt put away the evil from Israel.

13And all the people shall hear, and fear, and do no more presumptuously.

14When thou art come unto the land which the LORD thy God giveth thee, and shalt possess it, and shalt dwell therein, and shalt say, I will set a king over me, like as all the nations that *are* about me;

15Thou shalt in any wise set *him* king over thee, whom the LORD thy God shall choose: *one* from among thy brethren shalt thou set king over thee: thou mayest not set a stranger over thee, which *is* not thy brother.

16But he shall not multiply horses to himself, nor cause the people to return to Egypt, to the end that he should multiply horses: forasmuch as the LORD hath said unto you, Ye shall henceforth return no more that way.

17Neither shall he multiply wives to himself, that his heart turn not away: neither shall he greatly multiply to himself silver and gold.

18And it shall be, when he sitteth upon the throne of his kingdom, that he shall write him a copy of this law in a book out of *that which is* before the priests the Levites:

19And it shall be with him, and he shall read therein all the days of his life: that he may learn to fear the LORD his God, to keep all the words of this law and these statutes, to do them:

20That his heart be not lifted up above his brethren, and that he turn not aside from the commandment, *to* the right hand, or *to* the left: to the end that he may prolong *his* days in his kingdom, he, and his children, in the midst of Israel.

LUKE 9:7–27

Now Herod the tetrarch heard of all that was done by him [Jesus]: and he was perplexed, because that it was said of some, that John was risen from the dead;

8And of some, that Elias had appeared; and of others, that one of the old prophets was risen again.

9And Herod said, John have I beheaded: but who is this, of whom I hear such things? And he desired to see him.

10And the apostles, when they were returned, told him all that they had done. And he took them, and went aside privately into a desert place belonging to the city called Bethsaida.

11And the people, when they knew *it,* followed him: and he received them, and spake unto them of the kingdom of God, and healed them that had need of healing.

12And when the day began to wear away, then came the twelve, and said unto him, Send the multitude away, that they may go into the towns and country round about, and lodge, and get victuals: for we are here in a desert place.

13But he said unto them, Give ye them to eat. And they said, We have no more but five loaves and two fishes; except we should go and buy meat for all this people.

14For they were about five thousand men. And he said to his disciples, Make them sit down by fifties in a company.

15And they did so, and made them all sit down.

16Then he took the five loaves and the two fishes, and looking up to heaven, he blessed them, and brake, and gave to the disciples to set before the multitude.

17And they did eat, and were all filled: and there was taken up of fragments that remained to them twelve baskets.

18And it came to pass, as he was alone praying, his disciples were with him: and he asked them, saying, Whom say the people that I am?

19They answering said, John the Baptist; but some *say,* Elias; and others *say,* that one of the old prophets is risen again.

20He said unto them, But whom say ye that I am? Peter answering said, The Christ of God.

21And he straitly charged them, and commanded *them* to tell no man that thing;

22Saying, The Son of man must suffer many things, and be rejected of the elders and chief priests and scribes, and be slain, and be raised the third day.

23And he said to *them* all, If any *man* will come after me, let him deny himself, and take up his cross daily, and follow me.

24For whosoever will save his life shall lose it: but whosoever will lose his life for my sake, the same shall save it.

25For what is a man advantaged, if he gain the whole world, and lose himself, or be cast away?

26For whosoever shall be ashamed of me and of my words, of him shall the Son of man be ashamed, when he shall come in his own glory, and *in his* Father's, and of the holy angels.

27But I tell you of a truth, there be some standing here, which shall not taste of death, till they see the kingdom of God.

PSALM 72:1–20

GIVE the king thy judgments, O God, and thy righteousness unto the king's son.

2He shall judge thy people with righteousness, and thy poor with judgment.

3The mountains shall bring peace to the people, and the little hills, by righteousness.

4He shall judge the poor of the people, he shall save the children of the needy, and shall break in pieces the oppressor.

5They shall fear thee as long as the sun and moon endure, throughout all generations.

6He shall come down like rain upon the mown grass: as showers *that* water the earth.

7In his days shall the righteous flourish; and abundance of peace so long as the moon endureth.

8He shall have dominion also from sea to sea, and from the river unto the ends of the earth.

9They that dwell in the wilderness shall bow before him; and his enemies shall lick the dust.

10The kings of Tarshish and of the isles shall bring presents: the kings of Sheba and Seba shall offer gifts.

11Yea, all kings shall fall down before him: all nations shall serve him.

12For he shall deliver the needy when he crieth; the poor also, and *him* that hath no helper.

13He shall spare the poor and needy, and shall save the souls of the needy.

14He shall redeem their soul from deceit and violence: and precious shall their blood be in his sight.

15And he shall live, and to him shall be given of the gold of Sheba: prayer also shall be made for him continually; *and* daily shall he be praised.

16There shall be an handful of corn in the earth upon the top of the mountains; the fruit thereof shall shake like Lebanon: and *they* of the city shall flourish like grass of the earth.

17His name shall endure for ever: his name shall be continued as long as the sun: and *men* shall be blessed in him: all nations shall call him blessed.

18Blessed *be* the LORD God, the God of Israel, who only doeth wondrous things.

19And blessed *be* his glorious name for ever: and let the whole earth be filled *with* his glory; Amen, and Amen.

20The prayers of David the son of Jesse are ended.

PROVERBS FOR TODAY/ 12:8–9

A man shall be commended according to his wisdom: but he that is of a perverse heart shall be despised. □ He that is *despised, and hath a servant,* is *better than he that honoureth himself, and lacketh bread.*

APRIL 1

DEUTERONOMY 18:1—20:20

THE priests the Levites, *and* all the tribe of Levi, shall have no part nor inheritance with Israel: they shall eat the offerings of the LORD made by fire, and his inheritance.

2Therefore shall they have no inheritance among their brethren: the LORD *is* their inheritance, as he hath said unto them.

3And this shall be the priest's due from the people, from them that offer a sacrifice, whether *it be* ox or sheep; and they shall give unto the priest the shoulder, and the two cheeks, and the maw.

4The firstfruit *also* of thy corn, of thy wine, and of thine oil, and the first of the fleece of thy sheep, shalt thou give him.

5For the LORD thy God hath chosen him out of all thy tribes, to stand to minister in the name of the LORD, him and his sons for ever.

6And if a Levite come from any of thy gates out of all Israel, where he sojourned, and come with all the desire of his mind unto the place which the LORD shall choose;

7Then he shall minister in the name of the LORD his God, as all his brethren the Levites *do*, which stand there before the Lord.

8They shall have like portions to eat, beside that which cometh of the sale of his patrimony.

9When thou art come into the land which the Lord thy God giveth thee, thou shalt not learn to do after the abominations of those nations.

10There shall not be found among you *any one* that maketh his son or his daughter to pass through the fire, *or* that useth divination, *or* an observer of times, or an enchanter, or a witch.

11Or a charmer, or a consulter with familiar spirits, or a wizard, or a necromancer.

12For all that do these things *are* an abomination unto the Lord: and because of these abominations the Lord thy God doth drive them out from before thee.

13Thou shalt be perfect with the Lord thy God.

14For these nations, which thou shalt possess, hearkened unto observers of times, and unto diviners: but as for thee, the Lord thy God hath not suffered thee so *to do.*

15The Lord thy God will raise up unto thee a Prophet from the midst of thee, of thy brethren, like unto me; unto him ye shall hearken;

16According to all that thou desiredst of the Lord thy God in Horeb in the day of the assembly, saying, Let me not hear again the voice of the Lord my God, neither let me see this great fire any more, that I die not.

17And the Lord said unto me, They have well *spoken that* which they have spoken.

18I will raise them up a Prophet from among their brethren, like unto thee, and will put my words in his mouth; and he shall speak unto them all that I shall command him.

19And it shall come to pass, *that* whosoever will not hearken unto my words which he shall speak in my name, I will require *it* of him.

20But the prophet, which shall presume to speak a word in my name, which I have not commanded him to speak, or that shall speak in the name of other gods, even that prophet shall die.

21And if thou say in thine heart, How shall we know the word which the Lord hath not spoken?

22When a prophet speaketh in the name of the Lord, if the thing follow not, nor come to pass, that *is* the thing which the Lord hath not spoken, *but* the prophet hath spoken it presumptuously: thou shalt not be afraid of him.

When the Lord thy God hath cut off the nations, whose land the Lord thy God giveth thee, and thou succeedest them, and dwellest in their cities, and in their houses;

2Thou shalt separate three cities for thee in the midst of thy land, which the Lord thy God giveth thee to possess it.

3Thou shalt prepare thee a way, and divide the coasts of thy land, which the Lord thy God giveth thee to inherit, into three parts, that every slayer may flee thither.

4And this *is* the case of the slayer, which shall flee thither, that he may live: Whoso killeth his neighbour ignorantly, whom he hated not in time past;

5As when a man goeth into the wood with his neighbour to hew wood, and his hand fetcheth a stroke with the axe to cut down the tree, and the head slippeth from the helve, and lighteth upon his neighbour, that he die; he shall flee unto one of those cities, and live:

6Lest the avenger of the blood pursue the slayer, while his heart is hot, and overtake him, because the way is long, and slay him; whereas he *was* not worthy of death, inasmuch as he hated him not in time past.

7Wherefore I command thee, saying, Thou shalt separate three cities for thee.

⁸And if the LORD thy God enlarge thy coast, as he hath sworn unto thy fathers, and give thee all the land which he promised to give unto thy fathers;

⁹If thou shalt keep all these commandments to do them, which I command thee this day, to love the LORD thy God, and to walk ever in his ways; then shalt thou add three cities more for thee, beside these three:

¹⁰That innocent blood be not shed in thy land, which the LORD thy God giveth thee *for* an inheritance, and *so* blood be upon thee.

¹¹But if any man hate his neighbour, and lie in wait for him, and rise up against him, and smite him mortally that he die, and fleeth into one of these cities:

¹²Then the elders of his city shall send and fetch him thence, and deliver him into the hand of the avenger of blood, that he may die.

¹³Thine eye shall not pity him, but thou shalt put away *the guilt of* innocent blood from Israel, that it may go well with thee.

¹⁴Thou shalt not remove thy neighbour's landmark, which they of old time have set in thine inheritance, which thou shalt inherit in the land that the LORD thy God giveth thee to possess it.

¹⁵One witness shall not rise up against a man for any iniquity, or for any sin, in any sin that he sinneth: at the mouth of two witnesses, or at the mouth of three witnesses, shall the matter be established.

¹⁶If a false witness rise up against any man to testify against him *that which is* wrong;

¹⁷Then both the men, between whom the controversy *is,* shall stand before the LORD, before the priests and the judges, which shall be in those days;

¹⁸And the judges shall make diligent inquisition: and, behold, *if* the witness *be* a false witness, *and* hath testified falsely against his brother;

¹⁹Then shall ye do unto him, as he had thought to have done unto his brother: so shalt thou put the evil away from among you.

²⁰And those which remain shall hear, and fear, and shall henceforth commit no more any such evil among you.

²¹And thine eye shall not pity; *but* life *shall go* for life, eye for eye, tooth for tooth, hand for hand, foot for foot.

WHEN thou goest out to battle against thine enemies, and seest horses, and chariots, *and* a people more than thou, be not afraid of them: for the LORD thy God *is* with thee, which brought thee up out of the land of Egypt.

²And it shall be, when ye are come nigh unto the battle, that the priest shall approach and speak unto the people,

³And shall say unto them, Hear, O Israel, ye approach this day unto battle against your enemies: let not your hearts faint, fear not, and do not tremble, neither be ye terrified because of them;

⁴For the LORD your God *is* he that goeth with you, to fight for you against your enemies, to save you.

⁵And the officers shall speak unto the people, saying, What man *is there* that hath built a new house, and hath not dedicated it? let him go and return to his house, lest he die in the battle, and another man dedicate it.

⁶And what man *is he* that hath planted a vineyard, and hath not *yet* eaten of it? let him *also* go and return unto his house, lest he die in the battle, and another man eat of it.

⁷And what man *is there* that hath betrothed a wife, and hath not taken her? let him go and return unto his house, lest he die in the battle, and another man take her.

⁸And the officers shall speak further unto the people, and they shall say, What man *is there that is* fearful and fainthearted? let him go and return unto

his house, lest his brethren's heart faint as well as his heart.

9And it shall be, when the officers have made an end of speaking unto the people, that they shall make captains of the armies to lead the people.

10When thou comest nigh unto a city to fight against it, then proclaim peace unto it.

11And it shall be, if it make thee answer of peace, and open unto thee, then it shall be, *that* all the people *that is* found therein shall be tributaries unto thee, and they shall serve thee.

12And if it will make no peace with thee, but will make war against thee, then thou shalt besiege it:

13And when the Lord thy God hath delivered it into thine hands, thou shalt smite every male thereof with the edge of the sword:

14But the women, and the little ones, and the cattle, and all that is in the city, *even* all the spoil thereof, shalt thou take unto thyself; and thou shalt eat the spoil of thine enemies, which the Lord thy God hath given thee.

15Thus shalt thou do unto all the cities *which are* very far off from thee, which *are* not of the cities of these nations.

16But of the cities of these people, which the Lord thy God doth give thee *for* an inheritance, thou shalt save alive nothing that breatheth:

17But thou shalt utterly destroy them; *namely,* the Hittites, and the Amorites, the Canaanites, and the Perizzites, the Hivites, and the Jebusites; as the Lord thy God hath commanded thee:

18That they teach you not to do after all their abominations, which they have done unto their gods; so should ye sin against the Lord your God.

19When thou shalt besiege a city a long time, in making war against it to take it, thou shalt not destroy the trees thereof by forcing an axe against them: for thou mayest eat of them, and thou shalt not cut them down (for the tree of the field *is* man's *life*) to employ *them* in the siege:

20Only the trees which thou knowest that they *be* not trees for meat, thou shalt destroy and cut them down; and thou shalt build bulwarks against the city that maketh war with thee, until it be subdued.

LUKE 9:28–50

AND it came to pass about an eight days after these sayings, he [Jesus] took Peter and John and James, and went up into a mountain to pray.

29And as he prayed, the fashion of his countenance was altered, and his raiment *was* white *and* glistering.

30And, behold, there talked with him two men, which were Moses and Elias:

31Who appeared in glory, and spake of his decease which he should accomplish at Jerusalem.

32But Peter and they that were with him were heavy with sleep: and when they were awake, they saw his glory, and the two men that stood with him.

33And it came to pass, as they departed from him, Peter said unto Jesus, Master, it is good for us to be here: and let us make three tabernacles; one for thee, and one for Moses, and one for Elias: not knowing what he said.

34While he thus spake, there came a cloud, and overshadowed them: and they feared as they entered into the cloud.

35And there came a voice out of the cloud, saying, This is my beloved Son: hear him.

36And when the voice was past, Jesus was found alone. And they kept *it* close, and told no man in those days any of those things which they had seen.

37And it came to pass, that on the next day, when they were come down from the hill, much people met him.

38And, behold, a man of the company cried out, saying, Master, I beseech thee, look upon my son: for he is mine only child.

39And, lo, a spirit taketh him, and he suddenly crieth out; and it teareth him that he foameth again, and bruising him hardly departeth from him.

40And I besought thy disciples to cast him out; and they could not.

41And Jesus answering said, O faithless and perverse generation, how long shall I be with you, and suffer you? Bring thy son hither.

42And as he was yet a coming, the devil threw him down, and tare *him*. And Jesus rebuked the unclean spirit, and healed the child, and delivered him again to his father.

43And they were all amazed at the mighty power of God. But while they wondered every one at all things which Jesus did, he said unto his disciples,

44Let these sayings sink down into your ears: for the Son of man shall be delivered into the hands of men.

45But they understood not this saying, and it was hid from them, that they perceived it not: and they feared to ask him of that saying.

46Then there arose a reasoning among them, which of them should be greatest.

47And Jesus, perceiving the thought of their heart, took a child, and set him by him,

48And said unto them, Whosoever shall receive this child in my name receiveth me: and whosoever shall receive me receiveth him that sent me: for he that is least among you all, the same shall be great.

49And John answered and said, Master, we saw one casting out devils in thy name; and we forbad him, because he followeth not with us.

50And Jesus said unto him, Forbid *him* not: for he that is not against us is for us.

PSALM 73:1–28

Truly God *is* good to Israel, *even* to such as are of a clean heart.

2But as for me, my feet were almost gone; my steps had well nigh slipped.

3For I was envious at the foolish, *when* I saw the prosperity of the wicked.

4For *there are* no bands in their death: but their strength *is* firm.

5They *are* not in trouble *as other* men; neither are they plagued like *other* men.

6Therefore pride compasseth them about as a chain; violence covereth them *as* a garment.

7Their eyes stand out with fatness: they have more than heart could wish.

8They are corrupt, and speak wickedly *concerning* oppression: they speak loftily.

9They set their mouth against the heavens, and their tongue walketh through the earth.

10Therefore his people return hither: and waters of a full *cup* are wrung out to them.

11And they say, How doth God know? and is there knowledge in the most High?

12Behold, these *are* the ungodly, who prosper in the world; they increase *in* riches.

13Verily I have cleansed my heart *in* vain, and washed my hands in innocency.

14For all the day long have I been plagued, and chastened every morning.

15If I say, I will speak thus; behold, I should offend *against* the generation of thy children.

16When I thought to know this, it *was* too painful for me;

17Until I went into the sanctuary of God; *then* understood I their end.

18Surely thou didst set them in slippery places: thou castedst them down into destruction.

19How are they *brought* into desolation, as in a moment! they are utterly consumed with terrors.

20As a dream when *one* awaketh; *so,* O Lord, when thou awakest, thou shalt despise their image.

21Thus my heart was grieved, and I was pricked in my reins.

22So foolish *was* I, and ignorant: I was *as* a beast before thee.

23Nevertheless I *am* continually with thee: thou hast holden *me* by my right hand.

24Thou shalt guide me with thy counsel, and afterward receive me *to* glory.

25Whom have I in heaven *but thee?* and *there is* none upon earth *that* I desire beside thee.

26My flesh and my heart faileth: *but* God *is* the strength of my heart, and my portion for ever.

27For, lo, they that are far from thee shall perish: thou hast destroyed all them that go a whoring from thee.

28But *it is* good for me to draw near to God: I have put my trust in the Lord GOD, that I may declare all thy works.

PROVERBS FOR TODAY/ 12:10

A righteous man *regardeth the life of his beast: but the tender mercies of the wicked* are *cruel.*

APRIL 2

DEUTERONOMY 21:1—22:30

IF *one* be found slain in the land which the LORD thy God giveth thee to possess it, lying in the field, *and* it be not known who hath slain him:

2Then thy elders and thy judges shall come forth, and they shall measure unto the cities which *are* round about him that is slain:

3And it shall be, *that* the city *which is* next unto the slain man, even the elders of that city shall take an heifer, which hath not been wrought with, *and* which hath not drawn in the yoke;

4And the elders of that city shall bring down the heifer unto a rough valley, which is neither eared nor sown, and shall strike off the heifer's neck there in the valley:

5And the priests the sons of Levi shall come near; for them the LORD thy God hath chosen to minister unto him, and to bless in the name of the

LORD; and by their word shall every controversy and every stroke be *tried:*

6And all the elders of that city, *that are* next unto the slain *man,* shall wash their hands over the heifer that is beheaded in the valley:

7And they shall answer and say, Our hands have not shed this blood, neither have our eyes seen *it.*

8Be merciful, O LORD, unto thy people Israel, whom thou hast redeemed, and lay not innocent blood unto thy people of Israel's charge. And the blood shall be forgiven them.

9So shalt thou put away the *guilt of* innocent blood from among you, when thou shalt do *that which is* right in the sight of the LORD.

10When thou goest forth to war against thine enemies, and the LORD thy God hath delivered them into thine hands, and thou hast taken them captive,

11And seest among the captives a

beautiful woman, and hast a desire unto her, that thou wouldest have her to thy wife;

12Then thou shalt bring her home to thine house; and she shall shave her head, and pare her nails;

13And she shall put the raiment of her captivity from off her, and shall remain in thine house, and bewail her father and her mother a full month: and after that thou shalt go in unto her, and be her husband, and she shall be thy wife.

14And it shall be, if thou have no delight in her, then thou shalt let her go whither she will; but thou shalt not sell her at all for money, thou shalt not make merchandise of her, because thou hast humbled her.

15If a man have two wives, one beloved, and another hated, and they have born him children, *both* the beloved and the hated; and *if* the firstborn son be hers that was hated:

16Then it shall be, when he maketh his sons to inherit *that* which he hath, *that* he may not make the son of the beloved firstborn before the son of the hated, *which is indeed* the firstborn:

17But he shall acknowledge the son of the hated *for* the firstborn, by giving him a double portion of all that he hath: for he *is* the beginning of his strength; the right of the firstborn *is* his.

18If a man have a stubborn and rebellious son, which will not obey the voice of his father, or the voice of his mother, and *that,* when they have chastened him, will not hearken unto them:

19Then shall his father and his mother lay hold on him, and bring him out unto the elders of his city, and unto the gate of his place;

20And they shall say unto the elders of his city, This our son *is* stubborn and rebellious, he will not obey our voice; *he is* a glutton, and a drunkard.

21And all the men of his city shall stone him with stones, that he die: so shalt thou put evil away from among you; and all Israel shall hear, and fear.

22And if a man have committed a sin worthy of death, and he be to be put to death, and thou hang him on a tree:

23His body shall not remain all night upon the tree, but thou shalt in any wise bury him that day; (for he that is hanged *is* accursed of God;) that thy land be not defiled, which the LORD thy God giveth thee *for* an inheritance.

THOU shalt not see thy brother's ox or his sheep go astray, and hide thyself from them: thou shalt in any case bring them again unto thy brother.

2And if thy brother *be* not nigh unto thee, or if thou know him not, then thou shalt bring it unto thine own house, and it shall be with thee until thy brother seek after it, and thou shalt restore it to him again.

3In like manner shalt thou do with his ass; and so shalt thou do with his raiment; and with all lost things of thy brother's, which he hath lost, and thou hast found, shalt thou do likewise: thou mayest not hide thyself.

4Thou shalt not see thy brother's ass or his ox fall down by the way, and hide thyself from them: thou shalt surely help him to lift *them* up again.

5The woman shall not wear that which pertaineth unto a man, neither shall a man put on a woman's garment: for all that do so *are* abomination unto the LORD thy God.

6If a bird's nest chance to be before thee in the way in any tree, or on the ground, *whether they be* young ones, or eggs, and the dam sitting upon the young, or upon the eggs, thou shalt not take the dam with the young:

7But thou shalt in any wise let the dam go, and take the young to thee; that it may be well with thee, and *that* thou mayest prolong *thy* days.

8When thou buildest a new house, then thou shalt make a battlement for thy roof, that thou bring not blood upon thine house, if any man fall from thence.

9Thou shalt not sow thy vineyard with divers seeds: lest the fruit of thy seed which thou hast sown, and the fruit of thy vineyard, be defiled.

10Thou shalt not plow with an ox and an ass together.

11Thou shalt not wear a garment of divers sorts, *as* of woollen and linen together.

12Thou shalt make thee fringes upon the four quarters of thy vesture, wherewith thou coverest *thyself.*

13If any man take a wife, and go in unto her, and hate her,

14And give occasions of speech against her, and bring up an evil name upon her, and say, I took this woman, and when I came to her, I found her not a maid:

15Then shall the father of the damsel, and her mother, take and bring forth *the tokens of* the damsel's virginity unto the elders of the city in the gate:

16And the damsel's father shall say unto the elders, I gave my daughter unto this man to wife, and he hateth her;

17And, lo, he hath given occasions of speech *against her,* saying, I found not thy daughter a maid; and yet these *are the tokens of* my daughter's virginity. And they shall spread the cloth before the elders of the city.

18And the elders of that city shall take that man and chastise him;

19And they shall amerce him in an hundred *shekels* of silver, and give *them* unto the father of the damsel, because he hath brought up an evil name upon a virgin of Israel: and she shall be his wife; he may not put her away all his days.

20But if this thing be true, *and the tokens of* virginity be not found for the damsel:

21Then they shall bring out the damsel to the door of her father's house, and the men of her city shall stone her with stones that she die: because she hath wrought folly in Israel, to play the whore

in her father's house: so shalt thou put evil away from among you.

22If a man be found lying with a woman married to an husband, then they shall both of them die, *both* the man that lay with the woman, and the woman: so shalt thou put away evil from Israel.

23If a damsel *that is* a virgin be betrothed unto an husband, and the man find her in the city, and lie with her;

24Then ye shall bring them both out unto the gate of that city, and ye shall stone them with stones that they die; the damsel, because she cried not, *being* in the city; and the man, because he hath humbled his neighbour's wife: so thou shalt put away evil from among you.

25But if a man find a betrothed damsel in the field, and the man force her, and lie with her: then the man only that lay with her shall die:

26But unto the damsel thou shalt do nothing; *there is* in the damsel no sin *worthy* of death: for as when a man riseth against his neighbour, and slayeth him, even so *is* this matter:

27For he found her in the field, *and* the betrothed damsel cried, and *there was* none to save her.

28If a man find a damsel *that is* a virgin, which is not betrothed, and lay hold on her, and lie with her, and they be found;

29Then the man that lay with her shall give unto the damsel's father fifty *shekels* of silver, and she shall be his wife; because he hath humbled her, he may not put her away all his days.

30A man shall not take his father's wife, nor discover his father's skirt.

LUKE 9:51—10:12

AND it came to pass, when the time was come that he should be received up, he [Jesus] stedfastly set his face to go to Jerusalem,

52And sent messengers before his face: and they went, and entered into a village of the Samaritans, to make ready for him.

53And they did not receive him, because his face was as though he would go to Jerusalem.

54And when his disciples James and John saw *this,* they said, Lord, wilt thou that we command fire to come down from heaven, and consume them, even as Elias did?

55But he turned, and rebuked them, and said, Ye know not what manner of spirit ye are of.

56For the Son of man is not come to destroy men's lives, but to save *them.* And they went to another village.

57And it came to pass, that, as they went in the way, a certain *man* said unto him, Lord, I will follow thee whithersoever thou goest.

58And Jesus said unto him, Foxes have holes, and birds of the air *have* nests; but the Son of man hath not where to lay *his* head.

59And he said unto another, Follow me. But he said, Lord, suffer me first to go and bury my father.

60Jesus said unto him, Let the dead bury their dead: but go thou and preach the kingdom of God.

61And another also said, Lord, I will follow thee; but let me first go bid them farewell, which are at home at my house.

62And Jesus said unto him, No man, having put his hand to the plough, and looking back, is fit for the kingdom of God.

AFTER these things the Lord appointed other seventy also, and sent them two and two before his face into every city and place, whither he himself would come.

2Therefore said he unto them, The harvest truly *is* great, but the labourers *are* few: pray ye therefore the Lord of the harvest, that he would send forth labourers into his harvest.

3Go your ways: behold, I send you forth as lambs among wolves.

4Carry neither purse, nor scrip, nor shoes: and salute no man by the way.

5And into whatsoever house ye enter, first say, Peace *be* to this house.

6And if the son of peace be there, your peace shall rest upon it: if not, it shall turn to you again.

7And in the same house remain, eating and drinking such things as they give: for the labourer is worthy of his hire. Go not from house to house.

8And into whatsoever city ye enter, and they receive you, eat such things as are set before you:

9And heal the sick that are therein, and say unto them, The kingdom of God is come nigh unto you.

10But into whatsoever city ye enter, and they receive you not, go your ways out into the streets of the same, and say,

11Even the very dust of your city, which cleaveth on us, we do wipe off against you: notwithstanding be ye sure of this, that the kingdom of God is come nigh unto you.

12But I say unto you, that it shall be more tolerable in that day for Sodom, than for that city.

PSALM 74:1–23

O GOD, why hast thou cast *us* off for ever? *why* doth thine anger smoke against the sheep of thy pasture?

2Remember thy congregation, *which* thou hast purchased of old; the rod of thine inheritance, *which* thou hast redeemed; this mount Zion, wherein thou hast dwelt.

3Lift up thy feet unto the perpetual desolations: *even* all *that* the enemy hath done wickedly in the sanctuary.

4Thine enemies roar in the midst of thy congregations; they set up their ensigns *for* signs.

5A *man* was famous according as he had lifted up axes upon the thick trees.

6But now they break down the carved work thereof at once with axes and hammers.

7They have cast fire into thy sanctuary, they have defiled *by casting down* the dwelling place of thy name to the ground.

8They said in their hearts, Let us destroy them together: they have burned up all the synagogues of God in the land.

9We see not our signs: *there is* no more any prophet: neither *is there* among us any that knoweth how long.

10O God, how long shall the adversary reproach? shall the enemy blaspheme thy name for ever?

11Why withdrawest thou thy hand, even thy right hand? pluck *it* out of thy bosom.

12For God *is* my King of old, working salvation in the midst of the earth.

13Thou didst divide the sea by thy strength: thou brakest the heads of the dragons in the waters.

14Thou brakest the heads of leviathan in pieces, *and* gavest him *to be* meat to the people inhabiting the wilderness.

15Thou didst cleave the fountain and the flood: thou driedst up mighty rivers.

16The day *is* thine, the night also *is* thine: thou hast prepared the light and the sun.

17Thou hast set all the borders of the earth: thou hast made summer and winter.

18Remember this, *that* the enemy hath reproached, O LORD, and *that* the foolish people have blasphemed thy name.

19O deliver not the soul of thy turtledove unto the multitude *of the wicked:* forget not the congregation of thy poor for ever.

20Have respect unto the covenant: for the dark places of the earth are full of the habitations of cruelty.

21O let not the oppressed return ashamed: let the poor and needy praise thy name.

22Arise, O God, plead thine own cause: remember how the foolish man reproacheth thee daily.

23Forget not the voice of thine enemies: the tumult of those that rise up against thee increaseth continually.

PROVERBS FOR TODAY/ 12:11

He that tilleth his land shall be satisfied with bread: but he that followeth vain persons is *void of understanding.*

APRIL 3

DEUTERONOMY 23:1—25:19

HE that is wounded in the stones, or hath his privy member cut off, shall not enter into the congregation of the LORD.

2A bastard shall not enter into the congregation of the LORD; even to his tenth generation shall he not enter into the congregation of the LORD.

3An Ammonite or Moabite shall not enter into the congregation of the LORD; even to their tenth generation shall they not enter into the congregation of the LORD for ever:

4Because they met you not with bread and with water in the way, when ye came forth out of Egypt; and because they hired against thee Balaam the son of Beor of Pethor of Mesopotamia, to curse thee.

5Nevertheless the LORD thy God would not hearken unto Balaam; but the LORD thy God turned the curse into a blessing unto thee, because the LORD thy God loved thee.

6Thou shalt not seek their peace nor their prosperity all thy days for ever.

7Thou shalt not abhor an Edomite; for he *is* thy brother: thou shalt not abhor an Egyptian; because thou wast a stranger in his land.

8The children that are begotten of them shall enter into the congregation of the LORD in their third generation.

9When the host goeth forth against thine enemies, then keep thee from every wicked thing.

10If there be among you any man, that is not clean by reason of uncleanness that chanceth him by night, then shall he go abroad out of the camp, he shall not come within the camp:

11But it shall be, when evening cometh on, he shall wash *himself* with water: and when the sun is down, he shall come into the camp *again*.

12Thou shalt have a place also without the camp, whither thou shalt go forth abroad:

13And thou shalt have a paddle upon thy weapon; and it shall be, when thou wilt ease thyself abroad, thou shalt dig therewith, and shalt turn back and cover that which cometh from thee:

14For the LORD thy God walketh in the midst of thy camp, to deliver thee, and to give up thine enemies before thee; therefore shall thy camp be holy: that he see no unclean thing in thee, and turn away from thee.

15Thou shalt not deliver unto his master the servant which is escaped from his master unto thee:

16He shall dwell with thee, *even* among you, in that place which he shall choose in one of thy gates, where it liketh him best: thou shalt not oppress him.

17There shall be no whore of the daughters of Israel, nor a sodomite of the sons of Israel.

18Thou shalt not bring the hire of a whore, or the price of a dog, into the house of the LORD thy God for any vow: for even both these *are* abomination unto the LORD thy God.

19Thou shalt not lend upon usury to thy brother; usury of money, usury of victuals, usury of any thing that is lent upon usury:

20Unto a stranger thou mayest lend upon usury; but unto thy brother thou shalt not lend upon usury: that the LORD thy God may bless thee in all that thou settest thine hand to in the land whither thou goest to possess it.

21When thou shalt vow a vow unto the LORD thy God, thou shalt not slack to pay it: for the LORD thy God will surely require it of thee; and it would be sin in thee.

22But if thou shalt forbear to vow, it shall be no sin in thee.

23That which is gone out of thy lips thou shalt keep and perform; *even* a freewill offering, according as thou hast vowed unto the LORD thy God, which thou hast promised with thy mouth.

24When thou comest into thy neighbour's vineyard, then thou mayest eat grapes thy fill at thine own pleasure; but thou shalt not put *any* in thy vessel.

25When thou comest into the standing corn of thy neighbour, then thou mayest pluck the ears with thine hand; but thou shalt not move a sickle unto thy neighbour's standing corn.

WHEN a man hath taken a wife, and married her, and it come to pass that she find no favour in his eyes, because he hath found some uncleanness in her: then let him write her a bill of divorcement, and give *it* in her hand, and send her out of his house.

2And when she is departed out of his house, she may go and be another man's *wife*.

3And *if* the latter husband hate her, and write her a bill of divorcement, and giveth *it* in her hand, and sendeth her out of his house; or if the latter husband die, which took her *to be* his wife;

4Her former husband, which sent her away, may not take her again to be his wife, after that she is defiled; for that *is* abomination before the LORD: and thou shalt not cause the land to sin, which the LORD thy God giveth thee *for* an inheritance.

5When a man hath taken a new wife, he shall not go out to war, neither shall he be charged with any business: *but* he shall be free at home one year, and shall cheer up his wife which he hath taken.

6No man shall take the nether or the upper millstone to pledge: for he taketh *a man's* life to pledge.

7If a man be found stealing any of his brethren of the children of Israel, and maketh merchandise of him, or selleth him; then that thief shall die; and thou shalt put evil away from among you.

8Take heed in the plague of leprosy, that thou observe diligently, and do according to all that the priests the Levites shall teach you: as I commanded them, *so* ye shall observe to do.

9Remember what the LORD thy God did unto Miriam by the way, after that ye were come forth out of Egypt.

10When thou dost lend thy brother any thing, thou shalt not go into his house to fetch his pledge.

11Thou shalt stand abroad, and the man to whom thou dost lend shall bring out the pledge abroad unto thee.

12And if the man *be* poor, thou shalt not sleep with his pledge:

13In any case thou shalt deliver him the pledge again when the sun goeth down, that he may sleep in his own raiment, and bless thee: and it shall be righteousness unto thee before the LORD thy God.

14Thou shalt not oppress an hired servant *that is* poor and needy, *whether he be* of thy brethren, or of thy strangers that *are* in thy land within thy gates:

15At his day thou shalt give *him* his hire, neither shall the sun go down upon it; for he *is* poor, and setteth his heart upon it: lest he cry against thee unto the LORD: and it be sin unto thee.

16The fathers shall not be put to death for the children, neither shall the children be put to death for the fathers: every man shall be put to death for his own sin.

17Thou shalt not pervert the judgment of the stranger, *nor* of the fatherless; nor take a widow's raiment to pledge:

18But thou shalt remember that thou wast a bondman in Egypt, and the LORD thy God redeemed thee thence: therefore I command thee to do this thing.

19When thou cuttest down thine harvest in thy field, and hast forgot a sheaf in the field, thou shalt not go again to fetch it: it shall be for the stranger, for the fatherless, and for the widow: that the LORD thy God may bless thee in all the work of thine hands.

20When thou beatest thine olive tree, thou shalt not go over the boughs again: it shall be for the stranger, for the fatherless, and for the widow.

21When thou gatherest the grapes of thy vineyard, thou shalt not glean *it* afterward: it shall be for the stranger, for the fatherless, and for the widow.

22And thou shalt remember that thou wast a bondman in the land of Egypt: therefore I command thee to do this thing.

IF there be a controversy between men, and they come unto judgment, that *the judges* may judge them; then they shall justify the righteous, and condemn the wicked.

2And it shall be, if the wicked man *be* worthy to be beaten, that the judge shall cause him to lie down, and to be beaten before his face, according to his fault, by a certain number.

3Forty stripes he may give him, *and* not exceed: lest, *if* he should exceed, and beat him above these with many stripes, then thy brother should seem vile unto thee.

4Thou shalt not muzzle the ox when he treadeth out *the corn.*

5If brethren dwell together, and one of them die, and have no child, the wife of the dead shall not marry without unto a stranger: her husband's brother shall go in unto her, and take her to him to wife, and perform the duty of an husband's brother unto her.

6And it shall be, *that* the firstborn which she beareth shall succeed in the name of the brother *which is* dead, that his name be not put out of Israel.

7And if the man like not to take his brother's wife, then let his brother's wife go up to the gate unto the elders, and say, My husband's brother refuseth to raise up unto his brother a name in Israel, he will not perform the duty of my husband's brother.

8Then the elders of his city shall call him, and speak unto him: and *if* he stand *to it,* and say, I like not to take her;

9Then shall his brother's wife come unto him in the presence of the elders, and loose his shoe from off his foot, and spit in his face, and shall answer and say, So shall it be done unto that man that will not build up his brother's house.

10And his name shall be called in Israel, The house of him that hath his shoe loosed.

11When men strive together one with another, and the wife of the one draweth near for to deliver her husband out of the hand of him that smiteth him, and putteth forth her hand, and taketh him by the secrets:

12Then thou shalt cut off her hand, thine eye shall not pity *her.*

13Thou shalt not have in thy bag divers weights, a great and a small.

14Thou shalt not have in thine house divers measures, a great and a small.

15*But* thou shalt have a perfect and just weight, a perfect and just measure shalt thou have: that thy days may be lengthened in the land which the LORD thy God giveth thee.

16For all that do such things, *and* all that do unrighteously, *are* an abomination unto the LORD thy God.

17Remember what Amalek did unto thee by the way, when ye were come forth out of Egypt;

18How he met thee by the way, and smote the hindmost of thee, *even* all *that were* feeble behind thee, when thou *wast* faint and weary; and he feared not God.

19Therefore it shall be, when the LORD thy God hath given thee rest from all thine enemies round about, in the land which the LORD thy God giveth thee *for* an inheritance to possess it, *that* thou shalt blot out the remembrance of Amalek from under heaven; thou shalt not forget *it.*

LUKE 10:13–37

WOE unto thee, Chorazin! woe unto thee, Bethsaida! for if the mighty works had been done in Tyre and Sidon, which have been done in you, they had a great while ago repented, sitting in sackcloth and ashes.

14But it shall be more tolerable for Tyre and Sidon at the judgment, than for you.

15And thou, Capernaum, which art exalted to heaven, shalt be thrust down to hell.

16He that heareth you heareth me; and he that despiseth you despiseth me; and he that despiseth me despiseth him that sent me.

17And the seventy returned again with joy, saying, Lord, even the devils are subject unto us through thy name.

18And he said unto them, I beheld Satan as lightning fall from heaven.

19Behold, I give unto you power to tread on serpents and scorpions, and over all the power of the enemy: and nothing shall by any means hurt you.

20Notwithstanding in this rejoice not, that the spirits are subject unto you; but rather rejoice, because your names are written in heaven.

21In that hour Jesus rejoiced in spirit, and said, I thank thee, O Father, Lord of heaven and earth, that thou hast hid these things from the wise and prudent, and hast revealed them unto babes: even so, Father; for so it seemed good in thy sight.

22All things are delivered to me of my Father: and no man knoweth who the Son is, but the Father; and who the Father is, but the Son, and *he* to whom the Son will reveal *him.*

23And he turned him unto *his* disciples, and said privately, Blessed *are* the eyes which see the things that ye see:

24For I tell you, that many prophets and kings have desired to see those things which ye see, and have not seen *them;* and to hear those things which ye hear, and have not heard *them.*

25And, behold, a certain lawyer stood up, and tempted him, saying, Master, what shall I do to inherit eternal life?

26He said unto him, What is written in the law? how readest thou?

27And he answering said, Thou shalt love the Lord thy God with all thy heart, and with all thy soul, and with all thy strength, and with all thy mind; and thy neighbour as thyself.

28And he said unto him, Thou hast answered right: this do, and thou shalt live.

29But he, willing to justify himself, said unto Jesus, And who is my neighbour?

30And Jesus answering said, A certain *man* went down from Jerusalem to Jericho, and fell among thieves, which stripped him of his raiment, and wounded *him,* and departed, leaving *him* half dead.

31And by chance there came down a certain priest that way: and when he saw him, he passed by on the other side.

32And likewise a Levite, when he was at the place, came and looked *on him,* and passed by on the other side.

33But a certain Samaritan, as he journeyed, came where he was: and when he saw him, he had compassion *on him,*

34And went to *him,* and bound up his wounds, pouring in oil and wine, and set him on his own beast, and brought him to an inn, and took care of him.

35And on the morrow when he departed, he took out two pence, and gave *them* to the host, and said unto him, Take care of him; and whatsoever thou spendest more, when I come again, I will repay thee.

36Which now of these three, thinkest thou, was neighbour unto him that fell among the thieves?

37And he said, He that shewed mercy on him. Then said Jesus unto him, Go, and do thou likewise.

PSALM 75:1–10

Unto thee, O God, do we give thanks, *unto thee* do we give thanks: for *that* thy name is near thy wondrous works declare.

2When I shall receive the congregation I will judge uprightly.

3The earth and all the inhabitants thereof are dissolved: I bear up the pillars of it. Selah.

4I said unto the fools, Deal not foolishly: and to the wicked, Lift not up the horn:

5Lift not up your horn on high: speak *not with* a stiff neck.

6For promotion *cometh* neither from the east, nor from the west, nor from the south.

7But God *is* the judge: he putteth down one, and setteth up another.

8For in the hand of the LORD *there is* a cup, and the wine is red; it is full of mixture; and he poureth out of the same: but the dregs thereof, all the wicked of the earth shall wring *them* out, *and* drink *them*.

9But I will declare for ever; I will sing praises to the God of Jacob.

10All the horns of the wicked also will I cut off; *but* the horns of the righteous shall be exalted.

PROVERBS FOR TODAY/ 12:12–14

The wicked desireth the net of evil men: *but the root of the righteous yieldeth* fruit. □ *The wicked is snared by the transgression of* his *lips: but the just shall come out of trouble.* □ *A man shall be satisfied with good by the fruit of* his *mouth: and the recompence of a man's hands shall be rendered unto him.*

APRIL 4

DEUTERONOMY 26:1—27:26

AND it shall be, when thou *art* come in unto the land which the LORD thy God giveth thee *for* an inheritance, and possessest it, and dwellest therein;

2That thou shalt take of the first of all the fruit of the earth, which thou shalt bring of thy land that the LORD thy God giveth thee, and shalt put *it* in a basket, and shalt go unto the place which the LORD thy God shall choose to place his name there.

3And thou shalt go unto the priest that shall be in those days, and say unto him, I profess this day unto the LORD thy God, that I am come unto the country which the LORD sware unto our fathers for to give us.

4And the priest shall take the basket out of thine hand, and set it down before the altar of the LORD thy God.

5And thou shalt speak and say before the LORD thy God, A Syrian ready to perish *was* my father, and he went down into Egypt, and sojourned there with a few, and became there a nation, great, mighty, and populous:

6And the Egyptians evil entreated us, and afflicted us, and laid upon us hard bondage:

7And when we cried unto the LORD God of our fathers, the LORD heard our voice, and looked on our affliction, and our labour, and our oppression:

8And the LORD brought us forth out of Egypt with a mighty hand, and with an outstretched arm, and with great terribleness, and with signs, and with wonders:

9And he hath brought us into this place, and hath given us this land, *even* a land that floweth with milk and honey.

10And now, behold, I have brought the firstfruits of the land, which thou, O LORD, hast given me. And thou shalt set it before the LORD thy God, and worship before the LORD thy God:

11And thou shalt rejoice in every good *thing* which the LORD thy God hath given unto thee, and unto thine house, thou, and the Levite, and the stranger that *is* among you.

12When thou hast made an end of

tithing all the tithes of thine increase the third year, *which is* the year of tithing, and hast given *it* unto the Levite, the stranger, the fatherless, and the widow, that they may eat within thy gates, and be filled;

13Then thou shalt say before the LORD thy God, I have brought away the hallowed things out of *mine* house, and also have given them unto the Levite, and unto the stranger, to the fatherless, and to the widow, according to all thy commandments which thou hast commanded me: I have not transgressed thy commandments, neither have I forgotten *them:*

14I have not eaten thereof in my mourning, neither have I taken away *ought* thereof for *any* unclean *use,* nor given *ought* thereof for the dead: *but* I have hearkened to the voice of the LORD my God, *and* have done according to all that thou hast commanded me.

15Look down from thy holy habitation, from heaven, and bless thy people Israel, and the land which thou hast given us, as thou swarest unto our fathers, a land that floweth with milk and honey.

16This day the LORD thy God hath commanded thee to do these statutes and judgments: thou shalt therefore keep and do them with all thine heart, and with all thy soul.

17Thou hast avouched the LORD this day to be thy God, and to walk in his ways, and to keep his statutes, and his commandments, and his judgments, and to hearken unto his voice:

18And the LORD hath avouched thee this day to be his peculiar people, as he hath promised thee, and that *thou* shouldest keep all his commandments;

19And to make thee high above all nations which he hath made, in praise, and in name, and in honour; and that thou mayest be an holy people unto the LORD thy God, as he hath spoken.

AND Moses with the elders of Israel commanded the people, saying, Keep all the commandments which I command you this day.

2And it shall be on the day when ye shall pass over Jordan unto the land which the LORD thy God giveth thee, that thou shalt set thee up great stones, and plaister them with plaister:

3And thou shalt write upon them all the words of this law, when thou art passed over, that thou mayest go in unto the land which the LORD thy God giveth thee, a land that floweth with milk and honey; as the LORD God of thy fathers hath promised thee.

4Therefore it shall be when ye be gone over Jordan, *that* ye shall set up these stones, which I command you this day, in mount Ebal, and thou shalt plaister them with plaister.

5And there shalt thou build an altar unto the LORD thy God, an altar of stones: thou shalt not lift up *any* iron *tool* upon them.

6Thou shalt build the altar of the LORD thy God of whole stones: and thou shalt offer burnt offerings thereon unto the LORD thy God:

7And thou shalt offer peace offerings, and shalt eat there, and rejoice before the LORD thy God.

8And thou shalt write upon the stones all the words of this law very plainly.

9And Moses and the priests the Levites spake unto all Israel, saying, Take heed, and hearken, O Israel; this day thou art become the people of the LORD thy God.

10Thou shalt therefore obey the voice of the LORD thy God, and do his commandments and his statutes, which I command thee this day.

11And Moses charged the people the same day, saying,

12These shall stand upon mount Gerizim to bless the people, when ye are come over Jordan; Simeon, and Levi, and Judah, and Issachar, and Joseph, and Benjamin:

13And these shall stand upon mount Ebal to curse; Reuben, Gad, and Asher, and Zebulun, Dan, and Naphtali.

14And the Levites shall speak, and say unto all the men of Israel with a loud voice,

15Cursed *be* the man that maketh *any* graven or molten image, an abomination unto the LORD, the work of the hands of the craftsman, and putteth *it* in *a* secret *place*. And all the people shall answer and say, Amen.

16Cursed *be* he that setteth light by his father or his mother. And all the people shall say, Amen.

17Cursed *be* he that removeth his neighbour's landmark. And all the people shall say, Amen.

18Cursed *be* he that maketh the blind to wander out of the way. And all the people shall say, Amen.

19Cursed *be* he that perverteth the judgment of the stranger, fatherless, and widow. And all the people shall say, Amen.

20Cursed *be* he that lieth with his father's wife; because he uncovereth his father's skirt. And all the people shall say, Amen.

21Cursed *be* he that lieth with any manner of beast. And all the people shall say, Amen.

22Cursed *be* he that lieth with his sister, the daughter of his father, or the daughter of his mother. And all the people shall say, Amen.

23Cursed *be* he that lieth with his mother in law. And all the people shall say, Amen.

24Cursed *be* he that smiteth his neighbour secretly. And all the people shall say, Amen.

25Cursed *be* he that taketh reward to slay an innocent person. And all the people shall say, Amen.

26Cursed *be* he that confirmeth not *all* the words of the law to do them. And all the people shall say, Amen.

LUKE 10:38—11:13

Now it came to pass, as they went, that he [Jesus] entered into a certain village: and a certain woman named Martha received him into her house.

39And she had a sister called Mary, which also sat at Jesus' feet, and heard his word.

40But Martha was cumbered about much serving, and came to him, and said, Lord, dost thou not care that my sister hath left me to serve alone? bid her therefore that she help me.

41And Jesus answered and said unto her, Martha, Martha, thou art careful and troubled about many things:

42But one thing is needful: and Mary hath chosen that good part, which shall not be taken away from her.

AND it came to pass, that, as he was praying in a certain place, when he ceased, one of his disciples said unto him, Lord, teach us to pray, as John also taught his disciples.

2And he said unto them, When ye pray, say, Our Father which art in heaven, Hallowed be thy name. Thy kingdom come. Thy will be done, as in heaven, so in earth.

3Give us day by day our daily bread.

4And forgive us our sins; for we also forgive every one that is indebted to us. And lead us not into temptation; but deliver us from evil.

5And he said unto them, Which of you shall have a friend, and shall go unto him at midnight, and say unto him, Friend, lend me three loaves;

6For a friend of mine in his journey is come to me, and I have nothing to set before him?

7And he from within shall answer and say, Trouble me not: the door is now shut, and my children are with me in bed; I cannot rise and give thee.

8I say unto you, Though he will not rise and give him, because he is his friend, yet because of his importunity he will rise and give him as many as he needeth.

9And I say unto you, Ask, and it shall be given you; seek, and ye shall find; knock, and it shall be opened unto you.

10For every one that asketh receiveth; and he that seeketh findeth; and to him that knocketh it shall be opened.

11If a son shall ask bread of any of you that is a father, will he give him a stone? or if *he ask* a fish, will he for a fish give him a serpent?

12Or if he shall ask an egg, will he offer him a scorpion?

13If ye then, being evil, know how to give good gifts unto your children: how much more shall *your* heavenly Father give the Holy Spirit to them that ask him?

PSALM 76:1–12

IN Judah *is* God known: his name *is* great in Israel.

2In Salem also is his tabernacle, and his dwelling place in Zion.

3There brake he the arrows of the bow, the shield, and the sword, and the battle. Selah.

4Thou *art* more glorious *and* excellent than the mountains of prey.

5The stouthearted are spoiled, they have slept their sleep: and none of the men of might have found their hands.

6At thy rebuke, O God of Jacob, both the chariot and horse are cast into a dead sleep.

7Thou, *even* thou, *art* to be feared: and who may stand in thy sight when once thou art angry?

8Thou didst cause judgment to be heard from heaven; the earth feared, and was still,

9When God arose to judgment, to save all the meek of the earth. Selah.

10Surely the wrath of man shall praise thee: the remainder of wrath shalt thou restrain.

11Vow, and pay unto the LORD your God: let all that be round about him bring presents unto him that ought to be feared.

12He shall cut off the spirit of princes: *he is* terrible to the kings of the earth.

PROVERBS FOR TODAY/ 12:15–17

The way of a fool is *right in his own eyes: but he that hearkeneth unto counsel* is *wise.* □ *A fool's wrath is presently known: but a prudent* man *covereth shame.* □ He that *speaketh truth sheweth forth righteousness: but a false witness deceit.*

APRIL 5

DEUTERONOMY 28:1–68

AND it shall come to pass, if thou shalt hearken diligently unto the voice of the LORD thy God, to observe *and* to do all his commandments which I command thee this day, that the LORD thy God will set thee on high above all nations of the earth:

2And all these blessings shall come on thee, and overtake thee, if thou shalt hearken unto the voice of the LORD thy God.

3Blessed *shalt* thou *be* in the city, and blessed *shalt* thou *be* in the field.

4Blessed *shall be* the fruit of thy body, and the fruit of thy ground, and the fruit of thy cattle, the increase of thy kine, and the flocks of thy sheep.

5Blessed *shall be* thy basket and thy store.

6Blessed *shalt* thou *be* when thou comest in, and blessed *shalt* thou *be* when thou goest out.

7The Lord shall cause thine enemies that rise up against thee to be smitten before thy face: they shall come out against thee one way, and flee before thee seven ways.

8The Lord shall command the blessing upon thee in thy storehouses, and in all that thou settest thine hand unto; and he shall bless thee in the land which the Lord thy God giveth thee.

9The Lord shall establish thee an holy people unto himself, as he hath sworn unto thee, if thou shalt keep the commandments of the Lord thy God, and walk in his ways.

10And all the people of the earth shall see that thou art called by the name of the Lord; and they shall be afraid of thee.

11And the Lord shall make thee plenteous in goods, in the fruit of thy body, and in the fruit of thy cattle, and in the fruit of thy ground, in the land which the Lord sware unto thy fathers to give thee.

12The Lord shall open unto thee his good treasure, the heaven to give the rain unto thy land in his season, and to bless all the work of thine hand: and thou shalt lend unto many nations, and thou shalt not borrow.

13And the Lord shall make thee the head, and not the tail; and thou shalt be above only, and thou shalt not be beneath; if that thou hearken unto the commandments of the Lord thy God, which I command thee this day, to observe and to do *them:*

14And thou shalt not go aside from any of the words which I command thee this day, *to* the right hand, or *to* the left, to go after other gods to serve them.

15But it shall come to pass, if thou wilt not hearken unto the voice of the Lord thy God, to observe to do all his commandments and his statutes which I command thee this day; that all these curses shall come upon thee, and overtake thee:

16Cursed *shalt* thou *be* in the city, and cursed *shalt* thou *be* in the field.

17Cursed *shall be* thy basket and thy store.

18Cursed *shall be* the fruit of thy body, and the fruit of thy land, the increase of thy kine, and the flocks of thy sheep.

19Cursed *shalt* thou *be* when thou comest in, and cursed *shalt* thou *be* when thou goest out.

20The Lord shall send upon thee cursing, vexation, and rebuke, in all that thou settest thine hand unto for to do, until thou be destroyed, and until thou perish quickly; because of the wickedness of thy doings, whereby thou hast forsaken me.

21The Lord shall make the pestilence cleave unto thee, until he have consumed thee from off the land, whither thou goest to possess it.

22The Lord shall smite thee with a consumption, and with a fever, and with an inflammation, and with an extreme burning, and with the sword, and with blasting, and with mildew; and they shall pursue thee until thou perish.

23And thy heaven that *is* over thy head shall be brass, and the earth that *is* under thee *shall be* iron.

24The Lord shall make the rain of thy land powder and dust: from heaven shall it come down upon thee, until thou be destroyed.

25The Lord shall cause thee to be smitten before thine enemies: thou shalt go out one way against them, and flee seven ways before them: and shalt be removed into all the kingdoms of the earth.

26And thy carcase shall be meat unto all fowls of the air, and unto the beasts of the earth, and no man shall fray *them* away.

27The LORD will smite thee with the botch of Egypt, and with the emerods, and with the scab, and with the itch, whereof thou canst not be healed.

28The LORD shall smite thee with madness, and blindness, and astonishment of heart:

29And thou shalt grope at noonday, as the blind gropeth in darkness, and thou shalt not prosper in thy ways: and thou shalt be only oppressed and spoiled evermore, and no man shall save *thee*.

30Thou shalt betroth a wife, and another man shall lie with her: thou shalt build an house, and thou shalt not dwell therein: thou shalt plant a vineyard, and shalt not gather the grapes thereof.

31Thine ox *shall be* slain before thine eyes, and thou shalt not eat thereof: thine ass *shall be* violently taken away from before thy face, and shall not be restored to thee: thy sheep *shall be* given unto thine enemies, and thou shalt have none to rescue *them*.

32Thy sons and thy daughters *shall be* given unto another people, and thine eyes shall look, and fail *with longing* for them all the day long: and *there shall be* no might in thine hand.

33The fruit of thy land, and all thy labours, shall a nation which thou knowest not eat up; and thou shalt be only oppressed and crushed alway:

34So that thou shalt be mad for the sight of thine eyes which thou shalt see.

35The LORD shall smite thee in the knees, and in the legs, with a sore botch that cannot be healed, from the sole of thy foot unto the top of thy head.

36The LORD shall bring thee, and thy king which thou shalt set over thee, unto a nation which neither thou nor thy fathers have known; and there shalt thou serve other gods, wood and stone.

37And thou shalt become an astonishment, a proverb, and a byword, among all nations whither the LORD shall lead thee.

38Thou shalt carry much seed out into the field, and shalt gather *but* little in; for the locust shall consume it.

39Thou shalt plant vineyards, and dress *them,* but shalt neither drink *of* the wine, nor gather *the grapes;* for the worms shall eat them.

40Thou shalt have olive trees throughout all thy coasts, but thou shalt not anoint *thyself* with the oil; for thine olive shall cast *his fruit.*

41Thou shall beget sons and daughters, but thou shalt not enjoy them; for they shall go into captivity.

42And thy trees and fruit of thy land shall the locust consume.

43The stranger that *is* within thee shall get up above thee very high; and thou shalt come down very low.

44He shall lend to thee, and thou shalt not lend to him: he shall be the head, and thou shalt be the tail.

45Moreover all these curses shall come upon thee, and shall pursue thee, and overtake thee, till thou be destroyed; because thou hearkenedst not unto the voice of the LORD thy God, to keep his commandments and his statutes which he commanded thee:

46And they shall be upon thee for a sign and for a wonder, and upon thy seed for ever.

47Because thou servedst not the LORD thy God with joyfulness, and with gladness of heart, for the abundance of all *things;*

48Therefore shalt thou serve thine enemies which the LORD shall send against thee, in hunger, and in thirst, and in nakedness, and in want of all *things:* and he shall put a yoke of iron upon thy neck, until he have destroyed thee.

49The LORD shall bring a nation against thee from far, from the end of the earth, *as swift* as the eagle flieth;

a nation whose tongue thou shalt not understand;

50A nation of fierce countenance, which shall not regard the person of the old, nor shew favour to the young:

51And he shall eat the fruit of thy cattle, and the fruit of thy land, until thou be destroyed: which *also* shall not leave thee *either* corn, wine, or oil, *or* the increase of thy kine, or flocks of thy sheep, until he have destroyed thee.

52And he shall besiege thee in all thy gates, until thy high and fenced walls come down, wherein thou trustedst, throughout all thy land: and he shall besiege thee in all thy gates throughout all thy land, which the Lord thy God hath given thee.

53And thou shalt eat the fruit of thine own body, the flesh of thy sons and of thy daughters, which the Lord thy God hath given thee, in the siege, and in the straitness, wherewith thine enemies shall distress thee:

54*So that* the man *that is* tender among you, and very delicate, his eye shall be evil toward his brother, and toward the wife of his bosom, and toward the remnant of his children which he shall leave:

55So that he will not give to any of them of the flesh of his children whom he shall eat: because he hath nothing left him in the siege, and in the straitness, wherewith thine enemies shall distress thee in all thy gates.

56The tender and delicate woman among you, which would not adventure to set the sole of her foot upon the ground for delicateness and tenderness, her eye shall be evil toward the husband of her bosom, and toward her son, and toward her daughter,

57And toward her young one that cometh out from between her feet, and toward her children which she shall bear: for she shall eat them for want of all *things* secretly in the siege and straitness, wherewith thine enemy shall

distress thee in thy gates.

58If thou wilt not observe to do all the words of this law that are written in this book, that thou mayest fear this glorious and fearful name, THE LORD THY GOD;

59Then the Lord will make thy plagues wonderful, and the plagues of thy seed, *even* great plagues, and of long continuance, and sore sicknesses, and of long continuance.

60Moreover he will bring upon thee all the diseases of Egypt, which thou wast afraid of; and they shall cleave unto thee.

61Also every sickness, and every plague, which *is* not written in the book of this law, them will the Lord bring upon thee, until thou be destroyed.

62And ye shall be left few in number, whereas ye were as the stars of heaven for multitude; because thou wouldest not obey the voice of the Lord thy God.

63And it shall come to pass, *that* as the Lord rejoiced over you to do you good, and to multiply you; so the Lord will rejoice over you to destroy you, and to bring you to nought; and ye shall be plucked from off the land whither thou goest to possess it.

64And the Lord shall scatter thee among all people, from the one end of the earth even unto the other; and there thou shalt serve other gods, which neither thou nor thy fathers have known, *even* wood and stone.

65And among these nations shalt thou find no ease, neither shall the sole of thy foot have rest: but the Lord shall give thee there a trembling heart, and failing of eyes, and sorrow of mind:

66And thy life shall hang in doubt before thee; and thou shalt fear day and night, and shalt have none assurance of thy life:

67In the morning thou shalt say, Would God it were even! and at even thou shalt say, Would God it were morning! for the fear of thine heart wherewith thou shalt fear, and for the sight of thine eyes which thou shalt see.

68And the LORD shall bring thee into Egypt again with ships, by the way whereof I spake unto thee, Thou shalt see it no more again: and there ye shall be sold unto your enemies for bondmen and bondwomen, and no man shall buy *you.*

LUKE 11:14–36

AND he [Jesus] was casting out a devil, and it was dumb. And it came to pass, when the devil was gone out, the dumb spake; and the people wondered.

15But some of them said, He casteth out devils through Beelzebub the chief of the devils.

16And others, tempting *him,* sought of him a sign from heaven.

17But he, knowing their thoughts, said unto them, Every kingdom divided against itself is brought to desolation; and a house *divided* against a house falleth.

18If Satan also be divided against himself, how shall his kingdom stand? because ye say that I cast out devils through Beelzebub.

19And if I by Beelzebub cast out devils, by whom do your sons cast *them* out? therefore shall they be your judges.

20But if I with the finger of God cast out devils, no doubt the kingdom of God is come upon you.

21When a strong man armed keepeth his palace, his goods are in peace:

22But when a stronger than he shall come upon him, and overcome him, he taketh from him all his armour wherein he trusted, and divideth his spoils.

23He that is not with me is against me: and he that gathereth not with me scattereth.

24When the unclean spirit is gone out of a man, he walketh through dry places, seeking rest; and finding none, he saith, I will return unto my house whence I came out.

25And when he cometh, he findeth *it* swept and garnished.

26Then goeth he, and taketh *to him* seven other spirits more wicked than himself; and they enter in, and dwell there: and the last *state* of that man is worse than the first.

27And it came to pass, as he spake these things, a certain woman of the company lifted up her voice, and said unto him, Blessed *is* the womb that bare thee, and the paps which thou hast sucked.

28But he said, Yea rather, blessed *are* they that hear the word of God, and keep it.

29And when the people were gathered thick together, he began to say, This is an evil generation: they seek a sign; and there shall no sign be given it, but the sign of Jonas the prophet.

30For as Jonas was a sign unto the Ninevites, so shall also the Son of man be to this generation.

31The queen of the south shall rise up in the judgment with the men of this generation, and condemn them: for she came from the utmost parts of the earth to hear the wisdom of Solomon; and, behold, a greater than Solomon *is* here.

32The men of Nineve shall rise up in the judgment with this generation, and shall condemn it: for they repented at the preaching of Jonas; and, behold, a greater than Jonas *is* here.

33No man, when he hath lighted a candle, putteth *it* in a secret place, neither under a bushel, but on a candlestick, that they which come in may see the light.

34The light of the body is the eye: therefore when thine eye is single, thy whole body also is full of light; but when *thine eye* is evil, thy body also *is* full of darkness.

35Take heed therefore that the light which is in thee be not darkness.

36If thy whole body therefore *be* full of light, having no part dark, the whole shall be full of light, as when the bright shining of a candle doth give thee light.

PSALM 77:1–20

I CRIED unto God with my voice, *even* unto God with my voice; and he gave ear unto me.

2In the day of my trouble I sought the Lord: my sore ran in the night, and ceased not: my soul refused to be comforted.

3I remembered God, and was troubled: I complained, and my spirit was overwhelmed. Selah.

4Thou holdest mine eyes waking: I am so troubled that I cannot speak.

5I have considered the days of old, the years of ancient times.

6I call to remembrance my song in the night: I commune with mine own heart: and my spirit made diligent search.

7Will the Lord cast off for ever? and will he be favourable no more?

8Is his mercy clean gone for ever? doth *his* promise fail for evermore?

9Hath God forgotten to be gracious? hath he in anger shut up his tender mercies? Selah.

10And I said, This *is* my infirmity: *but I will remember* the years of the right hand of the most High.

11I will remember the works of the LORD: surely I will remember thy wonders of old.

12I will meditate also of all thy work, and talk of thy doings.

13Thy way, O God, *is* in the sanctuary: who *is so* great a God as *our* God?

14Thou *art* the God that doest wonders: thou hast declared thy strength among the people.

15Thou hast with *thine* arm redeemed thy people, the sons of Jacob and Joseph. Selah.

16The waters saw thee, O God, the waters saw thee; they were afraid: the depths also were troubled.

17The clouds poured out water: the skies sent out a sound: thine arrows also went abroad.

18The voice of thy thunder *was* in the heaven: the lightnings lightened the world: the earth trembled and shook.

19Thy way *is* in the sea, and thy path in the great waters, and thy footsteps are not known.

20Thou leddest thy people like a flock by the hand of Moses and Aaron.

PROVERBS FOR TODAY/ 12:18

There is that speaketh like the piercings of a sword: but the tongue of the wise is *health.*

APRIL 6

DEUTERONOMY 29:1—30:20

T HESE *are* the words of the covenant, which the LORD commanded Moses to make with the children of Israel in the land of Moab, beside the covenant which he made with them in Horeb.

2And Moses called unto all Israel, and said unto them, Ye have seen all that the LORD did before your eyes in the land of Egypt unto Pharaoh, and unto all his servants, and unto all his land;

3The great temptations which thine eyes have seen, the signs, and those great miracles:

4Yet the LORD hath not given you an heart to perceive, and eyes to see, and ears to hear, unto this day.

5And I have led you forty years in the wilderness: your clothes are not waxen old upon you, and thy shoe is not waxen old upon thy foot.

6Ye have not eaten bread, neither have ye drunk wine or strong drink: that ye might know that I *am* the LORD your God.

7And when ye came unto this place, Sihon the king of Heshbon, and Og the king of Bashan, came out against us unto battle, and we smote them:

8And we took their land, and gave it for an inheritance unto the Reubenites, and to the Gadites, and to the half tribe of Manasseh.

9Keep therefore the words of this covenant, and do them, that ye may prosper in all that ye do.

10Ye stand this day all of you before the LORD your God; your captains of your tribes, your elders, and your officers, *with* all the men of Israel,

11Your little ones, your wives, and thy stranger that *is* in thy camp, from the hewer of thy wood unto the drawer of thy water:

12That thou shouldest enter into covenant with the LORD thy God, and into his oath, which the LORD thy God maketh with thee this day:

13That he may establish thee to day for a people unto himself, and *that* he may be unto thee a God, as he hath said unto thee, and as he hath sworn unto thy fathers, to Abraham, to Isaac, and to Jacob.

14Neither with you only do I make this covenant and this oath;

15But with *him* that standeth here with us this day before the LORD our God, and also with *him* that *is* not here with us this day:

16(For ye know how we have dwelt in the land of Egypt; and how we came through the nations which ye passed by;

17And ye have seen their abominations, and their idols, wood and stone, silver and gold, which *were* among them:)

18Lest there should be among you man, or woman, or family, or tribe, whose heart turneth away this day from the LORD our God, to go *and* serve the gods of these nations; lest there should be among you a root that beareth gall and wormwood;

19And it came to pass, when he heareth the words of this curse, that he bless himself in his heart, saying, I shall have peace, though I walk in the imagination of mine heart, to add drunkenness to thirst:

20The LORD will not spare him, but then the anger of the LORD and his jealousy shall smoke against that man, and all the curses that are written in this book shall lie upon him, and the LORD shall blot out his name from under heaven.

21And the LORD shall separate him unto evil out of all the tribes of Israel, according to all the curses of the covenant that are written in this book of the law:

22So that the generation to come of your children that shall rise up after you, and the stranger that shall come from a far land, shall say, when they see the plagues of that land, and the sicknesses which the LORD hath laid upon it;

23*And that* the whole land thereof *is* brimstone, and salt, *and* burning, *that* it is not sown, nor beareth, nor any grass groweth therein, like the overthrow of Sodom, and Gomorrah, Admah, and Zeboim, which the LORD overthrew in his anger, and in his wrath:

24Even all nations shall say, Wherefore hath the LORD done thus unto this land? what *meaneth* the heat of this great anger?

25Then men shall say, Because they have forsaken the covenant of the LORD God of their fathers, which he made with them when he brought them forth out of the land of Egypt:

26For they went and served other gods, and worshipped them, gods whom they knew not, and *whom* he had not given unto them:

27And the anger of the LORD was kindled against this land, to bring upon it all the curses that are written in this book:

28And the LORD rooted them out of their land in anger, and in wrath, and in great indignation, and cast them into another land, as *it is* this day.

29The secret *things belong* unto the LORD our God: but those *things which are* revealed *belong* unto us and to our children for ever, that *we* may do all the words of this law.

AND it shall come to pass, when all these things are come upon thee, the blessing and the curse, which I have set before thee, and thou shalt call *them* to mind among all the nations, whither the LORD thy God hath driven thee,

2And shalt return unto the LORD thy God, and shalt obey his voice according to all that I command thee this day, thou and thy children, with all thine heart, and with all thy soul;

3That then the LORD thy God will turn thy captivity, and have compassion upon thee, and will return and gather thee from all the nations, whither the LORD thy God hath scattered thee.

4If *any* of thine be driven out unto the outmost *parts* of heaven, from thence will the LORD thy God gather thee, and from thence will he fetch thee:

5And the LORD thy God will bring thee into the land which thy fathers possessed, and thou shalt possess it;

and he will do thee good, and multiply thee above thy fathers.

6And the LORD thy God will circumcise thine heart, and the heart of thy seed, to love the LORD thy God with all thine heart, and with all thy soul, that thou mayest live.

7And the LORD thy God will put all these curses upon thine enemies, and on them that hate thee, which persecuted thee.

8And thou shalt return and obey the voice of the LORD, and do all his commandments which I command thee this day.

9And the LORD thy God will make thee plenteous in every work of thine hand, in the fruit of thy body, and in the fruit of thy cattle, and in the fruit of thy land, for good: for the LORD will again rejoice over thee for good, as he rejoiced over thy fathers:

10If thou shalt hearken unto the voice of the LORD thy God, to keep his commandments and his statutes which are written in this book of the law, *and if* thou turn unto the LORD thy God with all thine heart, and with all thy soul.

11For this commandment which I command thee this day, it *is* not hidden from thee, neither *is* it far off.

12It *is* not in heaven, that thou shouldest say, Who shall go up for us to heaven, and bring it unto us, that we may hear it, and do it?

13Neither *is* it beyond the sea, that thou shouldest say, Who shall go over the sea for us, and bring it unto us, that we may hear it, and do it?

14But the word *is* very nigh unto thee, in thy mouth, and in thy heart, that thou mayest do it.

15See, I have set before thee this day life and good, and death and evil;

16In that I command thee this day to love the LORD thy God, to walk in his ways, and to keep his commandments and his statutes and his judgments, that thou mayest live and multiply: and the LORD thy God shall bless thee in the land whither thou goest to possess it.

17But if thine heart turn away, so that thou wilt not hear, but shalt be drawn away, and worship other gods, and serve them;

18I denounce unto you this day, that ye shall surely perish, *and that* ye shall not prolong *your* days upon the land, whither thou passest over Jordan to go to possess it.

19I call heaven and earth to record this day against you, *that* I have set before you life and death, blessing and cursing: therefore choose life, that both thou and thy seed may live:

20That thou mayest love the LORD thy God, *and* that thou mayest obey his voice, and that thou mayest cleave unto him: for he *is* thy life, and the length of thy days: that thou mayest dwell in the land which the LORD sware unto thy fathers, to Abraham, to Isaac, and to Jacob, to give them.

LUKE 11:37—12:7

AND as he [Jesus] spake, a certain Pharisee besought him to dine with him: and he went in, and sat down to meat.

38And when the Pharisee saw *it,* he marvelled that he had not first washed before dinner.

39And the Lord said unto him, Now do ye Pharisees make clean the outside of the cup and the platter; but your inward part is full of ravening and wickedness.

40*Ye* fools, did not he that made that which is without make that which is within also?

41But rather give alms of such things as ye have; and, behold, all things are clean unto you.

42But woe unto you, Pharisees! for ye tithe mint and rue and all manner of herbs, and pass over judgment and the love of God: these ought ye to have done, and not to leave the other undone.

43Woe unto you, Pharisees! for ye love the uppermost seats in the synagogues, and greetings in the markets.

44Woe unto you, scribes and Pharisees, hypocrites! for ye are as graves which appear not, and the men that walk over *them* are not aware *of them.*

45Then answered one of the lawyers, and said unto him, Master, thus saying thou reproachest us also.

46And he said, Woe unto you also, *ye* lawyers! for ye lade men with burdens grievous to be borne, and ye yourselves touch not the burdens with one of your fingers.

47Woe unto you! for ye build the sepulchres of the prophets, and your fathers killed them.

48Truly ye bear witness that ye allow the deeds of your fathers: for they indeed killed them, and ye build their sepulchres.

49Therefore also said the wisdom of God, I will send them prophets and apostles, and *some* of them they shall slay and persecute:

50That the blood of all the prophets, which was shed from the foundation of the world, may be required of this generation;

51From the blood of Abel unto the blood of Zacharias, which perished between the altar and the temple: verily I say unto you, It shall be required of this generation.

52Woe unto you, lawyers! for ye have taken away the key of knowledge: ye entered not in yourselves, and them that were entering in ye hindered.

53And as he said these things unto them, the scribes and the Pharisees began to urge *him* vehemently, and to provoke him to speak of many things:

54Laying wait for him, and seeking to catch something out of his mouth, that they might accuse him.

IN the mean time, when there were gathered together an innumerable multitude of people, insomuch that they trode one upon another, he began to say unto his disciples first of all, Beware ye of the leaven of the Pharisees, which is hypocrisy.

2For there is nothing covered, that shall not be revealed; neither hid, that shall not be known.

3Therefore whatsoever ye have spoken in darkness shall be heard in the light; and that which ye have spoken in the ear in closets shall be proclaimed upon the housetops.

4And I say unto you my friends, Be not afraid of them that kill the body, and after that have no more that they can do.

5But I will forewarn you whom ye shall fear: Fear him, which after he hath killed hath power to cast into hell; yea, I say unto you, Fear him.

6Are not five sparrows sold for two farthings, and not one of them is forgotten before God?

7But even the very hairs of your head are all numbered. Fear not therefore: ye are of more value than many sparrows.

PSALM 78:1–25

GIVE ear, O my people, *to* my law: incline your ears to the words of my mouth.

2I will open my mouth in a parable: I will utter dark sayings of old:

3Which we have heard and known, and our fathers have told us.

4We will not hide *them* from their children, shewing to the generation to come the praises of the LORD, and his strength, and his wonderful works that he hath done.

5For he established a testimony in Jacob, and appointed a law in Israel, which he commanded our fathers, that they should make them known to their children:

6That the generation to come might know *them, even* the children *which* should be born; *who* should arise and declare *them* to their children:

7That they might set their hope in God, and not forget the works of God, but keep his commandments:

8And might not be as their fathers, a stubborn and rebellious generation; a generation *that* set not their heart aright, and whose spirit was not stedfast with God.

9The children of Ephraim, *being* armed, *and* carrying bows, turned back in the day of battle.

10They kept not the covenant of God, and refused to walk in his law;

11And forgat his works, and his wonders that he had shewed them.

12Marvellous things did he in the sight of their fathers, in the land of Egypt, *in* the field of Zoan.

13He divided the sea, and caused them to pass through; and he made the waters to stand as an heap.

14In the daytime also he led them with a cloud, and all the night with a light of fire.

15He clave the rocks in the wilderness, and gave *them* drink as *out of* the great depths.

16He brought streams also out of the rock, and caused waters to run down like rivers.

17And they sinned yet more against him by provoking the most High in the wilderness.

18And they tempted God in their heart by asking meat for their lust.

19Yea, they spake against God; they said, Can God furnish a table in the wilderness?

20Behold, he smote the rock, that the waters gushed out, and the streams overflowed; can he give bread also? can he provide flesh for his people?

21Therefore the LORD heard *this,* and was wroth; so a fire was kindled against Jacob, and anger also came up against Israel;

22Because they believed not in God, and trusted not in his salvation:

23Though he had commanded the clouds from above, and opened the doors of heaven,

24And had rained down manna upon them to eat, and had given them of the corn of heaven.

25Man did eat angels' food: he sent them meat to the full.

PROVERBS FOR TODAY/ 12:19–20

The lip of truth shall be established for ever: but a lying tongue is *but for a moment.* □ *Deceit* is *in the heart of them that imagine evil: but to the counsellors of peace* is *joy.*

APRIL 7

DEUTERONOMY 31:1—32:29

AND Moses went and spake these words unto all Israel. 2And he said unto them, I *am* an hundred and twenty years old this day; I can no more go out and come in: also the LORD hath said unto me, Thou shalt not go over this Jordan.

3The LORD thy God, he will go over before thee, *and* he will destroy these nations from before thee, and thou shalt possess them: *and* Joshua, he shall go over before thee, as the LORD hath said.

4And the LORD shall do unto them as he did to Sihon and to Og, kings of the Amorites, and unto the land of them, whom he destroyed.

5And the LORD shall give them up before your face, that ye may do unto them according unto all the commandments which I have commanded you.

6Be strong and of a good courage, fear not, nor be afraid of them: for the LORD thy God, he *it is* that doth go with thee; he will not fail thee, nor forsake thee.

7And Moses called unto Joshua, and said unto him in the sight of all Israel, Be strong and of a good courage: for thou must go with this people unto the land which the LORD hath sworn unto their fathers to give them; and thou shalt cause them to inherit it.

8And the LORD, he *it is* that doth go before thee; he will be with thee, he will not fail thee, neither forsake thee: fear not, neither be dismayed.

9And Moses wrote this law, and delivered it unto the priests the sons of Levi, which bare the ark of the covenant of the LORD, and unto all the elders of Israel.

10And Moses commanded them, saying, At the end of *every* seven years, in the solemnity of the year of release, in the feast of tabernacles,

11When all Israel is come to appear before the LORD thy God in the place which he shall choose, thou shalt read this law before all Israel in their hearing.

12Gather the people together, men, and women, and children, and thy stranger that *is* within thy gates, that they may hear, and that they may learn, and fear the LORD your God, and observe to do all the words of this law:

13And *that* their children, which have not known *any thing,* may hear, and learn to fear the LORD your God, as long as ye live in the land whither ye go over Jordan to possess it.

14And the LORD said unto Moses, Behold, thy days approach that thou must die: call Joshua, and present yourselves in the tabernacle of the congregation, that I may give him a charge. And Moses and Joshua went, and presented themselves in the tabernacle of the congregation.

15And the LORD appeared in the tabernacle in a pillar of a cloud: and the pillar of the cloud stood over the door of the tabernacle.

16And the LORD said unto Moses, Behold, thou shalt sleep with thy fathers; and this people will rise up, and go a whoring after the gods of the strangers of the land, whither they go *to be* among them, and will forsake me, and break my covenant which I have made with them.

17Then my anger shall be kindled against them in that day, and I will forsake them, and I will hide my face from them, and they shall be devoured, and many evils and troubles shall befall them; so that they will say in that day, Are not these evils come upon us, because our God *is* not among us?

18And I will surely hide my face in that day for all the evils which they shall have wrought, in that they are turned unto other gods.

19Now therefore write ye this song for you, and teach it the children of Israel: put it in their mouths, that this song may be a witness for me against the children of Israel.

20For when I shall have brought them into the land which I sware unto their fathers, that floweth with milk and honey; and they shall have eaten and filled themselves, and waxen fat; then will they turn unto other gods, and serve them, and provoke me, and break my covenant.

21And it shall come to pass, when many evils and troubles are befallen them, that this song shall testify against them as a witness; for it shall not be forgotten out of the mouths of their seed: for I know their imagination which they go about, even now, before I have brought them into the land which I sware.

22Moses therefore wrote this song the same day, and taught it the children of Israel.

23And he gave Joshua the son of Nun a charge, and said, Be strong and of a good courage: for thou shalt bring the children of Israel into the land which I sware unto them: and I will be with thee.

24And it came to pass, when Moses had made an end of writing the words of this law in a book, until they were finished,

25That Moses commanded the Levites, which bare the ark of the covenant of the LORD, saying,

26Take this book of the law, and put it in the side of the ark of the covenant of the LORD your God, that it may be there for a witness against thee.

27For I know thy rebellion, and thy stiff neck: behold, while I am yet alive with you this day, ye have been rebellious against the LORD; and how much more after my death?

28Gather unto me all the elders of your tribes, and your officers, that I may speak these words in their ears, and call heaven and earth to record against them.

29For I know that after my death ye will utterly corrupt *yourselves,* and turn aside from the way which I have commanded you; and evil will befall you in the latter days; because ye will do evil in the sight of the LORD, to provoke him to anger through the work of your hands.

30And Moses spake in the ears of all the congregation of Israel the words of this song, until they were ended.

GIVE ear, O ye heavens, and I will speak; and hear, O earth, the words of my mouth.

2My doctrine shall drop as the rain,

my speech shall distil as the dew, as the small rain upon the tender herb, and as the showers upon the grass:

3Because I will publish the name of the LORD: ascribe ye greatness unto our God.

4*He is* the Rock, his work *is* perfect: for all his ways *are* judgment: a God of truth and without iniquity, just and right *is* he.

5They have corrupted themselves, their spot *is* not *the spot* of his children: *they are* a perverse and crooked generation.

6Do ye thus requite the LORD, O foolish people and unwise? *is* not he thy father *that* hath bought thee? hath he not made thee, and established thee?

7Remember the days of old, consider the years of many generations: ask thy father, and he will shew thee; thy elders, and they will tell thee.

8When the Most High divided to the nations their inheritance, when he separated the sons of Adam, he set the bounds of the people according to the number of the children of Israel.

9For the LORD's portion *is* his people; Jacob *is* the lot of his inheritance.

10He found him in a desert land, and in the waste howling wilderness; he led him about, he instructed him, he kept him as the apple of his eye.

11As an eagle stirreth up her nest, fluttereth over her young, spreadeth abroad her wings, taketh them, beareth them on her wings:

12*So* the LORD alone did lead him, and *there was* no strange god with him.

13He made him ride on the high places of the earth, that he might eat the increase of the fields; and he made him to suck honey out of the rock, and oil out of the flinty rock;

14Butter of kine, and milk of sheep, with fat of lambs, and rams of the breed of Bashan, and goats, with the fat of kidneys of wheat; and thou didst drink the pure blood of the grape.

15But Jeshurun waxed fat, and kicked: thou art waxen fat, thou art grown thick, thou art covered *with fatness;* then he forsook God *which* made him, and lightly esteemed the Rock of his salvation.

16They provoked him to jealousy with strange *gods,* with abominations provoked they him to anger.

17They sacrificed unto devils, not to God; to gods whom they knew not, to new *gods that* came newly up, whom your fathers feared not.

18Of the Rock *that* begat thee thou art unmindful, and hast forgotten God that formed thee.

19And when the LORD saw *it,* he abhorred *them,* because of the provoking of his sons, and of his daughters.

20And he said, I will hide my face from them, I will see what their end *shall be:* for they *are* a very froward generation, children in whom *is* no faith.

21They have moved me to jealousy with *that which is* not God; they have provoked me to anger with their vanities: and I will move them to jealousy with *those which are* not a people; I will provoke them to anger with a foolish nation.

22For a fire is kindled in mine anger, and shall burn unto the lowest hell, and shall consume the earth with her increase, and set on fire the foundations of the mountains.

23I will heap mischiefs upon them; I will spend mine arrows upon them.

24*They shall be* burnt with hunger, and devoured with burning heat, and with bitter destruction: I will also send the teeth of beasts upon them, with the poison of serpents of the dust.

25The sword without, and terror within, shall destroy both the young man and the virgin, the suckling *also* with the man of gray hairs.

26I said, I would scatter them into corners, I would make the remembrance of them to cease from among men:

27Were it not that I feared the wrath

of the enemy, lest their adversaries should behave themselves strangely, *and* lest they should say, Our hand *is* high, and the LORD hath not done all this.

28For they *are* a nation void of counsel, neither *is there any* understanding in them.

29O that they were wise, *that* they understood this, *that* they would consider their latter end!

LUKE 12:8–34

ALSO I say unto you, Whosoever shall confess me before men, him shall the Son of man also confess before the angels of God:

9But he that denieth me before men shall be denied before the angels of God.

10And whosoever shall speak a word against the Son of man, it shall be forgiven him: but unto him that blasphemeth against the Holy Ghost it shall not be forgiven.

11And when they bring you unto the synagogues, and *unto* magistrats, and powers, take ye no thought how or what thing ye shall answer, or what ye shall say:

12For the Holy Ghost shall teach you in the same hour what ye ought to say.

13And one of the company said unto him, Master, speak to my brother, that he divide the inheritance with me.

14And he said unto him, Man, who made me a judge or a divider over you?

15And he said unto them, Take heed, and beware of covetousness: for a man's life consisteth not in the abundance of the things which he possesseth.

16And he spake a parable unto them, saying, The ground of a certain rich man brought forth plentifully:

17And he thought within himself, saying, What shall I do, because I have no room where to bestow my fruits?

18And he said, This will I do: I will pull down my barns, and build greater; and there will I bestow all my fruits and my goods.

19And I will say to my soul, Soul, thou hast much goods laid up for many years; take thine ease, eat, drink, *and* be merry.

20But God said unto him, *Thou* fool, this night thy soul shall be required of thee: then whose shall those things be, which thou hast provided?

21So *is* he that layeth up treasure for himself, and is not rich toward God.

22And he said unto his disciples, Therefore I say unto you, Take no thought for your life, what ye shall eat; neither for the body, what ye shall put on.

23The life is more than meat, and the body *is more* than raiment.

24Consider the ravens: for they neither sow nor reap; which neither have storehouse nor barn; and God feedeth them: how much more are ye better than the fowls?

25And which of you with taking thought can add to his stature one cubit?

26If ye then be not able to do that thing which is least, why take ye thought for the rest?

27Consider the lilies how they grow: they toil not, they spin not; and yet I say unto you, that Solomon in all his glory was not arrayed like one of these.

28If then God so clothe the grass, which is to day in the field, and to morrow is cast into the oven; how much more *will he clothe* you, O ye of little faith?

29And seek not ye what ye shall eat, or what ye shall drink, neither be ye of doubtful mind.

30For all these things do the nations of the world seek after: and your Father knoweth that ye have need of these things.

31But rather seek ye the kingdom of God; and all these things shall be added unto you.

32Fear not, little flock; for it is your

Father's good pleasure to give you the kingdom.

33Sell that ye have, and give alms; provide yourselves bags which wax not old, a treasure in the heavens that faileth not, where no thief approacheth, neither moth corrupteth.

34For where your treasure is, there will your heart be also.

PSALM 78:26–45

HE caused an east wind to blow in the heaven: and by his power he brought in the south wind.

27He rained flesh also upon them as dust, and feathered fowls like as the sand of the sea:

28And he let *it* fall in the midst of their camp, round about their habitations.

29So they did eat, and were well filled: for he gave them their own desire;

30They were not estranged from their lust. But while their meat *was* yet in their mouths,

31The wrath of God came upon them, and slew the fattest of them, and smote down the chosen *men* of Israel.

32For all this they sinned still, and believed not for his wondrous works.

33Therefore their days did he consume in vanity, and their years in trouble.

34When he slew them, then they sought him: and they returned and enquired early after God.

35And they remembered that God *was* their rock, and the high God their redeemer.

36Nevertheless they did flatter him with their mouth, and they lied unto him with their tongues.

37For their heart was not right with him, neither were they stedfast in his covenant.

38But he, *being* full of compassion, forgave *their* iniquity, and destroyed *them* not: yea, many a time turned he his anger away, and did not stir up all his wrath.

39For he remembered that they *were but* flesh; a wind that passeth away, and cometh not again.

40How oft did they provoke him in the wilderness, *and* grieve him in the desert!

41Yea, they turned back and tempted God, and limited the Holy One of Israel.

42They remembered not his hand, *nor* the day when he delivered them from the enemy.

43How he had wrought his signs in Egypt, and his wonders in the field of Zoan:

44And had turned their rivers into blood; and their floods that they could not drink.

45He sent divers sorts of flies among them, which devoured them; and frogs, which destroyed them.

PROVERBS FOR TODAY/ 12:21–23

There shall no evil happen to the just: but the wicked shall be filled with mischief. □ *Lying lips are abomination to the LORD: but they that deal truly are his delight.* □ *A prudent man concealeth knowledge: but the heart of fools proclaimeth foolishness.*

DEUTERONOMY 32:30–52

How should one chase a thousand, and two put ten thousand to flight, except their Rock had sold them, and the LORD had shut them up?

31For their rock *is* not as our Rock, even our enemies themselves *being* judges.

32For their vine *is* of the vine of Sodom, and of the fields of Gomorrah: their grapes *are* grapes of gall, their clusters *are* bitter:

33Their wine *is* the poison of dragons, and the cruel venom of asps.

34*Is* not this laid up in store with me, *and* sealed up among my treasures?

35To me *belongeth* vengeance, and recompence; their foot shall slide in *due* time: for the day of their calamity *is* at hand, and the things that shall come upon them make haste.

36For the LORD shall judge his people, and repent himself for his servants, when he seeth that *their* power is gone, and *there is* none shut up, or left.

37And he shall say, Where *are* their gods, *their* rock in whom they trusted,

38Which did eat the fat of their sacrifices, *and* drank the wine of their drink offerings? let them rise up and help you, *and* be your protection.

39See now that I, *even* I, *am* he, and *there is* no god with me: I kill, and I make alive; I wound, and I heal: neither *is there any* that can deliver out of my hand.

40For I lift up my hand to heaven, and say, I live for ever.

41If I whet my glittering sword, and mine hand take hold on judgment; I will render vengeance to mine enemies, and will reward them that hate me.

42I will make mine arrows drunk with blood, and my sword shall devour flesh; *and that* with the blood of the slain and of the captives, from the beginning of revenges upon the enemy.

43Rejoice, O ye nations, *with* his people: for he will avenge the blood of his servants, and will render vengeance to his adversaries, and will be merciful unto his land, *and* to his people.

44And Moses came and spake all the words of this song in the ears of the people, he, and Hoshea the son of Nun.

45And Moses made an end of speaking all these words to all Israel:

46And he said unto them, Set your hearts unto all the words which I testify among you this day, which ye shall command your children to observe to do, all the words of this law.

47For it *is* not a vain thing for you; because it *is* your life: and through this thing ye shall prolong *your* days in the land, whither ye go over Jordan to possess it.

48And the LORD spake unto Moses that selfsame day, saying,

49Get thee up into this mountain Abarim, *unto* mount Nebo, which *is* in the land of Moab, that *is* over against Jericho; and behold the land of Canaan, which I give unto the children of Israel for a possession:

50And die in the mount whither thou goest up, and be gathered unto thy people; as Aaron thy brother died in mount Hor, and was gathered unto his people:

51Because ye trespassed against me among the children of Israel at the waters of Meribah–Kadesh, in the wilderness of Zin; because ye sanctified me not in the midst of the children of Israel.

52Yet thou shalt see the land before *thee;* but thou shalt not go thither unto the land which I give the children of Israel.

LUKE 12:35–59

L ET your loins be girded about, and *your* lights burning;

36And ye yourselves like unto men that wait for their lord, when he will return from the wedding; that when he cometh and knocketh, they may open unto him immediately.

37Blessed *are* those servants, whom the lord when he cometh shall find watching: verily I say unto you, that he shall gird himself, and make them to sit down to meat, and will come forth and serve them.

38And if he shall come in the second watch, or come in the third watch, and find *them* so, blessed are those servants.

39And this know, that if the goodman of the house had known what hour the thief would come, he would have watched, and not have suffered his house to be broken through.

40Be ye therefore ready also: for the Son of man cometh at an hour when ye think not.

41Then Peter said unto him, Lord, speakest thou this parable unto us, or even to all?

42And the Lord said, Who then is that faithful and wise steward, whom *his* lord shall make ruler over his household, to give *them their* portion of meat in due season?

43Blessed *is* that servant, whom his lord when he cometh shall find so doing.

44Of a truth I say unto you, that he will make him ruler over all that he hath.

45But and if that servant say in his heart, My lord delayeth his coming; and shall begin to beat the menservants and maidens, and to eat and drink, and to be drunken;

46The lord of that servant will come in a day when he looketh not for *him,* and at an hour when he is not aware, and will cut him in sunder, and will appoint him his portion with the unbelievers.

47And that servant, which knew his lord's will, and prepared not *himself,* neither did according to his will, shall be beaten with many *stripes.*

48But he that knew not, and did commit things worthy of stripes, shall be beaten with few *stripes.* For unto whomsoever much is given, of him shall be much required: and to whom men have committed much, of him they will ask the more.

49I am come to send fire on the earth; and what will I, if it be already kindled?

50But I have a baptism to be baptized with; and how am I straitened till it be accomplished!

51Suppose ye that I am come to give peace on earth? I tell you, Nay; but rather division:

52For from henceforth there shall be five in one house divided, three against two and two against three.

53The father shall be divided against the son, and the son against the father; the mother against the daughter, and the daughter against the mother; the mother in law against her daughter in law, and the daughter in law against her mother in law.

54And he said also to the people, When ye see a cloud rise out of the west, straightway ye say, There cometh a shower; and so it is.

55And when *ye see* the south wind blow, ye say, There will be heat; and it cometh to pass.

56*Ye* hypocrites, ye can discern the face of the sky and of the earth; but how is it that ye do not discern this time?

57Yea, and why even of yourselves judge ye not what is right?

58When thou goest with thine adversary to the magistrate, *as thou art* in the way, give diligence that thou mayest be delivered from him; lest he hale thee to the judge, and the judge deliver thee to the officer, and the officer cast thee into prison.

59I tell thee, thou shalt not depart thence, till thou hast paid the very last mite.

PSALM 78:46–58

HE gave also their increase unto the caterpiller, and their labour unto the locust.

47He destroyed their vines with hail, and their sycomore trees with frost.

48He gave up their cattle also to the hail, and their flocks to hot thunderbolts.

49He cast upon them the fierceness of his anger, wrath, and indignation, and trouble, by sending evil angels *among them.*

50He made a way to his anger; he spared not their soul from death, but gave their life over to the pestilence;

51And smote all the firstborn in Egypt; the chief of *their* strength in the tabernacles of Ham:

52But made his own people to go forth like sheep, and guided them in the wilderness like a flock.

53And he led them on safely, so that they feared not: but the sea overwhelmed their enemies.

54And he brought them to the border of his sanctuary, *even to* this mountain, *which* his right hand had purchased.

55He cast out the heathen also before them, and divided them an inheritance by line, and made the tribes of Israel to dwell in their tents.

56Yet they tempted and provoked the most high God, and kept not his testimonies:

57But turned back, and dealt unfaithfully like their fathers: they were turned aside like a deceitful bow.

58For they provoked him to anger with their high places, and moved him to jealousy with their graven images.

PROVERBS FOR TODAY/ 12:24

The hand of the diligent shall bear rule: but the slothful shall be under tribute.

APRIL 9

DEUTERONOMY 33:1–29

AND this *is* the blessing, wherewith Moses the man of God blessed the children of Israel before his death.

2And he said, The LORD came from Sinai, and rose up from Seir unto them; he shined forth from mount Paran, and he came with ten thousands of saints: from his right hand *went* a fiery law for them.

3Yea, he loved the people; all his saints *are* in thy hand: and they sat down at thy feet; *every one* shall receive of thy words.

4Moses commanded us a law, *even* the inheritance of the congregation of Jacob.

5And he was king in Jeshurun, when the heads of the people *and* the tribes of Israel were gathered together.

6Let Reuben live, and not die; and let *not* his men be few.

7And this *is the blessing* of Judah: and he said, Hear, LORD, the voice of Judah, and bring him unto his people:

let his hands be sufficient for him; and be thou an help *to him* from his enemies.

8And of Levi he said, *Let* thy Thummim and thy Urim *be* with thy holy one, whom thou didst prove at Massah, *and with* whom thou didst strive at the waters of Meribah;

9Who said unto his father and to his mother, I have not seen him; neither did he acknowledge his brethren, nor knew his own children: for they have observed thy word, and kept thy covenant.

10They shall teach Jacob thy judgments, and Israel thy law: they shall put incense before thee, and whole burnt sacrifice upon thine altar.

11Bless, LORD, his substance, and accept the work of his hands: smite through the loins of them that rise against him, and of them that hate him, that they rise not again.

12*And* of Benjamin he said, The beloved of the LORD shall dwell in safety by him; *and the LORD* shall cover him all the day long, and he shall dwell between his shoulders.

13And of Joseph he said, Blessed of the LORD *be* his land, for the precious things of heaven, for the dew, and for the deep that coucheth beneath,

14And for the precious fruits *brought forth* by the sun, and for the precious things put forth by the moon,

15And for the chief things of the ancient mountains, and for the precious things of the lasting hills,

16And for the precious things of the earth and fulness thereof, and *for* the good will of him that dwelt in the bush: let *the blessing* come upon the head of Joseph, and upon the top of the head of him *that was* separated from his brethren.

17His glory *is like* the firstling of his bullock, and his horns *are like* the horns of unicorns: with them he shall push the people together to the ends of the earth: and they *are* the ten thousands of Ephraim, and they *are* the thousands of Manasseh.

18And of Zebulun he said, Rejoice, Zebulun, in thy going out; and, Issachar, in thy tents.

19They shall call the people unto the mountain; there they shall offer sacrifices of righteousness: for they shall suck *of* the abundance of the seas, and *of* treasures hid in the sand.

20And of Gad he said, Blessed *be* he that enlargeth Gad: he dwelleth as a lion, and teareth the arm with the crown of the head.

21And he provided the first part for himself, because there, *in* a portion of the lawgiver, *was he* seated; and he came with the heads of the people, he executed the justice of the LORD, and his judgments with Israel.

22And of Dan he said, Dan *is* a lion's whelp: he shall leap from Bashan.

23And of Naphtali he said, O Naphtali, satisfied with favour, and full with the blessing of the LORD: possess thou the west and the south.

24And of Asher he said, *Let* Asher *be* blessed with children; let him be acceptable to his brethren, and let him dip his foot in oil.

25Thy shoes *shall be* iron and brass; and as thy days, *so shall* thy strength *be*.

26There is none like unto the God of Jeshurun, *who* rideth upon the heaven in thy help, and in his excellency on the sky.

27The eternal God *is thy* refuge, and underneath *are* the everlasting arms: and he shall thrust out the enemy from before thee; and shall say, Destroy *them*.

28Israel then shall dwell in safety alone: the fountain of Jacob *shall be* upon a land of corn and wine; also his heavens shall drop down dew.

29Happy *art* thou, O Israel: who *is* like unto thee, O people saved by the LORD, the shield of thy help, and who *is* the sword of thy excellency! and thine enemies shall be found liars unto thee; and thou shalt tread upon their high places.

LUKE 13:1–22

THERE were present at that season some that told him [Jesus] of the Galilaeans, whose blood Pilate had mingled with their sacrifices.

2And Jesus answering said unto them, Suppose ye that these Galilaeans were sinners above all the Galilaeans, because they suffered such things?

3I tell you, Nay: but, except ye repent, ye shall all likewise perish.

4Or those eighteen, upon whom the tower in Siloam fell, and slew them, think ye that they were sinners above all men that dwelt in Jerusalem?

5I tell you, Nay: but, except ye repent, ye shall all likewise perish.

6He spake also this parable; A certain *man* had a fig tree planted in his vineyard; and he came and sought fruit thereon, and found none.

7Then said he unto the dresser of his vineyard, Behold, these three years I come seeking fruit on this fig tree, and find none: cut it down; why cumbereth it the ground?

8And he answering said unto him, Lord, let it alone this year also, till I shall dig about it, and dung *it:*

9And if it bear fruit, *well:* and if not, *then* after that thou shalt cut it down.

10And he was teaching in one of the synagogues on the sabbath.

11And, behold, there was a woman which had a spirit of infirmity eighteen years, and was bowed together, and could in no wise lift up *herself.*

12And when Jesus saw her, he called *her to him,* and said unto her, Woman, thou art loosed from thine infirmity.

13And he laid *his* hands on her: and immediately she was made straight, and glorified God.

14And the ruler of the synagogue answered with indignation, because that Jesus had healed on the sabbath day, and said unto the people, There are six days in which men ought to work: in them therefore come and be healed, and not on the sabbath day.

15The Lord then answered him, and said, *Thou* hypocrite, doth not each one of you on the sabbath loose his ox or *his* ass from the stall, and lead *him* away to watering?

16And ought not this woman, being a daughter of Abraham, whom Satan hath bound, lo, these eighteen years, be loosed from this bond on the sabbath day?

17And when he had said these things, all his adversaries were ashamed: and all the people rejoiced for all the glorious things that were done by him.

18Then said he, Unto what is the kingdom of God like? and whereunto shall I resemble it?

19It is like a grain of mustard seed, which a man took, and cast into his garden; and it grew, and waxed a great tree; and the fowls of the air lodged in the branches of it.

20And again he said, Whereunto shall I liken the kingdom of God?

21It is like leaven, which a woman took and hid in three measures of meal, till the whole was leavened.

22And he went through the cities and villages, teaching, and journeying toward Jerusalem.

PSALM 78:59–72

WHEN God heard *this,* he was wroth, and greatly abhorred Israel:

60So that he forsook the tabernacle of Shiloh, the tent *which* he placed among men;

61And delivered his strength into captivity, and his glory into the enemy's hand.

62He gave his people over also unto the sword; and was wroth with his inheritance.

63The fire consumed their young men; and their maidens were not given to marriage.

64Their priests fell by the sword; and their widows made no lamentation.

65Then the LORD awaked as one out of sleep, *and* like a mighty man that shouteth by reason of wine.

66And he smote his enemies in the hinder parts: he put them to a perpetual reproach.

67Moreover he refused the tabernacle of Joseph, and chose not the tribe of Ephraim:

68But chose the tribe of Judah, the mount Zion which he loved.

69And he built his sanctuary like high *palaces,* like the earth which he hath established for ever.

70He chose David also his servant, and took him from the sheepfolds:

71From following the ewes great with young he brought him to feed Jacob his people, and Israel his inheritance.

72So he fed them according to the integrity of his heart; and guided them by the skilfulness of his hands.

PROVERBS FOR TODAY/ 12:25

Heaviness in the heart of man maketh it stoop: but a good word maketh it glad.

APRIL 10

DEUTERONOMY 34:1—JOSHUA 2:24

AND Moses went up from the plains of Moab unto the mountain of Nebo, to the top of Pisgah, that *is* over against Jericho. And the LORD shewed him all the land of Gilead, unto Dan,

2And all Naphtali, and the land of Ephraim, and Manasseh, and all the land of Judah, unto the utmost sea,

3And the south, and the plain of the valley of Jericho, the city of palm trees, unto Zoar.

4And the LORD said unto him, This *is* the land which I sware unto Abraham, unto Isaac, and unto Jacob, saying, I will give it unto thy seed: I have caused thee to see *it* with thine eyes, but thou shalt not go over thither.

5So Moses the servant of the LORD died there in the land of Moab, according to the word of the LORD.

6And he buried him in a valley in the land of Moab, over against Beth–

peor: but no man knoweth of his sepulchre unto this day.

7And Moses *was* an hundred and twenty years old when he died: his eye was not dim, nor his natural force abated.

8And the children of Israel wept for Moses in the plains of Moab thirty days: so the days of weeping *and* mourning for Moses were ended.

9And Joshua the son of Nun was full of the spirit of wisdom; for Moses had laid his hands upon him: and the children of Israel hearkened unto him, and did as the LORD commanded Moses.

10And there arose not a prophet since in Israel like unto Moses, whom the LORD knew face to face,

11In all the signs and the wonders, which the LORD sent him to do in the land of Egypt to Pharaoh, and to all his servants, and to all his land,

12And in all that mighty hand, and

in all the great terror which Moses shewed in the sight of all Israel.

Now after the death of Moses the servant of the LORD it came to pass, that the LORD spake unto Joshua the son of Nun, Moses' minister, saying,

2Moses my servant is dead; now therefore arise, go over this Jordan, thou, and all this people, unto the land which I do give to them, *even* to the children of Israel.

3Every place that the sole of your foot shall tread upon, that have I given unto you, as I said unto Moses.

4From the wilderness and this Lebanon even unto the great river, the river Euphrates, all the land of the Hittites, and unto the great sea toward the going down of the sun, shall be your coast.

5There shall not any man be able to stand before thee all the days of thy life: as I was with Moses, *so* I will be with thee: I will not fail thee, nor forsake thee.

6Be strong and of a good courage: for unto this people shalt thou divide for an inheritance the land, which I sware unto their fathers to give them.

7Only be thou strong and very courageous, that thou mayest observe to do according to all the law, which Moses my servant commanded thee: turn not from it *to* the right hand or *to* the left, that thou mayest prosper whithersoever thou goest.

8This book of the law shall not depart out of thy mouth; but thou shalt meditate therein day and night, that thou mayest observe to do according to all that is written therein: for then thou shalt make thy way prosperous, and then thou shalt have good success.

9Have not I commanded thee? Be strong and of a good courage; be not afraid, neither be thou dismayed: for the LORD thy God *is* with thee whithersoever thou goest.

10Then Joshua commanded the officers of the people, saying,

11Pass through the host, and command the people, saying, Prepare you victuals; for within three days ye shall pass over this Jordan, to go in to possess the land, which the LORD your God giveth you to possess it.

12And to the Reubenites, and to the Gadites, and to half the tribe of Manasseh, spake Joshua, saying,

13Remember the word which Moses the servant of the LORD commanded you, saying, The LORD your God hath given you rest, and hath given you this land.

14Your wives, your little ones, and your cattle, shall remain in the land which Moses gave you on this side Jordan; but ye shall pass before your brethren armed, all the mighty men of valour, and help them;

15Until the LORD have given your brethren rest, as *he hath given* you, and they also have possessed the land which the LORD your God giveth them: then ye shall return unto the land of your possession, and enjoy it, which Moses the LORD'S servant gave you on this side Jordan toward the sunrising.

16And they answered Joshua, saying, All that thou commandest us we will do, and whithersoever thou sendest us, we will go.

17According as we hearkened unto Moses in all things, so will we hearken unto thee: only the LORD thy God be with thee, as he was with Moses.

18Whosoever *he be* that doth rebel against thy commandment, and will not hearken unto thy words in all that thou commandest him, he shall be put to death: only be strong and of a good courage.

AND Joshua the son of Nun sent out of Shittim two men to spy secretly, saying, Go view the land, even Jericho. And they went, and came into an harlot's house, named Rahab, and lodged there.

2And it was told the king of Jericho, saying, Behold, there came men in hither to night of the children of Israel to search out the country.

³And the king of Jericho sent unto Rahab, saying, Bring forth the men that are come to thee, which are entered into thine house: for they be come to search out all the country.

⁴And the woman took the two men, and hid them, and said thus, There came men unto me, but I wist not whence they *were:*

⁵And it came to pass *about the time* of shutting of the gate, when it was dark, that the men went out: whither the men went I wot not: pursue after them quickly; for ye shall overtake them.

⁶But she had brought them up to the roof of the house, and hid them with the stalks of flax, which she had laid in order upon the roof.

⁷And the men pursued after them the way to Jordan unto the fords: and as soon as they which pursued after them were gone out, they shut the gate.

⁸And before they were laid down, she came up unto them upon the roof;

⁹And she said unto the men, I know that the Lord hath given you the land, and that your terror is fallen upon us, and that all the inhabitants of the land faint because of you.

¹⁰For we have heard how the Lord dried up the water of the Red sea for you, when ye came out of Egypt; and what ye did unto the two kings of the Amorites, that *were* on the other side Jordan, Sihon and Og, whom ye utterly destroyed.

¹¹And as soon as we had heard *these things,* our hearts did melt, neither did there remain any more courage in any man, because of you: for the Lord your God, he *is* God in heaven above, and in earth beneath.

¹²Now therefore, I pray you, swear unto me by the Lord, since I have shewed you kindness, that ye will also shew kindness unto my father's house, and give me a true token:

¹³And *that* ye will save alive my father, and my mother, and my brethren, and my sisters, and all that they have, and deliver our lives from death.

¹⁴And the men answered her, Our life for yours, if ye utter not this our business. And it shall be, when the Lord hath given us the land, that we will deal kindly and truly with thee.

¹⁵Then she let them down by a cord through the window: for her house *was* upon the town wall, and she dwelt upon the wall.

¹⁶And she said unto them, Get you to the mountain, lest the pursuers meet you; and hide yourselves there three days, until the pursuers be returned: and afterward may ye go your way.

¹⁷And the men said unto her, We *will be* blameless of this thine oath which thou hast made us swear.

¹⁸Behold, *when* we come into the land, thou shalt bind this line of scarlet thread in the window which thou didst let us down by: and thou shalt bring thy father, and thy mother, and thy brethren, and all thy father's household, home unto thee.

¹⁹And it shall be, *that* whosoever shall go out of the doors of thy house into the street, his blood *shall be* upon his head, and we *will be* guiltless: and whosoever shall be with thee in the house, his blood *shall be* on our head, if *any* hand be upon him.

²⁰And if thou utter this our business, then we will be quit of thine oath which thou hast made us to swear.

²¹And she said, According unto your words, so *be* it. And she sent them away, and they departed: and she bound the scarlet line in the window.

²²And they went, and came unto the mountain, and abode there three days, until the pursuers were returned: and the pursuers sought *them* throughout all the way, but found *them* not.

²³So the two men returned, and descended from the mountain, and passed

over, and came to Joshua the son of Nun, and told him all *things* that befell them:

24And they said unto Joshua, Truly the LORD hath delivered into our hands all the land; for even all the inhabitants of the country do faint because of us.

LUKE 13:23—14:6

THEN said one unto him, Lord, are there few that be saved? And he said unto them, 24Strive to enter in at the strait gate: for many, I say unto you, will seek to enter in, and shall not be able.

25When once the master of the house is risen up, and hath shut to the door, and ye begin to stand without, and to knock at the door, saying, Lord, Lord, open unto us; and he shall answer and say unto you, I know you not whence ye are:

26Then shall ye begin to say, We have eaten and drunk in thy presence, and thou hast taught in our streets.

27But he shall say, I tell you, I know you not whence ye are; depart from me, all *ye* workers of iniquity.

28There shall be weeping and gnashing of teeth, when ye shall see Abraham, and Isaac, and Jacob, and all the prophets, in the kingdom of God, and you *yourselves* thrust out.

29And they shall come from the east, and *from* the west, and from the north, and *from* the south, and shall sit down in the kingdom of God.

30And, behold, there are last which shall be first, and there are first which shall be last.

31The same day there came certain of the Pharisees, saying unto him, Get thee out, and depart hence: for Herod will kill thee.

32And he said unto them, Go ye, and tell that fox, Behold, I cast out devils, and I do cures to day and to morrow, and the third *day* I shall be perfected.

33Nevertheless I must walk to day, and to morrow, and the *day* following: for it cannot be that a prophet perish out of Jerusalem.

34O Jerusalem, Jerusalem, which killest the prophets, and stonest them that are sent unto thee; how often would I have gathered thy children together, as a hen *doth gather* her brood under *her* wings, and ye would not!

35Behold, your house is left unto you desolate: and verily I say unto you, Ye shall not see me, until *the time* come when ye shall say, Blessed *is* he that cometh in the name of the Lord.

AND it came to pass, as he went into the house of one of the chief Pharisees to eat bread on the sabbath day, that they watched him.

2And, behold, there was a certain man before him which had the dropsy.

3And Jesus answering spake unto the lawyers and Pharisees, saying, Is it lawful to heal on the sabbath day?

4And they held their peace. And he took *him,* and healed him, and let him go;

5And answered them, saying, Which of you shall have an ass or an ox fallen into a pit, and will not straightway pull him out on the sabbath day?

6And they could not answer him again to these things.

PSALM 79:1–13

O GOD, the heathen are come into thine inheritance; thy holy temple have they defiled; they have laid Jerusalem on heaps.

2The dead bodies of thy servants have they given *to be* meat unto the fowls of the heaven, the flesh of thy saints unto the beasts of the earth.

3Their blood have they shed like water round about Jerusalem; and *there was* none to bury *them.*

4We are become a reproach to our neighbours, a scorn and derision to them that are round about us.

5How long, LORD? wilt thou be angry for ever? shall thy jealousy burn like fire?

6Pour out thy wrath upon the heathen that have not known thee, and upon the kingdoms that have not called upon thy name.

7For they have devoured Jacob, and laid waste his dwelling place.

8O remember not against us former iniquities: let thy tender mercies speedily prevent us: for we are brought very low.

9Help us, O God of our salvation, for the glory of thy name: and deliver us, and purge away our sins, for thy name's sake.

10Wherefore should the heathen say, Where is their God? let him be known among the heathen in our sight by the revenging of the blood of thy servants which is shed.

11Let the sighing of the prisoner come before thee; according to the greatness of thy power preserve thou those that are appointed to die;

12And render unto our neighbours sevenfold into their bosom their reproach, wherewith they have reproached thee, O Lord.

13So we thy people and sheep of thy pasture will give thee thanks for ever: we will shew forth thy praise to all generations.

PROVERBS FOR TODAY/ 12:26

The righteous is *more excellent than his neighbour: but the way of the wicked seduceth them.*

APRIL 11

JOSHUA 3:1—4:24

A ND Joshua rose early in the morning; and they removed from Shittim, and came to Jordan, he and all the children of Israel, and lodged there before they passed over.

2And it came to pass after three days, that the officers went through the host;

3And they commanded the people, saying, When ye see the ark of the covenant of the LORD your God, and the priests the Levites bearing it, then ye shall remove from your place, and go after it.

4Yet there shall be a space between you and it, about two thousand cubits by measure: come not near unto it, that ye may know the way by which ye must go: for ye have not passed

this way heretofore.

5And Joshua said unto the people, Sanctify yourselves: for to morrow the LORD will do wonders among you.

6And Joshua spake unto the priests, saying, Take up the ark of the covenant, and pass over before the people. And they took up the ark of the covenant, and went before the people.

7And the LORD said unto Joshua, This day will I begin to magnify thee in the sight of all Israel, that they may know that, as I was with Moses, *so* I will be with thee.

8And thou shalt command the priests that bear the ark of the covenant, saying, When ye are come to the brink of the water of Jordan, ye shall stand still in Jordan.

9And Joshua said unto the children of Israel, Come hither, and hear the words of the LORD your God.

10And Joshua said, Hereby ye shall know that the living God *is* among you, and *that* he will without fail drive out from before you the Canaanites, and the Hittites, and the Hivites, and the Perizzites, and the Girgashites, and the Amorites, and the Jebusites.

11Behold, the ark of the covenant of the Lord of all the earth passeth over before you into Jordan.

12Now therefore take you twelve men out of the tribes of Israel, out of every tribe a man.

13And it shall come to pass, as soon as the soles of the feet of the priests that bear the ark of the LORD, the Lord of all the earth, shall rest in the waters of Jordan, *that* the waters of Jordan shall be cut off *from* the waters that come down from above; and they shall stand upon an heap.

14And it came to pass, when the people removed from their tents, to pass over Jordan, and the priests bearing the ark of the covenant before the people;

15And as they that bare the ark were come unto Jordan, and the feet of the priests that bare the ark were dipped in the brim of the water, (for Jordan overfloweth all his banks all the time of harvest,)

16That the waters which came down from above stood *and* rose up upon an heap very far from the city Adam, that *is* beside Zaretan: and those that came down toward the sea of the plain, *even* the salt sea, failed, *and* were cut off: and the people passed over right against Jericho.

17And the priests that bare the ark of the covenant of the LORD stood firm on dry ground in the midst of Jordan, and all the Israelites passed over on dry ground, until all the people were passed clean over Jordan.

AND it came to pass, when all the people were clean passed over Jordan, that the LORD spake unto Joshua, saying,

2Take you twelve men out of the people, out of every tribe a man,

3And command ye them, saying, Take you hence out of the midst of Jordan, out of the place where the priests' feet stood firm, twelve stones, and ye shall carry them over with you, and leave them in the lodging place, where ye shall lodge this night.

4Then Joshua called the twelve men, whom he had prepared of the children of Israel, out of every tribe a man:

5And Joshua said unto them, Pass over before the ark of the LORD your God into the midst of Jordan, and take you up every man of you a stone upon his shoulder, according unto the number of the tribes of the children of Israel:

6That this may be a sign among you, *that* when your children ask *their fathers* in time to come, saying, What *mean* ye by these stones?

7Then ye shall answer them, That the waters of Jordan were cut off before the ark of the covenant of the LORD; when it passed over Jordan, the waters of Jordan were cut off: and these stones shall be for a memorial unto the children of Israel for ever.

8And the children of Israel did so as Joshua commanded, and took up twelve stones out of the midst of Jordan, as the LORD spake unto Joshua, according to the number of the tribes of the children of Israel, and carried them over with them unto the place where they lodged, and laid them down there.

9And Joshua set up twelve stones in the midst of Jordan, in the place where the feet of the priests which bare the ark of the covenant stood: and they are there unto this day.

10For the priests which bare the ark stood in the midst of Jordan, until everything was finished that the LORD commanded Joshua to speak unto the people, according to all that Moses commanded Joshua: and the people hasted and passed over.

11And it came to pass, when all the people were clean passed over, that the ark of the LORD passed over, and the priests, in the presence of the people.

12And the children of Reuben, and the children of Gad, and half the tribe of Manasseh, passed over armed before the children of Israel, as Moses spake unto them:

13About forty thousand prepared for war passed over before the LORD unto battle, to the plains of Jericho.

14On that day the LORD magnified Joshua in the sight of all Israel; and they feared him, as they feared Moses, all the days of his life.

15And the LORD spake unto Joshua, saying,

16Command the priests that bear the ark of the testimony, that they come up out of Jordan.

17Joshua therefore commanded the priests, saying, Come ye up out of Jordan.

18And it came to pass, when the priests that bare the ark of the covenant of the LORD were come up out of the midst of Jordan, *and* the soles of the priests' feet were lifted up unto the dry land, that the waters of Jordan returned unto their place, and flowed over all his banks, as *they did* before.

19And the people came up out of Jordan on the tenth *day* of the first month, and encamped in Gilgal, in the east border of Jericho.

20And those twelve stones, which they took out of Jordan, did Joshua pitch in Gilgal.

21And he spake unto the children of Israel, saying, When your children shall ask their fathers in time to come, saying, What *mean* these stones?

22Then ye shall let your children know, saying, Israel came over this Jordan on dry land.

23For the LORD your God dried up the waters of Jordan from before you, until ye were passed over, as the LORD your God did to the Red sea, which he dried up from before us, until we were gone over:

24That all the people of the earth might know the hand of the LORD, that it *is* mighty: that ye might fear the LORD your God for ever.

LUKE 14:7–35

AND he [Jesus] put forth a parable to those which were bidden, when he marked how they chose out the chief rooms; saying unto them,

8When thou art bidden of any *man* to a wedding, sit not down in the highest room; lest a more honourable man than thou be bidden of him;

9And he that bade thee and him come and say to thee, Give this man place; and thou begin with shame to take the lowest room.

10But when thou art bidden, go and sit down in the lowest room; that when he that bade thee cometh, he may say unto thee, Friend, go up higher: then shalt thou have worship in the presence of them that sit at meat with thee.

11For whosoever exalteth himself shall be abased; and he that humbleth himself shall be exalted.

12Then said he also to him that bade him, When thou makest a dinner or a supper, call not thy friends, nor thy brethren, neither thy kinsmen, nor *thy* rich neighbours; lest they also bid thee again, and a recompence be made thee.

13But when thou makest a feast, call the poor, the maimed, the lame, the blind:

14And thou shalt be blessed; for they cannot recompense thee: for thou shalt be recompensed at the resurrection of the just.

15And when one of them that sat at meat with him heard these things, he said unto him, Blessed *is* he that shall eat bread in the kingdom of God.

16Then said he unto him, A certain man made a great supper, and bade many:

17And sent his servant at supper time to say to them that were bidden, Come; for all things are now ready.

18And they all with one *consent* began to make excuse. The first said unto him, I have bought a piece of ground, and I must needs go and see it: I pray thee have me excused.

19And another said, I have bought five yoke of oxen, and I go to prove them: I pray thee have me excused.

20And another said, I have married a wife, and therefore I cannot come.

21So that servant came, and shewed his lord these things. Then the master of the house being angry said to his servant, Go out quickly into the streets and lanes of the city, and bring in hither the poor, and the maimed, and the halt, and the blind.

22And the servant said, Lord, it is done as thou hast commanded, and yet there is room.

23And the lord said unto the servant, Go out into the highways and hedges, and compel *them* to come in, that my house may be filled.

24For I say unto you, That none of those men which were bidden shall taste of my supper.

25And there went great multitudes with him: and he turned, and said unto them,

26If any *man* come to me, and hate not his father, and mother, and wife, and children, and brethren, and sisters, yea, and his own life also, he cannot be my disciple.

27And whosoever doth not bear his cross, and come after me, cannot be my disciple.

28For which of you, intending to build a tower, sitteth not down first, and counteth the cost, whether he have *sufficient* to finish *it?*

29Lest haply, after he hath laid the foundation, and is not able to finish *it,* all that behold *it* begin to mock him,

30Saying, This man began to build, and was not able to finish.

31Or what king, going to make war against another king, sitteth not down first, and consulteth whether he be able with ten thousand to meet him that cometh against him with twenty thousand?

32Or else, while the other is yet a great way off, he sendeth an ambassage, and desireth conditions of peace.

33So likewise, whosoever he be of you that forsaketh not all that he hath, he cannot be my disciple.

34Salt *is* good: but if the salt have lost his savour, wherewith shall it be seasoned?

35It is neither fit for the land, nor yet for the dunghill; *but* men cast it out. He that hath ears to hear, let him hear.

PSALM 80:1–19

GIVE ear, O Shepherd of Israel, thou that leadest Joseph like a flock; thou that dwellest *between* the cherubims, shine forth.

2Before Ephraim and Benjamin and Manasseh stir up thy strength, and come *and* save us.

3Turn us again, O God, and cause thy face to shine; and we shall be saved.

4O Lord God of hosts, how long wilt thou be angry against the prayer of thy people?

5Thou feedest them with the bread of tears; and givest them tears to drink in great measure.

6Thou makest us a strife unto our neighbours: and our enemies laugh among themselves.

7Turn us again, O God of hosts, and cause thy face to shine; and we shall be saved.

8Thou hast brought a vine out of Egypt: thou hast cast out the heathen, and planted it.

9Thou preparedst *room* before it, and didst cause it to take deep root, and it filled the land.

10The hills were covered with the shadow of it, and the boughs thereof *were like* the goodly cedars.

11She sent out her boughs unto the sea, and her branches unto the river.

12Why hast thou *then* broken down her hedges, so that all they which pass by the way do pluck her?

13The boar out of the wood doth waste it, and the wild beast of the field doth devour it.

14Return, we beseech thee, O God of hosts: look down from heaven, and behold, and visit this vine;

15And the vineyard which thy right hand hath planted, and the branch *that* thou madest strong for thyself.

16*It is* burned with fire, *it is* cut down: they perish at the rebuke of thy countenance.

17Let thy hand be upon the man of thy right hand, upon the son of man *whom* thou madest strong for thyself.

18So will not we go back from thee: quicken us, and we will call upon thy name.

19Turn us again, O Lord God of hosts, cause thy face to shine; and we shall be saved.

PROVERBS FOR TODAY/ 12:27–28

The slothful man *roasteth not that which he took in hunting: but the substance of a diligent man* is *precious.* □ *In the way of righteousness* is *life: and* in *the pathway* thereof there is *no death.*

APRIL 12

JOSHUA 5:1—7:15

And it came to pass, when all the kings of the Amorites, which *were* on the side of Jordan westward, and all the kings of the Canaanites, which *were* by the sea, heard that the Lord had dried up the waters of Jordan from before the children of Israel, until we were passed over, that their heart melted, neither was there spirit in them any more, because of the children of Israel.

2At that time the Lord said unto Joshua, Make thee sharp knives, and circumcise again the children of Israel the second time.

3And Joshua made him sharp knives, and circumcised the children of Israel at the hill of the foreskins.

4And this *is* the cause why Joshua did circumcise: All the people that came out of Egypt, *that were* males, *even* all the men of war, died in the wilderness by the way, after they came out of Egypt.

5Now all the people that came out were circumcised: but all the people *that were* born in the wilderness by the way as they came forth out of Egypt, *them* they had not circumcised.

6For the children of Israel walked forty years in the wilderness, till all the people *that were* men of war, which came out of Egypt, were consumed, because they obeyed not the voice of the Lord: unto whom the Lord sware that he would not shew them the land, which the Lord sware unto their fathers that he would give us, a land that floweth with milk and honey.

7And their children, *whom* he raised up in their stead, them Joshua circumcised: for they were uncircumcised, because they had not circumcised them by the way.

8And it came to pass, when they had done circumcising all the people, that they abode in their places in the camp, till they were whole.

9And the Lord said unto Joshua, This day have I rolled away the reproach of Egypt from off you. Wherefore the name of the place is called Gilgal unto this day.

10And the children of Israel encamped in Gilgal, and kept the passover on the fourteenth day of the month at even in the plains of Jericho.

11And they did eat of the old corn of the land on the morrow after the passover, unleavened cakes, and parched *corn* in the selfsame day.

12And the manna ceased on the morrow after they had eaten of the old corn of the land; neither had the children of Israel manna any more; but they did eat of the fruit of the land of Canaan that year.

13And it came to pass, when Joshua was by Jericho, that he lifted up his eyes and looked, and, behold, there stood a man over against him with his sword drawn in his hand: and Joshua went unto him, and said unto him, *Art* thou for us, or for our adversaries?

14And he said, Nay; but *as* captain of the host of the Lord am I now come. And Joshua fell on his face to the earth, and did worship, and said unto him, What saith my lord unto his servant?

15And the captain of the Lord's host said unto Joshua, Loose thy shoe from off thy foot; for the place whereon thou standest *is* holy. And Joshua did so.

Now Jericho was straitly shut up because of the children of Israel: none went out, and none came in.

2And the Lord said unto Joshua, See, I have given into thine hand Jericho, and the king thereof, *and* the mighty men of valour.

3And ye shall compass the city, all *ye* men of war, *and* go round about the city once. Thus shalt thou do six days.

4And seven priests shall bear before the ark seven trumpets of rams' horns: and the seventh day ye shall compass the city seven times, and the priests shall blow with the trumpets.

5And it shall come to pass, that when they make a long *blast* with the ram's horn, *and* when ye hear the sound of the trumpet, all the people shall shout with a great shout; and the wall of the city shall fall down flat, and the people shall ascend up every man straight before him.

6And Joshua the son of Nun called the priests, and said unto them, Take up the ark of the covenant, and let seven priests bear seven trumpets of rams' horns before the ark of the Lord.

7And he said unto the people, Pass on, and compass the city, and let him that is armed pass on before the ark of the Lord.

8And it came to pass, when Joshua had spoken unto the people, that the seven priests bearing the seven trumpets of rams' horns passed on before the Lord, and blew with the trumpets: and the ark of the covenant of the Lord followed them.

9And the armed men went before the priests that blew with the trumpets and the rereward came after the ark, *the priests* going on, and blowing with the trumpets.

10And Joshua had commanded the people, saying, Ye shall not shout, nor make any noise with your voice, neither shall *any* word proceed out of your mouth, until the day I bid you shout; then shall ye shout.

11So the ark of the Lord compassed the city, going about *it* once: and they came into the camp, and lodged in the camp.

¹²And Joshua rose early in the morning, and the priests took up the ark of the LORD.

¹³And seven priests bearing seven trumpets of rams' horns before the ark of the LORD went on continually, and blew with the trumpets: and the armed men went before them; but the rereward came after the ark of the LORD, *the priests* going on, and blowing with the trumpets.

¹⁴And the second day they compassed the city once, and returned into the camp: so they did six days.

¹⁵And it came to pass on the seventh day, that they rose early about the dawning of the day, and compassed the city after the same manner seven times: only on that day they compassed the city seven times.

¹⁶And it came to pass at the seventh time, when the priests blew with the trumpets, Joshua said unto the people, Shout; for the LORD hath given you the city.

¹⁷And the city shall be accursed, *even* it, and all that *are* therein, to the LORD: only Rahab the harlot shall live, she and all that *are* with her in the house, because she hid the messengers that we sent.

¹⁸And ye, in any wise keep *yourselves* from the accursed thing, lest ye make *yourselves* accursed, when ye take of the accursed thing, and make the camp of Israel a curse, and trouble it.

¹⁹But all the silver, and gold, and vessels of brass and iron, *are* consecrated unto the LORD: they shall come into the treasury of the LORD.

²⁰So the people shouted when *the priests* blew with the trumpets: and it came to pass, when the people heard the sound of the trumpet, and the people shouted with a great shout, that the wall fell down flat, so that the people went up into the city, every man straight before him, and they took the city.

²¹And they utterly destroyed all that *was* in the city, both man and woman, young and old, and ox, and sheep, and ass, with the edge of the sword.

²²But Joshua had said unto the two men that had spied out the country, Go into the harlot's house, and bring out thence the woman, and all that she hath, as ye sware unto her.

²³And the young men that were spies went in, and brought out Rahab, and her father, and her mother, and her brethren, and all that she had; and they brought out all her kindred, and left them without the camp of Israel.

²⁴And they burnt the city with fire, and all that *was* therein: only the silver, and the gold, and the vessels of brass and of iron, they put into the treasury of the house of the LORD.

²⁵And Joshua saved Rahab the harlot alive, and her father's household, and all that she had; and she dwelleth in Israel *even* unto this day; because she hid the messengers, which Joshua sent to spy out Jericho.

²⁶And Joshua adjured *them* at that time, saying, Cursed *be* the man before the LORD, that riseth up and buildeth this city Jericho: he shall lay the foundation thereof in his firstborn, and in his youngest *son* shall he set up the gates of it.

²⁷So the LORD was with Joshua; and his fame was *noised* throughout all the country.

BUT the children of Israel committed a trespass in the accursed thing: for Achan, the son of Carmi, the son of Zabdi, the son of Zerah, of the tribe of Judah, took of the accursed thing: and the anger of the LORD was kindled against the children of Israel.

²And Joshua sent men from Jericho to Ai, which *is* beside Beth–aven, on the east side of Beth–el, and spake unto them, saying, Go up and view the country. And the men went up and viewed Ai.

³And they returned to Joshua, and said unto him, Let not all the people

go up; but let about two or three thousand men go up and smite Ai; *and* make not all the people to labour thither; for they *are but* few.

4So there went up thither of the people about three thousand men: and they fled before the men of Ai.

5And the men of Ai smote of them about thirty and six men: for they chased them *from* before the gate *even* unto Shebarim, and smote them in the going down: wherefore the hearts of the people melted, and became as water.

6And Joshua rent his clothes, and fell to the earth upon his face before the ark of the LORD until the eventide, he and the elders of Israel, and put dust upon their heads.

7And Joshua said, Alas, O Lord God, wherefore hast thou at all brought this people over Jordan, to deliver us into the hand of the Amorites, to destroy us? would to God we had been content, and dwelt on the other side Jordan!

8O Lord, what shall I say, when Israel turneth their backs before their enemies!

9For the Canaanites and all the inhabitants of the land shall hear *of it,* and shall environ us round, and cut off our name from the earth: and what wilt thou do unto thy great name?

10And the LORD said unto Joshua, Get thee up, wherefore liest thou thus upon thy face?

11Israel hath sinned, and they have also transgressed my covenant which I commanded them: for they have even taken of the accursed thing, and have also stolen, and dissembled also, and they have put *it* even among their own stuff.

12Therefore the children of Israel could not stand before their enemies, *but* turned *their* backs before their enemies, because they were accursed: neither will I be with you any more, except ye destroy the accursed thing from among you.

13Up, sanctify the people, and say, Sanctify yourselves against to morrow: for thus saith the LORD God of Israel, *There* is an accursed thing in the midst of thee, O Israel: thou canst not stand before thine enemies, until ye take away the accursed thing from among you.

14In the morning therefore ye shall be brought according to your tribes: and it shall be, *that* the tribe which the LORD taketh shall come according to the families *thereof:* and the family which the LORD shall take shall come by households; and the household which the LORD shall take shall come man by man.

15And it shall be, *that* he that is taken with the accursed thing shall be burnt with fire, he and all that he hath: because he hath transgressed the covenant of the LORD, and because he hath wrought folly in Israel.

LUKE 15:1–32

THEN drew near unto him [Jesus] all the publicans and sinners for to hear him.

2And the Pharisees and scribes murmured, saying, This man receiveth sinners, and eateth with them.

3And he spake this parable unto them, saying,

4What man of you, having an hundred sheep, if he lose one of them, doth not leave the ninety and nine in the wilderness, and go after that which is lost, until he find it?

5And when he hath found *it,* he layeth *it* on his shoulders, rejoicing.

6And when he cometh home, he calleth together *his* friends and neighbours, saying unto them, Rejoice with me; for I have found my sheep which was lost.

7I say unto you, that likewise joy shall be in heaven over one sinner that repenteth, more than over ninety and nine just persons, which need no repentance.

8Either what woman having ten pieces of silver, if she lose one piece, doth not light a candle, and sweep the house, and seek diligently till she find *it?*

9And when she hath found *it,* she calleth *her* friends and *her* neighbours together, saying, Rejoice with me; for I have found the piece which I had lost.

10Likewise, I say unto you there is joy in the presence of the angels of God over one sinner that repenteth.

11And he said, A certain man had two sons:

12And the younger of them said to *his* father, Father, give me the portion of goods that falleth *to me.* And he divided unto them *his* living.

13And not many days after the younger son gathered all together, and took his journey into a far country, and there wasted his substance with riotous living.

14And when he had spent all, there arose a mighty famine in that land; and he began to be in want.

15And he went and joined himself to a citizen of that country; and he sent him into his fields to feed swine.

16And he would fain have filled his belly with the husks that the swine did eat: and no man gave unto him.

17And when he came to himself, he said, How many hired servants of my father's have bread enough and to spare, and I perish with hunger!

18I will arise and go to my father, and will say unto him, Father, I have sinned against heaven, and before thee,

19And am no more worthy to be called thy son: make me as one of thy hired servants.

20And he arose, and came to his father. But when he was yet a great way off, his father saw him, and had compassion, and ran, and fell on his neck, and kissed him.

21And the son said unto him, Father, I have sinned against heaven, and in thy sight, and am no more worthy to be called thy son.

22But the father said to his servants, Bring forth the best robe, and put *it* on him; and put a ring on his hand, and shoes on *his* feet:

23And bring hither the fatted calf, and kill *it;* and let us eat, and be merry:

24For this my son was dead, and is alive again; he was lost, and is found. And they began to be merry.

25Now his elder son was in the field: and as he came and drew nigh to the house, he heard musick and dancing.

26And he called one of the servants, and asked what these things meant.

27And he said unto him, Thy brother is come; and thy father hath killed the fatted calf, because he hath received him safe and sound.

28And he was angry, and would not go in: therefore came his father out, and intreated him.

29And he answering said to *his* father, Lo, these many years do I serve thee, neither transgressed I at any time thy commandment: and yet thou never gavest me a kid, that I might make merry with my friends:

30But as soon as this thy son was come, which hath devoured thy living with harlots, thou hast killed for him the fatted calf.

31And he said unto him, Son, thou art ever with me, and all that I have is thine.

32It was meet that we should make merry, and be glad: for this thy brother was dead, and is alive again; and was lost, and is found.

PSALM 81:1–16

SING aloud unto God our strength: make a joyful noise unto the God of Jacob.

2Take a psalm, and bring hither the timbrel, the pleasant harp with the psaltery.

3Blow up the trumpet in the new

moon, in the time appointed, on our solemn feast day.

4For this *was* a statute for Israel, *and* a law of the God of Jacob.

5This he ordained in Joseph *for* a testimony, when he went out through the land of Egypt: *where* I heard a language *that* I understood not.

6I removed his shoulder from the burden: his hands were delivered from the pots.

7Thou calledst in trouble, and I delivered thee; I answered thee in the secret place of thunder: I proved thee at the waters of Meribah. Selah.

8Hear, O my people, and I will testify unto thee: O Israel, if thou wilt hearken unto me;

9There shall no strange god be in thee; neither shalt thou worship any strange god.

10I *am* the LORD thy God, which brought thee out of the land of Egypt: open thy mouth wide, and I will fill it.

11But my people would not hearken to my voice; and Israel would none of me.

12So I gave them up unto their own hearts' lust: *and* they walked in their own counsels.

13Oh that my people had hearkened unto me, *and* Israel had walked in my ways!

14I should soon have subdued their enemies, and turned my hand against their adversaries.

15The haters of the LORD should have submitted themselves unto him: but their time should have endured for ever.

16He should have fed them also with the finest of the wheat: and with honey out of the rock should I have satisfied thee.

PROVERBS FOR TODAY/ 13:1

A wise son heareth *his father's instruction: but a scorner heareth not rebuke.*

APRIL 13

JOSHUA 7:16—9:2

So Joshua rose up early in the morning, and brought Israel by their tribes; and the tribe of Judah was taken:

17And he brought the family of Judah; and he took the family of the Zarhites: and he brought the family of the Zarhites man by man; and Zabdi was taken:

18And he brought his household man by man; and Achan, the son of Carmi, the son of Zabdi, the son of Zerah, of the tribe of Judah, was taken.

19And Joshua said unto Achan, My son, give, I pray thee, glory to the LORD God of Israel, and make confession unto him; and tell me now what thou hast done; hide *it* not from me.

20And Achan answered Joshua, and said, Indeed I have sinned against the LORD God of Israel, and thus and thus have I done:

21When I saw among the spoils a goodly Babylonish garment, and two hundred shekels of silver, and a wedge of gold of fifty shekels weight, then I coveted them, and took them; and, behold, they *are* hid in the earth in the midst of my tent, and the silver under it.

22So Joshua sent messengers, and they ran unto the tent; and, behold, *it was* hid in his tent, and the silver under it.

23And they took them out of the midst of the tent, and brought them unto Joshua, and unto all the children of Israel, and laid them out before the LORD.

24And Joshua, and all Israel with him, took Achan the son of Zerah, and the silver, and the garment, and the wedge of gold, and his sons, and his daughters, and his oxen, and his asses, and his sheep, and his tent, and all that he had: and they brought them unto the valley of Achor.

25And Joshua said, Why hast thou troubled us? the LORD shall trouble thee this day. And all Israel stoned him with stones, and burned them with fire, after they had stoned them with stones.

26And they raised over him a great heap of stones unto this day. So the LORD turned from the fierceness of his anger. Wherefore the name of that place was called, The valley of Achor, unto this day.

AND the LORD said unto Joshua, Fear not, neither be thou dismayed: take all the people of war with thee, and arise, go up to Ai: see, I have given into thy hand the king of Ai, and his people, and his city, and his land:

2And thou shalt do to Ai and her king as thou didst unto Jericho and her king: only the spoil thereof, and the cattle thereof, shall ye take for a prey unto yourselves: lay thee an ambush for the city behind it.

3So Joshua arose, and all the people of war, to go up against Ai: and Joshua chose out thirty thousand mighty men of valour, and sent them away by night.

4And he commanded them, saying, Behold, ye shall lie in wait against the city, *even* behind the city: go not very far from the city, but be ye all ready:

5And I, and all the people that *are* with me, will approach unto the city: and it shall come to pass, when they come out against us, as at the first, that we will flee before them,

6(For they will come out after us) till we have drawn them from the city; for they will say, They flee before us, as at the first: therefore we will flee before them.

7Then ye shall rise up from the ambush, and seize upon the city: for the LORD your God will deliver it into your hand.

8And it shall be, when ye have taken the city, *that* ye shall set the city on fire: according to the commandment of the LORD shall ye do. See, I have commanded you.

9Joshua therefore sent them forth: and they went to lie in ambush, and abode between Beth–el and Ai, on the west side of Ai: but Joshua lodged that night among the people.

10And Joshua rose up early in the morning, and numbered the people, and went up, he and the elders of Israel, before the people to Ai.

11And all the people, *even the people* of war that *were* with him, went up, and drew nigh, and came before the city, and pitched on the north side of Ai: now *there was* a valley between them and Ai.

12And he took about five thousand men, and set them to lie in ambush between Beth–el and Ai, on the west side of the city.

13And when they had set the people, *even* all the host that *was* on the north of the city, and their liers in wait on the west of the city, Joshua went that night into the midst of the valley.

14And it came to pass, when the king of Ai saw *it,* that they hasted and rose up early, and the men of the city went out against Israel to battle, he and all his people, at a time appointed, before the plain; but he wist not that *there were* liers in ambush against him behind the city.

15And Joshua and all Israel made as if they were beaten before them, and fled by the way of the wilderness.

16And all the people that *were* in Ai were called together to pursue after them: and they pursued after Joshua, and were drawn away from the city.

17And there was not a man left in Ai or Beth–el, that went not out after Israel: and they left the city open, and pursued after Israel.

18And the LORD said unto Joshua, Stretch out the spear that *is* in thy hand toward Ai; for I will give it into thine hand. And Joshua stretched out the spear that *he had* in his hand toward the city.

19And the ambush arose quickly out of their place, and they ran as soon as he had stretched out his hand: and they entered into the city, and took it, and hasted and set the city on fire.

20And when the men of Ai looked behind them, they saw, and, behold, the smoke of the city ascended up to heaven, and they had no power to flee this way or that way: and the people that fled to the wilderness turned back upon the pursuers.

21And when Joshua and all Israel saw that the ambush had taken the city, and that the smoke of the city ascended, then they turned again, and slew the men of Ai.

22And the other issued out of the city against them; so they were in the midst of Israel, some on this side, and some on that side: and they smote them, so that they let none of them remain or escape.

23And the king of Ai they took alive, and brought him to Joshua.

24And it came to pass, when Israel had made an end of slaying all the inhabitants of Ai in the field, in the wilderness wherein they chased them, and when they were all fallen on the edge of the sword, until they were consumed, that all the Israelites returned unto Ai, and smote it with the edge of the sword.

25And *so* it was, *that* all that fell that day, both of men and women, *were* twelve thousand, *even* all the men of Ai.

26For Joshua drew not his hand back, wherewith he stretched out the spear, until he had utterly destroyed all the inhabitants of Ai.

27Only the cattle and the spoil of that city Israel took for a prey unto themselves, according unto the word of the LORD which he commanded Joshua.

28And Joshua burnt Ai, and made it an heap for ever, *even* a desolation unto this day.

29And the king of Ai he hanged on a tree until eventide: and as soon as the sun was down, Joshua commanded that they should take his carcase down from the tree, and cast it at the entering of the gate of the city, and raise thereon a great heap of stones, *that remaineth* unto this day.

30Then Joshua built an altar unto the LORD God of Israel in mount Ebal,

31As Moses the servant of the LORD commanded the children of Israel, as it is written in the book of the law of Moses, an altar of whole stones, over which no man hath lift up *any* iron: and they offered thereon burnt offerings unto the LORD, and sacrificed peace offerings.

32And he wrote there upon the stones a copy of the law of Moses, which he wrote in the presence of the children of Israel.

33And all Israel, and their elders, and officers, and their judges, stood on this side the ark and on that side before the priests the Levites, which bare the ark of the covenant of the LORD, as well the stranger, as he that was born among them; half of them over against mount Gerizim, and half of them over against mount Ebal; as Moses the servant of the LORD had commanded before, that they should bless the people of Israel.

34And afterward he read all the words of the law, the blessings and cursings, according to all that is written in the book of the law.

35There was not a word of all that Moses commanded, which Joshua read not before all the congregation of Israel, with the women, and the little ones, and the strangers that were conversant among them.

AND it came to pass, when all the kings which *were* on this side Jordan, in the hills, and in the valleys, and in all the coasts of the great sea over against Lebanon, the Hittite, and the Amorite, the Canaanite, the Perizzite, the Hivite, and the Jebusite, heard *thereof;*

2That they gathered themselves together, to fight with Joshua and with Israel, with one accord.

LUKE 16:1–18

AND he [Jesus] said also unto his disciples, There was a certain rich man, which had a steward; and the same was accused unto him that he had wasted his goods.

2And he called him, and said unto him, How is it that I hear this of thee? give an account of thy stewardship; for thou mayest be no longer steward.

3Then the steward said within himself, What shall I do? for my lord taketh away from me the stewardship: I cannot dig; to beg I am ashamed.

4I am resolved what to do, that, when I am put out of the stewardship, they may receive me into their houses.

5So he called every one of his lord's debtors *unto him,* and said unto the first, how much owest thou unto my lord?

6And he said, An hundred measures of oil. And he said unto him, Take thy bill, and sit down quickly, and write fifty.

7Then said he to another, And how much owest thou? And he said, An hun-

dred measures of wheat. And he said unto him, Take thy bill, and write fourscore.

8And the lord commended the unjust steward, because he had done wisely: for the children of this world are in their generation wiser than the children of light.

9And I say unto you, Make to yourselves friends of the mammon of unrighteousness; that, when ye fail, they may receive you into everlasting habitations.

10He that is faithful in that which is least is faithful also in much: and he that is unjust in the least is unjust also in much.

11If therefore ye have not been faithful in the unrighteous mammon, who will commit to your trust the true *riches?*

12And if ye have not been faithful in that which is another man's, who shall give you that which is your own?

13No servant can serve two masters: for either he will hate the one, and love the other; or else he will hold to the one, and despise the other. Ye cannot serve God and mammon.

14And the Pharisees also, who were covetous, heard all these things: and they derided him.

15And he said unto them, Ye are they which justify yourselves before men; but God knoweth your hearts: for that which is highly esteemed among men is abomination in the sight of God.

16The law and the prophets *were* until John: since that time the kingdom of God is preached, and every man presseth into it.

17And it is easier for heaven and earth to pass, than one tittle of the law to fail.

18Whosoever putteth away his wife, and marrieth another, committeth adultery: and whosoever marrieth her that is put away from *her* husband committeth adultery.

PSALM 82:1–8

GOD standeth in the congregation of the mighty; he judgeth among the gods.

2How long will ye judge unjustly, and accept the persons of the wicked? Selah.

3Defend the poor and fatherless: do justice to the afflicted and needy.

4Deliver the poor and needy: rid *them* out of the hand of the wicked.

5They know not, neither will they understand; they walk on in darkness: all the foundations of the earth are out of course.

6I have said, Ye *are* gods; and all of you *are* children of the most High.

7But ye shall die like men, and fall like one of the princes.

8Arise, O God, judge the earth: for thou shalt inherit all nations.

PROVERBS FOR TODAY/ 13:2–3

A man shall eat good by the fruit of his *mouth: but the soul of the transgressors* shall eat *violence.* □ *He that keepeth his mouth keepeth his life:* but *he that openeth wide his lips shall have destruction.*

APRIL 14

JOSHUA 9:3—10:43

AND when the inhabitants of Gibeon heard what Joshua had done unto Jericho and to Ai,

4They did work wilily, and went and made as if they had been ambassadors, and took old sacks upon their asses, and wine bottles, old, and rent, and bound up;

5And old shoes and clouted upon their feet, and old garments upon them; and all the bread of their provision was dry *and* mouldy.

6And they went to Joshua unto the camp at Gilgal, and said unto him, and to the men of Israel, We be come from a far country: now therefore make ye a league with us.

7And the men of Israel said unto the Hivites, Peradventure ye dwell among us; and how shall we make a league with you?

8And they said unto Joshua, We *are* thy servants. And Joshua said unto them, Who *are* ye? and from whence come ye?

9And they said unto him, From a very far country thy servants are come because of the name of the LORD thy God: for we have heard the fame of him, and all that he did in Egypt,

10And all that he did to the two kings of the Amorites, that *were* beyond Jordan, to Sihon king of Heshbon, and to Og king of Bashan, which *was* at Ashtaroth.

11Wherefore our elders and all the inhabitants of our country spake to us, saying, Take victuals with you for the journey, and go to meet them, and say unto them, We *are* your servants: therefore now make ye a league with us.

12This our bread we took hot *for* our provision out of our houses on the day we came forth to go unto you; but now, behold, it is dry, and it is mouldy:

13And these bottles of wine, which *were* new; and, behold, they be rent: and these our garments and our shoes are become old by reason of the very long journey.

¹⁴And the men took of their victuals, and asked not *counsel* at the mouth of the LORD.

¹⁵And Joshua made peace with them, and made a league with them, to let them live: and the princes of the congregation sware unto them.

¹⁶And it came to pass at the end of three days after they had made a league with them, that they heard that they *were* their neighbours, and *that* they dwelt among them.

¹⁷And the children of Israel journeyed, and came unto their cities on the third day. Now their cities *were* Gibeon, and Chephirah, and Beeroth, and Kirjath–jearim.

¹⁸And the children of Israel smote them not, because the princes of the congregation had sworn unto them by the LORD God of Israel. And all the congregation murmured against the princes.

¹⁹But all the princes said unto all the congregation, We have sworn unto them by the LORD God of Israel: now therefore we may not touch them.

²⁰This we will do to them; we will even let them live, lest wrath be upon us, because of the oath which we sware unto them.

²¹And the princes said unto them, Let them live; but let them be hewers of wood and drawers of water unto all the congregation; as the princes had promised them.

²²And Joshua called for them, and he spake unto them, saying, Wherefore have ye beguiled us, saying, We *are* very far from you; when ye dwell among us?

²³Now therefore ye *are* cursed, and there shall none of you be freed from being bondmen, and hewers of wood and drawers of water for the house of my God.

²⁴And they answered Joshua, and said, Because it was certainly told thy servants, how that the LORD thy God commanded his servant Moses to give you all the land, and to destroy all the inhabitants of the land from before you, therefore we were sore afraid of our lives because of you, and have done this thing.

²⁵And now, behold, we *are* in thine hand: as it seemeth good and right unto thee to do unto us, do.

²⁶And so did he unto them, and delivered them out of the hand of the children of Israel, that they slew them not.

²⁷And Joshua made them that day hewers of wood and drawers of water for the congregation, and for the altar of the LORD, even unto this day, in the place which he should choose.

Now it came to pass, when Adoni–zedec king of Jerusalem had heard how Joshua had taken Ai, and had utterly destroyed it; as he had done to Jericho and her king, so he had done to Ai and her king; and how the inhabitants of Gibeon had made peace with Israel, and were among them;

²That they feared greatly, because Gibeon *was* a great city, as one of the royal cities, and because it *was* greater than Ai, and all the men thereof *were* mighty.

³Wherefore Adoni–zedec king of Jerusalem sent unto Hoham king of Hebron, and unto Piram king of Jarmuth, and unto Japhia king of Lachish, and unto Debir king of Eglon, saying,

⁴Come up unto me, and help me, that we may smite Gibeon: for it hath made peace with Joshua and with the children of Israel.

⁵Therefore the five kings of the Amorites, the king of Jerusalem, the king of Hebron, the king of Jarmuth, the king of Lachish, the king of Eglon, gathered themselves together, and went up, they and all their hosts, and encamped before Gibeon, and made war against it.

⁶And the men of Gibeon sent unto Joshua to the camp to Gilgal, saying, Slack not thy hand from thy servants;

come up to us quickly, and save us, and help us: for all the kings of the Amorites that dwell in the mountains are gathered together against us.

7So Joshua ascended from Gilgal, he, and all the people of war with him, and all the mighty men of valour.

8And the LORD said unto Joshua, Fear them not: for I have delivered them into thine hand; there shall not a man of them stand before thee.

9Joshua therefore came unto them suddenly, *and* went up from Gilgal all night.

10And the LORD discomfited them before Israel, and slew them with a great slaughter at Gibeon, and chased them along the way that goeth up to Beth–horon, and smote them to Azekah, and unto Makkedah.

11And it came to pass, as they fled from before Israel, *and* were in the going down to Beth–horon, that the LORD cast down great stones from heaven upon them unto Azekah, and they died: *they were* more which died with hailstones than *they* whom the children of Israel slew with the sword.

12Then spake Joshua to the LORD in the day when the LORD delivered up the Amorites before the children of Israel, and he said in the sight of Israel, Sun, stand thou still upon Gibeon; and thou, Moon, in the valley of Ajalon.

13And the sun stood still, and the moon stayed, until the people had avenged themselves upon their enemies. *Is* not this written in the book of Jasher? So the sun stood still in the midst of heaven, and hasted not to go down about a whole day.

14And there was no day like that before it or after it, that the LORD hearkened unto the voice of a man: for the LORD fought for Israel.

15And Joshua returned, and all Israel with him, unto the camp to Gilgal.

16But these five kings fled, and hid themselves in a cave at Makkedah.

17And it was told Joshua, saying, The five kings are found hid in a cave at Makkedah.

18And Joshua said, Roll great stones upon the mouth of the cave, and set men by it for to keep them:

19And stay ye not, *but* pursue after your enemies, and smite the hindmost of them; suffer them not to enter into their cities: for the LORD your God hath delivered them into your hand.

20And it came to pass, when Joshua and the children of Israel had made an end of slaying them with a very great slaughter, till they were consumed, that the rest *which* remained of them entered into fenced cities.

21And all the people returned to the camp to Joshua at Makkedah in peace: none moved his tongue against any of the children of Israel.

22Then said Joshua, Open the mouth of the cave, and bring out those five kings unto me out of the cave.

23And they did so, and brought forth those five kings unto him out of the cave, the king of Jerusalem, the king of Hebron, the king of Jarmuth, the king of Lachish, *and* the king of Eglon.

24And it came to pass, when they brought out those kings unto Joshua, that Joshua called for all the men of Israel, and said unto the captains of the men of war which went with him, Come near, put your feet upon the necks of these kings. And they came near, and put their feet upon the necks of them.

25And Joshua said unto them, Fear not, nor be dismayed, be strong and of good courage: for thus shall the LORD do to all your enemies against whom ye fight.

26And afterward Joshua smote them, and slew them, and hanged them on five trees: and they were hanging upon the trees until the evening.

27And it came to pass at the time of the going down of the sun, *that* Joshua commanded, and they took them down off the trees, and cast them into the cave wherein they had been hid, and laid great stones in the cave's mouth, *which remain* until this very day.

28And that day Joshua took Makkedah, and smote it with the edge of the sword, and the king thereof he utterly destroyed, them, and all the souls that *were* therein; he let none remain: and he did to the king of Makkedah as he did unto the king of Jericho.

29Then Joshua passed from Makkedah, and all Israel with him, unto Libnah, and fought against Libnah:

30And the LORD delivered it also, and the king thereof, into the hand of Israel; and he smote it with the edge of the sword, and all the souls that *were* therein; he let none remain in it; but did unto the king thereof as he did unto the king of Jericho.

31And Joshua passed from Libnah, and all Israel with him, unto Lachish, and encamped against it, and fought against it:

32And the LORD delivered Lachish into the hand of Israel, which took it on the second day, and smote it with the edge of the sword, and all the souls that *were* therein, according to all that he had done to Libnah.

33Then Horam king of Gezer came up to help Lachish; and Joshua smote him and his people, until he had left him none remaining.

34And from Lachish Joshua passed unto Eglon, and all Israel with him; and they encamped against it, and fought against it:

35And they took it on that day, and smote it with the edge of the sword, and all the souls that *were* therein he utterly destroyed that day, according to all that he had done to Lachish.

36And Joshua went up from Eglon, and all Israel with him, unto Hebron; and they fought against it:

37And they took it, and smote it with the edge of the sword, and the king thereof, and all the cities thereof, and all the souls that *were* therein; he left none remaining, according to all that he had done to Eglon; but destroyed it utterly, and all the souls that *were* therein.

38And Joshua returned, and all Israel with him, to Debir; and fought against it:

39And he took it, and the king thereof, and all the cities thereof; and they smote them with the edge of the sword, and utterly destroyed all the souls that *were* therein; he left none remaining: as he had done to Hebron, so he did to Debir, and to the king thereof; as he had done also to Libnah, and to her king.

40So Joshua smote all the country of the hills, and of the south, and of the vale, and of the springs, and all their kings: he left none remaining, but utterly destroyed all that breathed, as the LORD God of Israel commanded.

41And Joshua smote them from Kadesh–barnea even unto Gaza, and all the country of Goshen, even unto Gibeon.

42And all these kings and their land did Joshua take at one time, because the LORD God of Israel fought for Israel.

43And Joshua returned, and all Israel with him, unto the camp to Gilgal.

LUKE 16:19—17:10

THERE was a certain rich man, which was clothed in purple and fine linen, and fared sumptuously every day:

20And there was a certain beggar named Lazarus, which was laid at his gate, full of sores,

21And desiring to be fed with the crumbs which fell from the rich man's table: moreover the dogs came and licked his sores.

22And it came to pass, that the beggar died, and was carried by the angels into Abraham's bosom: the rich man also died, and was buried;

23And in hell he lift up his eyes, being

in torments, and seeth Abraham afar off, and Lazarus in his bosom.

24And he cried and said, Father Abraham, have mercy on me, and send Lazarus, that he may dip the tip of his finger in water, and cool my tongue; for I am tormented in this flame.

25But Abraham said, Son, remember that thou in thy lifetime receivedst thy good things, and likewise Lazarus evil things: but now he is comforted, and thou art tormented.

26And beside all this, between us and you there is a great gulf fixed: so that they which would pass from hence to you cannot; neither can they pass to us, that *would come* from thence.

27Then he said, I pray thee therefore, father, that thou wouldest send him to my father's house:

28For I have five brethren; that he may testify unto them, lest they also come into this place of torment.

29Abraham saith unto him, They have Moses and the prophets; let them hear them.

30And he said, Nay, father Abraham: but if one went unto them from the dead, they will repent.

31And he said unto him, If they hear not Moses and the prophets, neither will they be persuaded, though one rose from the dead.

THEN said he unto the disciples, It is impossible but that offences will come: but woe *unto him,* through whom they come!

2It were better for him that a millstone were hanged about his neck, and he cast into the sea, than that he should offend one of these little ones.

3Take heed to yourselves: If thy brother trespass against thee, rebuke him; and if he repent, forgive him.

4And if he trespass against thee seven times in a day, and seven times in a day turn again to thee, saying, I repent; thou shalt forgive him.

5And the apostles said unto the Lord, Increase our faith.

6And the Lord said, If ye had faith as a grain of mustard seed, ye might say unto this sycamine tree, Be thou plucked up by the root, and be thou planted in the sea; and it should obey you.

7But which of you, having a servant plowing or feeding cattle, will say unto him by and by, when he is come from the field, Go and sit down to meat?

8And will not rather say unto him, Make ready wherewith I may sup, and gird thyself, and serve me, till I have eaten and drunken; and afterward thou shalt eat and drink?

9Doth he thank that servant because he did the things that were commanded him? I trow not.

10So likewise ye, when ye shall have done all those things which are commanded you, say, We are unprofitable servants: we have done that which was our duty to do.

PSALM 83:1–18

KEEP not thou silence, O God: hold not thy peace, and be not still, O God.

2For, lo, thine enemies make a tumult: and they that hate thee have lifted up the head.

3They have taken crafty counsel against thy people, and consulted against thy hidden ones.

4They have said, Come, and let us cut them off from *being* a nation; that the name of Israel may be no more in remembrance.

5For they have consulted together with one consent: they are confederate against thee:

6The tabernacles of Edom, and the Ishmaelites; of Moab, and the Hagarenes;

7Gebal, and Ammon, and Amalek; the Philistines with the inhabitants of Tyre;

8Assur also is joined with them: they have holpen the children of Lot. Selah.

9Do unto them as *unto* the Midianites; as *to* Sisera, as *to* Jabin, at the brook of Kison:

10*Which* perished at En–dor: they became *as* dung for the earth.

11Make their nobles like Oreb, and like Zeeb: yea, all their princes as Zebah, and as Zalmunna:

12Who said, Let us take to ourselves the houses of God in possession.

13O my God, make them like a wheel; as the stubble before the wind.

14As the fire burneth a wood, and as the flame setteth the mountains on fire;

15So persecute them with thy tempest, and make them afraid with thy storm.

16Fill their faces with shame; that they may seek thy name, O LORD.

17Let them be confounded and troubled for ever; yea, let them be put to shame, and perish:

18That *men* may know that thou, whose name alone *is* JEHOVAH, *art* the most high over all the earth.

PROVERBS FOR TODAY/ 13:4

The soul of the sluggard desireth, and hath *nothing: but the soul of the diligent shall be made fat.*

APRIL 15

JOSHUA 11:1—12:24

AND it came to pass, when Jabin king of Hazor had heard *those things,* that he sent to Jobab king of Madon, and to the king of Shimron, and to the king of Achshaph,

2And to the kings that *were* on the north of the mountains, and of the plains south of Chinneroth, and in the valley, and in the borders of Dor on the west,

3*And to* the Canaanite on the east and on the west, and *to* the Amorite, and the Hittite, and the Perizzite, and the Jebusite in the mountains, and *to* the Hivite under Hermon in the land of Mizpeh.

4And they went out, they and all their hosts with them, much people, even as the sand that *is* upon the sea shore in multitude, with horses and chariots very many.

5And when all these kings were met together, they came and pitched together at the waters of Merom, to fight against Israel.

6And the LORD said unto Joshua, Be not afraid because of them: for tomorrow about this time will I deliver them up all slain before Israel: thou shalt hough their horses, and burn their chariots with fire.

7So Joshua came, and all the people of war with him, against them by the waters of Merom suddenly; and they fell upon them.

8And the LORD delivered them into the hand of Israel, who smote them, and chased them unto great Zidon, and unto Misrephoth–maim, and unto the valley of Mizpeh eastward; and they smote them, until they left them none remaining.

9And Joshua did unto them as the LORD bade him: he houghed their horses, and burnt their chariots with fire.

¹⁰And Joshua at that time turned back, and took Hazor, and smote the king thereof with the sword: for Hazor beforetime was the head of all those kingdoms.

¹¹And they smote all the souls that *were* therein with the edge of the sword, utterly destroying *them:* there was not any left to breathe: and he burnt Hazor with fire.

¹²And all the cities of those kings, and all the kings of them, did Joshua take, and smote them with the edge of the sword, *and* he utterly destroyed them, as Moses the servant of the LORD commanded.

¹³But *as for* the cities that stood still in their strength, Israel burned none of them, save Hazor only; *that* did Joshua burn.

¹⁴And all the spoil of these cities, and the cattle the children of Israel took for a prey unto themselves; but every man they smote with the edge of the sword, until they had destroyed them, neither left they any to breathe.

¹⁵As the LORD commanded Moses his servant, so did Moses command Joshua, and so did Joshua; he left nothing undone of all that the LORD commanded Moses.

¹⁶So Joshua took all that land, the hills, and all the south country, and all the land of Goshen, and the valley, and the plain, and the mountain of Israel, and the valley of the same;

¹⁷*Even* from the mount Halak, that goeth up to Seir, even unto Baal–gad in the valley of Lebanon under mount Hermon: and all their kings he took, and smote them, and slew them.

¹⁸Joshua made war a long time with all those kings.

¹⁹There was not a city that made peace with the children of Israel, save the Hivites the inhabitants of Gibeon: all *other* they took in battle.

²⁰For it was of the LORD to harden their hearts, that they should come against Israel in battle, that he might destroy them utterly, *and* that they might have no favour, but that he might destroy them, as the LORD commanded Moses.

²¹And at that time came Joshua, and cut off the Anakims from the mountains, from Hebron, from Debir, from Anab, and from all the mountains of Judah, and from all the mountains of Israel: Joshua destroyed them utterly with their cities.

²²There was none of the Anakims left in the land of the children of Israel: only in Gaza, in Gath, and in Ashdod, there remained.

²³So Joshua took the whole land, according to all that the LORD said unto Moses; and Joshua gave it for an inheritance unto Israel according to their divisions by their tribes. And the land rested from war.

Now these *are* the kings of the land, which the children of Israel smote, and possessed their land on the other side Jordan toward the rising of the sun, from the river Arnon unto mount Hermon, and all the plain on the east:

²Sihon king of the Amorites, who dwelt in Heshbon, *and* ruled from Aroer, which *is* upon the bank of the river Arnon, and from the middle of the river, and from half Gilead, even unto the river Jabbok, *which is* the border of the children of Ammon;

³And from the plain to the sea of Chinneroth on the east, and unto the sea of the plain, *even* the salt sea on the east, the way to Beth–jeshimoth; and from the south, under Ashdoth–pisgah:

⁴And the coast of Og king of Bashan, *which was* of the remnant of the giants, that dwelt at Ashtaroth and at Edrei,

⁵And reigned in mount Hermon, and in Salcah, and in all Bashan, unto the border of the Geshurites, and the Maachathites, and half Gilead, the border of Sihon king of Heshbon.

⁶Them did Moses the servant of the

LORD and the children of Israel smite: and Moses the servant of the LORD gave it *for* a possession unto the Reubenites, and the Gadites, and the half tribe of Manasseh.

7And these *are* the kings of the country which Joshua and the children of Israel smote on this side Jordan on the west, from Baal–gad in the valley of Lebanon even unto the mount Halak, that goeth up to Seir; which Joshua gave unto the tribes of Israel *for* a possession according to their divisions;

8In the mountains, and in the valleys, and in the plains, and in the springs, and in the wilderness, and in the south country; the Hittites, the Amorites, and the Canaanites, the Perizzites, the Hivites, and the Jebusites:

9The king of Jericho, one; the king of Ai, which *is* beside Beth–el, one;

10The king of Jerusalem, one; the king of Hebron, one;

11The king of Jarmuth, one; the king of Lachish, one;

12The king of Eglon, one; the king of Gezer, one;

13The king of Debir, one; the king of Geder, one;

14The king of Hormah, one; the king of Arad, one;

15The king of Libnah, one; the king of Adullam, one;

16The king of Makkedah, one; the king of Beth–el, one;

17The king of Tappuah, one; the king of Hepher, one;

18The king of Aphek, one; the king of Lasharon, one;

19The king of Madon, one; the king of Hazor, one;

20The king of Shimron–meron, one; the king of Achshaph, one;

21The king of Taanach, one; the king of Megiddo, one;

22The king of Kedesh, one; the king of Jokneam of Carmel, one;

23The king of Dor in the coast of Dor, one; the king of the nations of Gilgal, one;

24The king of Tirzah, one: all the kings thirty and one.

LUKE 17:11–37

AND it came to pass, as he [Jesus] went to Jerusalem, that he passed through the midst of Samaria and Galilee.

12And as he entered into a certain village, there met him ten men that were lepers, which stood afar off:

13And they lifted up *their* voices, and said, Jesus, Master, have mercy on us.

14And when he saw *them,* he said unto them, Go shew yourselves unto the priests. And it came to pass, that, as they went, they were cleansed.

15And one of them, when he saw that he was healed, turned back, and with a loud voice glorified God,

16And fell down on *his* face at his feet, giving him thanks: and he was a Samaritan.

17And Jesus answering said, Were there not ten cleansed? but where *are* the nine?

18There are not found that returned to give glory to God, save this stranger.

19And he said unto him, Arise, go thy way: thy faith hath made thee whole.

20And when he was demanded of the Pharisees, when the kingdom of God should come, he answered them and said, The kingdom of God cometh not with observation:

21Neither shall they say, Lo here! or, lo there! for, behold, the kingdom of God is within you.

22And he said unto the disciples, The days will come, when ye shall desire to see one of the days of the Son of man, and ye shall not see *it.*

23And they shall say to you, See here; or, see there: go not after *them,* nor follow *them.*

24For as the lightning, that lighteneth out of the one *part* under heaven, shineth unto the other *part* under heaven; so shall also the Son of man be in his day.

25But first must he suffer many things, and be rejected of this generation.

26And as it was in the days of Noe, so shall it be also in the days of the Son of man.

27They did eat, they drank, they married wives, they were given in marriage, until the day that Noe entered into the ark, and the flood came, and destroyed them all.

28Likewise also as it was in the days of Lot; they did eat, they drank, they bought, they sold, they planted, they builded;

29But the same day that Lot went out of Sodom it rained fire and brimstone from heaven, and destroyed *them* all.

30Even thus shall it be in the day when the Son of man is revealed.

31In that day, he which shall be upon the housetop, and his stuff in the house, let him not come down to take it away: and he that is in the field, let him likewise not return back.

32Remember Lot's wife.

33Whosoever shall seek to save his life shall lose it; and whosoever shall lose his life shall preserve it.

34I tell you, in that night there shall be two *men* in one bed; the one shall be taken, and the other shall be left.

35Two *women* shall be grinding together; the one shall be taken, and the other left.

36Two *men* shall be in the field; the one shall be taken, and the other left.

37And they answered and said unto him, Where, Lord? And he said unto them, Wheresoever the body *is*, thither will the eagles be gathered together.

PSALM 84:1–12

How amiable *are* thy tabernacles, O LORD of hosts!

2My soul longeth, yea, even fainteth for the courts of the LORD: my heart and my flesh crieth out for the living God.

3Yea, the sparrow hath found an house, and the swallow a nest for herself, where she may lay her young, *even* thine altars, O LORD of hosts, my King, and my God.

4Blessed *are* they that dwell in thy house: they will be still praising thee. Selah.

5Blessed *is* the man whose strength *is* in thee; in whose heart *are* the ways *of them.*

6*Who* passing through the valley of Baca make it a well; the rain also filleth the pools.

7They go from strength to strength, *every one of them* in Zion appeareth before God.

8O LORD God of hosts, hear my prayer: give ear, O God of Jacob. Selah.

9Behold, O God our shield, and look upon the face of thine anointed.

10For a day in thy courts *is* better than a thousand. I had rather be a doorkeeper in the house of my God, than to dwell in the tents of wickedness.

11For the LORD God *is* a sun and shield: the LORD will give grace and glory: no good *thing* will he withhold from them that walk uprightly.

12O LORD of hosts, blessed *is* the man that trusteth in thee.

PROVERBS FOR TODAY/ 13:5–6

A righteous man *hateth lying: but a wicked* man *is loathsome, and cometh to shame.* □ *Righteousness keepeth* him that is *upright in the way: but wickedness overthroweth the sinner.*

APRIL 16

JOSHUA 13:1—14:15

Now Joshua was old *and* stricken in years; and the LORD said unto him, Thou art old *and* stricken in years, and there remaineth yet very much land to be possessed.

2This *is* the land that yet remaineth: all the borders of the Philistines, and all Geshuri,

3From Sihor, which *is* before Egypt, even unto the borders of Ekron northward, *which* is counted to the Canaanite: five lords of the Philistines; the Gazathites, and the Ashdothites, the Eshkalonites, the Gittites, and the Ekronites; also the Avites:

4From the south, all the land of the Canaanites, and Mearah that *is* beside the Sidonians, unto Aphek, to the borders of the Amorites:

5And the land of the Giblites, and all Lebanon, toward the sunrising, from Baal–gad under mount Hermon unto the entering into Hamath.

6All the inhabitants of the hill country from Lebanon unto Misrephoth–maim, *and* all the Sidonians, them will I drive out from before the children of Israel: only divide thou it by lot unto the Israelites for an inheritance, as I have commanded thee.

7Now therefore divide this land for an inheritance unto the nine tribes, and the half tribe of Manasseh,

8With whom the Reubenites and the Gadites have received their inheritance, which Moses gave them, beyond Jordan eastward, *even* as Moses the servant of the LORD gave them;

9From Aroer, that *is* upon the bank of the river Arnon, and the city that *is* in the midst of the river, and all the plain of Medeba unto Dibon;

10And all the cities of Sihon king of the Amorites, which reigned in Heshbon, unto the border of the children of Ammon;

11And Gilead, and the border of the Geshurites and Maachathites, and all mount Hermon, and all Bashan unto Salcah;

12All the kingdom of Og in Bashan, which reigned in Ashtaroth and in Edrei, who remained of the remnant of the giants: for these did Moses smite, and cast them out.

13Nevertheless the children of Israel expelled not the Geshurites, nor the Maachathites: but the Geshurites and the Maachathites dwell among the Israelites until this day.

14Only unto the tribe of Levi he gave none inheritance; the sacrifices of the LORD God of Israel made by fire *are* their inheritance, as he said unto them.

15And Moses gave unto the tribe of the children of Reuben *inheritance* according to their families.

16And their coast was from Aroer, that *is* on the bank of the river Arnon, and the city that *is* in the midst of the river, and all the plain by Medeba;

17Heshbon, and all her cities that *are* in the plain; Dibon, and Bamoth–baal, and Beth–baal–meon,

18And Jahaza, and Kedemoth, and Mephaath,

19And Kirjathaim, and Sibmah, and Zareth–shahar in the mount of the valley,

20And Beth–peor, and Ashdoth–pisgah, and Beth–jeshimoth,

21And all the cities of the plain, and all the kingdom of Sihon king of the Amorites, which reigned in Heshbon, whom Moses smote with the princes of Midian, Evi, and Rekem, and Zur, and Hur, and Reba, *which were* dukes of Sihon, dwelling in the country.

22Balaam also the son of Beor, the

soothsayer, did the children of Israel slay with the sword among them that were slain by them.

23And the border of the children of Reuben was Jordan, and the border *thereof*. This *was* the inheritance of the children of Reuben after their families, the cities and the villages thereof.

24And Moses gave *inheritance* unto the tribe of Gad, *even* unto the children of Gad according to their families.

25And their coast was Jazer, and all the cities of Gilead, and half the land of the children of Ammon, unto Aroer that *is* before Rabbah;

26And from Heshbon unto Ramath–mizpeh, and Betonim; and from Mahanaim unto the border of Debir;

27And in the valley, Beth–aram, and Beth–nimrah, and Succoth, and Zaphon, the rest of the kingdom of Sihon king of Heshbon, Jordan and *his* border, *even* unto the edge of the sea of Chinnereth on the other side Jordan eastward.

28This *is* the inheritance of the children of Gad after their families, the cities, and their villages.

29And Moses gave *inheritance* unto the half tribe of Manasseh: and *this* was *the possession* of the half tribe of the children of Manasseh by their families.

30And their coast was from Mahanaim, all Bashan, all the kingdom of Og king of Bashan, and all the towns of Jair, which *are* in Bashan, threescore cities:

31And half Gilead, and Ashtaroth, and Edrei, cities of the kingdom of Og in Bashan, *were pertaining* unto the children of Machir the son of Manasseh, *even* to the one half of the children of Machir by their families.

32These *are the countries* which Moses did distribute for inheritance in the plains of Moab, on the other side Jordan, by Jericho, eastward.

33But unto the tribe of Levi Moses gave not *any* inheritance: the LORD God of Israel *was* their inheritance, as he said unto them.

AND these *are the countries* which the children of Israel inherited in the land of Canaan, which Eleazar the priest, and Joshua the son of Nun, and the heads of the fathers of the tribes of the children of Israel, distributed for inheritance to them.

2By lot *was* their inheritance, as the LORD commanded by the hand of Moses, for the nine tribes, and *for* the half tribe.

3For Moses had given the inheritance of two tribes and an half tribe on the other side Jordan: but unto the Levite he gave none inheritance among them.

4For the children of Joseph were two tribes, Manasseh and Ephraim: therefore they gave no part unto the Levites in the land, save cities to dwell *in,* with their suburbs for their cattle and for their substance.

5As the LORD commanded Moses, so the children of Israel did, and they divided the land.

6Then the children of Judah came unto Joshua in Gilgal: and Caleb the son of Jephunneh the Kenezite said unto him, Thou knowest the thing that the LORD said unto Moses the man of God concerning me and thee in Kadesh–barnea.

7Forty years old *was* I when Moses the servant of the LORD sent me from Kadesh–barnea to espy out the land; and I brought him word again as *it was* in mine heart.

8Nevertheless my brethren that went up with me made the heart of the people melt: but I wholly followed the LORD my God.

9And Moses sware on that day, saying, Surely the land whereon thy feet have trodden shall be thine inheritance, and thy children's for ever, because thou hast wholly followed the LORD my God.

10And now, behold, the LORD hath kept me alive, as he said, these forty and five years, even since the LORD spake this word unto Moses, while *the children of* Israel wandered in the wilderness: and now, lo, I *am* this day fourscore and five years old.

11As yet I *am as* strong this day as *I was* in the day that Moses sent me: as my strength *was* then, even so *is* my strength now, for war, both to go out, and to come in.

12Now therefore give me this mountain, whereof the LORD spake in that day; for thou heardest in that day how the Anakims *were* there, and *that* the cities *were* great *and* fenced: if so be the LORD *will be* with me, then I shall be able to drive them out, as the LORD said.

13And Joshua blessed him, and gave unto Caleb the son of Jephunneh Hebron for an inheritance.

14Hebron therefore became the inheritance of Caleb the son of Jephunneh the Kenezite unto this day, because that he wholly followed the LORD God of Israel.

15And the name of Hebron before *was* Kirjath–arba; *which Arba was* a great man among the Anakims. And the land had rest from war.

LUKE 18:1–17

AND he [Jesus] spake a parable unto them *to this end,* that men ought always to pray, and not to faint;

2Saying, There was in a city a judge, which feared not God, neither regarded man:

3And there was a widow in that city; and she came unto him, saying, Avenge me of mine adversary.

4And he would not for a while: but afterward he said within himself, Though I fear not God, nor regard man;

5Yet because this widow troubleth me, I will avenge her, lest by her continual coming she weary me.

6And the Lord said, Hear what the unjust judge saith.

7And shall not God avenge his own elect, which cry day and night unto him, though he bear long with them?

8I tell you that he will avenge them speedily. Nevertheless when the Son of man cometh, shall he find faith on the earth?

9And he spake this parable unto certain which trusted in themselves that they were righteous, and despised others:

10Two men went up into the temple to pray; the one a Pharisee, and the other a publican.

11The Pharisee stood and prayed thus with himself, God, I thank thee, that I am not as other men *are,* extortioners, unjust, adulterers, or even as this publican.

12I fast twice in the week, I give tithes of all that I possess.

13And the publican, standing afar off, would not lift up so much as *his* eyes unto heaven, but smote upon his breast, saying, God be merciful to me a sinner.

14I tell you, this man went down to his house justified *rather* than the other: for every one that exalteth himself shall be abased; and he that humbleth himself shall be exalted.

15And they brought unto him also infants, that he would touch them: but when *his* disciples saw *it,* they rebuked them.

16But Jesus called them *unto him,* and said, Suffer little children to come unto me, and forbid them not: for of such is the kingdom of God.

17Verily I say unto you, Whosoever shall not receive the kingdom of God as a little child shall in no wise enter therein.

PSALM 85:1–13

LORD, thou hast been favourable unto thy land: thou hast brought back the captivity of Jacob.

2Thou hast forgiven the iniquity of thy people, thou hast covered all their sin. Selah.

3Thou hast taken away all thy wrath: thou hast turned *thyself* from the fierceness of thine anger.

4Turn us, O God of our salvation, and cause thine anger toward us to cease.

5Wilt thou be angry with us for ever? wilt thou draw out thine anger to all generations?

6Wilt thou not revive us again: that thy people may rejoice in thee?

7Shew us thy mercy, O LORD, and grant us thy salvation.

8I will hear what God the LORD will speak: for he will speak peace unto his people, and to his saints: but let them not turn again to folly.

9Surely his salvation *is* nigh them that fear him; that glory may dwell in our land.

10Mercy and truth are met together; righteousness and peace have kissed *each other.*

11Truth shall spring out of the earth; and righteousness shall look down from heaven.

12Yea, the LORD shall give *that which is* good; and our land shall yield her increase.

13Righteousness shall go before him; and shall set *us* in the way of his steps.

PROVERBS FOR TODAY/ 13:7–8

There is that maketh himself rich, yet hath *nothing:* there is *that maketh himself poor, yet* hath *great riches.* □ *The ransom of a man's life* are *his riches: but the poor heareth not rebuke.*

APRIL 17

JOSHUA 15:1–63

THIS then was the lot of the tribe of the children of Judah by their families; *even* to the border of Edom the wilderness of Zin southward *was* the uttermost part of the south coast.

2And their south border was from the shore of the salt sea, from the bay that looketh southward:

3And it went out to the south side to Maaleh–acrabbim, and passed along to Zin, and ascended up on the south side unto Kadesh–barnea, and passed along to Hezron, and went up to Adar, and fetched a compass to Karkaa:

4*From thence* it passed toward Azmon, and went out unto the river of Egypt; and the goings out of that coast were at the sea: this shall be your south coast.

5And the east border *was* the salt sea, *even* unto the end of Jordan. And *their* border in the north quarter *was* from the bay of the sea at the uttermost part of Jordan:

6And the border went up to Beth–hogla, and passed along by the north of Beth–arabah; and the border went up to the stone of Bohan the son of Reuben:

7And the border went up toward Debir from the valley of Achor, and so northward, looking toward Gilgal, that *is* before the going up to Adummim, which *is* on the south side of the river: and the border passed toward the waters of En–shemesh, and the goings out thereof were at En–rogel:

8And the border went up by the valley of the son of Hinnom unto the south side of the Jebusite; the same *is* Jerusalem: and the border went up to the top of the mountain that *lieth* before the valley of Hinnom westward, which *is* at the end of the valley of the giants northward:

9And the border was drawn from the top of the hill unto the fountain of the water of Nephtoah, and went out to the cities of mount Ephron; and the border was drawn to Baalah, which *is* Kirjath–jearim:

10And the border compassed from Baalah westward unto mount Seir, and passed along unto the side of mount Jearim, which *is* Chesalon, on the north side, and went down to Beth–shemesh, and passed on to Timnah:

11And the border went out unto the side of Ekron northward: and the border was drawn to Shicron, and passed along to mount Baalah, and went out unto Jabneel; and the goings out of the border were at the sea.

12And the west border *was* to the great sea, and the coast *thereof.* This *is* the coast of the children of Judah round about according to their families.

13And unto Caleb the son of Jephunneh he gave a part among the children of Judah, according to the commandment of the LORD to Joshua, *even* the city of Arba the father of Anak, which *city is* Hebron.

14And Caleb drove thence the three sons of Anak, Sheshai, and Ahiman, and Talmai, the children of Anak.

15And he went up thence to the inhabitants of Debir: and the name of Debir before *was* Kirjath–sepher.

16And Caleb said, He that smiteth Kirjath–sepher, and taketh it, to him will I give Achsah my daughter to wife.

17And Othniel the son of Kenaz, the brother of Caleb, took it: and he gave him Achsah his daughter to wife.

18And it came to pass, as she came *unto him,* that she moved him to ask of her father a field: and she lighted off *her* ass; and Caleb said unto her, What wouldest thou?

19Who answered, Give me a blessing; for thou hast given me a south land; give me also springs of water. And he gave her the upper springs, and the nether springs.

20This *is* the inheritance of the tribe of the children of Judah according to their families.

21And the uttermost cities of the tribe of the children of Judah toward the coast of Edom southward were Kabzeel, and Eder, and Jagur,

22And Kinah, and Dimonah, and Adadah,

23And Kedesh, and Hazor, and Ithnan,

24Ziph, and Telem, and Bealoth,

25And Hazor, Hadattah, and Kerioth, *and* Hezron, which *is* Hazor,

26Amam, and Shema, and Moladah,

27And Hazar–gaddah, and Heshmon, and Beth–palet,

28And Hazar–shual, and Beer–sheba, and Bizjothjah,

29Baalah, and Iim, and Azem,

30And Eltolad, and Chesil, and Hormah,

31And Ziklag, and Madmannah, and Sansannah.

32And Lebaoth, and Shilhim, and Ain, and Rimmon: all the cities *are* twenty and nine, with their villages:

33*And* in the valley, Eshtaol, and Zoreah, and Ashnah,

34And Zanoah, and En–gannim, Tappuah, and Enam,

35Jarmuth, and Adullam, Socoh, and Azekah,

36And Sharaim, and Adithaim, and Gederah, and Gederothaim; fourteen cities with their villages:

37Zenan, and Hadashah, and Migdal–gad,

38And Dilean, and Mizpeh, and Joktheel,

39Lachish, and Bozkath, and Eglon,

40And Cabbon, and Lahmam, and Kithlish,

41And Gederoth, Beth–dagon, and Naamah, and Makkedah; sixteen cities with their villages:

42Libnah, and Ether, and Ashan,

43And Jiphtah, and Ashnah, and Nezib,

44And Keilah, and Achzib, and Mareshah; nine cities with their villages:

45Ekron, with her towns and her villages:

46From Ekron even unto the sea, all that *lay* near Ashdod, with their villages:

47Ashdod with her towns and her villages, Gaza with her towns and her villages, unto the river of Egypt, and the great sea, and the border *thereof:*

48And in the mountains, Shamir, and Jattir, and Socoh,

49And Dannah, and Kirjath–sannah, which *is* Debir,

50And Anab, and Eshtemoh, and Anim,

51And Goshen, and Holon, and Giloh; eleven cities with their villages:

52Arab, and Dumah, and Eshean,

53And Janum, and Beth–tappuah, and Aphekah,

54And Humtah, and Kirjath–arba, which *is* Hebron, and Zior; nine cities with their villages:

55Maon, Carmel, and Ziph, and Juttah,

56And Jezreel, and Jokdeam, and Zanoah,

57Cain, Gibeah, and Timnah; ten cities with their villages:

58Halhul, Beth–zur, and Gedor,

59And Maarath, and Beth–anoth, and Eltekon; six cities with their villages:

60Kirjath–baal, which *is* Kirjath–jearim, and Rabbah; two cities with their villages:

61In the wilderness, Beth–arabah, Middin, and Secacah,

62And Nibshan, and the city of Salt, and En–gedi; six cities with their villages.

63As for the Jebusites the inhabitants of Jerusalem, the children of Judah could not drive them out: but the Jebusites dwell with the children of Judah at Jerusalem unto this day.

LUKE 18:18–43

AND a certain ruler asked him [Jesus], saying, Good Master, what shall I do to inherit eternal life?

19And Jesus said unto him, Why callest thou me good? none *is* good, save one, *that is,* God.

20Thou knowest the commandments, Do not commit adultery, Do not kill, Do not steal, Do not bear false witness, Honour thy father and thy mother.

21And he said, All these have I kept from my youth up.

22Now when Jesus heard these things, he said unto him, Yet lackest thou one thing: sell all that thou hast, and distribute unto the poor, and thou shalt have treasure in heaven: and come, follow me.

23And when he heard this, he was very sorrowful: for he was very rich.

24And when Jesus saw that he was very sorrowful, he said, How hardly shall they that have riches enter into the kingdom of God!

25For it is easier for a camel to go through a needle's eye, than for a rich man to enter into the kingdom of God.

26And they that heard *it* said, Who then can be saved?

27And he said, The things which are impossible with men are possible with God.

28Then Peter said, Lo, we have left all, and followed thee,

29And he said unto them, Verily I say unto you, There is no man that hath left house, or parents, or brethren, or wife, or children, for the kingdom of God's sake,

30Who shall not receive manifold

more in this present time, and in the world to come life everlasting.

31Then he took *unto him* the twelve, and said unto them, Behold, we go up to Jerusalem, and all things that are written by the prophets concerning the Son of man shall be accomplished.

32For he shall be delivered unto the Gentiles, and shall be mocked, and spitefully entreated, and spitted on:

33And they shall scourge *him,* and put him to death: and the third day he shall rise again.

34And they understood none of these things: and this saying was hid from them, neither knew they the things which were spoken.

35And it came to pass, that as he was come nigh unto Jericho, a certain blind man sat by the way side begging:

36And hearing the multitude pass by, he asked what it meant.

37And they told him, that Jesus of Nazareth passeth by.

38And he cried, saying, Jesus, *thou* son of David, have mercy on me.

39And they which went before rebuked him, that he should hold his peace: but he cried so much the more, *Thou* son of David, have mercy on me.

40And Jesus stood, and commanded him to be brought unto him: and when he was come near, he asked him,

41Saying, What wilt thou that I shall do unto thee? And he said, Lord, that I may receive my sight.

42And Jesus said unto him, Receive thy sight: thy faith hath saved thee.

43And immediately he received his sight, and followed him, glorifying God: and all the people, when they saw *it,* gave praise unto God.

PSALM 86:1–17

Bow down thine ear, O Lord, hear me: for I *am* poor and needy.

2Preserve my soul; for I *am* holy: O thou my God, save thy servant that trusteth in thee.

3Be merciful unto me, O Lord: for I cry unto thee daily.

4Rejoice the soul of thy servant: for unto thee, O Lord, do I lift up my soul.

5For thou, Lord, *art* good, and ready to forgive; and plenteous in mercy unto all them that call upon thee.

6Give ear, O Lord, unto my prayer; and attend to the voice of my supplications.

7In the day of my trouble I will call upon thee: for thou wilt answer me.

8Among the gods *there is* none like unto thee, O Lord; neither *are there any works* like unto thy works.

9All nations whom thou hast made shall come and worship before thee, O Lord; and shall glorify thy name.

10For thou *art* great, and doest wondrous things: thou *art* God alone.

11Teach me thy way, O Lord; I will walk in thy truth: unite my heart to fear thy name.

12I will praise thee, O Lord my God, with all my heart: and I will glorify thy name for evermore.

13For great *is* thy mercy toward me: and thou hast delivered my soul from the lowest hell.

14O God, the proud are risen against me, and the assemblies of violent *men* have sought after my soul; and have not set thee before them.

15But thou, O Lord, *art* a God full of compassion, and gracious, longsuffering, and plenteous in mercy and truth.

16O turn unto me, and have mercy upon me; give thy strength unto thy servant, and save the son of thine handmaid.

17Shew me a token for good; that they which hate me may see *it,* and be ashamed: because thou, Lord, hast holpen me, and comforted me.

PROVERBS FOR TODAY/ 13:9–10

The light of the righteous rejoiceth: but the lamp of the wicked shall be put out. □ *Only by pride cometh contention: but with the well advised* is *wisdom.*

APRIL 18

JOSHUA 16:1—18:28

AND the lot of the children of Joseph fell from Jordan by Jericho, unto the water of Jericho on the east, to the wilderness that goeth up from Jericho throughout mount Beth–el,

2And goeth out from Beth–el to Luz, and passeth along unto the borders of Archi to Ataroth,

3And goeth down westward to the coast of Japhleti, unto the coast of Beth–horon the nether, and to Gezer; and the goings out thereof are at the sea.

4So the children of Joseph, Manasseh and Ephraim, took their inheritance.

5And the border of the children of Ephraim according to their families was *thus:* even the border of their inheritance on the east side was Ataroth–addar, unto Beth–horon the upper;

6And the border went out toward the sea to Michmethah on the north side; and the border went about eastward unto Taanath–shiloh, and passed by it on the east to Janohah;

7And it went down from Janohah to Ataroth, and to Naarath, and came to Jericho, and went out at Jordan.

8The border went out from Tappuah westward unto the river Kanah; and the goings out thereof were at the sea. This *is* the inheritance of the tribe of the children of Ephraim by their families.

9And the separate cities for the children of Ephraim *were* among the inheritance of the children of Manasseh, all the cities with their villages.

10And they drave not out the Canaanites that dwelt in Gezer: but the Canaanites dwell among the Ephraimites unto this day, and serve under tribute.

THERE was also a lot for the tribe of Manasseh; for he *was* the firstborn of Joseph; *to wit,* for Machir the firstborn of Manasseh, the father of Gilead: because he was a man of war, therefore he had Gilead and Bashan.

2There was also *a lot* for the rest of the children of Manasseh by their families; for the children of Abiezer, and for the children of Helek, and for the children of Asriel, and for the children of Shechem, and for the children of Hepher, and for the children of Shemida: these *were* the male children of Manasseh the son of Joseph by their families.

3But Zelophehad, the son of Hepher, the son of Gilead, the son of Machir, the son of Manasseh, had no sons, but daughters: and these *are* the names of his daughters, Mahlah, and Noah, Hoglah, Milcah, and Tirzah.

4And they came near before Eleazar the priest, and before Joshua the son of Nun, and before the princes, saying, The LORD commanded Moses to give us an inheritance among our brethren. Therefore according to the commandment of the LORD he gave them an inheritance among the brethren of their father.

5And there fell ten portions to Manasseh, beside the land of Gilead and Bashan, which *were* on the other side Jordan;

6Because the daughters of Manasseh had an inheritance among his sons: and the rest of Manasseh's sons had the land of Gilead.

7And the coast of Manasseh was from Asher to Michmethah, that *lieth* before Shechem; and the border went along on the right hand unto the inhabitants of En–tappuah.

8*Now* Manasseh had the land of Tappuah: but Tappuah on the border of Manasseh *belonged* to the children of Ephraim;

9And the coast descended unto the river Kanah, southward of the river: these cities of Ephraim *are* among the cities of Manasseh: the coast of Manasseh also *was* on the north side of the river, and the outgoings of it were at the sea:

10Southward *it was* Ephraim's, and northward *it was* Manasseh's, and the sea is his border; and they met together in Asher on the north, and in Issachar on the east.

11And Manasseh had in Issachar and in Asher Beth–shean and her towns, and Ibleam and her towns, and the inhabitants of Dor and her towns, and the inhabitants of En–dor and her towns, and the inhabitants of Taanach and her towns, and the inhabitants of Megiddo and her towns, *even* three countries.

12Yet the children of Manasseh could not drive out *the inhabitants of* those cities; but the Canaanites would dwell in that land.

13Yet it came to pass, when the children of Israel were waxen strong, that they put the Canaanites to tribute, but did not utterly drive them out.

14And the children of Joseph spake unto Joshua, saying, Why hast thou given me *but* one lot and one portion to inherit, seeing I *am* a great people,

forasmuch as the Lord hath blessed me hitherto?

15And Joshua answered them, If thou *be* a great people, *then* get thee up to the wood *country,* and cut down for thyself there in the land of the Perizzites and of the giants, if mount Ephraim be too narrow for thee.

16And the children of Joseph said, The hill is not enough for us: and all the Canaanites that dwell in the land of the valley have chariots of iron, *both they* who *are* of Beth–shean and her towns, and *they* who *are* of the valley of Jezreel.

17And Joshua spake unto the house of Joseph, *even* to Ephraim and to Manasseh, saying, Thou *art* a great people, and hast great power: thou shalt not have one lot *only:*

18But the mountain shall be thine; for it *is* a wood, and thou shalt cut it down: and the outgoings of it shall be thine: for thou shalt drive out the Canaanites, though they have iron chariots, *and* though they *be* strong.

AND the whole congregation of the children of Israel assembled together at Shiloh, and set up the tabernacle of the congregation there. And the land was subdued before them.

2And there remained among the children of Israel seven tribes, which had not yet received their inheritance.

3And Joshua said unto the children of Israel, How long *are* ye slack to go to possess the land, which the Lord God of your fathers hath given you?

4Give out from among you three men for *each* tribe: and I will send them, and they shall rise, and go through the land, and describe it according to the inheritance of them; and they shall come *again* to me.

5And they shall divide it into seven parts: Judah shall abide in their coast on the south, and the house of Joseph shall abide in their coasts on the north.

6Ye shall therefore describe the land

into seven parts, and bring *the description* hither to me, that I may cast lots for you here before the LORD our God.

7But the Levites have no part among you; for the priesthood of the LORD *is* their inheritance: and Gad, and Reuben, and half the tribe of Manasseh, have received their inheritance beyond Jordan on the east, which Moses the servant of the LORD gave them.

8And the men arose, and went away: and Joshua charged them that went to describe the land, saying, Go and walk through the land, and describe it, and come again to me, that I may here cast lots for you before the LORD in Shiloh.

9And the men went and passed through the land, and described it by cities into seven parts in a book, and came *again* to Joshua to the host at Shiloh.

10And Joshua cast lots for them in Shiloh before the LORD: and there Joshua divided the land unto the children of Israel according to their divisions.

11And the lot of the tribe of the children of Benjamin came up according to their families: and the coast of their lot came forth between the children of Judah and the children of Joseph.

12And their border on the north side was from Jordan; and the border went up to the side of Jericho on the north side, and went up through the mountains westward; and the goings out thereof were at the wilderness of Beth-aven.

13And the border went over from thence toward Luz, to the side of Luz, which *is* Beth-el, southward; and the border descended to Ataroth-adar, near the hill that *lieth* on the south side of the nether Beth-horon.

14And the border was drawn *thence,* and compassed the corner of the sea southward, from the hill that *lieth* before Beth-horon southward; and the goings out thereof were at Kirjath-baal, which *is* Kirjath-jearim, a city of the children of Judah: this *was* the west quarter.

15And the south quarter *was* from the end of Kirjath-jearim, and the border went out on the west, and went out to the well of waters of Nephtoah:

16And the border came down to the end of the mountain that *lieth* before the valley of the son of Hinnom, *and* which *is* in the valley of the giants on the north, and descended to the valley of Hinnom, to the side of Jebusi on the south, and descended to En-rogel,

17And was drawn from the north, and went forth to En-shemesh, and went forth toward Geliloth, which *is* over against the going up of Adummim, and descended to the stone of Bohan the son of Reuben,

18And passed along toward the side over against Arabah northward, and went down unto Arabah:

19And the border passed along to the side of Beth-hoglah northward: and the outgoings of the border were at the north bay of the salt sea at the south end of Jordan: this *was* the south coast.

20And Jordan was the border of it on the east side. This *was* the inheritance of the children of Benjamin, by the coasts thereof round about, according to their families.

21Now the cities of the tribe of the children of Benjamin according to their families were Jericho, and Beth-hoglah, and the valley of Keziz,

22And Beth-arabah, and Zemaraim, and Beth-el,

23And Avim, and Parah, and Ophrah,

24And Chephar-haammonai, and Ophni, and Gaba; twelve cities with their villages.

25Gibeon, and Ramah, and Beeroth,

26And Mizpeh, and Chephirah, and Mozah,

27And Rekem, and Irpeel, and Taralah,

28And Zelah, Eleph, and Jebusi, which *is* Jerusalem, Gibeath, *and* Kirjath; fourteen cities with their villages. This *is* the inheritance of the children of Benjamin according to their families.

LUKE 19:1–27

ND *Jesus* entered and passed through Jericho.

2And, behold, *there was* a man named Zacchaeus, which was the chief among the publicans, and he was rich.

3And he sought to see Jesus who he was; and could not for the press, because he was little of stature.

4And he ran before, and climbed up into a sycomore tree to see him: for he was to pass that *way.*

5And when Jesus came to the place, he looked up, and saw him, and said unto him, Zacchaeus, make haste, and come down; for to day I must abide at thy house.

6And he made haste, and came down, and received him joyfully.

7And when they saw *it,* they all murmured, saying, That he was gone to be guest with a man that is a sinner.

8And Zacchaeus stood, and said unto the Lord; Behold, Lord, the half of my goods I give to the poor; and if I have taken any thing from any man by false accusation, I restore *him* fourfold.

9And Jesus said unto him, This day is salvation come to this house forsomuch as he also is a son of Abraham.

10For the Son of man is come to seek and to save that which was lost.

11And as they heard these things, he added and spake a parable, because he was nigh to Jerusalem, and because they thought that the kingdom of God should immediately appear.

12He said therefore, A certain nobleman went into a far country to receive for himself a kingdom, and to return.

13And he called his ten servants, and delivered them ten pounds, and said unto them, Occupy till I come.

14But his citizens hated him, and sent a message after him, saying, We will not have this *man* to reign over us.

15And it came to pass, that when he was returned, having received the kingdom, then he commanded these servants to be called unto him, to whom he had given the money, that he might know how much every man had gained by trading.

16Then came the first, saying, Lord, thy pound hath gained ten pounds.

17And he said unto him, Well, thou good servant: because thou hast been faithful in a very little, have thou authority over ten cities.

18And the second came, saying, Lord, thy pound hath gained five pounds.

19And he said likewise to him, Be thou also over five cities.

20And another came, saying, Lord, behold, *here is* thy pound, which I have kept laid up in a napkin:

21For I feared thee, because thou art an austere man: thou takest up that thou layedst not down, and reapest that thou didst not sow.

22And he saith unto him, Out of thine own mouth will I judge thee, *thou* wicked servant. Thou knewest that I was an austere man, taking up that I laid not down, and reaping that I did not sow:

23Wherefore then gavest not thou my money into the bank, that at my coming I might have required mine own with usury?

24And he said unto them that stood by, Take from him the pound, and give *it* to him that hath ten pounds.

25(And they said unto him, Lord, he hath ten pounds.)

26For I say unto you, That unto every one which hath shall be given; and from him that hath not, even that he hath shall be taken away from him.

27But those mine enemies, which would not that I should reign over them, bring hither, and slay *them* before me.

PSALM 87:1–7

HIS foundation *is* in the holy mountains.

²The LORD loveth the gates of Zion more than all the dwellings of Jacob.

³Glorious things are spoken of thee, O city of God. Selah.

⁴I will make mention of Rahab and Babylon to them that know me: behold Philistia, and Tyre, with Ethiopia; this *man* was born there.

⁵And of Zion it shall be said, This and that man was born in her: and the highest himself shall establish her.

⁶The LORD shall count, when he writeth up the people, *that* this *man* was born there. Selah.

⁷As well the singers as the players on instruments *shall be there:* all my springs *are* in thee.

PROVERBS FOR TODAY/ 13:11

Wealth gotten *by vanity shall be diminished: but he that gathereth by labour shall increase.*

APRIL 19

JOSHUA 19:1—20:9

AND the second lot came forth to Simeon, *even* for the tribe of the children of Simeon according to their families: and their inheritance was within the inheritance of the children of Judah.

²And they had in their inheritance Beer-sheba, or Sheba, and Moladah,

³And Hazar–shual, and Balah, and Azem,

⁴And Eltolad, and Bethul, and Hormah,

⁵And Ziklag, and Beth–marcaboth, and Hazar–susah,

⁶And Beth–lebaoth, and Sharuhen; thirteen cities and their villages:

⁷Ain, Remmon, and Ether, and Ashan; four cities and their villages:

⁸And all the villages that *were* round about these cities to Baalath–beer, Ramath of the south. This *is* the inheritance of the tribe of the children of Simeon according to their families.

⁹Out of the portion of the children of Judah *was* the inheritance of the children of Simeon: for the part of the children of Judah was too much for them: therefore the children of Simeon had their inheritance within the inheritance of them.

¹⁰And the third lot came up for the children of Zebulun according to their families: and the border of their inheritance was unto Sarid:

¹¹And their border went up toward the sea, and Maralah, and reached to Dabbasheth, and reached to the river that *is* before Jokneam;

¹²And turned from Sarid eastward toward the sunrising unto the border of Chisloth–tabor, and then goeth out to Daberath, and goeth up to Japhia,

¹³And from thence passeth on along on the east to Gittah–hepher, to Ittah-kazin, and goeth out to Remmon–methoar to Neah;

¹⁴And the border compasseth it on the north side to Hannathon: and the outgoings thereof are in the valley of Jiphthah–el:

¹⁵And Kattath, and Nahallal, and

Shimron, and Idalah, and Beth–lehem: twelve cities with their villages.

16This *is* the inheritance of the children of Zebulun according to their families, these cities with their villages.

17*And* the fourth lot came out to Issachar, for the children of Issachar according to their families.

18And their border was toward Jezreel, and Chesulloth, and Shunem,

19And Hapharaim, and Shihon, and Anaharath,

20And Rabbith, and Kishion, and Abez,

21And Remeth, and En–gannim, and En–haddah, and Beth–pazzez;

22And the coast reacheth to Tabor, and Shahazimah, and Beth–shemesh; and the outgoings of their border were at Jordan: sixteen cities with their villages.

23This *is* the inheritance of the tribe of the children of Issachar according to their families, the cities and their villages.

24And the fifth lot came out for the tribe of the children of Asher according to their families.

25And their border was Helkath, and Hali, and Beten, and Achshaph,

26And Alammelech, and Amad, and Misheal; and reacheth to Carmel westward, and to Shihor–libnath;

27And turneth toward the sunrising to Beth–dagon, and reacheth to Zebulun, and to the valley of Jiphthah–el toward the north side of Beth–emek, and Neiel, and goeth out to Cabul on the left hand,

28And Hebron, and Rehob, and Hammon, and Kanah, *even* unto great Zidon;

29And *then* the coast turneth to Ramah, and to the strong city Tyre; and the coast turneth to Hosah; and the outgoings thereof are at the sea from the coast to Achzib:

30Ummah also, and Aphek, and Rehob; twenty and two cities with their villages.

31This *is* the inheritance of the tribe

of the children of Asher according to their families, these cities with their villages.

32The sixth lot came out to the children of Naphtali, *even* for the children of Naphtali according to their families.

33And their coast was from Heleph, from Allon to Zaanannim, and Adami, Nekeb, and Jabneel, unto Lakum; and the outgoings thereof were at Jordan:

34And *then* the coast turneth westward to Aznoth–tabor, and goeth out from thence to Hukkok, and reacheth to Zebulun on the south side, and reacheth to Asher on the west side, and to Judah upon Jordan toward the sunrising.

35And the fenced cities *are* Ziddim, Zer, and Hammath, Rakkath, and Chinnereth,

36And Adamah, and Ramah, and Hazor,

37And Kedesh, and Edrei, and En–hazor,

38And Iron, and Migdal–el, Horem, and Beth–anath, and Beth–shemesh; nineteen cities with their villages.

39This *is* the inheritance of the tribe of the children of Naphtali according to their families, the cities and their villages.

40*And* the seventh lot came out for the tribe of the children of Dan according to their families.

41And the coast of their inheritance was Zorah, and Eshtaol, and Ir–shemesh,

42And Shaalabbin, and Ajalon, and Jethlah,

43And Elon, and Thimnathah, and Ekron,

44And Eltekeh, and Gibbethon, and Baalath,

45And Jehud, and Bene–berak, and Gath–rimmon,

46And Me–jarkon, and Rakkon, with the border before Japho.

47And the coast of the children of Dan went out *too little* for them: therefore the children of Dan went up to fight against Leshem, and took it, and smote it with the edge of the sword, and possessed it, and dwelt therein, and called Leshem, Dan, after the name of Dan their father.

48This *is* the inheritance of the tribe of the children of Dan according to their families, these cities with their villages.

49When they had made an end of dividing the land for inheritance by their coasts, the children of Israel gave an inheritance to Joshua the son of Nun among them:

50According to the word of the LORD they gave him the city which he asked, *even* Timnath–serah in mount Ephraim: and he built the city, and dwelt therein.

51These *are* the inheritances, which Eleazar the priest, and Joshua the son of Nun, and the heads of the fathers of the tribes of the children of Israel, divided for an inheritance by lot in Shiloh before the LORD, at the door of the tabernacle of the congregation. So they made an end of dividing the country.

THE LORD also spake unto Joshua, saying,

2Speak to the children of Israel, saying, Appoint out for you cities of refuge, whereof I spake unto you by the hand of Moses:

3That the slayer that killeth *any* person unawares *and* unwittingly may flee thither: and they shall be your refuge from the avenger of blood.

4And when he that doth flee unto one of those cities shall stand at the entering of the gate of the city, and shall declare his cause in the ears of the elders of that city, they shall take him into the city unto them, and give him a place, that he may dwell among them.

5And if the avenger of blood pursue after him, then they shall not deliver the slayer up into his hand; because he smote his neighbour unwittingly, and hated him not beforetime.

6And he shall dwell in that city, until he stand before the congregation for judgment, *and* until the death of the high priest that shall be in those days: then shall the slayer return, and come unto his own city, and unto his own house, unto the city from whence he fled.

7And they appointed Kedesh in Galilee in mount Naphtali, and Shechem in mount Ephraim, and Kirjath–arba, which *is* Hebron, in the mountain of Judah.

8And on the other side Jordan by Jericho eastward, they assigned Bezer in the wilderness upon the plain out of the tribe of Reuben, and Ramoth in Gilead out of the tribe of Gad, and Golan in Bashan out of the tribe of Manasseh.

9These were the cities appointed for all the children of Israel, and for the stranger that sojourneth among them, that whosoever killeth *any* person at unawares might flee thither, and not die by the hand of the avenger of blood, until he stood before the congregation.

LUKE 19:28–48

AND when he [Jesus] had thus spoken, he went before, ascending up to Jerusalem.

29And it came to pass, when he was come nigh to Bethphage and Bethany, at the mount called *the mount* of Olives, he sent two of his disciples,

30Saying, Go ye into the village over against *you;* in the which at your entering ye shall find a colt tied, whereon yet never man sat: loose him, and bring *him hither.*

31And if any man ask you, Why do ye loose *him?* thus shall ye say unto him, Because the Lord hath need of him.

32And they that were sent went their way, and found even as he had said unto them.

33And as they were loosing the colt,

the owners thereof said unto them, Why loose ye the colt?

34And they said, The Lord hath need of him.

35And they brought him to Jesus: and they cast their garments upon the colt, and they set Jesus thereon.

36And as he went, they spread their clothes in the way.

37And when he was come nigh, even now at the descent of the mount of Olives, the whole multitude of the disciples began to rejoice and praise God with a loud voice for all the mighty works that they had seen;

38Saying, Blessed *be* the King that cometh in the name of the Lord: peace in heaven, and glory in the highest.

39And some of the Pharisees from among the multitude said unto him, Master, rebuke thy disciples.

40And he answered and said unto them, I tell you that, if these should hold their peace, the stones would immediately cry out.

41And when he was come near, he beheld the city, and wept over it,

42Saying, If thou hadst known, even thou, at least in this thy day, the things *which belong* unto thy peace! but now they are hid from thine eyes.

43For the days shall come upon thee, that thine enemies shall cast a trench about thee, and compass thee round, and keep thee in on every side,

44And shall lay thee even with the ground, and thy children within thee; and they shall not leave in thee one stone upon another; because thou knewest not the time of thy visitation.

45And he went into the temple, and began to cast out them that sold therein, and them that bought;

46Saying unto them, It is written, My house is the house of prayer: but ye have made it a den of thieves.

47And he taught daily in the temple. But the chief priests and the scribes and the chief of the people sought to destroy him,

48And could not find what they might do: for all the people were very attentive to hear him.

PSALM 88:1–18

O LORD God of my salvation, I have cried day *and* night before thee:

2Let my prayer come before thee: incline thine ear unto my cry;

3For my soul is full of troubles: and my life draweth nigh unto the grave.

4I am counted with them that go down into the pit: I am as a man *that hath* no strength:

5Free among the dead, like the slain that lie in the grave, whom thou rememberest no more: and they are cut off from thy hand.

6Thou hast laid me in the lowest pit, in darkness, in the deeps.

7Thy wrath lieth hard upon me, and thou hast afflicted *me* with all thy waves. Selah.

8Thou hast put away mine acquaintance far from me; thou hast made me an abomination unto them: *I am* shut up, and I cannot come forth.

9Mine eye mourneth by reason of affliction: LORD, I have called daily upon thee, I have stretched out my hands unto thee.

10Wilt thou shew wonders to the dead? shall the dead arise *and* praise thee? Selah.

11Shall thy lovingkindness be declared in the grave? *or* thy faithfulness in destruction?

12Shall thy wonders be known in the dark? and thy righteousness in the land of forgetfulness?

13But unto thee have I cried, O LORD; and in the morning shall my prayer prevent thee.

14LORD, why castest thou off my soul? *why* hidest thou thy face from me?

15I *am* afflicted and ready to die from

my youth up: *while* I suffer thy terrors I am distracted.

16Thy fierce wrath goeth over me; thy terrors have cut me off.

17They came round about me daily like water; they compassed me about together.

18Lover and friend hast thou put far from me, *and* mine acquaintance into darkness.

PROVERBS FOR TODAY/ 13:12–14

Hope deferred maketh the heart sick: but when *the desire cometh,* it is *a tree of life.* □ *Whoso despiseth the word shall be destroyed: but he that feareth the commandment shall be rewarded.* □ *The law of the wise* is *a fountain of life, to depart from the snares of death.*

APRIL 20

JOSHUA 21:1—22:20

THEN came near the heads of the fathers of the Levites unto Eleazar the priest, and unto Joshua the son of Nun, and unto the heads of the fathers of the tribes of the children of Israel;

2And they spake unto them at Shiloh in the land of Canaan, saying, The LORD commanded by the hand of Moses to give us cities to dwell in, with the suburbs thereof for our cattle.

3And the children of Israel gave unto the Levites out of their inheritance, at the commandment of the LORD, these cities and their suburbs.

4And the lot came out for the families of the Kohathites: and the children of Aaron the priest, *which were* of the Levites, had by lot out of the tribe of Judah, and out of the tribe of Simeon, and out of the tribe of Benjamin, thirteen cities.

5And the rest of the children of Kohath *had* by lot out of the families of the tribe of Ephraim, and out of the tribe of Dan, and out of the half tribe of Manasseh, ten cities.

6And the children of Gershon *had* by lot out of the families of the tribe of Issachar, and out of the tribe of Asher, and out of the tribe of Naphtali, and out of the half tribe of Manasseh in Bashan, thirteen cities.

7The children of Merari by their families *had* out of the tribe of Reuben, and out of the tribe of Gad, and out of the tribe of Zebulun, twelve cities.

8And the children of Israel gave by lot unto the Levites these cities with their suburbs, as the LORD commanded by the hand of Moses.

9And they gave out of the tribe of the children of Judah, and out of the tribe of the children of Simeon, these cities which are *here* mentioned by name,

10Which the children of Aaron, *being* of the families of the Kohathites, *who were* of the children of Levi, had: for theirs was the first lot.

11And they gave them the city of Arba the father of Anak, which *city is* Hebron, in the hill *country* of Judah, with the suburbs thereof round about it.

12But the fields of the city, and the villages thereof, gave they to Caleb the son of Jephunneh for his possession.

13Thus they gave to the children of

Aaron the priest Hebron with her suburbs, *to be* a city of refuge for the slayer; and Libnah with her suburbs,

14And Jattir with her suburbs, and Eshtemoa with her suburbs,

15And Holon with her suburbs, and Debir with her suburbs,

16And Ain with her suburbs, and Juttah with her suburbs, *and* Beth–shemesh with her suburbs; nine cities out of those two tribes.

17And out of the tribe of Benjamin, Gibeon with her suburbs, Geba with her suburbs,

18Anathoth with her suburbs, and Almon with her suburbs; four cities.

19All the cities of the children of Aaron, the priests, *were* thirteen cities with their suburbs.

20And the families of the children of Kohath, the Levites which remained of the children of Kohath, even they had the cities of their lot out of the tribe of Ephraim.

21For they gave them Shechem with her suburbs in mount Ephraim, *to be* a city of refuge for the slayer; and Gezer with her suburbs,

22And Kibzaim with her suburbs, and Beth–horon with her suburbs; four cities.

23And out of the tribe of Dan, Eltekeh with her suburbs, Gibbethon with her suburbs,

24Aijalon with her suburbs, Gath–rimmon with her suburbs; four cities.

25And out of the half tribe of Manasseh, Tanach with her suburbs, and Gath–rimmon with her suburbs; two cities.

26All the cities *were* ten with their suburbs for the families of the children of Kohath that remained.

27And unto the children of Gershon, of the families of the Levites, out of the *other* half tribe of Manasseh *they gave* Golan in Bashan with her suburbs, *to be* a city of refuge for the slayer; and Beesh–terah with her suburbs; two cities.

28And out of the tribe of Issachar, Kishon with her suburbs, Dabareh with her suburbs,

29Jarmuth with her suburbs, En–gannim with her suburbs; four cities.

30And out of the tribe of Asher, Mishal with her suburbs, Abdon with her suburbs,

31Helkath with her suburbs, and Rehob with her suburbs; four cities.

32And out of the tribe of Naphtali, Kedesh in Galilee with her suburbs, *to be* a city of refuge for the slayer; and Hammoth–dor with her suburbs, and Kartan with her suburbs; three cities.

33All the cities of the Gershonites according to their families *were* thirteen cities with their suburbs.

34And unto the families of the children of Merari, the rest of the Levites, out of the tribe of Zebulun, Jokneam with her suburbs, and Kartah with her suburbs,

35Dimnah with her suburbs, Nahalal with her suburbs; four cities.

36And out of the tribe of Reuben, Bezer with her suburbs, and Jahazah with her suburbs,

37Kedemoth with her suburbs, and Mephaath with her suburbs; four cities.

38And out of the tribe of Gad, Ramoth in Gilead with her suburbs, *to be* a city of refuge for the slayer; and Mahanaim with her suburbs,

39Heshbon with her suburbs, Jazer with her suburbs; four cities in all.

40So all the cities for the children of Merari by their families, which were remaining of the families of the Levites, were *by* their lot twelve cities.

41All the cities of the Levites within the possession of the children of Israel *were* forty and eight cities with their suburbs.

42These cities were every one with their suburbs round about them: thus *were* all these cities.

43And the LORD gave unto Israel all the land which he sware to give unto their fathers; and they possessed it, and dwelt therein.

44And the LORD gave them rest round about, according to all that he sware unto their fathers: and there stood not a man of all their enemies before them; the LORD delivered all their enemies into their hand.

45There failed not ought of any good thing which the LORD had spoken unto the house of Israel; all came to pass.

THEN Joshua called the Reubenites, and the Gadites, and the half tribe of Manasseh,

2And said unto them, Ye have kept all that Moses the servant of the LORD commanded you, and have obeyed my voice in all that I commanded you:

3Ye have not left your brethren these many days unto this day, but have kept the charge of the commandment of the LORD your God.

4And now the LORD your God hath given rest unto your brethren, as he promised them: therefore now return ye, and get you unto your tents, *and* unto the land of your possession, which Moses the servant of the LORD gave you on the other side Jordan.

5But take diligent heed to do the commandment and the law, which Moses the servant of the LORD charged you, to love the LORD your God, and to walk in all his ways, and to keep his commandments, and to cleave unto him, and to serve him with all your heart and with all your soul.

6So Joshua blessed them, and sent them away: and they went unto their tents.

7Now to the *one* half of the tribe of Manasseh Moses had given *possession* in Bashan: but unto the *other* half thereof gave Joshua among their brethren on this side Jordan westward. And when Joshua sent them away also unto their tents, then he blessed them,

8And he spake unto them, saying, Return with much riches unto your tents, and with very much cattle, with silver, and with gold, and with brass, and with iron, and with very much raiment: divide the spoil of your enemies with your brethren.

9And the children of Reuben and the children of Gad and the half tribe of Manasseh returned, and departed from the children of Israel out of Shiloh, which *is* in the land of Canaan, to go unto the country of Gilead, to the land of their possession, whereof they were possessed, according to the word of the LORD by the hand of Moses.

10And when they came unto the borders of Jordan, that *are* in the land of Canaan, the children of Reuben and the children of Gad and the half tribe of Manasseh built there an altar by Jordan, a great altar to see to.

11And the children of Israel heard say, Behold, the children of Reuben and the children of Gad and the half tribe of Manasseh have built an altar over against the land of Canaan, in the borders of Jordan, at the passage of the children of Israel.

12And when the children of Israel heard *of it,* the whole congregation of the children of Israel gathered themselves together at Shiloh, to go up to war against them.

13And the children of Israel sent unto the children of Reuben, and to the children of Gad, and to the half tribe of Manasseh, into the land of Gilead, Phinehas the son of Eleazar the priest,

14And with him ten princes, of each chief house a prince throughout all the tribes of Israel; and each one *was* an head of the house of their fathers among the thousands of Israel.

15And they came unto the children of Reuben, and to the children of Gad, and to the half tribe of Manasseh, unto the land of Gilead, and they spake with them, saying,

16Thus saith the whole congregation of the LORD, What trespass *is* this that ye have committed against the God of

Israel, to turn away this day from following the LORD, in that ye have builded you an altar, that ye might rebel this day against the LORD?

17Is the iniquity of Peor too little for us, from which we are not cleansed until this day, although there was a plague in the congregation of the LORD,

18But that ye must turn away this day from following the LORD? and it will be, *seeing* ye rebel to day against the LORD, that to morrow he will be wroth with the whole congregation of Israel.

19Notwithstanding, if the land of your possession *be* unclean, *then* pass ye over unto the land of the possession of the LORD, wherein the LORD's tabernacle dwelleth, and take possession among us: but rebel not against the LORD, nor rebel against us, in building you an altar beside the altar of the LORD our God.

20Did not Achan the son of Zerah commit a trespass in the accursed thing, and wrath fell on all the congregation of Israel? and that man perished not alone in his iniquity.

LUKE 20:1–26

AND it came to pass, *that* on one of those days, as he [Jesus] taught the people in the temple, and preached the gospel, the chief priests and the scribes came upon *him* with the elders,

2And spake unto him, saying, Tell us, by what authority doest thou these things? or who is he that gave thee this authority?

3And he answered and said unto them, I will also ask you one thing, and answer me:

4The baptism of John, was it from heaven, or of men?

5And they reasoned with themselves, saying, If we shall say, From heaven; he will say, Why then believed ye him not?

6But and if we say, Of men; all the people will stone us: for they be persuaded that John was a prophet.

7And they answered, that they could not tell whence *it was.*

8And Jesus said unto them, Neither tell I you by what authority I do these things.

9Then began he to speak to the people this parable; A certain man planted a vineyard, and let it forth to husbandmen, and went into a far country for a long time.

10And at the season he sent a servant to the husbandmen, that they should give him of the fruit of the vineyard: but the husbandmen beat him, and sent *him* away empty.

11And again he sent another servant: and they beat him also, and entreated *him* shamefully, and sent *him* away empty.

12And again he sent a third: and they wounded him also, and cast *him* out.

13Then said the lord of the vineyard, What shall I do? I will send my beloved son: it may be they will reverence *him* when they see him.

14But when the husbandmen saw him, they reasoned among themselves, saying, This is the heir: come, let us kill him, that the inheritance may be ours.

15So they cast him out of the vineyard, and killed *him.* What therefore shall the lord of the vineyard do unto them?

16He shall come and destroy these husbandmen, and shall give the vineyard to others. And when they heard *it,* they said, God forbid.

17And he beheld them, and said, What is this then that is written, The stone which the builders rejected, the same is become the head of the corner?

18Whosoever shall fall upon that stone shall be broken; but on whomsoever it shall fall, it will grind him to powder.

19And the chief priests and the scribes the same hour sought to lay hands on him; and they feared the people: for they perceived that he had spoken this parable against them.

20And they watched *him,* and sent forth spies, which should feign themselves just men, that they might take hold of his words, that so they might deliver him unto the power and authority of the governor.

21And they asked him, saying, Master, we know that thou sayest and teachest rightly, neither acceptest thou the person *of any,* but teachest the way of God truly:

22Is it lawful for us to give tribute unto Caesar, or no?

23But he perceived their craftiness, and said unto them, Why tempt ye me?

24Shew me a penny. Whose image and superscription hath it? They answered and said, Caesar's.

25And he said unto them, Render therefore unto Caesar the things which be Caesar's, and unto God the things which be God's.

26And they could not take hold of his words before the people: and they marvelled at his answer, and held their peace.

PSALM 89:1–13

I WILL sing of the mercies of the LORD for ever: with my mouth will I make known thy faithfulness to all generations.

2For I have said, Mercy shall be built up for ever: thy faithfulness shalt thou establish in the very heavens.

3I have made a covenant with my chosen, I have sworn unto David my servant,

4Thy seed will I establish for ever, and build up thy throne to all generations. Selah.

5And the heavens shall praise thy wonders, O LORD: thy faithfulness also in the congregation of the saints.

6For who in the heaven can be compared unto the LORD? *who* among the sons of the mighty can be likened unto the LORD?

7God is greatly to be feared in the assembly of the saints, and to be had in reverence of all *them that are* about him.

8O LORD God of hosts, who *is* a strong LORD like unto thee? or to thy faithfulness round about thee?

9Thou rulest the raging of the sea: when the waves thereof arise, thou stillest them.

10Thou hast broken Rahab in pieces, as one that is slain; thou hast scattered thine enemies with thy strong arm.

11The heavens *are* thine, the earth also *is* thine: *as for* the world and the fulness thereof, thou hast founded them.

12The north and the south thou hast created them: Tabor and Hermon shall rejoice in thy name.

13Thou hast a mighty arm: strong is thy hand, *and* high is thy right hand.

PROVERBS FOR TODAY/ 13:15–16

Good understanding giveth favour: but the way of transgressors is *hard.* □ *Every prudent* man *dealeth with knowledge: but a fool layeth open* his *folly.*

JOSHUA 22:21—23:16

THEN the children of Reuben and the children of Gad and the half tribe of Manasseh answered, and said unto the heads of the thousands of Israel,

22The LORD God of gods, the LORD God of gods, he knoweth, and Israel he shall know; if *it be* in rebellion, or if in transgression against the LORD, (save us not this day,)

23That we have built us an altar to turn from following the LORD, or if to offer thereon burnt offering or meat offering, or if to offer peace offerings thereon, let the LORD himself require *it;*

24And if we have not *rather* done it for fear of *this* thing, saying, In time to come your children might speak unto our children, saying, What have ye to do with the LORD God of Israel?

25For the LORD hath made Jordan a border between us and you, ye children of Reuben and children of Gad; ye have no part in the LORD: so shall your children make our children cease from fearing the LORD.

26Therefore we said, Let us now prepare to build us an altar, not for burnt offering, nor for sacrifice:

27But *that* it *may be* a witness between us and you, and our generations after us, that we might do the service of the LORD before him with our burnt offerings, and with our sacrifices, and with our peace offerings; that your children may not say to our children in time to come, Ye have no part in the LORD.

28Therefore said we, that it shall be, when they should *so* say to us or to our generations in time to come, that we may say *again,* Behold the pattern of the altar of the LORD, which our fathers made, not for burnt offerings,

nor for sacrifices; but it *is* a witness between us and you.

29God forbid that we should rebel against the LORD, and turn this day from following the LORD, to build an altar for burnt offerings, for meat offerings, or for sacrifices, beside the altar of the LORD our God that *is* before his tabernacle.

30And when Phinehas the priest, and the princes of the congregation and heads of the thousands of Israel which *were* with him, heard the words that the children of Reuben and the children of Gad and the children of Manasseh spake, it pleased them.

31And Phinehas the son of Eleazar the priest said unto the children of Reuben, and to the children of Gad, and to the children of Manasseh, This day we perceive that the LORD *is* among us, because ye have not committed this trespass against the LORD: now ye have delivered the children of Israel out of the hand of the LORD.

32And Phinehas the son of Eleazar the priest, and the princes, returned from the children of Reuben, and from the children of Gad, out of the land of Gilead, unto the land of Canaan, to the children of Israel, and brought them word again.

33And the thing pleased the children of Israel; and the children of Israel blessed God, and did not intend to go up against them in battle, to destroy the land wherein the children of Reuben and Gad dwelt.

34And the children of Reuben and the children of Gad called the altar *Ed:* for it *shall be* a witness between us that the LORD *is* God.

AND it came to pass a long time after that the LORD had given rest unto Israel from all their enemies round about, that Joshua waxed old *and* stricken in age.

2And Joshua called for all Israel, *and* for their elders, and for their heads, and for their judges, and for their officers, and said unto them, I am old *and* stricken in age:

3And ye have seen all that the LORD your God hath done unto all these nations because of you; for the LORD your God *is* he that hath fought for you.

4Behold, I have divided unto you by lot these nations that remain, to be an inheritance for your tribes, from Jordan, with all the nations that I have cut off, even unto the great sea westward.

5And the LORD your God, he shall expel them from before you, and drive them from out of your sight; and ye shall possess their land, as the LORD your God hath promised unto you.

6Be ye therefore very courageous to keep and to do all that is written in the book of the law of Moses, that ye turn not aside therefrom *to* the right hand or *to* the left;

7That ye come not among these nations, these that remain among you; neither make mention of the name of their gods, nor cause to swear *by them,* neither serve them, nor bow yourselves unto them:

8But cleave unto the LORD your God, as ye have done unto this day.

9For the LORD hath driven out from before you great nations and strong: but *as for* you, no man hath been able to stand before you unto this day.

10One man of you shall chase a thousand: for the LORD your God, he *it is* that fighteth for you, as he hath promised you.

11Take good heed therefore unto yourselves, that ye love the LORD your God.

12Else if ye do in any wise go back, and cleave unto the remnant of these nations, *even* these that remain among you, and shall make marriages with them, and go in unto them, and they to you:

13Know for a certainty that the LORD your God will no more drive out *any of* these nations from before you; but they shall be snares and traps unto you, and scourges in your sides, and thorns in your eyes, until ye perish from off this good land which the LORD your God hath given you.

14And, behold, this day I *am* going the way of all the earth: and ye know in all your hearts and in all your souls, that not one thing hath failed of all the good things which the LORD your God spake concerning you; all are come to pass unto you, *and* not one thing hath failed thereof.

15Therefore it shall come to pass, *that* as all good things are come upon you, which the LORD your God promised you; so shall the LORD bring upon you all evil things, until he have destroyed you from off this good land which the LORD your God hath given you.

16When ye have transgressed the covenant of the LORD your God, which he commanded you, and have gone and served other gods, and bowed yourselves to them; then shall the anger of the LORD be kindled against you, and ye shall perish quickly from off the good land which he hath given unto you.

LUKE 20:27–47

THEN came to *him* [Jesus] certain of the Sadducees, which deny that there is any resurrection: and they asked him,

28Saying, Master, Moses wrote unto us, If any man's brother die, having a wife, and he die without children, that his brother should take his wife, and raise up seed unto his brother.

29There were therefore seven brethren: and the first took a wife, and died without children.

30And the second took her to wife, and he died childless.

31And the third took her; and in like manner the seven also: and they left no children, and died.

32Last of all the woman died also.

33Therefore in the resurrection whose wife of them is she? for seven had her to wife.

34And Jesus answering said unto them, The children of this world marry, and are given in marriage:

35But they which shall be accounted worthy to obtain that world, and the resurrection from the dead, neither marry, nor are given in marriage:

36Neither can they die any more: for they are equal unto the angels; and are the children of God, being the children of the resurrection.

37Now that the dead are raised, even Moses shewed at the bush, when he calleth the Lord the God of Abraham, and the God of Isaac, and the God of Jacob.

38For he is not a God of the dead, but of the living: for all live unto him.

39Then certain of the scribes answering said, Master, thou hast well said.

40And after that they durst not ask him any *question at all.*

41And he said unto them, How say they that Christ is David's son?

42And David himself saith in the book of Psalms, The LORD said unto my Lord, Sit thou on my right hand,

43Till I make thine enemies thy footstool.

44David therefore calleth him Lord, how is he then his son?

45Then in the audience of all the people he said unto his disciples,

46Beware of the scribes, which desire to walk in long robes, and love greetings in the markets, and the highest seats in the synagogues, and the chief rooms at feasts;

47Which devour widows' houses, and for a shew make long prayers: the same shall receive greater damnation.

PSALM 89:14–37

JUSTICE and judgment *are* the habitation of thy throne: mercy and truth shall go before thy face.

15Blessed *is* the people that know the joyful sound: they shall walk, O LORD, in the light of thy countenance.

16In thy name shall they rejoice all the day: and in thy righteousness shall they be exalted.

17For thou *art* the glory of their strength: and in thy favour our horn shall be exalted.

18For the LORD *is* our defence; and the Holy One of Israel *is* our king.

19Then thou spakest in vision to thy holy one, and saidst, I have laid help upon *one that is* mighty; I have exalted *one* chosen out of the people.

20I have found David my servant; with my holy oil have I anointed him:

21With whom my hand shall be established: mine arm also shall strengthen him.

22The enemy shall not exact upon him; nor the son of wickedness afflict him.

23And I will beat down his foes before his face, and plague them that hate him.

24But my faithfulness and my mercy *shall be* with him: and in my name shall his horn be exalted.

25I will set his hand also in the sea, and his right hand in the rivers.

26He shall cry unto me, Thou *art* my father, my God, and the rock of my salvation.

27Also I will make him *my* firstborn, higher than the kings of the earth.

28My mercy will I keep for him for evermore, and my covenant shall stand fast with him.

29His seed also will I make *to endure* for ever, and his throne as the days of heaven.

30If his children forsake my law, and walk not in my judgments;

31If they break my statutes, and keep not my commandments;

32Then will I visit their transgression with the rod, and their iniquity with stripes.

33Nevertheless my lovingkindness will I not utterly take from him, nor suffer my faithfulness to fail.

34My covenant will I not break, nor alter the thing that is gone out of my lips.

35Once have I sworn by my holiness that I will not lie unto David.

36His seed shall endure for ever, and his throne as the sun before me.

37It shall be established for ever as the moon, and *as* a faithful witness in heaven. Selah.

PROVERBS FOR TODAY/ 13:17–19

A wicked messenger falleth into mischief: but a faithful ambassador is health. □ *Poverty and shame* shall be to *him that refuseth instruction: but he that regardeth reproof shall be honoured.* □ *The desire accomplished is sweet to the soul: but* it is *abomination to fools to depart from evil.*

APRIL 22

JOSHUA 24:1–33

AND Joshua gathered all the tribes of Israel to Shechem, and called for the elders of Israel, and for their heads, and for their judges, and for their officers; and they presented themselves before God.

2And Joshua said unto all the people, Thus saith the LORD God of Israel, Your fathers dwelt on the other side of the flood in old time, *even* Terah, the father of Abraham, and the father of Nachor: and they served other gods.

3And I took your father Abraham from the other side of the flood, and led him throughout all the land of Canaan, and multiplied his seed, and gave him Isaac.

4And I gave unto Isaac Jacob and Esau: and I gave unto Esau mount Seir, to possess it; but Jacob and his children went down into Egypt.

5I sent Moses also and Aaron, and I plagued Egypt, according to that which

I did among them: and afterward I brought you out.

6And I brought your fathers out of Egypt: and ye came unto the sea; and the Egyptians pursued after your fathers with chariots and horsemen unto the Red sea.

7And when they cried unto the LORD, he put darkness between you and the Egyptians, and brought the sea upon them, and covered them; and your eyes have seen what I have done in Egypt: and ye dwelt in the wilderness a long season.

8And I brought you into the land of the Amorites, which dwelt on the other side Jordan; and they fought with you: and I gave them into your hand, that ye might possess their land; and I destroyed them from before you.

9Then Balak the son of Zippor, king of Moab, arose and warred against Israel, and sent and called Balaam the son of Beor to curse you:

10But I would not hearken unto Balaam; therefore he blessed you still: so I delivered you out of his hand.

11And ye went over Jordan, and came unto Jericho: and the men of Jericho fought against you, the Amorites, and the Perizzites, and the Canaanites, and the Hittites, and the Girgashites, the Hivites, and the Jebusites; and I delivered them into your hand.

12And I sent the hornet before you, which drave them out from before you, *even* the two kings of the Amorites; *but* not with thy sword, nor with thy bow.

13And I have given you a land for which ye did not labour, and cities which ye built not, and ye dwell in them; of the vineyards and oliveyards which ye planted not do ye eat.

14Now therefore fear the LORD, and serve him in sincerity and in truth: and put away the gods which your fathers served on the other side of the flood, and in Egypt; and serve ye the LORD.

15And if it seem evil unto you to serve the LORD, choose you this day whom ye will serve; whether the gods which your fathers served that *were* on the other side of the flood, or the gods of the Amorites, in whose land ye dwell: but as for me and my house, we will serve the LORD.

16And the people answered and said, God forbid that we should forsake the LORD, to serve other gods;

17For the LORD our God, he *it is* that brought us up and our fathers out of the land of Egypt, from the house of bondage, and which did those great signs in our sight, and preserved us in all the way wherein we went, and among all the people through whom we passed:

18And the LORD drave out from before us all the people, even the Amorites which dwelt in the land: *therefore* will we also serve the LORD; for he *is* our God.

19And Joshua said unto the people,

Ye cannot serve the LORD: for he *is* an holy God; he *is* a jealous God; he will not forgive your transgressions nor your sins.

20If ye forsake the LORD, and serve strange gods, then he will turn and do you hurt, and consume you, after that he hath done you good.

21And the people said unto Joshua, Nay; but we will serve the LORD.

22And Joshua said unto the people, Ye *are* witnesses against yourselves that ye have chosen you the LORD, to serve him. And they said, *We are* witnesses.

23Now therefore put away, *said he,* the strange gods which *are* among you, and incline your heart unto the LORD God of Israel.

24And the people said unto Joshua, The LORD our God will we serve, and his voice will we obey.

25So Joshua made a covenant with the people that day, and set them a statute and an ordinance in Shechem.

26And Joshua wrote these words in the book of the law of God, and took a great stone, and set it up there under an oak, that *was* by the sanctuary of the LORD.

27And Joshua said unto all the people, Behold, this stone shall be a witness unto us; for it hath heard all the words of the LORD which he spake unto us: it shall be therefore a witness unto you, lest ye deny your God.

28So Joshua let the people depart, every man unto his inheritance.

29And it came to pass after these things, that Joshua the son of Nun, the servant of the LORD, died, *being* an hundred and ten years old.

30And they buried him in the border of his inheritance in Timnath–serah, which *is* in mount Ephraim, on the north side of the hill of Gaash.

31And Israel served the LORD all the days of Joshua, and all the days of the elders that overlived Joshua, and which had known all the works of the LORD, that he had done for Israel.

32And the bones of Joseph, which the children of Israel brought up out of Egypt, buried they in Shechem, in a parcel of ground which Jacob bought of the sons of Hamor the father of Shechem for an hundred pieces of silver: and it became the inheritance of the children of Joseph.

33And Eleazar the son of Aaron died; and they buried him in a hill *that pertained* to Phinehas his son, which was given him in mount Ephraim.

LUKE 21:1–28

AND he [Jesus] looked up, and saw the rich men casting their gifts into the treasury.

2And he saw also a certain poor widow casting in thither two mites.

3And he said, Of a truth I say unto you, that this poor widow hath cast in more than they all:

4For all these have of their abundance cast in unto the offerings of God: but she of her penury hath cast in all the living that she had.

5And as some spake of the temple, how it was adorned with goodly stones and gifts, he said,

6*As for* these things which ye behold, the days will come, in the which there shall not be left one stone upon another, that shall not be thrown down.

7And they asked him, saying, Master, but when shall these things be? and what sign *will there be* when these things shall come to pass?

8And he said, Take heed that ye be not deceived: for many shall come in my name, saying, I am *Christ;* and the time draweth near: go ye not therefore after them.

9But when ye shall hear of wars and commotions, be not terrified: for these things must first come to pass; but the end *is* not by and by.

10Then said he unto them, Nation shall rise against nation, and kingdom against kingdom:

11And great earthquakes shall be in divers places, and famines, and pestilences; and fearful sights and great signs shall there be from heaven.

12But before all these, they shall lay their hands on you, and persecute *you,* delivering *you* up to the synagogues, and into prisons, being brought before kings and rulers for my name's sake.

13And it shall turn to you for a testimony.

14Settle *it* therefore in your hearts, not to meditate before what ye shall answer:

15For I will give you a mouth and wisdom, which all your adversaries shall not be able to gainsay nor resist.

16And ye shall be betrayed both by parents, and brethren, and kinsfolks, and friends; and *some* of you shall they cause to be put to death.

17And ye shall be hated of all *men* for my name's sake.

18But there shall not an hair of your head perish.

19In your patience possess ye your souls.

20And when ye shall see Jerusalem compassed with armies, then know that the desolation thereof is nigh.

21Then let them which are in Judaea flee to the mountains; and let them which are in the midst of it depart out; and let not them that are in the countries enter thereinto.

22For these be the days of vengeance, that all things which are written may be fulfilled.

23But woe unto them that are with child, and to them that give suck, in those days! for there shall be great distress in the land, and wrath upon this people.

24And they shall fall by the edge of the sword, and shall be led away captive into all nations: and Jerusalem shall be trodden down of the Gentiles, until the times of the Gentiles be fulfilled.

25And there shall be signs in the sun, and in the moon, and in the stars; and upon the earth distress of nations, with perplexity; the sea and the waves roaring;

26Men's hearts failing them for fear, and for looking after those things which are coming on the earth: for the powers of heaven shall be shaken.

27And then shall they see the Son of man coming in a cloud with power and great glory.

28And when these things begin to come to pass, then look up, and lift up your heads; for your redemption draweth nigh.

PSALM 89:38–52

BUT thou hast cast off and abhorred, thou hast been wroth with thine anointed.

39Thou hast made void the covenant of thy servant: thou hast profaned his crown *by casting it* to the ground.

40Thou hast broken down all his hedges; thou hast brought his strong holds to ruin.

41All that pass by the way spoil him: he is a reproach to his neighbours.

42Thou hast set up the right hand of his adversaries; thou hast made all his enemies to rejoice.

43Thou hast also turned the edge of his sword, and hast not made him to stand in the battle.

44Thou hast made his glory to cease, and cast his throne down to the ground.

45The days of his youth hast thou shortened: thou hast covered him with shame. Selah.

46How long, LORD? wilt thou hide thyself for ever? shall thy wrath burn like fire?

47Remember how short my time is: wherefore hast thou made all men in vain?

48What man *is he that* liveth, and shall not see death? shall he deliver his soul from the hand of the grave? Selah.

49Lord, where *are* thy former lovingkindnesses, *which* thou swarest unto David in thy truth?

50Remember, Lord, the reproach of thy servants; *how* I do bear in my bosom *the reproach of* all the mighty people;

51Wherewith thine enemies have reproached, O LORD; wherewith they have reproached the footsteps of thine anointed.

52Blessed *be* the LORD for evermore. Amen, and Amen.

PROVERBS FOR TODAY/ 13:20–23

He that walketh with wise men *shall be wise: but a companion of fools shall be destroyed.* ☐ *Evil pursueth sinners: but to the righteous good shall be repayed.* ☐ *A good* man *leaveth an inheritance to his children's children: and the wealth of the sinner* is *laid up for the just.* ☐ *Much food* is in *the tillage of the poor but there* is *that is destroyed for want of judgment.*

APRIL 23

JUDGES 1:1—2:10

Now after the death of Joshua it came to pass, that the children of Israel asked the LORD, saying, Who shall go up for us against the Canaanites first, to fight against them?

2And the LORD said, Judah shall go up: behold, I have delivered the land into his hand.

3And Judah said unto Simeon his brother, Come up with me into my lot, that we may fight against the Canaanites; and I likewise will go with thee into thy lot. So Simeon went with him.

4And Judah went up; and the LORD delivered the Canaanites and the Perizzites into their hand: and they slew of them in Bezek ten thousand men.

5And they found Adoni–bezek in Bezek: and they fought against him, and they slew the Canaanites and the Perizzites.

6But Adoni–bezek fled; and they pursued after him, and caught him, and cut off his thumbs and his great toes.

7And Adoni–bezek said, Threescore and ten kings, having their thumbs and their great toes cut off, gathered *their meat* under my table: as I have done, so God hath requited me. And they brought him to Jerusalem, and there he died.

8Now the children of Judah had fought against Jerusalem, and had taken it, and smitten it with the edge of the sword, and set the city on fire.

9And afterward the children of Judah went down to fight against the Canaanites, that dwelt in the mountain, and in the south, and in the valley.

10And Judah went against the Canaanites that dwelt in Hebron: (now the name of Hebron before *was* Kirjath–arba:) and they slew Sheshai, and Ahiman, and Talmai.

11And from thence he went against the inhabitants of Debir: and the name of Debir before *was* Kirjath–sepher:

12And Caleb said, He that smiteth Kirjath–sepher, and taketh it, to him will I give Achsah my daughter to wife.

13And Othniel the son of Kenaz, Caleb's younger brother, took it: and he gave him Achsah his daughter to wife.

14And it came to pass, when she came *to him,* that she moved him to ask of her father a field: and she lighted from off *her* ass; and Caleb said unto her, What wilt thou?

15And she said unto him, Give me a blessing: for thou has given me a south land; give me also springs of water. And Caleb gave her the upper springs and the nether springs.

16And the children of the Kenite, Moses' father in law, went up out of the city of palm trees with the children of Judah into the wilderness of Judah, which *lieth* in the south of Arad; and they went and dwelt among the people.

17And Judah went with Simeon his brother, and they slew the Canaanites that inhabited Zephath, and utterly destroyed it. And the name of the city was called Hormah.

18Also Judah took Gaza with the coast thereof, and Askelon with the coast thereof, and Ekron with the coast thereof.

19And the LORD was with Judah; and he drave out *the inhabitants of* the mountain; but could not drive out the inhabitants of the valley, because they had chariots of iron.

20And they gave Hebron unto Caleb, as Moses said: and he expelled thence the three sons of Anak.

21And the children of Benjamin did not drive out the Jebusites that inhabited Jerusalem; but the Jebusites dwell with the children of Benjamin in Jerusalem unto this day.

22And the house of Joseph, they also went up against Beth–el: and the LORD *was* with them.

23And the house of Joseph sent to descry Beth–el. (Now the name of the city before *was* Luz.)

24And the spies saw a man come forth out of the city, and they said unto him, Shew us, we pray thee, the entrance into the city, and we will shew thee mercy.

25And when he shewed them the entrance into the city, they smote the city with the edge of the sword; but they let go the man and all his family.

26And the man went into the land of the Hittites, and built a city, and called the name thereof Luz: which *is* the name thereof unto this day.

27Neither did Manasseh drive out *the inhabitants of* Beth–shean and her towns, nor Taanach and her towns, nor the inhabitants of Dor and her towns, nor the inhabitants of Ibleam and her towns, nor the inhabitants of Megiddo and her towns: but the Canaanites would dwell in that land.

28And it came to pass, when Israel was strong, that they put the Canaanites to tribute, and did not utterly drive them out.

29Neither did Ephraim drive out the Canaanites that dwelt in Gezer; but the Canaanites dwelt in Gezer among them.

30Neither did Zebulun drive out the inhabitants of Kitron, nor the inhabitants of Nahalol; but the Canaanites dwelt among them, and became tributaries.

31Neither did Asher drive out the inhabitants of Accho, nor the inhabitants of Zidon, nor Ahlab, nor Achzib, nor of Helbah, nor of Aphik, nor of Rehob:

32But the Asherites dwelt among the Canaanites, the inhabitants of the land: for they did not drive them out.

33Neither did Naphtali drive out the inhabitants of Beth–shemesh, nor the inhabitants of Beth–anath; but he dwelt among the Canaanites, the inhabitants of the land: nevertheless the inhabitants of Beth–shemesh and of Beth–anath became tributaries unto them.

34And the Amorites forced the children of Dan into the mountain: for they would not suffer them to come down to the valley:

35But the Amorites would dwell in mount Heres in Aijalon, and in Shaalbim: yet the hand of the house of Joseph prevailed, so that they became tributaries.

36And the coast of the Amorites *was* from the going up to Akrabbim, from the rock, and upward.

AND an angel of the LORD came up from Gilgal to Bochim, and said, I made you to go up out of Egypt, and have brought you unto the land which I sware unto your fathers; and I said, I will never break my covenant with you.

2And ye shall make no league with the inhabitants of this land; ye shall throw down their altars: but ye have not obeyed my voice: why have ye done this?

3Wherefore I also said, I will not drive them out from before you; but they shall be *as thorns* in your sides, and their gods shall be a snare unto you.

4And it came to pass, when the angel of the LORD spake these words unto all the children of Israel, that the people lifted up their voice, and wept.

5And they called the name of that place Bochim: and they sacrificed there unto the LORD.

6And when Joshua had let the people go, the children of Israel went every man unto his inheritance to possess the land.

7And the people served the LORD all the days of Joshua, and all the days of the elders that outlived Joshua, who had seen all the great works of the

LORD, that he did for Israel.

8And Joshua the son of Nun, the servant of the LORD, died, *being* an hundred and ten years old.

9And they buried him in the border of his inheritance in Timnath–heres, in the mount of Ephraim, on the north side of the hill Gaash.

10And also all that generation were gathered unto their fathers: and there arose another generation after them, which knew not the LORD, nor yet the works which he had done for Israel.

LUKE 21:29—22:13

AND he [Jesus] spake to them a parable; Behold the fig tree, and all the trees;

30When they now shoot forth, ye see and know of your own selves that summer is now nigh at hand.

31So likewise ye, when ye see these things come to pass, know ye that the kingdom of God is nigh at hand.

32Verily I say unto you, This generation shall not pass away, till all be fulfilled.

33Heaven and earth shall pass away: but my words shall not pass away.

34And take heed to yourselves, lest at any time your hearts be overcharged with surfeiting, and drunkenness, and cares of this life, and *so* that day come upon you unawares.

35For as a snare shall it come on all them that dwell on the face of the whole earth.

36Watch ye therefore, and pray always, that ye may be accounted worthy to escape all these things that shall come to pass, and to stand before the Son of man.

37And in the day time he was teaching in the temple; and at night he went out, and abode in the mount that is called *the mount* of Olives.

38And all the people came early in the morning to him in the temple, for to hear him.

Now the feast of unleavened bread drew nigh, which is called the Passover.

2And the chief priests and scribes sought how they might kill him; for they feared the people.

3Then entered Satan into Judas surnamed Iscariot, being of the number of the twelve.

4And he went his way, and communed with the chief priests and captains, how he might betray him unto them.

5And they were glad, and covenanted to give him money.

6And he promised, and sought opportunity to betray him unto them in the absence of the multitude.

7Then came the day of unleavened bread, when the passover must be killed.

8And he sent Peter and John, saying, Go and prepare us the passover, that we may eat.

9And they said unto him, Where wilt thou that we prepare?

10And he said unto them, Behold, when ye are entered into the city, there shall a man meet you, bearing a pitcher of water; follow him into the house where he entereth in.

11And ye shall say unto the goodman of the house, The Master saith unto thee, Where is the guestchamber, where I shall eat the passover with my disciples?

12And he shall shew you a large upper room furnished: there make ready.

13And they went, and found as he had said unto them: and they made ready the passover.

PSALM 90:1—91:16

LORD, thou hast been our dwelling place in all generations.

2Before the mountains were brought forth, or ever thou hadst formed the earth and the world, even from everlasting to everlasting, thou *art* God.

3Thou turnest man to destruction; and sayest, Return, ye children of men.

4For a thousand years in thy sight *are but* as yesterday when it is past, and *as* a watch in the night.

5Thou carriest them away as with a flood; they are *as* a sleep: in the morning *they are* like grass *which* groweth up.

6In the morning it flourisheth, and groweth up; in the evening it is cut down, and withereth.

7For we are consumed by thine anger, and by thy wrath are we troubled.

8Thou hast set our iniquities before thee, our secret *sins* in the light of thy countenance.

9For all our days are passed away in thy wrath: we spend our years as a tale *that is told*.

10The days of our years *are* threescore years and ten; and if by reason of strength *they be* fourscore years, yet *is* their strength labour and sorrow; for it is soon cut off, and we fly away.

11Who knoweth the power of thine anger? even according to thy fear, *so is* thy wrath.

12So teach *us* to number our days, that we may apply *our* hearts unto wisdom.

13Return, O LORD, how long? and let it repent thee concerning thy servants.

14O satisfy us early with thy mercy; that we may rejoice and be glad all our days.

15Make us glad according to the days *wherein* thou hast afflicted us, *and* the years *wherein* we have seen evil.

16Let thy work appear unto thy servants, and thy glory unto their children.

17And let the beauty of the LORD our God be upon us: and establish thou the work of our hands upon us; yea, the work of our hands establish thou it.

HE that dwelleth in the secret place of the most High shall abide under the shadow of the Almighty.

2I will say of the LORD, *He is* my refuge and my fortress: my God; in him will I trust.

3Surely he shall deliver thee from the snare of the fowler, *and* from the noisome pestilence.

4He shall cover thee with his feathers, and under his wings shalt thou trust: his truth *shall be thy* shield and buckler.

5Thou shalt not be afraid for the terror by night; *nor* for the arrow *that* flieth by day;

6*Nor* for the pestilence *that* walketh in darkness; *nor* for the destruction *that* wasteth at noonday.

7A thousand shall fall at thy side, and ten thousand at thy right hand; *but* it shall not come nigh thee.

8Only with thine eyes shalt thou behold and see the reward of the wicked.

9Because thou hast made the LORD, *which is* my refuge, *even* the most High, thy habitation;

10There shall no evil befall thee, neither shall any plague come nigh thy dwelling.

11For he shall give his angels charge over thee, to keep thee in all thy ways.

12They shall bear thee up in *their* hands, lest thou dash thy foot against a stone.

13Thou shalt tread upon the lion and adder: the young lion and the dragon shalt thou trample under feet.

14Because he hath set his love upon me, therefore will I deliver him: I will set him on high, because he hath known my name.

15He shall call upon me, and I will answer him: I *will be* with him in trouble; I will deliver him, and honour him.

16With long life will I satisfy him, and shew him my salvation.

PROVERBS FOR TODAY/ 13:24–25

He that spareth his rod hateth his son: but he that loveth him chasteneth him betimes. □ *The righteous eateth to the satisfying of his soul: but the belly of the wicked shall want.*

APRIL 24

JUDGES 2:11—3:31

AND the children of Israel did evil in the sight of the LORD, and served Baalim:

12And they forsook the LORD God of their fathers, which brought them out of the land of Egypt, and followed other gods, of the gods of the people that *were* round about them, and bowed themselves unto them, and provoked the LORD to anger.

13And they forsook the LORD, and served Baal and Ashtaroth.

14And the anger of the LORD was hot against Israel, and he delivered them into the hands of spoilers that spoiled them, and he sold them into the hands of their enemies round about, so that they could not any longer stand before their enemies.

15Whithersoever they went out, the hand of the LORD was against them for evil, as the LORD had said, and as the LORD had sworn unto them: and they were greatly distressed.

16Nevertheless the LORD raised up judges, which delivered them out of the hand of those that spoiled them.

17And yet they would not hearken unto their judges, but they went a whoring after other gods, and bowed themselves unto them: they turned quickly out of the way which their fathers walked in, obeying the commandments of the LORD; *but* they did not so.

18And when the LORD raised them up judges, then the LORD was with the judge, and delivered them out of the hand of their enemies all the days of the judge: for it repented the LORD because of their groanings by reason of them that oppressed them and vexed them.

19And it came to pass, when the judge was dead, *that* they returned, and corrupted *themselves* more than their fathers, in following other gods to serve them, and to bow down unto them; they ceased not from their own doings, nor from their stubborn way.

20And the anger of the LORD was hot against Israel; and he said, Because that this people hath transgressed my covenant which I commanded their fathers, and have not hearkened unto my voice;

21I also will not henceforth drive out any from before them of the nations which Joshua left when he died:

22That through them I may prove Israel, whether they will keep the way of the LORD to walk therein, as their fathers did keep *it,* or not.

23Therefore the LORD left those nations, without driving them out hastily; neither delivered he them into the hand of Joshua.

Now these *are* the nations which the LORD left, to prove Israel by them, *even* as many *of Israel* as had not known all the wars of Canaan;

2Only that the generations of the children of Israel might know, to teach them war, at the least such as before knew nothing thereof;

3*Namely,* five lords of the Philistines, and all the Canaanites, and the Sidonians, and the Hivites that dwelt in mount Lebanon, from mount Baal–hermon unto the entering in of Hamath.

4And they were to prove Israel by them, to know whether they would hearken unto the commandments of the LORD, which he commanded their fathers by the hand of Moses.

5And the children of Israel dwelt among the Canaanites, Hittites, and Amorites, and Perizzites, and Hivites, and Jebusites:

6And they took their daughters to be their wives, and gave their daughters to their sons, and served their gods.

7And the children of Israel did evil in the sight of the LORD, and forgat the LORD their God, and served Baalim and the groves.

8Therefore the anger of the LORD was hot against Israel, and he sold them into the hand of Chushan–rishathaim king of Mesopotamia: and the children of Israel served Chushan–rishathaim eight years.

9And when the children of Israel cried unto the LORD, the LORD raised up a deliverer to the children of Israel, who delivered them, *even* Othniel the son of Kenaz, Caleb's younger brother.

10And the Spirit of the LORD came upon him, and he judged Israel, and went out to war: and the LORD delivered Chushan–rishathaim king of Mesopotamia into his hand; and his hand prevailed against Chushan–rishathaim.

11And the land had rest forty years. And Othniel the son of Kenaz died.

12And the children of Israel did evil again in the sight of the LORD: and the LORD strengthened Eglon the king of Moab against Israel, because they had done evil in the sight of the LORD.

13And he gathered unto him the children of Ammon and Amalek, and went and smote Israel, and possessed the city of palm trees.

14So the children of Israel served Eglon the king of Moab eighteen years.

15But when the children of Israel cried unto the LORD, the LORD raised them up a deliverer, Ehud the son of Gera, a Benjamite, a man left-handed: and by him the children of Israel sent a present unto Eglon the king of Moab.

16But Ehud made him a dagger which had two edges, of a cubit length; and he did gird it under his raiment upon his right thigh.

17And he brought the present unto Eglon king of Moab: and Eglon *was* a very fat man.

18And when he had made an end to offer the present, he sent away the people that bare the present.

19But he himself turned again from the quarries that *were* by Gilgal, and said, I have a secret errand unto thee, O king: who said, Keep silence. And all that stood by him went out from him.

20And Ehud came unto him; and he was sitting in a summer parlour, which he had for himself alone. And Ehud said, I have a message from God unto thee. And he arose out of *his* seat.

21And Ehud put forth his left hand, and took the dagger from his right thigh, and thrust it into his belly:

22And the haft also went in after the blade; and the fat closed upon the blade, so that he could not draw the dagger out of his belly; and the dirt came out.

23Then Ehud went forth through the porch, and shut the doors of the parlour upon him, and locked them.

24When he was gone out, his servants came; and when they saw that, behold, the doors of the parlour *were* locked, they said, Surely he covereth his feet in his summer chamber.

25And they tarried till they were ashamed: and, behold, he opened not the doors of the parlour; therefore they took a key, and opened *them:* and, behold, their lord *was* fallen down dead on the earth.

26And Ehud escaped while they tarried, and passed beyond the quarries, and escaped unto Seirath.

27And it came to pass, when he was come, that he blew a trumpet in the mountain of Ephraim, and the children of Israel went down with him from the mount, and he before them.

28And he said unto them, Follow after me: for the LORD hath delivered your enemies the Moabites into your hand. And they went down after him, and took the fords of Jordan toward Moab, and suffered not a man to pass over.

29And they slew of Moab at that time about ten thousand men, all lusty, and all men of valour; and there escaped not a man.

30So Moab was subdued that day under the hand of Israel. And the land had rest fourscore years.

31And after him was Shamgar the son of Anath, which slew of the Philistines six hundred men with an ox goad: and he also delivered Israel.

LUKE 22:14–34

A ND when the hour was come, he [Jesus] sat down, and the twelve apostles with him.

15And he said unto them, With desire I have desired to eat this passover with you before I suffer:

16For I say unto you, I will not any more eat thereof, until it be fulfilled in the kingdom of God.

17And he took the cup, and gave thanks, and said, Take this, and divide *it* among yourselves:

18For I say unto you, I will not drink of the fruit of the vine, until the kingdom of God shall come.

19And he took bread, and gave thanks, and brake *it,* and gave unto them, saying, This is my body which is given for you: this do in remembrance of me.

20Likewise also the cup after supper, saying, This cup *is* the new testament in my blood, which is shed for you.

21But, behold, the hand of him that betrayeth me *is* with me on the table.

22And truly the Son of man goeth, as it was determined: but woe unto that man by whom he is betrayed!

23And they began to enquire among themselves, which of them it was that should do this thing.

24And there was also a strife among them, which of them should be accounted the greatest.

25And he said unto them, The kings of the Gentiles exercise lordship over them; and they that exercise authority upon them are called benefactors.

26But ye *shall* not *be* so: but he that is greatest among you, let him be as the younger; and he that is chief, as he that doth serve.

27For whether *is* greater, he that sitteth at meat, or he that serveth? *is* not he that sitteth at meat? but I am among you as he that serveth.

28Ye are they which have continued with me in my temptations.

29And I appoint unto you a kingdom, as my Father hath appointed unto me;

30That ye may eat and drink at my table in my kingdom, and sit on thrones judging the twelve tribes of Israel.

31And the Lord said, Simon, Simon, behold, Satan hath desired *to have* you, that he may sift *you* as wheat:

32But I have prayed for thee, that thy faith fail not: and when thou art converted, strengthen thy brethren.

33And he said unto him, Lord, I am ready to go with thee, both into prison, and to death.

34And he said, I tell thee, Peter, the cock shall not crow this day, before that thou shalt thrice deny that thou knowest me.

PSALM 92:1—93:5

*I*T is a good *thing* to give thanks unto the LORD, and to sing praises unto thy name, O most High:

2To shew forth thy lovingkindness in the morning, and thy faithfulness every night,

3Upon an instrument of ten strings, and upon the psaltery; upon the harp with a solemn sound.

4For thou, LORD, hast made me glad through thy work: I will triumph in the works of thy hands.

5O LORD, how great are thy works! *and* thy thoughts are very deep.

6A brutish man knoweth not; neither doth a fool understand this.

7When the wicked spring as the grass, and when all the workers of iniquity do flourish; *it is* that they shall be destroyed for ever:

8But thou, LORD, *art most* high for evermore.

9For, lo, thine enemies, O LORD, for, lo, thine enemies shall perish; all the workers of iniquity shall be scattered.

10But my horn shalt thou exalt like *the horn of* an unicorn: I shall be anointed with fresh oil.

11Mine eye also shall see *my desire* on mine enemies, *and* mine ears shall hear *my desire* of the wicked that rise up against me.

12The righteous shall flourish like the palm tree: he shall grow like a cedar in Lebanon.

13Those that be planted in the house of the LORD shall flourish in the courts of our God.

14They shall still bring forth fruit in old age; they shall be fat and flourishing;

15To shew that the LORD *is* upright: *he is* my rock, and *there is* no unrighteousness in him.

THE LORD reigneth, he is clothed with majesty; the LORD is clothed with strength, *wherewith* he hath girded himself: the world also is stablished, that it cannot be moved.

2Thy throne *is* established of old: thou *art* from everlasting.

3The floods have lifted up, O LORD, the floods have lifted up their voice; the floods lift up their waves.

4The LORD on high *is* mightier than the noise of many waters, *yea, than* the mighty waves of the sea.

5Thy testimonies are very sure: holiness becometh thine house, O LORD, for ever.

PROVERBS FOR TODAY/ 14:1–2

Every wise woman buildeth her house: but the foolish plucketh it down with her hands. □ *He that walketh in his uprightness feareth the LORD: but* he that is *perverse in his ways despiseth him.*

APRIL 25

JUDGES 4:1—5:31

AND the children of Israel again did evil in the sight of the LORD, when Ehud was dead.

2And the LORD sold them into the hand of Jabin king of Canaan, that reigned in Hazor; the captain of whose host *was* Sisera, which dwelt in Harosheth of the Gentiles.

3And the children of Israel cried unto

the LORD: for he had nine hundred chariots of iron; and twenty years he mightily oppressed the children of Israel.

4And Deborah, a prophetess, the wife of Lapidoth, she judged Israel at that time.

5And she dwelt under the palm tree of Deborah between Ramah and Beth–el in mount Ephraim: and the children of Israel came up to her for judgment.

6And she sent and called Barak the son of Abinoam out of Kedesh–naphtali, and said unto him, Hath not the LORD God of Israel commanded, *saying*, Go and draw toward mount Tabor, and take with thee ten thousand men of the children of Naphtali and of the children of Zebulun?

7And I will draw unto thee to the river Kishon Sisera, the captain of Jabin's army, with his chariots and his multitude; and I will deliver him into thine hand.

8And Barak said unto her, If thou wilt go with me, then I will go: but if thou wilt not go with me, *then* I will not go.

9And she said, I will surely go with thee: notwithstanding the journey that thou takest shall not be for thine honour; for the LORD shall sell Sisera into the hand of a woman. And Deborah arose, and went with Barak to Kedesh.

10And Barak called Zebulun and Naphtali to Kedesh; and he went up with ten thousand men at his feet: and Deborah went up with him.

11Now Heber the Kenite, *which was* of the children of Hobab the father in law of Moses, had severed himself from the Kenites, and pitched his tent unto the plain of Zaanaim, which *is* by Kedesh.

12And they shewed Sisera that Barak the son of Abinoam was gone up to mount Tabor.

13And Sisera gathered together all his chariots, *even* nine hundred chariots of iron, and all the people that *were* with him, from Harosheth of the Gentiles unto the river of Kishon.

14And Deborah said unto Barak, Up; for this *is* the day in which the LORD hath delivered Sisera into thine hand: is not the LORD gone out before thee? So Barak went down from mount Tabor, and ten thousand men after him.

15And the LORD discomfited Sisera, and all *his* chariots, and all *his* host, with the edge of the sword before Barak; so that Sisera lighted down off *his* chariot, and fled away on his feet.

16But Barak pursued after the chariots, and after the host, unto Harosheth of the Gentiles: and all the host of Sisera fell upon the edge of the sword; *and* there was not a man left.

17Howbeit Sisera fled away on his feet to the tent of Jael the wife of Heber the Kenite: for *there was* peace between Jabin the king of Hazor and the house of Heber the Kenite.

18And Jael went out to meet Sisera, and said unto him, Turn in, my lord, turn in to me; fear not. And when he had turned in unto her into the tent, she covered him with a mantle.

19And he said unto her, Give me, I pray thee, a little water to drink; for I am thirsty. And she opened a bottle of milk, and gave him drink, and covered him.

20Again he said unto her, Stand in the door of the tent, and it shall be, when any man doth come and enquire of thee, and say, Is there any man here? that thou shalt say, No.

21Then Jael Heber's wife took a nail of the tent, and took an hammer in her hand, and went softly unto him, and smote the nail into his temples, and fastened it into the ground: for he was fast asleep and weary. So he died.

22And, behold, as Barak pursued Sisera, Jael came out to meet him, and said unto him, Come, and I will shew thee the man whom thou seekest. And when he came into her *tent,* behold, Sisera lay dead, and the nail *was* in his temples.

23So God subdued on that day Jabin the king of Canaan before the children of Israel.

24And the hand of the children of Israel prospered, and prevailed against Jabin the king of Canaan, until they had destroyed Jabin king of Canaan.

THEN sang Deborah and Barak the son of Abinoam on that day, saying,

2Praise ye the LORD for the avenging of Israel, when the people willingly offered themselves.

3Hear, O ye kings; give ear, O ye princes; I, *even* I, will sing unto the LORD; I will sing *praise* to the LORD God of Israel.

4LORD, when thou wentest out of Seir, when thou marchedst out of the field of Edom, the earth trembled, and the heavens dropped, the clouds also dropped water.

5The mountains melted from before the LORD, *even* that Sinai from before the LORD God of Israel.

6In the days of Shamgar the son of Anath, in the days of Jael, the highways were unoccupied, and the travellers walked through byways.

7*The inhabitants of* the villages ceased, they ceased in Israel, until that I Deborah arose, that I arose a mother in Israel.

8They chose new gods; then *was* war in the gates: was there a shield or spear seen among forty thousand in Israel?

9My heart *is* toward the governors of Israel, that offered themselves willingly among the people. Bless ye the LORD.

10Speak, ye that ride on white asses, ye that sit in judgment, and walk by the way.

11*They that are delivered* from the noise of archers in the places of drawing water, there shall they rehearse the righteous acts of the LORD, *even* the righteous acts *toward the inhabitants* of his villages in Israel: then shall the people of the LORD go down to the gates.

12Awake, awake, Deborah: awake, awake, utter a song: arise, Barak, and lead thy captivity captive, thou son of Abinoam.

13Then he made him that remaineth have dominion over the nobles among the people: the LORD made me have dominion over the mighty.

14Out of Ephraim *was there* a root of them against Amalek; after thee, Benjamin, among thy people; out of Machir came down governors, and out of Zebulun they that handle the pen of the writer.

15And the princes of Issachar *were* with Deborah; even Issachar, and also Barak: he was sent on foot into the valley. For the divisions of Reuben *there were* great thoughts of heart.

16Why abodest thou among the sheepfolds, to hear the bleatings of the flocks? For the divisions of Reuben *there were* great searchings of heart.

17Gilead abode beyond Jordan: and why did Dan remain in ships? Asher continued on the sea shore, and abode in his breaches.

18Zebulun and Naphtali *were* a people *that* jeoparded their lives unto the death in the high places of the field.

19The kings came *and* fought, then fought the kings of Canaan in Taanach by the waters of Megiddo; they took no gain of money.

20They fought from heaven; the stars in their courses fought against Sisera.

21The river of Kishon swept them away, that ancient river, the river Kishon. O my soul, thou hast trodden down strength.

22Then were the horsehoofs broken by the means of the pransings, the pransings of their mighty ones.

23Curse ye Meroz, said the angel of the LORD, curse ye bitterly the inhabitants thereof; because they came not to the help of the LORD, to the help of the LORD against the mighty.

24Blessed above women shall Jael the wife of Heber the Kenite be, blessed shall she be above women in the tent.

25He asked water, *and* she gave *him* milk; she brought forth butter in a lordly dish.

26She put her hand to the nail, and her right hand to the workmen's hammer; and with the hammer she smote Sisera, she smote off his head, when she had pierced and stricken through his temples.

27At her feet he bowed, he fell, he lay down: at her feet he bowed, he fell: where he bowed, there he fell down dead.

28The mother of Sisera looked out at a window, and cried through the lattice, Why is his chariot *so* long in coming? why tarry the wheels of his chariots?

29Her wise ladies answered her, yea, she returned answer to herself,

30Have they not sped? have they *not* divided the prey; to every man a damsel *or* two; to Sisera a prey of divers colours, a prey of divers colours of needlework, of divers colours of needlework on both sides, *meet* for the necks of *them that take* the spoil?

31So let all thine enemies perish, O LORD: but *let* them that love him *be* as the sun when he goeth forth in his might. And the land had rest forty years.

LUKE 22:35–54

AND he [Jesus] said unto them, When I sent you without purse, and scrip, and shoes, lacked ye any thing? And they said, Nothing.

36Then said he unto them, But now, he that hath a purse, let him take *it,* and likewise *his* scrip: and he that hath no sword, let him sell his garment, and buy one.

37For I say unto you, that this that is written must yet be accomplished in me, And he was reckoned among the transgressors: for the things concerning me have an end.

38And they said, Lord, behold, here *are* two swords. And he said unto them, It is enough.

39And he came out, and went, as he was wont, to the mount of Olives; and his disciples also followed him.

40And when he was at the place, he said unto them, Pray that ye enter not into temptation.

41And he was withdrawn from them about a stone's cast, and kneeled down, and prayed,

42Saying, Father, if thou be willing, remove this cup from me: nevertheless not my will, but thine, be done.

43And there appeared an angel unto him from heaven, strengthening him.

44And being in an agony he prayed more earnestly: and his sweat was as it were great drops of blood falling down to the ground.

45And when he rose up from prayer, and was come to his disciples, he found them sleeping for sorrow,

46And said unto them, Why sleep ye? rise and pray, lest ye enter into temptation.

47And while he yet spake, behold a multitude, and he that was called Judas, one of the twelve, went before them, and drew near unto Jesus to kiss him.

48But Jesus said unto him, Judas, betrayest thou the Son of man with a kiss?

49When they which were about him saw what would follow, they said unto him, Lord, shall we smite with the sword?

50And one of them smote the servant of the high priest, and cut off his right ear.

51And Jesus answered and said, Suffer ye thus far. And he touched his ear, and healed him.

52Then Jesus said unto the chief priests, and captains of the temple, and the elders, which were come to him, Be ye come out, as against a thief, with swords and staves?

53When I was daily with you in the temple, ye stretched forth no hands against me: but this is your hour, and the power of darkness.

54Then took they him, and led *him,* and brought him into the high priest's house. And Peter followed afar off.

PSALM 94:1–23

O LORD God, to whom vengeance belongeth; O God, to whom vengeance belongeth, shew thyself.

2Lift up thyself, thou judge of the earth: render a reward to the proud.

3LORD, how long shall the wicked, how long shall the wicked triumph?

4*How long* shall they utter *and* speak hard things? *and* all the workers of iniquity boast themselves?

5They break in pieces thy people, O LORD, and afflict thine heritage.

6They slay the widow and the stranger, and murder the fatherless.

7Yet they say, the LORD shall not see, neither shall the God of Jacob regard *it.*

8Understand, ye brutish among the people: and *ye* fools, when will ye be wise?

9He that planted the ear, shall he not hear? he that formed the eye, shall he not see?

10He that chastiseth the heathen, shall not he correct? he that teacheth man knowledge, *shall not he know?*

11The LORD knoweth the thoughts of man, that they *are* vanity.

12Blessed *is* the man whom thou chastenest, O LORD, and teachest him out of thy law;

13That thou mayest give him rest from the days of adversity, until the pit be digged for the wicked.

14For the LORD will not cast off his people, neither will he forsake his inheritance.

15But judgment shall return unto righteousness: and all the upright in heart shall follow it.

16Who will rise up for me against the evildoers? *or* who will stand up for me against the workers of iniquity?

17Unless the LORD *had been* my help, my soul had almost dwelt in silence.

18When I said, My foot slippeth; thy mercy, O LORD, held me up.

19In the multitude of my thoughts within me thy comforts delight my soul.

20Shall the throne of iniquity have fellowship with thee, which frameth mischief by a law?

21They gather themselves together against the soul of the righteous, and condemn the innocent blood.

22But the LORD is my defence; and my God *is* the rock of my refuge.

23And he shall bring upon them their own iniquity, and shall cut them off in their own wickedness; *yea,* the LORD our God shall cut them off.

PROVERBS FOR TODAY/ 14:3–4

In the mouth of the foolish is *a rod of pride: but the lips of the wise shall preserve them.*   □ *Where no oxen* are, *the crib* is *clean: but much increase* is *by the strength of the ox.*

APRIL 26

JUDGES 6:1–40

And the children of Israel did evil in the sight of the LORD: and the LORD delivered them into the hand of Midian seven years.

2And the hand of Midian prevailed against Israel: *and* because of the Midianites the children of Israel made them the dens which *are* in the mountains, and caves, and strong holds.

3And *so* it was, when Israel had sown, that the Midianites came up, and the Amalekites, and the children of the east, even they came up against them;

4And they encamped against them, and destroyed the increase of the earth, till thou come unto Gaza, and left no sustenance for Israel, neither sheep, nor ox, nor ass.

5For they came up with their cattle and their tents, and they came as grasshoppers for multitude; *for* both they and their camels were without number: and they entered into the land to destroy it.

6And Israel was greatly impoverished because of the Midianites; and the children of Israel cried unto the LORD.

7And it came to pass, when the children of Israel cried unto the LORD because of the Midianites,

8That the LORD sent a prophet unto the children of Israel, which said unto them, Thus saith the LORD God of Israel, I brought you up from Egypt, and brought you forth out of the house of bondage;

9And I delivered you out of the hand of the Egyptians, and out of the hand of all that oppressed you, and drave them out from before you, and gave you their land;

10And I said unto you, I *am* the LORD your God; fear not the gods of the Amorites, in whose land ye dwell: but ye have not obeyed my voice.

11And there came an angel of the LORD, and sat under an oak which *was* in Ophrah, that *pertained* unto Joash the Abi–ezrite: and his son Gideon threshed wheat by the winepress, to hide *it* from the Midianites.

12And the angel of the LORD appeared unto him, and said unto him, The LORD *is* with thee, thou mighty man of valour.

13And Gideon said unto him, Oh my Lord, if the LORD be with us, why then is all this befallen us? and where *be* all his miracles which our fathers told us of, saying, Did not the LORD bring us up from Egypt? but now the LORD hath forsaken us, and delivered us into the hands of the Midianites.

14And the LORD looked upon him, and said, Go in this thy might, and thou shalt save Israel from the hand of the Midianites: have not I sent thee?

15And he said unto him, Oh my Lord, wherewith shall I save Israel? behold, my family *is* poor in Manasseh, and I *am* the least in my father's house.

16And the LORD said unto him, Surely I will be with thee, and thou shalt smite the Midianites as one man.

17And he said unto him, If now I have found grace in thy sight, then shew me a sign that thou talkest with me.

18Depart not hence, I pray thee, until I come unto thee, and bring forth my present, and set *it* before thee. And he said, I will tarry until thou come again.

19And Gideon went in, and made ready a kid, and unleavened cakes of an ephah of flour: the flesh he put in a basket, and he put the broth in a pot, and brought *it* out unto him under the oak, and presented *it*.

20And the angel of God said unto him, Take the flesh and the unleavened cakes, and lay *them* upon this rock, and pour out the broth. And he did so.

21Then the angel of the LORD put forth the end of the staff that *was* in his hand, and touched the flesh and the unleavened cakes; and there rose up fire out of the rock, and consumed the flesh and the unleavened cakes. Then the angel of the LORD departed out of his sight.

22And when Gideon perceived that he *was* an angel of the LORD, Gideon said, Alas, O Lord GOD! for because I have seen an angel of the LORD face to face.

23And the LORD said unto him, Peace *be* unto thee; fear not: thou shalt not die.

24Then Gideon built an altar there unto the LORD, and called it Jehovah–shalom: unto this day it *is* yet in Ophrah of the Abi–ezrites.

25And it came to pass the same night, that the LORD said unto him, Take thy father's young bullock, even the second bullock of seven years old, and throw down the altar of Baal that thy father hath, and cut down the grove that *is* by it:

26And build an altar unto the LORD thy God upon the top of this rock, in the ordered place, and take the second bullock, and offer a burnt sacrifice with the wood of the grove which thou shalt cut down.

27Then Gideon took ten men of his servants, and did as the LORD had said unto him: and *so* it was, because he feared his father's household, and the men of the city, that he could not do *it* by day, that he did *it* by night.

28And when the men of the city arose early in the morning, behold, the altar of Baal was cast down, and the grove was cut down that *was* by it, and the second bullock was offered upon the altar *that was* built.

29And they said one to another, Who hath done this thing? And when they enquired and asked, they said, Gideon the son of Joash hath done this thing.

30Then the men of the city said unto Joash, Bring out thy son, that he may die: because he hath cast down the altar of Baal, and because he hath cut down the grove that *was* by it.

31And Joash said unto all that stood against him, Will ye plead for Baal? will ye save him? he that will plead for him, let him be put to death whilst *it is yet* morning: if he *be* a god, let him plead for himself, because *one* hath cast down his altar.

32Therefore on that day he called him Jerubbaal, saying, Let Baal plead against him, because he hath thrown down his altar.

33Then all the Midianites and the Amalekites and the children of the east were gathered together, and went over, and pitched in the valley of Jezreel.

34But the Spirit of the LORD came upon Gideon, and he blew a trumpet; and Abi–ezer was gathered after him.

35And he sent messengers throughout all Manasseh; who also was gathered after him: and he sent messengers unto Asher, and unto Zebulun, and unto Naphtali; and they came up to meet them.

36And Gideon said unto God, If thou wilt save Israel by mine hand, as thou hast said,

37Behold, I will put a fleece of wool in the floor; *and* if the dew be on the fleece only, and *it be* dry upon all the earth *beside,* then shall I know that thou wilt save Israel by mine hand, as thou hast said.

38And it was so: for he rose up early on the morrow, and thrust the fleece together, and wringed the dew out of the fleece, a bowl full of water.

39And Gideon said unto God, Let not thine anger be hot against me, and I will speak but this once: let me prove, I pray thee, but this once with the fleece; let it now be dry only upon the fleece, and upon all the ground let there be dew.

40And God did so that night: for it was dry upon the fleece only, and there was dew on all the ground.

LUKE 22:55—23:10

AND when they had kindled a fire in the midst of the hall, and were set down together, Peter sat down among them.

56But a certain maid beheld him as he sat by the fire, and earnestly looked upon him, and said, This man was also with him.

57And he denied him, saying, Woman, I know him not.

58And after a little while another saw him, and said, Thou art also of them. And Peter said, Man, I am not.

59And about the space of one hour after another confidently affirmed, saying, Of a truth this *fellow* also was with him: for he is a Galilaean.

60And Peter said, Man, I know not what thou sayest. And immediately, while he yet spake, the cock crew.

61And the Lord turned, and looked upon Peter. And Peter remembered the word of the Lord, how he had said unto him, Before the cock crow, thou shalt deny me thrice.

62And Peter went out and wept bitterly.

63And the men that held Jesus mocked him, and smote him.

64And when they had blindfolded him, they struck him on the face, and asked him, saying, Prophesy, who is it that smote thee?

65And many other things blasphemously spake they against him.

66And as soon as it was day, the elders of the people and the chief priests and the scribes came together, and led him into their council, saying,

67Art thou the Christ? tell us. And he said unto them, If I tell you, ye will not believe:

68And if I also ask *you*, ye will not answer me, nor let *me* go.

69Hereafter shall the Son of man sit on the right hand of the power of God.

70Then said they all, Art thou then the Son of God? And he said unto them, Ye say that I am.

71And they said, What need we any further witness? for we ourselves have heard of his own mouth.

AND the whole multitude of them arose, and led him unto Pilate.

2And they began to accuse him, saying, We found this *fellow* perverting the nation, and forbidding to give tribute to Caesar, saying that he himself is Christ a King.

3And Pilate asked him, saying, Art thou the King of the Jews? And he answered him and said, Thou sayest *it.*

4Then said Pilate to the chief priests and *to* the people, I find no fault in this man.

5And they were the more fierce, saying, He stirreth up the people, teaching throughout all Jewry, beginning from Galilee to this place.

6When Pilate heard of Galilee, he asked whether the man were a Galilaean.

7And as soon as he knew that he belonged unto Herod's jurisdiction, he sent him to Herod, who himself also was at Jerusalem at that time.

8And when Herod saw Jesus, he was exceeding glad: for he was desirous to see him of a long *season,* because he had heard many things of him; and he hoped to have seen some miracle done by him.

9Then he questioned with him in many words; but he answered him nothing.

10And the chief priests and scribes stood and vehemently accused him.

PSALM 95:1—96:13

O COME, let us sing unto the LORD: let us make a joyful noise to the rock of our salvation.

2Let us come before his presence with thanksgiving, and make a joyful noise unto him with psalms.

3For the LORD *is* a great God, and a great King above all gods.

4In his hand *are* the deep places of the earth: the strength of the hills *is* his also.

5The sea *is* his, and he made it: and his hands formed the dry *land.*

6O come, let us worship and bow down: let us kneel before the LORD our maker.

7For he *is* our God; and we *are* the people of his pasture, and the sheep of his hand. To day if ye will hear his voice,

8Harden not your heart, as in the provocation, *and* as *in* the day of temptation in the wilderness:

9When your fathers tempted me, proved me, and saw my work.

10Forty years long was I grieved with *this* generation, and said, It *is* a people that do err in their heart, and they have not known my ways:

11Unto whom I sware in my wrath that they should not enter into my rest.

O SING unto the LORD a new song: sing unto the LORD, all the earth.

2Sing unto the LORD, bless his name; shew forth his salvation from day to day.

3Declare his glory among the heathen, his wonders among all people.

4For the LORD *is* great, and greatly to be praised: he *is* to be feared above all gods.

5For all the gods of the nations *are* idols: but the LORD made the heavens.

6Honour and majesty *are* before him: strength and beauty *are* in his sanctuary.

7Give unto the LORD, O ye kindreds of the people, give unto the LORD glory and strength.

8Give unto the LORD the glory *due unto* his name: bring an offering, and come into his courts.

9O worship the LORD in the beauty of holiness: fear before him, all the earth.

10Say among the heathen *that* the LORD reigneth: the world also shall be established that it shall not be moved: he shall judge the people righteously.

11Let the heavens rejoice, and let the earth be glad; let the sea roar, and the fulness thereof.

12Let the field be joyful, and all that *is* therein: then shall all the trees of the wood rejoice

13Before the LORD: for he cometh, for he cometh to judge the earth: he shall judge the world with righteousness, and the people with his truth.

PROVERBS FOR TODAY/ 14:5–6

A faithful witness will not lie: but a false witness will utter lies. □*A scorner seeketh wisdom, and* findeth it *not: but knowledge* is *easy unto him that understandeth.*

APRIL 27

JUDGES 7:1—8:16

THEN Jerubbaal, who *is* Gideon, and all the people that *were* with him, rose up early, and pitched beside the well of Harod: so that the host of the Midianites were on the north side of them, by the hill of Moreh, in the valley.

2And the LORD said unto Gideon, The people that *are* with thee *are* too many for me to give the Midianites into their hands, lest Israel vaunt themselves against me, saying, Mine own hand hath saved me.

3Now therefore go to, proclaim in the ears of the people, saying, Whosoever *is* fearful and afraid, let him return and depart early from mount Gilead. And there returned of the people twenty and two thousand; and there remained ten thousand.

4And the LORD said unto Gideon, The people *are* yet *too* many; bring them down unto the water, and I will try them for thee there: and it shall be, *that* of whom I say unto thee, This shall go with thee, the same shall go with thee; and of whomsoever I say unto thee, This shall not go with thee, the same shall not go.

5So he brought down the people unto the water: and the LORD said unto Gideon, Every one that lappeth of the water with his tongue, as a dog lappeth, him shalt thou set by himself; likewise every one that boweth down upon his knees to drink.

6And the number of them that lapped, *putting* their hand to their mouth, were three hundred men: but all the rest of the people bowed down upon their knees to drink water.

7And the LORD said unto Gideon, By the three hundred men that lapped will I save you, and deliver the Midianites into thine hand: and let all the *other* people go every man unto his place.

8So the people took victuals in their hand, and their trumpets: and he sent all *the rest of* Israel every man unto his tent, and retained those three hundred men: and the host of Midian was beneath him in the valley.

9And it came to pass the same night, that the LORD said unto him, Arise, get thee down unto the host; for I have delivered it into thine hand.

10But if thou fear to go down, go thou with Phurah thy servant down to the host:

11And thou shalt hear what they say; and afterward shall thine hands be strengthened to go down unto the host. Then went he down with Phurah his servant unto the outside of the armed men that *were* in the host.

12And the Midianites and the Amalekites and all the children of the east lay along in the valley like grasshoppers for multitude; and their camels *were* without number, as the sand by the sea side for multitude.

13And when Gideon was come, behold, *there was* a man that told a dream unto his fellow, and said, Behold, I dreamed a dream, and, lo, a cake of barley bread tumbled into the host of Midian, and came unto a tent, and smote it that it fell, and overturned it, that the tent lay along.

14And his fellow answered and said, This *is* nothing else save the sword of Gideon the son of Joash, a man of Israel: *for* into his hand hath God delivered Midian, and all the host.

15And it was *so*, when Gideon heard the telling of the dream, and the interpretation thereof, that he worshipped, and returned into the host of Israel, and said, Arise; for the LORD hath delivered into your hand the host of Midian.

16And he divided the three hundred men *into* three companies, and he put a trumpet in every man's hand, with empty pitchers, and lamps within the pitchers.

17And he said unto them, Look on me, and do likewise: and, behold, when I come to the outside of the camp, it shall be *that,* as I do, so shall ye do.

18When I blow with a trumpet, I and all that *are* with me, then blow ye the trumpets also on every side of all the camp, and say, *The sword* of the LORD, and of Gideon.

19So Gideon, and the hundred men that *were* with him, came unto the outside of the camp in the beginning of the middle watch; and they had but newly set the watch: and they blew the trumpets, and brake the pitchers that *were* in their hands.

20And the three companies blew the trumpets, and brake the pitchers, and held the lamps in their left hands, and the trumpets in their right hands to blow *withal:* and they cried, The sword of the LORD, and of Gideon.

21And they stood every man in his place round about the camp: and all the host ran, and cried, and fled.

22And the three hundred blew the trumpets, and the LORD set every man's sword against his fellow, even throughout all the host: and the host fled to Beth–shittah in Zererath, *and* to the border of Abel–meholah, unto Tabbath.

23And the men of Israel gathered themselves together out of Naphtali, and out of Asher, and out of all Manasseh, and pursued after the Midianites.

24And Gideon sent messengers throughout all mount Ephraim, saying, Come down against the Midianites, and take before them the waters unto Beth–barah and Jordan. Then all the men of Ephraim gathered themselves together, and took the waters unto Beth–barah and Jordan.

25And they took two princes of the Midianites, Oreb and Zeeb; and they slew Oreb upon the rock Oreb, and Zeeb they slew at the winepress of Zeeb, and pursued Midian, and brought the heads of Oreb and Zeeb to Gideon on the other side Jordan.

AND the men of Ephraim said unto him, Why hast thou served us thus, that thou calledst us not, when thou wentest to fight with the Midianites? And they did chide with him sharply.

2And he said unto them, What have I done now in comparison of you? *Is* not the gleaning of the grapes of Ephraim better than the vintage of Abi–ezer?

3God hath delivered into your hands the princes of Midian, Oreb and Zeeb: and what was I able to do in comparison of you? Then their anger was abated toward him, when he had said that.

4And Gideon came to Jordan, *and* passed over, he, and the three hundred men that *were* with him, faint, yet pursuing *them.*

5And he said unto the men of Succoth, Give, I pray you, loaves of bread unto the people that follow me; for they *be* faint, and I am pursuing after Zebah and Zalmunna, kings of Midian.

6And the princes of Succoth said, *Are* the hands of Zebah and Zalmunna now in thine hand, that we should give bread unto thine army?

7And Gideon said, Therefore when the LORD hath delivered Zebah and Zalmunna into mine hand, then I will tear your flesh with the thorns of the wilderness and with briers.

8And he went up thence to Penuel, and spake unto them likewise: and the men of Penuel answered him as the men of Succoth had answered *him.*

9And he spake also unto the men of Penuel, saying, When I come again in peace, I will break down this tower.

10Now Zebah and Zalmunna *were* in Karkor, and their hosts with them, about fifteen thousand *men,* all that were left of all the hosts of the children of the east: for there fell an hundred and twenty thousand men that drew sword.

11And Gideon went up by the way of them that dwelt in tents on the east of Nobath and Jogbehah, and smote the host: for the host was secure.

12And when Zebah and Zalmunna fled, he pursued after them, and took the two kings of Midian, Zebah and Zalmunna, and discomfited all the host.

13And Gideon the son of Joash returned from battle before the sun *was up,*

14And caught a young man of the men of Succoth, and enquired of him: and he described unto him the princes of Succoth, and the elders thereof, *even* threescore and seventeen men.

15And he came unto the men of Succoth, and said, Behold Zebah and Zalmunna, with whom ye did upbraid me, saying, *Are* the hands of Zebah and Zalmunna now in thine hand, that we should give bread unto thy men *that are* weary?

16And he took the elders of the city, and thorns of the wilderness and briers, and with them he taught the men of Succoth.

LUKE 23:11–43

AND Herod with his men of war set him [Jesus] at nought, and mocked *him,* and arrayed him in a gorgeous robe, and sent him again to Pilate.

12And the same day Pilate and Herod were made friends together: for before they were at enmity between themselves.

13And Pilate, when he had called together the chief priests and the rulers and the people,

14Said unto them, Ye have brought this man unto me, as one that perverteth the people: and, behold, I, having examined *him* before you, have found no fault in this man touching those things whereof ye accuse him:

15No, nor yet Herod: for I sent you to him; and, lo, nothing worthy of death is done unto him.

16I will therefore chastise him, and release *him.*

17(For of necessity he must release one unto them at the feast.)

18And they cried out all at once, saying, Away with this *man,* and release unto us Barabbas:

19(Who for a certain sedition made in the city, and for murder, was cast into prison.)

20Pilate therefore, willing to release Jesus, spake again to them.

21But they cried, saying, Crucify *him,* crucify him.

22And he said unto them the third time, Why, what evil hath he done? I have found no cause of death in him: I will therefore chastise him, and let *him* go.

23And they were instant with loud voices, requiring that he might be crucified. And the voices of them and of the chief priests prevailed.

24And Pilate gave sentence that it should be as they required.

25And he released unto them him that for sedition and murder was cast into prison, whom they had desired; but he delivered Jesus to their will.

26And as they led him away, they laid hold upon one Simon, a Cyrenian, coming out of the country, and on him they laid the cross, that he might bear *it* after Jesus.

27And there followed him a great company of people, and of women, which also bewailed and lamented him.

28But Jesus turning unto them said, Daughters of Jerusalem, weep not for me, but weep for yourselves, and for your children.

29For, behold, the days are coming, in the which they shall say, Blessed *are* the barren, and the wombs that never bare, and the paps which never gave suck.

30Then shall they begin to say to the mountains, Fall on us; and to the hills, Cover us.

31For if they do these things in a green tree, what shall be done in the dry?

32And there were also two other, malefactors, led with him to be put to death.

33And when they were come to the place, which is called Calvary, there they crucified him, and the malefactors, one on the right hand, and the other on the left.

34Then said Jesus, Father, forgive them; for they know not what they do. And they parted his raiment, and cast lots.

35And the people stood beholding. And the rulers also with them derided *him,* saying, He saved others; let him save himself, if he be Christ, the chosen of God.

36And the soldiers also mocked him, coming to him, and offering him vinegar,

37And saying, If thou be the king of the Jews, save thyself.

38And a superscription also was written over him in letters of Greek, and Latin, and Hebrew, THIS IS THE KING OF THE JEWS.

39And one of the malefactors which were hanged railed on him, saying, If thou be Christ, save thyself and us.

40But the other answering rebuked him, saying, Dost not thou fear God, seeing thou art in the same condemnation?

41And we indeed justly; for we receive the due reward of our deeds: but this man hath done nothing amiss.

42And he said unto Jesus, Lord, remember me when thou comest into thy kingdom.

43And Jesus said unto him, Verily I say unto thee, To day shalt thou be with me in paradise.

PSALM 97:1—98:9

THE LORD reigneth; let the earth rejoice; let the multitude of isles be glad *thereof.*

2Clouds and darkness *are* round about him: righteousness and judgment *are* the habitation of his throne.

3A fire goeth before him, and burneth up his enemies round about.

4His lightnings enlightened the world: the earth saw, and trembled.

5The hills melted like wax at the presence of the LORD, at the presence of the LORD of the whole earth.

6The heavens declare his righteousness, and all the people see his glory.

7Confounded be all they that serve graven images, that boast themselves of idols: worship him, all *ye* gods.

8Zion heard, and was glad; and the daughters of Judah rejoiced because of thy judgments, O LORD.

9For thou, LORD, *art* high above all the earth: thou art exalted far above all gods.

10Ye that love the LORD, hate evil: he preserveth the souls of his saints; he delivereth them out of the hand of the wicked.

11Light is sown for the righteous, and gladness for the upright in heart.

12Rejoice in the LORD, ye righteous; and give thanks at the remembrance of his holiness.

O SING unto the LORD a new song; for he hath done marvellous things: his right hand, and his holy arm, hath gotten him the victory.

2The LORD hath made known his salvation: his righteousness hath he openly shewed in the sight of the heathen.

3He hath remembered his mercy and his truth toward the house of Israel: all the ends of the earth have seen the salvation of our God.

4Make a joyful noise unto the LORD, all the earth: make a loud noise, and rejoice, and sing praise.

⁵Sing unto the LORD with the harp; with the harp, and the voice of a psalm.

⁶With trumpets and sound of cornets make a joyful noise before the LORD, the King.

⁷Let the sea roar, and the fulness thereof; the world, and they that dwell therein.

⁸Let the floods clap *their* hands: let the hills be joyful together

⁹Before the LORD; for he cometh to judge the earth: with righteousness shall he judge the world, and the people with equity.

PROVERBS FOR TODAY/ 14:7–8

Go from the presence of a foolish man, when thou perceivest not in him *the lips of knowledge.* □ *The wisdom of the prudent is to understand his way: but the folly of fools* is *deceit.*

APRIL 28

JUDGES 8:17—9:21

A ND he [Gideon] beat down the tower of Penuel, and slew the men of the city.

¹⁸Then said he unto Zebah and Zalmunna, What manner of men *were they* whom ye slew at Tabor? And they answered, As thou *art,* so *were* they; each one resembled the children of a king.

¹⁹And he said, They *were* my brethren, *even* the sons of my mother: *as* the LORD liveth, if ye had saved them alive, I would not slay you.

²⁰And he said unto Jether his firstborn, Up, *and* slay them. But the youth drew not his sword: for he feared, because he *was* yet a youth.

²¹Then Zebah and Zalmunna said, Rise thou, and fall upon us: for as the man *is, so is* his strength. And Gideon arose, and slew Zebah and Zalmunna, and took away the ornaments that *were* on their camels' necks.

²²Then the men of Israel said unto Gideon, Rule thou over us, both thou, and thy son, and thy son's son also: for thou hast delivered us from the hand of Midian.

²³And Gideon said unto them, I will not rule over you, neither shall my son rule over you: the LORD shall rule over you.

²⁴And Gideon said unto them, I would desire a request of you, that ye would give me every man the earrings of his prey. (For they had golden earrings, because they *were* Ishmaelites.)

²⁵And they answered, We will willingly give *them.* And they spread a garment, and did cast therein every man the earrings of his prey.

²⁶And the weight of the golden earrings that he requested was a thousand and seven hundred *shekels* of gold; beside ornaments, and collars, and purple raiment that *was* on the kings of Midian, and beside the chains that *were* about their camels' necks.

²⁷And Gideon made an ephod thereof, and put it in his city, *even* in Ophrah: and all Israel went thither a whoring after it: which thing became a snare unto Gideon, and to his house.

²⁸Thus was Midian subdued before the children of Israel, so that they lifted up their heads no more. And the country

was in quietness forty years in the days of Gideon.

29And Jerubbaal the son of Joash went and dwelt in his own house.

30And Gideon had threescore and ten sons of his body begotten: for he had many wives.

31And his concubine that *was* in Shechem, she also bare him a son, whose name he called Abimelech.

32And Gideon the son of Joash died in a good old age, and was buried in the sepulchre of Joash his father, in Ophrah of the Abi–ezrites.

33And it came to pass, as soon as Gideon was dead, that the children of Israel turned again, and went a whoring after Baalim, and made Baal–berith their god.

34And the children of Israel remembered not the LORD their God, who had delivered them out of the hands of all their enemies on every side:

35Neither shewed they kindness to the house of Jerubbaal, *namely,* Gideon, according to all the goodness which he had shewed unto Israel.

AND Abimelech the son of Jerubbaal went to Shechem unto his mother's brethren, and communed with them, and with all the family of the house of his mother's father, saying,

2Speak, I pray you, in the ears of all the men of Shechem, Whether *is* better for you, either that all the sons of Jerubbaal, *which are* threescore and ten persons, reign over you, or that one reign over you? remember also that I *am* your bone and your flesh.

3And his mother's brethren spake of him in the ears of all the men of Shechem all these words: and their hearts inclined to follow Abimelech; for they said, He *is* our brother.

4And they gave him threescore and ten *pieces* of silver out of the house of Baal–berith, wherewith Abimelech hired vain and light persons, which followed him.

5And he went unto his father's house at Ophrah, and slew his brethren the sons of Jerubbaal, *being* threescore and ten persons, upon one stone: notwithstanding yet Jotham the youngest son of Jerubbaal was left; for he hid himself.

6And all the men of Shechem gathered together, and all the house of Millo, and went, and made Abimelech king, by the plain of the pillar that *was* in Shechem.

7And when they told *it* to Jotham, he went and stood in the top of mount Gerizim, and lifted up his voice, and cried, and said unto them, Hearken unto me, ye men of Shechem, that God may hearken unto you.

8The trees went forth *on a time* to anoint a king over them; and they said unto the olive tree, Reign thou over us.

9But the olive tree said unto them, Should I leave my fatness, wherewith by me they honour God and man, and go to be promoted over the trees?

10And the trees said to the fig tree, Come thou, *and* reign over us.

11But the fig tree said unto them, Should I forsake my sweetness, and my good fruit, and go to be promoted over the trees?

12Then said the trees unto the vine, Come thou, *and* reign over us.

13And the vine said unto them, Should I leave my wine, which cheereth God and man, and go to be promoted over the trees?

14Then said all the trees unto the bramble, Come thou, *and* reign over us.

15And the bramble said unto the trees, If in truth ye anoint me king over you, *then* come *and* put your trust in my shadow: and if not, let fire come out of the bramble, and devour the cedars of Lebanon.

16Now therefore, if ye have done truly and sincerely, in that ye have made Abimelech king, and if ye have dealt well with Jerubbaal and his house, and have done unto him according to the deserving of his hands;

17(For my father fought for you, and adventured his life far, and delivered you out of the hand of Midian:

18And ye are risen up against my father's house this day, and have slain his sons, threescore and ten persons, upon one stone, and have made Abimelech, the son of his maidservant, king over the men of Shechem, because he is your brother;)

19If ye then have dealt truly and sincerely with Jerubbaal and with his house this day, *then* rejoice ye in Abimelech, and let him also rejoice in you:

20But if not, let fire come out from Abimelech, and devour the men of Shechem, and the house of Millo; and let fire come out from the men of Shechem, and from the house of Millo, and devour Abimelech.

21And Jotham ran away, and fled, and went to Beer, and dwelt there, for fear of Abimelech his brother.

LUKE 23:44—24:12

And it was about the sixth hour, and there was a darkness over all the earth until the ninth hour.

45And the sun was darkened, and the vail of the temple was rent in the midst.

46And when Jesus had cried with a loud voice, he said, Father, into thy hands I commend my spirit: and having said thus, he gave up the ghost.

47Now when the centurion saw what was done, he glorified God, saying, Certainly this was a righteous man.

48And all the people that came together to that sight, beholding the things which were done, smote their breasts, and returned.

49And all his acquaintance, and the women that followed him from Galilee, stood afar off, beholding these things.

50And, behold, *there was* a man named Joseph, a counsellor; *and he was* a good man, and a just:

51(The same had not consented to the counsel and deed of them;) *he was* of Arimathaea, a city of the Jews: who also himself waited for the kingdom of God.

52This *man* went unto Pilate, and begged the body of Jesus.

53And he took it down, and wrapped it in linen, and laid it in a sepulchre that was hewn in stone, wherein never man before was laid.

54And that day was the preparation, and the sabbath drew on.

55And the women also, which came with him from Galilee, followed after, and beheld the sepulchre, and how his body was laid.

56And they returned, and prepared spices and ointments; and rested the sabbath day according to the commandment.

Now upon the first *day* of the week, very early in the morning, they came unto the sepulchre, bringing the spices which they had prepared, and certain *others* with them.

2And they found the stone rolled away from the sepulchre.

3And they entered in, and found not the body of the Lord Jesus.

4And it came to pass, as they were much perplexed thereabout, behold, two men stood by them in shining garments:

5And as they were afraid, and bowed down *their* faces to the earth, they said unto them, Why seek ye the living among the dead?

6He is not here, but is risen: remember how he spake unto you when he was yet in Galilee,

7Saying, the Son of man must be delivered into the hands of sinful men, and be crucified, and the third day rise again.

8And they remembered his words,

9And returned from the sepulchre,

and told all these things unto the eleven, and to all the rest.

10It was Mary Magdalene, and Joanna, and Mary *the mother* of James, and other *women that were* with them, which told these things unto the apostles.

11And their words seemed to them as idle tales, and they believed them not.

12Then arose Peter, and ran unto the sepulchre; and stooping down, he beheld the linen clothes laid by themselves, and departed, wondering in himself at that which was come to pass.

PSALM 99:1–9

THE LORD reigneth; let the people tremble: he sitteth *between* the cherubims; let the earth be moved.

2The LORD *is* great in Zion; and he *is* high above all the people.

3Let them praise thy great and terrible name; *for* it *is* holy.

4The king's strength also loveth judgment; thou dost establish equity, thou executest judgment and righteousness in Jacob.

5Exalt ye the LORD our God, and worship at his footstool; *for* he *is* holy.

6Moses and Aaron among his priests, and Samuel among them that call upon his name; they called upon the LORD, and he answered them.

7He spake unto them in the cloudy pillar: they kept his testimonies, and the ordinance *that* he gave them.

8Thou answeredst them, O LORD our God: thou wast a God that forgavest them, though thou tookest vengeance of their inventions.

9Exalt the LORD our God, and worship at his holy hill; for the LORD our God *is* holy.

PROVERBS FOR TODAY/ 14:9–10

Fools make a mock at sin: but among the righteous there is *favour.* □ *The heart knoweth his own bitterness; and a stranger doth not intermeddle with his joy.*

APRIL 29

JUDGES 9:22—10:18

WHEN Abimelech had reigned three years over Israel,

23Then God sent an evil spirit between Abimelech and the men of Shechem; and the men of Shechem dealt treacherously with Abimelech:

24That the cruelty *done* to the threescore and ten sons of Jerubbaal might come, and their blood be laid upon Abimelech their brother, which slew them; and upon the men of Shechem, which aided him in the killing of his brethren.

25And the men of Shechem set liers in wait for him in the top of the mountains, and they robbed all that came along that way by them: and it was told Abimelech.

26And Gaal the son of Ebed came with his brethren, and went over to Shechem: and the men of Shechem put their confidence in him.

27And they went out into the fields,

and gathered their vineyards, and trode *the grapes,* and made merry, and went into the house of their god, and did eat and drink, and cursed Abimelech.

28And Gaal the son of Ebed said, Who *is* Abimelech, and who *is* Shechem, that we should serve him? *is* not *he* the son of Jerubbaal? and Zebul his officer? serve the men of Hamor the father of Shechem: for why should we serve him?

29And would to God this people were under my hand! then would I remove Abimelech. And he said to Abimelech, Increase thine army, and come out.

30And when Zebul the ruler of the city heard the words of Gaal the son of Ebed, his anger was kindled.

31And he sent messengers unto Abimelech privily, saying, Behold, Gaal the son of Ebed and his brethren be come to Shechem; and, behold, they fortify the city against thee.

32Now therefore up by night, thou and the people that *is* with thee, and lie in wait in the field:

33And it shall be, *that* in the morning, as soon as the sun is up, thou shalt rise early, and set upon the city: and, behold, *when* he and the people that *is* with him come out against thee, then mayest thou do to them as thou shalt find occasion.

34And Abimelech rose up, and all the people that *were* with him, by night, and they laid wait against Shechem in four companies.

35And Gaal the son of Ebed went out, and stood in the entering of the gate of the city: and Abimelech rose up, and the people that *were* with him, from lying in wait.

36And when Gaal saw the people, he said to Zebul, Behold, there come people down from the top of the mountains. And Zebul said unto him, Thou seest the shadow of the mountains as *if they were* men.

37And Gaal spake again and said, See there come people down by the middle of the land, and another company come along by the plain of Meonenim.

38Then said Zebul unto him, Where *is* now thy mouth, wherewith thou saidst, Who *is* Abimelech, that we should serve him? *is* not this the people that thou hast despised? go out, I pray now, and fight with them.

39And Gaal went out before the men of Shechem, and fought with Abimelech.

40And Abimelech chased him, and he fled before him, and many were overthrown *and* wounded, *even* unto the entering of the gate.

41And Abimelech dwelt at Arumah: and Zebul thrust out Gaal and his brethren, that they should not dwell in Shechem.

42And it came to pass on the morrow, that the people went out into the field; and they told Abimelech.

43And he took the people, and divided them into three companies, and laid wait in the field, and looked, and, behold, the people *were* come forth out of the city; and he rose up against them, and smote them.

44And Abimelech, and the company that *was* with him, rushed forward, and stood in the entering of the gate of the city: and the two *other* companies ran upon all *the people* that *were* in the fields, and slew them.

45And Abimelech fought against the city all that day; and he took the city, and slew the people that *was* therein, and beat down the city, and sowed it with salt.

46And when all the men of the tower of Shechem heard *that,* they entered into an hold of the house of the god Berith.

47And it was told Abimelech, that all the men of the tower of Shechem were gathered together.

48And Abimelech gat him up to mount Zalmon, he and all the people that *were* with him; and Abimelech took an axe in his hand, and cut down a bough from the trees, and took it, and laid *it* on his shoulder, and said unto the people that *were* with him, What ye have seen me do, make haste, *and* do as I *have done.*

49And all the people likewise cut down every man his bough, and followed Abimelech, and put *them* to the hold, and set the hold on fire upon them; so that all the men of the tower of Shechem died also, about a thousand men and women.

50Then went Abimelech to Thebez, and encamped against Thebez, and took it.

51But there was a strong tower within the city, and thither fled all the men and women, and all they of the city, and shut *it* to them, and gat them up to the top of the tower.

52And Abimelech came unto the tower, and fought against it, and went hard unto the door of the tower to burn it with fire.

53And a certain woman cast a piece of a millstone upon Abimelech's head, and all to brake his skull.

54Then he called hastily unto the young man his armour-bearer, and said unto him, Draw thy sword, and slay me, that men say not of me, A woman slew him. And his young man thrust him through, and he died.

55And when the men of Israel saw that Abimelech was dead, they departed every man unto his place.

56Thus God rendered the wickedness of Abimelech, which he did unto his father, in slaying his seventy brethren:

57And all the evil of the men of Shechem did God render upon their heads: and upon them came the curse of Jotham the son of Jerubbaal.

AND after Abimelech there arose to defend Israel Tola the son of Puah, the son of Dodo, a man of Issachar; and he dwelt in Shamir in mount Ephraim.

2And he judged Israel twenty and three years, and died, and was buried in Shamir.

3And after him arose Jair, a Gileadite, and judged Israel twenty and two years.

4And he had thirty sons that rode on thirty ass colts, and they had thirty cities, which are called Havoth–jair unto this day, which *are* in the land of Gilead.

5And Jair died, and was buried in Camon.

6And the children of Israel did evil again in the sight of the LORD, and served Baalim, and Ashtaroth, and the gods of Syria, and the gods of Zidon, and the gods of Moab, and the gods of the children of Ammon, and the gods of the Philistines, and forsook the LORD, and served not him.

7And the anger of the LORD was hot against Israel, and he sold them into the hands of the Philistines, and into the hands of the children of Ammon.

8And that year they vexed and oppressed the children of Israel: eighteen years, all the children of Israel that *were* on the other side Jordan in the land of the Amorites, which *is* in Gilead.

9Moreover the children of Ammon passed over Jordan to fight also against Judah, and against Benjamin, and against the house of Ephraim; so that Israel was sore distressed.

10And the children of Israel cried unto the LORD, saying, We have sinned against thee, both because we have forsaken our God, and also served Baalim.

11And the LORD said unto the children of Israel, *Did* not *I deliver you* from the Egyptians, and from the Amorites, from the children of Ammon, and from the Philistines?

12The Zidonians also, and the Amalekites, and the Maonites, did oppress you; and ye cried to me, and I delivered you out of their hand.

13Yet ye have forsaken me, and served other gods: wherefore I will deliver you no more.

14Go and cry unto the gods which

ye have chosen; let them deliver you in the time of your tribulation.

15And the children of Israel said unto the LORD, We have sinned: do thou unto us whatsoever seemeth good unto thee; deliver us only, we pray thee, this day.

16And they put away the strange gods from among them, and served the LORD: and his soul was grieved for the misery of Israel.

17Then the children of Ammon were gathered together, and encamped in Gilead. And the children of Israel assembled themselves together, and encamped in Mizpeh.

18And the people *and* princes of Gilead said one to another, What man *is he* that will begin to fight against the children of Ammon? he shall be head over all the inhabitants of Gilead.

LUKE 24:13–53

AND, behold, two of them went that same day to a village called Emmaus, which was from Jerusalem *about* threescore furlongs.

14And they talked together of all these things which had happened.

15And it came to pass, that, while they communed *together* and reasoned, Jesus himself drew near, and went with them.

16But their eyes were holden that they should not know him.

17And he said unto them, What manner of communications *are* these that ye have one to another, as ye walk, and are sad?

18And the one of them, whose name was Cleopas, answering said unto him, Art thou only a stranger in Jerusalem, and hast not known the things which are come to pass there in these days?

19And he said unto them, What things? And they said unto him, Concerning Jesus of Nazareth, which was a prophet mighty in deed and word before God and all the people:

20And how the chief priests and our rulers delivered him to be condemned to death, and have crucified him.

21But we trusted that it had been he which should have redeemed Israel: and beside all this, to day is the third day since these things were done.

22Yea, and certain women also of our company made us astonished, which were early at the sepulchre;

23And when they found not his body, they came, saying, that they had also seen a vision of angels, which said that he was alive.

24And certain of them which were with us went to the sepulchre, and found *it* even so as the women had said: but him they saw not.

25Then he said unto them, O fools, and slow of heart to believe all that the prophets have spoken:

26Ought not Christ to have suffered these things, and to enter into his glory?

27And beginning at Moses and all the prophets, he expounded unto them in all the scriptures the things concerning himself.

28And they drew nigh unto the village, whither they went: and he made as though he would have gone further.

29But they constrained him, saying, Abide with us: for it is toward evening, and the day is far spent. And he went in to tarry with them.

30And it came to pass, as he sat at meat with them, he took bread, and blessed *it,* and brake, and gave to them.

31And their eyes were opened, and they knew him; and he vanished out of their sight.

32And they said one to another, Did not our heart burn within us, while he talked with us by the way, and while he opened to us the scriptures?

33And they rose up the same hour, and returned to Jerusalem, and found the eleven gathered together, and them that were with them,

34Saying, The Lord is risen indeed, and hath appeared to Simon.

35And they told what things *were done* in the way, and how he was known of them in breaking of bread.

36And as they thus spake, Jesus himself stood in the midst of them, and saith unto them, Peace *be* unto you.

37But they were terrified and affrighted, and supposed that they had seen a spirit.

38And he said unto them, Why are ye troubled? and why do thoughts arise in your hearts?

39Behold my hands and my feet, that it is I myself: handle me, and see; for a spirit hath not flesh and bones, as ye see me have.

40And when he had thus spoken, he shewed them *his* hands and *his* feet.

41And while they yet believed not for joy, and wondered, he said unto them, Have ye here any meat?

42And they gave him a piece of a broiled fish, and of an honeycomb.

43And he took *it,* and did eat before them.

44And he said unto them, These *are* the words which I spake unto you, while I was yet with you, that all things must be fulfilled, which were written in the law of Moses, and *in* the prophets, and *in* the psalms, concerning me.

45Then opened he their understanding, that they might understand the scriptures,

46And said unto them, Thus it is written, and thus it behoved Christ to suffer, and to rise from the dead the third day:

47And that repentance and remission of sins should be preached in his name among all nations, beginning at Jerusalem.

48And ye are witnesses of these things.

49And, behold, I send the promise of my Father upon you: but tarry ye in the city of Jerusalem, until ye be endued with power from on high.

50And he led them out as far as to Bethany, and he lifted up his hands, and blessed them.

51And it came to pass, while he blessed them, he was parted from them, and carried up into heaven.

52And they worshipped him, and returned to Jerusalem with great joy:

53And were continually in the temple, praising and blessing God. Amen.

PSALM 100:1–5

MAKE a joyful noise unto the LORD, all ye lands.

2Serve the LORD with gladness: come before his presence with singing.

3Know ye that the LORD he *is* God: *it is* he *that* hath made us, and not we ourselves; *we are* his people, and the sheep of his pasture.

4Enter into his gates with thanksgiving, *and* into his courts with praise: be thankful unto him, *and* bless his name.

5For the LORD *is* good; his mercy *is* everlasting; and his truth *endureth* to all generations.

PROVERBS FOR TODAY/ 14:11–12

The house of the wicked shall be overthrown: but the tabernacle of the upright shall flourish. □ *There is a way which seemeth right unto a man, but the end thereof* are *the ways of death.*

JUDGES 11:1—12:15

Now Jephthah the Gileadite was a mighty man of valour, and he *was* the son of an harlot: and Gilead begat Jephthah.

2And Gilead's wife bare him sons; and his wife's sons grew up, and they thrust out Jephthah, and said unto him, Thou shalt not inherit in our father's house; for thou *art* the son of a strange woman.

3Then Jephthah fled from his brethren, and dwelt in the land of Tob: and there were gathered vain men to Jephthah, and went out with him.

4And it came to pass in process of time, that the children of Ammon made war against Israel.

5And it was so, that when the children of Ammon made war against Israel, the elders of Gilead went to fetch Jephthah out of the land of Tob:

6And they said unto Jephthah, Come, and be our captain, that we may fight with the children of Ammon.

7And Jephthah said unto the elders of Gilead, Did not ye hate me, and expel me out of my father's house? and why are ye come unto me now when ye are in distress?

8And the elders of Gilead said unto Jephthah, Therefore we turn again to thee now, that thou mayest go with us, and fight against the children of Ammon, and be our head over all the inhabitants of Gilead.

9And Jephthah said unto the elders of Gilead, If ye bring me home again to fight against the children of Ammon, and the LORD deliver them before me, shall I be your head?

10And the elders of Gilead said unto Jephthah, The LORD be witness between us, if we do not so according to thy words.

11Then Jephthah went with the elders of Gilead, and the people made him head and captain over them: and Jephthah uttered all his words before the LORD in Mizpeh.

12And Jephthah sent messengers unto the king of the children of Ammon, saying, What hast thou to do with me, that thou art come against me to fight in my land?

13And the king of the children of Ammon answered unto the messengers of Jephthah, Because Israel took away my land, when they came up out of Egypt, from Arnon even unto Jabbok, and unto Jordan: now therefore restore those *lands* again peaceably.

14And Jephthah sent messengers again unto the king of the children of Ammon:

15And said unto him, Thus saith Jephthah, Israel took not away the land of Moab, nor the land of the children of Ammon:

16But when Israel came up from Egypt, and walked through the wilderness unto the Red sea, and came to Kadesh;

17Then Israel sent messengers unto the king of Edom, saying, Let me, I pray thee, pass through thy land: but the king of Edom would not hearken *thereto.* And in like manner they sent unto the king of Moab: but he would not *consent:* and Israel abode in Kadesh.

18Then they went along through the wilderness, and compassed the land of Edom, and the land of Moab, and came by the east side of the land of Moab, and pitched on the other side of Arnon, but came not within the border of Moab: for Arnon *was* the border of Moab.

19And Israel sent messengers unto Sihon king of the Amorites, the king of Heshbon; and Israel said unto him,

Let us pass, we pray thee, through thy land into my place.

20But Sihon trusted not Israel to pass through his coast: but Sihon gathered all his people together, and pitched in Jahaz, and fought against Israel.

21And the LORD God of Israel delivered Sihon and all his people into the hand of Israel, and they smote them: so Israel possessed all the land of the Amorites, the inhabitants of that country.

22And they possessed all the coasts of the Amorites, from Arnon even unto Jabbok, and from the wilderness even unto Jordan.

23So now the LORD God of Israel hath dispossessed the Amorites from before his people Israel, and shouldest thou possess it?

24Wilt not thou possess that which Chemosh thy god giveth thee to possess? So whomsoever the LORD our God shall drive out from before us, them will we possess.

25And now *art* thou any thing better than Balak the son of Zippor, king of Moab? did he ever strive against Israel, or did he ever fight against them,

26While Israel dwelt in Heshbon and her towns, and in Aroer and her towns, and in all the cities that *be* along by the coasts of Arnon, three hundred years? why therefore did ye not recover *them* within that time?

27Wherefore I have not sinned against thee, but thou doest me wrong to war against me: the LORD the Judge be judge this day between the children of Israel and the children of Ammon.

28Howbeit the king of the children of Ammon hearkened not unto the words of Jephthah which he sent him.

29Then the Spirit of the LORD came upon Jephthah, and he passed over Gilead, and Manasseh, and passed over Mizpeh of Gilead, and from Mizpeh of Gilead he passed over *unto* the children of Ammon.

30And Jephthah vowed a vow unto the LORD, and said, If thou shalt without fail deliver the children of Ammon into mine hands,

31Then it shall be, that whatsoever cometh forth of the doors of my house to meet me, when I return in peace from the children of Ammon, shall surely be the LORD'S, and I will offer it up for a burnt offering.

32So Jephthah passed over unto the children of Ammon to fight against them; and the LORD delivered them into his hands.

33And he smote them from Aroer, even till thou come to Minnith, *even* twenty cities, and unto the plain of the vineyards, with a very great slaughter. Thus the children of Ammon were subdued before the children of Israel.

34And Jephthah came to Mizpeh unto his house, and, behold, his daughter came out to meet him with timbrels and with dances: and she *was his* only child; beside her he had neither son nor daughter.

35And it came to pass, when he saw her, that he rent his clothes, and said, Alas, my daughter! thou hast brought me very low, and thou art one of them that trouble me: for I have opened my mouth unto the LORD, and I cannot go back.

36And she said unto him, My father, *if* thou hast opened thy mouth unto the LORD, do to me according to that which hath proceeded out of thy mouth; forasmuch as the LORD hath taken vengeance for thee of thine enemies, *even* of the children of Ammon.

37And she said unto her father, Let this thing be done for me: let me alone two months, that I may go up and down upon the mountains, and bewail my virginity, I and my fellows.

38And he said, Go. And he sent her away *for* two months: and she went with her companions, and bewailed her virginity upon the mountains.

39And it came to pass at the end of two months, that she returned unto her father, who did with her *according* to his vow which he had vowed: and she knew no man. And it was a custom in Israel,

40*That* the daughters of Israel went yearly to lament the daughter of Jephthah the Gileadite four days in a year.

AND the men of Ephraim gathered themselves together, and went northward, and said unto Jephthah, Wherefore passedst thou over to fight against the children of Ammon, and didst not call us to go with thee? we will burn thine house upon thee with fire.

2And Jephthah said unto them, I and my people were at great strife with the children of Ammon; and when I called you, ye delivered me not out of their hands.

3And when I saw that ye delivered *me* not, I put my life in my hands, and passed over against the children of Ammon, and the LORD delivered them into my hand: wherefore then are ye come up unto me this day, to fight against me?

4Then Jephthah gathered together all the men of Gilead, and fought with Ephraim: and the men of Gilead smote Ephraim, because they said, Ye Gileadites *are* fugitives of Ephraim among the Ephraimites, *and* among the Manassites.

5And the Gileadites took the passages of Jordan before the Ephraimites: and it was *so,* that when those Ephraimites which were escaped said, Let me go over; that the men of Gilead said unto him, *Art* thou an Ephraimite? If he said, Nay;

6Then said they unto him, Say now Shibboleth: and he said Sibboleth: for he could not frame to pronounce *it* right. Then they took him, and slew him at the passages of Jordan: and there fell at that time of the Ephraimites forty and two thousand.

7And Jephthah judged Israel six years. Then died Jephthah the Gileadite, and was buried in *one of* the cities of Gilead.

8And after him Ibzan of Beth–lehem judged Israel.

9And he had thirty sons, and thirty daughters, *whom* he sent abroad, and took in thirty daughters from abroad for his sons. And he judged Israel seven years.

10Then died Ibzan, and was buried at Beth–lehem.

11And after him Elon, a Zebulonite, judged Israel; and he judged Israel ten years.

12And Elon the Zebulonite died, and was buried in Aijalon in the country of Zebulun.

13And after him Abdon the son of Hillel, a Pirathonite, judged Israel.

14And he had forty sons and thirty nephews, that rode on threescore and ten ass colts: and he judged Israel eight years.

15And Abdon the son of Hillel the Pirathonite died, and was buried in Pirathon in the land of Ephraim, in the mount of the Amalekites.

JOHN 1:1–28

IN the beginning was the Word, and the Word was with God, and the Word was God.

2The same was in the beginning with God.

3All things were made by him; and without him was not any thing made that was made.

4In him was life; and the life was the light of men.

5And the light shineth in darkness; and the darkness comprehended it not.

6There was a man sent from God, whose name *was* John.

7The same came for a witness, to bear witness of the Light, that all *men* through him might believe.

8He was not that Light, but *was sent* to bear witness of that Light.

9*That* was the true Light, which lighteth every man that cometh into the world.

10He was in the world, and the world was made by him, and the world knew him not.

11He came unto his own, and his own received him not.

12But as many as received him, to them gave he power to become the sons of God, *even* to them that believe on his name:

13Which were born, not of blood, nor of the will of the flesh, nor of the will of man, but of God.

14And the Word was made flesh, and dwelt among us, (and we beheld his glory, the glory as of the only begotten of the Father,) full of grace and truth.

15John bare witness of him, and cried, saying, This was he of whom I spake, He that cometh after me is preferred before me: for he was before me.

16And of his fulness have all we received, and grace for grace.

17For the law was given by Moses, *but* grace and truth came by Jesus Christ.

18No man hath seen God at any time; the only begotten Son, which is in the bosom of the Father, he hath declared *him.*

19And this is the record of John, when the Jews sent priests and Levites from Jerusalem to ask him, Who art thou?

20And he confessed, and denied not; but confessed, I am not the Christ.

21And they asked him, What then? Art thou Elias? And he saith, I am not. Art thou that prophet? And he answered, No.

22Then said they unto him, Who art thou? that we may give an answer to them that sent us. What sayest thou of thyself?

23He said, I *am* the voice of one crying in the wilderness, Make straight the way of the Lord, as said the prophet Esaias.

24And they which were sent were of the Pharisees.

25And they asked him, and said unto him, Why baptizest thou then, if thou be not that Christ, nor Elias, neither that prophet?

26John answered them, saying, I baptize with water: but there standeth one among you, whom ye know not;

27He it is, who coming after me is preferred before me, whose shoe's latchet I am not worthy to unloose.

28These things were done in Bethabara beyond Jordan, where John was baptizing.

PSALM 101:1–8

I WILL sing of mercy and judgment: unto thee, O LORD, will I sing.

2I will behave myself wisely in a perfect way. O when wilt thou come unto me? I will walk within my house with a perfect heart.

3I will set no wicked thing before mine eyes: I hate the work of them that turn aside; *it* shall not cleave to me.

4A froward heart shall depart from me: I will not know a wicked *person.*

5Whoso privily slandereth his neighbour, him will I cut off: him that hath an high look and a proud heart will not I suffer.

6Mine eyes *shall be* upon the faithful of the land, that they may dwell with me: he that walketh in a perfect way, he shall serve me.

7He that worketh deceit shall not dwell within my house: he that telleth lies shall not tarry in my sight.

8I will early destroy all the wicked of the land: that I may cut off all wicked doers from the city of the LORD.

PROVERBS FOR TODAY/ 14:13–14

Even in laughter the heart is sorrowful; and the end of that mirth is heaviness. □ *The backslider in heart shall be filled with his own ways: and a good man shall be satisfied from himself.*

MAY 1

JUDGES 13:1—14:20

AND the children of Israel did evil again in the sight of the LORD; and the LORD delivered them into the hand of the Philistines forty years.

2And there was a certain man of Zorah, of the family of the Danites, whose name *was* Manoah; and his wife *was* barren, and bare not.

3And the angel of the LORD appeared unto the woman, and said unto her, Behold now, thou *art* barren, and bearest not: but thou shalt conceive, and bear a son.

4Now therefore beware, I pray thee, and drink not wine nor strong drink, and eat not any unclean *thing:*

5For, lo, thou shalt conceive, and bear a son; and no razor shall come on his head: for the child shall be a Nazarite unto God from the womb: and he shall begin to deliver Israel out of the hand of the Philistines.

6Then the woman came and told her husband, saying, A man of God came unto me, and his countenance *was* like the countenance of an angel of God, very terrible: but I asked him not whence he *was,* neither told he me his name:

7But he said unto me, Behold, thou shalt conceive, and bear a son; and now drink no wine nor strong drink, neither eat any unclean *thing:* for the child shall be a Nazarite to God from the womb to the day of his death.

8Then Manoah intreated the LORD, and said, O my Lord, let the man of God which thou didst send come again unto us, and teach us what we shall do unto the child that shall be born.

9And God hearkened to the voice of Manoah; and the angel of God came again unto the woman as she sat in the field: but Manoah her husband *was* not with her.

10And the woman made haste, and ran, and shewed her husband, and said unto him, Behold, the man hath appeared unto me, that came unto me the *other* day.

11And Manoah arose, and went after his wife, and came to the man, and said unto him, *Art* thou the man that spakest unto the woman? And he said, I *am.*

12And Manoah said, Now let thy words come to pass. How shall we order the child, and *how* shall we do unto him?

13And the angel of the LORD said unto Manoah, Of all that I said unto the woman let her beware.

14She may not eat of any *thing* that cometh of the vine, neither let her drink wine or strong drink, nor eat any unclean *thing:* all that I commanded her let her observe.

15And Manoah said unto the angel of the LORD, I pray thee, let us detain thee, until we shall have made ready a kid for thee.

16And the angel of the LORD said unto

Manoah, Though thou detain me, I will not eat of thy bread: and if thou wilt offer a burnt offering, thou must offer it unto the LORD. For Manoah knew not that he *was* an angel of the LORD.

17And Manoah said unto the angel of the LORD, What *is* thy name, that when thy sayings come to pass we may do thee honour?

18And the angel of the LORD said unto him, Why askest thou thus after my name, seeing it *is* secret?

19So Manoah took a kid with a meat offering, and offered *it* upon a rock unto the LORD: and *the angel* did wonderously; and Manoah and his wife looked on.

20For it came to pass, when the flame went up toward heaven from off the altar, that the angel of the LORD ascended in the flame of the altar. And Manoah and his wife looked on *it,* and fell on their faces to the ground.

21But the angel of the LORD did no more appear to Manoah and to his wife. Then Manoah knew that he *was* an angel of the LORD.

22And Manoah said unto his wife, We shall surely die, because we have seen God.

23But his wife said unto him, If the LORD were pleased to kill us, he would not have received a burnt offering and a meat offering at our hands, neither would he have shewed us all these *things,* nor would as at this time have told us *such things* as these.

24And the woman bare a son, and called his name Samson: and the child grew, and the LORD blessed him.

25And the Spirit of the LORD began to move him at times in the camp of Dan between Zorah and Eshtaol.

AND Samson went down to Timnath, and saw a woman in Timnath of the daughters of the Philistines.

2And he came up, and told his father and his mother, and said, I have seen a woman in Timnath of the daughters of the Philistines: now therefore get her for me to wife.

3Then his father and his mother said unto him, *Is there* never a woman among the daughters of thy brethren, or among all my people, that thou goest to take a wife of the uncircumcised Philistines? And Samson said unto his father, Get her for me; for she pleaseth me well.

4But his father and his mother knew not that it *was* of the LORD, that he sought an occasion against the Philistines: for at that time the Philistines had dominion over Israel.

5Then went Samson down, and his father and his mother, to Timnath, and came to the vineyards of Timnath: and, behold, a young lion roared against him.

6And the Spirit of the LORD came mightily upon him, and he rent him as he would have rent a kid, and *he had* nothing in his hand: but he told not his father or his mother what he had done.

7And he went down, and talked with the woman; and she pleased Samson well.

8And after a time he returned to take her, and he turned aside to see the carcase of the lion: and, behold, *there was* a swarm of bees and honey in the carcase of the lion.

9And he took thereof in his hands, and went on eating, and came to his father and mother, and he gave them, and they did eat: but he told not them that he had taken the honey out of the carcase of the lion.

10So his father went down unto the woman: and Samson made there a feast; for so used the young men to do.

11And it came to pass, when they saw him, that they brought thirty companions to be with him.

12And Samson said unto them, I will now put forth a riddle unto you: if ye can certainly declare it me within the seven days of the feast, and find *it* out, then I will give you thirty sheets and thirty change of garments:

13But if ye cannot declare *it* me, then shall ye give me thirty sheets and thirty change of garments. And they said unto him, Put forth thy riddle, that we may hear it.

14And he said unto them, Out of the eater came forth meat, and out of the strong came forth sweetness. And they could not in three days expound the riddle.

15And it came to pass on the seventh day, that they said unto Samson's wife, Entice thy husband, that he may declare unto us the riddle, lest we burn thee and thy father's house with fire: have ye called us to take that we have? *is it* not *so?*

16And Samson's wife wept before him, and said, Thou dost but hate me, and lovest me not: thou hast put forth a riddle unto the children of my people, and hast not told *it* me. And he said unto her, Behold, I have not told *it* my father nor my mother, and shall I tell *it* thee?

17And she wept before him the seven days, while their feast lasted: and it came to pass on the seventh day, that he told her, because she lay sore upon him: and she told the riddle to the children of her people.

18And the men of the city said unto him on the seventh day before the sun went down, What *is* sweeter than honey? and what *is* stronger than a lion? And he said unto them, If ye had not plowed with my heifer, ye had not found out my riddle.

19And the Spirit of the LORD came upon him, and he went down to Ashkelon, and slew thirty men of them, and took their spoil, and gave change of garments unto them which expounded the riddle. And his anger was kindled, and he went up to his father's house.

20But Samson's wife was *given* to his companion, whom he had used as his friend.

JOHN 1:29–51

THE next day John seeth Jesus coming unto him, and saith, Behold the Lamb of God, which taketh away the sin of the world.

30This is he of whom I said, After me cometh a man which is preferred before me: for he was before me.

31And I knew him not: but that he should be made manifest to Israel, therefore am I come baptizing with water.

32And John bare record, saying, I saw the Spirit descending from heaven like a dove, and it abode upon him.

33And I knew him not: but he that sent me to baptize with water, the same said unto me, Upon whom thou shalt see the Spirit descending, and remaining on him, the same is he which baptizeth with the Holy Ghost.

34And I saw, and bare record that this is the Son of God.

35Again the next day after John stood, and two of his disciples;

36And looking upon Jesus as he walked, he saith, Behold the Lamb of God!

37And the two disciples heard him speak, and they followed Jesus.

38Then Jesus turned, and saw them following, and saith unto them, What seek ye? They said unto him, Rabbi, (which is to say, being interpreted, Master,) where dwellest thou?

39He saith unto them, Come and see. They came and saw where he dwelt, and abode with him that day: for it was about the tenth hour.

40One of the two which heard John *speak,* and followed him, was Andrew, Simon Peter's brother.

41He first findeth his own brother Simon, and saith unto him, We have found the Messias, which is, being interpreted, the Christ.

42And he brought him to Jesus. And when Jesus beheld him, he said, Thou art Simon the son of Jona: thou shalt be called Cephas, which is by interpretation, A stone.

43The day following Jesus would go forth into Galilee, and findeth Philip, and saith unto him, Follow me.

44Now Philip was of Bethsaida, the city of Andrew and Peter.

45Philip findeth Nathanael, and saith unto him, We have found him, of whom Moses in the law, and the prophets, did write, Jesus of Nazareth, the son of Joseph.

46And Nathanael said unto him, Can there any good thing come out of Nazareth? Philip saith unto him, Come and see.

47Jesus saw Nathanael coming to him, and saith of him, Behold an Israelite indeed, in whom is no guile!

48Nathanael saith unto him, Whence knowest thou me? Jesus answered and said unto him, Before that Philip called thee, when thou wast under the fig tree, I saw thee.

49Nathanael answered and saith unto him, Rabbi, thou art the Son of God; thou art the King of Israel.

50Jesus answered and said unto him, Because I said unto thee, I saw thee under the fig tree, believest thou? thou shalt see greater things than these.

51And he saith unto him, Verily, verily, I say unto you, Hereafter ye shall see heaven open, and the angels of God ascending and descending upon the Son of man.

PSALM 102:1–28

Hear my prayer, O Lord, and let my cry come unto thee.

2Hide not thy face from me in the day *when* I am in trouble; incline thine ear unto me: in the day *when* I call answer me speedily.

3For my days are consumed like smoke, and my bones are burned as an hearth.

4My heart is smitten, and withered like grass; so that I forget to eat my bread.

5By reason of the voice of my groaning my bones cleave to my skin.

6I am like a pelican of the wilderness: I am like an owl of the desert.

7I watch, and am as a sparrow alone upon the house top.

8Mine enemies reproach me all the day; *and* they that are mad against me are sworn against me.

9For I have eaten ashes like bread, and mingled my drink with weeping,

10Because of thine indignation and thy wrath: for thou hast lifted me up, and cast me down.

11My days *are* like a shadow that declineth; and I am withered like grass.

12But thou, O Lord, shalt endure for ever; and thy remembrance unto all generations.

13Thou shalt arise, *and* have mercy upon Zion: for the time to favour her, yea, the set time, is come.

14For thy servants take pleasure in her stones, and favour the dust thereof.

15So the heathen shall fear the name of the Lord, and all the kings of the earth thy glory.

16When the Lord shall build up Zion, he shall appear in his glory.

17He will regard the prayer of the destitute, and not despise their prayer.

18This shall be written for the generation to come: and the people which shall be created shall praise the Lord.

19For he hath looked down from the height of his sanctuary; from heaven did the Lord behold the earth;

20To hear the groaning of the prisoner; to loose those that are appointed to death;

21To declare the name of the Lord in Zion, and his praise in Jerusalem;

22When the people are gathered together, and the kingdoms, to serve the Lord.

23He weakened my strength in the way; he shortened my days.

24I said, O my God, take me not

away in the midst of my days: thy years *are* throughout all generations.

25Of old hast thou laid the foundation of the earth: and the heavens *are* the work of thy hands.

26They shall perish, but thou shalt endure: yea, all of them shall wax old like a garment; as a vesture shalt thou change them, and they shall be changed:

27But thou *art* the same, and thy years shall have no end.

28The children of thy servants shall continue, and their seed shall be established before thee.

PROVERBS FOR TODAY/ 14:15–16

The simple believeth every word: but the prudent man *looketh well to his going.* ▢ *A wise* man *feareth, and departeth from evil: but the fool rageth, and is confident.*

MAY 2

JUDGES 15:1—16:31

BUT it came to pass within a while after, in the time of wheat harvest, that Samson visited his wife with a kid; and he said, I will go in to my wife into the chamber. But her father would not suffer him to go in.

2And her father said, I verily thought that thou hadst utterly hated her; therefore I gave her to thy companion: *is* not her younger sister fairer than she? take her, I pray thee, instead of her.

3And Samson said concerning them, Now shall I be more blameless than the Philistines, though I do them a displeasure.

4And Samson went and caught three hundred foxes, and took firebrands, and turned tail to tail, and put a firebrand in the midst between two tails.

5And when he had set the brands on fire, he let *them* go into the standing corn of the Philistines, and burnt up both the shocks, and also the standing corn, with the vineyards *and* olives.

6Then the Philistines said, Who hath done this? And they answered, Samson, the son in law of the Timnite, because he had taken his wife, and given her to his companion. And the Philistines came up, and burnt her and her father with fire.

7And Samson said unto them, Though ye have done this, yet will I be avenged of you, and after that I will cease.

8And he smote them hip and thigh with a great slaughter: and he went down and dwelt in the top of the rock Etam.

9Then the Philistines went up, and pitched in Judah, and spread themselves in Lehi.

10And the men of Judah said, Why are ye come up against us? And they answered, To bind Samson are we come up, to do to him as he hath done to us.

11Then three thousand men of Judah went to the top of the rock Etam, and said to Samson, Knowest thou not that the Philistines *are* rulers over us? what *is* this *that* thou hast done unto us? And he said unto them, As they did unto me, so have I done unto them.

12And they said unto him, We are come down to bind thee, that we may deliver thee into the hand of the Philistines. And Samson said unto them, Swear unto me, that ye will not fall upon me yourselves.

¹³And they spake unto him, saying, No; but we will bind thee fast, and deliver thee into their hand: but surely we will not kill thee. And they bound him with two new cords, and brought him up from the rock.

¹⁴*And* when he came unto Lehi, the Philistines shouted against him: and the Spirit of the LORD came mightily upon him, and the cords that *were* upon his arms became as flax that was burnt with fire, and his bands loosed from off his hands.

¹⁵And he found a new jawbone of an ass, and put forth his hand, and took it, and slew a thousand men therewith.

¹⁶And Samson said, With the jawbone of an ass, heaps upon heaps, with the jaw of an ass have I slain a thousand men.

¹⁷And it came to pass, when he had made an end of speaking, that he cast away the jawbone out of his hand, and called that place Ramath–lehi.

¹⁸And he was sore athirst, and called on the LORD, and said, Thou hast given this great deliverance into the hand of thy servant: and now shall I die for thirst, and fall into the hand of the uncircumcised?

¹⁹But God clave an hollow place that *was* in the jaw, and there came water thereout; and when he had drunk, his spirit came again, and he revived: wherefore he called the name thereof En–hakkore, which *is* in Lehi unto this day.

²⁰And he judged Israel in the days of the Philistines twenty years.

THEN went Samson to Gaza, and saw there an harlot, and went in unto her.

²*And it was told* the Gazites, saying, Samson is come hither. And they compassed *him* in, and laid wait for him all night in the gate of the city, and were quiet all the night, saying, In the morning, when it is day, we shall kill him.

³And Samson lay till midnight, and arose at midnight, and took the doors of the gate of the city, and the two posts, and went away with them, bar and all, and put *them* upon his shoulders, and carried them up to the top of an hill that *is* before Hebron.

⁴And it came to pass afterward, that he loved a woman in the valley of Sorek, whose name *was* Delilah.

⁵And the lords of the Philistines came up unto her, and said unto her, Entice him, and see wherein his great strength *lieth,* and by what *means* we may prevail against him, that we may bind him to afflict him: and we will give thee every one of us eleven hundred *pieces* of silver.

⁶And Delilah said to Samson, Tell me, I pray thee, wherein thy great strength *lieth,* and wherewith thou mightest be bound to afflict thee.

⁷And Samson said unto her, If they bind me with seven green withes that were never dried, then shall I be weak, and be as another man.

⁸Then the lords of the Philistines brought up to her seven green withes which had not been dried, and she bound him with them.

⁹Now *there were* men lying in wait, abiding with her in the chamber. And she said unto him, The Philistines *be* upon thee, Samson. And he brake the withes, as a thread of tow is broken when it toucheth the fire. So his strength was not known.

¹⁰And Delilah said unto Samson, Behold, thou hast mocked me, and told me lies: now tell me, I pray thee, wherewith thou mightest be bound.

¹¹And he said unto her, If they bind me fast with new ropes that never were occupied, then shall I be weak, and be as another man.

¹²Delilah therefore took new ropes, and bound him therewith, and said unto him, The Philistines *be* upon thee, Samson. And *there were* liers in wait abiding in the chamber. And he brake them from off his arms like a thread.

13And Delilah said unto Samson, Hitherto thou hast mocked me, and told me lies: tell me wherewith thou mightest be bound. And he said unto her, If thou weavest the seven locks of my head with the web.

14And she fastened *it* with the pin, and said unto him, The Philistines *be* upon thee, Samson. And he awaked out of his sleep, and went away with the pin of the beam, and with the web.

15And she said unto him, How canst thou say, I love thee, when thine heart *is* not with me? thou hast mocked me these three times, and hast not told me wherein thy great strength *lieth.*

16And it came to pass, when she pressed him daily with her words, and urged him, *so* that his soul was vexed unto death;

17That he told her all his heart, and said unto her, There hath not come a razor upon mine head; for I *have been* a Nazarite unto God from my mother's womb: if I be shaven, then my strength will go from me, and I shall become weak, and be like any *other* man.

18And when Delilah saw that he had told her all his heart, she sent and called for the lords of the Philistines, saying, Come up this once, for he hath shewed me all his heart. Then the lords of the Philistines came up unto her, and brought money in their hand.

19And she made him sleep upon her knees; and she called for a man, and she caused him to shave off the seven locks of his head; and she began to afflict him, and his strength went from him.

20And she said, The Philistines *be* upon thee, Samson. And he awoke out of his sleep, and said, I will go out as at other times before, and shake myself. And he wist not that the LORD was departed from him.

21But the Philistines took him, and put out his eyes, and brought him down to Gaza, and bound him with fetters of brass; and he did grind in the prison house.

22Howbeit the hair of his head began to grow again after he was shaven.

23Then the lords of the Philistines gathered them together for to offer a great sacrifice unto Dagon their god, and to rejoice: for they said, Our god hath delivered Samson our enemy into our hand.

24And when the people saw him, they praised their god: for they said, Our god hath delivered into our hands our enemy, and the destroyer of our country, which slew many of us.

25And it came to pass, when their hearts were merry, that they said, Call for Samson, that he may make us sport. And they called for Samson out of the prison house; and he made them sport: and they set him between the pillars.

26And Samson said unto the lad that held him by the hand, Suffer me that I may feel the pillars whereupon the house standeth, that I may lean upon them.

27Now the house was full of men and women; and all the lords of the Philistines *were* there; and *there were* upon the roof about three thousand men and women, that beheld while Samson made sport.

28And Samson called unto the LORD, and said, O Lord GOD, remember me, I pray thee, and strengthen me, I pray thee, only this once, O God, that I may be at once avenged of the Philistines for my two eyes.

29And Samson took hold of the two middle pillars upon which the house stood, and on which it was borne up, of the one with his right hand, and of the other with his left.

30And Samson said, Let me die with the Philistines. And he bowed himself with *all his* might; and the house fell upon the lords, and upon all the people that *were* therein. So the dead which he slew at his death were more than *they* which he slew in his life.

31Then his brethren and all the house of his father came down, and took him, and brought *him* up, and buried him between Zorah and Eshtaol in the buryingplace of Manoah his father. And he judged Israel twenty years.

JOHN 2:1–25

AND the third day there was a marriage in Cana of Galilee; and the mother of Jesus was there:

2And both Jesus was called, and his disciples, to the marriage.

3And when they wanted wine, the mother of Jesus saith unto him, They have no wine.

4Jesus saith unto her, Woman, what have I to do with thee? mine hour is not yet come.

5His mother saith unto the servants, Whatsoever he saith unto you, do *it*.

6And there were set there six waterpots of stone, after the manner of the purifying of the Jews, containing two or three firkins apiece.

7Jesus saith unto them, Fill the waterpots with water. And they filled them up to the brim.

8And he saith unto them, Draw out now, and bear unto the governor of the feast. And they bare *it*.

9When the ruler of the feast had tasted the water that was made wine, and knew not whence it was: (but the servants which drew the water knew;) the governor of the feast called the bridegroom,

10And saith unto him, Every man at the beginning doth set forth good wine; and when men have well drunk, then that which is worse: *but* thou hast kept the good wine until now.

11This beginning of miracles did Jesus in Cana of Galilee, and manifested forth his glory; and his disciples believed on him.

12After this he went down to Capernaum, he, and his mother, and his brethren, and his disciples: and they continued there not many days.

13And the Jews' passover was at hand, and Jesus went up to Jerusalem,

14And found in the temple those that sold oxen and sheep and doves, and the changers of money sitting:

15And when he had made a scourge of small cords, he drove them all out of the temple, and the sheep, and the oxen; and poured out the changers' money, and overthrew the tables;

16And said unto them that sold doves, Take these things hence; make not my Father's house an house of merchandise.

17And his disciples remembered that it was written, The zeal of thine house hath eaten me up.

18Then answered the Jews and said unto him, What sign shewest thou unto us, seeing that thou doest these things?

19Jesus answered and said unto them, Destroy this temple, and in three days I will raise it up.

20Then said the Jews, Forty and six years was this temple in building, and wilt thou rear it up in three days?

21But he spake of the temple of his body.

22When therefore he was risen from the dead, his disciples remembered that he had said this unto them; and they believed the scripture, and the word which Jesus had said.

23Now when he was in Jerusalem at the passover, in the feast *day,* many believed in his name, when they saw the miracles which he did.

24But Jesus did not commit himself unto them, because he knew all *men,*

25And needed not that any should testify of man: for he knew what was in man.

PSALM 103:1–22

BLESS the LORD, O my soul: and all that is within me, *bless* his holy name.

2Bless the LORD, O my soul, and

forget not all his benefits:

3Who forgiveth all thine iniquities; who healeth all thy diseases;

4Who redeemeth thy life from destruction; who crowneth thee with lovingkindness and tender mercies;

5Who satisfieth thy mouth with good *things; so that* thy youth is renewed like the eagle's.

6The LORD executeth righteousness and judgment for all that are oppressed.

7He made known his ways unto Moses, his acts unto the children of Israel.

8The LORD *is* merciful and gracious, slow to anger, and plenteous in mercy.

9He will not always chide: neither will he keep *his anger* for ever.

10He hath not dealt with us after our sins; nor rewarded us according to our iniquities.

11For as the heaven is high above the earth, *so* great is his mercy toward them that fear him.

12As far as the east is from the west, *so* far hath he removed our transgressions from us.

13Like as a father pitieth *his* children, *so* the LORD pitieth them that fear him.

14For he knoweth our frame; he remembereth that we *are* dust.

15*As for* man, his days *are* as grass; as a flower of the field, so he flourisheth.

16For the wind passeth over it, and it is gone; and the place thereof shall know it no more.

17But the mercy of the LORD *is* from everlasting to everlasting upon them that fear him, and his righteousness unto children's children;

18To such as keep his covenant, and to those that remember his commandments to do them.

19The LORD hath prepared his throne in the heavens; and his kingdom ruleth over all.

20Bless the LORD, ye his angels, that excel in strength, that do his commandments, hearkening unto the voice of his word.

21Bless ye the LORD, all *ye* his hosts; *ye* ministers of his, that do his pleasure.

22Bless the LORD, all his works in all places of his dominion: bless the LORD, O my soul.

PROVERBS FOR TODAY/ 14:17–19

He that is *soon angry dealeth foolishly: and a man of wicked devices is hated.* □ *The simple inherit folly: but the prudent are crowned with knowledge.* □ *The evil bow before the good; and the wicked at the gates of the righteous.*

MAY 3

JUDGES 17:1—18:31

AND there was a man of mount Ephraim, whose name *was* Micah.

2And he said unto his mother, The eleven hundred *shekels* of silver that were taken from thee, about which thou cursedst, and spakest of also in mine ears, behold, the silver *is* with me; I took it. And his mother said, Blessed *be thou* of the LORD, my son.

3And when he had restored the eleven hundred *shekels* of silver to his mother, his mother said, I had wholly dedicated the silver unto the LORD from my hand for my son, to make a graven image and a molten image: now therefore I will restore it unto thee.

4Yet he restored the money unto his mother; and his mother took two hundred *shekels* of silver, and gave them to the founder, who made thereof a graven image and a molten image: and they were in the house of Micah.

5And the man Micah had an house of gods, and made an ephod, and teraphim, and consecrated one of his sons, who became his priest.

6In those days *there was* no king in Israel, *but* every man did *that which was* right in his own eyes.

7And there was a young man out of Beth–lehem–judah of the family of Judah, who *was* a Levite, and he sojourned there.

8And the man departed out of the city from Beth–lehem–judah to sojourn where he could find *a place:* and he came to mount Ephraim to the house of Micah, as he journeyed.

9And Micah said unto him, Whence comest thou? And he said unto him, I *am* a Levite of Beth–lehem–judah, and I go to sojourn where I may find *a place.*

10And Micah said unto him, Dwell with me, and be unto me a father and a priest, and I will give thee ten *shekels* of silver by the year, and a suit of apparel, and thy victuals. So the Levite went in.

11And the Levite was content to dwell with the man; and the young man was unto him as one of his sons.

12And Micah consecrated the Levite; and the young man became his priest, and was in the house of Micah.

13Then said Micah, Now know I that the LORD will do me good, seeing I have a Levite to *my* priest.

IN those days *there was* no king in Israel: and in those days the tribe of the Danites sought them an inheritance to dwell in; for unto that day *all their* inheritance had not fallen unto them among the tribes of Israel.

2And the children of Dan sent of their family five men from their coasts, men of valour, from Zorah, and from Eshtaol, to spy out the land, and to search it; and they said unto them, Go, search the land: who when they came to mount Ephraim, to the house of Micah, they lodged there.

3When they *were* by the house of Micah, they knew the voice of the young man the Levite: and they turned in thither, and said unto him, Who brought thee hither? and what makest thou in this *place?* and what hast thou here?

4And he said unto them, Thus and thus dealeth Micah with me, and hath hired me, and I am his priest.

5And they said unto him, Ask counsel, we pray thee, of God, that we may know whether our way which we go shall be prosperous.

6And the priest said unto them, Go in peace: before the LORD *is* your way wherein ye go.

7Then the five men departed, and came to Laish, and saw the people that *were* therein, how they dwelt careless, after the manner of the Zidonians, quiet and secure; and *there was* no magistrate in the land, that might put *them* to shame in *any* thing; and they *were* far from the Zidonians, and had no business with *any* man.

8And they came unto their brethren to Zorah and Eshtaol: and their brethren said unto them, What *say* ye?

9And they said, Arise, that we may go up against them: for we have seen the land, and, behold, it *is* very good: and *are* ye still? be not slothful to go, *and* to enter to possess the land.

10When ye go, ye shall come unto a people secure, and to a large land: for God hath given it into your hands; a place where *there is* no want of any thing that *is* in the earth.

11And there went from thence of the family of the Danites, out of Zorah and out of Eshtaol, six hundred men appointed with weapons of war.

12And they went up, and pitched in

Kirjath–jearim, in Judah: wherefore they called that place Mahaneh–dan unto this day: behold, *it is* behind Kirjath–jearim.

¹³And they passed thence unto mount Ephraim, and came unto the house of Micah.

¹⁴Then answered the five men that went to spy out the country of Laish, and said unto their brethren, Do ye know that there is in these houses an ephod, and teraphim, and a graven image, and a molten image? now therefore consider what ye have to do.

¹⁵And they turned thitherward, and came to the house of the young man the Levite, *even* unto the house of Micah, and saluted him.

¹⁶And the six hundred men appointed with their weapons of war, which *were* of the children of Dan, stood by the entering of the gate.

¹⁷And the five men that went to spy out the land went up, *and* came in thither, *and* took the graven image, and the ephod, and the teraphim, and the molten image: and the priest stood in the entering of the gate with the six hundred men *that were* appointed with weapons of war.

¹⁸And these went into Micah's house, and fetched the carved image, the ephod, and the teraphim, and the molten image. Then said the priest unto them, What do ye?

¹⁹And they said unto him, Hold thy peace, lay thine hand upon thy mouth, and go with us, and be to us a father and a priest: *is it* better for thee to be a priest unto the house of one man, or that thou be a priest unto a tribe and a family in Israel?

²⁰And the priest's heart was glad, and he took the ephod, and the teraphim, and the graven image, and went in the midst of the people.

²¹So they turned and departed, and put the little ones and the cattle and the carriage before them.

²²*And* when they were a good way from the house of Micah, the men that *were* in the houses near to Micah's house were gathered together, and overtook the children of Dan.

²³And they cried unto the children of Dan. And they turned their faces, and said unto Micah, What aileth thee, that thou comest with such a company?

²⁴And he said, Ye have taken away my gods which I made, and the priest, and ye are gone away: and what have I more? and what *is* this *that* ye say unto me, What aileth thee?

²⁵And the children of Dan said unto him, Let not thy voice be heard among us, lest angry fellows run upon thee, and thou lose thy life, with the lives of thy household.

²⁶And the children of Dan went their way: and when Micah saw that they *were* too strong for him, he turned and went back unto his house.

²⁷And they took *the things* which Micah had made, and the priest which he had, and came unto Laish, unto a people *that were* at quiet and secure: and they smote them with the edge of the sword, and burnt the city with fire.

²⁸And *there was* no deliverer, because it *was* far from Zidon, and they had no business with *any* man; and it was in the valley that *lieth* by Beth–rehob. And they built a city, and dwelt therein.

²⁹And they called the name of the city Dan, after the name of Dan their father, who was born unto Israel: howbeit the name of the city *was* Laish at the first.

³⁰And the children of Dan set up the graven image: and Jonathan, the son of Gershom, the son of Manasseh, he and his sons were priests to the tribe of Dan until the day of the captivity of the land.

³¹And they set them up Micah's graven image, which he made, all the time that the house of God was in Shiloh.

JOHN 3:1–21

THERE was a man of the Pharisees, named Nicodemus, a ruler of the Jews:

2The same came to Jesus by night, and said unto him, Rabbi, we know that thou art a teacher come from God: for no man can do these miracles that thou doest, except God be with him.

3Jesus answered and said unto him, Verily, verily, I say unto thee, Except a man be born again, he cannot see the kingdom of God.

4Nicodemus saith unto him, How can a man be born when he is old? can he enter the second time into his mother's womb, and be born?

5Jesus answered, Verily, verily, I say unto thee, Except a man be born of water and *of* the Spirit, he cannot enter into the kingdom of God.

6That which is born of the flesh is flesh; and that which is born of the Spirit is spirit.

7Marvel not that I said unto thee, Ye must be born again.

8The wind bloweth where it listeth, and thou hearest the sound thereof, but canst not tell whence it cometh, and whither it goeth: so is every one that is born of the Spirit.

9Nicodemus answered and said unto him, How can these things be?

10Jesus answered and said unto him, Art thou a master of Israel, and knowest not these things?

11Verily, verily, I say unto thee, We speak that we do know, and testify that we have seen; and ye receive not our witness.

12If I have told you earthly things, and ye believe not, how shall ye believe, if I tell you *of* heavenly things?

13And no man hath ascended up to heaven, but he that came down from heaven, *even* the Son of man which is in heaven.

14And as Moses lifted up the serpent in the wilderness, even so must the Son of man be lifted up:

15That whosoever believeth in him should not perish, but have eternal life.

16For God so loved the world, that he gave his only begotten Son, that whosoever believeth in him should not perish, but have everlasting life.

17For God sent not his Son into the world to condemn the world; but that the world through him might be saved.

18He that believeth on him is not condemned: but he that believeth not is condemned already, because he hath not believed in the name of the only begotten Son of God.

19And this is the condemnation, that light is come into the world, and men loved darkness rather than light, because their deeds were evil.

20For every one that doeth evil hateth the light, neither cometh to the light, lest his deeds should be reproved.

21But he that doeth truth cometh to the light, that his deeds may be made manifest, that they are wrought in God.

PSALM 104:1–24

BLESS the LORD, O my soul. O LORD my God, thou art very great; thou art clothed with honour and majesty.

2Who coverest *thyself* with light as *with* a garment: who stretchest out the heavens like a curtain:

3Who layeth the beams of his chambers in the waters: who maketh the clouds his chariot: who walketh upon the wings of the wind:

4Who maketh his angels spirits; his ministers a flaming fire:

5*Who* laid the foundations of the earth, *that* it should not be removed for ever.

6Thou coveredst it with the deep as *with* a garment: the waters stood above the mountains.

7At thy rebuke they fled; at the voice of thy thunder they hasted away.

8They go up by the mountains; they

go down by the valleys unto the place which thou hast founded for them.

9Thou hast set a bound that they may not pass over; that they turn not again to cover the earth.

10He sendeth the springs into the valleys, *which* run among the hills.

11They give drink to every beast of the field: the wild asses quench their thirst.

12By them shall the fowls of the heaven have their habitation, *which* sing among the branches.

13He watereth the hills from his chambers: the earth is satisfied with the fruit of thy works.

14He causeth the grass to grow for the cattle, and herb for the service of man: that he may bring forth food out of the earth;

15And wine *that* maketh glad the heart of man, *and* oil to make *his* face to shine, and bread *which* strengtheneth man's heart.

16The trees of the LORD are full *of sap;* the cedars of Lebanon, which he hath planted;

17Where the birds make their nests: *as for* the stork, the fir trees *are* her house.

18The high hills *are* a refuge for the wild goats; *and* the rocks for the conies.

19He appointed the moon for seasons: the sun knoweth his going down.

20Thou makest darkness and it is night: wherein all the beasts of the forest do creep *forth.*

21The young lions roar after their prey, and seek their meat from God.

22The sun ariseth, they gather themselves together, and lay them down in their dens.

23Man goeth forth unto his work and to his labour until the evening.

24O LORD, how manifold are thy works! in wisdom hast thou made them all: the earth is full of thy riches.

PROVERBS FOR TODAY/ 14:20–21

The poor is hated even of his own neighbour: but the rich hath *many friends.* ☐ *He that despiseth his neighbour sinneth: but he that hath mercy on the poor, happy* is *he.*

MAY 4

JUDGES 19:1—20:48

AND it came to pass in those days, when *there was* no king in Israel, that there was a certain Levite sojourning on the side of mount Ephraim, who took to him a concubine out of Beth–lehem–judah.

2And his concubine played the whore against him, and went away from him unto her father's house to Beth–lehem–judah, and was there four whole months.

3And her husband arose, and went after her, to speak friendly unto her, *and* to bring her again, having his servant with him, and a couple of asses: and she brought him into her father's house: and when the father of the damsel saw him, he rejoiced to meet him.

4And his father in law, the damsel's father, retained him; and he abode with him three days: so they did eat and drink, and lodged there.

5And it came to pass on the fourth

day, when they arose early in the morning, that he rose up to depart: and the damsel's father said unto his son in law, Comfort thine heart with a morsel of bread, and afterward go your way.

6And they sat down, and did eat and drink both of them together: for the damsel's father had said unto the man, Be content, I pray thee, and tarry all night, and let thine heart be merry.

7And when the man rose up to depart, his father in law urged him: therefore he lodged there again.

8And he arose early in the morning on the fifth day to depart: and the damsel's father said, Comfort thine heart, I pray thee. And they tarried until afternoon, and they did eat both of them.

9And when the man rose up to depart, he, and his concubine, and his servant, his father in law, the damsel's father, said unto him, Behold, now the day draweth toward evening, I pray you tarry all night: behold, the day groweth to an end, lodge here, that thine heart may be merry; and to morrow get you early on your way, that thou mayest go home.

10But the man would not tarry that night, but he rose up and departed, and came over against Jebus, which *is* Jerusalem; and *there were* with him two asses saddled, his concubine also *was* with him.

11*And* when they *were* by Jebus, the day was far spent; and the servant said unto his master, Come, I pray thee, and let us turn in into this city of the Jebusites, and lodge in it.

12And his master said unto him, We will not turn aside hither into the city of a stranger, that *is* not of the children of Israel; we will pass over to Gibeah.

13And he said unto his servant, Come, and let us draw near to one of these places to lodge all night, in Gibeah, or in Ramah.

14And they passed on and went their way; and the sun went down upon them *when they were* by Gibeah, which *be-*

longeth to Benjamin.

15And they turned aside thither, to go in *and* to lodge in Gibeah: and when he went in, he sat him down in a street of the city: for *there was* no man that took them into his house to lodging.

16And, behold, there came an old man from his work out of the field at even, which *was* also of mount Ephraim; and he sojourned in Gibeah: but the men of the place *were* Benjamites.

17And when he had lifted up his eyes, he saw a wayfaring man in the street of the city: and the old man said, Whither goest thou? and whence comest thou?

18And he said unto him, We *are* passing from Beth–lehem–judah toward the side of mount Ephraim; from thence *am* I: and I went to Beth–lehem–judah, but I *am now* going to the house of the LORD; and there *is* no man that receiveth me to house.

19Yet there is both straw and provender for our asses; and there is bread and wine also for me, and for thy handmaid, and for the young man *which is* with thy servants: *there is* no want of any thing.

20And the old man said, Peace *be* with thee; howsoever *let* all thy wants *lie* upon me; only lodge not in the street.

21So he brought him into his house, and gave provender unto the asses: and they washed their feet, and did eat and drink.

22*Now* as they were making their hearts merry, behold, the men of the city, certain sons of Belial, beset the house round about, *and* beat at the door, and spake to the master of the house, the old man, saying, Bring forth the man that came into thine house, that we may know him.

23And the man, the master of the house, went out unto them, and said unto them, Nay, my brethren, *nay,* I pray you, do not *so* wickedly; seeing that this man is come into mine house, do not this folly.

24Behold, *here is* my daughter a

maiden, and his concubine; them I will bring out now, and humble ye them, and do with them what seemeth good unto you: but unto this man do not so vile a thing.

25But the men would not hearken to him: so the man took his concubine, and brought her forth unto them; and they knew her, and abused her all the night until the morning: and when the day began to spring, they let her go.

26Then came the woman in the dawning of the day, and fell down at the door of the man's house where her lord *was,* till it was light.

27And her lord rose up in the morning, and opened the doors of the house, and went out to go his way: and, behold, the woman his concubine was fallen down *at* the door of the house, and her hands *were* upon the threshold.

28And he said unto her, Up, and let us be going. But none answered. Then the man took her *up* upon an ass, and the man rose up, and gat him unto his place.

29And when he was come into his house, he took a knife, and laid hold on his concubine, and divided her, *together* with her bones, into twelve pieces, and sent her into all the coasts of Israel.

30And it was so, that all that saw it said, There was no such deed done nor seen from the day that the children of Israel came up out of the land of Egypt unto this day: consider of it, take advice, and speak *your minds.*

THEN all the children of Israel went out, and the congregation was gathered together as one man, from Dan even to Beer–sheba, with the land of Gilead, unto the LORD in Mizpeh.

2And the chief of all the people, *even* of all the tribes of Israel, presented themselves in the assembly of the people of God, four hundred thousand footmen that drew sword.

3(Now the children of Benjamin heard that the children of Israel were gone up to Mizpeh.) Then said the children of Israel, Tell *us,* how was this wickedness?

4And the Levite, the husband of the woman that was slain, answered and said, I came into Gibeah that *belongeth* to Benjamin, I and my concubine, to lodge.

5And the men of Gibeah rose against me, and beset the house round about upon me by night, *and* thought to have slain me: and my concubine have they forced, that she is dead.

6And I took my concubine, and cut her in pieces, and sent her throughout all the country of the inheritance of Israel: for they have committed lewdness and folly in Israel.

7Behold, ye *are* all children of Israel: give here your advice and counsel.

8And all the people arose as one man, saying, We will not any *of us* go to his tent, neither will we any *of us* turn into his house.

9But now this *shall be* the thing which we will do to Gibeah; *we will go up* by lot against it;

10And we will take ten men of an hundred throughout all the tribes of Israel, and an hundred of a thousand, and a thousand out of ten thousand, to fetch victual for the people, that they may do, when they come to Gibeah of Benjamin, according to all the folly that they have wrought in Israel.

11So all the men of Israel were gathered against the city, knit together as one man.

12And the tribes of Israel sent men through all the tribe of Benjamin, saying, What wickedness *is* this that is done among you?

13Now therefore deliver *us* the men, the children of Belial, which *are* in Gibeah, that we may put them to death, and put away evil from Israel. But the children of Benjamin would not hearken to the voice of their brethren the children of Israel:

14But the children of Benjamin gathered themselves together out of the cities unto Gibeah, to go out to battle against the children of Israel.

15And the children of Benjamin were numbered at that time out of the cities twenty and six thousand men that drew sword, beside the inhabitants of Gibeah, which were numbered seven hundred chosen men.

16Among all this people *there were* seven hundred chosen men lefthanded; every one could sling stones at an hair *breadth,* and not miss.

17And the men of Israel, beside Benjamin, were numbered four hundred thousand men that drew sword: all these *were* men of war.

18And the children of Israel arose, and went up to the house of God, and asked counsel of God, and said, Which of us shall go up first to the battle against the children of Benjamin? And the LORD said, Judah *shall go up* first.

19And the children of Israel rose up in the morning, and encamped against Gibeah.

20And the men of Israel went out to battle against Benjamin; and the men of Israel put themselves in array to fight against them at Gibeah.

21And the children of Benjamin came forth out of Gibeah, and destroyed down to the ground of the Israelites that day twenty and two thousand men.

22And the people the men of Israel encouraged themselves, and set their battle again in array in the place where they put themselves in array the first day.

23(And the children of Israel went up and wept before the LORD until even, and asked counsel of the LORD, saying, Shall I go up again to battle against the children of Benjamin my brother? And the LORD said, Go up against him.)

24And the children of Israel came near against the children of Benjamin the second day.

25And Benjamin went forth against

them out of Gibeah the second day, and destroyed down to the ground of the children of Israel again eighteen thousand men; all these drew the sword.

26Then all the children of Israel, and all the people, went up, and came unto the house of God, and wept, and sat there before the LORD, and fasted that day until even, and offered burnt offerings and peace offerings before the LORD.

27And the children of Israel enquired of the LORD, (for the ark of the covenant of God *was* there in those days,

28And Phinehas, the son of Eleazar, the son of Aaron, stood before it in those days,) saying, Shall I yet again go out to battle against the children of Benjamin my brother, or shall I cease? And the LORD said, Go up; for to morrow I will deliver them into thine hand.

29And Israel set liers in wait round about Gibeah.

30And the children of Israel went up against the children of Benjamin on the third day, and put themselves in array against Gibeah, as at other times.

31And the children of Benjamin went out against the people, *and* were drawn away from the city; and they began to smite of the people, *and* kill, as at other times, in the highways, of which one goeth up to the house of God, and the other to Gibeah in the field, about thirty men of Israel.

32And the children of Benjamin said, They *are* smitten down before us, as at the first. But the children of Israel said, Let us flee, and draw them from the city unto the highways.

33And all the men of Israel rose up out of their place, and put themselves in array at Baal-tamar: and the liers in wait of Israel came forth out of their places, *even* out of the meadows of Gibeah.

34And there came against Gibeah ten thousand chosen men out of all Israel, and the battle was sore: but they knew not that evil *was* near them.

35And the LORD smote Benjamin before Israel: and the children of Israel destroyed of the Benjamites that day twenty and five thousand and an hundred men: all these drew the sword.

36So the children of Benjamin saw that they were smitten: for the men of Israel gave place to the Benjamites, because they trusted unto the liers in wait which they had set beside Gibeah.

37And the liers in wait hasted, and rushed upon Gibeah; and the liers in wait drew *themselves* along, and smote all the city with the edge of the sword.

38Now there was an appointed sign between the men of Israel and the liers in wait, that they should make a great flame with smoke rise up out of the city.

39And when the men of Israel retired in the battle, Benjamin began to smite *and* kill of the men of Israel about thirty persons: for they said, Surely they are smitten down before us, as *in* the first battle.

40But when the flame began to arise up out of the city with a pillar of smoke, the Benjamites looked behind them, and, behold, the flame of the city ascended up to heaven.

41And when the men of Israel turned again, the men of Benjamin were amazed: for they saw that evil was coming upon them.

42Therefore they turned *their backs* before the men of Israel unto the way of the wilderness; but the battle overtook them; and them which *came* out of the cities they destroyed in the midst of them.

43*Thus* they inclosed the Benjamites round about, *and* chased them, *and* trode them down with ease over against Gibeah toward the sunrising.

44And there fell of Benjamin eighteen thousand men; all these *were* men of valour.

45And they turned and fled toward the wilderness unto the rock of Rimmon: and they gleaned of them in the highways five thousand men: and pursued hard after them unto Gidom, and slew two thousand men of them.

46So that all which fell that day of Benjamin were twenty and five thousand men that drew the sword; all these *were* men of valour.

47But six hundred men turned and fled to the wilderness unto the rock Rimmon, and abode in the rock Rimmon four months.

48And the men of Israel turned again upon the children of Benjamin, and smote them with the edge of the sword, as well the men of *every* city, as the beast, and all that came to hand: also they set on fire all the cities that they came to.

JOHN 3:22—4:4

AFTER these things came Jesus and his disciples into the land of Judaea; and there he tarried with them, and baptized.

23And John also was baptizing in Aenon near to Salim, because there was much water there: and they came, and were baptized.

24For John was not yet cast into prison.

25Then there arose a question between *some* of John's disciples and the Jews about purifying.

26And they came unto John, and said unto him, Rabbi, he that was with thee beyond Jordan, to whom thou barest witness, behold, the same baptizeth, and all *men* come to him.

27John answered and said, A man can receive nothing, except it be given him from heaven.

28Ye yourselves bear me witness, that I said, I am not the Christ, but that I am sent before him.

29He that hath the bride is the bridegroom: but the friend of the bridegroom, which standeth and heareth him, rejoiceth greatly because of the bridegroom's voice: this my joy therefore is fulfilled.

30He must increase, but I *must* decrease.

31He that cometh from above is above all: he that is of the earth is earthly, and speaketh of the earth: he that cometh from heaven is above all.

32And what he hath seen and heard, that he testifieth; and no man receiveth his testimony.

33He that hath received his testimony hath set to his seal that God is true.

34For he whom God hath sent speaketh the words of God: for God giveth not the Spirit by measure *unto him.*

35The Father loveth the Son, and hath given all things into his hand.

36He that believeth on the Son hath everlasting life: and he that believeth not the Son shall not see life; but the wrath of God abideth on him.

WHEN therefore the Lord knew how the Pharisees had heard that Jesus made and baptized more disciples than John,

2(Though Jesus himself baptized not, but his disciples,)

3He left Judaea, and departed again into Galilee.

4And he must needs go through Samaria.

PSALM 104:25–35

So is this great and wide sea, wherein *are* things creeping innumerable, both small and great beasts.

26There go the ships: *there is* that leviathan, *whom* thou hast made to play therein.

27These wait all upon thee; that thou mayest give *them* their meat in due season.

28*That* thou givest them they gather: thou openest thine hand, they are filled with good.

29Thou hidest thy face, they are troubled: thou takest away their breath, they die, and return to their dust.

30Thou sendest forth thy spirit, they are created: and thou renewest the face of the earth.

31The glory of the LORD shall endure for ever: the LORD shall rejoice in his works.

32He looketh on the earth, and it trembleth: he toucheth the hills, and they smoke.

33I will sing unto the LORD as long as I live: I will sing praise to my God while I have my being.

34My meditation of him shall be sweet: I will be glad in the LORD.

35Let the sinners be consumed out of the earth, and let the wicked be no more. Bless thou the LORD, O my soul. Praise ye the LORD.

PROVERBS FOR TODAY/ 14:22–24

Do they not err that devise evil? but mercy and truth shall be *to them that devise good.* □ *In all labour there is profit: but the talk of the lips* tendeth *only to penury.* □ *The crown of the wise* is *their riches:* but *the foolishness of fools* is *folly.*

JUDGES 21:1—RUTH 1:22

Now the men of Israel had sworn in Mizpeh, saying, There shall not any of us give his daughter unto Benjamin to wife.

2And the people came to the house of God, and abode there till even before God, and lifted up their voices, and wept sore;

3And said, O Lord God of Israel, why is this come to pass in Israel, that there should be to day one tribe lacking in Israel?

4And it came to pass on the morrow, that the people rose early, and built there an altar, and offered burnt offerings and peace offerings.

5And the children of Israel said, Who *is there* among all the tribes of Israel that came not up with the congregation unto the Lord? For they had made a great oath concerning him that came not up to the Lord to Mizpeh, saying, He shall surely be put to death.

6And the children of Israel repented them for Benjamin their brother, and said, There is one tribe cut off from Israel this day.

7How shall we do for wives for them that remain, seeing we have sworn by the Lord that we will not give them of our daughters to wives?

8And they said, What one *is there* of the tribes of Israel that came not up to Mizpeh to the Lord? And, behold, there came none to the camp from Jabesh–gilead to the assembly.

9For the people were numbered, and, behold, *there were* none of the inhabitants of Jabesh–gilead there.

10And the congregation sent thither twelve thousand men of the valiantest, and commanded them, saying, Go and smite the inhabitants of Jabesh–gilead with the edge of the sword, with the women and the children.

11And this *is* the thing that ye shall do, Ye shall utterly destroy every male, and every woman that hath lain by man.

12And they found among the inhabitants of Jabesh–gilead four hundred young virgins, that had known no man by lying with any male: and they brought them unto the camp to Shiloh, which *is* in the land of Canaan.

13And the whole congregation sent *some* to speak to the children of Benjamin that *were* in the rock Rimmon, and to call peaceably unto them.

14And Benjamin came again at that time; and they gave them wives which they had saved alive of the women of Jabesh–gilead: and yet so they sufficed them not.

15And the people repented them for Benjamin, because that the Lord had made a breach in the tribes of Israel.

16Then the elders of the congregation said, How shall we do for wives for them that remain, seeing the women are destroyed out of Benjamin?

17And they said, *There must be* an inheritance for them that be escaped of Benjamin, that a tribe be not destroyed out of Israel.

18Howbeit we may not give them wives of our daughters: for the children of Israel have sworn, saying, Cursed *be* he that giveth a wife to Benjamin.

19Then they said, Behold, *there is* a feast of the Lord in Shiloh yearly *in a place* which *is* on the north side of Beth–el, on the east side of the highway that goeth up from Beth–el to Shechem, and on the south of Lebonah.

20Therefore they commanded the children of Benjamin, saying, Go and lie in wait in the vineyards;

21And see, and, behold, if the daughters of Shiloh come out to dance in dances, then come ye out of the vineyards, and catch you every man his wife of the daughters of Shiloh, and go to the land of Benjamin.

22And it shall be, when their fathers or their brethren come unto us to complain, that we will say unto them, Be favourable unto them for our sakes: because we reserved not to each man his wife in the war: for ye did not give unto them at this time, *that* ye should be guilty.

23And the children of Benjamin did so, and took *them* wives, according to their number, of them that danced, whom they caught: and they went and returned unto their inheritance, and repaired the cities, and dwelt in them.

24And the children of Israel departed thence at that time, every man to his tribe and to his family, and they went out from thence every man to his inheritance.

25In those days *there was* no king in Israel: every man did *that which was* right in his own eyes.

Now it came to pass in the days when the judges ruled, that there was a famine in the land. And a certain man of Beth–lehem–judah went to sojourn in the country of Moab, he, and his wife, and his two sons.

2And the name of the man *was* Elimelech, and the name of his wife Naomi, and the name of his two sons Mahlon and Chilion, Ephrathites of Beth–lehem–judah. And they came into the country of Moab, and continued there.

3And Elimelech Naomi's husband died; and she was left, and her two sons.

4And they took them wives of the women of Moab; the name of the one *was* Orpah, and the name of the other Ruth: and they dwelled there about ten years.

5And Mahlon and Chilion died also both of them; and the woman was left of her two sons and her husband.

6Then she arose with her daughters in law, that she might return from the country of Moab: for she had heard in the country of Moab how that the LORD had visited his people in giving them bread.

7Wherefore she went forth out of the place where she was, and her two daughters in law with her; and they went on the way to return unto the land of Judah.

8And Naomi said unto her two daughters in law, Go, return each to her mother's house: the LORD deal kindly with you, as ye have dealt with the dead, and me.

9The LORD grant you that ye may find rest, each *of you* in the house of her husband. Then she kissed them; and they lifted up their voice, and wept.

10And they said unto her, Surely we will return with thee unto thy people.

11And Naomi said, Turn again, my daughters: why will ye go with me? *are* there yet *any more* sons in my womb, that they may be your husbands?

12Turn again, my daughters, go *your way;* for I am too old to have an husband. If I should say, I have hope, *if* I should have an husband also to night, and should also bear sons;

13Would ye tarry for them till they were grown? would ye stay for them from having husbands? nay, my daughters; for it grieveth me much for your sakes that the hand of the LORD is gone out against me.

14And they lifted up their voice, and wept again: and Orpah kissed her mother in law; but Ruth clave unto her.

15And she said, Behold, thy sister in law is gone back unto her people, and unto her gods: return thou after thy sister in law.

16And Ruth said, Entreat me not to leave thee, *or* to return from following after thee: for whither thou goest, I will go; and where thou lodgest, I will lodge: thy people *shall be* my people, and thy God my God:

17Where thou diest, will I die, and there will I be buried: the LORD do so to me, and more also, *if ought* but death part thee and me.

18When she saw that she was stedfastly minded to go with her, then she left speaking unto her.

19So they two went until they came to Beth–lehem. And it came to pass, when they were come to Beth–lehem, that all the city was moved about them, and they said, *Is* this Naomi?

20And she said unto them, Call me not Naomi, call me Mara: for the Almighty hath dealt very bitterly with me.

21I went out full, and the LORD hath brought me home again empty: why *then* call ye me Naomi, seeing the LORD hath testified against me, and the Almighty hath afflicted me?

22So Naomi returned, and Ruth the Moabitess, her daughter in law, with her, which returned out of the country of Moab: and they came to Beth–lehem in the beginning of barley harvest.

JOHN 4:5–42

THEN cometh he [Jesus] to a city of Samaria, which is called Sychar, near to the parcel of ground that Jacob gave to his son Joseph.

6Now Jacob's well was there. Jesus therefore, being wearied with *his* journey, sat thus on the well: *and* it was about the sixth hour.

7There cometh a woman of Samaria to draw water: Jesus saith unto her, Give me to drink.

8(For his disciples were gone away unto the city to buy meat.)

9Then saith the woman of Samaria unto him, How is it that thou, being a Jew, askest drink of me, which am a woman of Samaria? for the Jews have no dealings with the Samaritans.

10Jesus answered and said unto her, If thou knewest the gift of God, and who it is that saith to thee, Give me to drink; thou wouldest have asked of him, and he would have given thee living water.

11The woman saith unto him, Sir, thou hast nothing to draw with, and the well is deep: from whence then hast thou that living water?

12Art thou greater than our father Jacob, which gave us the well, and drank thereof himself, and his children, and his cattle?

13Jesus answered and said unto her, Whosoever drinketh of this water shall thirst again:

14But whosoever drinketh of the water that I shall give him shall never thirst; but the water that I shall give him shall be in him a well of water springing up into everlasting life.

15The woman saith unto him, Sir, give me this water, that I thirst not, neither come hither to draw.

16Jesus saith unto her, Go, call thy husband, and come hither.

17The woman answered and said, I have no husband. Jesus said unto her, Thou hast well said, I have no husband:

18For thou hast had five husbands; and he whom thou now hast is not thy husband: in that saidst thou truly.

19The woman saith unto him, Sir, I perceive that thou art a prophet.

20Our fathers worshipped in this mountain; and ye say, that in Jerusalem is the place where men ought to worship.

21Jesus saith unto her, Woman, believe me, the hour cometh, when ye shall neither in this mountain, nor yet at Jerusalem, worship the Father.

22Ye worship ye know not what: we know what we worship: for salvation is of the Jews.

23But the hour cometh, and now is, when the true worshippers shall worship the Father in spirit and in truth: for the Father seeketh such to worship him.

24God *is* a Spirit: and they that worship him must worship *him* in spirit and in truth.

25The woman saith unto him, I know that Messias cometh, which is called Christ: when he is come, he will tell us all things.

26Jesus saith unto her, I that speak unto thee am *he.*

27And upon this came his disciples, and marvelled that he talked with the woman: yet no man said, What seekest thou? or, Why talkest thou with her?

28The woman then left her waterpot, and went her way into the city, and saith to the men,

29Come, see a man, which told me all things that ever I did: is not this the Christ?

30Then they went out of the city, and came unto him.

31In the mean while his disciples prayed him, saying, Master, eat.

32But he said unto them, I have meat to eat that ye know not of.

33Therefore said the disciples one to another, Hath any man brought him *ought* to eat?

34Jesus saith unto them, My meat is to do the will of him that sent me, and to finish his work.

35Say not ye, There are yet four months, and *then* cometh harvest? behold, I say unto you, Lift up your eyes, and look on the fields; for they are white already to harvest.

36And he that reapeth receiveth wages, and gathereth fruit unto life eternal: that both he that soweth and he that reapeth may rejoice together.

37And herein is that saying true, One soweth, and another reapeth.

38I sent you to reap that whereon ye bestowed no labour: other men laboured, and ye are entered into their labours.

39And many of the Samaritans of that city believed on him for the saying of the woman, which testified, He told me all that ever I did.

40So when the Samaritans were come unto him, they besought him that he would tarry with them: and he

abode there two days.

41And many more believed because of his own word;

42And said unto the woman, Now we believe, not because of thy saying: for we have heard *him* ourselves, and know that this is indeed the Christ, the Saviour of the world.

PSALM 105:1–15

O GIVE thanks unto the LORD; call upon his name: make known his deeds among the people.

2Sing unto him, sing psalms unto him: talk ye of all his wondrous works.

3Glory ye in his holy name: let the heart of them rejoice that seek the LORD.

4Seek the LORD, and his strength: seek his face evermore.

5Remember his marvellous works that he hath done; his wonders, and the judgments of his mouth;

6O ye seed of Abraham his servant, ye children of Jacob his chosen.

7He *is* the LORD our God: his judgments *are* in all the earth.

8He hath remembered his covenant for ever, the word *which* he commanded to a thousand generations.

9Which *covenant* he made with Abraham, and his oath unto Isaac;

10And confirmed the same unto Jacob for a law, *and* to Israel *for* an everlasting covenant:

11Saying, Unto thee will I give the land of Canaan, the lot of your inheritance:

12When they were *but* a few men in number; yea, very few, and strangers in it.

13When they went from one nation to another, from *one* kingdom to another people;

14He suffered no man to do them wrong: yea, he reproved kings for their sakes;

15*Saying,* Touch not mine anointed, and do my prophets no harm.

PROVERBS FOR TODAY/ 14:25

A true witness delivereth souls: but a deceitful witness *speaketh lies.*

MAY 6

RUTH 2:1—4:22

AND Naomi had a kinsman of her husband's, a mighty man of wealth, of the family of Elimelech; and his name *was* Boaz.

2And Ruth the Moabitess said unto Naomi, Let me now go to the field, and glean ears of corn after *him* in whose sight I shall find grace. And she said unto her, Go, my daughter.

3And she went, and came, and gleaned in the field after the reapers: and her hap was to light on a part of the field *belonging* unto Boaz, who *was* of the kindred of Elimelech.

4And, behold, Boaz came from Beth–lehem, and said unto the reapers, The LORD *be* with you. And they answered him, The LORD bless thee.

5Then said Boaz unto his servant that was set over the reapers, Whose damsel *is* this?

6And the servant that was set over the reapers answered and said, It *is* the Moabitish damsel that came back with Naomi out of the country of Moab:

7And she said, I pray you, let me glean and gather after the reapers among the sheaves: so she came, and hath continued even from the morning until now, that she tarried a little in the house.

8Then said Boaz unto Ruth, Hearest thou not, my daughter? Go not to glean in another field, neither go from hence, but abide here fast by my maidens:

9*Let* thine eyes *be* on the field that they do reap, and go thou after them: have I not charged the young men that they shall not touch thee? and when thou art a thirst, go unto the vessels, and drink of *that* which the young men have drawn.

10Then she fell on her face, and bowed herself to the ground, and said unto him, Why have I found grace in thine eyes, that thou shouldest take knowledge of me, seeing I *am* a stranger?

11And Boaz answered and said unto her, It hath fully been shewed me, all that thou hast done unto thy mother in law since the death of thine husband: and *how* thou hast left thy father and thy mother, and the land of thy nativity, and art come unto a people which thou knewest not heretofore.

12The LORD recompense thy work, and a full reward be given thee of the LORD God of Israel, under whose wings thou art come to trust.

13Then she said, Let me find favour in thy sight, my lord; for that thou hast comforted me, and for that thou hast spoken friendly unto thine handmaid, though I be not like unto one of thine handmaidens.

14And Boaz said unto her, At mealtime come thou hither, and eat of the bread, and dip thy morsel in the vinegar. And she sat beside the reapers: and he reached her parched *corn,* and she did eat, and was sufficed, and left.

15And when she was risen up to glean, Boaz commanded his young men, saying, Let her glean even among the sheaves, and reproach her not:

16And let fall also *some* of the handfuls

of purpose for her, and leave *them,* that she may glean *them,* and rebuke her not.

17So she gleaned in the field until even, and beat out that she had gleaned: and it was about an ephah of barley.

18And she took *it* up, and went into the city: and her mother in law saw what she had gleaned: and she brought forth, and gave to her that she had reserved after she was sufficed.

19And her mother in law said unto her, Where hast thou gleaned today? and where wroughtest thou? blessed be he that did take knowledge of thee. And she shewed her mother in law with whom she had wrought, and said, The man's name with whom I wrought today *is* Boaz.

20And Naomi said unto her daughter in law, Blessed *be* he of the LORD, who hath not left off his kindness to the living and to the dead. And Naomi said unto her, The man *is* near of kin unto us, one of our next kinsmen.

21And Ruth the Moabitess said, He said unto me also, Thou shalt keep fast by my young men, until they have ended all my harvest.

22And Naomi said unto Ruth her daughter in law, *It is* good, my daughter, that thou go out with his maidens, that they meet thee not in any other field.

23So she kept fast by the maidens of Boaz to glean unto the end of barley harvest and of wheat harvest; and dwelt with her mother in law.

THEN Naomi her mother in law said unto her, My daughter, shall I not seek rest for thee, that it may be well with thee?

2And now *is* not Boaz of our kindred, with whose maidens thou wast? Behold, he winnoweth barley to night in the threshingfloor.

3Wash thyself therefore, and anoint thee, and put thy raiment upon thee, and get thee down to the floor: *but* make not thyself known unto the man,

until he shall have done eating and drinking.

4And it shall be, when he lieth down, that thou shalt mark the place where he shall lie, and thou shalt go in, and uncover his feet, and lay thee down; and he will tell thee what thou shalt do.

5And she said unto her, All that thou sayest unto me I will do.

6And she went down unto the floor, and did according to all that her mother in law bade her.

7And when Boaz had eaten and drunk, and his heart was merry, he went to lie down at the end of the heap of corn: and she came softly, and uncovered his feet, and laid her down.

8And it came to pass at midnight, that the man was afraid, and turned himself: and, behold, a woman lay at his feet.

9And he said, Who *art* thou? And she answered, I *am* Ruth thine handmaid: spread therefore thy skirt over thine handmaid; for thou *art* a near kinsman.

10And he said, Blessed *be* thou of the LORD, my daughter: *for* thou hast shewed more kindness in the latter end than at the beginning, inasmuch as thou followedst not young men, whether poor or rich.

11And now, my daughter, fear not; I will do to thee all that thou requirest: for all the city of my people doth know that thou *art* a virtuous woman.

12And now it is true that I *am thy* near kinsman: howbeit there is a kinsman nearer than I.

13Tarry this night, and it shall be in the morning, *that* if he will perform unto thee the part of a kinsman, well; let him do the kinsman's part: but if he will not do the part of a kinsman to thee, then will I do the part of a kinsman to thee, *as* the LORD liveth: lie down until the morning.

14And she lay at his feet until the morning: and she rose up before one could know another. And he said, Let it not be known that a woman came into the floor.

15Also he said, Bring the vail that *thou hast* upon thee, and hold it. And when she held it, he measured six *measures* of barley, and laid *it* on her: and she went into the city.

16And when she came to her mother in law, she said, Who *art* thou, my daughter? And she told her all that the man had done to her.

17And she said, These six *measures* of barley gave he me; for he said to me, Go not empty unto thy mother in law.

18Then said she, Sit still, my daughter, until thou know how the matter will fall: for the man will not be in rest, until he have finished the thing this day.

THEN went Boaz up to the gate, and sat him down there: and, behold, the kinsman of whom Boaz spake came by; unto whom he said, Ho, such a one! turn aside, sit down here. And he turned aside, and sat down.

2And he took ten men of the elders of the city, and said, Sit ye down here. And they sat down.

3And he said unto the kinsman, Naomi, that is come again out of the country of Moab, selleth a parcel of land, which *was* our brother Elimelech's:

4And I thought to advertise thee, saying, Buy *it* before the inhabitants, and before the elders of my people. If thou wilt redeem *it,* redeem *it:* but if thou wilt not redeem *it, then* tell me, that I may know: for *there is* none to redeem *it* beside thee; and I *am* after thee. And he said, I will redeem *it.*

5Then said Boaz, What day thou buyest the field of the hand of Naomi, thou must buy *it* also of Ruth the Moabitess, the wife of the dead, to raise up the name of the dead upon his inheritance.

6And the kinsman said, I cannot redeem *it* for myself, lest I mar mine own inheritance: redeem thou my right to thyself; for I cannot redeem *it.*

7Now this *was the manner* in former time in Israel concerning redeeming and concerning changing, for to confirm all things; a man plucked off his shoe, and gave *it* to his neighbour: and this *was* a testimony in Israel.

8Therefore the kinsman said unto Boaz, Buy *it* for thee. So he drew off his shoe.

9And Boaz said unto the elders, and *unto* all the people, Ye *are* witnesses this day, that I have bought all that *was* Elimelech's, and all that *was* Chilion's and Mahlon's, of the hand of Naomi.

10Moreover Ruth the Moabitess, the wife of Mahlon, have I purchased to be my wife, to raise up the name of the dead upon his inheritance, that the name of the dead be not cut off from among his brethren, and from the gate of his place: ye *are* witnesses this day.

11And all the people that *were* in the gate, and the elders, said, *We are* witnesses. The LORD make the woman that is come into thine house like Rachel and like Leah, which two did build the house of Israel: and do thou worthily in Ephratah, and be famous in Beth–lehem:

12And let thy house be like the house of Pharez, whom Tamar bare unto Judah, of the seed which the LORD shall give thee of this young woman.

13So Boaz took Ruth, and she was his wife: and when he went in unto her, the LORD gave her conception, and she bare a son.

14And the women said unto Naomi, Blessed *be* the LORD, which hath not left thee this day without a kinsman, that his name may be famous in Israel.

15And he shall be unto thee a restorer of *thy* life, and a nourisher of thine old age: for thy daughter in law, which loveth thee, which is better to thee than seven sons, hath born him.

16And Naomi took the child, and laid

it in her bosom, and became nurse unto it.

17And the women her neighbours gave it a name, saying, There is a son born to Naomi; and they called his name Obed: he *is* the father of Jesse, the father of David.

18Now these *are* the generations of Pharez: Pharez begat Hezron,

19And Hezron begat Ram, and Ram begat Amminadab,

20And Amminadab begat Nahshon, and Nahshon begat Salmon,

21And Salmon begat Boaz, and Boaz begat Obed,

22And Obed begat Jesse, and Jesse begat David.

JOHN 4:43–54

Now after two days he [Jesus] departed thence, and went into Galilee.

44For Jesus himself testified, that a prophet hath no honour in his own country.

45Then when he was come into Galilee, the Galilaeans received him, having seen all the things that he did at Jerusalem at the feast: for they also went unto the feast.

46So Jesus came again into Cana of Galilee, where he made the water wine. And there was a certain nobleman, whose son was sick at Capernaum.

47When he heard that Jesus was come out of Judaea into Galilee, he went unto him, and besought him that he would come down, and heal his son: for he was at the point of death.

48Then said Jesus unto him, Except ye see signs and wonders, ye will not believe.

49The nobleman saith unto him, Sir, come down ere my child die.

50Jesus saith unto him, Go thy way; thy son liveth. And the man believed the word that Jesus had spoken unto him, and he went his way.

51And as he was now going down,

his servants met him, and told *him,* saying, Thy son liveth.

52Then enquired he of them the hour when he began to amend. And they said unto him, Yesterday at the seventh hour the fever left him.

53So the father knew that *it was* at the same hour, in the which Jesus said unto him, Thy son liveth: and himself believed, and his whole house.

54This *is* again the second miracle *that* Jesus did, when he was come out of Judaea into Galilee.

PSALM 105:16–38

Moreover he called for a famine upon the land: he brake the whole staff of bread.

17He sent a man before them, *even* Joseph, *who* was sold for a servant:

18Whose feet they hurt with fetters: he was laid in iron:

19Until the time that his word came: the word of the LORD tried him.

20The king sent and loosed him; *even* the ruler of the people, and let him go free.

21He made him lord of his house, and ruler of all his substance:

22To bind his princes at his pleasure; and teach his senators wisdom.

23Israel also came into Egypt; and Jacob sojourned in the land of Ham.

24And he increased his people greatly; and made them stronger than their enemies.

25He turned their heart to hate his people, to deal subtilly with his servants.

26He sent Moses his servant; *and* Aaron whom he had chosen.

27They shewed his signs among them, and wonders in the land of Ham.

28He sent darkness, and made it dark; and they rebelled not against his word.

29He turned their waters into blood, and slew their fish.

30Their land brought forth frogs in

abundance, in the chambers of their kings.

31He spake, and there came divers sorts of flies, *and* lice in all their coasts.

32He gave them hail for rain, *and* flaming fire in their land.

33He smote their vines also and their fig trees; and brake the trees of their coasts.

34He spake, and the locusts came, and caterpillers, and that without number,

35And did eat up all the herbs in their land, and devoured the fruit of their ground.

36He smote also all the firstborn in their land, the chief of all their strength.

37He brought them forth also with silver and gold: and *there was* not one feeble *person* among their tribes.

38Egypt was glad when they departed: for the fear of them fell upon them.

PROVERBS FOR TODAY/ 14:26–27

In the fear of the Lord *is* strong confidence: and his children shall have a place *of refuge. The fear of the* Lord *is* a fountain of life, to depart from the snares of *death.*

MAY 7

1 SAMUEL 1:1—2:21

Now there was a certain man of Ramathaim–zophim, of mount Ephraim, and his name *was* Elkanah, the son of Jeroham, the son of Elihu, the son of Tohu, the son of Zuph, an Ephrathite:

2And he had two wives; the name of the one *was* Hannah, and the name of the other Peninnah: and Peninnah had children, but Hannah had no children.

3And this man went up out of his city yearly to worship and to sacrifice unto the Lord of hosts in Shiloh. And the two sons of Eli, Hophni and Phinehas, the priests of the Lord, *were* there.

4And when the time was that Elkanah offered, he gave to Peninnah his wife, and to all her sons and her daughters, portions:

5But unto Hannah he gave a worthy portion; for he loved Hannah: but the Lord had shut up her womb.

6And her adversary also provoked her sore, for to make her fret, because the Lord had shut up her womb.

7And *as* he did so year by year, when she went up to the house of the Lord, so she provoked her; therefore she wept, and did not eat.

8Then said Elkanah her husband to her, Hannah, why weepest thou? and why eatest thou not? and why is thy heart grieved? *am* not I better to thee than ten sons?

9So Hannah rose up after they had eaten in Shiloh, and after they had drunk. Now Eli the priest sat upon a seat by a post of the temple of the Lord.

10And she *was* in bitterness of soul, and prayed unto the Lord, and wept sore.

11And she vowed a vow, and said, O Lord of hosts, if thou wilt indeed look on the affliction of thine handmaid, and remember me, and not forget thine handmaid, but wilt give unto thine handmaid a man child, then I will give him unto the LORD all the days of his life, and there shall no razor come upon his head.

12And it came to pass, as she continued praying before the LORD, that Eli marked her mouth.

13Now Hannah, she spake in her heart; only her lips moved, but her voice was not heard: therefore Eli thought she had been drunken.

14And Eli said unto her, How long wilt thou be drunken? put away thy wine from thee.

15And Hannah answered and said, No, my lord, I *am* a woman of a sorrowful spirit: I have drunk neither wine nor strong drink, but have poured out my soul before the LORD.

16Count not thine handmaid for a daughter of Belial: for out of the abundance of my complaint and grief have I spoken hitherto.

17Then Eli answered and said, Go in peace: and the God of Israel grant *thee* thy petition that thou hast asked of him.

18And she said, Let thine handmaid find grace in thy sight. So the woman went her way, and did eat, and her countenance was no more *sad.*

19And they rose up in the morning early, and worshipped before the LORD, and returned, and came to their house to Ramah: and Elkanah knew Hannah his wife; and the LORD remembered her.

20Wherefore it came to pass, when the time was come about after Hannah had conceived, that she bare a son, and called his name Samuel, *saying,* Because I have asked him of the LORD.

21And the man Elkanah, and all his house, went up to offer unto the LORD the yearly sacrifice, and his vow.

22But Hannah went not up; for she said unto her husband, *I will not go up* until the child be weaned, and *then*

I will bring him, that he may appear before the LORD, and there abide for ever.

23And Elkanah her husband said unto her, Do what seemeth thee good; tarry until thou have weaned him; only the LORD establish his word. So the woman abode, and gave her son suck until she weaned him.

24And when she had weaned him, she took him up with her, with three bullocks, and one ephah of flour, and a bottle of wine, and brought him unto the house of the LORD in Shiloh: and the child *was* young.

25And they slew a bullock, and brought the child to Eli.

26And she said, Oh my lord, *as* thy soul liveth, my lord, I *am* the woman that stood by thee here, praying unto the LORD.

27For this child I prayed; and the LORD hath given me my petition which I asked of him:

28Therefore also I have lent him to the LORD; as long as he liveth he shall be lent to the LORD. And he worshipped the LORD there.

AND Hannah prayed, and said, My heart rejoiceth in the LORD, mine horn is exalted in the LORD: my mouth is enlarged over mine enemies; because I rejoice in thy salvation.

2*There is* none holy as the LORD: for *there is* none beside thee: neither *is there* any rock like our God.

3Talk no more so exceeding proudly; let *not* arrogancy come out of your mouth: for the LORD *is* a God of knowledge, and by him actions are weighed.

4The bows of the mighty men *are* broken, and they that stumbled are girded with strength.

5*They that were* full have hired out themselves for bread; and *they that were* hungry ceased: so that the barren hath born seven; and she that hath many children is waxed feeble.

6The LORD killeth, and maketh alive:

he bringeth down to the grave, and bringeth up.

7The LORD maketh poor, and maketh rich: he bringeth low, and lifteth up.

8He raiseth up the poor out of the dust, *and* lifteth up the beggar from the dunghill, to set *them* among princes, and to make them inherit the throne of glory: for the pillars of the earth *are* the LORD'S, and he hath set the world upon them.

9He will keep the feet of his saints, and the wicked shall be silent in darkness; for by strength shall no man prevail.

10The adversaries of the LORD shall be broken to pieces; out of heaven shall he thunder upon them: the LORD shall judge the ends of the earth; and he shall give strength unto his king, and exalt the horn of his anointed.

11And Elkanah went to Ramah to his house. And the child did minister unto the LORD before Eli the priest.

12Now the sons of Eli *were* sons of Belial; they knew not the LORD.

13And the priest's custom with the people *was, that,* when any man offered sacrifice, the priest's servant came, while the flesh was in seething, with a fleshhook of three teeth in his hand;

14And he struck *it* into the pan, or kettle, or caldron, or pot; all that the fleshhook brought up the priest took for himself. So they did in Shiloh unto all the Israelites that came thither.

15Also before they burnt the fat, the priest's servant came, and said to the man that sacrificed, Give flesh to roast for the priest; for he will not have sodden flesh of thee, but raw.

16And *if* any man said unto him, Let them not fail to burn the fat presently, and *then* take *as much* as thy soul desireth; then he would answer him, *Nay;* but thou shalt give *it me* now: and if not, I will take *it* by force.

17Wherefore the sin of the young men was very great before the LORD: for men abhorred the offering of the LORD.

18But Samuel ministered before the LORD, *being* a child, girded with a linen ephod.

19Moreover his mother made him a little coat, and brought *it* to him from year to year, when she came up with her husband to offer the yearly sacrifice.

20And Eli blessed Elkanah and his wife, and said, The LORD give thee seed of this woman for the loan which is lent to the LORD. And they went unto their own home.

21And the LORD visited Hannah, so that she conceived, and bare three sons and two daughters. And the child Samuel grew before the LORD.

JOHN 5:1–23

AFTER this there was a feast of the Jews; and Jesus went up to Jerusalem.

2Now there is at Jerusalem by the sheep *market* a pool, which is called in the Hebrew tongue Bethesda, having five porches.

3In these lay a great multitude of impotent folk, of blind, halt, withered, waiting for the moving of the water.

4For an angel went down at a certain season into the pool, and troubled the water: whosoever then first after the troubling of the water stepped in was made whole of whatsoever disease he had.

5And a certain man was there, which had an infirmity thirty and eight years.

6When Jesus saw him lie, and knew that he had been now a long time *in that case,* he saith unto him, Wilt thou be made whole?

7The impotent man answered him, Sir, I have no man, when the water is troubled, to put me into the pool: but while I am coming, another steppeth down before me.

8Jesus saith unto him, Rise, take up thy bed, and walk.

9And immediately the man was made

whole, and took up his bed, and walked: and on the same day was the sabbath.

10The Jews therefore said unto him that was cured, It is the sabbath day: it is not lawful for thee to carry *thy* bed.

11He answered them, He that made me whole, the same said unto me, Take up thy bed, and walk.

12Then asked they him, What man is that which said unto thee, Take up thy bed, and walk?

13And he that was healed wist not who it was: for Jesus had conveyed himself away, a multitude being in *that* place.

14Afterward Jesus findeth him in the temple, and said unto him, Behold, thou art made whole: sin no more, lest a worse thing come unto thee.

15The man departed, and told the Jews that it was Jesus, which had made him whole.

16And therefore did the Jews persecute Jesus, and sought to slay him, because he had done these things on the sabbath day.

17But Jesus answered them, My Father worketh hitherto, and I work.

18Therefore the Jews sought the more to kill him, because he not only had broken the sabbath, but said also that God was his Father, making himself equal with God.

19Then answered Jesus and said unto them, Verily, verily, I say unto you, The Son can do nothing of himself, but what he seeth the Father do: for what things soever he doeth, these also doeth the Son likewise.

20For the Father loveth the Son, and sheweth him all things that himself doeth: and he will shew him greater works than these, that ye may marvel.

21For as the Father raiseth up the dead, and quickeneth *them;* even so the Son quickeneth whom he will.

22For the Father judgeth no man, but hath committed all judgment unto the Son:

23That all *men* should honour the Son, even as they honour the Father. He that honoureth not the Son honoureth not the Father which hath sent him.

PSALM 105:39–45

HE spread a cloud for a covering; and fire to give light in the night.

40*The people* asked, and he brought quails, and satisfied them with the bread of heaven.

41He opened the rock, and the waters gushed out; they ran in the dry places *like* a river.

42For he remembered his holy promise, *and* Abraham his servant.

43And he brought forth his people with joy, *and* his chosen with gladness:

44And gave them the lands of the heathen: and they inherited the labour of the people;

45That they might observe his statutes, and keep his laws. Praise ye the LORD.

PROVERBS FOR TODAY/ 14:28–29

In the multitude of people is *the king's honour: but in the want of people* is *the destruction of the prince.* □ He that is *slow to wrath* is *of great understanding: but* he that is *hasty of spirit exalteth folly.*

MAY 8

1 SAMUEL 2:22—4:22

Now Eli was very old, and heard all that his sons did unto all Israel; and how they lay with the women that assembled *at* the door of the tabernacle of the congregation.

23And he said unto them, Why do ye such things? for I hear of your evil dealings by all this people.

24Nay, my sons; for *it is* no good report that I hear: ye make the LORD'S people to transgress.

25If one man sin against another, the judge shall judge him: but if a man sin against the LORD, who shall intreat for him? Notwithstanding they hearkened not unto the voice of their father, because the LORD would slay them.

26And the child Samuel grew on, and was in favour both with the LORD, and also with men.

27And there came a man of God unto Eli, and said unto him, Thus saith the LORD, Did I plainly appear unto the house of thy father, when they were in Egypt in Pharaoh's house?

28And did I choose him out of all the tribes of Israel *to be* my priest, to offer upon mine altar, to burn incense, to wear an ephod before me? and did I give unto the house of thy father all the offerings made by fire of the children of Israel?

29Wherefore kick ye at my sacrifice and at mine offering, which I have commanded *in my* habitation; and honourest thy sons above me, to make yourselves fat with the chiefest of all the offerings of Israel my people?

30Wherefore the LORD God of Israel saith, I said indeed *that* thy house, and the house of thy father, should walk before me for ever: but now the LORD saith, Be it far from me; for them that

honour me I will honour, and they that despise me shall be lightly esteemed.

31Behold, the days come, that I will cut off thine arm, and the arm of thy father's house, that there shall not be an old man in thine house.

32And thou shalt see an enemy *in my* habitation, in all *the wealth* which *God* shall give Israel: and there shall not be an old man in thine house for ever.

33And the man of thine, *whom* I shall not cut off from mine altar, *shall be* to consume thine eyes, and to grieve thine heart: and all the increase of thine house shall die in the flower of their age.

34And this *shall be* a sign unto thee, that shall come upon thy two sons, on Hophni and Phinehas; in one day they shall die both of them.

35And I will raise me up a faithful priest, *that* shall do according to *that* which *is* in mine heart and in my mind: and I will build him a sure house; and he shall walk before mine anointed for ever.

36And it shall come to pass, *that* every one that is left in thine house shall come *and* crouch to him for a piece of silver and a morsel of bread, and shall say, Put me, I pray thee, into one of the priests' offices, that I may eat a piece of bread.

AND the child Samuel ministered unto the LORD before Eli. And the word of the LORD was precious in those days; *there was* no open vision.

2And it came to pass at that time, when Eli *was* laid down in his place, and his eyes began to wax dim, *that* he could not see;

3And ere the lamp of God went out

in the temple of the LORD, where the ark of God *was,* and Samuel was laid down *to sleep;*

⁴That the LORD called Samuel: and he answered, Here *am* I.

⁵And he ran unto Eli, and said, Here *am* I; for thou calledst me. And he said, I called not; lie down again. And he went and lay down.

⁶And the LORD called yet again, Samuel. And Samuel arose and went to Eli, and said, Here *am* I; for thou didst call me. And he answered, I called not, my son; lie down again.

⁷Now Samuel did not yet know the LORD, neither was the word of the LORD yet revealed unto him.

⁸And the LORD called Samuel again the third time. And he arose and went to Eli, and said, Here *am* I; for thou didst call me. And Eli perceived that the LORD had called the child.

⁹Therefore Eli said unto Samuel, Go, lie down: and it shall be, if he call thee, that thou shalt say, Speak, LORD; for thy servant heareth. So Samuel went and lay down in his place.

¹⁰And the LORD came, and stood, and called as at other times, Samuel, Samuel. Then Samuel answered, Speak; for thy servant heareth.

¹¹And the LORD said to Samuel, Behold, I will do a thing in Israel, at which both the ears of every one that heareth it shall tingle.

¹²In that day I will perform against Eli all *things* which I have spoken concerning his house: when I begin, I will also make an end.

¹³For I have told him that I will judge his house for ever for the iniquity which he knoweth; because his sons made themselves vile, and he restrained them not.

¹⁴And therefore I have sworn unto the house of Eli, that the iniquity of Eli's house shall not be purged with sacrifice nor offering for ever.

¹⁵And Samuel lay until the morning, and opened the doors of the house of the LORD. And Samuel feared to shew Eli the vision.

¹⁶Then Eli called Samuel, and said, Samuel, my son. And he answered, Here *am* I.

¹⁷And he said, What *is* the thing that *the LORD hath said unto thee? I pray thee hide it* not from me: God do so to thee, and more also, if thou hide *any* thing from me of all the things that he said unto thee.

¹⁸And Samuel told him every whit, and hid nothing from him. And he said, It *is* the LORD: let him do what seemeth him good.

¹⁹And Samuel grew, and the LORD was with him, and did let none of his words fall to the ground.

²⁰And all Israel from Dan even to Beer–sheba knew that Samuel *was* established *to be* a prophet of the LORD.

²¹And the LORD appeared again in Shiloh: for the LORD revealed himself to Samuel in Shiloh by the word of the LORD.

AND the word of Samuel came to all Israel. Now Israel went out against the Philistines to battle, and pitched beside Eben–ezer: and the Philistines pitched in Aphek.

²And the Philistines put themselves in array against Israel: and when they joined battle, Israel was smitten before the Philistines: and they slew of the army in the field about four thousand men.

³And when the people were come into the camp, the elders of Israel said, Wherefore hath the LORD smitten us to day before the Philistines? Let us fetch the ark of the covenant of the LORD out of Shiloh unto us, that, when it cometh among us, it may save us out of the hand of our enemies.

⁴So the people sent to Shiloh, that they might bring from thence the ark of the covenant of the LORD of hosts, which dwelleth *between* the cherubims: and the two sons of Eli, Hophni and

Phinehas, *were* there with the ark of the covenant of God.

5And when the ark of the covenant of the LORD came into the camp, all Israel shouted with a great shout, so that the earth rang again.

6And when the Philistines heard the noise of the shout, they said, What *meaneth* the noise of this great shout in the camp of the Hebrews? And they understood that the ark of the LORD was come into the camp.

7And the Philistines were afraid, for they said, God is come into the camp. And they said, Woe unto us! for there hath not been such a thing heretofore.

8Woe unto us! who shall deliver us out of the hand of these mighty Gods? these *are* the Gods that smote the Egyptians with all the plagues in the wilderness.

9Be strong, and quit yourselves like men, O ye Philistines, that ye be not servants unto the Hebrews, as they have been to you: quit yourselves like men, and fight.

10And the Philistines fought, and Israel was smitten, and they fled every man into his tent: and there was a very great slaughter; for there fell of Israel thirty thousand footmen.

11And the ark of God was taken; and the two sons of Eli, Hophni and Phinehas, were slain.

12And there ran a man of Benjamin out of the army, and came to Shiloh the same day with his clothes rent, and with earth upon his head.

13And when he came, lo, Eli sat upon a seat by the wayside watching: for his heart trembled for the ark of God. And when the man came into the city, and told *it,* all the city cried out.

14And when Eli heard the noise of the crying, he said, What *meaneth* the noise of this tumult? And the man came in hastily, and told Eli.

15Now Eli was ninety and eight years old; and his eyes were dim, that he could not see.

16And the man said unto Eli, I *am* he that came out of the army, and I fled to day out of the army. And he said, What is there done, my son?

17And the messenger answered and said, Israel is fled before the Philistines, and there hath been also a great slaughter among the people, and thy two sons also, Hophni and Phinehas, are dead, and the ark of God is taken.

18And it came to pass, when he made mention of the ark of God, that he fell from off the seat backward by the side of the gate, and his neck brake, and he died: for he was an old man, and heavy. And he had judged Israel forty years.

19And his daughter in law, Phinehas' wife, was with child, *near* to be delivered: and when she heard the tidings that the ark of God was taken, and that her father in law and her husband were dead, she bowed herself and travailed; for her pains came upon her.

20And about the time of her death the women that stood by her said unto her, Fear not; for thou hast born a son. But she answered not, neither did she regard *it.*

21And she named the child I-chabod, saying, The glory is departed from Israel: because the ark of God was taken, and because of her father in law and her husband.

22And she said, The glory is departed from Israel: for the ark of God is taken.

JOHN 5:24–47

VERILY, verily, I say unto you, He that heareth my word, and believeth on him that sent me, hath everlasting life, and shall not come into condemnation; but is passed from death unto life.

25Verily, verily, I say unto you, The hour is coming, and now is, when the dead shall hear the voice of the Son of God: and they that hear shall live.

26For as the Father hath life in himself; so hath he given to the Son to have life in himself;

27And hath given him authority to execute judgment also, because he is the Son of man.

28Marvel not at this: for the hour is coming, in the which all that are in the graves shall hear his voice,

29And shall come forth; they that have done good, unto the resurrection of life; and they that have done evil, unto the resurrection of damnation.

30I can of mine own self do nothing: as I hear, I judge: and my judgment is just; because I seek not mine own will, but the will of the Father which hath sent me.

31If I bear witness of myself, my witness is not true.

32There is another that beareth witness of me; and I know that the witness which he witnesseth of me is true.

33Ye sent unto John, and he bare witness unto the truth.

34But I receive not testimony from man: but these things I say, that ye might be saved.

35He was a burning and a shining light: and ye were willing for a season to rejoice in his light.

36But I have greater witness than *that* of John: for the works which the Father hath given me to finish, the same works that I do, bear witness of me, that the Father hath sent me.

37And the Father himself, which hath sent me, hath borne witness of me. Ye have neither heard his voice at any time, nor seen his shape.

38And ye have not his word abiding in you: for whom he hath sent, him ye believe not.

39Search the scriptures; for in them ye think ye have eternal life: and they are they which testify of me.

40And ye will not come to me, that ye might have life.

41I receive not honour from men.

42But I know you, that ye have not the love of God in you.

43I am come in my Father's name, and ye receive me not: if another shall come in his own name, him ye will receive.

44How can ye believe, which receive honour one of another, and seek not the honour that *cometh* from God only?

45Do not think that I will accuse you to the Father: there is *one* that accuseth you, *even* Moses in whom ye trust.

46For had ye believed Moses, ye would have believed me: for he wrote of me.

47But if ye believe not his writings, how shall ye believe my words?

PSALM 106:1–12

Praise ye the Lord. O give thanks unto the Lord; for *he is* good: for his mercy *endureth* for ever.

2Who can utter the mighty acts of the Lord? who can shew forth all his praise?

3Blessed *are* they that keep judgment, *and* he that doeth righteousness at all times.

4Remember me, O Lord, with the favour *that thou bearest unto* thy people: O visit me with thy salvation;

5That I may see the good of thy chosen, that I may rejoice in the gladness of thy nation, that I may glory with thine inheritance.

6We have sinned with our fathers, we have committed iniquity, we have done wickedly.

7Our fathers understood not thy wonders in Egypt; they remembered not the multitude of thy mercies; but provoked *him* at the sea, *even* at the Red sea.

8Nevertheless he saved them for his name's sake, that he might make his mighty power to be known.

9He rebuked the Red sea also, and it was dried up: so he led them through the depths, as through the wilderness.

10And he saved them from the hand

of him that hated *them,* and redeemed them from the hand of the enemy.

¹¹And the waters covered their ene-

mies: there was not one of them left.

¹²Then believed they his words; they sang his praise.

PROVERBS FOR TODAY/ 14:30–31

A sound heart is *the life of the flesh: but envy the rottenness of the bones.* □ *He that oppresseth the poor reproacheth his Maker: but he that honoureth him hath mercy on the poor.*

MAY 9

1 SAMUEL 5:1—7:17

AND the Philistines took the ark of God, and brought it from Eben–ezer unto Ashdod.

²When the Philistines took the ark of God, they brought it into the house of Dagon, and set it by Dagon.

³And when they of Ashdod arose early on the morrow, behold, Dagon *was* fallen upon his face to the earth before the ark of the LORD. And they took Dagon, and set him in his place again.

⁴And when they arose early on the morrow morning, behold, Dagon *was* fallen upon his face to the ground before the ark of the LORD; and the head of Dagon and both the palms of his hands *were* cut off upon the threshold; only *the stump of* Dagon was left to him.

⁵Therefore neither the priests of Dagon, nor any that come into Dagon's house, tread on the threshold of Dagon in Ashdod unto this day.

⁶But the hand of the LORD was heavy upon them of Ashdod, and he destroyed them, and smote them with emerods, *even* Ashdod and the coasts thereof.

⁷And when the men of Ashdod saw that *it was* so, they said, The ark of the God of Israel shall not abide with

us: for his hand is sore upon us, and upon Dagon our god.

⁸They sent therefore and gathered all the lords of the Philistines unto them, and said, What shall we do with the ark of the God of Israel? And they answered, Let the ark of the God of Israel be carried about unto Gath. And they carried the ark of the God of Israel about *thither.*

⁹And it was *so,* that, after they had carried it about, the hand of the LORD was against the city with a very great destruction: and he smote the men of the city, both small and great, and they had emerods in their secret parts.

¹⁰Therefore they sent the ark of God to Ekron. And it came to pass, as the ark of God came to Ekron, that the Ekronites cried out, saying, They have brought about the ark of the God of Israel to us, to slay us and our people.

¹¹So they sent and gathered together all the lords of the Philistines, and said, Send away the ark of the God of Israel, and let it go again to his own place, that it slay us not, and our people: for there was a deadly destruction throughout all the city; the hand of God was very heavy there.

¹²And the men that died not were

smitten with the emerods: and the cry of the city went up to heaven.

AND the ark of the LORD was in the country of the Philistines seven months.

2And the Philistines called for the priests and the diviners, saying, What shall we do to the ark of the LORD? tell us wherewith we shall send it to his place.

3And they said, If ye send away the ark of the God of Israel, send it not empty; but in any wise return him a trespass offering: then ye shall be healed, and it shall be known to you why his hand is not removed from you.

4Then said they, What *shall be* the trespass offering which we shall return to him? They answered, Five golden emerods, and five golden mice, *according to* the number of the lords of the Philistines: for one plague *was* on you all, and on your lords.

5Wherefore ye shall make images of your emerods, and images of your mice that mar the land; and ye shall give glory unto the God of Israel: peradventure he will lighten his hand from off you, and from off your gods, and from off your land.

6Wherefore then do ye harden your hearts, as the Egyptians and Pharaoh hardened their hearts? when he had wrought wonderfully among them, did they not let the people go, and they departed?

7Now therefore make a new cart, and take two milch kine, on which there hath come no yoke, and tie the kine to the cart, and bring their calves home from them:

8And take the ark of the LORD, and lay it upon the cart; and put the jewels of gold, which ye return him *for* a trespass offering, in a coffer by the side thereof; and send it away, that it may go.

9And see, if it goeth up by the way of his own coast to Beth-shemesh, *then*

he hath done us this great evil: but if not, then we shall know that *it is* not his hand *that* smote us; it *was* a chance *that* happened to us.

10And the men did so; and took two milch kine, and tied them to the cart, and shut up their calves at home:

11And they laid the ark of the LORD upon the cart, and the coffer with the mice of gold and the images of their emerods.

12And the kine took the straight way to the way of Beth-shemesh, *and* went along the highway, lowing as they went, and turned not aside *to* the right hand or *to* the left; and the lords of the Philistines went after them unto the border of Beth-shemesh.

13And *they of* Beth-shemesh *were* reaping their wheat harvest in the valley: and they lifted up their eyes, and saw the ark, and rejoiced to see *it.*

14And the cart came into the field of Joshua, a Beth-shemite, and stood there, where *there was* a great stone: and they clave the wood of the cart, and offered the kine a burnt offering unto the LORD.

15And the Levites took down the ark of the LORD, and the coffer that *was* with it, wherein the jewels of gold *were,* and put *them* on the great stone: and the men of Beth-shemesh offered burnt offerings and sacrificed sacrifices the same day unto the LORD.

16And when the five lords of the Philistines had seen *it,* they returned to Ekron the same day.

17And these *are* the golden emerods which the Philistines returned *for* a trespass offering unto the LORD; for Ashdod one, for Gaza one, for Askelon one, for Gath one, for Ekron one;

18And the golden mice, *according to* the number of all the cities of the Philistines *belonging* to the five lords, *both* of fenced cities, and of country villages, even unto the great *stone of* Abel, whereon they set down the ark of the LORD: *which stone remaineth* unto this day in the field of Joshua, the Beth–shemite.

¹⁹And he smote the men of Beth–shemesh, because they had looked into the ark of the LORD, even he smote of the people fifty thousand and three-score and ten men: and the people lamented, because the LORD had smitten *many* of the people with a great slaughter.

²⁰And the men of Beth–shemesh said, Who is able to stand before this holy LORD God? and to whom shall he go up from us?

²¹And they sent messengers to the inhabitants of Kirjath–jearim, saying, The Philistines have brought again the ark of the LORD; come ye down, *and* fetch it up to you.

AND the men of Kirjath–jearim came, and fetched up the ark of the LORD, and brought it into the house of Abinadab in the hill, and sanctified Eleazar his son to keep the ark of the LORD.

²And it came to pass, while the ark abode in Kirjath–jearim, that the time was long; for it was twenty years: and all the house of Israel lamented after the LORD.

³And Samuel spake unto all the house of Israel, saying, If ye do return unto the LORD with all your hearts, *then* put away the strange gods and Ashtaroth from among you, and prepare your hearts unto the LORD, and serve him only: and he will deliver you out of the hand of the Philistines.

⁴Then the children of Israel did put away Baalim and Ashtaroth, and served the LORD only.

⁵And Samuel said, Gather all Israel to Mizpeh, and I will pray for you unto the LORD.

⁶And they gathered together to Mizpeh, and drew water, and poured *it* out before the LORD, and fasted on that day, and said there, We have sinned against the LORD. And Samuel judged the children of Israel in Mizpeh.

⁷And when the Philistines heard that the children of Israel were gathered together to Mizpeh, the lords of the Philistines went up against Israel. And when the children of Israel heard *it,* they were afraid of the Philistines.

⁸And the children of Israel said to Samuel, Cease not to cry unto the LORD our God for us, that he will save us out of the hand of the Philistines.

⁹And Samuel took a sucking lamb, and offered *it for* a burnt offering wholly unto the LORD: And Samuel cried unto the LORD for Israel; and the LORD heard him.

¹⁰And as Samuel was offering up the burnt offering, the Philistines drew near to battle against Israel: but the LORD thundered with a great thunder on that day upon the Philistines, and discomfited them; and they were smitten before Israel.

¹¹And the men of Israel went out of Mizpeh, and pursued the Philistines, and smote them, until *they came* under Beth–car.

¹²Then Samuel took a stone, and set *it* between Mizpeh and Shen, and called the name of it Eben–ezer, saying, Hitherto hath the LORD helped us.

¹³So the Philistines were subdued, and they came no more into the coast of Israel: and the hand of the LORD was against the Philistines all the days of Samuel.

¹⁴And the cities which the Philistines had taken from Israel were restored to Israel from Ekron even unto Gath; and the coasts thereof did Israel deliver out of the hands of the Philistines. And there was peace between Israel and the Amorites.

¹⁵And Samuel judged Israel all the days of his life.

¹⁶And he went from year to year in circuit to Beth–el, and Gilgal, and Mizpeh, and judged Israel in all those places.

¹⁷And his return *was* to Ramah; for there *was* his house; and there he

judged Israel; and there he built an altar unto the LORD.

JOHN 6:1–21

AFTER these things Jesus went over the sea of Galilee, which is *the sea* of Tiberias.

2And a great multitude followed him, because they saw his miracles which he did on them that were diseased.

3And Jesus went up into a mountain, and there he sat with his disciples.

4And the passover, a feast of the Jews, was nigh.

5When Jesus then lifted up *his* eyes, and saw a great company come unto him, he saith unto Philip, Whence shall we buy bread, that these may eat?

6And this he said to prove him: for he himself knew what he would do.

7Philip answered him, Two hundred pennyworth of bread is not sufficient for them, that every one of them may take a little.

8One of his disciples, Andrew, Simon Peter's brother, saith unto him,

9There is a lad here, which hath five barley loaves, and two small fishes: but what are they among so many?

10And Jesus said, Make the men sit down. Now there was much grass in the place. So the men sat down, in number about five thousand.

11And Jesus took the loaves; and when he had given thanks he distributed to the disciples, and the disciples to them that were set down; and likewise of the fishes as much as they would.

12When they were filled, he said unto his disciples, Gather up the fragments that remain, that nothing be lost.

13Therefore they gathered *them* together, and filled twelve baskets with the fragments of the five barley loaves, which remained over and above unto them that had eaten.

14Then those men, when they had seen the miracle that Jesus did, said, This is of a truth that prophet that should come into the world.

15When Jesus therefore perceived that they would come and take him by force, to make him a king, he departed again into a mountain himself alone.

16And when even was *now* come, his disciples went down unto the sea,

17And entered into a ship, and went over the sea toward Capernaum. And it was now dark, and Jesus was not come to them.

18And the sea arose by reason of a great wind that blew.

19So when they had rowed about five and twenty or thirty furlongs, they see Jesus walking on the sea, and drawing nigh unto the ship: and they were afraid.

20But he saith unto them, It is I; be not afraid.

21Then they willingly received him into the ship: and immediately the ship was at the land whither they went.

PSALM 106:13–31

THEY soon forgat his works; they waited not for his counsel:

14But lusted exceedingly in the wilderness, and tempted God in the desert.

15And he gave them their request; but sent leanness into their soul.

16They envied Moses also in the camp, *and* Aaron the saint of the LORD.

17The earth opened and swallowed up Dathan, and covered the company of Abiram.

18And a fire was kindled in their company; the flame burned up the wicked.

19They made a calf in Horeb, and worshipped the molten image.

20Thus they changed their glory into the similitude of an ox that eateth grass.

21They forgat God their saviour, which had done great things in Egypt;

22Wondrous works in the land of Ham, *and* terrible things by the Red sea.

23Therefore he said that he would destroy them, had not Moses his chosen stood before him in the breach, to turn away his wrath, lest he should destroy *them*.

24Yea, they despised the pleasant land, they believed not his word:

25But murmured in their tents, *and* hearkened not unto the voice of the LORD.

26Therefore he lifted up his hand against them, to overthrow them in the wilderness:

27To overthrow their seed also among the nations, and to scatter them in the lands.

28They joined themselves also unto Baal–peor, and ate the sacrifices of the dead.

29Thus they provoked *him* to anger with their inventions: and the plague brake in upon them.

30Then stood up Phinehas, and executed judgment: and *so* the plague was stayed.

31And that was counted unto him for righteousness unto all generations for evermore.

PROVERBS FOR TODAY/ 14:32–33

The wicked is driven away in his wickedness: but the righteous hath hope in his death. □ *Wisdom resteth in the heart of him that hath understanding: but* that which is *in the midst of fools is made known.*

MAY 10

1 SAMUEL 8:1—9:27

AND it came to pass, when Samuel was old, that he made his sons judges over Israel.

2Now the name of his firstborn was Joel; and the name of his second, Abiah: *they were* judges in Beer–sheba.

3And his sons walked not in his ways, but turned aside after lucre, and took bribes, and perverted judgment.

4Then all the elders of Israel gathered themselves together, and came to Samuel unto Ramah,

5And said unto him, Behold, thou art old, and thy sons walk not in thy ways: now make us a king to judge us like all the nations.

6But the thing displeased Samuel, when they said, Give us a king to judge us. And Samuel prayed unto the LORD.

7And the LORD said unto Samuel, Hearken unto the voice of the people in all that they say unto thee: for they have not rejected thee, but they have rejected me, that I should not reign over them.

8According to all the works which they have done since the day that I brought them up out of Egypt even unto this day, wherewith they have forsaken me, and served other gods, so do they also unto thee.

9Now therefore hearken unto their voice: howbeit yet protest solemnly unto them, and shew them the manner of the king that shall reign over them.

10And Samuel told all the words of the LORD unto the people that asked of him a king.

11And he said, This will be the manner of the king that shall reign over you: He will take your sons, and appoint *them* for himself, for his chariots, and *to be* his horsemen; and *some* shall run before his chariots.

12And he will appoint him captains over thousands, and captains over fifties; and *will set them* to ear his ground, and to reap his harvest, and to make his instruments of war, and instruments of his chariots.

13And he will take your daughters *to be* confectionaries, and *to be* cooks, and *to be* bakers.

14And he will take your fields, and your vineyards, and your oliveyards, *even* the best *of them,* and give *them* to his servants.

15And he will take the tenth of your seed, and of your vineyards, and give to his officers, and to his servants.

16And he will take your menservants, and your maidservants, and your goodliest young men, and your asses, and put *them* to his work.

17He will take the tenth of your sheep: and ye shall be his servants.

18And ye shall cry out in that day because of your king which ye shall have chosen you; and the LORD will not hear you in that day.

19Nevertheless the people refused to obey the voice of Samuel; and they said, Nay; but we will have a king over us;

20That we also may be like all the nations; and that our king may judge us, and go out before us, and fight our battles.

21And Samuel heard all the words of the people, and he rehearsed them in the ears of the LORD.

22And the LORD said to Samuel, Hearken unto their voice, and make them a king. And Samuel said unto the men of Israel, Go ye every man unto his city.

Now there was a man of Benjamin, whose name *was* Kish, the son of Abiel, the son of Zeror, the son of Bechorath, the son of Aphiah, a Benjamite, a mighty man of power.

2And he had a son, whose name *was* Saul, a choice young man, and a goodly: and *there was* not among the children of Israel a goodlier person than he: from his shoulders and upward *he was* higher than any of the people.

3And the asses of Kish Saul's father were lost. And Kish said to Saul his son, Take now one of the servants with thee, and arise, go seek the asses.

4And he passed through mount Ephraim, and passed through the land of Shalisha, but they found *them* not: then they passed through the land of Shalim, and *there they were* not: and he passed through the land of the Benjamites, but they found *them* not.

5*And* when they were come to the land of Zuph, Saul said to his servant that *was* with him, Come, and let us return; lest my father leave *caring* for the asses, and take thought for us.

6And he said unto him, Behold now, *there is* in this city a man of God, and *he is* an honourable man; all that he saith cometh surely to pass: now let us go thither; peradventure he can shew us our way that we should go.

7Then said Saul to his servant, But, behold, *if* we go, what shall we bring the man? for the bread is spent in our vessels, and *there is* not a present to bring to the man of God: what have we?

8And the servant answered Saul again, and said, Behold, I have here at hand the fourth part of a shekel of silver: *that* will I give to the man of God, to tell us our way.

9(Beforetime in Israel, when a man went to enquire of God, thus he spake, Come, and let us go to the seer: for *he that is* now *called* a Prophet was beforetime called a Seer.)

10Then said Saul to his servant, Well said; come, let us go. So they went unto the city where the man of God *was.*

11*And* as they went up the hill to the city, they found young maidens going out to draw water, and said unto them, Is the seer here?

12And they answered them, and said, He is; behold, *he is* before you: make haste now, for he came to day to the city; for *there is* a sacrifice of the people to day in the high place:

13As soon as ye be come into the city, ye shall straightway find him, before he go up to the high place to eat: for the people will not eat until he come, because he doth bless the sacrifice; *and* afterwards they eat that be bidden. Now therefore get you up; for about this time ye shall find him.

14And they went up into the city: *and* when they were come into the city, behold, Samuel came out against them, for to go up to the high place.

15Now the LORD had told Samuel in his ear a day before Saul came, saying,

16To morrow about this time I will send thee a man out of the land of Benjamin, and thou shalt anoint him *to be* captain over my people Israel, that he may save my people out of the hand of the Philistines: for I have looked upon my people, because their cry is come unto me.

17And when Samuel saw Saul, the LORD said unto him, Behold the man whom I spake to thee of! this same shall reign over my people.

18Then Saul drew near to Samuel in the gate, and said, Tell me, I pray thee, where the seer's house *is*.

19And Samuel answered Saul, and said, I *am* the seer: go up before me unto the high place; for ye shall eat with me to day, and to morrow I will let thee go, and will tell thee all that *is* in thine heart.

20And as for thine asses that were lost three days ago, set not thy mind on them; for they are found. And on whom *is* all the desire of Israel? *Is it* not on thee, and on all thy father's house?

21And Saul answered and said, *Am* not I a Benjamite, of the smallest of the tribes of Israel? and my family the least of all the families of the tribe of Benjamin? wherefore then speakest thou so to me?

22And Samuel took Saul and his servant, and brought them into the parlour, and made them sit in the chiefest place among them that were bidden, which *were* about thirty persons.

23And Samuel said unto the cook, Bring the portion which I gave thee, of which I said unto thee, Set it by thee.

24And the cook took up the shoulder, and *that* which *was* upon it, and set *it* before Saul. And Samuel said, Behold that which is left! set *it* before thee, *and* eat: for unto this time hath it been kept for thee since I said, I have invited the people. So Saul did eat with Samuel that day.

25And when they were come down from the high place into the city, *Samuel* communed with Saul upon the top of the house.

26And they arose early: and it came to pass about the spring of the day, that Samuel called Saul to the top of the house, saying, Up, that I may send thee away. And Saul arose, and they went out both of them, he and Samuel, abroad.

27*And* as they were going down to the end of the city, Samuel said to Saul, Bid the servant pass on before us, (and he passed on,) but stand thou still a while, that I may shew thee the word of God.

JOHN 6:22–46

THE day following, when the people which stood on the other side of the sea saw that there was none other boat there, save that one whereinto his disciples were entered, and that Jesus went not with his disciples into the boat, but *that* his disciples were gone away alone;

23(Howbeit there came other boats from Tiberias nigh unto the place where they did eat bread, after that the Lord had given thanks:)

24When the people therefore saw that Jesus was not there, neither his disciples, they also took shipping, and came to Capernaum, seeking for Jesus.

25And when they had found him on the other side of the sea, they said unto him, Rabbi, when camest thou hither?

26Jesus answered them and said, Verily, verily, I say unto you, Ye seek me, not because ye saw the miracles, but because ye did eat of the loaves, and were filled.

27Labour not for the meat which perisheth, but for that meat which endureth unto everlasting life, which the Son of man shall give unto you: for him hath God the Father sealed.

28Then said they unto him, What shall we do, that we might work the works of God?

29Jesus answered and said unto them, This is the work of God, that ye believe on him whom he hath sent.

30They said therefore unto him, What sign shewest thou then, that we may see, and believe thee? what dost thou work?

31Our fathers did eat manna in the desert; as it is written, He gave them bread from heaven to eat.

32Then Jesus said unto them, Verily, verily, I say unto you, Moses gave you not that bread from heaven; but my Father giveth you the true bread from heaven.

33For the bread of God is he which cometh down from heaven, and giveth life unto the world.

34Then said they unto him, Lord, evermore give us this bread.

35And Jesus said unto them, I am the bread of life: he that cometh to me shall never hunger; and he that believeth on me shall never thirst.

36But I said unto you, That ye also have seen me, and believe not.

37All that the Father giveth me shall come to me; and him that cometh to me I will in no wise cast out.

38For I came down from heaven, not to do mine own will, but the will of him that sent me.

39And this is the Father's will which hath sent me, that of all which he hath given me I should lose nothing, but should raise it up again at the last day.

40And this is the will of him that sent me, that every one which seeth the Son, and believeth on him, may have everlasting life: and I will raise him up at the last day.

41The Jews then murmured at him, because he said, I am the bread which came down from heaven.

42And they said, Is not this Jesus, the son of Joseph, whose father and mother we know? how is it then that he saith, I came down from heaven?

43Jesus therefore answered and said unto them, Murmur not among yourselves.

44No man can come to me, except the Father which hath sent me draw him: and I will raise him up at the last day.

45It is written in the prophets, And they shall be all taught of God. Every man therefore that hath heard, and hath learned of the Father, cometh unto me.

46Not that any man hath seen the Father, save he which is of God, he hath seen the Father.

PSALM 106:32–48

THEY angered *him* also at the waters of strife, so that it went ill with Moses for their sakes:

33Because they provoked his spirit, so that he spake unadvisedly with his lips.

34They did not destroy the nations, concerning whom the LORD commanded them:

35But were mingled among the heathen, and learned their works.

36And they served their idols: which

were a snare unto them.

37Yea, they sacrificed their sons and their daughters unto devils,

38And shed innocent blood, *even* the blood of their sons and of their daughters, whom they sacrificed unto the idols of Canaan: and the land was polluted with blood.

39Thus were they defiled with their own works, and went a whoring with their own inventions.

40Therefore was the wrath of the LORD kindled against his people, insomuch that he abhorred his own inheritance.

41And he gave them into the hand of the heathen; and they that hated them ruled over them.

42Their enemies also oppressed them, and they were brought into subjection under their hand.

43Many times did he deliver them; but they provoked *him* with their counsel, and were brought low for their iniquity.

44Nevertheless he regarded their affliction, when he heard their cry:

45And he remembered for them his covenant, and repented according to the multitude of his mercies.

46He made them also to be pitied of all those that carried them captives.

47Save us, O LORD our God, and gather us from among the heathen, to give thanks unto thy holy name, *and* to triumph in thy praise.

48Blessed *be* the LORD God of Israel from everlasting to everlasting: and let all the people say, Amen. Praise ye the LORD.

PROVERBS FOR TODAY/ 14:34–35

Righteousness exalteth a nation: but sin is *a reproach to any people.* □ *The king's favour* is *toward a wise servant: but his wrath is* against *him that causeth shame.*

MAY 11

1 SAMUEL 10:1—11:15

THEN Samuel took a vial of oil, and poured *it* upon his [Saul's] head, and kissed him, and said, *Is it* not because the LORD hath anointed thee *to be* captain over his inheritance?

2When thou art departed from me to day, then thou shalt find two men by Rachel's sepulchre in the border of Benjamin at Zelzah; and they will say unto thee, The asses which thou wentest to seek are found: and, lo, thy father hath left the care of the asses, and sorroweth for you, saying, What shall I do for my son?

3Then shalt thou go on forward from thence, and thou shalt come to the plain of Tabor, and there shall meet thee three men going up to God to Beth-el, one carrying three kids, and another carrying three loaves of bread, and another carrying a bottle of wine:

4And they will salute thee, and give thee two *loaves* of bread; which thou shalt receive of their hands.

5After that thou shalt come to the hill of God, where *is* the garrison of the Philistines: and it shall come to pass, when thou art come thither to the city, that thou shalt meet a company of prophets coming down from the high place with a psaltery, and a tabret, and a pipe, and a harp, before them; and they shall prophesy:

6And the Spirit of the Lord will come upon thee, and thou shalt prophesy with them, and shalt be turned into another man.

7And let it be, when these signs are come unto thee, *that* thou do as occasion serve thee; for God *is* with thee.

8And thou shalt go down before me to Gilgal; and, behold, I will come down unto thee, to offer burnt offerings, *and* to sacrifice sacrifices of peace offerings: seven days shalt thou tarry, till I come to thee, and shew thee what thou shalt do.

9And it was *so,* that when he had turned his back to go from Samuel, God gave him another heart: and all those signs came to pass that day.

10And when they came thither to the hill, behold, a company of prophets met him; and the Spirit of God came upon him, and he prophesied among them.

11And it came to pass, when all that knew him beforetime saw that, behold, he prophesied among the prophets, then the people said one to another, What *is* this *that* is come unto the son of Kish? *Is* Saul also among the prophets?

12And one of the same place answered and said, But who *is* their father? Therefore it became a proverb, *Is* Saul also among the prophets?

13And when he had made an end of prophesying, he came to the high place.

14And Saul's uncle said unto him and to his servant, Whither went ye? And he said, To seek the asses: and when we saw that *they were* no where, we came to Samuel.

15And Saul's uncle said, Tell me, I pray thee, what Samuel said unto you.

16And Saul said unto his uncle, He told us plainly that the asses were found. But of the matter of the kingdom, whereof Samuel spake, he told him not.

17And Samuel called the people together unto the Lord to Mizpeh;

18And said unto the children of Israel, Thus saith the Lord God of Israel, I brought up Israel out of Egypt, and delivered you out of the hand of the Egyptians, and out of the hand of all kingdoms, *and* of them that oppressed you:

19And ye have this day rejected your God, who himself saved you out of all your adversities and your tribulations; and ye have said unto him, *Nay,* but set a king over us. Now therefore present yourselves before the Lord by your tribes, and by your thousands.

20And when Samuel had caused all the tribes of Israel to come near, the tribe of Benjamin was taken.

21When he had caused the tribe of Benjamin to come near by their families, the family of Matri was taken, and Saul the son of Kish was taken: and when they sought him, he could not be found.

22Therefore they enquired of the Lord further, if the man should yet come thither. And the Lord answered, Behold, he hath hid himself among the stuff.

23And they ran and fetched him thence: and when he stood among the people, he was higher than any of the people from his shoulders and upward.

24And Samuel said to all the people, See ye him whom the Lord hath chosen, that *there is* none like him among all the people? And all the people shouted, and said, God save the king.

25Then Samuel told the people the manner of the kingdom, and wrote *it* in a book, and laid *it* up before the Lord. And Samuel sent all the people away, every man to his house.

26And Saul also went home to Gibeah; and there went with him a band of men, whose hearts God had touched.

27But the children of Belial said, How shall this man save us? And they despised him, and brought him no presents. But he held his peace.

THEN Nahash the Ammonite came up, and encamped against Jabesh–gilead: and all the men of Jabesh said unto Nahash, Make a covenant with us, and we will serve thee.

2And Nahash the Ammonite answered them, On this *condition* will I make *a covenant* with you, that I may thrust out all your right eyes, and lay it *for* a reproach upon all Israel.

3And the elders of Jabesh said unto him, Give us seven days' respite, that we may send messengers unto all the coasts of Israel: and then, if *there be* no man to save us, we will come out to thee.

4Then came the messengers to Gibeah of Saul, and told the tidings in the ears of the people: and all the people lifted up their voices, and wept.

5And, behold, Saul came after the herd out of the field; and Saul said, What *aileth* the people that they weep? And they told him the tidings of the men of Jabesh.

6And the Spirit of God came upon Saul when he heard those tidings, and his anger was kindled greatly.

7And he took a yoke of oxen, and hewed them in pieces, and sent *them* throughout all the coasts of Israel by the hands of messengers, saying, Whosoever cometh not forth after Saul and after Samuel, so shall it be done unto his oxen. And the fear of the LORD fell on the people, and they came out with one consent.

8And when he numbered them in Bezek, the children of Israel were three hundred thousand, and the men of Judah thirty thousand.

9And they said unto the messengers that came, Thus shall ye say unto the men of Jabesh–gilead, Tomorrow, by *that time* the sun be hot, ye shall have help. And the messengers came and shewed *it* to the men of Jabesh; and they were glad.

10Therefore the men of Jabesh said, To morrow we will come out unto you, and ye shall do with us all that seemeth good unto you.

11And it was *so* on the morrow, that Saul put the people in three companies; and they came into the midst of the host in the morning watch, and slew the Ammonites until the heat of the day: and it came to pass, that they which remained were scattered, so that two of them were not left together.

12And the people said unto Samuel, Who *is* he that said, Shall Saul reign over us? bring the men, that we may put them to death.

13And Saul said, There shall not a man be put to death this day: for to day the LORD hath wrought salvation in Israel.

14Then said Samuel to the people, Come, and let us go to Gilgal, and renew the kingdom there.

15And all the people went to Gilgal; and there they made Saul king before the LORD in Gilgal; and there they sacrificed sacrifices of peace offerings before the LORD; and there Saul and all the men of Israel rejoiced greatly.

JOHN 6:47–71

VERILY, verily, I say unto you, He that believeth on me hath everlasting life.

48I am that bread of life.

49Your fathers did eat manna in the wilderness, and are dead.

50This is the bread which cometh down from heaven, that a man may eat thereof, and not die.

51I am the living bread which came down from heaven: if any man eat of this bread, he shall live for ever: and the bread that I will give is my flesh, which I will give for the life of the world.

52The Jews therefore strove among themselves, saying, How can this man give us *his* flesh to eat?

53Then Jesus said unto them, Verily, verily, I say unto you, Except ye eat the flesh of the Son of man, and drink his blood, ye have no life in you.

54Whoso eateth my flesh, and drinketh my blood, hath eternal life; and I will raise him up at the last day.

55For my flesh is meat indeed, and my blood is drink indeed.

56He that eateth my flesh, and drinketh my blood, dwelleth in me, and I in him.

57As the living Father hath sent me, and I live by the Father: so he that eateth me, even he shall live by me.

58This is that bread which came down from heaven: not as your fathers did eat manna, and are dead: he that eateth of this bread shall live for ever.

59These things said he in the synagogue, as he taught in Capernaum.

60Many therefore of his disciples, when they had heard *this,* said, This is an hard saying; who can hear it?

61When Jesus knew in himself that his disciples murmured at it, he said unto them, Doth this offend you?

62*What* and if ye shall see the Son of man ascend up where he was before?

63It is the spirit that quickeneth; the flesh profiteth nothing: the words that I speak unto you, *they* are spirit, and *they* are life.

64But there are some of you that believe not. For Jesus knew from the beginning who they were that believed not, and who should betray him.

65And he said, Therefore said I unto you, that no man can come unto me, except it were given unto him of my Father.

66From that *time* many of his disciples went back, and walked no more with him.

67Then said Jesus unto the twelve, Will ye also go away?

68Then Simon Peter answered him, Lord, to whom shall we go? thou hast the words of eternal life.

69And we believe and are sure that thou art that Christ, the Son of the living God.

70Jesus answered them, Have not I chosen you twelve, and one of you is a devil?

71He spake of Judas Iscariot *the son* of Simon: for he it was that should betray him, being one of the twelve.

PSALM 107:1–43

O GIVE thanks unto the LORD, for *he is* good: for his mercy *endureth* for ever.

2Let the redeemed of the LORD say *so,* whom he hath redeemed from the hand of the enemy;

3And gathered them out of the lands, from the east, and from the west, from the north, and from the south.

4They wandered in the wilderness in a solitary way; they found no city to dwell in.

5Hungry and thirsty, their soul fainted in them.

6Then they cried unto the LORD in their trouble, *and* he delivered them out of their distresses.

7And he led them forth by the right way, that they might go to a city of habitation.

8Oh that *men* would praise the LORD *for* his goodness, and *for* his wonderful works to the children of men!

9For he satisfieth the longing soul, and filleth the hungry soul with goodness.

10Such as sit in darkness and in the shadow of death, *being* bound in affliction and iron;

11Because they rebelled against the words of God, and contemned the counsel of the most High:

12Therefore he brought down their heart with labour; they fell down and *there was* none to help.

13Then they cried unto the LORD in their trouble, *and* he saved them out of their distresses.

14He brought them out of darkness and the shadow of death, and brake their bands in sunder.

15Oh that *men* would praise the LORD

for his goodness, and *for* his wonderful works to the children of men!

16For he hath broken the gates of brass, and cut the bars of iron in sunder.

17Fools because of their transgression, and because of their iniquities, are afflicted.

18Their soul abhorreth all manner of meat; and they draw near unto the gates of death.

19Then they cry unto the LORD in their trouble, *and* he saveth them out of their distresses.

20He sent his word, and healed them, and delivered *them* from their destructions.

21Oh that *men* would praise the LORD *for* his goodness, and *for* his wonderful works to the children of men!

22And let them sacrifice the sacrifices of thanksgiving, and declare his works with rejoicing.

23They that go down to the sea in ships, that do business in great waters;

24These see the works of the LORD, and his wonders in the deep.

25For he commandeth, and raiseth the stormy wind, which lifteth up the waves thereof.

26They mount up to the heaven, they go down again to the depths: their soul is melted because of trouble.

27They reel to and fro, and stagger like a drunken man, and are at their wit's end.

28Then they cry unto the LORD in their trouble, and he bringeth them out of their distresses.

29He maketh the storm a calm, so that the waves thereof are still.

30Then are they glad because they be quiet; so he bringeth them unto their desired haven.

31Oh that *men* would praise the LORD *for* his goodness, and *for* his wonderful works to the children of men!

32Let them exalt him also in the congregation of the people, and praise him in the assembly of the elders.

33He turneth rivers into a wilderness, and the watersprings into dry ground;

34A fruitful land into barrenness, for the wickedness of them that dwell therein.

35He turneth the wilderness into a standing water, and dry ground into watersprings.

36And there he maketh the hungry to dwell, that they may prepare a city for habitation;

37And sow the fields, and plant vineyards, which may yield fruits of increase.

38He blesseth them also, so that they are multiplied greatly; and suffereth not their cattle to decrease.

39Again, they are minished and brought low through oppression, affliction, and sorrow.

40He poureth contempt upon princes, and causeth them to wander in the wilderness, *where there is* no way.

41Yet setteth he the poor on high from affliction, and maketh *him* families like a flock.

42The righteous shall see *it,* and rejoice: and all iniquity shall stop her mouth.

43Whoso *is* wise, and will observe these *things,* even they shall understand the lovingkindness of the LORD.

PROVERBS FOR TODAY/ 15:1–3

A soft answer turneth away wrath: but grievous words stir up anger. The tongue of the wise useth knowledge aright: but the mouth of fools poureth out foolishness. □ *The eyes of the LORD* are *in every place, beholding the evil and the good.*

MAY 12

A ND Samuel said unto all Israel, Behold, I have hearkened unto your voice in all that ye said unto me, and have made a king over you.

2And now, behold, the king walketh before you: and I am old and gray-headed; and, behold, my sons *are* with you: and I have walked before you from my childhood unto this day.

3Behold, here I *am:* witness against me before the LORD, and before his anointed: whose ox have I taken? or whose ass have I taken? or whom have I defrauded? whom have I oppressed? or of whose hand have I received *any* bribe to blind mine eyes therewith? and I will restore it you.

4And they said, Thou hast not defrauded us, nor oppressed us, neither hast thou taken ought of any man's hand.

5And he said unto them, The LORD *is* witness against you, and his anointed *is* witness this day, that ye have not found ought in my hand. And they answered, *He is* witness.

6And Samuel said unto the people, *It is* the LORD that advanced Moses and Aaron, and that brought your fathers up out of the land of Egypt.

7Now therefore stand still, that I may reason with you before the LORD of all the righteous acts of the LORD, which he did to you and to your fathers.

8When Jacob was come into Egypt, and your fathers cried unto the LORD, then the LORD sent Moses and Aaron, which brought forth your fathers out of Egypt, and made them dwell in this place.

9And when they forgat the LORD their God, he sold them into the hand of Sisera, captain of the host of Hazor, and into the hand of the Philistines, and into the hand of the king of Moab, and they fought against them.

10And they cried unto the LORD, and said, We have sinned, because we have forsaken the LORD, and have served Baalim and Ashtaroth: but now deliver us out of the hand of our enemies, and we will serve thee.

11And the LORD sent Jerubbaal, and Bedan, and Jephthah, and Samuel, and delivered you out of the hand of your enemies on every side, and ye dwelled safe.

12And when ye saw that Nahash the king of the children of Ammon came against you, ye said unto me, Nay; but a king shall reign over us: when the LORD your God *was* your king.

13Now therefore behold the king whom ye have chosen, *and* whom ye have desired! and, behold, the LORD hath set a king over you.

14If ye will fear the LORD, and serve him, and obey his voice, and not rebel against the commandment of the LORD, then shall both ye and also the king that reigneth over you continue following the LORD your God:

15But if ye will not obey the voice of the LORD, but rebel against the commandment of the LORD, then shall the hand of the LORD be against you, as *it was* against your fathers.

16Now therefore stand and see this great thing, which the LORD will do before your eyes.

17*Is it* not wheat harvest to day? I will call unto the LORD, and he shall send thunder and rain; that ye may perceive and see that your wickedness *is* great, which ye have done in the sight of the LORD, in asking you a king.

18So Samuel called unto the LORD; and the LORD sent thunder and rain that day: and all the people greatly feared the LORD and Samuel.

19And all the people said unto Samuel, Pray for thy servants unto the LORD thy God, that we die not: for we have added unto all our sins *this* evil, to ask us a king.

20And Samuel said unto the people, Fear not: ye have done all this wickedness: yet turn not aside from following the LORD, but serve the LORD with all your heart;

21And turn ye not aside: for *then should ye go* after vain *things,* which cannot profit nor deliver; for they *are* vain.

22For the LORD will not forsake his people for his great name's sake: because it hath pleased the LORD to make you his people.

23Moreover as for me, God forbid that I should sin against the LORD in ceasing to pray for you: but I will teach you the good and the right way:

24Only fear the LORD, and serve him in truth with all your heart: for consider how great *things* he hath done for you.

25But if ye shall still do wickedly, ye shall be consumed, both ye and your king.

SAUL reigned one year; and when he reigned two years over Israel,

2Saul chose him three thousand *men* of Israel; *whereof* two thousand were with Saul in Michmash and in mount Beth–el, and a thousand were with Jonathan in Gibeah of Benjamin: and the rest of the people he sent every man to his tent.

3And Jonathan smote the garrison of the Philistines that *was* in Geba, and the Philistines heard *of it.* And Saul blew the trumpet throughout all the land, saying, Let the Hebrews hear.

4And all Israel heard say *that* Saul had smitten a garrison of the Philistines, and *that* Israel also was had in abomination with the Philistines. And the people were called together after Saul to Gilgal.

5And the Philistines gathered themselves together to fight with Israel, thirty thousand chariots, and six thousand horsemen, and people as the sand which *is* on the sea shore in multitude: and they came up, and pitched in Michmash, eastward from Beth–aven.

6When the men of Israel saw that they were in a strait, (for the people were distressed,) then the people did hide themselves in caves, and in thickets, and in rocks, and in high places, and in pits.

7And *some of* the Hebrews went over Jordan to the land of Gad and Gilead. As for Saul, he *was* yet in Gilgal, and all the people followed him trembling.

8And he tarried seven days, according to the set time that Samuel *had appointed:* but Samuel came not to Gilgal; and the people were scattered from him.

9And Saul said, Bring hither a burnt offering to me, and peace offerings. And he offered the burnt offering.

10And it came to pass, that as soon as he had made an end of offering the burnt offering, behold, Samuel came; and Saul went out to meet him, that he might salute him.

11And Samuel said, What hast thou done? And Saul said, Because I saw that the people were scattered from me, and *that* thou camest not within the days appointed, and *that* the Philistines gathered themselves together at Michmash;

12Therefore said I, The Philistines will come down now upon me to Gilgal, and I have not made supplication unto the LORD: I forced myself therefore, and offered a burnt offering.

13And Samuel said to Saul, Thou hast done foolishly: thou hast not kept the commandment of the LORD thy God, which he commanded thee: for now would the LORD have established thy kingdom upon Israel for ever.

14But now thy kingdom shall not continue: the LORD hath sought him a man after his own heart, and the LORD hath commanded him *to be* captain over his people, because thou hast not kept *that* which the LORD commanded thee.

15And Samuel arose, and gat him up from Gilgal unto Gibeah of Benjamin. And Saul numbered the people *that were* present with him, about six hundred men.

16And Saul, and Jonathan his son, and the people *that were* present with them, abode in Gibeah of Benjamin: but the Philistines encamped in Michmash.

17And the spoilers came out of the camp of the Philistines in three companies: one company turned unto the way *that leadeth to* Ophrah, unto the land of Shual:

18And another company turned the way *to* Beth–horon: and another company turned *to* the way of the border that looketh to the valley of Zeboim toward the wilderness.

19Now there was no smith found throughout all the land of Israel: for the Philistines said, Lest the Hebrews make *them* swords or spears:

20But all the Israelites went down to the Philistines, to sharpen every man his share, and his coulter, and his axe, and his mattock.

21Yet they had a file for the mattocks, and for the coulters, and for the forks, and for the axes, and to sharpen the goads.

22So it came to pass in the day of battle, that there was neither sword nor spear found in the hand of any of the people that *were* with Saul and Jonathan: but with Saul and with Jonathan his son was there found.

23And the garrison of the Philistines went out to the passage of Michmash.

JOHN 7:1–30

After these things Jesus walked in Galilee: for he would not walk in Jewry, because the Jews sought to kill him.

2Now the Jews' feast of tabernacles was at hand.

3His brethren therefore said unto him, Depart hence, and go into Judaea, that thy disciples also may see the works that thou doest.

4For *there is* no man *that* doeth any thing in secret, and he himself seeketh to be known openly. If thou do these things, shew thyself to the world.

5For neither did his brethren believe in him.

6Then Jesus said unto them, My time is not yet come: but your time is alway ready.

7The world cannot hate you; but me it hateth, because I testify of it, that the works thereof are evil.

8Go ye up unto this feast: I go not up yet unto this feast; for my time is not yet full come.

9When he had said these words unto them, he abode *still* in Galilee.

10But when his brethren were gone up, then went he also up unto the feast, not openly, but as it were in secret.

11Then the Jews sought him at the feast, and said, Where is he?

12And there was much murmuring among the people concerning him: for some said, He is a good man: others said, Nay; but he deceiveth the people.

13Howbeit no man spake openly of him for fear of the Jews.

14Now about the midst of the feast Jesus went up into the temple, and taught.

15And the Jews marvelled, saying, How knoweth this man letters, having never learned?

16Jesus answered them, and said, My doctrine is not mine, but his that sent me.

17If any man will do his will, he shall know of the doctrine, whether it be of God, or *whether* I speak of myself.

18He that speaketh of himself seeketh his own glory: but he that seeketh his glory that sent him, the same is true, and no unrighteousness is in him.

19Did not Moses give you the law, and *yet* none of you keepeth the law? Why go ye about to kill me?

20The people answered and said, Thou hast a devil: who goeth about to kill thee?

21Jesus answered and said unto them, I have done one work, and ye all marvel.

22Moses therefore gave unto you circumcision; (not because it is of Moses, but of the fathers;) and ye on the sabbath day circumcise a man.

23If a man on the sabbath day receive circumcision, that the law of Moses should not be broken; are ye angry at me, because I have made a man every whit whole on the sabbath day?

24Judge not according to the appearance, but judge righteous judgment.

25Then said some of them of Jerusalem, Is not this he, whom they seek to kill?

26But, lo, he speaketh boldly, and they say nothing unto him. Do the rulers know indeed that this is the very Christ?

27Howbeit we know this man whence he is: but when Christ cometh, no man knoweth whence he is.

28Then cried Jesus in the temple as he taught, saying, Ye both know me, and ye know whence I am: and I am not come of myself, but he that sent me is true, whom ye know not.

29But I know him: for I am from him, and he hath sent me.

30Then they sought to take him: but no man laid hands on him, because his hour was not yet come.

PSALM 108:1–13

O GOD, my heart is fixed: I will sing and give praise, even with my glory.

2Awake, psaltery and harp: I *myself* will awake early.

3I will praise thee, O Lord, among the people: and I will sing praises unto thee among the nations.

4For thy mercy *is* great above the heavens: and thy truth *reacheth* unto the clouds.

5Be thou exalted, O God, above the heavens: and thy glory above all the earth;

6That thy beloved may be delivered: save *with* thy right hand, and answer me.

7God hath spoken in his holiness; I will rejoice, I will divide Shechem, and mete out the valley of Succoth.

8Gilead *is* mine; Manasseh *is* mine; Ephraim also *is* the strength of mine head; Judah *is* my lawgiver;

9Moab *is* my washpot; over Edom will I cast out my shoe; over Philistia will I triumph.

10Who will bring me into the strong city? who will lead me into Edom?

11*Wilt* not *thou,* O God, *who* hast cast us off? and wilt not thou, O God, go forth with our hosts?

12Give us help from trouble: for vain *is* the help of man.

13Through God we shall do valiantly: for he *it is that* shall tread down our enemies.

PROVERBS FOR TODAY/ 15:4

A wholesome tongue is *a tree of life: but perverseness therein* is *a breach in the spirit.*

MAY 13

1 SAMUEL 14:1–52

Now it came to pass upon a day, that Jonathan the son of Saul said unto the young man that bare his armour, Come, and let us go over to the Philistines' garrison, that *is* on the other side. But he told not his father.

2And Saul tarried in the uttermost part of Gibeah under a pomegranate tree which *is* in Migron: and the people that *were* with him *were* about six hundred men;

3And Ahiah, the son of Ahitub, I–chabod's brother, the son of Phinehas, the son of Eli, the LORD's priest in Shiloh, wearing an ephod. And the people knew not that Jonathan was gone.

4And between the passages, by which Jonathan sought to go over unto the Philistines' garrison, *there was* a sharp rock on the one side, and a sharp rock on the other side: and the name of the one *was* Bozez, and the name of the other Seneh.

5The forefront of the one *was* situate northward over against Michmash, and the other southward over against Gibeah.

6And Jonathan said to the young man that bare his armour, Come, and let us go over unto the garrison of these uncircumcised: it may be that the LORD will work for us: for *there is* no restraint to the LORD to save by many or by few.

7And his armourbearer said unto him, Do all that *is* in thine heart: turn thee; behold, I *am* with thee according to thy heart.

8Then said Jonathan, Behold, we will pass over unto *these* men, and we will discover ourselves unto them.

9If they say thus unto us, Tarry until we come to you; then we will stand still in our place, and will not go up unto them.

10But if they say thus, Come up unto us; then we will go up: for the LORD hath delivered them into our hand: and this *shall be* a sign unto us.

11And both of them discovered themselves unto the garrison of the Philistines: and the Philistines said, Behold, the Hebrews come forth out of the holes where they had hid themselves.

12And the men of the garrison answered Jonathan and his armourbearer, and said, Come up to us, and we will shew you a thing. And Jonathan said unto his armourbearer, Come up after me: for the LORD hath delivered them into the hand of Israel.

13And Jonathan climbed up upon his hands and upon his feet, and his armourbearer after him: and they fell before Jonathan; and his armourbearer slew after him.

14And that first slaughter, which Jonathan and his armourbearer made, was about twenty men, within as it were an half acre of land, *which* a yoke *of oxen might plow.*

15And there was trembling in the host, in the field, and among all the people: the garrison, and the spoilers, they also trembled, and the earth quaked: so it was a very great trembling.

16And the watchmen of Saul in Gibeah of Benjamin looked; and, behold, the multitude melted away, and they went on beating down *one another.*

17Then said Saul unto the people that *were* with him, Number now, and see who is gone from us. And when they had numbered, behold, Jonathan and his armourbearer *were* not *there.*

18And Saul said unto Ahiah, Bring hither the ark of God. For the ark of

God was at that time with the children of Israel.

19And it came to pass, while Saul talked unto the priest, that the noise that *was* in the host of the Philistines went on and increased: and Saul said unto the priest, Withdraw thine hand.

20And Saul and all the people that *were* with him assembled themselves, and they came to the battle: and, behold, every man's sword was against his fellow, *and there was* a very great discomfiture.

21Moreover the Hebrews *that* were with the Philistines before that time, which went up with them into the camp *from the country* round about, even they also *turned* to be with the Israelites that *were* with Saul and Jonathan.

22Likewise all the men of Israel which had hid themselves in mount Ephraim, *when* they heard that the Philistines fled, even they also followed hard after them in the battle.

23So the LORD saved Israel that day: and the battle passed over unto Beth–aven.

24And the men of Israel were distressed that day: for Saul had adjured the people, saying, Cursed *be* the man that eateth *any* food until evening, that I may be avenged on mine enemies. So none of the people tasted *any* food.

25And all *they of* the land came to a wood; and there was honey upon the ground.

26And when the people were come into the wood, behold, the honey dropped; but no man put his hand to his mouth: for the people feared the oath.

27But Jonathan heard not when his father charged the people with the oath: wherefore he put forth the end of the rod that *was* in his hand, and dipped it in an honeycomb, and put his hand to his mouth; and his eyes were enlightened.

28Then answered one of the people, and said, Thy father straitly charged the people with an oath, saying, Cursed *be* the man that eateth *any* food this day. And the people were faint.

29Then said Jonathan, My father hath troubled the land: see, I pray you, how mine eyes have been enlightened, because I tasted a little of this honey.

30How much more, if haply the people had eaten freely to day of the spoil of their enemies which they found? for had there not been now a much greater slaughter among the Philistines?

31And they smote the Philistines that day from Michmash to Aijalon: and the people were very faint.

32And the people flew upon the spoil, and took sheep, and oxen, and calves, and slew *them* on the ground: and the people did eat *them* with the blood.

33Then they told Saul, saying, Behold, the people sin against the LORD, in that they eat with the blood. And he said, Ye have transgressed: roll a great stone unto me this day.

34And Saul said, Disperse yourselves among the people, and say unto them, Bring me hither every man his ox, and every man his sheep, and slay *them* here, and eat; and sin not against the LORD in eating with the blood. And all the people brought every man his ox with him that night, and slew *them* there.

35And Saul built an altar unto the LORD: the same was the first altar that he built unto the LORD.

36And Saul said, Let us go down after the Philistines by night, and spoil them until the morning light, and let us not leave a man of them. And they said, Do whatsoever seemeth good unto thee. Then said the priest, Let us draw near hither unto God.

37And Saul asked counsel of God, Shall I go down after the Philistines? wilt thou deliver them into the hand of Israel? But he answered him not that day.

38And Saul said, Draw ye near hither, all the chief of the people: and know and see wherein this sin hath been this day.

39For, *as* the LORD liveth, which saveth Israel, though it be in Jonathan my son, he shall surely die. But *there was* not a man among all the people *that* answered him.

40Then said he unto all Israel, Be ye on one side, and I and Jonathan my son will be on the other side. And the people said unto Saul, Do what seemeth good unto thee.

41Therefore Saul said unto the LORD God of Israel, Give a perfect *lot.* And Saul and Jonathan were taken: but the people escaped.

42And Saul said, Cast *lots* between me and Jonathan my son. And Jonathan was taken.

43Then Saul said to Jonathan, Tell me what thou hast done. And Jonathan told him, and said, I did but taste a little honey with the end of the rod that *was* in mine hand, *and,* lo, I must die.

44And Saul answered, God do so and more also: for thou shalt surely die, Jonathan.

45And the people said unto Saul, Shall Jonathan die, who hath wrought this great salvation in Israel? God forbid: *as* the LORD liveth, there shall not one hair of his head fall to the ground; for he hath wrought with God this day. So the people rescued Jonathan, that he died not.

46Then Saul went up from following the Philistines: and the Philistines went to their own place.

47So Saul took the kingdom over Israel, and fought against all his enemies on every side, against Moab, and against the children of Ammon, and against Edom, and against the kings of Zobah, and against the Philistines: and whithersoever he turned himself, he vexed *them.*

48And he gathered an host, and smote the Amalekites, and delivered Israel out of the hands of them that spoiled them.

49Now the sons of Saul were Jonathan, and Ishui, and Melchishua: and the names of his two daughters *were these;* the name of the firstborn Merab, and the name of the younger Michal:

50And the name of Saul's wife *was* Ahinoam, the daughter of Ahimaaz: and the name of the captain of his host *was* Abner, the son of Ner, Saul's uncle.

51And Kish *was* the father of Saul; and Ner the father of Abner *was* the son of Abiel.

52And there was sore war against the Philistines all the days of Saul: and when Saul saw any strong man, or any valiant man, he took him unto him.

JOHN 7:31–53

AND many of the people believed on him [Jesus], and said, When Christ cometh, will he do more miracles than these which this *man* hath done?

32The Pharisees heard that the people murmured such things concerning him; and the Pharisees and the chief priests sent officers to take him.

33Then said Jesus unto them, Yet a little while am I with you, and *then* I go unto him that sent me.

34Ye shall seek me, and shall not find *me:* and where I am, *thither* ye cannot come.

35Then said the Jews among themselves, Whither will he go, that we shall not find him? will he go unto the dispersed among the Gentiles, and teach the Gentiles?

36What *manner of* saying is this that he said, Ye shall seek me, and shall not find *me:* and where I am, *thither* ye cannot come?

37In the last day, that great *day* of the feast, Jesus stood and cried, saying, If any man thirst, let him come unto me, and drink.

38He that believeth on me, as the scripture hath said, out of his belly shall flow rivers of living water.

39(But this spake he of the Spirit, which they that believe on him should receive: for the Holy Ghost was not yet *given;* because that Jesus was not yet glorified.)

40Many of the people therefore, when they heard this saying, said, Of a truth this is the Prophet.

41Others said, This is the Christ. But some said, Shall Christ come out of Galilee?

42Hath not the scripture said, That Christ cometh of the seed of David, and out of the town of Bethlehem, where David was?

43So there was a division among the people because of him.

44And some of them would have taken him; but no man laid hands on him.

45Then came the officers to the chief priests and Pharisees; and they said unto them, Why have ye not brought him?

46The officers answered, Never man spake like this man.

47Then answered them the Pharisees, Are ye also deceived?

48Have any of the rulers or of the Pharisees believed on him?

49But this people who knoweth not the law are cursed.

50Nicodemus saith unto them, (he that came to Jesus by night, being one of them,)

51Doth our law judge *any* man, before it hear him, and know what he doeth?

52They answered and said unto him, Art thou also of Galilee? Search, and look: for out of Galilee ariseth no prophet.

53And every man went unto his own house.

PSALM 109:1–31

HOLD not thy peace, O God of my praise;

2For the mouth of the wicked and the mouth of the deceitful are opened against me: they have spoken against me with a lying tongue.

3They compassed me about also with words of hatred; and fought against me without *a* cause.

4For my love they are my adversaries: but I *give myself unto* prayer.

5And they have rewarded me evil for good, and hatred for my love.

6Set thou a wicked man over him: and let Satan stand at his right hand.

7When he shall be judged, let him be condemned: and let his prayer become sin.

8Let his days be few; *and* let another take his office.

9Let his children be fatherless, and his wife a widow.

10Let his children be continually vagabonds, and beg: let them seek *their bread* also out of their desolate places.

11Let the extortioner catch all that he hath; and let the strangers spoil his labour.

12Let there be none to extend mercy unto him: neither let there be any to favour his fatherless children.

13Let his posterity be cut off; *and* in the generation following let their name be blotted out.

14Let the iniquity of his fathers be remembered with the LORD; and let not the sin of his mother be blotted out.

15Let them be before the LORD continually, that he may cut off the memory of them from the earth.

16Because that he remembered not to shew mercy, but persecuted the poor and needy man, that he might even slay the broken in heart.

17As he loved cursing, so let it come unto him: as he delighted not in blessing, so let it be far from him.

18As he clothed himself with cursing like as with his garment, so let it come into his bowels like water, and like oil into his bones.

19Let it be unto him as the garment

which covereth him, and for a girdle wherewith he is girded continually.

20*Let* this *be* the reward of mine adversaries from the LORD, and of them that speak evil against my soul.

21But do thou for me, O GOD the Lord, for thy name's sake: because thy mercy *is* good, deliver thou me.

22For I *am* poor and needy, and my heart is wounded within me.

23I am gone like the shadow when it declineth: I am tossed up and down as the locust.

24My knees are weak through fasting; and my flesh faileth of fatness.

25I became also a reproach unto them: *when* they looked upon me they shaked their heads.

26Help me, O LORD my God: O save me according to thy mercy:

27That they may know that this *is* thy hand; *that* thou, LORD, hast done it.

28Let them curse, but bless thou: when they arise, let them be ashamed; but let thy servant rejoice.

29Let mine adversaries be clothed with shame, and let them cover themselves with their own confusion, as with a mantle.

30I will greatly praise the LORD with my mouth; yea, I will praise him among the multitude.

31For he shall stand at the right hand of the poor, to save *him* from those that condemn his soul.

PROVERBS FOR TODAY/ 15:5–7

A fool despiseth his father's instruction: but he that regardeth reproof is prudent. □ *In the house of the righteous* is *much treasure: but in the revenues of the wicked is trouble.* □ *The lips of the wise disperse knowledge: but the heart of the foolish* doeth *not so.*

MAY 14

1 SAMUEL 15:1—16:23

SAMUEL also said unto Saul, The LORD sent me to anoint thee *to be* king over his people, over Israel: now therefore hearken thou unto the voice of the words of the LORD.

2Thus saith the LORD of hosts, I remember *that* which Amalek did to Israel, how he laid *wait* for him in the way, when he came up from Egypt.

3Now go and smite Amalek, and utterly destroy all that they have, and spare them not; but slay both man and woman, infant and suckling, ox and sheep, camel and ass.

4And Saul gathered the people together, and numbered them in Telaim, two hundred thousand footmen, and ten thousand men of Judah.

5And Saul came to a city of Amalek, and laid wait in the valley.

6And Saul said unto the Kenites, Go, depart, get you down from among the Amalekites, lest I destroy you with them: for ye shewed kindness to all the children of Israel, when they came up out of Egypt. So the Kenites departed from among the Amalekites.

7And Saul smote the Amalekites from Havilah *until* thou comest to Shur, that *is* over against Egypt.

8And he took Agag the king of the

Amalekites alive, and utterly destroyed all the people with the edge of the sword.

9But Saul and the people spared Agag, and the best of the sheep, and of the oxen, and of the fatlings, and the lambs, and all *that was* good, and would not utterly destroy them: but every thing *that was* vile and refuse, that they destroyed utterly.

10Then came the word of the LORD unto Samuel, saying,

11It repenteth me that I have set up Saul *to be* king: for he is turned back from following me, and hath not performed my commandments. And it grieved Samuel; and he cried unto the LORD all night.

12And when Samuel rose early to meet Saul in the morning, it was told Samuel, saying, Saul came to Carmel, and, behold, he set him up a place, and is gone about, and passed on, and gone down to Gilgal.

13And Samuel came to Saul: and Saul said unto him, Blessed *be* thou of the LORD: I have performed the commandment of the LORD.

14And Samuel said, What *meaneth* then this bleating of the sheep in mine ears, and the lowing of the oxen which I hear?

15And Saul said, They have brought them from the Amalekites: for the people spared the best of the sheep and of the oxen, to sacrifice unto the LORD thy God; and the rest we have utterly destroyed.

16Then Samuel said unto Saul, Stay, and I will tell thee what the LORD hath said to me this night. And he said unto him, Say on.

17And Samuel said, When thou *wast* little in thine own sight, *wast* thou not *made* the head of the tribes of Israel, and the LORD anointed thee king over Israel?

18And the LORD sent thee on a journey, and said, Go and utterly destroy the sinners the Amalekites, and fight against them until they be consumed.

19Wherefore then didst thou not obey the voice of the LORD, but didst fly upon the spoil, and didst evil in the sight of the LORD?

20And Saul said unto Samuel, Yea, I have obeyed the voice of the LORD, and have gone the way which the LORD sent me, and have brought Agag the king of Amalek, and have utterly destroyed the Amalekites.

21But the people took of the spoil, sheep and oxen, the chief of the things which should have been utterly destroyed, to sacrifice unto the LORD thy God in Gilgal.

22And Samuel said, Hath the LORD *as great* delight in burnt offerings and sacrifices, as in obeying the voice of the LORD? Behold, to obey *is* better than sacrifice, *and* to hearken than the fat of rams.

23For rebellion *is as* the sin of witchcraft, and stubbornness *is as* iniquity and idolatry. Because thou hast rejected the word of the LORD, he hath also rejected thee from *being* king.

24And Saul said unto Samuel, I have sinned: for I have transgressed the commandment of the LORD, and thy words: because I feared the people, and obeyed their voice.

25Now therefore, I pray thee, pardon my sin, and turn again with me, that I may worship the LORD.

26And Samuel said unto Saul, I will not return with thee: for thou hast rejected the word of the LORD, and the LORD hath rejected thee from being king over Israel.

27And as Samuel turned about to go away, he laid hold upon the skirt of his mantle, and it rent.

28And Samuel said unto him, The LORD hath rent the kingdom of Israel from thee this day, and hath given it to a neighbour of thine, *that is* better than thou.

29And also the Strength of Israel will not lie nor repent: for he *is* not a man, that he should repent.

30Then he said, I have sinned: yet honour me now, I pray thee, before the elders of my people, and before Israel, and turn again with me, that I may worship the LORD thy God.

31So Samuel turned again after Saul; and Saul worshipped the LORD.

32Then said Samuel, Bring ye hither to me Agag the king of the Amalekites. And Agag came unto him delicately. And Agag said, Surely the bitterness of death is past.

33And Samuel said, As thy sword hath made women childless, so shall thy mother be childless among women. And Samuel hewed Agag in pieces before the LORD in Gilgal.

34Then Samuel went to Ramah; and Saul went up to his house to Gibeah of Saul.

35And Samuel came no more to see Saul until the day of his death: nevertheless Samuel mourned for Saul: and the LORD repented that he had made Saul king over Israel.

AND the LORD said unto Samuel, How long wilt thou mourn for Saul, seeing I have rejected him from reigning over Israel? fill thine horn with oil, and go, I will send thee to Jesse the Beth–lehemite: for I have provided me a king among his sons.

2And Samuel said, How can I go? if Saul hear it, he will kill me. And the LORD said, Take an heifer with thee, and say, I am come to sacrifice to the LORD.

3And call Jesse to the sacrifice, and I will shew thee what thou shalt do: and thou shalt anoint unto me him whom I name unto thee.

4And Samuel did that which the LORD spake, and came to Beth–lehem. And the elders of the town trembled at his coming, and said, Comest thou peaceably?

5And he said, Peaceably: I am come to sacrifice unto the LORD: sanctify yourselves, and come with me to the sacrifice. And he sanctified Jesse and his sons, and called them to the sacrifice.

6And it came to pass, when they were come, that he looked on Eliab, and said, Surely the LORD's anointed is before him.

7But the LORD said unto Samuel, Look not on his countenance, or on the height of his stature: because I have refused him: for the LORD seeth not as man seeth; for man looketh on the outward appearance, but the LORD looketh on the heart.

8Then Jesse called Abinadab, and made him pass before Samuel. And he said, Neither hath the LORD chosen this.

9Then Jesse made Shammah to pass by. And he said, Neither hath the LORD chosen this.

10Again, Jesse made seven of his sons to pass before Samuel. And Samuel said unto Jesse, The LORD hath not chosen these.

11And Samuel said unto Jesse, Are here all thy children? And he said, There remaineth yet the youngest, and, behold, he keepeth the sheep. And Samuel said unto Jesse, Send and fetch him: for we will not sit down till he come hither.

12And he sent, and brought him in. Now he was ruddy, and withal of a beautiful countenance, and goodly to look to. And the LORD said, Arise, anoint him: for this is he.

13Then Samuel took the horn of oil, and anointed him in the midst of his brethren: and the Spirit of the LORD came upon David from that day forward. So Samuel rose up, and went to Ramah.

14But the Spirit of the LORD departed from Saul, and an evil spirit from the LORD troubled him.

15And Saul's servants said unto him, Behold now, an evil spirit from God troubleth thee.

16Let our lord now command thy servants, which are before thee, to seek out a man, *who is* a cunning player on an harp: and it shall come to pass, when the evil spirit from God is upon thee, that he shall play with his hand, and thou shalt be well.

17And Saul said unto his servants, Provide me now a man that can play well, and bring *him* to me.

18Then answered one of the servants, and said, Behold, I have seen a son of Jesse the Bethlehemite, *that is* cunning in playing, and a mighty valiant man, and a man of war, and prudent in matters, and a comely person, and the LORD *is* with him.

19Wherefore Saul sent messengers unto Jesse, and said, Send me David thy son, which *is* with the sheep.

20And Jesse took an ass *laden* with bread, and a bottle of wine, and a kid, and sent *them* by David his son unto Saul.

21And David came to Saul, and stood before him: and he loved him greatly; and he became his armourbearer.

22And Saul sent to Jesse, saying, Let David, I pray thee, stand before me; for he hath found favour in my sight.

23And it came to pass, when the *evil* spirit from God was upon Saul, that David took an harp, and played with his hand: so Saul was refreshed, and was well, and the evil spirit departed from him.

JOHN 8:1–20

JESUS went unto the mount of Olives.

2And early in the morning he came again into the temple, and all the people came unto him; and he sat down, and taught them.

3And the scribes and Pharisees brought unto him a woman taken in adultery; and when they had set her in the midst,

4They say unto him, Master, this woman was taken in adultery, in the very act.

5Now Moses in the law commanded us, that such should be stoned: but what sayest thou?

6This they said, tempting him, that they might have to accuse him. But Jesus stooped down, and with *his* finger wrote on the ground, *as though he heard them not.*

7So when they continued asking him, he lifted up himself, and said unto them, He that is without sin among you, let him first cast a stone at her.

8And again he stooped down, and wrote on the ground.

9And they which heard *it,* being convicted by *their own* conscience, went out one by one, beginning at the eldest, *even* unto the last: and Jesus was left alone, and the woman standing in the midst.

10When Jesus had lifted up himself, and saw none but the woman, he said unto her, Woman, where are those thine accusers? hath no man condemned thee?

11She said, No man, Lord. And Jesus said unto her, Neither do I condemn thee: go, and sin no more.

12Then spake Jesus again unto them, saying, I am the light of the world: he that followeth me shall not walk in darkness, but shall have the light of life.

13The Pharisees therefore said unto him, Thou bearest record of thyself; thy record is not true.

14Jesus answered and said unto them, Though I bear record of myself, *yet* my record is true: for I know whence I came, and whither I go; but ye cannot tell whence I come, and whither I go.

15Ye judge after the flesh; I judge no man.

16And yet if I judge, my judgment is true: for I am not alone, but I and the Father that sent me.

17It is also written in your law, that the testimony of two men is true.

18I am one that bear witness of myself, and the Father that sent me beareth witness of me.

19Then said they unto him, Where is thy Father? Jesus answered, Ye neither know me, nor my Father: if ye had known me, ye should have known my Father also.

20These words spake Jesus in the treasury, as he taught in the temple: and no man laid hands on him; for his hour was not yet come.

PSALM 110:1–7

THE LORD said unto my LORD, Sit thou at my right hand, until I make thine enemies thy footstool.

2The LORD shall send the rod of thy strength out of Zion: rule thou in the midst of thine enemies.

3Thy people *shall be* willing in the day of thy power, in the beauties of holiness from the womb of the morning: thou hast the dew of thy youth.

4The LORD hath sworn, and will not repent, Thou *art* a priest for ever after the order of Melchizedek.

5The LORD at thy right hand shall strike through kings in the day of his wrath.

6He shall judge among the heathen, he shall fill *the places* with the dead bodies; he shall wound the heads over many countries.

7He shall drink of the brook in the way: therefore shall he lift up the head.

PROVERBS FOR TODAY/ 15:8–10

The sacrifice of the wicked is *an abomination to the LORD: but the prayer of the upright* is *his delight. The way of the wicked* is *an abomination unto the LORD: but he loveth him that followeth after righteousness. Correction* is *grievous unto him that forsaketh the way:* and *he that hateth reproof shall die.*

MAY 15

1 SAMUEL 17:1—18:4

Now the Philistines gathered together their armies to battle, and were gathered together at Shochoh, which *belongeth* to Judah, and pitched between Shochoh and Azekah, in Ephesdammim.

2And Saul and the men of Israel were gathered together, and pitched by the valley of Elah, and set the battle in array against the Philistines.

3And the Philistines stood on a mountain on the one side, and Israel stood on a mountain on the other side: and *there was* a valley between them.

4And there went out a champion out of the camp of the Philistines named Goliath, of Gath, whose height *was* six cubits and a span.

5And *he had* an helmet of brass upon his head, and he *was* armed with a coat of mail; and the weight of the coat *was* five thousand shekels of brass.

6And *he had* greaves of brass upon his legs, and a target of brass between his shoulders.

7And the staff of his spear *was* like a weaver's beam; and his spear's head *weighed* six hundred shekels of iron: and one bearing a shield went before him.

8And he stood and cried unto the

armies of Israel, and said unto them, Why are ye come out to set *your* battle in array? *am* not I a Philistine, and ye servants to Saul? choose you a man for you, and let him come down to me.

9If he be able to fight with me, and to kill me, then will we be your servants: but if I prevail against him, and kill him, then shall ye be our servants, and serve us.

10And the Philistine said, I defy the armies of Israel this day; give me a man, that we may fight together.

11When Saul and all Israel heard those words of the Philistine, they were dismayed, and greatly afraid.

12Now David *was* the son of that Ephrathite of Beth–lehem–judah, whose name *was* Jesse; and he had eight sons: and the man went among men *for* an old man in the days of Saul.

13And the three eldest sons of Jesse went *and* followed Saul to the battle: and the names of his three sons that went to the battle *were* Eliab the first-born, and next unto him Abinadab, and the third Shammah.

14And David *was* the youngest: and the three eldest followed Saul.

15But David went and returned from Saul to feed his father's sheep at Beth–lehem.

16And the Philistine drew near morning and evening, and presented himself forty days.

17And Jesse said unto David his son, Take now for thy brethren an ephah of this parched *corn,* and these ten loaves, and run to the camp to thy brethren;

18And carry these ten cheeses unto the captain of *their* thousand, and look how thy brethren fare, and take their pledge.

19Now Saul, and they, and all the men of Israel, *were* in the valley of Elah, fighting with the Philistines.

20And David rose up early in the morning, and left the sheep with a keeper, and took, and went, as Jesse had commanded him; and he came to the trench, as the host was going forth to the fight, and shouted for the battle.

21For Israel and the Philistines had put the battle in array, army against army.

22And David left his carriage in the hand of the keeper of the carriage, and ran into the army, and came and saluted his brethren.

23And as he talked with them, behold, there came up the champion, the Philistine of Gath, Goliath by name, out of the armies of the Philistines, and spake according to the same words: and David heard *them.*

24And all the men of Israel, when they saw the man, fled from him, and were sore afraid.

25And the men of Israel said, Have ye seen this man that is come up? surely to defy Israel is he come up: and it shall be, *that* the man who killeth him, the king will enrich him with great riches, and will give him his daughter, and make his father's house free in Israel.

26And David spake to the men that stood by him, saying, What shall be done to the man that killeth this Philistine, and taketh away the reproach from Israel? For who *is* this uncircumcised Philistine, that he should defy the armies of the living God?

27And the people answered him after this manner, saying, So shall it be done to the man that killeth him.

28And Eliab his eldest brother heard when he spake unto the men; and Eliab's anger was kindled against David, and he said, Why camest thou down hither? and with whom hast thou left those few sheep in the wilderness? I know thy pride, and the naughtiness of thine heart; for thou art come down that thou mightest see the battle.

29And David said, What have I now done? *Is there* not a cause?

30And he turned from him toward another, and spake after the same manner: and the people answered him again after the former manner.

³¹And when the words were heard which David spake, they rehearsed *them* before Saul: and he sent for him.

³²And David said to Saul, Let no man's heart fail because of him; thy servant will go and fight with this Philistine.

³³And Saul said to David, Thou art not able to go against this Philistine to fight with him: for thou *art but* a youth, and he a man of war from his youth.

³⁴And David said unto Saul, Thy servant kept his father's sheep, and there came a lion, and a bear, and took a lamb out of the flock:

³⁵And I went out after him, and smote him, and delivered *it* out of his mouth: and when he arose against me, I caught *him* by his beard, and smote him, and slew him.

³⁶Thy servant slew both the lion and the bear: and this uncircumcised Philistine shall be as one of them, seeing he hath defied the armies of the living God.

³⁷David said moreover, The LORD that delivered me out of the paw of the lion, and out of the paw of the bear, he will deliver me out of the hand of this Philistine. And Saul said unto David, Go, and the LORD be with thee.

³⁸And Saul armed David with his armour, and he put an helmet of brass upon his head; also he armed him with a coat of mail.

³⁹And David girded his sword upon his armour, and he assayed to go; for he had not proved *it*. And David said unto Saul, I cannot go with these; for I have not proved *them*. And David put them off him.

⁴⁰And he took his staff in his hand, and chose him five smooth stones out of the brook, and put them in a shepherd's bag which he had, even in a scrip; and his sling *was* in his hand: and he drew near to the Philistine.

⁴¹And the Philistine came on and drew near unto David; and the man that bare the shield *went* before him.

⁴²And when the Philistine looked about, and saw David, he disdained him: for he was *but* a youth, and ruddy, and of a fair countenance.

⁴³And the Philistine said unto David, *Am* I a dog, that thou comest to me with staves? and the Philistine cursed David by his gods.

⁴⁴And the Philistine said to David, Come to me, and I will give thy flesh unto the fowls of the air, and to the beasts of the field.

⁴⁵Then said David to the Philistine, Thou comest to me with a sword, and with a spear, and with a shield: but I come to thee in the name of the LORD of hosts, the God of the armies of Israel, whom thou hast defied.

⁴⁶This day will the LORD deliver thee into mine hand; and I will smite thee, and take thine head from thee; and I will give the carcases of the host of the Philistines this day unto the fowls of the air, and to the wild beasts of the earth; that all the earth may know that there is a God in Israel.

⁴⁷And all this assembly shall know that the LORD saveth not with sword and spear: for the battle *is* the LORD'S, and he will give you into our hands.

⁴⁸And it came to pass, when the Philistine arose, and came and drew nigh to meet David, that David hasted, and ran toward the army to meet the Philistine.

⁴⁹And David put his hand in his bag, and took thence a stone, and slang *it,* and smote the Philistine in his forehead, that the stone sunk into his forehead; and he fell upon his face to the earth.

⁵⁰So David prevailed over the Philistine with a sling and with a stone, and smote the Philistine, and slew him; but *there was* no sword in the hand of David.

⁵¹Therefore David ran, and stood upon the Philistine, and took his sword, and drew it out of the sheath thereof,

and slew him, and cut off his head therewith. And when the Philistines saw their champion was dead, they fled.

52And the men of Israel and of Judah arose, and shouted, and pursued the Philistines, until thou come to the valley, and to the gates of Ekron. And the wounded of the Philistines fell down by the way to Shaaraim, even unto Gath, and unto Ekron.

53And the children of Israel returned from chasing after the Philistines, and they spoiled their tents.

54And David took the head of the Philistine, and brought it to Jerusalem; but he put his armour in his tent.

55And when Saul saw David go forth against the Philistine, he said unto Abner, the captain of the host, Abner, whose son *is* this youth? And Abner said, *As* thy soul liveth, O king, I cannot tell.

56And the king said, Enquire thou whose son the stripling *is*.

57And as David returned from the slaughter of the Philistine, Abner took him, and brought him before Saul with the head of the Philistine in his hand.

58And Saul said to him, Whose son *art* thou, *thou* young man? And David answered, I *am* the son of thy servant Jesse the Beth–lehemite.

AND it came to pass, when he had made an end of speaking unto Saul, that the soul of Jonathan was knit with the soul of David, and Jonathan loved him as his own soul.

2And Saul took him that day, and would let him go no more home to his father's house.

3Then Jonathan and David made a covenant, because he loved him as his own soul.

4And Jonathan stripped himself of the robe that *was* upon him, and gave it to David, and his garments, even to his sword, and to his bow, and to his girdle.

JOHN 8:21–30

THEN said Jesus again unto them, I go my way, and ye shall seek me, and shall die in your sins: whither I go, ye cannot come.

22Then said the Jews, Will he kill himself? because he saith, Whither I go, ye cannot come.

23And he said unto them, Ye are from beneath; I am from above: ye are of this world; I am not of this world.

24I said therefore unto you, that ye shall die in your sins: for if ye believe not that I am *he,* ye shall die in your sins.

25Then said they unto him, Who art thou? And Jesus saith unto them, Even *the same* that I said unto you from the beginning.

26I have many things to say and to judge of you: but he that sent me is true; and I speak to the world those things which I have heard of him.

27They understood not that he spake to them of the Father.

28Then said Jesus unto them, When ye have lifted up the Son of man, then shall ye know that I am *he,* and *that* I do nothing of myself; but as my Father hath taught me, I speak these things.

29And he that sent me is with me: the Father hath not left me alone; for I do always those things that please him.

30As he spake these words, many believed on him.

PSALM 111:1–10

PRAISE ye the LORD. I will praise the LORD with *my* whole heart, in the assembly of the upright, and *in* the congregation.

2The works of the LORD *are* great, sought out of all them that have pleasure therein.

3His work *is* honourable and glorious:

and his righteousness endureth for ever.

⁴He hath made his wonderful works to be remembered: the LORD *is* gracious and full of compassion.

⁵He hath given meat unto them that fear him: he will ever be mindful of his covenant.

⁶He hath shewed his people the power of his works, that he may give them the heritage of the heathen.

⁷The works of his hands *are* verity and judgment; all his commandments *are* sure.

⁸They stand fast for ever and ever, *and are* done in truth and uprightness.

⁹He sent redemption unto his people: he hath commanded his covenant for ever: holy and reverend *is* his name.

¹⁰The fear of the LORD *is* the beginning of wisdom: a good understanding have all they that do *his commandments:* his praise endureth for ever.

PROVERBS FOR TODAY/ 15:11

Hell and destruction are *before the* LORD: *how much more then the hearts of the children of men?*

MAY 16

1 SAMUEL 18:5—19:24

A ND David went out whithersoever Saul sent him, *and* behaved himself wisely: and Saul set him over the men of war, and he was accepted in the sight of all the people, and also in the sight of Saul's servants.

⁶And it came to pass as they came, when David was returned from the slaughter of the Philistine, that the women came out of all cities of Israel, singing and dancing, to meet king Saul, with tabrets, with joy, and with instruments of musick.

⁷And the women answered *one another* as they played, and said, Saul hath slain his thousands, and David his ten thousands.

⁸And Saul was very wroth, and the saying displeased him; and he said, They have ascribed unto David ten thousands, and to me they have ascribed *but* thousands: and *what* can he have more but the kingdom?

⁹And Saul eyed David from that day and forward.

¹⁰And it came to pass on the morrow, that the evil spirit from God came upon Saul, and he prophesied in the midst of the house: and David played with his hand, as at other times: and *there was* a javelin in Saul's hand.

¹¹And Saul cast the javelin; for he said, I will smite David even to the wall *with it.* And David avoided out of his presence twice.

¹²And Saul was afraid of David, because the LORD was with him, and was departed from Saul.

¹³Therefore Saul removed him from him, and made him his captain over a thousand; and he went out and came in before the people.

¹⁴And David behaved himself wisely in all his ways; and the LORD *was* with him.

¹⁵Wherefore when Saul saw that he behaved himself very wisely, he was afraid of him.

16But all Israel and Judah loved David, because he went out and came in before them.

17And Saul said to David, Behold my elder daughter Merab, her will I give thee to wife: only be thou valiant for me, and fight the LORD's battles. For Saul said, Let not mine hand be upon him, but let the hand of the Philistines be upon him.

18And David said unto Saul, Who *am* I? and what *is* my life, *or* my father's family in Israel, that I should be son in law to the king?

19But it came to pass at the time when Merab Saul's daughter should have been given to David, that she was given unto Adriel the Meholathite to wife.

20And Michal Saul's daughter loved David: and they told Saul, and the thing pleased him.

21And Saul said, I will give him her, that she may be a snare to him, and that the hand of the Philistines may be against him. Wherefore Saul said to David, Thou shalt this day be my son in law in *the one of* the twain.

22And Saul commanded his servants, *saying,* Commune with David secretly, and say, Behold, the king hath delight in thee, and all his servants love thee: now therefore be the king's son in law.

23And Saul's servants spake those words in the ears of David. And David said, Seemeth it to you *a* light *thing* to be a king's son in law, seeing that I *am* a poor man, and lightly esteemed?

24And the servants of Saul told him, saying, On this manner spake David.

25And Saul said, Thus shall ye say to David, The king desireth not any dowry, but an hundred foreskins of the Philistines, to be avenged of the king's enemies. But Saul thought to make David fall by the hand of the Philistines.

26And when his servants told David these words, it pleased David well to be the king's son in law: and the days were not expired.

27Wherefore David arose and went, he and his men, and slew of the Philistines two hundred men; and David brought their foreskins, and they gave them in full tale to the king, that he might be the king's son in law. And Saul gave him Michal his daughter to wife.

28And Saul saw and knew that the LORD *was* with David, and *that* Michal Saul's daughter loved him.

29And Saul was yet the more afraid of David; and Saul became David's enemy continually.

30Then the princes of the Philistines went forth: and it came to pass, after they went forth, *that* David behaved himself more wisely than all the servants of Saul; so that his name was much set by.

AND Saul spake to Jonathan his son, and to all his servants, that they should kill David.

2But Jonathan Saul's son delighted much in David: and Jonathan told David, saying, Saul my father seeketh to kill thee: now therefore, I pray thee, take heed to thyself until the morning, and abide in a secret *place,* and hide thyself:

3And I will go out and stand beside my father in the field where thou *art,* and I will commune with my father of thee; and what I see, that I will tell thee.

4And Jonathan spake good of David unto Saul his father, and said unto him, Let not the king sin against his servant, against David; because he hath not sinned against thee, and because his works *have been* to thee-ward very good:

5For he did put his life in his hand, and slew the Philistine, and the LORD wrought a great salvation for all Israel: thou sawest *it,* and didst rejoice: wherefore then wilt thou sin against innocent blood, to slay David without a cause?

6And Saul hearkened unto the voice of Jonathan: and Saul sware, *As* the LORD liveth, he shall not be slain.

7And Jonathan called David, and Jonathan shewed him all those things. And Jonathan brought David to Saul, and he was in his presence, as in times past.

8And there was war again: and David went out, and fought with the Philistines, and slew them with a great slaughter; and they fled from him.

9And the evil spirit from the LORD was upon Saul, as he sat in his house with his javelin in his hand: and David played with his hand.

10And Saul sought to smite David even to the wall with the javelin; but he slipped away out of Saul's presence, and he smote the javelin into the wall: and David fled, and escaped that night.

11Saul also sent messengers unto David's house, to watch him, and to slay him in the morning: and Michal David's wife told him, saying, If thou save not thy life to night, to morrow thou shalt be slain.

12So Michal let David down through a window: and he went, and fled, and escaped.

13And Michal took an image, and laid it in the bed, and put a pillow of goats' hair for his bolster, and covered it with a cloth.

14And when Saul sent messengers to take David, she said, He is sick.

15And Saul sent the messengers again to see David, saying, Bring him up to me in the bed, that I may slay him.

16And when the messengers were come in, behold, there was an image in the bed, with a pillow of goats' hair for his bolster.

17And Saul said unto Michal, Why hast thou deceived me so, and sent away mine enemy, that he is escaped? And Michal answered Saul, He said unto me, Let me go; why should I kill thee?

18So David fled, and escaped, and came to Samuel to Ramah, and told him all that Saul had done to him. And he and Samuel went and dwelt in Naioth.

19And it was told Saul, saying, Behold, David is at Naioth in Ramah.

20And Saul sent messengers to take David: and when they saw the company of the prophets prophesying, and Samuel standing as appointed over them, the Spirit of God was upon the messengers of Saul, and they also prophesied.

21And when it was told Saul, he sent other messengers, and they prophesied likewise, and Saul sent messengers again the third time, and they prophesied also.

22Then went he also to Ramah, and came to a great well that is in Sechu: and he asked and said, Where are Samuel and David? And one said, Behold, they be at Naioth in Ramah.

23And he went thither to Naioth in Ramah: and the Spirit of God was upon him also, and he went on, and prophesied, until he came to Naioth in Ramah.

24And he stripped off his clothes also, and prophesied before Samuel in like manner, and lay down naked all that day and all that night. Wherefore they say, Is Saul also among the prophets?

JOHN 8:31–59

THEN said Jesus to those Jews which believed on him, If ye continue in my word, then are ye my disciples indeed;

32And ye shall know the truth, and the truth shall make you free.

33They answered him, We be Abraham's seed, and were never in bondage to any man: how sayest thou, Ye shall be made free?

34Jesus answered them, Verily, verily, I say unto you, Whosoever committeth sin is the servant of sin.

35And the servant abideth not in the house for ever: but the Son abideth ever.

36If the Son therefore shall make you free, ye shall be free indeed.

37I know that ye are Abraham's seed; but ye seek to kill me, because my word hath no place in you.

38I speak that which I have seen with my Father: and ye do that which ye have seen with your father.

39They answered and said unto him, Abraham is our father. Jesus saith unto them, If ye were Abraham's children, ye would do the works of Abraham.

40But now ye seek to kill me, a man that hath told you the truth, which I have heard of God: this did not Abraham.

41Ye do the deeds of your father. Then said they to him, We be not born of fornication; we have one Father, *even* God.

42Jesus said unto them, If God were your Father, ye would love me: for I proceeded forth and came from God; neither came I of myself, but he sent me.

43Why do ye not understand my speech? *even* because ye cannot hear my word.

44Ye are of *your* father the devil, and the lusts of your father ye will do. He was a murderer from the beginning, and abode not in the truth, because there is no truth in him. When he speaketh a lie, he speaketh of his own: for he is a liar, and the father of it.

45And because I tell *you* the truth, ye believe me not.

46Which of you convinceth me of sin? And if I say the truth, why do ye not believe me?

47He that is of God heareth God's words: ye therefore hear *them* not, because ye are not of God.

48Then answered the Jews, and said unto him, Say we not well that thou art a Samaritan, and hast a devil?

49Jesus answered, I have not a devil; but I honour my Father, and ye do dishonour me.

50And I seek not mine own glory: there is one that seeketh and judgeth.

51Verily, verily, I say unto you, If a man keep my saying, he shall never see death.

52Then said the Jews unto him, Now we know that thou hast a devil. Abraham is dead, and the prophets; and thou sayest, If a man keep my saying, he shall never taste of death.

53Art thou greater than our father Abraham, which is dead? and the prophets are dead: whom makest thou thyself?

54Jesus answered, If I honour myself, my honour is nothing: it is my Father that honoureth me; of whom ye say, that he is your God:

55Yet ye have not known him; but I know him: and if I should say, I know him not, I shall be a liar like unto you: but I know him, and keep his saying.

56Your father Abraham rejoiced to see my day: and he saw *it*, and was glad.

57Then said the Jews unto him, Thou art not yet fifty years old, and hast thou seen Abraham?

58Jesus said unto them, Verily, verily, I say unto you, Before Abraham was, I am.

59Then took they up stones to cast at him: but Jesus hid himself, and went out of the temple, going through the midst of them, and so passed by.

PSALM 112:1–10

PRAISE ye the LORD. Blessed *is* the man *that* feareth the LORD, *that* delighteth greatly in his commandments.

2His seed shall be mighty upon earth: the generation of the upright shall be blessed.

3Wealth and riches *shall be* in his house: and his righteousness endureth for ever.

4Unto the upright there ariseth light in the darkness: *he is* gracious, and full of compassion, and righteous.

5A good man sheweth favour, and lendeth: he will guide his affairs with discretion.

6Surely he shall not be moved for

ever: the righteous shall be in everlasting remembrance.

7He shall not be afraid of evil tidings: his heart is fixed, trusting in the LORD.

8His heart *is* established, he shall not be afraid, until he see *his desire* upon his enemies.

9He hath dispersed, he hath given to the poor; his righteousness endureth for ever; his horn shall be exalted with honour.

10The wicked shall see *it,* and be grieved; he shall gnash with his teeth, and melt away: the desire of the wicked shall perish.

PROVERBS FOR TODAY/ 15:12–14

A scorner loveth not one that reproveth him: neither will he go unto the wise. □ *A merry heart maketh a cheerful countenance: but by sorrow of the heart the spirit is broken.* □ *The heart of him that hath understanding seeketh knowledge: but the mouth of fools feedeth on foolishness.*

MAY 17

1 SAMUEL 20:1—21:15

AND David fled from Naioth in Ramah, and came and said before Jonathan, What have I done? what *is* mine iniquity? and what *is* my sin before thy father, that he seeketh my life?

2And he said unto him, God forbid; thou shalt not die: behold, my father will do nothing either great or small, but that he will shew it me: and why should my father hide this thing from me? it *is* not *so.*

3And David sware moreover, and said, Thy father certainly knoweth that I have found grace in thine eyes; and he saith, Let not Jonathan know this, lest he be grieved: but truly *as* the LORD liveth, and *as* thy soul liveth, *there is* but a step between me and death.

4Then said Jonathan unto David, Whatsoever thy soul desireth, I will even do *it* for thee.

5And David said unto Jonathan, Behold, to morrow *is* the new moon, and I should not fail to sit with the king at meat: but let me go, that I may hide myself in the field unto the third *day* at even.

6If thy father at all miss me, then say, David earnestly asked *leave* of me that he might run to Beth–lehem his city: for *there is* a yearly sacrifice there for all the family.

7If he say thus, *It is* well; thy servant shall have peace: but if he be very wroth, *then* be sure that evil is determined by him.

8Therefore thou shalt deal kindly with thy servant; for thou hast brought thy servant into a covenant of the LORD with thee: notwithstanding, if there be in me iniquity, slay me thyself; for why shouldest thou bring me to thy father?

9And Jonathan said, Far be it from thee: for if I knew certainly that evil were determined by my father to come upon thee, then would not I tell it thee?

10Then said David to Jonathan, Who shall tell me? or what *if* thy father answer thee roughly?

11And Jonathan said unto David, Come, and let us go out into the field.

And they went out both of them into the field.

12And Jonathan said unto David, O Lord God of Israel, when I have sounded my father about to morrow any time, *or* the third *day,* and, behold, *if there be* good toward David, and I then send not unto thee, and shew it thee;

13The Lord do so and much more to Jonathan: but if it please my father *to do* thee evil, then I will shew it thee, and send thee away, that thou mayest go in peace: and the Lord be with thee, as he hath been with my father.

14And thou shalt not only while yet I live shew me the kindness of the Lord, that I die not:

15But *also* thou shalt not cut off thy kindness from my house for ever: no, not when the Lord hath cut off the enemies of David every one from the face of the earth.

16So Jonathan made *a covenant* with the house of David, *saying,* Let the Lord even require *it* at the hand of David's enemies.

17And Jonathan caused David to swear again, because he loved him: for he loved him as he loved his own soul.

18Then Jonathan said to David, To-morrow *is* the new moon: and thou shalt be missed, because thy seat will be empty.

19And *when* thou hast stayed three days, *then* thou shalt go down quickly, and come to the place where thou didst hide thyself when the business was *in hand,* and shalt remain by the stone Ezel.

20And I will shoot three arrows on the side *thereof,* as though I shot at a mark.

21And, behold, I will send a lad, *saying,* Go, find out the arrows. If I expressly say unto the lad, Behold, the arrows *are* on this side of thee, take them; then come thou: for *there is* peace to thee, and no hurt; *as* the Lord liveth.

22But if I say thus unto the young man, Behold, the arrows *are* beyond thee; go thy way: for the Lord hath sent thee away.

23And *as touching* the matter which thou and I have spoken of, behold, the Lord *be* between thee and me for ever.

24So David hid himself in the field: and when the new moon was come, the king sat him down to eat meat.

25And the king sat upon his seat, as at other times, *even* upon a seat by the wall: and Jonathan arose, and Abner sat by Saul's side, and David's place was empty.

26Nevertheless Saul spake not any thing that day: for he thought, Something hath befallen him, he *is* not clean; surely he *is* not clean.

27And it came to pass on the morrow, *which was* the second *day* of the month, that David's place was empty: and Saul said unto Jonathan his son, Wherefore cometh not the son of Jesse to meat, neither yesterday, nor to day?

28And Jonathan answered Saul, David earnestly asked *leave* of me *to go* to Beth–lehem:

29And he said, Let me go, I pray thee; for our family hath a sacrifice in the city; and my brother, he hath commanded me *to be there:* and now, if I have found favour in thine eyes, let me get away, I pray thee, and see my brethren. Therefore he cometh not unto the king's table.

30Then Saul's anger was kindled against Jonathan, and he said unto him, Thou son of the perverse rebellious *woman,* do not I know that thou hast chosen the son of Jesse to thine own confusion, and unto the confusion of thy mother's nakedness?

31For as long as the son of Jesse liveth upon the ground, thou shalt not be established, nor thy kingdom. Wherefore now send and fetch him unto me, for he shall surely die.

32And Jonathan answered Saul his father, and said unto him, Wherefore shall he be slain? what hath he done?

33And Saul cast a javelin at him to smite him: whereby Jonathan knew that it was determined of his father to slay David.

34So Jonathan arose from the table in fierce anger, and did eat no meat the second day of the month: for he was grieved for David, because his father had done him shame.

35And it came to pass in the morning, that Jonathan went out into the field at the time appointed with David, and a little lad with him.

36And he said unto his lad, Run, find out now the arrows which I shoot. *And* as the lad ran, he shot an arrow beyond him.

37And when the lad was come to the place of the arrow which Jonathan had shot, Jonathan cried after the lad, and said, *Is* not the arrow beyond thee?

38And Jonathan cried after the lad, Make speed, haste, stay not. And Jonathan's lad gathered up the arrows, and came to his master.

39But the lad knew not any thing: only Jonathan and David knew the matter.

40And Jonathan gave his artillery unto his lad, and said unto him, Go, carry *them* to the city.

41*And* as soon as the lad was gone, David arose out of *a place* toward the south, and fell on his face to the ground, and bowed himself three times: and they kissed one another, and wept one with another, until David exceeded.

42And Jonathan said to David, Go in peace, forasmuch as we have sworn both of us in the name of the LORD, saying, The LORD be between me and thee, and between my seed and thy seed for ever. And he arose and departed: and Jonathan went into the city.

THEN came David to Nob to Ahimelech the priest: and Ahimelech was afraid at the meeting of David, and said unto him, Why *art* thou alone, and no man with thee?

2And David said unto Ahimelech the priest, The king hath commanded me a business, and hath said unto me, Let no man know any thing of the business whereabout I send thee: and what I have commanded thee: and I have appointed *my* servants to such and such a place.

3Now therefore what is under thine hand? give *me* five *loaves of* bread in mine hand, or what there is present.

4And the priest answered David, and said, *There is* no common bread under mine hand, but there is hallowed bread; if the young men have kept themselves at least from women.

5And David answered the priest, and said unto him, Of a truth women *have been* kept from us about these three days, since I came out, and the vessels of the young men are holy, and *the bread is* in a manner common, yea, though it were sanctified this day in the vessel.

6So the priest gave him hallowed *bread:* for there was no bread there but the shewbread, that was taken from before the LORD, to put hot bread in the day when it was taken away.

7Now a certain man of the servants of Saul *was* there that day, detained before the LORD; and his name *was* Doeg, an Edomite, the chiefest of the herdmen that *belonged* to Saul.

8And David said unto Ahimelech, And is there not here under thine hand spear or sword? for I have neither brought my sword nor my weapons with me, because the king's business required haste.

9And the priest said, The sword of Goliath the Philistine, whom thou slewest in the valley of Elah, behold, it *is here* wrapped in a cloth behind the ephod: if thou wilt take that, take *it:* for *there is* no other save that here. And David said, *There is* none like that; give it me.

¹⁰And David arose, and fled that day for fear of Saul, and went to Achish the king of Gath.

¹¹And the servants of Achish said unto him, *Is* not this David the king of the land? did they not sing one to another of him in dances, saying, Saul hath slain his thousands, and David his ten thousands?

¹²And David laid up these words in his heart, and was sore afraid of Achish the king of Gath.

¹³And he changed his behavior before them, and feigned himself mad in their hands, and scrabbled on the doors of the gate, and let his spittle fall down upon his beard.

¹⁴Then said Achish unto his servants, Lo, ye see the man is mad: wherefore *then* have ye brought him to me?

¹⁵Have I need of mad men, that ye have brought this *fellow* to play the mad man in my presence? shall this *fellow* come into my house?

JOHN 9:1–41

AND as *Jesus* passed by, he saw a man which was blind from *his* birth.

²And his disciples asked him, saying, Master, who did sin, this man, or his parents, that he was born blind?

³Jesus answered, Neither hath this man sinned, nor his parents: but that the works of God should be made manifest in him.

⁴I must work the works of him that sent me, while it is day: the night cometh, when no man can work.

⁵As long as I am in the world, I am the light of the world.

⁶When he had thus spoken, he spat on the ground, and made clay of the spittle, and he anointed the eyes of the blind man with the clay,

⁷And said unto him, Go, wash in the pool of Siloam, (which is by interpretation, Sent.) He went his way therefore, and washed, and came seeing.

⁸The neighbours therefore, and they which before had seen him that he was blind, said, Is not this he that sat and begged?

⁹Some said, This is he: others *said,* He is like him: *but* he said, I am *he.*

¹⁰Therefore said they unto him, How were thine eyes opened?

¹¹He answered and said, A man that is called Jesus made clay, and anointed mine eyes, and said unto me, Go to the pool of Siloam, and wash: and I went and washed, and I received sight.

¹²Then said they unto him, Where is he? He said, I know not.

¹³They brought to the Pharisees him that aforetime was blind.

¹⁴And it was the sabbath day when Jesus made the clay, and opened his eyes.

¹⁵Then again the Pharisees also asked him how he had received his sight. He said unto them, He put clay upon mine eyes, and I washed, and do see.

¹⁶Therefore said some of the Pharisees, This man is not of God, because he keepeth not the sabbath day. Others said, How can a man that is a sinner do such miracles? And there was a division among them.

¹⁷They say unto the blind man again, What sayest thou of him, that he hath opened thine eyes? He said, He is a prophet.

¹⁸But the Jews did not believe concerning him, that he had been blind, and received his sight, until they called the parents of him that had received his sight.

¹⁹And they asked them, saying, Is this your son, who ye say was born blind? how then doth he now see?

²⁰His parents answered them and said, We know that this is our son, and that he was born blind:

²¹But by what means he now seeth, we know not; or who hath opened his eyes, we know not: he is of age; ask him: he shall speak for himself.

22These *words* spake his parents, because they feared the Jews: for the Jews had agreed already, that if any man did confess that he was Christ, he should be put out of the synagogue.

23Therefore said his parents, He is of age; ask him.

24Then again called they the man that was blind, and said unto him, Give God the praise: we know that this man is a sinner.

25He answered and said, Whether he be a sinner *or no,* I know not: one thing I know, that, whereas I was blind, now I see.

26Then said they to him again, What did he to thee? how opened he thine eyes?

27He answered them, I have told you already, and ye did not hear: wherefore would ye hear *it* again? will ye also be his disciples?

28Then they reviled him, and said, Thou art his disciple; but we are Moses' disciples.

29We know that God spake unto Moses: *as for* this *fellow,* we know not from whence he is.

30The man answered and said unto them, Why herein is a marvellous thing, that ye know not from whence he is, and *yet* he hath opened mine eyes.

31Now we know that God heareth not sinners: but if any man be a worshipper of God, and doeth his will, him he heareth.

32Since the world began was it not heard that any man opened the eyes of one that was born blind.

33If this man were not of God, he could do nothing.

34They answered and said unto him, Thou wast altogether born in sins, and dost thou teach us? And they cast him out.

35Jesus heard that they had cast him out; and when he had found him, he said unto him, Dost thou believe on the Son of God?

36He answered and said, Who is he,

Lord, that I might believe on him?

37And Jesus said unto him, Thou hast both seen him, and it is he that talketh with thee.

38And he said, Lord, I believe. And he worshipped him.

39And Jesus said, For judgment I am come into this world, that they which see not might see; and that they which see might be made blind.

40And *some* of the Pharisees which were with him heard these words and said unto him, Are we blind also?

41Jesus said unto them, If ye were blind, ye should have no sin: but now ye say, We see; therefore your sin remaineth.

PSALM 113:1—114:8

PRAISE ye the LORD. Praise, O ye servants of the LORD, praise the name of the LORD.

2Blessed be the name of the LORD from this time forth and for evermore.

3From the rising of the sun unto the going down of the same the LORD'S name *is* to be praised.

4The LORD *is* high above all nations, *and* his glory above the heavens.

5Who *is* like unto the LORD our God, who dwelleth on high,

6Who humbleth *himself* to behold *the things that are* in heaven, and in the earth!

7He raiseth up the poor out of the dust, *and* lifteth the needy out of the dunghill;

8That he may set *him* with princes, *even* with the princes of his people.

9He maketh the barren woman to keep house, *and to be* a joyful mother of children. Praise ye the LORD.

WHEN Israel went out of Egypt, the house of Jacob from a people of strange language;

2Judah was his sanctuary, *and* Israel his dominion.

3The sea saw *it,* and fled: Jordan was driven back.

4The mountains skipped like rams, *and* the little hills like lambs.

5What *ailed* thee, O thou sea, that thou fleddest? thou Jordan, *that* thou wast driven back?

6Ye mountains, *that* ye skipped like rams; *and* ye little hills, like lambs?

7Tremble, thou earth, at the presence of the LORD, at the presence of the God of Jacob;

8Which turned the rock *into* a standing water, the flint into a fountain of waters.

PROVERBS FOR TODAY/ 15:15–17

All the days of the afflicted are *evil: but he that is of a merry heart* hath *a continual feast.* □ *Better* is *little with the fear of the LORD than great treasure and trouble therewith.* □ *Better* is *a dinner of herbs where love is, than a stalled ox and hatred therewith.*

MAY 18

1 SAMUEL 22:1—23:29

DAVID therefore departed thence, and escaped to the cave Adullam: and when his brethren and all his father's house heard *it,* they went down thither to him.

2And every one *that was* in distress, and every one that *was* in debt, and every one *that was* discontented, gathered themselves unto him; and he became a captain over them: and there were with him about four hundred men.

3And David went thence to Mizpeh of Moab: and he said unto the king of Moab, Let my father and my mother, I pray thee, come forth, *and be* with you, till I know what God will do for me.

4And he brought them before the king of Moab: and they dwelt with him all the while that David was in the hold.

5And the prophet Gad said unto David, Abide not in the hold; depart, and get thee into the land of Judah. Then David departed, and came into the forest of Hareth.

6When Saul heard that David was discovered, and the men that *were* with him, (now Saul abode in Gibeah under a tree in Ramah, having his spear in his hand, and all his servants *were* standing about him;)

7Then Saul said unto his servants that stood about him, Hear now, ye Benjamites; will the son of Jesse give every one of you fields and vineyards, *and* make you all captains of thousands, and captains of hundreds;

8That all of you have conspired against me, and *there is* none that sheweth me that my son hath made a league with the son of Jesse, and *there is* none of you that is sorry for me, or sheweth unto me that my son hath stirred up my servant against me, to lie in wait, as at this day?

9Then answered Doeg the Edomite, which was set over the servants of Saul, and said, I saw the son of Jesse coming to Nob, to Ahimelech the son of Ahitub.

10And he enquired of the LORD for

him and gave him victuals, and gave him the sword of Goliath the Philistine.

11Then the king sent to call Ahimelech the priest, the son of Ahitub, and all his father's house, the priests that *were* in Nob: and they came all of them to the king.

12And Saul said, Hear now, thou son of Ahitub. And he answered, Here I *am,* my lord.

13And Saul said unto him, Why have ye conspired against me, thou and the son of Jesse, in that thou hast given him bread, and a sword, and hast enquired of God for him, that he should rise against me, to lie in wait, as at this day?

14Then Ahimelech answered the king, and said, And who *is so* faithful among all thy servants as David, which is the king's son in law, and goeth at thy bidding, and is honourable in thine house?

15Did I then begin to enquire of God for him? be it far from me: let not the king impute *any* thing unto his servant, *nor* to all the house of my father: for thy servant knew nothing of all this, less or more.

16And the king said, Thou shalt surely die, Ahimelech, thou, and all thy father's house.

17And the king said unto the footmen that stood about him, Turn, and slay the priests of the LORD; because their hand also *is* with David, and because they knew when he fled, and did not shew it to me. But the servants of the king would not put forth their hand to fall upon the priests of the LORD.

18And the king said to Doeg, Turn thou, and fall upon the priests. And Doeg the Edomite turned, and he fell upon the priests, and slew on that day fourscore and five persons that did wear a linen ephod.

19And Nob, the city of the priests, smote he with the edge of the sword, both men and women, children and sucklings, and oxen, and asses, and sheep, with the edge of the sword.

20And one of the sons of Ahimelech the son of Ahitub, named Abiathar, escaped, and fled after David.

21And Abiathar shewed David that Saul had slain the LORD's priests.

22And David said unto Abiathar, I knew *it* that day, when Doeg the Edomite *was* there, that he would surely tell Saul: I have occasioned *the death* of all the persons of thy father's house.

23Abide thou with me, fear not: for he that seeketh my life seeketh thy life: but with me thou *shalt* be in safeguard.

THEN they told David, saying, Behold, the Philistines fight against Keilah, and they rob the threshingfloors.

2Therefore David enquired of the LORD, saying, Shall I go and smite these Philistines? And the LORD said unto David, Go, and smite the Philistines, and save Keilah.

3And David's men said unto him, Behold, we be afraid here in Judah: how much more then if we come to Keilah against the armies of the Philistines?

4Then David enquired of the LORD yet again. And the LORD answered him and said, Arise, go down to Keilah; for I will deliver the Philistines into thine hand.

5So David and his men went to Keilah, and fought with the Philistines, and brought away their cattle, and smote them with a great slaughter. So David saved the inhabitants of Keilah.

6And it came to pass, when Abiathar the son of Ahimelech fled to David to Keilah, *that* he came down *with* an ephod in his hand.

7And it was told Saul that David was come to Keilah. And Saul said, God hath delivered him into mine hand; for he is shut in, by entering into a town that hath gates and bars.

8And Saul called all the people together to war, to go down to Keilah, to besiege David and his men.

9And David knew that Saul secretly practised mischief against him; and he said to Abiathar the priest, Bring hither the ephod.

10Then said David, O LORD God of Israel, thy servant hath certainly heard that Saul seeketh to come to Keilah, to destroy the city for my sake.

11Will the men of Keilah deliver me up into his hand? will Saul come down, as thy servant hath heard? O LORD God of Israel, I beseech thee, tell thy servant. And the LORD said, He will come down.

12Then said David, Will the men of Keilah deliver me and my men into the hand of Saul? And the LORD said, They will deliver *thee* up.

13Then David and his men, *which were* about six hundred, arose and departed out of Keilah, and went whithersoever they could go. And it was told Saul that David was escaped from Keilah; and he forbare to go forth.

14And David abode in the wilderness in strong holds, and remained in a mountain in the wilderness of Ziph. And Saul sought him every day, but God delivered him not into his hand.

15And David saw that Saul was come out to seek his life: and David *was* in the wilderness of Ziph in a wood.

16And Jonathan Saul's son arose, and went to David into the wood, and strengthened his hand in God.

17And he said unto him, Fear not: for the hand of Saul my father shall not find thee; and thou shalt be king over Israel, and I shall be next unto thee; and that also Saul my father knoweth.

18And they two made a covenant before the LORD: and David abode in the wood, and Jonathan went to his house.

19Then came up the Ziphites to Saul to Gibeah, saying, Doth not David hide himself with us in strong holds in the wood, in the hill of Hachilah, which *is* on the south of Jeshimon?

20Now therefore, O king, come down according to all the desire of thy soul to come down; and our part *shall be* to deliver him into the king's hand.

21And Saul said, Blessed *be* ye of the LORD; for ye have compassion on me.

22Go, I pray you, prepare yet, and know and see his place where his haunt is, *and* who hath seen him there: for it is told me *that* he dealeth very subtilly.

23See therefore, and take knowledge of all the lurking places where he hideth himself, and come ye again to me with the certainty, and I will go with you: and it shall come to pass, if he be in the land, that I will search him out throughout all the thousands of Judah.

24And they arose, and went to Ziph before Saul: but David and his men *were* in the wilderness of Maon, in the plain on the south of Jeshimon.

25Saul also and his men went to seek *him.* And they told David: wherefore he came down into a rock, and abode in the wilderness of Maon. And when Saul heard *that,* he pursued after David in the wilderness of Maon.

26And Saul went on this side of the mountain, and David and his men on that side of the mountain: and David made haste to get away for fear of Saul; for Saul and his men compassed David and his men round about to take them.

27But there came a messenger unto Saul, saying, Haste thee, and come; for the Philistines have invaded the land.

28Wherefore Saul returned from pursuing after David, and went against the Philistines: therefore they called that place Sela–hammahlekoth.

29And David went up from thence, and dwelt in strong holds at En–gedi.

JOHN 10:1–21

VERILY, verily, I say unto you, He that entereth not by the door into the sheepfold, but climbeth up some other way, the same is a thief and a robber.

2But he that entereth in by the door is the shepherd of the sheep.

3To him the porter openeth; and the sheep hear his voice: and he calleth his own sheep by name, and leadeth them out.

4And when he putteth forth his own sheep, he goeth before them, and the sheep follow him: for they know his voice.

5And a stranger will they not follow, but will flee from him: for they know not the voice of strangers.

6This parable spake Jesus unto them: but they understood not what things they were which he spake unto them.

7Then said Jesus unto them again, Verily, verily, I say unto you, I am the door of the sheep.

8All that ever came before me are thieves and robbers: but the sheep did not hear them.

9I am the door: by me if any man enter in, he shall be saved, and shall go in and out, and find pasture.

10The thief cometh not, but for to steal, and to kill, and to destroy: I am come that they might have life, and that they might have it more abundantly.

11I am the good shepherd: the good shepherd giveth his life for the sheep.

12But he that is an hireling, and not the shepherd, whose own the sheep are not, seeth the wolf coming, and leaveth the sheep, and fleeth: and the wolf catcheth them, and scattereth the sheep.

13The hireling fleeth, because he is an hireling, and careth not for the sheep.

14I am the good shepherd, and know my *sheep,* and am known of mine.

15As the Father knoweth me, even so know I the Father: and I lay down my life for the sheep.

16And other sheep I have, which are not of this fold: them also I must bring, and they shall hear my voice; and there shall be one fold, *and* one shepherd.

17Therefore doth my Father love me,

because I lay down my life, that I might take it again.

18No man taketh it from me, but I lay it down of myself. I have power to lay it down, and I have power to take it again. This commandment have I received of my Father.

19There was a division therefore again among the Jews for these sayings.

20And many of them said, He hath a devil, and is mad; why hear ye him?

21Others said, These are not the words of him that hath a devil. Can a devil open the eyes of the blind?

PSALM 115:1–18

Not unto us, O LORD, not unto us, but unto thy name give glory, for thy mercy, *and* for thy truth's sake.

2Wherefore should the heathen say, Where *is* now their God?

3But our God *is* in the heavens: he hath done whatsoever he hath pleased.

4Their idols *are* silver and gold, the work of men's hands.

5They have mouths, but they speak not: eyes have they, but they see not:

6They have ears, but they hear not: noses have they, but they smell not:

7They have hands, but they handle not: feet have they, but they walk not: neither speak they through their throat.

8They that make them are like unto them; *so is* every one that trusteth in them.

9O Israel, trust thou in the LORD: he *is* their help and their shield.

10O house of Aaron, trust in the LORD: he *is* their help and their shield.

11Ye that fear the LORD, trust in the LORD: he *is* their help and their shield.

12The LORD hath been mindful of us; he will bless *us;* he will bless the house of Israel; he will bless the house of Aaron.

13He will bless them that fear the LORD, *both* small and great.

14The LORD shall increase you more and more, you and your children.

15Ye *are* blessed of the LORD which made heaven and earth.

16The heaven, *even* the heavens, *are* the LORD'S: but the earth hath he given to the children of men.

17The dead praise not the LORD, neither any that go down into silence.

18But we will bless the LORD from this time forth and for evermore. Praise the LORD.

PROVERBS FOR TODAY/ 15:18–19

A wrathful man stirreth up strife: but he that is *slow to anger appeaseth strife.* ▢ *The way of the slothful* man is *as an hedge of thorns: but the way of the righteous* is *made plain.*

MAY 19

1 SAMUEL 24:1—25:44

AND it came to pass, when Saul was returned from following the Philistines, that it was told him, saying, Behold, David *is* in the wilderness of En–gedi.

2Then Saul took three thousand chosen men out of all Israel, and went to seek David and his men upon the rocks of the wild goats.

3And he came to the sheepcotes by the way, where *was* a cave; and Saul went in to cover his feet: and David and his men remained in the sides of the cave.

4And the men of David said unto him, Behold the day of which the LORD said unto thee, Behold, I will deliver thine enemy into thine hand, that thou mayest do to him as it shall seem good unto thee. Then David arose, and cut off the skirt of Saul's robe privily.

5And it came to pass afterward, that David's heart smote him, because he had cut off Saul's skirt.

6And he said unto his men, The LORD forbid that I should do this thing unto my master, the LORD'S anointed, to stretch forth mine hand against him, seeing he *is* the anointed of the LORD.

7So David stayed his servants with these words, and suffered them not to rise against Saul. But Saul rose up out of the cave, and went on *his* way.

8David also arose afterward, and went out of the cave, and cried after Saul, saying, My lord the king. And when Saul looked behind him, David stooped with his face to the earth, and bowed himself.

9And David said to Saul, Wherefore hearest thou men's words, saying, Behold, David seeketh thy hurt?

10Behold, this day thine eyes have seen how that the LORD had delivered thee to day into mine hand in the cave: and *some* bade *me* kill thee: but *mine eye* spared thee; and I said, I will not put forth mine hand against my lord; for he *is* the LORD'S anointed.

11Moreover, my father, see, yea, see the skirt of thy robe in my hand: for in that I cut off the skirt of thy robe, and killed thee not, know thou and see that *there is* neither evil nor transgression in mine hand, and I have not sinned against thee; yet thou huntest my soul to take it.

12The LORD judge between me and thee, and the LORD avenge me of thee:

but mine hand shall not be upon thee.

13As saith the proverb of the ancients, Wickedness proceedeth from the wicked: but mine hand shall not be upon thee.

14After whom is the king of Israel come out? after whom dost thou pursue? after a dead dog, after a flea.

15The LORD therefore be judge, and judge between me and thee, and see, and plead my cause, and deliver me out of thine hand.

16And it came to pass, when David had made an end of speaking these words unto Saul, that Saul said, *Is* this thy voice, my son David? And Saul lifted up his voice, and wept.

17And he said to David, Thou *art* more righteous than I: for thou hast rewarded me good, whereas I have rewarded thee evil.

18And thou hast shewed this day how that thou hast dealt well with me: forasmuch as when the LORD had delivered me into thine hand, thou killedst me not.

19For if a man find his enemy, will he let him go well away? wherefore the LORD reward thee good for that thou hast done unto me this day.

20And now, behold, I know well that thou shalt surely be king, and that the kingdom of Israel shall be established in thine hand.

21Swear now therefore unto me by the LORD, that thou wilt not cut off my seed after me, and that thou wilt not destroy my name out of my father's house.

22And David sware unto Saul. And Saul went home; but David and his men gat them up unto the hold.

AND Samuel died; and all the Israelites were gathered together, and lamented him, and buried him in his house at Ramah. And David arose, and went down to the wilderness of Paran.

2And *there was* a man in Maon, whose possessions *were* in Carmel; and the man *was* very great, and he had three thousand sheep, and a thousand goats: and he was shearing his sheep in Carmel.

3Now the name of the man *was* Nabal; and the name of his wife Abigail: and *she was* a woman of good understanding, and of a beautiful countenance: but the man *was* churlish and evil in his doings; and he *was* of the house of Caleb.

4And David heard in the wilderness that Nabal did shear his sheep.

5And David sent out ten young men, and David said unto the young men, Get you up to Carmel, and go to Nabal, and greet him in my name:

6And thus shall ye say to him that liveth *in prosperity,* Peace *be* both to thee, and peace *be* to thine house, and peace *be* unto all that thou hast.

7And now I have heard that thou hast shearers: now thy shepherds which were with us, we hurt them not, neither was there ought missing unto them, all the while they were in Carmel.

8Ask thy young men, and they will shew thee. Wherefore let the young men find favour in thine eyes: for we come in a good day: give, I pray thee, whatsoever cometh to thine hand unto thy servants, and to thy son David.

9And when David's young men came, they spake to Nabal according to all those words in the name of David, and ceased.

10And Nabal answered David's servants, and said, Who *is* David? and who *is* the son of Jesse? there be many servants now a days that break away every man from his master.

11Shall I then take my bread, and my water, and my flesh that I have killed for my shearers, and give *it* unto men, whom I know not whence they *be?*

12So David's young men turned their way, and went again, and came and told him all those sayings.

13And David said unto his men, Gird ye on every man his sword. And they girded on every man his sword; and David also girded on his sword: and there went up after David about four hundred men; and two hundred abode by the stuff.

14But one of the young men told Abigail, Nabal's wife, saying, Behold, David sent messengers out of the wilderness to salute our master; and he railed on them.

15But the men *were* very good unto us, and we were not hurt, neither missed we any thing, as long as we were conversant with them, when we were in the fields:

16They were a wall unto us both by night and day, all the while we were with them keeping the sheep.

17Now therefore know and consider what thou wilt do; for evil is determined against our master, and against all his household: for he *is such* a son of Belial, that *a man* cannot speak to him.

18Then Abigail made haste, and took two hundred loaves, and two bottles of wine, and five sheep ready dressed, and five measures of parched *corn,* and an hundred clusters of raisins, and two hundred cakes of figs, and laid *them* on asses.

19And she said unto her servants, Go on before me; behold, I come after you. But she told not her husband Nabal.

20And it was *so, as* she rode on the ass, that she came down by the covert of the hill, and, behold, David and his men came down against her; and she met them.

21Now David had said, Surely in vain have I kept all that this *fellow* hath in the wilderness, so that nothing was missed of all that *pertained* unto him: and he hath requited me evil for good.

22So and more also do God unto the enemies of David, if I leave of all that *pertain* to him by the morning light any that pisseth against the wall.

23And when Abigail saw David, she hasted, and lighted off the ass, and fell before David on her face, and bowed herself to the ground,

24And fell at his feet, and said, Upon me, my lord, *upon* me *let this* iniquity *be:* and let thine handmaid, I pray thee, speak in thine audience, and hear the words of thine handmaid.

25Let not my lord, I pray thee, regard this man of Belial, *even* Nabal: for as his name *is,* so *is* he; Nabal *is* his name, and folly *is* with him: but I thine handmaid saw not the young men of my lord, whom thou didst send.

26Now therefore, my lord, *as* the LORD liveth, and *as* thy soul liveth, seeing the LORD hath withholden thee from coming to *shed* blood, and from avenging thyself with thine own hand, now let thine enemies, and they that seek evil to my lord, be as Nabal.

27And now this blessing which thine handmaid hath brought unto my lord, let it even be given unto the young men that follow my lord.

28I pray thee, forgive the trespass of thine handmaid: for the LORD will certainly make my lord a sure house; because my lord fighteth the battles of the LORD, and evil hath not been found in thee *all* thy days.

29Yet a man is risen to pursue thee, and to seek thy soul: but the soul of my lord shall be bound in the bundle of life with the LORD thy God; and the souls of thine enemies, them shall he sling out, *as out* of the middle of a sling.

30And it shall come to pass, when the LORD shall have done to my lord according to all the good that he hath spoken concerning thee, and shall have appointed thee ruler over Israel;

31That this shall be no grief unto thee, nor offence of heart unto my lord, either that thou hast shed blood causeless, or that my lord hath avenged himself: but when the LORD shall have dealt well with my lord, then remember thine handmaid.

32And David said to Abigail, Blessed *be* the LORD God of Israel, which sent thee this day to meet me:

33And blessed *be* thy advice, and blessed *be* thou, which hast kept me this day from coming to *shed* blood, and from avenging myself with mine own hand.

34For in very deed, *as* the LORD God of Israel liveth, which hath kept me back from hurting thee, except thou hadst hasted and come to meet me, surely there had not been left unto Nabal by the morning light any that pisseth against the wall.

35So David received of her hand *that* which she had brought him, and said unto her, Go up in peace to thine house; see, I have hearkened to thy voice, and have accepted thy person.

36And Abigail came to Nabal; and, behold, he held a feast in his house, like the feast of a king; and Nabal's heart *was* merry within him, for he *was* very drunken: wherefore she told him nothing, less or more, until the morning light.

37But it came to pass in the morning, when the wine was gone out of Nabal, and his wife had told him these things, that his heart died within him, and he became *as* a stone.

38And it came to pass about ten days *after,* that the LORD smote Nabal, that he died.

39And when David heard that Nabal was dead, he said, Blessed *be* the LORD, that hath pleaded the cause of my reproach from the hand of Nabal, and hath kept his servant from evil: for the LORD hath returned the wickedness of Nabal upon his own head. And David sent and communed with Abigail, to take her to him to wife.

40And when the servants of David were come to Abigail to Carmel, they spake unto her, saying, David sent us unto thee, to take thee to him to wife.

41And she arose, and bowed herself on *her* face to the earth, and said, Behold, *let* thine handmaid *be* a servant to wash the feet of the servants of my lord.

42And Abigail hasted, and arose, and rode upon an ass, with five damsels of hers that went after her; and she went after the messengers of David, and became his wife.

43David also took Ahinoam of Jezreel; and they were also both of them his wives.

44But Saul had given Michal his daughter, David's wife, to Phalti the son of Laish, which *was* of Gallim.

JOHN 10:22–42

AND it was at Jerusalem the feast of the dedication, and it was winter.

23And Jesus walked in the temple in Solomon's porch.

24Then came the Jews round about him, and said unto him, How long dost thou make us to doubt? If thou be the Christ, tell us plainly.

25Jesus answered them, I told you, and ye believed not: the works that I do in my Father's name, they bear witness of me.

26But ye believe not, because ye are not of my sheep, as I said unto you.

27My sheep hear my voice, and I know them, and they follow me:

28And I give unto them eternal life; and they shall never perish, neither shall any *man* pluck them out of my hand.

29My Father, which gave *them* me, is greater than all; and no *man* is able to pluck *them* out of my Father's hand.

30I and *my* Father are one.

31Then the Jews took up stones again to stone him.

32Jesus answered them, Many good works have I shewed you from my Father; for which of those works do ye stone me?

33The Jews answered him, saying, For a good work we stone thee not; but for blasphemy; and because that thou, being a man, makest thyself God.

34Jesus answered them, Is it not written in your law, I said, Ye are gods?

35If he called them gods, unto whom the word of God came, and the scripture cannot be broken;

36Say ye of him, whom the Father hath sanctified, and sent into the world, Thou blasphemest; because I said, I am the Son of God?

37If I do not the works of my Father, believe me not.

38But if I do, though ye believe not me, believe the works: that ye may know, and believe, that the Father *is* in me, and I in him.

39Therefore they sought again to take him: but he escaped out of their hand,

40And went away again beyond Jordan into the place where John at first baptized; and there he abode.

41And many resorted unto him, and said, John did no miracle: but all things that John spake of this man were true.

42And many believed on him there.

PSALM 116:1–19

I LOVE the LORD, because he hath heard my voice *and* my supplications.

2Because he hath inclined his ear unto me, therefore will I call upon *him* as long as I live.

3The sorrows of death compassed me, and the pains of hell gat hold upon me: I found trouble and sorrow.

4Then called I upon the name of the LORD; O LORD, I beseech thee, deliver my soul.

5Gracious *is* the LORD, and righteous; yea, our God *is* merciful.

6The LORD preserveth the simple: I was brought low, and he helped me.

7Return unto thy rest, O my soul; for the LORD hath dealt bountifully with thee.

8For thou hast delivered my soul from death, mine eyes from tears, *and* my feet from falling.

9I will walk before the LORD in the land of the living.

10I believed, therefore have I spoken: I was greatly afflicted:

11I said in my haste, All men *are* liars.

12What shall I render unto the LORD *for* all his benefits toward me?

13I will take the cup of salvation, and call upon the name of the LORD.

14I will pay my vows unto the LORD now in the presence of all his people.

15Precious in the sight of the LORD *is* the death of his saints.

16O LORD, truly I *am* thy servant; I *am* thy servant, *and* the son of thine handmaid: thou hast loosed my bonds.

17I will offer to thee the sacrifice of thanksgiving, and will call upon the name of the LORD.

18I will pay my vows unto the LORD now in the presence of all his people,

19In the courts of the LORD's house, in the midst of thee, O Jerusalem. Praise ye the LORD.

PROVERBS FOR TODAY/ 15:20–21

A wise son maketh a glad father: but a foolish man despiseth his mother. □ *Folly is joy to him that is destitute of wisdom: but a man of understanding walketh uprightly.*

MAY 20

1 SAMUEL 26:1—28:25

AND the Ziphites came unto Saul to Gibeah, saying, Doth not David hide himself in the hill of Hachilah, *which is* before Jeshimon?

2Then Saul arose, and went down to the wilderness of Ziph, having three thousand chosen men of Israel with him, to seek David in the wilderness of Ziph.

3And Saul pitched in the hill of Hachilah, which *is* before Jeshimon, by the way. But David abode in the wilderness, and he saw that Saul came after him into the wilderness.

4David therefore sent out spies, and understood that Saul was come in very deed.

5And David arose, and came to the place where Saul had pitched: and David beheld the place where Saul lay, and Abner the son of Ner, the captain of his host: and Saul lay in the trench, and the people pitched round about him.

6Then answered David and said to Ahimelech the Hittite, and to Abishai the son of Zeruiah, brother to Joab, saying, Who will go down with me to Saul to the camp? And Abishai said, I will go down with thee.

7So David and Abishai came to the people by night: and, behold, Saul lay sleeping within the trench, and his spear stuck in the ground at his bolster: but Abner and the people lay round about him.

8Then said Abishai to David, God hath delivered thine enemy into thine hand this day: now therefore let me smite him, I pray thee, with the spear even to the earth at once, and I will not *smite* him the second time.

9And David said to Abishai, Destroy him not: for who can stretch forth his hand against the LORD'S anointed, and be guiltless?

10David said furthermore, As the LORD liveth, the LORD shall smite him; or his day shall come to die; or he shall descend into battle, and perish.

11The LORD forbid that I should stretch forth mine hand against the LORD'S anointed: but, I pray thee, take thou now the spear that *is* at his bolster, and the cruse of water, and let us go.

12So David took the spear and the cruse of water from Saul's bolster; and they gat them away, and no man saw *it,* nor knew *it,* neither awaked: for they *were* all asleep; because a deep sleep from the LORD was fallen upon them.

13Then David went over to the other side, and stood on the top of an hill afar off; a great space *being* between them:

14And David cried to the people, and to Abner the son of Ner, saying, Answerest thou not, Abner? Then Abner answered and said, Who *art* thou *that* criest to the king?

15And David said to Abner, *Art* not thou a *valiant* man? and who *is* like to thee in Israel? wherefore then hast thou not kept thy lord the king? for there came one of the people in to destroy the king thy lord.

16This thing *is* not good that thou hast done. *As* the LORD liveth, ye *are* worthy to die, because ye have not kept your master, the LORD'S anointed. And now see where the king's spear *is,* and the cruse of water that *was* at his bolster.

17And Saul knew David's voice, and said, *Is* this thy voice, my son David? And David said, *It is* my voice, my lord, O king.

18And he said, Wherefore doth my lord thus pursue after his servant? for what have I done? or what evil *is* in mine hand?

19Now therefore, I pray thee, let my lord the king hear the words of his servant. If the LORD have stirred thee up against me, let him accept an offering: but if *they be* the children of men, cursed *be* they before the LORD; for they have driven me out this day from abiding in the inheritance of the LORD, saying, Go, serve other gods.

20Now therefore, let not my blood fall to the earth before the face of the LORD: for the king of Israel is come out to seek a flea, as when one doth hunt a partridge in the mountains.

21Then said Saul, I have sinned: return, my son David: for I will no more do thee harm, because my soul was precious in thine eyes this day: behold, I have played the fool, and have erred exceedingly.

22And David answered and said, Behold the king's spear! and let one of the young men come over and fetch it.

23The LORD render to every man his righteousness and his faithfulness: for the LORD delivered thee into *my* hand to day, but I would not stretch forth mine hand against the LORD'S anointed.

24And, behold, as thy life was much set by this day in mine eyes, so let my life be much set by in the eyes of the LORD, and let him deliver me out of all tribulation.

25Then Saul said to David, Blessed *be* thou, my son David: thou shalt both do great *things,* and also shalt still prevail. So David went on his way, and Saul returned to his place.

AND David said in his heart, I shall now perish one day by the hand of Saul: *there is* nothing better for me than that I should speedily escape into the land of the Philistines; and Saul shall despair of me, to seek me any more in any coast of Israel: so shall I escape out of his hand.

2And David arose, and he passed over with the six hundred men that *were* with him unto Achish, the son of Maoch, king of Gath.

3And David dwelt with Achish at Gath, he and his men, every man with his household, *even* David with his two wives, Ahinoam the Jezreelitess, and Abigail the Carmelitess, Nabal's wife.

4And it was told Saul that David was fled to Gath: and he sought no more again for him.

5And David said unto Achish, If I have now found grace in thine eyes, let them give me a place in some town in the country, that I may dwell there: for why should thy servant dwell in the royal city with thee?

6Then Achish gave him Ziklag that day: wherefore Ziklag pertaineth unto the kings of Judah unto this day.

7And the time that David dwelt in the country of the Philistines was a full year and four months.

8And David and his men went up, and invaded the Geshurites, and the Gezrites, and the Amalekites: for those *nations were* of old the inhabitants of the land, as thou goest to Shur, even unto the land of Egypt.

9And David smote the land, and left neither man nor woman alive, and took away the sheep, and the oxen, and the asses, and the camels, and the apparel, and returned, and came to Achish.

10And Achish said, Whither have ye made a road to day? And David said, Against the south of Judah, and against the south of the Jerahmeelites, and against the south of the Kenites.

11And David saved neither man nor woman alive, to bring *tidings* to Gath, saying, Lest they should tell on us, saying, So did David, and so *will be* his manner all the while he dwelleth in the country of the Philistines.

12And Achish believed David, saying, He hath made his people Israel utterly to abhor him; therefore he shall be my servant for ever.

AND it came to pass in those days, that the Philistines gathered their armies together for warfare, to fight with Israel. And Achish said unto David, Know thou assuredly, that thou shalt go out with me to battle, thou and thy men.

2And David said to Achish, Surely thou shalt know what thy servant can do. And Achish said to David, Therefore will I make thee keeper of mine head for ever.

3Now Samuel was dead, and all Israel had lamented him, and buried him in Ramah, even in his own city. And Saul had put away those that had familiar spirits, and the wizards, out of the land.

4And the Philistines gathered themselves together, and came and pitched in Shunem: and Saul gathered all Israel together, and they pitched in Gilboa.

5And when Saul saw the host of the Philistines, he was afraid, and his heart greatly trembled.

6And when Saul enquired of the LORD, the LORD answered him not, neither by dreams, nor by Urim, nor by prophets.

7Then said Saul unto his servants, Seek me a woman that hath a familiar spirit, that I may go to her, and enquire of her. And his servants said to him, Behold, *there is* a woman that hath a familiar spirit at En–dor.

8And Saul disguised himself, and put on other raiment, and he went, and two men with him, and they came to the woman by night: and he said, I pray thee, divine unto me by the familiar spirit, and bring me *him* up, whom I shall name unto thee.

9And the woman said unto him, Behold, thou knowest what Saul hath done, how he hath cut off those that have familiar spirits, and the wizards, out of the land: wherefore then layest thou a snare for my life, to cause me to die?

10And Saul sware to her by the LORD, saying, *As* the LORD liveth, there shall no punishment happen to thee for this thing.

11Then said the woman, Whom shall I bring up unto thee? And he said, Bring me up Samuel.

12And when the woman saw Samuel, she cried with a loud voice: and the woman spake to Saul, saying, Why hast thou deceived me? for thou *art* Saul.

13And the king said unto her, Be not afraid: for what sawest thou? And the woman said unto Saul, I saw gods ascending out of the earth.

14And he said unto her, What form *is* he of? And she said, An old man cometh up; and he *is* covered with a mantle. And Saul perceived that it *was* Samuel, and he stooped with *his* face to the ground, and bowed himself.

15And Samuel said to Saul, Why hast thou disquieted me, to bring me up? And Saul answered, I am sore distressed; for the Philistines make war against me, and God is departed from me, and answereth me no more, neither by prophets, nor by dreams: therefore I have called thee, that thou mayest make known unto me what I shall do.

16Then said Samuel, Wherefore then dost thou ask of me, seeing the LORD is departed from thee, and is become thine enemy?

17And the LORD hath done to him, as he spake by me: for the LORD hath rent the kingdom out of thine hand, and given it to thy neighbour, *even* to David:

18Because thou obeyedst not the voice of the LORD, nor executedst his fierce wrath upon Amalek, therefore hath the LORD done this thing unto thee this day.

19Moreover the LORD will also deliver Israel with thee into the hand of the Philistines: and tomorrow *shalt* thou and thy sons *be* with me: the LORD also shall deliver the host of Israel into the hand of the Philistines.

20Then Saul fell straightway all along on the earth, and was sore afraid, because of the words of Samuel: and there was no strength in him; for he had eaten no bread all the day, nor all the night.

21And the woman came unto Saul, and saw that he was sore troubled, and said unto him, Behold, thine handmaid hath obeyed thy voice, and I have put my life in my hand, and have hearkened unto thy words which thou spakest unto me.

22Now therefore, I pray thee, hearken thou also unto the voice of thine handmaid, and let me set a morsel of bread before thee; and eat, that thou mayest have strength, when thou goest on thy way.

23But he refused, and said, I will not eat. But his servants, together with the woman, compelled him; and he hearkened unto their voice. So he arose from the earth, and sat upon the bed.

24And the woman had a fat calf in the house; and she hasted, and killed it, and took flour, and kneaded *it,* and did bake unleavened bread thereof:

25And she brought *it* before Saul, and before his servants; and they did eat. Then they rose up, and went away that night.

JOHN 11:1–53

Now a certain *man* was sick, *named* Lazarus, of Bethany, the town of Mary and her sister Martha.

2(It was *that* Mary which anointed the Lord with ointment, and wiped his feet with her hair, whose brother Lazarus was sick.)

3Therefore his sisters sent unto him, saying, Lord, behold, he whom thou lovest is sick.

4When Jesus heard *that,* he said, This sickness is not unto death, but for the glory of God, that the Son of God might be glorified thereby.

5Now Jesus loved Martha, and her sister, and Lazarus.

6When he had heard therefore that he was sick, he abode two days still in the same place where he was.

7Then after that saith he to *his* disciples, Let us go into Judaea again.

8*His* disciples say unto him, Master, the Jews of late sought to stone thee; and goest thou thither again?

9Jesus answered, Are there not twelve hours in the day? If any man walk in the day, he stumbleth not, because he seeth the light of this world.

10But if a man walk in the night, he stumbleth, because there is no light in him.

11These things said he: and after that he saith unto them, Our friend Lazarus sleepeth; but I go, that I may awake him out of sleep.

12Then said his disciples, Lord, if he sleep, he shall do well.

13Howbeit Jesus spake of his death: but they thought that he had spoken of taking of rest in sleep.

14Then said Jesus unto them plainly, Lazarus is dead.

15And I am glad for your sakes that I was not there, to the intent ye may believe; nevertheless let us go unto him.

16Then said Thomas, which is called Didymus, unto his fellowdisciples, Let us also go, that we may die with him.

17Then when Jesus came, he found that he had *lain* in the grave four days already.

18Now Bethany was nigh unto Jerusalem, about fifteen furlongs off:

19And many of the Jews came to Martha and Mary, to comfort them concerning their brother.

20Then Martha, as soon as she heard that Jesus was coming, went and met him: but Mary sat *still* in the house.

21Then said Martha unto Jesus, Lord, if thou hadst been here, my brother had not died.

22But I know, that even now, whatsoever thou wilt ask of God, God will give *it* thee.

23Jesus saith unto her, Thy brother shall rise again.

24Martha saith unto him, I know that he shall rise again in the resurrection at the last day.

25Jesus said unto her, I am the resurrection, and the life: he that believeth in me, though he were dead, yet shall he live:

26And whosoever liveth and believeth in me shall never die. Believest thou this?

27She saith unto him, Yea, Lord: I believe that thou art the Christ, the Son of God, which should come into the world.

28And when she had so said, she went her way, and called Mary her sister secretly, saying, The Master is come, and calleth for thee.

29As soon as she heard *that,* she arose quickly, and came unto him.

30Now Jesus was not yet come into the town, but was in that place where Martha met him.

31The Jews then which were with her in the house, and comforted her, when they saw Mary, that she rose up hastily and went out, followed her, saying, She goeth unto the grave to weep there.

32Then when Mary was come where Jesus was, and saw him, she fell down at his feet, saying unto him, Lord, if thou hadst been here, my brother had not died.

33When Jesus therefore saw her weeping, and the Jews also weeping which came with her, he groaned in the spirit, and was troubled,

34And said, Where have ye laid him? They said unto him, Lord, come and see.

35Jesus wept.

36Then said the Jews, Behold how he loved him!

37And some of them said, Could not this man, which opened the eyes of the blind, have caused that even this man should not have died?

38Jesus therefore again groaning in himself cometh to the grave. It was a cave, and a stone lay upon it.

39Jesus said, Take ye away the stone. Martha, the sister of him that was dead, saith unto him, Lord, by this time he stinketh: for he hath been *dead* four days.

40Jesus saith unto her, Said I not unto thee, that, if thou wouldest believe, thou shouldest see the glory of God?

41Then they took away the stone *from the place* where the dead was laid. And Jesus lifted up *his* eyes, and said, Father, I thank thee that thou hast heard me.

42And I knew that thou hearest me always: but because of the people which stand by I said *it,* that they may believe that thou hast sent me.

43And when he thus had spoken, he cried with a loud voice, Lazarus, come forth.

44And he that was dead came forth, bound hand and foot with graveclothes: and his face was bound about with a napkin. Jesus saith unto them, Loose him, and let him go.

45Then many of the Jews which came to Mary, and had seen the things which Jesus did, believed on him.

46But some of them went their ways to the Pharisees, and told them what things Jesus had done.

47Then gathered the chief priests and the Pharisees a council, and said, What do we? for this man doeth many miracles.

48If we let him thus alone, all *men* will believe on him: and the Romans shall come and take away both our place and nation.

49And one of them, *named* Caiaphas, being the high priest that same year, said unto them, Ye know nothing at all,

50Nor consider that it is expedient

for us, that one man should die for the people, and that the whole nation perish not.

51And this spake he not of himself: but being high priest that year, he prophesied that Jesus should die for that nation;

52And not for that nation only, but that also he should gather together in one the children of God that were scattered abroad.

53Then from that day forth they took counsel together for to put him to death.

PSALM 117:1–2

O PRAISE the LORD, all ye nations: praise him, all ye people.

2For his merciful kindness is great toward us: and the truth of the LORD *endureth* for ever. Praise ye the LORD.

PROVERBS FOR TODAY/ 15:22–23

Without counsel purposes are disappointed: but in the multitude of counsellors they are established. □*A man hath joy by the answer of his mouth: and a word* spoken *in due season, how good* is it!

MAY 21

1 SAMUEL 29:1—31:13

N ow the Philistines gathered together all their armies to Aphek: and the Israelites pitched by a fountain which *is* in Jezreel.

2And the lords of the Philistines passed on by hundreds, and by thousands: but David and his men passed on in the rereward with Achish.

3Then said the princes of the Philistines, What *do* these Hebrews *here?* And Achish said unto the princes of the Philistines, *Is* not this David, the servant of Saul the king of Israel, which hath been with me these days, or these years, and I have found no fault in him since he fell *unto me* unto this day?

4And the princes of the Philistines were wroth with him; and the princes of the Philistines said unto him, Make this fellow return, that he may go again to his place which thou hast appointed him, and let him not go down with us to battle, lest in the battle he be an adversary to us: for wherewith should

he reconcile himself unto his master? *should it* not *be* with the heads of these men?

5*Is* not this David, of whom they sang one to another in dances, saying, Saul slew his thousands, and David his ten thousands?

6Then Achish called David, and said unto him, Surely, *as* the LORD liveth, thou hast been upright, and thy going out and thy coming in with me in the host *is* good in my sight: for I have not found evil in thee since the day of thy coming unto me unto this day: nevertheless the lords favour thee not.

7Wherefore now return, and go in peace, that thou displease not the lords of the Philistines.

8And David said unto Achish, But what have I done? and what hast thou found in thy servant so long as I have been with thee unto this day, that I may not go fight against the enemies of my lord the king?

9And Achish answered and said to

David, I know that thou *art* good in my sight, as an angel of God: notwithstanding the princes of the Philistines have said, He shall not go up with us to the battle.

10Wherefore now rise up early in the morning with thy master's servants that are come with thee: and as soon as ye be up early in the morning, and have light, depart.

11So David and his men rose up early to depart in the morning, to return into the land of the Philistines. And the Philistines went up to Jezreel.

AND it came to pass, when David and his men were come to Ziklag on the third day, that the Amalekites had invaded the south, and Ziklag, and smitten Ziklag, and burned it with fire;

2And had taken the women captives, that *were* therein: they slew not any, either great or small, but carried *them* away, and went on their way.

3So David and his men came to the city, and, behold, *it was* burned with fire; and their wives, and their sons, and their daughters, were taken captives.

4Then David and the people that *were* with him lifted up their voice and wept, until they had no more power to weep.

5And David's two wives were taken captives, Ahinoam the Jezreelitess, and Abigail the wife of Nabal the Carmelite.

6And David was greatly distressed; for the people spake of stoning him, because the soul of all the people was grieved, every man for his sons and for his daughters: but David encouraged himself in the LORD his God.

7And David said to Abiathar the priest, Ahimelech's son, I pray thee, bring me hither the ephod. And Abiathar brought thither the ephod to David.

8And David enquired at the LORD, saying, Shall I pursue after this troop? shall I overtake them? And he answered him, Pursue: for thou shalt surely overtake *them,* and without fail recover *all.*

9So David went, he and the six hundred men that *were* with him, and came to the brook Besor, where those that were left behind stayed.

10But David pursued, he and four hundred men: for two hundred abode behind, which were so faint that they could not go over the brook Besor.

11And they found an Egyptian in the field, and brought him to David, and gave him bread, and he did eat; and they made him drink water;

12And they gave him a piece of a cake of figs, and two clusters of raisins: and when he had eaten, his spirit came again to him: for he had eaten no bread, nor drunk *any* water, three days and three nights.

13And David said unto him, To whom *belongest* thou? and whence *art* thou? And he said, I *am* a young man of Egypt, servant to an Amalekite; and my master left me, because three days agone I fell sick.

14We made an invasion *upon* the south of the Cherethites, and upon *the coast* which *belongeth* to Judah, and upon the south of Caleb; and we burned Ziklag with fire.

15And David said to him, Canst thou bring me down to this company? And he said, Swear unto me by God, that thou wilt neither kill me, nor deliver me into the hands of my master, and I will bring thee down to this company.

16And when he had brought him down, behold, *they were* spread abroad upon all the earth, eating and drinking, and dancing, because of all the great spoil that they had taken out of the land of the Philistines, and out of the land of Judah.

17And David smote them from the twilight even unto the evening of the next day: and there escaped not a man of them, save four hundred young men, which rode upon camels, and fled.

18And David recovered all that the Amalekites had carried away: and David rescued his two wives.

19And there was nothing lacking to them, neither small nor great, neither sons nor daughters, neither spoil, nor any *thing* that they had taken to them: David recovered all.

20And David took all the flocks and the herds, *which* they drave before those *other* cattle, and said, This *is* David's spoil.

21And David came to the two hundred men, which were so faint that they could not follow David, whom they had made also to abide at the brook Besor: and they went forth to meet David, and to meet the people that *were* with him: and when David came near to the people, he saluted them.

22Then answered all the wicked men and *men* of Belial, of those that went with David, and said, Because they went not with us, we will not give them *ought* of the spoil that we have recovered, save to every man his wife and his children, that they may lead *them* away, and depart.

23Then said David, Ye shall not do so, my brethren, with that which the LORD hath given us, who hath preserved us, and delivered the company that came against us into our hand.

24For who will hearken unto you in this matter? but as his part *is* that goeth down to the battle, so *shall* his part *be* that tarrieth by the stuff: they shall part alike.

25And it was *so* from that day forward, that he made it a statute and an ordinance for Israel unto this day.

26And when David came to Ziklag, he sent of the spoil unto the elders of Judah, *even* to his friends, saying, Behold a present for you of the spoil of the enemies of the LORD;

27To *them* which *were* in Beth–el, and to *them* which *were* in south Ramoth, and to *them* which *were* in Jattir,

28And to *them* which *were* in Aroer, and to *them* which *were* in Siphmoth, and to *them* which *were* in Eshtemoa,

29And to *them* which *were* in Rachal, and to *them* which *were* in the cities of the Jerahmeelites, and to *them* which *were* in the cities of the Kenites,

30And to *them* which *were* in Hormah, and to *them* which *were* in Chorashan, and to *them* which *were* in Athach,

31And to *them* which *were* in Hebron, and to all the places where David himself and his men were wont to haunt.

Now the Philistines fought against Israel: and the men of Israel fled from before the Philistines, and fell down slain in mount Gilboa.

2And the Philistines followed hard upon Saul and upon his sons; and the Philistines slew Jonathan, and Abinadab, and Melchishua, Saul's sons.

3And the battle went sore against Saul, and the archers hit him; and he was sore wounded of the archers.

4Then said Saul unto his armourbearer, Draw thy sword, and thrust me through therewith; lest these uncircumcised come and thrust me through, and abuse me. But his armourbearer would not; for he was sore afraid. Therefore Saul took a sword, and fell upon it.

5And when his armourbearer saw that Saul was dead, he fell likewise upon his sword, and died with him.

6So Saul died, and his three sons, and his armourbearer, and all his men, that same day together.

7And when the men of Israel that *were* on the other side of the valley, and *they* that *were* on the other side Jordan, saw that the men of Israel fled, and that Saul and his sons were dead, they forsook the cities, and fled; and the Philistines came and dwelt in them.

8And it came to pass on the morrow, when the Philistines came to strip the slain, that they found Saul and his three sons fallen in mount Gilboa.

9And they cut off his head, and stripped off his armour, and sent into the land of the Philistines round about, to publish *it in* the house of their idols, and among the people.

10And they put his armour in the house of Ashtaroth: and they fastened his body to the wall of Beth–shan.

11And when the inhabitants of Jabesh–gilead heard of that which the Philistines had done to Saul;

12All the valiant men arose, and went all night, and took the body of Saul and the bodies of his sons from the wall of Bethshan, and came to Jabesh, and burnt them there.

13And they took their bones, and buried *them* under a tree at Jabesh, and fasted seven days.

JOHN 11:54—12:19

Jesus therefore walked no more openly among the Jews; but went thence unto a country near to the wilderness, into a city called Ephraim, and there continued with his disciples.

55And the Jews' passover was nigh at hand: and many went out of the country up to Jerusalem before the passover, to purify themselves.

56Then sought they for Jesus, and spake among themselves, as they stood in the temple, What think ye, that he will not come to the feast?

57Now both the chief priests and the Pharisees had given a commandment, that, if any man knew where he were, he should shew *it,* that they might take him.

Then Jesus six days before the passover came to Bethany, where Lazarus was which had been dead, whom he raised from the dead.

2There they made him a supper; and Martha served: but Lazarus was one of them that sat at the table with him.

3Then took Mary a pound of ointment of spikenard, very costly, and anointed the feet of Jesus, and wiped his feet with her hair: and the house was filled with the odour of the ointment.

4Then saith one of his disciples, Judas Iscariot, Simon's *son,* which should betray him,

5Why was not this ointment sold for three hundred pence, and given to the poor?

6This he said, not that he cared for the poor; but because he was a thief, and had the bag, and bare what was put therein.

7Then said Jesus, Let her alone: against the day of my burying hath she kept this.

8For the poor always ye have with you; but me ye have not always.

9Much people of the Jews therefore knew that he was there: and they came not for Jesus' sake only, but that they might see Lazarus also, whom he had raised from the dead.

10But the chief priests consulted that they might put Lazarus also to death;

11Because that by reason of him many of the Jews went away, and believed on Jesus.

12On the next day much people that were come to the feast, when they heard that Jesus was coming to Jerusalem,

13Took branches of palm trees, and went forth to meet him, and cried, Hosanna: Blessed *is* the King of Israel that cometh in the name of the Lord.

14And Jesus, when he had found a young ass, sat thereon; as it is written,

15Fear not, daughter of Sion; behold, thy King cometh, sitting on an ass's colt.

16These things understood not his disciples at the first: but when Jesus was glorified, then remembered they that these things were written of him, and *that* they had done these things unto him.

17The people therefore that was with him when he called Lazarus out of his grave, and raised him from the dead, bare record.

18For this cause the people also met him, for that they heard that he had done this miracle.

¹⁹The Pharisees therefore said among themselves, Perceive ye how ye prevail nothing? behold, the world is gone after him.

PSALM 118:1–18

O GIVE thanks unto the LORD; for *he is* good: because his mercy *endureth* for ever.

²Let Israel now say, that his mercy *endureth* for ever.

³Let the house of Aaron now say, that his mercy *endureth* for ever.

⁴Let them now that fear the LORD say, that his mercy *endureth* for ever.

⁵I called upon the LORD in distress: the LORD answered me, *and set me* in a large place.

⁶The LORD *is* on my side; I will not fear: what can man do unto me?

⁷The LORD taketh my part with them that help me: therefore shall I see *my desire* upon them that hate me.

⁸*It is* better to trust in the LORD than to put confidence in man.

⁹*It is* better to trust in the LORD than to put confidence in princes.

¹⁰All nations compassed me about: but in the name of the LORD will I destroy them.

¹¹They compassed me about; yea, they compassed me about: but in the name of the LORD I will destroy them.

¹²They compassed me about like bees; they are quenched as the fire of thorns: for in the name of the LORD I will destroy them.

¹³Thou hast thrust sore at me that I might fall: but the LORD helped me.

¹⁴The LORD *is* my strength and song, and is become my salvation.

¹⁵The voice of rejoicing and salvation *is* in the tabernacles of the righteous: the right hand of the LORD doeth valiantly.

¹⁶The right hand of the LORD is exalted: the right hand of the LORD doeth valiantly.

¹⁷I shall not die, but live, and declare the works of the LORD.

¹⁸The LORD hath chastened me sore: but he hath not given me over unto death.

PROVERBS FOR TODAY/ 15:24–26

The way of life is *above to the wise, that he may depart from hell beneath.* □ *The* LORD *will destroy the house of the proud: but he will establish the border of the widow.* □ *The thoughts of the wicked* are *an abomination to the* LORD: *but* the words *of the pure* are *pleasant words.*

MAY 22

2 SAMUEL 1:1—2:11

N OW it came to pass after the death of Saul, when David was returned from the slaughter of the Amalekites, and David had abode two days in Ziklag;

²It came even to pass on the third day, that, behold, a man came out of the camp from Saul with his clothes rent, and earth upon his head: and *so* it was, when he came to David, that he fell to the earth, and did obeisance.

3And David said unto him, From whence comest thou? And he said unto him, Out of the camp of Israel am I escaped.

4And David said unto him, How went the matter? I pray thee, tell me. And he answered, That the people are fled from the battle, and many of the people also are fallen and dead; and Saul and Jonathan his son are dead also.

5And David said unto the young man that told him, How knowest thou that Saul and Jonathan his son be dead?

6And the young man that told him said, As I happened by chance upon mount Gilboa, behold, Saul leaned upon his spear; and, lo, the chariots and horsemen followed hard after him.

7And when he looked behind him, he saw me, and called unto me. And I answered, Here *am* I.

8And he said unto me, Who *art* thou? And I answered him, I *am* an Amalekite.

9He said unto me again, Stand, I pray thee, upon me, and slay me: for anguish is come upon me, because my life *is* yet whole in me.

10So I stood upon him, and slew him, because I was sure that he could not live after that he was fallen: and I took the crown that *was* upon his head, and the bracelet that *was* on his arm, and have brought them hither unto my lord.

11Then David took hold on his clothes, and rent them; and likewise all the men that *were* with him:

12And they mourned, and wept, and fasted until even, for Saul, and for Jonathan his son, and for the people of the Lord, and for the house of Israel; because they were fallen by the sword.

13And David said unto the young man that told him, Whence *art* thou? And he answered, I *am* the son of a stranger, an Amalekite.

14And David said unto him, How wast thou not afraid to stretch forth thine hand to destroy the Lord's anointed?

15And David called one of the young men, and said, Go near, *and* fall upon him. And he smote him that he died.

16And David said unto him, Thy blood *be* upon thy head; for thy mouth hath testified against thee, saying, I have slain the Lord's anointed.

17And David lamented with this lamentation over Saul and over Jonathan his son:

18(Also he bade them teach the children of Judah *the use of* the bow: behold, *it is* written in the book of Jasher.)

19The beauty of Israel is slain upon thy high places: how are the mighty fallen!

20Tell *it* not in Gath, publish *it* not in the streets of Askelon; lest the daughters of the Philistines rejoice, lest the daughters of the uncircumcised triumph.

21Ye mountains of Gilboa, *let there be* no dew, neither *let there be* rain, upon you, nor fields of offerings: for there the shield of the mighty is vilely cast away, the shield of Saul, *as though he had* not *been* anointed with oil.

22From the blood of the slain, from the fat of the mighty, the bow of Jonathan turned not back, and the sword of Saul returned not empty.

23Saul and Jonathan *were* lovely and pleasant in their lives, and in their death they were not divided: they were swifter than eagles, they were stronger than lions.

24Ye daughters of Israel, weep over Saul, who clothed you in scarlet, with *other* delights, who put on ornaments of gold upon your apparel.

25How are the mighty fallen in the midst of the battle! O Jonathan, *thou wast* slain in thine high places.

26I am distressed for thee, my brother Jonathan: very pleasant hast thou been unto me: thy love to me was wonderful, passing the love of women.

27How are the mighty fallen, and the weapons of war perished!

AND it came to pass after this, that David enquired of the LORD, saying, Shall I go up into any of the cities of Judah? And the LORD said unto him, Go up. And David said, Whither shall I go up? And he said, Unto Hebron.

2So David went up thither, and his two wives also, Ahinoam the Jezreelitess, and Abigail Nabal's wife the Carmelite.

3And his men that *were* with him did David bring up, every man with his household: and they dwelt in the cities of Hebron.

4And the men of Judah came, and there they anointed David king over the house of Judah. And they told David, saying, *That* the men of Jabesh–gilead *were they* that buried Saul.

5And David sent messengers unto the men of Jabesh–gilead, and said unto them, Blessed *be* ye of the LORD, that ye have shewed this kindness unto your lord, *even* unto Saul, and have buried him.

6And now the LORD shew kindness and truth unto you: and I also will requite you this kindness, because ye have done this thing.

7Therefore now let your hands be strengthened, and be ye valiant: for your master Saul is dead, and also the house of Judah have anointed me king over them.

8But Abner the son of Ner, captain of Saul's host, took Ish–bosheth the son of Saul, and brought him over to Mahanaim;

9And made him king over Gilead, and over the Ashurites, and over Jezreel, and over Ephraim, and over Benjamin, and over all Israel.

10Ish–bosheth Saul's son *was* forty years old when he began to reign over Israel, and reigned two years. But the house of Judah followed David.

11And the time that David was king in Hebron over the house of Judah was seven years and six months.

JOHN 12:20–50

AND there were certain Greeks among them that came up to worship at the feast:

21The same came therefore to Philip, which was of Bethsaida of Galilee, and desired him, saying, Sir, we would see Jesus.

22Philip cometh and telleth Andrew: and again Andrew and Philip tell Jesus.

23And Jesus answered them, saying, The hour is come, that the Son of man should be glorified.

24Verily, verily, I say unto you, Except a corn of wheat fall into the ground and die, it abideth alone: but if it die, it bringeth forth much fruit.

25He that loveth his life shall lose it; and he that hateth his life in this world shall keep it unto life eternal.

26If any man serve me, let him follow me; and where I am, there shall also my servant be: if any man serve me, him will *my* Father honour.

27Now is my soul troubled; and what shall I say? Father, save me from this hour: but for this cause came I unto this hour.

28Father, glorify thy name. Then came there a voice from heaven, *saying,* I have both glorified *it,* and will glorify *it* again.

29The people therefore, that stood by, and heard *it,* said that it thundered: others said, An angel spake to him.

30Jesus answered and said, This voice came not because of me, but for your sakes.

31Now is the judgment of this world: now shall the prince of this world be cast out.

32And I, if I be lifted up from the

earth, will draw all *men* unto me.

33This he said, signifying what death he should die.

34The people answered him, We have heard out of the law that Christ abideth forever: and how sayest thou, The Son of man must be lifted up? who is this Son of man?

35Then Jesus said unto them, Yet a little while is the light with you. Walk while ye have the light, lest darkness come upon you: for he that walketh in darkness knoweth not whither he goeth.

36While ye have light, believe in the light, that ye may be the children of light. These things spake Jesus, and departed, and did hide himself from them.

37But though he had done so many miracles before them, yet they believed not on him:

38That the saying of Esaias the prophet might be fulfilled, which he spake, Lord, who hath believed our report? and to whom hath the arm of the Lord been revealed?

39Therefore they could not believe, because that Esaias said again,

40He hath blinded their eyes, and hardened their heart; that they should not see with *their* eyes, nor understand with *their* heart, and be converted, and I should heal them.

41These things said Esaias, when he saw his glory, and spake of him.

42Nevertheless among the chief rulers also many believed on him; but because of the Pharisees they did not confess *him,* lest they should be put out of the synagogue:

43For they loved the praise of men more than the praise of God.

44Jesus cried and said, He that believeth on me, believeth not on me, but on him that sent me.

45And he that seeth me seeth him that sent me.

46I am come a light into the world, that whosoever believeth on me should not abide in darkness.

47And if any man hear my words, and believe not, I judge him not: for I came not to judge the world, but to save the world.

48He that rejecteth me, and receiveth not my words, hath one that judgeth him: the word that I have spoken, the same shall judge him in the last day.

49For I have not spoken of myself; but the Father which sent me, he gave me a commandment, what I should say, and what I should speak.

50And I know that his commandment is life everlasting: whatsoever I speak therefore, even as the Father said unto me, so I speak.

PSALM 118:19–29

O PEN to me the gates of righteousness: I will go into them, *and* I will praise the LORD:

20This gate of the LORD, into which the righteous shall enter.

21I will praise thee: for thou hast heard me, and art become my salvation.

22The stone *which* the builders refused is become the head *stone* of the corner.

23This is the LORD'S doing; *it is* marvellous in our eyes.

24This *is* the day *which* the LORD hath made; we will rejoice and be glad in it.

25Save now, I beseech thee, O LORD: O LORD, I beseech thee, send now prosperity.

26Blessed *be* he that cometh in the name of the LORD: we have blessed you out of the house of the LORD.

27God *is* the LORD, which hath shewed us light: bind the sacrifice with cords, *even* unto the horns of the altar.

28Thou *art* my God, and I will praise thee: *thou art* my God, I will exalt thee.

29O give thanks unto the LORD; for *he is* good: for his mercy *endureth* for ever.

He that is greedy of gain troubleth his own house; but he that hateth gifts shall live. □ *The heart of the righteous studieth to answer: but the mouth of the wicked poureth out evil things.*

MAY 23

2 SAMUEL 2:12—3:39

AND Abner the son of Ner, and the servants of Ish–bosheth the son of Saul, went out from Mahanaim to Gibeon.

13And Joab the son of Zeruiah, and the servants of David, went out, and met together by the pool of Gibeon: and they sat down, the one on the one side of the pool, and the other on the other side of the pool.

14And Abner said to Joab, Let the young men now arise, and play before us. And Joab said, Let them arise.

15Then there arose and went over by number twelve of Benjamin, which *pertained* to Ish–bosheth the son of Saul, and twelve of the servants of David.

16And they caught every one his fellow by the head, and *thrust* his sword in his fellow's side; so they fell down together: wherefore that place was called Helkath–hazzurim, which *is* in Gibeon.

17And there was a very sore battle that day; and Abner was beaten, and the men of Israel, before the servants of David.

18And there were three sons of Zeruiah there, Joab, and Abishai, and Asahel: and Asahel *was as* light of foot as a wild roe.

19And Asahel pursued after Abner; and in going he turned not to the right hand nor to the left from following Abner.

20Then Abner looked behind him, and said, *Art* thou Asahel? And he answered, I *am.*

21And Abner said to him, Turn thee aside to thy right hand or to thy left, and lay thee hold on one of the young men, and take thee his armour. But Asahel would not turn aside from following of him.

22And Abner said again to Asahel, Turn thee aside from following me: wherefore should I smite thee to the ground? how then should I hold up my face to Joab thy brother?

23Howbeit he refused to turn aside: wherefore Abner with the hinder end of the spear smote him under the fifth *rib,* that the spear came out behind him; and he fell down there, and died in the same place: and it came to pass, *that* as many as came to the place where Asahel fell down and died stood still.

24Joab also and Abishai pursued after Abner: and the sun went down when they were come to the hill of Ammah, that *lieth* before Giah by the way of the wilderness of Gibeon.

25And the children of Benjamin gathered themselves together after Abner, and became one troop, and stood on the top of an hill.

26Then Abner called to Joab, and said, Shall the sword devour for ever? knowest thou not that it will be bitterness in the latter end? how long shall it be then, ere thou bid the people return from following their brethren?

27And Joab said, *As* God liveth, unless

thou hadst spoken, surely then in the morning the people had gone up every one from following his brother.

28So Joab blew a trumpet, and all the people stood still, and pursued after Israel no more, neither fought they any more.

29And Abner and his men walked all that night through the plain, and passed over Jordan, and went through all Bithron, and they came to Mahanaim.

30And Joab returned from following Abner: and when he had gathered all the people together, there lacked of David's servants nineteen men and Asahel.

31But the servants of David had smitten of Benjamin, and of Abner's men, so that three hundred and threescore men died.

32And they took up Asahel, and buried him in the sepulchre of his father, which was in Beth-lehem. And Joab and his men went all night, and they came to Hebron at break of day.

Now there was long war between the house of Saul and the house of David: but David waxed stronger and stronger, and the house of Saul waxed weaker and weaker.

2And unto David were sons born in Hebron: and his firstborn was Amnon, of Ahinoam the Jezreelitess;

3And his second, Chileab, of Abigail the wife of Nabal the Carmelite; and the third, Absalom the son of Maacah the daughter of Talmai king of Geshur;

4And the fourth, Adonijah the son of Haggith; and the fifth, Shephatiah the son of Abital;

5And the sixth, Ithream, by Eglah David's wife. These were born to David in Hebron.

6And it came to pass, while there was war between the house of Saul and the house of David, that Abner made himself strong for the house of Saul.

7And Saul had a concubine, whose name was Rizpah, the daughter of Aiah: and Ish-bosheth said to Abner, Wherefore hast thou gone in unto my father's concubine?

8Then was Abner very wroth for the words of Ish-bosheth, and said, Am I a dog's head, which against Judah do shew kindness this day unto the house of Saul thy father, to his brethren, and to his friends, and have not delivered thee into the hand of David, that thou chargest me to day with a fault concerning this woman?

9So do God to Abner, and more also, except, as the LORD hath sworn to David, even so I do to him;

10To translate the kingdom from the house of Saul, and to set up the throne of David over Israel and over Judah, from Dan even to Beer-sheba.

11And he could not answer Abner a word again, because he feared him.

12And Abner sent messengers to David on his behalf, saying, Whose is the land? saying also, Make thy league with me, and, behold, my hand shall be with thee, to bring about all Israel unto thee.

13And he said, Well; I will make a league with thee: but one thing I require of thee, that is, Thou shalt not see my face, except thou first bring Michal Saul's daughter, when thou comest to see my face.

14And David sent messengers to Ish-bosheth Saul's son, saying, Deliver me my wife Michal, which I espoused to me for an hundred foreskins of the Philistines.

15And Ish-bosheth sent, and took her from her husband, even from Phaltiel the son of Laish.

16And her husband went with her along weeping behind her to Bahurim. Then said Abner unto him, Go, return. And he returned.

17And Abner had communication with the elders of Israel, saying, Ye sought for David in times past to be king over you:

18Now then do it: for the LORD hath

spoken of David, saying, By the hand of my servant David I will save my people Israel out of the hand of the Philistines, and out of the hand of all their enemies.

19And Abner also spake in the ears of Benjamin: and Abner went also to speak in the ears of David in Hebron all that seemed good to Israel, and that seemed good to the whole house of Benjamin.

20So Abner came to David to Hebron, and twenty men with him. And David made Abner and the men that *were* with him a feast.

21And Abner said unto David, I will arise and go, and will gather all Israel unto my lord the king, that they may make a league with thee, and that thou mayest reign over all that thine heart desireth. And David sent Abner away; and he went in peace.

22And, behold, the servants of David and Joab came from *pursuing* a troop, and brought in a great spoil with them: but Abner *was* not with David in Hebron: for he had sent him away, and he was gone in peace.

23When Joab and all the host that *was* with him were come, they told Joab, saying, Abner the son of Ner came to the king, and he hath sent him away, and he is gone in peace.

24Then Joab came to the king, and said, What hast thou done? behold, Abner came unto thee; why *is* it *that* thou hast sent him away, and he is quite gone?

25Thou knowest Abner the son of Ner, that he came to deceive thee, and to know thy going out and thy coming in, and to know all that thou doest.

26And when Joab was come out from David, he sent messengers after Abner, which brought him again from the well of Sirah: but David knew *it* not.

27And when Abner was returned to Hebron, Joab took him aside in the gate to speak with him quietly, and smote him there under the fifth *rib,* that he died, for the blood of Asahel his brother.

28And afterward when David heard *it,* he said, I and my kingdom *are* guiltless before the Lord for ever from the blood of Abner the son of Ner:

29Let it rest on the head of Joab, and on all his father's house; and let there not fail from the house of Joab one that hath an issue, or that is a leper, or that leaneth on a staff, or that falleth on the sword, or that lacketh bread.

30So Joab and Abishai his brother slew Abner, because he had slain their brother Asahel at Gibeon in the battle.

31And David said to Joab, and to all the people that *were* with him, Rend your clothes, and gird you with sackcloth, and mourn before Abner. And king David *himself* followed the bier.

32And they buried Abner in Hebron: and the king lifted up his voice, and wept at the grave of Abner; and all the people wept.

33And the king lamented over Abner, and said, Died Abner as a fool dieth?

34Thy hands *were* not bound, nor thy feet put into fetters: as a man falleth before wicked men, *so* fellest thou. And all the people wept again over him.

35And when all the people came to cause David to eat meat while it was yet day, David sware, saying, So do God to me, and more also, if I taste bread, or ought else, till the sun be down.

36And all the people took notice *of it,* and it pleased them: as whatsoever the king did pleased all the people.

37For all the people and all Israel understood that day that it was not of the king to slay Abner the son of Ner.

38And the king said unto his servants, Know ye not that there is a prince and a great man fallen this day in Israel?

39And I *am* this day weak, though anointed king; and these men the sons of Zeruiah *be* too hard for me: the Lord shall reward the doer of evil according to his wickedness.

JOHN 13:1–30

Now before the feast of the passover, when Jesus knew that his hour was come that he should depart out of this world unto the Father, having loved his own which were in the world, he loved them unto the end.

2And supper being ended, the devil having now put into the heart of Judas Iscariot, Simon's *son,* to betray him;

3Jesus knowing that the Father had given all things into his hands, and that he was come from God, and went to God;

4He riseth from supper, and laid aside his garments; and took a towel and girded himself.

5After that he poureth water into a bason, and began to wash the disciples' feet, and to wipe *them* with the towel wherewith he was girded.

6Then cometh he to Simon Peter: and Peter saith unto him, Lord, dost thou wash my feet?

7Jesus answered and said unto him, What I do thou knowest not now; but thou shalt know hereafter.

8Peter saith unto him, Thou shalt never wash my feet. Jesus answered him, If I wash thee not, thou hast no part with me.

9Simon Peter saith unto him, Lord, not my feet only, but also *my* hands and *my* head.

10Jesus saith to him, He that is washed needeth not save to wash *his* feet, but is clean every whit: and ye are clean, but not all.

11For he knew who should betray him; therefore said he, Ye are not all clean.

12So after he had washed their feet, and had taken his garments, and was set down again, he said unto them, Know ye what I have done to you?

13Ye call me Master and Lord: and ye say well; for *so* I am.

14If I then, *your* Lord and Master, have washed your feet; ye also ought to wash one another's feet.

15For I have given you an example, that ye should do as I have done to you.

16Verily, verily, I say unto you, The servant is not greater than his lord; neither he that is sent greater than he that sent him.

17If ye know these things, happy are ye if ye do them.

18I speak not of you all: I know whom I have chosen: but that the scripture may be fulfilled, He that eateth bread with me hath lifted up his heel against me.

19Now I tell you before it come, that, when it is come to pass, ye may believe that I am *he.*

20Verily, verily, I say unto you, He that receiveth whomsoever I send receiveth me; and he that receiveth me receiveth him that sent me.

21When Jesus had thus said, he was troubled in spirit, and testified, and said, Verily, verily, I say unto you, that one of you shall betray me.

22Then the disciples looked one on another, doubting of whom he spake.

23Now there was leaning on Jesus' bosom one of his disciples, whom Jesus loved.

24Simon Peter therefore beckoned to him, that he should ask who it should be of whom he spake.

25He then lying on Jesus' breast saith unto him, Lord, who is it?

26Jesus answered, He it is, to whom I shall give a sop, when I have dipped *it.* And when he had dipped the sop, he gave *it* to Judas Iscariot, *the son* of Simon.

27And after the sop Satan entered into him. Then said Jesus unto him, That thou doest, do quickly.

28Now no man at the table knew for what intent he spake this unto him.

29For some *of them* thought, because Judas had the bag, that Jesus had said unto him, Buy *those things* that we have need of against the feast; or, that he should give something to the poor.

30He then having received the sop went immediately out: and it was night.

PSALM 119:1–16

BLESSED *are* the undefiled in the way, who walk in the law of the LORD.

2Blessed *are* they that keep his testimonies, *and that* seek him with the whole heart.

3They also do no iniquity: they walk in his ways.

4Thou hast commanded *us* to keep thy precepts diligently.

5O that my ways were directed to keep thy statutes!

6Then shall I not be ashamed, when I have respect unto all thy commandments.

7I will praise thee with uprightness of heart, when I shall have learned thy righteous judgments.

8I will keep thy statutes: O forsake me not utterly.

9Wherewithal shall a young man cleanse his way? by taking heed *thereto* according to thy word.

10With my whole heart have I sought thee: O let me not wander from thy commandments.

11Thy word have I hid in mine heart, that I might not sin against thee.

12Blessed *art* thou, O LORD: teach me thy statutes.

13With my lips have I declared all the judgments of thy mouth.

14I have rejoiced in the way of thy testimonies, as *much as* in all riches.

15I will meditate in thy precepts, and have respect unto thy ways.

16I will delight myself in thy statutes: I will not forget thy word.

PROVERBS FOR TODAY/ 15:29–30

The LORD *is far from the wicked: but he heareth the prayer of the righteous.* □ *The light of the eyes rejoiceth the heart:* and *a good report maketh the bones fat.*

MAY 24

2 SAMUEL 4:1—6:23

AND when Saul's son heard that Abner was dead in Hebron, his hands were feeble, and all the Israelites were troubled.

2And Saul's son had two men *that were* captains of bands: the name of the one *was* Baanah, and the name of the other Rechab, the sons of Rimmon a Beerothite, of the children of Benjamin: (for Beeroth also was reckoned to Benjamin.

3And the Beerothites fled to Gittaim, and were sojourners there until this day.)

4And Jonathan, Saul's son, had a son *that was* lame of *his* feet. He was five years old when the tidings came of Saul and Jonathan out of Jezreel, and his nurse took him up, and fled: and it came to pass, as she made haste to flee, that he fell, and became lame. And his name *was* Mephibosheth.

5And the sons of Rimmon the Beerothite, Rechab and Baanah, went, and came about the heat of the day to the house of Ish–bosheth, who lay on a bed at noon.

6And they came thither into the midst of the house, *as though* they would have fetched wheat; and they smote him under the fifth *rib:* and Rechab and Baanah his brother escaped.

7For when they came into the house, he lay on his bed in his bedchamber, and they smote him, and slew him, and beheaded him, and took his head, and gat them away through the plain all night.

8And they brought the head of Ish–bosheth unto David to Hebron, and said to the king, Behold the head of Ish–bosheth the son of Saul thine enemy, which sought thy life; and the LORD hath avenged my lord the king this day of Saul, and of his seed.

9And David answered Rechab and Baanah his brother, the sons of Rimmon the Beerothite, and said unto them, *As* the LORD liveth, who hath redeemed my soul out of all adversity,

10When one told me, saying, Behold, Saul is dead, thinking to have brought good tidings, I took hold of him, and slew him in Ziklag, who *thought* that I would have given him a reward for his tidings:

11How much more, when wicked men have slain a righteous person in his own house upon his bed? shall I not therefore now require his blood of your hand, and take you away from the earth?

12And David commanded his young men, and they slew them, and cut off their hands and their feet, and hanged *them* up over the pool in Hebron. But they took the head of Ish–bosheth, and buried *it* in the sepulchre of Abner in Hebron.

THEN came all the tribes of Israel to David unto Hebron, and spake, saying, Behold, we *are* thy bone and thy flesh.

2Also in time past, when Saul was king over us, thou wast he that leddest out and broughtest in Israel: and the LORD said to thee, Thou shalt feed my people Israel, and thou shalt be a captain over Israel.

3So all the elders of Israel came to the king to Hebron; and king David made a league with them in Hebron before the LORD: and they anointed David king over Israel.

4David *was* thirty years old when he began to reign, *and* he reigned forty years.

5In Hebron he reigned over Judah seven years and six months: and in Jerusalem he reigned thirty and three years over all Israel and Judah.

6And the king and his men went to Jerusalem unto the Jebusites, the inhabitants of the land: which spake unto David, saying, Except thou take away the blind and the lame, thou shalt not come in hither: thinking, David cannot come in hither.

7Nevertheless David took the strong hold of Zion: the same *is* the city of David.

8And David said on that day, Whosoever getteth up to the gutter, and smiteth the Jebusites, and the lame and the blind, *that are* hated of David's soul, *he shall be chief and captain.* Wherefore they said, The blind and the lame shall not come into the house.

9So David dwelt in the fort, and called it the city of David. And David built round about from Millo and inward.

10And David went on, and grew great, and the LORD God of hosts *was* with him.

11And Hiram king of Tyre sent messengers to David, and cedar trees, and carpenters, and masons: and they built David an house.

12And David perceived that the LORD had established him king over Israel, and that he had exalted his kingdom for his people Israel's sake.

13And David took *him* more concubines and wives out of Jerusalem, after he was come from Hebron: and there were yet sons and daughters born to David.

14And these *be* the names of those that were born unto him in Jerusalem;

Shammuah, and Shobab, and Nathan, and Solomon,

15Ibhar also and Elishua, and Nepheg, and Japhia,

16And Elishama, and Eliada, and Eliphalet.

17But when the Philistines heard that they had anointed David king over Israel, all the Philistines came up to seek David; and David heard *of it,* and went down to the hold.

18The Philistines also came and spread themselves in the valley of Rephaim.

19And David enquired of the LORD, saying, Shall I go up to the Philistines? wilt thou deliver them into mine hand? And the LORD said unto David, Go up: for I will doubtless deliver the Philistines into thine hand.

20And David came to Baal–perazim, and David smote them there, and said, The LORD hath broken forth upon mine enemies before me, as the breach of waters. Therefore he called the name of that place Baal–perazim.

21And there they left their images, and David and his men burned them.

22And the Philistines came up yet again, and spread themselves in the valley of Rephaim.

23And when David enquired of the LORD, he said, Thou shalt not go up; *but* fetch a compass behind them, and come upon them over against the mulberry trees.

24And let it be, when thou hearest the sound of a going in the tops of the mulberry trees, that then thou shalt bestir thyself: for then shall the LORD go out before thee, to smite the host of the Philistines.

25And David did so, as the LORD had commanded him; and smote the Philistines from Geba until thou come to Gazer.

AGAIN, David gathered together all *the* chosen *men* of Israel, thirty thousand.

2And David arose, and went with all the people that *were* with him from Baale of Judah, to bring up from thence the ark of God, whose name is called by the name of the LORD of hosts that dwelleth *between* the cherubims.

3And they set the ark of God upon a new cart, and brought it out of the house of Abinadab that *was* in Gibeah: and Uzzah and Ahio, the sons of Abinadab, drave the new cart.

4And they brought it out of the house of Abinadab which *was* at Gibeah, accompanying the ark of God: and Ahio went before the ark.

5And David and all the house of Israel played before the LORD on all manner of *instruments made of* fir wood, even on harps, and on psalteries, and on timbrels, and on cornets, and on cymbals.

6And when they came to Nachon's threshingfloor, Uzzah put forth *his hand* to the ark of God, and took hold of it; for the oxen shook *it.*

7And the anger of the LORD was kindled against Uzzah; and God smote him there for *his* error; and there he died by the ark of God.

8And David was displeased, because the LORD had made a breach upon Uzzah: and he called the name of the place Perez–uzzah to this day.

9And David was afraid of the LORD that day, and said, How shall the ark of the LORD come to me?

10So David would not remove the ark of the LORD unto him into the city of David: but David carried it aside into the house of Obed–edom the Gittite.

11And the ark of the LORD continued in the house of Obed–edom the Gittite three months: and the LORD blessed Obed–edom, and all his household.

12And it was told king David, saying, The LORD hath blessed the house of Obed–edom, and all that *pertaineth* unto him, because of the ark of God. So David went and brought up the ark of God from the house of Obed–edom into the city of David with gladness.

13And it was *so,* that when they that bare the ark of the LORD had gone six paces, he sacrificed oxen and fatlings.

14And David danced before the LORD with all *his* might; and David *was* girded with a linen ephod.

15So David and all the house of Israel brought up the ark of the LORD with shouting, and with the sound of the trumpet.

16And as the ark of the LORD came into the city of David, Michal Saul's daughter looked through a window, and saw king David leaping and dancing before the LORD; and she despised him in her heart.

17And they brought in the ark of the LORD, and set it in his place, in the midst of the tabernacle that David had pitched for it: and David offered burnt offerings and peace offerings before the LORD.

18And as soon as David had made an end of offering burnt offerings and peace offerings, he blessed the people in the name of the LORD of hosts.

19And he dealt among all the people, *even* among the whole multitude of Israel, as well to the women as men, to every one a cake of bread, and a good piece *of flesh,* and a flagon *of wine.* So all the people departed every one to his house.

20Then David returned to bless his household. And Michal the daughter of Saul came out to meet David, and said, How glorious was the king of Israel to day, who uncovered himself to day in the eyes of the handmaids of his servants, as one of the vain fellows shamelessly uncovereth himself!

21And David said unto Michal, *It was* before the LORD, which chose me before thy father, and before all his house, to appoint me ruler of the people of the LORD, over Israel: therefore will I play before the LORD.

22And I will yet be more vile than thus, and will be base in mine own sight: and of the maidservants which thou hast spoken of, of them shall I be had in honour.

23Therefore Michal the daughter of Saul had no child unto the day of her death.

JOHN 13:31—14:14

Therefore, when he [Judas Iscariot] was gone out, Jesus said, Now is the Son of man glorified, and God is glorified in him.

32If God be glorified in him, God shall also glorify him in himself, and shall straightway glorify him.

33Little children, yet a little while I am with you. Ye shall seek me: and as I said unto the Jews, Whither I go, ye cannot come; so now I say to you.

34A new commandment I give unto you, That ye love one another; as I have loved you, that ye also love one another.

35By this shall all *men* know that ye are my disciples, if ye have love one to another.

36Simon Peter said unto him, Lord, whither goest thou? Jesus answered him, Whither I go, thou canst not follow me now; but thou shalt follow me afterwards.

37Peter said unto him, Lord, why cannot I follow thee now? I will lay down my life for thy sake.

38Jesus answered him, Wilt thou lay down thy life for my sake? Verily, verily, I say unto thee, The cock shall not crow, till thou hast denied me thrice.

LET not your heart be troubled: ye believe in God, believe also in me.

2In my Father's house are many mansions: if *it were* not *so,* I would have told you. I go to prepare a place for you.

3And if I go and prepare a place for you, I will come again, and receive you unto myself; that where I am, *there* ye may be also.

⁴And whither I go ye know, and the way ye know.

⁵Thomas saith unto him, Lord, we know not whither thou goest; and how can we know the way?

⁶Jesus saith unto him, I am the way, the truth, and the life: no man cometh unto the Father, but by me.

⁷If ye had known me, ye should have known my Father also: and from henceforth ye know him, and have seen him.

⁸Philip saith unto him, Lord, shew us the Father, and it sufficeth us.

⁹Jesus saith unto him, Have I been so long time with you, and yet hast thou not known me, Philip? he that hath seen me hath seen the Father; and how sayest thou *then,* Shew us the Father?

¹⁰Believest thou not that I am in the Father, and the Father in me? the words that I speak unto you I speak not of myself: but the Father that dwelleth in me, he doeth the works.

¹¹Believe me that I *am* in the Father, and the Father in me: or else believe me for the very works' sake.

¹²Verily, verily, I say unto you, He that believeth on me, the works that I do shall he do also; and greater *works* than these shall he do; because I go unto my Father.

¹³And whatsoever ye shall ask in my name, that will I do, that the Father may be glorified in the Son.

¹⁴If ye shall ask any thing in my name, I will do *it.*

PSALM 119:17–35

DEAL bountifully with thy servant, *that* I may live, and keep thy word.

¹⁸Open thou mine eyes, that I may behold wondrous things out of thy law.

¹⁹I am a stranger in the earth: hide not thy commandments from me.

²⁰My soul breaketh for the longing *that it hath* unto thy judgments at all times.

²¹Thou hast rebuked the proud *that are* cursed, which do err from thy commandments.

²²Remove from me reproach and contempt; for I have kept thy testimonies.

²³Princes also did sit *and* speak against me: *but* thy servant did meditate in thy statutes.

²⁴Thy testimonies also *are* my delight *and* my counsellors.

²⁵My soul cleaveth unto the dust: quicken thou me according to thy word.

²⁶I have declared my ways, and thou heardest me: teach me thy statutes.

²⁷Make me to understand the way of thy precepts: so shall I talk of thy wondrous works.

²⁸My soul melteth for heaviness: strengthen thou me according unto thy word.

²⁹Remove from me the way of lying: and grant me thy law graciously.

³⁰I have chosen the way of truth: thy judgments have I laid *before me.*

³¹I have stuck unto thy testimonies: O LORD, put me not to shame.

³²I will run the way of thy commandments, when thou shalt enlarge my heart.

³³Teach me, O LORD, the way of thy statutes; and I shall keep it *unto* the end.

³⁴Give me understanding, and I shall keep thy law; yea, I shall observe it with *my* whole heart.

³⁵Make me to go in the path of thy commandments; for therein do I delight.

PROVERBS FOR TODAY/ 15:31–32

The ear that heareth the reproof of life abideth among the wise. □ *He that refuseth instruction despiseth his own soul: but he that heareth reproof getteth understanding.*

2 SAMUEL 7:1—8:18

AND it came to pass, when the king [David] sat in his house, and the LORD had given him rest round about from all his enemies;

2That the king said unto Nathan the prophet, See now, I dwell in an house of cedar, but the ark of God dwelleth within curtains.

3And Nathan said to the king, Go, do all that *is* in thine heart; for the LORD *is* with thee.

4And it came to pass that night, that the word of the LORD came unto Nathan, saying,

5Go and tell my servant David, Thus saith the LORD, Shalt thou build me an house for me to dwell in?

6Whereas I have not dwelt in *any* house since the time that I brought up the children of Israel out of Egypt, even to this day, but have walked in a tent and in a tabernacle.

7In all *the places* wherein I have walked with all the children of Israel spake I a word with any of the tribes of Israel, whom I commanded to feed my people Israel, saying, Why build ye not me an house of cedar?

8Now therefore so shalt thou say unto my servant David, Thus saith the LORD of hosts, I took thee from the sheepcote, from following the sheep, to be ruler over my people, over Israel:

9And I was with thee whithersoever thou wentest, and have cut off all thine enemies out of thy sight, and have made thee a great name, like unto the name of the great *men* that *are* in the earth.

10Moreover I will appoint a place for my people Israel, and will plant them, that they may dwell in a place of their own, and move no more; neither shall the children of wickedness afflict them any more, as beforetime,

11And as since the time that I commanded judges *to be* over my people Israel, and have caused thee to rest from all thine enemies. Also the LORD telleth thee that he will make thee an house.

12And when thy days be fulfilled, and thou shalt sleep with thy fathers, I will set up thy seed after thee, which shall proceed out of thy bowels, and I will establish his kingdom.

13He shall build an house for my name, and I will stablish the throne of his kingdom for ever.

14I will be his father, and he shall be my son. If he commit iniquity, I will chasten him with the rod of men, and with the stripes of the children of men:

15But my mercy shall not depart away from him, as I took *it* from Saul, whom I put away before thee.

16And thine house and thy kingdom shall be established for ever before thee: thy throne shall be established for ever.

17According to all these words, and according to all this vision, so did Nathan speak unto David.

18Then went king David in, and sat before the LORD, and he said, Who *am* I, O Lord God? and what *is* my house, that thou hast brought me hitherto?

19And this was yet a small thing in thy sight, O Lord God; but thou hast spoken also of thy servant's house for a great while to come. And *is* this the manner of man, O Lord God?

20And what can David say more unto thee? for thou, Lord GOD, knowest thy servant.

21For thy word's sake, and according to thine own heart, hast thou done all these great things, to make thy servant know *them*.

22Wherefore thou art great, O LORD God: for *there is* none like thee, neither *is there any* God beside thee, according to all that we have heard with our ears.

23And what one nation in the earth *is* like thy people, *even* like Israel, whom God went to redeem for a people to himself, and to make him a name, and to do for you great things and terrible, for thy land, before thy people, which thou redeemedst to thee from Egypt, *from* the nations and their gods?

24For thou hast confirmed to thyself thy people Israel *to be* a people unto thee for ever: and thou, LORD, art become their God.

25And now, O LORD God, the word that thou hast spoken concerning thy servant, and concerning his house, establish *it* for ever, and do as thou hast said.

26And let thy name be magnified for ever, saying, The LORD of hosts *is* the God over Israel: and let the house of thy servant David be established before thee.

27For thou, O LORD of hosts, God of Israel, hast revealed to thy servant, saying, I will build thee an house: therefore hath thy servant found in his heart to pray this prayer unto thee.

28And now, O Lord GOD, thou *art* that God, and thy words be true, and thou hast promised this goodness unto thy servant:

29Therefore now let it please thee to bless the house of thy servant, that it may continue for ever before thee: for thou, O Lord GOD, hast spoken *it:* and with thy blessing let the house of thy servant be blessed for ever.

AND after this it came to pass, that David smote the Philistines, and subdued them: and David took Metheg–ammah out of the hand of the Philistines.

2And he smote Moab, and measured them with a line, casting them down to the ground; even with two lines measured he to put to death, and with one full line to keep alive. And *so* the Moabites became David's servants, *and* brought gifts.

3David smote also Hadadezer, the son of Rehob, king of Zobah, as he went to recover his border at the river Euphrates.

4And David took from him a thousand *chariots:* and seven hundred horsemen, and twenty thousand footmen: and David houghed all the chariot *horses,* but reserved of them *for* an hundred chariots.

5And when the Syrians of Damascus came to succour Hadadezer king of Zobah, David slew of the Syrians two and twenty thousand men.

6Then David put garrisons in Syria of Damascus: and the Syrians became servants to David, *and* brought gifts. And the LORD preserved David whithersoever he went.

7And David took the shields of gold that were on the servants of Hadadezer, and brought them to Jerusalem.

8And from Betah, and from Berothai, cities of Hadadezer, king David took exceeding much brass.

9When Toi king of Hamath heard that David had smitten all the host of Hadadezer,

10Then Toi sent Joram his son unto king David, to salute him, and to bless him, because he had fought against Hadadezer, and smitten him: for Hadadezer had wars with Toi. And *Joram* brought with him vessels of silver, and vessels of gold, and vessels of brass:

11Which also king David did dedicate unto the LORD, with the silver and gold that he had dedicated of all nations which he subdued;

12Of Syria, and Moab, and of the children of Ammon, and of the Philistines, and of Amalek, and of the spoil of Hadadezer, son of Rehob, king of Zobah.

13And David gat *him* a name when he returned from smiting of the Syrians in the valley of salt, *being* eighteen thousand *men.*

14And he put garrisons in Edom; throughout all Edom put he garrisons, and all they of Edom became David's servants. And the LORD preserved David withersoever he went.

15And David reigned over all Israel; and David executed judgment and justice unto all his people.

16And Joab the son of Zeruiah *was* over the host; and Jehoshaphat the son of Ahilud *was* recorder;

17And Zadok the son of Ahitub, and Ahimelech the son of Abiathar, *were* the priests; and Seraiah *was* the scribe;

18And Benaiah the son of Jehoiada *was over* both the Cherethites and the Pelethites; and David's sons were chief rulers.

JOHN 14:15–31

IF ye love me, keep my commandments.

16And I will pray the Father, and he shall give you another Comforter, that he may abide with you for ever;

17*Even* the Spirit of truth; whom the world cannot receive, because it seeth him not, neither knoweth him: but ye know him; for he dwelleth with you, and shall be in you.

18I will not leave you comfortless: I will come to you.

19Yet a little while, and the world seeth me no more; but ye see me: because I live, ye shall live also.

20At that day ye shall know that I *am* in my Father, and ye in me, and I in you.

21He that hath my commandments, and keepeth them, he it is that loveth me: and he that loveth me shall be loved of my Father, and I will love him, and will manifest myself to him.

22Judas saith unto him, not Iscariot, Lord, how is it that thou wilt manifest thyself unto us, and not unto the world?

23Jesus answered and said unto him, If a man love me, he will keep my words: and my Father will love him, and we will come unto him, and make our abode with him.

24He that loveth me not keepeth not my sayings: and the word which ye hear is not mine, but the Father's which sent me.

25These things have I spoken unto you, being *yet* present with you.

26But the Comforter, *which is* the Holy Ghost, whom the Father will send in my name, he shall teach you all things, and bring all things to your remembrance, whatsoever I have said unto you.

27Peace I leave with you, my peace I give unto you: not as the world giveth, give I unto you. Let not your heart be troubled, neither let it be afraid.

28Ye have heard how I said unto you, I go away, and come *again* unto you. If ye loved me, ye would rejoice, because I said, I go unto the Father: for my Father is greater than I.

29And now I have told you before it come to pass, that, when it is come to pass, ye might believe.

30Hereafter I will not talk much with you: for the prince of this world cometh, and hath nothing in me.

31But that the world may know that I love the Father; and as the Father gave me commandment, even so I do. Arise, let us go hence.

PSALM 119:36–52

INCLINE my heart unto thy testimonies, and not to covetousness.

37Turn away mine eyes from beholding vanity; *and* quicken thou me in thy way.

38Stablish thy word unto thy servant, who *is devoted* to thy fear.

39Turn away my reproach which I fear: for thy judgments *are* good.

40Behold, I have longed after thy precepts: quicken me in thy righteousness.

41Let thy mercies come also unto me, O LORD, *even* thy salvation, according to thy word.

42So shall I have wherewith to answer him that reproacheth me: for I trust in thy word.

43And take not the word of truth utterly out of my mouth; for I have hoped in thy judgments.

44So shall I keep thy law continually for ever and ever.

45And I will walk at liberty: for I seek thy precepts.

46I will speak of thy testimonies also before kings, and will not be ashamed.

47And I will delight myself in thy commandments, which I have loved.

48My hands also will I lift up unto thy commandments, which I have loved; and I will meditate in thy statutes.

49Remember the word unto thy servant, upon which thou hast caused me to hope.

50This *is* my comfort in my affliction: for thy word hath quickened me.

51The proud have had me greatly in derision: *yet* have I not declined from thy law.

52I remembered thy judgments of old, O LORD; and have comforted myself.

PROVERBS FOR TODAY/ 15:33

The fear of the LORD *is the instruction of wisdom; and before honour* is *humility.*

MAY 26

2 SAMUEL 9:1—11:27

AND David said, Is there yet any that is left of the house of Saul, that I may shew him kindness for Jonathan's sake?

2And *there was* of the house of Saul a servant whose name *was* Ziba. And when they had called him unto David, the king said unto him, *Art* thou Ziba? And he said, Thy servant *is he.*

3And the king said, *Is* there not yet any of the house of Saul, that I may shew the kindness of God unto him? And Ziba said unto the king, Jonathan hath yet a son, *which is* lame on *his* feet.

4And the king said unto him, Where *is* he? And Ziba said unto the king, Behold, he *is* in the house of Machir, the son of Ammiel, in Lo–debar.

5Then king David sent, and fetched him out of the house of Machir, the son of Ammiel, from Lo–debar.

6Now when Mephibosheth, the son of Jonathan, the son of Saul, was come unto David, he fell on his face, and did reverence. And David said, Mephibosheth. And he answered, Behold thy servant!

7And David said unto him, Fear not: for I will surely shew thee kindness for Jonathan thy father's sake, and will restore thee all the land of Saul thy father; and thou shalt eat bread at my table continually.

8And he bowed himself, and said, What *is* thy servant, that thou shouldest look upon such a dead dog as I *am?*

9Then the king called to Ziba, Saul's servant, and said unto him, I have given unto thy master's son all that pertained to Saul and to all his house.

10Thou therefore, and thy sons, and thy servants, shall till the land for him, and thou shalt bring in *the fruits,* that thy master's son may have food to eat: but Mephibosheth thy master's son shall eat bread alway at my table. Now

Ziba had fifteen sons and twenty servants.

11Then said Ziba unto the king, According to all that my lord the king hath commanded his servant, so shall thy servant do. As for Mephibosheth, *said the king,* he shall eat at my table, as one of the king's sons.

12And Mephibosheth had a young son, whose name *was* Micha. And all that dwelt in the house of Ziba *were* servants unto Mephibosheth.

13So Mephibosheth dwelt in Jerusalem: for he did eat continually at the king's table; and was lame on both his feet.

AND it came to pass after this, that the king of the children of Ammon died, and Hanun his son reigned in his stead.

2Then said David, I will shew kindness unto Hanun the son of Nahash, as his father shewed kindness unto me. And David sent to comfort him by the hand of his servants for his father. And David's servants came into the land of the children of Ammon.

3And the princes of the children of Ammon said unto Hanun their lord, Thinkest thou that David doth honour thy father, that he hath sent comforters unto thee? hath not David *rather* sent his servants unto thee to search the city, and to spy it out, and to overthrow it?

4Wherefore Hanun took David's servants, and shaved off the one half of their beards, and cut off their garments in the middle, *even* to their buttocks, and sent them away.

5When they told *it* unto David, he sent to meet them, because the men were greatly ashamed: and the king said, Tarry at Jericho until your beards be grown, and *then* return.

6And when the children of Ammon saw that they stank before David, the children of Ammon sent and hired the Syrians of Beth–rehob, and the Syrians of Zoba, twenty thousand footmen, and of king Maacah a thousand men, and of Ish–tob twelve thousand men.

7And when David heard of *it,* he sent Joab, and all the host of the mighty men.

8And the children of Ammon came out, and put the battle in array at the entering in of the gate: and the Syrians of Zoba, and of Rehob, and Ishtob, and Maacah, *were* by themselves in the field.

9When Joab saw that the front of the battle was against him before and behind, he chose of all the choice *men* of Israel, and put *them* in array against the Syrians:

10And the rest of the people he delivered into the hand of Abishai his brother, that he might put *them* in array against the children of Ammon.

11And he said, If the Syrians be too strong for me, then thou shalt help me: but if the children of Ammon be too strong for thee, then I will come and help thee.

12Be of good courage, and let us play the men for our people, and for the cities of our God: and the LORD do that which seemeth him good.

13And Joab drew nigh, and the people that *were* with him, unto the battle against the Syrians: and they fled before him.

14And when the children of Ammon saw that the Syrians were fled, then fled they also before Abishai, and entered into the city. So Joab returned from the children of Ammon, and came to Jerusalem.

15And when the Syrians saw that they were smitten before Israel, they gathered themselves together.

16And Hadarezer sent, and brought out the Syrians that *were* beyond the river: and they came to Helam; and Shobach the captain of the host of Hadarezer *went* before them.

17And when it was told David, he gathered all Israel together, and passed over Jordan, and came to Helam. And the Syrians set themselves in array against David, and fought with him.

18And the Syrians fled before Israel; and David slew *the men of* seven hundred chariots of the Syrians, and forty thousand horsemen, and smote Shobach the captain of their host, who died there.

19And when all the kings *that were* servants to Hadarezer saw that they were smitten before Israel, they made peace with Israel, and served them. So the Syrians feared to help the children of Ammon any more.

AND it came to pass, after the year was expired, at the time when kings go forth *to battle,* that David sent Joab, and his servants with him, and all Israel; and they destroyed the children of Ammon, and besieged Rabbah. But David tarried still at Jerusalem.

2And it came to pass in an eveningtide, that David arose from off his bed, and walked upon the roof of the king's house: and from the roof he saw a woman washing herself; and the woman *was* very beautiful to look upon.

3And David sent and enquired after the woman. And *one* said, *Is* not this Bath–sheba, the daughter of Eliam, the wife of Uriah the Hittite?

4And David sent messengers, and took her; and she came in unto him, and he lay with her; for she was purified from her uncleanness: and she returned unto her house.

5And the woman conceived, and sent and told David, and said, I *am* with child.

6And David sent to Joab, *saying,* Send me Uriah the Hittite. And Joab sent Uriah to David.

7And when Uriah was come unto him, David demanded *of him* how Joab did, and how the people did, and how the war prospered.

8And David said to Uriah, Go down to thy house, and wash thy feet. And Uriah departed out of the king's house, and there followed him a mess *of meat* from the king.

9But Uriah slept at the door of the king's house with all the servants of his lord, and went not down to his house.

10And when they had told David, saying, Uriah went not down unto his house, David said unto Uriah, Camest thou not from *thy* journey? why *then* didst thou not go down unto thine house?

11And Uriah said unto David, The ark, and Israel, and Judah, abide in tents; and my lord Joab, and the servants of my lord, are encamped in the open fields; shall I then go into mine house, to eat and to drink, and to lie with my wife? *as* thou livest, and *as* thy soul liveth, I will not do this thing.

12And David said to Uriah, Tarry here to day also, and tomorrow I will let thee depart. So Uriah abode in Jerusalem that day, and the morrow.

13And when David had called him, he did eat and drink before him; and he made him drunk: and at even he went out to lie on his bed with the servants of his lord, but went not down to his house.

14And it came to pass in the morning, that David wrote a letter to Joab, and sent *it* by the hand of Uriah.

15And he wrote in the letter, saying, Set ye Uriah in the forefront of the hottest battle, and retire ye from him, that he may be smitten, and die.

16And it came to pass, when Joab observed the city, that he assigned Uriah unto a place where he knew that valiant men *were.*

17And the men of the city went out, and fought with Joab: and there fell *some* of the people of the servants of David; and Uriah the Hittite died also.

18Then Joab sent and told David all the things concerning the war;

19And charged the messenger, saying, When thou hast made an end of telling the matters of the war unto the king,

20And if so be that the king's wrath arise, and he say unto thee, Wherefore approached ye so nigh unto the city when ye did fight? knew ye not that they would shoot from the wall?

21Who smote Abimelech the son of Jerubbesheth? did not a woman cast a piece of a millstone upon him from the wall, that he died in Thebez? why went ye nigh the wall? then say thou, Thy servant Uriah the Hittite is dead also.

22So the messenger went, and came and shewed David all that Joab had sent him for.

23And the messenger said unto David, Surely the men prevailed against us, and came out unto us into the field, and we were upon them even unto the entering of the gate.

24And the shooters shot from off the wall upon thy servants; and *some* of the king's servants be dead, and thy servant Uriah the Hittite is dead also.

25Then David said unto the messenger, Thus shalt thou say unto Joab, Let not this thing displease thee, for the sword devoureth one as well as another: make thy battle more strong against the city, and overthrow it: and encourage thou him.

26And when the wife of Uriah heard that Uriah her husband was dead, she mourned for her husband.

27And when the mourning was past, David sent and fetched her to his house, and she became his wife, and bare him a son. But the thing that David had done displeased the LORD.

JOHN 15:1–27

I AM the true vine, and my Father is the husbandman.

2Every branch in me that beareth not fruit he taketh away: and every *branch* that beareth fruit, he purgeth it, that it may bring forth more fruit.

3Now ye are clean through the word which I have spoken unto you.

4Abide in me, and I in you. As the branch cannot bear fruit of itself, except it abide in the vine; no more can ye, except ye abide in me.

5I am the vine, ye *are* the branches: He that abideth in me, and I in him, the same bringeth forth much fruit: for without me ye can do nothing.

6If a man abide not in me, he is cast forth as a branch, and is withered; and men gather them, and cast *them* into the fire, and they are burned.

7If ye abide in me, and my words abide in you, ye shall ask what ye will, and it shall be done unto you.

8Herein is my Father glorified, that ye bear much fruit; so shall ye be my disciples.

9As the Father hath loved me, so have I loved you: continue ye in my love.

10If ye keep my commandments, ye shall abide in my love; even as I have kept my Father's commandments, and abide in his love.

11These things have I spoken unto you, that my joy might remain in you, and *that* your joy might be full.

12This is my commandment, That ye love one another, as I have loved you.

13Greater love hath no man than this, that a man lay down his life for his friends.

14Ye are my friends, if ye do whatsoever I command you.

15Henceforth I call you not servants; for the servant knoweth not what his lord doeth: but I have called you friends; for all things that I have heard of my Father I have made known unto you.

16Ye have not chosen me, but I have chosen you, and ordained you, that ye should go and bring forth fruit, and *that* your fruit should remain: that whatsoever ye shall ask of the Father in my name, he may give it you.

17These things I command you, that ye love one another.

18If the world hate you, ye know that it hated me before *it hated* you.

19If ye were of the world, the world

would love his own: but because ye are not of the world, but I have chosen you out of the world, therefore the world hateth you.

20Remember the word that I said unto you, The servant is not greater than his lord. If they have persecuted me, they will also persecute you; if they have kept my saying, they will keep yours also.

21But all these things will they do unto you for my name's sake, because they know not him that sent me.

22If I had not come and spoken unto them, they had not had sin: but now they have no cloak for their sin.

23He that hateth me hateth my Father also.

24If I had not done among them the works which none other man did, they had not had sin: but now have they both seen and hated both me and my Father.

25But *this cometh to pass,* that the word might be fulfilled that is written in their law, They hated me without a cause.

26But when the Comforter is come, whom I will send unto you from the Father, *even* the Spirit of truth, which proceedeth from the Father, he shall testify of me:

27And ye also shall bear witness, because ye have been with me from the beginning.

PSALM 119:53–70

Horror hath taken hold upon me because of the wicked that forsake thy law.

54Thy statutes have been my songs in the house of my pilgrimage.

55I have remembered thy name, O Lord, in the night, and have kept thy law.

56This I had, because I kept thy precepts.

57*Thou art* my portion, O Lord: I have said that I would keep thy words.

58I intreated thy favour with *my* whole heart: be merciful unto me according to thy word.

59I thought on my ways, and turned my feet unto thy testimonies.

60I made haste, and delayed not to keep thy commandments.

61The bands of the wicked have robbed me: *but* I have not forgotten thy law.

62At midnight I will rise to give thanks unto thee because of thy righteous judgments.

63I *am* a companion of all *them* that fear thee, and of them that keep thy precepts.

64The earth, O Lord, is full of thy mercy: teach me thy statutes.

65Thou hast dealt well with thy servant, O Lord, according unto thy word.

66Teach me good judgment and knowledge: for I have believed thy commandments.

67Before I was afflicted I went astray: but now have I kept thy word.

68Thou *art* good, and doest good; teach me thy statutes.

69The proud have forged a lie against me: *but* I will keep thy precepts with *my* whole heart.

70Their heart is as fat as grease; *but* I delight in thy law.

PROVERBS FOR TODAY/ 16:1–3

The preparations of the heart in man, and the answer of the tongue, is *from the Lord.* □ *All the ways of a man* are *clean in his own eyes; but the Lord weigheth the spirits.* □ *Commit thy works unto the Lord, and thy thoughts shall be established.*

MAY 27

2 SAMUEL 12:1–31

And the Lord sent Nathan unto David. And he came unto him, and said unto him, There were two men in one city; the one rich, and the other poor.

2The rich *man* had exceeding many flocks and herds:

3But the poor *man* had nothing, save one little ewe lamb, which he had bought and nourished up: and it grew up together with him, and with his children; it did eat of his own meat, and drank of his own cup, and lay in his bosom, and was unto him as a daughter.

4And there came a traveller unto the rich man, and he spared to take of his own flock and of his own herd, to dress for the wayfaring man that was come unto him; but took the poor man's lamb, and dressed it for the man that was come to him.

5And David's anger was greatly kindled against the man; and he said to Nathan, *As* the Lord liveth, the man that hath done this *thing* shall surely die:

6And he shall restore the lamb fourfold, because he did this thing, and because he had no pity.

7And Nathan said to David, Thou *art* the man. Thus saith the Lord God of Israel, I anointed thee king over Israel, and I delivered thee out of the hand of Saul;

8And I gave thee thy master's house, and thy master's wives into thy bosom, and gave thee the house of Israel and of Judah; and if *that had been* too little, I would moreover have given unto thee such and such things.

9Wherefore hast thou despised the commandment of the Lord, to do evil in his sight? thou hast killed Uriah the Hittite with the sword, and hast taken his wife *to be* thy wife, and hast slain him with the sword of the children of Ammon.

10Now therefore the sword shall never depart from thine house; because thou hast despised me, and hast taken the wife of Uriah the Hittite to be thy wife.

11Thus saith the Lord, Behold, I will raise up evil against thee out of thine own house, and I will take thy wives before thine eyes, and give *them* unto thy neighbour, and he shall lie with thy wives in the sight of this sun.

12For thou didst *it* secretly: but I will do this thing before all Israel, and before the sun.

13And David said unto Nathan, I have sinned against the Lord. And Nathan said unto David, The Lord also hath put away thy sin; thou shalt not die.

14Howbeit, because by this deed thou hast given great occasion to the enemies of the Lord to blaspheme, the child also *that is* born unto thee shall surely die.

15And Nathan departed unto his house. And the Lord struck the child that Uriah's wife bare unto David, and it was very sick.

16David therefore besought God for the child; and David fasted, and went in, and lay all night upon the earth.

17And the elders of his house arose, *and went* to him, to raise him up from the earth: but he would not, neither did he eat bread with them.

18And it came to pass on the seventh day, that the child died. And the servants of David feared to tell him that the child was dead: for they said, Behold, while the child was yet alive, we spake unto him, and he would not hearken unto our voice: how will he then vex himself, if we tell him that the child is dead?

19But when David saw that his servants whispered, David perceived that the child was dead: therefore David said unto his servants, Is the child dead? And they said, He is dead.

20Then David arose from the earth, and washed, and anointed *himself,* and changed his apparel, and came into the house of the LORD, and worshipped: then he came to his own house; and when he required, they set bread before him, and he did eat.

21Then said his servants unto him, What thing *is* this that thou hast done? thou didst fast and weep for the child, *while it was* alive; but when the child was dead, thou didst rise and eat bread.

22And he said, While the child was yet alive, I fasted and wept: for I said, Who can tell *whether* God will be gracious to me, that the child may live?

23But now he is dead, wherefore should I fast? can I bring him back again? I shall go to him, but he shall not return to me.

24And David comforted Bath–sheba his wife, and went in unto her, and lay with her: and she bare a son, and he called his name Solomon: and the LORD loved him.

25And he sent by the hand of Nathan the prophet; and he called his name Jedidiah, because of the LORD.

26And Joab fought against Rabbah of the children of Ammon, and took the royal city.

27And Joab sent messengers to David, and said, I have fought against Rabbah, and have taken the city of waters.

28Now therefore gather the rest of the people together, and encamp against the city, and take it: lest I take the city, and it be called after my name.

29And David gathered all the people together, and went to Rabbah, and fought against it, and took it.

30And he took their king's crown from off his head, the weight whereof *was*

a talent of gold with the precious stones: and it was *set* on David's head. And he brought forth the spoil of the city in great abundance.

31And he brought forth the people that *were* therein, and put *them* under saws, and under harrows of iron, and under axes of iron, and made them pass through the brick-kiln: and thus did he unto all the cities of the children of Ammon. So David and all the people returned unto Jerusalem.

JOHN 16:1–33

THESE things have I spoken unto you, that ye should not be offended.

2They shall put you out of the synagogues: yea, the time cometh, that whosoever killeth you will think that he doeth God service.

3And these things will they do unto you, because they have not known the Father, nor me.

4But these things have I told you, that when the time shall come, ye may remember that I told you of them. And these things I said not unto you at the beginning, because I was with you.

5But now I go my way to him that sent me; and none of you asketh me, Whither goest thou?

6But because I have said these things unto you, sorrow hath filled your heart.

7Nevertheless I tell you the truth; It is expedient for you that I go away: for if I go not away, the Comforter will not come unto you; but if I depart, I will send him unto you.

8And when he is come, he will reprove the world of sin, and of righteousness, and of judgment:

9Of sin, because they believe not on me;

10Of righteousness, because I go to my Father, and ye see me no more;

11Of judgment, because the prince of this world is judged.

¹²I have yet many things to say unto you, but ye cannot bear them now.

¹³Howbeit when he, the Spirit of truth, is come, he will guide you into all truth: for he shall not speak of himself; but whatsoever he shall hear, *that* shall he speak: and he will shew you things to come.

¹⁴He shall glorify me: for he shall receive of mine, and shall shew *it* unto you.

¹⁵All things that the Father hath are mine: therefore said I, that he shall take of mine, and shall shew *it* unto you.

¹⁶A little while, and ye shall not see me: and again, a little while, and ye shall see me, because I go to the Father.

¹⁷Then said *some* of his disciples among themselves, What is this that he saith unto us, A little while, and ye shall not see me: and again, a little while, and ye shall see me: and, Because I go to the Father?

¹⁸They said therefore, What is this that he saith, A little while? we cannot tell what he saith.

¹⁹Now Jesus knew that they were desirous to ask him, and said unto them, Do ye enquire among yourselves of that I said, A little while, and ye shall not see me: and again, a little while, and ye shall see me?

²⁰Verily, verily, I say unto you, That ye shall weep and lament, but the world shall rejoice: and ye shall be sorrowful, but your sorrow shall be turned into joy.

²¹A woman when she is in travail hath sorrow, because her hour is come: but as soon as she is delivered of the child, she remembereth no more the anguish, for joy that a man is born into the world.

²²And ye now therefore have sorrow: but I will see you again, and your heart shall rejoice, and your joy no man taketh from you.

²³And in that day ye shall ask me nothing. Verily, verily, I say unto you, Whatsoever ye shall ask the Father in my name, he will give *it* you.

²⁴Hitherto have ye asked nothing in my name: ask, and ye shall receive, that your joy may be full.

²⁵These things have I spoken unto you in proverbs: but the time cometh, when I shall no more speak unto you in proverbs, but I shall shew you plainly of the Father.

²⁶At that day ye shall ask in my name: and I say not unto you, that I will pray the Father for you:

²⁷For the Father himself loveth you, because ye have loved me, and have believed that I came out from God.

²⁸I came forth from the Father, and am come into the world: again, I leave the world, and go to the Father.

²⁹His disciples said unto him, Lo, now speakest thou plainly, and speakest no proverb.

³⁰Now are we sure that thou knowest all things, and needest not that any man should ask thee: by this we believe that thou camest forth from God.

³¹Jesus answered them, Do ye now believe?

³²Behold, the hour cometh, yea, is now come, that ye shall be scattered, every man to his own, and shall leave me alone: and yet I am not alone, because the Father is with me.

³³These things I have spoken unto you, that in me ye might have peace. In the world ye shall have tribulation: but be of good cheer; I have overcome the world.

PSALM 119:71–80

I T is good for me that I have been afflicted; that I might learn thy statutes.

⁷²The law of thy mouth *is* better unto me than thousands of gold and silver.

⁷³Thy hands have made me and fashioned me: give me understanding, that

I may learn thy commandments.

74They that fear thee will be glad when they see me; because I have hoped in thy word.

75I know, O LORD, that thy judgments *are* right, and *that* thou in faithfulness hast afflicted me.

76Let, I pray thee, thy merciful kindness be for my comfort, according to thy word unto thy servant.

77Let thy tender mercies come unto me, that I may live: for thy law *is* my delight.

78Let the proud be ashamed; for they dealt perversely with me without a cause: *but* I will meditate in thy precepts.

79Let those that fear thee turn unto me, and those that have known thy testimonies.

80Let my heart be sound in thy statutes; that I be not ashamed.

PROVERBS FOR TODAY/ 16:4–5

The LORD hath made all things for himself: yea, even the wicked for the day of evil. □ *Every one that is proud in heart is an abomination to the LORD: though hand join in hand, he shall not be unpunished.*

MAY 28

2 SAMUEL 13:1–39

AND it came to pass after this, that Absalom the son of David had a fair sister, whose name *was* Tamar; and Amnon the son of David loved her.

2And Amnon was so vexed, that he fell sick for his sister Tamar; for she *was* a virgin; and Amnon thought it hard for him to do anything to her.

3But Amnon had a friend, whose name *was* Jonadab, the son of Shimeah David's brother: and Jonadab *was* a very subtil man.

4And he said unto him, Why *art* thou, *being* the king's son, lean from day to day? wilt thou not tell me? And Amnon said unto him, I love Tamar, my brother Absalom's sister.

5And Jonadab said unto him, Lay thee down on thy bed, and make thyself sick: and when thy father cometh to see thee, say unto him, I pray thee, let my sister Tamar come, and give

me meat, and dress the meat in my sight, that I may see *it,* and eat *it* at her hand.

6So Amnon lay down, and made himself sick: and when the king was come to see him, Amnon said unto the king, I pray thee, let Tamar my sister come, and make me a couple of cakes in my sight, that I may eat at her hand.

7Then David sent home to Tamar, saying, Go now to thy brother Amnon's house, and dress him meat.

8So Tamar went to her brother Amnon's house; and he was laid down. And she took flour, and kneaded *it,* and made cakes in his sight, and did bake the cakes.

9And she took a pan, and poured *them* out before him; but he refused to eat. And Amnon said, Have out all men from me. And they went out every man from him.

10And Amnon said unto Tamar, Bring the meat into the chamber, that I may eat of thine hand. And Tamar took the cakes which she had made, and brought *them* unto the chamber to Amnon her brother.

11And when she had brought *them* unto him to eat, he took hold of her, and said unto her, Come lie with me, my sister.

12And she answered him, Nay, my brother, do not force me; for no such thing ought to be done in Israel: do not thou this folly.

13And I, whither shall I cause my shame to go? and as for thee, thou shalt be as one of the fools in Israel. Now therefore, I pray thee, speak unto the king; for he will not withhold me from thee.

14Howbeit he would not hearken unto her voice: but, being stronger than she, forced her, and lay with her.

15Then Amnon hated her exceedingly; so that the hatred wherewith he hated her *was* greater than the love wherewith he had loved her. And Amnon said unto her, Arise, be gone.

16And she said unto him, *There is* no cause: this evil in sending me away *is* greater than the other that thou didst unto me. But he would not hearken unto her.

17Then he called his servant that ministered unto him, and said, Put now this *woman* out from me, and bolt the door after her.

18And *she had* a garment of divers colours upon her: for with such robes were the king's daughters *that were* virgins apparelled. Then his servant brought her out, and bolted the door after her.

19And Tamar put ashes on her head, and rent her garment of divers colours that *was* on her, and laid her hand on her head, and went on crying.

20And Absalom her brother said unto her, Hath Amnon thy brother been with thee? but hold now thy peace, my sister: he *is* thy brother; regard not this thing. So Tamar remained desolate in her brother Absalom's house.

21But when king David heard of all these things, he was very wroth.

22And Absalom spake unto his brother Amnon neither good nor bad: for Absalom hated Amnon, because he had forced his sister Tamar.

23And it came to pass after two full years, that Absalom had sheepshearers in Baalhazor, which *is* beside Ephraim: and Absalom invited all the king's sons.

24And Absalom came to the king, and said, Behold now, thy servant hath sheepshearers; let the king, I beseech thee, and his servants go with thy servant.

25And the king said to Absalom, Nay, my son, let us not all now go, lest we be chargeable unto thee. And he pressed him: howbeit he would not go, but blessed him.

26Then said Absalom, If not, I pray thee, let my brother Amnon go with us. And the king said unto him, Why should he go with thee?

27But Absalom pressed him, that he let Amnon and all the king's sons go with him.

28Now Absalom had commanded his servants, saying, Mark ye now when Amnon's heart is merry with wine, and when I say unto you, Smite Amnon; then kill him, fear not: have not I commanded you? be courageous, and be valiant.

29And the servants of Absalom did unto Amnon as Absalom had commanded. Then all the king's sons arose, and every man gat him up upon his mule, and fled.

30And it came to pass, while they were in the way, that tidings came to David, saying, Absalom hath slain all the king's sons, and there is not one of them left.

31Then the king arose, and tare his garments, and lay on the earth; and all his servants stood by with their clothes rent.

32And Jonadab, the son of Shimeah David's brother, answered and said, Let not my lord suppose *that* they have slain all the young men the king's sons; for Amnon only is dead: for by the appointment of Absalom this hath been determined from the day that he forced his sister Tamar.

33Now therefore let not my lord the king take the thing to his heart, to think that all the king's sons are dead: for Amnon only is dead.

34But Absalom fled. And the young man that kept the watch lifted up his eyes, and looked, and, behold, there came much people by the way of the hill side behind him.

35And Jonadab said unto the king, Behold, the king's sons come: as thy servant said, so it is.

36And it came to pass, as soon as he had made an end of speaking, that, behold, the king's sons came, and lifted up their voice and wept: and the king also and all his servants wept very sore.

37But Absalom fled, and went to Talmai, the son of Ammihud, king of Geshur. And *David* mourned for his son every day.

38So Absalom fled, and went to Geshur, and was there three years.

39And *the soul of* king David longed to go forth unto Absalom: for he was comforted concerning Amnon, seeing he was dead.

JOHN 17:1–26

THESE words spake Jesus, and lifted up his eyes to heaven, and said, Father, the hour is come; glorify thy Son, that thy Son also may glorify thee:

2As thou hast given him power over all flesh, that he should give eternal life to as many as thou hast given him.

3And this is life eternal, that they might know thee the only true God, and Jesus Christ, whom thou hast sent.

4I have glorified thee on the earth: I have finished the work which thou gavest me to do.

5And now, O Father, glorify thou me with thine own self with the glory which I had with thee before the world was.

6I have manifested thy name unto the men which thou gavest me out of the world: thine they were, and thou gavest them me; and they have kept thy word.

7Now they have known that all things whatsoever thou hast given me are of thee.

8For I have given unto them the words which thou gavest me; and they have received *them,* and have known surely that I came out from thee, and they have believed that thou didst send me.

9I pray for them: I pray not for the world, but for them which thou hast given me; for they are thine.

10And all mine are thine, and thine are mine; and I am glorified in them.

11And now I am no more in the world, but these are in the world, and I come to thee. Holy Father, keep through thine own name those whom thou hast given me, that they may be one, as we *are.*

12While I was with them in the world, I kept them in thy name: those that thou gavest me I have kept, and none of them is lost, but the son of perdition; that the scripture might be fulfilled.

13And now come I to thee; and these things I speak in the world, that they might have my joy fulfilled in themselves.

14I have given them thy word; and the world hath hated them, because they are not of the world, even as I am not of the world.

15I pray not that thou shouldest take

them out of the world, but that thou shouldest keep them from the evil.

16They are not of the world, even as I am not of the world.

17Sanctify them through thy truth: thy word is truth.

18As thou hast sent me into the world, even so have I also sent them into the world.

19And for their sakes I sanctify myself, that they also might be sanctified through the truth.

20Neither pray I for these alone, but for them also which shall believe on me through their word;

21That they all may be one; as thou, Father, *art* in me, and I in thee, that they also may be one in us: that the world may believe that thou hast sent me.

22And the glory which thou gavest me I have given them; that they may be one, even as we are one:

23I in them, and thou in me, that they may be made perfect in one; and that the world may know that thou hast sent me, and hast loved them, as thou hast loved me.

24Father, I will that they also, whom thou hast given me, be with me where I am; that they may behold my glory, which thou hast given me: for thou lovedst me before the foundation of the world.

25O righteous Father, the world hath not known thee: but I have known thee, and these have known that thou hast sent me.

26And I have declared unto them thy name, and will declare *it:* that the love wherewith thou hast loved me may be in them, and I in them.

PSALM 119:81–95

My soul fainteth for thy salvation: *but* I hope in thy word. 82Mine eyes fail for thy word, saying, When wilt thou comfort me?

83For I am become like a bottle in the smoke; *yet* do I not forget thy statutes.

84How many *are* the days of thy servant? when wilt thou execute judgment on them that persecute me?

85The proud have digged pits for me, which *are* not after thy law.

86All thy commandments *are* faithful: they persecute me wrongfully; help thou me.

87They had almost consumed me upon earth; but I forsook not thy precepts.

88Quicken me after thy lovingkindness; so shall I keep the testimony of thy mouth.

89For ever, O LORD, thy word is settled in heaven.

90Thy faithfulness *is* unto all generations: thou hast established the earth, and it abideth.

91They continue this day according to thine ordinances: for all *are* thy servants.

92Unless thy law *had been* my delights, I should then have perished in mine affliction.

93I will never forget thy precepts: for with them thou hast quickened me.

94I *am* thine, save me; for I have sought thy precepts.

95The wicked have waited for me to destroy me: *but* I will consider thy testimonies.

PROVERBS FOR TODAY/ 16:6–7

By mercy and truth iniquity is purged: and by the fear of the LORD men depart from evil. ☐ *When a man's ways please the LORD, he maketh even his enemies to be at peace with him.*

MAY 29

2 SAMUEL 14:1—15:22

Now Joab the son of Zeruiah perceived that the king's heart *was* toward Absalom.

2And Joab sent to Tekoah, and fetched thence a wise woman, and said unto her, I pray thee, feign thyself to be a mourner, and put on now mourning apparel, and anoint not thyself with oil, but be as a woman that had a long time mourned for the dead:

3And come to the king, and speak on this manner unto him. So Joab put the words in her mouth.

4And when the woman of Tekoah spake to the king, she fell on her face to the ground, and did obeisance, and said, Help, O king.

5And the king said unto her, What aileth thee? And she answered, I *am* indeed a widow woman, and mine husband is dead.

6And thy handmaid had two sons, and they two strove together in the field, and *there was* none to part them, but the one smote the other, and slew him.

7And, behold, the whole family is risen against thine handmaid, and they said, Deliver him that smote his brother, that we may kill him, for the life of his brother whom he slew; and we will destroy the heir also: and so they shall quench my coal which is left, and shall not leave to my husband *neither* name nor remainder upon the earth.

8And the king said unto the woman, Go to thine house, and I will give charge concerning thee.

9And the woman of Tekoah said unto the king, My lord, O king, the iniquity *be* on me, and on my father's house: and the king and his throne *be* guiltless.

10And the king said, Whosoever saith *ought* unto thee, bring him to me, and he shall not touch thee any more.

11Then said she, I pray thee, let the king remember the LORD thy God, that thou wouldest not suffer the revengers of blood to destroy any more, lest they destroy my son. And he said, *As* the LORD liveth, there shall not one hair of thy son fall to the earth.

12Then the woman said, Let thine handmaid, I pray thee, speak *one* word unto my lord the king. And he said, Say on.

13And the woman said, Wherefore then hast thou thought such a thing against the people of God? for the king doth speak this thing as one which is faulty, in that the king doth not fetch home again his banished.

14For we must needs die, and *are* as water spilt on the ground, which cannot be gathered up again; neither doth God respect *any* person: yet doth he devise means, that his banished be not expelled from him.

15Now therefore that I am come to speak of this thing unto my lord the king, *it is* because the people have made me afraid: and thy handmaid said, I will now speak unto the king; it may be that the king will perform the request of his handmaid.

16For the king will hear, to deliver his handmaid out of the hand of the man *that would* destroy me and my son together out of the inheritance of God.

17Then thine handmaid said, The word of my lord the king shall now be comfortable: for as an angel of God, so *is* my lord the king to discern good and bad: therefore the LORD thy God will be with thee.

18Then the king answered and said unto the woman, Hide not from me, I pray thee, the thing that I shall ask thee. And the woman said, Let my lord the king now speak.

19And the king said, *Is not* the hand of Joab with thee in all this? And the woman answered and said, *As* thy soul liveth, my lord the king, none can turn to the right hand or to the left from ought that my lord the king hath spoken: for thy servant Joab, he bade me, and he put all these words in the mouth of thine handmaid:

20To fetch about this form of speech hath thy servant Joab done this thing: and my lord *is* wise, according to the wisdom of an angel of God, to know all *things* that *are* in the earth.

21And the king said unto Joab, Behold now, I have done this thing: go therefore, bring the young man Absalom again.

22And Joab fell to the ground on his face, and bowed himself, and thanked the king: and Joab said, To day thy servant knoweth that I have found grace in thy sight, my lord, O king, in that the king hath fulfilled the request of his servant.

23So Joab arose and went to Geshur, and brought Absalom to Jerusalem.

24And the king said, Let him turn to his own house, and let him not see my face. So Absalom returned to his own house, and saw not the king's face.

25But in all Israel there was none to be so much praised as Absalom for his beauty: from the sole of his foot even to the crown of his head there was no blemish in him.

26And when he polled his head, (for it was at every year's end that he polled *it:* because *the hair* was heavy on him, therefore he polled it:) he weighed the hair of his head at two hundred shekels after the king's weight.

27And unto Absalom there were born three sons, and one daughter, whose name *was* Tamar: she was a woman of a fair countenance.

28So Absalom dwelt two full years in Jerusalem, and saw not the king's face.

29Therefore Absalom sent for Joab, to have sent him to the king; but he would not come to him: and when he sent again the second time, he would not come.

30Therefore he said unto his servants, See, Joab's field is near mine, and he hath barley there; go and set it on fire. And Absalom's servants set the field on fire.

31Then Joab arose, and came to Absalom unto *his* house, and said unto him, Wherefore have thy servants set my field on fire?

32And Absalom answered Joab, Behold, I sent unto thee, saying, Come hither, that I may send thee to the king, to say, Wherefore am I come from Geshur? *it had been* good for me *to have been* there still: now therefore let me see the king's face; and if there be *any* iniquity in me, let him kill me.

33So Joab came to the king, and told him: and when he had called for Absalom, he came to the king, and bowed himself on his face to the ground before the king: and the king kissed Absalom.

AND it came to pass after this, that Absalom prepared him chariots and horses, and fifty men to run before him.

2And Absalom rose up early, and stood beside the way of the gate: and it was *so,* that when any man that had a controversy came to the king for judgment, then Absalom called unto him, and said, Of what city *art* thou? And he said, Thy servant *is* of one of the tribes of Israel.

3And Absalom said unto him, See, thy matters *are* good and right; but *there is* no man *deputed* of the king to hear thee.

4Absalom said moreover, Oh that I were made judge in the land, that every man which hath any suit or cause might come unto me, and I would do him justice!

5And it was *so,* that when any man came nigh *to him* to do him obeisance, he put forth his hand, and took him, and kissed him.

6And on this manner did Absalom to all Israel that came to the king for judgment: so Absalom stole the hearts of the men of Israel.

7And it came to pass after forty years, that Absalom said unto the king, I pray thee, let me go and pay my vow, which I have vowed unto the LORD, in Hebron.

8For thy servant vowed a vow while I abode at Geshur in Syria, saying, If the LORD shall bring me again indeed to Jerusalem, then I will serve the LORD.

9And the king said unto him, Go in peace. So he arose, and went to Hebron.

10But Absalom sent spies throughout all the tribes of Israel, saying, As soon as ye hear the sound of the trumpet, then ye shall say, Absalom reigneth in Hebron.

11And with Absalom went two hundred men out of Jerusalem, *that were* called; and they went in their simplicity, and they knew not any thing.

12And Absalom sent for Ahithophel the Gilonite, David's counselor, from his city, *even* from Giloh, while he offered sacrifices. And the conspiracy was strong; for the people increased continually with Absalom.

13And there came a messenger to David, saying, The hearts of the men of Israel are after Absalom.

14And David said unto all his servants that *were* with him at Jerusalem, Arise, and let us flee; for we shall not *else* escape from Absalom: make speed to depart, lest he overtake us suddenly, and bring evil upon us, and smite the city with the edge of the sword.

15And the king's servants said unto the king, Behold, thy servants *are ready to do* whatsoever my lord the king shall appoint.

16And the king went forth, and all his household after him. And the king left ten women, *which were* concubines, to keep the house.

17And the king went forth, and all the people after him, and tarried in a place that was far off.

18And all his servants passed on beside him; and all the Cherethites, and all the Pelethites, and all the Gittites, six hundred men which came after him from Gath, passed on before the king.

19Then said the king to Ittai the Gittite, Wherefore goest thou also with us? return to thy place, and abide with the king: for thou *art* a stranger, and also an exile.

20Whereas thou camest *but* yesterday, should I this day make thee go up and down with us? seeing I go whither I may, return thou, and take back thy brethren: mercy and truth *be* with thee.

21And Ittai answered the king, and said, *As* the LORD liveth, and *as* my lord the king liveth, surely in what place my lord the king shall be, whether in death or life, even there also will thy servant be.

22And David said to Ittai, Go and pass over. And Ittai the Gittite passed over, and all his men, and all the little ones that *were* with him.

JOHN 18:1–24

WHEN Jesus had spoken these words, he went forth with his disciples over the brook Cedron, where was a garden, into the which he entered, and his disciples.

2And Judas also, which betrayed him, knew the place: for Jesus ofttimes resorted thither with his disciples.

3Judas then, having received a band *of men* and officers from the chief priests and Pharisees, cometh thither with lanterns and torches and weapons.

4Jesus therefore, knowing all things that should come upon him, went forth, and said unto them, Whom seek ye?

5They answered him, Jesus of Nazareth. Jesus saith unto them, I am *he.* And Judas also, which betrayed him, stood with them.

6As soon then as he had said unto them, I am *he,* they went backward, and fell to the ground.

7Then asked he them again, Whom seek ye? And they said, Jesus of Nazareth.

8Jesus answered, I have told you that I am *he:* if therefore ye seek me, let these go their way:

9That the saying might be fulfilled, which he spake, Of them which thou gavest me have I lost none.

10Then Simon Peter having a sword drew it, and smote the high priest's servant, and cut off his right ear. The servant's name was Malchus.

11Then said Jesus unto Peter, Put up thy sword into the sheath: the cup which my Father hath given me, shall I not drink it?

12Then the band and the captain and officers of the Jews took Jesus, and bound him,

13And led him away to Annas first; for he was father in law to Caiaphas, which was the high priest that same year.

14Now Caiaphas was he, which gave counsel to the Jews, that it was expedient that one man should die for the people.

15And Simon Peter followed Jesus, and *so did* another disciple: that disciple was known unto the high priest, and went in with Jesus into the palace of the high priest.

16But Peter stood at the door without. Then went out that other disciple, which was known unto the high priest, and spake unto her that kept the door, and brought in Peter.

17Then saith the damsel that kept the door unto Peter, Art not thou also *one* of this man's disciples? He saith, I am not.

18And the servants and officers stood there, who had made a fire of coals; for it was cold: and they warmed themselves: and Peter stood with them, and warmed himself.

19The high priest then asked Jesus of his disciples, and of his doctrine.

20Jesus answered him, I spake openly to the world; I ever taught in the synagogue, and in the temple, whither the Jews always resort; and in secret have I said nothing.

21Why askest thou me? ask them which heard me, what I have said unto them: behold, they know what I said.

22And when he had thus spoken, one of the officers which stood by struck Jesus with the palm of his hand, saying, Answerest thou the high priest so?

23Jesus answered him, If I have spoken evil, bear witness of the evil: but if well, why smitest thou me?

24Now Annas had sent him bound unto Caiaphas the high priest.

PSALM 119:96–112

I have seen an end of all perfection: *but* thy commandment *is* exceeding broad.

97O how love I thy law! it *is* my meditation all the day.

98Thou through thy commandments hast made me wiser than mine enemies: for they *are* ever with me.

99I have more understanding than all my teachers: for thy testimonies *are* my meditation.

100I understand more than the ancients, because I keep thy precepts.

101I have refrained my feet from every evil way, that I might keep thy word.

102I have not departed from thy judgments: for thou hast taught me.

103How sweet are thy words unto my taste! *yea, sweeter* than honey to my mouth!

104Through thy precepts I get understanding: therefore I hate every false way.

105Thy word *is* a lamp unto my feet, and a light unto my path.

106I have sworn, and I will perform *it,* that I will keep thy righteous judgments.

107I am afflicted very much: quicken me, O LORD, according unto thy word.

108Accept, I beseech thee, the freewill offerings of my mouth, O LORD, and teach me thy judgments.

109My soul *is* continually in my hand: yet do I not forget thy law.

110The wicked have laid a snare for me: yet I erred not from thy precepts.

111Thy testimonies have I taken as an heritage for ever: for they *are* the rejoicing of my heart.

112I have inclined mine heart to perform thy statutes alway, *even unto* the end.

PROVERBS FOR TODAY/ 16:8–9

Better is *a little with righteousness than great revenues without right.*   □*A man's heart deviseth his way: but the* LORD *directeth his steps.*

MAY 30

2 SAMUEL 15:23—16:23

AND all the country wept with a loud voice, and all the people passed over: the king also himself passed over the brook Kidron, and all the people passed over, toward the way of the wilderness.

24And lo Zadok also, and all the Levites *were* with him, bearing the ark of the covenant of God: and they set down the ark of God; and Abiathar went up, until all the people had done passing out of the city.

25And the king said unto Zadok, Carry back the ark of God into the city: if I shall find favour in the eyes of the LORD, he will bring me again, and shew me *both* it, and his habitation:

26But if he thus say, I have no delight in thee; behold, *here am* I, let him do to me as seemeth good unto him.

27The king said also unto Zadok the priest, *Art not* thou a seer? return into the city in peace, and your two sons with you, Ahimaaz thy son, and Jonathan the son of Abiathar.

28See, I will tarry in the plain of the wilderness, until there come word from you to certify me.

29Zadok therefore and Abiathar carried the ark of God again to Jerusalem: and they tarried there.

30And David went up by the ascent of *mount* Olivet, and wept as he went up, and had his head covered, and he went barefoot: and all the people that *was* with him covered every man his head, and they went up, weeping as they went up.

31And *one* told David, saying Ahithophel *is* among the conspirators with Absalom. And David said, O LORD, I pray thee, turn the counsel of Ahithophel into foolishness.

32And it came to pass, that *when* David was come to the top *of the mount,* where he worshipped God, behold, Hushai the Archite came to meet him with his coat rent, and earth upon his head:

33Unto whom David said, If thou passest on with me, then thou shalt be a burden unto me:

34But if thou return to the city, and say unto Absalom, I will be thy servant, O king; as I have been thy father's servant hitherto, so will I now also be thy servant: then mayest thou for me defeat the counsel of Ahithophel.

35And hast thou not there with thee Zadok and Abiathar the priests? therefore it shall be, that what thing soever thou shalt hear out of the king's house, thou shalt tell it to Zadok and Abiathar the priests.

36Behold, they have there with them their two sons, Ahimaaz Zadok's son, and Jonathan Abiathar's son; and by them ye shall send unto me every thing that ye can hear.

37So Hushai David's friend came into the city, and Absalom came into Jerusalem.

AND when David was a little past the top of the hill, behold, Ziba the servant of Mephibosheth met him, with a couple of asses saddled, and upon them two hundred loaves of bread, and an hundred bunches of raisins, and an hundred of summer fruits, and a bottle of wine.

2And the king said unto Ziba, What meanest thou by these? And Ziba said, The asses be for the king's household to ride on; and the bread and summer fruit for the young men to eat; and the wine, that such as be faint in the wilderness may drink.

3And the king said, And where is thy master's son? And Ziba said unto the king, Behold, he abideth at Jerusalem: for he said, To day shall the house of Israel restore me the kingdom of my father.

4Then said the king to Ziba, Behold, thine are all that pertained unto Mephibosheth. And Ziba said, I humbly beseech thee that I may find grace in thy sight, my lord, O king.

5And when king David came to Bahurim, behold, thence came out a man of the family of the house of Saul, whose name was Shimei, the son of Gera: he came forth, and cursed still as he came.

6And he cast stones at David, and at all the servants of king David: and all the people and all the mighty men were on his right hand and on his left.

7And thus said Shimei when he cursed, Come out, come out, thou bloody man, and thou man of Belial:

8The LORD hath returned upon thee all the blood of the house of Saul, in whose stead thou hast reigned; and the LORD hath delivered the kingdom into the hand of Absalom thy son: and, behold, thou art taken in thy mischief, because thou art a bloody man.

9Then said Abishai the son of Zeruiah unto the king, Why should this dead dog curse my lord the king? let me go over, I pray thee, and take off his head.

10And the king said, What have I to do with you, ye sons of Zeruiah? so let him curse, because the LORD hath said unto him, Curse David. Who shall then say, Wherefore hast thou done so?

11And David said to Abishai, and to all his servants, Behold, my son, which came forth of my bowels, seeketh my life: how much more now may this Benjamite do it? let him alone, and let him curse; for the LORD hath bidden him.

12It may be that the LORD will look on mine affliction, and that the LORD will requite me good for his cursing this day.

13And as David and his men went by the way, Shimei went along on the hill's side over against him, and cursed as he went, and threw stones at him, and cast dust.

14And the king, and all the people that were with him, came weary, and refreshed themselves there.

15And Absalom, and all the people the men of Israel, came to Jerusalem, and Ahithophel with him.

16And it came to pass, when Hushai

the Archite, David's friend, was come unto Absalom, that Hushai said unto Absalom, God save the king, God save the king.

17And Absalom said to Hushai, *Is* this thy kindness to thy friend? why wentest thou not with thy friend?

18And Hushai said unto Absalom, Nay; but whom the LORD, and this people, and all the men of Israel, choose, his will I be, and with him will I abide.

19And again, whom should I serve? *should I* not *serve* in the presence of his son? as I have served in thy father's presence, so will I be in thy presence.

20Then said Absalom to Ahithophel, Give counsel among you what we shall do.

21And Ahithophel said unto Absalom, Go in unto thy father's concubines, which he hath left to keep the house; and all Israel shall hear that thou art abhorred of thy father: then shall the hands of all that *are* with thee be strong.

22So they spread Absalom a tent upon the top of the house; and Absalom went in unto his father's concubines in the sight of all Israel.

23And the counsel of Ahithophel, which he counselled in those days, *was* as if a man had enquired at the oracle of God: so *was* all the counsel of Ahithophel both with David and with Absalom.

JOHN 18:25—19:22

AND Simon Peter stood and warmed himself. They said therefore unto him, Art not thou also *one* of his disciples? He denied *it,* and said, I am not.

26One of the servants of the high priest, being *his* kinsman whose ear Peter cut off, saith, Did not I see thee in the garden with him?

27Peter then denied again: and immediately the cock crew.

28Then led they Jesus from Caiaphas unto the hall of judgment: and it was early; and they themselves went not into the judgment hall, lest they should be defiled; but that they might eat the passover.

29Pilate then went out unto them, and said, What accusation bring ye against this man?

30They answered and said unto him, If he were not a malefactor, we would not have delivered him up unto thee.

31Then said Pilate unto them, Take ye him, and judge him according to your law. The Jews therefore said unto him, It is not lawful for us to put any man to death:

32That the saying of Jesus might be fulfilled, which he spake, signifying what death he should die.

33Then Pilate entered into the judgment hall again, and called Jesus, and said unto him, Art thou the King of the Jews?

34Jesus answered him, Sayest thou this thing of thyself, or did others tell it thee of me?

35Pilate answered, Am I a Jew? Thine own nation and the chief priests have delivered thee unto me: what hast thou done?

36Jesus answered, My kingdom is not of this world: if my kingdom were of this world, then would my servants fight, that I should not be delivered to the Jews: but now is my kingdom not from hence.

37Pilate therefore said unto him, Art thou a king then? Jesus answered, Thou sayest that I am a king. To this end was I born, and for this cause came I into the world, that I should bear witness unto the truth. Every one that is of the truth heareth my voice.

38Pilate saith unto him, What is truth? And when he had said this, he went out again unto the Jews, and saith unto them, I find in him no fault *at all.*

39But ye have a custom, that I should release unto you one at the passover: will ye therefore that I release unto you the King of the Jews?

40Then cried they all again, saying,

Not this man, but Barabbas. Now Barabbas was a robber.

THEN Pilate therefore took Jesus, and scourged *him*.

2And the soldiers platted a crown of thorns, and put *it* on his head, and they put on him a purple robe,

3And said, Hail, King of the Jews! and they smote him with their hands.

4Pilate therefore went forth again, and saith unto them, Behold, I bring him forth to you, that ye may know that I find no fault in him.

5Then came Jesus forth, wearing the crown of thorns, and the purple robe. And *Pilate* saith unto them, Behold the man!

6When the chief priests therefore and officers saw him, they cried out, saying, Crucify *him,* crucify *him*. Pilate saith unto them, Take ye him, and crucify *him:* for I find no fault in him.

7The Jews answered him, We have a law, and by our law he ought to die, because he made himself the Son of God.

8When Pilate therefore heard that saying, he was the more afraid;

9And went again into the judgment hall, and saith unto Jesus, Whence art thou? But Jesus gave him no answer.

10Then saith Pilate unto him, Speakest thou not unto me? knowest thou not that I have power to crucify thee, and have power to release thee?

11Jesus answered, Thou couldest have no power *at all* against me, except it were given thee from above: therefore he that delivered me unto thee hath the greater sin.

12And from thenceforth Pilate sought to release him: but the Jews cried out, saying, If thou let this man go, thou art not Caesar's friend: whosoever maketh himself a king speaketh against Caesar.

13When Pilate therefore heard that saying, he brought Jesus forth, and sat down in the judgment seat in a place that is called the Pavement, but in the Hebrew, Gabbatha.

14And it was the preparation of the passover, and about the sixth hour: and he saith unto the Jews, Behold your King!

15But they cried out, Away with *him,* away with *him,* crucify him. Pilate saith unto them, Shall I crucify your King? The chief priests answered, We have no king but Caesar.

16Then delivered he him therefore unto them to be crucified. And they took Jesus, and led *him* away.

17And he bearing his cross went forth into a place called *the place* of a skull, which is called in the Hebrew Golgotha:

18Where they crucified him, and two other with him, on either side one, and Jesus in the midst.

19And Pilate wrote a title, and put *it* on the cross. And the writing was, JESUS OF NAZARETH THE KING OF THE JEWS.

20This title then read many of the Jews: for the place where Jesus was crucified was nigh to the city: and it was written in Hebrew, *and* Greek, *and* Latin.

21Then said the chief priests of the Jews to Pilate, Write not, The king of the Jews; but that he said, I am King of the Jews.

22Pilate answered, What I have written I have written.

PSALM 119:113–131

I hate vain thoughts: but thy law do I love.

114Thou *art* my hiding place and my shield: I hope in thy word.

115Depart from me, ye evildoers: for I will keep the commandments of my God.

116Uphold me according unto thy word, that I may live: and let me not be ashamed of my hope.

117Hold thou me up, and I shall be safe: and I will have respect unto thy statutes continually.

118Thou hast trodden down all them that err from thy statutes: for their deceit *is* falsehood.

119Thou puttest away all the wicked of the earth *like* dross: therefore I love thy testimonies.

120My flesh trembleth for fear of thee; and I am afraid of thy judgments.

121I have done judgment and justice: leave me not to mine oppressors.

122Be surety for thy servant for good: let not the proud oppress me.

123Mine eyes fail for thy salvation, and for the word of thy righteousness.

124Deal with thy servant according unto thy mercy, and teach me thy statutes.

125I *am* thy servant; give me understanding, that I may know thy testimonies.

126*It is* time for *thee*, LORD, to work: *for* they have made void thy law.

127Therefore I love thy commandments above gold; yea, above fine gold.

128Therefore I esteem all *thy* precepts *concerning* all *things to be* right; *and* I hate every false way.

129Thy testimonies *are* wonderful: therefore doth my soul keep them.

130The entrance of thy words giveth light; it giveth understanding unto the simple.

131I opened my mouth, and panted: for I longed for thy commandments.

PROVERBS FOR TODAY/ 16:10–11

A divine sentence is *in the lips of the king: his mouth transgresseth not in judgment.* □*A just weight and balance* are *the LORD'S: all the weights of the bag* are *his work.*

MAY 31

2 SAMUEL 17:1–29

MOREOVER Ahithophel said unto Absalom, Let me now choose out twelve thousand men, and I will arise and pursue after David this night:

2And I will come upon him while he *is* weary and weak handed, and will make him afraid: and all the people that *are* with him shall flee; and I will smite the king only:

3And I will bring back all the people unto thee: the man whom thou seekest *is* as if all returned: *so* all the people shall be in peace.

4And the saying pleased Absalom well, and all the elders of Israel.

5Then said Absalom, Call now Hushai the Archite also, and let us hear likewise what he saith.

6And when Hushai was come to Absalom, Absalom spake unto him, saying, Ahithophel hath spoken after this manner: shall we do *after* his saying? if not; speak thou.

7And Hushai said unto Absalom, The counsel that Ahithophel hath given *is* not good at this time.

8For, said Hushai, thou knowest thy father and his men, that they *be* mighty men, and they *be* chafed in their minds, as a bear robbed of her whelps in the field: and thy father *is* a man of war, and will not lodge with the people.

9Behold, he is hid now in some pit, or in some *other* place: and it will come to pass, when some of them be overthrown at the first, that whosoever heareth it will say, There is a slaughter among the people that follow Absalom.

10And he also *that is* valiant, whose heart *is* as the heart of a lion, shall utterly melt: for all Israel knoweth that thy father *is* a mighty man, and *they* which *be* with him *are* valiant men.

11Therefore I counsel that all Israel be generally gathered unto thee, from Dan even to Beer–sheba, as the sand that *is* by the sea for multitude; and that thou go to battle in thine own person.

12So shall we come upon him in some place where he shall be found, and we will light upon him as the dew falleth on the ground: and of him and of all the men that *are* with him there shall not be left so much as one.

13Moreover, if he be gotten into a city, then shall all Israel bring ropes to that city, and we will draw it into the river, until there be not one small stone found there.

14And Absalom and all the men of Israel said, The counsel of Hushai the Archite *is* better than the counsel of Ahithophel. For the LORD had appointed to defeat the good counsel of Ahithophel, to the intent that the LORD might bring evil upon Absalom.

15Then said Hushai unto Zadok and to Abiathar the priests, Thus and thus did Ahithophel counsel Absalom and the elders of Israel; and thus and thus have I counselled.

16Now therefore send quickly, and tell David, saying, Lodge not this night in the plains of the wilderness, but speedily pass over; lest the king be swallowed up, and all the people that *are* with him.

17Now Jonathan and Ahimaaz stayed by En–rogel; for they might not be seen to come into the city: and a wench went and told them; and they went and told king David.

18Nevertheless a lad saw them, and told Absalom: but they went both of them away quickly, and came to a man's house in Bahurim, which had a well in his court; whither they went down.

19And the woman took and spread a covering over the well's mouth, and spread ground corn thereon; and the thing was not known.

20And when Absalom's servants came to the woman to the house, they said, Where *is* Ahimaaz and Jonathan? And the woman said unto them, They be gone over the brook of water. And when they had sought and could not find *them,* they returned to Jerusalem.

21And it came to pass, after they were departed, that they came up out of the well, and went and told king David, and said unto David, Arise, and pass quickly over the water: for thus hath Ahithophel counselled against you.

22Then David arose, and all the people that *were* with him, and they passed over Jordan: by the morning light there lacked not one of them that was not gone over Jordan.

23And when Ahithophel saw that his counsel was not followed, he saddled *his* ass, and arose, and gat him home to his house, to his city, and put his household in order, and hanged himself, and died, and was buried in the sepulchre of his father.

24Then David came to Mahanaim. And Absalom passed over Jordan, he and all the men of Israel with him.

25And Absalom made Amasa captain of the host instead of Joab: which Amasa *was* a man's son, whose name *was* Ithra an Israelite, that went in to Abigail the daughter of Nahash, sister to Zeruiah Joab's mother.

26So Israel and Absalom pitched in the land of Gilead.

27And it came to pass, when David was come to Mahanaim, that Shobi the son of Nahash of Rabbah of the children of Ammon, and Machir the son of Ammiel of Lo–debar, and Barzillai the Gileadite of Rogelim,

28Brought beds, and basons, and earthen vessels, and wheat, and barley, and flour, and parched *corn,* and beans, and lentiles, and parched *pulse,*

29And honey, and butter, and sheep, and cheese of kine, for David, and for the people that *were* with him, to eat: for they said, The people *is* hungry, and weary, and thirsty, in the wilderness.

JOHN 19:23–42

THEN the soldiers, when they had crucified Jesus, took his garments, and made four parts, to every soldier a part; and also *his* coat: now the coat was without seam, woven from the top throughout.

24They said therefore among themselves, Let us not rend it, but cast lots for it, whose it shall be: that the scripture might be fulfilled, which saith, They parted my raiment among them, and for my vesture they did cast lots. These things therefore the soldiers did.

25Now there stood by the cross of Jesus his mother, and his mother's sister, Mary the *wife* of Cleophas, and Mary Magdalene.

26When Jesus therefore saw his mother, and the disciple standing by, whom he loved, he saith unto his mother, Woman, behold thy son!

27Then saith he to the disciple, Behold thy mother! And from that hour that disciple took her unto his own *home.*

28After this, Jesus knowing that all things were now accomplished, that the scripture might be fulfilled, saith, I thirst.

29Now there was set a vessel full of vinegar: and they filled a spunge with vinegar, and put *it* upon hyssop, and put *it* to his mouth.

30When Jesus therefore had received the vinegar, he said, It is finished: and he bowed his head, and gave up the ghost.

31The Jews therefore, because it was the preparation, that the bodies should not remain upon the cross on the sabbath day, (for that sabbath day was an high day,) besought Pilate that their legs might be broken, and *that* they might be taken away.

32Then came the soldiers, and brake the legs of the first, and of the other which was crucified with him.

33But when they came to Jesus, and saw that he was dead already, they brake not his legs:

34But one of the soldiers with a spear pierced his side, and forthwith came there out blood and water.

35And he that saw *it* bare record, and his record is true: and he knoweth that he saith true, that ye might believe.

36For these things were done, that the scripture should be fulfilled, A bone of him shall not be broken.

37And again another scripture saith, They shall look on him whom they pierced.

38And after this Joseph of Arimathaea, being a disciple of Jesus, but secretly for fear of the Jews, besought Pilate that he might take away the body of Jesus: and Pilate gave *him* leave. He came therefore, and took the body of Jesus.

39And there came also Nicodemus, which at the first came to Jesus by night, and brought a mixture of myrrh and aloes, about an hundred pound *weight.*

40Then took they the body of Jesus, and wound it in linen clothes with the spices, as the manner of the Jews is to bury.

41Now in the place where he was crucified there was a garden; and in the garden a new sepulchre, wherein was never man yet laid.

42There laid they Jesus therefore because of the Jews' preparation *day;* for the sepulchre was nigh at hand.

PSALM 119:132-155

Look thou upon me, and be merciful unto me, as thou usest to do unto those that love thy name. 133Order my steps in thy word: and let not any iniquity have dominion over me.

134Deliver me from the oppression of man: so will I keep thy precepts.

135Make thy face to shine upon thy servant; and teach me thy statutes.

136Rivers of waters run down mine eyes, because they keep not thy law.

137Righteous *art* thou, O LORD, and upright *are* thy judgments.

138Thy testimonies *that* thou hast commanded *are* righteous and very faithful.

139My zeal hath consumed me, because mine enemies have forgotten thy words.

140Thy word *is* very pure: therefore thy servant loveth it.

141I *am* small and despised: *yet* do not I forget thy precepts.

142Thy righteousness *is* an everlasting righteousness, and thy law *is* the truth.

143Trouble and anguish have taken hold on me: *yet* thy commandments *are* my delights.

144The righteousness of thy testimonies *is* everlasting: give me understanding, and I shall live.

145I cried with *my* whole heart; hear me, O LORD: I will keep thy statutes.

146I cried unto thee; save me, and I shall keep thy testimonies.

147I prevented the dawning of the morning, and cried: I hoped in thy word.

148Mine eyes prevent the *night* watches, that I might meditate in thy word.

149Hear my voice according unto thy lovingkindness: O LORD, quicken me according to thy judgment.

150They draw nigh that follow after mischief: they are far from thy law.

151Thou *art* near, O LORD; and all thy commandments *are* truth.

152Concerning thy testimonies, I have known of old that thou hast founded them for ever.

153Consider mine affliction, and deliver me: for I do not forget thy law.

154Plead my cause, and deliver me: quicken me according to thy word.

155Salvation *is* far from the wicked: for they seek not thy statutes.

PROVERBS FOR TODAY/ 16:12-13

It is *an abomination to kings to commit wickedness: for the throne is established by righteousness. Righteous lips* are *the delight of kings; and they love him that speaketh right.*

JUNE 1

2 SAMUEL 18:1—19:10

And David numbered the people that *were* with him, and set captains of thousands and captains of hundreds over them.

2And David sent forth a third part of the people under the hand of Joab, and a third part under the hand of Abishai the son of Zeruiah, Joab's brother, and a third part under the hand of Ittai the

Gittite. And the king said unto the people, I will surely go forth with you myself also.

3But the people answered, Thou shalt not go forth: for if we flee away, they will not care for us; neither if half of us die, will they care for us: but now *thou art* worth ten thousand of us: therefore now *it is* better that thou succour us out of the city.

4And the king said unto them, What seemeth you best I will do. And the king stood by the gate side, and all the people came out by hundreds and by thousands.

5And the king commanded Joab and Abishai and Ittai, saying, *Deal* gently for my sake with the young man, *even* with Absalom. And all the people heard when the king gave all the captains charge concerning Absalom.

6So the people went out into the field against Israel: and the battle was in the wood of Ephraim;

7Where the people of Israel were slain before the servants of David, and there was there a great slaughter that day of twenty thousand *men*.

8For the battle was there scattered over the face of all the country: and the wood devoured more people that day than the sword devoured.

9And Absalom met the servants of David. And Absalom rode upon a mule, and the mule went under the thick boughs of a great oak, and his head caught hold of the oak, and he was taken up between the heaven and the earth; and the mule that *was* under him went away.

10And a certain man saw *it*, and told Joab, and said, Behold, I saw Absalom hanged in an oak.

11And Joab said unto the man that told him, And, behold, thou sawest *him,* and why didst thou not smite him there to the ground? and I would have given thee ten *shekels* of silver, and a girdle.

12And the man said unto Joab, Though I should receive a thousand *shekels* of silver in mine hand, *yet* would I not put forth mine hand against the king's son: for in our hearing the king charged thee and Abishai and Ittai, saying, Beware that none *touch* the young man Absalom.

13Otherwise I should have wrought falsehood against mine own life: for there is no matter hid from the king, and thou thyself wouldest have set thyself against *me.*

14Then said Joab, I may not tarry thus with thee. And he took three darts in his hand, and thrust them through the heart of Absalom, while he *was* yet alive in the midst of the oak.

15And ten young men that bare Joab's armour compassed about and smote Absalom, and slew him.

16And Joab blew the trumpet, and the people returned from pursuing after Israel: for Joab held back the people.

17And they took Absalom, and cast him into a great pit in the wood, and laid a very great heap of stones upon him: and all Israel fled every one to his tent.

18Now Absalom in his lifetime had taken and reared up for himself a pillar, which *is* in the king's dale: for he said, I have no son to keep my name in remembrance: and he called the pillar after his own name: and it is called unto this day, Absalom's place.

19Then said Ahimaaz the son of Zadok, Let me now run, and bear the king tidings, how that the LORD hath avenged him of his enemies.

20And Joab said unto him, Thou shalt not bear tidings this day, but thou shalt bear tidings another day: but this day thou shalt bear no tidings, because the king's son is dead.

21Then said Joab to Cushi, Go tell the king what thou hast seen. And Cushi bowed himself unto Joab, and ran.

22Then said Ahimaaz the son of Zadok yet again to Joab, But howsoever, let me, I pray thee, also run after Cushi. And Joab said, Wherefore wilt thou run, my son, seeing that thou hast no tidings ready?

23But howsoever, *said he,* let me run. And he said unto him, Run. Then Ahimaaz ran by the way of the plain, and overran Cushi.

24And David sat between the two gates: and the watchman went up to the roof over the gate unto the wall, and lifted up his eyes, and looked, and behold a man running alone.

25And the watchman cried, and told the king. And the king said, If he *be* alone, *there is* tidings in his mouth. And he came apace, and drew near.

26And the watchman saw another man running: and the watchman called unto the porter, and said, Behold *another* man running alone. And the king said, He also bringeth tidings.

27And the watchman said, Me thinketh the running of the foremost is like the running of Ahimaaz the son of Zadok. And the king said, He *is* a good man, and cometh with good tidings.

28And Ahimaaz called, and said unto the king, All is well. And he fell down to the earth upon his face before the king, and said, Blessed *be* the LORD thy God, which hath delivered up the men that lifted up their hand against my lord the king.

29And the king said, Is the young man Absalom safe? And Ahimaaz answered, When Joab sent the king's servant, and *me* thy servant, I saw a great tumult, but I knew not what *it was.*

30And the king said *unto him,* Turn aside, *and* stand here. And he turned aside, and stood still.

31And, behold, Cushi came; and Cushi said, Tidings, my lord the king: for the LORD hath avenged thee this day of all them that rose up against thee.

32And the king said unto Cushi, *Is* the young man Absalom safe? And Cushi answered, The enemies of my lord the king, and all that rise against thee to do *thee* hurt, be as *that* young man *is.*

33And the king was much moved, and went up to the chamber over the gate, and wept: and as he went, thus he said, O my son Absalom, my son, my son Absalom! would God I had died for thee, O Absalom, my son, my son!

AND it was told Joab, Behold, the king weepeth and mourneth for Absalom.

2And the victory that day was *turned* into mourning unto all the people: for the people heard say that day how the king was grieved for his son.

3And the people gat them by stealth that day into the city, as people being ashamed steal away when they flee in battle.

4But the king covered his face, and the king cried with a loud voice, O my son Absalom, O Absalom, my son, my son!

5And Joab came into the house to the king, and said, Thou hast shamed this day the faces of all thy servants, which this day have saved thy life, and the lives of thy sons and of thy daughters, and the lives of thy wives, and the lives of thy concubines;

6In that thou lovest thine enemies, and hatest thy friends. For thou hast declared this day, that thou regardest neither princes nor servants: for this day I perceive, that if Absalom had lived, and all we had died this day, then it had pleased thee well.

7Now therefore arise, go forth, and speak comfortably unto thy servants: for I swear by the LORD, if thou go not forth, there will not tarry one with thee this night: and that will be worse unto thee than all the evil that befell thee from thy youth until now.

8Then the king arose, and sat in the gate. And they told unto all the people, saying, Behold, the king doth sit in the gate. And all the people came before the king: for Israel had fled every man to his tent.

9And all the people were at strife throughout all the tribes of Israel, saying, The king saved us out of the hand of our enemies, and he delivered us out of the hand of the Philistines; and now he is fled out of the land for Absalom.

¹⁰And Absalom, whom we anointed over us, is dead in battle. Now therefore why speak ye not a word of bringing the king back?

JOHN 20:1–31

THE first *day* of the week cometh Mary Magdalene early, when it was yet dark, unto the sepulchre, and seeth the stone taken away from the sepulchre.

²Then she runneth, and cometh to Simon Peter, and to the other disciple, whom Jesus loved, and saith unto them, They have taken away the Lord out of the sepulchre, and we know not where they have laid him.

³Peter therefore went forth, and that other disciple, and came to the sepulchre.

⁴So they ran both together: and the other disciple did outrun Peter, and came first to the sepulchre.

⁵And he stooping down, *and looking in,* saw the linen clothes lying; yet went he not in.

⁶Then cometh Simon Peter following him, and went into the sepulchre, and seeth the linen clothes lie,

⁷And the napkin, that was about his head, not lying with the linen clothes, but wrapped together in a place by itself.

⁸Then went in also that other disciple, which came first to the sepulchre, and he saw, and believed.

⁹For as yet they knew not the scripture, that he must rise again from the dead.

¹⁰Then the disciples went away again unto their own home.

¹¹But Mary stood without at the sepulchre weeping: and as she wept, she stooped down, *and looked* into the sepulchre,

¹²And seeth two angels in white sitting, the one at the head, and the other at the feet, where the body of Jesus had lain.

¹³And they say unto her, Woman, why weepest thou? She saith unto them, Because they have taken away my Lord, and I know not where they have laid him.

¹⁴And when she had thus said, she turned herself back, and saw Jesus standing, and knew not that it was Jesus.

¹⁵Jesus saith unto her, Woman, why weepest thou? whom seekest thou? She, supposing him to be the gardener, saith unto him, Sir, if thou have borne him hence, tell me where thou hast laid him, and I will take him away.

¹⁶Jesus saith unto her, Mary. She turned herself, and saith unto him, Rabboni; which is to say, Master.

¹⁷Jesus saith unto her, Touch me not; for I am not yet ascended to my Father: but go to my brethren, and say unto them, I ascend unto my Father, and your Father; and *to* my God, and your God.

¹⁸Mary Magdalene came and told the disciples that she had seen the Lord, and *that* he had spoken these things unto her.

¹⁹Then the same day at evening, being the first *day* of the week, when the doors were shut where the disciples were assembled for fear of the Jews, came Jesus and stood in the midst, and saith unto them, Peace *be* unto you.

²⁰And when he had so said, he shewed unto them *his* hands and his side. Then were the disciples glad, when they saw the Lord.

²¹Then said Jesus to them again, Peace *be* unto you: as *my* Father hath sent me, even so send I you.

²²And when he had said this, he breathed on *them,* and saith unto them, Receive ye the Holy Ghost:

²³Whose soever sins ye remit, they are remitted unto them; *and* whose soever *sins* ye retain, they are retained.

24But Thomas, one of the twelve, called Didymus, was not with them when Jesus came.

25The other disciples therefore said unto him, We have seen the Lord. But he said unto them, Except I shall see in his hands the print of the nails, and put my finger into the print of the nails, and thrust my hand into his side, I will not believe.

26And after eight days again his disciples were within, and Thomas with them: *then* came Jesus, the doors being shut, and stood in the midst, and said, Peace *be* unto you.

27Then saith he to Thomas, Reach hither thy finger, and behold my hands; and reach hither thy hand, and thrust *it* into my side: and be not faithless, but believing.

28And Thomas answered and said unto him, My Lord and my God.

29Jesus saith unto him, Thomas, because thou hast seen me, thou hast believed: blessed *are* they that have not seen, and *yet* have believed.

30And many other signs truly did Jesus in the presence of his disciples, which are not written in this book:

31But these are written, that ye might believe that Jesus is the Christ, the Son of God; and that believing ye might have life through his name.

PSALM 119:156–176

GREAT *are* thy tender mercies, O LORD: quicken me according to thy judgments.

157Many *are* my persecutors and mine enemies; *yet* do I not decline from thy testimonies.

158I beheld the transgressors, and was grieved; because they kept not thy word.

159Consider how I love thy precepts: quicken me, O LORD, according to thy lovingkindness.

160Thy word *is* true *from* the beginning: and every one of thy righteous judgments *endureth* for ever.

161Princes have persecuted me without a cause: but my heart standeth in awe of thy word.

162I rejoice at thy word, as one that findeth great spoil.

163I hate and abhor lying: *but* thy law do I love.

164Seven times a day do I praise thee because of thy righteous judgments.

165Great peace have they which love thy law: and nothing shall offend them.

166LORD, I have hoped for thy salvation, and done thy commandments.

167My soul hath kept thy testimonies; and I love them exceedingly.

168I have kept thy precepts and thy testimonies: for all my ways *are* before thee.

169Let my cry come near before thee, O LORD: give me understanding according to thy word.

170Let my supplication come before thee: deliver me according to thy word.

171My lips shall utter praise, when thou hast taught me thy statutes.

172My tongue shall speak of thy word: for all thy commandments *are* righteousness.

173Let thine hand help me; for I have chosen thy precepts.

174I have longed for thy salvation, O LORD; and thy law *is* my delight.

175Let my soul live, and it shall praise thee; and let thy judgments help me.

176I have gone astray like a lost sheep; seek thy servant; for I do not forget thy commandments.

PROVERBS FOR TODAY/ 16:14–15

The wrath of a king is as *messengers of death: but a wise man will pacify it.* □ *In the light of the king's countenance* is *life; and his favour* is *as a cloud of the latter rain.*

JUNE 2

2 SAMUEL 19:11—20:13

A ND king David sent to Zadok and to Abiathar the priests, saying, Speak unto the elders of Judah, saying, Why are ye the last to bring the king back to his house? seeing the speech of all Israel is come to the king, *even* to his house.

12Ye *are* my brethren, ye *are* my bones and my flesh: wherefore then are ye the last to bring back the king?

13And say ye to Amasa, *Art* thou not of my bone, and of my flesh? God do so to me, and more also, if thou be not captain of the host before me continually in the room of Joab.

14And he bowed the heart of all the men of Judah, even as *the heart of* one man; so that they sent *this word* unto the king, Return thou, and all thy servants.

15So the king returned, and came to Jordan. And Judah came to Gilgal, to go to meet the king, to conduct the king over Jordan.

16And Shimei the son of Gera, a Benjamite, which *was* of Bahurim, hasted and came down with the men of Judah to meet king David.

17And *there were* a thousand men of Benjamin with him, and Ziba the servant of the house of Saul, and his fifteen sons and his twenty servants with him; and they went over Jordan before the king.

18And there went over a ferry boat to carry over the king's household, and to do what he thought good. And Shimei the son of Gera fell down before the king, as he was come over Jordan;

19And said unto the king, Let not my lord impute iniquity unto me, neither do thou remember that which thy servant did perversely the day that my lord the king went out of Jerusalem, that the king should take it to his heart.

20For thy servant doth know that I have sinned: therefore, behold, I am come the first this day of all the house of Joseph to go down to meet my lord the king.

21But Abishai the son of Zeruiah answered and said, Shall not Shimei be put to death for this, because he cursed the LORD's anointed?

22And David said, What have I to do with you, ye sons of Zeruiah, that ye should this day be adversaries unto me? shall there any man be put to death this day in Israel? for do not I know that I *am* this day king over Israel?

23Therefore the king said unto Shimei, Thou shalt not die. And the king sware unto him.

24And Mephibosheth the son of Saul came down to meet the king, and had neither dressed his feet, nor trimmed his beard, nor washed his clothes, from the day the king departed until the day he came *again* in peace.

25And it came to pass, when he was come to Jerusalem to meet the king, that the king said unto him, Wherefore wentest not thou with me, Mephibosheth?

26And he answered, My lord, O king, my servant deceived me: for thy servant said, I will saddle me an ass, that I may ride thereon, and go to the king; because thy servant *is* lame.

27And he hath slandered thy servant unto my lord the king; but my lord the king *is* as an angel of God: do therefore *what is* good in thine eyes.

28For all *of* my father's house were but dead men before my lord the king: yet didst thou set thy servant among them that did eat at thine own table. What right therefore have I yet to cry any more unto the king?

29And the king said unto him, Why speakest thou any more of thy matters? I have said, Thou and Ziba divide the land.

30And Mephibosheth said unto the king, Yea, let him take all, forasmuch as my lord the king is come again in peace unto his own house.

31And Barzillai the Gileadite came down from Rogelim, and went over Jordan with the king, to conduct him over Jordan.

32Now Barzillai was a very aged man, *even* fourscore years old: and he had provided the king of sustenance while he lay at Mahanaim; for he *was* a very great man.

33And the king said unto Barzillai, Come thou over with me, and I will feed thee with me in Jerusalem.

34And Barzillai said unto the king, How long have I to live, that I should go up with the king unto Jerusalem?

35I *am* this day fourscore years old: *and* can I discern between good and evil? can thy servant taste what I eat or what I drink? can I hear any more the voice of singing men and singing women? wherefore then should thy servant be yet a burden unto my lord the king?

36Thy servant will go a little way over Jordan with the king: and why should the king recompense it me with such a reward?

37Let thy servant, I pray thee, turn back again, that I may die in mine own city, *and be buried* by the grave of my father and of my mother. But behold thy servant Chimham; let him go over with my lord the king; and do to him what shall seem good unto thee.

38And the king answered, Chimham shall go over with me, and I will do to him that which shall seem good unto thee: and whatsoever thou shalt require of me, *that* will I do for thee.

39And all the people went over Jordan. And when the king was come over, the king kissed Barzillai, and blessed him; and he returned unto his own place.

40Then the king went on to Gilgal, and Chimham went on with him: and all the people of Judah conducted the king, and also half the people of Israel.

41And, behold, all the men of Israel came to the king, and said unto the king, Why have our brethren the men of Judah stolen thee away, and have brought the king, and his household, and all David's men with him, over Jordan?

42And all the men of Judah answered the men of Israel, Because the king *is* near of kin to us: wherefore then be ye angry for this matter? have we eaten at all of the king's *cost?* or hath he given us any gift?

43And the men of Israel answered the men of Judah, and said, We have ten parts in the king, and we have also more *right* in David than ye: why then did ye despise us, that our advice should not be first had in bringing back our king? And the words of the men of Judah were fiercer than the words of the men of Israel.

AND there happened to be there a man of Belial, whose name *was* Sheba, the son of Bichri, a Benjamite: and he blew a trumpet, and said, We have no part in David, neither have we inheritance in the son of Jesse: every man to his tents, O Israel.

2So every man of Israel went up from after David, *and* followed Sheba the son of Bichri: but the men of Judah clave unto their king, from Jordan even to Jerusalem.

3And David came to his house at Jerusalem; and the king took the ten women *his* concubines, whom he had left to keep the house, and put them in ward, and fed them, but went not in unto them. So they were shut up unto the day of their death, living in widowhood.

4Then said the king to Amasa, Assemble me the men of Judah within three days, and be thou here present.

5So Amasa went to assemble *the men of* Judah: but he tarried longer than the set time which he had appointed him.

6And David said to Abishai, Now shall Sheba the son of Bichri do us more harm than *did* Absalom: take thou thy lord's servants, and pursue after him, lest he get him fenced cities, and escape us.

7And there went out after him Joab's men, and the Cherethites, and the Pelethites, and all the mighty men: and they went out of Jerusalem, to pursue after Sheba the son of Bichri.

8When they *were* at the great stone which *is* in Gibeon, Amasa went before them. And Joab's garment that he had put on was girded unto him, and upon it a girdle *with* a sword fastened upon his loins in the sheath thereof; and as he went forth it fell out.

9And Joab said to Amasa, *Art* thou in health, my brother? And Joab took Amasa by the beard with the right hand to kiss him.

10But Amasa took no heed to the sword that *was* in Joab's hand: so he smote him therewith in the fifth *rib,* and shed out his bowels to the ground, and struck him not again; and he died. So Joab and Abishai his brother pursued after Sheba the son of Bichri.

11And one of Joab's men stood by him, and said, He that favoureth Joab, and he that *is* for David, *let him go* after Joab.

12And Amasa wallowed in blood in the midst of the highway. And when the man saw that all the people stood still, he removed Amasa out of the highway into the field, and cast a cloth upon him, when he saw that every one that came by him stood still.

13When he was removed out of the highway, all the people went on after Joab, to pursue after Sheba the son of Bichri.

JOHN 21:1–25

AFTER these things Jesus shewed himself again to the disciples at the sea of Tiberias; and on this wise shewed he *himself.*

2There were together Simon Peter, and Thomas called Didymus, and Nathanael of Cana in Galilee, and the *sons* of Zebedee, and two other of his disciples.

3Simon Peter saith unto them, I go a fishing. They say unto him, We also go with thee. They went forth, and entered into a ship immediately: and that night they caught nothing.

4But when the morning was now come, Jesus stood on the shore: but the disciples knew not that it was Jesus.

5Then Jesus saith unto them, Children, have ye any meat? They answered him, No.

6And he said unto them, Cast the net on the right side of the ship, and ye shall find. They cast therefore, and now they were not able to draw it for the multitude of fishes.

7Therefore that disciple whom Jesus loved saith unto Peter, It is the Lord. Now when Simon Peter heard that it was the Lord, he girt *his* fisher's coat *unto him,* (for he was naked,) and did cast himself into the sea.

8And the other disciples came in a little ship; (for they were not far from land, but as it were two hundred cubits,) dragging the net with fishes.

9As soon then as they were come to land, they saw a fire of coals there, and fish laid thereon, and bread.

10Jesus saith unto them, Bring of the fish which ye have now caught.

11Simon Peter went up, and drew the net to land full of great fishes, an hundred and fifty and three: and for all there were so many, yet was not the net broken.

12Jesus saith unto them, Come *and* dine. And none of the disciples durst ask him, Who art thou? knowing that it was the Lord.

13Jesus then cometh, and taketh bread, and giveth them, and fish likewise.

14This is now the third time that Jesus shewed himself to his disciples, after that he was risen from the dead.

15So when they had dined, Jesus saith to Simon Peter, Simon, *son* of Jonas, lovest thou me more than these? He saith unto him, Yea, Lord; thou knowest that I love thee. He saith unto him, Feed my lambs.

16He saith to him again the second time, Simon, *son* of Jonas, lovest thou me? He saith unto him, Yea, Lord; thou knowest that I love thee. He saith unto him, Feed my sheep.

17He saith unto him the third time, Simon, *son* of Jonas, lovest thou me? Peter was grieved because he said unto him the third time, Lovest thou me? And he said unto him, Lord, thou knowest all things; thou knowest that I love thee. Jesus saith unto him, Feed my sheep.

18Verily, verily, I say unto thee, When thou wast young, thou girdedst thyself, and walkedst whither thou wouldest: but when thou shalt be old, thou shalt stretch forth thy hands, and another shall gird thee, and carry *thee* whither thou wouldest not.

19This spake he, signifying by what death he should glorify God. And when he had spoken this, he saith unto him, Follow me.

20Then Peter, turning about, seeth the disciple whom Jesus loved following; which also leaned on his breast at supper, and said, Lord, which is he that betrayeth thee?

21Peter seeing him saith to Jesus, Lord, and what *shall* this man *do?*

22Jesus saith unto him, If I will that he tarry till I come, what *is that* to thee? follow thou me.

23Then went this saying abroad among the brethren, that that disciple should not die: yet Jesus said not unto him, He shall not die; but, If I will that he tarry till I come, what *is that* to thee?

24This is the disciple which testifieth of these things, and wrote these things: and we know that his testimony is true.

25And there are also many other things which Jesus did, the which, if they should be written every one, I suppose that even the world itself could not contain the books that should be written. Amen.

PSALM 120:1–7

IN my distress I cried unto the LORD, and he heard me.

2Deliver my soul, O LORD, from lying lips, *and* from a deceitful tongue.

3What shall be given unto thee? or what shall be done unto thee, thou false tongue?

4Sharp arrows of the mighty, with coals of juniper.

5Woe is me, that I sojourn in Mesech, *that* I dwell in the tents of Kedar!

6My soul hath long dwelt with him that hateth peace.

7I *am for* peace: but when I speak, they *are* for war.

PROVERBS FOR TODAY/ 16:16–17

How much better is it *to get wisdom than gold! and to get understanding rather to be chosen than silver!* □ *The highway of the upright* is *to depart from evil: he that keepeth his way preserveth his soul.*

JUNE 3

2 SAMUEL 20:14—22:20

AND he [Sheba] went through all the tribes of Israel unto Abel, and to Beth–maachah, and all the Berites: and they were gathered together, and went also after him.

15And they came and besieged him in Abel of Beth–maachah, and they cast up a bank against the city, and it stood in the trench: and all the people that *were* with Joab battered the wall, to throw it down.

16Then cried a wise woman out of the city, Hear, hear; say, I pray you, unto Joab, Come near hither, that I may speak with thee.

17And when he was come near unto her, the woman said, *Art* thou Joab? And he answered, I *am* he. Then she said unto him, Hear the words of thine handmaid. And he answered, I do hear.

18Then she spake, saying, They were wont to speak in old time, saying, They shall surely ask *counsel* at Abel: and so they ended *the matter.*

19I *am one of them that are* peaceable *and* faithful in Israel: thou seekest to destroy a city and a mother in Israel: why wilt thou swallow up the inheritance of the LORD?

20And Joab answered and said, Far be it, far be it from me, that I should swallow up or destroy.

21The matter *is* not so: but a man of mount Ephraim, Sheba the son of Bichri by name, hath lifted up his hand against the king, *even* against David: deliver him only, and I will depart from the city. And the woman said unto Joab, Behold, his head shall be thrown to thee over the wall.

22Then the woman went unto all the people in her wisdom. And they cut off the head of Sheba the son of Bichri, and cast *it* out to Joab. And he blew

a trumpet, and they retired from the city, every man to his tent. And Joab returned to Jerusalem unto the king.

23Now Joab *was* over all the host of Israel: and Benaiah the son of Jehoiada *was* over the Cherethites and over the Pelethites:

24And Adoram *was* over the tribute: and Jehoshaphat the son of Ahilud *was* recorder:

25And Sheva *was* scribe: and Zadok and Abiathar *were* the priests:

26And Ira also the Jairite was a chief ruler about David.

THEN there was a famine in the days of David three years, year after year; and David enquired of the LORD. And the LORD answered, *It is* for Saul, and for *his* bloody house, because he slew the Gibeonites.

2And the king called the Gibeonites, and said unto them; (now the Gibeonites *were* not of the children of Israel, but of the remnant of the Amorites; and the children of Israel had sworn unto them: and Saul sought to slay them in his zeal to the children of Israel and Judah.)

3Wherefore David said unto the Gibeonites, What shall I do for you? and wherewith shall I make the atonement, that ye may bless the inheritance of the LORD?

4And the Gibeonites said unto him, We will have no silver nor gold of Saul, nor of his house; neither for us shalt thou kill any man in Israel. And he said, What ye shall say, *that* will I do for you.

5And they answered the king, The man that consumed us, and that devised against us *that* we should be destroyed from remaining in any of the coasts of Israel,

⁶Let seven men of his sons be delivered unto us, and we will hang them up unto the LORD in Gibeah of Saul, *whom* the LORD did choose. And the king said, I will give *them.*

⁷But the king spared Mephibosheth, the son of Jonathan the son of Saul, because of the LORD's oath that *was* between them, between David and Jonathan the son of Saul.

⁸But the king took the two sons of Rizpah the daughter of Aiah, whom she bare unto Saul, Armoni and Mephibosheth; and the five sons of Michal the daughter of Saul, whom she brought up for Adriel the son of Barzillai the Meholathite:

⁹And he delivered them into the hands of the Gibeonites, and they hanged them in the hill before the LORD: and they fell *all* seven together, and were put to death in the days of harvest, in the first *days,* in the beginning of barley harvest.

¹⁰And Rizpah the daughter of Aiah took sackcloth, and spread it for her upon the rock, from the beginning of harvest until water dropped upon them out of heaven, and suffered neither the birds of the air to rest on them by day, nor the beasts of the field by night.

¹¹And it was told David what Rizpah the daughter of Aiah, the concubine of Saul, had done.

¹²And David went and took the bones of Saul and the bones of Jonathan his son from the men of Jabesh–gilead, which had stolen them from the street of Beth–shan, where the Philistines had hanged them, when the Philistines had slain Saul in Gilboa:

¹³And he brought up from thence the bones of Saul and the bones of Jonathan his son; and they gathered the bones of them that were hanged.

¹⁴And the bones of Saul and Jonathan his son buried they in the country of Benjamin in Zelah, in the sepulchre of Kish his father: and they performed all that the king commanded. And after

that God was intreated for the land.

¹⁵Moreover the Philistines had yet war again with Israel; and David went down, and his servants with him, and fought against the Philistines: and David waxed faint.

¹⁶And Ishbi–benob, which *was* of the sons of the giant, the weight of whose spear *weighed* three hundred *shekels* of brass in weight, he being girded with a new *sword,* thought to have slain David.

¹⁷But Abishai the son of Zeruiah succoured him, and smote the Philistine, and killed him. Then the men of David sware unto him, saying, Thou shalt go no more out with us to battle, that thou quench not the light of Israel.

¹⁸And it came to pass after this, that there was again a battle with the Philistines at Gob: then Sibbechai the Hushathite slew Saph, which *was* of the sons of the giant.

¹⁹And there was again a battle in Gob with the Philistines, where Elhanan the son of Jaare–oregim, a Beth–lehemite, slew *the brother of* Goliath the Gittite, the staff of whose spear *was* like a weaver's beam.

²⁰And there was yet a battle in Gath, where was a man of *great* stature, that had on every hand six fingers, and on every foot six toes, four and twenty in number; and he also was born to the giant.

²¹And when he defied Israel, Jonathan the son of Shimeah the brother of David slew him.

²²These four were born to the giant in Gath, and fell by the hand of David, and by the hand of his servants.

AND David spake unto the LORD the words of this song in the day *that* the LORD had delivered him out of the hand of all his enemies, and out of the hand of Saul:

²And he said, The LORD *is* my rock, and my fortress, and my deliverer;

³The God of my rock; in him will I

trust: *he is* my shield, and the horn of my salvation, my high tower, and my refuge, my saviour; thou savest me from violence.

4I will call on the LORD, *who is* worthy to be praised: so shall I be saved from mine enemies.

5When the waves of death compassed me, the floods of ungodly men made me afraid;

6The sorrows of hell compassed me about; the snares of death prevented me;

7In my distress I called upon the LORD, and cried to my God: and he did hear my voice out of his temple, and my cry *did enter* into his ears.

8Then the earth shook and trembled; the foundations of heaven moved and shook, because he was wroth.

9There went up a smoke out of his nostrils, and fire out of his mouth devoured: coals were kindled by it.

10He bowed the heavens also, and came down; and darkness *was* under his feet.

11And he rode upon a cherub, and did fly: and he was seen upon the wings of the wind.

12And he made darkness pavilions round about him, dark waters, *and* thick clouds of the skies.

13Through the brightness before him were coals of fire kindled.

14The LORD thundered from heaven, and the most High uttered his voice.

15And he sent out arrows, and scattered them; lightning, and discomfited them.

16And the channels of the sea appeared, the foundations of the world were discovered, at the rebuking of the LORD, at the blast of the breath of his nostrils.

17He sent from above, he took me; he drew me out of many waters;

18He delivered me from my strong enemy, *and* from them that hated me: for they were too strong for me.

19They prevented me in the day of my calamity: but the LORD was my stay.

20He brought me forth also into a large place: he delivered me, because he delighted in me.

ACTS 1:1–26

THE former treatise have I made, O Theophilus, of all that Jesus began both to do and teach,

2Until the day in which he was taken up, after that he through the Holy Ghost had given commandments unto the apostles whom he had chosen:

3To whom also he shewed himself alive after his passion by many infallible proofs, being seen of them forty days, and speaking of the things pertaining to the kingdom of God:

4And, being assembled together with *them,* commanded them that they should not depart from Jerusalem, but wait for the promise of the Father, which, *saith he,* ye have heard of me.

5For John truly baptized with water; but ye shall be baptized with the Holy Ghost not many days hence.

6When they therefore were come together, they asked of him, saying, Lord, wilt thou at this time restore again the kingdom to Israel?

7And he said unto them, It is not for you to know the times or the seasons, which the Father hath put in his own power.

8But ye shall receive power, after that the Holy Ghost is come upon you: and ye shall be witnesses unto me both in Jerusalem, and in all Judaea, and in Samaria, and unto the uttermost part of the earth.

9And when he had spoken these things, while they beheld, he was taken up; and a cloud received him out of their sight.

10And while they looked stedfastly toward heaven as he went up, behold, two men stood by them in white apparel;

11Which also said, Ye men of Galilee, why stand ye gazing up into heaven?

this same Jesus, which is taken up from you into heaven, shall so come in like manner as ye have seen him go into heaven.

12Then returned they unto Jerusalem from the mount called Olivet, which is from Jerusalem a sabbath day's journey.

13And when they were come in, they went up into an upper room, where abode both Peter, and James, and John, and Andrew, Philip, and Thomas, Bartholomew, and Matthew, James *the son* of Alphaeus, and Simon Zelotes, and Judas *the brother* of James.

14These all continued with one accord in prayer and supplication, with the women, and Mary the mother of Jesus, and with his brethren.

15And in those days Peter stood up in the midst of the disciples, and said, (the number of names together were about an hundred and twenty,)

16Men *and* brethren, this scripture must needs have been fulfilled, which the Holy Ghost by the mouth of David spake before concerning Judas, which was guide to them that took Jesus.

17For he was numbered with us, and had obtained part of this ministry.

18Now this man purchased a field with the reward of iniquity; and falling headlong, he burst asunder in the midst, and all his bowels gushed out.

19And it was known unto all the dwellers at Jerusalem; insomuch as that field is called in their proper tongue, A–celda–ma, that is to say, The field of blood.

20For it is written in the book of Psalms, Let his habitation be desolate, and let no man dwell therein: and his bishoprick let another take.

21Wherefore of these men which have companied with us all the time that the Lord Jesus went in and out among us,

22Beginning from the baptism of John, unto that same day that he was taken up from us, must one be ordained to be a witness with us of his resurrection.

23And they appointed two, Joseph called Barsabas, who was surnamed Justus, and Matthias.

24And they prayed, and said, Thou, Lord, which knowest the hearts of all *men,* shew whether of these two thou hast chosen,

25That he may take part of this ministry and apostleship, from which Judas by transgression fell, that he might go to his own place.

26And they gave forth their lots; and the lot fell upon Matthias; and he was numbered with the eleven apostles.

PSALM 121:1–8

I WILL lift up mine eyes unto the hills, from whence cometh my help.

2My help *cometh* from the LORD, which made heaven and earth.

3He will not suffer thy foot to be moved: he that keepeth thee will not slumber.

4Behold, he that keepeth Israel shall neither slumber nor sleep.

5The LORD *is* thy keeper: the LORD *is* thy shade upon thy right hand.

6The sun shall not smite thee by day, nor the moon by night.

7The LORD shall preserve thee from all evil: he shall preserve thy soul.

8The LORD shall preserve thy going out and thy coming in from this time forth, and even for evermore.

PROVERBS FOR TODAY/ 16:18

Pride goeth *before destruction, and an haughty spirit before a fall.*

JUNE 4

2 SAMUEL 22:21—23:23

THE LORD rewarded me according to my righteousness: according to the cleanness of my hands hath he recompensed me.

22For I have kept the ways of the LORD, and have not wickedly departed from my God.

23For all his judgments *were* before me: and *as for* his statutes, I did not depart from them.

24I was also upright before him, and have kept myself from mine iniquity.

25Therefore the LORD hath recompensed me according to my righteousness; according to my cleanness in his eye sight.

26With the merciful thou wilt shew thyself merciful, *and* with the upright man thou wilt shew thyself upright.

27With the pure thou wilt shew thyself pure; and with the froward thou wilt shew thyself unsavoury.

28And the afflicted people thou wilt save: but thine eyes *are* upon the haughty, *that* thou mayest bring *them* down.

29For thou *art* my lamp, O LORD; and the LORD will lighten my darkness.

30For by thee I have run through a troop: by my God have I leaped over a wall.

31*As for* God, his way *is* perfect; the word of the LORD *is* tried: he *is* a buckler to all them that trust in him.

32For who *is* God, save the LORD? and who *is* a rock, save our God?

33God *is* my strength *and* power: and he maketh my way perfect.

34He maketh my feet like hinds' *feet:* and setteth me upon my high places.

35He teacheth my hands to war; so that a bow of steel is broken by mine arms.

36Thou hast also given me the shield of thy salvation: and thy gentleness hath made me great.

37Thou hast enlarged my steps under me; so that my feet did not slip.

38I have pursued mine enemies, and destroyed them; and turned not again until I had consumed them.

39And I have consumed them, and wounded them, that they could not arise: yea, they are fallen under my feet.

40For thou hast girded me with strength to battle: them that rose up against me hast thou subdued under me.

41Thou hast also given me the necks of mine enemies, that I might destroy them that hate me.

42They looked, but *there was* none to save; *even* unto the LORD, but he answered them not.

43Then did I beat them as small as the dust of the earth, I did stamp them as the mire of the street, *and* did spread them abroad.

44Thou also hast delivered me from the strivings of my people, thou hast kept me *to be* head of the heathen: a people *which* I knew not shall serve me.

45Strangers shall submit themselves unto me: as soon as they hear, they shall be obedient unto me.

46Strangers shall fade away, and they shall be afraid out of their close places.

47The LORD liveth; and blessed *be* my rock; and exalted be the God of the rock of my salvation.

48It *is* God that avengeth me, and that bringeth down the people under me,

49And that bringeth me forth from mine enemies: thou also hast lifted me up on high above them that rose up against me: thou hast delivered me from the violent man.

50Therefore I will give thanks unto thee, O LORD, among the heathen, and I will sing praises unto thy name.

51*He is* the tower of salvation for his king: and sheweth mercy to his anointed, unto David, and to his seed for evermore.

Now these *be* the last words of David. David the son of Jesse said, and the man *who was* raised up on high, the anointed of the God of Jacob, and the sweet psalmist of Israel, said,

2The Spirit of the LORD spake by me, and his word *was* in my tongue.

3The God of Israel said, the Rock of Israel spake to me, He that ruleth over men *must be* just, ruling in the fear of God.

4And *he shall be* as the light of the morning, *when* the sun riseth, *even* a morning without clouds; *as* the tender grass *springing* out of the earth by clear shining after rain.

5Although my house *be* not so with God; yet he hath made with me an everlasting covenant, ordered in all *things,* and sure: for *this is* all my salvation, and all *my* desire, although he make *it* not to grow.

6But *the sons* of Belial *shall be* all of them as thorns thrust away, because they cannot be taken with hands:

7But the man *that* shall touch them must be fenced with iron and the staff of a spear; and they shall be utterly burned with fire in the *same* place.

8These *be* the names of the mighty men whom David had: The Tachmonite that sat in the seat, chief among the captains; the same *was* Adino the Eznite: *he lift up his spear* against eight hundred, whom he slew at one time.

9And after him *was* Eleazar the son of Dodo the Ahohite, *one* of the three mighty men with David, when they defied the Philistines *that* were there gathered together to battle, and the men of Israel were gone away:

10He arose, and smote the Philistines until his hand was weary, and his hand clave unto the sword: and the LORD wrought a great victory that day; and the people returned after him only to spoil.

11And after him *was* Shammah the son of Agee the Hararite. And the Philistines were gathered together into a troop, where was a piece of ground full of lentiles: and the people fled from the Philistines.

12But he stood in the midst of the ground, and defended it, and slew the Philistines: and the LORD wrought a great victory.

13And three of the thirty chief went down, and came to David in the harvest time unto the cave of Adullam: and the troop of the Philistines pitched in the valley of Rephaim.

14And David *was* then in an hold, and the garrison of the Philistines *was* then *in* Beth–lehem.

15And David longed, and said, Oh that one would give me drink of the water of the well of Beth–lehem, which *is* by the gate!

16And the three mighty men brake through the host of the Philistines, and drew water out of the well of Beth–lehem, that *was* by the gate, and took *it,* and brought *it* to David: nevertheless he would not drink thereof, but poured it out unto the LORD.

17And he said, Be it far from me, O LORD, that I should do this: *is not this* the blood of the men that went in jeopardy of their lives? therefore he would not drink it. These things did these three mighty men.

18And Abishai, the brother of Joab, the son of Zeruiah, was chief among three. And he lifted up his spear against three hundred, *and* slew *them,* and had the name among three.

19Was he not most honourable of three? therefore he was their captain: howbeit he attained not unto the *first* three.

20And Benaiah the son of Jehoiada,

the son of a valiant man, of Kabzeel, who had done many acts, he slew two lionlike men of Moab: he went down also and slew a lion in the midst of a pit in time of snow:

21And he slew an Egyptian, a goodly man: and the Egyptian had a spear in his hand; but he went down to him with a staff, and plucked the spear out of the Egyptian's hand, and slew him with his own spear.

22These *things* did Benaiah the son of Jehoiada, and had the name among three mighty men.

23He was more honourable than the thirty, but he attained not to the *first* three. And David set him over his guard.

ACTS 2:1-47

AND when the day of Pentecost was fully come, they were all with one accord in one place.

2And suddenly there came a sound from heaven as of a rushing mighty wind, and it filled all the house where they were sitting.

3And there appeared unto them cloven tongues like as of fire, and it sat upon each of them.

4And they were all filled with the Holy Ghost, and began to speak with other tongues, as the Spirit gave them utterance.

5And there were dwelling at Jerusalem Jews, devout men, out of every nation under heaven.

6Now when this was noised abroad, the multitude came together, and were confounded, because that every man heard them speak in his own language.

7And they were all amazed and marvelled, saying one to another, Behold, are not all these which speak Galilaeans?

8And how hear we every man in our own tongue, wherein we were born?

9Parthians, and Medes, and Elamites, and the dwellers in Mesopotamia,

and in Judaea, and Cappadocia, in Pontus, and Asia,

10Phrygia, and Pamphylia, in Egypt, and in the parts of Libya about Cyrene, and strangers of Rome, Jews and proselytes,

11Cretes and Arabians, we do hear them speak in our tongues the wonderful works of God.

12And they were all amazed, and were in doubt, saying one to another, What meaneth this?

13Others mocking said, These men are full of new wine.

14But Peter, standing up with the eleven, lifted up his voice, and said unto them, Ye men of Judaea, and all *ye* that dwell at Jerusalem, be this known unto you, and hearken to my words:

15For these are not drunken, as ye suppose, seeing it is *but* the third hour of the day.

16But this is that which was spoken by the prophet Joel;

17And it shall come to pass in the last days, saith God, I will pour out of my Spirit upon all flesh: and your sons and your daughters shall prophesy, and your young men shall see visions, and your old men shall dream dreams:

18And on my servants and on my handmaidens I will pour out in those days of my Spirit; and they shall prophesy:

19And I will shew wonders in heaven above, and signs in the earth beneath; blood, and fire, and vapour of smoke:

20The sun shall be turned into darkness, and the moon into blood, before that great and notable day of the Lord come:

21And it shall come to pass, *that* whosoever shall call on the name of the Lord shall be saved.

22Ye men of Israel, hear these words; Jesus of Nazareth, a man approved of God among you by miracles and wonders and signs, which God did by him in the midst of you, as ye yourselves also know:

23Him, being delivered by the determinate counsel and foreknowledge of God, ye have taken, and by wicked hands have crucified and slain:

24Whom God hath raised up, having loosed the pains of death: because it was not possible that he should be holden of it.

25For David speaketh concerning him, I foresaw the Lord always before my face, for he is on my right hand, that I should not be moved:

26Therefore did my heart rejoice, and my tongue was glad; moreover also my flesh shall rest in hope:

27Because thou wilt not leave my soul in hell, neither wilt thou suffer thine Holy One to see corruption.

28Thou hast made known to me the ways of life; thou shalt make me full of joy with thy countenance.

29Men *and* brethren, let me freely speak unto you of the patriarch David, that he is both dead and buried, and his sepulchre is with us unto this day.

30Therefore being a prophet, and knowing that God had sworn with an oath to him, that of the fruit of his loins, according to the flesh, he would raise up Christ to sit on his throne;

31He seeing this before spake of the resurrection of Christ, that his soul was not left in hell, neither his flesh did see corruption.

32This Jesus hath God raised up, whereof we all are witnesses.

33Therefore being by the right hand of God exalted, and having received of the Father the promise of the Holy Ghost, he hath shed forth this, which ye now see and hear.

34For David is not ascended into the heavens: but he saith himself, The LORD said unto my Lord, Sit thou on my right hand,

35Until I make thy foes thy footstool.

36Therefore let all the house of Israel know assuredly, that God hath made that same Jesus, whom ye have crucified, both Lord and Christ.

37Now when they heard *this*, they were pricked in their heart, and said unto Peter and to the rest of the apostles, Men *and* brethren, what shall we do?

38Then Peter said unto them, Repent, and be baptized every one of you in the name of Jesus Christ for the remission of sins, and ye shall receive the gift of the Holy Ghost.

39For the promise is unto you, and to your children, and to all that are afar off, *even* as many as the Lord our God shall call.

40And with many other words did he testify and exhort, saying, Save yourselves from this untoward generation.

41Then they that gladly received his word were baptized: and the same day there were added *unto them* about three thousand souls.

42And they continued stedfastly in the apostles' doctrine and fellowship, and in breaking of bread, and in prayers.

43And fear came upon every soul: and many wonders and signs were done by the apostles.

44And all that believed were together, and had all things common;

45And sold their possessions and goods, and parted them to all *men,* as every man had need.

46And they, continuing daily with one accord in the temple, and breaking bread from house to house, did eat their meat with gladness and singleness of heart,

47Praising God, and having favour with all the people. And the Lord added to the church daily such as should be saved.

PSALM 122:1–9

I WAS glad when they said unto me, Let us go into the house of the LORD.

2Our feet shall stand within thy gates, O Jerusalem.

3Jerusalem is builded as a city that is compact together:

4Whither the tribes go up, the tribes of the LORD, unto the testimony of Israel, to give thanks unto the name of the LORD.

5For there are set thrones of judgment, the thrones of the house of David.

6Pray for the peace of Jerusalem: they shall prosper that love thee.

7Peace be within thy walls, *and* prosperity within thy palaces.

8For my brethren and companions' sakes, I will now say, Peace *be* within thee.

9Because of the house of the LORD our God I will seek thy good.

PROVERBS FOR TODAY/ 16:19–20

Better it is to be *of an humble spirit with the lowly, than to divide the spoil with the proud.* □ *He that handleth a matter wisely shall find good: and whoso trusteth in the* LORD, *happy* is *he.*

JUNE 5

2 SAMUEL 23:24—24:25

ASAHEL the brother of Joab *was* one of the thirty; Elhanan the son of Dodo of Beth–lehem, 25Shammah the Harodite, Elika the Harodite,

26Helez the Paltite, Ira the son of Ikkesh the Tekoite,

27Abiezer the Anethothite, Mebunnai the Hushathite,

28Zalmon the Ahohite, Maharai the Netophathite,

29Heleb the son of Baanah, a Netophathite, Ittai the son of Ribai out of Gibeah of the children of Benjamin,

30Benaiah the Pirathonite, Hiddai of the brooks of Gaash,

31Abi–albon the Arbathite, Azmaveth the Barhumite,

32Eliahba the Shaalbonite, of the sons of Jashen, Jonathan,

33Shammah the Hararite, Ahiam the son of Sharar the Hararite,

34Eliphelet the son of Ahasbai, the son of the Maachathite, Eliam the son of Ahithophel the Gilonite,

35Hezrai the Carmelite, Paarai the Arbite,

36Igal the son of Nathan of Zobah, Bani the Gadite,

37Zelek the Ammonite, Nahari the Beerothite, armourbearer to Joab the son of Zeruiah,

38Ira an Ithrite, Gareb an Ithrite,

39Uriah the Hittite: thirty and seven in all.

AND again the anger of the LORD was kindled against Israel, and he moved David against them to say, Go, number Israel and Judah.

2For the king said to Joab the captain of the host, which *was* with him, Go now through all the tribes of Israel, from Dan even to Beer–sheba, and number ye the people, that I may know the number of the people.

3And Joab said unto the king, Now the LORD thy God add unto the people, how many soever they be, an hundredfold, and that the eyes of my lord the king may see *it:* but why doth my lord the king delight in this thing?

4Notwithstanding the king's word prevailed against Joab, and against the captains of the host. And Joab and the captains of the host went out from the presence of the king, to number the people of Israel.

5And they passed over Jordan, and pitched in Aroer, on the right side of the city that *lieth* in the midst of the river of Gad, and toward Jazer:

6Then they came to Gilead, and to the land of Tahtim–hodshi; and they came to Dan–jaan, and about to Zidon,

7And came to the strong hold of Tyre, and to all the cities of the Hivites, and of the Canaanites: and they went out to the south of Judah, *even* to Beer-sheba.

8So when they had gone through all the land, they came to Jerusalem at the end of nine months and twenty days.

9And Joab gave up the sum of the number of the people unto the king: and there were in Israel eight hundred thousand valiant men that drew the sword; and the men of Judah *were* five hundred thousand men.

10And David's heart smote him after that he had numbered the people. And David said unto the LORD, I have sinned greatly in that I have done: and now, I beseech thee, O LORD, take away the iniquity of thy servant; for I have done very foolishly.

11For when David was up in the morning, the word of the LORD came unto the prophet Gad, David's seer, saying,

12Go and say unto David, Thus saith the LORD, I offer thee three *things;* choose thee one of them, that I may *do it* unto thee.

13So Gad came to David, and told him, and said unto him, Shall seven years of famine come unto thee in thy land? or wilt thou flee three months before thine enemies, while they pursue thee? or that there be three days' pestilence in thy land? now advise, and see what answer I shall return to him that sent me.

14And David said unto Gad, I am in a great strait: let us fall now into the hand of the LORD; for his mercies *are* great: and let me not fall into the hand of man.

15So the LORD sent a pestilence upon Israel from the morning even to the time appointed: and there died of the people from Dan even to Beer–sheba seventy thousand men.

16And when the angel stretched out his hand upon Jerusalem to destroy it, the LORD repented him of the evil, and said to the angel that destroyed the people, It is enough: stay now thine hand. And the angel of the LORD was by the threshingplace of Araunah the Jebusite.

17And David spake unto the LORD when he saw the angel that smote the people, and said, Lo, I have sinned, and I have done wickedly: but these sheep, what have they done? let thine hand, I pray thee, be against me, and against my father's house.

18And Gad came that day to David, and said unto him, Go up, rear an altar unto the LORD in the threshingfloor of Araunah the Jebusite.

19And David, according to the saying of Gad, went up as the LORD commanded.

20And Araunah looked, and saw the king and his servants coming on toward him: and Araunah went out, and bowed himself before the king on his face upon the ground.

21And Araunah said, Wherefore is my lord the king come to his servant? And David said, To buy the threshingfloor of thee, to build an altar unto the LORD, that the plague may be stayed from the people.

22And Araunah said unto David, Let my lord the king take and offer up what *seemeth* good unto him: behold, *here be* oxen for burnt sacrifice, and threshing instruments and *other* instruments of the oxen for wood.

23All these *things* did Araunah, *as* a king, give unto the king. And Araunah said unto the king, The Lord thy God accept thee.

24And the king said unto Araunah, Nay; but I will surely buy *it* of thee at a price: neither will I offer burnt offerings unto the Lord my God of that which doth cost me nothing. So David bought the threshingfloor and the oxen for fifty shekels of silver.

25And David built there an altar unto the Lord, and offered burnt offerings and peace offerings. So the Lord was intreated for the land, and the plague was stayed from Israel.

ACTS 3:1–26

Now Peter and John went up together into the temple at the hour of prayer, *being* the ninth *hour.*

2And a certain man lame from his mother's womb was carried, whom they laid daily at the gate of the temple which is called Beautiful, to ask alms of them that entered into the temple;

3Who seeing Peter and John about to go into the temple asked an alms.

4And Peter, fastening his eyes upon him with John, said, Look on us.

5And he gave heed unto them, expecting to receive something of them.

6Then Peter said, Silver and gold have I none; but such as I have give I thee: In the name of Jesus Christ of Nazareth rise up and walk.

7And he took him by the right hand, and lifted *him* up: and immediately his feet and ankle bones received strength.

8And he leaping up stood, and walked, and entered with them into the temple, walking, and leaping, and praising God.

9And all the people saw him walking and praising God:

10And they knew that it was he which sat for alms at the Beautiful gate of the temple: and they were filled with wonder and amazement at that which had happened unto him.

11And as the lame man which was healed held Peter and John, all the people ran together unto them in the porch that is called Solomon's, greatly wondering.

12And when Peter saw *it,* he answered unto the people, Ye men of Israel, why marvel ye at this? or why look ye so earnestly on us, as though by our own power or holiness we had made this man to walk?

13The God of Abraham, and of Isaac, and of Jacob, the God of our fathers, hath glorified his Son Jesus; whom ye delivered up, and denied him in the presence of Pilate, when he was determined to let *him* go.

14But ye denied the Holy One and the Just, and desired a murderer to be granted unto you;

15And killed the Prince of life, whom God hath raised from the dead; whereof we are witnesses.

16And his name through faith in his name hath made this man strong, whom ye see and know: yea, the faith which is by him hath given him this perfect soundness in the presence of you all.

17And now, brethren, I wot that through ignorance ye did *it,* as *did* also your rulers.

18But those things, which God before had shewed by the mouth of all his prophets, that Christ should suffer, he hath so fulfilled.

19Repent ye therefore, and be converted, that your sins may be blotted out, when the times of refreshing shall come from the presence of the Lord;

20And he shall send Jesus Christ, which before was preached unto you:

21Whom the heaven must receive until the times of restitution of all things, which God hath spoken by the mouth of all his holy prophets since the world began.

22For Moses truly said unto the fathers, A prophet shall the Lord your God raise up unto you of your brethren, like unto me; him shall ye hear in all things whatsoever he shall say unto you.

23And it shall come to pass, *that* every soul, which will not hear that prophet, shall be destroyed from among the people.

24Yea, and all the prophets from Samuel and those that follow after, as many as have spoken, have likewise foretold of these days.

25Ye are the children of the prophets, and of the covenant which God made with our fathers, saying unto Abraham, And in thy seed shall all the kindreds of the earth be blessed.

26Unto you first God, having raised up his Son Jesus, sent him to bless you, in turning away every one of you from his iniquities.

PSALM 123:1–4

UNTO thee lift I up mine eyes, O thou that dwellest in the heavens.

2Behold, as the eyes of servants *look* unto the hand of their masters, *and* as the eyes of a maiden unto the hand of her mistress; so our eyes *wait* upon the LORD our God, until that he have mercy upon us.

3Have mercy upon us, O LORD, have mercy upon us: for we are exceedingly filled with contempt.

4Our soul is exceedingly filled with the scorning of those that are at ease, *and* with the contempt of the proud.

PROVERBS FOR TODAY/ 16:21–23

The wise in heart shall be called prudent: and the sweetness of the lips increaseth learning. □ *Understanding* is *a wellspring of life unto him that hath it: but the instruction of fools* is *folly.* □ *The heart of the wise teacheth his mouth, and addeth learning to his lips.*

JUNE 6

1 KINGS 1:1–53

NOW king David was old *and* stricken in years; and they covered him with clothes, but he gat no heat.

2Wherefore his servants said unto him, Let there be sought for my lord the king a young virgin: and let her stand before the king, and let her cherish him, and let her lie in thy bosom, that my lord the king may get heat.

3So they sought for a fair damsel throughout all the coasts of Israel, and found Abishag a Shunammite, and brought her to the king.

4And the damsel *was* very fair, and cherished the king, and ministered to him: but the king knew her not.

5Then Adonijah the son of Haggith exalted himself, saying, I will be king: and he prepared him chariots and horsemen, and fifty men to run before him.

6And his father had not displeased him at any time in saying, Why hast thou done so? and he also *was a* very goodly *man;* and *his mother* bare him after Absalom.

7And he conferred with Joab the son

of Zeruiah, and with Abiathar the priest: and they following Adonijah helped *him*.

8But Zadok the priest, and Benaiah the son of Jehoiada, and Nathan the prophet, and Shimei, and Rei, and the mighty men which *belonged* to David, were not with Adonijah.

9And Adonijah slew sheep and oxen and fat cattle by the stone of Zoheleth, which *is* by En–rogel, and called all his brethren the king's sons, and all the men of Judah the king's servants:

10But Nathan the prophet, and Benaiah, and the mighty men, and Solomon his brother, he called not.

11Wherefore Nathan spake unto Bath–sheba the mother of Solomon, saying, Hast thou not heard that Adonijah the son of Haggith doth reign, and David our lord knoweth *it* not?

12Now therefore come, let me, I pray thee, give thee counsel, that thou mayest save thine own life, and the life of thy son Solomon.

13Go and get thee in unto king David, and say unto him, Didst not thou, my lord, O king, swear unto thine handmaid, saying, Assuredly Solomon thy son shall reign after me, and he shall sit upon my throne? why then doth Adonijah reign?

14Behold, while thou yet talkest there with the king, I also will come in after thee, and confirm thy words.

15And Bath–sheba went in unto the king into the chamber: and the king was very old; and Abishag the Shunammite ministered unto the king.

16And Bath–sheba bowed, and did obeisance unto the king. And the king said, What wouldest thou?

17And she said unto him, My lord, thou swarest by the LORD thy God unto thine handmaid, *saying,* Assuredly Solomon thy son shall reign after me, and he shall sit upon my throne.

18And now, behold, Adonijah reigneth; and now, my lord the king, thou knowest *it* not:

19And he hath slain oxen and fat cattle and sheep in abundance, and hath called all the sons of the king, and Abiathar the priest, and Joab the captain of the host: but Solomon thy servant hath he not called.

20And thou, my lord, O king, the eyes of all Israel *are* upon thee, that thou shouldest tell them who shall sit on the throne of my lord the king after him.

21Otherwise it shall come to pass, when my lord the king shall sleep with his fathers, that I and my son Solomon shall be counted offenders.

22And, lo, while she yet talked with the king, Nathan the prophet also came in.

23And they told the king, saying, Behold Nathan the prophet. And when he was come in before the king, he bowed himself before the king with his face to the ground.

24And Nathan said, My lord, O king, hast thou said, Adonijah shall reign after me, and he shall sit upon my throne?

25For he is gone down this day, and hath slain oxen and fat cattle and sheep in abundance, and hath called all the king's sons, and the captains of the host, and Abiathar the priest; and, behold, they eat and drink before him, and say, God save king Adonijah.

26But me, *even* me thy servant, and Zadok the priest, and Benaiah the son of Jehoiada, and thy servant Solomon, hath he not called.

27Is this thing done by my lord the king, and thou hast not shewed *it* unto thy servant, who should sit on the throne of my lord the king after him?

28Then king David answered and said, Call me Bath–sheba. And she came into the king's presence, and stood before the king.

29And the king sware, and said, As the LORD liveth, that hath redeemed my soul out of all distress,

30Even as I sware unto thee by the LORD God of Israel, saying, Assuredly Solomon thy son shall reign after me, and he shall sit upon my throne in my stead; even so will I certainly do this day.

31Then Bath–sheba bowed with *her* face to the earth, and did reverence to the king, and said, Let my lord king David live for ever.

32And king David said, Call me Zadok the priest, and Nathan the prophet, and Benaiah the son of Jehoiada. And they came before the king.

33The king also said unto them, Take with you the servants of your lord, and cause Solomon my son to ride upon mine own mule, and bring him down to Gihon:

34And let Zadok the priest and Nathan the prophet anoint him there king over Israel: and blow ye with the trumpet, and say, God save king Solomon.

35Then ye shall come up after him, that he may come and sit upon my throne; for he shall be king in my stead: and I have appointed him to be ruler over Israel and over Judah.

36And Benaiah the son of Jehoiada answered the king, and said, Amen: the LORD God of my lord the king say so *too*.

37As the LORD hath been with my lord the king, even so be he with Solomon, and make his throne greater than the throne of my lord king David.

38So Zadok the priest, and Nathan the prophet, and Benaiah the son of Jehoiada, and the Cherethites, and the Pelethites, went down, and caused Solomon to ride upon king David's mule, and brought him to Gihon.

39And Zadok the priest took an horn of oil out of the tabernacle, and anointed Solomon. And they blew the trumpet; and all the people said, God save king Solomon.

40And all the people came up after him, and the people piped with pipes, and rejoiced with great joy, so that the earth rent with the sound of them.

41And Adonijah and all the guests that *were* with him heard *it* as they had made an end of eating. And when Joab heard the sound of the trumpet, he said, Wherefore *is this* noise of the city being in an uproar?

42And while he yet spake, behold, Jonathan the son of Abiathar the priest came; and Adonijah said unto him, Come in; for thou *art* a valiant man, and bringest good tidings.

43And Jonathan answered and said to Adonijah, Verily our lord king David hath made Solomon king.

44And the king hath sent with him Zadok the priest, and Nathan the prophet, and Benaiah the son of Jehoiada, and the Cherethites, and the Pelethites, and they have caused him to ride upon the king's mule:

45And Zadok the priest and Nathan the prophet have anointed him king in Gihon: and they are come up from thence rejoicing, so that the city rang again. This *is* the noise that ye have heard.

46And also Solomon sitteth on the throne of the kingdom.

47And moreover the king's servants came to bless our lord king David, saying, God make the name of Solomon better than thy name, and make his throne greater than thy throne. And the king bowed himself upon the bed.

48And also thus said the king, Blessed *be* the LORD God of Israel, which hath given *one* to sit on my throne this day, mine eyes even seeing *it*.

49And all the guests that *were* with Adonijah were afraid, and rose up, and went every man his way.

50And Adonijah feared because of Solomon, and arose, and went, and caught hold on the horns of the altar.

51And it was told Solomon, saying, Behold, Adonijah feareth king Solomon: for, lo, he hath caught hold on the horns of the altar, saying, Let king Solomon swear unto me today that he will not slay his servant with the sword.

52And Solomon said, If he will shew himself a worthy man, there shall not an hair of him fall to the earth: but if wickedness shall be found in him, he shall die.

53So king Solomon sent, and they brought him down from the altar. And he came and bowed himself to king Solomon: and Solomon said unto him, Go to thine house.

ACTS 4:1–37

AND as they [Peter and John] spake unto the people, the priests, and the captain of the temple, and the Sadducees, came upon them,

2Being grieved that they taught the people, and preached through Jesus the resurrection from the dead.

3And they laid hands on them, and put *them* in hold unto the next day: for it was now eventide.

4Howbeit many of them which heard the word believed; and the number of the men was about five thousand.

5And it came to pass on the morrow, that their rulers, and elders, and scribes,

6And Annas the high priest, and Caiaphas, and John, and Alexander, and as many as were of the kindred of the high priest, were gathered together at Jerusalem.

7And when they had set them in the midst, they asked, By what power, or by what name, have ye done this?

8Then Peter, filled with the Holy Ghost, said unto them, Ye rulers of the people, and elders of Israel,

9If we this day be examined of the good deed done to the impotent man, by what means he is made whole;

10Be it known unto you all, and to all the people of Israel, that by the name of Jesus Christ of Nazareth, whom ye crucified, whom God raised from the dead, *even* by him doth this man stand here before you whole.

11This is the stone which was set at nought of you builders, which is become the head of the corner.

12Neither is there salvation in any other: for there is none other name under heaven given among men, whereby we must be saved.

13Now when they saw the boldness of Peter and John, and perceived that they were unlearned and ignorant men, they marvelled; and they took knowledge of them, that they had been with Jesus.

14And beholding the man which was healed standing with them, they could say nothing against it.

15But when they had commanded them to go aside out of the council, they conferred among themselves,

16Saying, What shall we do to these men? for that indeed a notable miracle hath been done by them *is* manifest to all them that dwell in Jerusalem; and we cannot deny *it.*

17But that it spread no further among the people, let us straitly threaten them, that they speak henceforth to no man in this name.

18And they called them, and commanded them not to speak at all nor teach in the name of Jesus.

19But Peter and John answered and said unto them, Whether it be right in the sight of God to hearken unto you more than unto God, judge ye.

20For we cannot but speak the things which we have seen and heard.

21So when they had further threatened them, they let them go, finding nothing how they might punish them, because of the people: for all *men* glorified God for that which was done.

22For the man was above forty years old, on whom this miracle of healing was shewed.

23And being let go, they went to their own company, and reported all that the chief priests and elders had said unto them.

24And when they heard that, they lifted up their voice to God with one accord, and said, Lord, thou *art* God, which hast made heaven, and earth, and the sea, and all that in them is:

25Who by the mouth of thy servant David hast said, Why did the heathen rage, and the people imagine vain things?

26The kings of the earth stood up, and the rulers were gathered together against the Lord, and against his Christ.

27For a truth against thy holy child Jesus, whom thou hast anointed, both Herod, and Pontius Pilate, with the Gentiles, and the people of Israel, were gathered together,

28For to do whatsoever thy hand and thy counsel determined before to be done.

29And now, Lord, behold their threatenings: and grant unto thy servants, that with all boldness they may speak thy word,

30By stretching forth thine hand to heal; and that signs and wonders may be done by the name of thy holy child Jesus.

31And when they had prayed, the place was shaken where they were assembled together; and they were all filled with the Holy Ghost, and they spake the word of God with boldness.

32And the multitude of them that believed were of one heart and of one soul: neither said any *of them* that ought of the things which he possessed was his own; but they had all things common.

33And with great power gave the apostles witness of the resurrection of the Lord Jesus: and great grace was upon them all.

34Neither was there any among them that lacked: for as many as were possessors of lands or houses sold them, and brought the prices of the things that were sold,

35And laid *them* down at the apostles' feet: and distribution was made unto every man according as he had need.

36And Joses, who by the apostles was surnamed Barnabas, (which is, being interpreted, The son of consolation,) a Levite, *and* of the country of Cyprus,

37Having land, sold *it,* and brought the money, and laid *it* at the apostles' feet.

PSALM 124:1–8

IF *it had not been* the LORD who was on our side, now may Israel say;

2If *it had not been* the LORD who was on our side, when men rose up against us:

3Then they had swallowed us up quick, when their wrath was kindled against us:

4Then the waters had overwhelmed us, the stream had gone over our soul:

5Then the proud waters had gone over our soul.

6Blessed *be* the LORD, who hath not given us *as* a prey to their teeth.

7Our soul is escaped as a bird out of the snare of the fowlers: the snare is broken, and we are escaped.

8Our help *is* in the name of the LORD, who made heaven and earth.

PROVERBS FOR TODAY/ 16:24

Pleasant words are *as an honeycomb, sweet to the soul, and health to the bones.*

JUNE 7

1 KINGS 2:1—3:2

Now the days of David drew nigh that he should die; and he charged Solomon his son, saying,

2I go the way of all the earth: be thou strong therefore, and shew thyself a man;

3And keep the charge of the LORD thy God, to walk in his ways, to keep his statutes, and his commandments, and his judgments, and his testimonies, as it is written in the law of Moses, that thou mayest prosper in all that thou doest, and whithersoever thou turnest thyself:

4That the LORD may continue his word which he spake concerning me, saying, If thy children take heed to their way, to walk before me in truth with all their heart and with all their soul, there shall not fail thee (said he) a man on the throne of Israel.

5Moreover thou knowest also what Joab the son of Zeruiah did to me, *and* what he did to the two captains of the hosts of Israel, unto Abner the son of Ner, and unto Amasa the son of Jether, whom he slew, and shed the blood of war in peace, and put the blood of war upon his girdle that *was* about his loins, and in his shoes that *were* on his feet.

6Do therefore according to thy wisdom, and let not his hoar head go down to the grave in peace.

7But shew kindness unto the sons of Barzillai the Gileadite, and let them be of those that eat at thy table: for so they came to me when I fled because of Absalom thy brother.

8And, behold, *thou hast* with thee Shimei the son of Gera, a Benjamite of Bahurim, which cursed me with a grievous curse in the day when I went to Mahanaim: but he came down to meet me at Jordan, and I sware to him by the LORD, saying, I will not put thee to death with the sword.

9Now therefore hold him not guiltless: for thou *art* a wise man, and knowest what thou oughtest to do unto him; but his hoar head bring thou down to the grave with blood.

10So David slept with his fathers, and was buried in the city of David.

11And the days that David reigned over Israel *were* forty years: seven years reigned he in Hebron, and thirty and three years reigned he in Jerusalem.

12Then sat Solomon upon the throne of David his father; and his kingdom was established greatly.

13And Adonijah the son of Haggith came to Bath–sheba the mother of Solomon. And she said, Comest thou peaceably? And he said, Peaceably.

14He said moreover, I have somewhat to say unto thee. And she said, Say on.

15And he said, Thou knowest that the kingdom was mine, and *that* all Israel set their faces on me, that I should reign: howbeit the kingdom is turned about, and is become my brother's: for it was his from the LORD.

16And now I ask one petition of thee, deny me not. And she said unto him, Say on.

17And he said, Speak, I pray thee, unto Solomon the king, (for he will not say thee nay,) that he give me Abishag the Shunammite to wife.

18And Bath–sheba said, Well; I will speak for thee unto the king.

19Bath–sheba therefore went unto king Solomon, to speak unto him for Adonijah. And the king rose up to meet her, and bowed himself unto her, and sat down on his throne, and caused a seat to be set for the king's mother;

and she sat on his right hand.

20Then she said, I desire one small petition of thee; I *pray thee,* say me not nay. And the king said unto her, Ask on, my mother: for I will not say thee nay.

21And she said, Let Abishag the Shunammite be given to Adonijah thy brother to wife.

22And king Solomon answered and said unto his mother, And why dost thou ask Abishag the Shunammite for Adonijah? ask for him the kingdom also; for he *is* mine elder brother; even for him, and for Abiathar the priest, and for Joab the son of Zeruiah.

23Then king Solomon sware by the LORD, saying, God do so to me, and more also, if Adonijah have not spoken this word against his own life.

24Now therefore, *as* the LORD liveth, which hath established me, and set me on the throne of David my father, and who hath made me an house, as he promised, Adonijah shall be put to death this day.

25And king Solomon sent by the hand of Benaiah the son of Jehoiada; and he fell upon him that he died.

26And unto Abiathar the priest said the king, Get thee to Anathoth, unto thine own fields; for thou *art* worthy of death: but I will not at this time put thee to death, because thou barest the ark of the Lord GOD before David my father, and because thou hast been afflicted in all wherein my father was afflicted.

27So Solomon thrust out Abiathar from being priest unto the LORD; that he might fulfil the word of the LORD, which he spake concerning the house of Eli in Shiloh.

28Then tidings came to Joab: for Joab had turned after Adonijah, though he turned not after Absalom. And Joab fled unto the tabernacle of the LORD, and caught hold on the horns of the altar.

29And it was told king Solomon that Joab was fled unto the tabernacle of the LORD; and, behold, *he is* by the altar. Then Solomon sent Benaiah the son of Jehoiada, saying, Go, fall upon him.

30And Benaiah came to the tabernacle of the LORD, and said unto him, Thus saith the king, Come forth. And he said, Nay; but I will die here. And Benaiah brought the king word again, saying, Thus said Joab, and thus he answered me.

31And the king said unto him, Do as he hath said, and fall upon him, and bury him; that thou mayest take away the innocent blood, which Joab shed, from me, and from the house of my father.

32And the LORD shall return his blood upon his own head, who fell upon two men more righteous and better than he, and slew them with the sword, my father David not knowing *thereof, to wit,* Abner the son of Ner, captain of the host of Israel, and Amasa the son of Jether, captain of the host of Judah.

33Their blood shall therefore return upon the head of Joab, and upon the head of his seed for ever: but upon David, and upon his seed, and upon his house, and upon his throne, shall there be peace for ever from the LORD.

34So Benaiah the son of Jehoiada went up, and fell upon him, and slew him: and he was buried in his own house in the wilderness.

35And the king put Benaiah the son of Jehoiada in his room over the host: and Zadok the priest did the king put in the room of Abiathar.

36And the king sent and called for Shimei, and said unto him, Build thee an house in Jerusalem, and dwell there, and go not forth thence any whither.

37For it shall be, *that* on the day thou goest out, and passest over the brook Kidron, thou shalt know for certain that thou shalt surely die: thy blood shall be upon thine own head.

38And Shimei said unto the king, The

saying *is* good: as my lord the king hath said, so will thy servant do. And Shimei dwelt in Jerusalem many days.

39And it came to pass at the end of three years, that two of the servants of Shimei ran away unto Achish son of Maachah king of Gath. And they told Shimei, saying, Behold, thy servants *be* in Gath.

40And Shimei arose, and saddled his ass, and went to Gath to Achish to seek his servants: and Shimei went, and brought his servants from Gath.

41And it was told Solomon that Shimei had gone from Jerusalem to Gath, and was come again.

42And the king sent and called for Shimei, and said unto him, Did I not make thee to swear by the LORD, and protested unto thee, saying, Know for a certain, on the day thou goest out, and walkest abroad any whither, that thou shalt surely die? and thou saidst unto me, The word *that* I have heard *is* good.

43Why then hast thou not kept the oath of the LORD, and the commandment that I have charged thee with?

44The king said moreover to Shimei, Thou knowest all the wickedness which thine heart is privy to, that thou didst to David my father: therefore the LORD shall return thy wickedness upon thine own head;

45And king Solomon *shall be* blessed, and the throne of David shall be established before the LORD for ever.

46So the king commanded Benaiah the son of Jehoiada; which went out, and fell upon him, that he died. And the kingdom was established in the hand of Solomon.

AND Solomon made affinity with Pharaoh king of Egypt, and took Pharaoh's daughter, and brought her into the city of David, until he had made an end of building his own house, and the house of the LORD, and the wall of Jerusalem round about.

2Only the people sacrificed in high places, because there was no house built unto the name of the LORD, until those days.

ACTS 5:1–42

BUT a certain man named Ananias, with Sapphira his wife, sold a possession,

2And kept back *part* of the price, his wife also being privy *to it,* and brought a certain part, and laid *it* at the apostles' feet.

3But Peter said, Ananias, why hath Satan filled thine heart to lie to the Holy Ghost, and to keep back *part* of the price of the land?

4Whiles it remained, was it not thine own? and after it was sold, was it not in thine own power? why hast thou conceived this thing in thine heart? thou hast not lied unto men, but unto God.

5And Ananias hearing these words fell down, and gave up the ghost: and great fear came on all them that heard these things.

6And the young men arose, wound him up, and carried *him* out, and buried *him.*

7And it was about the space of three hours after, when his wife, not knowing what was done, came in.

8And Peter answered unto her, Tell me whether ye sold the land for so much? And she said, Yea, for so much.

9Then Peter said unto her, How is it that ye have agreed together to tempt the Spirit of the Lord? behold, the feet of them which have buried thy husband *are* at the door, and shall carry thee out.

10Then fell she down straightway at his feet, and yielded up the ghost: and the young men came in, and found her dead, and, carrying *her* forth, buried *her* by her husband.

11And great fear came upon all the church, and upon as many as heard these things.

12And by the hands of the apostles were many signs and wonders wrought among the people; (and they were all with one accord in Solomon's porch.

13And of the rest durst no man join himself to them: but the people magnified them.

14And believers were the more added to the Lord, multitudes both of men and women.)

15Insomuch that they brought forth the sick into the streets, and laid *them* on beds and couches, that at the least the shadow of Peter passing by might overshadow some of them.

16There came also a multitude *out* of the cities round about unto Jerusalem, bringing sick folks, and them which were vexed with unclean spirits: and they were healed every one.

17Then the high priest rose up, and all they that were with him, (which is the sect of the Sadducees,) and were filled with indignation,

18And laid their hands on the apostles, and put them in the common prison.

19But the angel of the Lord by night opened the prison doors, and brought them forth, and said,

20Go, stand and speak in the temple to the people all the words of this life.

21And when they heard *that,* they entered into the temple early in the morning, and taught. But the high priest came, and they that were with him, and called the council together, and all the senate of the children of Israel, and sent to the prison to have them brought.

22But when the officers came, and found them not in the prison, they returned, and told,

23Saying, The prison truly found we shut with all safety, and the keepers standing without before the doors: but when we had opened, we found no man within.

24Now when the high priest and the captain of the temple and the chief priests heard these things, they doubted of them whereunto this would grow.

25Then came one and told them, saying, Behold, the men whom ye put in prison are standing in the temple, and teaching the people.

26Then went the captain with the officers, and brought them without violence: for they feared the people, lest they should have been stoned.

27And when they had brought them, they set *them* before the council: and the high priest asked them,

28Saying, Did not we straitly command you that ye should not teach in this name? and, behold, ye have filled Jerusalem with your doctrine, and intend to bring this man's blood upon us.

29Then Peter and the *other* apostles answered and said, We ought to obey God rather than men.

30The God of our fathers raised up Jesus, whom ye slew and hanged on a tree.

31Him hath God exalted with his right hand *to be* a Prince and a Saviour, for to give repentance to Israel, and forgiveness of sins.

32And we are his witnesses of these things; and *so is* also the Holy Ghost, whom God hath given to them that obey him.

33When they heard *that,* they were cut *to the heart,* and took counsel to slay them.

34Then stood there up one in the council, a Pharisee, named Gamaliel, a doctor of the law, had in reputation among all the people, and commanded to put the apostles forth a little space;

35And said unto them, Ye men of Israel, take heed to yourselves what ye intend to do as touching these men.

36For before these days rose up Theudas, boasting himself to be somebody; to whom a number of men, about four hundred, joined themselves: who was slain; and all, as many as obeyed him, were scattered, and brought to nought.

37After this man rose up Judas of Galilee in the days of the taxing, and drew away much people after him: he also perished; and all, *even* as many as obeyed him, were dispersed.

38And now I say unto you, Refrain from these men, and let them alone: for if this counsel or this work be of men, it will come to nought:

39But if it be of God, ye cannot overthrow it; lest haply ye be found even to fight against God.

40And to him they agreed: and when they had called the apostles, and beaten *them,* they commanded that they should not speak in the name of Jesus, and let them go.

41And they departed from the presence of the council, rejoicing that they were counted worthy to suffer shame for his name.

42And daily in the temple, and in every house, they ceased not to teach and preach Jesus Christ.

PSALM 125:1–5

THEY that trust in the LORD *shall be* as mount Zion *which* cannot be removed, *but* abideth for ever.

2As the mountains *are* round about Jerusalem, so the LORD *is* round about his people from henceforth even for ever.

3For the rod of the wicked shall not rest upon the lot of the righteous; lest the righteous put forth their hands unto iniquity.

4Do good, O LORD, unto *those that be* good, and to *them that are* upright in their hearts.

5As for such as turn aside unto their crooked ways, the LORD shall lead them forth with the workers of iniquity: *but* peace *shall be* upon Israel.

PROVERBS FOR TODAY/ 16:25

There is a way that seemeth right unto a man, but the end thereof are *the ways of death.*

JUNE 8

1 KINGS 3:3—4:34

AND Solomon loved the LORD, walking in the statutes of David his father: only he sacrificed and burnt incense in high places.

4And the king went to Gibeon to sacrifice there; for that *was* the great high place: a thousand burnt offerings did Solomon offer upon that altar.

5In Gibeon the LORD appeared to Solomon in a dream by night: and God said, Ask what I shall give thee.

6And Solomon said, Thou hast shewed unto thy servant David my father great mercy, according as he walked before thee in truth, and in righteousness, and in uprightness of heart with thee; and thou hast kept for him this great kindness, that thou hast given him a son to sit on his throne, as *it is* this day.

7And now, O LORD my God, thou hast made thy servant king instead of David my father: and I *am but* a little child: I know not *how* to go out or come in.

8And thy servant *is* in the midst of thy people which thou hast chosen, a great people, that cannot be numbered nor counted for multitude.

9Give therefore thy servant an understanding heart to judge thy people, that I may discern between good and bad: for who is able to judge this thy so great a people?

10And the speech pleased the LORD, that Solomon had asked this thing.

11And God said unto him, Because thou hast asked this thing, and hast not asked for thyself long life; neither hast asked riches for thyself, nor hast asked the life of thine enemies; but hast asked for thyself understanding to discern judgment;

12Behold, I have done according to thy words: lo, I have given thee a wise and an understanding heart; so that there was none like thee before thee, neither after thee shall any arise like unto thee.

13And I have also given thee that which thou hast not asked, both riches, and honour: so that there shall not be any among the kings like unto thee all thy days.

14And if thou wilt walk in my ways, to keep my statutes and my commandments, as thy father David did walk, then I will lengthen thy days.

15And Solomon awoke; and, behold, *it was* a dream. And he came to Jerusalem, and stood before the ark of the covenant of the LORD, and offered up burnt offerings, and offered peace offerings, and made a feast to all his servants.

16Then came there two women, *that were* harlots, unto the king, and stood before him.

17And the one woman said, O my lord, I and this woman dwell in one house; and I was delivered of a child with her in the house.

18And it came to pass the third day after that I was delivered, that this woman was delivered also: and we *were* together; *there was* no stranger with us in the house, save we two in the house.

19And this woman's child died in the night; because she overlaid it.

20And she arose at midnight, and took my son from beside me, while thine handmaid slept, and laid it in her bosom, and laid her dead child in my bosom.

21And when I rose in the morning to give my child suck, behold, it was dead: but when I had considered it in the morning, behold, it was not my son, which I did bear.

22And the other woman said, Nay; but the living *is* my son, and the dead *is* thy son. And this said, No; but the dead *is* thy son, and the living *is* my son. Thus they spake before the king.

23Then said the king, The one saith, This *is* my son that liveth, and thy son *is* the dead: and the other saith, Nay; but thy son *is* the dead, and my son *is* the living.

24And the king said, Bring me a sword. And they brought a sword before the king.

25And the king said, Divide the living child in two, and give half to the one, and half to the other.

26Then spake the woman whose the living child *was* unto the king, for her bowels yearned upon her son, and she said, O my lord, give her the living child, and in no wise slay it. But the other said, Let it be neither mine nor thine, *but* divide *it.*

27Then the king answered and said, Give her the living child, and in no wise slay it: she *is* the mother thereof.

28And all Israel heard of the judgment which the king had judged; and they feared the king: for they saw that the wisdom of God *was* in him, to do judgment.

So king Solomon was king over all Israel.

2And these *were* the princes which

he had; Azariah the son of Zadok the priest,

3Elihoreph and Ahiah, the sons of Shisha, scribes; Jehoshaphat the son of Ahilud, the recorder.

4And Benaiah the son of Jehoiada *was* over the host: and Zadok and Abiathar *were* the priests:

5And Azariah the son of Nathan *was* over the officers: and Zabud the son of Nathan *was* principal officer, *and* the king's friend:

6And Ahishar *was* over the household: and Adoniram the son of Abda *was* over the tribute.

7And Solomon had twelve officers over all Israel, which provided victuals for the king and his household: each man his month in a year made provision.

8And these *are* their names: The son of Hur, in mount Ephraim:

9The son of Dekar, in Makaz, and in Shaalbim, and Beth–shemesh, and Elon–beth–hanan:

10The son of Hesed, in Aruboth; to him *pertained* Sochoh, and all the land of Hepher:

11The son of Abinadab, in all the region of Dor; which had Taphath the daughter of Solomon to wife:

12Baana the son of Ahilud; *to him pertained* Taanach and Megiddo, and all Beth–shean, which *is* by Zartanah beneath Jezreel, from Beth–shean to Abel–meholah, *even* unto *the place that is* beyond Jokneam:

13The son of Geber, in Ramoth–gilead; to him *pertained* the towns of Jair the son of Manasseh, which *are* in Gilead; to him *also pertained* the region of Argob, which *is* in Bashan, threescore great cities with walls and brasen bars:

14Ahinadab the son of Iddo *had* Mahanaim:

15Ahimaaz *was* in Naphtali; he also took Basmath the daughter of Solomon to wife:

16Baanah the son of Hushai *was* in Asher and in Aloth:

17Jehoshaphat the son of Paruah, in Issachar:

18Shimei the son of Elah, in Benjamin:

19Geber the son of Uri *was* in the country of Gilead, *in* the country of Sihon king of the Amorites, and of Og king of Bashan; and *he was* the only officer which *was* in the land.

20Judah and Israel *were* many, as the sand which *is* by the sea in multitude, eating and drinking, and making merry.

21And Solomon reigned over all kingdoms from the river unto the land of the Philistines, and unto the border of Egypt: they brought presents, and served Solomon all the days of his life.

22And Solomon's provision for one day was thirty measures of fine flour, and threescore measures of meal,

23Ten fat oxen, and twenty oxen out of the pastures, and an hundred sheep, beside harts, and roebucks, and fallowdeer, and fatted fowl.

24For he had dominion over all *the region* on this side the river, from Tiphsah even to Azzah, over all the kings on this side the river: and he had peace on all sides round about him.

25And Judah and Israel dwelt safely, every man under his vine and under his fig tree, from Dan even to Beersheba, all the days of Solomon.

26And Solomon had forty thousand stalls of horses for his chariots, and twelve thousand horsemen.

27And those officers provided victual for king Solomon, and for all that came unto king Solomon's table, every man in his month: they lacked nothing.

28Barley also and straw for the horses and dromedaries brought they unto the place where *the officers* were, every man according to his charge.

29And God gave Solomon wisdom and understanding exceeding much, and largeness of heart, even as the sand that *is* on the sea shore.

30And Solomon's wisdom excelled the wisdom of all the children of the east country, and all the wisdom of Egypt.

31For he was wiser than all men; than Ethan the Ezrahite, and Heman, and Chalcol, and Darda, the sons of Mahol: and his fame was in all nations round about.

32And he spake three thousand proverbs; and his songs were a thousand and five.

33And he spake of trees, from the cedar tree that *is* in Lebanon even unto the hyssop that springeth out of the wall: he spake also of beasts, and of fowl, and of creeping things, and of fishes.

34And there came of all people to hear the wisdom of Solomon, from all kings of the earth, which had heard of his wisdom.

ACTS 6:1–15

AND in those days, when the number of the disciples were multiplied, there arose a murmuring of the Grecians against the Hebrews, because their widows were neglected in the daily ministration.

2Then the twelve called the multitude of the disciples *unto them,* and said, It is not reason that we should leave the word of God, and serve tables.

3Wherefore, brethren, look ye out among you seven men of honest report, full of the Holy Ghost and wisdom, whom we may appoint over this business.

4But we will give ourselves continually to prayer, and to the ministry of the word.

5And the saying pleased the whole multitude: and they chose Stephen, a man full of faith and of the Holy Ghost, and Philip, and Prochorus, and Nicanor, and Timon, and Parmenas, and Nicolas a proselyte of Antioch:

6Whom they set before the apostles: and when they had prayed, they laid *their* hands on them.

7And the word of God increased; and the number of the disciples multiplied in Jerusalem greatly; and a great company of the priests were obedient to the faith.

8And Stephen, full of faith and power, did great wonders and miracles among the people.

9Then there arose certain of the synagogue, which is called *the synagogue* of the Libertines, and Cyrenians, and Alexandrians, and of them of Cilicia and of Asia, disputing with Stephen.

10And they were not able to resist the wisdom and the spirit by which he spake.

11Then they suborned men, which said, We have heard him speak blasphemous words against Moses, and *against* God.

12And they stirred up the people, and the elders, and the scribes, and came upon *him,* and caught him, and brought *him* to the council,

13And set up false witnesses, which said, This man ceaseth not to speak blasphemous words against this holy place, and the law:

14For we have heard him say, that this Jesus of Nazareth shall destroy this place, and shall change the customs which Moses delivered us.

15And all that sat in the council, looking stedfastly on him, saw his face as it had been the face of an angel.

PSALM 126:1–6

WHEN the LORD turned again the captivity of Zion, we were like them that dream.

2Then was our mouth filled with laughter, and our tongue with singing: then said they among the heathen, The LORD hath done great things for them.

3The LORD hath done great things for us; *whereof* we are glad.

4Turn again our captivity, O LORD, as the streams in the south.

5They that sow in tears shall reap in joy.

⁶He that goeth forth and weepeth, bearing precious seed, shall doubtless come again with rejoicing, bringing his sheaves *with him.*

PROVERBS FOR TODAY/ 16:26–27

He that laboureth laboureth for himself; for his mouth craveth it of him. □ *An ungodly man diggeth up evil: and in his lips* there is *as a burning fire.*

JUNE 9

1 KINGS 5:1—6:38

AND Hiram king of Tyre sent his servants unto Solomon; for he had heard that they had anointed him king in the room of his father: for Hiram was ever a lover of David.

²And Solomon sent to Hiram, saying,

³Thou knowest how that David my father could not build an house unto the name of the LORD his God for the wars which were about him on every side, until the LORD put them under the soles of his feet.

⁴But now the LORD my God hath given me rest on every side, *so that there is* neither adversary nor evil occurrent.

⁵And, behold, I purpose to build an house unto the name of the LORD my God, as the LORD spake unto David my father, saying, Thy son, whom I will set upon thy throne in thy room, he shall build an house unto my name.

⁶Now therefore command thou that they hew me cedar trees out of Lebanon; and my servants shall be with thy servants: and unto thee will I give hire for thy servants according to all that thou shalt appoint: for thou knowest that *there is* not among us any that can skill to hew timber like unto the Sidonians.

⁷And it came to pass, when Hiram heard the words of Solomon, that he rejoiced greatly, and said, Blessed *be* the LORD this day, which hath given unto David a wise son over this great people.

⁸And Hiram sent to Solomon, saying, I have considered the things which thou sentest to me for: *and* I will do all thy desire concerning timber of cedar, and concerning timber of fir.

⁹My servants shall bring *them* down from Lebanon unto the sea: and I will convey them by sea in floats unto the place that thou shalt appoint me, and will cause them to be discharged there, and thou shalt receive *them:* and thou shalt accomplish my desire, in giving food for my household.

¹⁰So Hiram gave Solomon cedar trees and fir trees *according to* all his desire.

¹¹And Solomon gave Hiram twenty thousand measures of wheat *for* food to his household, and twenty measures of pure oil: thus gave Solomon to Hiram year by year.

¹²And the LORD gave Solomon wisdom, as he promised him: and there was peace between Hiram and Solomon; and they two made a league together.

¹³And king Solomon raised a levy out of all Israel; and the levy was thirty thousand men.

¹⁴And he sent them to Lebanon, ten thousand a month by courses: a month

they were in Lebanon, *and* two months at home: and Adoniram *was* over the levy.

15And Solomon had threescore and ten thousand that bare burdens, and fourscore thousand hewers in the mountains;

16Beside the chief of Solomon's officers which *were* over the work, three thousand and three hundred, which ruled over the people that wrought in the work.

17And the king commanded, and they brought great stones, costly stones, *and* hewed stones, to lay the foundation of the house.

18And Solomon's builders and Hiram's builders did hew *them,* and the stonesquarers: so they prepared timber and stones to build the house.

AND it came to pass in the four hundred and eightieth year after the children of Israel were come out of the land of Egypt, in the fourth year of Solomon's reign over Israel, in the month Zif, which *is* the second month, that he began to build the house of the LORD.

2And the house which king Solomon built for the LORD, the length thereof *was* threescore cubits, and the breadth thereof twenty *cubits,* and the height thereof thirty cubits.

3And the porch before the temple of the house, twenty cubits *was* the length thereof, according to the breadth of the house; *and* ten cubits *was* the breadth thereof before the house.

4And for the house he made windows of narrow lights.

5And against the wall of the house he built chambers round about, *against* the walls of the house round about, *both* of the temple and of the oracle: and he made chambers round about:

6The nethermost chamber *was* five cubits broad, and the middle *was* six cubits broad, and the third *was* seven cubits broad: for without *in the wall* of the house he made narrowed rests

round about, that *the beams* should not be fastened in the walls of the house.

7And the house, when it was in building, was built of stone made ready before it was brought thither: so that there was neither hammer nor axe *nor* any tool of iron heard in the house, while it was in building.

8The door for the middle chamber *was* in the right side of the house: and they went up with winding stairs into the middle *chamber,* and out of the middle into the third.

9So he built the house, and finished it; and covered the house with beams and boards of cedar.

10And *then* he built chambers against all the house, five cubits high: and they rested on the house with timber of cedar.

11And the word of the LORD came to Solomon, saying,

12*Concerning* this house which thou art in building, if thou wilt walk in my statutes, and execute my judgments, and keep all my commandments to walk in them; then will I perform my word with thee, which I spake unto David thy father:

13And I will dwell among the children of Israel, and will not forsake my people Israel.

14So Solomon built the house, and finished it.

15And he built the walls of the house within with boards of cedar, both the floor of the house, and the walls of the ceiling: *and* he covered *them* on the inside with wood, and covered the floor of the house with planks of fir.

16And he built twenty cubits on the sides of the house, both the floor and the walls with boards of cedar: he even built *them* for it within, *even* for the oracle, *even* for the most holy *place.*

17And the house, that *is,* the temple before it, was forty cubits *long.*

18And the cedar of the house within *was* carved with knops and open flowers: all *was* cedar; there was no stone seen.

19And the oracle he prepared in the house within, to set there the ark of the covenant of the LORD.

20And the oracle in the forepart *was* twenty cubits in length, and twenty cubits in breadth, and twenty cubits in the height thereof: and he overlaid it with pure gold; and *so* covered the altar *which was of* cedar.

21So Solomon overlaid the house within with pure gold: and he made a partition by the chains of gold before the oracle; and he overlaid it with gold.

22And the whole house he overlaid with gold, until he had finished all the house: also the whole altar that *was* by the oracle he overlaid with gold.

23And within the oracle he made two cherubims *of* olive tree, *each* ten cubits high.

24And five cubits *was* the one wing of the cherub, and five cubits the other wing of the cherub: from the uttermost part of the one wing unto the uttermost part of the other *were* ten cubits.

25And the other cherub *was* ten cubits: both the cherubims *were* of one measure and one size.

26The height of the one cherub *was* ten cubits, and so *was it* of the other cherub.

27And he set the cherubims within the inner house: and they stretched forth the wings of the cherubims, so that the wing of the one touched the *one* wall, and the wing of the other cherub touched the other wall; and their wings touched one another in the midst of the house.

28And he overlaid the cherubims with gold.

29And he carved all the walls of the house round about with carved figures of cherubims and palm trees and open flowers, within and without.

30And the floor of the house he overlaid with gold, within and without.

31And for the entering of the oracle he made doors *of* olive tree: the lintel *and* side posts *were* a fifth part *of the wall.*

32The two doors also *were of* olive tree; and he carved upon them carvings of cherubims and palm trees and open flowers, and overlaid *them* with gold, and spread gold upon the cherubims, and upon the palm trees.

33So also made he for the door of the temple posts *of* olive tree, a fourth part *of the wall.*

34And the two doors *were of* fir tree: the two leaves of the one door *were* folding, and the two leaves of the other door *were* folding.

35And he carved *thereon* cherubims and palm trees and open flowers: and covered *them* with gold fitted upon the carved work.

36And he built the inner court with three rows of hewed stone, and a row of cedar beams.

37In the fourth year was the foundation of the house of the LORD laid, in the month Zif:

38And in the eleventh year, in the month Bul, which *is* the eighth month, was the house finished throughout all the parts thereof, and according to all the fashion of it. So was he seven years in building it.

ACTS 7:1–29

THEN said the high priest, Are these things so?

2And he [Stephen] said, Men, brethren, and fathers, hearken; The God of glory appeared unto our father Abraham, when he was in Mesopotamia, before he dwelt in Charran,

3And said unto him, Get thee out of thy country, and from thy kindred, and come into the land which I shall shew thee.

4Then came he out of the land of the Chaldaeans, and dwelt in Charran: and from thence, when his father was dead, he removed him into this land, wherein ye now dwell.

5And he gave him none inheritance in it, no, not *so much as* to set his foot on: yet he promised that he would give it to him for a possession, and to his seed after him, when *as yet* he had no child.

6And God spake on this wise, That his seed should sojourn in a strange land; and that they should bring them into bondage, and entreat *them* evil four hundred years.

7And the nation to whom they shall be in bondage will I judge, said God: and after that shall they come forth, and serve me in this place.

8And he gave him the covenant of circumcision: and so *Abraham* begat Isaac, and circumcised him the eighth day; and Isaac *begat* Jacob; and Jacob *begat* the twelve patriarchs.

9And the patriarchs, moved with envy, sold Joseph into Egypt: but God was with him,

10And delivered him out of all his afflictions, and gave him favour and wisdom in the sight of Pharaoh king of Egypt; and he made him governor over Egypt and all his house.

11Now there came a dearth over all the land of Egypt and Chanaan, and great affliction: and our fathers found no sustenance.

12But when Jacob heard that there was corn in Egypt, he sent out our fathers first.

13And at the second *time* Joseph was made known to his brethren; and Joseph's kindred was made known unto Pharaoh.

14Then sent Joseph, and called his father Jacob to *him,* and all his kindred, threescore and fifteen souls.

15So Jacob went down into Egypt, and died, he, and our fathers,

16And were carried over into Sychem, and laid in the sepulchre that Abraham bought for a sum of money of the sons of Emmor *the father* of Sychem.

17But when the time of the promise drew nigh, which God had sworn to Abraham, the people grew and multiplied in Egypt,

18Till another king arose, which knew not Joseph.

19The same dealt subtilly with our kindred, and evil entreated our fathers, so that they cast out their young children, to the end they might not live.

20In which time Moses was born, and was exceeding fair, and nourished up in his father's house three months:

21And when he was cast out, Pharaoh's daughter took him up, and nourished him for her own son.

22And Moses was learned in all the wisdom of the Egyptians, and was mighty in words and in deeds.

23And when he was full forty years old, it came into his heart to visit his brethren the children of Israel.

24And seeing one *of them* suffer wrong, he defended *him,* and avenged him that was oppressed, and smote the Egyptian:

25For he supposed his brethren would have understood how that God by his hand would deliver them: but they understood not.

26And the next day he shewed himself unto them as they strove, and would have set them at one again, saying, Sirs, ye are brethren; why do ye wrong one to another?

27But he that did his neighbour wrong thrust him away, saying, Who made thee a ruler and a judge over us?

28Wilt thou kill me, as thou diddest the Egyptian yesterday?

29Then fled Moses at this saying, and was a stranger in the land of Madian, where he begat two sons.

PSALM 127:1–5

EXCEPT the LORD build the house, they labour in vain that build it: except the LORD keep the city, the watchman waketh *but* in vain.

2*It is* vain for you to rise up early, to sit up late, to eat the bread of sorrows: *for* so he giveth his beloved sleep.

3Lo, children *are* an heritage of the Lord: *and* the fruit of the womb *is* his reward.

4As arrows *are* in the hand of a mighty man; so *are* children of the youth.

5Happy *is* the man that hath his quiver full of them: they shall not be ashamed, but they shall speak with the enemies in the gate.

PROVERBS FOR TODAY/ 16:28–30

A froward man soweth strife: and a whisperer separateth chief friends. □ *A violent man enticeth his neighbour, and leadeth him into the way* that is *not good. He shutteth his eyes to devise froward things: moving his lips he bringeth evil to pass.*

JUNE 10

1 KINGS 7:1–51

BUT Solomon was building his own house thirteen years, and he finished all his house.

2He built also the house of the forest of Lebanon; the length thereof *was* an hundred cubits, and the breadth thereof fifty cubits, and the height thereof thirty cubits, upon four rows of cedar pillars, with cedar beams upon the pillars.

3And *it was* covered with cedar above upon the beams, that *lay* on forty five pillars, fifteen *in* a row.

4And *there were* windows *in* three rows, and light *was* against light *in* three ranks.

5And all the doors and posts *were* square, with the windows: and light *was* against light *in* three ranks.

6And he made a porch of pillars; the length thereof *was* fifty cubits, and the breadth thereof thirty cubits: and the porch *was* before them: and the *other* pillars and the thick beam *were* before them.

7Then he made a porch for the throne where he might judge, *even* the porch of judgment: and *it was* covered with cedar from one side of the floor to the other.

8And his house where he dwelt *had* another court within the porch, *which* was of the like work. Solomon made also an house for Pharaoh's daughter, whom he had taken *to wife,* like unto this porch.

9All these *were of* costly stones, according to the measures of hewed stones, sawed with saws, within and without, even from the foundation unto the coping, and *so* on the outside toward the great court.

10And the foundation *was of* costly stones, even great stones, stones of ten cubits, and stones of eight cubits.

11And above *were* costly stones, after the measures of hewed stones, and cedars.

12And the great court round about *was* with three rows of hewed stones, and a row of cedar beams, both for the inner court of the house of the Lord, and for the porch of the house.

13And king Solomon sent and fetched Hiram out of Tyre.

14He *was* a widow's son of the tribe

of Naphtali, and his father *was* a man of Tyre, a worker in brass: and he was filled with wisdom, and understanding, and cunning to work all works in brass. And he came to king Solomon, and wrought all his work.

15For he cast two pillars of brass, of eighteen cubits high apiece: and a line of twelve cubits did compass either of them about.

16And he made two chapiters *of* molten brass, to set upon the tops of the pillars: the height of the one chapiter *was* five cubits, and the height of the other chapiter *was* five cubits:

17*And* nets of checker work, and wreaths of chain work, for the chapiters which *were* upon the top of the pillars; seven for the one chapiter, and seven for the other chapiter.

18And he made the pillars, and two rows round about upon the one network, to cover the chapiters that *were* upon the top, with pomegranates: and so did he for the other chapiter.

19And the chapiters that *were* upon the top of the pillars *were* of lily work in the porch, four cubits.

20And the chapiters upon the two pillars *had pomegranates* also above, over against the belly which *was* by the network: and the pomegranates *were* two hundred in rows round about upon the other chapiter.

21And he set up the pillars in the porch of the temple: and he set up the right pillar, and called the name thereof Jachin: and he set up the left pillar, and called the name thereof Boaz.

22And upon the top of the pillars *was* lily work: so was the work of the pillars finished.

23And he made a molten sea, ten cubits from the one brim to the other: *it was* round all about, and his height *was* five cubits: and a line of thirty cubits did compass it round about.

24And under the brim of it round about *there were* knops compassing it, ten in a cubit, compassing the sea round

about: the knops *were* cast in two rows, when it was cast.

25It stood upon twelve oxen, three looking toward the north, and three looking toward the west, and three looking toward the south, and three looking toward the east: and the sea *was set* above upon them, and all their hinder parts *were* inward.

26And it *was* an hand breadth thick, and the brim thereof was wrought like the brim of a cup, with flowers of lilies: it contained two thousand baths.

27And he made ten bases of brass; four cubits *was* the length of one base, and four cubits the breadth thereof, and three cubits the height of it.

28And the work of the bases *was* on this *manner:* they had borders, and the borders *were* between the ledges:

29And on the borders that *were* between the ledges *were* lions, oxen, and cherubims: and upon the ledges *there was* a base above: and beneath the lions and oxen *were* certain additions made of thin work.

30And every base had four brasen wheels, and plates of brass: and the four corners thereof had undersetters: under the laver *were* undersetters molten, at the side of every addition.

31And the mouth of it within the chapiter and above *was* a cubit: but the mouth thereof *was* round *after* the work of the base, a cubit and an half: and also upon the mouth of it *were* gravings with their borders, foursquare, not round.

32And under the borders *were* four wheels; and the axletrees of the wheels *were joined* to the base: and the height of a wheel *was* a cubit and half a cubit.

33And the work of the wheels *was* like the work of a chariot wheel: their axletrees, and their naves, and their felloes, and their spokes, *were* all molten.

34And *there were* four undersetters to the four corners of one base: *and* the undersetters *were* of the very base itself.

35And in the top of the base *was there* a round compass of half a cubit high: and on the top of the base the ledges thereof and the borders thereof *were* of the same.

36For on the plates of the ledges thereof, and on the borders thereof, he graved cherubims, lions, and palm trees, according to the proportion of every one, and additions round about.

37After this *manner* he made the ten bases: all of them had one casting, one measure, *and* one size.

38Then made he ten lavers of brass: one laver contained forty baths: *and* every laver was four cubits: *and* upon every one of the ten bases one laver.

39And he put five bases on the right side of the house, and five on the left side of the house: and he set the sea on the right side of the house eastward over against the south.

40And Hiram made the lavers, and the shovels, and the basons. So Hiram made an end of doing all the work that he made king Solomon for the house of the LORD:

41The two pillars, and the *two* bowls of the chapiters that *were* on the top of the two pillars; and the two networks, to cover the two bowls of the chapiters which *were* upon the top of the pillars;

42And four hundred pomegranates for the two networks, *even* two rows of pomegranates for one network, to cover the two bowls of the chapiters that *were* upon the pillars;

43And the ten bases, and ten lavers on the bases;

44And one sea, and twelve oxen under the sea;

45And the pots, and the shovels, and the basons: and all these vessels, which Hiram made to king Solomon for the house of the LORD, *were of* bright brass.

46In the plain of Jordan did the king cast them, in the clay ground between Succoth and Zarthan.

47And Solomon left all the vessels *unweighed,* because they were exceeding many: neither was the weight of the brass found out.

48And Solomon made all the vessels that *pertained* unto the house of the LORD: the altar of gold, and the table of gold, whereupon the shewbread *was,*

49And the candlesticks of pure gold, five on the right *side,* and five on the left, before the oracle, with the flowers, and the lamps, and the tongs *of* gold,

50And the bowls, and the snuffers, and the basons, and the spoons, and the censers *of* pure gold; and the hinges *of* gold, *both* for the doors of the inner house, the most holy *place, and* for the doors of the house, *to wit,* of the temple.

51So was ended all the work that king Solomon made for the house of the LORD. And Solomon brought in the things which David his father had dedicated; *even* the silver, and the gold, and the vessels, did he put among the treasures of the house of the LORD.

ACTS 7:30–50

AND when forty years were expired, there appeared to him [Moses] in the wilderness of mount Sina an angel of the Lord in a flame of fire in a bush.

31When Moses saw *it,* he wondered at the sight: and as he drew near to behold *it,* the voice of the Lord came unto him,

32*Saying, I am* the God of thy fathers, the God of Abraham, and the God of Isaac, and the God of Jacob. Then Moses trembled, and durst not behold.

33Then said the Lord to him, Put off thy shoes from thy feet: for the place where thou standest is holy ground.

34I have seen, I have seen the affliction of my people which is in Egypt, and I have heard their groaning, and am come down to deliver them. And now come, I will send thee into Egypt.

35This Moses whom they refused,

saying, Who made thee a ruler and a judge? the same did God send *to be* a ruler and a deliverer by the hand of the angel which appeared to him in the bush.

36He brought them out, after that he had shewed wonders and signs in the land of Egypt, and in the Red sea, and in the wilderness forty years.

37This is that Moses, which said unto the children of Israel, A prophet shall the Lord your God raise up unto you of your brethren, like unto me; him shall ye hear.

38This is he, that was in the church in the wilderness with the angel which spake to him in the mount Sina, and *with* our fathers: who received the lively oracles to give unto us:

39To whom our fathers would not obey, but thrust *him* from them, and in their hearts turned back again into Egypt,

40Saying unto Aaron, Make us gods to go before us: for *as for* this Moses, which brought us out of the land of Egypt, we wot not what is become of him.

41And they made a calf in those days, and offered sacrifice unto the idol, and rejoiced in the works of their own hands.

42Then God turned, and gave them up to worship the host of heaven; as it is written in the book of the prophets, O ye house of Israel, have ye offered to me slain beasts and sacrifices *by the space of* forty years in the wilderness?

43Yea, ye took up the tabernacle of Moloch, and the star of your god Remphan, figures which ye made to worship them: and I will carry you away beyond Babylon.

44Our fathers had the tabernacle of witness in the wilderness, as he had appointed, speaking unto Moses, that he should make it according to the fashion that he had seen.

45Which also our fathers that came after brought in with Jesus into the possession of the Gentiles, whom God drave out before the face of our fathers, unto the days of David;

46Who found favour before God, and desired to find a tabernacle for the God of Jacob.

47But Solomon built him an house.

48Howbeit the most High dwelleth not in temples made with hands; as saith the prophet,

49Heaven *is* my throne, and earth *is* my footstool: what house will ye build me? saith the Lord: or what *is* the place of my rest?

50Hath not my hand made all these things?

PSALM 128:1–6

BLESSED *is* every one that feareth the LORD; that walketh in his ways.

2For thou shalt eat the labour of thine hands: happy *shalt* thou *be,* and *it shall be* well with thee.

3Thy wife *shall be* as a fruitful vine by the sides of thine house: thy children like olive plants round about thy table.

4Behold, that thus shall the man be blessed that feareth the LORD.

5The LORD shall bless thee out of Zion: and thou shalt see the good of Jerusalem all the days of thy life.

6Yea, thou shalt see thy children's children, *and* peace upon Israel.

PROVERBS FOR TODAY/ 16:31–33

The hoary head is *a crown of glory,* if it *be found in the way of righteousness.* ▢ He that is *slow to anger* is *better than the mighty; and he that ruleth his spirit than he that taketh a city.* ▢ *The lot is cast into the lap; but the whole disposing thereof* is *of the* LORD.

JUNE 11

1 KINGS 8:1–66

THEN Solomon assembled the elders of Israel, and all the heads of the tribes, the chief of the fathers of the children of Israel, unto king Solomon in Jerusalem, that they might bring up the ark of the covenant of the LORD out of the city of David, which *is* Zion.

2And all the men of Israel assembled themselves unto king Solomon at the feast in the month Ethanim, which *is* the seventh month.

3And all the elders of Israel came, and the priests took up the ark.

4And they brought up the ark of the LORD, and the tabernacle of the congregation, and all the holy vessels that *were* in the tabernacle, even those did the priests and the Levites bring up.

5And king Solomon, and all the congregation of Israel, that were assembled unto him, *were* with him before the ark, sacrificing sheep and oxen, that could not be told nor numbered for multitude.

6And the priests brought in the ark of the covenant of the LORD unto his place, into the oracle of the house, to the most holy *place, even* under the wings of the cherubims.

7For the cherubims spread forth *their* two wings over the place of the ark, and the cherubims covered the ark and the staves thereof above.

8And they drew out the staves, that the ends of the staves were seen out in the holy *place* before the oracle, and they were not seen without: and there they are unto this day.

9*There was* nothing in the ark save the two tables of stone, which Moses put there at Horeb, when the LORD made *a covenant* with the children of Israel, when they came out of the land of Egypt.

10And it came to pass, when the priests were come out of the holy *place,* that the cloud filled the house of the LORD,

11So that the priests could not stand to minister because of the cloud: for the glory of the LORD had filled the house of the LORD.

12Then spake Solomon, The LORD said that he would dwell in the thick darkness.

13I have surely built thee an house to dwell in, a settled place for thee to abide in for ever.

14And the king turned his face about, and blessed all the congregation of Israel: (and all the congregation of Israel stood;)

15And he said, Blessed *be* the LORD God of Israel, which spake with his mouth unto David my father, and hath with his hand fulfilled *it,* saying,

16Since the day that I brought forth my people Israel out of Egypt, I chose no city out of all the tribes of Israel to build an house, that my name might be therein; but I chose David to be over my people Israel.

17And it was in the heart of David my father to build an house for the name of the LORD God of Israel.

18And the LORD said unto David my father, Whereas it was in thine heart to build an house unto my name, thou didst well that it was in thine heart.

19Nevertheless thou shalt not build the house; but thy son that shall come forth out of thy loins, he shall build the house unto my name.

20And the LORD hath performed his word that he spake, and I am risen up in the room of David my father, and sit on the throne of Israel, as the

LORD promised, and have built an house for the name of the LORD God of Israel.

21And I have set there a place for the ark, wherein *is* the covenant of the LORD, which he made with our fathers, when he brought them out of the land of Egypt.

22And Solomon stood before the altar of the LORD in the presence of all the congregation of Israel, and spread forth his hands toward heaven:

23And he said, LORD God of Israel, *there is* no God like thee, in heaven above, or on earth beneath, who keepest covenant and mercy with thy servants that walk before thee with all their heart:

24Who hast kept with thy servant David my father that thou promisedst him: thou spakest also with thy mouth, and hast fulfilled *it* with thine hand, as *it is* this day.

25Therefore now, LORD God of Israel, keep with thy servant David my father that thou promisedst him, saying, There shall not fail thee a man in my sight to sit on the throne of Israel; so that thy children take heed to their way, that they walk before me as thou hast walked before me.

26And now, O God of Israel, let thy word, I pray thee, be verified, which thou spakest unto thy servant David my father.

27But will God indeed dwell on the earth? behold, the heaven and heaven of heavens cannot contain thee; how much less this house that I have builded?

28Yet have thou respect unto the prayer of thy servant, and to his supplication, O LORD my God, to hearken unto the cry and to the prayer, which thy servant prayeth before thee to day:

29That thine eyes may be open toward this house night and day, *even* toward the place of which thou hast said, My name shall be there: that thou mayest hearken unto the prayer which thy servant shall make toward this place.

30And hearken thou to the supplication of thy servant, and of thy people Israel, when they shall pray toward this place: and hear thou in heaven thy dwelling place: and when thou hearest, forgive.

31If any man trespass against his neighbour, and an oath be laid upon him to cause him to swear, and the oath come before thine altar in this house:

32Then hear thou in heaven, and do, and judge thy servants, condemning the wicked, to bring his way upon his head; and justifying the righteous, to give him according to his righteousness.

33When thy people Israel be smitten down before the enemy, because they have sinned against thee, and shall turn again to thee, and confess thy name, and pray, and make supplication unto thee in this house:

34Then hear thou in heaven, and forgive the sin of thy people Israel, and bring them again unto the land which thou gavest unto their fathers.

35When heaven is shut up, and there is no rain, because they have sinned against thee; if they pray toward this place, and confess thy name, and turn from their sin, when thou afflictest them:

36Then hear thou in heaven, and forgive the sin of thy servants, and of thy people Israel, that thou teach them the good way wherein they should walk, and give rain upon thy land, which thou hast given to thy people for an inheritance.

37If there be in the land famine, if there be pestilence, blasting, mildew, locust, *or* if there be caterpiller; if their enemy besiege them in the land of their cities; whatsoever plague, whatsoever sickness *there be;*

38What prayer and supplication soever be *made* by any man, *or* by all thy people Israel, which shall know every man the plague of his own heart, and spread forth his hands toward this house:

³⁹Then hear thou in heaven thy dwelling place, and forgive, and do, and give to every man according to his ways, whose heart thou knowest; (for thou, *even* thou only, knowest the hearts of all the children of men;)

⁴⁰That they may fear thee all the days that they live in the land which thou gavest unto our fathers.

⁴¹Moreover concerning a stranger, that *is* not of thy people Israel, but cometh out of a far country for thy name's sake;

⁴²(For they shall hear of thy great name, and of thy strong hand, and of thy stretched out arm:) when he shall come and pray toward this house;

⁴³Hear thou in heaven thy dwelling place, and do according to all that the stranger calleth to thee for: that all people of the earth may know thy name, to fear thee, as *do* thy people Israel; and that they may know that this house, which I have builded, is called by thy name.

⁴⁴If thy people go out to battle against their enemy, whithersoever thou shalt send them, and shall pray unto the Lord toward the city which thou hast chosen, and *toward* the house that I have built for thy name:

⁴⁵Then hear thou in heaven their prayer and their supplication, and maintain their cause.

⁴⁶If they sin against thee, (for *there is* no man that sinneth not,) and thou be angry with them, and deliver them to the enemy, so that they carry them away captives unto the land of the enemy, far or near;

⁴⁷Yet if they shall bethink themselves in the land whither they were carried captives, and repent, and make supplication unto thee in the land of them that carried them captives, saying, We have sinned, and have done perversely, we have committed wickedness;

⁴⁸And *so* return unto thee with all their heart, and with all their soul, in the land of their enemies, which led them away captive, and pray unto thee toward their land, which thou gavest unto their fathers, the city which thou hast chosen, and the house which I have built for thy name:

⁴⁹Then hear thou their prayer and their supplication in heaven thy dwelling place, and maintain their cause,

⁵⁰And forgive thy people that have sinned against thee, and all their transgressions wherein they have transgressed against thee, and give them compassion before them who carried them captive, that they may have compassion on them:

⁵¹For they *be* thy people, and thine inheritance, which thou broughtest forth out of Egypt, from the midst of the furnace of iron:

⁵²That thine eyes may be open unto the supplication of thy servant, and unto the supplication of thy people Israel, to hearken unto them in all that they call for unto thee.

⁵³For thou didst separate them from among all the people of the earth, *to be* thine inheritance, as thou spakest by the hand of Moses thy servant, when thou broughtest our fathers out of Egypt, O Lord God.

⁵⁴And it was *so,* that when Solomon had made an end of praying all this prayer and supplication unto the Lord, he arose from before the altar of the Lord, from kneeling on his knees with his hands spread up to heaven.

⁵⁵And he stood, and blessed all the congregation of Israel with a loud voice, saying,

⁵⁶Blessed *be* the Lord, that hath given rest unto his people Israel, according to all that he promised: there hath not failed one word of all his good promise, which he promised by the hand of Moses his servant.

⁵⁷The Lord our God be with us, as he was with our fathers: let him not leave us, nor forsake us:

58That he may incline our hearts unto him, to walk in all his ways, and to keep his commandments, and his statutes, and his judgments, which he commanded our fathers.

59And let these my words, wherewith I have made supplication before the LORD, be nigh unto the LORD our God day and night, that he maintain the cause of his servant, and the cause of his people Israel at all times, as the matter shall require:

60That all the people of the earth may know that the LORD is God, *and that there is* none else.

61Let your heart therefore be perfect with the LORD our God, to walk in his statutes, and to keep his commandments, as at this day.

62And the king, and all Israel with him, offered sacrifice before the LORD.

63And Solomon offered a sacrifice of peace offerings, which he offered unto the LORD, two and twenty thousand oxen, and an hundred and twenty thousand sheep. So the king and all the children of Israel dedicated the house of the LORD.

64The same day did the king hallow the middle of the court that *was* before the house of the LORD: for there he offered burnt offerings, and meat offerings, and the fat of the peace offerings: because the brasen altar that *was* before the LORD *was* too little to receive the burnt offerings, and meat offerings, and the fat of the peace offerings.

65And at that time Solomon held a feast, and all Israel with him, a great congregation, from the entering in of Hamath unto the river of Egypt, before the LORD our God, seven days and seven days, *even* fourteen days.

66On the eighth day he sent the people away: and they blessed the king, and went unto their tents joyful and glad of heart for all the goodness that the LORD had done for David his servant, and for Israel his people.

ACTS 7:51—8:13

YE stiffnecked and uncircumcised in heart and ears, ye do always resist the Holy Ghost: as your fathers *did,* so *do* ye.

52Which of the prophets have not your fathers persecuted? and they have slain them which shewed before of the coming of the Just One; of whom ye have been now the betrayers and murderers:

53Who have received the law by the disposition of angels, and have not kept *it.*

54When they heard these things, they were cut to the heart, and they gnashed on him with *their* teeth.

55But he, being full of the Holy Ghost, looked up stedfastly into heaven, and saw the glory of God, and Jesus standing on the right hand of God,

56And said, Behold, I see the heavens opened, and the Son of man standing on the right hand of God.

57Then they cried out with a loud voice, and stopped their ears, and ran upon him with one accord,

58And cast *him* out of the city, and stoned *him:* and the witnesses laid down their clothes at a young man's feet, whose name was Saul.

59And they stoned Stephen, calling upon *God,* and saying, Lord Jesus, receive my spirit.

60And he kneeled down, and cried with a loud voice, Lord, lay not this sin to their charge. And when he had said this, he fell asleep.

AND Saul was consenting unto his death. And at that time there was a great persecution against the church which was at Jerusalem; and they were all scattered abroad throughout the regions of Judaea and Samaria, except the apostles.

2And devout men carried Stephen *to his burial,* and made great lamentation over him.

3As for Saul, he made havock of the

church, entering into every house, and haling men and women committed *them* to prison.

⁴Therefore they that were scattered abroad went every where preaching the word.

⁵Then Philip went down to the city of Samaria, and preached Christ unto them.

⁶And the people with one accord gave heed unto those things which Philip spake, hearing and seeing the miracles which he did.

⁷For unclean spirits, crying with loud voice, came out of many that were possessed *with them:* and many taken with palsies, and that were lame, were healed.

⁸And there was great joy in that city.

⁹But there was a certain man, called Simon, which beforetime in the same city used sorcery, and bewitched the people of Samaria, giving out that himself was some great one:

¹⁰To whom they all gave heed, from the least to the greatest, saying, This man is the great power of God.

¹¹And to him they had regard, because that of long time he had bewitched them with sorceries.

¹²But when they believed Philip preaching the things concerning the kingdom of God, and the name of Jesus Christ, they were baptized, both men and women.

¹³Then Simon himself believed also: and when he was baptized, he continued with Philip, and wondered, beholding the miracles and signs which were done.

PSALM 129:1–8

MANY a time have they afflicted me from my youth, may Israel now say:

²Many a time have they afflicted me from my youth: yet they have not prevailed against me.

³The plowers plowed upon my back: they made long their furrows.

⁴The LORD *is* righteous: he hath cut asunder the cords of the wicked.

⁵Let them all be confounded and turned back that hate Zion.

⁶Let them be as the grass *upon* the housetops, which withereth afore it groweth up:

⁷Wherewith the mower filleth not his hand; nor he that bindeth sheaves his bosom.

⁸Neither do they which go by say, The blessing of the LORD *be* upon you: we bless you in the name of the LORD.

PROVERBS FOR TODAY/ 17:1

Better is *a dry morsel, and quietness therewith, than an house full of sacrifices* with *strife.*

JUNE 12

1 KINGS 9:1—10:29

AND it came to pass, when Solomon had finished the building of the house of the LORD, and the king's house, and all Solomon's desire which he was pleased to do,

²That the LORD appeared to Solomon the second time, as he had appeared unto him at Gibeon.

³And the LORD said unto him, I have

heard thy prayer and thy supplication, that thou hast made before me: I have hallowed this house, which thou hast built, to put my name there for ever; and mine eyes and mine heart shall be there perpetually.

4And if thou wilt walk before me, as David thy father walked, in integrity of heart, and in uprightness, to do according to all that I have commanded thee, *and* wilt keep my statutes and my judgments:

5Then I will establish the throne of thy kingdom upon Israel for ever, as I promised to David thy father, saying, There shall not fail thee a man upon the throne of Israel.

6*But* if ye shall at all turn from following me, ye or your children, and will not keep my commandments *and* my statutes which I have set before you, but go and serve other gods, and worship them:

7Then will I cut off Israel out of the land which I have given them; and this house, which I have hallowed for my name, will I cast out of my sight; and Israel shall be a proverb and a byword among all people:

8And at this house, *which* is high, every one that passeth by it shall be astonished, and shall hiss; and they shall say, Why hath the LORD done thus unto this land, and to this house?

9And they shall answer, Because they forsook the LORD their God, who brought forth their fathers out of the land of Egypt, and have taken hold upon other gods, and have worshipped them, and served them: therefore hath the LORD brought upon them all this evil.

10And it came to pass at the end of twenty years, when Solomon had built the two houses, the house of the LORD, and the king's house,

11(*Now* Hiram the king of Tyre had furnished Solomon with cedar trees and fir trees, and with gold, according to all his desire,) that then king Solomon gave Hiram twenty cities in the land of Galilee.

12And Hiram came out from Tyre to see the cities which Solomon had given him; and they pleased him not.

13And he said, What cities *are* these which thou hast given me, my brother? And he called them the land of Cabul unto this day.

14And Hiram sent to the king sixscore talents of gold.

15And this *is* the reason of the levy which king Solomon raised; for to build the house of the LORD, and his own house, and Millo, and the wall of Jerusalem, and Hazor, and Megiddo, and Gezer.

16*For* Pharaoh king of Egypt had gone up, and taken Gezer, and burnt it with fire, and slain the Canaanites that dwelt in the city, and given it *for* a present unto his daughter, Solomon's wife.

17And Solomon built Gezer, and Beth–horon the nether,

18And Baalath, and Tadmor in the wilderness, in the land,

19And all the cities of store that Solomon had, and cities for his chariots, and cities for his horsemen, and that which Solomon desired to build in Jerusalem, and in Lebanon, and in all the land of his dominion.

20*And* all the people *that were* left of the Amorites, Hittites, Perizzites, Hivites, and Jebusites, which *were* not of the children of Israel,

21Their children that were left after them in the land, whom the children of Israel also were not able utterly to destroy, upon those did Solomon levy a tribute of bondservice unto this day.

22But of the children of Israel did Solomon make no bondmen: but they *were* men of war, and his servants, and his princes, and his captains, and rulers of his chariots, and his horsemen.

23These *were* the chief of the officers that *were* over Solomon's work, five hundred and fifty, which bare rule over the people that wrought in the work.

24But Pharaoh's daughter came up out of the city of David unto her house which *Solomon* had built for her: then did he build Millo.

25And three times in a year did Solomon offer burnt offerings and peace offerings upon the altar which he built unto the LORD, and he burnt incense upon the altar that *was* before the LORD. So he finished the house.

26And king Solomon made a navy of ships in Eziongeber, which *is* beside Eloth, on the shore of the Red sea, in the land of Edom.

27And Hiram sent in the navy his servants, shipmen that had knowledge of the sea, with the servants of Solomon.

28And they came to Ophir, and fetched from thence gold, four hundred and twenty talents, and brought *it* to king Solomon.

AND when the queen of Sheba heard of the fame of Solomon concerning the name of the LORD, she came to prove him with hard questions.

2And she came to Jerusalem with a very great train, with camels that bare spices, and very much gold, and precious stones: and when she was come to Solomon, she communed with him of all that was in her heart.

3And Solomon told her all her questions: there was not *any* thing hid from the king, which he told her not.

4And when the queen of Sheba had seen all Solomon's wisdom, and the house that he had built,

5And the meat of his table, and the sitting of his servants, and the attendance of his ministers, and their apparel, and his cupbearers, and his ascent by which he went up unto the house of the LORD; there was no more spirit in her.

6And she said to the king, It was a true report that I heard in mine own land of thy acts and of thy wisdom.

7Howbeit I believed not the words,

until I came, and mine eyes had seen *it:* and, behold, the half was not told me: thy wisdom and prosperity exceedeth the fame which I heard.

8Happy *are* thy men, happy *are* these thy servants, which stand continually before thee, *and* that hear thy wisdom.

9Blessed be the LORD thy God, which delighted in thee, to set thee on the throne of Israel: because the LORD loved Israel for ever, therefore made he thee king, to do judgment and justice.

10And she gave the king an hundred and twenty talents of gold, and of spices very great store, and precious stones: there came no more such abundance of spices as these which the queen of Sheba gave to king Solomon.

11And the navy also of Hiram, that brought gold from Ophir, brought in from Ophir great plenty of almug trees, and precious stones.

12And the king made of the almug trees pillars for the house of the LORD, and for the king's house, harps also and psalteries for singers: there came no such almug trees, nor were seen unto this day.

13And king Solomon gave unto the queen of Sheba all her desire, whatsoever she asked, beside *that* which Solomon gave her of his royal bounty. So she turned and went to her own country, she and her servants.

14Now the weight of gold that came to Solomon in one year was six hundred threescore and six talents of gold,

15Beside *that he had* of the merchantmen, and of the traffick of the spice merchants, and of all the kings of Arabia, and of the governors of the country.

16And king Solomon made two hundred targets *of* beaten gold: six hundred *shekels* of gold went to one target.

17And *he made* three hundred shields *of* beaten gold; three pound of gold went to one shield: and the king put them in the house of the forest of Lebanon.

18Moreover the king made a great

throne of ivory, and overlaid it with the best gold.

19The throne had six steps, and the top of the throne *was* round behind: and *there were* stays on either side on the place of the seat, and two lions stood beside the stays.

20And twelve lions stood there on the one side and on the other upon the six steps: there was not the like made in any kingdom.

21And all king Solomon's drinking vessels *were of* gold, and all the vessels of the house of the forest of Lebanon *were of* pure gold; none *were of* silver: it was nothing accounted of in the days of Solomon.

22For the king had at sea a navy of Tharshish with the navy of Hiram: once in three years came the navy of Tharshish, bringing gold, and silver, ivory, and apes, and peacocks.

23So king Solomon exceeded all the kings of the earth for riches and for wisdom.

24And all the earth sought to Solomon, to hear his wisdom, which God had put in his heart.

25And they brought every man his present, vessels of silver, and vessels of gold, and garments, and armour, and spices, horses, and mules, a rate year by year.

26And Solomon gathered together chariots and horsemen: and he had a thousand and four hundred chariots, and twelve thousand horsemen, whom he bestowed in the cities for chariots, and with the king at Jerusalem.

27And the king made silver *to be* in Jerusalem as stones, and cedars made he *to be* as the sycomore trees that *are* in the vale, for abundance.

28And Solomon had horses brought out of Egypt, and linen yarn: the king's merchants received the linen yarn at a price.

29And a chariot came up and went out of Egypt for six hundred *shekels* of silver, and an horse for an hundred

and fifty: and so for all the kings of the Hittites, and for the kings of Syria, did they bring *them* out by their means.

ACTS 8:14–40

Now when the apostles which were at Jerusalem heard that Samaria had received the word of God, they sent unto them Peter and John:

15Who, when they were come down, prayed for them, that they might receive the Holy Ghost:

16(For as yet he was fallen upon none of them: only they were baptized in the name of the Lord Jesus.)

17Then laid they *their* hands on them, and they received the Holy Ghost.

18And when Simon saw that through laying on of the apostles' hands the Holy Ghost was given, he offered them money,

19Saying, Give me also this power, that on whomsoever I lay hands, he may receive the Holy Ghost.

20But Peter said unto him, Thy money perish with thee, because thou hast thought that the gift of God may be purchased with money.

21Thou hast neither part nor lot in this matter: for thy heart is not right in the sight of God.

22Repent therefore of this thy wickedness, and pray God, if perhaps the thought of thine heart may be forgiven thee.

23For I perceive that thou art in the gall of bitterness, and *in* the bond of iniquity.

24Then answered Simon, and said, Pray ye to the Lord for me, that none of these things which ye have spoken come upon me.

25And they, when they had testified and preached the word of the Lord, returned to Jerusalem, and preached the gospel in many villages of the Samaritans.

26And the angel of the Lord spake

unto Philip, saying, Arise, and go toward the south unto the way that goeth down from Jerusalem unto Gaza, which is desert.

27And he arose and went: and, behold, a man of Ethiopia, an eunuch of great authority under Candace queen of the Ethiopians, who had the charge of all her treasure, and had come to Jerusalem for to worship,

28Was returning, and sitting in his chariot read Esaias the prophet.

29Then the Spirit said unto Philip, Go near, and join thyself to this chariot.

30And Philip ran thither to *him,* and heard him read the prophet Esaias, and said, Understandest thou what thou readest?

31And he said, How can I, except some man should guide me? And he desired Philip that he would come up and sit with him.

32The place of the scripture which he read was this, He was led as a sheep to the slaughter; and like a lamb dumb before his shearer, so opened he not his mouth:

33In his humiliation his judgment was taken away: and who shall declare his generation? for his life is taken from the earth.

34And the eunuch answered Philip, and said, I pray thee, of whom speaketh the prophet this? of himself, or of some other man?

35Then Philip opened his mouth, and began at the same scripture, and preached unto him Jesus.

36And as they went on *their* way, they came unto a certain water: and the eunuch said, See, *here is* water; what doth hinder me to be baptized?

37And Philip said, If thou believest with all thine heart, thou mayest. And he answered and said, I believe that Jesus Christ is the Son of God.

38And he commanded the chariot to stand still: and they went down both into the water, both Philip and the eunuch; and he baptized him.

39And when they were come up out of the water, the Spirit of the Lord caught away Philip, that the eunuch saw him no more: and he went on his way rejoicing.

40But Philip was found at Azotus: and passing through he preached in all the cities, till he came to Caesarea.

PSALM 130:1–8

Out of the depths have I cried unto thee, O LORD.

2Lord, hear my voice: let thine ears be attentive to the voice of my supplications.

3If thou, LORD, shouldest mark iniquities, O Lord, who shall stand?

4But *there is* forgiveness with thee, that thou mayest be feared.

5I wait for the LORD, my soul doth wait, and in his word do I hope.

6My soul *waiteth* for the Lord more than they that watch for the morning: *I say, more than* they that watch for the morning.

7Let Israel hope in the LORD: for with the LORD *there is* mercy, and with him *is* plenteous redemption.

8And he shall redeem Israel from all his iniquities.

PROVERBS FOR TODAY/ 17:2–3

A wise servant shall have rule over a son that causeth shame, and shall have part of the inheritance among the brethren. □ *The fining pot is for silver, and the furnace for gold: but the LORD trieth the hearts.*

JUNE 13

1 KINGS 11:1—12:19

BUT king Solomon loved many strange women, together with the daughter of Pharaoh, women of the Moabites, Ammonites, Edomites, Zidonians, *and* Hittites;

²Of the nations *concerning* which the LORD said unto the children of Israel, Ye shall not go in to them, neither shall they come in unto you: *for* surely they will turn away your heart after their gods: Solomon clave unto these in love.

³And he had seven hundred wives, princesses, and three hundred concubines: and his wives turned away his heart.

⁴For it came to pass, when Solomon was old, *that* his wives turned away his heart after other gods: and his heart was not perfect with the LORD his God, as *was* the heart of David his father.

⁵For Solomon went after Ashtoreth the goddess of the Zidonians, and after Milcom the abomination of the Ammonites.

⁶And Solomon did evil in the sight of the LORD, and went not fully after the LORD, as *did* David his father.

⁷Then did Solomon build an high place for Chemosh, the abomination of Moab, in the hill that *is* before Jerusalem, and for Molech, the abomination of the children of Ammon.

⁸And likewise did he for all his strange wives, which burnt incense and sacrificed unto their gods.

⁹And the LORD was angry with Solomon, because his heart was turned from the LORD God of Israel, which had appeared unto him twice,

¹⁰And had commanded him concerning this thing, that he should not go after other gods: but he kept not that which the LORD commanded.

¹¹Wherefore the LORD said unto Solomon, Forasmuch as this is done of thee, and thou hast not kept my covenant and my statutes, which I have commanded thee, I will surely rend the kingdom from thee, and will give it to thy servant.

¹²Notwithstanding in thy days I will not do it for David thy father's sake: *but* I will rend it out of the hand of thy son.

¹³Howbeit I will not rend away all the kingdom; *but* will give one tribe to thy son for David my servant's sake, and for Jerusalem's sake which I have chosen.

¹⁴And the LORD stirred up an adversary unto Solomon, Hadad the Edomite: he *was* of the king's seed in Edom.

¹⁵For it came to pass, when David was in Edom, and Joab the captain of the host was gone up to bury the slain, after he had smitten every male in Edom;

¹⁶(For six months did Joab remain there with all Israel, until he had cut off every male in Edom:)

¹⁷That Hadad fled, he and certain Edomites of his father's servants with him, to go into Egypt; Hadad *being* yet a little child.

¹⁸And they arose out of Midian, and came to Paran: and they took men with them out of Paran, and they came to Egypt, unto Pharaoh king of Egypt; which gave him an house, and appointed him victuals, and gave him land.

¹⁹And Hadad found great favour in the sight of Pharaoh, so that he gave him to wife the sister of his own wife, the sister of Tahpenes the queen.

²⁰And the sister of Tahpenes bare him Genubath his son, whom Tahpenes

weaned in Pharaoh's house: and Genubath was in Pharaoh's household among the sons of Pharaoh.

21And when Hadad heard in Egypt that David slept with his fathers, and that Joab the captain of the host was dead, Hadad said to Pharaoh, Let me depart, that I may go to mine own country.

22Then Pharaoh said unto him, But what hast thou lacked with me, that, behold, thou seekest to go to thine own country? And he answered, Nothing: howbeit let me go in any wise.

23And God stirred him up *another* adversary, Rezon the son of Eliadah, which fled from his lord Hadadezer king of Zobah:

24And he gathered men unto him, and became captain over a band, when David slew them *of Zobah:* and they went to Damascus, and dwelt therein, and reigned in Damascus.

25And he was an adversary to Israel all the days of Solomon, beside the mischief that Hadad *did:* and he abhorred Israel, and reigned over Syria.

26And Jeroboam the son of Nebat, an Ephrathite of Zereda, Solomon's servant, whose mother's name *was* Zeruah, a widow woman, even he lifted up *his* hand against the king.

27And this *was* the cause that he lifted up *his* hand against the king: Solomon built Millo, *and* repaired the breaches of the city of David his father.

28And the man Jeroboam *was* a mighty man of valour: and Solomon seeing the young man that he was industrious, he made him ruler over all the charge of the house of Joseph.

29And it came to pass at that time when Jeroboam went out of Jerusalem, that the prophet Ahijah the Shilonite found him in the way; and he had clad himself with a new garment; and they two *were* alone in the field:

30And Ahijah caught the new garment that *was* on him, and rent it *in* twelve pieces:

31And he said to Jeroboam, Take thee ten pieces: for thus saith the LORD, the God of Israel, Behold, I will rend the kingdom out of the hand of Solomon, and will give ten tribes to thee:

32(But he shall have one tribe for my servant David's sake, and for Jerusalem's sake, the city which I have chosen out of all the tribes of Israel:)

33Because that they have forsaken me, and have worshipped Ashtoreth the goddess of the Zidonians, Chemosh the god of the Moabites, and Milcom the god of the children of Ammon, and have not walked in my ways, to do *that which is* right in mine eyes, and *to keep* my statutes and my judgments, as *did* David his father.

34Howbeit I will not take the whole kingdom out of his hand: but I will make him prince all the days of his life for David my servant's sake, whom I chose, because he kept my commandments and my statutes:

35But I will take the kingdom out of his son's hand, and will give it unto thee, *even* ten tribes.

36And unto his son will I give one tribe, that David my servant may have a light alway before me in Jerusalem, the city which I have chosen me to put my name there.

37And I will take thee, and thou shalt reign according to all that thy soul desireth, and shalt be king over Israel.

38And it shall be, if thou wilt hearken unto all that I command thee, and wilt walk in my ways, and do *that is* right in my sight, to keep my statutes and my commandments, as David my servant did; that I will be with thee, and build thee a sure house, as I built for David, and will give Israel unto thee.

39And I will for this afflict the seed of David, but not for ever.

40Solomon sought therefore to kill Jeroboam. And Jeroboam arose, and fled into Egypt, unto Shishak king of

Egypt, and was in Egypt until the death of Solomon.

41And the rest of the acts of Solomon, and all that he did, and his wisdom, *are* they not written in the book of the acts of Solomon?

42And the time that Solomon reigned in Jerusalem over all Israel *was* forty years.

43And Solomon slept with his fathers, and was buried in the city of David his father: and Rehoboam his son reigned in his stead.

AND Rehoboam went to Shechem: for all Israel were come to Shechem to make him king.

2And it came to pass, when Jeroboam the son of Nebat, who was yet in Egypt, heard *of it,* (for he was fled from the presence of king Solomon, and Jeroboam dwelt in Egypt;)

3That they sent and called him. And Jeroboam and all the congregation of Israel came, and spake unto Rehoboam, saying,

4Thy father made our yoke grievous: now therefore make thou the grievous service of thy father, and his heavy yoke which he put upon us, lighter, and we will serve thee.

5And he said unto them, Depart yet *for* three days, then come again to me. And the people departed.

6And king Rehoboam consulted with the old men, that stood before Solomon his father while he yet lived, and said, How do ye advise that I may answer this people?

7And they spake unto him, saying, If thou wilt be a servant unto this people this day, and wilt serve them, and answer them, and speak good words to them, then they will be thy servants for ever.

8But he forsook the counsel of the old men, which they had given him, and consulted with the young men that were grown up with him, *and* which stood before him:

9And he said unto them, What counsel give ye that we may answer this people, who have spoken to me, saying, Make the yoke which thy father did put upon us lighter?

10And the young men that were grown up with him spake unto him, saying, Thus shalt thou speak unto this people that spake unto thee, saying, Thy father made our yoke heavy, but make thou *it* lighter unto us; thus shalt thou say unto them, My little *finger* shall be thicker than my father's loins.

11And now whereas my father did lade you with a heavy yoke, I will add to your yoke: my father hath chastised you with whips, but I will chastise you with scorpions.

12So Jeroboam and all the people came to Rehoboam the third day, as the king had appointed, saying, Come to me again the third day.

13And the king answered the people roughly, and forsook the old men's counsel that they gave him;

14And spake to them after the counsel of the young men, saying, My father made your yoke heavy, and I will add to your yoke: my father *also* chastised you with whips, but I will chastise you with scorpions.

15Wherefore the king hearkened not unto the people; for the cause was from the LORD, that he might perform his saying, which the LORD spake by Ahijah the Shilonite unto Jeroboam the son of Nebat.

16So when all Israel saw that the king hearkened not unto them, the people answered the king, saying, What portion have we in David? neither *have we* inheritance in the son of Jesse: to your tents, O Israel: now see to thine own house, David. So Israel departed unto their tents.

17But *as for* the children of Israel which dwelt in the cities of Judah, Rehoboam reigned over them.

18Then king Rehoboam sent Adoram,

who *was* over the tribute; and all Israel stoned him with stones, that he died. Therefore king Rehoboam made speed to get him up to his chariot, to flee to Jerusalem.

19So Israel rebelled against the house of David unto this day.

ACTS 9:1-25

AND Saul, yet breathing out threatenings and slaughter against the disciples of the Lord, went unto the high priest,

2And desired of him letters to Damascus to the synagogues, that if he found any of this way, whether they were men or women, he might bring them bound unto Jerusalem.

3And as he journeyed, he came near Damascus: and suddenly there shined round about him a light from heaven:

4And he fell to the earth, and heard a voice saying unto him, Saul, Saul, why persecutest thou me?

5And he said, Who art thou, Lord? And the Lord said, I am Jesus whom thou persecutest: *it is* hard for thee to kick against the pricks.

6And he trembling and astonished said, Lord, what wilt thou have me to do? And the Lord *said* unto him, Arise, and go into the city, and it shall be told thee what thou must do.

7And the men which journeyed with him stood speechless, hearing a voice, but seeing no man.

8And Saul arose from the earth; and when his eyes were opened, he saw no man: but they led him by the hand, and brought *him* into Damascus.

9And he was three days without sight, and neither did eat nor drink.

10And there was a certain disciple at Damascus, named Ananias; and to him said the Lord in a vision, Ananias. And he said, Behold, I *am here,* Lord.

11And the Lord *said* unto him, Arise, and go into the street which is called Straight, and enquire in the house of Judas for *one* called Saul of Tarsus: for, behold, he prayeth,

12And hath seen in a vision a man named Ananias coming in, and putting *his* hand on him, that he might receive his sight.

13Then Ananias answered, Lord, I have heard by many of this man, how much evil he hath done to thy saints at Jerusalem:

14And here he hath authority from the chief priests to bind all that call on thy name.

15But the Lord said unto him, Go thy way: for he is a chosen vessel unto me, to bear my name before the Gentiles, and kings, and the children of Israel:

16For I will shew him how great things he must suffer for my name's sake.

17And Ananias went his way, and entered into the house; and putting his hands on him said, Brother Saul, the Lord, *even* Jesus, that appeared unto thee in the way as thou camest, hath sent me, that thou mightest receive thy sight, and be filled with the Holy Ghost.

18And immediately there fell from his eyes as it had been scales: and he received sight forthwith, and arose, and was baptized.

19And when he had received meat, he was strengthened. Then was Saul certain days with the disciples which were at Damascus.

20And straightway he preached Christ in the synagogues, that he is the Son of God.

21But all that heard *him* were amazed, and said; Is not this he that destroyed them which called on this name in Jerusalem, and came hither for that intent, that he might bring them bound unto the chief priests?

22But Saul increased the more in

strength, and confounded the Jews which dwelt at Damascus, proving that this is very Christ.

23And after that many days were fulfilled, the Jews took counsel to kill him:

24But their laying await was known of Saul. And they watched the gates day and night to kill him.

25Then the disciples took him by night, and let *him* down by the wall in a basket.

PSALM 131:1–3

Lord, my heart is not haughty, nor mine eyes lofty: neither do I exercise myself in great matters, or in things too high for me.

2Surely I have behaved and quieted myself, as a child that is weaned of his mother: my soul *is* even as a weaned child.

3Let Israel hope in the Lord from henceforth and for ever.

PROVERBS FOR TODAY/ 17:4–5

A wicked doer giveth heed to false lips; and *a liar giveth ear to a naughty tongue.* □ *Whoso mocketh the poor reproacheth his Maker:* and *he that is glad at calamities shall not be unpunished.*

JUNE 14

1 KINGS 12:20—13:34

And it came to pass, when all Israel heard that Jeroboam was come again, that they sent and called him unto the congregation, and made him king over all Israel: there was none that followed the house of David, but the tribe of Judah only.

21And when Rehoboam was come to Jerusalem, he assembled all the house of Judah, with the tribe of Benjamin, an hundred and fourscore thousand chosen men, which were warriors, to fight against the house of Israel, to bring the kingdom again to Rehoboam the son of Solomon.

22But the word of God came unto Shemaiah the man of God, saying,

23Speak unto Rehoboam, the son of Solomon, king of Judah, and unto all the house of Judah and Benjamin, and to the remnant of the people, saying,

24Thus saith the Lord, Ye shall not go up, nor fight against your brethren the children of Israel: return every man to his house; for this thing is from me. They hearkened therefore to the word of the Lord, and returned to depart, according to the word of the Lord.

25Then Jeroboam built Shechem in mount Ephraim, and dwelt therein; and went out from thence, and built Penuel.

26And Jeroboam said in his heart, Now shall the kingdom return to the house of David:

27If this people go up to do sacrifice in the house of the Lord at Jerusalem, then shall the heart of this people turn again unto their lord, *even* unto Rehoboam king of Judah, and they shall kill me, and go again to Rehoboam king of Judah.

28Whereupon the king took counsel, and made two calves *of* gold, and said unto them, It is too much for you to go up to Jerusalem: behold thy gods,

O Israel, which brought thee up out of the land of Egypt.

29And he set the one in Beth–el, and the other put he in Dan.

30And this thing became a sin: for the people went *to worship* before the one, *even* unto Dan.

31And he made an house of high places, and made priests of the lowest of the people, which were not of the sons of Levi.

32And Jeroboam ordained a feast in the eighth month, on the fifteenth day of the month, like unto the feast that *is* in Judah, and he offered upon the altar. So did he in Beth–el, sacrificing unto the calves that he had made: and he placed in Beth–el the priests of the high places which he had made.

33So he offered upon the altar which he had made in Beth–el the fifteenth day of the eighth month, *even* in the month which he had devised of his own heart; and ordained a feast unto the children of Israel: and he offered upon the altar, and burnt incense.

AND, behold, there came a man of God out of Judah by the word of the LORD unto Beth–el: and Jeroboam stood by the altar to burn incense.

2And he cried against the altar in the word of the LORD, and said, O altar, altar, thus saith the LORD; Behold, a child shall be born unto the house of David, Josiah by name; and upon thee shall he offer the priests of the high places that burn incense upon thee, and men's bones shall be burnt upon thee.

3And he gave a sign the same day, saying, This *is* the sign which the LORD hath spoken; Behold, the altar shall be rent, and the ashes that *are* upon it shall be poured out.

4And it came to pass, when king Jeroboam heard the saying of the man of God, which had cried against the altar in Beth–el, that he put forth his hand from the altar, saying, Lay hold on him.

And his hand, which he put forth against him, dried up, so that he could not pull it in again to him.

5The altar also was rent, and the ashes poured out from the altar, according to the sign which the man of God had given by the word of the LORD.

6And the king answered and said unto the man of God, Intreat now the face of the LORD thy God, and pray for me, that my hand may be restored me again. And the man of God besought the LORD, and the king's hand was restored him again, and became as *it was* before.

7And the king said unto the man of God, Come home with me, and refresh thyself, and I will give thee a reward.

8And the man of God said unto the king, If thou wilt give me half thine house, I will not go in with thee, neither will I eat bread nor drink water in this place:

9For so was it charged me by the word of the LORD, saying, Eat no bread, nor drink water, nor turn again by the same way that thou camest.

10So he went another way, and returned not by the way that he came to Beth–el.

11Now there dwelt an old prophet in Beth–el; and his sons came and told him all the works that the man of God had done that day in Beth–el: the words which he had spoken unto the king, them they told also to their father.

12And their father said unto them, What way went he? For his sons had seen what way the man of God went, which came from Judah.

13And he said unto his sons, Saddle me the ass. So they saddled him the ass: and he rode thereon,

14And went after the man of God, and found him sitting under an oak: and he said unto him, *Art* thou the man of God that camest from Judah? And he said, I *am.*

15Then he said unto him, Come home with me, and eat bread.

16And he said, I may not return with

thee, nor go in with thee: neither will I eat bread nor drink water with thee in this place:

17For it was said to me by the word of the LORD, Thou shalt eat no bread nor drink water there, nor turn again to go by the way that thou camest.

18He said unto him, I *am* a prophet also as thou *art;* and an angel spake unto me by the word of the LORD, saying, Bring him back with thee into thine house, that he may eat bread and drink water. *But* he lied unto him.

19So he went back with him, and did eat bread in his house, and drank water.

20And it came to pass, as they sat at the table, that the word of the LORD came unto the prophet that brought him back:

21And he cried unto the man of God that came from Judah, saying, Thus saith the LORD, Forasmuch as thou hast disobeyed the mouth of the LORD, and hast not kept the commandment which the LORD thy God commanded thee,

22But camest back, and hast eaten bread and drunk water in the place, of the which *the LORD* did say to thee, Eat no bread, and drink no water; thy carcase shall not come unto the sepulchre of thy fathers.

23And it came to pass, after he had eaten bread, and after he had drunk, that he saddled for him the ass, *to wit,* for the prophet whom he had brought back.

24And when he was gone, a lion met him by the way, and slew him: and his carcase was cast in the way, and the ass stood by it, the lion also stood by the carcase.

25And, behold, men passed by, and saw the carcase cast in the way, and the lion standing by the carcase: and they came and told *it* in the city where the old prophet dwelt.

26And when the prophet that brought him back from the way heard *thereof,* he said, It *is* the man of God, who was disobedient unto the word of the LORD: therefore the LORD hath delivered him unto the lion, which hath torn him, and slain him, according to the word of the LORD, which he spake unto him.

27And he spake to his sons, saying, Saddle me the ass. And they saddled *him.*

28And he went and found his carcase cast in the way, and the ass and the lion standing by the carcase: the lion had not eaten the carcase, nor torn the ass.

29And the prophet took up the carcase of the man of God, and laid it upon the ass, and brought it back: and the old prophet came to the city, to mourn and to bury him.

30And he laid his carcase in his own grave; and they mourned over him, *saying,* Alas, my brother!

31And it came to pass, after he had buried him, that he spake to his sons, saying, When I am dead, then bury me in the sepulchre wherein the man of God *is* buried; lay my bones beside his bones:

32For the saying which he cried by the word of the LORD against the altar in Beth–el, and against all the houses of the high places which *are* in the cities of Samaria, shall surely come to pass.

33After this thing Jeroboam returned not from his evil way, but made again of the lowest of the people priests of the high places: whosoever would, he consecrated him, and he became *one* of the priests of the high places.

34And this thing became sin unto the house of Jeroboam, even to cut *it* off, and to destroy *it* from off the face of the earth.

ACTS 9:26–43

AND when Saul was come to Jerusalem, he assayed to join himself to the disciples: but they were all afraid of him, and believed not that he was a disciple.

27But Barnabas took him, and brought *him* to the apostles, and declared unto them how he had seen the Lord in the way, and that he had spoken to him, and how he had preached boldly at Damascus in the name of Jesus.

28And he was with them coming in and going out at Jerusalem.

29And he spake boldly in the name of the Lord Jesus, and disputed against the Grecians: but they went about to slay him.

30*Which* when the brethren knew, they brought him down to Caesarea, and sent him forth to Tarsus.

31Then had the churches rest throughout all Judaea and Galilee and Samaria, and were edified; and walking in the fear of the Lord, and in the comfort of the Holy Ghost, were multiplied.

32And it came to pass, as Peter passed throughout all *quarters,* he came down also to the saints which dwelt at Lydda.

33And there he found a certain man named Aeneas, which had kept his bed eight years, and was sick of the palsy.

34And Peter said unto him, Aeneas, Jesus Christ maketh thee whole: arise, and make thy bed. And he arose immediately.

35And all that dwelt at Lydda and Saron saw him, and turned to the Lord.

36Now there was at Joppa a certain disciple named Tabitha, which by interpretation is called Dorcas: this woman was full of good works and almsdeeds which she did.

37And it came to pass in those days, that she was sick, and died: whom when they had washed, they laid *her* in an upper chamber.

38And forasmuch as Lydda was nigh to Joppa, and the disciples had heard that Peter was there, they sent unto him two men, desiring *him* that he would not delay to come to them.

39Then Peter arose and went with them. When he was come, they brought him into the upper chamber: and all the widows stood by him weeping, and shewing the coats and garments which Dorcas made, while she was with them.

40But Peter put them all forth, and kneeled down, and prayed; and turning *him* to the body said, Tabitha, arise. And she opened her eyes: and when she saw Peter, she sat up.

41And he gave her *his* hand, and lifted her up, and when he had called the saints and widows, presented her alive.

42And it was known throughout all Joppa; and many believed in the Lord.

43And it came to pass, that he tarried many days in Joppa with one Simon a tanner.

PSALM 132:1–18

Lord, remember David, *and* all his afflictions:

2How he sware unto the Lord, *and* vowed unto the mighty *God* of Jacob;

3Surely I will not come into the tabernacle of my house, nor go up into my bed;

4I will not give sleep to mine eyes, *or* slumber to mine eyelids,

5Until I find out a place for the Lord, an habitation for the mighty *God* of Jacob.

6Lo, we heard of it at Ephratah: we found it in the fields of the wood.

7We will go into his tabernacles: we will worship at his footstool.

8Arise, O Lord, into thy rest; thou, and the ark of thy strength.

9Let thy priests be clothed with righteousness; and let thy saints shout for joy.

10For thy servant David's sake turn not away the face of thine anointed.

11The Lord hath sworn *in* truth unto David; he will not turn from it; Of the fruit of thy body will I set upon thy throne.

12If thy children will keep my covenant and my testimony that I shall teach them, their children shall also sit upon thy throne for evermore.

13For the LORD hath chosen Zion; he hath desired *it* for his habitation.

14This *is* my rest for ever: here will I dwell; for I have desired it.

15I will abundantly bless her provision: I will satisfy her poor with bread.

16I will also clothe her priests with salvation: and her saints shall shout aloud for joy.

17There will I make the horn of David to bud: I have ordained a lamp for mine anointed.

18His enemies will I clothe with shame: but upon himself shall his crown flourish.

PROVERBS FOR TODAY/ 17:6

Children's children are *the crown of old men; and the glory of children* are *their fathers.*

JUNE 15

1 KINGS 14:1—15:24

AT that time Abijah the son of Jeroboam fell sick.

2And Jeroboam said to his wife, Arise, I pray thee, and disguise thyself, that thou be not known to be the wife of Jeroboam; and get thee to Shiloh: behold, there *is* Ahijah the prophet, which told me that *I should be* king over this people.

3And take with thee ten loaves, and cracknels, and a cruse of honey, and go to him: he shall tell thee what shall become of the child.

4And Jeroboam's wife did so, and arose, and went to Shiloh, and came to the house of Ahijah. But Ahijah could not see; for his eyes were set by reason of his age.

5And the LORD said unto Ahijah, Behold, the wife of Jeroboam cometh to ask a thing of thee for her son; for he *is* sick: thus and thus shalt thou say unto her: for it shall be, when she cometh in, that she shall feign herself *to be* another *woman.*

6And it was *so,* when Ahijah heard the sound of her feet, as she came in at the door, that he said, Come in, thou wife of Jeroboam; why feignest thou thyself *to be* another? for *I am* sent to thee *with* heavy *tidings.*

7Go, tell Jeroboam, Thus saith the LORD God of Israel, Forasmuch as I exalted thee from among the people, and made thee prince over my people Israel,

8And rent the kingdom away from the house of David, and gave it thee: and *yet* thou hast not been as my servant David, who kept my commandments, and who followed me with all his heart, to do *that* only *which was* right in mine eyes;

9But hast done evil above all that were before thee: for thou hast gone and made thee other gods, and molten images, to provoke me to anger, and hast cast me behind thy back:

10Therefore, behold, I will bring evil upon the house of Jeroboam, and will cut off from Jeroboam him that pisseth against the wall, *and* him that is shut up and left in Israel, and will take away the remnant of the house of Jeroboam, as a man taketh away dung, till it be all gone.

11Him that dieth of Jeroboam in the city shall the dogs eat; and him that dieth in the field shall the fowls of the air eat: for the LORD hath spoken *it.*

12Arise thou therefore, get thee to thine own house: *and* when thy feet enter into the city, the child shall die.

13And all Israel shall mourn for him, and bury him: for he only of Jeroboam shall come to the grave, because in him there is found *some* good thing toward the LORD God of Israel in the house of Jeroboam.

14Moreover the LORD shall raise him up a king over Israel, who shall cut off the house of Jeroboam that day: but what? even now.

15For the LORD shall smite Israel, as a reed is shaken in the water, and he shall root up Israel out of this good land, which he gave to their fathers, and shall scatter them beyond the river, because they have made their groves, provoking the LORD to anger.

16And he shall give Israel up because of the sins of Jeroboam, who did sin, and who made Israel to sin.

17And Jeroboam's wife arose, and departed, and came to Tirzah: *and* when she came to the threshold of the door, the child died;

18And they buried him; and all Israel mourned for him, according to the word of the LORD, which he spake by the hand of his servant Ahijah the prophet.

19And the rest of the acts of Jeroboam, how he warred, and how he reigned, behold, they *are* written in the book of the chronicles of the kings of Israel.

20And the days which Jeroboam reigned *were* two and twenty years: and he slept with his fathers, and Nadab his son reigned in his stead.

21And Rehoboam the son of Solomon reigned in Judah. Rehoboam *was* forty and one years old when he began to reign, and he reigned seventeen years in Jerusalem, the city which the LORD did choose out of all the tribes of Israel, to put his name there. And his mother's name *was* Naamah an Ammonitess.

22And Judah did evil in the sight of the LORD, and they provoked him to jealousy with their sins which they had committed, above all that their fathers had done.

23For they also built them high places, and images, and groves, on every high hill, and under every green tree.

24And there were also sodomites in the land: *and* they did according to all the abominations of the nations which the LORD cast out before the children of Israel.

25And it came to pass in the fifth year of king Rehoboam, *that* Shishak king of Egypt came up against Jerusalem:

26And he took away the treasures of the house of the LORD, and the treasures of the king's house; he even took away all: and he took away all the shields of gold which Solomon had made.

27And king Rehoboam made in their stead brasen shields, and committed *them* unto the hands of the chief of the guard, which kept the door of the king's house.

28And it was *so,* when the king went into the house of the LORD, that the guard bare them, and brought them back into the guard chamber.

29Now the rest of the acts of Rehoboam, and all that he did, *are* they not written in the book of the chronicles of the kings of Judah?

30And there was war between Rehoboam and Jeroboam all *their* days.

31And Rehoboam slept with his fathers, and was buried with his fathers in the city of David. And his mother's name *was* Naamah an Ammonitess. And Abijam his son reigned in his stead.

Now in the eighteenth year of king Jeroboam the son of Nebat reigned Abijam over Judah.

2Three years reigned he in Jerusalem. And his mother's name *was* Maachah, the daughter of Abishalom.

3And he walked in all the sins of his father, which he had done before him: and his heart was not perfect with the LORD his God, as the heart of David his father.

4Nevertheless for David's sake did the LORD his God give him a lamp in Jerusalem, to set up his son after him, and to establish Jerusalem.

5Because David did *that which was* right in the eyes of the LORD, and turned not aside from any *thing* that he commanded him all the days of his life, save only in the matter of Uriah the Hittite.

6And there was war between Rehoboam and Jeroboam all the days of his life.

7Now the rest of the acts of Abijam, and all that he did, *are* they not written in the book of the chronicles of the kings of Judah? And there was war between Abijam and Jeroboam.

8And Abijam slept with his fathers; and they buried him in the city of David: and Asa his son reigned in his stead.

9And in the twentieth year of Jeroboam king of Israel reigned Asa over Judah.

10And forty and one years reigned he in Jerusalem. And his mother's name *was* Maachah, the daughter of Abishalom.

11And Asa did *that which was* right in the eyes of the LORD, as *did* David his father.

12And he took away the sodomites out of the land, and removed all the idols that his fathers had made.

13And also Maachah his mother, even her he removed from *being* queen, because she had made an idol in a grove; and Asa destroyed her idol, and burnt *it* by the brook Kidron.

14But the high places were not removed: nevertheless Asa's heart was perfect with the LORD all his days.

15And he brought in the things which his father had dedicated, and the things which himself had dedicated, into the house of the LORD, silver, and gold, and vessels.

16And there was war between Asa and Baasha king of Israel all their days.

17And Baasha king of Israel went up against Judah, and built Ramah, that he might not suffer any to go out or come in to Asa king of Judah.

18Then Asa took all the silver and the gold *that were* left in the treasures of the house of the LORD, and the treasures of the king's house, and delivered them into the hand of his servants: and king Asa sent them to Ben–hadad, the son of Tabrimon, the son of Hezion, king of Syria, that dwelt at Damascus, saying,

19*There is* a league between me and thee, *and* between my father and thy father: behold, I have sent unto thee a present of silver and gold; come and break thy league with Baasha king of Israel, that he may depart from me.

20So Ben–hadad hearkened unto king Asa, and sent the captains of the hosts which he had against the cities of Israel, and smote Ijon, and Dan, and Abel–beth–maachah, and all Cinneroth, with all the land of Naphtali.

21And it came to pass, when Baasha heard *thereof,* that he left off building of Ramah, and dwelt in Tirzah.

22Then king Asa made a proclamation throughout all Judah; none *was* exempted: and they took away the stones of Ramah, and the timber thereof, wherewith Baasha had builded; and king Asa built with them Geba of Benjamin, and Mizpah.

23The rest of all the acts of Asa, and all his might, and all that he did, and the cities which he built, *are* they not written in the book of the chronicles of the kings of Judah? Nevertheless in the time of his old age he was diseased in his feet.

24And Asa slept with his fathers, and was buried with his fathers in the city of David his father: and Jehoshaphat his son reigned in his stead.

ACTS 10:1–23

THERE was a certain man in Caesarea called Cornelius, a centurion of the band called the Italian *band,*

2A devout *man,* and one that feared God with all his house, which gave much alms to the people, and prayed to God alway.

3He saw in a vision evidently about the ninth hour of the day an angel of God coming in to him, and saying unto him, Cornelius.

4And when he looked on him, he was afraid, and said, What is it, Lord? And he said unto him, Thy prayers and thine alms are come up for a memorial before God.

5And now send men to Joppa, and call for *one* Simon, whose surname is Peter:

6He lodgeth with one Simon a tanner, whose house is by the sea side: he shall tell thee what thou oughtest to do.

7And when the angel which spake unto Cornelius was departed, he called two of his household servants, and a devout soldier of them that waited on him continually;

8And when he had declared all *these* things unto them, he sent them to Joppa.

9On the morrow, as they went on their journey, and drew nigh unto the city, Peter went up upon the housetop to pray about the sixth hour:

10And he became very hungry, and would have eaten: but while they made ready, he fell into a trance,

11And saw heaven opened, and a cer-tain vessel descending unto him, as it had been a great sheet knit at the four corners, and let down to the earth:

12Wherein were all manner of four-footed beasts of the earth, and wild beasts, and creeping things, and fowls of the air.

13And there came a voice to him, Rise, Peter; kill, and eat.

14But Peter said, Not so, Lord; for I have never eaten any thing that is common or unclean.

15And the voice *spake* unto him again the second time, What God hath cleansed, *that* call not thou common.

16This was done thrice: and the vessel was received up again into heaven.

17Now while Peter doubted in himself what this vision which he had seen should mean, behold, the men which were sent from Cornelius had made enquiry for Simon's house, and stood before the gate,

18And called, and asked whether Simon, which was surnamed Peter, were lodged there.

19While Peter thought on the vision, the Spirit said unto him, Behold, three men seek thee.

20Arise therefore, and get thee down, and go with them, doubting nothing: for I have sent them.

21Then Peter went down to the men which were sent unto him from Cornelius; and said, Behold, I am he whom ye seek: what *is* the cause wherefore ye are come?

22And they said, Cornelius the centurion, a just man, and one that feareth God, and of good report among all the nation of the Jews, was warned from God by an holy angel to send for thee into his house, and to hear words of thee.

23Then called he them in, and lodged *them.* And on the morrow Peter went away with them, and certain brethren from Joppa accompanied him.

PSALM 133:1–3

BEHOLD, how good and how pleasant *it is* for brethren to dwell together in unity!

²*It is* like the precious ointment upon the head, that ran down upon the beard, *even* Aaron's beard: that went down to the skirts of his garments;

³As the dew of Hermon, *and as the dew* that descended upon the mountains of Zion: for there the LORD commanded the blessing, *even* life for evermore.

PROVERBS FOR TODAY/ 17:7–8

Excellent speech becometh not a fool: much less do lying lips a prince. □ *A gift is as a precious stone in the eyes of him that hath it: whithersoever it turneth, it prospereth.*

JUNE 16

1 KINGS 15:25—17:24

AND Nadab the son of Jeroboam began to reign over Israel in the second year of Asa king of Judah, and reigned over Israel two years.

²⁶And he did evil in the sight of the LORD, and walked in the way of his father, and in his sin wherewith he made Israel to sin.

²⁷And Baasha the son of Ahijah, of the house of Issachar, conspired against him; and Baasha smote him at Gibbethon, which *belonged* to the Philistines; for Nadab and all Israel laid siege to Gibbethon.

²⁸Even in the third year of Asa king of Judah did Baasha slay him, and reigned in his stead.

²⁹And it came to pass, when he reigned, *that* he smote all the house of Jeroboam; he left not to Jeroboam any that breathed, until he had destroyed him, according unto the saying of the LORD, which he spake by his servant Ahijah the Shilonite:

³⁰Because of the sins of Jeroboam which he sinned, and which he made Israel sin, by his provocation wherewith he provoked the LORD God of Israel to anger.

³¹Now the rest of the acts of Nadab, and all that he did, *are* they not written in the book of the chronicles of the kings of Israel?

³²And there was war between Asa and Baasha king of Israel all their days.

³³In the third year of Asa king of Judah began Baasha the son of Ahijah to reign over all Israel in Tirzah, twenty and four years.

³⁴And he did evil in the sight of the LORD, and walked in the way of Jeroboam, and in his sin wherewith he made Israel to sin.

THEN the word of the LORD came to Jehu the son of Hanani against Baasha, saying,

²Forasmuch as I exalted thee out of the dust, and made thee prince over my people Israel; and thou hast walked in the way of Jeroboam, and hast made my people Israel to sin, to provoke me to anger with their sins;

³Behold, I will take away the posterity of Baasha, and the posterity of his house; and will make thy house like

the house of Jeroboam the son of Nebat.

4Him that dieth of Baasha in the city shall the dogs eat; and him that dieth of his in the fields shall the fowls of the air eat.

5Now the rest of the acts of Baasha, and what he did, and his might, *are* they not written in the book of the chronicles of the kings of Israel?

6So Baasha slept with his fathers, and was buried in Tirzah: and Elah his son reigned in his stead.

7And also by the hand of the prophet Jehu the son of Hanani came the word of the LORD against Baasha, and against his house, even for all the evil that he did in the sight of the LORD, in provoking him to anger with the work of his hands, in being like the house of Jeroboam; and because he killed him.

8In the twenty and sixth year of Asa king of Judah began Elah the son of Baasha to reign over Israel in Tirzah, two years.

9And his servant Zimri, captain of half *his* chariots, conspired against him, as he was in Tirzah, drinking himself drunk in the house of Arza steward of *his* house in Tirzah.

10And Zimri went in and smote him, and killed him, in the twenty and seventh year of Asa king of Judah, and reigned in his stead.

11And it came to pass, when he began to reign, as soon as he sat on his throne, *that* he slew all the house of Baasha: he left him not one that pisseth against a wall, neither of his kinsfolks, nor of his friends.

12Thus did Zimri destroy all the house of Baasha, according to the word of the LORD, which he spake against Baasha by Jehu the prophet,

13For all the sins of Baasha, and the sins of Elah his son, by which they sinned, and by which they made Israel to sin, in provoking the LORD God of Israel to anger with their vanities.

14Now the rest of the acts of Elah, and all that he did, *are* they not written in the book of the chronicles of the kings of Israel?

15In the twenty and seventh year of Asa king of Judah did Zimri reign seven days in Tirzah. And the people *were* encamped against Gibbethon, which *belonged* to the Philistines.

16And the people *that were* encamped heard say, Zimri hath conspired, and hath also slain the king: wherefore all Israel made Omri, the captain of the host, king over Israel that day in the camp.

17And Omri went up from Gibbethon, and all Israel with him, and they besieged Tirzah.

18And it came to pass, when Zimri saw that the city was taken, that he went into the palace of the king's house, and burnt the king's house over him with fire, and died,

19For his sins which he sinned in doing evil in the sight of the LORD, in walking in the way of Jeroboam, and in his sin which he did, to make Israel to sin.

20Now the rest of the acts of Zimri, and his treason that he wrought, *are* they not written in the book of the chronicles of the kings of Israel?

21Then were the people of Israel divided into two parts: half of the people followed Tibni the son of Ginath, to make him king; and half followed Omri.

22But the people that followed Omri prevailed against the people that followed Tibni the son of Ginath: so Tibni died, and Omri reigned.

23In the thirty and first year of Asa king of Judah began Omri to reign over Israel, twelve years: six years reigned he in Tirzah.

24And he bought the hill Samaria of Shemer for two talents of silver, and built on the hill, and called the name of the city which he built, after the name of Shemer, owner of the hill, Samaria.

25But Omri wrought evil in the eyes of the LORD, and did worse than all that *were* before him.

26For he walked in all the way of Jeroboam the son of Nebat, and in his sin wherewith he made Israel to sin, to provoke the LORD God of Israel to anger with their vanities.

27Now the rest of the acts of Omri which he did, and his might that he shewed, *are* they not written in the book of the chronicles of the kings of Israel?

28So Omri slept with his fathers, and was buried in Samaria: and Ahab his son reigned in his stead.

29And in the thirty and eighth year of Asa king of Judah began Ahab the son of Omri to reign over Israel: and Ahab the son of Omri reigned over Israel in Samaria twenty and two years.

30And Ahab the son of Omri did evil in the sight of the LORD above all that *were* before him.

31And it came to pass, as if it had been a light thing for him to walk in the sins of Jeroboam the son of Nebat, that he took to wife Jezebel the daughter of Ethbaal king of the Zidonians, and went and served Baal, and worshipped him.

32And he reared up an altar for Baal in the house of Baal, which he had built in Samaria.

33And Ahab made a grove; and Ahab did more to provoke the LORD God of Israel to anger than all the kings of Israel that were before him.

34In his days did Hiel the Bethelite build Jericho: he laid the foundation thereof in Abiram his firstborn, and set up the gates thereof in his youngest *son* Segub, according to the word of the LORD, which he spake by Joshua the son of Nun.

AND Elijah the Tishbite, *who was* of the inhabitants of Gilead, said unto Ahab, *As* the LORD God of Israel liveth, before whom I stand, there shall not be dew nor rain these years, but according to my word.

2And the word of the LORD came unto him, saying,

3Get thee hence, and turn thee eastward, and hide thyself by the brook Cherith, that *is* before Jordan.

4And it shall be, *that* thou shalt drink of the brook; and I have commanded the ravens to feed thee there.

5So he went and did according unto the word of the LORD; for he went and dwelt by the brook Cherith, that *is* before Jordan.

6And the ravens brought him bread and flesh in the morning, and bread and flesh in the evening; and he drank of the brook.

7And it came to pass after a while, that the brook dried up, because there had been no rain in the land.

8And the word of the LORD came unto him, saying,

9Arise, get thee to Zarephath, which *belongeth* to Zidon, and dwell there: behold, I have commanded a widow woman there to sustain thee.

10So he arose and went to Zarephath. And when he came to the gate of the city, behold, the widow woman *was* there gathering of sticks: and he called to her, and said, Fetch me, I pray thee, a little water in a vessel, that I may drink.

11And as she was going to fetch *it*, he called to her, and said, Bring me, I pray thee, a morsel of bread in thine hand.

12And she said, *As* the LORD thy God liveth, I have not a cake, but an handful of meal in a barrel, and a little oil in a cruse: and, behold, I *am* gathering two sticks, that I may go in and dress it for me and my son, that we may eat it, and die.

13And Elijah said unto her, Fear not; go *and* do as thou hast said: but make me thereof a little cake first, and bring *it* unto me, and after make for thee and for thy son.

14For thus saith the LORD God of Israel, The barrel of meal shall not waste, neither shall the cruse of oil fail, until the day *that* the LORD sendeth rain upon the earth.

15And she went and did according to the saying of Elijah: and she, and he, and her house, did eat *many* days.

16*And* the barrel of meal wasted not, neither did the cruse of oil fail, according to the word of the LORD, which he spake by Elijah.

17And it came to pass after these things, *that* the son of the woman, the mistress of the house, fell sick; and his sickness was so sore, that there was no breath left in him.

18And she said unto Elijah, What have I to do with thee, O thou man of God? art thou come unto me to call my sin to remembrance, and to slay my son?

19And he said unto her, Give me thy son. And he took him out of her bosom, and carried him up into a loft, where he abode, and laid him upon his own bed.

20And he cried unto the LORD, and said, O LORD my God, hast thou also brought evil upon the widow with whom I sojourn, by slaying her son?

21And he stretched himself upon the child three times, and cried unto the LORD, and said, O LORD my God, I pray thee, let this child's soul come into him again.

22And the LORD heard the voice of Elijah; and the soul of the child came into him again, and he revived.

23And Elijah took the child, and brought him down out of the chamber into the house, and delivered him unto his mother: and Elijah said, See, thy son liveth.

24And the woman said to Elijah, Now by this I know that thou *art* a man of God, *and* that the word of the LORD in thy mouth *is* truth.

ACTS 10:24–48

AND the morrow after they [Peter and companions] entered into Caesarea. And Cornelius waited for them, and had called together his kinsmen and near friends.

25And as Peter was coming in, Cornelius met him, and fell down at his feet, and worshipped *him.*

26But Peter took him up, saying, Stand up; I myself also am a man.

27And as he talked with him, he went in, and found many that were come together.

28And he said unto them, Ye know how that it is an unlawful thing for a man that is a Jew to keep company, or come unto one of another nation; but God hath shewed me that I should not call any man common or unclean.

29Therefore came I *unto you* without gainsaying, as soon as I was sent for: I ask therefore for what intent ye have sent for me?

30And Cornelius said, Four days ago I was fasting until this hour; and at the ninth hour I prayed in my house, and, behold, a man stood before me in bright clothing,

31And said, Cornelius, thy prayer is heard, and thine alms are had in remembrance in the sight of God.

32Send therefore to Joppa, and call hither Simon, whose surname is Peter; he is lodged in the house of *one* Simon a tanner by the sea side: who, when he cometh, shall speak unto thee.

33Immediately therefore I sent to thee; and thou hast well done that thou art come. Now therefore are we all here present before God, to hear all things that are commanded thee of God.

34Then Peter opened *his* mouth, and said, Of a truth I perceive that God is no respecter of persons:

35But in every nation he that feareth him, and worketh righteousness, is accepted with him.

36The word which *God* sent unto the

children of Israel, preaching peace by Jesus Christ: (he is Lord of all:)

37That word, *I say,* ye know, which was published throughout all Judaea, and began from Galilee, after the baptism which John preached;

38How God anointed Jesus of Nazareth with the Holy Ghost and with power: who went about doing good, and healing all that were oppressed of the devil; for God was with him.

39And we are witnesses of all things which he did both in the land of the Jews, and in Jerusalem; whom they slew and hanged on a tree:

40Him God raised up the third day, and shewed him openly;

41Not to all the people, but unto witnesses chosen before of God, *even* to us, who did eat and drink with him after he rose from the dead.

42And he commanded us to preach unto the people, and to testify that it is he which was ordained of God *to be* the Judge of quick and dead.

43To him give all the prophets witness, that through his name whosoever believeth in him shall receive remission of sins.

44While Peter yet spake these words, the Holy Ghost fell on all them which heard the word.

45And they of the circumcision which believed were astonished, as many as came with Peter, because that on the Gentiles also was poured out the gift of the Holy Ghost.

46For they heard them speak with tongues, and magnify God. Then answered Peter,

47Can any man forbid water, that these should not be baptized, which have received the Holy Ghost as well as we?

48And he commanded them to be baptized in the name of the Lord. Then prayed they him to tarry certain days.

PSALM 134:1–3

B EHOLD, bless ye the LORD, all *ye* servants of the LORD, which by night stand in the house of the LORD.

2Lift up your hands *in* the sanctuary, and bless the LORD.

3The LORD that made heaven and earth bless thee out of Zion.

PROVERBS FOR TODAY/ 17:9–11

He that covereth a transgression seeketh love; but he that repeateth a matter separateth very friends. □*A reproof entereth more into a wise man than an hundred stripes into a fool.* □*An evil* man *seeketh only rebellion: therefore a cruel messenger shall be sent against him.*

JUNE 17

1 KINGS 18:1–46

A ND it came to pass *after* many days, that the word of the LORD came to Elijah in the third year, saying, Go, shew thyself unto Ahab; and I will send rain upon the earth.

2And Elijah went to shew himself unto Ahab. And *there was* a sore famine in Samaria.

3And Ahab called Obadiah, which *was*

the governor of *his* house. (Now Obadiah feared the LORD greatly:

4For it was *so,* when Jezebel cut off the prophets of the LORD, that Obadiah took an hundred prophets, and hid them by fifty in a cave, and fed them with bread and water.)

5And Ahab said unto Obadiah, Go into the land, unto all fountains of water, and unto all brooks: peradventure we may find grass to save the horses and mules alive, that we lose not all the beasts.

6So they divided the land between them to pass throughout it: Ahab went one way by himself, and Obadiah went another way by himself.

7And as Obadiah was in the way, behold, Elijah met him: and he knew him, and fell on his face, and said, *Art* thou that my lord Elijah?

8And he answered him, I *am:* go, tell thy lord, Behold, Elijah *is here.*

9And he said, What have I sinned, that thou wouldest deliver thy servant into the hand of Ahab, to slay me?

10*As* the LORD thy God liveth, there is no nation or kingdom, whither my lord hath not sent to seek thee: and when they said, *He is* not *there;* he took an oath of the kingdom and nation, that they found thee not.

11And now thou sayest, Go, tell thy lord, Behold, Elijah *is here.*

12And it shall come to pass, *as soon as* I am gone from thee, that the Spirit of the LORD shall carry thee whither I know not; and *so* when I come and tell Ahab, and he cannot find thee, he shall slay me: but I thy servant fear the LORD from my youth.

13Was it not told my lord what I did when Jezebel slew the prophets of the LORD, how I hid an hundred men of the LORD's prophets by fifty in a cave, and fed them with bread and water?

14And now thou sayest, Go, tell thy lord, Behold, Elijah *is here:* and he shall slay me.

15And Elijah said, As the LORD of hosts liveth, before whom I stand, I will surely shew myself unto him to day.

16So Obadiah went to meet Ahab, and told him: and Ahab went to meet Elijah.

17And it came to pass, when Ahab saw Elijah, that Ahab said unto him, *Art* thou he that troubleth Israel?

18And he answered, I have not troubled Israel; but thou, and thy father's house, in that ye have forsaken the commandments of the LORD, and thou hast followed Baalim.

19Now therefore send, *and* gather to me all Israel unto mount Carmel, and the prophets of Baal four hundred and fifty, and the prophets of the groves four hundred, which eat at Jezebel's table.

20So Ahab sent unto all the children of Israel, and gathered the prophets together unto mount Carmel.

21And Elijah came unto all the people, and said, How long halt ye between two opinions? if the LORD *be* God, follow him: but if Baal, *then* follow him. And the people answered him not a word.

22Then said Elijah unto the people, I, *even* I only, remain a prophet of the LORD; but Baal's prophets *are* four hundred and fifty men.

23Let them therefore give us two bullocks; and let them choose one bullock for themselves, and cut it in pieces, and lay *it* on wood, and put no fire *under:* and I will dress the other bullock, and lay *it* on wood, and put no fire *under:*

24And call ye on the name of your gods, and I will call on the name of the LORD: and the God that answereth by fire, let him be God. And all the people answered and said, It is well spoken.

25And Elijah said unto the prophets of Baal, Choose you one bullock for yourselves, and dress *it* first; for ye *are* many; and call on the name of your gods, but put no fire *under.*

26And they took the bullock which was given them, and they dressed *it,* and called on the name of Baal from morning even until noon, saying, O Baal, hear us. But *there was* no voice, nor any that answered. And they leaped upon the altar which was made.

27And it came to pass at noon, that Elijah mocked them, and said, Cry aloud: for he *is* a god; either he is talking, or he is pursuing, or he is in a journey, *or* peradventure he sleepeth, and must be awaked.

28And they cried aloud, and cut themselves after their manner with knives and lancets, till the blood gushed out upon them.

29And it came to pass, when midday was past, and they prophesied until the *time* of the offering of the *evening* sacrifice, that *there was* neither voice, nor any to answer, nor any that regarded.

30And Elijah said unto all the people, Come near unto me. And all the people came near unto him. And he repaired the altar of the LORD *that was* broken down.

31And Elijah took twelve stones, according to the number of the tribes of the sons of Jacob, unto whom the word of the LORD came, saying, Israel shall be thy name:

32And with the stones he built an altar in the name of the LORD: and he made a trench about the altar, as great as would contain two measures of seed.

33And he put the wood in order, and cut the bullock in pieces, and laid *him* on the wood, and said, Fill four barrels with water, and pour *it* on the burnt sacrifice, and on the wood.

34And he said, Do *it* the second time. And they did *it* the second time. And he said, Do *it* the third time. And they did *it* the third time.

35And the water ran round about the altar; and he filled the trench also with water.

36And it came to pass at *the time of* the offering of the *evening* sacrifice, that Elijah the prophet came near, and said, LORD God of Abraham, Isaac, and of Israel, let it be known this day that thou *art* God in Israel, and *that I am* thy servant, and *that* I have done all these things at thy word.

37Hear me, O LORD, hear me, that this people may know that thou *art* the LORD God, and *that* thou hast turned their heart back again.

38Then the fire of the LORD fell, and consumed the burnt sacrifice, and the wood, and the stones, and the dust, and licked up the water that *was* in the trench.

39And when all the people saw *it,* they fell on their faces: and they said, The LORD, he *is* the God; the LORD, he *is* the God.

40And Elijah said unto them, Take the prophets of Baal; let not one of them escape. And they took them: and Elijah brought them down to the brook Kishon, and slew them there.

41And Elijah said unto Ahab, Get thee up, eat and drink; for *there is* a sound of abundance of rain.

42So Ahab went up to eat and to drink. And Elijah went up to the top of Carmel; and he cast himself down upon the earth, and put his face between his knees,

43And said to his servant, Go up now, look toward the sea. And he went up, and looked, and said, *There is* nothing. And he said, Go again seven times.

44And it came to pass at the seventh time, that he said, Behold, there ariseth a little cloud out of the sea, like a man's hand. And he said, Go up, say unto Ahab, Prepare *thy chariot,* and get thee down, that the rain stop thee not.

45And it came to pass in the mean while, that the heaven was black with clouds and wind, and there was a great rain. And Ahab rode, and went to Jezreel.

46And the hand of the LORD was on Elijah; and he girded up his loins, and ran before Ahab to the entrance of Jezreel.

ACTS 11:1–30

AND the apostles and brethren that were in Judaea heard that the Gentiles had also received the word of God.

2And when Peter was come up to Jerusalem, they that were of the circumcision contended with him,

3Saying, Thou wentest in to men uncircumcised, and didst eat with them.

4But Peter rehearsed *the matter* from the beginning, and expounded *it* by order unto them, saying,

5I was in the city of Joppa praying: and in a trance I saw a vision, A certain vessel descend, as it had been a great sheet, let down from heaven by four corners; and it came even to me:

6Upon the which when I had fastened mine eyes, I considered, and saw fourfooted beasts of the earth, and wild beasts, and creeping things, and fowls of the air.

7And I heard a voice saying unto me, Arise, Peter; slay and eat.

8But I said, Not so, Lord: for nothing common or unclean hath at any time entered into my mouth.

9But the voice answered me again from heaven, What God hath cleansed, *that* call not thou common.

10And this was done three times: and all were drawn up again into heaven.

11And, behold, immediately there were three men already come unto the house where I was, sent from Caesarea unto me.

12And the spirit bade me go with them, nothing doubting. Moreover these six brethren accompanied me, and we entered into the man's house:

13And he shewed us how he had seen an angel in his house, which stood and said unto him, Send men to Joppa, and call for Simon, whose surname is Peter;

14Who shall tell thee words, whereby thou and all thy house shall be saved.

15And as I began to speak, the Holy Ghost fell on them, as on us at the beginning.

16Then remembered I the word of the Lord, how that he said, John indeed baptized with water; but ye shall be baptized with the Holy Ghost.

17Forasmuch then as God gave them the like gift as *he did* unto us, who believed on the Lord Jesus Christ; what was I, that I could withstand God?

18When they heard these things, they held their peace, and glorified God, saying, Then hath God also to the Gentiles granted repentance unto life.

19Now they which were scattered abroad upon the persecution that arose about Stephen travelled as far as Phenice, and Cyprus, and Antioch, preaching the word to none but unto the Jews only.

20And some of them were men of Cyprus and Cyrene, which, when they were come to Antioch, spake unto the Grecians, preaching the Lord Jesus.

21And the hand of the Lord was with them: and a great number believed, and turned unto the Lord.

22Then tidings of these things came unto the ears of the church which was in Jerusalem: and they sent forth Barnabas, that he should go as far as Antioch.

23Who, when he came, and had seen the grace of God, was glad, and exhorted them all, that with purpose of heart they would cleave unto the Lord.

24For he was a good man, and full of the Holy Ghost and of faith: and much people was added unto the Lord.

25Then departed Barnabas to Tarsus, for to seek Saul:

26And when he had found him, he brought him unto Antioch. And it came to pass, that a whole year they assembled themselves with the church, and taught much people. And the disciples were called Christians first in Antioch.

27And in these days came prophets from Jerusalem unto Antioch.

28And there stood up one of them named Agabus, and signified by the spirit that there should be great dearth throughout all the world: which came to pass in the days of Claudius Caesar.

29Then the disciples, every man according to his ability, determined to send relief unto the brethren which dwelt in Judaea:

30Which also they did, and sent it to the elders by the hands of Barnabas and Saul.

PSALM 135:1–21

Praise ye the Lord. Praise ye the name of the Lord; praise *him,* O ye servants of the Lord.

2Ye that stand in the house of the Lord, in the courts of the house of our God,

3Praise the Lord; for the Lord *is* good: sing praises unto his name; for *it is* pleasant.

4For the Lord hath chosen Jacob unto himself, *and* Israel for his peculiar treasure.

5For I know that the Lord *is* great, and *that* our Lord *is* above all gods.

6Whatsoever the Lord pleased, *that* did he in heaven, and in earth, in the seas, and all deep places.

7He causeth the vapours to ascend from the ends of the earth; he maketh lightnings for the rain; he bringeth the wind out of his treasuries.

8Who smote the firstborn of Egypt, both of man and beast.

9*Who* sent tokens and wonders into the midst of thee, O Egypt, upon Pharaoh, and upon all his servants.

10Who smote great nations, and slew mighty kings;

11Sihon king of the Amorites, and Og king of Bashan, and all the kingdoms of Canaan:

12And gave their land *for* an heritage, an heritage unto Israel his people.

13Thy name, O Lord, *endureth* for ever, *and* thy memorial, O Lord, throughout all generations.

14For the Lord will judge his people, and he will repent himself concerning his servants.

15The idols of the heathen *are* silver and gold, the work of men's hands.

16They have mouths, but they speak not; eyes have they, but they see not;

17They have ears, but they hear not; neither is there *any* breath in their mouths.

18They that make them are like unto them: *so is* every one that trusteth in them.

19Bless the Lord, O house of Israel: bless the Lord, O house of Aaron:

20Bless the Lord, O house of Levi: ye that fear the Lord, bless the Lord.

21Blessed be the Lord out of Zion, which dwelleth at Jerusalem. Praise ye the Lord.

PROVERBS FOR TODAY/ 17:12–13

Let a bear robbed of her whelps meet a man, rather than a fool in his folly. ☐ *Whoso rewardeth evil for good, evil shall not depart from his house.*

JUNE 18

1 KINGS 19:1–21

AND Ahab told Jezebel all that Elijah had done, and withal how he had slain all the prophets with the sword.

2Then Jezebel sent a messenger unto Elijah, saying, So let the gods do to me, and more also, if I make not thy life as the life of one of them by to morrow about this time.

3And when he saw that, he arose, and went for his life, and came to Beer-sheba, which belongeth to Judah, and left his servant there.

4But he himself went a day's journey into the wilderness, and came and sat down under a juniper tree: and he requested for himself that he might die; and said, It is enough; now, O Lord, take away my life; for I am not better than my fathers.

5And as he lay and slept under a juniper tree, behold, then an angel touched him, and said unto him, Arise and eat.

6And he looked, and, behold, there was a cake baken on the coals, and a cruse of water at his head. And he did eat and drink, and laid him down again.

7And the angel of the Lord came again the second time, and touched him, and said, Arise and eat; because the journey is too great for thee.

8And he arose, and did eat and drink, and went in the strength of that meat forty days and forty nights unto Horeb the mount of God.

9And he came thither unto a cave, and lodged there; and, behold, the word of the Lord came to him, and he said unto him, What doest thou here, Elijah?

10And he said, I have been very jealous for the Lord God of hosts: for the children of Israel have forsaken thy covenant, thrown down thine altars, and slain thy prophets with the sword; and I, even I only, am left; and they seek my life, to take it away.

11And he said, Go forth, and stand upon the mount before the Lord. And, behold, the Lord passed by, and a great and strong wind rent the mountains, and brake in pieces the rocks before the Lord; but the Lord was not in the wind: and after the wind an earthquake; but the Lord was not in the earthquake:

12And after the earthquake a fire; but the Lord was not in the fire: and after the fire a still small voice.

13And it was so, when Elijah heard it, that he wrapped his face in his mantle, and went out, and stood in the entering in of the cave. And, behold, there came a voice unto him, and said, What doest thou here, Elijah?

14And he said, I have been very jealous for the Lord God of hosts: because the children of Israel have forsaken thy covenant, thrown down thine altars, and slain thy prophets with the sword; and I, even I only, am left; and they seek my life, to take it away.

15And the Lord said unto him, Go, return on thy way to the wilderness of Damascus: and when thou comest, anoint Hazael to be king over Syria:

16And Jehu the son of Nimshi shalt thou anoint to be king over Israel: and Elisha the son of Shaphat of Abel-meholah shalt thou anoint to be prophet in thy room.

17And it shall come to pass, that him that escapeth the sword of Hazael shall Jehu slay: and him that escapeth from the sword of Jehu shall Elisha slay.

18Yet I have left me seven thousand in Israel, all the knees which have not bowed unto Baal, and every mouth which hath not kissed him.

19So he departed thence, and found Elisha the son of Shaphat, who *was* plowing *with* twelve yoke *of oxen* before him, and he with the twelfth: and Elijah passed by him, and cast his mantle upon him.

20And he left the oxen, and ran after Elijah, and said, Let me, I pray thee, kiss my father and my mother, and *then* I will follow thee. And he said unto him, Go back again: for what have I done to thee?

21And he returned back from him, and took a yoke of oxen, and slew them, and boiled their flesh with the instruments of the oxen, and gave unto the people, and they did eat. Then he arose, and went after Elijah, and ministered unto him.

ACTS 12:1–23

Now about that time Herod the king stretched forth *his* hands to vex certain of the church.

2And he killed James the brother of John with the sword.

3And because he saw it pleased the Jews, he proceeded further to take Peter also. (Then were the days of unleavened bread.)

4And when he had apprehended him, he put *him* in prison, and delivered *him* to four quaternions of soldiers to keep him; intending after Easter to bring him forth to the people.

5Peter therefore was kept in prison: but prayer was made without ceasing of the church unto God for him.

6And when Herod would have brought him forth, the same night Peter was sleeping between two soldiers, bound with two chains: and the keepers before the door kept the prison.

7And, behold, the angel of the Lord came upon *him*, and a light shined in the prison: and he smote Peter on the side, and raised him up, saying, Arise up quickly. And his chains fell off from *his* hands.

8And the angel said unto him, Gird thyself, and bind on thy sandals. And so he did. And he saith unto him, Cast thy garment about thee, and follow me.

9And he went out, and followed him; and wist not that it was true which was done by the angel; but thought he saw a vision.

10When they were past the first and the second ward, they came unto the iron gate that leadeth unto the city; which opened to them of his own accord: and they went out, and passed on through one street; and forthwith the angel departed from him.

11And when Peter was come to himself, he said, Now I know of a surety, that the Lord hath sent his angel, and hath delivered me out of the hand of Herod, and *from* all the expectation of the people of the Jews.

12And when he had considered *the thing,* he came to the house of Mary the mother of John, whose surname was Mark; where many were gathered together praying.

13And as Peter knocked at the door of the gate, a damsel came to hearken, named Rhoda.

14And when she knew Peter's voice, she opened not the gate for gladness, but ran in, and told how Peter stood before the gate.

15And they said unto her, Thou art mad. But she constantly affirmed that it was even so. Then said they, It is his angel.

16But Peter continued knocking: and when they had opened *the door,* and saw him, they were astonished.

17But he, beckoning unto them with the hand to hold their peace, declared unto them how the Lord had brought him out of the prison. And he said, Go shew these things unto James, and to the brethren. And he departed, and went into another place.

18Now as soon as it was day, there was no small stir among the soldiers, what was become of Peter.

19And when Herod had sought for him, and found him not, he examined the keepers, and commanded that *they* should be put to death. And he went down from Judaea to Caesarea, and *there* abode.

20And Herod was highly displeased with them of Tyre and Sidon: but they came with one accord to him, and, having made Blastus the king's chamberlain their friend, desired peace; because their country was nourished by the king's *country*.

21And upon a set day Herod, arrayed in royal apparel, sat upon his throne, and made an oration unto them.

22And the people gave a shout, *saying, It is* the voice of a god, and not of a man.

23And immediately the angel of the Lord smote him, because he gave not God the glory: and he was eaten of worms, and gave up the ghost.

PSALM 136:1–26

O GIVE thanks unto the LORD; for *he is* good: for his mercy *endureth* for ever.

2O give thanks unto the God of gods: for his mercy *endureth* for ever.

3O give thanks to the Lord of lords: for his mercy *endureth* for ever.

4To him who alone doeth great wonders: for his mercy *endureth* for ever.

5To him that by wisdom made the heavens: for his mercy *endureth* for ever.

6To him that stretched out the earth above the waters: for his mercy *endureth* for ever.

7To him that made great lights: for his mercy *endureth* for ever:

8The sun to rule by day: for his mercy *endureth* for ever:

9The moon and stars to rule by night: for his mercy *endureth* for ever.

10To him that smote Egypt in their firstborn: for his mercy *endureth* for ever:

11And brought out Israel from among them: for his mercy *endureth* for ever:

12With a strong hand, and with a stretched out arm: for his mercy *endureth* for ever.

13To him which divided the Red sea into parts: for his mercy *endureth* for ever:

14And made Israel to pass through the midst of it: for his mercy *endureth* for ever:

15But overthrew Pharaoh and his host in the Red sea: for his mercy *endureth* for ever.

16To him which led his people through the wilderness: for his mercy *endureth* for ever.

17To him which smote great kings: for his mercy *endureth* for ever:

18And slew famous kings: for his mercy *endureth* for ever:

19Sihon king of the Amorites: for his mercy *endureth* for ever:

20And Og the king of Bashan: for his mercy *endureth* for ever:

21And gave their land for an heritage: for his mercy *endureth* for ever:

22*Even* an heritage unto Israel his servant: for his mercy *endureth* for ever.

23Who remembered us in our low estate: for his mercy *endureth* for ever:

24And hath redeemed us from our enemies: for his mercy *endureth* for ever.

25Who giveth food to all flesh: for his mercy *endureth* for ever.

26O give thanks unto the God of heaven: for his mercy *endureth* for ever.

PROVERBS FOR TODAY/ 17:14–15

The beginning of strife is as *when one letteth out water: therefore leave off contention, before it be meddled with.* □ *He that justifieth the wicked, and he that condemneth the just, even they both* are *abomination to the* LORD.

1 KINGS 20:1—21:29

AND Ben–hadad the king of Syria gathered all his host together: and *there were* thirty and two kings with him, and horses, and chariots: and he went up and besieged Samaria, and warred against it.

²And he sent messengers to Ahab king of Israel into the city, and said unto him, Thus saith Ben–hadad,

³Thy silver and thy gold *is* mine; thy wives also and thy children, *even* the goodliest, *are* mine.

⁴And the king of Israel answered and said, My lord, O king, according to thy saying, I *am* thine, and all that I have.

⁵And the messengers came again, and said, Thus speaketh Ben–hadad, saying, Although I have sent unto thee, saying, Thou shalt deliver me thy silver, and thy gold, and thy wives, and thy children;

⁶Yet I will send my servants unto thee to morrow about this time, and they shall search thine house, and the houses of thy servants; and it shall be, *that* whatsoever is pleasant in thine eyes, they shall put *it* in their hand, and take *it* away.

⁷Then the king of Israel called all the elders of the land, and said, Mark, I pray you, and see how this *man* seeketh mischief: for he sent unto me for my wives, and for my children, and for my silver, and for my gold; and I denied him not.

⁸And all the elders and all the people said unto him, Hearken not *unto him,* nor consent.

⁹Wherefore he said unto the messengers of Ben–hadad, Tell my lord the king, All that thou didst send for to thy servant at the first I will do: but this thing I may not do. And the messen-

gers departed, and brought him word again.

¹⁰And Ben–hadad sent unto him, and said, The gods do so unto me, and more also, if the dust of Samaria shall suffice for handfuls for all the people that follow me.

¹¹And the king of Israel answered and said, Tell *him,* Let not him that girdeth on *his harness* boast himself as he that putteth it off.

¹²And it came to pass, when *Ben–hadad* heard this message, as he *was* drinking, he and the kings in the pavilions, that he said unto his servants, Set *yourselves in array.* And they set *themselves in array* against the city.

¹³And, behold, there came a prophet unto Ahab king of Israel, saying, Thus saith the LORD, Hast thou seen all this great multitude? behold, I will deliver it into thine hand this day; and thou shalt know that I *am* the LORD.

¹⁴And Ahab said, By whom? And he said, Thus saith the LORD, *Even* by the young men of the princes of the provinces. Then he said, Who shall order the battle? And he answered, Thou.

¹⁵Then he numbered the young men of the princes of the provinces, and they were two hundred and thirty two: and after them he numbered all the people, *even* all the children of Israel, *being* seven thousand.

¹⁶And they went out at noon. But Ben–hadad *was* drinking himself drunk in the pavilions, he and the kings, the thirty and two kings that helped him.

¹⁷And the young men of the princes of the provinces went out first; and Ben–hadad sent out, and they told him, saying, There are men come out of Samaria.

¹⁸And he said, Whether they be come out for peace, take them alive; or

whether they be come out for war, take them alive.

19So these young men of the princes of the provinces came out of the city, and the army which followed them.

20And they slew every one his man: and the Syrians fled; and Israel pursued them: and Ben–hadad the king of Syria escaped on an horse with the horsemen.

21And the king of Israel went out, and smote the horses and chariots, and slew the Syrians with a great slaughter.

22And the prophet came to the king of Israel, and said unto him, Go, strengthen thyself, and mark, and see what thou doest: for at the return of the year the king of Syria will come up against thee.

23And the servants of the king of Syria said unto him, Their gods *are* gods of the hills; therefore they were stronger than we; but let us fight against them in the plain, and surely we shall be stronger than they.

24And do this thing, Take the kings away, every man out of his place, and put captains in their rooms:

25And number thee an army, like the army that thou hast lost, horse for horse, and chariot for chariot: and we will fight against them in the plain, *and* surely we shall be stronger than they. And he hearkened unto their voice, and did so.

26And it came to pass at the return of the year, that Ben–hadad numbered the Syrians, and went up to Aphek, to fight against Israel.

27And the children of Israel were numbered, and were all present, and went against them: and the children of Israel pitched before them like two little flocks of kids; but the Syrians filled the country.

28And there came a man of God, and spake unto the king of Israel, and said, Thus saith the LORD, Because the Syrians have said, The LORD *is* God of the hills, but he *is* not God of the valleys, therefore will I deliver all this great multitude into thine hand, and ye shall know that I *am* the LORD.

29And they pitched one over against the other seven days. And *so* it was, that in the seventh day the battle was joined: and the children of Israel slew of the Syrians an hundred thousand footmen in one day.

30But the rest fled to Aphek, into the city; and *there* a wall fell upon twenty and seven thousand of the men *that were* left. And Ben–hadad fled, and came into the city, into an inner chamber.

31And his servants said unto him, Behold now, we have heard that the kings of the house of Israel *are* merciful kings: let us, I pray thee, put sackcloth on our loins, and ropes upon our heads, and go out to the king of Israel: peradventure he will save thy life.

32So they girded sackcloth on their loins, and *put* ropes on their heads, and came to the king of Israel, and said, Thy servant Ben–hadad saith, I pray thee, let me live. And he said, *Is* he yet alive? he *is* my brother.

33Now the men did diligently observe whether *any thing would come* from him, and did hastily catch *it:* and they said, Thy brother Ben–hadad. Then he said, Go ye, bring him. Then Ben–hadad came forth to him; and he caused him to come up into the chariot.

34And *Ben–hadad* said unto him, The cities, which my father took from thy father, I will restore; and thou shalt make streets for thee in Damascus, as my father made in Samaria. Then *said Ahab,* I will send thee away with this covenant. So he made a covenant with him, and sent him away.

35And a certain man of the sons of the prophets said unto his neighbour in the word of the LORD, Smite me, I pray thee. And the man refused to smite him.

36Then said he unto him, Because thou hast not obeyed the voice of the LORD, behold, as soon as thou art departed from me, a lion shall slay thee.

And as soon as he was departed from him, a lion found him, and slew him.

37Then he found another man, and said, Smite me, I pray thee. And the man smote him, so that in smiting he wounded *him*.

38So the prophet departed, and waited for the king by the way, and disguised himself with ashes upon his face.

39And as the king passed by, he cried unto the king: and he said, Thy servant went out into the midst of the battle; and, behold, a man turned aside, and brought a man unto me, and said, Keep this man: if by any means he be missing, then shall thy life be for his life, or else thou shalt pay a talent of silver.

40And as thy servant was busy here and there, he was gone. And the king of Israel said unto him, So *shall* thy judgment *be;* thyself hast decided *it.*

41And he hasted, and took the ashes away from his face; and the king of Israel discerned him that he *was* of the prophets.

42And he said unto him, Thus saith the LORD, Because thou hast let go out of *thy* hand a man whom I appointed to utter destruction, therefore thy life shall go for his life, and thy people for his people.

43And the king of Israel went to his house heavy and displeased, and came to Samaria.

AND it came to pass after these things, *that* Naboth the Jezreelite had a vineyard, which *was* in Jezreel, hard by the palace of Ahab king of Samaria.

2And Ahab spake unto Naboth, saying, Give me thy vineyard, that I may have it for a garden of herbs, because it *is* near unto my house: and I will give thee for it a better vineyard than it; *or,* if it seem good to thee, I will give thee the worth of it in money.

3And Naboth said to Ahab, The LORD forbid it me, that I should give the inheritance of my fathers unto thee.

4And Ahab came into his house heavy and displeased because of the word which Naboth the Jezreelite had spoken to him: for he had said, I will not give thee the inheritance of my fathers. And he laid him down upon his bed, and turned away his face, and would eat no bread.

5But Jezebel his wife came to him, and said unto him, Why is thy spirit so sad, that thou eatest no bread?

6And he said unto her, Because I spake unto Naboth the Jezreelite, and said unto him, Give me thy vineyard for money; or else, if it please thee, I will give thee *another* vineyard for it: and he answered, I will not give thee my vineyard.

7And Jezebel his wife said unto him, Dost thou now govern the kingdom of Israel? arise, *and* eat bread, and let thine heart be merry: I will give thee the vineyard of Naboth the Jezreelite.

8So she wrote letters in Ahab's name, and sealed *them* with his seal, and sent the letters unto the elders and to the nobles that *were* in his city, dwelling with Naboth.

9And she wrote in the letters, saying, Proclaim a fast, and set Naboth on high among the people:

10And set two men, sons of Belial, before him, to bear witness against him, saying, Thou didst blaspheme God and the king. And *then* carry him out, and stone him, that he may die.

11And the men of his city, *even* the elders and the nobles who were the inhabitants in his city, did as Jezebel had sent unto them, *and* as it *was* written in the letters which she had sent unto them.

12They proclaimed a fast, and set Naboth on high among the people.

13And there came in two men, children of Belial, and sat before him: and the men of Belial witnessed against him, *even* against Naboth, in the presence of the people, saying, Naboth did blaspheme God and the king. Then they carried him forth out of the city, and stoned him with stones, that he died.

14Then they sent to Jezebel, saying, Naboth is stoned, and is dead.

15And it came to pass, when Jezebel heard that Naboth was stoned, and was dead, that Jezebel said to Ahab, Arise, take possession of the vineyard of Naboth the Jezreelite, which he refused to give thee for money: for Naboth is not alive, but dead.

16And it came to pass, when Ahab heard that Naboth was dead, that Ahab rose up to go down to the vineyard of Naboth the Jezreelite, to take possession of it.

17And the word of the LORD came to Elijah the Tishbite, saying,

18Arise, go down to meet Ahab king of Israel, which *is* in Samaria: behold, *he is* in the vineyard of Naboth, whither he is gone down to possess it.

19And thou shalt speak unto him, saying, Thus saith the LORD, Hast thou killed, and also taken possession? And thou shalt speak unto him, saying, Thus saith the LORD, In the place where dogs licked the blood of Naboth shall dogs lick thy blood, even thine.

20And Ahab said to Elijah, Hast thou found me, O mine enemy? And he answered, I have found *thee:* because thou hast sold thyself to work evil in the sight of the LORD.

21Behold, I will bring evil upon thee, and will take away thy posterity, and will cut off from Ahab him that pisseth against the wall, and him that is shut up and left in Israel,

22And will make thine house like the house of Jeroboam the son of Nebat, and like the house of Baasha the son of Ahijah, for the provocation wherewith thou hast provoked *me* to anger, and made Israel to sin.

23And of Jezebel also spake the LORD, saying, The dogs shall eat Jezebel by the wall of Jezreel.

24Him that dieth of Ahab in the city the dogs shall eat; and him that dieth

in the field shall the fowls of the air eat.

25But there was none like unto Ahab, which did sell himself to work wickedness in the sight of the LORD, whom Jezebel his wife stirred up.

26And he did very abominably in following idols, according to all *things* as did the Amorites, whom the LORD cast out before the children of Israel.

27And it came to pass, when Ahab heard those words, that he rent his clothes, and put sackcloth upon his flesh, and fasted, and lay in sackcloth, and went softly.

28And the word of the LORD came to Elijah the Tishbite, saying,

29Seest thou how Ahab humbleth himself before me? because he humbleth himself before me, I will not bring the evil in his days: *but* in his son's days will I bring the evil upon his house.

ACTS 12:24—13:15

BUT the word of God grew and multiplied.

25And Barnabas and Saul returned from Jerusalem, when they had fulfilled *their* ministry, and took with them John, whose surname was Mark.

Now there were in the church that was at Antioch certain prophets and teachers; as Barnabas, and Simeon that was called Niger, and Lucius of Cyrene, and Manaen, which had been brought up with Herod the tetrarch, and Saul.

2As they ministered to the Lord, and fasted, the Holy Ghost said, Separate me Barnabas and Saul for the work whereunto I have called them.

3And when they had fasted and prayed, and laid *their* hands on them, they sent *them* away.

4So they, being sent forth by the Holy Ghost, departed unto Seleucia; and from thence they sailed to Cyprus.

5And when they were at Salamis, they preached the word of God in the synagogues of the Jews: and they had also John to *their* minister.

6And when they had gone through the isle unto Paphos, they found a certain sorcerer, a false prophet, a Jew, whose name *was* Bar–jesus:

7Which was with the deputy of the country, Sergius Paulus, a prudent man; who called for Barnabas and Saul, and desired to hear the word of God.

8But Elymas the sorcerer (for so is his name by interpretation) withstood them, seeking to turn away the deputy from the faith.

9Then Saul, (who also *is called* Paul,) filled with the Holy Ghost, set his eyes on him,

10And said, O full of all subtilty and all mischief, *thou* child of the devil, *thou* enemy of all righteousness, wilt thou not cease to pervert the right ways of the Lord?

11And now, behold, the hand of the Lord *is* upon thee, and thou shalt be blind, not seeing the sun for a season. And immediately there fell on him a mist and a darkness; and he went about seeking some to lead him by the hand.

12Then the deputy, when he saw what was done, believed, being astonished at the doctrine of the Lord.

13Now when Paul and his company loosed from Paphos, they came to Perga in Pamphylia: and John departing from them returned to Jerusalem.

14But when they departed from Perga, they came to Antioch in Pisidia, and went into the synagogue on the sabbath day, and sat down.

15And after the reading of the law and the prophets the rulers of the synagogue sent unto them, saying, *Ye* men *and* brethren, if ye have any word of exhortation for the people, say on.

PSALM 137:1–9

BY the rivers of Babylon, there we sat down, yea, we wept, when we remembered Zion.

2We hanged our harps upon the willows in the midst thereof.

3For there they that carried us away captive required of us a song; and they that wasted us *required of us* mirth, *saying,* Sing us *one* of the songs of Zion.

4How shall we sing the LORD's song in a strange land?

5If I forget thee, O Jerusalem, let my right hand forget *her cunning.*

6If I do not remember thee, let my tongue cleave to the roof of my mouth; if I prefer not Jerusalem above my chief joy.

7Remember, O LORD, the children of Edom in the day of Jerusalem; who said, Rase *it,* rase *it, even* to the foundation thereof.

8O daughter of Babylon, who art to be destroyed; happy *shall he be,* that rewardeth thee as thou hast served us.

9Happy *shall he be,* that taketh and dasheth thy little ones against the stones.

PROVERBS FOR TODAY/ 17:16

Wherefore is there *a price in the hand of a fool to get wisdom, seeing* he hath *no heart to* it?

JUNE 20

1 KINGS 22:1–53

And they continued three years without war between Syria and Israel.

2And it came to pass in the third year, that Jehoshaphat the king of Judah came down to the king of Israel.

3And the king of Israel said unto his servants, Know ye that Ramoth in Gilead *is* ours, and we *be* still, *and* take it not out of the hand of the king of Syria?

4And he said unto Jehoshaphat, Wilt thou go with me to battle to Ramoth–gilead? And Jehoshaphat said to the king of Israel, I *am* as thou *art,* my people as thy people, my horses as thy horses.

5And Jehoshaphat said unto the king of Israel, Enquire, I pray thee, at the word of the LORD to day.

6Then the king of Israel gathered the prophets together, about four hundred men, and said unto them, Shall I go against Ramoth–gilead to battle, or shall I forbear? And they said, Go up; for the LORD shall deliver *it* into the hand of the king.

7And Jehoshaphat said, *Is there* not here a prophet of the LORD besides, that we might enquire of him?

8And the king of Israel said unto Jehoshaphat, *There is* yet one man, Micaiah the son of Imlah, by whom we may enquire of the LORD: but I hate him; for he doth not prophesy good concerning me, but evil. And Jehoshaphat said, Let not the king say so.

9Then the king of Israel called an officer, and said, Hasten *hither* Micaiah the son of Imlah.

10And the king of Israel and Jehoshaphat the king of Judah sat each on his throne, having put on their robes, in a void place in the entrance of the gate of Samaria; and all the prophets prophesied before them.

11And Zedekiah the son of Chenaanah made him horns of iron: and he said, Thus saith the LORD, With these shalt thou push the Syrians, until thou have consumed them.

12And all the prophets prophesied so, saying, Go up to Ramoth–gilead, and prosper: for the LORD shall deliver *it* into the king's hand.

13And the messenger that was gone to call Micaiah spake unto him, saying, Behold now, the words of the prophets *declare* good unto the king with one mouth: let thy word, I pray thee, be like the word of one of them, and speak *that which is* good.

14And Micaiah said, *As* the LORD liveth, what the LORD saith unto me, that will I speak.

15So he came to the king. And the king said unto him, Micaiah, shall we go against Ramoth–gilead to battle, or shall we forbear? And he answered him, Go, and prosper: for the LORD shall deliver *it* into the hand of the king.

16And the king said unto him, How many times shall I adjure thee that thou tell me nothing but *that which is* true in the name of the LORD?

17And he said, I saw all Israel scattered upon the hills, as sheep that have not a shepherd: and the LORD said, These have no master: let them return every man to his house in peace.

18And the king of Israel said unto Jehoshaphat, Did I not tell thee that he would prophesy no good concerning me, but evil?

19And he said, Hear thou therefore the word of the LORD: I saw the LORD sitting on his throne, and all the host of heaven standing by him on his right hand and on his left.

20And the LORD said, Who shall persuade Ahab, that he may go up and fall at Ramoth–gilead? And one said on this manner, and another said on that manner.

21And there came forth a spirit, and stood before the LORD, and said, I will persuade him.

22And the LORD said unto him, Wherewith? And he said, I will go forth, and I will be a lying spirit in the mouth of all his prophets. And he said, Thou shalt persuade *him,* and prevail also: go forth, and do so.

23Now therefore, behold, the LORD hath put a lying spirit in the mouth of all these thy prophets, and the LORD hath spoken evil concerning thee.

24But Zedekiah the son of Chenaanah went near, and smote Micaiah on the cheek, and said, Which way went the Spirit of the LORD from me to speak unto thee?

25And Micaiah said, Behold, thou shalt see in that day, when thou shalt go into an inner chamber to hide thyself.

26And the king of Israel said, Take Micaiah, and carry him back unto Amon the governor of the city, and to Joash the king's son;

27And say, Thus saith the king, Put this *fellow* in the prison, and feed him with bread of affliction and with water of affliction, until I come in peace.

28And Micaiah said, If thou return at all in peace, the LORD hath not spoken by me. And he said, Hearken, O people, every one of you.

29So the king of Israel and Jehoshaphat the king of Judah went up to Ramoth–gilead.

30And the king of Israel said unto Jehoshaphat, I will disguise myself, and enter into the battle; but put thou on thy robes. And the king of Israel disguised himself, and went into the battle.

31But the king of Syria commanded his thirty and two captains that had rule over his chariots, saying, Fight neither with small nor great, save only with the king of Israel.

32And it came to pass, when the captains of the chariots saw Jehoshaphat, that they said, Surely it *is* the king of Israel. And they turned aside to fight against him: and Jehoshaphat cried out.

33And it came to pass, when the captains of the chariots perceived that it *was* not the king of Israel, that they turned back from pursuing him.

34And a *certain* man drew a bow at a venture, and smote the king of Israel between the joints of the harness: wherefore he said unto the driver of his chariot, Turn thine hand, and carry me out of the host; for I am wounded.

35And the battle increased that day: and the king was stayed up in his chariot against the Syrians, and died at even: and the blood ran out of the wound into the midst of the chariot.

36And there went a proclamation throughout the host about the going down of the sun, saying, Every man to his city, and every man to his own country.

37So the king died, and was brought to Samaria; and they buried the king in Samaria.

38And *one* washed the chariot in the pool of Samaria; and the dogs licked up his blood; and they washed his armour; according unto the word of the LORD which he spake.

39Now the rest of the acts of Ahab, and all that he did, and the ivory house which he made, and all the cities that he built, *are* they not written in the book of the chronicles of the kings of Israel?

40So Ahab slept with his fathers; and Ahaziah his son reigned in his stead.

41And Jehoshaphat the son of Asa began to reign over Judah in the fourth year of Ahab king of Israel.

42Jehoshaphat *was* thirty and five years old when he began to reign; and he reigned twenty and five years in Jerusalem. And his mother's name *was* Azubah the daughter of Shilhi.

43And he walked in all the ways of

Asa his father; he turned not aside from it, doing *that which was* right in the eyes of the LORD: nevertheless the high places were not taken away; *for* the people offered and burnt incense yet in the high places.

⁴⁴And Jehoshaphat made peace with the king of Israel.

⁴⁵Now the rest of the acts of Jehoshaphat, and his might that he shewed, and how he warred, *are* they not written in the book of the chronicles of the kings of Judah?

⁴⁶And the remnant of the sodomites, which remained in the days of his father Asa, he took out of the land.

⁴⁷*There was* then no king in Edom: a deputy *was* king.

⁴⁸Jehoshaphat made ships of Tharshish to go to Ophir for gold: but they went not; for the ships were broken at Ezion–geber.

⁴⁹Then said Ahaziah the son of Ahab unto Jehoshaphat, Let my servants go with thy servants in the ships. But Jehoshaphat would not.

⁵⁰And Jehoshaphat slept with his fathers, and was buried with his fathers in the city of David his father: and Jehoram his son reigned in his stead.

⁵¹Ahaziah the son of Ahab began to reign over Israel in Samaria the seventeenth year of Jehoshaphat king of Judah, and reigned two years over Israel.

⁵²And he did evil in the sight of the LORD, and walked in the way of his father, and in the way of his mother, and in the way of Jeroboam the son of Nebat, who made Israel to sin:

⁵³For he served Baal, and worshipped him, and provoked to anger the LORD God of Israel, according to all that his father had done.

ACTS 13:16–41

THEN Paul stood up, and beckoning with *his* hand said, Men of Israel, and ye that fear God, give audience.

¹⁷The God of this people of Israel chose our fathers, and exalted the people when they dwelt as strangers in the land of Egypt, and with an high arm brought he them out of it.

¹⁸And about the time of forty years suffered he their manners in the wilderness.

¹⁹And when he had destroyed seven nations in the land of Chanaan, he divided their land to them by lot.

²⁰And after that he gave *unto them* judges about the space of four hundred and fifty years, until Samuel the prophet.

²¹And afterward they desired a king: and God gave unto them Saul the son of Cis, a man of the tribe of Benjamin, by the space of forty years.

²²And when he had removed him, he raised up unto them David to be their king; to whom also he gave testimony, and said, I have found David the *son* of Jesse, a man after mine own heart, which shall fulfil all my will.

²³Of this man's seed hath God according to *his* promise raised unto Israel a Saviour, Jesus:

²⁴When John had first preached before his coming the baptism of repentance to all the people of Israel.

²⁵And as John fulfilled his course, he said, Whom think ye that I am? I am not *he*. But, behold, there cometh one after me, whose shoes of *his* feet I am not worthy to loose.

²⁶Men *and* brethren, children of the stock of Abraham, and whosoever among you feareth God, to you is the word of this salvation sent.

²⁷For they that dwell at Jerusalem, and their rulers, because they knew him not, nor yet the voices of the prophets which are read every sabbath day, they have fulfilled *them* in condemning *him*.

²⁸And though they found no cause of death *in him,* yet desired they Pilate that he should be slain.

²⁹And when they had fulfilled all that

was written of him, they took *him* down from the tree, and laid *him* in a sepulchre.

30But God raised him from the dead:

31And he was seen many days of them which came up with him from Galilee to Jerusalem, who are his witnesses unto the people.

32And we declare unto you glad tidings, how that the promise which was made unto the fathers,

33God hath fulfilled the same unto us their children, in that he hath raised up Jesus again; as it is also written in the second psalm, Thou art my Son, this day have I begotten thee.

34And as concerning that he raised him up from the dead, *now* no more to return to corruption, he said on this wise, I will give you the sure mercies of David.

35Wherefore he saith also in another *psalm,* Thou shalt not suffer thine Holy One to see corruption.

36For David, after he had served his own generation by the will of God, fell on sleep, and was laid unto his fathers, and saw corruption:

37But he, whom God raised again, saw no corruption.

38Be it known unto you therefore, men *and* brethren, that through this man is preached unto you the forgiveness of sins:

39And by him all that believe are justified from all things, from which ye could not be justified by the law of Moses.

40Beware therefore, lest that come upon you, which is spoken of in the prophets;

41Behold, ye despisers, and wonder, and perish: for I work a work in your days, a work which ye shall in no wise believe, though a man declare it unto you.

PSALM 138:1–8

I WILL praise thee with my whole heart: before the gods will I sing praise unto thee.

2I will worship toward thy holy temple, and praise thy name for thy lovingkindness and for thy truth: for thou hast magnified thy word above all thy name.

3In the day when I cried thou answeredst me, *and* strengthenedst me *with* strength in my soul.

4All the kings of the earth shall praise thee, O LORD, when they hear the words of thy mouth.

5Yea, they shall sing in the ways of the LORD: for great *is* the glory of the LORD.

6Though the LORD *be* high, yet hath he respect unto the lowly: but the proud he knoweth afar off.

7Though I walk in the midst of trouble, thou wilt revive me: thou shalt stretch forth thine hand against the wrath of mine enemies, and thy right hand shall save me.

8The LORD will perfect *that which* concerneth me: thy mercy, O LORD, *endureth* for ever: forsake not the works of thine own hands.

PROVERBS FOR TODAY/ 17:17–18

A friend loveth at all times, and a brother is born for adversity. □ *A man void of understanding striketh hands,* and *becometh surety in the presence of his friend.*

JUNE 21

2 KINGS 1:1—2:25

THEN Moab rebelled against Israel after the death of Ahab.

2And Ahaziah fell down through a lattice in his upper chamber that *was* in Samaria, and was sick: and he sent messengers, and said unto them, Go, enquire of Baal–zebub the god of Ekron whether I shall recover of this disease.

3But the angel of the LORD said to Elijah the Tishbite, Arise, go up to meet the messengers of the king of Samaria, and say unto them, *Is it* not because *there is* not a God in Israel, *that* ye go to enquire of Baal–zebub the god of Ekron?

4Now therefore thus saith the LORD, Thou shalt not come down from that bed on which thou art gone up, but shalt surely die. And Elijah departed.

5And when the messengers turned back unto him, he said unto them, Why are ye now turned back?

6And they said unto him, There came a man up to meet us, and said unto us, Go, turn again unto the king that sent you, and say unto him, Thus saith the LORD, *Is it* not because *there is* not a God in Israel, *that* thou sendest to enquire of Baal–zebub the god of Ekron? therefore thou shalt not come down from that bed on which thou art gone up, but shalt surely die.

7And he said unto them, What manner of man *was he* which came up to meet you, and told you these words?

8And they answered him, *He was* an hairy man, and girt with a girdle of leather about his loins. And he said, It *is* Elijah the Tishbite.

9Then the king sent unto him a captain of fifty with his fifty. And he went up to him: and, behold, he sat on the top of an hill. And he spake unto him, Thou

man of God, the king hath said, Come down.

10And Elijah answered and said to the captain of fifty, If I *be* a man of God, then let fire come down from heaven, and consume thee and thy fifty. And there came down fire from heaven, and consumed him and his fifty.

11Again also he sent unto him another captain of fifty with his fifty. And he answered and said unto him, O man of God, thus hath the king said, Come down quickly.

12And Elijah answered and said unto them, If I *be* a man of God, let fire come down from heaven, and consume thee and thy fifty. And the fire of God came down from heaven, and consumed him and his fifty.

13And he sent again a captain of the third fifty with his fifty. And the third captain of fifty went up, and came and fell on his knees before Elijah, and besought him, and said unto him, O man of God, I pray thee, let my life, and the life of these fifty thy servants, be precious in thy sight.

14Behold, there came fire down from heaven, and burnt up the two captains of the former fifties with their fifties: therefore let my life now be precious in thy sight.

15And the angel of the LORD said unto Elijah, Go down with him: be not afraid of him. And he arose, and went down with him unto the king.

16And he said unto him, Thus saith the LORD, Forasmuch as thou hast sent messengers to enquire of Baal–zebub the God of Ekron, *is it* not because *there is* no God in Israel to enquire of his word? therefore thou shalt not come down off that bed on which thou art gone up, but shalt surely die.

17So he died according to the word

of the LORD which Elijah had spoken. And Jehoram reigned in his stead in the second year of Jehoram the son of Jehoshaphat king of Judah; because he had no son.

18Now the rest of the acts of Ahaziah which he did, *are* they not written in the book of the chronicles of the kings of Israel?

AND it came to pass, when the LORD would take up Elijah into heaven by a whirlwind, that Elijah went with Elisha from Gilgal.

2And Elijah said unto Elisha, Tarry here, I pray thee; for the LORD hath sent me to Beth–el. And Elisha said *unto him, As* the LORD liveth, and *as* thy soul liveth, I will not leave thee. So they went down to Beth–el.

3And the sons of the prophets that *were* at Beth–el came forth to Elisha, and said unto him, Knowest thou that the LORD will take away thy master from thy head to day? And he said, Yea, I know *it;* hold ye your peace.

4And Elijah said unto him, Elisha, tarry here, I pray thee; for the LORD hath sent me to Jericho. And he said, *As* the LORD liveth, and *as* thy soul liveth, I will not leave thee. So they came to Jericho.

5And the sons of the prophets that *were* at Jericho came to Elisha, and said unto him, Knowest thou that the LORD will take away thy master from thy head to day? And he answered, Yea, I know *it:* hold ye your peace.

6And Elijah said unto him, Tarry, I pray thee, here; for the LORD hath sent me to Jordan. And he said, *As* the LORD liveth, and *as* thy soul liveth, I will not leave thee. And they two went on.

7And fifty men of the sons of the prophets went, and stood to view afar off: and they two stood by Jordan.

8And Elijah took his mantle, and wrapped *it* together, and smote the waters, and they were divided hither and thither, so that they two went over on dry ground.

9And it came to pass, when they were gone over, that Elijah said unto Elisha, Ask what I shall do for thee, before I be taken away from thee. And Elisha said, I pray thee, let a double portion of thy spirit be upon me.

10And he said, Thou hast asked a hard thing: *nevertheless,* if thou see me *when I am* taken from thee, it shall be so unto thee; but if not, it shall not be *so.*

11And it came to pass, as they still went on, and talked, that, behold, *there appeared* a chariot of fire, and horses of fire, and parted them both asunder; and Elijah went up by a whirlwind into heaven.

12And Elisha saw *it,* and he cried, My father, my father, the chariot of Israel, and the horsemen thereof. And he saw him no more: and he took hold of his own clothes, and rent them in two pieces.

13He took up also the mantle of Elijah that fell from him, and went back, and stood by the bank of Jordan;

14And he took the mantle of Elijah that fell from him, and smote the waters, and said, Where *is* the LORD God of Elijah? and when he also had smitten the waters, they parted hither and thither: and Elisha went over.

15And when the sons of the prophets which *were* to view at Jericho saw him, they said, The spirit of Elijah doth rest on Elisha. And they came to meet him, and bowed themselves to the ground before him.

16And they said unto him, Behold now, there be with thy servants fifty strong men; let them go, we pray thee, and seek thy master: lest peradventure the Spirit of the LORD hath taken him up, and cast him upon some mountain, or into some valley. And he said, Ye shall not send.

17And when they urged him till he was ashamed, he said, Send. They sent therefore fifty men; and they sought three days, but found him not.

18And when they came again to him, (for he tarried at Jericho,) he said unto them, Did I not say unto you, Go not?

19And the men of the city said unto Elisha, Behold, I pray thee, the situation of this city is pleasant, as my lord seeth: but the water is naught, and the ground barren.

20And he said, Bring me a new cruse, and put salt therein. And they brought it to him.

21And he went forth unto the spring of the waters, and cast the salt in there, and said, Thus saith the LORD, I have healed these waters; there shall not be from thence any more death or barren land.

22So the waters were healed unto this day, according to the saying of Elisha which he spake.

23And he went up from thence unto Bethel: and as he was going up by the way, there came forth little children out of the city, and mocked him and said unto him, Go up, thou bald head; go up, thou bald head.

24And he turned back, and looked on them, and cursed them in the name of the LORD. And there came forth two she bears out of the wood, and tare forty and two children of them.

25And he went from thence to mount Carmel, and from thence he returned to Samaria.

ACTS 13:42—14:7

AND when the Jews were gone out of the synagogue, the Gentiles besought that these words might be preached to them the next sabbath.

43Now when the congregation was broken up, many of the Jews and religious proselytes followed Paul and Barnabas: who, speaking to them, persuaded them to continue in the grace of God.

44And the next sabbath day came almost the whole city together to hear the word of God.

45But when the Jews saw the multitudes, they were filled with envy, and spake against those things which were spoken by Paul, contradicting and blaspheming.

46Then Paul and Barnabas waxed bold, and said, It was necessary that the word of God should first have been spoken to you: but seeing ye put it from you, and judge yourselves unworthy of everlasting life, lo, we turn to the Gentiles.

47For so hath the Lord commanded us, saying, I have set thee to be a light of the Gentiles, that thou shouldest be for salvation unto the ends of the earth.

48And when the Gentiles heard this, they were glad, and glorified the word of the Lord: and as many as were ordained to eternal life believed.

49And the word of the Lord was published throughout all the region.

50But the Jews stirred up the devout and honourable women, and the chief men of the city, and raised persecution against Paul and Barnabas, and expelled them out of their coasts.

51But they shook off the dust of their feet against them, and came unto Iconium.

52And the disciples were filled with joy, and with the Holy Ghost.

AND it came to pass in Iconium, that they went both together into the synagogue of the Jews, and so spake, that a great multitude both of the Jews and also of the Greeks believed.

2But the unbelieving Jews stirred up the Gentiles, and made their minds evil affected against the brethren.

3Long time therefore abode they speaking boldly in the Lord, which gave testimony unto the word of his grace, and granted signs and wonders to be done by their hands.

4But the multitude of the city was divided: and part held with the Jews, and part with the apostles.

5And when there was an assault made both of the Gentiles, and also of the Jews with their rulers, to use *them* despitefully, and to stone them,

6They were ware of *it,* and fled unto Lystra and Derbe, cities of Lycaonia, and into the region that lieth round about:

7And there they preached the gospel.

PSALM 139:1–24

O LORD, thou hast searched me, and known *me.*

2Thou knowest my downsitting and mine uprising, thou understandest my thought afar off.

3Thou compassest my path and my lying down, and art acquainted *with* all my ways.

4For *there is* not a word in my tongue, *but,* lo, O LORD, thou knowest it altogether.

5Thou hast beset me behind and before, and laid thine hand upon me.

6*Such* knowledge *is* too wonderful for me; it is high, I cannot *attain* unto it.

7Whither shall I go from thy spirit? or whither shall I flee from thy presence?

8If I ascend up into heaven, thou *art* there: if I make my bed in hell, behold, thou *art there.*

9*If* I take the wings of the morning, *and* dwell in the uttermost parts of the sea;

10Even there shall thy hand lead me, and thy right hand shall hold me.

11If I say, Surely the darkness shall cover me; even the night shall be light about me.

12Yea, the darkness hideth not from thee; but the night shineth as the day: the darkness and the light *are* both alike *to thee.*

13For thou hast possessed my reins: thou hast covered me in my mother's womb.

14I will praise thee; for I am fearfully *and* wonderfully made: marvellous *are* thy works; and *that* my soul knoweth right well.

15My substance was not hid from thee, when I was made in secret, *and* curiously wrought in the lowest parts of the earth.

16Thine eyes did see my substance, yet being unperfect; and in thy book all *my members* were written, *which* in continuance were fashioned, when *as yet there was* none of them.

17How precious also are thy thoughts unto me, O God! how great is the sum of them!

18*If* I should count them, they are more in number than the sand: when I awake, I am still with thee.

19Surely thou wilt slay the wicked, O God: depart from me therefore, ye bloody men.

20For they speak against thee wickedly, *and* thine enemies take *thy name* in vain.

21Do not I hate them, O LORD, that hate thee? and am not I grieved with those that rise up against thee?

22I hate them with perfect hatred: I count them mine enemies.

23Search me, O God, and know my heart: try me, and know my thoughts:

24And see if *there be any* wicked way in me, and lead me in the way everlasting.

PROVERBS FOR TODAY/ 17:19–21

He loveth transgression that loveth strife: and *he that exalteth his gate seeketh destruction.* □ *He that hath a froward heart findeth no good: and he that hath a perverse tongue falleth into mischief.* □ *He that begetteth a fool* doeth it *to his sorrow: and the father of a fool hath no joy.*

2 KINGS 3:1—4:17

Now Jehoram the son of Ahab began to reign over Israel in Samaria the eighteenth year of Jehoshaphat king of Judah, and reigned twelve years.

2And he wrought evil in the sight of the LORD; but not like his father, and like his mother: for he put away the image of Baal that his father had made.

3Nevertheless he cleaved unto the sins of Jeroboam the son of Nebat, which made Israel to sin; he departed not therefrom.

4And Mesha king of Moab was a sheepmaster, and rendered unto the king of Israel an hundred thousand lambs, and an hundred thousand rams, with the wool.

5But it came to pass, when Ahab was dead, that the king of Moab rebelled against the king of Israel.

6And king Jehoram went out of Samaria the same time, and numbered all Israel.

7And he went and sent to Jehoshaphat the king of Judah, saying, The king of Moab hath rebelled against me: wilt thou go with me against Moab to battle? And he said, I will go up: I *am* as thou *art,* my people as thy people, *and* my horses as thy horses.

8And he said, Which way shall we go up? And he answered, the way through the wilderness of Edom.

9So the king of Israel went, and the king of Judah, and the king of Edom: and they fetched a compass of seven days' journey: and there was no water for the host, and for the cattle that followed them.

10And the king of Israel said, Alas! that the LORD hath called these three kings together, to deliver them into the hand of Moab!

11But Jehoshaphat said, *Is there* not here a prophet of the LORD, that we may enquire of the LORD by him? And one of the king of Israel's servants answered and said, Here *is* Elisha the son of Shaphat, which poured water on the hands of Elijah.

12And Jehoshaphat said, The word of the LORD is with him. So the king of Israel and Jehoshaphat and the king of Edom went down to him.

13And Elisha said unto the king of Israel, What have I to do with thee? get thee to the prophets of thy father, and to the prophets of thy mother. And the king of Israel said unto him, Nay: for the LORD hath called these three kings together, to deliver them into the hand of Moab.

14And Elisha said, *As* the LORD of hosts liveth, before whom I stand, surely, were it not that I regard the presence of Jehoshaphat the king of Judah, I would not look toward thee, nor see thee.

15But now bring me a minstrel. And it came to pass, when the minstrel played, that the hand of the LORD came upon him.

16And he said, Thus saith the LORD, Make this valley full of ditches.

17For thus saith the LORD, Ye shall not see wind, neither shall ye see rain; yet that valley shall be filled with water, that ye may drink, both ye, and your cattle, and your beasts.

18And this is *but* a light thing in the sight of the LORD: he will deliver the Moabites also into your hand.

19And ye shall smite every fenced city, and every choice city, and shall fell every good tree, and stop all wells of water, and mar every good piece of land with stones.

20And it came to pass in the morning, when the meat offering was offered, that, behold, there came water by the way of Edom, and the country was filled with water.

21And when all the Moabites heard that the kings were come up to fight against them, they gathered all that were able to put on armour, and upward, and stood in the border.

22And they rose up early in the morning, and the sun shone upon the water, and the Moabites saw the water on the other side *as* red as blood:

23And they said, This *is* blood: the kings are surely slain, and they have smitten one another: now therefore, Moab, to the spoil.

24And when they came to the camp of Israel, the Israelites rose up and smote the Moabites, so that they fled before them: but they went forward smiting the Moabites, even in *their* country.

25And they beat down the cities, and on every good piece of land cast every man his stone, and filled it; and they stopped all the wells of water, and felled all the good trees: only in Kirharaseth left they the stones thereof; howbeit the slingers went about *it,* and smote it.

26And when the king of Moab saw that the battle was too sore for him, he took with him seven hundred men that drew swords, to break through *even* unto the king of Edom: but they could not.

27Then he took his eldest son that should have reigned in his stead, and offered him *for* a burnt offering upon the wall. And there was great indignation against Israel: and they departed from him, and returned to *their own* land.

Now there cried a certain woman of the wives of the sons of the prophets unto Elisha, saying, Thy servant my husband is dead; and thou knowest that thy servant did fear the LORD: and the creditor is come to take unto him my two sons to be bondmen.

2And Elisha said unto her, What shall I do for thee? tell me, what hast thou in the house? And she said, Thine handmaid hath not any thing in the house, save a pot of oil.

3Then he said, Go, borrow thee vessels abroad of all thy neighbours, *even* empty vessels; borrow not a few.

4And when thou art come in, thou shalt shut the door upon thee and upon thy sons, and shalt pour out into all those vessels, and thou shalt set aside that which is full.

5So she went from him, and shut the door upon her and upon her sons, who brought *the vessels* to her; and she poured out.

6And it came to pass, when the vessels were full, that she said unto her son, Bring me yet a vessel. And he said unto her, *There is* not a vessel more. And the oil stayed.

7Then she came and told the man of God. And he said, Go, sell the oil, and pay thy debt, and live thou and thy children of the rest.

8And it fell on a day, that Elisha passed to Shunem, where *was* a great woman; and she constrained him to eat bread. And *so* it was, *that* as oft as he passed by, he turned in thither to eat bread.

9And she said unto her husband, Behold now, I perceive that this *is* an holy man of God, which passeth by us continually.

10Let us make a little chamber, I pray thee, on the wall; and let us set for him there a bed, and a table, and a stool, and a candlestick: and it shall be, when he cometh to us, that he shall turn in thither.

11And it fell on a day, that he came thither, and he turned into the chamber, and lay there.

12And he said to Gehazi his servant, Call this Shunammite. And when he had called her, she stood before him.

13And he said unto him, Say now unto her, Behold, thou hast been careful for us with all this care; what *is* to be done for thee? wouldest thou be spoken for to the king, or to the captain of the host? And she answered, I dwell among mine own people.

14And he said, What then *is* to be done for her? and Gehazi answered, Verily she hath no child, and her husband is old.

15And he said, Call her. And when he had called her, she stood in the door.

16And he said, About this season, according to the time of life, thou shalt embrace a son. And she said, Nay, my lord, *thou* man of God, do not lie unto thine handmaid.

17And the woman conceived, and bare a son at that season that Elisha had said unto her, according to the time of life.

ACTS 14:8–28

AND there sat a certain man at Lystra, impotent in his feet, being a cripple from his mother's womb, who never had walked:

9The same heard Paul speak: who stedfastly beholding him, and perceiving that he had faith to be healed,

10Said with a loud voice, Stand upright on thy feet. And he leaped and walked.

11And when the people saw what Paul had done, they lifted up their voices, saying in the speech of Lycaonia, The gods are come down to us in the likeness of men.

12And they called Barnabas, Jupiter; and Paul, Mercurius, because he was the chief speaker.

13Then the priest of Jupiter, which was before their city, brought oxen and garlands unto the gates, and would have done sacrifice with the people.

14*Which* when the apostles, Barnabas and Paul, heard *of,* they rent their clothes, and ran in among the people, crying out,

15And saying, Sirs, why do ye these things? We also are men of like passions with you, and preach unto you that ye should turn from these vanities unto the living God, which made heaven, and earth, and the sea, and all things that are therein:

16Who in times past suffered all nations to walk in their own ways.

17Nevertheless he left not himself without witness, in that he did good, and gave us rain from heaven, and fruitful seasons, filling our hearts with food and gladness.

18And with these sayings scarce restrained they the people, that they had not done sacrifice unto them.

19And there came thither *certain* Jews from Antioch and Iconium, who persuaded the people, and, having stoned Paul, drew *him* out of the city, supposing he had been dead.

20Howbeit, as the disciples stood round about him, he rose up, and came into the city: and the next day he departed with Barnabas to Derbe.

21And when they had preached the gospel to that city, and had taught many, they returned again to Lystra, and *to* Iconium, and Antioch,

22Confirming the souls of the disciples, *and* exhorting them to continue in the faith, and that we must through much tribulation enter into the kingdom of God.

23And when they had ordained them elders in every church, and had prayed with fasting, they commended them to the Lord, on whom they believed.

24And after they had passed throughout Pisidia, they came to Pamphylia.

25And when they had preached the word in Perga, they went down into Attalia:

26And thence sailed to Antioch, from whence they had been recommended to the grace of God for the work which they fulfilled.

27And when they were come, and had gathered the church together, they rehearsed all that God had done with them, and how he had opened the door of faith unto the Gentiles.

28And there they abode long time with the disciples.

PSALM 140:1–13

Deliver me, O Lord, from the evil man: preserve me from the violent man;

2Which imagine mischiefs in *their* heart; continually are they gathered together *for* war.

3They have sharpened their tongues like a serpent; adders' poison *is* under their lips. Selah.

4Keep me, O Lord, from the hands of the wicked; preserve me from the violent man; who have purposed to overthrow my goings.

5The proud have hid a snare for me, and cords; they have spread a net by the wayside; they have set gins for me. Selah.

6I said unto the Lord, Thou *art* my God: hear the voice of my supplications, O Lord.

7O God the Lord, the strength of my salvation, thou hast covered my head in the day of battle.

8Grant not, O Lord, the desires of the wicked: further not his wicked device; *lest* they exalt themselves. Selah.

9*As for* the head of those that compass me about, let the mischief of their own lips cover them.

10Let burning coals fall upon them: let them be cast into the fire; into deep pits, that they rise not up again.

11Let not an evil speaker be established in the earth: evil shall hunt the violent man to overthrow *him*.

12I know that the Lord will maintain the cause of the afflicted, *and* the right of the poor.

13Surely the righteous shall give thanks unto thy name: the upright shall dwell in thy presence.

PROVERBS FOR TODAY/ 17:22

A merry heart doeth good like *a medicine: but a broken spirit drieth the bones.*

JUNE 23

2 KINGS 4:18—5:27

And when the child was grown, it fell on a day, that he went out to his father to the reapers.

19And he said unto his father, My head, my head. And he said to a lad, Carry him to his mother.

20And when he had taken him, and brought him to his mother, he sat on her knees till noon, and *then* died.

21And she went up, and laid him on the bed of the man of God, and shut the door upon him, and went out.

22And she called unto her husband, and said, Send me, I pray thee, one of the young men, and one of the asses, that I may run to the man of God, and come again.

23And he said, Wherefore wilt thou go to him to day? *it is* neither new moon, nor sabbath. And she said, *It shall be* well.

24Then she saddled an ass, and said to her servant, Drive, and go forward;

slack not *thy* riding for me, except I bid thee.

25So she went and came unto the man of God to mount Carmel. And it came to pass, when the man of God saw her afar off, that he said to Gehazi his servant, Behold, *yonder is* that Shunammite:

26Run now, I pray thee, to meet her, and say unto her, *Is it* well with thee? *is it* well with thy husband? *is it* well with the child? And she answered, *It is* well.

27And when she came to the man of God to the hill, she caught him by the feet: but Gehazi came near to thrust her away. And the man of God said, Let her alone; for her soul *is* vexed within her: and the LORD hath hid *it* from me, and hath not told me.

28Then she said, Did I desire a son of my lord? did I not say, Do not deceive me?

29Then he said to Gehazi, Gird up thy loins, and take my staff in thine hand, and go thy way: if thou meet any man, salute him not; and if any salute thee, answer him not again: and lay my staff upon the face of the child.

30And the mother of the child said, As the LORD liveth, and *as* thy soul liveth, I will not leave thee. And he arose, and followed her.

31And Gehazi passed on before them, and laid the staff upon the face of the child; but *there was* neither voice, nor hearing. Wherefore he went again to meet him, and told him, saying, The child is not awaked.

32And when Elisha was come into the house, behold, the child was dead, *and* laid upon his bed.

33He went in therefore, and shut the door upon them twain, and prayed unto the LORD.

34And he went up, and lay upon the child, and put his mouth upon his mouth, and his eyes upon his eyes, and his hands upon his hands: and he stretched himself upon the child; and the flesh of the child waxed warm.

35Then he returned, and walked in the house to and fro; and went up, and stretched himself upon him: and the child sneezed seven times, and the child opened his eyes.

36And he called Gehazi, and said, Call this Shunammite. So he called her. And when she was come in unto him, he said, Take up thy son.

37Then she went in, and fell at his feet, and bowed herself to the ground, and took up her son, and went out.

38And Elisha came again to Gilgal: and *there was* a dearth in the land; and the sons of the prophets *were* sitting before him: and he said unto his servant, Set on the great pot, and seethe pottage for the sons of the prophets.

39And one went out into the field to gather herbs, and found a wild vine, and gathered thereof wild gourds his lap full, and came and shred *them* into the pot of pottage: for they knew *them* not.

40So they poured out for the men to eat. And it came to pass, as they were eating of the pottage, that they cried out, and said, O *thou* man of God, *there is* death in the pot. And they could not eat *thereof.*

41But he said, Then bring meal. And he cast *it* into the pot; and he said, Pour out for the people, that they may eat. And there was no harm in the pot.

42And there came a man from Baal-shalisha, and brought the man of God bread of the firstfruits, twenty loaves of barley, and full ears of corn in the husk thereof. And he said, Give unto the people, that they may eat.

43And his servitor said, What, should I set this before an hundred men? He said again, Give the people, that they may eat: for thus saith the LORD, They shall eat, and shall leave *thereof.*

44So he set *it* before them, and they

did eat, and left *thereof,* according to the word of the LORD.

Now Naaman, captain of the host of the king of Syria, was a great man with his master, and honourable, because by him the LORD had given deliverance unto Syria: he was also a mighty man in valour, *but he was* a leper.

2And the Syrians had gone out by companies, and had brought away captive out of the land of Israel a little maid; and she waited on Naaman's wife.

3And she said unto her mistress, Would God my lord *were* with the prophet that *is* in Samaria! for he would recover him of his leprosy.

4And *one* went in, and told his lord, saying, Thus and thus said the maid that *is* of the land of Israel.

5And the king of Syria said, Go to, go, and I will send a letter unto the king of Israel. And he departed, and took with him ten talents of silver, and six thousand *pieces* of gold, and ten changes of raiment.

6And he brought the letter to the king of Israel, saying, Now when this letter is come unto thee, behold, I have *therewith* sent Naaman my servant to thee, that thou mayest recover him of his leprosy.

7And it came to pass, when the king of Israel had read the letter, that he rent his clothes, and said, *Am* I God, to kill and to make alive, that this man doth send unto me to recover a man of his leprosy? wherefore consider, I pray you, and see how he seeketh a quarrel against me.

8And it was *so,* when Elisha the man of God had heard that the king of Israel had rent his clothes, that he sent to the king saying, Wherefore hast thou rent thy clothes? let him come now to me, and he shall know that there is a prophet in Israel.

9So Naaman came with his horses and with his chariot, and stood at the door of the house of Elisha.

10And Elisha sent a messenger unto him, saying, Go and wash in Jordan seven times, and thy flesh shall come again to thee, and thou shalt be clean.

11But Naaman was wroth, and went away, and said, Behold, I thought, He will surely come out to me, and stand, and call on the name of the LORD his God, and strike his hand over the place, and recover the leper.

12*Are* not Abana and Pharpar, rivers of Damascus, better than all the waters of Israel? may I not wash in them, and be clean? So he turned and went away in a rage.

13And his servants came near, and spake unto him, and said, My father, *if* the prophet had bid thee *do some* great thing, wouldest thou not have done *it?* how much rather then, when he saith to thee, Wash, and be clean?

14Then went he down, and dipped himself seven times in Jordan, according to the saying of the man of God: and his flesh came again like unto the flesh of a little child, and he was clean.

15And he returned to the man of God, he and all his company, and came, and stood before him: and he said, Behold, now I know that *there is* no God in all the earth, but in Israel: now therefore, I pray thee, take a blessing of thy servant.

16But he said, *As* the LORD liveth, before whom I stand, I will receive none. And he urged him to take *it;* but he refused.

17And Naaman said, Shall there not then, I pray thee, be given to thy servant two mules' burden of earth? for thy servant will henceforth offer neither burnt offering nor sacrifice unto other gods, but unto the LORD.

18In this thing the LORD pardon thy servant, *that* when my master goeth into the house of Rimmon to worship there, and he leaneth on my hand, and I bow myself in the house of

Rimmon: when I bow down myself in the house of Rimmon, the LORD pardon thy servant in this thing.

19And he said unto him, Go in peace. So he departed from him a little way.

20But Gehazi, the servant of Elisha the man of God, said, Behold, my master hath spared Naaman this Syrian, in not receiving at his hands that which he brought: but, *as* the LORD liveth, I will run after him, and take somewhat of him.

21So Gehazi followed after Naaman. And when Naaman saw *him* running after him, he lighted down from the chariot to meet him, and said, *Is* all well?

22And he said, All *is* well. My master hath sent me, saying, Behold, even now there be come to me from mount Ephraim two young men of the sons of the prophets: give them, I pray thee, a talent of silver, and two changes of garments.

23And Naaman said, Be content, take two talents. And he urged him, and bound two talents of silver in two bags, and with two changes of garments, and laid *them* upon two of his servants; and they bare *them* before him.

24And when he came to the tower, he took *them* from their hand, and bestowed *them* in the house: and he let the men go, and they departed.

25But he went in, and stood before his master. And Elisha said unto him, Whence *comest thou,* Gehazi? And he said, Thy servant went no whither.

26And he said unto him, Went not mine heart *with thee,* when the man turned again from his chariot to meet thee? *Is it* a time to receive money, and to receive garments, and olive-yards, and vineyards, and sheep, and oxen, and menservants, and maidservants?

27The leprosy therefore of Naaman shall cleave unto thee, and unto thy seed for ever. And he went out from his presence a leper *as white* as snow.

ACTS 15:1–31

AND certain men which came down from Judaea taught the brethren, *and said,* Except ye be circumcised after the manner of Moses, ye cannot be saved.

2When therefore Paul and Barnabas had no small dissension and disputation with them, they determined that Paul and Barnabas, and certain other of them, should go up to Jerusalem unto the apostles and elders about this question.

3And being brought on their way by the church, they passed through Phenice and Samaria, declaring the conversion of the Gentiles: and they caused great joy unto all the brethren.

4And when they were come to Jerusalem, they were received of the church, and *of* the apostles and elders, and they declared all things that God had done with them.

5But there rose up certain of the sect of the Pharisees which believed, saying, That it was needful to circumcise them, and to command *them* to keep the law of Moses.

6And the apostles and elders came together for to consider of this matter.

7And when there had been much disputing, Peter rose up, and said unto them, Men *and* brethren, ye know how that a good while ago God made choice among us, that the Gentiles by my mouth should hear the word of the gospel, and believe.

8And God, which knoweth the hearts, bare them witness, giving them the Holy Ghost, even as *he did* unto us;

9And put no difference between us and them, purifying their hearts by faith.

10Now therefore why tempt ye God, to put a yoke upon the neck of the disciples, which neither our fathers nor we were able to bear?

11But we believe that through the grace of the Lord Jesus Christ we shall be saved, even as they.

12Then all the multitude kept silence, and gave audience to Barnabas and Paul, declaring what miracles and wonders God had wrought among the Gentiles by them.

13And after they had held their peace, James answered, saying, Men *and* brethren, hearken unto me:

14Simeon hath declared how God at the first did visit the Gentiles, to take out of them a people for his name.

15And to this agree the words of the prophets; as it is written,

16After this I will return, and will build again the tabernacle of David, which is fallen down; and I will build again the ruins thereof, and I will set it up:

17That the residue of men might seek after the Lord, and all the Gentiles, upon whom my name is called, saith the Lord, who doeth all these things.

18Known unto God are all his works from the beginning of the world.

19Wherefore my sentence is, that we trouble not them, which from among the Gentiles are turned to God:

20But that we write unto them, that they abstain from pollutions of idols, and *from* fornication, and *from* things strangled, and *from* blood.

21For Moses of old time hath in every city them that preach him, being read in the synagogues every sabbath day.

22Then pleased it the apostles and elders, with the whole church, to send chosen men of their own company to Antioch with Paul and Barnabas: *namely,* Judas surnamed Barsabas, and Silas, chief men among the brethren:

23And they wrote *letters* by them after this manner; The apostles and elders and brethren *send* greeting unto the brethren which are of the Gentiles in Antioch and Syria and Cilicia.

24Forasmuch as we have heard, that certain which went out from us have troubled you with words, subverting your souls, saying, *Ye must* be circumcised, and keep the law: to whom we gave no *such* commandment:

25It seemed good unto us, being assembled with one accord, to send chosen men unto you with our beloved Barnabas and Paul,

26Men that have hazarded their lives for the name of our Lord Jesus Christ.

27We have sent therefore Judas and Silas, who shall also tell *you* the same things by mouth.

28For it seemed good to the Holy Ghost, and to us, to lay upon you no greater burden than these necessary things;

29That ye abstain from meats offered to idols, and from blood, and from things strangled, and from fornication: from which if ye keep yourselves, ye shall do well, Fare ye well.

30So when they were dismissed, they came to Antioch: and when they had gathered the multitude together, they delivered the epistle:

31*Which* when they had read, they rejoiced for the consolation.

PSALM 141:1–10

LORD, I cry unto thee: make haste unto me; give ear unto my voice, when I cry unto thee.

2Let my prayer be set forth before thee *as* incense; *and* the lifting up of my hands *as* the evening sacrifice.

3Set a watch, O LORD, before my mouth; keep the door of my lips.

4Incline not my heart to *any* evil thing, to practise wicked works with men that work iniquity: and let me not eat of their dainties.

5Let the righteous smite me; *it shall be* a kindness: and let him reprove me; *it shall be* an excellent oil, *which* shall not break my head: for yet my prayer also *shall be* in their calamities.

6When their judges are overthrown in stony places, they shall hear my words; for they are sweet.

7Our bones are scattered at the

grave's mouth, as when one cutteth and cleaveth *wood* upon the earth.

8But mine eyes *are* unto thee, O GOD the Lord: in thee is my trust; leave not my soul destitute.

9Keep me from the snares *which* they have laid for me, and the gins of the workers of iniquity.

10Let the wicked fall into their own nets, whilst that I withal escape.

PROVERBS FOR TODAY/ 17:23
A wicked man taketh a gift out of the bosom to pervert the ways of judgment.

JUNE 24

2 KINGS 6:1—7:20

AND the sons of the prophets said unto Elisha, Behold now, the place where we dwell with thee is too strait for us.

2Let us go, we pray thee, unto Jordan, and take thence every man a beam, and let us make us a place there, where we may dwell. And he answered, Go ye.

3And one said, Be content, I pray thee, and go with thy servants. And he answered, I will go.

4So he went with them. And when they came to Jordan, they cut down wood.

5But as one was felling a beam, the axe head fell into the water: and he cried, and said, Alas, master! for it was borrowed.

6And the man of God said, Where fell it? And he shewed him the place. And he cut down a stick, and cast *it* in thither; and the iron did swim.

7Therefore said he, Take *it* up to thee. And he put out his hand, and took it.

8Then the king of Syria warred against Israel, and took counsel with his servants, saying, In such and such a place *shall be* my camp.

9And the man of God sent unto the king of Israel, saying, Beware that thou pass not such a place; for thither the Syrians are come down.

10And the king of Israel sent to the place which the man of God told him and warned him of, and saved himself there, not once nor twice.

11Therefore the heart of the king of Syria was sore troubled for this thing; and he called his servants, and said unto them, Will ye not shew me which of us *is* for the king of Israel?

12And one of his servants said, None, my lord, O king: but Elisha, the prophet that *is* in Israel, telleth the king of Israel the words that thou speakest in thy bedchamber.

13And he said, Go and spy where he *is,* that I may send and fetch him. And it was told him, saying, Behold, *he is* in Dothan.

14Therefore sent he thither horses, and chariots, and a great host: and they came by night, and compassed the city about.

15And when the servant of the man of God was risen early, and gone forth, behold, an host compassed the city both with horses and chariots. And his servant said unto him, Alas, my master! how shall we do?

16And he answered, Fear not: for they that *be* with us *are* more than they that *be* with them.

17And Elisha prayed, and said, LORD, I pray thee, open his eyes, that he may see. And the LORD opened the eyes of the young man; and he saw: and, behold, the mountain *was* full of horses and chariots of fire round about Elisha.

18And when they came down to him, Elisha prayed unto the LORD, and said, Smite this people, I pray thee, with blindness. And he smote them with blindness according to the word of Elisha.

19And Elisha said unto them, This *is* not the way, neither *is* this the city: follow me, and I will bring you to the man whom ye seek. But he led them to Samaria.

20And it came to pass, when they were come into Samaria, that Elisha said, LORD, open the eyes of these *men,* that they may see. And the LORD opened their eyes, and they saw; and, behold, *they were* in the midst of Samaria.

21And the king of Israel said unto Elisha, when he saw them, My father, shall I smite *them?* shall I smite *them?*

22And he answered, Thou shalt not smite *them:* wouldest thou smite those whom thou hast taken captive with thy sword and with thy bow? set bread and water before them, that they may eat and drink, and go to their master.

23And he prepared great provision for them: and when they had eaten and drunk, he sent them away, and they went to their master. So the bands of Syria came no more into the land of Israel.

24And it came to pass after this, that Ben–hadad king of Syria gathered all his host, and went up, and besieged Samaria.

25And there was a great famine in Samaria: and, behold, they besieged it, until an ass's head was *sold* for fourscore *pieces* of silver, and the fourth part of a cab of dove's dung for five *pieces* of silver.

26And as the king of Israel was passing by upon the wall, there cried a woman unto him, saying, Help, my lord, O king.

27And he said, If the LORD do not help thee, whence shall I help thee? out of the barnfloor, or out of the winepress?

28And the king said unto her, What aileth thee? And she answered, This woman said unto me, Give thy son, that we may eat him to day, and we will eat my son to morrow.

29So we boiled my son, and did eat him: and I said unto her on the next day, Give thy son, that we may eat him: and she hath hid her son.

30And it came to pass, when the king heard the words of the woman, that he rent his clothes; and he passed by upon the wall, and the people looked, and, behold, *he had* sackcloth within upon his flesh.

31Then he said, God do so and more also to me, if the head of Elisha the son of Shaphat shall stand on him this day.

32But Elisha sat in his house, and the elders sat with him; and *the king* sent a man from before him: but ere the messenger came to him, he said to the elders, See ye how this son of a murderer hath sent to take away mine head? look, when the messenger cometh, shut the door, and hold him fast at the door: *is* not the sound of his master's feet behind him?

33And while he yet talked with them, behold, the messenger came down unto him: and he said, Behold, this evil *is* of the LORD; what should I wait for the LORD any longer?

THEN Elisha said, Hear ye the word of the LORD; Thus saith the LORD, To-morrow about this time *shall* a measure of fine flour *be sold* for a shekel, and two measures of barley for a shekel, in the gate of Samaria.

2Then a lord on whose hand the king

leaned answered the man of God, and said, Behold, *if* the LORD would make windows in heaven, might this thing be? And he said, Behold, thou shalt see *it* with thine eyes, but shalt not eat thereof.

3And there were four leprous men at the entering in of the gate: and they said one to another, Why sit we here until we die?

4If we say, We will enter into the city, then the famine *is* in the city, and we shall die there: and if we sit still here, we die also. Now therefore come, and let us fall unto the host of the Syrians: if they save us alive, we shall live; and if they kill us, we shall but die.

5And they rose up in the twilight, to go unto the camp of the Syrians: and when they were come to the uttermost part of the camp of Syria, behold, *there was* no man there.

6For the Lord had made the host of the Syrians to hear a noise of chariots, and a noise of horses, *even* the noise of a great host: and they said one to another, Lo, the king of Israel hath hired against us the kings of the Hittites, and the kings of the Egyptians, to come upon us.

7Wherefore they arose and fled in the twilight, and left their tents, and their horses, and their asses, even the camp as it *was,* and fled for their life.

8And when these lepers came to the uttermost part of the camp, they went into one tent, and did eat and drink, and carried thence silver, and gold, and raiment, and went and hid *it;* and came again, and entered into another tent, and carried thence *also,* and went and hid *it.*

9Then they said one to another, We do not well: this day *is* a day of good tidings, and we hold our peace: if we tarry till the morning light, some mischief will come upon us: now therefore come, that we may go and tell the king's household.

10So they came and called unto the porter of the city: and they told them, saying, We came to the camp of the Syrians, and, behold, *there was* no man there, neither voice of man, but horses tied, and asses tied, and the tents as they *were.*

11And he called the porters; and they told *it* to the king's house within.

12And the king arose in the night, and said unto his servants, I will now shew you what the Syrians have done to us. They know that we *be* hungry; therefore are they gone out of the camp to hide themselves in the field, saying, When they come out of the city, we shall catch them alive, and get into the city.

13And one of his servants answered and said, Let *some* take, I pray thee, five of the horses that remain, which are left in the city, (behold, they *are* as all the multitude of Israel that are left in it: behold, *I say,* they *are* even as all the multitude of the Israelites that are consumed:) and let us send and see.

14They took therefore two chariot horses; and the king sent after the host of the Syrians, saying, Go and see.

15And they went after them unto Jordan: and, lo, all the way *was* full of garments and vessels, which the Syrians had cast away in their haste. And the messengers returned, and told the king.

16And the people went out, and spoiled the tents of the Syrians. So a measure of fine flour was *sold* for a shekel, and two measures of barley for a shekel, according to the word of the LORD.

17And the king appointed the lord on whose hand he leaned to have the charge of the gate: and the people trode upon him in the gate, and he died, as the man of God had said, who spake when the king came down to him.

18And it came to pass as the man of God had spoken to the king, saying,

Two measures of barley for a shekel, and a measure of fine flour for a shekel, shall be to morrow about this time in the gate of Samaria:

19And that lord answered the man of God, and said, Now, behold, *if* the LORD should make windows in heaven, might such a thing be? And he said, Behold, thou shalt see it with thine eyes, but shalt not eat thereof.

20And so it fell out unto him: for the people trode upon him in the gate, and he died.

ACTS 15:32—16:15.

AND Judas and Silas, being prophets also themselves, exhorted the brethren with many words, and confirmed *them.*

33And after they had tarried *there* a space, they were let go in peace from the brethren unto the apostles.

34Notwithstanding it pleased Silas to abide there still.

35Paul also and Barnabas continued in Antioch, teaching and preaching the word of the Lord, with many others also.

36And some days after Paul said unto Barnabas, Let us go again and visit our brethren in every city where we have preached the word of the Lord, *and see* how they do.

37And Barnabas determined to take with them John, whose surname was Mark.

38But Paul thought not good to take him with them, who departed from them from Pamphylia, and went not with them to the work.

39And the contention was so sharp between them, that they departed asunder one from the other: and so Barnabas took Mark, and sailed unto Cyprus;

40And Paul chose Silas, and departed, being recommended by the brethren unto the grace of God.

41And he went through Syria and Cilicia, confirming the churches.

THEN came he to Derbe and Lystra: and, behold, a certain disciple was there, named Timotheus, the son of a certain woman, which was a Jewess, and believed; but his father *was* a Greek:

2Which was well reported of by the brethren that were at Lystra and Iconium.

3Him would Paul have to go forth with him; and took and circumcised him because of the Jews which were in those quarters: for they knew all that his father was a Greek.

4And as they went through the cities, they delivered them the decrees for to keep, that were ordained of the apostles and elders which were at Jerusalem.

5And so were the churches established in the faith, and increased in number daily.

6Now when they had gone throughout Phrygia and the region of Galatia, and were forbidden of the Holy Ghost to preach the word in Asia,

7After they were come to Mysia, they assayed to go into Bithynia: but the Spirit suffered them not.

8And they passing by Mysia came down to Troas.

9And a vision appeared to Paul in the night; there stood a man of Macedonia, and prayed him, saying, Come over into Macedonia, and help us.

10And after he had seen the vision, immediately we endeavoured to go into Macedonia, assuredly gathering that the Lord had called us for to preach the gospel unto them.

11Therefore loosing from Troas, we came with a straight course to Samothracia, and the next *day* to Neapolis;

12And from thence to Philippi, which is the chief city of that part of Macedonia, *and* a colony: and we were in that city abiding certain days.

13And on the sabbath we went out of the city by a river side, where prayer was wont to be made; and we sat down, and spake unto the women which resorted *thither.*

14And a certain woman named Lydia, a seller of purple, of the city of Thyatira, which worshipped God, heard *us:* whose heart the Lord opened, that she attended unto the things which were spoken of Paul.

15And when she was baptized, and her household, she besought *us,* saying, If ye have judged me to be faithful to the Lord, come into my house, and abide *there.* And she constrained us.

PSALM 142:1–7

I CRIED unto the LORD with my voice; with my voice unto the LORD did I make my supplication.

2I poured out my complaint before him; I shewed before him my trouble.

3When my spirit was overwhelmed within me, then thou knewest my path. In the way wherein I walked have they privily laid a snare for me.

4I looked on *my* right hand, and beheld, but *there was* no man that would know me: refuge failed me; no man cared for my soul.

5I cried unto thee, O LORD: I said, Thou *art* my refuge *and* my portion in the land of the living.

6Attend unto my cry; for I am brought very low: deliver me from my persecutors; for they are stronger than I.

7Bring my soul out of prison, that I may praise thy name: the righteous shall compass me about; for thou shalt deal bountifully with me.

PROVERBS FOR TODAY/ 17:24–25

Wisdom is *before him that hath understanding; but the eyes of a fool* are *in the ends of the earth.* □*A foolish son* is *a grief to his father, and bitterness to her that bare him.*

JUNE 25

2 KINGS 8:1—9:15

THEN spake Elisha unto the woman, whose son he had restored to life, saying, Arise, and go thou and thine household, and sojourn wheresoever thou canst sojourn: for the LORD hath called for a famine; and it shall also come upon the land seven years.

2And the woman arose, and did after the saying of the man of God: and she went with her household, and sojourned in the land of the Philistines seven years.

3And it came to pass at the seven years' end, that the woman returned out of the land of the Philistines: and she went forth to cry unto the king for her house and for her land.

4And the king talked with Gehazi the servant of the man of God, saying, Tell me, I pray thee, all the great things that Elisha hath done.

5And it came to pass, as he was telling the king how he had restored a dead body to life, that, behold, the woman, whose son he had restored to life, cried to the king for her house and for her land. And Gehazi said, My lord, O king, this *is* the woman, and this *is* her son, whom Elisha restored to life.

6And when the king asked the woman, she told him. So the king appointed unto her a certain officer, saying, Restore all that *was* hers, and all the fruits of the field since the day that she left the land, even until now.

7And Elisha came to Damascus; and Ben–hadad the king of Syria was sick; and it was told him, The man of God is come hither.

8And the king said unto Hazael, Take a present in thine hand, and go, meet the man of God, and enquire of the LORD by him, saying, Shall I recover of this disease?

9So Hazael went to meet him, and took a present with him, even of every good thing of Damascus, forty camels' burden, and came and stood before him, and said, Thy son Ben–hadad king of Syria hath sent me to thee, saying, Shall I recover of this disease?

10And Elisha said unto him, Go, say unto him, Thou mayest certainly recover: howbeit the LORD hath shewed me that he shall surely die.

11And he settled his countenance stedfastly, until he was ashamed: and the man of God wept.

12And Hazael said, Why weepeth my lord? and he answered, Because I know the evil that thou wilt do unto the children of Israel: their strong holds wilt thou set on fire, and their young men wilt thou slay with the sword, and wilt dash their children, and rip up their women with child.

13And Hazael said, But what, *is* thy servant a dog, that he should do this great thing? And Elisha answered, The LORD hath shewed me that thou *shalt be* king over Syria.

14So he departed from Elisha, and came to his master; who said to him, What said Elisha to thee? And he answered, He told me *that* thou shouldest surely recover.

15And it came to pass on the morrow, that he took a thick cloth, and dipped *it* in water, and spread *it* on his face, so that he died: and Hazael reigned in his stead.

16And in the fifth year of Joram the son of Ahab king of Israel, Jehoshaphat *being* then king of Judah, Jehoram the son of Jehoshaphat king of Judah began to reign.

17Thirty and two years old was he when he began to reign; and he reigned eight years in Jerusalem.

18And he walked in the way of the kings of Israel, as did the house of Ahab: for the daughter of Ahab was his wife: and he did evil in the sight of the LORD.

19Yet the LORD would not destroy Judah for David his servant's sake, as he promised him to give him alway a light, *and* to his children.

20In his days Edom revolted from under the hand of Judah, and made a king over themselves.

21So Joram went over to Zair, and all the chariots with him: and he rose by night, and smote the Edomites which compassed him about, and the captains of the chariots: and the people fled into their tents.

22Yet Edom revolted from under the hand of Judah unto this day. Then Libnah revolted at the same time.

23And the rest of the acts of Joram, and all that he did, *are* they not written in the book of the chronicles of the kings of Judah?

24And Joram slept with his fathers, and was buried with his fathers in the city of David: and Ahaziah his son reigned in his stead.

25In the twelfth year of Joram the son of Ahab king of Israel did Ahaziah the son of Jehoram king of Judah begin to reign.

26Two and twenty years old *was* Ahaziah when he began to reign; and he reigned one year in Jerusalem. And his mother's name *was* Athaliah, the daughter of Omri king of Israel.

27And he walked in the way of the house of Ahab, and did evil in the sight of the LORD, as *did* the house of

Ahab: for he *was* the son in law of the house of Ahab.

28And he went with Joram the son of Ahab to the war against Hazael king of Syria in Ramoth–gilead; and the Syrians wounded Joram.

29And king Joram went back to be healed in Jezreel of the wounds which the Syrians had given him at Ramah, when he fought against Hazael king of Syria. And Ahaziah the son of Jehoram king of Judah went down to see Joram the son of Ahab in Jezreel, because he was sick.

AND Elisha the prophet called one of the children of the prophets, and said unto him, Gird up thy loins, and take this box of oil in thine hand, and go to Ramoth–gilead:

2And when thou comest thither, look out there Jehu the son of Jehoshaphat the son of Nimshi, and go in, and make him arise up from among his brethren, and carry him to an inner chamber;

3Then take the box of oil, and pour *it* on his head, and say, Thus saith the LORD, I have anointed thee king over Israel. Then open the door, and flee, and tarry not.

4So the young man, *even* the young man the prophet, went to Ramoth–gilead.

5And when he came, behold, the captains of the host *were* sitting; and he said, I have an errand to thee, O captain. And Jehu said, Unto which of all us? And he said, To thee, O captain.

6And he arose, and went into the house; and he poured the oil on his head, and said unto him, Thus saith the LORD God of Israel, I have anointed thee king over the people of the LORD, *even* over Israel.

7And thou shalt smite the house of Ahab thy master, that I may avenge the blood of my servants the prophets, and the blood of all the servants of the LORD, at the hand of Jezebel.

8For the whole house of Ahab shall perish: and I will cut off from Ahab him that pisseth against the wall, and him that is shut up and left in Israel:

9And I will make the house of Ahab like the house of Jeroboam the son of Nebat, and like the house of Baasha the son of Ahijah:

10And the dogs shall eat Jezebel in the portion of Jezreel, and *there shall be* none to bury *her.* And he opened the door, and fled.

11Then Jehu came forth to the servants of his lord: and *one* said unto him, *Is* all well? wherefore came this mad *fellow* to thee? And he said unto them, Ye know the man, and his communication.

12And they said, *It is* false; tell us now. And he said, Thus and thus spake he to me, saying, Thus saith the LORD, I have anointed thee king over Israel.

13Then they hasted, and took every man his garment, and put *it* under him on the top of the stairs, and blew with trumpets, saying, Jehu is king.

14So Jehu the son of Jehoshaphat the son of Nimshi conspired against Joram. (Now Joram had kept Ramoth–gilead, he and all Israel, because of Hazael king of Syria.

15But king Joram was returned to be healed in Jezreel of the wounds which the Syrians had given him, when he fought with Hazael king of Syria.) And Jehu said, If it be your minds, *then* let none go forth *nor* escape out of the city to go to tell *it* in Jezreel.

ACTS 16:16–40

AND it came to pass, as we went to prayer, a certain damsel possessed with a spirit of divination met us, which brought her masters much gain by soothsaying:

17The same followed Paul and us, and cried, saying, These men are the servants of the most high God, which shew unto us the way of salvation.

18And this did she many days. But

Paul, being grieved, turned and said to the spirit, I command thee in the name of Jesus Christ to come out of her. And he came out the same hour.

19And when her masters saw that the hope of their gains was gone, they caught Paul and Silas, and drew *them* into the marketplace unto the rulers,

20And brought them to the magistrates, saying, These men, being Jews, do exceedingly trouble our city,

21And teach customs, which are not lawful for us to receive, neither to observe, being Romans.

22And the multitude rose up together against them: and the magistrates rent off their clothes, and commanded to beat *them*.

23And when they had laid many stripes upon them, they cast *them* into prison, charging the jailor to keep them safely:

24Who, having received such a charge, thrust them into the inner prison, and made their feet fast in the stocks.

25And at midnight Paul and Silas prayed, and sang praises unto God: and the prisoners heard them.

26And suddenly there was a great earthquake, so that the foundations of the prison were shaken: and immediately all the doors were opened, and every one's bands were loosed.

27And the keeper of the prison awaking out of his sleep, and seeing the prison doors open, he drew out his sword, and would have killed himself, supposing that the prisoners had been fled.

28But Paul cried with a loud voice, saying, Do thyself no harm: for we are all here.

29Then he called for a light, and sprang in, and came trembling, and fell down before Paul and Silas,

30And brought them out, and said, Sirs, what must I do to be saved?

31And they said, Believe on the Lord Jesus Christ, and thou shalt be saved, and thy house.

32And they spake unto him the word of the Lord, and to all that were in his house.

33And he took them the same hour of the night, and washed *their* stripes; and was baptized, he and all his, straightway.

34And when he had brought them into his house, he set meat before them, and rejoiced, believing in God with all his house.

35And when it was day, the magistrates sent the serjeants, saying, Let those men go.

36And the keeper of the prison told this saying to Paul, The magistrates have sent to let you go: now therefore depart, and go in peace.

37But Paul said unto them, They have beaten us openly uncondemned, being Romans, and have cast *us* into prison; and now do they thrust us out privily? nay verily; but let them come themselves and fetch us out.

38And the serjeants told these words unto the magistrates: and they feared, when they heard that they were Romans.

39And they came and besought them, and brought *them* out, and desired *them* to depart out of the city.

40And they went out of the prison, and entered into *the house of* Lydia: and when they had seen the brethren, they comforted them, and departed.

PSALM 143:1–12

HEAR my prayer, O LORD, give ear to my supplications: in thy faithfulness answer me, *and* in thy righteousness.

2And enter not into judgment with thy servant: for in thy sight shall no man living be justified.

3For the enemy hath persecuted my soul; he hath smitten my life down to the ground; he hath made me to dwell in darkness, as those that have been long dead.

4Therefore is my spirit overwhelmed within me; my heart within me is desolate.

5I remember the days of old; I meditate on all thy works; I muse on the work of thy hands.

6I stretch forth my hands unto thee: my soul *thirsteth* after thee, as a thirsty land. Selah.

7Hear me speedily, O LORD: my spirit faileth: hide not thy face from me, lest I be like unto them that go down into the pit.

8Cause me to hear thy lovingkindness in the morning; for in thee do I trust: cause me to know the way wherein I should walk; for I lift up my soul unto thee.

9Deliver me, O LORD, from mine enemies: I flee unto thee to hide me.

10Teach me to do thy will; for thou *art* my God: thy spirit *is* good; lead me into the land of uprightness.

11Quicken me, O LORD, for thy name's sake: for thy righteousness' sake bring my soul out of trouble.

12And of thy mercy cut off mine enemies, and destroy all them that afflict my soul: for I *am* thy servant.

PROVERBS FOR TODAY/ 17:26

Also to punish the just is *not good,* nor *to strike princes for equity.*

JUNE 26

2 KINGS 9:16—10:31

So Jehu rode in a chariot, and went to Jezreel; for Joram lay there. And Ahaziah king of Judah was come down to see Joram.

17And there stood a watchman on the tower in Jezreel, and he spied the company of Jehu as he came, and said, I see a company. And Joram said, Take an horseman, and send to meet them, and let him say, *Is it* peace?

18So there went one on horseback to meet him, and said, Thus saith the king, *Is it* peace? And Jehu said, What hast thou to do with peace? turn thee behind me. And the watchman told, saying, The messenger came to them, but he cometh not again.

19Then he sent out a second on horseback, which came to them, and said, Thus saith the king, *Is it* peace? And Jehu answered, What hast thou to do

with peace? turn thee behind me.

20And the watchman told, saying, He came even unto them, and cometh not again: and the driving *is* like the driving of Jehu the son of Nimshi; for he driveth furiously.

21And Joram said, Make ready. And his chariot was made ready. And Joram king of Israel and Ahaziah king of Judah went out, each in his chariot, and they went out against Jehu, and met him in the portion of Naboth the Jezreelite.

22And it came to pass, when Joram saw Jehu, that he said, *Is it* peace, Jehu? And he answered, What peace, so long as the whoredoms of thy mother Jezebel and her witchcrafts *are so* many?

23And Joram turned his hands, and fled, and said to Ahaziah, *There is* treachery, O Ahaziah.

24And Jehu drew a bow with his full strength, and smote Jehoram between his arms, and the arrow went out at his heart, and he sunk down in his chariot.

25Then said *Jehu* to Bidkar his captain, Take up, *and* cast him in the portion of the field of Naboth the Jezreelite: for remember how that, when I and thou rode together after Ahab his father, the LORD laid this burden upon him;

26Surely, I have seen yesterday the blood of Naboth, and the blood of his sons, saith the LORD; and I will requite thee in this plat, saith the LORD. Now therefore take *and* cast him into the plat *of ground,* according to the word of the LORD.

27But when Ahaziah the king of Judah saw *this,* he fled by the way of the garden house. And Jehu followed after him, and said, Smite him also in the chariot. *And they did so* at the going up to Gur, which *is* by Ibleam. And he fled to Megiddo, and died there.

28And his servants carried him in a chariot to Jerusalem, and buried him in his sepulchre with his fathers in the city of David.

29And in the eleventh year of Joram the son of Ahab began Ahaziah to reign over Judah.

30And when Jehu was come to Jezreel, Jezebel heard *of it;* and she painted her face, and tired her head, and looked out at a window.

31And as Jehu entered in at the gate, she said, *Had* Zimri peace, who slew his master?

32And he lifted up his face to the window, and said, Who *is* on my side? who? And there looked out to him two *or* three eunuchs.

33And he said, Throw her down. So they threw her down: and *some* of her blood was sprinkled on the wall, and on the horses: and he trode her under foot.

34And when he was come in, he did eat and drink, and said, Go, see now this cursed *woman,* and bury her: for she *is* a king's daughter.

35And they went to bury her: but they found no more of her than the skull, and the feet, and the palms of *her* hands.

36Wherefore they came again, and told him. And he said, This *is* the word of the LORD, which he spake by his servant Elijah the Tishbite, saying, In the portion of Jezreel shall dogs eat the flesh of Jezebel:

37And the carcase of Jezebel shall be as dung upon the face of the field in the portion of Jezreel; *so* that they shall not say, This *is* Jezebel.

AND Ahab had seventy sons in Samaria. And Jehu wrote letters, and sent to Samaria, unto the rulers of Jezreel, to the elders, and to them that brought up Ahab's *children,* saying,

2Now as soon as this letter cometh to you, seeing your master's sons *are* with you, and *there are* with you chariots and horses, a fenced city also, and armour;

3Look even out the best and meetest of your master's sons, and set *him* on his father's throne, and fight for your master's house.

4But they were exceedingly afraid, and said, Behold, two kings stood not before him: how then shall we stand?

5And he that *was* over the house, and he that *was* over the city, the elders also, and the bringers up *of the children,* sent to Jehu, saying, We *are* thy servants, and will do all that thou shalt bid us; we will not make any king: do thou *that which is* good in thine eyes.

6Then he wrote a letter the second time to them, saying, If ye *be* mine, and *if* ye will hearken unto my voice, take ye the heads of the men your master's sons, and come to me to Jezreel by to morrow this time. Now the king's sons, *being* seventy persons, *were* with the great men of the city, which brought them up.

7And it came to pass, when the letter

came to them, that they took the king's sons, and slew seventy persons, and put their heads in baskets, and sent him *them* to Jezreel.

8And there came a messenger, and told him, saying, They have brought the heads of the king's sons. And said, Lay ye them in two heaps at the entering in of the gate until the morning.

9And it came to pass in the morning, that he went out, and stood, and said to all the people, Ye *be* righteous: behold, I conspired against my master, and slew him: but who slew all these?

10Know now that there shall fall unto the earth nothing of the word of the LORD, which the LORD spake concerning the house of Ahab: for the LORD hath done *that* which he spake by his servant Elijah.

11So Jehu slew all that remained of the house of Ahab in Jezreel, and all his great men, and his kinsfolks, and his priests, until he left him none remaining.

12And he arose and departed, and came to Samaria. *And* as he *was* at the shearing house in the way,

13Jehu met with the brethren of Ahaziah king of Judah, and said, Who *are* ye? And they answered, We *are* the brethren of Ahaziah; and we go down to salute the children of the king and the children of the queen.

14And he said, Take them alive. And they took them alive, and slew them at the pit of the shearing house, *even* two and forty men; neither left he any of them.

15And when he was departed thence, he lighted on Jehonadab the son of Rechab *coming* to meet him: and he saluted him, and said to him, Is thine heart right, as my heart *is* with thy heart? And Jehonadab answered, It is. If it be, give *me* thine hand. And he gave *him* his hand; and he took him up to him into the chariot.

16And he said, Come with me, and see my zeal for the LORD. So they made him ride in his chariot.

17And when he came to Samaria, he slew all that remained unto Ahab in Samaria, till he had destroyed him, according to the saying of the LORD, which he spake to Elijah.

18And Jehu gathered all the people together, and said unto them, Ahab served Baal a little; *but* Jehu shall serve him much.

19Now therefore call unto me all the prophets of Baal, all his servants, and all his priests; let none be wanting: for I have a great sacrifice *to do* to Baal; whosoever shall be wanting, he shall not live. But Jehu did *it* in subtilty, to the intent that he might destroy the worshippers of Baal.

20And Jehu said, Proclaim a solemn assembly for Baal. And they proclaimed *it.*

21And Jehu sent through all Israel: and all the worshippers of Baal came, so that there was not a man left that came not. And they came into the house of Baal; and the house of Baal was full from one end to another.

22And he said unto him that *was* over the vestry, Bring forth vestments for all the worshippers of Baal. And he brought them forth vestments.

23And Jehu went, and Jehonadab the son of Rechab, into the house of Baal, and said unto the worshippers of Baal, Search, and look that there be here with you none of the servants of the LORD, but the worshippers of Baal only.

24And when they went in to offer sacrifices and burnt offerings, Jehu appointed fourscore men without, and said, *If* any of the men whom I have brought into your hands escape, *he that letteth him go,* his life *shall be* for the life of him.

25And it came to pass, as soon as he had made an end of offering the burnt offering, that Jehu said to the guard and to the captains, Go in, *and* slay them; let none come forth. And they smote them with the edge of the sword; and the guard and the captains cast *them* out, and went to the city of the house of Baal.

26And they brought forth the images out of the house of Baal, and burned them.

27And they brake down the image of Baal, and brake down the house of Baal, and made it a draught house unto this day.

28Thus Jehu destroyed Baal out of Israel.

29Howbeit *from* the sins of Jeroboam the son of Nebat, who made Israel to sin, Jehu departed not from after them, *to wit,* the golden calves that *were* in Beth–el, and that *were* in Dan.

30And the LORD said unto Jehu, Because thou hast done well in executing *that which is* right in mine eyes, *and* hast done unto the house of Ahab according to all that *was* in mine heart, thy children of the fourth *generation* shall sit on the throne of Israel.

31But Jehu took no heed to walk in the law of the LORD God of Israel with all his heart: for he departed not from the sins of Jeroboam, which made Israel to sin.

ACTS 17:1–34

Now when they [Paul and Silas] had passed through Amphipolis and Apollonia, they came to Thessalonica, where was a synagogue of the Jews:

2And Paul, as his manner was, went in unto them, and three sabbath days reasoned with them out of the scriptures,

3Opening and alleging, that Christ must needs have suffered, and risen again from the dead; and that this Jesus, whom I preach unto you, is Christ.

4And some of them believed, and consorted with Paul and Silas; and of the devout Greeks a great multitude, and of the chief women not a few.

5But the Jews which believed not, moved with envy, took unto them certain lewd fellows of the baser sort, and gathered a company, and set all the city on an uproar, and assaulted the house of Jason, and sought to bring them out to the people.

6And when they found them not, they drew Jason and certain brethren unto the rulers of the city, crying, These that have turned the world upside down are come hither also;

7Whom Jason hath received: and these all do contrary to the decrees of Caesar, saying that there is another king, *one* Jesus.

8And they troubled the people and the rulers of the city, when they heard these things.

9And when they had taken security of Jason, and of the other, they let them go.

10And the brethren immediately sent away Paul and Silas by night unto Berea: who coming *thither* went into the synagogue of the Jews.

11These were more noble than those in Thessalonica, in that they received the word with all readiness of mind, and searched the scriptures daily, whether those things were so.

12Therefore many of them believed; also of honourable women which were Greeks, and of men, not a few.

13But when the Jews of Thessalonica had knowledge that the word of God was preached of Paul at Berea, they came thither also, and stirred up the people.

14And then immediately the brethren sent away Paul to go as it were to the sea: but Silas and Timotheus abode there still.

15And they that conducted Paul brought him unto Athens: and receiving a commandment unto Silas and Timotheus for to come to him with all speed, they departed.

16Now while Paul waited for them at Athens, his spirit was stirred in him, when he saw the city wholly given to idolatry.

17Therefore disputed he in the synagogue with the Jews, and with the devout persons, and in the market daily with them that met with him.

18Then certain philosophers of the Epicureans, and of the Stoicks, encountered him. And some said, What will this babbler say? other some, He seemeth to be a setter forth of strange gods: because he preached unto them Jesus, and the resurrection.

19And they took him, and brought him unto Areopagus, saying, May we know what this new doctrine, whereof thou speakest, is?

20For thou bringest certain strange things to our ears: we would know therefore what these things mean.

21(For all the Athenians and strangers which were there spent their time in nothing else, but either to tell, or to hear some new thing.)

22Then Paul stood in the midst of Mars' hill, and said, *Ye* men of Athens, I perceive that in all things ye are too superstitious.

23For as I passed by, and beheld your devotions, I found an altar with this inscription, TO THE UNKNOWN GOD. Whom therefore ye ignorantly worship, him declare I unto you.

24God that made the world and all things therein, seeing that he is Lord of heaven and earth, dwelleth not in temples made with hands;

25Neither is worshipped with men's hands, as though he needed any thing, seeing he giveth to all life, and breath, and all things;

26And hath made of one blood all nations of men for to dwell on all the face of the earth, and hath determined the times before appointed, and the bounds of their habitation;

27That they should seek the Lord, if haply they might feel after him, and find him, though he be not far from every one of us:

28For in him we live, and move, and have our being; as certain also of your own poets have said, For we are also his offspring.

29Forasmuch then as we are the offspring of God, we ought not to think that the Godhead is like unto gold, or silver, or stone, graven by art and man's device.

30And the times of this ignorance God winked at; but now commandeth all men every where to repent:

31Because he hath appointed a day, in the which he will judge the world in righteousness by *that* man whom he hath ordained; *whereof* he hath given assurance unto all *men,* in that he hath raised him from the dead.

32And when they heard of the resurrection of the dead, some mocked: and others said, We will hear thee again of this *matter.*

33So Paul departed from among them.

34Howbeit certain men clave unto him, and believed: among the which *was* Dionysius the Areopagite, and a woman named Damaris, and others with them.

PSALM 144:1–15

BLESSED *be* the LORD my strength, which teacheth my hands to war, *and* my fingers to fight:

2My goodness, and my fortress; my high tower, and my deliverer; my shield, and *he* in whom I trust; who subdueth my people under me.

3LORD, what *is* man, that thou takest knowledge of him! *or* the son of man, that thou makest account of him!

4Man is like to vanity: his days *are* as a shadow that passeth away.

5Bow thy heavens, O LORD, and come down: touch the mountains, and they shall smoke.

6Cast forth lightning, and scatter them: shoot out thine arrows, and destroy them.

7Send thine hand from above: rid me, and deliver me out of great waters, from the hand of strange children;

8Whose mouth speaketh vanity, and their right hand *is* a right hand of falsehood.

9I will sing a new song unto thee, O God: upon a psaltery *and* an instrument of ten strings will I sing praises unto thee.

10*It is he* that giveth salvation unto kings: who delivereth David his servant from the hurtful sword.

11Rid me, and deliver me from the hand of strange children, whose mouth speaketh vanity, and their right hand

is a right hand of falsehood:

12That our sons *may be* as plants grown up in their youth; *that* our daughters *may be* as corner stones, polished *after* the similitude of a palace:

13*That* our garners *may be* full, affording all manner of store: *that* our sheep may bring forth thousands and ten thousands in our streets:

14*That* our oxen *may be* strong to labour; *that there be* no breaking in, nor going out; that *there be* no complaining in our streets:

15Happy *is that* people, that is in such a case: *yea,* happy *is that* people, whose God *is* the LORD.

PROVERBS FOR TODAY/ 17:27–28

He that hath knowledge spareth his words: and *a man of understanding is of an excellent spirit. Even a fool, when he holdeth his peace, is counted wise:* and *he that shutteth his lips* is esteemed *a man of understanding.*

JUNE 27

2 KINGS 10:32—12:21

IN those days the LORD began to cut Israel short: and Hazael smote them in all the coasts of Israel;

33From Jordan eastward, all the land of Gilead, the Gadites, and the Reubenites, and the Manassites, from Aroer, which *is* by the river Arnon, even Gilead and Bashan.

34Now the rest of the acts of Jehu, and all that he did, and all his might, *are* they not written in the book of the chronicles of the kings of Israel?

35And Jehu slept with his fathers: and they buried him in Samaria. And Jehoahaz his son reigned in his stead.

36And the time that Jehu reigned over Israel in Samaria *was* twenty and eight years.

AND when Athaliah the mother of Ahaziah saw that her son was dead, she arose and destroyed all the seed royal.

2But Jehosheba, the daughter of king Joram, sister of Ahaziah, took Joash the son of Ahaziah, and stole him from among the king's sons *which were* slain; and they hid him, *even* him and his nurse, in the bedchamber from Athaliah, so that he was not slain.

3And he was with her hid in the house of the LORD six years. And Athaliah did reign over the land.

4And the seventh year Jehoiada sent and fetched the rulers over hundreds, with the captains and the guard, and brought them to him into the house of the LORD, and made a covenant with them, and took an oath of them in the house of the LORD, and shewed them the king's son.

5And he commanded them, saying, This *is* the thing that ye shall do; A third part of you that enter in on the sabbath shall even be keepers of the watch of the king's house;

6And a third part *shall be* at the gate of Sur; and a third part at the gate behind the guard: so shall ye keep the watch of the house, that it be not broken down.

7And two parts of you that go forth on the sabbath, even they shall keep the watch of the house of the LORD about the king.

8And ye shall compass the king round about, every man with his weapons in his hand: and he that cometh within the ranges, let him be slain: and be ye with the king as he goeth out and as he cometh in.

9And the captains over the hundreds did according to all *things* that Jehoiada the priest commanded: and they took every man his men that were to come in on the sabbath, with them that should go on the sabbath, and came to Jehoiada the priest.

10And to the captains over hundreds did the priest give king David's spears and shields, that *were* in the temple of the LORD.

11And the guard stood, every man with his weapons in his hand, round about the king, from the right corner of the temple to the left corner of the temple, *along* by the altar and the temple.

12And he brought forth the king's son, and put the crown upon him, and *gave him* the testimony; and they made him king, and anointed him; and they clapped their hands, and said, God save the king.

13And when Athaliah heard the noise of the guard *and* of the people, she came to the people into the temple of the LORD.

14And when she looked, behold, the king stood by a pillar, as the manner *was,* and the princes and the trumpeters by the king, and all the people of the land rejoiced, and blew with trumpets: and Athaliah rent her clothes, and cried, Treason, Treason.

15But Jehoiada the priest commanded the captains of the hundreds, the officers of the host, and said unto them, Have her forth without the ranges: and him that followeth her kill with the sword. For the priest had said, Let her not be slain in the house of the LORD.

16And they laid hands on her; and she went by the way by the which the horses came into the king's house: and there was she slain.

17And Jehoiada made a covenant between the LORD and the king and the people, that they should be the LORD's people; between the king also and the people.

18And all the people of the land went into the house of Baal, and brake it down; his altars and his images brake they in pieces thoroughly, and slew Mattan the priest of Baal before the altars. And the priest appointed officers over the house of the LORD.

19And he took the rulers over hundreds, and the captains, and the guard, and all the people of the land; and they brought down the king from the house of the LORD, and came by the way of the gate of the guard to the king's house. And he sat on the throne of the kings.

20And all the people of the land rejoiced, and the city was in quiet: and they slew Athaliah with the sword *beside* the king's house.

21Seven years old *was* Jehoash when he began to reign.

IN the seventh year of Jehu Jehoash began to reign; and forty years reigned he in Jerusalem. And his mother's name *was* Zibiah of Beer–sheba.

2And Jehoash did *that which was* right

in the sight of the LORD all his days wherein Jehoiada the priest instructed him.

³But the high places were not taken away: the people still sacrificed and burnt incense in the high places.

⁴And Jehoash said to the priests, All the money of the dedicated things that is brought into the house of the LORD, *even* the money of every one that passeth *the account,* the money that every man is set at, *and* all the money that cometh into any man's heart to bring into the house of the LORD:

⁵Let the priests take *it* to them, every man of his acquaintance: and let them repair the breaches of the house, wheresoever any breach shall be found.

⁶But it was *so, that* in the three and twentieth year of king Jehoash the priests had not repaired the breaches of the house.

⁷Then king Jehoash called for Jehoiada the priest, and the *other* priests, and said unto them, Why repair ye not the breaches of the house? now therefore receive no *more* money of your acquaintance, but deliver it for the breaches of the house.

⁸And the priests consented to receive no *more* money of the people, neither to repair the breaches of the house.

⁹But Jehoiada the priest took a chest, and bored a hole in the lid of it, and set it beside the altar, on the right side as one cometh into the house of the LORD: and the priests that kept the door put therein all the money *that was* brought into the house of the LORD.

¹⁰And it was *so,* when they saw that *there was* much money in the chest, that the king's scribe and the high priest came up, and they put up in bags, and told the money that was found in the house of the LORD.

¹¹And they gave the money, being told, into the hands of them that did the work, that had the oversight of the house of the LORD: and they laid it out to the carpenters and builders, that wrought upon the house of the LORD,

¹²And to masons, and hewers of stone, and to buy timber and hewed stone to repair the breaches of the house of the LORD, and for all that was laid out for the house to repair *it.*

¹³Howbeit there were not made for the house of the LORD bowls of silver, snuffers, basons, trumpets, any vessels of gold, or vessels of silver, of the money *that was* brought into the house of the LORD:

¹⁴But they gave that to the workmen, and repaired therewith the house of the LORD.

¹⁵Moreover they reckoned not with the men, into whose hand they delivered the money to be bestowed on workmen: for they dealt faithfully.

¹⁶The trespass money and sin money was not brought into the house of the LORD: it was the priests'.

¹⁷Then Hazael king of Syria went up, and fought against Gath, and took it: and Hazael set his face to go up to Jerusalem.

¹⁸And Jehoash king of Judah took all the hallowed things that Jehoshaphat, and Jehoram, and Ahaziah, his fathers, kings of Judah, had dedicated, and his own hallowed things, and all the gold *that was* found in the treasures of the house of the LORD, and in the king's house, and sent *it* to Hazael king of Syria: and he went away from Jerusalem.

¹⁹And the rest of the acts of Joash, and all that he did, *are* they not written in the book of the chronicles of the kings of Judah?

²⁰And his servants arose, and made a conspiracy, and slew Joash in the house of Millo, which goeth down to Silla.

²¹For Jozachar the son of Shimeath, and Jehozabad the son of Shomer, his servants, smote him, and he died; and they buried him with his fathers in the

city of David: and Amaziah his son reigned in his stead.

ACTS 18:1–21

AFTER these things Paul departed from Athens and came to Corinth;

2And found a certain Jew named Aquila, born in Pontus, lately come from Italy, with his wife Priscilla; (because that Claudius had commanded all Jews to depart from Rome:) and came unto them.

3And because he was of the same craft, he abode with them, and wrought: for by their occupation they were tentmakers.

4And he reasoned in the synagogue every sabbath, and persuaded the Jews and the Greeks.

5And when Silas and Timotheus were come from Macedonia, Paul was pressed in the spirit, and testified to the Jews *that* Jesus *was* Christ.

6And when they opposed themselves, and blasphemed, he shook *his* raiment, and said unto them, Your blood *be* upon your own heads; I *am* clean: from henceforth I will go unto the Gentiles.

7And he departed thence, and entered into a certain *man's* house, named Justus, *one* that worshipped God, whose house joined hard to the synagogue.

8And Crispus, the chief ruler of the synagogue, believed on the Lord with all his house; and many of the Corinthians hearing believed, and were baptized.

9Then spake the Lord to Paul in the night by a vision, Be not afraid, but speak, and hold not thy peace:

10For I am with thee, and no man shall set on thee to hurt thee: for I have much people in this city.

11And he continued *there* a year and six months, teaching the word of God among them.

12And when Gallio was the deputy of Achaia, the Jews made insurrection with one accord against Paul, and brought him to the judgment seat,

13Saying, This *fellow* persuadeth men to worship God contrary to the law.

14And when Paul was now about to open *his* mouth, Gallio said unto the Jews, If it were a matter of wrong or wicked lewdness, O *ye* Jews, reason would that I should bear with you:

15But if it be a question of words and names, and *of* your law, look ye *to it;* for I will be no judge of such *matters.*

16And he drave them from the judgment seat.

17Then all the Greeks took Sosthenes, the chief ruler of the synagogue, and beat *him* before the judgment seat. And Gallio cared for none of those things.

18And Paul *after this* tarried *there* yet a good while, and then took his leave of the brethren, and sailed thence into Syria, and with him Priscilla and Aquila; having shorn *his* head in Cenchrea: for he had a vow.

19And he came to Ephesus, and left them there: but he himself entered into the synagogue, and reasoned with the Jews.

20When they desired *him* to tarry longer time with them, he consented not;

21But bade them farewell, saying, I must by all means keep this feast that cometh in Jerusalem: but I will return again unto you, if God will. And he sailed from Ephesus.

PSALM 145:1–21

I WILL extol thee, my God, O king; and I will bless thy name for ever and ever.

2Every day will I bless thee; and I will praise thy name for ever and ever.

3Great *is* the LORD, and greatly to

be praised; and his greatness *is* unsearchable.

4One generation shall praise thy works to another, and shall declare thy mighty acts.

5I will speak of the glorious honour of thy majesty, and of thy wondrous works.

6And *men* shall speak of the might of thy terrible acts: and I will declare thy greatness.

7They shall abundantly utter the memory of thy great goodness, and shall sing of thy righteousness.

8The LORD *is* gracious, and full of compassion; slow to anger, and of great mercy.

9The LORD *is* good to all: and his tender mercies *are* over all his works.

10All thy works shall praise thee, O LORD; and thy saints shall bless thee.

11They shall speak of the glory of thy kingdom, and talk of thy power;

12To make known to the sons of men his mighty acts, and the glorious majesty of his kingdom.

13Thy kingdom *is* an everlasting kingdom, and thy dominion *endureth* throughout all generations.

14The LORD upholdeth all that fall, and raiseth up all *those that be* bowed down.

15The eyes of all wait upon thee; and thou givest them their meat in due season.

16Thou openest thine hand, and satisfiest the desire of every living thing.

17The LORD *is* righteous in all his ways, and holy in all his works.

18The LORD *is* nigh unto all them that call upon him, to all that call upon him, in truth.

19He will fulfil the desire of them that fear him: he also will hear their cry, and will save them.

20The LORD preserveth all them that love him: but all the wicked will he destroy.

21My mouth shall speak the praise of the LORD: and let all flesh bless his holy name for ever and ever.

PROVERBS FOR TODAY/ 18:1

Through desire a man, having separated himself, seeketh and *intermeddleth with all wisdom.*

JUNE 28

2 KINGS 13:1—14:29

IN the three and twentieth year of Joash the son of Ahaziah king of Judah Jehoahaz the son of Jehu began to reign over Israel in Samaria, *and reigned* seventeen years.

2And he did *that which was* evil in the sight of the LORD, and followed the sins of Jeroboam the son of Nebat, which made Israel to sin; he departed not therefrom.

3And the anger of the LORD was kindled against Israel, and he delivered them into the hand of Hazael king of Syria, and into the hand of Ben–hadad the son of Hazael, all *their* days.

4And Jehoahaz besought the LORD, and the LORD hearkened unto him: for he saw the oppression of Israel, because the king of Syria oppressed them.

5(And the LORD gave Israel a saviour, so that they went out from under the hand of the Syrians: and the children of Israel dwelt in their tents, as beforetime.

⁶Nevertheless they departed not from the sins of the house of Jeroboam, who made Israel sin, *but* walked therein: and there remained the grove also in Samaria.)

⁷Neither did he leave of the people to Jehoahaz but fifty horsemen, and ten chariots, and ten thousand footmen; for the king of Syria had destroyed them, and had made them like the dust by threshing.

⁸Now the rest of the acts of Jehoahaz, and all that he did, and his might, *are* they not written in the book of the chronicles of the kings of Israel?

⁹And Jehoahaz slept with his fathers; and they buried him in Samaria: and Joash his son reigned in his stead.

¹⁰In the thirty and seventh year of Joash king of Judah began Jehoash the son of Jehoahaz to reign over Israel in Samaria, *and reigned* sixteen years.

¹¹And he did *that which was* evil in the sight of the LORD; he departed not from all the sins of Jeroboam the son of Nebat, who made Israel sin: *but* he walked therein.

¹²And the rest of the acts of Joash, and all that he did, and his might wherewith he fought against Amaziah king of Judah, *are* they not written in the book of the chronicles of the kings of Israel?

¹³And Joash slept with his fathers; and Jeroboam sat upon his throne: and Joash was buried in Samaria with the kings of Israel.

¹⁴Now Elisha was fallen sick of his sickness whereof he died. And Joash the king of Israel came down unto him, and wept over his face, and said, O my father, my father, the chariot of Israel, and the horsemen thereof.

¹⁵And Elisha said unto him, Take bow and arrows. And he took unto him bow and arrows.

¹⁶And he said to the king of Israel, Put thine hand upon the bow. And he put his hand *upon it:* and Elisha put his hands upon the king's hands.

¹⁷And he said, Open the window eastward. And he opened *it.* Then Elisha said, Shoot. And he shot. And he said, The arrow of the LORD's deliverance, and the arrow of deliverance from Syria: for thou shalt smite the Syrians in Aphek, till thou have consumed *them.*

¹⁸And he said, Take the arrows. And he took *them.* And he said unto the king of Israel, Smite upon the ground. And he smote thrice, and stayed.

¹⁹And the man of God was wroth with him, and said, Thou shouldest have smitten five or six times; then hadst thou smitten Syria till thou hadst consumed *it:* whereas now thou shalt smite Syria *but* thrice.

²⁰And Elisha died, and they buried him. And the bands of the Moabites invaded the land at the coming in of the year.

²¹And it came to pass, as they were burying a man, that, behold, they spied a band *of men;* and they cast the man into the sepulchre of Elisha: and when the man was let down, and touched the bones of Elisha, he revived, and stood up on his feet.

²²But Hazael king of Syria oppressed Israel all the days of Jehoahaz.

²³And the LORD was gracious unto them, and had compassion on them, and had respect unto them, because of his covenant with Abraham, Isaac, and Jacob, and would not destroy them, neither cast he them from his presence as yet.

²⁴So Hazael king of Syria died; and Ben–hadad his son reigned in his stead.

²⁵And Jehoash the son of Jehoahaz took again out of the hand of Ben–hadad the son of Hazael the cities, which he had taken out of the hand of Jehoahaz his father by war. Three times did Joash beat him, and recovered the cities of Israel.

IN the second year of Joash son of Jehoahaz king of Israel reigned Amaziah the son of Joash king of Judah.

2He was twenty and five years old when he began to reign, and reigned twenty and nine years in Jerusalem. And his mother's name *was* Jehoaddan of Jerusalem.

3And he did *that which was* right in the sight of the LORD, yet not like David his father: he did according to all things as Joash his father did.

4Howbeit the high places were not taken away: as yet the people did sacrifice and burnt incense on the high places.

5And it came to pass, as soon as the kingdom was confirmed in his hand, that he slew his servants which had slain the king his father.

6But the children of the murderers he slew not: according unto that which is written in the book of the law of Moses, wherein the LORD commanded, saying, The fathers shall not be put to death for the children, nor the children be put to death for the fathers; but every man shall be put to death for his own sin.

7He slew of Edom in the valley of salt ten thousand, and took Selah by war, and called the name of it Joktheel unto this day.

8Then Amaziah sent messengers to Jehoash, the son of Jehoahaz son of Jehu, king of Israel, saying, Come, let us look one another in the face.

9And Jehoash the king of Israel sent to Amaziah king of Judah, saying, The thistle that *was* in Lebanon sent to the cedar that *was* in Lebanon, saying, Give thy daughter to my son to wife: and there passed by a wild beast that *was* in Lebanon, and trode down the thistle.

10Thou hast indeed smitten Edom, and thine heart hath lifted thee up: glory *of this,* and tarry at home: for why shouldest thou meddle to *thy* hurt, that thou shouldest fall, *even* thou, and Judah with thee?

11But Amaziah would not hear. Therefore Jehoash king of Israel went up; and he and Amaziah king of Judah looked one another in the face at Beth–shemesh, which *belongeth* to Judah.

12And Judah was put to the worse before Israel; and they fled every man to their tents.

13And Jehoash king of Israel took Amaziah king of Judah, the son of Jehoash the son of Ahaziah, at Beth–shemesh, and came to Jerusalem, and brake down the wall of Jerusalem from the gate of Ephraim unto the corner gate, four hundred cubits.

14And he took all the gold and silver, and all the vessels that were found in the house of the LORD, and in the treasures of the king's house, and hostages, and returned to Samaria.

15Now the rest of the acts of Jehoash which he did, and his might, and how he fought with Amaziah king of Judah, *are* they not written in the book of the chronicles of the kings of Israel?

16And Jehoash slept with his fathers, and was buried in Samaria with the kings of Israel; and Jeroboam his son reigned in his stead.

17And Amaziah the son of Joash king of Judah lived after the death of Jehoash son of Jehoahaz king of Israel fifteen years.

18And the rest of the acts of Amaziah, *are* they not written in the book of the chronicles of the kings of Judah?

19Now they made a conspiracy against him in Jerusalem: and he fled to Lachish; but they sent after him to Lachish, and slew him there.

20And they brought him on horses: and he was buried at Jerusalem with his fathers in the city of David.

21And all the people of Judah took Azariah, which *was* sixteen years old, and made him king instead of his father Amaziah.

22He built Elath, and restored it to Judah, after that the king slept with his fathers.

23In the fifteenth year of Amaziah the son of Joash king of Judah Jeroboam the son of Joash king of Israel began to reign in Samaria, *and reigned* forty and one years.

24And he did *that which was* evil in the sight of the LORD: he departed not from all the sins of Jeroboam the son of Nebat, who made Israel to sin.

25He restored the coast of Israel from the entering of Hamath unto the sea of the plain, according to the word of the LORD God of Israel, which he spake by the hand of his servant Jonah, the son of Amittai, the prophet, which *was* of Gathhepher.

26For the LORD saw the affliction of Israel, *that it was* very bitter: for *there was* not any shut up, nor any left, nor any helper for Israel.

27And the LORD said not that he would blot out the name of Israel from under heaven: but he saved them by the hand of Jeroboam the son of Joash.

28Now the rest of the acts of Jeroboam, and all that he did, and his might, how he warred, and how he recovered Damascus, and Hamath, *which belonged* to Judah, for Israel, *are* they not written in the book of the chronicles of the kings of Israel?

29And Jeroboam slept with his fathers, *even* with the kings of Israel; and Zachariah his son reigned in his stead.

ACTS 18:22—19:12

AND when he [Paul] had landed at Caesarea, and gone up, and saluted the church, he went down to Antioch.

23And after he had spent some time *there,* he departed, and went over *all* the country of Galatia and Phrygia in order, strengthening all the disciples.

24And a certain Jew named Apollos, born at Alexandria, an eloquent man, *and* mighty in the scriptures, came to Ephesus.

25This man was instructed in the way of the Lord; and being fervent in the spirit, he spake and taught diligently the things of the Lord, knowing only the baptism of John.

26And he began to speak boldly in the synagogue: whom when Aquila and Priscilla had heard, they took him unto *them,* and expounded unto him the way of God more perfectly.

27And when he was disposed to pass into Achaia, the brethren wrote, exhorting the disciples to receive him: who, when he was come, helped them much which had believed through grace:

28For he mightily convinced the Jews, *and that* publickly, shewing by the scriptures that Jesus was Christ.

AND it came to pass, that, while Apollos was at Corinth, Paul having passed through the upper coasts came to Ephesus: and finding certain disciples,

2He said unto them, Have ye received the Holy Ghost since ye believed? And they said unto him, We have not so much as heard whether there be any Holy Ghost.

3And he said unto them, Unto what then were ye baptized? And they said, Unto John's baptism.

4Then said Paul, John verily baptized with the baptism of repentance, saying unto the people, that they should believe on him which should come after him, that is, on Christ Jesus.

5When they heard *this,* they were baptized in the name of the Lord Jesus.

6And when Paul had laid *his* hands upon them, the Holy Ghost came on them; and they spake with tongues, and prophesied.

7And all the men were about twelve.

8And he went into the synagogue, and spake boldly for the space of three months, disputing and persuading the things concerning the kingdom of God.

9But when divers were hardened, and believed not, but spake evil of that way before the multitude, he departed from them, and separated the disciples, disputing daily in the school of one Tyrannus.

10And this continued by the space of two years; so that all they which dwelt in Asia heard the word of the Lord Jesus, both Jews and Greeks.

11And God wrought special miracles by the hands of Paul:

12So that from his body were brought unto the sick handkerchiefs or aprons, and the diseases departed from them, and the evil spirits went out of them.

PSALM 146:1–10

P RAISE ye the LORD. Praise the LORD, O my soul.

2While I live will I praise the LORD: I will sing praises unto my God while I have any being.

3Put not your trust in princes, *nor* in the son of man, in whom *there is* no help.

4His breath goeth forth, he returneth to his earth; in that very day his thoughts perish.

5Happy *is he* that *hath* the God of Jacob for his help, whose hope *is* in the LORD his God:

6Which made heaven, and earth, the sea, and all that therein *is:* which keepeth truth for ever:

7Which executeth judgment for the oppressed: which giveth food to the hungry. The LORD looseth the prisoners:

8The LORD openeth *the eyes of* the blind: the LORD raiseth them that are bowed down: the LORD loveth the righteous:

9The LORD preserveth the strangers; he relieveth the fatherless and widow: but the way of the wicked he turneth upside down.

10The LORD shall reign for ever, *even* thy God, O Zion, unto all generations. Praise ye the LORD.

PROVERBS FOR TODAY/ 18:2–3

A fool hath no delight in understanding, but that his heart may discover itself. □ *When the wicked cometh,* then *cometh also contempt, and with ignominy reproach.*

JUNE 29

2 KINGS 15:1—16:20

I N the twenty and seventh year of Jeroboam king of Israel began Azariah son of Amaziah king of Judah to reign.

2Sixteen years old was he when he began to reign, and he reigned two and fifty years in Jerusalem. And his mother's name *was* Jecholiah of Jerusalem.

3And he did *that which was* right in

the sight of the LORD, according to all that his father Amaziah had done;

4Save that the high places were not removed: the people sacrificed and burnt incense still on the high places.

5And the LORD smote the king, so that he was a leper unto the day of his death, and dwelt in a several house. And Jotham the king's son *was* over the house, judging the people of the land.

6And the rest of the acts of Azariah, and all that he did, *are* they not written in the book of the chronicles of the kings of Judah?

7So Azariah slept with his fathers; and they buried him with his fathers in the city of David: and Jotham his son reigned in his stead.

8In the thirty and eighth year of Azariah king of Judah did Zachariah the son of Jeroboam reign over Israel in Samaria six months.

9And he did *that which was* evil in the sight of the LORD, as his fathers had done: he departed not from the sins of Jeroboam the son of Nebat, who made Israel to sin.

10And Shallum the son of Jabesh conspired against him, and smote him before the people, and slew him, and reigned in his stead.

11And the rest of the acts of Zachariah, behold, they *are* written in the book of the chronicles of the kings of Israel.

12This *was* the word of the LORD which he spake unto Jehu, saying, Thy sons shall sit on the throne of Israel unto the fourth *generation.* And so it came to pass.

13Shallum the son of Jabesh began to reign in the nine and thirtieth year of Uzziah king of Judah; and he reigned a full month in Samaria.

14For Menahem the son of Gadi went up from Tirzah, and came to Samaria, and smote Shallum the son of Jabesh in Samaria, and slew him, and reigned in his stead.

15And the rest of the acts of Shallum, and his conspiracy which he made, behold, they *are* written in the book of the chronicles of the kings of Israel.

16Then Menahem smote Tiphsah, and all that *were* therein, and the coasts thereof from Tirzah: because they opened not *to him,* therefore he smote *it; and* all the women therein that were with child he ripped up.

17In the nine and thirtieth year of Azariah king of Judah began Menahem the son of Gadi to reign over Israel, *and reigned* ten years in Samaria.

18And he did *that which was* evil in the sight of the LORD: he departed not all his days from the sins of Jeroboam the son of Nebat, who made Israel to sin.

19*And* Pul the king of Assyria came against the land: and Menahem gave Pul a thousand talents of silver, that his hand might be with him to confirm the kingdom in his hand.

20And Menahem exacted the money of Israel, *even* of all the mighty men of wealth, of each man fifty shekels of silver, to give to the king of Assyria. So the king of Assyria turned back, and stayed not there in the land.

21And the rest of the acts of Menahem, and all that he did, *are* they not written in the book of the chronicles of the kings of Israel?

22And Menahem slept with his fathers; and Pekahiah his son reigned in his stead.

23In the fiftieth year of Azariah king of Judah Pekahiah the son of Menahem began to reign over Israel in Samaria, *and reigned* two years.

24And he did *that which was* evil in the sight of the LORD: he departed not from the sins of Jeroboam the son of Nebat, who made Israel to sin.

25But Pekah the son of Remaliah, a captain of his, conspired against him, and smote him in Samaria, in the palace of the king's house, with Argob and Arieh, and with him fifty men of the Gileadites: and he killed him, and reigned in his room.

26And the rest of the acts of Pekahiah, and all that he did, behold, they *are* written in the book of the chronicles of the kings of Israel.

27In the two and fiftieth year of Azariah king of Judah Pekah the son of Remaliah began to reign over Israel in Samaria, *and reigned* twenty years.

28And he did *that which was* evil in

the sight of the LORD: he departed not from the sins of Jeroboam the son of Nebat, who made Israel to sin.

29In the days of Pekah king of Israel came Tiglath–pileser king of Assyria, and took Ijon, and Abel–beth–maachah, and Janoah, and Kedesh, and Hazor, and Gilead, and Galilee, all the land of Naphtali, and carried them captive to Assyria.

30And Hoshea the son of Elah made a conspiracy against Pekah the son of Remaliah, and smote him, and slew him, and reigned in his stead, in the twentieth year of Jotham the son of Uzziah.

31And the rest of the acts of Pekah, and all that he did, behold, they *are* written in the book of the chronicles of the kings of Israel.

32In the second year of Pekah the son of Remaliah king of Israel began Jotham the son of Uzziah king of Judah to reign.

33Five and twenty years old was he when he began to reign, and he reigned sixteen years in Jerusalem. And his mother's name *was* Jerusha, the daughter of Zadok.

34And he did *that which was* right in the sight of the LORD: he did according to all that his father Uzziah had done.

35Howbeit the high places were not removed: the people sacrificed and burned incense still in the high places. He built the higher gate of the house of the LORD.

36Now the rest of the acts of Jotham, and all that he did, *are* they not written in the book of the chronicles of the kings of Judah?

37In those days the LORD began to send against Judah Rezin the king of Syria, and Pekah the son of Remaliah.

38And Jotham slept with his fathers, and was buried with his fathers in the city of David his father: and Ahaz his son reigned in his stead.

IN the seventeenth year of Pekah the son of Remaliah Ahaz the son of Jotham king of Judah began to reign.

2Twenty years old *was* Ahaz when he began to reign, and reigned sixteen years in Jerusalem, and did not *that which was* right in the sight of the LORD his God, like David his father.

3But he walked in the way of the kings of Israel, yea, and made his son to pass through the fire, according to the abominations of the heathen, whom the LORD cast out from before the children of Israel.

4And he sacrificed and burnt incense in the high places, and on the hills, and under every green tree.

5Then Rezin king of Syria and Pekah son of Remaliah king of Israel came up to Jerusalem to war: and they besieged Ahaz, but could not overcome *him.*

6At that time Rezin king of Syria recovered Elath to Syria, and drave the Jews from Elath: and the Syrians came to Elath, and dwelt there unto this day.

7So Ahaz sent messengers to Tiglath–pileser king of Assyria, saying, I *am* thy servant and thy son: come up, and save me out of the hand of the king of Syria, and out of the hand of the king of Israel, which rise up against me.

8And Ahaz took the silver and gold that was found in the house of the LORD, and in the treasures of the king's house, and sent *it for* a present to the king of Assyria.

9And the king of Assyria hearkened unto him: for the king of Assyria went up against Damascus, and took it, and carried *the people of* it captive to Kir, and slew Rezin.

10And king Ahaz went to Damascus to meet Tiglath–pileser king of Assyria, and saw an altar that *was* at Damascus: and king Ahaz sent to Urijah the priest the fashion of the altar, and the pattern of it, according to all the workmanship thereof.

11And Urijah the priest built an altar according to all that king Ahaz had sent from Damascus: so Urijah the priest made *it* against king Ahaz came from Damascus.

12And when the king was come from Damascus, the king saw the altar: and the king approached to the altar, and offered thereon.

13And he burnt his burnt offering and his meat offering, and poured his drink offering, and sprinkled the blood of his peace offerings, upon the altar.

14And he brought also the brasen altar, which *was* before the LORD, from the forefront of the house, from between the altar and the house of the LORD, and put it on the north side of the altar.

15And king Ahaz commanded Urijah the priest, saying, Upon the great altar burn the morning burnt offering, and the evening meat offering, and the king's burnt sacrifice, and his meat offering, with the burnt offering of all the people of the land, and their meat offering, and their drink offerings; and sprinkle upon it all the blood of the burnt offering, and all the blood of the sacrifice: and the brasen altar shall be for me to enquire *by.*

16Thus did Urijah the priest, according to all that king Ahaz commanded.

17And king Ahaz cut off the borders of the bases, and removed the laver from off them; and took down the sea from off the brasen oxen that *were* under it, and put it upon a pavement of stones.

18And the covert for the sabbath that they had built in the house, and the king's entry without, turned he from the house of the LORD for the king of Assyria.

19Now the rest of the acts of Ahaz which he did, *are* they not written in the book of the chronicles of the kings of Judah?

20And Ahaz slept with his fathers, and was buried with his fathers in the city of David: and Hezekiah his son reigned in his stead.

ACTS 19:13–41

THEN certain of the vagabond Jews, exorcists, took upon them to call over them which had evil spirits the name of the Lord Jesus, saying, We adjure you by Jesus whom Paul preacheth.

14And there were seven sons of *one* Sceva, a Jew, *and* chief of the priests, which did so.

15And the evil spirit answered and said, Jesus I know, and Paul I know; but who are ye?

16And the man in whom the evil spirit was leaped on them, and overcame them, and prevailed against them, so that they fled out of that house naked and wounded.

17And this was known to all the Jews and Greeks also dwelling at Ephesus; and fear fell on them all, and the name of the Lord Jesus was magnified.

18And many that believed came, and confessed, and shewed their deeds.

19Many of them also which used curious arts brought their books together, and burned them before all *men:* and they counted the price of them, and found *it* fifty thousand *pieces* of silver.

20So mightily grew the word of God and prevailed.

21After these things were ended, Paul purposed in the spirit, when he had passed through Macedonia and Achaia, to go to Jerusalem, saying, After I have been there, I must also see Rome.

22So he sent into Macedonia two of them that ministered unto him, Timotheus and Erastus; but he himself stayed in Asia for a season.

23And the same time there arose no small stir about that way.

24For a certain *man* named Demetrius, a silversmith, which made silver shrines for Diana, brought no small gain unto the craftsmen;

25Whom he called together with the workmen of like occupation, and said,

Sirs, ye know that by this craft we have our wealth.

26Moreover ye see and hear, that not alone at Ephesus, but almost throughout all Asia, this Paul hath persuaded and turned away much people, saying that they be no gods, which are made with hands:

27So that not only this our craft is in danger to be set at nought; but also that the temple of the great goddess Diana should be despised, and her magnificence should be destroyed, whom all Asia and the world worshippeth.

28And when they heard *these sayings,* they were full of wrath, and cried out, saying, Great *is* Diana of the Ephesians.

29And the whole city was filled with confusion: and having caught Gaius and Aristarchus, men of Macedonia, Paul's companions in travel, they rushed with one accord into the theatre.

30And when Paul would have entered in unto the people, the disciples suffered him not.

31And certain of the chief of Asia, which were his friends, sent unto him, desiring *him* that he would not adventure himself into the theatre.

32Some therefore cried one thing, and some another: for the assembly was confused; and the more part knew not wherefore they were come together.

33And they drew Alexander out of the multitude, the Jews putting him forward. And Alexander beckoned with the hand, and would have made his defence unto the people.

34But when they knew that he was a Jew, all with one voice about the space of two hours cried out, Great *is* Diana of the Ephesians.

35And when the townclerk had appeased the people, he said, *Ye* men of Ephesus, what man is there that knoweth not how that the city of the Ephesians is a worshipper of the great goddess Diana, and of the *image* which fell down from Jupiter?

36Seeing then that these things cannot be spoken against, ye ought to be quiet, and to do nothing rashly.

37For ye have brought hither these men, which are neither robbers of churches, nor yet blasphemers of your goddess.

38Wherefore if Demetrius, and the craftsmen which are with him, have a matter against any man, the law is open, and there are deputies: let them implead one another.

39But if ye enquire any thing concerning other matters, it shall be determined in a lawful assembly.

40For we are in danger to be called in question for this day's uproar, there being no cause whereby we may give an account of this concourse.

41And when he had thus spoken, he dismissed the assembly.

PSALM 147:1–20

Praise ye the Lord: for *it is* good to sing praises unto our God; for *it is* pleasant; *and* praise is comely.

2The Lord doth build up Jerusalem: he gathereth together the outcasts of Israel.

3He healeth the broken in heart, and bindeth up their wounds.

4He telleth the number of the stars; he calleth them all by *their* names.

5Great *is* our Lord, and of great power: his understanding *is* infinite.

6The Lord lifteth up the meek: he casteth the wicked down to the ground.

7Sing unto the Lord with thanksgiving; sing praise upon the harp unto our God:

8Who covereth the heaven with clouds, who prepareth rain for the earth, who maketh grass to grow upon the mountains.

9He giveth to the beast his food, *and* to the young ravens which cry.

10He delighteth not in the strength of the horse: he taketh not pleasure in the legs of a man.

11The LORD taketh pleasure in them that fear him, in those that hope in his mercy.

12Praise the LORD, O Jerusalem; praise thy God, O Zion.

13For he hath strengthened the bars of thy gates; he hath blessed thy children within thee.

14He maketh peace *in* thy borders, *and* filleth thee with the finest of the wheat.

15He sendeth forth his commandment *upon* earth: his word runneth very swiftly.

16He giveth snow like wool: he scattereth the hoarfrost like ashes.

17He casteth forth his ice like morsels: who can stand before his cold?

18He sendeth out his word, and melteth them: he causeth his wind to blow, *and* the waters flow.

19He sheweth his word unto Jacob, his statutes and his judgments unto Israel.

20He hath not dealt so with any nation: and *as for his* judgments, they have not known them. Praise ye the LORD.

PROVERBS FOR TODAY/ 18:4–5

The words of a man's mouth are as *deep waters,* and *the wellspring of wisdom* as *a flowing brook.*   □ It is *not good to accept the person of the wicked, to overthrow the righteous in judgment.*

JUNE 30

2 KINGS 17:1—18:12

IN the twelfth year of Ahaz king of Judah began Hoshea the son of Elah to reign in Samaria over Israel nine years.

2And he did *that which was* evil in the sight of the LORD, but not as the kings of Israel that were before him.

3Against him came up Shalmaneser king of Assyria; and Hoshea became his servant, and gave him presents.

4And the king of Assyria found conspiracy in Hoshea: for he had sent messengers to So king of Egypt, and brought no present to the king of Assyria, as *he had done* year by year: therefore the king of Assyria shut him up, and bound him in prison.

5Then the king of Assyria came up throughout all the land, and went up to Samaria, and besieged it three years.

6In the ninth year of Hoshea the king of Assyria took Samaria, and carried Israel away into Assyria, and placed them in Halah and in Habor *by* the river of Gozan, and in the cities of the Medes.

7For *so* it was, that the children of Israel had sinned against the LORD their God, which had brought them up out of the land of Egypt, from under the hand of Pharaoh king of Egypt, and had feared other gods,

8And walked in the statutes of the heathen, whom the LORD cast out from before the children of Israel, and of the kings of Israel, which they had made.

9And the children of Israel did secretly *those* things that *were* not right against the LORD their God, and they built them high places in all their cities, from the tower of the watchmen to the fenced city.

10And they set them up images and groves in every high hill, and under every green tree:

11And there they burnt incense in all the high places, as *did* the heathen whom the LORD carried away before them; and wrought wicked things to provoke the LORD to anger:

12For they served idols, whereof the LORD had said unto them, Ye shall not do this thing.

13Yet the LORD testified against Israel, and against Judah, by all the prophets, *and by* all the seers, saying, Turn ye from your evil ways, and keep my commandments *and* my statutes, according to all the law which I commanded your fathers, and which I sent to you by my servants the prophets.

14Notwithstanding they would not hear, but hardened their necks, like to the neck of their fathers, that did not believe in the LORD their God.

15And they rejected his statutes, and his covenant that he made with their fathers, and his testimonies which he testified against them; and they followed vanity, and became vain, and went after the heathen that *were* round about them, *concerning* whom the LORD had charged them, that they should not do like them.

16And they left all the commandments of the LORD their God, and made them molten images, *even* two calves, and made a grove, and worshipped all the host of heaven, and served Baal.

17And they caused their sons and their daughters to pass through the fire, and used divination and enchantments, and sold themselves to do evil in the sight of the LORD, to provoke him to anger:

18Therefore the LORD was very angry with Israel, and removed them out of his sight: there was none left but the tribe of Judah only.

19Also Judah kept not the commandments of the LORD their God, but walked in the statutes of Israel which they made.

20And the LORD rejected all the seed of Israel, and afflicted them, and delivered them into the hand of spoilers, until he had cast them out of his sight.

21For he rent Israel from the house of David; and they made Jeroboam the son of Nebat king: and Jeroboam drave Israel from following the LORD, and made them sin a great sin.

22For the children of Israel walked in all the sins of Jeroboam which he did; they departed not from them;

23Until the LORD removed Israel out of his sight, as he had said by all his servants the prophets. So was Israel carried away out of their own land to Assyria unto this day.

24And the king of Assyria brought *men* from Babylon, and from Cuthah, and from Ava, and from Hamath, and from Sepharvaim, and placed *them* in the cities of Samaria instead of the children of Israel: and they possessed Samaria, and dwelt in the cities thereof.

25And *so* it was at the beginning of their dwelling there, *that* they feared not the LORD: therefore the LORD sent lions among them, which slew *some* of them.

26Wherefore they spake to the king of Assyria, saying, The nations which thou hast removed, and placed in the cities of Samaria, know not the manner of the God of the land: therefore he hath sent lions among them, and, behold, they slay them, because they know not the manner of the God of the land.

27Then the king of Assyria commanded, saying, Carry thither one of the priests whom ye brought from thence; and let them go and dwell there, and let him teach them the manner of the God of the land.

28Then one of the priests whom they had carried away from Samaria came and dwelt in Beth–el, and taught them how they should fear the LORD.

29Howbeit every nation made gods of their own, and put *them* in the houses of the high places which the Samaritans had made, every nation in their cities wherein they dwelt.

30And the men of Babylon made Succothbenoth, and the men of Cuth made Nergal, and the men of Hamath made Ashima,

31And the Avites made Nibhaz and Tartak, and the Sepharvites burnt their children in fire to Adrammelech and Anammelech, the gods of Sepharvaim.

32So they feared the LORD, and made unto themselves of the lowest of them priests of the high places, which sacrificed for them in the houses of the high places.

33They feared the LORD, and served their own gods, after the manner of the nations whom they carried away from thence.

34Unto this day they do after the former manners: they fear not the LORD, neither do they after their statutes, or after their ordinances, or after the law and commandment which the LORD commanded the children of Jacob, whom he named Israel;

35With whom the LORD had made a covenant, and charged them, saying, Ye shall not fear other gods, nor bow yourselves to them, nor serve them, nor sacrifice to them:

36But the LORD, who brought you up out of the land of Egypt with great power and a stretched out arm, him shall ye fear, and him shall ye worship, and to him shall ye do sacrifice.

37And the statutes, and the ordinances, and the law, and the commandment, which he wrote for you, ye shall observe to do for evermore; and ye shall not fear other gods.

38And the covenant that I have made with you ye shall not forget; neither shall ye fear other gods.

39But the LORD your God ye shall fear; and he shall deliver you out of the hand of all your enemies.

40Howbeit they did not hearken, but they did after their former manner.

41So these nations feared the LORD, and served their graven images, both their children, and their children's children: as did their fathers, so do they unto this day.

Now it came to pass in the third year of Hoshea son of Elah king of Israel, *that* Hezekiah the son of Ahaz king of Judah began to reign.

2Twenty and five years old was he when he began to reign; and he reigned twenty and nine years in Jerusalem. His mother's name also *was* Abi, the daughter of Zachariah.

3And he did *that which was* right in the sight of the LORD, according to all that David his father did.

4He removed the high places, and brake the images, and cut down the groves, and brake in pieces the brasen serpent that Moses had made: for unto those days the children of Israel did burn incense to it: and he called it Nehushtan.

5He trusted in the LORD God of Israel; so that after him was none like him among all the kings of Judah, nor *any* that were before him.

6For he clave to the LORD, *and* departed not from following him, but kept his commandments, which the LORD commanded Moses.

7And the LORD was with him; *and* he prospered whithersoever he went forth: and he rebelled against the king of Assyria, and served him not.

8He smote the Philistines, *even* unto Gaza, and the borders thereof, from the tower of the watchmen to the fenced city.

9And it came to pass in the fourth year of king Hezekiah, which *was* the seventh year of Hoshea son of Elah king of Israel, *that* Shalmaneser king of Assyria came up against Samaria, and besieged it.

10And at the end of three years they took it: *even* in the sixth year of Hezekiah, that *is* the ninth year of Hoshea king of Israel, Samaria was taken.

11And the king of Assyria did carry away Israel unto Assyria, and put them in Halah and in Habor *by* the river of Gozan, and in the cities of the Medes:

12Because they obeyed not the voice of the LORD their God, but transgressed his covenant, *and* all that Moses the servant of the LORD commanded, and would not hear *them,* nor do *them.*

ACTS 20:1–38

AND after the uproar was ceased, Paul called unto *him* the disciples, and embraced *them,* and departed for to go into Macedonia.

2And when he had gone over those parts, and had given them much exhortation, he came into Greece,

3And *there* abode three months. And when the Jews laid wait for him, as he was about to sail into Syria, he purposed to return through Macedonia.

4And there accompanied him into Asia Sopater of Berea; and of the Thessalonians, Aristarchus and Secundus; and Gaius of Derbe, and Timotheus; and of Asia, Tychicus and Trophimus.

5These going before tarried for us at Troas.

6And we sailed away from Philippi after the days of unleavened bread, and came unto them to Troas in five days; where we abode seven days.

7And upon the first *day* of the week, when the disciples came together to break bread, Paul preached unto them, ready to depart on the morrow; and continued his speech until midnight.

8And there were many lights in the upper chamber, where they were gathered together.

9And there sat in a window a certain young man named Eutychus, being fallen into a deep sleep: and as Paul was long preaching, he sunk down with sleep, and fell down from the third loft, and was taken up dead.

10And Paul went down, and fell on him, and embracing *him* said, Trouble not yourselves; for his life is in him.

11When he therefore was come up again, and had broken bread, and eaten, and talked a long while, even till break of day, so he departed.

12And they brought the young man alive, and were not a little comforted.

13And we went before to ship, and sailed unto Assos, there intending to take in Paul: for so had he appointed, minding himself to go afoot.

14And when he met with us at Assos, we took him in, and came to Mitylene.

15And we sailed thence, and came the next *day* over against Chios; and the next *day* we arrived at Samos, and tarried at Trogyllium; and the next *day* we came to Miletus.

16For Paul had determined to sail by Ephesus, because he would not spend the time in Asia: for he hasted, if it were possible for him, to be at Jerusalem the day of Pentecost.

17And from Miletus he sent to Ephesus, and called the elders of the church.

18And when they were come to him, he said unto them, Ye know, from the first day that I came into Asia, after what manner I have been with you at all seasons,

19Serving the Lord with all humility of mind, and with many tears, and temptations, which befell me by the lying in wait of the Jews:

20*And* how I kept back nothing that was profitable *unto you,* but have shewed you, and have taught you publickly, and from house to house,

21Testifying both to the Jews, and also to the Greeks, repentance toward God, and faith toward our Lord Jesus Christ.

22And now, behold, I go bound in the spirit unto Jerusalem, not knowing the things that shall befall me there:

23Save that the Holy Ghost witnesseth in every city, saying that bonds and afflictions abide me.

24But none of these things move me, neither count I my life dear unto myself, so that I might finish my course with joy, and the ministry, which I have received of the Lord Jesus, to testify the gospel of the grace of God.

25And now, behold, I know that ye all, among whom I have gone preaching the kingdom of God, shall see my face no more.

26Wherefore I take you to record this day, that I *am* pure from the blood of all *men*.

27For I have not shunned to declare unto you all the counsel of God.

28Take heed therefore unto yourselves, and to all the flock, over the which the Holy Ghost hath made you overseers, to feed the church of God, which he hath purchased with his own blood.

29For I know this, that after my departing shall grievous wolves enter in among you, not sparing the flock.

30Also of your own selves shall men arise, speaking perverse things, to draw away disciples after them.

31Therefore watch, and remember, that by the space of three years I ceased not to warn every one night and day with tears.

32And now, brethren, I commend you to God, and to the word of his grace, which is able to build you up, and to give you an inheritance among all them which are sanctified.

33I have coveted no man's silver, or gold, or apparel.

34Yea, ye yourselves know, that these hands have ministered unto my necessities, and to them that were with me.

35I have shewed you all things, how that so labouring ye ought to support the weak, and to remember the words of the Lord Jesus, how he said, It is more blessed to give than to receive.

36And when he had thus spoken, he kneeled down, and prayed with them all.

37And they all wept sore, and fell on Paul's neck, and kissed him,

38Sorrowing most of all for the words which he spake, that they should see his face no more. And they accompanied him unto the ship.

PSALM 148:1–14

Praise ye the Lord. Praise ye the Lord from the heavens: praise him in the heights.

2Praise ye him, all his angels: praise ye him, all his hosts.

3Praise ye him, sun and moon: praise him, all ye stars of light.

4Praise him, ye heavens of heavens, and ye waters that *be* above the heavens.

5Let them praise the name of the Lord: for he commanded, and they were created.

6He hath also stablished them for ever and ever: he hath made a decree which shall not pass.

7Praise the Lord from the earth, ye dragons, and all deeps:

8Fire, and hail; snow, and vapours; stormy wind fulfilling his word:

9Mountains, and all hills; fruitful trees, and all cedars:

10Beasts, and all cattle; creeping things, and flying fowl:

11Kings of the earth, and all people; princes, and all judges of the earth:

12Both young men, and maidens; old men, and children:

13Let them praise the name of the Lord: for his name alone is excellent; his glory *is* above the earth and heaven.

14He also exalteth the horn of his people, the praise of all his saints; *even* of the children of Israel, a people near unto him. Praise ye the Lord.

PROVERBS FOR TODAY/ 18:6–7

A fool's lips enter into contention, and his mouth calleth for strokes. A fool's mouth is *his destruction, and his lips* are *the snare of his soul.*

JULY 1

2 KINGS 18:13—19:37

Now in the fourteenth year of king Hezekiah did Sennacherib king of Assyria come up against all the fenced cities of Judah, and took them.

14And Hezekiah king of Judah sent to the king of Assyria to Lachish, saying, I have offended; return from me: that which thou puttest on me will I bear. And the king of Assyria appointed unto Hezekiah king of Judah three hundred talents of silver and thirty talents of gold.

15And Hezekiah gave *him* all the silver that was found in the house of the LORD, and in the treasures of the king's house.

16At that time did Hezekiah cut off *the gold from* the doors of the temple of the LORD, and *from* the pillars which Hezekiah king of Judah had overlaid, and gave it to the king of Assyria.

17And the king of Assyria sent Tartan and Rab–saris and Rab–shakeh from Lachish to king Hezekiah with a great host against Jerusalem. And they went up and came to Jerusalem. And when they were come up, they came and stood by the conduit of the upper pool, which *is* in the highway of the fuller's field.

18And when they had called to the king, there came out to them Eliakim the son of Hilkiah, which *was* over the household, and Shebna the scribe, and Joah the son of Asaph the recorder.

19And Rab–shakeh said unto them, Speak ye now to Hezekiah, Thus saith the great king, the king of Assyria, What confidence *is* this wherein thou trustest?

20Thou sayest, (but *they are but* vain words,) *I have* counsel and strength for the war. Now on whom dost thou trust, that thou rebellest against me?

21Now, behold, thou trustest upon the staff of this bruised reed, *even* upon Egypt, on which if a man lean, it will go into his hand, and pierce it: so *is* Pharaoh king of Egypt unto all that trust on him.

22But if ye say unto me, We trust in the LORD our God: *is* not that he, whose high places and whose altars Hezekiah hath taken away, and hath said to Judah and Jerusalem, Ye shall worship before this altar in Jerusalem?

23Now therefore, I pray thee, give pledges to my lord the king of Assyria, and I will deliver thee two thousand horses, if thou be able on thy part to set riders upon them.

24How then wilt thou turn away the face of one captain of the least of my master's servants, and put thy trust on Egypt for chariots and for horsemen?

25Am I now come up without the LORD against this place to destroy it? The LORD said to me, Go up against this land, and destroy it.

26Then said Eliakim the son of Hilkiah, and Shebna, and Joah, unto Rab–shakeh, Speak, I pray thee, to thy servants in the Syrian language; for we understand *it:* and talk not with us in the Jews' language in the ears of the people that *are* on the wall.

27But Rab–shakeh said unto them, Hath my master sent me to thy master, and to thee, to speak these words? *hath he* not *sent me* to the men which sit on the wall, that they may eat their own dung, and drink their own piss with you?

28Then Rab–shakeh stood and cried with a loud voice in the Jews' language, and spake, saying, Hear the word of the great king, the king of Assyria:

29Thus saith the king, Let not Hezekiah deceive you: for he shall not be able to deliver you out of his hand:

30Neither let Hezekiah make you trust in the LORD, saying, The LORD will surely deliver us, and this city shall not be delivered into the hand of the king of Assyria.

31Hearken not to Hezekiah: for thus saith the king of Assyria, Make *an agreement* with me by a present, and come out to me, and *then* eat ye every man of his own vine, and every one of his fig tree, and drink ye every one the waters of his cistern:

32Until I come and take you away to a land like your own land, a land of corn and wine, a land of bread and vineyards, a land of oil olive and of honey, that ye may live, and not die: and hearken not unto Hezekiah, when he persuadeth you, saying, The LORD will deliver us.

33Hath any of the gods of the nations delivered at all his land out of the hand of the king of Assyria?

34Where *are* the gods of Hamath, and of Arpad? where *are* the gods of Sepharvaim, Hena, and Ivah? have they delivered Samaria out of mine hand?

35Who *are* they among all the gods of the countries, that have delivered their country out of mine hand, that the LORD should deliver Jerusalem out of mine hand?

36But the people held their peace, and answered him not a word: for the king's commandment was, saying, Answer him not.

37Then came Eliakim the son of Hilkiah, which *was* over the household, and Shebna the scribe, and Joah the son of Asaph the recorder, to Hezekiah with *their* clothes rent, and told him the words of Rab–shakeh.

AND it came to pass, when king Hezekiah heard *it,* that he rent his clothes, and covered himself with sackcloth, and went into the house of the LORD.

2And he sent Eliakim, which *was* over the household, and Shebna the scribe, and the elders of the priests, covered with sackcloth, to Isaiah the prophet the son of Amoz.

3And they said unto him, Thus saith Hezekiah, This day *is* a day of trouble, and of rebuke, and blasphemy: for the children are come to the birth, and *there is* not strength to bring forth.

4It may be the LORD thy God will hear all the words of Rab–shakeh, whom the king of Assyria his master hath sent to reproach the living God; and will reprove the words which the LORD thy God hath heard: wherefore lift up *thy* prayer for the remnant that are left.

5So the servants of king Hezekiah came to Isaiah.

6And Isaiah said unto them, Thus shall ye say to your master, Thus saith the LORD, Be not afraid of the words which thou hast heard, with which the servants of the king of Assyria have blasphemed me.

7Behold, I will send a blast upon him, and he shall hear a rumour, and shall return to his own land; and I will cause him to fall by the sword in his own land.

8So Rab–shakeh returned, and found the king of Assyria warring against Libnah: for he had heard that he was departed from Lachish.

9And when he heard say of Tirhakah king of Ethiopia, Behold, he is come out to fight against thee: he sent messengers again unto Hezekiah, saying,

¹⁰Thus shall ye speak to Hezekiah king of Judah, saying, Let not thy God in whom thou trustest deceive thee, saying, Jerusalem shall not be delivered into the hand of the king of Assyria.

¹¹Behold, thou hast heard what the kings of Assyria have done to all lands, by destroying them utterly: and shalt thou be delivered?

¹²Have the gods of the nations delivered them which my fathers have destroyed; as Gozan, and Haran, and Rezeph, and the children of Eden which were in Thelasar?

¹³Where is the king of Hamath, and the king of Arpad, and the king of the city of Sepharvaim, of Hena, and Ivah?

¹⁴And Hezekiah received the letter of the hand of the messengers, and read it: and Hezekiah went up into the house of the LORD, and spread it before the LORD.

¹⁵And Hezekiah prayed before the LORD, and said, O LORD God of Israel, which dwellest between the cherubims, thou art the God, even thou alone, of all the kingdoms of the earth; thou hast made heaven and earth.

¹⁶LORD, bow down thine ear, and hear: open, LORD, thine eyes, and see: and hear the words of Sennacherib, which hath sent him to reproach the living God.

¹⁷Of a truth, LORD, the kings of Assyria have destroyed the nations and their lands,

¹⁸And have cast their gods into the fire: for they were no gods, but the work of men's hands, wood and stone: therefore they have destroyed them.

¹⁹Now therefore, O LORD our God, I beseech thee, save thou us out of his hand, that all the kingdoms of the earth may know that thou art the LORD God, even thou only.

²⁰Then Isaiah the son of Amoz sent to Hezekiah, saying, Thus saith the LORD God of Israel, That which thou hast prayed to me against Sennacherib

king of Assyria I have heard.

²¹This is the word that the LORD hath spoken concerning him; The virgin the daughter of Zion hath despised thee, and laughed thee to scorn; the daughter of Jerusalem hath shaken her head at thee.

²²Whom hast thou reproached and blasphemed? and against whom hast thou exalted thy voice, and lifted up thine eyes on high? even against the Holy One of Israel.

²³By thy messengers thou hast reproached the Lord, and hast said, With the multitude of my chariots I am come up to the height of the mountains, to the sides of Lebanon, and will cut down the tall cedar trees thereof, and the choice fir trees thereof: and I will enter into the lodgings of his borders, and into the forest of his Carmel.

²⁴I have digged and drunk strange waters, and with the sole of my feet have I dried up all the rivers of besieged places.

²⁵Hast thou not heard long ago how I have done it, and of ancient times that I have formed it? now have I brought it to pass, that thou shouldest be to lay waste fenced cities into ruinous heaps.

²⁶Therefore their inhabitants were of small power, they were dismayed and confounded; they were as the grass of the field, and as the green herb, as the grass on the house tops, and as corn blasted before it be grown up.

²⁷But I know thy abode, and thy going out, and thy coming in, and thy rage against me.

²⁸Because thy rage against me and thy tumult is come up into mine ears, therefore I will put my hook in thy nose, and my bridle in thy lips, and I will turn thee back by the way by which thou camest.

²⁹And this shall be a sign unto thee, Ye shall eat this year such things as grow of themselves, and in the second year that which springeth of the same;

and in the third year sow ye, and reap, and plant vineyards, and eat the fruits thereof.

30And the remnant that is escaped of the house of Judah shall yet again take root downward, and bear fruit upward.

31For out of Jerusalem shall go forth a remnant, and they that escape out of mount Zion: the zeal of the LORD *of hosts* shall do this.

32Therefore thus saith the LORD concerning the king of Assyria, He shall not come into this city, nor shoot an arrow there, nor come before it with shield, nor cast a bank against it.

33By the way that he came, by the same shall he return, and shall not come into this city, saith the LORD.

34For I will defend this city, to save it, for mine own sake, and for my servant David's sake.

35And it came to pass that night, that the angel of the LORD went out, and smote in the camp of the Assyrians an hundred fourscore and five thousand: and when they arose early in the morning, behold, they *were* all dead corpses.

36So Sennacherib king of Assyria departed, and went and returned, and dwelt at Nineveh.

37And it came to pass, as he was worshipping in the house of Nisroch his god, that Adrammelech and Sharezer his sons smote him with the sword: and they escaped into the land of Armenia. And Esar-haddon his son reigned in his stead.

ACTS 21:1–17

AND it came to pass, that after we were gotten from them, and had launched, we came with a straight course unto Coos, and the *day* following unto Rhodes, and from thence unto Patara:

2And finding a ship sailing over unto Phenicia, we went aboard, and set forth.

3Now when we had discovered Cyprus, we left it on the left hand, and sailed into Syria, and landed at Tyre: for there the ship was to unlade her burden.

4And finding disciples, we tarried there seven days: who said to Paul through the Spirit, that he should not go up to Jerusalem.

.5And when we had accomplished those days, we departed and went our way; and they all brought us on our way, with wives and children, till *we were* out of the city: and we kneeled down on the shore, and prayed.

6And when we had taken our leave one of another, we took ship; and they returned home again.

7And when we had finished *our* course from Tyre, we came to Ptolemais, and saluted the brethren, and abode with them one day.

8And the next *day* we that were of Paul's company departed, and came unto Caesarea: and we entered into the house of Philip the evangelist, which was *one* of the seven; and abode with him.

9And the same man had four daughters, virgins, which did prophesy.

10And as we tarried *there* many days, there came down from Judaea a certain prophet, named Agabus.

11And when he was come unto us, he took Paul's girdle, and bound his own hands and feet, and said, Thus saith the Holy Ghost, So shall the Jews at Jerusalem bind the man that owneth this girdle, and shall deliver *him* into the hands of the Gentiles.

12And when we heard these things, both we, and they of that place, besought him not to go up to Jerusalem.

13Then Paul answered, What mean ye to weep and to break mine heart? for I am ready not to be bound only, but also to die at Jerusalem for the name of the Lord Jesus.

14And when he would not be persuaded, we ceased, saying, The will of the Lord be done.

15And after those days we took up our carriages, and went up to Jerusalem.

16There went with us also *certain* of the disciples of Caesarea, and brought with them one Mnason of Cyprus, an old disciple, with whom we should lodge.

17And when we were come to Jerusalem, the brethren received us gladly.

PSALM 149:1–9

Praise ye the LORD. Sing unto the LORD a new song, *and* his praise in the congregation of saints.

2Let Israel rejoice in him that made him: let the children of Zion be joyful in their King.

3Let them praise his name in the dance: let them sing praises unto him with the timbrel and harp.

4For the LORD taketh pleasure in his people: he will beautify the meek with salvation.

5Let the saints be joyful in glory: let them sing aloud upon their beds.

6*Let* the high *praises* of God *be* in their mouth, and a two-edged sword in their hand;

7To execute vengeance upon the heathen, *and* punishments upon the people;

8To bind their kings with chains, and their nobles with fetters of iron;

9To execute upon them the judgment written: this honour have all his saints. Praise ye the LORD.

PROVERBS FOR TODAY/ 18:8

The words of a talebearer are *as wounds, and they go down into the innermost parts of the belly.*

JULY 2

2 KINGS 20:1—22:2

In those days was Hezekiah sick unto death. And the prophet Isaiah the son of Amoz came to him, and said unto him, Thus saith the LORD, Set thine house in order; for thou shalt die, and not live.

2Then he turned his face to the wall, and prayed unto the LORD, saying,

3I beseech thee, O LORD, remember now how I have walked before thee in truth and with a perfect heart, and have done *that which is* good in thy sight. And Hezekiah wept sore.

4And it came to pass, afore Isaiah was gone out into the middle court, that the word of the LORD came to him, saying,

5Turn again, and tell Hezekiah the captain of my people, Thus saith the LORD, the God of David thy father, I have heard thy prayer, I have seen thy tears: behold, I will heal thee: on the third day thou shalt go up unto the house of the LORD.

6And I will add unto thy days fifteen years; and I will deliver thee and this city out of the hand of the king of Assyria; and I will defend this city for mine own sake, and for my servant David's sake.

7And Isaiah said, Take a lump of figs.

And they took and laid *it* on the boil, and he recovered.

8And Hezekiah said unto Isaiah, What *shall be* the sign that the LORD will heal me, and that I shall go up into the house of the LORD the third day?

9And Isaiah said, This sign shalt thou have of the LORD, that the LORD will do the thing that he hath spoken: shall the shadow go forward ten degrees, or go back ten degrees?

10And Hezekiah answered, It is a light thing for the shadow to go down ten degrees: nay, but let the shadow return backward ten degrees.

11And Isaiah the prophet cried unto the LORD: and he brought the shadow ten degrees backward, by which it had gone down in the dial of Ahaz.

12At that time Berodach–baladan, the son of Baladan, king of Babylon, sent letters and a present unto Hezekiah: for he had heard that Hezekiah had been sick.

13And Hezekiah hearkened unto them, and shewed them all the house of his precious things, the silver, and the gold, and the spices, and the precious ointment, and *all* the house of his armour, and all that was found in his treasures: there was nothing in his house, nor in all his dominion, that Hezekiah shewed them not.

14Then came Isaiah the prophet unto king Hezekiah, and said unto him, What said these men? and from whence came they unto thee? And Hezekiah said, They are come from a far country, *even* from Babylon.

15And he said, What have they seen in thine house? And Hezekiah answered, All *the things* that *are* in mine house have they seen: there is nothing among my treasures that I have not shewed them.

16And Isaiah said unto Hezekiah, Hear the word of the LORD.

17Behold, the days come, that all that *is* in thine house, and that which thy fathers have laid up in store unto this day, shall be carried into Babylon: nothing shall be left, saith the LORD.

18And of thy sons that shall issue from thee, which thou shalt beget, shall they take away; and they shall be eunuchs in the palace of the king of Babylon.

19Then said Hezekiah unto Isaiah, Good *is* the word of the LORD which thou hast spoken. And he said, *Is it* not *good,* if peace and truth be in my days?

20And the rest of the acts of Hezekiah, and all his might, and how he made a pool, and a conduit, and brought water into the city, *are* they not written in the book of the chronicles of the kings of Judah?

21And Hezekiah slept with his fathers: and Manasseh his son reigned in his stead.

MANASSEH *was* twelve years old when he began to reign, and reigned fifty and five years in Jerusalem. And his mother's name *was* Hephzi–bah.

2And he did *that which was* evil in the sight of the LORD, after the abominations of the heathen, whom the LORD cast out before the children of Israel.

3For he built up again the high places which Hezekiah his father had destroyed; and he reared up altars for Baal, and made a grove, as did Ahab king of Israel; and worshipped all the host of heaven, and served them.

4And he built altars in the house of the LORD, of which the LORD said, In Jerusalem will I put my name.

5And he built altars for all the host of heaven in the two courts of the house of the LORD.

6And he made his son pass through the fire, and observed times, and used enchantments, and dealt with familiar spirits and wizards: he wrought much wickedness in the sight of the LORD, to provoke *him* to anger.

7And he set a graven image of the grove that he had made in the house, of which the LORD said to David, and to Solomon his son, In this house, and in Jerusalem, which I have chosen out of all tribes of Israel, will I put my name for ever:

8Neither will I make the feet of Israel move any more out of the land which I gave their fathers; only if they will observe to do according to all that I have commanded them, and according to all the law that my servant Moses commanded them.

9But they hearkened not: and Manasseh seduced them to do more evil than did the nations whom the LORD destroyed before the children of Israel.

10And the LORD spake by his servants the prophets, saying,

11Because Manasseh king of Judah hath done these abominations, *and* hath done wickedly above all that the Amorites did, which *were* before him, and hath made Judah also to sin with his idols:

12Therefore thus saith the LORD God of Israel, Behold, I *am* bringing *such* evil upon Jerusalem and Judah, that whosoever heareth of it, both his ears shall tingle.

13And I will stretch over Jerusalem the line of Samaria, and the plummet of the house of Ahab: and I will wipe Jerusalem as *a man* wipeth a dish, wiping *it,* and turning *it* upside down.

14And I will forsake the remnant of mine inheritance, and deliver them into the hand of their enemies; and they shall become a prey and a spoil to all their enemies;

15Because they have done *that which was* evil in my sight, and have provoked me to anger, since the day their fathers came forth out of Egypt, even unto this day.

16Moreover Manasseh shed innocent blood very much, till he had filled Jerusalem from one end to another; beside his sin wherewith he made Judah to sin, in doing *that which was* evil in the sight of the LORD.

17Now the rest of the acts of Manasseh, and all that he did, and his sin that he sinned, *are* they not written in the book of the chronicles of the kings of Judah?

18And Manasseh slept with his fathers, and was buried in the garden of his own house, in the garden of Uzza: and Amon his son reigned in his stead.

19Amon *was* twenty and two years old when he began to reign, and he reigned two years in Jerusalem. And his mother's name *was* Meshullemeth, the daughter of Haruz of Jotbah.

20And he did *that which was* evil in the sight of the LORD, as his father Manasseh did.

21And he walked in all the way that his father walked in, and served the idols that his father served, and worshipped them:

22And he forsook the LORD God of his fathers, and walked not in the way of the LORD.

23And the servants of Amon conspired against him, and slew the king in his own house.

24And the people of the land slew all them that had conspired against king Amon; and the people of the land made Josiah his son king in his stead.

25Now the rest of the acts of Amon which he did, *are* they not written in the book of the chronicles of the kings of Judah?

26And he was buried in his sepulchre in the garden of Uzza: and Josiah his son reigned in his stead.

JOSIAH *was* eight years old when he began to reign, and he reigned thirty and one years in Jerusalem. And his mother's name *was* Jedidah, the daughter of Adaiah of Boscath.

2And he did *that which was* right in the sight of the LORD, and walked in all the way of David his father, and turned not aside to the right hand or to the left.

ACTS 21:18–36

AND the *day* following Paul went in with us unto James; and all the elders were present.

19And when he had saluted them, he declared particularly what things God had wrought among the Gentiles by his ministry.

20And when they heard *it*, they glorified the Lord, and said unto him, Thou seest, brother, how many thousands of Jews there are which believe; and they are all zealous of the law:

21And they are informed of thee, that thou teachest all the Jews which are among the Gentiles to forsake Moses, saying that they ought not to circumcise *their* children, neither to walk after the customs.

22What is it therefore? the multitude must needs come together: for they will hear that thou art come.

23Do therefore this that we say to thee: We have four men which have a vow on them;

24Them take, and purify thyself with them, and be at charges with them, that they may shave *their* heads: and all may know that those things, whereof they were informed concerning thee, are nothing; but *that* thou thyself also walkest orderly, and keepest the law.

25As touching the Gentiles which believe, we have written *and* concluded that they observe no such thing, save only that they keep themselves from *things* offered to idols, and from blood, and from strangled, and from fornication.

26Then Paul took the men, and the next day purifying himself with them entered into the temple, to signify the accomplishment of the days of purification, until that an offering should be offered for every one of them.

27And when the seven days were almost ended, the Jews which were of Asia, when they saw him in the temple, stirred up all the people, and laid hands on him,

28Crying out, Men of Israel, help: This is the man, that teacheth all *men* every where against the people, and the law, and this place: and further brought Greeks also into the temple, and hath polluted this holy place.

29(For they had seen before with him in the city Trophimus an Ephesian, whom they supposed that Paul had brought into the temple.)

30And all the city was moved, and the people ran together: and they took Paul, and drew him out of the temple: and forthwith the doors were shut.

31And as they went about to kill him, tidings came unto the chief captain of the band, that all Jerusalem was in an uproar.

32Who immediately took soldiers and centurions, and ran down unto them: and when they saw the chief captain and the soldiers, they left beating of Paul.

33Then the chief captain came near, and took him, and commanded *him* to be bound with two chains; and demanded who he was, and what he had done.

34And some cried one thing, some another, among the multitude: and when he could not know the certainty for the tumult, he commanded him to be carried into the castle.

35And when he came upon the stairs, so it was, that he was borne of the soldiers for the violence of the people.

36For the multitude of the people followed after, crying, Away with him.

PSALM 150:1–6

PRAISE ye the LORD. Praise God in his sanctuary: praise him in the firmament of his power.

2Praise him for his mighty acts; praise him according to his excellent greatness.

3Praise him with the sound of the trumpet: praise him with the psaltery and harp.

⁴Praise him with the timbrel and dance: praise him with stringed instruments and organs.

⁵Praise him upon the loud cymbals: praise him upon the high sounding cymbals.

⁶Let every thing that hath breath praise the LORD. Praise ye the LORD.

PROVERBS FOR TODAY/ 18:9–10

He also that is slothful in his work is brother to him that is a great waster. ☐ *The name of the LORD is a strong tower: the righteous runneth into it, and is safe.*

JULY 3

2 KINGS 22:3—23:30

AND it came to pass in the eighteenth year of king Josiah, *that* the king sent Shaphan the son of Azaliah, the son of Meshullam, the scribe, to the house of the LORD, saying,

⁴Go up to Hilkiah the high priest, that he may sum the silver which is brought into the house of the LORD, which the keepers of the door have gathered of the people:

⁵And let them deliver it into the hand of the doers of the work, that have the oversight of the house of the LORD: and let them give it to the doers of the work which *is* in the house of the LORD, to repair the breaches of the house,

⁶Unto carpenters, and builders, and masons, and to buy timber and hewn stone to repair the house.

⁷Howbeit there was no reckoning made with them of the money that was delivered into their hand, because they dealt faithfully.

⁸And Hilkiah the high priest said unto Shaphan the scribe, I have found the book of the law in the house of the LORD. And Hilkiah gave the book to Shaphan, and he read it.

⁹And Shaphan the scribe came to the king, and brought the king word again, and said, Thy servants have gathered the money that was found in the house, and have delivered it into the hand of them that do the work, that have the oversight of the house of the LORD.

¹⁰And Shaphan the scribe shewed the king, saying, Hilkiah the priest hath delivered me a book. And Shaphan read it before the king.

¹¹And it came to pass, when the king had heard the words of the book of the law, that he rent his clothes.

¹²And the king commanded Hilkiah the priest, and Ahikam the son of Shaphan, and Achbor the son of Michaiah, and Shaphan the scribe, and Asahiah a servant of the king's, saying,

¹³Go ye, enquire of the LORD for me, and for the people, and for all Judah, concerning the words of this book that is found: for great *is* the wrath of the LORD that is kindled against us, because our fathers have not hearkened unto the words of this book, to do according unto all that which is written concerning us.

¹⁴So Hilkiah the priest, and Ahikam, and Achbor, and Shaphan, and Asahiah, went unto Huldah the prophetess, the wife of Shallum the son of Tikvah, the son of Harhas, keeper of the wardrobe; (now she dwelt in Jerusalem in her college;) and they communed with her.

¹⁵And she said unto them, Thus saith

the LORD God of Israel, Tell the man that sent you to me,

16Thus saith the LORD, Behold, I will bring evil upon this place, and upon the inhabitants thereof, *even* all the words of the book which the king of Judah hath read:

17Because they have forsaken me, and have burned incense unto other gods, that they might provoke me to anger with all the works of their hands; therefore my wrath shall be kindled against this place, and shall not be quenched.

18But to the king of Judah which sent you to enquire of the LORD, thus shall ye say to him, Thus saith the LORD God of Israel, *As touching* the words which thou hast heard;

19Because thine heart was tender, and thou hast humbled thyself before the LORD, when thou heardest what I spake against this place, and against the inhabitants thereof, that they should become a desolation and a curse, and hast rent thy clothes, and wept before me; I also have heard *thee,* saith the LORD.

20Behold therefore, I will gather thee unto thy fathers, and thou shalt be gathered into thy grave in peace; and thine eyes shall not see all the evil which I will bring upon this place. And they brought the king word again.

AND the king sent, and they gathered unto him all the elders of Judah and of Jerusalem.

2And the king went up into the house of the LORD, and all the men of Judah and all the inhabitants of Jerusalem with him, and the priests, and the prophets, and all the people, both small and great: and he read in their ears all the words of the book of the covenant which was found in the house of the LORD.

3And the king stood by a pillar, and made a covenant before the LORD, to walk after the LORD, and to keep his commandments and his testimonies and his statutes with all *their* heart and all *their* soul, to perform the words of this covenant that were written in this book. And all the people stood to the covenant.

4And the king commanded Hilkiah the high priest, and the priests of the second order, and the keepers of the door, to bring forth out of the temple of the LORD all the vessels that were made for Baal, and for the grove, and for all the host of heaven: and he burned them without Jerusalem in the fields of Kidron, and carried the ashes of them unto Beth–el.

5And he put down the idolatrous priests, whom the kings of Judah had ordained to burn incense in the high places in the cities of Judah, and in the places round about Jerusalem; them also that burned incense unto Baal, to the sun, and to the moon, and to the planets, and to all the host of heaven.

6And he brought out the grove from the house of the LORD, without Jerusalem, unto the brook Kidron, and burned it at the brook Kidron, and stamped *it* small to powder, and cast the powder thereof upon the graves of the children of the people.

7And he brake down the houses of the sodomites, that *were* by the house of the LORD, where the women wove hangings for the grove.

8And he brought all the priests out of the cities of Judah, and defiled the high places where the priests had burned incense, from Geba to Beer–sheba, and brake down the high places of the gates that *were* in the entering in of the gate of Joshua the governor of the city, which *were* on a man's left hand at the gate of the city.

9Nevertheless the priests of the high places came not up to the altar of the LORD in Jerusalem, but they did eat of the unleavened bread among their brethren.

10And he defiled Topheth, which *is* in the valley of the children of Hinnom, that no man might make his son or his daughter to pass through the fire to Molech.

11And he took away the horses that the kings of Judah had given to the sun, at the entering in of the house of the LORD, by the chamber of Nathan-melech the chamberlain, which *was* in the suburbs, and burned the chariots of the sun with fire.

12And the altars that *were* on the top of the upper chamber of Ahaz, which the kings of Judah had made, and the altars which Manasseh had made in the two courts of the house of the LORD, did the king beat down, and brake *them* down from thence, and cast the dust of them into the brook Kidron.

13And the high places that *were* before Jerusalem, which *were* on the right hand of the mount of corruption, which Solomon the king of Israel had builded for Ashtoreth the abomination of the Zidonians, and for Chemosh the abomination of the Moabites, and for Milcom the abomination of the children of Ammon, did the king defile.

14And he brake in pieces the images, and cut down the groves, and filled their places with the bones of men.

15Moreover the altar that *was* at Beth-el, *and* the high place which Jeroboam the son of Nebat, who made Israel to sin, had made, both that altar and the high place he brake down, and burned the high place, *and* stamped *it* small to powder, and burned the grove.

16And as Josiah turned himself, he spied the sepulchres that *were* there in the mount, and sent, and took the bones out of the sepulchres, and burned *them* upon the altar, and polluted it, according to the word of the LORD which the man of God proclaimed, who proclaimed these words.

17Then he said, What title *is* that that I see? And the men of the city told him, *It is* the sepulchre of the man of God, which came from Judah, and proclaimed these things that thou hast done against the altar of Beth-el.

18And he said, Let him alone; let no man move his bones. So they let his bones alone, with the bones of the prophet that came out of Samaria.

19And all the houses also of the high places that *were* in the cities of Samaria, which the kings of Israel had made to provoke *the LORD* to anger, Josiah took away, and did to them according to all the acts that he had done in Beth-el.

20And he slew all the priests of the high places that *were* there upon the altars, and burned men's bones upon them, and returned to Jerusalem.

21And the king commanded all the people, saying, Keep the passover unto the LORD your God, as *it is* written in the book of this covenant.

22Surely there was not holden such a passover from the days of the judges that judged Israel, nor in all the days of the kings of Israel, nor of the kings of Judah;

23But in the eighteenth year of king Josiah, *wherein* this passover was holden to the LORD in Jerusalem.

24Moreover the *workers with* familiar spirits, and the wizards, and the images, and the idols, and all the abominations that were spied in the land of Judah and in Jerusalem, did Josiah put away, that he might perform the words of the law which were written in the book that Hilkiah the priest found in the house of the LORD.

25And like unto him was there no king before him, that turned to the LORD with all his heart, and with all his soul, and with all his might, according to all the law of Moses; neither after him arose there *any* like him.

26Notwithstanding the LORD turned not from the fierceness of his great wrath, wherewith his anger was kindled against Judah, because of all the provocations that Manasseh had provoked him withal.

27And the LORD said, I will remove Judah also out of my sight, as I have removed Israel, and will cast off this city Jerusalem which I have chosen, and the house of which I said, My name shall be there.

28Now the rest of the acts of Josiah, and all that he did, *are* they not written in the book of the chronicles of the kings of Judah?

29In his days Pharaoh–nechoh king of Egypt went up against the king of Assyria to the river Euphrates: and king Josiah went against him; and he slew him at Megiddo, when he had seen him.

30And his servants carried him in a chariot dead from Megiddo, and brought him to Jerusalem, and buried him in his own sepulchre. And the people of the land took Jehoahaz the son of Josiah, and anointed him, and made him king in his father's stead.

ACTS 21:37—22:16

AND as Paul was to be led into the castle, he said unto the chief captain, May I speak unto thee? Who said, Canst thou speak Greek?

38Art not thou that Egyptian, which before these days madest an uproar, and leddest out into the wilderness four thousand men that were murderers?

39But Paul said, I am a man *which am* a Jew of Tarsus, *a city* in Cilicia, a citizen of no mean city: and, I beseech thee, suffer me to speak unto the people.

40And when he had given him licence, Paul stood on the stairs, and beckoned with the hand unto the people. And when there was made a great silence, he spake unto *them* in the Hebrew tongue, saying,

MEN, brethren, and fathers, hear ye my defence *which I make* now unto you.

2(And when they heard that he spake in the Hebrew tongue to them, they kept the more silence: and he saith,)

3I am verily a man *which am* a Jew, born in Tarsus, *a city* in Cilicia, yet brought up in this city at the feet of Gamaliel, *and* taught according to the perfect manner of the law of the fathers, and was zealous toward God, as ye all are this day.

4And I persecuted this way unto the death, binding and delivering into prisons both men and women.

5As also the high priest doth bear me witness, and all the estate of the elders: from whom also I received letters unto the brethren, and went to Damascus, to bring them which were there bound unto Jerusalem, for to be punished.

6And it came to pass, that, as I made my journey, and was come nigh unto Damascus about noon, suddenly there shone from heaven a great light round about me.

7And I fell unto the ground, and heard a voice saying unto me, Saul, Saul, why persecutest thou me?

8And I answered, Who art thou, Lord? And he said unto me, I am Jesus of Nazareth, whom thou persecutest.

9And they that were with me saw indeed the light, and were afraid; but they heard not the voice of him that spake to me.

10And I said, What shall I do, Lord? And the Lord said unto me, Arise, and go into Damascus; and there it shall be told thee of all things which are appointed for thee to do.

11And when I could not see for the glory of that light, being led by the hand of them that were with me, I came into Damascus.

12And one Ananias, a devout man according to the law, having a good report of all the Jews which dwelt *there,*

13Came unto me, and stood, and said unto me, Brother Saul, receive thy sight. And the same hour I looked up upon him.

14And he said, The God of our fathers hath chosen thee, that thou shouldest know his will, and see that Just One, and shouldest hear the voice of his mouth.

15For thou shalt be his witness unto all men of what thou hast seen and heard.

16And now why tarriest thou? arise, and be baptized, and wash away thy sins, calling on the name of the Lord.

PSALM 1:1–6

Blessed *is* the man that walk-eth not in the counsel of the ungodly, nor standeth in the way of sinners, nor sitteth in the seat of the scornful.

2But his delight *is* in the law of the Lord; and in his law doth he meditate day and night.

3And he shall be like a tree planted by the rivers of water, that bringeth forth his fruit in his season; his leaf also shall not wither; and whatsoever he doeth shall prosper.

4The ungodly *are* not so: but *are* like the chaff which the wind driveth away.

5Therefore the ungodly shall not stand in the judgment, nor sinners in the congregation of the righteous.

6For the Lord knoweth the way of the righteous: but the way of the ungodly shall perish.

PROVERBS FOR TODAY/ 18:11–12

The rich man's wealth is *his strong city, and as an high wall in his own conceit.* □ *Before destruction the heart of man is haughty, and before honour* is *humility.*

JULY 4

2 KINGS 23:31—25:30

Jehoahaz *was* twenty and three years old when he began to reign; and he reigned three months in Jerusalem. And his mother's name *was* Hamutal, the daughter of Jeremiah of Libnah.

32And he did *that which was* evil in the sight of the Lord, according to all that his fathers had done.

33And Pharaoh–nechoh put him in bands at Riblah in the land of Hamath, that he might not reign in Jerusalem; and put the land to a tribute of an hundred talents of silver, and a talent of gold.

34And Pharaoh–nechoh made Eliakim the son of Josiah king in the room of Josiah his father, and turned his name to Jehoiakim, and took Jehoahaz away: and he came to Egypt, and died there.

35And Jehoiakim gave the silver and the gold to Pharaoh; but he taxed the land to give the money according to the commandment of Pharaoh: he exacted the silver and the gold of the people of the land, of every one according to his taxation, to give *it* unto Pharaoh–nechoh.

36Jehoiakim *was* twenty and five years old when he began to reign; and he reigned eleven years in Jerusalem. And his mother's name *was* Zebudah, the daughter of Pedaiah of Rumah.

37And he did *that which was* evil in the sight of the LORD, according to all that his fathers had done.

In his days Nebuchadnezzar king of Babylon came up, and Jehoiakim became his servant three years: then he turned and rebelled against him.

2And the LORD sent against him bands of the Chaldees, and bands of the Syrians, and bands of the Moabites, and bands of the children of Ammon, and sent them against Judah to destroy it, according to the word of the LORD, which he spake by his servants the prophets.

3Surely at the commandment of the LORD came *this* upon Judah, to remove *them* out of his sight, for the sins of Manasseh, according to all that he did;

4And also for the innocent blood that he shed: for he filled Jerusalem with innocent blood; which the LORD would not pardon.

5Now the rest of the acts of Jehoiakim, and all that he did, *are* they not written in the book of the chronicles of the kings of Judah?

6So Jehoiakim slept with his fathers: and Jehoiachin his son reigned in his stead.

7And the king of Egypt came not again any more out of his land: for the king of Babylon had taken from the river of Egypt unto the river Euphrates all that pertained to the king of Egypt.

8Jehoiachin *was* eighteen years old when he began to reign, and he reigned in Jerusalem three months. And his mother's name *was* Nehushta, the daughter of Elnathan of Jerusalem.

9And he did *that which was* evil in the sight of the LORD, according to all that his father had done.

10At that time the servants of Nebuchadnezzar king of Babylon came up against Jerusalem, and the city was besieged.

11And Nebuchadnezzar king of Babylon came against the city, and his servants did besiege it.

12And Jehoiachin the king of Judah went out to the king of Babylon, he, and his mother, and his servants, and his princes, and his officers: and the king of Babylon took him in the eighth year of his reign.

13And he carried out thence all the treasures of the house of the LORD, and the treasures of the king's house, and cut in pieces all the vessels of gold which Solomon king of Israel had made in the temple of the LORD, as the LORD had said.

14And he carried away all Jerusalem, and all the princes, and all the mighty men of valour, *even* ten thousand captives, and all the craftsmen and smiths: none remained, save the poorest sort of the people of the land.

15And he carried away Jehoiachin to Babylon, and the king's mother, and the king's wives, and his officers, and the mighty of the land, *those* carried he into captivity from Jerusalem to Babylon.

16And all the men of might, *even* seven thousand, and craftsmen and smiths a thousand, all *that were* strong *and* apt for war, even them the king of Babylon brought captive to Babylon.

17And the king of Babylon made Mattaniah his father's brother king in his stead, and changed his name to Zedekiah.

18Zedekiah *was* twenty and one years old when he began to reign, and he reigned eleven years in Jerusalem. And his mother's name *was* Hamutal, the daughter of Jeremiah of Libnah.

19And he did *that which was* evil in the sight of the LORD, according to all that Jehoiakim had done.

20For through the anger of the LORD it came to pass in Jerusalem and Judah, until he had cast them out from his presence, that Zedekiah rebelled against the king of Babylon.

AND it came to pass in the ninth year of his reign, in the tenth month, in the tenth *day* of the month, *that* Nebuchadnezzar king of Babylon came, he, and all his host, against Jerusalem, and pitched against it; and they built forts against it round about.

2And the city was besieged unto the eleventh year of king Zedekiah.

3And on the ninth *day* of the *fourth* month the famine prevailed in the city, and there was no bread for the people of the land.

4And the city was broken up, and all the men of war *fled* by night by the way of the gate between two walls, which *is* by the king's garden: (now the Chaldees *were* against the city round about:) and *the king* went the way toward the plain.

5And the army of the Chaldees pursued after the king, and overtook him in the plains of Jericho: and all his army were scattered from him.

6So they took the king, and brought him up to the king of Babylon to Riblah; and they gave judgment upon him.

7And they slew the sons of Zedekiah before his eyes, and put out the eyes of Zedekiah, and bound him with fetters of brass, and carried him to Babylon.

8And in the fifth month, on the seventh *day* of the month, which *is* the nineteenth year of king Nebuchadnezzar king of Babylon, came Nebuzaradan, captain of the guard, a servant of the king of Babylon, unto Jerusalem:

9And he burnt the house of the LORD, and the king's house, and all the houses of Jerusalem, and every great *man's* house burnt he with fire.

10And all the army of the Chaldees, that *were with* the captain of the guard, brake down the walls of Jerusalem round about.

11Now the rest of the people *that were* left in the city, and the fugitives that fell away to the king of Babylon, with the remnant of the multitude, did Nebuzar–adan the captain of the guard carry away.

12But the captain of the guard left of the poor of the land *to be* vinedressers and husbandmen.

13And the pillars of brass that *were* in the house of the LORD, and the bases, and the brasen sea that *was* in the house of the LORD, did the Chaldees break in pieces, and carried the brass of them to Babylon.

14And the pots, and the shovels, and the snuffers, and the spoons, and all the vessels of brass wherewith they ministered, took they away.

15And the firepans, and the bowls, *and* such things as *were* of gold, *in* gold, and of silver, *in* silver, the captain of the guard took away.

16The two pillars, one sea, and the bases which Solomon had made for the house of the LORD; the brass of all these vessels was without weight.

17The height of the one pillar *was* eighteen cubits, and the chapiter upon it *was* brass: and the height of the chapiter three cubits: and the wreathen work, and pomegranates upon the chapiter round about, all of brass: and like unto these had the second pillar with wreathen work.

18And the captain of the guard took Seraiah the chief priest, and Zephaniah the second priest, and the three keepers of the door:

19And out of the city he took an officer that was set over the men of war, and five men of them that were in the king's presence, which were found in the city, and the principal scribe of the host, which mustered the people of the land, and threescore men of the people of the land *that were* found in the city:

20And Nebuzar–adan captain of the guard took these, and brought them to the king of Babylon to Riblah:

21And the king of Babylon smote them, and slew them at Riblah in the land of Hamath. So Judah was carried away out of their land.

22And *as for* the people that remained in the land of Judah, whom Nebuchadnezzar king of Babylon had left, even over them he made Gedaliah the son of Ahikam, the son of Shaphan, ruler.

23And when all the captains of the armies, they and their men, heard that the king of Babylon had made Gedaliah governor, there came to Gedaliah to Mizpah, even Ishmael the son of Nethaniah, and Johanan the son of Careah, and Seraiah the son of Tanhumeth the Netophathite, and Jaazaniah the son of a Maachathite, they and their men.

24And Gedaliah sware to them, and to their men, and said unto them, Fear not to be the servants of the Chaldees: dwell in the land, and serve the king of Babylon; and it shall be well with you.

25But it came to pass in the seventh month, that Ishmael the son of Nethaniah, the son of Elishama, of the seed royal, came, and ten men with him, and smote Gedaliah, that he died, and the Jews and the Chaldees, that were with him at Mizpah.

26And all the people, both small and great, and the captains of the armies, arose, and came to Egypt: for they were afraid of the Chaldees.

27And it came to pass in the seven and thirtieth year of the captivity of Jehoiachin king of Judah, in the twelfth month, on the seven and twentieth *day* of the month, *that* Evil–merodach king of Babylon in the year that he began to reign did lift up the head of Jehoiachin king of Judah out of prison;

28And he spake kindly to him, and set his throne above the throne of the kings that *were* with him in Babylon;

29And changed his prison garments: and he did eat bread continually before him all the days of his life.

30And his allowance *was* a continual allowance given him of the king, a daily rate for every day, all the days of his life.

ACTS 22:17—23:10

AND it came to pass, that, when I was come again to Jerusalem, even while I prayed in the temple, I was in a trance;

18And saw him saying unto me, Make haste, and get thee quickly out of Jerusalem: for they will not receive thy testimony concerning me.

19And I said, Lord, they know that I imprisoned and beat in every synagogue them that believed on thee:

20And when the blood of thy martyr Stephen was shed, I also was standing by, and consenting unto his death, and kept the raiment of them that slew him.

21And he said unto me, Depart: for I will send thee far hence unto the Gentiles.

22And they gave him audience unto this word, and *then* lifted up their voices, and said, Away with such a *fellow* from the earth: for it is not fit that he should live.

23And as they cried out, and cast off *their* clothes, and threw dust into the air,

24The chief captain commanded him to be brought into the castle, and bade that he should be examined by scourging; that he might know wherefore they cried so against him.

25And as they bound him with thongs, Paul said unto the centurion that stood by, Is it lawful for you to scourge a man that is a Roman, and uncondemned?

26When the centurion heard *that*, he went and told the chief captain, saying, Take heed what thou doest: for this man is a Roman.

27Then the chief captain came, and said unto him, Tell me, art thou a Roman? He said, Yea.

28And the chief captain answered, With a great sum obtained I this freedom. And Paul said, But I was *free* born.

29Then straightway they departed from him which should have examined him: and the chief captain also was afraid, after he knew that he was a Roman, and because he had bound him.

30On the morrow, because he would have known the certainty wherefore he was accused of the Jews, he loosed him from *his* bands, and commanded the chief priests and all their council to appear, and brought Paul down, and set him before them.

AND Paul, earnestly beholding the council, said, Men *and* brethren, I have lived in all good conscience before God unto this day.

2And the high priest Ananias commanded them that stood by him to smite him on the mouth.

3Then said Paul unto him, God shall smite thee, *thou* whited wall: for sittest thou to judge me after the law, and commandest me to be smitten contrary to the law?

4And they that stood by said, Revilest thou God's high priest?

5Then said Paul, I wist not, brethren, that he was the high priest: for it is written, Thou shalt not speak evil of the ruler of thy people.

6But when Paul perceived that the one part were Sadducees, and the other Pharisees, he cried out in the council, Men *and* brethren, I am a Pharisee, the son of a Pharisee: of the hope and resurrection of the dead I am called in question.

7And when he had so said, there arose a dissension between the Pharisees and the Sadducees: and the multitude was divided.

8For the Sadducees say that there is no resurrection, neither angel, nor spirit: but the Pharisees confess both.

9And there arose a great cry: and the scribes *that were* of the Pharisees' part arose, and strove, saying, We find no evil in this man: but if a spirit or an angel hath spoken to him, let us not fight against God.

10And when there arose a great dissension, the chief captain, fearing lest Paul should have been pulled in pieces of them, commanded the soldiers to go down, and to take him by force from among them, and to bring *him* into the castle.

PSALM 2:1–12

HY do the heathen rage, and the people imagine a vain thing?

2The kings of the earth set themselves, and the rulers take counsel together, against the LORD, and against his anointed, *saying,*

3Let us break their bands asunder, and cast away their cords from us.

4He that sitteth in the heavens shall laugh: the Lord shall have them in derision.

5Then shall he speak unto them in his wrath, and vex them in his sore displeasure.

6Yet have I set my king upon my holy hill of Zion.

7I will declare the decree: the LORD hath said unto me, Thou *art* my Son; this day have I begotten thee.

8Ask of me, and I shall give *thee* the heathen *for* thine inheritance, and the uttermost parts of the earth *for* thy possession.

9Thou shalt break them with a rod of iron; thou shalt dash them in pieces like a potter's vessel.

10Be wise now therefore, O ye kings: be instructed, ye judges of the earth.

11Serve the LORD with fear, and rejoice with trembling.

12Kiss the Son, lest he be angry, and ye perish *from* the way, when his wrath is kindled but a little. Blessed *are* all they that put their trust in him.

PROVERBS FOR TODAY/ 18:13
He that answereth a matter before he heareth it, *it is folly and shame unto him.*

JULY 5

1 CHRONICLES 1:1—2:17

ADAM, Sheth, Enosh,
²Kenan, Mahalaleel, Jered,
³Henoch, Methuselah, Lamech,

⁴Noah, Shem, Ham, and Japheth.

⁵The sons of Japheth; Gomer, and Magog, and Madai, and Javan, and Tubal, and Meshech, and Tiras.

⁶And the sons of Gomer; Ashchenaz, and Riphath, and Togarmah.

⁷And the sons of Javan; Elishah, and Tarshish, Kittim, and Dodanim.

⁸The sons of Ham; Cush, and Mizraim, Put, and Canaan.

⁹And the sons of Cush; Seba, and Havilah, and Sabta, and Raamah, and Sabtecha. And the sons of Raamah; Sheba, and Dedan.

¹⁰And Cush begat Nimrod: he began to be mighty upon the earth.

¹¹And Mizraim begat Ludim, and Anamim, and Lehabim, and Naphtuhim,

¹²And Pathrusim, and Casluhim, (of whom came the Philistines,) and Caphthorim.

¹³And Canaan begat Zidon his firstborn, and Heth,

¹⁴The Jebusite also, and the Amorite, and the Girgashite,

¹⁵And the Hivite, and the Arkite, and the Sinite,

¹⁶And the Arvadite, and the Zemarite, and the Hamathite.

¹⁷The sons of Shem; Elam, and Asshur, and Arphaxad, and Lud and Aram, and Uz, and Hul, and Gether, and Meshech.

¹⁸And Arphaxad begat Shelah, and Shelah begat Eber.

¹⁹And unto Eber were born two sons: the name of the one *was* Peleg; because in his days the earth was divided: and his brother's name *was* Joktan.

²⁰And Joktan begat Almodad, and Sheleph, and Hazar–maveth, and Jerah,

²¹Hadoram also, and Uzal, and Diklah,

²²And Ebal, and Abimael, and Sheba,

²³And Ophir, and Havilah, and Jobab. All these *were* the sons of Joktan.

²⁴Shem, Arphaxad, Shelah,

²⁵Eber, Peleg, Reu,

²⁶Serug, Nahor, Terah,

²⁷Abram; the same *is* Abraham.

²⁸The sons of Abraham; Isaac, and Ishmael.

²⁹These *are* their generations: The firstborn of Ishmael, Nebaioth; then Kedar, and Adbeel, and Mibsam,

³⁰Mishma, and Dumah, Massa, Hadad, and Tema,

³¹Jetur, Naphish, and Kedemah. These are the sons of Ishmael.

³²Now the sons of Keturah, Abraham's concubine: she bare Zimran, and Jokshan, and Medan, and Midian, and Ishbak, and Shuah. And the sons of Jokshan; Sheba, and Dedan.

³³And the sons of Midian; Ephah, and Epher, and Henoch, and Abida, and Eldaah. All these *are* the sons of Keturah.

³⁴And Abraham begat Isaac. The sons of Isaac; Esau and Israel.

³⁵The sons of Esau; Eliphaz, Reuel, and Jeush, and Jaalam, and Korah.

³⁶The sons of Eliphaz; Teman, and

Omar, Zephi, and Gatam, Kenaz, and Timna, and Amalek.

37The sons of Reuel; Nahath, Zerah, Shammah, and Mizzah.

38And the sons of Seir; Lotan, and Shobal, and Zibeon, and Anah, and Dishon, and Ezar, and Dishan.

39And the sons of Lotan; Hori, and Homam: and Timna *was* Lotan's sister.

40The sons of Shobal; Alian, and Manahath, and Ebal, Shephi, and Onam. And the sons of Zibeon; Aiah, and Anah.

41The sons of Anah; Dishon. And the sons of Dishon; Amram, and Eshban, and Ithran, and Cheran.

42The sons of Ezer; Bilhan, and Zavan, *and* Jakan. The sons of Dishan; Uz, and Aran.

43Now these *are* the kings that reigned in the land of Edom before *any* king reigned over the children of Israel; Bela the son of Beor: and the name of his city *was* Dinhabah.

44And when Bela was dead, Jobab the son of Zerah of Bozrah reigned in his stead.

45And when Jobab was dead, Husham of the land of the Temanites reigned in his stead.

46And when Husham was dead, Hadad the son of Bedad, which smote Midian in the field of Moab, reigned in his stead: and the name of his city *was* Avith.

47And when Hadad was dead, Samlah of Masrekah reigned in his stead.

48And when Samlah was dead, Shaul of Rehoboth by the river reigned in his stead.

49And when Shaul was dead, Baal–hanan the son of Achbor reigned in his stead.

50And when Baal–hanan was dead, Hadad reigned in his stead: and the name of his city *was* Pai; and his wife's name *was* Mehetabel, the daughter of Matred, the daughter of Mezahab.

51Hadad died also. And the dukes of Edom were; duke Timnah, duke Aliah, duke Jetheth,

52Duke Aholibamah, duke Elah, duke Pinon,

53Duke Kenaz, duke Teman, duke Mibzar,

54Duke Magdiel, duke Iram. These *are* the dukes of Edom.

THESE *are* the sons of Israel; Reuben, Simeon, Levi, and Judah, Issachar, and Zebulun,

2Dan, Joseph, and Benjamin, Naphtali, Gad, and Asher.

3The sons of Judah; Er, and Onan, and Shelah: *which* three were born unto him of the daughter of Shua the Canaanitess. And Er, the firstborn of Judah, was evil in the sight of the LORD; and he slew him.

4And Tamar his daughter in law bare him Pharez and Zerah. All the sons of Judah *were* five.

5The sons of Pharez; Hezron, and Hamul.

6And the sons of Zerah; Zimri, and Ethan, and Heman, and Calcol, and Dara: five of them in all.

7And the sons of Carmi; Achar, the troubler of Israel, who transgressed in the thing accursed.

8And the sons of Ethan; Azariah.

9The sons also of Hezron, that were born unto him; Jerahmeel, and Ram, and Chelubai.

10And Ram begat Amminadab; and Amminadab begat Nahshon, prince of the children of Judah;

11And Nahshon begat Salma, and Salma begat Boaz,

12And Boaz begat Obed, and Obed begat Jesse,

13And Jesse begat his firstborn Eliab, and Abinadab the second, and Shimma the third,

14Nethaneel the fourth, Raddai the fifth,

15Ozem the sixth, David the seventh:

16Whose sisters *were* Zeruiah, and Abigail. And the sons of Zeruiah; Abishai, and Joab, and Asahel, three.

17And Abigail bare Amasa: and the father of Amasa *was* Jether the Ishmeelite.

ACTS 23:11–35

A ND the night following the Lord stood by him, and said, Be of good cheer, Paul: for as thou hast testified of me in Jerusalem, so must thou bear witness also at Rome.

12And when it was day, certain of the Jews banded together, and bound themselves under a curse, saying that they would neither eat nor drink till they had killed Paul.

13And they were more than forty which had made this conspiracy.

14And they came to the chief priests and elders, and said, We have bound ourselves under a great curse, that we will eat nothing until we have slain Paul.

15Now therefore ye with the council signify to the chief captain that he bring him down unto you to morrow, as though ye would enquire something more perfectly concerning him: and we, or ever he come near, are ready to kill him.

16And when Paul's sister's son heard of their lying in wait, he went and entered into the castle, and told Paul.

17Then Paul called one of the centurions unto *him*, and said, Bring this young man unto the chief captain: for he hath a certain thing to tell him.

18So he took him, and brought *him* to the chief captain, and said, Paul the prisoner called me unto *him*, and prayed me to bring this young man unto thee, who hath something to say unto thee.

19Then the chief captain took him by the hand, and went *with him* aside privately, and asked *him,* What is that thou hast to tell me?

20And he said, The Jews have agreed to desire thee that thou wouldest bring down Paul to morrow into the council, as though they would enquire somewhat of him more perfectly.

21But do not thou yield unto them: for there lie in wait for him of them more than forty men, which have bound themselves with an oath, that they will neither eat nor drink till they have killed him: and now are they ready, looking for a promise from thee.

22So the chief captain *then* let the young man depart, and charged *him, See thou* tell no man that thou hast shewed these things to me.

23And he called unto *him* two centurions, saying, Make ready two hundred soldiers to go to Caesarea, and horsemen threescore and ten, and spearmen two hundred, at the third hour of the night;

24And provide *them* beasts, that they may set Paul on, and bring *him* safe unto Felix the governor.

25And he wrote a letter after this manner:

26Claudius Lysias unto the most excellent governor Felix *sendeth* greeting.

27This man was taken of the Jews, and should have been killed of them: then came I with an army, and rescued him, having understood that he was a Roman.

28And when I would have known the cause wherefore they accused him, I brought him forth into their council:

29Whom I perceived to be accused of questions of their law, but to have nothing laid to his charge worthy of death or of bonds.

30And when it was told me how that the Jews laid wait for the man, I sent straightway to thee, and gave commandment to his accusers also to say before thee what *they had* against him. Farewell.

31Then the soldiers, as it was commanded them, took Paul, and brought *him* by night to Antipatris.

32On the morrow they left the horsemen to go with him, and returned to the castle:

33Who, when they came to Caesarea, and delivered the epistle to the governor, presented Paul also before him.

34And when the governor had read *the letter,* he asked of what province he was. And when he understood that *he was* of Cilicia;

35I will hear thee, said he, when thine accusers are also come. And he commanded him to be kept in Herod's judgment hall.

PSALM 3:1–8

Lord, how are they increased that trouble me! many *are* they that rise up against me.

2Many *there be* which say of my soul, *There is* no help for him in God. Selah.

3But thou, O Lord, *art* a shield for me; my glory, and the lifter up of mine head.

4I cried unto the Lord with my voice, and he heard me out of his holy hill. Selah.

5I laid me down and slept; I awaked; for the Lord sustained me.

6I will not be afraid of ten thousands of people, that have set *themselves* against me round about.

7Arise, O Lord; save me, O my God: for thou hast smitten all mine enemies *upon* the cheek bone; thou hast broken the teeth of the ungodly.

8Salvation *belongeth* unto the Lord: thy blessing *is* upon thy people. Selah.

PROVERBS FOR TODAY/ 18:14–15

The spirit of a man will sustain his infirmity; but a wounded spirit who can bear? □ *The heart of the prudent getteth knowledge; and the ear of the wise seeketh knowledge.*

JULY 6

1 CHRONICLES 2:18—4:4

And Caleb the son of Hezron begat *children* of Azubah *his* wife, and of Jerioth: her sons *are* these; Jesher, and Shobab, and Ardon.

19And when Azubah was dead, Caleb took unto him Ephrath, which bare him Hur.

20And Hur begat Uri, and Uri begat Bezaleel.

21And afterward Hezron went in to the daughter of Machir the father of Gilead, whom he married when he *was* threescore years old; and she bare him Segub.

22And Segub begat Jair, who had three and twenty cities in the land of Gilead.

23And he took Geshur, and Aram, with the towns of Jair, from them, with Kenath, and the towns thereof, *even* threescore cities. All these *belonged* to the sons of Machir the father of Gilead.

24And after that Hezron was dead in Caleb–ephratah, then Abiah Hezron's wife bare him Ashur the father of Tekoa.

25And the sons of Jarahmeel the firstborn of Hezron were, Ram the firstborn, and Bunah, and Oren, and Ozem, *and* Ahijah.

26Jerahmeel had also another wife, whose name *was* Atarah; she *was* the mother of Onam.

27And the sons of Ram the firstborn of Jerahmeel were, Maaz, and Jamin, and Eker.

28And the sons of Onam were,

Shammai, and Jada. And the sons of Shammai; Nadab, and Abishur.

29And the name of the wife of Abishur *was* Abihail, and she bare him Ahban, and Molid.

30And the sons of Nadab; Seled, and Appaim: but Seled died without children.

31And the sons of Appaim; Ishi. And the sons of Ishi; Sheshan. And the children of Sheshan; Ahlai.

32And the sons of Jada the brother of Shammai; Jether, and Jonathan: and Jether died without children.

33And the sons of Jonathan; Peleth, and Zaza. These were the sons of Jerahmeel.

34Now Sheshan had no sons, but daughters. And Sheshan had a servant, an Egyptian, whose name *was* Jarha.

35And Sheshan gave his daughter to Jarha his servant to wife; and she bare him Attai.

36And Attai begat Nathan, and Nathan begat Zabad,

37And Zabad begat Ephlal, and Ephlal begat Obed,

38And Obed begat Jehu, and Jehu begat Azariah,

39And Azariah begat Helez, and Helez begat Eleasah,

40And Eleasah begat Sisamai, and Sisamai begat Shallum,

41And Shallum begat Jekamiah, and Jekamiah begat Elishama.

42Now the sons of Caleb the brother of Jerahmeel *were,* Mesha his firstborn, which *was* the father of Ziph; and the sons of Mareshah the father of Hebron.

43And the sons of Hebron; Korah, and Tappuah, and Rekem, and Shema.

44And Shema begat Raham, the father of Jorkoam: and Rekem begat Shammai.

45And the son of Shammai *was* Maon: and Maon *was* the father of Beth–zur.

46And Ephah, Caleb's concubine, bare Haran, and Moza, and Gazez: and Haran begat Gazez.

47And the sons of Jahdai; Regem, and Jotham, and Gesham, and Pelet, and Ephah, and Shaaph.

48Maachah, Caleb's concubine, bare Sheber, and Tirhanah.

49She bare also Shaaph the father of Madmannah, Sheva the father of Machbenah, and the father of Gibea: and the daughter of Caleb *was* Achsa.

50These were the sons of Caleb the son of Hur, the firstborn of Ephratah; Shobal the father of Kirjath–jearim,

51Salma the father of Beth–lehem, Hareph the father of Beth–gader.

52And Shobal the father of Kirjath–jearim had sons; Haroeh, *and* half of the Manahethites.

53And the families of Kirjath–jearim; the Ithrites, and the Puhites, and the Shumathites, and the Mishraites; of them came the Zareathites, and the Eshtaulites.

54The sons of Salma; Beth–lehem, and the Netophathites, Ataroth, the house of Joab, and half of the Manahethites, the Zorites.

55And the families of the scribes which dwelt at Jabez; the Tirathites, the Shimeathites, *and* Suchathites. These *are* the Kenites that came of Hemath, the father of the house of Rechab.

Now these were the sons of David, which were born unto him in Hebron; the firstborn Amnon, of Ahinoam the Jezreelitess; the second Daniel of Abigail the Carmelitess:

2The third, Absalom the son of Maachah the daughter of Talmai king of Geshur: the fourth, Adonijah the son of Haggith:

3The fifth, Shephatiah of Abital: the sixth, Ithream by Eglah his wife.

4*These* six were born unto him in Hebron; and there he reigned seven years and six months: and in Jerusalem he reigned thirty and three years.

5And these were born unto him in Jerusalem; Shimea, and Shobab, and

Nathan, and Solomon, four, of Bath–shua the daughter of Ammiel:

6Ibhar also, and Elishama, and Eliphelet,

7And Nogah, and Nepheg, and Japhia,

8And Elishama, and Eliada, and Eliphelet, nine.

9*These were* all the sons of David, beside the sons of the concubines, and Tamar their sister.

10And Solomon's son *was* Rehoboam, Abia his son, Asa his son, Jehoshaphat his son,

11Joram his son, Ahaziah his son, Joash his son,

12Amaziah his son, Azariah his son, Jotham his son,

13Ahaz his son, Hezekiah his son, Manasseh his son,

14Amon his son, Josiah his son.

15And the sons of Josiah *were,* the firstborn Johanan, the second Jehoiakim, the third Zedekiah, the fourth Shallum.

16And the sons of Jehoiakim: Jeconiah his son, Zedekiah his son.

17And the sons of Jeconiah; Assir, Salathiel his son,

18Malchiram also, and Pedaiah, and Shenazar, Jecamiah, Hoshama, and Nedabiah.

19And the sons of Pedaiah *were,* Zerubbabel, and Shimei: and the sons of Zerubbabel; Meshullam, and Hananiah, and Shelomith their sister:

20And Hashubah, and Ohel, and Berechiah, and Hasadiah, Jushab–hesed, five.

21And the sons of Hananiah; Pelatiah, and Jesaiah: the sons of Rephaiah, the sons of Arnan, the sons of Obadiah, the sons of Shechaniah.

22And the sons of Shechaniah; Shemaiah: and the sons of Shemaiah; Hattush, and Igeal, and Bariah, and Neariah, and Shaphat, six.

23And the sons of Neariah; Elioenai, and Hezekiah, and Azrikam, three.

24And the sons of Elioenai *were,* Hodaiah, and Eliashib, and Pelaiah, and

Akkub, and Johanan, and Dalaiah, and Anani, seven.

THE sons of Judah; Pharez, Hezron, and Carmi, and Hur, and Shobal.

2And Reaiah the son of Shobal begat Jahath; and Jahath begat Ahumai, and Lahad. These *are* the families of the Zorathites.

3And these *were of* the father of Etam; Jezreel, and Ishma, and Idbash: and the name of their sister *was* Hazelelponi:

4And Penuel the father of Gedor, and Ezer the father of Hushah. These *are* the sons of Hur, the firstborn of Ephratah, the father of Beth–lehem.

ACTS 24:1–27

AND after five days Ananias the high priest descended with the elders, and *with* a certain orator *named* Tertullus, who informed the governor against Paul.

2And when he was called forth, Tertullus began to accuse *him,* saying, Seeing that by thee we enjoy great quietness, and that very worthy deeds are done unto this nation by thy providence,

3We accept *it* always, and in all places, most noble Felix, with all thankfulness.

4Notwithstanding, that I be not further tedious unto thee, I pray thee that thou wouldest hear us of thy clemency a few words.

5For we have found this man *a* pestilent *fellow,* and a mover of sedition among all the Jews throughout the world, and a ringleader of the sect of the Nazarenes:

6Who also hath gone about to profane the temple: whom we took, and would have judged according to our law.

7But the chief captain Lysias came *upon us,* and with great violence took *him* away out of our hands,

8Commanding his accusers to come unto thee: by examining of whom thyself mayest take knowledge of all these things, whereof we accuse him.

9And the Jews also assented, saying that these things were so.

10Then Paul, after that the governor had beckoned unto him to speak, answered, Forasmuch as I know that thou hast been of many years a judge unto this nation, I do the more cheerfully answer for myself:

11Because that thou mayest understand, that there are yet but twelve days since I went up to Jerusalem for to worship.

12And they neither found me in the temple disputing with any man, neither raising up the people, neither in the synagogues, nor in the city:

13Neither can they prove the things whereof they now accuse me.

14But this I confess unto thee, that after the way which they call heresy, so worship I the God of my fathers, believing all things which are written in the law and in the prophets:

15And have hope toward God, which they themselves also allow, that there shall be a resurrection of the dead, both of the just and unjust.

16And herein do I exercise myself, to have always a conscience void of offence toward God, and *toward* men.

17Now after many years I came to bring alms to my nation, and offerings.

18Whereupon certain Jews from Asia found me purified in the temple, neither with multitude, nor with tumult.

19Who ought to have been here before thee, and object, if they had ought against me.

20Or else let these same *here* say, if they have found any evil doing in me, while I stood before the council,

21Except it be for this one voice, that I cried standing among them, Touching the resurrection of the dead I am called in question by you this day.

22And when Felix heard these things, having more perfect knowledge of *that* way, he deferred them, and said, When Lysias the chief captain shall come down, I will know the uttermost of your matter.

23And he commanded a centurion to keep Paul, and to let *him* have liberty, and that he should forbid none of his acquaintance to minister or come unto him.

24And after certain days, when Felix came with his wife Drusilla, which was a Jewess, he sent for Paul, and heard him concerning the faith in Christ.

25And as he reasoned of righteousness, temperance, and judgment to come, Felix trembled, and answered, Go thy way for this time; when I have a convenient season, I will call for thee.

26He hoped also that money should have been given him of Paul, that he might loose him: wherefore he sent for him the oftener, and communed with him.

27But after two years Porcius Festus came into Felix' room: and Felix, willing to shew the Jews a pleasure, left Paul bound.

PSALM 4:1–8

HEAR me when I call, O God of my righteousness: thou hast enlarged me *when I was* in distress; have mercy upon me, and hear my prayer.

2O ye sons of men, how long *will ye turn* my glory into shame? *how long* will ye love vanity, *and* seek after leasing? Selah.

3But know that the LORD hath set apart him that is godly for himself: the LORD will hear when I call unto him.

4Stand in awe, and sin not: commune with your own heart upon your bed, and be still. Selah.

5Offer the sacrifices of righteousness, and put your trust in the LORD.

6*There be* many that say, Who will shew us *any* good? LORD, lift thou up the light of thy countenance upon us.

7Thou hast put gladness in my heart, more than in the time *that* their corn and their wine increased.

8I will both lay me down in peace, and sleep: for thou, LORD, only makest me dwell in safety.

PROVERBS FOR TODAY/ 18:16–18

A man's gift maketh room for him, and bringeth him before great men. □ He that is *first in his own cause* seemeth *just; but his neighbour cometh and searcheth him.* □ *The lot causeth contentions to cease, and parteth between the mighty.*

JULY 7

1 CHRONICLES 4:5—5:17

AND Ashur the father of Tekoa had two wives, Helah and Naarah.

6And Naarah bare him Ahuzam, and Hepher, and Temeni, and Haahashtari. These *were* the sons of Naarah.

7And the sons of Helah *were*, Zereth, and Jezoar, and Ethnan.

8And Coz begat Anub, and Zobebah, and the families of Aharhel the son of Harum.

9And Jabez was more honourable than his brethren: and his mother called his name Jabez, saying, Because I bare him with sorrow.

10And Jabez called on the God of Israel, saying, Oh that thou wouldest bless me indeed, and enlarge my coast, and that thine hand might be with me, and that thou wouldest keep *me* from evil, that it may not grieve me! And God granted him that which he requested.

11And Chelub the brother of Shuah begat Mehir, which *was* the father of Eshton.

12And Eshton begat Beth–rapha, and Paseah, and Tehinnah the father of Irnahash. These *are* the men of Rechah.

13And the sons of Kenaz; Othniel, and Seraiah: and the sons of Othniel; Hathath.

14And Meonothai begat Ophrah: and Seraiah begat Joab, the father of the valley of Charashim; for they were craftsmen.

15And the sons of Caleb the son of Jephunneh; Iru, Elah, and Naam: and the sons of Elah, even Kenaz.

16And the sons of Jehaleleel; Ziph, and Ziphah, Tiria, and Asareel.

17And the sons of Ezra *were*, Jether, and Mered, and Epher, and Jalon: and she bare Miriam, and Shammai, and Ishbah the father of Eshtemoa.

18And his wife Jehudijah bare Jered the father of Gedor, and Heber the father of Socho, and Jekuthiel the father of Zanoah. And these *are* the sons of Bithiah the daughter of Pharaoh, which Mered took.

19And the sons of *his* wife Hodiah the sister of Naham, the father of Keilah the Garmite, and Eshtemoa the Maachathite.

20And the sons of Shimon *were*, Amnon, and Rinnah, Ben–hanan, and Tilon. And the sons of Ishi *were*, Zoheth, and Ben–zoheth.

21The sons of Shelah the son of Judah *were*, Er the father of Lecah, and Laadah the father of Mareshah, and the families of the house of them that wrought fine linen, of the house of Ashbea,

22And Jokim, and the men of

Chozeba, and Joash, and Saraph, who had the dominion in Moab, and Jashubi-lehem. And *these are* ancient things.

23These *were* the potters, and those that dwelt among plants and hedges: there they dwelt with the king for his work.

24The sons of Simeon *were,* Nemuel, and Jamin, Jarib, Zerah, *and* Shaul:

25Shallum his son, Mibsam his son, Mishma his son.

26And the sons of Mishma; Hamuel his son, Zacchur his son, Shimei his son.

27And Shimei had sixteen sons and six daughters; but his brethren had not many children, neither did all their family multiply, like to the children of Judah.

28And they dwelt at Beer–sheba, and Moladah, and Hazar–shual,

29And at Bilhah, and at Ezem, and at Tolad,

30And at Bethuel, and at Hormah, and at Ziklag,

31And at Beth–marcaboth, and Hazar–susim, and at Beth–birei, and at Shaaraim. These *were* their cities unto the reign of David.

32And their villages *were,* Etam, and Ain, Rimmon, and Tochen, and Ashan, five cities:

33And all their villages that *were* round about the same cities, unto Baal. These *were* their habitations, and their genealogy.

34And Meshobab, and Jamlech, and Joshah the son of Amaziah,

35And Joel, and Jehu the son of Josibiah, the son of Seraiah, the son of Asiel,

36And Elioenai, and Jaakobah, and Jeshohaiah, and Asaiah, and Adiel, and Jesimiel, and Benaiah,

37And Ziza the son of Shiphi, the son of Allon, the son of Jedaiah, the son of Shimri, the son of Shemaiah;

38These mentioned by *their* names *were* princes in their families: and the house of their fathers increased greatly.

39And they went to the entrance of Gedor, *even* unto the east side of the valley, to seek pasture for their flocks.

40And they found fat pasture and good, and the land *was* wide, and quiet, and peaceable; for *they* of Ham had dwelt there of old.

41And these written by name came in the days of Hezekiah king of Judah, and smote their tents, and the habitations that were found there, and destroyed them utterly unto this day, and dwelt in their rooms: because *there was* pasture there for their flocks.

42And *some* of them, *even* of the sons of Simeon, five hundred men, went to mount Seir, having for their captains Pelatiah, and Neariah, and Rephaiah, and Uzziel, the sons of Ishi.

43And they smote the rest of the Amalekites that were escaped, and dwelt there unto this day.

Now the sons of Reuben the firstborn of Israel, (for he *was* the firstborn; but, forasmuch as he defiled his father's bed, his birthright was given unto the sons of Joseph the son of Israel: and the genealogy is not to be reckoned after the birthright.

2For Judah prevailed above his brethren, and of him *came* the chief ruler; but the birthright *was* Joseph's:)

3The sons, *I say,* of Reuben the firstborn of Israel *were,* Hanoch, and Pallu, Hezron, and Carmi.

4The sons of Joel; Shemaiah his son, Gog his son, Shimei his son,

5Micah his son, Reaia his son, Baal his son,

6Beerah his son, whom Tilgath-pilneser king of Assyria carried away *captive:* he *was* prince of the Reubenites.

7And his brethren by their families, when the genealogy of their generations was reckoned, *were* the chief, Jeiel, and Zechariah,

8And Bela the son of Azaz, the son of Shema, the son of Joel, who dwelt in Aroer, even unto Nebo and Baal–meon:

9And eastward he inhabited unto the

entering in of the wilderness from the river Euphrates: because their cattle were multiplied in the land of Gilead.

10And in the days of Saul they made war with the Hagarites, who fell by their hand: and they dwelt in their tents throughout all the east *land* of Gilead.

11And the children of Gad dwelt over against them, in the land of Bashan unto Salcah:

12Joel the chief, and Shapham the next, and Jaanai, and Shaphat in Bashan.

13And their brethren of the house of their fathers *were,* Michael, and Meshullam, and Sheba, and Jorai, and Jachan, and Zia, and Heber, seven.

14These *are* the children of Abihail the son of Huri, the son of Jaroah, the son of Gilead, the son of Michael, the son of Jeshishai, the son of Jahdo, the son of Buz;

15Ahi the son of Abdiel, the son of Guni, chief of the house of their fathers.

16And they dwelt in Gilead in Bashan, and in her towns, and in all the suburbs of Sharon, upon their borders.

17All these were reckoned by genealogies in the days of Jotham king of Judah, and in the days of Jeroboam king of Israel.

ACTS 25:1–27

Now when Festus was come into the province, after three days he ascended from Caesarea to Jerusalem.

2Then the high priest and the chief of the Jews informed him against Paul, and besought him,

3And desired favour against him, that he would send for him to Jerusalem, laying wait in the way to kill him.

4But Festus answered, that Paul should be kept at Caesarea, and that he himself would depart shortly *thither.*

5Let them therefore, said he, which among you are able, go down with *me,* and accuse this man, if there be any wickedness in him.

6And when he had tarried among them more than ten days, he went down unto Caesarea; and the next day sitting on the judgment seat commanded Paul to be brought.

7And when he was come, the Jews which came down from Jerusalem stood round about, and laid many and grievous complaints against Paul, which they could not prove.

8While he answered for himself, Neither against the law of the Jews, neither against the temple, nor yet against Caesar, have I offended any thing at all.

9But Festus, willing to do the Jews a pleasure, answered Paul, and said, Wilt thou go up to Jerusalem, and there be judged of these things before me?

10Then said Paul, I stand at Caesar's judgment seat, where I ought to be judged: to the Jews have I done no wrong, as thou very well knowest.

11For if I be an offender, or have committed any thing worthy of death, I refuse not to die: but if there be none of these things whereof these accuse me, no man may deliver me unto them. I appeal unto Caesar.

12Then Festus, when he had conferred with the council, answered, Hast thou appealed unto Caesar? unto Caesar shalt thou go.

13And after certain days king Agrippa and Bernice came unto Caesarea to salute Festus.

14And when they had been there many days, Festus declared Paul's cause unto the king, saying, There is a certain man left in bonds by Felix:

15About whom, when I was at Jerusalem, the chief priests and the elders of the Jews informed *me,* desiring *to have* judgment against him.

16To whom I answered, It is not the manner of the Romans to deliver any man to die, before that he which is accused have the accusers face to face, and have licence to answer for himself concerning the crime laid against him.

17Therefore, when they were come

hither, without any delay on the morrow I sat on the judgment seat, and commanded the man to be brought forth.

18Against whom when the accusers stood up, they brought none accusation of such things as I supposed:

19But had certain questions against him of their own superstition, and of one Jesus, which was dead, whom Paul affirmed to be alive.

20And because I doubted of such manner of questions, I asked *him* whether he would go to Jerusalem, and there be judged of these matters.

21But when Paul had appealed to be reserved unto the hearing of Augustus, I commanded him to be kept till I might send him to Caesar.

22Then Agrippa said unto Festus, I would also hear the man myself. To morrow, said he, thou shalt hear him.

23And on the morrow, when Agrippa was come, and Bernice, with great pomp, and was entered into the place of hearing, with the chief captains, and principal men of the city, at Festus' commandment Paul was brought forth.

24And Festus said, King Agrippa, and all men which are here present with us, ye see this man, about whom all the multitude of the Jews have dealt with me, both at Jerusalem, and *also* here, crying that he ought not to live any longer.

25But when I found that he had committed nothing worthy of death, and that he himself hath appealed to Augustus, I have determined to send him.

26Of whom I have no certain thing to write unto my lord. Wherefore I have brought him forth before you, and specially before thee, O king Agrippa, that, after examination had, I might have somewhat to write.

27For it seemeth to me unreasonable to send a prisoner, and not withal to signify the crimes *laid* against him.

PSALM 5:1–12

Give ear to my words, O LORD, consider my meditation.

2Hearken unto the voice of my cry, my King, and my God: for unto thee will I pray.

3My voice shalt thou hear in the morning, O LORD; in the morning will I direct *my prayer* unto thee, and will look up.

4For thou *art* not a God that hath pleasure in wickedness: neither shall evil dwell with thee.

5The foolish shall not stand in thy sight: thou hatest all workers of iniquity.

6Thou shalt destroy them that speak leasing: the LORD will abhor the bloody and deceitful man.

7But as for me, I will come *into* thy house in the multitude of thy mercy: *and* in thy fear will I worship toward thy holy temple.

8Lead me, O LORD, in thy righteousness because of mine enemies; make thy way straight before my face.

9For *there is* no faithfulness in their mouth; their inward part *is* very wickedness; their throat *is* an open sepulchre; they flatter with their tongue.

10Destroy thou them, O God; let them fall by their own counsels; cast them out in the multitude of their transgressions; for they have rebelled against thee.

11But let all those that put their trust in thee rejoice: let them ever shout for joy, because thou defendest them: let them also that love thy name be joyful in thee.

12For thou, LORD, wilt bless the righteous; with favour wilt thou compass him as *with* a shield.

PROVERBS FOR TODAY/ 18:19

A brother offended is harder to be won *than a strong city: and* their *contentions* are *like the bars of a castle.*

1 CHRONICLES 5:18—6:81

THE sons of Reuben, and the Gadites, and half the tribe of Manasseh, of valiant men, men able to bear buckler and sword, and to shoot with bow, and skilful in war, *were* four and forty thousand seven hundred and threescore, that went out to the war.

19And they made war with the Hagarites, with Jetur, and Nephish, and Nodab.

20And they were helped against them, and the Hagarites were delivered into their hand, and all that *were* with them: for they cried to God in the battle, and he was intreated of them; because they put their trust in him.

21And they took away their cattle; of their camels fifty thousand, and of sheep two hundred and fifty thousand, and of asses two thousand, and of men an hundred thousand.

22For there fell down many slain, because the war *was* of God. And they dwelt in their steads until the captivity.

23And the children of the half tribe of Manasseh dwelt in the land: they increased from Bashan unto Baal–hermon and Senir, and unto mount Hermon.

24And these *were* the heads of the house of their fathers, even Epher, and Ishi, and Eliel, and Azriel, and Jeremiah, and Hodaviah, and Jahdiel, mighty men of valour, famous men, *and* heads of the house of their fathers.

25And they transgressed against the God of their fathers, and went a whoring after the gods of the people of the land, whom God destroyed before them.

26And the God of Israel stirred up the spirit of Pul king of Assyria, and the spirit of Tilgath–pilneser king of Assyria, and he carried them away, even the Reubenites, and the Gadites, and the half tribe of Manasseh, and brought them unto Halah, and Habor, and Hara, and to the river Gozan, unto this day.

THE sons of Levi; Gershon, Kohath, and Merari.

2And the sons of Kohath; Amram, Izhar, and Hebron, and Uzziel.

3And the children of Amram; Aaron, and Moses, and Miriam. The sons also of Aaron; Nadab, and Abihu, Eleazar, and Ithamar.

4Eleazar begat Phinehas, Phinehas begat Abishua,

5And Abishua begat Bukki, and Bukki begat Uzzi,

6And Uzzi begat Zerahiah, and Zerahiah begat Meraioth,

7Meraioth begat Amariah, and Amariah begat Ahitub,

8And Ahitub begat Zadok, and Zadok begat Ahimaaz,

9And Ahimaaz begat Azariah, and Azariah begat Johanan,

10And Johanan begat Azariah, (he *it is* that executed the priest's office in the temple that Solomon built in Jerusalem:)

11And Azariah begat Amariah, and Amariah begat Ahitub,

12And Ahitub begat Zadok, and Zadok begat Shallum,

13And Shallum begat Hilkiah, and Hilkiah begat Azariah,

14And Azariah begat Seraiah, and Seraiah begat Jehozadak,

15And Jehozadak went *into captivity,* when the LORD carried away Judah and Jerusalem by the hand of Nebuchadnezzar.

16The sons of Levi; Gershom, Kohath, and Merari.

17And these *be* the names of the sons of Gershom; Libni, and Shimei.

18And the sons of Kohath *were,* Amram, and Izhar, and Hebron, and Uzziel.

19The sons of Merari; Mahli, and Mushi. And these *are* the families of the Levites according to their fathers.

20Of Gershom; Libni his son, Jahath his son, Zimmah his son,

21Joah his son, Iddo his son, Zerah his son, Jeaterai his son.

22The sons of Kohath; Amminadab his son, Korah his son, Assir his son,

23Elkanah his son, and Ebiasaph his son, and Assir his son,

24Tahath his son, Uriel his son, Uzziah his son, and Shaul his son.

25And the sons of Elkanah; Amasai, and Ahimoth.

26*As for* Elkanah: the sons of Elkanah; Zophai his son, and Nahath his son,

27Eliab his son, Jeroham his son, Elkanah his son.

28And the sons of Samuel; the firstborn Vashni, and Abiah.

29The sons of Merari; Mahli, Libni his son, Shimei his son, Uzza his son,

30Shimea his son, Haggiah his son, Asaiah his son.

31And these *are they* whom David set over the service of song in the house of the LORD, after that the ark had rest.

32And they ministered before the dwelling place of the tabernacle of the congregation with singing, until Solomon had built the house of the LORD in Jerusalem: and *then* they waited on their office according to their order.

33And these *are* they that waited with their children. Of the sons of the Kohathites: Heman a singer, the son of Joel, the son of Shemuel,

34The son of Elkanah, the son of Jeroham, the son of Eliel, the son of Toah,

35The son of Zuph, the son of Elkanah, the son of Mahath, the son of Amasai,

36The son of Elkanah, the son of Joel, the son of Azariah, the son of Zephaniah,

37The son of Tahath, the son of Assir, the son of Ebiasaph, the son of Korah,

38The son of Izhar, the son of Kohath,

the son of Levi, the son of Israel.

39And his brother Asaph, who stood on his right hand, *even* Asaph the son of Berachiah, the son of Shimea,

40The son of Michael, the son of Baaseiah, the son of Malchiah,

41The son of Ethni, the son of Zerah, the son of Adaiah,

42The son of Ethan, the son of Zimmah, the son of Shimei,

43The son of Jahath, the son of Gershom, the son of Levi.

44And their brethren the sons of Merari *stood* on the left hand: Ethan the son of Kishi, the son of Abdi, the son of Malluch,

45The son of Hashabiah, the son of Amaziah, the son of Hilkiah,

46The son of Amzi, the son of Bani, the son of Shamer,

47The son of Mahli, the son of Mushi, the son of Merari, the son of Levi.

48Their brethren also the Levites *were* appointed unto all manner of service of the tabernacle of the house of God.

49But Aaron and his sons offered upon the altar of the burnt offering, and on the altar of incense, *and were appointed* for all the work of the *place* most holy, and to make an atonement for Israel, according to all that Moses the servant of God had commanded.

50And these *are* the sons of Aaron; Eleazar his son, Phinehas his son, Abishua his son,

51Bukki his son, Uzzi his son, Zerahiah his son,

52Meraioth his son, Amariah his son, Ahitub his son,

53Zadok his son, Ahimaaz his son.

54Now these *are* their dwelling places throughout their castles in their coasts, of the sons of Aaron, of the families of the Kohathites: for theirs was the lot.

55And they gave them Hebron in the land of Judah, and the suburbs thereof round about it.

56But the fields of the city, and the

villages thereof, they gave to Caleb the son of Jephunneh.

⁵⁷And to the sons of Aaron they gave the cities of Judah, *namely,* Hebron, *the city* of refuge, and Libnah with her suburbs, and Jattir, and Eshtemoa, with their suburbs,

⁵⁸And Hilen with her suburbs, Debir with her suburbs,

⁵⁹And Ashan with her suburbs, and Beth-shemesh with her suburbs:

⁶⁰And out of the tribe of Benjamin; Geba with her suburbs, and Alemeth with her suburbs, and Anathoth with her suburbs. All their cities throughout their families *were* thirteen cities.

⁶¹And unto the sons of Kohath, *which were* left of the family of that tribe, *were cities given* out of the half tribe, *namely, out of* the half *tribe* of Manasseh, by lot, ten cities.

⁶²And to the sons of Gershom throughout their families out of the tribe of Issachar, and out of the tribe of Asher, and out of the tribe of Naphtali, and out of the tribe of Manasseh in Bashan, thirteen cities.

⁶³Unto the sons of Merari *were given* by lot, throughout their families, out of the tribe of Reuben, and out of the tribe of Gad, and out of the tribe of Zebulun, twelve cities.

⁶⁴And the children of Israel gave to the Levites *these* cities with their suburbs.

⁶⁵And they gave by lot out of the tribe of the children of Judah, and out of the tribe of the children of Simeon, and out of the tribe of the children of Benjamin, these cities, which are called by *their* names.

⁶⁶And *the residue* of the families of the sons of Kohath had cities of their coasts out of the tribe of Ephraim.

⁶⁷And they gave unto them, *of the* cities of refuge, Shechem in mount Ephraim with her suburbs; *they gave* also Gezer with her suburbs,

⁶⁸And Jokmeam with her suburbs, and Beth-horon with her suburbs,

⁶⁹And Aijalon with her suburbs, and Gath-rimmon with her suburbs:

⁷⁰And out of the half tribe of Manasseh; Aner with her suburbs, and Bileam with her suburbs, for the family of the remnant of the sons of Kohath.

⁷¹Unto the sons of Gershom *were given* out of the family of the half tribe of Manasseh, Golan in Bashan with her suburbs, and Ashtaroth with her suburbs:

⁷²And out of the tribe of Issachar; Kedesh with her suburbs, Daberath with her suburbs,

⁷³And Ramoth with her suburbs, and Anem with her suburbs:

⁷⁴And out of the tribe of Asher; Mashal with her suburbs, and Abdon with her suburbs,

⁷⁵And Hukok with her suburbs, and Rehob with her suburbs:

⁷⁶And out of the tribe of Naphtali; Kedesh in Galilee with her suburbs, and Hammon with her suburbs, and Kirjathaim with her suburbs.

⁷⁷Unto the rest of the children of Merari *were given* out of the tribe of Zebulun, Rimmon with her suburbs, Tabor with her suburbs:

⁷⁸And on the other side Jordan by Jericho, on the east side of Jordan, *were given them* out of the tribe of Reuben, Bezer in the wilderness with her suburbs, and Jahzah with her suburbs,

⁷⁹Kedemoth also with her suburbs, and Mephaath with her suburbs:

⁸⁰And out of the tribe of Gad; Ramoth in Gilead with her suburbs, and Mahanaim with her suburbs,

⁸¹And Heshbon with her suburbs, and Jazer with her suburbs.

ACTS 26:1–32

THEN Agrippa said unto Paul, Thou art permitted to speak for thyself. Then Paul stretched forth the hand, and answered for himself:

2I think myself happy, king Agrippa, because I shall answer for myself this day before thee touching all the things whereof I am accused of the Jews:

3Especially *because I know* thee to be expert in all customs and questions which are among the Jews: wherefore I beseech thee to hear me patiently.

4My manner of life from my youth, which was at the first among mine own nation at Jerusalem, know all the Jews;

5Which knew me from the beginning, if they would testify, that after the most straitest sect of our religion I lived a Pharisee.

6And now I stand and am judged for the hope of the promise made of God unto our fathers:

7Unto which *promise* our twelve tribes, instantly serving *God* day and night, hope to come. For which hope's sake, king Agrippa, I am accused of the Jews.

8Why should it be thought a thing incredible with you, that God should raise the dead?

9I verily thought with myself, that I ought to do many things contrary to the name of Jesus of Nazareth.

10Which thing I also did in Jerusalem: and many of the saints did I shut up in prison, having received authority from the chief priests; and when they were put to death, I gave my voice against *them.*

11And I punished them oft in every synagogue, and compelled *them* to blaspheme; and being exceedingly mad against them, I persecuted *them* even unto strange cities.

12Whereupon as I went to Damascus with authority and commission from the chief priests,

13At midday, O king, I saw in the way a light from heaven, above the brightness of the sun, shining round about me and them which journeyed with me.

14And when we were all fallen to the earth, I heard a voice speaking unto me, and saying in the Hebrew tongue, Saul, Saul, why persecutest thou me? *it is* hard for thee to kick against the pricks.

15And I said, Who art thou, Lord? And he said, I am Jesus whom thou persecutest.

16But rise, and stand upon thy feet: for I have appeared unto thee for this purpose, to make thee a minister and a witness both of these things which thou hast seen, and of those things in the which I will appear unto thee;

17Delivering thee from the people, and *from* the Gentiles, unto whom now I send thee,

18To open their eyes, *and* to turn *them* from darkness to light, and *from* the power of Satan unto God, that they may receive forgiveness of sins, and inheritance among them which are sanctified by faith that is in me.

19Whereupon, O king Agrippa, I was not disobedient unto the heavenly vision:

20But shewed first unto them of Damascus, and at Jerusalem, and throughout all the coasts of Judaea, and *then* to the Gentiles, that they should repent and turn to God, and do works meet for repentance.

21For these causes the Jews caught me in the temple, and went about to kill *me.*

22Having therefore obtained help of God, I continue unto this day, witnessing both to small and great, saying none other things than those which the prophets and Moses did say should come:

23That Christ should suffer, *and* that he should be the first that should rise from the dead, and should shew light unto the people, and to the Gentiles.

24And as he thus spake for himself, Festus said with a loud voice, Paul, thou art beside thyself; much learning doth make thee mad.

25But he said, I am not mad, most noble Festus; but I speak forth the words of truth and soberness.

26For the king knoweth of these things, before whom also I speak freely: for I am persuaded that none of these things are hidden from him; for this thing was not done in a corner.

27King Agrippa, believest thou the prophets? I know that thou believest.

28Then Agrippa said unto Paul, Almost thou persuadest me to be a Christian.

29And Paul said, I would to God, that not only thou, but also all that hear me this day, were both almost, and altogether such as I am, except these bonds.

30And when he had thus spoken, the king rose up, and the governor, and Bernice, and they that sat with them:

31And when they were gone aside, they talked between themselves, saying, This man doeth nothing worthy of death or of bonds.

32Then said Agrippa unto Festus, This man might have been set at liberty, if he had not appealed unto Caesar.

PSALM 6:1–10

O LORD, rebuke me not in thine anger, neither chasten me in thy hot displeasure.

2Have mercy upon me, O LORD; for I am weak: O LORD, heal me; for my bones are vexed.

3My soul is also sore vexed: but thou, O LORD, how long?

4Return, O LORD, deliver my soul: oh save me for thy mercies' sake.

5For in death there is no remembrance of thee: in the grave who shall give thee thanks?

6I am weary with my groaning; all the night make I my bed to swim; I water my couch with my tears.

7Mine eye is consumed because of grief; it waxeth old because of all mine enemies.

8Depart from me, all ye workers of iniquity; for the LORD hath heard the voice of my weeping.

9The LORD hath heard my supplication; the LORD will receive my prayer.

10Let all mine enemies be ashamed and sore vexed: let them return and be ashamed suddenly.

PROVERBS FOR TODAY/ 18:20–21

A man's belly shall be satisfied with the fruit of his mouth; and *with the increase of his lips shall he be filled.* □ *Death and life* are *in the power of the tongue: and they that love it shall eat the fruit thereof.*

JULY 9

1 CHRONICLES 7:1—8:40

Now the sons of Issachar were, Tola, and Puah, Jashub, and Shimrom, four.

2And the sons of Tola; Uzzi, and Rephaiah, and Jeriel, and Jahmai, and Jibsam, and Shemuel, heads of their father's house, to wit, of Tola: they were valiant men of might in their generations; whose number was in the days of David two and twenty thousand and six hundred.

3And the sons of Uzzi; Izrahiah: and the sons of Izrahiah; Michael, and

Obadiah, and Joel, Ishiah, five: all of them chief men.

4And with them, by their generations, after the house of their fathers, *were* bands of soldiers for war, six and thirty thousand *men:* for they had many wives and sons.

5And their brethren among all the families of Issachar *were* valiant men of might, reckoned in all by their genealogies fourscore and seven thousand.

6*The sons* of Benjamin; Bela, and Becher, and Jediael, three.

7And the sons of Bela; Ezbon, and Uzzi, Uzziel, and Jerimoth, and Iri, five; heads of the house of *their* fathers, mighty men of valour; and were reckoned by their genealogies twenty and two thousand and thirty and four.

8And the sons of Becher; Zemira, and Joash, and Eliezer, and Elioenai, and Omri, and Jerimoth, and Abiah, and Anathoth, and Alameth. All these *are* the sons of Becher.

9And the number of them, after their genealogy by their generations, heads of the house of their fathers, mighty men of valour, *was* twenty thousand and two hundred.

10The sons also of Jediael; Bilhan: and the sons of Bilhan; Jeush, and Benjamin, and Ehud, and Chenaanah, and Zethan, and Tharshish, and Ahishahar.

11All these the sons of Jediael, by the heads of their fathers, mighty men of valour, *were* seventeen thousand and two hundred *soldiers,* fit to go out for war *and* battle.

12Shuppim also, and Huppim, the children of Ir, *and* Hushim, the sons of Aher.

13The sons of Naphtali; Jahziel, and Guni, and Jezer, and Shallum, the sons of Bilhah.

14The sons of Manasseh; Ashriel, whom she bare: (*but* his concubine the Aramitess bare Machir the father of Gilead:

15And Machir took to wife *the sister* of Huppim and Shuppim, whose sister's

name *was* Maachah;) and the name of the second *was* Zelophehad: and Zelophehad had daughters.

16And Maachah the wife of Machir bare a son, and she called his name Peresh; and the name of his brother *was* Sheresh; and his sons *were* Ulam and Rakem.

17And the sons of Ulam; Bedan. These *were* the sons of Gilead, the son of Machir, the son of Manasseh.

18And his sister Hammoleketh bare Ishod, and Abiezer, and Mahalah.

19And the sons of Shemidah were, Ahian, and Shechem, and Likhi, and Aniam.

20And the sons of Ephraim; Shuthelah, and Bered his son, and Tahath his son, and Eladah his son, and Tahath his son,

21And Zabad his son, and Shuthelah his son, and Ezer, and Elead, whom the men of Gath *that were* born in *that* land slew, because they came down to take away their cattle.

22And Ephraim their father mourned many days, and his brethren came to comfort him.

23And when he went in to his wife, she conceived, and bare a son, and he called his name Beriah, because it went evil with his house.

24(And his daughter *was* Sherah, who built Beth–horon the nether, and the upper, and Uzzen–sherah.)

25And Rephah *was* his son, also Resheph, and Telah his son, and Tahan his son,

26Laadan his son, Ammihud his son, Elishama his son,

27Non his son, Jehoshuah his son.

28And their possessions and habitations *were,* Beth–el and the towns thereof, and eastward Naaran, and westward Gezer, with the towns thereof; Shechem also and the towns thereof, unto Gaza and the towns thereof:

29And by the borders of the children of Manasseh, Beth–shean and her towns, Taanach and her towns, Megiddo and her towns, Dor and her towns. In these dwelt the children of Joseph the son of Israel.

30The sons of Asher; Imnah, and Isuah, and Ishuai, and Beriah, and Serah their sister.

31And the sons of Beriah; Heber, and Malchiel, who is the father of Birzavith.

32And Heber begat Japhlet, and Shomer, and Hotham, and Shua their sister.

33And the sons of Japhlet; Pasach, and Bimhal, and Ashvath. These are the children of Japhlet.

34And the sons of Shamer; Ahi, and Rohgah, Jehubbah, and Aram.

35And the sons of his brother Helem; Zophah, and Imna, and Shelesh, and Amal.

36The sons of Zophah; Suah, and Harnepher, and Shual, and Beri, and Imrah,

37Bezer, and Hod, and Shamma, and Shilshah, and Ithran, and Beera.

38And the sons of Jether; Jephunneh, and Pispah, and Ara.

39And the sons of Ulla; Arah, and Haniel, and Rezia.

40All these were the children of Asher, heads of their father's house, choice and mighty men of valour, chief of the princes. And the number throughout the genealogy of them that were apt to the war and to battle was twenty and six thousand men.

Now Benjamin begat Bela his firstborn, Ashbel the second, and Aharah the third,

2Nohah the fourth, and Rapha the fifth.

3And the sons of Bela were, Addar, and Gera, and Abihud,

4And Abishua, and Naaman, and Ahoah,

5And Gera, and Shephuphan, and Huram.

6And these are the sons of Ehud:

these are the heads of the fathers of the inhabitants of Geba, and they removed them to Manahath:

7And Naaman, and Ahiah, and Gera, he removed them, and begat Uzza, and Ahihud.

8And Shaharaim begat children in the country of Moab, after he had sent them away; Hushim and Baara were his wives.

9And he begat of Hodesh his wife, Jobab, and Zibia, and Mesha, and Malcham,

10And Jeuz, and Shachia, and Mirma. These were his sons, heads of the fathers.

11And of Hushim he begat Abitub, and Elpaal.

12The sons of Elpaal; Eber, and Misham, and Shamed, who built Ono, and Lod, with the towns thereof:

13Beriah also, and Shema, who were heads of the fathers of the inhabitants of Aijalon, who drove away the inhabitants of Gath:

14And Ahio, Shashak, and Jeremoth,

15And Zebadiah, and Arad and Ader,

16And Michael, and Ispah, and Joha, the sons of Beriah;

17And Zebadiah, and Meshullam, and Hezeki, and Heber,

18Ishmerai also, and Jezliah, and Jobab, the sons of Elpaal;

19And Jakim, and Zichri, and Zabdi,

20And Elienai, and Zilthai, and Eliel,

21And Adaiah, and Beraiah, and Shimrath, the sons of Shimhi;

22And Ishpan, and Heber, and Eliel,

23And Abdon, and Zichri, and Hanan,

24And Hananiah, and Elam, and Antothijah,

25And Iphedeiah, and Penuel, the sons of Shashak;

26And Shamsherai, and Shehariah, and Athaliah,

27And Jaresiah, and Eliah, and Zichri, the sons of Jeroham.

28These were heads of the fathers, by their generations, chief men. These dwelt in Jerusalem.

29And at Gibeon dwelt the father of

Gibeon; whose wife's name *was* Maachah:

30And his firstborn son Abdon, and Zur, and Kish, and Baal, and Nadab,

31And Gedor, and Ahio, and Zacher.

32And Mikloth begat Shimeah. And these also dwelt with their brethren in Jerusalem, over against them.

33And Ner begat Kish, and Kish begat Saul, and Saul begat Jonathan, and Malchi–shua, and Abinadab, and Esh–baal.

34And the son of Jonathan *was* Merib–baal; and Merib–baal begat Micah.

35And the sons of Micah *were*, Pithon, and Melech, and Tarea, and Ahaz.

36And Ahaz begat Jehoadah; and Jehoadah begat Alemeth, and Azmaveth, and Zimri; and Zimri begat Moza,

37And Moza begat Binea: Rapha *was* his son, Eleasah his son, Azel his son:

38And Azel had six sons, whose names *are* these, Azrikam, Bocheru, and Ishmael, and Sheariah, and Obadiah, and Hanan. All these *were* the sons of Azel.

39And the sons of Eshek his brother *were*, Ulam his firstborn, Jehush the second, and Eliphelet the third.

40And the sons of Ulam were mighty men of valour, archers, and had many sons, and sons' sons, an hundred and fifty. All these *are* of the sons of Benjamin.

ACTS 27:1–20

AND when it was determined that we should sail into Italy, they delivered Paul and certain other prisoners unto *one* named Julius a centurion of Augustus' band.

2And entering into a ship of Adramyttium, we launched, meaning to sail by the coasts of Asia; *one* Aristarchus, a Macedonian of Thessalonica, being with us.

3And the next *day* we touched at Sidon. And Julius courteously entreated Paul, and gave *him* liberty to go unto his friends to refresh himself.

4And when we had launched from thence, we sailed under Cyprus, because the winds were contrary.

5And when we had sailed over the sea of Cilicia and Pamphylia, we came to Myra, *a city* of Lycia.

6And there the centurion found a ship of Alexandria sailing into Italy; and he put us therein.

7And when we had sailed slowly many days, and scarce were come over against Cnidus, the wind not suffering us, we sailed under Crete, over against Salmone;

8And, hardly passing it, came unto a place which is called The fair havens; nigh whereunto was the city *of* Lasea.

9Now when much time was spent, and when sailing was now dangerous, because the fast was now already past, Paul admonished *them*,

10And said unto them, Sirs, I perceive that this voyage will be with hurt and much damage, not only of the lading and ship, but also of our lives.

11Nevertheless the centurion believed the master and the owner of the ship, more than those things which were spoken by Paul.

12And because the haven was not commodious to winter in, the more part advised to depart thence also, if by any means they might attain to Phenice, *and there* to winter; *which is* an haven of Crete, and lieth toward the south west and north west.

13And when the south wind blew softly, supposing that they had obtained *their* purpose, loosing *thence*, they sailed close by Crete.

14But not long after there arose against it a tempestuous wind, called Euroclydon.

15And when the ship was caught, and could not bear up into the wind, we let *her* drive.

16And running under a certain island which is called Clauda, we had much work to come by the boat:

17Which when they had taken up,

they used helps, undergirding the ship; and, fearing lest they should fall into the quicksands, strake sail, and so were driven.

18And we being exceedingly tossed with a tempest, the next *day* they lightened the ship;

19And the third *day* we cast out with our own hands the tackling of the ship.

20And when neither sun nor stars in many days appeared, and no small tempest lay on *us,* all hope that we should be saved was then taken away.

PSALM 7:1–17

O LORD my God, in thee do I put my trust: save me from all them that persecute me, and deliver me:

2Lest he tear my soul like a lion, rending *it* in pieces, while *there is* none to deliver.

3O LORD my God, if I have done this; if there be iniquity in my hands;

4If I have rewarded evil unto him that was at peace with me; (yea, I have delivered him that without cause is mine enemy:)

5Let the enemy persecute my soul, and take *it;* yea, let him tread down my life upon the earth, and lay mine honour in the dust. Selah.

6Arise, O LORD, in thine anger, lift up thyself because of the rage of mine enemies: and awake for me *to* the judgment *that* thou hast commanded.

7So shall the congregation of the people compass thee about: for their sakes therefore return thou on high.

8The LORD shall judge the people: judge me, O LORD, according to my righteousness, and according to mine integrity *that is* in me.

9Oh let the wickedness of the wicked come to an end; but establish the just: for the righteous God trieth the hearts and reins.

10My defence *is* of God, which saveth the upright in heart.

11God judgeth the righteous, and God is angry *with the wicked* every day.

12If he turn not, he will whet his sword; he hath bent his bow, and made it ready.

13He hath also prepared for him the instruments of death; he ordaineth his arrows against the persecutors.

14Behold, he travaileth with iniquity, and hath conceived mischief, and brought forth falsehood.

15He made a pit, and digged it, and is fallen into the ditch *which* he made.

16His mischief shall return upon his own head, and his violent dealing shall come down upon his own pate.

17I will praise the LORD according to his righteousness: and will sing praise to the name of the LORD most high.

PROVERBS FOR TODAY/ 18:22

Whoso *findeth a wife findeth a good* thing, *and obtaineth favour of the LORD.*

JULY 10

1 CHRONICLES 9:1—10:14

So all Israel were reckoned by genealogies; and, behold, they *were* written in the book of the kings of Israel and Judah, *who* were carried away to Babylon for their transgression.

2Now the first inhabitants that *dwelt* in their possessions in their cities *were,* the Israelites, the priests, Levites, and the Nethinims.

3And in Jerusalem dwelt of the children of Judah, and of the children of Benjamin, and of the children of Ephraim, and Manasseh;

4Uthai the son of Ammihud, the son of Omri, the son of Imri, the son of Bani, of the children of Pharez the son of Judah.

5And of the Shilonites; Asaiah the firstborn, and his sons.

6And of the sons of Zerah; Jeuel, and their brethren, six hundred and ninety.

7And of the sons of Benjamin; Sallu the son of Meshullam, the son of Hodaviah, the son of Hasenuah,

8And Ibneiah the son of Jeroham, and Elah the son of Uzzi, the son of Michri, and Meshullam the son of Shephathiah, the son of Reuel, the son of Ibnijah;

9And their brethren, according to their generations, nine hundred and fifty and six. All these men *were* chief of the fathers in the house of their fathers.

10And of the priests; Jedaiah, and Jehoiarib, and Jachin,

11And Azariah the son of Hilkiah, the son of Meshullam, the son of Zadok, the son of Meraioth, the son of Ahitub, the ruler of the house of God;

12And Adaiah the son of Jeroham, the son of Pashur, the son of Malchijah, and Maasiai the son of Adiel, the son

of Jahzerah, the son of Meshullam, the son of Meshillemith, the son of Immer;

13And their brethren, heads of the house of their fathers, a thousand and seven hundred and threescore; very able men for the work of the service of the house of God.

14And of the Levites; Shemaiah the son of Hasshub, the son of Azrikam, the son of Hashabiah, of the sons of Merari;

15And Bakbakkar, Heresh, and Galal, and Mattaniah the son of Micah, the son of Zichri, the son of Asaph;

16And Obadiah the son of Shemaiah, the son of Galal, the son of Jeduthun, and Berechiah the son of Asa, the son of Elkanah, that dwelt in the villages of the Netophathites.

17And the porters *were,* Shallum, and Akkub, and Talmon, and Ahiman, and their brethren: Shallum *was* the chief;

18Who hitherto *waited* in the king's gate eastward: they *were* porters in the companies of the children of Levi.

19And Shallum the son of Kore, the son of Ebiasaph, the son of Korah, and his brethren, of the house of his father, the Korahites, *were* over the work of the service, keepers of the gates of the tabernacle: and their fathers, *being* over the host of the LORD, *were* keepers of the entry.

20And Phinehas the son of Eleazar was the ruler over them in time past, *and* the LORD *was* with him.

21*And* Zechariah the son of Meshelemiah *was* porter of the door of the tabernacle of the congregation.

22All these *which were* chosen to be porters in the gates *were* two hundred and twelve. These were reckoned by their genealogy in their villages, whom David and Samuel the seer did ordain in their set office.

23So they and their children *had* the oversight of the gates of the house of the LORD, *namely,* the house of the tabernacle, by wards.

24In four quarters were the porters, toward the east, west, north, and south.

25And their brethren, *which were* in their villages, *were* to come after seven days from time to time with them.

26For these Levites, the four chief porters, were in *their* set office, and were over the chambers and treasuries of the house of God.

27And they lodged round about the house of God, because the charge *was* upon them, and the opening thereof every morning *pertained* to them.

28And *certain* of them had the charge of the ministering vessels, that they should bring them in and out by tale.

29*Some* of them also *were* appointed to oversee the vessels, and all the instruments of the sanctuary, and the fine flour, and the wine, and the oil, and the frankincense, and the spices.

30And *some* of the sons of the priests made the ointment of the spices.

31And Mattithiah, *one* of the Levites, who *was* the firstborn of Shallum the Korahite, had the set office over the things that were made in the pans.

32And *other* of their brethren, of the sons of the Kohathites, *were* over the shewbread, to prepare *it* every sabbath.

33And these *are* the singers, chief of the fathers of the Levites, *who remaining* in the chambers *were* free: for they were employed in *that* work day and night.

34These chief fathers of the Levites *were* chief throughout their generations; these dwelt at Jerusalem.

35And in Gibeon dwelt the father of Gibeon, Jehiel, whose wife's name *was* Maachah:

36And his firstborn son Abdon, then Zur, and Kish, and Baal, and Ner, and Nadab,

37And Gedor, and Ahio, and Zechariah, and Mikloth.

38And Mikloth begat Shimeam. And they also dwelt with their brethren at Jerusalem, over against their brethren.

39And Ner begat Kish; and Kish begat Saul; and Saul begat Jonathan, and Malchi–shua, and Abinadab, and Esh–baal.

40And the son of Jonathan *was* Merib–baal: and Merib–baal begat Micah.

41And the sons of Micah *were,* Pithon, and Melech, and Tahrea, *and Ahaz.*

42And Ahaz begat Jarah; and Jarah begat Alemeth, and Azmaveth, and Zimri; and Zimri begat Moza;

43And Moza begat Binea; and Rephaiah his son, Eleasah his son, Azel his son.

44And Azel had six sons, whose names *are* these, Azrikam, Bocheru, and Ishmael, and Sheariah, and Obadiah, and Hanan: these *were* the sons of Azel.

Now the Philistines fought against Israel; and the men of Israel fled from before the Philistines, and fell down slain in mount Gilboa.

2And the Philistines followed hard after Saul, and after his sons; and the Philistines slew Jonathan, and Abinadab, and Malchi–shua, the sons of Saul.

3And the battle went sore against Saul, and the archers hit him, and he was wounded of the archers.

4Then said Saul to his armourbearer, Draw thy sword, and thrust me through therewith; lest these uncircumcised come and abuse me. But his armourbearer would not; for he was sore afraid. So Saul took a sword, and fell upon it.

5And when his armourbearer saw that Saul was dead, he fell likewise on the sword, and died.

6So Saul died, and his three sons, and all his house died together.

7And when all the men of Israel that *were* in the valley saw that they fled, and that Saul and his sons were dead, then they forsook their cities, and fled:

and the Philistines came and dwelt in them.

8And it came to pass on the morrow, when the Philistines came to strip the slain, that they found Saul and his sons fallen in mount Gilboa.

9And when they had stripped him, they took his head, and his armour, and sent into the land of the Philistines round about, to carry tidings unto their idols, and to the people.

10And they put his armour in the house of their gods, and fastened his head in the temple of Dagon.

11And when all Jabesh–gilead heard all that the Philistines had done to Saul,

12They arose, all the valiant men, and took away the body of Saul, and the bodies of his sons, and brought them to Jabesh, and buried their bones under the oak in Jabesh, and fasted seven days.

13So Saul died for his transgression which he committed against the LORD, *even* against the word of the LORD, which he kept not, and also for asking *counsel* of *one that had* a familiar spirit, to enquire *of it;*

14And enquired not of the LORD: therefore he slew him, and turned the kingdom unto David the son of Jesse.

ACTS 27:21–44

BUT after long abstinence Paul stood forth in the midst of them, and said, Sirs, ye should have hearkened unto me, and not have loosed from Crete, and to have gained this harm and loss.

22And now I exhort you to be of good cheer: for there shall be no loss of *any man's* life among you, but of the ship.

23For there stood by me this night the angel of God, whose I am, and whom I serve,

24Saying, Fear not, Paul; thou must be brought before Caesar: and, lo, God hath given thee all them that sail with thee.

25Wherefore, sirs, be of good cheer: for I believe God, that it shall be even as it was told me.

26Howbeit we must be cast upon a certain island.

27But when the fourteenth night was come, as we were driven up and down in Adria, about midnight the shipmen deemed that they drew near to some country;

28And sounded, and found *it* twenty fathoms: and when they had gone a little further, they sounded again, and found *it* fifteen fathoms.

29Then fearing lest we should have fallen upon rocks, they cast four anchors out of the stern, and wished for the day.

30And as the shipmen were about to flee out of the ship, when they had let down the boat into the sea, under colour as though they would have cast anchors out of the foreship,

31Paul said to the centurion and to the soldiers, Except these abide in the ship, ye cannot be saved.

32Then the soldiers cut off the ropes of the boat, and let her fall off.

33And while the day was coming on, Paul besought *them* all to take meat, saying, This day is the fourteenth day that ye have tarried and continued fasting, having taken nothing.

34Wherefore I pray you to take *some* meat: for this is for your health: for there shall not an hair fall from the head of any of you.

35And when he had thus spoken, he took bread, and gave thanks to God in presence of them all: and when he had broken *it,* he began to eat.

36Then were they all of good cheer, and they also took *some* meat.

37And we were in all in the ship two hundred threescore and sixteen souls.

38And when they had eaten enough,

they lightened the ship, and cast out the wheat into the sea.

39And when it was day, they knew not the land: but they discovered a certain creek with a shore, into the which they were minded, if it were possible, to thrust in the ship.

40And when they had taken up the anchors, they committed *themselves* unto the sea, and loosed the rudder bands, and hoisted up the mainsail to the wind, and made toward shore.

41And falling into a place where two seas met, they ran the ship aground; and the forepart stuck fast, and remained unmoveable, but the hinder part was broken with the violence of the waves.

42And the soldiers' counsel was to kill the prisoners, lest any of them should swim out, and escape.

43But the centurion, willing to save Paul, kept them from *their* purpose; and commanded that they which could swim should cast *themselves* first *into the sea,* and get to land:

44And the rest, some on boards, and some on *broken pieces* of the ship. And so it came to pass, that they escaped all safe to land.

PSALM 8:1–9

O LORD our Lord, how excellent *is* thy name in all the earth! who hast set thy glory above the heavens.

2Out of the mouth of babes and sucklings hast thou ordained strength because of thine enemies, that thou mightest still the enemy and the avenger.

3When I consider thy heavens, the work of thy fingers, the moon and the stars, which thou hast ordained;

4What is man, that thou art mindful of him? and the son of man, that thou visitest him?

5For thou hast made him a little lower than the angels, and hast crowned him with glory and honour.

6Thou madest him to have dominion over the works of thy hands: thou hast put all *things* under his feet:

7All sheep and oxen, yea, and the beasts of the field;

8The fowl of the air, and the fish of the sea, *and whatsoever* passeth through the paths of the seas.

9O LORD our Lord, how excellent *is* thy name in all the earth!

PROVERBS FOR TODAY/ 18:23–24

The poor useth intreaties; but the rich answereth roughly. ☐ *A man* that hath *friends must shew himself friendly: and there is a friend* that *sticketh closer than a brother.*

JULY 11

1 CHRONICLES 11:1—12:18

THEN all Israel gathered themselves to David unto Hebron, saying, Behold, we *are* thy bone and thy flesh.

2And moreover in time past, even when Saul was king, thou *wast* he that leddest out and broughtest in Israel: and the LORD thy God said unto thee, Thou shalt feed my people Israel, and thou shalt be ruler over my people Israel.

3Therefore came all the elders of Israel to the king to Hebron; and David made a covenant with them in Hebron before the LORD; and they anointed David king over Israel, according to the word of the LORD by Samuel.

4And David and all Israel went to Jerusalem, which *is* Jebus; where the Jebusites *were,* the inhabitants of the land.

5And the inhabitants of Jebus said to David, Thou shalt not come hither. Nevertheless David took the castle of Zion, which *is* the city of David.

6And David said, Whosoever smiteth the Jebusites first shall be chief and captain. So Joab the son of Zeruiah went first up, and was chief.

7And David dwelt in the castle; therefore they called it the city of David.

8And he built the city round about, even from Millo round about: and Joab repaired the rest of the city.

9So David waxed greater and greater: for the LORD of hosts *was* with him.

10These also *are* the chief of the mighty men whom David had, who strengthened themselves with him in his kingdom, *and* with all Israel, to make him king, according to the word of the LORD concerning Israel.

11And this *is* the number of the mighty men whom David had; Jashobeam, an Hachmonite, the chief of the captains: he lifted up his spear against three hundred slain *by him* at one time.

12And after him *was* Eleazar the son of Dodo, the Ahohite, who *was one* of the three mighties.

13He was with David at Pasdammim, and there the Philistines were gathered together to battle, where was a parcel of ground full of barley; and the people fled from before the Philistines.

14And they set themselves in the midst of *that* parcel, and delivered it, and slew the Philistines; and the LORD saved *them* by a great deliverance.

15Now three of the thirty captains went down to the rock to David, into the cave of Adullam; and the host of the Philistines, encamped in the valley of Rephaim.

16And David *was* then in the hold, and the Philistines' garrison *was* then at Beth–lehem.

17And David longed, and said, Oh that one would give me drink of the water of the well of Beth–lehem, that *is* at the gate!

18And the three brake through the host of the Philistines, and drew water out of the well of Beth–lehem, that *was* by the gate, and took *it,* and brought *it* to David: but David would not drink *of* it, but poured it out to the LORD,

19And said, My God forbid it me, that I should do this thing: shall I drink the blood of these men that have put their lives in jeopardy? for with *the jeopardy of* their lives they brought it. Therefore he would not drink it. These things did these three mightiest.

20And Abishai the brother of Joab, he was chief of the three: for lifting up his spear against three hundred, he slew *them,* and had a name among the three.

21Of the three, he was more honourable than the two; for he was their captain: howbeit he attained not to the *first* three.

22Benaiah the son of Jehoiada, the son of a valiant man of Kabzeel, who had done many acts; he slew two lionlike men of Moab: also he went down and slew a lion in a pit in a snowy day.

23And he slew an Egyptian, a man of *great* stature, five cubits high; and in the Egyptian's hand *was* a spear like a weaver's beam; and he went down to him with a staff, and plucked the spear out of the Egyptian's hand, and slew him with his own spear.

24These *things* did Benaiah the son of Jehoiada, and had the name among the three mighties.

25Behold, he was honourable among

the thirty, but attained not to the *first* three: and David set him over his guard.

26Also the valiant men of the armies *were,* Asahel the brother of Joab, Elhanan the son of Dodo of Beth–lehem,

27Shammoth the Harorite, Helez the Pelonite,

28Ira the son of Ikkesh the Tekoite, Abi–ezer the Antothite,

29Sibbecai the Hushathite, Ilai the Ahohite,

30Maharai the Netophathite, Heled the son of Baanah the Netophathite,

31Ithai the son of Ribai of Gibeah, *that pertained* to the children of Benjamin, Benaiah the Pirathonite,

32Hurai of the brooks of Gaash, Abiel the Arbathite,

33Azmaveth the Baharumite, Eliahba the Shaalbonite,

34The sons of Hashem the Gizonite, Jonathan the son of Shage the Hararite,

35Ahiam the son of Sacar the Hararite, Eliphal the son of Ur,

36Hepher the Mecherathite, Ahijah the Pelonite,

37Hezro the Carmelite, Naarai the son of Ezbai,

38Joel the brother of Nathan, Mibhar the son of Haggeri,

39Zelek the Ammonite, Naharai the Berothite, the armourbearer of Joab the son of Zeruiah,

40Ira the Ithrite, Gareb the Ithrite,

41Uriah the Hittite, Zabad the son of Ahlai,

42Adina the son of Shiza the Reubenite, a captain of the Reubenites, and thirty with him,

43Hanan the son of Maachah, and Joshaphat the Mithnite,

44Uzzia the Ashterathite, Shama and Jehiel the sons of Hothan the Aroerite,

45Jediael the son of Shimri, and Joha his brother, the Tizite,

46Eliel the Mahavite, and Jeribai, and Joshaviah, the sons of Elnaam, and Ithmah the Moabite,

47Eliel, and Obed, and Jasiel the Mesobaite.

Now these *are* they that came to David to Ziklag, while he yet kept himself close because of Saul the son of Kish: and they *were* among the mighty men, helpers of the war.

2*They were* armed with bows, and could use both the right hand and the left in *hurling* stones and *shooting* arrows out of a bow, *even* of Saul's brethren of Benjamin.

3The chief *was* Ahiezer, then Joash, the sons of Shemaah the Gibeathite; and Jeziel, and Pelet, the sons of Azmaveth; and Berachah, and Jehu the Antothite,

4And Ismaiah the Gibeonite, a mighty man among the thirty, and over the thirty; and Jeremiah, and Jahaziel, and Johanan, and Josabad the Gederathite,

5Eluzai, and Jerimoth, and Bealiah, and Shemariah, and Shephatiah the Haruphite,

6Elkanah, and Jesiah, and Azareel, and Joezer, and Jashobeam, the Korhites,

7And Joelah, and Zebadiah, the sons of Jeroham of Gedor.

8And of the Gadites there separated themselves unto David into the hold to the wilderness men of might, *and* men of war *fit* for the battle, that could handle shield and buckler, whose faces *were like* the faces of lions, and *were* as swift as the roes upon the mountains;

9Ezer the first, Obadiah the second, Eliab the third,

10Mishmannah the fourth, Jeremiah the fifth,

11Attai the sixth, Eliel the seventh,

12Johanan the eighth, Elzabad the ninth,

13Jeremiah the tenth, Machbanai the eleventh.

14These *were* of the sons of Gad, captains of the host: one of the least *was* over an hundred, and the greatest over a thousand,

15These *are* they that went over Jordan in the first month, when it had overflown all his banks; and they put to flight all *them* of the valleys, *both* toward the east, and toward the west.

16And there came of the children of Benjamin and Judah to the hold unto David.

17And David went out to meet them, and answered and said unto them, If ye be come peaceably unto me to help me, mine heart shall be knit unto you: but if *ye be come* to betray me to mine enemies, seeing *there is* no wrong in mine hands, the God of our fathers look *thereon,* and rebuke *it.*

18Then the spirit came upon Amasai, *who was* chief of the captains, *and he said,* Thine *are we,* David, and on thy side, thou son of Jesse: peace, peace *be* unto thee, and peace *be* to thine helpers; for thy God helpeth thee. Then David received them and made them captains of the band.

ACTS 28:1–31

A ND when they [who were ship-wrecked] were escaped, then they knew that the island was called Melita.

2And the barbarous people shewed us no little kindness: for they kindled a fire, and received us every one, because of the present rain, and because of the cold.

3And when Paul had gathered a bundle of sticks, and laid *them* on the fire, there came a viper out of the heat, and fastened on his hand.

4And when the barbarians saw the *venomous* beast hang on his hand, they said among themselves, No doubt this man is a murderer, whom, though he hath escaped the sea, yet vengeance suffereth not to live.

5And he shook off the beast into the fire, and felt no harm.

6Howbeit they looked when he should have swollen, or fallen down dead suddenly: but after they had looked a great while, and saw no harm come to him,

they changed their minds, and said that he was a god.

7In the same quarters were possessions of the chief man of the island, whose name was Publius; who received us, and lodged us three days courteously.

8And it came to pass, that the father of Publius lay sick of a fever and of a bloody flux: to whom Paul entered in, and prayed, and laid his hands on him, and healed him.

9So when this was done, others also, which had diseases in the island, came, and were healed:

10Who also honoured us with many honours; and when we departed, they laded *us* with such things as were necessary.

11And after three months we departed in a ship of Alexandria, which had wintered in the isle, whose sign was Castor and Pollux.

12And landing at Syracuse, we tarried *there* three days.

13And from thence we fetched a compass, and came to Rhegium: and after one day the south wind blew, and we came the next day to Puteoli:

14Where we found brethren, and were desired to tarry with them seven days: and so we went toward Rome.

15And from thence, when the brethren heard of us, they came to meet us as far as Appii forum, and The three taverns: whom when Paul saw, he thanked God, and took courage.

16And when we came to Rome, the centurion delivered the prisoners to the captain of the guard: but Paul was suffered to dwell by himself with a soldier that kept him.

17And it came to pass, that after three days Paul called the chief of the Jews together: and when they were come together, he said unto them, Men *and* brethren, though I have committed nothing against the people, or customs of our fathers, yet was I delivered prisoner from Jerusalem into the hands of the Romans.

18Who, when they had examined me, would have let *me* go, because there was no cause of death in me.

19But when the Jews spake against *it,* I was constrained to appeal unto Caesar; not that I had ought to accuse my nation of.

20For this cause therefore have I called for you, to see *you,* and to speak with *you:* because that for the hope of Israel I am bound with this chain.

21And they said unto him, We neither received letters out of Judaea concerning thee, neither any of the brethren that came shewed or spake any harm of thee.

22But we desire to hear of thee what thou thinkest: for as concerning this sect, we know that every where it is spoken against.

23And when they had appointed him a day, there came many to him into *his* lodging; to whom he expounded and testified the kingdom of God, persuading them concerning Jesus, both out of the law of Moses, and *out of* the prophets, from morning till evening.

24And some believed the things which were spoken, and some believed not.

25And when they agreed not among themselves, they departed, after that Paul had spoken one word, Well spake the Holy Ghost by Esaias the prophet unto our fathers,

26Saying, Go unto this people, and say, Hearing ye shall hear, and shall not understand; and seeing ye shall see, and not perceive:

27For the heart of this people is waxed gross, and their ears are dull of hearing, and their eyes have they closed; lest they should see with *their* eyes, and hear with *their* ears, and understand with *their* heart, and should be converted, and I should heal them.

28Be it known therefore unto you, that the salvation of God is sent unto the Gentiles, and *that* they will hear it.

29And when he had said these words,

the Jews departed, and had great reasoning among themselves.

30And Paul dwelt two whole years in his own hired house, and received all that came in unto him,

31Preaching the kingdom of God, and teaching those things which concern the Lord Jesus Christ, with all confidence, no man forbidding him.

PSALM 9:1–12

I WILL praise *thee,* O LORD, with my whole heart; I will shew forth all thy marvellous works.

2I will be glad and rejoice in thee: I will sing praise to thy name, O thou most High.

3When mine enemies are turned back, they shall fall and perish at thy presence.

4For thou hast maintained my right and my cause; thou satest in the throne judging right.

5Thou hast rebuked the heathen, thou hast destroyed the wicked, thou hast put out their name for ever and ever.

6O thou enemy, destructions are come to a perpetual end: and thou hast destroyed cities; their memorial is perished with them.

7But the LORD shall endure for ever: he hath prepared his throne for judgment.

8And he shall judge the world in righteousness, he shall minister judgment to the people in uprightness.

9The LORD also will be a refuge for the oppressed, a refuge in times of trouble.

10And they that know thy name will put their trust in thee: for thou, LORD, hast not forsaken them that seek thee.

11Sing praises to the LORD, which dwelleth in Zion: declare among the people his doings.

12When he maketh inquisition for blood, he remembereth them: he forgetteth not the cry of the humble.

PROVERBS FOR TODAY/ 19:1–3

Better is *the poor that walketh in his integrity, than* he that is *perverse in his lips, and is a fool.* □ *Also,* that *the soul* be *without knowledge, it is not good; and he that hasteth with* his *feet sinneth.* □ *The foolishness of man perverteth his way: and his heart fretteth against the* LORD.

JULY 12

1 CHRONICLES 12:19—14:17

AND there fell *some* of Manasseh to David, when he came with the Philistines against Saul to battle: but they helped them not: for the lords of the Philistines upon advisement sent him away, saying, He will fall to his master Saul to *the jeopardy of* our heads.

20As he went to Ziklag, there fell to him of Manasseh, Adnah, and Jozabad, and Jediael, and Michael, and Jozabad, and Elihu, and Zilthai, captains of the thousands that *were* of Manasseh.

21And they helped David against the band *of the rovers* for they *were* all mighty men of valour, and were captains in the host.

22For at *that* time day by day there came to David to help him, until *it was* a great host, like the host of God.

23And these *are* the numbers of the bands *that were* ready armed to the war, *and* came to David to Hebron, to turn the kingdom of Saul to him, according to the word of the LORD.

24The children of Judah that bare shield and spear *were* six thousand and eight hundred, ready armed to the war.

25Of the children of Simeon, mighty men of valour for the war, seven thousand and one hundred.

26Of the children of Levi four thousand and six hundred.

27And Jehoiada *was* the leader of the Aaronites, and with him *were* three thousand and seven hundred;

28And Zadok, a young man mighty of valour, and of his father's house twenty and two captains.

29And of the children of Benjamin, the kindred of Saul, three thousand: for hitherto the greatest part of them had kept the ward of the house of Saul.

30And of the children of Ephraim twenty thousand and eight hundred, mighty men of valour, famous throughout the house of their fathers.

31And of the half tribe of Manasseh eighteen thousand, which were expressed by name, to come and make David king.

32And of the children of Issachar, *which were men* that had understanding of the times, to know what Israel ought to do; the heads of them *were* two hundred; and all their brethren *were* at their commandment.

33Of Zebulun, such as went forth to battle, expert in war, with all instruments of war, fifty thousand, which could keep rank: *they were* not of double heart.

34And of Naphtali a thousand captains, and with them with shield and spear thirty and seven thousand.

35And of the Danites expert in war twenty and eight thousand and six hundred.

36And of Asher, such as went forth to battle, expert in war, forty thousand.

37And on the other side of Jordan, of the Reubenites, and the Gadites, and of the half tribe of Manasseh, with all manner of instruments of war for the battle, an hundred and twenty thousand.

38All these men of war, that could keep rank, came with a perfect heart to Hebron, to make David king over all Israel and all the rest also of Israel *were* of one heart to make David king.

39And there they were with David three days, eating and drinking: for their brethren had prepared for them.

40Moreover they that were nigh them, *even* unto Issachar and Zebulun and Naphtali, brought bread on asses, and on camels, and on mules, and on oxen, *and* meat, meal, cakes of figs, and bunches of raisins, and wine, and oil, and oxen, and sheep abundantly: for *there was* joy in Israel.

AND David consulted with the captains of thousands and hundreds, *and* with every leader.

2And David said unto all the congregation of Israel, If *it seem* good unto you, and *that it be* of the LORD our God, let us send abroad unto our brethren every where, *that are* left in all the land of Israel, and with them *also* to the priests and Levites *which are* in their cities *and* suburbs, that they may gather themselves unto us:

3And let us bring again the ark of our God to us: for we enquired not at it in the days of Saul.

4And all the congregation said that they would do so: for the thing was right in the eyes of all the people.

5So David gathered all Israel together, from Shihor of Egypt even unto the entering of Hemath, to bring the ark of God from Kirjath–jearim.

6And David went up, and all Israel, to Baalah, *that is,* to Kirjath–jearim, which *belonged* to Judah, to bring up thence the ark of God the LORD, that dwelleth *between* the cherubims, whose name is called *on it*.

7And they carried the ark of God in a new cart out of the house of Abinadab: and Uzza and Ahio drave the cart.

8And David and all Israel played before God with all *their* might, and with singing, and with harps, and with psalteries, and with timbrels, and with cymbals, and with trumpets.

9And when they came unto the threshingfloor of Chidon, Uzza put forth his hand to hold the ark; for the oxen stumbled.

10And the anger of the LORD was kindled against Uzza, and he smote him, because he put his hand to the ark: and there he died before God.

11And David was displeased, because the LORD had made a breach upon Uzza: wherefore that place is called Perez–uzza to this day.

12And David was afraid of God that day, saying, How shall I bring the ark of God *home* to me?

13So David brought not the ark *home* to himself to the city of David, but carried it aside into the house of Obed–edom the Gittite.

14And the ark of God remained with the family of Obed–edom in his house three months. And the LORD blessed the house of Obed–edom, and all that he had.

Now Hiram king of Tyre sent messengers to David, and timber of cedars, with masons and carpenters, to build him an house.

2And David perceived that the LORD had confirmed him king over Israel, for his kingdom was lifted up on high, because of his people Israel.

3And David took more wives at Jerusalem: and David begat more sons and daughters.

4Now these *are* the names of *his*

children which he had in Jerusalem; Shammua, and Shobab, Nathan, and Solomon,

5And Ibhar, and Elishua, and Elpalet,

6And Nogah, and Nepheg, and Japhia,

7And Elishama, and Beeliada, and Eliphalet.

8And when the Philistines heard that David was anointed king over all Israel, all the Philistines went up to seek David. And David heard *of it,* and went out against them.

9And the Philistines came and spread themselves in the valley of Rephaim.

10And David enquired of God, saying, Shall I go up against the Philistines? And wilt thou deliver them into mine hand? And the Lord said unto him, Go up; for I will deliver them into thine hand.

11So they came up to Baal–perazim; and David smote them there. Then David said, God hath broken in upon mine enemies by mine hand like the breaking forth of waters: therefore they called the name of that place Baal–perazim.

12And when they had left their gods there, David gave a commandment, and they were burned with fire.

13And the Philistines yet again spread themselves abroad in the valley.

14Therefore David enquired again of God; and God said unto him, Go not up after them; turn away from them, and come upon them over against the mulberry trees.

15And it shall be, when thou shalt hear a sound of going in the tops of the mulberry trees, *that* then thou shalt go out to battle: for God is gone forth before thee to smite the host of the Philistines.

16David therefore did as God commanded him: and they smote the host of the Philistines from Gibeon even to Gazer.

17And the fame of David went out into all lands; and the Lord brought the fear of him upon all nations.

ROMANS 1:1–17

P AUL, a servant of Jesus Christ, called *to be* an apostle, separated unto the gospel of God,

2(Which he had promised afore by his prophets in the holy scriptures,)

3Concerning his Son Jesus Christ our Lord, which was made of the seed of David according to the flesh;

4And declared *to be* the Son of God with power, according to the spirit of holiness, by the resurrection from the dead:

5By whom we have received grace and apostleship, for obedience to the faith among all nations, for his name;

6Among whom are ye also the called of Jesus Christ:

7To all that be in Rome, beloved of God, called *to be* saints: Grace to you and peace from God our Father, and the Lord Jesus Christ.

8First, I thank my God through Jesus Christ for you all, that your faith is spoken of throughout the whole world.

9For God is my witness, whom I serve with my spirit in the gospel of his Son, that without ceasing I make mention of you always in my prayers;

10Making request, if by any means now at length I might have a prosperous journey by the will of God to come unto you.

11For I long to see you, that I may impart unto you some spiritual gift, to the end ye may be established;

12That is, that I may be comforted together with you by the mutual faith both of you and me.

13Now I would not have you ignorant, brethren, that oftentimes I purposed to come unto you, (but was let hitherto,) that I might have some fruit among you also, even as among other Gentiles.

14I am debtor both to the Greeks, and to the Barbarians; both to the wise, and to the unwise.

15So, as much as in me is, I am ready

to preach the gospel to you that are at Rome also.

16For I am not ashamed of the gospel of Christ: for it is the power of God unto salvation to every one that believeth; to the Jew first, and also to the Greek.

17For therein is the righteousness of God revealed from faith to faith: as it is written, The just shall live by faith.

PSALM 9:13–20

HAVE mercy upon me, O LORD; consider my trouble *which I suffer* of them that hate me, thou that liftest me up from the gates of death:

14That I may shew forth all thy praise in the gates of the daughter of Zion: I will rejoice in thy salvation.

15The heathen are sunk down in the pit *that* they made: in the net which they hid is their own foot taken.

16The LORD is known *by* the judgment *which* he executeth: the wicked is snared in the work of his own hands. Higgaion. Selah.

17The wicked shall be turned into hell, *and* all the nations that forget God.

18For the needy shall not alway be forgotten: the expectation of the poor shall *not* perish for ever.

19Arise, O LORD; let not man prevail: let the heathen be judged in thy sight.

20Put them in fear, O LORD: *that* the nations may know themselves *to be but* men. Selah.

PROVERBS FOR TODAY/ 19:4–5

Wealth maketh many friends; but the poor is separated from his neighbour. □ *A false witness shall not be unpunished, and* he that *speaketh lies shall not escape.*

JULY 13

1 CHRONICLES 15:1—16:36

AND *David* made him houses in the city of David, and prepared a place for the ark of God, and pitched for it a tent.

2Then David said, None ought to carry the ark of God but the Levites: for them hath the LORD chosen to carry the ark of God, and to minister unto him for ever.

3And David gathered all Israel together to Jerusalem, to bring up the ark of the LORD unto his place, which he had prepared for it.

4And David assembled the children of Aaron, and the Levites:

5Of the sons of Kohath; Uriel the

chief, and his brethren an hundred and twenty:

6Of the sons of Merari; Asaiah the chief, and his brethren two hundred and twenty:

7Of the sons of Gershom; Joel the chief, and his brethren an hundred and thirty:

8Of the sons of Elizaphan; Shemaiah the chief, and his brethren two hundred:

9Of the sons of Hebron; Eliel the chief, and his brethren fourscore:

10Of the sons of Uzziel; Amminadab the chief, and his brethren an hundred and twelve.

11And David called for Zadok and Abiathar the priests, and for the Levites, for Uriel, Asaiah, and Joel, Shemaiah, and Eliel, and Amminadab,

12And said unto them, Ye *are* the chief of the fathers of the Levites: sanctify yourselves, *both* ye and your brethren, that ye may bring up the ark of the LORD God of Israel unto *the place that* I have prepared for it.

13For because ye *did it* not at the first, the LORD our God made a breach upon us, for that we sought him not after the due order.

14So the priests and the Levites sanctified themselves to bring up the ark of the LORD God of Israel.

15And the children of the Levites bare the ark of God upon their shoulders with the staves thereon, as Moses commanded according to the word of the LORD.

16And David spake to the chief of the Levites to appoint their brethren *to be* the singers with instruments of musick, psalteries and harps and cymbals, sounding, by lifting up the voice with joy.

17So the Levites appointed Heman the son of Joel; and of his brethren, Asaph the son of Berechiah; and of the sons of Merari their brethren, Ethan the son of Kushaiah;

18And with them their brethren of the second *degree,* Zechariah, Ben, and Jaaziel, and Shemiramoth, and Jehiel, and Unni, Eliab, and Benaiah, and Maaseiah, and Mattithiah, and Elipheleh, and Mikneiah, and Obed–edom, and Jeiel, the porters.

19So the singers, Heman, Asaph, and Ethan, *were appointed* to sound with cymbals of brass;

20And Zechariah, and Aziel, and Shemiramoth, and Jehiel, and Unni, and Eliab, and Maaseiah, and Benaiah, with psalteries on Alamoth;

21And Mattithiah, and Elipheleh, and Mikneiah, and Obed–edom, and Jeiel, and Azaziah, with harps on the Sheminith to excel.

22And Chenaniah, chief of the Levites, *was* for song: he instructed about the song because he *was* skilful.

23And Berechiah and Elkanah *were* doorkeepers for the ark.

24And Shebaniah, and Jehoshaphat, and Nethaneel, and Amasai, and Zechariah, and Benaiah, and Eliezer, the priests, did blow with the trumpets before the ark of God: and Obed–edom and Jehiah *were* doorkeepers for the ark.

25So David, and the elders of Israel, and the captains over thousands, went to bring up the ark of the covenant of the LORD out of the house of Obed–edom with joy.

26And it came to pass, when God helped the Levites that bare the ark of the covenant of the LORD, that they offered seven bullocks and seven rams.

27And David *was* clothed with a robe of fine linen, and all the Levites that bare the ark, and the singers, and Chenaniah the master of the song with the singers: David also *had* upon him an ephod of linen.

28Thus all Israel brought up the ark of the covenant of the LORD with shouting, and with sound of the cornet, and with trumpets, and with cymbals, making a noise with psalteries and harps.

29And it came to pass, *as* the ark of the covenant of the LORD came to the city of David, that Michal the daughter of Saul looking out at a window saw king David dancing and playing: and she despised him in her heart.

So they brought the ark of God, and set it in the midst of the tent that David had pitched for it: and they offered burnt sacrifices and peace offerings before God.

2And when David had made an end of offering the burnt offerings and the peace offerings, he blessed the people in the name of the LORD.

3And he dealt to every one of Israel, both man and woman, to every one a loaf of bread, and a good piece of flesh, and a flagon *of wine.*

4And he appointed *certain* of the Levites to minister before the ark of the LORD, and to record, and to thank and praise the LORD God of Israel:

5Asaph the chief, and next to him Zechariah, Jeiel, and Shemiramoth, and Jehiel, and Mattithiah, and Eliab, and Benaiah, and Obed–edom: and Jeiel with psalteries and with harps; but Asaph made a sound with cymbals;

6Benaiah also and Jahaziel the priests with trumpets continually before the ark of the covenant of God.

7Then on that day David delivered first *this psalm* to thank the LORD into the hand of Asaph and his brethren.

8Give thanks unto the LORD, call upon his name, make known his deeds among the people.

9Sing unto him, sing psalms unto him, talk ye of all his wondrous works.

10Glory ye in his holy name: let the heart of them rejoice that seek the LORD.

11Seek the LORD and his strength, seek his face continually.

12Remember his marvellous works that he hath done, his wonders, and the judgments of his mouth;

13O ye seed of Israel his servant, ye children of Jacob, his chosen ones.

14He *is* the LORD our God; his judgments *are* in all the earth.

15Be ye mindful always of his covenant; the word *which* he commanded to a thousand generations;

16*Even of the covenant* which he made with Abraham, and of his oath unto Issac;

17And hath confirmed the same to Jacob for a law, *and* to Israel *for* an everlasting covenant,

18Saying, Unto thee will I give the land of Canaan, the lot of your inheritance;

19When ye were but few, even a few, and strangers in it.

20And *when* they went from nation to nation, and from *one* kingdom to another people;

21He suffered no man to do them wrong; yea, he reproved kings for their sakes,

22*Saying,* Touch not mine anointed, and do my prophets no harm.

23Sing unto the LORD, all the earth; shew forth from day to day his salvation.

24Declare his glory among the heathen: his marvellous works among all nations.

25For great *is* the LORD, and greatly to be praised: he also *is* to be feared above all gods.

26For all the gods of the people *are* idols: but the LORD made the heavens.

27Glory and honour *are* in his presence; strength and gladness *are* in his place.

28Give unto the LORD, ye kindreds of the people, give unto the LORD glory and strength.

29Give unto the LORD the glory *due* unto his name: bring an offering, and come before him: worship the LORD in the beauty of holiness.

30Fear before him, all the earth: the world also shall be stable, that it be not moved.

31Let the heavens be glad, and let the earth rejoice: and let *men* say among the nations, The LORD reigneth.

32Let the sea roar, and the fulness thereof: let the fields rejoice, and all that *is* therein.

33Then shall the trees of the wood sing out at the presence of the LORD, because he cometh to judge the earth.

34O give thanks unto the LORD; for *he is* good; for his mercy *endureth* for ever.

35And say ye, Save us, O God of our salvation, and gather us together, and deliver us from the heathen, that we may give thanks to thy holy name, *and* glory in thy praise.

36Blessed *be* the LORD God of Israel for ever and ever. And all the people said, Amen, and praised the LORD.

ROMAN 1:18-32

For the wrath of God is revealed from heaven against all ungodliness and unrighteousness of men, who hold the truth in unrighteousness;

19Because that which may be known of God is manifest in them; for God hath shewed *it* unto them.

20For the invisible things of him from the creation of the world are clearly seen, being understood by the things that are made, *even* his eternal power and Godhead; so that they are without excuse:

21Because that, when they knew God, they glorified *him* not as God, neither were thankful; but became vain in their imaginations, and their foolish heart was darkened.

22Professing themselves to be wise, they became fools,

23And changed the glory of the uncorruptible God into an image made like to corruptible man, and to birds, and fourfooted beasts, and creeping things.

24Wherefore God also gave them up to uncleanness through the lusts of their own hearts, to dishonour their own bodies between themselves:

25Who changed the truth of God into a lie, and worshipped and served the creature more than the Creator, who is blessed for ever. Amen.

26For this cause God gave them up unto vile affections: for even their women did change the natural use into that which is against nature:

27And likewise also the men, leaving the natural use of the woman, burned in their lust one toward another; men with men working that which is unseemly, and receiving in themselves that recompence of their error which was meet.

28And even as they did not like to retain God in *their* knowledge, God gave them over to a reprobate mind, to do those things which are not convenient;

29Being filled with all unrighteousness, fornication, wickedness, covetousness, maliciousness; full of envy, murder, debate, deceit, malignity; whisperers,

30Backbiters, haters of God, despiteful, proud, boasters, inventors of evil things, disobedient to parents,

31Without understanding, covenant breakers, without natural affection, implacable, unmerciful:

32Who knowing the judgment of God, that they which commit such things are worthy of death, not only do the same, but have pleasure in them that do them.

PSALM 10:1-15

Why standest thou afar off, O Lord? *why* hidest thou *thyself* in times of trouble?

2The wicked in *his* pride doth persecute the poor: let them be taken in the devices that they have imagined.

3For the wicked boasteth of his heart's desire, and blesseth the covetous, *whom* the Lord abhorreth.

4The wicked, through the pride of his countenance, will not seek *after God:* God *is* not in all his thoughts.

5His ways are always grievous; thy judgments *are* far above out of his sight: *as for* all his enemies, he puffeth at them.

6He hath said in his heart, I shall not be moved: for *I shall* never *be* in adversity.

7His mouth is full of cursing and deceit and fraud: under his tongue *is* mischief and vanity.

8He sitteth in the lurking places of the villages: in the secret places doth he murder the innocent: his eyes are privily set against the poor.

9He lieth in wait secretly as a lion in his den: he lieth in wait to catch the poor: he doth catch the poor, when he draweth him into his net.

10He croucheth, *and* humbleth himself, that the poor may fall by his strong ones.

11He hath said in his heart, God hath forgotten: he hideth his face; he will never see *it.*

12Arise, O LORD; O God, lift up thine hand: forget not the humble.

13Wherefore doth the wicked contemn God? he hath said in his heart, Thou wilt not require *it.*

14Thou hast seen *it;* for thou beholdest mischief and spite, to requite *it* with thy hand: the poor committeth himself unto thee; thou art the helper of the fatherless.

15Break thou the arm of the wicked and the evil *man:* seek out his wickedness *till* thou find none.

PROVERBS FOR TODAY/ 19:6–7

Many will intreat the favour of the prince: and every man is *a friend to him that giveth gifts.* □ *All the brethren of the poor do hate him: how much more do his friends go far from him? he pursueth* them with *words,* yet *they* are *wanting* to him.

JULY 14

1 CHRONICLES 16:37—18:17

So he [King David] left there before the ark of the covenant of the LORD Asaph and his brethren, to minister before the ark continually, as every day's work required:

38And Obed–edom with their brethren, threescore and eight; Obed–edom also the son of Jeduthun and Hosah *to be* porters:

39And Zadok the priest, and his brethren the priests, before the tabernacle of the LORD in the high place that *was* at Gibeon,

40To offer burnt offerings unto the LORD upon the altar of the burnt offering continually morning and evening, and *to do* according to all that is written in the law of the LORD, which he commanded Israel;

41And with them Heman and Jeduthun, and the rest that were chosen, who were expressed by name, to give thanks to the LORD, because his mercy *endureth* for ever;

42And with them Heman and Jeduthun with trumpets and cymbals for those that should make a sound, and with musical instruments of God. And the sons of Jeduthun *were* porters.

43And all the people departed every man to his house: and David returned to bless his house.

Now it came to pass, as David sat in his house, that David said to Nathan the prophet, Lo, I dwell in an house of cedars, but the ark of the covenant of the LORD *remaineth* under curtains.

2Then Nathan said unto David, Do all that *is* in thine heart; for God *is* with thee.

3And it came to pass the same night, that the word of God came to Nathan, saying,

4Go and tell David my servant, Thus saith the LORD, Thou shalt not build me an house to dwell in:

5For I have not dwelt in an house since the day that I brought up Israel unto this day; but have gone from tent to tent, and from *one* tabernacle *to another*.

6Wheresoever I have walked with all Israel, spake I a word to any of the judges of Israel, whom I commanded to feed my people, saying, Why have ye not built me an house of cedars?

7Now therefore thus shalt thou say unto my servant David, Thus saith the LORD of hosts, I took thee from the sheepcote, *even* from following the sheep, that thou shouldest be ruler over my people Israel:

8And I have been with thee whithersoever thou hast walked, and have cut off all thine enemies from before thee, and have made thee a name like the name of the great men that *are* in the earth.

9Also I will ordain a place for my people Israel, and will plant them, and they shall dwell in their place, and shall be moved no more; neither shall the children of wickedness waste them any more, as at the beginning,

10And since the time that I commanded judges *to be* over my people Israel. Moreover I will subdue all thine enemies. Furthermore I tell thee that the LORD will build thee an house.

11And it shall come to pass, when thy days be expired that thou must go *to be* with thy fathers, that I will raise up thy seed after thee, which shall be of thy sons; and I will establish his kingdom.

12He shall build me an house, and I will stablish his throne for ever.

13I will be his father, and he shall be my son: and I will not take my mercy away from him, as I took *it* from *him* that was before thee:

14But I will settle him in mine house and in my kingdom for ever: and his throne shall be established for evermore.

15According to all these words, and according to all this vision, so did Nathan speak unto David.

16And David the king came and sat before the LORD, and said, Who *am* I, O LORD God, and what *is* mine house, that thou hast brought me hitherto?

17And *yet* this was a small thing in thine eyes, O God; for thou hast *also* spoken of thy servant's house for a great while to come, and hast regarded me according to the estate of a man of high degree, O LORD God.

18What can David *speak* more to thee for the honour of thy servant? for thou knowest thy servant.

19O LORD, for thy servant's sake, and according to thine own heart, hast thou done all this greatness, in making known all *these* great things.

20O LORD, *there is* none like thee, neither *is there any* God beside thee, according to all that we have heard with our ears.

21And what one nation in the earth *is* like thy people Israel, whom God went to redeem *to be* his own people, to make thee a name of greatness and terribleness, by driving out nations from before thy people, whom thou hast redeemed out of Egypt?

22For thy people Israel didst thou make thine own people for ever; and thou, LORD, becamest their God.

23Therefore now, LORD, let the thing that thou hast spoken concerning thy servant and concerning his house be established for ever, and do as thou hast said.

24Let it even be established, that thy name may be magnified for ever, saying, The LORD of hosts *is* the God of Israel, *even* a God to Israel: and *let* the house of David thy servant *be* established before thee.

25For thou, O my God, hast told thy servant that thou wilt build him an house: therefore thy servant hath found *in his heart* to pray before thee.

26And now, LORD, thou art God, and hast promised this goodness unto thy servant:

27Now therefore let it please thee to bless the house of thy servant, that it may be before thee for ever: for thou blessest, O LORD, and *it shall be* blessed for ever.

Now after this it came to pass, that David smote the Philistines, and subdued them, and took Gath and her towns out of the hand of the Philistines.

2And he smote Moab; and the Moabites became David's servants, *and* brought gifts.

3And David smote Hadarezer king of Zobah unto Hamath, as he went to stablish his dominion by the river Euphrates.

4And David took from him a thousand chariots, and seven thousand horsemen, and twenty thousand footmen: David also houghed all the chariot *horses,* but reserved of them an hundred chariots.

5And when the Syrians of Damascus came to help Hadarezer king of Zobah, David slew of the Syrians two and twenty thousand men.

6Then David put *garrisons* in Syria-damascus; and the Syrians became David's servants, *and* brought gifts. Thus the LORD preserved David whithersoever he went.

7And David took the shields of gold that were on the servants of Hadarezer, and brought them to Jerusalem.

8Likewise from Tibhath, and from Chun, cities of Hadarezer, brought David very much brass, wherewith Solomon made the brasen sea, and the pillars, and the vessels of brass.

9Now when Tou king of Hamath heard how David had smitten all the host of Hadarezer king of Zobah;

10He sent Hadoram his son to king David, to enquire of his welfare, and to congratulate him, because he had fought against Hadarezer, and smitten him; (for Hadarezer had war with Tou;) and *with him* all manner of vessels of gold and silver and brass.

11Them also king David dedicated unto the LORD, with the silver and the gold that he brought from all *these* nations; from Edom, and from Moab, and from the children of Ammon, and from the Philistines, and from Amalek.

12Moreover Abishai the son of Zeruiah slew of the Edomites in the valley of salt eighteen thousand.

13And he put garrisons in Edom; and all the Edomites became David's servants. Thus the LORD preserved David whithersoever he went.

14So David reigned over all Israel, and executed judgment and justice among all his people.

15And Joab the son of Zeruiah *was* over the host; and Jehoshaphat the son of Ahilud, recorder.

16And Zadok the son of Ahitub, and Abimelech the son of Abiathar, *were* the priests; and Shavsha was scribe;

17And Benaiah the son of Jehoiada *was* over the Cherethites and the Pelethites; and the sons of David *were* chief about the king.

ROMANS 2:1–23

THEREFORE thou art inexcusable, O man, whosoever thou art that judgest: for wherein thou judgest another, thou condemnest thyself; for thou that judgest doest the same things.

2But we are sure that the judgment of God is according to truth against them which commit such things.

3And thinkest thou this, O man, that judgest them which do such things, and doest the same, that thou shalt escape the judgment of God?

4Or despisest thou the riches of his goodness and forbearance and longsuffering; not knowing that the goodness of God leadeth thee to repentance?

5But after thy hardness and impenitent heart treasurest up unto thyself wrath against the day of wrath and revelation of the righteous judgment of God;

6Who will render to every man according to his deeds:

7To them who by patient continuance in well doing seek for glory and honour and immortality, eternal life:

8But unto them that are contentious, and do not obey the truth, but obey unrighteousness, indignation and wrath,

9Tribulation and anguish, upon every soul of man that doeth evil, of the Jew first, and also of the Gentile;

10But glory, honour, and peace, to every man that worketh good, to the Jew first, and also to the Gentile:

11For there is no respect of persons with God.

12For as many as have sinned without law shall also perish without law: and as many as have sinned in the law shall be judged by the law;

13(For not the hearers of the law *are* just before God, but the doers of the law shall be justified.

14For when the Gentiles, which have not the law, do by nature the things contained in the law, these, having not the law, are a law unto themselves:

15Which shew the work of the law written in their hearts, their conscience also bearing witness, and *their* thoughts the mean while accusing or else excusing one another;)

16In the day when God shall judge the secrets of men by Jesus Christ according to my gospel.

17Behold, thou art called a Jew, and restest in the law, and makest thy boast of God,

18And knowest *his* will, and approvest the things that are more excellent, being instructed out of the law;

19And art confident that thou thyself art a guide of the blind, a light of them which are in darkness,

20An instructor of the foolish, a teacher of babes, which hast the form of knowledge and of the truth in the law.

21Thou therefore which teachest another, teachest thou not thyself? thou that preachest a man should not steal, dost thou steal?

22Thou that sayest a man should not commit adultery, dost thou commit adultery? thou that abhorrest idols, dost thou commit sacrilege?

23Thou that makest thy boast of the law, through breaking the law dishonourest thou God?

PSALM 10:16–18

THE LORD *is* King for ever and ever: the heathen are perished out of his land.

17LORD, thou hast heard the desire of the humble: thou wilt prepare their heart, thou wilt cause thine ear to hear:

18To judge the fatherless and the oppressed, that the man of the earth may no more oppress.

PROVERBS FOR TODAY/ 19:8–9

He that getteth wisdom loveth his own soul: he that keepeth understanding shall find good. ▫A false witness shall not be unpunished, and he that speaketh lies shall perish.

1 CHRONICLES 19:1—21:30

Now it came to pass after this, that Nahash the king of the children of Ammon died, and his son reigned in his stead.

2And David said, I will shew kindness unto Hanun the son of Nahash, because his father shewed kindness to me. And David sent messengers to comfort him concerning his father. So the servants of David came into the land of the children of Ammon to Hanun, to comfort him.

3But the princes of the children of Ammon said to Hanun, Thinkest thou that David doth honour thy father, that he hath sent comforters unto thee? are not his servants come unto thee for to search, and to overthrow, and to spy out the land?

4Wherefore Hanun took David's servants, and shaved them, and cut off their garments in the midst hard by their buttocks, and sent them away.

5Then there went *certain,* and told David how the men were served. And he sent to meet them: for the men were greatly ashamed. And the king said, Tarry at Jericho until your beards be grown, and *then* return.

6And when the children of Ammon saw that they had made themselves odious to David, Hanun and the children of Ammon sent a thousand talents of silver to hire them chariots and horsemen out of Mesopotamia and out of Syria–maachah, and out of Zobah.

7So they hired thirty and two thousand chariots, and the king of Maachah and his people; who came and pitched before Medeba. And the children of Ammon gathered themselves together from their cities, and came to battle.

8And when David heard *of it,* he sent Joab, and all the host of the mighty men.

9And the children of Ammon came out, and put the battle in array before the gate of the city: and the kings that were come *were* by themselves in the field.

10Now when Joab saw that the battle was set against him before and behind, he chose out of all the choice of Israel, and put *them* in array against the Syrians.

11And the rest of the people he delivered unto the hand of Abishai his brother, and they set *themselves* in array against the children of Ammon.

12And he said, If the Syrians be too strong for me, then thou shalt help me: but if the children of Ammon be too strong for thee, then I will help thee.

13Be of good courage, and let us behave ourselves valiantly for our people, and for the cities of our God: and let the LORD do *that which is* good in his sight.

14So Joab and the people that *were* with him drew nigh before the Syrians unto the battle; and they fled before him.

15And when the children of Ammon saw that the Syrians were fled, they likewise fled before Abishai his brother, and entered into the city. Then Joab came to Jerusalem.

16And when the Syrians saw that they were put to the worse before Israel, they sent messengers, and drew forth the Syrians that *were* beyond the river: and Shophach the captain of the host of Hadarezer *went* before them.

17And it was told David; and he gathered all Israel, and passed over Jordan, and came upon them, and set *the battle* in array against them. So when David had put the battle in array against the

Syrians, they fought with him.

18But the Syrians fled before Israel; and David slew of the Syrians seven thousand *men which fought in* chariots, and forty thousand footmen, and killed Shophach the captain of the host.

19And when the servants of Hadarezer saw that they were put to the worse before Israel, they made peace with David, and became his servants: neither would the Syrians help the children of Ammon any more.

AND it came to pass, that after the year was expired, at the time that kings go out *to battle,* Joab led forth the power of the army, and wasted the country of the children of Ammon, and came and besieged Rabbah. But David tarried at Jerusalem. And Joab smote Rabbah, and destroyed it.

2And David took the crown of their king from off his head, and found it to weigh a talent of gold, and *there were* precious stones in it; and it was set upon David's head: and he brought also exceeding much spoil out of the city.

3And he brought out the people that *were* in it, and cut *them* with saws, and with harrows of iron, and with axes. Even so dealt David with all the cities of the children of Ammon. And David and all the people returned to Jerusalem.

4And it came to pass after this, that there arose war at Gezer with the Philistines; at which time Sibbechai the Hushathite slew Sippai, *that was* of the children of the giant: and they were subdued.

5And there was war again with the Philistines; and Elhanan the son of Jair slew Lahmi the brother of Goliath the Gittite, whose spear staff *was* like a weaver's beam.

6And yet again there was war at Gath, where was a man of *great* stature whose fingers and toes *were* four and twenty, six *on each hand,* and six *on each foot:* and he also was the son of the giant.

7But when he defied Israel, Jonathan the son of Shimea David's brother slew him.

8These were born unto the giant in Gath; and they fell by the hand of David, and by the hand of his servants.

AND Satan stood up against Israel, and provoked David to number Israel.

2And David said to Joab and to the rulers of the people, Go, number Israel from Beer–sheba even to Dan; and bring the number of them to me, that I may know *it.*

3And Joab answered, The LORD make his people an hundred times so many more as they *be:* but, my lord the king, *are* they not all my lord's servants? why then doth my lord require this thing? why will he be a cause of trespass to Israel?

4Nevertheless the king's word prevailed against Joab. Wherefore Joab departed, and went throughout all Israel, and came to Jerusalem.

5And Joab gave the sum of the number of the people unto David. And all *they of* Israel were a thousand thousand and an hundred thousand men that drew sword: and Judah *was* four hundred threescore and ten thousand men that drew sword.

6But Levi and Benjamin counted he not among them: for the king's word was abominable to Joab.

7And God was displeased with this thing; therefore he smote Israel.

8And David said unto God, I have sinned greatly, because I have done this thing: but now, I beseech thee, do away the iniquity of thy servant; for I have done very foolishly.

9And the LORD spake unto Gad, David's seer, saying,

10Go and tell David, saying, Thus saith the LORD, I offer thee three *things:* choose thee one of them, that I may do *it* unto thee.

11So Gad came to David, and said

unto him, Thus saith the LORD, Choose thee

12Either three years' famine; or three months to be destroyed before thy foes, while that the sword of thine enemies overtaketh *thee;* or else three days the sword of the LORD, even the pestilence, in the land, and the angel of the LORD destroying throughout all the coasts of Israel. Now therefore advise thyself what word I shall bring again to him that sent me.

13And David said unto Gad, I am in a great strait: let me fall now into the hand of the LORD; for very great *are* his mercies: but let me not fall into the hand of man.

14So the LORD sent pestilence upon Israel: and there fell of Israel seventy thousand men.

15And God sent an angel unto Jerusalem to destroy it: and as he was destroying, the LORD beheld, and he repented him of the evil, and said to the angel that destroyed, It is enough, stay now thine hand. And the angel of the LORD stood by the threshingfloor of Ornan the Jebusite.

16And David lifted up his eyes, and saw the angel of the LORD stand between the earth and the heaven, having a drawn sword in his hand stretched out over Jerusalem. Then David and the elders *of Israel, who were* clothed in sackcloth, fell upon their faces.

17And David said unto God, *Is it* not I *that* commanded the people to be numbered? even I it is that have sinned and done evil indeed; but *as for* these sheep, what have they done? let thine hand, I pray thee, O LORD my God, be on me, and on my father's house; but not on thy people, that they should be plagued.

18Then the angel of the LORD commanded Gad to say to David, that David should go up, and set up an altar unto the LORD in the threshingfloor of Ornan the Jebusite.

19And David went up at the saying of Gad, which he spake in the name of the LORD.

20And Ornan turned back, and saw the angel; and his four sons with him hid themselves. Now Ornan was threshing wheat.

21And as David came to Ornan, Ornan looked and saw David, and went out of the threshingfloor, and bowed himself to David with *his* face to the ground.

22Then David said to Ornan, Grant me the place of *this* threshingfloor, that I may build an altar therein unto the LORD: thou shalt grant it me for the full price: that the plague may be stayed from the people.

23And Ornan said unto David, Take *it* to thee, and let my lord the king do *that which is* good in his eyes: lo, I give *thee* the oxen *also* for burnt offerings, and the threshing instruments for wood, and the wheat for the meat offering; I give it all.

24And king David said to Ornan, Nay; but I will verily buy it for the full price: for I will not take *that* which *is* thine for the LORD, nor offer burnt offerings without cost.

25So David gave to Ornan for the place six hundred shekels of gold by weight.

26And David built there an altar unto the LORD, and offered burnt offerings and peace offerings, and called upon the LORD; and he answered him from heaven by fire upon the altar of burnt offering.

27And the LORD commanded the angel; and he put up his sword again into the sheath thereof.

28At that time when David saw that the LORD had answered him in the threshingfloor of Ornan the Jebusite, then he sacrificed there.

29For the tabernacle of the LORD, which Moses made in the wilderness, and the altar of the burnt offering, *were* at that season in the high place at Gibeon.

30But David could not go before it

to enquire of God: for he was afraid because of the sword of the angel of the LORD.

ROMANS 2:24—3:8

FOR the name of God is blasphemed among the Gentiles through you, as it is written.

25For circumcision verily profiteth, if thou keep the law: but if thou be a breaker of the law, thy circumcision is made uncircumcision.

26Therefore if the uncircumcision keep the righteousness of the law, shall not his uncircumcision be counted for circumcision?

27And shall not uncircumcision which is by nature, if it fulfil the law, judge thee, who by the letter and circumcision dost transgress the law?

28For he is not a Jew, which is one outwardly; neither is that circumcision, which is outward in the flesh:

29But he is a Jew, which is one inwardly; and circumcision is that of the heart, in the spirit, and not in the letter; whose praise is not of men, but of God.

WHAT advantage then hath the Jew? or what profit is there of circumcision?

2Much every way: chiefly, because that unto them were committed the oracles of God.

3For what if some did not believe? shall their unbelief make the faith of God without effect?

4God forbid: yea, let God be true, but every man a liar; as it is written, That thou mightest be justified in thy sayings, and mightest overcome when thou art judged.

5But if our unrighteousness commend the righteousness of God, what shall we say? Is God unrighteous who taketh vengeance? (I speak as a man.)

6God forbid: for then how shall God judge the world?

7For if the truth of God hath more abounded through my lie unto his glory; why yet am I also judged as a sinner?

8And not rather, (as we be slanderously reported, and as some affirm that we say,) Let us do evil, that good may come? whose damnation is just.

PSALM 11:1–7

IN the LORD put I my trust: how say ye to my soul, Flee as a bird to your mountain?

2For, lo, the wicked bend their bow, they make ready their arrow upon the string, that they may privily shoot at the upright in heart.

3If the foundations be destroyed, what can the righteous do?

4The LORD is in his holy temple, the LORD'S throne is in heaven: his eyes behold, his eyelids try, the children of men.

5The LORD trieth the righteous: but the wicked and him that loveth violence his soul hateth.

6Upon the wicked he shall rain snares, fire and brimstone, and an horrible tempest: this shall be the portion of their cup.

7For the righteous LORD loveth righteousness; his countenance doth behold the upright.

PROVERBS FOR TODAY/ 19:10–12

Delight is not seemly for a fool; much less for a servant to have rule over princes. □ *The discretion of a man deferreth his anger; and* it is *his glory to pass over a transgression.* □ *The king's wrath* is *as the roaring of a lion; but his favour* is *as dew upon the grass.*

JULY 16

1 CHRONICLES 22:1—23:32

THEN David said, This *is* the house of the LORD God, and this *is* the altar of the burnt offering for Israel.

2And David commanded to gather together the strangers that *were* in the land of Israel; and he set masons to hew wrought stones to build the house of God.

3And David prepared iron in abundance for the nails for the doors of the gates, and for the joinings; and brass in abundance without weight;

4Also cedar trees in abundance: for the Zidonians and they of Tyre brought much cedar wood to David.

5And David said, Solomon my son *is* young and tender, and the house *that is* to be builded for the LORD *must be* exceeding magnifical, of fame and of glory throughout all countries: I will *therefore* now make preparation for it. So David prepared abundantly before his death.

6Then he called for Solomon his son, and charged him to build an house for the LORD God of Israel.

7And David said to Solomon, My son, as for me, it was in my mind to build an house unto the name of the LORD my God:

8But the word of the LORD came to me, saying, Thou hast shed blood abundantly, and hast made great wars: thou shalt not build an house unto my name, because thou hast shed much blood upon the earth in my sight.

9Behold, a son shall be born to thee, who shall be a man of rest; and I will give him rest from all his enemies round about: for his name shall be Solomon, and I will give peace and quietness unto Israel in his days.

10He shall build an house for my name; and he shall be my son, and I *will be* his father; and I will establish the throne of his kingdom over Israel for ever.

11Now, my son, the LORD be with thee; and prosper thou, and build the house of the LORD thy God, as he hath said of thee.

12Only the LORD give thee wisdom and understanding, and give thee charge concerning Israel, that thou mayest keep the law of the LORD thy God.

13Then shalt thou prosper, if thou takest heed to fulfil the statutes and judgments which the LORD charged Moses with concerning Israel: be strong, and of good courage; dread not, nor be dismayed.

14Now, behold, in my trouble I have prepared for the house of the LORD an hundred thousand talents of gold, and a thousand thousand talents of silver; and of brass and iron without weight; for it is in abundance: timber also and stone have I prepared; and thou mayest add thereto.

15Moreover *there are* workmen with thee in abundance, hewers and workers of stone and timber, and all manner of cunning men for every manner of work.

16Of the gold, the silver, and the brass, and the iron, *there is* no number. Arise *therefore,* and be doing, and the LORD be with thee.

17David also commanded all the princes of Israel to help Solomon his son, *saying,*

18*Is* not the LORD your God with you? and hath he *not* given you rest on every side? for he hath given the inhabitants of the land into mine hand; and the land is subdued before the LORD, and before his people.

¹⁹Now set your heart and your soul to seek the LORD your God; arise therefore, and build ye the sanctuary of the LORD God, to bring the ark of the covenant of the LORD, and the holy vessels of God, into the house that is to be built to the name of the LORD.

So when David was old and full of days, he made Solomon his son king over Israel.

²And he gathered together all the princes of Israel, with the priests and the Levites.

³Now the Levites were numbered from the age of thirty years and upward: and their number by their polls, man by man, was thirty and eight thousand.

⁴Of which, twenty and four thousand *were* to set forward the work of the house of the LORD; and six thousand *were* officers and judges:

⁵Moreover four thousand *were* porters; and four thousand praised the LORD with the instruments which I made, *said David* to praise *therewith.*

⁶And David divided them into courses among the sons of Levi, *namely,* Gershon, Kohath, and Merari.

⁷Of the Gershonites *were,* Laadan, and Shimei.

⁸The sons of Laadan; the chief *was* Jehiel, and Zetham, and Joel, three.

⁹The sons of Shimei; Shelomith, and Haziel, and Haran, three. These *were* the chief of the fathers of Laadan.

¹⁰And the sons of Shimei *were,* Jahath, Zina, and Jeush, and Beriah. These four *were* the sons of Shimei.

¹¹And Jahath was the chief, and Zizah the second: but Jeush and Beriah had not many sons; therefore they were in one reckoning, according to *their* father's house.

¹²The sons of Kohath; Amram, Izhar, Hebron, and Uzziel, four.

¹³The sons of Amram; Aaron and Moses: and Aaron was separated, that he should sanctify the most holy things,

he and his sons for ever, to burn incense before the LORD, to minister unto him, and to bless in his name for ever.

¹⁴Now *concerning* Moses the man of God, his sons were named of the tribe of Levi.

¹⁵The sons of Moses *were,* Gershom, and Eliezer.

¹⁶Of the sons of Gershom, Shebuel *was* the chief.

¹⁷And the sons of Eliezer *were,* Rehabiah the chief. And Eliezer had none other sons; but the sons of Rehabiah were very many.

¹⁸Of the sons of Izhar; Shelomith the chief.

¹⁹Of the sons of Hebron; Jeriah the first, Amariah the second, Jahaziel the third, and Jekameam the fourth.

²⁰Of the sons of Uzziel; Micah the first, and Jesiah the second.

²¹The sons of Merari; Mahli, and Mushi. The sons of Mahli; Eleazar, and Kish.

²²And Eleazar died, and had no sons, but daughters: and their brethren the sons of Kish took them.

²³The sons of Mushi; Mahli, and Eder, and Jeremoth, three.

²⁴These *were* the sons of Levi after the house of their fathers; *even* the chief of the fathers, as they were counted by number of names by their polls, that did the work for the service of the house of the LORD, from the age of twenty years and upward.

²⁵For David said, The LORD God of Israel hath given rest unto his people, that they may dwell in Jerusalem for ever:

²⁶And also unto the Levites; they shall no *more* carry the tabernacle, nor any vessels of it for the service thereof.

²⁷For by the last words of David the Levites *were* numbered from twenty years old and above:

²⁸Because their office *was* to wait on the sons of Aaron for the service of the house of the LORD, in the courts,

and in the chambers, and in the purifying of all holy things, and the work of the service of the house of God;

29Both for the shewbread, and for the fine flour for meat offering, and for the unleavened cakes, and for *that which is baked in* the pan, and for that which is fried, and for all manner of measure and size;

30And to stand every morning to thank and praise the LORD, and likewise at even;

31And to offer all burnt sacrifices unto the LORD in the sabbaths, in the new moons, and on the set feasts, by number, according to the order commanded unto them, continually before the LORD:

32And that they should keep the charge of the tabernacle of the congregation, and the charge of the holy *place,* and the charge of the sons of Aaron their brethren, in the service of the house of the LORD.

ROMANS 3:9–31

WHAT then? are we [Jews] better *than they?* No, in no wise: for we have before proved both Jews and Gentiles, that they are all under sin;

10As it is written, There is none righteous, no, not one:

11There is none that understandeth, there is none that seeketh after God.

12They are all gone out of the way, they are together become unprofitable; there is none that doeth good, no, not one.

13Their throat *is* an open sepulchre; with their tongues they have used deceit; the poison of asps *is* under their lips:

14Whose mouth *is* full of cursing and bitterness:

15Their feet *are* swift to shed blood:

16Destruction and misery *are* in their ways:

17And the way of peace have they not known:

18There is no fear of God before their eyes.

19Now we know that what things soever the law saith, it saith to them who are under the law: that every mouth may be stopped, and all the world may become guilty before God.

20Therefore by the deeds of the law there shall no flesh be justified in his sight: for by the law *is* the knowledge of sin.

21But now the righteousness of God without the law is manifested, being witnessed by the law and the prophets;

22Even the righteousness of God *which is* by faith of Jesus Christ unto all and upon all them that believe: for there is no difference:

23For all have sinned, and come short of the glory of God;

24Being justified freely by his grace through the redemption that is in Christ Jesus:

25Whom God hath set forth *to be* a propitiation through faith in his blood, to declare his righteousness for the remission of sins that are past, through the forbearance of God;

26To declare, *I say,* at this time his righteousness: that he might be just, and the justifier of him which believeth in Jesus.

27Where *is* boasting then? It is excluded. By what law? of works? Nay: but by the law of faith.

28Therefore we conclude that a man is justified by faith without the deeds of the law.

29*Is he* the God of the Jews only? *is he* not also of the Gentiles? Yes, of the Gentiles also:

30Seeing *it is* one God, which shall justify the circumcision by faith, and uncircumcision through faith.

31Do we then make void the law through faith? God forbid: yea, we establish the law.

PSALM 12:1–8

HELP, LORD; for the godly man ceaseth; for the faithful fail from among the children of men.

2They speak vanity every one with his neighbour: *with* flattering lips *and* with a double heart do they speak.

3The LORD shall cut off all flattering lips, *and* the tongue that speaketh proud things:

4Who have said, With our tongue will we prevail; our lips *are* our own:

who *is* lord over us?

5For the oppression of the poor, for the sighing of the needy, now will I arise, saith the LORD; I will set *him* in safety *from him that* puffeth at him.

6The words of the LORD *are* pure words: *as* silver tried in a furnace of earth, purified seven times.

7Thou shalt keep them, O LORD, thou shalt preserve them from this generation for ever.

8The wicked walk on every side, when the vilest men are exalted.

PROVERBS FOR TODAY/ 19:13–14

A foolish son is *the calamity of his father: and the contentions of a wife* are *a continual dropping.* □ *House and riches* are *the inheritance of fathers: and a prudent wife* is *from the LORD.*

JULY 17

1 CHRONICLES 24:1—26:11

NOW *these are* the divisions of the sons of Aaron. The sons of Aaron; Nadab, and Abihu, Eleazar, and Ithamar.

2But Nadab and Abihu died before their father, and had no children: therefore Eleazar and Ithamar executed the priest's office.

3And David distributed them, both Zadok of the sons of Eleazar, and Ahimelech of the sons of Ithamar, according to their offices in their service.

4And there were more chief men found of the sons of Eleazar than of the sons of Ithamar; and *thus* were they divided. Among the sons of Eleazar *there were* sixteen chief men of the house of *their* fathers, and eight among the sons of Ithamar according to the house of their fathers.

5Thus were they divided by lot, one

sort with another; for the governors of the sanctuary, and governors *of the house* of God, were of the sons of Eleazar, and of the sons of Ithamar.

6And Shemaiah the son of Nethaneel the scribe, *one* of the Levites, wrote them before the king, and the princes, and Zadok the priest, and Ahimelech the son of Abiathar, and *before* the chief of the fathers of the priests and Levites: one principal household being taken for Eleazar, and *one* taken for Ithamar.

7Now the first lot came forth to Jehoiarib, the second to Jedaiah,

8The third to Harim, the fourth to Seorim,

9The fifth to Malchijah, the sixth to Mijamin,

10The seventh to Hakkoz, the eighth to Abijah,

11The ninth to Jeshuah, the tenth to Shecaniah,

12The eleventh to Eliashib, the twelfth to Jakim,

13The thirteenth to Huppah, the fourteenth to Jeshebeab,

14The fifteenth to Bilgah, the sixteenth to Immer,

15The seventeenth to Hezir, the eighteenth to Aphses,

16The nineteenth to Pethahiah, the twentieth to Jehezekel,

17The one and twentieth to Jachin, the two and twentieth to Gamul,

18The three and twentieth to Delaiah, the four and twentieth to Maaziah.

19These *were* the orderings of them in their service to come into the house of the LORD, according to their manner, under Aaron their father, as the LORD God of Israel had commanded him.

20And the rest of the sons of Levi *were these:* Of the sons of Amram; Shubael: of the sons of Shubael; Jehdeiah.

21Concerning Rehabiah: of the sons of Rehabiah, the first *was* Isshiah.

22Of the Izharites; Shelomoth: of the sons of Shelomoth; Jahath.

23And the sons *of Hebron;* Jeriah *the first,* Amariah the second, Jahaziel the third, Jekameam the fourth.

24*Of* the sons of Uzziel; Micah: of the sons of Micah; Shamir.

25The brother of Micah *was* Isshiah: of the sons of Isshiah; Zechariah.

26The sons of Merari *were* Mahli and Mushi: the sons of Jaaziah; Beno.

27The sons of Merari by Jaaziah; Beno, and Shoham, and Zaccur, and Ibri.

28Of Mahli *came* Eleazar, who had no sons.

29Concerning Kish: the son of Kish *was* Jerahmeel.

30The sons also of Mushi; Mahli, and Eder, and Jerimoth. These *were* the sons of the Levites after the house of their fathers.

31These likewise cast lots over against their brethren the sons of Aaron in the presence of David the king, and Zadok, and Ahimelech, and the chief of the fathers of the priests and Levites, even the principal fathers over against their younger brethren.

MOREOVER David and the captains of the host separated to the service of the sons of Asaph, and of Heman, and of Jeduthun, who should prophesy with harps, with psalteries, and with cymbals: and the number of the workmen according to their service was:

2Of the sons of Asaph; Zaccur, and Joseph, and Nethaniah, and Asarelah, the sons of Asaph under the hands of Asaph, which prophesied according to the order of the king.

3Of Jeduthun: the sons of Jeduthun; Gedaliah, and Zeri, and Jeshaiah, Hashabiah, and Mattithiah, six, under the hands of their father Jeduthun, who prophesied with a harp, to give thanks and to praise the LORD.

4Of Heman: the sons of Heman; Bukkiah, Mattaniah, Uzziel, Shebuel, and Jerimoth, Hananiah, Hanani, Eliathah, Giddalti, and Romamti–ezer, Joshbekashah, Mallothi, Hothir, *and* Mahazioth:

5All these *were* the sons of Heman the king's seer in the words of God, to lift up the horn. And God gave to Heman fourteen sons and three daughters.

6All these *were* under the hands of their father for song *in* the house of the LORD, with cymbals, psalteries, and harps, for the service of the house of God, according to the king's order to Asaph, Jeduthun, and Heman.

7So the number of them, with their brethren that were instructed in the songs of the LORD, *even* all that were cunning, was two hundred fourscore and eight.

8And they cast lots, ward against *ward,* as well the small as the great, the teacher as the scholar.

9Now the first lot came forth for Asaph to Joseph: the second to

Gedaliah, who with his brethren and sons *were* twelve:

10The third to Zaccur, *he,* his sons, and his brethren, *were* twelve:

11The fourth to Izri, *he,* his sons, and his brethren, *were* twelve:

12The fifth to Nethaniah, *he,* his sons, and his brethren, *were* twelve:

13The sixth to Bukkiah, *he,* his sons, and his brethren, *were* twelve:

14The seventh to Jesharelah, *he,* his sons, and his brethren, *were* twelve:

15The eighth to Jeshaiah, *he,* his sons, and his brethren, *were* twelve:

16The ninth to Mattaniah, *he,* his sons, and his brethren, *were* twelve:

17The tenth to Shimei, *he,* his sons, and his brethren, *were* twelve:

18The eleventh to Azareel, *he,* his sons, and his brethren, *were* twelve:

19The twelfth to Hashabiah, *he,* his sons, and his brethren, *were* twelve:

20The thirteenth to Shubael, *he,* his sons, and his brethren, *were* twelve:

21The fourteenth to Mattithiah, *he,* his sons, and his brethren, *were* twelve:

22The fifteenth to Jeremoth, *he,* his sons, and his brethren, *were* twelve:

23The sixteenth to Hananiah, *he,* his sons, and his brethren, *were* twelve:

24The seventeenth to Joshbekashah, *he,* his sons, and his brethren, *were* twelve:

25The eighteenth to Hanani, *he,* his sons, and his brethren, *were* twelve:

26The nineteenth to Mallothi, *he,* his sons, and his brethren, *were* twelve:

27The twentieth to Eliathah, *he,* his sons, and his brethren, *were* twelve:

28The one and twentieth to Hothir, *he,* his sons, and his brethren, *were* twelve:

29The two and twentieth to Giddalti, *he,* his sons, and his brethren, *were* twelve:

30The three and twentieth to Mahazioth, *he,* his sons, and his brethren, *were* twelve:

31The four and twentieth to Ro-

mamti–ezer, *he,* his sons, and his brethren, *were* twelve.

CONCERNING the divisions of the porters: Of the Korhites *was* Meshelemiah the son of Kore, of the sons of Asaph.

2And the sons of Meshelemiah *were,* Zechariah the firstborn, Jediael the second, Zebadiah the third, Jathniel the fourth,

3Elam the fifth, Jehohanan the sixth, Elioenai the seventh.

4Moreover the sons of Obed–edom *were,* Shemaiah the firstborn, Jehozabad the second, Joah the third, and Sacar the fourth, and Nethaneel the fifth,

5Ammiel the sixth, Issachar the seventh, Peulthai the eighth: for God blessed him.

6Also unto Shemaiah his son were sons born, that ruled throughout the house of their father: for they *were* mighty men of valour.

7The sons of Shemaiah; Othni, and Rephael and Obed, Elzabad, whose brethren *were* strong men, Elihu, and Semachiah.

8All these of the sons of Obed–edom: they and their sons and their brethren, able men for strength for the service, *were* threescore and two of Obed–edom.

9And Meshelemiah had sons and brethren, strong men, eighteen.

10Also Hosah, of the children of Merari, had sons; Simri the chief, (for *though* he was not the firstborn, yet his father made him the chief;)

11Hilkiah the second, Tebaliah the third, Zechariah the fourth: all the sons and brethren of Hosah *were* thirteen.

ROMANS 4:1–13

WHAT shall we say then that Abraham our father, as pertaining to the flesh, hath found?

2For if Abraham were justified by

works, he hath *whereof* to glory; but not before God.

3For what saith the scripture? Abraham believed God, and it was counted unto him for righteousness.

4Now to him that worketh is the reward not reckoned of grace, but of debt.

5But to him that worketh not, but believeth on him that justifieth the ungodly, his faith is counted for righteousness.

6Even as David also describeth the blessedness of the man, unto whom God imputeth righteousness without works,

7*Saying,* Blessed *are* they whose iniquities are forgiven, and whose sins are covered.

8Blessed *is* the man to whom the Lord will not impute sin.

9*Cometh* this blessedness then upon the circumcision *only,* or upon the uncircumcision also? for we say that faith was reckoned to Abraham for righteousness.

10How was it then reckoned? when he was in circumcision, or in uncircumcision? Not in circumcision, but in uncircumcision.

11And he received the sign of circumcision, a seal of the righteousness of the faith which *he had yet* being uncircumcised: that he might be the father of all them that believe, though they be not circumcised; that righteousness might be imputed unto them also:

12And the father of circumcision to them who are not of the circumcision only, but who also walk in the steps of that faith of our father Abraham, which *he had* being *yet* uncircumcised.

13For the promise, that he should be the heir of the world, *was* not to Abraham, or to his seed, through the law, but through the righteousness of faith.

PSALM 13:1–6

How long wilt thou forget me, O Lord? for ever? how long wilt thou hide thy face from me?

2How long shall I take counsel in my soul, *having* sorrow in my heart daily? how long shall mine enemy be exalted over me?

3Consider *and* hear me, O Lord my God: lighten mine eyes, lest I sleep the *sleep of* death;

4Lest mine enemy say, I have prevailed against him; *and* those that troubled me rejoice when I am moved.

5But I have trusted in thy mercy; my heart shall rejoice in thy salvation.

6I will sing unto the Lord, because he hath dealt bountifully with me.

PROVERBS FOR TODAY/ 19:15–16

Slothfulness casteth into a deep sleep; and an idle soul shall suffer hunger. □ *He that keepeth the commandment keepeth his own soul; but he that despiseth his ways shall die.*

JULY 18

1 CHRONICLES 26:12—27:34

AMONG these *were* the divisions of the porters, *even* among the chief men, *having* wards one against another, to minister in the house of the LORD.

¹³And they cast lots, as well the small as the great, according to the house of their fathers, for every gate.

¹⁴And the lot eastward fell to Shelemiah. Then for Zechariah his son, a wise counsellor, they cast lots; and his lot came out northward.

¹⁵To Obed–edom southward; and to his sons the house of Asuppim.

¹⁶To Shuppim and Hosah *the lot came forth* westward, with the gate Shallecheth, by the causeway of the going up, ward against ward.

¹⁷Eastward *were* six Levites, northward four a day, southward four a day, and toward Asuppim two *and* two.

¹⁸At Parbar westward, four at the causeway, *and* two at Parbar.

¹⁹These *are* the divisions of the porters among the sons of Kore, and among the sons of Merari.

²⁰And of the Levites, Ahijah *was* over the treasures of the house of God, and over the treasures of the dedicated things.

²¹*As concerning* the sons of Laadan; the sons of the Gershonite Laadan, chief fathers, *even* of Laadan the Gershonite, *were* Jehieli.

²²The sons of Jehieli; Zetham, and Joel his brother, *which were* over the treasures of the house of the LORD.

²³Of the Amramites, *and* the Izharites, the Hebronites, *and* the Uzzielites:

²⁴And Shebuel the son of Gershom, the son of Moses, *was* ruler of the treasures.

²⁵And his brethren by Eliezer; Reha-

biah his son, and Jeshaiah his son, and Joram his son, and Zichri his son, and Shelomith his son.

²⁶Which Shelomith and his brethren *were* over all the treasures of the dedicated things, which David the king, and the chief fathers, the captains over thousands and hundreds, and the captains of the host, had dedicated.

²⁷Out of the spoils won in battles did they dedicate to maintain the house of the LORD.

²⁸And all that Samuel the seer, and Saul the son of Kish, and Abner the son of Ner, and Joab the son of Zeruiah, had dedicated; *and* whosoever had dedicated *any thing, it was* under the hand of Shelomith, and of his brethren.

²⁹Of the Izharites, Chenaniah and his sons *were* for the outward business over Israel, for officers and judges.

³⁰*And* of the Hebronites, Hashabiah and his brethren, men of valour, a thousand and seven hundred, *were* officers among them of Israel on this side Jordan westward in all the business of the LORD, and in the service of the king.

³¹Among the Hebronites *was* Jerijah the chief, *even* among the Hebronites, according to the generations of his fathers. In the fortieth year of the reign of David they were sought for, and there were found among them mighty men of valour at Jazer of Gilead.

³²And his brethren, men of valour, *were* two thousand and seven hundred chief fathers, whom king David made rulers over the Reubenites, the Gadites, and the half tribe of Manasseh, for every matter pertaining to God, and affairs of the king.

Now the children of Israel after their number, *to wit,* the chief fathers and captains of thousands and hundreds, and their officers that served the king in any matter of the courses, which came in and went out month by month throughout all the months of the year, of every course *were* twenty and four thousand.

2Over the first course for the first month *was* Jashobeam the son of Zabdiel: and in his course *were* twenty and four thousand.

3Of the children of Perez *was* the chief of all the captains of the host for the first month.

4And over the course of the second month *was* Dodai an Ahohite, and of his course *was* Mikloth also the ruler: in his course likewise *were* twenty and four thousand.

5The third captain of the host for the third month *was* Benaiah the son of Jehoiada, a chief priest: and in his course *were* twenty and four thousand.

6This *is that* Benaiah, *who was* mighty *among* the thirty, and above the thirty: and in his course *was* Ammizabad his son.

7The fourth *captain* for the fourth month *was* Asahel the brother of Joab, and Zebadiah his son after him: and in his course *were* twenty and four thousand.

8The fifth captain for the fifth month *was* Shamhuth the Izrahite: and in his course *were* twenty and four thousand.

9The sixth *captain* for the sixth month *was* Ira the son of Ikkesh the Tekoite: and in his course *were* twenty and four thousand.

10The seventh *captain* for the seventh month *was* Helez the Pelonite, of the children of Ephraim: and in his course *were* twenty and four thousand.

11The eighth *captain* for the eighth month *was* Sibbecai the Hushathite, of the Zarhites: and in his course *were* twenty and four thousand.

12The ninth *captain* for the ninth month *was* Abiezer the Anetothite, of the Benjamites: and in his course *were* twenty and four thousand.

13The tenth *captain* for the tenth month *was* Maharai the Netophathite, of the Zarhites: and in his course *were* twenty and four thousand.

14The eleventh *captain* for the eleventh month *was* Benaiah the Pirathonite, of the children of Ephraim: and in his course *were* twenty and four thousand.

15The twelfth *captain* for the twelfth month *was* Heldai the Netophathite, of Othniel: and in his course *were* twenty and four thousand.

16Furthermore over the tribes of Israel: the ruler of the Reubenites *was* Eliezer the son of Zichri: of the Simeonites, Shephatiah the son of Maachah:

17Of the Levites, Hashabiah the son of Kemuel: of the Aaronites, Zadok:

18Of Judah, Elihu, *one* of the brethren of David: of Issachar, Omri the son of Michael:

19Of Zebulun, Ishmaiah the son of Obadiah: of Naphtali, Jerimoth the son of Azriel:

20Of the children of Ephraim, Hoshea the son of Azaziah: of the half tribe of Manasseh, Joel the son of Pedaiah:

21Of the half *tribe* of Manasseh in Gilead, Iddo the son of Zechariah: of Benjamin, Jaasiel the son of Abner:

22Of Dan, Azareel the son of Jeroham. These were the princes of the tribes of Israel.

23But David took not the number of them from twenty years old and under: because the LORD had said he would increase Israel like to the stars of the heavens.

24Joab the son of Zeruiah began to number, but he finished not, because there fell wrath for it against Israel; neither was the number put in the account of the chronicles of king David.

25And over the king's treasures *was* Azmaveth the son of Adiel: and over the storehouses in the fields, in the cities, and in the villages, and in the castles, *was* Jehonathan the son of Uzziah:

26And over them that did the work of the field for tillage of the ground *was* Ezri the son of Chelub:

27And over the vineyards *was* Shimei the Ramathite: over the increase of the vineyards for the wine cellars *was* Zabdi the Shiphmite:

28And over the olive trees and the sycomore trees that *were* in the low plains *was* Baal–hanan the Gederite: and over the cellars of oil *was* Joash:

29And over the herds that fed in Sharon *was* Shitrai the Sharonite: and over the herds *that were* in the valleys *was* Shaphat the son of Adlai:

30Over the camels also *was* Obil the Ishmaelite: and over the asses *was* Jehdeiah the Meronothite:

31And over the flocks *was* Jaziz the Hagerite. All these *were* the rulers of the substance which *was* king David's.

32Also Jonathan David's uncle was a counsellor, a wise man, and a scribe: and Jehiel the son of Hachmoni *was* with the king's sons:

33And Ahithophel *was* the king's counsellor: and Hushai the Archite *was* the king's companion:

34And after Ahithophel *was* Jehoiada the son of Benaiah, and Abiathar: and the general of the king's army *was* Joab.

ROMANS 4:14—5:2

FOR if they which are of the law *be* heirs, faith is made void, and the promise made of none effect:

15Because the law worketh wrath: for where no law is, *there is* no transgression.

16Therefore *it is* of faith, that *it might be* by grace; to the end the promise might be sure to all the seed; not to that only which is of the law, but to that also which is of the faith of Abraham; who is the father of us all,

17(As it is written, I have made thee a father of many nations,) before him whom he believed, *even* God, who quickeneth the dead, and calleth those things which be not as though they were.

18Who against hope believed in hope, that he might become the father of many nations, according to that which was spoken, So shall thy seed be.

19And being not weak in faith, he considered not his own body now dead, when he was about an hundred years old, neither yet the deadness of Sarah's womb:

20He staggered not at the promise of God through unbelief; but was strong in faith, giving glory to God;

21And being fully persuaded that, what he had promised, he was able also to perform.

22And therefore it was imputed to him for righteousness.

23Now it was not written for his sake alone, that it was imputed to him;

24But for us also, to whom it shall be imputed, if we believe on him that raised up Jesus our Lord from the dead;

25Who was delivered for our offences, and was raised again for our justification.

THEREFORE being justified by faith, we have peace with God through our Lord Jesus Christ:

2By whom also we have access by faith into this grace wherein we stand, and rejoice in hope of the glory of God.

PSALM 14:1–7

THE fool hath said in his heart, *There is* no God. They are corrupt, they have done abominable works, *there is* none that doeth good.

2The LORD looked down from heaven upon the children of men, to see if there were any that did understand, *and* seek God.

3They are all gone aside, they are *all* together become filthy: *there is* none that doeth good, no, not one.

⁴Have all the workers of iniquity no knowledge? who eat up my people *as* they eat bread, and call not upon the LORD.

⁵There were they in great fear: for God *is* in the generation of the righteous.

⁶Ye have shamed the counsel of the poor, because the LORD *is* his refuge.

⁷Oh that the salvation of Israel *were come* out of Zion! when the LORD bringeth back the captivity of his people, Jacob shall rejoice, *and* Israel shall be glad.

PROVERBS FOR TODAY/ 19:17

He that hath pity upon the poor lendeth unto the LORD; and that which he hath given will he pay him again.

JULY 19

1 CHRONICLES 28:1—29:30

AND David assembled all the princes of Israel, the princes of the tribes, and the captains of the companies that ministered to the king by course, and the captains over the thousands, and captains over the hundreds, and the stewards over all the substance and possession of the king, and of his sons, with the officers, and with the mighty men, and with all the valiant men, unto Jerusalem.

²Then David the king stood up upon his feet, and said, Hear me, my brethren, and my people: *As for me,* I *had* in mine heart to build an house of rest for the ark of the covenant of the LORD, and for the footstool of our God, and had made ready for the building:

³But God said unto me, Thou shalt not build an house for my name, because thou *hast been* a man of war, and hast shed blood.

⁴Howbeit the LORD God of Israel chose me before all the house of my father to be king over Israel for ever: for he hath chosen Judah *to be* the ruler; and of the house of Judah, the house of my father; and among the sons of my father he liked me to make *me* king over all Israel:

⁵And of all my sons, (for the LORD hath given me many sons,) he hath chosen Solomon my son to sit upon the throne of the kingdom of the LORD over Israel.

⁶And he said unto me, Solomon thy son, he shall build my house and my courts: for I have chosen him *to be* my son, and I will be his father.

⁷Moreover I will establish his kingdom for ever, if he be constant to do my commandments and my judgments, as at this day.

⁸Now therefore in the sight of all Israel the congregation of the LORD, and in the audience of our God, keep and seek for all the commandments of the LORD your God: that ye may possess this good land, and leave *it* for an inheritance for your children after you for ever.

⁹And thou, Solomon my son, know thou the God of thy father, and serve him with a perfect heart and with a willing mind: for the LORD searcheth all hearts, and understandeth all the imaginations of the thoughts: if thou

seek him, he will be found of thee: but if thou forsake him, he will cast thee off for ever.

¹⁰Take heed now; for the LORD hath chosen thee to build an house for the sanctuary: be strong, and do *it*.

¹¹Then David gave to Solomon his son the pattern of the porch, and of the houses thereof, and of the treasuries thereof, and of the upper chambers thereof, and of the inner parlours thereof, and of the place of the mercy seat,

¹²And the pattern of all that he had by the spirit, of the courts of the house of the LORD, and of all the chambers round about, of the treasuries of the house of God, and of the treasuries of the dedicated things:

¹³Also for the courses of the priests and the Levites, and for all the work of the service of the house of the LORD, and for all the vessels of service in the house of the LORD.

¹⁴*He gave* of gold by weight for *things* of gold, for all instruments of all manner of service; *silver also* for all instruments of silver by weight, for all instruments of every kind of service:

¹⁵Even the weight for the candlesticks of gold, and for their lamps of gold, by weight for every candlestick, and for the lamps thereof: and for the candlesticks of silver by weight, *both* for the candlestick, and *also* for the lamps thereof, according to the use of every candlestick.

¹⁶And by weight *he gave* gold for the tables of shewbread, for every table; and *likewise* silver for the tables of silver:

¹⁷Also pure gold for the fleshhooks, and the bowls, and the cups: and for the golden basons *he gave gold* by weight for every bason; and *likewise silver* by weight for every bason of silver:

¹⁸And for the altar of incense refined gold by weight; and gold for the pattern of the chariot of the cherubims, that spread out *their wings,* and covered the ark of the covenant of the LORD.

¹⁹All *this, said David,* the LORD made me understand in writing by *his* hand upon me, *even* all the works of this pattern.

²⁰And David said to Solomon his son, Be strong and of good courage, and do *it:* fear not, nor be dismayed: for the LORD God, *even* my God, *will be* with thee; he will not fail thee, nor forsake thee, until thou hast finished all the work for the service of the house of the LORD.

²¹And, behold, the courses of the priests and the Levites, *even they shall be with thee* for all the service of the house of God: and *there shall be* with thee for all manner of workmanship every willing skilful man, for any manner of service: also the princes and all the people *will be* wholly at thy commandment.

FURTHERMORE David the king said unto all the congregation, Solomon my son, whom alone God hath chosen, *is yet* young and tender, and the work *is* great: for the palace *is* not for man, but for the LORD God.

²Now I have prepared with all my might for the house of my God the gold for *things to be made* of gold, and the silver for *things* of silver, and the brass for *things* of brass, the iron for *things* of iron, and wood for *things* of wood; onyx stones, and *stones* to be set, glistering stones, and of divers colours, and all manner of precious stones, and marble stones in abundance.

³Moreover, because I have set my affection to the house of my God, I have of mine own proper good, of gold and silver, *which* I have given to the house of my God, over and above all that I have prepared for the holy house,

⁴*Even* three thousand talents of gold, of the gold of Ophir, and seven thousand talents of refined silver, to overlay the walls of the houses *withal:*

⁵The gold for *things* of gold, and the

silver for *things* of silver, and for all manner of work *to be made* by the hands of artificers. And who *then* is willing to consecrate his service this day unto the LORD?

6Then the chief of the fathers and princes of the tribes of Israel, and the captains of thousands and of hundreds, with the rulers of the king's work, offered willingly,

7And gave for the service of the house of God of gold five thousand talents and ten thousand drams, and of silver ten thousand talents, and of brass eighteen thousand talents, and one hundred thousand talents of iron.

8And they with whom *precious* stones were found gave *them* to the treasure of the house of the LORD, by the hand of Jehiel the Gershonite.

9Then the people rejoiced, for that they offered willingly, because with perfect heart they offered willingly to the LORD: and David the king also rejoiced with great joy.

10Wherefore David blessed the LORD before all the congregation: and David said, Blessed *be* thou, LORD God of Israel our father, for ever and ever.

11Thine, O LORD, *is* the greatness, and the power, and the glory, and the victory, and the majesty: for all *that is* in the heaven and in the earth *is thine;* thine *is* the kingdom, O LORD, and thou art exalted as head above all.

12Both riches and honour *come* of thee, and thou reignest over all; and in thine hand *is* power and might; and in thine hand *it is* to make great, and to give strength unto all.

13Now therefore, our God, we thank thee, and praise thy glorious name.

14But who *am* I, and what *is* my people, that we should be able to offer so willingly after this sort? for all things *come* of thee, and of thine own have we given thee.

15For we *are* strangers before thee, and sojourners, as *were* all our fathers: our days on the earth *are* as a shadow, and *there is* none abiding.

16O LORD our God, all this store that we have prepared to build thee an house for thine holy name *cometh* of thine hand, and *is* all thine own.

17I know also, my God, that thou triest the heart, and hast pleasure in uprightness. As for me, in the uprightness of mine heart I have willingly offered all these things: and now have I seen with joy thy people, which are present here, to offer willingly unto thee.

18O LORD God of Abraham, Isaac, and of Israel, our fathers, keep this for ever in the imagination of the thoughts of the heart of thy people, and prepare their heart unto thee:

19And give unto Solomon my son a perfect heart, to keep thy commandments, thy testimonies, and thy statutes, and to do all *these things,* and to build the palace, *for* the which I have made provision.

20And David said to all the congregation, Now bless the LORD your God. And all the congregation blessed the LORD God of their fathers, and bowed down their heads, and worshipped the LORD, and the king.

21And they sacrificed sacrifices unto the LORD, and offered burnt offerings unto the LORD, on the morrow after that day, *even* a thousand bullocks, a thousand rams, *and* a thousand lambs, with their drink offerings, and sacrifices in abundance for all Israel:

22And did eat and drink before the LORD on that day with great gladness. And they made Solomon the son of David king the second time, and anointed *him* unto the LORD *to be* the chief governor, and Zadok *to be* priest.

23Then Solomon sat on the throne of the LORD as king instead of David his father, and prospered; and all Israel obeyed him.

24And all the princes, and the mighty men, and all the sons likewise of king

David, submitted themselves unto Solomon the king.

25And the LORD magnified Solomon exceedingly in the sight of all Israel, and bestowed upon him *such* royal majesty as had not been on any king before him in Israel.

26Thus David the son of Jesse reigned over all Israel.

27And the time that he reigned over Israel *was* forty years; seven years reigned he in Hebron, and thirty and three *years* reigned he in Jerusalem.

28And he died in a good old age, full of days, riches, and honour: and Solomon his son reigned in his stead.

29Now the acts of David the king, first and last, behold, they *are* written in the book of Samuel the seer, and in the book of Nathan the prophet, and in the book of Gad the seer,

30With all his reign and his might, and the times that went over him, and over Israel, and over all the kingdoms of the countries.

ROMANS 5:3–21

AND not only *so*, but we glory in tribulations also: knowing that tribulation worketh patience;

4And patience, experience; and experience, hope:

5And hope maketh not ashamed; because the love of God is shed abroad in our hearts by the Holy Ghost which is given unto us.

6For when we were yet without strength, in due time Christ died for the ungodly.

7For scarcely for a righteous man will one die: yet peradventure for a good man some would even dare to die.

8But God commendeth his love toward us, in that, while we were yet sinners, Christ died for us.

9Much more then, being now justified by his blood, we shall be saved from wrath through him.

10For if, when we were enemies, we were reconciled to God by the death of his Son, much more, being reconciled, we shall be saved by his life.

11And not only *so*, but we also joy in God through our Lord Jesus Christ, by whom we have now received the atonement.

12Wherefore, as by one man sin entered into the world, and death by sin; and so death passed upon all men, for that all have sinned:

13(For until the law sin was in the world: but sin is not imputed when there is no law.

14Nevertheless death reigned from Adam to Moses, even over them that had not sinned after the similitude of Adam's transgression, who is the figure of him that was to come.

15But not as the offence, so also *is* the free gift. For if through the offence of one many be dead, much more the grace of God, and the gift by grace, *which is* by one man, Jesus Christ, hath abounded unto many.

16And not as *it was* by one that sinned, *so is* the gift: for the judgment *was* by one to condemnation, but the free gift *is* of many offences unto justification.

17For if by one man's offence death reigned by one; much more they which receive abundance of grace and of the gift of righteousness shall reign in life by one, Jesus Christ.)

18Therefore as by the offence of one *judgment came* upon all men to condemnation; even so by the righteousness of one *the free gift came* upon all men unto justification of life.

19For as by one man's disobedience many were made sinners, so by the obedience of one shall many be made righteous.

20Moreover the law entered, that the offence might abound. But where sin abounded, grace did much more abound:

21That as sin hath reigned unto death,

even so might grace reign through righteousness unto eternal life by Jesus Christ our Lord.

PSALM 15:1–5

LORD, who shall abide in thy tabernacle? who shall dwell in thy holy hill?

2He that walketh uprightly, and worketh righteousness, and speaketh the truth in his heart.

3*He that* backbiteth not with his tongue, nor doeth evil to his neighbour, nor taketh up a reproach against his neighbour.

4In whose eyes a vile person is contemned; but he honoureth them that fear the LORD. *He that* sweareth to *his own* hurt, and changeth not.

5*He that* putteth not out his money to usury, nor taketh reward against the innocent. He that doeth these *things* shall never be moved.

PROVERBS FOR TODAY/ 19:18–19

Chasten thy son while there is hope, and let not thy soul spare for his crying. ☐ *A man of great wrath shall suffer punishment: for if thou deliver* him, *yet thou must do it again.*

JULY 20

2 CHRONICLES 1:1—3:17

AND Solomon the son of David was strengthened in his kingdom, and the LORD his God *was* with him, and magnified him exceedingly.

2Then Solomon spake unto all Israel, to the captains of thousands and of hundreds, and to the judges, and to every governor in all Israel, the chief of the fathers.

3So Solomon, and all the congregation with him, went to the high place that *was* at Gibeon; for there was the tabernacle of the congregation of God, which Moses the servant of the LORD had made in the wilderness.

4But the ark of God had David brought up from Kirjath–jearim to *the place which* David had prepared for it: for he had pitched a tent for it at Jerusalem.

5Moreover the brasen altar, that Bezaleel the son of Uri, the son of Hur, had made, he put before the tabernacle of the LORD: and Solomon and the congregation sought unto it.

6And Solomon went up thither to the brasen altar before the LORD, which *was* at the tabernacle of the congregation, and offered a thousand burnt offerings upon it.

7In that night did God appear unto Solomon, and said unto him, Ask what I shall give thee.

8And Solomon said unto God, Thou hast shewed great mercy unto David my father, and hast made me to reign in his stead.

9Now, O LORD God, let thy promise unto David my father be established: for thou hast made me king over a people like the dust of the earth in multitude.

10Give me now wisdom and knowledge, that I may go out and come in before this people: for who can judge this thy people, *that is so* great?

11And God said to Solomon, Because this was in thine heart, and thou hast not asked riches, wealth, or honour, nor the life of thine enemies, neither yet hast asked long life; but hast asked wisdom and knowledge for thyself, that thou mayest judge my people, over whom I have made thee king:

12Wisdom and knowledge *is* granted unto thee; and I will give thee riches, and wealth, and honour, such as none of the kings have had that *have been* before thee, neither shall there any after thee have the like.

13Then Solomon came *from his journey* to the high place that *was* at Gibeon to Jerusalem, from before the tabernacle of the congregation, and reigned over Israel.

14And Solomon gathered chariots and horsemen: and he had a thousand and four hundred chariots, and twelve thousand horsemen, which he placed in the chariot cities, and with the king at Jerusalem.

15And the king made silver and gold at Jerusalem *as plenteous* as stones, and cedar trees made he as the sycomore trees that *are* in the vale for abundance.

16And Solomon had horses brought out of Egypt, and linen yarn: the king's merchants received the linen yarn at a price.

17And they fetched up, and brought forth out of Egypt a chariot for six hundred *shekels* of silver, and an horse for an hundred and fifty: and so brought they out *horses* for all the kings of the Hittites, and for the kings of Syria, by their means.

AND Solomon determined to build an house for the name of the LORD, and an house for his kingdom.

2And Solomon told out threescore and ten thousand men to bear burdens, and fourscore thousand to hew in the mountain, and three thousand and six hundred to oversee them.

3And Solomon sent to Huram the king of Tyre, saying, As thou didst deal with David my father, and didst send him cedars to build him an house to dwell therein, *even so deal with me.*

4Behold, I build an house to the name of the LORD my God, to dedicate *it* to him, *and* to burn before him sweet incense, and for the continual shewbread, and for the burnt offerings morning and evening, on the sabbaths, and on the new moons, and on the solemn feasts of the LORD our God. This *is an ordinance* for ever to Israel.

5And the house which I build *is* great: for great *is* our God above all gods.

6But who is able to build him an house, seeing the heaven and heaven of heavens cannot contain him? who *am* I then, that I should build him an house, save only to burn sacrifice before him?

7Send me now therefore a man cunning to work in gold, and in silver, and in brass, and in iron, and in purple, and crimson, and blue, and that can skill to grave with the cunning men that *are* with me in Judah and in Jerusalem, whom David my father did provide.

8Send me also cedar trees, fir trees, and algum trees, out of Lebanon: for I know that thy servants can skill to cut timber in Lebanon; and, behold, my servants *shall be* with thy servants,

9Even to prepare me timber in abundance: for the house which I am about to build *shall be* wonderful great.

10And, behold, I will give to thy servants, the hewers that cut timber, twenty thousand measures of beaten wheat, and twenty thousand measures of barley, and twenty thousand baths of wine, and twenty thousand baths of oil.

11Then Huram the king of Tyre answered in writing, which he sent to Solomon, Because the LORD hath loved his people, he hath made thee king over them.

12Huram said moreover, Blessed *be*

the LORD God of Israel, that made heaven and earth, who hath given to David the king a wise son, endued with prudence and understanding, that might build an house for the LORD, and an house for his kingdom.

13And now I have sent a cunning man, endued with understanding, of Huram my father's,

14The son of a woman of the daughters of Dan, and his father *was* a man of Tyre, skilful to work in gold, and in silver, in brass, in iron, in stone, and in timber, in purple, in blue, and in fine linen, and in crimson; also to grave any manner of graving, and to find out every device which shall be put to him, with thy cunning men, and with the cunning men of my lord David thy father.

15Now therefore the wheat, and the barley, the oil, and the wine, which my lord hath spoken of, let him send unto his servants:

16And we will cut wood out of Lebanon, as much as thou shalt need: and we will bring it to thee in flotes by sea to Joppa; and thou shalt carry it up to Jerusalem.

17And Solomon numbered all the strangers that *were* in the land of Israel, after the numbering wherewith David his father had numbered them; and they were found an hundred and fifty thousand and three thousand and six hundred.

18And he set threescore and ten thousand of them *to be* bearers of burdens, and fourscore thousand *to be* hewers in the mountain, and three thousand and six hundred overseers to set the people a work.

THEN Solomon began to build the house of the LORD at Jerusalem in mount Moriah, where *the LORD* appeared unto David his father, in the place that David had prepared in the threshingfloor of Ornan the Jebusite.

2And he began to build in the second *day* of the second month, in the fourth year of his reign.

3Now these *are the things wherein* Solomon was instructed for the building of the house of God. The length by cubits after the first measure *was* threescore cubits, and the breadth twenty cubits.

4And the porch that *was* in the front *of the house,* the length *of it was* according to the breadth of the house, twenty cubits, and the height *was* an hundred and twenty: and he overlaid it within with pure gold.

5And the greater house he cieled with fir tree, which he overlaid with fine gold, and set thereon palm trees and chains.

6And he garnished the house with precious stones for beauty: and the gold *was* gold of Parvaim.

7He overlaid also the house, the beams, the posts. and the walls thereof, and the doors thereof, with gold; and graved cherubims on the walls.

8And he made the most holy house, the length whereof *was* according to the breadth of the house, twenty cubits, and the breadth thereof twenty cubits: and he overlaid it with fine gold, *amounting* to six hundred talents.

9And the weight of the nails *was* fifty shekels of gold. And he overlaid the upper chambers with gold.

10And in the most holy house he made two cherubims of image work, and overlaid them with gold.

11And the wings of the cherubims *were* twenty cubits long: one wing *of the one cherub was* five cubits, reaching to the wall of the house: and the other wing *was likewise* five cubits, reaching to the wing of the other cherub.

12And *one* wing of the other cherub *was* five cubits, reaching to the wall of the house: and the other wing *was* five cubits *also,* joining to the wing of the other cherub.

13The wings of these cherubims spread themselves forth twenty cubits: and they stood on their feet, and their faces *were* inward.

14And he made the vail *of* blue, and purple, and crimson, and fine linen, and wrought cherubims thereon.

15Also he made before the house two pillars of thirty and five cubits high, and the chapiter that *was* on the top of each of them *was* five cubits.

16And he made chains, *as* in the oracle, and put *them* on the heads of the pillars; and made an hundred pomegranates, and put *them* on the chains.

17And he reared up the pillars before the temple, one on the right hand, and the other on the left; and called the name of that on the right hand Jachin, and the name of that on the left Boaz.

ROMANS 6:1–23

WHAT shall we say then? Shall we continue in sin, that grace may abound?

2God forbid. How shall we, that are dead to sin, live any longer therein?

3Know ye not, that so many of us as were baptized into Jesus Christ were baptized into his death?

4Therefore we are buried with him by baptism into death: that like as Christ was raised up from the dead by the glory of the Father, even so we also should walk in newness of life.

5For if we have been planted together in the likeness of his death, we shall be also *in the likeness* of *his* resurrection:

6Knowing this, that our old man is crucified with *him,* that the body of sin might be destroyed, that henceforth we should not serve sin.

7For he that is dead is freed from sin.

8Now if we be dead with Christ, we believe that we shall also live with him:

9Knowing that Christ being raised from the dead dieth no more; death hath no more dominion over him.

10For in that he died, he died unto sin once: but in that he liveth, he liveth unto God.

11Likewise reckon ye also yourselves to be dead indeed unto sin, but alive unto God through Jesus Christ our Lord.

12Let not sin therefore reign in your mortal body, that ye should obey it in the lusts thereof.

13Neither yield ye your members *as* instruments of unrighteousness unto sin: but yield yourselves unto God, as those that are alive from the dead, and your members *as* instruments of righteousness unto God.

14For sin shall not have dominion over you: for ye are not under the law, but under grace.

15What then? shall we sin, because we are not under the law, but under grace? God forbid.

16Know ye not, that to whom ye yield yourselves servants to obey, his servants ye are to whom ye obey; whether of sin unto death, or of obedience unto righteousness?

17But God be thanked, that ye were the servants of sin, but ye have obeyed from the heart that form of doctrine which was delivered you.

18Being then made free from sin, ye became the servants of righteousness.

19I speak after the manner of men because of the infirmity of your flesh: for as ye have yielded your members servants to uncleanness and to iniquity unto iniquity; even so now yield your members servants to righteousness unto holiness.

20For when ye were the servants of sin, ye were free from righteousness.

21What fruit had ye then in those things whereof ye are now ashamed? for the end of those things *is* death.

22But now being made free from sin, and become servants to God, ye have your fruit unto holiness, and the end everlasting life.

23For the wages of sin *is* death; but the gift of God *is* eternal life through Jesus Christ our Lord.

PSALM 16:1–11

PRESERVE me, O God: for in thee do I put my trust.

2*O my soul,* thou hast said unto the LORD, Thou *art* my Lord: my goodness *extendeth* not to thee;

3*But* to the saints that *are* in the earth, and *to* the excellent, in whom *is* all my delight.

4Their sorrows shall be multiplied *that* hasten *after* another *god:* their drink offerings of blood will I not offer, nor take up their names into my lips.

5The LORD *is* the portion of mine inheritance and of my cup: thou maintainest my lot.

6The lines are fallen unto me in pleasant *places;* yea, I have a goodly heritage.

7I will bless the LORD, who hath given me counsel: my reins also instruct me in the night seasons.

8I have set the LORD always before me: because *he is* at my right hand, I shall not be moved.

9Therefore my heart is glad, and my glory rejoiceth: my flesh also shall rest in hope.

10For thou wilt not leave my soul in hell; neither wilt thou suffer thine Holy One to see corruption.

11Thou wilt shew me the path of life: in thy presence *is* fulness of joy; at thy right hand *there are* pleasures for evermore.

PROVERBS FOR TODAY/ 19:20–21

Hear counsel, and receive instruction, that thou mayest be wise in thy latter end. □ There are *many devices in a man's heart; nevertheless the counsel of the LORD, that shall stand.*

JULY 21

2 CHRONICLES 4:1—6:13

MOREOVER he [Solomon] made an altar of brass, twenty cubits the length thereof, and twenty cubits the breadth thereof, and ten cubits the height thereof.

2Also he made a molten sea of ten cubits from brim to brim, round in compass, and five cubits the height thereof; and a line of thirty cubits did compass it round about.

3And under it *was* the similitude of oxen, which did compass it round about: ten in a cubit, compassing the sea round about. Two rows of oxen *were* cast, when it was cast.

4It stood upon twelve oxen, three looking toward the north, and three looking toward the west, and three looking toward the south, and three looking toward the east: and the sea *was set* above upon them, and all their hinder parts *were* inward.

5And the thickness of it *was* an handbreadth, and the brim of it like the work of the brim of a cup, with flowers of lilies; *and* it received and held three thousand baths.

6He made also ten lavers, and put five on the right hand, and five on the left, to wash in them: such things as they offered for the burnt offering they washed in them; but the sea *was* for the priests to wash in.

7And he made ten candlesticks of gold according to their form, and set *them* in the temple, five on the right hand, and five on the left.

8He made also ten tables, and placed *them* in the temple, five on the right side, and five on the left. And he made an hundred basons of gold.

9Furthermore he made the court of the priests, and the great court, and doors for the court, and overlaid the doors of them with brass.

10And he set the sea on the right side of the east end, over against the south.

11And Huram made the pots, and the shovels, and the basons. And Huram finished the work that he was to make for king Solomon for the house of God;

12*To wit,* the two pillars, and the pommels, and the chapiters *which were* on the top of the two pillars, and the two wreaths to cover the two pommels of the chapiters which *were* on the top of the pillars;

13And four hundred pomegranates on the two wreaths; two rows of pomegranates on each wreath, to cover the two pommels of the chapiters which *were* upon the pillars.

14He made also bases, and lavers made he upon the bases;

15One sea, and twelve oxen under it.

16The pots also, and the shovels, and the fleshhooks, and all their instruments, did Huram his father make to king Solomon for the house of the LORD of bright brass.

17In the plain of Jordan did the king cast them, in the clay ground between Succoth and Zeredathah.

18Thus Solomon made all these vessels in great abundance: for the weight of the brass could not be found out.

19And Solomon made all the vessels that *were for* the house of God, the golden altar also, and the tables whereon the shewbread *was set;*

20Moreover the candlesticks with their lamps, that they should burn after the manner before the oracle, of pure gold;

21And the flowers, and the lamps, and the tongs, *made he of* gold, *and* that perfect gold;

22And the snuffers, and the basons, and the spoons, and the censers, *of* pure gold: and the entry of the house, the inner doors thereof for the most holy *place,* and the doors of the house of the temple, *were of* gold.

THUS all the work that Solomon made for the house of the LORD was finished: and Solomon brought in *all* the things that David his father had dedicated; and the silver, and the gold, and all the instruments, put he among the treasures of the house of God.

2Then Solomon assembled the elders of Israel, and all the heads of the tribes, the chief of the fathers of the children of Israel, unto Jerusalem, to bring up the ark of the covenant of the LORD out of the city of David, which *is* Zion.

3Wherefore all the men of Israel assembled themselves unto the king in the feast which *was* in the seventh month.

4And all the elders of Israel came; and the Levites took up the ark.

5And they brought up the ark, and the tabernacle of the congregation, and all the holy vessels that *were* in the tabernacle, these did the priests *and* the Levites bring up.

6Also king Solomon, and all the congregation of Israel that were assembled unto him before the ark, sacrificed sheep and oxen, which could not be told nor numbered for multitude.

7And the priests brought in the ark of the covenant of the LORD unto his place, to the oracle of the house, into the most holy *place, even* under the wings of the cherubims:

⁸For the cherubims spread forth *their* wings over the place of the ark, and the cherubims covered the ark and the staves thereof above.

⁹And they drew out the staves *of the ark,* that the ends of the staves were seen from the ark before the oracle; but they were not seen without. And there it is unto this day.

¹⁰*There was* nothing in the ark save the two tables which Moses put *therein* at Horeb, when the LORD made *a covenant* with the children of Israel, when they came out of Egypt.

¹¹And it came to pass, when the priests were come out of the holy *place:* (for all the priests *that were* present were sanctified, *and* did not *then* wait by course:

¹²Also the Levites *which were* the singers, all of them of Asaph, of Heman, of Jeduthun, with their sons and their brethren, *being* arrayed in white linen, having cymbals and psalteries and harps, stood at the east end of the altar, and with them an hundred and twenty priests sounding with trumpets:)

¹³It came even to pass, as the trumpeters and singers *were* as one, to make one sound to be heard in praising and thanking the LORD; and when they lifted up *their* voice with the trumpets and cymbals and instruments of musick, and praised the LORD, *saying,* For *he is* good; for his mercy *endureth* for ever: that *then* the house was filled with a cloud, *even* the house of the LORD;

¹⁴So that the priests could not stand to minister by reason of the cloud: for the glory of the LORD had filled the house of God.

THEN said Solomon, The LORD hath said that he would dwell in the thick darkness.

²But I have built an house of habitation for thee, and a place for thy dwelling for ever.

³And the king turned his face, and blessed the whole congregation of Israel: and all the congregation of Israel stood.

⁴And he said, Blessed *be* the LORD God of Israel, who hath with his hands fulfilled *that* which he spake with his mouth to my father David, saying,

⁵Since the day that I brought forth my people out of the land of Egypt I chose no city among all the tribes of Israel to build an house in, that my name might be there; neither chose I any man to be a ruler over my people Israel:

⁶But I have chosen Jerusalem, that my name might be there; and have chosen David to be over my people Israel.

⁷Now it was in the heart of David my father to build an house for the name of the LORD God of Israel.

⁸But the LORD said to David my father, Forasmuch as it was in thine heart to build an house for my name, thou didst well in that it was in thine heart:

⁹Notwithstanding thou shalt not build the house; but thy son which shall come forth out of thy loins, he shall build the house for my name.

¹⁰The LORD therefore hath performed his word that he hath spoken: for I am risen up in the room of David my father, and am set on the throne of Israel, as the LORD promised, and have built the house for the name of the LORD God of Israel.

¹¹And in it have I put the ark, wherein *is* the covenant of the LORD, that he made with the children of Israel.

¹²And he stood before the altar of the LORD in the presence of all the congregation of Israel, and spread forth his hands:

¹³For Solomon had made a brasen scaffold of five cubits long, and five cubits broad, and three cubits high, and had set it in the midst of the court: and upon it he stood, and kneeled down

upon his knees before all the congregation of Israel, and spread forth his hands toward heaven.

ROMANS 7:1-14

K NOW ye not, brethren, (for I speak to them that know the law,) how that the law hath dominion over a man as long as he liveth?

2For the woman which hath an husband is bound by the law to *her* husband so long as he liveth; but if the husband be dead, she is loosed from the law of *her* husband.

3So then if, while *her* husband liveth, she be married to another man, she shall be called an adulteress: but if her husband be dead, she is free from that law; so that she is no adulteress, though she be married to another man.

4Wherefore, my brethren, ye also are become dead to the law by the body of Christ; that ye should be married to another, *even* to him who is raised from the dead, that we should bring forth fruit unto God.

5For when we were in the flesh, the motions of sins, which were by the law, did work in our members to bring forth fruit unto death.

6But now we are delivered from the law, that being dead wherein we were held; that we should serve in newness of spirit, and not *in* the oldness of the letter.

7What shall we say then? *Is* the law sin? God forbid. Nay, I had not known sin, but by the law: for I had not known lust, except the law had said, Thou shalt not covet.

8But sin, taking occasion by the commandment, wrought in me all manner of concupiscence. For without the law sin *was* dead.

9For I was alive without the law once: but when the commandment came, sin revived, and I died.

10And the commandment, which *was* ordained to life, I found *to be* unto death.

11For sin, taking occasion by the commandment, deceived me, and by it slew *me*.

12Wherefore the law *is* holy, and the commandment holy, and just, and good.

13Was then that which is good made death unto me? God forbid. But sin, that it might appear sin, working death in me by that which is good; that sin by the commandment might become exceeding sinful.

14For we know that the law is spiritual: but I am carnal, sold under sin.

PSALM 17:1-15

H EAR the right, O LORD, attend unto my cry, give ear unto my prayer, *that goeth* not out of feigned lips.

2Let my sentence come forth from thy presence; let thine eyes behold the things that are equal.

3Thou hast proved mine heart; thou hast visited *me* in the night; thou hast tried me, *and* shalt find nothing; I am purposed *that* my mouth shall not transgress.

4Concerning the works of men, by the word of thy lips I have kept *me from* the paths of the destroyer.

5Hold up my goings in thy paths, *that* my footsteps slip not.

6I have called upon thee, for thou wilt hear me, O God: incline thine ear unto me, *and hear* my speech.

7Shew thy marvellous lovingkindness, O thou that savest by thy right hand them which put their trust *in thee* from those that rise up *against them*.

8Keep me as the apple of the eye, hide me under the shadow of thy wings,

9From the wicked that oppress me, *from* my deadly enemies, *who* compass me about.

10They are inclosed in their own fat: with their mouth they speak proudly.

11They have now compassed us in our steps: they have set their eyes bowing down to the earth;

12Like as a lion *that* is greedy of his prey, and as it were a young lion lurking in secret places.

13Arise, O LORD, disappoint him, cast him down: deliver my soul from the wicked, *which is* thy sword:

14From men *which are* thy hand, O LORD, from men of the world, *which* *have* their portion in *this* life, and whose belly thou fillest with thy hid *treasure:* they are full of children, and leave the rest of their *substance* to their babes.

15As for me, I will behold thy face in righteousness: I shall be satisfied, when I awake, with thy likeness.

PROVERBS FOR TODAY/ 19:22–23

The desire of a man is *his kindness: and a poor man* is *better than a liar.* □ *The fear of the LORD tendeth to life: and* he that hath it *shall abide satisfied; he shall not be visited with evil.*

JULY 22

2 CHRONICLES 6:14—8:10

AND [Solomon] said, O LORD God of Israel, *there is* no God like thee in the heaven, nor in the earth; which keepest covenant, and *shewest* mercy unto thy servants, that walk before thee with all their hearts:

15Thou which hast kept with thy servant David my father that which thou hast promised him; and spakest with thy mouth, and hast fulfilled *it* with thine hand, as *it is* this day.

16Now therefore, O LORD God of Israel, keep with thy servant David my father that which thou hast promised him, saying, There shall not fail thee a man in my sight to sit upon the throne of Israel; yet so that thy children take heed to their way to walk in my law, as thou hast walked before me.

17Now then, O LORD God of Israel, let thy word be verified, which thou hast spoken unto thy servant David.

18But will God in very deed dwell with men on the earth? behold, heaven and the heaven of heavens cannot contain thee; how much less this house which I have built!

19Have respect therefore to the prayer of thy servant, and to his supplication, O LORD my God, to hearken unto the cry and the prayer which thy servant prayeth before thee:

20That thine eyes may be open upon this house day and night, upon the place whereof thou hast said that thou wouldest put thy name there; to hearken unto the prayer which thy servant prayeth toward this place.

21Hearken therefore unto the supplications of thy servant, and of thy people Israel, which they shall make toward this place: hear thou from thy dwelling place, *even* from heaven; and when thou hearest, forgive.

22If a man sin against his neighbour, and an oath be laid upon him to make him swear, and the oath come before thine altar in this house;

23Then hear thou from heaven, and do, judge thy servants, by requiting the wicked, by recompensing his way upon his own head; and by justifying the righteous, by giving him according to his righteousness.

24And if thy people Israel be put to

the worse before the enemy, because they have sinned against thee; and shall return and confess thy name, and pray and make supplication before thee in this house;

25Then hear thou from the heavens, and forgive the sin of thy people Israel, and bring them again unto the land which thou gavest to them and to their fathers.

26When the heaven is shut up, and there is no rain, because they have sinned against thee; *yet* if they pray toward this place, and confess thy name, and turn from their sin, when thou dost afflict them;

27Then hear thou from heaven, and forgive the sin of thy servants, and of thy people Israel, when thou hast taught them the good way, wherein they should walk; and send rain upon thy land, which thou hast given unto thy people for an inheritance.

28If there be dearth in the land, if there be pestilence, if there be blasting, or mildew, locusts, or caterpillers; if their enemies besiege them in the cities of their land; whatsoever sore or whatsoever sickness *there be:*

29*Then* what prayer *or* what supplication soever shall be made of any man, or of all thy people Israel, when every one shall know his own sore and his own grief, and shall spread forth his hands in this house:

30Then hear thou from heaven thy dwelling place, and forgive, and render unto every man according unto all his ways, whose heart thou knowest; (for thou only knowest the hearts of the children of men:)

31That they may fear thee, to walk in thy ways, so long as they live in the land which thou gavest unto our fathers.

32Moreover concerning the stranger, which is not of thy people Israel, but is come from a far country for thy great name's sake, and thy mighty hand, and thy stretched out arm; if they come and pray in this house;

33Then hear thou from the heavens, *even* from thy dwelling place, and do according to all that the stranger calleth to thee for; that all people of the earth may know thy name, and fear thee, as *doth* thy people Israel, and may know that this house which I have built is called by thy name.

34If thy people go out to war against their enemies by the way that thou shalt send them, and they pray unto thee toward this city which thou hast chosen, and the house which I have built for thy name;

35Then hear thou from the heavens their prayer and their supplication, and maintain their cause.

36If they sin against thee, (for *there is* no man which sinneth not,) and thou be angry with them, and deliver them over before *their* enemies, and they carry them away captives unto a land far off or near;

37Yet *if* they bethink themselves in the land whither they are carried captive, and turn and pray unto thee in the land of their captivity, saying, We have sinned, we have done amiss, and have dealt wickedly;

38If they return to thee with all their heart and with all their soul in the land of their captivity, whither they have carried them captives, and pray toward their land, which thou gavest unto their fathers, and *toward* the city which thou hast chosen, and toward the house which I have built for thy name:

39Then hear thou from the heavens, *even* from thy dwelling place, their prayer and their supplications, and maintain their cause, and forgive thy people which have sinned against thee.

40Now, my God, let, I beseech thee, thine eyes be open, and *let* thine ears *be* attent unto the prayer *that is made* in this place.

41Now therefore arise, O Lord God, into thy resting place, thou, and the ark of thy strength: let thy priests, O Lord God, be clothed with salvation, and let thy saints rejoice in goodness.

42O LORD God, turn not away the face of thine anointed: remember the mercies of David thy servant.

Now when Solomon had made an end of praying, the fire came down from heaven, and consumed the burnt offering and the sacrifices; and the glory of the LORD filled the house.

2And the priests could not enter into the house of the LORD, because the glory of the LORD had filled the LORD'S house.

3And when all the children of Israel saw how the fire came down, and the glory of the LORD upon the house, they bowed themselves with their faces to the ground upon the pavement, and worshipped, and praised the LORD, *saying,* For *he is* good; for his mercy *endureth* for ever.

4Then the king and all the people offered sacrifices before the LORD.

5And king Solomon offered a sacrifice of twenty and two thousand oxen, and an hundred and twenty thousand sheep: so the king and all the people dedicated the house of God.

6And the priests waited on their offices: the Levites also with instruments of musick of the LORD, which David the king had made to praise the LORD, because his mercy *endureth* for ever, when David praised by their ministry; and the priests sounded trumpets before them, and all Israel stood.

7Moreover Solomon hallowed the middle of the court that *was* before the house of the LORD: for there he offered burnt offerings, and the fat of the peace offerings, because the brasen altar which Solomon had made was not able to receive the burnt offerings, and the meat offerings, and the fat.

8Also at the same time Solomon kept the feast seven days, and all Israel with him, a very great congregation, from the entering in of Hamath unto the river of Egypt.

9And in the eighth day they made a solemn assembly: for they kept the dedication of the altar seven days, and the feast seven days.

10And on the three and twentieth day of the seventh month he sent the people away into their tents, glad and merry in heart for the goodness that the LORD had shewed unto David, and to Solomon, and to Israel his people.

11Thus Solomon finished the house of the LORD, and the king's house: and all that came into Solomon's heart to make in the house of the LORD, and in his own house, he prosperously effected.

12And the LORD appeared to Solomon by night, and said unto him, I have heard thy prayer, and have chosen this place to myself for an house of sacrifice.

13If I shut up heaven that there be no rain, or if I command the locusts to devour the land, or if I send pestilence among my people;

14If my people, which are called by my name, shall humble themselves, and pray, and seek my face, and turn from their wicked ways; then will I hear from heaven, and will forgive their sin, and will heal their land.

15Now mine eyes shall be open, and mine ears attent unto the prayer *that is made* in this place.

16For now have I chosen and sanctified this house, that my name may be there for ever: and mine eyes and mine heart shall be there perpetually.

17And as for thee, if thou wilt walk before me, as David thy father walked, and do according to all that I have commanded thee, and shalt observe my statutes and my judgments;

18Then will I stablish the throne of thy kingdom, according as I have covenanted with David thy father, saying, There shall not fail thee a man *to be* ruler in Israel.

19But if ye turn away, and forsake my statutes and my commandments, which I have set before you, and shall go and serve other gods, and worship them;

20Then will I pluck them up by the roots out of my land which I have given them; and this house, which I have sanctified for my name, will I cast out of my sight, and will make it *to be* a proverb and a byword among all nations.

21And this house, which is high, shall be an astonishment to every one that passeth by it; so that he shall say, Why hath the LORD done thus unto this land, and unto this house?

22And it shall be answered, Because they forsook the LORD God of their fathers, which brought them forth out of the land of Egypt, and laid hold on other gods, and worshipped them, and served them: therefore hath he brought all this evil upon them.

AND it came to pass at the end of twenty years, wherein Solomon had built the house of the LORD, and his own house,

2That the cities which Huram had restored to Solomon, Solomon built them, and caused the children of Israel to dwell there.

3And Solomon went to Hamath–zobah, and prevailed against it.

4And he built Tadmor in the wilderness, and all the store cities, which he built in Hamath.

5Also he built Beth–horon the upper, and Beth–horon the nether, fenced cities, with walls, gates, and bars;

6And Baalath, and all the store cities that Solomon had, and all the chariot cities, and the cities of the horsemen, and all that Solomon desired to build in Jerusalem, and in Lebanon, and throughout all the land of his dominion.

7*As for* all the people *that were* left of the Hittites, and the Amorites, and the Perizzites, and the Hivites, and the Jebusites, which *were* not of Israel,

8*But* of their children, who were left after them in the land, whom the children of Israel consumed not, them did

Solomon make to pay tribute until this day.

9But of the children of Israel did Solomon make no servants for his work; but they *were* men of war, and chief of his captains, and captains of his chariots and horsemen.

10And these *were* the chief of king Solomon's officers, *even* two hundred and fifty, that bare rule over the people.

ROMANS 7:15—8:8

FOR that which I do I allow not: for what I would, that do I not; but what I hate, that do I.

16If then I do that which I would not, I consent unto the law that *it is* good.

17Now then it is no more I that do it, but sin that dwelleth in me.

18For I know that in me (that is, in my flesh,) dwelleth no good thing: for to will is present with me; but *how* to perform that which is good I find not.

19For the good that I would I do not: but the evil which I would not, that I do.

20Now if I do that I would not, it is no more I that do it, but sin that dwelleth in me.

21I find then a law, that, when I would do good, evil is present with me.

22For I delight in the law of God after the inward man:

23But I see another law in my members, warring against the law of my mind, and bringing me into captivity to the law of sin which is in my members.

24O wretched man that I am! who shall deliver me from the body of this death?

25I thank God through Jesus Christ our Lord. So then with the mind I myself serve the law of God; but with the flesh the law of sin.

THERE is therefore now no condemnation to them which are in Christ Jesus, who walk not after the flesh, but after the Spirit.

2For the law of the Spirit of life in Christ Jesus hath made me free from the law of sin and death.

3For what the law could not do, in that it was weak through the flesh, God sending his own Son in the likeness of sinful flesh, and for sin, condemned sin in the flesh:

4That the righteousness of the law might be fulfilled in us, who walk not after the flesh, but after the Spirit.

5For they that are after the flesh do mind the things of the flesh; but they that are after the Spirit the things of the Spirit.

6For to be carnally minded *is* death; but to be spiritually minded *is* life and peace.

7Because the carnal mind *is* enmity against God: for it is not subject to the law of God, neither indeed can be.

8So then they that are in the flesh cannot please God.

PSALM 18:1–15

I WILL love thee, O LORD, my strength.

2The LORD *is* my rock, and my fortress, and my deliverer; my God, my strength, in whom I will trust; my buckler, and the horn of my salvation, *and* my high tower.

3I will call upon the LORD, *who is worthy* to be praised: so shall I be saved from mine enemies.

4The sorrows of death compassed me, and the floods of ungodly men made me afraid.

5The sorrows of hell compassed me about: the snares of death prevented me.

6In my distress I called upon the LORD, and cried unto my God: he heard my voice out of his temple, and my cry came before him, *even* into his ears.

7Then the earth shook and trembled; the foundations also of the hills moved and were shaken, because he was wroth.

8There went up a smoke out of his nostrils, and fire out of his mouth devoured: coals were kindled by it.

9He bowed the heavens also, and came down: and darkness *was* under his feet.

10And he rode upon a cherub, and did fly: yea, he did fly upon the wings of the wind.

11He made darkness his secret place; his pavilion round about him *were* dark waters *and* thick clouds of the skies.

12At the brightness *that was* before him his thick clouds passed, hail *stones* and coals of fire.

13The LORD also thundered in the heavens, and the Highest gave his voice; hail *stones* and coals of fire.

14Yea, he sent out his arrows, and scattered them; and he shot out lightnings, and discomfited them.

15Then the channels of waters were seen, and the foundations of the world were discovered at thy rebuke, O LORD, at the blast of the breath of thy nostrils.

PROVERBS FOR TODAY/ 19:24–25

A slothful man hideth his hand in his bosom, and will not so much as bring it to his mouth again. □ *Smite a scorner, and the simple will beware: and reprove one that hath understanding, and he will understand knowledge.*

JULY 23

2 CHRONICLES 8:11—10:19

AND Solomon brought up the daughter of Pharaoh out of the city of David unto the house that he had built for her: for he said, My wife shall not dwell in the house of David king of Israel, because the places are holy, whereunto the ark of the LORD hath come.

12Then Solomon offered burnt offerings unto the LORD on the altar of the LORD, which he had built before the porch,

13Even after a certain rate every day, offering according to the commandment of Moses, on the sabbaths, and on the new moons, and on the solemn feasts, three times in the year, even in the feast of unleavened bread, and in the feast of weeks, and in the feast of tabernacles.

14And he appointed, according to the order of David his father, the courses of the priests to their service, and the Levites to their charges, to praise and minister before the priests, as the duty of every day required: the porters also by their courses at every gate: for so had David the man of God commanded.

15And they departed not from the commandment of the king unto the priests and Levites concerning any matter, or concerning the treasures.

16Now all the work of Solomon was prepared unto the day of the foundation of the house of the LORD, and until it was finished. So the house of the LORD was perfected.

17Then went Solomon to Ezion-geber, and to Eloth, at the sea side in the land of Edom.

18And Huram sent him by the hands of his servant ships, and servants that had knowledge of the sea; and they went with the servants of Solomon to Ophir, and took thence four hundred and fifty talents of gold, and brought them to king Solomon.

AND when the queen of Sheba heard of the fame of Solomon, she came to prove Solomon with hard questions at Jerusalem, with a very great company, and camels that bare spices, and gold in abundance, and precious stones: and when she was come to Solomon, she communed with him of all that was in her heart.

2And Solomon told her all her questions: and there was nothing hid from Solomon which he told her not.

3And when the queen of Sheba had seen the wisdom of Solomon, and the house that he had built,

4And the meat of his table, and the sitting of his servants, and the attendance of his ministers, and their apparel; his cupbearers also, and their apparel; and his ascent by which he went up into the house of the LORD; there was no more spirit in her.

5And she said to the king, It was a true report which I heard in mine own land of thine acts, and of thy wisdom:

6Howbeit I believed not their words, until I came, and mine eyes had seen it: and, behold, the one half of the greatness of thy wisdom was not told me: for thou exceedest the fame that I heard.

7Happy are thy men, and happy are these thy servants, which stand continually before thee, and hear thy wisdom.

8Blessed be the LORD thy God, which delighted in thee to set thee on his throne, to be king for the LORD thy God: because thy God loved Israel, to establish them for ever, therefore made he thee king over them, to do judgment and justice.

9And she gave the king an hundred and twenty talents of gold, and of spices great abundance, and precious stones: neither was there any such spice as the queen of Sheba gave king Solomon.

10And the servants also of Huram, and the servants of Solomon, which brought gold from Ophir, brought algum trees and precious stones.

11And the king made *of* the algum trees terraces to the house of the LORD, and to the king's palace, and harps and psalteries for singers: and there were none such seen before in the land of Judah.

12And king Solomon gave to the queen of Sheba all her desire, whatsoever she asked, beside *that* which she had brought unto the king. So she turned, and went away to her own land, she and her servants.

13Now the weight of gold that came to Solomon in one year was six hundred and three score and six talents of gold;

14Beside *that which* chapmen and merchants brought. And all the kings of Arabia and governors of the country brought gold and silver to Solomon.

15And king Solomon made two hundred targets *of* beaten gold: six hundred *shekels* of beaten gold went to one target.

16And three hundred shields *made he of* beaten gold: three hundred *shekels* of gold went to one shield. And the king put them in the house of the forest of Lebanon.

17Moreover the king made a great throne of ivory, and overlaid it with pure gold.

18And *there were* six steps to the throne, with a footstool of gold, *which were* fastened to the throne, and stays on each side of the sitting place, and two lions standing by the stays:

19And twelve lions stood there on the one side and on the other upon the six steps. There was not the like made in any kingdom.

20And all the drinking vessels of king Solomon *were of* gold, and all the vessels of the house of the forest of Lebanon *were of* pure gold: none *were of* silver; it was *not* any thing accounted of in the days of Solomon.

21For the king's ships went to Tarshish with the servants of Huram: every three years once came the ships of Tarshish bringing gold, and silver, ivory, and apes, and peacocks.

22And king Solomon passed all the kings of the earth in riches and wisdom.

23And all the kings of the earth sought the presence of Solomon, to hear his wisdom, that God had put in his heart.

24And they brought every man his present, vessels of silver, and vessels of gold, and raiment, harness, and spices, horses, and mules, a rate year by year.

25And Solomon had four thousand stalls for horses and chariots, and twelve thousand horsemen; whom he bestowed in the chariot cities, and with the king at Jerusalem.

26And he reigned over all the kings from the river even unto the land of the Philistines, and to the border of Egypt.

27And the king made silver in Jerusalem as stones, and cedar trees made he as the sycomore trees that *are* in the low plains in abundance.

28And they brought unto Solomon horses out of Egypt, and out of all lands.

29Now the rest of the acts of Solomon, first and last, *are* they not written in the book of Nathan the prophet, and in the prophecy of Ahijah the Shilonite, and in the visions of Iddo the seer against Jeroboam the son of Nebat?

30And Solomon reigned in Jerusalem over all Israel forty years.

31And Solomon slept with his fathers, and he was buried in the city of David his father: and Rehoboam his son reigned in his stead.

AND Rehoboam went to Shechem: for to Shechem were all Israel come to make him king.

2And it came to pass, when Jeroboam the son of Nebat, who *was* in Egypt, whither he had fled from the presence of Solomon the king, heard *it,* that Jeroboam returned out of Egypt.

3And they sent and called him. So Jeroboam and all Israel came and spake to Rehoboam, saying,

4Thy father made our yoke grievous: now therefore ease thou somewhat the grievous servitude of thy father, and his heavy yoke that he put upon us, and we will serve thee.

5And he said unto them, Come again unto me after three days. And the people departed.

6And king Rehoboam took counsel with the old men that had stood before Solomon his father while he yet lived, saying, What counsel give ye *me* to return answer to this people?

7And they spake unto him, saying, If thou be kind to this people, and please them, and speak good words to them, they will be thy servants for ever.

8But he forsook the counsel which the old men gave him, and took counsel with the young men that were brought up with him, that stood before him.

9And he said unto them, What advice give ye that we may return answer to this people, which have spoken to me, saying, Ease somewhat the yoke that thy father did put upon us?

10And the young men that were brought up with him spake unto him, saying, Thus shalt thou answer the people that spake unto thee, saying, Thy father made our yoke heavy, but make thou *it* somewhat lighter for us; thus shalt thou say unto them, My little *finger* shall be thicker than my father's loins.

11For whereas my father put a heavy yoke upon you, I will put more to your yoke: my father chastised you with whips, but I *will chastise you* with scorpions.

12So Jeroboam and all the people came to Rehoboam on the third day, as the king bade, saying, Come again to me on the third day.

13And the king answered them roughly; and king Rehoboam forsook the counsel of the old men,

14And answered them after the advice of the young men, saying, My father made your yoke heavy, but I will add thereto: my father chastised you with whips, but I *will chastise you* with scorpions.

15So the king hearkened not unto the people: for the cause was of God, that the LORD might perform his word, which he spake by the hand of Ahijah the Shilonite to Jeroboam the son of Nebat.

16And when all Israel *saw* that the king would not hearken unto them, the people answered the king, saying, What portion have we in David? and *we have* none inheritance in the son of Jesse: every man to your tents, O Israel: *and* now, David, see to thine own house. So all Israel went to their tents.

17But *as for* the children of Israel that dwelt in the cities of Judah, Rehoboam reigned over them.

18Then king Rehoboam sent Hadoram that *was* over the tribute; and the children of Israel stoned him with stones, that he died. But king Rehoboam made speed to get him up to *his* chariot, to flee to Jerusalem.

19And Israel rebelled against the house of David unto this day.

ROMANS 8:9–23

BUT ye are not in the flesh, but in the Spirit, if so be that the Spirit of God dwell in you. Now if any man have not the Spirit of Christ, he is none of his.

10And if Christ *be* in you, the body

is dead because of sin; but the Spirit *is* life because of righteousness.

11But if the Spirit of him that raised up Jesus from the dead dwell in you, he that raised up Christ from the dead shall also quicken your mortal bodies by his Spirit that dwelleth in you.

12Therefore, brethren, we are debtors, not to the flesh, to live after the flesh.

13For if ye live after the flesh, ye shall die: but if ye through the Spirit do mortify the deeds of the body, ye shall live.

14For as many as are led by the Spirit of God, they are the sons of God.

15For ye have not received the spirit of bondage again to fear; but ye have received the Spirit of adoption, whereby we cry, Abba, Father.

16The Spirit itself beareth witness with our spirit, that we are the children of God:

17And if children, then heirs; heirs of God, and joint-heirs with Christ; if so be that we suffer with *him,* that we may be also glorified together.

18For I reckon that the sufferings of this present time *are* not worthy *to be compared* with the glory which shall be revealed in us.

19For the earnest expectation of the creature waiteth for the manifestation of the sons of God.

20For the creature was made subject to vanity, not willingly, but by reason of him who hath subjected *the same* in hope,

21Because the creature itself also shall be delivered from the bondage of corruption into the glorious liberty of the children of God.

22For we know that the whole creation groaneth and travaileth in pain together until now.

23And not only *they,* but ourselves also, which have the firstfruits of the Spirit, even we ourselves groan within ourselves, waiting for the adoption, *to wit,* the redemption of our body.

PSALM 18:16–34

HE sent from above, he took me, he drew me out of many waters.

17He delivered me from my strong enemy, and from them which hated me: for they were too strong for me.

18They prevented me in the day of my calamity: but the LORD was my stay.

19He brought me forth also into a large place; he delivered me, because he delighted in me.

20The LORD rewarded me according to my righteousness; according to the cleanness of my hands hath he recompensed me.

21For I have. kept the ways of the LORD, and have not wickedly departed from my God.

22For all his judgments *were* before me, and I did not put away his statutes from me.

23I was also upright before him, and I kept myself from mine iniquity.

24Therefore hath the LORD recompensed me according to my righteousness, according to the cleanness of my hands in his eyesight.

25With the merciful thou wilt shew thyself merciful; with an upright man thou wilt shew thyself upright;

26With the pure thou wilt shew thyself pure; and with the froward thou wilt shew thyself froward.

27For thou wilt save the afflicted people; but wilt bring down high looks.

28For thou wilt light my candle: the LORD my God will enlighten my darkness.

29For by thee I have run through a troop; and by my God have I leaped over a wall.

30*As for* God, his way *is* perfect: the word of the LORD is tried: he *is* a buckler to all those that trust in him.

31For who *is* God save the LORD? or who *is* a rock save our God?

32*It is* God that girdeth me with

strength, and maketh my way perfect.

³³He maketh my feet like hinds' *feet,* and setteth me upon my high places.

³⁴He teacheth my hands to war, so that a bow of steel is broken by mine arms.

PROVERBS FOR TODAY/ 19:26

He that wasteth his *father,* and *chaseth away* his *mother,* is *a son that causeth shame, and bringeth reproach.*

JULY 24

2 CHRONICLES 11:1—13:22

AND when Rehoboam was come to Jerušalem, he gathered of the house of Judah and Benjamin an hundred and fourscore thousand chosen *men,* which were warriors, to fight against Israel, that he might bring the kingdom again to Rehoboam.

²But the word of the LORD came to Shemaiah the man of God, saying,

³Speak unto Rehoboam the son of Solomon, king of Judah, and to all Israel in Judah and Benjamin, saying,

⁴Thus saith the LORD, Ye shall not go up, nor fight against your brethren: return every man to his house: for this thing is done of me. And they obeyed the words of the LORD, and returned from going against Jeroboam.

⁵And Rehoboam dwelt in Jerusalem, and built cities for defence in Judah.

⁶He built even Beth–lehem, and Etam, and Tekoa,

⁷And Beth–zur, and Shoco, and Adullam,

⁸And Gath, and Mareshah, and Ziph,

⁹And Adoraim, and Lachish, and Azekah,

¹⁰And Zorah, and Aijalon, and Hebron, which *are* in Judah and in Benjamin fenced cities.

¹¹And he fortified the strong holds, and put captains in them, and store of victual, and of oil and wine.

¹²And in every several city *he put* shields and spears, and made them exceeding strong, having Judah and Benjamin on his side.

¹³And the priests and the Levites that *were* in all Israel resorted to him out of all their coasts.

¹⁴For the Levites left their suburbs and their possession, and came to Judah and Jerusalem: for Jeroboam and his sons had cast them off from executing the priest's office unto the LORD:

¹⁵And he ordained him priests for the high places, and for the devils, and for the calves which he had made.

¹⁶And after them out of all the tribes of Israel such as set their hearts to seek the LORD God of Israel came to Jerusalem, to sacrifice unto the LORD God of their fathers.

¹⁷So they strengthened the kingdom of Judah, and made Rehoboam the son of Solomon strong, three years: for three years they walked in the way of David and Solomon.

¹⁸And Rehoboam took him Mahalath the daughter of Jerimoth the son of David to wife, *and* Abihail the daughter of Eliab the son of Jesse;

¹⁹Which bare him children; Jeush, and Shemariah, and Zaham.

²⁰And after her he took Maachah the daughter of Absalom; which bare him

Abijah, and Attai, and Ziza, and Shelo-mith.

21And Rehoboam loved Maachah the daughter of Absalom above all his wives and his concubines: (for he took eighteen wives, and threescore concubines; and begat twenty and eight sons, and threescore daughters.)

22And Rehoboam made Abijah the son of Maachah the chief, *to be* ruler among his brethren: for *he thought* to make him king.

23And he dealt wisely, and dispersed of all his children throughout all the countries of Judah and Benjamin, unto every fenced city: and he gave them victual in abundance. And he desired many wives.

AND it came to pass, when Rehoboam had established the kingdom, and had strengthened himself, he forsook the law of the LORD, and all Israel with him.

2And it came to pass, *that* in the fifth year of king Rehoboam Shishak king of Egypt came up against Jerusalem, because they had transgressed against the LORD,

3With twelve hundred chariots, and threescore thousand horsemen: and the people *were* without number that came with him out of Egypt; the Lubims, the Sukkiims, and the Ethiopians.

4And he took the fenced cities which *pertained* to Judah, and came to Jerusalem.

5Then came Shemaiah the prophet to Rehoboam, and *to* the princes of Judah, that were gathered together to Jerusalem because of Shishak, and said unto them, Thus saith the LORD, Ye have forsaken me, and therefore have I also left you in the hand of Shishak.

6Whereupon the princes of Israel and the king humbled themselves; and they said, The LORD *is* righteous.

7And when the LORD saw that they humbled themselves, the word of the LORD came to Shemaiah, saying, They have humbled themselves; *therefore* I will not destroy them, but I will grant them some deliverance; and my wrath shall not be poured out upon Jerusalem by the hand of Shishak.

8Nevertheless they shall be his servants; that they may know my service, and the service of the kingdoms of the countries.

9So Shishak king of Egypt came up against Jerusalem, and took away the treasures of the house of the LORD, and the treasures of the king's house; he took all: he carried away also the shields of gold which Solomon had made.

10Instead of which king Rehoboam made shields of brass, and committed *them* to the hands of the chief of the guard, that kept the entrance of the king's house.

11And when the king entered into the house of the LORD, the guard came and fetched them, and brought them again into the guard chamber.

12And when he humbled himself, the wrath of the LORD turned from him, that he would not destroy *him* altogether: and also in Judah things went well.

13So king Rehoboam strengthened himself in Jerusalem, and reigned: for Rehoboam *was* one and forty years old when he began to reign, and he reigned seventeen years in Jerusalem, the city which the LORD had chosen out of all the tribes of Israel, to put his name there. And his mother's name *was* Naamah an Ammonitess.

14And he did evil, because he prepared not his heart to seek the LORD.

15Now the acts of Rehoboam, first and last, *are* they not written in the book of Shemaiah the prophet, and of Iddo the seer concerning genealogies? And *there were* wars between Rehoboam and Jeroboam continually.

16And Rehoboam slept with his fathers, and was buried in the city of

David: and Abijah his son reigned in his stead.

Now in the eighteenth year of king Jeroboam began Abijah to reign over Judah. 2He reigned three years in Jerusalem. His mother's name also *was* Michaiah the daughter of Uriel of Gibeah. And there was war between Abijah and Jeroboam.

3And Abijah set the battle in array with an army of valiant men of war, *even* four hundred thousand chosen men: Jeroboam also set the battle in array against him with eight hundred thousand chosen men, *being* mighty men of valour.

4And Abijah stood up upon mount Zemaraim, which *is* in mount Ephraim, and said, Hear me, thou Jeroboam, and all Israel;

5Ought ye not to know that the LORD God of Israel gave the kingdom over Israel to David for ever, *even* to him and to his sons by a covenant of salt?

6Yet Jeroboam the son of Nebat, the servant of Solomon the son of David, is risen up, and hath rebelled against his lord.

7And there are gathered unto him vain men, the children of Belial, and have strengthened themselves against Rehoboam the son of Solomon, when Rehoboam was young and tender-hearted, and could not withstand them.

8And now ye think to withstand the kingdom of the LORD in the hand of the sons of David; and ye *be* a great multitude, and *there are* with you golden calves, which Jeroboam made you for gods.

9Have ye not cast out the priests of the LORD, the sons of Aaron, and the Levites, and have made you priests after the manner of the nations of *other* lands? so that whosoever cometh to consecrate himself with a young bullock and seven rams, *the same* may be a priest of *them that are* no gods.

10But as for us, the LORD *is* our God, and we have not forsaken him; and the priests, which minister unto the LORD, *are* the sons of Aaron, and the Levites *wait* upon *their* business:

11And they burn unto the LORD every morning and every evening burnt sacrifices and sweet incense: the shewbread also *set they in order* upon the pure table; and the candlestick of gold with the lamps thereof, to burn every evening: for we keep the charge of the LORD our God; but ye have forsaken him.

12And, behold, God himself *is* with us for *our* captain, and his priests with sounding trumpets to cry alarm against you. O children of Israel, fight ye not against the LORD God of your fathers; for ye shall not prosper.

13But Jeroboam caused an ambushment to come about behind them: so they were before Judah, and the ambushment *was* behind them.

14And when Judah looked back, behold, the battle *was* before and behind: and they cried unto the LORD, and the priests sounded with the trumpets.

15Then the men of Judah gave a shout: and as the men of Judah shouted, it came to pass, that God smote Jeroboam and all Israel before Abijah and Judah.

16And the children of Israel fled before Judah: and God delivered them into their hand.

17And Abijah and his people slew them with a great slaughter: so there fell down slain of Israel five hundred thousand chosen men.

18Thus the children of Israel were brought under at that time, and the children of Judah prevailed, because they relied upon the LORD God of their fathers.

19And Abijah pursued after Jeroboam, and took cities from him, Beth-el with the towns thereof, and Jeshanah with the towns thereof, and Ephrain with the towns thereof.

20Neither did Jeroboam recover strength again in the days of Abijah:

and the LORD struck him, and he died.

21But Abijah waxed mighty, and married fourteen wives, and begat twenty and two sons, and sixteen daughters.

22And the rest of the acts of Abijah, and his ways, and his sayings, *are* written in the story of the prophet Iddo.

ROMANS 8:24–39

FOR we are saved by hope: but hope that is seen is not hope: for what a man seeth, why doth he yet hope for?

25But if we hope for that we see not, *then* do we with patience wait for *it*.

26Likewise the Spirit also helpeth our infirmities: for we know not what we should pray for as we ought: but the Spirit itself maketh intercession for us with groanings which cannot be uttered.

27And he that searcheth the hearts knoweth what *is* the mind of the Spirit, because he maketh intercession for the saints according to *the will of* God.

28And we know that all things work together for good to them that love God, to them who are the called according to *his* purpose.

29For whom he did foreknow, he also did predestinate *to be* conformed to the image of his Son, that he might be the firstborn among many brethren.

30Moreover whom he did predestinate, them he also called: and whom he called, them he also justified: and whom he justified, them he also glorified.

31What shall we then say to these things? If God *be* for us, who *can be* against us?

32He that spared not his own Son, but delivered him up for us all, how shall he not with him also freely give us all things?

33Who shall lay any thing to the charge of God's elect? *It is* God that justifieth.

34Who *is* he that condemneth? *It is* Christ that died, yea rather, that is

risen again, who is even at the right hand of God, who also maketh intercession for us.

35Who shall separate us from the love of Christ? *shall* tribulation, or distress, or persecution, or famine, or nakedness, or peril, or sword?

36As it is written, For thy sake we are killed all the day long; we are accounted as sheep for the slaughter.

37Nay, in all these things we are more than conquerors through him that loved us.

38For I am persuaded, that neither death, nor life, nor angels, nor principalities, nor powers, nor things present, nor things to come,

39Nor height, nor depth, nor any other creature, shall be able to separate us from the love of God, which is in Christ Jesus our Lord.

PSALM 18:35–50

THOU hast also given me the shield of thy salvation: and thy right hand hath holden me up, and thy gentleness hath made me great.

36Thou hast enlarged my steps under me, that my feet did not slip.

37I have pursued mine enemies, and overtaken them: neither did I turn again till they were consumed.

38I have wounded them that they were not able to rise: they are fallen under my feet.

39For thou hast girded me with strength unto the battle: thou hast subdued under me those that rose up against me.

40Thou hast also given me the necks of mine enemies; that I might destroy them that hate me.

41They cried, *but there was* none to save *them: even* unto the LORD, but he answered them not.

42Then did I beat them small as the dust before the wind: I did cast them out as the dirt in the streets.

43Thou hast delivered me from the

strivings of the people; *and* thou hast made me the head of the heathen: a people *whom* I have not known shall serve me.

⁴⁴As soon as they hear of me, they shall obey me: the strangers shall submit themselves unto me.

⁴⁵The strangers shall fade away, and be afraid out of their close places.

⁴⁶The LORD liveth; and blessed *be* my rock; and let the God of my salvation be exalted.

⁴⁷*It is* God that avengeth me, and subdueth the people under me.

⁴⁸He delivereth me from mine enemies: yea, thou liftest me up above those that rise up against me: thou hast delivered me from the violent man.

⁴⁹Therefore will I give thanks unto thee, O LORD, among the heathen, and sing praises unto thy name.

⁵⁰Great deliverance giveth he to his king; and sheweth mercy to his anointed, to David, and to his seed for evermore.

PROVERBS FOR TODAY/ 19:27–29

Cease, my son, to hear the instruction that causeth to err from the words of knowledge. ☐ *An ungodly witness scorneth judgment: and the mouth of the wicked devoureth iniquity.* ☐ *Judgments are prepared for scorners, and stripes for the back of fools.*

JULY 25

2 CHRONICLES 14:1—16:14

So Abijah slept with his fathers, and they buried him in the city of David: and Asa his son reigned in his stead. In his days the land was quiet ten years.

²And Asa did *that which was* good and right in the eyes of the LORD his God:

³For he took away the altars of the strange *gods,* and the high places, and brake down the images, and cut down the groves:

⁴And commanded Judah to seek the LORD God of their fathers, and to do the law and the commandment.

⁵Also he took away out of all the cities of Judah the high places and the images: and the kingdom was quiet before him.

⁶And he built fenced cities in Judah: for the land had rest, and he had no war in those years; because the LORD had given him rest.

⁷Therefore he said unto Judah, Let us build these cities, and make about *them* walls, and towers, gates, and bars, *while* the land *is* yet before us; because we have sought the LORD our God, we have sought *him,* and he hath given us rest on every side. So they built and prospered.

⁸And Asa had an army *of men* that bare targets and spears, out of Judah three hundred thousand; and out of Benjamin, that bare shields and drew bows, two hundred and fourscore thousand: all these *were* mighty men of valour.

⁹And there came out against them Zerah the Ethiopian with an host of a thousand thousand, and three hundred

chariots; and came unto Mareshah.

10Then Asa went out against him, and they set the battle in array in the valley of Zephathah at Mareshah.

11And Asa cried unto the LORD his God, and said, LORD, *it is* nothing with thee to help, whether with many, or with them that have no power: help us, O LORD our God; for we rest on thee, and in thy name we go against this multitude. O LORD, thou *art* our God; let not man prevail against thee.

12So the LORD smote the Ethiopians before Asa, and before Judah; and the Ethiopians fled.

13And Asa and the people that *were* with him pursued them unto Gerar: and the Ethiopians were overthrown, that they could not recover themselves; for they were destroyed before the LORD, and before his host; and they carried away very much spoil.

14And they smote all the cities round about Gerar; for the fear of the LORD came upon them: and they spoiled all the cities; for there was exceeding much spoil in them.

15They smote also the tents of cattle, and carried away sheep and camels in abundance, and returned to Jerusalem.

AND the Spirit of God came upon Azariah the son of Oded:

2And he went out to meet Asa, and said unto him, Hear ye me, Asa, and all Judah and Benjamin; The LORD *is* with you, while ye be with him; and if ye seek him, he will be found of you; but if ye forsake him, he will forsake you.

3Now for a long season Israel *hath been* without the true God, and without a teaching priest, and without law.

4But when they in their trouble did turn unto the LORD God of Israel, and sought him, he was found of them.

5And in those times *there was* no peace to him that went out, nor to him that came in, but great vexations *were* upon all the inhabitants of the countries.

6And nation was destroyed of nation, and city of city: for God did vex them with all adversity.

7Be ye strong therefore, and let not your hands be weak: for your work shall be rewarded.

8And when Asa heard these words, and the prophecy of Oded the prophet, he took courage, and put away the abominable idols out of the land of Judah and Benjamin, and out of the cities which he had taken from mount Ephraim, and renewed the altar of the LORD, that *was* before the porch of the LORD.

9And he gathered all Judah and Benjamin, and the strangers with them out of Ephraim and Manasseh, and out of Simeon: for they fell to him out of Israel in abundance, when they saw that the LORD his God *was* with him.

10So they gathered themselves together at Jerusalem in the third month, in the fifteenth year of the reign of Asa.

11And they offered unto the LORD the same time, of the spoil *which* they had brought, seven hundred oxen and seven thousand sheep.

12And they entered into a covenant to seek the LORD God of their fathers with all their heart and with all their soul;

13That whosoever would not seek the LORD God of Israel should be put to death, whether small or great, whether man or woman.

14And they sware unto the LORD with a loud voice, and with shouting, and with trumpets, and with cornets.

15And all Judah rejoiced at the oath: for they had sworn with all their heart, and sought him with their whole desire; and he was found of them: and the LORD gave them rest round about.

16And also *concerning* Maachah the mother of Asa the king, he removed her from *being* queen, because she had made an idol, in a grove: and Asa cut down her idol, and stamped *it,* and burnt *it* at the brook Kidron.

17But the high places were not taken away out of Israel: nevertheless the heart of Asa was perfect all his days.

18And he brought into the house of God the things that his father had dedicated, and that he himself had dedicated, silver, and gold, and vessels.

19And there was no *more* war unto the five and thirtieth year of the reign of Asa.

IN the six and thirtieth year of the reign of Asa Baasha king of Israel came up against Judah, and built Ramah, to the intent that he might let none go out or come in to Asa king of Judah.

2Then Asa brought out silver and gold out of the treasures of the house of the LORD and of the king's house, and sent to Ben–hadad king of Syria, that dwelt at Damascus, saying,

3*There is* a league between me and thee, as *there was* between my father and thy father: behold, I have sent thee silver and gold; go, break thy league with Baasha king of Israel, that he may depart from me.

4And Ben–hadad hearkened unto king Asa, and sent the captains of his armies against the cities of Israel; and they smote Ijon, and Dan, and Abel–maim, and all the store cities of Naphtali.

5And it came to pass, when Baasha heard *it,* that he left off building of Ramah, and let his work cease.

6Then Asa the king took all Judah; and they carried away the stones of Ramah, and the timber thereof, wherewith Baasha was building; and he built therewith Geba and Mizpah.

7And at that time Hanani the seer came to Asa king of Judah, and said unto him, Because thou hast relied on the king of Syria, and not relied on the LORD thy God, therefore is the host of the king of Syria escaped out of thine hand.

8Were not the Ethiopians and the Lubims a huge host, with very many chariots and horsemen? yet, because thou didst rely on the LORD, he delivered them into thine hand.

9For the eyes of the LORD run to and fro throughout the whole earth, to shew himself strong in the behalf of *them* whose heart *is* perfect toward him. Herein thou hast done foolishly: therefore from henceforth thou shalt have wars.

10Then Asa was wroth with the seer, and put him in a prison house; for *he was* in a rage with him because of this *thing.* And Asa oppressed *some* of the people the same time.

11And, behold, the acts of Asa, first and last, lo, they *are* written in the book of the kings of Judah and Israel.

12And Asa in the thirty and ninth year of his reign was diseased in his feet, until his disease *was* exceeding *great:* yet in his disease he sought not to the LORD, but to the physicians.

13And Asa slept with his fathers, and died in the one and fortieth year of his reign.

14And they buried him in his own sepulchres, which he had made for himself in the city of David, and laid him in the bed which was filled with sweet odours and divers kinds *of spices* prepared by the apothecaries' art: and they made a very great burning for him.

ROMANS 9:1–24

I SAY the truth in Christ, I lie not, my conscience also bearing me witness in the Holy Ghost,

2That I have great heaviness and continual sorrow in my heart.

3For I could wish that myself were accursed from Christ for my brethren, my kinsmen according to the flesh:

4Who are Israelites; to whom *pertaineth* the adoption, and the glory, and the covenants, and the giving of the law, and the service *of God,* and the promises;

5Whose *are* the fathers, and of whom as concerning the flesh Christ *came,* who is over all, God blessed for ever. Amen.

6Not as though the word of God hath taken none effect. For they *are* not all Israel, which are of Israel:

7Neither, because they are the seed of Abraham, *are they* all children: but, In Isaac shall thy seed be called.

8That is, They which are the children of the flesh, these *are* not the children of God: but the children of the promise are counted for the seed.

9For this *is* the word of promise, At this time will I come, and Sarah shall have a son.

10And not only *this;* but when Rebecca also had conceived by one, *even* by our father Isaac;

11(For *the children* being not yet born, neither having done any good or evil, that the purpose of God according to election might stand, not of works, but of him that calleth;)

12It was said unto her, The elder shall serve the younger.

13As it is written, Jacob have I loved, but Esau have I hated.

14What shall we say then? *Is there* unrighteousness with God? God forbid.

15For he saith to Moses, I will have mercy on whom I will have mercy, and I will have compassion on whom I will have compassion.

16So then *it is* not of him that willeth, nor of him that runneth, but of God that sheweth mercy.

17For the scripture saith unto Pharaoh, Even for this same purpose have I raised thee up, that I might shew my power in thee, and that my name might be declared throughout all the earth.

18Therefore hath he mercy on whom he will *have mercy,* and whom he will he hardeneth.

19Thou wilt say then unto me, Why doth he yet find fault? For who hath resisted his will?

20Nay but, O man, who art thou that repliest against God? Shall the thing formed say to him that formed *it,* Why hast thou made me thus?

21Hath not the potter power over the clay, of the same lump to make one vessel unto honour, and another unto dishonour?

22*What* if God, willing to shew *his* wrath, and to make his power known, endured with much longsuffering the vessels of wrath fitted to destruction:

23And that he might make known the riches of his glory on the vessels of mercy, which he had afore prepared unto glory,

24Even us, whom he hath called, not of the Jews only, but also of the Gentiles?

PSALM 19:1–14

THE heavens declare the glory of God; and the firmament sheweth his handywork.

2Day unto day uttereth speech, and night unto night sheweth knowledge.

3*There is* no speech nor language, *where* their voice is not heard.

4Their line is gone out through all the earth, and their words to the end of the world. In them hath he set a tabernacle for the sun,

5Which *is* as a bridegroom coming out of his chamber, *and* rejoiceth as a strong man to run a race.

6His going forth *is* from the end of the heaven, and his circuit unto the ends of it: and there is nothing hid from the heat thereof.

7The law of the LORD *is* perfect, converting the soul: the testimony of the LORD *is* sure, making wise the simple.

8The statutes of the LORD *are* right, rejoicing the heart: the commandment of the LORD *is* pure, enlightening the eyes.

9The fear of the LORD *is* clean, enduring for ever: the judgments of the LORD *are* true *and* righteous altogether.

10More to be desired *are they* than

gold, yea, than much fine gold: sweeter also than honey and the honeycomb.

11Moreover by them is thy servant warned: *and* in keeping of them *there is* great reward.

12Who can understand *his* errors? cleanse thou me from secret *faults.*

13Keep back thy servant also from presumptuous *sins;* let them not have dominion over me: then shall I be upright, and I shall be innocent from the great transgression.

14Let the words of my mouth, and the meditation of my heart, be acceptable in thy sight, O LORD, my strength, and my redeemer.

PROVERBS FOR TODAY/ 20:1

Wine is *a mocker, strong drink* is *raging: and whosoever is deceived thereby is not wise.*

JULY 26

2 CHRONICLES 17:1—18:34

AND Jehoshaphat his [Asa's] son reigned in his stead, and strengthened himself against Israel.

2And he placed forces in all the fenced cities of Judah, and set garrisons in the land of Judah, and in the cities of Ephraim, which Asa his father had taken.

3And the LORD was with Jehoshaphat, because he walked in the first ways of his father David, and sought not unto Baalim;

4But sought to the *LORD God of his father, and walked in his commandments, and not after the doings of Israel.*

5Therefore the LORD stablished the kingdom in his hand; and all Judah brought to Jehoshaphat presents; and he had riches and honour in abundance.

6And his heart was lifted up in the ways of the LORD: moreover he took away the high places and groves out of Judah.

7Also in the third year of his reign he sent to his princes, *even* to Benhail, and to Obadiah, and to Zechariah, and to Nethaneel, and to Michaiah, to teach the cities of Judah.

8And with them *he sent* Levites, *even* Shemaiah, and Nethaniah, and Zebadiah, and Asahel, and Shemiramoth, and Jehonathan, and Adonijah, and Tobijah, and Tob–adonijah, Levites; and with them Elishama and Jehoram, priests.

9And they taught in Judah, and *had* the book of the law of the LORD with them, and went about throughout all the cities of Judah, and taught the people.

10And the fear of the LORD fell upon all the kingdoms of the lands that *were* round about Judah, so that they made no war against Jehoshaphat.

11Also *some* of the Philistines brought Jehoshaphat presents, and tribute silver; and the Arabians brought him flocks, seven thousand and seven hundred rams, and seven thousand and seven hundred he goats.

12And Jehoshaphat waxed great exceedingly; and he built in Judah castles, and cities of store.

13And he had much business in the

cities of Judah: and the men of war, mighty men of valour, *were* in Jerusalem.

14And these *are* the numbers of them according to the house of their fathers: Of Judah, the captains of thousands; Adnah the chief, and with him mighty men of valour three hundred thousand.

15And next to him *was* Jehohanan the captain, and with him two hundred and fourscore thousand.

16And next to him *was* Amasiah the son of Zichri, who willingly offered himself unto the LORD; and with him two hundred thousand mighty men of valour.

17And of Benjamin; Eliada a mighty man of valour, and with him armed men with bow and shield two hundred thousand.

18And next him *was* Jehozabad, and with him an hundred and fourscore thousand ready prepared for the war.

19These waited on the king, beside *those* whom the king put in the fenced cities throughout all Judah.

Now Jehoshaphat had riches and honour in abundance, and joined affinity with Ahab.

2And after *certain* years he went down to Ahab to Samaria. And Ahab killed sheep and oxen for him in abundance, and for the people that *he had* with him, and persuaded him to go up *with him* to Ramoth–gilead.

3And Ahab king of Israel said unto Jehoshaphat king of Judah, Wilt thou go with me to Ramoth–gilead? And he answered him, I *am* as thou *art,* and my people as thy people; and *we will be* with thee in the war.

4And Jehoshaphat said unto the king of Israel, Enquire, I pray thee, at the word of the LORD to day.

5Therefore the king of Israel gathered together of prophets four hundred men, and said unto them, Shall we go to Ramoth–gilead to battle, or shall I forbear? And they said, Go up; for God

will deliver *it* into the king's hand.

6But Jehoshaphat said, *Is there* not here a prophet of the LORD besides, that we might enquire of him?

7And the king of Israel said unto Jehoshaphat, *There is* yet one man, by whom we may enquire of the LORD: but I hate him; for he never prophesied good unto me, but always evil: the same *is* Micaiah the son of Imla. And Jehoshaphat said, Let not the king say so.

8And the king of Israel called for one *of his* officers, and said, Fetch quickly Micaiah the son of Imla.

9And the king of Israel and Jehoshaphat king of Judah sat either of them on his throne, clothed in *their* robes, and they sat in a void place at the entering in of the gate of Samaria; and all the prophets prophesied before them.

10And Zedekiah the son of Chenaanah had made him horns of iron, and said, Thus saith the LORD, With these thou shalt push Syria until they be consumed.

11And all the prophets prophesied so, saying, Go up to Ramoth–gilead, and prosper: for the LORD shall deliver *it* into the hand of the king.

12And the messenger that went to call Micaiah spake to him, saying, Behold, the words of the prophets *declare* good to the king with one assent; let thy word therefore, I pray thee, be like one of theirs, and speak thou good.

13And Micaiah said, *As* the LORD liveth, even what my God saith, that will I speak.

14And when he was come to the king, the king said unto him, Micaiah, shall we go to Ramoth–gilead to battle, or shall I forbear? And he said, Go ye up, and prosper, and they shall be delivered into your hand.

15And the king said to him, How many times shall I adjure thee that thou say nothing but the truth to me in the name of the LORD?

16Then he said, I did see all Israel scattered upon the mountains, as sheep that have no shepherd: and the LORD said, These have no master; let them return *therefore* every man to his house in peace.

17And the king of Israel said to Jehoshaphat, Did I not tell thee *that* he would not prophesy good unto me, but evil?

18Again he said, Therefore hear the word of the LORD; I saw the LORD sitting upon his throne, and all the host of heaven standing on his right hand and *on* his left.

19And the LORD said, Who shall entice Ahab king of Israel, that he may go up and fall at Ramoth–gilead? And one spake saying after this manner, and another saying after that manner.

20Then there came out a spirit, and stood before the LORD, and said, I will entice him. And the LORD said unto him, Wherewith?

21And he said, I will go out, and be a lying spirit in the mouth of all his prophets. And *the LORD said, Thou shalt entice him,* and thou shalt also prevail: go out, and do *even* so.

22Now therefore, behold, the LORD hath put a lying spirit in the mouth of these thy prophets, and the LORD hath spoken evil against thee.

23Then Zedekiah the son of Chenaanah came near, and smote Micaiah upon the cheek, and said, Which way went the Spirit of the LORD from me to speak unto thee?

24And Micaiah said, Behold, thou shalt see on that day when thou shalt go into an inner chamber to hide thyself.

25Then the king of Israel said, Take ye Micaiah, and carry him back to Amon the governor of the city, and to Joash the king's son;

26And say, Thus saith the king, Put this *fellow* in the prison, and feed him with bread of affliction and with water of affliction, until I return in peace.

27And Micaiah said, If thou certainly return in peace, *then* hath not the LORD spoken by me. And he said, Hearken, all ye people.

28So the king of Israel and Jehoshaphat the king of Judah went up to Ramoth–gilead.

29And the king of Israel said unto Jehoshaphat, I will disguise myself, and will go to the battle; but put thou on thy robes. So the king of Israel disguised himself; and they went to the battle.

30Now the king of Syria had commanded the captains of the chariots that *were* with him, saying, Fight ye not with small or great, save only with the king of Israel.

31And it came to pass, when the captains of the chariots saw Jehoshaphat, that they said, It *is* the king of Israel. Therefore they compassed about him to fight: but Jehoshaphat cried out, and the LORD helped him; and God moved them *to depart* from him.

32For it came to pass, that, when the captains of the chariots perceived that it was not the king of Israel, they turned back again from pursuing him.

33And a *certain* man drew a bow at a venture, and smote the king of Israel between the joints of the harness: therefore he said to his chariot man, Turn thine hand, that thou mayest carry me out of the host; for I am wounded.

34And the battle increased that day: howbeit the king of Israel stayed *himself* up in *his* chariot against the Syrians until the even: and about the time of the sun going down he died.

ROMANS 9:25—10:12

As he saith also in Osee, I will call them my people, which were not my people; and her beloved, which was not beloved.

26And it shall come to pass, *that* in the place where it was said unto them, Ye *are* not my people; there shall they be called the children of the living God.

27Esaias also crieth concerning Israel, Though the number of the children of Israel be as the sand of the sea, a remnant shall be saved:

28For he will finish the work, and cut *it* short in righteousness: because a short work will the Lord make upon the earth.

29And as Esaias said before, Except the Lord of Sabaoth had left us a seed, we had been as Sodoma, and been made like unto Gomorrha.

30What shall we say then? That the Gentiles, which followed not after righteousness, have attained to righteousness, even the righteousness which is of faith.

31But Israel, which followed after the law of righteousness, hath not attained to the law of righteousness.

32Wherefore? Because *they sought it* not by faith, but as it were by the works of the law. For they stumbled at that stumblingstone;

33As it is written, Behold, I lay in Sion a stumblingstone and rock of offence: and whosoever believeth on him shall not be ashamed.

BRETHREN, my heart's desire and prayer to God for Israel is, that they might be saved.

2For I bear them record that they have a zeal of God, but not according to knowledge.

3For they being ignorant of God's righteousness, and going about to establish their own righteousness, have not submitted themselves unto the righteousness of God.

4For Christ *is* the end of the law for righteousness to every one that believeth.

5For Moses describeth the righteousness which is of the law, That the man which doeth those things shall live by them.

6But the righteousness which is of faith speaketh on this wise, Say not in thine heart, Who shall ascend into heaven? (that is, to bring Christ down *from above:*)

7Or, Who shall descend into the deep? (that is, to bring up Christ again from the dead.)

8But what saith it? The word is nigh thee, *even* in thy mouth, and in thy heart: that is, the word of faith, which we preach;

9That if thou shalt confess with thy mouth the Lord Jesus, and shalt believe in thine heart that God hath raised him from the dead, thou shalt be saved.

10For with the heart man believeth unto righteousness; and with the mouth confession is made unto salvation.

11For the scripture saith, Whosoever believeth on him shall not be ashamed.

12For there is no difference between the Jew and the Greek: for the same Lord over all is rich unto all that call upon him.

PSALM 20:1–9

THE LORD hear thee in the day of trouble; the name of the God of Jacob defend thee;

2Send thee help from the sanctuary, and strengthen thee out of Zion;

3Remember all thy offerings, and accept thy burnt sacrifice; Selah.

4Grant thee according to thine own heart, and fulfil all thy counsel.

5We will rejoice in thy salvation, and in the name of our God we will set up *our* banners: the LORD fulfil all thy petitions.

6Now know I that the LORD saveth his anointed; he will hear him from his holy heaven with the saving strength of his right hand.

7Some *trust* in chariots, and some in horses: but we will remember the name of the LORD our God.

8They are brought down and fallen: but we are risen, and stand upright.

9Save, LORD: let the king hear us when we call.

The fear of a king is *as the roaring of a lion:* whoso *provoketh him to anger sinneth* against *his own soul.* □ It is *an honour for a man to cease from strife: but every fool will be meddling.*

JULY 27

2 CHRONICLES 19:1—20:37

AND Jehoshaphat the king of Judah returned to his house in peace to Jerusalem.

2And Jehu the son of Hanani the seer went out to meet him, and said to king Jehoshaphat, Shouldest thou help the ungodly, and love them that hate the LORD? therefore *is* wrath upon thee from before the LORD.

3Nevertheless there are good things found in thee, in that thou hast taken away the groves out of the land, and hast prepared thine heart to seek God.

4And Jehoshaphat dwelt at Jerusalem: and he went out again through the people from Beer–sheba to mount Ephraim, and brought them back unto the LORD God of their fathers.

5And he set judges in the land throughout all the fenced cities of Judah, city by city,

6And said to the judges, Take heed what ye do: for ye judge not for man, but for the LORD, who *is* with you in the judgment.

7Wherefore now let the fear of the LORD be upon you; take heed and do *it:* for *there is* no iniquity with the LORD our God, nor respect of persons, nor taking of gifts.

8Moreover in Jerusalem did Jehoshaphat set of the Levites, and *of* the priests, and of the chief of the fathers of Israel, for the judgment of the LORD, and for controversies, when they returned to Jerusalem.

9And he charged them, saying, Thus shall ye do in the fear of the LORD, faithfully, and with a perfect heart.

10And what cause soever shall come to you of your brethren that dwell in their cities, between blood and blood, between law and commandment, statutes and judgments, ye shall even warn them that they trespass not against the LORD, and *so* wrath come upon you, and upon your brethren: this do, and ye shall not trespass.

11And, behold, Amariah the chief priest *is* over you in all matters of the LORD; and Zebadiah the son of Ishmael, the ruler of the house of Judah, for all the king's matters: also the Levites *shall be* officers before you. Deal courageously, and the LORD shall be with the good.

IT came to pass after this also, *that* the children of Moab, and the children of Ammon, and with them *other* beside the Ammonites, came against Jehoshaphat to battle.

2Then there came some that told Jehoshaphat, saying, There cometh a great multitude against thee from beyond the sea on this side Syria; and, behold, they *be* in Hazazon–tamar, which *is* En–gedi.

3And Jehoshaphat feared, and set himself to seek the LORD, and proclaimed a fast throughout all Judah.

4And Judah gathered themselves together, to ask *help* of the LORD: even out of all the cities of Judah they came to seek the LORD.

5And Jehoshaphat stood in the congregation of Judah and Jerusalem, in the house of the LORD, before the new court,

6And said, O LORD God of our fathers, *art* not thou God in heaven? and rulest *not* thou over all the kingdoms of the heathen? and in thine hand *is there not* power and might, so that none is able to withstand thee?

7*Art* not thou our God, *who* didst drive out the inhabitants of this land before thy people Israel, and gavest it to the seed of Abraham thy friend for ever?

8And they dwelt therein, and have built thee a sanctuary therein for thy name, saying,

9If, *when* evil cometh upon us, *as* the sword, judgment, or pestilence, or famine, we stand before this house, and in thy presence, (for thy name *is* in this house,) and cry unto thee in our affliction, then thou wilt hear and help.

10And now, behold, the children of Ammon and Moab and mount Seir, whom thou wouldest not let Israel invade, when they came out of the land of Egypt, but they turned from them, and destroyed them not;

11Behold, *I say, how* they reward us, to come to cast us out of thy possession, which thou hast given us to inherit.

12O our God, wilt thou not judge them? for we have no might against this great company that cometh against us; neither know we what to do: but our eyes *are* upon thee.

13And all Judah stood before the LORD, with their little ones, their wives, and their children.

14Then upon Jahaziel the son of Zechariah, the son of Benaiah, the son of Jeiel, the son of Mattaniah, a Levite of the sons of Asaph, came the Spirit of the LORD in the midst of the congregation;

15And he said, Hearken ye, all Judah, and ye inhabitants of Jerusalem, and thou king Jehoshaphat, Thus saith the LORD unto you, Be not afraid nor dismayed by reason of this great multitude; for the battle *is* not yours, but God's.

16To morrow go ye down against them: behold, they come up by the cliff of Ziz; and ye shall find them at the end of the brook, before the wilderness of Jeruel.

17Ye shall not *need* to fight in this *battle:* set yourselves, stand ye *still,* and see the salvation of the LORD with you, O Judah and Jerusalem: fear not, nor be dismayed; to morrow go out against them: for the LORD *will be* with you.

18And Jehoshaphat bowed his head with *his* face to the ground: and all Judah and the inhabitants of Jerusalem fell before the LORD, worshipping the LORD.

19And the Levites, of the children of the Kohathites, and of the children of the Korhites, stood up to praise the LORD God of Israel with a loud voice on high.

20And they rose early in the morning, and went forth into the wilderness of Tekoa: and as they went forth, Jehoshaphat stood and said, Hear me, O Judah, and ye inhabitants of Jerusalem; Believe in the LORD your God, so shall ye be established; believe his prophets, so shall ye prosper.

21And when he had consulted with the people, he appointed singers unto the LORD, and that should praise the beauty of holiness, as they went out before the army, and to say, Praise the LORD; for his mercy *endureth* for ever.

22And when they began to sing and to praise, the LORD set ambushments against the children of Ammon, Moab, and mount Seir, which were come against Judah; and they were smitten.

23For the children of Ammon and Moab stood up against the inhabitants of mount Seir, utterly to slay and destroy *them:* and when they had made an end of the inhabitants of Seir, every one helped to destroy another.

24And when Judah came toward the watch tower in the wilderness, they looked unto the multitude, and, behold, they *were* dead bodies fallen to the earth, and none escaped.

25And when Jehoshaphat and his people came to take away the spoil of them, they found among them in abundance both riches with the dead bodies, and precious jewels, which they stripped off for themselves, more than they could carry away: and they were three days in gathering of the spoil, it was so much.

26And on the fourth day they assembled themselves in the valley of Berachah; for there they blessed the LORD: therefore the name of the same place was called, The valley of Berachah, unto this day.

27Then they returned, every man of Judah and Jerusalem, and Jehoshaphat in the forefront of them, to go again to Jerusalem with joy; for the LORD had made them to rejoice over their enemies.

28And they came to Jerusalem with psalteries and harps and trumpets unto the house of the LORD.

29And the fear of God was on all the kingdoms of *those* countries, when they had heard that the LORD fought against the enemies of Israel.

30So the realm of Jehoshaphat was quiet: for his God gave him rest round about.

31And Jehoshaphat reigned over Judah: *he was* thirty and five years old when he began to reign, and he reigned twenty and five years in Jerusalem. And his mother's name *was* Azubah the daughter of Shilhi.

32And he walked in the way of Asa his father, and departed not from it, doing *that which was* right in the sight of the LORD.

33Howbeit the high places were not taken away: for as yet the people had not prepared their hearts unto the God of their fathers.

34Now the rest of the acts of Jehoshaphat, first and last, behold, they *are* written in the book of Jehu the son of Hanani, who *is* mentioned in the book of the kings of Israel.

35And after this did Jehoshaphat king of Judah join himself with Ahaziah king of Israel, who did very wickedly:

36And he joined himself with him to make ships to go to Tarshish: and they made the ships in Ezion–geber.

37Then Eliezer the son of Dodavah of Mareshah prophesied against Jehoshaphat, saying, Because thou hast joined thyself with Ahaziah, the LORD hath broken thy works. And the ships were broken, that they were not able to go to Tarshish.

ROMANS 10:13—11:12

FOR whosoever shall call upon the name of the Lord shall be saved.

14How then shall they call on him in whom they have not believed? and how shall they believe in him of whom they have not heard? and how shall they hear without a preacher?

15And how shall they preach, except they be sent? as it is written, How beautiful are the feet of them that preach the gospel of peace, and bring glad tidings of good things!

16But they have not all obeyed the gospel. For Esaias saith, Lord, who hath believed our report?

17So then faith *cometh* by hearing, and hearing by the word of God.

18But I say, Have they not heard? Yes verily, their sound went into all the earth, and their words unto the ends of the world.

19But I say, Did not Israel know? First Moses saith, I will provoke you to jealousy by *them that are* no people, *and* by a foolish nation I will anger you.

20But Esaias is very bold, and saith, I was found of them that sought me not; I was made manifest unto them that asked not after me.

21But to Israel he saith, All day long I have stretched forth my hands unto a disobedient and gainsaying people.

I SAY then, Hath God cast away his people? God forbid. For I also am an Israelite, of the seed of Abraham, *of* the tribe of Benjamin.

2God hath not cast away his people which he foreknew. Wot ye not what the scripture saith of Elias? how he maketh intercession to God against Israel, saying,

3Lord, they have killed thy prophets, and digged down thine altars; and I am left alone, and they seek my life.

4But what saith the answer of God unto him? I have reserved to myself seven thousand men, who have not bowed the knee to *the image of* Baal.

5Even so then at this present time also there is a remnant according to the election of grace.

6And if by grace, then *is it* no more of works: otherwise grace is no more grace. But if *it be* of works, then is it no more grace: otherwise work is no more work.

7What then? Israel hath not obtained that which he seeketh for; but the election hath obtained it, and the rest were blinded.

8(According as it is written, God hath given them the spirit of slumber, eyes that they should not see, and ears that they should not hear;) unto this day.

9And David saith, Let their table be made a snare, and a trap, and a stumblingblock, and a recompence unto them:

10Let their eyes be darkened, that they may not see, and bow down their back alway.

11I say then, Have they stumbled that they should fall? God forbid: but *rather* through their fall salvation *is come* unto the Gentiles, for to provoke them to jealousy.

12Now if the fall of them *be* the riches of the world, and the diminishing of them the riches of the Gentiles; how much more their fulness?

PSALM 21:1–13

THE king shall joy in thy strength, O LORD; and in thy salvation how greatly shall he rejoice!

2Thou hast given him his heart's desire, and hast not withholden the request of his lips. Selah.

3For thou preventest him with the blessings of goodness: thou settest a crown of pure gold on his head.

4He asked life of thee, *and* thou gavest *it* him, *even* length of days for ever and ever.

5His glory *is* great in thy salvation: honour and majesty hast thou laid upon him.

6For thou hast made him most blessed for ever: thou hast made him exceeding glad with thy countenance.

7For the king trusteth in the LORD, and through the mercy of the most High he shall not be moved.

8Thine hand shall find out all thine enemies: thy right hand shall find out those that hate thee.

9Thou shalt make them as a fiery oven in the time of thine anger: the LORD shall swallow them up in his wrath, and the fire shall devour them.

10Their fruit shalt thou destroy from the earth, and their seed from among the children of men.

11For they intended evil against thee: they imagined a mischievous device, *which* they are not able *to perform*.

12Therefore shalt thou make them turn their back, *when* thou shalt make ready *thine arrows* upon thy strings against the face of them.

13Be thou exalted, LORD, in thine own strength: *so* will we sing and praise thy power.

PROVERBS FOR TODAY/ 20:4–6

The sluggard will not plow by reason of the cold; therefore *shall he beg in harvest, and* have *nothing.* □ *Counsel in the heart of man* is like *deep water; but a man of understanding will draw it out.* □ *Most men will proclaim every one his own goodness: but a faithful man who can find?*

JULY 28

2 CHRONICLES 21:1—23:21

Now Jehoshaphat slept with his fathers, and was buried with his fathers in the city of David. And Jehoram his son reigned in his stead.

2And he had brethren the sons of Jehoshaphat, Azariah, and Jehiel, and Zechariah, and Azariah, and Michael, and Shephatiah: all these *were* the sons of Jehoshaphat king of Israel.

3And their father gave them great gifts of silver, and of gold, and of precious things, with fenced cities in Judah: but the kingdom gave he to Jehoram; because he *was* the firstborn.

4Now when Jehoram was risen up to the kingdom of his father, he strengthened himself, and slew all his brethren with the sword, and *divers* also of the princes of Israel.

5Jehoram *was* thirty and two years old when he began to reign, and he reigned eight years in Jerusalem.

6And he walked in the way of the kings of Israel, like as did the house of Ahab: for he had the daughter of Ahab to wife: and he wrought *that which was* evil in the eyes of the LORD.

7Howbeit the LORD would not destroy the house of David, because of the covenant that he had made with David, and as he promised to give a light to him and to his sons for ever.

8In his days the Edomites revolted from under the dominion of Judah, and made themselves a king.

9Then Jehoram went forth with his princes, and all his chariots with him: and he rose up by night, and smote the Edomites which compassed him in, and the captains of the chariots.

10So the Edomites revolted from under the hand of Judah unto this day. The same time *also* did Libnah revolt from under his hand; because he had forsaken the LORD God of his fathers.

11Moreover he made high places in the mountains of Judah, and caused the inhabitants of Jerusalem to commit fornication, and compelled Judah *thereto*.

12And there came a writing to him from Elijah the prophet, saying, Thus saith the LORD God of David thy father, Because thou hast not walked in the ways of Jehoshaphat thy father, nor in the ways of Asa king of Judah,

13But hast walked in the way of the kings of Israel, and hast made Judah and the inhabitants of Jerusalem to go a whoring, like to the whoredoms of the house of Ahab, and also hast slain thy brethren of thy father's house, *which were* better than thyself:

14Behold, with a great plague will the LORD smite thy people, and thy children, and thy wives, and all thy goods:

15And thou *shalt have* great sickness by disease of thy bowels, until thy bowels fall out by reason of the sickness day by day.

16Moreover the LORD stirred up

against Jehoram the spirit of the Philistines, and of the Arabians, that *were* near the Ethiopians:

17And they came up into Judah, and brake into it, and carried away all the substance that was found in the king's house, and his sons also, and his wives; so that there was never a son left him, save Jehoahaz, the youngest of his sons.

18And after all this the LORD smote him in his bowels with an incurable disease.

19And it came to pass, that in process of time, after the end of two years, his bowels fell out by reason of his sickness: so he died of sore diseases. And his people made no burning for him, like the burning of his fathers.

20Thirty and two years old was he when he began to reign, and he reigned in Jerusalem eight years, and departed without being desired. Howbeit they buried him in the city of David, but not in the sepulchres of the kings.

AND the inhabitants of Jerusalem made Ahaziah his youngest son king in his stead: for the band of men that came with the Arabians to the camp had slain all the eldest. So Ahaziah the son of Jehoram king of Judah reigned.

2Forty and two years old *was* Ahaziah when he began to reign, and he reigned one year in Jerusalem. His mother's name also *was* Athaliah the daughter of Omri.

3He also walked in the ways of the house of Ahab: for his mother was his counsellor to do wickedly.

4Wherefore he did evil in the sight of the LORD like the house of Ahab: for they were his counsellors after the death of his father to his destruction.

5He walked also after their counsel, and went with Jehoram the son of Ahab king of Israel to war against Hazael king of Syria at Ramoth–gilead: and the Syrians smote Joram.

6And he returned to be healed in Jezreel because of the wounds which were given him at Ramah, when he fought with Hazael king of Syria. And Azariah the son of Jehoram king of Judah went down to see Jehoram the son of Ahab at Jezreel, because he was sick.

7And the destruction of Ahaziah was of God by coming to Joram: for when he was come, he went out with Jehoram against Jehu the son of Nimshi, whom the LORD had anointed to cut off the house of Ahab.

8And it came to pass, that, when Jehu was executing judgment upon the house of Ahab, and found the princes of Judah, and the sons of the brethren of Ahaziah, that ministered to Ahaziah, he slew them.

9And he sought Ahaziah: and they caught him, (for he was hid in Samaria,) and brought him to Jehu: and when they had slain him, they buried him: Because, said they, he *is* the son of Jehoshaphat, who sought the LORD with all his heart. So the house of Ahaziah had no power to keep still the kingdom.

10But when Athaliah the mother of Ahaziah saw that her son was dead, she arose and destroyed all the seed royal of the house of Judah.

11But Jehoshabeath, the daughter of the king, took Joash the son of Ahaziah, and stole him from among the king's sons that were slain, and put him and his nurse in a bedchamber. So Jehoshabeath, the daughter of king Jehoram, the wife of Jehoiada the priest, (for she was the sister of Ahaziah,) hid him from Athaliah, so that she slew him not.

12And he was with them hid in the house of God six years: and Athaliah reigned over the land.

AND in the seventh year Jehoiada strengthened himself, and took the captains of hundreds, Azariah the son of Jeroham, and Ishmael the son of Jehohanan, and Azariah the son of Obed, and Maaseiah the son of Adaiah, and

Elishaphat the son of Zichri, into covenant with him.

2And they went about in Judah, and gathered the Levites out of all the cities of Judah, and the chief of the fathers of Israel, and they came to Jerusalem.

3And all the congregation made a covenant with the king in the house of God. And he said unto them, Behold, the king's son shall reign, as the LORD hath said of the sons of David.

4This *is* the thing that ye shall do; A third part of you entering on the sabbath, of the priests and of the Levites, *shall be* porters of the doors;

5And a third part *shall be* at the king's house; and a third part at the gate of the foundation: and all the people *shall be* in the courts of the house of the LORD.

6But let none come into the house of the LORD, save the priests, and they that minister of the Levites; they shall go in, for they *are* holy: but all the people shall keep the watch of the LORD.

7And the Levites shall compass the king round about, every man with his weapons in his hand; and whosoever *else* cometh into the house, he shall be put to death: but be ye with the king when he cometh in, and when he goeth out.

8So the Levites and all Judah did according to all things that Jehoiada the priest had commanded, and took every man his men that were to come in on the sabbath, with them that were to go *out* on the sabbath: for Jehoiada the priest dismissed not the courses.

9Moreover Jehoiada the priest delivered to the captains of hundreds spears, and bucklers, and shields, that *had been* king David's, which *were* in the house of God.

10And he set all the people, every man having his weapon in his hand, from the right side of the temple to the left side of the temple, along by the altar and the temple, by the king round about.

11Then they brought out the king's son, and put upon him the crown, and *gave him* the testimony, and made him king. And Jehoiada and his sons anointed him, and said, God save the king.

12Now when Athaliah heard the noise of the people running and praising the king, she came to the people into the house of the LORD:

13And she looked, and, behold, the king stood at his pillar at the entering in, and the princes and the trumpets by the king: and all the people of the land rejoiced, and sounded with trumpets, also the singers with instruments of musick, and such as taught to sing praise. Then Athaliah rent her clothes, and said, Treason, Treason.

14Then Jehoiada the priest brought out the captains of hundreds that were set over the host, and said unto them, Have her forth of the ranges: and whoso followeth her, let him be slain with the sword. For the priest said, Slay her not in the house of the LORD.

15So they laid hands on her; and when she was come to the entering of the horse gate by the king's house, they slew her there.

16And Jehoiada made a covenant between him, and between all the people, and between the king, that they should be the LORD's people.

17Then all the people went to the house of Baal, and brake it down, and brake his altars and his images in pieces, and slew Mattan the priest of Baal before the altars.

18Also Jehoiada appointed the offices of the house of the LORD by the hand of the priests the Levites, whom David had distributed in the house of the LORD, to offer the burnt offerings of the LORD, as *it is* written in the law of Moses, with rejoicing and with singing, *as it was ordained* by David.

19And he set the porters at the gates of the house of the LORD, that none *which was* unclean in any thing should enter in.

20And he took the captains of hundreds, and the nobles, and the governors of the people, and all the people of the land, and brought down the king from the house of the LORD: and they came through the high gate into the king's house, and set the king upon the throne of the kingdom.

21And all the people of the land rejoiced: and the city was quiet, after that they had slain Athaliah with the sword.

ROMANS 11:13–36

FOR I speak to you Gentiles, inasmuch as I am the apostle of the Gentiles, I magnify mine office:

14If by any means I may provoke to emulation *them which are* my flesh, and might save some of them.

15For if the casting away of them *be* the reconciling of the world, what *shall* the receiving *of them be,* but life from the dead?

16For if the firstfruit *be* holy, the lump *is* also *holy:* and if the root *be* holy, so *are* the branches.

17And if some of the branches be broken off, and thou, being a wild olive tree, wert graffed in among them, and with them partakest of the root and fatness of the olive tree;

18Boast not against the branches. But if thou boast, thou bearest not the root, but the root thee.

19Thou wilt say then, The branches were broken off, that I might be graffed in.

20Well; because of unbelief they were broken off, and thou standest by faith. Be not highminded, but fear:

21For if God spared not the natural branches, *take heed* lest he also spare not thee.

22Behold therefore the goodness and severity of God: on them which fell, severity; but toward thee, goodness, if thou continue in *his* goodness: otherwise thou also shalt be cut off.

23And they also, if they abide not still in unbelief, shall be graffed in: for God is able to graff them in again.

24For if thou wert cut out of the olive tree which is wild by nature, and wert graffed contrary to nature into a good olive tree: how much more shall these, which be the natural *branches,* be graffed into their own olive tree?

25For I would not, brethren, that ye should be ignorant of this mystery, lest ye should be wise in your own conceits; that blindness in part is happened to Israel, until the fulness of the Gentiles be come in.

26And so all Israel shall be saved: as it is written, There shall come out of Sion the Deliverer, and shall turn away ungodliness from Jacob:

27For this *is* my covenant unto them, when I shall take away their sins.

28As concerning the gospel, *they are* enemies for your sakes: but as touching the election, *they are* beloved for the fathers' sakes.

29For the gifts and calling of God *are* without repentance.

30For as ye in times past have not believed God, yet have now obtained mercy through their unbelief:

31Even so have these also now not believed, that through your mercy they also may obtain mercy.

32For God hath concluded them all in unbelief, that he might have mercy upon all.

33O the depth of the riches both of the wisdom and knowledge of God! how unsearchable *are* his judgments, and his ways past finding out!

34For who hath known the mind of the Lord? or who hath been his counsellor?

35Or who hath first given to him, and it shall be recompensed unto him again?

36For of him, and through him, and to him, *are* all things: to whom *be* glory for ever. Amen.

PSALM 22:1–18

MY God, my God, why hast thou forsaken me? *why art thou so far from helping me, and from* the words of my roaring?

2O my God, I cry in the daytime, but thou hearest not; and in the night season, and am not silent.

3But thou *art* holy, *O thou* that inhabitest the praises of Israel.

4Our fathers trusted in thee: they trusted, and thou didst deliver them.

5They cried unto thee, and were delivered: they trusted in thee, and were not confounded.

6But I *am* a worm, and no man; a reproach of men, and despised of the people.

7All they that see me laugh me to scorn: they shoot out the lip, they shake the head, *saying,*

8He trusted on the LORD *that* he would deliver him: let him deliver him, seeing he delighted in him.

9But thou *art* he that took me out of the womb: thou didst make me hope *when I was* upon my mother's breasts.

10I was cast upon thee from the womb: thou *art* my God from my mother's belly.

11Be not far from me; for trouble *is* near; for *there is* none to help.

12Many bulls have compassed me: strong *bulls* of Bashan have beset me round.

13They gaped upon me *with* their mouths, *as* a ravening and a roaring lion.

14I am poured out like water, and all my bones are out of joint: my heart is like wax; it is melted in the midst of my bowels.

15My strength is dried up like a potsherd; and my tongue cleaveth to my jaws; and thou hast brought me into the dust of death.

16For dogs have compassed me: the assembly of the wicked have inclosed me: they pierced my hands and my feet.

17I may tell all my bones: they look *and* stare upon me.

18They part my garments among them, and cast lots upon my vesture.

PROVERBS FOR TODAY/ 20:7

The just man *walketh in his integrity: his children* are *blessed after him.*

JULY 29

2 CHRONICLES 24:1—25:28

JOASH *was* seven years old when he began to reign, and he reigned forty years in Jerusalem. His mother's name also *was* Zibiah of Beersheba.

2And Joash did *that which was* right in the sight of the LORD all the days of Jehoiada the priest.

3And Jehoiada took for him two wives; and he begat sons and daughters.

4And it came to pass after this, *that* Joash was minded to repair the house of the LORD.

5And he gathered together the priests and the Levites, and said to them, Go out unto the cities of Judah, and gather of all Israel money to repair the house of your God from year to year, and see that ye hasten the matter.

Howbeit the Levites hastened *it* not.

6And the king called for Jehoiada the chief, and said unto him, Why hast thou not required of the Levites to bring in out of Judah and out of Jerusalem the collection, *according to the commandment* of Moses the servant of the LORD, and of the congregation of Israel, for the tabernacle of witness?

7For the sons of Athaliah, that wicked woman, had broken up the house of God; and also all the dedicated things of the house of the LORD did they bestow upon Baalim.

8And at the king's commandment they made a chest, and set it without at the gate of the house of the LORD.

9And they made a proclamation through Judah and Jerusalem, to bring in to the LORD the collection *that* Moses the servant of God *laid* upon Israel in the wilderness.

10And all the princes and all the people rejoiced, and brought in, and cast into the chest, until they had made an end.

11Now it came to pass, that at what time the chest was brought unto the king's office by the hand of the Levites, and when they saw that *there was* much money, the king's scribe and the high priest's officer came and emptied the chest, and took it, and carried it to his place again. Thus they did day by day, and gathered money in abundance.

12And the king and Jehoiada gave it to such as did the work of the service of the house of the LORD, and hired masons and carpenters to repair the house of the LORD, and also such as wrought iron and brass to mend the house of the LORD.

13So the workmen wrought, and the work was perfected by them, and they set the house of God in his state, and strengthened it.

14And when they had finished *it,* they brought the rest of the money before the king and Jehoiada, whereof were made vessels for the house of the LORD, *even* vessels to minister, and to offer *withal,* and spoons, and vessels of gold and silver. And they offered burnt offerings in the house of the LORD continually all the days of Jehoiada.

15But Jehoiada waxed old, and was full of days when he died; an hundred and thirty years old *was he* when he died.

16And they buried him in the city of David among the kings, because he had done good in Israel, both toward God, and toward his house.

17Now after the death of Jehoiada came the princes of Judah, and made obeisance to the king. Then the king hearkened unto them.

18And they left the house of the LORD God of their fathers, and served groves and idols: and wrath came upon Judah and Jerusalem for this their trespass.

19Yet he sent prophets to them, to bring them again unto the LORD; and they testified against them: but they would not give ear.

20And the Spirit of God came upon Zechariah the son of Jehoiada the priest, which stood above the people, and said unto them, Thus saith God, Why transgress ye the commandments of the LORD, that ye cannot prosper? because ye have forsaken the LORD, he hath also forsaken you.

21And they conspired against him, and stoned him with stones at the commandment of the king in the court of the house of the LORD.

22Thus Joash the king remembered not the kindness which Jehoiada his father had done to him, but slew his son. And when he died, he said, The LORD look upon *it,* and require *it.*

23And it came to pass at the end of the year, *that* the host of Syria came up against him: and they came to Judah and Jerusalem, and destroyed all the princes of the people from among the people, and sent all the spoil of them unto the king of Damascus.

24For the army of the Syrians came with a small company of men, and the

LORD delivered a very great host into their hand, because they had forsaken the LORD God of their fathers. So they executed judgment against Joash.

25And when they were departed from him, (for they left him in great diseases,) his own servants conspired against him for the blood of the sons of Jehoiada the priest, and slew him on his bed, and he died: and they buried him in the city of David, but they buried him not in the sepulchres of the kings.

26And these are they that conspired against him; Zabad the son of Shimeath an Ammonitess, and Jehozabad the son of Shimrith a Moabitess.

27Now *concerning* his sons, and the greatness of the burdens *laid* upon him, and the repairing of the house of God, behold, they *are* written in the story of the book of the kings. And Amaziah his son reigned in his stead.

AMAZIAH *was* twenty and five years old *when* he began to reign, and he reigned twenty and nine years in Jerusalem. And his mother's name *was* Jehoaddan of Jerusalem.

2And he did *that which was* right in the sight of the LORD, but not with a perfect heart.

3Now it came to pass, when the kingdom was established to him, that he slew his servants that had killed the king his father.

4But he slew not their children, but *did* as *it is* written in the law in the book of Moses, where the LORD commanded, saying, The fathers shall not die for the children, neither shall the children die for the fathers, but every man shall die for his own sin.

5Moreover Amaziah gathered Judah together, and made them captains over thousands, and captains over hundreds, according to the houses of *their* fathers, throughout all Judah and Benjamin: and he numbered them from twenty years old and above, and found them three hundred thousand choice *men, able* to go forth to war, that could handle spear and shield.

6He hired also an hundred thousand mighty men of valour out of Israel for an hundred talents of silver.

7But there came a man of God to him, saying, O king, let not the army of Israel go with thee; for the LORD *is* not with Israel, *to wit, with* all the children of Ephraim.

8But if thou wilt go, do *it,* be strong for the battle: God shall make thee fall before the enemy: for God hath power to help, and to cast down.

9And Amaziah said to the man of God, But what shall we do for the hundred talents which I have given to the army of Israel? And the man of God answered, The LORD is able to give thee much more than this.

10Then Amaziah separated them, *to wit,* the army that was come to him out of Ephraim, to go home again: wherefore their anger was greatly kindled against Judah, and they returned home in great anger.

11And Amaziah strengthened himself, and led forth his people, and went to the valley of salt, and smote of the children of Seir ten thousand.

12And *other* ten thousand *left* alive did the children of Judah carry away captive, and brought them unto the top of the rock, and cast them down from the top of the rock, that they all were broken in pieces.

13But the soldiers of the army which Amaziah sent back, that they should not go with him to battle, fell upon the cities of Judah, from Samaria even unto Beth–horon, and smote three thousand of them, and took much spoil.

14Now it came to pass, after that Amaziah was come from the slaughter of the Edomites, that he brought the gods of the children of Seir, and set them up *to be* his gods, and bowed down himself before them, and burned incense unto them.

15Wherefore the anger of the LORD

was kindled against Amaziah, and he sent unto him a prophet, which said unto him, Why hast thou sought after the gods of the people, which could not deliver their own people out of thine hand?

16And it came to pass, as he talked with him, that *the king* said unto him, Art thou made of the king's counsel? forbear; why shouldest thou be smitten? Then the prophet forbare, and said, I know that God hath determined to destroy thee, because thou hast done this, and hast not hearkened unto my counsel.

17Then Amaziah king of Judah took advice, and sent to Joash, the son of Jehoahaz, the son of Jehu, king of Israel, saying, Come, let us see one another in the face.

18And Joash king of Israel sent to Amaziah king of Judah, saying, The thistle that *was* in Lebanon sent to the cedar that *was* in Lebanon, saying, Give thy daughter to my son to wife: and there passed by a wild beast that *was* in Lebanon, and trode down the thistle.

19Thou sayest, Lo, thou hast smitten the Edomites; and thine heart lifteth thee up to boast: abide now at home; why shouldest thou meddle to *thine* hurt, and that thou shouldest fall, *even* thou, and Judah with thee?

20But Amaziah would not hear; for it *came* of God, that he might deliver them into the hand *of their enemies,* because they sought after the gods of Edom.

21So Joash the king of Israel went up; and they saw one another in the face, *both* he and Amaziah king of Judah, at Beth–shemesh, which *belongeth* to Judah.

22And Judah was put to the worse before Israel, and they fled every man to his tent.

23And Joash the king of Israel took Amaziah king of Judah, the son of Joash, the son of Jehoahaz, at Beth–shemesh, and brought him to Jerusalem, and brake

down the wall of Jerusalem from the gate of Ephraim to the corner gate, four hundred cubits.

24And *he took* all the gold and the silver, and all the vessels that were found in the house of God with Obed–edom, and the treasures of the king's house, the hostages also, and returned to Samaria.

25And Amaziah the son of Joash king of Judah lived after the death of Joash son of Jehoahaz king of Israel fifteen years.

26Now the rest of the acts of Amaziah, first and last, behold, *are* they not written in the book of the kings of Judah and Israel?

27Now after the time that Amaziah did turn away from following the LORD they made a conspiracy against him in Jerusalem; and he fled to Lachish: but they sent to Lachish after him, and slew him there.

28And they brought him upon horses, and buried him with his fathers in the city of Judah.

ROMANS 12:1–21

I BESEECH you therefore, brethren, by the mercies of God, that ye present your bodies a living sacrifice, holy, acceptable unto God, *which is* your reasonable service.

2And be not conformed to this world: but be ye transformed by the renewing of your mind, that ye may prove what *is* that good, and acceptable, and perfect, will of God.

3For I say, through the grace given unto me, to every man that is among you, not to think *of himself* more highly than he ought to think; but to think soberly, according as God hath dealt to every man the measure of faith.

4For as we have many members in one body, and all members have not the same office:

5So we, *being* many, are one body

king, and said unto him, *It appertaineth* not unto thee, Uzziah, to burn incense unto the LORD, but to the priests the sons of Aaron, that are consecrated to burn incense: go out of the sanctuary; for thou hast trespassed; neither *shall it be* for thine honour from the LORD God.

19Then Uzziah was wroth, and *had* a censer in his hand to burn incense: and while he was wroth with the priests, the leprosy even rose up in his forehead before the priests in the house of the LORD, from beside the incense altar.

20And Azariah the chief priest, and all the priests, looked upon him, and, behold, he *was* leprous in his forehead, and they thrust him out from thence; yea, himself hasted also to go out, because the LORD had smitten him.

21And Uzziah the king was a leper unto the day of his death, and dwelt in a several house, *being* a leper; for he was cut off from the house of the LORD: and Jotham his son *was* over the king's house, judging the people of the land.

22Now the rest of the acts of Uzziah, first and last, did Isaiah the prophet, the son of Amoz, write.

23So Uzziah slept with his fathers, and they buried him with his fathers in the field of the burial which *belonged* to the kings; for they said, He *is* a leper: and Jotham his son reigned in his stead.

JOTHAM *was* twenty and five years old when he began to reign, and he reigned sixteen years in Jerusalem. His mother's name also *was* Jerushah, the daughter of Zadok.

2And he did *that which was* right in the sight of the LORD, according to all that his father Uzziah did: howbeit he entered not into the temple of the LORD. And the people did yet corruptly.

3He built the high gate of the house of the LORD, and on the wall of Ophel he built much.

4Moreover he built cities in the mountains of Judah, and in the forests he built castles and towers.

5He fought also with the king of the Ammonites, and prevailed against them. And the children of Ammon gave him the same year an hundred talents of silver, and ten thousand measures of wheat, and ten thousand of barley. So much did the children of Ammon pay unto him, both the second year, and the third.

6So Jotham became mighty, because he prepared his ways before the LORD his God.

7Now the rest of the acts of Jotham, and all his wars, and his ways, lo, they *are* written in the book of the kings of Israel and Judah.

8He was five and twenty years old when he began to reign, and reigned sixteen years in Jerusalem.

9And Jotham slept with his fathers, and they buried him in the city of David: and Ahaz his son reigned in his stead.

AHAZ *was* twenty years old when he began to reign, and he reigned sixteen years in Jerusalem: but he did not *that which was* right in the sight of the LORD, like David his father:

2For he walked in the ways of the kings of Israel, and made also molten images for Baalim.

3Moreover he burnt incense in the valley of the son of Hinnom, and burnt his children in the fire, after the abominations of the heathen whom the LORD had cast out before the children of Israel.

4He sacrificed also and burnt incense in the high places, and on the hills, and under every green tree.

5Wherefore the LORD his God delivered him into the hand of the king of Syria; and they smote him, and carried away a great multitude of them captives, and brought *them* to Damascus. And he was also delivered into the hand of the king of Israel, who smote him with a great slaughter.

6For Pekah the son of Remaliah slew in Judah an hundred and twenty thousand in one day, *which were* all valiant men; because they had forsaken the LORD God of their fathers.

7And Zichri, a mighty man of Ephraim, slew Maaseiah the king's son, and Azrikam the governor of the house, and Elkanah *that was* next to the king.

8And the children of Israel carried away captive of their brethren two hundred thousand, women, sons, and daughters, and took also away much spoil from them, and brought the spoil to Samaria.

9But a prophet of the LORD was there, whose name *was* Oded: and he went out before the host that came to Samaria, and said unto them, Behold, because the LORD God of your fathers was wroth with Judah, he hath delivered them into your hand, and ye have slain them in a rage *that* reacheth up unto heaven.

10And now ye purpose to keep under the children of Judah and Jerusalem for bondmen and bondwomen unto you: *but are there* not with you, even with you, sins against the LORD your God?

11Now hear me therefore, and deliver the captives again, which ye have taken captive of your brethren: for the fierce wrath of the LORD *is* upon you.

12Then certain of the heads of the children of Ephraim, Azariah the son of Johanan, Berechiah the son of Meshillemoth, and Jehizkiah the son of Shallum, and Amasa the son of Hadlai, stood up against them that came from the war,

13And said unto them, Ye shall not bring in the captives hither: for whereas we have offended against the LORD *already,* ye intend to add *more* to our sins and to our trespass: for our trespass is great, and *there is* fierce wrath against Israel.

14So the armed men left the captives and the spoil before the princes and all the congregation.

15And the men which were expressed by name rose up, and took the captives, and with the spoil clothed all that were naked among them, and arrayed them, and shod them, and gave them to eat and to drink, and anointed them, and carried all the feeble of them upon asses, and brought them to Jericho, the city of palm trees, to their brethren: then they returned to Samaria.

16At that time did king Ahaz send unto the kings of Assyria to help him.

17For again the Edomites had come and smitten Judah, and carried away captives.

18The Philistines also had invaded the cities of the low country, and of the south of Judah, and had taken Beth-shemesh, and Ajalon, and Gederoth, and Shocho with the villages thereof, and Timnah with the villages thereof, Gimzo also and the villages thereof: and they dwelt there.

19For the LORD brought Judah low because of Ahaz king of Israel; for he made Judah naked, and transgressed sore against the LORD.

20And Tilgath-pilneser king of Assyria came unto him, and distressed him, but strengthened him not.

21For Ahaz took away a portion *out* of the house of the LORD, and *out* of the house of the king, and of the princes, and gave *it* unto the king of Assyria: but he helped him not.

22And in the time of his distress did he trespass yet more against the LORD: this *is that* king Ahaz.

23For he sacrificed unto the gods of Damascus, which smote him: and he said, Because the gods of the kings of Syria help them, *therefore* will I sacrifice to them, that they may help me. But they were the ruin of him, and of all Israel.

24And Ahaz gathered together the vessels of the house of God, and cut in pieces the vessels of the house of God, and shut up the doors of the house of the LORD, and he made him altars in every corner of Jerusalem.

25And in every several city of Judah he made high places to burn incense unto other gods, and provoked to anger the LORD God of his fathers.

26Now the rest of his acts and of all his ways, first and last, behold, they *are* written in the book of the kings of Judah and Israel.

27And Ahaz slept with his fathers, and they buried him in the city, *even* in Jerusalem: but they brought him not into the sepulchres of the kings of Israel: and Hezekiah his son reigned in his stead.

ROMANS 13:1-14

LET every soul be subject unto the higher powers. For there is no power but of God: the powers that be are ordained of God.

2Whosoever therefore resisteth the power, resisteth the ordinance of God: and they that resist shall receive to themselves damnation.

3For rulers are not a terror to good works, but to the evil. Wilt thou then not be afraid of the power? do that which is good, and thou shalt have praise of the same:

4For he is the minister of God to thee for good. But if thou do that which is evil, be afraid; for he beareth not the sword in vain: for he is the minister of God, a revenger to *execute* wrath upon him that doeth evil.

5Wherefore *ye* must needs be subject, not only for wrath, but also for conscience sake.

6For for this cause pay ye tribute also: for they are God's ministers, attending continually upon this very thing.

7Render therefore to all their dues: tribute to whom tribute *is due;* custom to whom custom; fear to whom fear; honour to whom honour.

8Owe no man any thing, but to love one another: for he that loveth another hath fulfilled the law.

9For this, Thou shalt not commit adultery, Thou shalt not kill, Thou shalt not steal, Thou shalt not bear false witness, Thou shalt not covet; and if *there be* any other commandment, it is briefly comprehended in this saying, namely, Thou shalt love thy neighbour as thyself.

10Love worketh no ill to his neighbour: therefore love *is* the fulfilling of the law.

11And that, knowing the time, that now *it is* high time to awake out of sleep: for now *is* our salvation nearer than when we believed.

12The night is far spent, the day is at hand: let us therefore cast off the works of darkness, and let us put on the armour of light.

13Let us walk honestly, as in the day; not in rioting and drunkenness, not in chambering and wantonness, not in strife and envying.

14But put ye on the Lord Jesus Christ, and make not provision for the flesh, to *fulfil* the lusts *thereof.*

PSALM 23:1-6

THE LORD *is* my shepherd; I shall not want.

2He maketh me to lie down in green pastures: he leadeth me beside the still waters.

3He restoreth my soul: he leadeth me in the paths of righteousness for his name's sake.

4Yea, though I walk through the valley of the shadow of death, I will fear no evil: for thou *art* with me; thy rod and thy staff they comfort me.

5Thou preparest a table before me in the presence of mine enemies: thou anointest my head with oil; my cup runneth over.

6Surely goodness and mercy shall follow me all the days of my life: and I will dwell in the house of the LORD for ever.

PROVERBS FOR TODAY/ 20:11

Even a child is known by his doings, whether his work be *pure, and whether* it
be *right.*

JULY 31

2 CHRONICLES 29:1–36

HEZEKIAH began to reign *when he was* five and twenty years old, and he reigned nine and twenty years in Jerusalem. And his mother's name *was* Abijah, the daughter of Zechariah.

2And he did *that which was* right in the sight of the LORD, according to all that David his father had done.

3He in the first year of his reign, in the first month, opened the doors of the house of the LORD, and repaired them.

4And he brought in the priests and the Levites, and gathered them together into the east street,

5And said unto them, Hear me, ye Levites, sanctify now yourselves, and sanctify the house of the LORD God of your fathers, and carry forth the filthiness out of the holy *place.*

6For our fathers have trespassed, and done *that which was* evil in the eyes of the LORD our God, and have forsaken him, and have turned away their faces from the habitation of the LORD, and turned *their* backs.

7Also they have shut up the doors of the porch, and put out the lamps, and have not burned incense nor offered burnt offerings in the holy *place* unto the God of Israel.

8Wherefore the wrath of the LORD was upon Judah and Jerusalem, and he hath delivered them to trouble, to astonishment, and to hissing, as ye see with your eyes.

9For, lo, our fathers have fallen by the sword, and our sons and our daughters and our wives *are* in captivity for this.

10Now *it is* in mine heart to make a covenant with the LORD God of Israel, that his fierce wrath may turn away from us.

11My sons, be not now negligent: for the LORD hath chosen you to stand before him, to serve him, and that ye should minister unto him, and burn incense.

12Then the Levites arose, Mahath the son of Amasai, and Joel the son of Azariah, of the sons of the Kohathites: and of the sons of Merari, Kish the son of Abdi, and Azariah the son of Jehalelel: and of the Gershonites; Joah the son of Zimmah, and Eden the son of Joah:

13And of the sons of Elizaphan; Shimri, and Jeiel: and of the sons of Asaph; Zechariah, and Mattaniah:

14And of the sons of Heman; Jehiel, and Shimei: and of the sons of Jeduthun; Shemaiah, and Uzziel.

15And they gathered their brethren, and sanctified themselves, and came, according to the commandment of the king, by the words of the LORD, to cleanse the house of the LORD.

16And the priests went into the inner part of the house of the LORD, to cleanse *it,* and brought out all the uncleanness that they found in the temple of the LORD into the court of the house of the LORD. And the Levites took *it,* to carry *it* out abroad into the brook Kidron.

17Now they began on the first *day* of the first month to sanctify, and on the eighth day of the month came they to the porch of the LORD: so they sanctified the house of the LORD in eight days; and in the sixteenth day of the first month they made an end.

18Then they went in to Hezekiah the king, and said, We have cleansed all the house of the LORD, and the altar of burnt offering, with all the vessels thereof, and the shewbread table, with all the vessels thereof.

19Moreover all the vessels, which king Ahaz in his reign did cast away in his transgression, have we prepared and sanctified, and, behold, they *are* before the altar of the LORD.

20Then Hezekiah the king rose early, and gathered the rulers of the city, and went up to the house of the LORD.

21And they brought seven bullocks, and seven rams, and seven lambs, and seven he goats, for a sin offering for the kingdom, and for the sanctuary, and for Judah. And he commanded the priests the sons of Aaron to offer *them* on the altar of the LORD.

22So they killed the bullocks, and the priests received the blood, and sprinkled *it* on the altar: likewise, when they had killed the rams, they sprinkled the blood upon the altar: they killed also the lambs, and they sprinkled the blood upon the altar.

23And they brought forth the he goats *for* the sin offering before the king and the congregation; and they laid their hands upon them:

24And the priests killed them, and they made reconciliation with their blood upon the altar, to make an atonement for all Israel: for the king commanded *that* the burnt offering and the sin offering *should be made* for all Israel.

25And he set the Levites in the house of the LORD with cymbals, with psalteries, and with harps, according to the commandment of David, and of Gad the king's seer, and Nathan the prophet: for *so was* the commandment of the LORD by his prophets.

26And the Levites stood with the instruments of David, and the priests with the trumpets.

27And Hezekiah commanded to offer the burnt offering upon the altar. And when the burnt offering began, the song of the LORD began *also* with the trumpets, and with the instruments *ordained* by David king of Israel.

28And all the congregation worshipped, and the singers sang, and the trumpeters sounded: *and* all *this continued* until the burnt offering was finished.

29And when they had made an end of offering, the king and all that were present with him bowed themselves, and worshipped.

30Moreover Hezekiah the king and the princes commanded the Levites to sing praise unto the LORD with the words of David, and of Asaph the seer. And they sang praises with gladness, and they bowed their heads and worshipped.

31Then Hezekiah answered and said, Now ye have consecrated yourselves unto the LORD, come near and bring sacrifices and thank offerings into the house of the LORD. And the congregation brought in sacrifices and thank offerings; and as many as were of a free heart burnt offerings.

32And the number of the burnt offerings, which the congregation brought, was threescore and ten bullocks, an hundred rams, *and* two hundred lambs: all these *were* for a burnt offering to the LORD.

33And the consecrated things *were* six hundred oxen and three thousand sheep.

34But the priests were too few, so that they could not flay all the burnt offerings: wherefore their brethren the Levites did help them, till the work was ended, and until the *other* priests had sanctified themselves: for the Levites *were* more upright in heart to sanctify themselves than the priests.

35And also the burnt offerings *were* in abundance, with the fat of the peace offerings, and the drink offerings for *every* burnt offering. So the service of the house of the LORD was set in order.

36And Hezekiah rejoiced, and all the people, that God had prepared the people: for the thing was *done* suddenly.

ROMANS 14:1–23

HIM that is weak in the faith receive ye, *but* not to doubtful disputations.

2For one believeth that he may eat all things: another, who is weak, eateth herbs.

3Let not him that eateth despise him that eateth not; and let not him which eateth not judge him that eateth: for God hath received him.

4Who art thou that judgest another man's servant? to his own master he standeth or falleth. Yea, he shall be holden up: for God is able to make him stand.

5One man esteemeth one day above another: another esteemeth every day *alike*. Let every man be fully persuaded in his own mind.

6He that regardeth the day, regardeth *it* unto the Lord; and he that regardeth not the day, to the Lord he doth not regard *it*. He that eateth, eateth to the Lord, for he giveth God thanks; and he that eateth not, to the Lord he eateth not, and giveth God thanks.

7For none of us liveth to himself, and no man dieth to himself.

8For whether we live, we live unto the Lord; and whether we die, we die unto the Lord: whether we live therefore, or die, we are the Lord's.

9For to this end Christ both died, and rose, and revived, that he might be Lord both of the dead and living.

10But why dost thou judge thy brother? or why dost thou set at nought thy brother? for we shall all stand before the judgment seat of Christ.

11For it is written, As I live, saith the Lord, every knee shall bow to me, and every tongue shall confess to God.

12So then every one of us shall give account of himself to God.

13Let us not therefore judge one another any more: but judge this rather, that no man put a stumblingblock or an occasion to fall in *his* brother's way.

14I know, and am persuaded by the Lord Jesus, that *there is* nothing unclean of itself: but to him that esteemeth any thing to be unclean, to him *it is* unclean.

15But if thy brother be grieved with *thy* meat, now walkest thou not charitably. Destroy not him with thy meat, for whom Christ died.

16Let not then your good be evil spoken of:

17For the kingdom of God is not meat and drink; but righteousness, and peace, and joy in the Holy Ghost.

18For he that in these things serveth Christ *is* acceptable to God, and approved of men.

19Let us therefore follow after the things which make for peace, and things wherewith one may edify another.

20For meat destroy not the work of God. All things indeed *are* pure; but *it is* evil for that man who eateth with offence.

21*It is* good neither to eat flesh, nor to drink wine, nor *any thing* whereby thy brother stumbleth, or is offended, or is made weak.

22Hast thou faith? have *it* to thyself before God. Happy *is* he that condemneth not himself in that thing which he alloweth.

23And he that doubteth is damned if he eat, because *he eateth* not of faith: for whatsoever *is* not of faith is sin.

PSALM 24:1–10

THE earth *is* the LORD'S, and the fulness thereof; the world, and they that dwell therein.

2For he hath founded it upon the seas, and established it upon the floods.

3Who shall ascend into the hill of the LORD? or who shall stand in his holy place?

4He that hath clean hands, and a pure heart; who hath not lifted up his soul unto vanity, nor sworn deceitfully.

5He shall receive the blessing from the LORD, and righteousness from the God of his salvation.

6This *is* the generation of them that seek him, that seek thy face, O Jacob. Selah.

7Lift up your heads, O ye gates; and be ye lift up, ye everlasting doors; and the King of glory shall come in.

8Who *is* this King of glory? The LORD strong and mighty, the LORD mighty in battle.

9Lift up your heads, O ye gates; even lift *them* up, ye everlasting doors; and the King of glory shall come in.

10Who is this King of glory? The LORD of hosts, he *is* the King of glory. Selah.

PROVERBS FOR TODAY/ 20:12

The hearing ear, and the seeing eye, the LORD hath made even both of them.

AUGUST 1

2 CHRONICLES 30:1—31:21

AND Hezekiah sent to all Israel and Judah, and wrote letters also to Ephraim and Manasseh, that they should come to the house of the LORD at Jerusalem, to keep the passover unto the LORD God of Israel.

2For the king had taken counsel, and his princes, and all the congregation in Jerusalem, to keep the passover in the second month.

3For they could not keep it at that time, because the priests had not sanctified themselves sufficiently, neither had the people gathered themselves together to Jerusalem.

4And the thing pleased the king and all the congregation.

5So they established a decree to make proclamation throughout all Israel, from Beer–sheba even to Dan, that they should come to keep the passover unto the LORD God of Israel at Jerusalem: for they had not done *it* of a long *time in such sort* as it was written.

6So the posts went with the letters from the king and his princes throughout all Israel and Judah, and according to the commandment of the king, saying, Ye children of Israel, turn again unto the LORD God of Abraham, Isaac, and Israel, and he will return to the remnant of you, that are escaped out of the hand of the kings of Assyria.

7And be not ye like your fathers, and like your brethren, which trespassed against the LORD God of their fathers, *who* therefore gave them up to desolation, as ye see.

8Now be ye not stiffnecked, as your fathers *were, but* yield yourselves unto the LORD, and enter into his sanctuary, which he hath sanctified for ever: and serve the LORD your God, that the fierceness of his wrath may turn away from you.

⁹For if ye turn again unto the Lord, your brethren and your children *shall find* compassion before them that lead them captive, so that they shall come again into this land: for the Lord your God *is* gracious and merciful, and will not turn away *his* face from you, if ye return unto him.

¹⁰So the posts passed from city to city through the country of Ephraim and Manasseh even unto Zebulun: but they laughed them to scorn, and mocked them.

¹¹Nevertheless divers of Asher and Manasseh and of Zebulun humbled themselves, and came to Jerusalem.

¹²Also in Judah the hand of God was to give them one heart to do the commandment of the king and of the princes, by the word of the Lord.

¹³And there assembled at Jerusalem much people to keep the feast of unleavened bread in the second month, a very great congregation.

¹⁴And they arose and took away the altars that *were* in Jerusalem, and all the altars for incense took they away, and cast *them* into the brook Kidron.

¹⁵Then they killed the passover on the fourteenth *day* of the second month: and the priests and the Levites were ashamed, and sanctified themselves, and brought in the burnt offerings into the house of the Lord.

¹⁶And they stood in their place after their manner, according to the law of Moses the man of God: the priests sprinkled the blood, *which they received* of the hand of the Levites.

¹⁷For *there were* many in the congregation that were not sanctified: therefore the Levites had the charge of the killing of the passovers for every one *that was* not clean, to sanctify *them* unto the Lord.

¹⁸For a multitude of the people, *even* many of Ephraim, and Manasseh, Issachar, and Zebulun, had not cleansed themselves, yet did they eat the passover otherwise than it was written. But Hezekiah prayed for them, saying, the good Lord pardon every one

¹⁹*That* prepareth his heart to seek God, the Lord God of his fathers, though *he be* not *cleansed* according to the purification of the sanctuary.

²⁰And the Lord hearkened to Hezekiah, and healed the people.

²¹And the children of Israel that were present at Jerusalem, kept the feast of unleavened bread seven days with great gladness: and the Levites and the priests praised the Lord day by day, *singing* with loud instruments unto the Lord.

²²And Hezekiah spake comfortably unto all the Levites that taught the good knowledge of the Lord: and they did eat throughout the feast seven days, offering peace offerings, and making confession to the Lord God of their fathers.

²³And the whole assembly took counsel to keep other seven days: and they kept *other* seven days with gladness.

²⁴For Hezekiah king of Judah did give to the congregation a thousand bullocks and seven thousand sheep; and the princes gave to the congregation a thousand bullocks and ten thousand sheep: and a great number of priests sanctified themselves.

²⁵And all the congregation of Judah, with the priests and the Levites, and all the congregation that came out of Israel, and the strangers that came out of the land of Israel, and that dwelt in Judah, rejoiced.

²⁶So there was great joy in Jerusalem: for since the time of Solomon the son of David king of Israel *there was* not the like in Jerusalem.

²⁷Then the priests the Levites arose and blessed the people: and their voice was heard, and their prayer came *up* to his holy dwelling place, *even* unto heaven.

Now when all this was finished, all Israel that were present went out to the cities of Judah, and brake the images in pieces, and cut down the groves, and threw down the high places and the altars out of all Judah and Benjamin, in Ephraim also and Manasseh, until they had utterly destroyed them all. Then all the children of Israel returned, every man to his possession, into their own cities.

2And Hezekiah appointed the courses of the priests and the Levites after their courses, every man according to his service, the priests and Levites for burnt offerings and for peace offerings, to minister, and to give thanks, and to praise in the gates of the tents of the LORD.

3*He appointed* also the king's portion of his substance for the burnt offerings, *to wit,* for the morning and evening burnt offerings, and the burnt offerings for the sabbaths, and for the new moons, and for the set feasts, as *it is* written in the law of the LORD.

4Moreover he commanded the people that dwelt in Jerusalem to give the portion of the priests and the Levites, that they might be encouraged in the law of the LORD.

5And as soon as the commandment came abroad, the children of Israel brought in abundance the firstfruits of corn, wine, and oil, and honey, and of all the increase of the field; and the tithe of all *things* brought they in abundantly.

6And *concerning* the children of Israel and Judah, that dwelt in the cities of Judah, they also brought in the tithe of oxen and sheep, and the tithe of holy things which were consecrated unto the LORD their God, and laid *them* by heaps.

7In the third month they began to lay the foundation of the heaps, and finished *them* in the seventh month.

8And when Hezekiah and the princes came and saw the heaps, they blessed the LORD, and his people Israel.

9Then Hezekiah questioned with the priests and the Levites concerning the heaps.

10And Azariah the chief priest of the house of Zadok answered him, and said, Since *the people* began to bring the offerings into the house of the LORD, we have had enough to eat, and have left plenty: for the LORD hath blessed his people; and that which is left *is* this great store.

11Then Hezekiah commanded to prepare chambers in the house of the LORD; and they prepared *them,*

12And brought in the offerings and the tithes and the dedicated *things* faithfully: over which Cononiah the Levite *was* ruler, and Shimei his brother *was* the next.

13And Jehiel, and Azaziah, and Nahath, and Asahel, and Jerimoth, and Jozabad, and Eliel, and Ismachiah, and Manath, and Benaiah, *were* overseers under the hand of Cononiah and Shimei his brother, at the commandment of Hezekiah the king, and Azariah the ruler of the house of God.

14And Kore the son of Imnah the Levite, the porter toward the east, *was* over the freewill offerings of God, to distribute the oblations of the LORD, and the most holy things.

15And next him *were* Eden, and Miniamin, and Jeshua, and Shemaiah, Amariah, and Shecaniah, in the cities of the priests, in *their* set office, to give to their brethren by courses, as well to the great as to the small:

16Beside their genealogy of males, from three years old and upward, *even* unto every one that entereth into the house of the LORD, his daily portion for their service in their charges according to their courses;

17Both to the genealogy of the priests by the house of their fathers, and the Levites from twenty years old and upward, in their charges by their courses;

18And to the genealogy of all their little ones, their wives, and their sons, and their daughters, through all the congregation: for in their set office they sanctified themselves in holiness:

19Also of the sons of Aaron the priests, *which were* in the fields of the suburbs of their cities, in every several city, the men that were expressed by name, to give portions to all the males among the priests, and to all that were reckoned by genealogies among the Levites.

20And thus did Hezekiah throughout all Judah, and wrought *that which was* good and right and truth before the LORD his God.

21And in every work that he began in the service of the house of God, and in the law, and in the commandments, to seek his God, he did *it* with all his heart, and prospered.

ROMANS 15:1–22

WE then that are strong ought to bear the infirmities of the weak, and not to please ourselves.

2Let every one of us please *his* neighbour for *his* good to edification.

3For even Christ pleased not himself: but, as it is written, The reproaches of them that reproached thee fell on me.

4For whatsoever things were written aforetime were written for our learning, that we through patience and comfort of the scriptures might have hope.

5Now the God of patience and consolation grant you to be likeminded one toward another according to Christ Jesus:

6That ye may with one mind *and* one mouth glorify God, even the Father of our Lord Jesus Christ.

7Wherefore receive ye one another, as Christ also received us to the glory of God.

8Now I say that Jesus Christ was a minister of the circumcision for the truth of God, to confirm the promises *made* unto the fathers:

9And that the Gentiles might glorify God for *his* mercy; as it is written, For this cause I will confess to thee among the Gentiles, and sing unto thy name.

10And again he saith, Rejoice, ye Gentiles, with his people.

11And again, Praise the Lord, all ye Gentiles; and laud him, all ye people.

12And again, Esaias saith, There shall be a root of Jesse, and he that shall rise to reign over the Gentiles; in him shall the Gentiles trust.

13Now the God of hope fill you with all joy and peace in believing, that ye may abound in hope, through the power of the Holy Ghost.

14And I myself also am persuaded of you, my brethren, that ye also are full of goodness, filled with all knowledge, able also to admonish one another.

15Nevertheless, brethren, I have written the more boldly unto you in some sort, as putting you in mind, because of the grace that is given to me of God,

16That I should be the minister of Jesus Christ to the Gentiles, ministering the gospel of God, that the offering up of the Gentiles might be acceptable, being sanctified by the Holy Ghost.

17I have therefore whereof I may glory through Jesus Christ in those things which pertain to God.

18For I will not dare to speak of any of those things which Christ hath not wrought by me, to make the Gentiles obedient, by word and deed,

19Through mighty signs and wonders, by the power of the Spirit of God; so that from Jerusalem, and round about unto Illyricum, I have fully preached the gospel of Christ.

20Yea, so have I strived to preach the gospel, not where Christ was named, lest I should build upon another man's foundation:

21But as it is written, To whom he was not spoken of, they shall see: and they that have not heard shall understand.

22For which cause also I have been much hindered from coming to you.

PSALM 25:1–11

UNTO thee, O LORD, do I lift up my soul.

2O my God, I trust in thee: let me not be ashamed, let not mine enemies triumph over me.

3Yea, let none that wait on thee be ashamed: let them be ashamed which transgress without cause.

4Shew me thy ways, O LORD; teach me thy paths.

5Lead me in thy truth, and teach me:

for thou *art* the God of my salvation; on thee do I wait all the day.

6Remember, O LORD, thy tender mercies and thy lovingkindnesses; for they *have been* ever of old.

7Remember not the sins of my youth, nor my transgressions: according to thy mercy remember thou me for thy goodness' sake, O LORD.

8Good and upright *is* the LORD: therefore will he teach sinners in the way.

9The meek will he guide in judgment: and the meek will he teach his way.

10All the paths of the LORD *are* mercy and truth unto such as keep his covenant and his testimonies.

11For thy name's sake, O LORD, pardon mine iniquity; for it *is* great.

PROVERBS FOR TODAY/ 20:13–15

Love not sleep, lest thou come to poverty; open thine eyes, and thou shalt be satisfied with bread. □ It is *naught, it is naught, saith the buyer: but when he is gone his way, then he boasteth.* □ *There is gold, and a multitude of rubies: but the lips of knowledge* are *a precious jewel.*

AUGUST 2

2 CHRONICLES 32:1—33:13

AFTER these things, and the establishment thereof, Sennacherib king of Assyria came, and entered into Judah, and encamped against the fenced cities, and thought to win them for himself.

2And when Hezekiah saw that Sennacherib was come, and that he was purposed to fight against Jerusalem,

3He took counsel with his princes and his mighty men to stop the waters of the fountains which *were* without the city: and they did help him.

4So there was gathered much people together, who stopped all the fountains, and the brook that ran through the midst

of the land, saying, Why should the kings of Assyria come, and find much water?

5Also he strengthened himself, and built up all the wall that was broken, and raised *it* up to the towers, and another wall without, and repaired Millo *in* the city of David, and made darts and shields in abundance.

6And he set captains of war over the people, and gathered them together to him in the street of the gate of the city, and spake comfortably to them, saying,

7Be strong and courageous, be not afraid nor dismayed for the king of Assyria, nor for all the multitude that *is* with him: for *there be* more with us than with him:

8With him *is* an arm of flesh; but with us *is* the LORD our God to help us, and to fight our battles. And the people rested themselves upon the words of Hezekiah king of Judah.

9After this did Sennacherib king of Assyria send his servants to Jerusalem, (but he *himself laid siege* against Lachish, and all his power with him,) unto Hezekiah king of Judah, and unto all Judah that *were* at Jerusalem, saying,

10Thus saith Sennacherib king of Assyria, Whereon do ye trust, that ye abide in the siege in Jerusalem?

11Doth not Hezekiah persuade you to give over yourselves to die by famine and by thirst, saying, The LORD our God shall deliver us out of the hand of the king of Assyria?

12Hath not the same Hezekiah taken away his high places and his altars, and commanded Judah and Jerusalem, saying, Ye shall worship before one altar, and burn incense upon it?

13Know ye not what I and my fathers have done unto all the people of *other* lands? were the gods of the nations of those lands any ways able to deliver their lands out of mine hand?

14Who *was there* among all the gods of those nations that my fathers utterly destroyed, that could deliver his people out of mine hand, that your God should be able to deliver you out of mine hand?

15Now therefore let not Hezekiah deceive you, nor persuade you on this manner, neither ye believe him: for no god of any nation or kingdom was able to deliver his people out of mine hand, and out of the hand of my fathers: how much less shall your God deliver you out of mine hand?

16And his servants spake yet *more* against the LORD God, and against his servant Hezekiah.

17He wrote also letters to rail on the LORD God of Israel, and to speak against him, saying, As the gods of the nations of *other* lands have not delivered their people out of mine hand, so shall not the God of Hezekiah deliver his people out of mine hand.

18Then they cried with a loud voice in the Jews' speech unto the people of Jerusalem that *were* on the wall, to affright them, and to trouble them; that they might take the city.

19And they spake against the God of Jerusalem, as against the gods of the people of the earth, *which were* the work of the hands of man.

20And for this *cause* Hezekiah the king, and the prophet Isaiah the son of Amoz, prayed and cried to heaven.

21And the LORD sent an angel, which cut off all the mighty men of valour, and the leaders and captains in the camp of the king of Assyria. So he returned with shame of face to his own land. And when he was come into the house of his god, they that came forth of his own bowels slew him there with the sword.

22Thus the LORD saved Hezekiah and the inhabitants of Jerusalem from the hand of Sennacherib the king of Assyria, and from the hand of all *other,* and guided them on every side.

23And many brought gifts unto the LORD to Jerusalem, and presents to Hezekiah king of Judah: so that he was magnified in the sight of all nations from thenceforth.

24In those days Hezekiah was sick to the death, and prayed unto the LORD: and he spake unto him, and he gave him a sign.

25But Hezekiah rendered not again according to the benefit *done* unto him; for his heart was lifted up: therefore there was wrath upon him, and upon Judah and Jerusalem.

26Notwithstanding Hezekiah humbled himself for the pride of his heart, *both* he and the inhabitants of Jerusalem, so that the wrath of the LORD came not upon them in the days of Hezekiah.

27And Hezekiah had exceeding much

riches and honour: and he made himself treasuries for silver, and for gold, and for precious stones, and for spices, and for shields, and for all manner of pleasant jewels;

28Storehouses also for the increase of corn, and wine, and oil; and stalls for all manner of beasts, and cotes for flocks.

29Moreover he provided him cities, and possessions of flocks and herds in abundance: for God had given him substance very much.

30This same Hezekiah also stopped the upper watercourse of Gihon, and brought it straight down to the west side of the city of David. And Hezekiah prospered in all his works.

31Howbeit in *the business of* the ambassadors of the princes of Babylon, who sent unto him to enquire of the wonder that was *done* in the land, God left him, to try him, that he might know all *that was* in his heart.

32Now the rest of the acts of Hezekiah, and his goodness, behold, they *are* written in the vision of Isaiah the prophet, the son of Amoz, *and* in the book of the kings of Judah and Israel.

33And Hezekiah slept with his fathers, and they buried him in the chiefest of the sepulchres of the sons of David: and all Judah and the inhabitants of Jerusalem did him honour at his death. And Manasseh his son reigned in his stead.

MANASSEH *was* twelve years old when he began to reign, and he reigned fifty and five years in Jerusalem:

2But did *that which was* evil in the sight of the LORD, like unto the abominations of the heathen, whom the LORD had cast out before the children of Israel.

3For he built again the high places which Hezekiah his father had broken down, and he reared up altars for Baalim, and made groves, and worshipped all the host of heaven, and served them.

4Also he built altars in the house of the LORD, whereof the LORD had said, In Jerusalem shall my name be for ever.

5And he built altars for all the host of heaven in the two courts of the house of the LORD.

6And he caused his children to pass through the fire in the valley of the son of Hinnom: also he observed times, and used enchantments, and used witchcraft, and dealt with a familiar spirit, and with wizards: he wrought much evil in the sight of the LORD, to provoke him to anger.

7And he set a carved image, the idol which he had made, in the house of God, of which God had said to David and to Solomon his son, In this house, and in Jerusalem, which I have chosen before all the tribes of Israel, will I put my name for ever:

8Neither will I any more remove the foot of Israel from out of the land which I have appointed for your fathers; so that they will take heed to do all that I have commanded them, according to the whole law and the statutes and the ordinances by the hand of Moses.

9So Manasseh made Judah and the inhabitants of Jerusalem to err, *and* to do worse than the heathen, whom the LORD had destroyed before the children of Israel.

10And the LORD spake to Manasseh, and to his people: but they would not hearken.

11Wherefore the LORD brought upon them the captains of the host of the king of Assyria, which took Manasseh among the thorns, and bound him with fetters, and carried him to Babylon.

12And when he was in affliction, he besought the LORD his God, and humbled himself greatly before the God of his fathers,

13And prayed unto him: and he was intreated of him, and heard his supplication, and brought him again to Jerusalem into his kingdom. Then Manasseh knew that the LORD he *was* God.

ROMANS 15:23—16:7

BUT now having no more place in these parts, and having a great desire these many years to come unto you;

24Whensoever I take my journey into Spain, I will come to you: for I trust to see you in my journey, and to be brought on my way thitherward by you, if first I be somewhat filled with your *company.*

25But now I go unto Jerusalem to minister unto the saints.

26For it hath pleased them of Macedonia and Achaia to make a certain contribution for the poor saints which are at Jerusalem.

27It hath pleased them verily; and their debtors they are. For if the Gentiles have been made partakers of their spiritual things, their duty is also to minister unto them in carnal things.

28When therefore I have performed this, and have sealed to them this fruit, I will come by you into Spain.

29And I am sure that, when I come unto you, I shall come in the fulness of the blessing of the gospel of Christ.

30Now I beseech you, brethren, for the Lord Jesus Christ's sake, and for the love of the Spirit, that ye strive together with me in *your* prayers to God for me;

31That I may be delivered from them that do not believe in Judaea; and that my service which *I have* for Jerusalem may be accepted of the saints;

32That I may come unto you with joy by the will of God, and may with you be refreshed.

33Now the God of peace *be* with you all. Amen.

I COMMEND unto you Phebe our sister, which is a servant of the church which is at Cenchrea:

2That ye receive her in the Lord, as becometh saints, and that ye assist her in whatsoever business she hath need of you: for she hath been a succourer of many, and of myself also.

3Greet Priscilla and Aquila my helpers in Christ Jesus:

4Who have for my life laid down their own necks: unto whom not only I give thanks, but also all the churches of the Gentiles.

5Likewise *greet* the church that is in their house. Salute my well beloved Epaenetus, who is the firstfruits of Achaia unto Christ.

6Greet Mary, who bestowed much labour on us.

7Salute Andronicus and Junia, my kinsmen, and my fellowprisoners, who are of note among the apostles, who also were in Christ before me.

PSALM 25:12–22

WHAT man *is* he that feareth the LORD? him shall he teach in the way *that* he shall choose.

13His soul shall dwell at ease; and his seed shall inherit the earth.

14The secret of the LORD *is* with them that fear him; and he will shew them his covenant.

15Mine eyes *are* ever toward the LORD; for he shall pluck my feet out of the net.

16Turn thee unto me, and have mercy upon me; for I *am* desolate and afflicted.

17The troubles of my heart are enlarged: *O* bring thou me out of my distresses.

18Look upon mine affliction and my pain; and forgive all my sins.

19Consider mine enemies; for they are many; and they hate me with cruel hatred.

20O keep my soul, and deliver me: let me not be ashamed; for I put my trust in thee.

21Let integrity and uprightness preserve me; for I wait on thee.

22Redeem Israel, O God, out of all
his troubles.

PROVERBS FOR TODAY/ 20:16–18

Take his garment that is surety for *a stranger: and take a pledge of him for a strange woman.* □ *Bread of deceit* is *sweet to a man; but afterwards his mouth shall be filled with gravel.* □ Every *purpose is established by counsel: and with good advice make war.*

AUGUST 3

2 CHRONICLES 33:14—34:33

Now after this he [Manasseh] built a wall without the city of David, on the west side of Gihon, in the valley, even to the entering in at the fish gate, and compassed about Ophel, and raised it up a very great height, and put captains of war in all the fenced cities of Judah.

15And he took away the strange gods, and the idol out of the house of the LORD, and all the altars that he had built in the mount of the house of the LORD, and in Jerusalem, and cast *them* out of the city.

16And he repaired the altar of the LORD, and sacrificed thereon peace offerings and thank offerings and commanded Judah to serve the LORD God of Israel.

17Nevertheless the people did sacrifice still in the high places, *yet* unto the LORD their God only.

18Now the rest of the acts of Manasseh, and his prayer unto his God, and the words of the seers that spake to him in the name of the LORD God of Israel, behold, they *are written* in the book of the kings of Israel.

19His prayer also, and *how God* was intreated of him, and all his sins, and his trespass, and the places wherein he built high places, and set up groves and graven images, before he was humbled: behold, they *are* written among the sayings of the seers.

20So Manasseh slept with his fathers, and they buried him in his own house: and Amon his son reigned in his stead.

21Amon *was* two and twenty years old when he began to reign, and reigned two years in Jerusalem.

22But he did *that which was* evil in the sight of the LORD, as did Manasseh his father: for Amon sacrificed unto all the carved images which Manasseh his father had made, and served them;

23And humbled not himself before the LORD, as Manasseh his father had humbled himself; but Amon trespassed more and more.

24And his servants conspired against him, and slew him in his own house.

25But the people of the land slew all them that had conspired against king Amon; and the people of the land made Josiah his son king in his stead.

JOSIAH *was* eight years old when he began to reign, and he reigned in Jerusalem one and thirty years.

2And he did *that which was* right in the sight of the LORD, and walked in the ways of David his father, and declined *neither* to the right hand, nor to the left.

3For in the eighth year of his reign, while he was yet young, he began to seek after the God of David his father: and in the twelfth year he began to purge Judah and Jerusalem from the high places, and the groves, and the carved images, and the molten images.

4And they brake down the altars of Baalim in his presence; and the images, that *were* on high above them, he cut down; and the groves, and the carved images, and the molten images, he brake in pieces, and made dust *of them,* and strowed *it* upon the graves of them that had sacrificed unto them.

5And he burnt the bones of the priests upon their altars, and cleansed Judah and Jerusalem.

6And *so did he* in the cities of Manasseh, and Ephraim, and Simeon, even unto Naphtali, with their mattocks round about.

7And when he had broken down the altars and the groves, and had beaten the graven images into powder, and cut down all the idols throughout all the land of Israel, he returned to Jerusalem.

8Now in the eighteenth year of his reign, when he had purged the land, and the house, he sent Shaphan the son of Azaliah, and Maaseiah the governor of the city, and Joah the son of Joahaz the recorder, to repair the house of the LORD his God.

9And when they came to Hilkiah the high priest, they delivered the money that was brought into the house of God, which the Levites that kept the doors had gathered of the hand of Manasseh and Ephraim, and of all the remnant of Israel, and of all Judah and Benjamin; and they returned to Jerusalem.

10And they put *it* in the hand of the workmen that had the oversight of the house of the LORD, and they gave it to the workmen that wrought in the house of the LORD, to repair and amend the house:

11Even to the artificers and builders gave they *it,* to buy hewn stone, and timber for couplings, and to floor the houses which the kings of Judah had destroyed.

12And the men did the work faithfully: and the overseers of them *were* Jahath and Obadiah, the Levites, of the sons of Merari; and Zechariah and Meshullam, of the sons of the Kohathites, to set *it* forward; and *other of* the Levites, all that could skill of instruments of musick.

13Also *they were* over the bearers of burdens, and *were* overseers of all that wrought the work in any manner of service: and of the Levites *there were* scribes, and officers, and porters.

14And when they brought out the money that was brought into the house of the LORD, Hilkiah the priest found a book of the law of the LORD *given* by Moses.

15And Hilkiah answered and said to Shaphan the scribe, I have found the book of the law in the house of the LORD. And Hilkiah delivered the book to Shaphan.

16And Shaphan carried the book to the king, and brought the king word back again, saying, All that was committed to thy servants, they do *it.*

17And they have gathered together the money that was found in the house of the LORD, and have delivered it into the hand of the overseers, and to the hand of the workmen.

18Then Shaphan the scribe told the king, saying, Hilkiah the priest hath given me a book. And Shaphan read it before the king.

19And it came to pass, when the king had heard the words of the law, that he rent his clothes.

20And the king commanded Hilkiah, and Ahikam the son of Shaphan, and Abdon the son of Micah, and Shaphan the scribe, and Asaiah a servant of the king's, saying,

21Go, enquire of the LORD for me, and for them that are left in Israel and in Judah, concerning the words of the book that is found: for great *is* the wrath of the LORD that is poured out upon us, because our fathers have not kept the word of the LORD, to do after all that is written in this book.

22And Hilkiah, and *they* that the king *had appointed,* went to Huldah the prophetess, the wife of Shallum the son of Tikvath, the son of Hasrah, keeper of the wardrobe; (now she dwelt in Jerusalem in the college:) and they spake to her to that *effect.*

23And she answered them, Thus saith the LORD God of Israel, Tell ye the man that sent you to me,

24Thus saith the LORD, Behold, I will bring evil upon this place, and upon the inhabitants thereof, *even* all the curses that are written in the book which they have read before the king of Judah:

25Because they have forsaken me, and have burned incense unto other gods, that they might provoke me to anger with all the works of their hands; therefore my wrath shall be poured out upon this place, and shall not be quenched.

26And as for the king of Judah, who sent you to enquire of the LORD, so shall ye say unto him, Thus saith the LORD God of Israel *concerning* the words which thou hast heard;

27Because thine heart was tender, and thou didst humble thyself before God, when thou heardest his words against this place, and against the inhabitants thereof, and humbledst thyself before me, and didst rend thy clothes, and weep before me; I have even heard *thee* also, saith the LORD.

28Behold, I will gather thee to thy fathers, and thou shalt be gathered to thy grave in peace, neither shall thine eyes see all the evil that I will bring

upon this place, and upon the inhabitants of the same. So they brought the king word again.

29Then the king sent and gathered together all the elders of Judah and Jerusalem.

30And the king went up into the house of the LORD, and all the men of Judah, and the inhabitants of Jerusalem, and the priests, and the Levites, and all the people, great and small: and he read in their ears all the words of the book of the covenant that was found in the house of the LORD.

31And the king stood in his place, and made a covenant before the LORD, to walk after the LORD, and to keep his commandments, and his testimonies, and his statutes, with all his heart, and with all his soul, to perform the words of the covenant which are written in this book.

32And he caused all that were present in Jerusalem and Benjamin to stand *to it.* And the inhabitants of Jerusalem did according to the covenant of God, the God of their fathers.

33And Josiah took away all the abominations out of all the countries that *pertained* to the children of Israel, and made all that were present in Israel to serve, *even* to serve the LORD their God. *And* all his days they departed not from following the LORD, the God of their fathers.

ROMANS 16:8–27

GREET Amplias my beloved in the Lord.

9Salute Urbane, our helper in Christ, and Stachys my beloved.

10Salute Apelles approved in Christ. Salute them which are of Aristobulus' *household.*

11Salute Herodion my kinsman. Greet them that be of the *household* of Narcissus, which are in the Lord.

12Salute Tryphena and Tryphosa, who labour in the Lord. Salute the beloved Persis, which laboured much in the Lord.

13Salute Rufus chosen in the Lord, and his mother and mine.

14Salute Asyncritus, Phlegon, Hermas, Patrobas, Hermes, and the brethren which are with them.

15Salute Philologus, and Julia, Nereus, and his sister, and Olympas, and all the saints which are with them.

16Salute one another with an holy kiss. The churches of Christ salute you.

17Now I beseech you, brethren, mark them which cause divisions and offences contrary to the doctrine which ye have learned; and avoid them.

18For they that are such serve not our Lord Jesus Christ, but their own belly; and by good words and fair speeches deceive the hearts of the simple.

19For your obedience is come abroad unto all *men*. I am glad therefore on your behalf: but yet I would have you wise unto that which is good, and simple concerning evil.

20And the God of peace shall bruise Satan under your feet shortly. The grace of our Lord Jesus Christ *be* with you. Amen.

21Timotheus my workfellow, and Lucius, and Jason, and Sosipater, my kinsmen, salute you.

22I Tertius, who wrote *this* epistle, salute you in the Lord.

23Gaius mine host, and of the whole church, saluteth you. Erastus the chamberlain of the city saluteth you, and Quartus a brother.

24The grace of our Lord Jesus Christ *be* with you all. Amen.

25Now to him that is of power to stablish you according to my gospel, and the preaching of Jesus Christ, according to the revelation of the mystery, which was kept secret since the world began,

26But now is made manifest, and by the scriptures of the prophets, according to the commandment of the everlasting God, made known to all nations for the obedience of faith:

27To God only wise, *be* glory through Jesus Christ for ever. Amen.

PSALM 26:1–12

JUDGE me, O LORD; for I have walked in mine integrity: I have trusted also in the LORD; *therefore* I shall not slide.

2Examine me, O LORD, and prove me; try my reins and my heart.

3For thy lovingkindness *is* before mine eyes: and I have walked in thy truth.

4I have not sat with vain persons, neither will I go in with dissemblers.

5I have hated the congregation of evil doers; and will not sit with the wicked.

6I will wash mine hands in innocency: so will I compass thine altar, O LORD:

7That I may publish with the voice of thanksgiving, and tell of all thy wondrous works.

8LORD, I have loved the habitation of thy house, and the place where thine honour dwelleth.

9Gather not my soul with sinners, nor my life with bloody men:

10In whose hands *is* mischief, and their right hand is full of bribes.

11But as for me, I will walk in mine integrity: redeem me, and be merciful unto me.

12My foot standeth in an even place: in the congregations will I bless the LORD.

PROVERBS FOR TODAY/ 20:19

He that goeth about as *a talebearer revealeth secrets: therefore meddle not with him that flattereth with his lips.*

AUGUST 4

2 CHRONICLES 35:1—36:23

MOREOVER Josiah kept a passover unto the LORD in Jerusalem: and they killed the passover on the fourteenth *day* of the first month.

2And he set the priests in their charges, and encouraged them to the service of the house of the LORD,

3And said unto the Levites that taught all Israel, which were holy unto the LORD, Put the holy ark in the house which Solomon the son of David king of Israel did build; *it shall* not *be* a burden upon *your* shoulders: serve now the LORD your God, and his people Israel,

4And prepare *yourselves* by the houses of your fathers, after your courses, according to the writing of David king of Israel, and according to the writing of Solomon his son.

5And stand in the holy *place* according to the divisions of the families of the fathers of your brethren the people, and *after* the division of the families of the Levites.

6So kill the passover, and sanctify yourselves, and prepare your brethren, that *they* may do according to the word of the LORD by the hand of Moses.

7And Josiah gave to the people, of the flock, lambs and kids, all for the passover offerings, for all that were present, to the number of thirty thousand, and three thousand bullocks: these *were* of the king's substance.

8And his princes gave willingly unto the people, to the priests, and to the Levites: Hilkiah and Zechariah and Jehiel, rulers of the house of God, gave unto the priests for the passover offerings two thousand and six hundred *small cattle,* and three hundred oxen.

9Conaniah also, and Shemaiah and Nethaneel, his brethren, and Hashabiah and Jeiel and Jozabad, chief of the Levites, gave unto the Levites for passover offerings five thousand *small cattle,* and five hundred oxen.

10So the service was prepared, and the priests stood in their place, and the Levites in their courses, according to the king's commandment.

11And they killed the passover, and the priests sprinkled *the blood* from their hands, and the Levites flayed *them.*

12And they removed the burnt offerings, that they might give according to the divisions of the families of the people, to offer unto the LORD, as *it is* written in the book of Moses. And so *did they* with the oxen.

13And they roasted the passover with fire according to the ordinance: but the *other* holy *offerings* sod they in pots, and in caldrons, and in pans, and divided *them* speedily among all the people.

14And afterward they made ready for themselves, and for the priests: because the priests the sons of Aaron *were busied* in offering of burnt offerings and the fat until night; therefore the Levites prepared for themselves, and for the priests the sons of Aaron.

15And the singers the sons of Asaph *were* in their place, according to the commandment of David, and Asaph, and Heman, and Jeduthun the king's seer; and the porters *waited* at every gate; they might not depart from their service; for their brethren the Levites prepared for them.

16So all the service of the LORD was prepared the same day, to keep the passover, and to offer burnt offerings upon the altar of the LORD, according to the commandment of king Josiah.

17And the children of Israel that were

present kept the passover at that time, and the feast of unleavened bread seven days.

18And there was no passover like to that kept in Israel from the days of Samuel the prophet; neither did all the kings of Israel keep such a passover as Josiah kept, and the priests, and the Levites, and all Judah and Israel that were present, and the inhabitants of Jerusalem.

19In the eighteenth year of the reign of Josiah was this passover kept.

20After all this, when Josiah had prepared the temple, Necho king of Egypt came up to fight against Charchemish by Euphrates: and Josiah went out against him.

21But he sent ambassadors to him, saying, What have I to do with thee, thou king of Judah? *I come* not against thee this day, but against the house wherewith I have war: for God commanded me to make haste: forbear thee from *meddling with* God, who *is* with me, that he destroy thee not.

22Nevertheless Josiah would not turn his face from him, but disguised himself, that he might fight with him, and hearkened not unto the words of Necho from the mouth of God, and came to fight in the valley of Megiddo.

23And the archers shot at king Josiah; and the king said to his servants, Have me away; for I am sore wounded.

24His servants therefore took him out of that chariot, and put him in the second chariot that he had; and they brought him to Jerusalem, and he died, and was buried in *one of* the sepulchres of his fathers. And all Judah and Jerusalem mourned for Josiah.

25And Jeremiah lamented for Josiah: and all the singing men and the singing women spake of Josiah in their lamentations to this day, and made them an ordinance in Israel: and, behold, they *are* written in the lamentations.

26Now the rest of the acts of Josiah, and his goodness, according to *that* *which was* written in the law of the LORD,

27And his deeds, first and last, behold, they *are* written in the book of the kings of Israel and Judah.

THEN the people of the land took Jehoahaz the son of Josiah, and made him king in his father's stead in Jerusalem.

2Jehoahaz *was* twenty and three years old when he began to reign, and he reigned three months in Jerusalem.

3And the king of Egypt put him down at Jerusalem, and condemned the land in an hundred talents of silver and a talent of gold.

4And the king of Egypt made Eliakim his brother king over Judah and Jerusalem, and turned his name to Jehoiakim. And Necho took Jehoahaz his brother, and carried him to Egypt.

5Jehoiakim *was* twenty and five years old when he began to reign, and he reigned eleven years in Jerusalem: and he did *that which was* evil in the sight of the LORD his God.

6Against him came up Nebuchadnezzar king of Babylon, and bound him in fetters, to carry him to Babylon.

7Nebuchadnezzar also carried of the vessels of the house of the LORD to Babylon, and put them in his temple at Babylon.

8Now the rest of the acts of Jehoiakim, and his abominations which he did, and that which was found in him, behold, they *are* written in the book of the kings of Israel and Judah: and Jehoiachin his son reigned in his stead.

9Jehoiachin *was* eight years old when he began to reign, and he reigned three months and ten days in Jerusalem: and he did *that which was* evil in the sight of the LORD.

10And when the year was expired, king Nebuchadnezzar sent, and brought him to Babylon, with the goodly vessels of the house of the LORD, and made

Zedekiah his brother king over Judah and Jerusalem.

11Zedekiah *was* one and twenty years old when he began to reign, and reigned eleven years in Jerusalem.

12And he did *that which was* evil in the sight of the LORD his God, *and* humbled not himself before Jeremiah the prophet *speaking* from the mouth of the LORD.

13And he also rebelled against king Nebuchadnezzar, who had made him swear by God: but he stiffened his neck, and hardened his heart from turning unto the LORD God of Israel.

14Moreover all the chief of the priests, and the people, transgressed very much after all the abominations of the heathen; and polluted the house of the LORD which he had hallowed in Jerusalem.

15And the LORD God of their fathers sent to them by his messengers, rising up betimes, and sending; because he had compassion on his people, and on his dwelling place:

16But they mocked the messengers of God, and despised his words, and misused his prophets, until the wrath of the LORD arose against his people, till *there was* no remedy.

17Therefore he brought upon them the king of the Chaldees, who slew their young men with the sword in the house of their sanctuary, and had no compassion upon young man or maiden, old man, or him that stooped for age: he gave *them* all into his hand.

18And all the vessels of the house of God, great and small, and the treasures of the house of the LORD, and the treasures of the king, and of his princes; all *these* he brought to Babylon.

19And they burnt the house of God, and brake down the wall of Jerusalem, and burnt all the palaces thereof with fire, and destroyed all the goodly vessels thereof.

20And them that had escaped from the sword carried he away to Babylon; where they were servants to him and his sons until the reign of the kingdom of Persia:

21To fulfil the word of the LORD by the mouth of Jeremiah, until the land had enjoyed her sabbaths: *for* as long as she lay desolate she kept sabbath, to fulfil threescore and ten years.

22Now in the first year of Cyrus king of Persia, that the word of the LORD *spoken* by the mouth of Jeremiah might be accomplished, the LORD stirred up the spirit of Cyrus king of Persia, that he made a proclamation throughout all his kingdom, and *put it* also in writing, saying,

23Thus saith Cyrus king of Persia, All the kingdoms of the earth hath the LORD God of heaven given me; and he hath charged me to build him an house in Jerusalem, which *is* in Judah. Who *is there* among you of all his people? The LORD his God *be* with him, and let him go up.

1 CORINTHIANS 1:1–17

PAUL, called *to be* an apostle of Jesus Christ through the will of God, and Sosthenes *our* brother,

2Unto the church of God which is at Corinth, to them that are sanctified in Christ Jesus, called *to be* saints, with all that in every place call upon the name of Jesus Christ our Lord, both theirs and ours:

3Grace *be* unto you, and peace, from God our Father, and *from* the Lord Jesus Christ.

4I thank my God always on your behalf, for the grace of God which is given you by Jesus Christ;

5That in every thing ye are enriched by him, in all utterance, and *in* all knowledge;

6Even as the testimony of Christ was confirmed in you:

7So that ye come behind in no gift; waiting for the coming of our Lord Jesus Christ:

8Who shall also confirm you unto the end, *that ye may be* blameless in the day of our Lord Jesus Christ.

9God *is* faithful, by whom ye were called unto the fellowship of his Son Jesus Christ our Lord.

10Now I beseech you, brethren, by the name of our Lord Jesus Christ, that ye all speak the same thing, and *that* there be no divisions among you; but *that* ye be perfectly joined together in the same mind and in the same judgment.

11For it hath been declared unto me of you, my brethren, by them *which are of the house* of Chloe, that there are contentions among you.

12Now this I say, that every one of you saith, I am of Paul; and I of Apollos; and I of Cephas; and I of Christ.

13Is Christ divided? was Paul crucified for you? or were ye baptized in the name of Paul?

14I thank God that I baptized none of you, but Crispus and Gaius;

15Lest any should say that I had baptized in mine own name.

16And I baptized also the household of Stephanas: besides, I know not whether I baptized any other.

17For Christ sent me not to baptize, but to preach the gospel: not with wisdom of words, lest the cross of Christ should be made of none effect.

PSALM 27:1–7

THE LORD *is* my light and my salvation; whom shall I fear? the LORD *is* the strength of my life; of whom shall I be afraid?

2When the wicked, *even* mine enemies and my foes, came upon me to eat up my flesh, they stumbled and fell.

3Though an host should encamp against me, my heart shall not fear: though war should rise against me, in this *will* I *be* confident.

4One *thing* have I desired of the LORD, that will I seek after; that I may dwell in the house of the LORD all the days of my life, to behold the beauty of the LORD, and to enquire in his temple.

5For in the time of trouble he shall hide me in his pavilion: in the secret of his tabernacle shall he hide me; he shall set me up upon a rock.

6And now shall mine head be lifted up above mine enemies round about me: therefore will I offer in his tabernacle sacrifices of joy; I will sing, yea, I will sing praises unto the LORD.

7Hear, O LORD, *when* I cry with my voice: have mercy also upon me, and answer me.

PROVERBS FOR TODAY/ 20:20–21

Whoso curseth his father or his mother, his lamp shall be put out in obscure darkness. □*An inheritance* may be *gotten hastily at the beginning; but the end thereof shall not be blessed.*

EZRA 1:1—2:70

Now in the first year of Cyrus king of Persia, that the word of the LORD by the mouth of Jeremiah might be fulfilled, the LORD stirred up the spirit of Cyrus king of Persia, that he made a proclamation throughout all his kingdom, and *put it* also in writing, saying,

2Thus saith Cyrus king of Persia, The LORD God of heaven hath given me all the kingdoms of the earth; and he hath charged me to build him an house at Jerusalem, which *is* in Judah.

3Who *is there* among you of all his people? his God be with him, and let him go up to Jerusalem, which *is* in Judah, and build the house of the LORD God of Israel, (he *is* the God,) which *is* in Jerusalem.

4And whosoever remaineth in any place where he sojourneth, let the men of his place help him with silver, and with gold, and with goods, and with beasts, beside the freewill offering for the house of God that *is* in Jerusalem.

5Then rose up the chief of the fathers of Judah and Benjamin, and the priests, and the Levites, with all *them* whose spirit God had raised, to go up to build the house of the LORD which *is* in Jerusalem.

6And all they that *were* about them strengthened their hands with vessels of silver, with gold, with goods, and with beasts, and with precious things, beside all *that* was willingly offered.

7Also Cyrus the king brought forth the vessels of the house of the LORD, which Nebuchadnezzar had brought forth out of Jerusalem, and had put them in the house of his gods;

8Even those did Cyrus king of Persia bring forth by the hand of Mithredath the treasurer, and numbered them unto Sheshbazzar, the prince of Judah.

9And this *is* the number of them: thirty chargers of gold, a thousand chargers of silver, nine and twenty knives,

10Thirty basons of gold, silver basons of a second *sort* four hundred and ten, *and* other vessels a thousand.

11All the vessels of gold and of silver *were* five thousand and four hundred. All *these* did Sheshbazzar bring up with *them* of the captivity that were brought up from Babylon unto Jerusalem.

Now these *are* the children of the province that went up out of the captivity, of those which had been carried away, whom Nebuchadnezzar the king of Babylon had carried away unto Babylon, and came again unto Jerusalem and Judah, every one unto his city;

2Which came with Zerubbabel: Jeshua, Nehemiah, Seraiah, Reelaiah, Mordecai, Bilshan, Mizpar, Bigvai, Rehum, Baanah. The number of the men of the people of Israel:

3The children of Parosh, two thousand an hundred seventy and two.

4The children of Shephatiah, three hundred seventy and two.

5The children of Arah, seven hundred seventy and five.

6The children of Pahath–moab, of the children of Jeshua *and* Joab, two thousand eight hundred and twelve.

7The children of Elam, a thousand two hundred fifty and four.

8The children of Zattu, nine hundred forty and five.

9The children of Zaccai, seven hundred and threescore.

10The children of Bani, six hundred forty and two.

11The children of Bebai, six hundred twenty and three.

12The children of Azgad, a thousand two hundred twenty and two.

13The children of Adonikam, six hundred sixty and six.

14The children of Bigvai, two thousand fifty and six.

15The children of Adin, four hundred fifty and four.

16The children of Ater of Hezekiah, ninety and eight.

17The children of Bezai, three hundred twenty and three.

18The children of Jorah, an hundred and twelve.

19The children of Hashum, two hundred twenty and three.

20The children of Gibbar, ninety and five.

21The children of Beth–lehem, an hundred twenty and three.

22The men of Netophah, fifty and six.

23The men of Anathoth, an hundred twenty and eight.

24The children of Azmaveth, forty and two.

25The children of Kirjath–arim, Chephirah, and Beeroth, seven hundred and forty and three.

26The children of Ramah and Gaba, six hundred twenty and one.

27The men of Michmas, an hundred twenty and two.

28The men of Beth–el and Ai, two hundred twenty and three.

29The children of Nebo, fifty and two.

30The children of Magbish, an hundred fifty and six.

31The children of the other Elam, a thousand two hundred fifty and four.

32The children of Harim, three hundred and twenty.

33The children of Lod, Hadid, and Ono, seven hundred twenty and five.

34The children of Jericho, three hundred forty and five.

35The children of Senaah, three thousand and six hundred and thirty.

36The priests: the children of Jedaiah, of the house of Jeshua, nine hundred seventy and three.

37The children of Immer, a thousand fifty and two.

38The children of Pashur, a thousand two hundred forty and seven.

39The children of Harim, a thousand and seventeen.

40The Levites: the children of Jeshua and Kadmiel, of the children of Hodaviah, seventy and four.

41The singers: the children of Asaph, an hundred twenty and eight.

42The children of the porters: the children of Shallum, the children of Ater, the children of Talmon, the children of Akkub, the children of Hatita, the children of Shobai, *in* all an hundred thirty and nine.

43The Nethinims: the children of Ziha, the children of Hasupha, the children of Tabbaoth,

44The children of Keros, the children of Siaha, the children of Padon.

45The children of Lebanah, the children of Hagabah, the children of Akkub,

46The children of Hagab, the children of Shalmai, the children of Hanan,

47The children of Giddel, the children of Gahar, the children of Reaiah,

48The children of Rezin, the children of Nekoda, the children of Gazzam,

49The children of Uzza, the children of Paseah, the children of Besai,

50The children of Asnah, the children of Mehunim, the children of Nephusim,

51The children of Bakbuk, the children of Hakupha, the children of Harhur,

52The children of Bazluth, the children of Mehida, the children of Harsha,

53The children of Barkos, the children of Sisera, the children of Thamah,

54The children of Neziah, the children of Hatipha.

55The children of Solomon's servants: the children of Sotai, the children of Sophereth, the children of Peruda,

56The children of Jaalah, the children of Darkon, the children of Giddel,

57The children of Shephatiah, the children of Hattil, the children of Pochereth of Zebaim, the children of Ami.

58All the Nethinims, and the children of Solomon's servants, *were* three hundred ninety and two.

59And these *were* they which went up from Tel–melah, Tel–harsa, Cherub, Addan, *and* Immer: but they could not shew their father's house, and their seed, whether they *were* of Israel.

60The children of Delaiah, the children of Tobiah, the children of Nekoda, six hundred fifty and two.

61And of the children of the priests: the children of Habaiah, the children of Koz, the children of Barzillai; which took a wife of the daughters of Barzillai the Gileadite, and was called after their name:

62These sought their register *among* those that were reckoned by genealogy, but they were not found: therefore were they, as polluted, put from the priesthood.

63And the Tirshatha said unto them, that they should not eat of the most holy things, till there stood up a priest with Urim and with Thummim.

64The whole congregation together *was* forty and two thousand three hundred *and* threescore,

65Beside their servants and their maids, of whom *there were* seven thousand three hundred thirty and seven: and *there were* among them two hundred singing men and singing women.

66Their horses *were* seven hundred thirty and six; their mules, two hundred forty and five;

67Their camels, four hundred thirty and five; *their* asses, six thousand seven hundred and twenty.

68And *some* of the chief of the fathers, when they came to the house of the LORD which *is* at Jerusalem, offered freely for the house of God to set it up in his place:

69They gave after their ability unto the treasure of the work threescore and one thousand drams of gold, and five thousand pound of silver, and one hundred priests' garments.

70So the priests, and the Levites, and *some* of the people, and the singers, and the porters, and the Nethinims, dwelt in their cities, and all Israel in their cities.

1 CORINTHIANS 1:18—2:5

FOR the preaching of the cross is to them that perish foolishness; but unto us which are saved it is the power of God.

19For it is written, I will destroy the wisdom of the wise, and will bring to nothing the understanding of the prudent.

20Where *is* the wise? where *is* the scribe? where *is* the disputer of this world? hath not God made foolish the wisdom of this world?

21For after that in the wisdom of God the world by wisdom knew not God, it pleased God by the foolishness of preaching to save them that believe.

22For the Jews require a sign, and the Greeks seek after wisdom:

23But we preach Christ crucified, unto the Jews a stumblingblock, and unto the Greeks foolishness;

24But unto them which are called, both Jews and Greeks, Christ the power of God, and the wisdom of God.

25Because the foolishness of God is wiser than men; and the weakness of God is stronger than men.

26For ye see your calling, brethren, how that not many wise men after the flesh, not many mighty, not many noble, *are called:*

27But God hath chosen the foolish things of the world to confound the wise; and God hath chosen the weak things of the world to confound the things which are mighty;

28And base things of the world, and things which are despised, hath God chosen, *yea,* and things which are not, to bring to nought things that are:

29That no flesh should glory in his presence.

30But of him are ye in Christ Jesus, who of God is made unto us wisdom, and righteousness, and sanctification, and redemption:

31That, according as it is written, He that glorieth, let him glory in the Lord.

AND I, brethren, when I came to you, came not with excellency of speech or of wisdom, declaring unto you the testimony of God.

2For I determined not to know any thing among you, save Jesus Christ, and him crucified.

3And I was with you in weakness, and in fear, and in much trembling.

4And my speech and my preaching *was* not with enticing words of man's wisdom, but in demonstration of the Spirit and of power:

5That your faith should not stand in the wisdom of men, but in the power of God.

PSALM 27:8–14

WHEN thou saidst, Seek ye my face; my heart said unto thee, Thy face, LORD, will I seek.

9Hide not thy face *far* from me; put not thy servant away in anger: thou hast been my help; leave me not, neither forsake me, O God of my salvation.

10When my father and my mother forsake me, then the LORD will take me up.

11Teach me thy way, O LORD, and lead me in a plain path, because of mine enemies.

12Deliver me not over unto the will of mine enemies: for false witnesses are risen up against me, and such as breathe out cruelty.

13*I had fainted,* unless I had believed to see the goodness of the LORD in the land of the living.

14Wait on the LORD: be of good courage, and he shall strengthen thine heart: wait, I say, on the LORD.

PROVERBS FOR TODAY/ 20:22–23

Say not thou, I will recompense evil; but *wait on the LORD, and he shall save thee.* □ *Divers weights are an abomination unto the LORD; and a false balance* is *not good.*

AUGUST 6

EZRA 3:1—4:24

AND when the seventh month was come, and the children of Israel *were* in the cities, the people gathered themselves together as one man to Jerusalem.

2Then stood up Jeshua the son of Jozadak, and his brethren the priests, and Zerubbabel the son of Shealtiel,

and his brethren, and builded the altar of the God of Israel, to offer burnt offerings thereon, as *it is* written in the law of Moses the man of God.

3And they set the altar upon his bases; for fear *was* upon them because of the people of those countries: and they offered burnt offerings thereon unto the Lord, *even* burnt offerings morning and evening.

4They kept also the feast of tabernacles, as *it is* written, and *offered* the daily burnt offerings by number, according to the custom, as the duty of every day required;

5And afterward *offered* the continual burnt offering, both of the new moons, and of all the set feasts of the LORD that were consecrated, and of every one that willingly offered a freewill offering unto the LORD.

6From the first day of the seventh month began they to offer burnt offerings unto the LORD. But the foundation of the temple of the LORD was not *yet* laid.

7They gave money also unto the masons, and to the carpenters; and meat, and drink, and oil, unto them of Zidon, and to them of Tyre, to bring cedar trees from Lebanon to the sea of Joppa, according to the grant that they had of Cyrus king of Persia.

8Now in the second year of their coming unto the house of God at Jerusalem, in the second month, began Zerubbabel the son of Shealtiel, and Jeshua the son of Jozadak, and the remnant of their brethren the priests and the Levites, and all they that were come out of the captivity unto Jerusalem; and appointed the Levites, from twenty years old and upward, to set forward the work of the house of the LORD.

9Then stood Jeshua *with* his sons and his brethren, Kadmiel and his sons, the sons of Judah, together, to set forward the workmen in the house of God: the sons of Henadad, *with* their sons and their brethren the Levites.

10And when the builders laid the foundation of the temple of the LORD, they set the priests in their apparel with trumpets, and the Levites the sons of Asaph with cymbals, to praise the LORD, after the ordinance of David king of Israel.

11And they sang together by course in praising and giving thanks unto the

LORD; because *he is* good, for his mercy *endureth* for ever toward Israel. And all the people shouted with a great shout, when they praised the LORD, because the foundation of the house of the LORD was laid.

12But many of the priests and Levites and chief of the fathers, *who were* ancient men, that had seen the first house, when the foundation of this house was laid before their eyes, wept with a loud voice; and many shouted aloud for joy:

13So that the people could not discern the noise of the shout of joy from the noise of the weeping of the people: for the people shouted with a loud shout, and the noise was heard afar off.

Now when the adversaries of Judah and Benjamin heard that the children of the captivity builded the temple unto the LORD God of Israel;

2Then they came to Zerubbabel, and to the chief of the fathers, and said unto them, Let us build with you: for we seek your God, as ye *do;* and we do sacrifice unto him since the days of Esar–haddon king of Assur, which brought us up hither.

3But Zerubbabel, and Jeshua, and the rest of the chief of the fathers of Israel, said unto them, Ye have nothing to do with us to build an house unto our God; but we ourselves together will build unto the LORD God of Israel, as king Cyrus the king of Persia hath commanded us.

4Then the people of the land weakened the hands of the people of Judah, and troubled them in building,

5And hired counsellors against them, to frustrate their purpose, all the days of Cyrus king of Persia, even until the reign of Darius king of Persia.

6And in the reign of Ahasuerus, in the beginning of his reign, wrote they *unto him* an accusation against the inhabitants of Judah and Jerusalem.

7And in the days of Artaxerxes wrote Bishlam, Mithredath, Tabeel, and the rest of their companions, unto Artaxerxes king of Persia; and the writing of the letter *was* written in the Syrian tongue, and interpreted in the Syrian tongue.

8Rehum the chancellor and Shimshai the scribe wrote a letter against Jerusalem to Artaxerxes the king in this sort:

9Then *wrote* Rehum the chancellor, and Shimshai the scribe, and the rest of their companions; the Dinaites, the Apharsathchites, the Tarpelites, the Apharsites, the Archevites, the Babylonians, the Susanchites, the Dehavites, *and* the Elamites,

10And the rest of the nations whom the great and noble Asnapper brought over, and set in the cities of Samaria, and the rest *that are* on this side the river, and at such a time.

11This *is* the copy of the letter that they sent unto him, *even* unto Artaxerxes the king; Thy servants the men on this side the river, and at such a time.

12Be it known unto the king, that the Jews which came up from thee to us are come unto Jerusalem, building the rebellious and the bad city, and have set up the walls *thereof,* and joined the foundations.

13Be it known now unto the king, that, if this city be builded, and the walls set up *again, then* will they not pay toll, tribute, and custom, and so thou shalt endamage the revenue of the kings.

14Now because we have maintenance from *the king's* palace, and it was not meet for us to see the king's dishonour, therefore have we sent and certified the king;

15That search may be made in the book of the records of thy fathers: so shalt thou find in the book of the records, and know that this city *is* a rebellious city, and hurtful unto kings and provinces, and that they have moved sedition within the same of old time: for which cause was this city destroyed.

16We certify the king that, if this city be builded *again,* and the walls thereof set up, by this means thou shalt have no portion on this side the river.

17*Then* sent the king an answer unto Rehum the chancellor, and *to* Shimshai the scribe, and *to* the rest of their companions that dwell in Samaria, and *unto* the rest beyond the river, Peace, and at such a time.

18The letter which ye sent unto us hath been plainly read before me.

19And I commanded, and search hath been made, and it is found that this city of old time hath made insurrection against kings, and *that* rebellion and sedition have been made therein.

20There have been mighty kings also over Jerusalem, which have ruled over all *countries* beyond the river; and toll, tribute, and custom, was paid unto them.

21Give ye now commandment to cause these men to cease, and that this city be not builded, until *another* commandment shall be given from me.

22Take heed now that ye fail not to do this: why should damage grow to the hurt of the kings?

23Now when the copy of king Artaxerxes' letter *was* read before Rehum, and Shimshai the scribe, and their companions, they went up in haste to Jerusalem unto the Jews, and made them to cease by force and power.

24Then ceased the work of the house of God which *is* at Jerusalem. So it ceased unto the second year of the reign of Darius king of Persia.

1 CORINTHIANS 2:6—3:4

Howbeit we speak wisdom among them that are perfect: yet not the wisdom of this world, nor of the princes of this world, that come to nought:

7But we speak the wisdom of God in a mystery, *even* the hidden *wisdom,* which God ordained before the world unto our glory:

8Which none of the princes of this world knew: for had they known *it*, they would not have crucified the Lord of glory.

9But as it is written, Eye hath not seen, nor ear heard, neither have entered into the heart of man, the things which God hath prepared for them that love him.

10But God hath revealed *them* unto us by his Spirit: for the Spirit searcheth all things, yea, the deep things of God.

11For what man knoweth the things of a man, save the spirit of man which is in him? even so the things of God knoweth no man, but the Spirit of God.

12Now we have received, not the spirit of the world, but the spirit which is of God; that we might know the things that are freely given to us of God.

13Which things also we speak, not in the words which man's wisdom teacheth, but which the Holy Ghost teacheth; comparing spiritual things with spiritual.

14But the natural man receiveth not the things of the Spirit of God: for they are foolishness unto him: neither can he know *them*, because they are spiritually discerned.

15But he that is spiritual judgeth all things, yet he himself is judged of no man.

16For who hath known the mind of the Lord, that he may instruct him? But we have the mind of Christ.

AND I, brethren, could not speak unto you as unto spiritual, but as unto carnal, *even* as unto babes in Christ.

2I have fed you with milk, and not with meat: for hitherto ye were not able *to bear it*, neither yet now are ye able.

3For ye are yet carnal: for whereas *there is* among you envying, and strife, and divisions, are ye not carnal, and walk as men?

4For while one saith, I am of Paul; and another, I *am* of Apollos; are ye not carnal?

PSALM 28:1–9

UNTO thee will I cry, O LORD my rock; be not silent to me: lest, *if* thou be silent to me, I become like them that go down into the pit.

2Hear the voice of my supplications, when I cry unto thee, when I lift up my hands toward thy holy oracle.

3Draw me not away with the wicked, and with the workers of iniquity, which speak peace to their neighbours, but mischief *is* in their hearts.

4Give them according to their deeds, and according to the wickedness of their endeavours: give them after the work of their hands; render to them their desert.

5Because they regard not the works of the LORD, nor the operation of his hands, he shall destroy them, and not build them up.

6Blessed *be* the LORD, because he hath heard the voice of my supplications.

7The LORD *is* my strength and my shield; my heart trusted in him, and I am helped: therefore my heart greatly rejoiceth; and with my song will I praise him.

8The LORD *is* their strength, and he *is* the saving strength of his anointed.

9Save thy people, and bless thine inheritance: feed them also, and lift them up for ever.

PROVERBS FOR TODAY/ 20:24–25

Man's goings are *of the LORD; how can a man then understand his own way?* □ It is *a snare to the man* who *devoureth* that which is *holy, and after vows to make enquiry.*

AUGUST 7

EZRA 5:1—6:22

THEN the prophets, Haggai the prophet, and Zechariah the son of Iddo, prophesied unto the Jews that *were* in Judah and Jerusalem in the name of the God of Israel, *even* unto them.

2Then rose up Zerubbabel the son of Shealtiel, and Jeshua the son of Jozadak, and began to build the house of God which *is* at Jerusalem: and with them *were* the prophets of God helping them.

3At the same time came to them Tatnai, governor on this side the river, and Shethar–boznai, and their companions, and said thus unto them, Who hath commanded you to build this house, and to make up this wall?

4Then said we unto them after this manner, What are the names of the men that make this building?

5But the eye of their God was upon the elders of the Jews, that they could not cause them to cease, till the matter came to Darius: and then they returned answer by letter concerning this *matter*.

6The copy of the letter that Tatnai, governor on this side the river, and Shethar–boznai, and his companions the Apharsachites, which *were* on this side the river, sent unto Darius the king:

7They sent a letter unto him, wherein was written thus; Unto Darius the king, all peace.

8Be it known unto the king, that we went into the province of Judea, to the house of the great God, which is builded with great stones, and timber is laid in the walls, and this work goeth fast on, and prospereth in their hands.

9Then asked we those elders, *and* said unto them thus, Who commanded you to build this house, and to make up these walls?

10We asked their names also, to certify thee, that we might write the names of the men that *were* the chief of them.

11And thus they returned us answer, saying, We are the servants of the God of heaven and earth, and build the house that was builded these many years ago, which a great king of Israel builded and set up.

12But after that our fathers had provoked the God of heaven unto wrath, he gave them into the hand of Nebuchadnezzar the king of Babylon, the Chaldean, who destroyed this house, and carried the people away into Babylon.

13But in the first year of Cyrus the king of Babylon *the same* king Cyrus made a decree to build this house of God.

14And the vessels also of gold and silver of the house of God, which Nebuchadnezzar took out of the temple that *was* in Jerusalem, and brought them into the temple of Babylon, those did Cyrus the king take out of the temple of Babylon, and they were delivered unto *one,* whose name *was* Sheshbazzar, whom he had made governor;

15And said unto him, Take these vessels, go, carry them into the temple that *is* in Jerusalem, and let the house of God be builded in his place.

16Then came the same Sheshbazzar, *and* laid the foundation of the house of God which *is* in Jerusalem: and since that time even until now hath it been in building, and *yet* it is not finished.

17Now therefore, if *it seem* good to the king, let there be search made in the king's treasure house, which *is* there at Babylon, whether it be *so,* that a decree was made of Cyrus the king to build this house of God at

Jerusalem, and let the king send his pleasure to us concerning this matter.

THEN Darius the king made a decree, and search was made in the house of the rolls, where the treasures were laid up in Babylon.

2And there was found at Achmetha, in the palace that *is* in the province of the Medes, a roll, and therein *was* a record thus written:

3In the first year of Cyrus the king *the same* Cyrus the king made a decree *concerning* the house of God at Jerusalem, Let the house be builded, the place where they offered sacrifices, and let the foundations thereof be strongly laid; the height thereof threescore cubits, *and* the breadth thereof threescore cubits;

4With three rows of great stones, and a row of new timber: and let the expenses be given out of the king's house:

5And also let the golden and silver vessels of the house of God, which Nebuchadnezzar took forth out of the temple which *is* at Jerusalem, and brought unto Babylon, be restored, and brought again unto the temple which *is* at Jerusalem, *every one* to his place, and place *them* in the house of God.

6Now *therefore* Tatnai, governor beyond the river, Shethar–boznai, and your companions the Apharsachites, which *are* beyond the river, be ye far from thence:

7Let the work of this house of God alone; let the governor of the Jews and the elders of the Jews build this house of God in his place.

8Moreover I make a decree what ye shall do to the elders of these Jews for the building of this house of God: that of the king's goods, *even* of the tribute beyond the river, forthwith expenses be given unto these men, that they be not hindered.

9And that which they have need of, both young bullocks, and rams, and lambs, for the burnt offerings of the God of heaven, wheat, salt, wine, and oil, according to the appointment of the priests which *are* at Jerusalem, let it be given them day by day without fail:

10That they may offer sacrifices of sweet savours unto the God of heaven, and pray for the life of the king, and of his sons.

11Also I have made a decree, that whosoever shall alter this word, let timber be pulled down from his house, and being set up, let him be hanged thereon; and let his house be made a dunghill for this.

12And the God that hath caused his name to dwell there destroy all kings and people, that shall put to their hand to alter *and* to destroy this house of God which is at Jerusalem. I Darius have made a decree; let it be done with speed.

13Then Tatnai, governor on this side the river, Shethar–boznai, and their companions, according to that which Darius the king had sent, so they did speedily.

14And the elders of the Jews builded, and they prospered through the prophesying of Haggai the prophet and Zechariah the son of Iddo. And they builded, and finished *it,* according to the commandment of the God of Israel, and according to the commandment of Cyrus, and Darius, and Artaxerxes king of Persia.

15And this house was finished on the third day of the month Adar, which was in the sixth year of the reign of Darius the king.

16And the children of Israel, the priests, and the Levites, and the rest of the children of the captivity, kept the dedication of this house of God with joy,

17And offered at the dedication of this house of God an hundred bullocks, two hundred rams, four hundred lambs; and for a sin offering for all Israel, twelve he goats, according to the number of the tribes of Israel.

18And they set the priests in their divisions, and the Levites in their courses, for the service of God, which *is* at Jerusalem; as it is written in the book of Moses.

19And the children of the captivity kept the passover upon the fourteenth *day* of the first month.

20For the priests and the Levites were purified together, all of them *were* pure, and killed the passover for all the children of the captivity, and for their brethren the priests, and for themselves.

21And the children of Israel, which were come again out of captivity, and all such as had separated themselves unto them from the filthiness of the heathen of the land, to seek the LORD God of Israel, did eat,

22And kept the feast of unleavened bread seven days with joy: for the LORD had made them joyful, and turned the heart of the king of Assyria unto them, to strengthen their hands in the work of the house of God, the God of Israel.

1 CORINTHIANS 3:5–23

WHO then is Paul, and who *is* Apollos, but ministers by whom ye believed, even as the Lord gave to every man?

6I have planted, Apollos watered; but God gave the increase.

7So then neither is he that planteth any thing, neither he that watereth; but God that giveth the increase.

8Now he that planteth and he that watereth are one: and every man shall receive his own reward according to his own labour.

9For we are labourers together with God: ye are God's husbandry, *ye are* God's building.

10According to the grace of God which is given unto me, as a wise masterbuilder, I have laid the foundation, and another buildeth thereon. But let every man take heed how he buildeth thereupon.

11For other foundation can no man lay than that is laid, which is Jesus Christ.

12Now if any man build upon this foundation gold, silver, precious stones, wood, hay, stubble;

13Every man's work shall be made manifest: for the day shall declare it, because it shall be revealed by fire; and the fire shall try every man's work of what sort it is.

14If any man's work abide which he hath built thereupon, he shall receive a reward.

15If any man's work shall be burned, he shall suffer loss: but he himself shall be saved; yet so as by fire.

16Know ye not that ye are the temple of God, and *that* the Spirit of God dwelleth in you?

17If any man defile the temple of God, him shall God destroy; for the temple of God is holy, which *temple* ye are.

18Let no man deceive himself. If any man among you seemeth to be wise in this world, let him become a fool, that he may be wise.

19For the wisdom of this world is foolishness with God. For it is written, He taketh the wise in their own craftiness.

20And again, The Lord knoweth the thoughts of the wise, that they are vain.

21Therefore let no man glory in men. For all things are yours;

22Whether Paul, or Apollos, or Cephas, or the world, or life, or death, or things present, or things to come; all are yours;

23And ye are Christ's; and Christ *is* God's.

PSALM 29:1–11

GIVE unto the LORD, O ye mighty, give unto the LORD glory and strength.

2Give unto the LORD the glory due

unto his name; worship the Lord in the beauty of holiness.

³The voice of the Lord *is* upon the waters: the God of glory thundereth: the Lord *is* upon many waters.

⁴The voice of the Lord *is* powerful; the voice of the Lord *is* full of majesty.

⁵The voice of the Lord breaketh the cedars; yea, the Lord breaketh the cedars of Lebanon.

⁶He maketh them also to skip like a calf; Lebanon and Sirion like a young unicorn.

⁷The voice of the Lord divideth the flames of fire.

⁸The voice of the Lord shaketh the wilderness; the Lord shaketh the wilderness of Kadesh.

⁹The voice of the Lord maketh the hinds to calve, and discovereth the forests: and in his temple doth every one speak of *his* glory.

¹⁰The Lord sitteth upon the flood; yea, the Lord sitteth King for ever.

¹¹The Lord will give strength unto his people; the Lord will bless his people with peace.

PROVERBS FOR TODAY/ 20:26–27

A wise king scattereth the wicked, and bringeth the wheel over them. □ *The spirit of man* is *the candle of the Lord, searching all the inward parts of the belly.*

AUGUST 8

EZRA 7:1—8:20

Now after these things, in the reign of Artaxerxes king of Persia, Ezra the son of Seraiah, the son of Azariah, the son of Hilkiah,

²The son of Shallum, the son of Zadok, the son of Ahitub,

³The son of Amariah, the son of Azariah, the son of Meraioth,

⁴The son of Zerahiah, the son of Uzzi, the son of Bukki,

⁵The son of Abishua, the son of Phinehas, the son of Eleazar, the son of Aaron the chief priest:

⁶This Ezra went up from Babylon; and he *was* a ready scribe in the law of Moses, which the Lord God of Israel had given: and the king granted him all his request, according to the hand of the Lord his God upon him.

⁷And there went up *some* of the children of Israel, and of the priests, and the Levites, and the singers, and the porters, and the Nethinims, unto Jerusalem, in the seventh year of Artaxerxes the king.

⁸And he came to Jerusalem in the fifth month, which *was* in the seventh year of the king.

⁹For upon the first *day* of the first month began he to go up from Babylon, and on the first *day* of the fifth month came he to Jerusalem, according to the good hand of his God upon him.

¹⁰For Ezra had prepared his heart to seek the law of the Lord, and to do *it*, and to teach in Israel statutes and judgments.

¹¹Now this *is* the copy of the letter that the king Artaxerxes gave unto Ezra the priest, the scribe, *even* a scribe of the words of the commandments of the Lord, and of his statutes to Israel.

¹²Artaxerxes, king of kings, unto

Ezra the priest, a scribe of the law of the God of heaven, perfect *peace,* and at such a time.

13I make a decree, that all they of the people of Israel, and *of* his priests and Levites, in my realm, which are minded of their own freewill to go up to Jerusalem, go with thee.

14Forasmuch as thou art sent of the king, and of his seven counsellors, to enquire concerning Judah and Jerusalem, according to the law of thy God which *is* in thine hand;

15And to carry the silver and gold, which the king and his counsellors have freely offered unto the God of Israel, whose habitation *is* in Jerusalem,

16And all the silver and gold that thou canst find in all the province of Babylon, with the freewill offering of the people, and of the priests, offering willingly for the house of their God which *is* in Jerusalem:

17That thou mayest buy speedily with this money bullocks, rams, lambs, with their meat offerings and their drink offerings, and offer them upon the altar of the house of your God which *is* in Jerusalem.

18And whatsoever shall seem good to thee, and to thy brethren, to do with the rest of the silver and the gold, that do after the will of your God.

19The vessels also that are given thee for the service of the house of thy God, *those* deliver thou before the God of Jerusalem.

20And whatsoever more shall be needful for the house of thy God, which thou shalt have occasion to bestow, bestow *it* out of the king's treasure house.

21And I, *even* I Artaxerxes the king, do make a decree to all the treasurers which *are* beyond the river, that whatsoever Ezra the priest, the scribe of the law of the God of heaven, shall require of you, it be done speedily,

22Unto an hundred talents of silver, and to an hundred measures of wheat, and to an hundred baths of wine, and to an hundred baths of oil, and salt without prescribing *how much.*

23Whatsoever is commanded by the God of heaven, let it be diligently done for the house of the God of heaven: for why should there be wrath against the realm of the king and his sons?

24Also we certify you, that touching any of the priests and Levites, singers, porters, Nethinims, or ministers of this house of God, it shall not be lawful to impose toll, tribute, or custom, upon them.

25And thou, Ezra, after the wisdom of thy God, that *is* in thine hand, set magistrates and judges, which may judge all the people that *are* beyond the river, all such as know the laws of thy God; and teach ye them that know *them* not.

26And whosoever will not do the law of thy God, and the law of the king, let judgment be executed speedily upon him, whether *it be* unto death, or to banishment, or to confiscation of goods, or to imprisonment.

27Blessed *be* the LORD God of our fathers, which hath put *such a thing* as this in the king's heart, to beautify the house of the LORD which *is* in Jerusalem:

28And hath extended mercy unto me before the king, and his counsellors, and before all the king's mighty princes. And I was strengthened as the hand of the LORD my God *was* upon me, and I gathered together out of Israel chief men to go up with me.

THESE *are* now the chief of their fathers, and *this is* the genealogy of them that went up with me from Babylon, in the reign of Artaxerxes the king.

2Of the sons of Phinehas; Gershom: of the sons of Ithamar; Daniel: of the sons of David; Hattush.

3Of the sons of Shechaniah, of the sons of Pharosh; Zechariah: and with him were reckoned by genealogy of the males an hundred and fifty.

4Of the sons of Pahath–moab; Elihoenai the son of Zerahiah, and with him two hundred males.

5Of the sons of Shechaniah; the son of Jahaziel, and with him three hundred males.

6Of the sons also of Adin; Ebed the son of Jonathan, and with him fifty males.

7And of the sons of Elam; Jeshaiah the son of Athaliah, and with him seventy males.

8And of the sons of Shephatiah; Zebadiah the son of Michael, and with him fourscore males.

9Of the sons of Joab; Obadiah the son of Jehiel, and with him two hundred and eighteen males.

10And of the sons of Shelomith; the son of Josiphiah, and with him an hundred and threescore males.

11And of the sons of Bebai; Zechariah the son of Bebai, and with him twenty and eight males.

12And of the sons of Azgad; Johanan the son of Hakkatan, and with him an hundred and ten males.

13And of the last sons of Adonikam, whose names are these, Eliphelet, Jeiel, and Shemaiah, and with them threescore males.

14Of the sons also of Bigvai; Uthai, and Zabbud, and with them seventy males.

15And I gathered them together to the river that runneth to Ahava; and there abode we in tents three days: and I viewed the people, and the priests, and found there none of the sons of Levi.

16Then sent I for Eliezer, for Ariel, for Shemaiah, and for Elnathan, and for Jarib, and for Elnathan, and for Nathan, and for Zechariah, and for Meshullam, chief men; also for Joiarib, and for Elnathan, men of understanding.

17And I sent them with commandment unto Iddo the chief at the place Casiphia, and I told them what they should say unto Iddo, and to his brethren the Nethinims, at the place Casiphia, that they should bring unto us ministers for the house of our God.

18And by the good hand of our God upon us they brought us a man of understanding, of the sons of Mahli, the son of Levi, the son of Israel; and Sherebiah, with his sons and his brethren, eighteen;

19And Hashabiah, and with him Jeshaiah of the sons of Merari, his brethren and their sons, twenty;

20Also of the Nethinims, whom David and the princes had appointed for the service of the Levites, two hundred and twenty Nethinims: all of them were expressed by name.

1 CORINTHIANS 4:1–21

LET a man so account of us, as of the ministers of Christ, and stewards of the mysteries of God.

2Moreover it is required in stewards, that a man be found faithful.

3But with me it is a very small thing that I should be judged of you, or of man's judgment: yea, I judge not mine own self.

4For I know nothing by myself; yet am I not hereby justified: but he that judgeth me is the Lord.

5Therefore judge nothing before the time, until the Lord come, who both will bring to light the hidden things of darkness, and will make manifest the counsels of the hearts: and then shall every man have praise of God.

6And these things, brethren, I have in a figure transferred to myself and to Apollos for your sakes; that ye might learn in us not to think of men above that which is written, that no one of you be puffed up for one against another.

7For who maketh thee to differ from another? and what hast thou that thou didst not receive? now if thou didst receive *it,* why dost thou glory, as if thou hadst not received *it?*

8Now ye are full, now ye are rich, ye have reigned as kings without us: and I would to God ye did reign, that we also might reign with you.

9For I think that God hath set forth us the apostles last, as it were appointed to death: for we are made a spectacle unto the world, and to angels, and to men.

10We *are* fools for Christ's sake, but ye *are* wise in Christ; we *are* weak, but ye *are* strong; ye *are* honourable, but we *are* despised.

11Even unto this present hour we both hunger, and thirst, and are naked, and are buffeted, and have no certain dwellingplace;

12And labour, working with our own hands: being reviled, we bless; being persecuted, we suffer it:

13Being defamed, we intreat: we are made as the filth of the world, *and are* the offscouring of all things unto this day.

14I write not these things to shame you, but as my beloved sons I warn *you.*

15For though ye have ten thousand instructors in Christ, yet *have ye* not many fathers: for in Christ Jesus I have begotten you through the gospel.

16Wherefore I beseech you, be ye followers of me.

17For this cause have I sent unto you Timotheus, who is my beloved son, and faithful in the Lord, who shall bring you into remembrance of my ways which be in Christ, as I teach every where in every church.

18Now some are puffed up, as though I would not come to you.

19But I will come to you shortly, if the Lord will, and will know, not the speech of them which are puffed up, but the power.

20For the kingdom of God *is* not in word, but in power.

21What will ye? shall I come unto you with a rod, or in love, and *in* the spirit of meekness?

PSALM 30:1–12

I WILL extol thee, O LORD; for thou hast lifted me up, and hast not made my foes to rejoice over me.

2O LORD my God, I cried unto thee, and thou hast healed me.

3O LORD, thou hast brought up my soul from the grave: thou hast kept me alive, that I should not go down to the pit.

4Sing unto the LORD, O ye saints of his, and give thanks at the remembrance of his holiness.

5For his anger *endureth but* a moment; in his favour *is* life: weeping may endure for a night, but joy *cometh* in the morning.

6And in my prosperity I said, I shall never be moved.

7LORD, by thy favour thou hast made my mountain to stand strong: thou didst hide thy face, *and* I was troubled.

8I cried to thee, O LORD; and unto the LORD I made supplication.

9What profit *is there* in my blood, when I go down to the pit? Shall the dust praise thee? shall it declare thy truth?

10Hear, O LORD, and have mercy upon me: LORD, be thou my helper.

11Thou hast turned for me my mourning into dancing: thou hast put off my sackcloth, and girded me with gladness;

12To the end that *my* glory may sing praise to thee, and not be silent. O LORD my God, I will give thanks unto thee for ever.

PROVERBS FOR TODAY/ 20:28–30

Mercy and truth preserve the king: and his throne is upholden by mercy. □ *The glory of young men* is *their strength: and the beauty of old men* is *the grey head.*

□ *The blueness of a wound cleanseth away evil: so* do *stripes the inward parts of the belly.*

AUGUST 9

EZRA 8:21—9:15

THEN I proclaimed a fast there, at the river of Ahava, that we might afflict ourselves before our God, to seek of him a right way for us, and for our little ones, and for all our substance.

22For I was ashamed to require of the king a band of soldiers and horsemen to help us against the enemy in the way: because we had spoken unto the king, saying, The hand of our God *is* upon all them for good that seek him; but his power and his wrath *is* against all them that forsake him.

23So we fasted and besought our God for this: and he was intreated of us.

24Then I separated twelve of the chief of the priests, Sherebiah, Hashabiah, and ten of their brethren with them,

25And weighed unto them the silver, and the gold, and the vessels, *even* the offering of the house of our God, which the king, and his counsellors, and his lords, and all Israel *there* present, had offered:

26I even weighed unto their hand six hundred and fifty talents of silver, and silver vessels an hundred talents, *and* of gold an hundred talents;

27Also twenty basons of gold, of a thousand drams; and two vessels of fine copper, precious as gold.

28And I said unto them, Ye *are* holy unto the LORD; the vessels *are* holy also; and the silver and the gold *are* a freewill offering unto the LORD God of your fathers.

29Watch ye, and keep *them,* until ye weigh *them* before the chief of the priests and the Levites, and chief of the fathers of Israel, at Jerusalem, in the chambers of the house of the LORD.

30So took the priests and the Levites the weight of the silver, and the gold, and the vessels, to bring *them* to Jerusalem unto the house of our God.

31Then we departed from the river of Ahava on the twelfth *day* of the first month, to go unto Jerusalem: and the hand of our God was upon us, and he delivered us from the hand of the enemy, and of such as lay in wait by the way.

32And we came to Jerusalem, and abode there three days.

33Now on the fourth day was the silver and the gold and the vessels weighed in the house of our God by the hand of Meremoth the son of Uriah the priest; and with him *was* Eleazar the son of Phinehas; and with them *was* Jozabad the son of Jeshua, and Noadiah the son of Binnui, Levites;

34By number *and* by weight of every one: and all the weight was written at that time.

35*Also* the children of those that had been carried away, which were come out of the captivity, offered burnt offerings unto the God of Israel, twelve bullocks for all Israel, ninety and six rams, seventy and seven lambs, twelve he goats *for* a sin offering: all *this was* a burnt offering unto the LORD.

36And they delivered the king's commissions unto the king's lieutenants, and to the governors on this side the river: and they furthered the people, and the house of God.

Now when these things were done, the princes came to me, saying, The people of Israel, and the priests, and the Levites, have not separated themselves from the people of the lands, *doing* according to their abominations, *even* of the Canaanites, the Hittites, the Perizzites, the Jebusites, the Ammonites, the Moabites, the Egyptians, and the Amorites.

2For they have taken of their daughters for themselves, and for their sons: so that the holy seed have mingled themselves with the people of *those* lands: yea, the hand of the princes and rulers hath been chief in this trespass.

3And when I heard this thing, I rent my garment and my mantle, and plucked off the hair of my head and of my beard, and sat down astonished.

4Then were assembled unto me every one that trembled at the words of the God of Israel, because of the transgression of those that had been carried away; and I sat astonished until the evening sacrifice.

5And at the evening sacrifice I arose up from my heaviness; and having rent my garment and my mantle, I fell upon my knees, and spread out my hands unto the LORD my God,

6And said, O my God, I am ashamed and blush to lift up my face to thee, my God: for our iniquities are increased over *our* head, and our trespass is grown up unto the heavens.

7Since the days of our fathers *have* we *been* in a great trespass unto this day; and for our iniquities have we, our kings, *and* our priests, been delivered into the hand of the kings of the lands, to the sword, to captivity, and to a spoil, and to confusion of face, as *it is* this day.

8And now for a little space grace hath been *shewed* from the LORD our God, to leave us a remnant to escape, and to give us a nail in his holy place, that our God may lighten our eyes, and give us a little reviving in our bondage.

9For we *were* bondmen; yet our God hath not forsaken us in our bondage, but hath extended mercy unto us in the sight of the kings of Persia, to give us a reviving, to set up the house of our God, and to repair the desolations thereof, and to give us a wall in Judah and in Jerusalem.

10And now, O our God, what shall we say after this? for we have forsaken thy commandments,

11Which thou hast commanded by thy servants the prophets, saying, The land, unto which ye go to possess it, is an unclean land with the filthiness of the people of the lands, with their abominations, which have filled it from one end to another with their uncleanness.

12Now therefore give not your daughters unto their sons, neither take their daughters unto your sons, nor seek their peace or their wealth for ever: that ye may be strong, and eat the good of the land, and leave *it* for an inheritance to your children for ever.

13And after all that is come upon us for our evil deeds, and for our great trespass, seeing that thou our God hast punished us less than our iniquities *deserve,* and hast given us *such* deliverance as this;

14Should we again break thy commandments, and join in affinity with the people of these abominations? wouldest not thou be angry with us till thou hadst consumed *us,* so that *there should be* no remnant nor escaping?

15O LORD God of Israel, thou *art* righteous: for we remain yet escaped, as *it is* this day: behold, we *are* before thee in our trespasses: for we cannot stand before thee because of this.

1 CORINTHIANS 5:1–13

I T is reported commonly *that there is* fornication among you, and such fornication as is not so much as named among the Gentiles, that one should have his father's wife.

2And ye are puffed up, and have not rather mourned, that he that hath done this deed might be taken away from among you.

3For I verily, as absent in body, but present in spirit, have judged already, as though I were present, *concerning* him that hath so done this deed.

4In the name of our Lord Jesus Christ, when ye are gathered together, and my spirit, with the power of our Lord Jesus Christ,

5To deliver such an one unto Satan for the destruction of the flesh, that the spirit may be saved in the day of the Lord Jesus.

6Your glorying *is* not good. Know ye not that a little leaven leaveneth the whole lump?

7Purge out therefore the old leaven, that ye may be a new lump, as ye are unleavened. For even Christ our passover is sacrificed for us:

8Therefore let us keep the feast, not with old leaven, neither with the leaven of malice and wickedness; but with the unleavened *bread* of sincerity and truth.

9I wrote unto you in an epistle not to company with fornicators:

10Yet not altogether the fornicators of this world, or with the covetous, or extortioners, or with idolaters; for then must ye needs go out of the world.

11But now I have written unto you not to keep company, if any man that is called a brother be a fornicator, or covetous, or an idolater, or a railer, or a drunkard, or an extortioner; with such an one no not to eat.

12For what have I to do to judge them also that are without? do not ye judge them that are within?

13But them that are without God judgeth. Therefore put away from among yourselves that wicked person.

PSALM 31:1–8

I N thee, O Lord, do I put my trust; let me never be ashamed: deliver me in thy righteousness.

2Bow down thine ear to me; deliver me speedily: be thou my strong rock, for an house of defence to save me.

3For thou *art* my rock and my fortress; therefore for thy name's sake lead me, and guide me.

4Pull me out of the net that they have laid privily for me: for thou *art* my strength.

5Into thine hand I commit my spirit: thou hast redeemed me, O Lord God of truth.

6I have hated them that regard lying vanities: but I trust in the Lord.

7I will be glad and rejoice in thy mercy: for thou hast considered my trouble; thou hast known my soul in adversities;

8And hast not shut me up into the hand of the enemy: thou hast set my feet in a large room.

PROVERBS FOR TODAY/ 21:1–2

The king's heart is *in the hand of the Lord,* as *the rivers of water: he turneth it whithersoever he will.* □ *Every way of a man* is *right in his own eyes: but the Lord pondereth the hearts.*

EZRA 10:1–44

Now when Ezra had prayed, and when he had confessed, weeping and casting himself down before the house of God, there assembled unto him out of Israel a very great congregation of men and women and children: for the people wept very sore.

2And Shechaniah the son of Jehiel, *one* of the sons of Elam, answered and said unto Ezra, We have trespassed against our God, and have taken strange wives of the people of the land: yet now there is hope in Israel concerning this thing.

3Now therefore let us make a covenant with our God to put away all the wives, and such as are born of them, according to the counsel of my lord, and of those that tremble at the commandment of our God; and let it be done according to the law.

4Arise; for *this* matter *belongeth* unto thee: we also *will be* with thee: be of good courage, and do *it.*

5Then arose Ezra, and made the chief priests, the Levites, and all Israel, to swear that they should do according to this word. And they sware.

6Then Ezra rose up from before the house of God, and went into the chamber of Johanan the son of Eliashib: and *when* he came thither, he did eat no bread, nor drink water: for he mourned because of the transgression of them that had been carried away.

7And they made proclamation throughout Judah and Jerusalem unto all the children of the captivity, that they should gather themselves together unto Jerusalem;

8And that whosoever would not come within three days, according to the counsel of the princes and the elders, all his substance should be forfeited, and himself separated from the congregation of those that had been carried away.

9Then all the men of Judah and Benjamin gathered themselves together unto Jerusalem within three days. It *was* the ninth month, on the twentieth *day* of the month; and all the people sat in the street of the house of God, trembling because of *this* matter, and for the great rain.

10And Ezra the priest stood up, and said unto them, Ye have transgressed, and have taken strange wives, to increase the trespass of Israel.

11Now therefore make confession unto the LORD God of your fathers, and do his pleasure: and separate yourselves from the people of the land, and from the strange wives.

12Then all the congregation answered and said with a loud voice, As thou hast said, so must we do.

13But the people *are* many, and *it is* a time of much rain, and we are not able to stand without, neither *is this* a work of one day or two: for we are many that have transgressed in this thing.

14Let now our rulers of all the congregation stand, and let all them which have taken strange wives in our cities come at appointed times, and with them the elders of every city, and the judges thereof, until the fierce wrath of our God for this matter be turned from us.

15Only Jonathan the son of Asahel and Jahaziah the son of Tikvah were employed about this *matter:* and Meshullam and Shabbethai the Levite helped them.

16And the children of the captivity did so. And Ezra the priest, *with* certain chief of the fathers, after the house of their fathers, and all of them by *their* names, were separated, and sat down in the first day of the tenth month to examine the matter.

17And they made an end with all the men that had taken strange wives by the first day of the first month.

18And among the sons of the priests there were found that had taken strange wives: *namely,* of the sons of Jeshua the son of Jozadak, and his brethren; Maaseiah, and Eliezer, and Jarib, and Gedaliah.

19And they gave their hands that they would put away their wives; and *being* guilty, *they offered* a ram of the flock for their trespass.

20And of the sons of Immer; Hanani, and Zebadiah.

21And of the sons of Harim; Maaseiah, and Elijah, and Shemaiah, and Jehiel, and Uzziah.

22And of the sons of Pashur; Elioenai, Maaseiah, Ishmael, Nethaneel, Jozabad, and Elasah.

23Also of the Levites; Jozabad, and Shimei, and Kelaiah, (the same *is* Kelita,) Pethahiah, Judah, and Eliezer.

24Of the singers also; Eliashib: and of the porters; Shallum, and Telem, and Uri.

25Moreover of Israel: of the sons of Parosh; Ramiah, and Jeziah, and Malchiah, and Miamin, and Eleazar, and Malchijah, and Benaiah.

26And of the sons of Elam; Mattaniah, Zechariah, and Jehiel, and Abdi, and Jeremoth, and Eliah.

27And of the sons of Zattu; Elioenai, Eliashib, Mattaniah, and Jeremoth, and Zabad, and Aziza.

28Of the sons also of Bebai; Jehohanan, Hananiah, Zabbai, *and* Athlai.

29And of the sons of Bani; Meshullam, Malluch, and Adaiah, Jashub, and Sheal, and Ramoth.

30And of the sons of Pahath–moab; Adna, and Chelal, Benaiah, Maaseiah, Mattaniah, Bezaleel, and Binnui, and Manasseh.

31And *of* the sons of Harim; Eliezer, Ishijah, Melchiah, Shemaiah, Shimeon,

32Benjamin, Malluch, *and* Shemariah.

33Of the sons of Hashum; Mattenai, Mattathah, Zabad, Eliphelet, Jeremai, Manasseh, *and* Shimei.

34Of the sons of Bani; Maadai, Amram, and Uel,

35Benaiah, Bedeiah, Chelluh,

36Vaniah, Meremoth, Eliashib,

37Mattaniah, Mattenai, and Jaasau,

38And Bani, and Binnui, Shimei,

39And Shelemiah, and Nathan, and Adaiah,

40Machnadebai, Shashai, Sharai,

41Azareel, and Shelemiah, Shemariah,

42Shallum, Amariah, *and* Joseph.

43Of the sons of Nebo; Jeiel, Mattithiah, Zabad, Zebina, Jadau, and Joel, Benaiah.

44All these had taken strange wives: and *some* of them had wives by whom they had children.

1 CORINTHIANS 6:1–20

Dare any of you, having a matter against another, go to law before the unjust, and not before the saints?

2Do ye not know that the saints shall judge the world? and if the world shall be judged by you, are ye unworthy to judge the smallest matters?

3Know ye not that we shall judge angels? how much more things that pertain to this life?

4If then ye have judgments of things pertaining to this life, set them to judge who are least esteemed in the church.

5I speak to your shame. Is it so, that there is not a wise man among you? no, not one that shall be able to judge between his brethren?

6But brother goeth to law with brother, and that before the unbelievers.

7Now therefore there is utterly a fault among you, because ye go to law one with another. Why do ye not rather take wrong? why do ye not rather *suffer yourselves* to be defrauded?

8Nay, ye do wrong, and defraud, and that *your* brethren.

9Know ye not that the unrighteous shall not inherit the kingdom of God? Be not deceived: neither fornicators, nor idolaters, nor adulterers, nor effeminate, nor abusers of themselves with mankind,

10Nor thieves, nor covetous, nor drunkards, nor revilers, nor extortioners, shall inherit the kingdom of God.

11And such were some of you: but ye are washed, but ye are sanctified, but ye are justified in the name of the Lord Jesus, and by the Spirit of our God.

12All things are lawful unto me, but all things are not expedient: all things are lawful for me, but I will not be brought under the power of any.

13Meats for the belly, and the belly for meats: but God shall destroy both it and them. Now the body *is* not for fornication, but for the Lord; and the Lord for the body.

14And God hath both raised up the Lord, and will also raise up us by his own power.

15Know ye not that your bodies are the members of Christ? shall I then take the members of Christ, and make *them* the members of an harlot? God forbid.

16What? know ye not that he which is joined to an harlot is one body? for two, saith he, shall be one flesh.

17But he that is joined unto the Lord is one spirit.

18Flee fornication. Every sin that a man doeth is without the body; but he that committeth fornication sinneth against his own body.

19What? know ye not that your body is the temple of the Holy Ghost *which is* in you, which ye have of God, and ye are not your own?

20For ye are bought with a price: therefore glorify God in your body, and in your spirit, which are God's.

PSALM 31:9–18

HAVE mercy upon me, O Lord, for I am in trouble: mine eye is consumed with grief, *yea* my soul and my belly.

10For my life is spent with grief, and my years with sighing: my strength faileth because of mine iniquity, and my bones are consumed.

11I was a reproach among all mine enemies, but especially among my neighbours, and a fear to mine acquaintance: they that did see me without fled from me.

12I am forgotten as a dead man out of mind: I am like a broken vessel.

13For I have heard the slander of many: fear *was* on every side: while they took counsel together against me, they devised to take away my life.

14But I trusted in thee, O Lord: I said, Thou *art* my God.

15My times *are* in thy hand: deliver me from the hand of mine enemies, and from them that persecute me.

16Make thy face to shine upon thy servant: save me for thy mercies' sake.

17Let me not be ashamed, O Lord; for I have called upon thee: let the wicked be ashamed, *and* let them be silent in the grave.

18Let the lying lips be put to silence; which speak grievous things proudly and contemptuously against the righteous.

PROVERBS FOR TODAY/ 21:3
To do justice and judgment is *more acceptable to the* Lord *than sacrifice.*

AUGUST 11

NEHEMIAH 1:1—3:14

THE words of Nehemiah the son of Hachaliah. And it came to pass in the month Chisleu, in the twentieth year, as I was in Shushan the palace,

2That Hanani, one of my brethren, came, he and *certain* men of Judah; and I asked them concerning the Jews that had escaped, which were left of the captivity, and concerning Jerusalem.

3And they said unto me, The remnant that are left of the captivity there in the province *are* in great affliction and reproach: the wall of Jerusalem also *is* broken down, and the gates thereof are burned with fire.

4And it came to pass, when I heard these words, that I sat down and wept, and mourned *certain* days, and fasted, and prayed before the God of heaven,

5And said, I beseech thee, O Lord God of heaven, the great and terrible God, that keepeth covenant and mercy for them that love him and observe his commandments:

6Let thine ear now be attentive, and thine eyes open, that thou mayest hear the prayer of thy servant, which I pray before thee now, day and night, for the children of Israel thy servants, and confess the sins of the children of Israel, which we have sinned against thee: both I and my father's house have sinned.

7We have dealt very corruptly against thee, and have not kept the commandments, nor the statutes, nor the judgments, which thou commandedst thy servant Moses.

8Remember, I beseech thee, the word that thou commandedst thy servant Moses, saying, *If* ye transgress, I will scatter you abroad among the nations:

9But *if* ye turn unto me, and keep my commandments, and do them; though there were of you cast out unto the uttermost part of the heaven, *yet* will I gather them from thence, and will bring them unto the place that I have chosen to set my name there.

10Now these *are* thy servants and thy people, whom thou hast redeemed by thy great power, and by thy strong hand.

11O Lord, I beseech thee, let now thine ear be attentive to the prayer of thy servant, and to the prayer of thy servants, who desire to fear thy name: and prosper, I pray thee, thy servant this day, and grant him mercy in the sight of this man. For I was the king's cupbearer.

And it came to pass in the month Nisan, in the twentieth year of Artaxerxes the king, *that* wine *was* before him: and I took up the wine, and gave *it* unto the king. Now I had not been *beforetime* sad in his presence.

2Wherefore the king said unto me, Why *is* thy countenance sad, seeing thou *art* not sick? this *is* nothing *else* but sorrow of heart. Then I was very sore afraid,

3And said unto the king, Let the king live for ever: why should not my countenance be sad, when the city, the place of my fathers' sepulchres, *lieth* waste, and the gates thereof are consumed with fire?

4Then the king said unto me, For what dost thou make request? So I prayed to the God of heaven.

5And I said unto the king, If it please the king, and if thy servant have found favour in thy sight, that thou wouldest send me unto Judah, unto the city of my fathers' sepulchres, that I may build it.

6And the king said unto me, (the queen also sitting by him,) For how long shall thy journey be? and when wilt thou return? So it pleased the king to send me; and I set him a time.

7Moreover I said unto the king, If it please the king, let letters be given me to the governors beyond the river, that they may convey me over till I come into Judah;

8And a letter unto Asaph the keeper of the king's forest, that he may give me timber to make beams for the gates of the palace which *appertained* to the house, and for the wall of the city, and for the house that I shall enter into. And the king granted me, according to the good hand of my God upon me.

9Then I came to the governors beyond the river, and gave them the king's letters. Now the king had sent captains of the army and horsemen with me.

10When Sanballat the Horonite, and Tobiah the servant, the Ammonite, heard *of it,* it grieved them exceedingly that there was come a man to seek the welfare of the children of Israel.

11So I came to Jerusalem, and was there three days.

12And I arose in the night, I and some few men with me; neither told I *any* man what my God had put in my heart to do at Jerusalem: neither *was there any* beast with me, save the beast that I rode upon.

13And I went out by night by the gate of the valley, even before the dragon well, and to the dung port, and viewed the walls of Jerusalem, which were broken down, and the gates thereof were consumed with fire.

14Then I went on to the gate of the fountain, and to the king's pool: but *there was* no place for the beast *that was* under me to pass.

15Then went I up in the night by the brook, and viewed the wall, and turned back, and entered by the gate of the valley, and *so* returned.

16And the rulers knew not whither I went, or what I did; neither had I as yet told *it* to the Jews, nor to the priests, nor to the nobles, nor to the rulers, nor to the rest that did the work.

17Then said I unto them, Ye see the distress that we *are* in, how Jerusalem *lieth* waste, and the gates thereof are burned with fire: come, and let us build up the wall of Jerusalem, that we be no more a reproach.

18Then I told them of the hand of my God which was good upon me; as also the king's words that he had spoken unto me. And they said, Let us rise up and build. So they strengthened their hands for *this* good *work.*

19But when Sanballat the Horonite, and Tobiah the servant, the Ammonite, and Geshem the Arabian, heard *it,* they laughed us to scorn, and despised us, and said, What *is* this thing that ye do? will ye rebel against the king?

20Then answered I them, and said unto them, the God of heaven, he will prosper us; therefore we his servants will arise and build: but ye have no portion, nor right, nor memorial, in Jerusalem.

THEN Eliashib the high priest rose up with his brethren the priests, and they builded the sheep gate; they sanctified it, and set up the doors of it; even unto the tower of Meah they sanctified it, unto the tower of Hananeel.

2And next unto him builded the men of Jericho. And next to them builded Zaccur the son of Imri.

3But the fish gate did the sons of Hassenaah build, who *also* laid the beams thereof, and set up the doors thereof, the locks thereof, and the bars thereof.

4And next unto them repaired Meremoth the son of Urijah, the son of Koz. And next unto them repaired Meshullam the son of Berechiah, the son of Meshezabeel. And next unto them repaired Zadok the son of Baana.

5And next unto them the Tekoites repaired; but their nobles put not their necks to the work of their Lord.

6Moreover the old gate repaired Jehoiada the son of Paseah, and Meshullam the son of Besodeiah; they laid the beams thereof, and set up the doors thereof, and the locks thereof, and the bars thereof.

7And next unto them repaired Melatiah the Gibeonite, and Jadon the Meronothite, the men of Gibeon, and of Mizpah, unto the throne of the governor on this side the river.

8Next unto him repaired Uzziel the son of Harhaiah, of the goldsmiths. Next unto him also repaired Hananiah the son of *one of* the apothecaries, and they fortified Jerusalem unto the broad wall.

9And next unto them repaired Rephaiah the son of Hur, the ruler of the half part of Jerusalem.

10And next unto them repaired Jedaiah the son of Harumaph, even over against his house. And next unto him repaired Hattush the son of Hashabniah.

11Malchijah the son of Harim, and Hashub the son of Pahathmoab, repaired the other piece, and the tower of the furnaces.

12And next unto him repaired Shallum the son of Halohesh, the ruler of the half part of Jerusalem, he and his daughters.

13The valley gate repaired Hanun, and the inhabitants of Zanoah; they built it, and set up the doors thereof, the locks thereof, and the bars thereof, and a thousand cubits on the wall unto the dung gate.

14But the dung gate repaired Malchiah the son of Rechab, the ruler of part of Beth–haccerem; he built it, and set up the doors thereof, the locks thereof, and the bars thereof.

1 CORINTHIANS 7:1–19

Now concerning the things whereof ye wrote unto me: *It is* good for a man not to touch a woman.

2Nevertheless, *to avoid* fornication, let every man have his own wife, and let every woman have her own husband.

3Let the husband render unto the wife due benevolence: and likewise also the wife unto the husband.

4The wife hath not power of her own body, but the husband: and likewise also the husband hath not power of his own body, but the wife.

5Defraud ye not one the other, except *it be* with consent for a time, that ye may give yourselves to fasting and prayer; and come together again, that Satan tempt you not for your incontinency.

6But I speak this by permission, *and* not of commandment.

7For I would that all men were even as I myself. But every man hath his proper gift of God, one after this manner, and another after that.

8I say therefore to the unmarried and widows, It is good for them if they abide even as I.

9But if they cannot contain, let them marry: for it is better to marry than to burn.

10And unto the married I command, *yet* not I, but the Lord, Let not the wife depart from *her* husband:

11But and if she depart, let her remain unmarried, or be reconciled to *her* husband: and let not the husband put away *his* wife.

12But to the rest speak I, not the Lord: If any brother hath a wife that believeth not, and she be pleased to dwell with him, let him not put her away.

13And the woman which hath an husband that believeth not, and if he be pleased to dwell with her, let her not leave him.

14For the unbelieving husband is sanctified by the wife, and the unbelieving wife is sanctified by the husband: else were your children unclean; but now are they holy.

15But if the unbelieving depart, let him depart. A brother or a sister is not under bondage in such *cases:* but God hath called us to peace.

16For what knowest thou, O wife, whether thou shalt save *thy* husband? or how knowest thou, O man, whether thou shalt save *thy* wife?

17But as God hath distributed to every man, as the Lord hath called every one, so let him walk. And so ordain I in all churches.

18Is any man called being circumcised? let him not become uncircumcised. Is any called in uncircumcision? let him not be circumcised.

19Circumcision is nothing, and uncircumcision is nothing, but the keeping of the commandments of God.

PSALM 31:19–24

OH how great *is* thy goodness, which thou hast laid up for them that fear thee; *which* thou hast wrought for them that trust in thee before the sons of men!

20Thou shalt hide them in the secret of thy presence from the pride of man: thou shalt keep them secretly in a pavilion from the strife of tongues.

21Blessed *be* the LORD: for he hath shewed me his marvellous kindness in a strong city.

22For I said in my haste, I am cut off from before thine eyes: nevertheless thou heardest the voice of my supplications when I cried unto thee.

23O love the LORD, all ye his saints: *for* the LORD preserveth the faithful, and plentifully rewardeth the proud doer.

24Be of good courage, and he shall strengthen your heart, all ye that hope in the LORD.

PROVERBS FOR TODAY/ 21:4

An high look, and a proud heart, and *the plowing of the wicked,* is *sin.*

AUGUST 12

NEHEMIAH 3:15—5:13

BUT the gate of the fountain repaired Shallun the son of Colhozeh, the ruler of part of Mizpah; he built it, and covered it, and set up the doors thereof, the locks thereof, and the bars thereof, and the wall of the pool of Siloah by the king's garden, and unto the stairs that go down from the city of David.

16After him repaired Nehemiah the son of Azbuk, the ruler of the half part of Bethzur, unto *the place* over against the sepulchres of David, and to the pool that was made, and unto the house of the mighty.

17After him repaired the Levites, Rehum the son of Bani. Next unto him repaired Hashabiah, the ruler of the half part of Keilah, in his part.

18After him repaired their brethren, Bavai the son of Henadad, the ruler of the half part of Keilah.

19And next to him repaired Ezer the son of Jeshua, the ruler of Mizpah, another piece over against the going up to the armoury at the turning *of the wall.*

20After him Baruch the son of Zabbai earnestly repaired the other piece, from the turning *of the wall* unto the door of the house of Eliashib the high priest.

21After him repaired Meremoth the son of Urijah the son of Koz another piece, from the door of the house of Eliashib even to the end of the house of Eliashib.

22And after him repaired the priests, the men of the plain.

23After him repaired Benjamin and Hashub over against their house. After him repaired Azariah the son of Maaseiah the son of Ananiah by his house.

24After him repaired Binnui the son of Henadad another piece, from the house of Azariah unto the turning *of the wall,* even unto the corner.

25Palal the son of Uzai, over against the turning *of the wall,* and the tower which lieth out from the king's high house, that *was* by the court of the prison. After him Pedaiah the son of Parosh.

26Moreover the Nethinims dwelt in Ophel, unto *the place* over against the water gate toward the east, and the tower that lieth out.

27After them the Tekoites repaired another piece, over against the great tower that lieth out, even unto the wall of Ophel.

28From above the horse gate repaired the priests, every one over against his house.

29After them repaired Zadok the son of Immer over against his house. After him repaired also Shemaiah the son of Shechaniah, the keeper of the east gate.

30After him repaired Hananiah the son of Shelemiah, and Hanun the sixth son of Zalaph, another piece. After him repaired Meshullam the son of Berechiah over against his chamber.

31After him repaired Malchiah the goldsmith's son unto the place of the Nethinims, and of the merchants, over against the gate Miphkad, and to the going up of the corner.

32And between the going up of the corner unto the sheep gate repaired the goldsmiths and the merchants.

But it came to pass, that when Sanballat heard that we builded the wall, he was wroth, and took great indignation, and mocked the Jews.

2And he spake before his brethren and the army of Samaria, and said, What do these feeble Jews? will they fortify themselves? will they sacrifice? will they make an end in a day? will they revive the stones out of the heaps of the rubbish which are burned?

3Now Tobiah the Ammonite *was* by him, and he said, Even that which they build, if a fox go up, he shall even break down their stone wall.

4Hear, O our God; for we are despised: and turn their reproach upon their own head, and give them for a prey in the land of captivity:

5And cover not their iniquity, and let not their sin be blotted out from before thee: for they have provoked *thee* to anger before the builders.

6So built we the wall; and all the wall was joined together unto the half thereof: for the people had a mind to work.

7But it came to pass, *that* when Sanballat, and Tobiah, and the Arabians, and the Ammonites, and the Ashdodites, heard that the walls of Jerusalem were made up, *and* that the breaches began to be stopped, then they were very wroth,

8And conspired all of them together to come *and* to fight against Jerusalem, and to hinder it.

9Nevertheless we made our prayer unto our God, and set a watch against them day and night, because of them.

10And Judah said, The strength of the bearers of burdens is decayed, and *there is* much rubbish; so that we are not able to build the wall.

11And our adversaries said, They shall not know, neither see, till we come in the midst among them, and slay them, and cause the work to cease.

12And it came to pass, that when the Jews which dwelt by them came, they said unto us ten times, From all places whence ye shall return unto us *they will be upon you.*

13Therefore set I in the lower places behind the wall, *and* on the higher places, I even set the people after their families with their swords, their spears, and their bows.

14And I looked, and rose up, and said unto the nobles, and to the rulers, and to the rest of the people, Be not ye afraid of them: remember the Lord, *which is* great and terrible, and fight for your brethren, your sons, and your daughters, your wives, and your houses.

15And it came to pass, when our enemies heard that it was known unto us, and God had brought their counsel to nought, that we returned all of us to the wall, every one unto his work.

16And it came to pass from that time forth, *that* the half of my servants wrought in the work, and the other half of them held both the spears, the shields, and the bows, and the habergeons; and the rulers *were* behind all the house of Judah.

17They which builded on the wall, and they that bare burdens, with those that laded, *every one* with one of his hands wrought in the work, and with the other *hand* held a weapon.

18For the builders, every one had his sword girded by his side, and *so* builded. And he that sounded the trumpet *was* by me.

19And I said unto the nobles, and to the rulers, and to the rest of the people, The work *is* great and large, and we are separated upon the wall, one far from another.

20In what place *therefore* ye hear the sound of the trumpet, resort ye thither unto us: our God shall fight for us.

21So we laboured in the work: and half of them held the spears from the rising of the morning till the stars appeared.

22Likewise at the same time said I unto the people, Let every one with his servant lodge within Jerusalem, that in the night they may be a guard to us, and labour on the day.

23So neither I, nor my brethren, nor my servants, nor the men of the guard which followed me, none of us put off our clothes, *saving that* every one put them off for washing.

AND there was a great cry of the people and of their wives against their brethren the Jews.

2For there were that said, We, our sons, and our daughters, *are* many: therefore we take up corn *for them,* that we may eat, and live.

3*Some* also there were that said, We have mortgaged our lands, vineyards, and houses, that we might buy corn, because of the dearth.

4There were also that said, We have borrowed money for the king's tribute, *and that upon* our lands and vineyards.

5Yet now our flesh *is* as the flesh

of our brethren, our children as their children: and, lo, we bring into bondage our sons and our daughters to be servants, and *some* of our daughters are brought unto bondage *already:* neither *is it* in our power to *redeem them;* for other men have our lands and vineyards.

⁶And I was very angry when I heard their cry and these words.

⁷Then I consulted with myself, and I rebuked the nobles, and the rulers, and said unto them, Ye exact usury, every one of his brother. And I set a great assembly against them.

⁸And I said unto them, We after our ability have redeemed our brethren the Jews, which were sold unto the heathen; and will ye even sell your brethren? or shall they be sold unto us? Then held they their peace, and found nothing *to answer.*

⁹Also I said, It *is* not good that ye do: ought ye not to walk in the fear of our God because of the reproach of the heathen our enemies?

¹⁰I likewise, *and* my brethren, and my servants, might exact of them money and corn: I pray you, let us leave off this usury.

¹¹Restore, I pray you, to them, even this day, their lands, their vineyards, their oliveyards, and their houses, also the hundredth *part* of the money, and of the corn, the wine, and the oil, that ye exact of them.

¹²Then said they, We will restore *them,* and will require nothing of them; so will we do as thou sayest. Then I called the priests, and took an oath of them, that they should do according to this promise.

¹³Also I shook my lap, and said, So God shake out every man from his house, and from his labour, that performeth not this promise, even thus be he shaken out, and emptied. And all the congregation said, Amen, and praised the LORD. And the people did according to this promise.

1 CORINTHIANS 7:20–40

LET every man abide in the same calling wherein he was called. ²¹Art thou called *being* a servant? care not for it: but if thou mayest be made free, use *it* rather.

²²For he that is called in the Lord, *being* a servant, is the Lord's freeman: likewise also he that is called, *being* free, is Christ's servant.

²³Ye are bought with a price; be not ye the servants of men.

²⁴Brethren, let every man, wherein he is called, therein abide with God.

²⁵Now concerning virgins I have no commandment of the Lord: yet I give my judgment, as one that hath obtained mercy of the Lord to be faithful.

²⁶I suppose therefore that this is good for the present distress, *I say,* that *it is* good for a man so to be.

²⁷Art thou bound unto a wife? seek not to be loosed. Art thou loosed from a wife? seek not a wife.

²⁸But and if thou marry, thou hast not sinned; and if a virgin marry, she hath not sinned. Nevertheless such shall have trouble in the flesh: but I spare you.

²⁹But this I say, brethren, the time *is* short: it remaineth, that both they that have wives be as though they had none;

³⁰And they that weep, as though they wept not; and they that rejoice, as though they rejoiced not; and they that buy, as though they possessed not;

³¹And they that use this world, as not abusing *it:* for the fashion of this world passeth away.

³²But I would have you without carefulness. He that is unmarried careth for the things that belong to the Lord, how he may please the Lord:

³³But he that is married careth for the things that are of the world, how he may please *his* wife.

³⁴There is difference *also* between a wife and a virgin. The unmarried woman careth for the things of the Lord,

that she may be holy both in body and in spirit: but she that is married careth for the things of the world, how she may please *her* husband.

35And this I speak for your own profit; not that I may cast a snare upon you, but for that which is comely, and that ye may attend upon the Lord without distraction.

36But if any man think that he behaveth himself uncomely toward his virgin, if she pass the flower of *her* age, and need so require, let him do what he will, he sinneth not: let them marry.

37Nevertheless he that standeth stedfast in his heart, having no necessity, but hath power over his own will, and hath so decreed in his heart that he will keep his virgin, doeth well.

38So then he that giveth *her* in marriage doeth well; but he that giveth *her* not in marriage doeth better.

39The wife is bound by the law as long as her husband liveth; but if her husband be dead, she is at liberty to be married to whom she will; only in the Lord.

40But she is happier if she so abide, after my judgment: and I think also that I have the Spirit of God.

PSALM 32:1–11

Blessed *is he whose* transgression is forgiven, *whose* sin *is* covered.

2Blessed *is* the man unto whom the Lord imputeth not iniquity, and in whose spirit *there is* no guile.

3When I kept silence, my bones waxed old through my roaring all the day long.

4For day and night thy hand was heavy upon me: my moisture is turned into the drought of summer. Selah.

5I acknowledged my sin unto thee, and mine iniquity have I not hid. I said, I will confess my transgressions unto the Lord; and thou forgavest the iniquity of my sin. Selah.

6For this shall every one that is godly pray unto thee in a time when thou mayest be found: surely in the floods of great waters they shall not come nigh unto him.

7Thou *art* my hiding place; thou shalt preserve me from trouble; thou shalt compass me about with songs of deliverance. Selah.

8I will instruct thee and teach thee in the way which thou shalt go: I will guide thee with mine eye.

9Be ye not as the horse, *or* as the mule, *which* have no understanding: whose mouth must be held in with bit and bridle, lest they come near unto thee.

10Many sorrows *shall be* to the wicked: but he that trusteth in the Lord, mercy shall compass him about.

11Be glad in the Lord, and rejoice, ye righteous: and shout for joy, all *ye that are* upright in heart.

PROVERBS FOR TODAY/ 21:5–7

The thoughts of the diligent tend *only to plenteousness; but of every one* that is *hasty only to want.* □ *The getting of treasures by a lying tongue* is *a vanity tossed to and fro of them that seek death.* □ *The robbery of the wicked shall destroy them; because they refuse to do judgment.*

AUGUST 13

NEHEMIAH 5:14—7:60

MOREOVER from the time that I was appointed to be their governor in the land of Judah, from the twentieth year even unto the two and thirtieth year of Artaxerxes the king, *that is,* twelve years, I and my brethren have not eaten the bread of the governor.

15But the former governors that *had been* before me were chargeable unto the people, and had taken of them bread and wine, beside forty shekels of silver; yea, even their servants bare rule over the people: but so did not I, because of the fear of God.

16Yea, also I continued in the work of this wall, neither bought we any land: and all my servants *were* gathered thither unto the work.

17Moreover *there were* at my table an hundred and fifty of the Jews and rulers, beside those that came unto us from among the heathen that *are* about us.

18Now *that* which was prepared *for me* daily *was* one ox *and* six choice sheep; also fowls were prepared for me and once in ten days store of all sorts of wine: yet for all this required not I the bread of the governor, because the bondage was heavy upon this people.

19Think upon me, my God, for good, *according* to all that I have done for this people.

Now it came to pass, when Sanballat, and Tobiah, and Geshem the Arabian, and the rest of our enemies, heard that I had builded the wall, and *that* there was no breach left therein; (though at that time I had not set up the doors upon the gates;)

2That Sanballat and Geshem sent unto me, saying, Come, let us meet together in *some one of* the villages in the plain of Ono. But they thought to do me mischief.

3And I sent messengers unto them, saying, I *am* doing a great work, so that I cannot come down: why should the work cease, whilst I leave it, and come down to you?

4Yet they sent unto me four times after this sort; and I answered them after the same manner.

5Then sent Sanballat his servant unto me in like manner the fifth time with an open letter in his hand;

6Wherein *was* written, It is reported among the heathen, and Gashmu saith *it, that* thou and the Jews think to rebel: for which cause thou buildest the wall, that thou mayest be their king, according to these words.

7And thou hast also appointed prophets to preach of thee at Jerusalem, saying, *There is* a king in Judah: and now shall it be reported to the king according to these words. Come now therefore, and let us take counsel together.

8Then I sent unto him, saying, There are no such things done as thou sayest, but thou feignest them out of thine own heart.

9For they all made us afraid, saying, Their hands shall be weakened from the work, that it be not done. Now therefore, *O God,* strengthen my hands.

10Afterward I came unto the house of Shemaiah the son of Delaiah the son of Mehetabeel, who *was* shut up; and he said, Let us meet together in the house of God, within the temple, and let us shut the doors of the temple: for they will come to slay thee; yea, in the night will they come to slay thee.

¹¹And I said, Should such a man as I flee? and who *is there,* that, *being* as I *am,* would go into the temple to save his life? I will not go in.

¹²And, lo, I perceived that God had not sent him; but that he pronounced this prophecy against me: for Tobiah and Sanballat had hired him.

¹³Therefore *was* he hired, that I should be afraid, and do so, and sin, and *that* they might have *matter* for an evil report, that they might reproach me.

¹⁴My God, think thou upon Tobiah and Sanballat according to these their works, and on the prophetess Noadiah, and the rest of the prophets, that would have put me in fear.

¹⁵So the wall was finished in the twenty and fifth *day* of *the month* Elul, in fifty and two days.

¹⁶And it came to pass, that when all our enemies heard *thereof,* and all the heathen that *were* about us saw *these things,* they were much cast down in their own eyes: for they perceived that this work was wrought of our God.

¹⁷Moreover in those days the nobles of Judah sent many letters unto Tobiah, and *the letters* of Tobiah came unto them.

¹⁸For *there were* many in Judah sworn unto him, because he *was* the son in law of Shechaniah the son of Arah; and his son Johanan had taken the daughter of Meshullam the son of Berechiah.

¹⁹Also they reported his good deeds before me, and uttered my words to him. *And* Tobiah sent letters to put me in fear.

Now it came to pass, when the wall was built, and I had set up the doors, and the porters and the singers and the Levites were appointed,

²That I gave my brother Hanani, and Hananiah the ruler of the palace, charge over Jerusalem: for he *was* a faithful man, and feared God above many.

³And I said unto them, Let not the gates of Jerusalem be opened until the sun be hot; and while they stand by, let them shut the doors, and bar *them:* and appoint watches of the inhabitants of Jerusalem, every one in his watch, and every one *to be* over against his house.

⁴Now the city *was* large and great: but the people *were* few therein, and the houses *were* not builded.

⁵And my God put into mine heart to gather together the nobles, and the rulers, and the people, that they might be reckoned by genealogy. And I found a register of the genealogy of them which came up at the first and found written therein,

⁶These *are* the children of the province, that went up out of the captivity, of those that had been carried away, whom Nebuchadnezzar the king of Babylon had carried away, and came again to Jerusalem and to Judah, every one unto his city;

⁷Who came with Zerubbabel, Jeshua, Nehemiah, Azariah, Raamiah, Nahamani, Mordecai, Bilshan, Mispereth, Bigvai, Nehum, Baanah. The number, *I say,* of the men of the people of Israel *was this;*

⁸The children of Parosh, two thousand an hundred seventy and two.

⁹The children of Shephatiah, three hundred seventy and two.

¹⁰The children of Arah, six hundred fifty and two.

¹¹The children of Pahath–moab, of the children of Jeshua and Joab, two thousand and eight hundred *and* eighteen.

¹²The children of Elam, a thousand two hundred fifty and four.

¹³The children of Zattu, eight hundred forty and five.

¹⁴The children of Zaccai, seven hundred and threescore.

¹⁵The children of Binnui, six hundred forty and eight.

16The children of Bebai, six hundred twenty and eight.

17The children of Azgad, two thousand three hundred twenty and two.

18The children of Adonikam, six hundred threescore and seven.

19The children of Bigvai, two thousand threescore and seven.

20The children of Adin, six hundred fifty and five.

21The children of Ater of Hezekiah, ninety and eight.

22The children of Hashum, three hundred twenty and eight.

23The children of Bezai, three hundred twenty and four.

24The children of Hariph, an hundred and twelve.

25The children of Gibeon, ninety and five.

26The men of Beth–lehem and Netophah, an hundred fourscore and eight.

27The men of Anathoth, an hundred twenty and eight.

28The men of Beth–azmaveth, forty and two.

29The men of Kirjath–jearim, Chephirah, and Beeroth, seven hundred forty and three.

30The men of Ramah and Gaba, six hundred twenty and one.

31The men of Michmas, an hundred and twenty and two.

32The men of Beth–el and Ai, an hundred twenty and three.

33The men of the other Nebo, fifty and two.

34The children of the other Elam, a thousand two hundred fifty and four.

35The children of Harim, three hundred and twenty.

36The children of Jericho, three hundred forty and five.

37The children of Lod, Hadid, and Ono, seven hundred twenty and one.

38The children of Senaah, three thousand nine hundred and thirty.

39The priests: the children of Jedaiah, of the house of Jeshua, nine hundred seventy and three.

40The children of Immer, a thousand fifty and two.

41The children of Pashur, a thousand two hundred forty and seven.

42The children of Harim, a thousand and seventeen.

43The Levites: the children of Jeshua, of Kadmiel, *and* of the children of Hodevah, seventy and four.

44The singers: the children of Asaph, an hundred forty and eight.

45The porters: the children of Shallum, the children of Ater, the children of Talmon, the children of Akkub, the children of Hatita, the children of Shobai, an hundred thirty and eight.

46The Nethinims: the children of Ziha, the children of Hashupha, the children of Tabbaoth,

47The children of Keros, the children of Sia, the children of Padon,

48The children of Lebana, the children of Hagaba, the children of Shalmai,

49The children of Hanan, the children of Giddel, the children of Gahar,

50The children of Reaiah, the children of Rezin, the children of Nekoda,

51The children of Gazzam, the children of Uzza, the children of Phaseah,

52The children of Besai, the children of Meunim, the children of Nephishesim,

53The children of Bakbuk, the children of Hakupha, the children of Harhur,

54The children of Bazlith, the children of Mehida, the children of Harsha,

55The children of Barkos, the children of Sisera, the children of Tamah,

56The children of Neziah, the children of Hatipha.

57The children of Solomon's servants: the children of Sotai, the children of Sophereth, the children of Perida,

58The children of Jaala, the children of Darkon, the children of Giddel,

59The children of Shephatiah, the children of Hattil, the children of Pochereth of Zebaim, the children of Amon.

60All the Nethinims, and the children

of Solomon's servants, *were* three hundred ninety and two.

1 CORINTHIANS 8:1–13

Now as touching things offered unto idols, we know that we all have knowledge. Knowledge puffeth up, but charity edifieth.

2And if any man think that he knoweth any thing, he knoweth nothing yet as he ought to know.

3But if any man love God, the same is known of him.

4As concerning therefore the eating of those things that are offered in sacrifice unto idols, we know that an idol *is* nothing in the world, and that *there is* none other God but one.

5For though there be that are called gods, whether in heaven or in earth, (as there be gods many, and lords many,)

6But to us *there is but* one God, the Father, of whom *are* all things, and we in him; and one Lord Jesus Christ, by whom *are* all things, and we by him.

7Howbeit *there is* not in every man that knowledge: for some with conscience of the idol unto this hour eat *it* as a thing offered unto an idol; and their conscience being weak is defiled.

8But meat commendeth us not to God: for neither, if we eat, are we the better; neither, if we eat not, are we the worse.

9But take heed lest by any means this liberty of yours become a stumblingblock to them that are weak.

10For if any man see thee which hast knowledge sit at meat in the idol's temple, shall not the conscience of him which is weak be emboldened to eat those things which are offered to idols;

11And through thy knowledge shall the weak brother perish, for whom Christ died?

12But when ye sin so against the brethren, and wound their weak conscience, ye sin against Christ.

13Wherefore, if meat make my brother to offend, I will eat no flesh while the world standeth, lest I make my brother to offend.

PSALM 33:1–11

Rejoice in the Lord, O ye righteous: *for* praise is comely for the upright.

2Praise the Lord with harp: sing unto him with the psaltery *and* an instrument of ten strings.

3Sing unto him a new song; play skilfully with a loud noise.

4For the word of the Lord *is* right; and all his works *are done* in truth.

5He loveth righteousness and judgment: the earth is full of the goodness of the Lord.

6By the word of the Lord were the heavens made; and all the host of them by the breath of his mouth.

7He gathereth the waters of the sea together as an heap: he layeth up the depth in storehouses.

8Let all the earth fear the Lord: let all the inhabitants of the world stand in awe of him.

9For he spake, and it was *done;* he commanded, and it stood fast.

10The Lord bringeth the counsel of the heathen to nought: he maketh the devices of the people of none effect.

11The counsel of the Lord standeth for ever, the thoughts of his heart to all generations.

PROVERBS FOR TODAY/ 21:8–10

The way of man is *froward and strange: but* as for *the pure, his work* is *right.* □ It is *better to dwell in a corner of the housetop, than with a brawling woman in a wide house.* □ *The soul of the wicked desireth evil: his neighbour findeth no favour in his eyes.*

AUGUST 14

NEHEMIAH 7:61—9:21

AND these *were* they which went up *also* from Tel–melah, Tel–haresha, Cherub, Addon, and Immer: but they could not shew their father's house, nor their seed, whether they *were* of Israel.

⁶²The children of Delaiah, the children of Tobiah, the children of Nekoda, six hundred forty and two.

⁶³And of the priests: the children of Habaiah, the children of Koz, the children of Barzillai, which took *one* of the daughters of Barzillai the Gileadite to wife, and was called after their name.

⁶⁴These sought their register *among* those that were reckoned by genealogy, but it was not found: therefore were they, as polluted, put from the priesthood.

⁶⁵And the Tirshatha said unto them, that they should not eat of the most holy things, till there stood *up* a priest with Urim and Thummim.

⁶⁶The whole congregation together *was* forty and two thousand three hundred and threescore,

⁶⁷Beside their manservants and their maidservants, of whom *there were* seven thousand three hundred thirty and seven: and they had two hundred forty and five singing men and singing women.

⁶⁸Their horses, seven hundred thirty and six: their mules, two hundred forty and five:

⁶⁹*Their* camels, four hundred thirty and five: six thousand seven hundred and twenty asses.

⁷⁰And some of the chief of the fathers gave unto the work. The Tirshatha gave to the treasure a thousand drams of gold, fifty basons, five hundred and thirty priests' garments.

⁷¹And *some* of the chief of the fathers gave to the treasure of the work twenty thousand drams of gold, and two thousand and two hundred pound of silver.

⁷²And *that* which the rest of the people gave *was* twenty thousand drams of gold, and two thousand pound of silver, and threescore and seven priests' garments.

⁷³So the priests, and the Levites, and the porters, and the singers, and *some* of the people, and the Nethinims, and all Israel, dwelt in their cities; and when the seventh month came, the children of Israel *were* in their cities.

AND all the people gathered themselves together as one man into the street that *was* before the water gate; and they spake unto Ezra the scribe to bring the book of the law of Moses, which the LORD had commanded to Israel.

²And Ezra the priest brought the law before the congregation both of men and women, and all that could hear with understanding, upon the first day of the seventh month.

³And he read therein before the street that *was* before the water gate from the morning until midday, before the men and the women, and those that could understand; and the ears of

all the people *were attentive* unto the book of the law.

4And Ezra the scribe stood upon a pulpit of wood, which they had made for the purpose; and beside him stood Mattithiah, and Shema, and Anaiah, and Urijah, and Hilkiah, and Maaseiah, on his right hand; and on his left hand, Pedaiah, and Mishael, and Malchiah, and Hashum, and Hashbadana, Zechariah, *and* Meshullam.

5And Ezra opened the book in the sight of all the people; (for he was above all the people;) and when he opened it, all the people stood up:

6And Ezra blessed the LORD, the great God. And all the people answered, Amen, Amen, with lifting up their hands: and they bowed their heads, and worshipped the LORD with *their* faces to the ground.

7Also Jeshua, and Bani, and Sherebiah, Jamin, Akkub, Shabbethai, Hodijah, Maaseiah, Kelita, Azariah, Jozabad, Hanan, Pelaiah, and the Levites, caused the people to understand the law: and the people *stood* in their place.

8So they read in the book in the law of God distinctly, and gave the sense, and caused *them* to understand the reading.

9And Nehemiah, which *is* the Tirshatha, and Ezra the priest the scribe, and the Levites that taught the people, said unto all the people, This day *is* holy unto the LORD your God; mourn not, nor weep. For all the people wept, when they heard the words of the law.

10Then he said unto them, Go your way, eat the fat, and drink the sweet, and send portions unto them for whom nothing is prepared: for *this* day *is* holy unto our Lord: neither be ye sorry; for the joy of the LORD is your strength.

11So the Levites stilled all the people, saying, Hold your peace, for the day *is* holy; neither be ye grieved.

12And all the people went their way to eat, and to drink, and to send portions, and to make great mirth, because they had understood the words that were declared unto them.

13And on the second day were gathered together the chief of the fathers of all the people, the priests, and the Levites, unto Ezra the scribe, even to understand the words of the law.

14And they found written in the law which the LORD had commanded by Moses, that the children of Israel should dwell in booths in the feast of the seventh month:

15And that they should publish and proclaim in all their cities, and in Jerusalem, saying, Go forth unto the mount, and fetch olive branches, and pine branches, and myrtle branches, and palm branches, and branches of thick trees, to make booths, as *it is* written.

16So the people went forth, and brought *them,* and made themselves booths, every one upon the roof of his house, and in their courts, and in the courts of the house of God, and in the street of the water gate, and in the street of the gate of Ephraim.

17And all the congregation of them that were come again out of the captivity made booths, and sat under the booths: for since the days of Jeshua the son of Nun unto that day had not the children of Israel done so. And there was very great gladness.

18Also day by day, from the first day unto the last day, he read in the book of the law of God. And they kept the feast seven days; and on the eighth day *was* a solemn assembly, according unto the manner.

Now in the twenty and fourth day of this month the children of Israel were assembled with fasting, and with sackclothes, and earth upon them.

2And the seed of Israel separated

themselves from all strangers, and stood and confessed their sins, and the iniquities of their fathers.

3And they stood up in their place, and read in the book of the law of the LORD their God *one* fourth part of the day; and *another* fourth part they confessed, and worshipped the LORD their God.

4Then stood up upon the stairs, of the Levites, Jeshua, and Bani, Kadmiel, Shebaniah, Bunni, Sherebiah, Bani *and* Chenani, and cried with a loud voice unto the LORD their God.

5Then the Levites, Jeshua, and Kadmiel, Bani, Hashabniah, Sherebiah, Hodijah, Shebaniah, *and* Pethahiah, said, Stand up *and* bless the LORD your God for ever and ever: and blessed be thy glorious name, which is exalted above all blessing and praise.

6Thou, *even* thou, *art* LORD alone; thou hast made heaven, the heaven of heavens, with all their host, the earth, and all *things* that *are* therein, the seas, and all that *is* therein, and thou preservest them all; and the host of heaven worshippeth thee.

7Thou *art* the LORD the God, who didst choose Abram, and broughtest him forth out of Ur of the Chaldees, and gavest him the name of Abraham;

8And foundest his heart faithful before thee, and madest a covenant with him to give the land of the Canaanites, the Hittites, the Amorites, and the Perizzites, and the Jebusites, and the Girgashites, to give *it, I say,* to his seed, and hast performed thy words; for thou *art* righteous:

9And didst see the affliction of our fathers in Egypt, and heardest their cry by the Red sea;

10And shewedst signs and wonders upon Pharaoh, and on all his servants, and on all the people of his land: for thou knewest that they dealt proudly against them. So didst thou get thee a name, as *it is* this day.

11And thou didst divide the sea before them, so that they went through the midst of the sea on the dry land; and their persecutors thou threwest into the deeps, as a stone into the mighty waters.

12Moreover thou leddest them in the day by a cloudy pillar; and in the night by a pillar of fire, to give them light in the way wherein they should go.

13Thou camest down also upon mount Sinai, and spakest with them from heaven, and gavest them right judgments, and true laws, good statutes and commandments:

14And madest known unto them thy holy sabbath, and commandedst them precepts, statutes, and laws, by the hand of Moses thy servant:

15And gavest them bread from heaven for their hunger, and broughtest forth water for them out of the rock for their thirst, and promisedst them that they should go in to possess the land which thou hadst sworn to give them.

16But they and our fathers dealt proudly, and hardened their necks, and hearkened not to thy commandments,

17And refused to obey, neither were mindful of thy wonders that thou didst among them; but hardened their necks, and in their rebellion appointed a captain to return to their bondage: but thou *art* a God ready to pardon, gracious and merciful, slow to anger, and of great kindness, and forsookest them not.

18Yea, when they had made them a molten calf, and said, This *is* thy god that brought thee up out of Egypt, and had wrought great provocations;

19Yet thou in thy manifold mercies forsookest them not in the wilderness: the pillar of the cloud departed not from them by day, to lead them in the way; neither the pillar of fire by night, to shew them light, and the way wherein they should go.

20Thou gavest also thy good spirit to instruct them, and withheldest not thy manna from their mouth, and gavest them water for their thirst.

21Yea, forty years didst thou sustain them in the wilderness, *so that* they lacked nothing; their clothes waxed not old, and their feet swelled not.

1 CORINTHIANS 9:1–19

A M I not an apostle? am I not free? have I not seen Jesus Christ our Lord? are not ye my work in the Lord?

2If I be not an apostle unto others, yet doubtless I am to you: for the seal of mine apostleship are ye in the Lord.

3Mine answer to them that do examine me is this,

4Have we not power to eat and to drink?

5Have we not power to lead about a sister, a wife, as well as other apostles, and *as* the brethren of the Lord, and Cephas?

6Or I only and Barnabas, have not we power to forbear working?

7Who goeth a warfare any time at his own charges? who planteth a vineyard, and eateth not of the fruit thereof? or who feedeth a flock, and eateth not of the milk of the flock?

8Say I these things as a man? or saith not the law the same also?

9For it is written in the law of Moses, Thou shalt not muzzle the mouth of the ox that treadeth out the corn. Doth God take care for oxen?

10Or saith he *it* altogether for our sakes? For our sakes, no doubt, *this* is written: that he that ploweth should plow in hope; and that he that thresheth in hope should be partaker of his hope.

11If we have sown unto you spiritual things, *is it* a great thing if we shall reap your carnal things?

12If others be partakers of *this* power over you, *are* not we rather? Nevertheless we have not used this power; but suffer all things, lest we should hinder the gospel of Christ.

13Do ye not know that they which minister about holy things live *of the things* of the temple? and they which wait at the altar are partakers with the altar?

14Even so hath the Lord ordained that they which preach the gospel should live of the gospel.

15But I have used none of these things: neither have I written these things, that it should be so done unto me: for *it were* better for me to die, than that any man should make my glorying void.

16For though I preach the gospel, I have nothing to glory of: for necessity is laid upon me; yea, woe is unto me, if I preach not the gospel!

17For if I do this thing willingly, I have a reward: but if against my will, a dispensation *of the gospel* is committed unto me.

18What is my reward then? *Verily* that, when I preach the gospel, I may make the gospel of Christ without charge, that I abuse not my power in the gospel.

19For though I be free from all *men,* yet have I made myself servant unto all, that I might gain the more.

PSALM 33:12–22

B LESSED *is* the nation whose God *is* the LORD: *and* the people *whom* he hath chosen for his own inheritance.

13The LORD looketh from heaven; he beholdeth all the sons of men.

14From the place of his habitation he looketh upon all the inhabitants of the earth.

15He fashioneth their hearts alike; he considereth all their works.

16There is no king saved by the multitude of an host: a mighty man is not delivered by much strength.

17An horse *is* a vain thing for safety: neither shall he deliver *any* by his great strength.

18Behold, the eye of the LORD *is* upon them that fear him, upon them that hope in his mercy;

19To deliver their soul from death, and to keep them alive in famine.

20Our soul waiteth for the LORD: he *is* our help and our shield.

21For our heart shall rejoice in him, because we have trusted in his holy name.

22Let thy mercy, O LORD, be upon us, according as we hope in thee.

PROVERBS FOR TODAY/ 21:11–12

When the scorner is punished, the simple is made wise: and when the wise is instructed, he receiveth knowledge. □ *The righteous* man *wisely considereth the house of the wicked:* but God *overthroweth the wicked for* their *wickedness.*

AUGUST 15

NEHEMIAH 9:22—10:39

MOREOVER thou gavest them kingdoms and nations, and didst divide them into corners: so they possessed the land of Sihon, and the land of the king of Heshbon, and the land of Og king of Bashan.

23Their children also multipliedst thou as the stars of heaven, and broughtest them into the land, concerning which thou hadst promised to their fathers, that they should go in to possess *it.*

24So the children went in and possessed the land, and thou subduedst before them the inhabitants of the land, the Canaanites, and gavest them into their hands, with their kings, and the people of the land, that they might do with them as they would.

25And they took strong cities, and a fat land, and possessed houses full of all goods, wells digged, vineyards, and oliveyards, and fruit trees in abundance: so they did eat, and were filled, and became fat, and delighted them-

selves in thy great goodness.

26Nevertheless they were disobedient, and rebelled against thee, and cast thy law behind their backs, and slew thy prophets which testified against them to turn them to thee, and they wrought great provocations.

27Therefore thou deliveredst them into the hand of their enemies, who vexed them: and in the time of their trouble, when they cried unto thee, thou heardest *them* from heaven; and according to thy manifold mercies thou gavest them saviours, who saved them out of the hand of their enemies.

28But after they had rest, they did evil again before thee: therefore leftest thou them in the hand of their enemies, so that they had the dominion over them: yet when they returned, and cried unto thee, thou heardest *them* from heaven; and many times didst thou deliver them according to thy mercies;

29And testifiedst against them, that thou mightest bring them again unto thy law: yet they dealt proudly, and hearkened not unto thy commandments, but sinned against thy judgments, (which if a man do, he shall live in them;) and withdrew the shoulder, and hardened their neck, and would not hear.

30Yet many years didst thou forbear them, and testifiedst against them by thy spirit in thy prophets: yet would they not give ear: therefore gavest thou them into the hand of the people of the lands.

31Nevertheless for thy great mercies' sake thou didst not utterly consume them, nor forsake them; for thou *art* a gracious and merciful God.

32Now therefore, our God, the great, the mighty, and the terrible God, who keepest covenant and mercy, let not all the trouble seem little before thee, that hath come upon us, on our kings, on our princes, and on our priests, and on our prophets, and on our fathers, and on all thy people, since the time of the kings of Assyria unto this day.

33Howbeit thou *art* just in all that is brought upon us; for thou hast done right, but we have done wickedly:

34Neither have our kings, our princes, our priests, nor our fathers, kept thy law, nor hearkened unto thy commandments and thy testimonies, wherewith thou didst testify against them.

35For they have not served thee in their kingdom, and in thy great goodness that thou gavest them, and in the large and fat land which thou gavest before them, neither turned they from their wicked works.

36Behold, we *are* servants this day, and *for* the land that thou gavest unto our fathers to eat the fruit thereof and the good thereof, behold, we *are* servants in it:

37And it yieldeth much increase unto the kings whom thou hast set over us because of our sins: also they have dominion over our bodies, and over our cattle, at their pleasure, and we *are* in great distress.

38And because of all this we make a sure *covenant,* and write *it;* and our princes, Levites, *and* priests, seal *unto it.*

Now those that sealed *were,* Nehemiah, the Tirshatha, the son of Hachaliah, and Zidkijah,

2Seraiah, Azariah, Jeremiah,

3Pashur, Amariah, Malchijah,

4Hattush, Shebaniah, Malluch,

5Harim, Meremoth, Obadiah,

6Daniel, Ginnethon, Baruch,

7Meshullam, Abijah, Mijamin,

8Maaziah, Bilgai, Shemaiah: these *were* the priests.

9And the Levites: both Jeshua the son of Azaniah, Binnui of the sons of Henadad, Kadmiel;

10And their brethren, Shebaniah, Hodijah, Kelita, Pelaiah, Hanan,

11Micha, Rehob, Hashabiah,

12Zaccur, Sherebiah, Shebaniah,

13Hodijah, Bani, Beninu.

14The chief of the people; Parosh, Pahath–moab, Elam, Zatthu, Bani,

15Bunni, Azgad, Bebai,

16Adonijah, Bigvai, Adin,

17Ater, Hizkijah, Azzur,

18Hodijah, Hashum, Bezai,

19Hariph, Anathoth, Nebai,

20Magpiash, Meshullam, Hezir,

21Meshezabeel, Zadok, Jaddua,

22Pelatiah, Hanan, Anaiah,

23Hoshea, Hananiah, Hashub,

24Hallohesh, Pileha, Shobek,

25Rehum, Hashabnah, Maaseiah,

26And Ahijah, Hanan, Anan,

27Malluch, Harim, Baanah.

28And the rest of the people, the priests, the Levites, the porters, the singers, the Nethinims, and all they that had separated themselves from the people of the lands unto the law of God, their wives, their sons, and their daughters, every one having knowledge, and having understanding;

29They clave to their brethren, their nobles, and entered into a curse, and into an oath, to walk in God's law, which was given by Moses the servant of God, and to observe and do all the commandments of the LORD our Lord, and his judgments and his statutes;

30And that we would not give our daughters unto the people of the land, nor take their daughters for our sons:

31And *if* the people of the land bring ware or any victuals on the sabbath day to sell, *that* we would not buy it of them on the sabbath, or on the holy day: and *that* we would leave the seventh year, and the exaction of every debt.

32Also we made ordinances for us, to charge ourselves yearly with the third part of a shekel for the service of the house of our God;

33For the shewbread, and for the continual meat offering, and for the continual burnt offering, of the sabbaths, of the new moons, for the set feasts, and for the holy *things*, and for the sin offerings to make an atonement for Israel, and *for* all the work of the house of our God.

34And we cast the lots among the priests, the Levites, and the people, for the wood offering, to bring *it* into the house of our God, after the houses of our fathers, at times appointed year by year, to burn upon the altar of the LORD our God, as *it is* written in the law:

35And to bring the firstfruits of our ground, and the firstfruits of all fruit of all trees, year by year, unto the house of the LORD:

36Also the firstborn of our sons, and of our cattle, as *it is* written in the law, and the firstlings of our herds and of our flocks, to bring to the house of our God, unto the priests that minister in the house of our God:

37And *that* we should bring the firstfruits of our dough, and our offerings, and the fruit of all manner of trees,

of wine and of oil, unto the priests, to the chambers of the house of our God; and the tithes of our ground unto the Levites, that the same Levites might have the tithes in all the cities of our tillage.

38And the priest the son of Aaron shall be with the Levites, when the Levites take tithes: and the Levites shall bring up the tithe of the tithes unto the house of our God, to the chambers, unto the treasure house.

39For the children of Israel and the children of Levi shall bring the offering of the corn, of the new wine, and the oil, unto the chambers, where *are* the vessels of the sanctuary, and the priests that minister, and the porters, and the singers: and we will not forsake the house of our God.

1 CORINTHIANS 9:20—10:14

AND unto the Jews I became as a Jew, that I might gain the Jews; to them that are under the law, as under the law, that I might gain them that are under the law;

21To them that are without law, as without law, (being not without law to God, but under the law to Christ,) that I might gain them that are without law.

22To the weak became I as weak, that I might gain the weak: I am made all things to all *men*, that I might by all means save some.

23And this I do for the gospel's sake, that I might be partaker thereof with *you.*

24Know ye not that they which run in a race run all, but one receiveth the prize? So run, that ye may obtain.

25And every man that striveth for the mastery is temperate in all things. Now they *do it* to obtain a corruptible crown; but we an incorruptible.

26I therefore so run, not as uncertainly; so fight I, not as one that beateth the air:

27But I keep under my body, and

bring *it* into subjection: lest that by any means, when I have preached to others, I myself should be a castaway.

MOREOVER, brethren, I would not that ye should be ignorant, how that all our fathers were under the cloud, and all passed through the sea;

2And were all baptized unto Moses in the cloud and in the sea;

3And did all eat the same spiritual meat;

4And did all drink the same spiritual drink: for they drank of that spiritual Rock that followed them: and that Rock was Christ.

5But with many of them God was not well pleased: for they were overthrown in the wilderness.

6Now these things were our examples, to the intent we should not lust after evil things, as they also lusted.

7Neither be ye idolaters, as *were* some of them; as it is written, The people sat down to eat and drink, and rose up to play.

8Neither let us commit fornication, as some of them committed, and fell in one day three and twenty thousand.

9Neither let us tempt Christ, as some of them also tempted, and were destroyed of serpents.

10Neither murmur ye, as some of them also murmured, and were destroyed of the destroyer.

11Now all these things happened unto them for ensamples: and they are written for our admonition, upon whom the ends of the world are come.

12Wherefore let him that thinketh he standeth take heed lest he fall.

13There hath no temptation taken you but such as is common to man: but God *is* faithful, who will not suffer you to be tempted above that ye are able; but will with the temptation also make a way to escape, that ye may be able to bear *it.*

14Wherefore, my dearly beloved, flee from idolatry.

PSALM 34:1–10

I WILL bless the LORD at all times: his praise *shall* continually *be* in my mouth.

2My soul shall make her boast in the LORD: the humble shall hear *thereof,* and be glad.

3O magnify the LORD with me, and let us exalt his name together.

4I sought the LORD, and he heard me, and delivered me from all my fears.

5They looked unto him, and were lightened: and their faces were not ashamed.

6This poor man cried, and the LORD heard *him,* and saved him out of all his troubles.

7The angel of the LORD encampeth round about them that fear him, and delivereth them.

8O taste and see that the LORD *is* good: blessed *is* the man *that* trusteth in him.

9O fear the LORD, ye his saints: for *there is* no want to them that fear him.

10The young lions do lack, and suffer hunger: but they that seek the LORD shall not want any good *thing.*

PROVERBS FOR TODAY/ 21:13

Whoso stoppeth his ears at the cry of the poor, he also shall cry himself, but shall not be heard.

AUGUST 16

NEHEMIAH 11:1—12:26

AND the rulers of the people dwelt at Jerusalem: the rest of the people also cast lots, to bring one of ten to dwell in Jerusalem the holy city, and nine parts to *dwell* in *other* cities.

2And the people blessed all the men, that willingly offered themselves to dwell at Jerusalem.

3Now these *are* the chief of the province that dwelt in Jerusalem: but in the cities of Judah dwelt every one in his possession in their cities, *to wit,* Israel, the priests, and the Levites, and the Nethinims, and the children of Solomon's servants.

4And at Jerusalem dwelt *certain* of the children of Judah, and of the children of Benjamin. Of the children of Judah; Athaiah the son of Uzziah, the son of Zechariah, the son of Amariah, the son of Shephatiah, the son of Mahalaleel, of the children of Perez;

5And Maaseiah the son of Baruch, the son of Colhozeh, the son of Hazaiah, the son of Adaiah, the son of Joiarib, the son of Zechariah, the son of Shiloni.

6All the sons of Perez that dwelt at Jerusalem *were* four hundred threescore and eight valiant men.

7And these *are* the sons of Benjamin; Sallu the son of Meshullam, the son of Joed, the son of Pedaiah, the son of Kolaiah, the son of Maaseiah, the son of Ithiel, the son of Jesaiah.

8And after him Gabbai, Sallai, nine hundred twenty and eight.

9And Joel the son of Zichri *was* their overseer: and Judah the son of Senuah *was* second over the city.

10Of the priests: Jedaiah the son of Joiarib, Jachin.

11Seraiah the son of Hilkiah, the son of Meshullam, the son of Zadok, the son of Meraioth, the son of Ahitub, *was* the ruler of the house of God.

12And their brethren that did the work of the house *were* eight hundred twenty and two: and Adaiah the son of Jeroham, the son of Pelaliah, the son of Amzi, the son of Zechariah, the son of Pashur, the son of Malchiah,

13And his brethren, chief of the fathers, two hundred forty and two: and Amashai the son of Azareel, the son of Ahasai, the son of Meshillemoth, the son of Immer,

14And their brethren, mighty men of valour, an hundred twenty and eight: and their overseer *was* Zabdiel, the son of *one of* the great men.

15Also of the Levites: Shemaiah the son of Hashub, the son of Azrikam, the son of Hashabiah, the son of Bunni;

16And Shabbethai and Jozabad, of the chief of the Levites, *had* the oversight of the outward business of the house of God.

17And Mattaniah the son of Micha, the son of Zabdi, the son of Asaph *was* the principal to begin the thanksgiving in prayer: and Bakbukiah the second among his brethren, and Abda the son of Shammua, the son of Galal, the son of Jeduthun.

18All the Levites in the holy city *were* two hundred fourscore and four.

19Moreover the porters, Akkub, Talmon, and their brethren that kept the gates, *were* an hundred seventy and two.

20And the residue of Israel, of the priests, *and* the Levites, *were* in all the cities of Judah, every one in his inheritance.

21But the Nethinims dwelt in Ophel: and Ziha and Gispa *were* over the Nethinims.

22The overseer also of the Levites

at Jerusalem *was* Uzzi the son of Bani, the son of Hashabiah, the son of Mattaniah, the son of Micha. Of the sons of Asaph, the singers *were* over the business of the house of God.

23For *it was* the king's commandment concerning them, that a certain portion should be for the singers, due for every day.

24And Pethahiah the son of Meshezabeel, of the children of Zerah the son of Judah, *was* at the king's hand in all matters concerning the people.

25And for the villages, with their fields, *some* of the children of Judah dwelt at Kirjath–arba, and *in* the villages thereof, and at Dibon, and *in* the villages thereof, and at Jekabzeel, and *in* the villages thereof,

26And at Jeshua, and at Moladah, and at Beth–phelet,

27And at Hazar–shual, and at Beer–sheba, and *in* the villages thereof,

28And at Ziklag, and at Mekonah, and in the villages thereof,

29And at En–rimmon, and at Zareah, and at Jarmuth,

30Zanoah, Adullam, and *in* their villages, at Lachish, and the fields thereof, at Azekah, and *in* the villages thereof. And they dwelt from Beer–sheba unto the valley of Hinnom.

31The children also of Benjamin from Geba *dwelt* at Michmash, and Aija, and Beth–el, and *in* their villages,

32*And* at Anathoth, Nob, Ananiah,

33Hazor, Ramah, Gittaim,

34Hadid, Zeboim, Neballat,

35Lod, and Ono, the valley of craftsmen.

36And of the Levites *were* divisions *in* Judah, *and* in Benjamin.

Now these *are* the priests and the Levites that went up with Zerubbabel the son of Shealtiel, and Jeshua: Seraiah, Jeremiah, Ezra,

2Amariah, Malluch, Hattush,

3Shechaniah, Rehum, Meremoth,

4Iddo, Ginnetho, Abijah,

5Miamin, Maadiah, Bilgah,

6Shemaiah, and Joiarib, Jedaiah,

7Sallu, Amok, Hilkiah, Jedaiah. These *were* the chief of the priests and of their brethren in the days of Jeshua.

8Moreover the Levites: Jeshua, Binnui, Kadmiel, Sherebiah, Judah, *and* Mattaniah, *which was* over the thanksgiving, he and his brethren.

9Also Bakbukiah and Unni, their brethren, *were* over against them in the watches.

10And Jeshua begat Joiakim, Joiakim also begat Eliashib, and Eliashib begat Joiada,

11And Joiada begat Jonathan, and Jonathan begat Jaddua.

12And in the days of Joiakim were priests, the chief of the fathers: of Seraiah, Meraiah; of Jeremiah, Hananiah;

13Of Ezra, Meshullam; of Amariah, Jehohanan;

14Of Melicu, Jonathan; of Shebaniah, Joseph;

15Of Harim, Adna; of Meraioth, Helkai;

16Of Iddo, Zechariah; of Ginnethon, Meshullam;

17Of Abijah, Zichri; of Miniamin, of Moadiah, Piltai;

18Of Bilgah, Shammua; of Shemaiah, Jehonathan;

19And of Joiarib, Mattenai; of Jedaiah, Uzzi;

20Of Sallai, Kallai; of Amok, Eber;

21Of Hilkiah, Hashabiah; of Jedaiah, Nethaneel.

22The Levites in the days of Eliashib, Joiada, and Johanan, and Jaddua, *were* recorded chief of the fathers: also the priests, to the reign of Darius the Persian.

23The sons of Levi the chief of the fathers, *were* written in the book of the chronicles, even until the days of Johanan the son of Eliashib.

24And the chief of the Levites: Hashabiah, Sherebiah, and Jeshua the son of Kadmiel, with their brethren over against them, to praise *and* to give thanks, according to the commandment of David the man of God, ward over against ward.

25Mattaniah, and Bakbukiah, Obadiah, Meshullam, Talmon, Akkub, *were* porters keeping the ward at the thresholds of the gates.

26These *were* in the days of Joiakim the son of Jeshua, the son of Jozadak, and in the days of Nehemiah the governor, and of Ezra the priest, the scribe.

1 CORINTHIANS 10:15—11:2

I speak as to wise men; judge ye what I say. 16The cup of blessing which we bless, is it not the communion of the blood of Christ? The bread which we break, is it not the communion of the body of Christ?

17For we *being* many are one bread, *and* one body: for we are all partakers of that one bread.

18Behold Israel after the flesh: are not they which eat of the sacrifices partakers of the altar?

19What say I then? that the idol is any thing, or that which is offered in sacrifice to idols is any thing?

20But *I say,* that the things which the Gentiles sacrifice, they sacrifice to devils, and not to God: and I would not that ye should have fellowship with devils.

21Ye cannot drink the cup of the Lord, and the cup of devils: ye cannot be partakers of the Lord's table, and of the table of devils.

22Do we provoke the Lord to jealousy? are we stronger than he?

23All things are lawful for me, but all things are not expedient: all things are lawful for me, but all things edify not.

24Let no man seek his own, but every man another's *wealth.*

25Whatsoever is sold in the shambles, *that* eat, asking no question for conscience sake:

26For the earth *is* the Lord's, and the fulness thereof.

27If any of them that believe not bid you *to a feast,* and ye be disposed to go; whatsoever is set before you, eat, asking no question for conscience sake.

28But if any man say unto you, This is offered in sacrifice unto idols, eat not for his sake that shewed it, and for conscience sake: for the earth *is* the Lord's, and the fulness thereof:

29Conscience, I say, not thine own, but of the other: for why is my liberty judged of another *man's* conscience?

30For if I by grace be a partaker, why am I evil spoken of for that for which I give thanks?

31Whether therefore ye eat, or drink, or whatsoever ye do, do all to the glory of God.

32Give none offence, neither to the Jews, nor to the Gentiles, nor to the church of God:

33Even as I please all *men* in all *things,* not seeking mine own profit, but the *profit* of many, that they may be saved.

Be ye followers of me, even as I also *am* of Christ. 2Now I praise you, brethren, that ye remember me in all things, and keep the ordinances, as I delivered *them* to you.

PSALM 34:11—22

Come, ye children, hearken unto me: I will teach you the fear of the Lord. 12What man *is* he *that* desireth life, *and* loveth *many* days, that he may see good?

13Keep thy tongue from evil, and thy lips from speaking guile.

14Depart from evil, and do good; seek peace, and pursue it.

15The eyes of the Lord *are* upon the righteous, and his ears *are open* unto their cry.

16The face of the Lord *is* against

them that do evil, to cut off the remembrance of them from the earth.

17The *righteous* cry, and the LORD heareth, and delivereth them out of all their troubles.

18The LORD *is* nigh unto them that are of a broken heart; and saveth such as be of a contrite spirit.

19Many *are* the afflictions of the righteous: but the LORD delivereth him out of them all.

20He keepeth all his bones: not one of them is broken.

21Evil shall slay the wicked: and they that hate the righteous shall be desolate.

22The LORD redeemeth the soul of his servants: and none of them that trust in him shall be desolate.

PROVERBS FOR TODAY/ 21:14-16

A gift in secret pacifieth anger: and a reward in the bosom strong wrath. ☐ It is *joy to the just to do judgment: but destruction* shall be *to the workers of iniquity.* ☐ *The man that wandereth out of the way of understanding shall remain in the congregation of the dead.*

AUGUST 17

NEHEMIAH 12:27—13:31

AND at the dedication of the wall of Jerusalem they sought the Levites out of all their places, to bring them to Jerusalem, to keep the dedication with gladness, both with thanksgivings, and with singing, *with* cymbals, psalteries, and with harps.

28And the sons of the singers gathered themselves together, both out of the plain country round about Jerusalem, and from the villages of Netophathi;

29Also from the house of Gilgal, and out of the fields of Geba and Azmaveth: for the singers had builded them villages round about Jerusalem.

30And the priests and the Levites purified themselves, and purified the people, and the gates, and the wall.

31Then I brought up the princes of Judah upon the wall, and appointed two great *companies of them that gave* thanks, *whereof one* went on the right hand upon the wall toward the dung gate:

32And after them went Hoshaiah, and half of the princes of Judah,

33And Azariah, Ezra, and Meshullam,

34Judah, and Benjamin, and Shemaiah, and Jeremiah,

35And *certain* of the priests' sons with trumpets; *namely,* Zechariah the son of Jonathan, the son of Shemaiah, the son of Mattaniah, the son of Michaiah, the son of Zaccur, the son of Asaph:

36And his brethren, Shemaiah, and Azarael, Milalai, Gilalai, Maai, Nethaneel, and Judah, Hanani, with the musical instruments of David the man of God, and Ezra the scribe before them.

37And at the fountain gate, which was over against them, they went up by the stairs of the city of David, at the going up of the wall, above the house of David, even unto the water gate eastward.

38And the other *company of them that gave* thanks went over against *them,* and I after them, and the half of the people upon the wall, from beyond the tower of the furnaces even unto the broad wall;

39And from above the gate of Ephraim, and above the old gate, and above the fish gate, and the tower of Hananeel, and the tower of Meah, even unto the sheep gate: and they stood still in the prison gate.

40So stood the two *companies of them that gave* thanks in the house of God, and I, and the half of the rulers with me:

41And the priests; Eliakim, Maaseiah, Miniamin, Michaiah, Elioenai, Zechariah, *and* Hananiah, with trumpets;

42And Maaseiah, and Shemaiah, and Eleazar, and Uzzi, and Jehohanan, and Malchijah, and Elam, and Ezer. And the singers sang loud, with Jezrahiah *their* overseer.

43Also that day they offered great sacrifices, and rejoiced: for God had made them rejoice with great joy: the wives also and the children rejoiced: so that the joy of Jerusalem was heard even afar off.

44And at that time were some appointed over the chambers for the treasures, for the offerings, for the firstfruits, and for the tithes, to gather into them out of the fields of the cities the portions of the law for the priests and Levites: for Judah rejoiced for the priests and for the Levites that waited.

45And both the singers and the porters kept the ward of their God, and the ward of the purification, according to the commandment of David, *and* of Solomon his son.

46For in the days of David and Asaph of old *there were* chief of the singers, and songs of praise and thanksgiving unto God.

47And all Israel in the days of Zerubbabel, and in the days of Nehemiah, gave the portions of the singers and the porters, every day his portion: and they sanctified *holy things* unto the Levites; and the Levites sanctified *them* unto the children of Aaron.

ON that day they read in the book of Moses in the audience of the people; and therein was found written, that the Ammonite and the Moabite should not come into the congregation of God for ever;

2Because they met not the children of Israel with bread and with water, but hired Balaam against them, that he should curse them: howbeit our God turned the curse into a blessing.

3Now it came to pass, when they had heard the law, that they separated from Israel all the mixed multitude.

4And before this, Eliashib the priest, having the oversight of the chamber of the house of our God, *was* allied unto Tobiah:

5And he had prepared for him a great chamber, where aforetime they laid the meat offerings, the frankincense, and the vessels, and the tithes of the corn, the new wine, and the oil, which was commanded *to be given* to the Levites, and the singers, and the porters; and the offerings of the priests.

6But in all this *time* was not I at Jerusalem: for in the two and thirtieth year of Artaxerxes king of Babylon came I unto the king, and after certain days obtained I leave of the king:

7And I came to Jerusalem, and understood of the evil that Eliashib did for Tobiah, in preparing him a chamber in the courts of the house of God.

8And it grieved me sore: therefore I cast forth all the household stuff of Tobiah out of the chamber.

9Then I commanded, and they cleansed the chambers: and thither brought I again the vessels of the house of God, with the meat offering and the frankincense.

10And I perceived that the portions of the Levites had not been given *them:* for the Levites and the singers, that did the work, were fled every one to his field.

11Then contended I with the rulers, and said, Why is the house of God forsaken? And I gathered them together, and set them in their place.

12Then brought all Judah the tithe of the corn and the new wine and the oil unto the treasuries.

13And I made treasurers over the treasuries, Shelemiah the priest, and Zadok the scribe, and of the Levites, Pedaiah: and next to them *was* Hanan the son of Zaccur, the son of Mattaniah: for they were counted faithful, and their office *was* to distribute unto their brethren.

14Remember me, O my God, concerning this, and wipe not out my good deeds that I have done for the house of my God, and for the offices thereof.

15In those days saw I in Judah *some* treading wine presses on the sabbath, and bringing in sheaves, and lading asses; as also wine, grapes, and figs, and all *manner of* burdens, which they brought into Jerusalem on the sabbath day: and I testified *against them* in the day wherein they sold victuals.

16There dwelt men of Tyre also therein, which brought fish, and all manner of ware, and sold on the sabbath unto the children of Judah, and in Jerusalem.

17Then I contended with the nobles of Judah, and said unto them, What evil thing *is* this that ye do, and profane the sabbath day?

18Did not your fathers thus, and did not our God bring all this evil upon us, and upon this city? yet ye bring more wrath upon Israel by profaning the sabbath.

19And it came to pass, that when the gates of Jerusalem began to be dark before the sabbath, I commanded that the gates should be shut, and charged that they should not be opened till after the sabbath: and *some* of my servants set I at the gates, *that* there should

no burden be brought in on the sabbath day.

20So the merchants and sellers of all kind of ware lodged without Jerusalem once or twice.

21Then I testified against them, and said unto them, Why lodge ye about the wall? if ye do *so* again, I will lay hands on you. From that time forth came they no *more* on the sabbath.

22And I commanded the Levites that they should cleanse themselves, and *that* they should come *and* keep the gates, to sanctify the sabbath day. Remember me, O my God, *concerning* this also, and spare me according to the greatness of thy mercy.

23In those days also saw I Jews *that* had married wives of Ashdod, of Ammon, *and* of Moab:

24And their children spake half in the speech of Ashdod, and could not speak in the Jews' language, but according to the language of each people.

25And I contended with them, and cursed them, and smote certain of them, and plucked off their hair, and made me swear by God, *saying,* Ye shall not give your daughters unto their sons, nor take their daughters unto your sons, or for yourselves.

26Did not Solomon king of Israel sin by these things? yet among many nations was there no king like him, who was beloved of his God, and God made him king over all Israel: nevertheless even him did outlandish women cause to sin.

27Shall we then hearken unto you to do all this great evil, to transgress against our God in marrying strange wives?

28And *one* of the sons of Joiada, the son of Eliashib the high priest, *was* son in law to Sanballat the Horonite; therefore I chased him from me.

29Remember them, O my God, because they have defiled the priesthood, and the covenant of the priesthood, and of the Levites.

30Thus cleansed I them from all strangers, and appointed the wards of the priests and the Levites, every one in his business;

31And for the wood offering, at times appointed, and for the firstfruits. Remember me, O my God, for good.

1 CORINTHIANS 11:3–16

Bᴜᴛ I would have you know, that the head of every man is Christ; and the head of the woman *is* the man; and the head of Christ *is* God.

4Every man praying or prophesying, having *his* head covered, dishonoureth his head.

5But every woman that prayeth or prophesieth with *her* head uncovered dishonoureth her head: for that is even all one as if she were shaven.

6For if the woman be not covered, let her also be shorn: but if it be a shame for a woman to be shorn or shaven, let her be covered.

7For a man indeed ought not to cover *his* head, forasmuch as he is the image and glory of God: but the woman is the glory of the man.

8For the man is not of the woman; but the woman of the man.

9Neither was the man created for the woman; but the woman for the man.

10For this cause ought the woman to have power on *her* head because of the angels.

11Nevertheless neither is the man without the woman, neither the woman without the man, in the Lord.

12For as the woman *is* of the man, even so *is* the man also by the woman; but all things of God.

13Judge in yourselves: is it comely that a woman pray unto God uncovered?

14Doth not even nature itself teach you, that, if a man have long hair, it is a shame unto him?

15But if a woman have long hair, it is a glory to her: for *her* hair is given her for a covering.

16But if any man seem to be contentious, we have no such custom, neither the churches of God.

PSALM 35:1–16

Pʟᴇᴀᴅ *my cause,* O Lᴏʀᴅ, with them that strive with me: fight against them that fight against me.

2Take hold of shield and buckler, and stand up for mine help.

3Draw out also the spear, and stop *the way* against them that persecute me: say unto my soul, I *am* thy salvation.

4Let them be confounded and put to shame that seek after my soul: let them be turned back and brought to confusion that devise my hurt.

5Let them be as chaff before the wind: and let the angel of the Lᴏʀᴅ chase *them.*

6Let their way be dark and slippery: and let the angel of the Lᴏʀᴅ persecute them.

7For without cause have they hid for me their net *in* a pit, *which* without cause they have digged for my soul.

8Let destruction come upon him at unawares; and let his net that he hath hid catch himself: into that very destruction let him fall.

9And my soul shall be joyful in the Lᴏʀᴅ: it shall rejoice in his salvation.

10All my bones shall say, Lᴏʀᴅ, who *is* like unto thee, which deliverest the poor from him that is too strong for him, yea, the poor and the needy from him that spoileth him?

11False witnesses did rise up; they laid to my charge *things* that I knew not.

12They rewarded me evil for good *to* the spoiling of my soul.

13But as for me, when they were sick, my clothing *was* sackcloth: I humbled my soul with fasting; and my prayer returned into mine own bosom.

14I behaved myself as though *he had*

been my friend *or* brother: I bowed down heavily, as one that mourneth *for his* mother.

¹⁵But in mine adversity they rejoiced, and gathered themselves together; *yea,* the abjects gathered themselves together against me, and I knew *it* not; they did tear *me,* and ceased not:

¹⁶With hypocritical mockers in feasts, they gnashed upon me with their teeth.

PROVERBS FOR TODAY/ 21:17–18

He that loveth pleasure shall be *a poor man: he that loveth wine and oil shall not be rich.* □ *The wicked* shall be *a ransom for the righteous, and the transgressor for the upright.*

AUGUST 18

ESTHER 1:1—3:15

Now it came to pass in the days of Ahasuerus, (this *is* Ahasuerus which reigned, from India even unto Ethiopia, *over* an hundred and seven and twenty provinces:)

²*That* in those days, when the king Ahasuerus sat on the throne of his kingdom, which *was* in Shushan the palace,

³In the third year of his reign, he made a feast unto all his princes and his servants; the power of Persia and Media, the nobles and princes of the provinces, *being* before him:

⁴When he shewed the riches of his glorious kingdom and the honour of his excellent majesty many days, *even* an hundred and fourscore days.

⁵And when these days were expired, the king made a feast unto all the people that were present in Shushan the palace, both unto great and small, seven days, in the court of the garden of the king's palace;

⁶*Where were* white, green, and blue, *hangings,* fastened with cords of fine linen and purple to silver rings and pillars of marble: the beds *were of* gold and silver, upon a pavement of red, and blue, and white, and black, marble.

⁷And they gave *them* drink in vessels of gold, (the vessels being diverse one from another,) and royal wine in abundance, according to the state of the king.

⁸And the drinking *was* according to the law; none did compel; for so the king had appointed to all the officers of his house, that they should do according to every man's pleasure.

⁹Also Vashti the queen made a feast for the women *in* the royal house which *belonged* to king Ahasuerus.

¹⁰On the seventh day, when the heart of the king was merry with wine, he commanded Mehuman, Biztha, Harbona, Bigtha, and Abagtha, Zethar, and Carcas, the seven chamberlains that served in the presence of Ahasuerus the king,

¹¹To bring Vashti the queen before the king with the crown royal, to shew the people and the princes her beauty: for she *was* fair to look on.

¹²But the queen Vashti refused to come at the king's commandment by *his* chamberlains: therefore was the king very wroth, and his anger burned in him.

¹³Then the king said to the wise men,

which knew the times, (for so *was* the king's manner toward all that knew law and judgment:

14And the next unto him *was* Carshena, Shethar, Admatha, Tarshish, Meres, Marsena, *and* Memucan, the seven princes of Persia and Media, which saw the king's face, *and* which sat the first in the kingdom;)

15What shall we do unto the queen Vashti according to law because she hath not performed the commandment of the king Ahasuerus by the chamberlains?

16And Memucan answered before the king and the princes, Vashti the queen hath not done wrong to the king only, but also to all the princes, and to all the people that *are* in all the provinces of the king Ahasuerus.

17For *this* deed of the queen shall come abroad unto all women, so that they shall despise their husbands in their eyes, when it shall be reported, The king Ahasuerus commanded Vashti the queen to be brought in before him, but she came not.

18*Likewise* shall the ladies of Persia and Media say this day unto all the king's princes, which have heard of the deed of the queen. Thus *shall there arise* too much contempt and wrath.

19If it please the king, let there go a royal commandment from him, and let it be written among the laws of the Persians and the Medes, that it be not altered, That Vashti come no more before king Ahasuerus; and let the king give her royal estate unto another that is better than she.

20And when the king's decree which he shall make shall be published throughout all his empire, (for it is great,) all the wives shall give to their husbands honour, both to great and small.

21And the saying pleased the king and the princes; and the king did according to the word of Memucan:

22For he sent letters into all the king's provinces, into every province according to the writing thereof, and to every people after their language, that every man should bear rule in his own house, and that *it* should be published according to the language of every people.

AFTER these things, when the wrath of king Ahasuerus was appeased, he remembered Vashti, and what she had done, and what was decreed against her.

2Then said the king's servants that ministered unto him, Let there be fair young virgins sought for the king:

3And let the king appoint officers in all the provinces of his kingdom, that they may gather together all the fair young virgins unto Shushan the palace, to the house of the women, unto the custody of Hege the king's chamberlain, keeper of the women; and let their things for purification be given *them:*

4And let the maiden which pleaseth the king be queen instead of Vashti. And the thing pleased the king; and he did so.

5*Now* in Shushan the palace there was a certain Jew, whose name *was* Mordecai, the son of Jair, the son of Shimei, the son of Kish, a Benjamite;

6Who had been carried away from Jerusalem with the captivity which had been carried away with Jeconiah king of Judah, whom Nebuchadnezzar the king of Babylon had carried away.

7And he brought up Hadassah, that *is,* Esther, his uncle's daughter: for she had neither father nor mother, and the maid *was* fair and beautiful; whom Mordecai, when her father and mother were dead, took for his own daughter.

8So it came to pass, when the king's commandment and his decree was heard, and when many maidens were gathered together unto Shushan the palace, to the custody of Hegai, that Esther was brought also unto the king's house, to the custody of Hegai, keeper of the women.

9And the maiden pleased him, and she obtained kindness of him; and he speedily gave her her things for purification, with such things as belonged to her, and seven maidens, *which were* meet to be given her, out of the king's house: and he preferred her and her maids unto the best *place* of the house of the women.

10Esther had not shewed her people nor her kindred: for Mordecai had charged her that she should not shew *it.*

11And Mordecai walked every day before the court of the women's house, to know how Esther did, and what should become of her.

12Now when every maid's turn was come to go in to king Ahasuerus, after that she had been twelve months, according to the manner of the women, (for so were the days of their purifications accomplished, *to wit,* six months with oil of myrrh, and six months with sweet odours, and with *other* things for the purifying of the women;)

13Then thus came *every* maiden unto the king; whatsoever she desired was given her to go with her out of the house of the women unto the king's house.

14In the evening she went, and on the morrow she returned into the second house of the women, to the custody of Shaashgaz, the king's chamberlain, which kept the concubines: she came in unto the king no more, except the king delighted in her, and that she were called by name.

15Now when the turn of Esther, the daughter of Abihail the uncle of Mordecai, who had taken her for his daughter, was come to go in unto the king, she required nothing but what Hegai the king's chamberlain, the keeper of the women, appointed. And Esther obtained favour in the sight of all them that looked upon her.

16So Esther was taken unto king Ahasuerus into his house royal in the tenth month, which *is* the month Tebeth, in the seventh year of his reign.

17And the king loved Esther above all the women, and she obtained grace and favour in his sight more than all the virgins; so that he set the royal crown upon her head, and made her queen instead of Vashti.

18Then the king made a great feast unto all his princes and his servants, *even* Esther's feast; and he made a release to the provinces, and gave gifts, according to the state of the king.

19And when the virgins were gathered together the second time, then Mordecai sat in the king's gate.

20Esther had not *yet* shewed her kindred nor her people; as Mordecai had charged her: for Esther did the commandment of Mordecai, like as when she was brought up with him.

21In those days, while Mordecai sat in the king's gate, two of the king's chamberlains, Bigthan and Teresh, of those which kept the door, were wroth, and sought to lay hand on the king Ahasuerus.

22And the thing was known to Mordecai, who told *it* unto Esther the queen; and Esther certified the king *thereof* in Mordecai's name.

23And when inquisition was made of the matter, it was found out; therefore they were both hanged on a tree: and it was written in the book of the chronicles before the king.

AFTER these things did king Ahasuerus promote Haman the son of Hammedatha the Agagite, and advanced him, and set his seat above all the princes that *were* with him.

2And all the king's servants, that *were* in the king's gate, bowed, and reverenced Haman: for the king had so commanded concerning him. But Mordecai bowed not, nor did *him* reverence.

3Then the king's servants, which *were* in the king's gate, said unto

Mordecai, Why transgressest thou the king's commandment?

4Now it came to pass, when they spake daily unto him, and he hearkened not unto them, that they told Haman, to see whether Mordecai's matters would stand: for he had told them that he *was* a Jew.

5And when Haman saw that Mordecai bowed not, nor did him reverence, then was Haman full of wrath.

6And he thought scorn to lay hands on Mordecai alone; for they had shewed him the people of Mordecai: wherefore Haman sought to destroy all the Jews that *were* throughout the whole kingdom of Ahasuerus, *even* the people of Mordecai.

7In the first month, that *is,* the month Nisan, in the twelfth year of king Ahasuerus, they cast Pur, that *is,* the lot, before Haman from day to day, and from month to month, *to* the twelfth *month,* that *is,* the month Adar.

8And Haman said unto king Ahasuerus, There is a certain people scattered abroad and dispersed among the people in all the provinces of thy kingdom; and their laws *are* diverse from all people; neither keep they the king's laws: therefore it *is* not for the king's profit to suffer them.

9If it please the king, let it be written that they may be destroyed: and I will pay ten thousand talents of silver to the hands of those that have the charge of the business, to bring *it* into the king's treasuries.

10And the king took his ring from his hand, and gave it unto Haman the son of Hammedatha the Agagite, the Jews' enemy.

11And the king said unto Haman, The silver *is* given to thee, the people also, to do with them as it seemeth good to thee.

12Then were the king's scribes called on the thirteenth day of the first month, and there was written according to all that Haman had commanded unto the king's lieutenants, and to the governors that *were* over every province, and to the rulers of every people of every province according to the writing thereof, and *to* every people after their language; in the name of king Ahasuerus was it written, and sealed with the king's ring.

13And the letters were sent by posts into all the king's provinces, to destroy, to kill, and to cause to perish, all Jews, both young and old, little children and women, in one day, *even* upon the thirteenth *day* of the twelfth month, which *is* the month Adar, and *to take* the spoil of them for a prey.

14The copy of the writing for a commandment to be given in every province was published unto all people, that they should be ready against that day.

15The posts went out, being hastened by the king's commandment, and the decree was given in Shushan the palace. And the king and Haman sat down to drink; but the city Shushan was perplexed.

1 CORINTHIANS 11:17–34

Now in this that I declare *unto you* I praise *you* not, that ye come together not for the better, but for the worse.

18For first of all, when ye come together in the church, I hear that there be divisions among you; and I partly believe it.

19For there must be also heresies among you, that they which are approved may be made manifest among you.

20When ye come together therefore into one place, *this* is not to eat the Lord's supper.

21For in eating every one taketh before *other* his own supper: and one is hungry, and another is drunken.

22What? have ye not houses to eat and to drink in? or despise ye the church of God, and shame them that have not?

What shall I say to you? shall I praise you in this? I praise *you* not.

23For I have received of the Lord that which also I delivered unto you, That the Lord Jesus the *same* night in which he was betrayed took bread:

24And when he had given thanks, he brake *it,* and said, Take, eat: this is my body, which is broken for you: this do in remembrance of me.

25After the same manner also *he took* the cup, when he had supped, saying, This cup is the new testament in my blood: this do ye, as oft as ye drink *it,* in remembrance of me.

26For as often as ye eat this bread, and drink this cup, ye do shew the Lord's death till he come.

27Wherefore whosoever shall eat this bread, and drink *this* cup of the Lord, unworthily, shall be guilty of the body and blood of the Lord.

28But let a man examine himself, and so let him eat of *that* bread, and drink of *that* cup.

29For he that eateth and drinketh unworthily, eateth and drinketh damnation to himself, not discerning the Lord's body.

30For this cause many *are* weak and sickly among you, and many sleep.

31For if we would judge ourselves, we should not be judged.

32But when we are judged, we are chastened of the Lord, that we should not be condemned with the world.

33Wherefore, my brethren, when ye come together to eat, tarry one for another.

34And if any man hunger, let him eat at home; that ye come not together unto condemnation. And the rest will I set in order when I come.

PSALM 35:17–28

Lord, how long wilt thou look on? rescue my soul from their destructions, my darling from the lions.

18I will give thee thanks in the great congregation: I will praise thee among much people.

19Let not them that are mine enemies wrongfully rejoice over me: *neither* let them wink with the eye that hate me without a cause.

20For they speak not peace: but they devise deceitful matters against *them that are* quiet in the land.

21Yea, they opened their mouth wide against me, *and* said, Aha, aha, our eye hath seen *it.*

22*This* thou hast seen, O Lord: keep not silence: O Lord, be not far from me.

23Stir up thyself, and awake to my judgment, *even* unto my cause, my God and my Lord.

24Judge me, O Lord my God, according to thy righteousness; and let them not rejoice over me.

25Let them not say in their hearts, Ah, so would we have it: let them not say, We have swallowed him up.

26Let them be ashamed and brought to confusion together that rejoice at mine hurt: let them be clothed with shame and dishonour that magnify *themselves* against me.

27Let them shout for joy, and be glad, that favour my righteous cause: yea, let them say continually, Let the Lord be magnified, which hath pleasure in the prosperity of his servant.

28And my tongue shall speak of thy righteousness *and* of thy praise all the day long.

PROVERBS FOR TODAY/ 21:19–20

It is *better to dwell in the wilderness, than with a contentious and an angry woman.* ☐ There is *treasure to be desired and oil in the dwelling of the wise; but a foolish man spendeth it up.*

AUGUST 19

ESTHER 4:1—7:10

WHEN Mordecai perceived all that was done, Mordecai rent his clothes, and put on sackcloth with ashes, and went out into the midst of the city, and cried with a loud and a bitter cry;

2And came even before the king's gate: for none *might* enter into the king's gate clothed with sackcloth.

3And in every province, whithersoever the king's commandment and his decree came, *there was* great mourning among the Jews, and fasting, and weeping, and wailing; and many lay in sackcloth and ashes.

4So Esther's maids and her chamberlains came and told *it* her. Then was the queen exceedingly grieved; and she sent raiment to clothe Mordecai, and to take away his sackcloth from him: but he received *it* not.

5Then called Esther for Hatach, *one* of the king's chamberlains, whom he had appointed to attend upon her, and gave him a commandment to Mordecai, to know what it *was,* and why it *was.*

6So Hatach went forth to Mordecai unto the street of the city, which *was* before the king's gate.

7And Mordecai told him of all that had happened unto him, and of the sum of the money that Haman had promised to pay to the king's treasuries for the Jews, to destroy them.

8Also he gave him the copy of the writing of the decree that was given at Shushan to destroy them, to shew *it* unto Esther, and to declare *it* unto her, and to charge her that she should go in unto the king, to make supplication unto him, and to make request before him for her people.

9And Hatach came and told Esther the words of Mordecai.

10Again Esther spake unto Hatach, and gave him commandment unto Mordecai;

11All the king's servants, and the people of the king's provinces, do know, that whosoever, whether man or woman, shall come unto the king into the inner court, who is not called, *there is* one law of his to put *him* to death, except such to whom the king shall hold out the golden sceptre, that he may live: but I have not been called to come in unto the king these thirty days.

12And they told to Mordecai Esther's words.

13Then Mordecai commanded to answer Esther, Think not with thyself that thou shalt escape in the king's house, more than all the Jews.

14For if thou altogether holdest thy peace at this time, *then* shall there enlargement and deliverance arise to the Jews from another place; but thou and thy father's house shall be destroyed: and who knoweth whether thou art come to the kingdom for *such* a time as this?

15Then Esther bade *them* return Mordecai *this answer,*

16Go, gather together all the Jews that are present in Shushan, and fast ye for me, and neither eat nor drink three days, night or day: I also and my maidens will fast likewise; and so will I go in unto the king, which *is* not according to the law: and if I perish, I perish.

17So Mordecai went his way, and did according to all that Esther had commanded him.

Now it came to pass on the third day, that Esther put on *her* royal *apparel,* and stood in the inner court of the king's house, over against the king's house: and the king sat upon his royal throne in the royal house, over against the gate of the house.

2And it was so, when the king saw Esther the queen standing in the court, *that* she obtained favour in his sight: and the king held out to Esther the golden sceptre that *was* in his hand. So Esther drew near, and touched the top of the sceptre.

3Then said the king unto her, What wilt thou, queen Esther? and what *is* thy request? it shall be even given thee to the half of the kingdom.

4And Esther answered, If *it seem* good unto the king, let the king and Haman come this day unto the banquet that I have prepared for him.

5Then the king said, Cause Haman to make haste, that he may do as Esther hath said. So the king and Haman came to the banquet that Esther had prepared.

6And the king said unto Esther at the banquet of wine, What *is* thy petition? and it shall be granted thee: and what *is* thy request? even to the half of the kingdom it shall be performed.

7Then answered Esther, and said, My petition and my request *is;*

8If I have found favour in the sight of the king, and if it please the king to grant my petition, and to perform my request, let the king and Haman come to the banquet that I shall prepare for them, and I will do to morrow as the king hath said.

9Then went Haman forth that day joyful and with a glad heart: but when Haman saw Mordecai in the king's gate, that he stood not up, nor moved for him, he was full of indignation against Mordecai.

10Nevertheless Haman refrained himself: and when he came home, he sent and called for his friends, and Zeresh his wife.

11And Haman told them of the glory of his riches, and the multitude of his children, and all *the things* wherein the king had promoted him, and how he had advanced him above the princes and servants of the king.

12Haman said moreover, Yea, Esther the queen did let no man come in with the king unto the banquet that she had prepared but myself; and to morrow am I invited unto her also with the king.

13Yet all this availeth me nothing, so long as I see Mordecai the Jew sitting at the king's gate.

14Then said Zeresh his wife and all his friends unto him, Let a gallows be made of fifty cubits high, and to morrow speak thou unto the king that Mordecai may be hanged thereon: then go thou in merrily with the king unto the banquet. And the thing pleased Haman; and he caused the gallows to be made.

On that night could not the king sleep, and he commanded to bring the book of records of the chronicles; and they were read before the king.

2And it was found written, that Mordecai had told of Bigthana and Teresh, two of the king's chamberlains, the keepers of the door, who sought to lay hand on the king Ahasuerus.

3And the king said, What honour and dignity hath been done to Mordecai for this? Then said the king's servants that ministered unto him, There is nothing done for him.

4And the king said, Who *is* in the court? Now Haman was come into the outward court of the king's house, to speak unto the king to hang Mordecai on the gallows that he had prepared for him.

5And the king's servants said unto him, Behold, Haman standeth in the court. And the king said, Let him come in.

6So Haman came in. And the king said unto him, What shall be done unto the man whom the king delighteth to honour? Now Haman thought in his heart, To whom would the king delight to do honour more than to myself?

7And Haman answered the king, For the man whom the king delighteth to honour,

8Let the royal apparel be brought which the king *useth* to wear, and the horse that the king rideth upon, and the crown royal which is set upon his head:

9And let this apparel and horse be delivered to the hand of one of the king's most noble princes, that they may array the man *withal* whom the king delighteth to honour, and bring him on horseback through the street of the city, and proclaim before him, Thus shall it be done to the man whom the king delighteth to honour.

10Then the king said to Haman, Make haste, *and* take the apparel and the horse, as thou hast said, and do even so to Mordecai the Jew, that sitteth at the king's gate: let nothing fail of all that thou hast spoken.

11Then took Haman the apparel and the horse, and arrayed Mordecai, and brought him on horseback through the street of the city, and proclaimed before him, Thus shall it be done unto the man whom the king delighteth to honour.

12And Mordecai came again to the king's gate. But Haman hasted to his house mourning, and having his head covered.

13And Haman told Zeresh his wife and all his friends every *thing* that had befallen him. Then said his wise men and Zeresh his wife unto him, If Mordecai *be* of the seed of the Jews, before whom thou hast begun to fall, thou shalt not prevail against him, but shalt surely fall before him.

14And while they *were* yet talking with him, came the king's chamberlains, and hasted to bring Haman unto the banquet that Esther had prepared.

So the king and Haman came to banquet with Esther the queen.

2And the king said again unto Esther on the second day at the banquet of wine, What *is* thy petition, queen Esther? and it shall be granted thee: and what *is* thy request? and it shall be performed, *even* to the half of the kingdom.

3Then Esther the queen answered and said, If I have found favour in thy sight, O king, and if it please the king, let my life be given me at my petition, and my people at my request:

4For we are sold, I and my people, to be destroyed, to be slain, and to perish. But if we had been sold for bondmen and bondwomen, I had held my tongue, although the enemy could not countervail the king's damage.

5Then the king Ahasuerus answered and said unto Esther the queen, Who is he, and where is he, that durst presume in his heart to do so?

6And Esther said, The adversary and enemy *is* this wicked Haman. Then Haman was afraid before the king and the queen.

7And the king arising from the banquet of wine in his wrath *went* into the palace garden: and Haman stood up to make request for his life to Esther the queen; for he saw that there was evil determined against him by the king.

8Then the king returned out of the palace garden into the place of the banquet of wine; and Haman was fallen upon the bed whereon Esther *was*. Then said the king, Will he force the queen also before me in the house? As the word went out of the king's mouth, they covered Haman's face.

9And Harbonah, one of the chamberlains, said before the king, Behold also, the gallows fifty cubits high, which Haman had made for Mordecai, who had spoken good for the king, standeth in the house of Haman. Then the king said, Hang him thereon.

10So they hanged Haman on the gallows that he had prepared for Mordecai. Then was the king's wrath pacified.

1 CORINTHIANS 12:1–26

Now concerning spiritual *gifts,* brethren, I would not have you ignorant.

2Ye know that ye were Gentiles, carried away unto these dumb idols, even as ye were led.

3Wherefore I give you to understand, that no man speaking by the Spirit of God calleth Jesus accursed: and *that* no man can say that Jesus is the Lord, but by the Holy Ghost.

4Now there are diversities of gifts, but the same Spirit.

5And there are differences of administrations, but the same Lord.

6And there are diversities of operations, but it is the same God which worketh all in all.

7But the manifestation of the Spirit is given to every man to profit withal.

8For to one is given by the Spirit the word of wisdom; to another the word of knowledge by the same Spirit;

9To another faith by the same Spirit; to another the gifts of healing by the same Spirit;

10To another the working of miracles; to another prophecy; to another discerning of spirits; to another *divers* kinds of tongues; to another the interpretation of tongues:

11But all these worketh that one and the selfsame Spirit, dividing to every man severally as he will.

12For as the body is one, and hath many members, and all the members of that one body, being many, are one body: so also *is* Christ.

13For by one Spirit are we all baptized into one body, whether *we be* Jews or Gentiles, whether *we be* bond or free; and have been all made to drink into one Spirit.

14For the body is not one member, but many.

15If the foot shall say, Because I am not the hand, I am not of the body; is it therefore not of the body?

16And if the ear shall say, Because I am not the eye, I am not of the body; is it therefore not of the body?

17If the whole body *were* an eye, where *were* the hearing? If the whole *were* hearing, where *were* the smelling?

18But now hath God set the members every one of them in the body, as it hath pleased him.

19And if they were all one member, where *were* the body?

20But now *are they* many members, yet but one body.

21And the eye cannot say unto the hand, I have no need of thee: nor again the head to the feet, I have no need of you.

22Nay, much more those members of the body, which seem to be more feeble, are necessary:

23And those *members* of the body, which we think to be less honourable, upon these we bestow more abundant honour; and our uncomely *parts* have more abundant comeliness.

24For our comely *parts* have no need: but God hath tempered the body together, having given more abundant honour to that *part* which lacked:

25That there should be no schism in the body; but *that* the members should have the same care one for another.

26And whether one member suffer, all the members suffer with it; or one member be honoured, all the members rejoice with it.

PSALM 36:1–12

THE transgression of the wicked saith within my heart, *that there is* no fear of God before his eyes.

2For he flattereth himself in his own eyes, until his iniquity be found to be hateful.

3The words of his mouth *are* iniquity and deceit: he hath left off to be wise, *and* to do good.

4He deviseth mischief upon his bed;

he setteth himself in a way *that is* not good; he abhorreth not evil.

⁵Thy mercy, O LORD, *is* in the heavens; *and* thy faithfulness *reacheth* unto the clouds.

⁶Thy righteousness *is* like the great mountains; thy judgments *are* a great deep: O LORD, thou preservest man and beast.

⁷How excellent *is* thy lovingkindness, O God! therefore the children of men put their trust under the shadow of thy wings.

⁸They shall be abundantly satisfied with the fatness of thy house; and thou shalt make them drink of the river of thy pleasures.

⁹For with thee *is* the fountain of life: in thy light shall we see light.

¹⁰O continue thy lovingkindness unto them that know thee; and thy righteousness to the upright in heart.

¹¹Let not the foot of pride come against me, and let not the hand of the wicked remove me.

¹²There are the workers of iniquity fallen: they are cast down, and shall not be able to rise.

PROVERBS FOR TODAY/ 21:21–22

He that followeth after righteousness and mercy findeth life; righteousness, and honour. □ *A wise* man *scaleth the city of the mighty, and casteth down the strength of the confidence thereof.*

AUGUST 20

ESTHER 8:1—10:3

ON that day did the king Ahasuerus give the house of Haman the Jews' enemy unto Esther the queen. And Mordecai came before the king; for Esther had told what he *was* unto her.

²And the king took off his ring, which he had taken from Haman, and gave it unto Mordecai. And Esther set Mordecai over the house of Haman.

³And Esther spake yet again before the king, and fell down at his feet, and besought him with tears to put away the mischief of Haman the Agagite, and his device that he had devised against the Jews.

⁴Then the king held out the golden sceptre toward Esther. So Esther arose, and stood before the king,

⁵And said, If it please the king, and if I have found favour in his sight, and the thing *seem* right before the king, and I *be* pleasing in his eyes, let it be written to reverse the letters devised by Haman the son of Hammedatha the Agagite, which he wrote to destroy the Jews which *are* in all the king's provinces:

⁶For how can I endure to see the evil that shall come unto my people? or how can I endure to see the destruction of my kindred?

⁷Then the king Ahasuerus said unto Esther the queen and to Mordecai the Jew, Behold, I have given Esther the house of Haman, and him they have hanged upon the gallows, because he laid his hand upon the Jews.

⁸Write ye also for the Jews, as it liketh you, in the king's name, and seal *it* with the king's ring: for the writing which is written in the king's name, and sealed with the king's ring,

may no man reverse.

⁹Then were the king's scribes called at that time in the third month, that *is,* the month Sivan, on the three and twentieth *day* thereof; and it was written according to all that Mordecai commanded unto the Jews, and to the lieutenants, and the deputies and rulers of the provinces which *are* from India unto Ethiopia, an hundred twenty and seven provinces, unto every province according to the writing thereof, and unto every people after their language, and to the Jews according to their writing, and according to their language.

¹⁰And he wrote in the king Ahasuerus' name, and sealed *it* with the king's ring, and sent letters by posts on horseback, *and* riders on mules, camels, *and* young dromedaries:

¹¹Wherein the king granted the Jews which *were* in every city to gather themselves together, and to stand for their life, to destroy, to slay, and to cause to perish, all the power of the people and province that would assault them, *both* little ones and women, and *to take* the spoil of them for a prey,

¹²Upon one day in all the provinces of king Ahasuerus, *namely,* upon the thirteenth *day* of the twelfth month, which *is* the month Adar.

¹³The copy of the writing for a commandment to be given in every province *was* published unto all people, and that the Jews should be ready against that day to avenge themselves on their enemies.

¹⁴*So* the posts that rode upon mules *and* camels went out, being hastened and pressed on by the king's commandment. And the decree was given at Shushan the palace.

¹⁵And Mordecai went out from the presence of the king in royal apparel of blue and white, and with a great crown of gold, and with a garment of fine linen and purple: and the city of Shushan rejoiced and was glad.

¹⁶The Jews had light, and gladness, and joy, and honour.

¹⁷And in every province, and in every city, whithersoever the king's commandment and his decree came, the Jews had joy and gladness, a feast and a good day. And many of the people of the land became Jews; for the fear of the Jews fell upon them.

Now in the twelfth month, that *is,* the month Adar, on the thirteenth day of the same, when the king's commandment and his decree drew near to be put in execution, in the day that the enemies of the Jews hoped to have power over them, (though it was turned to the contrary, that the Jews had rule over them that hated them;)

²The Jews gathered themselves together in their cities throughout all the provinces of the king Ahasuerus, to lay hand on such as sought their hurt: and no man could withstand them; for the fear of them fell upon all people.

³And all the rulers of the provinces, and the lieutenants, and the deputies, and officers of the king, helped the Jews; because the fear of Mordecai fell upon them.

⁴For Mordecai *was* great in the king's house, and his fame went out throughout all the provinces: for this man Mordecai waxed greater and greater.

⁵Thus the Jews smote all their enemies with the stroke of the sword, and slaughter, and destruction, and did what they would unto those that hated them.

⁶And in Shushan the palace the Jews slew and destroyed five hundred men.

⁷And Parshandatha, and Dalphon, and Aspatha,

⁸And Poratha, and Adalia, and Aridatha,

⁹And Parmashta, and Arisai, and Aridai, and Vajezatha,

¹⁰The ten sons of Haman the son of Hammedatha, the enemy of the Jews, slew they; but on the spoil laid they not their hand.

¹¹On that day the number of those

that were slain in Shushan the palace was brought before the king.

12And the king said unto Esther the queen, The Jews have slain and destroyed five hundred men in Shushan the palace, and the ten sons of Haman; what have they done in the rest of the king's provinces? now what *is* thy petition? and it shall be granted thee: or what *is* thy request further? and it shall be done.

13Then said Esther, If it please the king, let it be granted to the Jews which *are* in Shushan to do to morrow also according unto this day's decree, and let Haman's ten sons be hanged upon the gallows.

14And the king commanded it so to be done: and the decree was given at Shushan; and they hanged Haman's ten sons.

15For the Jews that *were* in Shushan gathered themselves together on the fourteenth day also of the month Adar, and slew three hundred men at Shushan; but on the prey they laid not their hand.

16But the other Jews that *were* in the king's provinces gathered themselves together, and stood for their lives, and had rest from their enemies, and slew of their foes seventy and five thousand, but they laid not their hands on the prey,

17On the thirteenth day of the month Adar; and on the fourteenth day of the same rested they, and made it a day of feasting and gladness.

18But the Jews that *were* at Shushan assembled together on the thirteenth *day* thereof, and on the fourteenth thereof; and on the fifteenth *day* of the same they rested, and made it a day of feasting and gladness.

19Therefore the Jews of the villages that dwelt in the unwalled towns, made the fourteenth day of the month Adar *a day of* gladness and feasting, and a good day, and of sending portions one to another.

20And Mordecai wrote these things, and sent letters unto all the Jews that *were* in all the provinces of the king Ahasuerus, *both* nigh and far,

21To stablish *this* among them, that they should keep the fourteenth day of the month Adar, and the fifteenth day of the same, yearly,

22As the days wherein the Jews rested from their enemies, and the month which was turned unto them from sorrow to joy, and from mourning into a good day: that they should make them days of feasting and joy, and of sending portions one to another, and gifts to the poor.

23And the Jews undertook to do as they had begun, and as Mordecai had written unto them;

24Because Haman the son of Hammedatha, the Agagite, the enemy of all the Jews, had devised against the Jews to destroy them, and had cast Pur, that *is*, the lot, to consume them, and to destroy them;

25But when *Esther* came before the king, he commanded by letters that his wicked device, which he devised against the Jews, should return upon his own head, and that he and his sons should be hanged on the gallows.

26Wherefore they called these days Purim after the name of Pur. Therefore for all the words of this letter, and *of that* which they had seen concerning this matter, and which had come unto them,

27The Jews ordained, and took upon them, and upon their seed, and upon all such as joined themselves unto them, so as it should not fail, that they would keep these two days according to their writing, and according to their *appointed* time every year;

28And *that* these days *should be* remembered and kept throughout every generation, every family, every province, and every city; and *that* these days of Purim should not fail from among the Jews, nor the memorial of them perish from their seed.

29Then Esther the queen, the daughter of Abihail, and Mordecai the Jew, wrote with all authority, to confirm this second letter of Purim.

30And he sent the letters unto all the Jews, to the hundred twenty and seven provinces of the kingdom of Ahasuerus, *with* words of peace and truth,

31To confirm these days of Purim in their times *appointed,* according as Mordecai the Jew and Esther the queen had enjoined them, and as they had decreed for themselves and for their seed, the matters of the fastings and their cry.

32And the decree of Esther confirmed these matters of Purim; and it was written in the book.

AND the king Ahasuerus laid a tribute upon the land, and *upon* the isles of the sea.

2And all the acts of his power and of his might, and the declaration of the greatness of Mordecai, whereunto the king advanced him, *are* they not written in the book of the chronicles of the kings of Media and Persia?

3For Mordecai the Jew *was* next unto the king Ahasuerus, and great among the Jews, and accepted of the multitude of his brethren, seeking the wealth of his people, and speaking peace to all his seed.

1 CORINTHIANS
12:27—13:13

Now ye are the body of Christ, and members in particular.

28And God hath set some in the church, first apostles, secondarily prophets, thirdly teachers, after that miracles, then gifts of healings, helps, governments, diversities of tongues.

29*Are* all apostles? *are* all prophets? *are* all teachers? *are* all workers of miracles?

30Have all the gifts of healing? do all speak with tongues? do all interpret?

31But covet earnestly the best gifts: and yet shew I unto you a more excellent way.

THOUGH I speak with the tongues of men and of angels, and have not charity, I am become *as* sounding brass, or a tinkling cymbal.

2And though I have *the gift of* prophecy, and understand all mysteries, and all knowledge; and though I have all faith, so that I could remove mountains, and have not charity, I am nothing.

3And though I bestow all my goods to feed *the poor,* and though I give my body to be burned, and have not charity, it profiteth me nothing.

4Charity suffereth long, *and* is kind; charity envieth not; charity vaunteth not itself, is not puffed up,

5Doth not behave itself unseemly, seeketh not her own, is not easily provoked, thinketh no evil;

6Rejoiceth not in iniquity, but rejoiceth in the truth;

7Beareth all things, believeth all things, hopeth all things, endureth all things.

8Charity never faileth: but whether *there be* prophecies, they shall fail; whether *there be* tongues, they shall cease; whether *there be* knowledge, it shall vanish away.

9For we know in part, and we prophesy in part.

10But when that which is perfect is come, then that which is in part shall be done away.

11When I was a child, I spake as a child, I understood as a child, I thought as a child: but when I became a man, I put away childish things.

12For now we see through a glass, darkly; but then face to face: now I know in part; but then shall I know even as also I am known.

13And now abideth faith, hope,

charity, these three; but the greatest of these *is* charity.

PSALM 37:1–11

FRET not thyself because of evildoers, neither be thou envious against the workers of iniquity.

2For they shall soon be cut down like the grass, and wither as the green herb.

3Trust in the LORD, and do good; *so* shalt thou dwell in the land, and verily thou shalt be fed.

4Delight thyself also in the LORD; and he shall give thee the desires of thine heart.

5Commit thy way unto the LORD; trust also in him; and he shall bring *it* to pass.

6And he shall bring forth thy righteousness as the light, and thy judgment as the noonday.

7Rest in the LORD, and wait patiently for him: fret not thyself because of him who prospereth in his way, because of the man who bringeth wicked devices to pass.

8Cease from anger, and forsake wrath: fret not thyself in any wise to do evil.

9For evildoers shall be cut off: but those that wait upon the LORD, they shall inherit the earth.

10For yet a little while, and the wicked *shall* not *be:* yea, thou shalt diligently consider his place, and it *shall* not *be.*

11But the meek shall inherit the earth; and shall delight themselves in the abundance of peace.

PROVERBS FOR TODAY/ 21:23–24

Whoso keepeth his mouth and his tongue keepeth his soul from troubles. ☐ *Proud* and *haughty scorner* is *his name, who dealeth in proud wrath.*

AUGUST 21

JOB 1:1—3:26

THERE was a man in the land of Uz, whose name *was* Job; and that man was perfect and upright, and one that feared God, and eschewed evil.

2And there were born unto him seven sons and three daughters.

3His substance also was seven thousand sheep, and three thousand camels, and five hundred yoke of oxen, and five hundred she asses, and a very great household; so that this man was the greatest of all the men of the east.

4And his sons went and feasted *in their* houses, every one his day; and sent and called for their three sisters to eat and to drink with them.

5And it was so, when the days of *their* feasting were gone about, that Job sent and sanctified them, and rose up early in the morning, and offered burnt offerings *according* to the number of them all: for Job said, It may be that my sons have sinned, and cursed God in their hearts. Thus did Job continually.

6Now there was a day when the sons of God came to present themselves before the LORD, and Satan came also among them.

7And the LORD said unto Satan, Whence comest thou? Then Satan answered the LORD, and said, From going to and fro in the earth, and from walking up and down in it.

8And the LORD said unto Satan, Hast thou considered my servant Job, that *there is* none like him in the earth, a perfect and an upright man, one that feareth God, and escheweth evil?

9Then Satan answered the LORD, and said, Doth Job fear God for nought?

10Hast not thou made an hedge about him, and about his house, and about all that he hath on every side? thou hast blessed the work of his hands, and his substance is increased in the land.

11But put forth thine hand now, and touch all that he hath, and he will curse thee to thy face.

12And the LORD said unto Satan, Behold, all that he hath *is* in thy power; only upon himself put not forth thine hand. So Satan went forth from the presence of the LORD.

13And there was a day when his sons and his daughters *were* eating and drinking wine in their eldest brother's house:

14And there came a messenger unto Job, and said, The oxen were plowing, and the asses feeding beside them:

15And the Sabeans fell *upon them,* and took them away; yea, they have slain the servants with the edge of the sword; and I only am escaped alone to tell thee.

16While he *was* yet speaking, there came also another, and said, The fire of God is fallen from heaven, and hath burned up the sheep, and the servants, and consumed them; and I only am escaped alone to tell thee.

17While he *was* yet speaking, there came also another, and said, The Chaldeans made out three bands, and fell upon the camels, and have carried them away, yea, and slain the servants with the edge of the sword; and I only am escaped alone to tell thee.

18While he *was* yet speaking, there came also another, and said, Thy sons and thy daughters *were* eating and drinking wine in their eldest brother's house:

19And, behold, there came a great wind from the wilderness, and smote the four corners of the house, and it fell upon the young men, and they are dead; and I only am escaped alone to tell thee.

20Then Job arose, and rent his mantle, and shaved his head, and fell down upon the ground, and worshipped,

21And said, Naked came I out of my mother's womb, and naked shall I return thither: the LORD gave, and the LORD hath taken away; blessed be the name of the LORD.

22In all this Job sinned not, nor charged God foolishly.

AGAIN there was a day when the sons of God came to present themselves before the LORD, and Satan came also among them to present himself before the LORD.

2And the LORD said unto Satan, From whence comest thou? And Satan answered the LORD, and said, From going to and fro in the earth, and from walking up and down in it.

3And the LORD said unto Satan, Hast thou considered my servant Job, that *there is* none like him in the earth, a perfect and an upright man, one that feareth God, and escheweth evil? and still he holdeth fast his integrity, although thou movedst me against him, to destroy him without cause.

4And Satan answered the LORD, and said, Skin for skin, yea, all that a man hath will he give for his life.

5But put forth thine hand now, and touch his bone and his flesh, and he will curse thee to thy face.

6And the LORD said unto Satan, Behold, he *is* in thine hand; but save his life.

7So went Satan forth from the presence of the LORD, and smote Job with sore boils from the sole of his foot unto his crown.

8And he took him a potsherd to scrape

himself withal; and he sat down among the ashes.

9Then said his wife unto him, Dost thou still retain thine integrity? curse God, and die.

10But he said unto her, Thou speakest as one of the foolish women speaketh. What? shall we receive good at the hand of God, and shall we not receive evil? In all this did not Job sin with his lips.

11Now when Job's three friends heard of all this evil that was come upon him, they came every one from his own place; Eliphaz the Temanite, and Bildad the Shuhite, and Zophar the Naamathite: for they had made an appointment together to come to mourn with him and to comfort him.

12And when they lifted up their eyes afar off, and knew him not, they lifted up their voice, and wept; and they rent every one his mantle, and sprinkled dust upon their heads toward heaven.

13So they sat down with him upon the ground seven days and seven nights, and none spake a word unto him: for they saw that *his* grief was very great.

AFTER this opened Job his mouth, and cursed his day.

2And Job spake, and said,

3Let the day perish wherein I was born, and the night *in which* it was said, There is a man child conceived.

4Let that day be darkness; let not God regard it from above, neither let the light shine upon it.

5Let darkness and the shadow of death stain it; let a cloud dwell upon it; let the blackness of the day terrify it.

6*As for* that night, let darkness seize upon it; let it not be joined unto the days of the year, let it not come into the number of the months.

7Lo, let that night be solitary, let no joyful voice come therein.

8Let them curse it that curse the day, who are ready to raise up their mourning.

9Let the stars of the twilight thereof be dark; let it look for light, but *have* none; neither let it see the dawning of the day:

10Because it shut not up the doors of my *mother's* womb, nor hid sorrow from mine eyes.

11Why died I not from the womb? *why* did I *not* give up the ghost when I came out of the belly?

12Why did the knees prevent me? or why the breasts that I should suck?

13For now should I have lain still and been quiet, I should have slept: then had I been at rest,

14With kings and counsellors of the earth, which built desolate places for themselves;

15Or with princes that had gold, who filled their houses with silver:

16Or as an hidden untimely birth I had not been; as infants *which* never saw light.

17There the wicked cease *from* troubling; and there the weary be at rest.

18*There* the prisoners rest together; they hear not the voice of the oppressor.

19The small and great are there; and the servant *is* free from his master.

20Wherefore is light given to him that is in misery, and life unto the bitter *in* soul;

21Which long for death, but it *cometh* not; and dig for it more than for hid treasures;

22Which rejoice exceedingly, *and* are glad, when they can find the grave?

23*Why is light given* to a man whose way is hid, and whom God hath hedged in?

24For my sighing cometh before I eat, and my roarings are poured out like the waters.

25For the thing which I greatly feared is come upon me, and that which I was afraid of is come unto me.

26I was not in safety, neither had I

rest, neither was I quiet; yet trouble came.

1 CORINTHIANS 14:1–17

FOLLOW after charity, and desire spiritual *gifts,* but rather that ye may prophesy.

2For he that speaketh in an *unknown* tongue speaketh not unto men, but unto God: for no man understandeth *him;* howbeit in the spirit he speaketh mysteries.

3But he that prophesieth speaketh unto men *to* edification, and exhortation, and comfort.

4He that speaketh in an *unknown* tongue edifieth himself; but he that prophesieth edifieth the church.

5I would that ye all spake with tongues, but rather that ye prophesied: for greater *is* he that prophesieth than he that speaketh with tongues, except he interpret, that the church may receive edifying.

6Now, brethren, if I come unto you speaking with tongues, what shall I profit you, except I shall speak to you either by revelation, or by knowledge, or by prophesying, or by doctrine?

7And even things without life giving sound, whether pipe or harp, except they give a distinction in the sounds, how shall it be known what is piped or harped?

8For if the trumpet give an uncertain sound, who shall prepare himself to the battle?

9So likewise ye, except ye utter by the tongue words easy to be understood, how shall it be known what is spoken? for ye shall speak into the air.

10There are, it may be, so many kinds of voices in the world, and none of them *is* without signification.

11Therefore if I know not the meaning of the voice, I shall be unto him that speaketh a barbarian, and he that speaketh *shall be* a barbarian unto me.

12Even so ye, forasmuch as ye are zealous of spiritual *gifts,* seek that ye may excel to the edifying of the church.

13Wherefore let him that speaketh in an *unknown* tongue pray that he may interpret.

14For if I pray in an *unknown* tongue, my spirit prayeth, but my understanding is unfruitful.

15What is it then? I will pray with the spirit, and I will pray with the understanding also: I will sing with the spirit, and I will sing with the understanding also.

16Else when thou shalt bless with the spirit, how shall he that occupieth the room of the unlearned say Amen at thy giving of thanks, seeing he understandeth not what thou sayest?

17For thou verily givest thanks well, but the other is not edified.

PSALM 37:12–28

THE wicked plotteth against the just, and gnasheth upon him with his teeth.

13The Lord shall laugh at him: for he seeth that his day is coming.

14The wicked have drawn out the sword, and have bent their bow, to cast down the poor and needy, *and* to slay such as be of upright conversation.

15Their sword shall enter into their own heart, and their bows shall be broken.

16A little that a righteous man hath *is* better than the riches of many wicked.

17For the arms of the wicked shall be broken: but the LORD upholdeth the righteous.

18The LORD knoweth the days of the upright: and their inheritance shall be for ever.

19They shall not be ashamed in the evil time: and in the days of famine they shall be satisfied.

20But the wicked shall perish, and the enemies of the LORD *shall be* as the fat of lambs: they shall consume;

into smoke shall they consume away.

21The wicked borroweth, and payeth not again: but the righteous sheweth mercy, and giveth.

22For *such as be* blessed of him shall inherit the earth; and *they that be* cursed of him shall be cut off.

23The steps of a *good* man are ordered by the LORD: and he delighteth in his way.

24Though he fall, he shall not be utterly cast down: for the LORD upholdeth *him with* his hand.

25I have been young, and *now* am old; yet have I not seen the righteous forsaken, nor his seed begging bread.

26*He is* ever merciful, and lendeth; and his seed *is* blessed.

27Depart from evil, and do good; and dwell for evermore.

28For the LORD loveth judgment, and forsaketh not his saints; they are preserved for ever: but the seed of the wicked shall be cut off.

PROVERBS FOR TODAY/ 21:25–26

The desire of the slothful killeth him; for his hands refuse to labour. He coveteth greedily all the day long: but the righteous giveth and spareth not.

AUGUST 22

JOB 4:1—7:21

THEN Eliphaz the Temanite answered and said,

2*If* we assay to commune with thee, wilt thou be grieved? but who can withhold himself from speaking?

3Behold, thou hast instructed many, and thou hast strengthened the weak hands.

4Thy words have upholden him that was falling, and thou hast strengthened the feeble knees.

5But now it is come upon thee, and thou faintest; it toucheth thee, and thou art troubled.

6*Is* not *this* thy fear, thy confidence, thy hope, and the uprightness of thy ways?

7Remember, I pray thee, who *ever* perished, being innocent? or where were the righteous cut off?

8Even as I have seen, they that plow iniquity, and sow wickedness, reap the same.

9By the blast of God they perish, and by the breath of his nostrils are they consumed.

10The roaring of the lion, and the voice of the fierce lion, and the teeth of the young lions, are broken.

11The old lion perisheth for lack of prey, and the stout lion's whelps are scattered abroad.

12Now a thing was secretly brought to me, and mine ear received a little thereof.

13In thoughts from the visions of the night, when deep sleep falleth on men,

14Fear came upon me, and trembling, which made all my bones to shake.

15Then a spirit passed before my face; the hair of my flesh stood up:

16It stood still, but I could not discern the form thereof: an image *was* before mine eyes, *there was* silence, and I heard a voice, *saying,*

17Shall mortal man be more just than God? shall a man be more pure than his maker?

18Behold, he put no trust in his servants; and his angels he charged with folly:

19How much less *in* them that dwell in houses of clay, whose foundation *is* in the dust, *which* are crushed before the moth?

20They are destroyed from morning to evening: they perish for ever without any regarding *it.*

21Doth not their excellency *which is* in them go away? they die, even without wisdom.

CALL now, if there be any that will answer thee; and to which of the saints wilt thou turn?

2For wrath killeth the foolish man, and envy slayeth the silly one.

3I have seen the foolish taking root: but suddenly I cursed his habitation.

4His children are far from safety, and they are crushed in the gate, neither *is there* any to deliver *them.*

5Whose harvest the hungry eateth up, and taketh it even out of the thorns, and the robber swalloweth up their substance.

6Although affliction cometh not forth of the dust, neither doth trouble spring out of the ground;

7Yet man is born unto trouble, as the sparks fly upward.

8I would seek unto God, and unto God would I commit my cause:

9Which doeth great things and unsearchable; marvellous things without number:

10Who giveth rain upon the earth, and sendeth waters upon the fields:

11To set up on high those that be low; that those which mourn may be exalted to safety.

12He disappointeth the devices of the crafty, so that their hands cannot perform *their* enterprise.

13He taketh the wise in their own craftiness: and the counsel of the froward is carried headlong.

14They meet with darkness in the daytime, and grope in the noonday as in the night.

15But he saveth the poor from the sword, from their mouth, and from the hand of the mighty.

16So the poor hath hope, and iniquity stoppeth her mouth.

17Behold, happy *is* the man whom God correcteth: therefore despise not thou the chastening of the Almighty:

18For he maketh sore, and bindeth up: he woundeth, and his hands make whole.

19He shall deliver thee in six troubles: yea, in seven there shall no evil touch thee.

20In famine he shall redeem thee from death: and in war from the power of the sword.

21Thou shalt be hid from the scourge of the tongue: neither shalt thou be afraid of destruction when it cometh.

22At destruction and famine thou shalt laugh: neither shalt thou be afraid of the beasts of the earth.

23For thou shalt be in league with the stones of the field: and the beasts of the field shall be at peace with thee.

24And thou shalt know that thy tabernacle *shall be* in peace; and thou shalt visit thy habitation, and shalt not sin.

25Thou shalt know also that thy seed *shall be* great, and thine offspring as the grass of the earth.

26Thou shalt come to *thy* grave in a full age, like as a shock of corn cometh in his season.

27Lo this, we have searched it, so it *is;* hear it, and know thou *it* for thy good.

BUT Job answered and said,

2Oh that my grief were throughly weighed, and my calamity laid in the balances together!

3For now it would be heavier than the sand of the sea: therefore my words are swallowed up.

4For the arrows of the Almighty *are* within me, the poison whereof drinketh up my spirit: the terrors of God do set themselves in array against me.

5Doth the wild ass bray when he hath grass? or loweth the ox over his fodder?

6Can that which is unsavoury be eaten without salt? or is there *any* taste in the white of an egg?

7The things *that* my soul refused to touch *are* as my sorrowful meat.

8Oh that I might have my request; and that God would grant *me* the thing that I long for!

9Even that it would please God to destroy me; that he would let loose his hand, and cut me off!

10Then should I yet have comfort; yea, I would harden myself in sorrow: let him not spare; for I have not concealed the words of the Holy One.

11What *is* my strength, that I should hope? and what *is* mine end, that I should prolong my life?

12*Is* my strength the strength of stones? or *is* my flesh of brass?

13*Is* not my help in me? and is wisdom driven quite from me?

14To him that is afflicted pity *should be shewed* from his friend; but he forsaketh the fear of the Almighty.

15My brethren have dealt deceitfully as a brook, *and* as the stream of brooks they pass away;

16Which are blackish by reason of the ice, *and* wherein the snow is hid:

17What time they wax warm, they vanish: when it is hot, they are consumed out of their place.

18The paths of their way are turned aside; they go to nothing, and perish.

19The troops of Tema looked, the companies of Sheba waited for them.

20They were confounded because they had hoped; they came thither, and were ashamed.

21For now ye are nothing; ye see *my* casting down, and are afraid.

22Did I say, Bring unto me? or, Give a reward for me of your substance?

23Or, Deliver me from the enemy's hand? or, Redeem me from the hand of the mighty?

24Teach me, and I will hold my tongue: and cause me to understand wherein I have erred.

25How forcible are right words! but what doth your arguing reprove?

26Do ye imagine to reprove words, and the speeches of one that is desperate, *which are* as wind?

27Yea, ye overwhelm the fatherless, and ye dig *a pit* for your friend.

28Now therefore be content, look upon me; for *it is* evident unto you if I lie.

29Return, I pray you, let it not be iniquity; yea, return again, my righteousness *is* in it.

30Is there iniquity in my tongue? cannot my taste discern perverse things?

Is *there* not an appointed time to man upon earth? *are not* his days also like the days of an hireling?

2As a servant earnestly desireth the shadow, and as an hireling looketh for *the reward of* his work:

3So am I made to possess months of vanity, and wearisome nights are appointed to me.

4When I lie down, I say, When shall I arise, and the night be gone? and I am full of tossings to and fro unto the dawning of the day.

5My flesh is clothed with worms and clods of dust; my skin is broken, and become loathsome.

6My days are swifter than a weaver's shuttle, and are spent without hope.

7O remember that my life *is* wind: mine eye shall no more see good.

8The eye of him that hath seen me shall see me no *more:* thine eyes *are* upon me, and I *am not.*

9*As* the cloud is consumed and vanisheth away: so he that goeth down to the grave shall come up no *more.*

10He shall return no more to his house, neither shall his place know him any more.

11Therefore I will not refrain my mouth; I will speak in the anguish of my spirit; I will complain in the bitterness of my soul.

12*Am* I a sea, or a whale, that thou settest a watch over me?

13When I say, My bed shall comfort me, my couch shall ease my complaint;

14Then thou scarest me with dreams, and terrifiest me through visions:

15So that my soul chooseth strangling, *and* death rather than my life.

16I loathe *it;* I would not live alway: let me alone; for my days *are* vanity.

17What *is* man, that thou shouldest magnify him? and that thou shouldest set thine heart upon him?

18And *that* thou shouldest visit him every morning, *and* try him every moment?

19How long wilt thou not depart from me, nor let me alone till I swallow down my spittle?

20I have sinned; what shall I do unto thee, O thou preserver of men? why hast thou set me as a mark against thee, so that I am a burden to myself?

21And why dost thou not pardon my transgression, and take away mine iniquity? for now shall I sleep in the dust; and thou shalt seek me in the morning, but I *shall* not *be.*

1 CORINTHIANS 14:18–40

I thank my God, I speak with tongues more than ye all:

19Yet in the church I had rather speak five words with my understanding, that *by my voice* I might teach others also, than ten thousand words in an *unknown* tongue.

20Brethren, be not children in understanding: howbeit in malice be ye children, but in understanding be men.

21In the law it is written, With *men* of other tongues and other lips will I speak unto this people; and yet for all that will they not hear me, saith the Lord.

22Wherefore tongues are for a sign, not to them that believe, but to them that believe not: but prophesying *serveth* not for them that believe not, but for them which believe.

23If therefore the whole church be come together into one place, and all speak with tongues, and there come in *those that are* unlearned, or unbelievers, will they not say that ye are mad?

24But if all prophesy, and there come in one that believeth not, or *one* unlearned, he is convinced of all, he is judged of all:

25And thus are the secrets of his heart made manifest; and so falling down on *his* face he will worship God, and report that God is in you of a truth.

26How is it then, brethren? when ye come together, every one of you hath a psalm, hath a doctrine, hath a tongue, hath a revelation, hath an interpretation. Let all things be done unto edifying.

27If any man speak in an *unknown* tongue, *let it be* by two, or at the most *by* three, and *that* by course; and let one interpret.

28But if there be no interpreter, let him keep silence in the church; and let him speak to himself, and to God.

29Let the prophets speak two or three, and let the other judge.

30If *any thing* be revealed to another that sitteth by, let the first hold his peace.

31For ye may all prophesy one by one, that all may learn, and all may be comforted.

32And the spirits of the prophets are subject to the prophets.

33For God is not *the author* of confusion, but of peace, as in all churches of the saints.

34Let your women keep silence in the churches: for it is not permitted unto them to speak; but *they are commanded* to be under obedience, as also saith the law.

35And if they will learn any thing,

let them ask their husbands at home: for it is a shame for women to speak in the church.

36What? came the word of God out from you? or came it unto you only?

37If any man think himself to be a prophet, or spiritual, let him acknowledge that the things that I write unto you are the commandments of the Lord.

38But if any man be ignorant, let him be ignorant.

39Wherefore, brethren, covet to prophesy, and forbid not to speak with tongues.

40Let all things be done decently and in order.

PSALM 37:29–40

THE righteous shall inherit the land, and dwell therein for ever. 30The mouth of the righteous speaketh wisdom, and his tongue talketh of judgment.

31The law of his God *is* in his heart; none of his steps shall slide.

32The wicked watcheth the righ-

teous, and seeketh to slay him.

33The LORD will not leave him in his hand, nor condemn him when he is judged.

34Wait on the LORD, and keep his way, and he shalt exalt thee to inherit the land: when the wicked are cut off, thou shall see *it*.

35I have seen the wicked in great power, and spreading himself like a green bay tree.

36Yet he passed away, and, lo, he *was* not: yea, I sought him, but he could not be found.

37Mark the perfect *man,* and behold the upright: for the end of *that* man *is* peace.

38But the transgressors shall be destroyed together: the end of the wicked shall be cut off.

39But the salvation of the righteous *is* of the LORD: he *is* their strength in the time of trouble.

40And the LORD shall help them, and deliver them: he shall deliver them from the wicked, and save them, because they trust in him.

PROVERBS FOR TODAY/ 21:27

The sacrifice of the wicked is *abomination: how much more,* when *he bringeth it with a wicked mind?*

AUGUST 23

JOB 8:1—11:20

THEN answered Bildad the Shuhite, and said, 2How long wilt thou speak these *things?* and *how long shall* the words of thy mouth *be like* a strong wind?

3Doth God pervert judgment? or doth the Almighty pervert justice?

4If thy children have sinned against

him, and he have cast them away for their transgression;

5If thou wouldest seek unto God betimes, and make thy supplication to the Almighty;

6If thou *wert* pure and upright; surely now he would awake for thee, and make the habitation of thy righteousness prosperous.

7Though thy beginning was small,

yet thy latter end should greatly increase.

⁸For enquire, I pray thee, of the former age, and prepare thyself to the search of their fathers:

⁹(For we *are but of* yesterday, and know nothing, because our days upon earth *are* a shadow:)

¹⁰Shall not they teach thee, *and* tell thee, and utter words out of their heart?

¹¹Can the rush grow up without mire? can the flag grow without water?

¹²Whilst it *is* yet in his greenness, *and* not cut down, it withereth before any *other* herb.

¹³So *are* the paths of all that forget God; and the hypocrite's hope shall perish:

¹⁴Whose hope shall be cut off, and whose trust *shall be* a spider's web.

¹⁵He shall lean upon his house, but it shall not stand: he shall hold it fast, but it shall not endure.

¹⁶He *is* green before the sun, and his branch shooteth forth in his garden.

¹⁷His roots are wrapped about the heap, *and* seeth the place of stones.

¹⁸If he destroy him from his place, then *it* shall deny him, *saying,* I have not seen thee.

¹⁹Behold, this *is* the joy of his way, and out of the earth shall others grow.

²⁰Behold, God will not cast away a perfect *man,* neither will he help the evil doers:

²¹Till he fill thy mouth with laughing, and thy lips with rejoicing.

²²They that hate thee shall be clothed with shame; and the dwelling place of the wicked shall come to nought.

THEN Job answered and said,

²I know *it is* so of a truth: but how should man be just with God?

³If he will contend with him, he cannot answer him one of a thousand.

⁴*He is* wise in heart, and mighty in strength: who hath hardened *himself* against him, and hath prospered?

⁵Which removeth the mountains, and they know not: which overturneth them in his anger.

⁶Which shaketh the earth out of her place, and the pillars thereof tremble.

⁷Which commandeth the sun, and it riseth not; and sealeth up the stars.

⁸Which alone spreadeth out the heavens, and treadeth upon the waves of the sea.

⁹Which maketh Arcturus, Orion, and Pleiades, and the chambers of the south.

¹⁰Which doeth great things past finding out; yea, and wonders without number.

¹¹Lo, he goeth by me, and I see *him* not: he passeth on also, but I perceive him not.

¹²Behold, he taketh away, who can hinder him? who will say unto him, What doest thou?

¹³*If* God will not withdraw his anger, the proud helpers do stoop under him.

¹⁴How much less shall I answer him, *and* choose out my words *to reason* with him?

¹⁵Whom, though I were righteous, *yet* would I not answer, *but* I would make supplication to my judge.

¹⁶If I had called, and he had answered me; *yet* would I not believe that he had hearkened unto my voice.

¹⁷For he breaketh me with a tempest, and multiplieth my wounds without cause.

¹⁸He will not suffer me to take my breath, but filleth me with bitterness.

¹⁹If *I speak* of strength, lo, *he is* strong: and if of judgment, who shall set me a time *to plead?*

²⁰If I justify myself, mine own mouth shall condemn me: *if I say,* I *am* perfect, it shall also prove me perverse.

²¹*Though* I *were* perfect, *yet* would I not know my soul: I would despise my life.

²²This *is* one *thing,* therefore I said *it,* He destroyeth the perfect and the wicked.

²³If the scourge slay suddenly, he

will laugh at the trial of the innocent.

24The earth is given into the hand of the wicked: he covereth the faces of the judges thereof; if not, where, *and* who *is* he?

25Now my days are swifter than a post: they flee away, they see no good.

26They are passed away as the swift ships: as the eagle *that* hasteth to the prey.

27If I say, I will forget my complaint, I will leave off my heaviness, and comfort *myself:*

28I am afraid of all my sorrows, I know that thou wilt not hold me innocent.

29*If* I be wicked, why then labour I in vain?

30If I wash myself with snow water, and make my hands never so clean;

31Yet shalt thou plunge me in the ditch, and mine own clothes shall abhor me.

32For *he is* not a man, as I *am, that* I should answer him, *and* we should come together in judgment.

33Neither is there any daysman betwixt us, *that* might lay his hand upon us both.

34Let him take his rod away from me, and let not his fear terrify me:

35*Then* would I speak, and not fear him; but *it is* not so with me.

My soul is weary of my life; I will leave my complaint upon myself; I will speak in the bitterness of my soul.

2I will say unto God, Do not condemn me; shew me wherefore thou contendest with me.

3*Is it* good unto thee that thou shouldest oppress, that thou shouldest despise the work of thine hands, and shine upon the counsel of the wicked?

4Hast thou eyes of flesh? or seest thou as man seeth?

5*Are* thy days as the days of man? *are* thy years as man's days,

6That thou enquirest after mine iniq-

uity, and searchest after my sin?

7Thou knowest that I am not wicked; and *there is* none that can deliver out of thine hand.

8Thine hands have made me and fashioned me together round about; yet thou dost destroy me.

9Remember, I beseech thee, that thou hast made me as the clay; and wilt thou bring me into dust again?

10Hast thou not poured me out as milk, and curdled me like cheese?

11Thou hast clothed me with skin and flesh, and hast fenced me with bones and sinews.

12Thou hast granted me life and favour, and thy visitation hath preserved my spirit.

13And these *things* hast thou hid in thine heart: I know that this *is* with thee.

14If I sin, then thou markest me, and thou wilt not acquit me from mine iniquity.

15If I be wicked, woe unto me; and *if* I be righteous, *yet* will I not lift up my head. *I am* full of confusion; therefore see thou mine affliction;

16For it increaseth. Thou huntest me as a fierce lion: and again thou shewest thyself marvellous upon me.

17Thou renewest thy witnesses against me, and increasest thine indignation upon me; changes and war *are* against me.

18Wherefore then hast thou brought me forth out of the womb? Oh that I had given up the ghost, and no eye had seen me!

19I should have been as though I had not been; I should have been carried from the womb to the grave.

20*Are* not my days few? cease *then, and* let me alone, that I may take comfort a little,

21Before I go *whence* I shall not return, *even* to the land of darkness and the shadow of death;

22A land of darkness, as darkness *itself; and* of the shadow of death, without any order, and *where* the light *is* as darkness.

THEN answered Zophar the Naamathite, and said,

2Should not the multitude of words be answered? and should a man full of talk be justified?

3Should thy lies make men hold their peace? and when thou mockest, shall no man make thee ashamed?

4For thou hast said, My doctrine *is* pure, and I am clean in thine eyes.

5But oh that God would speak, and open his lips against thee;

6And that he would shew thee the secrets of wisdom, that *they are* double to that which is! Know therefore that God exacteth of thee *less* than thine iniquity *deserveth.*

7Canst thou by searching find out God? canst thou find out the Almighty unto perfection?

8*It is* as high as heaven; what canst thou do? deeper than hell; what canst thou know?

9The measure thereof *is* longer than the earth, and broader than the sea.

10If he cut off, and shut up, or gather together, then who can hinder him?

11For he knoweth vain men: he seeth wickedness also; will he not then consider *it?*

12For vain man would be wise, though man be born *like* a wild ass's colt.

13If thou prepare thine heart, and stretch out thine hands toward him;

14If iniquity *be* in thine hand, put it far away, and let not wickedness dwell in thy tabernacles.

15For then shalt thou lift up thy face without spot; yea, thou shalt be stedfast, and shalt not fear:

16Because thou shalt forget *thy* misery, *and* remember *it* as waters *that* pass away:

17And *thine* age shall be clearer than the noonday; thou shalt shine forth, thou shalt be as the morning.

18And thou shalt be secure, because there is hope; yea, thou shalt dig *about thee, and* thou shalt take thy rest in safety.

19Also thou shalt lie down, and none shall make *thee* afraid; yea, many shall make suit unto thee.

20But the eyes of the wicked shall fail, and they shall not escape, and their hope *shall be as* the giving up of the ghost.

1 CORINTHIANS 15:1–28

MOREOVER, brethren, I declare unto you the gospel which I preached unto you, which also ye have received, and wherein ye stand;

2By which also ye are saved, if ye keep in memory what I preached unto you, unless ye have believed in vain.

3For I delivered unto you first of all that which I also received, how that Christ died for our sins according to the scriptures;

4And that he was buried, and that he rose again the third day according to the scriptures:

5And that he was seen of Cephas, then of the twelve:

6After that, he was seen of above five hundred brethren at once; of whom the greater part remain unto this present, but some are fallen asleep.

7After that, he was seen of James; then of all the apostles.

8And last of all he was seen of me also, as of one born out of due time.

9For I am the least of the apostles, that am not meet to be called an apostle, because I persecuted the church of God.

10But by the grace of God I am what I am: and his grace which *was bestowed* upon me was not in vain; but I laboured more abundantly than they all: yet not I, but the grace of God which was with me.

11Therefore whether *it were* I or they, so we preach, and so ye believed.

12Now if Christ be preached that he

rose from the dead, how say some among you that there is no resurrection of the dead?

¹³But if there be no resurrection of the dead, then is Christ not risen:

¹⁴And if Christ be not risen, then *is* our preaching vain, and your faith *is* also vain.

¹⁵Yea, and we are found false witnesses of God; because we have testified of God that he raised up Christ: whom he raised not up, if so be that the dead rise not.

¹⁶For if the dead rise not, then is not Christ raised:

¹⁷And if Christ be not raised, your faith *is* vain; ye are yet in your sins.

¹⁸Then they also which are fallen asleep in Christ are perished.

¹⁹If in this life only we have hope in Christ, we are of all men most miserable.

²⁰But now is Christ risen from the dead, *and* become the firstfruits of them that slept.

²¹For since by man *came* death, by man *came* also the resurrection of the dead.

²²For as in Adam all die, even so in Christ shall all be made alive.

²³But every man in his own order: Christ the firstfruits; afterward they that are Christ's at his coming.

²⁴Then *cometh* the end, when he shall have delivered up the kingdom to God, even the Father; when he shall have put down all rule and all authority and power.

²⁵For he must reign, till he hath put all enemies under his feet.

²⁶The last enemy *that* shall be destroyed *is* death.

²⁷For he hath put all things under his feet. But when he saith all things are put under *him, it is* manifest that he is excepted, which did put all things under him.

²⁸And when all things shall be subdued unto him, then shall the Son also himself be subject unto him that put all things under him, that God may be all in all.

PSALM 38:1–22

O LORD, rebuke me not in thy wrath: neither chasten me in thy hot displeasure.

²For thine arrows stick fast in me, and thy hand presseth me sore.

³*There is* no soundness in my flesh because of thine anger; neither *is there any* rest in my bones because of my sin.

⁴For mine iniquities are gone over mine head: as an heavy burden they are too heavy for me.

⁵My wounds stink *and* are corrupt because of my foolishness.

⁶I am troubled; I am bowed down greatly; I go mourning all the day long.

⁷For my loins are filled with a loathsome *disease:* and *there is* no soundness in my flesh.

⁸I am feeble and sore broken: I have roared by reason of the disquietness of my heart.

⁹Lord, all my desire *is* before thee; and my groaning is not hid from thee.

¹⁰My heart panteth, my strength faileth me: as for the light of mine eyes, it also is gone from me.

¹¹My lovers and my friends stand aloof from my sore; and my kinsmen stand afar off.

¹²They also that seek after my life lay snares *for me:* and they that seek my hurt speak mischievous things, and imagine deceits all the day long.

¹³But I, as a deaf *man,* heard not; and *I was* as a dumb man *that* openeth not his mouth.

¹⁴Thus I was as a man that heareth not, and in whose mouth *are* no reproofs.

¹⁵For in thee, O LORD, do I hope: thou wilt hear, O Lord my God.

¹⁶For I said, *Hear me,* lest *otherwise* they should rejoice over me: when my

foot slippeth, they magnify *themselves* against me.

17For I *am* ready to halt, and my sorrow *is* continually before me.

18For I will declare mine iniquity; I will be sorry for my sin.

19But mine enemies *are* lively, *and* they are strong: and they that hate me wrongfully are multiplied.

20They also that render evil for good are mine adversaries; because I follow *the thing that* good *is*.

21Forsake me not, O LORD: O my God, be not far from me.

22Make haste to help me, O Lord my salvation.

PROVERBS FOR TODAY/ 21:28–29

A false witness shall perish: but the man that heareth speaketh constantly.
□ *A wicked man hardeneth his face: but* as for *the upright, he directeth his way.*

AUGUST 24

JOB 12:1—15:35

AND Job answered and said,
2No doubt but ye *are* the people, and wisdom shall die with you.

3But I have understanding as well as you; I *am* not inferior to you: yea, who knoweth not such things as these?

4I am *as* one mocked of his neighbour, who calleth upon God, and he answereth him: the just upright *man is* laughed to scorn.

5He that is ready to slip with *his* feet *is as* a lamp despised in the thought of him that is at ease.

6The tabernacles of robbers prosper, and they that provoke God are secure; into whose hand God bringeth *abundantly*.

7But ask now the beasts, and they shall teach thee; and the fowls of the air, and they shall tell thee:

8Or speak to the earth, and it shall teach thee: and the fishes of the sea shall declare unto thee.

9Who knoweth not in all these that the hand of the LORD hath wrought this?

10In whose hand *is* the soul of every living thing, and the breath of all mankind.

11Doth not the ear try words? and the mouth taste his meat?

12With the ancient *is* wisdom; and in length of days understanding.

13With him *is* wisdom and strength, he hath counsel and understanding.

14Behold, he breaketh down, and it cannot be built again: he shutteth up a man, and there can be no opening.

15Behold, he withholdeth the waters, and they dry up: also he sendeth them out, and they overturn the earth.

16With him *is* strength and wisdom: the deceived and the deceiver *are* his.

17He leadeth counsellors away spoiled, and maketh the judges fools.

18He looseth the bond of kings, and girdeth their loins with a girdle.

19He leadeth princes away spoiled, and overthroweth the mighty.

20He removeth away the speech of the trusty, and taketh away the understanding of the aged.

21He poureth contempt upon princes, and weakeneth the strength of the mighty.

22He discovereth deep things out of darkness, and bringeth out to light the shadow of death.

23He increaseth the nations, and destroyeth them: he enlargeth the nations, and straiteneth them *again.*

24He taketh away the heart of the chief of the people of the earth, and causeth them to wander in a wilderness *where there is* no way.

25They grope in the dark without light, and he maketh them to stagger like *a* drunken *man.*

Lo, mine eye hath seen all *this,* mine ear hath heard and understood it.

2What ye know, *the same* do I know also: I *am* not inferior unto you.

3Surely I would speak to the Almighty, and I desire to reason with God.

4But ye *are* forgers of lies, ye *are* all physicians of no value.

5O that ye would altogether hold your peace! and it should be your wisdom.

6Hear now my reasoning, and hearken to the pleadings of my lips.

7Will ye speak wickedly for God? and talk deceitfully for him?

8Will ye accept his person? will ye contend for God?

9Is it good that he should search you out? or as one man mocketh another, do ye *so* mock him?

10He will surely reprove you, if ye do secretly accept persons.

11Shall not his excellency make you afraid? and his dread fall upon you?

12Your remembrances *are* like unto ashes, your bodies to bodies of clay.

13Hold your peace, let me alone, that I may speak, and let come on me what *will.*

14Wherefore do I take my flesh in my teeth, and put my life in mine hand?

15Though he slay me, yet will I trust in him: but I will maintain mine own ways before him.

16He also *shall be* my salvation: for an hypocrite shall not come before him.

17Hear diligently my speech, and my declaration with your ears.

18Behold now, I have ordered *my* cause; I know that I shall be justified.

19Who *is* he *that* will plead with me? for now, if I hold my tongue, I shall give up the ghost.

20Only do not two *things* unto me: then will I not hide myself from thee.

21Withdraw thine hand far from me: and let not thy dread make me afraid.

22Then call thou, and I will answer: or let me speak, and answer thou me.

23How many *are* mine iniquities and sins? make me to know my transgression and my sin.

24Wherefore hidest thou thy face, and holdest me for thine enemy?

25Wilt thou break a leaf driven to and fro? and wilt thou pursue the dry stubble?

26For thou writest bitter things against me, and makest me to possess the iniquities of my youth.

27Thou puttest my feet also in the stocks, and lookest narrowly unto all my paths; thou settest a print upon the heels of my feet.

28And he, as a rotten thing, consumeth, as a garment that is moth eaten.

MAN *that is* born of a woman *is* of few days, and full of trouble.

2He cometh forth like a flower, and is cut down: he fleeth also as a shadow, and continueth not.

3And dost thou open thine eyes upon such an one, and bringest me into judgment with thee?

4Who can bring a clean *thing* out of an unclean? not one.

5Seeing his days *are* determined, the number of his months *are* with thee, thou hast appointed his bounds that he cannot pass;

6Turn from him, that he may rest, till he shall accomplish, as an hireling, his day.

7For there is hope of a tree, if it be cut down, that it will sprout again, and that the tender branch thereof will not cease.

8Though the root thereof wax old in the earth, and the stock thereof die in the ground;

9*Yet* through the scent of water it will bud, and bring forth boughs like a plant.

10But man dieth, and wasteth away: yea, man giveth up the ghost, and where *is* he?

11*As* the waters fail from the sea, and the flood decayeth and drieth up:

12So man lieth down, and riseth not: till the heavens *be* no more, they shall not awake, nor be raised out of their sleep.

13O that thou wouldest hide me in the grave, that thou wouldest keep me secret, until thy wrath be past, that thou wouldest appoint me a set time, and remember me!

14If a man die, shall he live *again?* all the days of my appointed time will I wait, till my change come.

15Thou shalt call, and I will answer thee: thou wilt have a desire to the work of thine hands.

16For now thou numberest my steps: dost thou not watch over my sin?

17My transgression *is* sealed up in a bag, and thou sewest up mine iniquity.

18And surely the mountain falling cometh to nought, and the rock is removed out of his place.

19The waters wear the stones: thou washest away the things which grow *out* of the dust of the earth; and thou destroyest the hope of man.

20Thou prevailest for ever against him, and he passeth: thou changest his countenance, and sendest him away.

21His sons come to honour, and he knoweth *it* not; and they are brought low, but he perceiveth *it* not of them.

22But his flesh upon him shall have pain, and his soul within him shall mourn.

THEN answered Eliphaz the Temanite, and said,

2Should a wise man utter vain knowledge, and fill his belly with the east wind?

3Should he reason with unprofitable talk? or with speeches wherewith he can do no good?

4Yea, thou castest off fear, and restrainest prayer before God.

5For thy mouth uttereth thine iniquity, and thou choosest the tongue of the crafty.

6Thine own mouth condemneth thee, and not I: yea, thine own lips testify against thee.

7*Art* thou the first man *that* was born? or wast thou made before the hills?

8Hast thou heard the secret of God? and dost thou restrain wisdom to thyself?

9What knowest thou, that we know not? *what* understandest thou, which *is* not in us?

10With us *are* both the gray headed and very aged men, much elder than thy father.

11*Are* the consolations of God small with thee? is there any secret thing with thee?

12Why doth thine heart carry thee away? and what do thy eyes wink at,

13That thou turnest thy spirit against God, and lettest *such* words go out of thy mouth?

14What *is* man, that he should be clean? and *he which is* born of a woman, that he should be righteous?

15Behold, he putteth no trust in his saints; yea, the heavens are not clean in his sight.

16How much more abominable and filthy *is* man, which drinketh iniquity like water?

17I will shew thee, hear me; and that *which* I have seen I will declare;

18Which wise men have told from their fathers, and have not hid *it:*

19Unto whom alone the earth was

given, and no stranger passed among them.

20The wicked man travaileth with pain all *his* days, and the number of years is hidden to the oppressor.

21A dreadful sound *is* in his ears: in prosperity the destroyer shall come upon him.

22He believeth not that he shall return out of darkness, and he is waited for of the sword.

23He wandereth abroad for bread, *saying,* Where *is it?* he knoweth that the day of darkness is ready at his hand.

24Trouble and anguish shall make him afraid; they shall prevail against him, as a king ready to the battle.

25For he stretcheth out his hand against God, and strengtheneth himself against the Almighty.

26He runneth upon him, *even* on *his* neck, upon the thick bosses of his bucklers:

27Because he covereth his face with his fatness, and maketh collops of fat on *his* flanks.

28And he dwelleth in desolate cities, *and* in houses which no man inhabiteth, which are ready to become heaps.

29He shall not be rich, neither shall his substance continue, neither shall he prolong the perfection thereof upon the earth.

30He shall not depart out of darkness; the flame shall dry up his branches, and by the breath of his mouth shall he go away.

31Let not him that is deceived trust in vanity: for vanity shall be his recompence.

32It shall be accomplished before his time, and his branch shall not be green.

33He shall shake off his unripe grape as the vine, and shall cast off his flower as the olive.

34For the congregation of hypocrites *shall be* desolate, and fire shall consume the tabernacles of bribery.

35They conceive mischief, and bring forth vanity, and their belly prepareth deceit.

1 CORINTHIANS 15:29–58

ELSE what shall they do which are baptized for the dead, if the dead rise not at all? why are they then baptized for the dead?

30And why stand we in jeopardy every hour?

31I protest by your rejoicing which I have in Christ Jesus our Lord, I die daily.

32If after the manner of men I have fought with beasts at Ephesus, what advantageth it me, if the dead rise not? let us eat and drink; for to morrow we die.

33Be not deceived: evil communications corrupt good manners.

34Awake to righteousness, and sin not; for some have not the knowledge of God: I speak *this* to your shame.

35But some *man* will say, How are the dead raised up? and with what body do they come?

36*Thou* fool, that which thou sowest is not quickened, except it die:

37And that which thou sowest, thou sowest not that body that shall be, but bare grain, it may chance of wheat, or of some other *grain:*

38But God giveth it a body as it hath pleased him, and to every seed his own body.

39All flesh *is* not the same flesh: but *there is* one *kind of* flesh of men, another flesh of beasts, another of fishes, *and* another of birds.

40*There are* also celestial bodies, and bodies terrestrial: but the glory of the celestial *is* one, and the *glory* of the terrestrial *is* another.

41*There is* one glory of the sun, and another glory of the moon, and another glory of the stars: for *one* star differeth from *another* star in glory.

42So also *is* the resurrection of the dead. It is sown in corruption; it is raised in incorruption:

43It is sown in dishonour; it is raised in glory: it is sown in weakness; it is raised in power:

44It is sown a natural body; it is raised a spiritual body. There is a natural body, and there is a spiritual body.

45And so it is written, The first man Adam was made a living soul; the last Adam *was made* a quickening spirit.

46Howbeit that *was* not first which is spiritual, but that which is natural; and afterward that which is spiritual.

47The first man *is* of the earth, earthy: the second man *is* the Lord from heaven.

48*As is* the earthy, such *are* they also that are earthy: and as *is* the heavenly, such *are* they also that are heavenly.

49And as we have borne the image of the earthy, we shall also bear the image of the heavenly.

50Now this I say, brethren, that flesh and blood cannot inherit the kingdom of God; neither doth corruption inherit incorruption.

51Behold, I shew you a mystery; We shall not all sleep, but we shall all be changed,

52In a moment, in the twinkling of an eye, at the last trump: for the trumpet shall sound, and the dead shall be raised incorruptible, and we shall be changed.

53For this corruptible must put on incorruption, and this mortal *must* put on immortality.

54So when this corruptible shall have put on incorruption, and this mortal shall have put on immortality, then shall be brought to pass the saying that is written, Death is swallowed up in victory.

55O death, where *is* thy sting? O grave, where *is* thy victory?

56The sting of death *is* sin; and the strength of sin *is* the law.

57But thanks *be* to God, which giveth us the victory through our Lord Jesus Christ.

58Therefore, my beloved brethren, be ye stedfast, unmoveable, always abounding in the work of the Lord, forasmuch as ye know that your labour is not in vain in the Lord.

PSALM 39:1–13

I SAID, I will take heed to my ways, that I sin not with my tongue: I will keep my mouth with a bridle, while the wicked is before me.

2I was dumb with silence, I held my peace, *even* from good; and my sorrow was stirred.

3My heart was hot within me, while I was musing the fire burned: *then* spake I with my tongue,

4LORD, make me to know mine end, and the measure of my days, what it *is: that* I may know how frail I *am.*

5Behold, thou hast made my days *as* an handbreadth; and mine age *is* as nothing before thee: verily every man at his best state *is* altogether vanity. Selah.

6Surely every man walketh in a vain shew: surely they are disquieted in vain: he heapeth up *riches,* and knoweth not who shall gather them.

7And now, Lord, what wait I for? my hope *is* in thee.

8Deliver me from all my transgressions: make me not the reproach of the foolish.

9I was dumb, I opened not my mouth; because thou didst *it.*

10Remove thy stroke away from me: I am consumed by the blow of thine hand.

11When thou with rebukes dost correct man for iniquity, thou makest his beauty to consume away like a moth: surely every man *is* vanity. Selah.

12Hear my prayer, O LORD, and give ear unto my cry; hold not thy peace at my tears: for I *am* a stranger with thee, *and* a sojourner, as all my fathers *were.*

13O spare me, that I may recover strength, before I go hence, and be no more.

There is *no wisdom nor understanding nor counsel against the* LORD. ☐ *The horse* is *prepared against the day of battle: but safety* is *of the* LORD.

AUGUST 25

JOB 16:1—19:29

THEN Job answered and said,
²I have heard many such things: miserable comforters *are* ye all.

³Shall vain words have an end? or what emboldeneth thee that thou answerest?

⁴I also could speak as ye *do:* if your soul were in my soul's stead, I could heap up words against you, and shake mine head at you.

⁵*But* I would strengthen you with my mouth, and the moving of my lips should assuage *your grief.*

⁶Though I speak, my grief is not assuaged: and *though* I forbear, what am I eased?

⁷But now he hath made me weary: thou hast made desolate all my company.

⁸And thou hast filled me with wrinkles, *which* is a witness *against me:* and my leanness rising up in me beareth witness to my face.

⁹He teareth *me* in his wrath, who hateth me: he gnasheth upon me with his teeth; mine enemy sharpeneth his eyes upon me.

¹⁰They have gaped upon me with their mouth: they have smitten me upon the cheek reproachfully; they have gathered themselves together against me.

¹¹God hath delivered me to the ungodly, and turned me over into the hands of the wicked.

¹²I was at ease, but he hath broken me asunder: he hath also taken *me* by my neck, and shaken me to pieces, and set me up for his mark.

¹³His archers compass me round about, he cleaveth my reins asunder, and doth not spare; he poureth out my gall upon the ground.

¹⁴He breaketh me with breach upon breach, he runneth upon me like a giant.

¹⁵I have sewed sackcloth upon my skin, and defiled my horn in the dust.

¹⁶My face is foul with weeping, and on my eyelids *is* the shadow of death;

¹⁷Not for *any* injustice in mine hands: also my prayer *is* pure.

¹⁸O earth, cover not thou my blood, and let my cry have no place.

¹⁹Also now, behold, my witness *is* in heaven, and my record *is* on high.

²⁰My friends scorn me: *but* mine eye poureth out *tears* unto God.

²¹O that one might plead for a man with God, as a man *pleadeth* for his neighbour!

²²When a few years are come, then I shall go the way *whence* I shall not return.

My breath is corrupt, my days are extinct, the graves *are ready* for me.

²*Are there* not mockers with me? and doth not mine eye continue in their provocation?

³Lay down now, put me in a surety with thee; who *is* he *that* will strike hands with me?

⁴For thou hast hid their heart from

understanding: therefore shalt thou not exalt *them*.

5He that speaketh flattery to *his* friends, even the eyes of his children shall fail.

6He hath made me also a byword of the people; and aforetime I was as a tabret.

7Mine eye also is dim by reason of sorrow, and all my members *are* as a shadow.

8Upright *men* shall be astonied at this, and the innocent shall stir up himself against the hypocrite.

9The righteous also shall hold on his way, and he that hath clean hands shall be stronger and stronger.

10But as for you all, do ye return, and come now: for I cannot find *one* wise *man* among you.

11My days are past, my purposes are broken off, *even* the thoughts of my heart.

12They change the night into day: the light *is* short because of darkness.

13If I wait, the grave *is* mine house: I have made my bed in the darkness.

14I have said to corruption, Thou *art* my father: to the worm, *Thou art* my mother, and my sister.

15And where *is* now my hope? as for my hope, who shall see it?

16They shall go down to the bars of the pit, when *our* rest together *is* in the dust.

THEN answered Bildad the Shuhite, and said,

2How long *will it be ere* ye make an end of words? mark, and afterwards we will speak.

3Wherefore are we counted as beasts, *and* reputed vile in your sight?

4He teareth himself in his anger: shall the earth be forsaken for thee? and shall the rock be removed out of his place?

5Yea, the light of the wicked shall be put out, and the spark of his fire shall not shine.

6The light shall be dark in his tabernacle, and his candle shall be put out with him.

7The steps of his strength shall be straitened, and his own counsel shall cast him down.

8For he is cast into a net by his own feet, and he walketh upon a snare.

9The gin shall take *him* by the heel, *and* the robber shall prevail against him.

10The snare *is* laid for him in the ground, and a trap for him in the way.

11Terrors shall make him afraid on every side, and shall drive him to his feet.

12His strength shall be hungerbitten, and destruction *shall be* ready at his side.

13It shall devour the strength of his skin: *even* the firstborn of death shall devour his strength.

14His confidence shall be rooted out of his tabernacle, and it shall bring him to the king of terrors.

15It shall dwell in his tabernacle, because *it is* none of his: brimstone shall be scattered upon his habitation.

16His roots shall be dried up beneath, and above shall his branch be cut off.

17His remembrance shall perish from the earth, and he shall have no name in the street.

18He shall be driven from light into darkness, and chased out of the world.

19He shall neither have son nor nephew among his people, nor any remaining in his dwellings.

20They that come after *him* shall be astonied at his day, as they that went before were affrighted.

21Surely such *are* the dwellings of the wicked, and this *is* the place *of him that* knoweth not God.

THEN Job answered and said,

2How long will ye vex my soul, and break me in pieces with words?

3These ten times have ye reproached me: ye are not ashamed *that* ye make yourselves strange to me.

4And be it indeed *that* I have erred, mine error remaineth with myself.

5If indeed ye will magnify *yourselves* against me, and plead against me my reproach:

6Know now that God hath overthrown me, and hath compassed me with his net.

7Behold, I cry out of wrong, but I am not heard: I cry aloud, but *there is* no judgment.

8He hath fenced up my way that I cannot pass, and he hath set darkness in my paths.

9He hath stripped me of my glory, and taken the crown *from* my head.

10He hath destroyed me on every side, and I am gone: and mine hope hath he removed like a tree.

11He hath also kindled his wrath against me, and he counteth me unto him as *one of* his enemies.

12His troops come together, and raise up their way against me, and encamp round about my tabernacle.

13He hath put my brethren far from me, and mine acquaintance are verily estranged from me.

14My kinsfolk have failed, and my familiar friends have forgotten me.

15They that dwell in mine house, and my maids, count me for a stranger: I am an alien in their sight.

16I called my servant, and he gave *me* no answer; I intreated him with my mouth.

17My breath is strange to my wife, though I intreated for the children's *sake* of mine own body.

18Yea, young children despised me; I arose, and they spake against me.

19All my inward friends abhorred me: and they whom I loved are turned against me.

20My bone cleaveth to my skin and to my flesh, and I am escaped with the skin of my teeth.

21Have pity upon me, have pity upon me, O ye my friends; for the hand of God hath touched me.

22Why do ye persecute me as God, and are not satisfied with my flesh?

23Oh that my words were now written! oh that they were printed in a book!

24That they were graven with an iron pen and lead in the rock for ever!

25For I know *that* my redeemer liveth, and *that* he shall stand at the latter *day* upon the earth:

26And *though* after my skin *worms* destroy this *body,* yet in my flesh shall I see God:

27Whom I shall see for myself, and mine eyes shall behold, and not another; *though* my reins be consumed within me.

28But ye should say, Why persecute we him, seeing the root of the matter is found in me?

29Be ye afraid of the sword: for wrath *bringeth* the punishments of the sword, that ye may know *there is* a judgment.

1 CORINTHIANS 16:1–24

Now concerning the collection for the saints, as I have given order to the churches of Galatia, even so do ye.

2Upon the first *day* of the week let every one of you lay by him in store, as *God* hath prospered him, that there be no gatherings when I come.

3And when I come, whomsoever ye shall approve by *your* letters, them will I send to bring your liberality unto Jerusalem.

4And if it be meet that I go also, they shall go with me.

5Now I will come unto you, when I shall pass through Macedonia: for I do pass through Macedonia.

6And it may be that I will abide, yea, and winter with you, that ye may bring me on my journey whithersoever I go.

7For I will not see you now by the way; but I trust to tarry a while with you, if the Lord permit.

8But I will tarry at Ephesus until Pentecost.

9For a great door and effectual is opened unto me, and *there are* many adversaries.

10Now if Timotheus come, see that he may be with you without fear: for he worketh the work of the Lord, as I also *do*.

11Let no man therefore despise him: but conduct him forth in peace, that he may come unto me: for I look for him with the brethren.

12As touching *our* brother Apollos, I greatly desired him to come unto you with the brethren: but his will was not at all to come at this time; but he will come when he shall have convenient time.

13Watch ye, stand fast in the faith, quit you like men, be strong.

14Let all your things be done with charity.

15I beseech you, brethren, (ye know the house of Stephanas, that it is the firstfruits of Achaia, and *that* they have addicted themselves to the ministry of the saints,)

16That ye submit yourselves unto such, and to every one that helpeth with *us*, and laboureth.

17I am glad of the coming of Stephanas and Fortunatus and Achaicus: for that which was lacking on your part they have supplied.

18For they have refreshed my spirit and yours: therefore acknowledge ye them that are such.

19The churches of Asia salute you. Aquila and Priscilla salute you much in the Lord, with the church that is in their house.

20All the brethren greet you. Greet ye one another with an holy kiss.

21The salutation of *me* Paul with mine own hand.

22If any man love not the Lord Jesus Christ, let him be Anathema Maranatha.

23The grace of our Lord Jesus Christ *be* with you.

24My love *be* with you all in Christ Jesus. Amen.

PSALM 40:1–10

I WAITED patiently for the LORD; and he inclined unto me, and heard my cry.

2He brought me up also out of an horrible pit, out of the miry clay, and set my feet upon a rock, *and* established my goings.

3And he hath put a new song in my mouth, *even* praise unto our God: many shall see *it,* and fear, and shall trust in the LORD.

4Blessed *is* that man that maketh the LORD his trust, and respecteth not the proud, nor such as turn aside to lies.

5Many, O LORD my God, *are* thy wonderful works *which* thou hast done, and thy thoughts *which are* to us-ward: they cannot be reckoned up in order unto thee: *if* I would declare and speak *of them,* they are more than can be numbered.

6Sacrifice and offering thou didst not desire; mine ears hast thou opened: burnt offering and sin offering hast thou not required.

7Then said I, Lo, I come: in the volume of the book *it is* written of me,

8I delight to do thy will, O my God: yea, thy law *is* within my heart.

9I have preached righteousness in the great congregation: lo, I have not refrained my lips, O LORD, thou knowest.

10I have not hid thy righteousness within my heart; I have declared thy faithfulness and thy salvation: I have not concealed thy lovingkindness and thy truth from the great congregation.

PROVERBS FOR TODAY/ 22:1

A GOOD *name* is *rather to be chosen than great riches,* and *loving favour rather than silver and gold.*

AUGUST 26

JOB 20:1—22:30

THEN answered Zophar the Naamathite, and said,

²Therefore do my thoughts cause me to answer, and for *this* I make haste.

³I have heard the check of my reproach, and the spirit of my understanding causeth me to answer.

⁴Knowest thou *not* this of old, since man was placed upon earth,

⁵That the triumphing of the wicked *is* short, and the joy of the hypocrite *but* for a moment?

⁶Though his excellency mount up to the heavens, and his head reach unto the clouds;

⁷*Yet* he shall perish for ever like his own dung: they which have seen him shall say, Where *is* he?

⁸He shall fly away as a dream, and shall not be found: yea, he shall be chased away as a vision of the night.

⁹The eye also *which* saw him shall *see him* no more; neither shall his place any more behold him.

¹⁰His children shall seek to please the poor, and his hands shall restore their goods.

¹¹His bones are full *of the sin* of his youth, which shall lie down with him in the dust.

¹²Though wickedness be sweet in his mouth, *though* he hide it under his tongue;

¹³*Though* he spare it, and forsake it not; but keep it still within his mouth:

¹⁴*Yet* his meat in his bowels is turned, *it is* the gall of asps within him.

¹⁵He hath swallowed down riches, and he shall vomit them up again: God shall cast them out of his belly.

¹⁶He shall suck the poison of asps: the viper's tongue shall slay him.

¹⁷He shall not see the rivers, the floods, the brooks of honey and butter.

¹⁸That which he laboured for shall he restore, and shall not swallow *it* down: according to *his* substance *shall* the restitution *be,* and he shall not rejoice *therein.*

¹⁹Because he hath oppressed *and* hath forsaken the poor; *because* he hath violently taken away an house which he builded not;

²⁰Surely he shall not feel quietness in his belly, he shall not save of that which he desired.

²¹There shall none of his meat be left; therefore shall no man look for his goods.

²²In the fulness of his sufficiency he shall be in straits: every hand of the wicked shall come upon him.

²³*When* he is about to fill his belly, *God* shall cast the fury of his wrath upon him, and shall rain *it* upon him while he is eating.

²⁴He shall flee from the iron weapon, *and* the bow of steel shall strike him through.

²⁵It is drawn, and cometh out of the body; yea, the glittering sword cometh out of his gall: terrors *are* upon him.

²⁶All darkness *shall be* hid in his secret places: a fire not blown shall consume

him; it shall go ill with him that is left in his tabernacle.

27The heaven shall reveal his iniquity; and the earth shall rise up against him.

28The increase of his house shall depart, *and his goods* shall flow away in the day of his wrath.

29This *is* the portion of a wicked man from God, and the heritage appointed unto him by God.

BUT Job answered and said,

2Hear diligently my speech, and let this be your consolations.

3Suffer me that I may speak; and after that I have spoken, mock on.

4As for me, *is* my complaint to man? and if *it were so,* why should not my spirit be troubled?

5Mark me, and be astonished, and lay *your* hand upon *your* mouth.

6Even when I remember I am afraid, and trembling taketh hold on my flesh.

7Wherefore do the wicked live, become old, yea, are mighty in power?

8Their seed is established in their sight with them, and their offspring before their eyes.

9Their houses *are* safe from fear, neither *is* the rod of God upon them.

10Their bull gendereth, and faileth not; their cow calveth, and casteth not her calf,

11They send forth their little ones like a flock, and their children dance.

12They take the timbrel and harp, and rejoice at the sound of the organ.

13They spend their days in wealth, and in a moment go down to the grave.

14Therefore they say unto God, Depart from us; for we desire not the knowledge of thy ways.

15What *is* the Almighty, that we should serve him? and what profit should we have, if we pray unto him?

16Lo, their good *is* not in their hand: the counsel of the wicked is far from me.

17How oft is the candle of the wicked put out! and *how oft* cometh their destruction upon them! *God* distributeth sorrows in his anger.

18They are as stubble before the wind, and as chaff that the storm carrieth away.

19God layeth up his iniquity for his children: he rewardeth him, and he shall know *it.*

20His eyes shall see his destruction, and he shall drink of the wrath of the Almighty.

21For what pleasure *hath* he in his house after him, when the number of his months is cut off in the midst?

22Shall *any* teach God knowledge? seeing he judgeth those that are high.

23One dieth in his full strength, being wholly at ease and quiet.

24His breasts are full of milk, and his bones are moistened with marrow.

25And another dieth in the bitterness of his soul, and never eateth with pleasure.

26They shall lie down alike in the dust, and the worms shall cover them.

27Behold, I know your thoughts, and the devices *which* ye wrongfully imagine against me.

28For ye say, Where *is* the house of the prince? and where *are* the dwelling places of the wicked?

29Have ye not asked them that go by the way? and do ye not know their tokens,

30That the wicked is reserved to the day of destruction? they shall be brought forth to the day of wrath.

31Who shall declare his way to his face? and who shall repay him *what* he hath done?

32Yet shall he be brought to the grave, and shall remain in the tomb.

33The clods of the valley shall be sweet unto him, and every man shall draw after him, as *there are* innumerable before him.

34How then comfort ye me in vain, seeing in your answers there remaineth falsehood?

THEN Eliphaz the Temanite answered and said,

2Can a man be profitable unto God, as he that is wise may be profitable unto himself?

3*Is it* any pleasure to the Almighty, that thou art righteous? or *is it* gain *to him,* that thou makest thy ways perfect?

4Will he reprove thee for fear of thee? will he enter with thee into judgment?

5*Is* not thy wickedness great? and thine iniquities infinite?

6For thou hast taken a pledge from thy brother for nought, and stripped the naked of their clothing.

7Thou hast not given water to the weary to drink, and thou hast withholden bread from the hungry.

8But *as for* the mighty man, he had the earth; and the honourable man dwelt in it.

9Thou hast sent widows away empty, and the arms of the fatherless have been broken.

10Therefore snares *are* round about thee, and sudden fear troubleth thee;

11Or darkness, *that* thou canst not see; and abundance of waters cover thee.

12*Is* not God in the height of heaven? and behold the height of the stars, how high they are!

13And thou sayest, How doth God know? can he judge through the dark cloud?

14Thick clouds *are* a covering to him, that he seeth not; and he walketh in the circuit of heaven.

15Hast thou marked the old way which wicked men have trodden?

16Which were cut down out of time, whose foundation was overflown with a flood:

17Which said unto God, Depart from us: and what can the Almighty do for them?

18Yet he filled their houses with good *things:* but the counsel of the wicked is far from me.

19The righteous see *it,* and are glad: and the innocent laugh them to scorn.

20Whereas our substance is not cut down, but the remnant of them the fire consumeth.

21Acquaint now thyself with him, and be at peace: thereby good shall come unto thee,

22Receive, I pray thee, the law from his mouth, and lay up his words in thine heart.

23If thou return to the Almighty, thou shalt be built up, thou shalt put away iniquity far from thy tabernacles.

24Then shalt thou lay up gold as dust, and the *gold* of Ophir as the stones of the brooks.

25Yea, the Almighty shall be thy defence, and thou shalt have plenty of silver.

26For then shalt thou have thy delight in the Almighty, and shalt lift up thy face unto God.

27Thou shalt make thy prayer unto him, and he shall hear thee, and thou shalt pay thy vows.

28Thou shalt also decree a thing, and it shall be established unto thee: and the light shall shine upon thy ways.

29When *men* are cast down, then thou shalt say, *There is* lifting up; and he shall save the humble person.

30He shall deliver the island of the innocent: and it is delivered by the pureness of thine hands.

2 CORINTHIANS 1:1–11

PAUL, an apostle of Jesus Christ by the will of God, and Timothy *our* brother, unto the church of God which is at Corinth, with all the saints which are in all Achaia:

2Grace *be* to you and peace from God our Father, and *from* the Lord Jesus Christ.

3Blessed *be* God, even the Father of our Lord Jesus Christ, the Father of mercies, and the God of all comfort;

⁴Who comforteth us in all our tribulation, that we may be able to comfort them which are in any trouble, by the comfort wherewith we ourselves are comforted of God.

⁵For as the sufferings of Christ abound in us, so our consolation also aboundeth by Christ.

⁶And whether we be afflicted, *it is* for your consolation and salvation, which is effectual in the enduring of the same sufferings which we also suffer: or whether we be comforted, *it is* for your consolation and salvation.

⁷And our hope of you *is* stedfast, knowing, that as ye are partakers of the sufferings, so *shall ye be* also of the consolation.

⁸For we would not, brethren, have you ignorant of our trouble which came to us in Asia, that we were pressed out of measure, above strength, insomuch that we despaired even of life:

⁹But we had the sentence of death in ourselves, that we should not trust in ourselves, but in God which raiseth the dead:

¹⁰Who delivered us from so great a death, and doth deliver: in whom we trust that he will yet deliver *us;*

¹¹Ye also helping together by prayer for us, that for the gift *bestowed* upon us by the means of many persons thanks may be given by many on our behalf.

PSALM 40:11–17

WITHHOLD not thou thy tender mercies from me, O LORD: let thy lovingkindness and thy truth continually preserve me.

¹²For innumerable evils have compassed me about: mine iniquities have taken hold upon me, so that I am not able to look up; they are more than the hairs of mine head: therefore my heart faileth me.

¹³Be pleased, O LORD, to deliver me: O LORD, make haste to help me.

¹⁴Let them be ashamed and confounded together that seek after my soul to destroy it; let them be driven backward and put to shame that wish me evil.

¹⁵Let them be desolate for a reward of their shame that say unto me, Aha, aha.

¹⁶Let all those that seek thee rejoice and be glad in thee: let such as love thy salvation say continually, The LORD be magnified.

¹⁷But I *am* poor and needy; *yet* the Lord thinketh upon me: thou *art* my help and my deliverer; make no tarrying, O my God.

PROVERBS FOR TODAY/ 22:2–4

The rich and poor meet together: the LORD is the maker of them all. □*A prudent* man *foreseeth the evil, and hideth himself: but the simple pass on, and are punished.* □*By humility* and *the fear of the LORD* are *riches, and honour, and life.*

AUGUST 27

THEN Job answered and said,
²Even to day *is* my complaint
bitter: my stroke is heavier than
my groaning.

³Oh that I knew where I might find
him! *that* I might come *even* to his seat!

⁴I would order *my* cause before him,
and fill my mouth with arguments.

⁵I would know the words *which* he
would answer me, and understand what
he would say unto me.

⁶Will he plead against me with *his*
great power? No; but he would put
strength in me.

⁷There the righteous might dispute
with him; so should I be delivered for
ever from my judge.

⁸Behold, I go forward, but he *is* not
there; and backward, but I cannot perceive him:

⁹On the left hand, where he doth
work, but I cannot behold *him:* he hideth
himself on the right hand, that I cannot
see *him:*

¹⁰But he knoweth the way that I take:
when he hath tried me, I shall come
forth as gold.

¹¹My foot hath held his steps, his
way have I kept, and not declined.

¹²Neither have I gone back from the
commandment of his lips; I have esteemed the words of his mouth more
than my necessary *food.*

¹³But he *is* in one *mind,* and who
can turn him? and *what* his soul desireth,
even *that* he doeth.

¹⁴For he performeth *the thing that
is* appointed for me: and many such
things are with him.

¹⁵Therefore am I troubled at his presence: when I consider, I am afraid of
him.

¹⁶For God maketh my heart soft, and
the Almighty troubleth me:

¹⁷Because I was not cut off before
the darkness, *neither* hath he covered
the darkness from my face.

WHY, seeing times are not hidden from
the Almighty, do they that know him
not see his days?

²*Some* remove the landmarks; they
violently take away flocks, and feed
thereof.

³They drive away the ass of the fatherless, they take the widow's ox for
a pledge.

⁴They turn the needy out of the way:
the poor of the earth hide themselves
together.

⁵Behold, *as* wild asses in the desert,
go they forth to their work; rising betimes for a prey: the wilderness *yieldeth*
food for them *and* for *their* children.

⁶They reap *every one* his corn in the
field: and they gather the vintage of
the wicked.

⁷They cause the naked to lodge without clothing, that *they have* no covering
in the cold.

⁸They are wet with the showers of
the mountains, and embrace the rock
for want of a shelter.

⁹They pluck the fatherless from the
breast, and take a pledge of the poor.

¹⁰They cause *him* to go naked without
clothing, and they take away the sheaf
from the hungry;

¹¹*Which* make oil within their walls,
and tread *their* winepresses, and suffer
thirst.

¹²Men groan from out of the city,
and the soul of the wounded crieth out:
yet God layeth not folly *to them.*

¹³They are of those that rebel against
the light; they know not the ways
thereof, nor abide in the paths thereof.

¹⁴The murderer rising with the light
killeth the poor and needy, and in

the night is as a thief.

15The eye also of the adulterer waiteth for the twilight, saying, No eye shall see me: and disguiseth *his* face.

16In the dark they dig through houses, *which* they had marked for themselves in the daytime: they know not the light.

17For the morning *is* to them even as the shadow of death: if *one* know *them, they are in* the terrors of the shadow of death.

18He *is* swift as the waters; their portion is cursed in the earth: he beholdeth not the way of the vineyards.

19Drought and heat consume the snow waters: *so doth* the grave *those which* have sinned.

20The womb shall forget him; the worm shall feed sweetly on him; he shall be no more remembered; and wickedness shall be broken as a tree.

21He evil entreateth the barren *that* beareth not: and doeth not good to the widow.

22He draweth also the mighty with his power: he riseth up, and no *man* is sure of life.

23*Though* it be given him *to be* in safety, whereon he resteth; yet his eyes *are* upon their ways.

24They are exalted for a little while, but are gone and brought low; they are taken out of the way as all *other,* and cut off as the tops of the ears of corn.

25And if *it be* not *so* now, who will make me a liar, and make my speech nothing worth?

THEN answered Bildad the Shuhite, and said,

2Dominion and fear *are* with him, he maketh peace in his high places.

3Is there any number of his armies? and upon whom doth not his light arise?

4How then can man be justified with God? or how can he be clean *that is* born of a woman?

5Behold even to the moon, and it shineth not; yea, the stars are not pure in his sight.

6How much less man, *that is* a worm? and the son of man, *which is* a worm?

BUT Job answered and said,

2How hast thou helped *him that is* without power? *how* savest thou the arm *that hath* no strength?

3How hast thou counselled *him that hath* no wisdom? and *how* hast thou plentifully declared the thing as it is?

4To whom hast thou uttered words? and whose spirit came from thee?

5Dead *things* are formed from under the waters, and the inhabitants thereof.

6Hell *is* naked before him, and destruction hath no covering.

7He stretcheth out the north over the empty place, *and* hangeth the earth upon nothing.

8He bindeth up the waters in his thick clouds; and the cloud is not rent under them.

9He holdeth back the face of his throne, *and* spreadeth his cloud upon it.

10He hath compassed the waters with bounds, until the day and night come to an end.

11The pillars of heaven tremble and are astonished at his reproof.

12He divideth the sea with his power, and by his understanding he smiteth through the proud.

13By his spirit he hath garnished the heavens; his hand hath formed the crooked serpent.

14Lo, these *are* parts of his ways: but how little a portion is heard of him? but the thunder of his power who can understand?

MOREOVER Job continued his parable, and said,

2*As* God liveth, *who* hath taken away my judgment; and the Almighty, *who* hath vexed my soul;

3All the while my breath *is* in me, and the spirit of God *is* in my nostrils;

4My lips shall not speak wickedness, nor my tongue utter deceit.

5God forbid that I should justify you: till I die I will not remove mine integrity from me.

6My righteousness I hold fast, and will not let it go: my heart shall not reproach *me* so long as I live.

7Let mine enemy be as the wicked, and he that riseth up against me as the unrighteous.

8For what *is* the hope of the hypocrite, though he hath gained, when God taketh away his soul?

9Will God hear his cry when trouble cometh upon him?

10Will he delight himself in the Almighty? will he always call upon God?

11I will teach you by the hand of God: *that* which *is* with the Almighty will I not conceal.

12Behold, all ye yourselves have seen *it;* why then are ye thus altogether vain?

13This *is* the portion of a wicked man with God, and the heritage of oppressors, *which* they shall receive of the Almighty.

14If his children be multiplied, *it is* for the sword: and his offspring shall not be satisfied with bread.

15Those that remain of him shall be buried in death: and his widows shall not weep.

16Though he heap up silver as the dust, and prepare raiment as the clay;

17He may prepare *it,* but the just shall put *it* on, and the innocent shall divide the silver.

18He buildeth his house as a moth, and as a booth *that* the keeper maketh.

19The rich man shall lie down, but he shall not be gathered: he openeth his eyes, and he *is* not.

20Terrors take hold on him as waters, a tempest stealeth him away in the night.

21The east wind carrieth him away, and he departeth: and as a storm hurleth him out of his place.

22For *God* shall cast upon him, and not spare: he would fain flee out of his hand.

23*Men* shall clap their hands at him, and shall hiss him out of his place.

2 CORINTHIANS 1:12—2:8

FOR our rejoicing is this, the testimony of our conscience, that in simplicity and godly sincerity, not with fleshly wisdom, but by the grace of God, we have had our conversation in the world, and more abundantly to you-ward.

13For we write none other things unto you, than what ye read or acknowledge; and I trust ye shall acknowledge even to the end;

14As also ye have acknowledged us in part, that we are your rejoicing, even as ye also *are* ours in the day of the Lord Jesus.

15And in this confidence I was minded to come unto you before, that ye might have a second benefit;

16And to pass by you into Macedonia, and to come again out of Macedonia unto you, and of you to be brought on my way toward Judaea.

17When I therefore was thus minded, did I use lightness? or the things that I purpose, do I purpose according to the flesh, that with me there should be yea yea, and nay nay?

18But *as* God *is* true, our word toward you was not yea and nay.

19For the Son of God, Jesus Christ, who was preached among you by us, *even* by me and Silvanus and Timotheus, was not yea and nay, but in him was yea.

20For all the promises of God in him *are* yea, and in him Amen, unto the glory of God by us.

21Now he which stablisheth us with you in Christ, and hath anointed us, *is* God;

22Who hath also sealed us, and given the earnest of the Spirit in our hearts.

23Moreover I call God for a record

upon my soul, that to spare you I came not as yet unto Corinth.

24Not for that we have dominion over your faith, but are helpers of your joy: for by faith ye stand.

BUT I determined this with myself, that I would not come again to you in heaviness.

2For if I make you sorry, who is he then that maketh me glad, but the same which is made sorry by me?

3And I wrote this same unto you, lest, when I came, I should have sorrow from them of whom I ought to rejoice; having confidence in you all, that my joy is *the joy* of you all.

4For out of much affliction and anguish of heart I wrote unto you with many tears; not that ye should be grieved, but that ye might know the love which I have more abundantly unto you.

5But if any have caused grief, he hath not grieved me, but in part: that I may not overcharge you all.

6Sufficient to such a man *is* this punishment, which *was inflicted* of many.

7So that contrariwise ye *ought* rather to forgive *him,* and comfort *him,* lest perhaps such a one should be swallowed up with overmuch sorrow.

8Wherefore I beseech you that ye would confirm *your* love toward him.

PSALM 41:1–13

BLESSED *is* he that considereth the poor: the LORD will deliver him in time of trouble.

2The LORD will preserve him, and keep him alive; *and* he shall be blessed upon the earth: and thou wilt not deliver him unto the will of his enemies.

3The LORD will strengthen him upon the bed of languishing: thou wilt make all his bed in his sickness.

4I said, LORD, be merciful unto me: heal my soul; for I have sinned against thee.

5Mine enemies speak evil of me, When shall he die, and his name perish?

6And if he come to see *me,* he speaketh vanity: his heart gathereth iniquity to itself; *when* he goeth abroad, he telleth *it.*

7All that hate me whisper together against me: against me do they devise my hurt.

8An evil disease, *say they,* cleaveth fast unto him: and *now* that he lieth he shall rise up no more.

9Yea, mine own familiar friend, in whom I trusted, which did eat of my bread, hath lifted up *his* heel against me.

10But thou, O LORD, be merciful unto me, and raise me up, that I may requite them.

11By this I know that thou favourest me, because mine enemy doth not triumph over me.

12And as for me, thou upholdest me in mine integrity, and settest me before thy face for ever.

13Blessed *be* the LORD God of Israel from everlasting, and to everlasting. Amen, and Amen.

PROVERBS FOR TODAY/ 22:5–6

Thorns and *snares* are *in the way of the froward: he that doth keep his soul shall be far from them.*   □ *Train up a child in the way he should go: and when he is old, he will not depart from it.*

AUGUST 28

SURELY there is a vein for the silver, and a place for gold *where* they fine *it*.

2Iron is taken out of the earth, and brass *is* molten *out of* the stone.

3He setteth an end to darkness, and searcheth out all perfection: the stones of darkness, and the shadow of death.

4The flood breaketh out from the inhabitant: *even the waters* forgotten of the foot: they are dried up, they are gone away from men.

5*As for* the earth, out of it cometh bread: and under it is turned up as it were fire.

6The stones of it *are* the place of sapphires: and it hath dust of gold.

7*There is* a path which no fowl knoweth, and which the vulture's eye hath not seen:

8The lion's whelps have not trodden it, nor the fierce lion passed by it.

9He putteth forth his hand upon the rock; he overturneth the mountains by the roots.

10He cutteth out rivers among the rocks; and his eye seeth every precious thing.

11He bindeth the floods from overflowing; and *the thing that is* hid bringeth he forth to light.

12But where shall wisdom be found? and where *is* the place of understanding?

13Man knoweth not the price thereof; neither is it found in the land of the living.

14The depth saith, It *is* not in me: and the sea saith, *It is* not with me.

15It cannot be gotten for gold, neither shall silver be weighed *for* the price thereof.

16It cannot be valued with the gold of Ophir, with the precious onyx, or the sapphire.

17The gold and the crystal cannot equal it: and the exchange of it *shall not be for* jewels of fine gold.

18No mention shall be made of coral, or of pearls: for the price of wisdom *is* above rubies.

19The topaz of Ethiopia shall not equal it, neither shall it be valued with pure gold.

20Whence then cometh wisdom? and where *is* the place of understanding?

21Seeing it is hid from the eyes of all living, and kept close from the fowls of the air.

22Destruction and death say, We have heard the fame thereof with our ears.

23God understandeth the way thereof, and he knoweth the place thereof.

24For he looketh to the ends of the earth, *and* seeth under the whole heaven;

25To make the weight for the winds; and he weigheth the waters by measure.

26When he made a decree for the rain, and a way for the lightning of the thunder:

27Then did he see it, and declare it; he prepared it, yea, and searched it out.

28And unto man he said, Behold, the fear of the LORD, that *is* wisdom; and to depart from evil *is* understanding.

MOREOVER Job continued his parable, and said,

2Oh that I were as *in* months past, as *in* the days *when* God preserved me;

3When his candle shined upon my head, *and when* by his light I walked *through* darkness;

4As I was in the days of my youth,

when the secret of God *was* upon my tabernacle;

5When the Almighty *was* yet with me, *when* my children *were* about me;

6When I washed my steps with butter, and the rock poured me out rivers of oil;

7When I went out to the gate through the city, *when* I prepared my seat in the street!

8The young men saw me, and hid themselves: and the aged arose, *and* stood up.

9The princes refrained talking, and laid *their* hand on their mouth.

10The nobles held their peace, and their tongue cleaved to the roof of their mouth.

11When the ear heard *me,* then it blessed me; and when the eye saw *me,* it gave witness to me:

12Because I delivered the poor that cried, and the fatherless, and *him that had* none to help him.

13The blessing of him that was ready to perish came upon me: and I caused the widow's heart to sing for joy.

14I put on righteousness, and it clothed me: my judgment *was* as a robe and a diadem.

15I was eyes to the blind, and feet *was* I to the lame.

16I *was* a father to the poor: and the cause *which* I knew not I searched out.

17And I brake the jaws of the wicked, and plucked the spoil out of his teeth.

18Then I said, I shall die in my nest, and I shall multiply *my* days as the sand.

19My root *was* spread out by the waters, and the dew lay all night upon my branch.

20My glory *was* fresh in me, and my bow was renewed in my hand.

21Unto me *men* gave ear, and waited, and kept silence at my counsel.

22After my words they spake not again; and my speech dropped upon them.

23And they waited for me as for the rain; and they opened their mouth wide as for the latter rain.

24*If* I laughed on them, they believed *it* not; and the light of my countenance they cast not down.

25I chose out their way, and sat chief, and dwelt as a king in the army, as one *that* comforteth the mourners.

BUT now *they that are* younger than I have me in derision, whose fathers I would have disdained to have set with the dogs of my flock.

2Yea, whereto *might* the strength of their hands *profit* me, in whom old age was perished?

3For want and famine *they were* solitary; fleeing into the wilderness in former time desolate and waste.

4Who cut up mallows by the bushes, and juniper roots *for* their meat.

5They were driven forth from among *men,* (they cried after them as *after* a thief;)

6To dwell in the cliffs of the valleys, *in* caves of the earth, and *in* the rocks.

7Among the bushes they brayed; under the nettles they were gathered together.

8*They were* children of fools, yea, children of base men: they were viler than the earth.

9And now am I their song, yea, I am their byword.

10They abhor me, they flee far from me, and spare not to spit in my face.

11Because he hath loosed my cord, and afflicted me, they have also let loose the bridle before me.

12Upon *my* right *hand* rise the youth; they push away my feet, and they raise up against me the ways of their destruction.

13They mar my path, they set forward my calamity, they have no helper.

14They came *upon me* as a wide breaking in *of waters:* in the desolation they rolled themselves *upon me.*

15Terrors are turned upon me: they pursue my soul as the wind: and my welfare passeth away as a cloud.

16And now my soul is poured out upon me; the days of affliction have taken hold upon me.

17My bones are pierced in me in the night season: and my sinews take no rest.

18By the great force *of my disease* is my garment changed: it bindeth me about as the collar of my coat.

19He hath cast me into the mire, and I am become like dust and ashes.

20I cry unto thee, and thou dost not hear me: I stand up, and thou regardest me *not.*

21Thou art become cruel to me: with thy strong hand thou opposest thyself against me.

22Thou liftest me up to the wind; thou causest me to ride *upon it,* and dissolvest my substance.

23For I know *that* thou wilt bring me *to* death, and *to* the house appointed for all living.

24Howbeit he will not stretch out *his* hand to the grave, though they cry in his destruction.

25Did not I weep for him that was in trouble? was *not* my soul grieved for the poor?

26When I looked for good, then evil came *unto me:* and when I waited for light, there came darkness.

27My bowels boiled, and rested not: the days of affliction prevented me.

28I went mourning without the sun: I stood up, *and* I cried in the congregation.

29I am a brother to dragons, and a companion to owls.

30My skin is black upon me, and my bones are burned with heat.

31My harp also is *turned* to mourning, and my organ into the voice of them that weep.

2 CORINTHIANS 2:9–17

FOR to this end also did I write, that I might know the proof of you, whether ye be obedient in all things.

10To whom ye forgive any thing, I *forgive* also: for if I forgave any thing, to whom I forgave *it,* for your sakes *forgave I it* in the person of Christ;

11Lest Satan should get an advantage of us: for we are not ignorant of his devices.

12Furthermore, when I came to Troas to *preach* Christ's gospel, and a door was opened unto me of the Lord,

13I had no rest in my spirit, because I found not Titus my brother: but taking my leave of them, I went from thence into Macedonia.

14Now thanks *be* unto God, which always causeth us to triumph in Christ, and maketh manifest the savour of his knowledge by us in every place.

15For we are unto God a sweet savour of Christ, in them that are saved, and in them that perish:

16To the one *we are* the savour of death unto death; and to the other the savour of life unto life. And who *is* sufficient for these things?

17For we are not as many, which corrupt the word of God: but as of sincerity, but as of God, in the sight of God speak we in Christ.

PSALM 42:1–11

AS the hart panteth after the water brooks, so panteth my soul after thee, O God.

2My soul thirsteth for God, for the living God: when shall I come and appear before God?

3My tears have been my meat day and night, while they continually say unto me, Where *is* thy God?

4When I remember these *things,* I pour out my soul in me: for I had gone with the multitude, I went with them to the house of God, with the voice of joy and praise, with a multitude that kept holyday.

5Why art thou cast down, O my soul? and *why* art thou disquieted in me? hope thou in God: for I shall yet praise him *for* the help of his countenance.

6O my God, my soul is cast down within me: therefore will I remember thee from the land of Jordan, and of the Hermonites, from the hill Mizar.

7Deep calleth unto deep at the noise of thy waterspouts: all thy waves and thy billows are gone over me.

8*Yet* the LORD will command his lovingkindness in the daytime, and in the night his song *shall be* with me, *and* my prayer unto the God of my life.

9I will say unto God my rock, Why hast thou forgotten me? why go I mourning because of the oppression of the enemy?

10*As* with a sword in my bones, mine enemies reproach me; while they say daily unto me, Where *is* thy God?

11Why art thou cast down, O my soul? and why art thou disquieted within me? hope thou in God: for I shall yet praise him, *who is* the health of my countenance, and my God.

PROVERBS FOR TODAY/ 22:7

The rich ruleth over the poor, and the borrower is *servant to the lender.*

AUGUST 29

JOB 31:1—33:33

I MADE a covenant with mine eyes: why then should I think upon a maid?

2For what portion of God *is there* from above? and *what* inheritance of the Almighty from on high?

3*Is* not destruction to the wicked? and a strange *punishment* to the workers of iniquity?

4Doth not he see my ways, and count all my steps?

5If I have walked with vanity, or if my foot hath hasted to deceit;

6Let me be weighed in an even balance that God may know mine integrity.

7If my step hath turned out of the way, and mine heart walked after mine eyes, and if any blot hath cleaved to mine hands;

8*Then* let me sow, and let another eat; yea, let my offspring be rooted out.

9If mine heart have been deceived by a woman, or *if* I have laid wait at my neighbour's door;

10*Then* let my wife grind unto another, and let others bow down upon her.

11For this *is* an heinous crime; yea, it *is* an iniquity *to be punished by* the judges.

12For it *is* a fire *that* consumeth to destruction, and would root out all mine increase.

13If I did despise the cause of my manservant or of my maidservant, when they contended with me;

14What then shall I do when God riseth up? and when he visiteth, what shall I answer him?

15Did not he that made me in the womb make him? and did not one fashion us in the womb?

16If I have withheld the poor from *their* desire, or have caused the eyes of the widow to fail;

17Or have eaten my morsel myself alone, and the fatherless hath not eaten thereof;

18(For from my youth he was brought up with me, as *with* a father, and I have guided her from my mother's womb;)

19If I have seen any perish for want of clothing, or any poor without covering;

20If his loins have not blessed me, and *if* he were *not* warmed with the fleece of my sheep;

21If I have lifted up my hand against the fatherless, when I saw my help in the gate:

22*Then* let mine arm fall from my shoulder blade, and mine arm be broken from the bone.

23For destruction *from* God *was* a terror to me, and by reason of his highness I could not endure.

24If I have made gold my hope, or have said to the fine gold, *Thou art* my confidence;

25If I rejoiced because my wealth *was* great, and because mine hand had gotten much;

26If I beheld the sun when it shined, or the moon walking *in* brightness;

27And my heart hath been secretly enticed, or my mouth hath kissed my hand:

28This also *were* an iniquity *to be punished by* the judge: for I should have denied the God *that is* above.

29If I rejoiced at the destruction of him that hated me, or lifted up myself when evil found him:

30Neither have I suffered my mouth to sin by wishing a curse to his soul.

31If the men of my tabernacle said not, Oh that we had of his flesh! we cannot be satisfied.

32The stranger did not lodge in the street: *but* I opened my doors to the traveller.

33If I covered my transgressions as Adam, by hiding mine iniquity in my bosom:

34Did I fear a great multitude, or did the contempt of families terrify me, that I kept silence, *and* went not out of the door?

35Oh that one would hear me! behold, my desire *is, that* the Almighty would answer me, and *that* mine adversary had written a book.

36Surely I would take it upon my shoulder, *and* bind it *as* a crown to me.

37I would declare unto him the number of my steps; as a prince would I go near unto him.

38If my land cry against me, or that the furrows likewise thereof complain;

39If I have eaten the fruits thereof without money, or have caused the owners thereof to lose their life:

40Let thistles grow instead of wheat, and cockle instead of barley. The words of Job are ended.

So these three men ceased to answer Job, because he *was* righteous in his own eyes.

2Then was kindled the wrath of Elihu the son of Barachel the Buzite, of the kindred of Ram: against Job was his wrath kindled, because he justified himself rather than God.

3Also against his three friends was his wrath kindled, because they had found no answer, and *yet* had condemned Job.

4Now Elihu had waited till Job had spoken, because they *were* elder than he.

5When Elihu saw that *there was* no answer in the mouth of *these* three men, then his wrath was kindled.

6And Elihu the son of Barachel the Buzite answered and said, I *am* young, and ye *are* very old; wherefore I was afraid, and durst not shew you mine opinion.

7I said, Days should speak, and multitude of years should teach wisdom.

8But *there is* a spirit in man: and the inspiration of the Almighty giveth them understanding.

9Great men are not *always* wise: neither do the aged understand judgment.

10Therefore I said, Hearken to me; I also will shew mine opinion.

11Behold, I waited for your words; I gave ear to your reasons, whilst ye searched out what to say.

12Yea, I attended unto you, and, behold, *there was* none of you that convinced Job, *or* that answered his words:

13Lest ye should say, We have found out wisdom: God thrusteth him down, not man.

14Now he hath not directed *his* words against me: neither will I answer him with your speeches.

15They were amazed, they answered no more: they left off speaking.

16When I had waited, (for they spake not, but stood still, *and* answered no more;)

17*I said,* I will answer also my part, I also will shew mine opinion.

18For I am full of matter, the spirit within me constraineth me.

19Behold, my belly *is* as wine *which* hath no vent; it is ready to burst like new bottles.

20I will speak, that I may be refreshed: I will open my lips and answer.

21Let me not, I pray you, accept any man's person, neither let me give flattering titles unto man.

22For I know not to give flattering titles; *in so doing* my maker would soon take me away.

WHEREFORE, Job, I pray thee, hear my speeches, and hearken to all my words.

2Behold, now I have opened my mouth, my tongue hath spoken in my mouth.

3My words *shall be of* the uprightness of my heart: and my lips shall utter knowledge clearly.

4The spirit of God hath made me, and the breath of the Almighty hath given me life.

5If thou canst answer me, set *thy words* in order before me, stand up.

6Behold, I *am* according to thy wish in God's stead: I also am formed out of the clay.

7Behold, my terror shall not make thee afraid, neither shall my hand be heavy upon thee.

8Surely thou hast spoken in mine hearing, and I have heard the voice of *thy* words, *saying,*

9I am clean without transgression, I *am* innocent; neither *is there* iniquity in me.

10Behold, he findeth occasions against me, he counteth me for his enemy,

11He putteth my feet in the stocks, he marketh all my paths.

12Behold, *in* this thou art not just: I will answer thee, that God is greater than man.

13Why dost thou strive against him? for he giveth not account of any of his matters.

14For God speaketh once, yea twice, *yet man* perceiveth it not.

15In a dream, in a vision of the night, when deep sleep falleth upon men, in slumberings upon the bed;

16Then he openeth the ears of men, and sealeth their instruction,

17That he may withdraw man *from his* purpose, and hide pride from man.

18He keepeth back his soul from the pit, and his life from perishing by the sword.

19He is chastened also with pain upon his bed, and the multitude of his bones with strong *pain:*

20So that his life abhorreth bread, and his soul dainty meat.

21His flesh is consumed away, that it cannot be seen; and his bones *that* were not seen stick out.

22Yea, his soul draweth near unto the grave, and his life to the destroyers.

23If there be a messenger with him, an interpreter, one among a thousand, to shew unto man his uprightness:

24Then he is gracious unto him, and saith, Deliver him from going down to the pit: I have found a ransom.

25His flesh shall be fresher than a child's: he shall return to the days of his youth:

26He shall pray unto God, and he will be favourable unto him: and he shall see his face with joy: for he will render unto man his righteousness.

27He looketh upon men, and *if any* say, I have sinned, and perverted *that which was* right, and it profited me not;

28He will deliver his soul from going into the pit, and his life shall see the light.

29Lo, all these *things* worketh God oftentimes with man,

30To bring back his soul from the pit, to be enlightened with the light of the living.

31Mark well, O Job, hearken unto me: hold thy peace, and I will speak.

32If thou hast anything to say, answer me: speak, for I desire to justify thee.

33If not, hearken unto me: hold thy peace, and I shall teach thee wisdom.

2 CORINTHIANS 3:1–18

DO we begin again to commend ourselves? or need we, as some *others,* epistles of commendation to you, or *letters* of commendation from you?

2Ye are our epistle written in our hearts, known and read of all men:

3*Forasmuch as ye are* manifestly declared to be the epistle of Christ ministered by us, written not with ink, but with the Spirit of the living God; not in tables of stone, but in fleshy tables of the heart.

4And such trust have we through Christ to God-ward:

5Not that we are sufficient of our selves to think any thing as of ourselves; but our sufficiency *is* of God;

6Who also hath made us able ministers of the new testament; not of the letter, but of the spirit: for the letter killeth, but the spirit giveth life.

7But if the ministration of death, written *and* engraven in stones, was glorious, so that the children of Israel could not stedfastly behold the face of Moses for the glory of his countenance; which *glory* was to be done away:

8How shall not the ministration of the spirit be rather glorious?

9For if the ministration of condemnation *be* glory, much more doth the ministration of righteousness exceed in glory.

10For even that which was made glorious had no glory in this respect, by reason of the glory that excelleth.

11For if that which is done away *was* glorious, much more that which remaineth *is* glorious.

12Seeing then that we have such hope, we use great plainness of speech:

13And not as Moses, *which* put a vail over his face, that the children of Israel could not stedfastly look to the end of that which is abolished:

14But their minds were blinded: for until this day remaineth the same vail untaken away in the reading of the old testament; which *vail* is done away in Christ.

15But even unto this day, when Moses is read, the vail is upon their heart.

16Nevertheless when it shall turn to the Lord, the vail shall be taken away.

17Now the Lord is that Spirit: and where the Spirit of the Lord *is*, there *is* liberty.

18But we all, with open face beholding as in a glass the glory of the Lord, are changed into the same image from glory to glory, *even* as by the Spirit of the Lord.

PSALM 43:1–5

JUDGE me, O God, and plead my cause against an ungodly nation: O deliver me from the deceitful and unjust man.

2For thou *art* the God of my strength: why dost thou cast me off? why go I mourning because of the oppression of the enemy?

3O send out thy light and thy truth: let them lead me; let them bring me unto thy holy hill, and to thy tabernacles.

4Then will I go unto the altar of God, unto God my exceeding joy: yea, upon the harp will I praise thee, O God, my God.

5Why art thou cast down, O my soul? and why art thou disquieted within me? hope in God: for I shall yet praise him, *who is* the health of my countenance, and my God.

PROVERBS FOR TODAY/ 22:8–9

He that soweth iniquity shall reap vanity: and the rod of his anger shall fail. □ *He that hath a bountiful eye shall be blessed; for he giveth of his bread to the poor.*

AUGUST 30

JOB 34:1—36:33

FURTHERMORE Elihu answered and said,

2Hear my words, O ye wise *men;* and give ear unto me, ye that have knowledge.

3For the ear trieth words, as the mouth tasteth meat.

4Let us choose to us judgment: let us know among ourselves what *is* good.

5For Job hath said, I am righteous: and God hath taken away my judgment.

6Should I lie against my right? my wound *is* incurable without transgression.

7What man *is* like Job, *who* drinketh up scorning like water?

8Which goeth in company with the workers of iniquity, and walketh with wicked men.

9For he hath said, It profiteth a man nothing that he should delight himself with God.

10Therefore hearken unto me ye men of understanding: far be it from God, *that he should do* wickedness; and *from* the Almighty, *that he should commit* iniquity.

11For the work of a man shall he render unto him, and cause every man to find according to *his* ways.

12Yea, surely God will not do wickedly, neither will the Almighty pervert judgment.

13Who hath given him a charge over the earth? or who hath disposed the whole world?

14If he set his heart upon man *if* he gather unto himself his spirit and his breath;

15All flesh shall perish together, and man shall turn again unto dust.

16If now *thou hast* understanding, hear this: hearken to the voice of my words.

17Shall even he that hateth right govern? and wilt thou condemn him that is most just?

18*Is it fit* to say to a king, *Thou art* wicked? *and* to princes, *Ye are* ungodly?

19*How much less to him* that accepteth not the persons of princes, nor regardeth the rich more than the poor? for they all *are* the work of his hands.

20In a moment shall they die, and the people shall be troubled at midnight, and pass away: and the mighty shall be taken away without hand.

21For his eyes *are* upon the ways of man, and he seeth all his goings.

22*There is* no darkness, nor shadow of death, where the workers of iniquity may hide themselves.

23For he will not lay upon man more

than right; that he should enter into judgment with God.

24He shall break in pieces mighty men without number, and set others in their stead.

25Therefore he knoweth their works, and he overturneth *them* in the night, so that they are destroyed.

26He striketh them as wicked men in the open sight of others;

27Because they turned back from him, and would not consider any of his ways:

28So that they cause the cry of the poor to come unto him, and he heareth the cry of the afflicted.

29When he giveth quietness, who then can make trouble? and when he hideth *his* face, who then can behold him? whether *it be done* against a nation, or against a man only:

30That the hypocrite reign not, lest the people be ensnared.

31Surely it is meet to be said unto God, I have borne *chastisement,* I will not offend *any more:*

32That which I see not teach thou me: if I have done iniquity, I will do no more.

33*Should it be* according to thy mind? he will recompense it, whether thou refuse, or whether thou choose; and not I: therefore speak what thou knowest.

34Let men of understanding tell me, and let a wise man hearken unto me.

35Job hath spoken without knowledge, and his words *were* without wisdom.

36My desire *is that* Job may be tried unto the end because of *his* answers for wicked men.

37For he addeth rebellion unto his sin, he clappeth *his hands* among us, and multiplieth his words against God.

Elihu spake moreover, and said,

2Thinkest thou this to be right, *that* thou saidst, My righteousness *is* more than God's?

3For thou saidst, What advantage will it be unto thee? *and,* What profit shall I have, *if I be cleansed* from my sin?

4I will answer thee, and thy companions with thee.

5Look unto the heavens, and see; and behold the clouds *which* are higher than thou.

6If thou sinnest, what doest thou against him? or *if* thy transgressions be multiplied, what doest thou unto him?

7If thou be righteous, what givest thou him? or what receiveth he of thine hand?

8Thy wickedness *may hurt* a man as thou *art;* and thy righteousness *may profit* the son of man.

9By reason of the multitude of oppressions they make *the oppressed* to cry: they cry out by reason of the arm of the mighty.

10But none saith, Where *is* God my maker, who giveth songs in the night;

11Who teacheth us more than the beasts of the earth, and maketh us wiser than the fowls of heaven?

12There they cry, but none giveth answer, because of the pride of evil men.

13Surely God will not hear vanity, neither will the Almighty regard it.

14Although thou sayest thou shalt not see him, *yet* judgment *is* before him; therefore trust thou in him.

15But now, because *it is* not *so,* he hath visited in his anger; yet he knoweth *it* not in great extremity:

16Therefore doth Job open his mouth in vain; he multiplieth words without knowledge.

Elihu also proceeded, and said,

2Suffer me a little, and I will shew thee that *I have* yet to speak on God's behalf.

3I will fetch my knowledge from afar, and will ascribe righteousness to my Maker.

4For truly my words *shall* not *be* false:

he that is perfect in knowledge *is* with thee.

5Behold, God *is* mighty, and despiseth not *any: he is* mighty in strength *and* wisdom.

6He preserveth not the life of the wicked: but giveth right to the poor.

7He withdraweth not his eyes from the righteous: but with kings *are they* on the throne; yea, he doth establish them for ever, and they are exalted.

8And if *they be* bound in fetters, *and* be holden in cords of affliction;

9Then he sheweth them their work, and their transgressions that they have exceeded.

10He openeth also their ear to discipline, and commandeth that they return from iniquity.

11If they obey and serve *him,* they shall spend their days in prosperity, and their years in pleasures.

12But if they obey not, they shall perish by the sword, and they shall die without knowledge.

13But the hypocrites in heart heap up wrath: they cry not when he bindeth them.

14They die in youth, and their life *is* among the unclean.

15He delivereth the poor in his affliction, and openeth their ears in oppression.

16Even so would he have removed thee out of the strait *into* a broad place, where *there is* no straitness: and that which should be set on thy table *should be* full of fatness.

17But thou hast fulfilled the judgment of the wicked: judgment and justice take hold *on thee.*

18Because *there is* wrath, *beware* lest he take thee away with *his* stroke: then a great ransom cannot deliver thee.

19Will he esteem thy riches? *no,* not gold, nor all the forces of strength.

20Desire not the night, when people are cut off in their place.

21Take heed, regard not iniquity: for this hast thou chosen rather than affliction.

22Behold, God exalteth by his power: who teacheth like him?

23Who hath enjoined him his way? or who can say, Thou hast wrought iniquity?

24Remember that thou magnify his work, which men behold.

25Every man may see it; man may behold *it* afar off.

26Behold, God *is* great, and we know *him* not, neither can the number of his years be searched out.

27For he maketh small the drops of water: they pour down rain according to the vapour thereof:

28Which the clouds do drop *and* distil upon man abundantly.

29Also can *any* understand the spreadings of the clouds, *or* the noise of his tabernacle?

30Behold, he spreadeth his light upon it, and covereth the bottom of the sea.

31For by them judgeth he the people; he giveth meat in abundance.

32With clouds he covereth the light; and commandeth it *not to shine* by *the cloud* that cometh betwixt.

33The noise thereof sheweth concerning it, the cattle also concerning the vapour.

2 CORINTHIANS 4:1–12

THEREFORE seeing we have this ministry, as we have received mercy, we faint not;

2But have renounced the hidden things of dishonesty, not walking in craftiness, nor handling the word of God deceitfully; but by manifestation of the truth commending ourselves to every man's conscience in the sight of God.

3But if our gospel be hid, it is hid to them that are lost:

4In whom the god of this world hath blinded the minds of them which believe not, lest the light of the glorious gospel of Christ, who is the image of God, should shine unto them.

5For we preach not ourselves, but Christ Jesus the Lord; and ourselves your servants for Jesus' sake.

6For God, who commanded the light to shine out of darkness, hath shined in our hearts, to *give* the light of the knowledge of the glory of God in the face of Jesus Christ.

7But we have this treasure in earthen vessels, that the excellency of the power may be of God, and not of us.

8*We are* troubled on every side, yet not distressed; *we are* perplexed, but not in despair;

9Persecuted, but not forsaken; cast down, but not destroyed;

10Always bearing about in the body the dying of the Lord Jesus, that the life also of Jesus might be made manifest in our body.

11For we which live are alway delivered unto death for Jesus' sake, that the life also of Jesus might be made manifest in our mortal flesh.

12So then death worketh in us, but life in you.

PSALM 44:1–7

WE have heard with our ears, O God, our fathers have told us, *what* work thou didst in their days, in the times of old.

2*How* thou didst drive out the heathen with thy hand, and plantedst them; *how* thou didst afflict the people, and cast them out.

3For they got not the land in possession by their own sword, neither did their own arm save them: but thy right hand, and thine arm, and the light of thy countenance, because thou hadst a favour unto them.

4Thou art my King, O God: command deliverances for Jacob.

5Through thee will we push down our enemies: through thy name will we tread them under that rise up against us.

6For I will not trust in my bow, neither shall my sword save me.

7But thou hast saved us from our enemies, and hast put them to shame that hated us.

PROVERBS FOR TODAY/ 22:10–12

Cast out the scorner, and contention shall go out; yea, strife and reproach shall cease. □ *He that loveth pureness of heart,* for *the grace of his lips the king* shall be *his friend.* □ *The eyes of the* LORD *preserve knowledge, and he overthroweth the words of the transgressor.*

AUGUST 31

JOB 37:1—39:30

AT this also my heart trembleth, and is moved out of his place. 2Hear attentively the noise of his voice, and the sound *that* goeth out of his mouth.

3He directeth it under the whole

heaven, and his lightning unto the ends of the earth.

4After it a voice roareth: he thundereth with the voice of his excellency; and he will not stay them when his voice is heard.

5God thundereth marvellously with

his voice; great things doeth he, which we cannot comprehend.

6For he saith to the snow, Be thou *on* the earth; likewise to the small rain, and to the great rain of his strength.

7He sealeth up the hand of every man; that all men may know his work.

8Then the beasts go into dens, and remain in their places.

9Out of the south cometh the whirlwind: and cold out of the north.

10By the breath of God frost is given: and the breadth of the waters is straitened.

11Also by watering he wearieth the thick cloud: he scattereth his bright cloud:

12And it is turned round about by his counsels: that they may do whatsoever he commandeth them upon the face of the world in the earth.

13He causeth it to come, whether for correction, or for his land, or for mercy.

14Hearken unto this, O Job: stand still, and consider the wondrous works of God.

15Dost thou know when God disposed them, and caused the light of his cloud to shine?

16Dost thou know the balancings of the clouds, the wondrous works of him which is perfect in knowledge?

17How thy garments *are* warm, when he quieteth the earth by the south *wind?*

18Hast thou with him spread out the sky, *which is* strong, *and* as a molten looking glass?

19Teach us what we shall say unto him; *for* we cannot order *our speech* by reason of darkness.

20Shall it be told him that I speak? if a man speak, surely he shall be swallowed up.

21And now *men* see not the bright light which *is* in the clouds: but the wind passeth, and cleanseth them.

22Fair weather cometh out of the north: with God *is* terrible majesty.

23*Touching* the Almighty, we cannot find him out: *he is* excellent in power, and in judgment, and in plenty of justice: he will not afflict.

24Men do therefore fear him: he respecteth not any *that are* wise of heart.

THEN the LORD answered Job out of the whirlwind, and said,

2Who *is* this that darkeneth counsel by words without knowledge?

3Gird up now thy loins like a man: for I will demand of thee, and answer thou me.

4Where wast thou when I laid the foundations of the earth? declare, if thou hast understanding.

5Who hath laid the measures thereof, if thou knowest? or who hath stretched the line upon it?

6Whereupon are the foundations thereof fastened? or who laid the corner stone thereof;

7When the morning stars sang together, and all the sons of God shouted for joy?

8Or *who* shut up the sea with doors, when it brake forth, *as if* it had issued out of the womb?

9When I made the cloud the garment thereof, and thick darkness a swaddlingband for it,

10And brake up for it my decreed *place,* and set bars and doors,

11And said, Hitherto shalt thou come, but no further: and here shall thy proud waves be stayed?

12Hast thou commanded the morning since thy days; *and* caused the dayspring to know his place;

13That it might take hold of the ends of the earth, that the wicked might be shaken out of it?

14It is turned as clay *to* the seal; and they stand as a garment.

15And from the wicked their light is withholden, and the high arm shall be broken.

16Hast thou entered into the springs of the sea? or hast thou walked in the search of the depth?

17Have the gates of death been opened unto thee? or hast thou seen the doors of the shadow of death?

18Hast thou perceived the breadth of the earth? declare if thou knowest it all.

19Where *is* the way *where* light dwelleth? and *as for* darkness, where *is* the place thereof,

20That thou shouldest take it to the bound thereof, and that thou shouldest know the paths *to* the house thereof?

21Knowest thou *it,* because thou wast then born? or *because* the number of thy days *is* great?

22Hast thou entered into the treasures of the snow? or hast thou seen the treasures of the hail,

23Which I have reserved against the time of trouble, against the day of battle and war?

24By what way is the light parted, *which* scattereth the east wind upon the earth?

25Who hath divided a watercourse for the overflowing of waters, or a way for the lightning of thunder;

26To cause it to rain on the earth, *where* no man *is; on* the wilderness, wherein *there is* no man;

27To satisfy the desolate and waste *ground;* and to cause the bud of the tender herb to spring forth?

28Hath the rain a father? or who hath begotten the drops of dew?

29Out of whose womb came the ice? and the hoary frost of heaven, who hath gendered it?

30The waters are hid as *with* a stone, and the face of the deep is frozen.

31Canst thou bind the sweet influences of Pleiades, or loose the bands of Orion?

32Canst thou bring forth Mazzaroth in his season? or canst thou guide Arcturus with his sons?

33Knowest thou the ordinances of heaven? canst thou set the dominion thereof in the earth?

34Canst thou lift up thy voice to the clouds, that abundance of waters may cover thee?

35Canst thou send lightnings, that they may go, and say unto thee, Here we *are?*

36Who hath put wisdom in the inward parts? or who hath given understanding to the heart?

37Who can number the clouds in wisdom? or who can stay the bottles of heaven,

38When the dust groweth into hardness, and the clods cleave fast together?

39Wilt thou hunt the prey for the lion? or fill the appetite of the young lions,

40When they couch in *their* dens, *and* abide in the covert to lie in wait?

41Who provideth for the raven his food? when his young ones cry unto God, they wander for lack of meat.

KNOWEST thou the time when the wild goats of the rock bring forth? *or* canst thou mark when the hinds do calve?

2Canst thou number the months *that* they fulfil? or knowest thou the time when they bring forth?

3They bow themselves, they bring forth their young ones, they cast out their sorrows.

4Their young ones are in good liking, they grow up with corn; they go forth, and return not unto them.

5Who hath sent out the wild ass free? or who hath loosed the bands of the wild ass?

6Whose house I have made the wilderness, and the barren land his dwellings.

7He scorneth the multitude of the city, neither regardeth he the crying of the driver.

8The range of the mountains *is* his pasture, and he searcheth after every green thing.

9Will the unicorn be willing to serve thee, or abide by thy crib?

10Canst thou bind the unicorn with his band in the furrow? or will he harrow the valleys after thee?

11Wilt thou trust him, because his strength *is* great? or wilt thou leave thy labour to him?

12Wilt thou believe him, that he will bring home thy seed, and gather *it into* thy barn?

13*Gavest thou* the goodly wings unto the peacocks? or wings and feathers unto the ostrich?

14Which leaveth her eggs in the earth, and warmeth them in dust,

15And forgetteth that the foot may crush them, or that the wild beast may break them.

16She is hardened against her young ones, as though *they were* not hers: her labour is in vain without fear;

17Because God hath deprived her of wisdom, neither hath he imparted to her understanding.

18What time she lifteth up herself on high, she scorneth the horse and his rider.

19Hast thou given the horse strength? hast thou clothed his neck with thunder?

20Canst thou make him afraid as a grasshopper? the glory of his nostrils *is* terrible.

21He paweth in the valley, and rejoiceth in *his* strength: he goeth on to meet the armed men.

22He mocketh at fear, and is not affrighted; neither turneth he back from the sword.

23The quiver rattleth against him, the glittering spear and the shield.

24He swalloweth the ground with fierceness and rage: neither believeth he that *it is* the sound of the trumpet.

25He saith among the trumpets, Ha, ha; and he smelleth the battle afar off, the thunder of the captains, and the shouting.

26Doth the hawk fly by thy wisdom, *and* stretch her wings toward the south?

27Doth the eagle mount up at thy command, and make her nest on high?

28She dwelleth and abideth on the rock, upon the crag of the rock, and the strong place.

29From thence she seeketh the prey, *and* her eyes behold afar off.

30Her young ones also suck up blood: and where the slain *are,* there *is* she.

2 CORINTHIANS 4:13—5:11

WE having the same spirit of faith, according as it is written, I believed, and therefore have I spoken; we also believe, and therefore speak;

14Knowing that he which raised up the Lord Jesus shall raise up us also by Jesus, and shall present *us* with you.

15For all things *are* for your sakes, that the abundant grace might through the thanksgiving of many redound to the glory of God.

16For which cause we faint not; but though our outward man perish, yet the inward *man* is renewed day by day.

17For our light affliction, which is but for a moment, worketh for us a far more exceeding *and* eternal weight of glory;

18While we look not at the things which are seen, but at the things which are not seen: for the things which are seen *are* temporal; but the things which are not seen *are* eternal.

FOR we know that if our earthly house of *this* tabernacle were dissolved, we have a building of God, an house not made with hands, eternal in the heavens.

2For in this we groan, earnestly desiring to be clothed upon with our house which is from heaven:

3If so be that being clothed we shall not be found naked.

4For we that are in *this* tabernacle do groan, being burdened: not for that we would be unclothed, but clothed upon, that mortality might be swallowed up of life.

5Now he that hath wrought us for

the selfsame thing *is* God, who also hath given unto us the earnest of the Spirit.

6Therefore *we are* always confident, knowing that, whilst we are at home in the body, we are absent from the Lord:

7(For we walk by faith, not by sight:)

8We are confident, *I say,* and willing rather to be absent from the body, and to be present with the Lord.

9Wherefore we labour, that, whether present or absent, we may be accepted of him.

10For we must all appear before the judgment seat of Christ; that every one may receive the things *done* in *his* body, according to that he hath done, whether *it be* good or bad.

11Knowing therefore the terror of the Lord, we persuade men; but we are made manifest unto God; and I trust also are made manifest in your consciences.

PSALM 44:8–26

IN God we boast all the day long, and praise thy name for ever. Selah.

9But thou hast cast off, and put us to shame; and goest not forth with our armies.

10Thou makest us to turn back from the enemy: and they which hate us spoil for themselves.

11Thou hast given us like sheep *appointed* for meat; and hast scattered us among the heathen.

12Thou sellest thy people for nought, and dost not increase *thy wealth* by their price.

13Thou makest us a reproach to our neighbours, a scorn and a derision to them that are round about us.

14Thou makest us a byword among the heathen, a shaking of the head among the people.

15My confusion *is* continually before me, and the shame of my face hath covered me,

16For the voice of him that reproacheth and blasphemeth; by reason of the enemy and avenger.

17All this is come upon us; yet have we not forgotten thee, neither have we dealt falsely in thy covenant.

18Our heart is not turned back, neither have our steps declined from thy way;

19Though thou hast sore broken us in the place of dragons, and covered us with the shadow of death.

20If we have forgotten the name of our God, or stretched out our hands to a strange god;

21Shall not God search this out? for he knoweth the secrets of the heart.

22Yea, for thy sake are we killed all the day long; we are counted as sheep for the slaughter.

23Awake, why sleepest thou, O Lord? arise, cast *us* not off for ever.

24Wherefore hidest thou thy face, *and* forgettest our affliction and our oppression?

25For our soul is bowed down to the dust: our belly cleaveth unto the earth.

26Arise for our help, and redeem us for thy mercies' sake.

PROVERBS FOR TODAY/ 22:13

The slothful man *saith,* There is *a lion without, I shall be slain in the streets.*

SEPTEMBER 1

JOB 40:1—42:17

MOREOVER the LORD answered Job, and said,

²Shall he that contendeth with the Almighty instruct *him?* he that reproveth God, let him answer it.

³Then Job answered the LORD, and said,

⁴Behold, I am vile; what shall I answer thee? I will lay mine hand upon my mouth.

⁵Once have I spoken; but I will not answer: yea, twice; but I will proceed no further.

⁶Then answered the LORD unto Job out of the whirlwind, and said,

⁷Gird up thy loins now like a man: I will demand of thee, and declare thou unto me.

⁸Wilt thou also disannul my judgment? wilt thou condemn me, that thou mayest be righteous?

⁹Hast thou an arm like God? or canst thou thunder with a voice like him?

¹⁰Deck thyself now *with* majesty and excellency; and array thyself with glory and beauty.

¹¹Cast abroad the rage of thy wrath: and behold every one *that is* proud, and abase him.

¹²Look on every one *that is* proud, *and* bring him low; and tread down the wicked in their place.

¹³Hide them in the dust together; *and* bind their faces in secret.

¹⁴Then will I also confess unto thee that thine own right hand can save thee.

¹⁵Behold now behemoth, which I made with thee; he eateth grass as an ox.

¹⁶Lo now, his strength *is* in his loins, and his force *is* in the navel of his belly.

¹⁷He moveth his tail like a cedar: the sinews of his stones are wrapped together.

¹⁸His bones *are as* strong pieces of brass; his bones *are* like bars of iron.

¹⁹He *is* the chief of the ways of God: he that made him can make his sword to approach *unto him.*

²⁰Surely the mountains bring him forth food, where all the beasts of the field play.

²¹He lieth under the shady trees, in the covert of the reed, and fens.

²²The shady trees cover him *with* their shadow; the willows of the brook compass him about.

²³Behold, he drinketh up a river, *and* hasteth not: he trusteth that he can draw up Jordan into his mouth.

²⁴He taketh it with his eyes: *his* nose pierceth through snares.

CANST thou draw out leviathan with an hook? or his tongue with a cord *which* thou lettest down?

²Canst thou put an hook into his nose? or bore his jaw through with a thorn?

³Will he make many supplications unto thee? will he speak soft *words* unto thee?

⁴Will he make a covenant with thee? wilt thou take him for a servant for ever?

⁵Wilt thou play with him as *with* a bird? or wilt thou bind him for thy maidens?

⁶Shall the companions make a banquet of him? shall they part him among the merchants?

⁷Canst thou fill his skin with barbed irons? or his head with fish spears?

⁸Lay thine hand upon him, remember the battle, do no more.

⁹Behold, the hope of him is in vain: shall not *one* be cast down even at the sight of him?

¹⁰None *is so* fierce that dare stir him

up: who then is able to stand before me?

11Who hath prevented me, that I should repay *him? whatsoever is* under the whole heaven is mine.

12I will not conceal his parts, nor his power, nor his comely proportion.

13Who can discover the face of his garment? *or* who can come *to him* with his double bridle?

14Who can open the doors of his face? his teeth *are* terrible round about.

15*His* scales *are his* pride, shut up together *as with* a close seal.

16One is so near to another, that no air can come between them.

17They are joined one to another, they stick together, that they cannot be sundered.

18By his neesings a light doth shine, and his eyes *are* like the eyelids of the morning.

19Out of his mouth go burning lamps, *and* sparks of fire leap out.

20Out of his nostrils goeth smoke, as *out* of a seething pot or caldron.

21His breath kindleth coals, and a flame goeth out of his mouth.

22In his neck remaineth strength, and sorrow is turned into joy before him.

23The flakes of his flesh are joined together: they are firm in themselves; they cannot be moved.

24His heart is as firm as a stone; yea, as hard as a piece of the nether *millstone*.

25When he raiseth up himself, the mighty are afraid: by reason of break-ings they purify themselves.

26The sword of him that layeth at him cannot hold: the spear, the dart, nor the habergeon.

27He esteemeth iron as straw, *and* brass as rotten wood.

28The arrow cannot make him flee: slingstones are turned with him into stubble.

29Darts are counted as stubble: he laugheth at the shaking of a spear.

30Sharp stones *are* under him: he spreadeth sharp pointed things upon the mire.

31He maketh the deep to boil like a pot: he maketh the sea like a pot of ointment.

32He maketh a path to shine after him; *one* would think the deep *to be* hoary.

33Upon earth there is not his like, who is made without fear.

34He beholdeth all high *things:* he *is* a king over all the children of pride.

Then Job answered the Lord, and said,

2I know that thou canst do every *thing,* and *that* no thought can be with-holden from thee.

3Who *is* he that hideth counsel with-out knowledge? therefore have I ut-tered that I understood not; things too wonderful for me, which I knew not.

4Hear, I beseech thee, and I will speak: I will demand of thee, and declare thou unto me.

5I have heard of thee by the hearing of the ear: but now mine eye seeth thee.

6Wherefore I abhor *myself,* and re-pent in dust and ashes.

7And it was *so,* that after the Lord had spoken these words unto Job, the Lord said to Eliphaz the Temanite, My wrath is kindled against thee, and against thy two friends: for ye have not spoken of me *the thing that is* right, as my servant Job *hath.*

8Therefore take unto you now seven bullocks and seven rams, and go to my servant Job, and offer up for your-selves a burnt offering; and my servant Job shall pray for you: for him will I accept: lest I deal with you *after your* folly, in that ye have not spoken of me *the thing which is* right, like my servant Job.

9So Eliphaz the Temanite and Bildad the Shuhite *and* Zophar the Naamathite went, and did according as the Lord commanded them: the Lord also ac-cepted Job.

10And the LORD turned the captivity of Job, when he prayed for his friends: also the LORD gave Job twice as much as he had before.

11Then came there unto him all his brethren, and all his sisters, and all they that had been of his acquaintance before, and did eat bread with him in his house: and they bemoaned him, and comforted him over all the evil that the LORD had brought upon him: every man also gave him a piece of money, and every one an earring of gold.

12So the LORD blessed the latter end of Job more than his beginning: for he had fourteen thousand sheep, and six thousand camels, and a thousand yoke of oxen, and a thousand she asses.

13He had also seven sons and three daughters.

14And he called the name of the first, Jemima; and the name of the second, Kezia; and the name of the third, Keren-happuch.

15And in all the land were no women found *so* fair as the daughters of Job: and their father gave them inheritance among their brethren.

16After this lived Job an hundred and forty years, and saw his sons, and his sons' sons, *even* four generations.

17So Job died, *being* old and full of days.

2 CORINTHIANS 5:12–21

FOR we commend not ourselves again unto you, but give you occasion to glory on our behalf, that ye may have somewhat to *answer* them which glory in appearance, and not in heart.

13For whether we be beside ourselves, *it is* to God: or whether we be sober, *it is* for your cause.

14For the love of Christ constraineth us; because we thus judge, that if one died for all, then were all dead:

15And *that* he died for all, that they which live should not henceforth live unto themselves, but unto him which died for them, and rose again.

16Wherefore henceforth know we no man after the flesh: yea, though we have known Christ after the flesh, yet now henceforth know we *him* no more.

17Therefore if any man *be* in Christ, *he is* a new creature: old things are passed away; behold, all things are become new.

18And all things *are* of God, who hath reconciled us to himself by Jesus Christ, and hath given to us the ministry of reconciliation;

19To wit, that God was in Christ, reconciling the world unto himself, not imputing their trespasses unto them; and hath committed unto us the word of reconciliation.

20Now then we are ambassadors for Christ, as though God did beseech *you* by us; we pray *you* in Christ's stead, be ye reconciled to God.

21For he hath made him *to be* sin for us, who knew no sin; that we might be made the righteousness of God in him.

PSALM 45:1–17

MY heart is inditing a good matter: I speak of the things which I have made touching the king: my tongue *is* the pen of a ready writer.

2Thou art fairer than the children of men: grace is poured into thy lips: therefore God hath blessed thee for ever.

3Gird thy sword upon *thy* thigh, O *most* mighty, with thy glory and thy majesty.

4And in thy majesty ride prosperously because of truth and meekness *and* righteousness; and thy right hand shall teach thee terrible things.

5Thine arrows *are* sharp in the heart of the king's enemies; *whereby* the people fall under thee.

6Thy throne, O God, *is* for ever and

ever: the sceptre of thy kingdom *is* a right sceptre.

7Thou lovest righteousness, and hatest wickedness: therefore God, thy God, hath anointed thee with the oil of gladness above thy fellows.

8All thy garments *smell* of myrrh, and aloes, *and* cassia, out of the ivory palaces, whereby they have made thee glad.

9Kings' daughters *were* among thy honourable women: upon thy right hand did stand the queen in gold of Ophir.

10Hearken, O daughter, and consider, and incline thine ear; forget also thine own people, and thy father's house;

11So shall the king greatly desire thy beauty: for he *is* thy Lord; and worship thou him.

12And the daughter of Tyre *shall be there* with a gift; *even* the rich among the people shall intreat thy favour.

13The king's daughter *is* all glorious within: her clothing *is* of wrought gold.

14She shall be brought unto the king in raiment of needlework: the virgins her companions that follow her shall be brought unto thee.

15With gladness and rejoicing shall they be brought: they shall enter into the king's palace.

16Instead of thy fathers shall be thy children, whom thou mayest make princes in all the earth.

17I will make thy name to be remembered in all generations: therefore shall the people praise thee for ever and ever.

PROVERBS FOR TODAY/ 22:14

The mouth of strange women is *a deep pit: he that is abhorred of the* LORD *shall fall therein.*

SEPTEMBER 2

ECCLESIASTES 1:1—3:22

THE words of the Preacher, the son of David, king in Jerusalem.
2Vanity of vanities, saith the Preacher, vanity of vanities; all *is* vanity.

3What profit hath a man of all his labour which he taketh under the sun?

4*One* generation passeth away, and *another* generation cometh: but the earth abideth for ever.

5The sun also ariseth, and the sun goeth down, and hasteth to his place where he arose.

6The wind goeth toward the south, and turneth about unto the north; it whirleth about continually, and the wind returneth again according to his circuits.

7All the rivers run into the sea; yet the sea *is* not full; unto the place from whence the rivers come, thither they return again.

8All things *are* full of labour; man cannot utter *it:* the eye is not satisfied with seeing, nor the ear filled with hearing.

9The thing that hath been, it *is that* which shall be; and that which is done *is* that which shall be done: and *there is* no new *thing* under the sun.

10Is there *any* thing whereof it may be said, See, this *is* new? it hath been already of old time, which was before us.

11*There is* no remembrance of former *things;* neither shall there be *any* remembrance of *things* that are to come with *those* that shall come after.

12I the Preacher was king over Israel in Jerusalem.

13And I gave my heart to seek and search out by wisdom concerning all *things* that are done under heaven: this sore travail hath God given to the sons of man to be exercised therewith.

14I have seen all the works that are done under the sun; and, behold, all *is* vanity and vexation of spirit.

15*That which is* crooked cannot be made straight: and that which is wanting cannot be numbered.

16I communed with mine own heart, saying, Lo, I am come to great estate, and have gotten more wisdom than all *they* that have been before me in Jerusalem: yea, my heart had great experience of wisdom and knowledge.

17And I gave my heart to know wisdom, and to know madness and folly: I perceived that this also is vexation of spirit.

18For in much wisdom *is* much grief: and he that increaseth knowledge increaseth sorrow.

I SAID in mine heart, Go to now, I will prove thee with mirth, therefore enjoy pleasure: and, behold, this also *is* vanity.

2I said of laughter, *It is* mad: and of mirth, What doeth it?

3I sought in mine heart to give myself unto wine, yet acquainting mine heart with wisdom; and to lay hold on folly, till I might see what *was* that good for the sons of men, which they should do under the heaven all the days of their life.

4I made me great works; I builded me houses; I planted me vineyards:

5I made me gardens and orchards, and I planted trees in them of all *kind of* fruits:

6I made me pools of water, to water therewith the wood that bringeth forth trees:

7I got *me* servants and maidens, and had servants born in my house; also I had great possessions of great and small cattle above all that were in Jerusalem before me:

8I gathered me also silver and gold, and the peculiar treasure of kings and of the provinces: I gat me men singers and women singers, and the delights of the sons of men, *as* musical instruments, and that of all sorts.

9So I was great, and increased more than all that were before me in Jerusalem: also my wisdom remained with me.

10And whatsoever mine eyes desired I kept not from them, I withheld not my heart from any joy; for my heart rejoiced in all my labour: and this was my portion of all my labour.

11Then I looked on all the works that my hands had wrought, and on the labour that I had laboured to do: and, behold, all *was* vanity and vexation of spirit, and *there was* no profit under the sun.

12And I turned myself to behold wisdom, and madness, and folly: for what *can* the man *do* that cometh after the king? *even* that which hath been already done.

13Then I saw that wisdom excelleth folly, as far as light excelleth darkness.

14The wise man's eyes *are* in his head; but the fool walketh in darkness: and I myself perceived also that one event happeneth to them all.

15Then said I in my heart, As it happeneth to the fool, so it happeneth even to me; and why was I then more wise? Then I said in my heart, that this also *is* vanity.

16For *there is* no remembrance of the wise more than of the fool for ever; seeing that which now *is* in the days to come shall all be forgotten. And how dieth the wise *man?* as the fool.

17Therefore I hated life; because the work that is wrought under the sun *is* grievous unto me: for all *is* vanity and vexation of spirit.

18Yea, I hated all my labour which I had taken under the sun: because I should leave it unto the man that shall be after me.

19And who knoweth whether he shall be a wise *man* or a fool? yet shall he have rule over all my labour wherein I have laboured, and wherein I have shewed myself wise under the sun. This *is* also vanity.

20Therefore I went about to cause my heart to despair of all the labour which I took under the sun.

21For there is a man whose labour *is* in wisdom, and in knowledge, and in equity; yet to a man that hath not laboured therein shall he leave it *for* his portion. This also *is* vanity and a great evil.

22For what hath man of all his labour, and of the vexation of his heart, wherein he hath laboured under the sun?

23For all his days *are* sorrows, and his travail grief; yea, his heart taketh not rest in the night. This is also vanity.

24*There is* nothing better for a man, *than* that he should eat and drink, and *that* he should make his soul enjoy good in his labour. This also I saw, that it *was* from the hand of God.

25For who can eat, or who else can hasten *hereunto,* more than I?

26For *God* giveth to a man that *is* good in his sight wisdom, and knowledge, and joy: but to the sinner he giveth travail, to gather and to heap up, that he may give to *him that is* good before God. This also *is* vanity and vexation of spirit.

To every *thing there is* a season, and a time to every purpose under the heaven:

2A time to be born, and a time to die; a time to plant, and a time to pluck up *that which is* planted;

3A time to kill, and a time to heal; a time to break down, and a time to build up;

4A time to weep, and a time to laugh; a time to mourn, and a time to dance;

5A time to cast away stones, and a time to gather stones together; a time to embrace, and a time to refrain from embracing;

6A time to get, and a time to lose; a time to keep, and a time to cast away;

7A time to rend, and a time to sew; a time to keep silence, and a time to speak;

8A time to love, and a time to hate; a time of war, and a time of peace.

9What profit hath he that worketh in that wherein he laboureth?

10I have seen the travail, which God hath given to the sons of men to be exercised in it.

11He hath made every *thing* beautiful in his time: also he hath set the world in their heart, so that no man can find out the work that God maketh from the beginning to the end.

12I know that *there is* no good in them, but for *a man* to rejoice, and to do good in his life.

13And also that every man should eat and drink, and enjoy the good of all his labour, it *is* the gift of God.

14I know that, whatsoever God doeth, it shall be for ever: nothing can be put to it, nor any thing taken from it: and God doeth *it,* that *men* should fear before him.

15That which hath been is now; and that which is to be hath already been; and God requireth that which is past.

16And moreover I saw under the sun the place of judgment, *that* wickedness *was* there; and the place of righteousness, *that* iniquity *was* there.

17I said in mine heart, God shall judge the righteous and the wicked: for *there is* a time there for every purpose and for every work.

18I said in mine heart concerning the estate of the sons of men, that God might manifest them, and that they might see that they themselves are beasts.

19For that which befalleth the sons of men befalleth beasts; even one thing befalleth them: as the one dieth, so dieth the other; yea, they have all one breath; so that a man hath no preeminence above a beast: for all *is* vanity.

20All go unto one place; all are of the dust, and all turn to dust again.

21Who knoweth the spirit of man that goeth upward, and the spirit of the beast that goeth downward to the earth?

22Wherefore I perceive that *there is* nothing better, than that a man should rejoice in his own works; for that *is* his portion: for who shall bring him to see what shall be after him?

2 CORINTHIANS 6:1–13

WE then, as workers together *with him,* beseech *you* also that ye receive not the grace of God in vain.

2(For he saith, I have heard thee in a time accepted, and in the day of salvation have I succoured thee: behold, now *is* the accepted time; behold, now *is* the day of salvation.)

3Giving no offence in any thing, that the ministry be not blamed:

4But in all *things* approving ourselves as the ministers of God, in much patience, in afflictions, in necessities, in distresses,

5In stripes, in imprisonments, in tumults, in labours, in watchings, in fastings;

6By pureness, by knowledge, by longsuffering, by kindness, by the Holy Ghost, by love unfeigned,

7By the word of truth, by the power of God, by the armour of righteousness on the right hand and on the left,

8By honour and dishonour, by evil report and good report: as de-ceivers, and *yet* true;

9As unknown, and *yet* well known; as dying, and, behold, we live; as chastened, and not killed;

10As sorrowful, yet alway rejoicing; as poor, yet making many rich; as having nothing, and *yet* possessing all things.

11O *ye* Corinthians, our mouth is open unto you, our heart is enlarged.

12Ye are not straitened in us, but ye are straitened in your own bowels.

13Now for a recompence in the same, (I speak as unto *my* children,) be ye also enlarged.

PSALM 46:1–11

GOD *is* our refuge and strength, a very present help in trouble.

2Therefore will not we fear, though the earth be removed, and though the mountains be carried into the midst of the sea;

3*Though* the waters thereof roar *and* be troubled, *though* the mountains shake with the swelling thereof. Selah.

4*There is* a river, the streams whereof shall make glad the city of God, the holy *place* of the tabernacles of the most High.

5God *is* in the midst of her; she shall not be moved: God shall help her, *and that* right early.

6The heathen raged, the kingdoms were moved: he uttered his voice, the earth melted.

7The LORD of hosts *is* with us; the God of Jacob *is* our refuge. Selah.

8Come, behold the works of the LORD, what desolations he hath made in the earth.

9He maketh wars to cease unto the end of the earth; he breaketh the bow, and cutteth the spear in sunder; he burneth the chariot in the fire.

10Be still, and know that I *am* God: I will be exalted among the heathen, I will be exalted in the earth.

11The LORD of hosts *is* with us; the God of Jacob *is* our refuge. Selah.

PROVERBS FOR TODAY/ 22:15

Foolishness is *bound in the heart of a child;* but *the rod of correction shall drive it far from him.*

SEPTEMBER 3

ECCLESIASTES 4:1—6:12

So I returned, and considered all the oppressions that are done under the sun: and behold the tears of *such as were* oppressed, and they had no comforter; and on the side of their oppressors *there was* power; but they had no comforter.

2Wherefore I praised the dead which are already dead more than the living which are yet alive.

3Yea, better *is he* than both they, which hath not yet been, who hath not seen the evil work that is done under the sun.

4Again, I considered all travail, and every right work, that for this a man is envied of his neighbour. This *is* also vanity and vexation of spirit.

5The fool foldeth his hands together, and eateth his own flesh.

6Better *is* an handful *with* quietness, than both the hands full *with* travail and vexation of spirit.

7Then I returned, and I saw vanity under the sun.

8There is one *alone,* and *there is* not a second; yea, he hath neither child nor brother: yet *is there* no end of all his labour; neither is his eye satisfied with riches; neither *saith he,* For whom do I labour, and bereave my soul of good? This *is* also vanity, yea, it *is* a sore travail.

9Two *are* better than one; because they have a good reward for their labour.

10For if they fall, the one will lift up his fellow: but woe to him *that is* alone when he falleth; for *he hath* not another to help him up.

11Again, if two lie together, then they have heat: but how can one be warm *alone?*

12And if one prevail against him, two shall withstand him; and a threefold cord is not quickly broken.

13Better *is* a poor and a wise child than an old and foolish king, who will no more be admonished.

14For out of prison he cometh to reign; whereas also *he that is* born in his kingdom becometh poor.

15I considered all the living which walk under the sun, with the second child that shall stand up in his stead.

16*There is* no end of all the people, *even* of all that have been before them: they also that come after shall not rejoice in him. Surely this also *is* vanity and vexation of spirit.

Keep thy foot when thou goest to the house of God, and be more ready to hear, than to give the sacrifice of fools: for they consider not that they do evil.

2Be not rash with thy mouth, and let not thine heart be hasty to utter *any* thing before God: for God *is* in heaven, and thou upon earth: therefore let thy words be few.

3For a dream cometh through the multitude of business; and a fool's voice *is known* by multitude of words.

4When thou vowest a vow unto God, defer not to pay it; for *he hath* no pleasure in fools: pay that which thou hast vowed.

5Better *is it* that thou shouldest not vow, than that thou shouldest vow and not pay.

6Suffer not thy mouth to cause thy flesh to sin; neither say thou before the angel, that it *was* an error: wherefore should God be angry at thy voice, and destroy the work of thine hands?

7For in the multitude of dreams and many words *there are* also *divers* vanities: but fear thou God.

8If thou seest the oppression of the poor, and violent perverting of judgment and justice in a province, marvel not at the matter: for *he that is* higher than the highest regardeth; and *there be* higher than they.

9Moreover the profit of the earth is for all: the king *himself* is served by the field.

10He that loveth silver shall not be satisfied with silver; nor he that loveth abundance with increase: this *is* also vanity.

11When goods increase, they are increased that eat them: and what good *is there* to the owners thereof, saving the beholding *of them* with their eyes?

12The sleep of a labouring man *is* sweet, whether he eat little or much: but the abundance of the rich will not suffer him to sleep.

13There is a sore evil *which* I have seen under the sun, *namely* riches kept for the owners thereof to their hurt.

14But those riches perish by evil travail: and he begetteth a son, and *there is* nothing in his hand.

15As he came forth of his mother's womb, naked shall he return to go as he came, and shall take nothing of his labour, which he may carry away in his hand.

16And this also *is* a sore evil, *that* in all points as he came, so shall he go: and what profit hath he that hath laboured for the wind?

17All his days also he eateth in darkness, and *he hath* much sorrow and wrath with his sickness.

18Behold *that* which I have seen: *it is* good and comely *for one* to eat and to drink, and to enjoy the good of all his labour that he taketh under the sun all the days of his life, which God giveth him: for it *is* his portion.

19Every man also to whom God hath given riches and wealth, and hath given him power to eat thereof, and to take his portion, and to rejoice in his labour; this *is* the gift of God.

20For he shall not much remember the days of his life; because God answereth *him* in the joy of his heart.

THERE is an evil which I have seen under the sun, and it *is* common among men:

2A man to whom God hath given riches, wealth, and honour, so that he wanteth nothing for his soul of all that he desireth, yet God giveth him not power to eat thereof, but a stranger eateth it: this *is* vanity, and it *is* an evil disease.

3If a man beget an hundred *children,* and live many years, so that the days of his years be many, and his soul be not filled with good, and also *that* he have no burial; I say, *that* an untimely birth *is* better than he.

4For he cometh in with vanity, and departeth in darkness, and his name shall be covered with darkness.

5Moreover he hath not seen the sun, nor known *any thing:* this hath more rest than the other.

6Yea, though he live a thousand years twice *told,* yet hath he seen no good: do not all go to one place?

7All the labour of man *is* for his mouth, and yet the appetite is not filled.

8For what hath the wise more than the fool? what hath the poor, that knoweth to walk before the living?

9Better *is* the sight of the eyes than the wandering of the desire: this *is* also vanity and vexation of spirit.

10That which hath been is named already, and it is known that it *is* man: neither may he contend with him that is mightier than he.

11Seeing there be many things that increase vanity, what *is* man the better?

12For who knoweth what *is* good for man in *this* life, all the days of his vain life which he spendeth as a shadow? for who can tell a man what shall be after him under the sun?

2 CORINTHIANS 6:14—7:7

BE ye not unequally yoked together with unbelievers: for what fellowship hath righteousness with unrighteousness? and what communion hath light with darkness?

15And what concord hath Christ with Belial? or what part hath he that believeth with an infidel?

16And what agreement hath the temple of God with idols? for ye are the temple of the living God; as God hath said, I will dwell in them, and walk in *them;* and I will be their God, and they shall be my people.

17Wherefore come out from among them, and be ye separate, saith the Lord, and touch not the unclean *thing;* and I will receive you,

18And will be a Father unto you, and ye shall be my sons and daughters, saith the Lord Almighty.

HAVING therefore these promises, dearly beloved, let us cleanse ourselves from all filthiness of the flesh and spirit, perfecting holiness in the fear of God.

2Receive us; we have wronged no man, we have corrupted no man, we have defrauded no man.

3I speak not *this* to condemn *you:* for I have said before, that ye are in our hearts to die and live with *you.*

4Great *is* my boldness of speech toward you, great *is* my glorying of you: I am filled with comfort, I am exceeding joyful in all our tribulation.

5For, when we were come into Macedonia, our flesh had no rest, but we were troubled on every side; without *were* fightings, within *were* fears.

6Nevertheless God, that comforteth those that are cast down, comforted us by the coming of Titus;

7And not by his coming only, but by the consolation wherewith he was comforted in you, when he told us your earnest desire, your mourning, your fervent mind toward me; so that I rejoiced the more.

PSALM 47:1—9

O CLAP your hands, all ye people; shout unto God with the voice of triumph.

2For the LORD most high *is* terrible; *he is* a great King over all the earth.

3He shall subdue the people under us, and the nations under our feet.

4He shall choose our inheritance for us, the excellency of Jacob whom he loved. Selah.

5God is gone up with a shout, the LORD with the sound of a trumpet.

6Sing praises to God, sing praises: sing praises unto our King, sing praises.

7For God *is* the King of all the earth: sing ye praises with understanding.

8God reigneth over the heathen: God sitteth upon the throne of his holiness.

9The princes of the people are gathered together, *even* the people of the God of Abraham: for the shields of the earth *belong* unto God: he is greatly exalted.

PROVERBS FOR TODAY/ 22:16

He that oppresseth the poor to increase his riches, and *he that giveth to the rich,* shall *surely* come *to want.*

SEPTEMBER 4

ECCLESIASTES 7:1—9:18

AGOOD name *is* better than precious ointment; and the day of death than the day of one's birth.

2*It is* better to go to the house of mourning, than to go to the house of feasting: for that *is* the end of all men; and the living will lay *it* to his heart.

3Sorrow *is* better than laughter: for by the sadness of the countenance the heart is made better.

4The heart of the wise *is* in the house of mourning; but the heart of fools *is* in the house of mirth.

5*It is* better to hear the rebuke of the wise, than for a man to hear the song of fools.

6For as the crackling of thorns under a pot, so *is* the laughter of the fool: this also *is* vanity.

7Surely oppression maketh a wise man mad; and a gift destroyeth the heart.

8Better *is* the end of a thing than the beginning thereof: *and* the patient in spirit *is* better than the proud in spirit.

9Be not hasty in thy spirit to be angry: for anger resteth in the bosom of fools.

10Say not thou, What is *the cause* that the former days were better than these? for thou dost not enquire wisely concerning this.

11Wisdom *is* good with an inheritance: and *by it there is* profit to them that see the sun.

12For wisdom *is* a defence, *and* money *is* a defence: but the excellency of knowledge *is, that* wisdom giveth life to them that have it.

13Consider the work of God: for who can make *that* straight, which he hath made crooked?

14In the day of prosperity be joyful, but in the day of adversity consider: God also hath set the one over against the other, to the end that man should find nothing after him.

15All *things* have I seen in the days of my vanity: there is a just *man* that perisheth in his righteousness, and there is a wicked *man* that prolongeth *his life* in his wickedness.

16Be not righteous over much; neither make thyself over wise: why shouldest thou destroy thyself?

17Be not over much wicked, neither be thou foolish: why shouldest thou die before thy time?

18*It is* good that thou shouldest take hold of this; yea, also from this withdraw not thine hand: for he that feareth God shall come forth of them all.

19Wisdom strengtheneth the wise more than ten mighty *men* which are in the city.

20For *there is* not a just man upon earth, that doeth good, and sinneth not.

21Also take no heed unto all words that are spoken; lest thou hear thy servant curse thee:

22For oftentimes also thine own heart knoweth that thou thyself likewise hast cursed others.

23All this have I proved by wisdom: I said, I will be wise: but it *was* far from me.

24That which is far off, and exceeding deep, who can find it out?

25I applied mine heart to know and to search, and to seek out wisdom, and the reason *of things,* and to know the wickedness of folly, even of foolishness *and* madness:

26And I find more bitter than death the woman, whose heart *is* snares and nets, *and* her hands *as* bands: whoso pleaseth God shall escape from her; but the sinner shall be taken by her.

27Behold, this have I found, saith the

preacher, *counting* one by one, to find out the account.

28Which yet my soul seeketh, but I find not: one man among a thousand have I found; but a woman among all those have I not found.

29Lo, this only have I found, that God hath made man upright; but they have sought out many inventions.

WHO *is* as the wise *man?* and who knoweth the interpretation of a thing? a man's wisdom maketh his face to shine, and the boldness of his face shall be changed.

2I *counsel thee* to keep the king's commandment, and *that* in regard of the oath of God.

3Be not hasty to go out of his sight: stand not in an evil thing; for he doeth whatsoever pleaseth him.

4Where the word of a king *is, there is* power: and who may say unto him, What doest thou?

5Whoso keepeth the commandment shall feel no evil thing: and a wise man's heart discerneth both time and judgment.

6Because to every purpose there is time and judgment, therefore the misery of man *is* great upon him.

7For he knoweth not that which shall be: for who can tell him when it shall be?

8*There is* no man that hath power over the spirit to retain the spirit; neither *hath he* power in the day of death: and *there is* no discharge in *that* war; neither shall wickedness deliver those that are given to it.

9All this have I seen, and applied my heart unto every work that is done under the sun: *there is* a time wherein one man ruleth over another to his own hurt.

10And so I saw the wicked buried, who had come and gone from the place of the holy, and they were forgotten in the city where they had so done: this *is* also vanity.

11Because sentence against an evil work is not executed speedily, therefore the heart of the sons of men is fully set in them to do evil.

12Though a sinner do evil an hundred times, and his *days* be prolonged, yet surely I know that it shall be well with them that fear God, which fear before him:

13But it shall not be well with the wicked, neither shall he prolong *his* days, *which are* as a shadow; because he feareth not before God.

14There is a vanity which is done upon the earth; that there be just *men,* unto whom it happeneth according to the work of the wicked; again, there be wicked *men,* to whom it happeneth according to the work of the righteous: I said that this also *is* vanity.

15Then I commended mirth, because a man hath no better thing under the sun, than to eat, and to drink, and to be merry: for that shall abide with him of his labour the days of his life, which God giveth him under the sun.

16When I applied mine heart to know wisdom, and to see the business that is done upon the earth: (for also *there is that* neither day nor night seeth sleep with his eyes:)

17Then I beheld all the work of God, that a man cannot find out the work that is done under the sun: because though a man labor to seek *it* out, yet he shall not find *it;* yea further; though a wise *man* think to know *it,* yet shall he not be able to find *it.*

FOR all this I considered in my heart even to declare all this, that the righteous, and the wise, and their works, *are* in the hand of God: no man knoweth either love or hatred *by* all *that is* before them.

2All *things come* alike to all: *there is* one event to the righteous, and to the wicked; to the good and to the clean, and to the unclean; to him that sacrificeth, and to him that sacrificeth not:

as *is* the good, so *is* the sinner; *and* he that sweareth, as *he* that feareth an oath.

3This *is* an evil among all *things* that are done under the sun, that *there is* one event unto all: yea, also the heart of the sons of men is full of evil, and madness *is* in their heart while they live, and after that *they go* to the dead.

4For to him that is joined to all the living there is hope: for a living dog is better than a dead lion.

5For the living know that they shall die: but the dead know not any thing, neither have they any more a reward; for the memory of them is forgotten.

6Also their love, and their hatred, and their envy, is now perished; neither have they any more a portion for ever in any *thing* that is done under the sun.

7Go thy way, eat thy bread with joy, and drink thy wine with a merry heart; for God now accepteth thy works.

8Let thy garments be always white; and let thy head lack no ointment.

9Live joyfully with the wife whom thou lovest all the days of the life of thy vanity, which he hath given thee under the sun, all the days of thy vanity: for that *is* thy portion in *this* life, and in thy labour which thou takest under the sun.

10Whatsoever thy hand findeth to do, do *it* with thy might; for *there is* no work, nor device, nor knowledge, nor wisdom, in the grave, whither thou goest.

11I returned, and saw under the sun, that the race *is* not to the swift, nor the battle to the strong, neither yet bread to the wise, nor yet riches to men of understanding, nor yet favour to men of skill; but time and chance happeneth to them all.

12For man also knoweth not his time: as the fishes that are taken in an evil net, and as the birds that are caught in the snare; so *are* the sons of men snared in an evil time, when it falleth suddenly upon them.

13This wisdom have I seen also under the sun, and it *seemed* great unto me:

14*There was* a little city, and few men within it; and there came a great king against it, and besieged it, and built great bulwarks against it:

15Now there was found in it a poor wise man, and he by his wisdom delivered the city; yet no man remembered that same poor man.

16Then said I, Wisdom *is* better than strength: nevertheless the poor man's wisdom *is* despised, and his words are not heard.

17The words of wise *men are* heard in quiet more than the cry of him that ruleth among fools.

18Wisdom *is* better than weapons of war: but one sinner destroyeth much good.

2 CORINTHIANS 7:8–16

FOR though I made you sorry with a letter, I do not repent, though I did repent: for I perceive that the same epistle hath made you sorry, though *it were* but for a season.

9Now I rejoice, not that ye were made sorry, but that ye sorrowed to repentance: for ye were made sorry after a godly manner, that ye might receive damage by us in nothing.

10For godly sorrow worketh repentance to salvation not to be repented of: but the sorrow of the world worketh death.

11For behold this selfsame thing, that ye sorrowed after a godly sort, what carefulness it wrought in you, yea, *what* clearing of yourselves, yea, *what* indignation, yea, *what* fear, yea, *what* vehement desire, yea, *what* zeal, yea, *what* revenge! In all *things* ye have approved yourselves to be clear in this matter.

12Wherefore, though I wrote unto you, *I did it* not for his cause that had done the wrong, nor for his cause that suffered wrong, but that our care for you in the sight of God might appear unto you.

13Therefore we were comforted in your comfort: yea, and exceedingly the more joyed we for the joy of Titus, because his spirit was refreshed by you all.

14For if I have boasted any thing to him of you, I am not ashamed; but as we spake all things to you in truth, even so our boasting, which *I made* before Titus, is found a truth.

15And his inward affection is more abundant toward you, whilst he remembereth the obedience of you all, how with fear and trembling ye received him.

16I rejoice therefore that I have confidence in you in all *things*.

PSALM 48:1–14

GREAT *is* the LORD, and greatly to be praised in the city of our God, *in* the mountain of his holiness.

2Beautiful for situation, the joy of the whole earth, *is* mount Zion, *on* the sides of the north, the city of the great King.

3God is known in her palaces for a refuge.

4For, lo, the kings were assembled, they passed by together.

5They saw *it, and* so they marvelled; they were troubled, *and* hasted away.

6Fear took hold upon them there, *and* pain, as of a woman in travail.

7Thou breakest the ships of Tarshish with an east wind.

8As we have heard, so have we seen in the city of the LORD of hosts, in the city of our God: God will establish it for ever. Selah.

9We have thought of thy lovingkindness, O God, in the midst of thy temple.

10According to thy name, O God, so *is* thy praise unto the ends of the earth: thy right hand is full of righteousness.

11Let mount Zion rejoice, let the daughters of Judah be glad, because of thy judgments.

12Walk about Zion, and go round about her: tell the towers thereof.

13Mark ye well her bulwarks, consider her palaces; that ye may tell *it* to the generation following.

14For this God *is* our God for ever and ever: he will be our guide *even* unto death.

PROVERBS FOR TODAY/ 22:17–19

Bow down thine ear, and hear the words of the wise, and apply thine heart unto my knowledge. For it is a pleasant thing if thou keep them within thee; they shall withal be fitted in thy lips. That thy trust may be in the LORD, I have made known to thee this day, even to thee.

SEPTEMBER 5

ECCLESIASTES 10:1—12:14

DEAD flies cause the ointment of the apothecary to send forth a stinking savour: *so doth* a little folly him that is in reputation for wisdom *and* honour.

2A wise man's heart *is* at his right hand; but a fool's heart at his left.

3Yea also, when he that is a fool walketh by the way, his wisdom faileth *him,* and he saith to every one *that* he *is* a fool.

4If the spirit of the ruler rise up against thee, leave not thy place; for yielding pacifieth great offences.

5There is an evil *which* I have seen under the sun, as an error *which* proceedeth from the ruler:

6Folly is set in great dignity, and the rich sit in low place.

7I have seen servants upon horses, and princes walking as servants upon the earth.

8He that diggeth a pit shall fall into it; and whoso breaketh an hedge, a serpent shall bite him.

9Whoso removeth stones shall be hurt therewith; *and* he that cleaveth wood shall be endangered thereby.

10If the iron be blunt, and he do not whet the edge, then must he put to more strength: but wisdom *is* profitable to direct.

11Surely the serpent will bite without enchantment; and a babbler is no better.

12The words of a wise man's mouth *are* gracious; but the lips of a fool will swallow up himself.

13The beginning of the words of his mouth *is* foolishness: and the end of his talk *is* mischievous madness.

14A fool also is full of words: a man cannot tell what shall be; and what shall be after him, who can tell him?

15The labour of the foolish wearieth every one of them, because he knoweth not how to go to the city.

16Woe to thee, O land, when thy king *is* a child, and thy princes eat in the morning!

17Blessed *art* thou, O land, when thy king *is* the son of nobles, and thy princes eat in due season, for strength, and not for drunkenness!

18By much slothfulness the building decayeth; and through idleness of the hands the house droppeth through.

19A feast is made for laughter, and wine maketh merry: but money answereth all *things.*

20Curse not the king, no not in thy thought; and curse not the rich in thy bedchamber: for a bird of the air shall carry the voice, and that which hath wings shall tell the matter.

CAST thy bread upon the waters: for thou shalt find it after many days.

2Give a portion to seven, and also to eight; for thou knowest not what evil shall be upon the earth.

3If the clouds be full of rain, they empty *themselves* upon the earth: and if the tree fall toward the south, or toward the north, in the place where the tree falleth, there it shall be.

4He that observeth the wind shall not sow; and he that regardeth the clouds shall not reap.

5As thou knowest not what *is* the way of the spirit, *nor* how the bones *do grow* in the womb of her that is with child: even so thou knowest not the works of God who maketh all.

6In the morning sow thy seed, and in the evening withhold not thine hand: for thou knowest not whether shall prosper, either this or that, or whether they both *shall be* alike good.

7Truly the light *is* sweet, and a

pleasant *thing it is* for the eyes to behold the sun:

8But if a man live many years, *and* rejoice in them all; yet let him remember the days of darkness; for they shall be many. All that cometh *is* vanity.

9Rejoice, O young man, in thy youth; and let thy heart cheer thee in the days of thy youth, and walk in the ways of thine heart, and in the sight of thine eyes: but know thou, that for all these *things* God will bring thee into judgment.

10Therefore remove sorrow from thy heart, and put away evil from thy flesh: for childhood and youth *are* vanity.

REMEMBER now thy Creator in the days of thy youth, while the evil days come not, nor the years draw nigh, when thou shalt say, I have no pleasure in them;

2While the sun, or the light, or the moon, or the stars, be not darkened, nor the clouds return after the rain:

3In the day when the keepers of the house shall tremble, and the strong men shall bow themselves, and the grinders cease because they are few, and those that look out of the windows be darkened,

4And the doors shall be shut in the streets, when the sound of the grinding is low, and he shall rise up at the voice of the bird, and all the daughters of musick shall be brought low;

5Also *when* they shall be afraid of *that which is* high, and fears *shall be* in the way, and the almond tree shall flourish, and the grasshopper shall be a burden, and desire shall fail: because man goeth to his long home, and the mourners go about the streets:

6Or ever the silver cord be loosed, or the golden bowl be broken, or the pitcher be broken at the fountain, or the wheel broken at the cistern.

7Then shall the dust return to the earth as it was: and the spirit shall return unto God who gave it.

8Vanity of vanities, saith the preacher; all *is* vanity.

9And moreover, because the preacher was wise, he still taught the people knowledge; yea, he gave good heed, and sought out, *and* set in order many proverbs.

10The preacher sought to find out acceptable words: and *that which was* written *was* upright, *even* words of truth.

11The words of the wise *are* as goads, and as nails fastened *by* the masters of assemblies, *which* are given from one shepherd.

12And further, by these, my son, be admonished: of making many books *there is* no end; and much study *is* a weariness of the flesh.

13Let us hear the conclusion of the whole matter: Fear God, and keep his commandments: for this is the whole *duty* of man.

14For God shall bring every work into judgment, with every secret thing, whether *it be* good, or whether *it be* evil.

2 CORINTHIANS 8:1–15

MOREOVER, brethren, we do you to wit of the grace of God bestowed on the churches of Macedonia;

2How that in a great trial of affliction the abundance of their joy and their deep poverty abounded unto the riches of their liberality.

3For to *their* power, I bear record, yea, and beyond *their* power *they were* willing of themselves;

4Praying us with much entreaty that we would receive the gift, and *take upon us* the fellowship of the ministering to the saints.

5And *this they did,* not as we hoped, but first gave their own selves to the Lord, and unto us by the will of God.

6Insomuch that we desired Titus, that as he had begun, so he would also finish in you the same grace also.

7Therefore, as ye abound in every *thing, in* faith, and utterance, and knowledge, and *in* all diligence, and *in* your love to us, *see* that ye abound in this grace also.

8I speak not by commandment, but by occasion of the forwardness of others, and to prove the sincerity of your love.

9For ye know the grace of our Lord Jesus Christ, that, though he was rich, yet for your sakes he became poor, that ye through his poverty might be rich.

10And herein I give *my* advice: for this is expedient for you, who have begun before, not only to do, but also to be forward a year ago.

11Now therefore perform the doing *of it;* that as *there was* a readiness to will, so *there may be* a performance also out of that which ye have.

12For if there be first a willing mind, *it is* accepted according to that a man hath, *and* not according to that he hath not.

13For *I mean* not that other men be eased, and ye burdened:

14But by an equality, *that* now at this time your abundance *may be a supply* for their want, that their abundance also may be *a supply* for your want: that there may be equality:

15As it is written, He that *had gathered* much had nothing over; and he that *had gathered* little had no lack.

PSALM 49:1–20

HEAR this, all *ye* people; give ear, all *ye* inhabitants of the world: 2Both low and high, rich and poor, together.

3My mouth shall speak of wisdom; and the meditation of my heart *shall be* of understanding.

4I will incline mine ear to a parable: I will open my dark saying upon the harp.

5Wherefore should I fear in the days of evil, *when* the iniquity of my heels shall compass me about?

6They that trust in their wealth, and boast themselves in the multitude of their riches;

7None *of them* can by any means redeem his brother, nor give to God a ransom for him:

8(For the redemption of their soul *is* precious, and it ceaseth for ever:)

9That he should still live for ever, *and* not see corruption.

10For he seeth *that* wise men die, likewise the fool and the brutish person perish, and leave their wealth to others.

11Their inward thought *is, that* their houses *shall continue* for ever, *and* their dwelling places to all generations; they call *their* lands after their own names.

12Nevertheless man *being* in honour abideth not: he is like the beasts *that* perish.

13This their way *is* their folly: yet their posterity approve their sayings. Selah.

14Like sheep they are laid in the grave; death shall feed on them; and the upright shall have dominion over them in the morning; and their beauty shall consume in the grave from their dwelling.

15But God will redeem my soul from the power of the grave: for he shall receive me. Selah.

16Be not thou afraid when one is made rich, when the glory of his house is increased;

17For when he dieth he shall carry nothing away: his glory shall not descend after him.

18Though while he lived he blessed his soul: and *men* will praise thee, when thou doest well to thyself.

19He shall go to the generation of his fathers; they shall never see light.

20Man *that is* in honour, and understandeth not, is like the beasts *that* perish.

PROVERBS FOR TODAY/ 22:20–21

Have not I written to thee excellent things in counsels and knowledge, That I might make thee know the certainty of the words of truth; that thou mightest answer the words of truth to them that send unto thee?

SEPTEMBER 6

SONG OF SOLOMON 1:1—4:16

THE song of songs, which *is* Solomon's.

2Let him kiss me with the kisses of his mouth: for thy love *is* better than wine.

3Because of the savour of thy good ointments thy name *is as* ointment poured forth, therefore do the virgins love thee.

4Draw me, we will run after thee: the king hath brought me into his chambers: we will be glad and rejoice in thee, we will remember thy love more than wine: the upright love thee.

5I *am* black, but comely, O ye daughters of Jerusalem, as the tents of Kedar, as the curtains of Solomon.

6Look not upon me, because I *am* black, because the sun hath looked upon me: my mother's children were angry with me; they made me the keeper of the vineyards; *but* mine own vineyard have I not kept.

7Tell me, O thou whom my soul loveth, where thou feedest, where thou makest *thy flock* to rest at noon: for why should I be as one that turneth aside by the flocks of thy companions?

8If thou know not, O thou fairest among women, go thy way forth by the footsteps of the flock, and feed thy kids beside the shepherds' tents.

9I have compared thee, O my love, to a company of horses in Pharaoh's chariots.

10Thy cheeks are comely with rows *of jewels,* thy neck with chains *of gold.*

11We will make thee borders of gold with studs of silver.

12While the king *sitteth* at his table, my spikenard sendeth forth the smell thereof.

13A bundle of myrrh *is* my wellbeloved unto me; he shall lie all night betwixt my breasts.

14My beloved *is* unto me *as* a cluster of camphire in the vineyards of Engedi.

15Behold, thou *art* fair, my love; behold, thou *art* fair; thou *hast* doves' eyes.

16Behold, thou *art* fair, my beloved, yea, pleasant: also our bed *is* green.

17The beams of our house *are* cedar, *and* our rafters of fir.

I AM the rose of Sharon, *and* the lily of the valleys.

2As the lily among thorns, so *is* my love among the daughters.

3As the apple tree among the trees of the wood, so *is* my beloved among the sons. I sat down under his shadow with great delight, and his fruit *was* sweet to my taste.

4He brought me to the banqueting house, and his banner over me *was* love.

5Stay me with flagons, comfort me with apples: for I *am* sick of love.

6His left hand *is* under my head, and his right hand doth embrace me.

7I charge you, O ye daughters of Jerusalem, by the roes, and by the hinds of the field, that ye stir not up, nor awake *my* love, till he please.

8The voice of my beloved! behold, he cometh leaping upon the mountains, skipping upon the hills.

9My beloved is like a roe or a young hart: behold, he standeth behind our wall, he looketh forth at the windows, shewing himself through the lattice.

10My beloved spake, and said unto me, Rise up, my love, my fair one, and come away.

11For, lo, the winter is past, the rain is over *and* gone;

12The flowers appear on the earth; the time of the singing *of birds* is come, and the voice of the turtle is heard in our land;

13The fig tree putteth forth her green figs, and the vines *with* the tender grape give a *good* smell. Arise, my love, my fair one, and come away.

14O my dove, *that art* in the clefts of the rock, in the secret *places* of the stairs, let me see thy countenance, let me hear thy voice; for sweet *is* thy voice, and thy countenance *is* comely.

15Take us the foxes, the little foxes, that spoil the vines: for our vines *have* tender grapes.

16My beloved *is* mine, and I *am* his: he feedeth among the lilies.

17Until the day break, and the shadows flee away, turn, my beloved, and be thou like a roe or a young hart upon the mountains of Bether.

By night on my bed I sought him whom my soul loveth: I sought him, but I found him not.

2I will rise now, and go about the city in the streets, and in the broad ways I will seek him whom my soul loveth: I sought him, but I found him not.

3The watchmen that go about the city found me: *to whom I said,* Saw ye him whom my soul loveth?

4*It was* but a little that I passed from them, but I found him whom my soul loveth: I held him, and would not let him go, until I had brought him into my mother's house, and into the chamber of her that conceived me.

5I charge you, O ye daughters of Jerusalem, by the roes, and by the hinds of the field, that ye stir not up, nor awake *my* love, till he please.

6Who *is* this that cometh out of the wilderness like pillars of smoke, perfumed with myrrh and frankincense, with all powders of the merchant?

7Behold his bed, which is Solomon's; threescore valiant men *are* about it, of the valiant of Israel.

8They all hold swords, *being* expert in war: every man *hath* his sword upon his thigh because of fear in the night.

9King Solomon made himself a chariot of the wood of Lebanon.

10He made the pillars thereof *of* silver, the bottom thereof *of* gold, the covering of it *of* purple, the midst thereof being paved *with* love, for the daughters of Jerusalem.

11Go forth, O ye daughters of Zion, and behold king Solomon with the crown wherewith his mother crowned him in the day of his espousals, and in the day of the gladness of his heart.

Behold, thou *art* fair, my love; behold, thou *art* fair; thou *hast* doves' eyes within thy locks: thy hair *is* as a flock of goats, that appear from mount Gilead.

2Thy teeth *are* like a flock *of sheep that are even* shorn, which came up from the washing; whereof every one bear twins, and none *is* barren among them.

3Thy lips *are* like a thread of scarlet, and thy speech *is* comely: thy temples *are* like a piece of a pomegranate within thy locks.

4Thy neck *is* like the tower of David builded for an armoury, whereon there hang a thousand bucklers, all shields of mighty men.

5Thy two breasts *are* like two young roes that are twins, which feed among the lilies.

6Until the day break, and the shadows flee away, I will get me to the mountain of myrrh, and to the hill of frankincense.

7Thou *art* all fair, my love; *there is* no spot in thee.

8Come with me from Lebanon, *my* spouse, with me from Lebanon: look from the top of Amana, from the top of Shenir and Hermon, from the lions' dens, from the mountains of the leopards.

9Thou hast ravished my heart, my sister, *my* spouse; thou hast ravished my heart with one of thine eyes, with one chain of thy neck.

10How fair is thy love, my sister, *my* spouse! how much better is thy love than wine! and the smell of thine ointments than all spices!

11Thy lips, O *my* spouse, drop *as* the honeycomb: honey and milk *are* under thy tongue; and the smell of thy garments *is* like the smell of Lebanon.

12A garden inclosed *is* my sister, *my* spouse; a spring shut up, a fountain sealed.

13Thy plants *are* an orchard of pomegranates, with pleasant fruits; camphire, with spikenard,

14Spikenard and saffron; calamus and cinnamon, with all trees of frankincense; myrrh and aloes, with all the chief spices:

15A fountain of gardens, a well of living waters, and streams from Lebanon.

16Awake, O north wind; and come, thou south; blow upon my garden, *that* the spices thereof may flow out. Let my beloved come into his garden, and eat his pleasant fruits.

2 CORINTHIANS 8:16–24

Bᴜᴛ thanks *be* to God, which put the same earnest care into the heart of Titus for you.

17For indeed he accepted the exhortation; but being more forward, of his own accord he went unto you.

18And we have sent with him the brother, whose praise *is* in the gospel throughout all the churches;

19And not *that* only, but who was also chosen of the churches to travel with us with this grace, which is administered by us to the glory of the same Lord, and *declaration of* your ready mind:

20Avoiding this, that no man should blame us in this abundance which is administered by us:

21Providing for honest things, not only in the sight of the Lord, but also in the sight of men.

22And we have sent with them our brother, whom we have oftentimes proved diligent in many things, but now much more diligent, upon the great confidence which *I have* in you.

23Whether *any do enquire* of Titus, *he is* my partner and fellowhelper concerning you: or our brethren *be enquired of, they are* the messengers of the churches, *and* the glory of Christ.

24Wherefore shew ye to them, and before the churches, the proof of your love, and of our boasting on your behalf.

PSALM 50:1–23

Tʜᴇ mighty God, *even* the Lᴏʀᴅ, hath spoken, and called the earth from the rising of the sun unto the going down thereof.

2Out of Zion, the perfection of beauty, God hath shined.

3Our God shall come, and shall not keep silence: a fire shall devour before him, and it shall be very tempestuous round about him.

4He shall call to the heavens from above, and to the earth, that he may judge his people.

5Gather my saints together unto me; those that have made a covenant with me by sacrifice.

6And the heavens shall declare his

righteousness: for God *is* judge himself. Selah.

7Hear, O my people, and I will speak; O Israel, and I will testify against thee: I *am* God, *even* thy God.

8I will not reprove thee for thy sacrifices or thy burnt offerings, *to have been* continually before me.

9I will take no bullock out of thy house, *nor* he goats out of thy folds.

10For every beast of the forest *is* mine, *and* the cattle upon a thousand hills.

11I know all the fowls of the mountains: and the wild beasts of the field *are* mine.

12If I were hungry, I would not tell thee: for the world *is* mine, and the fulness thereof.

13Will I eat the flesh of bulls, or drink the blood of goats?

14Offer unto God thanksgiving; and pay thy vows unto the most High:

15And call upon me in the day of trouble: I will deliver thee, and thou shalt glorify me.

16But unto the wicked God saith, What hast thou to do to declare my statutes, or *that* thou shouldest take my covenant in thy mouth?

17Seeing thou hatest instruction, and casteth my words behind thee.

18When thou sawest a thief, then thou consentedst with him, and hast been partaker with adulterers.

19Thou givest thy mouth to evil, and thy tongue frameth deceit.

20Thou sittest *and* speakest against thy brother; thou slanderest thine own mother's son.

21These *things* hast thou done, and I kept silence; thou thoughtest that I was altogether *such an one* as thyself: *but* I will reprove thee, and set *them* in order before thine eyes.

22Now consider this, ye that forget God, lest I tear *you* in pieces, and *there be* none to deliver.

23Whoso offereth praise glorifieth me: and to him that ordereth *his* conversation *aright* will I shew the salvation of God.

PROVERBS FOR TODAY/ 22:22–23

Rob not the poor, because he is *poor: neither oppress the afflicted in the gate: For the* LORD *will plead their cause, and spoil the soul of those that spoiled them.*

SEPTEMBER 7

SONG OF SOLOMON 5:1—8:14

I AM come into my garden, my sister, *my* spouse: I have gathered my myrrh with my spice; I have eaten my honeycomb with my honey; I have drunk my wine with my milk: eat, O friends; drink, yea, drink abundantly, O beloved.

2I sleep, but my heart waketh: *it is* the voice of my beloved that knocketh, *saying,* Open to me, my sister, my love,

my dove, my undefiled: for my head is filled with dew, *and* my locks with the drops of the night.

3I have put off my coat; how shall I put it on? I have washed my feet; how shall I defile them?

4My beloved put in his hand by the hole *of the door,* and my bowels were moved for him.

5I rose up to open to my beloved;

and my hands dropped *with* myrrh, and my fingers *with* sweet smelling myrrh, upon the handles of the lock.

6I opened to my beloved; but my beloved had withdrawn himself, *and* was gone: my soul failed when he spake: I sought him, but I could not find him; I called him, but he gave me no answer.

7The watchmen that went about the city found me, they smote me, they wounded me; the keepers of the walls took away my veil from me.

8I charge you, O daughters of Jerusalem, if ye find my beloved, that ye tell him, that I *am* sick of love.

9What *is* thy beloved more than *another* beloved, O thou fairest among women? what *is* thy beloved more than *another* beloved, that thou dost so charge us?

10My beloved *is* white and ruddy, the chiefest among ten thousand.

11His head *is as* the most fine gold, his locks *are* bushy, *and* black as a raven.

12His eyes *are* as *the eyes* of doves by the rivers of waters, washed with milk, *and* fitly set.

13His cheeks *are* as a bed of spices, *as* sweet flowers: his lips *like* lilies, dropping sweet smelling myrrh.

14His hands *are as* gold rings set with the beryl: his belly *is as* bright ivory overlaid *with* sapphires.

15His legs *are as* pillars of marble, set upon sockets of fine gold: his countenance *is* as Lebanon, excellent as the cedars.

16His mouth *is* most sweet: yea, he *is* altogether lovely. This *is* my beloved, and this *is* my friend, O daughters of Jerusalem.

WHITHER is thy beloved gone, O thou fairest among women? whither is thy beloved turned aside? that we may seek him with thee.

2My beloved is gone down into his garden, to the beds of spices, to feed in the gardens, and to gather lilies.

3I *am* my beloved's, and my beloved *is* mine: he feedeth among the lilies.

4Thou *art* beautiful, O my love, as Tirzah, comely as Jerusalem, terrible as *an army* with banners.

5Turn away thine eyes from me, for they have overcome me: thy hair *is* as a flock of goats that appear from Gilead.

6Thy teeth *are* as a flock of sheep which go up from the washing, whereof every one beareth twins, and *there is* not one barren among them.

7As a piece of a pomegranate *are* thy temples within thy locks.

8There are threescore queens, and fourscore concubines, and virgins without number.

9My dove, my undefiled is *but* one; she *is* the *only* one of her mother, she *is* the choice *one* of her that bare her. The daughters saw her, and blessed her; *yea*, the queens and the concubines, and they praised her.

10Who *is* she *that* looketh forth as the morning, fair as the moon, clear as the sun, *and* terrible as *an army* with banners?

11I went down into the garden of nuts to see the fruits of the valley, *and* to see whether the vine flourished, *and* the pomegranates budded.

12Or ever I was aware, my soul made me *like* the chariots of Ammi–nadib.

13Return, return, O Shulamite; return, return, that we may look upon thee. What will ye see in the Shulamite? As it were the company of two armies.

How beautiful are thy feet with shoes, O prince's daughter! the joints of thy thighs *are* like jewels, the work of the hands of a cunning workman.

2Thy navel *is like* a round goblet, *which* wanteth not liquor: thy belly *is like* an heap of wheat set about with lilies.

3Thy two breasts *are* like two young roes *that are* twins.

4Thy neck *is* as a tower of ivory;

thine eyes *like* the fishpools in Heshbon, by the gate of Bath–rabbim: thy nose *is* as the tower of Lebanon which looketh toward Damascus.

5Thine head upon thee *is* like Carmel, and the hair of thine head like purple; the king *is* held in the galleries.

6How fair and how pleasant art thou, O love, for delights!

7This thy stature is like to a palm tree, and thy breasts to clusters *of grapes.*

8I said, I will go up to the palm tree, I will take hold of the boughs thereof: now also thy breasts shall be as clusters of the vine, and the smell of thy nose like apples;

9And the roof of thy mouth like the best wine for my beloved, that goeth *down* sweetly, causing the lips of those that are asleep to speak.

10I *am* my beloved's, and his desire *is* toward me.

11Come, my beloved, let us go forth into the field; let us lodge in the villages.

12Let us get up early to the vineyards; let us see if the vine flourish, *whether* the tender grape appear, *and* the pomegranates bud forth: there will I give thee my loves.

13The mandrakes give a smell, and at our gates *are* all manner of pleasant *fruits,* new and old, *which* I have laid up for thee, O my beloved.

O THAT thou *wert* as my brother, that sucked the breasts of my mother! *when* I should find thee without, I would kiss thee; yea, I should not be despised.

2I would lead thee, *and* bring thee into my mother's house, *who* would instruct me: I would cause thee to drink of spiced wine of the juice of my pomegranate.

3His left hand *should be* under my head, and his right hand should embrace me.

4I charge you, O daughters of Jerusalem, that ye stir not up, nor awake *my* love, until he please.

5Who *is* this that cometh up from the wilderness, leaning upon her beloved? I raised thee up under the apple tree: there thy mother brought thee forth: there she brought thee forth *that* bare thee.

6Set me as a seal upon thine heart, as a seal upon thine arm: for love *is* strong as death; jealousy *is* cruel as the grave: the coals thereof *are* coals of fire, *which hath* a most vehement flame.

7Many waters cannot quench love, neither can the floods drown it: if a man would give all the substance of his house for love, it would utterly be contemned.

8We have a little sister, and she hath no breasts: what shall we do for our sister in the day when she shall be spoken for?

9If she *be* a wall, we will build upon her a palace of silver: and if she *be* a door, we will inclose her with boards of cedar.

10I *am* a wall, and my breasts like towers: then was I in his eyes as one that found favour.

11Solomon had a vineyard at Baal–hamon; he let out the vineyard unto keepers; every one for the fruit thereof was to bring a thousand *pieces* of silver.

12My vineyard, which *is* mine, *is* before me: thou, O Solomon, *must have* a thousand, and those that keep the fruit thereof two hundred.

13Thou that dwellest in the gardens, the companions hearken to thy voice: cause me to hear *it.*

14Make haste, my beloved, and be thou like to a roe or to a young hart upon the mountains of spices.

2 CORINTHIANS 9:1–15

FOR as touching the ministering to the saints, it is superfluous for me to write to you:

2For I know the forwardness of your mind, for which I boast of you to them of Macedonia, that Achaia was ready a year ago; and your zeal hath provoked very many.

3Yet have I sent the brethren, lest our boasting of you should be in vain in this behalf; that, as I said, ye may be ready:

4Lest haply if they of Macedonia come with me, and find you unprepared, we (that we say not, ye) should be ashamed in this same confident boasting.

5Therefore I thought it necessary to exhort the brethren, and they would go before unto you, and make up beforehand your bounty, whereof ye had notice before, that the same might be ready, as *a matter of* bounty, and not as *of* covetousness.

6But this *I say,* He which soweth sparingly shall reap also sparingly; and he which soweth bountifully shall reap also bountifully.

7Every man according as he purposeth in his heart, *so let him give;* not grudgingly, or of necessity: for God loveth a cheerful giver.

8And God *is* able to make all grace abound toward you; that ye, always having all sufficiency in all *things,* may abound to every good work:

9(As it is written, He hath dispersed abroad; he hath given to the poor: his righteousness remaineth for ever.

10Now he that ministereth seed to the sower both minister bread for *your* food, and multiply your seed sown, and increase the fruits of your righteousness;)

11Being enriched in every thing to all bountifulness, which causeth through us thanksgiving to God.

12For the administration of this service not only supplieth the want of the saints, but is abundant also by many thanksgivings unto God;

13Whiles by the experiment of this ministration they glorify God for your professed subjection unto the gospel of Christ, and for *your* liberal distribution unto them, and unto all *men;*

14And by their prayer for you, which long after you for the exceeding grace of God in you.

15Thanks *be* unto God for his unspeakable gift.

PSALM 51:1–19

Have mercy upon me, O God, according to thy lovingkindness: according unto the multitude of thy tender mercies blot out my transgressions.

2Wash me throughly from mine iniquity, and cleanse me from my sin.

3For I acknowledge my transgressions: and my sin *is* ever before me.

4Against thee, thee only, have I sinned, and done *this* evil in thy sight: that thou mightest be justified when thou speakest, *and* be clear when thou judgest.

5Behold, I was shapen in iniquity; and in sin did my mother conceive me.

6Behold, thou desirest truth in the inward parts: and in the hidden *part* thou shalt make me to know wisdom.

7Purge me with hyssop, and I shall be clean: wash me, and I shall be whiter than snow.

8Make me to hear joy and gladness; *that* the bones *which* thou hast broken may rejoice.

9Hide thy face from my sins, and blot out all mine iniquities.

10Create in me a clean heart, O God; and renew a right spirit within me.

11Cast me not away from thy presence; and take not thy holy spirit from me.

12Restore unto me the joy of thy salvation; and uphold me *with thy* free spirit.

13*Then* will I teach transgressors thy ways; and sinners shall be converted unto thee.

14Deliver me from bloodguiltiness, O God, thou God of my salvation: *and* my tongue shall sing aloud of thy righteousness.

15O Lord, open thou my lips; and my mouth shall shew forth thy praise.

16For thou desirest not sacrifice; else would I give *it:* thou delightest not in burnt offering.

17The sacrifices of God *are* a broken spirit: a broken and a contrite heart, O God, thou wilt not despise.

18Do good in thy good pleasure unto Zion: build thou the walls of Jerusalem.

19Then shalt thou be pleased with the sacrifices of righteousness, with burnt offering and whole burnt offering: then shall they offer bullocks upon thine altar.

PROVERBS FOR TODAY/ 22:24–25

Make no friendship with an angry man; and with a furious man thou shalt not go: Lest thou learn his ways, and get a snare to thy soul.

SEPTEMBER 8

ISAIAH 1:1—2:22

THE vision of Isaiah the son of Amoz, which he saw concerning Judah and Jerusalem in the days of Uzziah, Jotham, Ahaz, *and* Hezekiah, kings of Judah.

2Hear, O heavens, and give ear, O earth: for the LORD hath spoken, I have nourished and brought up children, and they have rebelled against me.

3The ox knoweth his owner, and the ass his master's crib: *but* Israel doth not know, my people doth not consider.

4Ah sinful nation, a people laden with iniquity, a seed of evildoers, children that are corrupters: they have forsaken the LORD, they have provoked the Holy One of Israel unto anger, they are gone away backward.

5Why should ye be stricken any more? ye will revolt more and more: the whole head is sick, and the whole heart faint.

6From the sole of the foot even unto the head *there is* no soundness in it; *but* wounds, and bruises, and putrifying sores: they have not been closed, neither bound up, neither mollified with ointment.

7Your country *is* desolate, your cities *are* burned with fire: your land, strangers devour it in your presence, and *it is* desolate, as overthrown by strangers.

8And the daughter of Zion is left as a cottage in a vineyard, as a lodge in a garden of cucumbers, as a besieged city.

9Except the LORD of hosts had left unto us a very small remnant, we should have been as Sodom, *and* we should have been like unto Gomorrah.

10Hear the word of the LORD, ye rulers of Sodom; give ear unto the law of our God, ye people of Gomorrah.

11To what purpose *is* the multitude of your sacrifices unto me? saith the LORD: I am full of the burnt offerings of rams, and the fat of fed beasts; and I delight not in the blood of bullocks, or of lambs, or of he goats.

12When ye come to appear before me, who hath required this at your hand, to tread my courts?

13Bring no more vain oblations; incense is an abomination unto me; the new moons and sabbaths, the calling of assemblies, I cannot away with; *it is* iniquity, even the solemn meeting.

14Your new moons and your appointed feasts my soul hateth: they are a trouble unto me; I am weary to bear *them*.

15And when ye spread forth your hands, I will hide mine eyes from you: yea, when ye make many prayers, I will not hear: your hands are full of blood.

16Wash you, make you clean; put away the evil of your doings from before mine eyes; cease to do evil;

17Learn to do well; seek judgment, relieve the oppressed, judge the fatherless, plead for the widow.

18Come now, and let us reason together, saith the LORD: though your sins be as scarlet, they shall be as white as snow; though they be red like crimson, they shall be as wool.

19If ye be willing and obedient, ye shall eat the good of the land:

20But if ye refuse and rebel, ye shall be devoured with the sword: for the mouth of the LORD hath spoken *it*.

21How is the faithful city become an harlot! it was full of judgment; righteousness lodged in it; but now murderers.

22Thy silver is become dross, thy wine mixed with water:

23Thy princes *are* rebellious, and companions of thieves: every one loveth gifts, and followeth after rewards: they judge not the fatherless, neither doth the cause of the widow come unto them.

24Therefore saith the LORD, the LORD of hosts, the mighty One of Israel, Ah, I will ease me of mine adversaries, and avenge me of mine enemies:

25And I will turn my hand upon thee, and purely purge away thy dross, and take away all thy tin:

26And I will restore thy judges as at the first, and thy counsellors as at the beginning: afterward thou shalt be called, The city of righteousness, the faithful city.

27Zion shall be redeemed with judgment, and her converts with righteousness.

28And the destruction of the transgressors and of the sinners *shall be* together, and they that forsake the LORD shall be consumed.

29For they shall be ashamed of the oaks which ye have desired, and ye shall be confounded for the gardens that ye have chosen.

30For ye shall be as an oak whose leaf fadeth, and as a garden that hath no water.

31And the strong shall be as tow, and the maker of it as a spark, and they shall both burn together, and none shall quench *them*.

THE word that Isaiah the son of Amoz saw concerning Judah and Jerusalem.

2And it shall come to pass in the last days, *that* the mountain of the LORD's house shall be established in the top of the mountains, and shall be exalted above the hills; and all nations shall flow unto it.

3And many people shall go and say, Come ye, and let us go up to the mountain of the LORD, to the house of the God of Jacob; and he will teach us of his ways, and we will walk in his paths: for out of Zion shall go forth the law, and the word of the LORD from Jerusalem.

4And he shall judge among the nations, and shall rebuke many people: and they shall beat their swords into plowshares, and their spears into pruninghooks: nation shall not lift up sword against nation, neither shall they learn war any more.

5O house of Jacob, come ye, and let us walk in the light of the LORD.

6Therefore thou hast forsaken thy people the house of Jacob, because they be replenished from the east, and *are* soothsayers like the Philistines, and they please themselves in the children of strangers.

7Their land also is full of silver and gold, neither *is there any* end of their treasures; their land is also full of horses, neither *is there any* end of their chariots:

8Their land also is full of idols; they worship the work of their own hands, that which their own fingers have made:

9And the mean man boweth down, and the great man humbleth himself: therefore forgive them not.

10Enter into the rock, and hide thee in the dust, for fear of the LORD, and for the glory of his majesty.

11The lofty looks of man shall be humbled, and the haughtiness of men shall be bowed down, and the LORD alone shall be exalted in that day.

12For the day of the LORD of hosts *shall be* upon every *one that is* proud and lofty, and upon every *one that is* lifted up; and he shall be brought low:

13And upon all the cedars of Lebanon, *that are* high and lifted up, and upon all the oaks of Bashan,

14And upon all the high mountains, and upon all the hills *that are* lifted up,

15And upon every high tower, and upon every fenced wall,

16And upon all the ships of Tarshish, and upon all pleasant pictures.

17And the loftiness of man shall be bowed down, and the haughtiness of men shall be made low: and the LORD alone shall be exalted in that day.

18And the idols he shall utterly abolish.

19And they shall go into the holes of the rocks, and into the caves of the earth, for fear of the LORD, and for the glory of his majesty, when he ariseth to shake terribly the earth.

20In that day a man shall cast his idols of silver, and his idols of gold, which they made *each one* for himself to worship, to the moles and to the bats;

21To go into the clefts of the rocks, and into the tops of the ragged rocks, for fear of the LORD, and for the glory of his majesty, when he ariseth to shake terribly the earth.

22Cease ye from man, whose breath *is* in his nostrils: for wherein is he to be accounted of?

2 CORINTHIANS 10:1–18

Now I Paul myself beseech you by the meekness and gentleness of Christ, who in presence *am* base among you, but being absent am bold toward you:

2But I beseech *you,* that I may not be bold when I am present with that confidence, wherewith I think to be bold against some, which think of us as if we walked according to the flesh.

3For though we walk in the flesh, we do not war after the flesh:

4(For the weapons of our warfare *are* not carnal, but mighty through God to the pulling down of strong holds;)

5Casting down imaginations, and every high thing that exalteth itself against the knowledge of God, and bringing into captivity every thought to the obedience of Christ;

6And having in a readiness to revenge all disobedience, when your obedience is fulfilled.

7Do ye look on things after the outward appearance? If any man trust to himself that he is Christ's, let him of himself think this again, that, as he *is* Christ's, even so *are* we Christ's.

8For though I should boast somewhat more of our authority, which the Lord hath given us for edification, and not for your destruction, I should not be ashamed:

9That I may not seem as if I would terrify you by letters.

10For *his* letters, say they, *are* weighty and powerful; but *his* bodily presence *is* weak, and *his* speech contemptible.

11Let such an one think this, that, such as we are in word by letters when we are absent, such *will we be* also in deed when we are present.

12For we dare not make ourselves of the number, or compare ourselves with some that commend themselves: but they measuring themselves by themselves, and comparing themselves among themselves, are not wise.

13But we will not boast of things without *our* measure, but according to the measure of the rule which God hath distributed to us, a measure to reach even unto you.

14For we stretch not ourselves beyond *our measure,* as though we reached not unto you: for we are come as far as to you also in *preaching* the gospel of Christ:

15Not boasting of things without *our* measure, *that is,* of other men's labours; but having hope, when your faith is increased, that we shall be enlarged by you according to our rule abundantly,

16To preach the gospel in the *regions* beyond you, *and* not to boast in another man's line of things made ready to our hand.

17But he that glorieth, let him glory in the Lord.

18For not he that commendeth himself is approved, but whom the Lord commendeth.

PSALM 52:1–9

WHY boastest thou thyself in mischief, O mighty man? the goodness of God *endureth* continually.

2Thy tongue deviseth mischiefs; like a sharp razor, working deceitfully.

3Thou lovest evil more than good; *and* lying rather than to speak righteousness. Selah.

4Thou lovest all devouring words, O *thou* deceitful tongue.

5God shall likewise destroy thee for ever, he shall take thee away, and pluck thee out of *thy* dwelling place, and root thee out of the land of the living. Selah.

6The righteous also shall see, and fear, and shall laugh at him:

7Lo, *this is* the man *that* made not God his strength; but trusted in the abundance of his riches, *and* strengthened himself in his wickedness.

8But I *am* like a green olive tree in the house of God: I trust in the mercy of God for ever and ever.

9I will praise thee for ever, because thou hast done *it:* and I will wait on thy name; for *it is* good before thy saints.

PROVERBS FOR TODAY/ 22:26–27

Be not thou one *of them that strike hands,* or *of them that are sureties for debts. If thou hast nothing to pay, why should he take away thy bed from under thee?*

SEPTEMBER 9

ISAIAH 3:1—5:30

FOR, behold, the Lord, the LORD of hosts, doth take away from Jerusalem and from Judah the stay and the staff, the whole stay of bread, and the whole stay of water,

2The mighty man, and the man of war, the judge, and the prophet, and the prudent, and the ancient,

3The captain of fifty, and the honourable man, and the counsellor, and the cunning artificer, and the eloquent orator.

⁴And I will give children *to be* their princes, and babes shall rule over them.

⁵And the people shall be oppressed, every one by another, and every one by his neighbour: the child shall behave himself proudly against the ancient, and the base against the honourable.

⁶When a man shall take hold of his brother of the house of his father, *saying,* Thou hast clothing, be thou our ruler, and *let* this ruin *be* under thy hand:

⁷In that day shall he swear, saying, I will not be an healer; for in my house *is* neither bread nor clothing: make me not a ruler of the people.

⁸For Jerusalem is ruined, and Judah is fallen: because their tongue and their doings *are* against the LORD, to provoke the eyes of his glory.

⁹The shew of their countenance doth witness against them; and they declare their sin as Sodom, they hide *it* not. Woe unto their soul! for they have rewarded evil unto themselves.

¹⁰Say ye to the righteous, that *it shall be* well *with him:* for they shall eat the fruit of their doings.

¹¹Woe unto the wicked! *it shall be* ill *with him:* for the reward of his hands shall be given him.

¹²*As for* my people, children *are* their oppressors, and women rule over them. O my people, they which lead thee cause *thee* to err, and destroy the way of thy paths.

¹³The LORD standeth up to plead, and standeth to judge the people.

¹⁴The LORD will enter into judgment with the ancients of his people, and the princes thereof: for ye have eaten up the vineyard; the spoil of the poor *is* in your houses.

¹⁵What mean ye *that* ye beat my people to pieces, and grind the faces of the poor? saith the Lord GOD of hosts.

¹⁶Moreover the LORD saith, Because the daughters of Zion are haughty, and walk with stretched forth necks and wanton eyes, walking and mincing *as* they go, and making a tinkling with their feet:

¹⁷Therefore the Lord will smite with a scab the crown of the head of the daughters of Zion, and the LORD will discover their secret parts.

¹⁸In that day the Lord will take away the bravery of *their* tinkling ornaments *about their feet,* and *their* cauls, and *their* round tires like the moon,

¹⁹The chains, and the bracelets, and the mufflers,

²⁰The bonnets, and the ornaments of the legs, and the headbands, and the tablets, and the earrings,

²¹The rings, and nose jewels,

²²The changeable suits of apparel, and the mantles, and the wimples, and the crisping pins,

²³The glasses, and the fine linen, and the hoods, and the vails.

²⁴And it shall come to pass, *that* instead of sweet smell there shall be stink; and instead of a girdle a rent; and instead of well set hair baldness; and instead of a stomacher a girding of sackcloth; *and* burning instead of beauty.

²⁵Thy men shall fall by the sword, and thy mighty in the war.

²⁶And her gates shall lament and mourn; and she *being* desolate shall sit upon the ground.

AND in that day seven women shall take hold of one man, saying, We will eat our own bread, and wear our own apparel: only let us be called by thy name, to take away our reproach.

²In that day shall the branch of the LORD be beautiful and glorious, and the fruit of the earth *shall be* excellent and comely for them that are escaped of Israel.

³And it shall come to pass, *that he that is* left in Zion, and *he that* remaineth in Jerusalem, shall be called holy, *even*

every one that is written among the living in Jerusalem:

4When the Lord shall have washed away the filth of the daughters of Zion, and shall have purged the blood of Jerusalem from the midst thereof by the spirit of judgment, and by the spirit of burning.

5And the LORD will create upon every dwelling place of mount Zion, and upon her assemblies, a cloud and smoke by day, and the shining of a flaming fire by night: for upon all the glory *shall be* a defence.

6And there shall be a tabernacle for a shadow in the daytime from the heat, and for a place of refuge, and for a covert from storm and from rain.

Now will I sing to my wellbeloved a song of my beloved touching his vineyard. My wellbeloved hath a vineyard in a very fruitful hill:

2And he fenced it, and gathered out the stones thereof, and planted it with the choicest vine, and built a tower in the midst of it, and also made a winepress therein: and he looked that it should bring forth grapes, and it brought forth wild grapes.

3And now, O inhabitants of Jerusalem, and men of Judah, judge, I pray you, betwixt me and my vineyard.

4What could have been done more to my vineyard, that I have not done in it? wherefore, when I looked that it should bring forth grapes, brought it forth wild grapes?

5And now go to; I will tell you what I will do to my vineyard: I will take away the hedge thereof, and it shall be eaten up; *and* break down the wall thereof, and it shall be trodden down:

6And I will lay it waste: it shall not be pruned, nor digged; but there shall come up briers and thorns: I will also command the clouds that they rain no rain upon it.

7For the vineyard of the LORD of hosts *is* the house of Israel, and the men of Judah his pleasant plant: and he looked for judgment, but behold oppression; for righteousness, but behold a cry.

8Woe unto them that join house to house, *that* lay field to field, till *there be* no place, that they may be placed alone in the midst of the earth!

9In mine ears *said* the LORD of hosts, Of a truth many houses shall be desolate, *even* great and fair, without inhabitant.

10Yea, ten acres of vineyard shall yield one bath, and the seed of an homer shall yield an ephah.

11Woe unto them that rise up early in the morning, *that* they may follow strong drink; that continue until night, *till* wine inflame them!

12And the harp, and the viol, the tabret, and pipe, and wine, are in their feasts: but they regard not the work of the LORD, neither consider the operation of his hands.

13Therefore my people are gone into captivity, because *they have* no knowledge: and their honourable men *are* famished, and their multitude dried up with thirst.

14Therefore hell hath enlarged herself, and opened her mouth without measure: and their glory, and their multitude, and their pomp, and he that rejoiceth, shall descend into it.

15And the mean man shall be brought down, and the eyes of the lofty shall be humbled:

16But the LORD of hosts shall be exalted in judgment, and God that is holy shall be sanctified in righteousness.

17Then shall the lambs feed after their manner, and the waste places of the fat ones shall strangers eat.

18Woe unto them that draw iniquity with cords of vanity, and sin as it were with a cart rope:

19That say, Let him make speed, *and* hasten his work, that we may see *it:* and let the counsel of the Holy One of Israel draw nigh and come, that we may know *it!*

20Woe unto them that call evil good, and good evil; that put darkness for light, and light for darkness; that put bitter for sweet, and sweet for bitter!

21Woe unto *them that are* wise in their own eyes, and prudent in their own sight!

22Woe unto *them that are* mighty to drink wine, and men of strength to mingle strong drink:

23Which justify the wicked for reward, and take away the righteousness of the righteous from him!

24Therefore as the fire devoureth the stubble, and the flame consumeth the chaff, *so* their root shall be as rottenness, and their blossom shall go up as dust: because they have cast away the law of the LORD of hosts, and despised the word of the Holy One of Israel.

25Therefore is the anger of the LORD kindled against his people, and he hath stretched forth his hand against them, and hath smitten them: and the hills did tremble, and their carcases *were* torn in the midst of the streets. For all this his anger is not turned away, but his hand *is* stretched out still.

26And he will lift up an ensign to the nations from far, and will hiss unto them from the end of the earth: and, behold, they shall come with speed swiftly:

27None shall be weary nor stumble among them; none shall slumber nor sleep; neither shall the girdle of their loins be loosed, nor the latchet of their shoes be broken:

28Whose arrows *are* sharp, and all their bows bent, their horses' hoofs shall be counted like flint, and their wheels like a whirlwind:

29Their roaring *shall be* like a lion, they shall roar like young lions: yea, they shall roar, and lay hold of the prey, and shall carry *it* away safe, and none shall deliver *it.*

30And in that day they shall roar against them like the roaring of the sea: and if *one* look unto the land, behold, darkness *and* sorrow, and the light is darkened in the heavens thereof.

2 CORINTHIANS 11:1-15

WOULD to God ye could bear with me a little in *my* folly: and indeed bear with me.

2For I am jealous over you with godly jealousy: for I have espoused you to one husband, that I may present *you* as a chaste virgin to Christ.

3But I fear, lest by any means, as the serpent beguiled Eve through his subtilty, so your minds should be corrupted from the simplicity that is in Christ.

4For if he that cometh preacheth another Jesus, whom we have not preached, or *if* ye receive another spirit, which ye have not received, or another gospel, which ye have not accepted, ye might well bear with *him.*

5For I suppose I was not a whit behind the very chiefest apostles.

6But though *I be* rude in speech, yet not in knowledge; but we have been throughly made manifest among you in all things.

7Have I committed an offence in abasing myself that ye might be exalted, because I have preached to you the gospel of God freely?

8I robbed other churches, taking wages *of them,* to do you service.

9And when I was present with you, and wanted, I was chargeable to no man: for that which was lacking to me the brethren which came from Macedonia supplied: and in all *things* I have kept myself from being burdensome unto you, and *so* will I keep *myself.*

10As the truth of Christ is in me, no man shall stop me of this boasting in the regions of Achaia.

11Wherefore? because I love you not? God knoweth.

12But what I do, that I will do, that I may cut off occasion from them which desire occasion; that wherein they glory, they may be found even as we.

13For such *are* false apostles, deceitful workers, transforming themselves into the apostles of Christ.

14And no marvel; for Satan himself is transformed into an angel of light.

15Therefore *it is* no great thing if his ministers also be transformed as the ministers of righteousness; whose end shall be according to their works.

PSALM 53:1–6

THE fool hath said in his heart, *There is* no God. Corrupt are they, and have done abominable iniquity: *there is* none that doeth good.

2God looked down from heaven upon the children of men, to see if there were *any* that did understand, that did seek God.

3Every one of them is gone back: they are altogether become filthy; *there is* none that doeth good, no, not one.

4Have the workers of iniquity no knowledge? who eat up my people *as* they eat bread: they have not called upon God.

5There were they in great fear, *where* no fear was: for God hath scattered the bones of him that encampeth *against* thee: thou hast put *them* to shame, because God hath despised them.

6Oh that the salvation of Israel *were* come out of Zion! When God bringeth back the captivity of his people, Jacob shall rejoice, *and* Israel shall be glad.

PROVERBS FOR TODAY/ 22:28–29

Remove not the ancient landmark, which thy fathers have set. □ *Seest thou a man diligent in his business? he shall stand before kings; he shall not stand before mean men.*

SEPTEMBER 10

ISAIAH 6:1—7:25

IN the year that king Uzziah died I saw also the Lord sitting upon a throne, high and lifted up, and his train filled the temple.

2Above it stood the seraphims: each one had six wings; with twain he covered his face, and with twain he covered his feet, and with twain he did fly.

3And one cried unto another, and said, Holy, holy, holy, *is* the LORD of hosts: the whole earth *is* full of his glory.

4And the posts of the door moved at the voice of him that cried, and the house was filled with smoke.

5Then said I, Woe *is* me! for I am undone; because I *am* a man of unclean lips, and I dwell in the midst of a people of unclean lips: for mine eyes have seen the King, the LORD of hosts.

6Then flew one of the seraphims unto me, having a live coal in his hand, *which* he had taken with the tongs from off the altar:

7And he laid *it* upon my mouth, and said, Lo, this hath touched thy lips; and thine iniquity is taken away, and thy sin purged.

8Also I heard the voice of the Lord, saying, Whom shall I send, and who will go for us? Then said I, Here *am* I; send me.

9And he said, Go, and tell this people,

Hear ye indeed, but understand not; and see ye indeed, but perceive not.

10Make the heart of this people fat, and make their ears heavy, and shut their eyes; lest they see with their eyes, and hear with their ears, and understand with their heart, and convert, and be healed.

11Then said I, Lord, how long? And he answered, Until the cities be wasted without inhabitant, and the houses without man, and the land be utterly desolate,

12And the LORD have removed men far away, and *there be* a great forsaking in the midst of the land.

13But yet in it *shall be* a tenth, and *it* shall return, and shall be eaten: as a teil tree, and as an oak, whose substance *is* in them, when they cast *their leaves: so* the holy seed *shall be* the substance thereof.

AND it came to pass in the days of Ahaz the son of Jotham, the son of Uzziah, king of Judah, *that* Rezin the king of Syria, and Pekah the son of Remaliah, king of Israel, went up toward Jerusalem to war against it, but could not prevail against it.

2And it was told the house of David, saying, Syria is confederate with Ephraim. And his heart was moved, and the heart of his people, as the trees of the wood are moved with the wind.

3Then said the LORD unto Isaiah, Go forth now to meet Ahaz, thou, and Shear–jashub thy son, at the end of the conduit of the upper pool in the highway of the fuller's field;

4And say unto him, Take heed, and be quiet; fear not, neither be faint-hearted for the two tails of these smoking firebrands, for the fierce anger of Rezin with Syria, and of the son of Remaliah.

5Because Syria, Ephraim, and the son of Remaliah, have taken evil counsel against thee, saying,

6Let us go up against Judah, and vex it, and let us make a breach therein for us, and set a king in the midst of it, *even* the son of Tabeal:

7Thus saith the Lord GOD, It shall not stand, neither shall it come to pass.

8For the head of Syria *is* Damascus, and the head of Damascus *is* Rezin; and within threescore and five years shall Ephraim be broken, that it be not a people.

9And the head of Ephraim *is* Samaria, and the head of Samaria *is* Remaliah's son. If ye will not believe, surely ye shall not be established.

10Moreover the LORD spake again unto Ahaz, saying,

11Ask thee a sign of the LORD thy God; ask it either in the depth, or in the height above.

12But Ahaz said, I will not ask, neither will I tempt the LORD.

13And he said, Hear ye now, O house of David; *Is it* a small thing for you to weary men, but will ye weary my God also?

14Therefore the Lord himself shall give you a sign; Behold, a virgin shall conceive, and bear a son, and shall call his name Immanuel.

15Butter and honey shall he eat, that he may know to refuse the evil, and choose the good.

16For before the child shall know to refuse the evil, and choose the good, the land that thou abhorrest shall be forsaken of both her kings.

17The LORD shall bring upon thee, and upon thy people, and upon thy father's house, days that have not come, from the day that Ephraim departed from Judah; *even* the king of Assyria.

18And it shall come to pass in that day, *that* the LORD shall hiss for the fly that *is* in the uttermost part of the rivers of Egypt, and for the bee that *is* in the land of Assyria.

19And they shall come, and shall rest all of them in the desolate valleys, and in the holes of the rocks, and upon all thorns, and upon all bushes.

20In the same day shall the Lord shave with a razor that is hired, *namely,* by them beyond the river, by the king of Assyria, the head, and the hair of the feet: and it shall also consume the beard.

21And it shall come to pass in that day, *that* a man shall nourish a young cow, and two sheep;

22And it shall come to pass, for the abundance of milk *that* they shall give he shall eat butter: for butter and honey shall every one eat that is left in the land.

23And it shall come to pass in that day, *that* every place shall be, where there were a thousand vines at a thousand silverlings, it shall *even* be for briers and thorns.

24With arrows and with bows shall *men* come thither; because all the land shall become briers and thorns.

25And *on* all hills that shall be digged with the mattock, there shall not come thither the fear of briers and thorns: but it shall be for the sending forth of oxen, and for the treading of lesser cattle.

2 CORINTHIANS 11:16–33

I SAY again, Let no man think me a fool; if otherwise, yet as a fool receive me, that I may boast myself a little.

17That which I speak, I speak *it* not after the Lord, but as it were foolishly, in this confidence of boasting.

18Seeing that many glory after the flesh, I will glory also.

19For ye suffer fools gladly, seeing ye *yourselves* are wise.

20For ye suffer, if a man bring you into bondage, if a man devour *you,* if a man take *of you,* if a man exalt himself, if a man smite you on the face.

21I speak as concerning reproach, as though we had been weak. Howbeit whereinsoever any is bold, (I speak foolishly,) I am bold also.

22Are they Hebrews? so *am* I. Are they Israelites? so *am* I. Are they the seed of Abraham? so *am* I.

23Are they ministers of Christ? (I speak as a fool) I *am* more; in labours more abundant, in stripes above measure, in prisons more frequent, in deaths oft.

24Of the Jews five times received I forty *stripes* save one.

25Thrice was I beaten with rods, once was I stoned, thrice I suffered shipwreck, a night and a day I have been in the deep;

26*In* journeyings often, *in* perils of waters, *in* perils of robbers, *in* perils by *mine own* countrymen, *in* perils by the heathen, *in* perils in the city, *in* perils in the wilderness, *in* perils in the sea, *in* perils among false brethren;

27In weariness and painfulness, in watchings often, in hunger and thirst, in fastings often, in cold and nakedness.

28Beside those things that are without, that which cometh upon me daily, the care of all the churches.

29Who is weak, and I am not weak? who is offended, and I burn not?

30If I must needs glory, I will glory of the things which concern mine infirmities.

31The God and Father of our Lord Jesus Christ, which is blessed for evermore, knoweth that I lie not.

32In Damascus the governor under Aretas the king kept the city of the Damascenes with a garrison, desirous to apprehend me:

33And through a window in a basket was I let down by the wall, and escaped his hands.

PSALM 54:1–7

S AVE me, O God, by thy name, and judge me by thy strength.
2Hear my prayer, O God; give ear to the words of my mouth.

3For strangers are risen up against me, and oppressors seek after my soul:

they have not set God before them. Selah.

4Behold, God *is* mine helper: the Lord *is* with them that uphold my soul.

5He shall reward evil unto mine enemies: cut them off in thy truth.

PROVERBS FOR TODAY/ 23:1–3

When thou sittest to eat with a ruler, consider diligently what is *before thee: And put a knife to thy throat, if thou* be *a man given to appetite. Be not desirous of his dainties: for they* are *deceitful meat.*

6I will freely sacrifice unto thee: I will praise thy name, O LORD; for *it is* good.

7For he hath delivered me out of all trouble: and mine eye hath seen *his desire* upon mine enemies.

SEPTEMBER 11

ISAIAH 8:1—9:21

MOREOVER the LORD said unto me, Take thee a great roll, and write in it with a man's pen concerning Maher–shalal–hash–baz.

2And I took unto me faithful witnesses to record, Uriah the priest, and Zechariah the son of Jeberechiah.

3And I went unto the prophetess; and she conceived, and bare a son. Then said the LORD to me, Call his name Maher–shalal–hash–baz.

4For before the child shall have knowledge to cry, My father, and my mother, the riches of Damascus and the spoil of Samaria shall be taken away before the king of Assyria.

5The LORD spake also unto me again, saying,

6Forasmuch as this people refuseth the waters of Shiloah that go softly, and rejoice in Rezin and Remaliah's son;

7Now therefore, behold, the Lord bringeth up upon them the waters of the river, strong and many, *even* the king of Assyria, and all his glory: and he shall come up over all his channels, and go over all his banks:

8And he shall pass through Judah;

he shall overflow and go over, he shall reach *even* to the neck; and the stretching out of his wings shall fill the breadth of thy land, O Immanuel.

9Associate yourselves, O ye people, and ye shall be broken in pieces; and give ear, all ye of far countries: gird yourselves, and ye shall be broken in pieces; gird yourselves, and ye shall be broken in pieces.

10Take counsel together, and it shall come to nought; speak the word, and it shall not stand: for God *is* with us.

11For the LORD spake thus to me with a strong hand, and instructed me that I should not walk in the way of this people, saying,

12Say ye not, A confederacy, to all *them to* whom this people shall say, A confederacy; neither fear ye their fear, nor be afraid.

13Sanctify the LORD of hosts himself; and *let* him *be* your fear, and *let* him *be* your dread.

14And he shall be for a sanctuary; but for a stone of stumbling and for a rock of offence to both the houses of Israel, for a gin and for a snare to the inhabitants of Jerusalem.

15And many among them shall

stumble, and fall, and be broken, and be snared, and be taken.

16Bind up the testimony, seal the law among my disciples.

17And I will wait upon the LORD, that hideth his face from the house of Jacob, and I will look for him.

18Behold, I and the children whom the LORD hath given me *are* for signs and for wonders in Israel from the LORD of hosts, which dwelleth in mount Zion.

19And when they shall say unto you, Seek unto them that have familiar spirits, and unto wizards that peep, and that mutter: should not a people seek unto their God? for the living to the dead?

20To the law and to the testimony: if they speak not according to this word, *it is* because *there is* no light in them.

21And they shall pass through it, hardly bestead and hungry: and it shall come to pass, that when they shall be hungry, they shall fret themselves, and curse their king and their God, and look upward.

22And they shall look unto the earth; and behold trouble and darkness, dimness of anguish; and *they shall be* driven to darkness.

NEVERTHELESS the dimness *shall* not *be* such as *was* in her vexation, when at the first he lightly afflicted the land of Zebulun and the land of Naphtali, and afterward did more grievously afflict *her by* the way of the sea, beyond Jordan, in Galilee of the nations.

2The people that walked in darkness have seen a great light: they that dwell in the land of the shadow of death, upon them hath the light shined.

3Thou hast multiplied the nation, *and* not increased the joy: they joy before thee according to the joy in harvest, *and* as *men* rejoice when they divide the spoil.

4For thou hast broken the yoke of his burden, and the staff of his shoulder, the rod of his oppressor, as in the day of Midian.

5For every battle of the warrior *is* with confused noise, and garments rolled in blood; but *this* shall be with burning *and* fuel of fire.

6For unto us a child is born, unto us a son is given: and the government shall be upon his shoulder: and his name shall be called Wonderful, Counsellor, The mighty God, The everlasting Father, The Prince of Peace.

7Of the increase of *his* government and peace *there shall be* no end, upon the throne of David, and upon his kingdom, to order it, and to establish it with judgment and with justice from henceforth even for ever. The zeal of the LORD of hosts will perform this.

8The Lord sent a word into Jacob, and it hath lighted upon Israel.

9And all the people shall know, *even* Ephraim and the inhabitant of Samaria, that say in the pride and stoutness of heart,

10The bricks are fallen down, but we will build with hewn stones: the sycomores are cut down, but we will change *them into* cedars.

11Therefore the LORD shall set up the adversaries of Rezin against him, and join his enemies together;

12The Syrians before, and the Philistines behind; and they shall devour Israel with open mouth. For all this his anger is not turned away, but his hand *is* stretched out still.

13For the people turneth not unto him that smiteth them, neither do they seek the LORD of hosts.

14Therefore the LORD will cut off from Israel head and tail, branch and rush, in one day.

15The ancient and honourable, he *is* the head; and the prophet that teacheth lies, he *is* the tail.

16For the leaders of this people cause *them* to err; and *they that are* led of them *are* destroyed.

17Therefore the LORD shall have no

joy in their young men, neither shall have mercy on their fatherless and widows: for every one *is* an hypocrite and an evildoer, and every mouth speaketh folly. For all this his anger is not turned away, but his hand *is* stretched out still.

18For wickedness burneth as the fire: it shall devour the briers and thorns, and shall kindle in the thickets of the forest, and they shall mount up *like* the lifting up of smoke.

19Through the wrath of the LORD of hosts is the land darkened, and the people shall be as the fuel of the fire: no man shall spare his brother.

20And he shall snatch on the right hand, and be hungry; and he shall eat on the left hand, and they shall not be satisfied: they shall eat every man the flesh of his own arm:

21Manasseh, Ephraim; and Ephraim, Manasseh: *and* they together *shall be* against Judah. For all this his anger is not turned away, but his hand *is* stretched out still.

2 CORINTHIANS 12:1–10

IT is not expedient for me doubtless to glory. I will come to visions and revelations of the Lord.

2I knew a man in Christ above fourteen years ago, (whether in the body, I cannot tell; or whether out of the body, I cannot tell: God knoweth;) such an one caught up to the third heaven.

3And I knew such a man, (whether in the body, or out of the body, I cannot tell: God knoweth;)

4How that he was caught up into paradise, and heard unspeakable words, which it is not lawful for a man to utter.

5Of such an one will I glory: yet of myself I will not glory, but in mine infirmities.

6For though I would desire to glory, I shall not be a fool; for I will say the truth: but *now* I forbear, lest any man should think of me above that which

he seeth me *to be,* or *that* he heareth of me.

7And lest I should be exalted above measure through the abundance of the revelations, there was given to me a thorn in the flesh, the messenger of Satan to buffet me, lest I should be exalted above measure.

8For this thing I besought the Lord thrice, that it might depart from me.

9And he said unto me, My grace is sufficient for thee: for my strength is made perfect in weakness. Most gladly therefore will I rather glory in my infirmities, that the power of Christ may rest upon me.

10Therefore I take pleasure in infirmities, in reproaches, in necessities, in persecutions, in distresses for Christ's sake: for when I am weak, then am I strong.

PSALM 55:1–23

GIVE ear to my prayer, O God; and hide not thyself from my supplication.

2Attend unto me, and hear me: I mourn in my complaint, and make a noise;

3Because of the voice of the enemy, because of the oppression of the wicked: for they cast iniquity upon me, and in wrath they hate me.

4My heart is sore pained within me: and the terrors of death are fallen upon me.

5Fearfulness and trembling are come upon me, and horror hath overwhelmed me.

6And I said, Oh that I had wings like a dove! *for then* would I fly away, and be at rest.

7Lo, *then* would I wander far off, *and* remain in the wilderness. Selah.

8I would hasten my escape from the windy storm *and* tempest.

9Destroy, O Lord, *and* divide their tongues: for I have seen violence and strife in the city.

¹⁰Day and night they go about it upon the walls thereof: mischief also and sorrow *are* in the midst of it.

¹¹Wickedness *is* in the midst thereof: deceit and guile depart not from her streets.

¹²For *it was* not an enemy *that* reproached me; then I could have borne *it:* neither *was it* he that hated me *that* did magnify *himself* against me; then I would have hid myself from him:

¹³But *it was* thou, a man mine equal, my guide, and mine acquaintance.

¹⁴We took sweet counsel together, *and* walked unto the house of God in company.

¹⁵Let death seize upon them, *and* let them go down quick into hell: for wickedness *is* in their dwellings, *and* among them.

¹⁶As for me, I will call upon God; and the LORD shall save me.

¹⁷Evening, and morning, and at noon, will I pray, and cry aloud: and he shall hear my voice.

¹⁸He hath delivered my soul in peace from the battle *that was* against me: for there were many with me.

¹⁹God shall hear, and afflict them, even he that abideth of old. Selah. Because they have no changes, therefore they fear not God.

²⁰He hath put forth his hands against such as be at peace with him: he hath broken his covenant.

²¹*The words* of his mouth were smoother than butter, but war *was* in his heart: his words were softer than oil, yet *were* they drawn swords.

²²Cast thy burden upon the LORD, and he shall sustain thee: he shall never suffer the righteous to be moved.

²³But thou, O God, shalt bring them down into the pit of destruction: bloody and deceitful men shall not live out half their days; but I will trust in thee.

PROVERBS FOR TODAY/ 23:4–5

Labour not to be rich: cease from thine own wisdom. Wilt thou set thine eyes upon that which is not? for riches *certainly make themselves wings; they fly away as an eagle toward heaven.*

SEPTEMBER 12

ISAIAH 10:1—11:16

WOE unto them that decree unrighteous decrees, and that write grievousness *which* they have prescribed;

²To turn aside the needy from judgment, and to take away the right from the poor of my people, that widows may be their prey, and *that* they may rob the fatherless!

³And what will ye do in the day of visitation, and in the desolation *which* shall come from far? to whom will ye flee for help? and where will ye leave your glory?

⁴Without me they shall bow down under the prisoners, and they shall fall under the slain. For all this his anger is not turned away, but his hand *is* stretched out still.

⁵O Assyrian, the rod of mine anger, and the staff in their hand is mine indignation.

⁶I will send him against an hypocritical

nation, and against the people of my wrath will I give him a charge, to take the spoil, and to take the prey, and to tread them down like the mire of the streets.

7Howbeit he meaneth not so, neither doth his heart think so; but *it is* in his heart to destroy and cut off nations not a few.

. 8For he saith, *Are* not my princes altogether kings?

9*Is* not Calno as Carchemish? *is* not Hamath as Arpad? *is* not Samaria as Damascus?

10As my hand hath found the kingdoms of the idols, and whose graven images did excel them of Jerusalem and of Samaria;

11Shall I not, as I have done unto Samaria and her idols, so do to Jerusalem and her idols?

12Wherefore it shall come to pass, *that* when the Lord hath performed his whole work upon mount Zion and on Jerusalem, I will punish the fruit of the stout heart of the king of Assyria, and the glory of his high looks.

13For he saith, By the strength of my hand I have done *it,* and by my wisdom; for I am prudent: and I have removed the bounds of the people, and have robbed their treasures, and I have put down the inhabitants like a valiant *man:*

14And my hand hath found as a nest the riches of the people: and as one gathereth eggs *that are* left, have I gathered all the earth; and there was none that moved the wing, or opened the mouth, or peeped.

15Shall the axe boast itself against him that heweth therewith? *or* shall the saw magnify itself against him that shaketh it? as if the rod should shake *itself* against them that lift it up, *or* as if the staff should lift up *itself, as if it were* no wood.

16Therefore shall the Lord, the Lord of hosts, send among his fat ones leanness; and under his glory he shall kindle a burning like the burning of a fire.

17And the light of Israel shall be for a fire, and his Holy One for a flame: and it shall burn and devour his thorns and his briers in one day;

18And shall consume the glory of his forest, and of his fruitful field, both soul and body: and they shall be as when a standardbearer fainteth.

19And the rest of the trees of his forest shall be few, that a child may write them.

20And. it shall come to pass in that day, *that* the remnant of Israel, and such as are escaped of the house of Jacob, shall no more again stay upon him that smote them; but shall stay upon the LORD, the Holy One of Israel, in truth.

21The remnant shall return, *even* the remnant of Jacob, unto the mighty God.

22For though thy people Israel be as the sand of the sea, *yet* a remnant of them shall return: the consumption decreed shall overflow with righteousness.

23For the Lord GOD of hosts shall make a consumption, even determined, in the midst of all the land.

24Therefore thus saith the Lord GOD of hosts, O my people that dwellest in Zion, be not afraid of the Assyrian: he shall smite thee with a rod, and shall lift up his staff against thee, after the manner of Egypt.

25For yet a very little while, and the indignation shall cease, and mine anger in their destruction.

26And the LORD of hosts shall stir up a scourge for him according to the slaughter of Midian at the rock of Oreb: and *as* his rod *was* upon the sea, so shall he lift it up after the manner of Egypt.

27And it shall come to pass in that day, *that* his burden shall be taken away from off thy shoulder, and his yoke from off thy neck, and the yoke shall be destroyed because of the anointing.

28He is come to Aiath, he is passed

to Migron; at Michmash he hath laid up his carriages:

29They are gone over the passage: they have taken up their lodging at Geba; Ramah is afraid; Gibeah of Saul is fled.

30Lift up thy voice, O daughter of Gallim: cause it to be heard unto Laish, O poor Anathoth.

31Madmenah is removed; the inhabitants of Gebim gather themselves to flee.

32As yet shall he remain at Nob that day: he shall shake his hand *against* the mount of the daughter of Zion, the hill of Jerusalem.

33Behold, the Lord, the LORD of hosts, shall lop the bough with terror: and the high ones of stature *shall* be hewn down, and the haughty shall be humbled.

34And he shall cut down the thickets of the forest with iron, and Lebanon shall fall by a mighty one.

AND there shall come forth a rod out of the stem of Jesse, and a Branch shall grow out of his roots:

2And the spirit of the LORD shall rest upon him, the spirit of wisdom and understanding, the spirit of counsel and might, the spirit of knowledge and of the fear of the LORD;

3And shall make him of quick understanding in the fear of the LORD: and he shall not judge after the sight of his eyes, neither reprove after the hearing of his ears:

4But with righteousness shall he judge the poor, and reprove with equity for the meek of the earth: and he shall smite the earth with the rod of his mouth, and with the breath of his lips shall he slay the wicked.

5And righteousness shall be the girdle of his loins, and faithfulness the girdle of his reins.

6The wolf also shall dwell with the lamb, and the leopard shall lie down with the kid; and the calf and the young lion and the fatling together; and a little child shall lead them.

7And the cow and the bear shall feed; their young ones shall lie down together: and the lion shall eat straw like the ox.

8And the sucking child shall play on the hole of the asp, and the weaned child shall put his hand on the cockatrice den.

9They shall not hurt nor destroy in all my holy mountain: for the earth shall be full of the knowledge of the LORD, as the waters cover the sea.

10And in that day there shall be a root of Jesse, which shall stand for an ensign of the people; to it shall the Gentiles seek: and his rest shall be glorious.

11And it shall come to pass in that day, *that* the Lord shall set his hand again the second time to recover the remnant of his people, which shall be left, from Assyria, and from Egypt, and from Pathros, and from Cush, and from Elam, and from Shinar, and from Hamath, and from the islands of the sea.

12And he shall set up an ensign for the nations, and shall assemble the outcasts of Israel, and gather together the dispersed of Judah from the four corners of the earth.

13The envy also of Ephraim shall depart, and the adversaries of Judah shall be cut off: Ephraim shall not envy Judah, and Judah shall not vex Ephraim.

14But they shall fly upon the shoulders of the Philistines toward the west; they shall spoil them of the east together: they shall lay their hand upon Edom and Moab; and the children of Ammon shall obey them.

15And the LORD shall utterly destroy the tongue of the Egyptian sea; and with his mighty wind shall he shake his hand over the river, and shall smite it in the seven streams, and make *men* go over dryshod.

16And there shall be an highway for the remnant of his people, which shall be left, from Assyria; like as it was to Israel in the day that he came up out of the land of Egypt.

2 CORINTHIANS 12:11–21

I AM become a fool in glorying; ye have compelled me: for I ought to have been commended of you: for in nothing am I behind the very chiefest apostles, though I be nothing.

12Truly the signs of an apostle were wrought among you in all patience, in signs, and wonders, and mighty deeds.

13For what is it wherein ye were inferior to other churches, except *it be* that I myself was not burdensome to you? forgive me this wrong.

14Behold, the third time I am ready to come to you; and I will not be burdensome to you: for I seek not yours, but you: for the children ought not to lay up for the parents, but the parents for the children.

15And I will very gladly spend and be spent for you; though the more abundantly I love you, the less I be loved.

16But be it so, I did not burden you: nevertheless, being crafty, I caught you with guile.

17Did I make a gain of you by any of them whom I sent unto you?

18I desired Titus, and with *him* I sent a brother. Did Titus make a gain of you? walked we not in the same spirit? *walked we* not in the same steps?

19Again, think ye that we excuse ourselves unto you? we speak before God in Christ: but *we do* all things, dearly beloved, for your edifying.

20For I fear, lest when I come, I shall not find you such as I would, and *that* I shall be found unto you such as ye would not: lest *there be* debates, envyings, wraths, strifes, backbitings, whisperings, swellings, tumults:

21*And* lest, when I come again, my God will humble me among you, and *that* I shall bewail many which have sinned already, and have not repented of the uncleanness and fornication and lasciviousness which they have committed.

PSALM 56:1–13

B E merciful unto me, O God: for man would swallow me up; he fighting daily oppresseth me.

2Mine enemies would daily swallow *me* up: for *they be* many that fight against me, O thou most High.

3What time I am afraid, I will trust in thee.

4In God I will praise his word, in God I have put my trust; I will not fear what flesh can do unto me.

5Every day they wrest my words: all their thoughts *are* against me for evil.

6They gather themselves together, they hide themselves, they mark my steps, when they wait for my soul.

7Shall they escape by iniquity? in *thine* anger cast down the people, O God.

8Thou tellest my wanderings: put thou my tears into thy bottle: *are they* not in thy book?

9When I cry *unto thee,* then shall mine enemies turn back: this I know; for God *is* for me.

10In God will I praise *his* word: in the LORD will I praise *his* word.

11In God have I put my trust: I will not be afraid what man can do unto me.

12Thy vows *are* upon me, O God: I will render praises unto thee.

13For thou hast delivered my soul from death: *wilt* not *thou deliver* my feet from falling, that I may walk before God in the light of the living?

PROVERBS FOR TODAY/ 23:6–8

Eat thou not the bread of him that hath an evil eye, neither desire thou his dainty meats: For as he thinketh in his heart, so is *he: Eat and drink, saith he to thee; but his heart* is *not with thee. The morsel* which *thou hast eaten shalt thou vomit up, and lose thy sweet words.*

SEPTEMBER 13

ISAIAH 12:1—14:32

AND in that day thou shalt say, O LORD, I will praise thee: though thou wast angry with me, thine anger is turned away, and thou comfortedst me.

2Behold, God *is* my salvation; I will trust, and not be afraid: for the LORD JEHOVAH *is* my strength and *my* song; he also is become my salvation.

3Therefore with joy shall ye draw water out of the wells of salvation.

4And in that day shall ye say, Praise the LORD, call upon his name, declare his doings among the people, make mention that his name is exalted.

5Sing unto the LORD; for he hath done excellent things: this *is* known in all the earth.

6Cry out and shout, thou inhabitant of Zion: for great *is* the Holy One of Israel in the midst of thee.

THE burden of Babylon, which Isaiah the son of Amoz did see.

2Lift ye up a banner upon the high mountain, exalt the voice unto them, shake the hand, that they may go into the gates of the nobles.

3I have commanded my sanctified ones, I have also called my mighty ones for mine anger, *even* them that rejoice in my highness.

4The noise of a multitude in the mountains, like as of a great people; a tumultuous noise of the kingdoms of nations gathered together: the LORD of hosts mustereth the host of the battle.

5They come from a far country, from the end of heaven, *even* the LORD, and the weapons of his indignation, to destroy the whole land.

6Howl ye; for the day of the LORD *is* at hand; it shall come as a destruction from the Almighty.

7Therefore shall all hands be faint, and every man's heart shall melt:

8And they shall be afraid: pangs and sorrows shall take hold of them; they shall be in pain as a woman that travaileth: they shall be amazed one at another; their faces *shall be as* flames.

9Behold, the day of the LORD cometh, cruel both with wrath and fierce anger, to lay the land desolate: and he shall destroy the sinners thereof out of it.

10For the stars of heaven and the constellations thereof shall not give their light: the sun shall be darkened in his going forth, and the moon shall not cause her light to shine.

11And I will punish the world for *their* evil, and the wicked for their iniquity; and I will cause the arrogancy of the proud to cease, and will lay low the haughtiness of the terrible.

12I will make a man more precious than fine gold; even a man than the golden wedge of Ophir.

13Therefore I will shake the heavens, and the earth shall remove out of her place, in the wrath of the LORD of hosts, and in the day of his fierce anger.

14And it shall be as the chased roe, and as a sheep that no man taketh up: they shall every man turn to his own people, and flee every one into his own land.

15Every one that is found shall be thrust through; and every one that is joined *unto them* shall fall by the sword.

16Their children also shall be dashed to pieces before their eyes; their houses shall be spoiled, and their wives ravished.

17Behold, I will stir up the Medes against them, which shall not regard silver; and *as for* gold, they shall not delight in it.

18*Their* bows also shall dash the young men to pieces; and they shall have no pity on the fruit of the womb; their eye shall not spare children.

19And Babylon, the glory of kingdoms, the beauty of the Chaldees' excellency, shall be as when God overthrew Sodom and Gomorrah.

20It shall never be inhabited, neither shall it be dwelt in from generation to generation: neither shall the Arabian pitch tent there; neither shall the shepherds make their fold there.

21But wild beasts of the desert shall lie there; and their houses shall be full of doleful creatures; and owls shall dwell there, and satyrs shall dance there.

22And the wild beasts of the islands shall cry in their desolate houses, and dragons in *their* pleasant palaces: and her time *is* near to come, and her days shall not be prolonged.

For the Lord will have mercy on Jacob, and will yet choose Israel, and set them in their own land: and the strangers shall be joined with them, and they shall cleave to the house of Jacob.

2And the people shall take them, and bring them to their place: and the house of Israel shall possess them in the land of the Lord for servants and handmaids: and they shall take them captives, whose captives they were; and they shall rule over their oppressors.

3And it shall come to pass in the day that the Lord shall give thee rest from thy sorrow, and from thy fear, and from the hard bondage wherein thou wast made to serve,

4That thou shalt take up this proverb against the king of Babylon, and say, How hath the oppressor ceased! the golden city ceased!

5The Lord hath broken the staff of the wicked, *and* the sceptre of the rulers.

6He who smote the people in wrath with a continual stroke, he that ruled the nations in anger, is persecuted, *and* none hindereth.

7The whole earth is at rest, *and* is quiet: they break forth into singing.

8Yea, the fir trees rejoice at thee, *and* the cedars of Lebanon, *saying,* Since thou art laid down, no feller is come up against us.

9Hell from beneath is moved for thee to meet *thee* at thy coming: it stirreth up the dead for thee, *even* all the chief ones of the earth; it hath raised up from their thrones all the kings of the nations.

10All they shall speak and say unto thee, Art thou also become weak as we? art thou become like unto us?

11Thy pomp is brought down to the grave, *and* the noise of thy viols: the worm is spread under thee, and the worms cover thee.

12How art thou fallen from heaven, O Lucifer, son of the morning! *how* art thou cut down to the ground, which didst weaken the nations!

13For thou hast said in thine heart, I will ascend into heaven, I will exalt my throne above the stars of God: I will sit also upon the mount of the congregation, in the sides of the north:

14I will ascend above the heights of the clouds; I will be like the most High.

15Yet thou shalt be brought down to hell, to the sides of the pit.

16They that see thee shall narrowly look upon thee, *and* consider thee, *saying, Is* this the man that made the earth to tremble, that did shake kingdoms;

17*That* made the world as a wilderness, and destroyed the cities thereof; *that* opened not the house of his prisoners?

18All the kings of the nations, *even* all of them, lie in glory, every one in his own house.

19But thou art cast out of thy grave like an abominable branch, *and as* the raiment of those that are slain, thrust through with a sword, that go down to the stones of the pit; as a carcase trodden under feet.

20Thou shalt not be joined with them in burial, because thou hast destroyed thy land, *and* slain thy people: the seed of evildoers shall never be renowned.

21Prepare slaughter for his children for the iniquity of their fathers; that they do not rise, nor possess the land, nor fill the face of the world with cities.

22For I will rise up against them, saith the LORD of hosts, and cut off from Babylon the name, and remnant, and son, and nephew, saith the LORD.

23I will also make it a possession for the bittern, and pools of water: and I will sweep it with the besom of destruction, saith the LORD of hosts.

24The LORD of hosts hath sworn, saying, Surely as I have thought, so shall it come to pass; and as I have purposed, *so* shall it stand:

25That I will break the Assyrian in my land, and upon my mountains tread him under foot: then shall his yoke depart from off them, and his burden depart from off their shoulders.

26This *is* the purpose that is purposed upon the whole earth: and this *is* the hand that is stretched out upon all the nations.

27For the LORD of hosts hath purposed, and who shall disannul *it?* and his hand *is* stretched out, and who shall turn it back?

28In the year that king Ahaz died was this burden.

29Rejoice not thou, whole Palestina, because the rod of him that smote thee is broken: for out of the serpent's root shall come forth a cockatrice, and his fruit *shall be* a fiery flying serpent.

30And the firstborn of the poor shall feed, and the needy shall lie down in safety: and I will kill thy root with famine, and he shall slay thy remnant.

31Howl, O gate; cry, O city; thou, whole Palestina, *art* dissolved: for there shall come from the north a smoke, and none *shall be* alone in his appointed times.

32What shall *one* then answer the messengers of the nation? That the LORD hath founded Zion, and the poor of his people shall trust in it.

2 CORINTHIANS 13:1–14

THIS *is* the third *time* I am coming to you. In the mouth of two or three witnesses shall every word be established.

2I told you before, and foretell you, as if I were present, the second time; and being absent now I write to them which heretofore have sinned, and to all other, that, if I come again, I will not spare:

3Since ye seek a proof of Christ speaking in me, which to you-ward is not weak, but is mighty in you.

4For though he was crucified through weakness, yet he liveth by the power of God. For we also are weak in him, but we shall live with him by the power of God toward you.

5Examine yourselves, whether ye be in the faith; prove your own selves. Know ye not your own selves, how that Jesus Christ is in you, except ye be reprobates?

6But I trust that ye shall know that we are not reprobates.

7Now I pray to God that ye do no evil; not that we should appear approved, but that ye should do that which is honest, though we be as reprobates.

8For we can do nothing against the truth, but for the truth.

9For we are glad, when we are weak, and ye are strong: and this also we wish, *even* your perfection.

10Therefore I write these things being absent, lest being present I should use sharpness, according to the power which the Lord hath given me to edification, and not to destruction.

11Finally, brethren, farewell. Be perfect, be of good comfort, be of one mind, live in peace; and the God of love and peace shall be with you.

12Greet one another with an holy kiss.

13All the saints salute you.

14The grace of the Lord Jesus Christ, and the love of God, and the communion of the Holy Ghost, *be* with you all. Amen.

PSALM 57:1–11

BE merciful unto me, O God, be merciful unto me: for my soul trusteth in thee: yea, in the shadow of thy wings will I make my refuge, until *these* calamities be overpast.

2I will cry unto God most high; unto God that performeth *all things* for me.

3He shall send from heaven, and save me *from* the reproach of him that would swallow me up. Selah. God shall send forth his mercy and his truth.

4My soul *is* among lions: *and* I lie *even among* them that are set on fire, *even* the sons of men, whose teeth *are* spears and arrows, and their tongue a sharp sword.

5Be thou exalted, O God, above the heavens; *let* thy glory *be* above all the earth.

6They have prepared a net for my steps; my soul is bowed down: they have digged a pit before me, into the midst whereof they are fallen *themselves*. Selah.

7My heart is fixed, O God, my heart is fixed: I will sing and give praise.

8Awake up, my glory; awake, psaltery and harp: I *myself* will awake early.

9I will praise thee, O Lord, among the people: I will sing unto thee among the nations.

10For thy mercy *is* great unto the heavens, and thy truth unto the clouds.

11Be thou exalted, O God, above the heavens: *let* thy glory *be* above all the earth.

PROVERBS FOR TODAY/ 23:9–11

Speak not in the ears of a fool: for he will despise the wisdom of thy words. □ *Remove not the old landmark; and enter not into the fields of the fatherless: For their redeemer* is *mighty; he shall plead their cause with thee.*

SEPTEMBER 14

ISAIAH 15:1—18:7

THE burden of Moab. Because in the night Ar of Moab is laid waste, *and* brought to silence; because in the night Kir of Moab is laid waste, *and* brought to silence;

2He is gone up to Bajith, and to Dibon, the high places, to weep: Moab shall howl over Nebo, and over Medeba: on all their heads *shall be* baldness, *and* every beard cut off.

3In their streets they shall gird themselves with sackcloth: on the tops of their houses, and in their streets, every one shall howl, weeping abundantly.

4And Heshbon shall cry, and Elealeh: their voice shall be heard *even* unto Jahaz: therefore the armed soldiers of Moab shall cry out; his life shall be grievous unto him.

5My heart shall cry out for Moab; his fugitives *shall flee* unto Zoar, an heifer of three years old: for by the mounting up of Luhith with weeping shall they go it up; for in the way of Horonaim they shall raise up a cry of destruction.

6For the waters of Nimrim shall be desolate: for the hay is withered away, the grass faileth, there is no green thing.

7Therefore the abundance they have gotten, and that which they have laid up, shall they carry away to the brook of the willows.

8For the cry is gone round about the borders of Moab; the howling thereof unto Eglaim, and the howling thereof unto Beer–elim.

9For the waters of Dimon shall be full of blood: for I will bring more upon Dimon, lions upon him that escapeth of Moab, and upon the remnant of the land.

SEND ye the lamb to the ruler of the land from Sela to the wilderness, unto the mount of the daughter of Zion.

2For it shall be, *that*, as a wandering bird cast out of the nest, so the daughters of Moab shall be at the fords of Arnon.

3Take counsel, execute judgment; make thy shadow as the night in the midst of the noonday; hide the outcasts; bewray not him that wandereth.

4Let mine outcasts dwell with thee, Moab; be thou a covert to them from the face of the spoiler: for the extortioner is at an end, the spoiler ceaseth, the oppressors are consumed out of the land.

5And in mercy shall the throne be established: and he shall sit upon it in truth in the tabernacle of David, judging, and seeking judgment, and hasting righteousness.

6We have heard of the pride of Moab; *he is* very proud: *even* of his haughtiness, and his pride, and his wrath: *but* his lies *shall* not *be* so.

7Therefore shall Moab howl for Moab, every one shall howl: for the foundations of Kir–hareseth shall ye mourn; surely *they are* stricken.

8For the fields of Heshbon languish, *and* the vine of Sibmah: the lords of the heathen have broken down the principal plants thereof, they are come *even* unto Jazer, they wandered *through* the wilderness: her branches are stretched out, they are gone over the sea.

9Therefore I will bewail with the weeping of Jazer the vine of Sibmah: I will water thee with my tears, O Heshbon, and Elealeh: for the shouting for thy summer fruits and for thy harvest is fallen.

10And gladness is taken away, and joy out of the plentiful field; and in the vineyards there shall be no singing, neither shall there be shouting: the treaders shall tread out no wine in *their* presses; I have made *their vintage* shouting to cease.

11Wherefore my bowels shall sound like an harp for Moab, and mine inward parts for Kir–haresh.

12And it shall come to pass, when it is seen that Moab is weary on the high place, that he shall come to his sanctuary to pray; but he shall not prevail.

13This *is* the word that the LORD hath spoken concerning Moab since that time.

14But now the LORD hath spoken, saying, Within three years, as the years of an hireling, and the glory of Moab shall be contemned, with all that great multitude; and the remnant *shall be* very small *and* feeble.

THE burden of Damascus. Behold, Damascus is taken away from *being* a city, and it shall be a ruinous heap.

2The cities of Aroer *are* forsaken: they shall be for flocks, which shall lie down, and none shall make *them* afraid.

3The fortress also shall cease from Ephraim, and the kingdom from Damascus, and the remnant of Syria: they shall be as the glory of the children of Israel, saith the LORD of hosts.

4And in that day it shall come to pass, *that* the glory of Jacob shall be made thin, and the fatness of his flesh shall wax lean.

5And it shall be as when the harvestman gathereth the corn, and reapeth the ears with his arm; and it shall be as he that gathereth ears in the valley of Rephaim.

6Yet gleaning grapes shall be left in it, as the shaking of an olive tree, two *or* three berries in the top of the uppermost bough, four *or* five in the outmost fruitful branches thereof, saith the LORD God of Israel.

7At that day shall a man look to his Maker, and his eyes shall have respect to the Holy One of Israel.

8And he shall not look to the altars, the work of his hands, neither shall respect *that* which his fingers have made, either the groves, or the images.

9In that day shall his strong cities be as a forsaken bough, and an uppermost branch, which they left because of the children of Israel: and there shall be desolation.

10Because thou hast forgotten the God of thy salvation, and hast not been mindful of the rock of thy strength, therefore shalt thou plant pleasant plants, and shalt set it with strange slips:

11In the day shalt thou make thy plant to grow, and in the morning shalt thou make thy seed to flourish: *but* the harvest *shall be* a heap in the day of grief and of desperate sorrow.

12Woe to the multitude of many people, *which* make a noise like the noise of the seas; and to the rushing of nations, *that* make a rushing like the rushing of mighty waters!

13The nations shall rush like the rushing of many waters: but *God* shall rebuke them, and they shall flee far off, and shall be chased as the chaff of the mountains before the wind, and like a rolling thing before the whirlwind.

14And behold at eveningtide trouble; *and* before the morning he *is* not. This *is* the portion of them that spoil us, and the lot of them that rob us.

WOE to the land shadowing with wings, which *is* beyond the rivers of Ethiopia:

2That sendeth ambassadors by the sea, even in vessels of bulrushes upon the waters, *saying,* Go, ye swift messengers, to a nation scattered and peeled, to a people terrible from their beginning hitherto; a nation meted out and trodden down, whose land the rivers have spoiled!

3All ye inhabitants of the world, and dwellers on the earth, see ye, when he lifteth up an ensign on the mountains; and when he bloweth a trumpet, hear ye.

4For so the LORD said unto me, I will take my rest, and I will consider in my dwelling place like a clear heat upon herbs, *and* like a cloud of dew in the heat of harvest.

5For afore the harvest, when the bud is perfect, and the sour grape is ripening in the flower, he shall both cut off the sprigs with pruning hooks, and take away *and* cut down the branches.

6They shall be left together unto the fowls of the mountains, and to the beasts of the earth: and the fowls shall summer upon them, and all the beasts of the earth shall winter upon them.

7In that time shall the present be brought unto the LORD of hosts of a people scattered and peeled, and from a people terrible from their beginning hitherto; a nation meted out and trodden under foot, whose land the rivers have spoiled, to the place of the name of the LORD of hosts, the mount Zion.

GALATIANS 1:1–24

PAUL, an apostle, (not of men, neither by man, but by Jesus Christ, and God the Father, who raised him from the dead;)

2And all the brethren which are with me, unto the churches of Galatia:

3Grace *be* to you and peace from God the Father, and *from* our Lord Jesus Christ,

4Who gave himself for our sins, that he might deliver us from this present evil world, according to the will of God and our Father:

5To whom *be* glory for ever and ever. Amen.

6I marvel that ye are so soon removed from him that called you into the grace of Christ unto another gospel:

7Which is not another; but there be some that trouble you, and would pervert the gospel of Christ.

8But though we, or an angel from heaven, preach any other gospel unto you than that which we have preached unto you, let him be accursed.

9As we said before, so say I now again, if any *man* preach any other gospel unto you than that ye have received, let him be accursed.

10For do I now persuade men, or God? or do I seek to please men? for if I yet pleased men, I should not be the servant of Christ.

11But I certify you, brethren, that the gospel which was preached of me is not after man.

12For I neither received it of man, neither was I taught *it,* but by the revelation of Jesus Christ.

13For ye have heard of my conversation in time past in the Jews' religion, how that beyond measure I persecuted the church of God, and wasted it:

14And profited in the Jews' religion above many my equals in mine own nation, being more exceedingly zealous of the traditions of my fathers.

15But when it pleased God, who separated me from my mother's womb, and called *me* by his grace,

16To reveal his Son in me, that I might preach him among the heathen; immediately I conferred not with flesh and blood:

17Neither went I up to Jerusalem to them which were apostles before me; but I went into Arabia, and returned again unto Damascus.

18Then after three years I went up to Jerusalem to see Peter, and abode with him fifteen days.

19But other of the apostles saw I none, save James the Lord's brother.

20Now the things which I write unto you, behold, before God, I lie not.

21Afterwards I came into the regions of Syria and Cilicia;

22And was unknown by face unto the churches of Judaea which were in Christ:

23But they had heard only, That he which persecuted us in times past now preacheth the faith which once he destroyed.

24And they glorified God in me.

PSALM 58:1–11

DO ye indeed speak righteousness, O congregation? do ye judge uprightly, O ye sons of men?

2Yea, in heart ye work wickedness; ye weigh the violence of your hands in the earth.

3The wicked are estranged from the womb: they go astray as soon as they be born, speaking lies.

4Their poison *is* like the poison of a serpent: *they are* like the deaf adder *that* stoppeth her ear;

5Which will not hearken to the voice of charmers, charming never so wisely.

6Break their teeth, O God, in their mouth: break out the great teeth of the young lions, O LORD.

7Let them melt away as waters *which* run continually: *when* he bendeth *his bow to shoot* his arrows, let them be as cut in pieces.

8As a snail *which* melteth, let *every one of them* pass away: *like* the untimely birth of a woman, *that* they may not see the sun.

9Before your pots can feel the thorns, he shall take them away as with a whirlwind, both living, and in *his* wrath.

10The righteous shall rejoice when he seeth the vengeance: he shall wash his feet in the blood of the wicked.

11So that a man shall say, Verily *there is* a reward for the righteous; verily he is a God that judgeth in the earth.

PROVERBS FOR TODAY/ 23:12

Apply thine heart unto instruction, and thine ears to the words of knowledge.

SEPTEMBER 15

ISAIAH 19:1—21:17

THE burden of Egypt. Behold, the LORD rideth upon a swift cloud, and shall come into Egypt: and the idols of Egypt shall be moved at his presence, and the heart of Egypt shall melt in the midst of it.

2And I will set the Egyptians against the Egyptians: and they shall fight every one against his brother, and every one against his neighbour; city against city, *and* kingdom against kingdom.

3And the spirit of Egypt shall fail in the midst thereof; and I will destroy the counsel thereof: and they shall seek to the idols, and to the charmers, and to them that have familiar spirits, and to the wizards.

4And the Egyptians will I give over into the hand of a cruel lord; and a fierce king shall rule over them, saith the Lord, the LORD of hosts.

5And the waters shall fail from the sea, and the river shall be wasted and dried up.

6And they shall turn the rivers far away; *and* the brooks of defence shall be emptied and dried up: the reeds and flags shall wither.

7The paper reeds by the brooks, by the mouth of the brooks, and every thing sown by the brooks, shall wither, be driven away, and be no *more.*

8The fishers also shall mourn, and all they that cast angle into the brooks shall lament, and they that spread nets upon the waters shall languish.

9Moreover they that work in fine flax, and they that weave networks, shall be confounded.

10And they shall be broken in the purposes thereof, all that make sluices *and* ponds for fish.

11Surely the princes of Zoan *are* fools, the counsel of the wise counsellors of Pharaoh is become brutish: how say ye unto Pharaoh, I *am* the son of the wise, the son of ancient kings?

12Where *are* they? where *are* thy wise *men?* and let them tell thee now, and let them know what the LORD of hosts hath purposed upon Egypt.

13The princes of Zoan are become fools, the princes of Noph are deceived; they have also seduced Egypt, *even they that are* the stay of the tribes thereof.

14The LORD hath mingled a perverse spirit in the midst thereof: and they have caused Egypt to err in every work thereof, as a drunken *man* staggereth in his vomit.

15Neither shall there be *any* work for Egypt, which the head or tail, branch or rush, may do.

16In that day shall Egypt be like unto women: and it shall be afraid and fear because of the shaking of the hand of the LORD of hosts, which he shaketh over it.

17And the land of Judah shall be a terror unto Egypt, every one that maketh mention thereof shall be afraid in himself, because of the counsel of the LORD of hosts, which he hath determined against it.

18In that day shall five cities in the land of Egypt speak the language of Canaan, and swear to the LORD of hosts; one shall be called, The city of destruction.

19In that day shall there be an altar to the LORD in the midst of the land of Egypt, and a pillar at the border thereof to the LORD.

20And it shall be for a sign and for a witness unto the LORD of hosts in the land of Egypt: for they shall cry unto the LORD because of the oppressors, and he shall send them a saviour, and a great one, and he shall deliver them.

21And the LORD shall be known to Egypt, and the Egyptians shall know the LORD in that day, and shall do sacrifice and oblation; yea, they shall vow a vow unto the LORD, and perform *it.*

22And the LORD shall smite Egypt: he shall smite and heal *it:* and they shall return *even* to the LORD, and he shall be intreated of them, and shall heal them.

23In that day shall there be a highway out of Egypt to Assyria, and the Assyrian shall come into Egypt, and the Egyptian into Assyria, and the Egyptians shall serve with the Assyrians.

24In that day shall Israel be the third with Egypt and with Assyria, *even* a blessing in the midst of the land:

25Whom the LORD of hosts shall bless, saying, Blessed *be* Egypt my people, and Assyria the work of my hands, and Israel mine inheritance.

IN the year that Tartan came unto Ashdod, (when Sargon the king of Assyria sent him,) and fought against Ashdod, and took it;

2At the same time spake the LORD by Isaiah the son of Amoz, saying, Go and loose the sackcloth from off thy loins, and put off thy shoe from thy foot. And he did so, walking naked and barefoot.

3And the LORD said, Like as my servant Isaiah hath walked naked and barefoot three years *for* a sign and wonder upon Egypt and upon Ethiopia;

4So shall the king of Assyria lead away the Egyptians prisoners, and the Ethiopians captives, young and old, naked and barefoot, even with *their* buttocks uncovered, to the shame of Egypt.

5And they shall be afraid and ashamed of Ethiopia their expectation, and of Egypt their glory.

6And the inhabitant of this isle shall say in that day, Behold, such *is* our expectation, whither we flee for help to be delivered from the king of Assyria: and how shall we escape?

THE burden of the desert of the sea. As whirlwinds in the south pass through; *so* it cometh from the desert, from a terrible land.

2A grievous vision is declared unto me; the treacherous dealer dealeth treacherously, and the spoiler spoileth.

Go up, O Elam: besiege, O Media; all the sighing thereof have I made to cease.

3Therefore are my loins filled with pain: pangs have taken hold upon me, as the pangs of a woman that travaileth: I was bowed down at the hearing *of it;* I was dismayed at the seeing *of it.*

4My heart panted, fearfulness affrighted me: the night of my pleasure hath he turned into fear unto me.

5Prepare the table, watch in the watchtower, eat, drink: arise, ye princes, *and* anoint the shield.

6For thus hath the LORD said unto me, Go, set a watchman, let him declare what he seeth.

7And he saw a chariot *with* a couple of horsemen, a chariot of asses, *and* a chariot of camels; and he hearkened diligently with much heed:

8And he cried, A lion: My lord, I stand continually upon the watchtower in the daytime, and I am set in my ward whole nights:

9And, behold, here cometh a chariot of men, *with* a couple of horsemen. And he answered and said, Babylon is fallen, is fallen; and all the graven images of her gods he hath broken unto the ground.

10O my threshing, and the corn of my floor: that which I have heard of the LORD of hosts, the God of Israel, have I declared unto you.

11The burden of Dumah. He calleth to me out of Seir, Watchman, what of the night? Watchman, what of the night?

12The watchman said, The morning cometh, and also the night: if ye will enquire, enquire ye: return, come.

13The burden upon Arabia. In the forest in Arabia shall ye lodge, O ye travelling companies of Dedanim.

14The inhabitants of the land of Tema brought water to him that was thirsty, they prevented with their bread him that fled.

15For they fled from the swords, from the drawn sword, and from the bent bow, and from the grievousness of war.

16For thus hath the Lord said unto me, Within a year, according to the years of an hireling, and all the glory of Kedar shall fail:

17And the residue of the number of archers, the mighty men of the children of Kedar, shall be diminished: for the LORD God of Israel hath spoken *it.*

GALATIANS 2:1–16

THEN fourteen years after I went up again to Jerusalem with Barnabas, and took Titus with *me* also.

2And I went up by revelation, and communicated unto them that gospel which I preach among the Gentiles, but privately to them which were of reputation, lest by any means I should run, or had run, in vain.

3But neither Titus, who was with me, being a Greek, was compelled to be circumcised:

4And that because of false brethren unawares brought in, who came in privily to spy out our liberty which we have in Christ Jesus, that they might bring us into bondage:

5To whom we gave place by subjection, no, not for an hour; that the truth of the gospel might continue with you.

6But of these who seemed to be somewhat, (whatsoever they were, it maketh no matter to me: God accepteth no man's person:) for they who seemed *to be somewhat* in conference added nothing to me:

7But contrariwise, when they saw that the gospel of the uncircumcision was committed unto me, as *the gospel* of the circumcision *was* unto Peter;

8(For he that wrought effectually in Peter to the apostleship of the circumcision, the same was mighty in me toward the Gentiles:)

9And when James, Cephas, and John,

who seemed to be pillars, perceived the grace that was given unto me, they gave to me and Barnabas the right hands of fellowship; that we *should go* unto the heathen, and they unto the circumcision.

10Only *they would* that we should remember the poor; the same which I also was forward to do.

11But when Peter was come to Antioch, I withstood him to the face, because he was to be blamed.

12For before that certain came from James, he did eat with the Gentiles: but when they were come, he withdrew and separated himself, fearing them which were of the circumcision.

13And the other Jews dissembled likewise with him; insomuch that Barnabas also was carried away with their dissimulation.

14But when I saw that they walked not uprightly according to the truth of the gospel, I said unto Peter before *them* all, If thou, being a Jew, livest after the manner of Gentiles, and not as do the Jews, why compellest thou the Gentiles to live as do the Jews?

15We *who are* Jews by nature, and not sinners of the Gentiles,

16Knowing that a man is not justified by the works of the law, but by the faith of Jesus Christ, even we have believed in Jesus Christ, that we might be justified by the faith of Christ, and not by the works of the law: for by the works of the law shall no flesh be justified.

PSALM 59:1–17

Deliver me from mine enemies, O my God: defend me from them that rise up against me.

2Deliver me from the workers of iniquity, and save me from bloody men.

3For, lo, they lie in wait for my soul: the mighty are gathered against me; not *for* my transgression, nor *for* my sin, O Lord.

4They run and prepare themselves without *my* fault: awake to help me, and behold.

5Thou therefore, O Lord God of hosts, the God of Israel, awake to visit all the heathen: be not merciful to any wicked transgressors. Selah.

6They return at evening: they make a noise like a dog, and go round about the city.

7Behold, they belch out with their mouth: swords *are* in their lips: for who, *say they,* doth hear?

8But thou, O Lord, shalt laugh at them; thou shalt have all the heathen in derision.

9*Because of* his strength will I wait upon thee: for God *is* my defence.

10The God of my mercy shall prevent me: God shall let me see *my desire* upon mine enemies.

11Slay them not, lest my people forget: scatter them by thy power; and bring them down, O Lord our shield.

12*For* the sin of their mouth *and* the words of their lips let them even be taken in their pride: and for cursing and lying *which* they speak.

13Consume *them* in wrath, consume *them,* that they *may* not *be:* and let them know that God ruleth in Jacob unto the ends of the earth. Selah.

14And at evening let them return; *and* let them make a noise like a dog, and go round about the city.

15Let them wander up and down for meat, and grudge if they be not satisfied.

16But I will sing of thy power; yea, I will sing aloud of thy mercy in the morning: for thou hast been my defence and refuge in the day of my trouble.

17Unto thee, O my strength, will I sing: for God *is* my defence, *and* the God of my mercy.

PROVERBS FOR TODAY/ 23:13–14

Withhold not correction from the child: for if *thou beatest him with the rod, he shall not die. Thou shalt beat him with the rod, and shalt deliver his soul from hell.*

SEPTEMBER 16

ISAIAH 22:1—24:23

THE burden of the valley of vision. What aileth thee now, that thou art wholly gone up to the housetops?

2Thou that art full of stirs, a tumultuous city, a joyous city: thy slain *men are* not slain with the sword, nor dead in battle.

3All thy rulers are fled together, they are bound by the archers: all that are found in thee are bound together, *which* have fled from far.

4Therefore said I, Look away from me; I will weep bitterly, labour not to comfort me, because of the spoiling of the daughter of my people.

5For *it is* a day of trouble, and of treading down, and of perplexity by the Lord GOD of hosts in the valley of vision, breaking down the walls, and of crying to the mountains.

6And Elam bare the quiver with chariots of men *and* horsemen, and Kir uncovered the shield.

7And it shall come to pass, *that* thy choicest valleys shall be full of chariots, and the horsemen shall set themselves in array at the gate.

8And he discovered the covering of Judah, and thou didst look in that day to the armour of the house of the forest.

9Ye have seen also the breaches of the city of David, that they are many: and ye gathered together the waters of the lower pool.

10And ye have numbered the houses of Jerusalem, and the houses have ye broken down to fortify the wall.

11Ye made also a ditch between the two walls for the water of the old pool: but ye have not looked unto the maker thereof, neither had respect unto him that fashioned it long ago.

12And in that day did the Lord GOD of hosts call to weeping, and to mourning, and to baldness, and to girding with sackcloth:

13And behold joy and gladness, slaying oxen, and killing sheep, eating flesh, and drinking wine: let us eat and drink; for tomorrow we shall die.

14And it was revealed in mine ears by the LORD of hosts, Surely this iniquity shall not be purged from you till ye die, saith the Lord GOD of hosts.

15Thus saith the Lord GOD of hosts, Go, get thee unto this treasurer, *even* unto Shebna, which *is* over the house, *and say,*

16What hast thou here? and whom hast thou here, that thou hast hewed thee out a sepulchre here, *as* he that heweth him out a sepulchre on high, *and* that graveth an habitation for himself in a rock?

17Behold, the LORD will carry thee away with a mighty captivity, and will surely cover thee.

18He will surely violently turn and toss thee *like* a ball into a large country: there shalt thou die, and there the chariots of thy glory *shall be* the shame of thy lord's house.

19And I will drive thee from thy station, and from thy state shall he pull thee down.

20And it shall come to pass in that day, that I will call my servant Eliakim the son of Hilkiah:

21And I will clothe him with thy robe, and strengthen him with thy girdle, and I will commit thy government into his hand: and he shall be a father to the inhabitants of Jerusalem, and to the house of Judah.

22And the key of the house of David will I lay upon his shoulder; so he shall open, and none shall shut; and he shall shut, and none shall open.

23And I will fasten him *as* a nail in a sure place; and he shall be for a glorious throne to his father's house.

24And they shall hang upon him all the glory of his father's house, the offspring and the issue, all vessels of small quantity, from the vessels of cups, even to all the vessels of flagons.

25In that day, saith the LORD of hosts, shall the nail that is fastened in the sure place be removed, and be cut down, and fall; and the burden that *was* upon it shall be cut off: for the LORD hath spoken *it*.

THE burden of Tyre. Howl, ye ships of Tarshish; for it is laid waste, so that there is no house, no entering in: from the land of Chittim it is revealed to them.

2Be still, ye inhabitants of the isle; thou whom the merchants of Zidon, that pass over the sea, have replenished.

3And by great waters the seed of Sihor, the harvest of the river, *is* her revenue; and she is a mart of nations.

4Be thou ashamed, O Zidon: for the sea hath spoken, *even* the strength of the sea, saying, I travail not, nor bring forth children, neither do I nourish up young men, *nor* bring up virgins.

5As at the report concerning Egypt, *so* shall they be sorely pained at the report of Tyre.

6Pass ye over to Tarshish; howl, ye inhabitants of the isle.

7*Is* this your joyous *city*, whose antiquity *is* of ancient days? her own feet shall carry her afar off to sojourn.

8Who hath taken this counsel against Tyre, the crowning *city*, whose merchants *are* princes, whose traffickers *are* the honourable of the earth?

9The LORD of hosts hath purposed it, to stain the pride of all glory, *and* to bring into contempt all the honourable of the earth.

10Pass through thy land as a river, O daughter of Tarshish: *there is* no more strength.

11He stretched out his hand over the sea, he shook the kingdoms: the LORD hath given a commandment against the merchant *city*, to destroy the strong holds thereof.

12And he said, Thou shalt no more rejoice, O thou oppressed virgin, daughter of Zidon: arise, pass over to Chittim; there also shalt thou have no rest.

13Behold the land of the Chaldeans; this people was not, *till* the Assyrian founded it for them that dwell in the wilderness: they set up the towers thereof, they raised up the palaces thereof; *and* he brought it to ruin.

14Howl, ye ships of Tarshish: for your strength is laid waste.

15And it shall come to pass in that day, that Tyre shall be forgotten seventy years, according to the days of one king: after the end of seventy years shall Tyre sing as an harlot.

16Take an harp, go about the city, thou harlot that hast been forgotten; make sweet melody, sing many songs, that thou mayest be remembered.

17And it shall come to pass after the end of seventy years, that the LORD will visit Tyre, and she shall turn to her hire, and shall commit fornication with all the kingdoms of the world upon the face of the earth.

18And her merchandise and her hire shall be holiness to the Lord; it shall not be treasured nor laid up; for her merchandise shall be for them that dwell before the Lord, to eat sufficiently, and for durable clothing.

BEHOLD, the Lord maketh the earth empty, and maketh it waste, and turneth it upside down, and scattereth abroad the inhabitants thereof.

2And it shall be, as with the people, so with the priest; as with the servant, so with his master; as with the maid, so with her mistress; as with the buyer, so with the seller; as with the lender, so with the borrower; as with the taker of usury, so with the giver of usury to him.

3The land shall be utterly emptied, and utterly spoiled: for the Lord hath spoken this word.

4The earth mourneth *and* fadeth away, the world languisheth *and* fadeth away, the haughty people of the earth do languish.

5The earth also is defiled under the inhabitants thereof; because they have transgressed the laws, changed the ordinance, broken the everlasting covenant.

6Therefore hath the curse devoured the earth, and they that dwell therein are desolate: therefore the inhabitants of the earth are burned, and few men left.

7The new wine mourneth, the vine languisheth, all the merry-hearted do sigh.

8The mirth of tabrets ceaseth, the noise of them that rejoice endeth, the joy of the harp ceaseth.

9They shall not drink wine with a song; strong drink shall be bitter to them that drink it.

10The city of confusion is broken down: every house is shut up, that no man may come in.

11*There is* a crying for wine in the streets; all joy is darkened, the mirth of the land is gone.

12In the city is left desolation, and the gate is smitten with destruction.

13When thus it shall be in the midst of the land among the people, *there shall be* as the shaking of an olive tree, *and* as the gleaning grapes when the vintage is done.

14They shall lift up their voice, they shall sing for the majesty of the Lord, they shall cry aloud from the sea.

15Wherefore glorify ye the Lord in the fires, *even* the name of the Lord God of Israel in the isles of the sea.

16From the uttermost part of the earth have we heard songs, *even* glory to the righteous. But I said, My leanness, my leanness, woe unto me! the treacherous dealers have dealt treacherously; yea, the treacherous dealers have dealt very treacherously.

17Fear, and the pit, and the snare, *are* upon thee, O inhabitant of the earth.

18And it shall come to pass, *that* he who fleeth from the noise of the fear shall fall into the pit; and he that cometh up out of the midst of the pit shall be taken in the snare: for the windows from on high are open, and the foundations of the earth do shake.

19The earth is utterly broken down, the earth is clean dissolved, the earth is moved exceedingly.

20The earth shall reel to and fro like a drunkard, and shall be removed like a cottage; and the transgression thereof shall be heavy upon it; and it shall fall, and not rise again.

21And it shall come to pass in that day, *that* the Lord shall punish the host of the high ones *that are* on high, and the kings of the earth upon the earth.

22And they shall be gathered together, *as* prisoners are gathered in the pit, and shall be shut up in the prison, and after many days shall they be visited.

23Then the moon shall be confounded, and the sun ashamed, when the LORD of hosts shall reign in mount Zion, and in Jerusalem, and before his ancients gloriously.

GALATIANS 2:17—3:7

BUT if, while we seek to be justified by Christ, we ourselves also are found sinners, *is* therefore Christ the minister of sin? God forbid.

18For if I build again the things which I destroyed, I make myself a transgressor.

19For I through the law am dead to the law, that I might live unto God.

20I am crucified with Christ: nevertheless I live; yet not I, but Christ liveth in me: and the life which I now live in the flesh I live by the faith of the Son of God, who loved me, and gave himself for me.

21I do not frustrate the grace of God: for if righteousness *come* by the law, then Christ is dead in vain.

O FOOLISH Galatians, who hath bewitched you, that ye should not obey the truth, before whose eyes Jesus Christ hath been evidently set forth, crucified among you?

2This only would I learn of you, Received ye the Spirit by the works of the law, or by the hearing of faith?

3Are ye so foolish? having begun in the Spirit, are ye now made perfect by the flesh?

4Have ye suffered so many things in vain? if *it be* yet in vain.

5He therefore that ministereth to you the Spirit, and worketh miracles among you, *doeth he it* by the works of the law, or by the hearing of faith?

6Even as Abraham believed God, and

it was accounted to him for righteousness.

7Know ye therefore that they which are of faith, the same are the children of Abraham.

PSALM 60:1–12

O GOD, thou hast cast us off, thou hast scattered us, thou hast been displeased; O turn thyself to us again.

2Thou hast made the earth to tremble; thou hast broken it: heal the breaches thereof; for it shaketh.

3Thou hast shewed thy people hard things: thou hast made us to drink the wine of astonishment.

4Thou hast given a banner to them that fear thee, that it may be displayed because of the truth. Selah.

5That thy beloved may be delivered; save *with* thy right hand, and hear me.

6God hath spoken in his holiness; I will rejoice, I will divide Shechem, and mete out the valley of Succoth.

7Gilead *is* mine, and Manasseh *is* mine; Ephraim also *is* the strength of mine head; Judah *is* my lawgiver;

8Moab *is* my washpot; over Edom will I cast out my shoe: Philistia, triumph thou because of me.

9Who will bring me *into* the strong city? who will lead me into Edom?

10*Wilt* not thou, O God, *which* hadst cast us off? and *thou,* O God, *which* didst not go out with our armies?

11Give us help from trouble: for vain *is* the help of man.

12Through God we shall do valiantly: for he *it is that* shall tread down our enemies.

PROVERBS FOR TODAY/ 23:15–16

My son, if thine heart be wise, my heart shall rejoice, even mine. Yea, my reins shall rejoice, when thy lips speak right things.

SEPTEMBER 17

ISAIAH 25:1—28:13

O LORD, thou *art* my God; I will exalt thee, I will praise thy name; for thou hast done wonderful *things; thy* counsels of old *are* faithfulness *and* truth.

2For thou hast made of a city an heap; *of* a defenced city a ruin: a palace of strangers to be no city; it shall never be built.

3Therefore shall the strong people glorify thee, the city of the terrible nations shall fear thee.

4For thou hast been a strength to the poor, a strength to the needy in his distress, a refuge from the storm, a shadow from the heat, when the blast of the terrible ones *is* as a storm *against* the wall.

5Thou shalt bring down the noise of strangers, as the heat in a dry place; *even* the heat with the shadow of a cloud: the branch of the terrible ones shall be brought low.

6And in this mountain shall the LORD of hosts make unto all people a feast of fat things, a feast of wines on the lees, of fat things full of marrow, of wines on the lees well refined.

7And he will destroy in this mountain the face of the covering cast over all people, and the vail that is spread over all nations.

8He will swallow up death in victory; and the Lord GOD will wipe away tears from off all faces; and the rebuke of his people shall he take away from off all the earth: for the LORD hath spoken *it.*

9And it shall be said in that day, Lo, this *is* our God; we have waited for him, and he will save us: this *is* the LORD; we have waited for him, we will be glad and rejoice in his salvation.

10For in this mountain shall the hand of the LORD rest, and Moab shall be trodden down under him, even as straw is trodden down for the dunghill.

11And he shall spread forth his hands in the midst of them, as he that swimmeth spreadeth forth *his hands* to swim: and he shall bring down their pride together with the spoils of their hands.

12And the fortress of the high fort of thy walls shall he bring down, lay low, *and* bring to the ground, *even* to the dust.

IN that day shall this song be sung in the land of Judah; We have a strong city; salvation will *God* appoint *for* walls and bulwarks.

2Open ye the gates, that the righteous nation which keepeth the truth may enter in.

3Thou wilt keep *him* in perfect peace, *whose* mind *is* stayed *on thee:* because he trusteth in thee.

4Trust ye in the LORD for ever: for in the LORD JEHOVAH *is* everlasting strength:

5For he bringeth down them that dwell on high; the lofty city, he layeth it low; he layeth it low, *even* to the ground; he bringeth it *even* to the dust.

6The foot shall tread it down, *even* the feet of the poor, *and* the steps of the needy.

7The way of the just *is* uprightness: thou, most upright, dost weigh the path of the just.

8Yea, in the way of thy judgments, O LORD, have we waited for thee; the desire of *our* soul *is* to thy name, and to the remembrance of thee.

9With my soul have I desired thee in the night; yea, with my spirit within me will I seek thee early: for when thy judgments *are* in the earth, the inhabitants of the world will learn righteousness.

10Let favour be shewed to the wicked, *yet* will he not learn righteousness; in the land of uprightness will he deal unjustly, and will not behold the majesty of the LORD.

11LORD, *when* thy hand is lifted up, they will not see: *but* they shall see, and be ashamed for *their* envy at the people; yea, the fire of thine enemies shall devour them.

12LORD, thou wilt ordain peace for us: for thou also hast wrought all our works in us.

13O LORD our God, *other* lords beside thee have had dominion over us: *but* by thee only will we make mention of thy name.

14*They are* dead, they shall not live; *they are* deceased, they shall not rise: therefore hast thou visited and destroyed them, and made all their memory to perish.

15Thou hast increased the nation, O LORD, thou hast increased the nation: thou art glorified: thou hadst removed *it* far *unto* all the ends of the earth.

16LORD, in trouble have they visited thee, they poured out a prayer *when* thy chastening *was* upon them.

17Like as a woman with child, *that* draweth near the time of her delivery, is in pain, *and* crieth out in her pangs; so have we been in thy sight, O LORD.

18We have been with child, we have been in pain, we have as it were brought forth wind; we have not wrought any deliverance in the earth; neither have the inhabitants of the world fallen.

19Thy dead *men* shall live, *together with* my dead body shall they arise. Awake and sing, ye that dwell in dust: for thy dew *is as* the dew of herbs, and the earth shall cast out the dead.

20Come, my people, enter thou into thy chambers, and shut thy doors about thee: hide thyself as it were for a little moment, until the indignation be overpast.

21For, behold, the LORD cometh out of his place to punish the inhabitants of the earth for their iniquity: the earth also shall disclose her blood, and shall no more cover her slain.

IN that day the LORD with his sore and great and strong sword shall punish leviathan the piercing serpent, even leviathan that crooked serpent; and he shall slay the dragon that *is* in the sea.

2In that day sing ye unto her, A vineyard of red wine.

3I the LORD do keep it; I will water it every moment: lest *any* hurt it, I will keep it night and day.

4Fury *is* not in me: who would set the briers *and* thorns against me in battle? I would go through them, I would burn them together.

5Or let him take hold of my strength, *that* he may make peace with me; *and* he shall make peace with me.

6He shall cause them that come of Jacob to take root: Israel shall blossom and bud, and fill the face of the world with fruit.

7Hath he smitten him, as he smote those that smote him? *or* is he slain according to the slaughter of them that are slain by him?

8In measure, when it shooteth forth, thou wilt debate with it: he stayeth his rough wind in the day of the east wind.

9By this therefore shall the iniquity of Jacob be purged; and this *is* all the fruit to take away his sin; when he maketh all the stones of the altar as chalkstones that are beaten in sunder, the groves and images shall not stand up.

10Yet the defenced city *shall be* desolate, *and* the habitation forsaken, and left like a wilderness: there shall the calf feed, and there shall he lie down, and consume the branches thereof.

11When the boughs thereof are withered, they shall be broken off: the women come, *and* set them on fire:

for it *is* a people of no understanding: therefore he that made them will not have mercy on them, and he that formed them will shew them no favour.

12And it shall come to pass in that day, *that* the LORD shall beat off from the channel of the river unto the stream of Egypt, and ye shall be gathered one by one, O ye children of Israel.

13And it shall come to pass in that day, *that* the great trumpet shall be blown, and they shall come which were ready to perish in the land of Assyria, and the outcasts in the land of Egypt, and shall worship the LORD in the holy mount at Jerusalem.

WOE to the crown of pride, to the drunkards of Ephraim, whose glorious beauty *is* a fading flower, which *are* on the head of the fat valleys of them that are overcome with wine!

2Behold, the LORD hath a mighty and strong one, which as a tempest of hail *and* a destroying storm, as a flood of mighty waters overflowing, shall cast down to the earth with the hand.

3The crown of pride, the drunkards of Ephraim, shall be trodden under feet:

4And the glorious beauty, which *is* on the head of the fat valley, shall be a fading flower, *and* as the hasty fruit before the summer; which *when* he that looketh upon it seeth, while it is yet in his hand he eateth it up.

5In that day shall the LORD of hosts be for a crown of glory, and for a diadem of beauty, unto the residue of his people,

6And for a spirit of judgment to him that sitteth in judgment, and for strength to them that turn the battle to the gate.

7But they also have erred through wine, and through strong drink are out of the way; the priest and the prophet have erred through strong drink, they are swallowed up of wine, they are out of the way through strong drink;

they err in vision, they stumble *in* judgment.

8For all tables are full of vomit *and* filthiness, *so that there is* no place *clean.*

9Whom shall he teach knowledge? and whom shall he make to understand doctrine? *them that are* weaned from the milk, *and* drawn from the breasts.

10For precept *must be* upon precept, precept upon precept; line upon line, line upon line; here a little, *and* there a little:

11For with stammering lips and another tongue will he speak to this people.

12To whom he said, This *is* the rest *wherewith* ye may cause the weary to rest; and this *is* the refreshing: yet they would not hear.

13But the word of the LORD was unto them precept upon precept, precept upon precept; line upon line, line upon line; here a little, *and* there a little; that they might go, and fall backward, and be broken, and snared, and taken.

GALATIANS 3:8–22

AND the scripture, foreseeing that God would justify the heathen through faith, preached before the gospel unto Abraham, *saying,* In thee shall all nations be blessed.

9So then they which be of faith are blessed with faithful Abraham.

10For as many as are of the works of the law are under the curse: for it is written, Cursed *is* every one that continueth not in all things which are written in the book of the law to do them.

11But that no man is justified by the law in the sight of God, *it is* evident: for, The just shall live by faith.

12And the law is not of faith: but, The man that doeth them shall live in them.

13Christ hath redeemed us from the curse of the law, being made a curse for us: for it is written, Cursed *is* every one that hangeth on a tree:

14That the blessing of Abraham might come on the Gentiles through Jesus Christ; that we might receive the promise of the Spirit through faith.

15Brethren, I speak after the manner of men; Though *it be* but a man's covenant, yet *if it be* confirmed, no man disannulleth, or addeth thereto.

16Now to Abraham and his seed were the promises made. He saith not, And to seeds, as of many; but as of one, And to thy seed, which is Christ.

17And this I say, *that* the covenant, that was confirmed before of God in Christ, the law, which was four hundred and thirty years after, cannot disannul, that it should make the promise of none effect.

18For if the inheritance *be* of the law, *it is* no more of promise: but God gave *it* to Abraham by promise.

19Wherefore then *serveth* the law? It was added because of transgressions, till the seed should come to whom the promise was made; *and it was* ordained by angels in the hand of a mediator.

20Now a mediator is not *a mediator* of one, but God is one.

21*Is* the law then against the promises of God? God forbid: for if there had been a law given which could have given life, verily righteousness should have been by the law.

22But the scripture hath concluded all under sin, that the promise by faith of Jesus Christ might be given to them that believe.

PSALM 61:1–8

HEAR my cry, O God; attend unto my prayer.

2From the end of the earth will I cry unto thee, when my heart is overwhelmed: lead me to the rock *that* is higher than I.

3For thou hast been a shelter for me, *and* a strong tower from the enemy.

4I will abide in thy tabernacle for ever: I will trust in the covert of thy wings. Selah.

5For thou, O God, hast heard my vows: thou hast given *me* the heritage of those that fear thy name.

6Thou wilt prolong the king's life: *and* his years as many generations.

7He shall abide before God for ever: O prepare mercy and truth, *which* may preserve him.

8So will I sing praise unto thy name for ever, that I may daily perform my vows.

PROVERBS FOR TODAY/ 23:17–18

Let not thine heart envy sinners: but be thou *in the fear of the LORD all the day long. For surely there is an end; and thine expectation shall not be cut off.*

SEPTEMBER 18

ISAIAH 28:14—30:11

WHEREFORE hear the word of the LORD, ye scornful men, that rule this people which *is* in Jerusalem.

15Because ye have said, We have made a covenant with death, and with hell are we at agreement; when the overflowing scourge shall pass through, it shall not come unto us: for we have made lies our refuge, and under falsehood have we hid ourselves:

16Therefore thus saith the LORD GOD, Behold, I lay in Zion for a foundation a stone, a tried stone, a precious corner *stone,* a sure foundation; he that believeth shall not make haste.

17Judgment also will I lay to the line, and righteousness to the plummet: and the hail shall sweep away the refuge of lies, and the waters shall overflow the hiding place.

18And your covenant with death shall be disannulled, and your agreement with hell shall not stand; when the overflowing scourge shall pass through, then ye shall be trodden down by it.

19From the time that it goeth forth it shall take you: for morning by morning shall it pass over, by day and by night: and it shall be a vexation only *to* understand the report.

20For the bed is shorter than that *a man* can stretch himself *on it:* and the covering narrower than that he can wrap himself *in it.*

21For the LORD shall rise up as *in* mount Perazim, he shall be wroth as *in* the valley of Gibeon, that he may do his work, his strange work; and bring to pass his act, his strange act.

22Now therefore be ye not mockers, lest your bands be made strong: for I have heard from the Lord GOD of hosts a consumption, even determined upon the whole earth.

23Give ye ear, and hear my voice; hearken, and hear my speech.

24Doth the plowman plow all day to sow? doth he open and break the clods of his ground?

25When he hath made plain the face thereof, doth he not cast abroad the fitches, and scatter the cummin, and cast in the principal wheat and the appointed barley and the rie in their place?

26For his God doth instruct him to discretion, *and* doth teach him.

27For the fitches are not threshed with a threshing instrument, neither is a cart wheel turned about upon the cummin; but the fitches are beaten out with a staff, and the cummin with a rod.

28Bread *corn* is bruised; because he will not ever be threshing it, nor break *it with* the wheel of his cart, nor bruise it *with* his horsemen.

29This also cometh forth from the LORD of hosts, *which* is wonderful in counsel, *and* excellent in working.

WOE to Ariel, to Ariel, the city *where* David dwelt! add ye year to year; let them kill sacrifices.

2Yet I will distress Ariel, and there shall be heaviness and sorrow: and it shall be unto me as Ariel.

3And I will camp against thee round about, and will lay siege against thee with a mount, and I will raise forts against thee.

4And thou shalt be brought down, *and* shalt speak out of the ground, and thy speech shall be low out of the dust, and thy voice shall be, as of one that hath a familiar spirit, out of the ground, and thy speech shall whisper out of the dust.

5Moreover the multitude of thy strangers shall be like small dust, and the multitude of the terrible ones *shall be* as chaff that passeth away: yea, it shall be at an instant suddenly.

6Thou shalt be visited of the LORD of hosts with thunder, and with earthquake, and great noise, with storm and tempest, and the flame of devouring fire.

7And the multitude of all the nations that fight against Ariel, even all that fight against her and her munition, and that distress her, shall be as a dream of a night vision.

8It shall even be as when an hungry *man* dreameth, and, behold, he eateth; but he awaketh, and his soul is empty: or as when a thirsty man dreameth, and, behold, he drinketh; but he awaketh, and, behold, *he is* faint, and his soul hath appetite: so shall the multitude of all the nations be, that fight against mount Zion.

9Stay yourselves, and wonder; cry ye out, and cry: they are drunken, but not with wine; they stagger, but not with strong drink.

10For the LORD hath poured out upon you the spirit of deep sleep, and hath closed your eyes: the prophets and your rulers, the seers hath he covered.

11And the vision of all is become unto you as the words of a book that is sealed, which *men* deliver to one that is learned, saying, Read this, I pray thee: and he saith, I cannot; for it *is* sealed:

12And the book is delivered to him that is not learned, saying, Read this, I pray thee: and he saith, I am not learned.

13Wherefore the LORD said, Forasmuch as this people draw near *me* with their mouth, and with their lips do honour me, but have removed their heart far from me, and their fear toward me is taught by the precept of men:

14Therefore, behold, I will proceed to do a marvellous work among this people, *even* a marvellous work and a wonder: for the wisdom of their wise *men* shall perish, and the understanding of their prudent *men* shall be hid.

15Woe unto them that seek deep to hide their counsel from the LORD, and their works are in the dark, and they say, Who seeth us? and who knoweth us?

16Surely your turning of things upside down shall be esteemed as the potter's clay: for shall the work say of him that made it, He made me not? or shall the thing framed say of him that framed it, He had no understanding?

17*Is* it not yet a very little while, and Lebanon shall be turned into a fruitful field, and the fruitful field shall be esteemed as a forest?

18And in that day shall the deaf hear the words of the book, and the eyes of the blind shall see out of obscurity, and out of darkness.

19The meek also shall increase *their* joy in the LORD, and the poor among men shall rejoice in the Holy One of Israel.

20For the terrible one is brought to nought, and the scorner is consumed, and all that watch for iniquity are cut off:

21That make a man an offender for a word, and lay a snare for him that reproveth in the gate, and turn aside the just for a thing of nought.

22Therefore thus saith the LORD, who redeemed Abraham, concerning the house of Jacob, Jacob shall not now be ashamed, neither shall his face now wax pale.

23But when he seeth his children, the work of mine hands, in the midst of him, they shall sanctify my name, and sanctify the Holy One of Jacob, and shall fear the God of Israel.

24They also that erred in spirit shall come to understanding, and they that murmured shall learn doctrine.

WOE to the rebellious children, saith the LORD, that take counsel, but not of me; and that cover with a covering, but not of my spirit, that they may add sin to sin:

2That walk to go down into Egypt, and have not asked at my mouth; to strengthen themselves in the strength of Pharaoh, and to trust in the shadow of Egypt!

3Therefore shall the strength of Pharaoh be your shame, and the trust in the shadow of Egypt *your* confusion.

4For his princes were at Zoan, and his ambassadors came to Hanes.

5They were all ashamed of a people *that* could not profit them, nor be an help nor profit, but a shame, and also a reproach.

6The burden of the beasts of the south: into the land of trouble and anguish, from whence *come* the young and old lion, the viper and fiery flying serpent, they will carry their riches upon the shoulders of young asses, and their treasures upon the bunches of camels, to a people *that* shall not profit *them*.

7For the Egyptians shall help in vain, and to no purpose: therefore have I cried concerning this, Their strength *is* to sit still.

8Now go, write it before them in a table, and note it in a book, that it may be for the time to come for ever and ever:

9That this *is* a rebellious people, lying children, children *that* will not hear the law of the LORD:

10Which say to the seers, See not; and to the prophets, Prophesy not unto us right things, speak unto us smooth things, prophesy deceits:

11Get you out of the way, turn aside out of the path, cause the Holy One of Israel to cease from before us.

GALATIANS 3:23—4:31

BUT before faith came, we were kept under the law, shut up unto the faith which should afterwards be revealed.

24Wherefore the law was our schoolmaster *to bring us* unto Christ, that we might be justified by faith.

25But after that faith is come, we are no longer under a schoolmaster.

26For ye are all the children of God by faith in Christ Jesus.

27For as many of you as have been baptized into Christ have put on Christ.

28There is neither Jew nor Greek, there is neither bond nor free, there is neither male nor female: for ye are all one in Christ Jesus.

29And if ye *be* Christ's, then are ye Abraham's seed, and heirs according to the promise.

NOW I say, *That* the heir, as long as he is a child, differeth nothing from a servant, though he be lord of all;

2But is under tutors and governors until the time appointed of the father.

3Even so we, when we were children, were in bondage under the elements of the world:

4But when the fulness of the time was come, God sent forth his Son, made of a woman, made under the law,

5To redeem them that were under the law, that we might receive the adoption of sons.

6And because ye are sons, God hath sent forth the Spirit of his Son into your hearts, crying, Abba, Father.

7Wherefore thou art no more a servant, but a son; and if a son, then an heir of God through Christ.

8Howbeit then, when ye knew not God, ye did service unto them which by nature are no gods.

9But now, after that ye have known God, or rather are known of God, how turn ye again to the weak and beggarly elements, whereunto ye desire again to be in bondage?

10Ye observe days, and months, and times, and years.

11I am afraid of you, lest I have bestowed upon you labour in vain.

12Brethren, I beseech you, be as I *am;* for I *am* as ye *are:* ye have not injured me at all.

13Ye know how through infirmity of the flesh I preached the gospel unto you at the first.

14And my temptation which was in my flesh ye despised not, nor rejected; but received me as an angel of God, *even* as Christ Jesus.

15Where is then the blessedness ye spake of? for I bear you record, that, if *it had been* possible, ye would have plucked out your own eyes, and have given them to me.

16Am I therefore become your enemy, because I tell you the truth?

17They zealously affect you, *but* not well; yea, they would exclude you, that ye might affect them.

18But *it is* good to be zealously

affected always in *a* good *thing,* and not only when I am present with you.

19My little children, of whom I travail in birth again until Christ be formed in you,

20I desire to be present with you now, and to change my voice; for I stand in doubt of you.

21Tell me, ye that desire to be under the law, do ye not hear the law?

22For it is written, that Abraham had two sons, the one by a bondmaid, the other by a freewoman.

23But he *who was* of the bondwoman was born after the flesh; but he of the freewoman *was* by promise.

24Which things are an allegory: for these are the two covenants; the one from the mount Sinai, which gendereth to bondage, which is Agar.

25For this Agar is mount Sinai in Arabia, and answereth to Jerusalem which now is, and is in bondage with her children.

26But Jerusalem which is above is free, which is the mother of us all.

27For it is written, Rejoice, *thou* barren that bearest not; break forth and cry, thou that travailest not: for the desolate hath many more children than she which hath an husband.

28Now we, brethren, as Isaac was, are the children of promise.

29But as then he that was born after the flesh persecuted him *that was born* after the Spirit, even so *it is* now.

30Nevertheless what saith the scripture? Cast out the bondwoman and her son: for the son of the bondwoman shall not be heir with the son of the freewoman.

31So then, brethren, we are not children of the bondwoman, but of the free.

PSALM 62:1–12

TRULY my soul waiteth upon God: from him *cometh* my salvation.

2He only *is* my rock and my salvation; *he is* my defence; I shall not be greatly moved.

3How long will ye imagine mischief against a man? ye shall be slain all of you: as a bowing wall *shall ye be, and as* a tottering fence.

4They only consult to cast *him* down from his excellency: they delight in lies: they bless with their mouth, but they curse inwardly. Selah.

5My soul, wait thou only upon God; for my expectation *is* from him.

6He only *is* my rock and my salvation: *he is* my defence; I shall not be moved.

7In God *is* my salvation and my glory: the rock of my strength, *and* my refuge, *is* in God.

8Trust in him at all times; ye people, pour out your heart before him: God *is* a refuge for us. Selah.

9Surely men of low degree *are* vanity, *and* men of high degree *are* a lie: to be laid in the balance, they *are* altogether *lighter* than vanity.

10Trust not in oppression, and become not vain in robbery: if riches increase, set not your heart *upon them.*

11God hath spoken once; twice have I heard this; that power *belongeth* unto God.

12Also unto thee, O Lord, *belongeth* mercy: for thou renderest to every man according to his work.

PROVERBS FOR TODAY/ 23:19–21

Hear thou, my son, and be wise, and guide thine heart in the way. Be not among winebibbers; among riotous eaters of flesh: For the drunkard and the glutton shall come to poverty: and drowsiness shall clothe a man *with rags.*

SEPTEMBER 19

ISAIAH 30:12—33:12

WHEREFORE thus saith the Holy One of Israel, Because ye despise this word, and trust in oppression and perverseness, and stay thereon:

13Therefore this iniquity shall be to you as a breach ready to fall, swelling out in a high wall, whose breaking cometh suddenly at an instant.

14And he shall break it as the breaking of the potters' vessel that is broken in pieces; he shall not spare: so that there shall not be found in the bursting of it a sherd to take fire from the hearth, or to take water *withal* out of the pit.

15For thus saith the Lord GOD, the Holy One of Israel; In returning and rest shall ye be saved; in quietness and in confidence shall be your strength: and ye would not.

16But ye said, No; for we will flee upon horses; therefore shall ye flee: and, We will ride upon the swift; therefore shall they that pursue you be swift.

17One thousand *shall flee* at the rebuke of one; at the rebuke of five shall ye flee: till ye be left as a beacon upon the top of a mountain, and as an ensign on an hill.

18And therefore will the LORD wait, that he may be gracious unto you, and therefore will he be exalted, that he may have mercy upon you: for the LORD *is* a God of judgment: blessed *are* all they that wait for him.

19For the people shall dwell in Zion at Jerusalem: thou shalt weep no more: he will be very gracious unto thee at the voice of thy cry; when he shall hear it, he will answer thee.

20And *though* the Lord give you the bread of adversity, and the water of affliction, yet shall not thy teachers be removed into a corner any more, but thine eyes shall see thy teachers:

21And thine ears shall hear a word behind thee, saying, This *is* the way, walk ye in it, when ye turn to the right hand, and when ye turn to the left.

22Ye shall defile also the covering of thy graven images of silver, and the ornament of thy molten images of gold: thou shalt cast them away as a menstruous cloth; thou shalt say unto it, Get thee hence.

23Then shall he give the rain of thy seed, that thou shalt sow the ground withal; and bread of the increase of the earth, and it shall be fat and plenteous: in that day shall thy cattle feed in large pastures.

24The oxen likewise and the young asses that ear the ground shall eat clean provender, which hath been winnowed with the shovel and with the fan.

25And there shall be upon every high mountain, and upon every high hill, rivers *and* streams of waters in the day of the great slaughter, when the towers fall.

26Moreover the light of the moon shall be as the light of the sun, and the light of the sun shall be sevenfold, as the light of seven days, in the day that the LORD bindeth up the breach of his people, and healeth the stroke of their wound.

27Behold, the name of the LORD cometh from far, burning *with* his anger, and the burden *thereof is* heavy: his lips are full of indignation, and his tongue as a devouring fire:

28And his breath, as an overflowing stream, shall reach to the midst of the neck, to sift the nations with the sieve of vanity: and *there shall be* a bridle in the jaws of the people, causing *them* to err.

29Ye shall have a song, as in the night

when a holy solemnity is kept; and gladness of heart, as when one goeth with a pipe to come into the mountain of the LORD, to the mighty One of Israel.

30And the LORD shall cause his glorious voice to be heard, and shall shew the lighting down of his arm, with the indignation of *his* anger, and *with* the flame of a devouring fire, *with* scattering, and tempest, and hailstones.

31For through the voice of the LORD shall the Assyrian be beaten down, *which* smote with a rod.

32And *in* every place where the grounded staff shall pass, which the LORD shall lay upon him, *it* shall be with tabrets and harps: and in battles of shaking will he fight with it.

33For Tophet *is* ordained of old; yea, for the king it is prepared; he hath made *it* deep *and* large: the pile thereof *is* fire and much wood; the breath of the LORD, like a stream of brimstone, doth kindle it.

WOE to them that go down to Egypt for help; and stay on horses, and trust in chariots, because *they are* many; and in horsemen, because they are very strong; but they look not unto the Holy One of Israel, neither seek the LORD!

2Yet he also *is* wise, and will bring evil, and will not call back his words: but will arise against the house of the evildoers, and against the help of them that work iniquity.

3Now the Egyptians *are* men, and not God; and their horses flesh, and not spirit. When the LORD shall stretch out his hand, both he that helpeth shall fall, and he that is holpen shall fall down, and they all shall fail together.

4For thus hath the LORD spoken unto me, Like as the lion and the young lion roaring on his prey, when a multitude of shepherds is called forth against him, *he* will not be afraid of their voice, nor abase himself for the noise of them: so shall the LORD of hosts come down

to fight for mount Zion, and for the hill thereof.

5As birds flying, so will the LORD of hosts defend Jerusalem; defending also he will deliver *it; and* passing over he will preserve *it.*

6Turn ye unto *him from* whom the children of Israel have deeply revolted.

7For in that day every man shall cast away his idols of silver, and his idols of gold, which your own hands have made unto you *for* a sin.

8Then shall the Assyrian fall with the sword, not of a mighty man; and the sword, not of a mean man, shall devour him: but he shall flee from the sword, and his young men shall be discomfited.

9And he shall pass over to his strong hold for fear, and his princes shall be afraid of the ensign, saith the LORD, whose fire *is* in Zion, and his furnace in Jerusalem.

BEHOLD, a king shall reign in righteousness, and princes shall rule in judgment.

2And a man shall be as an hiding place from the wind, and a covert from the tempest; as rivers of water in a dry place, as the shadow of a great rock in a weary land.

3And the eyes of them that see shall not be dim, and the ears of them that hear shall hearken.

4The heart also of the rash shall understand knowledge, and the tongue of the stammerers shall be ready to speak plainly.

5The vile person shall be no more called liberal, nor the churl said *to be* bountiful.

6For the vile person will speak villany, and his heart will work iniquity, to practise hypocrisy, and to utter error against the LORD, to make empty the soul of the hungry, and he will cause the drink of the thirsty to fail.

7The instruments also of the churl *are* evil: he deviseth wicked devices to destroy the poor with lying words, even when the needy speaketh right.

8But the liberal deviseth liberal things; and by liberal things shall he stand.

9Rise up, ye women that are at ease; hear my voice, ye careless daughters; give ear unto my speech.

10Many days and years shall ye be troubled, ye careless women: for the vintage shall fail, the gathering shall not come.

11Tremble, ye women that are at ease; be troubled, ye careless ones: strip you, and make you bare, and gird *sackcloth* upon *your* loins.

12They shall lament for the teats, for the pleasant fields, for the fruitful vine.

13Upon the land of my people shall come up thorns *and* briers; yea, upon all the houses of joy *in* the joyous city:

14Because the palaces shall be forsaken; the multitude of the city shall be left; the forts and towers shall be for dens for ever, a joy of wild asses, a pasture of flocks;

15Until the spirit be poured upon us from on high, and the wilderness be a fruitful field, and the fruitful field be counted for a forest.

16Then judgment shall dwell in the wilderness, and righteousness remain in the fruitful field.

17And the work of righteousness shall be peace; and the effect of righteousness quietness and assurance for ever.

18And my people shall dwell in a peaceable habitation, and in sure dwellings, and in quiet resting places;

19When it shall hail, coming down on the forest; and the city shall be low in a low place.

20Blessed *are* ye that sow beside all waters, that send forth *thither* the feet of the ox and the ass.

WOE to thee that spoilest, and thou *wast* not spoiled; and dealest treacherously, and they dealt not treacherously with thee! when thou shalt cease to spoil, thou shalt be spoiled; *and* when thou shalt make an end to deal treacherously, they shall deal treacherously with thee.

2O LORD, be gracious unto us; we have waited for thee: be thou their arm every morning, our salvation also in the time of trouble.

3At the noise of the tumult the people fled; at the lifting up of thyself the nations were scattered.

4And your spoil shall be gathered *like* the gathering of the caterpiller: as the running to and fro of locusts shall he run upon them.

5The LORD is exalted; for he dwelleth on high: he hath filled Zion with judgment and righteousness.

6And wisdom and knowledge shall be the stability of thy times, *and* strength of salvation: the fear of the LORD *is* his treasure.

7Behold, their valiant ones shall cry without: the ambassadors of peace shall weep bitterly.

8The highways lie waste, the wayfaring man ceaseth: he hath broken the covenant, he hath despised the cities, he regardeth no man.

9The earth mourneth *and* languisheth: Lebanon is ashamed *and* hewn down: Sharon is like a wilderness; and Bashan and Carmel shake off *their fruits.*

10Now will I rise, saith the LORD; now will I be exalted; now will I lift up myself.

11Ye shall conceive chaff, ye shall bring forth stubble: your breath, *as* fire, shall devour you.

12And the people shall be *as* the burnings of lime: *as* thorns cut up shall they be burned in the fire.

GALATIANS 5:1–12

STAND fast therefore in the liberty wherewith Christ hath made us free, and be not entangled again with the yoke of bondage.

2Behold, I Paul say unto you, that if ye be circumcised, Christ shall profit you nothing.

3For I testify again to every man that is circumcised, that he is a debtor to do the whole law.

4Christ is become of no effect unto you, whosoever of you are justified by the law; ye are fallen from grace.

5For we through the Spirit wait for the hope of righteousness by faith.

6For in Jesus Christ neither circumcision availeth any thing, nor uncircumcision; but faith which worketh by love.

7Ye did run well; who did hinder you that ye should not obey the truth?

8This persuasion *cometh* not of him that calleth you.

9A little leaven leaveneth the whole lump.

10I have confidence in you through the Lord, that ye will be none otherwise minded: but he that troubleth you shall bear his judgment, whosoever he be.

11And I, brethren, if I yet preach circumcision, why do I yet suffer persecution? then is the offence of the cross ceased.

12I would they were even cut off which trouble you.

PSALM 63:1–11

O GOD, thou *art* my God; early will I seek thee: my soul thirsteth for thee, my flesh longeth for thee in a dry and thirsty land, where no water is;

2To see thy power and thy glory, so *as* I have seen thee in the sanctuary.

3Because thy lovingkindness *is* better than life, my lips shall praise thee.

4Thus will I bless thee while I live: I will lift up my hands in thy name.

5My soul shall be satisfied as *with* marrow and fatness; and my mouth shall praise *thee* with joyful lips:

6When I remember thee upon my bed, *and* meditate on thee in the *night* watches.

7Because thou hast been my help, therefore in the shadow of thy wings will I rejoice.

8My soul followeth hard after thee: thy right hand upholdeth me.

9But those *that* seek my soul, to destroy *it,* shall go into the lower parts of the earth.

10They shall fall by the sword: they shall be a portion for foxes.

11But the king shall rejoice in God; every one that sweareth by him shall glory: but the mouth of them that speak lies shall be stopped.

PROVERBS FOR TODAY/ 23:22

Hearken unto thy father that begat thee, and despise not thy mother when she is old.

SEPTEMBER 20

ISAIAH 33:13—36:22

HEAR, ye *that are* far off, what I have done; and, ye *that are* near, acknowledge my might.

14The sinners in Zion are afraid; fearfulness hath surprised the hypocrites. Who among us shall dwell with the devouring fire? who among us shall dwell with everlasting burnings?

15He that walketh righteously, and speaketh uprightly; he that despiseth the gain of oppressions, that shaketh his hands from holding of bribes, that stoppeth his ears from hearing of blood, and shutteth his eyes from seeing evil;

16He shall dwell on high: his place of defence *shall be* the munitions of rocks: bread shall be given him; his waters *shall be* sure.

17Thine eyes shall see the king in his beauty: they shall behold the land that is very far off.

18Thine heart shall meditate terror. Where *is* the scribe? where *is* the receiver? where *is* he that counted the towers?

19Thou shalt not see a fierce people, a people of a deeper speech than thou canst perceive; of a stammering tongue, *that thou canst* not understand.

20Look upon Zion, the city of our solemnities: thine eyes shall see Jerusalem a quiet habitation, a tabernacle *that* shall not be taken down; not one of the stakes thereof shall ever be removed, neither shall any of the cords thereof be broken.

21But there the glorious LORD *will be* unto us a place of broad rivers *and* streams; wherein shall go no galley with oars, neither shall gallant ship pass thereby.

22For the LORD *is* our judge, the LORD *is* our lawgiver, the LORD *is* our king; he will save us.

23Thy tacklings are loosed; they could not well strengthen their mast, they could not spread the sail: then is the prey of a great spoil divided; the lame take the prey.

24And the inhabitant shall not say, I am sick: the people that dwell therein *shall be* forgiven *their* iniquity.

COME near, ye nations, to hear; and hearken, ye people: let the earth hear, and all that is therein; the world, and all things that come forth of it.

2For the indignation of the LORD *is* upon all nations, and *his* fury upon all their armies: he hath utterly destroyed them, he hath delivered them to the slaughter.

3Their slain also shall be cast out, and their stink shall come up out of their carcases, and the mountains shall be melted with their blood.

4And all the host of heaven shall be dissolved, and the heavens shall be rolled together as a scroll: and all their host shall fall down, as the leaf falleth off from the vine, and as a falling *fig* from the fig tree.

5For my sword shall be bathed in heaven: behold, it shall come down upon Idumea, and upon the people of my curse, to judgment.

6The sword of the LORD is filled with blood, it is made fat with fatness, *and* with the blood of lambs and goats, with the fat of the kidneys of rams: for the LORD hath a sacrifice in Bozrah, and a great slaughter in the land of Idumea.

7And the unicorns shall come down with them, and the bullocks with the bulls; and their land shall be soaked with blood, and their dust made fat with fatness.

8For *it is* the day of the LORD'S

vengeance, *and* the year of recompences for the controversy of Zion.

9And the streams thereof shall be turned into pitch, and the dust thereof into brimstone, and the land thereof shall become burning pitch.

10It shall not be quenched night nor day; the smoke thereof shall go up for ever: from generation to generation it shall lie waste; none shall pass through it for ever and ever.

11But the cormorant and the bittern shall possess it; the owl also and the raven shall dwell in it: and he shall stretch out upon it the line of confusion, and the stones of emptiness.

12They shall call the nobles thereof to the kingdom, but none *shall be* there, and all her princes shall be nothing.

13And thorns shall come up in her palaces, nettles and brambles in the fortresses thereof: and it shall be an habitation of dragons, *and* a court for owls.

14The wild beasts of the desert shall also meet with the wild beasts of the island, and the satyr shall cry to his fellow; the screech owl also shall rest there, and find for herself a place of rest.

15There shall the great owl make her nest, and lay, and hatch, and gather under her shadow: there shall the vultures also be gathered, every one with her mate.

16Seek ye out of the book of the LORD, and read: no one of these shall fail, none shall want her mate: for my mouth it hath commanded, and his spirit it hath gathered them.

17And he hath cast the lot for them, and his hand hath divided it unto them by line: they shall possess it for ever, from generation to generation shall they dwell therein.

THE wilderness and the solitary place shall be glad for them; and the desert shall rejoice, and blossom as the rose.

2It shall blossom abundantly, and rejoice even with joy and singing: the glory of Lebanon shall be given unto it, the excellency of Carmel and Sharon, they shall see the glory of the LORD, *and* the excellency of our God.

3Strengthen ye the weak hands, and confirm the feeble knees.

4Say to them *that are* of a fearful heart, Be strong, fear not: behold, your God will come *with* vengeance, *even* God *with* a recompence; he will come and save you.

5Then the eyes of the blind shall be opened, and the ears of the deaf shall be unstopped.

6Then shall the lame *man* leap as an hart, and the tongue of the dumb sing: for in the wilderness shall waters break out, and streams in the desert.

7And the parched ground shall become a pool, and the thirsty land springs of water: in the habitation of dragons, where each lay, *shall be* grass with reeds and rushes.

8And an highway shall be there, and a way, and it shall be called The way of holiness; the unclean shall not pass over it; but it *shall be* for those: the wayfaring men, though fools, shall not err *therein.*

9No lion shall be there, nor *any* ravenous beast shall go up thereon, it shall not be found there; but the redeemed shall walk *there:*

10And the ransomed of the LORD shall return, and come to Zion with songs and everlasting joy upon their heads: they shall obtain joy and gladness, and sorrow and sighing shall flee away.

Now it came to pass in the fourteenth year of king Hezekiah, *that* Sennacherib king of Assyria came up against all the defenced cities of Judah, and took them.

2And the king of Assyria sent Rabshakeh from Lachish to Jerusalem unto king Hezekiah with a great army. And he stood by the conduit of the upper pool in the highway of the fuller's field.

³Then came forth unto him Eliakim, Hilkiah's son, which was over the house, and Shebna the scribe, and Joah, Asaph's son, the recorder.

⁴And Rabshakeh said unto them, Say ye now to Hezekiah, Thus saith the great king, the king of Assyria, What confidence *is* this wherein thou trustest?

⁵I say, *sayest thou,* (but *they are but* vain words) *I have* counsel and strength for war: now on whom dost thou trust, that thou rebellest against me?

⁶Lo, thou trustest in the staff of this broken reed, on Egypt; whereon if a man lean, it will go into his hand, and pierce it: so *is* Pharaoh king of Egypt to all that trust in him.

⁷But if thou say to me, We trust in the LORD our God: *is it* not he, whose high places and whose altars Hezekiah hath taken away, and said to Judah and to Jerusalem, Ye shall worship before this altar?

⁸Now therefore give pledges, I pray thee, to my master the king of Assyria, and I will give thee two thousand horses, if thou be able on thy part to set riders upon them.

⁹How then wilt thou turn away the face of one captain of the least of my master's servants, and put thy trust on Egypt for chariots and for horsemen?

¹⁰And am I now come up without the LORD against this land to destroy it? the LORD said unto me, Go up against this land, and destroy it.

¹¹Then said Eliakim and Shebna and Joah unto Rabshakeh, Speak, I pray thee, unto thy servants in the Syrian language; for we understand *it:* and speak not to us in the Jews' language, in the ears of the people that *are* on the wall.

¹²But Rabshakeh said, Hath my master sent me to thy master and to thee to speak these words? *hath he* not *sent* *me* to the men that sit upon the wall, that they may eat their own dung, and drink their own piss with you?

¹³Then Rabshakeh stood, and cried with a loud voice in the Jews' language, and said, Hear ye the words of the great king, the king of Assyria.

¹⁴Thus saith the king, Let not Hezekiah deceive you: for he shall not be able to deliver you.

¹⁵Neither let Hezekiah make you trust in the LORD, saying, The LORD will surely deliver us: this city shall not be delivered into the hand of the king of Assyria.

¹⁶Hearken not to Hezekiah: for thus saith the king of Assyria, Make *an agreement* with me *by* a present, and come out to me: and eat ye every one of his vine, and every one of his fig tree, and drink ye every one the waters of his own cistern;

¹⁷Until I come and take you away to a land like your own land, a land of corn and wine, a land of bread and vineyards.

¹⁸*Beware* lest Hezekiah persuade you, saying, The LORD will deliver us. Hath any of the gods of the nations delivered his land out of the hand of the king of Assyria?

¹⁹Where *are* the gods of Hamath and Arphad? where *are* the gods of Sepharvaim? and have they delivered Samaria out of my hand?

²⁰Who *are they* among all the gods of these lands, that have delivered their land out of my hand, that the LORD should deliver Jerusalem out of my hand?

²¹But they held their peace, and answered him not a word: for the king's commandment was, saying, Answer him not.

²²Then came Eliakim, the son of Hilkiah, that *was* over the household, and Shebna the scribe, and Joah, the son of Asaph, the recorder, to Hezekiah with their clothes rent, and told him the words of Rabshakeh.

GALATIANS 5:13–26

FOR, brethren, ye have been called unto liberty; only *use* not liberty for an occasion to the flesh, but by love serve one another.

14For all the law is fulfilled in one word, *even* in this; Thou shalt love thy neighbour as thyself.

15But if ye bite and devour one another, take heed that ye be not consumed one of another.

16*This* I say then, Walk in the Spirit, and ye shall not fulfil the lust of the flesh.

17For the flesh lusteth against the Spirit, and the Spirit against the flesh: and these are contrary the one to the other: so that ye cannot do the things that ye would.

18But if ye be led of the Spirit, ye are not under the law.

19Now the works of the flesh are manifest, which are *these;* Adultery, fornication, uncleanness, lasciviousness,

20Idolatry, witchcraft, hatred, variance, emulations, wrath, strife, seditions, heresies,

21Envyings, murders, drunkenness, revellings, and such like: of the which I tell you before, as I have also told *you* in time past, that they which do such things shall not inherit the kingdom of God.

22But the fruit of the Spirit is love, joy, peace, longsuffering, gentleness, goodness, faith,

23Meekness, temperance: against such there is no law.

24And they that are Christ's have crucified the flesh with the affections and lusts.

25If we live in the Spirit, let us also walk in the Spirit.

26Let us not be desirous of vain glory, provoking one another, envying one another.

PSALM 64:1–10

HEAR my voice, O God, in my prayer: preserve my life from fear of the enemy.

2Hide me from the secret counsel of the wicked; from the insurrection of the workers of iniquity:

3Who whet their tongue like a sword, *and* bend *their bows to shoot* their arrows, *even* bitter words:

4That they may shoot in secret at the perfect: suddenly do they shoot at him, and fear not.

5They encourage themselves *in* an evil matter: they commune of laying snares privily; they say, Who shall see them?

6They search out iniquities; they accomplish a diligent search: both the inward *thought* of every one *of them,* and the heart, *is* deep.

7But God shall shoot at them *with* an arrow; suddenly shall they be wounded.

8So they shall make their own tongue to fall upon themselves: all that see them shall flee away.

9And all men shall fear, and shall declare the work of God; for they shall wisely consider of his doing.

10The righteous shall be glad in the LORD, and shall trust in him; and all the upright in heart shall glory.

PROVERBS FOR TODAY/ 23:23

Buy the truth, and sell it *not; also wisdom, and instruction, and understanding.*

ISAIAH 37:1—38:22

AND it came to pass, when king Hezekiah heard *it,* that he rent his clothes, and covered himself with sackcloth, and went into the house of the LORD.

2And he sent Eliakim, who *was* over the household, and Shebna the scribe, and the elders of the priests covered with sackcloth, unto Isaiah the prophet the son of Amoz.

3And they said unto him, Thus saith Hezekiah, This day *is* a day of trouble, and of rebuke, and of blasphemy: for the children are come to the birth, and *there is* not strength to bring forth.

4It may be the LORD thy God will hear the words of Rabshakeh, whom the king of Assyria his master hath sent to reproach the living God, and will reprove the words which the LORD thy God hath heard: wherefore lift up *thy* prayer for the remnant that is left.

5So the servants of king Hezekiah came to Isaiah.

6And Isaiah said unto them, Thus shall ye say unto your master, Thus saith the LORD, Be not afraid of the words that thou hast heard, wherewith the servants of the king of Assyria have blasphemed me.

7Behold, I will send a blast upon him, and he shall hear a rumour, and return to his own land; and I will cause him to fall by the sword in his own land.

8So Rabshakeh returned, and found the king of Assyria warring against Libnah: for he had heard that he was departed from Lachish.

9And he heard say concerning Tirhakah king of Ethiopia, He is come forth to make war with thee. And when he heard *it,* he sent messengers to Hezekiah, saying,

10Thus shall ye speak to Hezekiah king of Judah, saying, Let not thy God, in whom thou trustest, deceive thee, saying, Jerusalem shall not be given into the hand of the king of Assyria.

11Behold, thou hast heard what the kings of Assyria have done to all lands by destroying them utterly; and shalt thou be delivered?

12Have the gods of the nations delivered them which my fathers have destroyed, *as* Gozan, and Haran, and Rezeph, and the children of Eden which *were* in Telassar?

13Where *is* the king of Hamath, and the king of Arphad, and the king of the city of Sepharvaim, Hena, and Ivah?

14And Hezekiah received the letter from the hand of the messengers, and read it: and Hezekiah went up unto the house of the LORD, and spread it before the LORD.

15And Hezekiah prayed unto the LORD, saying,

16O LORD of hosts, God of Israel, that dwellest *between* the cherubims, that *art* the God, *even* thou alone, of all the kingdoms of the earth: thou hast made heaven and earth.

17Incline thine ear, O LORD, and hear; open thine eyes, O LORD, and see: and hear all the words of Sennacherib, which hath sent to reproach the living God.

18Of a truth, LORD, the kings of Assyria have laid waste all the nations, and their countries.

19And have cast their gods into the fire: for they *were* no gods, but the work of men's hands, wood and stone: therefore they have destroyed them.

20Now therefore, O LORD our God, save us from his hand, that all the kingdoms of the earth may know that thou *art* the LORD, *even* thou only.

21Then Isaiah the son of Amoz sent unto Hezekiah, saying, Thus saith the

Lord God of Israel, Whereas thou hast prayed to me against Sennacherib king of Assyria:

22This *is* the word which the Lord hath spoken concerning him; The virgin, the daughter of Zion, hath despised thee, *and* laughed thee to scorn; the daughter of Jerusalem hath shaken her head at thee.

23Whom hast thou reproached and blasphemed? and against whom hast thou exalted *thy* voice, and lifted up thine eyes on high? *even* against the Holy One of Israel.

24By thy servants hast thou reproached the Lord, and hast said, By the multitude of my chariots am I come up to the height of the mountains, to the sides of Lebanon; and I will cut down the tall cedars thereof, *and* the choice fir trees thereof: and I will enter into the height of his border, *and* the forest of his Carmel.

25I have digged, and drunk water; and with the sole of my feet have I dried up all the rivers of the besieged places.

26Hast thou not heard long ago, *how* I have done it; *and* of ancient times, that I have formed it? now have I brought it to pass, that thou shouldest be to lay waste defenced cities *into* ruinous heaps.

27Therefore their inhabitants *were* of small power, they were dismayed and confounded: they were *as* the grass of the field, and *as* the green herb, *as* the grass on the housetops, and *as corn* blasted before it be grown up.

28But I know thy abode, and thy going out, and thy coming in, and thy rage against me.

29Because thy rage against me, and thy tumult, is come up into mine ears, therefore will I put my hook in thy nose, and my bridle in thy lips, and I will turn thee back by the way by which thou camest.

30And this *shall be* a sign unto thee, Ye shall eat *this* year such as groweth of itself; and the second year that which springeth of the same: and in the third year sow ye, and reap, and plant vineyards, and eat the fruit thereof.

31And the remnant that is escaped of the house of Judah shall again take root downward, and bear fruit upward:

32For out of Jerusalem shall go forth a remnant, and they that escape out of mount Zion: the zeal of the Lord of hosts shall do this.

33Therefore thus saith the Lord concerning the king of Assyria, He shall not come into this city, nor shoot an arrow there, nor come before it with shields, nor cast a bank against it.

34By the way that he came, by the same shall he return, and shall not come into this city, saith the Lord.

35For I will defend this city to save it for mine own sake, and for my servant David's sake.

36Then the angel of the Lord went forth, and smote in the camp of the Assyrians a hundred and fourscore and five thousand: and when they arose early in the morning, behold, they *were* all dead corpses.

37So Sennacherib king of Assyria departed, and went and returned, and dwelt at Nineveh.

38And it came to pass, as he was worshipping in the house of Nisroch his god, that Adrammelech and Sharezer his sons smote him with the sword; and they escaped into the land of Armenia: and Esar-haddon his son reigned in his stead.

In those days was Hezekiah sick unto death. And Isaiah the prophet the son of Amoz came unto him, and said unto him, Thus saith the Lord, Set thine house in order: for thou shalt die, and not live.

2Then Hezekiah turned his face toward the wall, and prayed unto the Lord,

3And said, Remember now, O Lord, I beseech thee, how I have walked before thee in truth and with a perfect heart, and have done *that which is* good in thy sight. And Hezekiah wept sore.

4Then came the word of the LORD to Isaiah, saying,

5Go, and say to Hezekiah, Thus saith the LORD, the God of David thy father, I have heard thy prayer, I have seen thy tears: behold, I will add unto thy days fifteen years.

6And I will deliver thee and this city out of the hand of the king of Assyria: and I will defend this city.

7And this *shall be* a sign unto thee from the LORD, that the LORD will do this thing that he hath spoken;

8Behold, I will bring again the shadow of the degrees, which is gone down in the sun dial of Ahaz, ten degrees backward. So the sun returned ten degrees, by which degrees it was gone down.

9The writing of Hezekiah king of Judah, when he had been sick, and was recovered of his sickness:

10I said in the cutting off of my days, I shall go to the gates of the grave: I am deprived of the residue of my years.

11I said, I shall not see the LORD, *even* the LORD, in the land of the living: I shall behold man no more with the inhabitants of the world.

12Mine age is departed, and is removed from me as a shepherd's tent: I have cut off like a weaver my life: he will cut me off with pining sickness: from day *even* to night wilt thou make an end of me.

13I reckoned till morning, *that,* as a lion, so will he break all my bones: from day *even* to night wilt thou make an end of me.

14Like a crane *or* a swallow, so did I chatter: I did mourn as a dove: mine eyes fail *with looking* upward: O LORD, I am oppressed; undertake for me.

15What shall I say? he hath both spoken unto me, and himself hath done *it:* I shall go softly all my years in the bitterness of my soul.

16O Lord, by these *things men* live, and in all these *things is* the life of my spirit: so wilt thou recover me, and make me to live.

17Behold, for peace I had great bitterness: but thou hast in love to my soul *delivered it* from the pit of corruption: for thou hast cast all my sins behind thy back.

18For the grave cannot praise thee, death can *not* celebrate thee: they that go down into the pit cannot hope for thy truth.

19The living, the living, he shall praise thee, as I *do* this day: the father to the children shall make known thy truth.

20The LORD *was ready* to save me: therefore we will sing my songs to the stringed instruments all the days of our life in the house of the LORD.

21For Isaiah had said, Let them take a lump of figs, and lay *it* for a plaister upon the boil, and he shall recover.

22Hezekiah also had said, What *is* the sign that I shall go up to the house of the LORD?

GALATIANS 6:1–18

BRETHREN, if a man be overtaken in a fault, ye which are spiritual, restore such an one in the spirit of meekness; considering thyself, lest thou also be tempted.

2Bear ye one another's burdens, and so fulfil the law of Christ.

3For if a man think himself to be something, when he is nothing, he deceiveth himself.

4But let every man prove his own work, and then shall he have rejoicing in himself alone, and not in another.

5For every man shall bear his own burden.

6Let him that is taught in the word communicate unto him that teacheth in all good things.

7Be not deceived; God is not mocked: for whatsoever a man soweth, that shall he also reap.

8For he that soweth to his flesh shall of the flesh reap corruption; but he that soweth to the Spirit shall of the Spirit reap life everlasting.

9And let us not be weary in well doing: for in due season we shall reap, if we faint not.

10As we have therefore opportunity, let us do good unto all *men,* especially unto them who are of the household of faith.

11Ye see how large a letter I have written unto you with mine own hand.

12As many as desire to make a fair shew in the flesh, they constrain you to be circumcised; only lest they should suffer persecution for the cross of Christ.

13For neither they themselves who are circumcised keep the law; but desire to have you circumcised, that they may glory in your flesh.

14But God forbid that I should glory, save in the cross of our Lord Jesus Christ, by whom the world is crucified unto me, and I unto the world.

15For in Christ Jesus neither circumcision availeth any thing, nor uncircumcision, but a new creature.

16And as many as walk according to this rule, peace *be* on them, and mercy, and upon the Israel of God.

17From henceforth let no man trouble me: for I bear in my body the marks of the Lord Jesus.

18Brethren, the grace of our Lord Jesus Christ *be* with your spirit. Amen.

PSALM 65:1–13

Praise waiteth for thee, O God, in Sion: and unto thee shall the vow be performed.

2O thou that hearest prayer, unto thee shall all flesh come.

3Iniquities prevail against me: *as for* our transgressions, thou shalt purge them away.

4Blessed *is the man whom* thou choosest, and causest to approach *unto thee, that* he may dwell in thy courts: we shall be satisfied with the goodness of thy house, *even* of thy holy temple.

5*By* terrible things in righteousness wilt thou answer us, O God of our salvation; *who art* the confidence of all the ends of the earth, and of them that are afar off *upon* the sea:

6Which by his strength setteth fast the mountains; *being* girded with power:

7Which stilleth the noise of the seas, the noise of their waves, and the tumult of the people.

8They also that dwell in the uttermost parts are afraid at thy tokens: thou makest the outgoings of the morning and evening to rejoice.

9Thou visitest the earth, and waterest it: thou greatly enrichest it with the river of God, *which* is full of water: thou preparest them corn, when thou hast so provided for it.

10Thou waterest the ridges thereof abundantly: thou settlest the furrows thereof: thou makest it soft with showers: thou blessest the springing thereof.

11Thou crownest the year with thy goodness; and thy paths drop fatness.

12They drop *upon* the pastures of the wilderness: and the little hills rejoice on every side.

13The pastures are clothed with flocks; the valleys also are covered over with corn; they shout for joy, they also sing.

PROVERBS FOR TODAY/ 23:24–25

The father of the righteous shall greatly rejoice: and he that begetteth a wise child *shall have joy of him. Thy father and thy mother shall be glad, and she that bare thee shall rejoice.*

SEPTEMBER 22

ISAIAH 39:1—41:16

A T that time Merodach–baladan, the son of Baladan, king of Babylon, sent letters and a present to Hezekiah: for he had heard that he had been sick, and was recovered.

2And Hezekiah was glad of them, and shewed them the house of his precious things, the silver, and the gold, and the spices, and the precious ointment, and all the house of his armour, and all that was found in his treasures: there was nothing in his house, nor in all his dominion, that Hezekiah shewed them not.

3Then came Isaiah the prophet unto king Hezekiah, and said unto him, What said these men? and from whence came they unto thee? And Hezekiah said, They are come from a far country unto me, *even* from Babylon.

4Then said he, What have they seen in thine house? And Hezekiah answered, All that *is* in mine house have they seen: there is nothing among my treasures that I have not shewed them.

5Then said Isaiah to Hezekiah, Hear the word of the LORD of hosts:

6Behold, the days come, that all that *is* in thine house, and *that* which thy fathers have laid up in store until this day, shall be carried to Babylon: nothing shall be left, saith the LORD.

7And of thy sons that shall issue from thee, which thou shalt beget, shall they take away; and they shall be eunuchs in the palace of the king of Babylon.

8Then said Hezekiah to Isaiah, Good *is* the word of the LORD which thou hast spoken. He said moreover, For there shall be peace and truth in my days.

COMFORT ye, comfort ye my people, saith your God.

2Speak ye comfortably to Jerusalem, and cry unto her, that her warfare is accomplished, that her iniquity is pardoned: for she hath received of the LORD's hand double for all her sins.

3The voice of him that crieth in the wilderness, Prepare ye the way of the LORD, make straight in the desert a highway for our God.

4Every valley shall be exalted, and every mountain and hill shall be made low: and the crooked shall be made straight, and the rough places plain:

5And the glory of the LORD shall be revealed, and all flesh shall see *it* together: for the mouth of the LORD hath spoken *it.*

6The voice said, Cry. And he said, What shall I cry? All flesh *is* grass, and all the goodliness thereof *is* as the flower of the field:

7The grass withereth, the flower fadeth: because the spirit of the LORD bloweth upon it: surely the people *is* grass.

8The grass withereth, the flower fadeth: but the word of our God shall stand for ever.

9O Zion, that bringest good tidings, get thee up into the high mountain; O Jerusalem, that bringest good tidings, lift up thy voice with strength; lift *it* up, be not afraid; say unto the cities of Judah, Behold your God!

10Behold, the Lord GOD will come with strong *hand,* and his arm shall rule for him: behold, his reward *is* with him, and his work before him.

11He shall feed his flock like a shepherd: he shall gather the lambs with his arm, and carry *them* in his bosom, *and* shall gently lead those that are with young.

12Who hath measured the waters in the hollow of his hand, and meted out heaven with the span, and comprehended the dust of the earth in a measure, and weighed the mountains in scales, and the hills in a balance?

13Who hath directed the Spirit of the LORD, or *being* his counsellor hath taught him?

14With whom took he counsel, and *who* instructed him, and taught him in the path of judgment, and taught him knowledge, and shewed to him the way of understanding?

15Behold, the nations *are* as a drop of a bucket, and are counted as the small dust of the balance: behold, he taketh up the isles as a very little thing.

16And Lebanon *is* not sufficient to burn, nor the beasts thereof sufficient for a burnt offering.

17All nations before him *are* as nothing; and they are counted to him less than nothing, and vanity.

18To whom then will ye liken God? or what likeness will ye compare unto him?

19The workman melteth a graven image, and the goldsmith spreadeth it over with gold, and casteth silver chains.

20He that *is* so impoverished that he hath no oblation chooseth a tree *that* will not rot; he seeketh unto him a cunning workman to prepare a graven image, *that* shall not be moved.

21Have ye not known? have ye not heard? hath it not been told you from the beginning? have ye not understood from the foundations of the earth?

22*It is* he that sitteth upon the circle of the earth, and the inhabitants thereof *are* as grasshoppers; that stretcheth out the heavens as a curtain, and spreadeth them out as a tent to dwell in:

23That bringeth the princes to nothing; he maketh the judges of the earth as vanity.

24Yea, they shall not be planted; yea, they shall not be sown: yea, their stock shall not take root in the earth: and he shall also blow upon them, and they shall wither, and the whirlwind shall take them away as stubble.

25To whom then will ye liken me, or shall I be equal? saith the Holy One.

26Lift up your eyes on high, and behold who hath created these *things,* that bringeth out their host by number: he calleth them all by names by the greatness of his might, for that *he is* strong in power; not one faileth.

27Why sayest thou, O Jacob, and speakest, O Israel, My way is hid from the LORD, and my judgment is passed over from my God?

28Hast thou not known? hast thou not heard, *that* the everlasting God, the LORD, the Creator of the ends of the earth, fainteth not, neither is weary? *there is* no searching of his understanding.

29He giveth power to the faint; and to *them that have* no might he increaseth strength.

30Even the youths shall faint and be weary, and the young men shall utterly fall:

31But they that wait upon the LORD shall renew their strength; they shall mount up with wings as eagles; they shall run, and not be weary; *and* they shall walk, and not faint.

KEEP silence before me, O islands; and let the people renew *their* strength: let them come near; then let them speak: let us come near together to judgment.

2Who raised up the righteous *man* from the east, called him to his foot, gave the nations before him, and made *him* rule over kings? he gave *them* as the dust to his sword, *and* as driven stubble to his bow.

3He pursued them, *and* passed safely; *even* by the way *that* he had not gone with his feet.

4Who hath wrought and done *it,* calling the generations from the beginning? I the LORD, the first, and with the last; I *am* he.

5The isles saw *it,* and feared; the ends of the earth were afraid, drew near, and came.

6They helped every one his neighbour; and *every one* said to his brother, Be of good courage.

7So the carpenter encouraged the goldsmith, *and* he that smootheth *with* the hammer him that smote the anvil, saying, It *is* ready for the sodering: and he fastened it with nails, *that it* should not be moved.

8But thou, Israel, *art* my servant, Jacob whom I have chosen, the seed of Abraham my friend.

9*Thou* whom I have taken from the ends of the earth, and called thee from the chief men thereof, and said unto thee, Thou *art* my servant; I have chosen thee, and not cast thee away.

10Fear thou not; for I *am* with thee: be not dismayed; for I *am* thy God: I will strengthen thee; yea, I will help thee; yea, I will uphold thee with the right hand of my righteousness.

11Behold, all they that were incensed against thee shall be ashamed and confounded: they shall be as nothing; and they that strive with thee shall perish.

12Thou shalt seek them, and shalt not find them, *even* them that contended with thee: they that war against thee shall be as nothing, and as a thing of nought.

13For I the LORD thy God will hold thy right hand, saying unto thee, Fear not; I will help thee.

14Fear not, thou worm Jacob, *and* ye men of Israel; I will help thee, saith the LORD, and thy redeemer, the Holy One of Israel.

15Behold, I will make thee a new sharp threshing instrument having teeth: thou shalt thresh the mountains, and beat *them* small, and shalt make the hills as chaff.

16Thou shalt fan them, and the wind shall carry them away, and the whirl-wind shall scatter them: and thou shalt rejoice in the LORD, *and* shalt glory in the Holy One of Israel.

EPHESIANS 1:1–23

PAUL, an apostle of Jesus Christ by the will of God, to the saints which are at Ephesus, and to the faithful in Christ Jesus:

2Grace *be* to you, and peace, from God our Father, and *from* the Lord Jesus Christ.

3Blessed *be* the God and Father of our Lord Jesus Christ, who hath blessed us with all spiritual blessings in heavenly *places* in Christ:

4According as he hath chosen us in him before the foundation of the world, that we should be holy and without blame before him in love:

5Having predestinated us unto the adoption of children by Jesus Christ to himself, according to the good pleasure of his will,

6To the praise of the glory of his grace, wherein he hath made us accepted in the beloved.

7In whom we have redemption through his blood, the forgiveness of sins, according to the riches of his grace;

8Wherein he hath abounded toward us in all wisdom and prudence;

9Having made known unto us the mystery of his will, according to his good pleasure which he hath purposed in himself:

10That in the dispensation of the fulness of times he might gather together in one all things in Christ, both which are in heaven, and which are on earth; *even* in him:

11In whom also we have obtained an inheritance, being predestinated according to the purpose of him who worketh all things after the counsel of his own will:

12That we should be to the praise

of his glory, who first trusted in Christ.

13In whom ye also *trusted,* after that ye heard the word of truth, the gospel of your salvation: in whom also after that ye believed, ye were sealed with that holy Spirit of promise,

14Which is the earnest of our inheritance until the redemption of the purchased possession, unto the praise of his glory.

15Wherefore I also, after I heard of your faith in the Lord Jesus, and love unto all the saints,

16Cease not to give thanks for you, making mention of you in my prayers,

17That the God of our Lord Jesus Christ, the Father of glory, may give unto you the spirit of wisdom and revelation in the knowledge of him:

18The eyes of your understanding being enlightened; that ye may know what is the hope of his calling, and what the riches of the glory of his inheritance in the saints,

19And what *is* the exceeding greatness of his power to us-ward who believe, according to the working of his mighty power,

20Which he wrought in Christ, when he raised him from the dead, and set *him* at his own right hand in the heavenly *places,*

21Far above all principality, and power, and might, and dominion, and every name that is named, not only in this world, but also in that which is to come:

22And hath put all *things* under his feet, and gave him *to be* the head over all *things* to the church,

23Which is his body, the fulness of him that filleth all in all.

PSALM 66:1–20

MAKE a joyful noise unto God, all ye lands:
2Sing forth the honour of his name: make his praise glorious.

3Say unto God, How terrible *art thou in* thy works! through the greatness of thy power shall thine enemies submit themselves unto thee.

4All the earth shall worship thee, and shall sing unto thee; they shall sing *to* thy name. Selah.

5Come and see the works of God: *he is* terrible *in his* doing toward the children of men.

6He turned the sea into dry *land:* they went through the flood on foot: there did we rejoice in him.

7He ruleth by his power for ever; his eyes behold the nations: let not the rebellious exalt themselves. Selah.

8O bless our God, ye people, and make the voice of his praise to be heard:

9Which holdeth our soul in life, and suffereth not our feet to be moved.

10For thou, O God, hast proved us: thou hast tried us, as silver is tried.

11Thou broughtest us into the net; thou laidst affliction upon our loins.

12Thou hast caused men to ride over our heads; we went through fire and through water: but thou broughtest us out into a wealthy *place.*

13I will go into thy house with burnt offerings: I will pay thee my vows,

14Which my lips have uttered, and my mouth hath spoken, when I was in trouble.

15I will offer unto thee burnt sacrifices of fatlings, with the incense of rams; I will offer bullocks with goats. Selah.

16Come *and* hear, all ye that fear God, and I will declare what he hath done for my soul.

17I cried unto him with my mouth, and he was extolled with my tongue.

18If I regard iniquity in my heart, the Lord will not hear *me:*

19*But* verily God hath heard *me;* he hath attended to the voice of my prayer.

20Blessed *be* God, which hath not turned away my prayer, nor his mercy from me.

PROVERBS FOR TODAY/ 23:26–28

My son, give me thine heart, and let thine eyes observe my ways. For a whore is *a deep ditch; and a strange woman* is *a narrow pit. She also lieth in wait as* for *a prey, and increaseth the transgressors among men.*

SEPTEMBER 23

ISAIAH 41:17—43:13

WHEN the poor and needy seek water, and *there is* none, *and* their tongue faileth for thirst, I the LORD will hear them, I the God of Israel will not forsake them.

18I will open rivers in high places, and fountains in the midst of the valleys: I will make the wilderness a pool of water, and the dry land springs of water.

19I will plant in the wilderness the cedar, the shittah tree, and the myrtle, and the oil tree; I will set in the desert the fir tree, *and* the pine, and the box tree together:

20That they may see, and know, and consider, and understand together, that the hand of the LORD hath done this, and the Holy One of Israel hath created it.

21Produce your cause, saith the LORD; bring forth your strong *reasons,* saith the King of Jacob.

22Let them bring *them* forth, and shew us what shall happen: let them shew the former things, what they *be,* that we may consider them, and know the latter end of them; or declare us things for to come.

23Shew the things that are to come hereafter, that we may know that ye *are* gods: yea, do good, or do evil, that we may be dismayed, and behold *it* together.

24Behold, ye *are* of nothing, and your work of nought: an abomination *is he that* chooseth you.

25I have raised up *one* from the north, and he shall come: from the rising of the sun shall he call upon my name: and he shall come upon princes as *upon* morter, and as the potter treadeth clay.

26Who hath declared from the beginning, that we may know? and before-time, that we may say, *He is* righteous? yea, *there is* none that sheweth, yea, *there is* none that declareth, yea, *there is* none that heareth your words.

27The first *shall say* to Zion, Behold, behold them: and I will give to Jerusalem one that bringeth good tidings.

28For I beheld, and *there was* no man; even among them, and *there was* no counsellor, that, when I asked of them, could answer a word.

29Behold, they *are* all vanity; their works *are* nothing: their molten images *are* wind and confusion.

BEHOLD my servant, whom I uphold; mine elect, *in whom* my soul delighteth; I have put my spirit upon him: he shall bring forth judgment to the Gentiles.

2He shall not cry, nor lift up, nor cause his voice to be heard in the street.

3A bruised reed shall he not break, and the smoking flax shall he not quench: he shall bring forth judgment unto truth.

4He shall not fail nor be discouraged, till he have set judgment in the earth: and the isles shall wait for his law.

5Thus saith God the LORD, he that created the heavens, and stretched them out; he that spread forth the earth, and that which cometh out of it; he that giveth breath unto the people upon it, and spirit to them that walk therein:

6I the LORD have called thee in righteousness, and will hold thine hand, and will keep thee, and give thee for a covenant of the people, for a light of the Gentiles;

7To open the blind eyes, to bring out the prisoners from the prison, *and* them that sit in darkness out of the prison house.

8I am the LORD: that *is* my name: and my glory will I not give to another, neither my praise to graven images.

9Behold, the former things are come to pass, and new things do I declare: before they spring forth I tell you of them.

10Sing unto the LORD a new song, *and* his praise from the end of the earth, ye that go down to the sea, and all that is therein; the isles, and the inhabitants thereof.

11Let the wilderness and the cities thereof lift up *their voice,* the villages *that* Kedar doth inhabit: let the inhabitants of the rock sing, let them shout from the top of the mountains.

12Let them give glory unto the LORD, and declare his praise in the islands.

13The LORD shall go forth as a mighty man, he shall stir up jealousy like a man of war: he shall cry, yea, roar; he shall prevail against his enemies.

14I have long time holden my peace; I have been still, *and* refrained myself: *now* will I cry like a travailing woman; I will destroy and devour at once.

15I will make waste mountains and hills, and dry up all their herbs; and I will make the rivers islands, and I will dry up the pools.

16And I will bring the blind by a way *that* they knew not; I will lead them in paths *that* they have not known: I will make darkness light before them, and crooked things straight. These

things will I do unto them, and not forsake them.

17They shall be turned back, they shall be greatly ashamed, that trust in graven images, that say to the molten images, Ye *are* our gods.

18Hear, ye deaf; and look, ye blind, that ye may see.

19Who *is* blind, but my servant? or deaf, as my messenger *that* I sent? who *is* blind as *he that is* perfect, and blind as the LORD'S servant?

20Seeing many things, but thou observest not; opening the ears, but he heareth not.

21The LORD is well pleased for his righteousness' sake; he will magnify the law, and make *it* honourable.

22But this *is* a people robbed and spoiled; *they are* all of them snared in holes, and they are hid in prison houses: they are for a prey, and none delivereth; for a spoil, and none saith, Restore.

23Who among you will give ear to this? *who* will hearken and hear for the time to come?

24Who gave Jacob for a spoil, and Israel to the robbers? did not the LORD, he against whom we have sinned? for they would not walk in his ways, neither were they obedient unto his law.

25Therefore he hath poured upon him the fury of his anger, and the strength of battle: and it hath set him on fire round about, yet he knew not; and it burned him, yet he laid *it* not to heart.

BUT now thus saith the LORD that created thee, O Jacob, and he that formed thee, O Israel, Fear not: for I have redeemed thee, I have called *thee* by thy name; thou *art* mine.

2When thou passest through the waters, I *will be* with thee; and through the rivers, they shall not overflow thee: when thou walkest through the fire, thou shalt not be burned; neither shall the flame kindle upon thee.

3For I *am* the LORD thy God, the Holy One of Israel, thy Saviour: I gave

Egypt *for* thy ransom, Ethiopia and Seba for thee.

4Since thou wast precious in my sight, thou hast been honourable, and I have loved thee: therefore will I give men for thee, and people for thy life.

5Fear not: for I *am* with thee: I will bring thy seed from the east, and gather thee from the west;

6I will say to the north, Give up; and to the south, Keep not back: bring my sons from far, and my daughters from the ends of the earth;

7*Even* every one that is called by my name: for I have created him for my glory, I have formed him; yea, I have made him.

8Bring forth the blind people that have eyes, and the deaf that have ears.

9Let all the nations be gathered together, and let the people be assembled: who among them can declare this, and shew us former things? let them bring forth their witnesses, that they may be justified: or let them hear, and say, *It is* truth.

10Ye *are* my witnesses, saith the LORD, and my servant whom I have chosen; that ye may know and believe me, and understand that I *am* he: before me there was no God formed, neither shall there be after me.

11I, *even* I, *am* the LORD; and beside me *there is* no saviour.

12I have declared, and have saved, and I have shewed, when *there was* no strange *god* among you: therefore ye *are* my witnesses, saith the LORD, that I *am* God.

13Yea, before the day *was* I *am* he; and *there is* none that can deliver out of my hand: I will work, and who shall let it?

EPHESIANS 2:1–22

A ND you *hath he quickened,* who were dead in trespasses and sins;

2Wherein in time past ye walked according to the course of this world, according to the prince of the power of the air, the spirit that now worketh in the children of disobedience:

3Among whom also we all had our conversation in times past in the lusts of our flesh, fulfilling the desires of the flesh and of the mind; and were by nature the children of wrath, even as others.

4But God, who is rich in mercy, for his great love wherewith he loved us,

5Even when we were dead in sins, hath quickened us together with Christ, (by grace ye are saved;)

6And hath raised *us* up together, and made *us* sit together in heavenly *places* in Christ Jesus:

7That in the ages to come he might shew the exceeding riches of his grace in *his* kindness toward us through Christ Jesus.

8For by grace are ye saved through faith; and that not of yourselves: *it is* the gift of God:

9Not of works, lest any man should boast.

10For we are his workmanship, created in Christ Jesus unto good works, which God hath before ordained that we should walk in them.

11Wherefore remember, that ye *being* in time past Gentiles in the flesh, who are called Uncircumcision by that which is called the Circumcision in the flesh made by hands;

12That at that time ye were without Christ, being aliens from the commonwealth of Israel, and strangers from the covenants of promise, having no hope, and without God in the world:

13But now in Christ Jesus ye who sometimes were far off are made nigh by the blood of Christ.

14For he is our peace, who hath made both one, and hath broken down the middle wall of partition *between us;*

15Having abolished in his flesh the

enmity, *even* the law of commandments *contained* in ordinances; for to make in himself of twain one new man, *so* making peace;

16And that he might reconcile both unto God in one body by the cross, having slain the enmity thereby:

17And came and preached peace to you which were afar off, and to them that were nigh.

18For through him we both have access by one Spirit unto the Father.

19Now therefore ye are no more strangers and foreigners, but fellow-citizens with the saints, and of the household of God;

20And are built upon the foundation of the apostles and prophets, Jesus Christ himself being the chief corner *stone;*

21In whom all the building fitly framed together groweth unto an holy temple in the Lord:

22In whom ye also are builded together for an habitation of God through the Spirit.

PSALM 67:1–7

GOD be merciful unto us, and bless us; *and* cause his face to shine upon us; Selah.

2That thy way may be known upon earth, thy saving health among all nations.

3Let the people praise thee, O God; let all the people praise thee.

4O let the nations be glad and sing for joy: for thou shalt judge the people righteously, and govern the nations upon earth. Selah.

5Let the people praise thee, O God; let all the people praise thee.

6*Then* shall the earth yield her increase; *and* God, *even* our own God, shall bless us.

7God shall bless us; and all the ends of the earth shall fear him.

PROVERBS FOR TODAY/ 23:29–35

Who hath woe? who hath sorrow? who hath contentions? who hath babbling? who hath wounds without cause? who hath redness of eyes? They that tarry long at the wine; they that go to seek mixed wine. Look not thou upon the wine when it is red, when it giveth his colour in the cup, when it moveth itself aright. At the last it biteth like a serpent, and stingeth like an adder. Thine eyes shall behold strange women, and thine heart shall utter perverse things. Yea, thou shalt be as he that lieth down in the midst of the sea, or as he that lieth upon the top of a mast. They have stricken me, shalt thou say, and I was not sick; they have beaten me, and I felt it not: when shall I awake? I will seek it yet again.

SEPTEMBER 24

ISAIAH 43:14—45:10

THUS saith the LORD, your redeemer, the Holy One of Israel; For your sake I have sent to Babylon, and have brought down all their nobles, and the Chaldeans, whose cry *is* in the ships.

15I *am* the LORD, your Holy One, the creator of Israel, your King.

16Thus saith the LORD, which maketh

a way in the sea, and a path in the mighty waters;

17Which bringeth forth the chariot and horse, the army and the power; they shall lie down together, they shall not rise: they are extinct, they are quenched as tow.

18Remember ye not the former things, neither consider the things of old.

19Behold, I will do a new thing; now it shall spring forth; shall ye not know it? I will even make a way in the wilderness, *and* rivers in the desert.

20The beast of the field shall honour me, the dragons and the owls: because I give waters in the wilderness, *and* rivers in the desert, to give drink to my people, my chosen.

21This people have I formed for myself; they shall shew forth my praise.

22But thou hast not called upon me, O Jacob; but thou hast been weary of me, O Israel.

23Thou hast not brought me the small cattle of thy burnt offerings; neither hast thou honoured me with thy sacrifices. I have not caused thee to serve with an offering, nor wearied thee with incense.

24Thou hast bought me no sweet cane with money, neither hast thou filled me with the fat of thy sacrifices: but thou hast made me to serve with thy sins, thou hast wearied me with thine iniquities.

25I, *even* I, *am* he that blotteth out thy transgressions for mine own sake, and will not remember thy sins.

26Put me in remembrance: let us plead together: declare thou, that thou mayest be justified.

27Thy first father hath sinned, and thy teachers have transgressed against me.

28Therefore I have profaned the princes of the sanctuary, and have given Jacob to the curse, and Israel to reproaches.

YET now hear, O Jacob my servant; and Israel, whom I have chosen:

2Thus saith the LORD that made thee, and formed thee from the womb, *which* will help thee; Fear not, O Jacob, my servant; and thou, Jesurun, whom I have chosen.

3For I will pour water upon him that is thirsty, and floods upon the dry ground: I will pour my spirit upon thy seed, and my blessing upon thine offspring:

4And they shall spring up *as* among the grass, as willows by the water courses.

5One shall say, I *am* the LORD's; and another shall call *himself* by the name of Jacob; and another shall subscribe *with* his hand unto the LORD, and surname *himself* by the name of Israel.

6Thus saith the LORD the King of Israel, and his redeemer the LORD of hosts; I *am* the first, and I am the last; and beside me *there is* no God.

7And who, as I, shall call, and shall declare it, and set it in order for me, since I appointed the ancient people? and the things that are coming, and shall come, let them shew unto them.

8Fear ye not, neither be afraid: have not I told thee from that time, and have declared *it?* ye *are* even my witnesses. Is there a God beside me? yea, *there is* no God; I know not *any.*

9They that make a graven image *are* all of them vanity; and their delectable things shall not profit; and they *are* their own witnesses; they see not, nor know; that they may be ashamed.

10Who hath formed a god, or molten a graven image *that* is profitable for nothing?

11Behold, all his fellows shall be ashamed: and the workmen, they *are* of men: let them all be gathered together, let them stand up; *yet* they shall fear, *and* they shall be ashamed together.

12The smith with the tongs both worketh in the coals, and fashioneth it with hammers, and worketh it with the strength of his arms: yea, he is hungry, and his strength faileth: he drinketh no water, and is faint.

¹³The carpenter stretcheth out *his* rule; he marketh it out with a line; he fitteth it with planes, and he marketh it out with the compass, and maketh it after the figure of a man, according to the beauty of a man; that it may remain in the house.

¹⁴He heweth him down cedars, and taketh the cypress and the oak, which he strengtheneth for himself among the trees of the forest: he planteth an ash, and the rain doth nourish *it*.

¹⁵Then shall it be for a man to burn: for he will take thereof, and warm himself; yea, he kindleth *it*, and baketh bread; yea, he maketh a god, and worshippeth *it*; he maketh it a graven image, and falleth down thereto.

¹⁶He burneth part thereof in the fire; with part thereof he eateth flesh; he roasteth roast, and is satisfied: yea, he warmeth *himself*, and saith, Aha, I am warm, I have seen the fire:

¹⁷And the residue thereof he maketh a god, *even* his graven image: he falleth down unto it, and worshippeth *it*, and prayeth unto it, and saith, Deliver me; for thou *art* my god.

¹⁸They have not known nor understood: for he hath shut their eyes, that they cannot see; *and* their hearts, that they cannot understand.

¹⁹And none considereth in his heart, neither *is there* knowledge nor understanding to say, I have burned part of it in the fire; yea, also I have baked bread upon the coals thereof; I have roasted flesh, and eaten *it*: and shall I make the residue thereof an abomination? shall I fall down to the stock of a tree?

²⁰He feedeth on ashes: a deceived heart hath turned him aside, that he cannot deliver his soul, nor say, *Is there* not a lie in my right hand?

²¹Remember these, O Jacob and Israel; for thou *art* my servant: I have formed thee; thou *art* my servant: O Israel, thou shalt not be forgotten of me.

²²I have blotted out, as a thick cloud, thy transgressions, and, as a cloud, thy sins: return unto me; for I have redeemed thee.

²³Sing, O ye heavens; for the LORD hath done *it*: shout, ye lower parts of the earth: break forth into singing, ye mountains, O forest, and every tree therein: for the LORD hath redeemed Jacob, and glorified himself in Israel.

²⁴Thus saith the LORD, thy redeemer, and he that formed thee from the womb, I *am* the LORD that maketh all *things*; that stretcheth forth the heavens alone; that spreadeth abroad the earth by myself;

²⁵That frustrateth the tokens of the liars, and maketh diviners mad; that turneth wise *men* backward, and maketh their knowledge foolish;

²⁶That confirmeth the word of his servant, and performeth the counsel of his messengers; that saith to Jerusalem, Thou shalt be inhabited; and to the cities of Judah, Ye shall be built, and I will raise up the decayed places thereof:

²⁷That saith to the deep, Be dry, and I will dry up thy rivers:

²⁸That saith of Cyrus, *He is* my shepherd, and shall perform all my pleasure: even saying to Jerusalem, Thou shalt be built; and to the temple, Thy foundation shall be laid.

THUS saith the LORD to his anointed, to Cyrus, whose right hand I have holden, to subdue nations before him; and I will loose the loins of kings, to open before him the two leaved gates; and the gates shall not be shut;

²I will go before thee, and make the crooked places straight: I will break in pieces the gates of brass, and cut in sunder the bars of iron:

³And I will give thee the treasures

of darkness, and hidden riches of secret places, that thou mayest know that I, the LORD, which call *thee* by thy name, *am* the God of Israel.

4For Jacob my servant's sake, and Israel mine elect, I have even called thee by thy name: I have surnamed thee, though thou hast not known me.

5I *am* the LORD, and *there is* none else, *there is* no God beside me: I girded thee, though thou hast not known me:

6That they may know from the rising of the sun, and from the west, that *there is* none beside me. I *am* the LORD, and *there is* none else.

7I form the light, and create darkness: I make peace, and create evil: I the LORD do all these *things*.

8Drop down, ye heavens, from above, and let the skies pour down righteousness: let the earth open, and let them bring forth salvation, and let righteousness spring up together; I the LORD have created it.

9Woe unto him that striveth with his Maker! *Let* the potsherd *strive* with the potsherds of the earth. Shall the clay say to him that fashioneth it, What makest thou? or thy work, He hath no hands?

10Woe unto him that saith unto *his* father, What begettest thou? or to the woman, What hast thou brought forth?

EPHESIANS 3:1–21

FOR this cause I Paul, the prisoner of Jesus Christ for you Gentiles,

2If ye have heard of the dispensation of the grace of God which is given me to you-ward:

3How that by revelation he made known unto me the mystery; (as I wrote afore in few words,

4Whereby, when ye read, ye may understand my knowledge in the mystery of Christ)

5Which in other ages was not made known unto the sons of men, as it is now revealed unto his holy apostles and prophets by the Spirit;

6That the Gentiles should be fellow-heirs, and of the same body, and partakers of his promise in Christ by the gospel:

7Whereof I was made a minister, according to the gift of the grace of God given unto me by the effectual working of his power.

8Unto me, who am less than the least of all saints, is this grace given, that I should preach among the Gentiles the unsearchable riches of Christ;

9And to make all *men* see what *is* the fellowship of the mystery, which from the beginning of the world hath been hid in God, who created all things by Jesus Christ:

10To the intent that now unto the principalities and powers in heavenly *places* might be known by the church the manifold wisdom of God,

11According to the eternal purpose which he purposed in Christ Jesus our Lord:

12In whom we have boldness and access with confidence by the faith of him.

13Wherefore I desire that ye faint not at my tribulations for you, which is your glory.

14For this cause I bow my knees unto the Father of our Lord Jesus Christ,

15Of whom the whole family in heaven and earth is named,

16That he would grant you, according to the riches of his glory, to be strengthened with might by his Spirit in the inner man;

17That Christ may dwell in your hearts by faith; that ye, being rooted and grounded in love,

18May be able to comprehend with all saints what *is* the breadth, and length, and depth, and height;

19And to know the love of Christ, which passeth knowledge, that ye might be filled with all the fulness of God.

20Now unto him that is able to do exceeding abundantly above all that we ask or think, according to the power that worketh in us,

21Unto him be glory in the church by Christ Jesus throughout all ages, world without end. Amen.

PSALM 68:1–18

Let God arise, let his enemies be scattered: let them also that hate him flee before him.

2As smoke is driven away, so drive them away: as wax melteth before the fire, so let the wicked perish at the presence of God.

3But let the righteous be glad; let them rejoice before God: yea, let them exceedingly rejoice.

4Sing unto God, sing praises to his name: extol him that rideth upon the heavens by his name JAH, and rejoice before him.

5A father of the fatherless, and a judge of the widows, is God in his holy habitation.

6God setteth the solitary in families: he bringeth out those which are bound with chains: but the rebellious dwell in a dry land.

7O God, when thou wentest forth before thy people, when thou didst march through the wilderness; Selah:

8The earth shook, the heavens also dropped at the presence of God: even Sinai itself was moved at the presence of God, the God of Israel.

9Thou, O God, didst send a plentiful rain, whereby thou didst confirm thine inheritance, when it was weary.

10Thy congregation hath dwelt therein: thou, O God, hast prepared of thy goodness for the poor.

11The Lord gave the word: great was the company of those that published it.

12Kings of armies did flee apace: and she that tarried at home divided the spoil.

13Though ye have lien among the pots, yet shall ye be as the wings of a dove covered with silver, and her feathers with yellow gold.

14When the Almighty scattered kings in it, it was white as snow in Salmon.

15The hill of God is as the hill of Bashan; an high hill as the hill of Bashan.

16Why leap ye, ye high hills? this is the hill which God desireth to dwell in; yea, the Lord will dwell in it for ever.

17The chariots of God are twenty thousand, even thousands of angels: the Lord is among them, as in Sinai, in the holy place.

18Thou hast ascended on high, thou hast led captivity captive: thou hast received gifts for men; yea, for the rebellious also, that the Lord God might dwell among them.

PROVERBS FOR TODAY/ 24:1–2

Be not thou envious against evil men, neither desire to be with them. For their heart studieth destruction, and their lips talk of mischief.

SEPTEMBER 25

THUS saith the LORD, the Holy One of Israel, and his Maker, Ask me of things to come concerning my sons, and concerning the work of my hands command ye me.

12I have made the earth, and created man upon it: I, *even* my hands, have stretched out the heavens, and all their host have I commanded.

13I have raised him up in righteousness, and I will direct all his ways: he shall build my city, and he shall let go my captives, not for price nor reward, saith the LORD of hosts.

14Thus saith the LORD, The labour of Egypt, and merchandise of Ethiopia and of the Sabeans, men of stature, shall come over unto thee, and they shall be thine: they shall come after thee; in chains they shall come over, and they shall fall down unto thee, they shall make supplication unto thee, *saying*, Surely God *is* in thee; and *there is* none else, *there is* no God.

15Verily thou *art* a God that hidest thyself, O God of Israel, the Saviour.

16They shall be ashamed, and also confounded, all of them: they shall go to confusion together *that are* makers of idols.

17*But* Israel shall be saved in the LORD with an everlasting salvation: ye shall not be ashamed nor confounded world without end.

18For thus saith the LORD that created the heavens; God himself that formed the earth and made it; he hath established it, he created it not in vain, he formed it to be inhabited: I *am* the LORD; and *there is* none else.

19I have not spoken in secret, in a dark place of the earth: I said not unto the seed of Jacob, Seek ye me in vain: I the LORD speak righteousness, I declare things that are right.

20Assemble yourselves and come; draw near together, ye *that are* escaped of the nations: they have no knowledge that set up the wood of their graven image, and pray unto a god *that* cannot save.

21Tell ye, and bring *them* near; yea, let them take counsel together: who hath declared this from ancient time? *who* hath told it from that time? *have* not I the LORD? and *there is* no God else beside me; a just God and a Saviour; *there is* none beside me.

22Look unto me, and be ye saved, all the ends of the earth: for I *am* God, and *there is* none else.

23I have sworn by myself, the word is gone out of my mouth *in* righteousness, and shall not return, That unto me every knee shall bow, every tongue shall swear.

24Surely, shall *one* say, in the LORD have I righteousness and strength: *even* to him shall *men* come; and all that are incensed against him shall be ashamed.

25In the LORD shall all the seed of Israel be justified, and shall glory.

BEL boweth down, Nebo stoopeth, their idols were upon the beasts, and upon the cattle: your carriages *were* heavy loaden; *they are* a burden to the weary *beast*.

2They stoop, they bow down together; they could not deliver the burden, but themselves are gone into captivity.

3Hearken unto me, O house of Jacob, and all the remnant of the house of Israel, which are borne *by me* from the belly, which are carried from the womb:

4And *even* to *your* old age I *am* he; and *even* to hoar hairs will I carry *you:*

I have made, and I will bear; even I will carry, and will deliver *you.*

5To whom will ye liken me, and make *me* equal, and compare me, that we may be like?

6They lavish gold out of the bag, and weigh silver in the balance, *and* hire a goldsmith; and he maketh it a god: they fall down, yea, they worship.

7They bear him upon the shoulder, they carry him, and set him in his place, and he standeth; from his place shall he not remove: yea, *one* shall cry unto him, yet can he not answer, nor save him out of his trouble.

8Remember this, and shew yourselves men: bring *it* again to mind, O ye transgressors.

9Remember the former things of old: for I *am* God, and *there is* none else; I *am* God, and *there is* none like me,

10Declaring the end from the beginning, and from ancient times *the things* that are not *yet* done, saying, My counsel shall stand, and I will do all my pleasure:

11Calling a ravenous bird from the east, the man that executeth my counsel from a far country: yea, I have spoken *it,* I will also bring it to pass; I have purposed *it,* I will also do it.

12Hearken unto me, ye stouthearted, that *are* far from righteousness:

13I bring near my righteousness: it shall not be far off, and my salvation shall not tarry: and I will place salvation in Zion for Israel my glory.

COME down, and sit in the dust, O virgin daughter of Babylon, sit on the ground: *there is* no throne, O daughter of the Chaldeans: for thou shalt no more be called tender and delicate.

2Take the millstones, and grind meal; uncover thy locks, make bare the leg, uncover the thigh, pass over the rivers.

3Thy nakedness shall be uncovered, yea, thy shame shall be seen: I will take vengeance, and I will not meet *thee as* a man.

4*As for* our redeemer, the LORD of hosts *is* his name, the Holy One of Israel.

5Sit thou silent, and get thee into darkness, O daughter of the Chaldeans: for thou shalt no more be called, The lady of kingdoms.

6I was wroth with my people, I have polluted mine inheritance, and given them into thine hand: thou didst shew them no mercy; upon the ancient hast thou very heavily laid thy yoke.

7And thou saidst, I shall be a lady for ever: so that thou didst not lay these *things* to thy heart, neither didst remember the latter end of it.

8Therefore hear now this, *thou that art* given to pleasures, that dwellest carelessly, that sayest in thine heart, I *am,* and none else beside me; I shall not sit *as* a widow, neither shall I know the loss of children:

9But these two *things* shall come to thee in a moment in one day, the loss of children, and widowhood: they shall come upon thee in their perfection for the multitude of thy sorceries, *and* for the great abundance of thine enchantments.

10For thou hast trusted in thy wickedness: thou hast said, None seeth me. Thy wisdom and thy knowledge, it hath perverted thee; and thou hast said in thine heart, I *am,* and none else beside me.

11Therefore shall evil come upon thee; thou shalt not know from whence it riseth: and mischief shall fall upon thee; thou shalt not be able to put it off: and desolation shall come upon thee suddenly, *which* thou shalt not know.

12Stand now with thine enchantments, and with the multitude of thy sorceries, wherein thou hast laboured from thy youth; if so be thou shalt be able to profit, if so be thou mayest prevail.

13Thou art wearied in the multitude of thy counsels. Let now the astrologers, the stargazers, the monthly prognosticators, stand up, and save thee from *these things* that shall come upon thee.

14Behold, they shall be as stubble; the fire shall burn them; they shall not deliver themselves from the power of the flame: *there shall* not *be* a coal to warm at, *nor* fire to sit before it.

15Thus shall they be unto thee with whom thou hast laboured, *even* thy merchants, from thy youth: they shall wander every one to his quarter; none shall save thee.

HEAR ye this, O house of Jacob, which are called by the name of Israel, and are come forth out of the waters of Judah, which swear by the name of the LORD, and make mention of the God of Israel, *but* not in truth, nor in righteousness.

2For they call themselves of the holy city, and stay themselves upon the God of Israel; The LORD of hosts *is* his name.

3I have declared the former things from the beginning; and they went forth out of my mouth, and I shewed them; I did *them* suddenly, and they came to pass.

4Because I knew that thou *art* obstinate, and thy neck *is* an iron sinew, and thy brow brass;

5I have even from the beginning declared *it* to thee; before it came to pass I shewed *it* thee: lest thou shouldest say, Mine idol hath done them, and my graven image, and my molten image, hath commanded them.

6Thou hast heard, see all this; and will not ye declare *it?* I have shewed thee new things from this time, even hidden things, and thou didst not know them.

7They are created now, and not from the beginning; even before the day when thou heardest them not; lest thou shouldest say, Behold, I knew them.

8Yea, thou heardest not; yea, thou knewest not; yea, from that time *that* thine ear was not opened: for I knew

that thou wouldest deal very treacherously, and wast called a transgressor from the womb.

9For my name's sake will I defer mine anger, and for my praise will I refrain for thee, that I cut thee not off.

10Behold, I have refined thee, but not with silver; I have chosen thee in the furnace of affliction.

11For mine own sake, *even* for mine own sake, will I do *it:* for how should *my name* be polluted? and I will not give my glory unto another.

EPHESIANS 4:1–16

I THEREFORE, the prisoner of the Lord, beseech you that ye walk worthy of the vocation wherewith ye are called,

2With all lowliness and meekness, with longsuffering, forbearing one another in love;

3Endeavouring to keep the unity of the Spirit in the bond of peace.

4*There is* one body, and one Spirit, even as ye are called in one hope of your calling;

5One Lord, one faith, one baptism,

6One God and Father of all, who *is* above all, and through all, and in you all.

7But unto every one of us is given grace according to the measure of the gift of Christ.

8Wherefore he saith, When he ascended up on high, he led captivity captive, and gave gifts unto men.

9(Now that he ascended, what is it but that he also descended first into the lower parts of the earth?

10He that descended is the same also that ascended up far above all heavens, that he might fill all things.)

11And he gave some, apostles; and some, prophets; and some, evangelists; and some, pastors and teachers;

12For the perfecting of the saints, for the work of the ministry, for the edifying of the body of Christ:

13Till we all come in the unity of the faith, and of the knowledge of the Son of God, unto a perfect man, unto the measure of the stature of the fulness of Christ:

14That we *henceforth* be no more children, tossed to and fro, and carried about with every wind of doctrine, by the sleight of men, *and* cunning craftiness, whereby they lie in wait to deceive;

15But speaking the truth in love, may grow up into him in all things, which is the head, *even* Christ:

16From whom the whole body fitly joined together and compacted by that which every joint supplieth, according to the effectual working in the measure of every part, maketh increase of the body unto the edifying of itself in love.

PSALM 68:19–35

B LESSED *be* the Lord, *who* daily loadeth us *with benefits, even* the God of our salvation. Selah.

20*He that is* our God *is* the God of salvation; and unto GOD the Lord *belong* the issues from death.

21But God shall wound the head of his enemies, *and* the hairy scalp of such an one as goeth on still in his trespasses.

22The Lord said, I will bring again from Bashan, I will bring *my people* again from the depths of the sea:

23That thy foot may be dipped in the blood of *thine* enemies, *and* the tongue of thy dogs in the same.

24They have seen thy goings, O God;

even the goings of my God, my King, in the sanctuary.

25The singers went before, the players on instruments *followed* after; among *them were* the damsels playing with timbrels.

26Bless ye God in the congregations, *even* the Lord, from the fountain of Israel.

27There *is* little Benjamin *with* their ruler, the princes of Judah *and* their council, the princes of Zebulun, *and* the princes of Naphtali.

28Thy God hath commanded thy strength: strengthen, O God, that which thou hast wrought for us.

29Because of thy temple at Jerusalem shall kings bring presents unto thee.

30Rebuke the company of spearmen, the multitude of the bulls, with the calves of the people, *till every one* submit himself with pieces of silver: scatter thou the people *that* delight in war.

31Princes shall come out of Egypt; Ethiopia shall soon stretch out her hands unto God.

32Sing unto God, ye kingdoms of the earth; O sing praises unto the Lord; Selah:

33To him that rideth upon the heavens of heavens, *which were* of old; lo, he doth send out his voice, *and that* a mighty voice.

34Ascribe ye strength unto God: his excellency *is* over Israel, and his strength *is* in the clouds.

35O God, *thou art* terrible out of thy holy places: the God of Israel *is* he that giveth strength and power unto *his* people. Blessed *be* God.

PROVERBS FOR TODAY/ 24:3–4

Through wisdom is an house builded; and by understanding it is established: And by knowledge shall the chambers be filled with all precious and pleasant riches.

SEPTEMBER 26

ISAIAH 48:12—50:11

Hearken unto me, O Jacob and Israel, my called; I *am* he; I *am* the first, I also *am* the last.

13Mine hand also hath laid the foundation of the earth, and my right hand hath spanned the heavens: *when* I call unto them, they stand up together.

14All ye, assemble yourselves, and hear; which among them hath declared these *things?* The Lord hath loved him: he will do his pleasure on Babylon, and his arm *shall be on* the Chaldeans.

15I, *even* I, have spoken; yea, I have called him: I have brought him, and he shall make his way prosperous.

16Come ye near unto me, hear ye this; I have not spoken in secret from the beginning; from the time that it was, there *am* I: and now the Lord God, and his Spirit, hath sent me.

17Thus saith the Lord, thy Redeemer, the Holy One of Israel; I *am* the Lord thy God which teacheth thee to profit, which leadeth thee by the way *that* thou shouldest go.

18O that thou hadst hearkened to my commandments! then had thy peace been as a river, and thy righteousness as the waves of the sea:

19Thy seed also had been as the sand, and the offspring of thy bowels like the gravel thereof; his name should not have been cut off nor destroyed from before me.

20Go ye forth of Babylon, flee ye from the Chaldeans, with a voice of singing declare ye, tell this, utter it *even* to the end of the earth; say ye, The Lord hath redeemed his servant Jacob.

21And they thirsted not *when* he led them through the deserts: he caused the waters to flow out of the rock for them: he clave the rock also, and the waters gushed out.

22*There is* no peace, saith the Lord, unto the wicked.

Listen, O isles, unto me; and hearken, ye people, from far; The Lord hath called me from the womb; from the bowels of my mother hath he made mention of my name.

2And he hath made my mouth like a sharp sword; in the shadow of his hand hath he hid me, and made me a polished shaft; in his quiver hath he hid me;

3And said unto me, Thou *art* my servant, O Israel, in whom I will be glorified.

4Then I said, I have laboured in vain, I have spent my strength for nought, and in vain: *yet* surely my judgment *is* with the Lord, and my work with my God.

5And now, saith the Lord that formed me from the womb *to be* his servant, to bring Jacob again to him, Though Israel be not gathered, yet shall I be glorious in the eyes of the Lord, and my God shall be my strength.

6And he said, It is a light thing that thou shouldest be my servant to raise up the tribes of Jacob, and to restore the preserved of Israel: I will also give thee for a light to the Gentiles, that thou mayest be my salvation unto the end of the earth.

7Thus saith the Lord, the Redeemer of Israel, *and* his Holy One, to him whom man despiseth, to him whom the nation abhorreth, to a servant of rulers, Kings shall see and arise, princes also shall worship, because of the Lord that is faithful, *and* the Holy One of Israel, and he shall choose thee.

8Thus saith the Lord, In an acceptable time have I heard thee, and in a day of salvation have I helped thee: and I will preserve thee, and give thee for a covenant of the people, to establish the earth, to cause to inherit the desolate heritages;

9That thou mayest say to the prisoners, Go forth; to them that *are* in darkness, Shew yourselves. They shall feed in the ways, and their pastures *shall be* in all high places.

10They shall not hunger nor thirst; neither shall the heat nor sun smite them: for he that hath mercy on them shall lead them, even by the springs of water shall he guide them.

11And I will make all my mountains a way, and my highways shall be exalted.

12Behold, these shall come from far: and, lo, these from the north and from the west; and these from the land of Sinim.

13Sing, O heavens; and be joyful, O earth; and break forth into singing, O mountains: for the LORD hath comforted his people, and will have mercy upon his afflicted.

14But Zion said, The LORD hath forsaken me, and my Lord hath forgotten me.

15Can a woman forget her sucking child, that she should not have compassion on the son of her womb? yea, they may forget, yet will I not forget thee.

16Behold, I have graven thee upon the palms of *my* hands; thy walls *are* continually before me.

17Thy children shall make haste; thy destroyers and they that made thee waste shall go forth of thee.

18Lift up thine eyes round about, and behold: all these gather themselves together, *and* come to thee. As I live, saith the LORD, thou shalt surely clothe thee with them all, as with an ornament, and bind them *on thee*, as a bride *doeth*.

19For thy waste and thy desolate places, and the land of thy destruction, shall even now be too narrow by reason of the inhabitants, and they that swallowed thee up shall be far away.

20The children which thou shalt have, after thou hast lost the other, shall say again in thine ears, The place *is* too strait for me: give place to me that I may dwell.

21Then shalt thou say in thine heart, who hath begotten me these, seeing I have lost my children, and am desolate, a captive, and removing to and fro? and who hath brought up these? Behold, I was left alone; these, where *had* they *been?*

22Thus saith the Lord GOD, Behold, I will lift up mine hand to the Gentiles, and set up my standard to the people: and they shall bring thy sons in *their* arms, and thy daughters shall be carried upon *their* shoulders.

23And kings shall be thy nursing fathers, and their queens thy nursing mothers: they shall bow down to thee with *their* face toward the earth, and lick up the dust of thy feet; and thou shalt know that I *am* the LORD: for they shall not be ashamed that wait for me.

24Shall the prey be taken from the mighty, or the lawful captive delivered?

25But thus saith the LORD, Even the captives of the mighty shall be taken away, and the prey of the terrible shall be delivered: for I will contend with him that contendeth with thee, and I will save thy children.

26And I will feed them that oppress thee with their own flesh; and they shall be drunken with their own blood, as with sweet wine: and all flesh shall know that I the LORD *am* thy Saviour and thy Redeemer, the mighty One of Jacob.

THUS saith the LORD, Where *is* the bill of your mother's divorcement, whom I have put away? or which of my creditors *is it* to whom I have sold you? Behold, for your iniquities have ye sold yourselves, and for your transgressions is your mother put away.

2Wherefore, when I came, *was there* no man? when I called, *was there* none to answer? Is my hand shortened at all, that it cannot redeem? or have I no power to deliver? behold, at my rebuke I dry up the sea, I make the rivers a wilderness: their fish stinketh, because *there is* no water, and dieth for thirst.

3I clothe the heavens with blackness, and I make sackcloth their covering.

4The Lord GOD hath given me the tongue of the learned, that I should know how to speak a word in season to *him that is* weary: he wakeneth morning by morning, he wakeneth mine ear to hear as the learned.

5The Lord GOD hath opened mine ear, and I was not rebellious, neither turned away back.

6I gave my back to the smiters, and my cheeks to them that plucked off the hair: I hid not my face from shame and spitting.

7For the Lord GOD will help me; therefore shall I not be confounded: therefore have I set my face like a flint, and I know that I shall not be ashamed.

8*He is* near that justifieth me; who will contend with me? let us stand together: who *is* mine adversary? let him come near to me.

9Behold, the Lord GOD will help me; who *is* he *that* shall condemn me? lo, they all shall wax old as a garment; the moth shall eat them up.

10Who *is* among you that feareth the LORD, that obeyeth the voice of his servant, that walketh *in* darkness, and hath no light? let him trust in the name of the LORD, and stay upon his God.

11Behold, all ye that kindle a fire, that compass *yourselves* about with sparks: walk in the light of your fire, and in the sparks *that* ye have kindled. This shall ye have of mine hand; ye shall lie down in sorrow.

EPHESIANS 4:17–32

THIS I say therefore, and testify in the Lord, that ye henceforth walk not as other Gentiles walk, in the vanity of their mind,

18Having the understanding darkened, being alienated from the life of God through the ignorance that is in them, because of the blindness of their heart:

19Who being past feeling have given themselves over unto lasciviousness, to work all uncleanness with greediness.

20But ye have not so learned Christ;

21If so be that ye have heard him, and have been taught by him, as the truth is in Jesus:

22That ye put off concerning the former conversation the old man, which is corrupt according to the deceitful lusts;

23And be renewed in the spirit of your mind;

24And that ye put on the new man, which after God is created in righteousness and true holiness.

25Wherefore putting away lying, speak every man truth with his neighbour: for we are members one of another.

26Be ye angry, and sin not: let not the sun go down upon your wrath:

27Neither give place to the devil.

28Let him that stole steal no more: but rather let him labour, working with *his* hands the thing which is good, that he may have to give to him that needeth.

29Let no corrupt communication proceed out of your mouth, but that which is good to the use of edifying, that it may minister grace unto the hearers.

30And grieve not the holy Spirit of God, whereby ye are sealed unto the day of redemption.

31Let all bitterness, and wrath, and anger, and clamour, and evil speaking, be put away from you, with all malice:

32And be ye kind one to another,

tenderhearted, forgiving one another, even as God for Christ's sake hath forgiven you.

PSALM 69:1–14

Save me, O God; for the waters are come in unto *my* soul.

2I sink in deep mire, where *there is* no standing: I am come into deep waters, where the floods overflow me.

3I am weary of my crying: my throat is dried: mine eyes fail while I wait for my God.

4They that hate me without a cause are more than the hairs of mine head: they that would destroy me, *being* mine enemies wrongfully, are mighty: then I restored *that* which I took not away.

5O God, thou knowest my foolishness; and my sins are not hid from thee.

6Let not them that wait on thee, O Lord God of hosts, be ashamed for my sake: let not those that seek thee

be confounded for my sake, O God of Israel.

7Because for thy sake I have borne reproach; shame hath covered my face.

8I am become a stranger unto my brethren, and an alien unto my mother's children.

9For the zeal of thine house hath eaten me up; and the reproaches of them that reproached thee are fallen upon me.

10When I wept, *and chastened* my soul with fasting, that was to my reproach.

11I made sackcloth also my garment; and I became a proverb to them.

12They that sit in the gate speak against me; and I *was* the song of the drunkards.

13But as for me, my prayer *is* unto thee, O Lord, *in* an acceptable time: O God, in the multitude of thy mercy hear me, in the truth of thy salvation.

14Deliver me out of the mire, and let me not sink: let me be delivered from them that hate me, and out of the deep waters.

PROVERBS FOR TODAY/ 24:5

A wise man is *strong; yea, a man of knowledge increaseth strength.*

SEPTEMBER 27

ISAIAH 51:1—53:12

Hearken to me, ye that follow after righteousness, ye that seek the Lord: look unto the rock *whence* ye are hewn, and to the hole of the pit *whence* ye are digged.

2Look unto Abraham your father, and unto Sarah *that* bare you: for I called him alone, and blessed him, and increased him.

3For the Lord shall comfort Zion:

he will comfort all her waste places; and he will make her wilderness like Eden, and her desert like the garden of the Lord; joy and gladness shall be found therein, thanksgiving, and the voice of melody.

4Hearken unto me, my people; and give ear unto me, O my nation: for a law shall proceed from me, and I will make my judgment to rest for a light of the people.

5My righteousness *is* near; my salvation is gone forth, and mine arms shall judge the people; the isles shall wait upon me, and on mine arm shall they trust.

6Lift up your eyes to the heavens, and look upon the earth beneath: for the heavens shall vanish away like smoke, and the earth shall wax old like a garment, and they that dwell therein shall die in like manner: but my salvation shall be for ever, and my righteousness shall not be abolished.

7Hearken unto me, ye that know righteousness, the people in whose heart *is* my law; fear ye not the reproach of men, neither be ye afraid of their revilings.

8For the moth shall eat them up like a garment, and the worm shall eat them like wool: but my righteousness shall be for ever, and my salvation from generation to generation.

9Awake, awake, put on strength, O arm of the LORD; awake, as in the ancient days, in the generations of old. *Art* thou not it that hath cut Rahab, *and* wounded the dragon?

10*Art* thou not it which hath dried the sea, the waters of the great deep; that hath made the depths of the sea a way for the ransomed to pass over?

11Therefore the redeemed of the LORD shall return, and come with singing unto Zion; and everlasting joy *shall be* upon their head: they shall obtain gladness and joy; *and* sorrow and mourning shall flee away.

12I, *even* I, *am* he that comforteth you: who *art* thou, that thou shouldest be afraid of a man *that* shall die, and of the son of man *which* shall be made *as* grass;

13And forgettest the LORD thy maker, that hath stretched forth the heavens, and laid the foundations of the earth; and hast feared continually every day because of the fury of the oppressor, as if he were ready to destroy? and where *is* the fury of the oppressor?

14The captive exile hasteneth that he may be loosed, and that he should not die in the pit, nor that his bread should fail.

15But I *am* the LORD thy God, that divided the sea, whose waves roared: The LORD of hosts *is* his name.

16And I have put my words in thy mouth, and I have covered thee in the shadow of mine hand, that I may plant the heavens, and lay the foundations of the earth, and say unto Zion, Thou *art* my people.

17Awake, awake, stand up, O Jerusalem, which hast drunk at the hand of the LORD the cup of his fury; thou hast drunken the dregs of the cup of trembling, *and* wrung *them* out.

18*There is* none to guide her among all the sons *whom* she hath brought forth; neither *is there any* that taketh her by the hand of all the sons *that* she hath brought up.

19These two *things* are come unto thee; who shall be sorry for thee? desolation, and destruction, and the famine, and the sword: by whom shall I comfort thee?

20Thy sons have fainted, they lie at the head of all the streets, as a wild bull in a net: they are full of the fury of the LORD, the rebuke of thy God.

21Therefore hear now this, thou afflicted, and drunken, but not with wine:

22Thus saith thy Lord the LORD, and thy God *that* pleadeth the cause of his people, Behold, I have taken out of thine hand the cup of trembling, *even* the dregs of the cup of my fury; thou shalt no more drink it again:

23But I will put it into the hand of them that afflict thee; which have said to thy soul, Bow down, that we may go over: and thou hast laid thy body as the ground, and as the street, to them that went over.

AWAKE, awake; put on thy strength, O Zion; put on thy beautiful garments, O Jerusalem, the holy city: for henceforth there shall no more come into thee the uncircumcised and the unclean.

2Shake thyself from the dust; arise, *and* sit down, O Jerusalem: loose thyself from the bands of thy neck, O captive daughter of Zion.

3For thus saith the LORD, Ye have sold yourselves for nought; and ye shall be redeemed without money.

4For thus saith the Lord GOD, My people went down aforetime into Egypt to sojourn there; and the Assyrian oppressed them without cause.

5Now therefore, what have I here, saith the LORD, that my people is taken away for nought? they that rule over them make them to howl, saith the LORD; and my name continually every day *is* blasphemed.

6Therefore my people shall know my name: therefore *they shall know* in that day that I *am* he that doth speak: behold, *it is* I.

7How beautiful upon the mountains are the feet of him that bringeth good tidings, that publisheth peace; that bringeth good tidings of good, that publisheth salvation; that saith unto Zion, Thy God reigneth!

8Thy watchmen shall lift up the voice; with the voice together shall they sing: for they shall see eye to eye, when the LORD shall bring again Zion.

9Break forth into joy, sing together, ye waste places of Jerusalem: for the LORD hath comforted his people, he hath redeemed Jerusalem.

10The LORD hath made bare his holy arm in the eyes of all the nations; and all the ends of the earth shall see the salvation of our God.

11Depart ye, depart ye, go ye out from thence, touch no unclean *thing;* go ye out of the midst of her; be ye clean, that bear the vessels of the LORD.

12For ye shall not go out with haste, nor go by flight: for the LORD will go before you; and the God of Israel *will be* your rereward.

13Behold, my servant shall deal prudently, he shall be exalted and extolled, and be very high.

14As many were astonied at thee; his visage was so marred more than any man, and his form more than the sons of men:

15So shall he sprinkle many nations; the kings shall shut their mouths at him: for *that* which had not been told them shall they see; and *that* which they had not heard shall they consider.

WHO hath believed our report? and to whom is the arm of the LORD revealed?

2For he shall grow up before him as a tender plant, and as a root out of a dry gound: he hath no form nor comeliness; and when we shall see him, *there is* no beauty that we should desire him.

3He is despised and rejected of men; a man of sorrows, and acquainted with grief: and we hid as it were *our* faces from him; he was despised, and we esteemed him not.

4Surely he hath borne our griefs, and carried our sorrows: yet we did esteem him stricken, smitten of God, and afflicted.

5But he *was* wounded for our transgressions, *he was* bruised for our iniquities: the chastisement of our peace *was* upon him; and with his stripes we are healed.

6All we like sheep have gone astray; we have turned every one to his own way; and the LORD hath laid on him the iniquity of us all.

7He was oppressed, and he was afflicted, yet he opened not his mouth: he is brought as a lamb to the slaughter, and as a sheep before her shearers is dumb, so he openeth not his mouth.

8He was taken from prison and from judgment: and who shall declare his generation? for he was cut off out of the land of the living: for the transgression of my people was he stricken.

9And he made his grave with the wicked, and with the rich in his death;

because he had done no violence, neither *was any* deceit in his mouth.

10Yet it pleased the LORD to bruise him; he hath put *him* to grief: when thou shalt make his soul an offering for sin, he shall see *his* seed, he shall prolong *his* days, and the pleasure of the LORD shall prosper in his hand.

11He shall see of the travail of his soul, *and* shall be satisfied: by his knowledge shall my righteous servant justify many; for he shall bear their iniquities.

12Therefore will I divide him *a portion* with the great, and he shall divide the spoil with the strong; because he hath poured out his soul unto death: and he was numbered with the transgressors; and he bare the sin of many, and made intercession for the transgressors.

EPHESIANS 5:1–33

BE ye therefore followers of God as dear children:
2And walk in love, as Christ also hath loved us, and hath given himself for us an offering and a sacrifice to God for a sweetsmelling savour.

3But fornication, and all uncleanness, or covetousness, let it not be once named among you, as becometh saints;

4Neither filthiness, nor foolish talking, nor jesting, which are not convenient: but rather giving of thanks.

5For this ye know, that no whoremonger, nor unclean person, nor covetous man, who is an idolater, hath any inheritance in the kingdom of Christ and of God.

6Let no man deceive you with vain words: for because of these things cometh the wrath of God upon the children of disobedience.

7Be not ye therefore partakers with them.

8For ye were sometimes darkness, but now *are ye* light in the Lord: walk as children of light:

9(For the fruit of the Spirit *is* in all goodness and righteousness and truth;)

10Proving what is acceptable unto the Lord.

11And have no fellowship with the unfruitful works of darkness, but rather reprove *them.*

12For it is a shame even to speak of those things which are done of them in secret.

13But all things that are reproved are made manifest by the light: for whatsoever doth make manifest is light.

14Wherefore he saith, Awake thou that sleepest, and arise from the dead, and Christ shall give thee light.

15See then that ye walk circumspectly, not as fools, but as wise,

16Redeeming the time, because the days are evil.

17Wherefore be ye not unwise, but understanding what the will of the Lord *is.*

18And be not drunk with wine, wherein is excess; but be filled with the Spirit;

19Speaking to yourselves in psalms and hymns and spiritual songs, singing and making melody in your heart to the Lord;

20Giving thanks always for all things unto God and the Father in the name of our Lord Jesus Christ;

21Submitting yourselves one to another in the fear of God.

22Wives, submit yourselves unto your own husbands, as unto the Lord.

23For the husband is the head of the wife, even as Christ is the head of the church: and he is the saviour of the body.

24Therefore as the church is subject unto Christ, so *let* the wives *be* to their own husbands in every thing.

25Husbands, love your wives, even as Christ also loved the church, and gave himself for it;

26That he might sanctify and cleanse it with the washing of water by the word,

27That he might present it to himself a glorious church, not having spot, or wrinkle, or any such thing; but that it should be holy and without blemish.

28So ought men to love their wives as their own bodies. He that loveth his wife loveth himself.

29For no man ever yet hated his own flesh; but nourisheth and cherisheth it, even as the Lord the church:

30For we are members of his body, of his flesh, and of his bones.

31For this cause shall a man leave his father and mother, and shall be joined unto his wife, and they two shall be one flesh.

32This is a great mystery: but I speak concerning Christ and the church.

33Nevertheless let every one of you in particular so love his wife even as himself; and the wife *see* that she reverence *her* husband.

PSALM 69:15–36

LET not the waterflood overflow me, neither let the deep swallow me up, and let not the pit shut her mouth upon me.

16Hear me, O LORD; for thy lovingkindness *is* good: turn unto me according to the multitude of thy tender mercies.

17And hide not thy face from thy servant; for I am in trouble; hear me speedily.

18Draw nigh unto my soul, *and* redeem it: deliver me because of mine enemies.

19Thou hast known my reproach, and my shame, and my dishonour: mine adversaries *are* all before thee.

20Reproach hath broken my heart; and I am full of heaviness: and I looked *for some* to take pity, but *there was* none; and for comforters, but I found none.

21They gave me also gall for my meat; and in my thirst they gave me vinegar to drink.

22Let their table become a snare before them: and *that which should have been* for *their* welfare, *let it become* a trap.

23Let their eyes be darkened, that they see not; and make their loins continually to shake.

24Pour out thine indignation upon them, and let thy wrathful anger take hold of them.

25Let their habitation be desolate; *and* let none dwell in their tents.

26For they persecute *him* whom thou hast smitten; and they talk to the grief of those whom thou hast wounded.

27Add iniquity unto their iniquity: and let them not come into thy righteousness.

28Let them be blotted out of the book of the living, and not be written with the righteous.

29But I *am* poor and sorrowful: let thy salvation, O God, set me up on high.

30I will praise the name of God with a song, and will magnify him with thanksgiving.

31*This* also shall please the LORD better than an ox *or* bullock that hath horns and hoofs.

32The humble shall see *this, and* be glad: and your heart shall live that seek God.

33For the LORD heareth the poor, and despiseth not his prisoners.

34Let the heaven and earth praise him, the seas, and every thing that moveth therein.

35For God will save Zion, and will build the cities of Judah: that they may dwell there, and have it in possession.

36The seed also of his servants shall inherit it: and they that love his name shall dwell therein.

PROVERBS FOR TODAY/ 24:6–7

For by wise counsel thou shalt make thy war: and in multitude of counsellors
there is safety. Wisdom is too high for a fool: he openeth not his mouth in the
gate.

SEPTEMBER 28

ISAIAH 54:1—57:14

SING, O barren, thou *that* didst not bear; break forth into singing, and cry aloud, thou *that* didst not travail with child: for more *are* the children of the desolate than the children of the married wife, saith the LORD.

2Enlarge the place of thy tent, and let them stretch forth the curtains of thine habitations: spare not, lengthen thy cords, and strengthen thy stakes;

3For thou shalt break forth on the right hand and on the left; and thy seed shall inherit the Gentiles, and make the desolate cities to be inhabited.

4Fear not; for thou shalt not be ashamed: neither be thou confounded; for thou shalt not be put to shame: for thou shalt forget the shame of thy youth, and shalt not remember the reproach of thy widowhood any more.

5For thy Maker *is* thine husband; the LORD of hosts *is* his name; and thy Redeemer the Holy One of Israel; The God of the whole earth shall he be called.

6For the LORD hath called thee as a woman forsaken and grieved in spirit, and a wife of youth, when thou wast refused, saith thy God.

7For a small moment have I forsaken thee; but with great mercies will I gather thee.

8In a little wrath I hid my face from thee for a moment; but with everlasting kindness will I have mercy on thee, saith the LORD thy Redeemer.

9For this *is as* the waters of Noah unto me: for *as* I have sworn that the waters of Noah should no more go over the earth; so have I sworn that I would not be wroth with thee, nor rebuke thee.

10For the mountains shall depart, and the hills be removed; but my kindness shall not depart from thee, neither shall the covenant of my peace be removed, saith the LORD that hath mercy on thee.

11O thou afflicted, tossed with tempest, *and* not comforted, behold, I will lay thy stones with fair colours, and lay thy foundations with sapphires.

12And I will make thy windows of agates, and thy gates of carbuncles, and all thy borders of pleasant stones.

13And all thy children *shall be* taught of the LORD; and great *shall be* the peace of thy children.

14In righteousness shalt thou be established: thou shalt be far from oppression; for thou shalt not fear: and from terror; for it shall not come near thee.

15Behold, they shall surely gather together, *but* not by me: whosoever shall gather together against thee shall fall for thy sake.

16Behold, I have created the smith that bloweth the coals in the fire, and that bringeth forth an instrument for his work; and I have created the waster to destroy.

17No weapon that is formed against thee shall prosper; and every tongue *that* shall rise against thee in judgment thou shalt condemn. This *is* the heritage of the servants of the LORD, and their righteousness *is* of me, saith the LORD.

Ho, every one that thirsteth, come ye to the waters, and he that hath no money; come ye, buy, and eat; yea, come, buy wine and milk without money and without price.

2Wherefore do ye spend money for *that which is* not bread? and your labour for *that which* satisfieth not? hearken diligently unto me, and eat ye *that which is* good, and let your soul delight itself in fatness.

3Incline your ear, and come unto me: hear, and your soul shall live; and I will make an everlasting covenant with you, *even* the sure mercies of David.

4Behold, I have given him *for* a witness to the people, a leader and commander to the people.

5Behold, thou shalt call a nation *that* thou knowest not, and nations *that* knew not thee shall run unto thee because of the LORD thy God, and for the Holy One of Israel; for he hath glorified thee.

6Seek ye the LORD while he may be found, call ye upon him while he is near:

7Let the wicked forsake his way, and the unrighteous man his thoughts: and let him return unto the LORD, and he will have mercy upon him; and to our God, for he will abundantly pardon.

8For my thoughts *are* not your thoughts, neither *are* your ways my ways, saith the LORD.

9For *as* the heavens are higher than the earth, so are my ways higher than your ways, and my thoughts than your thoughts.

10For as the rain cometh down, and the snow from heaven, and returneth not thither, but watereth the earth, and maketh it bring forth and bud, that it may give seed to the sower, and bread to the eater:

11So shall my word be that goeth forth out of my mouth: it shall not return unto me void, but it shall accomplish that which I please, and it shall prosper *in the thing* whereto I sent it.

12For ye shall go out with joy, and be led forth with peace: the mountains and the hills shall break forth before you into singing, and all the trees of the field shall clap *their* hands.

13Instead of the thorn shall come up the fir tree, and instead of the brier shall come up the myrtle tree: and it shall be to the LORD for a name, for an everlasting sign *that* shall not be cut off.

THUS saith the LORD, Keep ye judgment, and do justice: for my salvation *is* near to come, and my righteousness to be revealed.

2Blessed *is* the man *that* doeth this, and the son of man *that* layeth hold on it: that keepeth the sabbath from polluting it, and keepeth his hand from doing any evil.

3Neither let the son of the stranger, that hath joined himself to the LORD, speak, saying, The LORD hath utterly separated me from his people: neither let the eunuch say, Behold, I *am* a dry tree.

4For thus saith the LORD unto the eunuchs that keep my sabbaths, and choose *the things* that please me, and take hold of my covenant;

5Even unto them will I give in mine house and within my walls a place and a name better than of sons and of daughters: I will give them an everlasting name, that shall not be cut off.

6Also the sons of the stranger, that join themselves to the LORD, to serve him, and to love the name of the LORD, to be his servants, every one that keepeth the sabbath from polluting it, and taketh hold of my covenant;

7Even them will I bring to my holy mountain, and make them joyful in my house of prayer: their burnt offerings and their sacrifices *shall be* accepted upon mine altar; for mine house shall be called an house of prayer for all people.

⁸The Lord GOD which gathereth the outcasts of Israel saith, Yet will I gather *others* to him, beside those that are gathered unto him.

⁹All ye beasts of the field, come to devour, *yea,* all ye beasts in the forest.

¹⁰His watchmen *are* blind: they are all ignorant, they *are* all dumb dogs, they cannot bark; sleeping, lying down, loving to slumber.

¹¹Yea, *they are* greedy dogs *which* can never have enough, and they *are* shepherds *that* cannot understand: they all look to their own way, every one for his gain, from his quarter.

¹²Come ye, *say they,* I will fetch wine, and we will fill ourselves with strong drink; and to morrow shall be as this day, *and* much more abundant.

THE righteous perisheth, and no man layeth *it* to heart: and merciful men *are* taken away, none considering that the righteous is taken away from the evil *to come.*

²He shall enter into peace: they shall rest in their beds, *each one* walking *in* his uprightness.

³But draw near hither, ye sons of the sorceress, the seed of the adulterer and the whore.

⁴Against whom do ye sport yourselves? against whom make ye a wide mouth, *and* draw out the tongue? *are* ye not children of transgression, a seed of falsehood,

⁵Enflaming yourselves with idols under every green tree, slaying the children in the valleys under the clifts of the rocks?

⁶Among the smooth *stones* of the stream *is* thy portion; they, they *are* thy lot: even to them hast thou poured a drink offering, thou hast offered a meat offering. Should I receive comfort in these?

⁷Upon a lofty and high mountain hast thou set thy bed: even thither wentest thou up to offer sacrifice.

⁸Behind the doors also and the posts hast thou set up thy remembrance: for thou hast discovered *thyself to another* than me, and art gone up; thou hast enlarged thy bed, and made thee *a covenant* with them; thou lovedst their bed where thou sawest *it.*

⁹And thou wentest to the king with ointment, and didst increase thy perfumes, and didst send thy messengers far off, and didst debase *thyself even* unto hell.

¹⁰Thou art wearied in the greatness of thy way; *yet* saidst thou not, There is no hope: thou hast found the life of thine hand; therefore thou wast not grieved.

¹¹And of whom hast thou been afraid or feared, that thou hast lied, and hast not remembered me, nor laid *it* to thy heart? have not I held my peace even of old, and thou fearest me not?

¹²I will declare thy righteousness, and thy works; for they shall not profit thee.

¹³When thou criest, let thy companies deliver thee; but the wind shall carry them all away; vanity shall take *them:* but he that putteth his trust in me shall possess the land, and shall inherit my holy mountain;

¹⁴And shall say, Cast ye up, cast ye up, prepare the way, take up the stumblingblock out of the way of my people.

EPHESIANS 6:1-24

CHILDREN, obey your parents in the Lord: for this is right.

²Honour thy father and mother; which is the first commandment with promise;

³That it may be well with thee, and thou mayest live long on the earth.

⁴And, ye fathers, provoke not your children to wrath: but bring them up in the nurture and admonition of the Lord.

⁵Servants, be obedient to them that

are *your* masters according to the flesh, with fear and trembling, in singleness of your heart, as unto Christ;

6Not with eyeservice, as menpleasers; but as the servants of Christ, doing the will of God from the heart;

7With good will doing service, as to the Lord, and not to men:

8Knowing that whatsoever good thing any man doeth, the same shall he receive of the Lord, whether *he be* bond or free.

9And, ye masters, do the same things unto them, forbearing threatening: knowing that your Master also is in heaven; neither is there respect of persons with him.

10Finally, my brethren, be strong in the Lord, and in the power of his might.

11Put on the whole armour of God, that ye may be able to stand against the wiles of the devil.

12For we wrestle not against flesh and blood, but against principalities, against powers, against the rulers of the darkness of this world, against spiritual wickedness in high *places.*

13Wherefore take unto you the whole armour of God, that ye may be able to withstand in the evil day, and having done all, to stand.

14Stand therefore, having your loins girt about with truth, and having on the breastplate of righteousness;

15And your feet shod with the preparation of the gospel of peace;

16Above all, taking the shield of faith, wherewith ye shall be able to quench all the fiery darts of the wicked.

17And take the helmet of salvation, and the sword of the Spirit, which is the word of God:

18Praying always with all prayer and supplication in the Spirit, and watching thereunto with all perseverance and supplication for all saints;

19And for me, that utterance may be given unto me, that I may open my mouth boldly, to make known the mystery of the gospel,

20For which I am an ambassador in bonds: that therein I may speak boldly, as I ought to speak.

21But that ye also may know my affairs, *and* how I do, Tychicus, a beloved brother and faithful minister in the Lord, shall make known to you all things:

22Whom I have sent unto you for the same purpose, that ye might know our affairs, and *that* he might comfort your hearts.

23Peace *be* to the brethren, and love with faith, from God the Father and the Lord Jesus Christ.

24Grace *be* with all them that love our Lord Jesus Christ in sincerity. Amen.

PSALM 70:1–5

MAKE *haste,* O God, to deliver me; make haste to help me, O LORD.

2Let them be ashamed and confounded that seek after my soul: let them be turned backward, and put to confusion, that desire my hurt.

3Let them be turned back for a reward of their shame that say, Aha, aha.

4Let all those that seek thee rejoice and be glad in thee: and let such as love thy salvation say continually, Let God be magnified.

5But I *am* poor and needy: make haste unto me, O God: thou *art* my help and my deliverer; O LORD, make no tarrying.

PROVERBS FOR TODAY/ 24:8

He that deviseth to do evil shall be called a mischievous person.

ISAIAH 57:15—59:21

FOR thus saith the high and lofty One that inhabiteth eternity, whose name *is* Holy; I dwell in the high and holy *place,* with him also *that is* of a contrite and humble spirit, to revive the spirit of the humble, and to revive the heart of the contrite ones.

16For I will not contend for ever, neither will I be always wroth: for the spirit should fail before me, and the souls *which* I have made.

17For the iniquity of his covetousness was I wroth, and smote him: I hid me, and was wroth, and he went on frowardly in the way of his heart.

18I have seen his ways, and will heal him: I will lead him also, and restore comforts unto him and to his mourners.

19I create the fruit of the lips; Peace, peace to *him that is* far off, and to *him that is* near, saith the LORD; and I will heal him.

20But the wicked *are* like the troubled sea, when it cannot rest, whose waters cast up mire and dirt.

21*There is* no peace, saith my God, to the wicked.

CRY aloud, spare not, lift up thy voice like a trumpet, and shew my people their transgression, and the house of Jacob their sins.

2Yet they seek me daily, and delight to know my ways, as a nation that did righteousness, and forsook not the ordinance of their God: they ask of me the ordinances of justice; they take delight in approaching to God.

3Wherefore have we fasted, *say they,* and thou seest not? *wherefore* have we afflicted our soul, and thou takest no knowledge? Behold, in the day of your fast ye find pleasure, and exact all your labours.

4Behold, ye fast for strife and debate, and to smite with the fist of wickedness: ye shall not fast as *ye do this* day, to make your voice to be heard on high.

5Is it such a fast that I have chosen? a day for a man to afflict his soul? *is it* to bow down his head as a bulrush, and to spread sackcloth and ashes *under him?* wilt thou call this a fast, and an acceptable day to the LORD?

6*Is* not this the fast that I have chosen? to loose the bands of wickedness, to undo the heavy burdens, and to let the oppressed go free, and that ye break every yoke?

7*Is it* not to deal thy bread to the hungry, and that thou bring the poor that are cast out to thy house? when thou seest the naked, that thou cover him; and that thou hide not thyself from thine own flesh?

8Then shall thy light break forth as the morning, and thine health shall spring forth speedily: and thy righteousness shall go before thee; the glory of the LORD shall be thy rereward.

9Then shalt thou call, and the LORD shall answer; thou shalt cry, and he shall say, Here I *am.* If thou take away from the midst of thee the yoke, the putting forth of the finger, and speaking vanity;

10And *if* thou draw out thy soul to the hungry, and satisfy the afflicted soul; then shall thy light rise in obscurity, and thy darkness *be* as the noon day:

11And the LORD shall guide thee continually, and satisfy thy soul in drought, and make fat thy bones: and thou shalt be like a watered garden, and like a spring of water, whose waters fail not.

12And *they that shall be* of thee shall build the old waste places: thou shalt raise up the foundations of many generations; and thou shalt be called, The repairer of the breach, The restorer of paths to dwell in.

13If thou turn away thy foot from the sabbath, *from* doing thy pleasure on my holy day; and call the sabbath a delight, the holy of the LORD, honourable; and shalt honour him, not doing thine own ways, nor finding thine own pleasure, nor speaking *thine own* words:

14Then shalt thou delight thyself in the LORD; and I will cause thee to ride upon the high places of the earth, and feed thee with the heritage of Jacob thy father: for the mouth of the LORD hath spoken *it.*

BEHOLD, the LORD's hand is not shortened, that it cannot save; neither his ear heavy, that it cannot hear:

2But your iniquities have separated between you and your God, and your sins have hid *his* face from you, that he will not hear.

3For your hands are defiled with blood, and your fingers with iniquity; your lips have spoken lies, your tongue hath muttered perverseness.

4None calleth for justice, nor *any* pleadeth for truth: they trust in vanity, and speak lies; they conceive mischief, and bring forth iniquity.

5They hatch cockatrice eggs, and weave the spider's web: he that eateth of their eggs dieth, and that which is crushed breaketh out into a viper.

6Their webs shall not become garments, neither shall they cover themselves with their works: their works *are* works of iniquity, and the act of violence *is* in their hands.

7Their feet run to evil, and they make haste to shed innocent blood: their thoughts *are* thoughts of iniquity; wasting and destruction *are* in their paths.

8The way of peace they know not; and *there is* no judgment in their goings: they have made them crooked paths: whosoever goeth therein shall not know peace.

9Therefore is judgment far from us, neither doth justice overtake us: we wait for light, but behold obscurity; for brightness, *but* we walk in darkness.

10We grope for the wall like the blind, and we grope as if *we had* no eyes: we stumble at noon day as in the night; *we are* in desolate places as dead *men.*

11We roar all like bears, and mourn sore like doves: we look for judgment, but *there is* none; for salvation, *but* it is far off from us.

12For our transgressions are multiplied before thee, and our sins testify against us: for our transgressions *are* with us; and *as for* our iniquities, we know them;

13In transgressing and lying against the LORD, and departing away from our God, speaking oppression and revolt, conceiving and uttering from the heart words of falsehood.

14And judgment is turned away backward, and justice standeth afar off: for truth is fallen in the street, and equity cannot enter.

15Yea, truth faileth; and he *that* departeth from evil maketh himself a prey: and the LORD saw *it,* and it displeased him that *there was* no judgment.

16And he saw that *there was* no man, and wondered that *there was* no intercessor: therefore his arm brought salvation unto him; and his righteousness, it sustained him.

17For he put on righteousness as a breastplate, and an helmet of salvation upon his head; and he put on the garments of vengeance *for* clothing, and was clad with zeal as a cloak.

18According to *their* deeds, accordingly he will repay, fury to his adversaries, recompence to his enemies; to the islands he will repay recompence.

19So shall they fear the name of the LORD from the west, and his glory from the rising of the sun. When the enemy shall come in like a flood, the Spirit of the LORD shall lift up a standard against him.

20And the Redeemer shall come to Zion, and unto them that turn from transgression in Jacob, saith the LORD.

21As for me, this *is* my covenant with them, saith the LORD; My spirit that *is* upon thee, and my words which I have put in thy mouth, shall not depart out of thy mouth, nor out of the mouth of thy seed, nor out of the mouth of thy seed's seed, saith the LORD, from henceforth and for ever.

PHILIPPIANS 1:1–26

PAUL and Timotheus, the servants of Jesus Christ, to all the saints in Christ Jesus which are at Philippi, with the bishops and deacons:

2Grace *be* unto you, and peace, from God our Father, and *from* the Lord Jesus Christ.

3I thank my God upon every remembrance of you,

4Always in every prayer of mine for you all making request with joy,

5For your fellowship in the gospel from the first day until now;

6Being confident of this very thing, that he which hath begun a good work in you will perform *it* until the day of Jesus Christ:

7Even as it is meet for me to think this of you all, because I have you in my heart; inasmuch as both in my bonds, and in the defence and confirmation of the gospel, ye all are partakers of my grace.

8For God is my record, how greatly I long after you all in the bowels of Jesus Christ.

9And this I pray, that your love may abound yet more and more in knowledge and *in* all judgment;

10That ye may approve things that are excellent; that ye may be sincere and without offence till the day of Christ;

11Being filled with the fruits of righteousness, which are by Jesus Christ, unto the glory and praise of God.

12But I would ye should understand, brethren, that the things *which happened* unto me have fallen out rather unto the furtherance of the gospel;

13So that my bonds in Christ are manifest in all the palace, and in all other *places;*

14And many of the brethren in the Lord, waxing confident by my bonds, are much more bold to speak the word without fear.

15Some indeed preach Christ even of envy and strife; and some also of good will:

16The one preach Christ of contention, not sincerely, supposing to add affliction to my bonds:

17But the other of love, knowing that I am set for the defence of the gospel.

18What then? notwithstanding, every way, whether in pretence, or in truth, Christ is preached; and I therein do rejoice, yea, and will rejoice.

19For I know that this shall turn to my salvation through your prayer, and the supply of the Spirit of Jesus Christ,

20According to my earnest expectation and *my* hope, that in nothing I shall be ashamed, but *that* with all boldness, as always, *so* now also Christ shall be magnified in my body, whether *it be* by life, or by death.

21For to me to live *is* Christ, and to die *is* gain.

22But if I live in the flesh, this *is* the fruit of my labour: yet what I shall choose I wot not.

23For I am in a strait betwixt two, having a desire to depart, and to be with Christ; which is far better:

24Nevertheless to abide in the flesh *is* more needful for you.

25And having this confidence, I know that I shall abide and continue with you all for your furtherance and joy of faith;

26That your rejoicing may be more abundant in Jesus Christ for me by my coming to you again.

PSALM 71:1–24

IN thee, O LORD, do I put my trust: let me never be put to confusion. 2Deliver me in thy righteousness, and cause me to escape: incline thine ear unto me, and save me.

3Be thou my strong habitation, whereunto I may continually resort: thou hast given commandment to save me; for thou *art* my rock and my fortress.

4Deliver me, O my God, out of the hand of the wicked, out of the hand of the unrighteous and cruel man.

5For thou *art* my hope, O Lord GOD: *thou art* my trust from my youth.

6By thee have I been holden up from the womb: thou art he that took me out of my mother's bowels: my praise *shall be* continually of thee.

7I am as a wonder unto many; but thou *art* my strong refuge.

8Let my mouth be filled *with* thy praise *and with* thy honour all the day.

9Cast me not off in the time of old age; forsake me not when my strength faileth.

10For mine enemies speak against me; and they that lay wait for my soul take counsel together,

11Saying, God hath forsaken him: persecute and take him; for *there is* none to deliver *him.*

12O God, be not far from me: O my God, make haste for my help.

13Let them be confounded *and* consumed that are adversaries to my soul; let them be covered *with* reproach and dishonour that seek my hurt.

14But I will hope continually, and will yet praise thee more and more.

15My mouth shall shew forth thy righteousness *and* thy salvation all the day; for I know not the numbers *thereof.*

16I will go in the strength of the Lord GOD: I will make mention of thy righteousness, *even* of thine only.

17O God, thou hast taught me from my youth: and hitherto have I declared thy wondrous works.

18Now also when I am old and greyheaded, O God, forsake me not; until I have shewed thy strength unto *this* generation, *and* thy power to every one *that* is to come.

19Thy righteousness also, O God, *is* very high, who hast done great things: O God, who *is* like unto thee!

20*Thou,* which hast shewed me great and sore troubles, shalt quicken me again, and shalt bring me up again from the depths of the earth.

21Thou shalt increase my greatness, and comfort me on every side.

22I will also praise thee with the psaltery, *even* thy truth, O my God: unto thee will I sing with the harp, O thou Holy One of Israel.

23My lips shall greatly rejoice when I sing unto thee; and my soul, which thou hast redeemed.

24My tongue also shall talk of thy righteousness all the day long: for they are confounded, for they are brought unto shame, that seek my hurt.

PROVERBS FOR TODAY/ 24:9–10

The thought of foolishness is *sin: and the scorner* is *an abomination to men.* □ *If thou faint in the day of adversity, thy strength* is *small.*

SEPTEMBER 30

ISAIAH 60:1—62:7

ARISE, shine; for thy light is come, and the glory of the LORD is risen upon thee.

2For, behold, the darkness shall cover the earth, and gross darkness the people: but the LORD shall arise upon thee, and his glory shall be seen upon thee.

3And the Gentiles shall come to thy light, and kings to the brightness of thy rising.

4Lift up thine eyes round about, and see: all they gather themselves together, they come to thee: thy sons shall come from far, and thy daughters shall be nursed at *thy* side.

5Then thou shalt see, and flow together, and thine heart shall fear, and be enlarged; because the abundance of the sea shall be converted unto thee, the forces of the Gentiles shall come unto thee.

6The multitude of camels shall cover thee, the dromedaries of Midian and Ephah; all they from Sheba shall come: they shall bring gold and incense; and they shall shew forth the praises of the LORD.

7All the flocks of Kedar shall be gathered together unto thee, the rams of Nebaioth shall minister unto thee: they shall come up with acceptance on mine altar, and I will glorify the house of my glory.

8Who *are* these *that* fly as a cloud, and as the doves to their windows?

9Surely the isles shall wait for me, and the ships of Tarshish first, to bring thy sons from far, their silver and their gold with them, unto the name of the LORD thy God, and to the Holy One of Israel, because *he* hath glorified thee.

10And the sons of strangers shall build up thy walls, and their kings shall minister unto thee: for in my wrath I smote thee, but in my favour have I had mercy on thee.

11Therefore thy gates shall be open continually: they shall not be shut day nor night; that *men* may bring unto thee the forces of the Gentiles, and *that* their kings *may be* brought.

12For the nation and kingdom that will not serve thee shall perish; yea, *those* nations shall be utterly wasted.

13The glory of Lebanon shall come unto thee, the fir tree, the pine tree, and the box together, to beautify the place of my sanctuary; and I will make the place of my feet glorious.

14The sons also of them that afflicted thee shall come bending unto thee; and all they that despised thee shall bow themselves down at the soles of thy feet; and they shall call thee, The city of the LORD, The Zion of the Holy One of Israel.

15Whereas thou hast been forsaken and hated, so that no man went through *thee,* I will make thee an eternal excellency, a joy of many generations.

16Thou shalt also suck the milk of the Gentiles, and shalt suck the breast of kings: and thou shalt know that I the LORD *am* thy Saviour and thy Redeemer, the mighty One of Jacob.

17For brass I will bring gold, and for iron I will bring silver, and for wood brass, and for stones iron: I will also make thy officers peace, and thine exactors righteousness.

18Violence shall no more be heard in thy land, wasting nor destruction within thy borders; but thou shalt call thy walls Salvation, and thy gates Praise.

19The sun shall be no more thy light by day; neither for brightness shall the moon give light unto thee: but the LORD shall be unto thee an everlasting light, and thy God thy glory.

20Thy sun shall no more go down; neither shall thy moon withdraw itself: for the LORD shall be thine everlasting light, and the days of thy mourning shall be ended.

21Thy people also *shall be* all righteous: they shall inherit the land for ever, the branch of my planting, the work of my hands, that I may be glorified.

22A little one shall become a thousand, and a small one a strong nation: I the LORD will hasten it in his time.

THE Spirit of the Lord GOD *is* upon me; because the LORD hath anointed me to preach good tidings unto the meek; he hath sent me to bind up the brokenhearted, to proclaim liberty to the captives, and the opening of the prison to *them that are* bound;

2To proclaim the acceptable year of the LORD, and the day of vengeance of our God; to comfort all that mourn;

3To appoint unto them that mourn in Zion, to give unto them beauty for ashes, the oil of joy for mourning, the garment of praise for the spirit of heaviness; that they might be called trees of righteousness, the planting of the LORD, that he might be glorified.

4And they shall build the old wastes, they shall raise up the former desolations, and they shall repair the waste cities, the desolations of many generations.

5And strangers shall stand and feed your flocks, and the sons of the alien *shall be* your plowmen and your vinedressers.

6But ye shall be named the Priests of the LORD: *men* shall call you the Ministers of our God: ye shall eat the riches of the Gentiles, and in their glory shall ye boast yourselves.

7For your shame *ye shall have* double; and *for* confusion they shall rejoice in their portion: therefore in their land they shall possess the double: everlasting joy shall be unto them.

8For I the LORD love judgment, I hate robbery for burnt offering; and I will direct their work in truth, and I will make an everlasting covenant with them.

9And their seed shall be known among the Gentiles, and their offspring among the people: all that see them shall acknowledge them, that they *are* the seed *which* the LORD hath blessed.

10I will greatly rejoice in the LORD, my soul shall be joyful in my God; for he hath clothed me with the garments of salvation, he hath covered me with the robe of righteousness, as a bridegroom decketh *himself* with ornaments, and as a bride adorneth *herself* with her jewels.

11For as the earth bringeth forth her bud, and as the garden causeth the things that are sown in it to spring forth; so the Lord GOD will cause righteousness and praise to spring forth before all the nations.

FOR Zion's sake will I not hold my peace, and for Jerusalem's sake I will not rest, until the righteousness thereof go forth as brightness, and the salvation thereof as a lamp *that* burneth.

2And the Gentiles shall see thy righteousness, and all kings thy glory: and thou shalt be called by a new name, which the mouth of the LORD shall name.

3Thou shalt also be a crown of glory in the hand of the LORD, and a royal diadem in the hand of thy God.

4Thou shalt no more be termed Forsaken; neither shall thy land any more be termed Desolate: but thou shalt be called Hephzi–bah, and thy land Beulah: for the LORD delighteth in thee, and thy land shall be married.

5For *as* a young man marrieth a virgin, *so* shall thy sons marry thee: and *as* the bridegroom rejoiceth over the bride, *so* shall thy God rejoice over thee.

6I have set watchmen upon thy walls, O Jerusalem, *which* shall never hold their peace day nor night: ye that make mention of the LORD, keep not silence,

7And give him no rest, till he establish, and till he make Jerusalem a praise in the earth.

PHILIPPIANS 1:27—2:18

ONLY let your conversation be as it becometh the gospel of Christ: that whether I come and see you, or else be absent, I may hear of your affairs, that ye stand fast in one spirit, with one mind striving together for the faith of the gospel;

28And in nothing terrified by your adversaries: which is to them an evident token of perdition, but to you of salvation, and that of God.

29For unto you it is given in the behalf of Christ, not only to believe on him, but also to suffer for his sake;

30Having the same conflict which ye saw in me, and now hear *to be* in me.

IF *there be* therefore any consolation in Christ, if any comfort of love, if any fellowship of the Spirit, if any bowels and mercies,

2Fulfil ye my joy, that ye be likeminded, having the same love, *being* of one accord, of one mind.

3*Let* nothing *be done* through strife or vainglory; but in lowliness of mind let each esteem other better than themselves.

4Look not every man on his own things, but every man also on the things of others.

5Let this mind be in you, which was also in Christ Jesus:

6Who, being in the form of God, thought it not robbery to be equal with God:

7But made himself of no reputation, and took upon him the form of a servant, and was made in the likeness of men:

8And being found in fashion as a man, he humbled himself, and became obedient unto death, even the death of the cross.

9Wherefore God also hath highly exalted him, and given him a name which is above every name:

10That at the name of Jesus every knee should bow, of *things* in heaven, and *things* in earth, and *things* under the earth;

11And *that* every tongue should confess that Jesus Christ *is* Lord, to the glory of God the Father.

12Wherefore, my beloved, as ye have always obeyed, not as in my presence only, but now much more in my absence, work out your own salvation with fear and trembling.

13For it is God which worketh in you both to will and to do of *his* good pleasure.

14Do all things without murmurings and disputings:

15That ye may be blameless and harmless, the sons of God, without rebuke, in the midst of a crooked and perverse nation, among whom ye shine as lights in the world;

16Holding forth the word of life; that I may rejoice in the day of Christ, that I have not run in vain, neither laboured in vain.

17Yea, and if I be offered upon the sacrifice and service of your faith, I joy, and rejoice with you all.

18For the same cause also do ye joy, and rejoice with me.

PSALM 72:1–20

GIVE the king thy judgments, O God, and thy righteousness unto the king's son.

2He shall judge thy people with righteousness, and thy poor with judgment.

3The mountains shall bring peace to the people, and the little hills, by righteousness.

4He shall judge the poor of the people, he shall save the children of the needy, and shall break in pieces the oppressor.

5They shall fear thee as long as the sun and moon endure, throughout all generations.

6He shall come down like rain upon the mown grass: as showers *that* water the earth.

7In his days shall the righteous flourish; and abundance of peace so long as the moon endureth.

8He shall have dominion also from sea to sea, and from the river unto the ends of the earth.

9They that dwell in the wilderness shall bow before him; and his enemies shall lick the dust.

10The kings of Tarshish and of the isles shall bring presents: the kings of Sheba and Seba shall offer gifts.

11Yea, all kings shall fall down before him: all nations shall serve him.

12For he shall deliver the needy when he crieth; the poor also, and *him* that hath no helper.

13He shall spare the poor and needy, and shall save the souls of the needy.

14He shall redeem their soul from deceit and violence: and precious shall their blood be in his sight.

15And he shall live, and to him shall be given of the gold of Sheba: prayer also shall be made for him continually; *and* daily shall he be praised.

16There shall be an handful of corn in the earth upon the top of the mountains; the fruit thereof shall shake like Lebanon: and *they* of the city shall flourish like grass of the earth.

17His name shall endure for ever: his name shall be continued as long as the sun: and *men* shall be blessed in him: all nations shall call him blessed.

18Blessed *be* the Lord God, the God of Israel, who only doeth wondrous things.

19And blessed *be* his glorious name for ever: and let the whole earth be filled *with* his glory; Amen, and Amen.

20The prayers of David the son of Jesse are ended.

PROVERBS FOR TODAY/ 24:11–12

If thou forbear to deliver them that are drawn unto death, and those that are ready to be slain; If thou sayest, Behold, we knew it not; doth not he that pondereth the heart consider it? and he that keepeth thy soul, doth not he know it? and shall not he render to every man according to his works?

OCTOBER 1

ISAIAH 62:8—65:25

THE Lord hath sworn by his right hand, and by the arm of his strength, Surely I will no more give thy corn *to be* meat for thine enemies; and the sons of the stranger shall not drink thy wine, for the which thou hast laboured:

9But they that have gathered it shall eat it, and praise the Lord; and they that have brought it together shall drink it in the courts of my holiness.

10Go through, go through the gates; prepare ye the way of the people; cast up, cast up the highway; gather out the stones; lift up a standard for the people.

11Behold, the Lord hath proclaimed unto the end of the world, Say ye to the daughter of Zion, Behold, thy salvation cometh; behold, his reward *is* with him, and his work before him.

12And they shall call them, The holy people, The redeemed of the LORD: and thou shalt be called, Sought out, A city not forsaken.

WHO *is* this that cometh from Edom, with dyed garments from Bozrah? this *that is* glorious in his apparel, travelling in the greatness of his strength? I that speak in righteousness, mighty to save.

2Wherefore *art thou* red in thine apparel, and thy garments like him that treadeth in the winefat?

3I have trodden the winepress alone; and of the people *there was* none with me: for I will tread them in mine anger, and trample them in my fury; and their blood shall be sprinkled upon my garments, and I will stain all my raiment.

4For the day of vengeance *is* in mine heart, and the year of my redeemed is come.

5And I looked, and *there was* none to help; and I wondered that *there was* none to uphold: therefore mine own arm brought salvation unto me; and my fury, it upheld me.

6And I will tread down the people in mine anger, and make them drunk in my fury, and I will bring down their strength to the earth.

7I will mention the lovingkindnesses of the LORD, *and* the praises of the LORD, according to all that the LORD hath bestowed on us, and the great goodness toward the house of Israel, which he hath bestowed on them according to his mercies, and according to the multitude of his lovingkindnesses.

8For he said, Surely they *are* my people, children *that* will not lie: so he was their Saviour.

9In all their affliction he was afflicted, and the angel of his presence saved them: in his love and in his pity he redeemed them; and he bare them, and carried them all the days of old.

10But they rebelled, and vexed his holy Spirit: therefore he was turned to be their enemy, *and* he fought against them.

11Then he remembered the days of old, Moses *and* his people, *saying,* Where *is* he that brought them up out of the sea with the shepherd of his flock? where *is* he that put his holy Spirit within him?

12That led *them* by the right hand of Moses with his glorious arm, dividing the water before them, to make himself an everlasting name?

13That led them through the deep, as an horse in the wilderness, *that* they should not stumble?

14As a beast goeth down into the valley, the Spirit of the LORD caused him to rest: so didst thou lead thy people, to make thyself a glorious name.

15Look down from heaven, and behold from the habitation of thy holiness and of thy glory: where *is* thy zeal and thy strength, the sounding of thy bowels and of thy mercies toward me? are they restrained?

16Doubtless thou *art* our father, though Abraham be ignorant of us, and Israel acknowledge us not: thou, O LORD, *art* our father, our redeemer: thy name *is* from everlasting.

17O LORD, why hast thou made us to err from thy ways, *and* hardened our heart from thy fear? Return for thy servants' sake, the tribes of thine inheritance.

18The people of thy holiness have possessed *it* but a little while: our adversaries have trodden down thy sanctuary.

19We are *thine:* thou never barest rule over them; they were not called by thy name.

OH that thou wouldest rend the heavens, that thou wouldest come down, that the mountains might flow down at thy presence,

2As *when* the melting fire burneth, the fire causeth the waters to boil, to make thy name known to thine adversaries, *that* the nations may tremble at thy presence!

³When thou didst terrible things *which* we looked not for, thou camest down, the mountains flowed down at thy presence.

⁴For since the beginning of the world *men* have not heard, nor perceived by the ear, neither hath the eye seen, O God, beside thee, *what* he hath prepared for him that waiteth for him.

⁵Thou meetest him that rejoiceth and worketh righteousness, *those that* remember thee in thy ways: behold, thou art wroth; for we have sinned: in those is continuance, and we shall be saved.

⁶But we are all as an unclean *thing,* and all our righteousnesses *are* as filthy rags; and we all do fade as a leaf; and our iniquities, like the wind, have taken us away.

⁷And *there is* none that calleth upon thy name, that stirreth up himself to take hold of thee: for thou hast hid thy face from us, and hast consumed us, because of our iniquities.

⁸But now, O LORD, thou *art* our father; we *are* the clay, and thou our potter; and we all *are* the work of thy hand.

⁹Be not wroth very sore, O LORD, neither remember iniquity for ever: behold, see, we beseech thee, we *are* all thy people.

¹⁰Thy holy cities are a wilderness, Zion is a wilderness, Jerusalem a desolation.

¹¹Our holy and our beautiful house, where our fathers praised thee, is burned up with fire: and all our pleasant things are laid waste.

¹²Wilt thou refrain thyself for these *things,* O LORD? wilt thou hold thy peace, and afflict us very sore?

I AM sought of *them that* asked not *for me;* I am found of *them that* sought me not: I said, Behold me, behold me,

unto a nation *that* was not called by my name.

²I have spread out my hands all the day unto a rebellious people, which walketh in a way *that was* not good, after their own thoughts;

³A people that provoketh me to anger continually to my face; that sacrificeth in gardens, and burneth incense upon altars of brick;

⁴Which remain among the graves, and lodge in the monuments, which eat swine's flesh, and broth of abominable *things is in* their vessels;

⁵Which say, Stand by thyself, come not near to me: for I am holier than thou. These *are* a smoke in my nose, a fire that burneth all the day.

⁶Behold, *it is* written before me: I will not keep silence, but will recompense, even recompense into their bosom,

⁷Your iniquities, and the iniquities of your fathers together, saith the LORD, which have burned incense upon the mountains, and blasphemed me upon the hills: therefore will I measure their former work into their bosom.

⁸Thus saith the LORD, As the new wine is found in the cluster, and *one* saith, Destroy it not; for a blessing *is* in it: so will I do for my servants' sakes, that I may not destroy them all.

⁹And I will bring forth a seed out of Jacob, and out of Judah an inheritor of my mountains: and mine elect shall inherit it, and my servants shall dwell there.

¹⁰And Sharon shall be a fold of flocks, and the valley of Achor a place for the herds to lie down in, for my people that have sought me.

¹¹But ye *are* they that forsake the LORD, that forget my holy mountain, that prepare a table for that troop, and that furnish the drink offering unto that number.

¹²Therefore will I number you to the sword, and ye shall all bow down to the slaughter: because when I called,

ye did not answer; when I spake, ye did not hear; but did evil before mine eyes, and did choose *that* wherein I delighted not.

13Therefore thus saith the Lord GOD, Behold, my servants shall eat, but ye shall be hungry: behold, my servants shall drink, but ye shall be thirsty: behold, my servants shall rejoice, but ye shall be ashamed:

14Behold, my servants shall sing for joy of heart, but ye shall cry for sorrow of heart, and shall howl for vexation of spirit.

15And ye shall leave your name for a curse unto my chosen: for the Lord GOD shall slay thee, and call his servants by another name:

16That he who blesseth himself in the earth shall bless himself in the God of truth; and he that sweareth in the earth shall swear by the God of truth; because the former troubles are forgotten, and because they are hid from mine eyes.

17For, behold, I create new heavens and a new earth: and the former shall not be remembered, nor come into mind.

18But be ye glad and rejoice for ever *in that* which I create: for, behold, I create Jerusalem a rejoicing, and her people a joy.

19And I will rejoice in Jerusalem, and joy in my people: and the voice of weeping shall be no more heard in her, nor the voice of crying.

20There shall be no more thence an infant of days, nor an old man that hath not filled his days: for the child shall die an hundred years old; but the sinner *being* an hundred years old shall be accursed.

21And they shall build houses, and inhabit *them;* and they shall plant vineyards, and eat the fruit of them.

22They shall not build, and another inhabit; they shall not plant, and another eat: for as the days of a tree *are* the days of my people, and mine elect shall long enjoy the work of their hands.

23They shall not labour in vain, nor bring forth for trouble; for they *are* the seed of the blessed of the LORD, and their offspring with them.

24And it shall come to pass, that before they call, I will answer; and while they are yet speaking, I will hear.

25The wolf and the lamb shall feed together, and the lion shall eat straw like the bullock: and dust *shall be* the serpent's meat. They shall not hurt nor destroy in all my holy mountain, saith the LORD.

PHILIPPIANS 2:19—3:3

BUT I trust in the Lord Jesus to send Timotheus shortly unto you, that I also may be of good comfort, when I know your state.

20For I have no man likeminded, who will naturally care for your state.

21For all seek their own, not the things which are Jesus Christ's.

22But ye know the proof of him, that, as a son with the father, he hath served with me in the gospel.

23Him therefore I hope to send presently, so soon as I shall see how it will go with me.

24But I trust in the Lord that I also myself shall come shortly.

25Yet I supposed it necessary to send to you Epaphroditus, my brother, and companion in labour, and fellowsoldier, but your messenger, and he that ministered to my wants.

26For he longed after you all, and was full of heaviness, because that ye had heard that he had been sick.

27For indeed he was sick nigh unto death: but God had mercy on him; and not on him only, but on me also, lest I should have sorrow upon sorrow.

28I sent him therefore the more carefully, that, when ye see him again, ye may rejoice, and that I may be the less sorrowful.

29Receive him therefore in the Lord with all gladness; and hold such in reputation:

30Because for the work of Christ he was nigh unto death, not regarding his life, to supply your lack of service toward me.

FINALLY, my brethren, rejoice in the Lord. To write the same things to you, to me indeed *is* not grievous, but for you *it is* safe.

2Beware of dogs, beware of evil workers, beware of the concision.

3For we are the circumcision, which worship God in the spirit, and rejoice in Christ Jesus, and have no confidence in the flesh.

PSALM 73:1–28

TRULY God *is* good to Israel, *even* to such as are of a clean heart.

2But as for me, my feet were almost gone; my steps had well nigh slipped.

3For I was envious at the foolish, *when* I saw the prosperity of the wicked.

4For *there are* no bands in their death: but their strength *is* firm.

5They *are* not in trouble *as other* men; neither are they plagued like *other* men.

6Therefore pride compasseth them about as a chain; violence covereth them *as* a garment.

7Their eyes stand out with fatness: they have more than heart could wish.

8They are corrupt, and speak wickedly *concerning* oppression: they speak loftily.

9They set their mouth against the heavens, and their tongue walketh through the earth.

10Therefore his people return hither: and waters of a full *cup* are wrung out to them.

11And they say, How doth God know? and is there knowledge in the most High?

12Behold, these *are* the ungodly, who prosper in the world; they increase *in* riches.

13Verily I have cleansed my heart *in* vain, and washed my hands in innocency.

14For all the day long have I been plagued, and chastened every morning.

15If I say, I will speak thus; behold, I should offend *against* the generation of thy children.

16When I thought to know this, it *was* too painful for me;

17Until I went into the sanctuary of God; *then* understood I their end.

18Surely thou didst set them in slippery places: thou castedst them down into destruction.

19How are they *brought* into desolation, as in a moment! they are utterly consumed with terrors.

20As a dream when *one* awaketh; *so,* O Lord, when thou awakest, thou shalt despise their image.

21Thus my heart was grieved, and I was pricked in my reins.

22So foolish *was* I, and ignorant: I was *as* a beast before thee.

23Nevertheless I *am* continually with thee: thou hast holden *me* by my right hand.

24Thou shalt guide me with thy counsel, and afterward receive me *to* glory.

25Whom have I in heaven *but thee?* and *there is* none upon earth *that* I desire beside thee.

26My flesh and my heart faileth: *but* God *is* the strength of my heart, and my portion for ever.

27For, lo, they that are far from thee shall perish: thou hast destroyed all them that go a whoring from thee.

28But *it is* good for me to draw near to God: I have put my trust in the Lord GOD, that I may declare all thy works.

PROVERBS FOR TODAY/ 24:13–14

My son, eat thou honey, because it is *good; and the honeycomb,* which is *sweet to thy taste: So* shall *the knowledge of wisdom* be *unto thy soul: when thou hast found* it, *then there shall be a reward, and thy expectation shall not be cut off.*

OCTOBER 2

ISAIAH 66:1–24

Thus saith the LORD, The heaven *is* my throne, and the earth *is* my footstool: where *is* the house that ye build unto me? and where *is* the place of my rest?

2For all those *things* hath mine hand made, and all those *things* have been, saith the LORD: but to this *man* will I look, *even* to *him that is* poor and of a contrite spirit, and trembleth at my word.

3He that killeth an ox *is as if* he slew a man; he that sacrificeth a lamb, *as if* he cut off a dog's neck; he that offereth an oblation, *as if he offered* swine's blood; he that burneth incense, *as if* he blessed an idol. Yea, they have chosen their own ways, and their soul delighteth in their abominations.

4I also will choose their delusions, and will bring their fears upon them; because when I called, none did answer; when I spake, they did not hear: but they did evil before mine eyes, and chose *that* in which I delighted not.

5Hear the word of the LORD, ye that tremble at his word; Your brethren that hated you, that cast you out for my name's sake, said, Let the LORD be glorified: but he shall appear to your joy, and they shall be ashamed.

6A voice of noise from the city, a voice from the temple, a voice of the LORD that rendereth recompence to his enemies.

7Before she travailed, she brought forth; before her pain came, she was delivered of a man child.

8Who hath heard such a thing? who hath seen such things? Shall the earth be made to bring forth in one day? *or* shall a nation be born at once? for as soon as Zion travailed, she brought forth her children.

9Shall I bring to the birth, and not cause to bring forth? saith the LORD: shall I cause to bring forth, and shut *the womb?* saith thy God.

10Rejoice ye with Jerusalem, and be glad with her, all ye that love her: rejoice for joy with her, all ye that mourn for her:

11That ye may suck, and be satisfied with the breasts of her consolations; that ye may milk out, and be delighted with the abundance of her glory.

12For thus saith the LORD, Behold, I will extend peace to her like a river, and the glory of the Gentiles like a flowing stream: then shall ye suck, ye shall be borne upon *her* sides, and be dandled upon *her* knees.

13As one whom his mother comforteth, so will I comfort you; and ye shall be comforted in Jerusalem.

14And when ye see *this,* your heart shall rejoice, and your bones shall flourish like an herb: and the hand of the LORD shall be known toward his servants, and *his* indignation toward his enemies.

15For, behold, the LORD will come with fire, and with his chariots like a whirlwind, to render his anger with fury, and his rebuke with flames of fire.

16For by fire and by his sword will the Lord plead with all flesh: and the slain of the Lord shall be many.

17They that sanctify themselves, and purify themselves in the gardens behind one *tree* in the midst, eating swine's flesh, and the abomination, and the mouse, shall be consumed together, saith the Lord.

18For I *know* their works and their thoughts: it shall come, that I will gather all nations and tongues; and they shall come, and see my glory.

19And I will set a sign among them, and I will send those that escape of them unto the nations, *to* Tarshish, Pul, and Lud, that draw the bow, *to* Tubal, and Javan, *to* the isles afar off, that have not heard my fame, neither have seen my glory: and they shall declare my glory among the Gentiles.

20And they shall bring all your brethren *for* an offering unto the Lord out of all nations upon horses, and in chariots, and in litters, and upon mules, and upon swift beasts, to my holy mountain Jerusalem, saith the Lord, as the children of Israel bring an offering in a clean vessel into the house of the Lord.

21And I will also take of them for priests *and* for Levites, saith the Lord.

22For as the new heavens and the new earth, which I will make, shall remain before me, saith the Lord, so shall your seed and your name remain.

23And it shall come to pass, *that* from one new moon to another, and from one sabbath to another, shall all flesh come to worship before me, saith the Lord.

24And they shall go forth, and look upon the carcases of the men that have transgressed against me: for their worm shall not die, neither shall their fire be quenched; and they shall be an abhorring unto all flesh.

PHILIPPIANS 3:4–21

THOUGH I might also have confidence in the flesh. If any other man thinketh that he hath whereof he might trust in the flesh, I more:

5Circumcised the eighth day, of the stock of Israel, *of* the tribe of Benjamin, an Hebrew of the Hebrews; as touching the law, a Pharisee;

6Concerning zeal, persecuting the church; touching the righteousness which is in the law, blameless.

7But what things were gain to me, those I counted loss for Christ.

8Yea doubtless, and I count all things *but* loss for the excellency of the knowledge of Christ Jesus my Lord: for whom I have suffered the loss of all things, and do count them *but* dung, that I may win Christ,

9And be found in him, not having mine own righteousness, which is of the law, but that which is through the faith of Christ, the righteousness which is of God by faith:

10That I may know him, and the power of his resurrection, and the fellowship of his sufferings, being made conformable unto his death;

11If by any means I might attain unto the resurrection of the dead.

12Not as though I had already attained, either were already perfect: but I follow after, if that I may apprehend that for which also I am apprehended of Christ Jesus.

13Brethren, I count not myself to have apprehended: but *this* one thing *I do*, forgetting those things which are behind, and reaching forth unto those things which are before,

14I press toward the mark for the prize of the high calling of God in Christ Jesus.

15Let us therefore, as many as be perfect, be thus minded: and if in any thing ye be otherwise minded, God shall reveal even this unto you.

16Nevertheless, whereto we have already attained, let us walk by the same rule, let us mind the same thing.

17Brethren, be followers together of me, and mark them which walk so as ye have us for an ensample.

18(For many walk, of whom I have told you often, and now tell you even weeping, *that they are* the enemies of the cross of Christ:

19Whose end *is* destruction, whose God *is their* belly, and *whose* glory *is* in their shame, who mind earthly things.)

20For our conversation is in heaven; from whence also we look for the Saviour, the Lord Jesus Christ:

21Who shall change our vile body, that it may be fashioned like unto his glorious body, according to the working whereby he is able even to subdue all things unto himself.

PSALM 74:1–23

O GOD, why hast thou cast *us* off for ever? *why* doth thine anger smoke against the sheep of thy pasture?

2Remember thy congregation, *which* thou hast purchased of old; the rod of thine inheritance, *which* thou hast redeemed; this mount Zion, wherein thou hast dwelt.

3Lift up thy feet unto the perpetual desolations: *even* all *that* the enemy hath done wickedly in the sanctuary.

4Thine enemies roar in the midst of thy congregations; they set up their ensigns *for* signs.

5A *man* was famous according as he had lifted up axes upon the thick trees.

6But now they break down the carved work thereof at once with axes and hammers.

7They have cast fire into thy sanctuary, they have defiled *by casting down* the dwelling place of thy name to the ground.

8They said in their hearts, Let us destroy them together: they have burned up all the synagogues of God in the land.

9We see not our signs: *there is* no more any prophet: neither *is there* among us any that knoweth how long.

10O God, how long shall the adversary reproach? shall the enemy blaspheme thy name for ever?

11Why withdrawest thou thy hand, even thy right hand? pluck *it* out of thy bosom.

12For God *is* my King of old, working salvation in the midst of the earth.

13Thou didst divide the sea by thy strength: thou brakest the heads of the dragons in the waters.

14Thou brakest the heads of leviathan in pieces, *and* gavest him *to be* meat to the people inhabiting the wilderness.

15Thou didst cleave the fountain and the flood: thou driedst up mighty rivers.

16The day *is* thine, the night also *is* thine: thou hast prepared the light and the sun.

17Thou hast set all the borders of the earth: thou hast made summer and winter.

18Remember this, *that* the enemy hath reproached, O LORD, and *that* the foolish people have blasphemed thy name.

19O deliver not the soul of thy turtledove unto the multitude *of the wicked:* forget not the congregation of thy poor for ever.

20Have respect unto the covenant: for the dark places of the earth are full of the habitations of cruelty.

21O let not the oppressed return ashamed: let the poor and needy praise thy name.

22Arise, O God, plead thine own cause: remember how the foolish man reproacheth thee daily.

23Forget not the voice of thine enemies: the tumult of those that rise up against thee increaseth continually.

PROVERBS FOR TODAY/ 24:15–16

Lay not wait, O wicked man, *against the dwelling of the righteous; spoil not his resting place: For a just* man *falleth seven times, and riseth up again: but the wicked shall fall into mischief.*

OCTOBER 3

JEREMIAH 1:1—2:30

THE words of Jeremiah the son of Hilkiah, of the priests that *were* in Anathoth in the land of Benjamin:

2To whom the word of the LORD came in the days of Josiah the son of Amon king of Judah, in the thirteenth year of his reign.

3It came also in the days of Jehoiakim the son of Josiah king of Judah, unto the end of the eleventh year of Zedekiah the son of Josiah king of Judah, unto the carrying away of Jerusalem captive in the fifth month.

4Then the word of the LORD came unto me, saying,

5Before I formed thee in the belly I knew thee; and before thou camest forth out of the womb I sanctified thee, *and* I ordained thee a prophet unto the nations.

6Then said I, Ah, Lord GOD! behold, I cannot speak: for I *am* a child.

7But the LORD said unto me, Say not, I *am* a child: for thou shalt go to all that I shall send thee, and whatsoever I command thee thou shalt speak.

8Be not afraid of their faces: for I *am* with thee to deliver thee, saith the LORD.

9Then the LORD put forth his hand, and touched my mouth. And the LORD said unto me, Behold, I have put my words in thy mouth.

10See, I have this day set thee over the nations and over the kingdoms, to root out, and to pull down, and to destroy, and to throw down, to build, and to plant.

11Moreover the word of the LORD came unto me, saying, Jeremiah, what seest thou? And I said, I see a rod of an almond tree.

12Then said the LORD unto me, Thou hast well seen: for I will hasten my word to perform it.

13And the word of the LORD came unto me the second time, saying, What seest thou? And I said, I see a seething pot; and the face thereof *is* toward the north.

14Then the LORD said unto me, Out of the north an evil shall break forth upon all the inhabitants of the land.

15For, lo, I will call all the families of the kingdoms of the north, saith the LORD; and they shall come, and they shall set every one his throne at the entering of the gates of Jerusalem, and against all the walls thereof round about, and against all the cities of Judah.

16And I will utter my judgments against them touching all their wickedness, who have forsaken me, and have burned incense unto other gods, and worshipped the works of their own hands.

17Thou therefore gird up thy loins, and arise, and speak unto them all that I command thee: be not dismayed at their faces, lest I confound thee before them.

18For, behold, I have made thee this day a defenced city, and an iron pillar, and brasen walls against the whole land, against the kings of Judah, against the princes thereof, against the priests thereof, and against the people of the land.

19And they shall fight against thee; but they shall not prevail against thee; for I *am* with thee, saith the LORD, to deliver thee.

MOREOVER the word of the LORD came to me, saying,

2Go and cry in the ears of Jerusalem, saying, Thus saith the LORD; I remember thee, the kindness of thy youth, the love of thine espousals, when thou wentest after me in the wilderness, in a land *that was* not sown.

3Israel *was* holiness unto the LORD, *and* the firstfruits of his increase: all that devour him shall offend; evil shall come upon them, saith the LORD.

4Hear ye the word of the LORD, O house of Jacob, and all the families of the house of Israel:

5Thus saith the LORD, What iniquity have your fathers found in me, that they are gone far from me, and have walked after vanity, and are become vain?

6Neither said they, Where *is* the LORD that brought us up out of the land of Egypt, that led us through the wilderness, through a land of deserts and of pits, through a land of drought, and of the shadow of death, through a land that no man passed through, and where no man dwelt?

7And I brought you into a plentiful country, to eat the fruit thereof and the goodness thereof; but when ye entered, ye defiled my land, and made mine heritage an abomination.

8The priests said not, Where *is* the LORD? and they that handle the law knew me not: the pastors also transgressed against me, and the prophets prophesied by Baal, and walked after *things that* do not profit.

9Wherefore I will yet plead with you, saith the LORD, and with your children's children will I plead.

10For pass over the isles of Chittim, and see; and send unto Kedar, and consider diligently, and see if there be such a thing.

11Hath a nation changed *their* gods, which *are* yet no gods? but my people have changed their glory for *that which* doth not profit.

12Be astonished, O ye heavens, at this, and be horribly afraid, be ye very desolate, saith the LORD.

13For my people have committed two evils; they have forsaken me the fountain of living waters, *and* hewed them out cisterns, broken cisterns, that can hold no water.

14*Is* Israel a servant? *is* he a homeborn *slave?* why is he spoiled?

15The young lions roared upon him, *and* yelled, and they made his land waste: his cities are burned without inhabitant.

16Also the children of Noph and Tahapanes have broken the crown of thy head.

17Hast thou not procured this unto thyself, in that thou hast forsaken the LORD thy God, when he led thee by the way?

18And now what hast thou to do in the way of Egypt, to drink the waters of Sihor? or what hast thou to do in the way of Assyria, to drink the waters of the river?

19Thine own wickedness shall correct thee, and thy backslidings shall reprove thee: know therefore and see that *it is* an evil *thing* and bitter, that thou hast forsaken the LORD thy God, and that my fear *is* not in thee, saith the Lord GOD of hosts.

20For of old time I have broken thy yoke, *and* burst thy bands; and thou saidst, I will not transgress; when upon every high hill and under every green tree thou wanderest, playing the harlot.

21Yet I had planted thee a noble vine, wholly a right seed: how then art thou turned into the degenerate plant of a strange vine unto me?

22For though thou wash thee with nitre, and take thee much sope, *yet* thine iniquity is marked before me, saith the Lord GOD.

23How canst thou say, I am not polluted, I have not gone after Baalim? see thy way in the valley, know what thou hast done: *thou art* a swift dromedary traversing her ways;

24A wild ass used to the wilderness, *that* snuffeth up the wind at her pleasure; in her occasion who can turn her away? all they that seek her will not weary themselves; in her month they shall find her.

25Withhold thy foot from being unshod, and thy throat from thirst: but thou saidst, There is no hope: no; for I have loved strangers, and after them will I go.

26As the thief is ashamed when he is found, so is the house of Israel ashamed; they, their kings, their princes, and their priests, and their prophets,

27Saying to a stock, Thou *art* my father; and to a stone, Thou hast brought me forth: for they have turned *their* back unto me, and not *their* face: but in the time of their trouble they will say, Arise, and save us.

28But where *are* thy gods that thou hast made thee? let them arise, if they can save thee in the time of thy trouble: for *according* to the number of thy cities are thy gods, O Judah.

29Wherefore will ye plead with me? ye all have transgressed against me, saith the LORD.

30In vain have I smitten your children; they received no correction: your own sword hath devoured your prophets, like a destroying lion.

PHILIPPIANS 4:1–23

THEREFORE, my brethren dearly beloved and longed for, my joy and crown, so stand fast in the Lord, *my* dearly beloved.

2I beseech Euodias, and beseech Syntyche, that they be of the same mind in the Lord.

3And I intreat thee also, true yokefellow, help those women which laboured with me in the gospel, with Clement also, and *with* other my fellowlabourers, whose names *are* in the book of life.

4Rejoice in the Lord alway: *and* again I say, Rejoice.

5Let your moderation be known unto all men. The Lord *is* at hand.

6Be careful for nothing; but in every thing by prayer and supplication with thanksgiving let your requests be made known unto God.

7And the peace of God, which passeth all 'understanding, shall keep your hearts and minds through Christ Jesus.

8Finally, brethren, whatsoever things are true, whatsoever things *are* honest, whatsoever things *are* just, whatsoever things *are* pure, whatsoever things *are* lovely, whatsoever thing *are* of good report; if *there be* any virtue, and if *there be* any praise, think on these things.

9Those things, which ye have both learned, and received, and heard, and seen in me, do: and the God of peace shall be with you.

10But I rejoiced in the Lord greatly, that now at the last your care of me hath flourished again; wherein ye were also careful, but ye lacked opportunity.

11Not that I speak in respect of want: for I have learned, in whatsoever state I am, *therewith* to be content.

12I know both how to be abased, and I know how to abound: every where and in all things I am instructed both to be full and to be hungry, both to abound and to suffer need.

13I can do all things through Christ which strengtheneth me.

14Notwithstanding ye have well done, that ye did communicate with my affliction.

15Now ye Philippians know also, that in the beginning of the gospel, when I departed from Macedonia, no church communicated with me as concerning giving and receiving, but ye only.

16For even in Thessalonica ye sent once and again unto my necessity.

17Not because I desire a gift: but I desire fruit that may abound to your account.

18But I have all, and abound: I am full, having received of Epaphroditus the things *which were sent* from you, an odour of a sweet smell, a sacrifice acceptable, well-pleasing to God.

19But my God shall supply all your need according to his riches in glory by Christ Jesus.

20Now unto God and our Father *be* glory for ever and ever. Amen.

21Salute every saint in Christ Jesus. The brethren which are with me greet you.

22All the saints salute you, chiefly they that are of Caesar's household.

23The grace of our Lord Jesus Christ *be* with you all. Amen.

PSALM 75:1–10

UNTO thee, O God, do we give thanks, *unto thee* do we give thanks: for *that* thy name is near thy wondrous works declare.

2When I shall receive the congregation I will judge uprightly.

3The earth and all the inhabitants thereof are dissolved: I bear up the pillars of it. Selah.

4I said unto the fools, Deal not foolishly: and to the wicked, Lift not up the horn:

5Lift not up your horn on high: speak *not with* a stiff neck.

6For promotion *cometh* neither from the east, nor from the west, nor from the south.

7But God *is* the judge: he putteth down one, and setteth up another.

8For in the hand of the LORD *there is* a cup, and the wine is red; it is full of mixture; and he poureth out of the same: but the dregs thereof, all the wicked of the earth shall wring *them* out, *and* drink *them*.

9But I will declare for ever; I will sing praises to the God of Jacob.

10All the horns of the wicked also will I cut off; *but* the horns of the righteous shall be exalted.

PROVERBS FOR TODAY/ 24:17–20

Rejoice not when thine enemy falleth, and let not thine heart be glad when he stumbleth: Lest the LORD see it, *and it displease him, and he turn away his wrath from him. Fret not thyself because of evil* men, *neither be thou envious at the wicked; For there shall be no reward to the evil* man; *the candle of the wicked shall be put out.*

JEREMIAH 2:31—4:18

O GENERATION, see ye the word of the LORD. Have I been a wilderness unto Israel? a land of darkness? wherefore say my people, We are lords; we will come no more unto thee?

32Can a maid forget her ornaments, *or* a bride her attire? yet my people have forgotten me days without number.

33Why trimmest thou thy way to seek love? therefore hast thou also taught the wicked ones thy ways.

34Also in thy skirts is found the blood of the souls of the poor innocents: I have not found it by secret search, but upon all these.

35Yet thou sayest, Because I am innocent, surely his anger shall turn from me. Behold, I will plead with thee, because thou sayest, I have not sinned.

36Why gaddest thou about so much to change thy way? thou also shalt be ashamed of Egypt, as thou wast ashamed of Assyria.

37Yea, thou shalt go forth from him, and thine hands upon thine head: for the LORD hath rejected thy confidences, and thou shalt not prosper in them.

THEY say, If a man put away his wife, and she go from him, and become another man's, shall he return unto her again? shall not that land be greatly polluted? but thou hast played the harlot with many lovers; yet return again to me, saith the LORD.

2Lift up thine eyes unto the high places, and see where thou hast not been lien with. In the ways hast thou sat for them, as the Arabian in the wilderness; and thou hast polluted the land with thy whoredoms and with thy wickedness.

3Therefore the showers have been withholden, and there hath been no latter rain; and thou hadst a whore's forehead, thou refusedst to be ashamed.

4Wilt thou not from this time cry unto me, My father, thou *art* the guide of my youth?

5Will he reserve *his anger* for ever? will he keep *it* to the end? Behold, thou hast spoken and done evil things as thou couldest.

6The LORD said also unto me in the days of Josiah the king, Hast thou seen *that* which backsliding Israel hath done? she is gone up upon every high mountain and under every green tree, and there hath played the harlot.

7And I said after she had done all these *things,* Turn thou unto me. But she returned not. And her treacherous sister Judah saw *it.*

8And I saw, when for all the causes whereby backsliding Israel committed adultery I had put her away, and given her a bill of divorce; yet her treacherous sister Judah feared not, but went and played the harlot also.

9And it came to pass through the lightness of her whoredom, that she defiled the land, and committed adultery with stones and with stocks.

10And yet for all this her treacherous sister Judah hath not turned unto me with her whole heart, but feignedly, saith the LORD.

11And the LORD said unto me, The backsliding Israel hath justified herself more than treacherous Judah.

12Go and proclaim these words toward the north, and say, Return, thou backsliding Israel, saith the LORD; *and* I will not cause mine anger to fall upon you: for I *am* merciful, saith the LORD, *and* I will not keep *anger* for ever.

13Only acknowledge thine iniquity,

that thou hast transgressed against the LORD thy God, and hast scattered thy ways to the strangers under every green tree, and ye have not obeyed my voice, saith the LORD.

14Turn, O backsliding children, saith the LORD; for I am married unto you: and I will take you one of a city, and two of a family, and I will bring you to Zion:

15And I will give you pastors according to mine heart, which shall feed you with knowledge and understanding.

16And it shall come to pass, when ye be multiplied and increased in the land, in those days, saith the LORD, they shall say no more, The ark of the covenant of the LORD: neither shall it come to mind: neither shall they remember it; neither shall they visit *it;* neither shall *that* be done any more.

17At that time they shall call Jerusalem the throne of the LORD; and all the nations shall be gathered unto it, to the name of the LORD, to Jerusalem: neither shall they walk any more after the imagination of their evil heart.

18In those days the house of Judah shall walk with the house of Israel, and they shall come together out of the land of the north to the land that I have given for an inheritance unto your fathers.

19But I said, How shall I put thee among the children, and give thee a pleasant land, a goodly heritage of the hosts of nations? and I said, Thou shalt call me, My father; and shalt not turn away from me.

20Surely *as* a wife treacherously departeth from her husband, so have ye dealt treacherously with me, O house of Israel, saith the LORD.

21A voice was heard upon the high places, weeping *and* supplications of the children of Israel: for they have perverted their way, *and* they have forgotten the LORD their God.

22Return, ye backsliding children, *and* I will heal your backslidings. Behold, we come unto thee; for thou *art* the LORD our God.

23Truly in vain *is salvation hoped for* from the hills, *and from* the multitude of mountains: truly in the LORD our God *is* the salvation of Israel.

24For shame hath devoured the labour of our fathers from our youth; their flocks and their herds, their sons and their daughters.

25We lie down in our shame, and our confusion covereth us: for we have sinned against the LORD our God, we and our fathers, from our youth even unto this day, and have not obeyed the voice of the LORD our God.

IF thou wilt return, O Israel, saith the LORD, return unto me: and if thou wilt put away thine abominations out of my sight, then shalt thou not remove.

2And thou shalt swear, The LORD liveth, in truth, in judgment, and in righteousness; and the nations shall bless themselves in him, and in him shall they glory.

3For thus saith the LORD to the men of Judah and Jerusalem, Break up your fallow ground, and sow not among thorns.

4Circumcise yourselves to the LORD, and take away the foreskins of your heart, ye men of Judah and inhabitants of Jerusalem: lest my fury come forth like fire, and burn that none can quench *it,* because of the evil of your doings.

5Declare ye in Judah, and publish in Jerusalem; and say, Blow ye the trumpet in the land: cry, gather together, and say, Assemble yourselves, and let us go into the defenced cities.

6Set up the standard toward Zion: retire, stay not: for I will bring evil from the north, and a great destruction.

7The lion is come up from his thicket, and the destroyer of the Gentiles is on his way; he is gone forth from his place to make thy land desolate; *and* thy cities shall be laid waste, without an inhabitant.

8For this gird you with sackcloth, lament and howl: for the fierce anger of the LORD is not turned back from us.

9And it shall come to pass at that day, saith the LORD, *that* the heart of the king shall perish, and the heart of the princes; and the priests shall be astonished, and the prophets shall wonder.

10Then said I, Ah, Lord GOD! surely thou hast greatly deceived this people and Jerusalem, saying, Ye shall have peace; whereas the sword reacheth unto the soul.

11At that time shall it be said to this people and to Jerusalem, A dry wind of the high places in the wilderness toward the daughter of my people, not to fan, nor to cleanse,

12*Even* a full wind from those *places* shall come unto me: now also will I give sentence against them.

13Behold, he shall come up as clouds, and his chariots *shall be* as a whirlwind: his horses are swifter than eagles. Woe unto us! for we are spoiled.

14O Jerusalem, wash thine heart from wickedness, that thou mayest be saved. How long shall thy vain thoughts lodge within thee?

15For a voice declareth from Dan, and publisheth affliction from mount Ephraim.

16Make ye mention to the nations; behold, publish against Jerusalem, *that* watchers come from a far country, and give out their voice against the cities of Judah.

17As keepers of a field, are they against her round about; because she hath been rebellious against me, saith the LORD.

18Thy way and thy doings have procured these *things* unto thee; this *is* thy wickedness, because it is bitter, because it reacheth unto thine heart.

COLOSSIANS 1:1–19

PAUL, an apostle of Jesus Christ by the will of God, and Timotheus *our* brother,

2To the saints and faithful brethren in Christ which are at Colosse: Grace *be* unto you, and peace, from God our Father and the Lord Jesus Christ.

3We give thanks to God and the Father of our Lord Jesus Christ, praying always for you,

4Since we heard of your faith in Christ Jesus, and of the love *which ye have* to all the saints.

5For the hope which is laid up for you in heaven, whereof ye heard before in the word of the truth of the gospel;

6Which is come unto you, as *it is* in all the world; and bringeth forth fruit, as *it doth* also in you, since the day ye heard *of it,* and knew the grace of God in truth:

7As ye also learned of Epaphras our dear fellowservant, who is for you a faithful minister of Christ;

8Who also declared unto us your love in the Spirit.

9For this cause we also, since the day we heard *it,* do not cease to pray for you, and to desire that ye might be filled with the knowledge of his will in all wisdom and spiritual understanding;

10That ye might walk worthy of the Lord unto all pleasing, being fruitful in every good work, and increasing in the knowledge of God;

11Strengthened with all might, according to his glorious power, unto all patience and longsuffering with joyfulness;

12Giving thanks unto the Father, which hath made us meet to be partakers of the inheritance of the saints in light:

13Who hath delivered us from the power of darkness, and hath translated *us* into the kingdom of his dear Son:

14In whom we have redemption

through his blood, *even* the forgiveness of sins:

15Who is the image of the invisible God, the firstborn of every creature:

16For by him were all things created, that are in heaven, and that are in earth, visible and invisible, whether *they be* thrones, or dominions, or principalities, or powers: all things were created by him, and for him:

17And he is before all things, and by him all things consist.

18And he is the head of the body, the church: who is the beginning, the firstborn from the dead; that in all *things* he might have the preeminence.

19For it pleased *the Father* that in him should all fulness dwell;

PSALM 76:1–12

I N Judah *is* God known: his name *is* great in Israel.

2In Salem also is his tabernacle, and his dwelling place in Zion.

3There brake he the arrows of the bow, the shield, and the sword, and the battle. Selah.

4Thou *art* more glorious *and* excellent than the mountains of prey.

5The stouthearted are spoiled, they have slept their sleep: and none of the men of might have found their hands.

6At thy rebuke, O God of Jacob, both the chariot and horse are cast into a dead sleep.

7Thou, *even* thou, *art* to be feared: and who may stand in thy sight when once thou art angry?

8Thou didst cause judgment to be heard from heaven; the earth feared, and was still,

9When God arose to judgment, to save all the meek of the earth. Selah.

10Surely the wrath of man shall praise thee: the remainder of wrath shalt thou restrain.

11Vow, and pay unto the LORD your God: let all that be round about him bring presents unto him that ought to be feared.

12He shall cut off the spirit of princes: *he is* terrible to the kings of the earth.

PROVERBS FOR TODAY/ 24:21–22

My son, fear thou the LORD and the king: and meddle not with them that are given to change: For their calamity shall rise suddenly; and who knoweth the ruin of them both?

OCTOBER 5

JEREMIAH 4:19—6:14

M Y bowels, my bowels! I am pained at my very heart; my heart maketh a noise in me; I cannot hold my peace, because thou hast heard, O my soul, the sound of the trumpet, the alarm of war.

20Destruction upon destruction is cried; for the whole land is spoiled: suddenly are my tents spoiled, *and* my curtains in a moment.

21How long shall I see the standard, *and* hear the sound of the trumpet?

22For my people *is* foolish, they have not known me; they *are* sottish children, and they have none understanding: they *are* wise to do evil, but to do good they have no knowledge.

23I beheld the earth, and, lo, *it was* without form, and void; and the heavens, and they *had* no light.

24I beheld the mountains, and, lo, they trembled, and all the hills moved lightly.

25I beheld, and, lo, *there was* no man, and all the birds of the heavens were fled.

26I beheld, and, lo, the fruitful place *was* a wilderness, and all the cities thereof were broken down at the presence of the LORD, *and* by his fierce anger.

27For thus hath the LORD said, The whole land shall be desolate; yet will I not make a full end.

28For this shall the earth mourn, and the heavens above be black: because I have spoken *it,* I have purposed *it,* and will not repent, neither will I turn back from it.

29The whole city shall flee for the noise of the horsemen and bowmen; they shall go into thickets, and climb up upon the rocks: every city *shall be* forsaken, and not a man dwell therein.

30And *when* thou *art* spoiled, what wilt thou do? Though thou clothest thyself with crimson, though thou deckest thee with ornaments of gold, though thou rentest thy face with painting, in vain shalt thou make thyself fair; *thy* lovers will despise thee, they will seek thy life.

31For I have heard a voice as of a woman in travail, *and* the anguish as of her that bringeth forth her first child, the voice of the daughter of Zion, *that* bewaileth herself, *that* spreadeth her hands, *saying,* Woe *is* me now! for my soul is wearied because of murderers.

RUN ye to and fro through the streets of Jerusalem, and see now, and know, and seek in the broad places thereof, if ye can find a man, if there be *any* that executeth judgment, that seeketh the truth; and I will pardon it.

2And though they say, The LORD liveth; surely they swear falsely.

3O LORD, *are* not thine eyes upon the truth? thou hast stricken them, but they have not grieved; thou hast consumed them, *but* they have refused to receive correction: they have made their faces harder than a rock; they have refused to return.

4Therefore I said, Surely these *are* poor; they are foolish: for they know not the way of the LORD, *nor* the judgment of their God.

5I will get me unto the great men, and will speak unto them; for they have known the way of the LORD, *and* the judgment of their God: but these have altogether broken the yoke, *and* burst the bonds.

6Wherefore a lion out of the forest shall slay them, *and* a wolf of the evenings shall spoil them, a leopard shall watch over their cities: every one that goeth out thence shall be torn in pieces: because their transgressions are many, *and* their backslidings are increased.

7How shall I pardon thee for this? thy children have forsaken me, and sworn by *them that are* no gods: when I had fed them to the full, they then committed adultery, and assembled themselves by troops in the harlots' houses.

8They were *as* fed horses in the morning: every one neighed after his neighbour's wife.

9Shall I not visit for these *things?* saith the LORD: and shall not my soul be avenged on such a nation as this?

10Go ye up upon her walls, and destroy; but make not a full end: take away her battlements; for they *are* not the LORD'S.

11For the house of Israel and the house of Judah have dealt very treacherously against me, saith the LORD.

12They have belied the LORD, and said, *It is* not he; neither shall evil come upon us; neither shall we see sword nor famine:

13And the prophets shall become

wind, and the word *is* not in them: thus shall it be done unto them.

14Wherefore thus saith the LORD God of hosts, Because ye speak this word, behold, I will make my words in thy mouth fire, and this people wood, and it shall devour them.

15Lo, I will bring a nation upon you from far, O house of Israel, saith the LORD; it *is* a mighty nation, it *is* an ancient nation, a nation whose language thou knowest not, neither understandest what they say.

16Their quiver *is* as an open sepulchre, they *are* all mighty men.

17And they shall eat up thine harvest, and thy bread, *which* thy sons and thy daughters should eat: they shall eat up thy flocks and thine herds: they shall eat up thy vines and thy fig trees: they shall impoverish thy fenced cities, wherein thou trustedst, with the sword.

18Nevertheless in those days, saith the LORD, I will not make a full end with you.

19And it shall come to pass, when ye shall say, Wherefore doeth the LORD our God all these *things* unto us? then shalt thou answer them, Like as ye have forsaken me, and served strange gods in your land, so shall ye serve strangers in a land *that is* not yours.

20Declare this in the house of Jacob, and publish it in Judah, saying,

21Hear now this, O foolish people, and without understanding; which have eyes, and see not; which have ears, and hear not:

22Fear ye not me? saith the LORD: will ye not tremble at my presence, which have placed the sand *for* the bound of the sea by a perpetual decree, that it cannot pass it: and though the waves thereof toss themselves, yet can they not prevail; though they roar, yet can they not pass over it?

23But this people hath a revolting and a rebellious heart; they are revolted and gone.

24Neither say they in their heart, Let us now fear the LORD our God, that giveth rain, both the former and the latter, in his season: he reserveth unto us the appointed weeks of the harvest.

25Your iniquities have turned away these *things,* and your sins have withholden good *things* from you.

26For among my people are found wicked *men:* they lay wait, as he that setteth snares; they set a trap, they catch men.

27As a cage is full of birds, so *are* their houses full of deceit: therefore they are become great, and waxen rich.

28They are waxen fat, they shine: yea, they overpass the deeds of the wicked: they judge not the cause, the cause of the fatherless, yet they prosper; and the right of the needy do they not judge.

29Shall I not visit for these *things?* saith the LORD: shall not my soul be avenged on such a nation as this?

30A wonderful and horrible thing is committed in the land;

31The prophets prophesy falsely, and the priests bear rule by their means; and my people love *to have it* so: and what will ye do in the end thereof?

O YE children of Benjamin, gather yourselves to flee out of the midst of Jerusalem, and blow the trumpet in Tekoa, and set up a sign of fire in Beth–haccerem: for evil appeareth out of the north, and great destruction.

2I have likened the daughter of Zion to a comely and delicate *woman.*

3The shepherds with their flocks shall come unto her; they shall pitch *their* tents against her round about; they shall feed every one in his place.

4Prepare ye war against her; arise, and let us go up at noon. Woe unto us! for the day goeth away, for the shadows of the evening are stretched out.

5Arise, and let us go by night, and let us destroy her palaces.

6For thus hath the LORD of hosts

said, Hew ye down trees, and cast a mount against Jerusalem: this *is* the city to be visited; she *is* wholly oppression in the midst of her.

7As a fountain casteth out her waters, so she casteth out her wickedness: violence and spoil is heard in her; before me continually *is* grief and wounds.

8Be thou instructed, O Jerusalem, lest my soul depart from thee; lest I make thee desolate, a land not inhabited.

9Thus saith the LORD of hosts, They shall throughly glean the remnant of Israel as a vine: turn back thine hand as a grapegatherer into the baskets.

10To whom shall I speak, and give warning, that they may hear? behold, their ear *is* uncircumcised, and they cannot hearken: behold, the word of the LORD is unto them a reproach; they have no delight in it.

11Therefore I am full of the fury of the LORD; I am weary with holding in: I will pour it out upon the children abroad, and upon the assembly of young men together: for even the husband with the wife shall be taken, the aged with *him that is* full of days.

12And their houses shall be turned unto others, *with their* fields and wives together: for I will stretch out my hand upon the inhabitants of the land, saith the LORD.

13For from the least of them even unto the greatest of them every one *is* given to covetousness; and from the prophet even unto the priest every one dealeth falsely.

14They have healed also the hurt *of the daughter* of my people slightly, saying, Peace, peace; when *there is* no peace.

COLOSSIANS 1:20—2:7

AND, having made peace through the blood of his cross, by him to reconcile all things unto himself; by him, *I say*, whether *they be* things in earth, or things in heaven.

21And you, that were sometime alienated and enemies in *your* mind by wicked works, yet now hath he reconciled

22In the body of his flesh through death, to present you holy and unblameable and unreproveable in his sight:

23If ye continue in the faith grounded and settled, and *be* not moved away from the hope of the gospel, which ye have heard, *and* which was preached to every creature which is under heaven; whereof I Paul am made a minister;

24Who now rejoice in my sufferings for you, and fill up that which is behind of the afflictions of Christ in my flesh for his body's sake, which is the church:

25Whereof I am made a minister, according to the dispensation of God which is given to me for you, to fulfil the word of God;

26*Even* the mystery which hath been hid from ages and from generations, but now is made manifest to his saints:

27To whom God would make known what *is* the riches of the glory of this mystery among the Gentiles; which is Christ in you, the hope of glory:

28Whom we preach, warning every man, and teaching every man in all wisdom; that we may present every man perfect in Christ Jesus:

29Whereunto I also labour, striving according to his working, which worketh in me mightily.

FOR I would that ye knew what great conflict I have for you, and *for* them at Laodicea, and *for* as many as have not seen my face in the flesh;

2That their hearts might be comforted, being knit together in love, and unto all riches of the full assurance of understanding, to the acknowledgement of the mystery of God, and of the Father, and of Christ;

3In whom are hid all the treasures of wisdom and knowledge.

4And this I say, lest any man should

beguile you with enticing words.

5For though I be absent in the flesh, yet am I with you in the spirit, joying and beholding your order, and the stedfastness of your faith in Christ.

6As ye have therefore received Christ Jesus the Lord, *so* walk ye in him:

7Rooted and built up in him, and stablished in the faith, as ye have been taught, abounding therein with thanksgiving.

PSALM 77:1–20

I CRIED unto God with my voice, *even* unto God with my voice; and he gave ear unto me.

2In the day of my trouble I sought the Lord: my sore ran in the night, and ceased not: my soul refused to be comforted.

3I remembered God, and was troubled: I complained, and my spirit was overwhelmed. Selah.

4Thou holdest mine eyes waking: I am so troubled that I cannot speak.

5I have considered the days of old, the years of ancient times.

6I call to remembrance my song in the night: I commune with mine own heart: and my spirit made diligent search.

7Will the Lord cast off for ever? and will he be favourable no more?

8Is his mercy clean gone for ever? doth *his* promise fail for evermore?

9Hath God forgotten to be gracious? hath he in anger shut up his tender mercies? Selah.

10And I said, This *is* my infirmity: *but I will remember* the years of the right hand of the most High.

11I will remember the works of the LORD: surely I will remember thy wonders of old.

12I will meditate also of all thy work, and talk of thy doings.

13Thy way, O God, *is* in the sanctuary: who *is* so great a God as *our* God?

14Thou *art* the God that doest wonders: thou hast declared thy strength among the people.

15Thou hast with *thine* arm redeemed thy people, the sons of Jacob and Joseph. Selah.

16The waters saw thee, O God, the waters saw thee; they were afraid: the depths also were troubled.

17The clouds poured out water: the skies sent out a sound: thine arrows also went abroad.

18The voice of thy thunder *was* in the heaven: the lightnings lightened the world: the earth trembled and shook.

19Thy way *is* in the sea, and thy path in the great waters, and thy footsteps are not known.

20Thou leddest thy people like a flock by the hand of Moses and Aaron.

PROVERBS FOR TODAY/ 24:23–25

These things *also* belong *to the wise.* It is *not good to have respect of persons in judgment.* He that saith unto the wicked, Thou art *righteous; him shall the people curse, nations shall abhor him: But to them that rebuke* him *shall be delight, and a good blessing shall come upon them.*

OCTOBER 6

JEREMIAH 6:15—8:7

WERE they ashamed when they had committed abomination? nay, they were not at all ashamed, neither could they blush: therefore they shall fall among them that fall: at the time *that* I visit them they shall be cast down, saith the LORD.

16Thus saith the LORD, Stand ye in the ways, and see, and ask for the old paths, where *is* the good way, and walk therein, and ye shall find rest for your souls. But they said, We will not walk *therein.*

17Also I set watchmen over you, *saying,* Hearken to the sound of the trumpet. But they said, We will not hearken.

18Therefore hear, ye nations, and know, O congregation, what *is* among them.

19Hear, O earth: behold, I will bring evil upon this people, *even* the fruit of their thoughts, because they have not hearkened unto my words, nor to my law, but rejected it.

20To what purpose cometh there to me incense from Sheba, and the sweet cane from a far country? your burnt offerings *are* not acceptable, nor your sacrifices sweet unto me.

21Therefore thus saith the LORD, Behold, I will lay stumblingblocks before this people, and the fathers and the sons together shall fall upon them; the neighbour and his friend shall perish.

22Thus saith the LORD, Behold, a people cometh from the north country, and a great nation shall be raised from the sides of the earth.

23They shall lay hold on bow and spear; they *are* cruel, and have no mercy; their voice roareth like the sea; and they ride upon horses, set in array as men for war against thee, O daughter of Zion.

24We have heard the fame thereof: our hands wax feeble: anguish hath taken hold of us, *and* pain, as of a woman in travail.

25Go not forth into the field, nor walk by the way; for the sword of the enemy *and* fear *is* on every side.

26O daughter of my people, gird *thee* with sackcloth, and wallow thyself in ashes: make thee mourning, *as for* an only son, most bitter lamentation: for the spoiler shall suddenly come upon us.

27I have set thee *for* a tower *and* a fortress among my people, that thou mayest know and try their way.

28They *are* all grievous revolters, walking with slanders: *they are* brass and iron; they *are* all corrupters.

29The bellows are burned, the lead is consumed of the fire; the founder melteth in vain: for the wicked are not plucked away.

30Reprobate silver shall *men* call them, because the LORD hath rejected them.

THE word that came to Jeremiah from the LORD, saying,

2Stand in the gate of the LORD's house, and proclaim there this word, and say, Hear the word of the LORD, all *ye of* Judah, that enter in at these gates to worship the LORD.

3Thus saith the LORD of hosts, the God of Israel, Amend your ways and your doings, and I will cause you to dwell in this place.

4Trust ye not in lying words, saying, The temple of the LORD, The temple of the LORD, The temple of the LORD, *are* these.

5For if ye throughly amend your ways and your doings; if ye throughly execute judgment between a man and his neighbour;

⁶*If* ye oppress not the stranger, the fatherless, and the widow, and shed not innocent blood in this place, neither walk after other gods to your hurt:

⁷Then will I cause you to dwell in this place, in the land that I gave to your fathers, for ever and ever.

⁸Behold, ye trust in lying words, that cannot profit.

⁹Will ye steal, murder, and commit adultery, and swear falsely, and burn incense unto Baal, and walk after other gods whom ye know not;

¹⁰And come and stand before me in this house, which is called by my name, and say, We are delivered to do all these abominations?

¹¹Is this house, which is called by my name, become a den of robbers in your eyes? Behold, even I have seen *it,* saith the LORD.

¹²But go ye now unto my place which *was* in Shiloh, where I set my name at the first, and see what I did to it for the wickedness of my people Israel.

¹³And now, because ye have done all these works, saith the LORD, and I spake unto you, rising up early and speaking, but ye heard not; and I called you, but ye answered not;

¹⁴Therefore will I do unto *this* house, which is called by my name, wherein ye trust, and unto the place which I gave to you and to your fathers, as I have done to Shiloh.

¹⁵And I will cast you out of my sight, as I have cast out all your brethren, *even* the whole seed of Ephraim.

¹⁶Therefore pray not thou for this people, neither lift up cry nor prayer for them, neither make intercession to me: for I will not hear thee.

¹⁷Seest thou not what they do in the cities of Judah and in the streets of Jerusalem?

¹⁸The children gather wood, and the fathers kindle the fire, and the women knead *their* dough, to make cakes to the queen of heaven, and to pour out drink offerings unto other gods, that they may provoke me to anger.

¹⁹Do they provoke me to anger? saith the LORD: *do they* not *provoke* themselves to the confusion of their own faces?

²⁰Therefore thus saith the Lord GOD; Behold, mine anger and my fury shall be poured out upon this place, upon man, and upon beast, and upon the trees of the field, and upon the fruit of the ground, and it shall burn, and shall not be quenched.

²¹Thus saith the LORD of hosts, the God of Israel; Put your burnt offerings unto your sacrifices and eat flesh.

²²For I spake not unto your fathers, nor commanded them in the day that I brought them out of the land of Egypt, concerning burnt offerings or sacrifices:

²³But this thing commanded I them, saying, Obey my voice, and I will be your God, and ye shall be my people: and walk ye in all the ways that I have commanded you, that it may be well unto you.

²⁴But they hearkened not, nor inclined their ear, but walked in the counsels *and* in the imagination of their evil heart, and went backward, and not forward.

²⁵Since the day that your fathers came forth out of the land of Egypt unto this day I have even sent unto you all my servants the prophets, daily rising up early and sending *them:*

²⁶Yet they hearkened not unto me, nor inclined their ear, but hardened their neck: they did worse than their fathers.

²⁷Therefore thou shalt speak all these words unto them; but they will not hearken to thee: thou shalt also call unto them; but they will not answer thee.

²⁸But thou shalt say unto them, This *is* a nation that obeyeth not the voice of the LORD their God, nor receiveth correction: truth is perished, and is cut off from their mouth.

29Cut off thine hair, *O Jerusalem,* and cast *it* away, and take up a lamentation on high places; for the LORD hath rejected and forsaken the generation of his wrath.

30For the children of Judah have done evil in my sight, saith the LORD: they have set their abominations in the house which is called by my name, to pollute it.

31And they have built the high places of Tophet, which *is* in the valley of the son of Hinnom, to burn their sons and their daughters in the fire; which I commanded *them* not, neither came it into my heart.

32Therefore, behold, the days come, saith the LORD, that it shall no more be called Tophet, nor the valley of the son of Hinnom, but the valley of slaughter: for they shall bury in Tophet, till there be no place.

33And the carcases of this people shall be meat for the fowls of the heaven, and for the beasts of the earth; and none shall fray *them* away.

34Then will I cause to cease from the cities of Judah, and from the streets of Jerusalem, the voice of mirth, and the voice of gladness, the voice of the bridegroom, and the voice of the bride: for the land shall be desolate.

AT that time, saith the LORD, they shall bring out the bones of the kings of Judah, and the bones of his princes, and the bones of the priests, and the bones of the prophets, and the bones of the inhabitants of Jerusalem, out of their graves:

2And they shall spread them before the sun, and the moon, and all the host of heaven, whom they have loved, and whom they have served, and after whom they have walked, and whom they have sought, and whom they have worshipped: they shall not be gathered, nor be buried; they shall be for dung upon the face of the earth.

3And death shall be chosen rather than life by all the residue of them that remain of this evil family, which remain in all the places whither I have driven them, saith the LORD of hosts.

4Moreover thou shalt say unto them, Thus saith the LORD; Shall they fall, and not arise? shall he turn away, and not return?

5Why *then* is this people of Jerusalem slidden back by a perpetual backsliding? they hold fast deceit, they refuse to return.

6I hearkened and heard, *but* they spake not aright: no man repented him of his wickedness, saying, What have I done? every one turned to his course, as the horse rusheth into the battle.

7Yea, the stork in the heaven knoweth her appointed times; and the turtle and the crane and the swallow observe the time of their coming; but my people know not the judgment of the LORD.

COLOSSIANS 2:8–23

BEWARE lest any man spoil you through philosophy and vain deceit, after the tradition of men, after the rudiments of the world, and not after Christ.

9For in him dwelleth all the fulness of the Godhead bodily.

10And ye are complete in him, which is the head of all principality and power:

11In whom also ye are circumcised with the circumcision made without hands, in putting off the body of the sins of the flesh by the circumcision of Christ:

12Buried with him in baptism, wherein also ye are risen with *him* through the faith of the operation of God, who hath raised him from the dead.

13And you, being dead in your sins and the uncircumcision of your flesh, hath he quickened together with him, having forgiven you all trespasses;

14Blotting out the handwriting of ordinances that was against us, which was contrary to us, and took it out of the way, nailing it to his cross;

15*And* having spoiled principalities and powers, he made a shew of them openly, triumphing over them in it.

16Let no man therefore judge you in meat, or in drink, or in respect of an holyday, or of the new moon, or of the sabbath *days:*

17Which are a shadow of things to come; but the body *is* of Christ.

18Let no man beguile you of your reward in a voluntary humility and worshipping of angels, intruding into those things which he hath not seen, vainly puffed up by his fleshly mind,

19And not holding the Head, from which all the body by joints and bands having nourishment ministered, and knit together, increaseth with the increase of God.

20Wherefore if ye be dead with Christ from the rudiments of the world, why, as though living in the world, are ye subject to ordinances,

21(Touch not; taste not; handle not;

22Which all are to perish with the using;) after the commandments and doctrines of men?

23Which things have indeed a shew of wisdom in will worship, and humility, and neglecting of the body; not in any honour to the satisfying of the flesh.

PSALM 78:1–25

Give ear, O my people, *to* my law: incline your ears to the words of my mouth.

2I will open my mouth in a parable: I will utter dark sayings of old:

3Which we have heard and known, and our fathers have told us.

4We will not hide *them* from their children, shewing to the generation to come the praises of the Lord, and his strength, and his wonderful works that he hath done.

5For he established a testimony in Jacob, and appointed a law in Israel, which he commanded our fathers, that they should make them known to their children:

6That the generation to come might know *them, even* the children *which* should be born; *who* should arise and declare *them* to their children:

7That they might set their hope in God, and not forget the works of God, but keep his commandments:

8And might not be as their fathers, a stubborn and rebellious generation; a generation *that* set not their heart aright, and whose spirit was not stedfast with God.

9The children of Ephraim, *being* armed, *and* carrying bows, turned back in the day of battle.

10They kept not the covenant of God, and refused to walk in his law;

11And forgat his works, and his wonders that he had shewed them.

12Marvellous things did he in the sight of their fathers, in the land of Egypt, *in* the field of Zoan.

13He divided the sea, and caused them to pass through; and he made the waters to stand as an heap.

14In the daytime also he led them with a cloud, and all the night with a light of fire.

15He clave the rocks in the wilderness, and gave *them* drink as *out of* the great depths.

16He brought streams also out of the rock, and caused waters to run down like rivers.

17And they sinned yet more against him by provoking the most High in the wilderness.

18And they tempted God in their heart by asking meat for their lust.

19Yea, they spake against God; they said, Can God furnish a table in the wilderness?

20Behold, he smote the rock, that the waters gushed out, and the streams overflowed; can he give bread also? can he provide flesh for his people?

21Therefore the LORD heard *this,* and was wroth; so a fire was kindled against Jacob, and anger also came up against Israel;

22Because they believed not in God, and trusted not in his salvation:

23Though he had commanded the clouds from above, and opened the doors of heaven,

24And had rained down manna upon them to eat, and had given them of the corn of heaven.

25Man did eat angels' food: he sent them meat to the full.

PROVERBS FOR TODAY/ 24:26

Every man *shall kiss* his *lips that giveth a right answer.*

OCTOBER 7

JEREMIAH 8:8—9:26

How do ye say, We *are* wise, and the law of the LORD *is* with us? Lo, certainly in vain made he *it;* the pen of the scribes *is* in vain.

9The wise *men* are ashamed, they are dismayed and taken: lo, they have rejected the word of the LORD; and what wisdom *is* in them?

10Therefore will I give their wives unto others, *and* their fields to them that shall inherit *them:* for every one from the least even unto the greatest is given to covetousness, from the prophet even unto the priest every one dealeth falsely.

11For they have healed the hurt of the daughter of my people slightly, saying, Peace, peace; when *there is* no peace.

12Were they ashamed when they had committed abomination? nay, they were not at all ashamed, neither could they blush: therefore shall they fall among them that fall: in the time of their visitation they shall be cast down, saith the LORD.

13I will surely consume them, saith the LORD: *there shall be* no grapes on the vine, nor figs on the fig tree, and the leaf shall fade; and *the things* that I have given them shall pass away from them.

14Why do we sit still? assemble yourselves, and let us enter into the defenced cities, and let us be silent there: for the LORD our God hath put us to silence, and given us water of gall to drink, because we have sinned against the LORD.

15We looked for peace, but no good *came; and* for a time of health, and behold trouble!

16The snorting of his horses was heard from Dan: the whole land trembled at the sound of the neighing of his strong ones; for they are come, and have devoured the land, and all that is in it; the city, and those that dwell therein.

17For, behold, I will send serpents, cockatrices, among you, which *will* not *be* charmed, and they shall bite you, saith the LORD.

18*When* I would comfort myself against sorrow, my heart *is* faint in me.

19Behold the voice of the cry of the daughter of my people because of them that dwell in a far country: *Is* not the LORD in Zion? *is* not her king in her? Why have they provoked me to anger with their graven images, *and* with strange vanities?

20The harvest is past, the summer is ended, and we are not saved.

21For the hurt of the daughter of my people am I hurt; I am black; astonishment hath taken hold on me.

22Is there no balm in Gilead; is there no physician there? why then is not the health of the daughter of my people recovered?

OH that my head were waters, and mine eyes a fountain of tears, that I might weep day and night for the slain of the daughter of my people!

2Oh that I had in the wilderness a lodging place of wayfaring men; that I might leave my people, and go from them! for they be all adulterers, an assembly of treacherous men.

3And they bend their tongues like their bow for lies: but they are not valiant for the truth upon the earth; for they proceed from evil to evil, and they know not me, saith the LORD.

4Take ye heed every one of his neighbour, and trust ye not in any brother: for every brother will utterly supplant, and every neighbour will walk with slanders.

5And they will deceive every one his neighbour, and will not speak the truth: they have taught their tongue to speak lies, and weary themselves to commit iniquity.

6Thine habitation is in the midst of deceit; through deceit they refuse to know me, saith the LORD.

7Therefore thus saith the LORD of hosts, Behold, I will melt them, and try them; for how shall I do for the daughter of my people?

8Their tongue is as an arrow shot out; it speaketh deceit: one speaketh peaceably to his neighbour with his mouth, but in heart he layeth his wait.

9Shall I not visit them for these things? saith the LORD: shall not my soul be avenged on such a nation as this?

10For the mountains will I take up a weeping and wailing, and for the habitations of the wilderness a lamentation, because they are burned up, so that none can pass through them; neither can men hear the voice of the cattle; both the fowl of the heavens and the beast are fled; they are gone.

11And I will make Jerusalem heaps, and a den of dragons; and I will make the cities of Judah desolate, without an inhabitant.

12Who is the wise man, that may understand this? and who is he to whom the mouth of the LORD hath spoken, that he may declare it, for what the land perisheth and is burned up like a wilderness, that none passeth through?

13And the LORD saith, Because they have forsaken my law which I set before them, and have not obeyed my voice, neither walked therein;

14But have walked after the imagination of their own heart, and after Baalim, which their fathers taught them:

15Therefore thus saith the LORD of hosts, the God of Israel; Behold, I will feed them, even this people, with wormwood, and give them water of gall to drink.

16I will scatter them also among the heathen, whom neither they nor their fathers have known: and I will send a sword after them, till I have consumed them.

17Thus saith the LORD of hosts, Consider ye, and call for the mourning women, that they may come; and send for cunning women, that they may come:

18And let them make haste, and take up a wailing for us, that our eyes may run down with tears, and our eyelids gush out with waters.

19For a voice of wailing is heard out of Zion, How are we spoiled! we are greatly confounded, because we have forsaken the land, because our dwellings have cast us out.

20Yet hear the word of the LORD, O ye women, and let your ear receive the word of his mouth, and teach your daughters wailing, and every one her neighbour lamentation.

21For death is come up into our windows, *and* is entered into our palaces, to cut off the children from without, *and* the young men from the streets.

22Speak, Thus saith the LORD, Even the carcases of men shall fall as dung upon the open field, and as the handful after the harvestman, and none shall gather *them*.

23Thus saith the LORD, Let not the wise *man* glory in his wisdom, neither let the mighty *man* glory in his might, let not the rich *man* glory in his riches:

24But let him that glorieth glory in this, that he understandeth and knoweth me, that I *am* the LORD which exercise lovingkindness, judgment, and righteousness, in the earth: for in these *things* I delight, saith the LORD.

25Behold, the days come, saith the LORD, that I will punish all *them which are* circumcised with the uncircumcised;

26Egypt, and Judah, and Edom, and the children of Ammon, and Moab, and all *that are* in the utmost corners, that dwell in the wilderness: for all *these* nations *are* uncircumcised, and all the house of Israel *are* uncircumcised in the heart.

COLOSSIANS 3:1–17

IF ye then be risen with Christ, seek those things which are above, where Christ sitteth on the right hand of God.

2Set your affection on things above, not on things on the earth.

3For ye are dead, and your life is hid with Christ in God.

4When Christ, *who is* our life, shall appear, then shall ye also appear with him in glory.

5Mortify therefore your members which are upon the earth; fornication, uncleanness, inordinate affection, evil

concupiscence, and covetousness, which is idolatry:

6For which things' sake the wrath of God cometh on the children of disobedience:

7In the which ye also walked some time, when ye lived in them.

8But now ye also put off all these; anger, wrath, malice, blasphemy, filthy communication out of your mouth.

9Lie not one to another, seeing that ye have put off the old man with his deeds;

10And have put on the new *man*, which is renewed in knowledge after the image of him that created him:

11Where there is neither Greek nor Jew, circumcision nor uncircumcision, Barbarian, Scythian, bond *nor* free: but Christ *is* all, and in all.

12Put on therefore, as the elect of God, holy and beloved, bowels of mercies, kindness, humbleness of mind, meekness, longsuffering;

13Forbearing one another, and forgiving one another, if any man have a quarrel against any: even as Christ forgave you, so also *do* ye.

14And above all these things *put on* charity, which is the bond of perfectness.

15And let the peace of God rule in your hearts, to the which also ye are called in one body; and be ye thankful.

16Let the word of Christ dwell in you richly in all wisdom; teaching and admonishing one another in psalms and hymns and spiritual songs, singing with grace in your hearts to the Lord.

17And whatsoever ye do in word or deed, *do* all in the name of the Lord Jesus, giving thanks to God and the Father by him.

PSALM 78:26–58

HE caused an east wind to blow in the heaven: and by his power he brought in the south wind.

27He rained flesh also upon them as

dust, and feathered fowls like as the sand of the sea:

28And he let *it* fall in the midst of their camp, round about their habitations.

29So they did eat, and were well filled: for he gave them their own desire;

30They were not estranged from their lust. But while their meat *was* yet in their mouths,

31The wrath of God came upon them, and slew the fattest of them, and smote down the chosen *men* of Israel.

32For all this they sinned still, and believed not for his wondrous works.

33Therefore their days did he consume in vanity, and their years in trouble.

34When he slew them, then they sought him: and they returned and enquired early after God.

35And they remembered that God *was* their rock, and the high God their redeemer.

36Nevertheless they did flatter him with their mouth, and they lied unto him with their tongues.

37For their heart was not right with him, neither were they stedfast in his covenant.

38But he, *being* full of compassion, forgave *their* iniquity, and destroyed *them* not: yea, many a time turned he his anger away, and did not stir up all his wrath.

39For he remembered that they *were but* flesh; a wind that passeth away, and cometh not again.

40How oft did they provoke him in the wilderness, *and* grieve him in the desert!

41Yea, they turned back and tempted God, and limited the Holy One of Israel.

42They remembered not his hand, *nor* the day when he delivered them from the enemy.

43How he had wrought his signs in Egypt, and his wonders in the field of Zoan:

44And had turned their rivers into blood; and their floods that they could not drink.

45He sent divers sorts of flies among them, which devoured them; and frogs, which destroyed them.

46He gave also their increase unto the caterpiller, and their labour unto the locust.

47He destroyed their vines with hail, and their sycomore trees with frost.

48He gave up their cattle also to the hail, and their flocks to hot thunderbolts.

49He cast upon them the fierceness of his anger, wrath, and indignation, and trouble, by sending evil angels *among them.*

50He made a way to his anger; he spared not their soul from death, but gave their life over to the pestilence;

51And smote all the firstborn in Egypt; the chief of *their* strength in the tabernacles of Ham:

52But made his own people to go forth like sheep, and guided them in the wilderness like a flock.

53And he led them on safely, so that they feared not: but the sea overwhelmed their enemies.

54And he brought them to the border of his sanctuary, *even to* this mountain, *which* his right hand had purchased.

55He cast out the heathen also before them, and divided them an inheritance by line, and made the tribes of Israel to dwell in their tents.

56Yet they tempted and provoked the most high God, and kept not his testimonies:

57But turned back, and dealt unfaithfully like their fathers: they were turned aside like a deceitful bow.

58For they provoked him to anger with their high places, and moved him to jealousy with their graven images.

PROVERBS FOR TODAY/ 24:27

Prepare thy work without, and make it fit for thyself in the field; and afterwards build thine house.

OCTOBER 8

JEREMIAH 10:1—11:23

Hear ye the word which the Lord speaketh unto you, O house of Israel:

2Thus saith the Lord, Learn not the way of the heathen, and be not dismayed at the signs of heaven; for the heathen are dismayed at them.

3For the customs of the people *are* vain: for *one* cutteth a tree out of the forest, the work of the hands of the workman, with the axe.

4They deck it with silver and with gold; they fasten it with nails and with hammers, that it move not.

5They *are* upright as the palm tree, but speak not: they must needs be borne, because they cannot go. Be not afraid of them; for they cannot do evil, neither also *is it* in them to do good.

6Forasmuch as *there is* none like unto thee, O Lord; thou *art* great, and thy name *is* great in might.

7Who would not fear thee, O King of nations? for to thee doth it appertain: forasmuch as among all the wise *men* of the nations, and in all their kingdoms, *there is* none like unto thee.

8But they are altogether brutish and foolish: the stock *is* a doctrine of vanities.

9Silver spread into plates is brought from Tarshish, and gold from Uphaz, the work of the workman, and of the hands of the founder: blue and purple *is* their clothing: they *are* all the work of cunning *men*.

10But the Lord *is* the true God, he *is* the living God, and an everlasting king: at his wrath the earth shall tremble, and the nations shall not be able to abide his indignation.

11Thus shall ye say unto them, The gods that have not made the heavens and the earth, *even* they shall perish from the earth, and from under these heavens.

12He hath made the earth by his power, he hath established the world by his wisdom, and hath stretched out the heavens by his discretion.

13When he uttereth his voice, *there is* a multitude of waters in the heavens, and he causeth the vapours to ascend from the ends of the earth; he maketh lightnings with rain, and bringeth forth the wind out of his treasures.

14Every man is brutish in *his* knowledge: every founder is confounded by the graven image: for his molten image *is* falsehood, and *there is* no breath in them.

15They *are* vanity, *and* the work of errors: in the time of their visitation they shall perish.

16The portion of Jacob *is* not like them: for he *is* the former of all *things;* and Israel *is* the rod of his inheritance: The Lord of hosts *is* his name.

17Gather up thy wares out of the land, O inhabitant of the fortress.

18For thus saith the Lord, Behold, I will sling out the inhabitants of the land at this once, and will distress them, that they may find *it so.*

19Woe is me for my hurt! my wound

is grievous: but I said, Truly this *is* a grief, and I must bear it.

20My tabernacle is spoiled, and all my cords are broken: my children are gone forth of me, and they *are* not: *there is* none to stretch forth my tent any more, and to set up my curtains.

21For the pastors are become brutish, and have not sought the LORD: therefore they shall not prosper, and all their flocks shall be scattered.

22Behold, the noise of the bruit is come, and a great commotion out of the north country, to make the cities of Judah desolate, *and* a den of dragons.

23O LORD, I know that the way of man *is* not in himself: *it is* not in man that walketh to direct his steps.

24O LORD, correct me, but with judgment; not in thine anger, lest thou bring me to nothing.

25Pour out thy fury upon the heathen that know thee not, and upon the families that call not on thy name: for they have eaten up Jacob, and devoured him, and consumed him, and made his habitation desolate.

THE word that came to Jeremiah from the LORD, saying,

2Hear ye the words of this covenant, and speak unto the men of Judah, and to the inhabitants of Jerusalem;

3And say thou unto them, Thus saith the LORD God of Israel; Cursed *be* the man that obeyeth not the words of this covenant,

4Which I commanded your fathers in the day *that* I brought them forth out of the land of Egypt, from the iron furnace, saying, Obey my voice, and do them, according to all which I command you: so shall ye be my people, and I will be your God:

5That I may perform the oath which I have sworn unto your fathers, to give them a land flowing with milk and honey, as *it is* this day. Then answered I, and said, So be it, O LORD.

6Then the LORD said unto me, Proclaim all these words in the cities of Judah, and in the streets of Jerusalem, saying, Hear ye the words of this covenant, and do them.

7For I earnestly protested unto your fathers in the day *that* I brought them up out of the land of Egypt, *even* unto this day, rising early and protesting, saying, Obey my voice.

8Yet they obeyed not, nor inclined their ear, but walked every one in the imagination of their evil heart: therefore I will bring upon them all the words of this covenant, which I commanded *them* to do; but they did *them* not.

9And the LORD said unto me, A conspiracy is found among the men of Judah, and among the inhabitants of Jerusalem.

10They are turned back to the iniquities of their forefathers, which refused to hear my words; and they went after other gods to serve them: the house of Israel and the house of Judah have broken my covenant which I made with their fathers.

11Therefore thus saith the LORD, Behold, I will bring evil upon them, which they shall not be able to escape; and though they shall cry unto me, I will not hearken unto them.

12Then shall the cities of Judah and inhabitants of Jerusalem go, and cry unto the gods unto whom they offer incense: but they shall not save them at all in the time of their trouble.

13For *according to* the number of thy cities were thy gods, O Judah; and *according to* the number of the streets of Jerusalem have ye set up altars to *that* shameful thing, *even* altars to burn incense unto Baal.

14Therefore pray not thou for this people, neither lift up a cry or prayer for them: for I will not hear *them* in the time that they cry unto me for their trouble.

15What hath my beloved to do in mine house, *seeing* she hath wrought lewdness with many, and the holy flesh is passed from thee? when thou doest evil, then thou rejoicest.

16The LORD called thy name. A green olive tree, fair, *and* of goodly fruit: with the noise of a great tumult he hath kindled fire upon it, and the branches of it are broken.

17For the LORD of hosts, that planted thee, hath pronounced evil against thee, for the evil of the house of Israel and of the house of Judah, which they have done against themselves to provoke me to anger in offering incense unto Baal.

18And the LORD hath given me knowledge *of it,* and I know *it:* then thou shewedst me their doings.

19But I *was* like a lamb *or* an ox *that* is brought to the slaughter; and I knew not that they had devised devices against me, *saying,* Let us destroy the tree with the fruit thereof, and let us cut him off from the land of the living, that his name may be no more remembered.

20But, O LORD of hosts, that judgest righteously, that triest the reins and the heart, let me see thy vengeance on them: for unto thee have I revealed my cause.

21Therefore thus saith the LORD of the men of Anathoth, that seek thy life, saying, Prophesy not in the name of the LORD, that thou die not by our hand:

22Therefore thus saith the LORD of hosts, Behold, I will punish them: the young men shall die by the sword; their sons and their daughters shall die by famine:

23And there shall be no remnant of them: for I will bring evil upon the men of Anathoth, *even* the year of their visitation.

COLOSSIANS 3:18—4:18

WIVES, submit yourselves unto your own husbands, as it is fit in the Lord.

19Husbands, love *your* wives, and be not bitter against them.

20Children, obey *your* parents in all things: for this is well pleasing unto the Lord.

21Fathers, provoke not your children *to anger,* lest they be discouraged.

22Servants, obey in all things *your* masters according to the flesh; not with eyeservice, as menpleasers; but in singleness of heart, fearing God:

23And whatsoever ye do, do *it* heartily, as to the Lord, and not unto men;

24Knowing that of the Lord ye shall receive the reward of the inheritance; for ye serve the Lord Christ.

25But he that doeth wrong shall receive for the wrong which he hath done; and there is no respect of persons.

MASTERS, give unto *your* servants that which is just and equal; knowing that ye also have a Master in heaven.

2Continue in prayer, and watch in the same with thanksgiving;

3Withal praying also for us, that God would open unto us a door of utterance, to speak the mystery of Christ, for which I am also in bonds:

4That I may make it manifest, as I ought to speak.

5Walk in wisdom toward them that are without, redeeming the time.

6Let your speech *be* alway with grace, seasoned with salt, that ye may know how ye ought to answer every man.

7All my state shall Tychicus declare unto you, *who is* a beloved brother, and a faithful minister and fellowservant in the Lord:

8Whom I have sent unto you for the same purpose, that he might know your estate, and comfort your hearts;

9With Onesimus, a faithful and beloved brother, who is *one* of you. They shall make known unto you all things which *are done* here.

10Aristarchus my fellowprisoner saluteth you, and Marcus, sister's son to Barnabas, (touching whom ye received commandments: if he come unto you, receive him;)

11And Jesus, which is called Justus, who are of the circumcision. These only *are my* fellowworkers unto the kingdom of God, which have been a comfort unto me.

12Epaphras, who is *one* of you, a servant of Christ, saluteth you, always labouring fervently for you in prayers, that ye may stand perfect and complete in all the will of God.

13For I bear him record, that he hath a great zeal for you, and them *that are* in Laodicea, and them in Hierapolis.

14Luke, the beloved physician, and Demas, greet you.

15Salute the brethren which are in Laodicea, and Nymphas, and the church which is in his house.

16And when this epistle is read among you, cause that it be read also in the church of the Laodiceans; and that ye likewise read the *epistle* from Laodicea.

17And say to Archippus, Take heed to the ministry which thou hast received in the Lord, that thou fulfil it.

18The salutation by the hand of me Paul. Remember my bonds. Grace *be* with you. Amen.

PSALM 78:59–72

WHEN God heard *this,* he was wroth, and greatly abhorred Israel:

60So that he forsook the tabernacle of Shiloh, the tent *which* he placed among men;

61And delivered his strength into captivity, and his glory into the enemy's hand.

62He gave his people over also unto the sword; and was wroth with his inheritance.

63The fire consumed their young men; and their maidens were not given to marriage.

64Their priests fell by the sword; and their widows made no lamentation.

65Then the LORD awaked as one out of sleep, *and* like a mighty man that shouteth by reason of wine.

66And he smote his enemies in the hinder parts: he put them to a perpetual reproach.

67Moreover he refused the tabernacle of Joseph, and chose not the tribe of Ephraim:

68But chose the tribe of Judah, the mount Zion which he loved.

69And he built his sanctuary like high *palaces,* like the earth which he hath established for ever.

70He chose David also his servant, and took him from the sheepfolds:

71From following the ewes great with young he brought him to feed Jacob his people, and Israel his inheritance.

72So he fed them according to the integrity of his heart; and guided them by the skilfulness of his hands.

PROVERBS FOR TODAY/ 24:28–29

Be not a witness against thy neighbour without cause; and deceive not *with thy lips. Say not, I will do so to him as he hath done to me: I will render to the man according to his work.*

OCTOBER 9

JEREMIAH 12:1—14:10

RIGHTEOUS *art* thou, O LORD, when I plead with thee: yet let me talk with thee of *thy* judgments: Wherefore doth the way of the wicked prosper? *wherefore* are all they happy that deal very treacherously?

2Thou hast planted them, yea, they have taken root: they grow, yea, they bring forth fruit: thou *art* near in their mouth, and far from their reins.

3But thou, O LORD, knowest me: thou hast seen me, and tried mine heart toward thee: pull them out like sheep for the slaughter, and prepare them for the day of slaughter.

4How long shall the land mourn, and the herbs of every field wither, for the wickedness of them that dwell therein? the beasts are consumed, and the birds; because they said, He shall not see our last end.

5If thou hast run with the footmen, and they have wearied thee, then how canst thou contend with horses? and *if* in the land of peace, *wherein* thou trustedst, *they wearied thee,* then how wilt thou do in the swelling of Jordan?

6For even thy brethren, and the house of thy father, even they have dealt treacherously with thee; yea, they have called a multitude after thee: believe them not, though they speak fair words unto thee.

7I have forsaken mine house, I have left mine heritage; I have given the dearly beloved of my soul into the hand of her enemies.

8Mine heritage is unto me as a lion in the forest; it crieth out against me: therefore have I hated it.

9Mine heritage *is* unto me *as* a speckled bird, the birds round about *are* against her; come ye, assemble all the beasts of the field, come to devour.

10Many pastors have destroyed my vineyard, they have trodden my portion under foot, they have made my pleasant portion a desolate wilderness.

11They have made it desolate, *and being* desolate it mourneth unto me; the whole land is made desolate, because no man layeth *it* to heart.

12The spoilers are come upon all high places through the wilderness: for the sword of the LORD shall devour from the *one* end of the land even to the *other* end of the land: no flesh shall have peace.

13They have sown wheat, but shall reap thorns: they have put themselves to pain, *but* shall not profit: and they shall be ashamed of your revenues because of the fierce anger of the LORD.

14Thus saith the LORD against all mine evil neighbours, that touch the inheritance which I have caused my people Israel to inherit; Behold, I will pluck them out of their land, and pluck out the house of Judah from among them.

15And it shall come to pass, after that I have plucked them out I will return, and have compassion on them, and will bring them again, every man to his heritage, and every man to his land.

16And it shall come to pass, if they will diligently learn the ways of my people, to swear by my name, The LORD liveth; as they taught my people to swear by Baal; then shall they be built in the midst of my people.

17But if they will not obey, I will utterly pluck up and destroy that nation, saith the LORD.

THUS saith the LORD unto me, Go and get thee a linen girdle, and put it upon thy loins, and put it not in water.

2So I got a girdle according to the

word of the LORD, and put *it* on my loins.

3And· the word of the LORD came unto me the second time, saying,

4Take the girdle that thou hast got, which *is* upon thy loins, and arise, go to Euphrates, and hide it there in a hole of the rock.

5So I went, and hid it by Euphrates, as the LORD commanded me.

6And it came to pass after many days, that the LORD said unto me, Arise, go to Euphrates, and take the girdle from thence, which I commanded thee to hide there.

7Then I went to Euphrates, and digged, and took the girdle from the place where I had hid it: and, behold, the girdle was marred, it was profitable for nothing.

8Then the word of the LORD came unto me, saying,

9Thus saith the LORD, After this manner will I mar the pride of Judah, and the great pride of Jerusalem.

10This evil people, which refuse to hear my words, which walk in the imagination of their heart, and walk after other gods, to serve them, and to worship them, shall even be as this girdle, which is good for nothing.

11For as the girdle cleaveth to the loins of a man, so have I caused to cleave unto me the whole house of Israel and the whole house of Judah, saith the LORD; that they might be unto me for a people, and for a name, and for a praise, and for a glory: but they would not hear.

12Therefore thou shalt speak unto them this word; Thus saith the LORD God of Israel, Every bottle shall be filled with wine: and they shall say unto thee, Do we not certainly know that every bottle shall be filled with wine?

13Then shalt thou say unto them, Thus saith the LORD, Behold, I will fill all the inhabitants of this land, even the kings that sit upon David's throne, and the priests, and the prophets, and all the inhabitants of Jerusalem, with drunkenness.

14And I will dash them one against another, even the fathers and the sons together, saith the LORD: I will not pity, nor spare, nor have mercy, but destroy them.

15Hear ye, and give ear; be not proud: for the LORD hath spoken.

16Give glory to the LORD your God, before he cause darkness, and before your feet stumble upon the dark mountains, and, while ye look for light, he turn it into the shadow of death, *and* make *it* gross darkness.

17But if ye will not hear it, my soul shall weep in secret places for *your* pride; and mine eye shall weep sore, and run down with tears, because the LORD's flock is carried away captive.

18Say unto the king and to the queen, Humble yourselves, sit down: for your principalities shall come down, *even* the crown of your glory.

19The cities of the south shall be shut up, and none shall open *them:* Judah shall be carried away captive all of it, it shall be wholly carried away captive.

20Lift up your eyes, and behold them that come from the north: where *is* the flock *that* was given thee, thy beautiful flock?

21What wilt thou say when he shall punish thee? for thou hast taught them *to be* captains, *and* as chief over thee: shall not sorrows take thee, as a woman in travail?

22And if thou say in thine heart, Wherefore come these things upon me? For the greatness of thine iniquity are thy skirts discovered, *and* thy heels made bare.

23Can the Ethiopian change his skin, or the leopard his spots? *then* may ye also do good, that are accustomed to do evil.

24Therefore will I scatter them as the stubble that passeth away by the wind of the wilderness.

25This *is* thy lot, the portion of thy

measures from me, saith the LORD; because thou hast forgotten me, and trusted in falsehood.

26Therefore will I discover thy skirts upon thy face, that thy shame may appear.

27I have seen thine adulteries and thy neighings, the lewdness of thy whoredom, *and* thine abominations on the hills in the fields. Woe unto thee, O Jerusalem! wilt thou not be made clean? when *shall it* once *be?*

THE word of the LORD that came to Jeremiah concerning the dearth.

2Judah mourneth, and the gates thereof languish; they are black unto the ground; and the cry of Jerusalem is gone up.

3And their nobles have sent their little ones to the waters: they came to the pits, *and* found no water; they returned with their vessels empty; they were ashamed and confounded, and covered their heads.

4Because the ground is chapt, for there was no rain in the earth, the plowmen were ashamed, they covered their heads.

5Yea, the hind also calved in the field, and forsook *it,* because there was no grass.

6And the wild asses did stand in the high places, they snuffed up the wind like dragons; their eyes did fail, because *there was* no grass.

7O LORD, though our iniquities testify against us, do thou *it* for thy name's sake: for our backslidings are many; we have sinned against thee.

8O the hope of Israel, the saviour thereof in time of trouble, why shouldest thou be as a stranger in the land, and as a wayfaring man *that* turneth aside to tarry for a night?

9Why shouldest thou be as a man astonied, as a mighty man *that* cannot save? yet thou, O LORD, *art* in the midst of us, and we are called by thy name; leave us not.

10Thus saith the LORD unto this people, Thus have they loved to wander, they have not refrained their feet, therefore the LORD doth not accept them; he will now remember their iniquity, and visit their sins.

1 THESSALONIANS 1:1—2:8

PAUL, and Silvanus, and Timotheus, unto the church of the Thessalonians *which is* in God the Father and *in* the Lord Jesus Christ: Grace *be* unto you, and peace, from God our Father, and the Lord Jesus Christ.

2We give thanks to God always for you all, making mention of you in our prayers;

3Remembering without ceasing your work of faith, and labour of love, and patience of hope in our Lord Jesus Christ, in the sight of God and our Father;

4Knowing, brethren beloved, your election of God.

5For our gospel came not unto you in word only, but also in power, and in the Holy Ghost, and in much assurance; as ye know what manner of men we were among you for your sake.

6And ye became followers of us, and of the Lord, having received the word in much affliction, with joy of the Holy Ghost:

7So that ye were ensamples to all that believe in Macedonia and Achaia.

8For from you sounded out the word of the Lord not only in Macedonia and Achaia, but also in every place your faith to God-ward is spread abroad; so that we need not to speak any thing.

9For they themselves shew of us what manner of entering in we had unto you, and how ye turned to God from idols to serve the living and true God;

10And to wait for his Son from heaven, whom he raised from the dead, *even* Jesus, which delivered us from the wrath to come.

For yourselves, brethren, know our entrance in unto you, that it was not in vain:

2But even after that we had suffered before, and were shamefully entreated, as ye know, at Philippi, we were bold in our God to speak unto you the gospel of God with much contention.

3For our exhortation *was* not of deceit, nor of uncleanness, nor in guile:

4But as we were allowed of God to be put in trust with the gospel, even so we speak; not as pleasing men, but God, which trieth our hearts.

5For neither at any time used we flattering words, as ye know, nor a cloak of covetousness; God *is* witness:

6Nor of men sought we glory, neither of you, nor *yet* of others, when we might have been burdensome, as the apostles of Christ.

7But we were gentle among you, even as a nurse cherisheth her children:

8So being affectionately desirous of you, we were willing to have imparted unto you, not the gospel of God only, but also our own souls, because ye were dear unto us.

PSALM 79:1–13

O GOD, the heathen are come into thine inheritance; thy holy temple have they defiled; they have laid Jerusalem on heaps.

2The dead bodies of thy servants have they given *to be* meat unto the fowls of the heaven, the flesh of thy saints unto the beasts of the earth.

3Their blood have they shed like water round about Jerusalem; and *there was* none to bury *them.*

4We are become a reproach to our neighbours, a scorn and derision to them that are round about us.

5How long, LORD? wilt thou be angry for ever? shall thy jealousy burn like fire?

6Pour out thy wrath upon the heathen that have not known thee, and upon the kingdoms that have not called upon thy name.

7For they have devoured Jacob, and laid waste his dwelling place.

8O remember not against us former iniquities: let thy tender mercies speedily prevent us: for we are brought very low.

9Help us, O God of our salvation, for the glory of thy name: and deliver us, and purge away our sins, for thy name's sake.

10Wherefore should the heathen say, Where *is* their God? let him be known among the heathen in our sight *by* the revenging of the blood of thy servants *which is* shed.

11Let the sighing of the prisoner come before thee; according to the greatness of thy power preserve thou those that are appointed to die;

12And render unto our neighbours sevenfold into their bosom their reproach, wherewith they have reproached thee, O Lord.

13So we thy people and sheep of thy pasture will give thee thanks for ever: we will shew forth thy praise to all generations.

PROVERBS FOR TODAY/ 24:30–34

I went by the field of the slothful, and by the vineyard of the man void of understanding; And, lo, it was all grown over with thorns, and *nettles had covered the face thereof, and the stone wall thereof was broken down. Then I saw,* and *considered* it *well: I looked upon* it, and *received instruction. Yet a little sleep, a little slumber, a little folding of the hands to sleep: So shall thy poverty come* as *one that travelleth; and thy want as an armed man.*

OCTOBER 10

JEREMIAH 14:11—16:15

THEN said the LORD unto me, Pray not for this people for *their* good.

12When they fast, I will not hear their cry; and when they offer burnt offering and an oblation, I will not accept them: but I will consume them by the sword, and by the famine, and by the pestilence.

13Then said I, Ah, Lord GOD! behold, the prophets say unto them, Ye shall not see the sword, neither shall ye have famine; but I will give you assured peace in this place.

14Then the LORD said unto me, The prophets prophesy lies in my name: I sent them not, neither have I commanded them, neither spake unto them: they prophesy unto you a false vision and divination, and a thing of nought, and the deceit of their heart.

15Therefore thus saith the LORD concerning the prophets that prophesy in my name, and I sent them not, yet they say, Sword and famine shall not be in this land; By sword and famine shall those prophets be consumed.

16And the people to whom they prophesy shall be cast out in the streets of Jerusalem because of the famine and the sword; and they shall have none to bury them, them, their wives, nor their sons, nor their daughters: for I will pour their wickedness upon them.

17Therefore thou shalt say this word unto them; Let mine eyes run down with tears night and day, and let them not cease: for the virgin daughter of my people is broken with a great breach, with a very grievous blow.

18If I go forth into the field, then behold the slain with the sword! and if I enter into the city, then behold them that are sick with famine! yea, both the prophet and the priest go about into a land that they know not.

19Hast thou utterly rejected Judah? hath thy soul lothed Zion? why hast thou smitten us, and *there is* no healing for us? we looked for peace, and *there is* no good; and for the time of healing, and behold trouble!

20We acknowledge, O LORD, our wickedness, *and* the iniquity of our fathers: for we have sinned against thee.

21Do not abhor *us,* for thy name's sake, do not disgrace the throne of thy glory: remember, break not thy covenant with us.

22Are there *any* among the vanities of the Gentiles that can cause rain? or can the heavens give showers? *art* not thou he, O LORD our God? therefore we will wait upon thee: for thou hast made all these *things.*

THEN said the LORD unto me, Though Moses and Samuel stood before me, *yet* my mind *could* not *be* toward this people: cast *them* out of my sight, and let them go forth.

2And it shall come to pass, if they say unto thee, Whither shall we go forth? then thou shalt tell them, Thus saith the LORD; Such as *are* for death, to death; and such as *are* for the sword, to the sword; and such as *are* for the famine, to the famine; and such as *are* for the captivity, to the captivity.

3And I will appoint over them four kinds, saith the LORD: the sword to slay, and the dogs to tear, and the fowls of the heaven, and the beasts of the earth, to devour and destroy.

4And I will cause them to be removed into all kingdoms of the earth, because of Manasseh the son of Hezekiah king of Judah, for *that* which he did in Jerusalem.

5For who shall have pity upon thee,

O Jerusalem? or who shall bemoan thee? or who shall go aside to ask how thou doest?

⁶Thou hast forsaken me, saith the LORD, thou art gone backward: therefore will I stretch out my hand against thee, and destroy thee; I am weary with repenting.

⁷And I will fan them with a fan in the gates of the land; I will bereave *them* of children, I will destroy my people, *since* they return not from their ways.

⁸Their widows are increased to me above the sand of the seas: I have brought upon them against the mother of the young men a spoiler at noonday: I have caused *him* to fall upon it suddenly, and terrors upon the city.

⁹She that hath borne seven languisheth: she hath given up the ghost; her sun is gone down while *it was* yet day: she hath been ashamed and confounded: and the residue of them will I deliver to the sword before their enemies, saith the LORD.

¹⁰Woe is me, my mother, that thou hast borne me a man of strife and a man of contention to the whole earth! I have neither lent on usury, nor men have lent to me on usury; *yet* every one of them doth curse me.

¹¹The LORD said, Verily it shall be well with thy remnant; verily I will cause the enemy to entreat thee *well* in the time of evil and in the time of affliction.

¹²Shall iron break the northern iron and the steel?

¹³Thy substance and thy treasures will I give to the spoil without price, and *that* for all thy sins, even in all thy borders.

¹⁴And I will make *thee* to pass with thine enemies into a land *which* thou knowest not: for a fire is kindled in mine anger, *which* shall burn upon you.

¹⁵O LORD, thou knowest: remember me, and visit me, and revenge me of my persecutors; take me not away in thy longsuffering: know that for thy sake I have suffered rebuke.

¹⁶Thy words were found, and I did eat them; and thy word was unto me the joy and rejoicing of mine heart: for I am called by thy name, O LORD God of hosts.

¹⁷I sat not in the assembly of the mockers, nor rejoiced; I sat alone because of thy hand: for thou hast filled me with indignation.

¹⁸Why is my pain perpetual, and my wound incurable, *which* refuseth to be healed? wilt thou be altogether unto me as a liar, *and as* waters *that* fail?

¹⁹Therefore thus saith the LORD, If thou return, then will I bring thee again, *and* thou shalt stand before me: and if thou take forth the precious from the vile, thou shalt be as my mouth: let them return unto thee; but return not thou unto them.

²⁰And I will make thee unto this people a fenced brasen wall: and they shall fight against thee, but they shall not prevail against thee: for I *am* with thee to save thee and to deliver thee, saith the LORD.

²¹And I will deliver thee out of the hand of the wicked, and I will redeem thee out of the hand of the terrible.

THE word of the LORD came also unto me, saying,

²Thou shalt not take thee a wife, neither shalt thou have sons or daughters in this place.

³For thus saith the LORD concerning the sons and concerning the daughters that are born in this place, and concerning their mothers that bare them, and concerning their fathers that begat them in this land;

⁴They shall die of grievous deaths; they shall not be lamented; neither shall they be buried; *but* they shall be as dung upon the face of the earth: and they shall be consumed by the sword, and by famine; and their carcases shall be meat for the fowls of heaven, and for the beasts of the earth.

5For thus saith the LORD, Enter not into the house of mourning, neither go to lament nor bemoan them: for I have taken away my peace from this people, saith the LORD, *even* lovingkindness and mercies.

6Both the great and the small shall die in this land: they shall not be buried, neither shall *men* lament for them, nor cut themselves, nor make themselves bald for them:

7Neither shall *men* tear *themselves* for them in mourning, to comfort them for the dead; neither shall *men* give them the cup of consolation to drink for their father or for their mother.

8Thou shalt not also go into the house of feasting, to sit with them to eat and to drink.

9For thus saith the LORD of hosts, the God of Israel; Behold, I will cause to cease out of this place in your eyes, and in your days, the voice of mirth, and the voice of gladness, the voice of the bridegroom, and the voice of the bride.

10And it shall come to pass, when thou shalt shew this people all these words, and they shall say unto thee, Wherefore hath the LORD pronounced all this great evil against us? or what *is* our iniquity? or what *is* our sin that we have committed against the LORD our God?

11Then shalt thou say unto them, Because your fathers have forsaken me, saith the LORD, and have walked after other gods, and have served them, and have worshipped them, and have forsaken me, and have not kept my law;

12And ye have done worse than your fathers; for, behold, ye walk every one after the imagination of his evil heart, that they may not hearken unto me:

13Therefore will I cast you out of this land into a land that ye know not, *neither* ye nor your fathers; and there shall ye serve other gods day and night; where I will not shew you favour.

14Therefore, behold, the days come,

saith the LORD, that it shall no more be said, The LORD liveth, that brought up the children of Israel out of the land of Egypt;

15But, The LORD liveth, that brought up the children of Israel from the land of the north, and from all the lands whither he had driven them: and I will bring them again into their land that I gave unto their fathers.

1 THESSALONIANS 2:9—3:13

FOR ye remember, brethren, our labour and travail: for labouring night and day, because we would not be chargeable unto any of you, we preached unto you the gospel of God.

10Ye *are* witnesses, and God *also,* how holily and justly and unblameably we behaved ourselves among you that believe:

11As ye know how we exhorted and comforted and charged every one of you, as a father *doth* his children,

12That ye would walk worthy of God, who hath called you unto his kingdom and glory.

13For this cause also thank we God without ceasing, because, when ye received the word of God which ye heard of us, ye received *it* not *as* the word of men, but as it is in truth, the word of God, which effectually worketh also in you that believe.

14For ye, brethren, became followers of the churches of God which in Judaea are in Christ Jesus: for ye also have suffered like things of your own countrymen, even as they *have* of the Jews:

15Who both killed the Lord Jesus, and their own prophets, and have persecuted us; and they please not God, and are contrary to all men:

16Forbidding us to speak to the Gentiles that they might be saved, to fill up their sins alway: for the wrath is come upon them to the uttermost.

17But we, brethren, being taken from

you for a short time in presence, not in heart, endeavoured the more abundantly to see your face with great desire.

18Wherefore we would have come unto you, even I Paul, once and again; but Satan hindered us.

19For what *is* our hope, or joy, or crown of rejoicing? *Are* not even ye in the presence of our Lord Jesus Christ at his coming?

20For ye are our glory and joy.

WHEREFORE when we could no longer forbear, we thought it good to be left at Athens alone;

2And sent Timotheus, our brother, and minister of God, and our fellowlabourer in the gospel of Christ, to establish you, and to comfort you concerning your faith:

3That no man should be moved by these afflictions: for yourselves know that we are appointed thereunto.

4For verily, when we were with you, we told you before that we should suffer tribulation; even as it came to pass, and ye know.

5For this cause, when I could no longer forbear, I sent to know your faith, lest by some means the tempter have tempted you, and our labour be in vain.

6But now when Timotheus came from you unto us, and brought us good tidings of your faith and charity, and that ye have good remembrance of us always, desiring greatly to see us, as we also *to see* you:

7Therefore, brethren, we were comforted over you in all our affliction and distress by your faith:

8For now we live, if ye stand fast in the Lord.

9For what thanks can we render to God again for you, for all the joy wherewith we joy for your sakes before our God;

10Night and day praying exceedingly that we might see your face, and might

perfect that which is lacking in your faith?

11Now God himself and our Father, and our Lord Jesus Christ, direct our way unto you.

12And the Lord make you to increase and abound in love one toward another, and toward all *men,* even as we *do* toward you:

13To the end he may stablish your hearts unblameable in holiness before God, even our Father, at the coming of our Lord Jesus Christ with all his saints.

PSALM 80:1–19

GIVE ear, O Shepherd of Israel, thou that leadest Joseph like a flock; thou that dwellest *between* the cherubims, shine forth.

2Before Ephraim and Benjamin and Manasseh stir up thy strength, and come *and* save us.

3Turn us again, O God, and cause thy face to shine; and we shall be saved.

4O LORD God of hosts, how long wilt thou be angry against the prayer of thy people?

5Thou feedest them with the bread of tears; and givest them tears to drink in great measure.

6Thou makest us a strife unto our neighbours: and our enemies laugh among themselves.

7Turn us again, O God of hosts, and cause thy face to shine; and we shall be saved.

8Thou hast brought a vine out of Egypt: thou hast cast out the heathen, and planted it.

9Thou preparedst *room* before it, and didst cause it to take deep root, and it filled the land.

10The hills were covered with the shadow of it, and the boughs thereof *were like* the goodly cedars.

11She sent out her boughs unto the sea, and her branches unto the river.

12Why hast thou *then* broken down

her hedges, so that all they which pass by the way do pluck her?

¹³The boar out of the wood doth waste it, and the wild beast of the field doth devour it.

¹⁴Return, we beseech thee, O God of hosts: look down from heaven, and behold, and visit this vine;

¹⁵And the vineyard which thy right hand hath planted, and the branch *that* thou madest strong for thyself.

¹⁶*It is* burned with fire, *it is* cut down: they perish at the rebuke of thy countenance.

¹⁷Let thy hand be upon the man of thy right hand, upon the son of man *whom* thou madest strong for thyself.

¹⁸So will not we go back from thee: quicken us, and we will call upon thy name.

¹⁹Turn us again, O LORD God of hosts, cause thy face to shine; and we shall be saved.

PROVERBS FOR TODAY/ 25:1–5

These are *also proverbs of Solomon, which the men of Hezekiah king of Judah copied out. It is the glory of God to conceal a thing: but the honour of kings is to search out a matter. The heaven for height, and the earth for depth, and the heart of kings is unsearchable.* □ *Take away the dross from the silver, and there shall come forth a vessel for the finer. Take away the wicked* from *before the king, and his throne shall be established in righteousness.*

OCTOBER 11

JEREMIAH 16:16—18:23

BEHOLD, I will send for many fishers, saith the LORD, and they shall fish them; and after will I send for many hunters, and they shall hunt them from every mountain, and from every hill, and out of the holes of the rocks.

¹⁷For mine eyes *are* upon all their ways: they are not hid from my face, neither is their iniquity hid from mine eyes.

¹⁸And first I will recompense their iniquity and their sin double; because they have defiled my land, they have filled mine inheritance with the carcases of their detestable and abominable things.

¹⁹O LORD, my strength, and my fortress, and my refuge in the day of affliction, the Gentiles shall come unto thee from the ends of the earth, and shall say, Surely our fathers have inherited lies, vanity, and *things* wherein *there is* no profit.

²⁰Shall a man make gods unto himself, and they *are* no gods?

²¹Therefore, behold, I will this once cause them to know, I will cause them to know mine hand and my might; and they shall know that my name *is* The LORD.

THE sin of Judah *is* written with a pen of iron, *and* with the point of a diamond: *it is* graven upon the table of their heart, and upon the horns of your altars;

²Whilst their children remember their altars and their groves by the green trees upon the high hills.

³O my mountain in the field, I will give thy substance *and* all thy treasures

to the spoil, *and* thy high places for sin, throughout all thy borders.

⁴And thou, even thyself, shalt discontinue from thine heritage that I gave thee; and I will cause thee to serve thine enemies in the land which thou knowest not; for ye have kindled a fire in mine anger, *which* shall burn for ever.

⁵Thus saith the Lᴏʀᴅ; Cursed *be* the man that trusteth in man, and maketh flesh his arm, and whose heart departeth from the Lᴏʀᴅ.

⁶For he shall be like the heath in the desert, and shall not see when good cometh; but shall inhabit the parched places in the wilderness, *in* a salt land and not inhabited.

⁷Blessed *is* the man that trusteth in the Lᴏʀᴅ, and whose hope the Lᴏʀᴅ is.

⁸For he shall be as a tree planted by the waters, and *that* spreadeth out her roots by the river, and shall not see when heat cometh, but her leaf shall be green; and shall not be careful in the year of drought, neither shall cease from yielding fruit.

⁹The heart *is* deceitful above all *things,* and desperately wicked: who can know it?

¹⁰I the Lᴏʀᴅ search the heart, *I* try the reins, even to give every man according to his ways, *and* according to the fruit of his doings.

¹¹*As* the partridge sitteth *on eggs,* and hatcheth *them* not; *so* he that getteth riches, and not by right, shall leave them in the midst of his days, and at his end shall be a fool.

¹²A glorious high throne from the beginning *is* the place of our sanctuary.

¹³O Lᴏʀᴅ, the hope of Israel, all that forsake thee shall be ashamed, *and* they that depart from me shall be written in the earth, because they have forsaken the Lᴏʀᴅ, the fountain of living waters.

¹⁴Heal me, O Lᴏʀᴅ, and I shall be healed; save me, and I shall be saved: for thou *art* my praise.

¹⁵Behold, they say unto me, Where *is* the word of the Lᴏʀᴅ? let it come now.

¹⁶As for me, I have not hastened from *being* a pastor to follow thee: neither have I desired the woeful day; thou knowest: that which came out of my lips was *right* before thee.

¹⁷Be not a terror unto me: thou *art* my hope in the day of evil.

¹⁸Let them be confounded that persecute me, but let not me be confounded: let them be dismayed, but let not me be dismayed: bring upon them the day of evil, and destroy them with double destruction.

¹⁹Thus said the Lᴏʀᴅ unto me; Go and stand in the gate of the children of the people, whereby the kings of Judah come in, and by the which they go out, and in all the gates of Jerusalem;

²⁰And say unto them, Hear ye the word of the Lᴏʀᴅ, ye kings of Judah, and all Judah, and all the inhabitants of Jerusalem, that enter in by these gates:

²¹Thus saith the Lᴏʀᴅ; Take heed to yourselves, and bear no burden on the sabbath day, nor bring *it* in by the gates of Jerusalem;

²²Neither carry forth a burden out of your houses on the sabbath day, neither do ye any work, but hallow ye the sabbath day, as I commanded your fathers.

²³But they obeyed not, neither inclined their ear, but made their neck stiff, that they might not hear, nor receive instruction.

²⁴And it shall come to pass, if ye diligently hearken unto me, saith the Lᴏʀᴅ, to bring in no burden through the gates of this city on the sabbath day, but hallow the sabbath day, to do no work therein;

²⁵Then shall there enter into the gates of this city kings and princes sitting upon the throne of David, riding in chariots and on horses, they, and their princes, the men of Judah, and the inhabitants of Jerusalem: and this

city shall remain for ever.

26And they shall come from the cities of Judah, and from the places about Jerusalem, and from the land of Benjamin, and from the plain, and from the mountains, and from the south, bringing burnt offerings, and sacrifices, and meat offerings, and incense, and bringing sacrifices of praise, unto the house of the LORD.

27But if ye will not hearken unto me to hallow the sabbath day, and not to bear a burden, even entering in at the gates of Jerusalem on the sabbath day; then will I kindle a fire in the gates thereof, and it shall devour the palaces of Jerusalem, and it shall not be quenched.

THE word which came to Jeremiah from the LORD, saying,

2Arise, and go down to the potter's house, and there I will cause thee to hear my words.

3Then I went down to the potter's house, and, behold, he wrought a work on the wheels.

4And the vessel that he made of clay was marred in the hand of the potter: so he made it again another vessel, as seemed good to the potter to make it.

5Then the word of the LORD came to me, saying,

6O house of Israel, cannot I do with you as this potter? saith the LORD. Behold, as the clay is in the potter's hand, so are ye in mine hand, O house of Israel.

7At what instant I shall speak concerning a nation, and concerning a kingdom, to pluck up, and to pull down, and to destroy it;

8If that nation, against whom I have pronounced, turn from their evil, I will repent of the evil that I thought to do unto them.

9And at what instant I shall speak concerning a nation, and concerning a kingdom, to build and to plant it;

10If it do evil in my sight, that it obey not my voice, then I will repent of the good, wherewith I said I would benefit them.

11Now therefore go to, speak to the men of Judah, and to the inhabitants of Jerusalem, saying, Thus saith the LORD; Behold, I frame evil against you, and devise a device against you: return ye now every one from his evil way, and make your ways and your doings good.

12And they said, There is no hope: but we will walk after our own devices, and we will every one do the imagination of his evil heart.

13Therefore thus saith the LORD; Ask ye now among the heathen, who hath heard such things: the virgin of Israel hath done a very horrible thing.

14Will a man leave the snow of Lebanon which cometh from the rock of the field? or shall the cold flowing waters that come from another place be forsaken?

15Because my people hath forgotten me, they have burned incense to vanity, and they have caused them to stumble in their ways from the ancient paths, to walk in paths, in a way not cast up;

16To make their land desolate, and a perpetual hissing; every one that passeth thereby shall be astonished, and wag his head.

17I will scatter them as with an east wind before the enemy; I will shew them the back, and not the face, in the day of their calamity.

18Then said they, Come, and let us devise devices against Jeremiah; for the law shall not perish from the priest, nor counsel from the wise, nor the word from the prophet. Come, and let us smite him with the tongue, and let us not give heed to any of his words.

19Give heed to me, O LORD, and hearken to the voice of them that contend with me.

20Shall evil be recompensed for good?

for they have digged a pit for my soul. Remember that I stood before thee to speak good for them, *and* to turn away thy wrath from them.

21Therefore deliver up their children to the famine, and pour out their *blood* by the force of the sword; and let their wives be bereaved of their children, and *be* widows; and let their men be put to death; *let* their young men *be* slain by the sword in battle.

22Let a cry be heard from their houses, when thou shalt bring a troop suddenly upon them: for they have digged a pit to take me, and hid snares for my feet.

23Yet, LORD, thou knowest all their counsel against me to slay *me:* forgive not their iniquity, neither blot out their sin from thy sight, but let them be overthrown before thee; deal *thus* with them in the time of thine anger.

1 THESSALONIANS 4:1—5:3

Furthermore then we beseech you, brethren, and exhort *you* by the Lord Jesus, that as ye have received of us how ye ought to walk and to please God, *so* ye would abound more and more.

2For ye know what commandments we gave you by the Lord Jesus.

3For this is the will of God, *even* your sanctification, that ye should abstain from fornication:

4That every one of you should know how to possess his vessel in sanctification and honour;

5Not in the lust of concupiscence, even as the Gentiles which know not God:

6That no *man* go beyond and defraud his brother in *any* matter: because that the Lord *is* the avenger of all such, as we also have forewarned you and testified.

7For God hath not called us unto uncleanness, but unto holiness.

8He therefore that despiseth, despiseth not man, but God, who hath also given unto us his holy Spirit.

9But as touching brotherly love ye need not that I write unto you: for ye yourselves are taught of God to love one another.

10And indeed ye do it toward all the brethren which are in all Macedonia: but we beseech you, brethren, that ye increase more and more;

11And that ye study to be quiet, and to do your own business, and to work with your own hands, as we commanded you;

12That ye may walk honestly toward them that are without, and *that* ye may have lack of nothing.

13But I would not have you to be ignorant, brethren, concerning them which are asleep, that ye sorrow not, even as others which have no hope.

14For if we believe that Jesus died and rose again, even so them also which sleep in Jesus will God bring with him.

15For this we say unto you by the word of the Lord, that we which are alive *and* remain unto the coming of the Lord shall not prevent them which are asleep.

16For the Lord himself shall descend from heaven with a shout, with the voice of the archangel, and with the trump of God: and the dead in Christ shall rise first:

17Then we which are alive *and* remain shall be caught up together with them in the clouds to meet the Lord in the air: and so shall we ever be with the Lord.

18Wherefore comfort one another with these words.

But of the times and the seasons, brethren, ye have no need that I write unto you.

2For yourselves know perfectly that the day of the Lord so cometh as a thief in the night.

3For when they shall say, Peace and safety; then sudden destruction cometh upon them, as travail upon a woman with child; and they shall not escape.

PSALM 81:1–16

SING aloud unto God our strength: make a joyful noise unto the God of Jacob.

2Take a psalm, and bring hither the timbrel, the pleasant harp with the psaltery.

3Blow up the trumpet in the new moon, in the time appointed, on our solemn feast day.

4For this *was* a statute for Israel, *and* a law of the God of Jacob.

5This he ordained in Joseph *for* a testimony, when he went out through the land of Egypt: *where* I heard a language *that* I understood not.

6I removed his shoulder from the burden: his hands were delivered from the pots.

7Thou calledst in trouble, and I delivered thee; I answered thee in the secret place of thunder: I proved thee at the waters of Meribah. Selah.

8Hear, O my people, and I will testify unto thee: O Israel, if thou wilt hearken unto me;

9There shall no strange god be in thee; neither shalt thou worship any strange god.

10I *am* the LORD thy God, which brought thee out of the land of Egypt: open thy mouth wide, and I will fill it.

11But my people would not hearken to my voice; and Israel would none of me.

12So I gave them up unto their own hearts' lust: *and* they walked in their own counsels.

13Oh that my people had hearkened unto me, *and* Israel had walked in my ways!

14I should soon have subdued their enemies, and turned my hand against their adversaries.

15The haters of the LORD should have submitted themselves unto him: but their time should have endured for ever.

16He should have fed them also with the finest of the wheat: and with honey out of the rock should I have satisfied thee.

PROVERBS FOR TODAY/ 25:6–7

Put not forth thyself in the presence of the king, and stand not in the place of great men: *For better* it is *that it be said unto thee, Come up hither; than that thou shouldest be put lower in the presence of the prince whom thine eyes have seen.*

OCTOBER 12

JEREMIAH 19:1—21:14

THUS saith the LORD, Go and get a potter's earthen bottle, and *take* of the ancients of the people, and of the ancients of the priests;

2And go forth unto the valley of the son of Hinnom, which *is* by the entry

of the east gate, and proclaim there the words that I shall tell thee,

3And say, Hear ye the word of the LORD, O kings of Judah, and inhabitants of Jerusalem; Thus saith the LORD of hosts, the God of Israel; Behold, I will bring evil upon this place, the which whosoever heareth, his ears shall tingle.

4Because they have forsaken me, and have estranged this place, and have burned incense in it unto other gods, whom neither they nor their fathers have known, nor the kings of Judah, and have filled this place with the blood of innocents;

5They have built also the high places of Baal, to burn their sons with fire *for* burnt offerings unto Baal, which I commanded not, nor spake *it,* neither came *it* into my mind:

6Therefore, behold, the days come, saith the LORD, that this place shall no more be called Tophet, nor The valley of the son of Hinnom, but The valley of slaughter.

7And I will make void the counsel of Judah and Jerusalem in this place; and I will cause them to fall by the sword before their enemies, and by the hands of them that seek their lives: and their carcases will I give to be meat for the fowls of the heaven, and for the beasts of the earth.

8And I will make this city desolate, and an hissing; every one that passeth thereby shall be astonished and hiss because of all the plagues thereof.

9And I will cause them to eat the flesh of their sons and the flesh of their daughters, and they shall eat every one the flesh of his friend in the siege and straitness, wherewith their enemies, and they that seek their lives, shall straiten them.

10Then shalt thou break the bottle in the sight of the men that go with thee,

11And shalt say unto them, Thus saith the LORD of hosts; Even so will I break this people and this city, as *one* breaketh a potter's vessel, that cannot be made whole again: and they shall bury *them* in Tophet, till *there be* no place to bury.

12Thus will I do unto this place, saith the LORD, and to the inhabitants thereof, and *even* make this city as Tophet:

13And the houses of Jerusalem, and the houses of the kings of Judah, shall be defiled as the place of Tophet, because of all the houses upon whose roofs they have burned incense unto all the host of heaven, and have poured out drink offerings unto other gods.

14Then came Jeremiah from Tophet, whither the LORD had sent him to prophesy; and he stood in the court of the LORD's house; and said to all the people,

15Thus saith the LORD of hosts, the God of Israel; Behold, I will bring upon this city and upon all her towns all the evil that I have pronounced against it, because they have hardened their necks, that they might not hear my words.

Now Pashur the son of Immer the priest, who *was* also chief governor in the house of the LORD, heard that Jeremiah prophesied these things.

2Then Pashur smote Jeremiah the prophet, and put him in the stocks that *were* in the high gate of Benjamin, which *was* by the house of the LORD.

3And it came to pass on the morrow, that Pashur brought forth Jeremiah out of the stocks. Then said Jeremiah unto him, The LORD hath not called thy name Pashur, but Magor-missabib.

4For thus saith the LORD, Behold, I will make thee a terror to thyself, and to all thy friends: and they shall fall by the sword of their enemies, and thine eyes shall behold *it:* and I will give all Judah into the hand of the king of Babylon, and he shall carry them captive into Babylon, and shall slay them with the sword.

5Moreover I will deliver all the strength of this city, and all the labours thereof, and all the precious things thereof, and all the treasures of the kings of Judah will I give into the hand of their enemies, which shall spoil them, and take them, and carry them to Babylon.

6And thou, Pashur, and all that dwell in thine house shall go into captivity: and thou shalt come to Babylon, and there thou shalt die, and shalt be buried there, thou, and all thy friends, to whom thou hast prophesied lies.

7O LORD, thou hast deceived me, and I was deceived: thou art stronger than I, and hast prevailed: I am in derision daily, every one mocketh me.

8For since I spake, I cried out, I cried violence and spoil; because the word of the LORD was made a reproach unto me, and a derision, daily.

9Then I said, I will not make mention of him, nor speak any more in his name. But *his word* was in mine heart as a burning fire shut up in my bones, and I was weary with forbearing, and I could not *stay*.

10For I heard the defaming of many, fear on every side. Report, *say they,* and we will report it. All my familiars watched for my halting, *saying,* Peradventure he will be enticed, and we shall prevail against him, and we shall take our revenge on him.

11But the LORD *is* with me as a mighty terrible one: therefore my persecutors shall stumble, and they shall not prevail: they shall be greatly ashamed; for they shall not prosper: *their* everlasting confusion shall never be forgotten.

12But, O LORD of hosts, that triest the righteous, *and* seest the reins and the heart, let me see thy vengeance on them: for unto thee have I opened my cause.

13Sing unto the LORD, praise ye the LORD: for he hath delivered the soul of the poor from the hand of evildoers.

14Cursed *be* the day wherein I was born: let not the day wherein my mother bare me be blessed.

15Cursed *be* the man who brought tidings to my father, saying, A man child is born unto thee; making him very glad.

16And let that man be as the cities which the LORD overthrew, and repented not: and let him hear the cry in the morning, and the shouting at noontide;

17Because he slew me not from the womb; or that my mother might have been my grave, and her womb *to be* always great *with me.*

18Wherefore came I forth out of the womb to see labour and sorrow, that my days should be consumed with shame?

THE word which came unto Jeremiah from the LORD, when king Zedekiah sent him Pashur the son of Melchiah, and Zephaniah the son of Maaseiah the priest, saying,

2Enquire, I pray thee, of the LORD for us; for Nebuchadrezzar king of Babylon maketh war against us; if so be that the LORD will deal with us according to all his wondrous works, that he may go up from us.

3Then said Jeremiah unto them, Thus shall ye say to Zedekiah:

4Thus saith the LORD God of Israel; Behold, I will turn back the weapons of war that *are* in your hands, wherewith ye fight against the king of Babylon, and *against* the Chaldeans, which besiege you without the walls, and I will assemble them into the midst of this city.

5And I myself will fight against you with an outstretched hand and with a strong arm, even in anger, and in fury, and in great wrath.

6And I will smite the inhabitants of this city, both man and beast: they shall die of a great pestilence.

7And afterward, saith the LORD, I will deliver Zedekiah king of Judah, and his servants, and the people, and such as are left in this city from the pestilence, from the sword, and from the famine, into the hand of Nebuchadrezzar king of Babylon, and into the hand of their enemies, and into the hand of those that seek their life: and he shall smite them with the edge of the sword; he shall not spare them, neither have pity, nor have mercy.

⁸And unto this people thou shalt say, Thus saith the LORD; Behold, I set before you the way of life, and the way of death.

⁹He that abideth in this city shall die by the sword, and by the famine, and by the pestilence: but he that goeth out, and falleth to the Chaldeans that besiege you, he shall live, and his life shall be unto him for a prey.

¹⁰For I have set my face against this city for evil, and not for good, saith the LORD: it shall be given into the hand of the king of Babylon, and he shall burn it with fire.

¹¹And touching the house of the king of Judah, *say,* Hear ye the word of the LORD;

¹²O house of David, thus saith the LORD; Execute judgment in the morning, and deliver *him that is* spoiled out of the hand of the oppressor, lest my fury go out like fire, and burn that none can quench *it,* because of the evil of your doings.

¹³Behold, I *am* against thee, O inhabitant of the valley, *and* rock of the plain, saith the LORD; which say, Who shall come down against us? or who shall enter into our habitations?

¹⁴But I will punish you according to the fruit of your doings, saith the LORD: and I will kindle a fire in the forest thereof, and it shall devour all things round about it.

1 THESSALONIANS 5:4–28

BUT ye, brethren, are not in darkness, that that day should overtake you as a thief.

⁵Ye are all the children of light, and the children of the day: we are not of the night, nor of darkness.

⁶Therefore let us not sleep, as *do* others; but let us watch and be sober.

⁷For they that sleep sleep in the night; and they that be drunken are drunken in the night.

⁸But let us, who are of the day, be sober, putting on the breastplate of faith and love; and for an helmet, the hope of salvation.

⁹For God hath not appointed us to wrath, but to obtain salvation by our Lord Jesus Christ,

¹⁰Who died for us, that, whether we wake or sleep, we should live together with him.

¹¹Wherefore comfort yourselves together, and edify one another, even as also ye do.

¹²And we beseech you, brethren, to know them which labour among you, and are over you in the Lord, and admonish you;

¹³And to esteem them very highly in love for their work's sake. *And* be at peace among yourselves.

¹⁴Now we exhort you, brethren, warn them that are unruly, comfort the feebleminded, support the weak, be patient toward all *men.*

¹⁵See that none render evil for evil unto any *man;* but ever follow that which is good, both among yourselves, and to all *men.*

¹⁶Rejoice evermore.

¹⁷Pray without ceasing.

¹⁸In every thing give thanks: for this is the will of God in Christ Jesus concerning you.

¹⁹Quench not the Spirit.

²⁰Despise not prophesyings.

²¹Prove all things; hold fast that which is good.

²²Abstain from all appearance of evil.

²³And the very God of peace sanctify you wholly; and *I pray God* your whole spirit and soul and body be preserved blameless unto the coming of our Lord Jesus Christ.

²⁴Faithful *is* he that calleth you, who also will do *it.*

25Brethren, pray for us.

26Greet all the brethren with an holy kiss.

27I charge you by the Lord that this epistle be read unto all the holy brethren.

28The grace of our Lord Jesus Christ *be* with you. Amen.

PSALM 82:1–8

God standeth in the congregation of the mighty; he judgeth among the gods.

2How long will ye judge unjustly, and accept the persons of the wicked? Selah.

3Defend the poor and fatherless: do justice to the afflicted and needy.

4Deliver the poor and needy: rid *them* out of the hand of the wicked.

5They know not, neither will they understand; they walk on in darkness: all the foundations of the earth are out of course.

6I have said, Ye *are* gods; and all of you *are* children of the most High.

7But ye shall die like men, and fall like one of the princes.

8Arise, O God, judge the earth: for thou shalt inherit all nations.

PROVERBS FOR TODAY/ 25:8–10

Go not forth hastily to strive, lest thou know not *what to do in the end thereof, when thy neighbour hath put thee to shame. Debate thy cause with thy neighbour* himself; *and discover not a secret to another: Lest he that heareth* it *put thee to shame, and thine infamy turn not away.*

OCTOBER 13

JEREMIAH 22:1—23:20

Thus saith the Lord; Go down to the house of the king of Judah, and speak there this word,

2And say, Hear the word of the Lord, O king of Judah, that sittest upon the throne of David, thou, and thy servants, and thy people that enter in by these gates:

3Thus saith the Lord; Execute ye judgment and righteousness, and deliver the spoiled out of the hand of the oppressor: and do no wrong, do no violence to the stranger, the fatherless, nor the widow, neither shed innocent blood in this place.

4For if ye do this thing indeed, then shall there enter in by the gates of this house kings sitting upon the throne of David, riding in chariots and on horses, he, and his servants, and his people.

5But if ye will not hear these words, I swear by myself, saith the Lord, that this house shall become a desolation.

6For thus saith the Lord unto the king's house of Judah; thou *art* Gilead unto me, *and* the head of Lebanon: *yet* surely I will make thee a wilderness, *and* cities *which* are not inhabited.

7And I will prepare destroyers against thee, every one with his weapons: and they shall cut down thy choice cedars, and cast *them* into the fire.

8And many nations shall pass by this city, and they shall say every man to his neighbour, Wherefore hath the Lord done thus unto this great city?

9Then they shall answer, Because they have forsaken the covenant of the LORD their God, and worshipped other gods, and served them.

10Weep ye not for the dead, neither bemoan him: *but* weep sore for him that goeth away: for he shall return no more, nor see his native country.

11For thus saith the LORD touching Shallum the son of Josiah king of Judah, which reigned instead of Josiah his father, which went forth out of this place; He shall not return thither any more:

12But he shall die in the place whither they have led him captive, and shall see this land no more.

13Woe unto him that buildeth his house by unrighteousness, and his chambers by wrong; *that* useth his neighbour's service without wages, and giveth him not for his work;

14That saith, I will build me a wide house and large chambers, and cutteth him out windows; and *it is* cieled with cedar, and painted with vermilion.

15Shalt thou reign, because thou closest *thyself* in cedar? did not thy father eat and drink, and do judgment and justice, *and* then *it was* well with him?

16He judged the cause of the poor and needy; then *it was* well *with him: was* not this to know me? saith the LORD.

17But thine eyes and thine heart *are* not but for thy covetousness, and for to shed innocent blood, and for oppression, and for violence, to do *it.*

18Therefore thus saith the LORD concerning Jehoiakim the son of Josiah king of Judah; They shall not lament for him, *saying,* Ah my brother! or, Ah sister! they shall not lament for him, *saying,* Ah lord! or, Ah his glory!

19He shall be buried with the burial of an ass, drawn and cast forth beyond the gates of Jerusalem.

20Go up to Lebanon, and cry; and lift up thy voice in Bashan, and cry from the passages: for all thy lovers are destroyed.

21I spake unto thee in thy prosperity; *but* thou saidst, I will not hear. This *hath been* thy manner from thy youth, that thou obeyedst not my voice.

22The wind shall eat up all thy pastors, and thy lovers shall go into captivity: surely then shalt thou be ashamed and confounded for all thy wickedness.

23O inhabitant of Lebanon, that makest thy nest in the cedars, how gracious shalt thou be when pangs come upon thee, the pain as of a woman in travail!

24*As* I live, saith the LORD, though Coniah the son of Jehoiakim king of Judah were the signet upon my right hand, yet would I pluck thee thence;

25And I will give thee into the hand of them that seek thy life, and into the hand *of them* whose face thou fearest, even into the hand of Nebuchadrezzar king of Babylon, and into the hand of the Chaldeans.

26And I will cast thee out, and thy mother that bare thee, into another country, where ye were not born; and there shall ye die.

27But to the land whereunto they desire to return, thither shall they not return.

28*Is* this man Coniah a despised broken idol? *is he* a vessel wherein *is* no pleasure? wherefore are they cast out, he and his seed, and are cast into a land which they know not?

29O earth, earth, earth, hear the word of the LORD.

30Thus saith the LORD, Write ye this man childless, a man *that* shall not prosper in his days: for no man of his seed shall prosper, sitting upon the throne of David, and ruling any more in Judah.

WOE be unto the pastors that destroy and scatter the sheep of my pasture! saith the LORD.

2Therefore thus saith the LORD God of Israel against the pastors that feed my people; Ye have scattered my flock, and driven them away, and have not visited them: behold, I will visit upon you the evil of your doings, saith the Lord.

3And I will gather the remnant of my flock out of all countries whither I have driven them, and will bring them again to their folds; and they shall be fruitful and increase.

4And I will set up shepherds over them which shall feed them: and they shall fear no more, nor be dismayed, neither shall they be lacking, saith the Lord.

5Behold, the days come, saith the Lord, that I will raise unto David a righteous Branch, and a King shall reign and prosper, and shall execute judgment and justice in the earth.

6In his days Judah shall be saved, and Israel shall dwell safely: and this is his name whereby he shall be called, THE LORD OUR RIGHTEOUSNESS.

7Therefore, behold, the days come, saith the Lord, that they shall no more say, The Lord liveth, which brought up the children of Israel out of the land of Egypt;

8But, The Lord liveth, which brought up and which led the seed of the house of Israel out of the north country, and from all countries whither I had driven them; and they shall dwell in their own land.

9Mine heart within me is broken because of the prophets; all my bones shake; I am like a drunken man, and like a man whom wine hath overcome, because of the Lord, and because of the words of his holiness.

10For the land is full of adulterers; for because of swearing the land mourneth; the pleasant places of the wilderness are dried up, and their course is evil, and their force is not right.

11For both prophet and priest are profane; yea, in my house have I found their wickedness, saith the Lord.

12Wherefore their way shall be unto them as slippery ways in the darkness: they shall be driven on, and fall therein: for I will bring evil upon them, even the year of their visitation, saith the Lord.

13And I have seen folly in the prophets of Samaria; they prophesied in Baal, and caused my people Israel to err.

14I have seen also in the prophets of Jerusalem an horrible thing: they commit adultery, and walk in lies: they strengthen also the hands of evildoers, that none doth return from his wickedness: they are all of them unto me as Sodom, and the inhabitants thereof as Gomorrah.

15Therefore thus saith the Lord of hosts concerning the prophets; Behold, I will feed them with wormwood, and make them drink the water of gall: for from the prophets of Jerusalem is profaneness gone forth into all the land.

16Thus saith the Lord of hosts, Hearken not unto the words of the prophets that prophesy unto you: they make you vain: they speak a vision of their own heart, and not out of the mouth of the Lord.

17They say still unto them that despise me, The Lord hath said, Ye shall have peace; and they say unto every one that walketh after the imagination of his own heart, No evil shall come upon you.

18For who hath stood in the counsel of the Lord, and hath perceived and heard his word? who hath marked his word, and heard it?

19Behold, a whirlwind of the Lord is gone forth in fury, even a grievous whirlwind: it shall fall grievously upon the head of the wicked.

20The anger of the Lord shall not return, until he have executed, and till he have performed the thoughts of his heart: in the latter days ye shall consider it perfectly.

2 THESSALONIANS 1:1–12

Paul, and Silvanus, and Timotheus, unto the church of the Thessalonians in God our Father and the Lord Jesus Christ:

2Grace unto you, and peace, from God our Father and the Lord Jesus Christ.

3We are bound to thank God always for you, brethren, as it is meet, because that your faith groweth exceedingly, and the charity of every one of you all toward each other aboundeth;

4So that we ourselves glory in you in the churches of God for your patience and faith in all your persecutions and tribulations that ye endure:

5*Which is* a manifest token of the righteous judgment of God, that ye may be counted worthy of the kingdom of God, for which ye also suffer:

6Seeing *it is* a righteous thing with God to recompense tribulation to them that trouble you;

7And to you who are troubled rest with us, when the Lord Jesus shall be revealed from heaven with his mighty angels,

8In flaming fire taking vengeance on them that know not God, and that obey not the gospel of our Lord Jesus Christ:

9Who shall be punished with everlasting destruction from the presence of the Lord, and from the glory of his power;

10When he shall come to be glorified in his saints, and to be admired in all them that believe (because our testimony among you was believed) in that day.

11Wherefore also we pray always for you, that our God would count you worthy of *this* calling, and fulfil all the good pleasure of *his* goodness, and the work of faith with power:

12That the name of our Lord Jesus Christ may be glorified in you, and ye in him, according to the grace of our God and the Lord Jesus Christ.

PSALM 83:1–18

Keep not thou silence, O God: hold not thy peace, and be not still, O God.

2For, lo, thine enemies make a tumult: and they that hate thee have lifted up the head.

3They have taken crafty counsel against thy people, and consulted against thy hidden ones.

4They have said, Come, and let us cut them off from *being* a nation; that the name of Israel may be no more in remembrance.

5For they have consulted together with one consent: they are confederate against thee:

6The tabernacles of Edom, and the Ishmaelites; of Moab, and the Hagarenes;

7Gebal, and Ammon, and Amalek; the Philistines with the inhabitants of Tyre;

8Assur also is joined with them: they have holpen the children of Lot. Selah.

9Do unto them as *unto* the Midianites; as *to* Sisera, as *to* Jabin, at the brook of Kison:

10*Which* perished at En–dor: they became *as* dung for the earth.

11Make their nobles like Oreb, and like Zeeb: yea, all their princes as Zebah, and as Zalmunna:

12Who said, Let us take to ourselves the houses of God in possession.

13O my God, make them like a wheel; as the stubble before the wind.

14As the fire burneth a wood, and as the flame setteth the mountains on fire;

15So persecute them with thy tempest, and make them afraid with thy storm.

16Fill their faces with shame; that they may seek thy name, O Lord.

17Let them be confounded and troubled for ever; yea, let them be put to shame, and perish:

18That *men* may know that thou, whose name alone *is* JEHOVAH, *art* the most high over all the earth.

PROVERBS FOR TODAY/ 25:11–14

A word fitly spoken is like *apples of gold in pictures of silver. As an earring of gold, and an ornament of fine gold,* so is *a wise reprover upon an obedient ear.* □ *As the cold of snow in the time of harvest,* so is *a faithful messenger to them that send him: for he refresheth the soul of his masters.* □ *Whoso boasteth himself of a false gift* is like *clouds and wind without rain.*

OCTOBER 14

JEREMIAH 23:21—25:38

I HAVE not sent these prophets, yet they ran: I have not spoken to them, yet they prophesied.

22But if they had stood in my counsel, and had caused my people to hear my words, then they should have turned them from their evil way, and from the evil of their doings.

23*Am* I a God at hand, saith the LORD, and not a God afar off?

24Can any hide himself in secret places that I shall not see him? saith the LORD. Do not I fill heaven and earth? saith the LORD.

25I have heard what the prophets said, that prophesy lies in my name, saying, I have dreamed, I have dreamed.

26How long shall *this* be in the heart of the prophets that prophesy lies? yea, *they are* prophets of the deceit of their own heart;

27Which think to cause my people to forget my name by their dreams which they tell every man to his neighbour, as their fathers have forgotten my name for Baal.

28The prophet that hath a dream, let him tell a dream; and he that hath my word, let him speak my word faithfully. What *is* the chaff to the wheat? saith the LORD.

29*Is* not my word like as a fire? saith the LORD; and like a hammer *that* breaketh the rock in pieces?

30Therefore, behold, I *am* against the prophets, saith the LORD, that steal my words every one from his neighbour.

31Behold, I *am* against the prophets, saith the LORD, that use their tongues, and say, He saith.

32Behold, I *am* against them that prophesy false dreams, saith the LORD, and do tell them, and cause my people to err by their lies, and by their lightness; yet I sent them not, nor commanded them: therefore they shall not profit this people at all, saith the LORD.

33And when this people, or the prophet, or a priest, shall ask thee, saying, What *is* the burden of the LORD? thou shalt then say unto them, What burden? I will even forsake you, saith the LORD.

34And *as for* the prophet, and the priest, and the people, that shall say, The burden of the LORD, I will even punish that man and his house.

35Thus shall ye say every one to his neighbour, and every one to his brother,

What hath the LORD answered? and, What hath the LORD spoken?

36And the burden of the LORD shall ye mention no more: for every man's word shall be his burden; for ye have perverted the words of the living God, of the LORD of hosts our God.

37Thus shalt thou say to the prophet, What hath the LORD answered thee? and, What hath the LORD spoken?

38But since ye say, The burden of the LORD; therefore thus saith the LORD; Because ye say this word, The burden of the LORD, and I have sent unto you, saying, Ye shall not say, The burden of the LORD;

39Therefore, behold, I, even I, will utterly forget you, and I will forsake you, and the city that I gave you and your fathers, *and cast you* out of my presence:

40And I will bring an everlasting reproach upon you, and a perpetual shame, which shall not be forgotten.

THE LORD shewed me, and, behold, two baskets of figs *were* set before the temple of the LORD, after that Nebuchadrezzar king of Babylon had carried away captive Jeconiah the son of Jehoiakim king of Judah, and the princes of Judah, with the carpenters and smiths, from Jerusalem, and had brought them to Babylon.

2One basket *had* very good figs, *even* like the figs *that are* first ripe: and the other basket *had* very naughty figs, which could not be eaten, they were so bad.

3Then said the LORD unto me, What seest thou, Jeremiah? And I said, Figs; the good figs, very good; and the evil, very evil, that cannot be eaten, they are so evil.

4Again the word of the LORD came unto me, saying,

5Thus saith the LORD, the God of Israel; Like these good figs, so will I acknowledge them that are carried away captive of Judah, whom I have sent out of this place into the land of the Chaldeans for *their* good.

6For I will set mine eyes upon them for good, and I will bring them again to this land: and I will build them, and not pull *them* down; and I will plant them, and not pluck *them* up.

7And I will give them an heart to know me, that I *am* the LORD: and they shall be my people, and I will be their God: for they shall return unto me with their whole heart.

8And as the evil figs, which cannot be eaten, they are so evil; surely thus saith the LORD, So will I give Zedekiah the king of Judah, and his princes, and the residue of Jerusalem, that remain in this land, and them that dwell in the land of Egypt:

9And I will deliver them to be removed into all the kingdoms of the earth for *their* hurt, *to be* a reproach and a proverb, a taunt and a curse, in all places whither I shall drive them.

10And I will send the sword, the famine, and the pestilence, among them, till they be consumed from off the land that I gave unto them and to their fathers.

THE word that came to Jeremiah concerning all the people of Judah in the fourth year of Jehoiakim the son of Josiah king of Judah, that *was* the first year of Nebuchadrezzar king of Babylon;

2The which Jeremiah the prophet spake unto all the people of Judah, and to all the inhabitants of Jerusalem, saying,

3From the thirteenth year of Josiah the son of Amon king of Judah, even unto this day, that *is* the three and twentieth year, that the word of the LORD hath come unto me, and I have spoken unto you, rising early and speaking; but ye have not hearkened.

4And the LORD hath sent unto you all his servants the prophets, rising early and sending *them;* but ye have not hearkened, nor inclined your ear to hear.

5They said, Turn ye again now everyone from his evil way, and from the evil of your doings, and dwell in the land that the LORD hath given unto you and to your fathers for ever and ever:

6And go not after other gods to serve them, and to worship them, and provoke me not to anger with the works of your hands; and I will do you no hurt.

7Yet ye have not hearkened unto me, saith the LORD; that ye might provoke me to anger with the works of your hands to your own hurt.

8Therefore thus saith the LORD of hosts; Because ye have not heard my words,

9Behold, I will send and take all the families of the north, saith the LORD, and Nebuchadrezzar the king of Babylon, my servant, and will bring them against this land, and against the inhabitants thereof, and against all these nations round about, and will utterly destroy them, and make them an astonishment, and an hissing, and perpetual desolations.

10Moreover I will take from them the voice of mirth, and the voice of gladness, the voice of the bridegroom, and the voice of the bride, the sound of the millstones, and the light of the candle.

11And this whole land shall be a desolation, *and* an astonishment; and these nations shall serve the king of Babylon seventy years.

12And it shall come to pass, when seventy years are accomplished, *that* I will punish the king of Babylon, and that nation, saith the LORD, for their iniquity, and the land of the Chaldeans, and will make it perpetual desolations.

13And I will bring upon that land all my words which I have pronounced against it, *even* all that is written in this book, which Jeremiah hath prophesied against all the nations.

14For many nations and great kings shall serve themselves of them also: and I will recompense them according to their deeds, and according to the works of their own hands.

15For thus saith the LORD God of Israel unto me; Take the wine cup of this fury at my hand, and cause all the nations, to whom I send thee, to drink it.

16And they shall drink, and be moved, and be mad, because of the sword that I will send among them.

17Then took I the cup at the LORD's hand, and made all the nations to drink, unto whom the LORD had sent me:

18*To wit,* Jerusalem, and the cities of Judah, and the kings thereof, and the princes thereof, to make them a desolation, an astonishment, an hissing, and a curse; as *it is* this day;

19Pharaoh king of Egypt, and his servants, and his princes, and all his people;

20And all the mingled people, and all the kings of the land of Uz, and all the kings of the land of the Philistines, and Ashkelon, and Azzah, and Ekron, and the remnant of Ashdod,

21Edom, and Moab, and the children of Ammon,

22And all the kings of Tyrus, and all the kings of Zidon, and the kings of the isles which *are* beyond the sea,

23Dedan, and Tema, and Buz, and all *that are* in the utmost corners,

24And all the kings of Arabia, and all the kings of the mingled people that dwell in the desert,

25And all the kings of Zimri, and all the kings of Elam, and all the kings of the Medes,

26And all the kings of the north, far and near, one with another, and all the kingdoms of the world, which *are* upon the face of the earth: and the king of Sheshach shall drink after them.

27Therefore thou shalt say unto them, Thus saith the LORD of hosts, the God of Israel; Drink ye, and be drunken, and spue, and fall, and rise no more, because of the sword which I will send among you.

28And it shall be, if they refuse to take the cup at thine hand to drink, then shalt thou say unto them, Thus saith the LORD of hosts; Ye shall certainly drink.

29For, lo, I begin to bring evil on the city which is called by my name, and should ye be utterly unpunished? Ye shall not be unpunished: for I will call for a sword upon all the inhabitants of the earth, saith the LORD of hosts.

30Therefore prophesy thou against them all these words, and say unto them, The LORD shall roar from on high, and utter his voice from his holy habitation; he shall mightily roar upon his habitation; he shall give a shout, as they that tread *the grapes,* against all the inhabitants of the earth.

31A noise shall come *even* to the ends of the earth; for the LORD hath a controversy with the nations, he will plead with all flesh; he will give them *that are* wicked to the sword, saith the LORD.

32Thus saith the LORD of hosts, Behold, evil shall go forth from nation to nation, and a great whirlwind shall be raised up from the coasts of the earth.

33And the slain of the LORD shall be at that day from *one* end of the earth even unto the *other* end of the earth: they shall not be lamented, neither gathered, nor buried; they shall be dung upon the ground.

34Howl, ye shepherds, and cry; and wallow yourselves *in the ashes,* ye principal of the flock: for the days of your slaughter and of your dispersions are accomplished; and ye shall fall like a pleasant vessel.

35And the shepherds shall have no way to flee, nor the principal of the flock to escape.

36A voice of the cry of the shepherds, and an howling of the principal of the flock, *shall be heard:* for the LORD hath spoiled their pasture.

37And the peaceable habitations are cut down because of the fierce anger of the LORD.

38He hath forsaken his covert, as the lion: for their land is desolate because of the fierceness of the oppressor, and because of his fierce anger.

2 THESSALONIANS 2:1–17

Now we beseech you, brethren, by the coming of our Lord Jesus Christ, and *by* our gathering together unto him,

2That ye be not soon shaken in mind, or be troubled, neither by spirit, nor by word, nor by letter as from us, as that the day of Christ is at hand.

3Let no man deceive you by any means: for *that day shall not come,* except there come a falling away first, and that man of sin be revealed, the son of perdition;

4Who opposeth and exalteth himself above all that is called God, or that is worshipped; so that he as God sitteth in the temple of God, shewing himself that he is God.

5Remember ye not, that, when I was yet with you, I told you these things?

6And now ye know what withholdeth that he might be revealed in his time.

7For the mystery of iniquity doth already work: only he who now letteth *will let,* until he be taken out of the way.

8And then shall that Wicked be revealed, whom the Lord shall consume with the spirit of his mouth, and shall destroy with the brightness of his coming:

9*Even him,* whose coming is after the working of Satan with all power and signs and lying wonders,

10And with all deceivableness of unrighteousness in them that perish; because they received not the love of the truth, that they might be saved.

11And for this cause God shall send them strong delusion, that they should believe a lie:

12That they all might be damned who believed not the truth, but had pleasure in unrighteousness.

13But we are bound to give thanks alway to God for you, brethren beloved of the Lord, because God hath from the beginning chosen you to salvation through sanctification of the Spirit and belief of the truth:

14Whereunto he called you by our gospel, to the obtaining of the glory of our Lord Jesus Christ.

15Therefore, brethren, stand fast, and hold the traditions which ye have been taught, whether by word, or our epistle.

16Now our Lord Jesus Christ himself, and God, even our Father, which hath loved us, and hath given *us* everlasting consolation and good hope through grace,

17Comfort your hearts, and stablish you in every good word and work.

PSALM 84:1–12

How amiable *are* thy tabernacles, O LORD of hosts! 2My soul longeth, yea, even fainteth for the courts of the LORD: my heart and my flesh crieth out for the living God.

3Yea, the sparrow hath found an house, and the swallow a nest for herself, where she may lay her young, *even* thine altars, O LORD of hosts, my King, and my God.

4Blessed *are* they that dwell in thy house: they will be still praising thee. Selah.

5Blessed *is* the man whose strength *is* in thee; in whose heart *are* the ways *of them.*

6*Who* passing through the valley of Baca make it a well; the rain also filleth the pools.

7They go from strength to strength, *every one of them* in Zion appeareth before God.

8O LORD God of hosts, hear my prayer: give ear, O God of Jacob. Selah.

9Behold, O God our shield, and look upon the face of thine anointed.

10For a day in thy courts *is* better than a thousand. I had rather be a doorkeeper in the house of my God, than to dwell in the tents of wickedness.

11For the LORD God *is* a sun and shield: the LORD will give grace and glory: no good *thing* will he withhold from them that walk uprightly.

12O LORD of hosts, blessed *is* the man that trusteth in thee.

PROVERBS FOR TODAY/ 25:15

By long forbearing is a prince persuaded, and a soft tongue breaketh the bone.

OCTOBER 15

JEREMIAH 26:1—27:22

In the beginning of the reign of Jehoiakim the son of Josiah king of Judah came this word from the LORD, saying,

2Thus saith the LORD; Stand in the

court of the LORD's house, and speak unto all the cities of Judah, which come to worship in the LORD's house, all the words that I command thee to speak unto them; diminish not a word:

3If so be they will hearken, and turn

every man from his evil way, that I may repent me of the evil, which I purpose to do unto them because of the evil of their doings.

4And thou shalt say unto them, Thus saith the LORD; If ye will not hearken to me, to walk in my law, which I have set before you,

5To hearken to the words of my servants the prophets, whom I sent unto you, both rising up early, and sending *them,* but ye have not hearkened;

6Then will I make this house like Shiloh, and will make this city a curse to all the nations of the earth.

7So the priests and the prophets and all the people heard Jeremiah speaking these words in the house of the LORD.

8Now it came to pass, when Jeremiah had made an end of speaking all that the LORD had commanded *him* to speak unto all the people, that the priests and the prophets and all the people took him, saying, Thou shalt surely die.

9Why hast thou prophesied in the name of the LORD, saying, This house shall be like Shiloh, and this city shall be desolate without an inhabitant? And all the people were gathered against Jeremiah in the house of the LORD.

10When the princes of Judah heard these things, then they came up from the king's house unto the house of the LORD, and sat down in the entry of the new gate of the LORD's *house.*

11Then spake the priests and the prophets unto the princes and to all the people, saying, This man *is* worthy to die; for he hath prophesied against this city, as ye have heard with your ears.

12Then spake Jeremiah unto all the princes and to all the people, saying, The LORD sent me to prophesy against this house and against this city all the words that ye have heard.

13Therefore now amend your ways and your doings, and obey the voice of the LORD your God; and the LORD will repent him of the evil that he hath pronounced against you.

14As for me, behold, I *am* in your hand: do with me as seemeth good and meet unto you.

15But know ye for certain, that if ye put me to death, ye shall surely bring innocent blood upon yourselves, and upon this city, and upon the inhabitants thereof: for of a truth the LORD hath sent me unto you to speak all these words in your ears.

16Then said the princes and all the people unto the priests and to the prophets; This man *is* not worthy to die: for he hath spoken to us in the name of the LORD our God.

17Then rose up certain of the elders of the land, and spake to all the assembly of the people, saying,

18Micah the Morasthite prophesied in the days of Hezekiah king of Judah, and spake to all the people of Judah, saying, Thus saith the LORD of hosts; Zion shall be plowed *like* a field, and Jerusalem shall become heaps, and the mountain of the house as the high places of a forest.

19Did Hezekiah king of Judah and all Judah put him at all to death? did he not fear the LORD, and besought the LORD, and the LORD repented him of the evil which he had pronounced against them? Thus might we procure great evil against our souls.

20And there was also a man that prophesied in the name of the LORD, Urijah the son of Shemaiah of Kirjath–jearim, who prophesied against this city and against this land according to all the words of Jeremiah:

21And when Jehoiakim the king, with all his mighty men, and all the princes, heard his words, the king sought to put him to death: but when Urijah heard it, he was afraid, and fled, and went into Egypt;

22And Jehoiakim the king sent men into Egypt, *namely,* Elnathan the son of Achbor, and *certain* men with him into Egypt.

23And they fetched forth Urijah out of Egypt, and brought him unto Jehoiakim the king; who slew him with the sword, and cast his dead body into the graves of the common people.

24Nevertheless the hand of Ahikam the son of Shaphan was with Jeremiah, that they should not give him into the hand of the people to put him to death.

In the beginning of the reign of Jehoiakim the son of Josiah king of Judah came this word unto Jeremiah from the LORD, saying,

2Thus saith the LORD to me; Make thee bonds and yokes, and put them upon thy neck,

3And send them to the king of Edom, and to the king of Moab, and to the king of the Ammonites, and to the king of Tyrus, and to the king of Zidon, by the hand of the messengers which come to Jerusalem unto Zedekiah king of Judah;

4And command them to say unto their masters, Thus saith the LORD of hosts, the God of Israel; Thus shall ye say unto your masters;

5I have made the earth, the man and the beast that *are* upon the ground, by my great power and by my outstretched arm, and have given it unto whom it seemed meet unto me.

6And now have I given all these lands into the hand of Nebuchadnezzar the king of Babylon, my servant; and the beasts of the field have I given him also to serve him.

7And all nations shall serve him, and his son, and his son's son, until the very time of his land come: and then many nations and great kings shall serve themselves of him.

8And it shall come to pass, *that* the nation and kingdom which will not serve the same Nebuchadnezzar the king of Babylon, and that will not put their neck under the yoke of the king of Babylon, that nation will I punish, saith the LORD, with the sword, and with the famine, and with the pestilence, until I have consumed them by his hand.

9Therefore hearken not ye to your prophets, nor to your diviners, nor to your dreamers, nor to your enchanters, nor to your sorcerers, which speak unto you, saying, Ye shall not serve the king of Babylon:

10For they prophesy a lie unto you, to remove you far from your land; and that I should drive you out, and ye should perish.

11But the nations that bring their neck under the yoke of the king of Babylon, and serve him, those will I let remain still in their own land, saith the LORD; and they shall till it, and dwell therein.

12I spake also to Zedekiah king of Judah according to all these words, saying, Bring your necks under the yoke of the king of Babylon, and serve him and his people, and live.

13Why will ye die, thou and thy people, by the sword, by the famine, and by the pestilence, as the LORD hath spoken against the nation that will not serve the king of Babylon?

14Therefore hearken not unto the words of the prophets that speak unto you, saying, Ye shall not serve the king of Babylon: for they prophesy a lie unto you.

15For I have not sent them, saith the LORD, yet they prophesy a lie in my name; that I might drive you out, and that ye might perish, ye, and the prophets that prophesy unto you.

16Also I spake to the priests and to all this people, saying, Thus saith the LORD; Hearken not to the words of your prophets that prophesy unto you, saying, Behold, the vessels of the LORD's house shall now shortly be brought again from Babylon: for they prophesy a lie unto you.

17Hearken not unto them; serve the king of Babylon, and live: wherefore should this city be laid waste?

18But if they *be* prophets, and if the word of the LORD be with them, let them now make intercession to the LORD of hosts, that the vessels which are left in the house of the LORD, and *in* the house of the king of Judah, and at Jerusalem, go not to Babylon.

19For thus saith the LORD of hosts concerning the pillars, and concerning the sea, and concerning the bases, and concerning the residue of the vessels that remain in this city,

20Which Nebuchadnezzar king of Babylon took not, when he carried away captive Jeconiah the son of Jehoiakim king of Judah from Jerusalem to Babylon, and all the nobles of Judah and Jerusalem;

21Yea, thus saith the LORD of hosts, the God of Israel, concerning the vessels that remain *in* the house of the LORD, and *in* the house of the king of Judah and of Jerusalem;

22They shall be carried to Babylon, and there shall they be until the day that I visit them, saith the LORD; then will I bring them up, and restore them to this place.

2 THESSALONIANS 3:1-18

FINALLY, brethren, pray for us, that the word of the Lord may have *free* course, and be glorified, even as *it is* with you:

2And that we may be delivered from unreasonable and wicked men: for all *men* have not faith.

3But the Lord is faithful, who shall stablish you, and keep *you* from evil.

4And we have confidence in the Lord touching you, that ye both do and will do the things which we command you.

5And the Lord direct your hearts into the love of God, and into the patient waiting for Christ.

6Now we command you, brethren, in the name of our Lord Jesus Christ, that ye withdraw yourselves from every brother that walketh disorderly, and not after the tradition which he received of us.

7For yourselves know how ye ought to follow us: for we behaved not ourselves disorderly among you;

8Neither did we eat any man's bread for nought; but wrought with labour and travail night and day, that we might not be chargeable to any of you:

9Not because we have not power, but to make ourselves an ensample unto you to follow us.

10For even when we were with you, this we commanded you, that if any would not work, neither should he eat.

11For we hear that there are some which walk among you disorderly, working not at all, but are busybodies.

12Now them that are such we command and exhort by our Lord Jesus Christ, that with quietness they work, and eat their own bread.

13But ye, brethren, be not weary in well doing.

14And if any man obey not our word by this epistle, note that man, and have no company with him, that he may be ashamed.

15Yet count *him* not as an enemy, but admonish *him* as a brother.

16Now the Lord of peace himself give you peace always by all means. The Lord *be* with you all.

17The salutation of Paul with mine own hand, which is the token in every epistle: so I write.

18The grace of our Lord Jesus Christ *be* with you all. Amen.

PSALM 85:1-13

LORD, thou hast been favourable unto thy land: thou hast brought back the captivity of Jacob.

2Thou hast forgiven the iniquity of thy people, thou hast covered all their sin. Selah.

3Thou hast taken away all thy wrath: thou hast turned *thyself* from the fierceness of thine anger.

4Turn us, O God of our salvation,

and cause thine anger toward us to cease.

5Wilt thou be angry with us for ever? wilt thou draw out thine anger to all generations?

6Wilt thou not revive us again: that thy people may rejoice in thee?

7Shew us thy mercy, O LORD, and grant us thy salvation.

8I will hear what God the LORD will speak: for he will speak peace unto his people, and to his saints: but let them not turn again to folly.

9Surely his salvation is nigh them that fear him; that glory may dwell in our land.

10Mercy and truth are met together; righteousness and peace have kissed *each other.*

11Truth shall spring out of the earth; and righteousness shall look down from heaven.

12Yea, the LORD shall give *that which is* good; and our land shall yield her increase.

13Righteousness shall go before him; and shall set *us* in the way of his steps.

PROVERBS FOR TODAY/ 25:16

Hast thou found honey? eat so much as is sufficient for thee, lest thou be filled therewith, and vomit it.

OCTOBER 16

JEREMIAH 28:1—29:32

AND it came to pass the same year, in the beginning of the reign of Zedekiah king of Judah, in the fourth year, *and* in the fifth month, *that* Hananiah the son of Azur the prophet, which *was* of Gibeon, spake unto me in the house of the LORD, in the presence of the priests and of all the people, saying,

2Thus speaketh the LORD of hosts, the God of Israel, saying, I have broken the yoke of the king of Babylon.

3Within two full years will I bring again into this place all the vessels of the LORD's house, that Nebuchadnezzar king of Babylon took away from this place, and carried them to Babylon:

4And I will bring again to this place Jeconiah the son of Jehoiakim king of Judah, with all the captives of Judah, that went into Babylon, saith the LORD:

for I will break the yoke of the king of Babylon.

5Then the prophet Jeremiah said unto the prophet Hananiah in the presence of the priests, and in the presence of all the people that stood in the house of the LORD,

6Even the prophet Jeremiah said, Amen: the LORD do so: the LORD perform thy words which thou hast prophesied, to bring again the vessels of the LORD's house, and all that is carried away captive, from Babylon into this place.

7Nevertheless hear thou now this word that I speak in thine ears, and in the ears of all the people;

8The prophets that have been before me and before thee of old prophesied both against many countries, and against great kingdoms, of war, and of evil, and of pestilence.

9The prophet which prophesieth of peace, when the word of the prophet shall come to pass, *then* shall the prophet be known, that the LORD hath truly sent him.

10Then Hananiah the prophet took the yoke from off the prophet Jeremiah's neck, and brake it.

11And Hananiah spake in the presence of all the people, saying, Thus saith the LORD; Even so will I break the yoke of Nebuchadnezzar king of Babylon from the neck of all nations within the space of two full years. And the prophet Jeremiah went his way.

12Then the word of the LORD came unto Jeremiah *the prophet,* after that Hananiah the prophet had broken the yoke from off the neck of the prophet Jeremiah, saying,

13Go and tell Hananiah, saying, Thus saith the LORD; Thou hast broken the yokes of wood; but thou shalt make for them yokes of iron.

14For thus saith the LORD of hosts, the God of Israel; I have put a yoke of iron upon the neck of all these nations, that they may serve Nebuchadnezzar king of Babylon; and they shall serve him: and I have given him the beasts of the field also.

15Then said the prophet Jeremiah unto Hananiah the prophet, Hear now, Hananiah; The LORD hath not sent thee; but thou makest this people to trust in a lie.

16Therefore thus saith the LORD; Behold, I will cast thee from off the face of the earth: this year thou shalt die, because thou hast taught rebellion against the LORD.

17So Hananiah the prophet died the same year in the seventh month.

Now these *are* the words of the letter that Jeremiah the prophet sent from Jerusalem unto the residue of the elders which were carried away captives, and to the priests, and to the prophets, and to all the people whom Nebuchad-nezzar had carried away captive from Jerusalem to Babylon;

2(After that Jeconiah the king, and the queen, and the eunuchs, the princes of Judah and Jerusalem, and the carpenters, and the smiths, were departed from Jerusalem;)

3By the hand of Elasah the son of Shaphan, and Gemariah the son of Hilkiah, (whom Zedekiah king of Judah sent unto Babylon to Nebuchadnezzar king of Babylon) saying,

4Thus saith the LORD of hosts, the God of Israel, unto all that are carried away captives, whom I have caused to be carried away from Jerusalem unto Babylon;

5Build ye houses, and dwell *in them;* and plant gardens, and eat the fruit of them;

6Take ye wives, and beget sons and daughters; and take wives for your sons, and give your daughters to husbands, that they may bear sons and daughters; that ye may be increased there, and not diminished.

7And seek the peace of the city whither I have caused you to be carried away captives, and pray unto the LORD for it: for in the peace thereof shall ye have peace.

8For thus saith the LORD of hosts, the God of Israel; Let not your prophets and your diviners, that *be* in the midst of you, deceive you, neither hearken to your dreams which ye cause to be dreamed.

9For they prophesy falsely unto you in my name: I have not sent them, saith the LORD.

10For thus saith the LORD, That after seventy years be accomplished at Babylon I will visit you, and perform my good word toward you, in causing you to return to this place.

11For I know the thoughts that I think toward you, saith the LORD, thoughts of peace, and not of evil, to give you an expected end.

12Then shall ye call upon me, and

ye shall go and pray unto me, and I will hearken unto you.

13And ye shall seek me, and find *me*, when ye shall search for me with all your heart.

14And I will be found of you, saith the LORD: and I will turn away your captivity, and I will gather you from all the nations, and from all the places whither I have driven you, saith the LORD; and I will bring you again into the place whence I caused you to be carried away captive.

15Because ye have said, The LORD hath raised us up prophets in Babylon;

16*Know* that thus saith the LORD of the king that sitteth upon the throne of David, and of all the people that dwelleth in this city, *and* of your brethren that are not gone forth with you into captivity;

17Thus saith the LORD of hosts; Behold, I will send upon them the sword, the famine, and the pestilence, and will make them like vile figs, that cannot be eaten, they are so evil.

18And I will persecute them with the sword, with the famine, and with the pestilence, and will deliver them to be removed to all the kingdoms of the earth, to be a curse, and an astonishment, and an hissing, and a reproach, among all the nations whither I have driven them:

19Because they have not hearkened to my words, saith the LORD, which I sent unto them by my servants the prophets, rising up early and sending *them;* but ye would not hear, saith the LORD.

20Hear ye therefore the word of the LORD, all ye of the captivity, whom I have sent from Jerusalem to Babylon:

21Thus saith the LORD of hosts, the God of Israel, of Ahab the son of Kolaiah, and of Zedekiah the son of Maaseiah, which prophesy a lie unto you in my name; Behold, I will deliver them into the hand of Nebuchadrezzar king of Babylon; and he shall slay them before your eyes;

22And of them shall be taken up a curse by all the captivity of Judah which *are* in Babylon, saying, The LORD make thee like Zedekiah and like Ahab, whom the king of Babylon roasted in the fire;

23Because they have committed villany in Israel, and have committed adultery with their neighbours' wives, and have spoken lying words in my name, which I have not commanded them; even I know, and *am* a witness, saith the LORD.

24*Thus* shalt thou also speak to Shemaiah the Nehelamite, saying,

25Thus speaketh the LORD of hosts, the God of Israel, saying, Because thou hast sent letters in thy name unto all the people that *are* at Jerusalem, and to Zephaniah the son of Maaseiah the priest, and to all the priests, saying,

26The LORD hath made thee priest in the stead of Jehoiada the priest, that ye should be officers in the house of the LORD, for every man *that is* mad, and maketh himself a prophet, that thou shouldest put him in prison, and in the stocks.

27Now therefore why hast thou not reproved Jeremiah of Anathoth, which maketh himself a prophet to you?

28For therefore he sent unto us *in* Babylon, saying, This *captivity is* long: build ye houses, and dwell *in them;* and plant gardens, and eat the fruit of them.

29And Zephaniah the priest read this letter in the ears of Jeremiah the prophet.

30Then came the word of the LORD unto Jeremiah, saying,

31Send to all them of the captivity, saying, Thus saith the LORD concerning Shemaiah the Nehelamite; Because that Shemaiah hath prophesied unto you, and I sent him not, and he caused you to trust in a lie:

32Therefore thus saith the LORD; Behold, I will punish Shemaiah the Nehelamite, and his seed: he shall not have a man to dwell among this people; neither shall he behold the good that I will do for my people, saith the LORD; because he hath taught rebellion against the LORD.

1 TIMOTHY 1:1–20

PAUL, an apostle of Jesus Christ by the commandment of God our Saviour, and Lord Jesus Christ, *which is* our hope;

2Unto Timothy, *my* own son in the faith: Grace, mercy, *and* peace, from God our Father and Jesus Christ our Lord.

3As I besought thee to abide still at Ephesus, when I went into Macedonia, that thou mightest charge some that they teach no other doctrine,

4Neither give heed to fables and endless genealogies, which minister questions, rather than godly edifying which is in faith: *so do.*

5Now the end of the commandment is charity out of a pure heart, and *of* a good conscience, and *of* faith unfeigned:

6From which some having swerved have turned aside unto vain jangling;

7Desiring to be teachers of the law; understanding neither what they say, nor whereof they affirm.

8But we know that the law *is* good, if a man use it lawfully;

9Knowing this, that the law is not made for a righteous man, but for the lawless and disobedient, for the ungodly and for sinners, for unholy and profane, for murderers of fathers and murderers of mothers, for manslayers,

10For whoremongers, for them that defile themselves with mankind, for menstealers, for liars, for perjured persons, and if there be any other thing that is contrary to sound doctrine;

11According to the glorious gospel of the blessed God, which was committed to my trust.

12And I thank Christ Jesus our Lord,

who hath enabled me, for that he counted me faithful, putting me into the ministry;

13Who was before a blasphemer, and a persecutor, and injurious: but I obtained mercy, because I did *it* ignorantly in unbelief.

14And the grace of our Lord was exceeding abundant with faith and love which is in Christ Jesus.

15This *is* a faithful saying, and worthy of all acceptation, that Christ Jesus came into the world to save sinners; of whom I am chief.

16Howbeit for this cause I obtained mercy, that in me first Jesus Christ might shew forth all longsuffering, for a pattern to them which should hereafter believe on him to life everlasting.

17Now unto the King eternal, immortal, invisible, the only wise God, *be* honour and glory for ever and ever. Amen.

18This charge I commit unto thee, son Timothy, according to the prophecies which went before on thee, that thou by them mightest war a good warfare;

19Holding faith, and a good conscience; which some having put away concerning faith have made shipwreck:

20Of whom is Hymenaeus and Alexander; whom I have delivered unto Satan, that they may learn not to blaspheme.

PSALM 86:1–17

BOW down thine ear, O LORD, hear me: for I *am* poor and needy.

2Preserve my soul; for I *am* holy: O thou my God, save thy servant that trusteth in thee.

3Be merciful unto me, O Lord: for I cry unto thee daily.

4Rejoice the soul of thy servant: for unto thee, O Lord, do I lift up my soul.

5For thou, Lord, *art* good, and ready

to forgive; and plenteous in mercy unto all them that call upon thee.

6Give ear, O LORD, unto my prayer; and attend to the voice of my supplications.

7In the day of my trouble I will call upon thee: for thou wilt answer me.

8Among the gods *there is* none like unto thee, O Lord; neither *are there any works* like unto thy works.

9All nations whom thou hast made shall come and worship before thee, O Lord; and shall glorify thy name.

10For thou *art* great, and doest wondrous things: thou *art* God alone.

11Teach me thy way, O LORD; I will walk in thy truth: unite my heart to fear thy name.

12I will praise thee, O Lord my God, with all my heart: and I will glorify thy name for evermore.

13For great *is* thy mercy toward me: and thou hast delivered my soul from the lowest hell.

14O God, the proud are risen against me, and the assemblies of violent *men* have sought after my soul; and have not set thee before them.

15But thou, O Lord, *art* a God full of compassion, and gracious, longsuffering, and plenteous in mercy and truth.

16O turn unto me, and have mercy upon me; give thy strength unto thy servant, and save the son of thine handmaid.

17Shew me a token for good; that they which hate me may see *it,* and be ashamed: because thou, LORD, hast holpen me, and comforted me.

PROVERBS FOR TODAY/ 25:17

Withdraw thy foot from thy neighbour's house; lest he be weary of thee, and so *hate thee.*

OCTOBER 17

JEREMIAH 30:1—31:26

THE word that came to Jeremiah from the LORD, saying,

2Thus speaketh the LORD God of Israel, saying, Write thee all the words that I have spoken unto thee in a book.

3For, lo, the days come, saith the LORD, that I will bring again the captivity of my people Israel and Judah, saith the LORD: and I will cause them to return to the land that I gave to their fathers, and they shall possess it.

4And these *are* the words that the LORD spake concerning Israel and concerning Judah.

5For thus saith the LORD; We have heard a voice of trembling, of fear, and not of peace.

6Ask ye now, and see whether a man doth travail with child? wherefore do I see every man with his hands on his loins, as a woman in travail, and all faces are turned into paleness?

7Alas! for that day *is* great, so that none *is* like it: it *is* even the time of Jacob's trouble; but he shall be saved out of it.

8For it shall come to pass in that day, saith the LORD of hosts, *that* I will break his yoke from off thy neck, and will burst thy bonds, and strangers shall no more serve themselves of him:

9But they shall serve the LORD their

God, and David their king, whom I will raise up unto them.

¹⁰Therefore fear thou not, O my servant Jacob, saith the LORD; neither be dismayed, O Israel: for, lo, I will save thee from afar, and thy seed from the land of their captivity; and Jacob shall return, and shall be in rest, and be quiet, and none shall make *him* afraid.

¹¹For I *am* with thee, saith the LORD, to save thee: though I make a full end of all nations whither I have scattered thee, yet will I not make a full end of thee: but I will correct thee in measure, and will not leave thee altogether unpunished.

¹²For thus saith the LORD, Thy bruise *is* incurable, *and* thy wound *is* grievous.

¹³*There is* none to plead thy cause, that thou mayest be bound up: thou hast no healing medicines.

¹⁴All thy lovers have forgotten thee; they seek thee not; for I have wounded thee with the wound of an enemy, with the chastisement of a cruel one, for the multitude of thine iniquity; *because* thy sins were increased.

¹⁵Why criest thou for thine affliction? thy sorrow *is* incurable for the multitude of thine iniquity: *because* thy sins were increased, I have done these things unto thee.

¹⁶Therefore all they that devour thee shall be devoured; and all thine adversaries, every one of them, shall go into captivity; and they that spoil thee shall be a spoil, and all that prey upon thee will I give for a prey.

¹⁷For I will restore health unto thee, and I will heal thee of thy wounds, saith the LORD; because they called thee an Outcast, *saying,* This *is* Zion, whom no man seeketh after.

¹⁸Thus saith the LORD; Behold, I will bring again the captivity of Jacob's tents, and have mercy on his dwellingplaces; and the city shall be builded upon her own heap, and the palace shall remain after the manner thereof.

¹⁹And out of them shall proceed thanksgiving and the voice of them that make merry: and I will multiply them, and they shall not be few; I will also glorify them, and they shall not be small.

²⁰Their children also shall be as aforetime, and their congregation shall be established before me, and I will punish all that oppress them.

²¹And their nobles shall be of themselves, and their governor shall proceed from the midst of them; and I will cause him to draw near, and he shall approach unto me: for who *is* this that engaged his heart to approach unto me? saith the LORD.

²²And ye shall be my people, and I will be your God.

²³Behold, the whirlwind of the LORD goeth forth with fury, a continuing whirlwind: it shall fall with pain upon the head of the wicked.

²⁴The fierce anger of the LORD shall not return, until he have done *it,* and until he have performed the intents of his heart: in the latter days ye shall consider it.

AT the same time, saith the LORD, will I be the God of all the families of Israel, and they shall be my people.

²Thus saith the LORD, The people *which were* left of the sword found grace in the wilderness; *even* Israel, when I went to cause him to rest.

³The LORD hath appeared of old unto me, *saying,* Yea, I have loved thee with an everlasting love: therefore with lovingkindness have I drawn thee.

⁴Again I will build thee, and thou shalt be built, O virgin of Israel: thou shalt again be adorned with thy tabrets, and shalt go forth in the dances of them that make merry.

⁵Thou shalt yet plant vines upon the mountains of Samaria: the planters shall plant, and shall eat *them* as common things.

⁶For there shall be a day, *that* the watchman upon the mount Ephraim shall cry, Arise ye, and let us go up

to Zion unto the LORD our God.

7For thus saith the LORD; Sing with gladness for Jacob, and shout among the chief of the nations: publish ye, praise ye, and say, O LORD, save thy people, the remnant of Israel.

8Behold, I will bring them from the north country, and gather them from the coasts of the earth, *and* with them the blind and the lame, the woman with child and her that travaileth with child together: a great company shall return thither.

9They shall come with weeping, and with supplications will I lead them: I will cause them to walk by the rivers of waters in a straight way, wherein they shall not stumble: for I am a father to Israel, and Ephraim *is* my firstborn.

10Hear the word of the LORD, O ye nations, and declare *it* in the isles afar off, and say, He that scattered Israel will gather him, and keep him, as a shepherd *doth* his flock.

11For the LORD hath redeemed Jacob, and ransomed him from the hand of *him that was* stronger than he.

12Therefore they shall come and sing in the height of Zion, and shall flow together to the goodness of the LORD, for wheat, and for wine, and for oil, and for the young of the flock and of the herd: and their soul shall be as a watered garden; and they shall not sorrow any more at all.

13Then shall the virgin rejoice in the dance, both young men and old together: for I will turn their mourning into joy, and will comfort them, and make them rejoice from their sorrow.

14And I will satiate the soul of the priests with fatness, and my people shall be satisfied with my goodness, saith the LORD.

15Thus saith the LORD; A voice was heard in Ramah, lamentation, *and* bitter weeping; Rachel weeping for her children refused to be comforted for her children, because they *were* not.

16Thus saith the LORD; Refrain thy voice from weeping, and thine eyes from tears: for thy work shall be rewarded, saith the LORD; and they shall come again from the land of the enemy.

17And there is hope in thine end, saith the LORD, that thy children shall come again to their own border.

18I have surely heard Ephraim bemoaning himself *thus;* Thou hast chastised me, and I was chastised, as a bullock unaccustomed *to the yoke:* turn thou me, and I shall be turned; for thou *art* the LORD my God.

19Surely after that I was turned, I repented; and after that I was instructed, I smote upon *my* thigh: I was ashamed yea, even confounded, because I did bear the reproach of my youth.

20*Is* Ephraim my dear son? *is he* a pleasant child? for since I spake against him, I do earnestly remember him still: therefore my bowels are troubled for him; I will surely have mercy upon him, saith the LORD.

21Set thee up waymarks, make thee high heaps: set thine heart toward the highway, *even* the way *which* thou wentest: turn again, O virgin of Israel, turn again to these thy cities.

22How long wilt thou go about, O thou backsliding daughter? for the LORD hath created a new thing in the earth, A woman shall compass a man.

23Thus saith the LORD of hosts, the God of Israel; As yet they shall use this speech in the land of Judah and in the cities thereof, when I shall bring again their captivity; The LORD bless thee, O habitation of justice, *and* mountain of holiness.

24And there shall dwell in Judah itself, and in all the cities thereof together, husbandmen, and they *that* go forth with flocks.

25For I have satiated the weary soul, and I have replenished every sorrowful soul.

26Upon this I awaked, and beheld; and my sleep was sweet unto me.

1 TIMOTHY 2:1–15

I EXHORT therefore, that, first of all, supplications, prayers, intercessions, *and* giving of thanks, be made for all men;

2For kings, and *for* all that are in authority; that we may lead a quiet and peaceable life in all godliness and honesty.

3For this *is* good and acceptable in the sight of God our Saviour;

4Who will have all men to be saved, and to come unto the knowledge of the truth.

5For *there is* one God, and one mediator between God and men, the man Christ Jesus;

6Who gave himself a ransom for all, to be testified in due time.

7Whereunto I am ordained a preacher, and an apostle, (I speak the truth in Christ, *and* lie not;) a teacher of the Gentiles in faith and verity.

8I will therefore that men pray every where, lifting up holy hands, without wrath and doubting.

9In like manner also, that women adorn themselves in modest apparel, with shamefacedness and sobriety; not with broided hair, or gold, or pearls, or costly array.

10But (which becometh women professing godliness) with good works.

11Let the woman learn in silence with all subjection.

12But I suffer not a woman to teach, nor to usurp authority over the man, but to be in silence.

13For Adam was first formed, then Eve.

14And Adam was not deceived, but the woman being deceived was in the transgression.

15Notwithstanding she shall be saved in childbearing, if they continue in faith and charity and holiness with sobriety.

PSALM 87:1–7

H IS foundation *is* in the holy mountains.

2The LORD loveth the gates of Zion more than all the dwellings of Jacob.

3Glorious things are spoken of thee, O city of God. Selah.

4I will make mention of Rahab and Babylon to them that know me: behold Philistia, and Tyre, with Ethiopia; this *man* was born there.

5And of Zion it shall be said, This and that man was born in her: and the highest himself shall establish her.

6The LORD shall count, when he writeth up the people, *that* this *man* was born there. Selah.

7As well the singers as the players on instruments *shall be there:* all my springs *are* in thee.

PROVERBS FOR TODAY/ 25:18–19

A man that beareth false witness against his neighbour is *a maul, and a sword, and a sharp arrow.* □ *Confidence in an unfaithful man in time of trouble* is like *a broken tooth, and a foot out of joint.*

JEREMIAH 31:27—32:44

BEHOLD, the days come, saith the LORD, that I will sow the house of Israel and the house of Judah with the seed of man, and with the seed of beast.

28And it shall come to pass, *that* like as I have watched over them, to pluck up, and to break down, and to throw down, and to destroy, and to afflict; so will I watch over them, to build, and to plant, saith the LORD.

29In those days they shall say no more, The fathers have eaten a sour grape, and the children's teeth are set on edge.

30But every one shall die for his own iniquity: every man that eateth the sour grape, his teeth shall be set on edge.

31Behold, the days come, saith the LORD, that I will make a new covenant with the house of Israel and with the house of Judah:

32Not according to the covenant that I made with their fathers in the day *that* I took them by the hand to bring them out of the land of Egypt; which my covenant they brake, although I was an husband unto them, saith the LORD:

33But this *shall be* the covenant that I will make with the house of Israel; After those days, saith the LORD, I will put my law in their inward parts, and write it in their hearts; and will be their God, and they shall be my people.

34And they shall teach no more every man his neighbour, and every man his brother, saying, Know the LORD: for they shall all know me, from the least of them unto the greatest of them, saith the LORD: for I will forgive their iniquity, and I will remember their sin no more.

35Thus saith the LORD, which giveth the sun for a light by day, *and* the ordinances of the moon and of the stars for a light by night, which divideth the sea when the waves thereof roar; The LORD of hosts *is* his name:

36If those ordinances depart from before me, saith the LORD, *then* the seed of Israel also shall cease from being a nation before me for ever.

37Thus saith the LORD; If heaven above can be measured, and the foundations of the earth searched out beneath, I will also cast off all the seed of Israel for all that they have done, saith the LORD.

38Behold, the days come, saith the LORD, that the city shall be built to the LORD from the tower of Hananeel unto the gate of the corner.

39And the measuring line shall yet go forth over against it upon the hill Gareb, and shall compass about to Goath.

40And the whole valley of the dead bodies, and of the ashes, and all the fields unto the brook of Kidron, unto the corner of the horse gate toward the east, *shall be* holy unto the LORD; it shall not be plucked up, nor thrown down any more for ever.

THE word that came to Jeremiah from the LORD in the tenth year of Zedekiah king of Judah, which *was* the eighteenth year of Nebuchadrezzar.

2For then the king of Babylon's army besieged Jerusalem: and Jeremiah the prophet was shut up in the court of the prison, which *was* in the king of Judah's house.

3For Zedekiah king of Judah had shut him up, saying, Wherefore dost thou prophesy, and say, Thus saith the LORD, Behold, I will give this city into the hand of the king of Babylon, and he shall take it;

4And Zedekiah king of Judah shall not escape out of the hand of the Chaldeans, but shall surely be delivered into the hand of the king of Babylon, and shall speak with him mouth to mouth, and his eyes shall behold his eyes;

5And he shall lead Zedekiah to Babylon, and there shall he be until I visit him, saith the LORD: though ye fight with the Chaldeans, ye shall not prosper.

6And Jeremiah said, The word of the LORD came unto me, saying,

7Behold, Hanameel the son of Shallum thine uncle shall come unto thee, saying, Buy thee my field that *is* in Anathoth: for the right of redemption *is* thine to buy *it.*

8So Hanameel mine uncle's son came to me in the court of the prison according to the word of the LORD, and said unto me, Buy my field, I pray thee, that *is* in Anathoth, which *is* in the country of Benjamin: for the right of inheritance *is* thine, and the redemption *is* thine; buy *it* for thyself. Then I knew that this *was* the word of the LORD.

9And I bought the field of Hanameel my uncle's son, that *was* in Anathoth, and weighed him the money, *even* seventeen shekels of silver.

10And I subscribed the evidence, and sealed *it,* and took witnesses, and weighed *him* the money in the balances.

11So I took the evidence of the purchase, *both* that which was sealed *according* to the law and custom, and that which was open:

12And I gave the evidence of the purchase unto Baruch the son of Neriah, the son of Maaseiah, in the sight of Hanameel mine uncle's *son,* and in the presence of the witnesses that subscribed the book of the purchase, before all the Jews that sat in the court of the prison.

13And I charged Baruch before them, saying,

14Thus saith the LORD of hosts, the God of Israel; Take these evidences, this evidence of the purchase, both which is sealed, and this evidence which is open; and put them in an earthen vessel, that they may continue many days.

15For thus saith the LORD of hosts, the God of Israel; Houses and fields and vineyards shall be possessed again in this land.

16Now when I had delivered the evidence of the purchase unto Baruch the son of Neriah, I prayed unto the LORD, saying,

17Ah Lord GOD! behold, thou hast made the heaven and the earth by thy great power and stretched out arm, *and* there is nothing too hard for thee:

18Thou shewest lovingkindness unto thousands, and recompensest the iniquity of the fathers into the bosom of their children after them: the Great, the Mighty God, the LORD of hosts, *is* his name,

19Great in counsel, and mighty in work: for thine eyes *are* open upon all the ways of the sons of men: to give every one according to his ways, and according to the fruit of his doings:

20Which hast set signs and wonders in the land of Egypt, *even* unto this day, and in Israel, and among *other* men; and hast made thee a name, as at this day;

21And hast brought forth thy people Israel out of the land of Egypt with signs, and with wonders, and with a strong hand, and with a stretched out arm, and with great terror;

22And hast given them this land, which thou didst swear to their fathers to give them, a land flowing with milk and honey;

23And they came in, and possessed it; but they obeyed not thy voice, neither walked in thy law; they have done nothing of all that thou commandedst them to do: therefore thou hast caused all this evil to come upon them:

24Behold the mounts, they are come unto the city to take it: and the city is given into the hand of the Chaldeans, that fight against it, because of the sword, and of the famine, and of the pestilence: and what thou hast spoken is come to pass; and, behold, thou seest *it.*

25And thou hast said unto me, O Lord GOD, Buy thee the field for money, and take witnesses; for the city is given into the hand of the Chaldeans.

26Then came the word of the LORD unto Jeremiah, saying,

27Behold, I *am* the LORD, the God of all flesh: is there any thing too hard for me?

28Therefore thus saith the LORD; Behold, I will give this city into the hand of the Chaldeans, and into the hand of Nebuchadrezzar king of Babylon, and he shall take it:

29And the Chaldeans, that fight against this city, shall come and set fire on this city, and burn it with the houses, upon whose roofs they have offered incense unto Baal, and poured out drink offerings unto other gods, to provoke me to anger.

30For the children of Israel and the children of Judah have only done evil before me from their youth: for the children of Israel have only provoked me to anger with the work of their hands, saith the LORD.

31For this city hath been to me *as* a provocation of mine anger and of my fury from the day that they built it even unto this day; that I should remove it from before my face,

32Because of all the evil of the children of Israel and of the children of Judah, which they have done to provoke me to anger, they, their kings, their princes, their priests, and their prophets, and the men of Judah, and the inhabitants of Jerusalem.

33And they have turned unto me the back, and not the face: though I taught them, rising up early and teaching *them,* yet they have not hearkened to receive instruction.

34But they set their abominations in the house, which is called by my name, to defile it.

35And they built the high places of Baal, which *are* in the valley of the son of Hinnom, to cause their sons and their daughters to pass through *the fire* unto Molech; which I commanded them not, neither came it into my mind, that they should do this abomination, to cause Judah to sin.

36And now therefore thus saith the LORD, the God of Israel, concerning this city, whereof ye say, It shall be delivered into the hand of the king of Babylon by the sword, and by the famine, and by the pestilence;

37Behold, I will gather them out of all countries, whither I have driven them in mine anger, and in my fury, and in great wrath; and I will bring them again unto this place, and I will cause them to dwell safely:

38And they shall be my people, and I will be their God:

39And I will give them one heart, and one way, that they may fear me for ever, for the good of them, and of their children after them:

40And I will make an everlasting covenant with them, that I will not turn away from them, to do them good; but I will put my fear in their hearts, that they shall not depart from me.

41Yea, I will rejoice over them to do them good, and I will plant them in this land assuredly with my whole heart and with my whole soul.

42For thus saith the LORD; Like as I have brought all this great evil upon this people, so will I bring upon them all the good that I have promised them.

43And fields shall be bought in this land, whereof ye say, *It is* desolate without man or beast; it is given into the hand of the Chaldeans.

44Men shall buy fields for money, and subscribe evidences, and seal *them,* and take witnesses in the land of Benjamin, and in the places about Jerusalem, and in the cities of Judah, and in the cities of the mountains, and in the cities of the valley, and in the cities of the south: for I will cause their captivity to return, saith the LORD.

1 TIMOTHY 3:1–16

THIS *is* a true saying, If a man desire the office of a bishop, he desireth a good work.

2A bishop then must be blameless, the husband of one wife, vigilant, sober, of good behaviour, given to hospitality, apt to teach;

3Not given to wine, no striker, not greedy of filthy lucre; but patient, not a brawler, not covetous;

4One that ruleth well his own house, having his children in subjection with all gravity;

5(For if a man know not how to rule his own house, how shall he take care of the church of God?)

6Not a novice, lest being lifted up with pride he fall into the condemnation of the devil.

7Moreover he must have a good report of them which are without; lest he fall into reproach and the snare of the devil.

8Likewise *must* the deacons *be* grave, not doubletongued, not given to much wine, not greedy of filthy lucre;

9Holding the mystery of the faith in a pure conscience.

10And let these also first be proved; then let them use the office of a deacon, being *found* blameless.

11Even so *must their* wives *be* grave, not slanderers, sober, faithful in all things.

12Let the deacons be the husbands of one wife, ruling their children and their own houses well.

13For they that have used the office of a deacon well purchase to themselves a good degree, and great boldness in the faith which is in Christ Jesus.

14These things write I unto thee, hoping to come unto thee shortly:

15But if I tarry long, that thou mayest know how thou oughtest to behave thyself in the house of God, which is the church of the living God, the pillar and ground of the truth.

16And without controversy great is the mystery of godliness: God was manifest in the flesh, justified in the Spirit, seen of angels, preached unto the Gentiles, believed on in the world, received up into glory.

PSALM 88:1–18

O LORD God of my salvation, I have cried day *and* night before thee:

2Let my prayer come before thee: incline thine ear unto my cry;

3For my soul is full of troubles: and my life draweth nigh unto the grave.

4I am counted with them that go down into the pit: I am as a man *that hath* no strength:

5Free among the dead, like the slain that lie in the grave, whom thou rememberest no more: and they are cut off from thy hand.

6Thou hast laid me in the lowest pit, in darkness, in the deeps.

7Thy wrath lieth hard upon me, and thou hast afflicted *me* with all thy waves. Selah.

8Thou hast put away mine acquaintance far from me; thou hast made me an abomination unto them: *I am* shut up, and I cannot come forth.

9Mine eye mourneth by reason of affliction: LORD, I have called daily upon thee, I have stretched out my hands unto thee.

10Wilt thou shew wonders to the dead? shall the dead arise *and* praise thee? Selah.

11Shall thy lovingkindness be declared in the grave? *or* thy faithfulness in destruction?

12Shall thy wonders be known in the

dark? and thy righteousness in the land of forgetfulness?

13But unto thee have I cried, O Lord; and in the morning shall my prayer prevent thee.

14Lord, why castest thou off my soul? *why* hidest thou thy face from me?

15I *am* afflicted and ready to die from *my* youth up: *while* I suffer thy terrors I am distracted.

16Thy fierce wrath goeth over me; thy terrors have cut me off.

17They came round about me daily like water; they compassed me about together.

18Lover and friend hast thou put far from me, *and* mine acquaintance into darkness.

PROVERBS FOR TODAY/ 25:20–22

As he that taketh away a garment in cold weather, and as *vinegar upon nitre, so is he that singeth songs to an heavy heart.* □ *If thine enemy be hungry, give him bread to eat; and if he be thirsty, give him water to drink: For thou shalt heap coals of fire upon his head, and the Lord shall reward thee.*

OCTOBER 19

JEREMIAH 33:1—34:22

MOREOVER the word of the Lord came unto Jeremiah the second time, while he was yet shut up in the court of the prison, saying,

2Thus saith the Lord the maker thereof, the Lord that formed it, to establish it; the Lord *is* his name;

3Call unto me, and I will answer thee, and shew thee great and mighty things, which thou knowest not.

4For thus saith the Lord, the God of Israel, concerning the houses of this city, and concerning the houses of the kings of Judah, which are thrown down by the mounts, and by the sword;

5They come to fight with the Chaldeans, but *it is* to fill them with the dead bodies of men, whom I have slain in mine anger and in my fury, and for all whose wickedness I have hid my face from this city.

6Behold, I will bring it health and cure, and I will cure them, and will reveal unto them the abundance of peace and truth.

7And I will cause the captivity of Judah and the captivity of Israel to return, and will build them, as at the first.

8And I will cleanse them from all their iniquity, whereby they have sinned against me; and I will pardon all their iniquities, whereby they have sinned, and whereby they have transgressed against me.

9And it shall be to me a name of joy, a praise and an honour before all the nations of the earth, which shall hear all the good that I do unto them: and they shall fear and tremble for all the goodness and for all the prosperity that I procure unto it.

10Thus saith the Lord; Again there shall be heard in this place, which ye say *shall be* desolate without man and without beast, *even* in the cities of Judah, and in the streets of Jerusalem, that are desolate, without man, and without inhabitant, and without beast,

11The voice of joy, and the voice of gladness, the voice of the bridegroom, and the voice of the bride, the voice of them that shall say, Praise the LORD of hosts: for the LORD *is* good; for his mercy *endureth* for ever: *and* of them that shall bring the sacrifice of praise into the house of the LORD. For I will cause to return the captivity of the land, as at the first, saith the LORD.

12Thus saith the LORD of hosts; Again in this place, which is desolate without man and without beast, and in all the cities thereof, shall be an habitation of shepherds causing *their* flocks to lie down.

13In the cities of the mountains, in the cities of the vale, and in the cities of the south, and in the land of Benjamin, and in the places about Jerusalem, and in the cities of Judah, shall the flocks pass again under the hands of him that telleth *them,* saith the LORD.

14Behold, the days come, saith the LORD, that I will perform that good thing which I have promised unto the house of Israel and to the house of Judah.

15In those days, and at that time, will I cause the Branch of righteousness to grow up unto David; and he shall execute judgment and righteousness in the land.

16In those days shall Judah be saved, and Jerusalem shall dwell safely: and this *is the name* wherewith she shall be called, The LORD our righteousness.

17For thus saith the LORD; David shall never want a man to sit upon the throne of the house of Israel;

18Neither shall the priests the Levites want a man before me to offer burnt offerings, and to kindle meat offerings, and to do sacrifice continually.

19And the word of the LORD came unto Jeremiah, saying,

20Thus saith the LORD; If ye can break my covenant of the day, and my covenant of the night, and that there should not be day and night in their season;

21*Then* may also my covenant be broken with David my servant, that he should not have a son to reign upon his throne; and with the Levites the priests, my ministers.

22As the host of heaven cannot be numbered, neither the sand of the sea measured: so will I multiply the seed of David my servant, and the Levites that minister unto me.

23Moreover the word of the LORD came to Jeremiah, saying,

24Considerest thou not what this people have spoken, saying, The two families which the LORD hath chosen, he hath even cast them off? thus they have despised my people, that they should be no more a nation before them.

25Thus saith the LORD; If my covenant *be* not with day and night, *and if* I have not appointed the ordinances of heaven and earth;

26Then will I cast away the seed of Jacob, and David my servant, *so* that I will not take *any* of his seed *to be* rulers over the seed of Abraham, Isaac, and Jacob: for I will cause their captivity to return, and have mercy on them.

THE word which came unto Jeremiah from the LORD, when Nebuchadnezzar king of Babylon, and all his army, and all the kingdoms of the earth of his dominion, and all the people, fought against Jerusalem, and against all the cities thereof, saying,

2Thus saith the LORD, the God of Israel; Go and speak to Zedekiah king of Judah, and tell him, Thus saith the LORD; Behold, I will give this city into the hand of the king of Babylon, and he shall burn it with fire:

3And thou shalt not escape out of his hand, but shalt surely be taken, and delivered into his hand; and thine eyes shall behold the eyes of the king of Babylon, and he shall speak with thee mouth to mouth, and thou shalt go to Babylon.

4Yet hear the word of the LORD, O Zedekiah king of Judah; Thus saith the LORD of thee, Thou shalt not die by the sword:

5*But* thou shalt die in peace: and with

the burnings of thy fathers, the former kings which were before thee, so shall they burn *odours* for thee; and they will lament thee, *saying,* Ah lord! for I have pronounced the word, saith the LORD.

6Then Jeremiah the prophet spake all these words unto Zedekiah king of Judah in Jerusalem,

7When the king of Babylon's army fought against Jerusalem, and against all the cities of Judah that were left, against Lachish, and against Azekah: for these defenced cities remained of the cities of Judah.

8*This is* the word that came unto Jeremiah from the LORD, after that the king Zedekiah had made a covenant with all the people which *were* at Jerusalem, to proclaim liberty unto them;

9That every man should let his man-servant, and every man his maidservant, *being* an Hebrew or an Hebrewess, go free; that none should serve himself of them, *to wit,* of a Jew his brother.

10Now when all the princes, and all the people, which had entered into the covenant, heard that every one should let his manservant, and every one his maidservant, go free, that none should serve themselves of them any more, then they obeyed, and let *them* go.

11But afterward they turned, and caused the servants and the handmaids, whom they had let go free, to return, and brought them into subjection for servants and for handmaids.

12Therefore the word of the LORD came to Jeremiah from the LORD, saying,

13Thus saith the LORD, the God of Israel; I made a covenant with your fathers in the day that I brought them forth out of the land of Egypt, out of the house of bondmen, saying,

14At the end of seven years let ye go every man his brother an Hebrew, which hath been sold unto thee; and when he hath served thee six years,

thou shalt let him go free from thee: but your fathers hearkened not unto me, neither inclined their ear.

15And ye were now turned, and had done right in my sight, in proclaiming liberty every man to his neighbour; and ye had made a covenant before me in the house which is called by my name:

16But ye turned and polluted my name, and caused every man his servant, and every man his handmaid, whom he had set at liberty at their pleasure, to return, and brought them into subjection, to be unto you for servants and for handmaids.

17Therefore thus saith the LORD; Ye have not hearkened unto me, in proclaiming liberty, every one to his brother, and every man to his neighbour: behold, I proclaim a liberty for you, saith the LORD, to the sword, to the pestilence, and to the famine; and I will make you to be removed into all the kingdoms of the earth.

18And I will give the men that have transgressed my covenant, which have not performed the words of the covenant which they had made before me, when they cut the calf in twain, and passed between the parts thereof,

19The princes of Judah, and the princes of Jerusalem, the eunuchs, and the priests, and all the people of the land, which passed between the parts of the calf;

20I will even give them into the hand of their enemies, and into the hand of them that seek their life: and their dead bodies shall be for meat unto the fowls of the heaven, and to the beasts of the earth.

21And Zedekiah king of Judah and his princes will I give into the hand of their enemies, and into the hand of them that seek their life, and into the hand of the king of Babylon's army, which are gone up from you.

22Behold, I will command, saith the LORD, and cause them to return to this city; and they shall fight against it, and take it, and burn it with fire: and I will make the cities of Judah a desolation without an inhabitant.

1 TIMOTHY 4:1–16

Now the Spirit speaketh expressly, that in the latter times some shall depart from the faith, giving heed to seducing spirits, and doctrines of devils;

2Speaking lies in hypocrisy; having their conscience seared with a hot iron;

3Forbidding to marry, *and commanding* to abstain from meats, which God hath created to be received with thanksgiving of them which believe and know the truth.

4For every creature of God *is* good, and nothing to be refused, if it be received with thanksgiving:

5For it is sanctified by the word of God and prayer.

6If thou put the brethren in remembrance of these things, thou shalt be a good minister of Jesus Christ, nourished up in the words of faith and of good doctrine, whereunto thou hast attained.

7But refuse profane and old wives' fables, and exercise thyself *rather* unto godliness.

8For bodily exercise profiteth little: but godliness is profitable unto all things, having promise of the life that now is, and of that which is to come.

9This *is* a faithful saying and worthy of all acceptation.

10For therefore we both labour and suffer reproach, because we trust in the living God, who is the Saviour of all men, specially of those that believe.

11These things command and teach.

12Let no man despise thy youth; but be thou an example of the believers, in word, in conversation, in charity, in spirit, in faith, in purity.

13Till I come, give attendance to reading, to exhortation, to doctrine.

14Neglect not the gift that is in thee, which was given thee by prophecy, with the laying on of the hands of the presbytery.

15Meditate upon these things; give thyself wholly to them; that thy profiting may appear to all.

16Take heed unto thyself, and unto the doctrine; continue in them: for in doing this thou shalt both save thyself, and them that hear thee.

PSALM 89:1–13

I WILL sing of the mercies of the LORD for ever: with my mouth will I make known thy faithfulness to all generations.

2For I have said, Mercy shall be built up for ever: thy faithfulness shalt thou establish in the very heavens.

3I have made a covenant with my chosen, I have sworn unto David my servant,

4Thy seed will I establish for ever, and build up thy throne to all generations. Selah.

5And the heavens shall praise thy wonders, O LORD: thy faithfulness also in the congregation of the saints.

6For who in the heaven can be compared unto the LORD? *who* among the sons of the mighty can be likened unto the LORD?

7God is greatly to be feared in the assembly of the saints, and to be had in reverence of all *them that are* about him.

8O LORD God of hosts, who *is* a strong LORD like unto thee? or to thy faithfulness round about thee?

9Thou rulest the raging of the sea: when the waves thereof arise, thou stillest them.

10Thou hast broken Rahab in pieces, as one that is slain; thou hast scattered thine enemies with thy strong arm.

11The heavens *are* thine, the earth also *is* thine: *as for* the world and the fulness thereof, thou hast founded them.

12The north and the south thou hast created them: Tabor and Hermon shall rejoice in thy name.

13Thou hast a mighty arm: strong is thy hand, *and* high is thy right hand.

PROVERBS FOR TODAY/ 25:23–24

The north wind driveth away rain: so doth *an angry countenance a backbiting tongue.* □ It is *better to dwell in the corner of the housetop, than with a brawling woman and in a wide house.*

OCTOBER 20

JEREMIAH 35:1—36:32

THE word which came unto Jeremiah from the LORD in the days of Jehoiakim the son of Josiah king of Judah, saying,

2Go unto the house of the Rechabites, and speak unto them, and bring them into the house of the LORD, into one of the chambers, and give them wine to drink.

3Then I took Jaazaniah the son of Jeremiah, the son of Habaziniah, and his brethren, and all his sons, and the whole house of the Rechabites;

4And I brought them into the house of the LORD, into the chamber of the sons of Hanan, the son of Igdaliah, a man of God, which *was* by the chamber of the princes, which *was* above the chamber of Maaseiah the son of Shallum, the keeper of the door:

5And I set before the sons of the house of the Rechabites pots full of wine, and cups, and I said unto them, Drink ye wine.

6But they said, We will drink no wine: for Jonadab the son of Rechab our father commanded us, saying, Ye shall drink no wine, *neither* ye, nor your sons for ever:

7Neither shall ye build house, nor sow seed, nor plant vineyard, nor have *any:* but all your days ye shall dwell in tents; that ye may live many days in the land where ye *be* strangers.

8Thus have we obeyed the voice of Jonadab the son of Rechab our father in all that he hath charged us, to drink no wine all our days, we, our wives, our sons, nor our daughters;

9Nor to build houses for us to dwell in: neither have we vineyard, nor field, nor seed:

10But we have dwelt in tents, and have obeyed, and done according to all that Jonadab our father commanded us.

11But it came to pass, when Nebuchadrezzar king of Babylon came up into the land, that we said, Come, and let us go to Jerusalem for fear of the army of the Chaldeans, and for fear of the army of the Syrians: so we dwell at Jerusalem.

12Then came the word of the LORD unto Jeremiah, saying,

13Thus saith the LORD of hosts, the God of Israel; Go and tell the men of Judah and the inhabitants of Jerusalem, Will ye not receive instruction to hearken to my words? saith the LORD.

14The words of Jonadab the son of Rechab, that he commanded his sons not to drink wine, are performed; for unto this day they drink none, but obey their father's commandment: notwithstanding I have spoken unto you, rising early and speaking; but ye hearkened not unto me.

15I have sent also unto you all my servants the prophets, rising up early and sending *them,* saying, Return ye now every man from his evil way, and amend your doings, and go not after other gods to serve them, and ye shall dwell in the land which I have given to you and to your fathers: but ye have not inclined your ear, nor hearkened unto me.

16Because the sons of Jonadab the son of Rechab have performed the commandment of their father, which he commanded them; but this people hath not hearkened unto me:

17Therefore thus saith the LORD God of hosts, the God of Israel; Behold, I will bring upon Judah and upon all the inhabitants of Jerusalem all the evil that I have pronounced against them: because I have spoken unto them, but they have not heard; and I have called unto them, but they have not answered.

18And Jeremiah said unto the house of the Rechabites, Thus saith the LORD of hosts, the God of Israel; Because ye have obeyed the commandment of Jonadab your father, and kept all his precepts, and done according unto all that he hath commanded you:

19Therefore thus saith the LORD of hosts, the God of Israel; Jonadab the son of Rechab shall not want a man to stand before me for ever.

AND it came to pass in the fourth year of Jehoiakim the son of Josiah king of Judah, *that* this word came unto Jeremiah from the LORD, saying,

2Take thee a roll of a book, and write therein all the words that I have spoken unto thee against Israel, and against Judah, and against all the nations, from the day I spake unto thee, from the days of Josiah, even unto this day.

3It may be that the house of Judah will hear all the evil which I purpose to do unto them; that they may return every man from his evil way; that I may forgive their iniquity and their sin.

4Then Jeremiah called Baruch the son of Neriah: and Baruch wrote from the mouth of Jeremiah all the words of the LORD, which he had spoken unto him, upon a roll of a book.

5And Jeremiah commanded Baruch, saying, I *am* shut up; I cannot go into the house of the LORD:

6Therefore go thou, and read in the roll, which thou hast written from my mouth, the words of the LORD in the ears of the people in the LORD's house upon the fasting day: and also thou shalt read them in the ears of all Judah that come out of their cities.

7It may be they will present their supplication before the LORD, and will return every one from his evil way: for great *is* the anger and the fury that the LORD hath pronounced against this people.

8And Baruch the son of Neriah did according to all that Jeremiah the prophet commanded him, reading in the book the words of the LORD in the LORD's house.

9And it came to pass in the fifth year of Jehoiakim the son of Josiah king of Judah, in the ninth month, *that* they proclaimed a fast before the LORD to all the people in Jerusalem, and to all the people that came from the cities of Judah unto Jerusalem.

10Then read Baruch in the book the words of Jeremiah in the house of the LORD, in the chamber of Gemariah the son of Shaphan the scribe, in the higher court, at the entry of the new gate of the LORD's house, in the ears of all the people.

11When Michaiah the son of Gemariah, the son of Shaphan, had heard out of the book all the words of the LORD,

12Then he went down into the king's house, into the scribe's chamber: and, lo, all the princes sat there, *even*

Elishama the scribe, and Delaiah the son of Shemaiah, and Elnathan the son of Achbor, and Gemariah the son of Shaphan, and Zedekiah the son of Hananiah, and all the princes.

13Then Michaiah declared unto them all the words that he had heard, when Baruch read the book in the ears of the people.

14Therefore all the princes sent Jehudi the son of Nethaniah, the son of Shelemiah, the son of Cushi, unto Baruch, saying, Take in thine hand the roll wherein thou hast read in the ears of the people, and come. So Baruch the son of Neriah took the roll in his hand, and came unto them.

15And they said unto him, Sit down now, and read it in our ears. So Baruch read *it* in their ears.

16Now it came to pass, when they had heard all the words, they were afraid both one and other, and said unto Baruch, We will surely tell the king of all these words.

17And they asked Baruch, saying, Tell us now, How didst thou write all these words at his mouth?

18Then Baruch answered them, He pronounced all these words unto me with his mouth, and I wrote *them* with ink in the book.

19Then said the princes unto Baruch, Go, hide thee, thou and Jeremiah; and let no man know where ye be.

20And they went in to the king into the court, but they laid up the roll in the chamber of Elishama the scribe, and told all the words in the ears of the king.

21So the king sent Jehudi to fetch the roll: and he took it out of Elishama the scribe's chamber. And Jehudi read it in the ears of the king, and in the ears of all the princes which stood beside the king.

22Now the king sat in the winterhouse in the ninth month: and *there was a fire* on the hearth burning before him.

23And it came to pass, *that* when Jehudi had read three or four leaves, he cut it with the penknife, and cast *it* into the fire that *was* on the hearth, until all the roll was consumed in the fire that *was* on the hearth.

24Yet they were not afraid, nor rent their garments, *neither* the king, nor any of his servants that heard all these words.

25Nevertheless Elnathan and Delaiah and Gemariah had made intercession to the king that he would not burn the roll: but he would not hear them.

26But the king commanded Jerahmeel the son of Hammelech, and Seraiah the son of Azriel, and Shelemiah the son of Abdeel, to take Baruch the scribe and Jeremiah the prophet: but the LORD hid them.

27Then the word of the LORD came to Jeremiah, after that the king had burned the roll, and the words which Baruch wrote at the mouth of Jeremiah, saying,

28Take thee again another roll, and write in it all the former words that were in the first roll, which Jehoiakim the king of Judah hath burned.

29And thou shalt say to Jehoiakim king of Judah, Thus saith the LORD; Thou hast burned this roll, saying, Why hast thou written therein, saying, The king of Babylon shall certainly come and destroy this land, and shall cause to cease from thence man and beast?

30Therefore thus saith the LORD of Jehoiakim king of Judah; He shall have none to sit upon the throne of David: and his dead body shall be cast out in the day to the heat, and in the night to the frost.

31And I will punish him and his seed and his servants for their iniquity; and I will bring upon them, and upon the inhabitants of Jerusalem, and upon the men of Judah, all the evil that I have pronounced against them; but they hearkened not.

32Then took Jeremiah another roll, and gave it to Baruch the scribe, the son of Neriah; who wrote therein from the mouth of Jeremiah all the words of the book which Jehoiakim king of Judah had burned in the fire: and there were added besides unto them many like words.

1 TIMOTHY 5:1–25

Rᴇʙᴜᴋᴇ not an elder, but intreat *him* as a father; *and* the younger men as brethren;

2The elder women as mothers; the younger as sisters, with all purity.

3Honour widows that are widows indeed.

4But if any widow have children or nephews, let them learn first to shew piety at home, and to requite their parents: for that is good and acceptable before God.

5Now she that is a widow indeed, and desolate, trusteth in God, and continueth in supplications and prayers night and day.

6But she that liveth in pleasure is dead while she liveth.

7And these things give in charge, that they may be blameless.

8But if any provide not for his own, and specially for those of his own house, he hath denied the faith, and is worse than an infidel.

9Let not a widow be taken into the number under threescore years old, having been the wife of one man,

10Well reported of for good works; if she have brought up children, if she have lodged strangers, if she have washed the saints' feet, if she have relieved the afflicted, if she have diligently followed every good work.

11But the younger widows refuse: for when they have begun to wax wanton against Christ, they will marry;

12Having damnation, because they have cast off their first faith.

13And withal they learn *to be* idle, wandering about from house to house; and not only idle, but tattlers also and busybodies, speaking things which they ought not.

14I will therefore that the younger women marry, bear children, guide the house, give none occasion to the adversary to speak reproachfully.

15For some are already turned aside after Satan.

16If any man or woman that believeth have widows, let them relieve them, and let not the church be charged; that it may relieve them that are widows indeed.

17Let the elders that rule well be counted worthy of double honour, especially they who labour in the word and doctrine.

18For the scripture saith, Thou shalt not muzzle the ox that treadeth out the corn. And, The labourer *is* worthy of his reward.

19Against an elder receive not an accusation, but before two or three witnesses.

20Them that sin rebuke before all, that others also may fear.

21I charge *thee* before God, and the Lord Jesus Christ, and the elect angels, that thou observe these things without preferring one before another, doing nothing by partiality.

22Lay hands suddenly on no man, neither be partaker of other men's sins: keep thyself pure.

23Drink no longer water, but use a little wine for thy stomach's sake and thine often infirmities.

24Some men's sins are open beforehand, going before to judgment; and some *men* they follow after.

25Likewise also the good works *of some* are manifest beforehand; and they that are otherwise cannot be hid.

PSALM 89:14–37

Jᴜsᴛɪᴄᴇ and judgment *are* the habitation of thy throne: mercy and truth shall go before thy face.

15Blessed *is* the people that know

the joyful sound: they shall walk, O LORD, in the light of thy countenance.

16In thy name shall they rejoice all the day: and in thy righteousness shall they be exalted.

17For thou *art* the glory of their strength: and in thy favour our horn shall be exalted.

18For the LORD *is* our defence; and the Holy One of Israel *is* our king.

19Then thou spakest in vision to thy holy one, and saidst, I have laid help upon *one that is* mighty; I have exalted *one* chosen out of the people.

20I have found David my servant; with my holy oil have I anointed him:

21With whom my hand shall be established: mine arm also shall strengthen him.

22The enemy shall not exact upon him; nor the son of wickedness afflict him.

23And I will beat down his foes before his face, and plague them that hate him.

24But my faithfulness and my mercy *shall be* with him: and in my name shall his horn be exalted.

25I will set his hand also in the sea, and his right hand in the rivers.

26He shall cry unto me, Thou *art* my father, my God, and the rock of my salvation.

27Also I will make him *my* firstborn, higher than the kings of the earth.

28My mercy will I keep for him for evermore, and my covenant shall stand fast with him.

29His seed also will I make *to endure* for ever, and his throne as the days of heaven.

30If his children forsake my law, and walk not in my judgments;

31If they break my statutes, and keep not my commandments;

32Then will I visit their transgression with the rod, and their iniquity with stripes.

33Nevertheless my lovingkindness will I not utterly take from him, nor suffer my faithfulness to fail.

34My covenant will I not break, nor alter the thing that is gone out of my lips.

35Once have I sworn by my holiness that I will not lie unto David.

36His seed shall endure for ever, and his throne as the sun before me.

37It shall be established for ever as the moon, and *as* a faithful witness in heaven. Selah.

PROVERBS FOR TODAY/ 25:25–27

As *cold waters to a thirsty soul, so* is *good news from a far country.* □ *A righteous man falling down before the wicked* is as *a troubled fountain, and a corrupt spring.* □ It is *not good to eat much honey: so* for men *to search their own glory* is not *glory.*

OCTOBER 21

JEREMIAH 37:1—38:28

AND king Zedekiah the son of Josiah reigned instead of Coniah the son of Jehoiakim, whom Nebuchadrezzar king of Babylon made king in the land of Judah.

2But neither he, nor his servants, nor the people of the land, did hearken unto the words of the LORD, which he spake by the prophet Jeremiah.

3And Zedekiah the king sent Jehucal the son of Shelemiah and Zephaniah the son of Maaseiah the priest to the prophet Jeremiah, saying, Pray now unto the LORD our God for us.

⁴Now Jeremiah came in and went out among the people: for they had not put him into prison.

⁵Then Pharaoh's army was come forth out of Egypt: and when the Chaldeans that besieged Jerusalem heard tidings of them, they departed from Jerusalem.

⁶Then came the word of the LORD unto the prophet Jeremiah, saying,

⁷Thus saith the LORD, the God of Israel; Thus shall ye say to the king of Judah, that sent you unto me to enquire of me; Behold, Pharaoh's army, which is come forth to help you, shall return to Egypt into their own land.

⁸And the Chaldeans shall come again, and fight against this city, and take it, and burn it with fire.

⁹Thus saith the LORD; Deceive not yourselves, saying, The Chaldeans shall surely depart from us: for they shall not depart.

¹⁰For though ye had smitten the whole army of the Chaldeans that fight against you, and there remained *but* wounded men among them, *yet* should they rise up every man in his tent, and burn this city with fire.

¹¹And it came to pass, that when the army of the Chaldeans was broken up from Jerusalem for fear of Pharaoh's army,

¹²Then Jeremiah went forth out of Jerusalem to go into the land of Benjamin, to separate himself thence in the midst of the people.

¹³And when he was in the gate of Benjamin, a captain of the ward *was* there, whose name *was* Irijah, the son of Shelemiah, the son of Hananiah; and he took Jeremiah the prophet, saying, Thou fallest away to the Chaldeans.

¹⁴Then said Jeremiah, *It is* false; I fall not away to the Chaldeans. But he hearkened not to him: so Irijah took Jeremiah, and brought him to the princes.

¹⁵Wherefore the princes were wroth with Jeremiah, and smote him, and put him in prison in the house of Jonathan the scribe: for they had made that the prison.

¹⁶When Jeremiah was entered into the dungeon, and into the cabins, and Jeremiah had remained there many days;

¹⁷Then Zedekiah the king sent, and took him out: and the king asked him secretly in his house, and said, Is there *any* word from the LORD? And Jeremiah said, There is: for, said he, thou shalt be delivered into the hand of the king of Babylon.

¹⁸Moreover Jeremiah said unto king Zedekiah, What have I offended against thee, or against thy servants, or against this people, that ye have put me in prison?

¹⁹Where *are* now your prophets which prophesied unto you, saying, The king of Babylon shall not come against you, nor against this land?

²⁰Therefore hear now, I pray thee, O my lord the king: let my supplication, I pray thee, be accepted before thee; that thou cause me not to return to the house of Jonathan the scribe, lest I die there.

²¹Then Zedekiah the king commanded that they should commit Jeremiah into the court of the prison, and that they should give him daily a piece of bread out of the bakers' street, until all the bread in the city were spent. Thus Jeremiah remained in the court of the prison.

THEN Shephatiah the son of Mattan, and Gedaliah the son of Pashur, and Jucal the son of Shelemiah, and Pashur the son of Malchiah, heard the words that Jeremiah had spoken unto all the people, saying,

²Thus saith the LORD, He that remaineth in this city shall die by the

sword, by the famine, and by the pestilence: but he that goeth forth to the Chaldeans shall live; for he shall have his life for a prey, and shall live.

3Thus saith the LORD, This city shall surely be given into the hand of the king of Babylon's army, which shall take it.

4Therefore the princes said unto the king, We beseech thee, let this man be put to death: for thus he weakeneth the hands of the men of war that remain in this city, and the hands of all the people, in speaking such words unto them: for this man seeketh not the welfare of this people, but the hurt.

5Then Zedekiah the king said, Behold, he is in your hand: for the king is not he that can do any thing against you.

6Then took they Jeremiah, and cast him into the dungeon of Malchiah the son of Hammelech, that was in the court of the prison: and they let down Jeremiah with cords. And in the dungeon there was no water, but mire: so Jeremiah sunk in the mire.

7Now when Ebed–melech the Ethiopian, one of the eunuchs which was in the king's house, heard that they had put Jeremiah in the dungeon; the king then sitting in the gate of Benjamin;

8Ebed–melech went forth out of the king's house, and spake to the king, saying,

9My lord the king, these men have done evil in all that they have done to Jeremiah the prophet, whom they have cast into the dungeon; and he is like to die for hunger in the place where he is: for there is no more bread in the city.

10Then the king commanded Ebed–melech the Ethiopian, saying, Take from hence thirty men with thee, and take up Jeremiah the prophet out of the dungeon, before he die.

11So Ebed–melech took the men with him, and went into the house of the king under the treasury, and took thence old cast clouts and old rotten rags, and let them down by cords into the dungeon to Jeremiah.

12And Ebed–melech the Ethiopian said unto Jeremiah, Put now these old cast clouts and rotten rags under thine armholes under the cords. And Jeremiah did so.

13So they drew up Jeremiah with cords, and took him up out of the dungeon: and Jeremiah remained in the court of the prison.

14Then Zedekiah the king sent, and took Jeremiah the prophet unto him into the third entry that is in the house of the LORD: and the king said unto Jeremiah, I will ask thee a thing; hide nothing from me.

15Then Jeremiah said unto Zedekiah, If I declare it unto thee, wilt thou not surely put me to death? and if I give thee counsel, wilt thou not hearken unto me?

16So Zedekiah the king sware secretly unto Jeremiah, saying, As the LORD liveth, that made us this soul, I will not put thee to death, neither will I give thee into the hand of these men that seek thy life.

17Then said Jeremiah unto Zedekiah, Thus saith the LORD, the God of hosts, the God of Israel; If thou wilt assuredly go forth unto the king of Babylon's princes, then thy soul shall live, and this city shall not be burned with fire; and thou shalt live, and thine house:

18But if thou wilt not go forth to the king of Babylon's princes, then shall this city be given into the hand of the Chaldeans, and they shall burn it with fire, and thou shalt not escape out of their hand.

19And Zedekiah the king said unto Jeremiah, I am afraid of the Jews that are fallen to the Chaldeans, lest they deliver me into their hand, and they mock me.

20But Jeremiah said, They shall not deliver thee. Obey, I beseech thee, the voice of the LORD, which I speak unto thee: so it shall be well unto thee, and thy soul shall live.

21But if thou refuse to go forth, this *is* the word that the LORD hath shewed me:

22And, behold, all the women that are left in the king of Judah's house *shall be* brought forth to the king of Babylon's princes, and those *women* shall say, Thy friends have set thee on, and have prevailed against thee: thy feet are sunk in the mire, *and* they are turned away back.

23So they shall bring out all thy wives and thy children to the Chaldeans: and thou shalt not escape out of their hand, but shalt be taken by the hand of the king of Babylon: and thou shalt cause this city to be burned with fire.

24Then said Zedekiah unto Jeremiah, Let no man know of these words, and thou shalt not die.

25But if the princes hear that I have talked with thee, and they come unto thee, and say unto thee, Declare unto us now what thou hast said unto the king, hide it not from us, and we will not put thee to death; also what the king said unto thee:

26Then thou shalt say unto them, I presented my supplication before the king, that he would not cause me to return to Jonathan's house, to die there.

27Then came all the princes unto Jeremiah, and asked him: and he told them according to all these words that the king had commanded. So they left off speaking with him; for the matter was not perceived.

28So Jeremiah abode in the court of the prison until the day that Jerusalem was taken: and he was *there* when Jerusalem was taken.

1 TIMOTHY 6:1–21

L ET as many servants as are under the yoke count their own masters worthy of all honour, that the name of God and *his* doctrine be not blasphemed.

2And they that have believing masters, let them not despise *them,* because they are brethren; but rather do *them* service, because they are faithful and beloved, partakers of the benefit. These things teach and exhort.

3If any man teach otherwise, and consent not to wholesome words, *even* the words of our Lord Jesus Christ, and to the doctrine which is according to godliness;

4He is proud, knowing nothing, but doting about questions and strifes of words, whereof cometh envy, strife, railings, evil surmisings.

5Perverse disputings of men of corrupt minds, and destitute of the truth, supposing that gain is godliness: from such withdraw thyself.

6But godliness with contentment is great gain.

7For we brought nothing into *this* world, *and it is* certain we can carry nothing out.

8And having food and raiment let us be therewith content.

9But they that will be rich fall into temptation and a snare, and *into* many foolish and hurtful lusts, which drown men in destruction and perdition.

10For the love of money is the root of all evil: which while some coveted after, they have erred from the faith, and pierced themselves through with many sorrows.

11But thou, O man of God, flee these things; and follow after righteousness, godliness, faith, love, patience, meekness.

12Fight the good fight of faith, lay hold on eternal life, whereunto thou art also called, and hast professed a good profession before many witnesses.

13I give thee charge in the sight of God, who quickeneth all things, and *before* Christ Jesus, who before Pontius Pilate witnessed a good confession;

14That thou keep *this* commandment

without spot, unrebukeable, until the appearing of our Lord Jesus Christ:

15Which in his times he shall shew, *who is* the blessed and only Potentate, the King of kings, and Lord of lords;

16Who only hath immortality, dwelling in the light which no man can approach unto; whom no man hath seen, nor can see: to whom *be* honour and power everlasting. Amen.

17Charge them that are rich in this world, that they be not highminded; nor trust in uncertain riches, but in the living God, who giveth us richly all things to enjoy;

18That they do good, that they be rich in good works, ready to distribute, willing to communicate;

19Laying up in store for themselves a good foundation against the time to come, that they may lay hold on eternal life.

20O Timothy, keep that which is committed to thy trust, avoiding profane *and* vain babblings, and oppositions of science falsely so called:

21Which some professing have erred concerning the faith. Grace *be* with thee. Amen.

PSALM 89:38–52

BUT thou hast cast off and abhorred, thou hast been wroth with thine anointed.

39Thou hast made void the covenant of thy servant: thou hast profaned his crown *by casting it* to the ground.

40Thou hast broken down all his hedges; thou hast brought his strong holds to ruin.

41All that pass by the way spoil him: he is a reproach to his neighbours.

42Thou hast set up the right hand of his adversaries; thou hast made all his enemies to rejoice.

43Thou hast also turned the edge of his sword, and hast not made him to stand in the battle.

44Thou hast made his glory to cease, and cast his throne down to the ground.

45The days of his youth hast thou shortened: thou hast covered him with shame. Selah.

46How long, LORD? wilt thou hide thyself for ever? shall thy wrath burn like fire?

47Remember how short my time is: wherefore hast thou made all men in vain?

48What man *is he that* liveth, and shall not see death? shall he deliver his soul from the hand of the grave? Selah.

49Lord, where *are* thy former lovingkindnesses, *which* thou swarest unto David in thy truth?

50Remember, Lord, the reproach of thy servants; *how* I do bear in my bosom *the reproach of* all the mighty people;

51Wherewith thine enemies have reproached, O LORD; wherewith they have reproached the footsteps of thine anointed.

52Blessed *be* the LORD for evermore. Amen, and Amen.

PROVERBS FOR TODAY/ 25:28

He that hath *no rule over his own spirit* is like a *city* that is *broken down,* and *without walls.*

JEREMIAH 39:1—41:18

IN the ninth year of Zedekiah king of Judah, in the tenth month, came Nebuchadrezzar king of Babylon and all his army against Jerusalem, and they besieged it.

2*And* in the eleventh year of Zedekiah, in the fourth month, the ninth *day* of the month, the city was broken up.

3And all the princes of the king of Babylon came in, and sat in the middle gate, *even* Nergal–sharezer, Samgar-nebo, Sarsechim, Rab–saris, Nergal-sharezer, Rab–mag, with all the residue of the princes of the king of Babylon.

4And it came to pass, *that* when Zedekiah the king of Judah saw them, and all the men of war, then they fled, and went forth out of the city by night, by the way of the king's garden, by the gate betwixt the two walls: and he went out the way of the plain.

5But the Chaldeans' army pursued after them, and overtook Zedekiah in the plains of Jericho: and when they had taken him, they brought him up to Nebuchadnezzar king of Babylon to Riblah in the land of Hamath, where he gave judgment upon him.

6Then the king of Babylon slew the sons of Zedekiah in Riblah before his eyes: also the king of Babylon slew all the nobles of Judah.

7Moreover he put out Zedekiah's eyes, and bound him with chains, to carry him to Babylon.

8And the Chaldeans burned the king's house, and the houses of the people, with fire, and brake down the walls of Jerusalem.

9Then Nebuzar–adan the captain of the guard carried away captive into Babylon the remnant of the people that remained in the city, and those that fell away, that fell to him, with the rest of the people that remained.

10But Nebuzar–adan the captain of the guard left of the poor of the people, which had nothing, in the land of Judah, and gave them vineyards and fields at the same time.

11Now Nebuchadrezzar king of Babylon gave charge concerning Jeremiah to Nebuzar–adan the captain of the guard, saying,

12Take him, and look well to him, and do him no harm; but do unto him even as he shall say unto thee.

13So Nebuzar–adan the captain of the guard sent, and Nebushasban, Rab-saris, and Nergal–sharezer, Rab–mag, and all the king of Babylon's princes;

14Even they sent, and took Jeremiah out of the court of the prison, and committed him unto Gedaliah the son of Ahikam the son of Shaphan, that he should carry him home: so he dwelt among the people.

15Now the word of the LORD came unto Jeremiah, while he was shut up in the court of the prison, saying,

16Go and speak to Ebed–melech the Ethiopian, saying, Thus saith the LORD of hosts, the God of Israel; Behold, I will bring my words upon this city for evil, and not for good; and they shall be *accomplished* in that day before thee.

17But I will deliver thee in that day, saith the LORD: and thou shalt not be given into the hand of the men of whom thou *art* afraid.

18For I will surely deliver thee, and thou shalt not fall by the sword, but thy life shall be for a prey unto thee: because thou hast put thy trust in me, saith the LORD.

THE word that came to Jeremiah from the LORD, after that Nebuzar–adan the captain of the guard had let him go from Ramah, when he had taken him being bound in chains among all that were carried away captive of Jerusalem and Judah, which were carried away captive unto Babylon.

2And the captain of the guard took Jeremiah, and said unto him, The LORD thy God hath pronounced this evil upon this place.

3Now the LORD hath brought it, and done according as he hath said: because ye have sinned against the LORD, and have not obeyed his voice, therefore this thing is come upon you.

4And now, behold, I loose thee this day from the chains which were upon thine hand. If it seem good unto thee to come with me into Babylon, come; and I will look well unto thee: but if it seem ill unto thee to come with me into Babylon, forbear: behold, all the land is before thee: whither it seemeth good and convenient for thee to go, thither go.

5Now while he was not yet gone back, he said, Go back also to Gedaliah the son of Ahikam the son of Shaphan, whom the king of Babylon hath made governor over the cities of Judah, and dwell with him among the people: or go wheresoever it seemeth convenient unto thee to go. So the captain of the guard gave him victuals and a reward, and let him go.

6Then went Jeremiah unto Gedaliah the son of Ahikam to Mizpah; and dwelt with him among the people that were left in the land.

7Now when all the captains of the forces which were in the fields, even they and their men, heard that the king of Babylon had made Gedaliah the son of Ahikam governor in the land, and had committed unto him men, and women, and children, and of the poor of the land, of them that were not carried away captive to Babylon;

8Then they came to Gedaliah to Mizpah, even Ishmael the son of Netha-niah, and Johanan and Jonathan the sons of Kareah, and Seraiah the son of Tanhumeth, and the sons of Ephai the Netophathite, and Jezaniah the son of Maachathite, they and their men.

9And Gedaliah the son of Ahikam the son of Shaphan sware unto them and to their men, saying, Fear not to serve the Chaldeans: dwell in the land, and serve the king of Babylon, and it shall be well with you.

10As for me, behold, I will dwell at Mizpah, to serve the Chaldeans, which will come unto us: but ye, gather ye wine, and summer fruits, and oil, and put them in your vessels, and dwell in your cities that ye have taken.

11Likewise when all the Jews that were in Moab, and among the Ammonites, and in Edom, and that were in all the countries, heard that the king of Babylon had left a remnant of Judah, and that he had set over them Gedaliah the son of Ahikam the son of Shaphan;

12Even all the Jews returned out of all places whither they were driven, and came to the land of Judah, to Gedaliah, unto Mizpah, and gathered wine and summer fruits very much.

13Moreover Johanan the son of Kareah, and all the captains of the forces that were in the fields, came to Gedaliah to Mizpah,

14And said unto him, Dost thou certainly know that Baalis the king of the Ammonites hath sent Ishmael the son of Nethaniah to slay thee? But Gedaliah the son of Ahikam believed them not.

15Then Johanan the son of Kareah spake to Gedaliah in Mizpah secretly, saying, Let me go, I pray thee, and I will slay Ishmael the son of Nethaniah, and no man shall know it: wherefore should he slay thee, that all the Jews which are gathered unto thee should be scattered, and the remnant in Judah perish?

16But Gedaliah the son of Ahikam said unto Johanan the son of Kareah,

Thou shalt not do this thing: for thou speakest falsely of Ishmael.

Now it came to pass in the seventh month, that Ishmael the son of Nethaniah the son of Elishama, of the seed royal, and the princes of the king, even ten men with him, came unto Gedaliah the son of Ahikam to Mizpah; and there they did eat bread together in Mizpah.

²Then arose Ishmael the son of Nethaniah, and the ten men that were with him, and smote Gedaliah the son of Ahikam the son of Shaphan with the sword, and slew him, whom the king of Babylon had made governor over the land.

³Ishmael also slew all the Jews that were with him, even with Gedaliah, at Mizpah, and the Chaldeans that were found there, and the men of war.

⁴And it came to pass the second day after he had slain Gedaliah, and no man knew it,

⁵That there came certain from Shechem, from Shiloh, and from Samaria, even fourscore men, having their beards shaven, and their clothes rent, and having cut themselves, with offerings and incense in their hand, to bring them to the house of the LORD.

⁶And Ishmael the son of Nethaniah went forth from Mizpah to meet them, weeping all along as he went: and it came to pass, as he met them, he said unto them, Come to Gedaliah the son of Ahikam.

⁷And it was so, when they came into the midst of the city, that Ishmael the son of Nethaniah slew them, and cast them into the midst of the pit, he, and the men that were with him.

⁸But ten men were found among them that said unto Ishmael, Slay us not: for we have treasures in the field, of wheat, and of barley, and of oil, and of honey. So he forbare, and slew them not among their brethren.

⁹Now the pit wherein Ishmael had cast all the dead bodies of the men, whom he had slain because of Gedaliah, was it which Asa the king had made for fear of Baasha king of Israel: and Ishmael the son of Nethaniah filled it with them that were slain.

¹⁰Then Ishmael carried away captive all the residue of the people that were in Mizpah, even the king's daughters, and all the people that remained in Mizpah, whom Nebuzar–adan the captain of the guard had committed to Gedaliah the son of Ahikam: and Ishmael the son of Nethaniah carried them away captive, and departed to go over to the Ammonites.

¹¹But when Johanan the son of Kareah, and all the captains of the forces that were with him, heard of all the evil that Ishmael the son of Nethaniah had done,

¹²Then they took all the men, and went to fight with Ishmael the son of Nethaniah, and found him by the great waters that are in Gibeon.

¹³Now it came to pass, that when all the people which were with Ishmael saw Johanan the son of Kareah, and all the captains of the forces that were with him, then they were glad.

¹⁴So all the people that Ishmael had carried away captive from Mizpah cast about and returned, and went unto Johanan the son of Kareah.

¹⁵But Ishmael the son of Nethaniah escaped from Johanan with eight men, and went to the Ammonites.

¹⁶Then took Johanan the son of Kareah, and all the captains of the forces that were with him, all the remnant of the people whom he had recovered from Ishmael the son of Nethaniah, from Mizpah, after that he had slain Gedaliah the son of Ahikam, even mighty men of war, and the women, and the children, and the eunuchs, whom he had brought again from Gibeon:

¹⁷And they departed, and dwelt in the habitation of Chimham, which is by Beth–lehem, to go to enter into Egypt,

18Because of the Chaldeans: for they were afraid of them, because Ishmael the son of Nethaniah had slain Gedaliah the son of Ahikam, whom the king of Babylon made governor in the land.

2 TIMOTHY 1:1–18

PAUL, an apostle of Jesus Christ by the will of God, according to the promise of life which is in Christ Jesus,

2To Timothy, *my* dearly beloved son: Grace, mercy, *and* peace, from God the Father and Christ Jesus our Lord.

3I thank God, whom I serve from *my* forefathers with pure conscience, that without ceasing I have remembrance of thee in my prayers night and day;

4Greatly desiring to see thee, being mindful of thy tears, that I may be filled with joy;

5When I call to remembrance the unfeigned faith that is in thee, which dwelt first in thy grandmother Lois, and thy mother Eunice; and I am persuaded that in thee also.

6Wherefore I put thee in remembrance that thou stir up the gift of God, which is in thee by the putting on of my hands.

7For God hath not given us the spirit of fear; but of power, and of love, and of a sound mind.

8Be not thou therefore ashamed of the testimony of our Lord, nor of me his prisoner: but be thou partaker of the afflictions of the gospel according to the power of God;

9Who hath saved us, and called *us* with an holy calling, not according to our works, but according to his own purpose and grace, which was given us in Christ Jesus before the world began,

10But is now made manifest by the appearing of our Saviour Jesus Christ, who hath abolished death, and hath brought life and immortality to light through the gospel:

11Whereunto I am appointed a preacher, and an apostle, and a teacher of the Gentiles.

12For the which cause I also suffer these things: nevertheless I am not ashamed: for I know whom I have believed, and am persuaded that he is able to keep that which I have committed unto him against that day.

13Hold fast the form of sound words, which thou hast heard of me, in faith and love which is in Christ Jesus.

14That good thing which was committed unto thee keep by the Holy Ghost which dwelleth in us.

15This thou knowest, that all they which are in Asia be turned away from me; of whom are Phygellus and Hermogenes.

16The Lord give mercy unto the house of Onesiphorus; for he oft refreshed me, and was not ashamed of my chain:

17But, when he was in Rome, he sought me out very diligently, and found *me.*

18The Lord grant unto him that he may find mercy of the Lord in that day: and in how many things he ministered unto me at Ephesus, thou knowest very well.

PSALM 90:1—91:16

LORD, thou hast been our dwelling place in all generations.

2Before the mountains were brought forth, or ever thou hadst formed the earth and the world, even from everlasting to everlasting, thou *art* God.

3Thou turnest man to destruction; and sayest, Return, ye children of men.

4For a thousand years in thy sight *are but* as yesterday when it is past, and *as* a watch in the night.

5Thou carriest them away as with a flood; they are *as* a sleep: in the morning *they are* like grass *which* groweth up.

6In the morning it flourisheth, and groweth up; in the evening it is cut down, and withereth.

7For we are consumed by thine anger, and by thy wrath are we troubled.

8Thou hast set our iniquities before thee, our secret *sins* in the light of thy countenance.

9For all our days are passed away in thy wrath: we spend our years as a tale *that is told.*

10The days of our years *are* threescore years and ten; and if by reason of strength *they be* fourscore years, yet *is* their strength labour and sorrow; for it is soon cut off, and we fly away.

11Who knoweth the power of thine anger? even according to thy fear, *so is* thy wrath.

12So teach *us* to number our days, that we may apply *our* hearts unto wisdom.

13Return, O LORD, how long? and let it repent thee concerning thy servants.

14O satisfy us early with thy mercy; that we may rejoice and be glad all our days.

15Make us glad according to the days *wherein* thou hast afflicted us, *and* the years *wherein* we have seen evil.

16Let thy work appear unto thy servants, and thy glory unto their children.

17And let the beauty of the LORD our God be upon us: and establish thou the work of our hands upon us; yea, the work of our hands establish thou it.

HE that dwelleth in the secret place of the most High shall abide under the shadow of the Almighty.

2I will say of the LORD, *He is* my refuge and my fortress: my God; in him will I trust.

3Surely he shall deliver thee from the snare of the fowler, *and* from the noisome pestilence.

4He shall cover thee with his feathers, and under his wings shalt thou trust: his truth *shall be thy* shield and buckler.

5Thou shalt not be afraid for the terror by night; *nor* for the arrow *that* flieth by day;

6*Nor* for the pestilence *that* walketh in darkness; *nor* for the destruction *that* wasteth at noonday.

7A thousand shall fall at thy side, and ten thousand at thy right hand; *but* it shall not come nigh thee.

8Only with thine eyes shalt thou behold and see the reward of the wicked.

9Because thou hast made the LORD, *which is* my refuge, *even* the most High, thy habitation;

10There shall no evil befall thee, neither shall any plague come nigh thy dwelling.

11For he shall give his angels charge over thee, to keep thee in all thy ways.

12They shall bear thee up in *their* hands, lest thou dash thy foot against a stone.

13Thou shalt tread upon the lion and adder: the young lion and the dragon shalt thou trample under feet.

14Because he hath set his love upon me, therefore will I deliver him: I will set him on high, because he hath known my name.

15He shall call upon me, and I will answer him: I *will be* with him in trouble; I will deliver him, and honour him.

16With long life will I satisfy him, and shew him my salvation.

PROVERBS FOR TODAY/ 26:1–2

As snow in summer, and as rain in harvest, so honour is not seemly for a fool. As the bird by wandering, as the swallow by flying, so the curse causeless shall not come.

OCTOBER 23

JEREMIAH 42:1—44:23

THEN all the captains of the forces, and Johanan the son of Kareah, and Jezaniah the son of Hoshaiah, and all the people from the least even unto the greatest, came near,

2And said unto Jeremiah the prophet, Let, we beseech thee, our supplication be accepted before thee, and pray for us unto the LORD thy God, *even* for all this remnant; (for we are left *but* a few of many, as thine eyes do behold us:)

3That the LORD thy God may shew us the way wherein we may walk, and the thing that we may do.

4Then Jeremiah the prophet said unto them, I have heard *you;* behold, I will pray unto the LORD your God according to your words; and it shall come to pass, *that* whatsoever thing the LORD shall answer you, I will declare *it* unto you; I will keep nothing back from you.

5Then they said to Jeremiah, The LORD be a true and faithful witness between us, if we do not even according to all things for the which the LORD thy God shall send thee to us.

6Whether *it be* good, or whether *it be* evil, we will obey the voice of the LORD our God, to whom we send thee; that it may be well with us, when we obey the voice of the LORD our God.

7And it came to pass after ten days, that the word of the LORD came unto Jeremiah.

8Then called he Johanan the son of Kareah, and all the captains of the forces which *were* with him, and all the people from the least even to the greatest,

9And said unto them, Thus saith the LORD, the God of Israel, unto whom ye sent me to present your supplication before him;

10If ye will still abide in this land, then will I build you, and not pull *you* down, and I will plant you, and not pluck *you* up: for I repent me of the evil that I have done unto you.

11Be not afraid of the king of Babylon, of whom ye are afraid; be not afraid of him, saith the LORD: for I *am* with you to save you, and to deliver you from his hand.

12And I will shew mercies unto you, that he may have mercy upon you, and cause you to return to your own land.

13But if ye say, We will not dwell in this land, neither obey the voice of the LORD your God,

14Saying, No; but we will go into the land of Egypt, where we shall see no war, nor hear the sound of the trumpet, nor have hunger of bread; and there will we dwell:

15And now therefore hear the word of the LORD, ye remnant of Judah; Thus saith the LORD of hosts, the God of Israel; If ye wholly set your faces to enter into Egypt, and go to sojourn there;

16Then it shall come to pass, *that* the sword, which ye feared, shall overtake you there in the land of Egypt, and the famine, whereof ye were afraid, shall follow close after you there in Egypt; and there ye shall die.

17So shall it be with all the men that set their faces to go into Egypt to sojourn there; they shall die by the sword, by the famine, and by the pestilence: and none of them shall remain or escape from the evil that I will bring upon them.

18For thus saith the LORD of hosts, the God of Israel; As mine anger and my fury hath been poured forth upon the inhabitants of Jerusalem; so shall my fury be poured forth upon you, when ye shall enter into Egypt: and ye shall be an execration, and an astonishment, and a curse, and a reproach; and ye shall see this place no more.

19The LORD hath said concerning you, O ye remnant of Judah; Go ye not into Egypt: know certainly that I have admonished you this day.

20For ye dissembled in your hearts, when ye sent me unto the LORD your God, saying, Pray for us unto the LORD our God; and according unto all that the LORD our God shall say, so declare unto us, and we will do *it*.

21And *now* I have this day declared *it* to you; but ye have not obeyed the voice of the LORD your God, nor any *thing* for the which he hath sent me unto you.

22Now therefore know certainly that ye shall die by the sword, by the famine, and by the pestilence, in the place whither ye desire to go *and* to sojourn.

AND it came to pass, *that* when Jeremiah had made an end of speaking unto all the people all the words of the LORD their God, for which the LORD their God, had sent him to them, *even* all these words,

2Then spake Azariah the son of Hoshaiah, and Johanan the son of Kareah, and all the proud men, saying unto Jeremiah, Thou speakest falsely: the LORD our God hath not sent thee to say, Go not into Egypt to sojourn there:

3But Baruch the son of Neriah setteth thee on against us, for to deliver us into the hand of the Chaldeans, that they might put us to death, and carry us away captives into Babylon.

4So Johanan the son of Kareah, and all the captains of the forces, and all the people, obeyed not the voice of the LORD, to dwell in the land of Judah.

5But Johanan the son of Kareah, and all the captains of the forces, took all the remnant of Judah, that were returned from all nations, whither they had been driven, to dwell in the land of Judah;

6*Even* men, and women, and children, and the king's daughters, and every person that Nebuzar–adan the captain of the guard had left with Gedaliah the son of Ahikam the son of Shaphan, and Jeremiah the prophet, and Baruch the son of Neriah.

7So they came into the land of Egypt: for they obeyed not the voice of the LORD: thus came they *even* to Tahpanhes.

8Then came the word of the LORD unto Jeremiah in Tahpanhes, saying,

9Take great stones in thine hand and hide them in the clay in the brickkiln, which *is* at the entry of Pharaoh's house in Tahpanhes, in the sight of the men of Judah;

10And say unto them, Thus saith the LORD of hosts, the God of Israel; Behold, I will send and take Nebuchadrezzar the king of Babylon, my servant, and will set his throne upon these stones that I have hid; and he shall spread his royal pavilion over them.

11And when he cometh, he shall smite the land of Egypt, *and deliver* such *as are* for death to death; and such *as are* for captivity to captivity; and such *as are* for the sword to the sword.

12And I will kindle a fire in the houses of the gods of Egypt; and he shall burn them, and carry them away captives: and he shall array himself with the land of Egypt, as a shepherd putteth on his garment; and he shall go forth from thence in peace.

13He shall break also the images of Beth–shemesh, that *is* in the land of Egypt; and the houses of the gods of the Egyptians shall he burn with fire.

THE word that came to Jeremiah concerning all the Jews which dwell in the land of Egypt, which dwell at Migdol, and at Tahpanhes, and at Noph, and in the country of Pathros, saying,

2Thus saith the LORD of hosts, the God of Israel; Ye have seen all the evil that I have brought upon Jerusalem, and upon all the cities of Judah; and, behold, this day they *are* a desolation, and no man dwelleth therein,

³Because of their wickedness which they have committed to provoke me to anger, in that they went to burn incense, *and* to serve other gods, whom they knew not, *neither* they, ye, nor your fathers.

⁴Howbeit I sent unto you all my servants the prophets, rising early and sending *them,* saying, Oh, do not this abominable thing that I hate.

⁵But they hearkened not, nor inclined their ear to turn from their wickedness, to burn no incense unto other gods.

⁶Wherefore my fury and mine anger was poured forth, and was kindled in the cities of Judah and in the streets of Jerusalem; and they are wasted *and* desolate, as at this day.

⁷Therefore now thus saith the Lord, the God of hosts, the God of Israel; Wherefore commit ye *this* great evil against your souls, to cut off from you man and woman, child and suckling, out of Judah, to leave you none to remain;

⁸In that ye provoke me unto wrath with the works of your hands, burning incense unto other gods in the land of Egypt, whither ye be gone to dwell that ye might cut yourselves off, and that ye might be a curse and a reproach among all the nations of the earth?

⁹Have ye forgotten the wickedness of your fathers, and the wickedness of the kings of Judah, and the wickedness of their wives, and your own wickedness, and the wickedness of your wives, which they have committed in the land of Judah, and in the streets of Jerusalem?

¹⁰They are not humbled *even* unto this day, neither have they feared, nor walked in my law, nor in my statutes, that I set before you and before your fathers.

¹¹Therefore thus saith the Lord of hosts, the God of Israel; Behold, I will set my face against you for evil, and

to cut off all Judah.

¹²And I will take the remnant of Judah, that have set their faces to go into the land of Egypt to sojourn there, and they shall all be consumed, *and* fall in the land of Egypt; they shall *even* be consumed by the sword *and* by the famine; they shall die, from the least even unto the greatest, by the sword and by the famine: and they shall be an execration, *and* an astonishment, and a curse, and a reproach.

¹³For I will punish them that dwell in the land of Egypt, as I have punished Jerusalem, by the sword, by the famine, and by the pestilence:

¹⁴So that none of the remnant of Judah, which are gone into the land of Egypt to sojourn there, shall escape or remain, that they should return into the land of Judah, to the which they have a desire to return to dwell there: for none shall return but such as shall escape.

¹⁵Then all the men which knew that their wives had burned incense unto other gods, and all the women that stood by, a great multitude, even all the people that dwelt in the land of Egypt, in Pathros, answered Jeremiah, saying,

¹⁶*As for* the word that thou hast spoken unto us in the name of the Lord, we will not hearken unto thee.

¹⁷But we will certainly do whatsoever thing goeth forth out of our own mouth, to burn incense unto the queen of heaven, and to pour out drink offerings unto her, as we have done, we, and our fathers, our kings, and our princes, in the cities of Judah, and in the streets of Jerusalem: for *then* had we plenty of victuals, and were well, and saw no evil.

¹⁸But since we left off to burn incense to the queen of heaven, and to pour out drink offerings unto her, we have wanted all *things,* and have been consumed by the sword and by the famine.

¹⁹And when we burned incense to the queen of heaven, and poured out

drink offerings unto her, did we make her cakes to worship her, and pour out drink offerings unto her, without our men?

20Then Jeremiah said unto all the people, to the men, and to the women, and to all the people which had given him *that* answer, saying,

21The incense that ye burned in the cities of Judah, and in the streets of Jerusalem, ye, and your fathers, your kings, and your princes, and the people of the land, did not the Lord remember them, came it *not* into his mind?

22So that the Lord could no longer bear, because of the evil of your doings, *and* because of the abominations which ye have committed; therefore is your land a desolation, and an astonishment, and a curse, without an inhabitant, as at this day.

23Because ye have burned incense, and because ye have sinned against the Lord, and have not obeyed the voice of the Lord, nor walked in his law, nor in his statutes, nor in his testimonies; therefore this evil is happened unto you, as at this day.

2 TIMOTHY 2:1–21

THOU therefore, my son, be strong in the grace that is in Christ Jesus.

2And the things that thou hast heard of me among many witnesses, the same commit thou to faithful men, who shall be able to teach others also.

3Thou therefore endure hardness, as a good soldier of Jesus Christ.

4No man that warreth entangleth himself with the affairs of *this* life; that he may please him who hath chosen him to be a soldier.

5And if a man also strive for masteries, *yet* is he not crowned, except he strive lawfully.

6The husbandman that laboureth must be first partaker of the fruits.

7Consider what I say; and the Lord give thee understanding in all things.

8Remember that Jesus Christ of the seed of David was raised from the dead according to my gospel:

9Wherein I suffer trouble, as an evil doer, *even* unto bonds; but the word of God is not bound.

10Therefore I endure all things for the elect's sakes, that they may also obtain the salvation which is in Christ Jesus with eternal glory.

11*It is* a faithful saying: For if we be dead with *him,* we shall also live with *him:*

12If we suffer, we shall also reign with *him:* if we deny *him,* he also will deny us:

13If we believe not, *yet* he abideth faithful: he cannot deny himself.

14Of these things put *them* in remembrance, charging *them* before the Lord that they strive not about words to no profit, *but* to the subverting of the hearers.

15Study to shew thyself approved unto God, a workman that needeth not to be ashamed, rightly dividing the word of truth.

16But shun profane *and* vain babblings: for they will increase unto more ungodliness.

17And their word will eat as doth a canker: of whom is Hymenaeus and Philetus;

18Who concerning the truth have erred, saying that the resurrection is past already; and overthrow the faith of some.

19Nevertheless the foundation of God standeth sure, having this seal, The Lord knoweth them that are his. And, Let every one that nameth the name of Christ depart from iniquity.

20But in a great house there are not only vessels of gold and of silver, but also of wood and of earth; and some to honour, and some to dishonour.

21If a man therefore purge himself from these, he shall be a vessel unto honour, sanctified, and meet for the master's use, *and* prepared unto every good work.

PSALM 92:1—93:5

IT *is* a good *thing* to give thanks unto the LORD, and to sing praises unto thy name, O most High:

2To shew forth thy lovingkindness in the morning, and thy faithfulness every night,

3Upon an instrument of ten strings, and upon the psaltery; upon the harp with a solemn sound.

4For thou, LORD, hast made me glad through thy work: I will triumph in the works of thy hands.

5O LORD, how great are thy works! *and* thy thoughts are very deep.

6A brutish man knoweth not; neither doth a fool understand this.

7When the wicked spring as the grass, and when all the workers of iniquity do flourish; *it is* that they shall be destroyed for ever:

8But thou, LORD, *art most* high for evermore.

9For, lo, thine enemies, O LORD, for, lo, thine enemies shall perish; all the workers of iniquity shall be scattered.

10But my horn shalt thou exalt like *the horn of* an unicorn: I shall be anointed with fresh oil.

11Mine eye also shall see *my desire* on mine enemies, *and* mine ears shall hear *my desire* of the wicked that rise up against me.

12The righteous shall flourish like the palm tree: he shall grow like a cedar in Lebanon.

13Those that be planted in the house of the LORD shall flourish in the courts of our God.

14They shall still bring forth fruit in old age; they shall be fat and flourishing;

15To shew that the LORD *is* upright: *he is* my rock, and *there is* no unrighteousness in him.

THE LORD reigneth, he is clothed with majesty; the LORD is clothed with strength, *wherewith* he hath girded himself: the world also is stablished, that it cannot be moved.

2Thy throne *is* established of old: thou *art* from everlasting.

3The floods have lifted up, O LORD, the floods have lifted up their voice; the floods lift up their waves.

4The LORD on high *is* mightier than the noise of many waters, *yea, than* the mighty waves of the sea.

5Thy testimonies are very sure: holiness becometh thine house, O LORD, for ever.

PROVERBS FOR TODAY/ 26:3–5

A whip for the horse, a bridle for the ass, and a rod for the fool's back. Answer not a fool according to his folly, lest thou also be like unto him. Answer a fool according to his folly, lest he be wise in his own conceit.

JEREMIAH 44:24—47:7

MOREOVER Jeremiah said unto all the people, and to all the women, Hear the word of the LORD, all Judah that *are* in the land of Egypt:

25Thus saith the LORD of hosts, the God of Israel, saying; Ye and your wives have both spoken with your mouths, and fulfilled with your hand, saying, We will surely perform our vows that we have vowed, to burn incense to the queen of heaven, and to pour out drink offerings unto her: ye will surely accomplish your vows, and surely perform your vows.

26Therefore hear ye the word of the LORD, all Judah that dwell in the land of Egypt; Behold, I have sworn by my great name, saith the LORD, that my name shall no more be named in the mouth of any man of Judah in all the land of Egypt, saying, The Lord GOD liveth.

27Behold, I will watch over them for evil, and not for good: and all the men of Judah that *are* in the land of Egypt shall be consumed by the sword and by the famine, until there be an end of them.

28Yet a small number that escape the sword shall return out of the land of Egypt into the land of Judah, and all the remnant of Judah, that are gone into the land of Egypt to sojourn there, shall know whose words shall stand, mine, or theirs.

29And this *shall be* a sign unto you, saith the LORD, that I will punish you in this place, that ye may know that my words shall surely stand against you for evil:

30Thus saith the LORD; Behold, I will give Pharaoh–hophra king of Egypt into the hand of his enemies, and into the hand of them that seek his life; as I gave Zedekiah the king of Judah into the hand of Nebuchadrezzar king of Babylon, his enemy, and that sought his life.

THE word that Jeremiah the prophet spake unto Baruch the son of Neriah, when he had written these words in a book at the mouth of Jeremiah, in the fourth year of Jehoiakim the son of Josiah king of Judah, saying,

2Thus saith the LORD, the God of Israel, unto thee, O Baruch;

3Thou didst say, Woe is me now! for the LORD hath added grief to my sorrow; I fainted in my sighing, and I find no rest.

4Thus shalt thou say unto him, The LORD saith thus; Behold, *that* which I have built will I break down, and that which I have planted I will pluck up, even this whole land.

5And seekest thou great things for thyself? seek *them* not; for, behold, I will bring evil upon all flesh, saith the LORD: but thy life will I give unto thee for a prey in all places whither thou goest.

THE word of the LORD which came to Jeremiah the prophet against the Gentiles;

2Against Egypt, against the army of Pharaoh–necho king of Egypt, which was by the river Euphrates in Carchemish, which Nebuchadrezzar king of Babylon smote in the fourth year of Jehoiakim the son of Josiah king of Judah.

3Order ye the buckler and shield, and draw near to battle.

4Harness the horses; and get up, ye horsemen, and stand forth with *your* helmets; furbish the spears, *and* put on the brigandines.

5Wherefore have I seen them dismayed *and* turned away back? and their mighty ones are beaten down, and are fled apace, and look not back: *for* fear *was* round about, saith the LORD.

6Let not the swift flee away, nor the mighty man escape; they shall stumble, and fall toward the north by the river Euphrates.

7Who *is* this *that* cometh up as a flood, whose waters are moved as the rivers?

8Egypt riseth up like a flood, and *his* waters are moved like the rivers; and he saith, I will go up, *and* will cover the earth; I will destroy the city and the inhabitants thereof.

9Come up, ye horses; and rage, ye chariots; and let the mighty men come forth; the Ethiopians and the Libyans, that handle the shield; and the Lydians, that handle *and* bend the bow.

10For this *is* the day of the Lord GOD of hosts, a day of vengeance, that he may avenge him of his adversaries: and the sword shall devour, and it shall be satiate and made drunk with their blood: for the Lord GOD of hosts hath a sacrifice in the north country by the river Euphrates.

11Go up into Gilead, and take balm, O virgin, the daughter of Egypt: in vain shalt thou use many medicines; *for* thou shalt not be cured.

12The nations have heard of thy shame, and thy cry hath filled the land: for the mighty man hath stumbled against the mighty, *and* they are fallen both together.

13The word that the LORD spake to Jeremiah the prophet, how Nebuchadrezzar king of Babylon should come *and* smite the land of Egypt.

14Declare ye in Egypt, and publish in Migdol, and publish in Noph and in Tahpanhes: say ye, Stand fast, and prepare thee; for the sword shall devour round about thee.

15Why are thy valiant *men* swept away? they stood not, because the LORD did drive them.

16He made many to fall, yea, one fell upon another: and they said, Arise, and let us go again to our own people, and to the land of our nativity, from the oppressing sword.

17They did cry there, Pharaoh king of Egypt *is but* a noise; he hath passed the time appointed.

18*As* I live, saith the King, whose name *is* the LORD of hosts, Surely as Tabor *is* among the mountains, and as Carmel by the sea, *so* shall he come.

19O thou daughter dwelling in Egypt, furnish thyself to go into captivity: for Noph shall be waste and desolate without an inhabitant.

20Egypt *is like* a very fair heifer, *but* destruction cometh; it cometh out of the north.

21Also her hired men *are* in the midst of her like fatted bullocks; for they also are turned back, *and* are fled away together: they did not stand, because the day of their calamity was come upon them, *and* the time of their visitation.

22The voice thereof shall go like a serpent; for they shall march with an army, and come against her with axes, as hewers of wood.

23They shall cut down her forest, saith the LORD, though it cannot be searched; because they are more than the grasshoppers, and *are* innumerable.

24The daughter of Egypt shall be confounded; she shall be delivered into the hand of the people of the north.

25The LORD of hosts, the God of Israel, saith; Behold, I will punish the multitude of No, and Pharaoh, and Egypt, with their gods, and their kings; even Pharaoh, and *all* them that trust in him:

26And I will deliver them into the hand of those that seek their lives, and into the hand of Nebuchadrezzar king of Babylon, and into the hand of his servants: and afterward it shall be inhabited, as in the days of old, saith the LORD.

27But fear not thou, O my servant Jacob, and be not dismayed, O Israel: for, behold, I will save thee from afar off, and thy seed from the land of their captivity; and Jacob shall return, and be in rest and at ease, and none shall make *him* afraid.

28Fear thou not, O Jacob my servant, saith the LORD: for I *am* with thee; for I will make a full end of all the nations whither I have driven thee: but I will not make a full end of thee, but correct thee in measure; yet will I not leave thee wholly unpunished.

THE word of the LORD that came to Jeremiah the prophet against the Philistines, before that Pharaoh smote Gaza.

2Thus saith the LORD; Behold, waters rise up out of the north, and shall be an overflowing flood, and shall overflow the land, and all that is therein; the city, and them that dwell therein: then the men shall cry, and all the inhabitants of the land shall howl.

3At the noise of the stamping of the hoofs of his strong *horses,* at the rushing of his chariots, *and at* the rumbling of his wheels, the fathers shall not look back to *their* children for feebleness of hands;

4Because of the day that cometh to spoil all the Philistines, *and* to cut off from Tyrus and Zidon every helper that remaineth: for the LORD will spoil the Philistines, the remnant of the country of Caphtor.

5Baldness is come upon Gaza; Ashkelon is cut off *with* the remnant of their valley: how long wilt thou cut thyself?

6O thou sword of the LORD, how long *will it be* ere thou be quiet? put up thyself into thy scabbard, rest, and be still.

7How can it be quiet, seeing the LORD hath given it a charge against Ashkelon, and against the sea shore? there hath he appointed it.

2 TIMOTHY 2:22—3:17

FLEE also youthful lusts: but follow righteousness, faith, charity, peace, with them that call on the Lord out of a pure heart.

23But foolish and unlearned questions avoid, knowing that they do gender strifes.

24And the servant of the Lord must not strive; but be gentle unto all *men,* apt to teach, patient,

25In meekness instructing those that oppose themselves; if God peradventure will give them repentance to the acknowledging of the truth;

26And *that* they may recover themselves out of the snare of the devil, who are taken captive by him at his will.

THIS know also, that in the last days perilous times shall come.

2For men shall be lovers of their own selves, covetous, boasters, proud, blasphemers, disobedient to parents, unthankful, unholy,

3Without natural affection, trucebreakers, false accusers, incontinent, fierce, despisers of those that are good,

4Traitors, heady, highminded, lovers of pleasures more than lovers of God;

5Having a form of godliness, but denying the power thereof: from such turn away.

6For of this sort are they which creep into houses, and lead captive silly women laden with sins, led away with divers lusts,

7Ever learning, and never able to come to the knowledge of the truth.

8Now as Jannes and Jambres withstood Moses, so do these also resist the truth: men of corrupt minds, reprobate concerning the faith.

9But they shall proceed no further: for their folly shall be manifest unto all *men,* as theirs also was.

10But thou hast fully known my doctrine, manner of life, purpose, faith, longsuffering, charity, patience,

11Persecutions, afflictions, which came unto me at Antioch, at Iconium, at Lystra; what persecutions I endured: but out of *them* all the Lord delivered me.

12Yea, and all that will live godly in Christ Jesus shall suffer persecution.

13But evil men and seducers shall wax worse and worse, deceiving, and being deceived.

14But continue thou in the things which thou hast learned and hast been assured of, knowing of whom thou hast learned *them;*

15And that from a child thou hast known the holy scriptures, which are able to make thee wise unto salvation through faith which is in Christ Jesus.

16All scripture *is* given by inspiration of God, and *is* profitable for doctrine, for reproof, for correction, for instruction in righteousness:

17That the man of God may be perfect, throughly furnished unto all good works.

PSALM 94:1–23

O LORD God, to whom vengeance belongeth; O God, to whom vengeance belongeth, shew thyself.

2Lift up thyself, thou judge of the earth: render a reward to the proud.

3LORD, how long shall the wicked, how long shall the wicked triumph?

4*How long* shall they utter *and* speak hard things? *and* all the workers of iniquity boast themselves?

5They break in pieces thy people, O LORD, and afflict thine heritage.

6They slay the widow and the stranger, and murder the fatherless.

7Yet they say, the LORD shall not see, neither shall the God of Jacob regard *it.*

8Understand, ye brutish among the people: and *ye* fools, when will ye be wise?

9He that planted the ear, shall he not hear? he that formed the eye, shall he not see?

10He that chastiseth the heathen, shall not he correct? he that teacheth man knowledge, *shall not he know?*

11The LORD knoweth the thoughts of man, that they *are* vanity.

12Blessed *is* the man whom thou chastenest, O LORD, and teachest him out of thy law;

13That thou mayest give him rest from the days of adversity, until the pit be digged for the wicked.

14For the LORD will not cast off his people, neither will he forsake his inheritance.

15But judgment shall return unto righteousness: and all the upright in heart shall follow it.

16Who will rise up for me against the evildoers? *or* who will stand up for me against the workers of iniquity?

17Unless the LORD *had been* my help, my soul had almost dwelt in silence.

18When I said, My foot slippeth; thy mercy, O LORD, held me up.

19In the multitude of my thoughts within me thy comforts delight my soul.

20Shall the throne of iniquity have fellowship with thee, which frameth mischief by a law?

21They gather themselves together against the soul of the righteous, and condemn the innocent blood.

22But the LORD is my defence; and my God *is* the rock of my refuge.

23And he shall bring upon them their own iniquity, and shall cut them off in their own wickedness; *yea,* the LORD our God shall cut them off.

PROVERBS FOR TODAY/ 26:6–8

He that sendeth a message by the hand of a fool cutteth off the feet, and *drinketh damage. The legs of the lame are not equal: so* is *a parable in the mouth of fools. As he that bindeth a stone in a sling, so* is *he that giveth honour to a fool.*

OCTOBER 25

JEREMIAH 48:1—49:22

AGAINST Moab thus saith the LORD of hosts, the God of Israel; Woe unto Nebo! for it is spoiled: Kiriathaim is confounded *and* taken: Misgab is confounded and dismayed.

²*There shall be* no more praise of Moab: in Heshbon they have devised evil against it; come, and let us cut it off from *being* a nation. Also thou shalt be cut down, O Madmen; the sword shall pursue thee.

³A voice of crying *shall be* from Horonaim, spoiling and great destruction.

⁴Moab is destroyed; her little ones have caused a cry to be heard.

⁵For in the going up of Luhith continual weeping shall go up; for in the going down of Horonaim the enemies have heard a cry of destruction.

⁶Flee, save your lives, and be like the heath in the wilderness.

⁷For because thou hast trusted in thy works and in thy treasures, thou shalt also be taken: and Chemosh shall go forth into captivity *with* his priests and his princes together.

⁸And the spoiler shall come upon every city, and no city shall escape: the valley also shall perish, and the plain shall be destroyed, as the LORD hath spoken.

⁹Give wings unto Moab, that it may flee and get away: for the cities thereof shall be desolate, without any to dwell therein.

¹⁰Cursed *be* he that doeth the work of the LORD deceitfully, and cursed *be* he that keepeth back his sword from blood.

¹¹Moab hath been at ease from his youth, and he hath settled on his lees, and hath not been emptied from vessel to vessel, neither hath he gone into captivity: therefore his taste remained in him, and his scent is not changed.

¹²Therefore, behold, the days come, saith the LORD, that I will send unto him wanderers, that shall cause him to wander, and shall empty his vessels, and break their bottles.

¹³And Moab shall be ashamed of Chemosh, as the house of Israel was ashamed of Beth–el their confidence.

¹⁴How say ye, We *are* mighty and strong men for the war?

¹⁵Moab is spoiled, and gone up *out of* her cities, and his chosen young men are gone down to the slaughter, saith the King, whose name *is* the LORD of hosts.

¹⁶The calamity of Moab *is* near to come, and his affliction hasteth fast.

¹⁷All ye that are about him, bemoan him; and all ye that know his name, say, How is the strong staff broken, *and* the beautiful rod!

¹⁸Thou daughter that dost inhabit Dibon, come down from *thy* glory, and sit in thirst; for the spoiler of Moab shall come upon thee, *and* he shall destroy thy strong holds.

¹⁹O inhabitant of Aroer, stand by the way, and espy; ask him that fleeth,

and her that escapeth, *and* say, What is done?

20Moab is confounded; for it is broken down: howl and cry; tell ye it in Arnon, that Moab is spoiled,

21And judgment is come upon the plain country; upon Holon, and upon Jahazah, and upon Mephaath,

22And upon Dibon, and upon Nebo, and upon Beth–diblathaim,

23And upon Kiriathaim, and upon Beth–gamul, and upon Beth–meon,

24And upon Kerioth, and upon Bozrah, and upon all the cities of the land of Moab, far or near.

25The horn of Moab is cut off, and his arm is broken, saith the LORD.

26Make ye him drunken: for he magnified *himself* against the LORD: Moab also shall wallow in his vomit, and he also shall be in derision.

27For was not Israel a derision unto thee? was he found among thieves? for since thou spakest of him, thou skippedst for joy.

28O ye that dwell in Moab, leave the cities, and dwell in the rock, and be like the dove *that* maketh her nest in the sides of the hole's mouth.

29We have heard the pride of Moab, (he is exceeding proud) his loftiness, and his arrogancy, and his pride, and the haughtiness of his heart.

30I know his wrath, saith the LORD, but *it shall* not *be* so; his lies shall not so effect *it.*

31Therefore will I howl for Moab, and I will cry out for all Moab; *mine heart* shall mourn for the men of Kir–heres.

32O vine of Sibmah, I will weep for thee with the weeping of Jazer: thy plants are gone over the sea, they reach *even* to the sea of Jazer: the spoiler is fallen upon thy summer fruits and upon thy vintage.

33And joy and gladness is taken from the plentiful field, and from the land of Moab; and I have caused wine to fail from the winepresses: none shall tread with shouting; *their* shouting *shall be* no shouting.

34From the cry of Heshbon *even* unto Elealeh, *and even* unto Jahaz, have they uttered their voice, from Zoar *even* unto Horonaim, *as* an heifer of three years old: for the waters also of Nimrim shall be desolate.

35Moreover I will cause to cease in Moab, saith the LORD, him that offereth in the high places, and him that burneth incense to his gods.

36Therefore mine heart shall sound for Moab like pipes, and mine heart shall sound like pipes for the men of Kir–heres: because the riches *that* he hath gotten are perished.

37For every head *shall be* bald, and every beard clipped: upon all the hands *shall be* cuttings, and upon the loins sackcloth.

38*There shall be* lamentation generally upon all the housetops of Moab, and in the streets thereof: for I have broken Moab like a vessel wherein *is* no pleasure, saith the LORD.

39They shall howl, *saying,* How is it broken down! how hath Moab turned the back with shame! so shall Moab be a derision and a dismaying to all them about him.

40For thus saith the LORD; Behold, he shall fly as an eagle, and shall spread his wings over Moab.

41Kerioth is taken, and the strong holds are surprised, and the mighty men's hearts in Moab at that day shall be as the heart of a woman in her pangs.

42And Moab shall be destroyed from *being* a people, because he hath magnified *himself* against the LORD.

43Fear, and the pit, and the snare, *shall be* upon thee, O inhabitant of Moab, saith the LORD.

44He that fleeth from the fear shall fall into the pit; and he that getteth up out of the pit shall be taken in the snare: for I will bring upon it, *even* upon Moab, the year of their visitation, saith the LORD.

45They that fled stood under the shadow of Heshbon because of the force: but a fire shall come forth out of Heshbon, and a flame from the midst of Sihon, and shall devour the corner of Moab, and the crown of the head of the tumultuous ones.

46Woe be unto thee, O Moab! the people of Chemosh perisheth: for thy sons are taken captives, and thy daughters captives.

47Yet will I bring again the captivity of Moab in the latter days, saith the LORD. Thus far *is* the judgment of Moab.

CONCERNING the Ammonites, thus saith the LORD; Hath Israel no sons? hath he no heir? why *then* doth their king inherit Gad, and his people dwell in his cities?

2Therefore, behold, the days come, saith the LORD, that I will cause an alarm of war to be heard in Rabbah of the Ammonites; and it shall be a desolate heap, and her daughters shall be burned with fire: then shall Israel be heir unto them that were his heirs, saith the LORD.

3Howl, O Heshbon, for Ai is spoiled: cry, ye daughters of Rabbah, gird you with sackcloth; lament, and run to and fro by the hedges; for their king shall go into captivity, *and* his priests and his princes together.

4Wherefore gloriest thou in the valleys, thy flowing valley, O backsliding daughter? that trusted in her treasures, *saying*, Who shall come unto me?

5Behold, I will bring a fear upon thee, saith the Lord GOD of hosts, from all those that be about thee; and ye shall be driven out every man right forth; and none shall gather up him that wandereth.

6And afterward I will bring again the captivity of the children of Ammon, saith the LORD.

7Concerning Edom, thus saith the LORD of hosts; *Is* wisdom no more in Teman? is counsel perished from the prudent? is their wisdom vanished?

8Flee ye, turn back, dwell deep, O inhabitants of Dedan; for I will bring the calamity of Esau upon him, the time *that* I will visit him.

9If grapegatherers come to thee, would they not leave *some* gleaning grapes? if thieves by night, they will destroy till they have enough.

10But I have made Esau bare, I have uncovered his secret places, and he shall not be able to hide himself: his seed is spoiled, and his brethren, and his neighbours, and he *is* not.

11Leave thy fatherless children, I will preserve *them* alive; and let thy widows trust in me.

12For thus saith the LORD; Behold, they whose judgment *was* not to drink of the cup have assuredly drunken; and *art* thou he *that* shall altogether go unpunished? thou shalt not go unpunished, but thou shalt surely drink *of it.*

13For I have sworn by myself, saith the LORD, that Bozrah shall become a desolation, a reproach, a waste, and a curse; and all the cities thereof shall be perpetual wastes.

14I have heard a rumour from the LORD, and an ambassador is sent unto the heathen, *saying,* Gather ye together, and come against her, and rise up to the battle.

15For, lo, I will make thee small among the heathen, *and* despised among men.

16Thy terribleness hath deceived thee, *and* the pride of thine heart, O thou that dwellest in the clefts of the rock, that holdest the height of the hill: though thou shouldest make thy nest as high as the eagle, I will bring thee down from thence, saith the LORD.

17Also Edom shall be a desolation: every one that goeth by it shall be astonished, and shall hiss at all the plagues thereof.

18As in the overthrow of Sodom and Gomorrah and the neighbour *cities* thereof, saith the LORD, no man shall abide there, neither shall a son of man dwell in it.

19Behold, he shall come up like a lion from the swelling of Jordan against the habitation of the strong: but I will suddenly make him run away from her: and who *is* a chosen *man, that* I may appoint over her? for who *is* like me? and who will appoint me the time? and who *is* that shepherd that will stand before me?

20Therefore hear the counsel of the LORD, that he hath taken against Edom; and his purposes, that he hath purposed against the inhabitants of Teman: Surely the least of the flock shall draw them out: surely he shall make their habitations desolate with them.

21The earth is moved at the noise of their fall, at the cry the noise thereof was heard in the Red sea.

22Behold, he shall come up and fly as the eagle, and spread his wings over Bozrah: and at that day shall the heart of the mighty men of Edom be as the heart of a woman in her pangs.

2 TIMOTHY 4:1–22

I CHARGE *thee* therefore before God, and the Lord Jesus Christ, who shall judge the quick and the dead at his appearing and his kingdom;

2Preach the word; be instant in season, out of season; reprove, rebuke, exhort with all longsuffering and doctrine.

3For the time will come when they will not endure sound doctrine; but after their own lusts shall they heap to themselves teachers, having itching ears;

4And they shall turn away *their* ears from the truth, and shall be turned unto fables.

5But watch thou in all things, endure afflictions, do the work of an evangelist, make full proof of thy ministry.

6For I am now ready to be offered, and the time of my departure is at hand.

7I have fought a good fight, I have finished *my* course, I have kept the faith:

8Henceforth there is laid up for me a crown of righteousness, which the Lord, the righteous judge, shall give me at that day: and not to me only, but unto all them also that love his appearing.

9Do thy diligence to come 'shortly unto me:

10For Demas hath forsaken me, having loved this present world, and is departed unto Thessalonica; Crescens to Galatia, Titus unto Dalmatia.

11Only Luke is with me. Take Mark, and bring him with thee: for he is profitable to me for the ministry.

12And Tychicus have I sent to Ephesus.

13The cloak that I left at Troas with Carpus, when thou comest, bring *with thee,* and the books, *but* especially the parchments.

14Alexander the coppersmith did me much evil: the Lord reward him according to his works:

15Of whom be thou ware also; for he hath greatly withstood our words.

16At my first answer no man stood with me, but all *men* forsook me: *I pray God* that it may not be laid to their charge.

17Notwithstanding the Lord stood with me, and strengthened me; that by me the preaching might be fully known, and *that* all the Gentiles might hear: and I was delivered out of the mouth of the lion.

18And the Lord shall deliver me from every evil work, and will preserve *me* unto his heavenly kingdom: to whom *be* glory for ever and ever. Amen.

19Salute Prisca and Aquila, and the household of Onesiphorus.

20Erastus abode at Corinth: but Trophimus have I left at Miletum sick.

21Do thy diligence to come before winter. Eubulus greeteth thee and Pudens, and Linus, and Claudia, and all the brethren.

22The Lord Jesus Christ *be* with thy spirit. Grace *be* with you. Amen.

PSALM 95:1—96:13

O COME, let us sing unto the LORD: let us make a joyful noise to the rock of our salvation.

2Let us come before his presence with thanksgiving, and make a joyful noise unto him with psalms.

3For the LORD *is* a great God, and a great King above all gods.

4In his hand *are* the deep places of the earth: the strength of the hills *is* his also.

5The sea *is* his, and he made it: and his hands formed the dry *land*.

6O come, let us worship and bow down: let us kneel before the LORD our maker.

7For he *is* our God; and we *are* the people of his pasture, and the sheep of his hand. To day if ye will hear his voice,

8Harden not your heart, as in the provocation, *and* as *in* the day of temptation in the wilderness:

9When your fathers tempted me, proved me, and saw my work.

10Forty years long was I grieved with *this* generation, and said, It *is* a people that do err in their heart, and they have not known my ways:

11Unto whom I sware in my wrath that they should not enter into my rest.

O SING unto the LORD a new song: sing unto the LORD, all the earth.

2Sing unto the LORD, bless his name; shew forth his salvation from day to day.

3Declare his glory among the heathen, his wonders among all people.

4For the LORD *is* great, and greatly to be praised: he *is* to be feared above all gods.

5For all the gods of the nations *are* idols: but the LORD made the heavens.

6Honour and majesty *are* before him: strength and beauty *are* in his sanctuary.

7Give unto the LORD, O ye kindreds of the people, give unto the LORD glory and strength.

8Give unto the LORD the glory *due unto* his name: bring an offering, and come into his courts.

9O worship the LORD in the beauty of holiness: fear before him, all the earth.

10Say among the heathen *that* the LORD reigneth: the world also shall be established that it shall not be moved: he shall judge the people righteously.

11Let the heavens rejoice, and let the earth be glad; let the sea roar, and the fulness thereof.

12Let the field be joyful, and all that *is* therein: then shall all the trees of the wood rejoice

13Before the LORD: for he cometh, for he cometh to judge the earth: he shall judge the world with righteousness, and the people with his truth.

PROVERBS FOR TODAY/ 26:9–12

As *the thorn goeth up into the hand of a drunkard, so* is *a parable in the mouth of fools.* □ *The great* God *that formed all* things *both rewardeth the fool, and rewardeth transgressors.* □ *As a dog returneth to his vomit,* so *a fool returneth to his folly.* □ *Seest thou a man wise in his own conceit?* there is *more hope of a fool than of him.*

JEREMIAH 49:23—50:46

CONCERNING Damascus. Hamath is confounded, and Arpad: for they have heard evil tidings: they are fainthearted; *there is* sorrow on the sea; it cannot be quiet.

24Damascus is waxed feeble, *and* turneth herself to flee, and fear hath seized on *her:* anguish and sorrows have taken her, as a woman in travail.

25How is the city of praise not left, the city of my joy!

26Therefore her young men shall fall in her streets, and all the men of war shall be cut off in that day, saith the Lord of hosts.

27And I will kindle a fire in the wall of Damascus, and it shall consume the palaces of Ben–hadad.

28Concerning Kedar, and concerning the kingdoms of Hazor, which Nebuchadrezzar king of Babylon shall smite, thus saith the Lord; Arise ye, go up to Kedar, and spoil the men of the east.

29Their tents and their flocks shall they take away: they shall take to themselves their curtains, and all their vessels, and their camels; and they shall cry unto them, Fear *is* on every side.

30Flee, get you far off, dwell deep, O ye inhabitants of Hazor, saith the Lord; for Nebuchadrezzar king of Babylon hath taken counsel against you, and hath conceived a purpose against you.

31Arise, get you up unto the wealthy nation, that dwelleth without care, saith the Lord, which have neither gates nor bars, *which* dwell alone.

32And their camels shall be a booty, and the multitude of their cattle a spoil: and I will scatter into all winds them *that are* in the utmost corners; and I will bring their calamity from all sides thereof, saith the Lord.

33And Hazor shall be a dwelling for dragons, *and* a desolation for ever: there shall no man abide there, nor *any* son of man dwell in it.

34The word of the Lord that came to Jeremiah the prophet against Elam in the beginning of the reign of Zedekiah king of Judah, saying,

35Thus saith the Lord of hosts; Behold, I will break the bow of Elam, the chief of their might.

36And upon Elam will I bring the four winds from the four quarters of heaven, and will scatter them toward all those winds; and there shall be no nation whither the outcasts of Elam shall not come.

37For I will cause Elam to be dismayed before their enemies, and before them that seek their life: and I will bring evil upon them, *even* my fierce anger, saith the Lord; and I will send the sword after them, till I have consumed them:

38And I will set my throne in Elam, and will destroy from thence the king and the princes, saith the Lord.

39But it shall come to pass in the latter days, *that* I will bring again the captivity of Elam, saith the Lord.

THE word that the Lord spake against Babylon *and* against the land of the Chaldeans by Jeremiah the prophet.

2Declare ye among the nations, and publish, and set up a standard; publish, *and* conceal not: say, Babylon is taken, Bel is confounded, Merodach is broken in pieces: her idols are confounded, her images are broken in pieces.

3For out of the north there cometh up a nation against her, which shall make her land desolate, and none shall dwell therein: they shall remove, they shall depart, both man and beast.

4In those days, and in that time, saith the LORD, the children of Israel shall come, they and the children of Judah together, going and weeping: they shall go, and seek the LORD their God.

5They shall ask the way to Zion with their faces thitherward, *saying,* Come, and let us join ourselves to the LORD in a perpetual covenant *that* shall not be forgotten.

6My people hath been lost sheep: their shepherds have caused them to go astray, they have turned them away *on* the mountains: they have gone from mountain to hill, they have forgotten their restingplace.

7All that found them have devoured them: and their adversaries said, We offend not, because they have sinned against the LORD, the habitation of justice, even the LORD, the hope of their fathers.

8Remove out of the midst of Babylon, and go forth out of the land of the Chaldeans, and be as the he goats before the flocks.

9For, lo, I will raise and cause to come up against Babylon an assembly of great nations from the north country: and they shall set themselves in array against her; from thence she shall be taken: their arrows *shall be* as of a mighty expert man; none shall return in vain.

10And Chaldea shall be a spoil: all that spoil her shall be satisfied, saith the LORD.

11Because ye were glad, because ye rejoiced, O ye destroyers of mine heritage, because ye are grown fat as the heifer at grass, and bellow as bulls;

12Your mother shall be sore confounded; she that bare you shall be ashamed: behold, the hindermost of the nations *shall be* a wilderness, a dry land, and a desert.

13Because of the wrath of the LORD it shall not be inhabited, but it shall be wholly desolate: every one that goeth by Babylon shall be astonished, and hiss at all her plagues.

14Put yourselves in array against Babylon round about: all ye that bend the bow, shoot at her, spare no arrows: for she hath sinned against the LORD.

15Shout against her round about: she hath given her hand: her foundations are fallen, her walls are thrown down: for it *is* the vengeance of the LORD: take vengeance upon her; as she hath done, do unto her.

16Cut off the sower from Babylon, and him that handleth the sickle in the time of harvest: for fear of the oppressing sword they shall turn every one to his people, and they shall flee every one to his own land.

17Israel *is* a scattered sheep; the lions have driven *him* away: first the king of Assyria hath devoured him; and last this Nebuchadrezzar king of Babylon hath broken his bones.

18Therefore thus saith the LORD of hosts, the God of Israel; Behold, I will punish the king of Babylon and his land, as I have punished the king of Assyria.

19And I will bring Israel again to his habitation, and he shall feed on Carmel and Bashan, and his soul shall be satisfied upon mount Ephraim and Gilead.

20In those days, and in that time, saith the LORD, the iniquity of Israel shall be sought for, and *there shall be* none; and the sins of Judah, and they shall not be found: for I will pardon them whom I reserve.

21Go up against the land of Merathaim, *even* against it, and against the inhabitants of Pekod: waste and utterly destroy after them, saith the LORD, and do according to all that I have commanded thee.

22A sound of battle *is* in the land, and of great destruction.

23How is the hammer of the whole earth cut asunder and broken! how is Babylon become a desolation among the nations!

24I have laid a snare for thee, and thou art also taken, O Babylon, and thou wast not aware: thou art found, and also caught, because thou hast striven against the LORD.

25The LORD hath opened his armoury, and hath brought forth the weapons of his indignation: for this *is* the work of the Lord GOD of hosts in the land of the Chaldeans.

26Come against her from the utmost border, open her storehouses: cast her up as heaps, and destroy her utterly: let nothing of her be left.

27Slay all her bullocks; let them go down to the slaughter: woe unto them! for their day is come, the time of their visitation.

28The voice of them that flee and escape out of the land of Babylon, to declare in Zion the vengeance of the LORD our God, the vengeance of his temple.

29Call together the archers against Babylon: all ye that bend the bow, camp against it round about; let none thereof escape: recompense her according to her work; according to all that she hath done, do unto her: for she hath been proud against the LORD, against the Holy One of Israel.

30Therefore shall her young men fall in the streets, and all her men of war shall be cut off in that day, saith the LORD.

31Behold, I *am* against thee, O *thou* most proud, saith the Lord GOD of hosts: for thy day is come, the time *that* I will visit thee.

32And the most proud shall stumble and fall, and none shall raise him up: and I will kindle a fire in his cities, and it shall devour all round about him.

33Thus saith the LORD of hosts; The children of Israel and the children of Judah *were* oppressed together: and all that took them captives held them fast; they refused to let them go.

34Their Redeemer *is* strong; the LORD of hosts *is* his name: he shall throughly plead their cause, that he may give rest to the land, and disquiet the inhabitants of Babylon.

35A sword *is* upon the Chaldeans, saith the LORD, and upon the inhabitants of Babylon, and upon her princes, and upon her wise *men.*

36A sword *is* upon the liars; and they shall dote: a sword *is* upon her mighty men; and they shall be dismayed.

37A sword *is* upon their horses, and upon their chariots, and upon all the mingled people that *are* in the midst of her; and they shall become as women: a sword *is* upon her treasures; and they shall be robbed.

38A drought *is* upon her waters; and they shall be dried up: for it *is* the land of graven images, and they are mad upon *their* idols.

39Therefore the wild beasts of the desert with the wild beasts of the islands shall dwell *there,* and the owls shall dwell therein: and it shall be no more inhabited for ever; neither shall it be dwelt in from generation to generation.

40As God overthrew Sodom and Gomorrah and the neighbour *cities* thereof, saith the LORD; *so* shall no man abide there, neither shall any son of man dwell therein.

41Behold, a people shall come from the north, and a great nation, and many kings shall be raised up from the coasts of the earth.

42They shall hold the bow and the lance: they *are* cruel, and will not shew mercy: their voice shall roar like the sea, and they shall ride upon horses, *every one* put in array, like a man to the battle, against thee, O daughter of Babylon.

43The king of Babylon hath heard the report of them, and his hands waxed feeble: anguish took hold of him, *and* pangs as of a woman in travail.

44Behold, he shall come up like a lion from the swelling of Jordan unto the habitation of the strong: but I will make them suddenly run away from her: and who *is* a chosen *man, that* I may appoint over her? for who *is* like me? and who will appoint me the time? and who *is* that shepherd that will stand before me?

45Therefore hear ye the counsel of the LORD, that he hath taken against Babylon; and his purposes, that he hath purposed against the land of the Chaldeans: Surely the least of the flock shall draw them out: surely he shall make *their* habitation desolate with them.

46At the noise of the taking of Babylon the earth is moved, and the cry is heard among the nations.

TITUS 1:1–16

PAUL, a servant of God, and an apostle of Jesus Christ, according to the faith of God's elect, and the acknowledging of the truth which is after godliness;

2In hope of eternal life, which God, that cannot lie, promised before the world began;

3But hath in due times manifested his word through preaching, which is committed unto me according to the commandment of God our Saviour;

4To Titus, *mine* own son after the common faith: Grace, mercy, *and* peace, from God the Father and the Lord Jesus Christ our Saviour.

5For this cause left I thee in Crete, that thou shouldest set in order the things that are wanting, and ordain elders in every city, as I had appointed thee:

6If any be blameless, the husband of one wife, having faithful children not accused of riot or unruly.

7For a bishop must be blameless, as the steward of God; not selfwilled, not soon angry, not given to wine, no striker, not given to filthy lucre;

8But a lover of hospitality, a lover of good men, sober, just, holy, temperate;

9Holding fast the faithful word as he hath been taught, that he may be able by sound doctrine both to exhort and to convince the gainsayers.

10For there are many unruly and vain talkers and deceivers, specially they of the circumcision:

11Whose mouths must be stopped, who subvert whole houses, teaching things which they ought not, for filthy lucre's sake.

12One of themselves, *even* a prophet of their own, said, The Cretians *are* alway liars, evil beasts, slow bellies.

13This witness is true. Wherefore rebuke them sharply, that they may be sound in the faith;

14Not giving heed to Jewish fables, and commandments of men, that turn from the truth.

15Unto the pure all things *are* pure: but unto them that are defiled and unbelieving *is* nothing pure; but even their mind and conscience is defiled.

16They profess that they know God; but in works they deny *him,* being abominable, and disobedient, and unto every good work reprobate.

PSALM 97:1—98:9

THE LORD reigneth; let the earth rejoice; let the multitude of isles be glad *thereof.*

2Clouds and darkness *are* round about him: righteousness and judgment *are* the habitation of his throne.

3A fire goeth before him, and burneth up his enemies round about.

4His lightnings enlightened the world: the earth saw, and trembled.

5The hills melted like wax at the presence of the LORD, at the presence of the LORD of the whole earth.

6The heavens declare his righteousness, and all the people see his glory.

7Confounded be all they that serve graven images, that boast themselves of idols: worship him, all *ye* gods.

8Zion heard, and was glad; and the daughters of Judah rejoiced because of thy judgments, O LORD.

9For thou, LORD, *art* high above all

the earth: thou art exalted far above all gods.

10Ye that love the LORD, hate evil: he preserveth the souls of his saints; he delivereth them out of the hand of the wicked.

11Light is sown for the righteous, and gladness for the upright in heart.

12Rejoice in the LORD, ye righteous; and give thanks at the remembrance of his holiness.

O SING unto the LORD a new song; for he hath done marvellous things: his right hand, and his holy arm, hath gotten him the victory.

2The LORD hath made known his salvation: his righteousness hath he openly shewed in the sight of the heathen.

3He hath remembered his mercy and his truth toward the house of Israel: all the ends of the earth have seen the salvation of our God.

4Make a joyful noise unto the LORD, all the earth: make a loud noise, and rejoice, and sing praise.

5Sing unto the LORD with the harp; with the harp, and the voice of a psalm.

6With trumpets and sound of cornets make a joyful noise before the LORD, the King.

7Let the sea roar, and the fulness thereof; the world, and they that dwell therein.

8Let the floods clap *their* hands: let the hills be joyful together

9Before the LORD; for he cometh to judge the earth: with righteousness shall he judge the world, and the people with equity.

PROVERBS FOR TODAY/ 26:13–16

The slothful man *saith,* There is *a lion in the way; a lion* is *in the streets.* As *the door turneth upon his hinges, so* doth *the slothful upon his bed. The slothful hideth his hand in* his *bosom; it grieveth him to bring it again to his mouth. The sluggard* is *wiser in his own conceit than seven men that can render a reason.*

OCTOBER 27

JEREMIAH 51:1–53

THUS saith the LORD; Behold, I will raise up against Babylon, and against them that dwell in the midst of them that rise up against me, a destroying wind;

2And will send unto Babylon fanners, that shall fan her, and shall empty her land: for in the day of trouble they shall be against her round about.

3Against *him that* bendeth let the archer bend his bow, and against *him that* lifteth himself up in his brigandine: and spare ye not her young men; destroy ye utterly all her host.

4Thus the slain shall fall in the land of the Chaldeans, and *they that are* thrust through in her streets.

5For Israel *hath* not *been* forsaken, nor Judah of his God, of the LORD of hosts; though their land was filled with sin against the Holy One of Israel.

6Flee out of the midst of Babylon, and deliver every man his soul: be not cut off in her iniquity; for this *is* the time of the LORD'S vengeance; he will render unto her a recompence.

7Babylon *hath been* a golden cup in the LORD'S hand, that made all the earth drunken: the nations have drunken of her wine; therefore the nations are mad.

8Babylon is suddenly fallen and destroyed: howl for her; take balm for her pain, if so be she may be healed.

9We would have healed Babylon, but she is not healed: forsake her, and let us go every one into his own country: for her judgment reacheth unto heaven, and is lifted up *even* to the skies.

10The LORD hath brought forth our righteousness: come, and let us declare in Zion the work of the LORD our God.

11Make bright the arrows; gather the shields: the LORD hath raised up the spirit of the kings of the Medes: for his device *is* against Babylon, to destroy it; because it *is* the vengeance of the LORD, the vengeance of his temple.

12Set up the standard upon the walls of Babylon, make the watch strong, set up the watchmen, prepare the ambushes: for the LORD hath both devised and done that which he spake against the inhabitants of Babylon.

13O thou that dwellest upon many waters, abundant in treasures, thine end is come, *and* the measure of thy covetousness.

14The LORD of hosts hath sworn by himself, *saying,* Surely I will fill thee with men, as with caterpillers; and they shall lift up a shout against thee.

15He hath made the earth by his power, he hath established the world by his wisdom, and hath stretched out the heaven by his understanding.

16When he uttereth *his* voice, *there is* a multitude of waters in the heavens; and he causeth the vapours to ascend from the ends of the earth: he maketh lightnings with rain, and bringeth forth the wind out of his treasures.

17Every man is brutish by *his* knowledge; every founder is confounded by the graven image: for his molten image *is* falsehood, and *there is* no breath in them.

18They *are* vanity, the work of errors: in the time of their visitation they shall perish.

19The portion of Jacob *is* not like them; for he *is* the former of all things: and *Israel is* the rod of his inheritance: the LORD of hosts *is* his name.

20Thou *art* my battle axe *and* weapons of war: for with thee will I break in pieces the nations, and with thee will I destroy kingdoms;

21And with thee will I break in pieces the horse and his rider; and with thee will I break in pieces the chariot and his rider;

22With thee also will I break in pieces man and woman; and with thee will I break in pieces old and young; and with thee will I break in pieces the young man and the maid;

23I will also break in pieces with thee the shepherd and his flock; and with thee will I break in pieces the husbandman and his yoke of oxen; and with thee will I break in pieces captains and rulers.

24And I will render unto Babylon and to all the inhabitants of Chaldea all their evil that they have done in Zion in your sight, saith the LORD.

25Behold, I *am* against thee, O destroying mountain, saith the LORD, which destroyest all the earth: and I will stretch out mine hand upon thee, and roll thee down from the rocks, and will make thee a burnt mountain.

26And they shall not take of thee a stone for a corner, nor a stone for foundations; but thou shalt be desolate for ever, saith the LORD.

27Set ye up a standard in the land, blow the trumpet among the nations, prepare the nations against her, call together against her the kingdoms of Ararat, Minni, and Ashchenaz; appoint a captain against her; cause the horses to come up as the rough caterpillers.

28Prepare against her the nations with the kings of the Medes, the captains thereof, and all the rulers thereof, and all the land of his dominion.

29And the land shall tremble and sorrow: for every purpose of the LORD shall be performed against Babylon, to make the land of Babylon a desolation without an inhabitant.

30The mighty men of Babylon have forborn to fight, they have remained in *their* holds: their might hath failed; they became as women: they have burned her dwellingplaces; her bars are broken.

31One post shall run to meet another, and one messenger to meet another, to shew the king of Babylon that his city is taken at *one* end,

32And that the passages are stopped, and the reeds they have burned with fire, and the men of war are affrighted.

33For thus saith the LORD of hosts, the God of Israel; The daughter of Babylon *is* like a threshingfloor, *it is* time to thresh her: yet a little while, and the time of her harvest shall come.

34Nebuchadrezzar the king of Babylon hath devoured me, he hath crushed me, he hath made me an empty vessel, he hath swallowed me up like a dragon, he hath filled his belly with my delicates, he hath cast me out.

35The violence done to me and to my flesh *be* upon Babylon, shall the inhabitant of Zion say; and my blood upon the inhabitants of Chaldea, shall Jerusalem say.

36Therefore thus saith the LORD; Behold, I will plead thy cause, and take vengeance for thee; and I will dry up her sea, and make her springs dry.

37And Babylon shall become heaps, a dwellingplace for dragons, an astonishment, and an hissing, without an inhabitant.

38They shall roar together like lions: they shall yell as lions' whelps.

39In their heat I will make their feasts, and I will make them drunken, that they may rejoice, and sleep a perpetual sleep, and not wake, saith the LORD.

40I will bring them down like lambs to the slaughter, like rams with he goats.

41How is Sheshach taken! and how is the praise of the whole earth surprised! how is Babylon become an astonishment among the nations!

42The sea is come up upon Babylon: she is covered with the multitude of the waves thereof.

43Her cities are a desolation, a dry land, and a wilderness, a land wherein no man dwelleth, neither doth *any* son of man pass thereby.

44And I will punish Bel in Babylon, and I will bring forth out of his mouth that which he hath swallowed up: and the nations shall not flow together any more unto him: yea, the wall of Babylon shall fall.

45My people, go ye out of the midst of her, and deliver ye every man his soul from the fierce anger of the LORD.

46And lest your heart faint, and ye fear for the rumour that shall be heard in the land; a rumour shall both come *one* year, and after that in *another* year *shall come* a rumour, and violence in the land, ruler against ruler.

47Therefore behold, the days come, that I will do judgment upon the graven images of Babylon: and her whole land shall be confounded, and all her slain shall fall in the midst of her.

48Then the heaven and the earth, and all that *is* therein, shall sing for Babylon: for the spoilers shall come unto her from the north, saith the LORD.

49As Babylon *hath caused* the slain of Israel to fall, so at Babylon shall fall the slain of all the earth.

50Ye that have escaped the sword, go away, stand not still: remember the LORD afar off, and let Jerusalem come into your mind.

51We are confounded, because we have heard reproach: shame hath covered our faces: for strangers are come into the sanctuaries of the LORD's house.

52Wherefore, behold, the days come, saith the LORD, that I will do judgment upon her graven images: and through all her land the wounded shall groan.

53Though Babylon should mount up to heaven, and though she should fortify the height of her strength, *yet* from me shall spoilers come unto her, saith the LORD.

TITUS 2:1–15

BUT speak thou the things which become sound doctrine: 2That the aged men be sober, grave, temperate, sound in faith, in charity, in patience.

3The aged women likewise, that *they be* in behaviour as becometh holiness, not false accusers, not given to much wine, teachers of good things;

4That they may teach the young women to be sober, to love their husbands, to love their children,

5*To be* discreet, chaste, keepers at home, good, obedient to their own husbands, that the word of God be not blasphemed.

6Young men likewise exhort to be sober minded.

7In all things shewing thyself a pattern of good works: in doctrine *shewing* uncorruptness, gravity, sincerity,

8Sound speech, that cannot be condemned; that he that is of the contrary part may be ashamed, having no evil thing to say of you.

9*Exhort* servants to be obedient unto their own masters, *and* to please *them* well in all *things;* not answering again;

10Not purloining, but shewing all good fidelity; that they may adorn the doctrine of God our Saviour in all things.

11For the grace of God that bringeth salvation hath appeared to all men,

12Teaching us that, denying ungodliness and worldly lusts, we should live soberly, righteously, and godly, in this present world;

13Looking for that blessed hope, and the glorious appearing of the great God and our Saviour Jesus Christ;

14Who gave himself for us, that he might redeem us from all iniquity, and purify unto himself a peculiar people, zealous of good works.

15These things speak, and exhort, and rebuke with all authority. Let no man despise thee.

PSALM 99:1–9

THE LORD reigneth; let the people tremble: he sitteth *between* the cherubims; let the earth be moved.

2The LORD *is* great in Zion; and he *is* high above all the people.

3Let them praise thy great and terrible name; *for* it *is* holy.

4The king's strength also loveth judgment; thou dost establish equity, thou executest judgment and righteousness in Jacob.

5Exalt ye the LORD our God, and worship at his footstool; *for* he *is* holy.

6Moses and Aaron among his priests, and Samuel among them that call upon his name; they called upon the LORD, and he answered them.

7He spake unto them in the cloudy pillar: they kept his testimonies, and the ordinance *that* he gave them.

8Thou answeredst them, O LORD our God: thou wast a God that forgavest them, though thou tookest vengeance of their inventions.

9Exalt the LORD our God, and worship at his holy hill; for the LORD our God *is* holy.

PROVERBS FOR TODAY/ 26:17

He that passeth by, and *meddleth with strife* belonging *not to him,* is like *one that taketh a dog by the ears.*

JEREMIAH 51:54—52:34

A SOUND of a cry *cometh* from Babylon, and great destruction from the land of the Chaldeans:

⁵⁵Because the LORD hath spoiled Babylon, and destroyed out of her the great voice; when her waves do roar like great waters, a noise of their voice is uttered:

⁵⁶Because the spoiler is come upon her, *even* upon Babylon, and her mighty men are taken, every one of their bows is broken: for the LORD God of recompences shall surely requite.

⁵⁷And I will make drunk her princes, and her wise *men,* her captains, and her rulers, and her mighty men: and they shall sleep a perpetual sleep, and not wake, saith the King, whose name *is* the LORD of hosts.

⁵⁸Thus saith the LORD of hosts; The broad walls of Babylon shall be utterly broken, and her high gates shall be burned with fire; and the people shall labour in vain, and the folk in the fire, and they shall be weary.

⁵⁹The word which Jeremiah the prophet commanded Seraiah the son of Neriah, the son of Maaseiah, when he went with Zedekiah the king of Judah into Babylon in the fourth year of his reign. And *this* Seraiah *was* a quiet prince.

⁶⁰So Jeremiah wrote in a book all the evil that should come upon Babylon, *even* all these words that are written against Babylon.

⁶¹And Jeremiah said to Seraiah, When thou comest to Babylon, and shalt see, and shalt read all these words;

⁶²Then shalt thou say, O LORD, thou hast spoken against this place, to cut it off, that none shall remain in it, neither man nor beast, but that it shall be desolate for ever.

⁶³And it shall be, when thou hast made an end of reading this book, *that* thou shalt bind a stone to it, and cast it into the midst of Euphrates:

⁶⁴And thou shalt say, Thus shall Babylon sink, and shall not rise from the evil that I will bring upon her: and they shall be weary. Thus far *are* the words of Jeremiah.

ZEDEKIAH *was* one and twenty years old when he began to reign, and he reigned eleven years in Jerusalem. And his mother's name *was* Hamutal the daughter of Jeremiah of Libnah.

²And he did *that which was* evil in the eyes of the LORD, according to all that Jehoiakim had done.

³For through the anger of the LORD it came to pass in Jerusalem and Judah, till he had cast them out from his presence, that Zedekiah rebelled against the king of Babylon.

⁴And it came to pass in the ninth year of his reign, in the tenth month, in the tenth *day* of the month, *that* Nebuchadrezzar king of Babylon came, he and all his army, against Jerusalem, and pitched against it, and built forts against it round about.

⁵So the city was besieged unto the eleventh year of king Zedekiah.

⁶And in the fourth month, in the ninth *day* of the month, the famine was sore in the city, so that there was no bread for the people of the land.

⁷Then the city was broken up, and all the men of war fled, and went forth out of the city by night by the way of the gate between the two walls, which *was* by the king's garden; (now the Chaldeans *were* by the city round about:) and they went by the way of the plain.

⁸But the army of the Chaldeans pursued after the king, and overtook Zede-

kiah in the plains of Jericho; and all his army was scattered from him.

⁹Then they took the king, and carried him up unto the king of Babylon to Riblah in the land of Hamath; where he gave judgment upon him.

¹⁰And the king of Babylon slew the sons of Zedekiah before his eyes: he slew also all the princes of Judah in Riblah.

¹¹Then he put out the eyes of Zedekiah; and the king of Babylon bound him in chains, and carried him to Babylon, and put him in prison till the day of his death.

¹²Now in the fifth month, in the tenth *day* of the month, which *was* the nineteenth year of Nebuchadrezzar king of Babylon, came Nebuzar–adan, captain of the guard, *which* served the king of Babylon, into Jerusalem,

¹³And burned the house of the LORD, and the king's house; and all the houses of Jerusalem, and all the houses of the great *men,* burned he with fire:

¹⁴And all the army of the Chaldeans, that *were* with the captain of the guard, brake down all the walls of Jerusalem round about.

¹⁵Then Nebuzar–adan the captain of the guard carried away captive *certain* of the poor of the people, and the residue of the people that remained in the city, and those that fell away, that fell to the king of Babylon, and the rest of the multitude.

¹⁶But Nebuzar–adan the captain of the guard left *certain* of the poor of the land for vinedressers and for husbandmen.

¹⁷Also the pillars of brass that *were* in the house of the LORD, and the bases, and the brasen sea that *was* in the house of the LORD, the Chaldeans brake, and carried all the brass of them to Babylon.

¹⁸The caldrons also, and the shovels, and the snuffers, and the bowls, and the spoons, and all the vessels of brass wherewith they ministered, took they away.

¹⁹And the basons, and the firepans, and the bowls, and the caldrons, and the candlesticks, and the spoons, and the cups; *that* which *was* of gold *in* gold, and *that* which *was* of silver *in* silver, took the captain of the guard away.

²⁰The two pillars, one sea, and twelve brasen bulls that *were* under the bases, which king Solomon had made in the house of the LORD: the brass of all these vessels was without weight.

²¹And *concerning* the pillars, the height of one pillar *was* eighteen cubits; and a fillet of twelve cubits did compass it; and the thickness thereof *was* four fingers: *it was* hollow.

²²And a chapiter of brass *was* upon it; and the height of one chapiter *was* five cubits, with network and pomegranates upon the chapiters round about, all *of* brass. The second pillar also and the pomegranates *were* like unto these.

²³And there were ninety and six pomegranates on a side; *and* all the pomegranates upon the network *were* an hundred round about.

²⁴And the captain of the guard took Seraiah the chief priest, and Zephaniah the second priest, and the three keepers of the door:

²⁵He took also out of the city an eunuch, which had the charge of the men of war; and seven men of them that were near the king's person, which were found in the city; and the principal scribe of the host, who mustered the people of the land; and threescore men of the people of the land, that were found in the midst of the city.

²⁶So Nebuzar–adan the captain of the guard took them, and brought them to the king of Babylon to Riblah.

²⁷And the king of Babylon smote them, and put them to death in Riblah in the land of Hamath. Thus Judah was carried away captive out of his own land.

²⁸This *is* the people whom Nebuchadrezzar carried away captive: in the

seventh year three thousand Jews and three and twenty:

29In the eighteenth year of Nebuchadrezzar he carried away captive from Jerusalem eight hundred thirty and two persons:

30In the three and twentieth year of Nebuchadrezzar Nebuzar–adan the captain of the guard carried away captive of the Jews seven hundred forty and five persons: all the persons *were* four thousand and six hundred.

31And it came to pass in the seven and thirtieth year of the captivity of Jehoiachin king of Judah, in the twelfth month, in the five and twentieth *day* of the month, *that* Evil–merodach king of Babylon in the *first* year of his reign lifted up the head of Jehoiachin king of Judah, and brought him forth out of prison,

32And spake kindly unto him, and set his throne above the throne of the kings that *were* with him in Babylon,

33And changed his prison garments: and he did continually eat bread before him all the days of his life.

34And *for* his diet, there was a continual diet given him of the king of Babylon, every day a portion until the day of his death, all the days of his life.

TITUS 3:1–15

PUT them in mind to be subject to principalities and powers, to obey magistrates, to be ready to every good work,

2To speak evil of no man, to be no brawlers, *but* gentle, shewing all meekness unto all men.

3For we ourselves also were sometimes foolish, disobedient, deceived, serving divers lusts and pleasures, living in malice and envy, hateful, *and* hating one another.

4But after that the kindness and love of God our Saviour toward man appeared,

5Not by works of righteousness which we have done, but according to his mercy he saved us, by the washing of regeneration, and renewing of the Holy Ghost;

6Which he shed on us abundantly through Jesus Christ our Saviour;

7That being justified by his grace, we should be made heirs according to the hope of eternal life.

8*This is* a faithful saying, and these things I will that thou affirm constantly, that they which have believed in God might be careful to maintain good works. These things are good and profitable unto men.

9But avoid foolish questions, and genealogies, and contentions, and strivings about the law; for they are unprofitable and vain.

10A man that is an heretick after the first and second admonition reject;

11Knowing that he that is such is subverted, and sinneth, being condemned of himself.

12When I shall send Artemas unto thee, or Tychicus, be diligent to come unto me to Nicopolis: for I have determined there to winter.

13Bring Zenas the lawyer and Apollos on their journey diligently, that nothing be wanting unto them.

14And let ours also learn to maintain good works for necessary uses, that they be not unfruitful.

15All that are with me salute thee. Greet them that love us in the faith. Grace *be* with you all. Amen.

PSALM 100:1–5

MAKE a joyful noise unto the LORD, all ye lands.

2Serve the LORD with gladness: come before his presence with singing.

3Know ye that the LORD he *is* God: *it is* he *that* hath made us, and not we ourselves; *we are* his people, and the sheep of his pasture.

4Enter into his gates with thanksgiving, *and* into his courts with praise: be thankful unto him, *and* bless his name.

5For the LORD *is* good; his mercy *is* everlasting; and his truth *endureth* to all generations.

PROVERBS FOR TODAY/ 26:18–19

As a mad man *who casteth firebrands, arrows, and death, So* is *the man* that *deceiveth his neighbour, and saith, Am not I in sport?*

OCTOBER 29

LAMENTATIONS 1:1—2:19

How doth the city sit solitary, *that was* full of people! *how* is she become as a widow! she *that was* great among the nations, *and* princess among the provinces, *how* is she become tributary!

2She weepeth sore in the night, and her tears *are* on her cheeks: among all her lovers she hath none to comfort *her:* all her friends have dealt treacherously with her, they are become her enemies.

3Judah is gone into captivity because of affliction, and because of great servitude: she dwelleth among the heathen, she findeth no rest: all her persecutors overtook her between the straits.

4The ways of Zion do mourn, because none come to the solemn feasts: all her gates are desolate: her priests sigh, her virgins are afflicted, and she *is* in bitterness.

5Her adversaries are the chief, her enemies prosper; for the LORD hath afflicted her for the multitude of her transgressions: her children are gone into captivity before the enemy.

6And from the daughter of Zion all her beauty is departed: her princes are become like harts *that* find no pasture, and they are gone without strength before the pursuer.

7Jerusalem remembered in the days of her affliction and of her miseries all her pleasant things that she had in the days of old, when her people fell into the hand of the enemy, and none did help her: the adversaries saw her, *and* did mock at her sabbaths.

8Jerusalem hath grievously sinned; therefore she is removed: all that honoured her despise her, because they have seen her nakedness: yea, she sigheth, and turneth backward.

9Her filthiness *is* in her skirts; she remembereth not her last end; therefore she came down wonderfully: she had no comforter. O LORD, behold my affliction: for the enemy hath magnified *himself.*

10The adversary hath spread out his hand upon all her pleasant things: for she hath seen *that* the heathen entered into her sanctuary, whom thou didst command *that* they should not enter into thy congregation.

11All her people sigh, they seek bread; they have given their pleasant things for meat to relieve the soul: see, O LORD, and consider; for I am become vile.

12*Is it* nothing to you, all ye that pass by? behold, and see if there be any sorrow like unto my sorrow, which is done unto me, wherewith the LORD hath afflicted *me* in the day of his fierce anger.

¹³From above hath he sent fire into my bones, and it prevaileth against them: he hath spread a net for my feet, he hath turned me back: he hath made me desolate *and* faint all the day.

¹⁴The yoke of my transgressions is bound by his hand: they are wreathed, *and* come up upon my neck: he hath made my strength to fall, the Lord hath delivered me into *their* hands, *from whom* I am not able to rise up.

¹⁵The Lord hath trodden under foot all my mighty *men* in the midst of me: he hath called an assembly against me to crush my young men: the Lord hath trodden the virgin, the daughter of Judah, *as* in a winepress.

¹⁶For these *things* I weep; mine eye, mine eye runneth down with water, because the comforter that should relieve my soul is far from me: my children are desolate, because the enemy prevailed.

¹⁷Zion spreadeth forth her hands, *and there is* none to comfort her: the LORD hath commanded concerning Jacob, *that* his adversaries *should be* round about him: Jerusalem is as a menstruous woman among them.

¹⁸The LORD is righteous; for I have rebelled against his commandment: hear, I pray you, all people, and behold my sorrow: my virgins and my young men are gone into captivity.

¹⁹I called for my lovers, *but* they deceived me: my priests and mine elders gave up the ghost in the city, while they sought their meat to relieve their souls.

²⁰Behold, O LORD; for I *am* in distress: my bowels are troubled; mine heart is turned within me; for I have grievously rebelled: abroad the sword bereaveth, at home *there is* as death.

²¹They have heard that I sigh: *there is* none to comfort me: all mine enemies have heard of my trouble; they are glad that thou hast done *it:* thou wilt bring the day *that* thou hast called, and they shall be like unto me.

²²Let all their wickedness come before thee; and do unto them, as thou hast done unto me for all my transgressions: for my sighs *are* many, and my heart *is* faint.

How hath the Lord covered the daughter of Zion with a cloud in his anger, *and* cast down from heaven unto the earth the beauty of Israel, and remembered not his footstool in the day of his anger!

²The Lord hath swallowed up all the habitations of Jacob, and hath not pitied: he hath thrown down in his wrath the strong holds of the daughter of Judah; he hath brought *them* down to the ground: he hath polluted the kingdom and the princes thereof.

³He hath cut off in *his* fierce anger all the horn of Israel: he hath drawn back his right hand from before the enemy, and he burned against Jacob like a flaming fire, *which* devoureth round about.

⁴He hath bent his bow like an enemy: he stood with his right hand as an adversary, and slew all *that were* pleasant to the eye in the tabernacle of the daughter of Zion: he poured out his fury like fire.

⁵The Lord was as an enemy: he hath swallowed up Israel, he hath swallowed up all her palaces: he hath destroyed his strong holds, and hath increased in the daughter of Judah mourning and lamentation.

⁶And he hath violently taken away his tabernacle, as *if it were of* a garden: he hath destroyed his places of the assembly: the LORD hath caused the solemn feasts and sabbaths to be forgotten in Zion, and hath despised in the indignation of his anger the king and the priest.

⁷The Lord hath cast off his altar, he hath abhorred his sanctuary, he hath given up into the hand of the enemy the walls of her palaces; they have made a noise in the house of the LORD, as in the day of a solemn feast.

8The LORD hath purposed to destroy the wall of the daughter of Zion: he hath stretched out a line, he hath not withdrawn his hand from destroying: therefore he made the rampart and the wall to lament; they languished together.

9Her gates are sunk into the ground; he hath destroyed and broken her bars: her king and her princes *are* among the Gentiles: the law *is* no *more;* her prophets also find no vision from the LORD.

10The elders of the daughter of Zion sit upon the ground, *and* keep silence: they have cast up dust upon their heads; they have girded themselves with sackcloth: the virgins of Jerusalem hang down their heads to the ground.

11Mine eyes do fail with tears, my bowels are troubled, my liver is poured upon the earth, for the destruction of the daughter of my people; because the children and the sucklings swoon in the streets of the city.

12They say to their mothers, Where *is* corn and wine? when they swooned as the wounded in the streets of the city, when their soul was poured out into their mothers' bosom.

13What thing shall I take to witness for thee? what thing shall I liken to thee, O daughter of Jerusalem? what shall I equal to thee, that I may comfort thee, O virgin daughter of Zion? for thy breach *is* great like the sea: who can heal thee?

14Thy prophets have seen vain and foolish things for thee: and they have not discovered thine iniquity, to turn away thy captivity; but have seen for thee false burdens and causes of banishment.

15All that pass by clap *their* hands at thee; they hiss and wag their head at the daughter of Jerusalem, *saying, Is* this the city that *men* call The perfection of beauty, The joy of the whole earth?

16All thine enemies have opened their mouth against thee: they hiss and gnash the teeth: they say, We have swallowed *her* up: certainly this *is* the day that we looked for; we have found, we have seen *it.*

17The LORD hath done *that* which he had devised; he hath fulfilled his word that he had commanded in the days of old: he hath thrown down, and hath not pitied: and he hath caused *thine* enemy to rejoice over thee, he hath set up the horn of thine adversaries.

18Their heart cried unto the Lord, O wall of the daughter of Zion, let tears run down like a river day and night: give thyself no rest; let not the apple of thine eye cease.

19Arise, cry out in the night: in the beginning of the watches pour out thine heart like water before the face of the Lord: lift up thy hands toward him for the life of thy young children, that faint for hunger in the top of every street.

PHILEMON 1:1–25

Paul, a prisoner of Jesus Christ, and Timothy *our* brother, unto Philemon our dearly beloved, and fellowlabourer,

2And to *our* beloved Apphia, and Archippus our fellowsoldier, and to the church in thy house:

3Grace to you, and peace, from God our Father and the Lord Jesus Christ.

4I thank my God, making mention of thee always in my prayers,

5Hearing of thy love and faith, which thou hast toward the Lord Jesus, and toward all saints;

6That the communication of thy faith may become effectual by the acknowledging of every good thing which is in you in Christ Jesus.

7For we have great joy and consolation in thy love, because the bowels of the saints are refreshed by thee, brother.

8Wherefore, though I might be much

bold in Christ to enjoin thee that which is convenient,

9Yet for love's sake I rather beseech *thee*, being such an one as Paul the aged, and now also a prisoner of Jesus Christ.

10I beseech thee for my son Onesimus, whom I have begotten in my bonds:

11Which in time past was to thee unprofitable, but now profitable to thee and to me:

12Whom I have sent again: thou therefore receive him, that is, mine own bowels:

13Whom I would have retained with me, that in thy stead he might have ministered unto me in the bonds of the gospel:

14But without thy mind would I do nothing; that thy benefit should not be as it were of necessity, but willingly.

15For perhaps he therefore departed for a season, that thou shouldest receive him for ever;

16Not now as a servant, but above a servant, a brother beloved, specially to me, but how much more unto thee, both in the flesh and in the Lord?

17If thou count me therefore a partner, receive him as myself.

18If he hath wronged thee, or oweth *thee* ought, put that on mine account;

19I Paul have written *it* with mine own hand, I will repay *it:* albeit I do not say to thee how thou owest unto me even thine own self besides.

20Yea, brother, let me have joy of thee in the Lord: refresh my bowels in the Lord.

21Having confidence in thy obedience I wrote unto thee, knowing that thou wilt also do more than I say.

22But withal prepare me also a lodging: for I trust that through your prayers I shall be given unto you.

23There salute thee Epaphras, my fellowprisoner in Christ Jesus;

24Marcus, Aristarchus, Demas, Lucas, my fellowlabourers.

25The grace of our Lord Jesus Christ *be* with your spirit. Amen.

PSALM 101:1–8

I WILL sing of mercy and judgment: unto thee, O LORD, will I sing.

2I will behave myself wisely in a perfect way. O when wilt thou come unto me? I will walk within my house with a perfect heart.

3I will set no wicked thing before mine eyes: I hate the work of them that turn aside; *it* shall not cleave to me.

4A froward heart shall depart from me: I will not know a wicked *person*.

5Whoso privily slandereth his neighbour, him will I cut off: him that hath an high look and a proud heart will not I suffer.

6Mine eyes *shall be* upon the faithful of the land, that they may dwell with me: he that walketh in a perfect way, he shall serve me.

7He that worketh deceit shall not dwell within my house: he that telleth lies shall not tarry in my sight.

8I will early destroy all the wicked of the land: that I may cut off all wicked doers from the city of the LORD.

PROVERBS FOR TODAY/ 26:20

Where no wood is, there *the fire goeth out: so where* there is *no talebearer, the* strife ceaseth.

OCTOBER 30

LAMENTATIONS 2:20—3:66

BEHOLD, O LORD, and consider to whom thou hast done this. Shall the women eat their fruit, *and* children of a span long? shall the priest and the prophet be slain in the sanctuary of the Lord?

²¹The young and the old lie on the ground in the streets: my virgins and my young men are fallen by the sword; thou hast slain *them* in the day of thine anger; thou hast killed, *and* not pitied.

²²Thou hast called as in a solemn day my terrors round about, so that in the day of the LORD's anger none escaped nor remained: those that I have swaddled and brought up hath mine enemy consumed.

I AM the man *that* hath seen affliction by the rod of his wrath.

²He hath led me, and brought *me into* darkness, but not *into* light.

³Surely against me is he turned; he turneth his hand *against me* all the day.

⁴My flesh and my skin hath he made old; he hath broken my bones.

⁵He hath builded against me, and compassed *me* with gall and travail.

⁶He hath set me in dark places, as *they that be* dead of old.

⁷He hath hedged me about, that I cannot get out: he hath made my chain heavy.

⁸Also when I cry and shout, he shutteth out my prayer.

⁹He hath inclosed my ways with hewn stone, he hath made my paths crooked.

¹⁰He *was* unto me *as* a bear lying in wait, *and as* a lion in secret places.

¹¹He hath turned aside my ways, and pulled me in pieces: he hath made me desolate.

¹²He hath bent his bow, and set me as a mark for the arrow.

¹³He hath caused the arrows of his quiver to enter into my reins.

¹⁴I was a derision to all my people; *and* their song all the day.

¹⁵He hath filled me with bitterness, he hath made me drunken with wormwood.

¹⁶He hath also broken my teeth with gravel stones, he hath covered me with ashes.

¹⁷And thou hast removed my soul far off from peace: I forgat prosperity.

¹⁸And I said, My strength and my hope is perished from the LORD:

¹⁹Remembering mine affliction and my misery, the wormwood and the gall.

²⁰My soul hath *them* still in remembrance, and is humbled in me.

²¹This I recall to my mind, therefore have I hope.

²²*It is of* the LORD's mercies that we are not consumed, because his compassions fail not.

²³*They are* new every morning: great *is* thy faithfulness.

²⁴The LORD *is* my portion, saith my soul; therefore will I hope in him.

²⁵The LORD *is* good unto them that wait for him, to the soul *that* seeketh him.

²⁶*It is* good that *a man* should both hope and quietly wait for the salvation of the LORD.

²⁷*It is* good for a man that he bear the yoke in his youth.

²⁸He sitteth alone and keepeth silence, because he hath borne *it* upon him.

²⁹He putteth his mouth in the dust; if so be there may be hope.

³⁰He giveth *his* cheek to him that smiteth him: he is filled full with reproach.

³¹For the Lord will not cast off for ever:

32But though he cause grief, yet will he have compassion according to the multitude of his mercies.

33For he doth not afflict willingly nor grieve the children of men.

34To crush under his feet all the prisoners of the earth,

35To turn aside the right of a man before the face of the most High,

36To subvert a man in his cause, the Lord approveth not.

37Who *is* he *that* saith, and it cometh to pass, *when* the Lord commandeth *it* not?

38Out of the mouth of the most High proceedeth not evil and good?

39Wherefore doth a living man complain, a man for the punishment of his sins?

40Let us search and try our ways, and turn again to the LORD.

41Let us lift up our heart with *our* hands unto God in the heavens.

42We have transgressed and have rebelled: thou hast not pardoned.

43Thou hast covered with anger, and persecuted us: thou hast slain, thou hast not pitied.

44Thou hast covered thyself with a cloud, that *our* prayer should not pass through.

45Thou hast made us *as* the offscouring and refuse in the midst of the people.

46All our enemies have opened their mouths against us.

47Fear and a snare is come upon us, desolation and destruction.

48Mine eye runneth down with rivers of water for the destruction of the daughter of my people.

49Mine eye trickleth down, and ceaseth not, without any intermission,

50Till the LORD look down, and behold from heaven.

51Mine eye affecteth mine heart because of all the daughters of my city.

52Mine enemies chased me sore, like a bird, without cause.

53They have cut off my life in the dungeon, and cast a stone upon me.

54Waters flowed over mine head; *then* I said, I am cut off.

55I called upon thy name, O LORD, out of the low dungeon.

56Thou hast heard my voice: hide not thine ear at my breathing, at my cry.

57Thou drewest near in the day *that* I called upon thee: thou saidst, Fear not.

58O Lord, thou hast pleaded the causes of my soul; thou hast redeemed my life.

59O LORD, thou hast seen my wrong: judge thou my cause.

60Thou hast seen all their vengeance *and* all their imaginations against me.

61Thou hast heard their reproach, O LORD, *and* all their imaginations against me;

62The lips of those that rose up against me, and their device against me all the day.

63Behold their sitting down, and their rising up; I *am* their musick.

64Render unto them a recompence, O LORD, according to the work of their hands.

65Give them sorrow of heart, thy curse unto them.

66Persecute and destroy them in anger from under the heavens of the LORD.

HEBREWS 1:1–14

GOD, who at sundry times and in divers manners spake in time past unto the fathers by the prophets,

2Hath in these last days spoken unto us by *his* Son, whom he hath appointed heir of all things, by whom also he made the worlds;

3Who being the brightness of *his* glory, and the express image of his person, and upholding all things by the word of his power, when he had by himself purged our sins, sat down on the right hand of the Majesty on high;

4Being made so much better than

the angels, as he hath by inheritance obtained a more excellent name than they.

5For unto which of the angels said he at any time, Thou art my son, this day have I begotten thee? And again, I will be to him a Father, and he shall be to me a Son?

6And again, when he bringeth in the firstbegotten into the world, he saith, And let all the angels of God worship him.

7And of the angels he saith, Who maketh his angels spirits, and his ministers a flame of fire.

8But unto the Son *he saith,* Thy throne, O God, *is* for ever and ever: a sceptre of righteousness *is* the sceptre of thy kingdom.

9Thou hast loved righteousness, and hated iniquity; therefore God, *even* thy God, hath anointed thee with the oil of gladness above thy fellows.

10And, Thou, Lord, in the beginning hast laid the foundation of the earth; and the heavens are the works of thine hands:

11They shall perish; but thou remainest; and they all shall wax old as doth a garment;

12And as a vesture shalt thou fold them up, and they shall be changed: but thou art the same, and thy years shall not fail.

13But to which of the angels said he at any time, Sit on my right hand, until I make thine enemies thy footstool?

14Are they not all ministering spirits, sent forth to minister for them who shall be heirs of salvation?

PSALM 102:1–28

HEAR my prayer, O LORD, and let my cry come unto thee.
2Hide not thy face from me in the day *when* I am in trouble; incline thine ear unto me: in the day *when* I call answer me speedily.

3For my days are consumed like smoke, and my bones are burned as an hearth.

4My heart is smitten, and withered like grass; so that I forget to eat my bread.

5By reason of the voice of my groaning my bones cleave to my skin.

6I am like a pelican of the wilderness: I am like an owl of the desert.

7I watch, and am as a sparrow alone upon the house top.

8Mine enemies reproach me all the day; *and* they that are mad against me are sworn against me.

9For I have eaten ashes like bread, and mingled my drink with weeping,

10Because of thine indignation and thy wrath: for thou hast lifted me up, and cast me down.

11My days *are* like a shadow that declineth; and I am withered like grass.

12But thou, O LORD, shalt endure for ever; and thy remembrance unto all generations.

13Thou shalt arise, *and* have mercy upon Zion: for the time to favour her, yea, the set time, is come.

14For thy servants take pleasure in her stones, and favour the dust thereof.

15So the heathen shall fear the name of the LORD, and all the kings of the earth thy glory.

16When the LORD shall build up Zion, he shall appear in his glory.

17He will regard the prayer of the destitute, and not despise their prayer.

18This shall be written for the generation to come: and the people which shall be created shall praise the LORD.

19For he hath looked down from the height of his sanctuary; from heaven did the LORD behold the earth;

20To hear the groaning of the prisoner; to loose those that are appointed to death;

21To declare the name of the LORD in Zion, and his praise in Jerusalem;

22When the people are gathered together, and the kingdoms, to serve the LORD.

²³He weakened my strength in the way; he shortened my days.

²⁴I said, O my God, take me not away in the midst of my days: thy years *are* throughout all generations.

²⁵Of old hast thou laid the foundation of the earth: and the heavens *are* the work of thy hands.

²⁶They shall perish, but thou shalt endure: yea, all of them shall wax old like a garment; as a vesture shalt thou change them, and they shall be changed:

²⁷But thou *art* the same, and thy years shall have no end.

²⁸The children of thy servants shall continue, and their seed shall be established before thee.

PROVERBS FOR TODAY/ 26:21—22

As *coals* are *to burning coals, and wood to fire; so* is *a contentious man to kindle strife.* □ *The words of a talebearer* are *as wounds, and they go down into the innermost parts of the belly.*

OCTOBER 31

LAMENTATIONS 4:1—5:22

Ow is the gold become dim! *how* is the most fine gold changed! the stones of the sanctuary are poured out in the top of every street.

²The precious sons of Zion, comparable to fine gold, how are they esteemed as earthen pitchers, the work of the hands of the potter!

³Even the sea monsters draw out the breast, they give suck to their young ones: the daughter of my people *is become* cruel, like the ostriches in the wilderness.

⁴The tongue of the sucking child cleaveth to the roof of his mouth for thirst: the young children ask bread, *and* no man breaketh *it* unto them.

⁵They that did feed delicately are desolate in the streets: they that were brought up in scarlet embrace dunghills.

⁶For the punishment of the iniquity of the daughter of my people is greater than the punishment of the sin of Sodom, that was overthrown as in a moment, and no hands stayed on her.

⁷Her Nazarites were purer than snow, they were whiter than milk, they were more ruddy in body than rubies, their polishing *was* of sapphire:

⁸Their visage is blacker than a coal; they are not known in the streets: their skin cleaveth to their bones; it is withered, it is become like a stick.

⁹*They that be* slain with the sword are better than *they that be* slain with hunger: for these pine away, stricken through for *want of* the fruits of the field.

¹⁰The hands of the pitiful women have sodden their own children: they were their meat in the destruction of the daughter of my people.

¹¹The LORD hath accomplished his fury; he hath poured out his fierce anger, and hath kindled a fire in Zion, and it hath devoured the foundations thereof.

¹²The kings of the earth, and all the inhabitants of the world, would not have believed that the adversary and the enemy should have entered into the gates of Jerusalem.

¹³For the sins of her prophets, *and*

the iniquities of her priests, that have shed the blood of the just in the midst of her,

14They have wandered *as* blind *men* in the streets, they have polluted themselves with blood, so that men could not touch their garments.

15They cried unto them, Depart ye; *it is* unclean; depart, depart, touch not: when they fled away and wandered, they said among the heathen, They shall no more sojourn *there*.

16The anger of the LORD hath divided them; he will no more regard them: they respected not the persons of the priests, they favoured not the elders.

17As for us, our eyes as yet failed for our vain help: in our watching we have watched for a nation *that* could not save *us*.

18They hunt our steps, that we cannot go in our streets: our end is near, our days are fulfilled; for our end is come.

19Our persecutors are swifter than the eagles of the heaven: they pursued us upon the mountains, they laid wait for us in the wilderness.

20The breath of our nostrils, the anointed of the LORD, was taken in their pits, of whom we said, Under his shadow we shall live among the heathen.

21Rejoice and be glad, O daughter of Edom, that dwellest in the land of Uz; the cup also shall pass through unto thee: thou shalt be drunken, and shalt make thyself naked.

22The punishment of thine iniquity is accomplished, O daughter of Zion; he will no more carry thee away into captivity: he will visit thine iniquity, O daughter of Edom; he will discover thy sins.

REMEMBER, O LORD, what is come upon us: consider, and behold our reproach.

2Our inheritance is turned to strangers, our houses to aliens.

3We are orphans and fatherless, our mothers *are* as widows.

4We have drunken our water for money; our wood is sold unto us.

5Our necks *are* under persecution: we labour, *and* have no rest.

6We have given the hand *to* the Egyptians, *and to* the Assyrians, to be satisfied with bread.

7Our fathers have sinned, *and are* not; and we have borne their iniquities.

8Servants have ruled over us: *there is* none that doth deliver *us* out of their hand.

9We gat our bread with *the peril of* our lives because of the sword of the wilderness.

10Our skin was black like an oven because of the terrible famine.

11They ravished the women in Zion, *and* the maids in the cities of Judah.

12Princes are hanged up by their hand: the faces of elders were not honoured.

13They took the young men to grind, and the children fell under the wood.

14The elders have ceased from the gate, the young men from their musick.

15The joy of our heart is ceased; our dance is turned into mourning.

16The crown is fallen *from* our head: woe unto us, that we have sinned!

17For this our heart is faint; for these *things* our eyes are dim.

18Because of the mountain of Zion, which is desolate, the foxes walk upon it.

19Thou, O LORD, remainest for ever; thy throne from generation to generation.

20Wherefore dost thou forget us for ever, *and* forsake us so long time?

21Turn thou us unto thee, O LORD, and we shall be turned; renew our days as of old.

22But thou hast utterly rejected us; thou art very wroth against us.

HEBREWS 2:1–18

THEREFORE we ought to give the more earnest heed to the things which we have heard, lest at any time we should let *them* slip.

2For if the word spoken by angels was stedfast, and every transgression and disobedience received a just recompence of reward;

3How shall we escape, if we neglect so great salvation; which at the first began to be spoken by the Lord, and was confirmed unto us by them that heard *him;*

4God also bearing *them* witness, both with signs and wonders, and with divers miracles, and gifts of the Holy Ghost, according to his own will?

5For unto the angels hath he not put in subjection the world to come, whereof we speak.

6But one in a certain place testified, saying, What is man, that thou art mindful of him? or the son of man, that thou visitest him?

7Thou madest him a little lower than the angels; thou crownedst him with glory and honour, and didst set him over the works of thy hands:

8Thou hast put all things in subjection under his feet. For in that he put all in subjection under him, he left nothing *that is* not put under him. But now we see not yet all things put under him.

9But we see Jesus, who was made a little lower than the angels for the suffering of death, crowned with glory and honour; that he by the grace of God should taste death for every man.

10For it became him, for whom *are* all things, and by whom *are* all things, in bringing many sons unto glory, to make the captain of their salvation perfect through sufferings.

11For both he that sanctifieth and they who are sanctified *are* all of one: for which cause he is not ashamed to call them brethren,

12Saying, I will declare thy name unto my brethren, in the midst of the church will I sing praise unto thee.

13And again, I will put my trust in him. And again, Behold I and the children which God hath given me.

14Forasmuch then as the children are partakers of flesh and blood, he also himself likewise took part of the same; that through death he might destroy him that had the power of death, that is, the devil;

15And deliver them who through fear of death were all their lifetime subject to bondage.

16For verily he took not on *him the nature of* angels; but he took on *him* the seed of Abraham.

17Wherefore in all things it behoved him to be made like unto *his* brethren, that he might be a merciful and faithful high priest in things *pertaining* to God, to make reconciliation for the sins of the people.

18For in that he himself hath suffered being tempted, he is able to succour them that are tempted.

PSALM 103:1–22

BLESS the LORD, O my soul: and all that is within me, *bless* his holy name.

2Bless the LORD, O my soul, and forget not all his benefits:

3Who forgiveth all thine iniquities; who healeth all thy diseases;

4Who redeemeth thy life from destruction; who crowneth thee with lovingkindness and tender mercies;

5Who satisfieth thy mouth with good *things; so that* thy youth is renewed like the eagle's.

6The LORD executeth righteousness and judgment for all that are oppressed.

7He made known his ways unto Moses, his acts unto the children of Israel.

8The LORD *is* merciful and gracious, slow to anger, and plenteous in mercy.

9He will not always chide: neither

will he keep *his anger* for ever.

10He hath not dealt with us after our sins; nor rewarded us according to our iniquities.

11For as the heaven is high above the earth, *so* great is his mercy toward them that fear him.

12As far as the east is from the west, *so* far hath he removed our transgressions from us.

13Like as a father pitieth *his* children, *so* the LORD pitieth them that fear him.

14For he knoweth our frame; he remembereth that we *are* dust.

15*As for* man, his days *are* as grass; as a flower of the field, so he flourisheth.

16For the wind passeth over it, and it is gone; and the place thereof shall know it no more.

17But the mercy of the LORD *is* from everlasting to everlasting upon them that fear him, and his righteousness unto children's children;

18To such as keep his covenant, and to those that remember his commandments to do them.

19The LORD hath prepared his throne in the heavens; and his kingdom ruleth over all.

20Bless the LORD, ye his angels, that excel in strength, that do his commandments, hearkening unto the voice of his word.

21Bless ye the LORD, all *ye* his hosts; *ye* ministers of his, that do his pleasure.

22Bless the LORD, all his works in all places of his dominion: bless the LORD, O my soul.

PROVERBS FOR TODAY/ 26:23

Burning lips and a wicked heart are like *a potsherd covered with silver dross.*

NOVEMBER 1

EZEKIEL 1:1—3:15

Now it came to pass in the thirtieth year, in the fourth *month,* in the fifth *day* of the month, as I *was* among the captives by the river of Chebar, *that* the heavens were opened, and I saw visions of God.

2In the fifth *day* of the month, which *was* the fifth year of king Jehoiachin's captivity,

3The word of the LORD came expressly unto Ezekiel the priest, the son of Buzi, in the land of the Chaldeans by the river Chebar; and the hand of the LORD was there upon him.

4And I looked, and, behold, a whirlwind came out of the north, a great cloud, and a fire infolding itself, and a brightness *was* about it, and out of the midst thereof as the colour of amber, out of the midst of the fire.

5Also out of the midst thereof *came* the likeness of four living creatures. And this *was* their appearance; they had the likeness of a man.

6And every one had four faces, and every one had four wings.

7And their feet *were* straight feet; and the sole of their feet *was* like the sole of a calf's foot: and they sparkled like the colour of burnished brass.

8And *they had* the hands of a man under their wings on their four sides; and they four had their faces and their wings.

9Their wings *were* joined one to another; they turned not when they went; they went every one straight forward.

¹⁰As for the likeness of their faces, they four had the face of a man, and the face of a lion, on the right side: and they four had the face of an ox on the left side; they four also had the face of an eagle.

¹¹Thus *were* their faces: and their wings *were* stretched upward; two *wings* of every one *were* joined one to another, and two covered their bodies.

¹²And they went every one straight forward: whither the spirit was to go, they went; *and* they turned not when they went.

¹³As for the likeness of the living creatures, their appearance *was* like burning coals of fire, *and* like the appearance of lamps: it went up and down among the living creatures; and the fire was bright, and out of the fire went forth lightning.

¹⁴And the living creatures ran and returned as the appearance of a flash of lightning.

¹⁵Now as I beheld the living creatures, behold one wheel upon the earth by the living creatures, with his four faces.

¹⁶The appearance of the wheels and their work *was* like unto the colour of a beryl: and they four had one likeness: and their appearance and their work *was* as it were a wheel in the middle of a wheel.

¹⁷When they went, they went upon their four sides: *and* they turned not when they went.

¹⁸As for their rings, they were so high that they were dreadful; and their rings *were* full of eyes round about them four.

¹⁹And when the living creatures went, the wheels went by them: and when the living creatures were lifted up from the earth, the wheels were lifted up.

²⁰Whithersoever the spirit was to go, they went, thither *was their* spirit to go; and the wheels were lifted up over against them: for the spirit of the living creature *was* in the wheels.

²¹When those went, *these* went; and when those stood, *these* stood; and when those were lifted up from the earth, the wheels were lifted up over against them: for the spirit of the living creature *was* in the wheels.

²²And the likeness of the firmament upon the heads of the living creature *was* as the colour of the terrible crystal, stretched forth over their heads above.

²³And under the firmament *were* their wings straight, the one toward the other: every one had two, which covered on this side, and every one had two, which covered on that side, their bodies.

²⁴And when they went, I heard the noise of their wings, like the noise of great waters, as the voice of the Almighty, the voice of speech, as the noise of an host: when they stood, they let down their wings.

²⁵And there was a voice from the firmament that *was* over their heads, when they stood, *and* had let down their wings.

²⁶And above the firmament that *was* over their heads *was* the likeness of a throne, as the appearance of a sapphire stone: and upon the likeness of the throne *was* the likeness as the appearance of a man above upon it.

²⁷And I saw as the colour of amber, as the appearance of fire round about within it, from the appearance of his loins even upward, and from the appearance of his loins even downward, I saw as it were the appearance of fire, and it had brightness round about.

²⁸As the appearance of the bow that is in the cloud in the day of rain, so *was* the appearance of the brightness round about. This *was* the appearance of the likeness of the glory of the LORD. And when I saw *it*, I fell upon my face, and I heard a voice of one that spake.

AND he said unto me, Son of man, stand upon thy feet, and I will speak unto thee.

2And the spirit entered into me when he spake unto me, and set me upon my feet, that I heard him that spake unto me.

3And he said unto me, Son of man, I send thee to the children of Israel, to a rebellious nation that hath rebelled against me: they and their fathers have transgressed against me, *even* unto this very day.

4For *they are* impudent children and stiffhearted. I do send thee unto them; and thou shalt say unto them, Thus saith the Lord GOD.

5And they, whether they will hear, or whether they will forbear, (for they *are* a rebellious house,) yet shall know that there hath been a prophet among them.

6And thou, son of man, be not afraid of them, neither be afraid of their words, though briers and thorns *be* with thee, and thou dost dwell among scorpions: be not afraid of their words, nor be dismayed at their looks, though they *be* a rebellious house.

7And thou shalt speak my words unto them, whether they will hear, or whether they will forbear: for they *are* most rebellious.

8But thou, son of man, hear what I say unto thee; Be not thou rebellious like that rebellious house: open thy mouth, and eat that I give thee.

9And when I looked, behold, an hand *was* sent unto me; and, lo, a roll of a book *was* therein;

10And he spread it before me; and it *was* written within and without: and *there was* written therein lamentations, and mourning, and woe.

MOREOVER he said unto me, Son of man, eat that thou findest; eat this roll, and go speak unto the house of Israel.

2So I opened my mouth, and he caused me to eat that roll.

3And he said unto me, Son of man, cause thy belly to eat, and fill thy bowels with this roll that I give thee. Then did I eat *it;* and it was in my mouth as honey for sweetness.

4And he said unto me, Son of man, go, get thee unto the house of Israel, and speak with my words unto them.

5For thou *art* not sent to a people of a strange speech and of an hard language, *but* to the house of Israel;

6Not to many people of a strange speech and of an hard language, whose words thou canst not understand. Surely, had I sent thee to them, they would have hearkened unto thee.

7But the house of Israel will not hearken unto thee; for they will not hearken unto me: for all the house of Israel *are* impudent and hardhearted.

8Behold, I have made thy face strong against their faces, and thy forehead strong against their foreheads.

9As an adamant harder than flint have I made thy forehead: fear them not, neither be dismayed at their looks, though they *be* a rebellious house.

10Moreover he said unto me, Son of man, all my words that I shall speak unto thee receive in thine heart, and hear with thine ears.

11And go, get thee to them of the captivity, unto the children of thy people, and speak unto them, and tell them, Thus saith the Lord GOD; whether they will hear, or whether they will forbear.

12Then the spirit took me up, and I heard behind me a voice of a great rushing, *saying,* Blessed *be* the glory of the LORD from his place.

13*I heard* also the noise of the wings of the living creatures that touched one another, and the noise of the wheels over against them, and a noise of a great rushing.

14So the spirit lifted me up, and took me away, and I went in bitterness, in the heat of my spirit; but the hand of the LORD was strong upon me.

15Then I came to them of the captivity

at Tel–abib, that dwelt by the river of Chebar, and I sat where they sat, and remained there astonished among them seven days.

HEBREWS 3:1–19

Wherefore, holy brethren, partakers of the heavenly calling, consider the Apostle and High Priest of our profession, Christ Jesus;

2Who was faithful to him that appointed him, as also Moses *was faithful* in all his house.

3For this *man* was counted worthy of more glory than Moses, inasmuch as he who hath builded the house hath more honour than the house.

4For every house is builded by some *man;* but he that built all things *is* God.

5And Moses verily *was* faithful in all his house, as a servant, for a testimony of those things which were to be spoken after;

6But Christ as a son over his own house; whose house are we, if we hold fast the confidence and the rejoicing of the hope firm unto the end.

7Wherefore (as the Holy Ghost saith, To day if ye will hear his voice,

8Harden not your hearts, as in the provocation, in the day of temptation in the wilderness:

9When your fathers tempted me, proved me, and saw my works forty years.

10Wherefore I was grieved with that generation, and said, They do alway err in *their* heart; and they have not known my ways.

11So I sware in my wrath, They shall not enter into my rest.)

12Take heed, brethren, lest there be in any of you an evil heart of unbelief, in departing from the living God.

13But exhort one another daily, while it is called To day; lest any of you be hardened through the deceitfulness of sin.

14For we are made partakers of Christ, if we hold the beginning of our confidence stedfast unto the end;

15While it is said, To day if ye will hear his voice, harden not your hearts, as in the provocation.

16For some, when they had heard, did provoke: howbeit not all that came out of Egypt by Moses.

17But with whom was he grieved forty years? *was it* not with them that had sinned, whose carcases fell in the wilderness?

18And to whom sware he that they should not enter into his rest, but to them that believed not?

19So we see that they could not enter in because of unbelief.

PSALM 104:1–24

Bless the Lord, O my soul. O Lord my God, thou art very great; thou art clothed with honour and majesty.

2Who coverest *thyself* with light as *with* a garment: who stretchest out the heavens like a curtain:

3Who layeth the beams of his chambers in the waters: who maketh the clouds his chariot: who walketh upon the wings of the wind:

4Who maketh his angels spirits; his ministers a flaming fire:

5*Who* laid the foundations of the earth, *that* it should not be removed for ever.

6Thou coveredst it with the deep as *with* a garment: the waters stood above the mountains.

7At thy rebuke they fled; at the voice of thy thunder they hasted away.

8They go up by the mountains; they go down by the valleys unto the place which thou hast founded for them.

9Thou hast set a bound that they may not pass over; that they turn not again to cover the earth.

10He sendeth the springs into the valleys, *which* run among the hills.

11They give drink to every beast of the field: the wild asses quench their thirst.

12By them shall the fowls of the heaven have their habitation, *which* sing among the branches.

13He watereth the hills from his chambers: the earth is satisfied with the fruit of thy works.

14He causeth the grass to grow for the cattle, and herb for the service of man: that he may bring forth food out of the earth;

15And wine *that* maketh glad the heart of man, *and* oil to make *his* face to shine, and bread *which* strengtheneth man's heart.

16The trees of the LORD are full *of sap;* the cedars of Lebanon, which he hath planted;

17Where the birds make their nests: *as for* the stork, the fir trees *are* her house.

18The high hills *are* a refuge for the wild goats; *and* the rocks for the conies.

19He appointed the moon for seasons: the sun knoweth his going down.

20Thou makest darkness and it is night: wherein all the beasts of the forest do creep *forth.*

21The young lions roar after their prey, and seek their meat from God.

22The sun ariseth, they gather themselves together, and lay them down in their dens.

23Man goeth forth unto his work and to his labour until the evening.

24O LORD, how manifold are thy works! in wisdom hast thou made them all: the earth is full of thy riches.

PROVERBS FOR TODAY/ 26:24–26

He that hateth dissembleth with his lips, and layeth up deceit within him; When he speaketh fair, believe him not: for there are *seven abominations in his heart.* Whose *hatred is covered by deceit, his wickedness shall be shewed before the* whole *congregation.*

NOVEMBER 2

EZEKIEL 3:16—6:14

AND it came to pass at the end of seven days, that the word of the LORD came unto me, saying,

17Son of man, I have made thee a watchman unto the house of Israel: therefore hear the word at my mouth, and give them warning from me.

18When I say unto the wicked, Thou shalt surely die; and thou givest him not warning, nor speakest to warn the wicked from his wicked way, to save his life; the same wicked *man* shall die

in his iniquity; but his blood will I require at thine hand.

19Yet if thou warn the wicked, and he turn not from his wickedness, nor from his wicked way, he shall die in his iniquity; but thou hast delivered thy soul.

20Again, When a righteous *man* doth turn from his righteousness, and commit iniquity, and I lay a stumblingblock before him, he shall die: because thou hast not given him warning, he shall die in his sin, and his righteousness which he hath done shall not be remembered; but his blood will I require at thine hand.

21Nevertheless if thou warn the righteous *man,* that the righteous sin not, and he doth not sin, he shall surely live, because he is warned; also thou hast delivered thy soul.

22And the hand of the LORD was there upon me; and he said unto me, Arise, go forth into the plain, and I will there talk with thee.

23Then I arose, and went forth into the plain: and, behold, the glory of the LORD stood there, as the glory which I saw by the river of Chebar: and I fell on my face.

24Then the spirit entered into me, and set me upon my feet, and spake with me, and said unto me, Go, shut thyself within thine house.

25But thou, O son of man, behold, they shall put bands upon thee, and shall bind thee with them, and thou shalt not go out among them:

26And I will make thy tongue cleave to the roof of thy mouth, that thou shalt be dumb, and shalt not be to them a reprover: for they *are* a rebellious house.

27But when I speak with thee, I will open thy mouth, and thou shalt say unto them, Thus saith the Lord GOD; He that heareth, let him hear; and he that forbeareth, let him forbear: for they *are* a rebellious house.

THOU also, son of man, take thee a tile, and lay it before thee, and portray upon it the city, *even* Jerusalem:

2And lay siege against it, and build a fort against it, and cast a mount against it; set the camp also against it, and set *battering* rams against it round about.

3Moreover take thou unto thee an iron pan, and set it *for* a wall of iron between thee and the city: and set thy face against it, and it shall be besieged, and thou shalt lay siege against it. This *shall be* a sign to the house of Israel.

4Lie thou also upon thy left side, and lay the iniquity of the house of Israel upon it: *according* to the number of the days that thou shalt lie upon it thou shalt bear their iniquity.

5For I have laid upon thee the years of their iniquity, according to the number of the days, three hundred and ninety days: so shalt thou bear the iniquity of the house of Israel.

6And when thou hast accomplished them, lie again on thy right side, and thou shalt bear the iniquity of the house of Judah forty days: I have appointed thee each day for a year.

7Therefore thou shalt set thy face toward the siege of Jerusalem, and thine arm *shall be* uncovered, and thou shalt prophesy against it.

8And, behold, I will lay bands upon thee, and thou shalt not turn thee from one side to another, till thou hast ended the days of thy siege.

9Take thou also unto thee wheat, and barley, and beans, and lentiles, and millet, and fitches, and put them in one vessel, and make thee bread thereof, *according* to the number of the days that thou shalt lie upon thy side, three hundred and ninety days shalt thou eat thereof.

10And thy meat which thou shalt eat *shall be* by weight, twenty shekels a day: from time to time shalt thou eat it.

11Thou shalt drink also water by measure, the sixth part of an hin: from time to time shalt thou drink.

12And thou shalt eat it *as* barley cakes, and thou shalt bake it with dung that cometh out of man, in their sight.

13And the LORD said, Even thus shall the children of Israel eat their defiled bread among the Gentiles, whither I will drive them.

14Then said I, Ah Lord GOD! behold, my soul hath not been polluted; for from my youth up even till now have I not eaten of that which dieth of itself, or is torn in pieces; neither came there abominable flesh into my mouth.

15Then he said unto me, Lo, I have given thee cow's dung for man's dung, and thou shalt prepare thy bread therewith.

16Moreover he said unto me, Son of man, behold, I will break the staff of bread in Jerusalem: and they shall eat bread by weight, and with care; and they shall drink water by measure, and with astonishment:

17That they may want bread and water, and be astonied one with another, and consume away for their iniquity.

AND thou, son of man, take thee a sharp knife, take thee a barber's razor, and cause *it* to pass upon thine head and upon thy beard: then take thee balances to weigh, and divide the *hair.*

2Thou shalt burn with fire a third part in the midst of the city, when the days of the siege are fulfilled: and thou shalt take a third part, *and* smite about it with a knife: and a third part thou shalt scatter in the wind; and I will draw out a sword after them.

3Thou shalt also take thereof a few in number, and bind them in thy skirts.

4Then take of them again, and cast them into the midst of the fire, and burn them in the fire; *for* thereof shall a fire come forth into all the house of Israel.

5Thus saith the Lord GOD; This *is* Jerusalem: I have set it in the midst of the nations and countries *that are* round about her.

6And she hath changed my judgments into wickedness more than the nations, and my statutes more than the countries that *are* round about her: for they have refused my judgments and my statutes, they have not walked in them.

7Therefore thus saith the Lord GOD; Because ye multiplied more than the nations that *are* round about you, *and* have not walked in my statutes, neither have kept my judgments, neither have done according to the judgments of the nations that *are* round about you;

8Therefore thus saith the Lord GOD; Behold, I, even I, *am* against thee, and will execute judgments in the midst of thee in the sight of the nations.

9And I will do in thee that which I have not done, and whereunto I will not do any more the like, because of all thine abominations.

10Therefore the fathers shall eat the sons in the midst of thee, and the sons shall eat their fathers; and I will execute judgments in thee, and the whole remnant of thee will I scatter into all the winds.

11Wherefore, *as* I live, saith the Lord GOD; surely, because thou hast defiled my sanctuary with all thy detestable things, and with all thine abominations, therefore will I also diminish *thee;* neither shall mine eye spare, neither will I have any pity.

12A third part of thee shall die with the pestilence, and with famine shall they be consumed in the midst of thee: and a third part shall fall by the sword round about thee; and I will scatter a third part into all the winds, and I will draw out a sword after them.

13Thus shall mine anger be accomplished, and I will cause my fury to rest upon them, and I will be comforted: and they shall know that I the LORD have spoken *it* in my zeal, when I have accomplished my fury in them.

14Moreover I will make thee waste, and a reproach among the nations that *are* round about thee, in the sight of all that pass by.

15So it shall be a reproach and a taunt, an instruction and an astonishment unto the nations that *are* round about thee, when I shall execute judgments in thee in anger and in fury and in furious rebukes. I the LORD have spoken *it.*

16When I shall send upon them the evil arrows of famine, which shall be for *their* destruction, *and* which I will send to destroy you: and I will increase the famine upon you, and will break your staff of bread:

17So will I send upon you famine and evil beasts, and they shall bereave thee; and pestilence and blood shall pass through thee; and I will bring the sword upon thee. I the LORD have spoken *it*.

AND the word of the LORD came unto me, saying,

2Son of man, set thy face toward the mountains of Israel, and prophesy against them,

3And say, Ye mountains of Israel, hear the word of the Lord GOD; Thus saith the Lord GOD to the mountains, and to the hills, to the rivers, and to the valleys; Behold, I, *even* I, will bring a sword upon you, and I will destroy your high places.

4And your altars shall be desolate, and your images shall be broken: and I will cast down your slain *men* before your idols.

5And I will lay the dead carcases of the children of Israel before their idols; and I will scatter your bones round about your altars.

6In all your dwellingplaces the cities shall be laid waste, and the high places shall be desolate; that your altars may be laid waste and made desolate, and your idols may be broken and cease, and your images may be cut down, and your works may be abolished.

7And the slain shall fall in the midst of you, and ye shall know that I *am* the LORD.

8Yet will I leave a remnant, that ye may have *some* that shall escape the sword among the nations, when ye shall be scattered through the countries.

9And they that escape of you shall remember me among the nations whither they shall be carried captives, because I am broken with their whorish heart, which hath departed from me, and with their eyes, which go a whoring after their idols: and they shall lothe themselves for the evils which they have committed in all their abominations.

10And they shall know that I *am* the LORD, *and that* I have not said in vain that I would do this evil unto them.

11Thus saith the Lord GOD; Smite with thine hand, and stamp with thy foot, and say, Alas for all the evil abominations of the house of Israel! for they shall fall by the sword, by the famine, and by the pestilence.

12He that is far off shall die of the pestilence; and he that is near shall fall by the sword; and he that remaineth and is besieged shall die by the famine: thus will I accomplish my fury upon them.

13Then shall ye know that I *am* the LORD, when their slain *men* shall be among their idols round about their altars, upon every high hill, in all the tops of the mountains, and under every green tree, and under every thick oak, the place where they did offer sweet savour to all their idols.

14So will I stretch out my hand upon them, and make the land desolate, yea, more desolate than the wilderness toward Diblath, in all their habitations: and they shall know that I *am* the LORD.

HEBREWS 4:1–16

LET us therefore fear, lest, a promise being left *us* of entering into his rest, any of you should seem to come short of it.

2For unto us was the gospel preached, as well as unto them: but the word preached did not profit them, not being mixed with faith in them that heard *it*.

3For we which have believed do enter into rest, as he said, As I have sworn in my wrath, if they shall enter into my rest: although the works were finished from the foundation of the world.

4For he spake in a certain place of the seventh *day* on this wise, And God did rest the seventh day from all his works.

5And in this *place* again, If they shall enter into my rest.

6Seeing therefore it remaineth that some must enter therein, and they to whom it was first preached entered not in because of unbelief:

7Again, he limiteth a certain day, saying in David, To day, after so long a time; as it is said, To day if ye will hear his voice, harden not your hearts.

8For if Jesus had given them rest, then would he not afterward have spoken of another day.

9There remaineth therefore a rest to the people of God.

10For he that is entered into his rest, he also hath ceased from his own works, as God *did* from his.

11Let us labour therefore to enter into that rest, lest any man fall after the same example of unbelief.

12For the word of God *is* quick, and powerful, and sharper than any two-edged sword, piercing even to the dividing asunder of soul and spirit, and of the joints and marrow, and *is* a discerner of the thoughts and intents of the heart.

13Neither is there any creature that is not manifest in his sight: but all things *are* naked and opened unto the eyes of him with whom we have to do.

14Seeing then that we have a great high priest, that is passed into the heavens, Jesus the Son of God, let us hold fast *our* profession.

15For we have not an high priest which cannot be touched with the feeling of our infirmities; but was in all points tempted like as *we are, yet* without sin.

16Let us therefore come boldly unto the throne of grace, that we may obtain mercy, and find grace to help in time of need.

PSALM 104:25–35

So is this great and wide sea, wherein *are* things creeping innumerable, both small and great beasts.

26There go the ships: *there is* that leviathan, *whom* thou hast made to play therein.

27These wait all upon thee; that thou mayest give *them* their meat in due season.

28*That* thou givest them they gather: thou openest thine hand, they are filled with good.

29Thou hidest thy face, they are troubled: thou takest away their breath, they die, and return to their dust.

30Thou sendest forth thy spirit, they are created: and thou renewest the face of the earth.

31The glory of the LORD shall endure for ever: the LORD shall rejoice in his works.

32He looketh on the earth, and it trembleth: he toucheth the hills, and they smoke.

33I will sing unto the LORD as long as I live: I will sing praise to my God while I have my being.

34My meditation of him shall be sweet: I will be glad in the LORD.

35Let the sinners be consumed out of the earth, and let the wicked be no more. Bless thou the LORD, O my soul. Praise ye the LORD.

PROVERBS FOR TODAY/ 26:27

Whoso diggeth a pit shall fall therein: and he that rolleth a stone, it will return upon him.

EZEKIEL 7:1—9:11

MOREOVER the word of the LORD came unto me, saying,

2Also, thou son of man, thus saith the Lord GOD unto the land of Israel; An end, the end is come upon the four corners of the land.

3Now *is* the end *come* upon thee, and I will send mine anger upon thee, and will judge thee according to thy ways, and will recompense upon thee all thine abominations.

4And mine eye shall not spare thee, neither will I have pity: but I will recompense thy ways upon thee, and thine abominations shall be in the midst of thee: and ye shall know that I *am* the LORD.

5Thus saith the Lord GOD; An evil, an only evil, behold, is come.

6An end is come, the end is come: it watcheth for thee; behold, it is come.

7The morning is come unto thee, O thou that dwellest in the land: the time is come, the day of trouble *is* near, and not the sounding again of the mountains.

8Now will I shortly pour out my fury upon thee, and accomplish mine anger upon thee: and I will judge thee according to thy ways, and will recompense thee for all thine abominations.

9And mine eye shall not spare, neither will I have pity: I will recompense thee according to thy ways and thine abominations *that* are in the midst of thee; and ye shall know that I *am* the LORD that smiteth.

10Behold the day, behold, it is come: the morning is gone forth; the rod hath blossomed, pride hath budded.

11Violence is risen up into a rod of wickedness: none of them *shall remain,* nor of their multitude, nor of any of theirs: neither *shall there be* wailing for them.

12The time is come, the day draweth near: let not the buyer rejoice, nor the seller mourn: for wrath *is* upon all the multitude thereof.

13For the seller shall not return to that which is sold, although they were yet alive: for the vision *is* touching the whole multitude thereof, *which* shall not return; neither shall any strengthen himself in the iniquity of his life.

14They have blown the trumpet, even to make all ready; but none goeth to the battle: for my wrath *is* upon all the multitude thereof.

15The sword *is* without, and the pestilence and the famine within: he that *is* in the field shall die with the sword; and he that *is* in the city, famine and pestilence shall devour him.

16But they that escape of them shall escape, and shall be on the mountains like doves of the valleys, all of them mourning, every one for his iniquity.

17All hands shall be feeble, and all knees shall be weak *as* water.

18They shall also gird *themselves* with sackcloth, and horror shall cover them; and shame *shall be* upon all faces, and baldness upon all their heads.

19They shall cast their silver in the streets, and their gold shall be removed: their silver and their gold shall not be able to deliver them in the day of the wrath of the LORD: they shall not satisfy their souls, neither fill their bowels: because it is the stumblingblock of their iniquity.

20As for the beauty of his ornament, he set it in majesty: but they made the images of their abominations *and* of their detestable things therein: therefore have I set it far from them.

21And I will give it into the hands

of the strangers for a prey, and to the wicked of the earth for a spoil; and they shall pollute it.

22My face will I turn also from them, and they shall pollute my secret *place:* for the robbers shall enter into it, and defile it.

23Make a chain: for the land is full of bloody crimes, and the city is full of violence.

24Wherefore I will bring the worst of the heathen, and they shall possess their houses: I will also make the pomp of the strong to cease; and their holy places shall be defiled.

25Destruction cometh; and they shall seek peace, and *there shall be* none.

26Mischief shall come upon mischief, and rumour shall be upon rumour; then shall they seek a vision of the prophet; but the law shall perish from the priest, and counsel from the ancients.

27The king shall mourn, and the prince shall be clothed with desolation, and the hands of the people of the land shall be troubled: I will do unto them after their way, and according to their deserts will I judge them; and they shall know that I *am* the Lord.

And it came to pass in the sixth year, in the sixth *month,* in the fifth *day* of the month, *as* I sat in mine house, and the elders of Judah sat before me, that the hand of the Lord God fell there upon me.

2Then I beheld, and lo a likeness as the appearance of fire: from the appearance of his loins even downward, fire; and from his loins even upward, as the appearance of brightness, as the colour of amber.

3And he put forth the form of an hand, and took me by a lock of mine head; and the spirit lifted me up between the earth and the heaven, and brought me in the visions of God to Jerusalem, to the door of the inner gate that looketh toward the north; where *was* the seat of the image of jealousy, which pro-voketh to jealousy.

4And, behold, the glory of the God of Israel *was* there, according to the vision that I saw in the plain.

5Then said he unto me, Son of man, lift up thine eyes now the way toward the north. So I lifted up mine eyes the way toward the north, and behold northward at the gate of the altar this image of jealousy in the entry.

6He said furthermore unto me, Son of man, seest thou what they do? *even* the great abominations that the house of Israel committeth here, that I should go far off from my sanctuary? but turn thee yet again, *and* thou shalt see greater abominations.

7And he brought me to the door of the court; and when I looked, behold a hole in the wall.

8Then said he unto me, Son of man, dig now in the wall: and when I had digged in the wall, behold a door.

9And he said unto me, Go in, and behold the wicked abominations that they do here.

10So I went in and saw; and behold every form of creeping things, and abominable beasts, and all the idols of the house of Israel, pourtrayed upon the wall round about.

11And there stood before them seventy men of the ancients of the house of Israel, and in the midst of them stood Jaazaniah the son of Shaphan, with every man his censer in his hand; and a thick cloud of incense went up.

12Then said he unto me, Son of man, hast thou seen what the ancients of the house of Israel do in the dark, every man in the chambers of his imagery? for they say, The Lord seeth us not; the Lord hath forsaken the earth.

13He said also unto me, Turn thee yet again, *and* thou shalt see greater abominations that they do.

14Then he brought me to the door of the gate of the Lord's house which *was* toward the north; and, behold, there sat women weeping for Tammuz.

15Then said he unto me, Hast thou seen *this*, O son of man? turn thee yet again, *and* thou shalt see greater abominations than these.

16And he brought me into the inner court of the LORD'S house, and, behold, at the door of the temple of the LORD, between the porch and the altar, *were* about five and twenty men, with their backs toward the temple of the LORD, and their faces toward the east; and they worshipped the sun toward the east.

17Then he said unto me, Hast thou seen *this*, O son of man? Is it a light thing to the house of Judah that they commit the abominations which they commit here? for they have filled the land with violence, and have returned to provoke me to anger: and, lo, they put the branch to their nose.

18Therefore will I also deal in fury: mine eye shall not spare, neither will I have pity: and though they cry in mine ears with a loud voice, *yet* will I not hear them.

HE cried also in mine ears with a loud voice, saying, Cause them that have charge over the city to draw near, even every man *with* his destroying weapon in his hand.

2And, behold, six men came from the way of the higher gate, which lieth toward the north, and every man a slaughter weapon in his hand; and one man among them *was* clothed with linen, with a writer's inkhorn by his side: and they went in, and stood beside the brasen altar.

3And the glory of the God of Israel was gone up from the cherub, whereupon he was, to the threshold of the house. And he called to the man clothed with linen, which *had* the writer's inkhorn by his side;

4And the LORD said unto him, Go through the midst of the city, through the midst of Jerusalem, and set a mark upon the foreheads of the men that sigh and that cry for all the abominations that be done in the midst thereof.

5And to the others he said in mine hearing, Go ye after him through the city, and smite: let not your eye spare, neither have ye pity:

6Slay utterly old *and* young, both maids, and little children, and women: but come not near any man upon whom *is* the mark; and begin at my sanctuary. Then they began at the ancient men which *were* before the house.

7And he said unto them, Defile the house, and fill the courts with the slain: go ye forth. And they went forth, and slew in the city.

8And it came to pass, while they were slaying them, and I was left, that I fell upon my face, and cried, and said, Ah Lord GOD! wilt thou destroy all the residue of Israel in thy pouring out of thy fury upon Jerusalem?

9Then said he unto me, The iniquity of the house of Israel and Judah *is* exceeding great, and the land is full of blood, and the city full of perverseness: for they say, the LORD hath forsaken the earth, and the LORD seeth not.

10And as for me also, mine eye shall not spare, neither will I have pity, *but* I will recompense their way upon their head.

11And, behold, the man clothed with linen, which *had* the inkhorn by his side, reported the matter, saying, I have done as thou hast commanded me.

HEBREWS 5:1–14

FOR every high priest taken from among men is ordained for men in things *pertaining* to God, that he may offer both gifts and sacrifices for sins:

2Who can have compassion on the ignorant, and on them that are out of the way; for that he himself also is compassed with infirmity.

3And by reason hereof he ought, as

for the people, so also for himself, to offer for sins.

4And no man taketh this honour unto himself, but he that is called of God, as *was* Aaron.

5So also Christ glorified not himself to be made an high priest; but he that said unto him, Thou art my Son, to day have I begotten thee.

6As he saith also in another *place,* Thou *art* a priest for ever after the order of Melchisedec.

7Who in the days of his flesh, when he had offered up prayers and supplications with strong crying and tears unto him that was able to save him from death, and was heard in that he feared;

8Though he were a Son, yet learned he obedience by the things which he suffered;

9And being made perfect, he became the author of eternal salvation unto all them that obey him;

10Called of God an high priest after the order of Melchisedec.

11Of whom we have many things to say, and hard to be uttered, seeing ye are dull of hearing.

12For when for the time ye ought to be teachers, ye have need that one teach you again which *be* the first principles of the oracles of God; and are become such as have need of milk, and not of strong meat.

13For every one that useth milk *is* unskilful in the word of righteousness: for he is a babe.

14But strong meat belongeth to them that are of full age, *even* those who by reason of use have their senses exercised to discern both good and evil.

PSALM 105:1–15

O GIVE thanks unto the LORD; call upon his name: make known his deeds among the people.

2Sing unto him, sing psalms unto him: talk ye of all his wondrous works.

3Glory ye in his holy name: let the heart of them rejoice that seek the LORD.

4Seek the LORD, and his strength: seek his face evermore.

5Remember his marvellous works that he hath done; his wonders, and the judgments of his mouth;

6O ye seed of Abraham his servant, ye children of Jacob his chosen.

7He *is* the LORD our God: his judgments *are* in all the earth.

8He hath remembered his covenant for ever, the word *which* he commanded to a thousand generations.

9Which *covenant* he made with Abraham, and his oath unto Isaac;

10And confirmed the same unto Jacob for a law, *and* to Israel *for* an everlasting covenant:

11Saying, Unto thee will I give the land of Canaan, the lot of your inheritance:

12When they were *but* a few men in number; yea, very few, and strangers in it.

13When they went from one nation to another, from *one* kingdom to another people;

14He suffered no man to do them wrong: yea, he reproved kings for their sakes;

15*Saying,* Touch not mine anointed, and do my prophets no harm.

PROVERBS FOR TODAY/ 26:28

A lying tongue hateth those that are afflicted by it; and a flattering mouth worketh ruin.

NOVEMBER 4

EZEKIEL 10:1—11:25

THEN I looked, and, behold, in the firmament that was above the head of the cherubims there appeared over them as it were a sapphire stone, as the appearance of the likeness of a throne.

2And he spake unto the man clothed with linen, and said, Go in between the wheels, *even* under the cherub, and fill thine hand with coals of fire from between the cherubims, and scatter *them* over the city. And he went in in my sight.

3Now the cherubims stood on the right side of the house, when the man went in; and the cloud filled the inner court.

4Then the glory of the LORD went up from the cherub, *and stood* over the threshold of the house; and the house was filled with the cloud, and the court was full of the brightness of the LORD's glory.

5And the sound of the cherubims' wings was heard *even* to the outer court, as the voice of the Almighty God when he speaketh.

6And it came to pass, *that* when he had commanded the man clothed with linen, saying, Take fire from between the wheels, from between the cherubims; then he went in, and stood beside the wheels.

7And *one* cherub stretched forth his hand from between the cherubims unto the fire that *was* between the cherubims, and took *thereof,* and put *it* into the hands of *him that was* clothed with linen: who took *it,* and went out.

8And there appeared in the cherubims the form of a man's hand under their wings.

9And when I looked, behold the four wheels by the cherubims, one wheel by one cherub, and another wheel by another cherub: and the appearance of the wheels *was* as the colour of a beryl stone.

10And *as for* their appearances, they four had one likeness, as if a wheel had been in the midst of a wheel.

11When they went, they went upon their four sides; they turned not as they went, but to the place whither the head looked they followed it; they turned not as they went.

12And their whole body, and their backs, and their hands, and their wings, and the wheels, *were* full of eyes round about, *even* the wheels that they four had.

13As for the wheels, it was cried unto them in my hearing, O wheel.

14And every one had four faces: the first face *was* the face of a cherub, and the second face *was* the face of a man, and the third the face of a lion, and the fourth the face of an eagle.

15And the cherubims were lifted up. This *is* the living creature that I saw by the river of Chebar.

16And when the cherubims went, the wheels went by them: and when the cherubims lifted up their wings to mount up from the earth, the same wheels also turned not from beside them.

17When they stood, *these* stood; and when they were lifted up, *these* lifted up themselves *also:* for the spirit of the living creature *was* in them.

18Then the glory of the LORD departed from off the threshold of the house, and stood over the cherubims.

19And the cherubims lifted up their wings, and mounted up from the earth in my sight: when they went out, the wheels also *were* beside them, and *every one* stood at the door of the east gate of the LORD's house; and the glory of the God of Israel *was* over them above.

20This *is* the living creature that I saw under the God of Israel by the river of Chebar; and I knew that they *were* the cherubims.

21Every one had four faces apiece, and every one four wings; and the likeness of the hands of a man *was* under their wings.

22And the likeness of their faces *was* the same faces which I saw by the river of Chebar, their appearances and themselves: they went every one straight forward.

MOREOVER the spirit lifted me up, and brought me unto the east gate of the LORD'S house, which looketh eastward: and behold at the door of the gate five and twenty men; among whom I saw Jaazaniah the son of Azur, and Pelatiah the son of Benaiah, princes of the people.

2Then said he unto me, Son of man, these *are* the men that devise mischief, and give wicked counsel in this city:

3Which say, *It is* not near; let us build houses: this *city is* the caldron, and we *be* the flesh.

4Therefore prophesy against them, prophesy, O son of man.

5And the Spirit of the LORD fell upon me, and said unto me, Speak; thus saith the LORD; Thus have ye said, O house of Israel: for I know the things that come into your mind, *every one of* them.

6Ye have multiplied your slain in this city, and ye have filled the streets thereof with the slain.

7Therefore thus saith the LORD GOD; Your slain whom ye have laid in the midst of it, they *are* the flesh, and this *city is* the caldron: but I will bring you forth out of the midst of it.

8Ye have feared the sword; and I will bring a sword upon you, saith the Lord GOD.

9And I will bring you out of the midst thereof, and deliver you into the hands of strangers, and will execute judgments among you.

10Ye shall fall by the sword; I will judge you in the border of Israel; and ye shall know that I *am* the LORD.

11This *city* shall not be your caldron, neither shall ye be the flesh in the midst thereof; *but* I will judge you in the border of Israel:

12And ye shall know that I *am* the LORD: for ye have not walked in my statutes, neither executed my judgments, but have done after the manners of the heathen that *are* round about you.

13And it came to pass, when I prophesied, that Pelatiah the son of Benaiah died. Then fell I down upon my face, and cried with a loud voice, and said, Ah Lord GOD! wilt thou make a full end of the remnant of Israel?

14Again the word of the LORD came unto me, saying,

15Son of man, thy brethren, *even* thy brethren, the men of thy kindred, and all the house of Israel wholly, *are* they unto whom the inhabitants of Jerusalem have said, Get you far from the LORD: unto us is this land given in possession.

16Therefore say, Thus saith the Lord GOD; Although I have cast them far off among the heathen, and although I have scattered them among the countries, yet will I be to them as a little sanctuary in the countries where they shall come.

17Therefore say, Thus saith the Lord GOD; I will even gather you from the people, and assemble you out of the countries where ye have been scattered, and I will give you the land of Israel.

18And they shall come thither, and they shall take away all the detestable things thereof and all the abominations thereof from thence.

19And I will give them one heart, and I will put a new spirit within you; and I will take the stony heart out of their flesh, and will give them an heart of flesh:

20That they may walk in my statutes, and keep mine ordinances, and do them: and they shall be my people, and I will be their God.

21But *as for them* whose heart walketh after the heart of their detestable things and their abominations, I will recompense their way upon their own heads, saith the Lord GOD.

22Then did the cherubims lift up their wings, and the wheels beside them; and the glory of the God of Israel *was* over them above.

23And the glory of the LORD went up from the midst of the city, and stood upon the mountain which *is* on the east side of the city.

24Afterwards the spirit took me up, and brought me in a vision by the Spirit of God into Chaldea, to them of the captivity. So the vision that I had seen went up from me.

25Then I spake unto them of the captivity all the things that the LORD had shewed me.

HEBREWS 6:1–20

THEREFORE leaving the principles of the doctrine of Christ, let us go on unto perfection; not laying again the foundation of repentance from dead works, and of faith toward God,

2Of the doctrine of baptisms, and of laying on of hands, and of resurrection of the dead, and of eternal judgment.

3And this will we do, if God permit.

4For *it is* impossible for those who were once enlightened, and have tasted of the heavenly gift, and were made partakers of the Holy Ghost,

5And have tasted the good word of God, and the powers of the world to come,

6If they shall fall away, to renew them again unto repentance; seeing they crucify to themselves the Son of God afresh, and put *him* to an open shame.

7For the earth which drinketh in the rain that cometh oft upon it, and bringeth forth herbs meet for them by whom it is dressed, receiveth blessing from God:

8But that which beareth thorns and briers *is* rejected, and *is* nigh unto cursing; whose end *is* to be burned.

9But, beloved, we are persuaded better things of you, and things that accompany salvation, though we thus speak.

10For God *is* not unrighteous to forget your work and labour of love, which ye have shewed toward his name, in that ye have ministered to the saints, and do minister.

11And we desire that every one of you do shew the same diligence to the full assurance of hope unto the end:

12That ye be not slothful, but followers of them who through faith and patience inherit the promises.

13For when God made promise to Abraham, because he could swear by no greater, he sware by himself,

14Saying, Surely blessing I will bless thee, and multiplying I will multiply thee.

15And so, after he had patiently endured, he obtained the promise.

16For men verily swear by the greater: and an oath for confirmation *is* to them an end of all strife.

17Wherein God, willing more abundantly to shew unto the heirs of promise the immutability of his counsel, confirmed *it* by an oath:

18That by two immutable things, in which *it was* impossible for God to lie, we might have a strong consolation, who have fled for refuge to lay hold upon the hope set before us:

19Which *hope* we have as an anchor of the soul, both sure and stedfast, and which entereth into that within the veil;

20Whither the forerunner is for us entered, *even* Jesus, made an high priest for ever after the order of Melchisedec.

PSALM 105:16–38

MOREOVER he called for a famine upon the land: he brake the whole staff of bread.

17He sent a man before them, *even* Joseph, *who* was sold for a servant:

18Whose feet they hurt with fetters: he was laid in iron:

19Until the time that his word came: the word of the LORD tried him.

20The king sent and loosed him; *even* the ruler of the people, and let him go free.

21He made him lord of his house, and ruler of all his substance:

22To bind his princes at his pleasure; and teach his senators wisdom.

23Israel also came into Egypt; and Jacob sojourned in the land of Ham.

24And he increased his people greatly; and made them stronger than their enemies.

25He turned their heart to hate his people, to deal subtilely with his servants.

26He sent Moses his servant; *and* Aaron whom he had chosen.

27They shewed his signs among them, and wonders in the land of Ham.

28He sent darkness, and made it dark; and they rebelled not against his word.

29He turned their waters into blood, and slew their fish.

30Their land brought forth frogs in abundance, in the chambers of their kings.

31He spake, and there came divers sorts of flies, *and* lice in all their coasts.

32He gave them hail for rain, *and* flaming fire in their land.

33He smote their vines also and their fig trees; and brake the trees of their coasts.

34He spake, and the locusts came, and caterpillers, and that without number,

35And did eat up all the herbs in their land, and devoured the fruit of their ground.

36He smote also all the firstborn in their land, the chief of all their strength.

37He brought them forth also with silver and gold: and *there was* not one feeble *person* among their tribes.

38Egypt was glad when they departed: for the fear of them fell upon them.

PROVERBS FOR TODAY/ 27:1–2

Boast not thyself of tomorrow; for thou knowest not what a day may bring forth. □ *Let another man praise thee, and not thine own mouth; a stranger, and not thine own lips.*

NOVEMBER 5

EZEKIEL 12:1—14:11

THE word of the LORD also came unto me, saying,

2Son of man, thou dwellest in the midst of a rebellious house, which have eyes to see, and see not; they have ears to hear, and hear not: for they *are* a rebellious house.

3Therefore, thou son of man, prepare thee stuff for removing, and remove by day in their sight; and thou shalt remove from thy place to another place in their sight: it may be they will consider, though they *be* a rebellious house.

4Then shalt thou bring forth thy stuff by day in their sight, as stuff for removing: and thou shalt go forth at even in their sight, as they that go forth into captivity.

5Dig thou through the walls in their sight, and carry out thereby.

6In their sight shalt thou bear *it* upon *thy* shoulders, *and* carry *it* forth in the twilight: thou shalt cover thy face, that thou see not the ground: for I have set thee *for* a sign unto the house of Israel.

7And I did so as I was commanded: I brought forth my stuff by day, as stuff for captivity, and in the even I digged through the wall with mine hand; I brought *it* forth in the twilight, *and* I bare *it* upon *my* shoulder in their sight.

8And in the morning came the word of the LORD unto me, saying,

9Son of man, hath not the house of Israel, the rebellious house, said unto thee, What doest thou?

10Say thou unto them, Thus saith the Lord GOD; This burden *concerneth* the prince in Jerusalem, and all the house of Israel that *are* among them.

11Say, I *am* your sign: like as I have done, so shall it be done unto them: they shall remove *and* go into captivity.

12And the prince that *is* among them shall bear upon *his* shoulder in the twilight, and shall go forth: they shall dig through the wall to carry out thereby: he shall cover his face, that he see not the ground with *his* eyes.

13My net also will I spread upon him, and he shall be taken in my snare: and I will bring him to Babylon *to* the land of the Chaldeans; yet shall he not see it, though he shall die there.

14And I will scatter toward every wind all that *are* about him to help him, and all his bands; and I will draw out the sword after them.

15And they shall know that I *am* the LORD, when I shall scatter them among the nations, and disperse them in the countries.

16But I will leave a few men of them from the sword, from the famine, and from the pestilence; that they may declare all their abominations among the heathen whither they come; and they shall know that I *am* the LORD.

17Moreover the word of the LORD came to me, saying,

18Son of man, eat thy bread with quaking, and drink thy water with trembling and with carefulness;

19And say unto the people of the land, Thus saith the Lord GOD of the inhabitants of Jerusalem, *and* of the land of Israel; They shall eat their bread with carefulness, and drink their water with astonishment, that her land may be desolate from all that is therein, because of the violence of all them that dwell therein.

20And the cities that are inhabited shall be laid waste, and the land shall be desolate; and ye shall know that I *am* the LORD.

21And the word of the LORD came unto me, saying,

22Son of man, what *is* that proverb *that* ye have in the land of Israel, saying, The days are prolonged, and every vision faileth?

23Tell them therefore, Thus saith the Lord GOD; I will make this proverb to cease, and they shall no more use it as a proverb in Israel; but say unto them, The days are at hand, and the effect of every vision.

24For there shall be no more any vain vision nor flattering divination within the house of Israel.

25For I *am* the LORD: I will speak, and the word that I shall speak shall come to pass; it shall be no more prolonged: for in your days, O rebellious house, will I say the word, and will perform it, saith the Lord GOD.

26Again the word of the LORD came to me, saying,

27Son of man, behold, *they of* the house of Israel say, The vision that he seeth *is* for many days *to come,* and he prophesieth of the times *that are* far off.

28Therefore say unto them, Thus saith the Lord GOD; There shall none of my words be prolonged any more, but the word which I have spoken shall be done, saith the Lord GOD.

AND the word of the LORD came unto me, saying,

2Son of man, prophesy against the prophets of Israel that prophesy, and say thou unto them that prophesy out of their own hearts, Hear ye the word of the LORD;

3Thus saith the Lord GOD; Woe unto the foolish prophets, that follow their own spirit, and have seen nothing!

4O Israel, thy prophets are like the foxes in the deserts.

5Ye have not gone up into the gaps, neither made up the hedge for the house of Israel to stand in the battle in the day of the LORD.

6They have seen vanity and lying divination, saying, The LORD saith: and the LORD hath not sent them: and they have made *others* to hope that they would confirm the word.

7Have ye not seen a vain vision, and have ye not spoken a lying divination, whereas ye say, The LORD saith *it;* albeit I have not spoken?

8Therefore thus saith the Lord GOD; Because ye have spoken vanity, and seen lies, therefore, behold, I *am* against you, saith the Lord GOD.

9And mine hand shall be upon the prophets that see vanity, and that divine lies: they shall not be in the assembly of my people, neither shall they be written in the writing of the house of Israel, neither shall they enter into the land of Israel; and ye shall know that I *am* the Lord GOD.

10Because, even because they have seduced my people, saying, Peace; and *there was* no peace; and one built up a wall, and, lo, others daubed it with untempered *morter:*

11Say unto them which daub *it* with untempered *morter,* that it shall fall: there shall be an overflowing shower; and ye, O great hailstones, shall fall; and a stormy wind shall rend *it.*

12Lo, when the wall is fallen, shall it not be said unto you, Where *is* the daubing wherewith ye have daubed *it?*

13Therefore thus saith the Lord GOD; I will even rend *it* with a stormy wind in my fury; and there shall be an overflowing shower in mine anger, and great hailstones in *my* fury to consume *it.*

14So will I break down the wall that ye have daubed with untempered *morter,* and bring it down to the ground, so that the foundation thereof shall be discovered, and it shall fall, and ye shall be consumed in the midst thereof: and ye shall know that I *am* the LORD.

15Thus will I accomplish my wrath upon the wall, and upon them that have daubed it with untempered *morter,* and will say unto you, The wall *is* no *more,* neither they that daubed it;

16*To wit,* the prophets of Israel which prophesy concerning Jerusalem, and which see visions of peace for her, and *there is* no peace, saith the Lord GOD.

17Likewise, thou son of man, set thy face against the daughters of thy people, which prophesy out of their own heart; and prophesy thou against them,

18And say, Thus saith the Lord GOD; Woe to the *women* that sew pillows to all armholes, and make kerchiefs upon the head of every stature to hunt souls! Will ye hunt the souls of my people, and will ye save the souls alive *that come* unto you?

19And will ye pollute me among my people for handfuls of barley and for pieces of bread, to slay the souls that should not die, and to save the souls alive that should not live, by your lying to my people that hear *your* lies?

20Wherefore thus saith the Lord GOD; Behold, I *am* against your pillows, wherewith ye there hunt the souls to make *them* fly, and I will tear them from your arms, and will let the souls go, *even* the souls that ye hunt to make *them* fly.

21Your kerchiefs also will I tear, and deliver my people out of your hand, and they shall be no more in your hand to be hunted; and ye shall know that I *am* the LORD.

22Because with lies ye have made the heart of the righteous sad, whom I have not made sad; and strengthened the hands of the wicked, that he should not return from his wicked way, by promising him life:

23Therefore ye shall see no more vanity, nor divine divinations: for I will deliver my people out of your hand: and ye shall know that I *am* the LORD.

THEN came certain of the elders of Israel unto me, and sat before me.

2And the word of the LORD came unto me, saying,

3Son of man, these men have set up their idols in their heart, and put the stumblingblock of their iniquity before their face: should I be enquired of at all by them?

4Therefore speak unto them, and say unto them, Thus saith the Lord GOD; Every man of the house of Israel that setteth up his idols in his heart, and putteth the stumblingblock of his iniquity before his face, and cometh to the prophet; I the LORD will answer him that cometh according to the multitude of his idols;

5That I may take the house of Israel in their own heart, because they are all estranged from me through their idols.

6Therefore say unto the house of Israel, Thus saith the Lord GOD; Repent, and turn *yourselves* from your idols; and turn away your faces from all your abominations.

7For every one of the house of Israel, or of the stranger that sojourneth in Israel, which separateth himself from me, and setteth up his idols in his heart,

and putteth the stumblingblock of his iniquity before his face, and cometh to a prophet to enquire of him concerning me: I the LORD will answer him by myself:

8And I will set my face against that man, and will make him a sign and a proverb, and I will cut him off from the midst of my people; and ye shall know that I *am* the LORD.

9And if the prophet be deceived when he hath spoken a thing, I the LORD have deceived that prophet, and I will stretch out my hand upon him, and will destroy him from the midst of my people Israel.

10And they shall bear the punishment of their iniquity: the punishment of the prophet shall be even as the punishment of him that seeketh *unto him;*

11That the house of Israel may go no more astray from me, neither be polluted any more with all their transgressions; but that they may be my people, and I may be their God, saith the Lord GOD.

HEBREWS 7:1–17

FOR this Melchisedec, king of Salem, priest of the most high God, who met Abraham returning from the slaughter of the kings, and blessed him;

2To whom also Abraham gave a tenth part of all; first being by interpretation King of righteousness, and after that also King of Salem, which is, King of peace;

3Without father, without mother, without descent, having neither beginning of days, nor end of life; but made like unto the Son of God; abideth a priest continually.

4Now consider how great this man *was,* unto whom even the patriarch Abraham gave the tenth of the spoils.

5And verily they that are of the sons of Levi, who receive the office of the priesthood, have a commandment to take tithes of the people according to the law, that is, of their brethren, though they come out of the loins of Abraham:

6But he whose descent is not counted from them received tithes of Abraham, and blessed him that had the promises.

7And without all contradiction the less is blessed of the better.

8And here men that die receive tithes; but there he *receiveth them,* of whom it is witnessed that he liveth.

9And as I may so say, Levi also, who receiveth tithes, payed tithes in Abraham.

10For he was yet in the loins of his father, when Melchisedec met him.

11If therefore perfection were by the Levitical priesthood, (for under it the people received the law,) what further need *was there* that another priest should rise after the order of Melchisedec, and not be called after the order of Aaron?

12For the priesthood being changed, there is made of necessity a change also of the law.

13For he of whom these things are spoken pertaineth to another tribe, of which no man gave attendance at the altar.

14For *it is* evident that our Lord sprang out of Juda; of which tribe Moses spake nothing concerning priesthood.

15And it is yet far more evident: for that after the similitude of Melchisedec there ariseth another priest,

16Who is made, not after the law of a carnal commandment, but after the power of an endless life.

17For he testifieth, Thou *art* a priest for ever after the order of Melchisedec.

PSALM 105:39–45

HE spread a cloud for a covering; and fire to give light in the night.
40*The people* asked, and he brought quails, and satisfied them with the bread of heaven.

41He opened the rock, and the waters gushed out; they ran in the dry places *like* a river.

42For he remembered his holy promise, *and* Abraham his servant.

43And he brought forth his people with joy, *and* his chosen with gladness:

44And gave them the lands of the heathen: and they inherited the labour of the people;

45That they might observe his statutes, and keep his laws. Praise ye the LORD.

PROVERBS FOR TODAY/ 27:3

A stone is *heavy, and the sand weighty; but a fool's wrath* is *heavier than them both.*

NOVEMBER 6

EZEKIEL 14:12—16:42

THE word of the LORD came again to me, saying,
13Son of man, when the land sinneth against me by trespassing grievously, then will I stretch out mine hand upon it, and will break the staff of the bread thereof, and will send famine upon it, and will cut off man and beast from it:

14Though these three men, Noah, Daniel, and Job, were in it, they should deliver *but* their own souls by their righteousness, saith the LORD GOD.

15If I cause noisome beasts to pass through the land, and they spoil it, so that it be desolate, that no man may pass through because of the beasts:

16*Though* these three men *were* in it, *as* I live, saith the Lord GOD, they shall deliver neither sons nor daughters; they only shall be delivered, but the land shall be desolate.

17Or *if* I bring a sword upon that land, and say, Sword, go through the land; so that I cut off man and beast from it:

18Though these three men *were* in it, *as* I live, saith the Lord GOD, they shall deliver neither sons nor daughters, but they only shall be delivered themselves.

19Or *if* I send a pestilence into that land, and pour out my fury upon it in blood, to cut off from it man and beast:

20Though Noah, Daniel, and Job, *were* in it, *as* I live, saith the Lord GOD, they shall deliver neither son nor daughter; they shall *but* deliver their own souls by their righteousness.

21For thus saith the Lord GOD; How much more when I send my four sore judgments upon Jerusalem, the sword, and the famine, and the noisome beast, and the pestilence, to cut off from it man and beast?

22Yet, behold, therein shall be left a remnant that shall be brought forth, *both* sons and daughters: behold, they shall come forth unto you, and ye shall see their way and their doings: and ye shall be comforted concerning the evil that I have brought upon Jerusalem, *even* concerning all that I have brought upon it.

23And they shall comfort you, when ye see their ways and their doings: and ye shall know that I have not done without cause all that I have done in it, saith the Lord GOD.

AND the word of the LORD came unto me, saying,

2Son of man, What is the vine tree more than any tree, *or than* a branch which is among the trees of the forest?

3Shall wood be taken thereof to do any work? or will *men* take a pin of it to hang any vessel thereon?

4Behold, it is cast into the fire for fuel; the fire devoureth both the ends of it, and the midst of it is burned. Is it meet for *any* work?

5Behold, when it was whole, it was meet for no work: how much less shall it be meet yet for *any* work, when the fire hath devoured it, and it is burned?

6Therefore thus saith the Lord GOD; As the vine tree among the trees of the forest, which I have given to the fire for fuel, so will I give the inhabitants of Jerusalem.

7And I will set my face against them; they shall go out from *one* fire, and *another* fire shall devour them; and ye shall know that I *am* the LORD, when I set my face against them.

8And I will make the land desolate, because they have committed a trespass, saith the Lord GOD.

AGAIN the word of the LORD came unto me, saying,

2Son of man, cause Jerusalem to know her abominations,

3And say, Thus saith the Lord GOD unto Jerusalem; Thy birth and thy nativity *is* of the land of Canaan; thy father *was* an Amorite, and thy mother an Hittite.

4And *as for* thy nativity, in the day thou wast born thy navel was not cut, neither wast thou washed in water to supple *thee;* thou wast not salted at all, nor swaddled at all.

5None eye pitied thee, to do any of these unto thee, to have compassion upon thee; but thou wast cast out in the open field, to the lothing of thy person, in the day that thou wast born.

6And when I passed by thee, and

saw thee polluted in thine own blood, I said unto thee *when thou wast* in thy blood, Live; yea, I said unto thee *when thou wast* in thy blood, Live.

7I have caused thee to multiply as the bud of the field, and thou hast increased and waxen great, and thou art come to excellent ornaments: *thy* breasts are fashioned, and thine hair is grown, whereas thou *wast* naked and bare.

8Now when I passed by thee, and looked upon thee, behold, thy time *was* the time of love; and I spread my skirt over thee, and covered thy nakedness: yea, I sware unto thee, and entered into a covenant with thee, saith the Lord GOD, and thou becamest mine.

9Then washed I thee with water; yea, I throughly washed away thy blood from thee, and I anointed thee with oil.

10I clothed thee also with broidered work, and shod thee with badgers' skin, and I girded thee about with fine linen, and I covered thee with silk.

11I decked thee also with ornaments, and I put bracelets upon thy hands, and a chain on thy neck.

12And I put a jewel on thy forehead, and earrings in thine ears, and a beautiful crown upon thine head.

13Thus wast thou decked with gold and silver; and thy raiment *was of* fine linen, and silk, and broidered work; thou didst eat fine flour, and honey, and oil: and thou wast exceeding beautiful, and thou didst prosper into a kingdom.

14And thy renown went forth among the heathen for thy beauty: for it *was* perfect through my comeliness, which I had put upon thee, saith the Lord GOD.

15But thou didst trust in thine own beauty, and playedst the harlot because of thy renown, and pouredst out thy fornications on every one that passed by; his it was.

16And of thy garments thou didst take, and deckedst thy high places with divers colours, and playedst the harlot thereupon: *the like things* shall not come, neither shall it be so.

17Thou hast also taken thy fair jewels of my gold and of my silver, which I had given thee, and madest to thyself images of men, and didst commit whoredom with them,

18And tookest thy broidered garments, and coveredst them: and thou hast set mine oil and mine incense before them.

19My meat also which I gave thee, fine flour, and oil, and honey, *wherewith* I fed thee, thou hast even set it before them for a sweet savour: and *thus* it was, saith the Lord GOD.

20Moreover thou hast taken thy sons and thy daughters, whom thou hast borne unto me, and these hast thou sacrificed unto them to be devoured. *Is this* of thy whoredoms a small matter,

21That thou hast slain my children, and delivered them to cause them to pass through *the fire* for them?

22And in all thine abominations and thy whoredoms thou hast not remembered the days of thy youth, when thou wast naked and bare, *and* wast polluted in thy blood.

23And it came to pass after all thy wickedness, (woe, woe unto thee! saith the Lord GOD;)

24*That* thou hast also built unto thee an eminent place, and hast made thee an high place in every street.

25Thou hast built thy high place at every head of the way, and hast made thy beauty to be abhorred, and hast opened thy feet to every one that passed by, and multiplied thy whoredoms.

26Thou hast also committed fornication with the Egyptians thy neighbours, great of flesh; and hast increased thy whoredoms, to provoke me to anger.

27Behold, therefore I have stretched out my hand over thee, and have diminished thine ordinary *food,* and delivered thee unto the will of them that hate thee, the daughters of the Philistines, which are ashamed of thy lewd way.

28Thou hast played the whore also with the Assyrians, because thou wast unsatiable; yea, thou hast played the harlot with them, and yet couldest not be satisfied.

29Thou hast moreover multiplied thy fornication in the land of Canaan unto Chaldea; and yet thou wast not satisfied herewith.

30How weak is thine heart, saith the Lord GOD, seeing thou doest all these *things,* the work of an imperious whorish woman;

31In that thou buildest thine eminent place in the head of every way, and makest thine high place in every street; and hast not been as an harlot, in that thou scornest hire;

32*But as* a wife that committeth adultery, *which* taketh strangers instead of her husband!

33They give gifts to all whores: but thou givest thy gifts to all thy lovers, and hirest them, that they may come unto thee on every side for thy whoredom.

34And the contrary is in thee from *other* women in thy whoredoms, whereas none followeth thee to commit whoredoms: and in that thou givest a reward, and no reward is given unto thee, therefore thou art contrary.

35Wherefore, O harlot, hear the word of the LORD:

36Thus saith the LORD GOD; Because thy filthiness was poured out, and thy nakedness discovered through thy whoredoms with thy lovers, and with all the idols of thy abominations, and by the blood of thy children, which thou didst give unto them;

37Behold, therefore I will gather all thy lovers, with whom thou hast taken pleasure, and all *them* that thou hast loved, with all *them* that thou hast hated; I will even gather them round about against thee, and will discover thy nakedness unto them, that they may

see all thy nakedness.

38And I will judge thee, as women that break wedlock and shed blood are judged; and I will give thee blood in fury and jealousy.

39And I will also give thee into their hand, and they shall throw down thine eminent place, and shall break down thy high places: they shall strip thee also of thy clothes, and shall take thy fair jewels, and leave thee naked and bare.

40They shall also bring up a company against thee, and they shall stone thee with stones, and thrust thee through with their swords.

41And they shall burn thine houses with fire, and execute judgment upon thee in the sight of many women: and I will cause thee to cease from playing the harlot, and thou also shalt give no hire any more.

42So will I make my fury toward thee to rest, and my jealousy shall depart from thee, and I will be quiet, and will be no more angry.

HEBREWS 7:18–28

FOR there is verily a disannulling of the commandment going before for the weakness and unprofitableness thereof.

19For the law made nothing perfect, but the bringing in of a better hope *did;* by the which we draw nigh unto God.

20And inasmuch as not without an oath *he was made priest:*

21(For those priests were made without an oath; but this with an oath by him that said unto him, The Lord sware and will not repent, Thou *art* a priest for ever after the order of Melchisedec:)

22By so much was Jesus made a surety of a better testament.

23And they truly were many priests, because they were not suffered to continue by reason of death:

24But this *man,* because he continueth ever, hath an unchangeable priesthood.

25Wherefore he is able also to save them to the uttermost that come unto God by him, seeing he ever liveth to make intercession for them.

26For such an high priest became us, *who is* holy, harmless, undefiled, separate from sinners, and made higher than the heavens;

27Who needeth not daily, as those high priests, to offer up sacrifice, first for his own sins, and then for the people's: for this he did once, when he offered up himself.

28For the law maketh men high priests which have infirmity; but the word of the oath, which was since the law, *maketh* the Son, who is consecrated for evermore.

PSALM 106:1–12

PRAISE ye the LORD. O give thanks unto the LORD; for *he is* good: for his mercy *endureth* for ever.

2Who can utter the mighty acts of the LORD? *who* can shew forth all his praise?

3Blessed *are* they that keep judg-ment, *and* he that doeth righteousness at all times.

4Remember me, O LORD, with the favour *that thou bearest unto* thy people: O visit me with thy salvation;

5That I may see the good of thy chosen, that I may rejoice in the gladness of thy nation, that I may glory with thine inheritance.

6We have sinned with our fathers, we have committed iniquity, we have done wickedly.

7Our fathers understood not thy wonders in Egypt; they remembered not the multitude of thy mercies; but provoked *him* at the sea, *even* at the Red sea.

8Nevertheless he saved them for his name's sake, that he might make his mighty power to be known.

9He rebuked the Red sea also, and it was dried up: so he led them through the depths, as through the wilderness.

10And he saved them from the hand of him that hated *them,* and redeemed them from the hand of the enemy.

11And the waters covered their enemies: there was not one of them left.

12Then believed they his words; they sang his praise.

PROVERBS FOR TODAY/ 27:4–6

Wrath is *cruel, and anger* is *outrageous; but who* is *able to stand before envy?* □ *Open rebuke* is *better than secret love.* □ *Faithful* are *the wounds of a friend; but the kisses of an enemy* are *deceitful.*

NOVEMBER 7

EZEKIEL 16:43—17:24

BECAUSE thou hast not remembered the days of thy youth, but hast fretted me in all these *things;* behold, therefore I also will rec-ompense thy way upon *thine* head, saith the Lord GOD: and thou shalt not commit this lewdness above all thine abominations.

44Behold, every one that useth

proverbs shall use *this* proverb against thee, saying, As *is* the mother, *so is* her daughter.

45Thou *art* thy mother's daughter, that lotheth her husband and her children; and thou *art* the sister of thy sisters, which lothed their husbands and their children: your mother *was* an Hittite, and your father an Amorite.

46And thine elder sister *is* Samaria, she and her daughters that dwell at thy left hand: and thy younger sister, that dwelleth at thy right hand, *is* Sodom and her daughters.

47Yet hast thou not walked after their ways, nor done after their abominations: but, as *if that were* a very little *thing,* thou wast corrupted more than they in all thy ways.

48As I live, saith the Lord GOD, Sodom thy sister hath not done, she nor her daughters, as thou hast done, thou and thy daughters.

49Behold, this was the iniquity of thy sister Sodom, pride, fulness of bread, and abundance of idleness was in her and in her daughters, neither did she strengthen the hand of the poor and needy.

50And they were haughty, and committed abomination before me: therefore I took them away as I saw *good.*

51Neither hath Samaria committed half of thy sins; but thou hast multiplied thine abominations more than they, and hast justified thy sisters in all thine abominations which thou hast done.

52Thou also, which hast judged thy sisters, bear thine own shame for thy sins that thou hast committed more abominable than they: they are more righteous than thou: yea, be thou confounded also, and bear thy shame, in that thou hast justified thy sisters.

53When I shall bring again their captivity, the captivity of Sodom and her daughters, and the captivity of Samaria and her daughters, then *will I bring again* the captivity of thy captives in the midst of them:

54That thou mayest bear thine own shame, and mayest be confounded in all that thou hast done, in that thou art a comfort unto them.

55When thy sisters, Sodom and her daughters, shall return to their former estate, and Samaria and her daughters shall return to their former estate, then thou and thy daughters shall return to your former estate.

56For thy sister Sodom was not mentioned by thy mouth in the day of thy pride,

57Before thy wickedness was discovered, as at the time of *thy* reproach of the daughters of Syria, and all *that are* round about her, the daughters of the Philistines, which despise thee round about.

58Thou hast borne thy lewdness and thine abominations, saith the LORD.

59For thus saith the Lord GOD; I will even deal with thee as thou hast done, which hast despised the oath in breaking the covenant.

60Nevertheless I will remember my covenant with thee in the days of thy youth, and I will establish unto thee an everlasting covenant.

61Then thou shalt remember thy ways, and be ashamed, when thou shalt receive thy sisters, thine elder and thy younger: and I will give them unto thee for daughters, but not by thy covenant.

62And I will establish my covenant with thee; and thou shalt know that I *am* the LORD:

63That thou mayest remember, and be confounded, and never open thy mouth any more because of thy shame, when I am pacified toward thee for all that thou hast done, saith the Lord GOD.

AND the word of the LORD came unto me, saying,

2Son of man, put forth a riddle, and speak a parable unto the house of Israel;

3And say, Thus saith the Lord GOD; A great eagle with great wings, long-winged, full of feathers, which had divers colours, came unto Lebanon, and took the highest branch of the cedar:

4He cropped off the top of his young twigs, and carried it into a land of traffick; he set it in a city of merchants.

5He took also of the seed of the land, and planted it in a fruitful field; he placed *it* by great waters, *and* set it *as* a willow tree.

6And it grew, and became a spreading vine of low stature, whose branches turned toward him, and the roots thereof were under him: so it became a vine, and brought forth branches, and shot forth sprigs.

7There was also another great eagle with great wings and many feathers: and, behold, this vine did bend her roots toward him, and shot forth her branches toward him, that he might water it by the furrows of her plantation.

8It was planted in a good soil by great waters, that it might bring forth branches, and that it might bear fruit, that it might be a goodly vine.

9Say thou, Thus saith the Lord GOD; Shall it prosper? shall he not pull up the roots thereof, and cut off the fruit thereof, that it wither? it shall wither in all the leaves of her spring, even without great power or many people to pluck it up by the roots thereof.

10Yea, behold, *being* planted, shall it prosper? shall it not utterly wither, when the east wind toucheth it? it shall wither in the furrows where it grew.

11Moreover the word of the LORD came unto me, saying,

12Say now to the rebellious house, Know ye not what these *things mean?* tell *them,* Behold, the king of Babylon is come to Jerusalem, and hath taken the king thereof, and the princes thereof, and led them with him to Babylon;

13And hath taken of the king's seed, and made a covenant with him, and hath taken an oath of him: he hath also taken the mighty of the land:

14That the kingdom might be base, that it might not lift itself up, *but* that by keeping of his covenant it might stand.

15But he rebelled against him in sending his ambassadors into Egypt, that they might give him horses and much people. Shall he prosper? shall he escape that doeth such *things?* or shall he break the covenant, and be delivered?

16As I live, saith the Lord GOD, surely in the place *where* the king *dwelleth* that made him king, whose oath he despised, and whose covenant he brake, *even* with him in the midst of Babylon he shall die.

17Neither shall Pharaoh with *his* mighty army and great company make for him in the war, by casting up mounts, and building forts, to cut off many persons:

18Seeing he despised the oath by breaking the covenant, when, lo, he had given his hand, and hath done all these *things,* he shall not escape.

19Therefore thus saith the Lord GOD; As I live, surely mine oath that he hath despised, and my covenant that he hath broken, even it will I recompense upon his own head.

20And I will spread my net upon him, and he shall be taken in my snare, and I will bring him to Babylon, and will plead with him there for his trespass that he hath trespassed against me.

21And all his fugitives with all his bands shall fall by the sword, and they that remain shall be scattered toward all winds: and ye shall know that I the LORD have spoken *it.*

22Thus saith the Lord GOD; I will also take of the highest branch of the high cedar, and will set *it;* I will crop off from the top of his young twigs a tender one, and will plant *it* upon an high mountain and eminent:

23In the mountain of the height of Israel will I plant it: and it shall bring forth boughs, and bear fruit, and be a goodly cedar: and under it shall dwell all fowl of every wing; in the shadow of the branches thereof shall they dwell.

24And all the trees of the field shall know that I the LORD have brought down the high tree, have exalted the low tree, have dried up the green tree, and have made the dry tree to flourish: I the LORD have spoken and have done *it.*

HEBREWS 8:1–13

Now of the things which we have spoken *this is* the sum: We have such an high priest, who is set on the right hand of the throne of the Majesty in the heavens;

2A minister of the sanctuary, and of the true tabernacle, which the Lord pitched, and not man.

3For every high priest is ordained to offer gifts and sacrifices: wherefore *it is* of necessity that this man have somewhat also to offer.

4For if he were on earth, he should not be a priest, seeing that there are priests that offer gifts according to the law:

5Who serve unto the example and shadow of heavenly things, as Moses was admonished of God when he was about to make the tabernacle: for, See, saith he, *that* thou make all things according to the pattern shewed to thee in the mount.

6But now hath he obtained a more excellent ministry, by how much also he is the mediator of a better covenant, which was established upon better promises.

7For if that first *covenant* had been faultless, then should no place have been sought for the second.

8For finding fault with them, he saith, Behold, the days come, saith the Lord, when I will make a new covenant with the house of Israel and with the house of Judah:

9Not according to the covenant that I made with their fathers in the day when I took them by the hand to lead them out of the land of Egypt; because they continued not in my covenant, and I regarded them not, saith the Lord.

10For this *is* the covenant that I will make with the house of Israel after those days, saith the Lord; I will put my laws into their mind, and write them in their hearts: and I will be to them a God, and they shall be to me a people:

11And they shall not teach every man his neighbour, and every man his brother, saying, Know the Lord: for all shall know me, from the least to the greatest.

12For I will be merciful to their unrighteousness, and their sins and their iniquities will I remember no more.

13In that he saith, A new *covenant,* he hath made the first old. Now that which decayeth and waxeth old *is* ready to vanish away.

PSALM 106:13–31

They soon forgat his works; they waited not for his counsel:

14But lusted exceedingly in the wilderness, and tempted God in the desert.

15And he gave them their request; but sent leanness into their soul.

16They envied Moses also in the camp, *and* Aaron the saint of the LORD.

17The earth opened and swallowed up Dathan, and covered the company of Abiram.

18And a fire was kindled in their company; the flame burned up the wicked.

19They made a calf in Horeb, and worshipped the molten image.

20Thus they changed their glory into the similitude of an ox that eateth grass.

21They forgat God their saviour, which had done great things in Egypt;

22Wondrous works in the land of Ham, *and* terrible things by the Red sea.

23Therefore he said that he would destroy them, had not Moses his chosen stood before him in the breach, to turn away his wrath, lest he should destroy *them*.

24Yea, they despised the pleasant land, they believed not his word:

25But murmured in their tents, *and* hearkened not unto the voice of the LORD.

26Therefore he lifted up his hand against them, to overthrow them in the wilderness:

27To overthrow their seed also among the nations, and to scatter them in the lands.

28They joined themselves also unto Baal–peor, and ate the sacrifices of the dead.

29Thus they provoked *him* to anger with their inventions: and the plague brake in upon them.

30Then stood up Phinehas, and executed judgment: and *so* the plague was stayed.

31And that was counted unto him for righteousness unto all generations for evermore.

PROVERBS FOR TODAY/ 27:7–9

The full soul loatheth an honeycomb; but to the hungry soul every bitter thing is sweet. □ *As a bird that wandereth from her nest, so is a man that wandereth from his place.* □ *Ointment and perfume rejoice the heart: so* doth *the sweetness of a man's friend by hearty counsel.*

NOVEMBER 8

EZEKIEL 18:1—19:14

THE word of the LORD came unto me again, saying,

2What mean ye, that ye use this proverb concerning the land of Israel, saying, The fathers have eaten sour grapes, and the children's teeth are set on edge?

3As I live, saith the Lord GOD, ye shall not have *occasion* any more to use this proverb in Israel.

4Behold, all souls are mine; as the soul of the father, so also the soul of the son is mine: the soul that sinneth, it shall die.

5But if a man be just, and do that which is lawful and right,

6*And* hath not eaten upon the mountains, neither hath lifted up his eyes to the idols of the house of Israel, neither hath defiled his neighbour's wife, neither hath come near to a menstruous woman,

7And hath not oppressed any, *but* hath restored to the debtor his pledge, hath spoiled none by violence, hath given his bread to the hungry, and hath covered the naked with a garment;

8He *that* hath not given forth upon usury, neither hath taken any increase, *that* hath withdrawn his hand from iniquity, hath executed true judgment between man and man,

9Hath walked in statutes, and hath kept my judgments, to deal truly; he *is* just, he shall surely live, saith the Lord GOD.

10If he beget a son *that is* a robber, a shedder of blood, and *that* doeth the like to *any* one of these *things*,

11And that doeth not any of those *duties*, but even hath eaten upon the mountains, and defiled his neighbour's wife,

12Hath oppressed the poor and needy, hath spoiled by violence, hath not restored the pledge, and hath lifted up his eyes to the idols, hath committed abomination,

13Hath given forth upon usury, and hath taken increase: shall he then live? he shall not live; he hath done all these abominations; he shall surely die; his blood shall be upon him.

14Now, lo, *if* he beget a son, that seeth all his father's sins which he hath done, and considereth, and doeth not such like,

15*That* hath not eaten upon the mountains, neither hath lifted up his eyes to the idols of the house of Israel, hath not defiled his neighbour's wife,

16Neither hath oppressed any, hath not withholden the pledge, neither hath spoiled by violence, *but* hath given his bread to the hungry, and hath covered the naked with a garment,

17*That* hath taken off his hand from the poor, *that* hath not received usury nor increase, hath executed my judgments, hath walked in my statutes; he shall not die for the iniquity of his father, he shall surely live.

18As *for* his father, because he cruelly oppressed, spoiled his brother by violence, and did *that* which *is* not good among his people, lo, even he shall die in his iniquity.

19Yet say ye, Why? doth not the son bear the iniquity of the father? When the son hath done that which is lawful and right, *and* hath kept all my statutes, and hath done them, he shall surely live.

20The soul that sinneth, it shall die. The son shall not bear the iniquity of the father, neither shall the father bear the iniquity of the son: the righteousness of the righteous shall be upon him, and the wickedness of the wicked shall be upon him.

21But if the wicked will turn from all his sins that he hath committed, and keep all my statutes, and do that which is lawful and right, he shall surely live, he shall not die.

22All his transgressions that he hath committed, they shall not be mentioned unto him: in his righteousness that he hath done he shall live.

23Have I any pleasure at all that the wicked should die? saith the Lord GOD: *and* not that he should return from his ways, and live?

24But when the righteous turneth away from his righteousness, and committeth iniquity, *and* doeth according to all the abominations that the wicked *man* doeth, shall he live? All his righteousness that he hath done shall not be mentioned: in his trespass that he hath trespassed, and in his sin that he hath sinned, in them shall he die.

25Yet ye say, The way of the Lord is not equal. Hear now, O house of Israel; Is not my way equal? are not your ways unequal?

26When a righteous *man* turneth away from his righteousness, and committeth iniquity, and dieth in them; for his iniquity that he hath done shall he die.

27Again, when the wicked *man* turneth away from his wickedness that he hath committed, and doeth that which is lawful and right, he shall save his soul alive.

28Because he considereth, and turneth away from all his transgressions that he hath committed, he shall surely live, he shall not die.

29Yet saith the house of Israel, The way of the Lord is not equal. O house of Israel, are not my ways equal? are not your ways unequal?

30Therefore I will judge you, O house of Israel, every one according to his ways, saith the Lord GOD. Repent, and turn *yourselves* from all your transgressions; so iniquity shall not be your ruin.

31Cast away from you all your transgressions, whereby ye have transgressed; and make you a new heart and a new spirit: for why will ye die, O house of Israel?

32For I have no pleasure in the death of him that dieth, saith the Lord GOD: wherefore turn *yourselves,* and live ye.

MOREOVER take thou up a lamentation for the princes of Israel,

2And say, What *is* thy mother? A lioness: she lay down among lions, she nourished her whelps among young lions.

3And she brought up one of her whelps: it became a young lion, and it learned to catch the prey; it devoured men.

4The nations also heard of him; he was taken in their pit, and they brought him with chains unto the land of Egypt.

5Now when she saw that she had waited, *and* her hope was lost, then she took another of her whelps, *and* made him a young lion.

6And he went up and down among the lions, he became a young lion, and learned to catch the prey, *and* devoured men.

7And he knew their desolate palaces, and he laid waste their cities; and the land was desolate, and the fulness thereof, by the noise of his roaring.

8Then the nations set against him on every side from the provinces, and spread their net over him: he was taken in their pit.

9And they put him in ward in chains, and brought him to the king of Babylon: they brought him into holds, that his voice should no more be heard upon the mountains of Israel.

10Thy mother *is* like a vine in thy blood, planted by the waters: she was fruitful and full of branches by reason of many waters.

11And she had strong rods for the sceptres of them that bare rule, and her stature was exalted among the thick branches, and she appeared in her height with the multitude of her branches.

12But she was plucked up in fury, she was cast down to the ground, and the east wind dried up her fruit: her strong rods were broken and withered; the fire consumed them.

13And now she *is* planted in the wilderness, in a dry and thirsty ground.

14And fire is gone out of a rod of her branches, *which* hath devoured her fruit, so that she hath no strong rod *to be* a sceptre to rule. This *is* a lamentation, and shall be for a lamentation.

HEBREWS 9:1–12

THEN verily the first *covenant* had also ordinances of divine service, and a worldly sanctuary.

2For there was a tabernacle made; the first, wherein *was* the candlestick, and the table, and the shewbread; which is called the sanctuary.

3And after the second vail, the tabernacle which is called the Holiest of all;

4Which had the golden censer, and the ark of the covenant overlaid round about with gold, wherein *was* the golden pot that had manna, and Aaron's rod that budded, and the tables of the covenant;

5And over it the cherubims of glory shadowing the mercy seat; of which we cannot now speak particularly.

6Now when these things were thus ordained, the priests went always into the first tabernacle, accomplishing the service *of God.*

7But into the second *went* the high priest alone once every year, not without blood, which he offered for himself, and *for* the errors of the people:

8The Holy Ghost this signifying, that the way into the holiest of all was not yet made manifest, while as the first tabernacle was yet standing:

9Which *was* a figure for the time then present, in which were offered both gifts and sacrifices, that could not make him that did the service perfect, as pertaining to the conscience;

10*Which stood* only in meats and drinks, and divers washings, and carnal ordinances, imposed *on them* until the time of reformation.

11But Christ being come an high priest of good things to come, by a greater and more perfect tabernacle, not made with hands, that is to say, not of this building;

12Neither by the blood of goats and calves, but by his own blood he entered in once into the holy place, having obtained eternal redemption *for us.*

PSALM 106:32–48

THEY angered *him* also at the waters of strife, so that it went ill with Moses for their sakes:
33Because they provoked his spirit, so that he spake unadvisedly with his lips.

34They did not destroy the nations, concerning whom the LORD commanded them:

35But were mingled among the heathen, and learned their works.

36And they served their idols: which were a snare unto them.

37Yea, they sacrificed their sons and their daughters unto devils,

38And shed innocent blood, *even* the blood of their sons and of their daugh-

ters, whom they sacrificed unto the idols of Canaan: and the land was polluted with blood.

39Thus were they defiled with their own works, and went a whoring with their own inventions.

40Therefore was the wrath of the LORD kindled against his people, insomuch that he abhorred his own inheritance.

41And he gave them into the hand of the heathen; and they that hated them ruled over them.

42Their enemies also oppressed them, and they were brought into subjection under their hand.

43Many times did he deliver them; but they provoked *him* with their counsel, and were brought low for their iniquity.

44Nevertheless he regarded their affliction, when he heard their cry:

45And he remembered for them his covenant, and repented according to the multitude of his mercies.

46He made them also to be pitied of all those that carried them captives.

47Save us, O LORD our God, and gather us from among the heathen, to give thanks unto thy holy name, *and* to triumph in thy praise.

48Blessed *be* the LORD God of Israel from everlasting to everlasting: and let all the people say, Amen. Praise ye the LORD.

PROVERBS FOR TODAY/ 27:10

Thine own friend, and thy father's friend, forsake not; neither go into thy brother's house in the day of thy calamity: for better is a neighbour that is near than a brother far off.

NOVEMBER 9

EZEKIEL 20:1–49

AND it came to pass in the seventh year, in the fifth *month,* the tenth *day* of the month, *that* certain of the elders of Israel came to enquire of the LORD, and sat before me.

2Then came the word of the LORD unto me, saying,

3Son of man, speak unto the elders of Israel, and say unto them, Thus saith the Lord GOD; Are ye come to enquire of me? *As* I live saith the Lord GOD, I will not be enquired of by you.

4Wilt thou judge them, son of man, wilt thou judge *them?* cause them to know the abominations of their fathers:

5And say unto them, Thus saith the Lord GOD; In the day when I chose Israel, and lifted up mine hand unto the seed of the house of Jacob, and made myself known unto them in the land of Egypt, when I lifted up mine hand unto them, saying, I *am* the LORD your God;

6In the day *that* I lifted up mine hand unto them, to bring them forth of the land of Egypt into a land that I had espied for them, flowing with milk and honey, which *is* the glory of all lands:

7Then said I unto them, Cast ye away every man the abominations of his eyes, and defile not yourselves with the idols of Egypt: I *am* the LORD your God.

8But they rebelled against me, and would not hearken unto me: they did not every man cast away the abominations of their eyes, neither did they forsake the idols of Egypt: then I said, I will pour out my fury upon them, to accomplish my anger against them in the midst of the land of Egypt.

9But I wrought for my name's sake, that it should not be polluted before the heathen, among whom they *were,* in whose sight I made myself known unto them, in bringing them forth out of the land of Egypt.

10Wherefore I caused them to go forth out of the land of Egypt, and brought them into the wilderness.

11And I gave them my statutes, and shewed them my judgments, which *if* a man do, he shall even live in them.

12Moreover also I gave them my sabbaths, to be a sign between me and them, that they might know that I *am* the LORD that sanctify them.

13But the house of Israel rebelled against me in the wilderness: they walked not in my statutes, and they despised my judgments, which *if* a man do, he shall even live in them; and my sabbaths they greatly polluted: then I said, I would pour out my fury upon them in the wilderness, to consume them.

14But I wrought for my name's sake, that it should not be polluted before the heathen, in whose sight I brought them out.

15Yet also I lifted up my hand unto them in the wilderness, that I would not bring them into the land which I had given *them,* flowing with milk and honey, which *is* the glory of all lands;

16Because they despised my judgments, and walked not in my statutes, but polluted my sabbaths: for their heart went after their idols.

17Nevertheless mine eye spared them from destroying them, neither did I make an end of them in the wilderness.

18But I said unto their children in the wilderness, Walk ye not in the statutes of your fathers, neither observe their judgments, nor defile yourselves with their idols:

19I *am* the LORD your God; walk in

my statutes, and keep my judgments, and do them;

20And hallow my sabbaths; and they shall be a sign between me and you, that ye may know that I *am* the LORD your God.

21Notwithstanding the children rebelled against me: they walked not in my statutes, neither kept my judgments to do them, which *if* a man do, he shall even live in them; they polluted my sabbaths: then I said, I would pour out my fury upon them, to accomplish my anger against them in the wilderness.

22Nevertheless I withdrew mine hand, and wrought for my name's sake, that it should not be polluted in the sight of the heathen, in whose sight I brought them forth.

23I lifted up mine hand unto them also in the wilderness, that I would scatter them among the heathen, and disperse them through the countries;

24Because they had not executed my judgments, but had despised my statutes, and had polluted my sabbaths, and their eyes were after their fathers' idols.

25Wherefore I gave them also statutes *that were* not good, and judgments whereby they should not live;

26And I polluted them in their own gifts, in that they caused to pass through *the fire* all that openeth the womb, that I might make them desolate, to the end that they might know that I *am* the LORD.

27Therefore, son of man, speak unto the house of Israel, and say unto them, Thus saith the Lord GOD; Yet in this your fathers have blasphemed me, in that they have committed a trespass against me.

28*For* when I had brought them into the land, *for* the which I lifted up mine hand to give it to them, then they saw every high hill, and all the thick trees, and they offered there their sacrifices, and there they presented the provoca-tion of their offering: there also they made their sweet savour, and poured out there their drink offerings.

29Then I said unto them, What *is* the high place whereunto ye go? And the name thereof is called Bamah unto this day.

30Wherefore say unto the house of Israel, Thus saith the Lord GOD; Are ye polluted after the manner of your fathers? and commit ye whoredom after their abominations?

31For when ye offer your gifts, when ye make your sons to pass through the fire, ye pollute yourselves with all your idols, even unto this day: and shall I be enquired of by you, O house of Israel? *As* I live, saith the Lord GOD, I will not be enquired of by you.

32And that which cometh into your mind shall not be at all, that ye say, We will be as the heathen, as the families of the countries, to serve wood and stone.

33*As* I live, saith the Lord GOD, surely with a mighty hand, and with a stretched out arm, and with fury poured out, will I rule over you:

34And I will bring you out from the people, and will gather you out of the countries wherein ye are scattered, with a mighty hand, and with a stretched out arm, and with fury poured out.

35And I will bring you into the wilderness of the people, and there will I plead with you face to face.

36Like as I pleaded with your fathers in the wilderness of the land of Egypt, so will I plead with you, saith the Lord GOD.

37And I will cause you to pass under the rod, and I will bring you into the bond of the covenant:

38And I will purge out from among you the rebels, and them that transgress against me: I will bring them forth out of the country where they sojourn, and they shall not enter into the land of Israel; and ye shall know that I *am* the LORD.

39As for you, O house of Israel thus saith the Lord GOD: Go ye, serve ye every one his idols, and hereafter *also,* if ye will not hearken unto me: but pollute ye my holy name no more with your gifts, and with your idols.

40For in mine holy mountain, in the mountain of the height of Israel, saith the Lord GOD, there shall all the house of Israel, all of them in the land, serve me: there will I accept them, and there will I require your offerings, and the firstfruits of your oblations, with all your holy things.

41I will accept you with your sweet savour, when I bring you out from the people, and gather you out of the countries wherein ye have been scattered; and I will be sanctified in you before the heathen.

42And ye shall know that I *am* the LORD, when I shall bring you into the land of Israel, into the country *for* the which I lifted up mine hand to give it to your fathers.

43And there shall ye remember your ways, and all your doings, wherein ye have been defiled; and ye shall lothe yourselves in your own sight for all your evils that ye have committed.

44And ye shall know that I *am* the LORD, when I have wrought with you for my name's sake, not according to your wicked ways, nor according to your corrupt doings, O ye house of Israel, saith the Lord GOD.

45Moreover the word of the LORD came unto me, saying,

46Son of man, set thy face toward the south, and drop *thy word* toward the south, and prophesy against the forest of the south field;

47And say to the forest of the south, Hear the word of the LORD; Thus saith the Lord GOD; Behold, I will kindle a fire in thee, and it shall devour every green tree in thee, and every dry tree: the flaming flame shall not be quenched, and all faces from the south to the north shall be burned therein.

48And all flesh shall see that I the LORD have kindled it; it shall not be quenched.

49Then said I, Ah Lord GOD! they say of me, Doth he not speak parables?

HEBREWS 9:13–28

FOR if the blood of bulls and of goats, and the ashes of an heifer sprinkling the unclean, sanctifieth to the purifying of the flesh:

14How much more shall the blood of Christ, who through the eternal Spirit offered himself without spot to God, purge your conscience from dead works to serve the living God?

15And for this cause he is the mediator of the new testament, that by means of death, for the redemption of the transgressions *that were* under the first testament, they which are called might receive the promise of eternal inheritance.

16For where a testament *is,* there must also of necessity be the death of the testator.

17For a testament *is* of force after men are dead: otherwise it is of no strength at all while the testator liveth.

18Whereupon neither the first *testament* was dedicated without blood.

19For when Moses had spoken every precept to all the people according to the law, he took the blood of calves and of goats, with water, and scarlet wool, and hyssop, and sprinkled both the book, and all the people,

20Saying, This *is* the blood of the testament which God hath enjoined unto you.

21Moreover he sprinkled with blood both the tabernacle, and all the vessels of the ministry.

22And almost all things are by the law purged with blood; and without shedding of blood is no remission.

23*It was* therefore necessary that the patterns of things in the heavens should be purified with these; but the heavenly things themselves with better sacrifices than these.

24For Christ is not entered into the holy places made with hands, *which are* the figures of the true; but into heaven itself, now to appear in the presence of God for us:

25Nor yet that he should offer himself often, as the high priest entereth into the holy place every year with blood of others;

26For then must he often have suffered since the foundation of the world: but now once in the end of the world hath he appeared to put away sin by the sacrifice of himself.

27And as it is appointed unto men once to die, but after this the judgment:

28So Christ was once offered to bear the sins of many; and unto them that look for him shall he appear the second time without sin unto salvation.

PSALM 107:1–43

O GIVE thanks unto the LORD, for *he is* good: for his mercy *endureth* for ever.

2Let the redeemed of the LORD say *so,* whom he hath redeemed from the hand of the enemy;

3And gathered them out of the lands, from the east, and from the west, from the north, and from the south.

4They wandered in the wilderness in a solitary way; they found no city to dwell in.

5Hungry and thirsty, their soul fainted in them.

6Then they cried unto the LORD in their trouble, *and* he delivered them out of their distresses.

7And he led them forth by the right way, that they might go to a city of habitation.

8Oh that *men* would praise the LORD *for* his goodness, and *for* his wonderful works to the children of men!

9For he satisfieth the longing soul, and filleth the hungry soul with goodness.

10Such as sit in darkness and in the shadow of death, *being* bound in affliction and iron;

11Because they rebelled against the words of God, and contemned the counsel of the most High:

12Therefore he brought down their heart with labour; they fell down and *there was* none to help.

13Then they cried unto the LORD in their trouble, *and* he saved them out of their distresses.

14He brought them out of darkness and the shadow of death, and brake their bands in sunder.

15Oh that *men* would praise the LORD *for* his goodness, and *for* his wonderful works to the children of men!

16For he hath broken the gates of brass, and cut the bars of iron in sunder.

17Fools because of their transgression, and because of their iniquities, are afflicted.

18Their soul abhorreth all manner of meat; and they draw near unto the gates of death.

19Then they cry unto the LORD in their trouble, *and* he saveth them out of their distresses.

20He sent his word, and healed them, and delivered *them* from their destructions.

21Oh that *men* would praise the LORD *for* his goodness, and *for* his wonderful works to the children of men!

22And let them sacrifice the sacrifices of thanksgiving, and declare his works with rejoicing.

23They that go down to the sea in ships, that do business in great waters;

24These see the works of the LORD, and his wonders in the deep.

25For he commandeth, and raiseth the stormy wind, which lifteth up the waves thereof.

26They mount up to the heaven, they go down again to the depths: their soul is melted because of trouble.

27They reel to and fro, and stagger like a drunken man, and are at their wit's end.

28Then they cry unto the LORD in their trouble, and he bringeth them out of their distresses.

29He maketh the storm a calm, so that the waves thereof are still.

30Then are they glad because they be quiet; so he bringeth them unto their desired haven.

31Oh that *men* would praise the LORD *for* his goodness, and *for* his wonderful works to the children of men!

32Let them exalt him also in the congregation of the people, and praise him in the assembly of the elders.

33He turneth rivers into a wilderness, and the watersprings into dry ground;

34A fruitful land into barrenness, for the wickedness of them that dwell therein.

35He turneth the wilderness into a standing water, and dry ground into watersprings.

36And there he maketh the hungry to dwell, that they may prepare a city for habitation;

37And sow the fields, and plant vineyards, which may yield fruits of increase.

38He blesseth them also, so that they are multiplied greatly; and suffereth not their cattle to decrease.

39Again, they are minished and brought low through oppression, affliction, and sorrow.

40He poureth contempt upon princes, and causeth them to wander in the wilderness, *where there is* no way.

41Yet setteth he the poor on high from affliction, and maketh *him* families like a flock.

42The righteous shall see *it,* and rejoice: and all iniquity shall stop her mouth.

43Whoso *is* wise, and will observe these *things,* even they shall understand the lovingkindness of the LORD.

PROVERBS FOR TODAY/ 27:11

My son, be wise, and make my heart glad, that I may answer him that reproacheth me.

NOVEMBER 10

EZEKIEL 21:1—22:31

AND the word of the LORD came unto me, saying,

2Son of man, set thy face toward Jerusalem, and drop *thy word* toward the holy places, and prophesy against the land of Israel,

3And say to the land of Israel, Thus saith the LORD; Behold, I *am* against thee, and will draw forth my sword out of his sheath, and will cut off from thee the righteous and the wicked.

4Seeing then that I will cut off from thee the righteous and the wicked, therefore shall my sword go forth out of his sheath against all flesh from the south to the north:

5That all flesh may know that I the LORD have drawn forth my sword out of his sheath: it shall not return any more.

6Sigh therefore, thou son of man, with the breaking of *thy* loins; and with bitterness sigh before their eyes.

7And it shall be, when they say unto thee, Wherefore sighest thou? that thou shalt answer, For the tidings; because it cometh: and every heart shall melt, and all hands shall be feeble, and every spirit shall faint, and all knees shall be weak *as* water: behold, it cometh, and shall be brought to pass, saith the Lord GOD.

8Again the word of the LORD came unto me, saying,

9Son of man, prophesy, and say, Thus saith the LORD; Say, A sword, a sword is sharpened, and also furbished:

10It is sharpened to make a sore slaughter; it is furbished that it may glitter: should we then make mirth? it contemneth the rod of my son, *as* every tree.

11And he hath given it to be furbished, that it may be handled: this sword is sharpened, and it is furbished, to give it into the hand of the slayer.

12Cry and howl, son of man: for it shall be upon my people, it *shall be* upon all the princes of Israel: terrors by reason of the sword shall be upon my people: smite therefore upon *thy* thigh.

13Because *it is* a trial, and what if *the sword* contemn even the rod? it shall be no *more,* saith the Lord GOD.

14Thou therefore, son of man, prophesy, and smite *thine* hands together, and let the sword be doubled the third time, the sword of the slain: it *is* the sword of the great *men that are* slain, which entereth into their privy chambers.

15I have set the point of the sword against all their gates, that *their* heart may faint, and *their* ruins be multiplied: ah! *it is* made bright, *it is* wrapped up for the slaughter.

16Go thee one way or other, *either* on the right hand, *or* on the left, whithersoever thy face *is* set.

17I will also smite mine hands together, and I will cause my fury to rest: I the LORD have said *it.*

18The word of the LORD came unto me again, saying,

19Also, thou son of man, appoint thee two ways, that the sword of the king of Babylon may come: both twain shall come forth out of one land: and choose thou a place, choose *it* at the head of the way to the city.

20Appoint a way, that the sword may come to Rabbath of the Ammonites, and to Judah in Jerusalem the defenced.

21For the king of Babylon stood at the parting of the way, at the head of the two ways, to use divination: he made *his* arrows bright, he consulted with images, he looked in the liver.

22At his right hand was the divination for Jerusalem, to appoint captains, to open the mouth in the slaughter, to lift up the voice with shouting, to appoint *battering* rams against the gates, to cast a mount, *and* to build a fort.

23And it shall be unto them as a false divination in their sight, to them that have sworn oaths: but he will call to remembrance the iniquity, that they may be taken.

24Therefore thus saith the Lord GOD; Because ye have made your iniquity to be remembered, in that your transgressions are discovered, so that in all your doings your sins do appear; because, I *say,* that ye are come to remembrance, ye shall be taken with the hand.

25And thou, profane wicked prince of Israel, whose day is come, when iniquity *shall have* an end,

26Thus saith the Lord GOD; Remove the diadem, and take off the crown: this *shall* not *be* the same: exalt *him that is* low, and abase *him that is* high.

27I will overturn, overturn, overturn, it: and it shall be no *more,* until he come whose right it is; and I will give it *him.*

28And thou, son of man, prophesy and say, Thus saith the Lord GOD concerning the Ammonites, and concerning their reproach; even say thou, The sword, the sword *is* drawn: for the slaughter *it is* furbished, to consume because of the glittering:

29Whiles they see vanity unto thee, whiles they divine a lie unto thee, to bring thee upon the necks of *them that are* slain, of the wicked, whose day is come, when their iniquity *shall have* an end.

30Shall I cause *it* to return into his sheath? I will judge thee in the place where thou wast created, in the land of thy nativity.

31And I will pour out mine indignation upon thee, I will blow against thee in the fire of my wrath, and deliver thee into the hand of brutish men, *and* skilful to destroy.

32Thou shalt be for fuel to the fire; thy blood shall be in the midst of the land; thou shalt be no *more* remembered: for I the LORD have spoken *it*.

MOREOVER the word of the LORD came unto me, saying,

2Now, thou son of man, wilt thou judge, wilt thou judge the bloody city? yea, thou shalt shew her all her abominations.

3Then say thou, Thus saith the Lord GOD, The city sheddeth blood in the midst of it, that her time may come, and maketh idols against herself to defile herself.

4Thou art become guilty in thy blood that thou hast shed; and hast defiled thyself in thine idols which thou hast made; and thou hast caused thy days to draw near, and art come *even* unto thy years: therefore have I made thee a reproach unto the heathen, and a mocking to all countries.

5*Those that be* near, and *those that be* far from thee, shall mock thee, *which art* infamous *and* much vexed.

6Behold, the princes of Israel, every one were in thee to their power to shed blood.

7In thee have they set light by father and mother: in the midst of thee have they dealt by oppression with the stranger: in thee have they vexed the fatherless and the widow.

8Thou hast despised mine holy things, and hast profaned my sabbaths.

9In thee are men that carry tales to shed blood: and in thee they eat upon the mountains: in the midst of thee they commit lewdness.

10In thee have they discovered their fathers' nakedness: in thee have they humbled her that was set apart for pollution.

11And one hath committed abomination with his neighbour's wife; and another hath lewdly defiled his daughter in law; and another in thee hath humbled his sister, his father's daughter.

12In thee have they taken gifts to shed blood; thou hast taken usury and increase, and thou hast greedily gained of thy neighbours by extortion, and hast forgotten me, saith the Lord GOD.

13Behold, therefore I have smitten mine hand at thy dishonest gain which thou hast made, and at thy blood which hath been in the midst of thee.

14Can thine heart endure, or can thine hands be strong, in the days that I shall deal with thee? I the LORD have spoken *it*, and will do *it*.

15And I will scatter thee among the heathen, and disperse thee in the countries, and will consume thy filthiness out of thee.

16And thou shalt take thine inheritance in thyself in the sight of the heathen, and thou shalt know that I *am* the LORD.

17And the word of the LORD came unto me, saying,

18Son of man, the house of Israel is to me become dross: all they *are* brass, and tin, and iron, and lead, in the midst of the furnace; they are *even* the dross of silver.

19Therefore thus saith the Lord GOD; Because ye are all become dross, behold, therefore I will gather you into the midst of Jerusalem.

20As they gather silver, and brass, and iron, and lead, and tin, into the midst of the furnace, to blow the fire upon it, to melt *it;* so will I gather *you* in mine anger and in my fury, and I will leave *you there,* and melt you.

21Yea, I will gather you, and blow upon you in the fire of my wrath, and ye shall be melted in the midst thereof.

22As silver is melted in the midst of the furnace, so shall ye be melted in the midst thereof; and ye shall know that I the LORD have poured out my fury upon you.

23And the word of the LORD came unto me, saying,

24Son of man, say unto her, Thou *art* the land that is not cleansed, nor rained upon in the day of indignation.

25*There is* a conspiracy of her prophets in the midst thereof, like a roaring lion ravening the prey; they have devoured souls; they have taken the treasure and precious things; they have made her many widows in the midst thereof.

26Her priests have violated my law, and have profaned mine holy things: they have put no difference between the holy and profane, neither have they shewed *difference* between the unclean and the clean, and have hid their eyes from my sabbaths, and I am profaned among them.

27Her princes in the midst thereof *are* like wolves ravening the prey, to shed blood, *and* to destroy souls, to get dishonest gain.

28And her prophets have daubed them with untempered *morter,* seeing vanity, and divining lies unto them, saying, Thus saith the Lord GOD, when the LORD hath not spoken.

29The people of the land have used oppression, and exercised robbery, and have vexed the poor and needy: yea, they have oppressed the stranger wrongfully.

30And I sought for a man among them, that should make up the hedge, and stand in the gap before me for the land, that I should not destroy it: but I found none.

31Therefore have I poured out mine indignation upon them; I have consumed them with the fire of my wrath: their own way have I recompensed upon their heads, saith the Lord GOD.

HEBREWS 10:1–17

For the law having a shadow of good things to come, *and* not the very image of the things, can never with those sacrifices which they offered year by year continually make the comers thereunto perfect.

2For then would they not have ceased to be offered? because that the worshippers once purged should have had no more conscience of sins.

3But in those *sacrifices there is* a remembrance again *made* of sins every year.

4For *it is* not possible that the blood of bulls and of goats should take away sins.

5Wherefore when he cometh into the world, he saith, Sacrifice and offering thou wouldest not, but a body hast thou prepared me:

6In burnt offerings and *sacrifices* for sin thou hast had no pleasure.

7Then said I, Lo, I come (in the volume of the book it is written of me,) to do thy will, O God.

8Above when he said, Sacrifice and offering and burnt offerings and *offering* for sin thou wouldest not, neither hadst pleasure *therein;* which are offered by the law;

9Then said he, Lo, I come to do thy will, O God. He taketh away the first, that he may establish the second.

10By the which will we are sanctified through the offering of the body of Jesus Christ once *for all.*

11And every priest standeth daily ministering and offering oftentimes the same sacrifices, which can never take away sins:

12But this man, after he had offered one sacrifice for sins for ever, sat down on the right hand of God;

13From henceforth expecting till his enemies be made his footstool.

14For by one offering he hath perfected for ever them that are sanctified.

15*Whereof* the Holy Ghost also is a witness to us: for after that he had said before,

16This *is* the covenant that I will make with them after those days, saith the Lord, I will put my laws into their hearts, and in their minds will I write them;

17And their sins and iniquities will I remember no more.

PSALM 108:1–13

O GOD, my heart is fixed: I will sing and give praise, even with my glory.

2Awake, psaltery and harp: I *myself* will awake early.

3I will praise thee, O LORD, among the people: and I will sing praises unto thee among the nations.

4For thy mercy *is* great above the heavens: and thy truth *reacheth* unto the clouds.

5Be thou exalted, O God, above the heavens: and thy glory above all the earth;

6That thy beloved may be delivered: save *with* thy right hand, and answer me.

7God hath spoken in his holiness; I will rejoice, I will divide Shechem, and mete out the valley of Succoth.

8Gilead *is* mine: Manasseh *is* mine; Ephraim also *is* the strength of mine head; Judah *is* my lawgiver;

9Moab *is* my washpot; over Edom will I cast out my shoe; over Philistia will I triumph.

10Who will bring me into the strong city? who will lead me into Edom?

11*Wilt* not *thou,* O God, *who* hast cast us off? and wilt not thou, O God, go forth with our hosts?

12Give us help from trouble: for vain *is* the help of man.

13Through God we shall do valiantly: for he *it is that* shall tread down our enemies.

PROVERBS FOR TODAY/ 27:12

A prudent man *foreseeth the evil,* and *hideth himself;* but *the simple pass on,* and *are punished.*

NOVEMBER 11

EZEKIEL 23:1–49

THE word of the LORD came again unto me, saying,

2Son of man, there were two women, the daughters of one mother:

3And they committed whoredoms in Egypt; they committed whoredoms in their youth: there were their breasts pressed, and there they bruised the teats of their virginity.

4And the names of them *were* Aholah the elder, and Aholibah her sister: and they were mine, and they bare sons and daughters. Thus *were* their names; Samaria *is* Aholah, and Jerusalem Aholibah.

5And Aholah played the harlot when she was mine; and she doted on her lovers, on the Assyrians *her* neighbours,

6Which *were* clothed with blue, captains and rulers, all of them desirable young men, horsemen riding upon horses.

7Thus she committed her whoredoms with them, with all them *that were* the chosen men of Assyria, and with all on whom she doted: with all their idols she defiled herself.

8Neither left she her whoredoms *brought* from Egypt: for in her youth they lay with her, and they bruised the breasts of her virginity, and poured their whoredom upon her.

9Wherefore I have delivered her into the hand of her lovers, into the hand of the Assyrians, upon whom she doted.

10These discovered her nakedness: they took her sons and her daughters, and slew her with the sword: and she became famous among women; for they had executed judgment upon her.

11And when her sister Aholibah saw *this,* she was more corrupt in her inordinate love than she, and in her whoredoms more than her sister in *her* whoredoms.

12She doted upon the Assyrians *her* neighbours, captains and rulers clothed most gorgeously, horsemen riding upon horses, all of them desirable young men.

13Then I saw that she was defiled, *that* they *took* both one way,

14And *that* she increased her whoredoms: for when she saw men pourtrayed upon the wall, the images of the Chaldeans pourtrayed with vermilion,

15Girded with girdles upon their loins, exceeding in dyed attire upon their heads, all of them princes to look to, after the manner of the Babylonians of Chaldea, the land of their nativity:

16And as soon as she saw them with her eyes, she doted upon them, and sent messengers unto them into Chaldea.

17And the Babylonians came to her into the bed of love, and they defiled her with their whoredom, and she was polluted with them, and her mind was alienated from them.

18So she discovered her whoredoms, and discovered her nakedness: then my mind was alienated from her, like as my mind was alienated from her sister.

19Yet she multiplied her whoredoms, in calling to remembrance the days of her youth, wherein she had played the harlot in the land of Egypt.

20For she doted upon their paramours, whose flesh *is as* the flesh of asses, and whose issue *is like* the issue of horses.

21Thus thou calledst to remembrance the lewdness of thy youth, in bruising thy teats by the Egyptians for the paps of thy youth.

22Therefore, O Aholibah, thus saith the Lord GOD; Behold, I will raise up thy lovers against thee, from whom thy mind is alienated, and I will bring them against thee on every side;

23The Babylonians, and all the Chaldeans, Pekod, and Shoa, and Koa, *and* all the Assyrians with them: all of them desirable young men, captains and rulers, great lords and renowned, all of them riding upon horses.

24And they shall come against thee with chariots, wagons, and wheels, and with an assembly of people, *which* shall set against thee buckler and shield and helmet round about: and I will set judgment before them, and they shall judge thee according to their judgments.

25And I will set my jealousy against thee, and they shall deal furiously with thee: they shall take away thy nose and thine ears; and thy remnant shall fall by the sword: they shall take thy sons and thy daughters; and thy residue shall be devoured by the fire.

26They shall also strip thee out of

thy clothes, and take away thy fair jewels.

27Thus will I make thy lewdness to cease from thee, and thy whoredom *brought* from the land of Egypt: so that thou shalt not lift up thine eyes unto them, nor remember Egypt any more.

28For thus saith the Lord God; Behold, I will deliver thee into the hand *of them* whom thou hatest, into the hand *of them* from whom thy mind is alienated:

29And they shall deal with thee hatefully, and shall take away all thy labour, and shall leave thee naked and bare: and the nakedness of thy whoredoms shall be discovered, both thy lewdness and thy whoredoms.

30I will do these *things* unto thee, because thou hast gone a whoring after the heathen, *and* because thou art polluted with their idols.

31Thou hast walked in the way of thy sister; therefore will I give her cup into thine hand.

32Thus saith the Lord God; Thou shalt drink of thy sister's cup deep and large: thou shalt be laughed to scorn and had in derision; it containeth much.

33Thou shalt be filled with drunkenness and sorrow, with the cup of astonishment and desolation, with the cup of thy sister Samaria.

34Thou shalt even drink it and suck *it* out, and thou shalt break the sherds thereof, and pluck off thine own breasts: for I have spoken *it*, saith the Lord God.

35Therefore thus saith the Lord God; Because thou hast forgotten me, and cast me behind thy back, therefore bear thou also thy lewdness and thy whoredoms.

36The Lord said moreover unto me; Son of man, wilt thou judge Aholah and Aholibah? yea, declare unto them their abominations;

37That they have committed adultery, and blood *is* in their hands, and with their idols have they committed adultery, and have also caused their sons, whom they bare unto me, to pass for them through *the fire*, to devour *them*.

38Moreover this they have done unto me: they have defiled my sanctuary in the same day, and have profaned my sabbaths.

39For when they had slain their children to their idols, then they came the same day into my sanctuary to profane it; and, lo, thus have they done in the midst of mine house.

40And furthermore, that ye have sent for men to come from far, unto whom a messenger *was* sent; and, lo, they came: for whom thou didst wash thyself, paintedst thy eyes, and deckedst thyself with ornaments,

41And satest upon a stately bed, and a table prepared before it, whereupon thou hast set mine incense and mine oil.

42And a voice of a multitude being at ease *was* with her: and with the men of the common sort *were* brought Sabeans from the wilderness, which put bracelets upon their hands, and beautiful crowns upon their heads.

43Then said I unto *her that was* old in adulteries, Will they now commit whoredoms with her, and she *with them?*

44Yet they went in unto her, as they go in unto a woman that playeth the harlot: so went they in unto Aholah and unto Aholibah, the lewd women.

45And the righteous men, they shall judge them after the manner of adulteresses, and after the manner of women that shed blood; because they *are* adulteresses, and blood *is* in their hands.

46For thus saith the Lord God; I will bring up a company upon them, and will give them to be removed and spoiled.

47And the company shall stone them with stones, and dispatch them with their swords; they shall slay their sons and their daughters, and burn up their houses with fire.

48Thus will I cause lewdness to cease out of the land, that all women may be taught not to do after your lewdness.

49And they shall recompense your lewdness upon you, and ye shall bear the sins of your idols: and ye shall know that I *am* the Lord GOD.

HEBREWS 10:18–39

Now where remission of these *is, there is* no more offering for sin.

19Having therefore, brethren, boldness to enter into the holiest by the blood of Jesus,

20By a new and living way, which he hath consecrated for us, through the vail, that is to say, his flesh;

21And *having* an high priest over the house of God;

22Let us draw near with a true heart in full assurance of faith, having our hearts sprinkled from an evil conscience, and our bodies washed with pure water.

23Let us hold fast the profession of *our* faith without wavering; (for he *is* faithful that promised;)

24And let us consider one another to provoke unto love and to good works:

25Not forsaking the assembling of ourselves together, as the manner of some *is;* but exhorting *one another:* and so much the more, as ye see the day approaching.

26For if we sin wilfully after that we have received the knowledge of the truth, there remaineth no more sacrifice for sins,

27But a certain fearful looking for of judgment and fiery indignation, which shall devour the adversaries.

28He that despised Moses' law died without mercy under two or three witnesses:

29Of how much sorer punishment, suppose ye, shall he be thought worthy, who hath trodden under foot the Son

of God, and hath counted the blood of the covenant, wherewith he was sanctified, an unholy thing, and hath done despite unto the Spirit of grace?

30For we know him that hath said, Vengeance *belongeth* unto me, I will recompense, saith the Lord. And again, The Lord shall judge his people.

31*It is* a fearful thing to fall into the hands of the living God.

32But call to remembrance the former days, in which, after ye were illuminated, ye endured a great fight of afflictions;

33Partly, whilst ye were made a gazingstock both by reproaches and afflictions; and partly, whilst ye became companions of them that were so used.

34For ye had compassion of me in my bonds, and took joyfully the spoiling of your goods, knowing in yourselves that ye have in heaven a better and an enduring substance.

35Cast not away therefore your confidence, which hath great recompence of reward.

36For ye have need of patience, that, after ye have done the will of God, ye might receive the promise.

37For yet a little while, and he that shall come will come, and will not tarry.

38Now the just shall live by faith: but if *any man* draw back, my soul shall have no pleasure in him.

39But we are not of them who draw back unto perdition; but of them that believe to the saving of the soul.

PSALM 109:1–31

Hold not thy peace, O God of my praise;

2For the mouth of the wicked and the mouth of the deceitful are opened against me: they have spoken against me with a lying tongue.

3They compassed me about also with words of hatred; and fought against me without *a* cause.

4For my love they are my adversaries: but I *give myself unto* prayer.

5And they have rewarded me evil for good, and hatred for my love.

6Set thou a wicked man over him: and let Satan stand at his right hand.

7When he shall be judged, let him be condemned: and let his prayer become sin.

8Let his days be few; *and* let another take his office.

9Let his children be fatherless, and his wife a widow.

10Let his children be continually vagabonds, and beg: let them seek *their bread* also out of their desolate places.

11Let the extortioner catch all that he hath; and let the strangers spoil his labour.

12Let there be none to extend mercy unto him: neither let there be any to favour his fatherless children.

13Let his posterity be cut off; *and* in the generation following let their name be blotted out.

14Let the iniquity of his fathers be remembered with the LORD; and let not the sin of his mother be blotted out.

15Let them be before the LORD continually, that he may cut off the memory of them from the earth.

16Because that he remembered not to shew mercy, but persecuted the poor and needy man, that he might even slay the broken in heart.

17As he loved cursing, so let it come unto him: as he delighted not in blessing, so let it be far from him.

18As he clothed himself with cursing like as with his garment, so let it come into his bowels like water, and like oil into his bones.

19Let it be unto him as the garment *which* covereth him, and for a girdle wherewith he is girded continually.

20*Let* this *be* the reward of mine adversaries from the LORD, and of them that speak evil against my soul.

21But do thou for me, O GOD the Lord, for thy name's sake: because thy mercy *is* good, deliver thou me.

22For I *am* poor and needy, and my heart is wounded within me.

23I am gone like the shadow when it declineth: I am tossed up and down as the locust.

24My knees are weak through fasting; and my flesh faileth of fatness.

25I became also a reproach unto them: *when* they looked upon me they shaked their heads.

26Help me, O LORD my God: O save me according to thy mercy:

27That they may know that this *is* thy hand; *that* thou, LORD, hast done it.

28Let them curse, but bless thou: when they arise, let them be ashamed; but let thy servant rejoice.

29Let mine adversaries be clothed with shame, and let them cover themselves with their own confusion, as with a mantle.

30I will greatly praise the LORD with my mouth; yea, I will praise him among the multitude.

31For he shall stand at the right hand of the poor, to save *him* from those that condemn his soul.

PROVERBS FOR TODAY/ 27:13

Take his garment that is surety for a stranger, and take a pledge of him for a strange woman.

NOVEMBER 12

EZEKIEL 24:1—26:21

AGAIN in the ninth year, in the tenth month, in the tenth *day* of the month, the word of the LORD came unto me, saying,

2Son of man, write thee the name of the day, *even* of this same day: the king of Babylon set himself against Jerusalem this same day.

3And utter a parable unto the rebellious house, and say unto them, Thus saith the Lord GOD; Set on a pot, set *it* on, and also pour water into it:

4Gather the pieces thereof into it, *even* every good piece, the thigh, and the shoulder; fill *it* with the choice bones.

5Take the choice of the flock, and burn also the bones under it, *and* make it boil well, and let them seethe the bones of it therein.

6Wherefore thus saith the Lord GOD; Woe to the bloody city, to the pot whose scum *is* therein, and whose scum is not gone out of it! bring it out piece by piece; let no lot fall upon it.

7For her blood is in the midst of her; she set it upon the top of a rock; she poured it not upon the ground, to cover it with dust;

8That it might cause fury to come up to take vengeance; I have set her blood upon the top of a rock, that it should not be covered.

9Therefore thus saith the Lord GOD; Woe to the bloody city! I will even make the pile for fire great.

10Heap on wood, kindle the fire, consume the flesh, and spice it well, and let the bones be burned.

11Then set it empty upon the coals thereof, that the brass of it may be hot, and may burn, and *that* the filthiness of it may be molten in it, *that* the scum of it may be consumed.

12She hath wearied *herself* with lies, and her great scum went not forth out of her: her scum *shall be* in the fire.

13In thy filthiness *is* lewdness: because I have purged thee, and thou wast not purged, thou shalt not be purged from thy filthiness any more, till I have caused my fury to rest upon thee.

14I the LORD have spoken *it:* it shall come to pass, and I will do *it;* I will not go back, neither will I spare, neither will I repent; according to thy ways, and according to thy doings, shall they judge thee, saith the LORD GOD.

15Also the word of the LORD came unto me, saying,

16Son of man, behold, I take away from thee the desire of thine eyes with a stroke: yet neither shalt thou mourn nor weep, neither shall thy tears run down.

17Forbear to cry, make no mourning for the dead, bind the tire of thine head upon thee, and put on thy shoes upon thy feet, and cover not *thy* lips, and eat not the bread of men.

18So I spake unto the people in the morning: and at even my wife died; and I did in the morning as I was commanded.

19And the people said unto me, Wilt thou not tell us what these *things are* to us, that thou doest *so?*

20Then I answered them, The word of the LORD came unto me, saying,

21Speak unto the house of Israel, Thus saith the LORD GOD; Behold, I will profane my sanctuary, the excellency of your strength, the desire of your eyes, and that which your soul pitieth; and your sons and your daughters whom ye have left shall fall by the sword.

22And ye shall do as I have done:

ye shall not cover *your* lips, nor eat the bread of men.

23And your tires *shall be* upon your heads, and your shoes upon your feet: ye shall not mourn nor weep; but ye shall pine away for your iniquities, and mourn one toward another.

24Thus Ezekiel is unto you a sign: according to all that he hath done shall ye do: and when this cometh, ye shall know that I *am* the Lord GOD.

25Also, thou son of man, *shall it* not *be* in the day when I take from them their strength, the joy of their glory, the desire of their eyes, and that whereupon they set their minds, their sons and their daughters,

26*That* he that escapeth in that day shall come unto thee, to cause *thee* to hear *it* with *thine* ears?

27In that day shall thy mouth be opened to him which is escaped, and thou shalt speak, and be no more dumb: and thou shalt be a sign unto them; and they shall know that I *am* the LORD.

THE word of the LORD came again unto me, saying,

2Son of man, set thy face against the Ammonites, and prophesy against them;

3And say unto the Ammonites, Hear the word of the Lord GOD; Thus saith the Lord GOD; Because thou saidst, Aha, against my sanctuary, when it was profaned: and against the land of Israel, when it was desolate; and against the house of Judah, when they went into captivity;

4Behold, therefore I will deliver thee to the men of the east for a possession, and they shall set their palaces in thee, and make their dwellings in thee: they shall eat thy fruit, and they shall drink thy milk.

5And I will make Rabbah a stable for camels, and the Ammonites a couching place for flocks: and ye shall know that I *am* the LORD.

6For thus saith the Lord GOD; Because thou hast clapped *thine* hands, and stamped with the feet, and rejoiced in heart with all thy despite against the land of Israel;

7Behold, therefore I will stretch out mine hand upon thee, and will deliver thee for a spoil to the heathen; and I will cut thee off from the people, and I will cause thee to perish out of the countries: I will destroy thee; and thou shalt know that I *am* the LORD.

8Thus saith the Lord GOD; Because that Moab and Seir do say, Behold, the house of Judah *is* like unto all the heathen;

9Therefore, behold, I will open the side of Moab from the cities, from his cities *which are* on his frontiers, the glory of the country, Beth–jeshimoth, Baal–meon and Kiriathaim,

10Unto the men of the east with the Ammonites, and will give them in possession, that the Ammonites may not be remembered among the nations.

11And I will execute judgments upon Moab; and they shall know that I *am* the LORD.

12Thus saith the Lord GOD; Because that Edom hath dealt against the house of Judah by taking vengeance, and hath greatly offended, and revenged himself upon them;

13Therefore thus saith the Lord GOD; I will also stretch out mine hand upon Edom, and will cut off man and beast from it; and I will make it desolate from Teman; and they of Dedan shall fall by the sword.

14And I will lay my vengeance upon Edom by the hand of my people Israel: and they shall do in Edom according to mine anger and according to my fury; and they shall know my vengeance, saith the Lord GOD.

15Thus saith the Lord GOD; Because the Philistines have dealt by revenge, and have taken vengeance with a despiteful heart, to destroy *it* for the old hatred;

16Therefore thus saith the Lord GOD;

Behold, I will stretch out mine hand upon the Philistines, and I will cut off the Cherethims and destroy the remnant of the sea coast.

17And I will execute great vengeance upon them with furious rebukes; and they shall know that I *am* the LORD, when I shall lay my vengeance upon them.

AND it came to pass in the eleventh year, in the first *day* of the month, *that* the word of the LORD came unto me, saying,

2Son of man, because that Tyrus hath said against Jerusalem, Aha, she is broken *that was* the gates of the people: she is turned unto me: I shall be replenished, *now* she is laid waste:

3Therefore thus saith the Lord GOD; Behold, I *am* against thee, O Tyrus, and will cause many nations to come up against thee, as the sea causeth his waves to come up.

4And they shall destroy the walls of Tyrus, and break down her towers: I will also scrape her dust from her, and make her like the top of a rock.

5It shall be *a place for* the spreading of nets in the midst of the sea: for I have spoken *it,* saith the Lord GOD: and it shall become a spoil to the nations.

6And her daughters which *are* in the field shall be slain by the sword; and they shall know that I *am* the LORD.

7For thus saith the Lord GOD; Behold, I will bring upon Tyrus Nebuchadrezzar king of Babylon, a king of kings, from the north, with horses, and with chariots, and with horsemen, and companies, and much people.

8He shall slay with the sword thy daughters in the field: and he shall make a fort against thee, and cast a mount against thee, and lift up the buckler against thee.

9And he shall set engines of war against thy walls, and with his axes he shall break down thy towers.

10By reason of the abundance of his horses their dust shall cover thee: thy walls shall shake at the noise of the horsemen, and of the wheels, and of the chariots, when he shall enter into thy gates, as men enter into a city wherein is made a breach.

11With the hoofs of his horses shall he tread down all thy streets: he shall slay thy people by the sword, and thy strong garrisons shall go down to the ground.

12And they shall make a spoil of thy riches, and make a prey of thy merchandise: and they shall break down thy walls, and destroy thy pleasant houses: and they shall lay thy stones and thy timber and thy dust in the midst of the water.

13And I will cause the noise of thy songs to cease; and the sound of thy harps shall be no more heard.

14And I will make thee like the top of a rock: thou shalt be *a place* to spread nets upon; thou shalt be built no more: for I the LORD have spoken *it,* saith the Lord GOD.

15Thus saith the Lord GOD to Tyrus; Shall not the isles shake at the sound of thy fall, when the wounded cry, when the slaughter is made in the midst of thee?

16Then all the princes of the sea shall come down from their thrones, and lay away their robes, and put off their broidered garments: they shall clothe themselves with trembling; they shall sit upon the ground, and shall tremble at *every* moment, and be astonished at thee.

17And they shall take up a lamentation for thee, and say to thee, How art thou destroyed, *that wast* inhabited of seafaring men, the renowned city, which wast strong in the sea, she and her inhabitants, which cause their terror *to be* on all that haunt it!

18Now shall the isles tremble in the day of thy fall; yea, the isles that *are* in the sea shall be troubled at thy departure.

19For thus saith the Lord GOD; When I shall make thee a desolate city, like the cities that are not inhabited; when I shall bring up the deep upon thee, and great waters shall cover thee;

20When I shall bring thee down with them that descend into the pit, with the people of old time, and shall set thee in the low parts of the earth, in places desolate of old, with them that go down to the pit, that thou be not inhabited; and I shall set glory in the land of the living;

21I will make thee a terror, and thou *shalt be* no *more:* though thou be sought for, yet shalt thou never be found again, saith the Lord GOD.

HEBREWS 11:1–16

Now faith is the substance of things hoped for, the evidence of things not seen.

2For by it the elders obtained a good report.

3Through faith we understand that the worlds were framed by the word of God, so that things which are seen were not made of things which do appear.

4By faith Abel offered unto God a more excellent sacrifice than Cain, by which he obtained witness that he was righteous, God testifying of his gifts: and by it he being dead yet speaketh.

5By faith Enoch was translated that he should not see death; and was not found, because God had translated him: for before his translation he had this testimony, that he pleased God.

6But without faith *it is* impossible to please *him:* for he that cometh to God must believe that he is, and *that* he is a rewarder of them that diligently seek him.

7By faith Noah, being warned of God of things not seen as yet, moved with fear, prepared an ark to the saving of his house; by the which he condemned the world, and became heir of the righ-

teousness which is by faith.

8By faith Abraham, when he was called to go out into a place which he should after receive for an inheritance, obeyed; and he went out, not knowing whither he went.

9By faith he sojourned in the land of promise, as *in* a strange country, dwelling in tabernacles with Isaac and Jacob, the heirs with him of the same promise:

10For he looked for a city which hath foundations, whose builder and maker *is* God.

11Through faith also Sara herself received strength to conceive seed, and was delivered of a child when she was past age, because she judged him faithful who had promised.

12Therefore sprang there even of one, and him as good as dead, *so many* as the stars of the sky in multitude, and as the sand which is by the sea shore innumerable.

13These all died in faith, not having received the promises, but having seen them afar off, and were persuaded of *them,* and embraced *them,* and confessed that they were strangers and pilgrims on the earth.

14For they that say such things declare plainly that they seek a country.

15And truly, if they had been mindful of that *country* from whence they came out, they might have had opportunity to have returned.

16But now they desire a better *country,* that is, an heavenly: wherefore God is not ashamed to be called their God: for he hath prepared for them a city.

PSALM 110:1–7

The LORD said unto my LORD, Sit thou at my right hand, until I make thine enemies thy footstool.

2The LORD shall send the rod of thy strength out of Zion: rule thou in the midst of thine enemies.

3Thy people *shall be* willing in the day of thy power, in the beauties of holiness from the womb of the morning: thou hast the dew of thy youth.

4The LORD hath sworn, and will not repent, Thou *art* a priest for ever after the order of Melchizedek.

5The LORD at thy right hand shall strike through kings in the day of his wrath.

6He shall judge among the heathen, he shall fill *the places* with the dead bodies; he shall wound the heads over many countries.

7He shall drink of the brook in the way: therefore shall he lift up the head.

PROVERBS FOR TODAY/ 27:14

He that blesseth his friend with a loud voice, rising early in the morning, it shall be counted a curse to him.

NOVEMBER 13

EZEKIEL 27:1—28:26

THE word of the LORD came again unto me, saying,

2Now, thou son of man, take up a lamentation for Tyrus;

3And say unto Tyrus, O thou that art situate at the entry of the sea, *which art* a merchant of the people for many isles, Thus saith the Lord GOD; O Tyrus, thou hast said, I *am* of perfect beauty.

4Thy borders *are* in the midst of the seas, thy builders have perfected thy beauty.

5They have made all thy *ship* boards of fir trees of Senir: they have taken cedars from Lebanon to make masts for thee.

6*Of* the oaks of Bashan have they made thine oars; the company of the Ashurites have made thy benches *of* ivory, *brought* out of the isles of Chittim.

7Fine linen with broidered work from Egypt was that which thou spreadest forth to be thy sail; blue and purple from the isles of Elishah was that which covered thee.

8The inhabitants of Zidon and Arvad were thy mariners: thy wise *men,*

O Tyrus, *that* were in thee, were thy pilots.

9The ancients of Gebal and the wise *men* thereof were in thee thy calkers: and all the ships of the sea with their mariners were in thee to occupy thy merchandise.

10They of Persia and of Lud and of Phut were in thine army, thy men of war: they hanged the shield and helmet in thee; they set forth thy comeliness.

11The men of Arvad with thine army *were* upon thy walls round about, and the Gammadims were in thy towers: they hanged their shields upon thy walls round about; they have made thy beauty perfect.

12Tarshish *was* thy merchant by reason of the multitude of all *kind of* riches; with silver, iron, tin, and lead, they traded in thy fairs.

13Javan, Tubal, and Meshech, they *were* thy merchants: they traded the persons of men and vessels of brass in thy market.

14They of the house of Togarmah traded in thy fairs with horses and horsemen and mules.

15The men of Dedan *were* thy merchants; many isles *were* the merchandise of thine hand: they brought thee *for* a present horns of ivory and ebony.

16Syria *was* thy merchant by reason of the multitude of the wares of thy making: they occupied in thy fairs with emeralds, purple, and broidered work, and fine linen, and coral, and agate.

17Judah, and the land of Israel, they *were* thy merchants: they traded in thy market wheat of Minnith, and Pannag, and honey, and oil, and balm.

18Damascus *was* thy merchant in the multitude of the wares of thy making, for the multitude of all riches; in the wine of Helbon, and white wool.

19Dan also and Javan going to and fro occupied in thy fairs: bright iron, cassia, and calamus, were in thy market.

20Dedan *was* thy merchant in precious clothes for chariots.

21Arabia, and all the princes of Kedar, they occupied with thee in lambs, and rams, and goats: in these *were they* thy merchants.

22The merchants of Sheba and Raamah, they *were* thy merchants: they occupied in thy fairs with chief of all spices, and with all precious stones, and gold.

23Haran, and Canneh, and Eden, the merchants of Sheba, Asshur, *and* Chilmad, *were* thy merchants.

24These *were* thy merchants in all sorts *of things,* in blue clothes, and broidered work, and in chests of rich apparel, bound with cords, and made of cedar, among thy merchandise.

25The ships of Tarshish did sing of thee in thy market: and thou wast replenished, and made very glorious in the midst of the seas.

26Thy rowers have brought thee into great waters: the east wind hath broken thee in the midst of the seas.

27Thy riches, and thy fairs, thy merchandise, thy mariners, and thy pilots, thy calkers, and the occupiers of thy merchandise, and all thy men of war,

that *are* in thee, and in all thy company which *is* in the midst of thee, shall fall into the midst of the seas in the day of thy ruin.

28The suburbs shall shake at the sound of the cry of thy pilots.

29And all that handle the oar, the mariners, *and* all the pilots of the sea, shall come down from their ships, they shall stand upon the land;

30And shall cause their voice to be heard against thee, and shall cry bitterly, and shall cast up dust upon their heads, they shall wallow themselves in the ashes:

31And they shall make themselves utterly bald for thee, and gird them with sackcloth, and they shall weep for thee with bitterness of heart *and* bitter wailing.

32And in their wailing they shall take up a lamentation for thee, and lament over thee, *saying,* What *city is* like Tyrus, like the destroyed in the midst of the sea?

33When thy wares went forth out of the seas, thou filledst many people; thou didst enrich the kings of the earth with the multitude of thy riches and of thy merchandise.

34In the time *when* thou shalt be broken by the seas in the depths of the waters thy merchandise and all thy company in the midst of thee shall fall.

35All the inhabitants of the isles shall be astonished at thee, and their kings shall be sore afraid, they shall be troubled in *their* countenance.

36The merchants among the people shall hiss at thee; thou shalt be a terror, and never *shalt be* any more.

THE word of the LORD came again unto me, saying,

2Son of man, say unto the prince of Tyrus, Thus saith the Lord GOD; Because thine heart *is* lifted up, and thou hast said, I *am* a God, I sit *in* the seat of God, in the midst of the seas; yet thou *art* a man, and not God, though thou set thine heart as the heart of God:

3Behold, thou *art* wiser than Daniel; there is no secret that they can hide from thee:

4With thy wisdom and with thine understanding thou hast gotten thee riches, and hast gotten gold and silver into thy treasures:

5By thy great wisdom *and* by thy traffick hast thou increased thy riches, and thine heart is lifted up because of thy riches:

6Therefore thus saith the Lord GOD; Because thou hast set thine heart as the heart of God;

7Behold, therefore I will bring strangers upon thee, the terrible of the nations: and they shall draw their swords against the beauty of thy wisdom, and they shall defile thy brightness.

8They shall bring thee down to the pit, and thou shalt die the deaths of *them that are* slain in the midst of the seas.

9Wilt thou yet say before him that slayeth thee, I *am* God? but thou *shalt be* a man, and no God, in the hand of him that slayeth thee.

10Thou shalt die the deaths of the uncircumcised by the hand of strangers: for I have spoken *it,* saith the Lord GOD.

11Moreover the word of the LORD came unto me, saying,

12Son of man, take up a lamentation upon the king of Tyrus, and say unto him, Thus saith the Lord GOD; Thou sealest up the sum, full of wisdom, and perfect in beauty.

13Thou hast been in Eden the garden of God; every precious stone *was* thy covering, the sardius, topaz, and the diamond, the beryl, the onyx, and the jasper, the sapphire, the emerald, and the carbuncle, and gold: the workmanship of thy tabrets and of thy pipes was prepared in thee in the day that thou wast created.

14Thou *art* the anointed cherub that covereth; and I have set thee *so:* thou wast upon the holy mountain of God; thou hast walked up and down in the midst of the stones of fire.

15Thou *wast* perfect in thy ways from the day that thou wast created, till iniquity was found in thee.

16By the multitude of thy merchandise they have filled the midst of thee with violence, and thou hast sinned: therefore I will cast thee as profane out of the mountain of God: and I will destroy thee, O covering cherub, from the midst of the stones of fire.

17Thine heart was lifted up because of thy beauty, thou hast corrupted thy wisdom by reason of thy brightness: I will cast thee to the ground, I will lay thee before kings, that they may behold thee.

18Thou hast defiled thy sanctuaries by the multitude of thine iniquities, by the iniquity of thy traffick; therefore will I bring forth a fire from the midst of thee, it shall devour thee, and I will bring thee to ashes upon the earth in the sight of all them that behold thee.

19All they that know thee among the people shall be astonished at thee: thou shalt be a terror, and never *shalt* thou *be* any more.

20Again the word of the LORD came unto me, saying,

21Son of man, set thy face against Zidon, and prophesy against it,

22And say, Thus saith the Lord GOD; Behold, I *am* against thee, O Zidon; and I will be glorified in the midst of thee: and they shall know that I *am* the LORD, when I shall have executed judgments in her, and shall be sanctified in her.

23For I will send into her pestilence, and blood into her streets; and the wounded shall be judged in the midst of her by the sword upon her on every side; and they shall know that I *am* the LORD.

24And there shall be no more a pricking brier unto the house of Israel, nor *any* grieving thorn of all *that are* round about them, that despised them; and they shall know that I *am* the Lord GOD.

25Thus saith the Lord GOD; When I shall have gathered the house of Israel from the people among whom they are scattered, and shall be sanctified in them in the sight of the heathen, then shall they dwell in their land that I have given to my servant Jacob.

26And they shall dwell safely therein, and shall build houses, and plant vineyards; yea, they shall dwell with confidence, when I have executed judgments upon all those that despise them round about them; and they shall know that I *am* the LORD their God.

HEBREWS 11:17–31

BY faith Abraham, when he was tried, offered up Isaac: and he that had received the promises offered up his only begotten *son,*

18Of whom it was said, That in Isaac shall thy seed be called:

19Accounting that God *was* able to raise *him* up, even from the dead; from whence also he received him in a figure.

20By faith Isaac blessed Jacob and Esau concerning things to come.

21By faith Jacob, when he was a dying, blessed both the sons of Joseph; and worshipped, *leaning* upon the top of his staff.

22By faith Joseph, when he died, made mention of the departing of the children of Israel; and gave commandment concerning his bones.

23By faith Moses, when he was born, was hid three months of his parents, because they saw *he was* a proper child; and they were not afraid of the king's commandment.

24By faith Moses, when he was come to years, refused to be called the son of Pharaoh's daughter;

25Choosing rather to suffer affliction with the people of God, than to enjoy the pleasures of sin for a season;

26Esteeming the reproach of Christ greater riches than the treasures in Egypt: for he had respect unto the recompence of the reward.

27By faith he forsook Egypt, not fearing the wrath of the king: for he endured, as seeing him who is invisible.

28Through faith he kept the passover, and the sprinkling of blood, lest he that destroyed the firstborn should touch them.

29By faith they passed through the Red sea as by dry *land:* which the Egyptians assaying to do were drowned.

30By faith the walls of Jericho fell down, after they were compassed about seven days.

31By faith the harlot Rahab perished not with them that believed not, when she had received the spies with peace.

PSALM 111:1–10

PRAISE ye the LORD. I will praise the LORD with *my* whole heart, in the assembly of the upright, and *in* the congregation.

2The works of the LORD *are* great, sought out of all them that have pleasure therein.

3His work *is* honourable and glorious: and his righteousness endureth for ever.

4He hath made his wonderful works to be remembered: the LORD *is* gracious and full of compassion.

5He hath given meat unto them that fear him: he will ever be mindful of his covenant.

6He hath shewed his people the power of his works, that he may give them the heritage of the heathen.

7The works of his hands *are* verity and judgment; all his commandments *are* sure.

8They stand fast for ever and ever, *and are* done in truth and uprightness.

9He sent redemption unto his people:

he hath commanded his covenant for ever: holy and reverend *is* his name.

¹⁰The fear of the LORD *is* the begin-

ning of wisdom: a good understanding have all they that do *his commandments:* his praise endureth for ever.

PROVERBS FOR TODAY/ 27:15–16

A continual dropping in a very rainy day and a contentious woman are alike. Whosoever hideth her hideth the wind, and the ointment of his right hand, which *bewrayeth* itself.

NOVEMBER 14

EZEKIEL 29:1—30:26

IN the tenth year, in the tenth *month,* in the twelfth *day* of the month, the word of the LORD came unto me, saying,

²Son of man, set thy face against Pharaoh king of Egypt, and prophesy against him, and against all Egypt:

³Speak, and say, Thus saith the Lord GOD; Behold, I *am* against thee, Pharaoh king of Egypt, the great dragon that lieth in the midst of his rivers, which hath said, My river *is* mine own, and I have made *it* for myself.

⁴But I will put hooks in thy jaws, and I will cause the fish of thy rivers to stick unto thy scales, and I will bring thee up out of the midst of thy rivers, and all the fish of thy rivers shall stick unto thy scales.

⁵And I will leave thee *thrown* into the wilderness, thee and all the fish of thy rivers: thou shalt fall upon the open fields; thou shalt not be brought together, nor gathered: I have given thee for meat to the beasts of the field and to the fowls of the heaven.

⁶And all the inhabitants of Egypt shall know that I *am* the LORD, because they have been a staff of reed to the house of Israel.

⁷When they took hold of thee by thy hand, thou didst break, and rend all

their shoulder: and when they leaned upon thee, thou brakest, and madest all their loins to be at a stand.

⁸Therefore thus saith the Lord GOD; Behold, I will bring a sword upon thee, and cut off man and beast out of thee.

⁹And the land of Egypt shall be desolate and waste; and they shall know that I *am* the LORD: because he hath said, The river *is* mine, and I have made *it.*

¹⁰Behold, therefore I *am* against thee, and against thy rivers, and I will make the land of Egypt utterly waste *and* desolate, from the tower of Syene even unto the border of Ethiopia.

¹¹No foot of man shall pass through it, nor foot of beast shall pass through it, neither shall it be inhabited forty years.

¹²And I will make the land of Egypt desolate in the midst of the countries *that are* desolate, and her cities among the cities *that are* laid waste shall be desolate forty years: and I will scatter the Egyptians among the nations, and will disperse them through the countries.

¹³Yet thus saith the Lord GOD; At the end of forty years will I gather the Egyptians from the people whither they were scattered:

¹⁴And I will bring again the captivity

of Egypt, and will cause them to return *into* the land of Pathros, into the land of their habitation; and they shall be there a base kingdom.

15It shall be the basest of the kingdoms; neither shall it exalt itself any more above the nations: for I will diminish them, that they shall no more rule over the nations.

16And it shall be no more the confidence of the house of Israel, which bringeth *their* iniquity to remembrance, when they shall look after them: but they shall know that I *am* the Lord GOD.

17And it came to pass in the seven and twentieth year, in the first *month,* in the first *day* of the month, the word of the LORD came unto me, saying,

18Son of man, Nebuchadrezzar king of Babylon caused his army to serve a great service against Tyrus: every head *was* made bald, and every shoulder *was* peeled: yet had he no wages, nor his army, for Tyrus, for the service that he had served against it:

19Therefore thus saith the Lord GOD; Behold, I will give the land of Egypt unto Nebuchadrezzar king of Babylon; and he shall take her multitude, and take her spoil, and take her prey; and it shall be the wages for his army.

20I have given him the land of Egypt *for* his labour wherewith he served against it, because they wrought for me, saith the Lord GOD.

21In that day will I cause the horn of the house of Israel to bud forth, and I will give the opening of the mouth in the midst of them; and they shall know that I *am* the LORD.

THE word of the LORD came again unto me, saying,

2Son of man, prophesy and say, Thus saith the Lord GOD; Howl ye, Woe worth the day!

3For the day *is* near, even the day of the LORD *is* near, a cloudy day; it shall be the time of the heathen.

4And the sword shall come upon Egypt, and great pain shall be in Ethiopia, when the slain shall fall in Egypt, and they shall take away her multitude, and her foundations shall be broken down.

5Ethiopia, and Libya, and Lydia, and all the mingled people, and Chub, and the men of the land that is in league, shall fall with them by the sword.

6Thus saith the LORD; They also that uphold Egypt shall fall; and the pride of her power shall come down: from the tower of Syene shall they fall in it by the sword, saith the Lord GOD.

7And they shall be desolate in the midst of the countries *that are* desolate, and her cities shall be in the midst of the cities *that are* wasted.

8And they shall know that I *am* the LORD, when I have set a fire in Egypt, and *when* all her helpers shall be destroyed.

9In that day shall messengers go forth from me in ships to make the careless Ethiopians afraid, and great pain shall come upon them, as in the day of Egypt: for, lo, it cometh.

10Thus saith the Lord GOD; I will also make the multitude of Egypt to cease by the hand of Nebuchadrezzar king of Babylon.

11He and his people with him, the terrible of the nations, shall be brought to destroy the land: and they shall draw their swords against Egypt, and fill the land with the slain.

12And I will make the rivers dry, and sell the land into the hand of the wicked: and I will make the land waste, and all that is therein, by the hand of strangers: I the LORD have spoken *it.*

13Thus saith the Lord GOD; I will also destroy the idols, and I will cause *their* images to cease out of Noph; and there shall be no more a prince of the land of Egypt: and I will put a fear in the land of Egypt.

14And I will make Pathros desolate, and will set fire in Zoan, and will execute judgments in No.

15And I will pour my fury upon Sin, the strength of Egypt; and I will cut off the multitude of No.

16And I will set fire in Egypt: Sin shall have great pain, and No shall be rent asunder, and Noph *shall have* distresses daily.

17The young men of Aven and of Pibeseth shall fall by the sword: and these *cities* shall go into captivity.

18At Tehaphnehes also the day shall be darkened, when I shall break there the yokes of Egypt: and the pomp of her strength shall cease in her: as for her, a cloud shall cover her, and her daughters shall go into captivity.

19Thus will I execute judgments in Egypt: and they shall know that I *am* the LORD.

20And it came to pass in the eleventh year, in the first *month,* in the seventh *day* of the month, *that* the word of the LORD came unto me, saying,

21Son of man, I have broken the arm of Pharaoh king of Egypt; and, lo, it shall not be bound up to be healed, to put a roller to bind it, to make it strong to hold the sword.

22Therefore thus saith the Lord GOD; Behold, I *am* against Pharaoh king of Egypt, and will break his arms, the strong, and that which was broken; and I will cause the sword to fall out of his hand.

23And I will scatter the Egyptians among the nations, and will disperse them through the countries.

24And I will strengthen the arms of the king of Babylon, and put my sword in his hand: but I will break Pharaoh's arms, and he shall groan before him with the groanings of a deadly wounded *man.*

25But I will strengthen the arms of the king of Babylon, and the arms of Pharaoh shall fall down; and they shall know that I *am* the LORD, when I shall put my sword into the hand of the king of Babylon, and he shall stretch it out

upon the land of Egypt.

26And I will scatter the Egyptians among the nations, and disperse them among the countries; and they shall know that I *am* the LORD.

HEBREWS 11:32—12:13

AND what shall I more say? for the time would fail me to tell of Gedeon, and *of* Barak, and *of* Samson, and *of* Jephthae; *of* David also, and Samuel, and *of* the prophets:

33Who through faith subdued kingdoms, wrought righteousness, obtained promises, stopped the mouths of lions,

34Quenched the violence of fire, escaped the edge of the sword, out of weakness were made strong, waxed valiant in fight, turned to flight the armies of the aliens.

35Women received their dead raised to life again: and others were tortured, not accepting deliverance; that they might obtain a better resurrection:

36And others had trial of *cruel* mockings and scourgings, yea, moreover of bonds and imprisonment:

37They were stoned, they were sawn asunder, were tempted, were slain with the sword: they wandered about in sheepskins and goatskins; being destitute, afflicted, tormented;

38(Of whom the world was not worthy:) they wandered in deserts, and *in* mountains, and *in* dens and caves of the earth.

39And these all, having obtained a good report through faith, received not the promise:

40God having provided some better thing for us, that they without us should not be made perfect.

WHEREFORE seeing we also are compassed about with so great a cloud of witnesses, let us lay aside every weight, and the sin which doth so easily beset *us,* and let us run with patience the race that is set before us,

2Looking unto Jesus the author and finisher of *our* faith; who for the joy that was set before him endured the cross, despising the shame, and is set down at the right hand of the throne of God.

3For consider him that endured such contradiction of sinners against himself, lest ye be wearied and faint in your minds.

4Ye have not yet resisted unto blood, striving against sin.

5And ye have forgotten the exhortation which speaketh unto you as unto children, My son, despise not thou the chastening of the Lord, nor faint when thou art rebuked of him:

6For whom the Lord loveth he chasteneth, and scourgeth every son whom he receiveth.

7If ye endure chastening, God dealeth with you as with sons; for what son is he whom the father chasteneth not?

8But if ye be without chastisement, whereof all are partakers, then are ye bastards, and not sons.

9Furthermore we have had fathers of our flesh which corrected *us,* and we gave *them* reverence: shall we not much rather be in subjection unto the Father of spirits, and live?

10For they verily for a few days chastened *us* after their own pleasure; but he for *our* profit, that *we* might be partakers of his holiness.

11Now no chastening for the present seemeth to be joyous, but grievous: nevertheless afterward it yieldeth the peaceable fruit of righteousness unto them which are exercised thereby.

12Wherefore lift up the hands which hang down, and the feeble knees;

13And make straight paths for your feet, lest that which is lame be turned out of the way; but let it rather be healed.

PSALM 112:1–10

Praise ye the Lord. Blessed *is* the man *that* feareth the Lord, *that* delighteth greatly in his commandments.

2His seed shall be mighty upon earth: the generation of the upright shall be blessed.

3Wealth and riches *shall be* in his house: and his righteousness endureth for ever.

4Unto the upright there ariseth light in the darkness: *he is* gracious, and full of compassion, and righteous.

5A good man sheweth favour, and lendeth: he will guide his affairs with discretion.

6Surely he shall not be moved for ever: the righteous shall be in everlasting remembrance.

7He shall not be afraid of evil tidings: his heart is fixed, trusting in the Lord.

8His heart *is* established, he shall not be afraid, until he see *his desire* upon his enemies.

9He hath dispersed, he hath given to the poor; his righteousness endureth for ever; his horn shall be exalted with honour.

10The wicked shall see *it,* and be grieved; he shall gnash with his teeth, and melt away: the desire of the wicked shall perish.

PROVERBS FOR TODAY/ 27:17

Iron sharpeneth iron; so a man sharpeneth the countenance of his friend.

NOVEMBER 15

EZEKIEL 31:1—32:32

AND it came to pass in the eleventh year, in the third *month,* in the first *day* of the month, *that* the word of the LORD came unto me, saying,

2Son of man, speak unto Pharaoh king of Egypt, and to his multitude; Whom art thou like in thy greatness?

3Behold, the Assyrian *was* a cedar in Lebanon with fair branches, and with a shadowing shroud, and of an high stature; and his top was among the thick boughs.

4The waters made him great, the deep set him up on high with her rivers running round about his plants, and sent out her little rivers unto all the trees of the field.

5Therefore his height was exalted above all the trees of the field, and his boughs were multiplied, and his branches became long because of the multitude of waters, when he shot forth.

6All the fowls of heaven made their nests in his boughs, and under his branches did all the beasts of the field bring forth their young, and under his shadow dwelt all great nations.

7Thus was he fair in his greatness, in the length of his branches: for his root was by great waters.

8The cedars in the garden of God could not hide him: the fir trees were not like his boughs, and the chesnut trees were not like his branches; nor any tree in the garden of God was like unto him in his beauty.

9I have made him fair by the multitude of his branches: so that all the trees of Eden, that *were* in the garden of God, envied him.

10Therefore thus saith the Lord GOD; Because thou hast lifted up thyself in height, and he hath shot up his top among the thick boughs, and his heart is lifted up in his height;

11I have therefore delivered him into the hand of the mighty one of the heathen; he shall surely deal with him: I have driven him out for his wickedness.

12And strangers, the terrible of the nations, have cut him off, and have left him: upon the mountains and in all the valleys his branches are fallen, and his boughs are broken by all the rivers of the land; and all the people of the earth are gone down from his shadow, and have left him.

13Upon his ruin shall all the fowls of the heaven remain, and all the beasts of the field shall be upon his branches:

14To the end that none of all the trees by the waters exalt themselves for their height, neither shoot up their top among the thick boughs, neither their trees stand up in their height, all that drink water: for they are all delivered unto death, to the nether parts of the earth, in the midst of the children of men, with them that go down to the pit.

15Thus saith the Lord GOD; In the day when he went down to the grave I caused a mourning: I covered the deep for him, and I restrained the floods thereof, and the great waters were stayed: and I caused Lebanon to mourn for him, and all the trees of the field fainted for him.

16I made the nations to shake at the sound of his fall, when I cast him down to hell with them that descend into the pit: and all the trees of Eden, the choice and best of Lebanon, all that drink water, shall be comforted in the nether parts of the earth.

17They also went down into hell with him unto *them that be* slain with the sword; and *they that were* his arm, *that* dwelt under his shadow in the midst of the heathen.

18To whom art thou thus like in glory and in greatness among the trees of Eden? yet shalt thou be brought down with the trees of Eden unto the nether parts of the earth: thou shalt lie in the midst of the uncircumcised with *them that be* slain by the sword. This *is* Pharaoh and all his multitude, saith the Lord GOD.

AND it came to pass in the twelfth year, in the twelfth month, in the first *day* of the month, *that* the word of the LORD came unto me, saying,

2Son of man, take up a lamentation for Pharaoh king of Egypt, and say unto him, Thou art like a young lion of the nations, and thou *art* as a whale in the seas: and thou camest forth with thy rivers, and troubledst the waters with thy feet, and fouledst their rivers.

3Thus saith the Lord GOD; I will therefore spread out my net over thee with a company of many people; and they shall bring thee up in my net.

4Then will I leave thee upon the land, I will cast thee forth upon the open field, and will cause all the fowls of the heaven to remain upon thee, and I will fill the beasts of the whole earth with thee.

5And I will lay thy flesh upon the mountains, and fill the valleys with thy height.

6I will also water with thy blood the land wherein thou swimmest, *even* to the mountains; and the rivers shall be full of thee.

7And when I shall put thee out, I will cover the heaven, and make the stars thereof dark; I will cover the sun with a cloud, and the moon shall not give her light.

8All the bright lights of heaven will I make dark over thee, and set darkness upon thy land, saith the Lord GOD.

9I will also vex the hearts of many people, when I shall bring thy destruction among the nations, into the countries which thou hast not known.

10Yea, I will make many people amazed at thee, and their kings shall be horribly afraid for thee, when I shall brandish my sword before them; and they shall tremble at *every* moment, every man for his own life, in the day of thy fall.

11For thus saith the Lord GOD; The sword of the king of Babylon shall come upon thee.

12By the swords of the mighty will I cause thy multitude to fall, the terrible of the nations, all of them: and they shall spoil the pomp of Egypt, and all the multitude thereof shall be destroyed.

13I will destroy also all the beasts thereof from beside the great waters; neither shall the foot of man trouble them any more, nor the hoofs of beasts trouble them.

14Then will I make their waters deep, and cause their rivers to run like oil, saith the Lord GOD.

15When I shall make the land of Egypt desolate, and the country shall be destitute of that whereof it was full, when I shall smite all them that dwell therein, then shall they know that I *am* the LORD.

16This *is* the lamentation wherewith they shall lament her: the daughters of the nations shall lament her: they shall lament for her, *even* for Egypt, and for all her multitude, saith the Lord GOD.

17It came to pass also in the twelfth year, in the fifteenth *day* of the month, *that* the word of the LORD came unto me, saying,

18Son of man, wail for the multitude of Egypt, and cast them down, *even* her, and the daughters of the famous nations, unto the nether parts of the earth, with them that go down into the pit.

¹⁹Whom dost thou pass in beauty? go down, and be thou laid with the uncircumcised.

²⁰They shall fall in the midst of *them that are* slain by the sword: she is delivered to the sword: draw her and all her multitudes.

²¹The strong among the mighty shall speak to him out of the midst of hell with them that help him: they are gone down, they lie uncircumcised, slain by the sword.

²²Asshur *is* there and all her company: his graves *are* about him: all of them slain, fallen by the sword:

²³Whose graves are set in the sides of the pit, and her company is round about her grave: all of them slain, fallen by the sword, which caused terror in the land of the living.

²⁴There *is* Elam and all her multitude round about her grave, all of them slain, fallen by the sword, which are gone down uncircumcised into the nether parts of the earth, which caused their terror in the land of the living; yet have they borne their shame with them that go down to the pit.

²⁵They have set her a bed in the midst of the slain with all her multitude: her graves *are* round about him: all of them uncircumcised, slain by the sword: though their terror was caused in the land of the living, yet have they borne their shame with them that go down to the pit: he is put in the midst of *them that be* slain.

²⁶There *is* Meshech, Tubal, and all her multitude: her graves *are* round about him: all of them uncircumcised, slain by the sword, though they caused their terror in the land of the living.

²⁷And they shall not lie with the mighty *that are* fallen of the uncircumcised, which are gone down to hell with their weapons of war: and they have laid their swords under their heads, but their iniquities shall be upon their bones, though *they were* the terror of the mighty in the land of the living.

²⁸Yea, thou shalt be broken in the midst of the uncircumcised, and shalt lie with *them that are* slain with the sword.

²⁹There *is* Edom, her kings, and all her princes, which with their might are laid by *them that were* slain by the sword: they shall lie with the uncircumcised, and with them that go down to the pit.

³⁰There *be* the princes of the north, all of them, and all the Zidonians, which are gone down with the slain; with their terror they are ashamed of their might; and they lie uncircumcised with *them that be* slain by the sword, and bear their shame with them that go down to the pit.

³¹Pharaoh shall see them, and shall be comforted over all his multitude, *even* Pharaoh and all his army slain by the sword, saith the Lord God.

³²For I have caused my terror in the land of the living: and he shall be laid in the midst of the uncircumcised with *them that are* slain with the sword, *even* Pharaoh and all his multitude, saith the Lord God.

HEBREWS 12:14–29

FOLLOW peace with all *men,* and holiness, without which no man shall see the Lord:

¹⁵Looking diligently lest any man fail of the grace of God; lest any root of bitterness springing up trouble *you,* and thereby many be defiled;

¹⁶Lest there *be* any fornicator, or profane person, as Esau, who for one morsel of meat sold his birthright.

¹⁷For ye know how that afterward, when he would have inherited the blessing, he was rejected: for he found no place of repentance, though he sought it carefully with tears.

¹⁸For ye are not come unto the mount

that might be touched, and that burned with fire, nor unto blackness, and darkness, and tempest,

19And the sound of a trumpet, and the voice of words; which *voice* they that heard entreated that the word should not be spoken to them any more:

20(For they could not endure that which was commanded, And if so much as a beast touch the mountain, it shall be stoned, or thrust through with a dart:

21And so terrible was the sight, *that* Moses said, I exceedingly fear and quake:)

22But ye are come unto mount Sion, and unto the city of the living God, the heavenly Jerusalem, and to an innumerable company of angels,

23To the general assembly and church of the firstborn, which are written in heaven, and to God the Judge of all, and to the spirits of just men made perfect,

24And to Jesus the mediator of the new covenant, and to the blood of sprinkling, that speaketh better things than *that of* Abel.

25See that ye refuse not him that speaketh. For if they escaped not who refused him that spake on earth, much more *shall not* we *escape,* if we turn away from him that *speaketh* from heaven:

26Whose voice then shook the earth: but now he hath promised, saying, Yet once more I shake not the earth only, but also heaven.

27And this *word,* Yet once more, signifieth the removing of those things that are shaken, as of things that are made, that those things which cannot be shaken may remain.

28Wherefore we receiving a kingdom which cannot be moved, let us have grace, whereby we may serve God acceptably with reverence and godly fear:

29For our God *is* a consuming fire.

PSALM 113:1—114:8

PRAISE ye the LORD. Praise, O ye servants of the LORD, praise the name of the LORD.

2Blessed be the name of the LORD from this time forth and for evermore.

3From the rising of the sun unto the going down of the same the LORD'S name *is* to be praised.

4The LORD *is* high above all nations, *and* his glory above the heavens.

5Who *is* like unto the LORD our God, who dwelleth on high,

6Who humbleth *himself* to behold *the things that are* in heaven, and in the earth!

7He raiseth up the poor out of the dust, *and* lifteth the needy out of the dunghill;

8That he may set *him* with princes, *even* with the princes of his people.

9He maketh the barren woman to keep house, *and to be* a joyful mother of children. Praise ye the LORD.

WHEN Israel went out of Egypt, the house of Jacob from a people of strange language;

2Judah was his sanctuary, *and* Israel his dominion.

3The sea saw *it,* and fled: Jordan was driven back.

4The mountains skipped like rams, *and* the little hills like lambs.

5What *ailed* thee, O thou sea, that thou fleddest? thou Jordan, *that* thou wast driven back?

6Ye mountains, *that* ye skipped like rams; *and* ye little hills, like lambs?

7Tremble, thou earth, at the presence of the LORD, at the presence of the God of Jacob;

8Which turned the rock *into* a standing water, the flint into a fountain of waters.

PROVERBS FOR TODAY/ 27:18–20

Whoso keepeth the fig tree shall eat the fruit thereof: so he that waiteth on his master shall be honoured. □ *As in water face* answereth *to face, so the heart of man to man.* □ *Hell and destruction are never full; so the eyes of man are never satisfied.*

NOVEMBER 16

EZEKIEL 33:1—34:31

AGAIN the word of the LORD came unto me, saying,

2Son of man, speak to the children of thy people, and say unto them, When I bring the sword upon a land, if the people of the land take a man of their coasts, and set him for their watchman:

3If when he seeth the sword come upon the land, he blow the trumpet, and warn the people;

4Then whosoever heareth the sound of the trumpet, and taketh not warning; if the sword come, and take him away, his blood shall be upon his own head.

5He heard the sound of the trumpet, and took not warning; his blood shall be upon him. But he that taketh warning shall deliver his soul.

6But if the watchman see the sword come, and blow not the trumpet, and the people be not warned; if the sword come, and take *any* person from among them, he is taken away in his iniquity; but his blood will I require at the watchman's hand.

7So thou, O son of man, I have set thee a watchman unto the house of Israel; therefore thou shalt hear the word at my mouth, and warn them from me.

8When I say unto the wicked, O wicked *man,* thou shalt surely die; if thou dost not speak to warn the wicked from his way, that wicked *man* shall die in his iniquity; but his blood will I require at thine hand.

9Nevertheless, if thou warn the wicked of his way to turn from it; if he do not turn from his way, he shall die in his iniquity; but thou hast delivered thy soul.

10Therefore, O thou son of man, speak unto the house of Israel; Thus ye speak, saying, If our transgressions and our sins *be* upon us, and we pine away in them, how should we then live?

11Say unto them, As I live, saith the Lord GOD, I have no pleasure in the death of the wicked; but that the wicked turn from his way and live: turn ye, turn ye from your evil ways; for why will ye die, O house of Israel?

12Therefore, thou son of man, say unto the children of thy people, The righteousness of the righteous shall not deliver him in the day of his transgression: as for the wickedness of the wicked, he shall not fall thereby in the day that he turneth from his wickedness; neither shall the righteous be able to live for his *righteousness* in the day that he sinneth.

13When I shall say to the righteous, *that* he shall surely live; if he trust to his own righteousness, and commit iniquity, all his righteousnesses shall not be remembered; but for his iniquity that he hath committed, he shall die for it.

14Again, when I say unto the wicked,

Thou shalt surely die; if he turn from his sin, and do that which is lawful and right;

15If the wicked restore the pledge, give again that he had robbed, walk in the statutes of life, without committing iniquity; he shall surely live, he shall not die.

16None of his sins that he hath committed shall be mentioned unto him: he hath done that which is lawful and right; he shall surely live.

17Yet the children of thy people say, The way of the Lord is not equal: but as for them, their way is not equal.

18When the righteous turneth from his righteousness, and committeth iniquity, he shall even die thereby.

19But if the wicked turn from his wickedness, and do that which is lawful and right, he shall live thereby.

20Yet ye say, The way of the Lord is not equal. O ye house of Israel, I will judge you every one after his ways.

21And it came to pass in the twelfth year of our captivity, in the tenth *month*, in the fifth *day* of the month, *that* one that had escaped out of Jerusalem came unto me, saying, The city is smitten.

22Now the hand of the LORD was upon me in the evening, afore he that was escaped came; and had opened my mouth, until he came to me in the morning; and my mouth was opened, and I was no more dumb.

23Then the word of the LORD came unto me, saying,

24Son of man, they that inhabit those wastes of the land of Israel speak, saying, Abraham was one, and he inherited the land: but we *are* many; the land is given us for inheritance.

25Wherefore say unto them, Thus saith the Lord GOD; Ye eat with the blood, and lift up your eyes toward your idols, and shed blood: and shall ye possess the land?

26Ye stand upon your sword, ye work abomination, and ye defile every one his neighbour's wife: and shall ye possess the land?

27Say thou thus unto them, Thus saith the Lord GOD; *As* I live, surely they that *are* in the wastes shall fall by the sword, and him that *is* in the open field will I give to the beasts to be devoured, and they that *be* in the forts and in the caves shall die of the pestilence.

28For I will lay the land most desolate, and the pomp of her strength shall cease; and the mountains of Israel shall be desolate, that none shall pass through.

29Then shall they know that I *am* the LORD, when I have laid the land most desolate because of all their abominations which they have committed.

30Also, thou son of man, the children of thy people still are talking against thee by the walls and in the doors of the houses, and speak one to another, every one to his brother, saying, Come, I pray you, and hear what is the word that cometh forth from the LORD.

31And they come unto thee as the people cometh, and they sit before thee *as* my people, and they hear thy words, but they will not do them; for with their mouth they shew much love, *but* their heart goeth after their covetousness.

32And, lo, thou *art* unto them as a very lovely song of one that hath a pleasant voice, and can play well on an instrument: for they hear thy words, but they do them not.

33And when this cometh to pass, (lo, it will come,) then shall they know that a prophet hath been among them.

AND the word of the LORD came unto me, saying,

2Son of man, prophesy against the shepherds of Israel, prophesy, and say unto them, Thus saith the Lord GOD unto the shepherds; Woe *be* to the shepherds of Israel that do feed themselves! should not the shepherds feed the flocks?

3Ye eat the fat, and ye clothe you

with the wool, ye kill them that are fed: *but* ye feed not the flock.

⁴The diseased have ye not strengthened, neither have ye healed that which was sick, neither have ye bound up *that which was* broken, neither have ye brought again that which was driven away, neither have ye sought that which was lost; but with force and with cruelty have ye ruled them.

⁵And they were scattered, because *there is* no shepherd: and they became meat to all the beasts of the field, when they were scattered.

⁶My sheep wandered through all the mountains, and upon every high hill: yea, my flock was scattered upon all the face of the earth, and none did search or seek *after them.*

⁷Therefore, ye shepherds, hear the word of the LORD;

⁸As I live, saith the Lord GOD, surely because my flock became a prey, and my flock became meat to every beast of the field, because *there was* no shepherd, neither did my shepherds search for my flock, but the shepherds fed themselves, and fed not my flock;

⁹Therefore, O ye shepherds, hear the word of the LORD;

¹⁰Thus saith the Lord GOD; Behold, I *am* against the shepherds; and I will require my flock at their hand, and cause them to cease from feeding the flock; neither shall the shepherds feed themselves any more; for I will deliver my flock from their mouth, that they may not be meat for them.

¹¹For thus saith the Lord GOD; Behold, I, *even* I, will both search my sheep, and seek them out.

¹²As a shepherd seeketh out his flock in the day that he is among his sheep *that are* scattered; so will I seek out my sheep, and will deliver them out of all places where they have been scattered in the cloudy and dark day.

¹³And I will bring them out from the people, and gather them from the countries, and will bring them to their own land, and feed them upon the mountains of Israel by the rivers, and in all the inhabited places of the country.

¹⁴I will feed them in a good pasture, and upon the high mountains of Israel shall their fold be: there shall they lie in a good fold, and *in* a fat pasture shall they feed upon the mountains of Israel.

¹⁵I will feed my flock, and I will cause them to lie down, saith the Lord GOD.

¹⁶I will seek that which was lost, and bring again that which was driven away, and will bind up *that which was* broken, and will strengthen that which was sick: but I will destroy the fat and the strong; I will feed them with judgment.

¹⁷And *as for* you, O my flock, thus saith the Lord GOD; Behold, I judge between cattle and cattle, between the rams and the he goats.

¹⁸*Seemeth it* a small thing unto you to have eaten up the good pasture, but ye must tread down with your feet the residue of your pastures? and to have drunk of the deep waters, but ye must foul the residue with your feet?

¹⁹And *as for* my flock, they eat that which ye have trodden with your feet; and they drink that which ye have fouled with your feet.

²⁰Therefore thus saith the Lord GOD unto them; Behold, I, *even* I, will judge between the fat cattle and between the lean cattle.

²¹Because ye have thrust with side and with shoulder, and pushed all the diseased with your horns, till ye have scattered them abroad;

²²Therefore will I save my flock, and they shall no more be a prey; and I will judge between cattle and cattle.

²³And I will set up one shepherd over them, and he shall feed them, *even* my servant David; he shall feed them, and he shall be their shepherd.

²⁴And I the LORD will be their God, and my servant David a prince among them; I the LORD have spoken *it.*

²⁵And I will make with them a cov-

enant of peace, and will cause the evil beasts to cease out of the land: and they shall dwell safely in the wilderness, and sleep in the woods.

26And I will make them and the places round about my hill a blessing; and I will cause the shower to come down in his season; there shall be showers of blessing.

27And the tree of the field shall yield her fruit, and the earth shall yield her increase, and they shall be safe in their land, and shall know that I *am* the LORD, when I have broken the bands of their yoke, and delivered them out of the hand of those that served themselves of them.

28And they shall no more be a prey to the heathen, neither shall the beast of the land devour them; but they shall dwell safely, and none shall make *them* afraid.

29And I will raise up for them a plant of renown, and they shall be no more consumed with hunger in the land, neither bear the shame of the heathen any more.

30Thus shall they know that I the LORD their God *am* with them, and *that* they, *even* the house of Israel, *are* my people, saith the Lord GOD.

31And ye my flock, the flock of my pasture, *are* men, *and I am* your God, saith the Lord GOD.

HEBREWS 13:1–25

LET brotherly love continue.
2Be not forgetful to entertain strangers: for thereby some have entertained angels unawares.

3Remember them that are in bonds, as bound with them; *and* them which suffer adversity, as being yourselves also in the body.

4Marriage *is* honourable in all, and the bed undefiled: but whoremongers and adulterers God will judge.

5*Let your* conversation *be* without covetousness; *and be* content with such things as ye have: for he hath said, I will never leave thee, nor forsake thee.

6So that we may boldly say, The Lord *is* my helper, and I will not fear what man shall do unto me.

7Remember them which have the rule over you, who have spoken unto you the word of God: whose faith follow, considering the end of *their* conversation.

8Jesus Christ the same yesterday, and to day, and for ever.

9Be not carried about with divers and strange doctrines. For *it is* a good thing that the heart be established with grace; not with meats, which have not profited them that have been occupied therein.

10We have an altar, whereof they have no right to eat which serve the tabernacle.

11For the bodies of those beasts, whose blood is brought into the sanctuary by the high priest for sin, are burned without the camp.

12Wherefore Jesus also, that he might sanctify the people with his own blood, suffered without the gate.

13Let us go forth therefore unto him without the camp, bearing his reproach.

14For here have we no continuing city, but we seek one to come.

15By him therefore let us offer the sacrifice of praise to God continually, that is, the fruit of *our* lips giving thanks to his name.

16But to do good and to communicate forget not: for with such sacrifices God is well pleased.

17Obey them that have the rule over you, and submit yourselves: for they watch for your souls, as they that must give account, that they may do it with joy, and not with grief: for that *is* unprofitable for you.

18Pray for us: for we trust we have a good conscience, in all things willing to live honestly.

19But I beseech *you* the rather to

do this, that I may be restored to you the sooner.

20Now the God of peace, that brought again from the dead our Lord Jesus, that great shepherd of the sheep, through the blood of the everlasting covenant,

21Make you perfect in every good work to do his will, working in you that which is wellpleasing in his sight, through Jesus Christ; to whom *be* glory for ever and ever. Amen.

22And I beseech you, brethren, suffer the word of exhortation: for I have written a letter unto you in few words.

23Know ye that *our* brother Timothy is set at liberty; with whom, if he come shortly, I will see you.

24Salute all them that have the rule over you, and all the saints. They of Italy salute you.

25Grace *be* with you all. Amen.

PSALM 115:1–18

NOT unto us, O LORD, not unto us, but unto thy name give glory, for thy mercy, *and* for thy truth's sake.

2Wherefore should the heathen say, Where *is* now their God?

3But our God *is* in the heavens: he hath done whatsoever he hath pleased.

4Their idols *are* silver and gold, the work of men's hands.

5They have mouths, but they speak not: eyes have they, but they see not:

6They have ears, but they hear not: noses have they, but they smell not:

7They have hands, but they handle not: feet have they, but they walk not: neither speak they through their throat.

8They that make them are like unto them; *so is* every one that trusteth in them.

9O Israel, trust thou in the LORD: he *is* their help and their shield.

10O house of Aaron, trust in the LORD: he *is* their help and their shield.

11Ye that fear the LORD, trust in the LORD: he *is* their help and their shield.

12The LORD hath been mindful of us; he will bless *us;* he will bless the house of Israel; he will bless the house of Aaron.

13He will bless them that fear the LORD, *both* small and great.

14The LORD shall increase you more and more, you and your children.

15Ye *are* blessed of the LORD which made heaven and earth.

16The heaven, *even* the heavens, *are* the LORD's: but the earth hath he given to the children of men.

17The dead praise not the LORD, neither any that go down into silence.

18But we will bless the LORD from this time forth and for evermore. Praise the LORD.

PROVERBS FOR TODAY/ 27:21–22

As *the fining pot for silver, and the furnace for gold; so* is *a man to his praise.* □ *Though thou shouldest bray a fool in a mortar among wheat with a pestle, yet will not his foolishness depart from him.*

EZEKIEL 35:1—36:38

MOREOVER the word of the LORD came unto me, saying,

2Son of man, set thy face against mount Seir, and prophesy against it,

3And say unto it, Thus saith the Lord GOD; Behold, O mount Seir, I *am* against thee, and I will stretch out mine hand against thee, and I will make thee most desolate.

4I will lay thy cities waste, and thou shalt be desolate, and thou shalt know that I *am* the LORD.

5Because thou hast had a perpetual hatred, and hast shed *the blood of* the children of Israel by the force of the sword in the time of their calamity, in the time *that their* iniquity *had* an end:

6Therefore, as I live, saith the Lord GOD, I will prepare thee unto blood, and blood shall pursue thee: sith thou hast not hated blood, even blood shall pursue thee.

7Thus will I make mount Seir most desolate, and cut off from it him that passeth out and him that returneth.

8And I will fill his mountains with his slain *men:* in thy hills, and in thy valleys, and in all thy rivers, shall they fall that are slain with the sword.

9I will make thee perpetual desolation, and thy cities shall not return: and ye shall know that I *am* the LORD.

10Because thou hast said, These two nations and these two countries shall be mine, and we will possess it; whereas the LORD was there:

11Therefore, *as* I live, saith the Lord GOD, I will even do according to thine anger, and according to thine envy which thou hast used out of thy hatred against them; and I will make myself known among them, when I have judged thee.

12And thou shalt know that I *am* the LORD, *and that* I have heard all thy blasphemies which thou hast spoken against the mountains of Israel, saying, They are laid desolate, they are given us to consume.

13Thus with your mouth ye have boasted against me, and have multiplied your words against me: I have heard *them.*

14Thus saith the Lord GOD; When the whole earth rejoiceth, I will make thee desolate.

15As thou didst rejoice at the inheritance of the house of Israel, because it was desolate, so will I do unto thee: thou shalt be desolate, O mount Seir, and all Idumea, *even* all of it: and they shall know that I *am* the LORD.

ALSO, thou son of man, prophesy unto the mountains of Israel, and say, Ye mountains of Israel, hear the word of the LORD:

2Thus saith the Lord GOD; Because the enemy hath said against you, Aha, even the ancient high places are ours in possession:

3Therefore prophesy and say, Thus saith the Lord GOD; Because they have made *you* desolate, and swallowed you up on every side, that ye might be a possession unto the residue of the heathen, and ye are taken up in the lips of talkers, and *are* an infamy of the people:

4Therefore, ye mountains of Israel, hear the word of the Lord GOD; Thus saith the Lord GOD to the mountains, and to the hills, to the rivers, and to the valleys, to the desolate wastes, and to the cities that are forsaken, which became a prey and derision to the residue of the heathen that *are* round about;

5Therefore thus saith the Lord GOD;

Surely in the fire of my jealousy have I spoken against the residue of the heathen, and against all Idumea, which have appointed my land into their possession with the joy of all *their* heart, with despiteful minds, to cast it out for a prey.

6Prophesy therefore concerning the land of Israel, and say unto the mountains, and to the hills, to the rivers, and to the valleys, Thus saith the Lord GOD; Behold, I have spoken in my jealousy and in my fury, because ye have borne the shame of the heathen:

7Therefore thus saith the Lord GOD; I have lifted up mine hand, Surely the heathen that *are* about you, they shall bear their shame.

8But ye, O mountains of Israel, ye shall shoot forth your branches, and yield your fruit to my people of Israel; for they are at hand to come.

9For, behold, I *am* for you, and I will turn unto you, and ye shall be tilled and sown:

10And I will multiply men upon you, all the house of Israel, *even* all of it: and the cities shall be inhabited, and the wastes shall be builded:

11And I will multiply upon you man and beast; and they shall increase and bring fruit: and I will settle you after your old estates, and will do better *unto you* than at your beginnings: and ye shall know that I *am* the LORD.

12Yea, I will cause men to walk upon you, *even* my people Israel; and they shall possess thee, and thou shalt be their inheritance, and thou shalt no more henceforth bereave them *of men*.

13Thus saith the Lord GOD; Because they say unto you, Thou *land* devourest up men, and hast bereaved thy nations;

14Therefore thou shalt devour men no more, neither bereave thy nations any more, saith the Lord GOD.

15Neither will I cause *men* to hear in thee the shame of the heathen any more, neither shalt thou bear the reproach of the people any more, neither shalt thou cause thy nations to fall any more, saith the Lord GOD.

16Moreover the word of the LORD came unto me, saying,

17Son of man, when the house of Israel dwelt in their own land, they defiled it by their own way and by their doings: their way was before me as the uncleanness of a removed woman.

18Wherefore I poured my fury upon them for the blood that they had shed upon the land, and for their idols *wherewith* they had polluted it:

19And I scattered them among the heathen, and they were dispersed through the countries: according to their way and according to their doings I judged them.

20And when they entered unto the heathen, whither they went, they profaned my holy name, when they said to them, These *are* the people of the LORD, and are gone forth out of his land.

21But I had pity for mine holy name, which the house of Israel had profaned among the heathen, whither they went.

22Therefore say unto the house of Israel, Thus saith the Lord GOD; I do not *this* for your sakes, O house of Israel, but for mine holy name's sake, which ye have profaned among the heathen, whither ye went.

23And I will sanctify my great name, which was profaned among the heathen, which ye have profaned in the midst of them; and the heathen shall know that I *am* the LORD, saith the Lord GOD, when I shall be sanctified in you before their eyes.

24For I will take you from among the heathen, and gather you out of all countries, and will bring you into your own land.

25Then will I sprinkle clean water upon you, and ye shall be clean: from all your filthiness, and from all your idols, will I cleanse you.

26A new heart also will I give you, and a new spirit will I put within you:

and I will take away the stony heart out of your flesh, and I will give you an heart of flesh.

27And I will put my spirit within you, and cause you to walk in my statutes, and ye shall keep my judgments, and do *them.*

28And ye shall dwell in the land that I gave to your fathers; and ye shall be my people, and I will be your God.

29I will also save you from all your uncleannesses: and I will call for the corn, and will increase it, and lay no famine upon you.

30And I will multiply the fruit of the tree, and the increase of the field, that ye shall receive no more reproach of famine among the heathen.

31Then shall ye remember your own evil ways, and your doings that *were* not good, and shall lothe yourselves in your own sight for your iniquities and for your abominations.

32Not for your sakes do I *this,* saith the Lord GOD, be it known unto you: be ashamed and confounded for your own ways, O house of Israel.

33Thus saith the Lord GOD; In the day that I shall have cleansed you from all your iniquities I will also cause *you* to dwell in the cities, and the wastes shall be builded.

34And the desolate land shall be tilled, whereas it lay desolate in the sight of all that passed by.

35And they shall say, This land that was desolate is become like the garden of Eden; and the waste and desolate and ruined cities *are become* fenced, *and* are inhabited.

36Then the heathen that are left round about you shall know that I the LORD build the ruined *places, and* plant that that was desolate: I the LORD have spoken *it,* and I will do *it.*

37Thus saith the Lord GOD; I will yet *for* this be enquired of by the house of Israel, to do *it* for them; I will increase them with men like a flock.

38As the holy flock, as the flock of Jerusalem in her solemn feasts; so shall the waste cities be filled with flocks of men: and they shall know that I *am* the LORD.

JAMES 1:1–18

JAMES, a servant of God and of the Lord Jesus Christ, to the twelve tribes which are scattered abroad, greeting.

2My brethren, count it all joy when ye fall into divers temptations;

3Knowing *this,* that the trying of your faith worketh patience.

4But let patience have *her* perfect work, that ye may be perfect and entire, wanting nothing.

5If any of you lack wisdom, let him ask of God, that giveth to all *men* liberally, and upbraideth not; and it shall be given him.

6But let him ask in faith, nothing wavering. For he that wavereth is like a wave of the sea driven with the wind and tossed.

7For let not that man think that he shall receive any thing of the Lord.

8A double minded man *is* unstable in all his ways.

9Let the brother of low degree rejoice in that he is exalted:

10But the rich, in that he is made low: because as the flower of the grass he shall pass away.

11For the sun is no sooner risen with a burning heat, but it withereth the grass, and the flower thereof falleth, and the grace of the fashion of it perisheth: so also shall the rich man fade away in his ways.

12Blessed *is* the man that endureth temptation: for when he is tried, he shall receive the crown of life, which the Lord hath promised to them that love him.

13Let no man say when he is tempted, I am tempted of God: for God cannot be tempted with evil, neither tempteth he any man:

14But every man is tempted, when he is drawn away of his own lust, and enticed.

15Then when lust hath conceived, it bringeth forth sin: and sin, when it is finished, bringeth forth death.

16Do not err, my beloved brethren.

17Every good gift and every perfect gift is from above, and cometh down from the Father of lights, with whom is no variableness, neither shadow of turning.

18Of his own will begat he us with the word of truth, that we should be a kind of firstfruits of his creatures.

PSALM 116:1–19

I LOVE the LORD, because he hath heard my voice *and* my supplications.

2Because he hath inclined his ear unto me, therefore will I call upon *him* as long as I live.

3The sorrows of death compassed me, and the pains of hell gat hold upon me: I found trouble and sorrow.

4Then called I upon the name of the LORD; O LORD, I beseech thee, deliver my soul.

5Gracious *is* the LORD, and righteous; yea, our God *is* merciful.

6The LORD preserveth the simple: I was brought low, and he helped me.

7Return unto thy rest, O my soul; for the LORD hath dealt bountifully with thee.

8For thou hast delivered my soul from death, mine eyes from tears, *and* my feet from falling.

9I will walk before the LORD in the land of the living.

10I believed, therefore have I spoken: I was greatly afflicted:

11I said in my haste, All men *are* liars.

12What shall I render unto the LORD *for* all his benefits toward me?

13I will take the cup of salvation, and call upon the name of the LORD.

14I will pay my vows unto the LORD now in the presence of all his people.

15Precious in the sight of the LORD *is* the death of his saints.

16O LORD, truly I *am* thy servant; I *am* thy servant, *and* the son of thine handmaid: thou hast loosed my bonds.

17I will offer to thee the sacrifice of thanksgiving, and will call upon the name of the LORD.

18I will pay my vows unto the LORD now in the presence of all his people,

19In the courts of the LORD's house, in the midst of thee, O Jerusalem. Praise ye the LORD.

PROVERBS FOR TODAY/ 27:23–27

Be thou diligent to know the state of thy flocks, and *look well to thy herds. For riches* are *not for ever: and doth the crown* endure *to every generation? The hay appeareth, and the tender grass sheweth itself, and herbs of the mountains are gathered. The lambs* are *for thy clothing, and the goats* are *the price of the field. And thou shalt have goats' milk enough for thy food, for the food of thy household, and* for *the maintenance for thy maidens.*

EZEKIEL 37:1—38:23

THE hand of the LORD was upon me, and carried me out in the spirit of the LORD, and set me down in the midst of the valley which *was* full of bones,

2And caused me to pass by them round about: and, behold, *there were* very many in the open valley; and, lo, *they were* very dry.

3And he said unto me, Son of man, can these bones live? And I answered, O Lord GOD, thou knowest.

4Again he said unto me, Prophesy upon these bones, and say unto them, O ye dry bones, hear the word of the LORD.

5Thus saith the Lord GOD unto these bones; Behold, I will cause breath to enter into you, and ye shall live:

6And I will lay sinews upon you, and will bring up flesh upon you, and cover you with skin, and put breath in you, and ye shall live; and ye shall know that I *am* the LORD.

7So I prophesied as I was commanded: and as I prophesied, there was a noise, and behold a shaking, and the bones came together, bone to his bone.

8And when I beheld, lo, the sinews and the flesh came up upon them, and the skin covered them above: but *there was* no breath in them.

9Then said he unto me, Prophesy unto the wind, prophesy, son of man, and say to the wind, thus saith the Lord GOD; Come from the four winds, O breath, and breathe upon these slain, that they may live.

10So I prophesied as he commanded me, and the breath came into them, and they lived, and stood up upon their feet, an exceeding great army.

11Then he said unto me, Son of man,

these bones are the whole house of Israel: behold, they say, Our bones are dried, and our hope is lost: we are cut off for our parts.

12Therefore prophesy and say unto them, Thus saith the Lord GOD; Behold, O my people, I will open your graves, and cause you to come up out of your graves, and bring you into the land of Israel.

13And ye shall know that I *am* the LORD, when I have opened your graves, O my people, and brought you up out of your graves,

14And shall put my spirit in you, and ye shall live, and I shall place you in your own land: then shall ye know that I the LORD have spoken *it,* and performed *it,* saith the LORD.

15The word of the LORD came again unto me, saying,

16Moreover, thou son of man, take thee one stick, and write upon it, For Judah, and for the children of Israel his companions: then take another stick, and write upon it, For Joseph, the stick of Ephraim, and *for* all the house of Israel his companions:

17And join them one to another into one stick; and they shall become one in thine hand.

18And when the children of thy people shall speak unto thee, saying, Wilt thou not shew us what thou *meanest* by these?

19Say unto them, Thus saith the Lord GOD; Behold, I will take the stick of Joseph, which *is* in the hand of Ephraim, and the tribes of Israel his fellows, and will put them with him, *even* with the stick of Judah, and make them one stick, and they shall be one in mine hand.

20And the sticks whereon thou writest shall be in thine hand before their eyes.

21And say unto them, Thus saith the Lord GOD; Behold, I will take the children of Israel from among the heathen, whither they be gone, and will gather them on every side, and bring them into their own land:

22And I will make them one nation in the land upon the mountains of Israel; and one king shall be king to them all: and they shall be no more two nations, neither shall they be divided into two kingdoms any more at all:

23Neither shall they defile themselves any more with their idols, nor with their detestable things, nor with any of their transgressions: but I will save them out of all their dwelling-places, wherein they have sinned, and will cleanse them: so shall they be my people, and I will be their God.

24And David my servant *shall be* king over them; and they all shall have one shepherd: they shall also walk in my judgments, and observe my statutes, and do them.

25And they shall dwell in the land that I have given unto Jacob my servant, wherein your fathers have dwelt; and they shall dwell therein, *even* they, and their children, and their children's children for ever: and my servant David *shall be* their prince for ever.

26Moreover I will make a covenant of peace with them; it shall be an everlasting covenant with them: and I will place them, and multiply them, and will set my sanctuary in the midst of them for evermore.

27My tabernacle also shall be with them: yea, I will be their God, and they shall be my people.

28And the heathen shall know that I the LORD do sanctify Israel, when my sanctuary shall be in the midst of them for evermore.

AND the word of the LORD came unto me, saying,

2Son of man, set thy face against Gog, the land of Magog, the chief prince of Meshech and Tubal, and prophesy against him,

3And say, Thus saith the Lord GOD: Behold, I *am* against thee, O Gog, the chief prince of Meshech and Tubal:

4And I will turn thee back, and put hooks into thy jaws, and I will bring thee forth, and all thine army, horses and horsemen, all of them clothed with all sorts of *armour, even* a great company *with* bucklers and shields, all of them handling swords:

5Persia, Ethiopia, and Libya with them; all of them with shield and helmet:

6Gomer, and all his bands; the house of Togarmah of the north quarters, and all his bands: *and* many people with thee.

7Be thou prepared, and prepare for thyself, thou, and all thy company that are assembled unto thee, and be thou a guard unto them.

8After many days thou shalt be visited: in the latter years thou shalt come into the land *that is* brought back from the sword, *and is* gathered out of many people, against the mountains of Israel, which have been always waste: but it is brought forth out of the nations, and they shall dwell safely all of them.

9Thou shalt ascend and come like a storm, thou shalt be like a cloud to cover the land, thou, and all thy bands, and many people with thee.

10Thus saith the Lord GOD; It shall also come to pass, *that* at the same time shall things come into thy mind, and thou shalt think an evil thought:

11And thou shalt say, I will go up to the land of unwalled villages; I will go to them that are at rest, that dwell safely, all of them dwelling without walls, and having neither bars nor gates,

12To take a spoil, and to take a prey; to turn thine hand upon the desolate places *that are now* inhabited, and upon the people *that are* gathered out of the nations, which have gotten cattle and goods, that dwell in the midst of the land.

13Sheba, and Dedan, and the merchants of Tarshish, with all the young lions thereof, shall say unto thee, Art thou come to take a spoil? hast thou gathered thy company to take a prey? to carry away silver and gold, to take away cattle and goods, to take a great spoil?

14Therefore, son of man, prophesy and say unto Gog, Thus saith the Lord GOD; In that day when my people of Israel dwelleth safely, shalt thou not know *it?*

15And thou shalt come from thy place out of the north parts, thou, and many people with thee, all of them riding upon horses, a great company, and a mighty army:

16And thou shalt come up against my people of Israel, as a cloud to cover the land; it shall be in the latter days, and I will bring thee against my land, that the heathen may know me, when I shall be sanctified in thee, O Gog, before their eyes.

17Thus saith the Lord GOD; *Art* thou he of whom I have spoken in old time by my servants the prophets of Israel, which prophesied in those days *many* years that I would bring thee against them?

18And it shall come to pass at the same time when Gog shall come against the land of Israel, saith the Lord GOD, *that* my fury shall come up in my face.

19For in my jealousy *and* in the fire of my wrath have I spoken, Surely in that day there shall be a great shaking in the land of Israel;

20So that the fishes of the sea, and the fowls of the heaven, and the beasts of the field, and all creeping things that creep upon the earth, and all the men that *are* upon the face of the earth, shall shake at my presence, and the mountains shall be thrown down, and the steep places shall fall, and every wall shall fall to the ground.

21And I will call for a sword against him throughout all my mountains, saith the Lord GOD: every man's sword shall be against his brother.

22And I will plead against him with pestilence and with blood; and I will rain upon him, and upon his bands, and upon the many people that *are* with him, an overflowing rain, and great hailstones, fire, and brimstone.

23Thus will I magnify myself, and sanctify myself; and I will be known in the eyes of many nations, and they shall know that I *am* the LORD.

JAMES 1:19—2:17

WHEREFORE, my beloved brethren, let every man be swift to hear, slow to speak, slow to wrath:

20For the wrath of man worketh not the righteousness of God.

21Wherefore lay apart all filthiness and superfluity of naughtiness, and receive with meekness the engrafted word, which is able to save your souls.

22But be ye doers of the word, and not hearers only, deceiving your own selves.

23For if any be a hearer of the word, and not a doer, he is like unto a man beholding his natural face in a glass:

24For he beholdeth himself, and goeth his way, and straightway forgetteth what manner of man he was.

25But whoso looketh into the perfect law of liberty, and continueth *therein,* he being not a forgetful hearer, but a doer of the work, this man shall be blessed in his deed.

26If any man among you seem to be religious, and bridleth not his tongue, but deceiveth his own heart, this man's religion *is* vain.

27Pure religion and undefiled before God and the Father is this, To visit the fatherless and widows in their affliction, *and* to keep himself unspotted from the world.

MY brethren, have not the faith of our Lord Jesus Christ, *the Lord* of glory, with respect of persons.

2For if there come unto your assembly a man with a gold ring, in goodly apparel, and there come in also a poor man in vile raiment;

3And ye have respect to him that weareth the gay clothing, and say unto him, Sit thou here in a good place; and say to the poor, Stand thou there, or sit here under my footstool:

4Are ye not then partial in yourselves, and are become judges of evil thoughts?

5Hearken, my beloved brethren, Hath not God chosen the poor of this world rich in faith, and heirs of the kingdom which he hath promised to them that love him?

6But ye have despised the poor. Do not rich men oppress you, and draw you before the judgment seats?

7Do not they blaspheme that worthy name by the which ye are called?

8If ye fulfil the royal law according to the scripture, Thou shalt love thy neighbour as thyself, ye do well:

9But if ye have respect to persons, ye commit sin, and are convinced of the law as transgressors.

10For whosoever shall keep the whole law, and yet offend in one *point,* he is guilty of all.

11For he that said, Do not commit adultery, said also, Do not kill. Now if thou commit no adultery, yet if thou kill, thou art become a transgressor of the law.

12So speak ye, and so do, as they that shall be judged by the law of liberty.

13For he shall have judgment without mercy, that hath shewed no mercy; and mercy rejoiceth against judgment.

14What *doth it* profit, my brethren, though a man say he hath faith, and have not works? can faith save him?

15If a brother or sister be naked, and destitute of daily food,

16And one of you say unto them, Depart in peace, be *ye* warmed and filled; notwithstanding ye give them not those things which are needful to the body; what *doth it* profit?

17Even so faith, if it hath not works, is dead, being alone.

PSALM 117:1–2

O PRAISE the LORD, all ye nations: praise him, all ye people.

2For his merciful kindness is great toward us: and the truth of the LORD *endureth* for ever. Praise ye the LORD.

PROVERBS FOR TODAY/ 28:1

The wicked flee when no man pursueth: but the righteous are bold as a lion.

NOVEMBER 19

EZEKIEL 39:1—40:27

T HEREFORE, thou son of man, prophesy against Gog, and say, Thus saith the Lord GOD; Behold, I *am* against thee, O Gog, the chief prince of Meshech and Tubal:

2And I will turn thee back, and leave but the sixth part of thee, and will cause thee to come up from the north parts, and will bring thee upon the mountains of Israel:

3And I will smite thy bow out of thy

left hand, and will cause thine arrows to fall out of thy right hand.

4Thou shalt fall upon the mountains of Israel, thou, and all thy bands, and the people that *is* with thee: I will give thee unto the ravenous birds of every sort, and *to* the beasts of the field to be devoured.

5Thou shalt fall upon the open field: for I have spoken *it,* saith the Lord GOD.

6And I will send a fire on Magog, and among them that dwell carelessly in the isles: and they shall know that I *am* the LORD.

7So will I make my holy name known in the midst of my people Israel; and I will not *let them* pollute my holy name any more: and the heathen shall know that I *am* the LORD, the Holy One in Israel.

8Behold, it is come, and it is done, saith the Lord GOD; this *is* the day whereof I have spoken.

9And they that dwell in the cities of Israel shall go forth, and shall set on fire and burn the weapons, both the shields and the bucklers, the bows and the arrows, and the handstaves, and the spears, and they shall burn them with fire seven years:

10So that they shall take no wood out of the field, neither cut down *any* out of the forests; for they shall burn the weapons with fire: and they shall spoil those that spoiled them, and rob those that robbed them, saith the Lord GOD.

11And it shall come to pass in that day, *that* I will give unto Gog a place there of graves in Israel, the valley of the passengers on the east of the sea: and it shall stop the *noses* of the passengers: and there shall they bury Gog and all his multitude: and they shall call *it* The valley of Hamongog.

12And seven months shall the house of Israel be burying of them, that they may cleanse the land.

13Yea, all the people of the land shall bury *them;* and it shall be to them a renown the day that I shall be glorified, saith the Lord GOD.

14And they shall sever out men of continual employment, passing through the land to bury with the passengers those that remain upon the face of the earth, to cleanse it: after the end of seven months shall they search.

15And the passengers *that* pass through the land, when *any* seeth a man's bone, then shall he set up a sign by it, till the buriers have buried it in the valley of Hamongog.

16And also the name of the city *shall be* Hamonah. Thus shall they cleanse the land.

17And, thou son of man, thus saith the Lord GOD; Speak unto every feathered fowl, and to every beast of the field, Assemble yourselves, and come; gather yourselves on every side to my sacrifice that I do sacrifice for you, *even* a great sacrifice upon the mountains of Israel, that ye may eat flesh, and drink blood.

18Ye shall eat the flesh of the mighty, and drink the blood of the princes of the earth, of rams, of lambs, and of goats, of bullocks, all of them fatlings of Bashan.

19And ye shall eat fat till ye be full, and drink blood till ye be drunken, of my sacrifice which I have sacrificed for you.

20Thus ye shall be filled at my table with horses and chariots, with mighty men, and with all men of war, saith the Lord GOD.

21And I will set my glory among the heathen, and all the heathen shall see my judgment that I have executed, and my hand that I have laid upon them.

22So the house of Israel shall know that I *am* the LORD their God from that day and forward.

23And the heathen shall know that the house of Israel went into captivity for their iniquity: because they trespassed against me, therefore hid I my face from them, and gave them into the hand of their enemies: so fell they all by the sword.

24According to their uncleanness and according to their transgressions have I done unto them, and hid my face from them.

25Therefore thus saith the Lord GOD; Now will I bring again the captivity of Jacob, and have mercy upon the whole house of Israel, and will be jealous for my holy name;

26After that they have borne their shame, and all their trespasses whereby they have trespassed against me, when they dwelt safely in their land, and none made *them* afraid.

27When I have brought them again from the people, and gathered them out of their enemies' lands, and am sanctified in them in the sight of many nations;

28Then shall they know that I *am* the LORD their God, which caused them to be led into captivity among the heathen: but I have gathered them unto their own land, and have left none of them any more there.

29Neither will I hide my face any more from them: for I have poured out my spirit upon the house of Israel, saith the Lord GOD.

IN the five and twentieth year of our captivity, in the beginning of the year, in the tenth *day* of the month, in the fourteenth year after that the city was smitten, in the selfsame day the hand of the LORD was upon me, and brought me thither.

2In the visions of God brought he me into the land of Israel, and set me upon a very high mountain, by which *was* as the frame of a city on the south.

3And he brought me thither, and, behold, *there was* a man, whose appearance *was* like the appearance of brass, with a line of flax in his hand, and a measuring reed; and he stood in the gate.

4And the man said unto me, Son of man, behold with thine eyes, and hear with thine ears, and set thine heart upon all that I shall shew thee; for to the intent that I might shew *them* unto thee *art* thou brought hither: declare all that thou seest to the house of Israel.

5And behold a wall on the outside of the house round about, and in the man's hand a measuring reed of six cubits *long* by the cubit and an hand breadth: so he measured the breadth of the building, one reed; and the height, one reed.

6Then came he unto the gate which looketh toward the east, and went up the stairs thereof, and measured the threshold of the gate, *which was* one reed broad; and the other threshold *of the gate, which was* one reed broad.

7And *every* little chamber *was* one reed long, and one reed broad; and between the little chambers *were* five cubits; and the threshold of the gate by the porch of the gate within *was* one reed.

8He measured also the porch of the gate within, one reed.

9Then measured he the porch of the gate, eight cubits; and the posts thereof, two cubits; and the porch of the gate *was* inward.

10And the little chambers of the gate eastward *were* three on this side, and three on that side; they three *were* of one measure: and the posts had one measure on this side and on that side.

11And he measured the breadth of the entry of the gate, ten cubits; *and* the length of the gate, thirteen cubits.

12The space also before the little chambers *was* one cubit *on this side,* and the space *was* one cubit on that side: and the little chambers *were* six cubits on this side, and six cubits on that side.

13He measured then the gate from the roof of *one* little chamber to the roof of another: the breadth *was* five and twenty cubits, door against door.

14He made also posts of threescore cubits, even unto the post of the court round about the gate.

15And from the face of the gate of the entrance unto the face of the porch of the inner gate *were* fifty cubits.

16And *there were* narrow windows to the little chambers, and to their posts within the gate round about, and likewise to the arches: and windows *were* round about inward: and upon *each* post *were* palm trees.

17Then brought he me into the outward court, and, lo, *there were* chambers, and a pavement made for the court round about: thirty chambers *were* upon the pavement.

18And the pavement by the side of the gates over against the length of the gates *was* the lower pavement.

19Then he measured the breadth from the forefront of the lower gate unto the forefront of the inner court without, an hundred cubits eastward and northward.

20And the gate of the outward court that looked toward the north, he measured the length thereof, and the breadth thereof.

21And the little chambers thereof *were* three on this side and three on that side; and the posts thereof and the arches thereof were after the measure of the first gate: the length thereof *was* fifty cubits, and the breadth five and twenty cubits.

22And their windows, and their arches, and their palm trees, *were* after the measure of the gate that looketh toward the east; and they went up unto it by seven steps; and the arches thereof *were* before them.

23And the gate of the inner court *was* over against the gate toward the north, and toward the east; and he measured from gate to gate an hundred cubits.

24After that he brought me toward the south, and behold a gate toward the south: and he measured the posts thereof and the arches thereof according to these measures.

25And *there were* windows in it and in the arches thereof round about, like those windows: the length *was* fifty cubits, and the breadth five and twenty cubits.

26And *there were* seven steps to go up to it, and the arches thereof *were* before them: and it had palm trees, one on this side, and another on that side, upon the posts thereof.

27And *there was* a gate in the inner court toward the south: and he measured from gate to gate toward the south an hundred cubits.

JAMES 2:18—3:18

YEA, a man may say, Thou hast faith, and I have works: shew me thy faith without thy works, and I will shew thee my faith by my works.

19Thou believest that there is one God; thou doest well: the devils also believe, and tremble.

20But wilt thou know, O vain man, that faith without works is dead?

21Was not Abraham our father justified by works, when he had offered Isaac his son upon the altar?

22Seest thou how faith wrought with his works, and by works was faith made perfect?

23And the scripture was fulfilled which saith, Abraham believed God, and it was imputed unto him for righteousness: and he was called the Friend of God.

24Ye see then how that by works a man is justified, and not by faith only.

25Likewise also was not Rahab the harlot justified by works, when she had received the messengers, and had sent *them* out another way?

26For as the body without the spirit is dead, so faith without works is dead also.

My brethren, be not many masters, knowing that we shall receive the greater condemnation.

2For in many things we offend all. If any man offend not in word, the same *is* a perfect man, *and* able also to bridle the whole body.

3Behold, we put bits in the horses' mouths, that they may obey us; and we turn about their whole body.

4Behold also the ships, which though *they be* so great, and *are* driven of fierce winds, yet are they turned about with a very small helm, whithersoever the governor listeth.

5Even so the tongue is a little member, and boasteth great things. Behold, how great a matter a little fire kindleth!

6And the tongue *is* a fire, a world of iniquity; so is the tongue among our members, that it defileth the whole body, and setteth on fire the course of nature; and it is set on fire of hell.

7For every kind of beasts, and of birds, and of serpents, and of things in the sea, is tamed, and hath been tamed of mankind:

8But the tongue can no man tame; *it is* an unruly evil, full of deadly poison.

9Therewith bless we God, even the Father; and therewith curse we men, which are made after the similitude of God.

10Out of the same mouth proceedeth blessing and cursing. My brethren, these things ought not so to be.

11Doth a fountain send forth at the same place sweet *water* and bitter?

12Can the fig tree, my brethren, bear olive berries? either a vine, figs? so *can* no fountain both yield salt water and fresh.

13Who *is* a wise man and endued with knowledge among you? let him shew out of a good conversation his works with meekness of wisdom.

14But if ye have bitter envying and strife in your hearts, glory not, and lie not against the truth.

15This wisdom descendeth not from above, but *is* earthly, sensual, devilish.

16For where envying and strife *is,* there *is* confusion and every evil work.

17But the wisdom that is from above is first pure, then peaceable, gentle, *and* easy to be intreated, full of mercy and good fruits, without partiality, and without hypocrisy.

18And the fruit of righteousness is sown in peace of them that make peace.

PSALM 118:1–18

O GIVE thanks unto the LORD; for *he is* good: because his mercy *endureth* for ever.

2Let Israel now say, that his mercy *endureth* for ever.

3Let the house of Aaron now say, that his mercy *endureth* for ever.

4Let them now that fear the LORD say, that his mercy *endureth* for ever.

5I called upon the LORD in distress: the LORD answered me, *and set me* in a large place.

6The LORD *is* on my side; I will not fear: what can man do unto me?

7The LORD taketh my part with them that help me: therefore shall I see *my desire* upon them that hate me.

8*It is* better to trust in the LORD than to put confidence in man.

9*It is* better to trust in the LORD than to put confidence in princes.

10All nations compassed me about: but in the name of the LORD will I destroy them.

11They compassed me about; yea, they compassed me about: but in the name of the LORD I will destroy them.

12They compassed me about like bees; they are quenched as the fire of thorns: for in the name of the LORD I will destroy them.

13Thou hast thrust sore at me that I might fall: but the LORD helped me.

14The LORD *is* my strength and song, and is become my salvation.

15The voice of rejoicing and salvation *is* in the tabernacles of the righteous:

the right hand of the Lord doeth valiantly.

16The right hand of the Lord is exalted: the right hand of the Lord doeth valiantly.

17I shall not die, but live, and declare the works of the Lord.

18The Lord hath chastened me sore: but he hath not given me over unto death.

PROVERBS FOR TODAY/ 28:2

For the transgression of a land many are *the princes thereof: but by a man of understanding* and *knowledge the state* thereof *shall be prolonged.*

NOVEMBER 20

EZEKIEL 40:28—41:26

And he brought me to the inner court by the south gate: and he measured the south gate according to these measures;

29And the little chambers thereof, and the posts thereof, and the arches thereof, according to these measures: and *there were* windows in it and in the arches thereof round about: *it was* fifty cubits long, and five and twenty cubits broad.

30And the arches round about *were* five and twenty cubits long, and five cubits broad.

31And the arches thereof *were* toward the utter court; and palm trees *were* upon the posts thereof: and the going up to it *had* eight steps.

32And he brought me into the inner court toward the east: and he measured the gate according to these measures.

33And the little chambers thereof, and the posts thereof, and the arches thereof, *were* according to these measures: and *there were* windows therein and in the arches thereof round about: *it was* fifty cubits long, and five and twenty cubits broad.

34And the arches thereof *were* toward the outward court; and palm trees *were* upon the posts thereof, on this side,

and on that side: and the going up to it *had* eight steps.

35And he brought me to the north gate, and measured *it* according to these measures;

36The little chambers thereof, the posts thereof, and the arches thereof, and the windows to it round about: the length *was* fifty cubits, and the breadth five and twenty cubits.

37And the posts thereof *were* toward the utter court; and palm trees *were* upon the posts thereof, on this side, and on that side: and the going up to it *had* eight steps.

38And the chambers and the entries thereof *were* by the posts of the gates, where they washed the burnt offering.

39And in the porch of the gate *were* two tables on this side, and two tables on that side, to slay thereon the burnt offering and the sin offering and the trespass offering.

40And at the side without as one goeth up to the entry of the north gate, *were* two tables; and on the other side, which *was* at the porch of the gate, *were* two tables.

41Four tables *were* on this side, and four tables on that side, by the side of the gate; eight tables, whereupon they slew *their sacrifices.*

⁴²And the four tables *were* of hewn stone for the burnt offering, of a cubit and an half long, and a cubit and an half broad, and one cubit high: whereupon also they laid the instruments wherewith they slew the burnt offering and the sacrifice.

⁴³And within *were* hooks, an hand broad, fastened round about: and upon the tables *was* the flesh of the offering.

⁴⁴And without the inner gate *were* the chambers of the singers in the inner court, which *was* at the side of the north gate; and their prospect *was* toward the south: one at the side of the east gate *having* the prospect toward the north.

⁴⁵And he said unto me, This chamber, whose prospect *is* toward the south, *is* for the priests, the keepers of the charge of the house.

⁴⁶And the chamber whose prospect *is* toward the north *is* for the priests, the keepers of the charge of the altar: these *are* the sons of Zadok among the sons of Levi, which come near to the Lord to minister unto him.

⁴⁷So he measured the court, an hundred cubits long, and an hundred cubits broad, foursquare; and the altar *that was* before the house.

⁴⁸And he brought me to the porch of the house, and measured *each* post of the porch, five cubits on this side, and five cubits on that side: and the breadth of the gate *was* three cubits on this side, and three cubits on that side.

⁴⁹The length of the porch *was* twenty cubits, and the breadth eleven cubits; and *he brought me* by the steps whereby they went up to it: and *there were* pillars by the posts, one on this side, and another on that side.

AFTERWARD he brought me to the temple, and measured the posts, six cubits broad on the one side, and six cubits broad on the other side, *which* was the breadth of the tabernacle.

²And the breadth of the door *was* ten cubits; and the sides of the door *were* five cubits on the one side, and five cubits on the other side: and he measured the length thereof, forty cubits: and the breadth, twenty cubits.

³Then went he inward, and measured the post of the door, two cubits; and the door, six cubits; and the breadth of the door, seven cubits.

⁴So he measured the length thereof, twenty cubits; and the breadth, twenty cubits, before the temple: and he said unto me, This *is* the most holy *place.*

⁵After he measured the wall of the house, six cubits; and the breadth of *every* side chamber, four cubits, round about the house on every side.

⁶And the side chambers *were* three, one over another, and thirty in order; and they entered into the wall which *was* of the house for the side chambers round about, that they might have hold, but they had not hold in the wall of the house.

⁷And *there was* an enlarging, and a winding about still upward to the side chambers: for the winding about of the house went still upward round about the house: therefore the breadth of the house *was still* upward, and so increased *from* the lowest *chamber* to the highest by the midst.

⁸I saw also the height of the house round about: the foundations of the side chambers *were* a full reed of six great cubits.

⁹The thickness of the wall, which *was* for the side chamber without, *was* five cubits: and *that* which *was* left *was* the place of the side chambers that *were* within.

¹⁰And between the chambers *was* the wideness of twenty cubits round about the house on every side.

¹¹And the doors of the side chambers *were* toward *the place that was* left, one door toward the north, and another door toward the south: and the breadth of

the place that was left *was* five cubits round about.

12Now the building that *was* before the separate place at the end toward the west *was* seventy cubits broad; and the wall of the building *was* five cubits thick round about, and the length thereof ninety cubits.

13So he measured the house, an hundred cubits long; and the separate place, and the building, with the walls thereof, an hundred cubits long;

14Also the breadth of the face of the house, and of the separate place toward the east, an hundred cubits.

15And he measured the length of the building over against the separate place which *was* behind it, and the galleries thereof on the one side and on the other side, an hundred cubits, with the inner temple, and the porches of the court;

16The door posts, and the narrow windows, and the galleries round about on their three stories, over against the door, cieled with wood round about, and from the ground up to the windows, and the windows *were* covered;

17To that above the door, even unto the inner house, and without, and by all the wall round about within and without, by measure.

18And *it was* made with cherubims and palm trees, so that a palm tree *was* between a cherub and a cherub; and *every* cherub had two faces;

19So that the face of a man *was* toward the palm tree on the one side, and the face of a young lion toward the palm tree on the other side: *it was* made through all the house round about.

20From the ground unto above the door *were* cherubims and palm trees made, and *on* the wall of the temple.

21The posts of the temple *were* squared, *and* the face of the sanctuary; the appearance *of the one* as the appearance *of the other*.

22The altar of wood *was* three cubits high, and the length thereof two cubits; and the corners thereof, and the length

thereof, and the walls thereof, *were* of wood: and he said unto me, This *is* the table that *is* before the LORD.

23And the temple and the sanctuary had two doors.

24And the doors had two leaves *apiece,* two turning leaves; two *leaves* for the one door, and two leaves for the other *door.*

25And *there were* made on them, on the doors of the temple, cherubims and palm trees, like as *were* made upon the walls; and *there were* thick planks upon the face of the porch without.

26And *there were* narrow windows and palm trees on the one side and on the other side, on the sides of the porch, and *upon* the side chambers of the house, and thick planks.

JAMES 4:1–17

FROM whence *come* wars and fightings among you? *come they* not hence, *even* of your lusts that war in your members?

2Ye lust, and have not: ye kill, and desire to have, and cannot obtain: ye fight and war, yet ye have not, because ye ask not.

3Ye ask, and receive not, because ye ask amiss, that ye may consume *it* upon your lusts.

4Ye adulterers and adulteresses, know ye not that the friendship of the world is enmity with God? whosoever therefore will be a friend of the world is the enemy of God.

5Do ye think that the scripture saith in vain, The spirit that dwelleth in us lusteth to envy?

6But he giveth more grace. Wherefore he saith, God resisteth the proud, but giveth grace unto the humble.

7Submit yourselves therefore to God. Resist the devil, and he will flee from you.

8Draw nigh to God, and he will draw nigh to you. Cleanse *your* hands, *ye* sinners; and purify *your* hearts, *ye* double minded.

9Be afflicted, and mourn, and weep: let your laughter be turned to mourning, and *your* joy to heaviness.

10Humble yourselves in the sight of the Lord, and he shall lift you up.

11Speak not evil one of another, brethren. He that speaketh evil of *his* brother, and judgeth his brother, speaketh evil of the law, and judgeth the law: but if thou judge the law, thou art not a doer of the law, but a judge.

12There is one lawgiver, who is able to save and to destroy: who art thou that judgest another?

13Go to now, ye that say, To day or to morrow we will go into such a city, and continue there a year, and buy and sell, and get gain:

14Whereas ye know not what *shall be* on the morrow. For what *is* your life? It is even a vapour, that appeareth for a little time, and then vanisheth away.

15For that ye *ought* to say, If the Lord will, we shall live, and do this, or that.

16But now ye rejoice in your boastings: all such rejoicing is evil.

17Therefore to him that knoweth to do good, and doeth *it* not, to him it is sin.

PSALM 118:19–29

OPEN to me the gates of righteousness: I will go into them, *and* I will praise the LORD:

20This gate of the LORD, into which the righteous shall enter.

21I will praise thee: for thou hast heard me, and art become my salvation.

22The stone *which* the builders refused is become the head *stone* of the corner.

23This is the LORD'S doing; *it is* marvellous in our eyes.

24This *is* the day *which* the LORD hath made; we will rejoice and be glad in it.

25Save now, I beseech thee, O LORD: O LORD, I beseech thee, send now prosperity.

26Blessed *be* he that cometh in the name of the LORD: we have blessed you out of the house of the LORD.

27God *is* the LORD, which hath shewed us light: bind the sacrifice with cords, *even* unto the horns of the altar.

28Thou *art* my God, and I will praise thee: *thou art* my God, I will exalt thee.

29O give thanks unto the LORD; for *he is* good: for his mercy *endureth* for ever.

PROVERBS FOR TODAY/ 28:3–5

A poor man that oppresseth the poor is like *a sweeping rain which leaveth no food.* □ *They that forsake the law praise the wicked: but such as keep the law contend with them.* □ *Evil men understand not judgment: but they that seek the* LORD *understand all* things.

EZEKIEL 42:1—43:27

THEN he brought me forth into the utter court, the way toward the north: and he brought me into the chamber that *was* over against the separate place, and which *was* before the building toward the north.

2Before the length of an hundred cubits *was* the north door, and the breadth *was* fifty cubits.

3Over against the twenty *cubits* which *were* for the inner court, and over against the pavement which *was* for the utter court, *was* gallery against gallery in three *stories*.

4And before the chambers *was* a walk of ten cubits breadth inward, a way of one cubit; and their doors toward the north.

5Now the upper chambers *were* shorter: for the galleries were higher than these, than the lower, and than the middlemost of the building.

6For they *were* in three *stories*, but had not pillars as the pillars of the courts: therefore *the building* was straitened more than the lowest and the middlemost from the ground.

7And the wall that *was* without over against the chambers, toward the utter court on the forepart of the chambers, the length thereof *was* fifty cubits.

8For the length of the chambers that *were* in the utter court *was* fifty cubits: and, lo, before the temple *were* an hundred cubits.

9And from under these chambers *was* the entry on the east side, as one goeth into them from the utter court.

10The chambers *were* in the thickness of the wall of the court toward the east, over against the separate place, and over against the building.

11And the way before them *was* like the appearance of the chambers which *were* toward the north, as long as they, *and* as broad as they: and all their goings out *were* both according to their fashions, and according to their doors.

12And according to the doors of the chambers that *were* toward the south *was* a door in the head of the way, *even* the way directly before the wall toward the east, as one entereth into them.

13Then said he unto me, The north chambers *and* the south chambers, which *are* before the separate place, they *be* holy chambers, where the priests that approach unto the LORD shall eat the most holy things: there shall they lay the most holy things, and the meat offering, and the sin offering, and the trespass offering; for the place *is* holy.

14When the priests enter therein, then shall they not go out of the holy *place* into the utter court, but there they shall lay their garments wherein they minister; for they *are* holy; and shall put on other garments, and shall approach to *those things* which *are* for the people.

15Now when he had made an end of measuring the inner house, he brought me forth toward the gate whose prospect *is* toward the east, and measured it round about.

16He measured the east side with the measuring reed, five hundred reeds, with the measuring reed round about.

17He measured the north side, five hundred reeds, with the measuring reed round about.

18He measured the south side, five hundred reeds, with the measuring reed.

19He turned about to the west side, *and* measured five hundred reeds with the measuring reed.

20He measured it by the four sides: it had a wall round about, five hundred *reeds* long, and five hundred broad, to make a separation between the sanctuary and the profane place.

AFTERWARD he brought me to the gate, *even* the gate that looketh toward the east:

2And, behold, the glory of the God of Israel came from the way of the east: and his voice *was* like a noise of many waters: and the earth shined with his glory.

3And *it was* according to the appearance of the vision which I saw, *even* according to the vision that I saw when I came to destroy the city: and the visions *were* like the vision that I saw by the river Chebar; and I fell upon my face.

4And the glory of the LORD came into the house by the way of the gate whose prospect *is* toward the east.

5So the spirit took me up, and brought me into the inner court; and, behold, the glory of the LORD filled the house.

6And I heard *him* speaking unto me out of the house; and the man stood by me.

7And he said unto me, Son of man, the place of my throne, and the place of the soles of my feet, where I will dwell in the midst of the children of Israel for ever, and my holy name, shall the house of Israel no more defile, *neither* they, nor their kings, by their whoredom, nor by the carcases of their kings in their high places.

8In their setting of their threshold by my thresholds, and their post by my posts, and the wall between me and them, they have even defiled my holy name by their abominations that they have committed: wherefore I have consumed them in mine anger.

9Now let them put away their whoredom, and the carcases of their kings, far from me, and I will dwell in the midst of them for ever.

10Thou son of man, shew the house to the house of Israel, that they may be ashamed of their iniquities: and let them measure the pattern.

11And if they be ashamed of all that they have done, shew them the form of the house, and the fashion thereof, and the goings out thereof, and the comings in thereof, and all the forms thereof, and all the ordinances thereof, and all the forms thereof, and all the laws thereof: and write *it* in their sight, that they may keep the whole form thereof, and all the ordinances thereof, and do them.

12This *is* the law of the house; Upon the top of the mountain the whole limit thereof round about *shall be* most holy. Behold, this *is* the law of the house.

13And these *are* the measures of the altar after the cubits: The cubit *is* a cubit and an hand breadth; even the bottom *shall be* a cubit, and the breadth a cubit, and the border thereof by the edge thereof round about *shall be* a span: and this *shall be* the higher place of the altar.

14And from the bottom *upon* the ground *even* to the lower settle *shall be* two cubits, and the breadth one cubit; and from the lesser settle *even* to the greater settle *shall be* four cubits, and the breadth *one* cubit.

15So the altar *shall be* four cubits; and from the altar and upward *shall be* four horns.

16And the altar *shall be* twelve *cubits* long, twelve broad, square in the four squares thereof.

17And the settle *shall be* fourteen *cubits* long and fourteen broad in the four squares thereof; and the border about it *shall be* half a cubit; and the bottom thereof *shall be* a cubit about; and his stairs shall look toward the east.

18And he said unto me, Son of man, thus saith the Lord GOD; These *are* the ordinances of the altar in the day when they shall make it, to offer burnt offerings thereon, and to sprinkle blood thereon.

19And thou shalt give to the priests the Levites that be of the seed of Zadok, which approach unto me, to minister unto me, saith the Lord GOD, a young bullock for a sin offering.

20And thou shalt take of the blood thereof, and put *it* on the four horns of it, and on the four corners of the settle, and upon the border round about: thus shalt thou cleanse and purge it.

21Thou shalt take the bullock also of the sin offering, and he shall burn it in the appointed place of the house, without the sanctuary.

22And on the second day thou shalt offer a kid of the goats without blemish for a sin offering; and they shall cleanse the altar, as they did cleanse *it* with the bullock.

23When thou hast made an end of cleansing *it,* thou shalt offer a young bullock without blemish, and a ram out of the flock without blemish.

24And thou shalt offer them before the LORD, and the priests shall cast salt upon them, and they shall offer them up *for* a burnt offering unto the LORD.

25Seven days shalt thou prepare every day a goat *for* a sin offering: they shall also prepare a young bullock, and a ram out of the flock, without blemish.

26Seven days shall they purge the altar and purify it; and they shall consecrate themselves.

27And when these days are expired, it shall be, *that* upon the eighth day, and *so* forward, the priests shall make your burnt offerings upon the altar, and your peace offerings; and I will accept you, saith the Lord GOD.

JAMES 5:1–20

Go to now, *ye* rich men, weep and howl for your miseries that shall come upon *you.*

2Your riches are corrupted, and your garments are motheaten.

3Your gold and silver is cankered; and the rust of them shall be a witness against you, and shall eat your flesh as it were fire. Ye have heaped treasure together for the last days.

4Behold, the hire of the labourers who have reaped down your fields, which is of you kept back by fraud, crieth: and the cries of them which have reaped are entered into the ears of the Lord of Sabaoth.

5Ye have lived in pleasure on the earth, and been wanton; ye have nourished your hearts, as in a day of slaughter.

6Ye have condemned *and* killed the just; *and* he doth not resist you.

7Be patient therefore, brethren, unto the coming of the Lord. Behold, the husbandman waiteth for the precious fruit of the earth, and hath long patience for it, until he receive the early and latter rain.

8Be ye also patient; stablish your hearts: for the coming of the Lord draweth nigh.

9Grudge not one against another, brethren, lest ye be condemned: behold, the judge standeth before the door.

10Take, my brethren, the prophets, who have spoken in the name of the Lord, for an example of suffering affliction, and of patience.

11Behold, we count them happy which endure. Ye have heard of the patience of Job, and have seen the end of the Lord; that the Lord is very pitiful, and of tender mercy.

12But above all things, my brethren, swear not, neither by heaven, neither by the earth, neither by any other oath: but let your yea be yea; and *your* nay, nay; lest ye fall into condemnation.

13Is any among you afflicted? let him pray. Is any merry? let him sing psalms.

14Is any sick among you? let him call for the elders of the church; and let them pray over him, anointing him with oil in the name of the Lord:

15And the prayer of faith shall save the sick, and the Lord shall raise him up; and if he have committed sins, they shall be forgiven him.

16Confess *your* faults one to another, and pray one for another, that ye may be healed. The effectual fervent prayer of a righteous man availeth much.

17Elias was a man subject to like passions as we are, and he prayed earnestly that it might not rain: and it rained not on the earth by the space of three years and six months.

18And he prayed again, and the heaven gave rain, and the earth brought forth her fruit.

19Brethren, if any of you do err from the truth, and one convert him;

20Let him know, that he which converteth the sinner from the error of his way shall save a soul from death, and shall hide a multitude of sins.

PSALM 119:1–16

BLESSED *are* the undefiled in the way, who walk in the law of the LORD.

2Blessed *are* they that keep his testimonies, *and that* seek him with the whole heart.

3They also do no iniquity: they walk in his ways.

4Thou hast commanded *us* to keep thy precepts diligently.

5O that my ways were directed to keep thy statutes!

6Then shall I not be ashamed, when I have respect unto all thy commandments.

7I will praise thee with uprightness of heart, when I shall have learned thy righteous judgments.

8I will keep thy statutes: O forsake me not utterly.

9Wherewithal shall a young man cleanse his way? by taking heed *thereto* according to thy word.

10With my whole heart have I sought thee: O let me not wander from thy commandments.

11Thy word have I hid in mine heart, that I might not sin against thee.

12Blessed *art* thou, O LORD: teach me thy statutes.

13With my lips have I declared all the judgments of thy mouth.

14I have rejoiced in the way of thy testimonies, as *much as* in all riches.

15I will meditate in thy precepts, and have respect unto thy ways.

16I will delight myself in thy statutes: I will not forget thy word.

PROVERBS FOR TODAY/ 28:6–7

Better is *the poor that walketh in his uprightness, than* he that is *perverse* in his *ways, though* he be *rich*. □ *Whoso keepeth the law* is *a wise son: but he that is a companion of riotous* men *shameth his father*.

NOVEMBER 22

EZEKIEL 44:1—45:12

THEN he brought me back the way of the gate of the outward sanctuary which looketh toward the east; and it *was* shut.

2Then said the LORD unto me; This gate shall be shut, it shall not be opened, and no man shall enter in by it; because the LORD, the God of Israel, hath entered in by it, therefore it shall be shut.

3*It is* for the prince; the prince, he shall sit in it to eat bread before the LORD; he shall enter by the way of the porch of *that* gate, and shall go out by the way of the same.

4Then brought he me the way of the north gate before the house: and I looked, and, behold, the glory of the LORD filled the house of the LORD: and I fell upon my face.

5And the LORD said unto me, Son of man, mark well, and behold with thine eyes, and hear with thine ears all that I say unto thee concerning all the ordinances of the house of the LORD, and all the laws thereof; and mark well the entering in of the house, with every going forth of the sanctuary.

6And thou shalt say to the rebellious, *even* to the house of Israel, Thus saith the Lord GOD; O ye house of Israel, let it suffice you of all your abominations,

7In that ye have brought *into my sanctuary* strangers, uncircumcised in heart, and uncircumcised in flesh, to be in my sanctuary, to pollute it, *even* my house, when ye offer my bread, the fat and the blood, and they have broken my covenant because of all your abominations.

8And ye have not kept the charge of mine holy things: but ye have set keepers of my charge in my sanctuary for yourselves.

9Thus saith the Lord GOD; No stranger, uncircumcised in heart, nor uncircumcised in flesh, shall enter into my sanctuary, of any stranger that *is* among the children of Israel.

10And the Levites that are gone away far from me, when Israel went astray, which went astray away from me after their idols; they shall even bear their iniquity.

11Yet they shall be ministers in my sanctuary, *having* charge at the gates of the house, and ministering to the house: they shall slay the burnt offering and the sacrifice for the people, and they shall stand before them to minister unto them.

12Because they ministered unto them before their idols, and caused the house of Israel to fall into iniquity; therefore have I lifted up mine hand against them, saith the Lord GOD, and they shall bear their iniquity.

13And they shall not come near unto me, to do the office of a priest unto me, nor to come near to any of my holy things, in the most holy *place:* but they shall bear their shame, and their abominations which they have committed.

14But I will make them keepers of the charge of the house, for all the service thereof, and for all that shall be done therein.

15But the priests the Levites, the sons of Zadok, that kept the charge of my sanctuary when the children of Israel went astray from me, they shall come near to me to minister unto me, and they shall stand before me to offer unto me the fat and the blood, saith the Lord GOD:

16They shall enter into my sanctuary, and they shall come near to my table, to minister unto me, and they shall keep my charge.

17And it shall come to pass, *that* when they enter in at the gates of the inner court, they shall be clothed with linen garments; and no wool shall come upon them, whiles they minister in the gates of the inner court, and within.

18They shall have linen bonnets upon their heads, and shall have linen breeches upon their loins; they shall not gird *themselves* with any thing that causeth sweat.

19And when they go forth into the utter court, *even* into the utter court to the people, they shall put off their garments wherein they ministered, and lay them in the holy chambers, and they shall put on other garments; and they shall not sanctify the people with their garments.

20Neither shall they shave their heads, nor suffer their locks to grow long; they shall only poll their heads.

21Neither shall any priest drink wine, when they enter into the inner court.

22Neither shall they take for their wives a widow, nor her that is put away: but they shall take maidens of the seed of the house of Israel, or a widow that had a priest before.

23And they shall teach my people *the difference* between the holy and profane, and cause them to discern between the unclean and the clean.

24And in controversy they shall stand in judgment; *and* they shall judge it according to my judgments: and they shall keep my laws and my statutes in all mine assemblies; and they shall hallow my sabbaths.

25And they shall come at no dead person to defile themselves: but for father, or for mother, or for son, or for daughter, for brother, or for sister that hath had no husband, they may defile themselves.

26And after he is cleansed, they shall reckon unto him seven days.

27And in the day that he goeth into the sanctuary, unto the inner court, to minister in the sanctuary, he shall offer his sin offering, saith the Lord God.

28And it shall be unto them for an inheritance: I *am* their inheritance: and ye shall give them no possession in Israel: I *am* their possession.

29They shall eat the meat offering, and the sin offering, and the trespass offering; and every dedicated thing in Israel shall be theirs.

30And the first of all the firstfruits of all *things,* and every oblation of all, of every *sort* of your oblations, shall be the priest's: ye shall also give unto the priest the first of your dough, that he may cause the blessing to rest in thine house.

31The priests shall not eat of any thing that is dead of itself, or torn, whether it be fowl or beast.

Moreover, when ye shall divide by lot the land for inheritance, ye shall offer an oblation unto the Lord, an holy portion of the land: the length *shall be* the length of five and twenty thousand *reeds,* and the breadth *shall be* ten thousand. This *shall be* holy in all the borders thereof round about.

2Of this there shall be for the sanctuary five hundred *in length,* with five hundred *in breadth,* square round about; and fifty cubits round about for the suburbs thereof.

3And of this measure shalt thou measure the length of five and twenty thousand, and the breadth of ten thousand: and in it shall be the sanctuary *and* the most holy *place.*

4The holy *portion* of the land shall be for the priests the ministers of the sanctuary, which shall come near to minister unto the Lord: and it shall be a place for their houses, and an holy place for the sanctuary.

5And the five and twenty thousand of length, and the ten thousand of breadth, shall also the Levites, the ministers of the house, have for themselves, for a possession for twenty chambers.

6And ye shall appoint the possession of the city five thousand broad, and five and twenty thousand long, over against the oblation of the holy *portion:* it shall be for the whole house of Israel.

7And *a portion shall be* for the prince on the one side and on the other side of the oblation of the holy *portion,* and of the possession of the city, before the oblation of the holy *portion,* and before the possession of the city, from the west side westward, and from the east side eastward: and the length *shall be* over against one of the portions, from the west border unto the east border.

8In the land shall be his possession

in Israel: and my princes shall no more oppress my people; and *the rest of* the land shall they give to the house of Israel according to their tribes.

9Thus saith the Lord GOD; Let it suffice you, O princes of Israel: remove violence and spoil, and execute judgment and justice, take away your exactions from my people, saith the Lord GOD.

10Ye shall have just balances, and a just ephah, and a just bath.

11The ephah and the bath shall be of one measure, that the bath may contain the tenth part of an homer, and the ephah the tenth part of an homer: the measure thereof shall be after the homer.

12And the shekel *shall be* twenty gerahs: twenty shekels, five and twenty shekels, fifteen shekels, shall be your maneh.

1 PETER 1:1–13

PETER, an apostle of Jesus Christ, to the strangers scattered throughout Pontus, Galatia, Cappadocia, Asia, and Bithynia,

2Elect according to the foreknowledge of God the Father, through sanctification of the Spirit, unto obedience and sprinkling of the blood of Jesus Christ: Grace unto you, and peace, be multiplied.

3Blessed *be* the God and Father of our Lord Jesus Christ, which according to his abundant mercy hath begotten us again unto a lively hope by the resurrection of Jesus Christ from the dead,

4To an inheritance incorruptible, and undefiled, and that fadeth not away, reserved in heaven for you,

5Who are kept by the power of God through faith unto salvation ready to be revealed in the last time.

6Wherein ye greatly rejoice, though now for a season, if need be, ye are in heaviness through manifold temptations:

7That the trial of your faith, being much more precious than of gold that perisheth, though it be tried with fire, might be found unto praise and honour and glory at the appearing of Jesus Christ:

8Whom having not seen, ye love; in whom, though now ye see *him* not, yet believing, ye rejoice with joy unspeakable and full of glory:

9Receiving the end of your faith, *even* the salvation of *your* souls.

10Of which salvation the prophets have enquired and searched diligently, who prophesied of the grace *that should come* unto you:

11Searching what, or what manner of time the Spirit of Christ which was in them did signify, when it testified beforehand the sufferings of Christ, and the glory that should follow.

12Unto whom it was revealed, that not unto themselves, but unto us they did minister the things, which are now reported unto you by them that have preached the gospel unto you with the Holy Ghost sent down from heaven; which things the angels desire to look into.

13Wherefore gird up the loins of your mind, be sober, and hope to the end for the grace that is to be brought unto you at the revelation of Jesus Christ;

PSALM 119:17–35

DEAL bountifully with thy servant, *that* I may live, and keep thy word.

18Open thou mine eyes, that I may behold wondrous things out of thy law.

19I am a stranger in the earth: hide not thy commandments from me.

20My soul breaketh for the longing *that it hath* unto thy judgments at all times.

21Thou hast rebuked the proud *that are* cursed, which do err from thy commandments.

22Remove from me reproach and

contempt; for I have kept thy testimonies.

23Princes also did sit *and* speak against me: *but* thy servant did meditate in thy statutes.

24Thy testimonies also *are* my delight *and* my counsellors.

25My soul cleaveth unto the dust: quicken thou me according to thy word.

26I have declared my ways, and thou heardest me: teach me thy statutes.

27Make me to understand the way of thy precepts: so shall I talk of thy wondrous works.

28My soul melteth for heaviness: strengthen thou me according unto thy word.

29Remove from me the way of lying: and grant me thy law graciously.

30I have chosen the way of truth: thy judgments have I laid *before me.*

31I have stuck unto thy testimonies: O LORD, put me not to shame.

32I will run the way of thy commandments, when thou shalt enlarge my heart.

33Teach me, O LORD, the way of thy statutes; and I shall keep it *unto* the end.

34Give me understanding, and I shall keep thy law; yea, I shall observe it with *my* whole heart.

35Make me to go in the path of thy commandments; for therein do I delight.

PROVERBS FOR TODAY/ 28:8–10

He that by usury and unjust gain increaseth his substance, he shall gather it for him that will pity the poor. □ *He that turneth away his ear from hearing the law, even his prayer* shall be *abomination.* □ *Whoso causeth the righteous to go astray in an evil way, he shall fall himself into his own pit: but the upright shall have good* things *in possession.*

NOVEMBER 23

EZEKIEL 45:13—46:24

THIS *is* the oblation that ye shall offer; the sixth part of an ephah of an homer of wheat, and ye shall give the sixth part of an ephah of an homer of barley:

14Concerning the ordinance of oil, the bath of oil, *ye shall offer* the tenth part of a bath out of the cor, *which is* an homer of ten baths; for ten baths *are* an homer:

15And one lamb out of the flock, out of two hundred, out of the fat pastures of Israel; for a meat offering, and for a burnt offering, and for peace offerings, to make reconciliation for them, saith the Lord GOD.

16All the people of the land shall give this oblation for the prince in Israel.

17And it shall be the prince's part *to give* burnt offerings, and meat offerings, and drink offerings, in the feasts, and in the new moons, and in the sabbaths, in all solemnities of the house of Israel: he shall prepare the sin offering, and the meat offering, and the burnt offering, and the peace offerings, to make reconciliation for the house of Israel.

18Thus saith the Lord GOD; In the first *month,* in the first *day* of the month, thou shalt take a young bullock without blemish, and cleanse the sanctuary:

19And the priest shall take of the blood

of the sin offering, and put *it* upon the posts of the house, and upon the four corners of the settle of the altar, and upon the posts of the gate of the inner court.

20And so thou shalt do the seventh *day* of the month for every one that erreth, and for *him that is* simple: so shall ye reconcile the house.

21In the first *month,* in the fourteenth day of the month, ye shall have the passover, a feast of seven days; unleavened bread shall be eaten.

22And upon that day shall the prince prepare for himself and for all the people of the land a bullock *for* a sin offering.

23And seven days of the feast he shall prepare a burnt offering to the LORD, seven bullocks and seven rams without blemish daily the seven days; and a kid of the goats daily *for* a sin offering.

24And he shall prepare a meat offering of an ephah for a bullock, and an ephah for a ram, and an hin of oil for an ephah.

25In the seventh *month,* in the fifteenth day of the month, shall he do the like in the feast of the seven days, according to the sin offering, according to the burnt offering, and according to the meat offering, and according to the oil.

THUS saith the Lord GOD; The gate of the inner court that looketh toward the east shall be shut the six working days; but on the sabbath it shall be opened, and in the day of the new moon it shall be opened.

2And the prince shall enter by the way of the porch of *that* gate without, and shall stand by the post of the gate, and the priests shall prepare his burnt offering and his peace offerings, and he shall worship at the threshold of the gate: then he shall go forth; but the gate shall not be shut until the evening.

3Likewise the people of the land shall worship at the door of this gate before the LORD in the sabbaths and in the new moons.

4And the burnt offering that the prince shall offer unto the LORD in the sabbath day *shall be* six lambs without blemish, and a ram without blemish.

5And the meat offering *shall be* an ephah for a ram, and the meat offering for the lambs as he shall be able to give, and an hin of oil to an ephah.

6And in the day of the new moon *it shall be* a young bullock without blemish, and six lambs, and a ram: they shall be without blemish.

7And he shall prepare a meat offering, an ephah for a bullock, and an ephah for a ram, and for the lambs according as his hand shall attain unto, and an hin of oil to an ephah.

8And when the prince shall enter, he shall go in by the way of the porch of *that* gate, and he shall go forth by the way thereof.

9But when the people of the land shall come before the LORD in the solemn feasts, he that entereth in by the way of the north gate to worship shall go out by the way of the south gate; and he that entereth by the way of the south gate shall go forth by the way of the north gate: he shall not return by the way of the gate whereby he came in, but shall go forth over against it.

10And the prince in the midst of them, when they go in, shall go in; and when they go forth, shall go forth.

11And in the feasts and in the solemnities the meat offering shall be an ephah to a bullock, and an ephah to a ram, and to the lambs as he is able to give, and an hin of oil to an ephah.

12Now when the prince shall prepare a voluntary burnt offering or peace offerings voluntarily unto the LORD, *one* shall then open him the gate that looketh toward the east, and he shall prepare his burnt offering and his peace offerings, as he did on the sabbath day: then he shall go forth; and after his going forth *one* shall shut the gate.

13Thou shalt daily prepare a burnt offering unto the LORD *of* a lamb of the first year without blemish: thou shalt prepare it every morning.

14And thou shalt prepare a meat offering for it every morning, the sixth part of an ephah, and the third part of an hin of oil, to temper with the fine flour; a meat offering continually by a perpetual ordinance unto the LORD.

15Thus shall they prepare the lamb, and the meat offering, and the oil, every morning *for* a continual burnt offering.

16Thus saith the Lord GOD; If the prince give a gift unto any of his sons, the inheritance thereof shall be his sons'; it *shall be* their possession by inheritance.

17But if he give a gift of his inheritance to one of his servants, then it shall be his to the year of liberty; after it shall return to the prince: but his inheritance shall be his sons' for them.

18Moreover the prince shall not take of the people's inheritance by oppression, to thrust them out of their possession; *but* he shall give his sons inheritance out of his own possession: that my people be not scattered every man from his possession.

19After he brought me through the entry, which *was* at the side of the gate, into the holy chambers of the priests, which looked toward the north: and, behold, there *was* a place on the two sides westward.

20Then said he unto me, This *is* the place where the priests shall boil the trespass offering and the sin offering, where they shall bake the meat offering; that they bear *them* not out into the utter court, to sanctify the people.

21Then he brought me forth into the utter court, and caused me to pass by the four corners of the court; and, behold, in every corner of the court *there was* a court.

22In the four corners of the court *there were* courts joined of forty *cubits* long and thirty broad: these four corners *were* of one measure.

23And *there was* a row *of building* round about in them, round about them four, and *it was* made with boiling places under the rows round about.

24Then said he unto me, these *are* the places of them that boil, where the ministers of the house shall boil the sacrifice of the people.

1 PETER 1:14—2:10

As obedient children, not fashioning yourselves according to the former lusts in your ignorance: 15But as he which hath called you is holy, so be ye holy in all manner of conversation;

16Because it is written, Be ye holy; for I am holy.

17And if ye call on the Father, who without respect of persons judgeth according to every man's work, pass the time of your sojourning *here* in fear:

18Forasmuch as ye know that ye were not redeemed with corruptible things, *as* silver and gold, from your vain conversation *received* by tradition from your fathers;

19But with the precious blood of Christ, as of a lamb without blemish and without spot:

20Who verily was foreordained before the foundation of the world, but was manifest in these last times for you,

21Who by him do believe in God, that raised him up from the dead, and gave him glory; that your faith and hope might be in God.

22Seeing ye have purified your souls in obeying the truth through the Spirit unto unfeigned love of the brethren, *see that ye* love one another with a pure heart fervently:

23Being born again, not of corruptible seed, but of incorruptible, by the word of God, which liveth and abideth for ever.

24For all flesh *is* as grass, and all the glory of man as the flower of grass. The grass withereth, and the flower thereof falleth away:

25But the word of the Lord endureth for ever. And this is the word which by the gospel is preached unto you.

WHEREFORE laying aside all malice, and all guile, and hypocrisies, and envies, and all evil speakings,

2As newborn babes, desire the sincere milk of the word, that ye may grow thereby:

3If so be ye have tasted that the Lord *is* gracious.

4To whom coming, *as unto* a living stone, disallowed indeed of men, but chosen of God, *and* precious,

5Ye also, as lively stones, are built up a spiritual house, an holy priesthood, to offer up spiritual sacrifices, acceptable to God by Jesus Christ.

6Wherefore also it is contained in the scripture, Behold, I lay in Sion a chief corner stone, elect, precious: and he that believeth on him shall not be confounded.

7Unto you therefore which believe *he is* precious: but unto them which be disobedient, the stone which the builders disallowed, the same is made the head of the corner,

8And a stone of stumbling, and a rock of offence, *even to them* which stumble at the word, being disobedient: whereunto also they were appointed.

9But ye *are* a chosen generation, a royal priesthood, an holy nation, a peculiar people; that ye should shew forth the praises of him who hath called you out of darkness into his marvellous light:

10Which in time past *were* not a people, but *are* now the people of God: which had not obtained mercy, but now have obtained mercy.

PSALM 119:36–52

INCLINE my heart unto thy testimonies, and not to covetousness. 37Turn away mine eyes from beholding vanity; *and* quicken thou me in thy way.

38Stablish thy word unto thy servant, who *is devoted* to thy fear.

39Turn away my reproach which I fear: for thy judgments *are* good.

40Behold, I have longed after thy precepts: quicken me in thy righteousness.

41Let thy mercies come also unto me, O LORD, *even* thy salvation, according to thy word.

42So shall I have wherewith to answer him that reproacheth me: for I trust in thy word.

43And take not the word of truth utterly out of my mouth; for I have hoped in thy judgments.

44So shall I keep thy law continually for ever and ever.

45And I will walk at liberty: for I seek thy precepts.

46I will speak of thy testimonies also before kings, and will not be ashamed.

47And I will delight myself in thy commandments, which I have loved.

48My hands also will I lift up unto thy commandments, which I have loved; and I will meditate in thy statutes.

49Remember the word unto thy servant, upon which thou hast caused me to hope.

50This *is* my comfort in my affliction: for thy word hath quickened me.

51The proud have had me greatly in derision: *yet* have I not declined from thy law.

52I remembered thy judgments of old, O LORD; and have comforted myself.

PROVERBS FOR TODAY/ 28:11

The rich man is *wise in his own conceit; but the poor that hath understanding searcheth him out.*

EZEKIEL 47:1—48:35

AFTERWARD he brought me again unto the door of the house; and, behold, waters issued out from under the threshold of the house eastward: for the forefront of the house *stood toward* the east, and the waters came down from under from the right side of the house, at the south *side* of the altar.

2Then brought he me out of the way of the gate northward, and led me about the way without unto the utter gate by the way that looketh eastward; and, behold, there ran out waters on the right side.

3And when the man that had the line in his hand went forth eastward, he measured a thousand cubits, and he brought me through the waters; the waters *were* to the ancles.

4Again he measured a thousand, and brought me through the waters; the waters *were* to the knees. Again he measured a thousand, and brought me through; the waters *were* to the loins.

5Afterward he measured a thousand; *and it was* a river that I could not pass over: for the waters were risen, waters to swim in, a river that could not be passed over.

6And he said unto me, Son of man, hast thou seen *this?* Then he brought me, and caused me to return to the brink of the river.

7Now when I had returned, behold, at the bank of the river *were* very many trees on the one side and on the other.

8Then said he unto me, These waters issue out toward the east country, and go down into the desert, and go into the sea: *which being* brought forth into the sea, the waters shall be healed.

9And it shall come to pass, *that* every thing that liveth, which moveth, whith-ersoever the rivers shall come, shall live: and there shall be a very great multitude of fish, because these waters shall come thither: for they shall be healed; and every thing shall live whither the river cometh.

10And it shall come to pass, *that* the fishers shall stand upon it from En—gedi even unto En—eglaim; they shall be a *place* to spread forth nets; their fish shall be according to their kinds, as the fish of the great sea, exceeding many.

11But the miry places thereof and the marishes thereof shall not be healed; they shall be given to salt.

12And by the river upon the bank thereof, on this side and on that side, shall grow all trees for meat, whose leaf shall not fade, neither shall the fruit thereof be consumed: it shall bring forth new fruit according to his months, because their waters they issued out of the sanctuary: and the fruit thereof shall be for meat, and the leaf thereof for medicine.

13Thus saith the Lord GOD; This *shall be* the border, whereby ye shall inherit the land according to the twelve tribes of Israel: Joseph *shall have two* portions.

14And ye shall inherit it, one as well as another: *concerning* the which I lifted up mine hand to give it unto your fathers: and this land shall fall unto you for inheritance.

15And this *shall be* the border of the land toward the north side, from the great sea, the way of Hethlon, as men go to Zedad;

16Hamath, Berothah, Sibraim, which *is* between the border of Damascus and the border of Hamath; Hazar—hatticon, which *is* by the coast of Hauran.

17And the border from the sea shall be Hazar—enan, the border of Damascus, and the north northward, and the border of Hamath. And *this is* the north side.

18And the east side ye shall measure from Hauran, and from Damascus, and from Gilead, and from the land of Israel *by* Jordan, from the border unto the east sea. And *this is* the east side.

19And the south side southward, from Tamar *even* to the waters of strife *in* Kadesh, the river to the great sea. And *this is* the south side southward.

20The west side also *shall be* the great sea from the border, till a man come over against Hamath. This *is* the west side.

21So shall ye divide this land unto you according to the tribes of Israel.

22And it shall come to pass, *that* ye shall divide it by lot for an inheritance unto you, and to the strangers that sojourn among you, which shall beget children among you: and they shall be unto you as born in the country among the children of Israel; they shall have inheritance with you among the tribes of Israel.

23And it shall come to pass, *that* in what tribe the stranger sojourneth, there shall ye give *him* his inheritance, saith the Lord God.

Now these *are* the names of the tribes. From the north end to the coast of the way of Hethlon, as one goeth to Hamath, Hazar–enan, the border of Damascus northward, to the coast of Hamath; for these are his sides east *and* west; a *portion for* Dan.

2And by the border of Dan, from the east side unto the west side, a *portion for* Asher.

3And by the border of Asher, from the east side even unto the west side, a *portion for* Naphtali.

4And by the border of Naphtali, from the east side unto the west side, a *portion for* Manasseh.

5And by the border of Manasseh, from the east side unto the west side, a *portion for* Ephraim.

6And by the border of Ephraim, from the east side even unto the west side, a *portion for* Reuben.

7And by the border of Reuben, from the east side unto the west side, a *portion for* Judah.

8And by the border of Judah, from the east side unto the west side, shall be the offering which ye shall offer of five and twenty thousand *reeds in* breadth, and *in* length as one of the *other* parts, from the east side unto the west side: and the sanctuary shall be in the midst of it.

9The oblation that ye shall offer unto the Lord *shall be* of five and twenty thousand in length, and of ten thousand in breadth.

10And for them, *even* for the priests, shall be *this* holy oblation; toward the north five and twenty thousand *in length,* and toward the west ten thousand in breadth, and toward the east ten thousand in breadth, and toward the south five and twenty thousand in length: and the sanctuary of the Lord shall be in the midst thereof.

11*It shall be* for the priests that are sanctified of the sons of Zadok; which have kept my charge, which went not astray when the children of Israel went astray, as the Levites went astray.

12And *this* oblation of the land that is offered shall be unto them a thing most holy by the border of the Levites.

13And over against the border of the priests the Levites *shall have* five and twenty thousand in length, and ten thousand in breadth: all the length *shall be* five and twenty thousand, and the breadth ten thousand.

14And they shall not sell of it, neither exchange, nor alienate the firstfruits of the land: for *it is* holy unto the Lord.

15And the five thousand, that are left

in the breadth over against the five and twenty thousand, shall be a profane *place* for the city, for dwelling, and for suburbs: and the city shall be in the midst thereof.

16And these *shall be* the measures thereof; the north side four thousand and five hundred, and the south side four thousand and five hundred, and on the east side four thousand and five hundred, and the west side four thousand and five hundred.

17And the suburbs of the city shall be toward the north two hundred and fifty, and toward the south two hundred and fifty, and toward the east two hundred and fifty, and toward the west two hundred and fifty.

18And the residue in length over against the oblation of the holy *portion shall be* ten thousand eastward, and ten thousand westward: and it shall be over against the oblation of the holy *portion;* and the increase thereof shall be for food unto them that serve the city.

19And they that serve the city shall serve it out of all the tribes of Israel.

20All the oblation *shall be* five and twenty thousand by five and twenty thousand: ye shall offer the holy oblation foursquare, with the possession of the city.

21And the residue *shall be* for the prince, on the one side and on the other of the holy oblation, and of the possession of the city, over against the five and twenty thousand of the oblation toward the east border, and westward over against the five and twenty thousand toward the west border, over against the portions for the prince: and it shall be the holy oblation; and the sanctuary of the house *shall be* in the midst thereof.

22Moreover from the possession of the Levites, and from the possession of the city, *being* in the midst *of that* which is the prince's, between the border of Judah and the border of Benjamin, shall be for the prince.

23As for the rest of the tribes, from the east side unto the west side, Benjamin *shall have* a *portion.*

24And by the border of Benjamin, from the east side unto the west side, Simeon *shall have* a *portion.*

25And by the border of Simeon, from the east side unto the west side, Issachar a *portion.*

26And by the border of Issachar, from the east side unto the west side, Zebulun a *portion.*

27And by the border of Zebulun, from the east side unto the west side, Gad a *portion.*

28And by the border of Gad, at the south side southward, the border shall be even from Tamar *unto* the waters of strife *in* Kadesh, *and* to the river toward the great sea.

29This *is* the land which ye shall divide by lot unto the tribes of Israel for inheritance, and these *are* their portions, saith the Lord GOD.

30And these *are* the goings out of the city on the north side, four thousand and five hundred measures.

31And the gates of the city *shall be* after the names of the tribes of Israel: three gates northward; one gate of Reuben, one gate of Judah, one gate of Levi.

32And at the east side four thousand and five hundred: and three gates; and one gate of Joseph, one gate of Benjamin, one gate of Dan.

33And at the south side four thousand and five hundred measures: and three gates; one gate of Simeon, one gate of Issachar, one gate of Zebulun.

34At the west side four thousand and five hundred, *with* their three gates; one gate of Gad, one gate of Asher, one gate of Naphtali.

35*It was* round about eighteen thousand *measures:* and the name of the city from *that* day *shall be,* The LORD *is* there.

1 PETER 2:11—3:9

DEARLY beloved, I beseech *you* as strangers and pilgrims, abstain from fleshly lusts, which war against the soul;

12Having your conversation honest among the Gentiles: that, whereas they speak against you as evildoers, they may by *your* good works, which they shall behold, glorify God in the day of visitation.

13Submit yourselves to every ordinance of man for the Lord's sake: whether it be to the king, as supreme;

14Or unto governors, as unto them that are sent by him for the punishment of evildoers, and for the praise of them that do well.

15For so is the will of God, that with well doing ye may put to silence the ignorance of foolish men:

16As free, and not using *your* liberty for a cloak of maliciousness, but as the servants of God.

17Honour all *men.* Love the brotherhood. Fear God. Honour the king.

18Servants, *be* subject to *your* masters with all fear; not only to the good and gentle, but also to the froward.

19For this *is* thankworthy, if a man for conscience toward God endure grief, suffering wrongfully.

20For what glory *is it,* if, when ye be buffeted for your faults, ye shall take it patiently? but if, when ye do well, and suffer *for it,* ye take it patiently, this *is* acceptable with God.

21For even hereunto were ye called: because Christ also suffered for us, leaving us an example, that ye should follow his steps:

22Who did no sin, neither was guile found in his mouth:

23Who, when he was reviled, reviled not again; when he suffered, he threatened not; but committed *himself* to him that judgeth righteously:

24Who his own self bare our sins in his own body on the tree, that we, being dead to sins, should live unto righteousness: by whose stripes ye were healed.

25For ye were as sheep going astray; but are now returned unto the Shepherd and Bishop of your souls.

LIKEWISE, ye wives, *be* in subjection to your own husbands; that, if any obey not the word, they also may without the word be won by the conversation of the wives;

2While they behold your chaste conversation *coupled* with fear.

3Whose adorning let it not be that outward *adorning* of plaiting the hair, and of wearing of gold, or of putting on of apparel;

4But *let it be* the hidden man of the heart, in that which is not corruptible, *even the ornament* of a meek and quiet spirit, which is in the sight of God of great price.

5For after this manner in the old time the holy women also, who trusted in God, adorned themselves, being in subjection unto their own husbands:

6Even as Sara obeyed Abraham, calling him lord: whose daughters ye are, as long as ye do well, and are not afraid with any amazement.

7Likewise, ye husbands, dwell with *them* according to knowledge, giving honour unto the wife, as unto the weaker vessel, and as being heirs together of the grace of life; that your prayers be not hindered.

8Finally, *be ye* all of one mind, having compassion one of another, love as brethren, *be* pitiful, *be* courteous:

9Not rendering evil for evil, or railing for railing: but contrariwise blessing; knowing that ye are thereunto called, that ye should inherit a blessing.

PSALM 119:53–70

HORROR hath taken hold upon me because of the wicked that forsake thy law.

54Thy statutes have been my songs in the house of my pilgrimage.

55I have remembered thy name, O LORD, in the night, and have kept thy law.

56This I had, because I kept thy precepts.

57*Thou art* my portion, O LORD: I have said that I would keep thy words.

58I intreated thy favour with *my* whole heart: be merciful unto me according to thy word.

59I thought on my ways, and turned my feet unto thy testimonies.

60I made haste, and delayed not to keep thy commandments.

61The bands of the wicked have robbed me: *but* I have not forgotten thy law.

62At midnight I will rise to give thanks unto thee because of thy righteous judgments.

63I *am* a companion of all *them* that fear thee, and of them that keep thy precepts.

64The earth, O LORD, is full of thy mercy: teach me thy statutes.

65Thou hast dealt well with thy servant, O LORD, according unto thy word.

66Teach me good judgment and knowledge: for I have believed thy commandments.

67Before I was afflicted I went astray: but now have I kept thy word.

68Thou *art* good, and doest good; teach me thy statutes.

69The proud have forged a lie against me: *but* I will keep thy precepts with *my* whole heart.

70Their heart is as fat as grease; *but* I delight in thy law.

PROVERBS FOR TODAY/ 28:12–13

When righteous men *do rejoice,* there is *great glory: but when the wicked rise, a* man *is hidden.* □ *He that covereth his sins shall not prosper: but whoso confesseth and forsaketh* them *shall have mercy.*

NOVEMBER 25

DANIEL 1:1—2:23

IN the third year of the reign of Jehoiakim king of Judah came Nebuchadnezzar king of Babylon unto Jerusalem, and besieged it.

2And the Lord gave Jehoiakim king of Judah into his hand, with part of the vessels of the house of God: which he carried into the land of Shinar to the house of his god; and he brought the vessels into the treasure house of his god.

3And the king spake unto Ashpenaz the master of his eunuchs, that he should bring *certain* of the children of Israel, and of the king's seed, and of the princes;

4Children in whom *was* no blemish, but well favoured, and skilful in all wisdom, and cunning in knowledge, and understanding science, and such as *had* ability in them to stand in the king's palace, and whom they might teach the learning and the tongue of the Chaldeans.

5And the king appointed them a daily provision of the king's meat, and of the wine which he drank: so nourishing them three years, that at the end thereof they might stand before the king.

6Now among these were of the children of Judah, Daniel, Hananiah, Mishael, and Azariah:

7Unto whom the prince of the eunuchs gave names: for he gave unto Daniel *the name* of Belteshazzar; and to Hananiah, of Shadrach; and to Mishael, of Meshach; and to Azariah, of Abed–nego.

8But Daniel purposed in his heart that he would not defile himself with the portion of the king's meat, nor with the wine which he drank: therefore he requested of the prince of the eunuchs that he might not defile himself.

9Now God had brought Daniel into favour and tender love with the prince of the eunuchs.

10And the prince of the eunuchs said unto Daniel, I fear my lord the king, who hath appointed your meat and your drink: for why should he see your faces worse liking than the children which *are* of your sort? then shall ye make *me* endanger my head to the king.

11Then said Daniel to Melzar, whom the prince of the eunuchs had set over Daniel, Hananiah, Mishael, and Azariah,

12Prove thy servants, I beseech thee, ten days; and let them give us pulse to eat, and water to drink.

13Then let our countenances be looked upon before thee, and the countenance of the children that eat of the portion of the king's meat: and as thou seest, deal with thy servants.

14So he consented to them in this matter, and proved them ten days.

15And at the end of ten days their countenances appeared fairer and fatter in flesh than all the children which did eat the portion of the king's meat.

16Thus Melzar took away the portion of their meat, and the wine that they should drink; and gave them pulse.

17As for these four children, God gave them knowledge and skill in all learning and wisdom: and Daniel had understanding in all visions and dreams.

18Now at the end of the days that the king had said he should bring them in, then the prince of the eunuchs brought them in before Nebuchadnezzar.

19And the king communed with them; and among them all was found none like Daniel, Hananiah, Mishael, and Azariah: therefore stood they before the king.

20And in all matters of wisdom *and* understanding, that the king enquired of them, he found them ten times better than all the magicians *and* astrologers that *were* in all his realm.

21And Daniel continued *even* unto the first year of king Cyrus.

AND in the second year of the reign of Nebuchadnezzar, Nebuchadnezzar dreamed dreams, wherewith his spirit was troubled, and his sleep brake from him.

2Then the king commanded to call the magicians, and the astrologers, and the sorcerers, and the Chaldeans, for to shew the king his dreams. So they came and stood before the king.

3And the king said unto them, I have dreamed a dream, and my spirit was troubled to know the dream.

4Then spake the Chaldeans to the king in Syriack, O king, live for ever: tell thy servants the dream, and we will shew the interpretation.

5The king answered and said to the Chaldeans, The thing is gone from me: if ye will not make known unto me the dream, with the interpretation thereof, ye shall be cut in pieces, and your houses shall be made a dunghill.

6But if ye shew the dream, and the interpretation thereof, ye shall receive of me gifts and rewards and great honour: therefore shew me the dream, and the interpretation thereof.

7They answered again and said, Let

the king tell his servants the dream, and we will shew the interpretation of it.

8The king answered and said, I know of certainty that ye would gain the time, because ye see the thing is gone from me.

9But if ye will not make known unto me the dream, *there is but* one decree for you: for ye have prepared lying and corrupt words to speak before me, till the time be changed: therefore tell me the dream, and I shall know that ye can shew me the interpretation thereof.

10The Chaldeans answered before the king, and said, There is not a man upon the earth that can shew the king's matter: therefore *there is* no king, lord, nor ruler, *that* asked such things at any magician, or astrologer, or Chaldean.

11And *it is* a rare thing that the king requireth, and there is none other that can shew it before the king, except the gods, whose dwelling is not with flesh.

12For this cause the king was angry and very furious, and commanded to destroy all the wise *men* of Babylon.

13And the decree went forth that the wise *men* should be slain; and they sought Daniel and his fellows to be slain.

14Then Daniel answered with counsel and wisdom to Arioch the captain of the king's guard, which was gone forth to slay the wise *men* of Babylon:

15He answered and said to Arioch the king's captain, Why *is* the decree *so* hasty from the king? Then Arioch made the thing known to Daniel.

16Then Daniel went in, and desired of the king that he would give him time, and that he would shew the king the interpretation.

17Then Daniel went to his house, and made the thing known to Hananiah, Mishael, and Azariah, his companions:

18That they would desire mercies of the God of heaven concerning this secret; that Daniel and his fellows should not perish with the rest of the wise *men* of Babylon.

19Then was the secret revealed unto Daniel in a night vision. Then Daniel blessed the God of heaven.

20Daniel answered and said, Blessed be the name of God for ever and ever: for wisdom and might are his:

21And he changeth the times and the seasons: he removeth kings, and setteth up kings: he giveth wisdom unto the wise, and knowledge to them that know understanding:

22He revealeth the deep and secret things: he knoweth what *is* in the darkness, and the light dwelleth with him.

23I thank thee, and praise thee, O thou God of my fathers, who hast given me wisdom and might, and hast made known unto me now what we desired of thee: for thou hast *now* made known unto us the king's matter.

1 PETER 3:10—4:6

FOR he that will love life, and see good days, let him refrain his tongue from evil, and his lips that they speak no guile:

11Let him eschew evil, and do good; let him seek peace, and ensue it.

12For the eyes of the Lord *are* over the righteous, and his ears *are open* unto their prayers: but the face of the Lord *is* against them that do evil.

13And who *is* he that will harm you, if ye be followers of that which is good?

14But and if ye suffer for righteousness' sake, happy *are ye:* and be not afraid of their terror, neither be troubled;

15But sanctify the Lord God in your hearts: and *be* ready always to *give* an answer to every man that asketh you a reason of the hope that is in you with meekness and fear:

16Having a good conscience; that, whereas they speak evil of you, as of evildoers, they may be ashamed that falsely accuse your good conversation in Christ.

17For *it is* better, if the will of God be so, that ye suffer for well doing, than for evil doing.

18For Christ also hath once suffered for sins, the just for the unjust, that he might bring us to God, being put to death in the flesh, but quickened by the Spirit:

19By which also he went and preached unto the spirits in prison;

20Which sometime were disobedient, when once the longsuffering of God waited in the days of Noah, while the ark was a preparing, wherein few, that is, eight souls were saved by water.

21The like figure whereunto *even* baptism doth also now save us (not the putting away of the filth of the flesh, but the answer of a good conscience toward God,) by the resurrection of Jesus Christ:

22Who is gone into heaven, and is on the right hand of God; angels and authorities and powers being made subject unto him.

FORASMUCH then as Christ hath suffered for us in the flesh, arm yourselves likewise with the same mind: for he that hath suffered in the flesh hath ceased from sin;

2That he no longer should live the rest of *his* time in the flesh to the lusts of men, but to the will of God.

3For the time past of *our* life may suffice us to have wrought the will of the Gentiles, when we walked in lasciviousness, lusts, excess of wine, revellings, banquetings, and abominable idolatries:

4Wherein they think it strange that ye run not with *them* to the same excess of riot, speaking evil of *you:*

5Who shall give account to him that is ready to judge the quick and the dead.

6For for this cause was the gospel preached also to them that are dead, that they might be judged according to men in the flesh, but live according to God in the spirit.

PSALM 119:71–80

I T *is* good for me that I have been afflicted; that I might learn thy statutes.

72The law of thy mouth *is* better unto me than thousands of gold and silver.

73Thy hands have made me and fashioned me: give me understanding, that I may learn thy commandments.

74They that fear thee will be glad when they see me; because I have hoped in thy word.

75I know, O LORD, that thy judgments *are* right, and *that* thou in faithfulness hast afflicted me.

76Let, I pray thee, thy merciful kindness be for my comfort, according to thy word unto thy servant.

77Let thy tender mercies come unto me, that I may live: for thy law *is* my delight.

78Let the proud be ashamed; for they dealt perversely with me without a cause: *but* I will meditate in thy precepts.

79Let those that fear thee turn unto me, and those that have known thy testimonies.

80Let my heart be sound in thy statutes; that I be not ashamed.

PROVERBS FOR TODAY/ 28:14

Happy is *the man that feareth alway: but he that hardeneth his heart shall fall into mischief.*

NOVEMBER 26

DANIEL 2:24—3:30

THEREFORE Daniel went in unto Arioch, whom the king had ordained to destroy the wise *men* of Babylon: he went and said thus unto him; Destroy not the wise *men* of Babylon: bring me in before the king, and I will shew unto the king the interpretation.

25Then Arioch brought in Daniel before the king in haste, and said thus unto him, I have found a man of the captives of Judah, that will make known unto the king the interpretation.

26The king answered and said to Daniel, whose name *was* Belteshazzar, Art thou able to make known unto me the dream which I have seen, and the interpretation thereof?

27Daniel answered in the presence of the king, and said, The secret which the king hath demanded cannot the wise *men,* the astrologers, the magicians, the soothsayers, shew unto the king;

28But there is a God in heaven that revealeth secrets, and maketh known to the king Nebuchadnezzar what shall be in the latter days. Thy dream, and the visions of thy head upon thy bed, are these;

29As for thee, O king, thy thoughts came *into thy mind* upon thy bed, what should come to pass hereafter: and he that revealeth secrets maketh known to thee what shall come to pass.

30But as for me, this secret is not revealed to me for *any* wisdom that I have more than any living, but for *their* sakes that shall make known the interpretation to the king, and that thou mightest know the thoughts of thy heart.

31Thou, O king, sawest, and behold a great image. This great image, whose brightness *was* excellent, stood before thee; and the form thereof *was* terrible.

32This image's head *was* of fine gold, his breast and his arms of silver, his belly and his thighs of brass,

33His legs of iron, his feet part of iron and part of clay.

34Thou sawest till that a stone was cut out without hands, which smote the image upon his feet *that were* of iron and clay, and brake them to pieces.

35Then was the iron, the clay, the brass, the silver, and the gold, broken to pieces together, and became like the chaff of the summer threshingfloors; and the wind carried them away, that no place was found for them: and the stone that smote the image became a great mountain, and filled the whole earth.

36This *is* the dream; and we will tell the interpretation thereof before the king.

37Thou, O king, *art* a king of kings: for the God of heaven hath given thee a kingdom, power, and strength, and glory.

38And wheresoever the children of men dwell, the beasts of the field and the fowls of the heaven hath he given into thine hand, and hath made thee ruler over them all. Thou *art* this head of gold.

39And after thee shall arise another kingdom inferior to thee, and another third kingdom of brass, which shall bear rule over all the earth.

40And the fourth kingdom shall be strong as iron: forasmuch as iron breaketh in pieces and subdueth all *things:* and as iron that breaketh all these, shall it break in pieces and bruise.

41And whereas thou sawest the feet and toes, part of potters' clay, and part of iron, the kingdom shall be divided; but there shall be in it of the strength of the iron, forasmuch as thou sawest the iron mixed with miry clay.

⁴²And *as* the toes of the feet *were* part of iron, and part of clay, *so* the kingdom shall be partly strong, and partly broken.

⁴³And whereas thou sawest iron mixed with miry clay, they shall mingle themselves with the seed of men: but they shall not cleave one to another, even as iron is not mixed with clay.

⁴⁴And in the days of these kings shall the God of heaven set up a kingdom, which shall never be destroyed: and the kingdom shall not be left to other people, *but* it shall break in pieces and consume all these kingdoms, and it shall stand for ever.

⁴⁵Forasmuch as thou sawest that the stone was cut out of the mountain without hands, and that it brake in pieces the iron, the brass, the clay, the silver, and the gold; the great God hath made known to the king what shall come to pass hereafter: and the dream *is* certain, and the interpretation thereof sure.

⁴⁶Then the king Nebuchadnezzar fell upon his face, and worshipped Daniel, and commanded that they should offer an oblation and sweet odours unto him.

⁴⁷The king answered unto Daniel, and said, Of a truth *it is,* that your God *is* a God of gods, and a Lord of kings, and a revealer of secrets, seeing thou couldest reveal this secret.

⁴⁸Then the king made Daniel a great man, and gave him many great gifts, and made him ruler over the whole province of Babylon, and chief of the governors over all the wise *men* of Babylon.

⁴⁹Then Daniel requested of the king, and he set Shadrach, Meshach, and Abed–nego, over the affairs of the province of Babylon: but Daniel *sat* in the gate of the king.

NEBUCHADNEZZAR the king made an image of gold, whose height *was* threescore cubits, *and* the breadth thereof six cubits: he set it up in the plain of Dura, in the province of Babylon.

²Then Nebuchadnezzar the king sent to gather together the princes, the governors, and the captains, the judges, the treasurers, the counsellors, the sheriffs, and all the rulers of the provinces, to come to the dedication of the image which Nebuchadnezzar the king had set up.

³Then the princes, the governors, and captains, the judges, the treasurers, the counsellors, the sheriffs, and all the rulers of the provinces, were gathered together unto the dedication of the image that Nebuchadnezzar the king had set up; and they stood before the image that Nebuchadnezzar had set up.

⁴Then an herald cried aloud, To you it is commanded, O people, nations, and languages,

⁵*That* at what time ye hear the sound of the cornet, flute, harp, sackbut, psaltery, dulcimer, and all kinds of musick, ye fall down and worship the golden image that Nebuchadnezzar the king hath set up:

⁶And whoso falleth not down and worshippeth shall the same hour be cast into the midst of a burning fiery furnace.

⁷Therefore at that time, when all the people heard the sound of the cornet, flute, harp, sackbut, psaltery, and all kinds of musick, all the people, the nations, and the languages, fell down *and* worshipped the golden image that Nebuchadnezzar the king had set up.

⁸Wherefore at that time certain Chaldeans came near, and accused the Jews.

⁹They spake and said to the king Nebuchadnezzar, O king, live for ever.

¹⁰Thou, O king, hast made a decree, that every man that shall hear the sound of the cornet, flute, harp, sackbut, psaltery, and dulcimer, and all kinds of musick, shall fall down and worship the golden image:

¹¹And whoso falleth not down and worshippeth, *that* he should be cast

into the midst of a burning fiery furnace.

¹²There are certain Jews whom thou hast set over the affairs of the province of Babylon, Shadrach, Meshach, and Abed–nego; these men, O king, have not regarded thee: they serve not thy gods, nor worship the golden image which thou hast set up.

¹³Then Nebuchadnezzar in *his* rage and fury commanded to bring Shadrach, Meshach, and Abed–nego. Then they brought these men before the king.

¹⁴Nebuchadnezzar spake and said unto them, *Is it* true, O Shadrach, Meshach, and Abed–nego, do not ye serve my gods, nor worship the golden image which I have set up?

¹⁵Now if ye be ready that at what time ye hear the sound of the cornet, flute, harp, sackbut, psaltery, and dulcimer, and all kinds of musick, ye fall down and worship the image which I have made; *well:* but if ye worship not, ye shall be cast the same hour into the midst of a burning fiery furnace; and who *is* that God that shall deliver you out of my hands?

¹⁶Shadrach, Meshach, and Abed–nego, answered and said to the king, O Nebuchadnezzar, we *are* not careful to answer thee in this matter.

¹⁷If it be *so,* our God whom we serve is able to deliver us from the burning fiery furnace, and he will deliver *us* out of thine hand, O king.

¹⁸But if not, be it known unto thee, O king, that we will not serve thy gods, nor worship the golden image which thou hast set up.

¹⁹Then was Nebuchadnezzar full of fury, and the form of his visage was changed against Shadrach, Meshach, and Abed–nego: *therefore* he spake, and commanded that they should heat the furnace one seven times more than it was wont to be heated.

²⁰And he commanded the most mighty men that *were* in his army to bind Shadrach, Meshach, and Abed–

nego, *and* to cast *them* into the burning fiery furnace.

²¹Then these men were bound in their coats, their hosen, and their hats, and their *other* garments, and were cast into the midst of the burning fiery furnace.

²²Therefore because the king's commandment was urgent, and the furnace exceeding hot, the flame of the fire slew those men that took up Shadrach, Meshach, and Abed–nego.

²³And these three men Shadrach, Meshach, and Abed–nego, fell down bound into the midst of the burning fiery furnace.

²⁴Then Nebuchadnezzar the king was astonied, and rose up in haste, *and* spake, and said unto his counsellors, Did not we cast three men bound into the midst of the fire? They answered and said unto the king, True, O king.

²⁵He answered and said, Lo, I see four men loose, walking in the midst of the fire, and they have no hurt; and the form of the fourth is like the Son of God.

²⁶Then Nebuchadnezzar came near to the mouth of the burning fiery furnace, *and* spake, and said, Shadrach, Meshach, and Abed–nego, ye servants of the most high God, come forth, and come *hither.* Then Shadrach, Meshach, and Abed–nego, came forth of the midst of the fire.

²⁷And the princes, governors, and captains, and the king's counsellors, being gathered together, saw these men, upon whose bodies the fire had no power, nor was an hair of their head singed, neither were their coats changed, nor the smell of fire had passed on them.

²⁸*Then* Nebuchadnezzar spake, and said, Blessed *be* the God of Shadrach, Meshach, and Abed–nego, who hath sent his angel, and delivered his servants that trusted in him, and have changed the king's word, and yielded their bodies, that they might not serve

nor worship any god, except their own God.

29Therefore I make a decree, That every people, nation, and language, which speak any thing amiss against the God of Shadrach, Meshach, and Abed–nego, shall be cut in pieces, and their houses shall be made a dunghill: because there is no other God that can deliver after this sort.

30Then the king promoted Shadrach, Meshach, and Abed–nego, in the province of Babylon.

1 PETER 4:7—5:14

BUT the end of all things is at hand: be ye therefore sober, and watch unto prayer.

8And above all things have fervent charity among yourselves: for charity shall cover the multitude of sins.

9Use hospitality one to another without grudging.

10As every man hath received the gift, *even so* minister the same one to another, as good stewards of the manifold grace of God.

11If any man speak, *let him speak* as the oracles of God; if any man minister, *let him do it* as of the ability which God giveth: that God in all things may be glorified through Jesus Christ, to whom be praise and dominion for ever and ever. Amen.

12Beloved, think it not strange concerning the fiery trial which is to try you, as though some strange thing happened unto you:

13But rejoice, inasmuch as ye are partakers of Christ's sufferings; that, when his glory shall be revealed, ye may be glad also with exceeding joy.

14If ye be reproached for the name of Christ, happy *are ye;* for the spirit of glory and of God resteth upon you: on their part he is evil spoken of, but on your part he is glorified.

15But let none of you suffer as a murderer, or *as* a thief, or *as* an evildoer, or as a busybody in other men's matters.

16Yet if *any man suffer* as a Christian, let him not be ashamed; but let him glorify God on this behalf.

17For the time *is come* that judgment must begin at the house of God: and if *it* first *begin* at us, what shall the end *be* of them that obey not the gospel of God?

18And if the righteous scarcely be saved, where shall the ungodly and the sinner appear?

19Wherefore let them that suffer according to the will of God commit the keeping of their souls *to him* in well doing, as unto a faithful Creator.

THE elders which are among you I exhort, who am also an elder, and a witness of the sufferings of Christ, and also a partaker of the glory that shall be revealed:

2Feed the flock of God which is among you, taking the oversight *thereof,* not by constraint, but willingly; not for filthy lucre, but of a ready mind;

3Neither as being lords over *God's* heritage, but being ensamples to the flock.

4And when the chief Shepherd shall appear, ye shall receive a crown of glory that fadeth not away.

5Likewise, ye younger, submit yourselves unto the elder. Yea, all *of you* be subject one to another, and be clothed with humility: for God resisteth the proud, and giveth grace to the humble.

6Humble yourselves therefore under the mighty hand of God, that he may exalt you in due time:

7Casting all your care upon him; for he careth for you.

8Be sober, be vigilant; because your adversary the devil, as a roaring lion, walketh about, seeking whom he may devour:

9Whom resist stedfast in the faith, knowing that the same afflictions are accomplished in your brethren that are in the world.

10But the God of all grace, who hath called us unto his eternal glory by Christ Jesus, after that ye have suffered a while, make you perfect, stablish, strengthen, settle *you*.

11To him *be* glory and dominion for ever and ever. Amen.

12By Silvanus, a faithful brother unto you, as I suppose, I have written briefly, exhorting, and testifying that this is the true grace of God wherein ye stand.

13The *church that is* at Babylon, elected together with *you*, saluteth you; and *so doth* Marcus my son.

14Greet ye one another with a kiss of charity. Peace *be* with you all that are in Christ Jesus. Amen.

PSALM 119:81–95

MY soul fainteth for thy salvation: *but* I hope in thy word. 82Mine eyes fail for thy word, saying, When wilt thou comfort me?

83For I am become like a bottle in the smoke; *yet* do I not forget thy statutes.

84How many *are* the days of thy ser-vant? when wilt thou execute judgment on them that persecute me?

85The proud have digged pits for me, which *are* not after thy law.

86All thy commandments *are* faithful: they persecute me wrongfully; help thou me.

87They had almost consumed me upon earth; but I forsook not thy precepts.

88Quicken me after thy lovingkindness; so shall I keep the testimony of thy mouth.

89For ever, O LORD, thy word is settled in heaven.

90Thy faithfulness *is* unto all generations: thou hast established the earth, and it abideth.

91They continue this day according to thine ordinances: for all *are* thy servants.

92Unless thy law *had been* my delights, I should then have perished in mine affliction.

93I will never forget thy precepts: for with them thou hast quickened me.

94I *am* thine, save me; for I have sought thy precepts.

95The wicked have waited for me to destroy me: *but* I will consider thy testimonies.

PROVERBS FOR TODAY/ 28:15–16

As a roaring lion, and a ranging bear; so is a wicked ruler over the poor people. □ *The prince that wanteth understanding* is *also a great oppressor:* but *he that hateth covetousness shall prolong* his *days.*

NOVEMBER 27

DANIEL 4:1–37

NEBUCHADNEZZAR the king, unto all people, nations, and languages, that dwell in all the earth; Peace be multiplied unto you.

2I thought it good to shew the signs and wonders that the high God hath wrought toward me.

3How great *are* his signs! and how mighty *are* his wonders! his kingdom *is* an everlasting kingdom, and his dominion *is* from generation to generation.

4I Nebuchadnezzar was at rest in mine house, and flourishing in my palace:

5I saw a dream which made me afraid, and the thoughts upon my bed and the visions of my head troubled me.

6Therefore made I a decree to bring in all the wise *men* of Babylon before me, that they might make known unto me the interpretation of the dream.

7Then came in the magicians, the astrologers, the Chaldeans, and the soothsayers: and I told the dream before them; but they did not make known unto me the interpretation thereof.

8But at the last Daniel came in before me, whose name *was* Belteshazzar, according to the name of my god, and in whom *is* the spirit of the holy gods: and before him I told the dream, *saying,*

9O Belteshazzar, master of the magicians, because I know that the spirit of the holy gods *is* in thee, and no secret troubleth thee, tell me the visions of my dream that I have seen, and the interpretation thereof.

10Thus *were* the visions of mine head in my bed; I saw, and behold a tree in the midst of the earth, and the height thereof *was* great.

11The tree grew, and was strong, and the height thereof reached unto heaven, and the sight thereof to the end of all the earth:

12The leaves thereof *were* fair, and the fruit thereof much, and in it *was* meat for all: the beasts of the field had shadow under it, and the fowls of the heaven dwelt in the boughs thereof, and all flesh was fed of it.

13I saw in the visions of my head upon my bed, and, behold, a watcher and an holy one came down from heaven;

14He cried aloud, and said thus, Hew down the tree, and cut off his branches, shake off his leaves, and scatter his fruit: let the beasts get away from under it, and the fowls from his branches:

15Nevertheless leave the stump of his roots in the earth, even with a band of iron and brass, in the tender grass of the field; and let it be wet with the dew of heaven, and *let* his portion *be* with the beasts in the grass of the earth:

16Let his heart be changed from man's, and let a beast's heart be given unto him: and let seven times pass over him.

17This matter *is* by the decree of the watchers, and the demand by the word of the holy ones: to the intent that the living may know that the most High ruleth in the kingdom of men, and giveth it to whomsoever he will, and setteth up over it the basest of men.

18This dream I king Nebuchadnezzar have seen. Now thou, O Belteshazzar, declare the interpretation thereof, forasmuch as all the wise *men* of my kingdom are not able to make known unto me the interpretation: but thou *art* able; for the spirit of the holy gods *is* in thee.

19Then Daniel, whose name *was* Belteshazzar, was astonied for one hour, and his thoughts troubled him. The king spake, and said, Belteshazzar, let not the dream, or the interpretation thereof, trouble thee. Belteshazzar answered and said, My lord, the dream *be* to them that hate thee, and the interpretation thereof to thine enemies.

20The tree that thou sawest, which grew, and was strong, whose height reached unto the heaven, and the sight thereof to all the earth;

21Whose leaves *were* fair, and the fruit thereof much, and in it *was* meat for all; under which the beasts of the field dwelt, and upon whose branches the fowls of the heaven had their habitation:

22It *is* thou, O king, that art grown and become strong: for thy greatness is grown, and reacheth unto heaven, and thy dominion to the end of the earth.

23And whereas the king saw a

watcher and an holy one coming down from heaven, and saying, Hew the tree down, and destroy it; yet leave the stump of the roots thereof in the earth, even with a band of iron and brass, in the tender grass of the field; and let it be wet with the dew of heaven, and *let* his portion *be* with the beasts of the field, till seven times pass over him;

24This *is* the interpretation, O king, and this *is* the decree of the most High, which is come upon my lord the king:

25That they shall drive thee from men, and thy dwelling shall be with the beasts of the field, and they shall make thee to eat grass as oxen, and they shall wet thee with the dew of heaven, and seven times shall pass over thee, till thou know that the most High ruleth in the kingdom of men, and giveth it to whomsoever he will.

26And whereas they commanded to leave the stump of the tree roots; thy kingdom shall be sure unto thee, after that thou shalt have known that the heavens do rule.

27Wherefore, O king, let my counsel be acceptable unto thee, and break off thy sins by righteousness, and thine iniquities by shewing mercy to the poor; if it may be a lengthening of thy tranquillity.

28All this came upon the king Nebuchadnezzar.

29At the end of twelve months he walked in the palace of the kingdom of Babylon.

30The king spake, and said, Is not this great Babylon, that I have built for the house of the kingdom by the might of my power, and for the honour of my majesty?

31While the word *was* in the king's mouth, there fell a voice from heaven, *saying,* O king Nebuchadnezzar, to thee it is spoken; The kingdom is departed from thee.

32And they shall drive thee from men, and thy dwelling *shall be* with the beasts of the field: they shall make thee to eat grass as oxen, and seven times shall pass over thee, until thou know that the most High ruleth in the kingdom of men, and giveth it to whomsoever he will.

33The same hour was the thing fulfilled upon Nebuchadnezzar: and he was driven from men, and did eat grass as oxen, and his body was wet with the dew of heaven, till his hairs were grown like eagles' *feathers,* and his nails like birds' *claws.*

34And at the end of the days I Nebuchadnezzar lifted up mine eyes unto heaven, and mine understanding returned unto me, and I blessed the most High, and I praised and honoured him that liveth for ever, whose dominion *is* an everlasting dominion, and his kingdom is from generation to generation:

35And all the inhabitants of the earth *are* reputed as nothing: and he doeth according to his will in the army of heaven, and *among* the inhabitants of the earth: and none can stay his hand, or say unto him, What doest thou?

36At the same time my reason returned unto me; and for the glory of my kingdom, mine honour and brightness returned unto me; and my counsellors and my lords sought unto me; and I was established in my kingdom, and excellent majesty was added unto me.

37Now I Nebuchadnezzar praise and extol and honour the King of heaven, all whose works *are* truth, and his ways judgment: and those that walk in pride he is able to abase.

2 PETER 1:1–21

SIMON Peter, a servant and an apostle of Jesus Christ, to them that have obtained like precious faith with us through the righteousness of God and our Saviour Jesus Christ:

2Grace and peace be multiplied unto you through the knowledge of God, and of Jesus our Lord,

3According as his divine power hath given unto us all things that *pertain* unto life and godliness, through the knowledge of him that hath called us to glory and virtue:

4Whereby are given unto us exceeding great and precious promises: that by these ye might be partakers of the divine nature, having escaped the corruption that is in the world through lust.

5And beside this, giving all diligence, add to your faith virtue; and to virtue knowledge;

6And to knowledge temperance; and to temperance patience; and to patience godliness;

7And to godliness brotherly kindness; and to brotherly kindness charity.

8For if these things be in you, and abound, they make *you that ye shall* neither *be* barren nor unfruitful in the knowledge of our Lord Jesus Christ.

9But he that lacketh these things is blind, and cannot see afar off, and hath forgotten that he was purged from his old sins.

10Wherefore the rather, brethren, give diligence to make your calling and election sure: for if ye do these things, ye shall never fall:

11For so an entrance shall be ministered unto you abundantly into the everlasting kingdom of our Lord and Saviour Jesus Christ.

12Wherefore I will not be negligent to put you always in remembrance of these things, though ye know *them,* and be established in the present truth.

13Yea, I think it meet, as long as I am in this tabernacle, to stir you up by putting *you* in remembrance;

14Knowing that shortly I must put off *this* my tabernacle, even as our Lord Jesus Christ hath shewed me.

15Moreover I will endeavour that ye may be able after my decease to have these things always in remembrance.

16For we have not followed cunningly devised fables, when we made known unto you the power and coming of our Lord Jesus Christ, but were eyewitnesses of his majesty.

17For he received from God the Father honour and glory, when there came such a voice to him from the excellent glory, This is my beloved Son, in whom I am well pleased.

18And this voice which came from heaven we heard, when we were with him in the holy mount.

19We have also a more sure word of prophecy; whereunto ye do well that ye take heed, as unto a light that shineth in a dark place, until the day dawn, and the day star arise in your hearts:

20Knowing this first, that no prophecy of the scripture is of any private interpretation.

21For the prophecy came not in old time by the will of man: but holy men of God spake *as they were* moved by the Holy Ghost.

PSALM 119:96–112

I HAVE seen an end of all perfection: *but* thy commandment *is* exceeding broad.

97O how love I thy law! it *is* my meditation all the day.

98Thou through thy commandments hast made me wiser than mine enemies: for they *are* ever with me.

99I have more understanding than all my teachers: for thy testimonies *are* my meditation.

100I understand more than the ancients, because I keep thy precepts.

101I have refrained my feet from every evil way, that I might keep thy word.

102I have not departed from thy judgments: for thou hast taught me.

103How sweet are thy words unto my taste! *yea, sweeter* than honey to my mouth!

104Through thy precepts I get understanding: therefore I hate every false way.

105Thy word *is* a lamp unto my feet, and a light unto my path.

106I have sworn, and I will perform *it,* that I will keep thy righteous judgments.

107I am afflicted very much: quicken me, O LORD, according unto thy word.

108Accept, I beseech thee, the free-will offerings of my mouth, O LORD, and teach me thy judgments.

109My soul *is* continually in my hand: yet do I not forget thy law.

110The wicked have laid a snare for me: yet I erred not from thy precepts.

111Thy testimonies have I taken as an heritage for ever: for they *are* the rejoicing of my heart.

112I have inclined mine heart to perform thy statutes alway, *even unto* the end.

PROVERBS FOR TODAY/ 28:17–18

A man that doeth violence to the blood of any *person shall flee to the pit; let no man stay him.* □ *Whoso walketh uprightly shall be saved: but* he that is *perverse* in his *ways shall fall at once.*

NOVEMBER 28

DANIEL 5:1–31

BELSHAZZAR the king made a great feast to a thousand of his lords, and drank wine before the thousand.

2Belshazzar, whiles he tasted the wine, commanded to bring the golden and silver vessels which his father Nebuchadnezzar had taken out of the temple which *was* in Jerusalem; that the king, and his princes, his wives, and his concubines, might drink therein.

3Then they brought the golden vessels that were taken out of the temple of the house of God which *was* at Jerusalem; and the king, and his princes, his wives, and his concubines, drank in them.

4They drank wine, and praised the gods of gold, and of silver, of brass, of iron, of wood, and of stone.

5In the same hour came forth fingers of a man's hand, and wrote over against the candlestick upon the plaister of the wall of the king's palace: and the king saw the part of the hand that wrote.

6Then the king's countenance was changed, and his thoughts troubled him, so that the joints of his loins were loosed, and his knees smote one against another.

7The king cried aloud to bring in the astrologers, the Chaldeans, and the soothsayers. *And* the king spake, and said to the wise *men* of Babylon, Whosoever shall read this writing, and shew me the interpretation thereof, shall be clothed with scarlet, and *have* a chain of gold about his neck, and shall be the third ruler in the kingdom.

8Then came in all the king's wise *men:* but they could not read the writing, nor make known to the king the interpretation thereof.

9Then was king Belshazzar greatly troubled, and his countenance was changed in him, and his lords were astonished.

10*Now* the queen by reason of the words of the king and his lords came into the banquet house: *and* the queen spake and said, O king, live for ever:

let not thy thoughts trouble thee, nor let thy countenance be changed:

11There is a man in thy kingdom, in whom *is* the spirit of the holy gods; and in the days of thy father light and understanding and wisdom, like the wisdom of the gods, was found in him; whom the king Nebuchadnezzar thy father, the king, *I say,* thy father, made master of the magicians, astrologers, Chaldeans, *and* soothsayers;

12Forasmuch as an excellent spirit, and knowledge, and understanding, interpreting of dreams, and shewing of hard sentences, and dissolving of doubts, were found in the same Daniel, whom the king named Belteshazzar: now let Daniel be called, and he will shew the interpretation.

13Then was Daniel brought in before the king. *And* the king spake and said unto Daniel, *Art* thou that Daniel, which *art* of the children of the captivity of Judah, whom the king my father brought out of Jewry?

14I have even heard of thee, that the spirit of the gods *is* in thee, and *that* light and understanding and excellent wisdom is found in thee.

15And now the wise *men,* the astrologers, have been brought in before me, that they should read this writing, and make known unto me the interpretation thereof: but they could not shew the interpretation of the thing:

16And I have heard of thee, that thou canst make interpretations, and dissolve doubts: now if thou canst read the writing, and make known to me the interpretation thereof, thou shalt be clothed with scarlet, and *have* a chain of gold about thy neck, and shalt be the third ruler in the kingdom.

17Then Daniel answered and said before the king, Let thy gifts be to thyself, and give thy rewards to another; yet I will read the writing unto the king, and make known to him the interpretation.

18O thou king, the most high God

gave Nebuchadnezzar thy father a kingdom, and majesty, and glory, and honour:

19And for the majesty that he gave him, all people, nations, and languages, trembled and feared before him: whom he would he slew; and whom he would he kept alive; and whom he would he set up; and whom he would he put down.

20But when his heart was lifted up, and his mind hardened in pride, he was deposed from his kingly throne, and they took his glory from him:

21And he was driven from the sons of men; and his heart was made like the beasts, and his dwelling *was* with the wild asses: they fed him with grass like oxen, and his body was wet with the dew of heaven; till he knew that the most high God ruled in the kingdom of men, and *that* he appointeth over it whomsoever he will.

22And thou his son, O Belshazzar, hast not humbled thine heart, though thou knewest all this;

23But hast lifted up thyself against the Lord of heaven; and they have brought the vessels of his house before thee, and thou, and thy lords, thy wives, and thy concubines, have drunk wine in them; and thou hast praised the gods of silver, and gold, of brass, iron, wood, and stone, which see not, nor hear, nor know: and the God in whose hand thy breath *is,* and whose *are* all thy ways, hast thou not glorified:

24Then was the part of the hand sent from him; and this writing was written.

25And this *is* the writing that was written, MENE, MENE, TEKEL, UPHARSIN.

26This *is* the interpretation of the thing: MENE; God hath numbered thy kingdom, and finished it.

27TEKEL; Thou art weighed in the balances, and art found wanting.

28PERES; Thy kingdom is divided, and given to the Medes and Persians.

29Then commanded Belshazzar, and

they clothed Daniel with scarlet, and *put* a chain of gold about his neck, and made a proclamation concerning him, that he should be the third ruler in the kingdom.

30In that night was Belshazzar the king of the Chaldeans slain.

31And Darius the Median took the kingdom, *being* about threescore and two years old.

2 PETER 2:1–22

BUT there were false prophets also among the people, even as there shall be false teachers among you, who privily shall bring in damnable heresies, even denying the Lord that bought them, and bring upon themselves swift destruction.

2And many shall follow their pernicious ways; by reason of whom the way of truth shall be evil spoken of.

3And through covetousness shall they with feigned words make merchandise of you: whose judgment now of a long time lingereth not, and their damnation slumbereth not.

4For if God spared not the angels that sinned, but cast *them* down to hell, and delivered *them* into chains of darkness, to be reserved unto judgment;

5And spared not the old world, but saved Noah the eighth *person,* a preacher of righteousness, bringing in the flood upon the world of the ungodly;

6And turning the cities of Sodom and Gomorrha into ashes condemned *them* with an overthrow, making *them* an ensample unto those that after should live ungodly;

7And delivered just Lot, vexed with the filthy conversation of the wicked:

8(For that righteous man dwelling among them, in seeing and hearing, vexed *his* righteous soul from day to day with *their* unlawful deeds);

9The Lord knoweth how to deliver the godly out of temptations, and to reserve the unjust unto the day of judgment to be punished:

10But chiefly them that walk after the flesh in the lust of uncleanness, and despise government. Presumptuous *are they,* selfwilled, they are not afraid to speak evil of dignities.

11Whereas angels, which are greater in power and might, bring not railing accusation against them before the Lord.

12But these, as natural brute beasts, made to be taken and destroyed, speak evil of the things that they understand not; and shall utterly perish in their own corruption;

13And shall receive the reward of unrighteousness, *as* they that count it pleasure to riot in the day time. Spots *they are* and blemishes, sporting themselves with their own deceivings while they feast with you;

14Having eyes full of adultery, and that cannot cease from sin; beguiling unstable souls: an heart they have exercised with covetous practices; cursed children:

15Which have forsaken the right way, and are gone astray, following the way of Balaam *the son* of Bosor, who loved the wages of unrighteousness;

16But was rebuked for his iniquity: the dumb ass speaking with man's voice forbad the madness of the prophet.

17These are wells without water, clouds that are carried with a tempest: to whom the mist of darkness is reserved for ever.

18For when they speak great swelling *words* of vanity, they allure through the lusts of the flesh, *through much* wantonness, those that were clean escaped from them who live in error.

19While they promise them liberty, they themselves are the servants of corruption: for of whom a man is overcome, of the same is he brought in bondage.

20For if after they have escaped the pollutions of the world through the knowledge of the Lord and Saviour Jesus Christ, they are again entangled therein, and overcome, the latter end is worse with them than the beginning.

21For it had been better for them not to have known the way of righteousness, than, after they have known *it*, to turn from the holy commandment delivered unto them.

22But it is happened unto them according to the true proverb, The dog *is* turned to his own vomit again; and the sow that was washed to her wallowing in the mire.

PSALM 119:113–131

I HATE vain thoughts: but thy law do I love.

114Thou *art* my hiding place and my shield: I hope in thy word.

115Depart from me, ye evildoers: for I will keep the commandments of my God.

116Uphold me according unto thy word, that I may live: and let me not be ashamed of my hope.

117Hold thou me up, and I shall be safe: and I will have respect unto thy statutes continually.

118Thou hast trodden down all them that err from thy statutes: for their deceit *is* falsehood.

119Thou puttest away all the wicked of the earth *like* dross: therefore I love thy testimonies.

120My flesh trembleth for fear of thee; and I am afraid of thy judgments.

121I have done judgment and justice: leave me not to mine oppressors.

122Be surety for thy servant for good: let not the proud oppress me.

123Mine eyes fail for thy salvation, and for the word of thy righteousness.

124Deal with thy servant according unto thy mercy, and teach me thy statutes.

125I *am* thy servant; give me understanding, that I may know thy testimonies.

126*It is* time for *thee,* LORD, to work: *for* they have made void thy law.

127Therefore I love thy commandments above gold; yea, above fine gold.

128Therefore I esteem all *thy* precepts *concerning* all *things to be* right; *and* I hate every false way.

129Thy testimonies *are* wonderful: therefore doth my soul keep them.

130The entrance of thy words giveth light; it giveth understanding unto the simple.

131I opened my mouth, and panted: for I longed for thy commandments.

PROVERBS FOR TODAY/ 28:19–20

He that tilleth his land shall have plenty of bread: but he that followeth after vain persons *shall have poverty enough.* □ *A faithful man shall abound with blessings: but he that maketh haste to be rich shall not be innocent.*

NOVEMBER 29

DANIEL 6:1–28

I T pleased Darius to set over the kingdom an hundred and twenty princes, which should be over the whole kingdom;

2And over these three presidents; of whom Daniel *was* first: that the princes might give accounts unto them, and the king should have no damage.

3Then this Daniel was preferred

above the presidents and princes, because an excellent spirit *was* in him; and the king thought to set him over the whole realm.

4Then the presidents and princes sought to find occasion against Daniel concerning the kingdom; but they could find none occasion nor fault; forasmuch as he *was* faithful, neither was there any error or fault found in him.

5Then said these men, We shall not find any occasion against this Daniel, except we find *it* against him concerning the law of his God.

6Then these presidents and princes assembled together to the king, and said thus unto him, King Darius, live for ever.

7All the presidents of the kingdom, the governors, and the princes, the counsellors, and the captains, have consulted together to establish a royal statute, and to make a firm decree, that whosoever shall ask a petition of any God or man for thirty days, save of thee, O king, he shall be cast into the den of lions.

8Now, O king, establish the decree, and sign the writing, that it be not changed, according to the law of the Medes and Persians, which altereth not.

9Wherefore king Darius signed the writing and the decree.

10Now when Daniel knew that the writing was signed, he went into his house; and his windows being open in his chamber toward Jerusalem, he kneeled upon his knees three times a day, and prayed, and gave thanks before his God, as he did aforetime.

11Then these men assembled, and found Daniel praying and making supplication before his God.

12Then they came near, and spake before the king concerning the king's decree; Hast thou not signed a decree, that every man that shall ask *a petition* of any God or man within thirty days, save of thee, O king, shall be cast into

the den of lions? The king answered and said, The thing *is* true, according to the law of the Medes and Persians, which altereth not.

13Then answered they and said before the king, That Daniel, which *is* of the children of the captivity of Judah, regardeth not thee, O king, nor the decree that thou hast signed, but maketh his petition three times a day.

14Then the king, when he heard *these* words, was sore displeased with himself, and set *his* heart on Daniel to deliver him: and he laboured till the going down of the sun to deliver him.

15Then these men assembled unto the king, and said unto the king, Know, O king, that the law of the Medes and Persians *is,* That no decree nor statute which the king establisheth may be changed.

16Then the king commanded, and they brought Daniel, and cast *him* into the den of lions. *Now* the king spake and said unto Daniel, Thy God whom thou servest continually, he will deliver thee.

17And a stone was brought, and laid upon the mouth of the den; and the king sealed it with his own signet, and with the signet of his lords; that the purpose might not be changed concerning Daniel.

18Then the king went to his palace, and passed the night fasting: neither were instruments of musick brought before him: and his sleep went from him.

19Then the king arose very early in the morning, and went in haste unto the den of lions.

20And when he came to the den, he cried with a lamentable voice unto Daniel: *and* the king spake and said to Daniel, O Daniel, servant of the living God, is thy God, whom thou servest continually, able to deliver thee from the lions?

21Then said Daniel unto the king, O king, live for ever.

22My God hath sent his angel, and

hath shut the lions' mouths, that they have not hurt me: forasmuch as before him innocency was found in me; and also before thee, O king, have I done no hurt.

23Then was the king exceeding glad for him, and commanded that they should take Daniel up out of the den. So Daniel was taken up out of the den, and no manner of hurt was found upon him, because he believed in his God.

24And the king commanded, and they brought those men which had accused Daniel, and they cast *them* into the den of lions, them, their children, and their wives; and the lions had the mastery of them, and brake all their bones in pieces or ever they came at the bottom of the den.

25Then king Darius wrote unto all people, nations, and languages, that dwell in all the earth; Peace be multiplied unto you.

26I make a decree, That in every dominion of my kingdom men tremble and fear before the God of Daniel: for he *is* the living God, and stedfast for ever, and his kingdom *that* which shall not be destroyed, and his dominion *shall be even* unto the end.

27He delivereth and rescueth, and he worketh signs and wonders in heaven and in earth, who hath delivered Daniel from the power of the lions.

28So this Daniel prospered in the reign of Darius, and in the reign of Cyrus the Persian.

2 PETER 3:1–18

THIS second epistle, beloved, I now write unto you; in *both* which I stir up your pure minds by way of remembrance:

2That ye may be mindful of the words which were spoken before by the holy prophets, and of the commandment of us the apostles of the Lord and Saviour:

3Knowing this first, that there shall come in the last days scoffers, walking after their own lusts,

4And saying, Where is the promise of his coming? for since the fathers fell asleep, all things continue as *they were* from the beginning of the creation.

5For this they willingly are ignorant of, that by the word of God the heavens were of old, and the earth standing out of the water and in the water:

6Whereby the world that then was, being overflowed with water, perished.

7But the heavens and the earth, which are now, by the same word are kept in store, reserved unto fire against the day of judgment and perdition of ungodly men.

8But, beloved, be not ignorant of this one thing, that one day *is* with the Lord as a thousand years, and a thousand years as one day.

9The Lord is not slack concerning his promise, as some men count slackness; but is longsuffering to us-ward, not willing that any should perish, but that all should come to repentance.

10But the day of the Lord will come as a thief in the night; in the which the heavens shall pass away with a great noise, and the elements shall melt with fervent heat, the earth also and the works that are therein shall be burned up.

11*Seeing* then *that* all these things shall be dissolved, what manner *of persons* ought ye to be in *all* holy conversation and godliness,

12Looking for and hasting unto the coming of the day of God, wherein the heavens being on fire shall be dissolved, and the elements shall melt with fervent heat?

13Nevertheless we, according to his promise, look for new heavens and a new earth, wherein dwelleth righteousness.

14Wherefore, beloved, seeing that ye look for such things, be diligent that ye may be found of him in peace, without spot, and blameless.

15And account *that* the longsuffering

of our Lord *is* salvation; even as our beloved brother Paul also according to the wisdom given unto him hath written unto you;

16As also in all *his* epistles, speaking in them of these things; in which are some things hard to be understood, which they that are unlearned and unstable wrest, as *they do* also the other scriptures, unto their own destruction.

17Ye therefore, beloved, seeing ye know *these things* before, beware lest ye also, being led away with the error of the wicked, fall from your own stedfastness.

18But grow in grace, and *in* the knowledge of our Lord and Saviour Jesus Christ. To him *be* glory both now and for ever. Amen.

PSALM 119:132–155

Look thou upon me, and be merciful unto me, as thou usest to do unto those that love thy name.

133Order my steps in thy word: and let not any iniquity have dominion over me.

134Deliver me from the oppression of man: so will I keep thy precepts.

135Make thy face to shine upon thy servant; and teach me thy statutes.

136Rivers of waters run down mine eyes, because they keep not thy law.

137Righteous *art* thou, O LORD, and upright *are* thy judgments.

138Thy testimonies *that* thou hast commanded *are* righteous and very faithful.

139My zeal hath consumed me, because mine enemies have forgotten thy words.

140Thy word *is* very pure: therefore thy servant loveth it.

141I *am* small and despised: *yet* do not I forget thy precepts.

142Thy righteousness *is* an everlasting righteousness, and thy law *is* the truth.

143Trouble and anguish have taken hold on me: *yet* thy commandments *are* my delights.

144The righteousness of thy testimonies *is* everlasting: give me understanding, and I shall live.

145I cried with *my* whole heart; hear me, O LORD: I will keep thy statutes.

146I cried unto thee; save me, and I shall keep thy testimonies.

147I prevented the dawning of the morning, and cried: I hoped in thy word.

148Mine eyes prevent the *night* watches, that I might meditate in thy word.

149Hear my voice according unto thy lovingkindness: O LORD, quicken me according to thy judgment.

150They draw nigh that follow after mischief: they are far from thy law.

151Thou *art* near, O LORD; and all thy commandments *are* truth.

152Concerning thy testimonies, I have known of old that thou hast founded them for ever.

153Consider mine affliction, and deliver me: for I do not forget thy law.

154Plead my cause, and deliver me: quicken me according to thy word.

155Salvation *is* far from the wicked: for they seek not thy statutes.

PROVERBS FOR TODAY/ 28:21–22

To have respect of persons is *not good: for for a piece of bread* that *man will transgress.* □ *He that hasteth to be rich* hath *an evil eye, and considereth not that poverty shall come upon him.*

DANIEL 7:1–28

IN the first year of Belshazzar king of Babylon Daniel had a dream and visions of his head upon his bed: then he wrote the dream, *and* told the sum of the matters.

2Daniel spake and said, I saw in my vision by night, and, behold, the four winds of the heaven strove upon the great sea.

3And four great beasts came up from the sea, diverse one from another.

4The first *was* like a lion, and had eagle's wings: I beheld till the wings thereof were plucked, and it was lifted up from the earth, and made stand upon the feet as a man, and a man's heart was given to it.

5And behold another beast, a second, like to a bear, and it raised up itself on one side, and *it had* three ribs in the mouth of it between the teeth of it: and they said thus unto it, Arise, devour much flesh.

6After this I beheld, and lo another, like a leopard, which had upon the back of it four wings of a fowl; the beast had also four heads; and dominion was given to it.

7After this I saw in the night visions, and behold a fourth beast, dreadful and terrible, and strong exceedingly; and it had great iron teeth: it devoured and brake in pieces, and stamped the residue with the feet of it: and it *was* diverse from all the beasts that *were* before it; and it had ten horns.

8I considered the horns, and, behold, there came up among them another little horn, before whom there were three of the first horns plucked up by the roots: and, behold, in this horn *were* eyes like the eyes of man, and a mouth speaking great things.

9I beheld till the thrones were cast down, and the Ancient of days did sit, whose garment *was* white as snow, and the hair of his head like the pure wool: his throne *was like* the fiery flame, *and* his wheels *as* burning fire.

10A fiery stream issued and came forth from before him: thousand thousands ministered unto him, and ten thousand times ten thousand stood before him: the judgment was set, and the books were opened.

11I beheld then because of the voice of the great words which the horn spake: I beheld *even* till the beast was slain, and his body destroyed, and given to the burning flame.

12As concerning the rest of the beasts, they had their dominion taken away: yet their lives were prolonged for a season and time.

13I saw in the night visions, and, behold, *one* like the Son of man came with the clouds of heaven, and came to the Ancient of days, and they brought him near before him.

14And there was given him dominion, and glory, and a kingdom, that all people, nations, and languages, should serve him: his dominion *is* an everlasting dominion, which shall not pass away, and his kingdom *that* which shall not be destroyed.

15I Daniel was grieved in my spirit in the midst of *my* body, and the visions of my head troubled me.

16I came near unto one of them that stood by, and asked him the truth of all this. So he told me, and made me know the interpretation of the things.

17These great beasts, which are four, *are* four kings, *which* shall arise out of the earth.

18But the saints of the most High shall take the kingdom, and possess the kingdom for ever, even for ever and ever.

19Then I would know the truth of the fourth beast, which was diverse from all the others, exceeding dreadful, whose teeth *were of* iron, and his nails *of* brass; *which* devoured, brake in pieces, and stamped the residue with his feet;

20And of the ten horns that *were* in his head, and *of* the other which came up, and before whom three fell; even *of* that horn that had eyes, and a mouth that spake very great things, whose look *was* more stout than his fellows.

21I beheld, and the same horn made war with the saints, and prevailed against them;

22Until the Ancient of days came, and judgment was given to the saints of the most High; and the time came that the saints possessed the kingdom.

23Thus he said, The fourth beast shall be the fourth kingdom upon earth, which shall be diverse from all kingdoms, and shall devour the whole earth, and shall tread it down, and break it in pieces.

24And the ten horns out of this kingdom *are* ten kings *that* shall arise: and another shall rise after them; and he shall be diverse from the first, and he shall subdue three kings.

25And he shall speak *great* words against the most High, and shall wear out the saints of the most High, and think to change times and laws: and they shall be given into his hand until a time and times and the dividing of time.

26But the judgment shall sit, and they shall take away his dominion, to consume and to destroy *it* unto the end.

27And the kingdom and dominion, and the greatness of the kingdom under the whole heaven, shall be given to the people of the saints of the most High, whose kingdom *is* an everlasting kingdom, and all dominions shall serve and obey him.

28Hitherto *is* the end of the matter. As for me Daniel, my cogitations much troubled me, and my countenance changed in me: but I kept the matter in my heart.

1 JOHN 1:1–10

THAT which was from the beginning, which we have heard, which we have seen with our eyes, which we have looked upon, and our hands have handled, of the Word of life;

2(For the life was manifested, and we have seen *it,* and bear witness, and shew unto you that eternal life, which was with the Father, and was manifested unto us;)

3That which we have seen and heard declare we unto you, that ye also may have fellowship with us: and truly our fellowship *is* with the Father, and with his Son Jesus Christ.

4And these things write we unto you, that your joy may be full.

5This then is the message which we have heard of him, and declare unto you, that God is light, and in him is no darkness at all.

6If we say that we have fellowship with him, and walk in darkness, we lie, and do not the truth:

7But if we walk in the light, as he is in the light, we have fellowship one with another, and the blood of Jesus Christ his Son cleanseth us from all sin.

8If we say that we have no sin, we deceive ourselves, and the truth is not in us.

9If we confess our sins, he is faithful and just to forgive us *our* sins, and to cleanse us from all unrighteousness.

10If we say that we have not sinned, we make him a liar, and his word is not in us.

PSALM 119:156–176

GREAT *are* thy tender mercies, O LORD: quicken me according to thy judgments.

157Many *are* my persecutors and mine enemies; *yet* do I not decline from thy testimonies.

158I beheld the transgressors, and was grieved; because they kept not thy word.

159Consider how I love thy precepts: quicken me, O LORD, according to thy lovingkindness.

160Thy word *is* true *from* the beginning: and every one of thy righteous judgments *endureth* for ever.

161Princes have persecuted me without a cause: but my heart standeth in awe of thy word.

162I rejoice at thy word, as one that findeth great spoil.

163I hate and abhor lying: *but* thy law do I love.

164Seven times a day do I praise thee because of thy righteous judgments.

165Great peace have they which love thy law: and nothing shall offend them.

166LORD, I have hoped for thy salvation, and done thy commandments.

167My soul hath kept thy testimonies; and I love them exceedingly.

168I have kept thy precepts and thy testimonies: for all my ways *are* before thee.

169Let my cry come near before thee, O LORD: give me understanding according to thy word.

170Let my supplication come before thee: deliver me according to thy word.

171My lips shall utter praise, when thou hast taught me thy statutes.

172My tongue shall speak of thy word: for all thy commandments *are* righteousness.

173Let thine hand help me; for I have chosen thy precepts.

174I have longed for thy salvation, O LORD; and thy law *is* my delight.

175Let my soul live, and it shall praise thee; and let thy judgments help me.

176I have gone astray like a lost sheep; seek thy servant; for I do not forget thy commandments.

PROVERBS FOR TODAY/ 28:23–24

He that rebuketh a man afterwards shall find more favour than he that flattereth with the tongue. □ *Whoso robbeth his father or his mother and saith, It is no transgression; the same is the companion of a destroyer.*

DECEMBER 1

DANIEL 8:1–27

IN the third year of the reign of king Belshazzar a vision appeared unto me, *even unto* me Daniel, after that which appeared unto me at the first.

2And I saw in a vision; and it came to pass, when I saw, that I *was* at Shushan *in* the palace, which *is* in the province of Elam; and I saw in a vision, and I was by the river of Ulai.

3Then I lifted up mine eyes, and saw, and, behold, there stood before the river a ram which had *two* horns: and the *two* horns *were* high; but one *was* higher than the other, and the higher came up last.

4I saw the ram pushing westward,

and northward, and southward; so that no beasts might stand before him, neither *was there any* that could deliver out of his hand; but he did according to his will, and became great.

5And as I was considering, behold, an he goat came from the west on the face of the whole earth, and touched not the ground: and the goat *had* a notable horn between his eyes.

6And he came to the ram that had *two* horns, which I had seen standing before the river, and ran unto him in the fury of his power.

7And I saw him come close unto the ram, and he was moved with choler against him, and smote the ram, and brake his two horns: and there was no power in the ram to stand before him, but he cast him down to the ground, and stamped upon him: and there was none that could deliver the ram out of his hand.

8Therefore the he goat waxed very great: and when he was strong, the great horn was broken; and for it came up four notable ones toward the four winds of heaven.

9And out of one of them came forth a little horn, which waxed exceeding great, toward the south, and toward the east, and toward the pleasant *land*.

10And it waxed great, *even* to the host of heaven; and it cast down *some* of the host and of the stars to the ground, and stamped upon them.

11Yea, he magnified *himself* even to the prince of the host, and by him the daily *sacrifice* was taken away, and the place of his sanctuary was cast down.

12And an host was given *him* against the daily *sacrifice* by reason of transgression, and it cast down the truth to the ground; and it practised, and prospered.

13Then I heard one saint speaking, and another saint said unto that certain *saint* which spake, How long *shall be* the vision *concerning* the daily *sacrifice*, and the transgression of desolation, to give both the sanctuary and the host to be trodden under foot?

14And he said unto me, Unto two thousand and three hundred days; then shall the sanctuary be cleansed.

15And it came to pass, when I, *even* I Daniel, had seen the vision, and sought for the meaning, then, behold, there stood before me as the appearance of a man.

16And I heard a man's voice between *the banks of* Ulai, which called, and said, Gabriel, make this *man* to understand the vision.

17So he came near where I stood: and when he came, I was afraid, and fell upon my face: but he said unto me, Understand, O son of man: for at the time of the end *shall be* the vision.

18Now as he was speaking with me, I was in a deep sleep on my face toward the ground: but he touched me, and set me upright.

19And he said, Behold, I will make thee know what shall be in the last end of the indignation: for at the time appointed the end *shall be*.

20The ram which thou sawest having *two* horns *are* the kings of Media and Persia.

21And the rough goat *is* the king of Grecia: and the great horn that *is* between his eyes *is* the first king.

22Now that being broken, whereas four stood up for it, four kingdoms shall stand up out of the nation, but not in his power.

23And in the latter time of their kingdom, when the transgressors are come to the full, a king of fierce countenance, and understanding dark sentences, shall stand up.

24And his power shall be mighty, but not by his own power: and he shall destroy wonderfully, and shall prosper, and practise, and shall destroy the mighty and the holy people.

25And through his policy also he shall cause craft to prosper in his hand; and he shall magnify *himself* in his heart, and by peace shall destroy many: he shall also stand up against the Prince of princes; but he shall be broken without hand.

26And the vision of the evening and the morning which was told *is* true: wherefore shut thou up the vision; for it *shall be* for many days.

27And I Daniel fainted, and was sick *certain* days; afterward I rose up, and did the king's business; and I was astonished at the vision, but none understood *it.*

1 JOHN 2:1–17

My little children, these things write I unto you, that ye sin not. And if any man sin, we have an advocate with the Father, Jesus Christ the righteous:

2And he is the propitiation for our sins: and not for ours only, but also for *the sins of* the whole world.

3And hereby we do know that we know him, if we keep his commandments.

4He that saith, I know him, and keepeth not his commandments, is a liar, and the truth is not in him.

5But whoso keepeth his word, in him verily is the love of God perfected: hereby know we that we are in him.

6He that saith he abideth in him ought himself also so to walk, even as he walked.

7Brethren, I write no new commandment unto you, but an old commandment which ye had from the beginning. The old commandment is the word which ye have heard from the beginning.

8Again, a new commandment I write unto you, which thing is true in him and in you: because the darkness is past, and the true light now shineth.

9He that saith he is in the light, and hateth his brother, is in darkness even until now.

10He that loveth his brother abideth in the light, and there is none occasion of stumbling in him.

11But he that hateth his brother is in darkness, and walketh in darkness, and knoweth not whither he goeth, because that darkness hath blinded his eyes.

12I write unto you, little children, because your sins are forgiven you for his name's sake.

13I write unto you, fathers, because ye have known him *that is* from the beginning. I write unto you, young men, because ye have overcome the wicked one. I write unto you, little children, because ye have known the Father.

14I have written unto you, fathers, because ye have known him *that is* from the beginning. I have written unto you, young men, because ye are strong, and the word of God abideth in you, and ye have overcome the wicked one.

15Love not the world, neither the things *that are* in the world. If any man love the world, the love of the Father is not in him.

16For all that *is* in the world, the lust of the flesh, and the lust of the eyes, and the pride of life, is not of the Father, but is of the world.

17And the world passeth away, and the lust thereof: but he that doeth the will of God abideth for ever.

PSALM 120:1–7

In my distress I cried unto the LORD, and he heard me.

2Deliver my soul, O LORD, from lying lips, *and* from a deceitful tongue.

3What shall be given unto thee? or what shall be done unto thee, thou false tongue?

4Sharp arrows of the mighty, with coals of juniper.

5Woe is me, that I sojourn in Mesech, *that* I dwell in the tents of Kedar!

6My soul hath long dwelt with him that hateth peace.

7I *am for* peace: but when I speak, they *are* for war.

PROVERBS FOR TODAY/ 28:25–26

He that is of a proud heart stirreth up strife: but he that putteth his trust in the LORD *shall be made fat.* □ *He that trusteth in his own heart is a fool: but whoso walketh wisely, he shall be delivered.*

DECEMBER 2

DANIEL 9:1—10:21

IN the first year of Darius the son of Ahasuerus, of the seed of the Medes, which was made king over the realm of the Chaldeans;

2In the first year of his reign I Daniel understood by books the number of the years, whereof the word of the LORD came to Jeremiah the prophet, that he would accomplish seventy years in the desolations of Jersualem.

3And I set my face unto the Lord God, to seek by prayer and supplications, with fasting, and sackcloth, and ashes:

4And I prayed unto the LORD my God, and made my confession, and said, O Lord, the great and dreadful God, keeping the covenant and mercy to them that love him, and to them that keep his commandments;

5We have sinned, and have committed iniquity, and have done wickedly, and have rebelled, even by departing from thy precepts and from thy judgments:

6Neither have we hearkened unto thy servants the prophets, which spake in thy name to our kings, our princes, and our fathers, and to all the people of the land.

7O Lord, righteousness *belongeth* unto thee, but unto us confusion of faces, as at this day; to the men of Judah, and to the inhabitants of Jerusalem, and unto all Israel, *that are* near, and *that are* far off, through all the countries whither thou hast driven them, because of their trespass that they have trespassed against thee.

8O Lord, to us *belongeth* confusion of face, to our kings, to our princes, and to our fathers, because we have sinned against thee.

9To the Lord our God *belong* mercies and forgiveness, though we have rebelled against him;

10Neither have we obeyed the voice of the LORD our God, to walk in his laws, which he set before us by his servants the prophets.

11Yea, all Israel have transgressed thy law, even by departing, that they might not obey thy voice; therefore the curse is poured upon us, and the oath that *is* written in the law of Moses the servant of God, because we have sinned against him.

12And he hath confirmed his words, which he spake against us, and against our judges that judged us, by bringing upon us a great evil: for under the whole heaven hath not been done as hath been done upon Jerusalem.

13As *it is* written in the law of Moses, all this evil is come upon us: yet made we not our prayer before the LORD our God, that we might turn from our iniquities, and understand thy truth.

14Therefore hath the LORD watched upon the evil, and brought it upon us: for the LORD our God *is* righteous in all his works which he doeth: for we obeyed not his voice.

15And now, O Lord our God, that hast brought thy people forth out of the land of Egypt with a mighty hand, and hast gotten thee renown, as at this day; we have sinned, we have done wickedly.

16O Lord, according to all thy righteousness, I beseech thee, let thine anger and thy fury be turned away from thy city Jerusalem, thy holy mountain: because for our sins, and for the iniquities of our fathers, Jerusalem and thy people *are become* a reproach to all *that are* about us.

17Now therefore, O our God, hear the prayer of thy servant, and his supplications, and cause thy face to shine upon thy sanctuary that is desolate, for the Lord's sake.

18O my God, incline thine ear, and hear; open thine eyes, and behold our desolations, and the city which is called by thy name: for we do not present our supplications before thee for our righteousnesses, but for thy great mercies.

19O Lord, hear; O Lord, forgive; O Lord, hearken and do; defer not, for thine own sake, O my God: for thy city and thy people are called by thy name.

20And whiles I *was* speaking, and praying, and confessing my sin and the sin of my people Israel, and presenting my supplication before the Lord my God for the holy mountain of my God;

21Yea, whiles I *was* speaking in prayer, even the man Gabriel, whom I had seen in the vision at the beginning, being caused to fly swiftly, touched me about the time of the evening oblation.

22And he informed *me,* and talked with me, and said, O Daniel, I am now come forth to give thee skill and understanding.

23At the beginning of thy supplications the commandment came forth, and I am come to shew *thee;* for thou *art* greatly beloved: therefore understand the matter, and consider the vision.

24Seventy weeks are determined upon thy people and upon thy holy city, to finish the transgression, and to make an end of sins, and to make reconciliation for iniquity, and to bring in everlasting righteousness, and to seal up the vision and prophecy, and to anoint the most Holy.

25Know therefore and understand, *that* from the going forth of the commandment to restore and to build Jerusalem unto the Messiah the Prince *shall be* seven weeks, and threescore and two weeks: the street shall be built again, and the wall, even in troublous times.

26And after threescore and two weeks shall Messiah be cut off, but not for himself: and the people of the prince that shall come shall destroy the city and the sanctuary; and the end thereof *shall be* with a flood, and unto the end of the war desolations are determined.

27And he shall confirm the covenant with many for one week: and in the midst of the week he shall cause the sacrifice and the oblation to cease, and for the overspreading of abominations he shall make *it* desolate, even until the consummation, and that determined shall be poured upon the desolate.

In the third year of Cyrus king of Persia a thing was revealed unto Daniel, whose name was called Belteshazzar; and the thing *was* true, but the time appointed *was* long: and he understood the thing, and had understanding of the vision.

2In those days I Daniel was mourning three full weeks.

3I ate no pleasant bread, neither came flesh nor wine in my mouth, neither did I anoint myself at all, till three whole weeks were fulfilled.

4And in the four and twentieth day of the first month, as I was by the side of the great river, which *is* Hiddekel;

⁵Then I lifted up mine eyes, and looked, and behold, a certain man clothed in linen, whose loins *were* girded with fine gold of Uphaz:

⁶His body also *was* like the beryl, and his face as the appearance of lightning, and his eyes as lamps of fire, and his arms and his feet like in colour to polished brass, and the voice of his words like the voice of a multitude.

⁷And I Daniel alone saw the vision: for the men that were with me saw not the vision; but a great quaking fell upon them, so that they fled to hide themselves.

⁸Therefore I was left alone, and saw this great vision, and there remained no strength in me: for my comeliness was turned in me into corruption, and I retained no strength.

⁹Yet heard I the voice of his words: and when I heard the voice of his words, then was I in a deep sleep on my face, and my face toward the ground.

¹⁰And, behold, an hand touched me, which set me upon my knees and *upon* the palms of my hands.

¹¹And he said unto me, O Daniel, a man greatly beloved, understand the words that I speak unto thee, and stand upright: for unto thee am I now sent. And when he had spoken this word unto me, I stood trembling.

¹²Then said he unto me, Fear not, Daniel: for from the first day that thou didst set thine heart to understand, and to chasten thyself before thy God, thy words were heard, and I am come for thy words.

¹³But the prince of the kingdom of Persia withstood me one and twenty days: but, lo, Michael, one of the chief princes, came to help me; and I remained there with the kings of Persia.

¹⁴Now I am come to make thee understand what shall befall thy people in the latter days: for yet the vision *is* for *many* days.

¹⁵And when he had spoken such words unto me, I set my face toward the ground, and I became dumb.

¹⁶And, behold, *one* like the similitude of the sons of men touched my lips: then I opened my mouth, and spake, and said unto him that stood before me, O my lord, by the vision my sorrows are turned upon me, and I have retained no strength.

¹⁷For how can the servant of this my lord talk with this my lord? for as for me, straightway there remained no strength in me, neither is there breath left in me.

¹⁸Then there came again and touched me *one* like the appearance of a man, and he strengthened me.

¹⁹And said, O man greatly beloved, fear not: peace *be* unto thee, be strong, yea, be strong. And when he had spoken unto me, I was strengthened, and said, Let my lord speak; for thou hast strengthened me.

²⁰Then said he, Knowest thou wherefore I come unto thee? and now will I return to fight with the prince of Persia: and when I am gone forth, lo, the prince of Grecia shall come.

²¹But I will shew thee that which is noted in the scripture of truth: and *there is* none that holdeth with me in these things, but Michael your prince.

1 JOHN 2:18—3:6

LITTLE children, it is the last time: and as ye have heard that antichrist shall come, even now are there many antichrists; whereby we know that it is the last time.

¹⁹They went out from us, but they were not of us: for if they had been of us, they would *no doubt* have continued with us: but *they went out,* that they might be made manifest that they were not all of us.

²⁰But ye have an unction from the Holy One, and ye know all things.

²¹I have not written unto you because

ye know not the truth, but because ye know it, and that no lie is of the truth.

22Who is a liar but he that denieth that Jesus is the Christ? He is antichrist, that denieth the Father and the Son.

23Whosoever denieth the Son, the same hath not the Father: [but] *he that acknowledgeth the Son hath the Father also.*

24Let that therefore abide in you, which ye have heard from the beginning. If that which ye have heard from the beginning shall remain in you, ye also shall continue in the Son, and in the Father.

25And this is the promise that he hath promised us, *even* eternal life,

26These *things* have I written unto you concerning them that seduce you.

27But the anointing which ye have received of him abideth in you, and ye need not that any man teach you: but as the same anointing teacheth you of all things, and is truth, and is no lie, and even as it hath taught you, ye shall abide in him.

28And now, little children, abide in him; that, when he shall appear, we may have confidence, and not be ashamed before him at his coming.

29If ye know that he is righteous, ye know that every one that doeth righteousness is born of him.

BEHOLD, what manner of love the Father hath bestowed upon us, that we should be called the sons of God: therefore the world knoweth us not, because it knew him not.

2Beloved, now are we the sons of God, and it doth not yet appear what we shall be: but we know that, when he shall appear, we shall be like him; for we shall see him as he is.

3And every man that hath this hope in him purifieth himself, even as he is pure.

4Whosoever committeth sin transgresseth also the law: for sin is the transgression of the law.

5And ye know that he was manifested to take away our sins; and in him is no sin.

6Whosoever abideth in him sinneth not: whosoever sinneth hath not seen him, neither known him.

PSALM 121:1–8

I WILL lift up mine eyes unto the hills, from whence cometh my help.

2My help *cometh* from the LORD, which made heaven and earth.

3He will not suffer thy foot to be moved: he that keepeth thee will not slumber.

4Behold, he that keepeth Israel shall neither slumber nor sleep.

5The LORD *is* thy keeper: the LORD *is* thy shade upon thy right hand.

6The sun shall not smite thee by day, nor the moon by night.

7The LORD shall preserve thee from all evil: he shall preserve thy soul.

8The LORD shall preserve thy going out and thy coming in from this time forth, and even for evermore.

PROVERBS FOR TODAY/ 28:27–28

He that giveth unto the poor shall not lack: but he that hideth his eyes shall have many a curse. □ When the wicked rise, men hide themselves: but when they perish, the righteous increase.

DECEMBER 3

DANIEL 11:1–34

ALSO I in the first year of Darius the Mede, *even* I, stood to confirm and to strengthen him.

2And now will I shew thee the truth. Behold, there shall stand up yet three kings in Persia; and the fourth shall be far richer than *they* all: and by his strength through his riches he shall stir up all against the realm of Grecia.

3And a mighty king shall stand up, that shall rule with great dominion, and do according to his will.

4And when he shall stand up, his kingdom shall be broken, and shall be divided toward the four winds of heaven; and not to his posterity, nor according to his dominion which he ruled: for his kingdom shall be plucked up, even for others beside those.

5And the king of the south shall be strong, and *one* of his princes; and he shall be strong above him, and have dominion; his dominion *shall be* a great dominion.

6And in the end of years they shall join themselves together; for the king's daughter of the south shall come to the king of the north to make an agreement: but she shall not retain the power of the arm; neither shall he stand, nor his arm: but she shall be given up, and they that brought her, and he that begat her, and he that strengthened her in *these* times.

7But out of a branch of her roots shall *one* stand up in his estate, which shall come with an army, and shall enter into the fortress of the king of the north, and shall deal against them, and shall prevail:

8And shall also carry captives into Egypt their gods, with their princes, *and* with their precious vessels of silver and of gold; and he shall continue *more* years than the king of the north.

9So the king of the south shall come into *his* kingdom, and shall return into his own land.

10But his sons shall be stirred up, and shall assemble a multitude of great forces: and *one* shall certainly come, and overflow, and pass through: then shall he return, and be stirred up, *even* to his fortress.

11And the king of the south shall be moved with choler, and shall come forth and fight with him, *even* with the king of the north: and he shall set forth a great multitude; but the multitude shall be given into his hand.

12*And* when he hath taken away the multitude, his heart shall be lifted up; and he shall cast down *many* ten thousands: but he shall not be strengthened *by it.*

13For the king of the north shall return, and shall set forth a multitude greater than the former, and shall certainly come after certain years with a great army and with much riches.

14And in those times there shall many stand up against the king of the south: also the robbers of thy people shall exalt themselves to establish the vision; but they shall fall.

15So the king of the north shall come, and cast up a mount, and take the most fenced cities: and the arms of the south shall not withstand, neither his chosen people, neither *shall there be any* strength to withstand.

16But he that cometh against him shall do according to his own will, and none shall stand before him: and he shall stand in the glorious land, which by his hand shall be consumed.

17He shall also set his face to enter with the strength of his whole kingdom, and upright ones with him; thus shall he do: and he shall give him the daughter of women, corrupting her: but she shall not stand *on his side,* neither be for him.

18After this shall he turn his face unto the isles, and shall take many: but a prince for his own behalf shall cause the reproach offered by him to cease; without his own reproach he shall cause *it* to turn upon him.

19Then he shall turn his face toward the fort of his own land: but he shall stumble and fall, and not be found.

20Then shall stand up in his estate a raiser of taxes *in* the glory of the kingdom: but within few days he shall be destroyed, neither in anger, nor in battle.

21And in his estate shall stand up a vile person, to whom they shall not give the honour of the kingdom: but he shall come in peaceably, and obtain the kingdom by flatteries.

22And with the arms of a flood shall they be overflown from before him, and shall be broken; yea, also the prince of the covenant.

23And after the league *made* with him he shall work deceitfully: for he shall come up, and shall become strong with a small people.

24He shall enter peaceably even upon the fattest places of the province; and he shall do *that* which his fathers have not done, nor his fathers' fathers; he shall scatter among them the prey, and spoil, and riches: *yea,* and he shall forecast his devices against the strong holds, even for a time.

25And he shall stir up his power and his courage against the king of the south with a great army; and the king of the south shall be stirred up to battle with a very great and mighty army; but he shall not stand: for they shall forecast devices against him.

26Yea, they that feed of the portion of his meat shall destroy him, and his army shall overflow: and many shall fall down slain.

27And both these kings' hearts *shall be* to do mischief, and they shall speak lies at one table; but it shall not prosper: for yet the end *shall be* at the time appointed.

28Then shall he return into his land with great riches; and his heart *shall be* against the holy covenant; and he shall do *exploits,* and return to his own land.

29At the time appointed he shall return, and come toward the south; but it shall not be as the former, or as the latter.

30For the ships of Chittim shall come against him: therefore he shall be grieved, and return, and have indignation against the holy covenant: so shall he do; he shall even return, and have intelligence with them that forsake the holy covenant.

31And arms shall stand on his part, and they shall pollute the sanctuary of strength, and shall take away the daily *sacrifice,* and they shall place the abomination that maketh desolate.

32And such as do wickedly against the covenant shall he corrupt by flatteries: but the people that do know their God shall be strong, and do *exploits.*

33And they that understand among the people shall instruct many: yet they shall fall by the sword, and by flame, by captivity, and by spoil, *many* days.

34Now when they shall fall, they shall be holpen with a little help: but many shall cleave to them with flatteries.

1 JOHN 3:7–24

L ITTLE children, let no man deceive you: he that doeth righteousness is righteous, even as he is righteous.

8He that committeth sin is of the devil; for the devil sinneth from the beginning. For this purpose the Son of God was manifested, that he might destroy the works of the devil.

9Whosoever is born of God doth not

commit sin; for his seed remaineth in him: and he cannot sin, because he is born of God.

10In this the children of God are manifest, and the children of the devil: whosoever doeth not righteousness is not of God, neither he that loveth not his brother.

11For this is the message that ye heard from the beginning, that we should love one another.

12Not as Cain, *who* was of that wicked one, and slew his brother. And wherefore slew he him? Because his own works were evil, and his brother's righteous.

13Marvel not, my brethren, if the world hate you.

14We know that we have passed from death unto life, because we love the brethren. He that loveth not *his* brother abideth in death.

15Whosoever hateth his brother is a murderer: and ye know that no murderer hath eternal life abiding in him.

16Hereby perceive we the love *of God,* because he laid down his life for us: and we ought to lay down *our* lives for the brethren.

17But whoso hath this world's good, and seeth his brother have need, and shutteth up his bowels *of compassion* from him, how dwelleth the love of God in him?

18My little children, let us not love in word, neither in tongue; but in deed and in truth.

19And hereby we know that we are of the truth, and shall assure our hearts before him.

20For if our heart condemn us, God is greater than our heart, and knoweth all things.

21Beloved, if our heart condemn us not, *then* have we confidence toward God.

22And whatsoever we ask, we receive of him, because we keep his commandments, and do those things that are pleasing in his sight.

23And this is his commandment, That we should believe on the name of his Son Jesus Christ, and love one another, as he gave us commandment.

24And he that keepeth his commandments dwelleth in him, and he in him. And hereby we know that he abideth in us, by the Spirit which he hath given us.

PSALM 122:1–9

I was glad when they said unto me, Let us go into the house of the Lord.

2Our feet shall stand within thy gates, O Jerusalem.

3Jerusalem is builded as a city that is compact together:

4Whither the tribes go up, the tribes of the Lord, unto the testimony of Israel, to give thanks unto the name of the Lord.

5For there are set thrones of judgment, the thrones of the house of David.

6Pray for the peace of Jerusalem: they shall prosper that love thee.

7Peace be within thy walls, *and* prosperity within thy palaces.

8For my brethren and companions' sakes, I will now say, Peace *be* within thee.

9Because of the house of the Lord our God I will seek thy good.

PROVERBS FOR TODAY/ 29:1

He, that being often reproved hardeneth his neck, shall suddenly be destroyed, and that without remedy.

DECEMBER 4

DANIEL 11:35—12:13

Aᴺᴰ *some* of them of understanding shall fall, to try them, and to purge, and to make *them* white, *even* to the time of the end: because *it is* yet for a time appointed.

³⁶And the king shall do according to his will; and he shall exalt himself, and magnify himself above every god, and shall speak marvellous things against the God of gods, and shall prosper till the indignation be accomplished: for that that is determined shall be done.

³⁷Neither shall he regard the God of his fathers, nor the desire of women, nor regard any god: for he shall magnify himself above all.

³⁸But in his estate shall he honour the God of forces: and a god whom his fathers knew not shall he honour with gold, and silver, and with precious stones, and pleasant things.

³⁹Thus shall he do in the most strong holds with a strange god, whom he shall acknowledge *and* increase with glory: and he shall cause them to rule over many, and shall divide the land for gain.

⁴⁰And at the time of the end shall the king of the south push at him: and the king of the north shall come against him like a whirlwind, with chariots, and with horsemen, and with many ships; and he shall enter into the countries, and shall overflow and pass over.

⁴¹He shall enter also into the glorious land, and many *countries* shall be overthrown: but these shall escape out of his hand, *even* Edom, and Moab, and the chief of the children of Ammon.

⁴²He shall stretch forth his hand also upon the countries: and the land of Egypt shall not escape.

⁴³But he shall have power over the treasures of gold and of silver, and over all the precious things of Egypt; and the Libyans and the Ethiopians *shall be* at his steps.

⁴⁴But tidings out of the east and out of the north shall trouble him: therefore he shall go forth with great fury to destroy, and utterly to make away many.

⁴⁵And he shall plant the tabernacles of his palace between the seas in the glorious holy mountain; yet he shall come to his end, and none shall help him.

Aɴᴅ at that time shall Michael stand up, the great prince which standeth for the children of thy people: and there shall be a time of trouble, such as never was since there was a nation *even* to that same time: and at that time thy people shall be delivered, every one that shall be found written in the book.

²And many of them that sleep in the dust of the earth shall awake, some to everlasting life, and some to shame *and* everlasting contempt.

³And they that be wise shall shine as the brightness of the firmament; and they that turn many to righteousness as the stars for ever and ever.

⁴But thou, O Daniel, shut up the words, and seal the book, *even* to the time of the end: many shall run to and fro, and knowledge shall be increased.

⁵Then I Daniel looked, and, behold, there stood other two, the one on this side of the bank of the river, and the other on that side of the bank of the river.

⁶And *one* said to the man clothed in linen, which *was* upon the waters of the river, How long *shall it be to* the end of these wonders?

⁷And I heard the man clothed in linen, which *was* upon the waters of the river, when he held up his right hand and

his left hand unto heaven, and sware by him that liveth for ever that *it shall be* for a time, times, and an half; and when he shall have accomplished to scatter the power of the holy people, all these *things* shall be finished.

8And I heard, but I understood not: then said I, O my Lord, what *shall be* the end of these *things?*

9And he said, Go thy way, Daniel: for the words *are* closed up and sealed till the time of the end.

10Many shall be purified, and made white, and tried; but the wicked shall do wickedly: and none of the wicked shall understand; but the wise shall understand.

11And from the time *that* the daily *sacrifice* shall be taken away, and the abomination that maketh desolate set up, *there shall be* a thousand two hundred and ninety days.

12Blessed *is* he that waiteth, and cometh to the thousand three hundred and five and thirty days.

13But go thou thy way till the end *be:* for thou shalt rest, and stand in thy lot at the end of the days.

1 JOHN 4:1–21

BELOVED, believe not every spirit, but try the spirits whether they are of God: because many false prophets are gone out into the world.

2Hereby know ye the Spirit of God: Every spirit that confesseth that Jesus Christ is come in the flesh is of God:

3And every spirit that confesseth not that Jesus Christ is come in the flesh is not of God: and this is that *spirit* of antichrist, whereof ye have heard that it should come; and even now already is it in the world.

4Ye are of God, little children, and have overcome them: because greater is he that is in you, than he that is in the world.

5They are of the world: therefore speak they of the world, and the world heareth them.

6We are of God: he that knoweth God heareth us; he that is not of God heareth not us. Hereby know we the spirit of truth, and the spirit of error.

7Beloved, let us love one another: for love is of God; and every one that loveth is born of God, and knoweth God.

8He that loveth not knoweth not God; for God is love.

9In this was manifested the love of God toward us, because that God sent his only begotten Son into the world, that we might live through him.

10Herein is love, not that we loved God, but that he loved us, and sent his Son *to be* the propitiation for our sins.

11Beloved, if God so loved us, we ought also to love one another.

12No man hath seen God at any time. If we love one another, God dwelleth in us, and his love is perfected in us.

13Hereby know we that we dwell in him, and he in us, because he hath given us of his Spirit.

14And we have seen and do testify that the Father sent the Son *to be* the Saviour of the world.

15Whosoever shall confess that Jesus is the Son of God, God dwelleth in him, and he in God.

16And we have known and believed the love that God hath to us. God is love; and he that dwelleth in love dwelleth in God, and God in him.

17Herein is our love made perfect, that we may have boldness in the day of judgment: because as he is, so are we in this world.

18There is no fear in love; but perfect love casteth out fear: because fear hath torment. He that feareth is not made perfect in love.

19We love him, because he first loved us.

20If a man say, I love God, and hateth his brother, he is a liar: for he that loveth not his brother whom he hath seen, how can he love God whom he hath not seen?

21And this commandment have we from him, That he who loveth God love his brother also.

PSALM 123:1–4

UNTO thee lift I up mine eyes, O thou that dwellest in the heavens.

2Behold, as the eyes of servants *look* unto the hand of their masters, *and* as the eyes of a maiden unto the hand of her mistress; so our eyes *wait* upon the LORD our God, until that he have mercy upon us.

3Have mercy upon us, O LORD, have mercy upon us: for we are exceedingly filled with contempt.

4Our soul is exceedingly filled with the scorning of those that are at ease, *and* with the contempt of the proud.

PROVERBS FOR TODAY/ 29:2–4

When the righteous are in authority, the people rejoice: but when the wicked beareth rule, the people mourn. □ *Whoso loveth wisdom rejoiceth his father: but he that keepeth company with harlots spendeth his substance.* □ *The king by judgment establisheth the land: but he that receiveth gifts overthroweth it.*

DECEMBER 5

HOSEA 1:1—3:5

THE word of the LORD that came unto Hosea, the son of Beeri, in the days of Uzziah, Jotham, Ahaz, *and* Hezekiah, kings of Judah, and in the days of Jeroboam the son of Joash, king of Israel.

2The beginning of the word of the LORD by Hosea. And the LORD said to Hosea, Go, take unto thee a wife of whoredoms and children of whoredoms: for the land hath committed great whoredom, *departing* from the LORD.

3So he went and took Gomer the daughter of Diblaim; which conceived, and bare him a son.

4And the LORD said unto him, Call his name Jezreel; for yet a little *while,* and I will avenge the blood of Jezreel upon the house of Jehu, and will cause to cease the kingdom of the house of Israel.

5And it shall come to pass at that day, that I will break the bow of Israel in the valley of Jezreel.

6And she conceived again, and bare a daughter. And *God* said unto him, Call her name Lo–ruhamah: for I will no more have mercy upon the house of Israel; but I will utterly take them away.

7But I will have mercy upon the house of Judah, and will save them by the LORD their God, and will not save them by bow, nor by sword, nor by battle, by horses, nor by horsemen.

8Now when she had weaned Lo–ruhamah, she conceived, and bare a son.

9Then said *God,* Call his name Lo–ammi: for ye *are* not my people, and I will not be your *God.*

10Yet the number of the children of Israel shall be as the sand of the sea, which cannot be measured nor numbered; and it shall come to pass, *that* in the place where it was said unto them, Ye *are* not my people, *there* it shall be said unto them, *Ye are* the sons of the living God.

11Then shall the children of Judah and the children of Israel be gathered together, and appoint themselves one head, and they shall come up out of the land: for great *shall be* the day of Jezreel.

SAY ye unto your brethren, Ammi; and to your sisters, Ruhamah.

2Plead with your mother, plead: for she *is* not my wife, neither *am* I her husband: let her therefore put away her whoredoms out of her sight, and her adulteries from between her breasts;

3Lest I strip her naked, and set her as in the day that she was born, and make her as a wilderness, and set her like a dry land, and slay her with thirst.

4And I will not have mercy upon her children; for they *be* the children of whoredoms.

5For their mother hath played the harlot: she that conceived them hath done shamefully: for she said, I will go after my lovers, that give *me* my bread and my water, my wool and my flax, mine oil and my drink.

6Therefore, behold, I will hedge up thy way with thorns, and make a wall, that she shall not find her paths.

7And she shall follow after her lovers, but she shall not overtake them; and she shall seek them, but shall not find *them:* then shall she say, I will go and return to my first husband; for then *was it* better with me than now.

8For she did not know that I gave her corn, and wine, and oil, and multiplied her silver and gold, *which* they prepared for Baal.

9Therefore will I return, and take away my corn in the time thereof, and my wine in the season thereof, and will recover my wool and my flax *given*

to cover her nakedness.

10And now will I discover her lewdness in the sight of her lovers, and none shall deliver her out of mine hand.

11I will also cause all her mirth to cease, her feast days, her new moons, and her sabbaths, and all her solemn feasts.

12And I will destroy her vines, and her fig trees, whereof she hath said, These *are* my rewards that my lovers have given me: and I will make them a forest, and the beasts of the field shall eat them.

13And I will visit upon her the days of Baalim, wherein she burned incense to them, and she decked herself with her earrings and her jewels, and she went after her lovers, and forgat me, saith the LORD.

14Therefore, behold, I will allure her, and bring her into the wilderness, and speak comfortably unto her.

15And I will give her her vineyards from thence, and the valley of Achor for a door of hope: and she shall sing there, as in the days of her youth, and as in the day when she came up out of the land of Egypt.

16And it shall be at that day, saith the LORD, *that* thou shalt call me Ishi; and shalt call me no more Baali.

17For I will take away the names of Baalim out of her mouth, and they shall no more be remembered by their name.

18And in that day will I make a covenant for them with the beasts of the field, and with the fowls of heaven, and *with* the creeping things of the ground: and I will break the bow and the sword and the battle out of the earth, and will make them to lie down safely.

19And I will betroth thee unto me for ever; yea, I will betroth thee unto me in righteousness, and in judgment, and in lovingkindness, and in mercies.

20I will even betroth thee unto me in faithfulness: and thou shalt know the LORD.

21And it shall come to pass in that day, I will hear, saith the LORD, I will hear the heavens, and they shall hear the earth;

22And the earth shall hear the corn, and the wine, and the oil; and they shall hear Jezreel.

23And I will sow her unto me in the earth; and I will have mercy upon her that had not obtained mercy; and I will say to *them which were* not my people, Thou *art* my people; and they shall say, *Thou art* my God.

THEN said the LORD unto me, Go yet, love a woman beloved of *her* friend, yet an adulteress, according to the love of the LORD toward the children of Israel, who look to other gods, and love flagons of wine.

2So I bought her to me for fifteen *pieces* of silver, and *for* an homer of barley, and an half homer of barley:

3And I said unto her, Thou shalt abide for me many days; thou shalt not play the harlot, and thou shalt not be for *another* man: so *will* I also *be* for thee.

4For the children of Israel shall abide many days without a king, and without a prince, and without a sacrifice, and without an image, and without an ephod, and *without* teraphim:

5Afterward shall the children of Israel return, and seek the LORD their God, and David their king; and shall fear the LORD and his goodness in the latter days.

1 JOHN 5:1–21

WHOSOEVER believeth that Jesus is the Christ is born of God: and every one that loveth him that begat loveth him also that is begotten of him.

2By this we know that we love the children of God, when we love God, and keep his commandments.

3For this is the love of God, that we keep his commandments: and his commandments are not grievous.

4For whatsoever is born of God overcometh the world: and this is the victory that overcometh the world, *even* our faith.

5Who is he that overcometh the world, but he that believeth that Jesus is the Son of God?

6This is he that came by water and blood, *even* Jesus Christ; not by water only, but by water and blood. And it is the Spirit that beareth witness, because the Spirit is truth.

7For there are three that bear record in heaven, the Father, the Word, and the Holy Ghost: and these three are one.

8And there are three that bear witness in earth, the spirit, and the water, and the blood: and these three agree in one.

9If we receive the witness of men, the witness of God is greater: for this is the witness of God which he hath testified of his Son.

10He that believeth on the Son of God hath the witness in himself: he that believeth not God hath made him a liar; because he believeth not the record that God gave of his Son.

11And this is the record, that God hath given to us eternal life, and this life is in his Son.

12He that hath the Son hath life: *and* he that hath not the Son of God hath not life.

13These things have I written unto you that believe on the name of the Son of God; that ye may know that ye have eternal life, and that ye may believe on the name of the Son of God.

14And this is the confidence that we have in him, that, if we ask any thing according to his will, he heareth us:

15And if we know that he hear us, whatsoever we ask, we know that we have the petitions that we desired of him.

16If any man see his brother sin a sin *which is* not unto death, he shall ask, and he shall give him life for them that sin not unto death. There is a sin unto death: I do not say that he shall pray for it.

17All unrighteousness is sin: and there is a sin not unto death.

18We know that whosoever is born of God sinneth not; but he that is begotten of God keepeth himself, and that wicked one toucheth him not.

19*And* we know that we are of God, and the whole world lieth in wickedness.

20And we know that the Son of God is come, and hath given us an understanding, that we may know him that is true, and we are in him that is true, *even* in his Son Jesus Christ. This is the true God, and eternal life.

21Little children, keep yourselves from idols. Amen.

PSALM 124:1–8

IF *it had not been* the LORD who was on our side, now may Israel say;

2If *it had not been* the LORD who was on our side, when men rose up against us:

3Then they had swallowed us up quick, when their wrath was kindled against us:

4Then the waters had overwhelmed us, the stream had gone over our soul:

5Then the proud waters had gone over our soul.

6Blessed *be* the LORD, who hath not given us *as* a prey to their teeth.

7Our soul is escaped as a bird out of the snare of the fowlers: the snare is broken, and we are escaped.

8Our help *is* in the name of the LORD, who made heaven and earth.

PROVERBS FOR TODAY/ 29:5–8

A man that flattereth his neighbour spreadeth a net for his feet. □ *In the transgression of an evil man* there is *a snare: but the righteous doth sing and rejoice.* □ *The righteous considereth the cause of the poor:* but *the wicked regardeth not to know* it. □ *Scornful men bring a city into a snare: but wise* men *turn away wrath.*

DECEMBER 6

HOSEA 4:1—5:15

HEAR the word of the LORD, ye children of Israel: for the LORD hath a controversy with the inhabitants of the land, because *there is* no truth, nor mercy, nor knowledge of God in the land.

2By swearing, and lying, and killing, and stealing, and committing adultery, they break out, and blood toucheth blood.

3Therefore shall the land mourn, and every one that dwelleth therein shall languish, with the beasts of the field, and with the fowls of heaven; yea, the fishes of the sea also shall be taken away.

4Yet let no man strive, nor reprove another: for thy people *are* as they that strive with the priest.

5Therefore shalt thou fall in the day, and the prophet also shall fall with thee in the night, and I will destroy thy mother.

6My people are destroyed for lack of knowledge: because thou hast rejected knowledge, I will also reject thee, that thou shalt be no priest to me: seeing thou hast forgotten the law of thy God, I will also forget thy children.

7As they were increased, so they sinned against me: *therefore* will I change their glory into shame.

8They eat up the sin of my people, and they set their heart on their iniquity.

9And there shall be, like people, like priest: and I will punish them for their ways, and reward them their doings.

10For they shall eat, and not have enough: they shall commit whoredom, and shall not increase: because they have left off to take heed to the LORD.

11Whoredom and wine and new wine take away the heart.

12My people ask counsel at their stocks, and their staff declareth unto them: for the spirit of whoredoms hath caused *them* to err, and they have gone a whoring from under their God.

13They sacrifice upon the tops of the mountains, and burn incense upon the hills, under oaks and poplars and elms, because the shadow thereof *is* good: therefore your daughters shall commit whoredom, and your spouses shall commit adultery.

14I will not punish your daughters when they commit whoredom, nor your spouses when they commit adultery: for themselves are separated with whores, and they sacrifice with harlots: therefore the people *that* doth not understand shall fall.

15Though thou, Israel, play the harlot, *yet* let not Judah offend; and come not ye unto Gilgal, neither go ye up to Beth–aven, nor swear, The LORD liveth.

16For Israel slideth back as a backsliding heifer: now the LORD will feed them as a lamb in a large place.

17Ephraim *is* joined to idols: let him alone.

18Their drink is sour: they have committed whoredom continually: her rulers *with* shame do love, Give ye.

19The wind hath bound her up in her wings, and they shall be ashamed because of their sacrifices.

HEAR ye this, O priests; and hearken, ye house of Israel; and give ye ear, O house of the king; for judgment *is* toward you, because ye have been a snare on Mizpah, and a net spread upon Tabor.

2And the revolters are profound to make slaughter, though I *have been* a rebuker of them all.

3I know Ephraim, and Israel is not hid from me: for now, O Ephraim, thou committest whoredom, *and* Israel is defiled.

4They will not frame their doings to turn unto their God: for the spirit of whoredoms *is* in the midst of them, and they have not known the LORD.

5And the pride of Israel doth testify to his face: therefore shall Israel and Ephraim fall in their iniquity; Judah also shall fall with them.

6They shall go with their flocks and with their herds to seek the LORD; but they shall not find *him;* he hath withdrawn himself from them.

7They have dealt treacherously against the LORD: for they have begotten strange children: now shall a month devour them with their portions.

8Blow ye the cornet in Gibeah, *and* the trumpet in Ramah: cry aloud *at* Beth–aven, after thee, O Benjamin.

9Ephraim shall be desolate in the day of rebuke: among the tribes of Israel have I made known that which shall surely be.

10The princes of Judah were like them that remove the bound: *therefore* I will pour out my wrath upon them like water.

11Ephraim *is* oppressed *and* broken in judgment, because he willingly walked after the commandment.

12Therefore *will* I *be* unto Ephraim as a moth, and to the house of Judah as rottenness.

13When Ephraim saw his sickness, and Judah *saw* his wound, then went Ephraim to the Assyrian, and sent to king Jareb: yet could he not heal you, nor cure you of your wound.

14For I *will be* unto Ephraim as a lion, and as a young lion to the house of Judah: I, *even* I, will tear and go away; I will take away, and none shall rescue *him.*

15I will go *and* return to my place, till they acknowledge their offence, and seek my face: in their affliction they will seek me early.

2 JOHN 1:1–13

THE elder unto the elect lady and her children, whom I love in the truth; and not I only, but also all they that have known the truth;

2For the truth's sake, which dwelleth in us, and shall be with us for ever.

3Grace be with you, mercy, *and* peace, from God the Father, and from the Lord Jesus Christ, the Son of the Father, in truth and love.

4I rejoiced greatly that I found of thy children walking in truth, as we have received a commandment from the Father.

5And now I beseech thee, lady, not as though I wrote a new commandment unto thee, but that which we had from the beginning, that we love one another.

6And this is love, that we walk after his commandments. This is the commandment, That, as ye have heard from the beginning, ye should walk in it.

7For many deceivers are entered into the world, who confess not that Jesus Christ is come in the flesh. This is a deceiver and an antichrist.

8Look to yourselves, that we lose not those things which we have wrought, but that we receive a full reward.

9Whosoever transgresseth, and abideth not in the doctrine of Christ, hath not God. He that abideth in the doctrine of Christ, he hath both the Father and the Son.

10If there come any unto you, and bring not this doctrine, receive him not into *your* house, neither bid him God speed:

11For he that biddeth him God speed is partaker of his evil deeds.

12Having many things to write unto you, I would not *write* with paper and ink: but I trust to come unto you, and speak face to face, that our joy may be full.

13The children of thy elect sister greet thee. Amen.

PSALM 125:1–5

THEY that trust in the LORD *shall be* as mount Zion *which* cannot be removed, *but* abideth for ever.

2As the mountains *are* round about Jerusalem, so the LORD *is* round about his people from henceforth even for ever.

3For the rod of the wicked shall not rest upon the lot of the righteous; lest the righteous put forth their hands unto iniquity.

4Do good, O LORD, unto *those that be* good, and to *them that are* upright in their hearts.

5As for such as turn aside unto their crooked ways, the LORD shall lead them forth with the workers of iniquity: *but* peace *shall be* upon Israel.

PROVERBS FOR TODAY/ 29:9–11

If *a wise man contendeth with a foolish man, whether he rage or laugh,* there is *no rest.* ☐ *The bloodthirsty hate the upright: but the just seek his soul. A fool uttereth all his mind: but a wise* man *keepeth it in till afterwards.*

DECEMBER 7

HOSEA 6:1—9:17

COME, and let us return unto the LORD: for he hath torn, and he will heal us; he hath smitten, and he will bind us up.

2After two days will he revive us: in the third day he will raise us up, and we shall live in his sight.

3Then shall we know, *if* we follow on to know the LORD: his going forth is prepared as the morning; and he shall come unto us as the rain, as the latter *and* former rain unto the earth.

4O Ephraim, what shall I do unto thee? O Judah, what shall I do unto thee? for your goodness *is* as a morning cloud, and as the early dew it goeth away.

5Therefore have I hewed *them* by the prophets; I have slain them by the words of my mouth: and thy judgments *are as* the light *that* goeth forth.

6For I desired mercy, and not sacrifice; and the knowledge of God more than burnt offerings.

7But they like men have transgressed the covenant: there have they dealt treacherously against me.

8Gilead *is* a city of them that work iniquity, *and is* polluted with blood.

9And as troops of robbers wait for a man, *so* the company of priests murder in the way by consent: for they commit lewdness.

10I have seen an horrible thing in the house of Israel: there *is* the whoredom of Ephraim, Israel is defiled.

11Also, O Judah, he hath set an harvest for thee, when I returned the captivity of my people.

WHEN I would have healed Israel, then the iniquity of Ephraim was discovered, and the wickedness of Samaria: for they commit falsehood; and the thief cometh in, *and* the troop of robbers spoileth without.

2And they consider not in their hearts *that* I remember all their wickedness: now their own doings have beset them about; they are before my face.

3They make the king glad with their wickedness, and the princes with their lies.

4They *are* all adulterers, as an oven heated by the baker, *who* ceaseth from raising after he hath kneaded the dough, until it be leavened.

5In the day of our king the princes have made *him* sick with bottles of wine; he stretched out his hand with scorners.

6For they have made ready their heart like an oven, whiles they lie in wait: their baker sleepeth all the night; in the morning it burneth as a flaming fire.

7They are all hot as an oven, and have devoured their judges; all their kings are fallen: *there is* none among them that calleth unto me.

8Ephraim, he hath mixed himself among the people; Ephraim is a cake not turned.

9Strangers have devoured his strength, and he knoweth *it* not: yea, gray hairs are here and there upon him, yet he knoweth not.

10And the pride of Israel testifieth to his face: and they do not return to the LORD their God, nor seek him for all this.

11Ephraim also is like a silly dove without heart: they call to Egypt, they go to Assyria.

12When they shall go, I will spread my net upon them; I will bring them down as the fowls of the heaven; I will chastise them, as their congregation hath heard.

13Woe unto them! for they have fled

from me: destruction unto them! because they have transgressed against me: though I have redeemed them, yet they have spoken lies against me.

14And they have not cried unto me with their heart, when they howled upon their beds: they assemble themselves for corn and wine, *and* they rebel against me.

15Though I have bound *and* strengthened their arms, yet do they imagine mischief against me.

16They return, *but* not to the most High: they are like a deceitful bow: their princes shall fall by the sword for the rage of their tongue: this *shall be* their derision in the land of Egypt.

SET the trumpet to thy mouth. *He shall come* as an eagle against the house of the LORD, because they have transgressed my covenant, and trespassed against my law.

2Israel shall cry unto me, My God, we know thee.

3Israel hath cast off *the thing that is* good: the enemy shall pursue him.

4They have set up kings, but not by me: they have made princes, and I knew *it* not: of their silver and their gold have they made them idols, that they may be cut off.

5Thy calf, O Samaria, hath cast *thee* off; mine anger is kindled against them: how long *will it be* ere they attain to innocency?

6For from Israel *was* it also: the workman made it; therefore it *is* not God: but the calf of Samaria shall be broken in pieces.

7For they have sown the wind, and they shall reap the whirlwind: it hath no stalk: the bud shall yield no meal: if so be it yield, the strangers shall swallow it up.

8Israel is swallowed up: now shall they be among the Gentiles as a vessel wherein *is* no pleasure.

9For they are gone up to Assyria, a wild ass alone by himself: Ephraim hath hired lovers.

10Yea, though they have hired among the nations, now will I gather them, and they shall sorrow a little for the burden of the king of princes.

11Because Ephraim hath made many altars to sin, altars shall be unto him to sin.

12I have written to him the great things of my law, *but* they were counted as a strange thing.

13They sacrifice flesh *for* the sacrifices of mine offerings, and eat *it; but* the LORD accepteth them not; now will he remember their iniquity, and visit their sins: they shall return to Egypt.

14For Israel hath forgotten his Maker, and buildeth temples; and Judah hath multiplied fenced cities: but I will send a fire upon his cities, and it shall devour the palaces thereof.

REJOICE not, O Israel, for joy, as *other* people: for thou hast gone a whoring from thy God, thou hast loved a reward upon every cornfloor.

2The floor and the winepress shall not feed them, and the new wine shall fail in her.

3They shall not dwell in the LORD's land; but Ephraim shall return to Egypt, and they shall eat unclean *things* in Assyria.

4They shall not offer wine *offerings* to the LORD, neither shall they be pleasing unto him: their sacrifices *shall be* unto them as the bread of mourners; all that eat thereof shall be polluted: for their bread for their soul shall not come into the house of the LORD.

5What will ye do in the solemn day, and in the day of the feast of the LORD?

6For, lo, they are gone because of destruction: Egypt shall gather them up, Memphis shall bury them: the pleasant *places* for their silver, nettles shall possess them: thorns *shall be* in their tabernacles.

7The days of visitation are come, the days of recompence are come; Israel shall know *it:* the prophet *is* a fool, the spiritual man *is* mad, for the multitude of thine iniquity, and the great hatred.

8The watchman of Ephraim *was* with my God: *but* the prophet *is* a snare of a fowler in all his ways, *and* hatred in the house of his God.

9They have deeply corrupted *themselves,* as in the days of Gibeah: *therefore* he will remember their iniquity, he will visit their sins.

10I found Israel like grapes in the wilderness; I saw your fathers as the firstripe in the fig tree at her first time: *but* they went to Baalpeor, and separated themselves unto *that* shame; and *their* abominations were according as they loved.

11*As for* Ephraim, their glory shall fly away like a bird, from the birth, and from the womb, and from the conception.

12Though they bring up their children, yet will I bereave them, *that there shall* not *be* a man *left:* yea, woe also to them when I depart from them!

13Ephraim, as I saw Tyrus, *is* planted in a pleasant place: but Ephraim shall bring forth his children to the murderer.

14Give them, O LORD: what wilt thou give? give them a miscarrying womb and dry breasts.

15All their wickedness *is* in Gilgal: for there I hated them: for the wickedness of their doings I will drive them out of mine house, I will love them no more: all their princes *are* revolters.

16Ephraim is smitten, their root is dried up, they shall bear no fruit: yea, though they bring forth, yet will I slay *even* the beloved *fruit* of their womb.

17My God will cast them away, because they did not hearken unto him: and they shall be wanderers among the nations.

3 JOHN 1:1–14

THE elder unto the wellbeloved Gaius, whom I love in the truth.

2Beloved, I wish above all things that thou mayest prosper and be in health, even as thy soul prospereth.

3For I rejoiced greatly, when the brethren came and testified of the truth that is in thee, even as thou walkest in the truth.

4I have no greater joy than to hear that my children walk in truth.

5Beloved, thou doest faithfully whatsoever thou doest to the brethren, and to strangers;

6Which have borne witness of thy charity before the church: whom if thou bring forward on their journey after a godly sort, thou shalt do well:

7Because that for his name's sake they went forth, taking nothing of the Gentiles.

8We therefore ought to receive such, that we might be fellowhelpers to the truth.

9I wrote unto the church: but Diotrephes, who loveth to have the preeminence among them, receiveth us not.

10Wherefore, if I come, I will remember his deeds which he doeth, prating against us with malicious words: and not content therewith, neither doth he himself receive the brethren, and forbiddeth them that would, and casteth *them* out of the church.

11Beloved, follow not that which is evil, but that which is good. He that doeth good is of God: but he that doeth evil hath not seen God.

12Demetrius hath good report of all *men,* and of the truth itself: yea, and we *also* bear record; and ye know that our record is true.

13I had many things to write, but I will not with ink and pen write unto thee:

14But I trust I shall shortly see thee, and we shall speak face to face. Peace *be* to thee. *Our* friends salute thee. Greet the friends by name.

PSALM 126:1–6

WHEN the LORD turned again the captivity of Zion, we were like them that dream. 2Then was our mouth filled with laughter, and our tongue with singing: then said they among the heathen, The LORD hath done great things for them. 3The LORD hath done great things for us; *whereof* we are glad. 4Turn again our captivity, O LORD, as the streams in the south. 5They that sow in tears shall reap in joy. 6He that goeth forth and weepeth, bearing precious seed, shall doubtless come again with rejoicing, bringing his sheaves *with him.*

PROVERBS FOR TODAY/ 29:12–14

If a ruler hearken to lies, all his servants are *wicked.* □ *The poor and the deceitful man meet together: the* LORD *lighteneth both their eyes.* □ *The king that faithfully judgeth the poor, his throne shall be established for ever.*

DECEMBER 8

HOSEA 10:1—14:9

ISRAEL *is* an empty vine, he bringeth forth fruit unto himself: according to the multitude of his fruit he hath increased the altars; according to the goodness of his land they have made goodly images. 2Their heart is divided; now shall they be found faulty: he shall break down their altars, he shall spoil their images. 3For now they shall say, We have no king, because we feared not the LORD; what then should a king do to us? 4They have spoken words, swearing falsely in making a covenant: thus judgment springeth up as hemlock in the furrows of the field. 5The inhabitants of Samaria shall fear because of the calves of Beth–aven: for the people thereof shall mourn over it, and the priests thereof *that* rejoiced on it, for the glory thereof, because it is departed from it. 6It shall be also carried unto Assyria *for* a present to king Jareb: Ephraim shall receive shame, and Israel shall be ashamed of his own counsel. 7*As for* Samaria, her king is cut off as the foam upon the water. 8The high places also of Aven, the sin of Israel, shall be destroyed: the thorn and the thistle shall come up on their altars; and they shall say to the mountains, Cover us; and to the hills, Fall on us. 9O Israel, thou hast sinned from the days of Gibeah: there they stood: the battle in Gibeah against the children of iniquity did not overtake them. 10*It is* in my desire that I should chastise them; and the people shall be gathered against them, when they shall bind themselves in their two furrows. 11And Ephraim *is as* an heifer *that is* taught, *and* loveth to tread out *the corn;* but I passed over upon her fair neck: I will make Ephraim to ride; Judah shall plow, *and* Jacob shall break his clods.

¹²Sow to yourselves in righteousness, reap in mercy; break up your fallow ground: for *it is* time to seek the LORD, till he come and rain righteousness upon you.

¹³Ye have plowed wickedness, ye have reaped iniquity; ye have eaten the fruit of lies: because thou didst trust in thy way, in the multitude of thy mighty men.

¹⁴Therefore shall a tumult arise among thy people, and all thy fortresses shall be spoiled, as Shalman spoiled Beth–arbel in the day of battle: the mother was dashed in pieces upon *her* children.

¹⁵So shall Beth–el do unto you because of your great wickedness: in a morning shall the king of Israel utterly be cut off.

WHEN Israel *was* a child, then I loved him, and called my son out of Egypt.

²*As* they called them, so they went from them: they sacrificed unto Baalim, and burned incense to graven images.

³I taught Ephraim also to go, taking them by their arms; but they knew not that I healed them.

⁴I drew them with cords of a man, with bands of love: and I was to them as they that take off the yoke on their jaws, and I laid meat unto them.

⁵He shall not return into the land of Egypt, but the Assyrian shall be his king, because they refused to return.

⁶And the sword shall abide on his cities, and shall consume his branches, and devour *them,* because of their own counsels.

⁷And my people are bent to backsliding from me: though they called them to the most High, none at all would exalt *him.*

⁸How shall I give thee up, Ephraim? *how* shall I deliver thee, Israel? how shall I make thee as Admah? *how* shall I set thee as Zeboim? mine heart is turned within me, my repentings are kindled together.

⁹I will not execute the fierceness of mine anger, I will not return to destroy Ephraim: for I *am* God, and not man; the Holy One in the midst of thee: and I will not enter into the city.

¹⁰They shall walk after the LORD: he shall roar like a lion: when he shall roar, then the children shall tremble from the west.

¹¹They shall tremble as a bird out of Egypt, and as a dove out of the land of Assyria: and I will place them in their houses, saith the LORD.

¹²Ephraim compasseth me about with lies, and the house of Israel with deceit: but Judah yet ruleth with God, and is faithful with the saints.

EPHRAIM feedeth on wind, and followeth after the east wind: he daily increaseth lies and desolation; and they do make a covenant with the Assyrians, and oil is carried into Egypt.

²The LORD hath also a controversy with Judah, and will punish Jacob according to his ways; according to his doings will he recompense him.

³He took his brother by the heel in the womb, and by his strength he had power with God:

⁴Yea, he had power over the angel, and prevailed: he wept, and made supplication unto him: he found him *in* Beth–el, and there he spake with us;

⁵Even the LORD God of hosts; the LORD *is* his memorial.

⁶Therefore turn thou to thy God: keep mercy and judgment, and wait on thy God continually.

⁷*He is* a merchant, the balances of deceit *are* in his hand: he loveth to oppress.

⁸And Ephraim said, Yet I am become rich, I have found me out substance: *in* all my labours they shall find none iniquity in me that *were* sin.

⁹And I *that am* the LORD thy God from the land of Egypt will yet make thee to dwell in tabernacles, as in the days of the solemn feast.

10I have also spoken by the prophets, and I have multiplied visions, and used similitudes, by the ministry of the prophets.

11*Is there* iniquity *in* Gilead? surely they are vanity: they sacrificed bullocks in Gilgal; yea, their altars *are* as heaps in the furrows of the fields.

12And Jacob fled into the country of Syria, and Israel served for a wife, and for a wife he kept *sheep*.

13And by a prophet the LORD brought Israel out of Egypt, and by a prophet was he preserved.

14Ephraim provoked *him* to anger most bitterly: therefore shall he leave his blood upon him, and his reproach shall his Lord return unto him.

WHEN Ephraim spake trembling, he exalted himself in Israel; but when he offended in Baal, he died.

2And now they sin more and more, and have made them molten images of their silver, *and* idols according to their own understanding, all of it the work of the craftsmen: they say of them, Let the men that sacrifice kiss the calves.

3Therefore they shall be as the morning cloud, and as the early dew that passeth away, as the chaff *that* is driven with the whirlwind out of the floor, and as the smoke out of the chimney.

4Yet I *am* the LORD thy God from the land of Egypt, and thou shalt know no god but me: for *there is* no saviour beside me.

5I did know thee in the wilderness, in the land of great drought.

6According to their pasture, so were they filled; they were filled, and their heart was exalted; therefore have they forgotten me.

7Therefore I will be unto them as a lion: as a leopard by the way will I observe *them:*

8I will meet them as a bear *that is* bereaved *of her whelps,* and will rend the caul of their heart, and there will

I devour them like a lion: the wild beast shall tear them.

9O Israel, thou hast destroyed thyself; but in me *is* thine help.

10I will be thy king: where *is any other* that may save thee in all thy cities? and thy judges of whom thou saidst, Give me a king and princes?

11I gave thee a king in mine anger, and took *him* away in my wrath.

12The iniquity of Ephraim *is* bound up; his sin *is* hid.

13The sorrows of a travailing woman shall come upon him: he *is* an unwise son; for he should not stay long in *the place of* the breaking forth of children.

14I will ransom them from the power of the grave; I will redeem them from death: O death, I will be thy plagues; O grave, I will be thy destruction: repentance shall be hid from mine eyes.

15Though he be fruitful among *his* brethren, an east wind shall come, the wind of the LORD shall come up from the wilderness, and his spring shall become dry, and his fountain shall be dried up: he shall spoil the treasure of all pleasant vessels.

16Samaria shall become desolate; for she hath rebelled against her God: they shall fall by the sword: their infants shall be dashed in pieces, and their women with child shall be ripped up.

O ISRAEL, return unto the LORD thy God; for thou hast fallen by thine iniquity.

2Take with you words, and turn to the LORD: say unto him, Take away all iniquity, and receive *us* graciously: so will we render the calves of our lips.

3Asshur shall not save us; we will not ride upon horses: neither will we say any more to the work of our hands, *Ye are* our gods: for in thee the fatherless findeth mercy.

4I will heal their backsliding, I will love them freely; for mine anger is turned away from him.

5I will be as the dew unto Israel: he shall grow as the lily, and cast forth his roots as Lebanon.

6His branches shall spread, and his beauty shall be as the olive tree, and his smell as Lebanon.

7They that dwell under his shadow shall return; they shall revive *as* the corn, and grow as the vine: the scent thereof *shall be* as the wine of Lebanon.

8Ephraim *shall say,* What have I to do any more with idols? I have heard *him,* and observed him: I *am* like a green fir tree. From me is thy fruit found.

9Who *is* wise, and he shall understand these *things?* prudent, and he shall know them? for the ways of the LORD *are* right, and the just shall walk in them: but the transgressors shall fall therein.

JUDE 1:1–25

JUDE, the servant of Jesus Christ, and brother of James, to them that are sanctified by God the Father, and preserved in Jesus Christ, *and* called.

2Mercy unto you, and peace, and love, be multiplied.

3Beloved, when I gave all diligence to write unto you of the common salvation, it was needful for me to write unto you, and exhort *you* that ye should earnestly contend for the faith which was once delivered unto the saints.

4For there are certain men crept in unawares, who were before of old ordained to this condemnation, ungodly men, turning the grace of our God into lasciviousness, and denying the only Lord God, and our Lord Jesus Christ.

5I will therefore put you in remembrance, though ye once knew this, how that the Lord, having saved the people out of the land of Egypt, afterward destroyed them that believed not.

6And the angels which kept not their first estate, but left their own habitation, he hath reserved in everlasting chains under darkness unto the judgment of the great day.

7Even as Sodom and Gomorrha, and the cities about them in like manner, giving themselves over to fornication, and going after strange flesh, are set forth for an example, suffering the vengeance of eternal fire.

8Likewise also these *filthy* dreamers defile the flesh, despise dominion, and speak evil of dignities.

9Yet Michael the archangel, when contending with the devil he disputed about the body of Moses, durst not bring against him a railing accusation, but said, The Lord rebuke thee.

10But these speak evil of those things which they know not: but what they know naturally, as brute beasts, in those things they corrupt themselves.

11Woe unto them! for they have gone in the way of Cain, and ran greedily after the error of Balaam for reward, and perished in the gainsaying of Core.

12These are spots in your feasts of charity, when they feast with you, feeding themselves without fear: clouds *they are* without water, carried about of winds; trees whose fruit withereth, without fruit, twice dead, plucked up by the roots;

13Raging waves of the sea, foaming out their own shame; wandering stars, to whom is reserved the blackness of darkness for ever.

14And Enoch also, the seventh from Adam, prophesied of these, saying, Behold, the Lord cometh with ten thousands of his saints,

15To execute judgment upon all, and to convince all that are ungodly among them of all their ungodly deeds which they have ungodly committed, and of all their hard *speeches* which ungodly sinners have spoken against him.

16These are murmurers, complainers, walking after their own lusts; and their mouth speaketh great swelling *words,* having men's persons in admiration because of advantage.

17But, beloved, remember ye the words which were spoken before of the apostles of our Lord Jesus Christ;

18How that they told you there should be mockers in the last time, who should walk after their own ungodly lusts.

19These be they who separate themselves, sensual, having not the Spirit.

20But ye, beloved, building up yourselves on your most holy faith, praying in the Holy Ghost,

21Keep yourselves in the love of God, looking for the mercy of our Lord Jesus Christ unto eternal life.

22And of some have compassion, making a difference:

23And others save with fear, pulling *them* out of the fire; hating even the garment spotted by the flesh.

24Now unto him that is able to keep you from falling, and to present *you* faultless before the presence of his glory with exceeding joy,

25To the only wise God our Saviour, *be* glory and majesty, dominion and power, both now and ever. Amen.

PSALM 127:1–5

EXCEPT the LORD build the house, they labour in vain that build it: except the LORD keep the city, the watchman waketh *but* in vain.

2*It is* vain for you to rise up early, to sit up late, to eat the bread of sorrows: *for* so he giveth his beloved sleep.

3Lo, children *are* an heritage of the LORD: *and* the fruit of the womb *is his* reward.

4As arrows *are* in the hand of a mighty man; so *are* children of the youth.

5Happy *is* the man that hath his quiver full of them: they shall not be ashamed, but they shall speak with the enemies in the gate.

PROVERBS FOR TODAY/ 29:15–17

The rod and reproof give wisdom: but a child left to himself *bringeth his mother to shame.* □ *When the wicked are multiplied, transgression increaseth: but the righteous shall see their fall.* □ *Correct thy son, and he shall give thee rest; yea, he shall give delight unto thy soul.*

DECEMBER 9

JOEL 1:1—3:21

THE word of the LORD that came to Joel the son of Pethuel.

2Hear this, ye old men, and give ear, all ye inhabitants of the land. Hath this been in your days, or even in the days of your fathers?

3Tell ye your children of it, and *let* your children *tell* their children, and their children another generation.

4That which the palmerworm hath left hath the locust eaten; and that which the locust hath left hath the cankerworm eaten; and that which the cankerworm hath left hath the caterpiller eaten.

5Awake, ye drunkards, and weep; and howl, all ye drinkers of wine, because of the new wine; for it is cut off from your mouth.

6For a nation is come up upon my land, strong, and without number, whose teeth *are* the teeth of a lion, and he hath the cheek teeth of a great lion.

7He hath laid my vine waste, and barked my fig tree: he hath made it clean bare, and cast *it* away; the branches thereof are made white.

8Lament like a virgin girded with sackcloth for the husband of her youth.

9The meat offering and the drink offering is cut off from the house of the LORD; the priests, the LORD's ministers, mourn.

10The field is wasted, the land mourneth; for the corn is wasted: the new wine is dried up, the oil languisheth.

11Be ye ashamed, O ye husbandmen; howl, O ye vinedressers, for the wheat and for the barley; because the harvest of the field is perished.

12The vine is dried up, and the fig tree languisheth; the pomegranate tree, the palm tree also, and the apple tree, *even* all the trees of the field, are withered: because joy is withered away from the sons of men.

13Gird yourselves, and lament, ye priests: howl, ye ministers of the altar: come, lie all night in sackcloth, ye ministers of my God: for the meat offering and the drink offering is withholden from the house of your God.

14Sanctify ye a fast, call a solemn assembly, gather the elders *and* all the inhabitants of the land *into* the house of the LORD your God, and cry unto the LORD.

15Alas for the day! for the day of the LORD *is* at hand, and as a destruction from the Almighty shall it come.

16Is not the meat cut off before our eyes, *yea,* joy and gladness from the house of our God?

17The seed is rotten under their clods, the garners are laid desolate, the barns are broken down; for the corn is withered.

18How do the beasts groan! the herds of cattle are perplexed, because they have no pasture; yea, the flocks of sheep are made desolate.

19O LORD, to thee will I cry: for the fire hath devoured the pastures of the wilderness, and the flame hath burned all the trees of the field.

20The beasts of the field cry also unto thee: for the rivers of waters are dried up, and the fire hath devoured the pastures of the wilderness.

BLOW ye the trumpet in Zion, and sound an alarm in my holy mountain: let all the inhabitants of the land tremble: for the day of the LORD cometh, for *it is* nigh at hand;

2A day of darkness and of gloominess, a day of clouds and of thick darkness, as the morning spread upon the mountains: a great people and a strong; there hath not been ever the like, neither shall be any more after it, *even* to the years of many generations.

3A fire devoureth before them; and behind them a flame burneth: the land *is* as the garden of Eden before them, and behind them a desolate wilderness; yea, and nothing shall escape them.

4The appearance of them *is* as the appearance of horses; and as horsemen, so shall they run.

5Like the noise of chariots on the tops of mountains shall they leap, like the noise of a flame of fire that devoureth the stubble, as a strong people set in battle array.

6Before their face the people shall be much pained: all faces shall gather blackness.

7They shall run like mighty men; they shall climb the wall like men of war; and they shall march every one on his ways, and they shall not break their ranks:

8Neither shall one thrust another; they shall walk every one in his path: and *when* they fall upon the sword, they shall not be wounded.

9They shall run to and fro in the city; they shall run upon the wall, they shall climb up upon the houses; they shall enter in at the windows like a thief.

10The earth shall quake before them; the heavens shall tremble: the sun and the moon shall be dark, and the stars shall withdraw their shining:

11And the LORD shall utter his voice before his army: for his camp *is* very great: for *he is* strong that executeth his word: for the day of the LORD *is* great and very terrible; and who can abide it?

12Therefore also now, saith the LORD, Turn ye *even* to me with all your heart, and with fasting, and with weeping, and with mourning:

13And rend your heart, and not your garments, and turn unto the LORD your God: for he *is* gracious and merciful, slow to anger, and of great kindness, and repenteth him of the evil.

14Who knoweth *if* he will return and repent, and leave a blessing behind him; *even* a meat offering and a drink offering unto the LORD your God?

15Blow the trumpet in Zion, sanctify a fast, call a solemn assembly:

16Gather the people, sanctify the congregation, assemble the elders, gather the children, and those that suck the breasts: let the bridegroom go forth of his chamber, and the bride out of her closet.

17Let the priests, the ministers of the LORD, weep between the porch and the altar, and let them say, Spare thy people, O LORD, and give not thine heritage to reproach, that the heathen should rule over them: wherefore should they say among the people, Where *is* their God?

18Then will the LORD be jealous for his land, and pity his people.

19Yea, the LORD will answer and say unto his people, Behold, I will send you corn, and wine, and oil, and ye shall be satisfied therewith: and I will no more make you a reproach among the heathen:

20But I will remove far off from you the northern *army*, and will drive him into a land barren and desolate, with his face toward the east sea, and his hinder part toward the utmost sea, and

his stink shall come up, and his ill savour shall come up, because he hath done great things.

21Fear not, O land; be glad and rejoice: for the LORD will do great things.

22Be not afraid, ye beasts of the field: for the pastures of the wilderness do spring, for the tree beareth her fruit, the fig tree and the vine do yield their strength.

23Be glad then, ye children of Zion, and rejoice in the LORD your God: for he hath given you the former rain moderately, and he will cause to come down for you the rain, the former rain, and the latter rain in the first *month*.

24And the floors shall be full of wheat, and the fats shall overflow with wine and oil.

25And I will restore to you the years that the locust hath eaten, the cankerworm, and the caterpiller, and the palmerworm, my great army which I sent among you.

26And ye shall eat in plenty, and be satisfied, and praise the name of the LORD your God, that hath dealt wondrously with you: and my people shall never be ashamed.

27And ye shall know that I *am* in the midst of Israel, and *that I am* the LORD your God, and none else: and my people shall never be ashamed.

28And it shall come to pass afterward, *that* I will pour out my spirit upon all flesh; and your sons and your daughters shall prophesy, your old men shall dream dreams, your young men shall see visions:

29And also upon the servants and upon the handmaids in those days will I pour out my spirit.

30And I will shew wonders in the heavens and in the earth, blood, and fire, and pillars of smoke.

31The sun shall be turned into darkness, and the moon into blood, before the great and the terrible day of the LORD come.

32And it shall come to pass, *that* whosoever shall call on the name of the LORD shall be delivered: for in mount Zion and in Jerusalem shall be deliverance, as the LORD hath said, and in the remnant whom the LORD shall call.

FOR, behold, in those days, and in that time, when I shall bring again the captivity of Judah and Jerusalem,

2I will also gather all nations, and will bring them down into the valley of Jehoshaphat, and will plead with them there for my people and *for* my heritage Israel, whom they have scattered among the nations, and parted my land.

3And they have cast lots for my people; and have given a boy for an harlot, and sold a girl for wine, that they might drink.

4Yea, and what have ye to do with me, O Tyre, and Zidon, and all the coasts of Palestine? will ye render me a recompence? and if ye recompense me, swiftly *and* speedily will I return your recompence upon your own head;

5Because ye have taken my silver and my gold, and have carried into your temples my goodly pleasant things:

6The children also of Judah and the children of Jerusalem have ye sold unto the Grecians, that ye might remove them far from their border.

7Behold, I will raise them out of the place whither ye have sold them, and will return your recompence upon your own head:

8And I will sell your sons and your daughters into the hand of the children of Judah, and they shall sell them to the Sabeans, to a people far off: for the LORD hath spoken *it*.

9Proclaim ye this among the Gentiles; Prepare war, wake up the mighty men, let all the men of war draw near; let them come up:

10Beat your plowshares into swords, and your pruninghooks into spears: let the weak say, I *am* strong.

11Assemble yourselves, and come, all ye heathen, and gather yourselves together round about: thither cause thy mighty ones to come down, O LORD.

12Let the heathen be wakened, and come up to the valley of Jehoshaphat: for there will I sit to judge all the heathen round about.

13Put ye in the sickle, for the harvest is ripe: come, get you down; for the press is full, the fats overflow; for their wickedness *is* great.

14Multitudes, multitudes in the valley of decision: for the day of the LORD *is* near in the valley of decision.

15The sun and the moon shall be darkened, and the stars shall withdraw their shining.

16The LORD also shall roar out of Zion, and utter his voice from Jerusalem; and the heavens and the earth shall shake: but the LORD *will be* the hope of his people, and the strength of the children of Israel.

17So shall ye know that I *am* the LORD your God dwelling in Zion, my holy mountain: then shall Jerusalem be holy, and there shall no strangers pass through her any more.

18And it shall come to pass in that day, *that* the mountains shall drop down new wine, and the hills shall flow with milk, and all the rivers of Judah shall flow with waters, and a fountain shall come forth of the house of the LORD, and shall water the valley of Shittim.

19Egypt shall be a desolation, and Edom shall be a desolate wilderness, for the violence *against* the children of Judah, because they have shed innocent blood in their land.

20But Judah shall dwell for ever, and Jerusalem from generation to generation.

21For I will cleanse their blood *that* I have not cleansed: for the LORD dwelleth in Zion.

REVELATION 1:1–20

THE Revelation of Jesus Christ, which God gave unto him, to shew unto his servants things which must shortly come to pass; and he sent and signified *it* by his angel unto his servant John:

2Who bare record of the word of God, and of the testimony of Jesus Christ, and of all things that he saw.

3Blessed *is* he that readeth, and they that hear the words of this prophecy, and keep those things which are written therein: for the time *is* at hand.

4John to the seven churches which are in Asia: Grace *be* unto you, and peace, from him which is, and which was, and which is to come; and from the seven Spirits which are before his throne;

5And from Jesus Christ, *who is* the faithful witness, *and* the first begotten of the dead, and the prince of the kings of the earth. Unto him that loved us, and washed us from our sins in his own blood,

6And hath made us kings and priests unto God and his Father; to him *be* glory and dominion for ever and ever. Amen.

7Behold, he cometh with clouds; and every eye shall see him, and they *also* which pierced him: and all kindreds of the earth shall wail because of him. Even so, Amen.

8I am Alpha and Omega, the beginning and the ending, saith the Lord, which is, and which was, and which is to come, the Almighty.

9I John, who also am your brother, and companion in tribulation, and in the kingdom and patience of Jesus Christ, was in the isle that is called Patmos, for the word of God, and for the testimony of Jesus Christ.

10I was in the Spirit on the Lord's day, and heard behind me a great voice, as of a trumpet,

11Saying, I am Alpha and Omega, the first and the last: and, What thou seest, write in a book, and send *it* unto the seven churches which are in Asia; unto Ephesus, and unto Smyrna, and unto Pergamos, and unto Thyatira, and unto Sardis, and unto Philadelphia, and unto Laodicea.

12And I turned to see the voice that spake with me. And being turned, I saw seven golden candlesticks;

13And in the midst of the seven candlesticks *one* like unto the Son of man, clothed with a garment down to the foot, and girt about the paps with a golden girdle.

14His head and *his* hairs *were* white like wool, as white as snow; and his eyes *were* as a flame of fire;

15And his feet like unto fine brass, as if they burned in a furnace; and his voice as the sound of many waters.

16And he had in his right hand seven stars: and out of his mouth went a sharp twoedged sword: and his countenance *was* as the sun shineth in his strength.

17And when I saw him, I fell at his feet as dead. And he laid his right hand upon me, saying unto me, Fear not; I am the first and the last:

18*I am* he that liveth, and was dead; and, behold, I am alive for evermore, Amen; and have the keys of hell and of death.

19Write the things which thou hast seen, and the things which are, and the things which shall be hereafter;

20The mystery of the seven stars which thou sawest in my right hand, and the seven golden candlesticks. The seven stars are the angels of the seven churches: and the seven candlesticks which thou sawest are the seven churches.

PSALM 128:1–6

BLESSED *is* every one that feareth the LORD; that walketh in his ways.

2For thou shalt eat the labour of thine

hands: happy *shalt* thou *be,* and *it shall be* well with thee.

3Thy wife *shall be* as a fruitful vine by the sides of thine house: thy children like olive plants round about thy table.

4Behold, that thus shall the man be blessed that feareth the LORD.

5The LORD shall bless thee out of Zion: and thou shalt see the good of Jerusalem all the days of thy life.

6Yea, thou shalt see thy children's children, *and* peace upon Israel.

PROVERBS FOR TODAY/ 29:18

Where there is *no vision, the people perish: but he that keepeth the law, happy* is *he.*

DECEMBER 10

AMOS 1:1—3:15

THE words of Amos, who was among the herdmen of Tekoa, which he saw concerning Israel in the days of Uzziah king of Judah, and in the days of Jeroboam the son of Joash king of Israel, two years before the earthquake.

2And he said, The LORD will roar from Zion, and utter his voice from Jerusalem; and the habitations of the shepherds shall mourn, and the top of Carmel shall wither.

3Thus saith the LORD; For three transgressions of Damascus, and for four, I will not turn away *the punishment* thereof; because they have threshed Gilead with threshing instruments of iron:

4But I will send a fire into the house of Hazael, which shall devour the palaces of Ben–hadad.

5I will break also the bar of Damascus, and cut off the inhabitant from the plain of Aven, and him that holdeth the sceptre from the house of Eden: and the people of Syria shall go into captivity unto Kir, saith the LORD.

6Thus saith the LORD; For three transgressions of Gaza, and for four, I will not turn away *the punishment* thereof; because they carried away captive the whole captivity, to deliver *them* up to Edom:

7But I will send a fire on the wall of Gaza, which shall devour the palaces thereof:

8And I will cut off the inhabitant from Ashdod, and him that holdeth the sceptre from Ashkelon, and I will turn mine hand against Ekron: and the remnant of the Philistines shall perish, saith the Lord GOD.

9Thus saith the LORD; For three transgressions of Tyrus, and for four, I will not turn away *the punishment* thereof; because they delivered up the whole captivity to Edom, and remembered not the brotherly covenant:

10But I will send a fire on the wall of Tyrus, which shall devour the palaces thereof.

11Thus saith the LORD; For three transgressions of Edom, and for four, I will not turn away *the punishment* thereof; because he did pursue his brother with the sword, and did cast off all pity, and his anger did tear perpetually, and he kept his wrath for ever:

12But I will send a fire upon Teman, which shall devour the palaces of Bozrah.

13Thus saith the LORD; For three transgressions of the children of Ammon, and for four, I will not turn away *the punishment* thereof; because they have ripped up the women with child of Gilead, that they might enlarge their border:

14But I will kindle a fire in the wall of Rabbah, and it shall devour the palaces thereof, with shouting in the day of battle, with a tempest in the day of the whirlwind:

15And their king shall go into captivity, he and his princes together, saith the LORD.

THUS saith the LORD; For three transgressions of Moab, and for four, I will not turn away *the punishment* thereof; because he burned the bones of the king of Edom into lime:

2But I will send a fire upon Moab, and it shall devour the palaces of Kirioth: and Moab shall die with tumult, with shouting, *and* with the sound of the trumpet:

3And I will cut off the judge from the midst thereof, and will slay all the princes thereof with him, saith the LORD.

4Thus saith the LORD; For three transgressions of Judah, and for four, I will not turn away *the punishment* thereof; because they have despised the law of the LORD, and have not kept his commandments, and their lies caused them to err, after the which their fathers have walked:

5But I will send a fire upon Judah, and it shall devour the palaces of Jerusalem.

6Thus saith the LORD; For three transgressions of Israel, and for four, I will not turn away *the punishment* thereof; because they sold the righteous for silver, and the poor for a pair of shoes;

7That pant after the dust of the earth on the head of the poor, and turn aside the way of the meek: and a man and his father will go in unto the *same* maid, to profane my holy name:

8And they lay *themselves* down upon clothes laid to pledge by every altar, and they drink the wine of the condemned *in* the house of their god.

9Yet destroyed I the Amorite before them, whose height *was* like the height of the cedars, and he *was* strong as the oaks; yet I destroyed his fruit from above, and his roots from beneath.

10Also I brought you up from the land of Egypt, and led you forty years through the wilderness, to possess the land of the Amorite.

11And I raised up of your sons for prophets, and of your young men for Nazarites. *Is it* not even thus, O ye children of Israel? saith the LORD.

12But ye gave the Nazarites wine to drink; and commanded the prophets, saying, Prophesy not.

13Behold, I am pressed under you, as a cart is pressed *that is* full of sheaves.

14Therefore the flight shall perish from the swift, and the strong shall not strengthen his force, neither shall the mighty deliver himself:

15Neither shall he stand that handleth the bow; and *he that is* swift of foot shall not deliver *himself:* neither shall he that rideth the horse deliver himself.

16And *he that is* courageous among the mighty shall flee away naked in that day, saith the LORD.

HEAR this word that the LORD hath spoken against you, O children of Israel, against the whole family which I brought up from the land of Egypt, saying,

2You only have I known of all the families of the earth: therefore I will punish you for all your iniquities.

3Can two walk together, except they be agreed?

4Will a lion roar in the forest, when he hath no prey? will a young lion cry out of his den, if he have taken nothing?

5Can a bird fall in a snare upon the earth, where no gin *is* for him? shall *one* take up a snare from the earth, and have taken nothing at all?

6Shall a trumpet be blown in the city, and the people not be afraid? shall there be evil in a city, and the LORD hath not done *it?*

7Surely the Lord GOD will do nothing but he revealeth his secret unto his servants the prophets.

8The lion hath roared, who will not fear? the Lord GOD hath spoken, who can but prophesy?

9Publish in the palaces at Ashdod, and in the palaces in the land of Egypt, and say, Assemble yourselves upon the mountains of Samaria, and behold the great tumults in the midst thereof, and the oppressed in the midst thereof.

10For they know not to do right, saith the LORD, who store up violence and robbery in their palaces.

11Therefore thus saith the Lord GOD; An adversary *there shall be* even round about the land; and he shall bring down thy strength from thee, and thy palaces shall be spoiled.

12Thus saith the LORD; As the shepherd taketh out of the mouth of the lion two legs, or a piece of an ear; so shall the children of Israel be taken out that dwell in Samaria in the corner of a bed, and in Damascus *in* a couch.

13Hear ye, and testify in the house of Jacob, saith the Lord GOD, the God of hosts,

14That in the day that I shall visit the transgressions of Israel upon him I will also visit the altars of Beth–el: and the horns of the altar shall be cut off, and fall to the ground.

15And I will smite the winter house with the summer house; and the houses of ivory shall perish, and the great houses shall have an end, saith the LORD.

REVELATION 2:1–17

UNTO the angel of the church of Ephesus write; These things saith he that holdeth the seven stars in his right hand, who walketh in the midst of the seven golden candlesticks;

2I know thy works, and thy labour, and thy patience, and how thou canst not bear them which are evil: and thou hast tried them which say they are apostles, and are not, and hast found them liars:

3And hast borne, and hast patience, and for my name's sake hast laboured, and hast not fainted.

4Nevertheless I have *somewhat* against thee, because thou hast left thy first love.

5Remember therefore from whence thou art fallen, and repent, and do the first works; or else I will come unto thee quickly, and will remove thy candlestick out of his place, except thou repent.

6But this thou hast, that thou hatest the deeds of the Nicolaitanes, which I also hate.

7He that hath an ear, let him hear what the Spirit saith unto the churches; To him that overcometh will I give to eat of the tree of life, which is in the midst of the paradise of God.

8And unto the angel of the church in Smyrna write; These things saith the first and the last, which was dead, and is alive;

9I know thy works, and tribulation, and poverty, (but thou art rich) and *I know* the blasphemy of them which say they are Jews, and are not, but *are* the synagogue of Satan.

10Fear none of those things which thou shalt suffer: behold, the devil shall cast *some* of you into prison, that ye may be tried; and ye shall have tribulation ten days; be thou faithful unto death, and I will give thee a crown of life.

11He that hath an ear, let him hear what the Spirit saith unto the churches; He that overcometh shall not be hurt of the second death.

12And to the angel of the church in Pergamos write; These things saith he which hath the sharp sword with two edges;

13I know thy works, and where thou dwellest, *even* where Satan's seat *is:* and thou holdest fast my name, and hast not denied my faith, even in those days wherein Antipas *was* my faithful martyr, who was slain among you, where Satan dwelleth.

14But I have a few things against thee, because thou hast there them that hold the doctrine of Balaam, who taught Balac to cast a stumblingblock before the children of Israel, to eat things sacrificed unto idols, and to commit fornication.

15So hast thou also them that hold the doctrine of the Nicolaitanes, which thing I hate.

16Repent; or else I will come unto thee quickly, and will fight against them with the sword of my mouth.

17He that hath an ear, let him hear what the Spirit saith unto the churches; To him that overcometh will I give to eat of the hidden manna, and will give him a white stone, and in the stone a new name written, which no man knoweth saving he that receiveth *it.*

PSALM 129:1–8

MANY a time have they afflicted me from my youth, may Israel now say:

2Many a time have they afflicted me from my youth: yet they have not prevailed against me.

3The plowers plowed upon my back: they made long their furrows.

4The LORD *is* righteous: he hath cut asunder the cords of the wicked.

5Let them all be confounded and turned back that hate Zion.

6Let them be as the grass *upon* the housetops, which withereth afore it groweth up:

7Wherewith the mower filleth not his hand; nor he that bindeth sheaves his bosom.

8Neither do they which go by say, The blessing of the LORD *be* upon you: we bless you in the name of the LORD.

PROVERBS FOR TODAY/ 29:19–20

A servant will not be corrected by words: for though he understand he will not answer. □ *Seest thou a man* that is *hasty in his words?* There is *more hope of a fool than of him.*

DECEMBER 11

AMOS 4:1—6:14

HEAR this word, ye kine of Bashan, that *are* in the mountain of Samaria, which oppress the poor, which crush the needy, which say to their masters, Bring, and let us drink.

2The Lord GOD hath sworn by his holiness, that, lo, the days shall come upon you, that he will take you away with hooks, and your posterity with fishhooks.

3And ye shall go out at the breaches, every *cow at that which is* before her; and ye shall cast *them* into the palace, saith the LORD.

4Come to Beth–el, and transgress; at Gilgal multiply transgression; and bring your sacrifices every morning, *and* your tithes after three years:

5And offer a sacrifice of thanksgiving with leaven, and proclaim *and* publish the free offerings: for this liketh you, O ye children of Israel, saith the Lord GOD.

6And I also have given you cleanness of teeth in all your cities, and want of bread in all your places: yet have ye not returned unto me, saith the LORD.

7And also I have withholden the rain from you, when *there were* yet three months to the harvest: and I caused it to rain upon one city, and caused it not to rain upon another city: one piece was rained upon, and the piece whereupon it rained not withered.

8So two *or* three cities wandered unto one city, to drink water; but they were not satisfied: yet have ye not returned unto me, saith the LORD.

9I have smitten you with blasting and mildew: when your gardens and your vineyards and your fig trees and your olive trees increased, the palmerworm devoured *them:* yet have ye not returned unto me, saith the LORD.

10I have sent among you the pestilence after the manner of Egypt: your young men have I slain with the sword, and have taken away your horses; and I have made the stink of your camps to come up unto your nostrils: yet have ye not returned unto me, saith the LORD.

11I have overthrown *some* of you, as God overthrew Sodom and Gomorrah, and ye were as a firebrand plucked out of the burning: yet have ye not returned unto me, saith the LORD.

12Therefore thus will I do unto thee, O Israel: *and* because I will do this unto thee, prepare to meet thy God, O Israel.

13For, lo, he that formeth the mountains, and createth the wind, and declareth unto man what *is* his thought, that maketh the morning darkness, and treadeth upon the high places of the earth, The LORD, The God of hosts, *is* his name.

HEAR ye this word which I take up against you, *even* a lamentation, O house of Israel.

2The virgin of Israel is fallen; she shall no more rise: she is forsaken upon her land; *there is* none to raise her up.

3For thus saith the Lord GOD; The city that went out *by* a thousand shall leave an hundred, and that which went forth *by* an hundred shall leave ten, to the house of Israel.

4For thus saith the LORD unto the house of Israel, Seek ye me, and ye shall live:

5But seek not Beth–el, nor enter into Gilgal, and pass not to Beer–sheba: for Gilgal shall surely go into captivity, and Beth–el shall come to nought.

6Seek the LORD, and ye shall live; lest he break out like fire in the house of Joseph, and devour *it,* and *there be* none to quench *it* in Beth–el.

7Ye who turn judgment to wormwood, and leave off righteousness in the earth,

8*Seek him* that maketh the seven stars and Orion, and turneth the shadow of death into the morning, and maketh the day dark with night: that calleth for the waters of the sea, and poureth them out upon the face of the earth: The LORD *is* his name:

9That strengtheneth the spoiled against the strong, so that the spoiled shall come against the fortress.

10They hate him that rebuketh in the gate, and they abhor him that speaketh uprightly.

11Forasmuch therefore as your

treading *is* upon the poor, and ye take from him burdens of wheat: ye have built houses of hewn stone, but ye shall not dwell in them; ye have planted pleasant vineyards, but ye shall not drink wine of them.

¹²For I know your manifold transgressions and your mighty sins: they afflict the just, they take a bribe, and they turn aside the poor in the gate *from their right.*

¹³Therefore the prudent shall keep silence in that time: for it *is* an evil time.

¹⁴Seek good, and not evil, that ye may live: and so the LORD, the God of hosts, shall be with you, as ye have spoken.

¹⁵Hate the evil, and love the good, and establish judgment in the gate: it may be that the LORD God of hosts will be gracious unto the remnant of Joseph.

¹⁶Therefore the LORD, the God of hosts, the Lord, saith thus; Wailing *shall be* in all streets; and they shall say in all the highways, Alas! alas! and they shall call the husbandman to mourning, and such as are skilful of lamentation to wailing.

¹⁷And in all vineyards *shall be* wailing: for I will pass through thee, saith the LORD.

¹⁸Woe unto you that desire the day of the LORD! to what end *is* it for you? the day of the LORD *is* darkness, and not light.

¹⁹As if a man did flee from a lion, and a bear met him; or went into the house, and leaned his hand on the wall, and a serpent bit him.

²⁰*Shall* not the day of the LORD *be* darkness, and not light? even very dark, and no brightness in it?

²¹I hate, I despise your feast days, and I will not smell in your solemn assemblies.

²²Though ye offer me burnt offerings and your meat offerings, I will not accept *them:* neither will I regard the peace offerings of your fat beasts.

²³Take thou away from me the noise of thy songs; for I will not hear the melody of thy viols.

²⁴But let judgment run down as waters, and righteousness as a mighty stream.

²⁵Have ye offered unto me sacrifices and offerings in the wilderness forty years, O house of Israel?

²⁶But ye have borne the tabernacle of your Moloch and Chiun your images, the star of your god, which ye made to yourselves.

²⁷Therefore will I cause you to go into captivity beyond Damascus, saith the LORD, whose name *is* The God of hosts.

WOE to them *that are* at ease in Zion, and trust in the mountain of Samaria, *which are* named chief of the nations, to whom the house of Israel came!

²Pass ye unto Calneh, and see; and from thence go ye to Hamath the great: then go down to Gath of the Philistines: *be they* better than these kingdoms? or their border greater than your border?

³Ye that put far away the evil day, and cause the seat of violence to come near;

⁴That lie upon beds of ivory, and stretch themselves upon their couches, and eat the lambs out of the flock, and the calves out of the midst of the stall;

⁵That chant to the sound of the viol, *and* invent to themselves instruments of musick, like David;

⁶That drink wine in bowls, and anoint themselves with the chief ointments: but they are not grieved for the affliction of Joseph.

⁷Therefore now shall they go captive with the first that go captive, and the banquet of them that stretched themselves shall be removed.

⁸The Lord GOD hath sworn by himself, saith the LORD the God of hosts, I abhor the excellency of Jacob, and

hate his palaces: therefore will I deliver up the city with all that is therein.

9And it shall come to pass, if there remain ten men in one house, that they shall die.

10And a man's uncle shall take him up, and he that burneth him, to bring out the bones out of the house, and shall say unto him that *is* by the sides of the house, *Is there* yet *any* with thee? and he shall say, No. Then shall he say, Hold thy tongue: for we may not make mention of the name of the LORD.

11For, behold, the LORD commandeth, and he will smite the great house with breaches, and the little house with clefts.

12Shall horses run upon the rock? will *one* plow *there* with oxen? for ye have turned judgment into gall, and the fruit of righteousness into hemlock:

13Ye which rejoice in a thing of nought, which say, Have we not taken to us horns by our own strength?

14But, behold, I will raise up against you a nation, O house of Israel, saith the LORD the God of hosts; and they shall afflict you from the entering in of Hemath unto the river of the wilderness.

REVELATION 2:18—3:6

AND unto the angel of the church in Thyatira write; These things saith the Son of God, who hath his eyes like unto a flame of fire, and his feet *are* like fine brass;

19I know thy works, and charity, and service, and faith, and thy patience, and thy works; and the last *to be* more than the first.

20Notwithstanding I have a few things against thee, because thou sufferest that woman Jezebel, which calleth herself a prophetess, to teach and to seduce my servants to commit fornication, and to eat things sacrificed unto idols.

21And I gave her space to repent of her fornication; and she repented not.

22Behold, I will cast her into a bed, and them that commit adultery with her into great tribulation, except they repent of their deeds.

23And I will kill her children with death; and all the churches shall know that I am he which searcheth the reins and hearts: and I will give unto every one of you according to your works.

24But unto you I say, and unto the rest in Thyatira, as many as have not this doctrine, and which have not known the depths of Satan, as they speak; I will put upon you none other burden.

25But that which ye have *already* hold fast till I come.

26And he that overcometh, and keepeth my works unto the end, to him will I give power over the nations:

27And he shall rule them with a rod of iron; as the vessels of a potter shall they be broken to shivers: even as I received of my Father.

28And I will give him the morning star.

29He that hath an ear, let him hear what the Spirit saith unto the churches.

AND unto the angel of the church in Sardis write; These things saith he that hath the seven Spirits of God, and the seven stars; I know thy works, that thou hast a name that thou livest, and art dead.

2Be watchful, and strengthen the things which remain that are ready to die: for I have not found thy works perfect before God.

3Remember therefore how thou hast received and heard, and hold fast, and repent. If therefore thou shalt not watch, I will come on thee as a thief, and thou shalt not know what hour I will come upon thee.

4Thou hast a few names even in Sardis which have not defiled their garments; and they shall walk with me in white: for they are worthy.

5He that overcometh, the same shall be clothed in white raiment; and I will not blot out his name out of the book of life, but I will confess his name before my Father, and before his angels.

6He that hath an ear, let him hear what the Spirit saith unto the churches.

PSALM 130:1–8

OUT of the depths have I cried unto thee, O LORD.
2Lord, hear my voice: let thine ears be attentive to the voice of my supplications.

3If thou, LORD, shouldest mark iniquities, O Lord, who shall stand?

4But *there is* forgiveness with thee, that thou mayest be feared.

5I wait for the LORD, my soul doth wait, and in his word do I hope.

6My soul *waiteth* for the Lord more than they that watch for the morning: *I say, more than* they that watch for the morning.

7Let Israel hope in the LORD: for with the LORD *there is* mercy, and with him *is* plenteous redemption.

8And he shall redeem Israel from all his iniquities.

PROVERBS FOR TODAY/ 29:21–22

He that delicately bringeth up his servant from a child shall have him become his *son at the length.* □*An angry man stirreth up strife, and a furious man aboundeth in transgression.*

DECEMBER 12

AMOS 7:1—9:15

THUS hath the Lord GOD shewed unto me; and, behold, he formed grasshoppers in the beginning of the shooting up of the latter growth; and, lo, *it was* the latter growth after the king's mowings.

2And it came to pass, *that* when they had made an end of eating the grass of the land, then I said, O Lord GOD, forgive, I beseech thee: by whom shall Jacob arise? for he *is* small.

3The LORD repented for this: It shall not be, saith the LORD.

4Thus hath the Lord GOD shewed unto me: and, behold, the Lord GOD called to contend by fire, and it devoured the great deep, and did eat up a part.

5Then said I, O Lord GOD, cease, I beseech thee: by whom shall Jacob arise? for he *is* small.

6The LORD repented for this: This also shall not be, saith the Lord GOD.

7Thus he shewed me: and, behold, the Lord stood upon a wall *made* by a plumbline, with a plumbline in his hand.

8And the LORD said unto me, Amos, what seest thou? And I said, A plumbline. Then said the Lord, Behold, I will set a plumbline in the midst of my people Israel: I will not again pass by them any more:

9And the high places of Isaac shall be desolate, and the sanctuaries of Israel shall be laid waste; and I will rise against the house of Jeroboam with the sword.

10Then Amaziah the priest of Bethel sent to Jeroboam king of Israel, saying, Amos hath conspired against thee in the midst of the house of Israel: the land is not able to bear all his words.

11For thus Amos saith, Jeroboam shall die by the sword, and Israel shall surely be led away captive out of their own land.

12Also Amaziah said unto Amos, O thou seer, go, flee thee away into the land of Judah, and there eat bread, and prophesy there:

13But prophesy not again any more at Beth–el: for it *is* the king's chapel, and it *is* the king's court.

14Then answered Amos, and said to Amaziah, I *was* no prophet, neither *was* I a prophet's son; but I *was* an herdman, and a gatherer of sycomore fruit:

15And the LORD took me as I followed the flock, and the LORD said unto me, Go, prophesy unto my people Israel.

16Now therefore hear thou the word of the LORD: Thou sayest, Prophesy not against Israel, and drop not *thy word* against the house of Isaac.

17Therefore thus saith the LORD; Thy wife shall be an harlot in the city, and thy sons and thy daughters shall fall by the sword, and thy land shall be divided by line; and thou shalt die in a polluted land: and Israel shall surely go into captivity forth of his land.

THUS hath the Lord GOD shewed unto me: and behold a basket of summer fruit.

2And he said, Amos, what seest thou? And I said, A basket of summer fruit. Then said the LORD unto me, The end is come upon my people of Israel; I will not again pass by them any more.

3And the songs of the temple shall be howlings in that day, saith the Lord GOD: *there shall be* many dead bodies in every place; they shall cast *them* forth with silence.

4Hear this, O ye that swallow up the needy, even to make the poor of the land to fail,

5Saying, When will the new moon be gone, that we may sell corn? and the sabbath, that we may set forth wheat, making the ephah small, and the shekel great, and falsifying the balances by deceit?

6That we may buy the poor for silver, and the needy for a pair of shoes; *yea,* and sell the refuse of the wheat?

7The LORD hath sworn by the excellency of Jacob, Surely I will never forget any of their works.

8Shall not the land tremble for this, and every one mourn that dwelleth therein? and it shall rise up wholly as a flood; and it shall be cast out and drowned, as *by* the flood of Egypt.

9And it shall come to pass in that day, saith the Lord GOD, that I will cause the sun to go down at noon, and I will darken the earth in the clear day:

10And I will turn your feasts into mourning, and all your songs into lamentation; and I will bring up sackcloth upon all loins, and baldness upon every head; and I will make it as the mourning of an only *son,* and the end thereof as a bitter day.

11Behold, the days come, saith the Lord GOD, that I will send a famine in the land, not a famine of bread, nor a thirst for water, but of hearing the words of the LORD:

12And they shall wander from sea to sea, and from the north even to the east, they shall run to and fro to seek the word of the LORD, and shall not find *it.*

13In that day shall the fair virgins and young men faint for thirst.

14They that swear by the sin of Samaria, and say, Thy God, O Dan, liveth; and, The manner of Beer–sheba liveth; even they shall fall, and never rise up again.

I SAW the Lord standing upon the altar: and he said, Smite the lintel of the door, that the posts may shake: and cut them in the head, all of them; and I will slay the last of them with the sword: he that fleeth of them shall not flee away, and he that escapeth of them shall not be delivered.

2Though they dig into hell, thence shall mine hand take them; though they climb up to heaven, thence will I bring them down:

3And though they hide themselves in the top of Carmel, I will search and take them out thence; and though they be hid from my sight in the bottom of the sea, thence will I command the serpent, and he shall bite them:

4And though they go into captivity before their enemies, thence will I command the sword, and it shall slay them: and I will set mine eyes upon them for evil, and not for good.

5And the Lord GOD of hosts *is* he that toucheth the land, and it shall melt, and all that dwell therein shall mourn: and it shall rise up wholly like a flood; and shall be drowned, as *by* the flood of Egypt.

6*It is* he that buildeth his stories in the heaven, and hath founded his troop in the earth; he that calleth for the waters of the sea, and poureth them out upon the face of the earth: The LORD *is* his name.

7*Are* ye not as children of the Ethiopians unto me, O children of Israel? saith the LORD. Have not I brought up Israel out of the land of Egypt? and the Philistines from Caphtor, and the Syrians from Kir?

8Behold, the eyes of the Lord GOD *are* upon the sinful kingdom, and I will destroy it from off the face of the earth; saving that I will not utterly destroy the house of Jacob, saith the LORD.

9For, lo, I will command, and I will sift the house of Israel among all nations, like as *corn* is sifted in a sieve, yet shall not the least grain fall upon the earth.

10All the sinners of my people shall die by the sword, which say, The evil shall not overtake nor prevent us.

11In that day will I raise up the tabernacle of David that is fallen, and close up the breaches thereof; and I will raise up his ruins, and I will build it as in the days of old:

12That they may possess the remnant of Edom, and of all the heathen, which are called by my name, saith the LORD that doeth this.

13Behold, the days come, saith the LORD, that the plowman shall overtake the reaper, and the treader of grapes him that soweth seed; and the mountains shall drop sweet wine, and all the hills shall melt.

14And I will bring again the captivity of my people of Israel, and they shall build the waste cities, and inhabit *them;* and they shall plant vineyards, and drink the wine thereof; they shall also make gardens, and eat the fruit of them.

15And I will plant them upon their land, and they shall no more be pulled up out of their land which I have given them, saith the LORD thy God.

REVELATION 3:7–22

AND to the angel of the church in Philadelphia write; These things saith he that is holy, he that is true, he that hath the key of David, he that openeth, and no man shutteth; and shutteth, and no man openeth;

8I know thy works: behold, I have set before thee an open door, and no man can shut it: for thou hast a little strength, and hast kept my word, and hast not denied my name.

9Behold, I will make them of the synagogue of Satan, which say they are Jews, and are not, but do lie; behold, I will make them to come and worship before thy feet, and to know that I have loved thee.

10Because thou hast kept the word of my patience, I also will keep thee from the hour of temptation, which shall come upon all the world, to try them that dwell upon the earth.

11Behold, I come quickly: hold that

fast which thou hast, that no man take thy crown.

12Him that overcometh will I make a pillar in the temple of my God, and he shall go no more out: and I will write upon him the name of my God, and the name of the city of my God, *which is* new Jerusalem, which cometh down out of heaven from my God: and *I will write upon him* my new name.

13He that hath an ear, let him hear what the Spirit saith unto the churches.

14And unto the angel of the church of the Laodiceans write; These things saith the Amen, the faithful and true witness, the beginning of the creation of God;

15I know thy works, that thou art neither cold nor hot: I would thou wert cold or hot.

16So then because thou art lukewarm, and neither cold nor hot, I will spue thee out of my mouth.

17Because thou sayest, I am rich, and increased with goods, and have need of nothing; and knowest not that thou art wretched, and miserable, and poor, and blind, and naked:

18I counsel thee to buy of me gold tried in the fire, that thou mayest be rich; and white raiment, that thou may-est be clothed, and *that* the shame of thy nakedness do not appear; and anoint thine eyes with eyesalve, that thou mayest see.

19As many as I love, I rebuke and chasten: be zealous therefore, and repent.

20Behold, I stand at the door, and knock: if any man hear my voice, and open the door, I will come in to him, and will sup with him, and he with me.

21To him that overcometh will I grant to sit with me in my throne, even as I also overcame, and am set down with my Father in his throne.

22He that hath an ear, let him hear what the Spirit saith unto the churches.

PSALM 131:1–3

Lord, my heart is not haughty, nor mine eyes lofty: neither do I exercise myself in great matters, or in things too high for me.

2Surely I have behaved and quieted myself, as a child that is weaned of his mother: my soul *is* even as a weaned child.

3Let Israel hope in the Lord from henceforth and for ever.

PROVERBS FOR TODAY/ 29:23

A man's pride shall bring him low: but honour shall uphold the humble in spirit.

DECEMBER 13

OBADIAH 1:1–21

The vision of Obadiah. Thus saith the Lord God concerning Edom; We have heard a rumour from the Lord, and an ambassador is sent among the heathen, Arise ye, and let us rise up against her in battle.

2Behold, I have made thee small among the heathen: thou art greatly despised.

3The pride of thine heart hath deceived thee, thou that dwellest in the clefts of the rock, whose habitation *is* high; that saith in his heart, Who shall bring me down to the ground?

4Though thou exalt *thyself* as the eagle, and though thou set thy nest among the stars, thence will I bring thee down, saith the LORD.

5If thieves came to thee, if robbers by night, (how art thou cut off!) would they not have stolen till they had enough? if the grapegatherers came to thee, would they not leave *some* grapes?

6How are *the things* of Esau searched out! *how* are his hidden things sought up!

7All the men of thy confederacy have brought thee *even* to the border: the men that were at peace with thee have deceived thee, *and* prevailed against thee; *they that eat* thy bread have laid a wound under thee: *there is* none understanding in him.

8Shall I not in that day, saith the LORD, even destroy the wise *men* out of Edom, and understanding out of the mount of Esau?

9And thy mighty *men,* O Teman, shall be dismayed, to the end that every one of the mount of Esau may be cut off by slaughter.

10For *thy* violence against thy brother Jacob shame shall cover thee, and thou shalt be cut off for ever.

11In the day that thou stoodest on the other side, in the day that the strangers carried away captive his forces, and foreigners entered into his gates, and cast lots upon Jerusalem, even thou *wast* as one of them.

12But thou shouldest not have looked on the day of thy brother in the day that he became a stranger; neither shouldest thou have rejoiced over the children of Judah in the day of their destruction; neither shouldest thou have spoken proudly in the day of distress.

13Thou shouldest not have entered into the gate of my people in the day of their calamity; yea, thou shouldest not have looked on their affliction in the day of their calamity, nor have laid *hands* on their substance in the day of their calamity;

14Neither shouldest thou have stood in the crossway, to cut off those of his that did escape; neither shouldest thou have delivered up those of his that did remain in the day of distress.

15For the day of the LORD *is* near upon all the heathen: as thou hast done, it shall be done unto thee: thy reward shall return upon thine own head.

16For as ye have drunk upon my holy mountain, *so* shall all the heathen drink continually, yea, they shall drink, and they shall swallow down, and they shall be as though they had not been.

17But upon mount Zion shall be deliverance, and there shall be holiness; and the house of Jacob shall possess their possessions.

18And the house of Jacob shall be a fire, and the house of Joseph a flame, and the house of Esau for stubble, and they shall kindle in them, and devour them; and there shall not be *any* remaining of the house of Esau; for the LORD hath spoken it.

19And *they of* the south shall possess the mount of Esau; and *they of* the plain the Philistines: and they shall possess the fields of Ephraim, and the fields of Samaria: and Benjamin *shall possess* Gilead.

20And the captivity of this host of the children of Israel *shall possess* that of the Canaanites, *even* unto Zarephath; and the captivity of Jerusalem, which *is* in Sepharad, shall possess the cities of the south.

21And saviours shall come up on mount Zion to judge the mount of Esau; and the kingdom shall be the LORD'S.

REVELATION 4:1–11

AFTER this I looked, and, behold, a door *was* opened in heaven: and the first voice which I heard *was* as it were of a trumpet talking with me; which said, Come up hither, and I will shew thee things which must be hereafter.

2And immediately I was in the spirit: and, behold, a throne was set in heaven, and *one* sat on the throne.

3And he that sat was to look upon like a jasper and a sardine stone: and *there was* a rainbow round about the throne, in sight like unto an emerald.

4And round about the throne *were* four and twenty seats: and upon the seats I saw four and twenty elders sitting, clothed in white raiment; and they had on their heads crowns of gold.

5And out of the throne proceeded lightnings and thunderings and voices: and *there were* seven lamps of fire burning before the throne, which are the seven Spirits of God.

6And before the throne *there was* a sea of glass like unto crystal: and in the midst of the throne, and round about the throne, *were* four beasts full of eyes before and behind.

7And the first beast *was* like a lion, and the second beast like a calf, and the third beast had a face as a man, and the fourth beast *was* like a flying eagle.

8And the four beasts had each of them six wings about *him;* and *they were* full of eyes within: and they rest not day and night, saying, Holy, holy, holy, Lord God Almighty, which was, and is, and is to come.

9And when those beasts give glory and honour and thanks to him that sat on the throne, who liveth for ever and ever,

10The four and twenty elders fall down before him that sat on the throne, and worship him that liveth for ever and ever, and cast their crowns before the throne, saying,

11Thou art worthy, O Lord, to receive glory and honour and power: for thou hast created all things, and for thy pleasure they are and were created.

PSALM 132:1–18

LORD, remember David, *and* all his afflictions:

2How he sware unto the LORD, *and* vowed unto the mighty *God* of Jacob;

3Surely I will not come into the tabernacle of my house, nor go up into my bed;

4I will not give sleep to mine eyes, *or* slumber to mine eyelids,

5Until I find out a place for the LORD, an habitation for the mighty *God* of Jacob.

6Lo, we heard of it at Ephratah: we found it in the fields of the wood.

7We will go into his tabernacles: we will worship at his footstool.

8Arise, O LORD, into thy rest; thou, and the ark of thy strength.

9Let thy priests be clothed with righteousness; and let thy saints shout for joy.

10For thy servant David's sake turn not away the face of thine anointed.

11The LORD hath sworn *in* truth unto David; he will not turn from it; Of the fruit of thy body will I set upon thy throne.

12If thy children will keep my covenant and my testimony that I shall teach them, their children shall also sit upon thy throne for evermore.

13For the LORD hath chosen Zion; he hath desired *it* for his habitation.

14This *is* my rest for ever: here will I dwell; for I have desired it.

15I will abundantly bless her provision: I will satisfy her poor with bread.

16I will also clothe her priests with salvation: and her saints shall shout aloud for joy.

17There will I make the horn of David to bud: I have ordained a lamp for mine anointed.

18His enemies will I clothe with shame: but upon himself shall his crown flourish.

PROVERBS FOR TODAY/ 29:24–25

Whoso is partner with a thief hateth his own soul: he heareth cursing, and bewrayeth it not. □ *The fear of man bringeth a snare: but whoso putteth his trust in the* LORD *shall be safe.*

DECEMBER 14

JONAH 1:1—4:11

Now the word of the LORD came unto Jonah the son of Amittai, saying,

2Arise, go to Nineveh, that great city, and cry against it; for their wickedness is come up before me.

3But Jonah rose up to flee unto Tarshish from the presence of the LORD, and went down to Joppa; and he found a ship going to Tarshish: so he paid the fare thereof, and went down into it, to go with them unto Tarshish from the presence of the LORD.

4But the LORD sent out a great wind into the sea, and there was a mighty tempest in the sea, so that the ship was like to be broken.

5Then the mariners were afraid, and cried every man unto his god, and cast forth the wares that *were* in the ship into the sea, to lighten *it* of them. But Jonah was gone down into the sides of the ship; and he lay, and was fast asleep.

6So the shipmaster came to him, and said unto him, What meanest thou, O sleeper? arise, call upon thy God, if so be that God will think upon us, that we perish not.

7And they said every one to his fellow, Come, and let us cast lots, that we may know for whose cause this evil *is* upon us. So they cast lots, and the lot fell upon Jonah.

8Then said they unto him, Tell us, we pray thee, for whose cause this evil *is* upon us; What *is* thine occupation? and whence comest thou? what *is* thy country? and of what people *art* thou?

9And he said unto them, I *am* an Hebrew; and I fear the LORD, the God of heaven, which hath made the sea and the dry *land*.

10Then were the men exceedingly afraid, and said unto him, Why hast thou done this? For the men knew that he fled from the presence of the LORD, because he had told them.

11Then said they unto him, What shall we do unto thee, that the sea may be calm unto us? for the sea wrought, and was tempestuous.

12And he said unto them, Take me up, and cast me forth into the sea; so shall the sea be calm unto you: for I know that for my sake this great tempest *is* upon you.

13Nevertheless the men rowed hard to bring *it* to the land; but they could not: for the sea wrought, and was tempestuous against them.

14Wherefore they cried unto the LORD, and said, We beseech thee, O LORD, we beseech thee, let us not perish for this man's life, and lay not upon us innocent blood: for thou, O LORD, hast done as it pleased thee.

15So they took up Jonah, and cast him forth into the sea: and the sea ceased from her raging.

16Then the men feared the LORD exceedingly, and offered a sacrifice unto the LORD, and made vows.

17Now the LORD had prepared a great fish to swallow up Jonah. And Jonah was in the belly of the fish three days and three nights.

THEN Jonah prayed unto the LORD his God out of the fish's belly,

2And said, I cried by reason of mine affliction unto the LORD, and he heard me; out of the belly of hell cried I, *and* thou heardest my voice.

3For thou hadst cast me into the deep, in the midst of the seas; and the floods compassed me about: all thy billows and thy waves passed over me.

4Then I said, I am cast out of thy sight; yet I will look again toward thy holy temple.

5The waters compassed me about, *even* to the soul: the depth closed me round about, the weeds were wrapped about my head.

6I went down to the bottoms of the mountains; the earth with her bars *was* about me for ever: yet hast thou brought up my life from corruption, O LORD my God.

7When my soul fainted within me I remembered the LORD: and my prayer came in unto thee, into thine holy temple.

8They that observe lying vanities forsake their own mercy.

9But I will sacrifice unto thee with the voice of thanksgiving; I will pay *that* that I have vowed. Salvation *is* of the LORD.

10And the LORD spake unto the fish, and it vomited out Jonah upon the dry *land*.

AND the word of the LORD came unto Jonah the second time, saying,

2Arise, go unto Nineveh, that great city, and preach unto it the preaching that I bid thee.

3So Jonah arose, and went unto Nineveh, according to the word of the LORD. Now Nineveh was an exceeding great city of three days' journey.

4And Jonah began to enter into the city a day's journey, and he cried, and said, yet forty days, and Nineveh shall be overthrown.

5So the people of Nineveh believed God, and proclaimed a fast, and put on sackcloth, from the greatest of them even to the least of them.

6For word came unto the king of Nineveh, and he arose from his throne, and he laid his robe from him, and covered *him* with sackcloth, and sat in ashes.

7And he caused *it* to be proclaimed and published through Nineveh by the decree of the king and his nobles, saying, let neither man nor beast, herd nor flock, taste anything: let them not feed, nor drink water:

8But let man and beast be covered with sackcloth, and cry mightily unto God: yea, let them turn every one from his evil way, and from the violence that *is* in their hands.

9Who can tell *if* God will turn and repent, and turn away from his fierce anger, that we perish not?

10And God saw their works, that they turned from their evil way; and God repented of the evil, that he had said that he would do unto them; and he did *it* not.

BUT it displeased Jonah exceedingly, and he was very angry.

2And he prayed unto the LORD, and said, I pray thee, O LORD, *was* not this my saying, when I was yet in my country? Therefore I fled before unto Tarshish: for I knew that thou *art* a gracious God, and merciful, slow to anger, and of great kindness, and repentest thee of the evil.

3Therefore now, O LORD, take, I beseech thee, my life from me; for *it is* better for me to die than to live.

4Then said the LORD, Doest thou well to be angry?

5So Jonah went out of the city, and sat on the east side of the city, and there made him a booth, and sat under it in the shadow, till he might see what would become of the city.

6And the LORD God prepared a gourd, and made *it* to come up over Jonah, that it might be a shadow over his head, to deliver him from his grief. So Jonah was exceeding glad of the gourd.

7But God prepared a worm when the morning rose the next day, and it smote the gourd that it withered.

8And it came to pass, when the sun did arise, that God prepared a vehement east wind; and the sun beat upon the head of Jonah, that he fainted, and wished in himself to die, and said, *It is* better for me to die than to live.

9And God said to Jonah, Doest thou well to be angry for the gourd? And he said, I do well to be angry, *even* unto death.

10Then said the LORD, Thou hast had pity on the gourd, for the which thou hast not laboured, neither madest it grow; which came up in a night, and perished in a night:

11And should not I spare Nineveh, that great city, wherein are more than sixscore thousand persons that cannot discern between their right hand and their left hand; and *also* much cattle?

REVELATION 5:1–14

AND I saw in the right hand of him that sat on the throne a book written within and on the backside, sealed with seven seals.

2And I saw a strong angel proclaiming with a loud voice, Who is worthy to open the book, and to loose the seals thereof?

3And no man in heaven, nor in earth, neither under the earth, was able to open the book, neither to look thereon.

4And I wept much, because no man was found worthy to open and to read the book, neither to look thereon.

5And one of the elders saith unto me, Weep not: behold, the Lion of the tribe of Juda, the Root of David, hath prevailed to open the book, and to loose the seven seals thereof.

6And I beheld, and, lo, in the midst of the throne and of the four beasts, and in the midst of the elders, stood a Lamb as it had been slain, having seven horns and seven eyes, which are the seven Spirits of God sent forth into all the earth.

7And he came and took the book out of the right hand of him that sat upon the throne.

8And when he had taken the book, the four beasts and four *and* twenty elders fell down before the Lamb, having every one of them harps, and golden vials full of odours, which are the prayers of saints.

9And they sung a new song, saying, Thou art worthy to take the book, and to open the seals thereof: for thou wast slain, and hast redeemed us to God by thy blood out of every kindred, and tongue, and people, and nation;

10And hast made us unto our God kings and priests: and we shall reign on the earth.

11And I beheld, and I heard the voice of many angels round about the throne and the beasts and the elders: and the number of them was ten thousand times ten thousand, and thousands of thousands;

12Saying with a loud voice, Worthy is the Lamb that was slain to receive power, and riches, and wisdom, and strength, and honour, and glory, and blessing.

13And every creature which is in heaven, and on the earth, and under the earth, and such as are in the sea, and all that are in them, heard I saying, Blessing, and honour, and glory, and power, *be* unto him that sitteth upon the throne, and unto the Lamb for ever and ever.

14And the four beasts said, Amen. And the four *and* twenty elders fell down and worshipped him that liveth for ever and ever.

PSALM 133:1–3

BEHOLD, how good and how pleasant *it is* for brethren to dwell together in unity!

²*It is* like the precious ointment upon the head, that ran down upon the beard, *even* Aaron's beard: that went down to the skirts of his garments;

³As the dew of Hermon, *and as the dew* that descended upon the mountains of Zion: for there the LORD commanded the blessing, *even* life for evermore.

PROVERBS FOR TODAY/ 29:26–27

Many seek the ruler's favour; but every *man's judgment* cometh *from the* LORD. □*An unjust man* is *an abomination to the just: and* he that is *upright in the way* is *abomination to the wicked.*

DECEMBER 15

MICAH 1:1—4:13

THE word of the LORD that came to Micah the Morasthite in the days of Jotham, Ahaz, *and* Hezekiah, kings of Judah, which he saw concerning Samaria and Jerusalem.

²Hear, all ye people; hearken, O earth, and all that therein is: and let the Lord GOD be witness against you, the LORD from his holy temple.

³For, behold, the LORD cometh forth out of his place, and will come down, and tread upon the high places of the earth.

⁴And the mountains shall be molten under him, and the valleys shall be cleft, as wax before the fire, *and* as the waters *that are* poured down a steep place.

⁵For the transgression of Jacob *is* all this, and for the sins of the house of Israel. What *is* the transgression of Jacob? *is it* not Samaria? and what *are* the high places of Judah? *are they* not Jerusalem?

⁶Therefore I will make Samaria as an heap of the field, *and* as plantings of a vineyard: and I will pour down the stones thereof into the valley, and I will discover the foundations thereof.

⁷And all the graven images thereof shall be beaten to pieces, and all the hires thereof shall be burned with the fire, and all the idols thereof will I lay desolate: for she gathered *it* of the hire of an harlot, and they shall return to the hire of an harlot.

⁸Therefore I will wail and howl, I will go stripped and naked: I will make a wailing like the dragons, and mourning as the owls.

⁹For her wound *is* incurable; for it is come unto Judah; he is come unto the gate of my people, *even* to Jerusalem.

¹⁰Declare ye *it* not at Gath, weep ye not at all: in the house of Aphrah roll thyself in the dust.

¹¹Pass ye away, thou inhabitant of Saphir, having thy shame naked: the inhabitant of Zaanan came not forth in the mourning of Beth–ezel; he shall receive of you his standing.

¹²For the inhabitant of Maroth waited carefully for good: but evil came down

from the LORD unto the gate of Jerusalem.

13O thou inhabitant of Lachish, bind the chariot to the swift beast: she *is* the beginning of the sin to the daughter of Zion: for the transgressions of Israel were found in thee.

14Therefore shalt thou give presents to Moresheth–gath: the houses of Achzib *shall be* a lie to the kings of Israel.

15Yet will I bring an heir unto thee, O inhabitant of Mareshah: he shall come unto Adullam the glory of Israel.

16Make thee bald, and poll thee for thy delicate children; enlarge thy baldness as the eagle; for they are gone into captivity from thee.

WOE to them that devise iniquity, and work evil upon their beds! when the morning is light, they practise it, because it is in the power of their hand.

2And they covet fields, and take *them* by violence; and houses, and take *them* away: so they oppress a man and his house, even a man and his heritage.

3Therefore thus saith the LORD; Behold, against this family do I devise an evil, from which ye shall not remove your necks; neither shall ye go haughtily: for this time *is* evil.

4In that day shall *one* take up a parable against you, and lament with a doleful lamentation, *and* say, We be utterly spoiled: he hath changed the portion of my people: how hath he removed *it* from me! turning away he hath divided our fields.

5Therefore thou shalt have none that shall cast a cord by lot in the congregation of the LORD.

6Prophesy ye not, *say they to them that* prophesy: they shall not prophesy to them, *that* they shall not take shame.

7O *thou that art* named the house of Jacob, is the spirit of the LORD straitened? *are* these his doings? do not my words do good to him that walketh uprightly?

8Even of late my people is risen up as an enemy: ye pull off the robe with the garment from them that pass by securely as men averse from war.

9The women of my people have ye cast out from their pleasant houses; from their children have ye taken away my glory for ever.

10Arise ye, and depart; for this *is* not *your* rest: because it is polluted, it shall destroy *you,* even with a sore destruction.

11If a man walking in the spirit and falsehood do lie, *saying,* I will prophesy unto thee of wine and of strong drink; he shall even be the prophet of this people.

12I will surely assemble, O Jacob, all of thee; I will surely gather the remnant of Israel; I will put them together as the sheep of Bozrah, as the flock in the midst of their fold: they shall make great noise by reason of *the multitude of* men.

13The breaker is come up before them: they have broken up, and have passed through the gate, and are gone out by it: and their king shall pass before them, and the LORD on the head of them.

AND I said, Hear, I pray you, O heads of Jacob, and ye princes of the house of Israel; *Is it* not for you to know judgment?

2Who hate the good, and love the evil; who pluck off their skin from off them, and their flesh from off their bones;

3Who also eat the flesh of my people, and flay their skin from off them; and they break their bones, and chop them in pieces, as for the pot, and as flesh within the caldron.

4Then shall they cry unto the LORD, but he will not hear them: he will even hide his face from them at that time, as they have behaved themselves ill in their doings.

5Thus saith the LORD concerning the

prophets that make my people err, that bite with their teeth, and cry, Peace; and he that putteth not into their mouths, they even prepare war against him.

6Therefore night *shall be* unto you, that ye shall not have a vision; and it shall be dark unto you, that ye shall not divine; and the sun shall go down over the prophets, and the day shall be dark over them.

7Then shall the seers be ashamed, and the diviners confounded: yea, they shall all cover their lips; for *there is* no answer of God.

8But truly I am full of power by the spirit of the LORD, and of judgment, and of might, to declare unto Jacob his transgression, and to Israel his sin.

9Hear this, I pray you, ye heads of the house of Jacob, and princes of the house of Israel, that abhor judgment, and pervert all equity.

10They build up Zion with blood, and Jerusalem with iniquity.

11The heads thereof judge for reward, and the priests thereof teach for hire, and the prophets thereof divine for money: yet will they lean upon the LORD, and say, *Is* not the LORD among us? none evil can come upon us.

12Therefore shall Zion for your sake be plowed *as* a field, and Jerusalem shall become heaps, and the mountain of the house as the high places of the forest.

BUT in the last days it shall come to pass, *that* the mountain of the house of the LORD shall be established in the top of the mountains, and it shall be exalted above the hills; and people shall flow unto it.

2And many nations shall come, and say, Come, and let us go up to the mountain of the LORD, and to the house of the God of Jacob; and he will teach us of his ways, and we will walk in his paths: for the law shall go forth of Zion, and the word of the LORD from Jerusalem.

3And he shall judge among many people, and rebuke strong nations afar off; and they shall beat their swords into plowshares, and their spears into pruninghooks: nation shall not lift up a sword against nation, neither shall they learn war any more.

4But they shall sit every man under his vine and under his fig tree; and none shall make *them* afraid: for the mouth of the LORD of hosts hath spoken *it.*

5For all people will walk every one in the name of his god, and we will walk in the name of the LORD our God for ever and ever.

6In that day, saith the LORD, will I assemble her that halteth, and I will gather her that is driven out, and her that I have afflicted;

7And I will make her that halted a remnant, and her that was cast far off a strong nation: and the LORD shall reign over them in mount Zion from henceforth, even for ever.

8And thou, O tower of the flock, the strong hold of the daughter of Zion, unto thee shall it come, even the first dominion; the kingdom shall come to the daughter of Jerusalem.

9Now why dost thou cry out aloud? *is there* no king in thee? is thy counsellor perished? for pangs have taken thee as a woman in travail.

10Be in pain, and labour to bring forth, O daughter of Zion, like a woman in travail: for now shalt thou go forth out of the city, and thou shalt dwell in the field, and thou shalt go *even* to Babylon; there shalt thou be delivered; there the LORD shall redeem thee from the hand of thine enemies.

11Now also many nations are gathered against thee, that say, Let her be defiled, and let our eye look upon Zion.

12But they know not the thoughts of the LORD, neither understand they his counsel: for he shall gather them as the sheaves into the floor.

13Arise and thresh, O daughter of Zion: for I will make thine horn iron, and I will make thy hoofs brass: and thou shalt beat in pieces many people: and I will consecrate their gain unto the LORD, and their substance unto the LORD of the whole earth.

REVELATION 6:1–17

AND I saw when the Lamb opened one of the seals, and I heard, as it were the noise of thunder, one of the four beasts saying, Come and see.

2And I saw, and behold a white horse: and he that sat on him had a bow; and a crown was given unto him: and he went forth conquering, and to conquer.

3And when he had opened the second seal, I heard the second beast say, Come and see.

4And there went out another horse *that was* red: and *power* was given to him that sat thereon to take peace from the earth, and that they should kill one another: and there was given unto him a great sword.

5And when he had opened the third seal, I heard the third beast say, Come and see. And I beheld, and lo a black horse; and he that sat on him had a pair of balances in his hand.

6And I heard a voice in the midst of the four beasts say, A measure of wheat for a penny, and three measures of barley for a penny; and *see* thou hurt not the oil and the wine.

7And when he had opened the fourth seal, I heard the voice of the fourth beast say, Come and see.

8And I looked, and behold a pale horse: and his name that sat on him was Death, and Hell followed with him. And power was given unto them over the fourth part of the earth, to kill with sword, and with hunger, and with death, and with the beasts of the earth.

9And when he had opened the fifth seal, I saw under the altar the souls of them that were slain for the word of God, and for the testimony which they held:

10And they cried with a loud voice, saying, How long, O Lord, holy and true, dost thou not judge and avenge our blood on them that dwell on the earth?

11And white robes were given unto every one of them; and it was said unto them, that they should rest yet for a little season, until their fellowservants also and their brethren, that should be killed as they *were*, should be fulfilled.

12And I beheld when he had opened the sixth seal, and, lo, there was a great earthquake; and the sun became black as sackcloth of hair, and the moon became as blood;

13And the stars of heaven fell unto the earth, even as a fig tree casteth her untimely figs, when she is shaken of a mighty wind.

14And the heaven departed as a scroll when it is rolled together; and every mountain and island were moved out of their places.

15And the kings of the earth, and the great men, and the rich men, and the chief captains, and the mighty men, and every bondman, and every free man, hid themselves in the dens and in the rocks of the mountains;

16And said to the mountains and rocks, Fall on us, and hide us from the face of him that sitteth on the throne, and from the wrath of the Lamb:

17For the great day of his wrath is come; and who shall be able to stand?

PSALM 134:1–3

BEHOLD, bless ye the LORD, all *ye* servants of the LORD, which by night stand in the house of the LORD.

2Lift up your hands *in* the sanctuary, and bless the LORD.

3The LORD that made heaven and earth bless thee out of Zion.

PROVERBS FOR TODAY/ 30:1–4

The words of Agur the son of Jakeh, even *the prophecy: the man spake unto Ithiel, even unto Ithiel and Ucal, Surely I* am *more brutish than* any *man, and have not the understanding of a man. I neither learned wisdom, nor have the knowledge of the holy. Who hath ascended up into heaven, or descended? Who hath gathered the wind in his fists? Who hath bound the waters in a garment? Who hath established all the ends of the earth? What* is *his name, and what* is *his son's name, if thou canst tell?*

DECEMBER 16

MICAH 5:1—7:20

Now gather thyself in troops, O daughter of troops: he hath laid siege against us: they shall smite the judge of Israel with a rod upon the cheek.

2But thou, Beth–lehem Ephratah, *though* thou be little among the thousands of Judah, *yet* out of thee shall he come forth unto me *that is* to be ruler in Israel; whose goings forth *have been* from of old, from everlasting.

3Therefore will he give them up, until the time *that* she which travaileth hath brought forth: then the remnant of his brethren shall return unto the children of Israel.

4And he shall stand and feed in the strength of the LORD, in the majesty of the name of the LORD his God; and they shall abide: for now shall he be great unto the ends of the earth.

5And this *man* shall be the peace, when the Assyrian shall come into our land: and when he shall tread in our palaces, then shall we raise against him seven shepherds, and eight principal men.

6And they shall waste the land of Assyria with the sword, and the land of Nimrod in the entrances thereof: thus shall he deliver *us* from the Assyrian, when he cometh into our land, and when he treadeth within our borders.

7And the remnant of Jacob shall be in the midst of many people as a dew from the LORD, as the showers upon the grass, that tarrieth not for man, nor waiteth for the sons of men.

8And the remnant of Jacob shall be among the Gentiles in the midst of many people as a lion among the beasts of the forest, as a young lion among the flocks of sheep: who, if he go through, both treadeth down, and teareth in pieces, and none can deliver.

9Thine hand shall be lifted up upon thine adversaries, and all thine enemies shall be cut off.

10And it shall come to pass in that day, saith the LORD, that I will cut off thy horses out of the midst of thee, and I will destroy thy chariots:

11And I will cut off the cities of thy land, and throw down all thy strong holds:

12And I will cut off witchcrafts out of thine hand; and thou shalt have no *more* soothsayers:

13Thy graven images also will I cut off, and thy standing images out of the midst of thee; and thou shalt no more worship the work of thine hands.

14And I will pluck up thy groves out of the midst of thee: so will I destroy thy cities.

15And I will execute vengeance in anger and fury upon the heathen, such as they have not heard.

Hear ye now what the LORD saith; Arise, contend thou before the mountains, and let the hills hear thy voice.

2Hear ye, O mountains, the LORD's controversy, and ye strong foundations of the earth: for the LORD hath a controversy with his people, and he will plead with Israel.

3O my people, what have I done unto thee? and wherein have I wearied thee? testify against me.

4For I brought thee up out of the land of Egypt, and redeemed thee out of the house of servants; and I sent before thee Moses, Aaron, and Miriam.

5O my people, remember now what Balak king of Moab consulted, and what Balaam the son of Beor answered him from Shittim unto Gilgal; that ye may know the righteousness of the LORD.

6Wherewith shall I come before the LORD, and bow myself before the high God? shall I come before him with burnt offerings, with calves of a year old?

7Will the LORD be pleased with thousands of rams, or with ten thousands of rivers of oil? shall I give my firstborn for my transgression, the fruit of my body for the sin of my soul?

8He hath shewed thee, O man, what is good; and what doth the LORD require of thee, but to do justly, and to love mercy, and to walk humbly with thy God?

9The LORD's voice crieth unto the city, and the man of wisdom shall see thy name: hear ye the rod, and who hath appointed it.

10Are there yet the treasures of wickedness in the house of the wicked, and the scant measure that is abominable?

11Shall I count them pure with the wicked balances, and with the bag of deceitful weights?

12For the rich men thereof are full of violence, and the inhabitants thereof have spoken lies, and their tongue is deceitful in their mouth.

13Therefore also will I make thee sick in smiting thee, in making thee desolate because of thy sins.

14Thou shalt eat, but not be satisfied; and thy casting down shall be in the midst of thee; and thou shalt take hold, but shalt not deliver; and that which thou deliverest will I give up to the sword.

15Thou shalt sow, but thou shalt not reap; thou shalt tread the olives, but thou shalt not anoint thee with oil; and sweet wine, but shalt not drink wine.

16For the statutes of Omri are kept, and all the works of the house of Ahab, and ye walk in their counsels; that I should make thee a desolation, and the inhabitants thereof an hissing; therefore ye shall bear the reproach of my people.

Woe is me! for I am as when they have gathered the summer fruits, as the grapegleanings of the vintage: there is no cluster to eat: my soul desired the firstripe fruit.

2The good man is perished out of the earth: and there is none upright among men: they all lie in wait for blood; they hunt every man his brother with a net.

3That they may do evil with both hands earnestly, the prince asketh, and the judge asketh for a reward; and the great man, he uttereth his mischievous desire: so they wrap it up.

4The best of them is as a brier: the most upright is sharper than a thorn hedge: the day of thy watchmen and thy visitation cometh; now shall be their perplexity.

5Trust ye not in a friend, put ye not confidence in a guide: keep the doors of thy mouth from her that lieth in thy bosom.

6For the son dishonoureth the father, the daughter riseth up against her mother, the daughter in law against her mother in law; a man's enemies *are* the men of his own house.

7Therefore I will look unto the LORD; I will wait for the God of my salvation: my God will hear me.

8Rejoice not against me, O mine enemy: when I fall, I shall arise; when I sit in darkness, the LORD *shall be* a light unto me.

9I will bear the indignation of the LORD, because I have sinned against him, until he plead my cause, and execute judgment for me: he will bring me forth to the light, *and* I shall behold his righteousness.

10Then *she that is* mine enemy shall see *it,* and shame shall cover her which said unto me, Where is the LORD thy God? mine eyes shall behold her: now shall she be trodden down as the mire of the streets.

11*In* the day that thy walls are to be built, *in* that day shall the decree be far removed.

12*In* that day *also* he shall come even to thee from Assyria, and *from* the fortified cities, and from the fortress even to the river, and from sea to sea, and *from* mountain to mountain.

13Notwithstanding the land shall be desolate because of them that dwell therein, for the fruit of their doings.

14Feed thy people with thy rod, the flock of thine heritage, which dwell solitarily *in* the wood, in the midst of Carmel: let them feed *in* Bashan and Gilead, as in the days of old.

15According to the days of thy coming out of the land of Egypt will I shew unto him marvellous *things.*

16The nations shall see and be confounded at all their might: they shall lay *their* hand upon *their* mouth, their ears shall be deaf.

17They shall lick the dust like a serpent, they shall move out of their holes like worms of the earth: they shall be afraid of the LORD our God, and shall fear because of thee.

18Who *is* a God like unto thee, that pardoneth iniquity, and passeth by the transgression of the remnant of his heritage? he retaineth not his anger for ever, because he delighteth *in* mercy.

19He will turn again, he will have compassion upon us; he will subdue our iniquities; and thou wilt cast all their sins into the depths of the sea.

20Thou wilt perform the truth to Jacob, *and* the mercy to Abraham, which thou hast sworn unto our fathers from the days of old.

REVELATION 7:1–17

AND after these things I saw four angels standing on the four corners of the earth, holding the four winds of the earth, that the wind should not blow on the earth, nor on the sea, nor on any tree.

2And I saw another angel ascending from the east, having the seal of the living God: and he cried with a loud voice to the four angels, to whom it was given to hurt the earth and the sea,

3Saying, Hurt not the earth, neither the sea, nor the trees, till we have sealed the servants of our God in their foreheads.

4And I heard the number of them which were sealed: *and there were* sealed an hundred *and* forty *and* four thousand of all the tribes of the children of Israel.

5Of the tribe of Juda *were* sealed twelve thousand. Of the tribe of Reuben *were* sealed twelve thousand. Of the tribe of Gad *were* sealed twelve thousand.

6Of the tribe of Aser *were* sealed twelve thousand. Of the tribe of

Nephthalim *were* sealed twelve thousand. Of the tribe of Manasses *were* sealed twelve thousand.

7Of the tribe of Simeon *were* sealed twelve thousand. Of the tribe of Levi *were* sealed twelve thousand. Of the tribe of Issachar *were* sealed twelve thousand.

8Of the tribe of Zabulon *were* sealed twelve thousand. Of the tribe of Joseph *were* sealed twelve thousand. Of the tribe of Benjamin *were* sealed twelve thousand.

9After this I beheld, and, lo, a great multitude, which no man could number, of all nations, and kindreds, and people, and tongues, stood before the throne, and before the Lamb, clothed with white robes, and palms in their hands;

10And cried with a loud voice, saying, Salvation to our God which sitteth upon the throne, and unto the Lamb.

11And all the angels stood round about the throne, and *about* the elders and the four beasts, and fell before the throne on their faces, and worshipped God,

12Saying, Amen: Blessing, and glory, and wisdom, and thanksgiving, and honour, and power, and might, *be* unto our God for ever and ever. Amen.

13And one of the elders answered, saying unto me, What are these which are arrayed in white robes? and whence came they?

14And I said unto him, Sir, thou knowest. And he said to me, These are they which came out of great tribulation, and have washed their robes, and made them white in the blood of the Lamb.

15Therefore are they before the throne of God, and serve him day and night in his temple: and he that sitteth on the throne shall dwell among them.

16They shall hunger no more, neither thirst any more; neither shall the sun light on them, nor any heat.

17For the Lamb which is in the midst of the throne shall feed them, and shall lead them unto living fountains of waters: and God shall wipe away all tears from their eyes.

PSALM 135:1–21

PRAISE ye the LORD. Praise ye the name of the LORD; praise *him,* O ye servants of the LORD.

2Ye that stand in the house of the LORD, in the courts of the house of our God,

3Praise the LORD; for the LORD *is* good: sing praises unto his name; for *it is* pleasant.

4For the LORD hath chosen Jacob unto himself, *and* Israel for his peculiar treasure.

5For I know that the LORD *is* great, and *that* our Lord *is* above all gods.

6Whatsoever the LORD pleased, *that* did he in heaven, and in earth, in the seas, and all deep places.

7He causeth the vapours to ascend from the ends of the earth; he maketh lightnings for the rain; he bringeth the wind out of his treasuries.

8Who smote the firstborn of Egypt, both of man and beast.

9*Who* sent tokens and wonders into the midst of thee, O Egypt, upon Pharaoh, and upon all his servants.

10Who smote great nations, and slew mighty kings;

11Sihon king of the Amorites, and Og king of Bashan, and all the kingdoms of Canaan:

12And gave their land *for* an heritage, an heritage unto Israel his people.

13Thy name, O LORD, *endureth* for ever, *and* thy memorial, O LORD, throughout all generations.

14For the LORD will judge his people, and he will repent himself concerning his servants.

15The idols of the heathen *are* silver and gold, the work of men's hands.

16They have mouths, but they speak not; eyes have they, but they see not;

17They have ears, but they hear not;

neither is there *any* breath in their mouths.

18They that make them are like unto them: *so is* every one that trusteth in them.

19Bless the LORD, O house of Israel:

bless the LORD, O house of Aaron:

20Bless the LORD, O house of Levi: ye that fear the LORD, bless the LORD.

21Blessed be the LORD out of Zion, which dwelleth at Jerusalem. Praise ye the LORD.

PROVERBS FOR TODAY/ 30:5–6

Every word of God is *pure: he* is *a shield unto them that put their trust in him. Add thou not unto his words, lest he reprove thee, and thou be found a liar.*

DECEMBER 17

NAHUM 1:1—3:19

THE burden of Nineveh. The book of the vision of Nahum the El-koshite.

2God *is* jealous, and the LORD revengeth; the LORD revengeth, and *is* furious; the LORD will take vengeance on his adversaries, and he reserveth *wrath* for his enemies.

3The LORD *is* slow to anger, and great in power, and will not at all acquit *the wicked:* the LORD *hath* his way in the whirlwind and in the storm, and the clouds *are* the dust of his feet.

4He rebuketh the sea, and maketh it dry, and drieth up all the rivers; Bashan languisheth, and Carmel, and the flower of Lebanon languisheth.

5The mountains quake at him, and the hills melt, and the earth is burned at his presence, yea, the world, and all that dwell therein.

6Who can stand before his indignation? and who can abide in the fierceness of his anger? his fury is poured out like fire, and the rocks are thrown down by him.

7The LORD *is* good, a strong hold in the day of trouble; and he knoweth them that trust in him.

8But with an overrunning flood he

will make an utter end of the place thereof, and darkness shall pursue his enemies.

9What do ye imagine against the LORD? he will make an utter end: affliction shall not rise up the second time.

10For while *they be* folden together *as* thorns, and while they are drunken *as* drunkards, they shall be devoured as stubble fully dry.

11There is *one* come out of thee, that imagineth evil against the LORD, a wicked counsellor.

12Thus saith the LORD; Though *they be* quiet, and likewise many, yet thus shall they be cut down, when he shall pass through. Though I have afflicted thee, I will afflict thee no more.

13For now will I break his yoke from off thee, and will burst thy bonds in sunder.

14And the LORD hath given a commandment concerning thee, *that* no more of thy name be sown: out of the house of thy gods will I cut off the graven image and the molten image: I will make thy grave; for thou art vile.

15Behold upon the mountains the feet of him that bringeth good tidings, that publisheth peace! O Judah, keep thy solemn feasts, perform thy vows: for the wicked shall no more pass through thee; he is utterly cut off.

HE that dasheth in pieces is come up before thy face: keep the munition, watch the way, make *thy* loins strong, fortify *thy* power mightily.

2For the LORD hath turned away the excellency of Jacob, as the excellency of Israel: for the emptiers have emptied them out, and marred their vine branches.

3The shield of his mighty men is made red, the valiant men *are* in scarlet: the chariots *shall be* with flaming torches in the day of his preparation, and the fir trees shall be terribly shaken.

4The chariots shall rage in the streets, they shall justle one against another in the broad ways: they shall seem like torches, they shall run like the lightnings.

5He shall recount his worthies: they shall stumble in their walk; they shall make haste to the wall thereof, and the defence shall be prepared.

6The gates of the rivers shall be opened, and the palace shall be dissolved.

7And Huzzab shall be led away captive, she shall be brought up, and her maids shall lead *her* as with the voice of doves, tabering upon their breasts.

8But Nineveh *is* of old like a pool of water: yet they shall flee away. Stand, stand, *shall they cry;* but none shall look back.

9Take ye the spoil of silver, take the spoil of gold: for *there is* none end of the store *and* glory out of all the pleasant furniture.

10She is empty, and void, and waste: and the heart melteth, and the knees smite together, and much pain *is* in all loins, and the faces of them all gather blackness.

11Where *is* the dwelling of the lions, and the feedingplace of the young lions, where the lion, *even* the old lion, walked, *and* the lion's whelp, and none made *them* afraid?

12The lion did tear in pieces enough for his whelps, and strangled for his lionesses, and filled his holes with prey, and his dens with ravin.

13Behold, I *am* against thee, saith the LORD of hosts, and I will burn her chariots in the smoke, and the sword shall devour thy young lions: and I will cut off thy prey from the earth, and the voice of thy messengers shall no more be heard.

WOE to the bloody city! it *is* all full of lies *and* robbery; the prey departeth not;

2The noise of a whip, and the noise of the rattling of the wheels, and of the pransing horses, and of the jumping chariots.

3The horseman lifteth up both the bright sword and the glittering spear: and *there is* a multitude of slain, and a great number of carcases; and *there is* none end of *their* corpses; they stumble upon their corpses:

4Because of the multitude of the whoredoms of the wellfavoured harlot, the mistress of witchcrafts, that selleth nations through her whoredoms, and families through her witchcrafts.

5Behold, I *am* against thee, saith the LORD of hosts; and I will discover thy skirts upon thy face, and I will shew the nations thy nakedness, and the kingdoms thy shame.

6And I will cast abominable filth upon thee, and make thee vile, and will set thee as a gazingstock.

7And it shall come to pass, *that* all they that look upon thee shall flee from thee, and say, Nineveh is laid waste: who will bemoan her? whence shall I seek comforters for thee?

8Art thou better than populous No, that was situate among the rivers, *that had* the waters round about it, whose rampart *was* the sea, *and* her wall *was* from the sea?

9Ethiopia and Egypt *were* her strength, and *it was* infinite; Put and Lubim were thy helpers.

10Yet *was* she carried away, she went into captivity: her young children also were dashed in pieces at the top of all the streets: and they cast lots for her honourable men, and all her great men were bound in chains.

11Thou also shalt be drunken: thou shalt be hid, thou also shalt seek strength because of the enemy.

12All thy strong holds *shall be like* fig trees with the firstripe figs: if they be shaken, they shall even fall into the mouth of the eater.

13Behold, thy people in the midst of thee *are* women: the gates of thy land shall be set wide open unto thine enemies: the fire shall devour thy bars.

14Draw thee waters for the siege, fortify thy strong holds: go into clay, and tread the morter, make strong the brickkiln.

15There shall the fire devour thee; the sword shall cut thee off, it shall eat thee up like the cankerworm: make thyself many as the cankerworm, make thyself many as the locusts.

16Thou hast multiplied thy merchants above the stars of heaven: the cankerworm spoileth, and fleeth away.

17Thy crowned *are* as the locusts, and thy captains as the great grasshoppers, which camp in the hedges in the cold day, *but* when the sun ariseth they flee away, and their place is not known where they *are*.

18Thy shepherds slumber, O king of Assyria: thy nobles shall dwell *in the dust:* thy people is scattered upon the mountains, and no man gathereth *them*.

19*There is* no healing of thy bruise; thy wound is grievous: all that hear the bruit of thee shall clap the hands over thee: for upon whom hath not thy wickedness passed continually?

REVELATION 8:1–13

AND when he had opened the seventh seal, there was silence in heaven about the space of half an hour.

2And I saw the seven angels which stood before God; and to them were given seven trumpets.

3And another angel came and stood at the altar, having a golden censer; and there was given unto him much incense, that he should offer *it* with the prayers of all saints upon the golden altar which was before the throne.

4And the smoke of the incense *which came* with the prayers of the saints, ascended up before God out of the angel's hand.

5And the angel took the censer, and filled it with fire of the altar, and cast *it* into the earth: and there were voices, and thunderings, and lightnings, and an earthquake.

6And the seven angels which had the seven trumpets prepared themselves to sound.

7The first angel sounded, and there followed hail and fire mingled with blood, and they were cast upon the earth: and the third part of trees was burnt up, and all green grass was burnt up.

8And the second angel sounded, and as it were a great mountain burning with fire was cast into the sea: and the third part of the sea became blood;

9And the third part of the creatures which were in the sea, and had life, died; and the third part of the ships were destroyed.

10And the third angel sounded, and there fell a great star from heaven, burning as it were a lamp, and it fell upon the third part of the rivers, and upon the fountains of waters;

11And the name of the star is called Wormwood: and the third part of the waters became wormwood; and many men died of the waters, because they were made bitter.

12And the fourth angel sounded, and the third part of the sun was smitten, and the third part of the moon, and the third part of the stars; so as the third part of them was darkened, and the day shone not for a third part of it, and the night likewise.

13And I beheld, and heard an angel flying through the midst of heaven, saying with a loud voice, Woe, woe, woe, to the inhabiters of the earth by reason of the other voices of the trumpet of the three angels, which are yet to sound!

PSALM 136:1–26

O GIVE thanks unto the LORD; for *he is* good: for his mercy *endureth* for ever.

2O give thanks unto the God of gods: for his mercy *endureth* for ever.

3O give thanks to the Lord of lords: for his mercy *endureth* for ever.

4To him who alone doeth great wonders: for his mercy *endureth* for ever.

5To him that by wisdom made the heavens: for his mercy *endureth* for ever.

6To him that stretched out the earth above the waters: for his mercy *endureth* for ever.

7To him that made great lights: for his mercy *endureth* for ever:

8The sun to rule by day: for his mercy *endureth* for ever:

9The moon and stars to rule by night: for his mercy *endureth* for ever.

10To him that smote Egypt in their firstborn: for his mercy *endureth* for ever:

11And brought out Israel from among them: for his mercy *endureth* for ever:

12With a strong hand, and with a stretched out arm: for his mercy *endureth* for ever.

13To him which divided the Red sea into parts: for his mercy *endureth* for ever:

14And made Israel to pass through the midst of it: for his mercy *endureth* for ever:

15But overthrew Pharaoh and his host in the Red sea: for his mercy *endureth* for ever.

16To him which led his people through the wilderness: for his mercy *endureth* for ever.

17To him which smote great kings: for his mercy *endureth* for ever:

18And slew famous kings: for his mercy *endureth* for ever:

19Sihon king of the Amorites: for his mercy *endureth* for ever:

20And Og the king of Bashan: for his mercy *endureth* for ever:

21And gave their land for an heritage: for his mercy *endureth* for ever:

22*Even* an heritage unto Israel his servant: for his mercy *endureth* for ever.

23Who remembered us in our low estate: for his mercy *endureth* for ever:

24And hath redeemed us from our enemies: for his mercy *endureth* for ever.

25Who giveth food to all flesh: for his mercy *endureth* for ever.

26O give thanks unto the God of heaven: for his mercy *endureth* for ever.

PROVERBS FOR TODAY/ 30:7–9

Two things have I required of thee; deny me them not before I die: Remove far from me vanity and lies: give me neither poverty nor riches; feed me with food convenient for me: Lest I be full, and deny thee, and say, Who is the LORD? or lest I be poor, and steal, and take the name of my God in vain.

DECEMBER 18

HABAKKUK 1:1—3:19

THE burden which Habakkuk the prophet did see.

2O LORD, how long shall I cry, and thou wilt not hear! *even* cry out unto thee *of* violence, and thou wilt not save!

3Why dost thou shew me iniquity, and cause *me* to behold grievance? for spoiling and violence *are* before me: and there are *that* raise up strife and contention.

4Therefore the law is slacked, and judgment doth never go forth: for the wicked doth compass about the righteous; therefore wrong judgment proceedeth.

5Behold ye among the heathen, and regard, and wonder marvellously: for *I* will work a work in your days, *which* ye will not believe, though it be told *you*.

6For, lo, I raise up the Chaldeans, *that* bitter and hasty nation, which shall march through the breadth of the land, to possess the dwellingplaces *that are* not theirs.

7They *are* terrible and dreadful: their judgment and their dignity shall proceed of themselves.

8Their horses also are swifter than the leopards, and are more fierce than the evening wolves: and their horsemen shall spread themselves, and their horsemen shall come from far; they shall fly as the eagle *that* hasteth to eat.

9They shall come all for violence: their faces shall sup up *as* the east wind, and they shall gather the captivity as the sand.

10And they shall scoff at the kings, and the princes shall be a scorn unto them: they shall deride every strong hold; for they shall heap dust, and take it.

11Then shall *his* mind change, and he shall pass over, and offend, *imputing* this his power unto his god.

12*Art* thou not from everlasting, O LORD my God, mine Holy One? we shall not die. O LORD, thou hast ordained them for judgment; and, O mighty God, thou hast established them for correction.

13*Thou art* of purer eyes than to behold evil, and canst not look on iniquity: wherefore lookest thou upon them that deal treacherously, *and* holdest thy tongue when the wicked devoureth *the man that is* more righteous than he?

14And makest men as the fishes of the sea, as the creeping things, *that have* no ruler over them?

15They take up all of them with the angle, they catch them in their net, and gather them in their drag: therefore they rejoice and are glad.

16Therefore they sacrifice unto their net, and burn incense unto their drag; because by them their portion *is* fat, and their meat plenteous.

17Shall they therefore empty their net, and not spare continually to slay the nations?

I WILL stand upon my watch, and set me upon the tower, and will watch to see what he will say unto me, and what I shall answer when I am reproved.

2And the LORD answered me, and said, Write the vision, and make *it* plain upon tables, that he may run that readeth it.

3For the vision *is* yet for an appointed time, but at the end it shall speak, and not lie: though it tarry, wait for it; because it will surely come, it will not tarry.

⁴Behold, his soul *which* is lifted up is not upright in him: but the just shall live by his faith.

⁵Yea also, because he transgresseth by wine, *he is* a proud man, neither keepeth at home, who enlargeth his desire as hell, and *is* as death, and cannot be satisfied, but gathereth unto him all nations, and heapeth unto him all people:

⁶Shall not all these take up a parable against him, and a taunting proverb against him, and say, Woe to him that increaseth *that which is* not his! how long? and to him that ladeth himself with thick clay!

⁷Shall they not rise up suddenly that shall bite thee, and awake that shall vex thee, and thou shalt be for booties unto them?

⁸Because thou hast spoiled many nations, all the remnant of the people shall spoil thee; because of men's blood, and *for* the violence of the land, of the city, and of all that dwell therein.

⁹Woe to him that coveteth an evil covetousness to his house, that he may set his nest on high, that he may be delivered from the power of evil!

¹⁰Thou hast consulted shame to thy house by cutting off many people, and hast sinned *against* thy soul.

¹¹For the stone shall cry out of the wall, and the beam out of the timber shall answer it.

¹²Woe to him that buildeth a town with blood, and stablisheth a city by iniquity!

¹³Behold, *is it* not of the LORD of hosts that the people shall labour in the very fire, and the people shall weary themselves for very vanity?

¹⁴For the earth shall be filled with the knowledge of the glory of the LORD, as the waters cover the sea.

¹⁵Woe unto him that giveth his neighbour drink, that puttest thy bottle to *him,* and makest *him* drunken also, that thou mayest look on their nakedness!

¹⁶Thou art filled with shame for glory: drink thou also, and let thy foreskin be uncovered: the cup of the LORD's right hand shall be turned unto thee, and shameful spewing *shall be* on thy glory.

¹⁷For the violence of Lebanon shall cover thee, and the spoil of beasts, *which* made them afraid, because of men's blood, and for the violence of the land, of the city, and of all that dwell therein.

¹⁸What profiteth the graven image that the maker thereof hath graven it; the molten image, and a teacher of lies, that the maker of his work trusteth therein, to make dumb idols?

¹⁹Woe unto him that saith to the wood, Awake; to the dumb stone, Arise, it shall teach! Behold, it *is* laid over with gold and silver, and *there is* no breath at all in the midst of it.

²⁰But the LORD *is* in his holy temple: let all the earth keep silence before him.

A PRAYER of Habakkuk the prophet upon Shigionoth.

²O LORD, I have heard thy speech, *and* was afraid: O LORD, revive thy work in the midst of the years, in the midst of the years make known; in wrath remember mercy.

³God came from Teman, and the Holy One from mount Paran. Selah. His glory covered the heavens, and the earth was full of his praise.

⁴And *his* brightness was as the light; he had horns *coming* out of his hand: and there *was* the hiding of his power.

⁵Before him went the pestilence, and burning coals went forth at his feet.

⁶He stood, and measured the earth: he beheld, and drove asunder the nations; and the everlasting mountains were scattered, the perpetual hills did bow: his ways *are* everlasting.

⁷I saw the tents of Cushan in affliction:

and the curtains of the land of Midian did tremble.

8Was the LORD displeased against the rivers? *was* thine anger against the rivers? *was* thy wrath against the sea, that thou didst ride upon thine horses *and* thy chariots of salvation?

9Thy bow was made quite naked, *according* to the oaths of the tribes, *even thy* word. Selah. Thou didst cleave the earth with rivers.

10The mountains saw thee, *and* they trembled: the overflowing of the water passed by: the deep uttered his voice, *and* lifted up his hands on high.

11The sun *and* moon stood still in their habitation: at the light of thine arrows they went, *and* at the shining of thy glittering spear.

12Thou didst march through the land in indignation, thou didst thresh the heathen in anger.

13Thou wentest forth for the salvation of thy people, *even* for salvation with thine anointed; thou woundedst the head out of the house of the wicked, by discovering the foundation unto the neck. Selah.

14Thou didst strike through with his staves the head of his villages: they came out as a whirlwind to scatter me: their rejoicing *was* as to devour the poor secretly.

15Thou didst walk through the sea with thine horses, *through* the heap of great waters.

16When I heard, my belly trembled; my lips quivered at the voice: rottenness entered into my bones, and I trembled in myself, that I might rest in the day of trouble: when he cometh up unto the people, he will invade them with his troops.

17Although the fig tree shall not blossom, neither *shall* fruit *be* in the vines; the labour of the olive shall fail, and the fields shall yield no meat; the flock shall be cut off from the fold, and *there shall be* no herd in the stalls:

18Yet I will rejoice in the LORD, I will joy in the God of my salvation.

19The LORD God *is* my strength, and he will make my feet like hinds' *feet,* and he will make me to walk upon mine high places. To the chief singer on my stringed instruments.

REVELATION 9:1–21

AND the fifth angel sounded, and I saw a star fall from heaven unto the earth: and to him was given the key of the bottomless pit.

2And he opened the bottomless pit; and there arose a smoke out of the pit, as the smoke of a great furnace; and the sun and the air were darkened by reason of the smoke of the pit.

3And there came out of the smoke locusts upon the earth: and unto them was given power, as the scorpions of the earth have power.

4And it was commanded them that they should not hurt the grass of the earth, neither any green thing, neither any tree; but only those men which have not the seal of God in their foreheads.

5And to them it was given that they should not kill them, but that they should be tormented five months: and their torment *was* as the torment of a scorpion, when he striketh a man.

6And in those days shall men seek death, and shall not find it; and shall desire to die, and death shall flee from them.

7And the shapes of the locusts *were* like unto horses prepared unto battle; and on their heads *were* as it were crowns like gold, and their faces *were* as the faces of men.

8And they had hair as the hair of women, and their teeth were as *the teeth* of lions.

9And they had breastplates, as it were breastplates of iron; and the sound of their wings *was* as the sound of chariots of many horses running to battle.

10And they had tails like unto

scorpions, and there were stings in their tails: and their power *was* to hurt men five months.

11And they had a king over them, *which is* the angel of the bottomless pit, whose name in the Hebrew tongue *is* Abaddon, but in the Greek tongue hath *his* name Apollyon.

12One woe is past; *and,* behold, there come two woes more hereafter.

13And the sixth angel sounded, and I heard a voice from the four horns of the golden altar which is before God,

14Saying to the sixth angel which had the trumpet, Loose the four angels which are bound in the great river Euphrates.

15And the four angels were loosed, which were prepared for an hour, and a day, and a month, and a year, for to slay the third part of men.

16And the number of the army of the horsemen *were* two hundred thousand thousand: and I heard the number of them.

17And thus I saw the horses in the vision, and them that sat on them, having breastplates of fire, and of jacinth, and brimstone: and the heads of the horses *were* as the heads of lions; and out of their mouths issued fire and smoke and brimstone.

18By these three was the third part of men killed, by the fire, and by the smoke, and by the brimstone, which issued out of their mouths.

19For their power is in their mouth, and in their tails: for their tails *were* like unto serpents, and had heads, and with them they do hurt.

20And the rest of the men which were not killed by these plagues yet repented not of the works of their hands, that they should not worship devils, and idols of gold, and silver, and brass, and stone, and of wood: which neither can see, nor hear, nor walk:

21Neither repented they of their murders, nor of their sorceries, nor of their fornication, nor of their thefts.

PSALM 137:1–9

BY the rivers of Babylon, there we sat down, yea, we wept, when we remembered Zion.

2We hanged our harps upon the willows in the midst thereof.

3For there they that carried us away captive required of us a song; and they that wasted us *required of us* mirth, *saying,* Sing us *one* of the songs of Zion.

4How shall we sing the LORD'S song in a strange land?

5If I forget thee, O Jerusalem, let my right hand forget *her cunning.*

6If I do not remember thee, let my tongue cleave to the roof of my mouth; if I prefer not Jerusalem above my chief joy.

7Remember, O LORD, the children of Edom in the day of Jerusalem; who said, Rase *it,* rase *it, even* to the foundation thereof.

8O daughter of Babylon, who art to be destroyed; happy *shall he be,* that rewardeth thee as thou hast served us.

9Happy *shall he be,* that taketh and dasheth thy little ones against the stones.

PROVERBS FOR TODAY/ 30:10

Accuse not a servant unto his master, lest he curse thee, and thou be found guilty.

DECEMBER 19

ZEPHANIAH 1:1—3:20

THE word of the LORD which came unto Zephaniah the son of Cushi, the son of Gedaliah, the son of Amariah, the son of Hizkiah, in the days of Josiah the son of Amon, king of Judah.

2I will utterly consume all *things* from off the land, saith the LORD.

3I will consume man and beast; I will consume the fowls of the heaven, and the fishes of the sea, and the stumblingblocks with the wicked; and I will cut off man from off the land, saith the LORD.

4I will also stretch out mine hand upon Judah, and upon all the inhabitants of Jerusalem; and I will cut off the remnant of Baal from this place, *and* the name of the Chemarims with the priests;

5And them that worship the host of heaven upon the housetops; and them that worship *and* that swear by the LORD, and that swear by Malcham;

6And them that are turned back from the LORD; and *those* that have not sought the LORD, nor enquired for him.

7Hold thy peace at the presence of the Lord GOD: for the day of the LORD *is* at hand: for the LORD hath prepared a sacrifice, he hath bid his guests.

8And it shall come to pass in the day of the LORD'S sacrifice, that I will punish the princes, and the king's children, and all such as are clothed with strange apparel.

9In the same day also will I punish all those that leap on the threshold, which fill their masters' houses with violence and deceit.

10And it shall come to pass in that day, saith the LORD, *that there shall be* the noise of a cry from the fish gate, and an howling from the second, and a great crashing from the hills.

11Howl, ye inhabitants of Maktesh, for all the merchant people are cut down; all they that bear silver are cut off.

12And it shall come to pass at that time, *that* I will search Jerusalem with candles, and punish the men that are settled on their lees: that say in their heart, The LORD will not do good, neither will he do evil.

13Therefore their goods shall become a booty, and their houses a desolation: they shall also build houses, but not inhabit *them;* and they shall plant vineyards, but not drink the wine thereof.

14The great day of the LORD *is* near, *it is* near, and hasteth greatly, *even* the voice of the day of the LORD: the mighty man shall cry there bitterly.

15That day *is* a day of wrath, a day of trouble and distress, a day of wasteness and desolation, a day of darkness and gloominess, a day of clouds and thick darkness,

16A day of the trumpet and alarm against the fenced cities, and against the high towers.

17And I will bring distress upon men, that they shall walk like blind men, because they have sinned against the LORD: and their blood shall be poured out as dust, and their flesh as the dung.

18Neither their silver nor their gold shall be able to deliver them in the day of the LORD'S wrath; but the whole land shall be devoured by the fire of his jealousy: for he shall make even a speedy riddance of all them that dwell in the land.

GATHER yourselves together, yea, gather together, O nation not desired;

2Before the decree bring forth, *before* the day pass as the chaff, before the fierce anger of the LORD come upon you, before the day of the LORD's anger come upon you.

3Seek ye the LORD, all ye meek of the earth, which have wrought his judgment; seek righteousness, seek meekness: it may be ye shall be hid in the day of the LORD's anger.

4For Gaza shall be forsaken, and Ashkelon a desolation: they shall drive out Ashdod at the noon day, and Ekron shall be rooted up.

5Woe unto the inhabitants of the sea coast, the nation of the Cherethites! the word of the LORD is against you; O Canaan, the land of the Philistines, I will even destroy thee, that there shall be no inhabitant.

6And the sea coast shall be dwellings and cottages for shepherds, and folds for flocks.

7And the coast shall be for the remnant of the house of Judah; they shall feed thereupon: in the houses of Ashkelon shall they lie down in the evening: for the LORD their God shall visit them and turn away their captivity.

8I have heard the reproach of Moab, and the revilings of the children of Ammon, whereby they have reproached my people, and magnified themselves against their border.

9Therefore as I live, saith the LORD of hosts, the God of Israel, Surely Moab shall be as Sodom, and the children of Ammon as Gomorrah, even the breeding of nettles, and saltpits, and a perpetual desolation: the residue of my people shall spoil them, and the remnant of my people shall possess them.

10This shall they have for their pride, because they have reproached and magnified themselves against the people of the LORD of hosts.

11The LORD will be terrible unto them: for he will famish all the gods of the earth; and men shall worship him, every one from his place, even all the isles of the heathen.

12Ye Ethiopians also, ye shall be slain by my sword.

13And he will stretch out his hand against the north, and destroy Assyria; and will make Nineveh a desolation, and dry like a wilderness.

14And flocks shall lie down in the midst of her, all the beasts of the nations: both the cormorant and the bittern shall lodge in the upper lintels of it; their voice shall sing in the windows; desolation shall be in the thresholds: for he shall uncover the cedar work.

15This is the rejoicing city that dwelt carelessly, that said in her heart, I am, and there is none beside me: how is she become a desolation, a place for beasts to lie down in! every one that passeth by her shall hiss, and wag his hand.

WOE to her that is filthy and polluted, to the oppressing city!

2She obeyed not the voice; she received not correction; she trusted not in the LORD; she drew not near to her God.

3Her princes within her are roaring lions; her judges are evening wolves; they gnaw not the bones till the morrow.

4Her prophets are light and treacherous persons: her priests have polluted the sanctuary, they have done violence to the law.

5The just LORD is in the midst thereof; he will not do iniquity: every morning doth he bring his judgment to light, he faileth not; but the unjust knoweth no shame.

6I have cut off the nations: their towers are desolate; I made their streets waste, that none passeth by: their cities are destroyed, so that there is no man, that there is none inhabitant.

7I said, Surely thou wilt fear me, thou wilt receive instruction; so their dwelling should not be cut off, howsoever I punished them: but they rose early, and corrupted all their doings.

8Therefore wait ye upon me, saith

the LORD, until the day that I rise up to the prey: for my determination *is* to gather the nations, that I may assemble the kingdoms, to pour upon them mine indignation, *even* all my fierce anger: for all the earth shall be devoured with the fire of my jealousy.

9For then will I turn to the people a pure language, that they may all call upon the name of the LORD, to serve him with one consent.

10From beyond the rivers of Ethiopia my suppliants, *even* the daughter of my dispersed, shall bring mine offering.

11In that day shalt thou not be ashamed for all thy doings, wherein thou hast transgressed against me: for then I will take away out of the midst of thee them that rejoice in thy pride, and thou shalt no more be haughty because of my holy mountain.

12I will also leave in the midst of thee an afflicted and poor people, and they shall trust in the name of the LORD.

13The remnant of Israel shall not do iniquity, nor speak lies; neither shall a deceitful tongue be found in their mouth: for they shall feed and lie down, and none shall make *them* afraid.

14Sing, O daughter of Zion; shout, O Israel; be glad and rejoice with all thy heart, O daughter of Jerusalem.

15The LORD hath taken away thy judgments, he hath cast out thine enemy: the king of Israel, *even* the LORD, *is* in the midst of thee: thou shalt not see evil any more.

16In that day it shall be said to Jerusalem, Fear thou not: *and to* Zion, Let not thine hands be slack.

17The LORD thy God in the midst of thee *is* mighty; he will save, he will rejoice over thee with joy; he will rest in his love, he will joy over thee with singing.

18I will gather *them that are* sorrowful for the solemn assembly, *who* are of thee, *to whom* the reproach of it *was* a burden.

19Behold, at that time I will undo all that afflict thee: and I will save her that halteth, and gather her that was driven out; and I will get them praise and fame in every land where they have been put to shame.

20At that time will I bring you *again,* even in the time that I gather you: for I will make you a name and a praise among all people of the earth, when I turn back your captivity before your eyes, saith the LORD.

REVELATION 10:1–11

AND I saw another mighty angel come down from heaven, clothed with a cloud: and a rainbow *was* upon his head, and his face *was* as it were the sun, and his feet as pillars of fire:

2And he had in his hand a little book open: and he set his right foot upon the sea, and *his* left *foot* on the earth,

3And cried with a loud voice, as *when* a lion roareth: and when he had cried, seven thunders uttered their voices.

4And when the seven thunders had uttered their voices, I was about to write: and I heard a voice from heaven saying unto me, Seal up those things which the seven thunders uttered, and write them not.

5And the angel which I saw stand upon the sea and upon the earth lifted up his hand to heaven,

6And sware by him that liveth for ever and ever, who created heaven, and the things that therein are, and the earth, and the things that therein are, and the sea, and the things which are therein, that there should be time no longer:

7But in the days of the voice of the seventh angel, when he shall begin to sound, the mystery of God should be finished, as he hath declared to his servants the prophets.

8And the voice which I heard from heaven spake unto me again, and said, Go *and* take the little book which is open in the hand of the angel which standeth upon the sea and upon the earth.

9And I went unto the angel, and said unto him, Give me the little book. And he said unto me, Take *it,* and eat it up; and it shall make thy belly bitter, but it shall be in thy mouth sweet as honey.

10And I took the little book out of the angel's hand, and ate it up; and it was in my mouth sweet as honey: and as soon as I had eaten it, my belly was bitter.

11And he said unto me, Thou must prophesy again before many peoples, and nations, and tongues, and kings.

PSALM 138:1–8

I WILL praise thee with my whole heart: before the gods will I sing praise unto thee.

2I will worship toward thy holy tem-ple, and praise thy name for thy loving-kindness and for thy truth: for thou hast magnified thy word above all thy name.

3In the day when I cried thou answeredst me, *and* strengthenedst me *with* strength in my soul.

4All the kings of the earth shall praise thee, O LORD, when they hear the words of thy mouth.

5Yea, they shall sing in the ways of the LORD: for great *is* the glory of the LORD.

6Though the LORD *be* high, yet hath he respect unto the lowly: but the proud he knoweth afar off.

7Though I walk in the midst of trouble, thou wilt revive me: thou shalt stretch forth thine hand against the wrath of mine enemies, and thy right hand shall save me.

8The LORD will perfect *that which* concerneth me: thy mercy, O LORD, *endureth* for ever: forsake not the works of thine own hands.

PROVERBS FOR TODAY/ 30:11–14

There is *a generation* that *curseth their father, and doth not bless their mother.* There is *a generation* that are *pure in their own eyes, and* yet *is not washed from their filthiness.* There is *a generation, O how lofty are their eyes! and their eyelids are lifted up.* There is *a generation, whose teeth* are as *swords, and their jaw teeth* as *knives, to devour the poor from off the earth, and the needy from* among *men.*

DECEMBER 20

HAGGAI 1:1—2:23

I N the second year of Darius the king, in the sixth month, in the first day of the month, came the word of the LORD by Haggai the prophet unto Zerubbabel the son of Shealtiel, governor of Judah, and to Joshua the son of Josedech, the high priest, saying,

2Thus speaketh the LORD of hosts, saying, This people say, The time is not come, the time that the LORD'S house should be built.

3Then came the word of the LORD by Haggai the prophet, saying,

⁴*Is it* time for you, O ye, to dwell in your cieled houses, and this house *lie* waste?

⁵Now therefore thus saith the LORD of hosts; Consider your ways.

⁶Ye have sown much, and bring in little; ye eat, but ye have not enough; ye drink, but ye are not filled with drink; ye clothe you, but there is none warm; and he that earneth wages earneth wages *to put it* into a bag with holes.

⁷Thus saith the LORD of hosts; Consider your ways.

⁸Go up to the mountain, and bring wood, and build the house; and I will take pleasure in it, and I will be glorified, saith the LORD.

⁹Ye looked for much, and lo, *it came* to little; and when ye brought *it* home, I did blow upon it. Why? saith the LORD of hosts. Because of mine house that *is* waste, and ye run every man unto his own house.

¹⁰Therefore the heaven over you is stayed from dew, and the earth is stayed *from* her fruit.

¹¹And I called for a drought upon the land, and upon the mountains, and upon the corn, and upon the new wine, and upon the oil, and upon *that* which the ground bringeth forth, and upon men, and upon cattle, and upon all the labour of the hands.

¹²Then Zerubbabel the son of Shealtiel, and Joshua the son of Josedech, the high priest, with all the remnant of the people, obeyed the voice of the LORD their God, and the words of Haggai the prophet, as the LORD their God had sent him, and the people did fear before the LORD.

¹³Then spake Haggai the LORD's messenger in the LORD's message unto the people, saying, I *am* with you, saith the LORD.

¹⁴And the LORD stirred up the spirit of Zerubbabel the son of Shealtiel, governor of Judah, and the spirit of Joshua the son of Josedech, the high priest, and the spirit of all the remnant of the people; and they came and did work in the house of the LORD of hosts, their God,

¹⁵In the four and twentieth day of the sixth month, in the second year of Darius the king.

IN the seventh *month,* in the one and twentieth *day* of the month, came the word of the LORD by the prophet Haggai, saying,

²Speak now to Zerubbabel the son of Shealtiel, governor of Judah, and to Joshua the son of Josedech, the high priest, and to the residue of the people, saying,

³Who *is* left among you that saw this house in her first glory? and how do ye see it now? *is it* not in your eyes in comparison of it as nothing?

⁴Yet now be strong, O Zerubbabel, saith the LORD; and be strong, O Joshua, son of Josedech, the high priest; and be strong, all ye people of the land, saith the LORD, and work: for I *am* with you, saith the LORD of hosts:

⁵*According to* the word that I covenanted with you when ye came out of Egypt, so my spirit remaineth among you: fear ye not.

⁶For thus saith the LORD of hosts; Yet once, it *is* a little while, and I will shake the heavens, and the earth, and the sea, and the dry *land;*

⁷And I will shake all nations, and the desire of all nations shall come: and I will fill this house with glory, saith the LORD of hosts.

⁸The silver *is* mine, and the gold *is* mine, saith the LORD of hosts.

⁹The glory of this latter house shall be greater than of the former, saith the LORD of hosts: and in this place will I give peace, saith the LORD of hosts.

¹⁰In the four and twentieth *day* of the ninth *month,* in the second year of Darius, came the word of the LORD by Haggai the prophet, saying,

¹¹Thus saith the LORD of hosts; Ask

now the priests *concerning* the law, saying,

12If one bear holy flesh in the skirt of his garment, and with his skirt do touch bread, or pottage, or wine, or oil, or any meat, shall it be holy? And the priests answered and said, No.

13Then said Haggai, if *one that is* unclean by a dead body touch any of these, shall it be unclean? And the priests answered and said, It shall be unclean.

14Then answered Haggai, and said, So *is* this people, and so *is* this nation before me, saith the LORD; and so *is* every work of their hands; and that which they offer there *is* unclean.

15And now, I pray you, consider from this day and upward, from before a stone was laid upon a stone in the temple of the LORD:

16Since those *days* were, when *one* came to an heap of twenty *measures,* there were *but* ten: when *one* came to the pressfat for to draw out fifty *vessels* out of the press, there were *but* twenty.

17I smote you with blasting and with mildew and with hail in all the labours of your hands; yet ye *turned* not to me, saith the LORD.

18Consider now from this day and upward, from the four and twentieth day of the ninth *month, even* from the day that the foundation of the LORD'S temple was laid, consider *it.*

19Is the seed yet in the barn? yea, as yet the vine, and the fig tree, and the pomegranate, and the olive tree, hath not brought forth: from this day will I bless *you.*

20And again the word of the LORD came unto Haggai in the four and twentieth *day* of the month, saying,

21Speak to Zerubbabel, governor of Judah, saying, I will shake the heavens and the earth;

22And I will overthrow the throne of kingdoms, and I will destroy the strength of the kingdoms of the heathen; and I will overthrow the chariots, and those that ride in them; and the horses and their riders shall come down, every one by the sword of his brother.

23In that day, saith the LORD of hosts, will I take thee, O Zerubbabel, my servant, the son of Shealtiel, saith the LORD, and will make thee as a signet: for I have chosen thee, saith the LORD of hosts.

REVELATION 11:1–19

AND there was given me a reed like unto a rod: and the angel stood, saying, Rise, and measure the temple of God, and the altar, and them that worship therein.

2But the court which is without the temple leave out, and measure it not; for it is given unto the Gentiles: and the holy city shall they tread under foot forty and two months.

3And I will give *power* unto my two witnesses, and they shall prophesy a thousand two hundred *and* threescore days, clothed in sackcloth.

4These are the two olive trees, and the two candlesticks standing before the God of the earth.

5And if any man will hurt them, fire proceedeth out of their mouth, and devoureth their enemies: and if any man will hurt them, he must in this manner be killed.

6These have power to shut heaven, that it rain not in the days of their prophecy: and have power over waters to turn them to blood, and to smite the earth with all plagues, as often as they will.

7And when they shall have finished their testimony, the beast that ascendeth out of the bottomless pit shall make war against them, and shall overcome them, and kill them.

8And their dead bodies *shall lie* in the street of the great city, which spiritually is called Sodom and Egypt, where also our Lord was crucified.

9And they of the people and kindreds and tongues and nations shall see their dead bodies three days and an half, and shall not suffer their dead bodies to be put in graves.

10And they that dwell upon the earth shall rejoice over them, and make merry, and shall send gifts one to another; because these two prophets tormented them that dwelt on the earth.

11And after three days and an half the Spirit of life from God entered into them, and they stood upon their feet; and great fear fell upon them which saw them.

12And they heard a great voice from heaven saying unto them, Come up hither. And they ascended up to heaven in a cloud; and their enemies beheld them.

13And the same hour was there a great earthquake, and the tenth part of the city fell, and in the earthquake were slain of men seven thousand: and the remnant were affrighted, and gave glory to the God of heaven.

14The second woe is past; *and,* behold, the third woe cometh quickly.

15And the seventh angel sounded; and there were great voices in heaven, saying, The kingdoms of this world are become *the kingdoms* of our Lord, and of his Christ; and he shall reign for ever and ever.

16And the four and twenty elders, which sat before God on their seats, fell upon their faces, and worshipped God,

17Saying, We give thee thanks, O Lord God Almighty, which art, and wast, and art to come; because thou hast taken to thee thy great power, and hast reigned.

18And the nations were angry, and thy wrath is come, and the time of the dead, that they should be judged, and that thou shouldest give reward unto thy servants the prophets, and to the saints, and them that fear thy name, small and great; and shouldest

destroy them which destroy the earth.

19And the temple of God was opened in heaven, and there was seen in his temple the ark of his testament: and there were lightnings, and voices, and thunderings, and an earthquake, and great hail.

PSALM 139:1–24

O LORD, thou hast searched me, and known *me.*

2Thou knowest my downsitting and mine uprising, thou understandest my thought afar off.

3Thou compassest my path and my lying down, and art acquainted *with* all my ways.

4For *there is* not a word in my tongue, *but,* lo, O LORD, thou knowest it altogether.

5Thou hast beset me behind and before, and laid thine hand upon me.

6*Such* knowledge *is* too wonderful for me; it is high, I cannot *attain* unto it.

7Whither shall I go from thy spirit? or whither shall I flee from thy presence?

8If I ascend up into heaven, thou *art* there: if I make my bed in hell, behold, thou *art there.*

9*If* I take the wings of the morning, *and* dwell in the uttermost parts of the sea;

10Even there shall thy hand lead me, and thy right hand shall hold me.

11If I say, Surely the darkness shall cover me; even the night shall be light about me.

12Yea, the darkness hideth not from thee; but the night shineth as the day: the darkness and the light *are* both alike *to thee.*

13For thou hast possessed my reins: thou hast covered me in my mother's womb.

14I will praise thee; for I am fearfully *and* wonderfully made: marvellous *are* thy works; and *that* my soul knoweth right well.

15My substance was not hid from thee, when I was made in secret, *and* curiously wrought in the lowest parts of the earth.

16Thine eyes did see my substance, yet being unperfect; and in thy book all *my members* were written, *which* in continuance were fashioned, when *as yet there was* none of them.

17How precious also are thy thoughts unto me, O God! how great is the sum of them!

18*If* I should count them, they are more in number than the sand: when I awake, I am still with thee.

19Surely thou wilt slay the wicked, O God: depart from me therefore, ye bloody men.

20For they speak against thee wickedly, *and* thine enemies take *thy name* in vain.

21Do not I hate them, O LORD, that hate thee? and am not I grieved with those that rise up against thee?

22I hate them with perfect hatred: I count them mine enemies.

23Search me, O God, and know my heart: try me, and know my thoughts:

24And see if *there be any* wicked way in me, and lead me in the way everlasting.

PROVERBS FOR TODAY/ 30:15–16

The horseleach hath two daughters, crying, *Give, give. There are three* things that *are never satisfied,* yea, *four* things *say not,* It is *enough: The grave; and the barren womb; the earth* that is *not filled with water; and the fire* that *saith not,* It is *enough.*

DECEMBER 21

ZECHARIAH 1:1–21

IN the eighth month, in the second year of Darius, came the word of the LORD unto Zechariah, the son of Berechiah, the son of Iddo the prophet, saying,

2The LORD hath been sore displeased with your fathers.

3Therefore say thou unto them, Thus saith the LORD of hosts; Turn ye unto me, saith the LORD of hosts, and I will turn unto you, saith the LORD of hosts.

4Be ye not as your fathers, unto whom the former prophets have cried, saying, Thus saith the LORD of hosts; Turn ye now from your evil ways, and *from* your evil doings: but they did not

hear, nor hearken unto me, saith the LORD.

5Your fathers, where *are* they? and the prophets, do they live for ever?

6But my words and my statutes, which I commanded my servants the prophets, did they not take hold of your fathers? and they returned and said, Like as the LORD of hosts thought to do unto us, according to our ways, and according to our doings, so hath he dealt with us.

7Upon the four and twentieth day of the eleventh month, which *is* the month Sebat, in the second year of Darius, came the word of the LORD unto Zechariah, the son of Berechiah, the son of Iddo the prophet, saying,

8I saw by night, and behold a man riding upon a red horse, and he stood among the myrtle trees that *were* in the bottom; and behind him *were there* red horses, speckled, and white.

9Then said I, O my lord, what *are* these? And the angel that talked with me said unto me, I will shew thee what these *be.*

10And the man that stood among the myrtle trees answered and said, These *are they* whom the LORD hath sent to walk to and fro through the earth.

11And they answered the angel of the LORD that stood among the myrtle trees, and said, We have walked to and fro through the earth, and, behold, all the earth sitteth still, and is at rest.

12Then the angel of the LORD answered and said, O LORD of hosts, how long wilt thou not have mercy on Jerusalem and on the cities of Judah, against which thou hast had indignation these threescore and ten years?

13And the LORD answered the angel that talked with me *with* good words *and* comfortable words.

14So the angel that communed with me said unto me, Cry thou, saying, Thus saith the LORD of hosts; I am jealous for Jerusalem and for Zion with a great jealousy.

15And I am very sore displeased with the heathen *that are* at ease: for I was but a little displeased, and they helped forward the affliction.

16Therefore thus saith the LORD; I am returned to Jerusalem with mercies: my house shall be built in it, saith the LORD of hosts, and a line shall be stretched forth upon Jerusalem.

17Cry yet, saying, Thus saith the LORD of hosts; My cities through prosperity shall yet be spread abroad; and the LORD shall yet comfort Zion, and shall yet choose Jerusalem.

18Then lifted I up mine eyes, and saw, and behold four horns.

19And I said unto the angel that talked with me, What *be* these? And he answered me, These *are* the horns which have scattered Judah, Israel, and Jerusalem.

20And the LORD shewed me four carpenters.

21Then said I, What come these to do? And he spake, saying, These *are* the horns which have scattered Judah, so that no man did lift up his head: but these are come to fray them, to cast out the horns of the Gentiles, which lifted up *their* horn over the land of Judah to scatter it.

REVELATION 12:1–17

AND there appeared a great wonder in heaven; a woman clothed with the sun, and the moon under her feet, and upon her head a crown of twelve stars:

2And she being with child cried, travailing in birth, and pained to be delivered.

3And there appeared another wonder in heaven; and behold a great red dragon, having seven heads and ten horns, and seven crowns upon his heads.

4And his tail drew the third part of the stars of heaven, and did cast them to the earth: and the dragon stood before the woman which was ready to be delivered, for to devour her child as soon as it was born.

5And she brought forth a man child, who was to rule all nations with a rod of iron: and her child was caught up unto God, and *to* his throne.

6And the woman fled into the wilderness, where she hath a place prepared of God, that they should feed her there a thousand two hundred *and* threescore days.

7And there was war in heaven: Michael and his angels fought against the dragon; and the dragon fought and his angels,

8And prevailed not; neither was their

place found any more in heaven.

9And the great dragon was cast out, that old serpent, called the Devil, and Satan, which deceiveth the whole world: he was cast out into the earth, and his angels were cast out with him.

10And I heard a loud voice saying in heaven, Now is come salvation, and strength, and the kingdom of our God, and the power of his Christ: for the accuser of our brethren is cast down, which accused them before our God day and night.

11And they overcame him by the blood of the Lamb, and by the word of their testimony; and they loved not their lives unto the death.

12Therefore rejoice, *ye* heavens, and ye that dwell in them. Woe to the inhabitants of the earth and of the sea! for the devil is come down unto you, having great wrath, because he knoweth that he hath but a short time.

13And when the dragon saw that he was cast unto the earth, he persecuted the woman which brought forth the man *child.*

14And to the woman were given two wings of a great eagle, that she might fly into the wilderness, into her place, where she is nourished for a time, and times, and half a time, from the face of the serpent.

15And the serpent cast out of his mouth water as a flood after the woman, that he might cause her to be carried away of the flood.

16And the earth helped the woman, and the earth opened her mouth, and swallowed up the flood which the dragon cast out of his mouth.

17And the dragon was wroth with the woman, and went to make war with the remnant of her seed, which keep the commandments of God,

and have the testimony of Jesus Christ.

PSALM 140:1–13

DELIVER me, O LORD, from the evil man: preserve me from the violent man;

2Which imagine mischiefs in *their* heart; continually are they gathered together *for* war.

3They have sharpened their tongues like a serpent; adders' poison *is* under their lips. Selah.

4Keep me, O LORD, from the hands of the wicked; preserve me from the violent man; who have purposed to overthrow my goings.

5The proud have hid a snare for me, and cords; they have spread a net by the wayside; they have set gins for me. Selah.

6I said unto the LORD, Thou *art* my God: hear the voice of my supplications, O LORD.

7O GOD the Lord, the strength of my salvation, thou hast covered my head in the day of battle.

8Grant not, O LORD, the desires of the wicked: further not his wicked device; *lest* they exalt themselves. Selah.

9*As for* the head of those that compass me about, let the mischief of their own lips cover them.

10Let burning coals fall upon them: let them be cast into the fire; into deep pits, that they rise not up again.

11Let not an evil speaker be established in the earth: evil shall hunt the violent man to overthrow *him.*

12I know that the LORD will maintain the cause of the afflicted, *and* the right of the poor.

13Surely the righteous shall give thanks unto thy name: the upright shall dwell in thy presence.

PROVERBS FOR TODAY/ 30:17

The eye that mocketh at his father, and despiseth to obey his mother, the ravens of the valley shall pick it out, and the young eagles shall eat it.

DECEMBER 22

ZECHARIAH 2:1—3:10

I LIFTED up mine eyes again, and looked, and behold a man with a measuring line in his hand.

2Then said I, Whither goest thou? And he said unto me, To measure Jerusalem, to see what *is* the breadth thereof, and what *is* the length thereof.

3And, behold, the angel that talked with me went forth, and another angel went out to meet him,

4And said unto him, Run, speak to this young man, saying, Jerusalem shall be inhabited *as* towns without walls for the multitude of men and cattle therein:

5For I, saith the LORD, will be unto her a wall of fire round about, and will be the glory in the midst of her.

6Ho, ho, *come forth,* and flee from the land of the north, saith the LORD: for I have spread you abroad as the four winds of the heaven, saith the LORD.

7Deliver thyself, O Zion, that dwellest *with* the daughter of Babylon.

8For thus saith the LORD of hosts; After the glory hath he sent me unto the nations which spoiled you: for he that toucheth you toucheth the apple of his eye.

9For, behold, I will shake mine hand upon them, and they shall be a spoil to their servants: and ye shall know that the LORD of hosts hath sent me.

10Sing and rejoice, O daughter of Zion: for, lo, I come, and I will dwell in the midst of thee, saith the LORD.

11And many nations shall be joined to the LORD in that day, and shall be my people: and I will dwell in the midst of thee, and thou shalt know that the LORD of hosts hath sent me unto thee.

12And the LORD shall inherit Judah his portion in the holy land, and shall choose Jerusalem again.

13Be silent, O all flesh, before the LORD: for he is raised up out of his holy habitation.

AND he shewed me Joshua the high priest standing before the angel of the LORD, and Satan standing at his right hand to resist him.

2And the LORD said unto Satan, The LORD rebuke thee, O Satan; even the LORD that hath chosen Jerusalem rebuke thee: *is* not this a brand plucked out of the fire?

3Now Joshua was clothed with filthy garments, and stood before the angel.

4And he answered and spake unto those that stood before him, saying, Take away the filthy garments from him. And unto him he said, Behold, I have caused thine iniquity to pass from thee, and I will clothe thee with change of raiment.

5And I said, Let them set a fair mitre upon his head. So they set a fair mitre upon his head, and clothed him with garments. And the angel of the LORD stood by.

6And the angel of the LORD protested unto Joshua, saying,

7Thus saith the LORD of hosts; If thou wilt walk in my ways, and if thou wilt keep my charge, then thou shalt also judge my house, and shalt also keep my courts, and I will give thee places to walk among these that stand by.

8Hear now, O Joshua the high priest, thou, and thy fellows that sit before thee: for they *are* men wondered at: for, behold, I will bring forth my servant the BRANCH.

9For behold the stone that I have laid before Joshua; upon one stone *shall be* seven eyes: behold, I will engrave the graving thereof, saith the LORD of hosts, and I will remove the iniquity of that land in one day.

10In that day, saith the LORD of hosts, shall ye call every man his neighbour under the vine and under the fig tree.

REVELATION 13:1–18

AND I stood upon the sand of the sea, and saw a beast rise up out of the sea, having seven heads and ten horns, and upon his horns ten crowns, and upon his heads the name of blasphemy.

2And the beast which I saw was like unto a leopard, and his feet were as *the feet* of a bear, and his mouth as the mouth of a lion: and the dragon gave him his power, and his seat, and great authority.

3And I saw one of his heads as it were wounded to death; and his deadly wound was healed: and all the world wondered after the beast.

4And they worshipped the dragon which gave power unto the beast: and they worshipped the beast, saying, Who *is* like unto the beast? who is able to make war with him?

5And there was given unto him a mouth speaking great things and blasphemies; and power was given unto him to continue forty *and* two months.

6And he opened his mouth in blasphemy against God, to blaspheme his name, and his tabernacle, and them that dwell in heaven.

7And it was given unto him to make war with the saints, and to overcome them: and power was given him over all kindreds, and tongues, and nations.

8And all that dwell upon the earth shall worship him, whose names are not written in the book of life of the Lamb slain from the foundation of the world.

9If any man have an ear, let him hear.

10He that leadeth into captivity shall go into captivity: he that killeth with the sword must be killed with the sword. Here is the patience and the faith of the saints.

11And I beheld another beast coming up out of the earth; and he had two horns like a lamb, and he spake as a dragon.

12And he exerciseth all the power of the first beast before him, and causeth the earth and them which dwell therein to worship the first beast, whose deadly wound was healed.

13And he doeth great wonders, so that he maketh fire come down from heaven on the earth in the sight of men,

14And deceiveth them that dwell on the earth by *the means of* those miracles which he had power to do in the sight of the beast; saying to them that dwell on the earth, that they should make an image to the beast, which had the wound by a sword, and did live.

15And he had power to give life unto the image of the beast, that the image of the beast should both speak, and cause that as many as would not worship the image of the beast should be killed.

16And he causeth all, both small and great, rich and poor, free and bond, to receive a mark in their right hand, or in their foreheads:

17And that no man might buy or sell, save he that had the mark, or the name of the beast, or the number of his name.

18Here is wisdom. Let him that hath understanding count the number of the beast: for it is the number of a man; and his number *is* Six hundred threescore *and* six.

PSALM 141:1–10

LORD, I cry unto thee: make haste unto me; give ear unto my voice, when I cry unto thee.

2Let my prayer be set forth before thee *as* incense; *and* the lifting up of my hands *as* the evening sacrifice.

3Set a watch, O LORD, before my mouth; keep the door of my lips.

4Incline not my heart to *any* evil thing,

to practise wicked works with men that work iniquity: and let me not eat of their dainties.

5Let the righteous smite me; *it shall be* a kindness: and let him reprove me; *it shall be* an excellent oil, *which* shall not break my head: for yet my prayer also *shall be* in their calamities.

6When their judges are overthrown in stony places, they shall hear my words; for they are sweet.

7Our bones are scattered at the grave's mouth, as when one cutteth and cleaveth *wood* upon the earth.

8But mine eyes *are* unto thee, O GOD the Lord: in thee is my trust; leave not my soul destitute.

9Keep me from the snares *which* they have laid for me, and the gins of the workers of iniquity.

10Let the wicked fall into their own nets, whilst that I withal escape.

PROVERBS FOR TODAY/ 30:18–20

There be three things which *are too wonderful for me, yea, four which I know not: The way of an eagle in the air; the way of a serpent upon a rock; the way of a ship in the midst of the sea; and the way of a man with a maid.* □ *Such* is *the way of an adulterous woman; she eateth, and wipeth her mouth, and saith, I have done no wickedness.*

DECEMBER 23

ZECHARIAH 4:1—5:11

AND the angel that talked with me came again, and waked me, as a man that is wakened out of his sleep,

2And said unto me, What seest thou? And I said, I have looked, and behold a candlestick all *of* gold, with a bowl upon the top of it, and his seven lamps thereon, and seven pipes to the seven lamps, which *are* upon the top thereof:

3And two olive trees by it, one upon the right *side* of the bowl, and the other upon the left *side* thereof.

4So I answered and spake to the angel that talked with me, saying, What *are* these, my lord?

5Then the angel that talked with me answered and said unto me, Knowest thou not what these be? And I said, No, my lord.

6Then he answered and spake unto me, saying, This *is* the word of the LORD unto Zerubbabel, saying, Not by might, nor by power, but by my spirit, saith the LORD of hosts.

7Who *art* thou, O great mountain? before Zerubbabel *thou shalt become* a plain: and he shall bring forth the headstone *thereof with* shoutings, *crying,* Grace, grace unto it.

8Moreover the word of the LORD came unto me, saying,

9The hands of Zerubbabel have laid the foundation of this house; his hands shall also finish it; and thou shalt know that the LORD of hosts hath sent me unto you.

10For who hath despised the day of small things? for they shall rejoice, and shall see the plummet in the hand of Zerubbabel *with* those seven; they *are* the eyes of the LORD, which run to and fro through the whole earth.

11Then answered I, and said unto him, What *are* these two olive trees upon the right *side* of the candlestick and upon the left *side* thereof?

12And I answered again, and said unto him, What *be these* two olive branches which through the two golden pipes empty the golden *oil* out of themselves?

13And he answered me and said, Knowest thou not what these *be?* And I said, No, my lord.

14Then said he, These *are* the two anointed ones, that stand by the Lord of the whole earth.

THEN I turned, and lifted up mine eyes, and looked, and behold a flying roll.

2And he said unto me, What seest thou? And I answered, I see a flying roll; the length thereof *is* twenty cubits, and the breadth thereof ten cubits.

3Then said he unto me, This *is* the curse that goeth forth over the face of the whole earth: for every one that stealeth shall be cut off *as* on this side according to it; and every one that sweareth shall be cut off *as* on that side according to it.

4I will bring it forth, saith the LORD of hosts, and it shall enter into the house of the thief, and into the house of him that sweareth falsely by my name: and it shall remain in the midst of his house, and shall consume it with the timber thereof and the stones thereof.

5Then the angel that talked with me went forth, and said unto me, Lift up now thine eyes, and see what *is* this that goeth forth.

6And I said, What *is* it? And he said, This *is* an ephah that goeth forth. He said moreover, This *is* their resemblance through all the earth.

7And, behold, there was lifted up a talent of lead: and this *is* a woman that sitteth in the midst of the ephah.

8And he said, This *is* wickedness. And he cast it into the midst of the ephah; and he cast the weight of lead upon the mouth thereof.

9Then lifted I up mine eyes, and looked, and, behold, there came out two women, and the wind *was* in their wings; for they had wings like the wings of a stork: and they lifted up the ephah between the earth and the heaven.

10Then said I to the angel that talked with me, Whither do these bear the ephah?

11And he said unto me, To build it an house in the land of Shinar: and it shall be established, and set there upon her own base.

REVELATION 14:1–20

AND I looked, and, lo, a Lamb stood on the mount Sion, and with him an hundred forty *and* four thousand, having his Father's name written in their foreheads.

2And I heard a voice from heaven, as the voice of many waters, and as the voice of a great thunder: and I heard the voice of harpers harping with their harps:

3And they sung as it were a new song before the throne, and before the four beasts, and the elders: and no man could learn that song but the hundred *and* forty *and* four thousand, which were redeemed from the earth.

4These are they which were not defiled with women; for they are virgins. These are they which follow the Lamb whithersoever he goeth. These were redeemed from among men, *being* the firstfruits unto God and to the Lamb.

5And in their mouth was found no guile: for they are without fault before the throne of God.

6And I saw another angel fly in the midst of heaven, having the everlasting gospel to preach unto them that dwell on the earth, and to every nation, and kindred, and tongue, and people,

7Saying with a loud voice, Fear God, and give glory to him; for the hour of his judgment is come: and worship him that made heaven, and earth, and the sea, and the fountains of waters.

8And there followed another angel,

saying, Babylon is fallen, is fallen, that great city, because she made all nations drink of the wine of the wrath of her fornication.

9And the third angel followed them, saying with a loud voice, If any man worship the beast and his image, and receive *his* mark in his forehead, or in his hand,

10The same shall drink of the wine of the wrath of God, which is poured out without mixture into the cup of his indignation; and he shall be tormented with fire and brimstone in the presence of the holy angels, and in the presence of the Lamb:

11And the smoke of their torment ascendeth up for ever and ever: and they have no rest day nor night, who worship the beast and his image, and whosoever receiveth the mark of his name.

12Here is the patience of the saints: here *are* they that keep the commandments of God, and the faith of Jesus.

13And I heard a voice from heaven saying unto me, Write, Blessed *are* the dead which die in the Lord from henceforth: Yea, saith the Spirit, that they may rest from their labours; and their works do follow them.

14And I looked, and behold a white cloud, and upon the cloud *one* sat like unto the Son of man, having on his head a golden crown, and in his hand a sharp sickle.

15And another angel came out of the temple, crying with a loud voice to him that sat on the cloud, Thrust in thy sickle, and reap: for the time is come for thee to reap; for the harvest of the earth is ripe.

16And he that sat on the cloud thrust in his sickle on the earth; and the earth was reaped.

17And another angel came out of the temple which is in heaven, he also having a sharp sickle.

18And another angel came out from the altar, which had power over fire; and cried with a loud cry to him that had the sharp sickle, saying, Thrust in thy sharp sickle, and gather the clusters of the vine of the earth; for her grapes are fully ripe.

19And the angel thrust in his sickle into the earth, and gathered the vine of the earth, and cast *it* into the great winepress of the wrath of God.

20And the winepress was trodden without the city, and blood came out of the winepress, even unto the horse bridles, by the space of a thousand *and* six hundred furlongs.

PSALM 142:1–7

I CRIED unto the LORD with my voice; with my voice unto the LORD did I make my supplication.

2I poured out my complaint before him; I shewed before him my trouble.

3When my spirit was overwhelmed within me, then thou knewest my path. In the way wherein I walked have they privily laid a snare for me.

4I looked on *my* right hand, and beheld, but *there was* no man that would know me: refuge failed me; no man cared for my soul.

5I cried unto thee, O LORD: I said, Thou *art* my refuge *and* my portion in the land of the living.

6Attend unto my cry; for I am brought very low: deliver me from my persecutors; for they are stronger than I.

7Bring my soul out of prison, that I may praise thy name: the righteous shall compass me about; for thou shalt deal bountifully with me.

PROVERBS FOR TODAY/ 30:21–23

For three things *the earth is disquieted, and for four* which *it cannot bear: For a servant when he reigneth; and a fool when he is filled with meat; For an odious* woman *when she is married; and an handmaid that is heir to her mistress.*

ZECHARIAH 6:1—7:14

AND I turned, and lifted up mine eyes, and looked, and, behold, there came four chariots out from between two mountains; and the mountains *were* mountains of brass.

2In the first chariot *were* red horses; and in the second chariot black horses;

3And in the third chariot white horses; and in the fourth chariot grisled and bay horses.

4Then I answered and said unto the angel that talked with me, What *are* these, my lord?

5And the angel answered and said unto me, These *are* the four spirits of the heavens, which go forth from standing before the Lord of all the earth.

6The black horses which *are* therein go forth into the north country; and the white go forth after them; and the grisled go forth toward the south country.

7And the bay went forth, and sought to go that they might walk to and fro through the earth: and he said, Get you hence, walk to and fro through the earth. So they walked to and fro through the earth.

8Then cried he upon me, and spake unto me, saying, Behold, these that go toward the north country have quieted my spirit in the north country.

9And the word of the Lord came unto me, saying,

10Take of *them of* the captivity, *even* of Heldai, of Tobijah, and of Jedaiah, which are come from Babylon, and come thou the same day, and go into the house of Josiah the son of Zephaniah;

11Then take silver and gold, and make crowns, and set *them* upon the head of Joshua the son of Josedech, the high priest;

12And speak unto him, saying, Thus speaketh the Lord of hosts, saying, Behold the man whose name *is* The BRANCH; and he shall grow up out of his place, and he shall build the temple of the Lord:

13Even he shall build the temple of the Lord; and he shall bear the glory, and shall sit and rule upon his throne; and he shall be a priest upon his throne: and the counsel of peace shall be between them both.

14And the crowns shall be to Helem, and to Tobijah, and to Jedaiah, and to Hen the son of Zephaniah, for a memorial in the temple of the Lord.

15And they *that are* far off shall come and build in the temple of the Lord, and ye shall know that the Lord of hosts hath sent me unto you. And *this* shall come to pass, if ye will diligently obey the voice of the Lord your God.

AND it came to pass in the fourth year of king Darius, *that* the word of the Lord came unto Zechariah in the fourth *day* of the ninth month, *even* in Chisleu;

2When they had sent unto the house of God Sherezer and Regem–melech, and their men, to pray before the Lord,

3*And* to speak unto the priests which *were* in the house of the Lord of hosts, and to the prophets, saying, Should I weep in the fifth month, separating myself, as I have done these so many years?

4Then came the word of the Lord of hosts unto me, saying,

5Speak unto all the people of the land, and to the priests, saying, When ye fasted and mourned in the fifth and seventh *month,* even those seventy years, did ye at all fast unto me, *even* to me?

6And when ye did eat, and when ye did drink, did not ye eat *for yourselves,* and drink *for yourselves?*

7*Should ye* not *hear* the words which the LORD hath cried by the former prophets, when Jerusalem was inhabited and in prosperity, and the cities thereof round about her, when *men* inhabited the south and the plain?

8And the word of the LORD came unto Zechariah, saying,

9Thus speaketh the LORD of hosts, saying, Execute true judgment, and shew mercy and compassions every man to his brother:

10And oppress not the widow, nor the fatherless, the stranger, nor the poor; and let none of you imagine evil against his brother in your heart.

11But they refused to hearken, and pulled away the shoulder, and stopped their ears, that they should not hear.

12Yea, they made their hearts *as* an adamant stone, lest they should hear the law, and the words which the LORD of hosts hath sent in his spirit by the former prophets: therefore came a great wrath from the LORD of hosts.

13Therefore it is come to pass, *that* as he cried, and they would not hear; so they cried, and I would not hear, saith the LORD of hosts:

14But I scattered them with a whirlwind among all the nations whom they knew not. Thus the land was desolate after them, that no man passed through nor returned: for they laid the pleasant land desolate.

REVELATION 15:1–8

AND I saw another sign in heaven, great and marvellous, seven angels having the seven last plagues; for in them is filled up the wrath of God.

2And I saw as it were a sea of glass mingled with fire: and them that had gotten the victory over the beast, and over his image, and over his mark, *and* over the number of his name, stand on the sea of glass, having the harps of God.

3And they sing the song of Moses the servant of God, and the song of the Lamb, saying, Great and marvellous *are* thy works, Lord God Almighty; just and true *are* thy ways, thou King of saints.

4Who shall not fear thee, O Lord, and glorify thy name? for *thou* only *art* holy: for all nations shall come and worship before thee; for thy judgments are made manifest.

5And after that I looked, and, behold, the temple of the tabernacle of the testimony in heaven was opened:

6And the seven angels came out of the temple, having the seven plagues, clothed in pure and white linen, and having their breasts girded with golden girdles.

7And one of the four beasts gave unto the seven angels seven golden vials full of the wrath of God, who liveth for ever and ever.

8And the temple was filled with smoke from the glory of God, and from his power; and no man was able to enter into the temple, till the seven plagues of the seven angels were fulfilled.

PSALM 143:1–12

HEAR my prayer, O LORD, give ear to my supplications: in thy faithfulness answer me, *and* in thy righteousness.

2And enter not into judgment with thy servant: for in thy sight shall no man living be justified.

3For the enemy hath persecuted my soul; he hath smitten my life down to the ground; he hath made me to dwell in darkness, as those that have been long dead.

4Therefore is my spirit overwhelmed within me; my heart within me is desolate.

5I remember the days of old; I meditate on all thy works; I muse on the work of thy hands.

⁶I stretch forth my hands unto thee: my soul *thirsteth* after thee, as a thirsty land. Selah.

⁷Hear me speedily, O LORD: my spirit faileth: hide not thy face from me, lest I be like unto them that go down into the pit.

⁸Cause me to hear thy lovingkindness in the morning; for in thee do I trust: cause me to know the way wherein I should walk; for I lift up my soul unto thee.

⁹Deliver me, O LORD, from mine enemies: I flee unto thee to hide me.

¹⁰Teach me to do thy will; for thou *art* my God: thy spirit *is* good; lead me into the land of uprightness.

¹¹Quicken me, O LORD, for thy name's sake: for thy righteousness' sake bring my soul out of trouble.

¹²And of thy mercy cut off mine enemies, and destroy all them that afflict my soul: for I *am* thy servant.

PROVERBS FOR TODAY/ 30:24–28

There be four things which are *little upon the earth, but they* are *exceeding wise: The ants* are *a people not strong, yet they prepare their meat in the summer; The conies* are but *a feeble folk, yet make they their houses in the rocks; The locusts have no king, yet go they forth all of them by bands; The spider taketh hold with her hands, and is in kings' palaces.*

DECEMBER 25

ZECHARIAH 8:1–23

A GAIN the word of the LORD of hosts came *to me,* saying,

²Thus saith the LORD of hosts; I was jealous for Zion with great jealousy, and I was jealous for her with great fury.

³Thus saith the LORD; I am returned unto Zion, and will dwell in the midst of Jerusalem: and Jerusalem shall be called a city of truth; and the mountain of the LORD of hosts the holy mountain.

⁴Thus saith the LORD of hosts; There shall yet old men and old women dwell in the streets of Jerusalem, and every man with his staff in his hand for very age.

⁵And the streets of the city shall be full of boys and girls playing in the streets thereof.

⁶Thus saith the LORD of hosts; If it be marvellous in the eyes of the remnant of this people in these days, should it also be marvellous in mine eyes? saith the LORD of hosts.

⁷Thus saith the LORD of hosts; Behold, I will save my people from the east country, and from the west country;

⁸And I will bring them, and they shall dwell in the midst of Jerusalem: and they shall be my people, and I will be their God, in truth and in righteousness.

⁹Thus saith the LORD of hosts; Let your hands be strong, ye that hear in these days these words by the mouth of the prophets, which *were* in the day *that* the foundation of the house of the LORD of hosts was laid, that the temple might be built.

¹⁰For before these days there was no hire for man, nor any hire for beast; neither *was there any* peace to him that went out or came in because of the

affliction: for I set all men every one against his neighbour.

11But now I *will* not *be* unto the residue of this people as in the former days, saith the LORD of hosts.

12For the seed *shall be* prosperous; the vine shall give her fruit, and the ground shall give her increase, and the heavens shall give their dew; and I will cause the remnant of this people to possess all these *things*.

13And it shall come to pass, *that* as ye were a curse among the heathen, O house of Judah, and house of Israel; so will I save you, and ye shall be a blessing: fear not, *but* let your hands be strong.

14For thus saith the LORD of hosts; As I thought to punish you, when your fathers provoked me to wrath, saith the LORD of hosts, and I repented not:

15So again have I thought in these days to do well unto Jerusalem and to the house of Judah: fear ye not.

16These *are* the things that ye shall do; Speak ye every man the truth to his neighbour; execute the judgment of truth and peace in your gates:

17And let none of you imagine evil in your hearts against his neighbour; and love no false oath: for all these *are things* that I hate, saith the LORD.

18And the word of the LORD of hosts came unto me, saying,

19Thus saith the LORD of hosts; The fast of the fourth *month*, and the fast of the fifth, and the fast of the seventh, and the fast of the tenth, shall be to the house of Judah joy and gladness, and cheerful feasts; therefore love the truth and peace.

20Thus saith the LORD of hosts; *It shall* yet *come to pass,* that there shall come people, and the inhabitants of many cities:

21And the inhabitants of one *city* shall go to another, saying, Let us go speedily to pray before the LORD, and to seek the LORD of hosts: I will go also.

22Yea, many people and strong nations shall come to seek the LORD of hosts in Jerusalem, and to pray before the LORD.

23Thus saith the LORD of hosts; In those days *it shall come to pass,* that ten men shall take hold out of all languages of the nations, even shall take hold of the skirt of him that is a Jew, saying, We will go with you: for we have heard *that* God *is* with you.

REVELATION 16:1–21

AND I heard a great voice out of the temple saying to the seven angels, Go your ways, and pour out the vials of the wrath of God upon the earth.

2And the first went, and poured out his vial upon the earth; and there fell a noisome and grievous sore upon the men which had the mark of the beast, and *upon* them which worshipped his image.

3And the second angel poured out his vial upon the sea; and it became as the blood of a dead *man:* and every living soul died in the sea.

4And the third angel poured out his vial upon the rivers and fountains of waters; and they became blood.

5And I heard the angel of the waters say, Thou art righteous, O Lord, which art, and wast, and shalt be, because thou hast judged thus.

6For they have shed the blood of saints and prophets, and thou hast given them blood to drink; for they are worthy.

7And I heard another out of the altar say, Even so, Lord God Almighty, true and righteous *are* thy judgments.

8And the fourth angel poured out his vial upon the sun; and power was given unto him to scorch men with fire.

9And men were scorched with great heat, and blasphemed the name of God, which hath power over these plagues: and they repented not to give him glory.

10And the fifth angel poured out his

vial upon the seat of the beast; and his kingdom was full of darkness; and they gnawed their tongues for pain,

11And blasphemed the God of heaven because of their pains and their sores, and repented not of their deeds.

12And the sixth angel poured out his vial upon the great river Euphrates; and the water thereof was dried up, that the way of the kings of the east might be prepared.

13And I saw three unclean spirits like frogs *come* out of the mouth of the dragon, and out of the mouth of the beast, and out of the mouth of the false prophet.

14For they are the spirits of devils, working miracles, *which* go forth unto the kings of the earth and of the whole world, to gather them to the battle of that great day of God Almighty.

15Behold, I come as a thief. Blessed *is* he that watcheth, and keepeth his garments, lest he walk naked, and they see his shame.

16And he gathered them together into a place called in the Hebrew tongue Armageddon.

17And the seventh angel poured out his vial into the air; and there came a great voice out of the temple of heaven, from the throne, saying, It is done.

18And there were voices, and thunders, and lightnings; and there was a great earthquake, such as was not since men were upon the earth, so mighty an earthquake, *and* so great.

19And the great city was divided into three parts, and the cities of the nations fell: and great Babylon came in remembrance before God, to give unto her the cup of the wine of the fierceness of his wrath.

20And every island fled away, and the mountains were not found.

21And there fell upon men a great hail out of heaven, *every stone* about the weight of a talent: and men blasphemed God because of the plague of the hail; for the plague thereof was exceeding great.

PSALM 144:1–15

BLESSED *be* the LORD my strength, which teacheth my hands to war, *and* my fingers to fight:

2My goodness, and my fortress; my high tower, and my deliverer; my shield, and *he* in whom I trust; who subdueth my people under me.

3LORD, what *is* man, that thou takest knowledge of him! *or* the son of man, that thou makest account of him!

4Man is like to vanity: his days *are* as a shadow that passeth away.

5Bow thy heavens, O LORD, and come down: touch the mountains, and they shall smoke.

6Cast forth lightning, and scatter them: shoot out thine arrows, and destroy them.

7Send thine hand from above: rid me, and deliver me out of great waters, from the hand of strange children;

8Whose mouth speaketh vanity, and their right hand *is* a right hand of falsehood.

9I will sing a new song unto thee, O God: upon a psaltery *and* an instrument of ten strings will I sing praises unto thee.

10*It is he* that giveth salvation unto kings: who delivereth David his servant from the hurtful sword.

11Rid me, and deliver me from the hand of strange children, whose mouth speaketh vanity, and their right hand *is* a right hand of falsehood:

12That our sons *may be* as plants grown up in their youth; *that* our daughters *may be* as corner stones, polished *after* the similitude of a palace:

13*That* our garners *may be* full, affording all manner of store: *that* our sheep may bring forth thousands and ten thousands in our streets:

14*That* our oxen *may be* strong to

labour; *that there be* no breaking in, nor going out; that *there be* no complaining in our streets.

15Happy *is that* people, that is in such a case: *yea,* happy *is that* people, whose God *is* the LORD.

PROVERBS FOR TODAY/ 30:29–31

There be three things *which go well, yea, four are comely in going: A lion* which is *strongest among beasts, and turneth not away for any; A greyhound; an he goat also; and a king, against whom* there is *no rising up.*

DECEMBER 26

ZECHARIAH 9:1–17

THE burden of the word of the LORD in the land of Hadrach, and Damascus *shall be* the rest thereof: when the eyes of man, as of all the tribes of Israel, *shall be* toward the LORD.

2And Hamath also shall border thereby; Tyrus, and Zidon, though it be very wise.

3And Tyrus did build herself a strong hold, and heaped up silver as the dust, and fine gold as the mire of the streets.

4Behold, the LORD will cast her out, and he will smite her power in the sea; and she shall be devoured with fire.

5Ashkelon shall see *it,* and fear; Gaza also *shall see it,* and be very sorrowful, and Ekron; for her expectation shall be ashamed; and the king shall perish from Gaza, and Ashkelon shall not be inhabited.

6And a bastard shall dwell in Ashdod, and I will cut off the pride of the Philistines.

7And I will take away his blood out of his mouth, and his abominations from between his teeth: but he that remaineth, even he, *shall be* for our God, and he shall be as a governor in Judah, and Ekron as a Jebusite.

8And I will encamp about mine house because of the army, because of him that passeth by, and because of him that returneth: and no oppressor shall pass through them any more: for now have I seen with mine eyes.

9Rejoice greatly, O daughter of Zion; shout, O daughter of Jerusalem: behold, thy King cometh unto thee: he *is* just, and having salvation; lowly, and riding upon an ass, and upon a colt the foal of an ass.

10And I will cut off the chariot from Ephraim, and the horse from Jerusalem, and the battle bow shall be cut off: and he shall speak peace unto the heathen: and his dominion *shall be* from sea *even* to sea, and from the river *even* to the ends of the earth.

11As for thee also, by the blood of thy covenant I have sent forth thy prisoners out of the pit wherein *is* no water.

12Turn you to the strong hold, ye prisoners of hope: even to day do I declare *that* I will render double unto thee;

13When I have bent Judah for me, filled the bow with Ephraim, and raised up thy sons, O Zion, against thy sons, O Greece, and made thee as the sword of a mighty man.

14And the LORD shall be seen over them, and his arrow shall go forth as the lightning: and the Lord GOD shall blow the trumpet, and shall go with whirlwinds of the south.

15The LORD of hosts shall defend them; and they shall devour, and subdue with sling stones; and they shall drink, *and* make a noise as through wine; and they shall be filled like bowls, *and* as the corners of the altar.

16And the LORD their God shall save them in that day as the flock of his people: for *they shall be as* the stones of a crown, lifted up as an ensign upon his land.

17For how great *is* his goodness, and how great *is* his beauty! corn shall make the young men cheerful, and new wine the maids.

REVELATION 17:1–18

AND there came one of the seven angels which had the seven vials, and talked with me, saying unto me, Come hither; I will shew unto thee the judgment of the great whore that sitteth upon many waters:

2With whom the kings of the earth have committed fornication, and the inhabitants of the earth have been made drunk with the wine of her fornication.

3So he carried me away in the spirit into the wilderness: and I saw a woman sit upon a scarlet coloured beast, full of names of blasphemy, having seven heads and ten horns.

4And the woman was arrayed in purple and scarlet colour, and decked with gold and precious stones and pearls, having a golden cup in her hand full of abominations and filthiness of her fornication:

5And upon her forehead *was* a name written, MYSTERY, BABYLON THE GREAT, THE MOTHER OF HARLOTS AND ABOMINATIONS OF THE EARTH.

6And I saw the woman drunken with the blood of the saints, and with the blood of the martyrs of Jesus: and when I saw her, I wondered with great admiration.

7And the angel said unto me, Wherefore didst thou marvel? I will tell thee the mystery of the woman, and of the beast that carrieth her, which hath the seven heads and ten horns.

8The beast that thou sawest was, and is not; and shall ascend out of the bottomless pit, and go into perdition: and they that dwell on the earth shall wonder, whose names were not written in the book of life from the foundation of the world, when they behold the beast that was, and is not, and yet is.

9And here *is* the mind which hath wisdom. The seven heads are seven mountains, on which the woman sitteth.

10And there are seven kings: five are fallen, and one is, *and* the other is not yet come; and when he cometh, he must continue a short space.

11And the beast that was, and is not, even he is the eighth, and is of the seven, and goeth into perdition.

12And the ten horns which thou sawest are ten kings, which have received no kingdom as yet; but receive power as kings one hour with the beast.

13These have one mind, and shall give their power and strength unto the beast.

14These shall make war with the Lamb, and the Lamb shall overcome them: for he is Lord of lords, and King of kings: and they that are with him *are* called, and chosen, and faithful.

15And he saith unto me, The waters which thou sawest, where the whore sitteth, are peoples, and multitudes, and nations, and tongues.

16And the ten horns which thou sawest upon the beast, these shall hate the whore, and shall make her desolate and naked, and shall eat her flesh, and burn her with fire.

17For God hath put in their hearts to fulfil his will, and to agree, and give their kingdom unto the beast, until the words of God shall be fulfilled.

18And the woman which thou sawest

is that great city, which reigneth over the kings of the earth.

PSALM 145:1–21

I WILL extol thee, my God, O king; and I will bless thy name for ever and ever.

2Every day will I bless thee; and I will praise thy name for ever and ever.

3Great *is* the LORD, and greatly to be praised; and his greatness *is* unsearchable.

4One generation shall praise thy works to another, and shall declare thy mighty acts.

5I will speak of the glorious honour of thy majesty, and of thy wondrous works.

6And *men* shall speak of the might of thy terrible acts: and I will declare thy greatness.

7They shall abundantly utter the memory of thy great goodness, and shall sing of thy righteousness.

8The LORD *is* gracious, and full of compassion; slow to anger, and of great mercy.

9The LORD *is* good to all: and his tender mercies *are* over all his works.

10All thy works shall praise thee,

O LORD; and thy saints shall bless thee.

11They shall speak of the glory of thy kingdom, and talk of thy power;

12To make known to the sons of men his mighty acts, and the glorious majesty of his kingdom.

13Thy kingdom *is* an everlasting kingdom, and thy dominion *endureth* throughout all generations.

14The LORD upholdeth all that fall, and raiseth up all *those that be* bowed down.

15The eyes of all wait upon thee; and thou givest them their meat in due season.

16Thou openest thine hand, and satisfiest the desire of every living thing.

17The LORD *is* righteous in all his ways, and holy in all his works.

18The LORD *is* nigh unto all them that call upon him, to all that call upon him, in truth.

19He will fulfil the desire of them that fear him: he also will hear their cry, and will save them.

20The LORD preserveth all them that love him: but all the wicked will he destroy.

21My mouth shall speak the praise of the LORD: and let all flesh bless his holy name for ever and ever.

PROVERBS FOR TODAY/ 30:32

If thou hast done foolishly in lifting up thyself, or if thou hast thought evil, lay thine hand upon thy mouth.

DECEMBER 27

ZECHARIAH 10:1—11:17

ASK ye of the LORD rain in the time of the latter rain; *so* the LORD shall make bright clouds, and give them showers of rain, to every one grass in the field.

2For the idols have spoken vanity, and the diviners have seen a lie, and have told false dreams; they comfort in vain: therefore they went their way as a flock, they were troubled, because *there was* no shepherd.

3Mine anger was kindled against the shepherds, and I punished the goats: for the LORD of hosts hath visited his flock the house of Judah, and hath made them as his goodly horse in the battle.

4Out of him came forth the corner, out of him the nail, out of him the battle bow, out of him every oppressor together.

5And they shall be as mighty *men*, which tread down *their enemies* in the mire of the streets in the battle: and they shall fight, because the LORD *is* with them, and the riders on horses shall be confounded.

6And I will strengthen the house of Judah, and I will save the house of Joseph, and I will bring them again to place them; for I have mercy upon them: and they shall be as though I had not cast them off: for I *am* the LORD their God, and will hear them.

7And *they of* Ephraim shall be like a mighty *man,* and their heart shall rejoice as through wine: yea, their children shall see *it,* and be glad; their heart shall rejoice in the LORD.

8I will hiss for them, and gather them; for I have redeemed them: and they shall increase as they have increased.

9And I will sow them among the people: and they shall remember me in far countries; and they shall live with their children, and turn again.

10I will bring them again also out of the land of Egypt, and gather them out of Assyria; and I will bring them into the land of Gilead and Lebanon; and *place* shall not be found for them.

11And he shall pass through the sea with affliction, and shall smite the waves in the sea, and all the deeps of the river shall dry up: and the pride of Assyria shall be brought down, and the sceptre of Egypt shall depart away.

12And I will strengthen them in the LORD; and they shall walk up and down in his name, saith the LORD.

OPEN thy doors, O Lebanon, that the fire may devour thy cedars.

2Howl, fir tree; for the cedar is fallen; because the mighty are spoiled: howl, O ye oaks of Bashan; for the forest of the vintage is come down.

3*There is* a voice of the howling of the shepherds; for their glory is spoiled: a voice of the roaring of young lions; for pride of Jordan is spoiled.

4Thus saith the LORD my God; Feed the flock of the slaughter;

5Whose possessors slay them, and hold themselves not guilty: and they that sell them say, Blessed *be* the LORD; for I am rich: and their own shepherds pity them not.

6For I will no more pity the inhabitants of the land, saith the LORD: but, lo, I will deliver the men every one into his neighbour's hand, and into the hand of his king: and they shall smite the land, and out of their hand I will not deliver *them.*

7And I will feed the flock of slaughter, *even* you, O poor of the flock. And I took unto me two staves; the one I called Beauty, and the other I called Bands; and I fed the flock.

8Three shepherds also I cut off in one month; and my soul loathed them, and their soul also abhorred me.

9Then said I, I will not feed you: that that dieth, let it die; and that that is to be cut off, let it be cut off; and let the rest eat every one the flesh of another.

10And I took my staff, *even* Beauty, and cut it asunder, that I might break my covenant which I had made with all the people.

11And it was broken in that day: and so the poor of the flock that waited upon me knew that it *was* the word of the LORD.

12And I said unto them, If ye think good, give *me* my price; and if not, forbear. So they weighed for my price thirty *pieces* of silver.

13And the LORD said unto me, Cast

it unto the potter: a goodly price that I was prised at of them. And I took the thirty *pieces* of silver, and cast them to the potter in the house of the LORD.

14Then I cut asunder mine other staff, *even* Bands, that I might break the brotherhood between Judah and Israel.

15And the LORD said unto me, Take unto thee yet the instruments of a foolish shepherd.

16For, lo, I will raise up a shepherd in the land, *which* shall not visit those that be cut off, neither shall seek the young one, nor heal that that is broken, nor feed that that standeth still: but he shall eat the flesh of the fat, and tear their claws in pieces.

17Woe to the idle shepherd that leaveth the flock! the sword *shall be* upon his arm, and upon his right eye: his arm shall be clean dried up, and his right eye shall be utterly darkened.

REVELATION 18:1–24

AND after these things I saw another angel come down from heaven, having great power; and the earth was lightened with his glory.

2And he cried mightily with a strong voice, saying, Babylon the great is fallen, is fallen, and is become the habitation of devils, and the hold of every foul spirit, and a cage of every unclean and hateful bird.

3For all nations have drunk of the wine of the wrath of her fornication, and the kings of the earth have committed fornication with her, and the merchants of the earth are waxed rich through the abundance of her delicacies.

4And I heard another voice from heaven, saying, Come out of her, my people, that ye be not partakers of her sins, and that ye receive not of her plagues.

5For her sins have reached unto heaven, and God hath remembered her iniquities.

6Reward her even as she rewarded you, and double unto her double according to her works: in the cup which she hath filled fill to her double.

7How much she hath glorified herself, and lived deliciously, so much torment and sorrow give her: for she saith in her heart, I sit a queen, and am no widow, and shall see no sorrow.

8Therefore shall her plagues come in one day, death, and mourning, and famine; and she shall be utterly burned with fire: for strong *is* the Lord God who judgeth her.

9And the kings of the earth, who have committed fornication and lived deliciously with her, shall bewail her, and lament for her, when they shall see the smoke of her burning,

10Standing afar off for the fear of her torment, saying, Alas, alas that great city Babylon, that mighty city! for in one hour is thy judgment come.

11And the merchants of the earth shall weep and mourn over her; for no man buyeth their merchandise any more:

12The merchandise of gold, and silver, and precious stones, and of pearls, and fine linen, and purple, and silk, and scarlet, and all thyine wood, and all manner vessels of ivory, and all manner vessels of most precious wood, and of brass, and iron, and marble,

13And cinnamon, and odours, and ointments, and frankincense, and wine, and oil, and fine flour, and wheat, and beasts, and sheep, and horses, and chariots, and slaves, and souls of men.

14And the fruits that thy soul lusted after are departed from thee, and all things which were dainty and goodly are departed from thee, and thou shalt find them no more at all.

15The merchants of these things, which were made rich by her, shall stand afar off for the fear of her torment, weeping and wailing,

16And saying, Alas, alas that great city, that was clothed in fine linen, and purple, and scarlet, and decked with gold, and precious stones, and pearls!

17For in one hour so great riches is come to nought. And every shipmaster, and all the company in ships, and sailors, and as many as trade by sea, stood afar off,

18And cried when they saw the smoke of her burning, saying, What *city is* like unto this great city!

19And they cast dust on their heads, and cried, weeping and wailing, saying, Alas, alas, that great city, wherein were made rich all that had ships in the sea by reason of her costliness! for in one hour is she made desolate.

20Rejoice over her, *thou* heaven, and *ye* holy apostles and prophets; for God hath avenged you on her.

21And a mighty angel took up a stone like a great millstone, and cast *it* into the sea, saying, Thus with violence shall that great city Babylon be thrown down, and shall be found no more at all.

22And the voice of harpers, and musicians, and of pipers, and trumpeters, shall be heard no more at all in thee; and no craftsman, of whatsoever craft *he be,* shall be found any more in thee; and the sound of a millstone shall be heard no more at all in thee;

23And the light of a candle shall shine no more at all in thee; and the voice of the bridegroom and of the bride shall be heard no more at all in thee: for thy merchants were the great men of the earth; for by thy sorceries were all nations deceived.

24And in her was found the blood of prophets, and of saints, and of all that were slain upon the earth.

PSALM 146:1–10

Praise ye the Lord. Praise the Lord, O my soul.

2While I live will I praise the Lord: I will sing praises unto my God while I have any being.

3Put not your trust in princes, *nor* in the son of man, in whom *there is* no help.

4His breath goeth forth, he returneth to his earth; in that very day his thoughts perish.

5Happy *is he* that *hath* the God of Jacob for his help, whose hope *is* in the Lord his God:

6Which made heaven, and earth, the sea, and all that therein *is:* which keepeth truth for ever:

7Which executeth judgment for the oppressed: which giveth food to the hungry. The Lord looseth the prisoners:

8The Lord openeth *the eyes of* the blind: the Lord raiseth them that are bowed down: the Lord loveth the righteous:

9The Lord preserveth the strangers; he relieveth the fatherless and widow: but the way of the wicked he turneth upside down.

10The Lord shall reign for ever, *even* thy God, O Zion, unto all generations. Praise ye the Lord.

PROVERBS FOR TODAY/ 30:33

Surely the churning of milk bringeth forth butter, and the wringing of the nose bringeth forth blood: so the forcing of wrath bringeth forth strife.

DECEMBER 28

ZECHARIAH 12:1—13:9

THE burden of the word of the LORD for Israel, saith the LORD, which stretcheth forth the heavens, and layeth the foundation of the earth, and formeth the spirit of man within him.

2Behold, I will make Jerusalem a cup of trembling unto all the people round about, when they shall be in the siege both against Judah *and* against Jerusalem.

3And in that day will I make Jerusalem a burdensome stone for all people: all that burden themselves with it shall be cut in pieces, though all the people of the earth be gathered together against it.

4In that day, saith the LORD, I will smite every horse with astonishment, and his rider with madness: and I will open mine eyes upon the house of Judah, and will smite every horse of the people with blindness.

5And the governors of Judah shall say in their heart, The inhabitants of Jerusalem *shall be* my strength in the LORD of hosts their God.

6In that day will I make the governors of Judah like an hearth of fire among the wood, and like a torch of fire in a sheaf; and they shall devour all the people round about, on the right hand and on the left: and Jerusalem shall be inhabited again in her own place, *even* in Jerusalem.

7The LORD also shall save the tents of Judah first, that the glory of the house of David and the glory of the inhabitants of Jerusalem do not magnify *themselves* against Judah.

8In that day shall the LORD defend the inhabitants of Jerusalem; and he that is feeble among them at that day shall be as David; and the house of David *shall be* as God, as the angel of the LORD before them.

9And it shall come to pass in that day, *that* I will seek to destroy all the nations that come against Jerusalem.

10And I will pour upon the house of David, and upon the inhabitants of Jerusalem, the spirit of grace and of supplications: and they shall look upon me whom they have pierced, and they shall mourn for him, as one mourneth for *his* only *son,* and shall be in bitterness for him, as one that is in bitterness for *his* firstborn.

11In that day shall there be a great mourning in Jerusalem, as the mourning of Hadad–rimmon in the valley of Megiddon.

12And the land shall mourn, every family apart; the family of the house of David apart, and their wives apart; the family of the house of Nathan apart, and their wives apart;

13The family of the house of Levi apart, and their wives apart; the family of Shimei apart, and their wives apart;

14All the families that remain, every family apart, and their wives apart.

IN that day there shall be a fountain opened to the house of David and to the inhabitants of Jerusalem for sin and for uncleanness.

2And it shall come to pass in that day, saith the LORD of hosts, *that* I will cut off the names of the idols out of the land, and they shall no more be remembered: and also I will cause the prophets and the unclean spirit to pass out of the land.

3And it shall come to pass, *that* when any shall yet prophesy, then his father and his mother that begat him shall say unto him, Thou shalt not live; for thou speakest lies in the name of the

LORD: and his father and his mother that begat him shall thrust him through when he prophesieth.

4And it shall come to pass in that day, *that* the prophets shall be ashamed every one of his vision, when he hath prophesied; neither shall they wear a rough garment to deceive:

5But he shall say, I *am* no prophet, I *am* an husbandman; for man taught me to keep cattle from my youth.

6And *one* shall say unto him, What *are* these wounds in thine hands? Then he shall answer, *Those* with which I was wounded *in* the house of my friends.

7Awake, O sword, against my shepherd, and against the man *that is* my fellow, saith the LORD of hosts: smite the shepherd, and the sheep shall be scattered: and I will turn mine hand upon the little ones.

8And it shall come to pass, *that* in all the land, saith the LORD, two parts therein shall be cut off *and* die; but the third shall be left therein.

9And I will bring the third part through the fire, and will refine them as silver is refined, and will try them as gold is tried: they shall call on my name, and I will hear them: I will say, It *is* my people: and they shall say, The LORD *is* my God.

REVELATION 19:1–21

AND after these things I heard a great voice of much people in heaven, saying, Alleluia; Salvation, and glory, and honour, and power, unto the Lord our God:

2For true and righteous *are* his judgments: for he hath judged the great whore, which did corrupt the earth with her fornication, and hath avenged the blood of his servants at her hand.

3And again they said, Alleluia. And her smoke rose up for ever and ever.

4And the four and twenty elders and the four beasts fell down and worshipped God that sat on the throne, saying, Amen; Alleluia.

5And a voice came out of the throne, saying, Praise our God, all ye his servants, and ye that fear him, both small and great.

6And I heard as it were the voice of a great multitude, and as the voice of many waters, and as the voice of mighty thunderings, saying, Alleluia: for the Lord God omnipotent reigneth.

7Let us be glad and rejoice, and give honour to him: for the marriage of the Lamb is come, and his wife hath made herself ready.

8And to her was granted that she should be arrayed in fine linen, clean and white: for the fine linen is the righteousness of saints.

9And he saith unto me, Write, Blessed *are* they which are called unto the marriage supper of the Lamb. And he saith unto me, These are the true sayings of God.

10And I fell at his feet to worship him. And he said unto me, See *thou do it* not: I am thy fellowservant, and of thy brethren that have the testimony of Jesus: worship God: for the testimony of Jesus is the spirit of prophecy.

11And I saw heaven opened, and behold a white horse; and he that sat upon him *was* called Faithful and True, and in righteousness he doth judge and make war.

12His eyes *were* as a flame of fire, and on his head *were* many crowns; and he had a name written, that no man knew, but he himself.

13And he *was* clothed with a vesture dipped in blood: and his name is called The Word of God.

14And the armies *which were* in heaven followed him upon white horses, clothed in fine linen, white and clean.

15And out of his mouth goeth a sharp sword, that with it he should smite the nations: and he shall rule them with a rod of iron: and he treadeth the winepress of the fierceness and wrath of Almighty God.

16And he hath on *his* vesture and on his thigh a name written, KING OF KINGS, AND LORD OF LORDS.

17And I saw an angel standing in the sun; and he cried with a loud voice, saying to all the fowls that fly in the midst of heaven, Come and gather yourselves together unto the supper of the great God;

18That ye may eat the flesh of kings, and the flesh of captains, and the flesh of mighty men, and the flesh of horses, and of them that sit on them, and the flesh of all *men, both* free and bond, both small and great.

19And I saw the beast, and the kings of the earth, and their armies, gathered together to make war against him that sat on the horse, and against his army.

20And the beast was taken, and with him the false prophet that wrought miracles before him, with which he deceived them that had received the mark of the beast, and them that worshipped his image. These both were cast alive into a lake of fire burning with brimstone.

21And the remnant were slain with the sword of him that sat upon the horse, which *sword* proceeded out of his mouth: and all the fowls were filled with their flesh.

PSALM 147:1–20

PRAISE ye the LORD: for *it is* good to sing praises unto our God; for *it is* pleasant; *and* praise is comely.

2The LORD doth build up Jerusalem: he gathereth together the outcasts of Israel.

3He healeth the broken in heart, and bindeth up their wounds.

4He telleth the number of the stars; he calleth them all by *their* names.

5Great *is* our Lord, and of great power: his understanding *is* infinite.

6The LORD lifteth up the meek: he casteth the wicked down to the ground.

7Sing unto the LORD with thanksgiving; sing praise upon the harp unto our God:

8Who covereth the heaven with clouds, who prepareth rain for the earth, who maketh grass to grow upon the mountains.

9He giveth to the beast his food, *and* to the young ravens which cry.

10He delighteth not in the strength of the horse: he taketh not pleasure in the legs of a man.

11The LORD taketh pleasure in them that fear him, in those that hope in his mercy.

12Praise the LORD, O Jerusalem; praise thy God, O Zion.

13For he hath strengthened the bars of thy gates; he hath blessed thy children within thee.

14He maketh peace *in* thy borders, *and* filleth thee with the finest of the wheat.

15He sendeth forth his commandment *upon* earth: his word runneth very swiftly.

16He giveth snow like wool: he scattereth the hoarfrost like ashes.

17He casteth forth his ice like morsels: who can stand before his cold?

18He sendeth out his word, and melteth them: he causeth his wind to blow, *and* the waters flow.

19He sheweth his word unto Jacob, his statutes and his judgments unto Israel.

20He hath not dealt so with any nation: and *as for his* judgments, they have not known them. Praise ye the LORD.

PROVERBS FOR TODAY/ 31:1–7

The words of king Lemuel, the prophecy that his mother taught him. What, my son? and what, the son of my womb? and what, the son of my vows? Give not thy strength unto women, nor thy ways to that which destroyeth kings. ☐ It is *not for kings, O Lemuel, it is not for kings to drink wine; nor for princes strong drink: Lest they drink, and forget the law, and pervert the judgment of any of the afflicted. Give strong drink unto him that is ready to perish, and wine unto those that be of heavy hearts. Let him drink, and forget his poverty, and remember his misery no more.*

DECEMBER 29

ZECHARIAH 14:1–21

BEHOLD, the day of the LORD cometh, and thy spoil shall be divided in the midst of thee.

2For I will gather all nations against Jerusalem to battle; and the city shall be taken, and the houses rifled, and the women ravished; and half of the city shall go forth into captivity, and the residue of the people shall not be cut off from the city.

3Then shall the LORD go forth, and fight against those nations, as when he fought in the day of battle.

4And his feet shall stand in that day upon the mount of Olives, which *is* before Jerusalem on the east, and the mount of Olives shall cleave in the midst thereof toward the east and toward the west, *and there shall be* a very great valley; and half of the mountain shall remove toward the north, and half of it toward the south.

5And ye shall flee *to* the valley of the mountains; for the valley of the mountains shall reach unto Azal: yea, ye shall flee, like as ye fled from before the earthquake in the days of Uzziah king of Judah: and the LORD my God shall come, *and* all the saints with thee.

6And it shall come to pass in that day, *that* the light shall not be clear, *nor* dark:

7But it shall be one day which shall be known to the LORD, nor day, nor night: but it shall come to pass, *that* at evening time it shall be light.

8And it shall be in that day, *that* living waters shall go out from Jerusalem; half of them toward the former sea, and half of them toward the hinder sea: in summer and in winter shall it be.

9And the LORD shall be king over all the earth: in that day shall there be one LORD, and his name one.

10All the land shall be turned as a plain from Geba to Rimmon south of Jerusalem: and it shall be lifted up, and inhabited in her place, from Benjamin's gate unto the place of the first gate, unto the corner gate, and *from* the tower of Hananeel unto the king's winepresses.

11And *men* shall dwell in it, and there shall be no more utter destruction; but Jerusalem shall be safely inhabited.

12And this shall be the plague wherewith the LORD will smite all the people that have fought against Jerusalem; Their flesh shall consume away while they stand upon their feet, and their eyes shall consume away in their holes, and their tongue shall consume away in their mouth.

13And it shall come to pass in that day, *that* a great tumult from the LORD shall be among them; and they shall lay hold every one on the hand of his neighbour, and his hand shall rise up against the hand of his neighbour.

14And Judah also shall fight at Jerusalem; and the wealth of all the heathen round about shall be gathered together, gold, and silver, and apparel, in great abundance.

15And so shall be the plague of the horse, of the mule, of the camel, and of the ass, and of all the beasts that shall be in these tents, as this plague.

16And it shall come to pass, *that* every one that is left of all the nations which came against Jerusalem shall even go up from year to year to worship the King, the LORD of hosts, and to keep the feast of tabernacles.

17And it shall be, *that* whoso will not come up of *all* the families of the earth unto Jerusalem to worship the King, the LORD of hosts, even upon them shall be no rain.

18And if the family of Egypt go not up, and come not, that *have* no *rain;* there shall be the plague, wherewith the LORD will smite the heathen that come not up to keep the feast of tabernacles.

19This shall be the punishment of Egypt, and the punishment of all nations that come not up to keep the feast of tabernacles.

20In that day shall there be upon the bells of the horses, HOLINESS UNTO THE LORD; and the pots in the LORD's house shall be like the bowls before the altar.

21Yea, every pot in Jerusalem and in Judah shall be holiness unto the LORD of hosts: and all they that sacrifice shall come and take of them, and seethe therein: and in that day there shall be no more the Canaanite in the house of the LORD of hosts.

REVELATION 20:1–15

A ND I saw an angel come down from heaven, having the key of the bottomless pit and a great chain in his hand.

2And he laid hold on the dragon, that old serpent, which is the Devil, and Satan, and bound him a thousand years,

3And cast him into the bottomless pit, and shut him up, and set a seal upon him, that he should deceive the nations no more, till the thousand years should be fulfilled: and after that he must be loosed a little season.

4And I saw thrones, and they sat upon them, and judgment was given unto them: and *I saw* the souls of them that were beheaded for the witness of Jesus, and for the word of God, and which had not worshipped the beast, neither his image, neither had received *his* mark upon their foreheads, or in their hands; and they lived and reigned with Christ a thousand years.

5But the rest of the dead lived not again until the thousand years were finished. This *is* the first resurrection.

6Blessed and holy *is* he that hath part in the first resurrection: on such the second death hath no power, but they shall be priests of God and of Christ, and shall reign with him a thousand years.

7And when the thousand years are expired, Satan shall be loosed out of his prison,

8And shall go out to deceive the nations which are in the four quarters of the earth, Gog and Magog, to gather them together to battle: the number of whom *is* as the sand of the sea.

9And they went up on the breadth of the earth, and compassed the camp of the saints about, and the beloved city: and fire came down from God out of heaven, and devoured them.

10And the devil that deceived them was cast into the lake of fire and brimstone, where the beast and the false prophet *are,* and shall be tormented day and night for ever and ever.

11And I saw a great white throne, and him that sat on it, from whose face the earth and the heaven fled away; and there was found no place for them.

12And I saw the dead, small and great,

stand before God; and the books were opened: and another book was opened, which is *the book* of life: and the dead were judged out of those things which were written in the books, according to their works.

13And the sea gave up the dead which were in it; and death and hell delivered up the dead which were in them: and they were judged every man according to their works.

14And death and hell were cast into the lake of fire. This is the second death.

15And whosoever was not found written in the book of life was cast into the lake of fire.

PSALM 148:1–14

PRAISE ye the LORD. Praise ye the LORD from the heavens: praise him in the heights.

2Praise ye him, all his angels: praise ye him, all his hosts.

3Praise ye him, sun and moon: praise him, all ye stars of light.

4Praise him, ye heavens of heavens, and ye waters that *be* above the heavens.

5Let them praise the name of the LORD: for he commanded, and they were created.

6He hath also stablished them for ever and ever: he hath made a decree which shall not pass.

7Praise the LORD from the earth, ye dragons, and all deeps:

8Fire, and hail; snow, and vapours; stormy wind fulfilling his word:

9Mountains, and all hills; fruitful trees, and all cedars:

10Beasts, and all cattle; creeping things, and flying fowl:

11Kings of the earth, and all people; princes, and all judges of the earth:

12Both young men, and maidens; old men, and children:

13Let them praise the name of the LORD: for his name alone is excellent; his glory *is* above the earth and heaven.

14He also exalteth the horn of his people, the praise of all his saints; *even* of the children of Israel, a people near unto him. Praise ye the LORD.

PROVERBS FOR TODAY/ 31:8–9

Open thy mouth for the dumb in the cause of all such as are appointed to destruction.
Open thy mouth, judge righteously, and plead the cause of the poor and needy.

DECEMBER 30

MALACHI 1:1—2:17

THE burden of the word of the LORD to Israel by Malachi.

2I have loved you, saith the LORD. Yet ye say, Wherein hast thou loved us? *Was* not Esau Jacob's brother? saith the LORD: yet I loved Jacob,

3And I hated Esau, and laid his mountains and his heritage waste for the dragons of the wilderness.

4Whereas Edom saith, We are impoverished, but we will return and build the desolate places; thus saith the LORD of hosts, They shall build, but I will throw down; and they shall call them, The border of wickedness, and, The people against whom the LORD hath indignation for ever.

5And your eyes shall see, and ye shall say, The LORD will be magnified from the border of Israel.

6A son honoureth *his* father, and a servant his master: if then I *be* a father, where *is* mine honour? and if I *be* a master, where *is* my fear? saith the LORD of hosts unto you, O priests, that despise my name. And ye say, Wherein have we despised thy name?

7Ye offer polluted bread upon mine altar; and ye say, Wherein have we polluted thee? In that ye say, The table of the LORD *is* contemptible.

8And if ye offer the blind for sacrifice, *is it* not evil? and if ye offer the lame and sick, *is it* not evil? offer it now unto thy governor; will he be pleased with thee, or accept thy person? saith the LORD of hosts.

9And now, I pray you, beseech God that he will be gracious unto us: this hath been by your means: will he regard your persons? saith the LORD of hosts.

10Who *is there* even among you that would shut the doors *for nought?* neither do ye kindle *fire* on mine altar for nought. I have no pleasure in you, saith the LORD of hosts, neither will I accept an offering at your hand.

11For from the rising of the sun even unto the going down of the same my name *shall be* great among the Gentiles; and in every place incense *shall be* offered unto my name, and a pure offering: for my name *shall be* great among the heathen, saith the LORD of hosts.

12But ye have profaned it, in that ye say, The table of the LORD *is* polluted; and the fruit thereof, *even* his meat, *is* contemptible.

13Ye said also, Behold, what a weariness *is it!* and ye have snuffed at it, saith the LORD of hosts; and ye brought *that which was* torn, and the lame, and the sick; thus ye brought an offering: should I accept this of your hand? saith the LORD.

14But cursed *be* the deceiver, which hath in his flock a male, and voweth, and sacrificeth unto the LORD a corrupt thing: for I *am* a great King, saith the LORD of hosts, and my name *is* dreadful among the heathen.

AND now, O ye priests, this commandment *is* for you.

2If ye will not hear, and if ye will not lay *it* to heart, to give glory unto my name, saith the LORD of hosts, I will even send a curse upon you, and I will curse your blessings: yea, I have cursed them already, because ye do not lay *it* to heart.

3Behold, I will corrupt your seed, and spread dung upon your faces, *even* the dung of your solemn feasts; and *one* shall take you away with it.

4And ye shall know that I have sent this commandment unto you, that my covenant might be with Levi, saith the LORD of hosts.

5My covenant was with him of life and peace; and I gave them to him *for* the fear wherewith he feared me, and was afraid before my name.

6The law of truth was in his mouth, and iniquity was not found in his lips: he walked with me in peace and equity, and did turn many away from iniquity.

7For the priest's lips should keep knowledge, and they should seek the law at his mouth: for he *is* the messenger of the LORD of hosts.

8But ye are departed out of the way; ye have caused many to stumble at the law; ye have corrupted the covenant of Levi, saith the LORD of hosts.

9Therefore have I also made you contemptible and base before all the people, according as ye have not kept my ways, but have been partial in the law.

10Have we not all one father? hath not one God created us? why do we deal treacherously every man against his brother, by profaning the covenant of our fathers?

11Judah hath dealt treacherously, and an abomination is committed in Israel and in Jerusalem; for Judah hath profaned the holiness of the LORD which he loved, and hath married the daughter of a strange god.

12The Lord will cut off the man that doeth this, the master and the scholar, out of the tabernacles of Jacob, and him that offereth an offering unto the Lord of hosts.

13And this have ye done again, covering the altar of the Lord with tears, with weeping, and with crying out, insomuch that he regardeth not the offering any more, or receiveth *it* with good will at your hand.

14Yet ye say, Wherefore? Because the Lord hath been witness between thee and the wife of thy youth, against whom thou hast dealt treacherously: yet *is* she thy companion, and the wife of thy covenant.

15And did not he make one? Yet had he the residue of the spirit. And wherefore one? That he might seek a godly seed. Therefore take heed to your spirit, and let none deal treacherously against the wife of his youth.

16For the Lord, the God of Israel, saith that he hateth putting away: for *one* covereth violence with his garment, saith the Lord of hosts: therefore take heed to your spirit, that ye deal not treacherously.

17Ye have wearied the Lord with your words. Yet ye say, Wherein have we wearied *him?* When ye say, Every one that doeth evil *is* good in the sight of the Lord, and he delighteth in them; or, Where *is* the God of Judgment?

REVELATION 21:1–27

AND I saw a new heaven and a new earth: for the first heaven and the first earth were passed away; and there was no more sea.

2And I John saw the holy city, new Jerusalem, coming down from God out of heaven, prepared as a bride adorned for her husband.

3And I heard a great voice out of heaven saying, Behold, the tabernacle of God *is* with men, and he will dwell with them, and they shall be his people, and God himself shall be with them, *and be* their God.

4And God shall wipe away all tears from their eyes; and there shall be no more death, neither sorrow, nor crying, neither shall there be any more pain: for the former things are passed away.

5And he that sat upon the throne said, Behold, I make all things new. And he said unto me, Write: for these words are true and faithful.

6And he said unto me, It is done. I am Alpha and Omega, the beginning and the end. I will give unto him that is athirst of the fountain of the water of life freely.

7He that overcometh shall inherit all things; and I will be his God, and he shall be my son.

8But the fearful, and unbelieving, and the abominable, and murderers, and whoremongers, and sorcerers, and idolaters, and all liars, shall have their part in the lake which burneth with fire and brimstone: which is the second death.

9And there came unto me one of the seven angels which had the seven vials full of the seven last plagues, and talked with me, saying, Come hither, I will shew thee the bride, the Lamb's wife.

10And he carried me away in the spirit to a great and high mountain, and shewed me that great city, the holy Jerusalem, descending out of heaven from God,

11Having the glory of God: and her light *was* like unto a stone most precious, even like a jasper stone, clear as crystal;

12And had a wall great and high, *and* had twelve gates, and at the gates twelve angels, and names written thereon, which are *the names* of the twelve tribes of the children of Israel:

13On the east three gates; on the north three gates; on the south three gates; and on the west three gates.

14And the wall of the city had twelve foundations, and in them the names of the twelve apostles of the Lamb.

15And he that talked with me had a golden reed to measure the city, and the gates thereof, and the wall thereof.

16And the city lieth foursquare, and the length is as large as the breadth: and he measured the city with the reed, twelve thousand furlongs. The length and the breadth and the height of it are equal.

17And he measured the wall thereof, an hundred *and* forty *and* four cubits, *according to* the measure of a man, that is, of the angel.

18And the building of the wall of it was *of* jasper: and the city *was* pure gold, like unto clear glass.

19And the foundations of the wall of the city *were* garnished with all manner of precious stones. The first foundation was jasper; the second, sapphire; the third, a chalcedony; the fourth, an emerald;

20The fifth, sardonyx; the sixth, sardius; the seventh, chrysolyte; the eighth, beryl; the ninth, a topaz; the tenth, a chrysoprasus; the eleventh, a jacinth; the twelfth, an amethyst.

21And the twelve gates *were* twelve pearls; every several gate was of one pearl: and the street of the city *was* pure gold, as it were transparent glass.

22And I saw no temple therein: for the Lord God Almighty and the Lamb are the temple of it.

23And the city had no need of the sun, neither of the moon, to shine in it: for the glory of God did lighten it, and the Lamb *is* the light thereof.

24And the nations of them which are saved shall walk in the light of it: and the kings of the earth do bring their glory and honour into it.

25And the gates of it shall not be shut at all by day: for there shall be no night there.

26And they shall bring the glory and honour of the nations into it.

27And there shall in no wise enter into it any thing that defileth, neither *whatsoever* worketh abomination, or *maketh* a lie: but they which are written in the Lamb's book of life.

PSALM 149:1–9

PRAISE ye the LORD. Sing unto the LORD a new song, *and* his praise in the congregation of saints.

2Let Israel rejoice in him that made him: let the children of Zion be joyful in their King.

3Let them praise his name in the dance: let them sing praises unto him with the timbrel and harp.

4For the LORD taketh pleasure in his people: he will beautify the meek with salvation.

5Let the saints be joyful in glory: let them sing aloud upon their beds.

6*Let* the high *praises* of God *be* in their mouth, and a two-edged sword in their hand;

7To execute vengeance upon the heathen, *and* punishments upon the people;

8To bind their kings with chains, and their nobles with fetters of iron;

9To execute upon them the judgment written: this honour have all his saints. Praise ye the LORD.

PROVERBS FOR TODAY/ 31:10–24

Who can find a virtuous woman? for her price is *far above rubies. The heart of her husband doth safely trust in her, so that he shall have no need of spoil. She will do him good and not evil all the days of her life. She seeketh wool, and flax, and worketh willingly with her hands. She is like the merchants' ships; she bringeth her food from afar. She riseth also while it is yet night, and giveth meat to her household, and a portion to her maidens. She considereth a field, and buyeth it:*

with the fruit of her hands she planteth a vineyard. She girdeth her loins with strength, and strengtheneth her arms. She perceiveth that her merchandise is good: her candle goeth not out by night. She layeth her hands to the spindle, and her hands hold the distaff. She stretcheth out her hand to the poor; yea, she reacheth forth her hands to the needy. She is not afraid of the snow for her household: for all her household are clothed with scarlet. She maketh herself coverings of tapestry; her clothing is silk and purple. Her husband is known in the gates, when he sitteth among the elders of the land. She maketh fine linen, and selleth it; and delivereth girdles unto the merchant.

DECEMBER 31

MALACHI 3:1—4:6

BEHOLD, I will send my messenger, and he shall prepare the way before me: and the Lord, whom ye seek, shall suddenly come to his temple, even the messenger of the covenant, whom ye delight in: behold, he shall come, saith the LORD of hosts.

2But who may abide the day of his coming? and who shall stand when he appeareth? for he *is* like a refiner's fire, and like fullers' soap:

3And he shall sit *as* a refiner and purifier of silver: and he shall purify the sons of Levi, and purge them as gold and silver, that they may offer unto the LORD an offering in righteousness.

4Then shall the offering of Judah and Jerusalem be pleasant unto the LORD, as in the days of old, and as in former years.

5And I will come near to you to judgment; and I will be a swift witness against the sorcerers, and against the adulterers, and against false swearers, and against those that oppress the hireling in *his* wages, the widow, and the fatherless, and that turn aside the stranger *from his right,* and fear not me, saith the LORD of hosts.

6For I *am* the LORD, I change not; therefore ye sons of Jacob are not consumed.

7Even from the days of your fathers ye are gone away from mine ordinances, and have not kept *them*. Return unto me, and I will return unto you, saith the LORD of hosts. But ye said, Wherein shall we return?

8Will a man rob God? Yet ye have robbed me. But ye say, Wherein have we robbed thee? In tithes and offerings.

9Ye *are* cursed with a curse: for ye have robbed me, *even* this whole nation.

10Bring ye all the tithes into the storehouse, that there may be meat in mine house, and prove me now herewith, saith the LORD of hosts, if I will not open you the windows of heaven, and pour you out a blessing, that *there shall* not *be room* enough *to receive it.*

11And I will rebuke the devourer for your sakes, and he shall not destroy the fruits of your ground; neither shall your vine cast her fruit before the time in the field, saith the LORD of hosts.

12And all nations shall call you blessed: for ye shall be a delightsome land, saith the LORD of hosts.

13Your words have been stout against me, saith the LORD. Yet ye say, What have we spoken *so much* against thee?

14Ye have said, It *is* vain to serve God: and what profit *is it* that we have kept his ordinance, and that we have walked mournfully before the LORD of hosts?

15And now we call the proud happy; yea, they that work wickedness are set up; yea, *they that* tempt God are even delivered.

16Then they that feared the LORD spake often one to another: and the LORD hearkened, and heard *it,* and a book of remembrance was written before him for them that feared the LORD, and that thought upon his name.

17And they shall be mine, saith the LORD of hosts, in that day when I make up my jewels; and I will spare them, as a man spareth his own son that serveth him.

18Then shall ye return, and discern between the righteous and the wicked, between him that serveth God and him that serveth him not.

FOR, behold, the day cometh, that shall burn as an oven; and all the proud, yea, and all that do wickedly, shall be stubble: and the day that cometh shall burn them up, saith the LORD of hosts, that it shall leave them neither root nor branch.

2But unto you that fear my name shall the Sun of righteousness arise with healing in his wings; and ye shall go forth, and grow up as calves of the stall.

3And ye shall tread down the wicked; for they shall be ashes under the soles of your feet in the day that I shall do *this,* saith the LORD of hosts.

4Remember ye the law of Moses my servant, which I commanded unto him in Horeb for all Israel, *with* the statutes and judgments.

5Behold, I will send you Elijah the prophet before the coming of the great and dreadful day of the LORD:

6And he shall turn the heart of the fathers to the children, and the heart of the children to their fathers, lest I come and smite the earth with a curse.

REVELATION 22:1–21

AND he shewed me a pure river of water of life, clear as crystal, proceeding out of the throne of God and of the Lamb.

2In the midst of the street of it, and on either side of the river, *was there* the tree of life, which bare twelve *manner of* fruits, *and* yielded her fruit every month: and the leaves of the tree *were* for the healing of the nations.

3And there shall be no more curse: but the throne of God and of the Lamb shall be in it; and his servants shall serve him:

4And they shall see his face; and his name *shall be* in their foreheads.

5And there shall be no night there; and they need no candle, neither light of the sun; for the Lord God giveth them light: and they shall reign for ever and ever.

6And he said unto me, These sayings *are* faithful and true: and the Lord God of the holy prophets sent his angel to shew unto his servants the things which must shortly be done.

7Behold, I come quickly: blessed *is* he that keepeth the saying of the prophecy of this book.

8And I John saw these things, and heard *them.* And when I had heard and seen, I fell down to worship before the feet of the angel which shewed me these things.

9Then saith he unto me, See *thou do it* not: for I am thy fellowservant, and of thy brethren the prophets, and of them which keep the sayings of this book: worship God.

10And he saith unto me, Seal not the sayings of the prophecy of this book: for the time is at hand.

11He that is unjust, let him be unjust still: and he which is filthy, let him be filthy still: and he that is righteous, let him be righteous still: and he that is holy, let him be holy still.

12And, behold, I come quickly; and my reward *is* with me, to give every man according as his work shall be.

13I am Alpha and Omega, the beginning and the end, the first and the last.

14Blessed *are* they that do his commandments, that they may have right to the tree of life, and may enter in through the gates into the city.

15For without *are* dogs, and sorcerers, and whoremongers, and murderers, and idolaters, and whosoever loveth and maketh a lie.

16I Jesus have sent mine angel to testify unto you these things in the churches. I am the root and the offspring of David, *and* the bright and morning star.

17And the Spirit and the bride say, Come. And let him that heareth say, Come. And let him that is athirst come. And whosoever will, let him take the water of life freely.

18For I testify unto every man that heareth the words of the prophecy of this book, If any man shall add unto these things, God shall add unto him the plagues that are written in this book:

19And if any man shall take away from the words of the book of this prophecy, God shall take away his part out of the book of life, and out of the holy city, and *from* the things which are written in this book.

20He which testifieth these things saith, Surely I come quickly. Amen. Even so, come, Lord Jesus.

21The grace of our Lord Jesus Christ *be* with you all. Amen.

PSALM 150:1–6

PRAISE ye the LORD. Praise God in his sanctuary: praise him in the firmament of his power.

2Praise him for his mighty acts; praise him according to his excellent greatness.

3Praise him with the sound of the trumpet: praise him with the psaltery and harp.

4Praise him with the timbrel and dance: praise him with stringed instruments and organs.

5Praise him upon the loud cymbals: praise him upon the high sounding cymbals.

6Let every thing that hath breath praise the LORD. Praise ye the LORD.

PROVERBS FOR TODAY/ 31:25–31

Strength and honour are *her clothing; and she shall rejoice in time to come. She openeth her mouth with wisdom; and in her tongue* is *the law of kindness. She looketh well to the ways of her household, and eateth not the bread of idleness. Her children arise up, and call her blessed; her husband* also, *and he praiseth her. Many daughters have done virtuously, but thou excellest them all. Favour is deceitful, and beauty* is *vain:* but *a woman that feareth the LORD, she shall be praised. Give her of the fruit of her hands; and let her own works praise her in the gates.*

Now that you have reached your goal of reading through the Bible in this version, you may want to use *The Living Bible* edition of *The One Year Bible* for your daily reading next year. It is available at your Christian bookstore.

The Bible Talks about Life

Casting all your care upon him; for he careth for you. *1 Peter 5:7*

AGITATION

Peace I leave with you, my peace I give unto you: not as the world giveth, give I unto you. Let not your heart be troubled, neither let it be afraid. *John 14:27*

Be careful for nothing; but in every thing by prayer and supplication with thanksgiving let your requests be made known unto God. And the peace of God, which passeth all understanding, shall keep your hearts and minds through Christ Jesus. *Philippians 4:6, 7*

ANGER

Be ye angry, and sin not: let not the sun go down upon your wrath: Neither give place to the devil. *Ephesians 4:26, 27*

Wherefore, my beloved brethren, let every man be swift to hear, slow to speak, slow to wrath: For the wrath of man worketh not the righteousness of God. *James 1:19, 20*

DEPRESSION

I waited patiently for the LORD: and he inclined unto me, and heard my cry. He brought me up also out of an horrible pit, out of the miry clay, and set my feet upon a rock, *and* established my goings. And he hath put a new song in my mouth, *even* praise unto our God: many shall see *it,* and fear, and shall trust in the LORD. *Psalm 40:1-3*

The *righteous* cry, and the LORD heareth, and delivereth them out of all their troubles. The LORD *is* nigh unto them that are of a broken heart; and saveth such as be of a contrite spirit. Many *are* the afflictions of the righteous: but the LORD delivereth him out of them all. *Psalm 34:17, 19*

DISCOURAGEMENT

Let not your heart be troubled: ye believe in God, believe also in me. In my Father's house are many mansions: if *it were* not *so,* I would have told you. I go to prepare a place for you. And if I go and prepare a place for you, I will come again, and receive you unto myself; that where I am, *there* ye may be also. *John 14:1-3*

Be strong and of a good courage, fear not, nor be afraid of them: for the LORD thy God, he *it is* that doth go with thee; he will not fail thee, nor forsake thee. *Deuteronomy 31:6*

Note: Words beginning with an initial capital letter, following punctuation other than a period indicate a new verse in accordance with the system used in the King James Version.

ETERNAL LIFE
Jesus said unto her, I am the resurrection, and the life: he that believeth in me, though he were dead, yet shall he live: And whosoever liveth and believeth in me shall never die. Believest thou this? *John 11:25, 26*

For we know that if our earthly house of *this* tabernacle were dissolved, we have a building of God, an house not made with hands, eternal in the heavens. For in this we groan, earnestly desiring to be clothed upon with our house which is from heaven: If so be that being clothed we shall not be found naked. For we that are in *this* tabernacle do groan, being burdened: not for that we would be unclothed, but clothed upon, that mortality might be swallowed up of life. Now he that hath wrought us for the selfsame thing *is* God, who also hath given unto us the earnest of the Spirit. *2 Corinthians 5:1-5*

FEAR
Fear thou not; for I *am* with thee: be not dismayed; for I *am* thy God: I will strengthen thee; yea, I will help thee; yea, I will uphold thee with the right hand of my righteousness. *Isaiah 41:10*

He shall not be afraid of evil tidings: his heart is fixed, trusting in the LORD. His heart *is* established, he shall not be afraid, until he see *his desire* upon his enemies. *Psalm 112:7, 8*

FRUSTRATION
For ye have need of patience, that, after ye have done the will of God, ye might receive the promise. *Hebrews 10:36*

Thou wilt keep *him* in perfect peace, *whose* mind *is* stayed *on thee:* because he trusteth in thee. Trust ye in the LORD for ever: for in the LORD JEHOVAH *is* everlasting strength. *Isaiah 26:3, 4*

GUILT
If we confess our sins, he is faithful and just to forgive us *our* sins, and to cleanse us from all unrighteousness. *1 John 1:9*

Come now, and let us reason together, saith the LORD: though your sins be as scarlet, they shall be as white as snow; though they be red like crimson, they shall be as wool. *Isaiah 1:18*

For I will be merciful to their unrighteousness, and their sins and their iniquities will I remember no more. *Hebrews 8:12*

IMPATIENCE
Rest in the LORD, and wait patiently for him: fret not thyself because of him who prospereth in his way, because of the man who bringeth wicked devices to pass. *Psalm 37:7*

Be patient therefore, brethren, unto the coming of the Lord. Behold, the husbandman waiteth for the precious fruit of the earth, and hath long patience for it, until he receive the early and latter rain. Be ye also patient; stablish your hearts: for the coming of the Lord draweth nigh. *James 5:7, 8*

INSECURITY
What shall we then say to these things? If God *be* for us, who *can be* against us? He that spared not his own Son, but delivered him up for us all, how shall he not with him also freely give us all things? *Romans 8:31, 32*

For I the LORD thy God will hold thy right hand, saying unto thee, Fear not; I will help thee. *Isaiah 41:13*

So that we may boldly say, The Lord *is* my helper, and I will not fear what man shall do unto me. *Hebrews 13:6*

JEALOUSY
But if ye have bitter envying and strife in your hearts, glory not, and lie not against the truth. This wisdom descendeth not from above, but *is* earthly, sensual, devilish. For where envying and strife *is,* there *is* confusion and every evil work. *James 3:14-16*

Be not thou afraid when one is made rich, when the glory of his house is increased; For when he dieth he shall carry nothing away: his glory shall not descend after him. *Psalm 49:16, 17*

LOW SELF-ESTEEM
So God created man in his *own* image, in the image of God created he him; male and female created he them. *Genesis 1:27*

For I say, through the grace given unto me, to every man that is among you, not to think *of himself* more highly than he ought to think; but to think soberly, according as God hath dealt to every man the measure of faith. For as we have many members in one body, and all members have not the same office: So we, *being* many, are one body in Christ, and every one members one of another. *Romans 12:3-5*

PAIN
For our light affliction, which is but for a moment, worketh for us a far more exceeding *and* eternal weight of glory; While we look not at the things which are seen, but at the things which are not seen: for the things which are seen *are* temporal; but the things which are not seen *are* eternal.
2 Corinthians 4:17, 18

And lest I should be exalted above measure through the abundance of the revelations, there was given to me a thorn in the flesh, the messenger of Satan to buffet me, lest I should be exalted above measure. For this thing I besought the Lord thrice, that it might depart from me. And he said unto me, My grace is sufficient for thee: for my strength is made perfect in weakness. Most gladly therefore will I rather glory in my infirmities, that the power of Christ may rest upon me. Therefore I take pleasure in infirmities, in reproaches, in necessities, in persecutions, in distresses for Christ's sake: for when I am weak, then am I strong. *2 Corinthians 12:7-10*

PERSECUTION
Blessed *are* they which are persecuted for righteousness' sake: for theirs is the kingdom of heaven. Blessed are ye, when *men* shall revile you, and persecute *you,* and shall say all manner of evil against you falsely, for my sake. Rejoice, and be exceeding glad: for great *is* your reward in heaven: for so persecuted they the prophets which were before you. *Matthew 5:10-12*

But I say unto you, Love your enemies, bless them that curse you, do good to them that hate you, and pray for them which despitefully use you, and persecute you; That ye may be the children of your Father which is in heaven: for he maketh his sun to rise on the evil and on the good, and sendeth rain on the just and on the unjust. *Matthew 5:44, 45*

SICKNESS
Is any sick among you? let him call for the elders of the church; and let them pray over him, anointing him with oil in the name of the Lord: And the prayer of faith shall save the sick, and the Lord shall raise him up; and if he have committed sins, they shall be forgiven him. *James 5:14, 15*

SUFFERING AND DEATH
But I would not have you to be ignorant, brethren, concerning them which are asleep, that ye sorrow not, even as others which have no hope. For if we believe that Jesus died and rose again, even so them also which sleep in Jesus will God bring with him. *1 Thessalonians 4:13, 14*

The LORD *is* nigh unto them that are of a broken heart; and saveth such as be of a contrite spirit. Many *are* the afflictions of the righteous: but the LORD delivereth him out of them all. *Psalm 34:18, 19*

Behold, I shew you a mystery; We shall not all sleep, but we shall all be changed, In a moment, in the twinkling of an eye, at the last trump: for the trumpet shall sound, and the dead shall be raised incorruptible, and we shall be changed. For this corruptible must put on incorruption, and this mortal *must* put on immortality. So when this corruptible shall have put on incorruption, and this mortal shall have put on immortality, then shall be brought to pass the saying that is written, Death is swallowed up in victory. O death, where *is* thy sting? O grave, where *is* thy victory? *1 Corthians 15:51-55*

TEMPTATION
There hath no temptation taken you but such as is common to man: but God *is* faithful, who will not suffer you to be tempted above that ye are able; but will with the temptation also make a way to escape, that ye may be able to bear *it. 1 Corinthians 10:13*

For in that he himself hath suffered being tempted, he is able to succor them that are tempted. *Hebrews 2:18*

Blessed *is* the man that endureth temptation: for when he is tried, he shall receive the crown of life, which the Lord hath promised to them that love him. Let no man say when he is tempted, I am tempted of God: for God cannot be tempted with evil, neither tempteth he any man: But every man is tempted, when he is drawn away of his own lust, and enticed. *James 1:12-14*

WEARINESS
But they that wait upon the LORD shall renew their strength; they shall mount up with wings as eagles; they shall run, and not be weary; *and* they shall walk, and not faint. *Isaiah 40:31*

Come unto me, all *ye* that labour and are heavy laden, and I will give you rest. Take my yoke upon you, and learn of me; for I am meek and lowly in heart: and ye shall find rest unto your souls. For my yoke *is* easy, and my burden is light. *Matthew 11:28-30*

WORRY
Thou wilt keep *him* in perfect peace, *whose* mind *is* stayed *on thee:* because he trusteth in thee. Trust ye in the LORD for ever: for in the LORD JEHOVAH *is* everlasting strength. *Isaiah 26:3, 4*

Casting all your care upon him; for he careth for you. *1 Peter 5:7*

And he said unto his disciples, Therefore I say unto you, Take no thought for your life, what ye shall eat; neither for the body, what ye shall put on. The life is more than meat, and the body *is more* than raiment. Consider the ravens: for they neither sow nor reap; which neither have storehouse nor barn; and God feedeth them: how much more are ye better than the fowls? And which of you with taking thought can add to his stature one cubit? *Luke 12:22-28*

The Bible Talks about Relationships
A man *that hath* friends must shew himself friendly: and there is a friend *that* sticketh closer than a brother. *Proverbs 18:24*

FRIENDS
He that walketh with wise men shall be wise: but a companion of fools shall be destroyed. *Proverbs 13:20*

Let nothing be done through strife or vainglory; but in lowliness of mind let each esteem other better than themselves. Look not every man on his own things, but every man also on the things of others. *Philippians 2:3, 4*

INJUSTICE
For *it is* better, if the will of God be so, that ye suffer for well doing, than for evil doing. *1 Peter 3:17*

But the God of all grace, who hath called us unto his eternal glory by Christ Jesus, after that ye have suffered a while, make you perfect, stablish, strengthen, settle you. *1 Peter 5:10*

LOVE

This is my commandment, That ye love one another, as I have loved you. Greater love hath no man than this, that a man lay down his life for his friends. Ye are my friends, if ye do whatsoever I command you. Henceforth I call you not servants; for the servant knoweth not what his lord doeth: but I have called you friends; for all things that I have heard of my Father I have made known unto you. Ye have not chosen me, but I have chosen you, and ordained you, that ye should go and bring forth fruit, and *that* your fruit should remain: that whatsoever ye shall ask of the Father in my name, he may give it you. These things I command you, that ye love one another. *John 15:12-17*

For God so loved the world, that he gave his only begotten Son, that whosoever believeth in him should not perish, but have everlasting life. *John 3:16*

Beloved, let us love one another: for love is of God; and every one that loveth is born of God, and knoweth God. He that loveth not knoweth not God for God is love. In this was manifested the love of God toward us, because that God sent his only begotten Son into the world, that we might live through him. Herein is love, not that we loved God, but that he loved us, and sent his Son *to be* the propitiation for our sins. Beloved, if God so loved us, we ought also to love one another. No man hath seen God at any time. If we love one another, God dwelleth in us, and his love is perfected in us. *1 John 4:7-12*

Charity suffereth long, *and* is kind; charity envieth now; charity vaunteth not itself, is not puffed up, Doth not behave itself unseemly, seeketh not her own, is not easily provoked, thinketh no evil; Rejoiceth not in iniquity, but rejoiceth in the truth; Beareth all things, believeth all things, hopeth all things, endureth all things. *1 Corinthians 13:4-7*

MARRIAGE

Submitting yourself one to another in the fear of God. Wives, submit yourselves unto your own husbands, as unto the Lord. For the husband is the head of the wife, even as Christ is the head of the church: and he is the saviour of the body. Therefore as the church is subject unto Christ, so let the wives be to their own husbands in every thing. Husbands, love your wives, even as Christ also loved the church, and gave himself for it; That he might sanctify and cleanse it with the washing of water by the word, That he might present it to himself a glorious church, not having spot, or wrinkle, or any such thing; but that it should be holy and without blemish. So ought men to love their wives as their own bodies. He that loveth his wife loveth himself. *Ephesians 5:21-28*

Likewise, ye wives, be in subjection to your own husbands; that, if any obey not the word, they also may without the word be won by the conversation of the wives; While they behold your chaste conversation *coupled* with fear. . . . Likewise, ye husbands, dwell with *them* according to knowledge, giving honour unto the wife, as unto the weaker vessel, and as being heirs together of the grace of life; that your prayers be not hindered. *1 Peter 3:1, 2, 7*

And said, For this cause shall a man leave father and mother, and shall cleave to his wife: and they twain shall be one flesh? Wherefore they are no more twain, but one flesh. What therefore God hath joined together, let not man put asunder. *Matthew 19: 5, 6*

And I say unto you, Whosoever shall put away his wife, except *it* be for fornication, and shall marry another, committeth adultery: and whoso marrieth her which is put away doth commit adultery. *Matthew 19:9*

And he saith unto them, Whosoever shall put away his wife, and marry another, committeth adultery against her. And if a woman shall put away her husband, and be married to another, she committeth audltery. *Mark 10: 11, 12*

PARENTS AND CHILDREN
Children, obey your parents in the Lord: for this is right. Honour thy father and mother; which is the first commandment with promise; That it may be well with thee, and thou mayest live long on the earth. And, ye fathers, provoke not your children to wrath: but bring them up in the nurture and admonition of the Lord. *Ephesians 6:1-4*

The Bible Talks about the Future
Thy word *is* a lamp unto my feet, and a light unto my path. *Psalm 119:105*

ASTROLOGY, HOROSCOPES, AND THE OCCULT
And when they shall say unto you, Seek unto them that have familiar spirits, and unto wizards that peep, and that mutter: should not a people seek unto their God? for the living to the dead? *Isaiah 8:19*

Stand now with thine enchantments, and with the multitude of thy sorceries, wherein thou hast laboured from thy youth; if so be thou shalt be able to profit, if so be thou mayest prevail. Thou art wearied in the multitude of thy counsels. Let now the astrologers, the stargazers, the monthly prognosticators, stand up, and save thee from *these things* that shall come upon thee. Behold, they shall be as stubble; the fire shall burn them; they shall not deliver themselves from the power of the flame: *there shall* not *be* a coal to warm at, *nor* fire to sit before it. *Isaiah 47:12*

DIRECTION FOR LIFE
But be ye doers of the word, and not hearers only, deceiving your own selves. For if any be a hearer of the word, and not a doer, he is like unto a man beholding his natural face in a glass: For he beholdeth himself, and goeth his way, and straightway forgetteth what manner of man he was. But whoso looketh into the perfect law of liberty, and continueth *therein,* he being not a forgetful hearer, but a doer of the work, this man shall be blessed in his deed. *James 1:22-25*

MONEY MANAGEMENT

But my God shall supply all your need according to his riches in glory by Christ Jesus. *Philippians 4:19*

He that loveth silver shall not be satisfied with silver; nor he that loveth abundance with increase: this *is* also vanity. *Ecclesiastes 5:10*

But godliness with contentment is great gain. For we brought nothing into *this* world, *and it is* certain we can carry nothing out. And having food and raiment let us be therewith content. But they that will be rich fall into temptation and a snare, and *into* many foolish and hurtful lusts, which drown men in destruction and perdition. For the love of money is the root of all evil: which while some coveted after, they have erred from the faith, and pierced themselves through with many sorrows. *1 Timothy 6:6-10*

TRUST

Trust in the LORD with all thine heart; and lean not unto thine own understanding. In all thy ways acknowledge him, and he shall direct thy paths. *Proverbs 3:5, 6*

I know both how to be abased, and I know how to abound: every where and in all things I am instructed both to be full and to be hungry, both to abound and to suffer need. I can do all things through Christ which strengtheneth me. *Philippians 4:12, 13*

The Bible Talks about Faith

So then faith *cometh* by hearing, and hearing by the word of God. *Romans 10:17*

BEING BORN AGAIN

Jesus answered and said unto him, Verily, verily, I say unto thee, Except a man be born again, he cannot see the kingdom of God. Nicodemus saith unto him, How can a man be born when he is old? can he enter the second time into his mother's womb, and be born? Jesus answered, Verily, verily, I say unto thee, Except a man be born of water and *of* the Spirit, he cannot enter into the kingdom of God. *John 3:3-5*

Blessed *be* the God and Father of our Lord Jesus Christ, which according to his abundant mercy hath begotten us again unto a lively hope by the resurrection of Jesus Christ from the dead. *1 Peter 1:3*

FINDING GOD

That they should seek the Lord, if haply they might feel after him, and find him, though he be not far from every one of us: For in him we live, and move, and have our being; as certain also of your own poets have said, For we are also his offspring. *Acts 17:27, 28*

For I know the thoughts that I think toward you, saith the LORD, thoughts of peace, and not of evil, to give you an expected end. Then shall ye call upon me, and ye shall go and pray unto me, and I will hearken unto you. And ye shall seek me, and find *me,* when ye shall search for me with all your heart. *Jeremiah 29:11-13*

KNOWING GOD

To whom then will ye liken God? or what likeness will ye compare unto him? *It is* he that sitteth upon the circle of the earth, and the inhabitants thereof *are* as grasshoppers; that stretcheth out the heavens as a curtain, and spreadeth them out as a tent to dwell in: That bringeth the princes to nothing; he maketh the judges of the earth as vanity. Yea, they shall not be planted; yea, they shall not be sown: yea, their stock shall not take root in the earth: and he shall also blow upon them, and they shall wither, and the whirlwind shall take them away as stubble. To whom then will ye liken me, or shall I be equal? saith the Holy One. Lift up your eyes on high, and behold who hath created these *things,* that bringeth out their host by number: he calleth them all by names by the greatness of his might, for that *he is* strong in power; not one faileth. *Isaiah 40:18, 22-26*

Beloved, let us love one another: for love is of God; and every one that loveth is born of God, and knoweth God. He that loveth not knoweth not God; for God is love. *1 John 4:7, 8*

KNOWING JESUS CHRIST

In the beginning was the Word, and the Word was with God, and the Word was God. The same was in the beginning with God. All things were made by him; and without him was not any thing made that was made. In him was life; and the life was the light of men. And the light shineth in darkness; and the darkness comprehended it not. There was a man sent from God, whose name was John. The same came for a witness, to bear witness of the Light, that all *men* through him might believe. He was not that Light, but *was sent* to bear witness of that Light. That was the true Light, which lighteth every man that cometh into the world. He was in the world, and the world was made by him, and the world knew him not. He came unto his own, and his own received him not. But as many as received him, to them gave he power to become the sons of God, *even* to them that believe on his name: Which were born, not of blood, nor of the will of the flesh, nor of the will of man, but of God. And the Word was made flesh, and dwelt among us (and we beheld his glory, the glory as of the only begotten of the Father) full of grace and truth. *John 1:1-14*

Giving thanks unto the Father, which hath made us meet to be partakers of the inheritance of the saints in light: Who hath delivered us from the power of darkness, and hath translated *us* into the kingdom of his dear Son: In whom we have redemption through his blood, *even* the forgiveness of sins: Who is the image of the invisible God, the firstborn of every creature: For by him were all things created, that are in heaven, and that are in earth, visible and invisible, whether *they be* thrones, or dominions, or principalities, or power: all things were created by him, and for him: And he is before all things, and by him all things consist. And he is the head of the body, the church: who is the beginning, the firstborn from the dead; that in all *things* he might have the preeminence. For it pleased *the Father* that in him should all fulness dwell. *Colossians 1:12-19*

KNOWING THE HOLY SPIRIT

So then they that are in the flesh cannot please God. But ye are not in the flesh, but in the Spirit, if so be that the Spirit of God dwell in you. Now if any man have not the Spirit of Christ, he is none of his. And if Christ *be* in you, the body *is* dead because of sin; but the Spirit *is* life because of righteousness. But if the Spirit of him that raised up Jesus from the dead dwell in you, he that raised up Christ from the dead shall also quicken your mortal bodies by his Spirit that dwelleth in you. *Romans 8:8-11*

And I will pray the Father, and he shall give you another Comforter, that he may abide with you for ever; *Even* the Spirit of truth; whom the world cannot receive, because it seeth him not, neither knoweth him: but ye know him; for he dwelleth with you, and shall be in you. . . . But the Comforter, *which is* the Holy Ghost, whom the Father will send in my name, he shall teach you all things, and bring all things to your remembrance, whatsoever I have said unto you. *John 14:16, 17, 26*

PRAYER

Confess *your* faults one to another, and pray one for another, that ye may be healed. The effectual fervent prayer of a righteous man availeth much. *James 5:16*

If ye abide in me, and my words abide in you, ye shall ask what ye will, and it shall be done unto you. *John 15:7*

Ask, and it shall be given you; seek, and ye shall find; knock, and it shall be opened unto you: For every one that asketh receiveth; and he that seeketh findeth; and to him that knocketh it shall opened. *Matthew 7:7, 8*

If we confess our sins, he is faithful and just to forgive us *our* sins, and to cleanse us from all unrighteousness. *1 John 1:9*